A2 ALTITUDE CORRECTION TABLES 10°–90°—SUN, STARS, PLANETS

OCT.–MAR. SUN APR.–SEPT.

App. Alt.	Lower Limb	Upper Limb	App. Alt.	Lower Limb	Upper Limb
° ′	′	′	° ′	′	′
9 33	+10·8	−21·5	9 39	+10·6	−21·2
9 45	+10·9	−21·4	9 50	+10·7	−21·1
9 56	+11·0	−21·3	10 02	+10·8	−21·0
10 08	+11·1	−21·2	10 14	+10·9	−20·9
10 20	+11·2	−21·1	10 27	+11·0	−20·8
10 33	+11·3	−21·0	10 40	+11·1	−20·7
10 46	+11·4	−20·9	10 53	+11·2	−20·6
11 00	+11·5	−20·8	11 07	+11·3	−20·5
11 15	+11·6	−20·7	11 22	+11·4	−20·4
11 30	+11·7	−20·6	11 37	+11·5	−20·3
11 45	+11·8	−20·5	11 53	+11·6	−20·2
12 01	+11·9	−20·4	12 10	+11·7	−20·1
12 18	+12·0	−20·3	12 27	+11·8	−20·0
12 36	+12·1	−20·2	12 45	+11·9	−19·9
12 54	+12·2	−20·1	13 04	+12·0	−19·8
13 14	+12·3	−20·0	13 24	+12·1	−19·7
13 34	+12·4	−19·9	13 44	+12·2	−19·6
13 55	+12·5	−19·8	14 06	+12·3	−19·5
14 17	+12·6	−19·7	14 29	+12·4	−19·4
14 41	+12·7	−19·6	14 53	+12·5	−19·3
15 05	+12·8	−19·5	15 18	+12·6	−19·2
15 31	+12·9	−19·4	15 45	+12·7	−19·1
15 59	+13·0	−19·3	16 13	+12·8	−19·0
16 27	+13·1	−19·2	16 43	+12·9	−18·9
16 58	+13·2	−19·1	17 14	+13·0	−18·8
17 30	+13·3	−19·0	17 47	+13·1	−18·7
18 05	+13·4	−18·9	18 23	+13·2	−18·6
18 41	+13·5	−18·8	19 00	+13·3	−18·5
19 20	+13·6	−18·7	19 41	+13·4	−18·4
20 02	+13·7	−18·6	20 24	+13·5	−18·3
20 46	+13·8	−18·5	21 10	+13·6	−18·2
21 34	+13·9	−18·4	21 59	+13·7	−18·1
22 25	+14·0	−18·3	22 52	+13·8	−18·0
23 20	+14·1	−18·2	23 49	+13·9	−17·9
24 20	+14·2	−18·1	24 51	+14·0	−17·8
25 24	+14·3	−18·0	25 58	+14·1	−17·7
26 34	+14·4	−17·9	27 11	+14·2	−17·6
27 50	+14·5	−17·8	28 31	+14·3	−17·5
29 13	+14·6	−17·7	29 58	+14·4	−17·4
30 44	+14·7	−17·6	31 33	+14·5	−17·3
32 24	+14·8	−17·5	33 18	+14·6	−17·2
34 15	+14·9	−17·4	35 15	+14·7	−17·1
36 17	+15·0	−17·3	37 24	+14·8	−17·0
38 34	+15·1	−17·2	39 48	+14·9	−16·9
41 06	+15·2	−17·1	42 28	+15·0	−16·8
43 56	+15·3	−17·0	45 29	+15·1	−16·7
47 07	+15·4	−16·9	48 52	+15·2	−16·6
50 43	+15·5	−16·8	52 41	+15·3	−16·5
54 46	+15·6	−16·7	56 59	+15·4	−16·4
59 21	+15·7	−16·6	61 50	+15·5	−16·3
64 28	+15·8	−16·5	67 15	+15·6	−16·2
70 10	+15·9	−16·4	73 14	+15·7	−16·1
76 24	+16·0	−16·3	79 42	+15·8	−16·0
83 05	+16·1	−16·2	86 31	+15·9	−15·9
90 00			90 00		

STARS AND PLANETS

App. Alt.	Corrⁿ	App. Alt.	Additional Corrⁿ
° ′	′		**2019**
9 55	−5·3		**VENUS**
10 07	−5·2		Jan. 1–Feb. 15
10 20	−5·1	°	′
10 32	−5·0	41	+0·2
10 46	−5·0	76	+0·1
10 59	−4·8		Feb. 16–Dec. 31
11 14	−4·7	°	′
11 29	−4·6	60	+0·1
11 44	−4·5		
12 00	−4·4		**MARS**
12 17	−4·3		Jan. 1–Dec. 31
12 35	−4·2	°	′
12 53	−4·1	60	+0·1
13 12	−4·0		
13 32	−3·9		
13 53	−3·8		
14 16	−3·7		
14 39	−3·6		
15 03	−3·5		
15 29	−3·4		
15 56	−3·3		
16 25	−3·2		
16 55	−3·1		
17 27	−3·0		
18 01	−2·9		
18 37	−2·8		
19 16	−2·7		
19 56	−2·6		
20 40	−2·5		
21 27	−2·4		
22 17	−2·3		
23 11	−2·2		
24 09	−2·1		
25 12	−2·0		
26 20	−1·9		
27 34	−1·8		
28 54	−1·7		
30 22	−1·6		
31 58	−1·5		
33 43	−1·4		
35 38	−1·3		
37 45	−1·2		
40 06	−1·1		
42 42	−1·0		
45 34	−0·9		
48 45	−0·8		
52 16	−0·7		
56 09	−0·6		
60 26	−0·5		
65 06	−0·4		
70 09	−0·3		
75 32	−0·2		
81 12	−0·1		
87 03	0·0		
90 00			

DIP

Ht. of Eye	Corrⁿ	Ht. of Eye	Ht. of Eye	Corrⁿ
m	′	ft.	m	′
2·4	−2·8	8·0	1·0 − 1·8	
2·6	−2·9	8·6	1·5 − 2·2	
2·8	−3·0	9·2	2·0 − 2·5	
3·0	−3·1	9·8	2·5 − 2·8	
3·2	−3·2	10·5	3·0 − 3·0	
3·4	−3·3	11·2	See table ←	
3·6	−3·4	11·9		
3·8	−3·5	12·6	m ′	
4·0	−3·6	13·3	20 − 7·9	
4·3	−3·7	14·1	22 − 8·3	
4·5	−3·8	14·9	24 − 8·6	
4·7	−3·9	15·7	26 − 9·0	
5·0	−4·0	16·5	28 − 9·3	
5·2	−4·1	17·4		
5·5	−4·2	18·3	30 − 9·6	
5·8	−4·3	19·1	32 − 10·0	
6·1	−4·4	20·1	34 − 10·3	
6·3	−4·5	21·0	36 − 10·6	
6·6	−4·6	22·0	38 − 10·8	
6·9	−4·7	22·9		
7·2	−4·8	23·9	40 − 11·1	
7·5	−4·9	24·9	42 − 11·4	
7·9	−5·0	26·0	44 − 11·7	
8·2	−5·1	27·1	46 − 11·9	
8·5	−5·2	28·1	48 − 12·2	
8·8	−5·3	29·2		
9·2	−5·4	30·4	ft. ′	
9·5	−5·5	31·5	2 − 1·4	
9·9	−5·6	32·7	4 − 1·9	
10·3	−5·7	33·9	6 − 2·4	
10·6	−5·8	35·1	8 − 2·7	
11·0	−5·9	36·3	10 − 3·1	
11·4	−6·0	37·6	See table ←	
11·8	−6·1	38·9		
12·2	−6·2	40·1	ft. ′	
12·6	−6·3	41·5	70 − 8·1	
13·0	−6·4	42·8	75 − 8·4	
13·4	−6·5	44·2	80 − 8·7	
13·8	−6·6	45·5	85 − 8·9	
14·2	−6·7	46·9	90 − 9·2	
14·7	−6·8	48·4	95 − 9·5	
15·1	−6·9	49·8		
15·5	−7·0	51·3	100 − 9·7	
16·0	−7·1	52·8	105 − 9·9	
16·5	−7·2	54·3	110 − 10·2	
16·9	−7·3	55·8	115 − 10·4	
17·4	−7·4	57·4	120 − 10·6	
17·9	−7·5	58·9	125 − 10·8	
18·4	−7·6	60·5		
18·8	−7·7	62·1	130 − 11·1	
19·3	−7·8	63·8	135 − 11·3	
19·8	−7·9	65·4	140 − 11·5	
20·4	−8·0	67·1	145 − 11·7	
20·9	−8·1	68·8	150 − 11·9	
21·4		70·5	155 − 12·1	

App. Alt. = Apparent altitude = Sextant altitude corrected for index error and dip.

© British Crown Copyright 2018. All rights reserved.

D1286669

App. Alt.	OCT.–MAR. SUN		APR.–SEPT.		STARS PLANETS
	Lower Limb	Upper Limb	Lower Limb	Upper Limb	
° ′	′	′	′	′	′
0 00	−17·5	−49·8	−17·8	−49·6	−33·8
0 03	16·9	49·2	17·2	49·0	33·2
0 06	16·3	48·6	16·6	48·4	32·6
0 09	15·7	48·0	16·0	47·8	32·0
0 12	15·2	47·5	15·4	47·2	31·5
0 15	14·6	46·9	14·8	46·6	30·9
0 18	−14·1	−46·4	−14·3	−46·1	−30·4
0 21	13·5	45·8	13·8	45·6	29·8
0 24	13·0	45·3	13·3	45·1	29·3
0 27	12·5	44·8	12·8	44·6	28·8
0 30	12·0	44·3	12·3	44·1	28·3
0 33	11·6	43·9	11·8	43·6	27·9
0 36	−11·1	−43·4	−11·3	−43·1	−27·4
0 39	10·6	42·9	10·9	42·7	26·9
0 42	10·2	42·5	10·5	42·3	26·5
0 45	9·8	42·1	10·0	41·8	26·1
0 48	9·4	41·7	9·6	41·4	25·7
0 51	9·0	41·3	9·2	41·0	25·3
0 54	−8·6	−40·9	−8·8	−40·6	−24·9
0 57	8·2	40·5	8·4	40·2	24·5
1 00	7·8	40·1	8·0	39·8	24·1
1 03	7·4	39·7	7·7	39·5	23·7
1 06	7·1	39·4	7·3	39·1	23·4
1 09	6·7	39·0	7·0	38·8	23·0
1 12	−6·4	−38·7	−6·6	−38·4	−22·7
1 15	6·0	38·3	6·3	38·1	22·3
1 18	5·7	38·0	6·0	37·8	22·0
1 21	5·4	37·7	5·7	37·5	21·7
1 24	5·1	37·4	5·3	37·1	21·4
1 27	4·8	37·1	5·0	36·8	21·1
1 30	−4·5	−36·8	−4·7	−36·5	−20·8
1 35	4·0	36·3	4·3	36·1	20·3
1 40	3·6	35·9	3·8	35·6	19·9
1 45	3·1	35·4	3·4	35·2	19·4
1 50	2·7	35·0	2·9	34·7	19·0
1 55	2·3	34·6	2·5	34·3	18·6
2 00	−1·9	−34·2	−2·1	−33·9	−18·2
2 05	1·5	33·8	1·7	33·5	17·8
2 10	1·1	33·4	1·4	33·2	17·4
2 15	0·8	33·1	1·0	32·8	17·1
2 20	0·4	32·7	0·7	32·5	16·7
2 25	−0·1	32·4	−0·3	32·1	16·4
2 30	+0·2	−32·1	0·0	−31·8	−16·1
2 35	0·5	31·8	+0·3	31·5	15·8
2 40	0·8	31·5	0·6	31·2	15·4
2 45	1·1	31·2	0·9	30·9	15·2
2 50	1·4	30·9	1·2	30·6	14·9
2 55	1·7	30·6	1·4	30·4	14·6
3 00	+2·0	−30·3	+1·7	−30·1	−14·3
3 05	2·2	30·1	2·0	29·8	14·1
3 10	2·5	29·8	2·2	29·6	13·8
3 15	2·7	29·6	2·5	29·3	13·6
3 20	2·9	29·4	2·7	29·1	13·4
3 25	3·2	29·1	2·9	28·9	13·1
3 30	+3·4	−28·9	+3·1	−28·7	−12·9

App. Alt.	OCT.–MAR. SUN		APR.–SEPT.		STARS PLANETS
	Lower Limb	Upper Limb	Lower Limb	Upper Limb	
° ′	′	′	′	′	′
3 30	+3·4	−28·9	+3·1	−28·7	−12·9
3 35	3·6	28·7	3·3	28·5	12·7
3 40	3·8	28·5	3·6	28·2	12·5
3 45	4·0	28·3	3·8	28·0	12·3
3 50	4·2	28·1	4·0	27·8	12·1
3 55	4·4	27·9	4·1	27·7	11·9
4 00	+4·6	−27·7	+4·3	−27·5	−11·7
4 05	4·8	27·5	4·5	27·3	11·5
4 10	4·9	27·4	4·7	27·1	11·4
4 15	5·1	27·2	4·9	26·9	11·2
4 20	5·3	27·0	5·0	26·8	11·0
4 25	5·4	26·9	5·2	26·6	10·9
4 30	+5·6	−26·7	+5·3	−26·5	−10·7
4 35	5·7	26·6	5·5	26·3	10·6
4 40	5·9	26·4	5·6	26·2	10·4
4 45	6·0	26·3	5·8	26·0	10·3
4 50	6·2	26·1	5·9	25·9	10·1
4 55	6·3	26·0	6·1	25·7	10·0
5 00	+6·4	−25·9	+6·2	−25·6	−9·8
5 05	6·6	25·7	6·3	25·5	9·7
5 10	6·7	25·6	6·5	25·3	9·6
5 15	6·8	25·5	6·6	25·2	9·5
5 20	7·0	25·3	6·7	25·1	9·3
5 25	7·1	25·2	6·8	25·0	9·2
5 30	+7·2	−25·1	+6·9	−24·9	−9·1
5 35	7·3	25·0	7·1	24·7	9·0
5 40	7·4	24·9	7·2	24·6	8·9
5 45	7·5	24·8	7·3	24·5	8·8
5 50	7·6	24·7	7·4	24·4	8·7
5 55	7·7	24·6	7·5	24·3	8·6
6 00	+7·8	−24·5	+7·6	−24·2	−8·5
6 10	8·0	24·3	7·8	24·0	8·3
6 20	8·2	24·1	8·0	23·8	8·1
6 30	8·4	23·9	8·2	23·6	7·9
6 40	8·6	23·7	8·3	23·5	7·7
6 50	8·7	23·6	8·5	23·3	7·6
7 00	+8·9	−23·4	+8·7	−23·1	−7·4
7 10	9·1	23·2	8·8	23·0	7·2
7 20	9·2	23·1	9·0	22·8	7·1
7 30	9·3	23·0	9·1	22·7	6·9
7 40	9·5	22·8	9·2	22·6	6·8
7 50	9·6	22·7	9·4	22·4	6·7
8 00	+9·7	−22·6	+9·5	−22·3	−6·6
8 10	9·9	22·4	9·6	22·2	6·4
8 20	10·0	22·3	9·7	22·1	6·3
8 30	10·1	22·2	9·9	21·9	6·2
8 40	10·2	22·1	10·0	21·8	6·1
8 50	10·3	22·0	10·1	21·7	6·0
9 00	+10·4	−21·9	+10·2	−21·6	−5·9
9 10	10·5	21·8	10·3	21·5	5·8
9 20	10·6	21·7	10·4	21·4	5·7
9 30	10·7	21·6	10·5	21·3	5·6
9 40	10·8	21·5	10·6	21·2	5·5
9 50	10·9	21·4	10·6	21·2	5·4
10 00	+11·0	−21·3	+10·7	−21·1	−5·3

Additional corrections for temperature and pressure are given on the following page.

For bubble sextant observations ignore dip and use the star corrections for Sun, planets and stars.

© British Crown Copyright 2018. All rights reserved.

A4 ALTITUDE CORRECTION TABLES—ADDITIONAL CORRECTIONS
ADDITIONAL REFRACTION CORRECTIONS FOR NON-STANDARD CONDITIONS

App. Alt.	A	B	C	D	E	F	G	H	J	K	L	M	N	P	App. Alt.
° ′	′	′	′	′	′	′	′	′	′	′	′	′	′	′	° ′
00 00	−7·3	−5·9	−4·6	−3·4	−2·2	−1·1	0·0	+1·0	+2·0	+3·0	+4·0	+4·9	+5·9	+6·9	00 00
00 30	5·5	4·5	3·5	2·6	1·7	0·8	0·0	0·8	1·6	2·3	3·1	3·8	4·5	5·3	00 30
01 00	4·4	3·5	2·8	2·0	1·3	0·7	0·0	0·6	1·2	1·8	2·4	3·0	3·6	4·2	01 00
01 30	3·5	2·9	2·2	1·7	1·1	0·5	0·0	0·5	1·0	1·5	2·0	2·5	2·9	3·4	01 30
02 00	2·9	2·4	1·9	1·4	0·9	0·4	0·0	0·4	0·8	1·3	1·7	2·0	2·4	2·8	02 00
02 30	−2·5	−2·0	−1·6	−1·2	−0·8	−0·4	0·0	+0·4	+0·7	+1·1	+1·4	+1·7	+2·1	+2·4	02 30
03 00	2·1	1·7	1·4	1·0	0·7	0·3	0·0	0·3	0·6	0·9	1·2	1·5	1·8	2·1	03 00
03 30	1·9	1·5	1·2	0·9	0·6	0·3	0·0	0·3	0·5	0·8	1·1	1·3	1·6	1·8	03 30
04 00	1·6	1·3	1·1	0·8	0·5	0·3	0·0	0·2	0·5	0·7	0·9	1·2	1·4	1·6	04 00
04 30	1·5	1·2	0·9	0·7	0·5	0·2	0·0	0·2	0·4	0·6	0·8	1·0	1·3	1·5	04 30
05 00	−1·3	−1·1	−0·9	−0·6	−0·4	−0·2	0·0	+0·2	+0·4	+0·6	+0·8	+0·9	+1·1	+1·3	05 00
06	1·1	0·9	0·7	0·5	0·3	0·2	0·0	0·2	0·3	0·5	0·6	0·8	0·9	1·1	06
07	1·0	0·8	0·6	0·5	0·3	0·1	0·0	0·1	0·3	0·4	0·5	0·7	0·8	0·9	07
08	0·8	0·7	0·5	0·4	0·3	0·1	0·0	0·1	0·2	0·4	0·5	0·6	0·7	0·8	08
09	0·7	0·6	0·5	0·4	0·2	0·1	0·0	0·1	0·2	0·3	0·4	0·5	0·6	0·7	09
10 00	−0·7	−0·5	−0·4	−0·3	−0·2	−0·1	0·0	+0·1	+0·2	+0·3	+0·4	+0·5	+0·6	+0·7	10 00
12	0·6	0·5	0·4	0·3	0·2	0·1	0·1	0·0	0·1	0·2	0·3	0·3	0·4	0·5	12
14	0·5	0·4	0·3	0·2	0·1	0·1	0·0	0·1	0·1	0·2	0·3	0·3	0·4	0·5	14
16	0·4	0·3	0·3	0·2	0·1	0·1	0·0	0·1	0·1	0·2	0·2	0·3	0·3	0·4	16
18	0·4	0·3	0·2	0·2	0·1	−0·1	0·0	+0·1	0·1	0·2	0·2	0·3	0·3	0·4	18
20 00	−0·3	−0·3	−0·2	−0·2	−0·1	0·0	0·0	0·0	+0·1	+0·1	+0·2	+0·2	+0·3	+0·3	20 00
25	0·3	0·2	0·2	0·1	0·1	0·0	0·0	0·0	0·1	0·1	0·1	0·2	0·2	0·2	25
30	0·2	0·2	0·1	0·1	0·1	0·0	0·0	0·0	+0·1	0·1	0·1	0·1	0·1	0·2	30
35	0·2	0·1	0·1	0·1	−0·1	0·0	0·0	0·0	0·0	0·0	0·1	0·1	0·1	0·2	35
40	0·1	0·1	0·1	−0·1	0·0	0·0	0·0	0·0	0·0	+0·1	0·1	0·1	0·1	0·1	40
50 00	−0·1	−0·1	−0·1	0·0	0·0	0·0	0·0	0·0	0·0	0·0	+0·1	+0·1	+0·1	+0·1	50 00

The graph is entered with arguments temperature and pressure to find a zone letter; using as arguments this zone letter and apparent altitude (sextant altitude corrected for index error and dip), a correction is taken from the table. This correction is to be applied to the sextant altitude in addition to the corrections for standard conditions (for the Sun, stars and planets from page A2-A3 and for the Moon from pages xxxiv and xxxv).

© British Crown Copyright 2018. All rights reserved.

2019
Nautical Almanac
COMMERCIAL EDITION

All rights reserved. No part of this publication may be
reproduced, stored in a retrieval system, or transmitted in any form or
by any means, electronic, mechanical, photocopying or otherwise,
without the prior permission of the copyright owner.

© Copyright 2018 by Snowball Publishing

www.snowballpublishing.com

info@snowballpublishing.com

For information regarding special discounts for bulk purchases, please contact
Snowball Publishing at

sales@snowballpublishing.com

THE NAUTICAL ALMANAC 2019
Commercial Edition

LIST OF CONTENTS

© British Crown Copyright 2018. All rights reserved.

CALENDAR, 2019

RELIGIOUS CALENDARS

Epiphany	Jan. 6	Low Sunday	Apr. 28
Septuagesima Sunday	Feb. 17	Rogation Sunday	May 26
Quinquagesima Sunday	Mar. 3	Ascension Day—Holy Thursday	May 30
Ash Wednesday	Mar. 6	Whit Sunday—Pentecost	June 9
Quadragesima Sunday	Mar. 10	Trinity Sunday	June 16
Palm Sunday	Apr. 14	Corpus Christi	June 20
Good Friday	Apr. 19	First Sunday in Advent	Dec. 1
Easter Day	Apr. 21	Christmas Day (Wednesday)	Dec. 25
First Day of Passover (Pesach)	Apr. 20	Day of Atonement (Yom Kippur)	Oct. 9
Feast of Weeks (Shavuot)	June 9	First day of Tabernacles (Succoth)	Oct. 14
Jewish New Year 5780 (Rosh Hashanah)	Sept. 30		
Ramadân, First day of (tabular)	May 6	Islamic New Year (1441)	Sept. 1

The Jewish and Islamic dates above are tabular dates, which begin at sunset on the previous evening and end at sunset on the date tabulated. In practice, the dates of Islamic fasts and festivals are determined by an actual sighting of the appropriate new moon.

CIVIL CALENDAR—UNITED KINGDOM

Accession of Queen Elizabeth II	Feb. 6	The Queen's Official Birthday†	June 8
St David (Wales)	Mar. 1	Birthday of Prince Philip, Duke of	
Commonwealth Day	Mar. 11	Edinburgh	June 10
St Patrick (Ireland)	Mar. 17	Remembrance Sunday	Nov. 10
Birthday of Queen Elizabeth II	Apr. 21	Birthday of the Prince of Wales	Nov. 14
St George (England)	Apr. 23	St Andrew (Scotland)	Nov. 30
Coronation Day	June 2		

PUBLIC HOLIDAYS

England and Wales—Jan. 1†, Apr. 19, Apr. 22, May 6†, May 27, Aug. 26, Dec. 25, Dec. 26

Northern Ireland—Jan. 1†, Mar. 18, Apr. 19, Apr. 22, May 6†, May 27, July 12†, Aug. 26, Dec. 25, Dec. 26

Scotland—Jan. 1, Jan. 2, Apr. 19, May 6, May 27†, Aug. 5, Dec. 25, Dec. 26†

CIVIL CALENDAR—UNITED STATES OF AMERICA

New Year's Day	Jan. 1	Labor Day	Sept. 2
Martin Luther King's Birthday	Jan. 21	Columbus Day	Oct. 14
Washington's Birthday	Feb. 18	Election Day (in certain States)	Nov. 5
Memorial Day	May 27	Veterans Day	Nov. 11
Independence Day	July 4	Thanksgiving Day	Nov. 28

†Dates subject to confirmation

PHASES OF THE MOON

	New Moon				First Quarter				Full Moon				Last Quarter		
	d	h	m		d	h	m		d	h	m		d	h	m
Jan.	6	01	28	Jan.	14	06	46	Jan.	21	05	16	Jan.	27	21	10
Feb.	4	21	04	Feb.	12	22	26	Feb.	19	15	54	Feb.	26	11	28
Mar.	6	16	04	Mar.	14	10	27	Mar.	21	01	43	Mar.	28	04	10
Apr.	5	08	50	Apr.	12	19	06	Apr.	19	11	12	Apr.	26	22	18
May	4	22	46	May	12	01	12	May	18	21	11	May	26	16	34
June	3	10	02	June	10	05	59	June	17	08	31	June	25	09	46
July	2	19	16	July	9	10	55	July	16	21	38	July	25	01	18
Aug.	1	03	12	Aug.	7	17	31	Aug.	15	12	29	Aug.	23	14	56
Aug.	30	10	37	Sept.	6	03	10	Sept.	14	04	33	Sept.	22	02	41
Sept.	28	18	26	Oct.	5	16	47	Oct.	13	21	08	Oct.	21	12	39
Oct.	28	03	38	Nov.	4	10	23	Nov.	12	13	34	Nov.	19	21	11
Nov.	26	15	06	Dec.	4	06	58	Dec.	12	05	12	Dec.	19	04	57
Dec.	26	05	13												

© British Crown Copyright 2018. All rights reserved.

DAYS OF THE WEEK AND DAYS OF THE YEAR

Day	JAN. Wk Yr	FEB. Wk Yr	MAR. Wk Yr	APR. Wk Yr	MAY Wk Yr	JUNE Wk Yr	JULY Wk Yr	AUG. Wk Yr	SEPT. Wk Yr	OCT. Wk Yr	NOV. Wk Yr	DEC. Wk Yr
1	Tu. 1	F. 32	F. 60	M. 91	W. 121	Sa. 152	M. 182	Th. 213	Su. 244	Tu. 274	F. 305	Su. 335
2	W. 2	Sa. 33	Sa. 61	Tu. 92	Th. 122	Su. 153	Tu. 183	F. 214	M. 245	W. 275	Sa. 306	M. 336
3	Th. 3	Su. 34	Su. 62	W. 93	F. 123	M. 154	W. 184	Sa. 215	Tu. 246	Th. 276	Su. 307	Tu. 337
4	F. 4	M. 35	M. 63	Th. 94	Sa. 124	Tu. 155	Th. 185	Su. 216	W. 247	F. 277	M. 308	W. 338
5	Sa. 5	Tu. 36	Tu. 64	F. 95	Su. 125	W. 156	F. 186	M. 217	Th. 248	Sa. 278	Tu. 309	Th. 339
6	Su. 6	W. 37	W. 65	Sa. 96	M. 126	Th. 157	Sa. 187	Tu. 218	F. 249	Su. 279	W. 310	F. 340
7	M. 7	Th. 38	Th. 66	Su. 97	Tu. 127	F. 158	Su. 188	W. 219	Sa. 250	M. 280	Th. 311	Sa. 341
8	Tu. 8	F. 39	F. 67	M. 98	W. 128	Sa. 159	M. 189	Th. 220	Su. 251	Tu. 281	F. 312	Su. 342
9	W. 9	Sa. 40	Sa. 68	Tu. 99	Th. 129	Su. 160	Tu. 190	F. 221	M. 252	W. 282	Sa. 313	M. 343
10	Th. 10	Su. 41	Su. 69	W. 100	F. 130	M. 161	W. 191	Sa. 222	Tu. 253	Th. 283	Su. 314	Tu. 344
11	F. 11	M. 42	M. 70	Th. 101	Sa. 131	Tu. 162	Th. 192	Su. 223	W. 254	F. 284	M. 315	W. 345
12	Sa. 12	Tu. 43	Tu. 71	F. 102	Su. 132	W. 163	F. 193	M. 224	Th. 255	Sa. 285	Tu. 316	Th. 346
13	Su. 13	W. 44	W. 72	Sa. 103	M. 133	Th. 164	Sa. 194	Tu. 225	F. 256	Su. 286	W. 317	F. 347
14	M. 14	Th. 45	Th. 73	Su. 104	Tu. 134	F. 165	Su. 195	W. 226	Sa. 257	M. 287	Th. 318	Sa. 348
15	Tu. 15	F. 46	F. 74	M. 105	W. 135	Sa. 166	M. 196	Th. 227	Su. 258	Tu. 288	F. 319	Su. 349
16	W. 16	Sa. 47	Sa. 75	Tu. 106	Th. 136	Su. 167	Tu. 197	F. 228	M. 259	W. 289	Sa. 320	M. 350
17	Th. 17	Su. 48	Su. 76	W. 107	F. 137	M. 168	W. 198	Sa. 229	Tu. 260	Th. 290	Su. 321	Tu. 351
18	F. 18	M. 49	M. 77	Th. 108	Sa. 138	Tu. 169	Th. 199	Su. 230	W. 261	F. 291	M. 322	W. 352
19	Sa. 19	Tu. 50	Tu. 78	F. 109	Su. 139	W. 170	F. 200	M. 231	Th. 262	Sa. 292	Tu. 323	Th. 353
20	Su. 20	W. 51	W. 79	Sa. 110	M. 140	Th. 171	Sa. 201	Tu. 232	F. 263	Su. 293	W. 324	F. 354
21	M. 21	Th. 52	Th. 80	Su. 111	Tu. 141	F. 172	Su. 202	W. 233	Sa. 264	M. 294	Th. 325	Sa. 355
22	Tu. 22	F. 53	F. 81	M. 112	W. 142	Sa. 173	M. 203	Th. 234	Su. 265	Tu. 295	F. 326	Su. 356
23	W. 23	Sa. 54	Sa. 82	Tu. 113	Th. 143	Su. 174	Tu. 204	F. 235	M. 266	W. 296	Sa. 327	M. 357
24	Th. 24	Su. 55	Su. 83	W. 114	F. 144	M. 175	W. 205	Sa. 236	Tu. 267	Th. 297	Su. 328	Tu. 358
25	F. 25	M. 56	M. 84	Th. 115	Sa. 145	Tu. 176	Th. 206	Su. 237	W. 268	F. 298	M. 329	W. 359
26	Sa. 26	Tu. 57	Tu. 85	F. 116	Su. 146	W. 177	F. 207	M. 238	Th. 269	Sa. 299	Tu. 330	Th. 360
27	Su. 27	W. 58	W. 86	Sa. 117	M. 147	Th. 178	Sa. 208	Tu. 239	F. 270	Su. 300	W. 331	F. 361
28	M. 28	Th. 59	Th. 87	Su. 118	Tu. 148	F. 179	Su. 209	W. 240	Sa. 271	M. 301	Th. 332	Sa. 362
29	Tu. 29		F. 88	M. 119	W. 149	Sa. 180	M. 210	Th. 241	Su. 272	Tu. 302	F. 333	Su. 363
30	W. 30		Sa. 89	Tu. 120	Th. 150	Su. 181	Tu. 211	F. 242	M. 273	W. 303	Sa. 334	M. 364
31	Th. 31		Su. 90		F. 151		W. 212	Sa. 243		Th. 304		Tu. 365

ECLIPSES

There are three eclipses of the Sun and two of the Moon.

1. *A partial eclipse of the Sun*, January 5-6. See map on page 6. The eclipse begins at $23^h 34^m$ on January 5 and ends at $03^h 49^m$ on January 6. The time of greatest eclipse is $01^h 41^m$ on January 6, when 0.71 of the Sun's diameter is obscured.

2. *A total eclipse of the Moon*, January 21. The umbral eclipse begins at $03^h 34^m$ and ends at $06^h 51^m$. Totality lasts from $04^h 41^m$ to $05^h 44^m$. It is is visible from western Asia, most of Africa, Europe, the Americas and the eastern part of Russia.

3. *A total eclipse of the Sun*, July 2. See map on page 7. The eclipse begins at $16^h 55^m$ and ends at $21^h 51^m$; the total phase begins at $18^h 02^m$ and ends at $20^h 44^m$. The maximum duration of totality is $4^m 38^s$.

4. *A partial eclipse of the Moon*, July 16-17. The eclipse begins at $20^h 01^m$ on July 16 and ends at $23^h 00^m$ on July 16. The time of maximum eclipse is $21^h 31^m$ when 0·66 of the Moon's diameter is obscured. It is visible from most of Australasia, Indonesia, most of Asia, Africa, Europe and South America.

5. *An annular eclipse of the Sun*, December 26. See map on page 7. The eclipse begins at $02^h 30^m$ and ends at $08^h 06^m$; the annular phase begins at $03^h 36^m$ and ends at $07^h 00^m$. The maximum duration of annularity is $3^m 34^s$.

© British Crown Copyright 2018. All rights reserved.

PARTIAL SOLAR ECLIPSE OF 2019 JANUARY 5–6

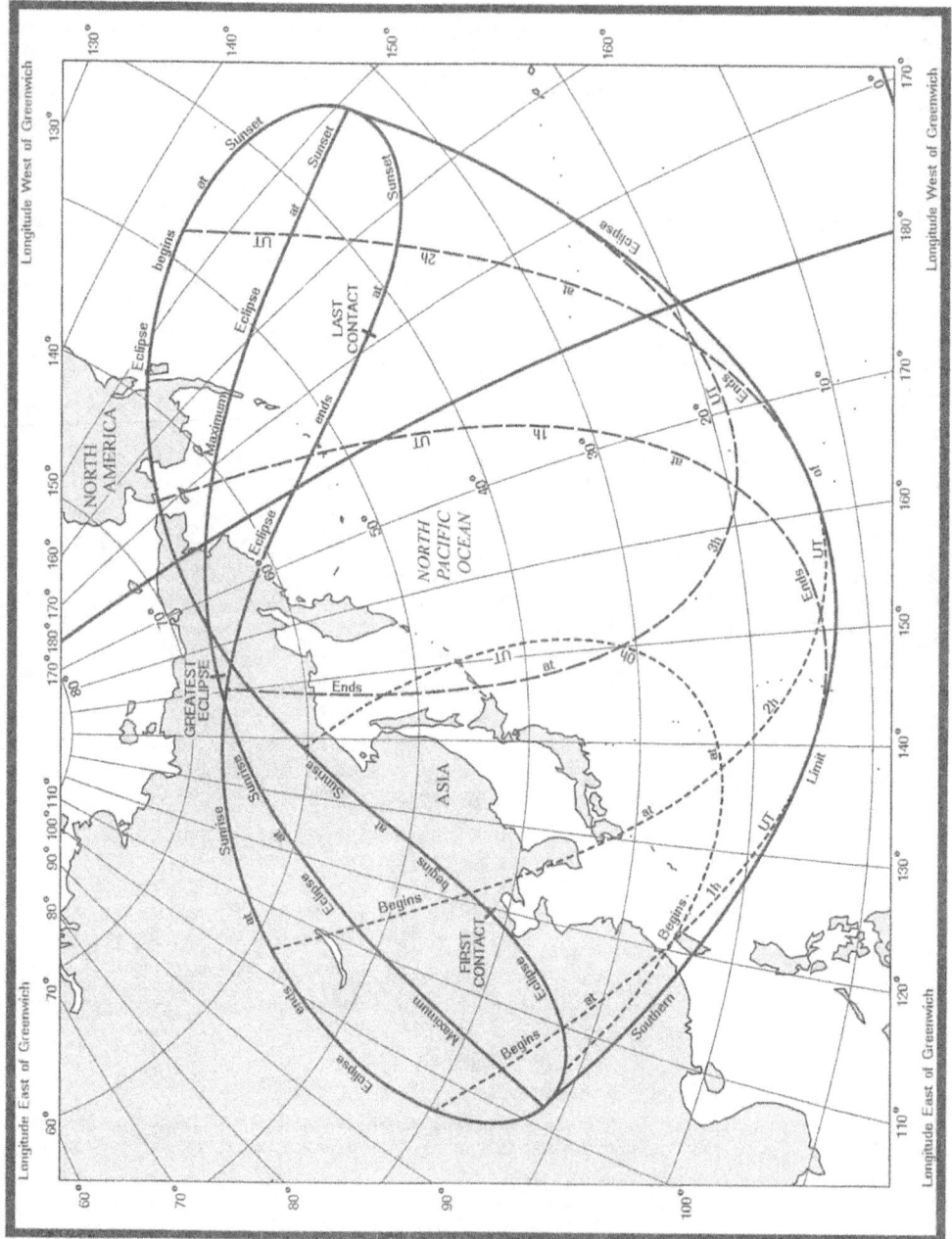

SOLAR ECLIPSE DIAGRAMS

The principal features shown on these diagrams are: the paths of total and annular eclipses; the northern and southern limits of partial eclipse; the sunrise and sunset curves; dashed lines which show the times of beginning and end of partial eclipse at hourly intervals. Further details of the paths and times of central eclipse are given in *The Astronomical Almanac*.

© British Crown Copyright 2018. All rights reserved.

TOTAL SOLAR ECLIPSE OF 2019 JULY 2

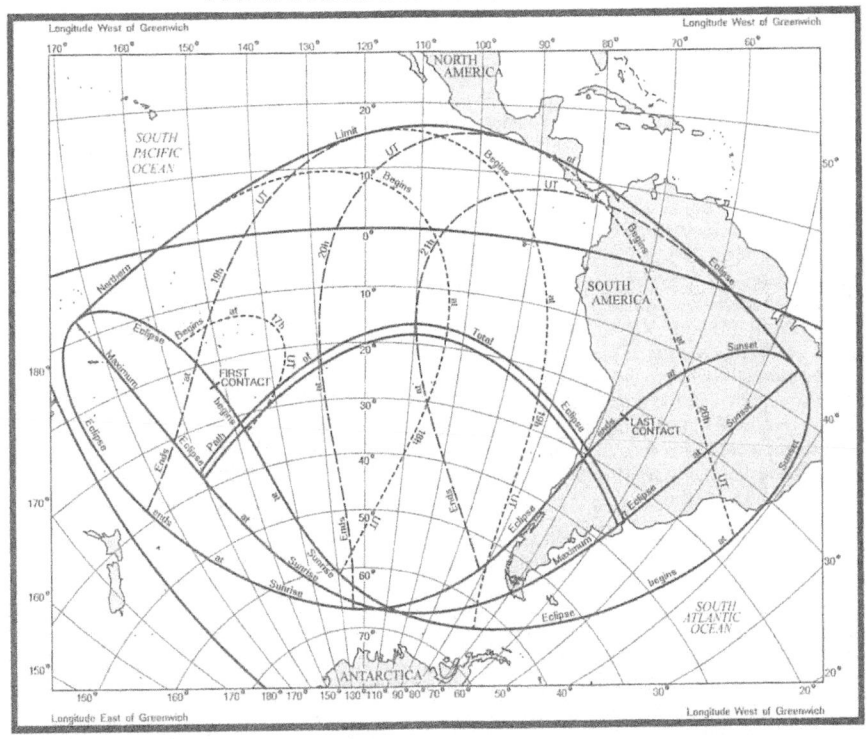

ANNULAR SOLAR ECLIPSE OF 2019 DECEMBER 26

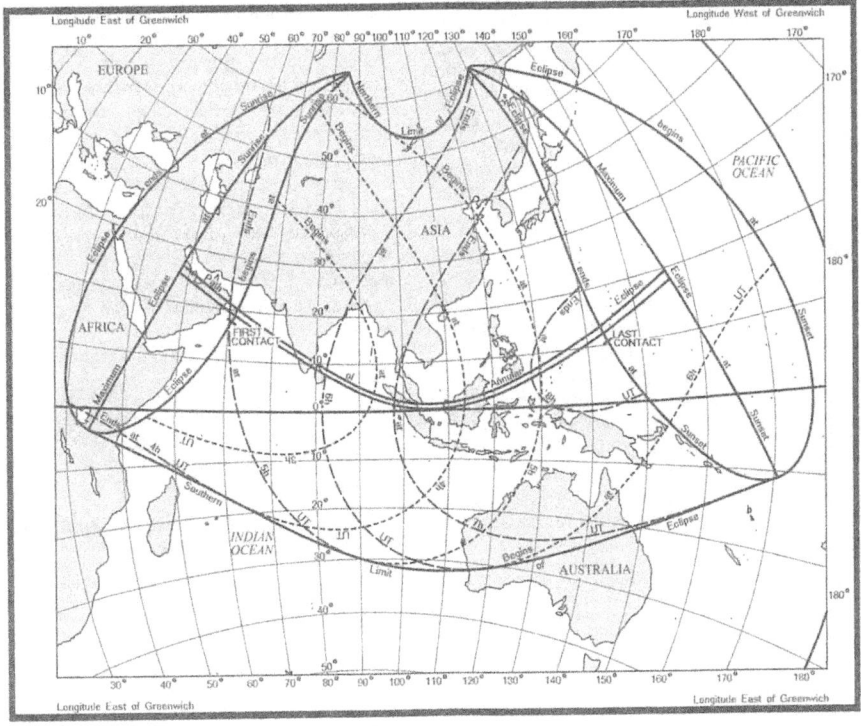

© British Crown Copyright 2018. All rights reserved.

VISIBILITY OF PLANETS

VENUS is a brilliant object in the morning sky from the beginning of the year until the second week of July when it becomes too close to the Sun for observation. It reappears in the second half of Sept. in the evening sky where it stays until the end of the year. Venus is in conjunction with Mercury on Oct. 30, with Jupiter on Jan. 22 and Nov. 24 and with Saturn on Feb. 18 and Dec. 11.

MARS is visible as a reddish object in Pisces in the evening sky at the beginning of the year. Its eastward elongation decreases as it moves through Aries from mid-Feb., Taurus from late March (passing 7° N. of *Aldebaran* on April 16), into Gemini from mid-May (passing 6° S. of *Pollux* on June 23) and into Cancer in late June. It becomes too close to the Sun for observation in mid-July. It reappears in the morning sky during the third week of Oct. in Virgo (passing 3° N. of *Spica* on Nov. 8) and then moves into Libra early in Dec., where it remains for the rest of the year. Mars is in conjunction with Mercury on June 18 and July 7.

JUPITER is visible in the morning sky in Ophiuchus at the beginning of the year. Its westward elongation increases and from mid-March it can be seen for more than half the night. It is at opposition on June 10 when it is visible throughout the night. By early Sept. it can only be seen in the evening sky. It moves into Sagittarius in mid-Nov. and from mid-Dec. becomes too close to the Sun for observation. Jupiter is in conjunction with Venus on Jan. 22 and Nov. 24.

SATURN is too close to the Sun for observation from the beginning of the year until the third week of Jan. when it rises just before sunrise in Sagittarius, in which constellation it remains throughout the year. Its westward elongation increases and in mid-April it becomes visible for more than half the night. It is at opposition on July 9 when it can be seen throughout the night. From early Oct. until late Dec. it can only be seen in the evening sky and then becomes too close to the Sun for observation for the remainder of the year. Saturn is in conjunction with Venus on Feb. 18 and Dec. 11.

MERCURY can only be seen low in the east before sunrise, or low in the west after sunset (about the time of beginning or end of civil twilight). It is visible in the mornings between the following approximate dates: Jan. 1 (−0·4) to Jan. 15 (−0·7), Mar. 22 (+2·9) to May 14 (−1·3), July 30 (+2·7) to Aug. 26 (−1·4) and Nov. 18 (+1·3) to Dec. 25 (−0·7); the planet is brighter at the end of each period. It is visible in the evenings between the following approximate dates: Feb. 11 (−1·2) to Mar. 8 (+2·0), May 29 (−1·4) to July 13 (+3·1) and Sept. 15 (−0·9) to Nov. 6 (+2·1); the planet is brighter at the beginning of each period. The figures in parentheses are the magnitudes.

PLANET DIAGRAM

General Description. The diagram on the opposite page shows, in graphical form for any date during the year, the local mean time of meridian passage of the Sun, of the five planets Mercury, Venus, Mars, Jupiter, and Saturn, and of each 30° of SHA; intermediate lines corresponding to particular stars, may be drawn in by the user if desired. It is intended to provide a general picture of the availability of planets and stars for observation.

On each side of the line marking the time of meridian passage of the Sun a band, 45^m wide, is shaded to indicate that planets and most stars crossing the meridian within 45^m of the Sun are too close to the Sun for observation.

Method of use and interpretation. For any date, the diagram provides immediately the local mean times of meridian passage of the Sun, planets and stars, and thus the following information:

(a) whether a planet or star is too close to the Sun for observation;

(b) some indication of its position in the sky, especially during twilight;

(c) the proximity of other planets.

When the meridian passage of an outer planet occurs at midnight, the body is in opposition to the Sun and is visible all night; a planet may then be observable during both morning and evening twilights. As the time of meridian passage decreases, the body eventually ceases to be observable in the morning, but its altitude above the eastern horizon at sunset gradually increases; this continues until the body is on the meridian during evening twilight. From then onwards, the body is observable above the western horizon and its altitude at sunset gradually decreases; eventually the body becomes too close to the Sun for observation. When the body again becomes visible it is seen low in the east during morning twilight; its altitude at sunrise increases until meridian passage occurs during morning twilight. Then, as the time of meridian passage decreases to 0^h, the body is observable in the west during morning twilight with a gradually decreasing altitude, until it once again reaches opposition.

DO NOT CONFUSE

Venus with Jupiter in late January and late November, with Saturn in mid-February and mid-December and with Mercury in mid-April, late September and late October to early November; on all occasions Venus is the brighter object.

Mercury with Mars from mid-June to mid-July when Mercury is the brighter object.

© British Crown Copyright 2018. All rights reserved.

LOCAL MEAN TIME OF MERIDIAN PASSAGE

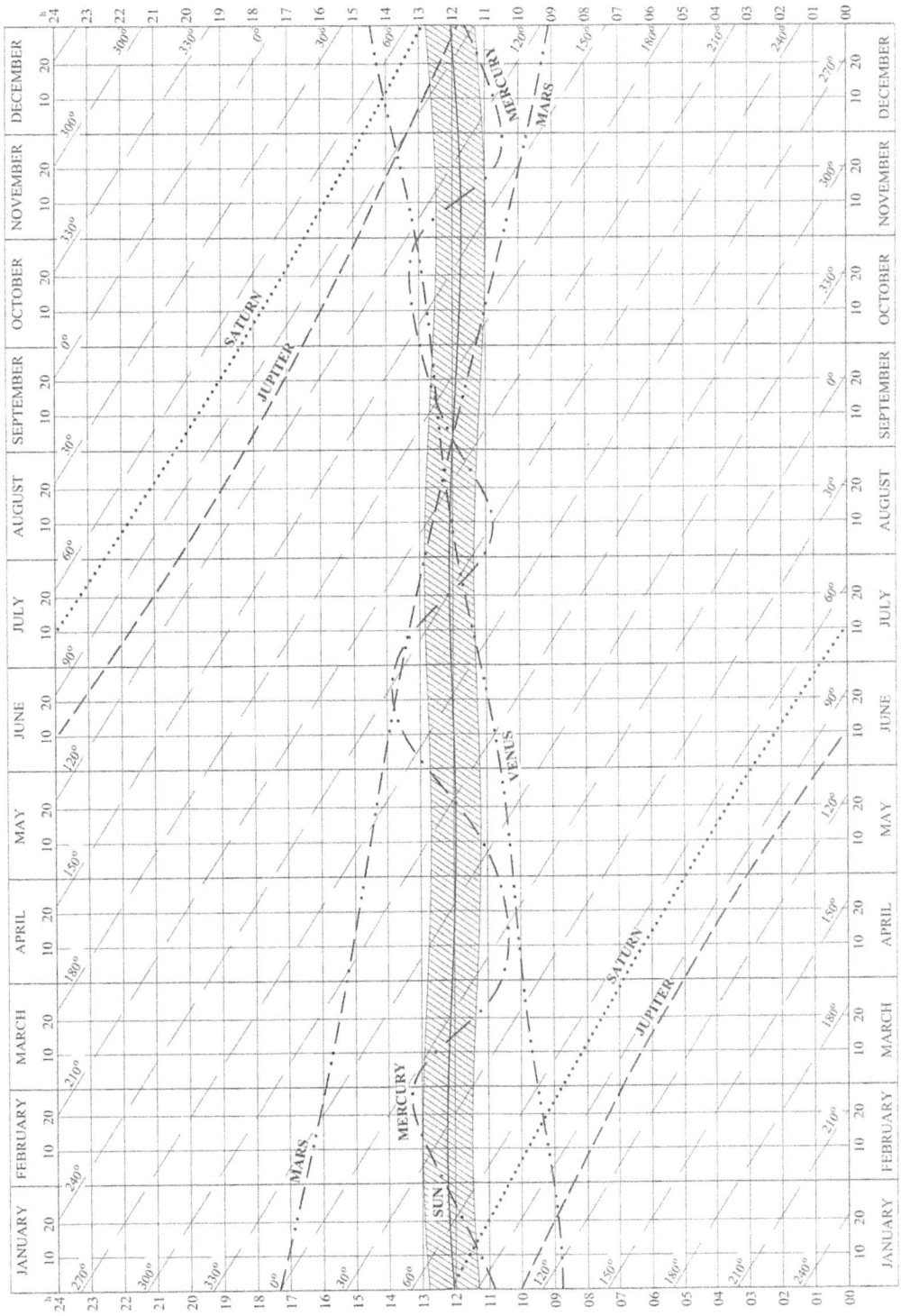

LOCAL MEAN TIME OF MERIDIAN PASSAGE

© British Crown Copyright 2018. All rights reserved.

UT	ARIES GHA	VENUS −4.6 GHA	Dec	MARS +0.5 GHA	Dec	JUPITER −1.8 GHA	Dec	SATURN +0.5 GHA	Dec	Name	SHA	Dec
1 00	100 21.4	228 21.4	S15 18.7	100 17.9	S 0 18.0	210 00.8	S21 34.3	178 01.9	S22 28.0	Acamar	315 15.2	S40 14.1
01	115 23.9	243 21.4	19.3	115 18.8	17.2	225 02.7	34.4	193 04.1	28.0	Achernar	335 23.8	S57 08.9
02	130 26.3	258 21.4	19.8	130 19.8	16.5	240 04.6	34.5	208 06.2	28.0	Acrux	173 05.0	S63 11.9
03	145 28.8	273 21.4 ..	20.4	145 20.7 ..	15.8	255 06.5 ..	34.5	223 08.3 ..	28.0	Adhara	255 09.2	S29 00.0
04	160 31.3	288 21.4	21.0	160 21.7	15.1	270 08.4	34.6	238 10.5	27.9	Aldebaran	290 44.7	N16 32.7
05	175 33.7	303 21.4	21.6	175 22.6	14.4	285 10.3	34.7	253 12.6	27.9			
06	190 36.2	318 21.3	S15 22.2	190 23.6	S 0 13.6	300 12.2	S21 34.7	268 14.8	S22 27.9	Alioth	166 17.4	N55 51.2
07	205 38.6	333 21.3	22.8	205 24.5	12.9	315 14.1	34.8	283 16.9	27.9	Alkaid	152 56.1	N49 13.0
T 08	220 41.1	348 21.3	23.3	220 25.4	12.2	330 16.1	34.9	298 19.1	27.8	Alnair	27 39.3	S46 52.4
U 09	235 43.6	3 21.3 ..	23.9	235 26.4 ..	11.5	345 18.0 ..	35.0	313 21.2 ..	27.8	Alnilam	275 42.2	S 1 11.6
E 10	250 46.0	18 21.3	24.5	250 27.3	10.8	0 19.9	35.0	328 23.4	27.8	Alphard	217 52.1	S 8 44.5
S 11	265 48.5	33 21.3	25.1	265 28.3	10.0	15 21.8	35.1	343 25.5	27.8			
D 12	280 51.0	48 21.3	S15 25.7	280 29.2	S 0 09.3	30 23.7	S21 35.2	358 27.7	S22 27.7	Alphecca	126 08.1	N26 39.1
A 13	295 53.4	63 21.3	26.2	295 30.2	08.6	45 25.6	35.2	13 29.8	27.7	Alpheratz	357 39.6	N29 11.8
Y 14	310 55.9	78 21.3	26.8	310 31.1	07.9	60 27.5	35.3	28 31.9	27.7	Altair	62 04.9	N 8 55.2
15	325 58.4	93 21.2 ..	27.4	325 32.1 ..	07.2	75 29.4 ..	35.4	43 34.1 ..	27.7	Ankaa	353 12.0	S42 12.5
16	341 00.8	108 21.2	28.0	340 33.0	06.4	90 31.3	35.5	58 36.2	27.7	Antares	112 21.9	S26 28.2
17	356 03.3	123 21.2	28.6	355 34.0	05.7	105 33.2	35.5	73 38.4	27.6			
18	11 05.8	138 21.2	S15 29.2	10 34.9	S 0 05.0	120 35.1	S21 35.6	88 40.5	S22 27.6	Arcturus	145 52.4	N19 05.0
19	26 08.2	153 21.2	29.7	25 35.8	04.3	135 37.0	35.7	103 42.7	27.6	Atria	107 20.9	S69 03.3
20	41 10.7	168 21.1	30.3	40 36.8	03.6	150 38.9	35.7	118 44.8	27.6	Avior	234 15.9	S59 34.2
21	56 13.1	183 21.1 ..	30.9	55 37.7 ..	02.8	165 40.8 ..	35.8	133 47.0 ..	27.5	Bellatrix	278 27.6	N 6 21.8
22	71 15.6	198 21.1	31.5	70 38.7	02.1	180 42.7	35.9	148 49.1	27.5	Betelgeuse	270 56.9	N 7 24.4
23	86 18.1	213 21.1	32.1	85 39.6	01.4	195 44.6	35.9	163 51.3	27.5			
2 00	101 20.5	228 21.0	S15 32.6	100 40.6	S 0 00.7	210 46.5	S21 36.0	178 53.4	S22 27.5	Canopus	263 53.9	S52 42.5
01	116 23.0	243 21.0	33.2	115 41.5	00.0	225 48.5	36.1	193 55.5	27.4	Capella	280 28.4	N46 00.9
02	131 25.5	258 21.0	33.8	130 42.5	N 00.8	240 50.4	36.2	208 57.7	27.4	Deneb	49 29.3	N45 21.0
03	146 27.9	273 21.0 ..	34.4	145 43.4 ..	01.5	255 52.3 ..	36.2	223 59.8 ..	27.4	Denebola	182 29.8	N14 27.9
04	161 30.4	288 20.9	35.0	160 44.3	02.2	270 54.2	36.3	239 02.0	27.4	Diphda	348 52.1	S17 53.2
05	176 32.9	303 20.9	35.5	175 45.3	02.9	285 56.1	36.4	254 04.1	27.4			
06	191 35.3	318 20.9	S15 36.1	190 46.2	N 0 03.6	300 58.0	S21 36.4	269 06.3	S22 27.3	Dubhe	193 46.8	N61 38.7
W 07	206 37.8	333 20.8	36.7	205 47.2	04.4	315 59.9	36.5	284 08.4	27.3	Elnath	278 07.5	N28 37.2
E 08	221 40.3	348 20.8	37.3	220 48.1	05.1	331 01.8	36.6	299 10.6	27.3	Eltanin	90 44.9	N51 29.2
D 09	236 42.7	3 20.8 ..	37.9	235 49.1 ..	05.8	346 03.7 ..	36.7	314 12.7 ..	27.3	Enif	33 43.7	N 9 57.7
N 10	251 45.2	18 20.7	38.4	250 50.0	06.5	1 05.6	36.7	329 14.9	27.2	Fomalhaut	15 20.0	S29 31.5
E 11	266 47.6	33 20.7	39.0	265 50.9	07.2	16 07.5	36.8	344 17.0	27.2			
S 12	281 50.1	48 20.7	S15 39.6	280 51.9	N 0 08.0	31 09.4	S21 36.9	359 19.2	S22 27.2	Gacrux	171 56.6	S57 12.8
D 13	296 52.6	63 20.6	40.2	295 52.8	08.7	46 11.3	36.9	14 21.3	27.2	Gienah	175 48.4	S17 38.7
A 14	311 55.0	78 20.6	40.8	310 53.8	09.4	61 13.2	37.0	29 23.4	27.2	Hadar	148 42.7	S60 27.4
Y 15	326 57.5	93 20.5 ..	41.3	325 54.7 ..	10.1	76 15.2 ..	37.1	44 25.6 ..	27.1	Hamal	327 56.4	N23 33.1
16	342 00.0	108 20.5	41.9	340 55.7	10.8	91 17.1	37.1	59 27.7	27.1	Kaus Aust.	83 39.2	S34 22.4
17	357 02.4	123 20.5	42.5	355 56.6	11.6	106 19.0	37.2	74 29.9	27.1			
18	12 04.9	138 20.4	S15 43.1	10 57.6	N 0 12.3	121 20.9	S21 37.3	89 32.0	S22 27.1	Kochab	137 20.8	N74 04.5
19	27 07.4	153 20.4	43.7	25 58.5	13.0	136 22.8	37.3	104 34.2	27.1	Markab	13 34.7	N15 18.4
20	42 09.8	168 20.3	44.2	40 59.4	13.7	151 24.7	37.4	119 36.3	27.0	Menkar	314 10.9	N 4 09.7
21	57 12.3	183 20.3 ..	44.8	56 00.4 ..	14.4	166 26.6 ..	37.5	134 38.5 ..	27.0	Menkent	148 03.3	S36 27.5
22	72 14.8	198 20.2	45.4	71 01.3	15.2	181 28.5	37.6	149 40.6	27.0	Miaplacidus	221 38.1	S69 47.5
23	87 17.2	213 20.2	46.0	86 02.3	15.9	196 30.4	37.6	164 42.8	27.0			
3 00	102 19.7	228 20.1	S15 46.5	101 03.2	N 0 16.6	211 32.3	S21 37.7	179 44.9	S22 26.9	Mirfak	308 34.6	N49 55.7
01	117 22.1	243 20.1	47.1	116 04.2	17.3	226 34.2	37.8	194 47.0	26.9	Nunki	75 54.0	S26 16.3
02	132 24.6	258 20.0	47.7	131 05.1	18.0	241 36.1	37.8	209 49.2	26.9	Peacock	53 13.9	S56 40.5
03	147 27.1	273 20.0 ..	48.3	146 06.0 ..	18.8	256 38.1 ..	37.9	224 51.3 ..	26.9	Pollux	243 22.8	N27 58.6
04	162 29.5	288 19.9	48.9	161 07.0	19.5	271 40.0	38.0	239 53.5	26.8	Procyon	244 55.5	N 5 10.4
05	177 32.0	303 19.9	49.4	176 07.9	20.2	286 41.9	38.0	254 55.6	26.8			
06	192 34.5	318 19.8	S15 50.0	191 08.9	N 0 20.9	301 43.8	S21 38.1	269 57.8	S22 26.8	Rasalhague	96 03.3	N12 32.9
07	207 36.9	333 19.8	50.6	206 09.8	21.6	316 45.7	38.2	284 59.9	26.8	Regulus	207 39.3	N11 52.4
T 08	222 39.4	348 19.7	51.2	221 10.8	22.4	331 47.6	38.3	300 02.1	26.8	Rigel	281 08.1	S 8 11.0
H 09	237 41.9	3 19.6 ..	51.7	236 11.7 ..	23.1	346 49.5 ..	38.3	315 04.2 ..	26.7	Rigil Kent.	139 46.9	S60 54.3
U 10	252 44.3	18 19.6	52.3	251 12.6	23.8	1 51.4	38.4	330 06.3	26.7	Sabik	102 08.5	S15 44.7
R 11	267 46.8	33 19.5	52.9	266 13.6	24.5	16 53.3	38.5	345 08.5	26.7			
S 12	282 49.2	48 19.5	S15 53.5	281 14.5	N 0 25.2	31 55.2	S21 38.5	0 10.6	S22 26.7	Schedar	349 36.2	N56 38.6
D 13	297 51.7	63 19.4	54.1	296 15.5	26.0	46 57.1	38.6	15 12.8	26.6	Shaula	96 17.2	S37 06.8
A 14	312 54.2	78 19.3	54.6	311 16.4	26.7	61 59.1	38.7	30 14.9	26.6	Sirius	258 30.0	S16 44.7
Y 15	327 56.6	93 19.3 ..	55.2	326 17.4 ..	27.4	77 01.0 ..	38.7	45 17.1 ..	26.6	Spica	158 27.3	S11 15.4
16	342 59.1	108 19.2	55.8	341 18.3	28.1	92 02.9	38.8	60 19.2	26.6	Suhail	222 49.3	S43 30.5
17	358 01.6	123 19.1	56.4	356 19.2	28.8	107 04.8	38.9	75 21.4	26.6			
18	13 04.0	138 19.1	S15 56.9	11 20.2	N 0 29.6	122 06.7	S21 38.9	90 23.5	S22 26.5	Vega	80 36.8	N38 48.2
19	28 06.5	153 19.0	57.5	26 21.1	30.3	137 08.6	39.0	105 25.7	26.5	Zuben'ubi	137 01.4	S16 07.0
20	43 09.0	168 18.9	58.1	41 22.1	31.0	152 10.5	39.1	120 27.8	26.5			
21	58 11.4	183 18.9 ..	58.7	56 23.0 ..	31.7	167 12.4 ..	39.1	135 29.9 ..	26.5		SHA	Mer.Pass.
22	73 13.9	198 18.8	59.2	71 23.9	32.4	182 14.3	39.2	150 32.1	26.4	Venus	127 00.5	8 47
23	88 16.4	213 18.7	59.8	86 24.9	33.2	197 16.3	39.3	165 34.2	26.4	Mars	359 20.0	17 16
Mer.Pass. 17 11.8		v 0.0	d 0.6	v 0.9	d 0.7	v 1.9	d 0.1	v 2.1	d 0.0	Jupiter	109 26.0	9 56
										Saturn	77 32.9	12 03

© British Crown Copyright 2018. All rights reserved.

UT	SUN GHA	SUN Dec	MOON GHA	v	Dec	d	HP
d h	° ′	° ′	° ′	′	° ′	′	′
1 00	179 11.9	S23 02.3	238 51.3	12.3	S10 42.3	10.4	56.6
01	194 11.6	02.1	253 22.6	12.2	10 52.7	10.3	56.6
02	209 11.3	01.9	267 53.8	12.3	11 03.0	10.3	56.6
03	224 11.0	.. 01.7	282 25.1	12.2	11 13.3	10.3	56.6
04	239 10.7	01.5	296 56.3	12.2	11 23.6	10.1	56.6
05	254 10.4	01.3	311 27.5	12.2	11 33.7	10.1	56.5
06	269 10.1	S23 01.1	325 58.7	12.2	S11 43.8	10.1	56.5
07	284 09.8	00.9	340 29.9	12.1	11 53.9	9.9	56.5
T 08	299 09.5	00.7	355 01.0	12.2	12 03.8	9.9	56.5
U 09	314 09.2	.. 00.5	9 32.2	12.1	12 13.7	9.9	56.4
E 10	329 08.9	00.3	24 03.3	12.1	12 23.6	9.7	56.4
S 11	344 08.6	23 00.1	38 34.4	12.1	12 33.3	9.7	56.4
D 12	359 08.3	S22 59.9	53 05.5	12.1	S12 43.0	9.7	56.4
A 13	14 08.0	59.7	67 36.6	12.1	12 52.7	9.5	56.3
Y 14	29 07.7	59.5	82 07.7	12.0	13 02.2	9.5	56.3
15	44 07.4	.. 59.3	96 38.7	12.1	13 11.7	9.5	56.3
16	59 07.1	59.1	111 09.8	12.0	13 21.2	9.3	56.3
17	74 06.8	58.9	125 40.8	12.0	13 30.5	9.3	56.2
18	89 06.5	S22 58.7	140 11.8	12.0	S13 39.8	9.2	56.2
19	104 06.2	58.5	154 42.8	11.9	13 49.0	9.1	56.2
20	119 05.9	58.3	169 13.7	12.0	13 58.1	9.1	56.2
21	134 05.7	.. 58.0	183 44.7	11.9	14 07.2	9.0	56.2
22	149 05.4	57.8	198 15.6	11.9	14 16.2	8.9	56.1
23	164 05.1	57.6	212 46.5	11.9	14 25.1	8.8	56.1
2 00	179 04.8	S22 57.4	227 17.4	11.9	S14 33.9	8.8	56.1
01	194 04.5	57.2	241 48.3	11.8	14 42.7	8.7	56.1
02	209 04.2	57.0	256 19.1	11.8	14 51.4	8.6	56.0
03	224 03.9	.. 56.7	270 49.9	11.8	15 00.0	8.5	56.0
04	239 03.6	56.5	285 20.7	11.8	15 08.5	8.5	56.0
05	254 03.3	56.3	299 51.5	11.8	15 17.0	8.3	56.0
06	269 03.0	S22 56.1	314 22.3	11.7	S15 25.3	8.3	56.0
W 07	284 02.7	55.9	328 53.0	11.7	15 33.6	8.2	55.9
E 08	299 02.4	55.7	343 23.7	11.7	15 41.8	8.1	55.9
D 09	314 02.1	.. 55.4	357 54.4	11.7	15 49.9	8.1	55.9
N 10	329 01.8	55.2	12 25.1	11.6	15 58.0	7.9	55.9
E 11	344 01.5	55.0	26 55.7	11.7	16 05.9	7.9	55.9
S 12	359 01.2	S22 54.8	41 26.4	11.6	S16 13.8	7.8	55.8
D 13	14 01.0	54.5	55 57.0	11.6	16 21.6	7.7	55.8
A 14	29 00.7	54.3	70 27.6	11.5	16 29.3	7.6	55.8
Y 15	44 00.4	.. 54.1	84 58.1	11.6	16 36.9	7.6	55.8
16	59 00.1	53.9	99 28.7	11.5	16 44.5	7.4	55.8
17	73 59.8	53.6	113 59.2	11.5	16 51.9	7.4	55.7
18	88 59.5	S22 53.4	128 29.7	11.5	S16 59.3	7.2	55.7
19	103 59.2	53.2	143 00.2	11.5	17 06.5	7.2	55.7
20	118 58.9	52.9	157 30.7	11.4	17 13.7	7.1	55.7
21	133 58.6	.. 52.7	172 01.1	11.4	17 20.8	7.0	55.7
22	148 58.3	52.5	186 31.5	11.4	17 27.8	6.9	55.6
23	163 58.0	52.2	201 01.9	11.4	17 34.7	6.9	55.6
3 00	178 57.8	S22 52.0	215 32.3	11.3	S17 41.6	6.7	55.6
01	193 57.5	51.8	230 02.6	11.4	17 48.3	6.7	55.6
02	208 57.2	51.5	244 33.0	11.3	17 55.0	6.5	55.6
03	223 56.9	.. 51.3	259 03.3	11.3	18 01.5	6.5	55.5
04	238 56.6	51.1	273 33.6	11.2	18 08.0	6.3	55.5
05	253 56.3	50.8	288 03.8	11.3	18 14.3	6.3	55.5
06	268 56.0	S22 50.6	302 34.1	11.2	S18 20.6	6.2	55.5
07	283 55.7	50.3	317 04.3	11.2	18 26.8	6.0	55.5
T 08	298 55.4	50.1	331 34.5	11.2	18 32.9	6.0	55.4
H 09	313 55.1	.. 49.9	346 04.7	11.2	18 38.9	5.9	55.4
U 10	328 54.9	49.6	0 34.9	11.2	18 44.8	5.8	55.4
R 11	343 54.6	49.4	15 05.1	11.1	18 50.6	5.7	55.4
S 12	358 54.3	S22 49.1	29 35.2	11.1	S18 56.3	5.6	55.4
D 13	13 54.0	48.9	44 05.3	11.1	19 01.9	5.5	55.4
A 14	28 53.7	48.6	58 35.4	11.1	19 07.4	5.4	55.3
Y 15	43 53.4	.. 48.4	73 05.5	11.1	19 12.8	5.3	55.3
16	58 53.1	48.2	87 35.6	11.1	19 18.1	5.2	55.3
17	73 52.8	47.9	102 05.7	11.0	19 23.3	5.2	55.3
18	88 52.5	S22 47.7	116 35.7	11.0	S19 28.5	5.0	55.3
19	103 52.3	47.4	131 05.7	11.0	19 33.5	4.9	55.3
20	118 52.0	47.2	145 35.7	11.0	19 38.4	4.8	55.2
21	133 51.7	.. 46.9	160 05.7	11.0	19 43.2	4.7	55.2
22	148 51.4	46.7	174 35.7	10.9	19 47.9	4.7	55.2
23	163 51.1	46.4	189 05.6	11.0	S19 52.6	4.5	55.2
	SD 16.3 d 0.2		SD 15.4		15.2		15.1

Lat.	Twilight Naut.	Civil	Sunrise	Moonrise 1	2	3	4
°	h m	h m	h m	h m	h m	h m	h m
N 72	08 23	10 40	▉▉▉	04 52	07 04	▉▉▉	▉▉▉
N 70	08 04	09 48	▉▉▉	04 31	06 24	08 28	▉▉▉
68	07 49	09 16	▉▉▉	04 14	05 56	07 39	09 21
66	07 37	08 52	10 26	04 01	05 36	07 08	08 34
64	07 26	08 34	09 49	03 51	05 19	06 45	08 03
62	07 17	08 18	09 22	03 41	05 06	06 27	07 41
60	07 09	08 05	09 02	03 34	04 54	06 12	07 23
N 58	07 02	07 54	08 45	03 27	04 44	05 59	07 07
56	06 55	07 44	08 31	03 21	04 36	05 48	06 54
54	06 50	07 35	08 19	03 15	04 28	05 38	06 43
52	06 44	07 28	08 08	03 10	04 21	05 30	06 33
50	06 39	07 20	07 58	03 06	04 15	05 22	06 24
45	06 28	07 05	07 38	02 57	04 02	05 06	06 06
N 40	06 18	06 52	07 22	02 49	03 51	04 52	05 51
35	06 09	06 40	07 08	02 42	03 42	04 41	05 38
30	06 00	06 30	06 56	02 36	03 34	04 31	05 26
20	05 44	06 11	06 35	02 26	03 20	04 14	05 07
N 10	05 28	05 54	06 17	02 17	03 08	03 59	04 51
0	05 12	05 38	06 00	02 09	02 57	03 46	04 35
S 10	04 53	05 20	05 43	02 01	02 46	03 32	04 20
20	04 31	05 00	05 25	01 52	02 34	03 18	04 03
30	04 02	04 36	05 03	01 43	02 21	03 01	03 45
35	03 44	04 21	04 50	01 37	02 13	02 51	03 34
40	03 22	04 03	04 35	01 31	02 04	02 41	03 21
45	02 52	03 41	04 18	01 23	01 54	02 28	03 06
S 50	02 08	03 12	03 56	01 15	01 41	02 12	02 48
52	01 42	02 57	03 45	01 11	01 36	02 05	02 40
54	01 03	02 40	03 34	01 06	01 29	01 57	02 30
56	////	02 19	03 20	01 01	01 22	01 48	02 20
58	////	01 51	03 05	00 56	01 15	01 38	02 07
S 60	////	01 08	02 44	00 50	01 06	01 26	01 53

Lat.	Sunset	Twilight Civil	Naut.	Moonset 1	2	3	4
°	h m	h m	h m	h m	h m	h m	h m
N 72	▉▉▉	13 28	15 45	11 30	10 58	▉▉▉	▉▉▉
N 70	▉▉▉	14 20	16 04	11 53	11 40	11 17	▉▉▉
68	▉▉▉	14 52	16 19	12 10	12 08	12 07	12 09
66	13 42	15 16	16 31	12 25	12 30	12 39	12 56
64	14 19	15 34	16 42	12 36	12 47	13 02	13 26
62	14 46	15 50	16 51	12 46	13 01	13 21	13 49
60	15 06	16 03	16 59	12 55	13 13	13 36	14 08
N 58	15 23	16 14	17 06	13 03	13 24	13 50	14 23
56	15 37	16 24	17 13	13 10	13 33	14 01	14 36
54	15 49	16 33	17 19	13 16	13 41	14 11	14 48
52	16 00	16 41	17 24	13 21	13 48	14 20	14 58
50	16 10	16 48	17 29	13 26	13 55	14 28	15 07
45	16 30	17 03	17 40	13 37	14 09	14 45	15 26
N 40	16 46	17 16	17 50	13 46	14 21	14 59	15 42
35	17 00	17 28	17 59	13 53	14 31	15 11	15 55
30	17 12	17 38	18 08	14 00	14 39	15 21	16 06
20	17 33	17 56	18 24	14 12	14 55	15 39	16 26
N 10	17 51	18 13	18 40	14 22	15 08	15 55	16 43
0	18 08	18 30	18 56	14 32	15 20	16 09	16 59
S 10	18 25	18 48	19 15	14 42	15 33	16 24	17 15
20	18 43	19 08	19 37	14 52	15 46	16 40	17 33
30	19 05	19 32	20 05	15 04	16 02	16 58	17 52
35	19 17	19 47	20 23	15 11	16 11	17 08	18 04
40	19 32	20 05	20 46	15 19	16 21	17 21	18 17
45	19 50	20 27	21 15	15 28	16 33	17 35	18 33
S 50	20 11	20 55	21 59	15 39	16 47	17 52	18 52
52	20 22	21 10	22 24	15 45	16 54	18 00	19 01
54	20 34	21 27	23 03	15 50	17 02	18 10	19 11
56	20 47	21 48	////	15 57	17 10	18 20	19 23
58	21 03	22 15	////	16 04	17 20	18 32	19 36
S 60	21 23	22 57	////	16 12	17 31	18 46	19 52

Day	SUN Eqn. of Time 00h	12h	Mer. Pass.	MOON Mer. Pass. Upper	Lower	Age	Phase
d	m s	m s	h m	h m	h m	d	%
1	03 12	03 26	12 03	08 21	20 45	25	19
2	03 40	03 54	12 04	09 09	21 33	26	12
3	04 08	04 22	12 04	09 58	22 22	27	6

© British Crown Copyright 2018. All rights reserved.

2019 JANUARY 4, 5, 6 (FRI., SAT., SUN.)

UT	ARIES GHA	VENUS −4.6 GHA	Dec	MARS +0.5 GHA	Dec	JUPITER −1.8 GHA	Dec	SATURN +0.5 GHA	Dec	STARS Name	SHA	Dec
4 00	103 18.8	228 18.7	S16 00.4	101 25.8	N 0 33.9	212 18.2	S21 39.3	180 36.4	S22 26.4	Acamar	315 15.2	S40 14.1
01	118 21.3	243 18.6	01.0	116 26.8	34.6	227 20.1	39.4	195 38.5	26.4	Achernar	335 23.9	S57 08.9
02	133 23.7	258 18.5	01.5	131 27.7	35.3	242 22.0	39.5	210 40.7	26.3	Acrux	173 04.9	S63 11.9
03	148 26.2	273 18.4	.. 02.1	146 28.6	.. 36.0	257 23.9	.. 39.6	225 42.8	.. 26.3	Adhara	255 09.2	S29 00.0
04	163 28.7	288 18.4	02.7	161 29.6	36.8	272 25.8	39.6	240 45.0	26.3	Aldebaran	290 44.7	N16 32.7
05	178 31.1	303 18.3	03.3	176 30.5	37.5	287 27.7	39.7	255 47.1	26.3			
06	193 33.6	318 18.2	S16 03.8	191 31.5	N 0 38.2	302 29.6	S21 39.8	270 49.3	S22 26.3	Alioth	166 17.4	N55 51.2
07	208 36.1	333 18.1	04.4	206 32.4	38.9	317 31.5	39.8	285 51.4	26.2	Alkaid	152 56.1	N49 13.0
08	223 38.5	348 18.0	05.0	221 33.4	39.6	332 33.4	39.9	300 53.5	26.2	Alnair	27 39.3	S46 52.4
F 09	238 41.0	3 18.0	.. 05.6	236 34.3	.. 40.4	347 35.4	.. 40.0	315 55.7	.. 26.2	Alnilam	275 42.2	S 1 11.6
R 10	253 43.5	18 17.9	06.1	251 35.2	41.1	2 37.3	40.0	330 57.8	26.2	Alphard	217 52.1	S 8 44.5
I 11	268 45.9	33 17.8	06.7	266 36.2	41.8	17 39.2	40.1	346 00.0	26.1			
D 12	283 48.4	48 17.7	S16 07.3	281 37.1	N 0 42.5	32 41.1	S21 40.2	1 02.1	S22 26.1	Alphecca	126 08.1	N26 39.1
A 13	298 50.9	63 17.6	07.9	296 38.1	43.2	47 43.0	40.2	16 04.3	26.1	Alpheratz	357 39.6	N29 11.8
Y 14	313 53.3	78 17.5	08.4	311 39.0	44.0	62 44.9	40.3	31 06.4	26.1	Altair	62 04.9	N 8 55.2
15	328 55.8	93 17.5	.. 09.0	326 39.9	.. 44.7	77 46.8	.. 40.4	46 08.6	.. 26.0	Ankaa	353 12.0	S42 12.5
16	343 58.2	108 17.4	09.6	341 40.9	45.4	92 48.7	40.4	61 10.7	26.0	Antares	112 21.9	S26 28.2
17	359 00.7	123 17.3	10.1	356 41.8	46.1	107 50.7	40.5	76 12.9	26.0			
18	14 03.2	138 17.2	S16 10.7	11 42.8	N 0 46.8	122 52.6	S21 40.6	91 15.0	S22 26.0	Arcturus	145 52.4	N19 05.0
19	29 05.6	153 17.1	11.3	26 43.7	47.5	137 54.5	40.6	106 17.1	26.0	Atria	107 20.8	S69 03.3
20	44 08.1	168 17.0	11.9	41 44.6	48.3	152 56.4	40.7	121 19.3	25.9	Avior	234 15.8	S59 34.2
21	59 10.6	183 16.9	.. 12.4	56 45.6	.. 49.0	167 58.3	.. 40.8	136 21.4	.. 25.9	Bellatrix	278 27.6	N 6 21.8
22	74 13.0	198 16.8	13.0	71 46.5	49.7	183 00.2	40.8	151 23.6	25.9	Betelgeuse	270 56.9	N 7 24.4
23	89 15.5	213 16.7	13.6	86 47.5	50.4	198 02.1	40.9	166 25.7	25.9			
5 00	104 18.0	228 16.6	S16 14.1	101 48.4	N 0 51.1	213 04.0	S21 41.0	181 27.9	S22 25.8	Canopus	263 53.9	S52 42.5
01	119 20.4	243 16.5	14.7	116 49.3	51.9	228 06.0	41.0	196 30.0	25.8	Capella	280 28.4	N46 00.9
02	134 22.9	258 16.4	15.3	131 50.3	52.6	243 07.9	41.1	211 32.2	25.8	Deneb	49 29.3	N45 21.0
03	149 25.4	273 16.3	.. 15.9	146 51.2	.. 53.3	258 09.8	.. 41.2	226 34.3	.. 25.8	Denebola	182 29.7	N14 27.9
04	164 27.8	288 16.2	16.4	161 52.2	54.0	273 11.7	41.2	241 36.5	25.7	Diphda	348 52.1	S17 53.2
05	179 30.3	303 16.1	17.0	176 53.1	54.7	288 13.6	41.3	256 38.6	25.7			
06	194 32.7	318 16.0	S16 17.6	191 54.0	N 0 55.5	303 15.5	S21 41.4	271 40.7	S22 25.7	Dubhe	193 46.8	N61 38.7
07	209 35.2	333 15.9	18.1	206 55.0	56.2	318 17.4	41.4	286 42.9	25.7	Elnath	278 07.5	N28 37.2
S 08	224 37.7	348 15.8	18.7	221 55.9	56.9	333 19.3	41.5	301 45.0	25.7	Eltanin	90 44.9	N51 29.2
A 09	239 40.1	3 15.7	.. 19.3	236 56.9	.. 57.6	348 21.3	.. 41.6	316 47.2	.. 25.6	Enif	33 43.7	N 9 57.7
T 10	254 42.6	18 15.6	19.8	251 57.8	58.3	3 23.2	41.6	331 49.3	25.6	Fomalhaut	15 20.0	S29 31.5
U 11	269 45.1	33 15.5	20.4	266 58.7	59.1	18 25.1	41.7	346 51.5	25.6			
R 12	284 47.5	48 15.4	S16 21.0	281 59.7	N 0 59.8	33 27.0	S21 41.8	1 53.6	S22 25.6	Gacrux	171 56.6	S57 12.8
D 13	299 50.0	63 15.3	21.5	297 00.6	1 00.5	48 28.9	41.8	16 55.8	25.5	Gienah	175 48.3	S17 38.7
A 14	314 52.5	78 15.2	22.1	312 01.6	01.2	63 30.8	41.9	31 57.9	25.5	Hadar	148 42.7	S60 27.4
Y 15	329 54.9	93 15.1	.. 22.7	327 02.5	.. 01.9	78 32.7	.. 42.0	47 00.1	.. 25.5	Hamal	327 56.4	N23 33.1
16	344 57.4	108 15.0	23.3	342 03.4	02.6	93 34.7	42.0	62 02.2	25.5	Kaus Aust.	83 39.2	S34 22.4
17	359 59.9	123 14.9	23.8	357 04.4	03.4	108 36.6	42.1	77 04.3	25.4			
18	15 02.3	138 14.8	S16 24.4	12 05.3	N 1 04.1	123 38.5	S21 42.2	92 06.5	S22 25.4	Kochab	137 20.8	N74 04.5
19	30 04.8	153 14.6	25.0	27 06.2	04.8	138 40.4	42.2	107 08.6	25.4	Markab	13 34.7	N15 18.4
20	45 07.2	168 14.5	25.5	42 07.2	05.5	153 42.3	42.3	122 10.8	25.4	Menkar	314 10.9	N 4 09.7
21	60 09.7	183 14.4	.. 26.1	57 08.1	.. 06.2	168 44.2	.. 42.4	137 12.9	.. 25.3	Menkent	148 03.2	S36 27.5
22	75 12.2	198 14.3	26.7	72 09.1	07.0	183 46.1	42.4	152 15.1	25.3	Miaplacidus	221 38.0	S69 47.5
23	90 14.6	213 14.2	27.2	87 10.0	07.7	198 48.1	42.5	167 17.2	25.3			
6 00	105 17.1	228 14.1	S16 27.8	102 10.9	N 1 08.4	213 50.0	S21 42.6	182 19.4	S22 25.3	Mirfak	308 34.6	N49 55.7
01	120 19.6	243 13.9	28.4	117 11.9	09.1	228 51.9	42.6	197 21.5	25.3	Nunki	75 54.0	S26 16.3
02	135 22.0	258 13.8	28.9	132 12.8	09.8	243 53.8	42.7	212 23.7	25.2	Peacock	53 13.9	S56 40.5
03	150 24.5	273 13.7	.. 29.5	147 13.8	.. 10.6	258 55.7	.. 42.8	227 25.8	.. 25.2	Pollux	243 22.8	N27 58.6
04	165 27.0	288 13.6	30.1	162 14.7	11.3	273 57.6	42.8	242 27.9	25.2	Procyon	244 55.5	N 5 10.4
05	180 29.4	303 13.5	30.6	177 15.6	12.0	288 59.6	42.9	257 30.1	25.2			
06	195 31.9	318 13.3	S16 31.2	192 16.6	N 1 12.7	304 01.5	S21 43.0	272 32.2	S22 25.1	Rasalhague	96 03.3	N12 32.9
07	210 34.4	333 13.2	31.7	207 17.5	13.4	319 03.4	43.0	287 34.4	25.1	Regulus	207 39.3	N11 52.4
08	225 36.8	348 13.1	32.3	222 18.4	14.1	334 05.3	43.1	302 36.5	25.1	Rigel	281 08.1	S 8 11.0
S 09	240 39.3	3 13.0	.. 32.9	237 19.4	.. 14.9	349 07.2	.. 43.2	317 38.7	.. 25.1	Rigil Kent.	139 46.9	S60 54.3
U 10	255 41.7	18 12.8	33.4	252 20.3	15.6	4 09.1	43.2	332 40.8	25.0	Sabik	102 08.5	S15 44.7
N 11	270 44.2	33 12.7	34.0	267 21.3	16.3	19 11.0	43.3	347 43.0	25.0			
D 12	285 46.7	48 12.6	S16 34.6	282 22.2	N 1 17.0	34 13.0	S21 43.4	2 45.1	S22 25.0	Schedar	349 36.2	N56 38.6
A 13	300 49.1	63 12.4	35.1	297 23.1	17.7	49 14.9	43.4	17 47.3	25.0	Shaula	96 17.2	S37 06.8
Y 14	315 51.6	78 12.3	35.7	312 24.1	18.5	64 16.8	43.5	32 49.4	24.9	Sirius	258 30.0	S16 44.7
15	330 54.1	93 12.2	.. 36.3	327 25.0	.. 19.2	79 18.7	.. 43.6	47 51.5	.. 24.9	Spica	158 27.3	S11 15.4
16	345 56.5	108 12.1	36.8	342 25.9	19.9	94 20.6	43.6	62 53.7	24.9	Suhail	222 49.3	S43 30.5
17	0 59.0	123 11.9	37.4	357 26.9	20.6	109 22.5	43.7	77 55.8	24.9			
18	16 01.5	138 11.8	S16 37.9	12 27.8	N 1 21.3	124 24.5	S21 43.8	92 58.0	S22 24.9	Vega	80 36.8	N38 48.2
19	31 03.9	153 11.6	38.5	27 28.8	22.1	139 26.4	43.8	108 00.1	24.8	Zuben'ubi	137 01.4	S16 07.0
20	46 06.4	168 11.5	39.1	42 29.7	22.8	154 28.3	43.9	123 02.3	24.8		SHA	Mer.Pass.
21	61 08.8	183 11.4	.. 39.6	57 30.6	.. 23.5	169 30.2	.. 44.0	138 04.4	.. 24.8			h m
22	76 11.3	198 11.2	40.2	72 31.6	24.2	184 32.1	44.0	153 06.6	24.8	Venus	123 58.7	8 47
23	91 13.8	213 11.1	40.7	87 32.5	24.9	199 34.0	44.1	168 08.7	24.7	Mars	357 30.4	17 12
	h m									Jupiter	108 46.1	9 46
Mer. Pass.	17 00.0	v −0.1	d 0.6	v 0.9	d 0.7	v 1.9	d 0.1	v 2.1	d 0.0	Saturn	77 09.9	11 52

© British Crown Copyright 2018. All rights reserved.

UT	SUN GHA	SUN Dec	MOON GHA	v	MOON Dec	d	HP
4 00	178 50.8	S22 46.2	203 35.6	10.9	S19 57.1	4.4	55.2
01	193 50.5	45.9	218 05.5	11.0	20 01.5	4.3	55.1
02	208 50.2	45.6	232 35.5	10.9	20 05.8	4.2	55.1
03	223 50.0	.. 45.4	247 05.4	10.9	20 10.0	4.2	55.1
04	238 49.7	45.1	261 35.3	10.9	20 14.2	4.0	55.1
05	253 49.4	44.9	276 05.2	10.8	20 18.2	3.9	55.1
F 06	268 49.1	S22 44.6	290 35.0	10.9	S20 22.1	3.8	55.1
R 07	283 48.8	44.4	305 04.9	10.9	20 25.9	3.7	55.1
I 08	298 48.5	44.1	319 34.8	10.8	20 29.6	3.6	55.0
D 09	313 48.2	.. 43.8	334 04.6	10.9	20 33.2	3.5	55.0
A 10	328 48.0	43.6	348 34.5	10.8	20 36.7	3.4	55.0
Y 11	343 47.7	43.3	3 04.3	10.8	20 40.1	3.3	55.0
12	358 47.4	S22 43.1	17 34.1	10.8	S20 43.4	3.2	55.0
13	13 47.1	42.8	32 03.9	10.9	20 46.6	3.0	55.0
14	28 46.8	42.5	46 33.8	10.8	20 49.6	3.0	54.9
15	43 46.5	.. 42.3	61 03.6	10.8	20 52.6	2.9	54.9
16	58 46.3	42.0	75 33.4	10.8	20 55.5	2.8	54.9
17	73 46.0	41.7	90 03.2	10.8	20 58.3	2.6	54.9
18	88 45.7	S22 41.5	104 33.0	10.8	S21 00.9	2.6	54.9
19	103 45.4	41.2	119 02.8	10.8	21 03.5	2.4	54.9
20	118 45.1	40.9	133 32.6	10.8	21 05.9	2.4	54.9
21	133 44.8	.. 40.7	148 02.4	10.8	21 08.3	2.2	54.8
22	148 44.6	40.4	162 32.2	10.7	21 10.5	2.2	54.8
23	163 44.3	40.1	177 01.9	10.8	21 12.7	2.0	54.8
5 00	178 44.0	S22 39.9	191 31.7	10.8	S21 14.7	1.9	54.8
01	193 43.7	39.6	206 01.5	10.8	21 16.6	1.8	54.8
02	208 43.4	39.3	220 31.3	10.8	21 18.4	1.7	54.8
03	223 43.1	.. 39.0	235 01.1	10.8	21 20.1	1.6	54.7
04	238 42.9	38.8	249 30.9	10.8	21 21.7	1.5	54.7
05	253 42.6	38.5	264 00.7	10.8	21 23.2	1.4	54.7
S 06	268 42.3	S22 38.2	278 30.5	10.8	S21 24.6	1.3	54.7
A 07	283 42.0	37.9	293 00.3	10.9	21 25.9	1.2	54.7
T 08	298 41.7	37.7	307 30.2	10.8	21 27.1	1.1	54.7
U 09	313 41.5	.. 37.4	322 00.0	10.8	21 28.2	1.0	54.7
R 10	328 41.2	37.1	336 29.8	10.9	21 29.2	0.8	54.7
D 11	343 40.9	36.8	350 59.7	10.8	21 30.0	0.8	54.6
A 12	358 40.6	S22 36.5	5 29.5	10.9	S21 30.8	0.6	54.6
Y 13	13 40.3	36.3	19 59.4	10.9	21 31.4	0.6	54.6
14	28 40.1	36.0	34 29.3	10.8	21 32.0	0.4	54.6
15	43 39.8	.. 35.7	48 59.1	10.9	21 32.4	0.4	54.6
16	58 39.5	35.4	63 29.0	10.9	21 32.8	0.2	54.6
17	73 39.2	35.1	77 58.9	11.0	21 33.0	0.1	54.6
18	88 38.9	S22 34.8	92 28.9	10.9	S21 33.1	0.1	54.6
19	103 38.7	34.5	106 58.8	10.9	21 33.2	0.1	54.5
20	118 38.4	34.3	121 28.7	11.0	21 33.1	0.2	54.5
21	133 38.1	.. 34.0	135 58.7	11.0	21 32.9	0.3	54.5
22	148 37.8	33.7	150 28.7	11.0	21 32.6	0.4	54.5
23	163 37.5	33.4	164 58.7	11.0	S21 32.2	0.5	54.5
6 00	178 37.3	S22 33.1					
01	193 37.0	32.8					
02	208 36.7	32.5					
03	223 36.4	.. 32.2					
04	238 36.2	31.9					
05	253 35.9	31.6					
S 06	268 35.6	S22 31.3	266 29.2	11.1	S21 26.5	1.2	54.4
U 07	283 35.3	31.0	280 59.3	11.2	21 25.3	1.4	54.4
N 08	298 35.0	30.8	295 29.5	11.2	21 23.9	1.4	54.4
D 09	313 34.8	.. 30.5	309 59.7	11.2	21 22.5	1.5	54.4
A 10	328 34.5	30.2	324 29.9	11.3	21 21.0	1.7	54.4
Y 11	343 34.2	29.9	339 00.2	11.3	21 19.3	1.7	54.4
12	358 33.9	S22 29.6	353 30.5	11.2	S21 17.6	1.8	54.3
13	13 33.7	29.3	8 00.7	11.4	21 15.8	2.0	54.3
14	28 33.4	29.0	22 31.1	11.3	21 13.8	2.0	54.3
15	43 33.1	.. 28.7	37 01.4	11.4	21 11.8	2.1	54.3
16	58 32.8	28.4	51 31.8	11.4	21 09.7	2.3	54.3
17	73 32.6	28.1	66 02.2	11.4	21 07.4	2.3	54.3
18	88 32.3	S22 27.7	80 32.6	11.5	S21 05.1	2.5	54.3
19	103 32.0	27.4	95 03.1	11.5	21 02.6	2.5	54.3
20	118 31.7	27.1	109 33.6	11.5	21 00.1	2.6	54.3
21	133 31.5	.. 26.8	124 04.1	11.6	20 57.5	2.8	54.3
22	148 31.2	26.5	138 34.7	11.6	20 54.7	2.8	54.3
23	163 30.9	26.2	153 05.3	11.6	S20 51.9	2.9	54.2
	SD 16.3	d 0.3	SD 15.0		14.9		14.8

A partial eclipse of the Sun occurs on this date. See page 5.

Twilight / Moonrise

Lat.	Naut.	Civil	Sunrise	4	5	6	7
N 72	08 20	10 30	■	■	■	■	■
N 70	08 02	09 43	■	■	■	■	■
68	07 47	09 12	11 31	09 21	10 49	11 29	11 35
66	07 35	08 50	10 20	08 34	09 44	10 30	10 55
64	07 25	08 32	09 45	08 03	09 09	09 57	10 27
62	07 16	08 17	09 20	07 41	08 44	09 32	10 06
60	07 08	08 04	09 00	07 23	08 24	09 12	09 49
N 58	07 01	07 53	08 44	07 07	08 07	08 56	09 34
56	06 55	07 43	08 30	06 54	07 53	08 42	09 22
54	06 49	07 35	08 18	06 43	07 41	08 30	09 11
52	06 44	07 27	08 07	06 33	07 30	08 20	09 01
50	06 39	07 20	07 58	06 24	07 21	08 10	08 52
45	06 28	07 05	07 38	06 06	07 01	07 51	08 34
N 40	06 18	06 52	07 22	05 51	06 45	07 35	08 19
35	06 09	06 41	07 08	05 38	06 31	07 21	08 06
30	06 01	06 30	06 57	05 26	06 19	07 09	07 55
20	05 45	06 12	06 36	05 07	05 59	06 49	07 36
N 10	05 29	05 56	06 18	04 51	05 42	06 31	07 19
0	05 13	05 39	06 02	04 35	05 25	06 15	07 04
S 10	04 55	05 22	05 45	04 20	05 09	05 59	06 48
20	04 33	05 02	05 26	04 03	04 51	05 41	06 32
30	04 05	04 38	05 05	03 45	04 31	05 21	06 12
35	03 47	04 23	04 53	03 34	04 20	05 09	06 01
40	03 25	04 06	04 38	03 21	04 06	04 55	05 48
45	02 56	03 44	04 21	03 06	03 50	04 39	05 33
S 50	02 13	03 16	03 59	02 48	03 31	04 20	05 14
52	01 48	03 02	03 49	02 40	03 21	04 10	05 06
54	01 12	02 45	03 37	02 30	03 11	04 00	04 56
56	////	02 24	03 24	02 20	02 59	03 48	04 45
58	////	01 58	03 08	02 07	02 46	03 34	04 32
S 60	////	01 18	02 49	01 53	02 30	03 18	04 17

Sunset / Twilight / Moonset

Lat.	Sunset	Civil	Naut.	4	5	6	7
N 72	■	13 41	15 51	■	■	■	■
N 70	■	14 28	16 09	■	■	■	■
68	12 40	14 59	16 24	12 09	12 24	13 28	15 02
66	13 51	15 21	16 36	12 56	13 29	14 26	15 42
64	14 26	15 39	16 46	13 26	14 05	15 00	16 09
62	14 51	15 54	16 55	13 49	14 30	15 24	16 30
60	15 11	16 07	17 03	14 08	14 50	15 44	16 47
N 58	15 27	16 18	17 11	14 23	15 07	16 00	17 01
56	15 41	16 27	17 16	14 36	15 21	16 13	17 14
54	15 53	16 36	17 22	14 48	15 33	16 25	17 24
52	16 04	16 44	17 27	14 58	15 43	16 36	17 34
50	16 13	16 51	17 32	15 07	15 53	16 45	17 42
45	16 33	17 06	17 43	15 26	16 13	17 04	18 00
N 40	16 49	17 19	17 53	15 42	16 29	17 20	18 15
35	17 02	17 30	18 02	15 55	16 43	17 34	18 27
30	17 14	17 40	18 10	16 06	16 55	17 45	18 38
20	17 34	17 58	18 26	16 26	17 15	18 05	18 56
N 10	17 52	18 15	18 41	16 43	17 33	18 23	19 12
0	18 09	18 31	18 57	16 59	17 49	18 39	19 27
S 10	18 26	18 49	19 16	17 15	18 06	18 55	19 42
20	18 44	19 08	19 37	17 33	18 23	19 12	19 57
30	19 05	19 32	20 05	17 52	18 44	19 32	20 16
35	19 18	19 47	20 23	18 04	18 56	19 43	20 26
40	19 32	20 05	20 45	18 17	19 09	19 56	20 38
45	19 49	20 26	21 14	18 33	19 25	20 12	20 52
S 50	20 11	20 54	21 56	18 52	19 45	20 31	21 09
52	20 21	21 08	22 21	19 01	19 55	20 40	21 17
54	20 33	21 25	22 56	19 11	20 05	20 50	21 26
56	20 46	21 45	////	19 23	20 17	21 01	21 36
58	21 01	22 11	////	19 36	20 31	21 14	21 48
S 60	21 20	22 50	////	19 52	20 47	21 30	22 01

SUN / MOON

Day	Eqn. of Time 00h	Eqn. of Time 12h	Mer. Pass.	Mer. Pass. Upper	Mer. Pass. Lower	Age	Phase
	m s	m s	h m	h m	h m	d	%
4	04 36	04 50	12 05	10 47	23 12	28	2
5	05 03	05 17	12 05	11 37	24 02	29	0
6	05 30	05 44	12 06	12 27	00 02	00	0

© British Crown Copyright 2018. All rights reserved.

UT	ARIES GHA	VENUS −4.5 GHA	Dec	MARS +0.6 GHA	Dec	JUPITER −1.8 GHA	Dec	SATURN +0.5 GHA	Dec
7 00	106 16.2	228 11.0	S16 41.3	102 33.4	N 1 25.6	214 36.0	S21 44.2	183 10.9	S22 24.7
01	121 18.7	243 10.8	41.9	117 34.4	26.4	229 37.9	44.2	198 13.0	24.7
02	136 21.2	258 10.7	42.4	132 35.3	27.1	244 39.8	44.3	213 15.2	24.7
03	151 23.6	273 10.5 ..	43.0	147 36.3 ..	27.8	259 41.7 ..	44.3	228 17.3 ..	24.6
04	166 26.1	288 10.4	43.5	162 37.2	28.5	274 43.6	44.4	243 19.4	24.6
05	181 28.6	303 10.2	44.1	177 38.1	29.2	289 45.6	44.5	258 21.6	24.6
06	196 31.0	318 10.1	S16 44.7	192 39.1	N 1 29.9	304 47.5	S21 44.5	273 23.7	S22 24.6
07	211 33.5	333 10.0	45.2	207 40.0	30.7	319 49.4	44.6	288 25.9	24.5
M 08	226 36.0	348 09.8	45.8	222 40.9	31.4	334 51.3	44.7	303 28.0	24.5
O 09	241 38.4	3 09.7 ..	46.3	237 41.9 ..	32.1	349 53.2 ..	44.7	318 30.2 ..	24.5
N 10	256 40.9	18 09.5	46.9	252 42.8	32.8	4 55.1	44.8	333 32.3	24.5
D 11	271 43.3	33 09.4	47.5	267 43.7	33.5	19 57.1	44.9	348 34.5	24.4
A 12	286 45.8	48 09.2	S16 48.0	282 44.7	N 1 34.3	34 59.0	S21 44.9	3 36.6	S22 24.4
Y 13	301 48.3	63 09.1	48.6	297 45.6	35.0	50 00.9	45.0	18 38.8	24.4
14	316 50.7	78 08.9	49.1	312 46.6	35.7	65 02.8	45.1	33 40.9	24.4
15	331 53.2	93 08.8 ..	49.7	327 47.5 ..	36.4	80 04.7 ..	45.1	48 43.1 ..	24.4
16	346 55.7	108 08.6	50.2	342 48.4	37.1	95 06.7	45.2	63 45.2	24.3
17	1 58.1	123 08.5	50.8	357 49.4	37.8	110 08.6	45.2	78 47.3	24.3
18	17 00.6	138 08.3	S16 51.3	12 50.3	N 1 38.6	125 10.5	S21 45.3	93 49.5	S22 24.3
19	32 03.1	153 08.1	51.9	27 51.2	39.3	140 12.4	45.4	108 51.6	24.3
20	47 05.5	168 08.0	52.5	42 52.2	40.0	155 14.3	45.4	123 53.8	24.2
21	62 08.0	183 07.8 ..	53.0	57 53.1 ..	40.7	170 16.3 ..	45.5	138 55.9 ..	24.2
22	77 10.5	198 07.7	53.6	72 54.0	41.4	185 18.2	45.6	153 58.1	24.2
23	92 12.9	213 07.5	54.1	87 55.0	42.1	200 20.1	45.6	169 00.2	24.2
8 00	107 15.4	228 07.3	S16 54.7	102 55.9	N 1 42.9	215 22.0	S21 45.7	184 02.4	S22 24.1
01	122 17.8	243 07.2	55.2	117 56.8	43.6	230 23.9	45.8	199 04.5	24.1
02	137 20.3	258 07.0	55.8	132 57.8	44.3	245 25.9	45.8	214 06.7	24.1
03	152 22.8	273 06.9 ..	56.3	147 58.7 ..	45.0	260 27.8 ..	45.9	229 08.8 ..	24.1
04	167 25.2	288 06.7	56.9	162 59.6	45.7	275 29.7	46.0	244 11.0	24.0
05	182 27.7	303 06.5	57.4	178 00.6	46.5	290 31.6	46.0	259 13.1	24.0
06	197 30.2	318 06.4	S16 58.0	193 01.5	N 1 47.2	305 33.5	S21 46.1	274 15.2	S22 24.0
07	212 32.6	333 06.2	58.5	208 02.5	47.9	320 35.5	46.1	289 17.4	24.0
T 08	227 35.1	348 06.0	59.1	223 03.4	48.6	335 37.4	46.2	304 19.5	23.9
U 09	242 37.6	3 05.9	16 59.6	238 04.3 ..	49.3	350 39.3 ..	46.3	319 21.7 ..	23.9
E 10	257 40.0	18 05.7	17 00.2	253 05.3	50.0	5 41.2	46.3	334 23.8	23.9
S 11	272 42.5	33 05.5	00.7	268 06.2	50.8	20 43.1	46.4	349 26.0	23.9
D 12	287 45.0	48 05.3	S17 01.3	283 07.1	N 1 51.5	35 45.1	S21 46.5	4 28.1	S22 23.8
A 13	302 47.4	63 05.2	01.8	298 08.1	52.2	50 47.0	46.5	19 30.3	23.8
Y 14	317 49.9	78 05.0	02.4	313 09.0	52.9	65 48.9	46.6	34 32.4	23.8
15	332 52.3	93 04.8 ..	02.9	328 09.9 ..	53.6	80 50.8 ..	46.7	49 34.6 ..	23.8
16	347 54.8	108 04.6	03.5	343 10.9	54.3	95 52.7	46.7	64 36.7	23.7
17	2 57.3	123 04.5	04.0	358 11.8	55.1	110 54.7	46.8	79 38.9	23.7
18	17 59.7	138 04.3	S17 04.6	13 12.7	N 1 55.8	125 56.6	S21 46.8	94 41.0	S22 23.7
19	33 02.2	153 04.1	05.1	28 13.7	56.5	140 58.5	46.9	109 43.2	23.7
20	48 04.7	168 03.9	05.7	43 14.6	57.2	156 00.4	47.0	124 45.3	23.7
21	63 07.1	183 03.8 ..	06.2	58 15.5 ..	57.9	171 02.3 ..	47.0	139 47.4 ..	23.6
22	78 09.6	198 03.6	06.8	73 16.5	58.6	186 04.3	47.1	154 49.6	23.6
23	93 12.1	213 03.4	07.3	88 17.4	1 59.4	201 06.2	47.2	169 51.7	23.6
9 00	108 14.5	228 03.2	S17 07.9	103 18.3	N 2 00.1	216 08.1	S21 47.2	184 53.9	S22 23.6
01	123 17.0	243 03.0	08.4	118 19.3	00.8	231 10.0	47.3	199 56.0	23.5
02	138 19.4	258 02.8	09.0	133 20.2	01.5	246 12.0	47.3	214 58.2	23.5
03	153 21.9	273 02.7 ..	09.5	148 21.1 ..	02.2	261 13.9 ..	47.4	230 00.3 ..	23.5
04	168 24.4	288 02.5	10.1	163 22.1	02.9	276 15.8	47.5	245 02.5	23.5
05	183 26.8	303 02.3	10.6	178 23.0	03.7	291 17.7	47.5	260 04.6	23.4
06	198 29.3	318 02.1	S17 11.2	193 23.9	N 2 04.4	306 19.7	S21 47.6	275 06.8	S22 23.4
W 07	213 31.8	333 01.9	11.7	208 24.9	05.1	321 21.6	47.7	290 08.9	23.4
E 08	228 34.2	348 01.7	12.2	223 25.8	05.8	336 23.5	47.7	305 11.1	23.4
D 09	243 36.7	3 01.5 ..	12.8	238 26.7 ..	06.5	351 25.4 ..	47.8	320 13.2 ..	23.3
N 10	258 39.2	18 01.3	13.3	253 27.7	07.2	6 27.3	47.8	335 15.4	23.3
E 11	273 41.6	33 01.2	13.9	268 28.6	08.0	21 29.3	47.9	350 17.5	23.3
S 12	288 44.1	48 01.0	S17 14.4	283 29.5	N 2 08.7	36 31.2	S21 48.0	5 19.6	S22 23.3
D 13	303 46.6	63 00.8	15.0	298 30.5	09.4	51 33.1	48.0	20 21.8	23.2
A 14	318 49.0	78 00.6	15.5	313 31.4	10.1	66 35.0	48.1	35 23.9	23.2
Y 15	333 51.5	93 00.4 ..	16.0	328 32.3 ..	10.8	81 37.0 ..	48.2	50 26.1 ..	23.2
16	348 53.9	108 00.2	16.6	343 33.3	11.5	96 38.9	48.2	65 28.2	23.2
17	3 56.4	123 00.0	17.1	358 34.2	12.3	111 40.8	48.3	80 30.4	23.1
18	18 58.9	137 59.8	S17 17.7	13 35.1	N 2 13.0	126 42.7	S21 48.3	95 32.5	S22 23.1
19	34 01.3	152 59.6	18.2	28 36.1	13.7	141 44.7	48.4	110 34.7	23.1
20	49 03.8	167 59.4	18.7	43 37.0	14.4	156 46.6	48.5	125 36.8	23.1
21	64 06.3	182 59.2 ..	19.3	58 37.9 ..	15.1	171 48.5 ..	48.5	140 39.0 ..	23.0
22	79 08.7	197 59.0	19.8	73 38.9	15.8	186 50.4	48.6	155 41.1	23.0
23	94 11.2	212 58.8	20.4	88 39.8	16.5	201 52.4	48.7	170 43.3	23.0
Mer. Pass. 16 48.2		v −0.2	d 0.6	v 0.9	d 0.7	v 1.9	d 0.1	v 2.1	d 0.0

STARS

Name	SHA	Dec
Acamar	315 15.3	S40 14.1
Achernar	335 23.9	S57 08.9
Acrux	173 04.9	S63 11.9
Adhara	255 09.2	S29 00.0
Aldebaran	290 44.7	N16 32.7
Alioth	166 17.4	N55 51.2
Alkaid	152 56.0	N49 13.0
Alnair	27 39.3	S46 52.3
Alnilam	275 42.2	S 1 11.6
Alphard	217 52.1	S 8 44.5
Alphecca	126 08.0	N26 39.1
Alpheratz	357 39.7	N29 11.7
Altair	62 04.9	N 8 55.2
Ankaa	353 12.0	S42 12.5
Antares	112 21.9	S26 28.2
Arcturus	145 52.4	N19 05.0
Atria	107 20.8	S69 03.3
Avior	234 15.8	S59 34.2
Bellatrix	278 27.6	N 6 21.8
Betelgeuse	270 56.9	N 7 24.4
Canopus	263 53.9	S52 42.5
Capella	280 28.4	N46 00.9
Deneb	49 29.3	N45 21.0
Denebola	182 29.7	N14 27.9
Diphda	348 52.1	S17 53.2
Dubhe	193 46.8	N61 38.7
Elnath	278 07.5	N28 37.2
Eltanin	90 44.9	N51 29.2
Enif	33 43.7	N 9 57.7
Fomalhaut	15 20.0	S29 31.5
Gacrux	171 56.5	S57 12.8
Gienah	175 48.3	S17 38.7
Hadar	148 42.6	S60 27.4
Hamal	327 56.4	N23 33.1
Kaus Aust.	83 39.2	S34 22.4
Kochab	137 20.7	N74 04.5
Markab	13 34.7	N15 18.4
Menkar	314 10.9	N 4 09.7
Menkent	148 03.2	S36 27.5
Miaplacidus	221 38.0	S69 47.6
Mirfak	308 34.6	N49 55.7
Nunki	75 54.0	S26 16.3
Peacock	53 13.9	S56 40.5
Pollux	243 22.7	N27 58.6
Procyon	244 55.4	N 5 10.4
Rasalhague	96 03.3	N12 32.9
Regulus	207 39.3	N11 52.4
Rigel	281 08.1	S 8 11.0
Rigil Kent.	139 46.8	S60 54.4
Sabik	102 08.5	S15 44.7
Schedar	349 36.2	N56 38.6
Shaula	96 17.2	S37 06.8
Sirius	258 30.0	S16 44.7
Spica	158 27.3	S11 15.5
Suhail	222 49.2	S43 30.5
Vega	80 36.8	N38 48.1
Zuben'ubi	137 01.4	S16 07.0

	SHA	Mer. Pass.
Venus	120 52.0	8 48
Mars	355 40.5	17 07
Jupiter	108 06.6	9 37
Saturn	76 47.0	11 42

© British Crown Copyright 2018. All rights reserved.

UT	SUN GHA	Dec	MOON GHA	v	Dec	d	HP
d h	° ′	° ′	° ′	′	° ′	′	′
7 00	178 30.6	S22 25.9	167 35.9	11.6	S20 49.0	3.0	54.2
01	193 30.4	25.6	182 06.5	11.7	20 46.0	3.2	54.2
02	208 30.1	25.3	196 37.2	11.7	20 42.8	3.2	54.2
03	223 29.8	.. 25.0	211 07.9	11.8	20 39.6	3.3	54.2
04	238 29.6	24.7	225 38.7	11.8	20 36.3	3.4	54.2
05	253 29.3	24.4	240 09.5	11.8	20 32.9	3.5	54.2
06	268 29.0	S22 24.0	254 40.3	11.8	S20 29.4	3.6	54.2
07	283 28.7	23.7	269 11.1	11.9	20 25.8	3.7	54.2
08	298 28.5	23.4	283 42.0	11.9	20 22.1	3.8	54.2
M 09	313 28.2	.. 23.1	298 12.9	12.0	20 18.3	3.8	54.2
O 10	328 27.9	22.8	312 43.9	12.0	20 14.5	4.0	54.2
N 11	343 27.7	22.5	327 14.9	12.0	20 10.5	4.1	54.1
D 12	358 27.4	S22 22.1	341 45.9	12.1	S20 06.4	4.1	54.1
A 13	13 27.1	21.8	356 17.0	12.1	20 02.3	4.3	54.1
Y 14	28 26.8	21.5	10 48.1	12.1	19 58.0	4.3	54.1
15	43 26.6	.. 21.2	25 19.2	12.2	19 53.7	4.4	54.1
16	58 26.3	20.9	39 50.4	12.2	19 49.3	4.5	54.1
17	73 26.0	20.5	54 21.6	12.3	19 44.8	4.6	54.1
18	88 25.8	S22 20.2	68 52.9	12.3	S19 40.2	4.7	54.1
19	103 25.5	19.9	83 24.2	12.3	19 35.5	4.8	54.1
20	118 25.2	19.6	97 55.5	12.4	19 30.7	4.8	54.1
21	133 25.0	.. 19.2	112 26.9	12.4	19 25.9	5.0	54.1
22	148 24.7	18.9	126 58.3	12.5	19 20.9	5.0	54.1
23	163 24.4	18.6	141 29.8	12.5	19 15.9	5.2	54.1
8 00	178 24.2	S22 18.3	156 01.3	12.5	S19 10.7	5.2	54.1
01	193 23.9	17.9	170 32.8	12.6	19 05.5	5.3	54.1
02	208 23.6	17.6	185 04.4	12.6	19 00.2	5.3	54.1
03	223 23.3	.. 17.3	199 36.0	12.7	18 54.9	5.5	54.1
04	238 23.1	17.0	214 07.7	12.7	18 49.4	5.5	54.0
05	253 22.8	16.6	228 39.4	12.7	18 43.9	5.6	54.0
06	268 22.5	S22 16.3	243 11.1	12.8	S18 38.3	5.8	54.0
07	283 22.3	16.0	257 42.9	12.8	18 32.5	5.7	54.0
T 08	298 22.0	15.6	272 14.7	12.9	18 26.8	5.9	54.0
U 09	313 21.7	.. 15.3	286 46.6	12.9	18 20.9	6.0	54.0
E 10	328 21.5	15.0	301 18.5	12.9	18 14.9	6.0	54.0
S 11	343 21.2	14.6	315 50.4	13.0	18 08.9	6.1	54.0
D 12	358 21.0	S22 14.3	330 22.4	13.0	S18 02.8	6.2	54.0
A 13	13 20.7	13.9	344 54.4	13.1	17 56.6	6.2	54.0
Y 14	28 20.4	13.6	359 26.5	13.1	17 50.4	6.4	54.0
15	43 20.2	.. 13.3	13 58.6	13.2	17 44.0	6.4	54.0
16	58 19.9	12.9	28 30.8	13.1	17 37.6	6.5	54.0
17	73 19.6	12.6	43 02.9	13.3	17 31.1	6.5	54.0
18	88 19.4	S22 12.2	57 35.2	13.3	S17 24.6	6.7	54.0
19	103 19.1	11.9	72 07.5	13.3	17 17.9	6.7	54.0
20	118 18.8	11.6	86 39.8	13.3	17 11.2	6.8	54.0
21	133 18.6	.. 11.2	101 12.1	13.4	17 04.4	6.8	54.0
22	148 18.3	10.9	115 44.5	13.5	16 57.6	7.0	54.0
23	163 18.0	10.5	130 17.0	13.4	16 50.6	7.0	54.0
9 00	178 17.8	S22 10.2	144 49.4	13.6	S16 43.6	7.1	54.0
01	193 17.5	09.8	159 22.0	13.5	16 36.5	7.1	54.0
02	208 17.3	09.5	173 54.5	13.6	16 29.4	7.2	54.0
03	223 17.0	.. 09.1	188 27.1	13.6	16 22.2	7.3	54.0
04	238 16.7	08.8	202 59.7	13.7	16 14.9	7.4	54.0
05	253 16.5	08.5	217 32.4	13.7	16 07.5	7.4	54.0
06	268 16.2	S22 08.1	232 05.1	13.8	S16 00.1	7.5	54.0
W 07	283 16.0	07.8	246 37.9	13.8	15 52.6	7.5	54.0
E 08	298 15.7	07.4	261 10.7	13.8	15 45.1	7.7	54.0
D 09	313 15.4	.. 07.0	275 43.5	13.9	15 37.4	7.6	54.0
N 10	328 15.2	06.7	290 16.4	13.9	15 29.8	7.8	54.0
E 11	343 14.9	06.3	304 49.3	14.0	15 22.0	7.8	54.0
S 12	358 14.6	S22 06.0	319 22.3	14.0	S15 14.2	7.9	54.0
D 13	13 14.4	05.6	333 55.3	14.0	15 06.3	7.9	54.0
A 14	28 14.1	05.3	348 28.3	14.0	14 58.4	8.1	54.0
Y 15	43 13.9	.. 04.9	3 01.3	14.1	14 50.3	8.0	54.0
16	58 13.6	04.6	17 34.4	14.2	14 42.3	8.2	54.0
17	73 13.4	04.2	32 07.6	14.1	14 34.1	8.1	54.0
18	88 13.1	S22 03.8	46 40.7	14.2	S14 26.0	8.3	54.0
19	103 12.8	03.5	61 13.9	14.3	14 17.7	8.3	54.0
20	118 12.6	03.1	75 47.2	14.3	14 09.4	8.4	54.0
21	133 12.3	.. 02.8	90 20.5	14.3	14 01.0	8.4	54.0
22	148 12.1	02.4	104 53.8	14.3	13 52.6	8.5	54.0
23	163 11.8	02.0	119 27.1	14.4	S13 44.1	8.5	54.0
	SD 16.3	d 0.3	SD 14.8		14.7		14.7

Lat.	Twilight Naut.	Civil	Sunrise	Moonrise 7	8	9	10
°	h m	h m	h m	h m	h m	h m	h m
N 72	08 15	10 20	▓▓	▓▓	13 45	12 32	12 07
N 70	07 58	09 37	▓▓	▓▓	12 15	11 58	11 47
68	07 44	09 08	11 11	11 35	11 35	11 33	11 31
66	07 33	08 46	10 13	10 55	11 08	11 14	11 18
64	07 23	08 29	09 40	10 27	10 47	10 59	11 07
62	07 14	08 14	09 16	10 06	10 29	10 46	10 58
60	07 07	08 02	08 57	09 49	10 15	10 35	10 50
N 58	07 00	07 51	08 41	09 34	10 03	10 25	10 43
56	06 54	07 42	08 28	09 22	09 52	10 17	10 37
54	06 48	07 34	08 16	09 11	09 43	10 09	10 31
52	06 43	07 26	08 06	09 01	09 35	10 03	10 26
50	06 38	07 19	07 57	08 52	09 27	09 57	10 22
45	06 28	07 04	07 38	08 34	09 11	09 43	10 12
N 40	06 18	06 52	07 22	08 19	08 58	09 33	10 04
35	06 09	06 41	07 09	08 06	08 47	09 23	09 57
30	06 01	06 31	06 57	07 55	08 37	09 15	09 50
20	05 46	06 13	06 37	07 36	08 20	09 01	09 39
N 10	05 31	05 57	06 19	07 19	08 05	08 48	09 30
0	05 15	05 41	06 03	07 04	07 51	08 37	09 21
S 10	04 57	05 23	05 46	06 48	07 37	08 25	09 12
20	04 35	05 04	05 28	06 32	07 22	08 13	09 02
30	04 08	04 40	05 07	06 12	07 05	07 58	08 51
35	03 50	04 26	04 55	06 01	06 55	07 50	08 45
40	03 28	04 09	04 41	05 48	06 44	07 40	08 37
45	03 00	03 48	04 24	05 33	06 30	07 29	08 29
S 50	02 19	03 20	04 03	05 14	06 14	07 15	08 19
52	01 55	03 06	03 53	05 06	06 06	07 09	08 14
54	01 22	02 50	03 42	04 56	05 57	07 02	08 09
56	////	02 30	03 29	04 45	05 47	06 54	08 03
58	////	02 05	03 13	04 32	05 36	06 45	07 56
S 60	////	01 29	02 55	04 17	05 24	06 35	07 49

Lat.	Sunset	Twilight Civil	Naut.	Moonset 7	8	9	10
°	h m	h m	h m	h m	h m	h m	h m
N 72	▓▓	13 54	15 59	▓▓	14 31	17 18	19 14
N 70	▓▓	14 37	16 16	▓▓	16 00	17 51	19 33
68	13 03	15 06	16 30	15 02	16 39	18 15	19 47
66	14 00	15 28	16 41	15 42	17 06	18 33	19 59
64	14 33	15 45	16 51	16 09	17 27	18 47	20 09
62	14 57	15 59	16 59	16 30	17 43	19 00	20 17
60	15 16	16 12	17 07	16 47	17 57	19 10	20 24
N 58	15 32	16 22	17 14	17 01	18 09	19 19	20 30
56	15 46	16 31	17 20	17 14	18 19	19 27	20 36
54	15 57	16 40	17 25	17 24	18 28	19 34	20 41
52	16 07	16 47	17 30	17 34	18 36	19 40	20 45
50	16 17	16 54	17 35	17 42	18 43	19 46	20 49
45	16 36	17 09	17 46	18 00	18 58	19 58	20 58
N 40	16 52	17 22	17 55	18 15	19 11	20 08	21 05
35	17 05	17 33	18 04	18 27	19 21	20 16	21 11
30	17 16	17 43	18 12	18 38	19 31	20 24	21 17
20	17 36	18 00	18 27	18 56	19 47	20 37	21 27
N 10	17 54	18 16	18 43	19 12	20 00	20 48	21 34
0	18 10	18 33	18 59	19 27	20 13	20 58	21 42
S 10	18 27	18 50	19 17	19 42	20 26	21 09	21 49
20	18 45	19 09	19 38	19 57	20 40	21 20	21 57
30	19 06	19 33	20 05	20 16	20 56	21 32	22 06
35	19 18	19 47	20 23	20 26	21 05	21 39	22 11
40	19 32	20 04	20 45	20 38	21 15	21 48	22 17
45	19 49	20 25	21 13	20 52	21 27	21 57	22 24
S 50	20 10	20 52	21 53	21 09	21 41	22 08	22 32
52	20 20	21 06	22 17	21 17	21 48	22 14	22 36
54	20 31	21 22	22 49	21 26	21 56	22 20	22 40
56	20 44	21 42	////	21 36	22 04	22 26	22 44
58	20 59	22 07	////	21 48	22 13	22 33	22 50
S 60	21 17	22 42	////	22 01	22 24	22 41	22 55

Day	SUN Eqn. of Time 00ʰ	12ʰ	Mer. Pass.	MOON Mer. Pass. Upper	Lower	Age	Phase
d	m s	m s	h m	h m	h m	d	%
7	05 57	06 10	12 06	13 15	00 51	01	2
8	06 23	06 36	12 07	14 02	01 39	02	5
9	06 48	07 01	12 07	14 48	02 25	03	10

© British Crown Copyright 2018. All rights reserved.

UT	ARIES GHA	VENUS −4.5 GHA	Dec	MARS +0.6 GHA	Dec	JUPITER −1.8 GHA	Dec	SATURN +0.5 GHA	Dec	STARS Name	SHA	Dec
10 00	109 13.7	227 58.6	S17 20.9	103 40.7	N 2 17.3	216 54.3	S21 48.7	185 45.4	S22 23.0	Acamar	315 15.3	S40 14.1
01	124 16.1	242 58.4	21.4	118 41.7	18.0	231 56.2	48.8	200 47.6	22.9	Achernar	335 23.9	S57 08.9
02	139 18.6	257 58.2	22.0	133 42.6	18.7	246 58.1	48.8	215 49.7	22.9	Acrux	173 04.8	S63 11.9
03	154 21.1	272 58.0	.. 22.5	148 43.5	.. 19.4	262 00.1	.. 48.9	230 51.9	.. 22.9	Adhara	255 09.2	S29 00.0
04	169 23.5	287 57.8	23.1	163 44.5	20.1	277 02.0	49.0	245 54.0	22.9	Aldebaran	290 44.7	N16 32.7
05	184 26.0	302 57.6	23.6	178 45.4	20.8	292 03.9	49.0	260 56.1	22.8			
T 06	199 28.4	317 57.4	S17 24.1	193 46.3	N 2 21.6	307 05.8	S21 49.1	275 58.3	S22 22.8	Alioth	166 17.3	N55 51.2
H 07	214 30.9	332 57.1	24.7	208 47.2	22.3	322 07.8	49.2	291 00.4	22.8	Alkaid	152 56.0	N49 13.0
U 08	229 33.4	347 56.9	25.2	223 48.2	23.0	337 09.7	49.2	306 02.6	22.8	Alnair	27 39.4	S46 52.3
R 09	244 35.8	2 56.7	.. 25.7	238 49.1	.. 23.7	352 11.6	.. 49.3	321 04.7	.. 22.7	Alnilam	275 42.2	S 1 11.6
S 10	259 38.3	17 56.5	26.3	253 50.0	24.4	7 13.5	49.3	336 06.9	22.7	Alphard	217 52.1	S 8 44.5
D 11	274 40.8	32 56.3	26.8	268 51.0	25.1	22 15.5	49.4	351 09.0	22.7			
A 12	289 43.2	47 56.1	S17 27.3	283 51.9	N 2 25.8	37 17.4	S21 49.5	6 11.2	S22 22.7	Alphecca	126 08.0	N26 39.0
Y 13	304 45.7	62 55.9	27.9	298 52.8	26.6	52 19.3	49.5	21 13.3	22.7	Alpheratz	357 39.7	N29 11.7
14	319 48.2	77 55.7	28.4	313 53.8	27.3	67 21.2	49.6	36 15.5	22.6	Altair	62 04.9	N 8 55.2
15	334 50.6	92 55.4	.. 28.9	328 54.7	.. 28.0	82 23.2	.. 49.6	51 17.6	.. 22.6	Ankaa	353 12.1	S42 12.5
16	349 53.1	107 55.2	29.5	343 55.6	28.7	97 25.1	49.7	66 19.8	22.6	Antares	112 21.9	S26 28.2
17	4 55.5	122 55.0	30.0	358 56.6	29.4	112 27.0	49.8	81 21.9	22.6			
18	19 58.0	137 54.8	S17 30.5	13 57.5	N 2 30.1	127 28.9	S21 49.8	96 24.1	S22 22.5	Arcturus	145 52.4	N19 05.0
19	35 00.5	152 54.6	31.1	28 58.4	30.9	142 30.9	49.9	111 26.2	22.5	Atria	107 20.7	S69 03.3
20	50 02.9	167 54.4	31.6	43 59.4	31.6	157 32.8	49.9	126 28.4	22.5	Avior	234 15.8	S59 34.2
21	65 05.4	182 54.1	.. 32.1	59 00.3	.. 32.3	172 34.7	.. 50.0	141 30.5	.. 22.5	Bellatrix	278 27.6	N 6 21.8
22	80 07.9	197 53.9	32.7	74 01.2	33.0	187 36.7	50.1	156 32.7	22.4	Betelgeuse	270 56.9	N 7 24.4
23	95 10.3	212 53.7	33.2	89 02.1	33.7	202 38.6	50.1	171 34.8	22.4			
11 00	110 12.8	227 53.5	S17 33.7	104 03.1	N 2 34.4	217 40.5	S21 50.2	186 36.9	S22 22.4	Canopus	263 53.9	S52 42.6
01	125 15.3	242 53.2	34.2	119 04.0	35.1	232 42.4	50.3	201 39.1	22.4	Capella	280 28.4	N46 00.9
02	140 17.7	257 53.0	34.8	134 04.9	35.9	247 44.4	50.3	216 41.2	22.3	Deneb	49 29.3	N45 21.0
03	155 20.2	272 52.8	.. 35.3	149 05.9	.. 36.6	262 46.3	.. 50.4	231 43.4	.. 22.3	Denebola	182 29.7	N14 27.9
04	170 22.7	287 52.6	35.8	164 06.8	37.3	277 48.2	50.4	246 45.5	22.3	Diphda	348 52.1	S17 53.2
05	185 25.1	302 52.3	36.4	179 07.7	38.0	292 50.1	50.5	261 47.7	22.3			
F 06	200 27.6	317 52.1	S17 36.9	194 08.7	N 2 38.7	307 52.1	S21 50.6	276 49.8	S22 22.2	Dubhe	193 46.7	N61 38.7
R 07	215 30.0	332 51.9	37.4	209 09.6	39.4	322 54.0	50.6	291 52.0	22.2	Elnath	278 07.5	N28 37.3
I 08	230 32.5	347 51.7	37.9	224 10.5	40.1	337 55.9	50.7	306 54.1	22.2	Eltanin	90 44.9	N51 29.2
D 09	245 35.0	2 51.4	.. 38.5	239 11.5	.. 40.9	352 57.9	.. 50.7	321 56.3	.. 22.2	Enif	33 43.7	N 9 57.7
A 10	260 37.4	17 51.2	39.0	254 12.4	41.6	7 59.8	50.8	336 58.4	22.1	Fomalhaut	15 20.0	S29 31.5
Y 11	275 39.9	32 51.0	39.5	269 13.3	42.3	23 01.7	50.9	352 00.6	22.1			
12	290 42.4	47 50.7	S17 40.0	284 14.2	N 2 43.0	38 03.6	S21 50.9	7 02.7	S22 22.1	Gacrux	171 56.5	S57 12.8
13	305 44.8	62 50.5	40.6	299 15.2	43.7	53 05.6	51.0	22 04.9	22.1	Gienah	175 48.3	S17 38.7
14	320 47.3	77 50.3	41.1	314 16.1	44.4	68 07.5	51.0	37 07.0	22.0	Hadar	148 42.6	S60 27.4
15	335 49.8	92 50.0	.. 41.6	329 17.0	.. 45.1	83 09.4	.. 51.1	52 09.2	.. 22.0	Hamal	327 56.4	N23 33.1
16	350 52.2	107 49.8	42.1	344 18.0	45.9	98 11.4	51.2	67 11.3	22.0	Kaus Aust.	83 39.2	S34 22.4
17	5 54.7	122 49.6	42.7	359 18.9	46.6	113 13.3	51.2	82 13.5	22.0			
18	20 57.2	137 49.3	S17 43.2	14 19.8	N 2 47.3	128 15.2	S21 51.3	97 15.6	S22 21.9	Kochab	137 20.7	N74 04.5
19	35 59.6	152 49.1	43.7	29 20.7	48.0	143 17.1	51.3	112 17.8	21.9	Markab	13 34.7	N15 18.4
20	51 02.1	167 48.8	44.2	44 21.7	48.7	158 19.1	51.4	127 19.9	21.9	Menkar	314 10.9	N 4 09.7
21	66 04.5	182 48.6	.. 44.8	59 22.6	.. 49.4	173 21.0	.. 51.5	142 22.1	.. 21.9	Menkent	148 03.2	S36 27.5
22	81 07.0	197 48.4	45.3	74 23.5	50.1	188 22.9	51.5	157 24.2	21.8	Miaplacidus	221 38.0	S69 47.6
23	96 09.5	212 48.1	45.8	89 24.5	50.8	203 24.9	51.6	172 26.3	21.8			
12 00	111 11.9	227 47.9	S17 46.3	104 25.4	N 2 51.6	218 26.8	S21 51.6	187 28.5	S22 21.8	Mirfak	308 34.6	N49 55.7
01	126 14.4	242 47.6	46.8	119 26.3	52.3	233 28.7	51.7	202 30.6	21.8	Nunki	75 54.0	S26 16.3
02	141 16.9	257 47.4	47.4	134 27.3	53.0	248 30.7	51.8	217 32.8	21.7	Peacock	53 13.9	S56 40.5
03	156 19.3	272 47.1	.. 47.9	149 28.2	.. 53.7	263 32.6	.. 51.8	232 34.9	.. 21.7	Pollux	243 22.7	N27 58.6
04	171 21.8	287 46.9	48.4	164 29.1	54.4	278 34.5	51.9	247 37.1	21.7	Procyon	244 55.4	N 5 10.4
05	186 24.3	302 46.6	48.9	179 30.0	55.1	293 36.4	51.9	262 39.2	21.7			
S 06	201 26.7	317 46.4	S17 49.4	194 31.0	N 2 55.8	308 38.4	S21 52.0	277 41.4	S22 21.6	Rasalhague	96 03.2	N12 32.9
A 07	216 29.2	332 46.1	50.0	209 31.9	56.6	323 40.3	52.1	292 43.5	21.6	Regulus	207 39.2	N11 52.4
T 08	231 31.6	347 45.9	50.5	224 32.8	57.3	338 42.2	52.1	307 45.7	21.6	Rigel	281 08.1	S 8 11.0
U 09	246 34.1	2 45.6	.. 51.0	239 33.8	.. 58.0	353 44.2	.. 52.2	322 47.8	.. 21.6	Rigil Kent.	139 46.8	S60 54.4
R 10	261 36.6	17 45.4	51.5	254 34.7	58.7	8 46.1	52.2	337 50.0	21.5	Sabik	102 08.5	S15 44.7
D 11	276 39.0	32 45.1	52.0	269 35.6	2 59.4	23 48.0	52.3	352 52.1	21.5			
A 12	291 41.5	47 44.9	S17 52.5	284 36.5	N 3 00.1	38 50.0	S21 52.3	7 54.3	S22 21.5	Schedar	349 36.2	N56 38.6
Y 13	306 44.0	62 44.6	53.0	299 37.5	00.8	53 51.9	52.4	22 56.4	21.5	Shaula	96 17.1	S37 06.8
14	321 46.4	77 44.4	53.5	314 38.4	01.5	68 53.8	52.5	37 58.6	21.4	Sirius	258 30.0	S16 44.7
15	336 48.9	92 44.1	.. 54.1	329 39.3	.. 02.3	83 55.8	.. 52.5	53 00.7	.. 21.4	Spica	158 27.3	S11 15.5
16	351 51.4	107 43.9	54.6	344 40.2	03.0	98 57.7	52.6	68 02.9	21.4	Suhail	222 49.2	S43 30.5
17	6 53.8	122 43.6	55.1	359 41.2	03.7	113 59.6	52.6	83 05.0	21.4			
18	21 56.3	137 43.4	S17 55.6	14 42.1	N 3 04.4	129 01.6	S21 52.7	98 07.2	S22 21.3	Vega	80 36.8	N38 48.1
19	36 58.8	152 43.1	56.1	29 43.0	05.1	144 03.5	52.8	113 09.3	21.3	Zuben'ubi	137 01.4	S16 07.0
20	52 01.2	167 42.8	56.6	44 44.0	05.8	159 05.4	52.8	128 11.5	21.3		SHA	Mer.Pass.
21	67 03.7	182 42.6	.. 57.2	59 44.9	.. 06.5	174 07.4	.. 52.9	143 13.6	.. 21.3	Venus	117 40.7	8 49
22	82 06.1	197 42.3	57.7	74 45.8	07.2	189 09.3	52.9	158 15.8	21.2	Mars	353 50.3	17 03
23	97 08.6	212 42.1	58.2	89 46.7	08.0	204 11.2	53.0	173 17.9	21.2	Jupiter	107 27.7	9 28
Mer.Pass. 16 36.4		v −0.2	d 0.5	v 0.9	d 0.7	v 1.9	d 0.1	v 2.1	d 0.0	Saturn	76 24.1	11 32

© British Crown Copyright 2018. All rights reserved.

UT	SUN GHA	SUN Dec	MOON GHA	v	MOON Dec	d	HP
d h	° ′	° ′	° ′	′	° ′	′	′
10 00	178 11.5	S22 01.7	134 00.5	14.4	S13 35.6	8.6	54.0
01	193 11.3	01.3	148 33.9	14.5	13 27.0	8.7	54.0
02	208 11.0	00.9	163 07.4	14.4	13 18.3	8.7	54.0
03	223 10.8	.. 00.6	177 40.8	14.5	13 09.6	8.8	54.0
04	238 10.5	22 00.2	192 14.3	14.6	13 00.8	8.8	54.1
05	253 10.3	21 59.8	206 47.9	14.6	12 52.0	8.9	54.1
06	268 10.0	S21 59.5	221 21.5	14.6	S12 43.1	8.9	54.1
T 07	283 09.8	59.1	235 55.1	14.6	12 34.2	9.0	54.1
H 08	298 09.5	58.7	250 28.7	14.7	12 25.2	9.0	54.1
U 09	313 09.2	.. 58.4	265 02.4	14.7	12 16.2	9.1	54.1
R 10	328 09.0	58.0	279 36.1	14.7	12 07.1	9.1	54.1
S 11	343 08.7	57.6	294 09.8	14.7	11 58.0	9.2	54.1
D 12	358 08.5	S21 57.3	308 43.5	14.8	S11 48.8	9.3	54.1
A 13	13 08.2	56.9	323 17.3	14.8	11 39.5	9.2	54.1
Y 14	28 08.0	56.5	337 51.1	14.8	11 30.3	9.4	54.1
15	43 07.7	.. 56.1	352 24.9	14.9	11 20.9	9.4	54.1
16	58 07.5	55.8	6 58.8	14.9	11 11.5	9.4	54.1
17	73 07.2	55.4	21 32.7	14.9	11 02.1	9.5	54.1
18	88 07.0	S21 55.0	36 06.6	14.9	S10 52.6	9.5	54.1
19	103 06.7	54.6	50 40.5	15.0	10 43.1	9.5	54.2
20	118 06.5	54.3	65 14.5	14.9	10 33.6	9.6	54.2
21	133 06.2	.. 53.9	79 48.4	15.0	10 24.0	9.7	54.2
22	148 06.0	53.5	94 22.4	15.0	10 14.3	9.7	54.2
23	163 05.7	53.1	108 56.4	15.1	10 04.6	9.7	54.2
11 00	178 05.5	S21 52.7	123 30.5	15.0	S 9 54.9	9.8	54.2
01	193 05.2	52.4	138 04.5	15.1	9 45.1	9.8	54.2
02	208 05.0	52.0	152 38.6	15.1	9 35.3	9.9	54.2
03	223 04.7	.. 51.6	167 12.7	15.1	9 25.4	9.9	54.2
04	238 04.5	51.2	181 46.8	15.2	9 15.5	10.0	54.2
05	253 04.2	50.8	196 21.0	15.1	9 05.5	9.9	54.3
06	268 04.0	S21 50.4	210 55.1	15.2	S 8 55.6	10.1	54.3
07	283 03.7	50.0	225 29.3	15.2	8 45.5	10.0	54.3
08	298 03.5	49.7	240 03.5	15.2	8 35.5	10.1	54.3
F 09	313 03.2	.. 49.3	254 37.7	15.2	8 25.4	10.2	54.3
R 10	328 03.0	48.9	269 11.9	15.2	8 15.2	10.1	54.3
I 11	343 02.7	48.5	283 46.1	15.3	8 05.1	10.3	54.3
D 12	358 02.5	S21 48.1	298 20.4	15.2	S 7 54.8	10.2	54.3
A 13	13 02.2	47.7	312 54.6	15.3	7 44.6	10.3	54.3
Y 14	28 02.0	47.3	327 28.9	15.3	7 34.3	10.3	54.4
15	43 01.7	.. 46.9	342 03.2	15.3	7 24.0	10.4	54.4
16	58 01.5	46.5	356 37.5	15.2	7 13.6	10.3	54.4
17	73 01.2	46.1	11 11.7	15.4	7 03.3	10.5	54.4
18	88 01.0	S21 45.7	25 46.1	15.3	S 6 52.8	10.4	54.4
19	103 00.7	45.4	40 20.4	15.3	6 42.4	10.5	54.4
20	118 00.5	45.0	54 54.7	15.3	6 31.9	10.5	54.4
21	133 00.3	.. 44.6	69 29.0	15.3	6 21.4	10.5	54.4
22	148 00.0	44.2	84 03.3	15.4	6 10.9	10.6	54.5
23	162 59.8	43.8	98 37.7	15.3	6 00.3	10.6	54.5
12 00	177 59.5	S21 43.4	113 12.0	15.4	S 5 49.7	10.6	54.5
01	192 59.3	43.0	127 46.4	15.3	5 39.1	10.7	54.5
02	207 59.0	42.6	142 20.7	15.3	5 28.4	10.7	54.5
03	222 58.8	.. 42.2	156 55.0	15.4	5 17.7	10.7	54.6
04	237 58.5	41.8	171 29.4	15.3	5 07.0	10.7	54.6
05	252 58.3	41.4	186 03.7	15.4	4 56.3	10.8	54.6
06	267 58.1	S21 41.0	200 38.1	15.3	S 4 45.5	10.8	54.6
07	282 57.8	40.6	215 12.4	15.4	4 34.7	10.8	54.6
S 08	297 57.6	40.1	229 46.8	15.3	4 23.9	10.8	54.6
A 09	312 57.3	.. 39.7	244 21.1	15.3	4 13.1	10.9	54.7
T 10	327 57.1	39.3	258 55.4	15.4	4 02.2	10.9	54.7
U 11	342 56.8	38.9	273 29.8	15.3	3 51.3	10.9	54.7
R 12	357 56.6	S21 38.5	288 04.1	15.3	S 3 40.4	10.9	54.7
D 13	12 56.4	38.1	302 38.4	15.3	3 29.5	11.0	54.7
A 14	27 56.1	37.7	317 12.7	15.3	3 18.5	11.0	54.8
Y 15	42 55.9	.. 37.3	331 47.0	15.3	3 07.5	10.9	54.8
16	57 55.6	36.9	346 21.3	15.3	2 56.6	11.1	54.8
17	72 55.4	36.5	0 55.6	15.2	2 45.5	11.0	54.8
18	87 55.2	S21 36.1	15 29.8	15.3	S 2 34.5	11.0	54.8
19	102 54.9	35.6	30 04.1	15.2	2 23.5	11.1	54.9
20	117 54.7	35.2	44 38.3	15.2	2 12.4	11.1	54.9
21	132 54.4	.. 34.8	59 12.5	15.3	2 01.3	11.1	54.9
22	147 54.2	34.4	73 46.8	15.2	1 50.2	11.1	54.9
23	162 54.0	34.0	88 21.0	15.1	S 1 39.1	11.1	55.0
	SD 16.3	d 0.4	SD 14.7	14.8			14.9

Lat.	Twilight Naut.	Twilight Civil	Sunrise	Moonrise 10	11	12	13
°	h m	h m	h m	h m	h m	h m	h m
N 72	08 10	10 08	■■	12 07	11 49	11 35	11 21
N 70	07 54	09 29	■■	11 47	11 38	11 30	11 22
68	07 40	09 02	10 54	11 31	11 28	11 25	11 23
66	07 29	08 42	10 05	11 18	11 20	11 22	11 23
64	07 20	08 25	09 35	11 07	11 14	11 19	11 24
62	07 12	08 11	09 12	10 58	11 08	11 16	11 24
60	07 05	08 00	08 54	10 50	11 03	11 14	11 24
N 58	06 58	07 49	08 39	10 43	10 58	11 12	11 25
56	06 52	07 40	08 26	10 37	10 54	11 10	11 25
54	06 47	07 32	08 14	10 31	10 51	11 08	11 25
52	06 42	07 25	08 04	10 26	10 47	11 07	11 25
50	06 37	07 18	07 55	10 22	10 44	11 05	11 26
45	06 27	07 04	07 37	10 12	10 38	11 02	11 26
N 40	06 18	06 51	07 21	10 04	10 32	10 59	11 26
35	06 09	06 41	07 08	09 57	10 28	10 57	11 27
30	06 01	06 31	06 57	09 50	10 23	10 55	11 27
20	05 46	06 14	06 39	09 39	10 16	10 52	11 28
N 10	05 32	05 58	06 20	09 30	10 10	10 49	11 28
0	05 16	05 42	06 04	09 21	10 04	10 46	11 29
S 10	04 58	05 25	05 48	09 12	09 58	10 43	11 29
20	04 37	05 06	05 30	09 02	09 51	10 40	11 30
30	04 10	04 43	05 10	08 51	09 44	10 37	11 30
35	03 53	04 29	04 58	08 45	09 40	10 35	11 31
40	03 32	04 12	04 44	08 37	09 35	10 32	11 31
45	03 04	03 51	04 28	08 29	09 29	10 30	11 32
S 50	02 25	03 25	04 07	08 19	09 22	10 27	11 32
52	02 02	03 11	03 57	08 14	09 19	10 25	11 32
54	01 32	02 55	03 46	08 09	09 16	10 24	11 33
56	00 28	02 37	03 34	08 03	09 12	10 22	11 33
58	////	02 13	03 19	07 56	09 08	10 20	11 34
S 60	////	01 40	03 01	07 49	09 03	10 18	11 34

Lat.	Sunset	Twilight Civil	Twilight Naut.	Moonset 10	11	12	13
°	h m	h m	h m	h m	h m	h m	h m
N 72	■■	14 08	16 07	19 14	21 01	22 44	24 28
N 70	■■	14 47	16 23	19 33	21 10	22 46	24 24
68	13 22	15 14	16 36	19 47	21 18	22 48	24 20
66	14 11	15 34	16 47	19 59	21 25	22 50	24 17
64	14 41	15 51	16 56	20 09	21 30	22 52	24 15
62	15 04	16 05	17 04	20 17	21 35	22 53	24 13
60	15 22	16 17	17 11	20 24	21 39	22 54	24 11
N 58	15 38	16 27	17 18	20 30	21 42	22 55	24 09
56	15 50	16 36	17 24	20 36	21 45	22 56	24 08
54	16 02	16 44	17 29	20 41	21 48	22 57	24 06
52	16 12	16 51	17 34	20 45	21 51	22 57	24 05
50	16 20	16 58	17 39	20 49	21 53	22 58	24 04
45	16 39	17 12	17 49	20 58	21 58	22 59	24 02
N 40	16 55	17 25	17 58	21 05	22 03	23 01	24 00
35	17 08	17 35	18 06	21 11	22 06	23 02	23 58
30	17 19	17 45	18 14	21 17	22 09	23 02	23 57
20	17 38	18 02	18 29	21 26	22 15	23 04	23 54
N 10	17 55	18 18	18 44	21 34	22 20	23 05	23 52
0	18 12	18 34	19 00	21 42	22 24	23 06	23 49
S 10	18 28	18 51	19 17	21 49	22 29	23 08	23 47
20	18 45	19 09	19 38	21 57	22 33	23 09	23 45
30	19 05	19 32	20 05	22 06	22 39	23 10	23 42
35	19 17	19 46	20 22	22 11	22 42	23 11	23 41
40	19 31	20 03	20 43	22 17	22 45	23 12	23 39
45	19 48	20 24	21 11	22 24	22 49	23 13	23 37
S 50	20 08	20 50	21 50	22 32	22 54	23 14	23 35
52	20 18	21 04	22 12	22 36	22 56	23 15	23 34
54	20 29	21 19	22 41	22 40	22 58	23 15	23 33
56	20 41	21 38	23 37	22 44	23 01	23 16	23 31
58	20 56	22 01	////	22 50	23 04	23 17	23 30
S 60	21 13	22 33	////	22 55	23 07	23 17	23 28

Day	SUN Eqn. of Time 00h	12h	Mer. Pass.	MOON Mer. Pass. Upper	Lower	Age	Phase
d	m s	m s	h m	h m	h m	d %	
10	07 13	07 26	12 07	15 31	03 10	04 17	
11	07 38	07 50	12 08	16 14	03 55	05 24	
12	08 01	08 13	12 08	16 56	04 35	06 33	

© British Crown Copyright 2018. All rights reserved.

UT	ARIES GHA	VENUS −4·5 GHA	Dec	MARS +0·7 GHA	Dec	JUPITER −1·8 GHA	Dec	SATURN +0·5 GHA	Dec	STARS Name	SHA	Dec
13 00	112 11.1	227 41.8	S17 58.7	104 47.7	N 3 08.7	219 13.2	S21 53.1	188 20.1	S22 21.2	Acamar	315 15.3	S40 14.1
01	127 13.5	242 41.5	59.2	119 48.6	09.4	234 15.1	53.1	203 22.2	21.2	Achernar	335 23.9	S57 08.9
02	142 16.0	257 41.3	17 59.7	134 49.5	10.1	249 17.0	53.2	218 24.4	21.1	Acrux	173 04.8	S63 11.9
03	157 18.5	272 41.0	18 00.2	149 50.5 ..	10.8	264 19.0 ..	53.2	233 26.5 ..	21.1	Adhara	255 09.2	S29 00.1
04	172 20.9	287 40.7	00.7	164 51.4	11.5	279 20.9	53.3	248 28.7	21.1	Aldebaran	290 44.8	N16 32.7
05	187 23.4	302 40.5	01.2	179 52.3	12.2	294 22.8	53.3	263 30.8	21.1			
06	202 25.9	317 40.2	S18 01.7	194 53.2	N 3 12.9	309 24.8	S21 53.4	278 33.0	S22 21.0	Alioth	166 17.3	N55 51.2
07	217 28.3	332 39.9	02.2	209 54.2	13.7	324 26.7	53.5	293 35.1	21.0	Alkaid	152 56.0	N49 12.9
08	232 30.8	347 39.7	02.8	224 55.1	14.4	339 28.6	53.5	308 37.2	21.0	Alnair	27 39.4	S46 52.3
S 09	247 33.3	2 39.4 ..	03.3	239 56.0 ..	15.1	354 30.6 ..	53.6	323 39.4 ..	21.0	Alnilam	275 42.2	S 1 11.6
U 10	262 35.7	17 39.1	03.8	254 56.9	15.8	9 32.5	53.6	338 41.5	20.9	Alphard	217 52.1	S 8 44.5
N 11	277 38.2	32 38.9	04.3	269 57.9	16.5	24 34.4	53.7	353 43.7	20.9			
D 12	292 40.6	47 38.6	S18 04.8	284 58.8	N 3 17.2	39 36.4	S21 53.8	8 45.8	S22 20.9	Alphecca	126 08.0	N26 39.0
A 13	307 43.1	62 38.3	05.3	299 59.7	17.9	54 38.3	53.8	23 48.0	20.8	Alpheratz	357 39.7	N29 11.7
Y 14	322 45.6	77 38.0	05.8	315 00.6	18.6	69 40.2	53.9	38 50.1	20.8	Altair	62 04.9	N 8 55.2
15	337 48.0	92 37.8 ..	06.3	330 01.6 ..	19.4	84 42.2 ..	53.9	53 52.3 ..	20.8	Ankaa	353 12.1	S42 12.5
16	352 50.5	107 37.5	06.8	345 02.5	20.1	99 44.1	54.0	68 54.4	20.8	Antares	112 21.9	S26 28.2
17	7 53.0	122 37.2	07.3	0 03.4	20.8	114 46.0	54.0	83 56.6	20.7			
18	22 55.4	137 36.9	S18 07.8	15 04.4	N 3 21.5	129 48.0	S21 54.1	98 58.7	S22 20.7	Arcturus	145 52.4	N19 05.0
19	37 57.9	152 36.7	08.3	30 05.3	22.2	144 49.9	54.2	114 00.9	20.7	Atria	107 20.7	S69 03.3
20	53 00.4	167 36.4	08.8	45 06.2	22.9	159 51.8	54.2	129 03.0	20.7	Avior	234 15.8	S59 34.2
21	68 02.8	182 36.1 ..	09.3	60 07.1 ..	23.6	174 53.8 ..	54.3	144 05.2 ..	20.6	Bellatrix	278 27.6	N 6 21.8
22	83 05.3	197 35.8	09.8	75 08.1	24.3	189 55.7	54.3	159 07.3	20.6	Betelgeuse	270 56.9	N 7 24.4
23	98 07.7	212 35.5	10.3	90 09.0	25.0	204 57.6	54.4	174 09.5	20.6			
14 00	113 10.2	227 35.3	S18 10.8	105 09.9	N 3 25.8	219 59.6	S21 54.4	189 11.6	S22 20.6	Canopus	263 53.9	S52 42.6
01	128 12.7	242 35.0	11.3	120 10.8	26.5	235 01.5	54.5	204 13.8	20.5	Capella	280 28.4	N46 00.9
02	143 15.1	257 34.7	11.8	135 11.8	27.2	250 03.4	54.6	219 15.9	20.5	Deneb	49 29.3	N45 21.0
03	158 17.6	272 34.4 ..	12.3	150 12.7 ..	27.9	265 05.4 ..	54.6	234 18.1 ..	20.5	Denebola	182 29.7	N14 27.9
04	173 20.1	287 34.1	12.8	165 13.6	28.6	280 07.3	54.7	249 20.2	20.5	Diphda	348 52.1	S17 53.2
05	188 22.5	302 33.8	13.3	180 14.5	29.3	295 09.3	54.7	264 22.4	20.4			
06	203 25.0	317 33.6	S18 13.8	195 15.5	N 3 30.0	310 11.2	S21 54.8	279 24.5	S22 20.4	Dubhe	193 46.7	N61 38.7
07	218 27.5	332 33.3	14.3	210 16.4	30.7	325 13.1	54.9	294 26.7	20.4	Elnath	278 07.5	N28 37.3
08	233 29.9	347 33.0	14.8	225 17.3	31.4	340 15.1	54.9	309 28.8	20.4	Eltanin	90 44.9	N51 29.2
M 09	248 32.4	2 32.7 ..	15.3	240 18.2 ..	32.2	355 17.0 ..	55.0	324 31.0 ..	20.3	Enif	33 43.7	N 9 57.7
O 10	263 34.9	17 32.4	15.8	255 19.2	32.9	10 18.9	55.0	339 33.1	20.3	Fomalhaut	15 20.0	S29 31.5
N 11	278 37.3	32 32.1	16.3	270 20.1	33.6	25 20.9	55.1	354 35.3	20.3			
D 12	293 39.8	47 31.8	S18 16.8	285 21.0	N 3 34.3	40 22.8	S21 55.1	9 37.4	S22 20.3	Gacrux	171 56.5	S57 12.8
A 13	308 42.2	62 31.5	17.2	300 21.9	35.0	55 24.7	55.2	24 39.6	20.2	Gienah	175 48.3	S17 38.7
Y 14	323 44.7	77 31.2	17.7	315 22.9	35.7	70 26.7	55.3	39 41.7	20.2	Hadar	148 42.6	S60 27.4
15	338 47.2	92 30.9 ..	18.2	330 23.8 ..	36.4	85 28.6 ..	55.3	54 43.9 ..	20.2	Hamal	327 56.4	N23 33.1
16	353 49.6	107 30.7	18.7	345 24.7	37.1	100 30.6	55.4	69 46.0	20.2	Kaus Aust.	83 39.2	S34 22.4
17	8 52.1	122 30.4	19.2	0 25.6	37.8	115 32.5	55.4	84 48.2	20.1			
18	23 54.6	137 30.1	S18 19.7	15 26.6	N 3 38.5	130 34.4	S21 55.5	99 50.3	S22 20.1	Kochab	137 20.6	N74 04.5
19	38 57.0	152 29.8	20.2	30 27.5	39.3	145 36.4	55.5	114 52.5	20.1	Markab	13 34.7	N15 18.4
20	53 59.5	167 29.5	20.7	45 28.4	40.0	160 38.3	55.6	129 54.6	20.1	Menkar	314 10.9	N 4 09.6
21	69 02.0	182 29.2 ..	21.2	60 29.3 ..	40.7	175 40.3 ..	55.6	144 56.8 ..	20.0	Menkent	148 03.1	S36 27.5
22	84 04.4	197 28.9	21.7	75 30.3	41.4	190 42.2	55.7	159 58.9	20.0	Miaplacidus	221 38.0	S69 47.6
23	99 06.9	212 28.6	22.2	90 31.2	42.1	205 44.1	55.8	175 01.1	20.0			
15 00	114 09.3	227 28.3	S18 22.6	105 32.1	N 3 42.8	220 46.1	S21 55.8	190 03.2	S22 20.0	Mirfak	308 34.6	N49 55.7
01	129 11.8	242 28.0	23.1	120 33.0	43.5	235 48.0	55.9	205 05.4	19.9	Nunki	75 54.0	S26 16.3
02	144 14.3	257 27.7	23.6	135 34.0	44.2	250 49.9	55.9	220 07.5	19.9	Peacock	53 13.9	S56 40.4
03	159 16.7	272 27.4 ..	24.1	150 34.9 ..	44.9	265 51.9 ..	56.0	235 09.7 ..	19.9	Pollux	243 22.7	N27 58.6
04	174 19.2	287 27.1	24.6	165 35.8	45.6	280 53.8	56.0	250 11.8	19.9	Procyon	244 55.4	N 5 10.4
05	189 21.7	302 26.8	25.1	180 36.7	46.3	295 55.8	56.1	265 14.0	19.8			
06	204 24.1	317 26.5	S18 25.6	195 37.7	N 3 47.1	310 57.7	S21 56.2	280 16.1	S22 19.8	Rasalhague	96 03.2	N12 32.8
07	219 26.6	332 26.2	26.0	210 38.6	47.8	325 59.6	56.2	295 18.3	19.8	Regulus	207 39.2	N11 52.4
08	234 29.1	347 25.8	26.5	225 39.5	48.5	341 01.6	56.3	310 20.4	19.7	Rigel	281 08.1	S 8 11.0
T 09	249 31.5	2 25.5 ..	27.0	240 40.4 ..	49.2	356 03.5 ..	56.3	325 22.6 ..	19.7	Rigil Kent.	139 46.7	S60 54.4
U 10	264 34.0	17 25.2	27.5	255 41.3	49.9	11 05.5	56.4	340 24.7	19.7	Sabik	102 08.5	S15 44.7
E 11	279 36.5	32 24.9	28.0	270 42.3	50.6	26 07.4	56.4	355 26.9	19.7			
S 12	294 38.9	47 24.6	S18 28.5	285 43.2	N 3 51.3	41 09.3	S21 56.5	10 29.0	S22 19.6	Schedar	349 36.3	N56 38.6
D 13	309 41.4	62 24.3	28.9	300 44.1	52.0	56 11.3	56.5	25 31.2	19.6	Shaula	96 17.1	S37 06.8
A 14	324 43.8	77 24.0	29.4	315 45.0	52.7	71 13.2	56.6	40 33.3	19.6	Sirius	258 30.0	S16 44.7
Y 15	339 46.3	92 23.7 ..	29.9	330 46.0 ..	53.4	86 15.2 ..	56.7	55 35.5 ..	19.6	Spica	158 27.2	S11 15.5
16	354 48.8	107 23.4	30.4	345 46.9	54.1	101 17.1	56.7	70 37.6	19.5	Suhail	222 49.2	S43 30.5
17	9 51.2	122 23.1	30.9	0 47.8	54.9	116 19.0	56.8	85 39.8	19.5			
18	24 53.7	137 22.7	S18 31.3	15 48.7	N 3 55.6	131 21.0	S21 56.8	100 41.9	S22 19.5	Vega	80 36.8	N38 48.1
19	39 56.2	152 22.4	31.8	30 49.7	56.3	146 22.9	56.9	115 44.1	19.5	Zuben'ubi	137 01.3	S16 07.0
20	54 58.6	167 22.1	32.3	45 50.6	57.0	161 24.9	56.9	130 46.2	19.4			
21	70 01.1	182 21.8 ..	32.8	60 51.5 ..	57.7	176 26.8 ..	57.0	145 48.4 ..	19.4		SHA	Mer. Pass.
22	85 03.6	197 21.5	33.3	75 52.4	58.4	191 28.7	57.0	160 50.5	19.4	Venus	114 25.1	8 50
23	100 06.0	212 21.2	33.7	90 53.3	59.1	206 30.7	57.1	175 52.7	19.4	Mars	351 59.7	16 58
	h m									Jupiter	106 49.4	9 19
Mer. Pass. 16 24.6		v −0.3	d 0.5	v 0.9	d 0.7	v 1.9	d 0.1	v 2.1	d 0.0	Saturn	76 01.4	11 22

© British Crown Copyright 2018. All rights reserved.

UT	SUN GHA	SUN Dec	MOON GHA	v	Dec	d	HP
13 00	177 53.7	S21 33.6	102 55.1	15.2	S 1 28.0	11.2	55.0
01	192 53.5	33.2	117 29.3	15.1	1 16.8	11.1	55.0
02	207 53.3	32.7	132 03.4	15.2	1 05.7	11.2	55.0
03	222 53.0	.. 32.3	146 37.6	15.1	0 54.5	11.2	55.0
04	237 52.8	31.9	161 11.7	15.1	0 43.3	11.2	55.1
05	252 52.5	31.5	175 45.8	15.0	0 32.1	11.2	55.1
06	267 52.3	S21 31.1	190 19.8	15.1	S 0 20.9	11.2	55.1
07	282 52.1	30.6	204 53.9	15.0	S 0 09.7	11.3	55.1
08	297 51.8	30.2	219 27.9	15.0	N 0 01.6	11.2	55.2
S 09	312 51.6	.. 29.8	234 01.9	14.9	0 12.8	11.3	55.2
U 10	327 51.4	29.4	248 35.8	15.0	0 24.1	11.2	55.2
N 11	342 51.1	28.9	263 09.8	14.9	0 35.3	11.3	55.2
D 12	357 50.9	S21 28.5	277 43.7	14.9	N 0 46.6	11.3	55.3
A 13	12 50.7	28.1	292 17.6	14.8	0 57.9	11.2	55.3
Y 14	27 50.4	27.7	306 51.4	14.8	1 09.1	11.3	55.3
15	42 50.2	.. 27.2	321 25.2	14.8	1 20.4	11.3	55.3
16	57 50.0	26.8	335 59.0	14.8	1 31.7	11.3	55.4
17	72 49.7	26.4	350 32.8	14.7	1 43.0	11.3	55.4
18	87 49.5	S21 26.0	5 06.5	14.7	N 1 54.3	11.3	55.4
19	102 49.3	25.5	19 40.2	14.6	2 05.6	11.3	55.5
20	117 49.0	25.1	34 13.8	14.6	2 16.9	11.3	55.5
21	132 48.8	.. 24.7	48 47.4	14.6	2 28.2	11.3	55.5
22	147 48.6	24.2	63 21.0	14.6	2 39.5	11.3	55.5
23	162 48.3	23.8	77 54.6	14.5	2 50.8	11.3	55.6
14 00	177 48.1	S21 23.4	92 28.1	14.4	N 3 02.1	11.3	55.6
01	192 47.9	22.9	107 01.5	14.4	3 13.4	11.3	55.6
02	207 47.6	22.5	121 34.9	14.4	3 24.7	11.3	55.7
03	222 47.4	.. 22.1	136 08.3	14.4	3 36.0	11.3	55.7
04	237 47.2	21.6	150 41.7	14.2	3 47.3	11.3	55.7
05	252 46.9	21.2	165 14.9	14.3	3 58.6	11.3	55.8
06	267 46.7	S21 20.8	179 48.2	14.2	N 4 09.9	11.3	55.8
07	282 46.5	20.3	194 21.4	14.1	4 21.2	11.3	55.8
08	297 46.3	19.9	208 54.5	14.1	4 32.5	11.3	55.8
M 09	312 46.0	.. 19.4	223 27.6	14.1	4 43.8	11.2	55.9
O 10	327 45.8	19.0	238 00.7	14.0	4 55.0	11.3	55.9
N 11	342 45.6	18.6	252 33.7	13.9	5 06.3	11.2	55.9
D 12	357 45.3	S21 18.1	267 06.6	13.9	N 5 17.5	11.3	56.0
A 13	12 45.1	17.7	281 39.5	13.9	5 28.8	11.2	56.0
Y 14	27 44.9	17.2	296 12.4	13.8	5 40.0	11.2	56.0
15	42 44.7	.. 16.8	310 45.2	13.7	5 51.2	11.2	56.1
16	57 44.4	16.3	325 17.9	13.7	6 02.4	11.2	56.1
17	72 44.2	15.9	339 50.6	13.6	6 13.6	11.1	56.1
18	87 44.0	S21 15.4	354 23.2	13.6	N 6 24.7	11.2	56.2
19	102 43.8	15.0	8 55.8	13.5	6 35.9	11.1	56.2
20	117 43.5	14.5	23 28.3	13.4	6 47.0	11.2	56.2
21	132 43.3	.. 14.1	38 00.7	13.4	6 58.2	11.1	56.3
22	147 43.1	13.6	52 33.1	13.3	7 09.3	11.1	56.3
23	162 42.9	13.2	67 05.4	13.3	7 20.4	11.0	56.3
15 00	177 42.6	S21 12.7	81 37.7	13.2	N 7 31.4	11.1	56.4
01	192 42.4	12.3	96 09.3	13.1	7 42.5	11.0	56.4
02	207 42.2	11.8	110 42.0	13.1	7 53.5	11.0	56.4
03	222 42.0	.. 11.4	125 14.1	13.0	8 04.5	11.0	56.5
04	237 41.7	10.9	139 46.1	12.9	8 15.5	10.9	56.5
05	252 41.5	10.5	154 18.0	12.9	8 26.4	11.0	56.6
06	267 41.3	S21 10.0	168 49.9	12.8	N 8 37.4	10.9	56.6
07	282 41.1	09.6	183 21.7	12.7	8 48.3	10.8	56.6
08	297 40.9	09.1	197 53.4	12.6	8 59.1	10.9	56.7
T 09	312 40.6	.. 08.7	212 25.0	12.6	9 10.0	10.8	56.7
U 10	327 40.4	08.2	226 56.6	12.5	9 20.8	10.8	56.7
E 11	342 40.2	07.7	241 28.1	12.5	9 31.6	10.8	56.8
S 12	357 40.0	S21 07.3	255 59.6	12.3	N 9 42.4	10.7	56.8
D 13	12 39.7	06.8	270 30.9	12.3	9 53.1	10.7	56.9
A 14	27 39.5	06.4	285 02.2	12.2	10 03.8	10.6	56.9
Y 15	42 39.3	.. 05.9	299 33.4	12.1	10 14.4	10.7	56.9
16	57 39.1	05.4	314 04.5	12.1	10 25.1	10.5	57.0
17	72 38.9	05.0	328 35.6	11.9	10 35.6	10.6	57.0
18	87 38.6	S21 04.5	343 06.5	11.9	N10 46.2	10.5	57.0
19	102 38.4	04.1	357 37.4	11.8	10 56.7	10.5	57.1
20	117 38.2	03.6	12 08.2	11.7	11 07.2	10.4	57.1
21	132 38.0	.. 03.1	26 38.9	11.7	11 17.6	10.4	57.1
22	147 37.8	02.7	41 09.6	11.5	11 28.0	10.3	57.2
23	162 37.6	02.2	55 40.1	11.5	N11 38.3	10.3	57.2
SD	16.3	d 0.4	15.1		15.3		15.5

Lat.	Twilight Naut.	Twilight Civil	Sunrise	Moonrise 13	14	15	16
N 72	08 04	09 57	■■■■	11 21	11 07	10 52	10 31
N 70	07 48	09 21	■■■■	11 22	11 14	11 06	10 56
68	07 36	08 56	10 39	11 23	11 20	11 17	11 15
66	07 26	08 37	09 57	11 23	11 25	11 27	11 31
64	07 17	08 21	09 28	11 24	11 29	11 35	11 44
62	07 09	08 08	09 07	11 24	11 32	11 42	11 55
60	07 02	07 56	08 50	11 24	11 35	11 48	12 04
N 58	06 56	07 47	08 35	11 25	11 38	11 53	12 12
56	06 50	07 38	08 23	11 25	11 41	11 58	12 19
54	06 45	07 30	08 12	11 25	11 43	12 02	12 26
52	06 41	07 23	08 02	11 25	11 45	12 06	12 32
50	06 36	07 17	07 54	11 26	11 47	12 10	12 37
45	06 26	07 03	07 35	11 26	11 51	12 18	12 48
N 40	06 17	06 51	07 21	11 26	11 54	12 24	12 58
35	06 09	06 40	07 08	11 27	11 57	12 30	13 06
30	06 02	06 31	06 57	11 27	12 00	12 35	13 13
20	05 47	06 14	06 38	11 28	12 04	12 43	13 26
N 10	05 33	05 59	06 21	11 28	12 09	12 51	13 37
0	05 17	05 43	06 05	11 29	12 12	12 58	13 48
S 10	05 00	05 27	05 49	11 29	12 16	13 06	13 58
20	04 40	05 08	05 32	11 30	12 20	13 14	14 09
30	04 13	04 46	05 12	11 30	12 25	13 22	14 22
35	03 56	04 32	05 01	11 31	12 28	13 28	14 30
40	03 36	04 16	04 47	11 31	12 31	13 34	14 39
45	03 09	03 55	04 31	11 32	12 35	13 41	14 49
S 50	02 31	03 29	04 11	11 32	12 39	13 49	15 01
52	02 10	03 17	04 02	11 32	12 41	13 53	15 07
54	01 42	03 01	03 51	11 33	12 44	13 57	15 13
56	00 55	02 43	03 39	11 33	12 46	14 02	15 20
58	////	02 21	03 25	11 34	12 49	14 07	15 28
S 60	////	01 51	03 08	11 34	12 52	14 13	15 38

Lat.	Sunset	Twilight Civil	Twilight Naut.	Moonset 13	14	15	16
N 72	■■■■	14 22	16 15	24 28	00 28	02 18	04 18
N 70	■■■■	14 57	16 30	24 24	00 24	02 06	03 55
68	13 40	15 22	16 43	24 20	00 20	01 56	03 37
66	14 22	15 42	16 53	24 17	00 17	01 48	03 23
64	14 50	15 58	17 02	24 15	00 15	01 41	03 11
62	15 12	16 11	17 10	24 13	00 13	01 35	03 01
60	15 29	16 22	17 16	24 11	00 11	01 30	02 53
N 58	15 43	16 32	17 23	24 09	00 09	01 26	02 45
56	15 56	16 41	17 28	24 08	00 08	01 22	02 39
54	16 07	16 48	17 33	24 06	00 06	01 18	02 33
52	16 16	16 55	17 38	24 05	00 05	01 15	02 28
50	16 25	17 02	17 42	24 04	00 04	01 12	02 23
45	16 43	17 16	17 52	24 02	00 02	01 06	02 13
N 40	16 58	17 28	18 01	24 00	00 00	01 01	02 04
35	17 10	17 38	18 09	23 58	24 56	00 56	01 57
30	17 21	17 47	18 17	23 57	24 52	00 52	01 51
20	17 40	18 04	18 31	23 54	24 46	00 46	01 40
N 10	17 57	18 19	18 45	23 52	24 40	00 40	01 30
0	18 13	18 35	19 01	23 49	24 34	00 34	01 21
S 10	18 28	18 51	19 18	23 47	24 28	00 28	01 13
20	18 45	19 10	19 38	23 45	24 23	00 23	01 03
30	19 05	19 32	20 04	23 42	24 16	00 16	00 52
35	19 17	19 46	20 21	23 41	24 12	00 12	00 46
40	19 30	20 02	20 42	23 39	24 08	00 08	00 39
45	19 46	20 22	21 08	23 37	24 02	00 02	00 31
S 50	20 06	20 48	21 45	23 35	23 56	24 21	00 21
52	20 15	21 00	22 06	23 34	23 54	24 17	00 17
54	20 26	21 15	22 33	23 32	23 51	24 12	00 12
56	20 38	21 33	23 17	23 31	23 47	24 06	00 06
58	20 52	21 55	////	23 30	23 44	24 00	00 00
S 60	21 08	22 24	////	23 28	23 39	23 53	24 11

Day	SUN Eqn. of Time 00h	12h	Mer. Pass.	MOON Mer. Pass. Upper	Lower	Age	Phase
13	08 25	08 36	12 09	17 39	05 17	07	42
14	08 47	08 58	12 09	18 23	06 01	08	52
15	09 09	09 20	12 09	19 10	06 46	09	62

© British Crown Copyright 2018. All rights reserved.

UT	ARIES GHA	VENUS −4.5 GHA	Dec	MARS +0.7 GHA	Dec	JUPITER −1.8 GHA	Dec	SATURN +0.5 GHA	Dec	STARS Name	SHA	Dec
16 00	115 08.5	227 20.8	S18 34.2	105 54.3	N 3 59.8	221 32.6	S21 57.2	190 54.8	S22 19.3	Acamar	315 15.3	S40 14.1
01	130 11.0	242 20.5	34.7	120 55.2	4 00.5	236 34.6	57.2	205 57.0	19.3	Achernar	335 24.0	S57 08.9
02	145 13.4	257 20.2	35.2	135 56.1	01.2	251 36.5	57.3	220 59.1	19.3	Acrux	173 04.7	S63 11.9
03	160 15.9	272 19.9 ..	35.6	150 57.0 ..	01.9	266 38.5 ..	57.3	236 01.3 ..	19.3	Adhara	255 09.2	S29 00.1
04	175 18.3	287 19.6	36.1	165 58.0	02.6	281 40.4	57.4	251 03.4	19.2	Aldebaran	290 44.8	N16 32.7
05	190 20.8	302 19.2	36.6	180 58.9	03.4	296 42.3	57.4	266 05.6	19.2			
06	205 23.3	317 18.9	S18 37.0	195 59.8	N 4 04.1	311 44.3	S21 57.5	281 07.7	S22 19.2	Alioth	166 17.2	N55 51.2
W 07	220 25.7	332 18.6	37.5	211 00.7	04.8	326 46.2	57.5	296 09.9	19.2	Alkaid	152 55.9	N49 12.9
E 08	235 28.2	347 18.3	38.0	226 01.6	05.5	341 48.2	57.6	311 12.0	19.1	Alnair	27 39.4	S46 52.3
D 09	250 30.7	2 17.9 ..	38.5	241 02.6 ..	06.2	356 50.1 ..	57.7	326 14.2 ..	19.1	Alnilam	275 42.2	S 1 11.6
N 10	265 33.1	17 17.6	38.9	256 03.5	06.9	11 52.1	57.7	341 16.4	19.1	Alphard	217 52.1	S 8 44.5
E 11	280 35.6	32 17.3	39.4	271 04.4	07.6	26 54.0	57.8	356 18.5	19.1			
S 12	295 38.1	47 17.0	S18 39.9	286 05.3	N 4 08.3	41 55.9	S21 57.8	11 20.7	S22 19.0	Alphecca	126 08.0	N26 39.0
D 13	310 40.5	62 16.6	40.3	301 06.3	09.0	56 57.9	57.9	26 22.8	19.0	Alpheratz	357 39.7	N29 11.7
A 14	325 43.0	77 16.3	40.8	316 07.2	09.7	71 59.8	57.9	41 25.0	19.0	Altair	62 04.9	N 8 55.1
Y 15	340 45.5	92 16.0 ..	41.3	331 08.1 ..	10.4	87 01.8 ..	58.0	56 27.1 ..	18.9	Ankaa	353 12.1	S42 12.5
16	355 47.9	107 15.6	41.7	346 09.0	11.1	102 03.7	58.0	71 29.3	18.9	Antares	112 21.8	S26 28.2
17	10 50.4	122 15.3	42.2	1 09.9	11.8	117 05.7	58.1	86 31.4	18.9			
18	25 52.8	137 15.0	S18 42.7	16 10.9	N 4 12.6	132 07.6	S21 58.1	101 33.6	S22 18.9	Arcturus	145 52.3	N19 05.0
19	40 55.3	152 14.6	43.1	31 11.8	13.3	147 09.5	58.2	116 35.7	18.8	Atria	107 20.7	S69 03.3
20	55 57.8	167 14.3	43.6	46 12.7	14.0	162 11.5	58.3	131 37.9	18.8	Avior	234 15.8	S59 34.3
21	71 00.2	182 14.0 ..	44.1	61 13.6 ..	14.7	177 13.4 ..	58.3	146 40.0 ..	18.8	Bellatrix	278 27.6	N 6 21.8
22	86 02.7	197 13.6	44.5	76 14.5	15.4	192 15.4	58.4	161 42.2	18.8	Betelgeuse	270 56.9	N 7 24.4
23	101 05.2	212 13.3	45.0	91 15.5	16.1	207 17.3	58.4	176 44.3	18.7			
17 00	116 07.6	227 13.0	S18 45.5	106 16.4	N 4 16.8	222 19.3	S21 58.5	191 46.5	S22 18.7	Canopus	263 53.9	S52 42.6
01	131 10.1	242 12.6	45.9	121 17.3	17.5	237 21.2	58.5	206 48.6	18.7	Capella	280 28.4	N46 00.9
02	146 12.6	257 12.3	46.4	136 18.2	18.2	252 23.2	58.6	221 50.8	18.7	Deneb	49 29.3	N45 21.0
03	161 15.0	272 12.0 ..	46.8	151 19.2 ..	18.9	267 25.1 ..	58.6	236 52.9 ..	18.6	Denebola	182 29.6	N14 27.9
04	176 17.5	287 11.6	47.3	166 20.1	19.6	282 27.0	58.7	251 55.1	18.6	Diphda	348 52.2	S17 53.2
05	191 19.9	302 11.3	47.8	181 21.0	20.3	297 29.0	58.7	266 57.2	18.6			
06	206 22.4	317 10.9	S18 48.2	196 21.9	N 4 21.0	312 30.9	S21 58.8	281 59.4	S22 18.6	Dubhe	193 46.6	N61 38.7
T 07	221 24.9	332 10.6	48.7	211 22.8	21.7	327 32.9	58.9	297 01.5	18.5	Elnath	278 07.5	N28 37.3
H 08	236 27.3	347 10.2	49.1	226 23.8	22.4	342 34.8	58.9	312 03.7	18.5	Eltanin	90 44.9	N51 29.2
U 09	251 29.8	2 09.9 ..	49.6	241 24.7 ..	23.1	357 36.8 ..	59.0	327 05.8 ..	18.5	Enif	33 43.7	N 9 57.7
R 10	266 32.3	17 09.6	50.1	256 25.6	23.9	12 38.7	59.0	342 08.0	18.4	Fomalhaut	15 20.1	S29 31.5
S 11	281 34.7	32 09.2	50.5	271 26.5	24.6	27 40.7	59.1	357 10.1	18.4			
D 12	296 37.2	47 08.9	S18 51.0	286 27.4	N 4 25.3	42 42.6	S21 59.1	12 12.3	S22 18.4	Gacrux	171 56.4	S57 12.8
A 13	311 39.7	62 08.5	51.4	301 28.4	26.0	57 44.6	59.2	27 14.4	18.4	Gienah	175 48.3	S17 38.7
Y 14	326 42.1	77 08.2	51.9	316 29.3	26.7	72 46.5	59.2	42 16.6	18.3	Hadar	148 42.5	S60 27.4
15	341 44.6	92 07.8 ..	52.3	331 30.2 ..	27.4	87 48.4 ..	59.3	57 18.8 ..	18.3	Hamal	327 56.4	N23 33.1
16	356 47.1	107 07.5	52.8	346 31.1	28.1	102 50.4	59.3	72 20.9	18.3	Kaus Aust.	83 39.2	S34 22.4
17	11 49.5	122 07.1	53.2	1 32.0	28.8	117 52.3	59.4	87 23.1	18.3			
18	26 52.0	137 06.8	S18 53.7	16 33.0	N 4 29.5	132 54.3	S21 59.4	102 25.2	S22 18.2	Kochab	137 20.5	N74 04.4
19	41 54.4	152 06.4	54.2	31 33.9	30.2	147 56.2	59.5	117 27.4	18.2	Markab	13 34.8	N15 18.4
20	56 56.9	167 06.1	54.6	46 34.8	30.9	162 58.2	59.6	132 29.5	18.2	Menkar	314 10.9	N 4 09.6
21	71 59.4	182 05.7 ..	55.1	61 35.7 ..	31.6	178 00.1 ..	59.6	147 31.7 ..	18.1	Menkent	148 03.1	S36 27.5
22	87 01.8	197 05.4	55.5	76 36.6	32.3	193 02.1	59.7	162 33.8	18.1	Miaplacidus	221 38.0	S69 47.6
23	102 04.3	212 05.0	56.0	91 37.6	33.0	208 04.0	59.7	177 36.0	18.1			
18 00	117 06.8	227 04.7	S18 56.4	106 38.5	N 4 33.7	223 06.0	S21 59.8	192 38.1	S22 18.1	Mirfak	308 34.6	N49 55.7
01	132 09.2	242 04.3	56.9	121 39.4	34.4	238 07.9	59.8	207 40.3	18.1	Nunki	75 54.0	S26 16.3
02	147 11.7	257 04.0	57.3	136 40.3	35.1	253 09.9	59.9	222 42.4	18.0	Peacock	53 13.9	S56 40.4
03	162 14.2	272 03.6 ..	57.8	151 41.2 ..	35.8	268 11.8 21 59.9		237 44.6 ..	18.0	Pollux	243 22.7	N27 58.6
04	177 16.6	287 03.2	58.2	166 42.2	36.5	283 13.8 22 00.0		252 46.7	18.0	Procyon	244 55.4	N 5 10.4
05	192 19.1	302 02.9	58.6	181 43.1	37.3	298 15.7	00.0	267 48.9	17.9			
06	207 21.6	317 02.5	S18 59.1	196 44.0	N 4 38.0	313 17.7	S22 00.1	282 51.0	S22 17.9	Rasalhague	96 03.2	N12 32.8
F 07	222 24.0	332 02.2	18 59.5	211 44.9	38.7	328 19.6	00.1	297 53.2	17.9	Regulus	207 39.2	N11 52.4
R 08	237 26.5	347 01.8	19 00.0	226 45.8	39.4	343 21.6	00.2	312 55.3	17.9	Rigel	281 08.1	S 8 11.0
I 09	252 28.9	2 01.4 ..	00.4	241 46.7 ..	40.1	358 23.5 ..	00.2	327 57.5 ..	17.8	Rigil Kent.	139 46.7	S60 54.4
10	267 31.4	17 01.1	00.9	256 47.7	40.8	13 25.5	00.3	342 59.6	17.8	Sabik	102 08.5	S15 44.7
11	282 33.9	32 00.7	01.3	271 48.6	41.5	28 27.4	00.4	358 01.8	17.8			
D 12	297 36.3	47 00.4	S19 01.8	286 49.5	N 4 42.2	43 29.4	S22 00.4	13 04.0	S22 17.8	Schedar	349 36.3	N56 38.6
A 13	312 38.8	62 00.0	02.2	301 50.4	42.9	58 31.3	00.5	28 06.1	17.7	Shaula	96 17.1	S37 06.8
Y 14	327 41.3	76 59.6	02.6	316 51.3	43.6	73 33.3	00.5	43 08.3	17.7	Sirius	258 30.0	S16 44.8
15	342 43.7	91 59.3 ..	03.1	331 52.3 ..	44.3	88 35.2 ..	00.6	58 10.4 ..	17.7	Spica	158 27.2	S11 15.5
16	357 46.2	106 58.9	03.5	346 53.2	45.0	103 37.2	00.6	73 12.6	17.7	Suhail	222 49.2	S43 30.5
17	12 48.7	121 58.5	04.0	1 54.1	45.7	118 39.1	00.7	88 14.7	17.6			
18	27 51.1	136 58.2	S19 04.4	16 55.0	N 4 46.4	133 41.1	S22 00.7	103 16.9	S22 17.6	Vega	80 36.8	N38 48.1
19	42 53.6	151 57.8	04.8	31 55.9	47.1	148 43.0	00.8	118 19.0	17.6	Zuben'ubi	137 01.3	S16 07.0
20	57 56.1	166 57.4	05.3	46 56.9	47.8	163 45.0	00.8	133 21.2	17.6		SHA	Mer.Pass.
21	72 58.5	181 57.1 ..	05.7	61 57.8 ..	48.5	178 46.9 ..	00.9	148 23.3 ..	17.5			h m
22	88 01.0	196 56.7	06.2	76 58.7	49.2	193 48.9	00.9	163 25.5	17.5	Venus	111 05.3	8 51
23	103 03.4	211 56.3	06.6	91 59.6	49.9	208 50.8	01.0	178 27.6	17.5	Mars	350 08.8	16 54
Mer. Pass. 16 12.8		v −0.3 d 0.5		v 0.9 d 0.7		v 1.9 d 0.1		v 2.2 d 0.0		Jupiter	106 11.6	9 10
										Saturn	75 38.8	11 11

© British Crown Copyright 2018. All rights reserved.

UT	SUN GHA	SUN Dec	MOON GHA	v	Dec	d	HP
d h	° '	° '	° '	'	° '	'	'
16 00	177 37.3	S21 01.7	70 10.6	11.3	N11 48.6	10.3	57.3
01	192 37.1	01.3	84 40.9	11.3	11 58.9	10.2	57.3
02	207 36.9	00.8	99 11.2	11.2	12 09.1	10.2	57.4
03	222 36.7	21 00.3	113 41.4	11.2	12 19.3	10.1	57.4
04	237 36.5	20 59.8	128 11.6	11.0	12 29.4	10.0	57.4
05	252 36.3	59.4	142 41.6	10.9	12 39.4	10.1	57.5
06	267 36.0	S20 58.9	157 11.5	10.9	N12 49.5	9.9	57.5
W 07	282 35.8	58.4	171 41.4	10.7	12 59.4	9.9	57.6
E 08	297 35.6	58.0	186 11.1	10.7	13 09.3	9.9	57.6
D 09	312 35.4	.. 57.5	200 40.8	10.6	13 19.2	9.8	57.6
N 10	327 35.2	57.0	215 10.4	10.5	13 29.0	9.7	57.7
E 11	342 35.0	56.5	229 39.9	10.4	13 38.7	9.7	57.7
S 12	357 34.8	S20 56.1	244 09.3	10.2	N13 48.4	9.6	57.8
D 13	12 34.5	55.6	258 38.5	10.2	13 58.0	9.6	57.8
A 14	27 34.3	55.1	273 07.7	10.2	14 07.6	9.5	57.8
Y 15	42 34.1	.. 54.6	287 36.9	10.0	14 17.1	9.4	57.9
16	57 33.9	54.1	302 05.9	9.9	14 26.5	9.4	57.9
17	72 33.7	53.7	316 34.8	9.8	14 35.9	9.3	58.0
18	87 33.5	S20 53.2	331 03.6	9.7	N14 45.2	9.2	58.0
19	102 33.3	52.7	345 32.3	9.6	14 54.4	9.2	58.0
20	117 33.1	52.2	0 00.9	9.5	15 03.6	9.1	58.1
21	132 32.9	.. 51.7	14 29.4	9.5	15 12.7	9.0	58.1
22	147 32.6	51.3	28 57.9	9.3	15 21.7	9.0	58.2
23	162 32.4	50.8	43 26.2	9.2	15 30.7	8.8	58.2
17 00	177 32.2	S20 50.3	57 54.4	9.1	N15 39.5	8.8	58.2
01	192 32.0	49.8	72 22.5	9.0	15 48.3	8.8	58.3
02	207 31.8	49.3	86 50.5	8.9	15 57.1	8.6	58.3
03	222 31.6	.. 48.8	101 18.4	8.9	16 05.7	8.6	58.4
04	237 31.4	48.3	115 46.3	8.7	16 14.3	8.5	58.4
05	252 31.2	47.9	130 14.0	8.6	16 22.8	8.4	58.4
06	267 31.0	S20 47.4	144 41.6	8.5	N16 31.2	8.3	58.5
T 07	282 30.8	46.9	159 09.1	8.4	16 39.5	8.2	58.5
H 08	297 30.6	46.4	173 36.5	8.3	16 47.7	8.2	58.6
U 09	312 30.4	.. 45.9	188 03.8	8.2	16 55.9	8.0	58.6
R 10	327 30.1	45.4	202 31.0	8.1	17 03.9	8.0	58.7
11	342 29.9	44.9	216 58.1	8.0	17 11.9	7.8	58.7
S 12	357 29.7	S20 44.4	231 25.1	7.9	N17 19.7	7.8	58.7
D 13	12 29.5	43.9	245 52.0	7.8	17 27.5	7.7	58.8
A 14	27 29.3	43.4	260 18.8	7.7	17 35.2	7.6	58.8
Y 15	42 29.1	.. 42.9	274 45.5	7.6	17 42.8	7.5	58.9
16	57 28.9	42.5	289 12.1	7.5	17 50.3	7.4	58.9
17	72 28.7	42.0	303 38.6	7.4	17 57.7	7.3	58.9
18	87 28.5	S20 41.5	318 05.0	7.3	N18 05.0	7.2	59.0
19	102 28.3	41.0	332 31.3	7.2	18 12.2	7.1	59.0
20	117 28.1	40.5	346 57.5	7.0	18 19.3	7.0	59.1
21	132 27.9	.. 40.0	1 23.5	7.0	18 26.3	6.8	59.1
22	147 27.7	39.5	15 49.5	6.9	18 33.1	6.8	59.1
23	162 27.5	39.0	30 15.4	6.8	18 39.9	6.7	59.2
18 00	177 27.3	S20 38.5	44 41.2	6.7	N18 46.6	6.5	59.2
01	192 27.1	38.0	59 06.9	6.5	18 53.1	6.5	59.3
02	207 26.9	37.5	73 32.4	6.5	18 59.6	6.3	59.3
03	222 26.7	.. 37.0	87 57.9	6.4	19 05.9	6.2	59.3
04	237 26.5	36.5	102 23.3	6.3	19 12.1	6.1	59.4
05	252 26.3	36.0	116 48.6	6.2	19 18.2	6.0	59.4
06	267 26.1	S20 35.4	131 13.8	6.1	N19 24.2	5.9	59.4
07	282 25.9	34.9	145 38.9	6.0	19 30.1	5.7	59.5
08	297 25.7	34.4	160 03.9	5.9	19 35.8	5.6	59.5
F 09	312 25.5	.. 33.9	174 28.8	5.8	19 41.4	5.5	59.6
R 10	327 25.3	33.4	188 53.6	5.7	19 46.9	5.4	59.6
I 11	342 25.1	32.9	203 18.3	5.6	19 52.3	5.2	59.6
D 12	357 24.9	S20 32.4	217 42.9	5.6	N19 57.5	5.2	59.7
A 13	12 24.7	31.9	232 07.5	5.4	20 02.7	4.9	59.7
Y 14	27 24.5	31.4	246 31.9	5.4	20 07.6	4.9	59.7
15	42 24.3	.. 30.9	260 56.3	5.2	20 12.5	4.7	59.8
16	57 24.1	30.4	275 20.5	5.2	20 17.2	4.6	59.8
17	72 23.9	29.9	289 44.7	5.1	20 21.8	4.5	59.8
18	87 23.7	S20 29.3	304 08.8	5.0	N20 26.3	4.3	59.9
19	102 23.5	28.8	318 32.8	4.9	20 30.6	4.2	59.9
20	117 23.3	28.3	332 56.7	4.8	20 34.8	4.1	60.0
21	132 23.1	.. 27.8	347 20.5	4.8	20 38.9	3.9	60.0
22	147 22.9	27.3	1 44.3	4.7	20 42.8	3.8	60.0
23	162 22.7	26.8	16 08.0	4.6	N20 46.6	3.6	60.1
	SD 16.3	d 0.5	SD 15.7		16.0		16.3

Lat.	Twilight Naut.	Twilight Civil	Sunrise	Moonrise 16	Moonrise 17	Moonrise 18	Moonrise 19
°	h m	h m	h m	h m	h m	h m	h m
N 72	07 56	09 44	▬	10 31	09 53	▭	▭
N 70	07 42	09 12	11 47	10 56	10 43	10 10	▭
68	07 31	08 49	10 25	11 15	11 15	11 17	11 32
66	07 21	08 31	09 48	11 31	11 38	11 53	12 26
64	07 13	08 16	09 22	11 44	11 57	12 19	12 59
62	07 05	08 03	09 01	11 55	12 12	12 40	13 23
60	06 59	07 53	08 45	12 04	12 25	12 56	13 42
N 58	06 53	07 43	08 31	12 12	12 37	13 10	13 58
56	06 48	07 35	08 19	12 19	12 46	13 23	14 12
54	06 43	07 28	08 09	12 26	12 55	13 33	14 24
52	06 39	07 21	08 00	12 32	13 03	13 43	14 34
50	06 34	07 15	07 51	12 37	13 10	13 51	14 44
45	06 25	07 01	07 34	12 48	13 25	14 09	15 04
N 40	06 16	06 50	07 19	12 58	13 37	14 24	15 20
35	06 09	06 40	07 07	13 06	13 48	14 37	15 33
30	06 01	06 31	06 56	13 13	13 57	14 48	15 45
20	05 47	06 14	06 38	13 26	14 13	15 06	16 05
N 10	05 33	05 59	06 22	13 37	14 28	15 23	16 23
0	05 19	05 44	06 06	13 48	14 41	15 38	16 40
S 10	05 02	05 28	05 51	13 58	14 54	15 54	16 56
20	04 42	05 10	05 34	14 09	15 09	16 11	17 14
30	04 16	04 48	05 15	14 22	15 25	16 30	17 35
35	04 00	04 35	05 04	14 30	15 35	16 41	17 47
40	03 40	04 19	04 51	14 39	15 46	16 54	18 01
45	03 14	04 00	04 35	14 49	15 59	17 10	18 17
S 50	02 38	03 35	04 16	15 01	16 15	17 29	18 37
52	02 18	03 22	04 07	15 07	16 23	17 38	18 47
54	01 52	03 08	03 57	15 13	16 31	17 48	18 58
56	01 13	02 51	03 45	15 20	16 41	17 59	19 10
58	////	02 30	03 31	15 28	16 51	18 12	19 24
S 60	////	02 02	03 16	15 38	17 04	18 27	19 41

Lat.	Sunset	Twilight Civil	Twilight Naut.	Moonset 16	Moonset 17	Moonset 18	Moonset 19
°	h m	h m	h m	h m	h m	h m	h m
N 72	▬	14 37	16 25	04 18	06 45	▭	▭
N 70	12 34	15 08	16 39	03 55	05 56	08 26	▭
68	13 56	15 32	16 50	03 37	05 25	07 20	09 12
66	14 33	15 50	17 00	03 23	05 03	06 45	08 18
64	14 59	16 05	17 08	03 11	04 45	06 19	07 45
62	15 19	16 17	17 15	03 01	04 30	05 59	07 21
60	15 36	16 28	17 22	02 53	04 18	05 43	07 02
N 58	15 49	16 37	17 27	02 45	04 07	05 29	06 46
56	16 01	16 46	17 33	02 39	03 58	05 17	06 33
54	16 12	16 53	17 37	02 33	03 50	05 07	06 21
52	16 21	17 00	17 42	02 28	03 43	04 58	06 10
50	16 29	17 06	17 46	02 23	03 36	04 50	06 01
45	16 47	17 19	17 56	02 13	03 22	04 33	05 42
N 40	17 01	17 31	18 04	02 04	03 11	04 18	05 26
35	17 13	17 41	18 12	01 57	03 01	04 06	05 12
30	17 24	17 50	18 19	01 51	02 52	03 56	05 01
20	17 42	18 06	18 33	01 40	02 37	03 38	04 41
N 10	17 58	18 21	18 47	01 30	02 25	03 22	04 23
0	18 14	18 36	19 01	01 21	02 12	03 08	04 07
S 10	18 29	18 52	19 18	01 13	02 00	02 53	03 51
20	18 46	19 10	19 38	01 03	01 48	02 38	03 34
30	19 05	19 31	20 03	00 52	01 33	02 20	03 14
35	19 16	19 45	20 20	00 46	01 25	02 10	03 02
40	19 29	20 00	20 40	00 39	01 15	01 58	02 49
45	19 44	20 20	21 05	00 31	01 04	01 44	02 33
S 50	20 03	20 44	21 41	00 21	00 50	01 27	02 13
52	20 12	20 57	22 00	00 17	00 44	01 19	02 04
54	20 22	21 11	22 25	00 12	00 37	01 10	01 54
56	20 34	21 28	23 02	00 06	00 30	01 00	01 42
58	20 47	21 48	////	00 00	00 21	00 49	01 29
S 60	21 03	22 15	////	24 11	00 11	00 36	01 13

Day	SUN Eqn. of Time 00h	SUN Eqn. of Time 12h	SUN Mer. Pass.	MOON Mer. Pass. Upper	MOON Mer. Pass. Lower	Age	Phase
d	m s	m s	h m	h m	h m	d	%
16	09 30	09 41	12 10	20 00	07 34	10	72
17	09 51	10 01	12 10	20 54	08 27	11	82
18	10 10	10 20	12 10	21 53	09 23	12	90

© British Crown Copyright 2018. All rights reserved.

UT	ARIES GHA	VENUS −4·4 GHA	Dec	MARS +0·7 GHA	Dec	JUPITER −1·8 GHA	Dec	SATURN +0·5 GHA	Dec	STARS Name	SHA	Dec
19 00	118 05.9	226 55.9	S19 07.0	107 00.5	N 4 50.6	223 52.8	S22 01.0	193 29.8	S22 17.4	Acamar	315 15.3	S40 14.1
01	133 08.4	241 55.6	.. 07.5	122 01.4	51.3	238 54.7	01.1	208 31.9	17.4	Achernar	335 24.0	S57 08.9
02	148 10.8	256 55.2	07.9	137 02.4	52.0	253 56.7	01.1	223 34.1	17.4	Acrux	173 04.7	S63 11.9
03	163 13.3	271 54.8	.. 08.3	152 03.3	.. 52.7	268 58.6	.. 01.2	238 36.3	.. 17.4	Adhara	255 09.2	S29 00.1
04	178 15.8	286 54.4	08.8	167 04.2	53.4	284 00.6	01.2	253 38.4	17.3	Aldebaran	290 44.8	N16 32.7
05	193 18.2	301 54.1	09.2	182 05.1	54.1	299 02.5	01.3	268 40.6	17.3			
06	208 20.7	316 53.7	S19 09.6	197 06.0	N 4 54.8	314 04.5	S22 01.3	283 42.7	S22 17.3	Alioth	166 17.2	N55 51.2
S 07	223 23.2	331 53.3	10.1	212 06.9	55.5	329 06.4	01.4	298 44.9	17.3	Alkaid	152 55.9	N49 12.9
A 08	238 25.6	346 52.9	10.5	227 07.9	56.2	344 08.4	01.5	313 47.0	17.2	Alnair	27 39.4	S46 52.3
T 09	253 28.1	1 52.6	.. 10.9	242 08.8	.. 56.9	359 10.3	.. 01.5	328 49.2	.. 17.2	Alnilam	275 42.2	S 1 11.6
U 10	268 30.6	16 52.2	11.3	257 09.7	57.7	14 12.3	01.6	343 51.3	17.2	Alphard	217 52.0	S 8 44.5
R 11	283 33.0	31 51.8	11.8	272 10.6	58.4	29 14.2	01.6	358 53.5	17.2			
D 12	298 35.5	46 51.4	S19 12.2	287 11.5	N 4 59.1	44 16.2	S22 01.7	13 55.6	S22 17.1	Alphecca	126 07.9	N26 39.0
A 13	313 37.9	61 51.0	12.6	302 12.5	4 59.8	59 18.1	01.7	28 57.8	17.1	Alpheratz	357 39.7	N29 11.7
Y 14	328 40.4	76 50.7	13.1	317 13.4	5 00.5	74 20.1	01.8	43 59.9	17.1	Altair	62 04.9	N 8 55.1
15	343 42.9	91 50.3	.. 13.5	332 14.3	.. 01.2	89 22.0	.. 01.8	59 02.1	.. 17.0	Ankaa	353 12.1	S42 12.5
16	358 45.3	106 49.9	13.9	347 15.2	01.9	104 24.0	01.9	74 04.3	17.0	Antares	112 21.8	S26 28.2
17	13 47.8	121 49.5	14.3	2 16.1	02.6	119 25.9	01.9	89 06.4	17.0			
18	28 50.3	136 49.1	S19 14.8	17 17.0	N 5 03.3	134 27.9	S22 02.0	104 08.6	S22 17.0	Arcturus	145 52.3	N19 05.0
19	43 52.7	151 48.7	15.2	32 18.0	04.0	149 29.8	02.0	119 10.7	16.9	Atria	107 20.6	S69 03.3
20	58 55.2	166 48.4	15.6	47 18.9	04.7	164 31.8	02.1	134 12.9	16.9	Avior	234 15.8	S59 34.3
21	73 57.7	181 48.0	.. 16.0	62 19.8	.. 05.4	179 33.8	.. 02.1	149 15.0	.. 16.9	Bellatrix	278 27.6	N 6 21.8
22	89 00.1	196 47.6	16.5	77 20.7	06.1	194 35.7	02.2	164 17.2	16.9	Betelgeuse	270 56.9	N 7 24.4
23	104 02.6	211 47.2	16.9	92 21.6	06.8	209 37.7	02.2	179 19.3	16.8			
20 00	119 05.1	226 46.8	S19 17.3	107 22.5	N 5 07.5	224 39.6	S22 02.3	194 21.5	S22 16.8	Canopus	263 53.9	S52 42.6
01	134 07.5	241 46.4	17.7	122 23.4	08.2	239 41.6	02.3	209 23.6	16.8	Capella	280 28.4	N46 00.9
02	149 10.0	256 46.0	18.1	137 24.4	08.9	254 43.5	02.4	224 25.8	16.8	Deneb	49 29.3	N45 20.9
03	164 12.4	271 45.6	.. 18.6	152 25.3	.. 09.6	269 45.5	.. 02.4	239 27.9	.. 16.7	Denebola	182 29.6	N14 27.9
04	179 14.9	286 45.2	19.0	167 26.2	10.3	284 47.4	02.5	254 30.1	16.7	Diphda	348 52.2	S17 53.2
05	194 17.4	301 44.8	19.4	182 27.1	11.0	299 49.4	02.5	269 32.3	16.7			
06	209 19.8	316 44.5	S19 19.8	197 28.0	N 5 11.7	314 51.3	S22 02.6	284 34.4	S22 16.6	Dubhe	193 46.6	N61 38.7
07	224 22.3	331 44.1	20.2	212 28.9	12.4	329 53.3	02.6	299 36.6	16.6	Elnath	278 07.5	N28 37.3
08	239 24.8	346 43.7	20.6	227 29.9	13.1	344 55.3	02.7	314 38.7	16.6	Eltanin	90 44.8	N51 29.1
S 09	254 27.2	1 43.3	.. 21.1	242 30.8	.. 13.8	359 57.2	.. 02.7	329 40.9	.. 16.6	Enif	33 43.7	N 9 57.7
U 10	269 29.7	16 42.9	21.5	257 31.7	14.5	14 59.2	02.8	344 43.0	16.5	Fomalhaut	15 20.1	S29 31.5
N 11	284 32.2	31 42.5	21.9	272 32.6	15.2	30 01.1	02.8	359 45.2	16.5			
D 12	299 34.6	46 42.1	S19 22.3	287 33.5	N 5 15.9	45 03.1	S22 02.9	14 47.3	S22 16.5	Gacrux	171 56.4	S57 12.8
A 13	314 37.1	61 41.7	22.7	302 34.4	16.6	60 05.0	02.9	29 49.5	16.5	Gienah	175 48.2	S17 38.7
Y 14	329 39.5	76 41.3	23.1	317 35.4	17.3	75 07.0	03.0	44 51.6	16.4	Hadar	148 42.5	S60 27.5
15	344 42.0	91 40.9	.. 23.5	332 36.3	.. 18.0	90 08.9	.. 03.0	59 53.8	.. 16.4	Hamal	327 56.4	N23 33.1
16	359 44.5	106 40.5	23.9	347 37.2	18.7	105 10.9	03.1	74 56.0	16.4	Kaus Aust.	83 39.1	S34 22.4
17	14 46.9	121 40.1	24.4	2 38.1	19.4	120 12.9	03.1	89 58.1	16.4			
18	29 49.4	136 39.7	S19 24.8	17 39.0	N 5 20.1	135 14.8	S22 03.2	105 00.3	S22 16.3	Kochab	137 20.5	N74 04.4
19	44 51.9	151 39.3	25.2	32 39.9	20.8	150 16.8	03.2	120 02.4	16.3	Markab	13 34.8	N15 18.4
20	59 54.3	166 38.9	25.6	47 40.8	21.5	165 18.7	03.3	135 04.6	16.3	Menkar	314 10.9	N 4 09.6
21	74 56.8	181 38.5	.. 26.0	62 41.8	.. 22.2	180 20.7	.. 03.3	150 06.7	.. 16.2	Menkent	148 03.1	S36 27.5
22	89 59.3	196 38.1	26.4	77 42.7	22.9	195 22.6	03.4	165 08.9	16.2	Miaplacidus	221 38.0	S69 47.6
23	105 01.7	211 37.7	26.8	92 43.6	23.6	210 24.6	03.4	180 11.0	16.2			
21 00	120 04.2	226 37.3	S19 27.2	107 44.5	N 5 24.3	225 26.6	S22 03.5	195 13.2	S22 16.2	Mirfak	308 34.6	N49 55.7
01	135 06.7	241 36.9	27.6	122 45.4	25.0	240 28.5	03.5	210 15.4	16.1	Nunki	75 54.0	S26 16.3
02	150 09.1	256 36.5	28.0	137 46.3	25.7	255 30.5	03.6	225 17.5	16.1	Peacock	53 13.9	S56 40.4
03	165 11.6	271 36.0	.. 28.4	152 47.2	.. 26.4	270 32.4	.. 03.6	240 19.7	.. 16.1	Pollux	243 22.7	N27 58.6
04	180 14.0	286 35.6	28.8	167 48.2	27.1	285 34.4	03.7	255 21.8	16.1	Procyon	244 55.4	N 5 10.4
05	195 16.5	301 35.2	29.2	182 49.1	27.8	300 36.3	03.7	270 24.0	16.0			
06	210 19.0	316 34.8	S19 29.6	197 50.0	N 5 28.5	315 38.3	S22 03.8	285 26.1	S22 16.0	Rasalhague	96 03.2	N12 32.8
07	225 21.4	331 34.4	30.0	212 50.9	29.2	330 40.3	03.8	300 28.3	16.0	Regulus	207 39.2	N11 52.3
08	240 23.9	346 34.0	30.4	227 51.8	29.9	345 42.2	03.9	315 30.4	16.0	Rigel	281 08.1	S 8 11.0
M 09	255 26.4	1 33.6	.. 30.8	242 52.7	.. 30.6	0 44.2	.. 03.9	330 32.6	.. 15.9	Rigil Kent.	139 46.6	S60 54.4
O 10	270 28.8	16 33.2	31.2	257 53.6	31.3	15 46.1	04.0	345 34.8	15.9	Sabik	102 08.4	S15 44.7
N 11	285 31.3	31 32.8	31.6	272 54.6	32.0	30 48.1	04.0	0 36.9	15.9			
D 12	300 33.8	46 32.3	S19 32.0	287 55.5	N 5 32.7	45 50.1	S22 04.1	15 39.1	S22 15.8	Schedar	349 36.3	N56 38.6
A 13	315 36.2	61 31.9	32.4	302 56.4	33.4	60 52.0	04.1	30 41.2	15.8	Shaula	96 17.1	S37 06.8
Y 14	330 38.7	76 31.5	32.8	317 57.3	34.1	75 54.0	04.2	45 43.4	15.8	Sirius	258 30.0	S16 44.8
15	345 41.2	91 31.1	.. 33.2	332 58.2	.. 34.8	90 55.9	.. 04.2	60 45.5	.. 15.8	Spica	158 27.2	S11 15.5
16	0 43.6	106 30.7	33.6	347 59.1	35.5	105 57.9	04.3	75 47.7	15.7	Suhail	222 49.2	S43 30.6
17	15 46.1	121 30.3	34.0	3 00.0	36.2	120 59.9	04.3	90 49.8	15.7			
18	30 48.5	136 29.9	S19 34.4	18 01.0	N 5 36.9	136 01.8	S22 04.4	105 52.0	S22 15.7	Vega	80 36.8	N38 48.1
19	45 51.0	151 29.4	34.8	33 01.9	37.6	151 03.8	04.4	120 54.2	15.7	Zuben'ubi	137 01.3	S16 07.0
20	60 53.5	166 29.0	35.2	48 02.8	38.2	166 05.7	04.5	135 56.3	15.6		SHA	Mer.Pass.
21	75 55.9	181 28.6	.. 35.6	63 03.7	.. 38.9	181 07.7	.. 04.5	150 58.5	.. 15.6			h m
22	90 58.4	196 28.2	36.0	78 04.6	39.6	196 09.7	04.6	166 00.6	15.6	Venus	107 41.8	8 53
23	106 00.9	211 27.8	36.4	93 05.5	40.3	211 11.6	04.6	181 02.8	15.5	Mars	348 17.5	16 49
	h m									Jupiter	105 34.6	9 00
Mer. Pass. 16 01.0	v −0.4 d 0.4			v 0.9 d 0.7		v 2.0 d 0.1		v 2.2 d 0.0		Saturn	75 16.4	11 01

© British Crown Copyright 2018. All rights reserved.

UT	SUN GHA	SUN Dec	MOON GHA	v	MOON Dec	d	HP
d h	° ′	° ′	° ′	′	° ′	′	′
19 00	177 22.5	S20 26.2	30 31.6	4.5	N20 50.2	3.5	60.1
01	192 22.3	25.7	44 55.1	4.4	20 53.7	3.3	60.1
02	207 22.1	25.2	59 18.5	4.4	20 57.0	3.3	60.2
03	222 21.9	.. 24.7	73 41.9	4.3	21 00.3	3.0	60.2
04	237 21.8	24.2	88 05.2	4.2	21 03.3	2.9	60.2
05	252 21.6	23.7	102 28.4	4.2	21 06.2	2.8	60.3
06	267 21.4	S20 23.1	116 51.6	4.1	N21 09.0	2.6	60.3
07	282 21.2	22.6	131 14.7	4.0	21 11.6	2.5	60.3
S 08	297 21.0	22.1	145 37.7	4.0	21 14.1	2.3	60.4
A 09	312 20.8	.. 21.6	160 00.7	3.9	21 16.4	2.2	60.4
T 10	327 20.6	21.0	174 23.6	3.8	21 18.6	2.0	60.4
U 11	342 20.4	20.5	188 46.4	3.8	21 20.6	1.8	60.5
R 12	357 20.2	S20 20.0	203 09.2	3.7	N21 22.4	1.7	60.5
D 13	12 20.0	19.5	217 31.9	3.6	21 24.1	1.6	60.5
A 14	27 19.8	18.9	231 54.5	3.7	21 25.7	1.4	60.5
Y 15	42 19.6	.. 18.4	246 17.2	3.5	21 27.1	1.3	60.6
16	57 19.5	17.9	260 39.7	3.5	21 28.3	1.1	60.6
17	72 19.3	17.4	275 02.2	3.5	21 29.4	1.0	60.6
18	87 19.1	S20 16.8	289 24.7	3.4	N21 30.4	0.7	60.7
19	102 18.9	16.3	303 47.1	3.4	21 31.1	0.6	60.7
20	117 18.7	15.8	318 09.5	3.3	21 31.7	0.5	60.7
21	132 18.5	.. 15.2	332 31.8	3.3	21 32.2	0.3	60.7
22	147 18.3	14.7	346 54.1	3.3	21 32.5	0.1	60.8
23	162 18.1	14.2	1 16.4	3.2	21 32.6	0.0	60.8
20 00	177 18.0	S20 13.6	15 38.6	3.2	N21 32.6	0.2	60.8
01	192 17.8	13.1	30 00.8	3.1	21 32.4	0.4	60.8
02	207 17.6	12.6	44 22.9	3.1	21 32.0	0.5	60.9
03	222 17.4	.. 12.0	58 45.0	3.2	21 31.5	0.7	60.9
04	237 17.2	11.5	73 07.2	3.0	21 30.8	0.8	60.9
05	252 17.0	11.0	87 29.2	3.1	21 30.0	1.0	60.9
06	267 16.8	S20 10.4	101 51.3	3.0	N21 29.0	1.2	60.9
07	282 16.7	09.9	116 13.3	3.0	21 27.8	1.3	61.0
08	297 16.5	09.4	130 35.3	3.0	21 26.5	1.5	61.0
S 09	312 16.3	.. 08.8	144 57.3	3.0	21 25.0	1.6	61.0
U 10	327 16.1	08.3	159 19.3	3.0	21 23.4	1.9	61.0
N 11	342 15.9	07.7	173 41.3	3.0	21 21.5	1.9	61.0
D 12	357 15.7	S20 07.2	188 03.3	2.9	N21 19.6	2.2	61.1
A 13	12 15.6	06.7	202 25.2	3.0	21 17.4	2.3	61.1
Y 14	27 15.4	06.1	216 47.2	3.0	21 15.1	2.5	61.1
15	42 15.2	.. 05.6	231 09.2	2.9	21 12.6	2.6	61.1
16	57 15.0	05.0	245 31.1	3.0	21 10.0	2.8	61.1
17	72 14.8	04.5	259 53.1	2.9	21 07.2	2.9	61.1
18	87 14.6	S20 03.9	274 15.0	3.0	N21 04.3	3.1	61.2
19	102 14.5	03.4	288 37.0	3.0	21 01.2	3.3	61.2
20	117 14.3	02.9	302 59.0	3.0	20 57.9	3.5	61.2
21	132 14.1	.. 02.3	317 21.0	3.0	20 54.4	3.6	61.2
22	147 13.9	01.8	331 43.0	3.0	20 50.8	3.7	61.2
23	162 13.7	01.2	346 05.0	3.1	20 47.1	3.9	61.2
21 00	177 13.6	S20 00.7	0 27.1	3.0	N20 43.2	4.1	61.2
01	192 13.4	20 00.1	14 49.1	3.1	20 39.1	4.2	61.3
02	207 13.2	19 59.6	29 11.2	3.1	20 34.9	4.4	61.3
03	222 13.0	.. 59.0	43 33.3	3.1	20 30.5	4.6	61.3
04	237 12.9	58.5	57 55.4	3.2	20 25.9	4.7	61.3
05	252 12.7	57.9	72 17.6	3.2	20 21.2	4.9	61.3
06	267 12.5	S19 57.4	86 39.8	3.2	N20 16.3	5.0	61.3
07	282 12.3	56.8	101 02.0	3.3	20 11.3	5.1	61.3
08	297 12.1	56.3	115 24.3	3.3	20 06.2	5.4	61.3
M 09	312 12.0	.. 55.7	129 46.6	3.3	20 00.8	5.4	61.3
O 10	327 11.8	55.1	144 08.9	3.4	19 55.4	5.7	61.3
N 11	342 11.6	54.6	158 31.3	3.4	19 49.7	5.7	61.3
D 12	357 11.4	S19 54.0	172 53.7	3.4	N19 44.0	6.0	61.3
A 13	12 11.3	53.5	187 16.1	3.5	19 38.0	6.0	61.3
Y 14	27 11.1	52.9	201 38.6	3.6	19 32.0	6.3	61.4
15	42 10.9	.. 52.4	216 01.2	3.6	19 25.7	6.3	61.4
16	57 10.7	51.8	230 23.8	3.6	19 19.4	6.5	61.4
17	72 10.6	51.2	244 46.4	3.7	19 12.9	6.7	61.4
18	87 10.4	S19 50.7	259 09.1	3.7	N19 06.2	6.8	61.4
19	102 10.2	50.1	273 31.8	3.8	18 59.4	6.9	61.4
20	117 10.1	49.6	287 54.6	3.9	18 52.5	7.1	61.4
21	132 09.9	.. 49.0	302 17.5	3.9	18 45.4	7.2	61.4
22	147 09.7	48.4	316 40.4	4.0	18 38.2	7.4	61.4
23	162 09.5	47.9	331 03.4	4.0	N18 30.8	7.4	61.4
	SD 16.3	d 0.5	SD 16.5		16.6		16.7

Lat.	Twilight Naut.	Twilight Civil	Sunrise	Moonrise 19	Moonrise 20	Moonrise 21	Moonrise 22
°	h m	h m	h m	h m	h m	h m	h m
N 72	07 48	09 32	■■■■	□	□	□	15 28
N 70	07 36	09 03	11 07	□	□	13 30	16 12
68	07 25	08 42	10 11	11 32	12 37	14 35	16 41
66	07 16	08 25	09 38	12 26	13 31	15 10	17 02
64	07 08	08 11	09 14	12 59	14 04	15 35	17 19
62	07 01	07 59	08 55	13 23	14 29	15 55	17 33
60	06 55	07 48	08 40	13 42	14 48	16 11	17 45
N 58	06 50	07 40	08 27	13 58	15 04	16 25	17 55
56	06 45	07 32	08 15	14 12	15 17	16 37	18 04
54	06 40	07 25	08 05	14 24	15 29	16 47	18 12
52	06 36	07 18	07 57	14 34	15 39	16 56	18 19
50	06 32	07 12	07 49	14 44	15 49	17 04	18 26
45	06 23	06 59	07 32	15 04	16 08	17 22	18 39
N 40	06 15	06 48	07 18	15 20	16 24	17 36	18 50
35	06 08	06 39	07 06	15 33	16 38	17 48	19 00
30	06 01	06 30	06 56	15 45	16 49	17 58	19 08
20	05 47	06 14	06 38	16 05	17 09	18 16	19 23
N 10	05 34	06 00	06 22	16 23	17 27	18 31	19 35
0	05 20	05 45	06 07	16 40	17 43	18 46	19 47
S 10	05 03	05 30	05 52	16 56	17 59	19 01	19 58
20	04 44	05 12	05 36	17 14	18 17	19 16	20 11
30	04 19	04 51	05 18	17 35	18 37	19 34	20 25
35	04 03	04 38	05 07	17 47	18 48	19 44	20 33
40	03 44	04 23	04 54	18 01	19 02	19 56	20 42
45	03 19	04 04	04 39	18 17	19 18	20 10	20 53
S 50	02 45	03 40	04 21	18 37	19 37	20 27	21 06
52	02 26	03 28	04 12	18 47	19 46	20 35	21 12
54	02 03	03 14	04 02	18 58	19 57	20 43	21 19
56	01 29	02 58	03 51	19 10	20 08	20 53	21 27
58	////	02 39	03 38	19 24	20 22	21 04	21 35
S 60	////	02 13	03 23	19 41	20 38	21 17	21 44

Lat.	Sunset	Twilight Civil	Twilight Naut.	Moonset 19	Moonset 20	Moonset 21	Moonset 22
°	h m	h m	h m	h m	h m	h m	h m
N 72	■■■■	14 51	16 35	□	□	11 52	
N 70	13 15	15 20	16 47	□	□	11 39	11 07
68	14 12	15 41	16 58	09 12	10 19	10 34	10 37
66	14 45	15 58	17 07	08 18	09 24	09 58	10 14
64	15 09	16 12	17 14	07 45	08 51	09 32	09 56
62	15 27	16 24	17 21	07 21	08 27	09 12	09 41
60	15 43	16 34	17 27	07 02	08 07	08 55	09 28
N 58	15 56	16 43	17 33	06 46	07 51	08 41	09 18
56	16 07	16 51	17 37	06 33	07 38	08 29	09 08
54	16 17	16 58	17 42	06 21	07 26	08 18	08 59
52	16 26	17 04	17 46	06 10	07 15	08 09	08 52
50	16 34	17 10	17 50	06 01	07 06	08 01	08 45
45	16 51	17 23	17 59	05 42	06 46	07 43	08 30
N 40	17 04	17 34	18 07	05 26	06 30	07 28	08 18
35	17 16	17 43	18 14	05 12	06 16	07 15	08 08
30	17 26	17 52	18 21	05 01	06 04	07 04	07 58
20	17 44	18 08	18 35	04 41	05 44	06 45	07 42
N 10	18 00	18 22	18 48	04 23	05 26	06 29	07 28
0	18 15	18 37	19 02	04 07	05 10	06 13	07 15
S 10	18 29	18 52	19 18	03 51	04 53	05 58	07 02
20	18 45	19 09	19 37	03 34	04 35	05 41	06 48
30	19 04	19 30	20 02	03 14	04 15	05 21	06 31
35	19 15	19 43	20 18	03 02	04 03	05 10	06 22
40	19 27	19 58	20 37	02 49	03 49	04 57	06 11
45	19 42	20 17	21 02	02 33	03 32	04 42	05 58
S 50	20 00	20 41	21 36	02 13	03 12	04 23	05 42
52	20 09	20 52	21 54	02 04	03 02	04 14	05 34
54	20 19	21 06	22 17	01 54	02 52	04 04	05 26
56	20 30	21 22	22 49	01 42	02 39	03 52	05 17
58	20 42	21 41	////	01 29	02 25	03 39	05 06
S 60	20 57	22 06	////	01 13	02 08	03 24	04 54

Day	SUN Eqn. of Time 00h	SUN Eqn. of Time 12h	SUN Mer. Pass.	MOON Mer. Pass. Upper	MOON Mer. Pass. Lower	Age	Phase
d	m s	m s	h m	h m	h m	d	%
19	10 30	10 39	12 11	22 55	10 23	13	96
20	10 48	10 57	12 11	23 58	11 26	14	99
21	11 05	11 14	12 11	25 01	12 30	15	100

© British Crown Copyright 2018. All rights reserved.

UT	ARIES GHA	VENUS −4.4 GHA	Dec	MARS +0.8 GHA	Dec	JUPITER −1.8 GHA	Dec	SATURN +0.5 GHA	Dec	STARS Name	SHA	Dec
22 00	121 03.3	226 27.3	S19 36.8	108 06.4	N 5 41.0	226 13.6	S22 04.7	196 04.9	S22 15.5	Acamar	315 15.3	S40 14.1
01	136 05.8	241 26.9	37.1	123 07.3	41.7	241 15.5	04.7	211 07.1	15.5	Achernar	335 24.0	S57 08.9
02	151 08.3	256 26.5	37.5	138 08.3	42.4	256 17.5	04.8	226 09.3	15.5	Acrux	173 04.7	S63 11.9
03	166 10.7	271 26.1 ..	37.9	153 09.2 ..	43.1	271 19.5 ..	04.8	241 11.4 ..	15.4	Adhara	255 09.2	S29 00.1
04	181 13.2	286 25.6	38.3	168 10.1	43.8	286 21.4	04.9	256 13.6	15.4	Aldebaran	290 44.8	N16 32.7
05	196 15.7	301 25.2	38.7	183 11.0	44.5	301 23.4	04.9	271 15.7	15.4			
06	211 18.1	316 24.8	S19 39.1	198 11.9	N 5 45.2	316 25.3	S22 05.0	286 17.9	S22 15.4	Alioth	166 17.2	N55 51.2
07	226 20.6	331 24.4	39.5	213 12.8	45.9	331 27.3	05.0	301 20.0	15.3	Alkaid	152 55.9	N49 12.9
08	241 23.0	346 23.9	39.9	228 13.7	46.6	346 29.3	05.1	316 22.2	15.3	Alnair	27 39.4	S46 52.3
09	256 25.5	1 23.5 ..	40.2	243 14.6 ..	47.3	1 31.2 ..	05.1	331 24.3 ..	15.3	Alnilam	275 42.2	S 1 11.6
10	271 28.0	16 23.1	40.6	258 15.6	48.0	16 33.2	05.2	346 26.5	15.3	Alphard	217 52.0	S 8 44.5
11	286 30.4	31 22.6	41.0	273 16.5	48.7	31 35.2	05.2	1 28.7	15.2			
12	301 32.9	46 22.2	S19 41.4	288 17.4	N 5 49.4	46 37.1	S22 05.3	16 30.8	S22 15.2	Alphecca	126 07.9	N26 39.0
13	316 35.4	61 21.8	41.8	303 18.3	50.1	61 39.1	05.3	31 33.0	15.2	Alpheratz	357 39.7	N29 11.7
14	331 37.8	76 21.4	42.1	318 19.2	50.8	76 41.0	05.4	46 35.1	15.1	Altair	62 04.8	N 8 55.1
15	346 40.3	91 20.9 ..	42.5	333 20.1 ..	51.5	91 43.0 ..	05.4	61 37.3 ..	15.1	Ankaa	353 12.1	S42 12.5
16	1 42.8	106 20.5	42.9	348 21.0	52.2	106 45.0	05.5	76 39.4	15.1	Antares	112 21.8	S26 28.2
17	16 45.2	121 20.1	43.3	3 21.9	52.9	121 46.9	05.5	91 41.6	15.1			
18	31 47.7	136 19.6	S19 43.7	18 22.8	N 5 53.6	136 48.9	S22 05.6	106 43.8	S22 15.0	Arcturus	145 52.3	N19 05.0
19	46 50.2	151 19.2	44.0	33 23.8	54.3	151 50.9	05.6	121 45.9	15.0	Atria	107 20.5	S69 03.3
20	61 52.6	166 18.8	44.4	48 24.7	55.0	166 52.8	05.7	136 48.1	15.0	Avior	234 15.8	S59 34.3
21	76 55.1	181 18.3 ..	44.8	63 25.6 ..	55.7	181 54.8 ..	05.7	151 50.2 ..	15.0	Bellatrix	278 27.6	N 6 21.8
22	91 57.5	196 17.9	45.2	78 26.5	56.4	196 56.8	05.8	166 52.4	14.9	Betelgeuse	270 56.9	N 7 24.4
23	107 00.0	211 17.5	45.5	93 27.4	57.0	211 58.7	05.8	181 54.5	14.9			
23 00	122 02.5	226 17.0	S19 45.9	108 28.3	N 5 57.7	227 00.7	S22 05.9	196 56.7	S22 14.9	Canopus	263 53.9	S52 42.6
01	137 04.9	241 16.6	46.3	123 29.2	58.4	242 02.6	05.9	211 58.9	14.8	Capella	280 28.4	N46 00.9
02	152 07.4	256 16.1	46.7	138 30.1	59.1	257 04.6	06.0	227 01.0	14.8	Deneb	49 29.3	N45 20.9
03	167 09.9	271 15.7 ..	47.0	153 31.0	5 59.8	272 06.6 ..	06.0	242 03.2 ..	14.8	Denebola	182 29.6	N14 27.9
04	182 12.3	286 15.3	47.4	168 32.0	6 00.5	287 08.5	06.1	257 05.3	14.8	Diphda	348 52.2	S17 53.2
05	197 14.8	301 14.8	47.8	183 32.9	01.2	302 10.5	06.1	272 07.5	14.7			
06	212 17.3	316 14.4	S19 48.1	198 33.8	N 6 01.9	317 12.5	S22 06.2	287 09.6	S22 14.7	Dubhe	193 46.6	N61 38.7
07	227 19.7	331 13.9	48.5	213 34.7	02.6	332 14.4	06.2	302 11.8	14.7	Elnath	278 07.5	N28 37.3
08	242 22.2	346 13.5	48.9	228 35.6	03.3	347 16.4	06.2	317 14.0	14.7	Eltanin	90 44.8	N51 29.1
09	257 24.6	1 13.0 ..	49.2	243 36.5 ..	04.0	2 18.4 ..	06.3	332 16.1 ..	14.6	Enif	33 43.7	N 9 57.7
10	272 27.1	16 12.6	49.6	258 37.4	04.7	17 20.3	06.3	347 18.3	14.6	Fomalhaut	15 20.1	S29 31.5
11	287 29.6	31 12.2	50.0	273 38.3	05.4	32 22.3	06.4	2 20.4	14.6			
12	302 32.0	46 11.7	S19 50.3	288 39.2	N 6 06.1	47 24.3	S22 06.4	17 22.6	S22 14.5	Gacrux	171 56.4	S57 12.9
13	317 34.5	61 11.3	50.7	303 40.2	06.8	62 26.2	06.5	32 24.8	14.5	Gienah	175 48.2	S17 38.7
14	332 37.0	76 10.8	51.1	318 41.1	07.5	77 28.2	06.5	47 26.9	14.5	Hadar	148 42.4	S60 27.5
15	347 39.4	91 10.4 ..	51.4	333 42.0 ..	08.2	92 30.2 ..	06.6	62 29.1 ..	14.5	Hamal	327 56.4	N23 33.1
16	2 41.9	106 09.9	51.8	348 42.9	08.8	107 32.1	06.6	77 31.2	14.4	Kaus Aust.	83 39.1	S34 22.4
17	17 44.4	121 09.5	52.2	3 43.8	09.5	122 34.1	06.7	92 33.4	14.4			
18	32 46.8	136 09.0	S19 52.5	18 44.7	N 6 10.2	137 36.1	S22 06.7	107 35.5	S22 14.4	Kochab	137 20.4	N74 04.4
19	47 49.3	151 08.6	52.9	33 45.6	10.9	152 38.0	06.8	122 37.7	14.4	Markab	13 34.8	N15 18.4
20	62 51.8	166 08.1	53.2	48 46.5	11.6	167 40.0	06.8	137 39.9	14.3	Menkar	314 11.0	N 4 09.6
21	77 54.2	181 07.7 ..	53.6	63 47.4 ..	12.3	182 42.0 ..	06.9	152 42.0 ..	14.3	Menkent	148 03.1	S36 27.5
22	92 56.7	196 07.2	54.0	78 48.3	13.0	197 43.9	06.9	167 44.2	14.3	Miaplacidus	221 37.9	S69 47.7
23	107 59.1	211 06.8	54.3	93 49.2	13.7	212 45.9	07.0	182 46.3	14.2			
24 00	123 01.6	226 06.3	S19 54.7	108 50.2	N 6 14.4	227 47.9	S22 07.0	197 48.5	S22 14.2	Mirfak	308 34.7	N49 55.7
01	138 04.1	241 05.9	55.0	123 51.1	15.1	242 49.8	07.1	212 50.7	14.2	Nunki	75 53.9	S26 16.3
02	153 06.5	256 05.4	55.4	138 52.0	15.8	257 51.8	07.1	227 52.8	14.2	Peacock	53 13.9	S56 40.4
03	168 09.0	271 05.0 ..	55.7	153 52.9 ..	16.5	272 53.8 ..	07.1	242 55.0 ..	14.1	Pollux	243 22.7	N27 58.6
04	183 11.5	286 04.5	56.1	168 53.8	17.2	287 55.7	07.2	257 57.1	14.1	Procyon	244 55.4	N 5 10.4
05	198 13.9	301 04.0	56.4	183 54.7	17.9	302 57.7	07.2	272 59.3	14.1			
06	213 16.4	316 03.6	S19 56.8	198 55.6	N 6 18.5	317 59.7	S22 07.3	288 01.4	S22 14.1	Rasalhague	96 03.2	N12 32.8
07	228 18.9	331 03.1	57.2	213 56.5	19.2	333 01.6	07.3	303 03.6	14.0	Regulus	207 39.2	N11 52.3
08	243 21.3	346 02.7	57.5	228 57.4	19.9	348 03.6	07.4	318 05.8	14.0	Rigel	281 08.1	S 8 11.0
09	258 23.8	1 02.2 ..	57.9	243 58.3 ..	20.6	3 05.6 ..	07.4	333 07.9 ..	14.0	Rigil Kent.	139 46.6	S60 54.4
10	273 26.3	16 01.8	58.2	258 59.2	21.3	18 07.6	07.5	348 10.1	13.9	Sabik	102 08.4	S15 44.7
11	288 28.7	31 01.3	58.6	274 00.2	22.0	33 09.5	07.5	3 12.2	13.9			
12	303 31.2	46 00.8	S19 58.9	289 01.1	N 6 22.7	48 11.5	S22 07.6	18 14.4	S22 13.9	Schedar	349 36.3	N56 38.6
13	318 33.6	61 00.4	59.2	304 02.0	23.4	63 13.5	07.6	33 16.6	13.9	Shaula	96 17.1	S37 06.8
14	333 36.1	75 59.9	59.6	319 02.9	24.1	78 15.4	07.7	48 18.7	13.8	Sirius	258 30.0	S16 44.8
15	348 38.6	90 59.5	19 59.9	334 03.8 ..	24.8	93 17.4 ..	07.7	63 20.9 ..	13.8	Spica	158 27.2	S11 15.5
16	3 41.0	105 59.0	20 00.3	349 04.7	25.5	108 19.4	07.8	78 23.0	13.8	Suhail	222 49.2	S43 30.6
17	18 43.5	120 58.5	00.6	4 05.6	26.2	123 21.3	07.8	93 25.2	13.8			
18	33 46.0	135 58.1	S20 01.0	19 06.5	N 6 26.8	138 23.3	S22 07.9	108 27.4	S22 13.7	Vega	80 36.8	N38 48.1
19	48 48.4	150 57.6	01.3	34 07.4	27.5	153 25.3	07.9	123 29.5	13.7	Zuben'ubi	137 01.2	S16 07.1
20	63 50.9	165 57.1	01.7	49 08.3	28.2	168 27.3	07.9	138 31.7	13.7		SHA	Mer. Pass.
21	78 53.4	180 56.7 ..	02.0	64 09.2 ..	28.9	183 29.2 ..	08.0	153 33.8 ..	13.6			h m
22	93 55.8	195 56.2	02.3	79 10.1	29.6	198 31.2	08.0	168 36.0	13.6	Venus	104 14.5	8 55
23	108 58.3	210 55.7	02.7	94 11.1	30.3	213 33.2	08.1	183 38.2	13.6	Mars	346 25.8	16 45
	h m									Jupiter	104 58.2	8 51
Mer. Pass.	15 49.2	v −0.4	d 0.4	v 0.9	d 0.7	v 2.0	d 0.0	v 2.2	d 0.0	Saturn	74 54.2	10 51

© British Crown Copyright 2018. All rights reserved.

UT	SUN GHA	SUN Dec	MOON GHA	v	MOON Dec	d	HP
22 00	177 09.4	S19 47.3	345 26.4	4.1	N18 23.4	7.7	61.4
01	192 09.2	46.7	359 49.5	4.2	18 15.7	7.7	61.4
02	207 09.0	46.2	14 12.7	4.2	18 08.0	7.9	61.4
03	222 08.9	.. 45.6	28 35.9	4.3	18 00.1	8.0	61.3
04	237 08.7	45.0	42 59.2	4.3	17 52.1	8.2	61.3
05	252 08.5	44.5	57 22.5	4.5	17 43.9	8.2	61.3
06	267 08.3	S19 43.9	71 46.0	4.5	N17 35.7	8.4	61.3
07	282 08.2	43.3	86 09.5	4.5	17 27.3	8.6	61.3
T 08	297 08.0	42.8	100 33.0	4.7	17 18.7	8.6	61.3
U 09	312 07.8	.. 42.2	114 56.7	4.7	17 10.1	8.8	61.3
E 10	327 07.7	41.6	129 20.4	4.7	17 01.3	8.9	61.3
S 11	342 07.5	41.1	143 44.1	4.9	16 52.4	9.0	61.3
D 12	357 07.3	S19 40.5	158 08.0	4.9	N16 43.4	9.1	61.3
A 13	12 07.2	39.9	172 31.9	5.0	16 34.3	9.2	61.3
Y 14	27 07.0	39.4	186 55.9	5.1	16 25.1	9.4	61.3
15	42 06.8	.. 38.8	201 20.0	5.1	16 15.7	9.4	61.3
16	57 06.7	38.2	215 44.1	5.3	16 06.3	9.6	61.2
17	72 06.5	37.6	230 08.4	5.3	15 56.7	9.7	61.2
18	87 06.3	S19 37.1	244 32.7	5.4	N15 47.0	9.7	61.2
19	102 06.2	36.5	258 57.1	5.4	15 37.3	9.9	61.2
20	117 06.0	35.9	273 21.5	5.6	15 27.4	10.0	61.2
21	132 05.8	.. 35.3	287 46.1	5.6	15 17.4	10.1	61.2
22	147 05.7	34.7	302 10.7	5.7	15 07.3	10.2	61.2
23	162 05.5	34.2	316 35.4	5.8	14 57.1	10.3	61.2
23 00	177 05.4	S19 33.6	331 00.2	5.9	N14 46.8	10.4	61.1
01	192 05.2	33.0	345 25.1	5.9	14 36.4	10.4	61.1
02	207 05.0	32.4	359 50.0	6.0	14 26.0	10.6	61.1
03	222 04.9	.. 31.8	14 15.0	6.2	14 15.4	10.7	61.1
04	237 04.7	31.3	28 40.2	6.2	14 04.7	10.7	61.1
05	252 04.5	30.7	43 05.4	6.2	13 54.0	10.9	61.1
06	267 04.4	S19 30.1	57 30.6	6.4	N13 43.1	10.9	61.0
W 07	282 04.2	29.5	71 56.0	6.4	13 32.2	11.0	61.0
E 08	297 04.1	28.9	86 21.4	6.6	13 21.2	11.1	61.0
D 09	312 03.9	.. 28.3	100 47.0	6.6	13 10.1	11.1	61.0
N 10	327 03.7	27.8	115 12.6	6.7	12 59.0	11.3	61.0
E 11	342 03.6	27.2	129 38.3	6.7	12 47.7	11.3	60.9
S 12	357 03.4	S19 26.6	144 04.0	6.9	N12 36.4	11.4	60.9
D 13	12 03.3	26.0	158 29.9	6.9	12 25.0	11.5	60.9
A 14	27 03.1	25.4	172 55.8	7.0	12 13.5	11.5	60.9
Y 15	42 03.0	.. 24.8	187 21.8	7.1	12 02.0	11.6	60.8
16	57 02.8	24.2	201 47.9	7.2	11 50.4	11.7	60.8
17	72 02.6	23.6	216 14.1	7.3	11 38.7	11.7	60.8
18	87 02.5	S19 23.1	230 40.4	7.3	N11 27.0	11.8	60.8
19	102 02.3	22.5	245 06.7	7.5	11 15.2	11.9	60.8
20	117 02.2	21.9	259 33.2	7.5	11 03.3	11.9	60.7
21	132 02.0	.. 21.3	273 59.7	7.6	10 51.4	12.0	60.7
22	147 01.9	20.7	288 26.3	7.6	10 39.4	12.0	60.7
23	162 01.7	20.1	302 52.9	7.8	10 27.4	12.1	60.7
24 00	177 01.5	S19 19.5	317 19.7	7.8	N10 15.3	12.2	60.6
01	192 01.4	18.9	331 46.5	7.9	10 03.1	12.2	60.6
02	207 01.2	18.3	346 13.4	8.0	9 50.9	12.2	60.6
03	222 01.1	.. 17.7	0 40.4	8.1	9 38.7	12.3	60.5
04	237 00.9	17.1	15 07.5	8.1	9 26.4	12.4	60.5
05	252 00.8	16.5	29 34.6	8.2	9 14.0	12.4	60.5
06	267 00.6	S19 15.9	44 01.8	8.3	N 9 01.6	12.4	60.5
07	282 00.5	15.3	58 29.1	8.4	8 49.2	12.5	60.4
T 08	297 00.3	14.7	72 56.5	8.4	8 36.7	12.5	60.4
H 09	312 00.2	.. 14.1	87 23.9	8.6	8 24.2	12.6	60.4
U 10	327 00.0	13.5	101 51.5	8.6	8 11.6	12.6	60.3
R 11	341 59.9	12.9	116 19.1	8.6	7 59.0	12.6	60.3
S 12	356 59.7	S19 12.3	130 46.7	8.8	N 7 46.4	12.6	60.3
D 13	11 59.6	11.7	145 14.5	8.8	7 33.8	12.7	60.3
A 14	26 59.4	11.1	159 42.3	8.9	7 21.1	12.7	60.2
Y 15	41 59.3	.. 10.5	174 10.2	8.9	7 08.3	12.7	60.2
16	56 59.1	09.9	188 38.1	9.0	6 55.6	12.8	60.2
17	71 59.0	09.3	203 06.1	9.1	6 42.8	12.8	60.1
18	86 58.8	S19 08.7	217 34.2	9.2	N 6 30.0	12.8	60.1
19	101 58.7	08.1	232 02.4	9.2	6 17.2	12.9	60.1
20	116 58.5	07.5	246 30.6	9.3	6 04.3	12.8	60.0
21	131 58.4	.. 06.9	260 58.9	9.4	5 51.5	12.9	60.0
22	146 58.2	06.3	275 27.3	9.4	5 38.6	12.9	60.0
23	161 58.1	05.7	289 55.7	9.5	N 5 25.7	13.0	59.9
	SD 16.3	d 0.6	SD 16.7		16.6		16.4

Lat.	Twilight Naut.	Twilight Civil	Sunrise	Moonrise 22	23	24	25
N 72	07 40	09 19	■■	15 28	18 06	20 21	22 26
N 70	07 28	08 53	10 43	16 12	18 27	20 30	22 26
68	07 18	08 33	09 58	16 41	18 42	20 37	22 27
66	07 10	08 18	09 28	17 02	18 55	20 43	22 27
64	07 03	08 04	09 06	17 19	19 05	20 48	22 27
62	06 57	07 53	08 49	17 33	19 14	20 52	22 27
60	06 51	07 44	08 34	17 45	19 22	20 56	22 27
N 58	06 46	07 35	08 22	17 55	19 28	20 59	22 27
56	06 42	07 28	08 11	18 04	19 34	21 02	22 28
54	06 37	07 21	08 01	18 12	19 39	21 05	22 28
52	06 33	07 15	07 53	18 19	19 44	21 07	22 28
50	06 30	07 09	07 45	18 26	19 48	21 09	22 28
45	06 21	06 57	07 29	18 39	19 58	21 14	22 28
N 40	06 14	06 47	07 16	18 50	20 05	21 18	22 28
35	06 07	06 38	07 05	19 00	20 12	21 21	22 28
30	06 00	06 29	06 55	19 08	20 17	21 24	22 28
20	05 47	06 14	06 38	19 23	20 27	21 29	22 29
N 10	05 35	06 00	06 22	19 35	20 36	21 34	22 29
0	05 21	05 46	06 08	19 47	20 44	21 38	22 29
S 10	05 05	05 31	05 54	19 58	20 52	21 42	22 29
20	04 46	05 15	05 38	20 11	21 01	21 47	22 30
30	04 22	04 54	05 20	20 25	21 11	21 52	22 30
35	04 07	04 41	05 10	20 33	21 16	21 55	22 30
40	03 48	04 27	04 58	20 42	21 23	21 58	22 31
45	03 24	04 09	04 43	20 53	21 30	22 02	22 31
S 50	02 52	03 46	04 26	21 06	21 39	22 06	22 31
52	02 34	03 34	04 17	21 12	21 43	22 08	22 32
54	02 13	03 21	04 08	21 19	21 47	22 11	22 32
56	01 43	03 06	03 57	21 27	21 52	22 13	22 32
58	00 52	02 48	03 45	21 35	21 58	22 16	22 32
S 60	////	02 25	03 31	21 44	22 04	22 19	22 32

Lat.	Sunset	Twilight Civil	Twilight Naut.	Moonset 22	23	24	25
N 72	■■	15 06	16 45	11 52	11 15	10 55	10 38
N 70	13 42	15 31	16 56	11 07	10 53	10 43	10 35
68	14 27	15 51	17 06	10 37	10 36	10 34	10 32
66	14 56	16 07	17 14	10 14	10 22	10 26	10 29
64	15 18	16 20	17 21	09 56	10 10	10 20	10 27
62	15 36	16 31	17 27	09 41	10 00	10 14	10 25
60	15 50	16 40	17 33	09 28	09 52	10 09	10 23
N 58	16 03	16 49	17 38	09 18	09 44	10 05	10 22
56	16 13	16 56	17 43	09 08	09 37	10 01	10 20
54	16 23	17 03	17 47	08 59	09 31	09 57	10 19
52	16 31	17 09	17 51	08 52	09 26	09 54	10 18
50	16 39	17 15	17 54	08 45	09 21	09 51	10 17
45	16 55	17 27	18 03	08 30	09 10	09 44	10 15
N 40	17 08	17 37	18 10	08 18	09 01	09 39	10 13
35	17 19	17 47	18 19	08 08	08 54	09 34	10 11
30	17 29	17 55	18 24	07 58	08 47	09 30	10 10
20	17 46	18 10	18 36	07 42	08 35	09 23	10 07
N 10	18 01	18 23	18 49	07 28	08 24	09 16	10 05
0	18 15	18 37	19 03	07 15	08 14	09 10	10 03
S 10	18 30	18 52	19 18	07 02	08 04	09 04	10 00
20	18 45	19 09	19 37	06 48	07 54	08 57	09 58
30	19 03	19 29	20 01	06 31	07 41	08 50	09 55
35	19 13	19 42	20 16	06 22	07 34	08 45	09 54
40	19 25	19 56	20 34	06 11	07 26	08 40	09 52
45	19 40	20 14	20 58	05 58	07 16	08 34	09 50
S 50	19 57	20 37	21 30	05 42	07 05	08 27	09 47
52	20 05	20 48	21 47	05 34	06 59	08 24	09 46
54	20 14	21 01	22 08	05 26	06 53	08 20	09 44
56	20 25	21 16	22 36	05 17	06 46	08 16	09 43
58	20 37	21 34	23 23	05 06	06 39	08 12	09 41
S 60	20 51	21 56	////	04 54	06 30	08 06	09 40

Day	SUN Eqn. of Time 00h	12h	Mer. Pass.	MOON Mer. Pass. Upper	Lower	Age	Phase
d	m s	m s	h m	h m	h m	d	%
22	11 22	11 30	12 12	01 01	13 31	16	97
23	11 38	11 46	12 12	02 01	14 29	17	92
24	11 54	12 01	12 12	02 57	15 24	18	85

© British Crown Copyright 2018. All rights reserved.

2019 JANUARY 25, 26, 27 (FRI., SAT., SUN.)

UT	ARIES GHA	VENUS −4.4 GHA	Dec	MARS +0.8 GHA	Dec	JUPITER −1.9 GHA	Dec	SATURN +0.6 GHA	Dec	STARS Name	SHA	Dec
25 00	124 00.7	225 55.3	S20 03.0	109 12.0	N 6 31.0	228 35.1	S22 08.1	198 40.3	S22 13.6	Acamar	315 15.4	S40 14.1
01	139 03.2	240 54.8	03.4	124 12.9	31.7	243 37.1	08.2	213 42.5	13.5	Achernar	335 24.0	S57 08.9
02	154 05.7	255 54.3	03.7	139 13.8	32.4	258 39.1	08.2	228 44.6	13.5	Acrux	173 04.6	S63 11.9
03	169 08.1	270 53.9 ..	04.0	154 14.7 ..	33.1	273 41.1 ..	08.3	243 46.8 ..	13.5	Adhara	255 09.2	S29 00.1
04	184 10.6	285 53.4	04.4	169 15.6	33.7	288 43.0	08.3	258 49.0	13.5	Aldebaran	290 44.8	N16 32.7
05	199 13.1	300 52.9	04.7	184 16.5	34.4	303 45.0	08.4	273 51.1	13.4			
06	214 15.5	315 52.4	S20 05.0	199 17.4	N 6 35.1	318 47.0	S22 08.4	288 53.3	S22 13.4	Alioth	166 17.1	N55 51.2
07	229 18.0	330 52.0	05.4	214 18.3	35.8	333 48.9	08.5	303 55.4	13.4	Alkaid	152 55.8	N49 12.9
08	244 20.5	345 51.5	05.7	229 19.2	36.5	348 50.9	08.5	318 57.6	13.3	Alnair	27 39.4	S46 52.3
F 09	259 22.9	0 51.0 ..	06.0	244 20.1 ..	37.2	3 52.9 ..	08.5	333 59.8 ..	13.3	Alnilam	275 42.2	S 1 11.6
R 10	274 25.4	15 50.6	06.4	259 21.0	37.9	18 54.9	08.6	349 01.9	13.3	Alphard	217 52.0	S 8 44.6
I 11	289 27.9	30 50.1	06.7	274 21.9	38.6	33 56.8	08.6	4 04.1	13.3			
D 12	304 30.3	45 49.6	S20 07.0	289 22.8	N 6 39.3	48 58.8	S22 08.7	19 06.2	S22 13.2	Alphecca	126 07.9	N26 39.0
A 13	319 32.8	60 49.1	07.4	304 23.7	40.0	64 00.8	08.7	34 08.4	13.2	Alpheratz	357 39.7	N29 11.7
Y 14	334 35.2	75 48.6	07.7	319 24.7	40.6	79 02.8	08.8	49 10.6	13.2	Altair	62 04.8	N 8 55.1
15	349 37.7	90 48.2 ..	08.0	334 25.6 ..	41.3	94 04.7 ..	08.8	64 12.7 ..	13.1	Ankaa	353 12.1	S42 12.5
16	4 40.2	105 47.7	08.4	349 26.5	42.0	109 06.7	08.9	79 14.9	13.1	Antares	112 21.8	S26 28.2
17	19 42.6	120 47.2	08.7	4 27.4	42.7	124 08.7	08.9	94 17.0	13.1			
18	34 45.1	135 46.7	S20 09.0	19 28.3	N 6 43.4	139 10.7	S22 09.0	109 19.2	S22 13.1	Arcturus	145 52.2	N19 05.0
19	49 47.6	150 46.3	09.3	34 29.2	44.1	154 12.6	09.0	124 21.4	13.0	Atria	107 20.5	S69 03.3
20	64 50.0	165 45.8	09.7	49 30.1	44.8	169 14.6	09.0	139 23.5	13.0	Avior	234 15.8	S59 34.3
21	79 52.5	180 45.3 ..	10.0	64 31.0 ..	45.5	184 16.6 ..	09.1	154 25.7 ..	13.0	Bellatrix	278 27.7	N 6 21.8
22	94 55.0	195 44.8	10.3	79 31.9	46.2	199 18.5	09.1	169 27.8	13.0	Betelgeuse	270 56.9	N 7 24.4
23	109 57.4	210 44.3	10.6	94 32.8	46.8	214 20.5	09.2	184 30.0	12.9			
26 00	124 59.9	225 43.9	S20 10.9	109 33.7	N 6 47.5	229 22.5	S22 09.2	199 32.2	S22 12.9	Canopus	263 54.0	S52 42.6
01	140 02.3	240 43.4	11.3	124 34.6	48.2	244 24.5	09.3	214 34.3	12.9	Capella	280 28.4	N46 00.9
02	155 04.8	255 42.9	11.6	139 35.5	48.9	259 26.5	09.3	229 36.5	12.8	Deneb	49 29.3	N45 20.9
03	170 07.3	270 42.4 ..	11.9	154 36.4 ..	49.6	274 28.4 ..	09.4	244 38.6 ..	12.8	Denebola	182 29.6	N14 27.9
04	185 09.7	285 41.9	12.2	169 37.3	50.3	289 30.4	09.4	259 40.8	12.8	Diphda	348 52.2	S17 53.2
05	200 12.2	300 41.4	12.5	184 38.2	51.0	304 32.4	09.5	274 43.0	12.8			
06	215 14.7	315 40.9	S20 12.9	199 39.1	N 6 51.7	319 34.4	S22 09.5	289 45.1	S22 12.7	Dubhe	193 46.5	N61 38.7
07	230 17.1	330 40.5	13.2	214 40.0	52.3	334 36.3	09.5	304 47.3	12.7	Elnath	278 07.5	N28 37.3
08	245 19.6	345 40.0	13.5	229 40.9	53.0	349 38.3	09.6	319 49.5	12.7	Eltanin	90 44.8	N51 29.1
S 09	260 22.1	0 39.5 ..	13.8	244 41.9 ..	53.7	4 40.3 ..	09.6	334 51.6 ..	12.7	Enif	33 43.7	N 9 57.7
A 10	275 24.5	15 39.0	14.1	259 42.8	54.4	19 42.3	09.7	349 53.8	12.6	Fomalhaut	15 20.1	S29 31.5
T 11	290 27.0	30 38.5	14.4	274 43.7	55.1	34 44.2	09.7	4 55.9	12.6			
U 12	305 29.5	45 38.0	S20 14.7	289 44.6	N 6 55.8	49 46.2	S22 09.8	19 58.1	S22 12.6	Gacrux	171 56.3	S57 12.9
R 13	320 31.9	60 37.5	15.1	304 45.5	56.5	64 48.2	09.8	35 00.3	12.5	Gienah	175 48.2	S17 38.8
D 14	335 34.4	75 37.0	15.4	319 46.4	57.1	79 50.2	09.9	50 02.4	12.5	Hadar	148 42.4	S60 27.5
A 15	350 36.8	90 36.6 ..	15.7	334 47.3 ..	57.8	94 52.1 ..	09.9	65 04.6 ..	12.5	Hamal	327 56.4	N23 33.0
Y 16	5 39.3	105 36.1	16.0	349 48.2	58.5	109 54.1	09.9	80 06.7	12.5	Kaus Aust.	83 39.1	S34 22.4
17	20 41.8	120 35.6	16.3	4 49.1	59.2	124 56.1	10.0	95 08.9	12.4			
18	35 44.2	135 35.1	S20 16.6	19 50.0	N 6 59.9	139 58.1	S22 10.0	110 11.1	S22 12.4	Kochab	137 20.3	N74 04.4
19	50 46.7	150 34.6	16.9	34 50.9	7 00.6	155 00.1	10.1	125 13.2	12.4	Markab	13 34.8	N15 18.4
20	65 49.2	165 34.1	17.2	49 51.8	01.3	170 02.0	10.1	140 15.4	12.3	Menkar	314 11.0	N 4 09.6
21	80 51.6	180 33.6 ..	17.5	64 52.7 ..	02.0	185 04.0 ..	10.2	155 17.6 ..	12.3	Menkent	148 03.0	S36 27.5
22	95 54.1	195 33.1	17.8	79 53.6	02.7	200 06.0	10.2	170 19.7	12.3	Miaplacidus	221 37.9	S69 47.7
23	110 56.6	210 32.6	18.1	94 54.5	03.3	215 08.0	10.3	185 21.9	12.3			
27 00	125 59.0	225 32.1	S20 18.4	109 55.4	N 7 04.0	230 09.9	S22 10.3	200 24.0	S22 12.2	Mirfak	308 34.7	N49 55.7
01	141 01.5	240 31.6	18.7	124 56.3	04.7	245 11.9	10.3	215 26.2	12.2	Nunki	75 53.9	S26 16.3
02	156 04.0	255 31.1	19.0	139 57.2	05.4	260 13.9	10.4	230 28.4	12.2	Peacock	53 13.8	S56 40.4
03	171 06.4	270 30.6 ..	19.3	154 58.1 ..	06.1	275 15.9 ..	10.4	245 30.5 ..	12.2	Pollux	243 22.7	N27 58.6
04	186 08.9	285 30.1	19.6	169 59.0	06.8	290 17.9	10.5	260 32.7	12.1	Procyon	244 55.4	N 5 10.4
05	201 11.3	300 29.6	19.9	184 59.9	07.4	305 19.8	10.5	275 34.9	12.1			
06	216 13.8	315 29.1	S20 20.2	200 00.8	N 7 08.1	320 21.8	S22 10.6	290 37.0	S22 12.1	Rasalhague	96 03.2	N12 32.8
07	231 16.3	330 28.6	20.5	215 01.7	08.8	335 23.8	10.6	305 39.2	12.0	Regulus	207 39.2	N11 52.3
08	246 18.7	345 28.1	20.8	230 02.6	09.5	350 25.8	10.7	320 41.3	12.0	Rigel	281 08.1	S 8 11.1
S 09	261 21.2	0 27.6 ..	21.1	245 03.5 ..	10.2	5 27.8 ..	10.7	335 43.5 ..	12.0	Rigil Kent.	139 46.6	S60 54.4
U 10	276 23.7	15 27.1	21.4	260 04.4	10.9	20 29.7	10.7	350 45.7	12.0	Sabik	102 08.4	S15 44.7
N 11	291 26.1	30 26.6	21.7	275 05.3	11.5	35 31.7	10.8	5 47.8	11.9			
D 12	306 28.6	45 26.1	S20 22.0	290 06.2	N 7 12.2	50 33.7	S22 10.8	20 50.0	S22 11.9	Schedar	349 36.4	N56 38.6
A 13	321 31.1	60 25.6	22.3	305 07.1	12.9	65 35.7	10.9	35 52.2	11.9	Shaula	96 17.0	S37 06.8
Y 14	336 33.5	75 25.1	22.6	320 08.1	13.6	80 37.7	10.9	50 54.3	11.8	Sirius	258 30.0	S16 44.8
15	351 36.0	90 24.6 ..	22.9	335 09.0 ..	14.3	95 39.7 ..	11.0	65 56.5 ..	11.8	Spica	158 27.1	S11 15.5
16	6 38.4	105 24.1	23.2	350 09.9	15.0	110 41.6	11.0	80 58.6	11.8	Suhail	222 49.2	S43 30.6
17	21 40.9	120 23.6	23.5	5 10.8	15.6	125 43.6	11.0	96 00.8	11.8			
18	36 43.4	135 23.1	S20 23.8	20 11.7	N 7 16.3	140 45.6	S22 11.1	111 03.0	S22 11.7	Vega	80 36.8	N38 48.0
19	51 45.8	150 22.6	24.0	35 12.6	17.0	155 47.6	11.1	126 05.1	11.7	Zuben'ubi	137 01.2	S16 07.1
20	66 48.3	165 22.1	24.3	50 13.5	17.7	170 49.6	11.2	141 07.3	11.7			
21	81 50.8	180 21.6 ..	24.6	65 14.4 ..	18.4	185 51.5 ..	11.2	156 09.5 ..	11.7		SHA	Mer. Pass.
22	96 53.2	195 21.0	24.9	80 15.3	19.1	200 53.5	11.3	171 11.6	11.6	Venus	100 44.0	8 57
23	111 55.7	210 20.5	25.2	95 16.2	19.7	215 55.5	11.3	186 13.8	11.6	Mars	344 33.8	16 41
Mer. Pass.	15 37.4	v −0.5	d 0.3	v 0.9	d 0.7	v 2.0	d 0.0	v 2.2	d 0.0	Jupiter	104 22.6	8 41
										Saturn	74 32.3	10 40

© British Crown Copyright 2018. All rights reserved.

UT	SUN GHA	SUN Dec	MOON GHA	v	Dec	d	HP
d h	° '	° '	° '	'	° '	'	'
25 00	176 57.9	S19 05.1	304 24.2	9.6	N 5 12.7	12.9	59.9
01	191 57.8	04.5	318 52.8	9.6	4 59.8	12.9	59.9
02	206 57.6	03.8	333 21.4	9.7	4 46.9	13.0	59.8
03	221 57.5	.. 03.2	347 50.1	9.7	4 33.9	13.0	59.8
04	236 57.3	02.6	2 18.8	9.8	4 20.9	13.0	59.8
05	251 57.2	02.0	16 47.6	9.9	4 07.9	13.0	59.7
06	266 57.0	S19 01.4	31 16.5	9.9	N 3 54.9	13.0	59.7
07	281 56.9	00.8	45 45.4	10.0	3 41.9	13.0	59.7
F 08	296 56.8	19 00.2	60 14.4	10.1	3 28.9	13.0	59.6
R 09	311 56.6	18 59.6	74 43.5	10.1	3 15.9	13.0	59.6
I 10	326 56.5	58.9	89 12.6	10.1	3 02.9	13.0	59.5
D 11	341 56.3	58.3	103 41.7	10.2	2 49.9	13.0	59.5
A 12	356 56.2	S18 57.7	118 10.9	10.3	N 2 36.9	13.0	59.5
Y 13	11 56.0	57.1	132 40.2	10.3	2 23.9	13.0	59.4
14	26 55.9	56.5	147 09.5	10.3	2 10.9	13.0	59.4
15	41 55.7	.. 55.9	161 38.8	10.5	1 57.9	13.0	59.4
16	56 55.6	55.2	176 08.3	10.4	1 44.9	13.0	59.3
17	71 55.5	54.6	190 37.7	10.5	1 31.9	13.0	59.3
18	86 55.3	S18 54.0	205 07.2	10.6	N 1 18.9	12.9	59.3
19	101 55.2	53.4	219 36.8	10.6	1 06.0	13.0	59.2
20	116 55.0	52.8	234 06.4	10.7	0 53.0	12.9	59.2
21	131 54.9	.. 52.1	248 36.1	10.7	0 40.1	13.0	59.2
22	146 54.8	51.5	263 05.8	10.7	0 27.1	12.9	59.1
23	161 54.6	50.9	277 35.5	10.8	0 14.2	12.9	59.1
26 00	176 54.5	S18 50.3	292 05.3	10.9	N 0 01.3	12.9	59.0
01	191 54.3	49.6	306 35.2	10.8	S 0 11.6	12.8	59.0
02	206 54.2	49.0	321 05.0	11.0	0 24.4	12.9	59.0
03	221 54.1	.. 48.4	335 35.0	10.9	0 37.3	12.8	58.9
04	236 53.9	47.8	350 04.9	11.0	0 50.1	12.8	58.9
05	251 53.8	47.1	4 34.9	11.1	1 02.9	12.8	58.9
06	266 53.7	S18 46.5	19 05.0	11.0	S 1 15.7	12.8	58.8
07	281 53.5	45.9	33 35.0	11.1	1 28.5	12.7	58.8
S 08	296 53.4	45.3	48 05.1	11.2	1 41.2	12.7	58.7
A 09	311 53.2	.. 44.6	62 35.3	11.2	1 53.9	12.7	58.7
T 10	326 53.1	44.0	77 05.5	11.2	2 06.6	12.6	58.7
U 11	341 53.0	43.4	91 35.7	11.2	2 19.2	12.7	58.6
R 12	356 52.8	S18 42.7	106 05.9	11.3	S 2 31.9	12.6	58.6
D 13	11 52.7	42.1	120 36.2	11.3	2 44.5	12.5	58.6
A 14	26 52.6	41.5	135 06.5	11.4	2 57.0	12.6	58.5
Y 15	41 52.4	.. 40.9	149 36.9	11.3	3 09.6	12.5	58.5
16	56 52.3	40.2	164 07.2	11.4	3 22.1	12.4	58.4
17	71 52.2	39.6	178 37.6	11.5	3 34.5	12.5	58.4
18	86 52.0	S18 39.0	193 08.1	11.4	S 3 47.0	12.4	58.4
19	101 51.9	38.3	207 38.5	11.5	3 59.4	12.3	58.3
20	116 51.8	37.7	222 09.0	11.5	4 11.7	12.3	58.3
21	131 51.6	.. 37.0	236 39.5	11.5	4 24.0	12.3	58.3
22	146 51.5	36.4	251 10.0	11.6	4 36.3	12.3	58.2
23	161 51.4	35.8	265 40.6	11.6	4 48.6	12.2	58.2
27 00	176 51.2	S18 35.1	280 11.2	11.6	S 5 00.8	12.1	58.1
01	191 51.1	34.5	294 41.8	11.6	5 12.9	12.1	58.1
02	206 51.0	33.9	309 12.4	11.6	5 25.0	12.1	58.1
03	221 50.9	.. 33.2	323 43.0	11.7	5 37.1	12.0	58.0
04	236 50.7	32.6	338 13.7	11.7	5 49.1	12.0	58.0
05	251 50.6	31.9	352 44.4	11.7	6 01.1	12.0	58.0
06	266 50.5	S18 31.3	7 15.1	11.7	S 6 13.1	11.9	57.9
07	281 50.3	30.7	21 45.8	11.7	6 25.0	11.8	57.9
08	296 50.2	30.0	36 16.5	11.8	6 36.8	11.8	57.9
S 09	311 50.1	.. 29.4	50 47.3	11.7	6 48.6	11.7	57.8
U 10	326 50.0	28.7	65 18.0	11.8	7 00.3	11.7	57.8
N 11	341 49.8	28.1	79 48.8	11.8	7 12.0	11.7	57.7
D 12	356 49.7	S18 27.4	94 19.6	11.8	S 7 23.7	11.6	57.7
A 13	11 49.6	26.8	108 50.4	11.8	7 35.3	11.5	57.7
Y 14	26 49.4	26.1	123 21.2	11.8	7 46.8	11.5	57.6
15	41 49.3	.. 25.5	137 52.0	11.8	7 58.3	11.4	57.6
16	56 49.2	24.9	152 22.8	11.9	8 09.7	11.4	57.6
17	71 49.1	24.2	166 53.7	11.8	8 21.1	11.3	57.5
18	86 48.9	S18 23.6	181 24.5	11.9	S 8 32.4	11.3	57.5
19	101 48.8	22.9	195 55.4	11.9	8 43.7	11.2	57.5
20	116 48.7	22.3	210 26.2	11.9	8 54.9	11.1	57.4
21	131 48.6	.. 21.6	224 57.1	11.9	9 06.0	11.1	57.4
22	146 48.5	21.0	239 28.0	11.9	9 17.1	11.1	57.3
23	161 48.3	20.3	253 58.9	11.9	S 9 28.2	10.9	57.3
	SD 16.3	d 0.6	SD 16.2		16.0		15.7

Lat.	Twilight Naut.	Twilight Civil	Sunrise	Moonrise 25	Moonrise 26	Moonrise 27	Moonrise 28
°	h m	h m	h m	h m	h m	h m	h m
N 72	07 31	09 06	11 45	22 26	24 26	00 26	02 26
N 70	07 20	08 43	10 22	22 26	24 18	00 18	02 08
68	07 11	08 25	09 44	22 27	24 12	00 12	01 55
66	07 04	08 10	09 18	22 27	24 07	00 07	01 44
64	06 58	07 58	08 58	22 27	24 02	00 02	01 35
62	06 52	07 48	08 42	22 27	23 58	25 27	01 27
60	06 47	07 39	08 28	22 27	23 55	25 20	01 20
N 58	06 42	07 31	08 16	22 27	23 52	25 14	01 14
56	06 38	07 24	08 06	22 28	23 50	25 09	01 09
54	06 34	07 17	07 57	22 28	23 47	25 04	01 04
52	06 30	07 12	07 49	22 28	23 45	25 00	01 00
50	06 27	07 06	07 42	22 28	23 43	24 56	00 56
45	06 19	06 55	07 27	22 28	23 39	24 48	00 48
N 40	06 12	06 45	07 14	22 28	23 36	24 41	00 41
35	06 06	06 36	07 03	22 28	23 33	24 35	00 35
30	05 59	06 28	06 54	22 28	23 30	24 30	00 30
20	05 47	06 14	06 37	22 29	23 26	24 22	00 22
N 10	05 35	06 00	06 23	22 29	23 22	24 14	00 14
0	05 22	05 47	06 09	22 29	23 18	24 07	00 07
S 10	05 07	05 33	05 55	22 29	23 15	24 00	00 00
20	04 49	05 17	05 40	22 30	23 11	23 52	24 34
30	04 25	04 57	05 23	22 30	23 07	23 44	24 21
35	04 11	04 45	05 13	22 30	23 05	23 39	24 14
40	03 53	04 31	05 01	22 31	23 02	23 33	24 06
45	03 30	04 13	04 48	22 31	22 59	23 27	23 57
S 50	02 59	03 51	04 31	22 31	22 55	23 19	23 46
52	02 43	03 41	04 23	22 31	22 53	23 16	23 40
54	02 23	03 28	04 14	22 32	22 52	23 12	23 35
56	01 57	03 14	04 04	22 32	22 50	23 08	23 28
58	01 17	02 57	03 52	22 32	22 47	23 03	23 21
S 60	////	02 36	03 39	22 32	22 45	22 58	23 13

Lat.	Sunset	Twilight Civil	Twilight Naut.	Moonset 25	Moonset 26	Moonset 27	Moonset 28
°	h m	h m	h m	h m	h m	h m	h m
N 72	12 41	15 20	16 56	10 38	10 23	10 08	09 50
N 70	14 04	15 43	17 06	10 35	10 27	10 18	10 09
68	14 41	16 01	17 15	10 32	10 29	10 26	10 24
66	15 08	16 16	17 22	10 29	10 31	10 33	10 36
64	15 28	16 28	17 28	10 27	10 33	10 39	10 47
62	15 44	16 38	17 34	10 25	10 35	10 44	10 55
60	15 58	16 47	17 39	10 23	10 36	10 49	11 03
N 58	16 09	16 55	17 44	10 22	10 37	10 53	11 10
56	16 19	17 02	17 48	10 20	10 39	10 57	11 16
54	16 28	17 08	17 52	10 19	10 40	11 00	11 21
52	16 36	17 14	17 55	10 18	10 40	11 03	11 26
50	16 44	17 19	17 59	10 17	10 41	11 05	11 30
45	16 59	17 31	18 06	10 15	10 43	11 11	11 40
N 40	17 11	17 41	18 13	10 13	10 45	11 16	11 48
35	17 22	17 49	18 20	10 11	10 46	11 20	11 55
30	17 32	17 57	18 26	10 10	10 47	11 24	12 01
20	17 48	18 11	18 38	10 07	10 49	11 30	12 12
N 10	18 02	18 25	18 50	10 05	10 51	11 36	12 21
0	18 16	18 38	19 03	10 03	10 53	11 42	12 30
S 10	18 30	18 52	19 18	10 00	10 54	11 47	12 39
20	18 45	19 08	19 36	09 58	10 56	11 53	12 48
30	19 02	19 28	19 59	09 55	10 58	11 59	12 59
35	19 12	19 40	20 14	09 54	10 59	12 03	13 05
40	19 23	19 54	20 31	09 52	11 01	12 07	13 13
45	19 37	20 11	20 54	09 50	11 02	12 12	13 20
S 50	19 53	20 32	21 24	09 47	11 04	12 18	13 30
52	20 01	20 43	21 40	09 46	11 05	12 21	13 35
54	20 10	20 55	22 00	09 44	11 06	12 24	13 40
56	20 20	21 09	22 25	09 43	11 07	12 28	13 46
58	20 31	21 26	23 02	09 41	11 08	12 31	13 52
S 60	20 44	21 47	////	09 40	11 09	12 36	13 59

Day	SUN Eqn. of Time 00h	SUN Eqn. of Time 12h	SUN Mer. Pass.	MOON Mer. Pass. Upper	MOON Mer. Pass. Lower	Age	Phase
d	m s	m s	h m	h m	h m	d %	
25	12 08	12 15	12 12	03 50	16 16	19 75	
26	12 22	12 28	12 12	04 41	17 06	20 65	
27	12 35	12 41	12 13	05 30	17 54	21 54	

© British Crown Copyright 2018. All rights reserved.

UT	ARIES GHA	VENUS −4.3 GHA	Dec	MARS +0.8 GHA	Dec	JUPITER −1.9 GHA	Dec	SATURN +0.6 GHA	Dec	STARS Name	SHA	Dec
28 00	126 58.2	225 20.0	S20 25.5	110 17.1	N 7 20.4	230 57.5	S22 11.3	201 16.0	S22 11.6	Acamar	315 15.4	S40 14.1
01	142 00.6	240 19.5	25.8	125 18.0	21.1	245 59.5	11.4	216 18.1	11.5	Achernar	335 24.1	S57 08.9
02	157 03.1	255 19.0	26.0	140 18.9	21.8	261 01.5	11.4	231 20.3	11.5	Acrux	173 04.6	S63 12.0
03	172 05.6	270 18.5 ..	26.3	155 19.8 ..	22.5	276 03.4 ..	11.5	246 22.4 ..	11.5	Adhara	255 09.2	S29 00.1
04	187 08.0	285 18.0	26.6	170 20.7	23.2	291 05.4	11.5	261 24.6	11.5	Aldebaran	290 44.8	N16 32.7
05	202 10.5	300 17.5	26.9	185 21.6	23.8	306 07.4	11.6	276 26.8	11.4			
06	217 12.9	315 17.0	S20 27.2	200 22.5	N 7 24.5	321 09.4	S22 11.6	291 28.9	S22 11.4	Alioth	166 17.1	N55 51.2
07	232 15.4	330 16.4	27.4	215 23.4	25.2	336 11.4	11.7	306 31.1	11.4	Alkaid	152 55.8	N49 12.9
08	247 17.9	345 15.9	27.7	230 24.3	25.9	351 13.4	11.7	321 33.3	11.3	Alnair	27 39.4	S46 52.3
M 09	262 20.3	0 15.4 ..	28.0	245 25.2 ..	26.6	6 15.3 ..	11.7	336 35.4 ..	11.3	Alnilam	275 42.2	S 1 11.6
O 10	277 22.8	15 14.9	28.3	260 26.1	27.3	21 17.3	11.8	351 37.6	11.3	Alphard	217 52.0	S 8 44.6
N 11	292 25.3	30 14.4	28.5	275 27.0	27.9	36 19.3	11.8	6 39.8	11.3			
D 12	307 27.7	45 13.9	S20 28.8	290 27.9	N 7 28.6	51 21.3	S22 11.9	21 41.9	S22 11.2	Alphecca	126 07.9	N26 39.0
A 13	322 30.2	60 13.4	29.1	305 28.8	29.3	66 23.3	11.9	36 44.1	11.2	Alpheratz	357 39.7	N29 11.7
Y 14	337 32.7	75 12.8	29.4	320 29.7	30.0	81 25.3	12.0	51 46.2	11.2	Altair	62 04.8	N 8 55.1
15	352 35.1	90 12.3 ..	29.6	335 30.6 ..	31.3	96 27.2 ..	12.0	66 48.4 ..	11.2	Ankaa	353 12.1	S42 12.5
16	7 37.6	105 11.8	29.9	350 31.5	31.3	111 29.2	12.0	81 50.6	11.1	Antares	112 21.7	S26 28.2
17	22 40.1	120 11.3	30.2	5 32.4	32.0	126 31.2	12.1	96 52.7	11.1			
18	37 42.5	135 10.8	S20 30.5	20 33.3	N 7 32.7	141 33.2	S22 12.1	111 54.9	S22 11.1	Arcturus	145 52.2	N19 05.0
19	52 45.0	150 10.2	30.7	35 34.2	33.4	156 35.2	12.2	126 57.1	11.0	Atria	107 20.4	S69 03.3
20	67 47.4	165 09.7	31.0	50 35.1	34.1	171 37.2	12.2	141 59.2	11.0	Avior	234 15.8	S59 34.3
21	82 49.9	180 09.2 ..	31.3	65 36.0 ..	34.7	186 39.2 ..	12.2	157 01.4 ..	11.0	Bellatrix	278 27.7	N 6 21.8
22	97 52.4	195 08.7	31.5	80 36.9	35.4	201 41.1	12.3	172 03.6	11.0	Betelgeuse	270 56.9	N 7 24.4
23	112 54.8	210 08.2	31.8	95 37.8	36.1	216 43.1	12.3	187 05.7	10.9			
29 00	127 57.3	225 07.6	S20 32.1	110 38.7	N 7 36.8	231 45.1	S22 12.4	202 07.9	S22 10.9	Canopus	263 54.0	S52 42.6
01	142 59.8	240 07.1	32.3	125 39.6	37.5	246 47.1	12.4	217 10.1	10.9	Capella	280 28.4	N46 01.0
02	158 02.2	255 06.6	32.6	140 40.5	38.2	261 49.1	12.5	232 12.2	10.8	Deneb	49 29.3	N45 20.9
03	173 04.7	270 06.1 ..	32.8	155 41.4 ..	38.8	276 51.1 ..	12.5	247 14.4 ..	10.8	Denebola	182 29.5	N14 27.9
04	188 07.2	285 05.5	33.1	170 42.3	39.5	291 53.1	12.5	262 16.6	10.8	Diphda	348 52.2	S17 53.2
05	203 09.6	300 05.0	33.4	185 43.2	40.2	306 55.1	12.6	277 18.7	10.8			
06	218 12.1	315 04.5	S20 33.6	200 44.1	N 7 40.9	321 57.0	S22 12.6	292 20.9	S22 10.7	Dubhe	193 46.5	N61 38.7
07	233 14.5	330 04.0	33.9	215 45.0	41.5	336 59.0	12.7	307 23.0	10.7	Elnath	278 07.5	N28 37.3
T 08	248 17.0	345 03.4	34.1	230 45.9	42.2	352 01.0	12.7	322 25.2	10.7	Eltanin	90 44.8	N51 29.1
U 09	263 19.5	0 02.9 ..	34.4	245 46.8 ..	42.9	7 03.0 ..	12.8	337 27.4 ..	10.6	Enif	33 43.7	N 9 57.7
E 10	278 21.9	15 02.4	34.7	260 47.7	43.6	22 05.0	12.8	352 29.5	10.6	Fomalhaut	15 20.1	S29 31.5
S 11	293 24.4	30 01.9	34.9	275 48.6	44.3	37 07.0	12.8	7 31.7	10.6			
D 12	308 26.9	45 01.3	S20 35.2	290 49.5	N 7 44.9	52 09.0	S22 12.9	22 33.9	S22 10.6	Gacrux	171 56.3	S57 12.9
A 13	323 29.3	60 00.8	35.4	305 50.4	45.6	67 11.0	12.9	37 36.0	10.5	Gienah	175 48.2	S17 38.8
Y 14	338 31.8	75 00.3	35.7	320 51.2	46.3	82 13.0	13.0	52 38.2	10.5	Hadar	148 42.3	S60 27.5
15	353 34.3	89 59.7 ..	35.9	335 52.1 ..	47.0	97 14.9 ..	13.0	67 40.4 ..	10.5	Hamal	327 56.4	N23 33.0
16	8 36.7	104 59.2	36.2	350 53.0	47.7	112 16.9	13.0	82 42.5	10.5	Kaus Aust.	83 39.1	S34 22.3
17	23 39.2	119 58.7	36.4	5 53.9	48.3	127 18.9	13.1	97 44.7	10.4			
18	38 41.7	134 58.2	S20 36.7	20 54.8	N 7 49.0	142 20.9	S22 13.1	112 46.9	S22 10.4	Kochab	137 20.3	N74 04.4
19	53 44.1	149 57.6	36.9	35 55.7	49.7	157 22.9	13.2	127 49.0	10.4	Markab	13 34.8	N15 18.4
20	68 46.6	164 57.1	37.2	50 56.6	50.4	172 24.9	13.2	142 51.2	10.3	Menkar	314 11.0	N 4 09.6
21	83 49.0	179 56.6 ..	37.4	65 57.5 ..	51.1	187 26.9 ..	13.3	157 53.4 ..	10.3	Menkent	148 03.0	S36 27.5
22	98 51.5	194 56.0	37.7	80 58.4	51.7	202 28.9	13.3	172 55.5	10.3	Miaplacidus	221 37.9	S69 47.7
23	113 54.0	209 55.5	37.9	95 59.3	52.4	217 30.9	13.3	187 57.7	10.3			
30 00	128 56.4	224 55.0	S20 38.2	111 00.2	N 7 53.1	232 32.9	S22 13.4	202 59.9	S22 10.2	Mirfak	308 34.7	N49 55.7
01	143 58.9	239 54.4	38.4	126 01.1	53.8	247 34.8	13.4	218 02.0	10.2	Nunki	75 53.9	S26 16.3
02	159 01.4	254 53.9	38.7	141 02.0	54.4	262 36.8	13.5	233 04.2	10.2	Peacock	53 13.8	S56 40.4
03	174 03.8	269 53.3 ..	38.9	156 02.9 ..	55.1	277 38.8 ..	13.5	248 06.4 ..	10.1	Pollux	243 22.7	N27 58.6
04	189 06.3	284 52.8	39.1	171 03.8	55.8	292 40.8	13.5	263 08.5	10.1	Procyon	244 55.4	N 5 10.4
05	204 08.8	299 52.3	39.4	186 04.7	56.5	307 42.8	13.6	278 10.7	10.1			
06	219 11.2	314 51.7	S20 39.6	201 05.6	N 7 57.2	322 44.8	S22 13.6	293 12.9	S22 10.1	Rasalhague	96 03.1	N12 32.8
W 07	234 13.7	329 51.2	39.9	216 06.5	57.8	337 46.8	13.7	308 15.0	10.0	Regulus	207 39.1	N11 52.3
E 08	249 16.2	344 50.7	40.1	231 07.4	58.5	352 48.8	13.7	323 17.2	10.0	Rigel	281 08.1	S 8 11.1
D 09	264 18.6	359 50.1 ..	40.3	246 08.3 ..	59.2	7 50.8 ..	13.7	338 19.4 ..	10.0	Rigil Kent.	139 46.5	S60 54.4
N 10	279 21.1	14 49.6	40.6	261 09.2	7 59.9	22 52.8	13.8	353 21.5	09.9	Sabik	102 08.4	S15 44.7
E 11	294 23.5	29 49.0	40.8	276 10.1	8 00.5	37 54.8	13.8	8 23.7	09.9			
S 12	309 26.0	44 48.5	S20 41.0	291 11.0	N 8 01.2	52 56.8	S22 13.9	23 25.9	S22 09.9	Schedar	349 36.4	N56 38.6
D 13	324 28.5	59 48.0	41.3	306 11.9	01.9	67 58.7	13.9	38 28.0	09.9	Shaula	96 17.0	S37 06.8
A 14	339 30.9	74 47.4	41.5	321 12.8	02.6	83 00.7	14.0	53 30.2	09.8	Sirius	258 30.0	S16 44.8
Y 15	354 33.4	89 46.9 ..	41.7	336 13.7 ..	03.2	98 02.7 ..	14.0	68 32.4 ..	09.8	Spica	158 27.1	S11 15.5
16	9 35.9	104 46.3	42.0	351 14.6	03.9	113 04.7	14.0	83 34.5	09.8	Suhail	222 49.2	S43 30.6
17	24 38.3	119 45.8	42.2	6 15.5	04.6	128 06.7	14.1	98 36.7	09.7			
18	39 40.8	134 45.2	S20 42.4	21 16.4	N 8 05.3	143 08.7	S22 14.1	113 38.9	S22 09.7	Vega	80 36.7	N38 48.0
19	54 43.3	149 44.7	42.7	36 17.2	05.9	158 10.7	14.2	128 41.0	09.7	Zuben'ubi	137 01.2	S16 07.1
20	69 45.7	164 44.2	42.9	51 18.1	06.6	173 12.7	14.2	143 43.2	09.7		SHA	Mer.Pass.
21	84 48.2	179 43.6 ..	43.1	66 19.0 ..	07.3	188 14.7 ..	14.2	158 45.4 ..	09.6			h m
22	99 50.6	194 43.1	43.3	81 19.9	08.0	203 16.7	14.3	173 47.5	09.6	Venus	97 10.3	9 00
23	114 53.1	209 42.5	43.6	96 20.8	08.6	218 18.7	14.3	188 49.7	09.6	Mars	342 41.4	16 36
	h m									Jupiter	103 47.8	8 32
Mer.Pass. 15 25.6	v −0.5	d 0.3	v 0.9	d 0.7	v 2.0	d 0.0	v 2.2	d 0.0	Saturn	74 10.6	10 30

© British Crown Copyright 2018. All rights reserved.

UT	SUN GHA	Dec	MOON GHA	v	Dec	d	HP
d h	° '	° '	° '	'	° '	'	'
28 00	176 48.2	S18 19.7	268 29.8	11.9	S 9 39.1	10.9	57.3
01	191 48.1	19.0	283 00.7	11.8	9 50.0	10.9	57.2
02	206 48.0	18.4	297 31.5	11.9	10 00.9	10.8	57.2
03	221 47.8	.. 17.7	312 02.4	11.9	10 11.7	10.7	57.2
04	236 47.7	17.0	326 33.3	11.9	10 22.4	10.6	57.1
05	251 47.6	16.4	341 04.2	12.0	10 33.0	10.6	57.1
06	266 47.5	S18 15.7	355 35.2	11.9	S10 43.6	10.6	57.1
07	281 47.4	15.1	10 06.1	11.9	10 54.2	10.4	57.0
08	296 47.2	14.4	24 37.0	11.9	11 04.6	10.4	57.0
M 09	311 47.1	.. 13.8	39 07.9	11.9	11 15.0	10.3	57.0
O 10	326 47.0	13.1	53 38.8	11.9	11 25.3	10.3	56.9
N 11	341 46.9	12.5	68 09.7	11.9	11 35.6	10.2	56.9
D 12	356 46.8	S18 11.8	82 40.6	11.8	S11 45.8	10.1	56.9
A 13	11 46.6	11.1	97 11.4	11.9	11 55.9	10.0	56.8
Y 14	26 46.5	10.5	111 42.3	11.9	12 05.9	10.0	56.8
15	41 46.4	.. 09.8	126 13.2	11.9	12 15.9	9.9	56.8
16	56 46.3	09.2	140 44.1	11.9	12 25.8	9.9	56.7
17	71 46.2	08.5	155 15.0	11.8	12 35.7	9.7	56.7
18	86 46.1	S18 07.8	169 45.8	11.9	S12 45.4	9.7	56.7
19	101 45.9	07.2	184 16.7	11.9	12 55.1	9.6	56.6
20	116 45.8	06.5	198 47.6	11.8	13 04.7	9.6	56.6
21	131 45.7	.. 05.8	213 18.4	11.9	13 14.3	9.4	56.6
22	146 45.6	05.2	227 49.3	11.8	13 23.7	9.4	56.5
23	161 45.5	04.5	242 20.1	11.8	13 33.1	9.3	56.5
29 00	176 45.4	S18 03.9	256 50.9	11.9	S13 42.4	9.3	56.5
01	191 45.2	03.2	271 21.8	11.8	13 51.7	9.1	56.5
02	206 45.1	02.5	285 52.6	11.8	14 00.8	9.1	56.4
03	221 45.0	.. 01.9	300 23.4	11.8	14 09.9	9.0	56.4
04	236 44.9	01.2	314 54.2	11.7	14 18.9	9.0	56.4
05	251 44.8	18 00.5	329 24.9	11.8	14 27.9	8.8	56.3
06	266 44.7	S17 59.9	343 55.7	11.8	S14 36.7	8.8	56.3
07	281 44.6	59.2	358 26.5	11.7	14 45.5	8.6	56.3
T 08	296 44.5	58.5	12 57.2	11.8	14 54.1	8.6	56.2
U 09	311 44.3	.. 57.8	27 28.0	11.7	15 02.7	8.6	56.2
E 10	326 44.2	57.2	41 58.7	11.7	15 11.3	8.4	56.2
S 11	341 44.1	56.5	56 29.4	11.7	15 19.7	8.4	56.2
D 12	356 44.0	S17 55.8	71 00.1	11.7	S15 28.1	8.2	56.1
A 13	11 43.9	55.2	85 30.8	11.7	15 36.3	8.2	56.1
Y 14	26 43.8	54.5	100 01.5	11.7	15 44.5	8.1	56.1
15	41 43.7	.. 53.8	114 32.2	11.6	15 52.6	8.0	56.0
16	56 43.6	53.1	129 02.8	11.7	16 00.6	8.0	56.0
17	71 43.5	52.5	143 33.5	11.6	16 08.6	7.8	56.0
18	86 43.4	S17 51.8	158 04.1	11.7	S16 16.4	7.8	56.0
19	101 43.2	51.1	172 34.8	11.6	16 24.2	7.6	55.9
20	116 43.1	50.4	187 05.4	11.6	16 31.8	7.6	55.9
21	131 43.0	.. 49.8	201 36.0	11.5	16 39.4	7.5	55.9
22	146 42.9	49.1	216 06.5	11.6	16 46.9	7.4	55.9
23	161 42.8	48.4	230 37.1	11.6	16 54.3	7.4	55.8
30 00	176 42.7	S17 47.7	245 07.7	11.5	S17 01.7	7.2	55.8
01	191 42.6	47.0	259 38.2	11.5	17 08.9	7.1	55.8
02	206 42.5	46.4	274 08.7	11.5	17 16.0	7.1	55.8
03	221 42.4	.. 45.7	288 39.2	11.5	17 23.1	6.9	55.7
04	236 42.3	45.0	303 09.7	11.5	17 30.0	6.9	55.7
05	251 42.2	44.3	317 40.2	11.5	17 36.9	6.8	55.7
06	266 42.1	S17 43.6	332 10.7	11.5	S17 43.7	6.7	55.6
W 07	281 42.0	43.0	346 41.2	11.4	17 50.4	6.6	55.6
E 08	296 41.9	42.3	1 11.6	11.4	17 57.0	6.5	55.6
D 09	311 41.8	.. 41.6	15 42.0	11.4	18 03.5	6.4	55.6
N 10	326 41.7	40.9	30 12.4	11.5	18 09.9	6.3	55.6
E 11	341 41.6	40.2	44 42.9	11.3	18 16.2	6.2	55.5
S 12	356 41.5	S17 39.5	59 13.2	11.4	S18 22.4	6.0	55.5
D 13	11 41.4	38.9	73 43.6	11.4	18 28.5	6.0	55.5
A 14	26 41.3	38.2	88 14.0	11.3	18 34.5	6.0	55.5
Y 15	41 41.2	.. 37.5	102 44.3	11.4	18 40.5	5.8	55.4
16	56 41.1	36.8	117 14.7	11.3	18 46.3	5.8	55.4
17	71 41.0	36.1	131 45.0	11.3	18 52.1	5.6	55.4
18	86 40.9	S17 35.4	146 15.3	11.3	S18 57.7	5.6	55.4
19	101 40.8	34.7	160 45.6	11.3	19 03.3	5.4	55.3
20	116 40.7	34.0	175 15.9	11.3	19 08.7	5.4	55.3
21	131 40.6	.. 33.3	189 46.2	11.2	19 14.1	5.2	55.3
22	146 40.5	32.7	204 16.4	11.3	19 19.3	5.2	55.3
23	161 40.4	32.0	218 46.7	11.2	S19 24.5	5.0	55.3
	SD 16.3	d 0.7	SD 15.5		15.3		15.1

Lat.	Twilight Naut.	Civil	Sunrise	Moonrise 28	29	30	31
°	h m	h m	h m	h m	h m	h m	h m
N 72	07 21	08 53	10 58	02 26	04 33	▬▬	▬▬
N 70	07 12	08 32	10 04	02 08	04 00	06 00	▬▬
68	07 04	08 16	09 31	01 55	03 37	05 20	07 02
66	06 57	08 02	09 08	01 44	03 19	04 52	06 20
64	06 51	07 51	08 49	01 35	03 05	04 32	05 52
62	06 46	07 41	08 34	01 27	02 53	04 15	05 31
60	06 42	07 33	08 21	01 20	02 42	04 01	05 14
N 58	06 38	07 26	08 10	01 14	02 33	03 49	04 59
56	06 34	07 19	08 01	01 09	02 26	03 39	04 47
54	06 30	07 13	07 53	01 04	02 19	03 30	04 36
52	06 27	07 08	07 45	01 00	02 12	03 22	04 27
50	06 24	07 03	07 38	00 56	02 07	03 14	04 18
45	06 17	06 52	07 24	00 48	01 55	02 59	04 00
N 40	06 10	06 43	07 12	00 41	01 45	02 46	03 45
35	06 04	06 34	07 01	00 35	01 36	02 36	03 33
30	05 58	06 27	06 52	00 30	01 29	02 26	03 22
20	05 47	06 13	06 36	00 22	01 16	02 10	03 03
N 10	05 35	06 01	06 23	00 14	01 05	01 56	02 47
0	05 23	05 48	06 10	00 07	00 55	01 43	02 32
S 10	05 08	05 34	05 56	00 00	00 45	01 30	02 17
20	04 51	05 19	05 42	24 34	00 34	01 17	02 01
30	04 29	05 00	05 26	24 21	00 21	01 01	01 43
35	04 14	04 48	05 16	24 14	00 14	00 52	01 33
40	03 57	04 35	05 05	24 06	00 06	00 42	01 21
45	03 35	04 18	04 52	23 57	24 30	00 30	01 06
S 50	03 06	03 57	04 36	23 46	24 15	00 15	00 49
52	02 51	03 47	04 28	23 40	24 08	00 08	00 41
54	02 33	03 35	04 20	23 35	24 01	00 01	00 22
56	02 09	03 22	04 10	23 28	23 52	24 22	00 22
58	01 37	03 06	04 00	23 21	23 43	24 10	00 10
S 60	////	02 47	03 47	23 13	23 32	23 57	24 30

Lat.	Sunset	Twilight Civil	Naut.	Moonset 28	29	30	31
°	h m	h m	h m	h m	h m	h m	h m
N 72	13 29	15 35	17 07	09 50	09 23	▬▬	▬▬
N 70	14 23	15 55	17 16	10 09	09 57	09 39	▬▬
68	14 56	16 12	17 23	10 24	10 21	10 20	10 20
66	15 19	16 25	17 30	10 36	10 40	10 48	11 02
64	15 38	16 36	17 36	10 47	10 56	11 09	11 30
62	15 53	16 46	17 41	10 55	11 09	11 27	11 52
60	16 06	16 54	17 45	11 03	11 20	11 41	12 10
N 58	16 16	17 01	17 49	11 10	11 29	11 54	12 24
56	16 26	17 08	17 53	11 16	11 38	12 04	12 37
54	16 34	17 14	17 57	11 21	11 45	12 14	12 48
52	16 42	17 19	18 00	11 26	11 52	12 22	12 58
50	16 49	17 24	18 03	11 30	11 58	12 30	13 07
45	17 03	17 35	18 10	11 40	12 11	12 46	13 25
N 40	17 15	17 44	18 16	11 48	12 22	12 59	13 40
35	17 25	17 52	18 23	11 55	12 32	13 11	13 53
30	17 34	18 00	18 28	12 01	12 40	13 21	14 04
20	17 50	18 13	18 40	12 12	12 54	13 38	14 24
N 10	18 04	18 26	18 51	12 21	13 06	13 53	14 40
0	18 17	18 38	19 04	12 30	13 18	14 07	14 56
S 10	18 30	18 52	19 18	12 39	13 30	14 21	15 12
20	18 44	19 07	19 35	12 48	13 42	14 36	15 29
30	19 00	19 26	19 57	12 59	13 57	14 53	15 48
35	19 10	19 37	20 11	13 05	14 05	15 03	15 59
40	19 21	19 51	20 28	13 12	14 15	15 15	16 12
45	19 33	20 07	20 49	13 20	14 26	15 29	16 27
S 50	19 49	20 28	21 18	13 30	14 39	15 45	16 46
52	19 57	20 38	21 33	13 35	14 46	15 53	16 55
54	20 05	20 49	21 51	13 40	14 53	16 02	17 05
56	20 14	21 02	22 14	13 46	15 01	16 12	17 16
58	20 25	21 18	22 45	13 52	15 10	16 23	17 29
S 60	20 37	21 37	23 46	13 59	15 20	16 36	17 45

Day	SUN Eqn. of Time 00ʰ	12ʰ	Mer. Pass.	MOON Mer. Pass. Upper	Lower	Age	Phase
d	m s	m s	h m	h m	h m	d	%
28	12 47	12 53	12 13	06 18	18 42	22	44
29	12 58	13 04	12 13	07 06	19 31	23	34
30	13 09	13 14	12 13	07 55	20 20	24	24

© British Crown Copyright 2018. All rights reserved.

UT	ARIES GHA	VENUS −4.3 GHA	Dec	MARS +0.9 GHA	Dec	JUPITER −1.9 GHA	Dec	SATURN +0.6 GHA	Dec	STARS Name	SHA	Dec
31 00	129 55.6	224 42.0	S20 43.8	111 21.7	N 8 09.3	233 20.7	S22 14.4	203 51.9	S22 09.6	Acamar	315 15.4	S40 14.1
01	144 58.0	239 41.4	44.0	126 22.6	10.0	248 22.7	14.4	218 54.0	09.5	Achernar	335 24.1	S57 08.9
02	160 00.5	254 40.9	44.2	141 23.5	10.7	263 24.7	14.4	233 56.2	09.5	Acrux	173 04.5	S63 12.0
03	175 03.0	269 40.3	.. 44.5	156 24.4	.. 11.3	278 26.7	.. 14.5	248 58.4	.. 09.5	Adhara	255 09.2	S29 00.1
04	190 05.4	284 39.8	44.7	171 25.3	12.0	293 28.7	14.5	264 00.6	09.4	Aldebaran	290 44.8	N16 32.7
05	205 07.9	299 39.2	44.9	186 26.2	12.7	308 30.7	14.6	279 02.7	09.4			
06	220 10.4	314 38.7	S20 45.1	201 27.1	N 8 13.4	323 32.6	S22 14.6	294 04.9	S22 09.4	Alioth	166 17.1	N55 51.2
07	235 12.8	329 38.1	45.3	216 28.0	14.0	338 34.6	14.6	309 07.1	09.4	Alkaid	152 55.8	N49 12.9
T 08	250 15.3	344 37.6	45.6	231 28.9	14.7	353 36.6	14.7	324 09.2	09.3	Alnair	27 39.4	S46 52.3
H 09	265 17.8	359 37.0	.. 45.8	246 29.8	.. 15.4	8 38.6	.. 14.7	339 11.4	.. 09.3	Alnilam	275 42.2	S 1 11.6
U 10	280 20.2	14 36.5	46.0	261 30.7	16.1	23 40.6	14.8	354 13.6	09.3	Alphard	217 52.0	S 8 44.6
R 11	295 22.7	29 35.9	46.2	276 31.6	16.7	38 42.6	14.8	9 15.7	09.2			
S 12	310 25.1	44 35.4	S20 46.4	291 32.4	N 8 17.4	53 44.6	S22 14.8	24 17.9	S22 09.2	Alphecca	126 07.8	N26 39.0
D 13	325 27.6	59 34.8	46.6	306 33.3	18.1	68 46.6	14.9	39 20.1	09.2	Alpheratz	357 39.7	N29 11.7
A 14	340 30.1	74 34.3	46.9	321 34.2	18.8	83 48.6	14.9	54 22.2	09.2	Altair	62 04.8	N 8 55.1
Y 15	355 32.5	89 33.7	.. 47.1	336 35.1	.. 19.4	98 50.6	.. 15.0	69 24.4	.. 09.1	Ankaa	353 12.2	S42 12.5
16	10 35.0	104 33.2	47.3	351 36.0	20.1	113 52.6	15.0	84 26.6	09.1	Antares	112 21.7	S26 28.2
17	25 37.5	119 32.6	47.5	6 36.9	20.8	128 54.6	15.0	99 28.7	09.1			
18	40 39.9	134 32.1	S20 47.7	21 37.8	N 8 21.4	143 56.6	S22 15.1	114 30.9	S22 09.0	Arcturus	145 52.2	N19 04.9
19	55 42.4	149 31.5	47.9	36 38.7	22.1	158 58.6	15.1	129 33.1	09.0	Atria	107 20.4	S69 03.3
20	70 44.9	164 30.9	48.1	51 39.6	22.8	174 00.6	15.2	144 35.2	09.0	Avior	234 15.8	S59 34.3
21	85 47.3	179 30.4	.. 48.3	66 40.5	.. 23.5	189 02.6	.. 15.2	159 37.4	.. 09.0	Bellatrix	278 27.7	N 6 21.8
22	100 49.8	194 29.8	48.5	81 41.4	24.1	204 04.6	15.2	174 39.6	08.9	Betelgeuse	270 56.9	N 7 24.4
23	115 52.3	209 29.3	48.7	96 42.3	24.8	219 06.6	15.3	189 41.8	08.9			
1 00	130 54.7	224 28.7	S20 48.9	111 43.2	N 8 25.5	234 08.6	S22 15.3	204 43.9	S22 08.9	Canopus	263 54.0	S52 42.7
01	145 57.2	239 28.2	49.1	126 44.1	26.2	249 10.6	15.4	219 46.1	08.8	Capella	280 28.5	N46 01.0
02	160 59.6	254 27.6	49.3	141 44.9	26.8	264 12.6	15.4	234 48.3	08.8	Deneb	49 29.3	N45 20.9
03	176 02.1	269 27.0	.. 49.5	156 45.8	.. 27.5	279 14.6	.. 15.4	249 50.4	.. 08.8	Denebola	182 29.5	N14 27.9
04	191 04.6	284 26.5	49.7	171 46.7	28.2	294 16.6	15.5	264 52.6	08.8	Diphda	348 52.2	S17 53.2
05	206 07.0	299 25.9	49.9	186 47.6	28.8	309 18.6	15.5	279 54.8	08.7			
06	221 09.5	314 25.4	S20 50.1	201 48.5	N 8 29.5	324 20.6	S22 15.6	294 56.9	S22 08.7	Dubhe	193 46.5	N61 38.7
07	236 12.0	329 24.8	50.3	216 49.4	30.2	339 22.6	15.6	309 59.1	08.7	Elnath	278 07.5	N28 37.3
08	251 14.4	344 24.2	50.5	231 50.3	30.9	354 24.6	15.6	325 01.3	08.6	Eltanin	90 44.8	N51 29.1
F 09	266 16.9	359 23.7	.. 50.7	246 51.2	.. 31.5	9 26.6	.. 15.7	340 03.5	.. 08.6	Enif	33 43.7	N 9 57.7
R 10	281 19.4	14 23.1	50.9	261 52.1	32.2	24 28.6	15.7	355 05.6	08.6	Fomalhaut	15 20.1	S29 31.5
I 11	296 21.8	29 22.6	51.1	276 53.0	32.9	39 30.6	15.7	10 07.8	08.6			
D 12	311 24.3	44 22.0	S20 51.3	291 53.9	N 8 33.5	54 32.6	S22 15.8	25 10.0	S22 08.5	Gacrux	171 56.3	S57 12.0
A 13	326 26.8	59 21.4	51.5	306 54.8	34.2	69 34.6	15.8	40 12.1	08.5	Gienah	175 48.1	S17 38.8
Y 14	341 29.2	74 20.9	51.7	321 55.6	34.9	84 36.6	15.9	55 14.3	08.5	Hadar	148 42.3	S60 27.5
15	356 31.7	89 20.3	.. 51.9	336 56.5	.. 35.5	99 38.6	.. 15.9	70 16.5	.. 08.5	Hamal	327 56.5	N23 33.0
16	11 34.1	104 19.7	52.1	351 57.4	36.2	114 40.6	15.9	85 18.6	08.4	Kaus Aust.	83 39.1	S34 22.3
17	26 36.6	119 19.2	52.3	6 58.3	36.9	129 42.6	16.0	100 20.8	08.4			
18	41 39.1	134 18.6	S20 52.5	21 59.2	N 8 37.6	144 44.6	S22 16.0	115 23.0	S22 08.4	Kochab	137 20.2	N74 04.4
19	56 41.5	149 18.0	52.7	37 00.1	38.2	159 46.6	16.1	130 25.2	08.3	Markab	13 34.8	N15 18.4
20	71 44.0	164 17.5	52.8	52 01.0	38.9	174 48.6	16.1	145 27.3	08.3	Menkar	314 11.0	N 4 09.6
21	86 46.5	179 16.9	.. 53.0	67 01.9	.. 39.6	189 50.6	.. 16.1	160 29.5	.. 08.3	Menkent	148 03.0	S36 27.5
22	101 48.9	194 16.3	53.2	82 02.8	40.2	204 52.6	16.2	175 31.7	08.3	Miaplacidus	221 37.9	S69 47.7
23	116 51.4	209 15.8	53.4	97 03.7	40.9	219 54.6	16.2	190 33.8	08.2			
2 00	131 53.9	224 15.2	S20 53.6	112 04.6	N 8 41.6	234 56.6	S22 16.3	205 36.0	S22 08.2	Mirfak	308 34.7	N49 55.7
01	146 56.3	239 14.6	53.8	127 05.4	42.2	249 58.6	16.3	220 38.2	08.2	Nunki	75 53.9	S26 16.3
02	161 58.8	254 14.1	53.9	142 06.3	42.9	265 00.6	16.3	235 40.4	08.1	Peacock	53 13.8	S56 40.4
03	177 01.3	269 13.5	.. 54.1	157 07.2	.. 43.6	280 02.6	.. 16.4	250 42.5	.. 08.1	Pollux	243 22.7	N27 58.7
04	192 03.7	284 12.9	54.3	172 08.1	44.3	295 04.6	16.4	265 44.7	08.1	Procyon	244 55.4	N 5 10.4
05	207 06.2	299 12.4	54.5	187 09.0	44.9	310 06.7	16.4	280 46.9	08.1			
06	222 08.6	314 11.8	S20 54.7	202 09.9	N 8 45.6	325 08.7	S22 16.5	295 49.0	S22 08.0	Rasalhague	96 03.1	N12 32.8
07	237 11.1	329 11.2	54.8	217 10.8	46.3	340 10.7	16.5	310 51.2	08.0	Regulus	207 39.1	N11 52.3
S 08	252 13.6	344 10.7	55.0	232 11.7	46.9	355 12.7	16.6	325 53.4	08.0	Rigel	281 08.2	S 8 11.1
A 09	267 16.0	359 10.1	.. 55.2	247 12.6	.. 47.6	10 14.7	.. 16.6	340 55.6	.. 07.9	Rigil Kent.	139 46.5	S60 54.4
T 10	282 18.5	14 09.5	55.4	262 13.4	48.3	25 16.7	16.6	355 57.7	07.9	Sabik	102 08.3	S15 44.7
U 11	297 21.0	29 08.9	55.5	277 14.3	48.9	40 18.7	16.7	10 59.9	07.9			
R 12	312 23.4	44 08.4	S20 55.7	292 15.2	N 8 49.6	55 20.7	S22 16.7	26 02.1	S22 07.9	Schedar	349 36.4	N56 38.6
D 13	327 25.9	59 07.8	55.9	307 16.1	50.3	70 22.7	16.7	41 04.2	07.8	Shaula	96 17.0	S37 06.8
A 14	342 28.4	74 07.2	56.1	322 17.0	50.9	85 24.7	16.8	56 06.4	07.8	Sirius	258 30.0	S16 44.8
Y 15	357 30.8	89 06.6	.. 56.2	337 17.9	.. 51.6	100 26.7	.. 16.8	71 08.6	.. 07.8	Spica	158 27.1	S11 15.5
16	12 33.3	104 06.1	56.4	352 18.8	52.3	115 28.7	16.9	86 10.8	07.7	Suhail	222 49.2	S43 30.6
17	27 35.7	119 05.5	56.6	7 19.7	52.9	130 30.7	16.9	101 12.9	07.7			
18	42 38.2	134 04.9	S20 56.7	22 20.6	N 8 53.6	145 32.7	S22 16.9	116 15.1	S22 07.7	Vega	80 36.7	N38 48.0
19	57 40.7	149 04.3	56.9	37 21.4	54.3	160 34.7	17.0	131 17.3	07.7	Zuben'ubi	137 01.2	S16 07.1
20	72 43.1	164 03.8	57.1	52 22.3	54.9	175 36.7	17.0	146 19.4	07.6		SHA	Mer.Pass.
21	87 45.6	179 03.2	.. 57.2	67 23.2	.. 55.6	190 38.7	.. 17.1	161 21.6	.. 07.6			h m
22	102 48.1	194 02.6	57.4	82 24.1	56.3	205 40.7	17.1	176 23.8	07.6	Venus	93 34.0	9 02
23	117 50.5	209 02.0	57.6	97 25.0	56.9	220 42.8	17.1	191 26.0	07.5	Mars	340 48.4	16 32
	h m									Jupiter	103 13.9	8 22
Mer. Pass.	15 13.9	v −0.6	d 0.2	v 0.9	d 0.7	v 2.0	d 0.0	v 2.2	d 0.0	Saturn	73 49.2	10 20

© British Crown Copyright 2018. All rights reserved.

UT	SUN GHA	SUN Dec	MOON GHA	v	MOON Dec	d	HP
31 00	176 40.3	S17 31.3	233 16.9	11.3	S19 29.5	5.0	55.2
01	191 40.2	30.6	247 47.2	11.2	19 34.5	4.9	55.2
02	206 40.1	29.9	262 17.4	11.2	19 39.4	4.7	55.2
03	221 40.0	.. 29.2	276 47.6	11.2	19 44.1	4.7	55.2
04	236 39.9	28.5	291 17.8	11.2	19 48.8	4.6	55.1
05	251 39.8	27.8	305 48.0	11.2	19 53.4	4.4	55.1
06	266 39.7	S17 27.1	320 18.2	11.1	S19 57.8	4.4	55.1
07	281 39.6	26.4	334 48.3	11.2	20 02.2	4.3	55.1
T 08	296 39.5	25.7	349 18.5	11.1	20 06.5	4.1	55.1
H 09	311 39.4	.. 25.0	3 48.6	11.2	20 10.6	4.1	55.0
U 10	326 39.3	24.3	18 18.8	11.1	20 14.7	4.0	55.0
R 11	341 39.2	23.6	32 48.9	11.2	20 18.7	3.8	55.0
S 12	356 39.1	S17 22.9	47 19.1	11.1	S20 22.5	3.8	55.0
D 13	11 39.0	22.2	61 49.2	11.1	20 26.3	3.6	55.0
A 14	26 38.9	21.5	76 19.3	11.1	20 29.9	3.6	55.0
Y 15	41 38.8	.. 20.8	90 49.4	11.1	20 33.5	3.5	54.9
16	56 38.7	20.1	105 19.5	11.1	20 37.0	3.3	54.9
17	71 38.7	19.4	119 49.6	11.1	20 40.3	3.2	54.9
18	86 38.6	S17 18.7	134 19.7	11.1	S20 43.5	3.2	54.9
19	101 38.5	18.0	148 49.8	11.1	20 46.7	3.0	54.9
20	116 38.4	17.3	163 19.9	11.0	20 49.7	3.0	54.8
21	131 38.3	.. 16.6	177 49.9	11.1	20 52.7	2.8	54.8
22	146 38.2	15.9	192 20.0	11.1	20 55.5	2.7	54.8
23	161 38.1	15.2	206 50.1	11.0	20 58.2	2.7	54.8
1 00	176 38.0	S17 14.5	221 20.1	11.1	S21 00.9	2.5	54.8
01	191 37.9	13.8	235 50.2	11.1	21 03.4	2.4	54.8
02	206 37.8	13.1	250 20.3	11.1	21 05.8	2.3	54.7
03	221 37.8	.. 12.4	264 50.4	11.0	21 08.1	2.3	54.7
04	236 37.7	11.7	279 20.4	11.1	21 10.4	2.1	54.7
05	251 37.6	11.0	293 50.5	11.0	21 12.5	2.0	54.7
06	266 37.5	S17 10.3	308 20.5	11.1	S21 14.5	1.9	54.7
07	281 37.4	09.6	322 50.6	11.1	21 16.4	1.8	54.7
F 08	296 37.3	08.9	337 20.7	11.1	21 18.2	1.7	54.6
R 09	311 37.2	.. 08.1	351 50.8	11.0	21 19.9	1.6	54.6
I 10	326 37.1	07.4	6 20.8	11.1	21 21.5	1.4	54.6
D 11	341 37.1	06.7	20 50.9	11.1	21 22.9	1.4	54.6
A 12	356 37.0	S17 06.0	35 21.0	11.1	S21 24.3	1.3	54.6
Y 13	11 36.9	05.3	49 51.1	11.1	21 25.6	1.2	54.6
14	26 36.8	04.6	64 21.2	11.1	21 26.8	1.0	54.6
15	41 36.7	.. 03.9	78 51.3	11.1	21 27.8	1.0	54.5
16	56 36.6	03.2	93 21.4	11.1	21 28.8	0.9	54.5
17	71 36.6	02.5	107 51.5	11.1	21 29.7	0.7	54.5
18	86 36.5	S17 01.7	122 21.6	11.1	S21 30.4	0.7	54.5
19	101 36.4	01.0	136 51.7	11.2	21 31.1	0.5	54.5
20	116 36.3	17 00.3	151 21.9	11.1	21 31.6	0.4	54.5
21	131 36.2	16 59.6	165 52.0	11.2	21 32.0	0.4	54.5
22	146 36.1	58.9	180 22.2	11.1	21 32.4	0.2	54.5
23	161 36.1	58.2	194 52.3	11.2	21 32.6	0.2	54.4
2 00	176 36.0	S16 57.4	209 22.5	11.2	S21 32.8	0.0	54.4
01	191 35.9	56.7	223 52.7	11.2	21 32.8	0.1	54.4
02	206 35.8	56.0	238 22.9	11.2	21 32.7	0.2	54.4
03	221 35.7	.. 55.3	252 53.1	11.2	21 32.5	0.3	54.4
04	236 35.7	54.6	267 23.3	11.2	21 32.2	0.3	54.4
05	251 35.6	53.8	281 53.6	11.2	21 31.9	0.5	54.4
06	266 35.5	S16 53.1	296 23.8	11.3	S21 31.4	0.6	54.4
07	281 35.4	52.4	310 54.1	11.3	21 30.8	0.7	54.3
S 08	296 35.3	51.7	325 24.4	11.3	21 30.1	0.8	54.3
A 09	311 35.3	.. 51.0	339 54.7	11.3	21 29.3	0.9	54.3
T 10	326 35.2	50.2	354 25.0	11.3	21 28.4	1.0	54.3
U 11	341 35.1	49.5	8 55.3	11.4	21 27.4	1.1	54.3
R 12	356 35.0	S16 48.8	23 25.7	11.3	S21 26.3	1.2	54.3
D 13	11 35.0	48.1	37 56.0	11.4	21 25.1	1.3	54.3
A 14	26 34.9	47.3	52 26.4	11.4	21 23.8	1.5	54.3
Y 15	41 34.8	.. 46.6	66 56.8	11.5	21 22.3	1.5	54.3
16	56 34.7	45.9	81 27.3	11.4	21 20.8	1.6	54.2
17	71 34.6	45.2	95 57.7	11.5	21 19.2	1.7	54.2
18	86 34.6	S16 44.4	110 28.2	11.5	S21 17.5	1.8	54.2
19	101 34.5	43.7	124 58.7	11.5	21 15.7	1.9	54.2
20	116 34.4	43.0	139 29.2	11.5	21 13.8	2.0	54.2
21	131 34.4	.. 42.3	153 59.7	11.6	21 11.8	2.1	54.2
22	146 34.3	41.5	168 30.3	11.6	21 09.7	2.2	54.2
23	161 34.2	40.8	183 00.9	11.6	S21 07.5	2.4	54.2
	SD 16.3	d 0.7	SD 15.0		14.9		14.8

Moonrise

Lat.	Twilight Naut.	Twilight Civil	Sunrise	31	1	2	3
N 72	07 10	08 40	10 29	▬	▬	▬	▬
N 70	07 02	08 21	09 47	▬	▬	▬	▬
68	06 56	08 06	09 19	07 02	08 36	09 34	09 46
66	06 50	07 54	08 57	06 20	07 36	08 30	09 01
64	06 45	07 44	08 40	05 52	07 02	07 55	08 31
62	06 40	07 35	08 26	05 31	06 37	07 30	08 08
60	06 36	07 27	08 15	05 14	06 18	07 10	07 50
N 58	06 33	07 20	08 04	04 59	06 02	06 54	07 35
56	06 29	07 14	07 55	04 47	05 48	06 40	07 22
54	06 26	07 09	07 48	04 36	05 36	06 28	07 10
52	06 23	07 04	07 40	04 27	05 25	06 17	07 00
50	06 20	06 59	07 34	04 18	05 16	06 07	06 51
45	06 14	06 49	07 20	04 00	04 56	05 48	06 33
N 40	06 08	06 40	07 09	03 45	04 41	05 31	06 17
35	06 02	06 32	06 59	03 33	04 27	05 18	06 04
30	05 57	06 25	06 50	03 22	04 15	05 06	05 53
20	05 46	06 13	06 36	03 03	03 55	04 45	05 33
N 10	05 35	06 01	06 22	02 47	03 38	04 28	05 16
0	05 23	05 48	06 10	02 32	03 22	04 11	05 00
S 10	05 10	05 35	05 57	02 17	03 06	03 55	04 44
20	04 53	05 21	05 44	02 01	02 48	03 37	04 27
30	04 32	05 02	05 28	01 43	02 29	03 17	04 07
35	04 18	04 52	05 19	01 33	02 17	03 05	03 56
40	04 01	04 39	05 09	01 21	02 04	02 51	03 43
45	03 41	04 23	04 56	01 06	01 48	02 35	03 27
S 50	03 13	04 03	04 41	00 49	01 29	02 15	03 08
52	02 59	03 53	04 34	00 41	01 20	02 06	02 59
54	02 42	03 42	04 26	00 32	01 10	01 55	02 49
56	02 21	03 30	04 17	00 22	00 58	01 44	02 37
58	01 53	03 15	04 07	00 10	00 45	01 30	02 24
S 60	01 07	02 57	03 55	24 30	00 30	01 13	02 08

Moonset

Lat.	Sunset	Twilight Civil	Twilight Naut.	31	1	2	3
N 72	13 59	15 49	17 18	▬	▬	▬	▬
N 70	14 41	16 07	17 26	▬	▬	▬	▬
68	15 10	16 22	17 33	10 20	10 29	11 14	12 42
66	15 31	16 34	17 38	11 02	11 29	12 17	13 28
64	15 48	16 44	17 43	11 30	12 03	12 52	13 57
62	16 02	16 53	17 48	11 52	12 28	13 18	14 20
60	16 13	17 01	17 52	12 10	12 48	13 37	14 38
N 58	16 23	17 08	17 55	12 24	13 04	13 54	14 53
56	16 32	17 14	17 59	12 37	13 18	14 08	15 05
54	16 40	17 19	18 02	12 48	13 30	14 20	15 16
52	16 47	17 24	18 05	12 58	13 40	14 30	15 26
50	16 54	17 29	18 07	13 07	13 50	14 40	15 35
45	17 07	17 39	18 14	13 25	14 10	14 59	15 54
N 40	17 19	17 47	18 20	13 40	14 26	15 16	16 09
35	17 28	17 55	18 25	13 53	14 39	15 29	16 21
30	17 37	18 02	18 31	14 04	14 51	15 41	16 32
20	17 52	18 15	18 41	14 24	15 12	16 01	16 51
N 10	18 05	18 27	18 52	14 40	15 29	16 19	17 08
0	18 17	18 39	19 04	14 56	15 46	16 35	17 23
S 10	18 29	18 52	19 17	15 12	16 02	16 51	17 39
20	18 43	19 06	19 34	15 29	16 20	17 09	17 55
30	18 58	19 24	19 55	15 48	16 40	17 29	18 14
35	19 07	19 35	20 08	15 59	16 52	17 40	18 25
40	19 18	19 48	20 24	16 12	17 05	17 54	18 37
45	19 30	20 03	20 45	16 27	17 21	18 10	18 52
S 50	19 45	20 23	21 12	16 46	17 41	18 29	19 09
52	19 52	20 32	21 26	16 55	17 51	18 38	19 18
54	20 00	20 43	21 42	17 05	18 01	18 48	19 27
56	20 08	20 55	22 03	17 16	18 13	19 00	19 38
58	20 18	21 10	22 30	17 29	18 27	19 14	19 50
S 60	20 30	21 27	23 11	17 45	18 43	19 29	20 04

Day	SUN Eqn. of Time 00h	SUN Eqn. of Time 12h	SUN Mer. Pass.	MOON Mer. Pass. Upper	MOON Mer. Pass. Lower	Age	Phase
31	13 19	13 23	12 13	08 44	21 09	25	17
1	13 28	13 32	12 14	09 34	21 58	26	10
2	13 36	13 40	12 14	10 23	22 48	27	5

© British Crown Copyright 2018. All rights reserved.

UT	ARIES GHA	VENUS −4.3 GHA	Dec	MARS +0.9 GHA	Dec	JUPITER −1.9 GHA	Dec	SATURN +0.6 GHA	Dec	Name	SHA	Dec
3 00	132 53.0	224 01.5	S20 57.7	112 25.9	N 8 57.6	235 44.8	S22 17.2	206 28.1	S22 07.5	Acamar	315 15.4	S40 14.1
01	147 55.5	239 00.9	57.9	127 26.8	58.3	250 46.8	17.2	221 30.3	07.5	Achernar	335 24.1	S57 08.8
02	162 57.9	254 00.3	58.0	142 27.7	58.9	265 48.8	17.2	236 32.5	07.5	Acrux	173 04.5	S63 12.0
03	178 00.4	268 59.7 ..	58.2	157 28.5	8 59.6	280 50.8 ..	17.3	251 34.7 ..	07.4	Adhara	255 09.2	S29 00.1
04	193 02.9	283 59.1	58.4	172 29.4	9 00.3	295 52.8	17.3	266 36.8	07.4	Aldebaran	290 44.8	N16 32.7
05	208 05.3	298 58.6	58.5	187 30.3	00.9	310 54.8	17.3	281 39.0	07.4			
06	223 07.8	313 58.0	S20 58.7	202 31.2	N 9 01.6	325 56.8	S22 17.4	296 41.2	S22 07.3	Alioth	166 17.0	N55 51.2
07	238 10.2	328 57.4	58.8	217 32.1	02.3	340 58.8	17.4	311 43.3	07.3	Alkaid	152 55.7	N49 12.9
08	253 12.7	343 56.8	59.0	232 33.0	02.9	356 00.8	17.5	326 45.5	07.3	Alnair	27 39.4	S46 52.3
S 09	268 15.2	358 56.2 ..	59.1	247 33.9 ..	03.6	11 02.8 ..	17.5	341 47.7 ..	07.3	Alnilam	275 42.2	S 1 11.6
U 10	283 17.6	13 55.7	59.3	262 34.8	04.3	26 04.8	17.5	356 49.9	07.2	Alphard	217 52.0	S 8 44.6
N 11	298 20.1	28 55.1	59.4	277 35.6	04.9	41 06.9	17.6	11 52.0	07.2			
D 12	313 22.6	43 54.5	S20 59.6	292 36.5	N 9 05.6	56 08.9	S22 17.6	26 54.2	S22 07.2	Alphecca	126 07.8	N26 39.0
A 13	328 25.0	58 53.9	59.7	307 37.4	06.2	71 10.9	17.7	41 56.4	07.1	Alpheratz	357 39.7	N29 11.7
Y 14	343 27.5	73 53.3	20 59.9	322 38.3	06.9	86 12.9	17.7	56 58.6	07.1	Altair	62 04.8	N 8 55.1
15	358 30.0	88 52.7	21 00.0	337 39.2 ..	07.6	101 14.9 ..	17.7	72 00.7 ..	07.1	Ankaa	353 12.2	S42 12.5
16	13 32.4	103 52.2	00.2	352 40.1	08.2	116 16.9	17.8	87 02.9	07.1	Antares	112 21.7	S26 28.2
17	28 34.9	118 51.6	00.3	7 41.0	08.9	131 18.9	17.8	102 05.1	07.0			
18	43 37.4	133 51.0	S21 00.5	22 41.8	N 9 09.6	146 20.9	S22 17.8	117 07.3	S22 07.0	Arcturus	145 52.2	N19 04.9
19	58 39.8	148 50.4	00.6	37 42.7	10.2	161 22.9	17.9	132 09.4	07.0	Atria	107 20.3	S69 03.3
20	73 42.3	163 49.8	00.8	52 43.6	10.9	176 25.0	17.9	147 11.6	06.9	Avior	234 15.8	S59 34.4
21	88 44.7	178 49.2 ..	00.9	67 44.5 ..	11.6	191 27.0 ..	17.9	162 13.8 ..	06.9	Bellatrix	278 27.7	N 6 21.8
22	103 47.2	193 48.6	01.1	82 45.4	12.2	206 29.0	18.0	177 15.9	06.9	Betelgeuse	270 56.9	N 7 24.4
23	118 49.7	208 48.1	01.2	97 46.3	12.9	221 31.0	18.0	192 18.1	06.9			
4 00	133 52.1	223 47.5	S21 01.3	112 47.2	N 9 13.5	236 33.0	S22 18.1	207 20.3	S22 06.8	Canopus	263 54.0	S52 42.7
01	148 54.6	238 46.9	01.5	127 48.0	14.2	251 35.0	18.1	222 22.5	06.8	Capella	280 28.5	N46 01.0
02	163 57.1	253 46.3	01.6	142 48.9	14.9	266 37.0	18.1	237 24.6	06.8	Deneb	49 29.3	N45 20.9
03	178 59.5	268 45.7 ..	01.8	157 49.8 ..	15.5	281 39.0 ..	18.2	252 26.8 ..	06.7	Denebola	182 29.5	N14 27.9
04	194 02.0	283 45.1	01.9	172 50.7	16.2	296 41.1	18.2	267 29.0	06.7	Diphda	348 52.2	S17 53.2
05	209 04.5	298 44.5	02.0	187 51.6	16.9	311 43.1	18.2	282 31.2	06.7			
06	224 06.9	313 43.9	S21 02.2	202 52.5	N 9 17.5	326 45.1	S22 18.3	297 33.3	S22 06.7	Dubhe	193 46.4	N61 38.7
07	239 09.4	328 43.3	02.3	217 53.3	18.2	341 47.1	18.3	312 35.5	06.6	Elnath	278 07.5	N28 37.3
08	254 11.9	343 42.8	02.4	232 54.2	18.8	356 49.1	18.3	327 37.7	06.6	Eltanin	90 44.7	N51 29.1
M 09	269 14.3	358 42.2 ..	02.6	247 55.1 ..	19.5	11 51.1 ..	18.4	342 39.9 ..	06.6	Enif	33 43.7	N 9 57.7
O 10	284 16.8	13 41.6	02.7	262 56.0	20.2	26 53.1	18.4	357 42.0	06.6	Fomalhaut	15 20.1	S29 31.5
N 11	299 19.2	28 41.0	02.8	277 56.9	20.8	41 55.1	18.5	12 44.2	06.5			
D 12	314 21.7	43 40.4	S21 02.9	292 57.8	N 9 21.5	56 57.2	S22 18.5	27 46.4	S22 06.5	Gacrux	171 56.2	S57 12.9
A 13	329 24.2	58 39.8	03.1	307 58.7	22.2	71 59.2	18.5	42 48.6	06.5	Gienah	175 48.1	S17 38.8
Y 14	344 26.6	73 39.2	03.2	322 59.5	22.8	87 01.2	18.6	57 50.7	06.4	Hadar	148 42.3	S60 27.5
15	359 29.1	88 38.6 ..	03.3	338 00.4 ..	23.5	102 03.2 ..	18.6	72 52.9 ..	06.4	Hamal	327 56.5	N23 33.0
16	14 31.6	103 38.0	03.5	353 01.3	24.1	117 05.2	18.6	87 55.1	06.4	Kaus Aust.	83 39.0	S34 22.3
17	29 34.0	118 37.4	03.6	8 02.2	24.8	132 07.2	18.7	102 57.3	06.4			
18	44 36.5	133 36.8	S21 03.7	23 03.1	N 9 25.5	147 09.3	S22 18.7	117 59.4	S22 06.3	Kochab	137 20.1	N74 04.4
19	59 39.0	148 36.2	03.8	38 04.0	26.1	162 11.3	18.7	133 01.6	06.3	Markab	13 34.8	N15 18.4
20	74 41.4	163 35.6	04.0	53 04.8	26.8	177 13.3	18.8	148 03.8	06.3	Menkar	314 11.0	N 4 09.6
21	89 43.9	178 35.1 ..	04.1	68 05.7 ..	27.4	192 15.3 ..	18.8	163 06.0 ..	06.2	Menkent	148 02.9	S36 27.6
22	104 46.3	193 34.5	04.2	83 06.6	28.1	207 17.3	18.9	178 08.2	06.2	Miaplacidus	221 37.9	S69 47.7
23	119 48.8	208 33.9	04.3	98 07.5	28.8	222 19.3	18.9	193 10.3	06.2			
5 00	134 51.3	223 33.3	S21 04.4	113 08.4	N 9 29.4	237 21.3	S22 18.9	208 12.5	S22 06.2	Mirfak	308 34.7	N49 55.7
01	149 53.7	238 32.7	04.5	128 09.3	30.1	252 23.4	19.0	223 14.7	06.1	Nunki	75 53.9	S26 16.3
02	164 56.2	253 32.1	04.7	143 10.1	30.7	267 25.4	19.0	238 16.9	06.1	Peacock	53 13.8	S56 40.4
03	179 58.7	268 31.5 ..	04.8	158 11.0 ..	31.4	282 27.4 ..	19.0	253 19.0 ..	06.1	Pollux	243 22.7	N27 58.7
04	195 01.1	283 30.9	04.9	173 11.9	32.1	297 29.4	19.1	268 21.2	06.0	Procyon	244 55.4	N 5 10.4
05	210 03.6	298 30.3	05.0	188 12.8	32.7	312 31.4	19.1	283 23.4	06.0			
06	225 06.1	313 29.7	S21 05.1	203 13.7	N 9 33.4	327 33.5	S22 19.1	298 25.6	S22 06.0	Rasalhague	96 03.1	N12 32.8
07	240 08.5	328 29.1	05.2	218 14.5	34.0	342 35.5	19.2	313 27.7	06.0	Regulus	207 39.1	N11 52.3
T 08	255 11.0	343 28.5	05.3	233 15.4	34.7	357 37.5	19.2	328 29.9	05.9	Rigel	281 08.2	S 8 11.1
U 09	270 13.5	358 27.9 ..	05.5	248 16.3 ..	35.4	12 39.5 ..	19.2	343 32.1 ..	05.9	Rigil Kent.	139 46.4	S60 54.4
E 10	285 15.9	13 27.3	05.6	263 17.2	36.0	27 41.5	19.3	358 34.3	05.9	Sabik	102 08.3	S15 44.8
S 11	300 18.4	28 26.7	05.7	278 18.1	36.7	42 43.5	19.3	13 36.4	05.8			
D 12	315 20.8	43 26.1	S21 05.8	293 19.0	N 9 37.3	57 45.6	S22 19.4	28 38.6	S22 05.8	Schedar	349 36.4	N56 38.6
A 13	330 23.3	58 25.5	05.9	308 19.8	38.0	72 47.6	19.4	43 40.8	05.8	Shaula	96 17.0	S37 06.8
Y 14	345 25.8	73 24.9	06.0	323 20.7	38.6	87 49.6	19.4	58 43.0	05.8	Sirius	258 30.0	S16 44.8
15	0 28.2	88 24.3 ..	06.1	338 21.6 ..	39.3	102 51.6 ..	19.5	73 45.2 ..	05.7	Spica	158 27.1	S11 15.6
16	15 30.7	103 23.7	06.2	353 22.5	40.0	117 53.6	19.5	88 47.3	05.7	Suhail	222 49.2	S43 30.6
17	30 33.2	118 23.1	06.3	8 23.4	40.6	132 55.7	19.5	103 49.5	05.7			
18	45 35.6	133 22.5	S21 06.4	23 24.2	N 9 41.3	147 57.7	S22 19.6	118 51.7	S22 05.6	Vega	80 36.7	N38 48.0
19	60 38.1	148 21.9	06.5	38 25.1	41.9	162 59.7	19.6	133 53.9	05.6	Zuben'ubi	137 01.2	S16 07.1
20	75 40.6	163 21.3	06.6	53 26.0	42.6	178 01.7	19.6	148 56.0	05.6		SHA	Mer. Pass.
21	90 43.0	178 20.7 ..	06.7	68 26.9 ..	43.2	193 03.7 ..	19.7	163 58.2 ..	05.6	Venus	89 55.3	9 05
22	105 45.5	193 20.1	06.8	83 27.8	43.9	208 05.8	19.7	179 00.4	05.5	Mars	338 55.0	16 28
23	120 48.0	208 19.5	06.9	98 28.6	44.6	223 07.8	19.7	194 02.6	05.5	Jupiter	102 40.9	8 13
Mer. Pass. 15 02.1		v −0.6	d 0.1	v 0.9	d 0.7	v 2.0	d 0.0	v 2.2	d 0.0	Saturn	73 28.2	10 09

© British Crown Copyright 2018. All rights reserved.

UT	SUN GHA	SUN Dec	MOON GHA	v	MOON Dec	d	HP
d h	° ′	° ′	° ′	′	° ′	′	′
3 00	176 34.1	S16 40.1	197 31.5	11.6	S21 05.1	2.4	54.2
01	191 34.1	39.3	212 02.1	11.7	21 02.7	2.5	54.2
02	206 34.0	38.6	226 32.8	11.6	21 00.2	2.6	54.2
03	221 33.9	.. 37.9	241 03.4	11.8	20 57.6	2.7	54.2
04	236 33.8	37.2	255 34.2	11.7	20 54.9	2.8	54.1
05	251 33.8	36.4	270 04.9	11.8	20 52.1	2.9	54.1
06	266 33.7	S16 35.7	284 35.7	11.8	S20 49.2	3.0	54.1
07	281 33.6	35.0	299 06.5	11.8	20 46.2	3.1	54.1
08	296 33.6	34.2	313 37.3	11.8	20 43.1	3.1	54.1
S 09	311 33.5	.. 33.5	328 08.1	11.9	20 40.0	3.3	54.1
U 10	326 33.4	32.8	342 39.0	11.9	20 36.7	3.4	54.1
N 11	341 33.4	32.0	357 09.9	12.0	20 33.3	3.5	54.1
D 12	356 33.3	S16 31.3	11 40.9	11.9	S20 29.8	3.5	54.1
A 13	11 33.2	30.5	26 11.8	12.0	20 26.3	3.7	54.1
Y 14	26 33.1	29.8	40 42.8	12.1	20 22.6	3.7	54.1
15	41 33.1	.. 29.1	55 13.9	12.0	20 18.9	3.9	54.1
16	56 33.0	28.3	69 44.9	12.1	20 15.0	3.9	54.1
17	71 32.9	27.6	84 16.0	12.2	20 11.1	4.0	54.1
18	86 32.9	S16 26.9	98 47.2	12.1	S20 07.1	4.2	54.0
19	101 32.8	26.1	113 18.3	12.2	20 02.9	4.2	54.0
20	116 32.7	25.4	127 49.5	12.2	19 58.7	4.3	54.0
21	131 32.7	.. 24.6	142 20.7	12.3	19 54.4	4.4	54.0
22	146 32.6	23.9	156 52.0	12.3	19 50.0	4.4	54.0
23	161 32.6	23.2	171 23.3	12.3	19 45.6	4.6	54.0
4 00	176 32.5	S16 22.4	185 54.6	12.4	S19 41.0	4.7	54.0
01	191 32.4	21.7	200 26.0	12.4	19 36.3	4.7	54.0
02	206 32.4	20.9	214 57.4	12.4	19 31.6	4.8	54.0
03	221 32.3	.. 20.2	229 28.8	12.5	19 26.8	5.0	54.0
04	236 32.2	19.4	244 00.3	12.5	19 21.8	5.0	54.0
05	251 32.2	18.7	258 31.8	12.5	19 16.8	5.1	54.0
06	266 32.1	S16 18.0	273 03.3	12.6	S19 11.7	5.2	54.0
07	281 32.0	17.2	287 34.9	12.6	19 06.5	5.2	54.0
08	296 32.0	16.5	302 06.5	12.7	19 01.3	5.4	54.0
M 09	311 31.9	.. 15.7	316 38.2	12.7	18 55.9	5.4	54.0
O 10	326 31.9	15.0	331 09.9	12.7	18 50.5	5.5	54.0
N 11	341 31.8	14.2	345 41.6	12.7	18 45.0	5.6	54.0
D 12	356 31.7	S16 13.5	0 13.3	12.8	S18 39.4	5.7	54.0
A 13	11 31.7	12.7	14 45.1	12.9	18 33.7	5.8	54.0
Y 14	26 31.6	12.0	29 17.0	12.8	18 27.9	5.8	54.0
15	41 31.6	.. 11.2	43 48.8	13.0	18 22.1	6.0	54.0
16	56 31.5	10.5	58 20.8	12.9	18 16.1	6.0	54.0
17	71 31.4	09.7	72 52.7	13.0	18 10.1	6.1	54.0
18	86 31.4	S16 09.0	87 24.7	13.0	S18 04.0	6.1	54.0
19	101 31.3	08.2	101 56.7	13.1	17 57.9	6.3	53.9
20	116 31.3	07.5	116 28.8	13.1	17 51.6	6.3	53.9
21	131 31.2	.. 06.7	131 00.9	13.1	17 45.3	6.4	53.9
22	146 31.2	06.0	145 33.0	13.2	17 38.9	6.5	53.9
23	161 31.1	05.2	160 05.2	13.2	17 32.4	6.5	53.9
5 00	176 31.1	S16 04.5	174 37.4	13.3	S17 25.9	6.7	53.9
01	191 31.0	03.7	189 09.7	13.2	17 19.2	6.7	53.9
02	206 30.9	03.0	203 41.9	13.4	17 12.5	6.8	53.9
03	221 30.9	.. 02.2	218 14.3	13.3	17 05.7	6.8	53.9
04	236 30.8	01.5	232 46.6	13.4	16 58.9	6.9	53.9
05	251 30.8	16 00.7	247 19.0	13.5	16 52.0	7.0	53.9
06	266 30.7	S15 59.9	261 51.5	13.5	S16 45.0	7.1	53.9
07	281 30.7	59.2	276 24.0	13.5	16 37.9	7.2	53.9
T 08	296 30.6	58.4	290 56.5	13.5	16 30.7	7.2	53.9
U 09	311 30.6	.. 57.7	305 29.0	13.6	16 23.5	7.3	53.9
E 10	326 30.5	56.9	320 01.6	13.7	16 16.2	7.3	53.9
S 11	341 30.5	56.2	334 34.3	13.6	16 08.9	7.5	53.9
D 12	356 30.4	S15 55.4	349 06.9	13.7	S16 01.4	7.4	53.9
A 13	11 30.4	54.6	3 39.6	13.8	15 54.0	7.6	53.9
Y 14	26 30.3	53.9	18 12.4	13.8	15 46.4	7.6	53.9
15	41 30.3	.. 53.1	32 45.2	13.8	15 38.8	7.7	53.9
16	56 30.2	52.4	47 18.0	13.8	15 31.1	7.8	53.9
17	71 30.2	51.6	61 50.8	13.9	15 23.3	7.8	53.9
18	86 30.1	S15 50.8	76 23.7	14.0	S15 15.5	7.9	53.9
19	101 30.1	50.1	90 56.7	13.9	15 07.6	8.0	53.9
20	116 30.0	49.3	105 29.6	14.0	14 59.6	8.0	53.9
21	131 30.0	.. 48.6	120 02.6	14.1	14 51.6	8.1	53.9
22	146 29.9	47.8	134 35.7	14.0	14 43.5	8.1	53.9
23	161 29.9	47.0	149 08.7	14.1	S14 35.4	8.2	53.9
	SD 16.3	d 0.7	SD 14.7		14.7		14.7

Lat.	Twilight Naut.	Twilight Civil	Sunrise	Moonrise 3	4	5	6
°	h m	h m	h m	h m	h m	h m	h m
N 72	07 00	08 26	10 06	■■	■■	10 57	10 26
N 70	06 53	08 10	09 31	■■	10 36	10 15	10 02
68	06 47	07 56	09 06	09 46	09 48	09 46	09 44
66	06 42	07 45	08 47	09 01	09 17	09 25	09 29
64	06 38	07 36	08 31	08 31	08 53	09 08	09 17
62	06 34	07 28	08 18	08 08	08 35	08 53	09 07
60	06 31	07 21	08 07	07 50	08 19	08 41	08 58
N 58	06 27	07 15	07 58	07 35	08 06	08 31	08 50
56	06 24	07 09	07 50	07 22	07 55	08 22	08 43
54	06 22	07 04	07 42	07 10	07 45	08 13	08 37
52	06 19	06 59	07 36	07 00	07 36	08 06	08 31
50	06 16	06 55	07 30	06 51	07 29	08 00	08 26
45	06 11	06 46	07 17	06 33	07 12	07 45	08 15
N 40	06 05	06 38	07 06	06 17	06 58	07 34	08 06
35	06 00	06 30	06 57	06 04	06 46	07 24	07 58
30	05 55	06 24	06 49	05 53	06 36	07 15	07 51
20	05 45	06 12	06 35	05 33	06 18	07 00	07 39
N 10	05 35	06 00	06 22	05 16	06 02	06 46	07 29
0	05 24	05 49	06 10	05 00	05 48	06 34	07 19
S 10	05 11	05 37	05 59	04 44	05 33	06 21	07 09
20	04 55	05 22	05 46	04 27	05 18	06 08	06 58
30	04 35	05 05	05 31	04 07	05 00	05 53	06 46
35	04 22	04 55	05 22	03 56	04 49	05 44	06 39
40	04 06	04 43	05 12	03 43	04 37	05 34	06 31
45	03 47	04 28	05 01	03 27	04 23	05 22	06 21
S 50	03 21	04 09	04 46	03 08	04 06	05 07	06 10
52	03 07	04 00	04 40	02 59	03 58	05 00	06 05
54	02 52	03 50	04 32	02 49	03 49	04 52	05 59
56	02 33	03 38	04 24	02 37	03 38	04 44	05 52
58	02 08	03 24	04 15	02 24	03 26	04 34	05 45
S 60	01 33	03 08	04 04	02 08	03 13	04 23	05 36

Lat.	Sunset	Twilight Civil	Twilight Naut.	Moonset 3	4	5	6
°	h m	h m	h m	h m	h m	h m	h m
N 72	14 23	16 03	17 30	■■	■■	14 47	16 50
N 70	14 58	16 20	17 36	■■	13 32	15 28	17 12
68	15 23	16 33	17 42	12 42	14 19	15 56	17 29
66	15 42	16 44	17 47	13 28	14 50	16 16	17 43
64	15 58	16 53	17 51	13 57	15 13	16 33	17 54
62	16 10	17 01	17 55	14 20	15 31	16 46	18 04
60	16 21	17 08	17 58	14 38	15 46	16 58	18 12
N 58	16 31	17 14	18 01	14 53	15 58	17 08	18 19
56	16 39	17 20	18 04	15 05	16 09	17 16	18 25
54	16 46	17 25	18 07	15 16	16 19	17 24	18 31
52	16 53	17 29	18 10	15 26	16 27	17 31	18 36
50	16 59	17 33	18 12	15 35	16 35	17 37	18 40
45	17 12	17 43	18 18	15 54	16 51	17 50	18 50
N 40	17 22	17 51	18 23	16 09	17 04	18 01	18 58
35	17 31	17 58	18 28	16 22	17 15	18 10	19 05
30	17 39	18 04	18 33	16 32	17 25	18 18	19 11
20	17 53	18 16	18 43	16 51	17 42	18 32	19 22
N 10	18 06	18 28	18 53	17 08	17 57	18 44	19 31
0	18 17	18 39	19 04	17 23	18 10	18 56	19 40
S 10	18 29	18 51	19 17	17 39	18 24	19 07	19 48
20	18 42	19 05	19 32	17 55	18 38	19 19	19 57
30	18 56	19 22	19 52	18 14	18 55	19 33	20 07
35	19 05	19 32	20 05	18 25	19 04	19 40	20 13
40	19 15	19 44	20 21	18 37	19 15	19 49	20 21
45	19 26	19 59	20 40	18 52	19 28	20 00	20 28
S 50	19 40	20 18	21 06	19 09	19 43	20 12	20 37
52	19 47	20 26	21 19	19 18	19 51	20 18	20 41
54	19 54	20 37	21 34	19 28	19 59	20 24	20 46
56	20 02	20 48	21 52	19 38	20 08	20 31	20 51
58	20 12	21 01	22 16	19 50	20 18	20 39	20 57
S 60	20 22	21 17	22 49	20 04	20 29	20 48	21 03

Day	SUN Eqn. of Time 00h	SUN Eqn. of Time 12h	SUN Mer. Pass.	MOON Mer. Pass. Upper	MOON Mer. Pass. Lower	Age	Phase
d	m s	m s	h m	h m	h m	d	%
3	13 43	13 47	12 14	11 12	23 36	28	2
4	13 50	13 53	12 14	11 59	24 22	29	0
5	13 56	13 58	12 14	12 45	00 22	01	0

© British Crown Copyright 2018. All rights reserved.

UT	ARIES GHA	VENUS −4.3 GHA	Dec	MARS +1.0 GHA	Dec	JUPITER −1.9 GHA	Dec	SATURN +0.6 GHA	Dec	STARS Name	SHA	Dec
6 00	135 50.4	223 18.9	S21 07.0	113 29.5	N 9 45.2	238 09.8	S22 19.8	209 04.8	S22 05.5	Acamar	315 15.4	S40 14.1
01	150 52.9	238 18.3	07.1	128 30.4	45.9	253 11.8	19.8	224 06.9	05.4	Achernar	335 24.1	S57 08.8
02	165 55.3	253 17.6	07.2	143 31.3	46.5	268 13.8	19.8	239 09.1	05.4	Acrux	173 04.5	S63 12.0
03	180 57.8	268 17.0 ..	07.3	158 32.2 ..	47.2	283 15.9 ..	19.9	254 11.3 ..	05.4	Adhara	255 09.2	S29 00.2
04	196 00.3	283 16.4	07.4	173 33.1	47.8	298 17.9	19.9	269 13.5	05.4	Aldebaran	290 44.8	N16 32.7
05	211 02.7	298 15.8	07.5	188 33.9	48.5	313 19.9	19.9	284 15.6	05.3			
W 06	226 05.2	313 15.2	S21 07.5	203 34.8	N 9 49.2	328 21.9	S22 20.0	299 17.8	S22 05.3	Alioth	166 17.0	N55 51.2
E 07	241 07.7	328 14.6	07.6	218 35.7	49.8	343 24.0	20.0	314 20.0	05.3	Alkaid	152 55.7	N49 12.9
D 08	256 10.1	343 14.0	07.7	233 36.6	50.5	358 26.0	20.0	329 22.2	05.2	Alnair	27 39.4	S46 52.3
N 09	271 12.6	358 13.4 ..	07.8	248 37.4 ..	51.1	13 28.0 ..	20.1	344 24.4 ..	05.2	Alnilam	275 42.3	S 1 11.6
E 10	286 15.1	13 12.8	07.9	263 38.3	51.8	28 30.0	20.1	359 26.5	05.2	Alphard	217 52.0	S 8 44.6
S 11	301 17.5	28 12.2	08.0	278 39.2	52.4	43 32.1	20.2	14 28.7	05.2			
D 12	316 20.0	43 11.6	S21 08.1	293 40.1	N 9 53.1	58 34.1	S22 20.2	29 30.9	S22 05.1	Alphecca	126 07.8	N26 39.0
A 13	331 22.4	58 11.0	08.2	308 41.0	53.7	73 36.1	20.2	44 33.1	05.1	Alpheratz	357 39.8	N29 11.7
Y 14	346 24.9	73 10.4	08.2	323 41.8	54.4	88 38.1	20.3	59 35.2	05.1	Altair	62 04.8	N 8 55.1
15	1 27.4	88 09.8 ..	08.3	338 42.7 ..	55.1	103 40.1 ..	20.3	74 37.4 ..	05.0	Ankaa	353 12.2	S42 12.5
16	16 29.8	103 09.1	08.4	353 43.6	55.7	118 42.2	20.3	89 39.6	05.0	Antares	112 21.7	S26 28.2
17	31 32.3	118 08.5	08.5	8 44.5	56.4	133 44.2	20.4	104 41.8	05.0			
18	46 34.8	133 07.9	S21 08.6	23 45.4	N 9 57.0	148 46.2	S22 20.4	119 44.0	S22 05.0	Arcturus	145 52.2	N19 04.9
19	61 37.2	148 07.3	08.6	38 46.2	57.7	163 48.2	20.4	134 46.1	04.9	Atria	107 20.3	S69 03.3
20	76 39.7	163 06.7	08.7	53 47.1	58.3	178 50.3	20.5	149 48.3	04.9	Avior	234 15.8	S59 34.4
21	91 42.2	178 06.1 ..	08.8	68 48.0 ..	59.0	193 52.3 ..	20.5	164 50.5 ..	04.9	Bellatrix	278 27.7	N 6 21.8
22	106 44.6	193 05.5	08.9	83 48.9	9 59.6	208 54.3	20.5	179 52.7	04.8	Betelgeuse	270 56.9	N 7 24.4
23	121 47.1	208 04.9	08.9	98 49.8	10 00.3	223 56.3	20.6	194 54.9	04.8			
7 00	136 49.6	223 04.3	S21 09.0	113 50.6	N10 00.9	238 58.4	S22 20.6	209 57.0	S22 04.8	Canopus	263 54.0	S52 42.7
01	151 52.0	238 03.7	09.1	128 51.5	01.6	254 00.4	20.6	224 59.2	04.8	Capella	280 28.5	N46 01.0
02	166 54.5	253 03.0	09.2	143 52.4	02.2	269 02.4	20.7	240 01.4	04.7	Deneb	49 29.3	N45 20.9
03	181 56.9	268 02.4 ..	09.2	158 53.3 ..	02.9	284 04.5 ..	20.7	255 03.6 ..	04.7	Denebola	182 29.5	N14 27.9
04	196 59.4	283 01.8	09.3	173 54.1	03.5	299 06.5	20.7	270 05.8	04.7	Diphda	348 52.2	S17 53.2
05	212 01.9	298 01.2	09.4	188 55.0	04.2	314 08.5	20.8	285 07.9	04.6			
T 06	227 04.3	313 00.6	S21 09.4	203 55.9	N10 04.9	329 10.5	S22 20.8	300 10.1	S22 04.6	Dubhe	193 46.4	N61 38.7
H 07	242 06.8	328 00.0	09.5	218 56.8	05.5	344 12.6	20.8	315 12.3	04.6	Elnath	278 07.5	N28 37.3
U 08	257 09.3	342 59.4	09.6	233 57.7	06.2	359 14.6	20.9	330 14.5	04.6	Eltanin	90 44.7	N51 29.1
R 09	272 11.7	357 58.7 ..	09.6	248 58.5 ..	06.8	14 16.6 ..	20.9	345 16.7 ..	04.5	Enif	33 43.7	N 9 57.7
S 10	287 14.2	12 58.1	09.7	263 59.4	07.5	29 18.6	20.9	0 18.8	04.5	Fomalhaut	15 20.1	S29 31.5
D 11	302 16.7	27 57.5	09.8	279 00.3	08.1	44 20.7	21.0	15 21.0	04.5			
A 12	317 19.1	42 56.9	S21 09.8	294 01.2	N10 08.8	59 22.7	S22 21.0	30 23.2	S22 04.4	Gacrux	171 56.2	S57 12.9
Y 13	332 21.6	57 56.3	09.9	309 02.0	09.4	74 24.7	21.0	45 25.4	04.4	Gienah	175 48.1	S17 38.8
14	347 24.0	72 55.7	09.9	324 02.9	10.1	89 26.8	21.1	60 27.6	04.4	Hadar	148 42.2	S60 27.5
15	2 26.5	87 55.1 ..	10.0	339 03.8 ..	10.7	104 28.8 ..	21.1	75 29.7 ..	04.4	Hamal	327 56.5	N23 33.0
16	17 29.0	102 54.4	10.1	354 04.7	11.4	119 30.8	21.1	90 31.9	04.3	Kaus Aust.	83 39.0	S34 22.3
17	32 31.4	117 53.8	10.1	9 05.5	12.0	134 32.8	21.2	105 34.1	04.3			
18	47 33.9	132 53.2	S21 10.2	24 06.4	N10 12.7	149 34.9	S22 21.2	120 36.3	S22 04.3	Kochab	137 20.1	N74 04.4
19	62 36.4	147 52.6	10.2	39 07.3	13.3	164 36.9	21.2	135 38.5	04.2	Markab	13 34.8	N15 18.4
20	77 38.8	162 52.0	10.3	54 08.2	14.0	179 38.9	21.3	150 40.7	04.2	Menkar	314 11.0	N 4 09.6
21	92 41.3	177 51.3 ..	10.3	69 09.0 ..	14.6	194 41.0 ..	21.3	165 42.8 ..	04.2	Menkent	148 02.9	S36 27.6
22	107 43.8	192 50.7	10.4	84 09.9	15.3	209 43.0	21.3	180 45.0	04.2	Miaplacidus	221 37.9	S69 47.8
23	122 46.2	207 50.1	10.4	99 10.8	15.9	224 45.0	21.4	195 47.2	04.1			
8 00	137 48.7	222 49.5	S21 10.5	114 11.7	N10 16.6	239 47.1	S22 21.4	210 49.4	S22 04.1	Mirfak	308 34.8	N49 55.7
01	152 51.2	237 48.9	10.5	129 12.5	17.2	254 49.1	21.4	225 51.6	04.1	Nunki	75 53.9	S26 16.3
02	167 53.6	252 48.3	10.6	144 13.4	17.9	269 51.1	21.5	240 53.7	04.0	Peacock	53 13.8	S56 40.3
03	182 56.1	267 47.6 ..	10.6	159 14.3 ..	18.5	284 53.2 ..	21.5	255 55.9 ..	04.0	Pollux	243 22.7	N27 58.7
04	197 58.5	282 47.0	10.7	174 15.2	19.2	299 55.2	21.5	270 58.1	04.0	Procyon	244 55.4	N 5 10.4
05	213 01.0	297 46.4	10.7	189 16.0	19.8	314 57.2	21.6	286 00.3	04.0			
F 06	228 03.5	312 45.8	S21 10.8	204 16.9	N10 20.5	329 59.2	S22 21.6	301 02.5	S22 03.9	Rasalhague	96 03.1	N12 32.8
R 07	243 05.9	327 45.2	10.8	219 17.8	21.1	345 01.3	21.6	316 04.7	03.9	Regulus	207 39.1	N11 52.3
I 08	258 08.4	342 44.5	10.9	234 18.7	21.8	0 03.3	21.7	331 06.8	03.9	Rigel	281 08.2	S 8 11.1
D 09	273 10.9	357 43.9 ..	10.9	249 19.5 ..	22.4	15 05.3 ..	21.7	346 09.0 ..	03.8	Rigil Kent.	139 46.4	S60 54.4
A 10	288 13.3	12 43.3	10.9	264 20.4	23.1	30 07.4	21.7	1 11.2	03.8	Sabik	102 08.3	S15 44.8
Y 11	303 15.8	27 42.7	11.0	279 21.3	23.7	45 09.4	21.8	16 13.4	03.8			
12	318 18.3	42 42.0	S21 11.0	294 22.2	N10 24.4	60 11.4	S22 21.8	31 15.6	S22 03.8	Schedar	349 36.4	N56 38.6
13	333 20.7	57 41.4	11.1	309 23.0	25.0	75 13.5	21.8	46 17.7	03.7	Shaula	96 16.9	S37 06.8
14	348 23.2	72 40.8	11.1	324 23.9	25.7	90 15.5	21.9	61 19.9	03.7	Sirius	258 30.1	S16 44.8
15	3 25.7	87 40.2 ..	11.2	339 24.8 ..	26.3	105 17.5 ..	21.9	76 22.1 ..	03.7	Spica	158 27.0	S11 15.6
16	18 28.1	102 39.6	11.2	354 25.7	26.9	120 19.6	21.9	91 24.3	03.6	Suhail	222 49.2	S43 30.7
17	33 30.6	117 38.9	11.2	9 26.5	27.6	135 21.6	22.0	106 26.5	03.6			
18	48 33.0	132 38.3	S21 11.2	24 27.4	N10 28.2	150 23.6	S22 22.0	121 28.7	S22 03.6	Vega	80 36.7	N38 48.0
19	63 35.5	147 37.7	11.3	39 28.3	28.9	165 25.7	22.0	136 30.8	03.6	Zuben'ubi	137 01.1	S16 07.1
20	78 38.0	162 37.1	11.3	54 29.2	29.5	180 27.7	22.1	151 33.0	03.5		SHA	Mer.Pass.
21	93 40.4	177 36.4 ..	11.3	69 30.0 ..	30.2	195 29.7 ..	22.1	166 35.2 ..	03.5		° ′	h m
22	108 42.9	192 35.8	11.4	84 30.9	30.8	210 31.8	22.1	181 37.4	03.5	Venus	86 14.7	9 08
23	123 45.4	207 35.2	11.4	99 31.8	31.5	225 33.8	22.2	196 39.6	03.4	Mars	337 01.1	16 24
Mer. Pass.	h m 14 50.3	v −0.6	d 0.1	v 0.9	d 0.7	v 2.0	d 0.0	v 2.2	d 0.0	Jupiter	102 08.8	8 03
										Saturn	73 07.5	9 59

© British Crown Copyright 2018. All rights reserved.

UT	SUN GHA	SUN Dec	MOON GHA	v	MOON Dec	d	HP
d h	° ′	° ′	° ′	′	° ′	′	′
6 00	176 29.8	S15 46.3	163 41.8	14.2	S14 27.2	8.3	54.0
01	191 29.8	45.5	178 15.0	14.2	14 18.9	8.3	54.0
02	206 29.7	44.7	192 48.2	14.2	14 10.6	8.4	54.0
03	221 29.7	.. 44.0	207 21.4	14.2	14 02.2	8.5	54.0
04	236 29.6	43.2	221 54.6	14.3	13 53.7	8.5	54.0
05	251 29.6	42.4	236 27.9	14.3	13 45.2	8.5	54.0
06	266 29.5	S15 41.7	251 01.2	14.4	S13 36.7	8.7	54.0
W 07	281 29.5	40.9	265 34.6	14.3	13 28.0	8.6	54.0
E 08	296 29.4	40.1	280 07.9	14.4	13 19.4	8.8	54.0
D 09	311 29.4	.. 39.4	294 41.3	14.5	13 10.6	8.8	54.0
N 10	326 29.4	38.6	309 14.8	14.5	13 01.8	8.8	54.0
E 11	341 29.3	37.8	323 48.3	14.5	12 53.0	8.9	54.0
S 12	356 29.3	S15 37.0	338 21.8	14.5	S12 44.1	9.0	54.0
D 13	11 29.2	36.3	352 55.3	14.6	12 35.1	9.0	54.0
A 14	26 29.2	35.5	7 28.9	14.6	12 26.1	9.0	54.0
Y 15	41 29.1	.. 34.7	22 02.5	14.6	12 17.1	9.1	54.0
16	56 29.1	34.0	36 36.1	14.7	12 08.0	9.2	54.0
17	71 29.1	33.2	51 09.8	14.7	11 58.8	9.2	54.0
18	86 29.0	S15 32.4	65 43.5	14.7	S11 49.6	9.2	54.0
19	101 29.0	31.6	80 17.2	14.7	11 40.4	9.4	54.0
20	116 28.9	30.9	94 50.9	14.8	11 31.0	9.3	54.0
21	131 28.9	.. 30.1	109 24.7	14.8	11 21.7	9.4	54.0
22	146 28.9	29.3	123 58.5	14.8	11 12.3	9.5	54.0
23	161 28.8	28.5	138 32.3	14.9	11 02.8	9.5	54.0
7 00	176 28.8	S15 27.8	153 06.2	14.9	S10 53.3	9.5	54.0
01	191 28.7	27.0	167 40.1	14.9	10 43.8	9.6	54.1
02	206 28.7	26.2	182 14.0	14.9	10 34.2	9.6	54.1
03	221 28.7	.. 25.4	196 47.9	15.0	10 24.6	9.7	54.1
04	236 28.6	24.7	211 21.9	14.9	10 14.9	9.7	54.1
05	251 28.6	23.9	225 55.8	15.1	10 05.2	9.8	54.1
06	266 28.6	S15 23.1	240 29.9	15.0	S 9 55.4	9.8	54.1
T 07	281 28.5	22.3	255 03.9	15.0	9 45.6	9.8	54.1
H 08	296 28.5	21.5	269 37.9	15.1	9 35.8	9.9	54.1
U 09	311 28.4	.. 20.8	284 12.0	15.1	9 25.9	9.9	54.1
R 10	326 28.4	20.0	298 46.1	15.1	9 16.0	10.0	54.1
S 11	341 28.4	19.2	313 20.2	15.1	9 06.0	10.0	54.1
D 12	356 28.3	S15 18.4	327 54.3	15.2	S 8 56.0	10.0	54.1
A 13	11 28.3	17.6	342 28.5	15.2	8 46.0	10.1	54.1
Y 14	26 28.3	16.9	357 02.7	15.2	8 35.9	10.1	54.1
15	41 28.2	.. 16.1	11 36.9	15.2	8 25.8	10.2	54.2
16	56 28.2	15.3	26 11.1	15.2	8 15.6	10.2	54.2
17	71 28.2	14.5	40 45.3	15.2	8 05.4	10.2	54.2
18	86 28.1	S15 13.7	55 19.5	15.3	S 7 55.2	10.3	54.2
19	101 28.1	12.9	69 53.8	15.3	7 44.9	10.3	54.2
20	116 28.1	12.2	84 28.1	15.3	7 34.6	10.3	54.2
21	131 28.0	.. 11.4	99 02.4	15.3	7 24.3	10.3	54.2
22	146 28.0	10.6	113 36.7	15.3	7 14.0	10.4	54.2
23	161 28.0	09.8	128 11.0	15.3	7 03.6	10.5	54.2
8 00	176 27.9	S15 09.0	142 45.3	15.4	S 6 53.1	10.4	54.2
01	191 27.9	08.2	157 19.7	15.3	6 42.7	10.5	54.3
02	206 27.9	07.4	171 54.0	15.4	6 32.2	10.5	54.3
03	221 27.9	.. 06.7	186 28.4	15.4	6 21.7	10.5	54.3
04	236 27.8	05.9	201 02.8	15.4	6 11.2	10.6	54.3
05	251 27.8	05.1	215 37.2	15.4	6 00.6	10.6	54.3
06	266 27.8	S15 04.3	230 11.6	15.4	S 5 50.0	10.6	54.3
07	281 27.7	03.5	244 46.0	15.4	5 39.4	10.7	54.3
08	296 27.7	02.7	259 20.4	15.4	5 28.7	10.6	54.3
F 09	311 27.7	.. 01.9	273 54.8	15.4	5 18.1	10.7	54.3
R 10	326 27.7	01.1	288 29.2	15.5	5 07.4	10.8	54.4
I 11	341 27.6	15 00.3	303 03.6	15.5	4 56.6	10.7	54.4
D 12	356 27.6	S14 59.5	317 38.1	15.4	S 4 45.9	10.8	54.4
A 13	11 27.6	58.8	332 12.5	15.5	4 35.1	10.8	54.4
Y 14	26 27.6	58.0	346 47.0	15.4	4 24.3	10.8	54.4
15	41 27.5	.. 57.2	1 21.4	15.5	4 13.5	10.8	54.4
16	56 27.5	56.4	15 55.9	15.4	4 02.7	10.9	54.4
17	71 27.5	55.6	30 30.3	15.5	3 51.8	10.9	54.4
18	86 27.5	S14 54.8	45 04.8	15.4	S 3 40.9	10.8	54.5
19	101 27.4	54.0	59 39.2	15.5	3 30.1	11.0	54.5
20	116 27.4	53.2	74 13.7	15.4	3 19.1	10.9	54.5
21	131 27.4	.. 52.4	88 48.1	15.4	3 08.2	10.9	54.5
22	146 27.4	51.6	103 22.5	15.5	2 57.3	11.0	54.5
23	161 27.3	50.8	117 57.0	15.4	2 46.3	11.0	54.5
	SD 16.2	d 0.8	SD 14.7		14.7		14.8

Lat.	Twilight Naut.	Twilight Civil	Sunrise	Moonrise 6	7	8	9
°	h m	h m	h m	h m	h m	h m	h m
N 72	06 48	08 13	09 45	10 26	10 07	09 51	09 38
N 70	06 43	07 58	09 15	10 02	09 53	09 44	09 36
68	06 38	07 46	08 53	09 44	09 41	09 38	09 35
66	06 34	07 36	08 36	09 29	09 32	09 33	09 35
64	06 31	07 28	08 22	09 17	09 24	09 29	09 34
62	06 27	07 21	08 10	09 07	09 17	09 25	09 33
60	06 24	07 14	08 00	08 58	09 11	09 22	09 33
N 58	06 22	07 09	07 51	08 50	09 06	09 19	09 32
56	06 19	07 03	07 44	08 43	09 01	09 17	09 32
54	06 17	06 59	07 37	08 37	08 57	09 14	09 31
52	06 15	06 55	07 31	08 31	08 53	09 12	09 31
50	06 12	06 51	07 25	08 26	08 49	09 10	09 31
45	06 07	06 42	07 13	08 15	08 42	09 06	09 30
N 40	06 02	06 35	07 03	08 06	08 35	09 03	09 29
35	05 58	06 28	06 54	07 58	08 30	09 00	09 29
30	05 53	06 22	06 47	07 51	08 25	08 57	09 28
20	05 44	06 11	06 33	07 39	08 16	08 52	09 28
N 10	05 35	06 00	06 22	07 29	08 09	08 48	09 27
0	05 24	05 49	06 11	07 19	08 02	08 44	09 26
S 10	05 12	05 38	05 59	07 09	07 55	08 40	09 26
20	04 57	05 24	05 47	06 58	07 47	08 36	09 25
30	04 38	05 08	05 33	06 46	07 39	08 31	09 24
35	04 26	04 58	05 25	06 39	07 34	08 29	09 24
40	04 11	04 47	05 16	06 31	07 28	08 26	09 23
45	03 52	04 33	05 05	06 21	07 22	08 22	09 23
S 50	03 28	04 15	04 52	06 10	07 14	08 18	09 22
52	03 15	04 06	04 45	06 05	07 10	08 16	09 22
54	03 01	03 57	04 39	05 59	07 06	08 14	09 21
56	02 44	03 46	04 31	05 52	07 01	08 11	09 21
58	02 22	03 33	04 22	05 45	06 56	08 08	09 21
S 60	01 52	03 18	04 12	05 36	06 51	08 05	09 21

Lat.	Sunset	Twilight Civil	Twilight Naut.	Moonset 6	7	8	9
°	h m	h m	h m	h m	h m	h m	h m
N 72	14 45	16 17	17 42	16 50	18 39	20 22	22 05
N 70	15 15	16 32	17 47	17 12	18 51	20 27	22 03
68	15 36	16 43	17 51	17 29	19 01	20 31	22 01
66	15 54	16 53	17 55	17 43	19 09	20 34	22 00
64	16 08	17 02	17 59	17 54	19 16	20 37	21 59
62	16 19	17 09	18 02	18 04	19 21	20 39	21 58
60	16 29	17 15	18 05	18 12	19 26	20 41	21 57
N 58	16 38	17 21	18 07	18 19	19 31	20 43	21 56
56	16 46	17 26	18 10	18 25	19 35	20 45	21 55
54	16 52	17 30	18 12	18 31	19 38	20 46	21 55
52	16 58	17 34	18 14	18 36	19 42	20 48	21 54
50	17 04	17 38	18 17	18 40	19 44	20 49	21 54
45	17 16	17 47	18 22	18 50	19 51	20 51	21 53
N 40	17 26	17 54	18 26	18 58	19 56	20 54	21 52
35	17 34	18 01	18 31	19 05	20 00	20 55	21 51
30	17 42	18 07	18 35	19 11	20 04	20 57	21 50
20	17 55	18 18	18 44	19 22	20 11	21 00	21 49
N 10	18 07	18 28	18 53	19 31	20 17	21 02	21 48
0	18 18	18 39	19 04	19 40	20 22	21 05	21 47
S 10	18 29	18 50	19 16	19 48	20 28	21 07	21 46
20	18 41	19 04	19 31	19 57	20 34	21 09	21 45
30	18 54	19 20	19 50	20 07	20 40	21 12	21 43
35	19 02	19 29	20 02	20 13	20 44	21 13	21 43
40	19 12	19 41	20 17	20 20	20 48	21 15	21 42
45	19 22	19 55	20 35	20 28	20 53	21 17	21 41
S 50	19 35	20 12	20 59	20 37	20 59	21 19	21 40
52	19 42	20 20	21 11	20 41	21 02	21 21	21 39
54	19 48	20 30	21 25	20 46	21 04	21 22	21 38
56	19 56	20 41	21 42	20 51	21 08	21 23	21 38
58	20 05	20 53	22 03	20 57	21 11	21 24	21 37
S 60	20 14	21 08	22 31	21 03	21 15	21 26	21 36

Day	SUN Eqn. of Time 00ʰ	12ʰ	SUN Mer. Pass.	MOON Mer. Pass. Upper	Lower	Age	Phase
d	m s	m s	h m	h m	h m	d	%
6	14 01	14 03	12 14	13 29	01 07	02	2
7	14 05	14 07	12 14	14 12	01 51	03	6
8	14 08	14 10	12 14	14 54	02 33	04	11

© British Crown Copyright 2018. All rights reserved.

UT	ARIES GHA	VENUS −4.2 GHA	VENUS Dec	MARS +1.0 GHA	MARS Dec	JUPITER −1.9 GHA	JUPITER Dec	SATURN +0.6 GHA	SATURN Dec	Star Name	SHA	Dec
9 00	138 47.8	222 34.6	S21 11.4	114 32.7	N10 32.1	240 35.9	S22 22.2	211 41.8	S22 03.4	Acamar	315 15.4	S40 14.1
01	153 50.3	237 33.9	11.4	129 33.5	32.8	255 37.9	22.2	226 43.9	03.4	Achernar	335 24.1	S57 08.8
02	168 52.8	252 33.3	11.5	144 34.4	33.4	270 39.9	22.2	241 46.1	03.4	Acrux	173 04.5	S63 12.0
03	183 55.2	267 32.7 ..	11.5	159 35.3 ..	34.1	285 42.0 ..	22.3	256 48.3 ..	03.3	Adhara	255 09.2	S29 00.2
04	198 57.7	282 32.1	11.5	174 36.1	34.7	300 44.0	22.3	271 50.5	03.3	Aldebaran	290 44.8	N16 32.7
05	214 00.1	297 31.4	11.5	189 37.0	35.4	315 46.0	22.3	286 52.7	03.3			
06	229 02.6	312 30.8	S21 11.6	204 37.9	N10 36.0	330 48.1	S22 22.4	301 54.9	S22 03.2	Alioth	166 17.0	N55 51.2
07	244 05.1	327 30.2	11.6	219 38.8	36.6	345 50.1	22.4	316 57.1	03.2	Alkaid	152 55.7	N49 12.9
S 08	259 07.5	342 29.5	11.6	234 39.6	37.3	0 52.1	22.4	331 59.2	03.2	Alnair	27 39.4	S46 52.2
A 09	274 10.0	357 28.9 ..	11.6	249 40.5 ..	37.9	15 54.2 ..	22.5	347 01.4 ..	03.2	Alnilam	275 42.3	S 1 11.7
T 10	289 12.5	12 28.3	11.6	264 41.4	38.6	30 56.2	22.5	2 03.6	03.1	Alphard	217 52.0	S 8 44.6
U 11	304 14.9	27 27.7	11.7	279 42.2	39.2	45 58.3	22.5	17 05.8	03.1			
R 12	319 17.4	42 27.0	S21 11.7	294 43.1	N10 39.9	61 00.3	S22 22.6	32 08.0	S22 03.1	Alphecca	126 07.8	N26 38.9
D 13	334 19.9	57 26.4	11.7	309 44.0	40.5	76 02.3	22.6	47 10.2	03.0	Alpheratz	357 39.8	N29 11.7
A 14	349 22.3	72 25.8	11.7	324 44.9	41.2	91 04.4	22.6	62 12.3	03.0	Altair	62 04.8	N 8 55.1
Y 15	4 24.8	87 25.2 ..	11.7	339 45.7 ..	41.8	106 06.4 ..	22.7	77 14.5 ..	03.0	Ankaa	353 12.2	S42 12.5
16	19 27.3	102 24.5	11.7	354 46.6	42.5	121 08.5	22.7	92 16.7	03.0	Antares	112 21.6	S26 28.2
17	34 29.7	117 23.9	11.7	9 47.5	43.1	136 10.5	22.7	107 18.9	02.9			
18	49 32.2	132 23.3	S21 11.8	24 48.3	N10 43.7	151 12.5	S22 22.8	122 21.1	S22 02.9	Arcturus	145 52.1	N19 04.9
19	64 34.6	147 22.6	11.8	39 49.2	44.4	166 14.6	22.8	137 23.3	02.9	Atria	107 20.2	S69 03.3
20	79 37.1	162 22.0	11.8	54 50.1	45.0	181 16.6	22.8	152 25.5	02.8	Avior	234 15.8	S59 34.4
21	94 39.6	177 21.4 ..	11.8	69 51.0 ..	45.7	196 18.7 ..	22.9	167 27.6 ..	02.8	Bellatrix	278 27.7	N 6 21.8
22	109 42.0	192 20.7	11.8	84 51.8	46.3	211 20.7	22.9	182 29.8	02.8	Betelgeuse	270 56.9	N 7 24.4
23	124 44.5	207 20.1	11.8	99 52.7	46.9	226 22.7	22.9	197 32.0	02.8			
10 00	139 47.0	222 19.5	S21 11.8	114 53.6	N10 47.6	241 24.8	S22 22.9	212 34.2	S22 02.7	Canopus	263 54.0	S52 42.7
01	154 49.4	237 18.9	11.8	129 54.4	48.2	256 26.8	23.0	227 36.4	02.7	Capella	280 28.5	N46 01.0
02	169 51.9	252 18.2	11.8	144 55.3	48.9	271 28.9	23.0	242 38.6	02.7	Deneb	49 29.3	N45 20.8
03	184 54.4	267 17.6 ..	11.8	159 56.2 ..	49.5	286 30.9 ..	23.0	257 40.8 ..	02.6	Denebola	182 29.5	N14 27.8
04	199 56.8	282 17.0	11.8	174 57.1	50.2	301 32.9	23.1	272 42.9	02.6	Diphda	348 52.2	S17 53.2
05	214 59.3	297 16.3	11.8	189 57.9	50.8	316 35.0	23.1	287 45.1	02.6			
06	230 01.7	312 15.7	S21 11.8	204 58.8	N10 51.4	331 37.0	S22 23.1	302 47.3	S22 02.6	Dubhe	193 46.4	N61 38.7
07	245 04.2	327 15.1	11.8	219 59.7	52.1	346 39.1	23.2	317 49.5	02.5	Elnath	278 07.5	N28 37.3
08	260 06.7	342 14.4	11.8	235 00.5	52.7	1 41.1	23.2	332 51.7	02.5	Eltanin	90 44.7	N51 29.0
S 09	275 09.1	357 13.8 ..	11.8	250 01.4 ..	53.3	16 43.1 ..	23.2	347 53.9 ..	02.5	Enif	33 43.7	N 9 57.7
U 10	290 11.6	12 13.2	11.8	265 02.3	54.0	31 45.2	23.3	2 56.1	02.4	Fomalhaut	15 20.1	S29 31.5
N 11	305 14.1	27 12.5	11.8	280 03.1	54.6	46 47.2	23.3	17 58.2	02.4			
D 12	320 16.5	42 11.9	S21 11.8	295 04.0	N10 55.3	61 49.3	S22 23.3	33 00.4	S22 02.4	Gacrux	171 56.2	S57 12.9
A 13	335 19.0	57 11.3	11.8	310 04.9	55.9	76 51.3	23.3	48 02.6	02.4	Gienah	175 48.1	S17 38.8
Y 14	350 21.5	72 10.6	11.8	325 05.8	56.6	91 53.4	23.4	63 04.8	02.3	Hadar	148 42.2	S60 27.5
15	5 23.9	87 10.0 ..	11.7	340 06.6 ..	57.2	106 55.4 ..	23.4	78 07.0 ..	02.3	Hamal	327 56.5	N23 33.0
16	20 26.4	102 09.4	11.7	355 07.5	57.8	121 57.5	23.4	93 09.2	02.3	Kaus Aust.	83 39.0	S34 22.3
17	35 28.9	117 08.7	11.7	10 08.4	58.5	136 59.5	23.5	108 11.4	02.2			
18	50 31.3	132 08.1	S21 11.7	25 09.2	N10 59.1	152 01.5	S22 23.5	123 13.6	S22 02.2	Kochab	137 20.0	N74 04.4
19	65 33.8	147 07.5	11.7	40 10.1	10 59.8	167 03.6	23.5	138 15.7	02.2	Markab	13 34.8	N15 18.4
20	80 36.2	162 06.8	11.7	55 11.0	11 00.4	182 05.6	23.6	153 17.9	02.2	Menkar	314 11.0	N 4 09.6
21	95 38.7	177 06.2 ..	11.7	70 11.8 ..	01.0	197 07.7 ..	23.6	168 20.1 ..	02.1	Menkent	148 02.9	S36 27.6
22	110 41.2	192 05.5	11.6	85 12.7	01.7	212 09.7	23.6	183 22.3	02.1	Miaplacidus	221 37.9	S69 47.8
23	125 43.6	207 04.9	11.6	100 13.6	02.3	227 11.8	23.7	198 24.5	02.1			
11 00	140 46.1	222 04.3	S21 11.6	115 14.4	N11 03.0	242 13.8	S22 23.7	213 26.7	S22 02.0	Mirfak	308 34.8	N49 55.7
01	155 48.6	237 03.6	11.6	130 15.3	03.6	257 15.9	23.7	228 28.9	02.0	Nunki	75 53.8	S26 16.3
02	170 51.0	252 03.0	11.6	145 16.2	04.2	272 17.9	23.7	243 31.1	02.0	Peacock	53 13.8	S56 40.3
03	185 53.5	267 02.4 ..	11.5	160 17.0 ..	04.9	287 19.9 ..	23.8	258 33.2 ..	02.0	Pollux	243 22.7	N27 58.7
04	200 56.0	282 01.7	11.5	175 17.9	05.5	302 22.0	23.8	273 35.4	01.9	Procyon	244 55.4	N 5 10.4
05	215 58.4	297 01.1	11.5	190 18.8	06.2	317 24.0	23.8	288 37.6	01.9			
06	231 00.9	312 00.4	S21 11.5	205 19.6	N11 06.8	332 26.1	S22 23.9	303 39.8	S22 01.9	Rasalhague	96 03.1	N12 32.8
07	246 03.3	326 59.8	11.4	220 20.5	07.4	347 28.1	23.9	318 42.0	01.8	Regulus	207 39.1	N11 52.3
08	261 05.8	341 59.2	11.4	235 21.4	08.1	2 30.2	23.9	333 44.2	01.8	Rigel	281 08.2	S 8 11.1
M 09	276 08.3	356 58.5 ..	11.4	250 22.2 ..	08.7	17 32.2 ..	24.0	348 46.4 ..	01.8	Rigil Kent.	139 46.4	S60 54.4
O 10	291 10.7	11 57.9	11.4	265 23.1	09.3	32 34.3	24.0	3 48.6	01.8	Sabik	102 08.3	S15 44.8
N 11	306 13.2	26 57.3	11.3	280 24.0	10.0	47 36.3	24.0	18 50.7	01.7			
D 12	321 15.7	41 56.6	S21 11.3	295 24.8	N11 10.6	62 38.4	S22 24.0	33 52.9	S22 01.7	Schedar	349 36.5	N56 38.6
A 13	336 18.1	56 56.0	11.3	310 25.7	11.3	77 40.4	24.1	48 55.1	01.7	Shaula	96 16.9	S37 06.8
Y 14	351 20.6	71 55.3	11.2	325 26.6	11.9	92 42.5	24.1	63 57.3	01.6	Sirius	258 30.1	S16 44.8
15	6 23.1	86 54.7 ..	11.2	340 27.4 ..	12.5	107 44.5 ..	24.1	78 59.5 ..	01.6	Spica	158 27.0	S11 15.6
16	21 25.5	101 54.1	11.2	355 28.3	13.2	122 46.6	24.2	94 01.7	01.6	Suhail	222 49.2	S43 30.7
17	36 28.0	116 53.4	11.1	10 29.2	13.8	137 48.6	24.2	109 03.9	01.6			
18	51 30.5	131 52.8	S21 11.1	25 30.0	N11 14.4	152 50.7	S22 24.2	124 06.1	S22 01.5	Vega	80 36.7	N38 48.0
19	66 32.9	146 52.1	11.1	40 30.9	15.1	167 52.7	24.3	139 08.3	01.5	Zuben'ubi	137 01.1	S16 07.1
20	81 35.4	161 51.5	11.0	55 31.8	15.7	182 54.8	24.3	154 10.4	01.5			
21	96 37.8	176 50.9 ..	11.0	70 32.6 ..	16.3	197 56.8 ..	24.3	169 12.6 ..	01.4		SHA	Mer.Pass.
22	111 40.3	191 50.2	10.9	85 33.5	17.0	212 58.9	24.3	184 14.8	01.4	Venus	82 32.5	9 11
23	126 42.8	206 49.6	10.9	100 34.4	17.6	228 00.9	24.4	199 17.0	01.4	Mars	335 06.6	16 19
Mer.Pass.	h m 14 38.5	v −0.6	d 0.0	v 0.9	d 0.6	v 2.0	d 0.0	v 2.2	d 0.0	Jupiter	101 37.8	7 53
										Saturn	72 47.2	9 48

© British Crown Copyright 2018. All rights reserved.

UT	SUN GHA	SUN Dec	MOON GHA	v	MOON Dec	d	HP
d h	° ′	° ′	° ′	′	° ′	′	′
9 00	176 27.3	S14 50.0	132 31.4	15.5	S 2 35.3	11.0	54.5
01	191 27.3	49.2	147 05.9	15.4	2 24.3	11.0	54.6
02	206 27.3	48.4	161 40.3	15.4	2 13.3	11.0	54.6
03	221 27.3	.. 47.6	176 14.7	15.4	2 02.3	11.1	54.6
04	236 27.2	46.8	190 49.1	15.4	1 51.2	11.0	54.6
05	251 27.2	46.0	205 23.5	15.4	1 40.2	11.1	54.6
06	266 27.2	S14 45.2	219 57.9	15.4	S 1 29.1	11.1	54.6
07	281 27.2	44.4	234 32.3	15.4	1 18.0	11.0	54.7
S 08	296 27.2	43.6	249 06.7	15.4	1 07.0	11.1	54.7
A 09	311 27.1	.. 42.8	263 41.1	15.3	0 55.9	11.2	54.7
T 10	326 27.1	42.0	278 15.4	15.3	0 44.7	11.1	54.7
U 11	341 27.1	41.2	292 49.7	15.4	0 33.6	11.1	54.7
R 12	356 27.1	S14 40.4	307 24.1	15.3	S 0 22.5	11.1	54.7
D 13	11 27.1	39.6	321 58.4	15.3	0 11.4	11.2	54.8
A 14	26 27.0	38.8	336 32.7	15.3	S 0 00.2	11.1	54.8
Y 15	41 27.0	.. 38.0	351 07.0	15.2	N 0 10.9	11.2	54.8
16	56 27.0	37.2	5 41.2	15.3	0 22.1	11.1	54.8
17	71 27.0	36.4	20 15.5	15.2	0 33.2	11.2	54.8
18	86 27.0	S14 35.6	34 49.7	15.2	N 0 44.4	11.2	54.9
19	101 27.0	34.8	49 23.9	15.2	0 55.6	11.1	54.9
20	116 26.9	34.0	63 58.1	15.2	1 06.7	11.2	54.9
21	131 26.9	.. 33.2	78 32.3	15.1	1 17.9	11.2	54.9
22	146 26.9	32.4	93 06.4	15.1	1 29.1	11.2	54.9
23	161 26.9	31.6	107 40.5	15.1	1 40.3	11.1	55.0
10 00	176 26.9	S14 30.7	122 14.6	15.1	N 1 51.4	11.2	55.0
01	191 26.9	29.9	136 48.7	15.1	2 02.6	11.2	55.0
02	206 26.9	29.1	151 22.8	15.0	2 13.8	11.2	55.0
03	221 26.8	.. 28.3	165 56.8	15.0	2 25.0	11.1	55.0
04	236 26.8	27.5	180 30.8	15.0	2 36.1	11.2	55.1
05	251 26.8	26.7	195 04.8	14.9	2 47.3	11.2	55.1
06	266 26.8	S14 25.9	209 38.7	14.9	N 2 58.5	11.1	55.1
07	281 26.8	25.1	224 12.6	14.9	3 09.6	11.2	55.1
08	296 26.8	24.3	238 46.5	14.8	3 20.8	11.1	55.1
S 09	311 26.8	.. 23.5	253 20.3	14.8	3 31.9	11.2	55.2
U 10	326 26.8	22.7	267 54.1	14.8	3 43.1	11.1	55.2
N 11	341 26.8	21.8	282 27.9	14.8	3 54.2	11.1	55.2
D 12	356 26.7	S14 21.0	297 01.7	14.7	N 4 05.3	11.2	55.2
A 13	11 26.7	20.2	311 35.4	14.7	4 16.5	11.1	55.3
Y 14	26 26.7	19.4	326 09.1	14.6	4 27.6	11.1	55.3
15	41 26.7	.. 18.6	340 42.7	14.6	4 38.7	11.1	55.3
16	56 26.7	17.8	355 16.3	14.6	4 49.8	11.0	55.3
17	71 26.7	17.0	9 49.9	14.5	5 00.8	11.1	55.4
18	86 26.7	S14 16.1	24 23.4	14.5	N 5 11.9	11.1	55.4
19	101 26.7	15.3	38 56.9	14.4	5 23.0	11.0	55.4
20	116 26.7	14.5	53 30.3	14.4	5 34.0	11.0	55.4
21	131 26.7	.. 13.7	68 03.7	14.4	5 45.0	11.0	55.4
22	146 26.7	12.9	82 37.1	14.3	5 56.0	11.0	55.5
23	161 26.7	12.1	97 10.4	14.2	6 07.0	11.0	55.5
11 00	176 26.7	S14 11.2	111 43.6	14.3	N 6 18.0	11.0	55.5
01	191 26.6	10.4	126 16.9	14.1	6 29.0	10.9	55.6
02	206 26.6	09.6	140 50.0	14.2	6 39.9	10.9	55.6
03	221 26.6	.. 08.8	155 23.2	14.0	6 50.8	10.9	55.6
04	236 26.6	08.0	169 56.2	14.1	7 01.7	10.9	55.6
05	251 26.6	07.2	184 29.3	13.9	7 12.6	10.9	55.7
06	266 26.6	S14 06.3	199 02.2	14.0	N 7 23.5	10.8	55.7
07	281 26.6	05.5	213 35.2	13.9	7 34.3	10.8	55.7
08	296 26.6	04.7	228 08.1	13.8	7 45.1	10.8	55.7
M 09	311 26.6	.. 03.9	242 40.9	13.7	7 55.9	10.8	55.8
O 10	326 26.6	03.1	257 13.6	13.8	8 06.7	10.7	55.8
N 11	341 26.6	02.2	271 46.4	13.6	8 17.4	10.8	55.8
D 12	356 26.6	S14 01.4	286 19.0	13.6	N 8 28.2	10.6	55.9
A 13	11 26.6	14 00.6	300 51.6	13.6	8 38.8	10.7	55.9
Y 14	26 26.6	13 59.8	315 24.2	13.4	8 49.5	10.6	55.9
15	41 26.6	.. 58.9	329 56.6	13.5	9 00.1	10.6	55.9
16	56 26.6	58.1	344 29.1	13.3	9 10.7	10.6	56.0
17	71 26.6	57.3	359 01.4	13.3	9 21.3	10.5	56.0
18	86 26.6	S13 56.5	13 33.7	13.3	N 9 31.8	10.5	56.0
19	101 26.6	55.6	28 06.0	13.2	9 42.3	10.5	56.1
20	116 26.6	54.8	42 38.2	13.1	9 52.8	10.5	56.1
21	131 26.6	.. 54.0	57 10.3	13.0	10 03.3	10.4	56.1
22	146 26.6	53.2	71 42.3	13.0	10 13.7	10.3	56.1
23	161 26.6	52.3	86 14.3	12.9	N10 24.0	10.4	56.2
	SD 16.2	d 0.8	SD 14.9	15.0			15.2

Lat.	Twilight Naut.	Civil	Sunrise	Moonrise 9	10	11	12
°	h m	h m	h m	h m	h m	h m	h m
N 72	06 36	07 59	09 25	09 38	09 24	09 09	08 51
N 70	06 32	07 46	09 00	09 36	09 29	09 21	09 11
68	06 29	07 36	08 40	09 35	09 33	09 30	09 27
66	06 26	07 27	08 25	09 35	09 36	09 38	09 40
64	06 23	07 19	08 12	09 34	09 39	09 44	09 51
62	06 20	07 13	08 01	09 33	09 41	09 50	10 01
60	06 18	07 07	07 52	09 33	09 43	09 55	10 09
N 58	06 16	07 02	07 44	09 32	09 45	09 59	10 16
56	06 14	06 58	07 37	09 32	09 47	10 03	10 22
54	06 12	06 53	07 31	09 31	09 48	10 07	10 28
52	06 10	06 50	07 25	09 31	09 50	10 10	10 33
50	06 08	06 46	07 20	09 31	09 51	10 13	10 37
45	06 04	06 38	07 09	09 30	09 54	10 19	10 47
N 40	05 59	06 31	06 59	09 29	09 56	10 25	10 56
35	05 55	06 25	06 51	09 29	09 58	10 29	11 03
30	05 51	06 20	06 44	09 28	10 00	10 34	11 09
20	05 43	06 09	06 32	09 28	10 03	10 41	11 21
N 10	05 34	05 59	06 21	09 27	10 06	10 47	11 30
0	05 25	05 49	06 11	09 26	10 09	10 53	11 40
S 10	05 13	05 39	06 00	09 26	10 12	10 59	11 49
20	04 59	05 26	05 49	09 25	10 15	11 06	11 59
30	04 41	05 11	05 36	09 24	10 18	11 13	12 10
35	04 29	05 01	05 28	09 24	10 20	11 18	12 17
40	04 15	04 51	05 20	09 24	10 22	11 23	12 25
45	03 58	04 37	05 09	09 23	10 25	11 28	12 34
S 50	03 35	04 21	04 57	09 22	10 28	11 35	12 44
52	03 23	04 13	04 51	09 22	10 29	11 38	12 49
54	03 10	04 04	04 45	09 22	10 31	11 42	12 55
56	02 54	03 54	04 38	09 21	10 33	11 46	13 01
58	02 34	03 42	04 30	09 21	10 35	11 50	13 08
S 60	02 09	03 28	04 20	09 21	10 37	11 55	13 16

Lat.	Sunset	Twilight Civil	Naut.	Moonset 9	10	11	12
°	h m	h m	h m	h m	h m	h m	h m
N 72	15 05	16 31	17 54	22 05	23 50	25 43	01 43
N 70	15 30	16 44	17 58	22 03	23 41	25 25	01 25
68	15 49	16 54	18 01	22 01	23 34	25 10	01 10
66	16 05	17 03	18 04	22 00	23 28	24 58	00 58
64	16 17	17 10	18 07	21 59	23 22	24 49	00 49
62	16 28	17 17	18 09	21 58	23 18	24 40	00 40
60	16 37	17 22	18 12	21 57	23 14	24 33	00 33
N 58	16 45	17 27	18 14	21 56	23 11	24 27	00 27
56	16 52	17 32	18 16	21 55	23 07	24 21	00 21
54	16 58	17 36	18 18	21 55	23 05	24 16	00 16
52	17 04	17 40	18 19	21 54	23 02	24 12	00 12
50	17 09	17 43	18 21	21 54	23 00	24 08	00 08
45	17 20	17 51	18 25	21 53	22 55	23 59	25 05
N 40	17 29	17 58	18 30	21 52	22 51	23 52	24 55
35	17 37	18 04	18 33	21 51	22 48	23 46	24 46
30	17 44	18 09	18 37	21 50	22 45	23 40	24 39
20	17 57	18 19	18 45	21 49	22 39	23 31	24 25
N 10	18 07	18 29	18 54	21 48	22 34	23 23	24 14
0	18 18	18 39	19 04	21 47	22 30	23 15	24 03
S 10	18 28	18 50	19 15	21 46	22 26	23 07	23 52
20	18 39	19 02	19 29	21 45	22 21	22 59	23 41
30	18 52	19 17	19 47	21 43	22 16	22 50	23 28
35	18 59	19 26	19 59	21 43	22 13	22 45	23 20
40	19 08	19 37	20 12	21 42	22 09	22 39	23 11
45	19 18	19 50	20 30	21 41	22 05	22 32	23 01
S 50	19 30	20 06	20 52	21 40	22 00	22 23	22 49
52	19 36	20 14	21 03	21 39	21 58	22 19	22 44
54	19 42	20 23	21 16	21 38	21 56	22 15	22 38
56	19 49	20 33	21 32	21 38	21 53	22 10	22 31
58	19 57	20 44	21 51	21 37	21 50	22 05	22 23
S 60	20 06	20 58	22 15	21 36	21 47	21 59	22 15

Day	SUN Eqn. of Time 00ʰ	12ʰ	Mer. Pass.	MOON Mer. Pass. Upper	Lower	Age	Phase
d	m s	m s	h m	h m	h m	d	%
9	14 11	14 12	12 14	15 37	03 15	05	18
10	14 12	14 13	12 14	16 19	03 58	06	26
11	14 13	14 14	12 14	17 04	04 41	07	36

© British Crown Copyright 2018. All rights reserved.

UT	ARIES GHA	VENUS −4.2 GHA	Dec	MARS +1.0 GHA	Dec	JUPITER −1.9 GHA	Dec	SATURN +0.6 GHA	Dec	STARS Name	SHA	Dec
12 00	141 45.2	221 48.9	S21 10.9	115 35.2	N11 18.3	243 03.0	S22 24.4	214 19.2	S22 01.4	Acamar	315 15.5	S40 14.1
01	156 47.7	236 48.3	10.8	130 36.1	18.9	258 05.0	24.4	229 21.4	01.3	Achernar	335 24.2	S57 08.8
02	171 50.2	251 47.7	10.8	145 37.0	19.5	273 07.1	24.5	244 23.6	01.3	Acrux	173 04.4	S63 12.0
03	186 52.6	266 47.0 ..	10.7	160 37.8 ..	20.2	288 09.1 ..	24.5	259 25.8 ..	01.3	Adhara	255 09.2	S29 00.2
04	201 55.1	281 46.4	10.7	175 38.7	20.8	303 11.2	24.5	274 28.0	01.2	Aldebaran	290 44.8	N16 32.7
05	216 57.6	296 45.7	10.6	190 39.6	21.4	318 13.2	24.6	289 30.2	01.2			
06	232 00.0	311 45.1	S21 10.6	205 40.4	N11 22.1	333 15.3	S22 24.6	304 32.3	S22 01.2	Alioth	166 16.9	N55 51.2
07	247 02.5	326 44.4	10.5	220 41.3	22.7	348 17.3	24.6	319 34.5	01.2	Alkaid	152 55.6	N49 12.9
T 08	262 05.0	341 43.8	10.5	235 42.2	23.3	3 19.4	24.6	334 36.7	01.1	Alnair	27 39.4	S46 52.2
U 09	277 07.4	356 43.2 ..	10.4	250 43.0 ..	24.0	18 21.4 ..	24.7	349 38.9 ..	01.1	Alnilam	275 42.3	S 1 11.7
E 10	292 09.9	11 42.5	10.4	265 43.9	24.6	33 23.5	24.7	4 41.1	01.1	Alphard	217 52.0	S 8 44.6
S 11	307 12.3	26 41.9	10.3	280 44.8	25.2	48 25.5	24.7	19 43.3	01.0			
D 12	322 14.8	41 41.2	S21 10.3	295 45.6	N11 25.9	63 27.6	S22 24.8	34 45.5	S22 01.0	Alphecca	126 07.7	N26 38.9
A 13	337 17.3	56 40.6	10.2	310 46.5	26.5	78 29.6	24.8	49 47.7	01.0	Alpheratz	357 39.8	N29 11.7
Y 14	352 19.7	71 39.9	10.2	325 47.3	27.1	93 31.7	24.8	64 49.9	01.0	Altair	62 04.8	N 8 55.1
15	7 22.2	86 39.3 ..	10.1	340 48.2 ..	27.8	108 33.8 ..	24.8	79 52.1 ..	00.9	Ankaa	353 12.2	S42 12.5
16	22 24.7	101 38.7	10.0	355 49.1	28.4	123 35.8	24.9	94 54.3	00.9	Antares	112 21.6	S26 28.2
17	37 27.1	116 38.0	10.0	10 49.9	29.0	138 37.9	24.9	109 56.4	00.9			
18	52 29.6	131 37.4	S21 09.9	25 50.8	N11 29.7	153 39.9	S22 24.9	124 58.6	S22 00.8	Arcturus	145 52.1	N19 04.9
19	67 32.1	146 36.7	09.9	40 51.7	30.3	168 42.0	25.0	140 00.8	00.8	Atria	107 20.2	S69 03.3
20	82 34.5	161 36.1	09.8	55 52.5	30.9	183 44.0	25.0	155 03.0	00.8	Avior	234 15.8	S59 34.4
21	97 37.0	176 35.4 ..	09.7	70 53.4 ..	31.6	198 46.1 ..	25.0	170 05.2 ..	00.8	Bellatrix	278 27.7	N 6 21.8
22	112 39.4	191 34.8	09.7	85 54.3	32.2	213 48.1	25.0	185 07.4	00.7	Betelgeuse	270 56.9	N 7 24.4
23	127 41.9	206 34.1	09.6	100 55.1	32.8	228 50.2	25.1	200 09.6	00.7			
13 00	142 44.4	221 33.5	S21 09.5	115 56.0	N11 33.4	243 52.2	S22 25.1	215 11.8	S22 00.7	Canopus	263 54.1	S52 42.7
01	157 46.8	236 32.9	09.5	130 56.8	34.1	258 54.3	25.1	230 14.0	00.6	Capella	280 28.5	N46 01.0
02	172 49.3	251 32.2	09.4	145 57.7	34.7	273 56.4	25.2	245 16.2	00.6	Deneb	49 29.3	N45 20.8
03	187 51.8	266 31.6 ..	09.3	160 58.6 ..	35.3	288 58.4 ..	25.2	260 18.4 ..	00.6	Denebola	182 29.5	N14 27.8
04	202 54.2	281 30.9	09.3	175 59.4	36.0	304 00.5	25.2	275 20.6	00.6	Diphda	348 52.2	S17 53.2
05	217 56.7	296 30.3	09.2	191 00.3	36.6	319 02.5	25.2	290 22.8	00.5			
06	232 59.2	311 29.6	S21 09.1	206 01.2	N11 37.2	334 04.6	S22 25.3	305 24.9	S22 00.5	Dubhe	193 46.4	N61 38.8
W 07	248 01.6	326 29.0	09.0	221 02.0	37.9	349 06.6	25.3	320 27.1	00.5	Elnath	278 07.6	N28 37.3
E 08	263 04.1	341 28.3	09.0	236 02.9	38.5	4 08.7	25.3	335 29.3	00.4	Eltanin	90 44.7	N51 29.0
D 09	278 06.6	356 27.7 ..	08.9	251 03.7 ..	39.1	19 10.8 ..	25.4	350 31.5 ..	00.4	Enif	33 43.7	N 9 57.7
N 10	293 09.0	11 27.0	08.8	266 04.6	39.7	34 12.8	25.4	5 33.7	00.4	Fomalhaut	15 20.1	S29 31.5
E 11	308 11.5	26 26.4	08.7	281 05.5	40.4	49 14.9	25.4	20 35.9	00.4			
S 12	323 13.9	41 25.8	S21 08.7	296 06.3	N11 41.0	64 16.9	S22 25.4	35 38.1	S22 00.3	Gacrux	171 56.2	S57 13.0
D 13	338 16.4	56 25.1	08.6	311 07.2	41.6	79 19.0	25.5	50 40.3	00.3	Gienah	175 48.1	S17 38.8
A 14	353 18.9	71 24.5	08.5	326 08.1	42.3	94 21.1	25.5	65 42.5	00.3	Hadar	148 42.1	S60 27.5
Y 15	8 21.3	86 23.8 ..	08.4	341 08.9 ..	42.9	109 23.1 ..	25.5	80 44.7 ..	00.2	Hamal	327 56.5	N23 33.0
16	23 23.8	101 23.2	08.3	356 09.8	43.5	124 25.2	25.6	95 46.9	00.2	Kaus Aust.	83 39.0	S34 22.3
17	38 26.3	116 22.5	08.3	11 10.6	44.2	139 27.2	25.6	110 49.1	00.2			
18	53 28.7	131 21.9	S21 08.2	26 11.5	N11 44.8	154 29.3	S22 25.6	125 51.3	S22 00.2	Kochab	137 19.9	N74 04.4
19	68 31.2	146 21.2	08.1	41 12.4	45.4	169 31.4	25.6	140 53.5	00.1	Markab	13 34.8	N15 18.4
20	83 33.7	161 20.6	08.0	56 13.2	46.0	184 33.4	25.7	155 55.6	00.1	Menkar	314 11.0	N 4 09.6
21	98 36.1	176 19.9 ..	07.9	71 14.1 ..	46.7	199 35.5 ..	25.7	170 57.8 ..	00.1	Menkent	148 02.9	S36 27.6
22	113 38.6	191 19.3	07.8	86 14.9	47.3	214 37.5	25.7	186 00.0	00.0	Miaplacidus	221 37.9	S69 47.8
23	128 41.1	206 18.6	07.7	101 15.8	47.9	229 39.6	25.8	201 02.2	00.0			
14 00	143 43.5	221 18.0	S21 07.6	116 16.7	N11 48.5	244 41.7	S22 25.8	216 04.4	S22 00.0	Mirfak	308 34.8	N49 55.7
01	158 46.0	236 17.3	07.6	131 17.5	49.2	259 43.7	25.8	231 06.6	22 00.0	Nunki	75 53.8	S26 16.3
02	173 48.4	251 16.7	07.5	146 18.4	49.8	274 45.8	25.8	246 08.8	21 59.9	Peacock	53 13.8	S56 40.3
03	188 50.9	266 16.0 ..	07.4	161 19.2 ..	50.4	289 47.8 ..	25.9	261 11.0 ..	59.9	Pollux	243 22.7	N27 58.7
04	203 53.4	281 15.4	07.3	176 20.1	51.1	304 49.9	25.9	276 13.2	59.9	Procyon	244 55.4	N 5 10.4
05	218 55.8	296 14.7	07.2	191 21.0	51.7	319 52.0	25.9	291 15.4	59.8			
06	233 58.3	311 14.1	S21 07.1	206 21.8	N11 52.3	334 54.0	S22 26.0	306 17.6	S21 59.8	Rasalhague	96 03.0	N12 32.7
07	249 00.8	326 13.4	07.0	221 22.7	52.9	349 56.1	26.0	321 19.8	59.8	Regulus	207 39.1	N11 52.3
T 08	264 03.2	341 12.8	06.9	236 23.5	53.6	4 58.2	26.0	336 22.0	59.8	Rigel	281 08.2	S 8 11.1
H 09	279 05.7	356 12.1 ..	06.8	251 24.4 ..	54.2	20 00.2 ..	26.0	351 24.2 ..	59.7	Rigil Kent.	139 46.3	S60 54.4
U 10	294 08.2	11 11.5	06.7	266 25.3	54.8	35 02.3	26.1	6 26.4	59.7	Sabik	102 08.3	S15 44.8
R 11	309 10.6	26 10.8	06.6	281 26.1	55.4	50 04.3	26.1	21 28.6	59.7			
S 12	324 13.1	41 10.2	S21 06.5	296 27.0	N11 56.1	65 06.4	S22 26.1	36 30.8	S21 59.6	Schedar	349 36.5	N56 38.6
D 13	339 15.6	56 09.5	06.4	311 27.8	56.7	80 08.5	26.1	51 33.0	59.6	Shaula	96 16.9	S37 06.8
A 14	354 18.0	71 08.9	06.3	326 28.7	57.3	95 10.5	26.2	66 35.2	59.6	Sirius	258 30.1	S16 44.8
Y 15	9 20.5	86 08.2 ..	06.2	341 29.6 ..	57.9	110 12.6 ..	26.2	81 37.3 ..	59.6	Spica	158 27.0	S11 15.6
16	24 22.9	101 07.6	06.1	356 30.4	58.6	125 14.7	26.2	96 39.5	59.5	Suhail	222 49.2	S43 30.7
17	39 25.4	116 06.9	06.0	11 31.3	59.2	140 16.7	26.3	111 41.7	59.5			
18	54 27.9	131 06.3	S21 05.8	26 32.1	N11 59.8	155 18.8	S22 26.3	126 43.9	S21 59.5	Vega	80 36.7	N38 48.0
19	69 30.3	146 05.6	05.7	41 33.0	12 00.4	170 20.9	26.3	141 46.1	59.4	Zuben'ubi	137 01.1	S16 07.1
20	84 32.8	161 05.0	05.6	56 33.9	01.1	185 22.9	26.3	156 48.3	59.4		SHA	Mer.Pass.
21	99 35.3	176 04.3 ..	05.5	71 34.7 ..	01.7	200 25.0 ..	26.4	171 50.5 ..	59.4			h m
22	114 37.7	191 03.7	05.4	86 35.6	02.3	215 27.1	26.4	186 52.7	59.4	Venus	78 49.1	9 14
23	129 40.2	206 03.0	05.3	101 36.4	02.9	230 29.1	26.4	201 54.9	59.3	Mars	333 11.6	16 15
	h m									Jupiter	101 07.9	7 43
Mer.Pass. 14 26.7	v −0.6 d 0.1	v 0.9 d 0.6		v 2.1 d 0.0		v 2.2 d 0.0				Saturn	72 27.4	9 38

© British Crown Copyright 2018. All rights reserved.

UT	SUN GHA	Dec	MOON GHA	v	Dec	d	HP
d h	° '	° '	° '	'	° '	'	'
12 00	176 26.6	S13 51.5	100 46.2	12.9	N10 34.4	10.2	56.2
01	191 26.6	50.7	115 18.1	12.8	10 44.6	10.3	56.2
02	206 26.6	49.9	129 49.9	12.7	10 54.9	10.2	56.3
03	221 26.6 ..	49.0	144 21.6	12.6	11 05.1	10.2	56.3
04	236 26.6	48.2	158 53.2	12.6	11 15.3	10.1	56.3
05	251 26.6	47.4	173 24.8	12.5	11 25.4	10.1	56.4
06	266 26.6	S13 46.5	187 56.3	12.5	N11 35.5	10.0	56.4
07	281 26.6	45.7	202 27.8	12.3	11 45.5	10.0	56.4
08	296 26.6	44.9	216 59.1	12.3	11 55.5	10.0	56.5
09	311 26.7 ..	44.1	231 30.4	12.2	12 05.5	9.9	56.5
10	326 26.7	43.2	246 01.6	12.2	12 15.4	9.9	56.5
11	341 26.7	42.4	260 32.8	12.0	12 25.3	9.8	56.6
12	356 26.7	S13 41.6	275 03.8	12.0	N12 35.1	9.7	56.6
13	11 26.7	40.7	289 34.8	11.9	12 44.8	9.7	56.6
14	26 26.7	39.9	304 05.7	11.8	12 54.5	9.7	56.7
15	41 26.7 ..	39.1	318 36.5	11.8	13 04.2	9.6	56.7
16	56 26.7	38.2	333 07.3	11.7	13 13.8	9.6	56.7
17	71 26.7	37.4	347 38.0	11.6	13 23.4	9.5	56.8
18	86 26.7	S13 36.6	2 08.6	11.5	N13 32.9	9.4	56.8
19	101 26.7	35.7	16 39.1	11.4	13 42.3	9.4	56.8
20	116 26.7	34.9	31 09.5	11.4	13 51.7	9.3	56.9
21	131 26.7 ..	34.1	45 39.9	11.2	14 01.0	9.3	56.9
22	146 26.8	33.2	60 10.1	11.2	14 10.3	9.2	56.9
23	161 26.8	32.4	74 40.3	11.1	14 19.5	9.1	57.0
13 00	176 26.8	S13 31.6	89 10.4	11.0	N14 28.6	9.1	57.0
01	191 26.8	30.7	103 40.4	10.9	14 37.7	9.0	57.0
02	206 26.8	29.9	118 10.3	10.9	14 46.7	9.0	57.1
03	221 26.8 ..	29.0	132 40.2	10.7	14 55.7	8.9	57.1
04	236 26.8	28.2	147 09.9	10.7	15 04.6	8.8	57.2
05	251 26.8	27.4	161 39.6	10.6	15 13.4	8.7	57.2
06	266 26.8	S13 26.5	176 09.2	10.4	N15 22.1	8.7	57.2
07	281 26.9	25.7	190 38.6	10.4	15 30.8	8.6	57.3
08	296 26.9	24.8	205 08.0	10.4	15 39.4	8.6	57.3
09	311 26.9 ..	24.0	219 37.4	10.2	15 48.0	8.4	57.3
10	326 26.9	23.2	234 06.6	10.1	15 56.4	8.4	57.4
11	341 26.9	22.3	248 35.7	10.0	16 04.8	8.4	57.4
12	356 26.9	S13 21.5	263 04.7	10.0	N16 13.2	8.2	57.5
13	11 26.9	20.6	277 33.7	9.9	16 21.4	8.2	57.5
14	26 27.0	19.8	292 02.6	9.7	16 29.6	8.1	57.5
15	41 27.0 ..	19.0	306 31.3	9.7	16 37.7	8.0	57.6
16	56 27.0	18.1	321 00.0	9.6	16 45.7	7.9	57.6
17	71 27.0	17.3	335 28.6	9.5	16 53.6	7.8	57.6
18	86 27.0	S13 16.4	349 57.1	9.4	N17 01.4	7.8	57.7
19	101 27.0	15.6	4 25.5	9.3	17 09.2	7.7	57.7
20	116 27.1	14.7	18 53.8	9.2	17 16.9	7.5	57.8
21	131 27.1 ..	13.9	33 22.0	9.1	17 24.4	7.5	57.8
22	146 27.1	13.1	47 50.1	9.0	17 31.9	7.4	57.8
23	161 27.1	12.2	62 18.1	8.9	17 39.3	7.4	57.9
14 00	176 27.1	S13 11.4	76 46.0	8.9	N17 46.7	7.2	57.9
01	191 27.1	10.5	91 13.9	8.7	17 53.9	7.1	57.9
02	206 27.2	09.7	105 41.6	8.6	18 01.0	7.1	58.0
03	221 27.2 ..	08.8	120 09.2	8.6	18 08.1	6.9	58.0
04	236 27.2	08.0	134 36.8	8.4	18 15.0	6.9	58.1
05	251 27.2	07.1	149 04.2	8.4	18 21.9	6.7	58.1
06	266 27.2	S13 06.3	163 31.6	8.3	N18 28.6	6.7	58.1
07	281 27.3	05.4	177 58.9	8.1	18 35.3	6.5	58.2
08	296 27.3	04.6	192 26.0	8.1	18 41.8	6.5	58.2
09	311 27.3 ..	03.7	206 53.1	8.0	18 48.3	6.3	58.3
10	326 27.3	02.9	221 20.1	7.9	18 54.6	6.3	58.3
11	341 27.4	02.0	235 47.0	7.8	19 00.9	6.1	58.3
12	356 27.4	S13 01.2	250 13.8	7.7	N19 07.0	6.1	58.4
13	11 27.4	13 00.3	264 40.5	7.6	19 13.1	5.9	58.4
14	26 27.4	12 59.5	279 07.1	7.5	19 19.0	5.8	58.5
15	41 27.4 ..	58.6	293 33.6	7.4	19 24.8	5.7	58.5
16	56 27.5	57.8	308 00.0	7.3	19 30.5	5.6	58.5
17	71 27.5	56.9	322 26.3	7.3	19 36.1	5.5	58.6
18	86 27.5	S12 56.1	336 52.6	7.1	N19 41.6	5.4	58.6
19	101 27.5	55.2	351 18.7	7.1	19 47.0	5.2	58.6
20	116 27.6	54.4	5 44.8	6.9	19 52.2	5.2	58.7
21	131 27.6 ..	53.5	20 10.7	6.9	19 57.4	5.0	58.7
22	146 27.6	52.7	34 36.6	6.8	20 02.4	4.9	58.8
23	161 27.6	51.8	49 02.4	6.7	N20 07.3	4.8	58.8
	SD 16.2	d 0.8	SD 15.4		15.7		15.9

TUESDAY (12), WEDNESDAY (13), THURSDAY (14)

Twilight, Sunrise, Moonrise

Lat.	Naut.	Civil	Sunrise	12	13	14	15
°	h m	h m	h m	h m	h m	h m	h m
N 72	06 24	07 45	09 07	08 51	08 24	▭	▭
N 70	06 21	07 34	08 45	09 11	09 00	08 40	▭
68	06 19	07 25	08 28	09 27	09 26	09 26	09 31
66	06 17	07 17	08 14	09 40	09 46	09 56	10 17
64	06 15	07 11	08 02	09 51	10 02	10 18	10 47
62	06 13	07 05	07 53	10 01	10 15	10 36	11 10
60	06 11	07 00	07 44	10 09	10 27	10 52	11 28
N 58	06 09	06 56	07 37	10 16	10 36	11 04	11 44
56	06 08	06 51	07 31	10 22	10 45	11 16	11 57
54	06 06	06 48	07 25	10 28	10 53	11 25	12 08
52	06 05	06 44	07 20	10 33	11 00	11 34	12 18
50	06 03	06 41	07 15	10 37	11 06	11 42	12 27
45	06 00	06 34	07 04	10 47	11 20	11 59	12 46
N 40	05 56	06 28	06 56	10 56	11 31	12 13	13 02
35	05 53	06 22	06 48	11 03	11 41	12 24	13 15
30	05 49	06 17	06 42	11 09	11 49	12 35	13 27
20	05 42	06 08	06 31	11 21	12 04	12 53	13 47
N 10	05 34	05 59	06 20	11 30	12 17	13 08	14 04
0	05 25	05 50	06 11	11 40	12 29	13 23	14 20
S 10	05 14	05 39	06 01	11 49	12 42	13 37	14 36
20	05 01	05 28	05 51	11 59	12 55	13 53	14 54
30	04 44	05 13	05 38	12 10	13 10	14 11	15 14
35	04 33	05 05	05 31	12 17	13 19	14 22	15 26
40	04 19	04 54	05 23	12 25	13 29	14 34	15 39
45	04 03	04 42	05 14	12 34	13 41	14 49	15 56
S 50	03 41	04 27	05 02	12 44	13 55	15 06	16 15
52	03 31	04 19	04 57	12 49	14 02	15 15	16 25
54	03 19	04 11	04 51	12 55	14 10	15 24	16 35
56	03 04	04 01	04 44	13 01	14 18	15 35	16 47
58	02 46	03 51	04 37	13 08	14 28	15 47	17 01
S 60	02 24	03 38	04 29	13 16	14 39	16 01	17 18

Sunset, Twilight, Moonset

Lat.	Sunset	Civil	Naut.	12	13	14	15
°	h m	h m	h m	h m	h m	h m	h m
N 72	15 23	16 45	18 06	01 43	03 52	▭	▭
N 70	15 45	16 56	18 09	01 25	03 17	05 25	▭
68	16 02	17 05	18 11	01 10	02 52	04 41	06 33
66	16 16	17 12	18 13	00 58	02 33	04 11	05 47
64	16 27	17 19	18 15	00 49	02 18	03 49	05 18
62	16 37	17 24	18 17	00 40	02 05	03 32	04 55
60	16 45	17 29	18 18	00 33	01 55	03 17	04 37
N 58	16 52	17 34	18 20	00 27	01 45	03 05	04 22
56	16 59	17 38	18 22	00 21	01 37	02 54	04 09
54	17 04	17 42	18 23	00 16	01 30	02 45	03 58
52	17 10	17 45	18 25	00 12	01 24	02 36	03 48
50	17 14	17 48	18 26	00 08	01 18	02 29	03 39
45	17 25	17 55	18 29	25 05	01 05	02 13	03 20
N 40	17 33	18 01	18 33	24 55	00 55	02 00	03 05
35	17 40	18 06	18 36	24 46	00 46	01 49	02 52
30	17 47	18 11	18 40	24 39	00 39	01 39	02 41
20	17 58	18 21	18 47	24 25	00 25	01 22	02 22
N 10	18 08	18 30	18 55	24 14	00 14	01 08	02 05
0	18 18	18 39	19 04	24 03	00 03	00 54	01 50
S 10	18 27	18 49	19 14	23 52	24 41	00 41	01 34
20	18 38	19 00	19 27	23 41	24 26	00 26	01 17
30	18 49	19 14	19 44	23 28	24 08	00 10	00 58
35	18 56	19 23	19 55	23 20	24 00	00 00	00 47
40	19 04	19 33	20 08	23 11	23 49	24 34	00 34
45	19 14	19 45	20 24	23 01	23 37	24 19	00 19
S 50	19 25	20 01	20 45	22 49	23 21	24 01	00 01
52	19 30	20 08	20 56	22 44	23 14	23 52	24 42
54	19 36	20 16	21 08	22 38	23 06	23 43	24 31
56	19 42	20 25	21 22	22 31	22 57	23 32	24 19
58	19 50	20 36	21 39	22 23	22 47	23 19	24 05
S 60	19 58	20 48	22 00	22 15	22 35	23 05	23 49

Day	SUN Eqn. of Time 00h	SUN Eqn. of Time 12h	Mer. Pass.	MOON Mer. Pass. Upper	MOON Mer. Pass. Lower	Age	Phase
d	m s	m s	h m	h m	h m	d	%
12	14 14	14 13	12 14	17 51	05 27	08	46
13	14 13	14 12	12 14	18 42	06 16	09	56
14	14 12	14 11	12 14	19 36	07 08	10	67

© British Crown Copyright 2018. All rights reserved.

UT	ARIES	VENUS −4.2		MARS +1.1		JUPITER −2.0		SATURN +0.6		STARS		
	GHA	GHA	Dec	GHA	Dec	GHA	Dec	GHA	Dec	Name	SHA	Dec
d h	° ′	° ′	° ′	° ′	° ′	° ′	° ′	° ′	° ′		° ′	° ′
15 00	144 42.7	221 02.4	S21 05.2	116 37.3	N12 03.5	245 31.2	S22 26.4	216 57.1	S21 59.3	Acamar	315 15.5	S40 14.1
01	159 45.1	236 01.7	05.1	131 38.1	04.2	260 33.3	26.5	231 59.3	59.3	Achernar	335 24.2	S57 08.8
02	174 47.6	251 01.1	04.9	146 39.0	04.8	275 35.3	26.5	247 01.5	59.2	Acrux	173 04.4	S63 12.1
03	189 50.0	266 00.4	.. 04.8	161 39.9	.. 05.4	290 37.4	.. 26.5	262 03.7	.. 59.2	Adhara	255 09.2	S29 00.2
04	204 52.5	280 59.8	04.7	176 40.7	06.0	305 39.5	26.6	277 05.9	59.2	Aldebaran	290 44.8	N16 32.7
05	219 55.0	295 59.1	04.6	191 41.6	06.7	320 41.5	26.6	292 08.1	59.2			
06	234 57.4	310 58.5	S21 04.5	206 42.4	N12 07.3	335 43.6	S22 26.6	307 10.3	S21 59.1	Alioth	166 16.9	N55 51.2
07	249 59.9	325 57.8	04.4	221 43.3	07.9	350 45.7	26.6	322 12.5	59.1	Alkaid	152 55.6	N49 12.9
08	265 02.4	340 57.2	04.2	236 44.1	08.5	5 47.7	26.7	337 14.7	59.1	Alnair	27 39.4	S46 52.2
F 09	280 04.8	355 56.5	.. 04.1	251 45.0	.. 09.1	20 49.8	.. 26.7	352 16.9	.. 59.1	Alnilam	275 42.3	S 1 11.7
R 10	295 07.3	10 55.8	04.0	266 45.9	09.8	35 51.9	26.7	7 19.1	59.0	Alphard	217 52.0	S 8 44.6
I 11	310 09.8	25 55.2	03.9	281 46.7	10.4	50 53.9	26.7	22 21.3	59.0			
D 12	325 12.2	40 54.5	S21 03.7	296 47.6	N12 11.0	65 56.0	S22 26.8	37 23.5	S21 59.0	Alphecca	126 07.7	N26 38.9
A 13	340 14.7	55 53.9	03.6	311 48.4	11.6	80 58.1	26.8	52 25.7	58.9	Alpheratz	357 39.8	N29 11.7
Y 14	355 17.2	70 53.2	03.5	326 49.3	12.3	96 00.1	26.8	67 27.9	58.9	Altair	62 04.8	N 8 55.1
15	10 19.6	85 52.6	.. 03.3	341 50.1	.. 12.9	111 02.2	.. 26.8	82 30.1	.. 58.9	Ankaa	353 12.2	S42 12.5
16	25 22.1	100 51.9	03.2	356 51.0	13.5	126 04.3	26.9	97 32.3	58.9	Antares	112 21.6	S26 28.2
17	40 24.5	115 51.3	03.1	11 51.9	14.1	141 06.4	26.9	112 34.5	58.8			
18	55 27.0	130 50.6	S21 03.0	26 52.7	N12 14.7	156 08.4	S22 26.9	127 36.7	S21 58.8	Arcturus	145 52.1	N19 04.9
19	70 29.5	145 50.0	02.8	41 53.6	15.4	171 10.5	27.0	142 38.9	58.8	Atria	107 20.1	S69 03.3
20	85 31.9	160 49.3	02.7	56 54.4	16.0	186 12.6	27.0	157 41.1	58.7	Avior	234 15.8	S59 34.4
21	100 34.4	175 48.7	.. 02.5	71 55.3	.. 16.6	201 14.6	.. 27.0	172 43.3	.. 58.7	Bellatrix	278 27.7	N 6 21.8
22	115 36.9	190 48.0	02.4	86 56.1	17.2	216 16.7	27.0	187 45.5	58.7	Betelgeuse	270 56.9	N 7 24.4
23	130 39.3	205 47.3	02.3	101 57.0	17.8	231 18.8	27.1	202 47.7	58.7			
16 00	145 41.8	220 46.7	S21 02.1	116 57.8	N12 18.5	246 20.9	S22 27.1	217 49.9	S21 58.6	Canopus	263 54.1	S52 42.7
01	160 44.3	235 46.0	02.0	131 58.7	19.1	261 22.9	27.1	232 52.1	58.6	Capella	280 28.5	N46 01.0
02	175 46.7	250 45.4	01.9	146 59.6	19.7	276 25.0	27.1	247 54.3	58.6	Deneb	49 29.3	N45 20.8
03	190 49.2	265 44.7	.. 01.7	162 00.4	.. 20.3	291 27.1	.. 27.2	262 56.4	.. 58.5	Denebola	182 29.4	N14 27.8
04	205 51.7	280 44.1	01.6	177 01.3	20.9	306 29.1	27.2	277 58.6	58.5	Diphda	348 52.2	S17 53.2
05	220 54.1	295 43.4	01.4	192 02.1	21.5	321 31.2	27.2	293 00.8	58.5			
06	235 56.6	310 42.8	S21 01.3	207 03.0	N12 22.2	336 33.3	S22 27.2	308 03.0	S21 58.5	Dubhe	193 46.4	N61 38.8
07	250 59.0	325 42.1	01.1	222 03.8	22.8	351 35.4	27.3	323 05.2	58.4	Elnath	278 07.6	N28 37.3
S 08	266 01.5	340 41.5	01.0	237 04.7	23.4	6 37.4	27.3	338 07.4	58.4	Eltanin	90 44.6	N51 29.0
A 09	281 04.0	355 40.8	.. 00.8	252 05.5	.. 24.0	21 39.5	.. 27.3	353 09.6	.. 58.3	Enif	33 43.7	N 9 57.7
T 10	296 06.4	10 40.1	00.7	267 06.4	24.6	36 41.6	27.3	8 11.8	58.3	Fomalhaut	15 20.1	S29 31.5
U 11	311 08.9	25 39.5	00.6	282 07.3	25.2	51 43.7	27.4	23 14.0	58.3			
R 12	326 11.4	40 38.8	S21 00.4	297 08.1	N12 25.9	66 45.7	S22 27.4	38 16.2	S21 58.3	Gacrux	171 56.1	S57 13.0
D 13	341 13.8	55 38.2	00.2	312 09.0	26.5	81 47.8	27.4	53 18.4	58.3	Gienah	175 48.1	S17 38.8
A 14	356 16.3	70 37.5	21 00.1	327 09.8	27.1	96 49.9	27.5	68 20.6	58.2	Hadar	148 42.1	S60 27.5
Y 15	11 18.8	85 36.9	20 59.9	342 10.7	.. 27.7	111 52.0	.. 27.5	83 22.8	.. 58.2	Hamal	327 56.5	N23 33.0
16	26 21.2	100 36.2	59.8	357 11.5	28.3	126 54.0	27.5	98 25.0	58.2	Kaus Aust.	83 38.9	S34 22.3
17	41 23.7	115 35.6	59.6	12 12.4	28.9	141 56.1	27.5	113 27.2	58.1			
18	56 26.2	130 34.9	S20 59.5	27 13.2	N12 29.6	156 58.2	S22 27.6	128 29.4	S21 58.1	Kochab	137 19.9	N74 04.4
19	71 28.6	145 34.2	59.3	42 14.1	30.2	172 00.3	27.6	143 31.6	58.1	Markab	13 34.8	N15 18.4
20	86 31.1	160 33.6	59.2	57 14.9	30.8	187 02.3	27.6	158 33.8	58.1	Menkar	314 11.0	N 4 09.6
21	101 33.5	175 32.9	.. 59.0	72 15.8	.. 31.4	202 04.4	.. 27.6	173 36.0	.. 58.0	Menkent	148 02.8	S36 27.6
22	116 36.0	190 32.3	58.8	87 16.6	32.0	217 06.5	27.7	188 38.2	58.0	Miaplacidus	221 38.0	S69 47.8
23	131 38.5	205 31.6	58.7	102 17.5	32.6	232 08.6	27.7	203 40.4	58.0			
17 00	146 40.9	220 31.0	S20 58.5	117 18.4	N12 33.3	247 10.6	S22 27.7	218 42.6	S21 57.9	Mirfak	308 34.8	N49 55.7
01	161 43.4	235 30.4	58.4	132 19.2	33.9	262 12.7	27.7	233 44.9	57.9	Nunki	75 53.8	S26 16.3
02	176 45.9	250 29.7	58.2	147 20.1	34.5	277 14.8	27.8	248 47.1	57.9	Peacock	53 13.7	S56 40.3
03	191 48.3	265 29.0	.. 58.0	162 20.9	.. 35.1	292 16.9	.. 27.8	263 49.3	.. 57.9	Pollux	243 22.7	N27 58.7
04	206 50.8	280 28.3	57.9	177 21.8	35.7	307 19.0	27.8	278 51.5	57.8	Procyon	244 55.4	N 5 10.4
05	221 53.3	295 27.7	57.7	192 22.6	36.3	322 21.0	27.8	293 53.7	57.8			
06	236 55.7	310 27.0	S20 57.6	207 23.5	N12 36.9	337 23.1	S22 27.9	308 55.9	S21 57.7	Rasalhague	96 03.0	N12 32.7
07	251 58.2	325 26.4	57.4	222 24.3	37.6	352 25.2	27.9	323 58.1	57.7	Regulus	207 39.1	N11 52.3
08	267 00.7	340 25.7	57.2	237 25.2	38.2	7 27.3	27.9	339 00.3	57.7	Rigel	281 08.2	S 8 11.1
S 09	282 03.1	355 25.1	.. 57.0	252 26.0	.. 38.8	22 29.4	.. 27.9	354 02.5	.. 57.7	Rigil Kent.	139 46.3	S60 54.4
U 10	297 05.6	10 24.4	56.8	267 26.9	39.4	37 31.4	28.0	9 04.7	57.6	Sabik	102 08.2	S15 44.8
N 11	312 08.0	25 23.7	56.7	282 27.7	40.0	52 33.5	28.0	24 06.9	57.6			
D 12	327 10.5	40 23.1	S20 56.5	297 28.6	N12 40.6	67 35.6	S22 28.0	39 09.1	S21 57.6	Schedar	349 36.5	N56 38.5
A 13	342 13.0	55 22.4	56.3	312 29.4	41.2	82 37.7	28.0	54 11.3	57.6	Shaula	96 16.9	S37 06.8
Y 14	357 15.4	70 21.8	56.1	327 30.3	41.8	97 39.8	28.1	69 13.5	57.6	Sirius	258 30.1	S16 44.8
15	12 17.9	85 21.1	.. 56.0	342 31.1	.. 42.5	112 41.8	.. 28.1	84 15.7	.. 57.5	Spica	158 27.0	S11 15.6
16	27 20.4	100 20.5	55.8	357 32.0	43.1	127 43.9	28.1	99 17.9	57.5	Suhail	222 49.2	S43 30.7
17	42 22.8	115 19.8	55.6	12 32.8	43.7	142 46.0	28.1	114 20.1	57.5			
18	57 25.3	130 19.1	S20 55.4	27 33.7	N12 44.3	157 48.1	S22 28.2	129 22.3	S21 57.4	Vega	80 36.6	N38 48.0
19	72 27.8	145 18.5	55.2	42 34.5	44.9	172 50.2	28.2	144 24.5	57.4	Zuben'ubi	137 01.1	S16 07.1
20	87 30.2	160 17.8	55.1	57 35.4	45.5	187 52.2	28.2	159 26.7	57.4		SHA	Mer. Pass.
21	102 32.7	175 17.2	.. 54.9	72 36.2	.. 46.1	202 54.3	.. 28.2	174 28.9	57.4		° ′	h m
22	117 35.1	190 16.5	54.7	87 37.1	46.7	217 56.4	28.3	189 31.1	57.3	Venus	75 04.9	9 17
23	132 37.6	205 15.9	54.5	102 37.9	47.3	232 58.5	28.3	204 33.3	57.3	Mars	331 16.1	16 11
	h m									Jupiter	100 39.1	7 34
Mer. Pass. 14 14.9		v −0.7	d 0.2	v 0.9	d 0.6	v 2.1	d 0.0	v 2.2	d 0.0	Saturn	72 08.1	9 27

© British Crown Copyright 2018. All rights reserved.

UT	SUN GHA	SUN Dec	MOON GHA	v	Dec	d	HP
d h	° ′	° ′	° ′	′	° ′	′	′
15 00	176 27.7	S12 51.0	63 28.1	6.6	N20 12.1	4.6	58.8
01	191 27.7	50.1	77 53.7	6.5	20 16.7	4.6	58.9
02	206 27.7	49.3	92 19.2	6.4	20 21.3	4.4	58.9
03	221 27.8	.. 48.4	106 44.6	6.4	20 25.7	4.3	59.0
04	236 27.8	47.5	121 10.0	6.2	20 30.0	4.1	59.0
05	251 27.8	46.7	135 35.2	6.2	20 34.1	4.1	59.0
06	266 27.8	S12 45.8	150 00.4	6.1	N20 38.2	3.9	59.1
07	281 27.9	45.0	164 25.5	6.0	20 42.1	3.8	59.1
F 08	296 27.9	44.1	178 50.5	5.9	20 45.9	3.6	59.2
R 09	311 27.9	.. 43.3	193 15.4	5.9	20 49.5	3.5	59.2
I 10	326 28.0	42.4	207 40.3	5.7	20 53.0	3.4	59.2
11	341 28.0	41.6	222 05.0	5.7	20 56.4	3.2	59.3
D 12	356 28.0	S12 40.7	236 29.7	5.6	N20 59.6	3.2	59.3
A 13	11 28.0	39.8	250 54.3	5.6	21 02.8	2.9	59.3
Y 14	26 28.1	39.0	265 18.9	5.4	21 05.7	2.9	59.4
15	41 28.1	.. 38.1	279 43.3	5.4	21 08.6	2.7	59.4
16	56 28.1	37.3	294 07.7	5.3	21 11.3	2.5	59.5
17	71 28.2	36.4	308 32.0	5.2	21 13.8	2.5	59.5
18	86 28.2	S12 35.5	322 56.2	5.2	N21 16.3	2.3	59.5
19	101 28.2	34.7	337 20.4	5.1	21 18.6	2.1	59.6
20	116 28.3	33.8	351 44.5	5.0	21 20.7	2.0	59.6
21	131 28.3	.. 33.0	6 08.5	5.0	21 22.7	1.8	59.6
22	146 28.3	32.1	20 32.5	4.8	21 24.5	1.8	59.7
23	161 28.4	31.2	34 56.3	4.9	21 26.3	1.5	59.7
16 00	176 28.4	S12 30.4	49 20.2	4.7	N21 27.8	1.4	59.8
01	191 28.4	29.5	63 43.9	4.7	21 29.2	1.3	59.8
02	206 28.5	28.6	78 07.6	4.7	21 30.5	1.1	59.8
03	221 28.5	.. 27.8	92 31.3	4.5	21 31.6	1.0	59.9
04	236 28.5	26.9	106 54.8	4.6	21 32.6	0.8	59.9
05	251 28.6	26.0	121 18.4	4.4	21 33.4	0.7	59.9
06	266 28.6	S12 25.2	135 41.8	4.4	N21 34.1	0.5	60.0
07	281 28.6	24.3	150 05.2	4.4	21 34.6	0.4	60.0
S 08	296 28.7	23.5	164 28.6	4.3	21 35.0	0.2	60.0
A 09	311 28.7	.. 22.6	178 51.9	4.3	21 35.2	0.1	60.1
T 10	326 28.8	21.7	193 15.2	4.2	21 35.3	0.1	60.1
U 11	341 28.8	20.9	207 38.4	4.2	21 35.2	0.2	60.1
R 12	356 28.8	S12 20.0	222 01.6	4.1	N21 35.0	0.4	60.2
D 13	11 28.9	19.1	236 24.7	4.1	21 34.6	0.6	60.2
A 14	26 28.9	18.3	250 47.8	4.0	21 34.0	0.7	60.2
Y 15	41 28.9	.. 17.4	265 10.8	4.0	21 33.3	0.9	60.3
16	56 29.0	16.5	279 33.8	4.0	21 32.4	1.0	60.3
17	71 29.0	15.6	293 56.8	3.9	21 31.4	1.1	60.3
18	86 29.1	S12 14.8	308 19.7	3.9	N21 30.3	1.4	60.4
19	101 29.1	13.9	322 42.6	3.9	21 28.9	1.5	60.4
20	116 29.1	13.0	337 05.5	3.8	21 27.4	1.6	60.4
21	131 29.2	.. 12.2	351 28.3	3.9	21 25.8	1.8	60.5
22	146 29.2	11.3	5 51.2	3.7	21 24.0	2.0	60.5
23	161 29.3	10.4	20 13.9	3.8	21 22.0	2.1	60.5
17 00	176 29.3	S12 09.6	34 36.7	3.8	N21 19.9	2.3	60.6
01	191 29.4	08.7	48 59.5	3.7	21 17.6	2.4	60.6
02	206 29.4	07.8	63 22.2	3.7	21 15.2	2.6	60.6
03	221 29.4	.. 06.9	77 44.9	3.7	21 12.6	2.7	60.6
04	236 29.5	06.1	92 07.6	3.6	21 09.9	2.9	60.7
05	251 29.5	05.2	106 30.2	3.7	21 07.0	3.1	60.7
06	266 29.6	S12 04.3	120 52.9	3.7	N21 03.9	3.2	60.7
07	281 29.6	03.5	135 15.6	3.6	21 00.7	3.4	60.8
S 08	296 29.7	02.6	149 38.2	3.6	20 57.3	3.5	60.8
U 09	311 29.7	.. 01.7	164 00.8	3.7	20 53.8	3.7	60.8
N 10	326 29.7	00.8	178 23.5	3.6	20 50.1	3.9	60.8
11	341 29.8	12 00.0	192 46.1	3.6	20 46.2	4.0	60.9
D 12	356 29.8	S11 59.1	207 08.7	3.7	N20 42.2	4.2	60.9
A 13	11 29.9	58.2	221 31.4	3.6	20 38.0	4.3	60.9
Y 14	26 29.9	57.3	235 54.0	3.6	20 33.7	4.5	60.9
15	41 30.0	.. 56.5	250 16.6	3.7	20 29.2	4.6	61.0
16	56 30.0	55.6	264 39.3	3.6	20 24.6	4.8	61.0
17	71 30.1	54.7	279 01.9	3.7	20 19.8	4.9	61.0
18	86 30.1	S11 53.8	293 24.6	3.7	N20 14.9	5.1	61.0
19	101 30.2	53.0	307 47.3	3.7	20 09.8	5.3	61.0
20	116 30.2	52.1	322 10.0	3.7	20 04.5	5.4	61.1
21	131 30.3	.. 51.2	336 32.7	3.7	19 59.1	5.5	61.1
22	146 30.3	50.3	350 55.4	3.7	19 53.6	5.7	61.1
23	161 30.4	49.4	5 18.1	3.8	N19 47.9	5.9	61.1
	SD 16.2	d 0.9	SD 16.2		16.4		16.6

Lat.	Twilight Naut.	Civil	Sunrise	Moonrise 15	16	17	18
°	h m	h m	h m	h m	h m	h m	h m
N 72	06 12	07 31	08 49	▭	▭	▭	▭
N 70	06 10	07 22	08 30	▭	▭	▭	13 00
68	06 09	07 14	08 15	09 31	10 02	11 38	13 42
66	06 07	07 07	08 03	10 17	11 02	12 24	14 11
64	06 06	07 02	07 53	10 47	11 37	12 54	14 32
62	06 05	06 57	07 44	11 10	12 02	13 17	14 49
60	06 04	06 53	07 36	11 28	12 22	13 35	15 04
N 58	06 03	06 49	07 30	11 44	12 38	13 50	15 16
56	06 02	06 45	07 24	11 57	12 52	14 03	15 27
54	06 01	06 42	07 18	12 08	13 04	14 14	15 36
52	05 59	06 39	07 14	12 18	13 15	14 24	15 44
50	05 58	06 36	07 09	12 27	13 24	14 33	15 51
45	05 56	06 30	07 00	12 46	13 44	14 52	16 07
N 40	05 53	06 24	06 52	13 02	14 00	15 07	16 20
35	05 50	06 19	06 45	13 15	14 14	15 20	16 31
30	05 47	06 15	06 39	13 27	14 26	15 31	16 41
20	05 40	06 06	06 29	13 47	14 46	15 51	16 57
N 10	05 33	05 58	06 20	14 04	15 04	16 07	17 12
0	05 25	05 50	06 11	14 20	15 21	16 23	17 25
S 10	05 15	05 40	06 02	14 36	15 37	16 39	17 38
20	05 03	05 29	05 52	14 54	15 55	16 55	17 53
30	04 46	05 16	05 41	15 14	16 16	17 15	18 09
35	04 36	05 08	05 34	15 26	16 28	17 26	18 18
40	04 24	04 58	05 27	15 39	16 42	17 39	18 29
45	04 08	04 47	05 18	15 56	16 58	17 54	18 42
S 50	03 48	04 32	05 08	16 15	17 18	18 12	18 57
52	03 38	04 26	05 03	16 25	17 28	18 21	19 04
54	03 27	04 18	04 57	16 35	17 39	18 31	19 12
56	03 14	04 09	04 51	16 47	17 51	18 42	19 21
58	02 58	03 59	04 44	17 01	18 05	18 54	19 31
S 60	02 38	03 48	04 37	17 18	18 22	19 09	19 42

Lat.	Sunset	Twilight Civil	Naut.	Moonset 15	16	17	18
°	h m	h m	h m	h m	h m	h m	h m
N 72	15 40	16 59	18 19	▭	▭	▭	▭
N 70	15 59	17 08	18 20	▭	▭	▭	09 31
68	16 14	17 16	18 21	06 33	08 07	08 42	08 48
66	16 27	17 22	18 22	05 47	07 07	07 55	08 18
64	16 37	17 28	18 23	05 18	06 33	07 25	07 56
62	16 45	17 32	18 24	04 55	06 07	07 02	07 38
60	16 53	17 37	18 25	04 37	05 48	06 43	07 23
N 58	16 59	17 41	18 27	04 22	05 31	06 28	07 10
56	17 05	17 44	18 28	04 09	05 17	06 15	06 59
54	17 11	17 47	18 29	03 58	05 05	06 03	06 50
52	17 15	17 50	18 30	03 48	04 55	05 53	06 41
50	17 20	17 53	18 31	03 39	04 45	05 44	06 33
45	17 29	17 59	18 33	03 20	04 25	05 25	06 16
N 40	17 37	18 04	18 36	03 05	04 09	05 09	06 03
35	17 43	18 09	18 39	02 52	03 55	04 56	05 51
30	17 49	18 14	18 42	02 41	03 44	04 44	05 41
20	18 00	18 22	18 48	02 22	03 23	04 24	05 23
N 10	18 09	18 30	18 55	02 05	03 05	04 07	05 07
0	18 17	18 39	19 03	01 50	02 49	03 50	04 53
S 10	18 26	18 48	19 13	01 34	02 32	03 34	04 38
20	18 36	18 59	19 25	01 17	02 14	03 16	04 22
30	18 47	19 12	19 41	00 58	01 54	02 56	04 04
35	18 53	19 20	19 51	00 47	01 42	02 44	03 53
40	19 01	19 29	20 03	00 34	01 28	02 31	03 41
45	19 09	19 40	20 19	00 19	01 12	02 15	03 26
S 50	19 19	19 55	20 38	00 01	00 52	01 55	03 09
52	19 24	20 01	20 48	24 42	00 42	01 45	03 00
54	19 30	20 09	20 59	24 31	00 31	01 34	02 51
56	19 35	20 17	21 12	24 19	00 19	01 22	02 40
58	19 42	20 27	21 27	24 05	00 05	01 08	02 28
S 60	19 50	20 38	21 46	23 49	24 52	00 52	02 14

Day	SUN Eqn. of Time 00h	12h	Mer. Pass.	MOON Mer. Pass. Upper	Lower	Age	Phase
d	m s	m s	h m	h m	h m	d	%
15	14 09	14 08	12 14	20 34	08 05	11	77
16	14 06	14 05	12 14	21 36	09 05	12	86
17	14 03	14 01	12 14	22 38	10 07	13	93

© British Crown Copyright 2018. All rights reserved.

UT	ARIES	VENUS −4.2		MARS +1.1		JUPITER −2.0		SATURN +0.6		STARS		
	GHA	GHA	Dec	GHA	Dec	GHA	Dec	GHA	Dec	Name	SHA	Dec
d h	° ′	° ′	° ′	° ′	° ′	° ′	° ′	° ′	° ′		° ′	° ′
18 00	147 40.1	220 15.2	S20 54.3	117 38.8	N12 48.0	248 00.6	S22 28.3	219 35.5	S21 57.3	Acamar	315 15.5	S40 14.1
01	162 42.5	235 14.5	54.1	132 39.6	48.6	263 02.7	28.3	234 37.7	57.2	Achernar	335 24.2	S57 08.8
02	177 45.0	250 13.9	53.9	147 40.5	49.2	278 04.7	28.4	249 39.9	57.2	Acrux	173 04.4	S63 12.1
03	192 47.5	265 13.2 ..	53.8	162 41.3 ..	49.8	293 06.8 ..	28.4	264 42.1 ..	57.2	Adhara	255 09.2	S29 00.2
04	207 49.9	280 12.6	53.6	177 42.2	50.4	308 08.9	28.4	279 44.3	57.2	Aldebaran	290 44.9	N16 32.7
05	222 52.4	295 11.9	53.4	192 43.0	51.0	323 11.0	28.4	294 46.5	57.1			
06	237 54.9	310 11.2	S20 53.2	207 43.9	N12 51.6	338 13.1	S22 28.5	309 48.7	S21 57.1	Alioth	166 16.9	N55 51.2
07	252 57.3	325 10.6	53.0	222 44.7	52.2	353 15.2	28.5	324 50.9	57.1	Alkaid	152 55.6	N49 12.9
M 08	267 59.8	340 09.9	52.8	237 45.6	52.8	8 17.2	28.5	339 53.1	57.0	Alnair	27 39.3	S46 52.2
O 09	283 02.3	355 09.3 ..	52.6	252 46.4 ..	53.4	23 19.3 ..	28.5	354 55.3 ..	57.0	Alnilam	275 42.3	S 1 11.7
N 10	298 04.7	10 08.6	52.4	267 47.3	54.0	38 21.4	28.6	9 57.5	57.0	Alphard	217 52.0	S 8 44.6
D 11	313 07.2	25 08.0	52.2	282 48.1	54.7	53 23.5	28.6	24 59.7	57.0			
A 12	328 09.6	40 07.3	S20 52.0	297 49.0	N12 55.3	68 25.6	S22 28.6	40 02.0	S21 56.9	Alphecca	126 07.7	N26 38.9
Y 13	343 12.1	55 06.6	51.8	312 49.8	55.9	83 27.7	28.6	55 04.2	56.9	Alpheratz	357 39.8	N29 11.6
14	358 14.6	70 06.0	51.6	327 50.7	56.5	98 29.8	28.7	70 06.4	56.9	Altair	62 04.7	N 8 55.1
15	13 17.0	85 05.3 ..	51.4	342 51.5 ..	57.1	113 31.8 ..	28.7	85 08.6 ..	56.8	Ankaa	353 12.2	S42 12.5
16	28 19.5	100 04.7	51.2	357 52.4	57.7	128 33.9	28.7	100 10.8	56.8	Antares	112 21.6	S26 28.2
17	43 22.0	115 04.0	51.0	12 53.2	58.3	143 36.0	28.7	115 13.0	56.8			
18	58 24.4	130 03.3	S20 50.8	27 54.1	N12 58.9	158 38.1	S22 28.8	130 15.2	S21 56.8	Arcturus	145 52.1	N19 04.9
19	73 26.9	145 02.7	50.6	42 54.9	12 59.5	173 40.2	28.8	145 17.4	56.7	Atria	107 20.0	S69 03.3
20	88 29.4	160 02.0	50.4	57 55.8	13 00.1	188 42.3	28.8	160 19.6	56.7	Avior	234 15.9	S59 34.4
21	103 31.8	175 01.4 ..	50.2	72 56.6 ..	00.7	203 44.4 ..	28.8	175 21.8 ..	56.7	Bellatrix	278 27.7	N 6 21.8
22	118 34.3	190 00.7	50.0	87 57.5	01.3	218 46.5	28.9	190 24.0	56.6	Betelgeuse	270 56.9	N 7 24.4
23	133 36.8	205 00.1	49.8	102 58.3	01.9	233 48.5	28.9	205 26.2	56.6			
19 00	148 39.2	219 59.4	S20 49.5	117 59.2	N13 02.5	248 50.6	S22 28.9	220 28.4	S21 56.6	Canopus	263 54.1	S52 42.7
01	163 41.7	234 58.7	49.3	133 00.0	03.2	263 52.7	28.9	235 30.6	56.6	Capella	280 28.5	N46 01.0
02	178 44.1	249 58.1	49.1	148 00.9	03.8	278 54.8	29.0	250 32.8	56.5	Deneb	49 29.3	N45 20.8
03	193 46.6	264 57.4 ..	48.9	163 01.7 ..	04.4	293 56.9 ..	29.0	265 35.0 ..	56.5	Denebola	182 29.4	N14 27.8
04	208 49.1	279 56.8	48.7	178 02.6	05.0	308 59.0	29.0	280 37.2	56.5	Diphda	348 52.2	S17 53.2
05	223 51.5	294 56.1	48.5	193 03.4	05.6	324 01.1	29.0	295 39.4	56.5			
06	238 54.0	309 55.4	S20 48.3	208 04.3	N13 06.2	339 03.2	S22 29.0	310 41.7	S21 56.4	Dubhe	193 46.3	N61 38.8
07	253 56.5	324 54.8	48.0	223 05.1	06.8	354 05.3	29.1	325 43.9	56.4	Elnath	278 07.6	N28 37.3
T 08	268 58.9	339 54.1	47.8	238 06.0	07.4	9 07.3	29.1	340 46.1	56.4	Eltanin	90 44.6	N51 29.0
U 09	284 01.4	354 53.5 ..	47.6	253 06.8 ..	08.0	24 09.4 ..	29.1	355 48.3 ..	56.3	Enif	33 43.6	N 9 57.6
E 10	299 03.9	9 52.8	47.4	268 07.6	08.6	39 11.5	29.1	10 50.5	56.3	Fomalhaut	15 20.1	S29 31.5
S 11	314 06.3	24 52.1	47.2	283 08.5	09.2	54 13.6	29.2	25 52.7	56.3			
D 12	329 08.8	39 51.5	S20 46.9	298 09.3	N13 09.8	69 15.7	S22 29.2	40 54.9	S21 56.3	Gacrux	171 56.1	S57 13.0
A 13	344 11.2	54 50.8	46.7	313 10.2	10.4	84 17.8	29.2	55 57.1	56.2	Gienah	175 48.0	S17 38.8
Y 14	359 13.7	69 50.2	46.5	328 11.0	11.0	99 19.9	29.2	70 59.3	56.2	Hadar	148 42.1	S60 27.6
15	14 16.2	84 49.5 ..	46.3	343 11.9 ..	11.6	114 22.0 ..	29.3	86 01.5 ..	56.2	Hamal	327 56.5	N23 33.0
16	29 18.6	99 48.9	46.0	358 12.7	12.2	129 24.1	29.3	101 03.7	56.1	Kaus Aust.	83 38.9	S34 22.3
17	44 21.1	114 48.2	45.8	13 13.6	12.8	144 26.2	29.3	116 05.9	56.1			
18	59 23.6	129 47.5	S20 45.6	28 14.4	N13 13.4	159 28.3	S22 29.3	131 08.1	S21 56.1	Kochab	137 19.8	N74 04.4
19	74 26.0	144 46.9	45.3	43 15.3	14.0	174 30.4	29.4	146 10.3	56.1	Markab	13 34.8	N15 18.3
20	89 28.5	159 46.2	45.1	58 16.1	14.6	189 32.4	29.4	161 12.6	56.0	Menkar	314 11.1	N 4 09.6
21	104 31.0	174 45.6 ..	44.9	73 17.0 ..	15.2	204 34.5 ..	29.4	176 14.8 ..	56.0	Menkent	148 02.8	S36 27.6
22	119 33.4	189 44.9	44.7	88 17.8	15.8	219 36.6	29.4	191 17.0	56.0	Miaplacidus	221 38.0	S69 47.8
23	134 35.9	204 44.2	44.4	103 18.6	16.4	234 38.7	29.4	206 19.2	55.9			
20 00	149 38.4	219 43.6	S20 44.2	118 19.5	N13 17.0	249 40.8	S22 29.5	221 21.4	S21 55.9	Mirfak	308 34.8	N49 55.7
01	164 40.8	234 42.9	44.0	133 20.3	17.6	264 42.9	29.5	236 23.6	55.9	Nunki	75 53.8	S26 16.3
02	179 43.3	249 42.3	43.7	148 21.2	18.2	279 45.0	29.5	251 25.8	55.9	Peacock	53 13.7	S56 40.3
03	194 45.7	264 41.6 ..	43.5	163 22.0 ..	18.8	294 47.1 ..	29.5	266 28.0 ..	55.8	Pollux	243 22.7	N27 58.7
04	209 48.2	279 40.9	43.2	178 22.9	19.4	309 49.2	29.6	281 30.2	55.8	Procyon	244 55.4	N 5 10.4
05	224 50.7	294 40.3	43.0	193 23.7	20.0	324 51.3	29.6	296 32.4	55.8			
06	239 53.1	309 39.6	S20 42.8	208 24.6	N13 20.6	339 53.4	S22 29.6	311 34.6	S21 55.8	Rasalhague	96 03.0	N12 32.7
W 07	254 55.6	324 39.0	42.5	223 25.4	21.2	354 55.5	29.6	326 36.8	55.7	Regulus	207 39.1	N11 52.3
E 08	269 58.1	339 38.3	42.3	238 26.3	21.8	9 57.6	29.7	341 39.1	55.7	Rigel	281 08.2	S 8 11.1
D 09	285 00.5	354 37.6 ..	42.0	253 27.1 ..	22.4	24 59.7 ..	29.7	356 41.3 ..	55.7	Rigil Kent.	139 46.2	S60 54.4
N 10	300 03.0	9 37.0	41.8	268 27.9	23.0	40 01.8	29.7	11 43.5	55.6	Sabik	102 08.2	S15 44.8
E 11	315 05.5	24 36.3	41.5	283 28.8	23.6	55 03.9	29.7	26 45.7	55.6			
S 12	330 07.9	39 35.7	S20 41.3	298 29.6	N13 24.2	70 06.0	S22 29.7	41 47.9	S21 55.6	Schedar	349 36.5	N56 38.5
D 13	345 10.4	54 35.0	41.1	313 30.5	24.8	85 08.1	29.8	56 50.1	55.6	Shaula	96 16.8	S37 06.8
A 14	0 12.9	69 34.3	40.8	328 31.3	25.4	100 10.2	29.8	71 52.3	55.5	Sirius	258 30.1	S16 44.8
Y 15	15 15.3	84 33.7 ..	40.6	343 32.2 ..	26.0	115 12.3 ..	29.8	86 54.5 ..	55.5	Spica	158 27.0	S11 15.6
16	30 17.8	99 33.0	40.3	358 33.0	26.6	130 14.4	29.8	101 56.7	55.5	Suhail	222 49.2	S43 30.7
17	45 20.2	114 32.4	40.1	13 33.8	27.2	145 16.5	29.9	116 58.9	55.4			
18	60 22.7	129 31.7	S20 39.8	28 34.7	N13 27.8	160 18.6	S22 29.9	132 01.1	S21 55.4	Vega	80 36.6	N38 47.9
19	75 25.2	144 31.1	39.5	43 35.5	28.4	175 20.7	29.9	147 03.4	55.4	Zuben'ubi	137 01.0	S16 07.1
20	90 27.6	159 30.4	39.3	58 36.4	29.0	190 22.8	29.9	162 05.6	55.4		SHA	Mer.Pass.
21	105 30.1	174 29.7 ..	39.0	73 37.2 ..	29.6	205 24.9 ..	30.0	177 07.8 ..	55.3		° ′	h m
22	120 32.6	189 29.1	38.8	88 38.1	30.2	220 27.0	30.0	192 10.0	55.3	Venus	71 20.2	9 20
23	135 35.0	204 28.4	38.5	103 38.9	30.8	235 29.1	30.0	207 12.3	55.3	Mars	329 20.0	16 07
	h m									Jupiter	100 11.4	7 24
Mer. Pass. 14 03.1	v −0.7	d 0.2		v 0.8	d 0.6	v 2.1	d 0.0	v 2.2	d 0.0	Saturn	71 49.2	9 17

© British Crown Copyright 2018. All rights reserved.

UT	SUN GHA	SUN Dec	MOON GHA	v	MOON Dec	d	HP
d h	° ′	° ′	° ′	′	° ′	′	′
18 00	176 30.4	S11 48.6	19 40.9	3.8	N19 42.0	6.0	61.1
01	191 30.5	47.7	34 03.7	3.8	19 36.0	6.1	61.2
02	206 30.5	46.8	48 26.5	3.8	19 29.9	6.3	61.2
03	221 30.6	.. 45.9	62 49.3	3.9	19 23.6	6.5	61.2
04	236 30.6	45.0	77 12.2	3.9	19 17.1	6.6	61.2
05	251 30.7	44.2	91 35.1	3.9	19 10.5	6.7	61.2
06	266 30.7	S11 43.3	105 58.0	3.9	N19 03.8	6.9	61.2
07	281 30.8	42.4	120 20.9	4.0	18 56.9	7.0	61.3
M 08	296 30.8	41.5	134 43.9	4.0	18 49.9	7.2	61.3
O 09	311 30.9	.. 40.6	149 06.9	4.1	18 42.7	7.3	61.3
N 10	326 30.9	39.8	163 30.0	4.1	18 35.4	7.5	61.3
D 11	341 31.0	38.9	177 53.1	4.1	18 27.9	7.6	61.3
A 12	356 31.0	S11 38.0	192 16.2	4.2	N18 20.3	7.7	61.3
Y 13	11 31.1	37.1	206 39.4	4.2	18 12.6	7.9	61.3
14	26 31.1	36.2	221 02.6	4.3	18 04.7	8.0	61.4
15	41 31.2	.. 35.3	235 25.9	4.3	17 56.7	8.1	61.4
16	56 31.2	34.5	249 49.2	4.4	17 48.6	8.3	61.4
17	71 31.3	33.6	264 12.6	4.4	17 40.3	8.4	61.4
18	86 31.3	S11 32.7	278 36.0	4.4	N17 31.9	8.5	61.4
19	101 31.4	31.8	292 59.4	4.5	17 23.4	8.6	61.4
20	116 31.4	30.9	307 22.9	4.5	17 14.8	8.8	61.4
21	131 31.5	.. 30.0	321 46.4	4.6	17 06.0	8.9	61.4
22	146 31.6	29.2	336 10.0	4.7	16 57.1	9.1	61.4
23	161 31.6	28.3	350 33.7	4.7	16 48.0	9.1	61.4
19 00	176 31.7	S11 27.4	4 57.4	4.8	N16 38.9	9.3	61.4
01	191 31.7	26.5	19 21.2	4.8	16 29.6	9.4	61.4
02	206 31.8	25.6	33 45.0	4.8	16 20.2	9.6	61.5
03	221 31.8	.. 24.7	48 08.8	5.0	16 10.6	9.6	61.5
04	236 31.9	23.8	62 32.8	4.9	16 01.0	9.7	61.5
05	251 32.0	22.9	76 56.7	5.1	15 51.3	9.9	61.5
06	266 32.0	S11 22.1	91 20.8	5.1	N15 41.4	10.0	61.5
07	281 32.1	21.2	105 44.9	5.2	15 31.4	10.1	61.5
T 08	296 32.1	20.3	120 09.1	5.2	15 21.3	10.2	61.5
U 09	311 32.2	.. 19.4	134 33.3	5.3	15 11.1	10.3	61.5
E 10	326 32.2	18.5	148 57.6	5.3	15 00.8	10.4	61.5
S 11	341 32.3	17.6	163 21.9	5.4	14 50.4	10.5	61.5
D 12	356 32.4	S11 16.7	177 46.3	5.5	N14 39.9	10.7	61.5
A 13	11 32.4	15.8	192 10.8	5.5	14 29.2	10.7	61.5
Y 14	26 32.5	14.9	206 35.3	5.6	14 18.5	10.8	61.5
15	41 32.5	.. 14.1	220 59.9	5.7	14 07.7	10.9	61.5
16	56 32.6	13.2	235 24.6	5.7	13 56.8	11.0	61.4
17	71 32.7	12.3	249 49.3	5.8	13 45.8	11.2	61.4
18	86 32.7	S11 11.4	264 14.1	5.9	N13 34.6	11.2	61.4
19	101 32.8	10.5	278 39.0	5.9	13 23.4	11.3	61.4
20	116 32.9	09.6	293 03.9	6.0	13 12.1	11.3	61.4
21	131 32.9	.. 08.7	307 28.9	6.1	13 00.8	11.5	61.4
22	146 33.0	07.8	321 54.0	6.1	12 49.3	11.6	61.4
23	161 33.0	06.9	336 19.1	6.2	12 37.7	11.6	61.4
20 00	176 33.1	S11 06.0	350 44.3	6.3	N12 26.1	11.7	61.4
01	191 33.2	05.1	5 09.6	6.3	12 14.4	11.8	61.4
02	206 33.2	04.2	19 34.9	6.4	12 02.6	11.9	61.4
03	221 33.3	.. 03.3	34 00.3	6.5	11 50.7	11.9	61.4
04	236 33.4	02.4	48 25.8	6.5	11 38.8	12.1	61.4
05	251 33.4	01.6	62 51.3	6.6	11 26.7	12.1	61.3
06	266 33.5	S11 00.7	77 16.9	6.7	N11 14.6	12.1	61.3
W 07	281 33.6	10 59.8	91 42.6	6.7	11 02.5	12.3	61.3
E 08	296 33.6	58.9	106 08.3	6.8	10 50.2	12.3	61.3
D 09	311 33.7	.. 58.0	120 34.1	6.9	10 37.9	12.4	61.3
N 10	326 33.8	57.1	135 00.0	6.9	10 25.5	12.4	61.3
E 11	341 33.8	56.2	149 25.9	7.0	10 13.1	12.5	61.3
S 12	356 33.9	S10 55.3	163 51.9	7.1	N10 00.6	12.5	61.2
D 13	11 34.0	54.4	178 18.0	7.2	9 48.1	12.6	61.2
A 14	26 34.0	53.5	192 44.2	7.2	9 35.5	12.7	61.2
Y 15	41 34.1	.. 52.6	207 10.4	7.2	9 22.8	12.7	61.2
16	56 34.2	51.7	221 36.6	7.4	9 10.1	12.8	61.2
17	71 34.2	50.8	236 03.0	7.4	8 57.3	12.8	61.2
18	86 34.3	S10 49.9	250 29.4	7.4	N 8 44.5	12.9	61.1
19	101 34.4	49.0	264 55.8	7.6	8 31.6	12.9	61.1
20	116 34.4	48.1	279 22.4	7.6	8 18.7	13.0	61.1
21	131 34.5	.. 47.2	293 49.0	7.6	8 05.7	13.0	61.1
22	146 34.6	46.3	308 15.6	7.8	7 52.7	13.0	61.1
23	161 34.6	45.4	322 42.4	7.8	N 7 39.7	13.1	61.0
	SD 16.2	d 0.9	SD 16.7		16.7		16.7

Lat.	Twilight Naut.	Twilight Civil	Sunrise	Moonrise 18	19	20	21
°	h m	h m	h m	h m	h m	h m	h m
N 72	05 58	07 17	08 32	▭	14 56	17 24	19 38
N 70	05 58	07 09	08 16	13 00	15 26	17 39	19 42
68	05 58	07 03	08 03	13 42	15 48	17 50	19 46
66	05 58	06 57	07 52	14 11	16 05	17 59	19 49
64	05 57	06 53	07 43	14 32	16 19	18 07	19 51
62	05 57	06 49	07 35	14 49	16 31	18 13	19 53
60	05 56	06 45	07 28	15 04	16 41	18 19	19 55
N 58	05 56	06 41	07 22	15 16	16 49	18 24	19 57
56	05 55	06 38	07 17	15 27	16 57	18 28	19 58
54	05 55	06 36	07 12	15 36	17 03	18 32	19 59
52	05 54	06 33	07 08	15 44	17 09	18 36	20 01
50	05 53	06 31	07 04	15 51	17 15	18 39	20 02
45	05 51	06 25	06 55	16 07	17 26	18 46	20 04
N 40	05 49	06 21	06 48	16 20	17 36	18 52	20 06
35	05 47	06 16	06 42	16 31	17 44	18 57	20 08
30	05 44	06 12	06 37	16 41	17 51	19 01	20 09
20	05 39	06 05	06 27	16 57	18 04	19 09	20 12
N 10	05 32	05 57	06 19	17 12	18 15	19 16	20 14
0	05 25	05 49	06 10	17 25	18 25	19 22	20 16
S 10	05 16	05 41	06 02	17 38	18 35	19 28	20 18
20	05 04	05 31	05 53	17 53	18 46	19 35	20 21
30	04 49	05 18	05 43	18 09	18 58	19 42	20 23
35	04 40	05 11	05 37	18 18	19 05	19 47	20 25
40	04 28	05 02	05 30	18 29	19 13	19 51	20 26
45	04 13	04 51	05 23	18 42	19 22	19 57	20 28
S 50	03 55	04 38	05 13	18 57	19 33	20 04	20 31
52	03 46	04 32	05 08	19 04	19 38	20 07	20 32
54	03 35	04 25	05 03	19 12	19 44	20 10	20 33
56	03 23	04 17	04 58	19 21	19 50	20 14	20 34
58	03 09	04 08	04 52	19 31	19 57	20 18	20 36
S 60	02 51	03 57	04 45	19 42	20 05	20 23	20 37

Lat.	Sunset	Twilight Civil	Twilight Naut.	Moonset 18	19	20	21
°	h m	h m	h m	h m	h m	h m	h m
N 72	15 57	17 12	18 32	▭	09 43	09 16	08 57
N 70	16 13	17 20	18 31	09 31	09 11	08 59	08 50
68	16 27	17 26	18 31	08 48	08 48	08 46	08 44
66	16 37	17 32	18 31	08 18	08 30	08 35	08 39
64	16 46	17 36	18 32	07 56	08 15	08 26	08 35
62	16 54	17 40	18 32	07 38	08 02	08 18	08 31
60	17 01	17 44	18 33	07 23	07 51	08 11	08 27
N 58	17 07	17 47	18 33	07 10	07 42	08 05	08 25
56	17 12	17 50	18 34	06 59	07 33	08 00	08 22
54	17 17	17 53	18 34	06 50	07 26	07 55	08 20
52	17 21	17 55	18 35	06 41	07 19	07 51	08 17
50	17 25	17 58	18 35	06 33	07 13	07 47	08 15
45	17 33	18 03	18 37	06 16	07 00	07 38	08 11
N 40	17 40	18 08	18 39	06 03	06 50	07 31	08 07
35	17 46	18 12	18 41	05 51	06 40	07 24	08 04
30	17 52	18 16	18 44	05 41	06 32	07 19	08 01
20	18 01	18 23	18 49	05 23	06 18	07 09	07 56
N 10	18 09	18 31	18 55	05 07	06 05	07 00	07 52
0	18 17	18 38	19 03	04 53	05 54	06 52	07 48
S 10	18 25	18 47	19 12	04 38	05 42	06 44	07 44
20	18 34	18 57	19 23	04 22	05 29	06 35	07 39
30	18 44	19 09	19 38	04 04	05 14	06 25	07 34
35	18 50	19 16	19 47	03 53	05 06	06 19	07 31
40	18 56	19 25	19 59	03 41	04 56	06 12	07 27
45	19 04	19 35	20 13	03 26	04 44	06 04	07 23
S 50	19 14	19 48	20 31	03 09	04 30	05 55	07 18
52	19 18	19 55	20 40	03 00	04 24	05 50	07 16
54	19 23	20 02	20 51	02 51	04 16	05 45	07 13
56	19 28	20 09	21 02	02 40	04 08	05 40	07 11
58	19 34	20 18	21 16	02 28	03 59	05 34	07 08
S 60	19 41	20 29	21 33	02 14	03 48	05 27	07 04

Day	SUN Eqn. of Time 00h	12h	SUN Mer. Pass.	MOON Mer. Pass. Upper	Lower	Age	Phase
d	m s	m s	h m	h m	h m	d	%
18	13 58	13 56	12 14	23 39	11 09	14	98
19	13 53	13 51	12 14	24 39	12 09	15	100
20	13 48	13 45	12 14	00 39	13 07	16	99

© British Crown Copyright 2018. All rights reserved.

UT	ARIES GHA	VENUS −4.1 GHA	Dec	MARS +1.1 GHA	Dec	JUPITER −2.0 GHA	Dec	SATURN +0.6 GHA	Dec
21 00	150 37.5	219 27.8	S20 38.3	118 39.7	N13 31.4	250 31.2	S22 30.0	222 14.4	S21 55.3
01	165 40.0	234 27.1	38.0	133 40.6	32.0	265 33.3	30.0	237 16.6	55.2
02	180 42.4	249 26.4	37.7	148 41.4	32.6	280 35.4	30.1	252 18.8	55.2
03	195 44.9	264 25.8	37.5	163 42.3	33.2	295 37.5	30.1	267 21.0	55.2
04	210 47.3	279 25.1	37.2	178 43.1	33.8	310 39.6	30.1	282 23.3	55.1
05	225 49.8	294 24.5	37.0	193 44.0	34.4	325 41.7	30.1	297 25.5	55.1
06	240 52.3	309 23.8	S20 36.7	208 44.8	N13 35.0	340 43.8	S22 30.2	312 27.7	S21 55.1
07	255 54.7	324 23.1	36.4	223 45.6	35.6	355 45.9	30.2	327 29.9	55.1
T 08	270 57.2	339 22.5	36.2	238 46.5	36.2	10 48.0	30.2	342 32.1	55.0
H 09	285 59.7	354 21.8	35.9	253 47.3	36.8	25 50.1	30.2	357 34.3	55.0
U 10	301 02.1	9 21.2	35.6	268 48.2	37.4	40 52.2	30.2	12 36.5	55.0
R 11	316 04.6	24 20.5	35.3	283 49.0	38.0	55 54.3	30.3	27 38.7	54.9
S 12	331 07.1	39 19.8	S20 35.1	298 49.9	N13 38.6	70 56.4	S22 30.3	42 40.9	S21 54.9
D 13	346 09.5	54 19.2	34.8	313 50.7	39.2	85 58.5	30.3	57 43.2	54.9
A 14	1 12.0	69 18.5	34.5	328 51.5	39.7	101 00.6	30.3	72 45.4	54.9
Y 15	16 14.5	84 17.9	34.3	343 52.4	40.3	116 02.7	30.4	87 47.6	54.8
16	31 16.9	99 17.2	34.0	358 53.2	40.9	131 04.8	30.4	102 49.8	54.8
17	46 19.4	114 16.5	33.7	13 54.1	41.5	146 06.9	30.4	117 52.0	54.8
18	61 21.8	129 15.9	S20 33.4	28 54.9	N13 42.1	161 09.0	S22 30.4	132 54.2	S21 54.8
19	76 24.3	144 15.2	33.2	43 55.7	42.7	176 11.1	30.4	147 56.4	54.7
20	91 26.8	159 14.6	32.9	58 56.6	43.3	191 13.2	30.5	162 58.6	54.7
21	106 29.2	174 13.9	32.6	73 57.4	43.9	206 15.3	30.5	178 00.9	54.7
22	121 31.7	189 13.3	32.3	88 58.3	44.5	221 17.4	30.5	193 03.1	54.6
23	136 34.2	204 12.6	32.0	103 59.1	45.1	236 19.5	30.5	208 05.3	54.6
22 00	151 36.6	219 11.9	S20 31.7	118 59.9	N13 45.7	251 21.6	S22 30.6	223 07.5	S21 54.6
01	166 39.1	234 11.3	31.5	134 00.8	46.3	266 23.7	30.6	238 09.7	54.6
02	181 41.6	249 10.6	31.2	149 01.6	46.9	281 25.8	30.6	253 11.9	54.5
03	196 44.0	264 10.0	30.9	164 02.5	47.5	296 27.9	30.6	268 14.1	54.5
04	211 46.5	279 09.3	30.6	179 03.3	48.0	311 30.0	30.6	283 16.4	54.5
05	226 48.9	294 08.6	30.3	194 04.1	48.6	326 32.2	30.7	298 18.6	54.4
06	241 51.4	309 08.0	S20 30.0	209 05.0	N13 49.2	341 34.3	S22 30.7	313 20.8	S21 54.4
07	256 53.9	324 07.3	29.7	224 05.8	49.8	356 36.4	30.7	328 23.0	54.4
F 08	271 56.3	339 06.7	29.4	239 06.7	50.4	11 38.5	30.7	343 25.2	54.4
R 09	286 58.8	354 06.0	29.2	254 07.5	51.0	26 40.6	30.8	358 27.4	54.3
I 10	302 01.3	9 05.4	28.9	269 08.3	51.6	41 42.7	30.8	13 29.6	54.3
11	317 03.7	24 04.7	28.6	284 09.2	52.2	56 44.8	30.8	28 31.9	54.3
D 12	332 06.2	39 04.0	S20 28.3	299 10.0	N13 52.8	71 46.9	S22 30.8	43 34.1	S21 54.3
A 13	347 08.7	54 03.4	28.0	314 10.9	53.4	86 49.0	30.8	58 36.3	54.2
Y 14	2 11.1	69 02.7	27.7	329 11.7	53.9	101 51.1	30.9	73 38.5	54.2
15	17 13.6	84 02.1	27.4	344 12.5	54.5	116 53.2	30.9	88 40.7	54.2
16	32 16.1	99 01.4	27.1	359 13.4	55.1	131 55.3	30.9	103 42.9	54.1
17	47 18.5	114 00.7	26.8	14 14.2	55.7	146 57.5	30.9	118 45.1	54.1
18	62 21.0	129 00.1	S20 26.5	29 15.0	N13 56.3	161 59.6	S22 30.9	133 47.4	S21 54.1
19	77 23.4	143 59.4	26.2	44 15.9	56.9	177 01.7	31.0	148 49.6	54.1
20	92 25.9	158 58.8	25.9	59 16.7	57.5	192 03.8	31.0	163 51.8	54.0
21	107 28.4	173 58.1	25.6	74 17.6	58.1	207 05.9	31.0	178 54.0	54.0
22	122 30.8	188 57.5	25.3	89 18.4	58.7	222 08.0	31.0	193 56.2	54.0
23	137 33.3	203 56.8	25.0	104 19.2	59.2	237 10.1	31.0	208 58.4	53.9
23 00	152 35.8	218 56.1	S20 24.7	119 20.1	N13 59.8	252 12.2	S22 31.1	224 00.7	S21 53.9
01	167 38.2	233 55.5	24.3	134 20.9	14 00.4	267 14.3	31.1	239 02.9	53.9
02	182 40.7	248 54.8	24.0	149 21.7	01.0	282 16.5	31.1	254 05.1	53.9
03	197 43.2	263 54.2	23.7	164 22.6	01.6	297 18.6	31.1	269 07.3	53.8
04	212 45.6	278 53.5	23.4	179 23.4	02.2	312 20.7	31.2	284 09.5	53.8
05	227 48.1	293 52.9	23.1	194 24.3	02.8	327 22.8	31.2	299 11.7	53.8
06	242 50.5	308 52.2	S20 22.8	209 25.1	N14 03.4	342 24.9	S22 31.2	314 13.9	S21 53.8
07	257 53.0	323 51.5	22.5	224 25.9	03.9	357 27.0	31.2	329 16.2	53.7
S 08	272 55.5	338 50.9	22.2	239 26.8	04.5	12 29.1	31.2	344 18.4	53.7
A 09	287 57.9	353 50.2	21.8	254 27.6	05.1	27 31.2	31.3	359 20.6	53.7
T 10	303 00.4	8 49.6	21.5	269 28.4	05.7	42 33.4	31.3	14 22.8	53.6
U 11	318 02.9	23 48.9	21.2	284 29.3	06.3	57 35.5	31.3	29 25.0	53.6
R 12	333 05.3	38 48.2	S20 20.9	299 30.1	N14 06.9	72 37.6	S22 31.3	44 27.3	S21 53.6
D 13	348 07.8	53 47.6	20.6	314 30.9	07.4	87 39.7	31.3	59 29.5	53.6
A 14	3 10.3	68 46.9	20.3	329 31.8	08.0	102 41.8	31.4	74 31.7	53.5
Y 15	18 12.7	83 46.3	19.9	344 32.6	08.6	117 43.9	31.4	89 33.9	53.5
16	33 15.2	98 45.6	19.6	359 33.5	09.2	132 46.1	31.4	104 36.1	53.5
17	48 17.7	113 45.0	19.3	14 34.3	09.8	147 48.2	31.4	119 38.3	53.5
18	63 20.1	128 44.3	S20 19.0	29 35.1	N14 10.4	162 50.3	S22 31.4	134 40.6	S21 53.4
19	78 22.6	143 43.7	18.6	44 36.0	11.0	177 52.4	31.5	149 42.8	53.4
20	93 25.0	158 43.0	18.3	59 36.8	11.5	192 54.5	31.5	164 45.0	53.4
21	108 27.5	173 42.3	18.0	74 37.6	12.1	207 56.6	31.5	179 47.2	53.3
22	123 30.0	188 41.7	17.7	89 38.5	12.7	222 58.8	31.5	194 49.4	53.3
23	138 32.4	203 41.0	17.3	104 39.3	13.3	238 00.9	31.5	209 51.6	53.3
Mer.Pass.	h m 13 51.3	v −0.7	d 0.3	v 0.8	d 0.6	v 2.1	d 0.0	v 2.2	d 0.0

STARS

Name	SHA	Dec
Acamar	315 15.5	S40 14.1
Achernar	335 24.2	S57 08.8
Acrux	173 04.4	S63 12.1
Adhara	255 09.2	S29 00.2
Aldebaran	290 44.9	N16 32.7
Alioth	166 16.9	N55 51.2
Alkaid	152 55.6	N49 12.9
Alnair	27 39.3	S46 52.2
Alnilam	275 42.3	S 1 11.7
Alphard	217 52.0	S 8 44.6
Alphecca	126 07.7	N26 38.9
Alpheratz	357 39.8	N29 11.6
Altair	62 04.7	N 8 55.1
Ankaa	353 12.2	S42 12.4
Antares	112 21.5	S26 28.3
Arcturus	145 52.0	N19 04.9
Atria	107 20.0	S69 03.3
Avior	234 15.9	S59 34.5
Bellatrix	278 27.7	N 6 21.8
Betelgeuse	270 56.9	N 7 24.4
Canopus	263 54.1	S52 42.7
Capella	280 28.6	N46 01.0
Deneb	49 29.3	N45 20.8
Denebola	182 29.4	N14 27.8
Diphda	348 52.3	S17 53.2
Dubhe	193 46.3	N61 38.8
Elnath	278 07.6	N28 37.3
Eltanin	90 44.6	N51 29.0
Enif	33 43.6	N 9 57.6
Fomalhaut	15 20.1	S29 31.4
Gacrux	171 56.1	S57 13.0
Gienah	175 48.0	S17 38.8
Hadar	148 42.0	S60 27.6
Hamal	327 56.5	N23 33.0
Kaus Aust.	83 38.9	S34 22.3
Kochab	137 19.7	N74 04.4
Markab	13 34.8	N15 18.3
Menkar	314 11.1	N 4 09.6
Menkent	148 02.8	S36 27.6
Miaplacidus	221 38.0	S69 47.8
Mirfak	308 34.9	N49 55.7
Nunki	75 53.8	S26 16.3
Peacock	53 13.7	S56 40.3
Pollux	243 22.7	N27 58.7
Procyon	244 55.4	N 5 10.4
Rasalhague	96 03.0	N12 32.7
Regulus	207 39.1	N11 52.3
Rigel	281 08.2	S 8 11.1
Rigil Kent.	139 46.2	S60 54.5
Sabik	102 08.2	S15 44.8
Schedar	349 36.5	N56 38.5
Shaula	96 16.8	S37 06.8
Sirius	258 30.1	S16 44.8
Spica	158 27.0	S11 15.6
Suhail	222 49.2	S43 30.7
Vega	80 36.6	N38 47.9
Zuben'ubi	137 01.0	S16 07.1

	SHA	Mer.Pass.
	° ′	h m
Venus	67 35.3	9 24
Mars	327 23.3	16 03
Jupiter	99 45.0	7 14
Saturn	71 30.9	9 06

© British Crown Copyright 2018. All rights reserved.

INDEX TO SELECTED STARS, 2019

Name	No	Mag	SHA	Dec		No	Name	Mag	SHA	Dec
			°	°						°
Acamar	7	3·2	315	S 40		1	Alpheratz	2·1	358	N 29
Achernar	5	0·5	335	S 57		2	Ankaa	2·4	353	S 42
Acrux	30	1·3	173	S 63		3	Schedar	2·2	350	N 57
Adhara	19	1·5	255	S 29		4	Diphda	2·0	349	S 18
Aldebaran	10	0·9	291	N 17		5	Achernar	0·5	335	S 57
Alioth	32	1·8	166	N 56		6	Hamal	2·0	328	N 24
Alkaid	34	1·9	153	N 49		7	Acamar	3·2	315	S 40
Alnair	55	1·7	28	S 47		8	Menkar	2·5	314	N 4
Alnilam	15	1·7	276	S 1		9	Mirfak	1·8	309	N 50
Alphard	25	2·0	218	S 9		10	Aldebaran	0·9	291	N 17
Alphecca	41	2·2	126	N 27		11	Rigel	0·1	281	S 8
Alpheratz	1	2·1	358	N 29		12	Capella	0·1	280	N 46
Altair	51	0·8	62	N 9		13	Bellatrix	1·6	278	N 6
Ankaa	2	2·4	353	S 42		14	Elnath	1·7	278	N 29
Antares	42	1·0	112	S 26		15	Alnilam	1·7	276	S 1
Arcturus	37	0·0	146	N 19		16	Betelgeuse	Var.*	271	N 7
Atria	43	1·9	107	S 69		17	Canopus	−0·7	264	S 53
Avior	22	1·9	234	S 60		18	Sirius	−1·5	259	S 17
Bellatrix	13	1·6	278	N 6		19	Adhara	1·5	255	S 29
Betelgeuse	16	Var.*	271	N 7		20	Procyon	0·4	245	N 5
Canopus	17	−0·7	264	S 53		21	Pollux	1·1	243	N 28
Capella	12	0·1	280	N 46		22	Avior	1·9	234	S 60
Deneb	53	1·3	49	N 45		23	Suhail	2·2	223	S 44
Denebola	28	2·1	182	N 14		24	Miaplacidus	1·7	222	S 70
Diphda	4	2·0	349	S 18		25	Alphard	2·0	218	S 9
Dubhe	27	1·8	194	N 62		26	Regulus	1·4	208	N 12
Elnath	14	1·7	278	N 29		27	Dubhe	1·8	194	N 62
Eltanin	47	2·2	91	N 51		28	Denebola	2·1	182	N 14
Enif	54	2·4	34	N 10		29	Gienah	2·6	176	S 18
Fomalhaut	56	1·2	15	S 30		30	Acrux	1·3	173	S 63
Gacrux	31	1·6	172	S 57		31	Gacrux	1·6	172	S 57
Gienah	29	2·6	176	S 18		32	Alioth	1·8	166	N 56
Hadar	35	0·6	149	S 60		33	Spica	1·0	158	S 11
Hamal	6	2·0	328	N 24		34	Alkaid	1·9	153	N 49
Kaus Australis	48	1·9	84	S 34		35	Hadar	0·6	149	S 60
Kochab	40	2·1	137	N 74		36	Menkent	2·1	148	S 36
Markab	57	2·5	14	N 15		37	Arcturus	0·0	146	N 19
Menkar	8	2·5	314	N 4		38	Rigil Kentaurus	−0·3	140	S 61
Menkent	36	2·1	148	S 36		39	Zubenelgenubi	2·8	137	S 16
Miaplacidus	24	1·7	222	S 70		40	Kochab	2·1	137	N 74
Mirfak	9	1·8	309	N 50		41	Alphecca	2·2	126	N 27
Nunki	50	2·0	76	S 26		42	Antares	1·0	112	S 26
Peacock	52	1·9	53	S 57		43	Atria	1·9	107	S 69
Pollux	21	1·1	243	N 28		44	Sabik	2·4	102	S 16
Procyon	20	0·4	245	N 5		45	Shaula	1·6	96	S 37
Rasalhague	46	2·1	96	N 13		46	Rasalhague	2·1	96	N 13
Regulus	26	1·4	208	N 12		47	Eltanin	2·2	91	N 51
Rigel	11	0·1	281	S 8		48	Kaus Australis	1·9	84	S 34
Rigil Kentaurus	38	−0·3	140	S 61		49	Vega	0·0	81	N 39
Sabik	44	2·4	102	S 16		50	Nunki	2·0	76	S 26
Schedar	3	2·2	350	N 57		51	Altair	0·8	62	N 9
Shaula	45	1·6	96	S 37		52	Peacock	1·9	53	S 57
Sirius	18	−1·5	259	S 17		53	Deneb	1·3	49	N 45
Spica	33	1·0	158	S 11		54	Enif	2·4	34	N 10
Suhail	23	2·2	223	S 44		55	Alnair	1·7	28	S 47
Vega	49	0·0	81	N 39		56	Fomalhaut	1·2	15	S 30
Zubenelgenubi	39	2·8	137	S 16		57	Markab	2·5	14	N 15

*0·1 — 1·2

xxxiii

© British Crown Copyright 2018. All rights reserved.

ALTITUDE CORRECTION TABLES 0°–35°— MOON

App. Alt.	0°–4° Corrⁿ	5°–9° Corrⁿ	10°–14° Corrⁿ	15°–19° Corrⁿ	20°–24° Corrⁿ	25°–29° Corrⁿ	30°–34° Corrⁿ	App. Alt.
00	0 34·5	5 58·2	10 62·1	15 62·8	20 62·2	25 60·8	30 58·9	00
10	36·5	58·5	62·2	62·8	62·2	60·8	58·8	10
20	38·3	58·7	62·2	62·8	62·1	60·7	58·8	20
30	40·0	58·9	62·3	62·8	62·1	60·7	58·7	30
40	41·5	59·1	62·3	62·8	62·0	60·6	58·6	40
50	42·9	59·3	62·4	62·7	62·0	60·6	58·5	50
00	1 44·2	6 59·5	11 62·4	16 62·7	21 62·0	26 60·5	31 58·5	00
10	45·4	59·7	62·4	62·7	61·9	60·4	58·4	10
20	46·5	59·9	62·5	62·7	61·9	60·4	58·3	20
30	47·5	60·0	62·5	62·7	61·9	60·3	58·2	30
40	48·4	60·2	62·5	62·7	61·8	60·3	58·2	40
50	49·3	60·3	62·6	62·7	61·8	60·2	58·1	50
00	2 50·1	7 60·5	12 62·6	17 62·7	22 61·7	27 60·1	32 58·0	00
10	50·8	60·6	62·6	62·6	61·7	60·1	57·9	10
20	51·5	60·7	62·6	62·6	61·6	60·0	57·8	20
30	52·2	60·9	62·7	62·6	61·6	59·9	57·8	30
40	52·8	61·0	62·7	62·6	61·6	59·9	57·7	40
50	53·4	61·1	62·7	62·6	61·5	59·8	57·6	50
00	3 53·9	8 61·2	13 62·7	18 62·5	23 61·5	28 59·7	33 57·5	00
10	54·4	61·3	62·7	62·5	61·4	59·7	57·4	10
20	54·9	61·4	62·7	62·5	61·4	59·6	57·4	20
30	55·3	61·5	62·8	62·5	61·3	59·5	57·3	30
40	55·7	61·6	62·8	62·4	61·3	59·5	57·2	40
50	56·1	61·6	62·8	62·4	61·2	59·4	57·1	50
00	4 56·4	9 61·7	14 62·8	19 62·4	24 61·2	29 59·3	34 57·0	00
10	56·8	61·8	62·8	62·4	61·1	59·3	56·9	10
20	57·1	61·9	62·8	62·3	61·1	59·2	56·9	20
30	57·4	61·9	62·8	62·3	61·0	59·1	56·8	30
40	57·7	62·0	62·8	62·3	61·0	59·1	56·7	40
50	58·0	62·1	62·8	62·2	60·9	59·0	56·6	50

HP	L	U	L	U	L	U	L	U	L	U	L	U	L	U	HP
54·0	0·3	0·9	0·3	0·9	0·4	1·0	0·5	1·1	0·6	1·2	0·7	1·3	0·9	1·5	54·0
54·3	0·7	1·1	0·7	1·2	0·8	1·2	0·8	1·3	0·9	1·4	1·1	1·5	1·2	1·7	54·3
54·6	1·1	1·4	1·1	1·4	1·1	1·4	1·2	1·5	1·3	1·6	1·4	1·7	1·5	1·8	54·6
54·9	1·4	1·6	1·5	1·6	1·5	1·6	1·6	1·7	1·6	1·8	1·8	1·9	1·9	2·0	54·9
55·2	1·8	1·8	1·8	1·8	1·9	1·8	1·9	1·9	2·0	2·0	2·1	2·1	2·2	2·2	55·2
55·5	2·2	2·0	2·2	2·0	2·3	2·1	2·3	2·1	2·4	2·2	2·4	2·3	2·5	2·4	55·5
55·8	2·6	2·2	2·6	2·2	2·6	2·3	2·7	2·3	2·7	2·4	2·8	2·4	2·9	2·5	55·8
56·1	3·0	2·4	3·0	2·5	3·0	2·5	3·0	2·5	3·1	2·6	3·1	2·6	3·2	2·7	56·1
56·4	3·3	2·7	3·4	2·7	3·4	2·7	3·4	2·7	3·4	2·8	3·5	2·8	3·5	2·9	56·4
56·7	3·7	2·9	3·7	2·9	3·8	2·9	3·8	2·9	3·8	3·0	3·8	3·0	3·9	3·0	56·7
57·0	4·1	3·1	4·1	3·1	4·1	3·1	4·1	3·1	4·2	3·2	4·2	3·2	4·2	3·2	57·0
57·3	4·5	3·3	4·5	3·3	4·5	3·3	4·5	3·3	4·5	3·3	4·5	3·4	4·6	3·4	57·3
57·6	4·9	3·5	4·9	3·5	4·9	3·5	4·9	3·5	4·9	3·5	4·9	3·5	4·9	3·6	57·6
57·9	5·3	3·8	5·3	3·8	5·2	3·8	5·2	3·7	5·2	3·7	5·2	3·7	5·2	3·7	57·9
58·2	5·6	4·0	5·6	4·0	5·6	4·0	5·6	4·0	5·6	3·9	5·6	3·9	5·6	3·9	58·2
58·5	6·0	4·2	6·0	4·2	6·0	4·2	6·0	4·2	6·0	4·1	5·9	4·1	5·9	4·1	58·5
58·8	6·4	4·4	6·4	4·4	6·4	4·4	6·3	4·4	6·3	4·3	6·3	4·3	6·2	4·2	58·8
59·1	6·8	4·6	6·8	4·6	6·7	4·6	6·7	4·6	6·7	4·5	6·6	4·5	6·6	4·4	59·1
59·4	7·2	4·8	7·1	4·8	7·1	4·8	7·1	4·8	7·0	4·7	7·0	4·7	6·9	4·6	59·4
59·7	7·5	5·1	7·5	5·0	7·5	5·0	7·5	5·0	7·4	4·9	7·3	4·8	7·2	4·8	59·7
60·0	7·9	5·3	7·9	5·3	7·9	5·2	7·8	5·2	7·8	5·1	7·7	5·0	7·6	4·9	60·0
60·3	8·3	5·5	8·3	5·5	8·2	5·4	8·2	5·4	8·1	5·3	8·0	5·2	7·9	5·1	60·3
60·6	8·7	5·7	8·7	5·7	8·6	5·7	8·6	5·6	8·5	5·5	8·4	5·4	8·2	5·3	60·6
60·9	9·1	5·9	9·0	5·9	9·0	5·9	8·9	5·8	8·8	5·7	8·7	5·6	8·6	5·4	60·9
61·2	9·5	6·2	9·4	6·1	9·4	6·1	9·3	6·0	9·2	5·9	9·1	5·8	8·9	5·6	61·2
61·5	9·8	6·4	9·8	6·3	9·7	6·3	9·7	6·2	9·5	6·1	9·4	5·8	9·2	5·8	61·5

DIP

Ht. of Eye	Corrⁿ	Ht. of Eye	Ht. of Eye	Corrⁿ	Ht. of Eye
m		ft.	m		ft.
2·4	−2·8	8·0	9·5	−5·5	31·5
2·6	−2·9	8·6	9·9	−5·6	32·7
2·8	−3·0	9·2	10·3	−5·7	33·9
3·0	−3·1	9·8	10·6	−5·8	35·1
3·2	−3·2	10·5	11·0	−5·9	36·3
3·4	−3·3	11·2	11·4	−6·0	37·6
3·6	−3·4	11·9	11·8	−6·1	38·9
3·8	−3·5	12·6	12·2	−6·2	40·1
4·0	−3·6	13·3	12·6	−6·3	41·5
4·3	−3·7	14·1	13·0	−6·4	42·8
4·5	−3·8	14·9	13·4	−6·5	44·2
4·7	−3·9	15·7	13·8	−6·6	45·5
5·0	−4·0	16·5	14·2	−6·7	46·9
5·2	−4·1	17·4	14·7	−6·8	48·4
5·5	−4·2	18·3	15·1	−6·9	49·8
5·8	−4·3	19·1	15·5	−7·0	51·3
6·1	−4·4	20·1	16·0	−7·1	52·8
6·3	−4·5	21·0	16·5	−7·2	54·3
6·6	−4·6	22·0	16·9	−7·3	55·8
6·9	−4·7	22·9	17·4	−7·4	57·4
7·2	−4·8	23·9	17·9	−7·5	58·9
7·5	−4·9	24·9	18·4	−7·6	60·5
7·9	−5·0	26·0	18·8	−7·7	62·1
8·2	−5·1	27·1	19·3	−7·8	63·8
8·5	−5·2	28·1	19·8	−7·9	65·4
8·8	−5·3	29·2	20·4	−8·0	67·1
9·2	−5·4	30·4	20·9	−8·1	68·8
9·5		31·5	21·4		70·5

MOON CORRECTION TABLE

The correction is in two parts; the first correction is taken from the upper part of the table with argument apparent altitude, and the second from the lower part, with argument HP, in the same column as that from which the first correction was taken. Separate corrections are given in the lower part for lower (L) and upper(U) limbs. All corrections are to be **added** to apparent altitude, *but 30′ is to be subtracted from the altitude of the upper limb.*

For corrections for pressure and temperature see page A4.

For bubble sextant observations ignore dip, take the mean of upper and lower limb corrections and subtract 15′ from the altitude.

App. Alt. = Apparent altitude = Sextant altitude corrected for index error and dip.

© British Crown Copyright 2018. All rights reserved.

UT	SUN GHA	SUN Dec	MOON GHA	v	Dec	d	HP
d h	° ′	° ′	° ′	′	° ′	′	′
21 00	176 34.7	S10 44.5	337 09.2	7.8	N 7 26.6	13.2	61.0
01	191 34.8	43.6	351 36.0	7.9	7 13.4	13.1	61.0
02	206 34.8	42.7	6 02.9	8.0	7 00.3	13.2	61.0
03	221 34.9	.. 41.8	20 29.9	8.0	6 47.1	13.2	60.9
04	236 35.0	40.9	34 56.9	8.1	6 33.9	13.3	60.9
05	251 35.1	40.0	49 24.0	8.2	6 20.6	13.3	60.9
06	266 35.1	S10 39.1	63 51.2	8.2	N 6 07.3	13.3	60.9
07	281 35.2	38.2	78 18.4	8.3	5 54.0	13.3	60.8
T 08	296 35.3	37.3	92 45.7	8.4	5 40.7	13.4	60.8
H 09	311 35.3	.. 36.4	107 13.1	8.4	5 27.3	13.4	60.8
U 10	326 35.4	35.5	121 40.5	8.4	5 13.9	13.4	60.8
R 11	341 35.5	34.6	136 07.9	8.5	5 00.5	13.4	60.7
S 12	356 35.6	S10 33.7	150 35.4	8.6	N 4 47.1	13.4	60.7
D 13	11 35.6	32.8	165 03.0	8.6	4 33.7	13.5	60.7
A 14	26 35.7	31.9	179 30.6	8.7	4 20.2	13.5	60.7
Y 15	41 35.8	.. 30.9	193 58.3	8.8	4 06.7	13.4	60.6
16	56 35.9	30.0	208 26.1	8.8	3 53.3	13.5	60.6
17	71 35.9	29.1	222 53.9	8.8	3 39.8	13.5	60.6
18	86 36.0	S10 28.2	237 21.7	8.9	N 3 26.3	13.5	60.5
19	101 36.1	27.3	251 49.6	9.0	3 12.8	13.5	60.5
20	116 36.2	26.4	266 17.6	9.0	2 59.3	13.6	60.5
21	131 36.2	.. 25.5	280 45.6	9.0	2 45.7	13.5	60.4
22	146 36.3	24.6	295 13.6	9.1	2 32.2	13.5	60.4
23	161 36.4	23.7	309 41.7	9.2	2 18.7	13.5	60.4
22 00	176 36.5	S10 22.8	324 09.9	9.2	N 2 05.2	13.5	60.4
01	191 36.5	21.9	338 38.1	9.2	1 51.7	13.5	60.3
02	206 36.6	21.0	353 06.3	9.3	1 38.2	13.5	60.3
03	221 36.7	.. 20.1	7 34.6	9.4	1 24.7	13.5	60.3
04	236 36.8	19.2	22 03.0	9.4	1 11.2	13.5	60.2
05	251 36.9	18.2	36 31.4	9.4	0 57.7	13.5	60.2
06	266 36.9	S10 17.3	50 59.8	9.5	N 0 44.2	13.4	60.2
07	281 37.0	16.4	65 28.3	9.5	0 30.8	13.5	60.1
F 08	296 37.1	15.5	79 56.8	9.6	0 17.3	13.4	60.1
R 09	311 37.2	.. 14.6	94 25.4	9.6	N 0 03.9	13.4	60.0
I 10	326 37.3	13.7	108 54.0	9.7	S 0 09.5	13.4	60.0
11	341 37.3	12.8	123 22.7	9.7	0 22.9	13.4	60.0
D 12	356 37.4	S10 11.9	137 51.4	9.7	S 0 36.3	13.4	59.9
A 13	11 37.5	11.0	152 20.1	9.8	0 49.7	13.3	59.9
Y 14	26 37.6	10.1	166 48.9	9.8	1 03.0	13.3	59.9
15	41 37.7	.. 09.1	181 17.7	9.9	1 16.3	13.3	59.8
16	56 37.7	08.2	195 46.6	9.9	1 29.6	13.3	59.8
17	71 37.8	07.3	210 15.5	9.9	1 42.9	13.2	59.8
18	86 37.9	S10 06.4	224 44.4	10.0	S 1 56.1	13.3	59.7
19	101 38.0	05.5	239 13.4	10.0	2 09.4	13.1	59.7
20	116 38.1	04.6	253 42.4	10.0	2 22.5	13.2	59.6
21	131 38.1	.. 03.7	268 11.4	10.1	2 35.7	13.1	59.6
22	146 38.2	02.8	282 40.5	10.1	2 48.8	13.1	59.6
23	161 38.3	01.8	297 09.6	10.1	3 01.9	13.0	59.5
23 00	176 38.4	S10 00.9	311 38.7	10.2	S 3 14.9	13.0	59.5
01	191 38.5	10 00.0	326 07.9	10.2	3 27.9	13.0	59.5
02	206 38.6	9 59.1	340 37.1	10.2	3 40.9	13.0	59.4
03	221 38.6	.. 58.2	355 06.3	10.2	3 53.9	12.9	59.4
04	236 38.7	57.3	9 35.5	10.3	4 06.8	12.8	59.3
05	251 38.8	56.4	24 04.8	10.3	4 19.6	12.8	59.3
06	266 38.9	S 9 55.4	38 34.1	10.4	S 4 32.4	12.8	59.3
07	281 39.0	54.5	53 03.5	10.3	4 45.2	12.7	59.2
S 08	296 39.1	53.6	67 32.8	10.4	4 57.9	12.7	59.2
A 09	311 39.1	.. 52.7	82 02.2	10.5	5 10.6	12.7	59.1
T 10	326 39.2	51.8	96 31.7	10.4	5 23.3	12.5	59.1
U 11	341 39.3	50.9	111 01.1	10.5	5 35.8	12.6	59.1
R 12	356 39.4	S 9 49.9	125 30.6	10.5	S 5 48.4	12.5	59.0
D 13	11 39.5	49.0	140 00.1	10.5	6 00.9	12.4	59.0
A 14	26 39.6	48.1	154 29.6	10.5	6 13.3	12.4	58.9
Y 15	41 39.7	.. 47.2	168 59.1	10.5	6 25.7	12.3	58.9
16	56 39.7	46.3	183 28.6	10.6	6 38.0	12.3	58.9
17	71 39.8	45.3	197 58.2	10.6	6 50.3	12.3	58.8
18	86 39.9	S 9 44.4	212 27.8	10.6	S 7 02.6	12.1	58.8
19	101 40.0	43.5	226 57.4	10.7	7 14.7	12.1	58.7
20	116 40.1	42.6	241 27.1	10.6	7 26.8	12.1	58.7
21	131 40.2	.. 41.7	255 56.7	10.7	7 38.9	12.0	58.7
22	146 40.3	40.8	270 26.4	10.7	7 50.9	11.9	58.6
23	161 40.4	39.8	284 56.1	10.7	S 8 02.8	11.9	58.6
	SD 16.2	d 0.9	SD 16.5		16.3		16.1

Lat.	Twilight Naut.	Twilight Civil	Sunrise	Moonrise 21	22	23	24
°	h m	h m	h m	h m	h m	h m	h m
N 72	05 45	07 03	08 16	19 38	21 45	23 49	25 58
N 70	05 46	06 57	08 02	19 42	21 41	23 36	25 32
68	05 47	06 52	07 50	19 46	21 37	23 26	25 12
66	05 48	06 47	07 40	19 49	21 34	23 17	24 57
64	05 48	06 43	07 32	19 51	21 32	23 10	24 44
62	05 49	06 40	07 26	19 53	21 30	23 03	24 34
60	05 49	06 37	07 20	19 55	21 28	22 58	24 25
N 58	05 49	06 34	07 14	19 57	21 27	22 53	24 17
56	05 49	06 32	07 10	19 58	21 25	22 49	24 10
54	05 48	06 29	07 05	19 59	21 24	22 45	24 04
52	05 48	06 27	07 02	20 01	21 23	22 42	23 58
50	05 48	06 25	06 58	20 02	21 22	22 39	23 53
45	05 47	06 21	06 50	20 04	21 19	22 32	23 42
N 40	05 45	06 17	06 44	20 06	21 18	22 27	23 34
35	05 43	06 13	06 38	20 08	21 16	22 22	23 26
30	05 42	06 09	06 34	20 09	21 15	22 18	23 19
20	05 37	06 03	06 25	20 12	21 12	22 11	23 08
N 10	05 31	05 56	06 17	20 14	21 10	22 05	22 58
0	05 25	05 49	06 10	20 16	21 08	21 59	22 49
S 10	05 16	05 41	06 03	20 18	21 06	21 53	22 39
20	05 06	05 32	05 55	20 21	21 04	21 47	22 30
30	04 52	05 21	05 46	20 23	21 02	21 40	22 19
35	04 43	05 14	05 40	20 25	21 01	21 36	22 12
40	04 32	05 06	05 34	20 26	20 59	21 32	22 05
45	04 19	04 56	05 27	20 28	20 58	21 27	21 57
S 50	04 01	04 44	05 18	20 31	20 56	21 21	21 47
52	03 53	04 38	05 14	20 32	20 55	21 18	21 42
54	03 43	04 31	05 10	20 33	20 54	21 15	21 37
56	03 32	04 24	05 05	20 34	20 53	21 12	21 32
58	03 19	04 16	04 59	20 36	20 52	21 08	21 25
S 60	03 03	04 06	04 53	20 37	20 50	21 04	21 18

Lat.	Sunset	Twilight Civil	Twilight Naut.	Moonset 21	22	23	24
°	h m	h m	h m	h m	h m	h m	h m
N 72	16 13	17 26	18 45	08 57	08 41	08 25	08 08
N 70	16 27	17 32	18 43	08 50	08 41	08 33	08 23
68	16 39	17 37	18 42	08 44	08 41	08 38	08 36
66	16 48	17 41	18 41	08 39	08 41	08 43	08 46
64	16 56	17 45	18 40	08 35	08 41	08 48	08 54
62	17 03	17 48	18 40	08 31	08 41	08 51	09 02
60	17 09	17 51	18 40	08 27	08 41	08 54	09 08
N 58	17 14	17 54	18 40	08 25	08 41	08 57	09 14
56	17 18	17 56	18 40	08 22	08 41	09 00	09 19
54	17 23	17 59	18 40	08 20	08 41	09 02	09 24
52	17 26	18 01	18 40	08 17	08 41	09 04	09 28
50	17 30	18 03	18 40	08 15	08 41	09 06	09 32
45	17 37	18 07	18 41	08 11	08 41	09 10	09 40
N 40	17 44	18 11	18 42	08 07	08 41	09 14	09 47
35	17 49	18 15	18 44	08 04	08 41	09 17	09 53
30	17 54	18 18	18 46	08 01	08 41	09 20	09 58
20	18 02	18 25	18 50	07 56	08 41	09 24	10 07
N 10	18 10	18 31	18 56	07 52	08 41	09 28	10 15
0	18 17	18 38	19 02	07 48	08 41	09 32	10 23
S 10	18 24	18 45	19 10	07 44	08 41	09 36	10 30
20	18 32	18 54	19 21	07 39	08 41	09 40	10 38
30	18 41	19 06	19 35	07 34	08 41	09 45	10 47
35	18 46	19 12	19 43	07 31	08 40	09 48	10 53
40	18 52	19 20	19 54	07 27	08 40	09 51	10 59
45	18 59	19 30	20 07	07 23	08 40	09 54	11 06
S 50	19 08	19 42	20 24	07 18	08 40	09 59	11 15
52	19 12	19 48	20 33	07 16	08 40	10 01	11 19
54	19 16	19 54	20 42	07 14	08 40	10 03	11 23
56	19 21	20 01	20 53	07 11	08 40	10 05	11 28
58	19 26	20 09	21 06	07 08	08 39	10 08	11 33
S 60	19 32	20 19	21 21	07 04	08 39	10 11	11 39

Day	SUN Eqn. of Time 00h	SUN Eqn. of Time 12h	SUN Mer. Pass.	MOON Mer. Pass. Upper	MOON Mer. Pass. Lower	Age	Phase
d	m s	m s	h m	h m	h m	d	%
21	13 41	13 38	12 14	01 35	14 02	17	95
22	13 34	13 31	12 14	02 29	14 55	18	88
23	13 27	13 23	12 13	03 20	15 46	19	80

© British Crown Copyright 2018. All rights reserved.

UT	ARIES GHA	VENUS −4.1 GHA	Dec	MARS +1.1 GHA	Dec	JUPITER −2.0 GHA	Dec	SATURN +0.6 GHA	Dec	STARS Name	SHA	Dec
24 00	153 34.9	218 40.4	S20 17.0	119 40.1	N14 13.9	253 03.0	S22 31.6	224 53.9	S21 53.3	Acamar	315 15.5	S40 14.1
01	168 37.4	233 39.7	16.7	134 41.0	14.5	268 05.1	31.6	239 56.1	53.2	Achernar	335 24.2	S57 08.8
02	183 39.8	248 39.1	16.3	149 41.8	15.0	283 07.2	31.6	254 58.3	53.2	Acrux	173 04.3	S63 12.1
03	198 42.3	263 38.4 ..	16.0	164 42.6 ..	15.6	298 09.3 ..	31.6	270 00.5 ..	53.2	Adhara	255 09.2	S29 00.2
04	213 44.8	278 37.7	15.7	179 43.5	16.2	313 11.5	31.7	285 02.7	53.1	Aldebaran	290 44.9	N16 32.7
05	228 47.2	293 37.1	15.3	194 44.3	16.8	328 13.6	31.7	300 05.0	53.1			
06	243 49.7	308 36.4	S20 15.0	209 45.1	N14 17.4	343 15.7	S22 31.7	315 07.2	S21 53.1	Alioth	166 16.8	N55 51.2
07	258 52.2	323 35.8	14.6	224 46.0	17.9	358 17.8	31.7	330 09.4	53.1	Alkaid	152 55.5	N49 12.9
S 08	273 54.6	338 35.1	14.3	239 46.8	18.5	13 19.9	31.7	345 11.6	53.0	Alnair	27 39.3	S46 52.2
U 09	288 57.1	353 34.5 ..	14.0	254 47.6 ..	19.1	28 22.1 ..	31.8	0 13.8 ..	53.0	Alnilam	275 42.3	S 1 11.7
N 10	303 59.5	8 33.8	13.6	269 48.5	19.7	43 24.2	31.8	15 16.1	53.0	Alphard	217 52.0	S 8 44.6
D 11	319 02.0	23 33.2	13.3	284 49.3	20.3	58 26.3	31.8	30 18.3	53.0			
A 12	334 04.5	38 32.5	S20 12.9	299 50.1	N14 20.8	73 28.4	S22 31.8	45 20.5	S21 52.9	Alphecca	126 07.7	N26 38.9
Y 13	349 06.9	53 31.8	12.6	314 51.0	21.4	88 30.5	31.8	60 22.7	52.9	Alpheratz	357 39.8	N29 11.6
14	4 09.4	68 31.2	12.3	329 51.8	22.0	103 32.7	31.9	75 24.9	52.9	Altair	62 04.7	N 8 55.1
15	19 11.9	83 30.5 ..	11.9	344 52.6 ..	22.6	118 34.8 ..	31.9	90 27.2 ..	52.8	Ankaa	353 12.2	S42 12.4
16	34 14.3	98 29.9	11.6	359 53.5	23.2	133 36.9	31.9	105 29.4	52.8	Antares	112 21.5	S26 28.3
17	49 16.8	113 29.2	11.2	14 54.3	23.7	148 39.0	31.9	120 31.6	52.8			
18	64 19.3	128 28.6	S20 10.9	29 55.1	N14 24.3	163 41.1	S22 31.9	135 33.8	S21 52.8	Arcturus	145 52.0	N19 04.9
19	79 21.7	143 27.9	10.5	44 56.0	24.9	178 43.3	32.0	150 36.0	52.7	Atria	107 19.9	S69 03.3
20	94 24.2	158 27.3	10.2	59 56.8	25.5	193 45.4	32.0	165 38.3	52.7	Avior	234 15.9	S59 34.5
21	109 26.7	173 26.6 ..	09.8	74 57.6 ..	26.1	208 47.5 ..	32.0	180 40.5 ..	52.7	Bellatrix	278 27.7	N 6 21.8
22	124 29.1	188 26.0	09.5	89 58.5	26.6	223 49.6	32.0	195 42.7	52.7	Betelgeuse	270 57.0	N 7 24.4
23	139 31.6	203 25.3	09.1	104 59.3	27.2	238 51.8	32.0	210 44.9	52.6			
25 00	154 34.0	218 24.6	S20 08.7	120 00.1	N14 27.8	253 53.9	S22 32.1	225 47.1	S21 52.6	Canopus	263 54.1	S52 42.7
01	169 36.5	233 24.0	08.4	135 01.0	28.4	268 56.0	32.1	240 49.4	52.6	Capella	280 28.6	N46 01.0
02	184 39.0	248 23.3	08.0	150 01.8	28.9	283 58.1	32.1	255 51.6	52.5	Deneb	49 29.3	N45 20.8
03	199 41.4	263 22.7 ..	07.7	165 02.6 ..	29.5	299 00.3 ..	32.1	270 53.8 ..	52.5	Denebola	182 29.4	N14 27.8
04	214 43.9	278 22.0	07.3	180 03.4	30.1	314 02.4	32.1	285 56.0	52.5	Diphda	348 52.3	S17 53.2
05	229 46.4	293 21.4	07.0	195 04.3	30.7	329 04.5	32.1	300 58.2	52.5			
06	244 48.8	308 20.7	S20 06.6	210 05.1	N14 31.3	344 06.6	S22 32.2	316 00.5	S21 52.4	Dubhe	193 46.3	N61 38.8
07	259 51.3	323 20.1	06.2	225 05.9	31.8	359 08.8	32.2	331 02.7	52.4	Elnath	278 07.6	N28 37.3
M 08	274 53.8	338 19.4	05.9	240 06.8	32.4	14 10.9	32.2	346 04.9	52.4	Eltanin	90 44.6	N51 29.0
O 09	289 56.2	353 18.8 ..	05.5	255 07.6 ..	33.0	29 13.0 ..	32.2	1 07.1 ..	52.4	Enif	33 43.6	N 9 57.6
N 10	304 58.7	8 18.1	05.1	270 08.4	33.6	44 15.1	32.2	16 09.4	52.3	Fomalhaut	15 20.1	S29 31.4
D 11	320 01.1	23 17.5	04.8	285 09.3	34.1	59 17.3	32.3	31 11.6	52.3			
A 12	335 03.6	38 16.8	S20 04.4	300 10.1	N14 34.7	74 19.4	S22 32.3	46 13.8	S21 52.3	Gacrux	171 56.1	S57 13.0
Y 13	350 06.1	53 16.1	04.0	315 10.9	35.3	89 21.5	32.3	61 16.0	52.2	Gienah	175 48.0	S17 38.9
14	5 08.5	68 15.5	03.7	330 11.8	35.9	104 23.6	32.3	76 18.2	52.2	Hadar	148 42.0	S60 27.6
15	20 11.0	83 14.8 ..	03.3	345 12.6 ..	36.4	119 25.8 ..	32.3	91 20.5 ..	52.2	Hamal	327 56.6	N23 33.0
16	35 13.5	98 14.2	02.9	0 13.4	37.0	134 27.9	32.4	106 22.7	52.2	Kaus Aust.	83 38.9	S34 22.3
17	50 15.9	113 13.5	02.6	15 14.2	37.6	149 30.0	32.4	121 24.9	52.1			
18	65 18.4	128 12.9	S20 02.2	30 15.1	N14 38.2	164 32.2	S22 32.4	136 27.1	S21 52.1	Kochab	137 19.7	N74 04.4
19	80 20.9	143 12.2	01.8	45 15.9	38.7	179 34.3	32.4	151 29.4	52.1	Markab	13 34.8	N15 18.3
20	95 23.3	158 11.6	01.4	60 16.7	39.3	194 36.4	32.4	166 31.6	52.1	Menkar	314 11.1	N 4 09.6
21	110 25.8	173 10.9 ..	01.1	75 17.6 ..	39.9	209 38.5 ..	32.5	181 33.8 ..	52.0	Menkent	148 02.8	S36 27.6
22	125 28.3	188 10.3	00.7	90 18.4	40.5	224 40.7	32.5	196 36.0	52.0	Miaplacidus	221 38.0	S69 47.9
23	140 30.7	203 09.6	20 00.3	105 19.2	41.0	239 42.8	32.5	211 38.3	52.0			
26 00	155 33.2	218 09.0	S19 59.9	120 20.0	N14 41.6	254 44.9	S22 32.5	226 40.5	S21 51.9	Mirfak	308 34.9	N49 55.7
01	170 35.6	233 08.3	59.6	135 20.9	42.2	269 47.1	32.5	241 42.7	51.9	Nunki	75 53.7	S26 16.2
02	185 38.1	248 07.7	59.2	150 21.7	42.7	284 49.2	32.6	256 44.9	51.9	Peacock	53 13.7	S56 40.3
03	200 40.6	263 07.0 ..	58.8	165 22.5 ..	43.3	299 51.3 ..	32.6	271 47.2 ..	51.9	Pollux	243 22.7	N27 58.7
04	215 43.0	278 06.4	58.4	180 23.4	43.9	314 53.5	32.6	286 49.4	51.8	Procyon	244 55.4	N 5 10.4
05	230 45.5	293 05.7	58.0	195 24.2	44.5	329 55.6	32.6	301 51.6	51.8			
06	245 48.0	308 05.1	S19 57.6	210 25.0	N14 45.0	344 57.7	S22 32.6	316 53.8	S21 51.8	Rasalhague	96 03.0	N12 32.7
07	260 50.4	323 04.4	57.3	225 25.8	45.6	359 59.8	32.6	331 56.1	51.8	Regulus	207 39.1	N11 52.3
T 08	275 52.9	338 03.8	56.9	240 26.7	46.2	15 02.0	32.7	346 58.3	51.7	Rigel	281 08.2	S 8 11.1
U 09	290 55.4	353 03.1 ..	56.5	255 27.5 ..	46.7	30 04.1 ..	32.7	2 00.5 ..	51.7	Rigil Kent.	139 46.2	S60 54.5
E 10	305 57.8	8 02.5	56.1	270 28.3	47.3	45 06.2	32.7	17 02.7	51.7	Sabik	102 08.2	S15 44.8
S 11	321 00.3	23 01.8	55.7	285 29.2	47.9	60 08.4	32.7	32 05.0	51.6			
D 12	336 02.7	38 01.2	S19 55.3	300 30.0	N14 48.5	75 10.5	S22 32.7	47 07.2	S21 51.6	Schedar	349 36.6	N56 38.5
A 13	351 05.2	53 00.5	54.9	315 30.8	49.0	90 12.6	32.8	62 09.4	51.6	Shaula	96 16.8	S37 06.8
Y 14	6 07.7	67 59.9	54.5	330 31.6	49.6	105 14.8	32.8	77 11.6	51.6	Sirius	258 30.1	S16 44.9
15	21 10.1	82 59.2 ..	54.1	345 32.5 ..	50.2	120 16.9 ..	32.8	92 13.9 ..	51.5	Spica	158 26.9	S11 15.6
16	36 12.6	97 58.6	53.7	0 33.3	50.7	135 19.0	32.8	107 16.1	51.5	Suhail	222 49.2	S43 30.8
17	51 15.1	112 57.9	53.3	15 34.1	51.3	150 21.2	32.8	122 18.3	51.5			
18	66 17.5	127 57.3	S19 53.0	30 34.9	N14 51.9	165 23.3	S22 32.9	137 20.5	S21 51.5	Vega	80 36.6	N38 47.9
19	81 20.0	142 56.6	52.6	45 35.8	52.4	180 25.4	32.9	152 22.8	51.4	Zuben'ubi	137 01.0	S16 07.1
20	96 22.5	157 56.0	52.2	60 36.6	53.0	195 27.6	32.9	167 25.0	51.4		SHA	Mer.Pass.
21	111 24.9	172 55.3 ..	51.8	75 37.4 ..	53.6	210 29.7 ..	32.9	182 27.2 ..	51.4			
22	126 27.4	187 54.7	51.4	90 38.3	54.1	225 31.9	32.9	197 29.4	51.4	Venus	63 50.6	9 27
23	141 29.9	202 54.0	51.0	105 39.1	54.7	240 34.0	32.9	212 31.7	51.3	Mars	325 26.1	15 59
Mer.Pass. 13 39.5		v −0.7	d 0.4	v 0.8	d 0.6	v 2.1	d 0.0	v 2.2	d 0.0	Jupiter	99 19.8	7 03
										Saturn	71 13.1	8 56

© British Crown Copyright 2018. All rights reserved.

UT	SUN GHA	SUN Dec	MOON GHA	v	MOON Dec	d	HP
d h	° ′	° ′	° ′	′	° ′	′	′
24 00	176 40.5	S 9 38.9	299 25.8	10.7	S 8 14.7	11.8	58.5
01	191 40.5	38.0	313 55.5	10.7	8 26.5	11.8	58.5
02	206 40.6	37.1	328 25.2	10.7	8 38.3	11.7	58.4
03	221 40.7	.. 36.2	342 54.9	10.8	8 50.0	11.6	58.4
04	236 40.8	35.2	357 24.7	10.8	9 01.6	11.6	58.4
05	251 40.9	34.3	11 54.5	10.7	9 13.2	11.5	58.3
06	266 41.0	S 9 33.4	26 24.2	10.8	S 9 24.7	11.4	58.3
07	281 41.1	32.5	40 54.0	10.8	9 36.1	11.3	58.2
08	296 41.2	31.5	55 23.8	10.9	9 47.4	11.3	58.2
09	311 41.3	.. 30.6	69 53.7	10.8	9 58.7	11.3	58.2
10	326 41.4	29.7	84 23.5	10.8	10 10.0	11.1	58.1
11	341 41.5	28.8	98 53.3	10.9	10 21.1	11.1	58.1
12	356 41.5	S 9 27.9	113 23.2	10.8	S10 32.2	11.0	58.0
13	11 41.6	26.9	127 53.0	10.9	10 43.2	10.9	58.0
14	26 41.7	26.0	142 22.9	10.8	10 54.1	10.9	58.0
15	41 41.8	.. 25.1	156 52.7	10.9	11 05.0	10.8	57.9
16	56 41.9	24.2	171 22.6	10.9	11 15.8	10.7	57.9
17	71 42.0	23.2	185 52.5	10.9	11 26.5	10.7	57.8
18	86 42.1	S 9 22.3	200 22.4	10.9	S11 37.2	10.5	57.8
19	101 42.2	21.4	214 52.3	10.9	11 47.7	10.5	57.8
20	116 42.3	20.5	229 22.2	10.9	11 58.2	10.4	57.7
21	131 42.4	.. 19.5	243 52.1	10.9	12 08.6	10.4	57.7
22	146 42.5	18.6	258 22.0	10.9	12 19.0	10.2	57.6
23	161 42.6	17.7	272 51.9	10.9	12 29.2	10.2	57.6
25 00	176 42.7	S 9 16.8	287 21.8	10.9	S12 39.4	10.1	57.6
01	191 42.8	15.8	301 51.7	11.0	12 49.5	10.0	57.5
02	206 42.9	14.9	316 21.7	10.9	12 59.5	9.9	57.5
03	221 43.0	.. 14.0	330 51.6	10.9	13 09.4	9.9	57.4
04	236 43.1	13.0	345 21.5	11.0	13 19.3	9.7	57.4
05	251 43.1	12.1	359 51.5	10.9	13 29.0	9.7	57.4
06	266 43.2	S 9 11.2	14 21.4	10.9	S13 38.7	9.6	57.3
07	281 43.3	10.3	28 51.3	10.9	13 48.3	9.5	57.3
08	296 43.4	09.3	43 21.2	11.0	13 57.8	9.5	57.2
09	311 43.5	.. 08.4	57 51.2	10.9	14 07.3	9.3	57.2
10	326 43.6	07.5	72 21.1	11.0	14 16.6	9.3	57.2
11	341 43.7	06.5	86 51.1	10.9	14 25.9	9.1	57.1
12	356 43.8	S 9 05.6	101 21.0	10.9	S14 35.0	9.1	57.1
13	11 43.9	04.7	115 50.9	10.9	14 44.1	9.0	57.1
14	26 44.0	03.8	130 20.8	11.0	14 53.1	8.9	57.0
15	41 44.1	.. 02.8	144 50.8	10.9	15 02.0	8.8	57.0
16	56 44.2	01.9	159 20.7	10.9	15 10.8	8.8	56.9
17	71 44.3	01.0	173 50.6	11.0	15 19.6	8.6	56.9
18	86 44.4	S 9 00.0	188 20.6	10.9	S15 28.2	8.6	56.9
19	101 44.5	8 59.1	202 50.5	10.9	15 36.8	8.4	56.8
20	116 44.6	58.2	217 20.4	10.9	15 45.2	8.4	56.8
21	131 44.7	.. 57.2	231 50.3	11.0	15 53.6	8.3	56.8
22	146 44.8	56.3	246 20.3	10.9	16 01.9	8.1	56.7
23	161 44.9	55.4	260 50.2	10.9	16 10.0	8.1	56.7
26 00	176 45.0	S 8 54.4	275 20.1	10.9	S16 18.1	8.0	56.6
01	191 45.1	53.5	289 50.0	10.9	16 26.1	7.9	56.6
02	206 45.2	52.6	304 19.9	10.9	16 34.0	7.8	56.6
03	221 45.3	.. 51.7	318 49.8	10.9	16 41.8	7.7	56.5
04	236 45.4	50.7	333 19.7	10.9	16 49.5	7.7	56.5
05	251 45.5	49.8	347 49.6	10.9	16 57.2	7.5	56.5
06	266 45.6	S 8 48.9	2 19.5	10.9	S17 04.7	7.4	56.4
07	281 45.7	47.9	16 49.4	10.9	17 12.1	7.3	56.4
08	296 45.8	47.0	31 19.3	10.9	17 19.4	7.3	56.4
09	311 45.9	.. 46.0	45 49.2	10.9	17 26.7	7.1	56.3
10	326 46.0	45.1	60 19.1	10.8	17 33.8	7.0	56.3
11	341 46.2	44.2	74 48.9	10.9	17 40.8	7.0	56.3
12	356 46.3	S 8 43.2	89 18.8	10.9	S17 47.8	6.8	56.2
13	11 46.4	42.3	103 48.7	10.9	17 54.6	6.8	56.2
14	26 46.5	41.4	118 18.6	10.8	18 01.4	6.6	56.2
15	41 46.6	.. 40.4	132 48.4	10.9	18 08.0	6.6	56.1
16	56 46.7	39.5	147 18.3	10.8	18 14.6	6.4	56.1
17	71 46.8	38.6	161 48.1	10.9	18 21.0	6.4	56.1
18	86 46.9	S 8 37.6	176 18.0	10.9	S18 27.4	6.2	56.0
19	101 47.0	36.7	190 47.9	10.8	18 33.6	6.2	56.0
20	116 47.1	35.8	205 17.7	10.9	18 39.8	6.0	56.0
21	131 47.2	.. 34.8	219 47.6	10.8	18 45.8	5.9	55.9
22	146 47.3	33.9	234 17.4	10.8	18 51.7	5.9	55.9
23	161 47.4	32.9	248 47.2	10.9	S18 57.6	5.7	55.9
	SD 16.2	d 0.9	SD 15.8		15.6		15.3

(Left margin day labels: 24 = SUNDAY; 25 = MONDAY; 26 = TUESDAY)

Lat.	Twilight Naut.	Twilight Civil	Sunrise	Moonrise 24	Moonrise 25	Moonrise 26	Moonrise 27
°	h m	h m	h m	h m	h m	h m	h m
N 72	05 31	06 49	08 00	25 58	01 58	04 29	▬
N 70	05 34	06 44	07 47	25 32	01 32	03 32	05 57
68	05 36	06 40	07 37	25 12	01 12	02 58	04 43
66	05 38	06 37	07 29	24 57	00 57	02 34	04 07
64	05 39	06 34	07 22	24 44	00 44	02 15	03 41
62	05 40	06 31	07 16	24 34	00 34	02 00	03 20
60	05 41	06 29	07 11	24 25	00 25	01 47	03 04
N 58	05 41	06 27	07 06	24 17	00 17	01 36	02 50
56	05 42	06 25	07 02	24 10	00 10	01 27	02 38
54	05 42	06 23	06 59	24 04	00 04	01 18	02 28
52	05 42	06 21	06 55	23 58	25 11	01 11	02 19
50	05 42	06 20	06 52	23 53	25 04	01 04	02 10
45	05 42	06 16	06 45	23 42	24 50	00 50	01 53
N 40	05 41	06 13	06 40	23 34	24 38	00 38	01 39
35	05 40	06 09	06 35	23 26	24 28	00 28	01 27
30	05 39	06 06	06 31	23 19	24 19	00 19	01 16
20	05 35	06 01	06 23	23 08	24 04	00 04	00 58
N 10	05 30	05 55	06 16	22 58	23 51	24 43	00 43
0	05 24	05 49	06 10	22 49	23 38	24 28	00 28
S 10	05 17	05 42	06 03	22 39	23 26	24 14	00 14
20	05 07	05 34	05 56	22 30	23 13	23 58	24 45
30	04 54	05 23	05 48	22 19	22 59	23 41	24 26
35	04 46	05 17	05 43	22 12	22 50	23 31	24 14
40	04 36	05 09	05 37	22 05	22 41	23 19	24 01
45	04 24	05 00	05 31	21 57	22 29	23 05	23 46
S 50	04 08	04 49	05 23	21 47	22 16	22 49	23 27
52	04 00	04 44	05 20	21 42	22 09	22 41	23 18
54	03 51	04 38	05 16	21 37	22 02	22 32	23 08
56	03 41	04 31	05 11	21 32	21 55	22 23	22 57
58	03 29	04 24	05 06	21 25	21 46	22 12	22 44
S 60	03 15	04 15	05 01	21 18	21 35	21 59	22 29

Lat.	Sunset	Twilight Civil	Twilight Naut.	Moonset 24	Moonset 25	Moonset 26	Moonset 27
°	h m	h m	h m	h m	h m	h m	h m
N 72	16 28	17 40	18 58	08 08	07 44	06 58	▬
N 70	16 40	17 44	18 55	08 23	08 12	07 56	07 15
68	16 50	17 48	18 52	08 36	08 33	08 30	08 29
66	16 58	17 51	18 50	08 46	08 49	08 55	09 07
64	17 05	17 54	18 49	08 54	09 03	09 15	09 33
62	17 11	17 56	18 48	09 02	09 14	09 31	09 54
60	17 16	17 59	18 47	09 08	09 24	09 44	10 11
N 58	17 21	18 01	18 46	09 14	09 33	09 56	10 25
56	17 25	18 03	18 46	09 19	09 41	10 06	10 37
54	17 28	18 04	18 45	09 24	09 47	10 15	10 48
52	17 32	18 06	18 45	09 28	09 54	10 23	10 57
50	17 35	18 08	18 45	09 32	09 59	10 30	11 06
45	17 41	18 11	18 45	09 40	10 11	10 45	11 24
N 40	17 47	18 14	18 46	09 47	10 21	10 58	11 38
35	17 52	18 17	18 47	09 53	10 30	11 09	11 51
30	17 56	18 20	18 48	09 58	10 37	11 18	12 02
20	18 03	18 26	18 51	10 07	10 50	11 35	12 21
N 10	18 10	18 31	18 55	10 15	11 02	11 49	12 37
0	18 16	18 37	19 02	10 23	11 12	12 02	12 52
S 10	18 23	18 44	19 09	10 30	11 23	12 16	13 08
20	18 30	18 52	19 18	10 38	11 35	12 30	13 24
30	18 38	19 02	19 31	10 47	11 48	12 47	13 43
35	18 43	19 09	19 39	10 53	11 56	12 56	13 54
40	18 48	19 16	19 49	10 59	12 05	13 07	14 07
45	18 54	19 25	20 01	11 06	12 15	13 20	14 22
S 50	19 02	19 36	20 17	11 15	12 27	13 36	14 40
52	19 05	19 41	20 25	11 19	12 33	13 44	14 49
54	19 09	19 47	20 33	11 23	12 40	13 52	14 58
56	19 13	19 53	20 43	11 28	12 47	14 01	15 09
58	19 18	20 01	20 55	11 33	12 55	14 12	15 22
S 60	19 24	20 09	21 09	11 39	13 04	14 24	15 37

Day	SUN Eqn. of Time 00h	SUN Eqn. of Time 12h	SUN Mer. Pass.	MOON Mer. Pass. Upper	MOON Mer. Pass. Lower	Age	Phase
d	m s	m s	h m	h m	h m	d	%
24	13 18	13 14	12 13	04 11	16 36	20	70
25	13 10	13 05	12 13	05 01	17 25	21	60
26	13 00	12 55	12 13	05 50	18 15	22	50

© British Crown Copyright 2018. All rights reserved.

UT	ARIES GHA	VENUS −4.1 GHA	Dec	MARS +1.2 GHA	Dec	JUPITER −2.0 GHA	Dec	SATURN +0.6 GHA	Dec	STARS Name	SHA	Dec
27 00	156 32.3	217 53.4	S19 50.6	120 39.9	N14 55.3	255 36.1	S22 33.0	227 33.9	S21 51.3	Acamar	315 15.5	S40 14.1
01	171 34.8	232 52.7	50.2	135 40.7	55.9	270 38.3	33.0	242 36.1	51.3	Achernar	335 24.3	S57 08.8
02	186 37.2	247 52.1	49.7	150 41.6	56.4	285 40.4	33.0	257 38.3	51.2	Acrux	173 04.3	S63 12.1
03	201 39.7	262 51.4 ..	49.3	165 42.4 ..	57.0	300 42.5 ..	33.0	272 40.6 ..	51.2	Adhara	255 09.3	S29 00.2
04	216 42.2	277 50.8	48.9	180 43.2	57.6	315 44.7	33.0	287 42.8	51.2	Aldebaran	290 44.9	N16 32.7
05	231 44.6	292 50.1	48.5	195 44.0	58.1	330 46.8	33.1	302 45.0	51.2			
06	246 47.1	307 49.5	S19 48.1	210 44.9	N14 58.7	345 48.9	S22 33.1	317 47.3	S21 51.1	Alioth	166 16.8	N55 51.2
W 07	261 49.6	322 48.8	47.7	225 45.7	59.3	0 51.1	33.1	332 49.5	51.1	Alkaid	152 55.5	N49 12.9
E 08	276 52.0	337 48.2	47.3	240 46.5	14 59.8	15 53.2	33.1	347 51.7	51.1	Alnair	27 39.3	S46 52.2
D 09	291 54.5	352 47.5 ..	46.9	255 47.3	15 00.4	30 55.4 ..	33.1	2 53.9 ..	51.1	Alnilam	275 42.3	S 1 11.7
N 10	306 57.0	7 46.9	46.5	270 48.2	01.0	45 57.5	33.1	17 56.2	51.0	Alphard	217 52.0	S 8 44.6
E 11	321 59.4	22 46.2	46.1	285 49.0	01.5	60 59.6	33.2	32 58.4	51.0			
S 12	337 01.9	37 45.6	S19 45.7	300 49.8	N15 02.1	76 01.8	S22 33.2	48 00.6	S21 51.0	Alphecca	126 07.6	N26 38.9
D 13	352 04.4	52 44.9	45.2	315 50.6	02.6	91 03.9	33.2	63 02.8	50.9	Alpheratz	357 39.8	N29 11.6
A 14	7 06.8	67 44.3	44.8	330 51.5	03.2	106 06.1	33.2	78 05.1	50.9	Altair	62 04.7	N 8 55.1
Y 15	22 09.3	82 43.7 ..	44.4	345 52.3 ..	03.8	121 08.2 ..	33.2	93 07.3 ..	50.9	Ankaa	353 12.2	S42 12.4
16	37 11.7	97 43.0	44.0	0 53.1	04.3	136 10.3	33.3	108 09.5	50.9	Antares	112 21.5	S26 28.3
17	52 14.2	112 42.4	43.6	15 53.9	04.9	151 12.5	33.3	123 11.8	50.8			
18	67 16.7	127 41.7	S19 43.1	30 54.8	N15 05.5	166 14.6	S22 33.3	138 14.0	S21 50.8	Arcturus	145 52.0	N19 04.9
19	82 19.1	142 41.1	42.7	45 55.6	06.0	181 16.8	33.3	153 16.2	50.8	Atria	107 19.9	S69 03.3
20	97 21.6	157 40.4	42.3	60 56.4	06.6	196 18.9	33.3	168 18.4	50.8	Avior	234 15.9	S59 34.5
21	112 24.1	172 39.8 ..	41.9	75 57.2 ..	07.2	211 21.0 ..	33.3	183 20.7 ..	50.7	Bellatrix	278 27.8	N 6 21.8
22	127 26.5	187 39.1	41.5	90 58.0	07.7	226 23.2	33.4	198 22.9	50.7	Betelgeuse	270 57.0	N 7 24.4
23	142 29.0	202 38.5	41.0	105 58.9	08.3	241 25.3	33.4	213 25.1	50.7			
28 00	157 31.5	217 37.8	S19 40.6	120 59.7	N15 08.9	256 27.5	S22 33.4	228 27.4	S21 50.7	Canopus	263 54.2	S52 42.8
01	172 33.9	232 37.2	40.2	136 00.5	09.4	271 29.6	33.4	243 29.6	50.6	Capella	280 28.6	N46 01.0
02	187 36.4	247 36.5	39.8	151 01.3	10.0	286 31.8	33.4	258 31.8	50.6	Deneb	49 29.2	N45 20.8
03	202 38.9	262 35.9 ..	39.3	166 02.2 ..	10.5	301 33.9 ..	33.5	273 34.1 ..	50.6	Denebola	182 29.4	N14 27.8
04	217 41.3	277 35.3	38.9	181 03.0	11.1	316 36.0	33.5	288 36.3	50.5	Diphda	348 52.3	S17 53.2
05	232 43.8	292 34.6	38.5	196 03.8	11.7	331 38.2	33.5	303 38.5	50.5			
06	247 46.2	307 34.0	S19 38.0	211 04.6	N15 12.2	346 40.3	S22 33.5	318 40.7	S21 50.5	Dubhe	193 46.3	N61 38.8
T 07	262 48.7	322 33.3	37.6	226 05.4	12.8	1 42.5	33.5	333 43.0	50.5	Elnath	278 07.6	N28 37.3
H 08	277 51.2	337 32.7	37.2	241 06.3	13.3	16 44.6	33.5	348 45.2	50.4	Eltanin	90 44.5	N51 29.0
U 09	292 53.6	352 32.0 ..	36.7	256 07.1 ..	13.9	31 46.8 ..	33.6	3 47.4 ..	50.4	Enif	33 43.6	N 9 57.6
R 10	307 56.1	7 31.4	36.3	271 07.9	14.5	46 48.9	33.6	18 49.7	50.4	Fomalhaut	15 20.1	S29 31.4
S 11	322 58.6	22 30.7	35.9	286 08.7	15.0	61 51.1	33.6	33 51.9	50.4			
D 12	338 01.0	37 30.1	S19 35.4	301 09.6	N15 15.6	76 53.2	S22 33.6	48 54.1	S21 50.3	Gacrux	171 56.1	S57 13.0
A 13	353 03.5	52 29.5	35.0	316 10.4	16.2	91 55.3	33.6	63 56.4	50.3	Gienah	175 48.0	S17 38.9
Y 14	8 06.0	67 28.8	34.5	331 11.2	16.7	106 57.5	33.6	78 58.6	50.3	Hadar	148 42.0	S60 27.6
15	23 08.4	82 28.2 ..	34.1	346 12.0 ..	17.3	121 59.6 ..	33.7	94 00.8 ..	50.2	Hamal	327 56.6	N23 33.0
16	38 10.9	97 27.5	33.7	1 12.8	17.8	137 01.8	33.7	109 03.0	50.2	Kaus Aust.	83 38.8	S34 22.3
17	53 13.3	112 26.9	33.2	16 13.7	18.4	152 03.9	33.7	124 05.3	50.2			
18	68 15.8	127 26.2	S19 32.8	31 14.5	N15 18.9	167 06.1	S22 33.7	139 07.5	S21 50.2	Kochab	137 19.6	N74 04.4
19	83 18.3	142 25.6	32.3	46 15.3	19.5	182 08.2	33.7	154 09.7	50.1	Markab	13 34.8	N15 18.3
20	98 20.7	157 25.0	31.9	61 16.1	20.1	197 10.4	33.8	169 12.0	50.1	Menkar	314 11.1	N 4 09.6
21	113 23.2	172 24.3 ..	31.4	76 16.9 ..	20.6	212 12.5 ..	33.8	184 14.2 ..	50.1	Menkent	148 02.8	S36 27.6
22	128 25.7	187 23.7	31.0	91 17.8	21.2	227 14.7	33.8	199 16.4	50.1	Miaplacidus	221 38.0	S69 47.9
23	143 28.1	202 23.0	30.6	106 18.6	21.7	242 16.8	33.8	214 18.7	50.0			
1 00	158 30.6	217 22.4	S19 30.1	121 19.4	N15 22.3	257 19.0	S22 33.8	229 20.9	S21 50.0	Mirfak	308 34.9	N49 55.7
01	173 33.1	232 21.8	29.7	136 20.2	22.9	272 21.1	33.8	244 23.1	50.0	Nunki	75 53.7	S26 16.2
02	188 35.5	247 21.1	29.2	151 21.0	23.4	287 23.3	33.9	259 25.4	50.0	Peacock	53 13.6	S56 40.3
03	203 38.0	262 20.5 ..	28.8	166 21.9 ..	24.0	302 25.4 ..	33.9	274 27.6 ..	49.9	Pollux	243 22.7	N27 58.7
04	218 40.5	277 19.8	28.3	181 22.7	24.5	317 27.6	33.9	289 29.8	49.9	Procyon	244 55.4	N 5 10.4
05	233 42.9	292 19.2	27.8	196 23.5	25.1	332 29.7	33.9	304 32.1	49.9			
06	248 45.4	307 18.6	S19 27.4	211 24.3	N15 25.6	347 31.9	S22 33.9	319 34.3	S21 49.9	Rasalhague	96 02.9	N12 32.7
07	263 47.8	322 17.9	26.9	226 25.1	26.2	2 34.0	33.9	334 36.5	49.8	Regulus	207 39.1	N11 52.3
F 08	278 50.3	337 17.3	26.5	241 26.0	26.8	17 36.2	34.0	349 38.8	49.8	Rigel	281 08.3	S 8 11.1
R 09	293 52.8	352 16.6 ..	26.0	256 26.8 ..	27.3	32 38.3 ..	34.0	4 41.0 ..	49.8	Rigil Kent.	139 46.1	S60 54.5
I 10	308 55.2	7 16.0	25.6	271 27.6	27.9	47 40.5	34.0	19 43.2	49.7	Sabik	102 08.1	S15 44.8
11	323 57.7	22 15.4	25.1	286 28.4	28.4	62 42.6	34.0	34 45.5	49.7			
D 12	339 00.2	37 14.7	S19 24.6	301 29.2	N15 29.0	77 44.8	S22 34.0	49 47.7	S21 49.7	Schedar	349 36.6	N56 38.5
A 13	354 02.6	52 14.1	24.2	316 30.1	29.5	92 46.9	34.0	64 49.9	49.7	Shaula	96 16.7	S37 06.8
Y 14	9 05.1	67 13.4	23.7	331 30.9	30.1	107 49.1	34.1	79 52.2	49.6	Sirius	258 30.1	S16 44.9
15	24 07.6	82 12.8 ..	23.3	346 31.7 ..	30.6	122 51.2 ..	34.1	94 54.4 ..	49.6	Spica	158 26.9	S11 15.6
16	39 10.0	97 12.2	22.8	1 32.5	31.2	137 53.4	34.1	109 56.6	49.6	Suhail	222 49.2	S43 30.8
17	54 12.5	112 11.5	22.3	16 33.3	31.7	152 55.5	34.1	124 58.9	49.6			
18	69 15.0	127 10.9	S19 21.9	31 34.1	N15 32.3	167 57.7	S22 34.1	140 01.1	S21 49.5	Vega	80 36.5	N38 47.9
19	84 17.4	142 10.2	21.4	46 35.0	32.9	182 59.9	34.1	155 03.3	49.5	Zuben'ubi	137 01.0	S16 07.2
20	99 19.9	157 09.6	20.9	61 35.8	33.4	198 02.0	34.2	170 05.6	49.5		SHA	Mer.Pass.
21	114 22.3	172 09.0 ..	20.5	76 36.6 ..	34.0	213 04.2 ..	34.2	185 07.8 ..	49.5			h m
22	129 24.8	187 08.3	20.0	91 37.4	34.5	228 06.3	34.2	200 10.0	49.4	Venus	60 06.4	9 30
23	144 27.3	202 07.7	19.5	106 38.2	35.1	243 08.5	34.2	215 12.3	49.4	Mars	323 28.2	15 55
Mer.Pass.	h m 13 27.7	v −0.6	d 0.4	v 0.8	d 0.6	v 2.1	d 0.0	v 2.2	d 0.0	Jupiter	98 56.0	6 53
										Saturn	70 55.9	8 45

© British Crown Copyright 2018. All rights reserved.

SUN / MOON

UT (d h)	SUN GHA	SUN Dec	MOON GHA	v	Dec	d	HP
27 00	176 47.5	S 8 32.0	263 17.1	10.8	S19 03.3	5.7	55.8
01	191 47.6	31.1	277 46.9	10.9	19 09.0	5.5	55.8
02	206 47.7	30.1	292 16.8	10.8	19 14.5	5.4	55.8
03	221 47.8	.. 29.2	306 46.6	10.8	19 19.9	5.4	55.8
04	236 47.9	28.3	321 16.4	10.9	19 25.3	5.2	55.7
05	251 48.1	27.3	335 46.3	10.8	19 30.5	5.1	55.7
06	266 48.2	S 8 26.4	350 16.1	10.8	S19 35.6	5.1	55.7
W 07	281 48.3	25.4	4 45.9	10.9	19 40.7	4.9	55.6
E 08	296 48.4	24.5	19 15.8	10.8	19 45.6	4.8	55.6
D 09	311 48.5	.. 23.6	33 45.6	10.8	19 50.4	4.7	55.6
N 10	326 48.6	22.6	48 15.4	10.8	19 55.1	4.6	55.6
E 11	341 48.7	21.7	62 45.2	10.9	19 59.7	4.5	55.5
S 12	356 48.8	S 8 20.7	77 15.1	10.8	S20 04.2	4.4	55.5
D 13	11 48.9	19.8	91 44.9	10.8	20 08.6	4.3	55.5
A 14	26 49.0	18.9	106 14.7	10.9	20 12.9	4.2	55.4
Y 15	41 49.1	.. 17.9	120 44.6	10.8	20 17.1	4.1	55.4
16	56 49.3	17.0	135 14.4	10.8	20 21.2	4.0	55.4
17	71 49.4	16.0	149 44.2	10.9	20 25.2	3.9	55.4
18	86 49.5	S 8 15.1	164 14.1	10.8	S20 29.1	3.8	55.3
19	101 49.6	14.2	178 43.9	10.8	20 32.9	3.6	55.3
20	116 49.7	13.2	193 13.7	10.9	20 36.5	3.6	55.3
21	131 49.8	.. 12.3	207 43.6	10.8	20 40.1	3.5	55.3
22	146 49.9	11.3	222 13.4	10.9	20 43.6	3.3	55.2
23	161 50.0	10.4	236 43.3	10.8	20 46.9	3.3	55.2
28 00	176 50.1	S 8 09.4	251 13.1	10.9	S20 50.2	3.1	55.2
01	191 50.3	08.5	265 43.0	10.9	20 53.3	3.0	55.2
02	206 50.4	07.6	280 12.9	10.8	20 56.3	3.0	55.1
03	221 50.5	.. 06.6	294 42.7	10.9	20 59.3	2.8	55.1
04	236 50.6	05.7	309 12.6	10.9	21 02.1	2.7	55.1
05	251 50.7	04.7	323 42.5	10.9	21 04.8	2.6	55.1
06	266 50.8	S 8 03.8	338 12.4	10.9	S21 07.4	2.5	55.0
T 07	281 50.9	02.8	352 42.3	10.8	21 09.9	2.4	55.0
H 08	296 51.1	01.9	7 12.1	11.0	21 12.3	2.3	55.0
U 09	311 51.2	.. 01.0	21 42.1	10.9	21 14.6	2.2	55.0
R 10	326 51.3	8 00.0	36 12.0	10.9	21 16.8	2.1	55.0
S 11	341 51.4	7 59.1	50 41.9	10.9	21 18.9	2.0	54.9
D 12	356 51.5	S 7 58.1	65 11.8	11.0	S21 20.9	1.9	54.9
A 13	11 51.6	57.2	79 41.8	10.9	21 22.8	1.7	54.9
Y 14	26 51.7	56.2	94 11.7	11.0	21 24.5	1.7	54.9
15	41 51.9	.. 55.3	108 41.7	10.9	21 26.2	1.6	54.8
16	56 52.0	54.3	123 11.6	11.0	21 27.8	1.4	54.8
17	71 52.1	53.4	137 41.6	11.0	21 29.2	1.3	54.8
18	86 52.2	S 7 52.4	152 11.6	11.0	S21 30.5	1.3	54.8
19	101 52.3	51.5	166 41.6	11.0	21 31.8	1.1	54.8
20	116 52.4	50.5	181 11.6	11.1	21 32.9	1.0	54.7
21	131 52.6	.. 49.6	195 41.7	11.0	21 33.9	1.0	54.7
22	146 52.7	48.7	210 11.7	11.1	21 34.9	0.8	54.7
23	161 52.8	47.7	224 41.8	11.0	21 35.7	0.7	54.7
1 00	176 52.9	S 7 46.8	239 11.8	11.1	S21 36.4	0.6	54.7
01	191 53.0	45.8	253 41.9	11.1	21 37.0	0.5	54.7
02	206 53.1	44.9	268 12.0	11.1	21 37.5	0.4	54.6
03	221 53.3	.. 43.9	282 42.1	11.1	21 37.9	0.3	54.6
04	236 53.4	43.0	297 12.2	11.2	21 38.2	0.2	54.6
05	251 53.5	42.0	311 42.4	11.1	21 38.4	0.2	54.6
06	266 53.6	S 7 41.1	326 12.5	11.2	S21 38.5	0.1	54.6
07	281 53.7	40.1	340 42.7	11.2	21 38.4	0.1	54.6
08	296 53.8	39.2	355 12.9	11.2	21 38.3	0.2	54.5
F 09	311 54.0	.. 38.2	9 43.1	11.3	21 38.1	0.3	54.5
R 10	326 54.1	37.3	24 13.4	11.2	21 37.8	0.5	54.5
I 11	341 54.2	36.3	38 43.6	11.3	21 37.3	0.5	54.5
D 12	356 54.3	S 7 35.4	53 13.9	11.3	S21 36.8	0.7	54.5
A 13	11 54.4	34.4	67 44.2	11.3	21 36.1	0.7	54.5
Y 14	26 54.6	33.5	82 14.5	11.3	21 35.4	0.9	54.4
15	41 54.7	.. 32.5	96 44.8	11.4	21 34.5	0.9	54.4
16	56 54.8	31.6	111 15.2	11.3	21 33.6	1.1	54.4
17	71 54.9	30.6	125 45.5	11.4	21 32.5	1.1	54.4
18	86 55.1	S 7 29.7	140 15.9	11.5	S21 31.4	1.3	54.4
19	101 55.2	28.7	154 46.4	11.4	21 30.1	1.3	54.4
20	116 55.3	27.8	169 16.8	11.5	21 28.8	1.5	54.4
21	131 55.4	.. 26.8	183 47.3	11.4	21 27.3	1.5	54.3
22	146 55.5	25.9	198 17.7	11.6	21 25.8	1.7	54.3
23	161 55.7	24.9	212 48.3	11.5	S21 24.1	1.8	54.3
	SD 16.2 d 0.9		SD 15.1		15.0		14.8

Twilight / Sunrise / Moonrise

Lat.	Naut.	Civil	Sunrise	27	28	1	2
N 72	05 16	06 34	07 44	▪	▪	▪	▪
N 70	05 21	06 31	07 33	05 57	▪	▪	▪
68	05 24	06 28	07 25	04 43	06 25	07 41	08 00
66	05 27	06 26	07 18	04 07	05 29	06 30	07 07
64	05 29	06 24	07 12	03 41	04 55	05 54	06 35
62	05 31	06 22	07 07	03 20	04 31	05 28	06 11
60	05 32	06 20	07 02	03 04	04 12	05 08	05 52
N 58	05 34	06 19	06 58	02 50	03 56	04 52	05 36
56	05 35	06 17	06 55	02 38	03 42	04 37	05 22
54	05 35	06 16	06 52	02 28	03 31	04 25	05 11
52	05 36	06 15	06 49	02 19	03 20	04 14	05 00
50	05 36	06 14	06 46	02 10	03 11	04 05	04 51
45	05 37	06 11	06 40	01 53	02 52	03 45	04 32
N 40	05 37	06 08	06 35	01 39	02 36	03 28	04 16
35	05 36	06 06	06 31	01 27	02 23	03 15	04 02
30	05 36	06 03	06 27	01 16	02 11	03 03	03 51
20	05 33	05 59	06 21	00 58	01 51	02 42	03 31
N 10	05 29	05 54	06 15	00 43	01 34	02 24	03 13
0	05 24	05 48	06 09	00 28	01 18	02 08	02 57
S 10	05 17	05 42	06 03	00 14	01 02	01 51	02 41
20	05 09	05 35	05 57	24 45	00 45	01 34	02 23
30	04 57	05 26	05 50	24 26	00 26	01 13	02 03
35	04 49	05 20	05 46	24 14	00 14	01 01	01 51
40	04 40	05 13	05 41	24 01	00 01	00 48	01 38
45	04 28	05 05	05 35	23 46	24 32	00 32	01 22
S 50	04 14	04 55	05 28	23 27	24 12	00 12	01 02
52	04 06	04 50	05 25	23 18	24 02	00 02	00 53
54	03 58	04 45	05 22	23 08	23 52	24 43	00 43
56	03 49	04 38	05 18	22 57	23 40	24 31	00 31
58	03 38	04 32	05 14	22 44	23 26	24 17	00 17
S 60	03 25	04 24	05 09	22 29	23 10	24 01	00 01

Sunset / Twilight / Moonset

Lat.	Sunset	Civil	Naut.	27	28	1	2
N 72	16 43	17 53	19 12	▪	▪	▪	▪
N 70	16 54	17 56	19 07	07 15	▪	▪	▪
68	17 02	17 59	19 03	08 29	08 32	08 59	10 21
66	17 09	18 01	19 00	09 07	09 28	10 09	11 14
64	17 15	18 03	18 58	09 33	10 02	10 46	11 46
62	17 20	18 04	18 56	09 54	10 26	11 11	12 10
60	17 24	18 06	18 54	10 11	10 46	11 32	12 29
N 58	17 28	18 07	18 53	10 25	11 02	11 48	12 44
56	17 31	18 09	18 52	10 37	11 15	12 02	12 58
54	17 34	18 10	18 51	10 48	11 27	12 15	13 09
52	17 37	18 11	18 50	10 57	11 38	12 25	13 20
50	17 40	18 12	18 50	11 06	11 47	12 35	13 29
45	17 46	18 15	18 49	11 24	12 07	12 55	13 48
N 40	17 50	18 18	18 49	11 38	12 23	13 11	14 03
35	17 54	18 20	18 49	11 51	12 36	13 25	14 16
30	17 58	18 22	18 50	12 02	12 48	13 37	14 28
20	18 05	18 27	18 52	12 21	13 08	13 57	14 47
N 10	18 10	18 32	18 56	12 37	13 26	14 15	15 04
0	18 16	18 37	19 01	12 52	13 42	14 32	15 20
S 10	18 22	18 43	19 07	13 08	13 59	14 48	15 36
20	18 28	18 50	19 16	13 24	14 16	15 06	15 53
30	18 35	18 59	19 28	13 43	14 36	15 26	16 12
35	18 39	19 05	19 35	13 54	14 48	15 38	16 23
40	18 44	19 11	19 44	14 07	15 02	15 52	16 36
45	18 49	19 19	19 56	14 22	15 18	16 08	16 51
S 50	18 56	19 29	20 10	14 40	15 37	16 28	17 10
52	18 59	19 34	20 17	14 49	15 47	16 37	17 19
54	19 02	19 39	20 25	14 58	15 57	16 47	17 29
56	19 06	19 45	20 34	15 09	16 09	16 59	17 40
58	19 10	19 52	20 45	15 22	16 23	17 13	17 52
S 60	19 15	19 59	20 57	15 37	16 39	17 29	18 07

SUN / MOON

Day	SUN Eqn. of Time 00h	12h	Mer. Pass.	MOON Mer. Pass. Upper	Lower	Age	Phase
	m s	m s	h m	h m	h m	d	%
27	12 50	12 45	12 13	06 40	19 05	23	40
28	12 40	12 34	12 13	07 30	19 55	24	31
1	12 29	12 23	12 12	08 20	20 44	25	22

© British Crown Copyright 2018. All rights reserved.

UT	ARIES GHA	VENUS −4·1 GHA	Dec	MARS +1·2 GHA	Dec	JUPITER −2·0 GHA	Dec	SATURN +0·6 GHA	Dec	STARS Name	SHA	Dec
2 00	159 29.7	217 07.1	S19 19.0	121 39.1	N15 35.6	258 10.6	S22 34.2	230 14.5	S21 49.4	Acamar	315 15.6	S40 14.1
01	174 32.2	232 06.4	18.6	136 39.9	36.2	273 12.8	34.2	245 16.8	49.3	Achernar	335 24.3	S57 08.8
02	189 34.7	247 05.8	18.1	151 40.7	36.7	288 14.9	34.3	260 19.0	49.3	Acrux	173 04.3	S63 12.1
03	204 37.1	262 05.1	.. 17.6	166 41.5	.. 37.3	303 17.1	.. 34.3	275 21.2	.. 49.3	Adhara	255 09.3	S29 00.2
04	219 39.6	277 04.5	17.1	181 42.3	37.8	318 19.3	34.3	290 23.5	49.3	Aldebaran	290 44.9	N16 32.7
05	234 42.1	292 03.9	16.7	196 43.1	38.4	333 21.4	34.3	305 25.7	49.2			
06	249 44.5	307 03.2	S19 16.2	211 44.0	N15 38.9	348 23.6	S22 34.3	320 27.9	S21 49.2	Alioth	166 16.8	N55 51.3
07	264 47.0	322 02.6	15.7	226 44.8	39.5	3 25.7	34.3	335 30.2	49.2	Alkaid	152 55.5	N49 12.9
S 08	279 49.4	337 02.0	15.2	241 45.6	40.0	18 27.9	34.4	350 32.4	49.2	Alnair	27 39.3	S46 52.2
A 09	294 51.9	352 01.3	.. 14.8	256 46.4	.. 40.6	33 30.0	.. 34.4	5 34.6	.. 49.1	Alnilam	275 42.3	S 1 11.7
T 10	309 54.4	7 00.7	14.3	271 47.2	41.1	48 32.2	34.4	20 36.9	49.1	Alphard	217 52.0	S 8 44.7
U 11	324 56.8	22 00.1	13.8	286 48.0	41.7	63 34.4	34.4	35 39.1	49.1			
R 12	339 59.3	36 59.4	S19 13.3	301 48.8	N15 42.2	78 36.5	S22 34.4	50 41.3	S21 49.1	Alphecca	126 07.6	N26 38.9
D 13	355 01.8	51 58.8	12.8	316 49.7	42.8	93 38.7	34.4	65 43.6	49.0	Alpheratz	357 39.8	N29 11.6
A 14	10 04.2	66 58.2	12.3	331 50.5	43.3	108 40.8	34.5	80 45.8	49.0	Altair	62 04.7	N 8 55.0
Y 15	25 06.7	81 57.5	.. 11.9	346 51.3	.. 43.9	123 43.0	.. 34.5	95 48.1	.. 49.0	Ankaa	353 12.2	S42 12.4
16	40 09.2	96 56.9	11.4	1 52.1	44.4	138 45.2	34.5	110 50.3	49.0	Antares	112 21.5	S26 28.3
17	55 11.6	111 56.3	10.9	16 52.9	45.0	153 47.3	34.5	125 52.5	48.9			
18	70 14.1	126 55.6	S19 10.4	31 53.7	N15 45.5	168 49.5	S22 34.5	140 54.8	S21 48.9	Arcturus	145 52.0	N19 04.9
19	85 16.6	141 55.0	09.9	46 54.6	46.1	183 51.6	34.5	155 57.0	48.9	Atria	107 19.8	S69 03.3
20	100 19.0	156 54.4	09.4	61 55.4	46.6	198 53.8	34.5	170 59.2	48.8	Avior	234 15.9	S59 34.5
21	115 21.5	171 53.7	.. 08.9	76 56.2	.. 47.2	213 56.0	.. 34.6	186 01.5	.. 48.8	Bellatrix	278 27.8	N 6 21.8
22	130 23.9	186 53.1	08.4	91 57.0	47.7	228 58.1	34.6	201 03.7	48.8	Betelgeuse	270 57.0	N 7 24.4
23	145 26.4	201 52.5	07.9	106 57.8	48.3	244 00.3	34.6	216 06.0	48.8			
3 00	160 28.9	216 51.8	S19 07.4	121 58.6	N15 48.8	259 02.4	S22 34.6	231 08.2	S21 48.7	Canopus	263 54.2	S52 42.8
01	175 31.3	231 51.2	06.9	136 59.4	49.4	274 04.6	34.6	246 10.4	48.7	Capella	280 28.6	N46 01.0
02	190 33.8	246 50.6	06.4	152 00.3	49.9	289 06.8	34.6	261 12.7	48.7	Deneb	49 29.2	N45 20.7
03	205 36.3	261 49.9	.. 05.9	167 01.1	.. 50.5	304 08.9	.. 34.7	276 14.9	.. 48.7	Denebola	182 29.4	N14 27.8
04	220 38.7	276 49.3	05.4	182 01.9	51.0	319 11.1	34.7	291 17.2	48.6	Diphda	348 52.3	S17 53.2
05	235 41.2	291 48.7	04.9	197 02.7	51.5	334 13.3	34.7	306 19.4	48.6			
06	250 43.7	306 48.0	S19 04.4	212 03.5	N15 52.1	349 15.4	S22 34.7	321 21.6	S21 48.6	Dubhe	193 46.3	N61 38.8
07	265 46.1	321 47.4	03.9	227 04.3	52.6	4 17.6	34.7	336 23.9	48.6	Elnath	278 07.6	N28 37.3
S 08	280 48.6	336 46.8	03.4	242 05.1	53.2	19 19.7	34.7	351 26.1	48.5	Eltanin	90 44.5	N51 29.0
U 09	295 51.1	351 46.1	.. 02.9	257 05.9	.. 53.7	34 21.9	.. 34.8	6 28.3	.. 48.5	Enif	33 43.6	N 9 57.6
N 10	310 53.5	6 45.5	02.4	272 06.8	54.3	49 24.1	34.8	21 30.6	48.5	Fomalhaut	15 20.0	S29 31.4
D 11	325 56.0	21 44.9	01.9	287 07.6	54.8	64 26.2	34.8	36 32.8	48.5			
A 12	340 58.4	36 44.3	S19 01.4	302 08.4	N15 55.4	79 28.4	S22 34.8	51 35.1	S21 48.4	Gacrux	171 56.0	S57 13.1
Y 13	356 00.9	51 43.6	00.9	317 09.2	55.9	94 30.6	34.8	66 37.3	48.4	Gienah	175 48.0	S17 38.9
14	11 03.4	66 43.0	19 00.4	332 10.0	56.5	109 32.7	34.8	81 39.5	48.4	Hadar	148 41.9	S60 27.6
15	26 05.8	81 42.4	18 59.9	347 10.8	.. 57.0	124 34.9	.. 34.8	96 41.8	.. 48.4	Hamal	327 56.6	N23 33.0
16	41 08.3	96 41.7	59.4	2 11.6	57.5	139 37.1	34.9	111 44.0	48.3	Kaus Aust.	83 38.8	S34 22.3
17	56 10.8	111 41.1	58.9	17 12.4	58.1	154 39.2	34.9	126 46.3	48.3			
18	71 13.2	126 40.5	S18 58.4	32 13.3	N15 58.6	169 41.4	S22 34.9	141 48.5	S21 48.3	Kochab	137 19.6	N74 04.4
19	86 15.7	141 39.9	57.9	47 14.1	59.2	184 43.6	34.9	156 50.7	48.2	Markab	13 34.8	N15 18.3
20	101 18.2	156 39.2	57.3	62 14.9	15 59.7	199 45.7	34.9	171 53.0	48.2	Menkar	314 11.1	N 4 09.6
21	116 20.6	171 38.6	.. 56.8	77 15.7	16 00.3	214 47.9	.. 34.9	186 55.2	.. 48.2	Menkent	148 02.7	S36 27.6
22	131 23.1	186 38.0	56.3	92 16.5	00.8	229 50.1	35.0	201 57.5	48.2	Miaplacidus	221 38.0	S69 47.9
23	146 25.5	201 37.3	55.8	107 17.3	01.3	244 52.2	35.0	216 59.7	48.1			
4 00	161 28.0	216 36.7	S18 55.3	122 18.1	N16 01.9	259 54.4	S22 35.0	232 01.9	S21 48.1	Mirfak	308 34.9	N49 55.7
01	176 30.5	231 36.1	54.8	137 18.9	02.4	274 56.6	35.0	247 04.2	48.1	Nunki	75 53.7	S26 16.2
02	191 32.9	246 35.5	54.2	152 19.7	03.0	289 58.8	35.0	262 06.4	48.1	Peacock	53 13.6	S56 40.3
03	206 35.4	261 34.8	.. 53.7	167 20.6	.. 03.5	305 00.9	.. 35.0	277 08.7	.. 48.0	Pollux	243 22.7	N27 58.7
04	221 37.9	276 34.2	53.2	182 21.4	04.0	320 03.1	35.0	292 10.9	48.0	Procyon	244 55.5	N 5 10.4
05	236 40.3	291 33.6	52.7	197 22.2	04.6	335 05.3	35.1	307 13.2	48.0			
06	251 42.8	306 33.0	S18 52.2	212 23.0	N16 05.1	350 07.4	S22 35.1	322 15.4	S21 48.0	Rasalhague	96 02.9	N12 32.7
07	266 45.3	321 32.3	51.6	227 23.8	05.7	5 09.6	35.1	337 17.6	47.9	Regulus	207 39.1	N11 52.3
08	281 47.7	336 31.7	51.1	242 24.6	06.2	20 11.8	35.1	352 19.9	47.9	Rigel	281 08.3	S 8 11.1
M 09	296 50.2	351 31.1	.. 50.6	257 25.4	.. 06.7	35 13.9	.. 35.1	7 22.1	.. 47.9	Rigil Kent.	139 46.1	S60 54.5
O 10	311 52.7	6 30.5	50.0	272 26.2	07.3	50 16.1	35.1	22 24.4	47.9	Sabik	102 08.1	S15 44.8
N 11	326 55.1	21 29.8	49.5	287 27.0	07.8	65 18.3	35.2	37 26.6	47.8			
D 12	341 57.6	36 29.2	S18 49.0	302 27.8	N16 08.4	80 20.5	S22 35.2	52 28.9	S21 47.8	Schedar	349 36.6	N56 38.5
A 13	357 00.0	51 28.6	48.5	317 28.7	08.9	95 22.6	35.2	67 31.1	47.8	Shaula	96 16.7	S37 06.8
Y 14	12 02.5	66 28.0	47.9	332 29.5	09.4	110 24.8	35.2	82 33.3	47.8	Sirius	258 30.1	S16 44.9
15	27 05.0	81 27.3	.. 47.4	347 30.3	.. 10.0	125 27.0	.. 35.2	97 35.6	.. 47.7	Spica	158 26.9	S11 15.6
16	42 07.4	96 26.7	46.9	2 31.1	10.5	140 29.1	35.2	112 37.8	47.7	Suhail	222 49.2	S43 30.8
17	57 09.9	111 26.1	46.3	17 31.9	11.1	155 31.3	35.2	127 40.1	47.7			
18	72 12.4	126 25.5	S18 45.8	32 32.7	N16 11.6	170 33.5	S22 35.3	142 42.3	S21 47.7	Vega	80 36.5	N38 47.9
19	87 14.8	141 24.9	45.3	47 33.5	12.1	185 35.7	35.3	157 44.6	47.6	Zuben'ubi	137 00.9	S16 07.2
20	102 17.3	156 24.2	44.7	62 34.3	12.7	200 37.8	35.3	172 46.8	47.6		SHA	Mer.Pass.
21	117 19.8	171 23.6	.. 44.2	77 35.1	.. 13.2	215 40.0	.. 35.3	187 49.0	.. 47.6			
22	132 22.2	186 23.0	43.7	92 35.9	13.7	230 42.2	35.3	202 51.3	47.6	Venus	56 23.0	9 33
23	147 24.7	201 22.4	43.1	107 36.7	14.3	245 44.4	35.3	217 53.5	47.5	Mars	321 29.7	15 51
Mer.Pass.	13 15.9	v −0.6	d 0.5	v 0.8	d 0.5	v 2.2	d 0.0	v 2.2	d 0.0	Jupiter	98 33.6	6 43
										Saturn	70 39.3	8 34

© British Crown Copyright 2018. All rights reserved.

UT	SUN GHA	SUN Dec	MOON GHA	v	MOON Dec	d	HP
2 00	176 55.8	S 7 24.0	227 18.8	11.5	S21 22.3	1.8	54.3
01	191 55.9	23.0	241 49.3	11.6	21 20.5	2.0	54.3
02	206 56.0	22.1	256 19.9	11.6	21 18.5	2.1	54.3
03	221 56.2	.. 21.1	270 50.5	11.7	21 16.4	2.1	54.3
04	236 56.3	20.2	285 21.2	11.6	21 14.3	2.3	54.3
05	251 56.4	19.2	299 51.8	11.7	21 12.0	2.3	54.2
06	266 56.5	S 7 18.2	314 22.5	11.8	S21 09.7	2.5	54.2
07	281 56.6	17.3	328 53.3	11.7	21 07.2	2.5	54.2
S 08	296 56.8	16.3	343 24.0	11.8	21 04.7	2.7	54.2
A 09	311 56.9	.. 15.4	357 54.8	11.8	21 02.0	2.7	54.2
T 10	326 57.0	14.4	12 25.6	11.8	20 59.3	2.9	54.2
U 11	341 57.1	13.5	26 56.4	11.9	20 56.4	2.9	54.2
R 12	356 57.3	S 7 12.5	41 27.3	11.8	S20 53.5	3.1	54.2
D 13	11 57.4	11.6	55 58.1	12.0	20 50.4	3.1	54.2
A 14	26 57.5	10.6	70 29.1	11.9	20 47.3	3.2	54.2
Y 15	41 57.6	.. 09.7	85 00.0	12.0	20 44.1	3.3	54.1
16	56 57.8	08.7	99 31.0	12.0	20 40.8	3.5	54.1
17	71 57.9	07.7	114 02.0	12.0	20 37.3	3.5	54.1
18	86 58.0	S 7 06.8	128 33.0	12.1	S20 33.8	3.6	54.1
19	101 58.1	05.8	143 04.1	12.1	20 30.2	3.7	54.1
20	116 58.3	04.9	157 35.2	12.1	20 26.5	3.8	54.1
21	131 58.4	.. 03.9	172 06.3	12.2	20 22.7	3.9	54.1
22	146 58.5	03.0	186 37.5	12.2	20 18.8	3.9	54.1
23	161 58.7	02.0	201 08.7	12.2	20 14.9	4.1	54.1
3 00	176 58.8	S 7 01.1	215 39.9	12.3	S20 10.8	4.2	54.1
01	191 58.9	7 00.1	230 11.2	12.3	20 06.6	4.2	54.1
02	206 59.0	6 59.1	244 42.5	12.3	20 02.4	4.4	54.1
03	221 59.2	.. 58.2	259 13.8	12.4	19 58.0	4.4	54.1
04	236 59.3	57.2	273 45.2	12.4	19 53.6	4.5	54.0
05	251 59.4	56.3	288 16.6	12.4	19 49.1	4.6	54.0
06	266 59.6	S 6 55.3	302 48.0	12.5	S19 44.5	4.7	54.0
07	281 59.7	54.4	317 19.5	12.5	19 39.8	4.8	54.0
S 08	296 59.8	53.4	331 51.0	12.5	19 35.0	4.9	54.0
U 09	311 59.9	.. 52.4	346 22.5	12.6	19 30.1	5.0	54.0
N 10	327 00.1	51.5	0 54.1	12.6	19 25.1	5.0	54.0
D 11	342 00.2	50.5	15 25.7	12.6	19 20.1	5.2	54.0
A 12	357 00.3	S 6 49.6	29 57.3	12.7	S19 14.9	5.2	54.0
Y 13	12 00.5	48.6	44 29.0	12.7	19 09.7	5.3	54.0
14	27 00.6	47.6	59 00.7	12.7	19 04.4	5.4	54.0
15	42 00.7	.. 46.7	73 32.4	12.8	18 59.0	5.5	54.0
16	57 00.9	45.7	88 04.2	12.8	18 53.5	5.5	54.0
17	72 01.0	44.8	102 36.0	12.8	18 48.0	5.7	54.0
18	87 01.1	S 6 43.8	117 07.8	12.9	S18 42.3	5.7	54.0
19	102 01.2	42.8	131 39.7	12.9	18 36.6	5.8	54.0
20	117 01.4	41.9	146 11.6	13.0	18 30.8	5.9	54.0
21	132 01.5	.. 40.9	160 43.6	13.0	18 24.9	6.0	54.0
22	147 01.6	40.0	175 15.6	13.0	18 18.9	6.0	54.0
23	162 01.8	39.0	189 47.6	13.1	18 12.9	6.2	54.0
4 00	177 01.9	S 6 38.0	204 19.7	13.1	S18 06.7	6.2	54.0
01	192 02.0	37.1	218 51.8	13.1	18 00.5	6.3	54.0
02	207 02.2	36.1	233 23.9	13.2	17 54.2	6.3	54.0
03	222 02.3	.. 35.2	247 56.1	13.2	17 47.9	6.5	54.0
04	237 02.4	34.2	262 28.3	13.2	17 41.4	6.5	54.0
05	252 02.6	33.2	277 00.5	13.3	17 34.9	6.6	54.0
06	267 02.7	S 6 32.3	291 32.8	13.3	S17 28.3	6.7	54.0
07	282 02.8	31.3	306 05.1	13.3	17 21.6	6.7	54.0
08	297 03.0	30.4	320 37.4	13.4	17 14.9	6.9	54.0
M 09	312 03.1	.. 29.4	335 09.8	13.4	17 08.0	6.9	54.0
O 10	327 03.2	28.4	349 42.2	13.5	17 01.1	7.0	54.0
N 11	342 03.4	27.5	4 14.7	13.5	16 54.1	7.0	54.0
D 12	357 03.5	S 6 26.5	18 47.2	13.5	S16 47.1	7.1	54.0
A 13	12 03.6	25.5	33 19.7	13.6	16 40.0	7.2	54.0
Y 14	27 03.8	24.6	47 52.3	13.5	16 32.8	7.3	54.0
15	42 03.9	.. 23.6	62 24.8	13.7	16 25.5	7.4	54.0
16	57 04.1	22.7	76 57.5	13.6	16 18.1	7.4	54.0
17	72 04.2	21.7	91 30.1	13.7	16 10.7	7.4	54.0
18	87 04.3	S 6 20.7	106 02.8	13.8	S16 03.3	7.6	54.0
19	102 04.5	19.8	120 35.6	13.7	15 55.7	7.6	54.0
20	117 04.6	18.8	135 08.3	13.8	15 48.1	7.7	54.0
21	132 04.7	.. 17.8	149 41.1	13.9	15 40.4	7.8	54.0
22	147 04.9	16.9	164 14.0	13.8	15 32.6	7.8	54.0
23	162 05.0	15.9	178 46.8	13.9	S15 24.8	7.9	54.0
	SD 16.2	d 1.0	SD 14.8		14.7		14.7

Lat.	Twilight Naut.	Civil	Sunrise	Moonrise 2	3	4	5
°	h m	h m	h m	h m	h m	h m	h m
N 72	05 01	06 20	07 28	▪▪▪▪	▪▪▪▪	09 28	08 46
N 70	05 07	06 18	07 19	▪▪▪▪	09 06	08 33	08 18
68	05 12	06 16	07 12	08 00	08 02	08 00	07 57
66	05 16	06 15	07 07	07 07	07 26	07 35	07 41
64	05 19	06 14	07 02	06 35	07 00	07 16	07 27
62	05 22	06 13	06 57	06 11	06 40	07 01	07 15
60	05 24	06 12	06 54	05 52	06 24	06 47	07 05
N 58	05 26	06 11	06 51	05 36	06 10	06 36	06 56
56	05 27	06 10	06 47	05 22	05 58	06 26	06 49
54	05 28	06 09	06 45	05 11	05 48	06 18	06 42
52	05 29	06 08	06 42	05 00	05 38	06 10	06 36
50	05 30	06 08	06 40	04 51	05 30	06 03	06 30
45	05 32	06 06	06 35	04 32	05 12	05 47	06 18
N 40	05 33	06 04	06 31	04 16	04 58	05 35	06 08
35	05 33	06 02	06 27	04 02	04 45	05 24	06 00
30	05 32	06 00	06 24	03 51	04 35	05 15	05 52
20	05 31	05 56	06 19	03 31	04 16	04 59	05 39
N 10	05 28	05 52	06 14	03 13	04 00	04 45	05 27
0	05 24	05 48	06 09	02 57	03 45	04 31	05 17
S 10	05 18	05 43	06 04	02 41	03 30	04 18	05 06
20	05 10	05 36	05 58	02 23	03 14	04 04	04 54
30	04 59	05 28	05 52	02 03	02 55	03 48	04 41
35	04 52	05 23	05 48	01 51	02 44	03 38	04 33
40	04 44	05 17	05 44	01 38	02 32	03 27	04 24
45	04 33	05 09	05 39	01 22	02 17	03 14	04 14
S 50	04 20	05 00	05 33	01 02	01 59	02 59	04 01
52	04 13	04 56	05 31	00 53	01 50	02 52	03 56
54	04 06	04 51	05 28	00 43	01 41	02 43	03 49
56	03 57	04 45	05 24	00 31	01 30	02 34	03 42
58	03 47	04 39	05 21	00 17	01 17	02 24	03 34
S 60	03 36	04 32	05 17	00 01	01 03	02 12	03 25

Lat.	Sunset	Twilight Civil	Naut.	Moonset 2	3	4	5
°	h m	h m	h m	h m	h m	h m	h m
N 72	16 58	18 07	19 25	▪▪▪▪	▪▪▪▪	12 10	14 25
N 70	17 06	18 08	19 19	▪▪▪▪	10 55	13 04	14 51
68	17 13	18 09	19 14	10 21	11 59	13 36	15 11
66	17 19	18 11	19 10	11 14	12 34	14 00	15 27
64	17 24	18 12	19 07	11 46	12 59	14 18	15 43
62	17 28	18 12	19 04	12 10	13 19	14 33	15 51
60	17 32	18 13	19 02	12 29	13 35	14 46	16 00
N 58	17 35	18 14	19 00	12 44	13 48	14 57	16 08
56	17 38	18 15	18 58	12 58	14 00	15 06	16 15
54	17 40	18 16	18 57	13 09	14 10	15 15	16 21
52	17 43	18 17	18 56	13 20	14 19	15 22	16 27
50	17 45	18 17	18 55	13 29	14 27	15 29	16 32
45	17 50	18 19	18 53	13 48	14 44	15 43	16 43
N 40	17 54	18 21	18 52	14 03	14 58	15 55	16 52
35	17 57	18 22	18 52	14 16	15 10	16 05	17 00
30	18 00	18 24	18 52	14 28	15 20	16 13	17 07
20	18 06	18 28	18 53	14 47	15 38	16 28	17 18
N 10	18 11	18 32	18 57	15 04	15 53	16 41	17 28
0	18 15	18 36	19 00	15 20	16 08	16 53	17 38
S 10	18 20	18 41	19 06	15 36	16 22	17 06	17 47
20	18 25	18 48	19 14	15 53	16 37	17 18	17 57
30	18 31	18 56	19 24	16 12	16 54	17 33	18 09
35	18 35	19 01	19 31	16 23	17 04	17 41	18 15
40	18 39	19 07	19 39	16 36	17 16	17 51	18 23
45	18 44	19 14	19 50	16 51	17 29	18 02	18 31
S 50	18 49	19 23	20 03	17 10	17 46	18 16	18 41
52	18 52	19 27	20 09	17 19	17 53	18 22	18 46
54	18 55	19 32	20 17	17 29	18 02	18 29	18 51
56	18 58	19 37	20 25	17 40	18 11	18 37	18 57
58	19 02	19 43	20 34	17 52	18 22	18 45	19 04
S 60	19 06	19 50	20 46	18 07	18 35	18 55	19 11

Day	SUN Eqn. of Time 00h	12h	Mer. Pass.	MOON Mer. Pass. Upper	Lower	Age	Phase
d	m s	m s	h m	h m	h m	d	%
2	12 17	12 11	12 12	09 09	21 33	26	15
3	12 05	11 59	12 12	09 56	22 20	27	9
4	11 53	11 46	12 12	10 42	23 05	28	4

© British Crown Copyright 2018. All rights reserved.

UT	ARIES GHA	VENUS −4.1 GHA	Dec	MARS +1.2 GHA	Dec	JUPITER −2.1 GHA	Dec	SATURN +0.6 GHA	Dec	STARS Name	SHA	Dec
5 00	162 27.2	216 21.7	S18 42.6	122 37.6	N16 14.8	260 46.5	S22 35.3	232 55.8	S21 47.5	Acamar	315 15.6	S40 14.1
01	177 29.6	231 21.1	42.0	137 38.4	15.4	275 48.7	35.4	247 58.0	47.5	Achernar	335 24.3	S57 08.8
02	192 32.1	246 20.5	41.5	152 39.2	15.9	290 50.9	35.4	263 00.3	47.4	Acrux	173 04.3	S63 12.2
03	207 34.5	261 19.9	.. 41.0	167 40.0	.. 16.4	305 53.1	.. 35.4	278 02.5	.. 47.4	Adhara	255 09.3	S29 00.2
04	222 37.0	276 19.3	40.4	182 40.8	17.0	320 55.3	35.4	293 04.8	47.4	Aldebaran	290 44.9	N16 32.7
05	237 39.5	291 18.6	39.9	197 41.6	17.5	335 57.4	35.4	308 07.0	47.4			
06	252 41.9	306 18.0	S18 39.3	212 42.4	N16 18.0	350 59.6	S22 35.4	323 09.2	S21 47.3	Alioth	166 16.8	N55 51.3
07	267 44.4	321 17.4	38.8	227 43.2	18.6	6 01.8	35.5	338 11.5	47.3	Alkaid	152 55.5	N49 12.9
T 08	282 46.9	336 16.8	38.2	242 44.0	19.1	21 04.0	35.5	353 13.7	47.3	Alnair	27 39.3	S46 52.1
U 09	297 49.3	351 16.2	.. 37.7	257 44.8	.. 19.6	36 06.1	.. 35.5	8 16.0	.. 47.3	Alnilam	275 42.4	S 1 11.7
E 10	312 51.8	6 15.5	37.1	272 45.6	20.2	51 08.3	35.5	23 18.2	47.2	Alphard	217 52.0	S 8 44.7
S 11	327 54.3	21 14.9	36.6	287 46.4	20.7	66 10.5	35.5	38 20.5	47.2			
D 12	342 56.7	36 14.3	S18 36.0	302 47.2	N16 21.2	81 12.7	S22 35.5	53 22.7	S21 47.2	Alphecca	126 07.6	N26 38.9
A 13	357 59.2	51 13.7	35.5	317 48.0	21.8	96 14.9	35.5	68 25.0	47.2	Alpheratz	357 39.8	N29 11.6
Y 14	13 01.6	66 13.1	34.9	332 48.9	22.3	111 17.0	35.6	83 27.2	47.1	Altair	62 04.7	N 8 55.0
15	28 04.1	81 12.4	.. 34.4	347 49.7	.. 22.8	126 19.2	.. 35.6	98 29.5	.. 47.1	Ankaa	353 12.2	S42 12.4
16	43 06.6	96 11.8	33.8	2 50.5	23.4	141 21.4	35.6	113 31.7	47.1	Antares	112 21.4	S26 28.3
17	58 09.0	111 11.2	33.3	17 51.3	23.9	156 23.6	35.6	128 33.9	47.1			
18	73 11.5	126 10.6	S18 32.7	32 52.1	N16 24.4	171 25.8	S22 35.6	143 36.2	S21 47.0	Arcturus	145 52.0	N19 04.9
19	88 14.0	141 10.0	32.1	47 52.9	25.0	186 27.9	35.6	158 38.4	47.0	Atria	107 19.7	S69 03.3
20	103 16.4	156 09.4	31.6	62 53.7	25.5	201 30.1	35.6	173 40.7	47.0	Avior	234 16.0	S59 34.5
21	118 18.9	171 08.7	.. 31.0	77 54.5	.. 26.0	216 32.3	.. 35.7	188 42.9	.. 47.0	Bellatrix	278 27.8	N 6 21.8
22	133 21.4	186 08.1	30.5	92 55.3	26.6	231 34.5	35.7	203 45.2	46.9	Betelgeuse	270 57.0	N 7 24.4
23	148 23.8	201 07.5	29.9	107 56.1	27.1	246 36.7	35.7	218 47.4	46.9			
6 00	163 26.3	216 06.9	S18 29.3	122 56.9	N16 27.6	261 38.8	S22 35.7	233 49.7	S21 46.9	Canopus	263 54.2	S52 42.8
01	178 28.8	231 06.3	28.8	137 57.7	28.2	276 41.0	35.7	248 51.9	46.9	Capella	280 28.6	N46 01.0
02	193 31.2	246 05.7	28.2	152 58.5	28.7	291 43.2	35.7	263 54.2	46.8	Deneb	49 29.2	N45 20.7
03	208 33.7	261 05.1	.. 27.7	167 59.3	.. 29.2	306 45.4	.. 35.7	278 56.4	.. 46.8	Denebola	182 29.4	N14 27.8
04	223 36.1	276 04.4	27.1	183 00.1	29.7	321 47.6	35.8	293 58.7	46.8	Diphda	348 52.3	S17 53.2
05	238 38.6	291 03.8	26.5	198 00.9	30.3	336 49.8	35.8	309 00.9	46.8			
06	253 41.1	306 03.2	S18 26.0	213 01.7	N16 30.8	351 51.9	S22 35.8	324 03.2	S21 46.7	Dubhe	193 46.3	N61 38.8
W 07	268 43.5	321 02.6	25.4	228 02.5	31.3	6 54.1	35.8	339 05.4	46.7	Elnath	278 07.6	N28 37.3
E 08	283 46.0	336 02.0	24.8	243 03.3	31.9	21 56.3	35.8	354 07.7	46.7	Eltanin	90 44.5	N51 29.0
D 09	298 48.5	351 01.4	.. 24.2	258 04.2	.. 32.4	36 58.5	.. 35.8	9 09.9	.. 46.7	Enif	33 43.6	N 9 57.6
N 10	313 50.9	6 00.8	23.7	273 05.0	32.9	52 00.7	35.8	24 12.2	46.6	Fomalhaut	15 20.0	S29 31.4
E 11	328 53.4	21 00.1	23.1	288 05.8	33.5	67 02.9	35.8	39 14.4	46.6			
S 12	343 55.9	35 59.5	S18 22.5	303 06.6	N16 34.0	82 05.1	S22 35.9	54 16.7	S21 46.6	Gacrux	171 56.0	S57 13.1
D 13	358 58.3	50 58.9	22.0	318 07.4	34.5	97 07.2	35.9	69 18.9	46.6	Gienah	175 48.0	S17 38.9
A 14	14 00.8	65 58.3	21.4	333 08.2	35.0	112 09.4	35.9	84 21.2	46.5	Hadar	148 41.9	S60 27.6
Y 15	29 03.2	80 57.7	.. 20.8	348 09.0	.. 35.6	127 11.6	.. 35.9	99 23.4	.. 46.5	Hamal	327 56.6	N23 33.0
16	44 05.7	95 57.1	20.2	3 09.8	36.1	142 13.8	35.9	114 25.6	46.5	Kaus Aust.	83 38.8	S34 22.3
17	59 08.2	110 56.5	19.7	18 10.6	36.6	157 16.0	35.9	129 27.9	46.5			
18	74 10.6	125 55.9	S18 19.1	33 11.4	N16 37.1	172 18.2	S22 35.9	144 30.1	S21 46.4	Kochab	137 19.5	N74 04.4
19	89 13.1	140 55.2	18.5	48 12.2	37.7	187 20.4	36.0	159 32.4	46.4	Markab	13 34.8	N15 18.3
20	104 15.6	155 54.6	17.9	63 13.0	38.2	202 22.5	36.0	174 34.6	46.4	Menkar	314 11.1	N 4 09.6
21	119 18.0	170 54.0	.. 17.3	78 13.8	.. 38.7	217 24.7	.. 36.0	189 36.9	.. 46.4	Menkent	148 02.7	S36 27.7
22	134 20.5	185 53.4	16.8	93 14.6	39.2	232 26.9	36.0	204 39.1	46.3	Miaplacidus	221 38.1	S69 47.9
23	149 23.0	200 52.8	16.2	108 15.4	39.8	247 29.1	36.0	219 41.4	46.3			
7 00	164 25.4	215 52.2	S18 15.6	123 16.2	N16 40.3	262 31.3	S22 36.0	234 43.6	S21 46.3	Mirfak	308 34.9	N49 55.7
01	179 27.9	230 51.6	15.0	138 17.0	40.8	277 33.5	36.0	249 45.9	46.3	Nunki	75 53.7	S26 16.2
02	194 30.4	245 51.0	14.4	153 17.8	41.3	292 35.7	36.1	264 48.2	46.2	Peacock	53 13.6	S56 40.2
03	209 32.8	260 50.4	.. 13.8	168 18.6	.. 41.9	307 37.9	.. 36.1	279 50.4	.. 46.2	Pollux	243 22.7	N27 58.7
04	224 35.3	275 49.8	13.2	183 19.4	42.4	322 40.1	36.1	294 52.7	46.2	Procyon	244 55.5	N 5 10.4
05	239 37.7	290 49.2	12.7	198 20.2	42.9	337 42.3	36.1	309 54.9	46.2			
06	254 40.2	305 48.5	S18 12.1	213 21.0	N16 43.4	352 44.4	S22 36.1	324 57.2	S21 46.1	Rasalhague	96 02.9	N12 32.7
07	269 42.7	320 47.9	11.5	228 21.8	44.0	7 46.6	36.1	339 59.4	46.1	Regulus	207 39.1	N11 52.3
T 08	284 45.1	335 47.3	10.9	243 22.6	44.5	22 48.8	36.1	355 01.7	46.1	Rigel	281 08.3	S 8 11.1
H 09	299 47.6	350 46.7	.. 10.3	258 23.4	.. 45.0	37 51.0	.. 36.1	10 03.9	.. 46.1	Rigil Kent.	139 46.1	S60 54.5
U 10	314 50.1	5 46.1	09.7	273 24.2	45.5	52 53.2	36.2	25 06.2	46.0	Sabik	102 08.1	S15 44.8
R 11	329 52.5	20 45.5	09.1	288 25.0	46.1	67 55.4	36.2	40 08.4	46.0			
S 12	344 55.0	35 44.9	S18 08.5	303 25.8	N16 46.6	82 57.6	S22 36.2	55 10.7	S21 46.0	Schedar	349 36.6	N56 38.5
D 13	359 57.5	50 44.3	07.9	318 26.6	47.1	97 59.8	36.2	70 12.9	46.0	Shaula	96 16.7	S37 06.8
A 14	14 59.9	65 43.7	07.3	333 27.4	47.6	113 02.0	36.2	85 15.2	45.9	Sirius	258 30.1	S16 44.9
Y 15	30 02.4	80 43.1	.. 06.7	348 28.2	.. 48.2	128 04.2	.. 36.2	100 17.4	.. 45.9	Spica	158 26.9	S11 15.6
16	45 04.9	95 42.5	06.1	3 29.0	48.7	143 06.4	36.2	115 19.7	45.9	Suhail	222 49.2	S43 30.8
17	60 07.3	110 41.9	05.5	18 29.8	49.2	158 08.6	36.3	130 21.9	45.9			
18	75 09.8	125 41.3	S18 04.9	33 30.6	N16 49.7	173 10.8	S22 36.3	145 24.2	S21 45.8	Vega	80 36.5	N38 47.9
19	90 12.2	140 40.7	04.3	48 31.4	50.2	188 13.0	36.3	160 26.4	45.8	Zuben'ubi	137 00.9	S16 07.2
20	105 14.7	155 40.1	03.7	63 32.2	50.8	203 15.2	36.3	175 28.7	45.8		SHA	Mer.Pass.
21	120 17.2	170 39.5	.. 03.1	78 33.0	.. 51.3	218 17.3	.. 36.3	190 30.9	.. 45.8			h m
22	135 19.6	185 38.9	02.5	93 33.8	51.8	233 19.5	36.3	205 33.2	45.7	Venus	52 40.6	9 36
23	150 22.1	200 38.3	01.9	108 34.6	52.3	248 21.7	36.3	220 35.4	45.7	Mars	319 30.6	15 47
	h m									Jupiter	98 12.6	6 32
Mer. Pass. 13 04.1		v −0.6	d 0.6	v 0.8	d 0.5	v 2.2	d 0.0	v 2.2	d 0.0	Saturn	70 23.4	8 23

© British Crown Copyright 2018. All rights reserved.

UT	SUN GHA	SUN Dec	MOON GHA	v	Dec	d	HP
5 d h	° ′	° ′	° ′	′	° ′	′	′
00	177 05.1	S 6 14.9	193 19.7	14.0	S15 16.9	7.9	54.0
01	192 05.3	14.0	207 52.7	13.9	15 09.0	8.1	54.0
02	207 05.4	13.0	222 25.6	14.0	15 00.9	8.1	54.0
03	222 05.6	.. 12.1	236 58.6	14.1	14 52.8	8.1	54.0
04	237 05.7	11.1	251 31.7	14.0	14 44.7	8.2	54.0
05	252 05.8	10.1	266 04.7	14.1	14 36.5	8.3	54.0
06	267 06.0	S 6 09.2	280 37.8	14.2	S14 28.2	8.3	54.0
07	282 06.1	08.2	295 11.0	14.1	14 19.9	8.4	54.0
T 08	297 06.2	07.2	309 44.1	14.2	14 11.5	8.5	54.0
U 09	312 06.4	.. 06.3	324 17.3	14.3	14 03.0	8.5	54.0
E 10	327 06.5	05.3	338 50.6	14.2	13 54.5	8.6	54.0
S 11	342 06.7	04.3	353 23.8	14.3	13 45.9	8.6	54.0
D 12	357 06.8	S 6 03.4	7 57.1	14.3	S13 37.3	8.7	54.0
A 13	12 06.9	02.4	22 30.4	14.4	13 28.6	8.8	54.0
Y 14	27 07.1	01.4	37 03.8	14.3	13 19.8	8.8	54.0
15	42 07.2	6 00.5	51 37.1	14.4	13 11.0	8.9	54.0
16	57 07.4	5 59.5	66 10.5	14.5	13 02.1	8.9	54.0
17	72 07.5	58.5	80 44.0	14.4	12 53.2	9.0	54.0
18	87 07.6	S 5 57.6	95 17.4	14.5	S12 44.2	9.0	54.0
19	102 07.8	56.6	109 50.9	14.5	12 35.2	9.1	54.0
20	117 07.9	55.6	124 24.4	14.6	12 26.1	9.2	54.0
21	132 08.1	.. 54.7	138 58.0	14.6	12 16.9	9.2	54.0
22	147 08.2	53.7	153 31.6	14.6	12 07.7	9.2	54.0
23	162 08.3	52.7	168 05.2	14.6	11 58.5	9.3	54.1
6 00	177 08.5	S 5 51.8	182 38.8	14.6	S11 49.2	9.4	54.1
01	192 08.6	50.8	197 12.4	14.7	11 39.8	9.4	54.1
02	207 08.8	49.8	211 46.1	14.7	11 30.4	9.5	54.1
03	222 08.9	.. 48.9	226 19.8	14.8	11 20.9	9.5	54.1
04	237 09.1	47.9	240 53.6	14.7	11 11.4	9.5	54.1
05	252 09.2	46.9	255 27.3	14.8	11 01.9	9.6	54.1
06	267 09.3	S 5 45.9	270 01.1	14.8	S10 52.3	9.7	54.1
W 07	282 09.5	45.0	284 34.9	14.8	10 42.6	9.7	54.1
E 08	297 09.6	44.0	299 08.7	14.9	10 32.9	9.7	54.1
D 09	312 09.8	.. 43.0	313 42.6	14.8	10 23.2	9.8	54.1
N 10	327 09.9	42.1	328 16.4	14.9	10 13.4	9.8	54.1
E 11	342 10.1	41.1	342 50.3	14.9	10 03.6	9.9	54.1
S 12	357 10.2	S 5 40.1	357 24.2	15.0	S 9 53.7	9.9	54.1
D 13	12 10.3	39.2	11 58.2	14.9	9 43.8	10.0	54.2
A 14	27 10.5	38.2	26 32.1	15.0	9 33.8	10.0	54.2
Y 15	42 10.6	.. 37.2	41 06.1	15.0	9 23.8	10.0	54.2
16	57 10.8	36.3	55 40.1	15.0	9 13.8	10.1	54.2
17	72 10.9	35.3	70 14.1	15.0	9 03.7	10.1	54.2
18	87 11.1	S 5 34.3	84 48.1	15.1	S 8 53.6	10.2	54.2
19	102 11.2	33.3	99 22.2	15.0	8 43.4	10.2	54.2
20	117 11.4	32.4	113 56.2	15.1	8 33.2	10.2	54.2
21	132 11.5	.. 31.4	128 30.3	15.1	8 23.0	10.3	54.2
22	147 11.6	30.4	143 04.4	15.1	8 12.7	10.3	54.2
23	162 11.8	29.5	157 38.5	15.1	8 02.4	10.4	54.2
7 00	177 11.9	S 5 28.5	172 12.6	15.2	S 7 52.0	10.3	54.2
01	192 12.1	27.5	186 46.8	15.1	7 41.7	10.5	54.3
02	207 12.2	26.5	201 20.9	15.2	7 31.2	10.4	54.3
03	222 12.4	.. 25.6	215 55.1	15.2	7 20.8	10.5	54.3
04	237 12.5	24.6	230 29.3	15.2	7 10.3	10.5	54.3
05	252 12.7	23.6	245 03.5	15.2	6 59.8	10.6	54.3
06	267 12.8	S 5 22.7	259 37.7	15.2	S 6 49.2	10.6	54.3
07	282 13.0	21.7	274 11.9	15.2	6 38.6	10.6	54.3
T 08	297 13.1	20.7	288 46.1	15.3	6 28.0	10.6	54.3
H 09	312 13.3	.. 19.7	303 20.4	15.2	6 17.4	10.7	54.3
U 10	327 13.4	18.8	317 54.6	15.3	6 06.7	10.7	54.3
R 11	342 13.5	17.8	332 28.9	15.2	5 56.0	10.7	54.4
S 12	357 13.7	S 5 16.8	347 03.1	15.3	S 5 45.3	10.8	54.4
D 13	12 13.8	15.9	1 37.4	15.3	5 34.5	10.8	54.4
A 14	27 14.0	14.9	16 11.7	15.3	5 23.7	10.8	54.4
Y 15	42 14.1	.. 13.9	30 46.0	15.3	5 12.9	10.8	54.4
16	57 14.3	12.9	45 20.3	15.3	5 02.1	10.9	54.4
17	72 14.4	12.0	59 54.6	15.3	4 51.2	10.8	54.4
18	87 14.6	S 5 11.0	74 28.9	15.3	S 4 40.4	11.0	54.4
19	102 14.7	10.0	89 03.2	15.3	4 29.4	10.9	54.4
20	117 14.9	09.0	103 37.5	15.3	4 18.5	10.9	54.5
21	132 15.0	.. 08.1	118 11.8	15.3	4 07.6	11.0	54.5
22	147 15.2	07.1	132 46.1	15.3	3 56.6	11.0	54.5
23	162 15.3	06.1	147 20.4	15.3	S 3 45.6	11.0	54.5
	SD 16.1 d 1.0		SD 14.7	14.8			14.8

Lat.	Twilight Naut.	Twilight Civil	Sunrise	Moonrise 5	6	7	8
°	h m	h m	h m	h m	h m	h m	h m
N 72	04 46	06 05	07 12	08 46	08 24	08 08	07 53
N 70	04 54	06 05	07 05	08 18	08 08	07 59	07 50
68	05 00	06 04	07 00	07 57	07 54	07 51	07 48
66	05 05	06 04	06 55	07 41	07 43	07 45	07 46
64	05 09	06 04	06 51	07 27	07 34	07 39	07 44
62	05 12	06 04	06 48	07 15	07 26	07 35	07 43
60	05 15	06 03	06 45	07 05	07 19	07 31	07 41
N 58	05 18	06 03	06 42	06 56	07 13	07 27	07 40
56	05 20	06 03	06 40	06 49	07 08	07 24	07 39
54	05 21	06 02	06 38	06 42	07 03	07 21	07 38
52	05 23	06 02	06 36	06 36	06 58	07 18	07 37
50	05 24	06 01	06 34	06 30	06 54	07 16	07 36
45	05 27	06 00	06 30	06 18	06 46	07 11	07 35
N 40	05 28	05 59	06 26	06 08	06 38	07 06	07 33
35	05 29	05 58	06 23	06 00	06 32	07 02	07 32
30	05 29	05 57	06 21	05 52	06 26	06 59	07 31
20	05 29	05 54	06 16	05 39	06 17	06 53	07 29
N 10	05 27	05 51	06 12	05 27	06 08	06 48	07 27
0	05 23	05 47	06 08	05 17	06 00	06 43	07 25
S 10	05 18	05 43	06 04	05 06	05 52	06 38	07 24
20	05 11	05 37	05 59	04 54	05 44	06 33	07 22
30	05 02	05 30	05 54	04 41	05 34	06 27	07 20
35	04 55	05 25	05 51	04 33	05 28	06 24	07 19
40	04 48	05 20	05 48	04 24	05 22	06 20	07 18
45	04 38	05 14	05 43	04 14	05 14	06 15	07 16
S 50	04 25	05 05	05 38	04 01	05 05	06 10	07 15
52	04 19	05 02	05 36	03 56	05 01	06 07	07 14
54	04 13	04 57	05 34	03 49	04 56	06 04	07 13
56	04 05	04 52	05 31	03 42	04 51	06 01	07 12
58	03 56	04 47	05 28	03 34	04 46	05 58	07 11
S 60	03 46	04 41	05 24	03 25	04 39	05 54	07 10

Lat.	Sunset	Twilight Civil	Twilight Naut.	Moonset 5	6	7	8
°	h m	h m	h m	h m	h m	h m	h m
N 72	17 13	18 20	19 40	14 25	16 17	18 03	19 46
N 70	17 19	18 20	19 32	14 51	16 32	18 10	19 46
68	17 24	18 20	19 25	15 11	16 44	18 15	19 46
66	17 29	18 20	19 20	15 27	16 54	18 20	19 46
64	17 33	18 20	19 16	15 40	17 02	18 24	19 46
62	17 36	18 21	19 12	15 51	17 09	18 27	19 46
60	17 39	18 21	19 09	16 00	17 15	18 30	19 46
N 58	17 42	18 21	19 06	16 08	17 20	18 33	19 46
56	17 44	18 21	19 04	16 15	17 25	18 35	19 46
54	17 46	18 21	19 02	16 21	17 29	18 37	19 46
52	17 48	18 22	19 01	16 27	17 33	18 39	19 46
50	17 50	18 22	19 00	16 32	17 36	18 41	19 46
45	17 54	18 23	18 57	16 43	17 44	18 45	19 46
N 40	17 57	18 24	18 55	16 52	17 50	18 48	19 46
35	18 00	18 25	18 54	17 00	17 55	18 50	19 46
30	18 02	18 26	18 54	17 07	18 00	18 53	19 46
20	18 07	18 29	18 54	17 18	18 08	18 57	19 46
N 10	18 11	18 32	18 56	17 28	18 15	19 00	19 46
0	18 15	18 35	18 59	17 38	18 21	19 04	19 46
S 10	18 19	18 40	19 04	17 47	18 27	19 07	19 46
20	18 23	18 45	19 11	17 57	18 34	19 10	19 46
30	18 28	18 52	19 20	18 09	18 42	19 14	19 46
35	18 31	18 57	19 27	18 15	18 46	19 16	19 45
40	18 34	19 02	19 34	18 23	18 51	19 19	19 45
45	18 38	19 08	19 44	18 31	18 57	19 22	19 45
S 50	18 43	19 16	19 56	18 41	19 04	19 25	19 45
52	18 45	19 20	20 02	18 46	19 07	19 27	19 45
54	18 48	19 24	20 08	18 51	19 11	19 28	19 45
56	18 51	19 29	20 16	18 57	19 15	19 30	19 45
58	18 54	19 34	20 24	19 04	19 19	19 32	19 45
S 60	18 57	19 40	20 35	19 11	19 24	19 35	19 45

Day	SUN Eqn. of Time 00h	12h	SUN Mer. Pass.	MOON Mer. Pass. Upper	Lower	Age	Phase
d	m s	m s	h m	h m	h m	d	%
5	11 40	11 33	12 12	11 27	23 49	29	1
6	11 26	11 20	12 11	12 11	24 32	30	0
7	11 13	11 06	12 11	12 53	00 32	01	1

© British Crown Copyright 2018. All rights reserved.

UT (d h)	ARIES GHA	VENUS −4.0 GHA	VENUS Dec	MARS +1.3 GHA	MARS Dec	JUPITER −2.1 GHA	JUPITER Dec	SATURN +0.6 GHA	SATURN Dec	STARS Name	SHA	Dec
8 FRIDAY												
00	165 24.6	215 37.7	S18 01.3	123 35.4	N16 52.8	263 23.9	S22 36.3	235 37.7	S21 45.7	Acamar	315 15.6	S40 14.1
01	180 27.0	230 37.1	00.7	138 36.2	53.4	278 26.1	36.4	250 40.0	45.7	Achernar	335 24.3	S57 08.7
02	195 29.5	245 36.5	18 00.1	153 37.0	53.9	293 28.3	36.4	265 42.2	45.6	Acrux	173 04.3	S63 12.2
03	210 32.0	260 35.8	17 59.5	168 37.8 ..	54.4	308 30.5 ..	36.4	280 44.5 ..	45.6	Adhara	255 09.3	S29 00.2
04	225 34.4	275 35.2	58.9	183 38.6	54.9	323 32.7	36.4	295 46.7	45.6	Aldebaran	290 44.9	N16 32.7
05	240 36.9	290 34.6	58.3	198 39.4	55.4	338 34.9	36.4	310 49.0	45.6			
06	255 39.3	305 34.0	S17 57.7	213 40.2	N16 56.0	353 37.1	S22 36.4	325 51.2	S21 45.5	Alioth	166 16.7	N55 51.3
07	270 41.8	320 33.4	57.0	228 41.0	56.5	8 39.3	36.4	340 53.5	45.5	Alkaid	152 55.4	N49 13.0
08	285 44.3	335 32.8	56.4	243 41.8	57.0	23 41.5	36.4	355 55.7	45.5	Alnair	27 39.3	S46 52.1
09	300 46.7	350 32.2 ..	55.8	258 42.6 ..	57.5	38 43.7 ..	36.5	10 58.0 ..	45.5	Alnilam	275 42.4	S 1 11.7
10	315 49.2	5 31.6	55.2	273 43.4	58.0	53 45.9	36.5	26 00.2	45.4	Alphard	217 52.0	S 8 44.7
11	330 51.7	20 31.0	54.6	288 44.2	58.5	68 48.1	36.5	41 02.5	45.4			
12	345 54.1	35 30.4	S17 54.0	303 45.0	N16 59.1	83 50.3	S22 36.5	56 04.8	S21 45.4	Alphecca	126 07.6	N26 38.9
13	0 56.6	50 29.8	53.4	318 45.8	16 59.6	98 52.5	36.5	71 07.0	45.4	Alpheratz	357 39.8	N29 11.6
14	15 59.1	65 29.2	52.7	333 46.6	17 00.1	113 54.7	36.5	86 09.3	45.3	Altair	62 04.6	N 8 55.0
15	31 01.5	80 28.6 ..	52.1	348 47.4 ..	00.6	128 56.9 ..	36.5	101 11.5 ..	45.3	Ankaa	353 12.2	S42 12.4
16	46 04.0	95 28.0	51.5	3 48.2	01.1	143 59.1	36.6	116 13.8	45.3	Antares	112 21.4	S26 28.3
17	61 06.5	110 27.4	50.9	18 49.0	01.6	159 01.3	36.6	131 16.0	45.3			
18	76 08.9	125 26.9	S17 50.3	33 49.8	N17 02.2	174 03.5	S22 36.6	146 18.3	S21 45.2	Arcturus	145 51.9	N19 04.9
19	91 11.4	140 26.3	49.6	48 50.6	02.7	189 05.7	36.6	161 20.5	45.2	Atria	107 19.7	S69 03.3
20	106 13.8	155 25.7	49.0	63 51.4	03.2	204 07.9	36.6	176 22.8	45.2	Avior	234 16.0	S59 34.5
21	121 16.3	170 25.1 ..	48.4	78 52.2 ..	03.7	219 10.1 ..	36.6	191 25.1 ..	45.2	Bellatrix	278 27.8	N 6 21.8
22	136 18.8	185 24.5	47.8	93 53.0	04.2	234 12.3	36.6	206 27.3	45.1	Betelgeuse	270 57.0	N 7 24.4
23	151 21.2	200 23.9	47.1	108 53.8	04.7	249 14.5	36.6	221 29.6	45.1			
9 SATURDAY												
00	166 23.7	215 23.3	S17 46.5	123 54.6	N17 05.2	264 16.7	S22 36.7	236 31.8	S21 45.1	Canopus	263 54.3	S52 42.8
01	181 26.2	230 22.7	45.9	138 55.4	05.8	279 18.9	36.7	251 34.1	45.1	Capella	280 28.7	N46 01.0
02	196 28.6	245 22.1	45.3	153 56.1	06.3	294 21.1	36.7	266 36.3	45.0	Deneb	49 29.2	N45 20.7
03	211 31.1	260 21.5 ..	44.6	168 56.9 ..	06.8	309 23.3 ..	36.7	281 38.6 ..	45.0	Denebola	182 29.4	N14 27.8
04	226 33.6	275 20.9	44.0	183 57.7	07.3	324 25.5	36.7	296 40.9	45.0	Diphda	348 52.3	S17 53.2
05	241 36.0	290 20.3	43.4	198 58.5	07.8	339 27.8	36.7	311 43.1	45.0			
06	256 38.5	305 19.7	S17 42.7	213 59.3	N17 08.3	354 30.0	S22 36.7	326 45.4	S21 44.9	Dubhe	193 46.3	N61 38.9
07	271 40.9	320 19.1	42.1	229 00.1	08.8	9 32.2	36.7	341 47.6	44.9	Elnath	278 07.7	N28 37.3
08	286 43.4	335 18.5	41.5	244 00.9	09.3	24 34.4	36.7	356 49.9	44.9	Eltanin	90 44.4	N51 29.0
09	301 45.9	350 17.9 ..	40.8	259 01.7 ..	09.9	39 36.6 ..	36.8	11 52.1 ..	44.9	Enif	33 43.6	N 9 57.6
10	316 48.3	5 17.3	40.2	274 02.5	10.4	54 38.8	36.8	26 54.4	44.8	Fomalhaut	15 20.0	S29 31.4
11	331 50.8	20 16.7	39.6	289 03.3	10.9	69 41.0	36.8	41 56.7	44.8			
12	346 53.3	35 16.1	S17 38.9	304 04.1	N17 11.4	84 43.2	S22 36.8	56 58.9	S21 44.8	Gacrux	171 56.0	S57 13.1
13	1 55.7	50 15.5	38.3	319 04.9	11.9	99 45.4	36.8	72 01.2	44.8	Gienah	175 48.0	S17 38.9
14	16 58.2	65 15.0	37.6	334 05.7	12.4	114 47.6	36.8	87 03.4	44.7	Hadar	148 41.9	S60 27.6
15	32 00.7	80 14.4 ..	37.0	349 06.5 ..	12.9	129 49.8 ..	36.8	102 05.7 ..	44.7	Hamal	327 56.6	N23 33.0
16	47 03.1	95 13.8	36.4	4 07.3	13.4	144 52.0	36.8	117 08.0	44.7	Kaus Aust.	83 38.8	S34 22.3
17	62 05.6	110 13.2	35.7	19 08.1	13.9	159 54.2	36.9	132 10.2	44.7			
18	77 08.1	125 12.6	S17 35.1	34 08.9	N17 14.5	174 56.4	S22 36.9	147 12.5	S21 44.6	Kochab	137 19.4	N74 04.4
19	92 10.5	140 12.0	34.4	49 09.7	15.0	189 58.7	36.9	162 14.7	44.6	Markab	13 34.8	N15 18.3
20	107 13.0	155 11.4	33.8	64 10.5	15.5	205 00.9	36.9	177 17.0	44.6	Menkar	314 11.1	N 4 09.6
21	122 15.4	170 10.8 ..	33.2	79 11.2 ..	16.0	220 03.1 ..	36.9	192 19.3 ..	44.6	Menkent	148 02.7	S36 27.7
22	137 17.9	185 10.2	32.5	94 12.0	16.5	235 05.3	36.9	207 21.5	44.5	Miaplacidus	221 38.1	S69 47.9
23	152 20.4	200 09.6	31.9	109 12.8	17.0	250 07.5	36.9	222 23.8	44.5			
10 SUNDAY												
00	167 22.8	215 09.1	S17 31.2	124 13.6	N17 17.5	265 09.7	S22 36.9	237 26.0	S21 44.5	Mirfak	308 35.0	N49 55.7
01	182 25.3	230 08.5	30.6	139 14.4	18.0	280 11.9	37.0	252 28.3	44.5	Nunki	75 53.6	S26 16.2
02	197 27.8	245 07.9	29.9	154 15.2	18.5	295 14.1	37.0	267 30.6	44.5	Peacock	53 13.5	S56 40.2
03	212 30.2	260 07.3 ..	29.3	169 16.0 ..	19.0	310 16.3 ..	37.0	282 32.8 ..	44.4	Pollux	243 22.8	N27 58.7
04	227 32.7	275 06.7	28.6	184 16.8	19.5	325 18.5	37.0	297 35.1	44.4	Procyon	244 55.5	N 5 10.4
05	242 35.2	290 06.1	28.0	199 17.6	20.0	340 20.8	37.0	312 37.3	44.4			
06	257 37.6	305 05.5	S17 27.3	214 18.4	N17 20.6	355 23.0	S22 37.0	327 39.6	S21 44.4	Rasalhague	96 02.9	N12 32.7
07	272 40.1	320 04.9	26.7	229 19.2	21.1	10 25.2	37.0	342 41.9	44.3	Regulus	207 39.1	N11 52.3
08	287 42.5	335 04.4	26.0	244 20.0	21.6	25 27.4	37.0	357 44.1	44.3	Rigel	281 08.3	S 8 11.1
09	302 45.0	350 03.8 ..	25.3	259 20.8 ..	22.1	40 29.6 ..	37.0	12 46.4 ..	44.3	Rigil Kent.	139 46.0	S60 54.5
10	317 47.5	5 03.2	24.7	274 21.6	22.6	55 31.8	37.1	27 48.6	44.3	Sabik	102 08.1	S15 44.8
11	332 49.9	20 02.6	24.0	289 22.3	23.1	70 34.0	37.1	42 50.9	44.2			
12	347 52.4	35 02.0	S17 23.4	304 23.1	N17 23.6	85 36.2	S22 37.1	57 53.2	S21 44.2	Schedar	349 36.6	N56 38.5
13	2 54.9	50 01.4	22.7	319 23.9	24.1	100 38.5	37.1	72 55.4	44.2	Shaula	96 16.7	S37 06.8
14	17 57.3	65 00.8	22.1	334 24.7	24.6	115 40.7	37.1	87 57.7	44.2	Sirius	258 30.2	S16 44.9
15	32 59.8	80 00.3 ..	21.4	349 25.5 ..	25.1	130 42.9 ..	37.1	103 00.0 ..	44.1	Spica	158 26.9	S11 15.6
16	48 02.3	94 59.7	20.7	4 26.3	25.6	145 45.1	37.1	118 02.2	44.1	Suhail	222 49.2	S43 30.8
17	63 04.7	109 59.1	20.1	19 27.1	26.1	160 47.3	37.1	133 04.5	44.1			
18	78 07.2	124 58.5	S17 19.4	34 27.9	N17 26.6	175 49.5	S22 37.2	148 06.7	S21 44.1	Vega	80 36.5	N38 47.9
19	93 09.7	139 57.9	18.8	49 28.7	27.1	190 51.8	37.2	163 09.0	44.0	Zuben'ubi	137 00.9	S16 07.2
20	108 12.1	154 57.3	18.1	64 29.5	27.6	205 54.0	37.2	178 11.3	44.0		SHA	Mer.Pass.
21	123 14.6	169 56.8 ..	17.4	79 30.3 ..	28.1	220 56.2 ..	37.2	193 13.5 ..	44.0			
22	138 17.0	184 56.2	16.7	94 31.0	28.6	235 58.4	37.2	208 15.8	44.0	Venus	48 59.6	9 39
23	153 19.5	199 55.6	16.1	109 31.8	29.1	251 00.6	37.2	223 18.1	43.9	Mars	317 30.9	15 44
Mer. Pass. 12 52.3		v −0.6 d 0.6		v 0.8 d 0.5		v 2.2 d 0.0		v 2.3 d 0.0		Jupiter	97 53.0	6 22
										Saturn	70 08.1	8 13

© British Crown Copyright 2018. All rights reserved.

UT	SUN GHA	SUN Dec	MOON GHA	v	MOON Dec	d	HP
8 d h	° ′	° ′	° ′	′	° ′	′	′
00	177 15.5	S 5 05.1	161 54.7	15.3	S 3 34.6	11.0	54.5
01	192 15.6	04.2	176 29.0	15.3	3 23.6	11.1	54.5
02	207 15.8	03.2	191 03.3	15.4	3 12.5	11.1	54.5
03	222 15.9	.. 02.2	205 37.7	15.3	3 01.4	11.1	54.5
04	237 16.1	01.3	220 12.0	15.3	2 50.3	11.1	54.6
05	252 16.2	5 00.3	234 46.3	15.3	2 39.2	11.1	54.6
06	267 16.4	S 4 59.3	249 20.6	15.3	S 2 28.1	11.1	54.6
07	282 16.5	58.3	263 54.9	15.3	2 17.0	11.2	54.6
08	297 16.7	57.4	278 29.2	15.3	2 05.8	11.1	54.6
F 09	312 16.8	.. 56.4	293 03.5	15.2	1 54.7	11.2	54.6
R 10	327 17.0	55.4	307 37.7	15.3	1 43.5	11.2	54.6
I 11	342 17.1	54.4	322 12.0	15.3	1 32.3	11.2	54.6
D 12	357 17.3	S 4 53.5	336 46.3	15.3	S 1 21.1	11.2	54.7
A 13	12 17.4	52.5	351 20.6	15.2	1 09.9	11.2	54.7
Y 14	27 17.6	51.5	5 54.8	15.2	0 58.7	11.2	54.7
15	42 17.8	.. 50.5	20 29.0	15.3	0 47.5	11.3	54.7
16	57 17.9	49.6	35 03.3	15.2	0 36.2	11.2	54.7
17	72 18.1	48.6	49 37.5	15.2	0 25.0	11.3	54.7
18	87 18.2	S 4 47.6	64 11.7	15.2	S 0 13.7	11.2	54.7
19	102 18.4	46.6	78 45.9	15.2	S 0 02.5	11.3	54.8
20	117 18.5	45.6	93 20.1	15.2	N 0 08.8	11.2	54.8
21	132 18.7	.. 44.7	107 54.3	15.1	0 20.0	11.3	54.8
22	147 18.8	43.7	122 28.4	15.2	0 31.3	11.3	54.8
23	162 19.0	42.7	137 02.6	15.1	0 42.6	11.3	54.8
9 00	177 19.1	S 4 41.7	151 36.7	15.1	N 0 53.9	11.3	54.8
01	192 19.3	40.8	166 10.8	15.1	1 05.2	11.2	54.9
02	207 19.4	39.8	180 44.9	15.1	1 16.4	11.3	54.9
03	222 19.6	.. 38.8	195 19.0	15.0	1 27.7	11.3	54.9
04	237 19.7	37.8	209 53.0	15.0	1 39.0	11.3	54.9
05	252 19.9	36.9	224 27.0	15.1	1 50.3	11.3	54.9
06	267 20.1	S 4 35.9	239 01.1	14.9	N 2 01.6	11.3	54.9
07	282 20.2	34.9	253 35.0	15.0	2 12.9	11.2	54.9
S 08	297 20.4	33.9	268 09.0	15.0	2 24.1	11.3	55.0
A 09	312 20.5	.. 32.9	282 43.0	14.9	2 35.4	11.3	55.0
T 10	327 20.7	32.0	297 16.9	14.9	2 46.7	11.2	55.0
U 11	342 20.8	31.0	311 50.8	14.9	2 57.9	11.3	55.0
R 12	357 21.0	S 4 30.0	326 24.7	14.8	N 3 09.2	11.3	55.0
D 13	12 21.1	29.0	340 58.5	14.8	3 20.5	11.2	55.0
A 14	27 21.3	28.1	355 32.3	14.8	3 31.7	11.2	55.1
Y 15	42 21.5	.. 27.1	10 06.1	14.8	3 42.9	11.3	55.1
16	57 21.6	26.1	24 39.9	14.7	3 54.2	11.2	55.1
17	72 21.8	25.1	39 13.6	14.7	4 05.4	11.2	55.1
18	87 21.9	S 4 24.1	53 47.3	14.7	N 4 16.6	11.2	55.1
19	102 22.1	23.2	68 21.0	14.7	4 27.8	11.2	55.2
20	117 22.2	22.2	82 54.7	14.6	4 39.0	11.1	55.2
21	132 22.4	.. 21.2	97 28.3	14.6	4 50.1	11.2	55.2
22	147 22.6	20.2	112 01.9	14.5	5 01.3	11.1	55.2
23	162 22.7	19.3	126 35.4	14.5	5 12.4	11.2	55.2
10 00	177 22.9	S 4 18.3	141 08.9	14.5	N 5 23.6	11.1	55.2
01	192 23.0	17.3	155 42.4	14.4	5 34.7	11.1	55.3
02	207 23.2	16.3	170 15.8	14.5	5 45.8	11.0	55.3
03	222 23.3	.. 15.3	184 49.3	14.3	5 56.8	11.1	55.3
04	237 23.5	14.4	199 22.6	14.4	6 07.9	11.0	55.3
05	252 23.7	13.4	213 56.0	14.3	6 18.9	11.1	55.3
06	267 23.8	S 4 12.4	228 29.3	14.2	N 6 30.0	11.0	55.4
07	282 24.0	11.4	243 02.5	14.2	6 41.0	10.9	55.4
08	297 24.1	10.4	257 35.7	14.2	6 51.9	11.0	55.4
S 09	312 24.3	.. 09.5	272 08.9	14.1	7 02.9	10.9	55.4
U 10	327 24.5	08.5	286 42.0	14.1	7 13.8	10.9	55.4
N 11	342 24.6	07.5	301 15.1	14.1	7 24.7	10.9	55.5
D 12	357 24.8	S 4 06.5	315 48.2	14.0	N 7 35.6	10.9	55.5
A 13	12 24.9	05.5	330 21.2	13.9	7 46.5	10.8	55.5
Y 14	27 25.1	04.6	344 54.1	14.0	7 57.3	10.8	55.5
15	42 25.3	.. 03.6	359 27.1	13.8	8 08.1	10.8	55.5
16	57 25.4	02.6	13 59.9	13.8	8 18.9	10.7	55.6
17	72 25.6	01.6	28 32.7	13.8	8 29.6	10.8	55.6
18	87 25.7	S 4 00.6	43 05.5	13.7	N 8 40.4	10.6	55.6
19	102 25.9	3 59.7	57 38.2	13.7	8 51.0	10.7	55.6
20	117 26.1	58.7	72 10.9	13.6	9 01.7	10.6	55.6
21	132 26.2	.. 57.7	86 43.5	13.6	9 12.3	10.6	55.7
22	147 26.4	56.7	101 16.1	13.5	9 22.9	10.6	55.7
23	162 26.5	55.7	115 48.6	13.5	N 9 33.5	10.5	55.7
	SD 16.1	d 1.0	SD 14.9		15.0		15.1

Lat.	Twilight Naut.	Twilight Civil	Sunrise	Moonrise 8	9	10	11
°	h m	h m	h m	h m	h m	h m	h m
N 72	04 30	05 50	06 57	07 53	07 39	07 24	07 07
N 70	04 39	05 51	06 52	07 50	07 42	07 34	07 25
68	04 47	05 52	06 47	07 48	07 45	07 41	07 38
66	04 53	05 53	06 44	07 46	07 47	07 48	07 50
64	04 58	05 54	06 41	07 44	07 49	07 53	08 00
62	05 03	05 54	06 38	07 43	07 50	07 58	08 08
60	05 06	05 55	06 36	07 41	07 51	08 02	08 15
N 58	05 09	05 55	06 34	07 40	07 53	08 06	08 21
56	05 12	05 55	06 32	07 39	07 54	08 09	08 27
54	05 14	05 55	06 30	07 38	07 55	08 12	08 32
52	05 16	05 55	06 29	07 37	07 56	08 15	08 36
50	05 18	05 55	06 27	07 36	07 57	08 18	08 41
45	05 21	05 55	06 24	07 35	07 58	08 23	08 50
N 40	05 23	05 55	06 22	07 33	08 00	08 28	08 57
35	05 25	05 54	06 19	07 32	08 01	08 31	09 04
30	05 26	05 54	06 17	07 31	08 02	08 35	09 10
20	05 26	05 52	06 14	07 29	08 04	08 41	09 20
N 10	05 25	05 49	06 11	07 27	08 06	08 46	09 29
0	05 23	05 47	06 07	07 25	08 08	08 52	09 37
S 10	05 18	05 43	06 04	07 24	08 10	08 57	09 45
20	05 12	05 38	06 00	07 22	08 12	09 02	09 54
30	05 04	05 32	05 56	07 20	08 14	09 09	10 05
35	04 58	05 28	05 54	07 19	08 15	09 12	10 11
40	04 51	05 23	05 51	07 18	08 17	09 16	10 18
45	04 42	05 18	05 47	07 16	08 18	09 21	10 26
S 50	04 31	05 11	05 43	07 15	08 20	09 27	10 35
52	04 26	05 07	05 42	07 14	08 21	09 30	10 40
54	04 20	05 03	05 39	07 13	08 22	09 33	10 45
56	04 13	04 59	05 37	07 12	08 24	09 36	10 51
58	04 04	04 54	05 35	07 11	08 25	09 40	10 57
S 60	03 55	04 49	05 32	07 10	08 26	09 44	11 04

Lat.	Sunset	Twilight Civil	Twilight Naut.	Moonset 8	9	10	11
°	h m	h m	h m	h m	h m	h m	h m
N 72	17 27	18 34	19 55	19 46	21 31	23 22	25 23
N 70	17 32	18 32	19 45	19 46	21 24	23 06	24 55
68	17 36	18 31	19 37	19 46	21 18	22 54	24 33
66	17 39	18 30	19 30	19 46	21 14	22 43	24 17
64	17 42	18 29	19 25	19 46	21 10	22 35	24 03
62	17 44	18 29	19 21	19 46	21 06	22 28	23 52
60	17 47	18 28	19 17	19 46	21 03	22 22	23 42
N 58	17 49	18 28	19 13	19 46	21 00	22 16	23 33
56	17 50	18 27	19 11	19 46	20 58	22 11	23 26
54	17 52	18 27	19 08	19 46	20 56	22 07	23 20
52	17 53	18 27	19 06	19 46	20 54	22 03	23 14
50	17 55	18 27	19 04	19 46	20 52	22 00	23 08
45	17 58	18 27	19 01	19 46	20 48	21 52	22 57
N 40	18 00	18 27	18 59	19 46	20 45	21 46	22 47
35	18 02	18 28	18 57	19 46	20 43	21 40	22 39
30	18 04	18 28	18 56	19 46	20 40	21 35	22 32
20	18 08	18 30	18 55	19 46	20 36	21 27	22 20
N 10	18 11	18 32	18 56	19 46	20 32	21 20	22 09
0	18 14	18 35	18 59	19 46	20 29	21 13	21 59
S 10	18 17	18 38	19 03	19 46	20 25	21 06	21 50
20	18 21	18 43	19 08	19 46	20 22	20 59	21 39
30	18 25	18 49	19 17	19 46	20 18	20 51	21 27
35	18 27	18 52	19 22	19 45	20 15	20 46	21 20
40	18 30	18 57	19 29	19 45	20 12	20 41	21 12
45	18 33	19 03	19 38	19 45	20 09	20 35	21 03
S 50	18 37	19 09	19 49	19 45	20 06	20 27	20 52
52	18 39	19 13	19 54	19 45	20 04	20 24	20 47
54	18 41	19 16	20 00	19 45	20 02	20 20	20 41
56	18 43	19 21	20 07	19 45	20 00	20 16	20 35
58	18 45	19 25	20 15	19 45	19 58	20 12	20 28
S 60	18 48	19 31	20 24	19 45	19 55	20 07	20 20

	SUN Eqn. of Time 00h	SUN Eqn. of Time 12h	SUN Mer. Pass.	MOON Mer. Pass. Upper	MOON Mer. Pass. Lower	Age	Phase
Day	m s	m s	h m	h m	h m	d	%
8	10 58	10 51	12 11	13 36	01 14	02	3
9	10 44	10 36	12 11	14 18	01 57	03	8
10	10 29	10 21	12 10	15 02	02 40	04	14

© British Crown Copyright 2018. All rights reserved.

UT	ARIES GHA	VENUS −4.0 GHA	Dec	MARS +1.3 GHA	Dec	JUPITER −2.1 GHA	Dec	SATURN +0.6 GHA	Dec	STARS Name	SHA	Dec
11 00	168 22.0	214 55.0	S17 15.4	124 32.6	N17 29.6	266 02.8	S22 37.2	238 20.3	S21 43.9	Acamar	315 15.6	S40 14.1
01	183 24.4	229 54.4	14.7	139 33.4	30.1	281 05.1	37.2	253 22.6	43.9	Achernar	335 24.3	S57 08.7
02	198 26.9	244 53.8	14.1	154 34.2	30.6	296 07.3	37.2	268 24.8	43.9	Acrux	173 04.2	S63 12.2
03	213 29.4	259 53.3	.. 13.4	169 35.0	.. 31.1	311 09.5	.. 37.3	283 27.1	.. 43.8	Adhara	255 09.3	S29 00.2
04	228 31.8	274 52.7	12.7	184 35.8	31.6	326 11.7	37.3	298 29.4	43.8	Aldebaran	290 45.0	N16 32.7
05	243 34.3	289 52.1	12.1	199 36.6	32.1	341 13.9	37.3	313 31.6	43.8			
06	258 36.8	304 51.5	S17 11.4	214 37.4	N17 32.6	356 16.2	S22 37.3	328 33.9	S21 43.8	Alioth	166 16.7	N55 51.3
07	273 39.2	319 50.9	10.7	229 38.2	33.1	11 18.4	37.3	343 36.2	43.8	Alkaid	152 55.4	N49 13.0
08	288 41.7	334 50.4	10.0	244 38.9	33.6	26 20.6	37.3	358 38.4	43.7	Alnair	27 39.3	S46 52.1
M 09	303 44.1	349 49.8	.. 09.4	259 39.7	.. 34.1	41 22.8	.. 37.3	13 40.7	.. 43.7	Alnilam	275 42.4	S 1 11.7
O 10	318 46.6	4 49.2	08.7	274 40.5	34.6	56 25.0	37.3	28 43.0	43.7	Alphard	217 52.0	S 8 44.7
N 11	333 49.1	19 48.6	08.0	289 41.3	35.1	71 27.3	37.3	43 45.2	43.7			
D 12	348 51.5	34 48.1	S17 07.3	304 42.1	N17 35.6	86 29.5	S22 37.4	58 47.5	S21 43.6	Alphecca	126 07.5	N26 38.9
A 13	3 54.0	49 47.5	06.6	319 42.9	36.1	101 31.7	37.4	73 49.8	43.6	Alpheratz	357 39.8	N29 11.6
Y 14	18 56.5	64 46.9	06.0	334 43.7	36.6	116 33.9	37.4	88 52.0	43.6	Altair	62 04.6	N 8 55.0
15	33 58.9	79 46.3	.. 05.3	349 44.5	.. 37.1	131 36.1	.. 37.4	103 54.3	.. 43.6	Ankaa	353 12.2	S42 12.4
16	49 01.4	94 45.7	04.6	4 45.3	37.6	146 38.4	37.4	118 56.6	43.5	Antares	112 21.4	S26 28.3
17	64 03.9	109 45.2	03.9	19 46.0	38.1	161 40.6	37.4	133 58.8	43.5			
18	79 06.3	124 44.6	S17 03.2	34 46.8	N17 38.6	176 42.8	S22 37.4	149 01.1	S21 43.5	Arcturus	145 51.9	N19 04.9
19	94 08.8	139 44.0	02.6	49 47.6	39.1	191 45.0	37.4	164 03.3	43.5	Atria	107 19.6	S69 03.3
20	109 11.3	154 43.4	01.9	64 48.4	39.6	206 47.3	37.4	179 05.6	43.4	Avior	234 16.0	S59 34.5
21	124 13.7	169 42.9	.. 01.2	79 49.2	.. 40.1	221 49.5	.. 37.5	194 07.9	.. 43.4	Bellatrix	278 27.8	N 6 21.8
22	139 16.2	184 42.3	17 00.5	94 50.0	40.6	236 51.7	37.5	209 10.1	43.4	Betelgeuse	270 57.0	N 7 24.4
23	154 18.6	199 41.7	16 59.8	109 50.8	41.1	251 53.9	37.5	224 12.4	43.4			
12 00	169 21.1	214 41.1	S16 59.1	124 51.6	N17 41.6	266 56.2	S22 37.5	239 14.7	S21 43.3	Canopus	263 54.3	S52 42.8
01	184 23.6	229 40.6	58.4	139 52.3	42.1	281 58.4	37.5	254 16.9	43.3	Capella	280 28.7	N46 01.0
02	199 26.0	244 40.0	57.7	154 53.1	42.6	297 00.6	37.5	269 19.2	43.3	Deneb	49 29.2	N45 20.7
03	214 28.5	259 39.4	.. 57.1	169 53.9	.. 43.1	312 02.8	.. 37.5	284 21.5	.. 43.3	Denebola	182 29.4	N14 27.8
04	229 31.0	274 38.8	56.4	184 54.7	43.6	327 05.1	37.5	299 23.7	43.3	Diphda	348 52.3	S17 53.2
05	244 33.4	289 38.3	55.7	199 55.5	44.1	342 07.3	37.5	314 26.0	43.2			
06	259 35.9	304 37.7	S16 55.0	214 56.3	N17 44.6	357 09.5	S22 37.6	329 28.3	S21 43.2	Dubhe	193 46.3	N61 38.9
07	274 38.4	319 37.1	54.3	229 57.1	45.1	12 11.7	37.6	344 30.6	43.2	Elnath	278 07.7	N28 37.3
T 08	289 40.8	334 36.6	53.6	244 57.9	45.6	27 14.0	37.6	359 32.8	43.2	Eltanin	90 44.4	N51 29.0
U 09	304 43.3	349 36.0	.. 52.9	259 58.6	.. 46.1	42 16.2	.. 37.6	14 35.1	.. 43.1	Enif	33 43.6	N 9 57.6
E 10	319 45.8	4 35.4	52.2	274 59.4	46.6	57 18.4	37.6	29 37.4	43.1	Fomalhaut	15 20.0	S29 31.4
S 11	334 48.2	19 34.8	51.5	290 00.2	47.1	72 20.6	37.6	44 39.6	43.1			
D 12	349 50.7	34 34.3	S16 50.8	305 01.0	N17 47.6	87 22.9	S22 37.6	59 41.9	S21 43.1	Gacrux	171 56.0	S57 13.1
A 13	4 53.1	49 33.7	50.1	320 01.8	48.0	102 25.1	37.6	74 44.2	43.0	Gienah	175 48.0	S17 38.9
Y 14	19 55.6	64 33.1	49.4	335 02.6	48.5	117 27.3	37.6	89 46.4	43.0	Hadar	148 41.9	S60 27.6
15	34 58.1	79 32.6	.. 48.7	350 03.4	.. 49.0	132 29.6	.. 37.6	104 48.7	.. 43.0	Hamal	327 56.6	N23 33.0
16	50 00.5	94 32.0	48.0	5 04.1	49.5	147 31.8	37.7	119 51.0	43.0	Kaus Aust.	83 38.7	S34 22.3
17	65 03.0	109 31.4	47.3	20 04.9	50.0	162 34.0	37.7	134 53.2	42.9			
18	80 05.5	124 30.9	S16 46.6	35 05.7	N17 50.5	177 36.3	S22 37.7	149 55.5	S21 42.9	Kochab	137 19.4	N74 04.5
19	95 07.9	139 30.3	45.9	50 06.5	51.0	192 38.5	37.7	164 57.8	42.9	Markab	13 34.8	N15 18.3
20	110 10.4	154 29.7	45.2	65 07.3	51.5	207 40.7	37.7	180 00.0	42.9	Menkar	314 11.1	N 4 09.6
21	125 12.9	169 29.2	.. 44.5	80 08.1	.. 52.0	222 42.9	.. 37.7	195 02.3	.. 42.9	Menkent	148 02.7	S36 27.7
22	140 15.3	184 28.6	43.8	95 08.9	52.5	237 45.2	37.7	210 04.6	42.8	Miaplacidus	221 38.1	S69 47.9
23	155 17.8	199 28.0	43.1	110 09.6	53.0	252 47.4	37.7	225 06.9	42.8			
13 00	170 20.2	214 27.5	S16 42.3	125 10.4	N17 53.5	267 49.6	S22 37.7	240 09.1	S21 42.8	Mirfak	308 35.0	N49 55.7
01	185 22.7	229 26.9	41.6	140 11.2	53.9	282 51.9	37.8	255 11.4	42.8	Nunki	75 53.6	S26 16.2
02	200 25.2	244 26.3	40.9	155 12.0	54.4	297 54.1	37.8	270 13.7	42.7	Peacock	53 13.5	S56 40.2
03	215 27.6	259 25.8	.. 40.2	170 12.8	.. 54.9	312 56.3	.. 37.8	285 15.9	.. 42.7	Pollux	243 22.8	N27 58.7
04	230 30.1	274 25.2	39.5	185 13.6	55.4	327 58.6	37.8	300 18.2	42.7	Procyon	244 55.5	N 5 10.4
05	245 32.6	289 24.6	38.8	200 14.3	55.9	343 00.8	37.8	315 20.5	42.7			
06	260 35.0	304 24.1	S16 38.1	215 15.1	N17 56.4	358 03.0	S22 37.8	330 22.7	S21 42.6	Rasalhague	96 02.9	N12 32.7
W 07	275 37.5	319 23.5	37.4	230 15.9	56.9	13 05.3	37.8	345 25.0	42.6	Regulus	207 39.1	N11 52.3
E 08	290 40.0	334 22.9	36.7	245 16.7	57.4	28 07.5	37.8	0 27.3	42.6	Rigel	281 08.3	S 8 11.1
D 09	305 42.4	349 22.4	.. 35.9	260 17.5	.. 57.9	43 09.7	.. 37.8	15 29.6	.. 42.6	Rigil Kent.	139 46.0	S60 54.5
N 10	320 44.9	4 21.8	35.2	275 18.3	58.3	58 12.0	37.8	30 31.8	42.6	Sabik	102 08.0	S15 44.8
E 11	335 47.4	19 21.2	34.5	290 19.0	58.8	73 14.2	37.9	45 34.1	42.5			
S 12	350 49.8	34 20.7	S16 33.8	305 19.8	N17 59.3	88 16.5	S22 37.9	60 36.4	S21 42.5	Schedar	349 36.6	N56 38.4
D 13	5 52.3	49 20.1	33.1	320 20.6	17 59.8	103 18.7	37.9	75 38.6	42.5	Shaula	96 16.6	S37 06.8
A 14	20 54.7	64 19.6	32.3	335 21.4	18 00.3	118 20.9	37.9	90 40.9	42.5	Sirius	258 30.2	S16 44.9
Y 15	35 57.2	79 19.0	.. 31.6	350 22.2	.. 00.8	133 23.2	.. 37.9	105 43.2	.. 42.4	Spica	158 26.9	S11 15.6
16	50 59.7	94 18.4	30.9	5 23.0	01.3	148 25.4	37.9	120 45.5	42.4	Suhail	222 49.2	S43 30.8
17	66 02.1	109 17.9	30.2	20 23.7	01.8	163 27.6	37.9	135 47.7	42.4			
18	81 04.6	124 17.3	S16 29.5	35 24.5	N18 02.2	178 29.9	S22 37.9	150 50.0	S21 42.4	Vega	80 36.4	N38 47.9
19	96 07.1	139 16.8	28.7	50 25.3	02.7	193 32.1	37.9	165 52.3	42.3	Zuben'ubi	137 00.9	S16 07.2
20	111 09.5	154 16.2	28.0	65 26.1	03.2	208 34.4	37.9	180 54.6	42.3		SHA	Mer.Pass.
21	126 12.0	169 15.6	.. 27.3	80 26.9	.. 03.7	223 36.6	.. 38.0	195 56.8	.. 42.3	Venus	45 20.0	9 42
22	141 14.5	184 15.1	26.6	95 27.7	04.2	238 38.8	38.0	210 59.1	42.3	Mars	315 30.5	15 40
23	156 16.9	199 14.5	25.8	110 28.4	04.7	253 41.1	38.0	226 01.4	42.2	Jupiter	97 35.0	6 11
Mer.Pass. 12 40.5		v −0.6	d 0.7	v 0.8	d 0.5	v 2.2	d 0.0	v 2.3	d 0.0	Saturn	69 53.6	8 02

© British Crown Copyright 2018. All rights reserved.

SUN and MOON

UT	SUN GHA	SUN Dec	MOON GHA	v	MOON Dec	d	HP
d h	° ′	° ′	° ′	′	° ′	′	′
11 00	177 26.7	S 3 54.7	130 21.1	13.4	N 9 44.0	10.5	55.7
01	192 26.9	53.8	144 53.5	13.4	9 54.5	10.4	55.8
02	207 27.0	52.8	159 25.9	13.3	10 04.9	10.4	55.8
03	222 27.2	.. 51.8	173 58.2	13.3	10 15.3	10.4	55.8
04	237 27.3	50.8	188 30.5	13.2	10 25.7	10.3	55.8
05	252 27.5	49.8	203 02.7	13.1	10 36.0	10.3	55.9
06	267 27.7	S 3 48.9	217 34.8	13.1	N10 46.3	10.3	55.9
07	282 27.8	47.9	232 06.9	13.0	10 56.6	10.2	55.9
M 08	297 28.0	46.9	246 38.9	13.0	11 06.8	10.1	55.9
O 09	312 28.2	.. 45.9	261 10.9	12.9	11 16.9	10.0	55.9
N 10	327 28.3	44.9	275 42.8	12.9	11 27.1	10.0	56.0
D 11	342 28.5	44.0	290 14.7	12.8	11 37.1	10.1	56.0
A 12	357 28.6	S 3 43.0	304 46.5	12.7	N11 47.2	9.9	56.0
Y 13	12 28.8	42.0	319 18.2	12.7	11 57.1	10.0	56.0
14	27 29.0	41.0	333 49.9	12.6	12 07.1	9.9	56.1
15	42 29.1	.. 40.0	348 21.5	12.5	12 17.0	9.8	56.1
16	57 29.3	39.0	2 53.0	12.5	12 26.8	9.8	56.1
17	72 29.5	38.1	17 24.5	12.4	12 36.6	9.7	56.1
18	87 29.6	S 3 37.1	31 55.9	12.4	N12 46.3	9.7	56.2
19	102 29.8	36.1	46 27.3	12.2	12 56.0	9.6	56.2
20	117 30.0	35.1	60 58.5	12.3	13 05.6	9.6	56.2
21	132 30.1	.. 34.1	75 29.8	12.1	13 15.2	9.5	56.2
22	147 30.3	33.1	90 00.9	12.1	13 24.7	9.5	56.3
23	162 30.4	32.2	104 32.0	12.0	13 34.2	9.4	56.3
12 00	177 30.6	S 3 31.2	119 03.0	12.0	N13 43.6	9.3	56.3
01	192 30.8	30.2	133 34.0	11.9	13 52.9	9.3	56.3
02	207 30.9	29.2	148 04.9	11.8	14 02.2	9.2	56.4
03	222 31.1	.. 28.2	162 35.7	11.7	14 11.4	9.2	56.4
04	237 31.3	27.2	177 06.4	11.7	14 20.6	9.1	56.4
05	252 31.4	26.3	191 37.1	11.6	14 29.7	9.0	56.4
06	267 31.6	S 3 25.3	206 07.7	11.5	N14 38.7	9.0	56.5
07	282 31.8	24.3	220 38.2	11.5	14 47.7	8.9	56.5
T 08	297 31.9	23.3	235 08.7	11.3	14 56.6	8.9	56.5
U 09	312 32.1	.. 22.3	249 39.0	11.3	15 05.5	8.7	56.6
E 10	327 32.3	21.3	264 09.3	11.3	15 14.2	8.8	56.6
S 11	342 32.4	20.4	278 39.6	11.1	15 23.0	8.6	56.6
D 12	357 32.6	S 3 19.4	293 09.7	11.1	N15 31.6	8.6	56.6
A 13	12 32.8	18.4	307 39.8	11.0	15 40.2	8.5	56.7
Y 14	27 32.9	17.4	322 09.8	11.0	15 48.7	8.4	56.7
15	42 33.1	.. 16.4	336 39.8	10.8	15 57.1	8.3	56.7
16	57 33.3	15.4	351 09.6	10.8	16 05.4	8.3	56.7
17	72 33.4	14.5	5 39.4	10.7	16 13.7	8.2	56.8
18	87 33.6	S 3 13.5	20 09.1	10.7	N16 21.9	8.1	56.8
19	102 33.8	12.5	34 38.8	10.5	16 30.0	8.1	56.8
20	117 33.9	11.5	49 08.3	10.5	16 38.1	7.9	56.9
21	132 34.1	.. 10.5	63 37.8	10.4	16 46.0	7.9	56.9
22	147 34.3	09.5	78 07.2	10.3	16 53.9	7.8	56.9
23	162 34.4	08.6	92 36.5	10.3	17 01.7	7.8	56.9
13 00	177 34.6	S 3 07.6	107 05.8	10.2	N17 09.5	7.6	57.0
01	192 34.8	06.6	121 35.0	10.1	17 17.1	7.5	57.0
02	207 34.9	05.6	136 04.1	10.0	17 24.6	7.5	57.0
03	222 35.1	.. 04.6	150 33.1	9.9	17 32.1	7.4	57.1
04	237 35.3	03.6	165 02.0	9.9	17 39.5	7.3	57.1
05	252 35.5	02.6	179 30.9	9.7	17 46.8	7.2	57.1
06	267 35.6	S 3 01.7	193 59.6	9.7	N17 54.0	7.1	57.1
W 07	282 35.8	3 00.7	208 28.3	9.6	18 01.1	7.1	57.2
E 08	297 36.0	2 59.7	222 56.9	9.6	18 08.2	6.9	57.2
D 09	312 36.1	.. 58.7	237 25.5	9.4	18 15.1	6.8	57.2
N 10	327 36.3	57.7	251 53.9	9.4	18 21.9	6.8	57.3
E 11	342 36.5	56.7	266 22.3	9.3	18 28.7	6.6	57.3
S 12	357 36.6	S 2 55.7	280 50.6	9.2	N18 35.3	6.6	57.3
D 13	12 36.8	54.8	295 18.8	9.2	18 41.9	6.5	57.4
A 14	27 37.0	53.8	309 47.0	9.0	18 48.4	6.3	57.4
Y 15	42 37.1	.. 52.8	324 15.0	9.0	18 54.7	6.3	57.4
16	57 37.3	51.8	338 43.0	8.9	19 01.0	6.2	57.5
17	72 37.5	50.8	353 10.9	8.8	19 07.2	6.0	57.5
18	87 37.7	S 2 49.8	7 38.7	8.8	N19 13.2	6.0	57.5
19	102 37.8	48.9	22 06.5	8.6	19 19.2	5.8	57.5
20	117 38.0	47.9	36 34.1	8.6	19 25.0	5.8	57.6
21	132 38.2	.. 46.9	51 01.7	8.5	19 30.8	5.6	57.6
22	147 38.3	45.9	65 29.2	8.5	19 36.4	5.6	57.6
23	162 38.5	44.9	79 56.7	8.3	N19 42.0	5.4	57.7
	SD 16.1	d 1.0	SD 15.3		15.4		15.6

Twilight, Sunrise and Moonrise

Lat.	Naut.	Civil	Sunrise	Moonrise 11	12	13	14
°	h m	h m	h m	h m	h m	h m	h m
N 72	04 13	05 34	06 41	07 07	06 43	05 44	▭▭
N 70	04 25	05 37	06 38	07 25	07 13	06 56	▭▭
68	04 34	05 40	06 35	07 38	07 36	07 34	07 34
66	04 41	05 42	06 32	07 50	07 54	08 01	08 15
64	04 48	05 43	06 30	08 00	08 08	08 21	08 43
62	04 53	05 45	06 29	08 08	08 20	08 38	09 05
60	04 57	05 46	06 27	08 15	08 31	08 52	09 23
N 58	05 01	05 47	06 25	08 21	08 40	09 04	09 37
56	05 04	05 47	06 24	08 27	08 48	09 15	09 50
54	05 07	05 48	06 23	08 32	08 55	09 24	10 01
52	05 09	05 48	06 22	08 36	09 02	09 32	10 11
50	05 11	05 49	06 21	08 41	09 07	09 40	10 20
45	05 16	05 50	06 19	08 50	09 20	09 56	10 38
N 40	05 19	05 50	06 17	08 57	09 30	10 09	10 53
35	05 21	05 50	06 15	09 04	09 39	10 20	11 06
30	05 22	05 50	06 14	09 10	09 47	10 30	11 18
20	05 24	05 49	06 11	09 20	10 01	10 47	11 37
N 10	05 24	05 48	06 09	09 29	10 13	11 02	11 54
0	05 22	05 46	06 07	09 37	10 25	11 16	12 10
S 10	05 19	05 43	06 04	09 45	10 36	11 30	12 26
20	05 14	05 39	06 01	09 54	10 48	11 45	12 43
30	05 06	05 34	05 58	10 05	11 03	12 02	13 03
35	05 01	05 31	05 56	10 11	11 11	12 12	13 14
40	04 55	05 27	05 54	10 18	11 20	12 24	13 28
45	04 47	05 22	05 51	10 26	11 31	12 38	13 43
S 50	04 37	05 16	05 48	10 35	11 45	12 55	14 03
52	04 32	05 13	05 47	10 40	11 51	13 03	14 12
54	04 26	05 09	05 45	10 45	11 58	13 11	14 22
56	04 20	05 06	05 44	10 50	12 06	13 21	14 34
58	04 13	05 02	05 42	10 57	12 15	13 33	14 47
S 60	04 04	04 57	05 39	11 04	12 25	13 46	15 03

Sunset, Twilight and Moonset

Lat.	Sunset	Civil	Naut.	Moonset 11	12	13	14
°	h m	h m	h m	h m	h m	h m	h m
N 72	17 41	18 48	20 10	25 23	01 23	04 07	▭▭
N 70	17 44	18 45	19 58	24 55	00 55	02 55	▭▭
68	17 47	18 42	19 49	24 33	00 33	02 18	04 09
66	17 49	18 40	19 41	24 17	00 17	01 53	03 29
64	17 51	18 38	19 34	24 03	00 03	01 33	03 01
62	17 53	18 37	19 29	23 52	25 17	01 17	02 40
60	17 54	18 36	19 24	23 42	25 03	01 03	02 22
N 58	17 55	18 34	19 20	23 33	24 52	00 52	02 08
56	17 57	18 34	19 17	23 26	24 42	00 42	01 56
54	17 58	18 33	19 14	23 20	24 33	00 33	01 45
52	17 59	18 32	19 12	23 14	24 25	00 25	01 35
50	18 00	18 32	19 09	23 08	24 18	00 18	01 27
45	18 02	18 31	19 05	22 57	24 03	00 03	01 09
N 40	18 03	18 30	19 02	22 47	23 51	24 54	00 54
35	18 05	18 30	18 59	22 39	23 40	24 42	00 42
30	18 06	18 30	18 58	22 32	23 31	24 31	00 31
20	18 09	18 31	18 56	22 20	23 15	24 12	00 12
N 10	18 11	18 32	18 58	22 09	23 01	23 56	24 53
0	18 13	18 34	18 58	21 59	22 49	23 41	24 37
S 10	18 15	18 36	19 01	21 50	22 36	23 26	24 20
20	18 18	18 40	19 06	21 39	22 22	23 10	24 03
30	18 21	18 45	19 13	21 27	22 07	22 52	23 42
35	18 23	18 48	19 18	21 20	21 58	22 41	23 31
40	18 25	18 52	19 24	21 12	21 47	22 29	23 17
45	18 27	18 57	19 32	21 03	21 35	22 14	23 01
S 50	18 30	19 03	19 42	20 52	21 21	21 57	22 41
52	18 32	19 06	19 46	20 47	21 14	21 48	22 32
54	18 33	19 09	19 52	20 41	21 07	21 39	22 21
56	18 35	19 12	19 58	20 35	20 58	21 29	22 09
58	18 37	19 16	20 05	20 28	20 49	21 17	21 56
S 60	18 39	19 21	20 13	20 20	20 38	21 03	21 39

SUN and MOON

Day	SUN Eqn. of Time 00ʰ	12ʰ	Mer. Pass.	MOON Mer. Pass. Upper	Lower	Age	Phase
d	m s	m s	h m	h m	h m	d	%
11	10 14	10 06	12 10	15 48	03 25	05	21
12	09 58	09 50	12 10	16 37	04 12	06	30
13	09 42	09 34	12 10	17 28	05 02	07	40

© British Crown Copyright 2018. All rights reserved.

UT	ARIES GHA	VENUS −4.0 GHA	Dec	MARS +1.3 GHA	Dec	JUPITER −2.1 GHA	Dec	SATURN +0.6 GHA	Dec	STARS Name	SHA	Dec
14 00	171 19.4	214 14.0	S16 25.1	125 29.2	N18 05.1	268 43.3	S22 38.0	241 03.7	S21 42.2	Acamar	315 15.6	S40 14.1
01	186 21.9	229 13.4	24.4	140 30.0	05.6	283 45.5	38.0	256 05.9	42.2	Achernar	335 24.3	S57 08.7
02	201 24.3	244 12.8	23.6	155 30.8	06.1	298 47.8	38.0	271 08.2	42.2	Acrux	173 04.2	S63 12.2
03	216 26.8	259 12.3	.. 22.9	170 31.6	.. 06.6	313 50.0	.. 38.0	286 10.5	.. 42.2	Adhara	255 09.3	S29 00.2
04	231 29.2	274 11.7	22.2	185 32.3	07.1	328 52.3	38.0	301 12.7	42.1	Aldebaran	290 45.0	N16 32.7
05	246 31.7	289 11.2	21.4	200 33.1	07.6	343 54.5	38.0	316 15.0	42.1			
06	261 34.2	304 10.6	S16 20.7	215 33.9	N18 08.0	358 56.8	S22 38.0	331 17.3	S21 42.1	Alioth	166 16.7	N55 51.3
07	276 36.6	319 10.1	20.0	230 34.7	08.5	13 59.0	38.1	346 19.6	42.1	Alkaid	152 55.4	N49 13.0
T 08	291 39.1	334 09.5	19.2	245 35.5	09.0	29 01.2	38.1	1 21.8	42.0	Alnair	27 39.3	S46 52.1
H 09	306 41.6	349 08.9	.. 18.5	260 36.2	.. 09.5	44 03.5	.. 38.1	16 24.1	.. 42.0	Alnilam	275 42.4	S 1 11.7
U 10	321 44.0	4 08.4	17.8	275 37.0	10.0	59 05.7	38.1	31 26.4	42.0	Alphard	217 52.0	S 8 44.7
R 11	336 46.5	19 07.8	17.0	290 37.8	10.5	74 08.0	38.1	46 28.7	42.0			
S 12	351 49.0	34 07.3	S16 16.3	305 38.6	N18 10.9	89 10.2	S22 38.1	61 30.9	S21 42.0	Alphecca	126 07.5	N26 38.9
D 13	6 51.4	49 06.7	15.6	320 39.4	11.4	104 12.5	38.1	76 33.2	41.9	Alpheratz	357 39.8	N29 11.6
A 14	21 53.9	64 06.2	14.8	335 40.2	11.9	119 14.7	38.1	91 35.5	41.9	Altair	62 04.6	N 8 55.0
Y 15	36 56.4	79 05.6	.. 14.1	350 40.9	.. 12.4	134 16.9	.. 38.1	106 37.8	.. 41.9	Ankaa	353 12.2	S42 12.4
16	51 58.8	94 05.1	13.3	5 41.7	12.9	149 19.2	38.1	121 40.0	41.9	Antares	112 21.4	S26 28.3
17	67 01.3	109 04.5	12.6	20 42.5	13.3	164 21.4	38.1	136 42.3	41.8			
18	82 03.7	124 04.0	S16 11.9	35 43.3	N18 13.8	179 23.7	S22 38.2	151 44.6	S21 41.8	Arcturus	145 51.9	N19 04.9
19	97 06.2	139 03.4	11.1	50 44.0	14.3	194 25.9	38.2	166 46.9	41.8	Atria	107 19.6	S69 03.3
20	112 08.7	154 02.8	10.4	65 44.8	14.8	209 28.2	38.2	181 49.2	41.8	Avior	234 16.0	S59 34.6
21	127 11.1	169 02.3	.. 09.6	80 45.6	.. 15.3	224 30.4	.. 38.2	196 51.4	.. 41.7	Bellatrix	278 27.8	N 6 21.8
22	142 13.6	184 01.7	08.9	95 46.4	15.7	239 32.7	38.2	211 53.7	41.7	Betelgeuse	270 57.0	N 7 24.4
23	157 16.1	199 01.2	08.1	110 47.2	16.2	254 34.9	38.2	226 56.0	41.7			
15 00	172 18.5	214 00.6	S16 07.4	125 47.9	N18 16.7	269 37.2	S22 38.2	241 58.3	S21 41.7	Canopus	263 54.3	S52 42.8
01	187 21.0	229 00.1	06.6	140 48.7	17.2	284 39.4	38.2	257 00.5	41.7	Capella	280 28.7	N46 01.0
02	202 23.5	243 59.5	05.9	155 49.5	17.7	299 41.6	38.2	272 02.8	41.6	Deneb	49 29.1	N45 20.7
03	217 25.9	258 59.0	.. 05.1	170 50.3	.. 18.1	314 43.9	.. 38.2	287 05.1	.. 41.6	Denebola	182 29.4	N14 27.8
04	232 28.4	273 58.4	04.4	185 51.1	18.6	329 46.1	38.3	302 07.4	41.6	Diphda	348 52.3	S17 53.2
05	247 30.8	288 57.9	03.6	200 51.8	19.1	344 48.4	38.3	317 09.6	41.6			
06	262 33.3	303 57.3	S16 02.9	215 52.6	N18 19.6	359 50.6	S22 38.3	332 11.9	S21 41.5	Dubhe	193 46.3	N61 38.9
07	277 35.8	318 56.8	02.1	230 53.4	20.0	14 52.9	38.3	347 14.2	41.5	Elnath	278 07.7	N28 37.3
08	292 38.2	333 56.2	01.4	245 54.2	20.5	29 55.1	38.3	2 16.5	41.5	Eltanin	90 44.4	N51 29.0
F 09	307 40.7	348 55.7	16 00.6	260 55.0	.. 21.0	44 57.4	.. 38.3	17 18.8	.. 41.5	Enif	33 43.6	N 9 57.6
R 10	322 43.2	3 55.2	15 59.9	275 55.7	21.5	59 59.6	38.3	32 21.0	41.5	Fomalhaut	15 20.0	S29 31.4
I 11	337 45.6	18 54.6	59.1	290 56.5	21.9	75 01.9	38.3	47 23.3	41.4			
D 12	352 48.1	33 54.1	S15 58.4	305 57.3	N18 22.4	90 04.1	S22 38.3	62 25.6	S21 41.4	Gacrux	171 56.0	S57 13.1
A 13	7 50.6	48 53.5	57.6	320 58.1	22.9	105 06.4	38.3	77 27.9	41.4	Gienah	175 48.0	S17 38.9
Y 14	22 53.0	63 53.0	56.8	335 58.8	23.4	120 08.6	38.3	92 30.2	41.4	Hadar	148 41.8	S60 27.7
15	37 55.5	78 52.4	.. 56.1	350 59.6	.. 23.8	135 10.9	.. 38.4	107 32.4	.. 41.3	Hamal	327 56.6	N23 33.0
16	52 58.0	93 51.9	55.3	6 00.4	24.3	150 13.1	38.4	122 34.7	41.3	Kaus Aust.	83 38.7	S34 22.3
17	68 00.4	108 51.3	54.6	21 01.2	24.8	165 15.4	38.4	137 37.0	41.3			
18	83 02.9	123 50.8	S15 53.8	36 01.9	N18 25.3	180 17.7	S22 38.4	152 39.3	S21 41.3	Kochab	137 19.4	N74 04.5
19	98 05.3	138 50.2	53.0	51 02.7	25.7	195 19.9	38.4	167 41.5	41.2	Markab	13 34.8	N15 18.3
20	113 07.8	153 49.7	52.3	66 03.5	26.2	210 22.2	38.4	182 43.8	41.2	Menkar	314 11.2	N 4 09.6
21	128 10.3	168 49.1	.. 51.5	81 04.3	.. 26.7	225 24.4	.. 38.4	197 46.1	.. 41.2	Menkent	148 02.7	S36 27.7
22	143 12.7	183 48.6	50.7	96 05.1	27.2	240 26.7	38.4	212 48.4	41.2	Miaplacidus	221 38.1	S69 48.0
23	158 15.2	198 48.1	50.0	111 05.8	27.6	255 28.9	38.4	227 50.7	41.2			
16 00	173 17.7	213 47.5	S15 49.2	126 06.6	N18 28.1	270 31.2	S22 38.4	242 53.0	S21 41.1	Mirfak	308 35.0	N49 55.7
01	188 20.1	228 47.0	48.5	141 07.4	28.6	285 33.4	38.4	257 55.2	41.1	Nunki	75 53.6	S26 16.2
02	203 22.6	243 46.4	47.7	156 08.2	29.0	300 35.7	38.5	272 57.5	41.1	Peacock	53 13.5	S56 40.2
03	218 25.1	258 45.9	.. 46.9	171 08.9	.. 29.5	315 37.9	.. 38.5	287 59.8	.. 41.1	Pollux	243 22.8	N27 58.7
04	233 27.5	273 45.4	46.1	186 09.7	30.0	330 40.2	38.5	303 02.1	41.0	Procyon	244 55.5	N 5 10.3
05	248 30.0	288 44.8	45.4	201 10.5	30.4	345 42.5	38.5	318 04.4	41.0			
06	263 32.5	303 44.3	S15 44.6	216 11.3	N18 30.9	0 44.7	S22 38.5	333 06.6	S21 41.0	Rasalhague	96 02.8	N12 32.7
07	278 34.9	318 43.7	43.8	231 12.0	31.4	15 47.0	38.5	348 08.9	41.0	Regulus	207 39.1	N11 52.3
S 08	293 37.4	333 43.2	43.1	246 12.8	31.9	30 49.2	38.5	3 11.2	41.0	Rigel	281 08.3	S 8 11.1
A 09	308 39.8	348 42.6	.. 42.3	261 13.6	.. 32.3	45 51.5	.. 38.5	18 13.5	.. 40.9	Rigil Kent.	139 46.0	S60 54.5
T 10	323 42.3	3 42.1	41.5	276 14.4	32.8	60 53.7	38.5	33 15.8	40.9	Sabik	102 08.0	S15 44.8
U 11	338 44.8	18 41.6	40.7	291 15.1	33.3	75 56.0	38.5	48 18.0	40.9			
R 12	353 47.2	33 41.0	S15 40.0	306 15.9	N18 33.7	90 58.3	S22 38.5	63 20.3	S21 40.9	Schedar	349 36.6	N56 38.4
D 13	8 49.7	48 40.5	39.2	321 16.7	34.2	106 00.5	38.5	78 22.6	40.8	Shaula	96 16.6	S37 06.8
A 14	23 52.2	63 40.0	38.4	336 17.5	34.7	121 02.8	38.6	93 24.9	40.8	Sirius	258 30.2	S16 44.9
Y 15	38 54.6	78 39.4	.. 37.6	351 18.2	.. 35.1	136 05.0	.. 38.6	108 27.2	.. 40.8	Spica	158 26.8	S11 15.6
16	53 57.1	93 38.9	36.9	6 19.0	35.6	151 07.3	38.6	123 29.5	40.8	Suhail	222 49.2	S43 30.8
17	68 59.6	108 38.3	36.1	21 19.8	36.1	166 09.5	38.6	138 31.7	40.8			
18	84 02.0	123 37.8	S15 35.3	36 20.6	N18 36.5	181 11.8	S22 38.6	153 34.0	S21 40.7	Vega	80 36.4	N38 47.9
19	99 04.5	138 37.3	34.5	51 21.3	37.0	196 14.1	38.6	168 36.3	40.7	Zuben'ubi	137 00.9	S16 07.2
20	114 07.0	153 36.7	33.7	66 22.1	37.5	211 16.3	38.6	183 38.6	40.7		SHA	Mer.Pass.
21	129 09.4	168 36.2	.. 33.0	81 22.9	.. 37.9	226 18.6	.. 38.6	198 40.9	.. 40.7			
22	144 11.9	183 35.7	32.2	96 23.7	38.4	241 20.9	38.6	213 43.2	40.7	Venus	41 42.1	9 44
23	159 14.3	198 35.1	31.4	111 24.4	38.9	256 23.1	38.6	228 45.4	40.6	Mars	313 29.4	15 36
Mer.Pass. 12 28.7		v −0.5	d 0.8	v 0.8	d 0.5	v 2.3	d 0.0	v 2.3	d 0.0	Jupiter	97 18.6	6 01
										Saturn	69 39.7	7 51

© British Crown Copyright 2018. All rights reserved.

UT	SUN GHA	SUN Dec	MOON GHA	v	MOON Dec	d	HP
d h	° ′	° ′	° ′	′	° ′	′	′
14 00	177 38.7	S 2 43.9	94 24.0	8.3	N19 47.4	5.3	57.7
01	192 38.8	42.9	108 51.3	8.2	19 52.7	5.3	57.7
02	207 39.0	42.0	123 18.5	8.1	19 58.0	5.1	57.8
03	222 39.2	.. 41.0	137 45.6	8.1	20 03.1	5.0	57.8
04	237 39.4	40.0	152 12.7	7.9	20 08.1	4.8	57.8
05	252 39.5	39.0	166 39.6	7.9	20 12.9	4.8	57.9
06	267 39.7	S 2 38.0	181 06.5	7.8	N20 17.7	4.7	57.9
07	282 39.9	37.0	195 33.3	7.8	20 22.4	4.5	57.9
T 08	297 40.0	36.0	210 00.1	7.7	20 26.9	4.4	58.0
H 09	312 40.2	.. 35.0	224 26.8	7.6	20 31.3	4.3	58.0
U 10	327 40.4	34.1	238 53.4	7.5	20 35.6	4.2	58.0
R 11	342 40.6	33.1	253 19.9	7.4	20 39.8	4.1	58.1
S 12	357 40.7	S 2 32.1	267 46.3	7.4	N20 43.9	3.9	58.1
D 13	12 40.9	31.1	282 12.7	7.3	20 47.8	3.8	58.1
A 14	27 41.1	30.1	296 39.0	7.2	20 51.6	3.7	58.2
Y 15	42 41.3	.. 29.1	311 05.2	7.2	20 55.3	3.6	58.2
16	57 41.4	28.1	325 31.4	7.1	20 58.9	3.4	58.2
17	72 41.6	27.2	339 57.5	7.0	21 02.3	3.4	58.2
18	87 41.8	S 2 26.2	354 23.5	7.0	N21 05.7	3.2	58.3
19	102 41.9	25.2	8 49.5	6.9	21 08.9	3.0	58.3
20	117 42.1	24.2	23 15.4	6.8	21 11.9	3.0	58.3
21	132 42.3	.. 23.2	37 41.2	6.8	21 14.9	2.8	58.4
22	147 42.5	22.2	52 07.0	6.7	21 17.7	2.7	58.4
23	162 42.6	21.2	66 32.7	6.6	21 20.4	2.5	58.4
15 00	177 42.8	S 2 20.2	80 58.3	6.6	N21 22.9	2.4	58.5
01	192 43.0	19.3	95 23.9	6.5	21 25.3	2.3	58.5
02	207 43.2	18.3	109 49.4	6.4	21 27.6	2.2	58.5
03	222 43.3	.. 17.3	124 14.8	6.4	21 29.8	2.0	58.6
04	237 43.5	16.3	138 40.2	6.3	21 31.8	1.9	58.6
05	252 43.7	15.3	153 05.5	6.3	21 33.7	1.8	58.6
06	267 43.9	S 2 14.3	167 30.8	6.2	N21 35.5	1.6	58.7
07	282 44.0	13.3	181 56.0	6.2	21 37.1	1.5	58.7
08	297 44.2	12.4	196 21.2	6.1	21 38.6	1.3	58.7
F 09	312 44.4	.. 11.4	210 46.3	6.0	21 39.9	1.2	58.8
R 10	327 44.6	10.4	225 11.3	6.0	21 41.1	1.1	58.8
I 11	342 44.7	09.4	239 36.3	6.0	21 42.2	0.9	58.8
D 12	357 44.9	S 2 08.4	254 01.3	5.9	N21 43.1	0.8	58.9
A 13	12 45.1	07.4	268 26.2	5.8	21 43.9	0.6	58.9
Y 14	27 45.3	06.4	282 51.0	5.8	21 44.5	0.5	58.9
15	42 45.4	.. 05.4	297 15.8	5.8	21 45.0	0.4	59.0
16	57 45.6	04.5	311 40.6	5.7	21 45.4	0.2	59.0
17	72 45.8	03.5	326 05.3	5.6	21 45.6	0.1	59.0
18	87 46.0	S 2 02.5	340 29.9	5.6	N21 45.7	0.1	59.1
19	102 46.1	01.5	354 54.5	5.6	21 45.6	0.2	59.1
20	117 46.3	2 00.5	9 19.1	5.6	21 45.4	0.3	59.1
21	132 46.5	1 59.5	23 43.7	5.5	21 45.1	0.5	59.2
22	147 46.7	58.5	38 08.2	5.4	21 44.6	0.7	59.2
23	162 46.8	57.5	52 32.6	5.4	21 43.9	0.8	59.2
16 00	177 47.0	S 1 56.6	66 57.0	5.4	N21 43.1	0.9	59.3
01	192 47.2	55.6	81 21.4	5.4	21 42.2	1.1	59.3
02	207 47.4	54.6	95 45.8	5.3	21 41.1	1.2	59.3
03	222 47.6	.. 53.6	110 10.1	5.3	21 39.9	1.4	59.3
04	237 47.7	52.6	124 34.4	5.3	21 38.5	1.5	59.4
05	252 47.9	51.6	138 58.7	5.2	21 37.0	1.7	59.4
06	267 48.1	S 1 50.6	153 22.9	5.2	N21 35.3	1.8	59.4
S 07	282 48.3	49.6	167 47.1	5.2	21 33.5	2.0	59.5
A 08	297 48.4	48.7	182 11.3	5.2	21 31.5	2.1	59.5
T 09	312 48.6	.. 47.7	196 35.5	5.1	21 29.4	2.2	59.5
U 10	327 48.8	46.7	210 59.6	5.1	21 27.2	2.5	59.6
R 11	342 49.0	45.7	225 23.7	5.1	21 24.7	2.5	59.6
D 12	357 49.1	S 1 44.7	239 47.8	5.1	N21 22.2	2.7	59.6
A 13	12 49.3	43.7	254 11.9	5.1	21 19.5	2.9	59.7
Y 14	27 49.5	42.7	268 36.0	5.1	21 16.6	3.0	59.7
15	42 49.7	.. 41.7	283 00.1	5.0	21 13.6	3.1	59.7
16	57 49.9	40.8	297 24.1	5.0	21 10.5	3.3	59.7
17	72 50.0	39.8	311 48.1	5.0	21 07.2	3.5	59.8
18	87 50.2	S 1 38.8	326 12.1	5.0	N21 03.7	3.6	59.8
19	102 50.4	37.8	340 36.1	5.0	21 00.1	3.7	59.8
20	117 50.6	36.8	355 00.1	5.0	20 56.4	3.9	59.9
21	132 50.8	.. 35.8	9 24.1	5.0	20 52.5	4.0	59.9
22	147 50.9	34.8	23 48.1	5.0	20 48.5	4.2	59.9
23	162 51.1	33.8	38 12.1	5.0	N20 44.3	4.4	59.9
	SD 16.1	d 1.0	SD 15.8		16.0		16.2

Lat.	Twilight Naut.	Twilight Civil	Sunrise	Moonrise 14	15	16	17
°	h m	h m	h m	h m	h m	h m	h m
N 72	03 55	05 19	06 26	▭	▭	▭	▭
N 70	04 09	05 23	06 24	▭	▭	▭	09 35
68	04 20	05 27	06 22	07 34	07 46	08 52	10 49
66	04 29	05 30	06 21	08 15	08 47	09 51	11 26
64	04 36	05 33	06 20	08 43	09 22	10 25	11 53
62	04 42	05 35	06 19	09 05	09 47	10 50	12 13
60	04 48	05 37	06 18	09 23	10 07	11 10	12 29
N 58	04 52	05 38	06 17	09 37	10 24	11 26	12 43
56	04 56	05 39	06 16	09 50	10 38	11 40	12 55
54	04 59	05 41	06 16	10 01	10 50	11 51	13 06
52	05 02	05 42	06 15	10 11	11 00	12 02	13 15
50	05 05	05 42	06 15	10 20	11 10	12 11	13 23
45	05 10	05 44	06 13	10 38	11 30	12 31	13 41
N 40	05 14	05 45	06 12	10 53	11 46	12 47	13 55
35	05 17	05 46	06 11	11 06	12 00	13 01	14 07
30	05 19	05 47	06 10	11 18	12 12	13 12	14 18
20	05 21	05 47	06 09	11 37	12 33	13 33	14 36
N 10	05 22	05 46	06 07	11 54	12 50	13 50	14 52
0	05 21	05 45	06 06	12 10	13 07	14 07	15 07
S 10	05 19	05 43	06 04	12 26	13 24	14 23	15 21
20	05 15	05 40	06 02	12 43	13 42	14 40	15 37
30	05 08	05 36	06 00	13 03	14 03	15 01	15 55
35	05 04	05 33	05 59	13 14	14 15	15 12	16 05
40	04 58	05 30	05 57	13 27	14 29	15 26	16 17
45	04 51	05 26	05 55	13 43	14 45	15 42	16 31
S 50	04 42	05 21	05 53	14 03	15 06	16 02	16 49
52	04 38	05 18	05 52	14 12	15 16	16 11	16 57
54	04 33	05 15	05 51	14 22	15 27	16 21	17 05
56	04 27	05 12	05 50	14 34	15 39	16 33	17 16
58	04 21	05 09	05 48	14 47	15 53	16 47	17 27
S 60	04 13	05 05	05 47	15 03	16 10	17 03	17 40

Lat.	Sunset	Twilight Civil	Twilight Naut.	Moonset 14	15	16	17
°	h m	h m	h m	h m	h m	h m	h m
N 72	17 55	19 02	20 27	▭	▭	▭	▭
N 70	17 56	18 57	20 12	▭	▭	▭	08 17
68	17 58	18 53	20 01	04 09	05 56	06 53	07 02
66	17 59	18 50	19 51	03 29	04 54	05 54	06 24
64	18 00	18 47	19 44	03 01	04 20	05 20	05 57
62	18 01	18 45	19 38	02 40	03 55	04 55	05 36
60	18 01	18 43	19 32	02 22	03 35	04 35	05 19
N 58	18 02	18 41	19 28	02 08	03 19	04 18	05 05
56	18 03	18 40	19 24	01 56	03 05	04 05	04 53
54	18 03	18 39	19 20	01 45	02 53	03 53	04 42
52	18 04	18 38	19 17	01 35	02 42	03 42	04 32
50	18 04	18 37	19 14	01 27	02 33	03 32	04 24
45	18 05	18 35	19 09	01 09	02 13	03 12	04 05
N 40	18 06	18 33	19 05	00 54	01 57	02 56	03 50
35	18 07	18 33	19 02	00 42	01 43	02 42	03 38
30	18 08	18 32	19 00	00 31	01 31	02 30	03 27
20	18 10	18 32	18 57	00 12	01 11	02 10	03 08
N 10	18 11	18 33	18 57	24 53	00 53	01 52	02 51
0	18 12	18 33	18 57	24 37	00 37	01 35	02 35
S 10	18 14	18 35	18 59	24 20	00 20	01 19	02 19
20	18 15	18 37	19 03	24 03	00 03	01 01	02 02
30	18 17	18 41	19 09	23 42	24 40	00 40	01 43
35	18 19	18 44	19 14	23 31	24 28	00 28	01 32
40	18 20	18 47	19 19	23 17	24 14	00 14	01 18
45	18 22	18 51	19 26	23 01	23 57	25 03	01 03
S 50	18 24	18 56	19 35	22 41	23 37	24 44	00 44
52	18 25	18 59	19 39	22 32	23 27	24 35	00 35
54	18 26	19 01	19 44	22 21	23 16	24 24	00 24
56	18 27	19 04	19 49	22 09	23 04	24 13	00 13
58	18 28	19 08	19 56	21 56	22 49	23 59	25 23
S 60	18 30	19 12	20 03	21 39	22 32	23 44	25 11

Day	SUN Eqn. of Time 00h	SUN Eqn. of Time 12h	SUN Mer. Pass.	MOON Mer. Pass. Upper	MOON Mer. Pass. Lower	Age	Phase
d	m s	m s	h m	h m	h m	d %	
14	09 26	09 17	12 09	18 23	05 55	08 51	
15	09 09	09 01	12 09	19 21	06 52	09 62	
16	08 52	08 44	12 09	20 21	07 51	10 73	

© British Crown Copyright 2018. All rights reserved.

UT (d h)	ARIES GHA	VENUS −4.0 GHA	Dec	MARS +1.3 GHA	Dec	JUPITER −2.1 GHA	Dec	SATURN +0.6 GHA	Dec	STARS Name	SHA	Dec
17 00	174 16.8	213 34.6	S15 30.6	126 25.2	N18 39.3	271 25.4	S22 38.6	243 47.7	S21 40.6	Acamar	315 15.6	S40 14.1
01	189 19.3	228 34.1	29.8	141 26.0	39.8	286 27.6	38.7	258 50.0	40.6	Achernar	335 24.4	S57 08.7
02	204 21.7	243 33.5	29.0	156 26.7	40.3	301 29.9	38.7	273 52.3	40.6	Acrux	173 04.2	S63 12.2
03	219 24.2	258 33.0 ..	28.2	171 27.5 ..	40.7	316 32.2 ..	38.7	288 54.6 ..	40.5	Adhara	255 09.3	S29 00.2
04	234 26.7	273 32.5	27.5	186 28.3	41.2	331 34.4	38.7	303 56.9	40.5	Aldebaran	290 45.0	N16 32.7
05	249 29.1	288 31.9	26.7	201 29.1	41.7	346 36.7	38.7	318 59.1	40.5			
06	264 31.6	303 31.4	S15 25.9	216 29.8	N18 42.1	1 39.0	S22 38.7	334 01.4	S21 40.5	Alioth	166 16.7	N55 51.3
07	279 34.1	318 30.9	25.1	231 30.6	42.6	16 41.2	38.7	349 03.7	40.5	Alkaid	152 55.4	N49 13.0
08	294 36.5	333 30.3	24.3	246 31.4	43.1	31 43.5	38.7	4 06.0	40.4	Alnair	27 39.2	S46 52.1
S 09	309 39.0	348 29.8 ..	23.5	261 32.2 ..	43.5	46 45.8 ..	38.7	19 08.3 ..	40.4	Alnilam	275 42.4	S 1 11.7
U 10	324 41.4	3 29.3	22.7	276 32.9	44.0	61 48.0	38.7	34 10.6	40.4	Alphard	217 52.0	S 8 44.7
N 11	339 43.9	18 28.7	21.9	291 33.7	44.4	76 50.3	38.7	49 12.9	40.4			
D 12	354 46.4	33 28.2	S15 21.1	306 34.5	N18 44.9	91 52.5	S22 38.7	64 15.1	S21 40.3	Alphecca	126 07.5	N26 38.9
A 13	9 48.8	48 27.7	20.3	321 35.2	45.4	106 54.8	38.8	79 17.4	40.3	Alpheratz	357 39.8	N29 11.6
Y 14	24 51.3	63 27.1	19.5	336 36.0	45.8	121 57.1	38.8	94 19.7	40.3	Altair	62 04.6	N 8 55.0
15	39 53.8	78 26.6 ..	18.7	351 36.8 ..	46.3	136 59.3 ..	38.8	109 22.0 ..	40.3	Ankaa	353 12.2	S42 12.3
16	54 56.2	93 26.1	17.9	6 37.6	46.8	152 01.6	38.8	124 24.3	40.3	Antares	112 21.3	S26 28.3
17	69 58.7	108 25.6	17.1	21 38.3	47.2	167 03.9	38.8	139 26.6	40.2			
18	85 01.2	123 25.0	S15 16.3	36 39.1	N18 47.7	182 06.1	S22 38.8	154 28.9	S21 40.2	Arcturus	145 51.9	N19 04.9
19	100 03.6	138 24.5	15.5	51 39.9	48.1	197 08.4	38.8	169 31.1	40.2	Atria	107 19.5	S69 03.3
20	115 06.1	153 24.0	14.7	66 40.6	48.6	212 10.7	38.8	184 33.4	40.2	Avior	234 16.1	S59 34.6
21	130 08.6	168 23.4 ..	13.9	81 41.4 ..	49.1	227 13.0 ..	38.8	199 35.7 ..	40.2	Bellatrix	278 27.8	N 6 21.8
22	145 11.0	183 22.9	13.1	96 42.2	49.5	242 15.2	38.8	214 38.0	40.1	Betelgeuse	270 57.0	N 7 24.4
23	160 13.5	198 22.4	12.3	111 43.0	50.0	257 17.5	38.8	229 40.3	40.1			
18 00	175 15.9	213 21.9	S15 11.5	126 43.7	N18 50.4	272 19.8	S22 38.8	244 42.6	S21 40.1	Canopus	263 54.3	S52 42.8
01	190 18.4	228 21.3	10.7	141 44.5	50.9	287 22.0	38.9	259 44.9	40.1	Capella	280 28.7	N46 01.0
02	205 20.9	243 20.8	09.9	156 45.3	51.4	302 24.3	38.9	274 47.2	40.0	Deneb	49 29.1	N45 20.7
03	220 23.3	258 20.3 ..	09.1	171 46.0 ..	51.8	317 26.6 ..	38.9	289 49.4 ..	40.0	Denebola	182 29.4	N14 27.8
04	235 25.8	273 19.8	08.3	186 46.8	52.3	332 28.8	38.9	304 51.7	40.0	Diphda	348 52.3	S17 53.2
05	250 28.3	288 19.2	07.5	201 47.6	52.7	347 31.1	38.9	319 54.0	40.0			
06	265 30.7	303 18.7	S15 06.7	216 48.3	N18 53.2	2 33.4	S22 38.9	334 56.3	S21 40.0	Dubhe	193 46.3	N61 38.9
07	280 33.2	318 18.2	05.9	231 49.1	53.6	17 35.7	38.9	349 58.6	39.9	Elnath	278 07.7	N28 37.3
08	295 35.7	333 17.7	05.1	246 49.9	54.1	32 37.9	38.9	5 00.9	39.9	Eltanin	90 44.3	N51 29.0
M 09	310 38.1	348 17.1 ..	04.3	261 50.7 ..	54.6	47 40.2 ..	38.9	20 03.2 ..	39.9	Enif	33 43.6	N 9 57.6
O 10	325 40.6	3 16.6	03.5	276 51.4	55.0	62 42.5	38.9	35 05.5	39.9	Fomalhaut	15 20.0	S29 31.4
N 11	340 43.1	18 16.1	02.7	291 52.2	55.5	77 44.7	38.9	50 07.8	39.8			
D 12	355 45.5	33 15.6	S15 01.9	306 53.0	N18 56.0	92 47.0	S22 38.9	65 10.0	S21 39.8	Gacrux	171 56.0	S57 13.1
A 13	10 48.0	48 15.0	01.0	321 53.7	56.4	107 49.3	38.9	80 12.3	39.8	Gienah	175 47.9	S17 38.9
Y 14	25 50.4	63 14.5	15 00.2	336 54.5	56.8	122 51.6	39.0	95 14.6	39.8	Hadar	148 41.8	S60 27.7
15	40 52.9	78 14.0	14 59.4	351 55.3 ..	57.3	137 53.8 ..	39.0	110 16.9 ..	39.8	Hamal	327 56.6	N23 33.0
16	55 55.4	93 13.5	58.6	6 56.0	57.8	152 56.1	39.0	125 19.2	39.7	Kaus Aust.	83 38.7	S34 22.3
17	70 57.8	108 13.0	57.8	21 56.8	58.2	167 58.4	39.0	140 21.5	39.7			
18	86 00.3	123 12.4	S14 57.0	36 57.6	N18 58.7	183 00.7	S22 39.0	155 23.8	S21 39.7	Kochab	137 19.3	N74 04.5
19	101 02.8	138 11.9	56.1	51 58.3	59.1	198 02.9	39.0	170 26.1	39.7	Markab	13 34.8	N15 18.3
20	116 05.2	153 11.4	55.3	66 59.1	18 59.6	213 05.2	39.0	185 28.4	39.7	Menkar	314 11.2	N 4 09.6
21	131 07.7	168 10.9 ..	54.5	81 59.9	19 00.0	228 07.5 ..	39.0	200 30.7 ..	39.6	Menkent	148 02.6	S36 27.7
22	146 10.2	183 10.4	53.7	97 00.7	00.5	243 09.8	39.0	215 32.9	39.6	Miaplacidus	221 38.2	S69 48.0
23	161 12.6	198 09.8	52.9	112 01.4	00.9	258 12.1	39.0	230 35.2	39.6			
19 00	176 15.1	213 09.3	S14 52.1	127 02.2	N19 01.4	273 14.3	S22 39.0	245 37.5	S21 39.6	Mirfak	308 35.0	N49 55.7
01	191 17.5	228 08.8	51.2	142 03.0	01.8	288 16.6	39.0	260 39.8	39.6	Nunki	75 53.6	S26 16.2
02	206 20.0	243 08.3	50.4	157 03.7	02.3	303 18.9	39.0	275 42.1	39.5	Peacock	53 13.5	S56 40.2
03	221 22.5	258 07.8 ..	49.6	172 04.5 ..	02.7	318 21.2 ..	39.1	290 44.4 ..	39.5	Pollux	243 22.8	N27 58.7
04	236 24.9	273 07.2	48.8	187 05.3	03.2	333 23.4	39.1	305 46.7	39.5	Procyon	244 55.5	N 5 10.3
05	251 27.4	288 06.7	47.9	202 06.0	03.6	348 25.7	39.1	320 49.0	39.5			
06	266 29.9	303 06.2	S14 47.1	217 06.8	N19 04.1	3 28.0	S22 39.1	335 51.3	S21 39.4	Rasalhague	96 02.8	N12 32.7
07	281 32.3	318 05.7	46.3	232 07.6	04.5	18 30.3	39.1	350 53.6	39.4	Regulus	207 39.1	N11 52.3
T 08	296 34.8	333 05.2	45.5	247 08.3	05.0	33 32.6	39.1	5 55.9	39.4	Rigel	281 08.3	S 8 11.1
U 09	311 37.3	348 04.7 ..	44.6	262 09.1 ..	05.4	48 34.8 ..	39.1	20 58.2 ..	39.4	Rigil Kent.	139 45.9	S60 54.5
E 10	326 39.7	3 04.1	43.8	277 09.9	05.9	63 37.1	39.1	36 00.4	39.4	Sabik	102 08.0	S15 44.8
S 11	341 42.2	18 03.6	43.0	292 10.6	06.3	78 39.4	39.1	51 02.7	39.3			
D 12	356 44.7	33 03.1	S14 42.2	307 11.4	N19 06.8	93 41.7	S22 39.1	66 05.0	S21 39.3	Schedar	349 36.6	N56 38.4
A 13	11 47.1	48 02.6	41.3	322 12.2	07.2	108 44.0	39.1	81 07.3	39.3	Shaula	96 16.6	S37 06.8
Y 14	26 49.6	63 02.1	40.5	337 12.9	07.7	123 46.2	39.1	96 09.6	39.3	Sirius	258 30.2	S16 44.9
15	41 52.0	78 01.6 ..	39.7	352 13.7 ..	08.1	138 48.5 ..	39.1	111 11.9 ..	39.3	Spica	158 26.8	S11 15.7
16	56 54.5	93 01.1	38.8	7 14.5	08.6	153 50.8	39.2	126 14.2	39.2	Suhail	222 49.2	S43 30.8
17	71 57.0	108 00.5	38.0	22 15.2	09.0	168 53.1	39.2	141 16.5	39.2			
18	86 59.4	123 00.0	S14 37.2	37 16.0	N19 09.5	183 55.4	S22 39.2	156 18.8	S21 39.2	Vega	80 36.4	N38 47.9
19	102 01.9	137 59.5	36.3	52 16.8	09.9	198 57.7	39.2	171 21.1	39.2	Zuben'ubi	137 00.9	S16 07.2
20	117 04.4	152 59.0	35.5	67 17.5	10.4	213 59.9	39.2	186 23.4	39.2		SHA	Mer.Pass.
21	132 06.8	167 58.5 ..	34.7	82 18.3 ..	10.8	229 02.2 ..	39.2	201 25.7 ..	39.1			h m
22	147 09.3	182 58.0	33.8	97 19.1	11.3	244 04.5	39.2	216 28.0	39.1	Venus	38 05.9	9 47
23	162 11.8	197 57.5	33.0	112 19.8	11.7	259 06.8	39.2	231 30.3	39.1	Mars	311 27.8	15 32
Mer. Pass.	h m 12 16.9	v −0.5	d 0.8	v 0.8	d 0.5	v 2.3	d 0.0	v 2.3	d 0.0	Jupiter	97 03.8	5 50
										Saturn	69 26.6	7 40

© British Crown Copyright 2018. All rights reserved.

UT	SUN GHA	SUN Dec	MOON GHA	v	MOON Dec	d	HP
d h	° ′	° ′	° ′	′	° ′	′	′
17 00	177 51.3	S 1 32.8	52 36.1	5.0	N20 39.9	4.4	60.0
01	192 51.5	31.9	67 00.1	4.9	20 35.5	4.7	60.0
02	207 51.6	30.9	81 24.0	5.0	20 30.8	4.7	60.0
03	222 51.8	.. 29.9	95 48.0	5.0	20 26.1	5.0	60.0
04	237 52.0	28.9	110 12.0	5.0	20 21.1	5.0	60.1
05	252 52.2	27.9	124 36.0	5.0	20 16.1	5.2	60.1
06	267 52.4	S 1 26.9	139 00.0	5.0	N20 10.9	5.4	60.1
07	282 52.5	25.9	153 24.0	5.0	20 05.5	5.5	60.2
08	297 52.7	24.9	167 48.0	5.1	20 00.0	5.6	60.2
S 09	312 52.9	.. 24.0	182 12.1	5.0	19 54.4	5.8	60.2
U 10	327 53.1	23.0	196 36.1	5.0	19 48.6	5.9	60.2
N 11	342 53.3	22.0	211 00.1	5.1	19 42.7	6.1	60.3
D 12	357 53.4	S 1 21.0	225 24.2	5.1	N19 36.6	6.2	60.3
A 13	12 53.6	20.0	239 48.3	5.1	19 30.4	6.4	60.3
Y 14	27 53.8	19.0	254 12.4	5.1	19 24.0	6.5	60.3
15	42 54.0	.. 18.0	268 36.5	5.1	19 17.5	6.6	60.4
16	57 54.2	17.0	283 00.6	5.2	19 10.9	6.7	60.4
17	72 54.3	16.0	297 24.8	5.1	19 04.2	7.0	60.4
18	87 54.5	S 1 15.1	311 48.9	5.2	N18 57.2	7.0	60.4
19	102 54.7	14.1	326 13.1	5.3	18 50.2	7.2	60.4
20	117 54.9	13.1	340 37.4	5.2	18 43.0	7.3	60.5
21	132 55.1	.. 12.1	355 01.6	5.3	18 35.7	7.4	60.5
22	147 55.2	11.1	9 25.9	5.3	18 28.3	7.6	60.5
23	162 55.4	10.1	23 50.2	5.3	18 20.7	7.7	60.5
18 00	177 55.6	S 1 09.1	38 14.5	5.3	N18 13.0	7.9	60.5
01	192 55.8	08.1	52 38.8	5.4	18 05.1	8.0	60.6
02	207 56.0	07.2	67 03.2	5.4	17 57.1	8.1	60.6
03	222 56.2	.. 06.2	81 27.6	5.5	17 49.0	8.2	60.6
04	237 56.3	05.2	95 52.1	5.5	17 40.8	8.4	60.6
05	252 56.5	04.2	110 16.6	5.5	17 32.4	8.4	60.6
06	267 56.7	S 1 03.2	124 41.1	5.5	N17 24.0	8.7	60.7
07	282 56.9	02.2	139 05.6	5.6	17 15.3	8.7	60.7
08	297 57.1	01.2	153 30.2	5.6	17 06.6	8.9	60.7
M 09	312 57.2	1 00.2	167 54.8	5.6	16 57.7	8.9	60.7
O 10	327 57.4	0 59.2	182 19.4	5.7	16 48.8	9.1	60.7
N 11	342 57.6	58.3	196 44.1	5.8	16 39.7	9.3	60.7
D 12	357 57.8	S 0 57.3	211 08.9	5.7	N16 30.4	9.3	60.8
A 13	12 58.0	56.3	225 33.6	5.8	16 21.1	9.5	60.8
Y 14	27 58.2	55.3	239 58.4	5.9	16 11.6	9.6	60.8
15	42 58.3	.. 54.3	254 23.3	5.9	16 02.0	9.6	60.8
16	57 58.5	53.3	268 48.2	5.9	15 52.4	9.8	60.8
17	72 58.7	52.3	283 13.1	5.9	15 42.6	10.0	60.8
18	87 58.9	S 0 51.3	297 38.0	6.1	N15 32.6	10.0	60.8
19	102 59.1	50.4	312 03.1	6.0	15 22.6	10.1	60.9
20	117 59.2	49.4	326 28.1	6.1	15 12.5	10.3	60.9
21	132 59.4	.. 48.4	340 53.2	6.1	15 02.2	10.3	60.9
22	147 59.6	47.4	355 18.3	6.2	14 51.9	10.5	60.9
23	162 59.8	46.4	9 43.5	6.3	14 41.4	10.5	60.9
19 00	178 00.0	S 0 45.4	24 08.8	6.2	N14 30.9	10.7	60.9
01	193 00.2	44.4	38 34.0	6.4	14 20.2	10.8	60.9
02	208 00.3	43.4	52 59.4	6.3	14 09.4	10.8	60.9
03	223 00.5	.. 42.4	67 24.7	6.4	13 58.6	11.0	60.9
04	238 00.7	41.5	81 50.1	6.5	13 47.6	11.0	61.0
05	253 00.9	40.5	96 15.6	6.5	13 36.6	11.2	61.0
06	268 01.1	S 0 39.5	110 41.1	6.5	N13 25.4	11.2	61.0
07	283 01.3	38.5	125 06.6	6.6	13 14.2	11.4	61.0
T 08	298 01.4	37.5	139 32.2	6.7	13 02.8	11.4	61.0
U 09	313 01.6	.. 36.5	153 57.9	6.7	12 51.4	11.5	61.0
E 10	328 01.8	35.5	168 23.6	6.7	12 39.9	11.6	61.0
S 11	343 02.0	34.5	182 49.3	6.8	12 28.3	11.7	61.0
D 12	358 02.2	S 0 33.6	197 15.1	6.9	N12 16.6	11.7	61.0
A 13	13 02.4	32.6	211 41.0	6.8	12 04.9	11.9	61.0
Y 14	28 02.5	31.6	226 06.8	7.0	11 53.0	11.9	61.0
15	43 02.7	.. 30.6	240 32.8	6.9	11 41.1	12.0	61.0
16	58 02.9	29.6	254 58.7	7.1	11 29.1	12.1	61.0
17	73 03.1	28.6	269 24.8	7.1	11 17.0	12.2	61.0
18	88 03.3	S 0 27.6	283 50.9	7.1	N11 04.8	12.2	61.0
19	103 03.5	26.6	298 17.0	7.2	10 52.6	12.3	61.0
20	118 03.7	25.6	312 43.2	7.2	10 40.3	12.4	61.0
21	133 03.8	.. 24.7	327 09.4	7.2	10 27.9	12.5	61.0
22	148 04.0	23.7	341 35.6	7.4	10 15.4	12.5	61.0
23	163 04.2	22.7	356 02.0	7.3	N10 02.9	12.6	61.0
	SD 16.1	d 1.0	SD 16.4		16.6		16.6

Lat.	Twilight Naut.	Twilight Civil	Sunrise	Moonrise 17	Moonrise 18	Moonrise 19	Moonrise 20
°	h m	h m	h m	h m	h m	h m	h m
N 72	03 37	05 03	06 10	▭	11 35	14 19	16 39
N 70	03 53	05 09	06 10	09 35	12 23	14 40	16 48
68	04 06	05 14	06 10	10 49	12 54	14 57	16 56
66	04 16	05 19	06 09	11 26	13 16	15 10	17 02
64	04 25	05 22	06 09	11 53	13 34	15 21	17 07
62	04 32	05 25	06 09	12 13	13 49	15 30	17 11
60	04 38	05 27	06 09	12 29	14 01	15 38	17 15
N 58	04 43	05 30	06 09	12 43	14 12	15 45	17 19
56	04 48	05 32	06 08	12 55	14 21	15 51	17 22
54	04 52	05 33	06 08	13 06	14 29	15 56	17 24
52	04 55	05 35	06 08	13 15	14 36	16 01	17 27
50	04 58	05 36	06 08	13 23	14 43	16 05	17 29
45	05 04	05 38	06 08	13 41	14 56	16 15	17 34
N 40	05 09	05 40	06 07	13 55	15 08	16 23	17 38
35	05 12	05 42	06 07	14 07	15 18	16 30	17 41
30	05 15	05 43	06 07	14 18	15 26	16 36	17 44
20	05 19	05 44	06 06	14 36	15 41	16 46	17 50
N 10	05 20	05 45	06 06	14 52	15 54	16 55	17 54
0	05 20	05 44	06 05	15 07	16 06	17 03	17 59
S 10	05 19	05 43	06 04	15 21	16 18	17 12	18 03
20	05 16	05 41	06 03	15 37	16 30	17 20	18 08
30	05 10	05 38	06 02	15 55	16 45	17 31	18 13
35	05 06	05 36	06 01	16 05	16 53	17 36	18 16
40	05 01	05 33	06 00	16 17	17 03	17 43	18 19
45	04 55	05 30	05 59	16 31	17 14	17 51	18 23
S 50	04 47	05 26	05 58	16 49	17 27	18 00	18 28
52	04 43	05 24	05 57	16 57	17 34	18 04	18 30
54	04 39	05 21	05 57	17 05	17 40	18 09	18 32
56	04 34	05 19	05 56	17 16	17 48	18 14	18 35
58	04 28	05 16	05 55	17 27	17 57	18 19	18 38
S 60	04 22	05 12	05 54	17 40	18 06	18 26	18 41

Lat.	Sunset	Twilight Civil	Twilight Naut.	Moonset 17	Moonset 18	Moonset 19	Moonset 20
°	h m	h m	h m	h m	h m	h m	h m
N 72	18 08	19 16	20 44	▭	08 23	07 41	07 18
N 70	18 08	19 10	20 27	08 17	07 34	07 18	07 06
68	18 09	19 04	20 13	07 02	07 02	07 02	06 57
66	18 09	19 00	20 03	06 24	06 38	06 45	06 49
64	18 09	18 56	19 54	05 57	06 19	06 33	06 42
62	18 09	18 53	19 46	05 36	06 04	06 22	06 36
60	18 09	18 50	19 40	05 19	05 51	06 14	06 31
N 58	18 09	18 48	19 35	05 05	05 40	06 06	06 26
56	18 09	18 46	19 30	04 53	05 30	05 59	06 22
54	18 09	18 44	19 26	04 42	05 21	05 53	06 18
52	18 09	18 43	19 23	04 32	05 13	05 47	06 15
50	18 09	18 41	19 19	04 24	05 06	05 42	06 12
45	18 09	18 39	19 13	04 05	04 51	05 31	06 05
N 40	18 10	18 37	19 08	03 50	04 39	05 21	06 00
35	18 10	18 35	19 04	03 38	04 28	05 14	05 55
30	18 10	18 34	19 02	03 27	04 19	05 06	05 50
20	18 10	18 32	18 58	03 08	04 03	04 54	05 43
N 10	18 11	18 32	18 56	02 51	03 48	04 43	05 36
0	18 11	18 32	18 56	02 35	03 35	04 33	05 30
S 10	18 12	18 33	18 57	02 19	03 21	04 23	05 23
20	18 13	18 35	19 00	02 02	03 07	04 12	05 16
30	18 14	18 38	19 06	01 43	02 50	03 59	05 08
35	18 15	18 40	19 09	01 32	02 40	03 52	05 04
40	18 15	18 42	19 14	01 18	02 29	03 43	04 59
45	18 16	18 45	19 20	01 03	02 16	03 33	04 52
S 50	18 17	18 50	19 28	00 44	02 00	03 21	04 45
52	18 18	18 52	19 32	00 35	01 52	03 16	04 42
54	18 18	18 54	19 36	00 24	01 44	03 09	04 38
56	18 19	18 56	19 41	00 13	01 34	03 03	04 34
58	18 20	18 59	19 46	25 23	01 23	02 55	04 29
S 60	18 21	19 02	19 53	25 11	01 11	02 46	04 23

	SUN Eqn. of Time 00ʰ	SUN Eqn. of Time 12ʰ	SUN Mer. Pass.	MOON Mer. Pass. Upper	MOON Mer. Pass. Lower	Age	Phase
Day	m s	m s	h m	h m	h m	d	%
17	08 35	08 27	12 08	21 21	08 51	11	82
18	08 18	08 09	12 08	22 20	09 50	12	90
19	08 00	07 52	12 08	23 16	10 48	13	96

© British Crown Copyright 2018. All rights reserved.

UT	ARIES	VENUS −4·0		MARS +1·4		JUPITER −2·2		SATURN +0·6		STARS		
	GHA	GHA	Dec	GHA	Dec	GHA	Dec	GHA	Dec	Name	SHA	Dec
d h	° ′	° ′	° ′	° ′	° ′	° ′	° ′	° ′	° ′		° ′	° ′
20 00	177 14.2	212 57.0	S14 32.1	127 20.6	N19 12.2	274 09.1	S22 39.2	246 32.6	S21 39.1	Acamar	315 15.7	S40 14.1
01	192 16.7	227 56.5	31.3	142 21.4	12.6	289 11.4	39.2	261 34.9	39.1	Achernar	335 24.4	S57 08.7
02	207 19.2	242 55.9	30.5	157 22.1	13.1	304 13.7	39.2	276 37.2	39.0	Acrux	173 04.2	S63 12.2
03	222 21.6	257 55.4 . .	29.6	172 22.9 . .	13.5	319 15.9 . .	39.2	291 39.4 . .	39.0	Adhara	255 09.4	S29 00.2
04	237 24.1	272 54.9	28.8	187 23.6	13.9	334 18.2	39.2	306 41.7	39.0	Aldebaran	290 45.0	N16 32.7
05	252 26.5	287 54.4	27.9	202 24.4	14.4	349 20.5	39.2	321 44.0	39.0			
06	267 29.0	302 53.9	S14 27.1	217 25.2	N19 14.8	4 22.8	S22 39.3	336 46.3	S21 38.9	Alioth	166 16.7	N55 51.3
W 07	282 31.5	317 53.4	26.3	232 25.9	15.3	19 25.1	39.3	351 48.6	38.9	Alkaid	152 55.4	N49 13.0
E 08	297 33.9	332 52.9	25.4	247 26.7	15.7	34 27.4	39.3	6 50.9	38.9	Alnair	27 39.2	S46 52.1
D 09	312 36.4	347 52.4 . .	24.6	262 27.5 . .	16.2	49 29.7 . .	39.3	21 53.2 . .	38.9	Alnilam	275 42.4	S 1 11.7
N 10	327 38.9	2 51.9	23.7	277 28.2	16.6	64 31.9	39.3	36 55.5	38.9	Alphard	217 52.0	S 8 44.7
E 11	342 41.3	17 51.4	22.9	292 29.0	17.1	79 34.2	39.3	51 57.8	38.8			
S 12	357 43.8	32 50.9	S14 22.0	307 29.8	N19 17.5	94 36.5	S22 39.3	67 00.1	S21 38.8	Alphecca	126 07.5	N26 38.9
D 13	12 46.3	47 50.4	21.2	322 30.5	17.9	109 38.8	39.3	82 02.4	38.8	Alpheratz	357 39.8	N29 11.6
A 14	27 48.7	62 49.9	20.3	337 31.3	18.4	124 41.1	39.3	97 04.7	38.8	Altair	62 04.6	N 8 55.0
Y 15	42 51.2	77 49.3 . .	19.5	352 32.1 . .	18.8	139 43.4 . .	39.3	112 07.0 . .	38.8	Ankaa	353 12.2	S42 12.3
16	57 53.6	92 48.8	18.6	7 32.8	19.3	154 45.7	39.3	127 09.3	38.7	Antares	112 21.3	S26 28.3
17	72 56.1	107 48.3	17.8	22 33.6	19.7	169 48.0	39.3	142 11.6	38.7			
18	87 58.6	122 47.8	S14 16.9	37 34.3	N19 20.2	184 50.3	S22 39.3	157 13.9	S21 38.7	Arcturus	145 51.9	N19 04.9
19	103 01.0	137 47.3	16.1	52 35.1	20.6	199 52.6	39.3	172 16.2	38.7	Atria	107 19.5	S69 03.3
20	118 03.5	152 46.8	15.2	67 35.9	21.0	214 54.8	39.3	187 18.5	38.7	Avior	234 16.1	S59 34.6
21	133 06.0	167 46.3 . .	14.4	82 36.6 . .	21.5	229 57.1 . .	39.4	202 20.8 . .	38.6	Bellatrix	278 27.9	N 6 21.8
22	148 08.4	182 45.8	13.5	97 37.4	21.9	244 59.4	39.4	217 23.1	38.6	Betelgeuse	270 57.1	N 7 24.4
23	163 10.9	197 45.3	12.7	112 38.2	22.4	260 01.7	39.4	232 25.4	38.6			
21 00	178 13.4	212 44.8	S14 11.8	127 38.9	N19 22.8	275 04.0	S22 39.4	247 27.7	S21 38.6	Canopus	263 54.4	S52 42.8
01	193 15.8	227 44.3	11.0	142 39.7	23.2	290 06.3	39.4	262 30.0	38.6	Capella	280 28.7	N46 01.0
02	208 18.3	242 43.8	10.1	157 40.4	23.7	305 08.6	39.4	277 32.3	38.5	Deneb	49 29.1	N45 20.7
03	223 20.8	257 43.3 . .	09.3	172 41.2 . .	24.1	320 10.9 . .	39.4	292 34.6 . .	38.5	Denebola	182 29.4	N14 27.8
04	238 23.2	272 42.8	08.4	187 42.0	24.5	335 13.2	39.4	307 36.9	38.5	Diphda	348 52.3	S17 53.1
05	253 25.7	287 42.3	07.5	202 42.7	25.0	350 15.5	39.4	322 39.2	38.5			
06	268 28.1	302 41.8	S14 06.7	217 43.5	N19 25.4	5 17.8	S22 39.4	337 41.5	S21 38.5	Dubhe	193 46.3	N61 38.9
07	283 30.6	317 41.3	05.8	232 44.3	25.9	20 20.1	39.4	352 43.8	38.4	Elnath	278 07.7	N28 37.3
T 08	298 33.1	332 40.8	05.0	247 45.0	26.3	35 22.4	39.4	7 46.1	38.4	Eltanin	90 44.3	N51 29.0
H 09	313 35.5	347 40.3 . .	04.1	262 45.8 . .	26.7	50 24.7 . .	39.4	22 48.4 . .	38.4	Enif	33 43.5	N 9 57.6
U 10	328 38.0	2 39.8	03.2	277 46.5	27.2	65 27.0	39.4	37 50.7	38.4	Fomalhaut	15 20.0	S29 31.4
R 11	343 40.5	17 39.3	02.4	292 47.3	27.6	80 29.3	39.5	52 53.0	38.4			
S 12	358 42.9	32 38.8	S14 01.5	307 48.1	N19 28.0	95 31.6	S22 39.5	67 55.3	S21 38.3	Gacrux	171 56.0	S57 13.2
D 13	13 45.4	47 38.3	14 00.7	322 48.8	28.5	110 33.9	39.5	82 57.6	38.3	Gienah	175 47.9	S17 38.9
A 14	28 47.9	62 37.8	13 59.8	337 49.6	28.9	125 36.1	39.5	97 59.9	38.3	Hadar	148 41.8	S60 27.7
Y 15	43 50.3	77 37.3 . .	58.9	352 50.4 . .	29.4	140 38.4 . .	39.5	113 02.2 . .	38.3	Hamal	327 56.6	N23 33.0
16	58 52.8	92 36.8	58.1	7 51.1	29.8	155 40.7	39.5	128 04.5	38.3	Kaus Aust.	83 38.7	S34 22.3
17	73 55.2	107 36.3	57.2	22 51.9	30.2	170 43.0	39.5	143 06.8	38.2			
18	88 57.7	122 35.8	S13 56.3	37 52.6	N19 30.7	185 45.3	S22 39.5	158 09.1	S21 38.2	Kochab	137 19.3	N74 04.5
19	104 00.2	137 35.3	55.5	52 53.4	31.1	200 47.6	39.5	173 11.4	38.2	Markab	13 34.7	N15 18.3
20	119 02.6	152 34.8	54.6	67 54.2	31.5	215 49.9	39.5	188 13.7	38.2	Menkar	314 11.2	N 4 09.6
21	134 05.1	167 34.3 . .	53.7	82 54.9 . .	32.0	230 52.2 . .	39.5	203 16.0 . .	38.2	Menkent	148 02.6	S36 27.7
22	149 07.6	182 33.8	52.8	97 55.7	32.4	245 54.5	39.5	218 18.3	38.1	Miaplacidus	221 38.2	S69 48.0
23	164 10.0	197 33.3	52.0	112 56.4	32.8	260 56.8	39.5	233 20.6	38.1			
22 00	179 12.5	212 32.9	S13 51.1	127 57.2	N19 33.3	275 59.1	S22 39.5	248 22.9	S21 38.1	Mirfak	308 35.0	N49 55.7
01	194 15.0	227 32.4	50.2	142 58.0	33.7	291 01.4	39.5	263 25.2	38.1	Nunki	75 53.5	S26 16.2
02	209 17.4	242 31.9	49.4	157 58.7	34.1	306 03.7	39.5	278 27.5	38.1	Peacock	53 13.4	S56 40.2
03	224 19.9	257 31.4 . .	48.5	172 59.5 . .	34.6	321 06.0 . .	39.6	293 29.8 . .	38.0	Pollux	243 22.8	N27 58.7
04	239 22.4	272 30.9	47.6	188 00.2	35.0	336 08.3	39.6	308 32.1	38.0	Procyon	244 55.5	N 5 10.4
05	254 24.8	287 30.4	46.7	203 01.0	35.4	351 10.6	39.6	323 34.4	38.0			
06	269 27.3	302 29.9	S13 45.9	218 01.8	N19 35.9	6 13.0	S22 39.6	338 36.7	S21 38.0	Rasalhague	96 02.8	N12 32.7
07	284 29.7	317 29.4	45.0	233 02.5	36.3	21 15.3	39.6	353 39.0	38.0	Regulus	207 39.1	N11 52.3
08	299 32.2	332 28.9	44.1	248 03.3	36.7	36 17.6	39.6	8 41.3	37.9	Rigel	281 08.4	S 8 11.1
F 09	314 34.7	347 28.4 . .	43.2	263 04.0 . .	37.1	51 19.9 . .	39.6	23 43.6 . .	37.9	Rigil Kent.	139 45.9	S60 54.6
R 10	329 37.1	2 27.9	42.4	278 04.8	37.6	66 22.2	39.6	38 45.9	37.9	Sabik	102 08.0	S15 44.8
I 11	344 39.6	17 27.4	41.5	293 05.5	38.0	81 24.5	39.6	53 48.2	37.9			
D 12	359 42.1	32 26.9	S13 40.6	308 06.3	N19 38.4	96 26.8	S22 39.6	68 50.5	S21 37.9	Schedar	349 36.6	N56 38.4
A 13	14 44.5	47 26.5	39.7	323 07.1	38.9	111 29.1	39.6	83 52.8	37.8	Shaula	96 16.6	S37 06.8
Y 14	29 47.0	62 26.0	38.8	338 07.8	39.3	126 31.4	39.6	98 55.1	37.8	Sirius	258 30.2	S16 44.9
15	44 49.5	77 25.5 . .	38.0	353 08.6 . .	39.7	141 33.7 . .	39.6	113 57.4 . .	37.8	Spica	158 26.8	S11 15.7
16	59 51.9	92 25.0	37.1	8 09.3	40.2	156 36.0	39.6	128 59.7	37.8	Suhail	222 49.3	S43 30.9
17	74 54.4	107 24.5	36.2	23 10.1	40.6	171 38.3	39.6	144 02.0	37.8			
18	89 56.8	122 24.0	S13 35.3	38 10.9	N19 41.0	186 40.6	S22 39.6	159 04.3	S21 37.7	Vega	80 36.4	N38 47.9
19	104 59.3	137 23.5	34.4	53 11.6	41.4	201 42.9	39.7	174 06.7	37.7	Zuben'ubi	137 00.8	S16 07.2
20	120 01.8	152 23.0	33.5	68 12.4	41.9	216 45.2	39.7	189 09.0	37.7		SHA	Mer. Pass.
21	135 04.2	167 22.5 . .	32.7	83 13.1 . .	42.3	231 47.5 . .	39.7	204 11.3 . .	37.7		° ′	h m
22	150 06.7	182 22.1	31.8	98 13.9	42.7	246 49.8	39.7	219 13.6	37.7	Venus	34 31.5	9 49
23	165 09.2	197 21.6	30.9	113 14.6	43.1	261 52.1	39.7	234 15.9	37.6	Mars	309 25.6	15 29
	h m									Jupiter	96 50.7	5 39
Mer. Pass. 12 05.1		v −0.5	d 0.9	v 0.8	d 0.4	v 2.3	d 0.0	v 2.3	d 0.0	Saturn	69 14.3	7 29

© British Crown Copyright 2018. All rights reserved.

UT	SUN GHA	SUN Dec	MOON GHA	v	MOON Dec	d	HP
d h	° ′	° ′	° ′	′	° ′	′	′
20 00	178 04.4	S 0 21.7	10 28.3	7.4	N 9 50.3	12.6	61.0
01	193 04.6	20.7	24 54.7	7.5	9 37.7	12.7	61.0
02	208 04.8	19.7	39 21.2	7.5	9 25.0	12.8	61.0
03	223 04.9	.. 18.7	53 47.7	7.6	9 12.2	12.8	61.0
04	238 05.1	17.7	68 14.3	7.6	8 59.4	12.9	61.0
05	253 05.3	16.8	82 40.9	7.6	8 46.5	12.9	61.0
06	268 05.5	S 0 15.8	97 07.5	7.7	N 8 33.6	13.0	61.0
W 07	283 05.7	14.8	111 34.2	7.7	8 20.6	13.0	61.0
E 08	298 05.9	13.8	126 00.9	7.8	8 07.6	13.1	61.0
D 09	313 06.1	.. 12.8	140 27.7	7.8	7 54.5	13.2	61.0
N 10	328 06.2	11.8	154 54.5	7.9	7 41.3	13.2	61.0
E 11	343 06.4	10.8	169 21.4	7.9	7 28.1	13.2	61.0
S 12	358 06.6	S 0 09.8	183 48.3	8.0	N 7 14.9	13.3	60.9
D 13	13 06.8	08.9	198 15.3	8.0	7 01.6	13.3	60.9
A 14	28 07.0	07.9	212 42.3	8.1	6 48.3	13.3	60.9
Y 15	43 07.2	.. 06.9	227 09.4	8.0	6 35.0	13.4	60.9
16	58 07.4	05.9	241 36.4	8.2	6 21.6	13.5	60.9
17	73 07.5	04.9	256 03.6	8.2	6 08.1	13.4	60.9
18	88 07.7	S 0 03.9	270 30.8	8.2	N 5 54.7	13.5	60.9
19	103 07.9	02.9	284 58.0	8.2	5 41.2	13.5	60.9
20	118 08.1	01.9	299 25.2	8.3	5 27.7	13.6	60.9
21	133 08.3	S 01.0	313 52.5	8.4	5 14.1	13.6	60.8
22	148 08.5	00.0	328 19.9	8.4	5 00.5	13.6	60.8
23	163 08.7	N 01.0	342 47.3	8.4	4 46.9	13.6	60.8
21 00	178 08.8	N 0 02.0	357 14.7	8.5	N 4 33.3	13.7	60.8
01	193 09.0	03.0	11 42.2	8.5	4 19.6	13.6	60.8
02	208 09.2	04.0	26 09.7	8.5	4 06.0	13.7	60.8
03	223 09.4	.. 05.0	40 37.2	8.6	3 52.3	13.7	60.8
04	238 09.6	06.0	55 04.8	8.6	3 38.6	13.7	60.7
05	253 09.8	06.9	69 32.4	8.6	3 24.9	13.8	60.7
06	268 10.0	N 0 07.9	84 00.0	8.7	N 3 11.1	13.7	60.7
07	283 10.1	08.9	98 27.7	8.7	2 57.4	13.8	60.7
T 08	298 10.3	09.9	112 55.4	8.8	2 43.6	13.8	60.7
H 09	313 10.5	.. 10.9	127 23.2	8.8	2 29.8	13.7	60.7
U 10	328 10.7	11.9	141 51.0	8.8	2 16.1	13.8	60.6
R 11	343 10.9	12.9	156 18.8	8.9	2 02.3	13.8	60.6
S 12	358 11.1	N 0 13.9	170 46.7	8.9	N 1 48.5	13.8	60.6
D 13	13 11.3	14.8	185 14.6	8.9	1 34.7	13.8	60.6
A 14	28 11.5	15.8	199 42.5	9.0	1 20.9	13.7	60.6
Y 15	43 11.6	.. 16.8	214 10.5	8.9	1 07.2	13.8	60.5
16	58 11.8	17.8	228 38.4	9.1	0 53.4	13.8	60.5
17	73 12.0	18.8	243 06.5	9.0	0 39.6	13.8	60.5
18	88 12.2	N 0 19.8	257 34.5	9.1	N 0 25.8	13.7	60.5
19	103 12.4	20.8	272 02.6	9.1	N 0 12.1	13.8	60.4
20	118 12.6	21.8	286 30.7	9.1	S 0 01.7	13.7	60.4
21	133 12.8	.. 22.7	300 58.8	9.2	0 15.4	13.8	60.4
22	148 12.9	23.7	315 27.0	9.2	0 29.2	13.7	60.4
23	163 13.1	24.7	329 55.2	9.2	0 42.9	13.7	60.3
22 00	178 13.3	N 0 25.7	344 23.4	9.2	S 0 56.6	13.6	60.3
01	193 13.5	26.7	358 51.6	9.3	1 10.2	13.7	60.3
02	208 13.7	27.7	13 19.9	9.3	1 23.9	13.6	60.3
03	223 13.9	.. 28.7	27 48.2	9.3	1 37.5	13.7	60.2
04	238 14.1	29.7	42 16.5	9.4	1 51.2	13.6	60.2
05	253 14.3	30.6	56 44.9	9.3	2 04.8	13.5	60.2
06	268 14.4	N 0 31.6	71 13.2	9.4	S 2 18.3	13.6	60.2
07	283 14.6	32.6	85 41.6	9.4	2 31.9	13.5	60.1
08	298 14.8	33.6	100 10.0	9.5	2 45.4	13.5	60.1
F 09	313 15.0	.. 34.6	114 38.5	9.4	2 58.9	13.4	60.1
R 10	328 15.2	35.6	129 06.9	9.5	3 12.3	13.5	60.0
I 11	343 15.4	36.6	143 35.4	9.5	3 25.8	13.4	60.0
D 12	358 15.6	N 0 37.5	158 03.9	9.5	S 3 39.2	13.3	60.0
A 13	13 15.8	38.5	172 32.4	9.5	3 52.5	13.3	59.9
Y 14	28 15.9	39.5	187 00.9	9.5	4 05.8	13.3	59.9
15	43 16.1	.. 40.5	201 29.4	9.6	4 19.1	13.2	59.9
16	58 16.3	41.5	215 58.0	9.6	4 32.3	13.3	59.9
17	73 16.5	42.5	230 26.6	9.6	4 45.6	13.1	59.8
18	88 16.7	N 0 43.5	244 55.2	9.6	S 4 58.7	13.1	59.8
19	103 16.9	44.4	259 23.8	9.6	5 11.8	13.1	59.8
20	118 17.1	45.4	273 52.4	9.7	5 24.9	13.0	59.7
21	133 17.3	.. 46.4	288 21.1	9.6	5 37.9	13.0	59.7
22	148 17.4	47.4	302 49.7	9.7	5 50.9	12.9	59.7
23	163 17.6	48.4	317 18.4	9.7	S 6 03.8	12.9	59.6
	SD 16.1	d 1.0	SD 16.6		16.5		16.3

Lat.	Twilight Naut.	Twilight Civil	Sunrise	Moonrise 20	21	22	23
°	h m	h m	h m	h m	h m	h m	h m
N 72	03 17	04 47	05 55	16 39	18 51	20 59	23 10
N 70	03 36	04 55	05 56	16 48	18 51	20 51	22 50
68	03 51	05 01	05 57	16 56	18 51	20 44	22 35
66	04 03	05 07	05 58	17 02	18 51	20 38	22 23
64	04 13	05 11	05 59	17 07	18 51	20 33	22 13
62	04 21	05 15	05 59	17 11	18 51	20 29	22 04
60	04 28	05 18	06 00	17 15	18 51	20 25	21 56
N 58	04 34	05 21	06 00	17 19	18 51	20 22	21 50
56	04 39	05 24	06 01	17 22	18 51	20 19	21 44
54	04 44	05 26	06 01	17 24	18 51	20 16	21 39
52	04 48	05 28	06 01	17 27	18 51	20 14	21 35
50	04 51	05 29	06 02	17 29	18 51	20 12	21 30
45	04 58	05 33	06 02	17 34	18 52	20 08	21 21
N 40	05 04	05 36	06 03	17 38	18 52	20 04	21 14
35	05 08	05 38	06 03	17 41	18 52	20 01	21 08
30	05 12	05 39	06 03	17 44	18 52	19 58	21 02
20	05 16	05 42	06 04	17 50	18 52	19 53	20 52
N 10	05 19	05 43	06 04	17 54	18 52	19 49	20 44
0	05 19	05 43	06 04	17 59	18 52	19 45	20 36
S 10	05 19	05 43	06 04	18 03	18 52	19 41	20 29
20	05 16	05 42	06 04	18 08	18 53	19 37	20 20
30	05 12	05 40	06 04	18 13	18 53	19 32	20 11
35	05 09	05 38	06 04	18 16	18 53	19 29	20 06
40	05 05	05 36	06 03	18 19	18 53	19 26	20 00
45	04 59	05 34	06 03	18 23	18 53	19 23	19 53
S 50	04 52	05 31	06 03	18 28	18 54	19 19	19 45
52	04 49	05 29	06 03	18 30	18 54	19 17	19 41
54	04 45	05 27	06 02	18 32	18 54	19 15	19 37
56	04 41	05 25	06 02	18 35	18 54	19 13	19 32
58	04 36	05 23	06 02	18 38	18 54	19 10	19 27
S 60	04 30	05 20	06 02	18 41	18 55	19 08	19 21

Lat.	Sunset	Twilight Civil	Twilight Naut.	Moonset 20	21	22	23
°	h m	h m	h m	h m	h m	h m	h m
N 72	18 22	19 31	21 03	07 18	07 00	06 44	06 27
N 70	18 21	19 22	20 42	07 06	06 57	06 47	06 38
68	18 19	19 16	20 26	06 57	06 54	06 50	06 47
66	18 18	19 10	20 14	06 49	06 51	06 53	06 55
64	18 18	19 05	20 04	06 42	06 49	06 55	07 01
62	18 17	19 01	19 55	06 36	06 47	06 57	07 07
60	18 16	18 58	19 48	06 31	06 45	06 58	07 12
N 58	18 16	18 55	19 42	06 26	06 44	07 00	07 16
56	18 15	18 52	19 37	06 22	06 42	07 01	07 20
54	18 15	18 50	19 32	06 18	06 41	07 02	07 24
52	18 14	18 48	19 28	06 15	06 40	07 03	07 27
50	18 14	18 46	19 24	06 12	06 39	07 04	07 30
45	18 13	18 43	19 17	06 05	06 37	07 06	07 36
N 40	18 13	18 40	19 11	06 00	06 35	07 08	07 41
35	18 12	18 37	19 07	05 55	06 33	07 10	07 46
30	18 12	18 36	19 04	05 50	06 31	07 11	07 50
20	18 11	18 33	18 59	05 43	06 29	07 13	07 57
N 10	18 11	18 31	18 55	05 36	06 26	07 15	08 03
0	18 11	18 31	18 55	05 30	06 24	07 17	08 09
S 10	18 10	18 31	18 56	05 23	06 22	07 19	08 15
20	18 10	18 32	18 58	05 16	06 19	07 21	08 21
30	18 10	18 34	19 02	05 08	06 17	07 23	08 29
35	18 10	18 36	19 05	05 04	06 15	07 25	08 33
40	18 10	18 38	19 09	04 59	06 13	07 26	08 37
45	18 11	18 40	19 14	04 52	06 11	07 28	08 43
S 50	18 11	18 43	19 21	04 45	06 08	07 30	08 50
52	18 11	18 45	19 24	04 42	06 07	07 31	08 53
54	18 11	18 46	19 28	04 38	06 06	07 32	08 56
56	18 11	18 48	19 32	04 34	06 04	07 33	09 00
58	18 11	18 50	19 37	04 29	06 02	07 34	09 04
S 60	18 12	18 53	19 43	04 23	06 01	07 36	09 08

Day	SUN Eqn. of Time 00ʰ	SUN Eqn. of Time 12ʰ	SUN Mer. Pass.	MOON Mer. Pass. Upper	MOON Mer. Pass. Lower	Age	Phase
d	m s	m s	h m	h m	h m	d	%
20	07 43	07 34	12 08	24 11	11 44	14	99
21	07 25	07 16	12 07	00 11	12 38	15	100
22	07 07	06 58	12 07	01 05	13 31	16	97

© British Crown Copyright 2018. All rights reserved.

UT	ARIES GHA	VENUS −4.0 GHA	Dec	MARS +1.4 GHA	Dec	JUPITER −2.2 GHA	Dec	SATURN +0.6 GHA	Dec	STARS Name	SHA	Dec
23 00	180 11.6	212 21.1	S13 30.0	128 15.4	N19 43.6	276 54.5	S22 39.7	249 18.2	S21 37.6	Acamar	315 15.7	S40 14.1
01	195 14.1	227 20.6	29.1	143 16.2	44.0	291 56.8	39.7	264 20.5	37.6	Achernar	335 24.4	S57 08.7
02	210 16.6	242 20.1	28.2	158 16.9	44.4	306 59.1	39.7	279 22.8	37.6	Acrux	173 04.2	S63 12.3
03	225 19.0	257 19.6 ..	27.3	173 17.7 ..	44.8	322 01.4 ..	39.7	294 25.1 ..	37.6	Adhara	255 09.4	S29 00.2
04	240 21.5	272 19.1	26.4	188 18.4	45.3	337 03.7	39.7	309 27.4	37.5	Aldebaran	290 45.0	N16 32.7
05	255 24.0	287 18.7	25.5	203 19.2	45.7	352 06.0	39.7	324 29.7	37.5			
06	270 26.4	302 18.2	S13 24.7	218 19.9	N19 46.1	7 08.3	S22 39.7	339 32.0	S21 37.5	Alioth	166 16.7	N55 51.3
07	285 28.9	317 17.7	23.8	233 20.7	46.5	22 10.6	39.7	354 34.3	37.5	Alkaid	152 55.4	N49 13.0
S 08	300 31.3	332 17.2	22.9	248 21.5	47.0	37 12.9	39.7	9 36.6	37.5	Alnair	27 39.2	S46 52.1
A 09	315 33.8	347 16.7 ..	22.0	263 22.2 ..	47.4	52 15.2 ..	39.7	24 38.9 ..	37.4	Alnilam	275 42.4	S 1 11.7
T 10	330 36.3	2 16.2	21.1	278 23.0	47.8	67 17.6	39.7	39 41.2	37.4	Alphard	217 52.0	S 8 44.7
U 11	345 38.7	17 15.7	20.2	293 23.7	48.2	82 19.9	39.7	54 43.6	37.4			
R 12	0 41.2	32 15.3	S13 19.3	308 24.5	N19 48.7	97 22.2	S22 39.8	69 45.9	S21 37.4	Alphecca	126 07.5	N26 38.9
D 13	15 43.7	47 14.8	18.4	323 25.2	49.1	112 24.5	39.8	84 48.2	37.4	Alpheratz	357 39.8	N29 11.6
A 14	30 46.1	62 14.3	17.5	338 26.0	49.5	127 26.8	39.8	99 50.5	37.3	Altair	62 04.5	N 8 55.0
Y 15	45 48.6	77 13.8 ..	16.6	353 26.7 ..	49.9	142 29.1 ..	39.8	114 52.8 ..	37.3	Ankaa	353 12.2	S42 12.3
16	60 51.1	92 13.3	15.7	8 27.5	50.4	157 31.4	39.8	129 55.1	37.3	Antares	112 21.3	S26 28.3
17	75 53.5	107 12.9	14.8	23 28.3	50.8	172 33.7	39.8	144 57.4	37.3			
18	90 56.0	122 12.4	S13 13.9	38 29.0	N19 51.2	187 36.1	S22 39.8	159 59.7	S21 37.3	Arcturus	145 51.9	N19 04.9
19	105 58.4	137 11.9	13.0	53 29.8	51.6	202 38.4	39.8	175 02.0	37.3	Atria	107 19.4	S69 03.3
20	121 00.9	152 11.4	12.1	68 30.5	52.0	217 40.7	39.8	190 04.3	37.2	Avior	234 16.1	S59 34.6
21	136 03.4	167 10.9 ..	11.2	83 31.3 ..	52.5	232 43.0 ..	39.8	205 06.6 ..	37.2	Bellatrix	278 27.9	N 6 21.8
22	151 05.8	182 10.5	10.3	98 32.0	52.9	247 45.3	39.8	220 08.9	37.2	Betelgeuse	270 57.1	N 7 24.4
23	166 08.3	197 10.0	09.4	113 32.8	53.3	262 47.6	39.8	235 11.3	37.2			
24 00	181 10.8	212 09.5	S13 08.5	128 33.5	N19 53.7	277 50.0	S22 39.8	250 13.6	S21 37.2	Canopus	263 54.4	S52 42.8
01	196 13.2	227 09.0	07.6	143 34.3	54.1	292 52.3	39.8	265 15.9	37.1	Capella	280 28.8	N46 01.0
02	211 15.7	242 08.5	06.7	158 35.1	54.6	307 54.6	39.8	280 18.2	37.1	Deneb	49 29.1	N45 20.7
03	226 18.2	257 08.1 ..	05.8	173 35.8 ..	55.0	322 56.9 ..	39.8	295 20.5 ..	37.1	Denebola	182 29.4	N14 27.9
04	241 20.6	272 07.6	04.9	188 36.6	55.4	337 59.2	39.8	310 22.8	37.1	Diphda	348 52.3	S17 53.1
05	256 23.1	287 07.1	04.0	203 37.3	55.8	353 01.5	39.8	325 25.1	37.1			
06	271 25.6	302 06.6	S13 03.1	218 38.1	N19 56.2	8 03.9	S22 39.9	340 27.4	S21 37.0	Dubhe	193 46.3	N61 38.9
07	286 28.0	317 06.2	02.2	233 38.8	56.6	23 06.2	39.9	355 29.7	37.0	Elnath	278 07.7	N28 37.3
S 08	301 30.5	332 05.7	01.3	248 39.6	57.1	38 08.5	39.9	10 32.0	37.0	Eltanin	90 44.3	N51 29.0
U 09	316 32.9	347 05.2 ..	13 00.3	263 40.3 ..	57.5	53 10.8 ..	39.9	25 34.4 ..	37.0	Enif	33 43.5	N 9 57.6
N 10	331 35.4	2 04.7	12 59.4	278 41.1	57.9	68 13.1	39.9	40 36.7	37.0	Fomalhaut	15 20.0	S29 31.4
D 11	346 37.9	17 04.3	58.5	293 41.8	58.3	83 15.5	39.9	55 39.0	36.9			
A 12	1 40.3	32 03.8	S12 57.6	308 42.6	N19 58.7	98 17.8	S22 39.9	70 41.3	S21 36.9	Gacrux	171 56.0	S57 13.2
Y 13	16 42.8	47 03.3	56.7	323 43.3	59.1	113 20.1	39.9	85 43.6	36.9	Gienah	175 47.9	S17 38.9
14	31 45.3	62 02.8	55.8	338 44.1	19 59.6	128 22.4	39.9	100 45.9	36.9	Hadar	148 41.8	S60 27.7
15	46 47.7	77 02.4 ..	54.9	353 44.8	20 00.0	143 24.7 ..	39.9	115 48.2 ..	36.9	Hamal	327 56.6	N23 33.0
16	61 50.2	92 01.9	54.0	8 45.6	00.4	158 27.1	39.9	130 50.5	36.9	Kaus Aust.	83 38.6	S34 22.3
17	76 52.7	107 01.4	53.0	23 46.4	00.8	173 29.4	39.9	145 52.8	36.8			
18	91 55.1	122 00.9	S12 52.1	38 47.1	N20 01.2	188 31.7	S22 39.9	160 55.2	S21 36.8	Kochab	137 19.2	N74 04.5
19	106 57.6	137 00.5	51.2	53 47.9	01.6	203 34.0	39.9	175 57.5	36.8	Markab	13 34.7	N15 18.3
20	122 00.1	152 00.0	50.3	68 48.6	02.1	218 36.3	39.9	190 59.8	36.8	Menkar	314 11.2	N 4 09.6
21	137 02.5	166 59.5 ..	49.4	83 49.4 ..	02.5	233 38.7 ..	39.9	206 02.1 ..	36.8	Menkent	148 02.6	S36 27.7
22	152 05.0	181 59.1	48.5	98 50.1	02.9	248 41.0	39.9	221 04.4	36.7	Miaplacidus	221 38.3	S69 48.0
23	167 07.4	196 58.6	47.5	113 50.9	03.3	263 43.3	39.9	236 06.7	36.7			
25 00	182 09.9	211 58.1	S12 46.6	128 51.6	N20 03.7	278 45.6	S22 39.9	251 09.0	S21 36.7	Mirfak	308 35.1	N49 55.7
01	197 12.4	226 57.6	45.7	143 52.4	04.1	293 48.0	40.0	266 11.3	36.7	Nunki	75 53.5	S26 16.2
02	212 14.8	241 57.2	44.8	158 53.1	04.5	308 50.3	40.0	281 13.7	36.7	Peacock	53 13.4	S56 40.2
03	227 17.3	256 56.7 ..	43.9	173 53.9 ..	04.9	323 52.6 ..	40.0	296 16.0 ..	36.6	Pollux	243 22.8	N27 58.7
04	242 19.8	271 56.2	43.0	188 54.6	05.4	338 54.9	40.0	311 18.3	36.6	Procyon	244 55.5	N 5 10.4
05	257 22.2	286 55.8	42.0	203 55.4	05.8	353 57.3	40.0	326 20.6	36.6			
06	272 24.7	301 55.3	S12 41.1	218 56.1	N20 06.2	8 59.6	S22 40.0	341 22.9	S21 36.6	Rasalhague	96 02.8	N12 32.7
07	287 27.2	316 54.8	40.2	233 56.9	06.6	24 01.9	40.0	356 25.2	36.6	Regulus	207 39.1	N11 52.3
08	302 29.6	331 54.4	39.3	248 57.6	07.0	39 04.3	40.0	11 27.5	36.6	Rigel	281 08.4	S 8 11.1
M 09	317 32.1	346 53.9 ..	38.3	263 58.4 ..	07.4	54 06.6 ..	40.0	26 29.9 ..	36.5	Rigil Kent.	139 45.9	S60 54.6
O 10	332 34.5	1 53.4	37.4	278 59.1	07.8	69 08.9	40.0	41 32.2	36.5	Sabik	102 08.0	S15 44.8
N 11	347 37.0	16 53.0	36.5	293 59.9	08.2	84 11.2	40.0	56 34.5	36.5			
D 12	2 39.5	31 52.5	S12 35.6	309 00.6	N20 08.6	99 13.6	S22 40.0	71 36.8	S21 36.5	Schedar	349 36.6	N56 38.4
A 13	17 41.9	46 52.0	34.6	324 01.4	09.0	114 15.9	40.0	86 39.1	36.5	Shaula	96 16.5	S37 06.8
Y 14	32 44.4	61 51.6	33.7	339 02.1	09.5	129 18.2	40.0	101 41.4	36.4	Sirius	258 30.2	S16 44.9
15	47 46.9	76 51.1 ..	32.8	354 02.9 ..	09.9	144 20.5 ..	40.0	116 43.7 ..	36.4	Spica	158 26.8	S11 15.7
16	62 49.3	91 50.6	31.8	9 03.6	10.3	159 22.9	40.0	131 46.1	36.4	Suhail	222 49.3	S43 30.9
17	77 51.8	106 50.2	30.9	24 04.4	10.7	174 25.2	40.0	146 48.4	36.4			
18	92 54.3	121 49.7	S12 30.0	39 05.1	N20 11.1	189 27.5	S22 40.0	161 50.7	S21 36.4	Vega	80 36.3	N38 47.9
19	107 56.7	136 49.2	29.1	54 05.9	11.5	204 29.9	40.0	176 53.0	36.4	Zuben'ubi	137 00.8	S16 07.2
20	122 59.2	151 48.8	28.1	69 06.6	11.9	219 32.2	40.1	191 55.3	36.3		SHA	Mer. Pass.
21	138 01.7	166 48.3 ..	27.2	84 07.4 ..	12.3	234 34.5 ..	40.1	206 57.6 ..	36.3		° '	h m
22	153 04.1	181 47.8	26.3	99 08.1	12.7	249 36.9	40.1	222 00.0	36.3	Venus	30 58.7	9 52
23	168 06.6	196 47.4	25.3	114 08.9	13.1	264 39.2	40.1	237 02.3	36.3	Mars	307 22.8	15 25
	h m									Jupiter	96 39.2	5 28
Mer. Pass. 11 53.3	v −0.5	d 0.9	v 0.8	d 0.4	v 2.3	d 0.0	v 2.3	d 0.0	Saturn	69 02.8	7 18

© British Crown Copyright 2018. All rights reserved.

UT	SUN GHA	SUN Dec	MOON GHA	v	MOON Dec	d	HP
d h	° '	° '	° '	'	° '	'	'
23 00	178 17.8	N 0 49.4	331 47.1	9.7	S 6 16.7	12.8	59.6
01	193 18.0	50.4	346 15.8	9.7	6 29.5	12.8	59.6
02	208 18.2	51.3	0 44.5	9.7	6 42.3	12.7	59.5
03	223 18.4	.. 52.3	15 13.2	9.7	6 55.0	12.7	59.5
04	238 18.6	53.3	29 41.9	9.8	7 07.7	12.6	59.5
05	253 18.8	54.3	44 10.7	9.7	7 20.3	12.6	59.4
06	268 19.0	N 0 55.3	58 39.4	9.8	S 7 32.9	12.5	59.4
07	283 19.1	56.3	73 08.2	9.8	7 45.4	12.4	59.3
S 08	298 19.3	57.3	87 37.0	9.8	7 57.8	12.4	59.3
A 09	313 19.5	.. 58.2	102 05.8	9.8	8 10.2	12.3	59.3
T 10	328 19.7	0 59.2	116 34.6	9.8	8 22.5	12.2	59.2
U 11	343 19.9	1 00.2	131 03.4	9.8	8 34.7	12.2	59.2
R 12	358 20.1	N 1 01.2	145 32.2	9.8	S 8 46.9	12.2	59.2
D 13	13 20.3	02.2	160 01.0	9.8	8 59.1	12.0	59.1
A 14	28 20.5	03.2	174 29.8	9.8	9 11.1	12.0	59.1
Y 15	43 20.6	.. 04.2	188 58.6	9.9	9 23.1	11.9	59.1
16	58 20.8	05.1	203 27.5	9.8	9 35.0	11.9	59.0
17	73 21.0	06.1	217 56.3	9.8	9 46.9	11.7	59.0
18	88 21.2	N 1 07.1	232 25.1	9.9	S 9 58.6	11.8	58.9
19	103 21.4	08.1	246 54.0	9.8	10 10.4	11.6	58.9
20	118 21.6	09.1	261 22.8	9.9	10 22.0	11.6	58.9
21	133 21.8	.. 10.1	275 51.7	9.9	10 33.6	11.4	58.8
22	148 22.0	11.1	290 20.6	9.8	10 45.0	11.5	58.8
23	163 22.2	12.0	304 49.4	9.9	10 56.5	11.3	58.8
24 00	178 22.3	N 1 13.0	319 18.3	9.9	S11 07.8	11.2	58.7
01	193 22.5	14.0	333 47.2	9.9	11 19.0	11.2	58.7
02	208 22.7	15.0	348 16.0	9.9	11 30.2	11.1	58.6
03	223 22.9	.. 16.0	2 44.9	9.9	11 41.3	11.0	58.6
04	238 23.1	17.0	17 13.8	9.9	11 52.3	11.0	58.6
05	253 23.3	17.9	31 42.7	9.9	12 03.3	10.8	58.5
06	268 23.5	N 1 18.9	46 11.6	9.9	S12 14.1	10.8	58.5
07	283 23.7	19.9	60 40.5	9.8	12 24.9	10.7	58.4
08	298 23.9	20.9	75 09.3	9.9	12 35.6	10.6	58.4
S 09	313 24.0	.. 21.9	89 38.2	9.9	12 46.2	10.5	58.4
U 10	328 24.2	22.9	104 07.1	9.9	12 56.7	10.5	58.3
N 11	343 24.4	23.9	118 36.0	9.9	13 07.2	10.3	58.3
D 12	358 24.6	N 1 24.8	133 04.9	9.9	S13 17.5	10.3	58.3
A 13	13 24.8	25.8	147 33.8	9.9	13 27.8	10.1	58.2
Y 14	28 25.0	26.8	162 02.7	9.9	13 37.9	10.1	58.2
15	43 25.2	.. 27.8	176 31.6	9.9	13 48.0	10.0	58.1
16	58 25.4	28.8	191 00.5	9.9	13 58.0	9.9	58.1
17	73 25.6	29.8	205 29.4	9.8	14 07.9	9.8	58.1
18	88 25.7	N 1 30.7	219 58.2	9.9	S14 17.7	9.7	58.0
19	103 25.9	31.7	234 27.1	9.9	14 27.4	9.7	58.0
20	118 26.1	32.7	248 56.0	9.9	14 37.1	9.5	57.9
21	133 26.3	.. 33.7	263 24.9	9.9	14 46.6	9.4	57.9
22	148 26.5	34.7	277 53.8	9.9	14 56.0	9.4	57.9
23	163 26.7	35.7	292 22.7	9.9	15 05.4	9.2	57.8
25 00	178 26.9	N 1 36.6	306 51.6	9.9	S15 14.6	9.2	57.8
01	193 27.1	37.6	321 20.5	9.8	15 23.8	9.0	57.7
02	208 27.3	38.6	335 49.3	9.9	15 32.8	9.0	57.7
03	223 27.4	.. 39.6	350 18.2	9.9	15 41.8	8.8	57.7
04	238 27.6	40.6	4 47.1	9.9	15 50.6	8.8	57.6
05	253 27.8	41.6	19 16.0	9.9	15 59.4	8.7	57.6
06	268 28.0	N 1 42.5	33 44.9	9.9	S16 08.1	8.5	57.5
07	283 28.2	43.5	48 13.8	9.9	16 16.6	8.5	57.5
08	298 28.4	44.5	62 42.6	9.9	16 25.1	8.3	57.5
M 09	313 28.6	.. 45.5	77 11.5	9.9	16 33.4	8.3	57.4
O 10	328 28.8	46.5	91 40.4	9.9	16 41.7	8.1	57.4
N 11	343 29.0	47.5	106 09.3	9.9	16 49.8	8.1	57.4
D 12	358 29.1	N 1 48.4	120 38.2	9.8	S16 57.9	8.0	57.3
A 13	13 29.3	49.4	135 07.0	9.9	17 05.9	7.8	57.3
Y 14	28 29.5	50.4	149 35.9	9.9	17 13.7	7.8	57.2
15	43 29.7	.. 51.4	164 04.8	9.9	17 21.5	7.6	57.2
16	58 29.9	52.4	178 33.7	9.9	17 29.1	7.5	57.2
17	73 30.1	53.3	193 02.6	9.8	17 36.6	7.5	57.1
18	88 30.3	N 1 54.3	207 31.4	9.9	S17 44.1	7.3	57.1
19	103 30.5	55.3	222 00.3	9.9	17 51.4	7.2	57.0
20	118 30.7	56.3	236 29.2	9.9	17 58.6	7.1	57.0
21	133 30.8	.. 57.3	250 58.1	9.9	18 05.7	7.0	57.0
22	148 31.0	58.3	265 27.0	9.9	18 12.7	6.9	56.9
23	163 31.2	59.2	279 55.9	9.8	S18 19.6	6.8	56.9
	SD 16.1	d 1.0	SD 16.1		15.9		15.6

Lat.	Twilight Naut.	Twilight Civil	Sunrise	Moonrise 23	24	25	26
°	h m	h m	h m	h m	h m	h m	h m
N 72	02 55	04 30	05 39	23 10	25 33	01 33	▨▨▨
N 70	03 19	04 40	05 42	22 50	24 53	00 53	03 10
68	03 36	04 48	05 45	22 35	24 26	00 26	02 17
66	03 50	04 55	05 46	22 23	24 06	00 06	01 45
64	04 01	05 00	05 48	22 13	23 49	25 21	01 21
62	04 10	05 05	05 49	22 04	23 36	25 03	01 03
60	04 18	05 09	05 51	21 56	23 24	24 47	00 47
N 58	04 25	05 12	05 52	21 50	23 15	24 34	00 34
56	04 31	05 15	05 53	21 44	23 06	24 23	00 23
54	04 36	05 18	05 54	21 39	22 59	24 13	00 13
52	04 40	05 21	05 54	21 35	22 52	24 05	00 05
50	04 44	05 23	05 55	21 30	22 46	23 57	25 02
45	04 53	05 27	05 56	21 21	22 33	23 40	24 43
N 40	04 59	05 31	05 58	21 14	22 22	23 27	24 27
35	05 04	05 33	05 59	21 08	22 13	23 15	24 14
30	05 08	05 36	06 00	21 02	22 05	23 05	24 03
20	05 13	05 39	06 01	20 52	21 51	22 48	23 43
N 10	05 17	05 41	06 02	20 44	21 39	22 33	23 27
0	05 18	05 42	06 03	20 36	21 28	22 19	23 11
S 10	05 19	05 43	06 04	20 29	21 17	22 06	22 55
20	05 17	05 43	06 05	20 20	21 05	21 51	22 38
30	05 14	05 42	06 06	20 11	20 52	21 34	22 19
35	05 11	05 41	06 06	20 06	20 44	21 25	22 08
40	05 08	05 39	06 07	20 00	20 35	21 14	21 55
45	05 03	05 38	06 07	19 53	20 25	21 01	21 40
S 50	04 57	05 35	06 08	19 45	20 13	20 45	21 22
52	04 55	05 34	06 08	19 41	20 07	20 38	21 13
54	04 51	05 33	06 08	19 37	20 01	20 30	21 04
56	04 47	05 31	06 08	19 32	19 54	20 21	20 53
58	04 43	05 29	06 09	19 27	19 47	20 10	20 40
S 60	04 38	05 27	06 09	19 21	19 38	19 59	20 26

Lat.	Sunset	Twilight Civil	Twilight Naut.	Moonset 23	24	25	26
°	h m	h m	h m	h m	h m	h m	h m
N 72	18 36	19 46	21 23	06 27	06 05	05 30	▨▨
N 70	18 33	19 35	20 59	06 38	06 27	06 12	05 43
68	18 30	19 27	20 40	06 47	06 43	06 40	06 36
66	18 28	19 20	20 26	06 55	06 57	07 01	07 09
64	18 26	19 15	20 14	07 01	07 09	07 19	07 34
62	18 25	19 10	20 05	07 07	07 18	07 33	07 53
60	18 23	19 05	19 57	07 12	07 27	07 45	08 09
N 58	18 22	19 02	19 50	07 16	07 34	07 55	08 22
56	18 21	18 59	19 44	07 20	07 41	08 05	08 34
54	18 20	18 56	19 38	07 24	07 46	08 13	08 44
52	18 19	18 53	19 34	07 27	07 52	08 20	08 53
50	18 19	18 51	19 30	07 30	07 57	08 27	09 01
45	18 17	18 46	19 21	07 36	08 07	08 41	09 18
N 40	18 16	18 43	19 15	07 41	08 16	08 53	09 33
35	18 15	18 40	19 10	07 46	08 23	09 03	09 45
30	18 14	18 38	19 06	07 50	08 30	09 11	09 55
20	18 12	18 34	19 00	07 57	08 41	09 27	10 13
N 10	18 11	18 32	18 56	08 03	08 51	09 40	10 29
0	18 10	18 30	18 54	08 09	09 01	09 53	10 44
S 10	18 09	18 30	18 54	08 15	09 10	10 05	10 59
20	18 08	18 30	18 55	08 21	09 21	10 19	11 15
30	18 07	18 30	18 58	08 29	09 32	10 34	11 33
35	18 06	18 31	19 01	08 33	09 39	10 43	11 44
40	18 06	18 33	19 04	08 37	09 47	10 53	11 56
45	18 05	18 34	19 08	08 43	09 56	11 05	12 11
S 50	18 04	18 36	19 14	08 50	10 07	11 20	12 28
52	18 04	18 38	19 17	08 53	10 12	11 27	12 37
54	18 04	18 39	19 20	08 56	10 17	11 35	12 46
56	18 03	18 40	19 24	09 00	10 23	11 43	12 57
58	18 03	18 42	19 28	09 04	10 30	11 53	13 09
S 60	18 02	18 44	19 33	09 08	10 38	12 04	13 23

	SUN			MOON		
Day	Eqn. of Time 00h	Eqn. of Time 12h	Mer. Pass.	Mer. Pass. Upper	Mer. Pass. Lower	Age Phase
d	m s	m s	h m	h m	h m	d %
23	06 49	06 40	12 07	01 57	14 23	17 92
24	06 31	06 22	12 06	02 49	15 14	18 85
25	06 13	06 04	12 06	03 40	16 06	19 76

© British Crown Copyright 2018. All rights reserved.

UT	ARIES GHA	VENUS −4.0 GHA	Dec	MARS +1.4 GHA	Dec	JUPITER −2.2 GHA	Dec	SATURN +0.6 GHA	Dec	STARS Name	SHA	Dec
26 00	183 09.0	211 46.9	S12 24.4	129 09.6	N20 13.5	279 41.5	S22 40.1	252 04.6	S21 36.3	Acamar	315 15.7	S40 14.0
01	198 11.5	226 46.4	23.5	144 10.4	13.9	294 43.9	40.1	267 06.9	36.2	Achernar	335 24.4	S57 08.6
02	213 14.0	241 46.0	22.5	159 11.1	14.3	309 46.2	40.1	282 09.2	36.2	Acrux	173 04.2	S63 12.3
03	228 16.4	256 45.5 ..	21.6	174 11.9 ..	14.7	324 48.5 ..	40.1	297 11.5 ..	36.2	Adhara	255 09.4	S29 00.3
04	243 18.9	271 45.1	20.7	189 12.6	15.1	339 50.9	40.1	312 13.9	36.2	Aldebaran	290 45.0	N16 32.7
05	258 21.4	286 44.6	19.7	204 13.4	15.6	354 53.2	40.1	327 16.2	36.2			
06	273 23.8	301 44.1	S12 18.8	219 14.1	N20 16.0	9 55.5	S22 40.1	342 18.5	S21 36.1	Alioth	166 16.7	N55 51.3
07	288 26.3	316 43.7	17.8	234 14.9	16.4	24 57.9	40.1	357 20.8	36.1	Alkaid	152 55.3	N49 13.0
08	303 28.8	331 43.2	16.9	249 15.6	16.8	40 00.2	40.1	12 23.1	36.1	Alnair	27 39.2	S46 52.1
09	318 31.2	346 42.8 ..	16.0	264 16.4 ..	17.2	55 02.5 ..	40.1	27 25.5 ..	36.1	Alnilam	275 42.5	S 1 11.7
10	333 33.7	1 42.3	15.0	279 17.1	17.6	70 04.9	40.1	42 27.8	36.1	Alphard	217 52.0	S 8 44.7
11	348 36.2	16 41.8	14.1	294 17.9	18.0	85 07.2	40.1	57 30.1	36.1			
12	3 38.6	31 41.4	S12 13.2	309 18.6	N20 18.4	100 09.5	S22 40.1	72 32.4	S21 36.0	Alphecca	126 07.4	N26 38.9
13	18 41.1	46 40.9	12.2	324 19.4	18.8	115 11.9	40.1	87 34.7	36.0	Alpheratz	357 39.8	N29 11.6
14	33 43.5	61 40.5	11.3	339 20.1	19.2	130 14.2	40.1	102 37.0	36.0	Altair	62 04.5	N 8 55.0
15	48 46.0	76 40.0 ..	10.3	354 20.9 ..	19.6	145 16.6 ..	40.1	117 39.4 ..	36.0	Ankaa	353 12.2	S42 12.3
16	63 48.5	91 39.5	09.4	9 21.6	20.0	160 18.9	40.1	132 41.7	36.0	Antares	112 21.3	S26 28.3
17	78 50.9	106 39.1	08.4	24 22.4	20.4	175 21.2	40.2	147 44.0	36.0			
18	93 53.4	121 38.6	S12 07.5	39 23.1	N20 20.8	190 23.6	S22 40.2	162 46.3	S21 35.9	Arcturus	145 51.9	N19 04.9
19	108 55.9	136 38.2	06.6	54 23.8	21.2	205 25.9	40.2	177 48.6	35.9	Atria	107 19.4	S69 03.3
20	123 58.3	151 37.7	05.6	69 24.6	21.6	220 28.2	40.2	192 51.0	35.9	Avior	234 16.1	S59 34.6
21	139 00.8	166 37.3 ..	04.7	84 25.3 ..	22.0	235 30.6 ..	40.2	207 53.3 ..	35.9	Bellatrix	278 27.9	N 6 21.8
22	154 03.3	181 36.8	03.7	99 26.1	22.4	250 32.9	40.2	222 55.6	35.9	Betelgeuse	270 57.1	N 7 24.4
23	169 05.7	196 36.3	02.8	114 26.8	22.8	265 35.3	40.2	237 57.9	35.8			
27 00	184 08.2	211 35.9	S12 01.8	129 27.6	N20 23.2	280 37.6	S22 40.2	253 00.3	S21 35.8	Canopus	263 54.4	S52 42.8
01	199 10.7	226 35.4	12 00.9	144 28.3	23.6	295 39.9	40.2	268 02.6	35.8	Capella	280 28.8	N46 01.0
02	214 13.1	241 35.0	11 59.9	159 29.1	24.0	310 42.3	40.2	283 04.9	35.8	Deneb	49 29.1	N45 20.7
03	229 15.6	256 34.5 ..	59.0	174 29.8 ..	24.4	325 44.6 ..	40.2	298 07.2 ..	35.8	Denebola	182 29.3	N14 27.9
04	244 18.0	271 34.1	58.0	189 30.6	24.8	340 47.0	40.2	313 09.5	35.8	Diphda	348 52.3	S17 53.1
05	259 20.5	286 33.6	57.1	204 31.3	25.2	355 49.3	40.2	328 11.9	35.7			
06	274 23.0	301 33.2	S11 56.1	219 32.1	N20 25.6	10 51.7	S22 40.2	343 14.2	S21 35.7	Dubhe	193 46.3	N61 38.9
07	289 25.4	316 32.7	55.2	234 32.8	26.0	25 54.0	40.2	358 16.5	35.7	Elnath	278 07.7	N28 37.3
08	304 27.9	331 32.3	54.2	249 33.6	26.4	40 56.3	40.2	13 18.8	35.7	Eltanin	90 44.3	N51 29.0
09	319 30.4	346 31.8 ..	53.3	264 34.3 ..	26.8	55 58.7 ..	40.2	28 21.1 ..	35.7	Enif	33 43.5	N 9 57.6
10	334 32.8	1 31.3	52.3	279 35.0	27.2	71 01.0	40.2	43 23.5	35.7	Fomalhaut	15 20.0	S29 31.3
11	349 35.3	16 30.9	51.4	294 35.8	27.6	86 03.4	40.2	58 25.8	35.6			
12	4 37.8	31 30.4	S11 50.4	309 36.5	N20 27.9	101 05.7	S22 40.2	73 28.1	S21 35.6	Gacrux	171 55.9	S57 13.2
13	19 40.2	46 30.0	49.4	324 37.3	28.3	116 08.1	40.2	88 30.4	35.6	Gienah	175 47.9	S17 38.9
14	34 42.7	61 29.5	48.5	339 38.0	28.7	131 10.4	40.2	103 32.8	35.6	Hadar	148 41.7	S60 27.7
15	49 45.1	76 29.1 ..	47.5	354 38.8 ..	29.1	146 12.8 ..	40.2	118 35.1 ..	35.6	Hamal	327 56.6	N23 33.0
16	64 47.6	91 28.6	46.6	9 39.5	29.5	161 15.1	40.3	133 37.4	35.5	Kaus Aust.	83 38.6	S34 22.3
17	79 50.1	106 28.2	45.6	24 40.3	29.9	176 17.4	40.3	148 39.7	35.5			
18	94 52.5	121 27.7	S11 44.7	39 41.0	N20 30.3	191 19.8	S22 40.3	163 42.1	S21 35.5	Kochab	137 19.2	N74 04.5
19	109 55.0	136 27.3	43.7	54 41.7	30.7	206 22.1	40.3	178 44.4	35.5	Markab	13 34.7	N15 18.3
20	124 57.5	151 26.8	42.7	69 42.5	31.1	221 24.5	40.3	193 46.7	35.5	Menkar	314 11.2	N 4 09.6
21	139 59.9	166 26.4 ..	41.8	84 43.2 ..	31.5	236 26.8 ..	40.3	208 49.0 ..	35.5	Menkent	148 02.6	S36 27.7
22	155 02.4	181 25.9	40.8	99 44.0	31.9	251 29.2	40.3	223 51.3	35.4	Miaplacidus	221 38.3	S69 48.0
23	170 04.9	196 25.5	39.9	114 44.7	32.3	266 31.5	40.3	238 53.7	35.4			
28 00	185 07.3	211 25.0	S11 38.9	129 45.5	N20 32.7	281 33.9	S22 40.3	253 56.0	S21 35.4	Mirfak	308 35.1	N49 55.7
01	200 09.8	226 24.6	37.9	144 46.2	33.1	296 36.2	40.3	268 58.3	35.4	Nunki	75 53.5	S26 16.2
02	215 12.3	241 24.2	37.0	159 47.0	33.5	311 38.6	40.3	284 00.6	35.4	Peacock	53 13.4	S56 40.2
03	230 14.7	256 23.7 ..	36.0	174 47.7 ..	33.8	326 40.9 ..	40.3	299 03.0 ..	35.4	Pollux	243 22.8	N27 58.7
04	245 17.2	271 23.3	35.0	189 48.4	34.2	341 43.3	40.3	314 05.3	35.3	Procyon	244 55.5	N 5 10.3
05	260 19.6	286 22.8	34.1	204 49.2	34.6	356 45.6	40.3	329 07.6	35.3			
06	275 22.1	301 22.4	S11 33.1	219 49.9	N20 35.0	11 48.0	S22 40.3	344 09.9	S21 35.3	Rasalhague	96 02.7	N12 32.7
07	290 24.6	316 21.9	32.1	234 50.7	35.4	26 50.3	40.3	359 12.3	35.3	Regulus	207 39.1	N11 52.3
08	305 27.0	331 21.5	31.2	249 51.4	35.8	41 52.7	40.3	14 14.6	35.3	Rigel	281 08.4	S 8 11.1
09	320 29.5	346 21.0 ..	30.2	264 52.2 ..	36.2	56 55.0 ..	40.3	29 16.9 ..	35.3	Rigil Kent.	139 45.9	S60 54.6
10	335 32.0	1 20.6	29.2	279 52.9	36.6	71 57.4	40.3	44 19.3	35.2	Sabik	102 07.9	S15 44.8
11	350 34.4	16 20.1	28.3	294 53.6	37.0	86 59.7	40.3	59 21.6	35.2			
12	5 36.9	31 19.7	S11 27.3	309 54.4	N20 37.4	102 02.1	S22 40.3	74 23.9	S21 35.2	Schedar	349 36.6	N56 38.4
13	20 39.4	46 19.3	26.3	324 55.1	37.7	117 04.4	40.3	89 26.2	35.2	Shaula	96 16.5	S37 06.8
14	35 41.8	61 18.8	25.4	339 55.9	38.1	132 06.8	40.3	104 28.6	35.2	Sirius	258 30.2	S16 44.9
15	50 44.3	76 18.4 ..	24.4	354 56.6 ..	38.5	147 09.1 ..	40.3	119 30.9 ..	35.1	Spica	158 26.8	S11 15.7
16	65 46.8	91 17.9	23.4	9 57.4	38.9	162 11.5	40.3	134 33.2	35.1	Suhail	222 49.3	S43 30.9
17	80 49.2	106 17.5	22.5	24 58.1	39.3	177 13.9	40.4	149 35.5	35.1			
18	95 51.7	121 17.0	S11 21.5	39 58.8	N20 39.7	192 16.2	S22 40.4	164 37.9	S21 35.1	Vega	80 36.3	N38 47.9
19	110 54.1	136 16.6	20.5	54 59.6	40.1	207 18.6	40.4	179 40.2	35.1	Zuben'ubi	137 00.8	S16 07.2
20	125 56.6	151 16.2	19.5	70 00.3	40.5	222 20.9	40.4	194 42.5	35.1		SHA	Mer. Pass.
21	140 59.1	166 15.7 ..	18.6	85 01.1 ..	40.8	237 23.3 ..	40.4	209 44.9 ..	35.0	Venus	27 27.7	9 54
22	156 01.5	181 15.3	17.6	100 01.8	41.2	252 25.6	40.4	224 47.2	35.0	Mars	305 19.4	15 21
23	171 04.0	196 14.8	16.6	115 02.5	41.6	267 28.0	40.4	239 49.5	35.0	Jupiter	96 29.4	5 17
Mer. Pass. 11 41.5		v −0.5	d 1.0	v 0.7	d 0.4	v 2.3	d 0.0	v 2.3	d 0.0	Saturn	68 52.1	7 07

© British Crown Copyright 2018. All rights reserved.

UT	SUN GHA	Dec	MOON GHA	v	Dec	d	HP
26 00	178 31.4	N 2 00.2	294 24.7	9.9	S18 26.4	6.7	56.9
01	193 31.6	01.2	308 53.6	9.9	18 33.1	6.6	56.8
02	208 31.8	02.2	323 22.5	9.9	18 39.7	6.5	56.8
03	223 32.0	.. 03.2	337 51.4	9.9	18 46.2	6.3	56.7
04	238 32.2	04.1	352 20.3	9.9	18 52.5	6.3	56.7
05	253 32.4	05.1	6 49.2	9.9	18 58.8	6.1	56.7
06	268 32.5	N 2 06.1	21 18.1	9.9	S19 04.9	6.1	56.6
07	283 32.7	07.1	35 47.0	9.9	19 11.0	5.9	56.6
T 08	298 32.9	08.1	50 15.9	9.9	19 16.9	5.8	56.6
U 09	313 33.1	.. 09.1	64 44.8	10.0	19 22.7	5.7	56.5
E 10	328 33.3	10.0	79 13.8	9.9	19 28.4	5.6	56.5
S 11	343 33.5	11.0	93 42.7	9.9	19 34.0	5.5	56.5
D 12	358 33.7	N 2 12.0	108 11.6	9.9	S19 39.5	5.4	56.4
A 13	13 33.9	13.0	122 40.5	10.0	19 44.9	5.3	56.4
Y 14	28 34.1	14.0	137 09.5	9.9	19 50.2	5.1	56.4
15	43 34.3	.. 14.9	151 38.4	10.0	19 55.3	5.1	56.3
16	58 34.4	15.9	166 07.4	9.9	20 00.4	4.9	56.3
17	73 34.6	16.9	180 36.3	10.0	20 05.3	4.8	56.3
18	88 34.8	N 2 17.9	195 05.3	10.0	S20 10.1	4.7	56.2
19	103 35.0	18.9	209 34.3	10.0	20 14.8	4.6	56.2
20	118 35.2	19.8	224 03.3	10.0	20 19.4	4.5	56.2
21	133 35.4	.. 20.8	238 32.3	10.0	20 23.9	4.4	56.1
22	148 35.6	21.8	253 01.3	10.0	20 28.3	4.2	56.1
23	163 35.8	22.8	267 30.3	10.0	20 32.5	4.2	56.1
27 00	178 36.0	N 2 23.8	281 59.3	10.0	S20 36.7	4.0	56.0
01	193 36.1	24.7	296 28.3	10.1	20 40.7	4.0	56.0
02	208 36.3	25.7	310 57.4	10.0	20 44.7	3.8	56.0
03	223 36.5	.. 26.7	325 26.4	10.1	20 48.5	3.7	55.9
04	238 36.7	27.7	339 55.5	10.0	20 52.2	3.6	55.9
05	253 36.9	28.7	354 24.5	10.1	20 55.8	3.5	55.9
06	268 37.1	N 2 29.6	8 53.6	10.1	S20 59.3	3.3	55.8
W 07	283 37.3	30.6	23 22.7	10.1	21 02.6	3.3	55.8
E 08	298 37.5	31.6	37 51.8	10.2	21 05.9	3.1	55.8
D 09	313 37.7	.. 32.6	52 21.0	10.1	21 09.0	3.1	55.7
N 10	328 37.8	33.6	66 50.1	10.2	21 12.1	2.9	55.7
E 11	343 38.0	34.5	81 19.3	10.1	21 15.0	2.8	55.7
S 12	358 38.2	N 2 35.5	95 48.4	10.2	S21 17.8	2.7	55.6
D 13	13 38.4	36.5	110 17.6	10.2	21 20.5	2.6	55.6
A 14	28 38.6	37.5	124 46.8	10.2	21 23.1	2.4	55.6
Y 15	43 38.8	.. 38.4	139 16.0	10.3	21 25.5	2.4	55.6
16	58 39.0	39.4	153 45.3	10.3	21 27.9	2.2	55.5
17	73 39.2	40.4	168 14.5	10.3	21 30.1	2.2	55.5
18	88 39.4	N 2 41.4	182 43.8	10.3	S21 32.3	2.0	55.5
19	103 39.5	42.4	197 13.1	10.3	21 34.3	1.9	55.4
20	118 39.7	43.3	211 42.4	10.3	21 36.2	1.8	55.4
21	133 39.9	.. 44.3	226 11.7	10.3	21 38.0	1.7	55.4
22	148 40.1	45.3	240 41.0	10.4	21 39.7	1.6	55.4
23	163 40.3	46.3	255 10.4	10.4	21 41.3	1.4	55.3
28 00	178 40.5	N 2 47.2	269 39.8	10.4	S21 42.7	1.4	55.3
01	193 40.7	48.2	284 09.2	10.4	21 44.1	1.2	55.3
02	208 40.9	49.2	298 38.6	10.5	21 45.3	1.2	55.3
03	223 41.1	.. 50.2	313 08.1	10.4	21 46.5	1.0	55.2
04	238 41.2	51.2	327 37.5	10.5	21 47.5	0.9	55.2
05	253 41.4	52.1	342 07.0	10.6	21 48.4	0.8	55.2
06	268 41.6	N 2 53.1	356 36.6	10.5	S21 49.2	0.7	55.2
07	283 41.8	54.1	11 06.1	10.6	21 49.9	0.6	55.1
T 08	298 42.0	55.1	25 35.7	10.6	21 50.5	0.5	55.1
H 09	313 42.2	.. 56.0	40 05.3	10.6	21 51.0	0.4	55.1
U 10	328 42.4	57.0	54 34.9	10.6	21 51.4	0.2	55.1
R 11	343 42.6	58.0	69 04.5	10.7	21 51.6	0.2	55.0
S 12	358 42.8	N 2 59.0	83 34.2	10.7	S21 51.8	0.0	55.0
D 13	13 42.9	3 00.0	98 03.9	10.7	21 51.8	0.0	55.0
A 14	28 43.1	00.9	112 33.6	10.7	21 51.8	0.2	55.0
Y 15	43 43.3	.. 01.9	127 03.3	10.8	21 51.6	0.3	54.9
16	58 43.5	02.9	141 33.1	10.8	21 51.3	0.4	54.9
17	73 43.7	03.9	156 02.9	10.9	21 50.9	0.5	54.9
18	88 43.9	N 3 04.8	170 32.8	10.8	S21 50.4	0.6	54.9
19	103 44.1	05.8	185 02.6	10.9	21 49.8	0.7	54.9
20	118 44.3	06.8	199 32.5	10.9	21 49.1	0.8	54.8
21	133 44.4	.. 07.8	214 02.4	11.0	21 48.3	0.9	54.8
22	148 44.6	08.7	228 32.4	11.0	21 47.4	1.0	54.8
23	163 44.8	09.7	243 02.4	11.0	S21 46.4	1.1	54.8
	SD 16.1	d 1.0	SD 15.4		15.2		15.0

Lat.	Twilight Naut.	Civil	Sunrise	Moonrise 26	27	28	29
N 72	02 31	04 13	05 24	■■■■	■■■■	■■■■	■■■■
N 70	02 59	04 25	05 28	03 10	■■■■	■■■■	■■■■
68	03 20	04 35	05 32	02 17	04 07	■■■■	■■■■
66	03 36	04 43	05 35	01 45	03 16	05 53	06 22
64	03 49	04 49	05 37	01 21	02 44	04 29	05 14
62	03 59	04 55	05 40	01 03	02 20	03 51	04 39
60	04 08	05 00	05 42	00 47	02 02	03 25	04 13
N 58	04 16	05 04	05 43	00 34	01 46	03 04	03 53
56	04 22	05 07	05 45	00 23	01 33	02 47	03 36
54	04 28	05 11	05 46	00 13	01 21	02 33	03 22
52	04 33	05 13	05 47	00 05	01 11	02 20	03 10
50	04 37	05 16	05 48	25 02	01 02	02 09	02 59
45	04 47	05 21	05 51	24 43	00 43	01 39	02 29
N 40	04 54	05 26	05 53	24 27	00 27	01 23	02 13
35	04 59	05 29	05 54	24 14	00 14	01 09	01 59
30	05 04	05 32	05 56	24 03	00 03	00 57	01 47
20	05 11	05 36	05 58	23 43	24 36	00 36	01 27
N 10	05 15	05 39	06 00	23 27	24 19	00 19	01 09
0	05 17	05 42	06 02	23 11	24 02	00 02	00 52
S 10	05 19	05 43	06 04	22 55	23 45	24 35	00 35
20	05 18	05 44	06 06	22 38	23 27	24 17	00 17
30	05 16	05 44	06 07	22 19	23 07	23 57	24 49
35	05 14	05 43	06 08	22 08	22 55	23 45	24 37
40	05 11	05 42	06 10	21 55	22 41	23 31	24 24
45	05 07	05 42	06 11	21 40	22 25	23 15	24 09
S 50	05 02	05 40	06 12	21 22	22 05	22 55	23 50
52	05 00	05 39	06 13	21 13	21 56	22 45	23 41
54	04 57	05 38	06 14	21 04	21 45	22 34	23 31
56	04 54	05 37	06 14	20 53	21 33	22 22	23 19
58	04 50	05 36	06 15	20 40	21 19	22 08	23 06
S 60	04 46	05 35	06 16	20 26	21 03	21 51	22 51

Lat.	Sunset	Twilight Civil	Naut.	Moonset 26	27	28	29
N 72	18 50	20 01	21 46	■■■■	■■■■	■■■■	■■■■
N 70	18 45	19 49	21 16	05 43	■■■■	■■■■	■■■■
68	18 41	19 39	20 55	06 36	06 33	06 34	07 49
66	18 38	19 31	20 38	07 09	07 25	07 58	08 56
64	18 35	19 24	20 25	07 34	07 58	08 36	09 32
62	18 33	19 18	20 14	07 53	08 21	09 03	09 57
60	18 31	19 13	20 05	08 09	08 41	09 23	10 18
N 58	18 29	19 09	19 57	08 22	08 56	09 40	10 34
56	18 27	19 05	19 50	08 34	09 10	09 55	10 48
54	18 26	19 02	19 45	08 44	09 22	10 07	11 00
52	18 25	18 59	19 39	08 53	09 32	10 18	11 11
50	18 23	18 56	19 35	09 01	09 41	10 28	11 20
45	18 21	18 50	19 25	09 18	10 01	10 48	11 40
N 40	18 19	18 46	19 18	09 33	10 17	11 05	11 56
35	18 17	18 42	19 11	09 45	10 30	11 19	12 10
30	18 15	18 39	19 07	09 55	10 42	11 31	12 22
20	18 13	18 35	19 01	10 13	11 02	11 51	12 42
N 10	18 11	18 32	18 55	10 29	11 19	12 09	12 59
0	18 09	18 29	18 53	10 44	11 35	12 26	13 16
S 10	18 07	18 28	18 52	10 59	11 52	12 43	13 32
20	18 05	18 27	18 53	11 15	12 09	13 01	13 49
30	18 03	18 27	18 55	11 33	12 29	13 22	14 09
35	18 02	18 27	18 56	11 44	12 41	13 34	14 21
40	18 01	18 28	18 59	11 56	12 55	13 47	14 34
45	17 59	18 29	19 03	12 11	13 11	14 04	14 50
S 50	17 58	18 30	19 07	12 28	13 30	14 24	15 10
52	17 57	18 31	19 10	12 37	13 40	14 34	15 19
54	17 56	18 31	19 13	12 46	13 50	14 44	15 29
56	17 55	18 32	19 16	12 57	14 02	14 57	15 41
58	17 54	18 33	19 19	13 09	14 16	15 11	15 54
S 60	17 53	18 35	19 23	13 23	14 32	15 28	16 10

	SUN Eqn. of Time 00h	12h	Mer. Pass.	MOON Mer. Pass. Upper	Lower	Age	Phase
Day	m s	m s	h m	h m	h m	d %	
26	05 55	05 46	12 06	04 32	16 57	20 67	
27	05 37	05 27	12 05	05 23	17 49	21 57	
28	05 18	05 09	12 05	06 14	18 39	22 47	

© British Crown Copyright 2018. All rights reserved.

UT	ARIES GHA	VENUS −3.9 GHA	Dec	MARS +1.4 GHA	Dec	JUPITER −2.2 GHA	Dec	SATURN +0.6 GHA	Dec	Name	SHA	Dec
29 00	186 06.5	211 14.4	S11 15.6	130 03.3	N20 42.0	282 30.3	S22 40.4	254 51.8	S21 35.0	Acamar	315 15.7	S40 14.0
01	201 08.9	226 14.0	14.7	145 04.0	42.4	297 32.7	40.4	269 54.2	35.0	Achernar	335 24.4	S57 08.6
02	216 11.4	241 13.5	13.7	160 04.8	42.8	312 35.1	40.4	284 56.5	35.0	Acrux	173 04.2	S63 12.3
03	231 13.9	256 13.1	.. 12.7	175 05.5	.. 43.2	327 37.4	.. 40.4	299 58.8	.. 34.9	Adhara	255 09.4	S29 00.3
04	246 16.3	271 12.6	11.7	190 06.3	43.5	342 39.8	40.4	315 01.2	34.9	Aldebaran	290 45.0	N16 32.7
05	261 18.8	286 12.2	10.8	205 07.0	43.9	357 42.1	40.4	330 03.5	34.9			
06	276 21.2	301 11.8	S11 09.8	220 07.7	N20 44.3	12 44.5	S22 40.4	345 05.8	S21 34.9	Alioth	166 16.7	N55 51.4
07	291 23.7	316 11.3	08.8	235 08.5	44.7	27 46.9	40.4	0 08.1	34.9	Alkaid	152 55.3	N49 13.0
08	306 26.2	331 10.9	07.8	250 09.2	45.1	42 49.2	40.4	15 10.5	34.9	Alnair	27 39.2	S46 52.0
F 09	321 28.6	346 10.4	.. 06.8	265 10.0	.. 45.5	57 51.6	.. 40.4	30 12.8	.. 34.8	Alnilam	275 42.5	S 1 11.7
R 10	336 31.1	1 10.0	05.9	280 10.7	45.8	72 53.9	40.4	45 15.1	34.8	Alphard	217 52.0	S 8 44.7
I 11	351 33.6	16 09.6	04.9	295 11.4	46.2	87 56.3	40.4	60 17.5	34.8			
D 12	6 36.0	31 09.1	S11 03.9	310 12.2	N20 46.6	102 58.7	S22 40.4	75 19.8	S21 34.8	Alphecca	126 07.4	N26 38.9
A 13	21 38.5	46 08.7	02.9	325 12.9	47.0	118 01.0	40.4	90 22.1	34.8	Alpheratz	357 39.8	N29 11.6
Y 14	36 41.0	61 08.3	01.9	340 13.7	47.4	133 03.4	40.4	105 24.5	34.8	Altair	62 04.5	N 8 55.0
15	51 43.4	76 07.8	.. 00.9	355 14.4	.. 47.7	148 05.7	.. 40.4	120 26.8	.. 34.7	Ankaa	353 12.2	S42 12.3
16	66 45.9	91 07.4	11 00.0	10 15.1	48.1	163 08.1	40.4	135 29.1	34.7	Antares	112 21.2	S26 28.3
17	81 48.4	106 06.9	10 59.0	25 15.9	48.5	178 10.5	40.4	150 31.4	34.7			
18	96 50.8	121 06.5	S10 58.0	40 16.6	N20 48.9	193 12.8	S22 40.4	165 33.8	S21 34.7	Arcturus	145 51.8	N19 04.9
19	111 53.3	136 06.1	57.0	55 17.4	49.3	208 15.2	40.5	180 36.1	34.7	Atria	107 19.3	S69 03.3
20	126 55.7	151 05.6	56.0	70 18.1	49.6	223 17.6	40.5	195 38.4	34.7	Avior	234 16.2	S59 34.6
21	141 58.2	166 05.2	.. 55.0	85 18.8	.. 50.0	238 19.9	.. 40.5	210 40.8	.. 34.6	Bellatrix	278 27.9	N 6 21.8
22	157 00.7	181 04.8	54.0	100 19.6	50.4	253 22.3	40.5	225 43.1	34.6	Betelgeuse	270 57.1	N 7 24.4
23	172 03.1	196 04.3	53.1	115 20.3	50.8	268 24.7	40.5	240 45.4	34.6			
30 00	187 05.6	211 03.9	S10 52.1	130 21.0	N20 51.2	283 27.0	S22 40.5	255 47.8	S21 34.6	Canopus	263 54.4	S52 42.8
01	202 08.1	226 03.5	51.1	145 21.8	51.5	298 29.4	40.5	270 50.1	34.6	Capella	280 28.8	N46 01.0
02	217 10.5	241 03.0	50.1	160 22.5	51.9	313 31.7	40.5	285 52.4	34.6	Deneb	49 29.0	N45 20.7
03	232 13.0	256 02.6	.. 49.1	175 23.3	.. 52.3	328 34.1	.. 40.5	300 54.8	.. 34.6	Denebola	182 29.3	N14 27.9
04	247 15.5	271 02.2	48.1	190 24.0	52.7	343 36.5	40.5	315 57.1	34.5	Diphda	348 52.3	S17 53.1
05	262 17.9	286 01.7	47.1	205 24.7	53.0	358 38.8	40.5	330 59.4	34.5			
06	277 20.4	301 01.3	S10 46.1	220 25.5	N20 53.4	13 41.2	S22 40.5	346 01.8	S21 34.5	Dubhe	193 46.3	N61 38.9
S 07	292 22.9	316 00.9	45.1	235 26.2	53.8	28 43.6	40.5	1 04.1	34.5	Elnath	278 07.8	N28 37.3
A 08	307 25.3	331 00.5	44.1	250 27.0	54.2	43 45.9	40.5	16 06.4	34.5	Eltanin	90 44.2	N51 29.0
T 09	322 27.8	346 00.0	.. 43.1	265 27.7	.. 54.5	58 48.3	.. 40.5	31 08.8	.. 34.5	Enif	33 43.5	N 9 57.6
U 10	337 30.2	0 59.6	42.2	280 28.4	54.9	73 50.7	40.5	46 11.1	34.4	Fomalhaut	15 20.0	S29 31.3
R 11	352 32.7	15 59.2	41.2	295 29.2	55.3	88 53.1	40.5	61 13.4	34.4			
D 12	7 35.2	30 58.7	S10 40.2	310 29.9	N20 55.7	103 55.4	S22 40.5	76 15.8	S21 34.4	Gacrux	171 55.9	S57 13.2
A 13	22 37.6	45 58.3	39.2	325 30.6	56.0	118 57.8	40.5	91 18.1	34.4	Gienah	175 47.9	S17 38.9
Y 14	37 40.1	60 57.9	38.2	340 31.4	56.4	134 00.2	40.5	106 20.4	34.4	Hadar	148 41.7	S60 27.7
15	52 42.6	75 57.4	.. 37.2	355 32.1	.. 56.8	149 02.5	.. 40.5	121 22.8	.. 34.4	Hamal	327 56.6	N23 33.0
16	67 45.0	90 57.0	36.2	10 32.9	57.2	164 04.9	40.5	136 25.1	34.3	Kaus Aust.	83 38.6	S34 22.3
17	82 47.5	105 56.6	35.2	25 33.6	57.5	179 07.3	40.5	151 27.4	34.3			
18	97 50.0	120 56.2	S10 34.2	40 34.3	N20 57.9	194 09.6	S22 40.5	166 29.8	S21 34.3	Kochab	137 19.1	N74 04.5
19	112 52.4	135 55.7	33.2	55 35.1	58.3	209 12.0	40.5	181 32.1	34.3	Markab	13 34.7	N15 18.3
20	127 54.9	150 55.3	32.2	70 35.8	58.7	224 14.4	40.5	196 34.5	34.3	Menkar	314 11.2	N 4 09.6
21	142 57.3	165 54.9	.. 31.2	85 36.5	.. 59.0	239 16.8	.. 40.5	211 36.8	.. 34.3	Menkent	148 02.6	S36 27.7
22	157 59.8	180 54.5	30.2	100 37.3	59.4	254 19.1	40.5	226 39.1	34.2	Miaplacidus	221 38.3	S69 48.0
23	173 02.3	195 54.0	29.2	115 38.0	20 59.8	269 21.5	40.5	241 41.5	34.2			
31 00	188 04.7	210 53.6	S10 28.2	130 38.7	N21 00.1	284 23.9	S22 40.5	256 43.8	S21 34.2	Mirfak	308 35.1	N49 55.7
01	203 07.2	225 53.2	27.2	145 39.5	00.5	299 26.3	40.5	271 46.1	34.2	Nunki	75 53.5	S26 16.2
02	218 09.7	240 52.8	26.2	160 40.2	00.9	314 28.6	40.6	286 48.5	34.2	Peacock	53 13.3	S56 40.2
03	233 12.1	255 52.3	.. 25.2	175 41.0	.. 01.3	329 31.0	.. 40.6	301 50.8	.. 34.2	Pollux	243 22.8	N27 58.7
04	248 14.6	270 51.9	24.2	190 41.7	01.6	344 33.4	40.6	316 53.1	34.2	Procyon	244 55.6	N 5 10.4
05	263 17.1	285 51.5	23.2	205 42.4	02.0	359 35.8	40.6	331 55.5	34.1			
06	278 19.5	300 51.1	S10 22.2	220 43.2	N21 02.4	14 38.1	S22 40.6	346 57.8	S21 34.1	Rasalhague	96 02.7	N12 32.7
07	293 22.0	315 50.6	21.2	235 43.9	02.8	29 40.5	40.6	2 00.2	34.1	Regulus	207 39.1	N11 52.3
08	308 24.5	330 50.2	20.2	250 44.6	03.1	44 42.9	40.6	17 02.5	34.1	Rigel	281 08.4	S 8 11.1
S 09	323 26.9	345 49.8	.. 19.2	265 45.4	.. 03.5	59 45.3	.. 40.6	32 04.8	.. 34.1	Rigil Kent.	139 45.8	S60 54.6
U 10	338 29.4	0 49.4	18.1	280 46.1	03.8	74 47.6	40.6	47 07.2	34.1	Sabik	102 07.9	S15 44.8
N 11	353 31.8	15 48.9	17.1	295 46.8	04.2	89 50.0	40.6	62 09.5	34.0			
D 12	8 34.3	30 48.5	S10 16.1	310 47.6	N21 04.6	104 52.4	S22 40.6	77 11.8	S21 34.0	Schedar	349 36.6	N56 38.4
A 13	23 36.8	45 48.1	15.1	325 48.3	04.9	119 54.8	40.6	92 14.2	34.0	Shaula	96 16.5	S37 06.8
Y 14	38 39.2	60 47.7	14.1	340 49.0	05.3	134 57.1	40.6	107 16.5	34.0	Sirius	258 30.3	S16 44.9
15	53 41.7	75 47.3	.. 13.1	355 49.8	.. 05.7	149 59.5	.. 40.6	122 18.9	.. 34.0	Spica	158 26.8	S11 15.7
16	68 44.2	90 46.8	12.1	10 50.5	06.0	165 01.9	40.6	137 21.2	34.0	Suhail	222 49.3	S43 30.9
17	83 46.6	105 46.4	11.1	25 51.2	06.4	180 04.3	40.6	152 23.5	33.9			
18	98 49.1	120 46.0	S10 10.1	40 52.0	N21 06.8	195 06.7	S22 40.6	167 25.9	S21 34.0	Vega	80 36.3	N38 47.9
19	113 51.6	135 45.6	09.1	55 52.7	07.1	210 09.0	40.6	182 28.2	33.9	Zuben'ubi	137 00.8	S16 07.2
20	128 54.0	150 45.1	08.1	70 53.4	07.5	225 11.4	40.6	197 30.6	33.9		SHA	Mer.Pass.
21	143 56.5	165 44.7	.. 07.0	85 54.2	.. 07.9	240 13.8	.. 40.6	212 32.9	.. 33.9	Venus	23 58.3	9 56
22	158 59.0	180 44.3	06.0	100 54.9	08.2	255 16.2	40.6	227 35.2	33.9	Mars	303 15.4	15 18
23	174 01.4	195 43.9	05.0	115 55.6	08.6	270 18.6	40.6	242 37.6	33.9	Jupiter	96 21.4	5 05
Mer.Pass. 11 29.7		v −0.4	d 1.0	v 0.7	d 0.4	v 2.4	d 0.0	v 2.3	d 0.0	Saturn	68 42.2	6 56

© British Crown Copyright 2018. All rights reserved.

UT	SUN GHA	Dec	MOON GHA	v	Dec	d	HP
d h	° ′	° ′	° ′	′	° ′	′	′
29 00	178 45.0	N 3 10.7	257 32.4	11.0	S21 45.3	1.3	54.8
01	193 45.2	11.7	272 02.4	11.1	21 44.0	1.3	54.7
02	208 45.4	12.6	286 32.5	11.1	21 42.7	1.4	54.7
03	223 45.6 ..	13.6	301 02.6	11.2	21 41.3	1.6	54.7
04	238 45.8	14.6	315 32.8	11.1	21 39.7	1.6	54.7
05	253 46.0	15.6	330 02.9	11.2	21 38.1	1.8	54.7
06	268 46.1	N 3 16.5	344 33.1	11.3	S21 36.3	1.8	54.6
07	283 46.3	17.5	359 03.4	11.3	21 34.5	2.0	54.6
08	298 46.5	18.5	13 33.7	11.3	21 32.5	2.0	54.6
F 09	313 46.7 ..	19.5	28 04.0	11.3	21 30.5	2.2	54.6
R 10	328 46.9	20.4	42 34.3	11.4	21 28.3	2.2	54.6
I 11	343 47.1	21.4	57 04.7	11.4	21 26.1	2.4	54.5
D 12	358 47.3	N 3 22.4	71 35.1	11.5	S21 23.7	2.5	54.5
A 13	13 47.5	23.4	86 05.6	11.4	21 21.2	2.5	54.5
Y 14	28 47.6	24.3	100 36.0	11.6	21 18.7	2.7	54.5
15	43 47.8 ..	25.3	115 06.6	11.5	21 16.0	2.7	54.5
16	58 48.0	26.3	129 37.1	11.6	21 13.3	2.9	54.5
17	73 48.2	27.3	144 07.7	11.6	21 10.4	2.9	54.5
18	88 48.4	N 3 28.2	158 38.3	11.7	S21 07.5	3.1	54.4
19	103 48.6	29.2	173 09.0	11.7	21 04.4	3.1	54.4
20	118 48.8	30.2	187 39.7	11.7	21 01.3	3.3	54.4
21	133 49.0 ..	31.1	202 10.4	11.8	20 58.0	3.3	54.4
22	148 49.1	32.1	216 41.2	11.8	20 54.7	3.5	54.4
23	163 49.3	33.1	231 12.0	11.9	20 51.2	3.5	54.4
30 00	178 49.5	N 3 34.1	245 42.9	11.9	S20 47.7	3.6	54.4
01	193 49.7	35.0	260 13.8	11.9	20 44.1	3.7	54.3
02	208 49.9	36.0	274 44.7	12.0	20 40.4	3.8	54.3
03	223 50.1 ..	37.0	289 15.7	12.0	20 36.6	4.0	54.3
04	238 50.3	38.0	303 46.7	12.0	20 32.6	4.0	54.3
05	253 50.5	38.9	318 17.7	12.1	20 28.6	4.1	54.3
06	268 50.6	N 3 39.9	332 48.8	12.2	S20 24.5	4.1	54.3
07	283 50.8	40.9	347 20.0	12.1	20 20.4	4.3	54.3
S 08	298 51.0	41.8	1 51.1	12.2	20 16.1	4.4	54.3
A 09	313 51.2 ..	42.8	16 22.3	12.3	20 11.7	4.5	54.3
T 10	328 51.4	43.8	30 53.6	12.2	20 07.2	4.5	54.3
U 11	343 51.6	44.8	45 24.8	12.4	20 02.7	4.6	54.2
R 12	358 51.8	N 3 45.7	59 56.2	12.3	S19 58.1	4.8	54.2
D 13	13 52.0	46.7	74 27.5	12.4	19 53.3	4.8	54.2
A 14	28 52.1	47.7	88 58.9	12.5	19 48.5	4.9	54.2
Y 15	43 52.3 ..	48.6	103 30.4	12.4	19 43.6	5.0	54.2
16	58 52.5	49.6	118 01.8	12.6	19 38.6	5.1	54.2
17	73 52.7	50.6	132 33.4	12.5	19 33.5	5.1	54.2
18	88 52.9	N 3 51.6	147 04.9	12.6	S19 28.4	5.3	54.2
19	103 53.1	52.5	161 36.5	12.6	19 23.1	5.3	54.2
20	118 53.3	53.5	176 08.1	12.7	19 17.8	5.5	54.2
21	133 53.5 ..	54.5	190 39.8	12.7	19 12.3	5.5	54.2
22	148 53.6	55.4	205 11.5	12.8	19 06.8	5.6	54.2
23	163 53.8	56.4	219 43.3	12.8	19 01.2	5.7	54.1
31 00	178 54.0	N 3 57.4	234 15.1	12.8	S18 55.5	5.7	54.1
01	193 54.2	58.3	248 46.9	12.9	18 49.8	5.9	54.1
02	208 54.4	3 59.3	263 18.8	12.9	18 43.9	5.9	54.1
03	223 54.6	4 00.3	277 50.7	13.0	18 38.0	6.0	54.1
04	238 54.8	01.3	292 22.7	13.0	18 32.0	6.1	54.1
05	253 54.9	02.2	306 54.7	13.0	18 25.9	6.2	54.1
06	268 55.1	N 4 03.2	321 26.7	13.1	S18 19.7	6.2	54.1
07	283 55.3	04.2	335 58.8	13.1	18 13.5	6.4	54.1
08	298 55.5	05.1	350 30.9	13.1	18 07.1	6.4	54.1
S 09	313 55.7 ..	06.1	5 03.0	13.2	18 00.7	6.5	54.1
U 10	328 55.9	07.1	19 35.2	13.3	17 54.2	6.5	54.1
N 11	343 56.1	08.0	34 07.5	13.2	17 47.7	6.7	54.1
D 12	358 56.3	N 4 09.0	48 39.7	13.3	S17 41.0	6.7	54.1
A 13	13 56.4	10.0	63 12.0	13.4	17 34.3	6.8	54.1
Y 14	28 56.6	10.9	77 44.4	13.3	17 27.5	6.8	54.1
15	43 56.8 ..	11.9	92 16.7	13.5	17 20.7	7.0	54.1
16	58 57.0	12.9	106 49.2	13.4	17 13.7	7.0	54.1
17	73 57.2	13.8	121 21.6	13.5	17 06.7	7.1	54.1
18	88 57.4	N 4 14.8	135 54.1	13.5	S16 59.6	7.2	54.1
19	103 57.6	15.8	150 26.6	13.6	16 52.4	7.2	54.1
20	118 57.7	16.7	164 59.2	13.6	16 45.2	7.3	54.1
21	133 57.9 ..	17.7	179 31.8	13.6	16 37.9	7.4	54.1
22	148 58.1	18.7	194 04.4	13.7	16 30.5	7.5	54.1
23	163 58.3	19.6	208 37.1	13.7	S16 23.0	7.5	54.1
	SD 16.0	d 1.0	SD 14.9		14.8		14.7

Lat.	Twilight Naut.	Twilight Civil	Sunrise	Moonrise 29	30	31	1
°	h m	h m	h m	h m	h m	h m	h m
N 72	02 04	03 55	05 08	■■	■■	■■	07 12
N 70	02 39	04 10	05 14	■■	■■	06 58	06 38
68	03 03	04 21	05 19	06 22	06 20	06 16	06 13
66	03 21	04 30	05 23	05 14	05 37	05 48	05 53
64	03 36	04 38	05 27	04 39	05 08	05 26	05 37
62	03 48	04 44	05 30	04 13	04 46	05 09	05 24
60	03 58	04 50	05 32	03 53	04 28	04 54	05 13
N 58	04 06	04 55	05 35	03 36	04 14	04 42	05 03
56	04 13	04 59	05 37	03 22	04 01	04 31	04 55
54	04 20	05 03	05 39	03 10	03 50	04 22	04 47
52	04 25	05 06	05 40	02 59	03 40	04 13	04 41
50	04 30	05 09	05 42	02 49	03 31	04 05	04 34
45	04 41	05 16	05 45	02 29	03 12	03 49	04 21
N 40	04 49	05 21	05 48	02 13	02 57	03 36	04 10
35	04 55	05 25	05 50	01 59	02 44	03 24	04 01
30	05 00	05 28	05 52	01 47	02 33	03 14	03 52
20	05 08	05 34	05 56	01 27	02 13	02 57	03 38
N 10	05 13	05 38	05 59	01 09	01 57	02 42	03 25
0	05 17	05 41	06 01	00 52	01 41	02 28	03 14
S 10	05 18	05 43	06 04	00 35	01 25	02 14	03 02
20	05 19	05 44	06 06	00 17	01 08	01 59	02 49
30	05 18	05 45	06 09	24 49	00 49	01 41	02 35
35	05 16	05 46	06 11	24 37	00 37	01 31	02 26
40	05 14	05 46	06 13	24 24	00 24	01 20	02 16
45	05 11	05 45	06 15	24 09	00 09	01 06	02 05
S 50	05 07	05 45	06 17	23 50	24 49	00 49	01 51
52	05 05	05 44	06 18	23 41	24 41	00 41	01 45
54	05 03	05 44	06 19	23 31	24 32	00 32	01 38
56	05 00	05 43	06 20	23 19	24 23	00 23	01 30
58	04 57	05 43	06 22	23 06	24 11	00 11	01 21
S 60	04 53	05 42	06 23	22 51	23 58	25 10	01 10

Lat.	Sunset	Twilight Civil	Twilight Naut.	Moonset 29	30	31	1
°	h m	h m	h m	h m	h m	h m	h m
N 72	19 04	20 18	22 14	■■	■■	■■	11 52
N 70	18 57	20 03	21 36	■■	■■	10 31	12 25
68	18 52	19 51	21 10	07 49	09 32	11 12	12 49
66	18 48	19 41	20 51	08 56	10 14	11 40	13 08
64	18 44	19 33	20 36	09 32	10 42	12 01	13 23
62	18 41	19 27	20 24	09 57	11 04	12 18	13 35
60	18 38	19 21	20 14	10 18	11 22	12 32	13 46
N 58	18 36	19 16	20 05	10 34	11 36	12 44	13 55
56	18 33	19 11	19 58	10 48	11 49	12 54	14 03
54	18 32	19 07	19 51	11 00	11 59	13 03	14 10
52	18 30	19 04	19 45	11 11	12 09	13 11	14 16
50	18 28	19 01	19 40	11 20	12 18	13 19	14 22
45	18 25	18 54	19 29	11 40	12 36	13 34	14 34
N 40	18 22	18 49	19 21	11 56	12 51	13 47	14 44
35	18 19	18 45	19 15	12 10	13 03	13 58	14 53
30	18 17	18 41	19 09	12 22	13 14	14 07	15 00
20	18 14	18 36	19 02	12 42	13 33	14 23	15 13
N 10	18 11	18 32	18 56	12 59	13 49	14 37	15 24
0	18 08	18 29	18 53	13 16	14 04	14 50	15 35
S 10	18 05	18 26	18 51	13 32	14 19	15 03	15 46
20	18 02	18 24	18 50	13 49	14 35	15 17	15 57
30	17 59	18 23	18 51	14 09	14 53	15 33	16 09
35	17 58	18 23	18 52	14 21	15 04	15 42	16 17
40	17 56	18 23	18 57	14 34	15 16	15 52	16 25
45	17 54	18 23	18 57	14 50	15 30	16 05	16 34
S 50	17 51	18 23	19 01	15 10	15 48	16 19	16 46
52	17 50	18 24	19 03	15 19	15 56	16 26	16 51
54	17 49	18 24	19 05	15 29	16 05	16 34	16 57
56	17 48	18 24	19 08	15 41	16 15	16 42	17 04
58	17 46	18 25	19 11	15 54	16 27	16 52	17 11
S 60	17 44	18 26	19 14	16 10	16 40	17 03	17 19

Day	SUN Eqn. of Time 00h	12h	Mer. Pass.	MOON Mer. Pass. Upper	Lower	Age	Phase
d	m s	m s	h m	h m	h m	d %	
29	05 00	04 51	12 05	07 04	19 28	23 37	
30	04 42	04 33	12 05	07 52	20 16	24 29	
31	04 24	04 15	12 04	08 39	21 02	25 20	

© British Crown Copyright 2018. All rights reserved.

UT	ARIES GHA	VENUS −3.9 GHA	Dec	MARS +1.5 GHA	Dec	JUPITER −2.3 GHA	Dec	SATURN +0.6 GHA	Dec	STARS Name	SHA	Dec
1 00	189 03.9	210 43.5	S10 04.0	130 56.4	N21 09.0	285 20.9	S22 40.6	257 39.9	S21 33.8	Acamar	315 15.7	S40 14.0
01	204 06.3	225 43.1	03.0	145 57.1	09.3	300 23.3	40.6	272 42.3	33.8	Achernar	335 24.4	S57 08.6
02	219 08.8	240 42.6	02.0	160 57.8	09.7	315 25.7	40.6	287 44.6	33.8	Acrux	173 04.2	S63 12.3
03	234 11.3	255 42.2	10 01.0	175 58.6 ..	10.0	330 28.1 ..	40.6	302 46.9 ..	33.8	Adhara	255 09.4	S29 00.2
04	249 13.7	270 41.8	9 59.9	190 59.3	10.4	345 30.5	40.6	317 49.3	33.8	Aldebaran	290 45.0	N16 32.7
05	264 16.2	285 41.4	58.9	206 00.0	10.8	0 32.9	40.6	332 51.6	33.8			
06	279 18.7	300 41.0	S 9 57.9	221 00.8	N21 11.1	15 35.2	S22 40.6	347 54.0	S21 33.8	Alioth	166 16.7	N55 51.4
07	294 21.1	315 40.5	56.9	236 01.5	11.5	30 37.6	40.6	2 56.3	33.7	Alkaid	152 55.3	N49 13.0
08	309 23.6	330 40.1	55.9	251 02.2	11.9	45 40.0	40.6	17 58.7	33.7	Alnair	27 39.1	S46 52.0
M 09	324 26.1	345 39.7 ..	54.9	266 03.0 ..	12.2	60 42.4 ..	40.6	33 01.0 ..	33.7	Alnilam	275 42.5	S 1 11.7
O 10	339 28.5	0 39.3	53.8	281 03.7	12.6	75 44.8	40.6	48 03.3	33.7	Alphard	217 52.0	S 8 44.7
N 11	354 31.0	15 38.9	52.8	296 04.4	12.9	90 47.2	40.6	63 05.7	33.7			
D 12	9 33.4	30 38.5	S 9 51.8	311 05.2	N21 13.3	105 49.6	S22 40.7	78 08.0	S21 33.7	Alphecca	126 07.4	N26 38.9
A 13	24 35.9	45 38.1	50.8	326 05.9	13.7	120 51.9	40.7	93 10.4	33.6	Alpheratz	357 39.8	N29 11.5
Y 14	39 38.4	60 37.6	49.8	341 06.6	14.0	135 54.3	40.7	108 12.7	33.6	Altair	62 04.5	N 8 55.0
15	54 40.8	75 37.2 ..	48.7	356 07.4 ..	14.4	150 56.7 ..	40.7	123 15.0 ..	33.6	Ankaa	353 12.2	S42 12.3
16	69 43.3	90 36.8	47.7	11 08.1	14.7	165 59.1	40.7	138 17.4	33.6	Antares	112 21.2	S26 28.3
17	84 45.8	105 36.4	46.7	26 08.8	15.1	181 01.5	40.7	153 19.7	33.6			
18	99 48.2	120 36.0	S 9 45.7	41 09.6	N21 15.5	196 03.9	S22 40.7	168 22.1	S21 33.6	Arcturus	145 51.8	N19 04.9
19	114 50.7	135 35.6	44.7	56 10.3	15.8	211 06.3	40.7	183 24.4	33.6	Atria	107 19.3	S69 03.3
20	129 53.2	150 35.2	43.6	71 11.0	16.2	226 08.7	40.7	198 26.8	33.5	Avior	234 16.2	S59 34.6
21	144 55.6	165 34.7 ..	42.6	86 11.8 ..	16.5	241 11.0 ..	40.7	213 29.1 ..	33.5	Bellatrix	278 27.9	N 6 21.8
22	159 58.1	180 34.3	41.6	101 12.5	16.9	256 13.4	40.7	228 31.5	33.5	Betelgeuse	270 57.1	N 7 24.4
23	175 00.6	195 33.9	40.6	116 13.2	17.2	271 15.8	40.7	243 33.8	33.5			
2 00	190 03.0	210 33.5	S 9 39.5	131 14.0	N21 17.6	286 18.2	S22 40.7	258 36.1	S21 33.5	Canopus	263 54.5	S52 42.8
01	205 05.5	225 33.1	38.5	146 14.7	18.0	301 20.6	40.7	273 38.5	33.5	Capella	280 28.8	N46 01.0
02	220 07.9	240 32.7	37.5	161 15.4	18.3	316 23.0	40.7	288 40.8	33.5	Deneb	49 29.0	N45 20.7
03	235 10.4	255 32.3 ..	36.5	176 16.1 ..	18.7	331 25.4 ..	40.7	303 43.2 ..	33.4	Denebola	182 29.3	N14 27.9
04	250 12.9	270 31.9	35.4	191 16.9	19.0	346 27.8	40.7	318 45.5	33.4	Diphda	348 52.3	S17 53.1
05	265 15.3	285 31.4	34.4	206 17.6	19.4	1 30.2	40.7	333 47.9	33.4			
06	280 17.8	300 31.0	S 9 33.4	221 18.3	N21 19.7	16 32.6	S22 40.7	348 50.2	S21 33.4	Dubhe	193 46.3	N61 39.0
07	295 20.3	315 30.6	32.3	236 19.1	20.1	31 35.0	40.7	3 52.6	33.4	Elnath	278 07.8	N28 37.3
T 08	310 22.7	330 30.2	31.3	251 19.8	20.4	46 37.4	40.7	18 54.9	33.4	Eltanin	90 44.2	N51 29.0
U 09	325 25.2	345 29.8 ..	30.3	266 20.5 ..	20.8	61 39.7 ..	40.7	33 57.3 ..	33.3	Enif	33 43.5	N 9 57.6
E 10	340 27.7	0 29.4	29.3	281 21.3	21.1	76 42.1	40.7	48 59.6	33.3	Fomalhaut	15 20.0	S29 31.3
S 11	355 30.1	15 29.0	28.2	296 22.0	21.5	91 44.5	40.7	64 01.9	33.3			
D 12	10 32.6	30 28.6	S 9 27.2	311 22.7	N21 21.9	106 46.9	S22 40.7	79 04.3	S21 33.3	Gacrux	171 55.9	S57 13.2
A 13	25 35.1	45 28.2	26.2	326 23.4	22.2	121 49.3	40.7	94 06.6	33.3	Gienah	175 47.9	S17 39.0
Y 14	40 37.5	60 27.8	25.1	341 24.2	22.6	136 51.7	40.7	109 09.0	33.3	Hadar	148 41.7	S60 27.8
15	55 40.0	75 27.4 ..	24.1	356 24.9 ..	22.9	151 54.1 ..	40.7	124 11.3 ..	33.3	Hamal	327 56.6	N23 33.0
16	70 42.4	90 27.0	23.1	11 25.6	23.3	166 56.5	40.7	139 13.7	33.2	Kaus Aust.	83 38.5	S34 22.3
17	85 44.9	105 26.5	22.0	26 26.4	23.6	181 58.9	40.7	154 16.0	33.2			
18	100 47.4	120 26.1	S 9 21.0	41 27.1	N21 24.0	197 01.3	S22 40.7	169 18.4	S21 33.2	Kochab	137 19.1	N74 04.5
19	115 49.8	135 25.7	20.0	56 27.8	24.3	212 03.7	40.7	184 20.7	33.2	Markab	13 34.7	N15 18.3
20	130 52.3	150 25.3	18.9	71 28.6	24.7	227 06.1	40.7	199 23.1	33.2	Menkar	314 11.2	N 4 09.6
21	145 54.8	165 24.9 ..	17.9	86 29.3 ..	25.0	242 08.5 ..	40.7	214 25.4 ..	33.2	Menkent	148 02.6	S36 27.8
22	160 57.2	180 24.5	16.9	101 30.0	25.4	257 10.9	40.7	229 27.8	33.2	Miaplacidus	221 38.4	S69 48.0
23	175 59.7	195 24.1	15.8	116 30.7	25.7	272 13.3	40.7	244 30.1	33.1			
3 00	191 02.2	210 23.7	S 9 14.8	131 31.5	N21 26.1	287 15.7	S22 40.7	259 32.5	S21 33.1	Mirfak	308 35.1	N49 55.6
01	206 04.6	225 23.3	13.8	146 32.2	26.4	302 18.1	40.7	274 34.8	33.1	Nunki	75 53.5	S26 16.2
02	221 07.1	240 22.9	12.7	161 32.9	26.8	317 20.5	40.7	289 37.2	33.1	Peacock	53 13.3	S56 40.2
03	236 09.5	255 22.5 ..	11.7	176 33.7 ..	27.1	332 22.9 ..	40.7	304 39.5 ..	33.1	Pollux	243 22.9	N27 58.7
04	251 12.0	270 22.1	10.6	191 34.4	27.5	347 25.3	40.7	319 41.9	33.1	Procyon	244 55.6	N 5 10.4
05	266 14.5	285 21.7	09.6	206 35.1	27.8	2 27.7	40.7	334 44.2	33.1			
06	281 16.9	300 21.3	S 9 08.6	221 35.8	N21 28.2	17 30.1	S22 40.7	349 46.6	S21 33.0	Rasalhague	96 02.7	N12 32.7
W 07	296 19.4	315 20.9	07.5	236 36.6	28.5	32 32.5	40.8	4 48.9	33.0	Regulus	207 39.1	N11 52.3
E 08	311 21.9	330 20.5	06.5	251 37.3	28.8	47 34.9	40.8	19 51.3	33.0	Rigel	281 08.4	S 8 11.1
D 09	326 24.3	345 20.1 ..	05.4	266 38.0 ..	29.2	62 37.3 ..	40.8	34 53.6 ..	33.0	Rigil Kent.	139 45.8	S60 54.6
N 10	341 26.8	0 19.7	04.4	281 38.7	29.5	77 39.7	40.8	49 56.0	33.0	Sabik	102 07.9	S15 44.8
E 11	356 29.3	15 19.3	03.4	296 39.5	29.9	92 42.1	40.8	64 58.3	33.0			
S 12	11 31.7	30 18.9	S 9 02.3	311 40.2	N21 30.2	107 44.5	S22 40.8	80 00.7	S21 33.0	Schedar	349 36.6	N56 38.4
D 13	26 34.2	45 18.5	01.3	326 40.9	30.6	122 46.9	40.8	95 03.0	33.0	Shaula	96 16.4	S37 06.8
A 14	41 36.7	60 18.1	9 00.2	341 41.7	30.9	137 49.3	40.8	110 05.4	32.9	Sirius	258 30.3	S16 44.9
Y 15	56 39.1	75 17.7	8 59.2	356 42.4 ..	31.3	152 51.7 ..	40.8	125 07.7 ..	32.9	Spica	158 26.8	S11 15.7
16	71 41.6	90 17.3	58.2	11 43.1	31.6	167 54.1	40.8	140 10.1	32.9	Suhail	222 49.3	S43 30.9
17	86 44.0	105 16.9	57.1	26 43.8	32.0	182 56.5	40.8	155 12.4	32.9			
18	101 46.5	120 16.5	S 8 56.1	41 44.6	N21 32.3	197 58.9	S22 40.8	170 14.8	S21 32.9	Vega	80 36.3	N38 47.9
19	116 49.0	135 16.1	55.0	56 45.3	32.6	213 01.3	40.8	185 17.1	32.9	Zuben'ubi	137 00.8	S16 07.2
20	131 51.4	150 15.7	54.0	71 46.0	33.0	228 03.7	40.8	200 19.5	32.9		SHA	Mer. Pass.
21	146 53.9	165 15.3 ..	52.9	86 46.7 ..	33.3	243 06.1 ..	40.8	215 21.8 ..	32.8		° '	h m
22	161 56.4	180 14.9	51.9	101 47.5	33.7	258 08.5	40.8	230 24.2	32.8	Venus	20 30.5	9 58
23	176 58.8	195 14.5	50.8	116 48.2	34.0	273 10.9	40.8	245 26.5	32.8	Mars	301 10.9	15 14
Mer. Pass.	h m 11 17.9	v −0.4	d 1.0	v 0.7	d 0.4	v 2.4	d 0.0	v 2.3	d 0.0	Jupiter	96 15.2	4 54
										Saturn	68 33.1	6 45

© British Crown Copyright 2018. All rights reserved.

UT	SUN GHA	SUN Dec	MOON GHA	v	MOON Dec	d	HP
d h	° ′	° ′	° ′	′	° ′	′	′
1 00	178 58.5	N 4 20.6	223 09.8	13.8	S16 15.5	7.6	54.1
01	193 58.7	21.6	237 42.6	13.8	16 07.9	7.7	54.1
02	208 58.9	22.5	252 15.4	13.8	16 00.2	7.7	54.1
03	223 59.0	.. 23.5	266 48.2	13.8	15 52.5	7.8	54.1
04	238 59.2	24.5	281 21.0	13.9	15 44.7	7.9	54.1
05	253 59.4	25.4	295 53.9	13.9	15 36.8	7.9	54.1
06	268 59.6	N 4 26.4	310 26.8	14.0	S15 28.9	8.0	54.1
07	283 59.8	27.4	324 59.8	14.0	15 20.9	8.1	54.1
M 08	299 00.0	28.3	339 32.8	14.0	15 12.8	8.1	54.1
O 09	314 00.2	.. 29.3	354 05.8	14.1	15 04.7	8.2	54.1
N 10	329 00.3	30.3	8 38.9	14.1	14 56.5	8.3	54.1
D 11	344 00.5	31.2	23 12.0	14.1	14 48.2	8.3	54.1
A 12	359 00.7	N 4 32.2	37 45.1	14.1	S14 39.9	8.4	54.1
Y 13	14 00.9	33.2	52 18.2	14.2	14 31.5	8.5	54.1
14	29 01.1	34.1	66 51.4	14.2	14 23.0	8.5	54.1
15	44 01.3	.. 35.1	81 24.6	14.3	14 14.5	8.6	54.1
16	59 01.4	36.1	95 57.9	14.2	14 05.9	8.6	54.1
17	74 01.6	37.0	110 31.1	14.3	13 57.3	8.7	54.1
18	89 01.8	N 4 38.0	125 04.4	14.4	S13 48.6	8.8	54.1
19	104 02.0	39.0	139 37.8	14.3	13 39.8	8.8	54.1
20	119 02.2	39.9	154 11.1	14.4	13 31.0	8.9	54.1
21	134 02.4	.. 40.9	168 44.5	14.5	13 22.1	8.9	54.1
22	149 02.6	41.8	183 18.0	14.4	13 13.2	9.0	54.1
23	164 02.7	42.8	197 51.4	14.5	13 04.2	9.1	54.1
2 00	179 02.9	N 4 43.8	212 24.9	14.5	S12 55.1	9.1	54.1
01	194 03.1	44.7	226 58.4	14.5	12 46.0	9.1	54.1
02	209 03.3	45.7	241 31.9	14.6	12 36.9	9.3	54.1
03	224 03.5	.. 46.7	256 05.5	14.6	12 27.6	9.2	54.1
04	239 03.7	47.6	270 39.1	14.6	12 18.4	9.4	54.2
05	254 03.8	48.6	285 12.7	14.6	12 09.0	9.3	54.2
06	269 04.0	N 4 49.6	299 46.3	14.7	S11 59.7	9.5	54.2
07	284 04.2	50.5	314 20.0	14.6	11 50.2	9.5	54.2
T 08	299 04.4	51.5	328 53.6	14.7	11 40.7	9.5	54.2
U 09	314 04.6	.. 52.4	343 27.3	14.8	11 31.2	9.6	54.2
E 10	329 04.8	53.4	358 01.1	14.7	11 21.6	9.6	54.2
S 11	344 04.9	54.4	12 34.8	14.8	11 12.0	9.7	54.2
D 12	359 05.1	N 4 55.3	27 08.6	14.8	S11 02.3	9.7	54.2
A 13	14 05.3	56.3	41 42.4	14.8	10 52.6	9.8	54.2
Y 14	29 05.5	57.2	56 16.2	14.8	10 42.8	9.8	54.2
15	44 05.7	.. 58.2	70 50.0	14.9	10 33.0	9.9	54.2
16	59 05.9	4 59.2	85 23.9	14.9	10 23.1	9.9	54.2
17	74 06.1	5 00.1	99 57.8	14.8	10 13.2	10.0	54.2
18	89 06.2	N 5 01.1	114 31.6	15.0	S10 03.2	10.0	54.3
19	104 06.4	02.0	129 05.6	14.9	9 53.2	10.1	54.3
20	119 06.6	03.0	143 39.5	14.9	9 43.1	10.1	54.3
21	134 06.8	.. 04.0	158 13.4	15.0	9 33.0	10.1	54.3
22	149 07.0	04.9	172 47.4	15.0	9 22.9	10.2	54.3
23	164 07.2	05.9	187 21.4	15.0	9 12.7	10.2	54.3
3 00	179 07.3	N 5 06.9	201 55.4	15.0	S 9 02.5	10.3	54.3
01	194 07.5	07.8	216 29.4	15.0	8 52.2	10.3	54.3
02	209 07.7	08.8	231 03.4	15.0	8 41.9	10.4	54.3
03	224 07.9	.. 09.7	245 37.4	15.1	8 31.5	10.4	54.3
04	239 08.1	10.7	260 11.5	15.0	8 21.1	10.4	54.4
05	254 08.2	11.6	274 45.5	15.1	8 10.7	10.4	54.4
06	269 08.4	N 5 12.6	289 19.6	15.1	S 8 00.3	10.6	54.4
W 07	284 08.6	13.6	303 53.7	15.1	7 49.7	10.5	54.4
E 08	299 08.8	14.5	318 27.8	15.1	7 39.2	10.6	54.4
D 09	314 09.0	.. 15.5	333 01.9	15.1	7 28.6	10.6	54.4
N 10	329 09.2	16.4	347 36.0	15.1	7 18.0	10.6	54.4
E 11	344 09.3	17.4	2 10.1	15.2	7 07.4	10.7	54.4
S 12	359 09.5	N 5 18.4	16 44.3	15.1	S 6 56.7	10.7	54.4
D 13	14 09.7	19.3	31 18.4	15.2	6 46.0	10.8	54.5
A 14	29 09.9	20.3	45 52.6	15.2	6 35.2	10.8	54.5
Y 15	44 10.1	.. 21.2	60 26.7	15.2	6 24.4	10.8	54.5
16	59 10.3	22.2	75 00.9	15.2	6 13.6	10.8	54.5
17	74 10.4	23.1	89 35.1	15.2	6 02.8	10.9	54.5
18	89 10.6	N 5 24.1	104 09.2	15.2	S 5 51.9	10.9	54.5
19	104 10.8	25.1	118 43.4	15.2	5 41.0	10.9	54.5
20	119 11.0	26.0	133 17.6	15.2	5 30.1	11.0	54.5
21	134 11.2	.. 27.0	147 51.8	15.2	5 19.1	11.0	54.5
22	149 11.3	27.9	162 26.0	15.1	5 08.1	11.0	54.6
23	164 11.5	28.9	177 00.1	15.2	S 4 57.1	11.0	54.6
	SD 16.0	d 1.0	SD 14.7		14.8		14.8

Lat.	Twilight Naut.	Twilight Civil	Sunrise	Moonrise 1	2	3	4
°	h m	h m	h m	h m	h m	h m	h m
N 72	01 29	03 37	04 52	07 12	06 45	06 26	06 11
N 70	02 16	03 54	05 00	06 38	06 25	06 15	06 06
68	02 45	04 07	05 06	06 13	06 09	06 05	06 01
66	03 06	04 18	05 12	05 53	05 56	05 57	05 58
64	03 22	04 27	05 16	05 37	05 45	05 51	05 55
62	03 36	04 34	05 20	05 24	05 36	05 45	05 52
60	03 47	04 40	05 23	05 13	05 28	05 40	05 50
N 58	03 56	04 46	05 26	05 03	05 21	05 35	05 48
56	04 04	04 51	05 29	04 55	05 14	05 31	05 46
54	04 12	04 55	05 31	04 47	05 09	05 28	05 45
52	04 18	04 59	05 33	04 41	05 04	05 24	05 43
50	04 23	05 03	05 35	04 34	04 59	05 21	05 42
45	04 35	05 10	05 40	04 21	04 49	05 15	05 39
N 40	04 44	05 16	05 45	04 10	04 41	05 09	05 36
35	04 51	05 21	05 46	04 01	04 34	05 05	05 34
30	04 56	05 25	05 49	03 52	04 27	05 00	05 32
20	05 05	05 31	05 53	03 38	04 16	04 53	05 29
N 10	05 11	05 36	05 57	03 25	04 07	04 47	05 26
0	05 16	05 40	06 00	03 14	03 58	04 41	05 23
S 10	05 18	05 43	06 04	03 02	03 49	04 35	05 21
20	05 20	05 45	06 07	02 49	03 39	04 28	05 18
30	05 19	05 47	06 11	02 35	03 28	04 21	05 14
35	05 19	05 48	06 13	02 26	03 21	04 17	05 12
40	05 17	05 49	06 16	02 16	03 14	04 12	05 10
45	05 15	05 49	06 18	02 05	03 05	04 06	05 08
S 50	05 12	05 49	06 22	01 51	02 55	03 59	05 05
52	05 10	05 49	06 23	01 45	02 50	03 56	05 03
54	05 08	05 49	06 25	01 38	02 45	03 53	05 02
56	05 06	05 49	06 27	01 30	02 39	03 49	05 00
58	05 04	05 49	06 28	01 21	02 32	03 45	04 58
S 60	05 01	05 49	06 31	01 10	02 25	03 40	04 56

Lat.	Sunset	Twilight Civil	Twilight Naut.	Moonset 1	2	3	4
°	h m	h m	h m	h m	h m	h m	h m
N 72	19 18	20 35	22 51	11 52	13 50	15 39	17 24
N 70	19 10	20 17	21 58	12 25	14 09	15 48	17 26
68	19 03	20 03	21 27	12 49	14 24	15 56	17 28
66	18 58	19 52	21 05	13 08	14 35	16 02	17 29
64	18 53	19 43	20 48	13 23	14 45	16 08	17 31
62	18 49	19 35	20 34	13 35	14 53	16 12	17 32
60	18 45	19 29	20 23	13 46	15 01	16 16	17 33
N 58	18 42	19 23	20 13	13 55	15 07	16 20	17 34
56	18 40	19 18	20 05	14 03	15 12	16 23	17 35
54	18 37	19 13	19 57	14 10	15 17	16 26	17 35
52	18 35	19 09	19 51	14 16	15 22	16 28	17 36
50	18 33	19 06	19 45	14 22	15 26	16 31	17 36
45	18 29	18 58	19 34	14 34	15 35	16 36	17 38
N 40	18 25	18 52	19 25	14 44	15 42	16 40	17 39
35	18 22	18 47	19 17	14 53	15 48	16 44	17 40
30	18 19	18 43	19 11	15 00	15 53	16 47	17 40
20	18 14	18 37	19 02	15 13	16 03	16 52	17 42
N 10	18 11	18 32	18 56	15 24	16 11	16 57	17 43
0	18 07	18 28	18 52	15 35	16 19	17 01	17 44
S 10	18 03	18 24	18 49	15 46	16 26	17 06	17 45
20	18 00	18 22	18 47	15 57	16 34	17 10	17 46
30	17 56	18 20	18 47	16 09	16 43	17 16	17 47
35	17 54	18 19	18 48	16 17	16 48	17 19	17 48
40	17 51	18 18	18 49	16 25	16 54	17 22	17 49
45	17 48	18 17	18 51	16 34	17 01	17 26	17 50
S 50	17 45	18 17	18 54	16 46	17 09	17 31	17 51
52	17 43	18 17	18 56	16 51	17 13	17 33	17 51
54	17 42	18 17	18 58	16 57	17 17	17 35	17 52
56	17 40	18 17	19 00	17 04	17 22	17 38	17 52
58	17 38	18 17	19 02	17 11	17 27	17 40	17 53
S 60	17 35	18 17	19 05	17 19	17 32	17 44	17 54

	SUN			MOON			
Day	Eqn. of Time 00ʰ	12ʰ	Mer. Pass.	Mer. Pass. Upper	Lower	Age	Phase
d	m s	m s	h m	h m	h m	d	%
1	04 06	03 58	12 04	09 24	21 46	26	13
2	03 49	03 40	12 04	10 08	22 30	27	8
3	03 31	03 22	12 03	10 51	23 12	28	3

© British Crown Copyright 2018. All rights reserved.

UT	ARIES GHA	VENUS −3.9 GHA	Dec	MARS +1.5 GHA	Dec	JUPITER −2.3 GHA	Dec	SATURN +0.6 GHA	Dec	STARS Name	SHA	Dec
4 00	192 01.3	210 14.1	S 8 49.8	131 48.9	N21 34.4	288 13.4	S22 40.8	260 28.9	S21 32.8	Acamar	315 15.7	S40 14.0
01	207 03.8	225 13.7	48.7	146 49.7	34.7	303 15.8	40.8	275 31.2	32.8	Achernar	335 24.4	S57 08.6
02	222 06.2	240 13.3	47.7	161 50.4	35.0	318 18.2	40.8	290 33.6	32.8	Acrux	173 04.2	S63 12.3
03	237 08.7	255 12.9	.. 46.6	176 51.1	.. 35.4	333 20.6	.. 40.8	305 35.9	.. 32.8	Adhara	255 09.4	S29 00.2
04	252 11.1	270 12.5	45.6	191 51.8	35.7	348 23.0	40.8	320 38.3	32.7	Aldebaran	290 45.1	N16 32.7
05	267 13.6	285 12.1	44.5	206 52.6	36.1	3 25.4	40.8	335 40.6	32.7			
06	282 16.1	300 11.7	S 8 43.5	221 53.3	N21 36.4	18 27.8	S22 40.8	350 43.0	S21 32.7	Alioth	166 16.7	N55 51.4
07	297 18.5	315 11.3	42.4	236 54.0	36.7	33 30.2	40.8	5 45.3	32.7	Alkaid	152 55.3	N49 13.0
T 08	312 21.0	330 10.9	41.4	251 54.7	37.1	48 32.6	40.8	20 47.7	32.7	Alnair	27 39.1	S46 52.0
H 09	327 23.5	345 10.5	.. 40.3	266 55.5	.. 37.4	63 35.0	.. 40.8	35 50.1	.. 32.7	Alnilam	275 42.5	S 1 11.7
U 10	342 25.9	0 10.1	39.3	281 56.2	37.8	78 37.4	40.8	50 52.4	32.7	Alphard	217 52.0	S 8 44.7
R 11	357 28.4	15 09.7	38.2	296 56.9	38.1	93 39.9	40.8	65 54.8	32.6			
S 12	12 30.9	30 09.3	S 8 37.2	311 57.6	N21 38.4	108 42.3	S22 40.8	80 57.1	S21 32.6	Alphecca	126 07.4	N26 39.0
D 13	27 33.3	45 08.9	36.1	326 58.4	38.8	123 44.7	40.8	95 59.5	32.6	Alpheratz	357 39.8	N29 11.5
A 14	42 35.8	60 08.5	35.1	341 59.1	39.1	138 47.1	40.8	111 01.8	32.6	Altair	62 04.5	N 8 55.0
Y 15	57 38.3	75 08.1	.. 34.0	356 59.8	.. 39.5	153 49.5	.. 40.8	126 04.2	.. 32.6	Ankaa	353 12.2	S42 12.3
16	72 40.7	90 07.7	33.0	12 00.5	39.8	168 51.9	40.8	141 06.5	32.6	Antares	112 21.2	S26 28.3
17	87 43.2	105 07.3	31.9	27 01.3	40.1	183 54.3	40.8	156 08.9	32.6			
18	102 45.6	120 06.9	S 8 30.9	42 02.0	N21 40.5	198 56.7	S22 40.8	171 11.3	S21 32.6	Arcturus	145 51.8	N19 04.9
19	117 48.1	135 06.5	29.8	57 02.7	40.8	213 59.2	40.8	186 13.6	32.5	Atria	107 19.2	S69 03.3
20	132 50.6	150 06.1	28.8	72 03.4	41.1	229 01.6	40.8	201 16.0	32.5	Avior	234 16.2	S59 34.6
21	147 53.0	165 05.7	.. 27.7	87 04.2	.. 41.5	244 04.0	.. 40.8	216 18.3	.. 32.5	Bellatrix	278 27.9	N 6 21.8
22	162 55.5	180 05.3	26.6	102 04.9	41.8	259 06.4	40.8	231 20.7	32.5	Betelgeuse	270 57.1	N 7 24.4
23	177 58.0	195 05.0	25.6	117 05.6	42.1	274 08.8	40.8	246 23.0	32.5			
5 00	193 00.4	210 04.6	S 8 24.5	132 06.3	N21 42.5	289 11.2	S22 40.8	261 25.4	S21 32.5	Canopus	263 54.5	S52 42.8
01	208 02.9	225 04.2	23.5	147 07.0	42.8	304 13.6	40.8	276 27.7	32.5	Capella	280 28.8	N46 01.0
02	223 05.4	240 03.8	22.4	162 07.8	43.2	319 16.1	40.8	291 30.1	32.4	Deneb	49 29.0	N45 20.7
03	238 07.8	255 03.4	.. 21.3	177 08.5	.. 43.5	334 18.5	.. 40.8	306 32.5	.. 32.4	Denebola	182 29.4	N14 27.9
04	253 10.3	270 03.0	20.3	192 09.2	43.8	349 20.9	40.8	321 34.8	32.4	Diphda	348 52.3	S17 53.1
05	268 12.7	285 02.6	19.2	207 09.9	44.2	4 23.3	40.8	336 37.2	32.4			
06	283 15.2	300 02.2	S 8 18.2	222 10.7	N21 44.5	19 25.7	S22 40.8	351 39.5	S21 32.4	Dubhe	193 46.3	N61 39.0
07	298 17.7	315 01.8	17.1	237 11.4	44.8	34 28.1	40.8	6 41.9	32.4	Elnath	278 07.8	N28 37.3
F 08	313 20.1	330 01.4	16.0	252 12.1	45.1	49 30.6	40.8	21 44.2	32.4	Eltanin	90 44.2	N51 29.0
R 09	328 22.6	345 01.0	.. 15.0	267 12.8	.. 45.5	64 33.0	.. 40.8	36 46.6	.. 32.4	Enif	33 43.5	N 9 57.6
I 10	343 25.1	0 00.6	13.9	282 13.6	45.8	79 35.4	40.8	51 49.0	32.3	Fomalhaut	15 19.9	S29 31.3
D 11	358 27.5	15 00.3	12.9	297 14.3	46.1	94 37.8	40.8	66 51.3	32.3			
A 12	13 30.0	29 59.9	S 8 11.8	312 15.0	N21 46.5	109 40.2	S22 40.8	81 53.7	S21 32.3	Gacrux	171 55.9	S57 13.2
Y 13	28 32.5	44 59.5	10.7	327 15.7	46.8	124 42.7	40.8	96 56.0	32.3	Gienah	175 47.9	S17 39.0
14	43 34.9	59 59.1	09.7	342 16.4	47.1	139 45.1	40.8	111 58.4	32.3	Hadar	148 41.7	S60 27.8
15	58 37.4	74 58.7	.. 08.6	357 17.2	.. 47.5	154 47.5	.. 40.8	127 00.8	.. 32.3	Hamal	327 56.6	N23 33.0
16	73 39.9	89 58.3	07.5	12 17.9	47.8	169 49.9	40.8	142 03.1	32.3	Kaus Aust.	83 38.5	S34 22.3
17	88 42.3	104 57.9	06.5	27 18.6	48.1	184 52.3	40.8	157 05.5	32.3			
18	103 44.8	119 57.5	S 8 05.4	42 19.3	N21 48.5	199 54.8	S22 40.8	172 07.8	S21 32.2	Kochab	137 19.1	N74 04.5
19	118 47.2	134 57.2	04.4	57 20.1	48.8	214 57.2	40.8	187 10.2	32.2	Markab	13 34.7	N15 18.3
20	133 49.7	149 56.8	03.3	72 20.8	49.1	229 59.6	40.8	202 12.6	32.2	Menkar	314 11.2	N 4 09.6
21	148 52.2	164 56.4	.. 02.2	87 21.5	.. 49.4	245 02.0	.. 40.8	217 14.9	.. 32.2	Menkent	148 02.6	S36 27.8
22	163 54.6	179 56.0	01.2	102 22.2	49.8	260 04.5	40.8	232 17.3	32.2	Miaplacidus	221 38.4	S69 48.0
23	178 57.1	194 55.6	8 00.1	117 22.9	50.1	275 06.9	40.8	247 19.6	32.2			
6 00	193 59.6	209 55.2	S 7 59.0	132 23.7	N21 50.4	290 09.3	S22 40.9	262 22.0	S21 32.2	Mirfak	308 35.1	N49 55.6
01	209 02.0	224 54.8	57.9	147 24.4	50.8	305 11.7	40.9	277 24.4	32.2	Nunki	75 53.4	S26 16.2
02	224 04.5	239 54.4	56.9	162 25.1	51.1	320 14.2	40.9	292 26.7	32.1	Peacock	53 13.3	S56 40.2
03	239 07.0	254 54.1	.. 55.8	177 25.8	.. 51.4	335 16.6	.. 40.9	307 29.1	.. 32.1	Pollux	243 22.9	N27 58.7
04	254 09.4	269 53.7	54.7	192 26.6	51.7	350 19.0	40.9	322 31.4	32.1	Procyon	244 55.6	N 5 10.4
05	269 11.9	284 53.3	53.7	207 27.3	52.1	5 21.4	40.9	337 33.8	32.1			
06	284 14.3	299 52.9	S 7 52.6	222 28.0	N21 52.4	20 23.9	S22 40.9	352 36.2	S21 32.1	Rasalhague	96 02.7	N12 32.7
07	299 16.8	314 52.5	51.5	237 28.7	52.7	35 26.3	40.9	7 38.5	32.1	Regulus	207 39.1	N11 52.3
S 08	314 19.3	329 52.1	50.5	252 29.4	53.0	50 28.7	40.9	22 40.9	32.1	Rigel	281 08.4	S 8 11.1
A 09	329 21.7	344 51.7	.. 49.4	267 30.2	.. 53.4	65 31.1	.. 40.9	37 43.3	.. 32.1	Rigil Kent.	139 45.8	S60 54.6
T 10	344 24.2	359 51.4	48.3	282 30.9	53.7	80 33.6	40.9	52 45.6	32.0	Sabik	102 07.9	S15 44.8
U 11	359 26.7	14 51.0	47.2	297 31.6	54.0	95 36.0	40.9	67 48.0	32.0			
R 12	14 29.1	29 50.6	S 7 46.2	312 32.3	N21 54.3	110 38.4	S22 40.9	82 50.3	S21 32.0	Schedar	349 36.6	N56 38.3
D 13	29 31.6	44 50.2	45.1	327 33.0	54.7	125 40.8	40.9	97 52.7	32.0	Shaula	96 16.4	S37 06.8
A 14	44 34.1	59 49.8	44.0	342 33.8	55.0	140 43.3	40.9	112 55.1	32.0	Sirius	258 30.3	S16 44.9
Y 15	59 36.5	74 49.4	.. 43.0	357 34.5	.. 55.3	155 45.7	.. 40.9	127 57.4	.. 32.0	Spica	158 26.8	S11 15.7
16	74 39.0	89 49.1	41.9	12 35.2	55.6	170 48.1	40.9	142 59.8	32.0	Suhail	222 49.3	S43 30.9
17	89 41.5	104 48.7	40.8	27 35.9	55.9	185 50.6	40.9	158 02.2	32.0			
18	104 43.9	119 48.3	S 7 39.7	42 36.6	N21 56.3	200 53.0	S22 40.9	173 04.5	S21 31.9	Vega	80 36.2	N38 47.9
19	119 46.4	134 47.9	38.7	57 37.4	56.6	215 55.4	40.9	188 06.9	31.9	Zuben'ubi	137 00.8	S16 07.2
20	134 48.8	149 47.5	37.6	72 38.1	56.9	230 57.9	40.9	203 09.3	31.9		SHA	Mer.Pass.
21	149 51.3	164 47.2	.. 36.5	87 38.8	.. 57.2	246 00.3	.. 40.9	218 11.6	.. 31.9	Venus	17 04.1	10 00
22	164 53.8	179 46.8	35.4	102 39.5	57.5	261 02.7	40.9	233 14.0	31.9	Mars	299 05.9	15 11
23	179 56.2	194 46.4	34.4	117 40.2	57.9	276 05.2	40.9	248 16.3	31.9	Jupiter	96 10.8	4 42
Mer.Pass.	h m 11 06.1	v −0.4	d 1.1	v 0.7	d 0.3	v 2.4	d 0.0	v 2.4	d 0.0	Saturn	68 25.0	6 33

© British Crown Copyright 2018. All rights reserved.

UT	SUN GHA	SUN Dec	MOON GHA	v	MOON Dec	d	HP
4 00	179 11.7	N 5 29.8	191 34.3	15.2	S 4 46.1	11.1	54.6
01	194 11.9	30.8	206 08.5	15.2	4 35.0	11.1	54.6
02	209 12.1	31.7	220 42.7	15.2	4 23.9	11.1	54.6
03	224 12.3	.. 32.7	235 16.9	15.2	4 12.8	11.2	54.6
04	239 12.4	33.7	249 51.1	15.2	4 01.6	11.1	54.6
05	254 12.6	34.6	264 25.3	15.1	3 50.5	11.2	54.7
06	269 12.8	N 5 35.6	278 59.4	15.2	S 3 39.3	11.2	54.7
07	284 13.0	36.5	293 33.6	15.2	3 28.1	11.2	54.7
T 08	299 13.2	37.5	308 07.8	15.2	3 16.9	11.3	54.7
H 09	314 13.3	.. 38.4	322 42.0	15.1	3 05.6	11.3	54.7
U 10	329 13.5	39.4	337 16.1	15.2	2 54.3	11.2	54.7
R 11	344 13.7	40.3	351 50.3	15.1	2 43.1	11.3	54.7
S 12	359 13.9	N 5 41.3	6 24.4	15.2	S 2 31.8	11.4	54.8
D 13	14 14.1	42.3	20 58.6	15.1	2 20.4	11.3	54.8
A 14	29 14.2	43.2	35 32.7	15.1	2 09.1	11.3	54.8
Y 15	44 14.4	.. 44.2	50 06.8	15.1	1 57.8	11.4	54.8
16	59 14.6	45.1	64 40.9	15.1	1 46.4	11.4	54.8
17	74 14.8	46.1	79 15.0	15.1	1 35.0	11.4	54.8
18	89 15.0	N 5 47.0	93 49.1	15.1	S 1 23.6	11.4	54.8
19	104 15.1	48.0	108 23.2	15.1	1 12.2	11.4	54.9
20	119 15.3	48.9	122 57.3	15.0	1 00.8	11.4	54.9
21	134 15.5	.. 49.9	137 31.3	15.1	0 49.4	11.5	54.9
22	149 15.7	50.8	152 05.4	15.0	0 37.9	11.4	54.9
23	164 15.9	51.8	166 39.4	15.0	0 26.5	11.5	54.9
5 00	179 16.0	N 5 52.7	181 13.4	15.0	S 0 15.0	11.5	54.9
01	194 16.2	53.7	195 47.4	15.0	S 0 03.5	11.4	55.0
02	209 16.4	54.6	210 21.4	15.0	N 0 07.9	11.5	55.0
03	224 16.6	.. 55.6	224 55.4	14.9	0 19.4	11.5	55.0
04	239 16.8	56.5	239 29.3	14.9	0 30.9	11.5	55.0
05	254 16.9	57.5	254 03.2	14.9	0 42.4	11.5	55.0
06	269 17.1	N 5 58.4	268 37.1	14.9	N 0 53.9	11.5	55.0
07	284 17.3	5 59.4	283 11.0	14.9	1 05.4	11.5	55.1
08	299 17.5	6 00.3	297 44.9	14.8	1 16.9	11.5	55.1
F 09	314 17.7	.. 01.3	312 18.7	14.9	1 28.4	11.5	55.1
R 10	329 17.8	02.2	326 52.6	14.8	1 39.9	11.5	55.1
I 11	344 18.0	03.2	341 26.4	14.7	1 51.4	11.5	55.1
D 12	359 18.2	N 6 04.1	356 00.1	14.8	N 2 02.9	11.5	55.2
A 13	14 18.4	05.1	10 33.9	14.7	2 14.4	11.5	55.2
Y 14	29 18.5	06.0	25 07.6	14.7	2 25.9	11.6	55.2
15	44 18.7	.. 07.0	39 41.3	14.7	2 37.5	11.4	55.2
16	59 18.9	07.9	54 15.0	14.6	2 48.9	11.5	55.2
17	74 19.1	08.9	68 48.6	14.6	3 00.4	11.5	55.2
18	89 19.3	N 6 09.8	83 22.2	14.6	N 3 11.9	11.5	55.2
19	104 19.4	10.8	97 55.8	14.6	3 23.4	11.5	55.2
20	119 19.6	11.7	112 29.4	14.5	3 34.9	11.5	55.3
21	134 19.8	.. 12.7	127 02.9	14.5	3 46.4	11.4	55.3
22	149 20.0	13.6	141 36.4	14.5	3 57.8	11.5	55.3
23	164 20.2	14.6	156 09.9	14.4	4 09.3	11.4	55.3
6 00	179 20.3	N 6 15.5	170 43.3	14.4	N 4 20.7	11.4	55.3
01	194 20.5	16.5	185 16.7	14.4	4 32.1	11.5	55.4
02	209 20.7	17.4	199 50.1	14.3	4 43.6	11.4	55.4
03	224 20.9	.. 18.4	214 23.4	14.3	4 55.0	11.4	55.4
04	239 21.0	19.3	228 56.7	14.3	5 06.4	11.3	55.4
05	254 21.2	20.3	243 30.0	14.2	5 17.7	11.4	55.4
06	269 21.4	N 6 21.2	258 03.2	14.2	N 5 29.1	11.3	55.5
07	284 21.6	22.1	272 36.4	14.2	5 40.4	11.4	55.5
S 08	299 21.8	23.1	287 09.6	14.1	5 51.8	11.3	55.5
A 09	314 21.9	.. 24.0	301 42.7	14.1	6 03.1	11.3	55.5
T 10	329 22.1	25.0	316 15.8	14.0	6 14.4	11.3	55.5
U 11	344 22.3	25.9	330 48.8	14.0	6 25.7	11.2	55.6
R 12	359 22.5	N 6 26.9	345 21.8	14.0	N 6 36.9	11.2	55.6
D 13	14 22.6	27.8	359 54.8	13.9	6 48.1	11.2	55.6
A 14	29 22.8	28.8	14 27.7	13.9	6 59.3	11.2	55.6
Y 15	44 23.0	.. 29.7	29 00.6	13.8	7 10.5	11.2	55.6
16	59 23.2	30.7	43 33.4	13.8	7 21.7	11.1	55.6
17	74 23.3	31.6	58 06.2	13.7	7 32.8	11.1	55.7
18	89 23.5	N 6 32.5	72 38.9	13.7	N 7 43.9	11.1	55.7
19	104 23.7	33.5	87 11.6	13.7	7 55.0	11.1	55.7
20	119 23.9	34.4	101 44.3	13.6	8 06.1	11.0	55.7
21	134 24.0	.. 35.4	116 16.9	13.5	8 17.1	11.0	55.7
22	149 24.2	36.3	130 49.4	13.5	8 28.1	11.0	55.8
23	164 24.4	37.3	145 22.0	13.4	N 8 39.1	10.9	55.8
	SD 16.0	d 0.9	SD 14.9		15.0		15.1

Lat.	Twilight Naut.	Civil	Sunrise	Moonrise 4	5	6	7
°	h m	h m	h m	h m	h m	h m	h m
N 72	00 29	03 18	04 36	06 11	05 56	05 41	05 23
N 70	01 49	03 37	04 46	06 06	05 57	05 48	05 38
68	02 25	03 53	04 54	06 01	05 58	05 54	05 50
66	02 50	04 05	05 00	05 58	05 58	05 59	06 00
64	03 08	04 15	05 06	05 55	05 59	06 03	06 09
62	03 24	04 24	05 10	05 52	06 00	06 07	06 16
60	03 36	04 31	05 14	05 50	06 00	06 10	06 22
N 58	03 46	04 37	05 18	05 48	06 01	06 13	06 28
56	03 55	04 43	05 21	05 46	06 01	06 16	06 33
54	04 03	04 48	05 24	05 45	06 01	06 18	06 37
52	04 10	04 52	05 27	05 43	06 02	06 21	06 41
50	04 16	04 56	05 29	05 42	06 02	06 22	06 45
45	04 29	05 04	05 34	05 39	06 03	06 27	06 53
N 40	04 38	05 11	05 38	05 36	06 03	06 30	07 00
35	04 46	05 16	05 42	05 34	06 04	06 34	07 05
30	04 53	05 21	05 45	05 32	06 04	06 36	07 10
20	05 02	05 28	05 51	05 29	06 05	06 41	07 19
N 10	05 10	05 34	05 55	05 26	06 05	06 46	07 27
0	05 15	05 39	06 00	05 23	06 06	06 50	07 35
S 10	05 18	05 43	06 04	05 21	06 07	06 54	07 42
20	05 20	05 46	06 08	05 18	06 08	06 58	07 50
30	05 21	05 49	06 13	05 14	06 08	07 03	08 00
35	05 21	05 50	06 16	05 12	06 09	07 06	08 05
40	05 20	05 52	06 19	05 10	06 09	07 10	08 11
45	05 19	05 53	06 22	05 08	06 10	07 14	08 18
S 50	05 17	05 54	06 26	05 05	06 11	07 18	08 27
52	05 15	05 54	06 28	05 03	06 11	07 20	08 31
54	05 12	05 55	06 30	05 02	06 12	07 23	08 35
56	05 12	05 55	06 33	05 00	06 12	07 25	08 40
58	05 10	05 56	06 35	04 58	06 13	07 28	08 46
S 60	05 08	05 56	06 38	04 56	06 13	07 32	08 52

Lat.	Sunset	Twilight Civil	Naut.	Moonset 4	5	6	7
°	h m	h m	h m	h m	h m	h m	h m
N 72	19 32	20 53	////	17 24	19 10	21 00	23 00
N 70	19 22	20 32	22 26	17 26	19 05	20 47	22 35
68	19 14	20 16	21 46	17 28	19 01	20 37	22 17
66	19 08	20 03	21 20	17 29	18 58	20 28	22 02
64	19 02	19 53	21 00	17 31	18 55	20 21	21 50
62	18 57	19 44	20 45	17 32	18 53	20 15	21 40
60	18 53	19 37	20 32	17 33	18 51	20 10	21 31
N 58	18 49	19 30	20 21	17 34	18 49	20 05	21 23
56	18 46	19 24	20 12	17 35	18 47	20 01	21 17
54	18 43	19 19	20 04	17 35	18 46	19 57	21 11
52	18 40	19 15	19 57	17 36	18 44	19 54	21 05
50	18 38	19 11	19 51	17 36	18 43	19 51	21 00
45	18 32	19 02	19 38	17 38	18 40	19 44	20 50
N 40	18 28	18 55	19 28	17 39	18 38	19 39	20 41
35	18 24	18 50	19 20	17 40	18 36	19 34	20 34
30	18 21	18 45	19 14	17 40	18 35	19 30	20 27
20	18 15	18 38	19 03	17 42	18 32	19 23	20 16
N 10	18 10	18 32	18 51	17 43	18 29	19 17	20 06
0	18 06	18 27	18 51	17 44	18 27	19 11	19 57
S 10	18 02	18 23	18 47	17 45	18 25	19 05	19 48
20	17 57	18 19	18 45	17 46	18 22	18 59	19 38
30	17 52	18 16	18 44	17 47	18 19	18 52	19 27
35	17 49	18 15	18 44	17 48	18 17	18 48	19 21
40	17 46	18 13	18 45	17 49	18 16	18 44	19 14
45	17 43	18 12	18 46	17 50	18 13	18 38	19 06
S 50	17 38	18 11	18 48	17 51	18 11	18 32	18 55
52	17 36	18 10	18 49	17 51	18 10	18 29	18 51
54	17 34	18 10	18 50	17 52	18 08	18 26	18 46
56	17 32	18 09	18 52	17 52	18 07	18 22	18 40
58	17 29	18 09	18 54	17 53	18 05	18 19	18 34
S 60	17 26	18 08	18 56	17 54	18 04	18 14	18 27

Day	SUN Eqn. of Time 00h	12h	Mer. Pass.	MOON Mer. Pass. Upper	Lower	Age	Phase
d	m s	m s	h m	h m	h m	d	%
4	03 14	03 05	12 03	11 34	23 55	29	1
5	02 56	02 48	12 03	12 16	24 38	00	0
6	02 39	02 31	12 03	13 00	00 38	01	1

© British Crown Copyright 2018. All rights reserved.

UT	ARIES GHA	VENUS −3.9 GHA	Dec	MARS +1.5 GHA	Dec	JUPITER −2.3 GHA	Dec	SATURN +0.6 GHA	Dec	Star Name	SHA	Dec
7 00	194 58.7	209 46.0	S 7 33.3	132 41.0	N21 58.2	291 07.6	S22 40.9	263 18.7	S21 31.9	Acamar	315 15.7	S40 14.0
01	210 01.2	224 45.6	32.2	147 41.7	58.5	306 10.0	40.9	278 21.1	31.9	Achernar	335 24.4	S57 08.6
02	225 03.6	239 45.3	31.1	162 42.4	58.8	321 12.5	40.9	293 23.4	31.8	Acrux	173 04.2	S63 12.3
03	240 06.1	254 44.9 ..	30.0	177 43.1 ..	59.1	336 14.9 ..	40.9	308 25.8 ..	31.8	Adhara	255 09.5	S29 00.2
04	255 08.6	269 44.5	29.0	192 43.8	59.5	351 17.3	40.9	323 28.2	31.8	Aldebaran	290 45.1	N16 32.6
05	270 11.0	284 44.1	27.9	207 44.5	21 59.8	6 19.8	40.9	338 30.5	31.8			
06	285 13.5	299 43.7	S 7 26.8	222 45.3	N22 00.1	21 22.2	S22 40.9	353 32.9	S21 31.8	Alioth	166 16.7	N55 51.4
07	300 16.0	314 43.4	25.7	237 46.0	00.4	36 24.6	40.9	8 35.3	31.8	Alkaid	152 55.3	N49 13.1
08	315 18.4	329 43.0	24.7	252 46.7	00.7	51 27.1	40.9	23 37.6	31.8	Alnair	27 39.1	S46 52.0
S 09	330 20.9	344 42.6 ..	23.6	267 47.4 ..	01.1	66 29.5 ..	40.9	38 40.0 ..	31.8	Alnilam	275 42.5	S 1 11.7
U 10	345 23.3	359 42.2	22.5	282 48.1	01.4	81 31.9	40.9	53 42.4	31.7	Alphard	217 52.1	S 8 44.7
N 11	0 25.8	14 41.8	21.4	297 48.9	01.7	96 34.4	40.9	68 44.7	31.7			
D 12	15 28.3	29 41.5	S 7 20.3	312 49.6	N22 02.0	111 36.8	S22 40.9	83 47.1	S21 31.7	Alphecca	126 07.4	N26 39.0
A 13	30 30.7	44 41.1	19.2	327 50.3	02.3	126 39.2	40.9	98 49.5	31.7	Alpheratz	357 39.8	N29 11.5
Y 14	45 33.2	59 40.7	18.2	342 51.0	02.6	141 41.7	40.9	113 51.8	31.7	Altair	62 04.4	N 8 55.0
15	60 35.7	74 40.3 ..	17.1	357 51.7 ..	02.9	156 44.1 ..	40.9	128 54.2 ..	31.7	Ankaa	353 12.2	S42 12.3
16	75 38.1	89 40.0	16.0	12 52.5	03.3	171 46.6	40.9	143 56.6	31.7	Antares	112 21.2	S26 28.3
17	90 40.6	104 39.6	14.9	27 53.2	03.6	186 49.0	40.9	158 58.9	31.7			
18	105 43.1	119 39.2	S 7 13.8	42 53.9	N22 03.9	201 51.4	S22 40.9	174 01.3	S21 31.7	Arcturus	145 51.8	N19 04.9
19	120 45.5	134 38.8	12.7	57 54.6	04.2	216 53.9	40.9	189 03.7	31.6	Atria	107 19.2	S69 03.3
20	135 48.0	149 38.5	11.7	72 55.3	04.5	231 56.3	40.9	204 06.1	31.6	Avior	234 16.3	S59 34.6
21	150 50.4	164 38.1 ..	10.6	87 56.0 ..	04.8	246 58.7 ..	40.9	219 08.4 ..	31.6	Bellatrix	278 27.9	N 6 21.8
22	165 52.9	179 37.7	09.5	102 56.8	05.1	262 01.2	40.9	234 10.8	31.6	Betelgeuse	270 57.1	N 7 24.4
23	180 55.4	194 37.3	08.4	117 57.5	05.5	277 03.6	40.9	249 13.2	31.6			
8 00	195 57.8	209 37.0	S 7 07.3	132 58.2	N22 05.8	292 06.1	S22 40.9	264 15.5	S21 31.6	Canopus	263 54.5	S52 42.8
01	211 00.3	224 36.6	06.2	147 58.9	06.1	307 08.5	40.9	279 17.9	31.6	Capella	280 28.9	N46 01.0
02	226 02.8	239 36.2	05.1	162 59.6	06.4	322 11.0	40.9	294 20.3	31.6	Deneb	49 29.0	N45 20.7
03	241 05.2	254 35.8 ..	04.1	178 00.3 ..	06.7	337 13.4 ..	40.9	309 22.6 ..	31.5	Denebola	182 29.4	N14 27.9
04	256 07.7	269 35.5	03.0	193 01.1	07.0	352 15.8	40.9	324 25.0	31.5	Diphda	348 52.3	S17 53.1
05	271 10.2	284 35.1	01.9	208 01.8	07.3	7 18.3	40.9	339 27.4	31.5			
06	286 12.6	299 34.7	S 7 00.8	223 02.5	N22 07.6	22 20.7	S22 40.9	354 29.7	S21 31.5	Dubhe	193 46.3	N61 39.0
07	301 15.1	314 34.3	6 59.7	238 03.2	08.0	37 23.2	40.9	9 32.1	31.5	Elnath	278 07.8	N28 37.3
08	316 17.6	329 34.0	58.6	253 03.9	08.3	52 25.6	40.9	24 34.5	31.5	Eltanin	90 44.1	N51 29.0
M 09	331 20.0	344 33.6 ..	57.5	268 04.6 ..	08.6	67 28.1 ..	40.9	39 36.9 ..	31.5	Enif	33 43.5	N 9 57.6
O 10	346 22.5	359 33.2	56.4	283 05.4	08.9	82 30.5	40.9	54 39.2	31.5	Fomalhaut	15 19.9	S29 31.3
N 11	1 24.9	14 32.8	55.4	298 06.1	09.2	97 32.9	40.9	69 41.6	31.5			
D 12	16 27.4	29 32.5	S 6 54.3	313 06.8	N22 09.5	112 35.4	S22 40.9	84 44.0	S21 31.4	Gacrux	171 55.9	S57 13.3
A 13	31 29.9	44 32.1	53.2	328 07.5	09.8	127 37.8	40.9	99 46.3	31.4	Gienah	175 47.9	S17 39.0
Y 14	46 32.3	59 31.7	52.1	343 08.2	10.1	142 40.3	40.9	114 48.7	31.4	Hadar	148 41.7	S60 27.8
15	61 34.8	74 31.4 ..	51.0	358 08.9 ..	10.4	157 42.7 ..	40.9	129 51.1 ..	31.4	Hamal	327 56.6	N23 32.9
16	76 37.3	89 31.0	49.9	13 09.7	10.7	172 45.2	40.9	144 53.5	31.4	Kaus Aust.	83 38.5	S34 22.3
17	91 39.7	104 30.6	48.8	28 10.4	11.0	187 47.6	40.9	159 55.8	31.4			
18	106 42.2	119 30.2	S 6 47.7	43 11.1	N22 11.3	202 50.1	S22 40.9	174 58.2	S21 31.4	Kochab	137 19.0	N74 04.6
19	121 44.7	134 29.9	46.6	58 11.8	11.6	217 52.5	40.9	190 00.6	31.4	Markab	13 34.7	N15 18.3
20	136 47.1	149 29.5	45.5	73 12.5	12.0	232 55.0	40.9	205 02.9	31.4	Menkar	314 11.2	N 4 09.6
21	151 49.6	164 29.1 ..	44.4	88 13.2 ..	12.3	247 57.4 ..	40.9	220 05.3 ..	31.3	Menkent	148 02.5	S36 27.8
22	166 52.0	179 28.8	43.3	103 13.9	12.6	262 59.9	40.9	235 07.7	31.3	Miaplacidus	221 38.4	S69 48.1
23	181 54.5	194 28.4	42.2	118 14.7	12.9	278 02.3	40.9	250 10.1	31.3			
9 00	196 57.0	209 28.0	S 6 41.2	133 15.4	N22 13.2	293 04.8	S22 40.9	265 12.4	S21 31.3	Mirfak	308 35.1	N49 55.6
01	211 59.4	224 27.6	40.1	148 16.1	13.5	308 07.2	40.9	280 14.8	31.3	Nunki	75 53.4	S26 16.2
02	227 01.9	239 27.3	39.0	163 16.8	13.8	323 09.7	40.9	295 17.2	31.3	Peacock	53 13.2	S56 40.1
03	242 04.4	254 26.9 ..	37.9	178 17.5 ..	14.1	338 12.1 ..	40.9	310 19.6 ..	31.3	Pollux	243 22.9	N27 58.7
04	257 06.8	269 26.5	36.8	193 18.2	14.4	353 14.6	40.9	325 21.9	31.3	Procyon	244 55.6	N 5 10.4
05	272 09.3	284 26.2	35.7	208 18.9	14.7	8 17.0	40.9	340 24.3	31.3			
06	287 11.8	299 25.8	S 6 34.6	223 19.7	N22 15.0	23 19.5	S22 40.9	355 26.7	S21 31.2	Rasalhague	96 02.7	N12 32.7
07	302 14.2	314 25.4	33.5	238 20.4	15.3	38 21.9	40.9	10 29.1	31.2	Regulus	207 39.1	N11 52.3
08	317 16.7	329 25.1	32.4	253 21.1	15.6	53 24.4	40.9	25 31.4	31.2	Rigel	281 08.4	S 8 11.1
T 09	332 19.2	344 24.7 ..	31.3	268 21.8 ..	15.9	68 26.8 ..	40.9	40 33.8 ..	31.2	Rigil Kent.	139 45.8	S60 54.6
U 10	347 21.6	359 24.3	30.2	283 22.5	16.2	83 29.3	40.9	55 36.2	31.2	Sabik	102 07.8	S15 44.8
E 11	2 24.1	14 24.0	29.1	298 23.2	16.5	98 31.7	40.9	70 38.6	31.2			
S 12	17 26.5	29 23.6	S 6 28.0	313 23.9	N22 16.8	113 34.2	S22 40.9	85 40.9	S21 31.2	Schedar	349 36.6	N56 38.3
D 13	32 29.0	44 23.2	26.9	328 24.7	17.1	128 36.6	40.9	100 43.3	31.2	Shaula	96 16.4	S37 06.8
A 14	47 31.5	59 22.9	25.8	343 25.4	17.4	143 39.1	40.9	115 45.7	31.2	Sirius	258 30.3	S16 44.9
Y 15	62 33.9	74 22.5 ..	24.7	358 26.1 ..	17.7	158 41.5 ..	40.9	130 48.1 ..	31.1	Spica	158 26.8	S11 15.7
16	77 36.4	89 22.1	23.6	13 26.8	18.0	173 44.0	40.9	145 50.4	31.1	Suhail	222 49.4	S43 30.9
17	92 38.9	104 21.8	22.5	28 27.5	18.3	188 46.5	40.9	160 52.8	31.1			
18	107 41.3	119 21.4	S 6 21.4	43 28.2	N22 18.6	203 48.9	S22 40.9	175 55.2	S21 31.1	Vega	80 36.2	N38 47.9
19	122 43.8	134 21.0	20.3	58 28.9	18.9	218 51.4	40.9	190 57.6	31.1	Zuben'ubi	137 00.8	S16 07.2
20	137 46.3	149 20.7	19.2	73 29.7	19.2	233 53.8	40.9	205 59.9	31.1		SHA	Mer.Pass.
21	152 48.7	164 20.3 ..	18.1	88 30.4 ..	19.5	248 56.3 ..	40.9	221 02.3 ..	31.1	Venus	13 39.1	10 02
22	167 51.2	179 19.9	17.0	103 31.1	19.8	263 58.7	40.9	236 04.7	31.1	Mars	297 00.4	15 07
23	182 53.7	194 19.6	15.9	118 31.8	20.1	279 01.2	40.9	251 07.1	31.1	Jupiter	96 08.2	4 31
Mer. Pass. 10 54.4		v −0.4	d 1.1	v 0.7	d 0.3	v 2.4	d 0.0	v 2.4	d 0.0	Saturn	68 17.7	6 22

© British Crown Copyright 2018. All rights reserved.

UT	SUN GHA	SUN Dec	MOON GHA	v	Dec	d	HP
d h	° ′	° ′	° ′	′	° ′	′	′
7 00	179 24.6	N 6 38.2	159 54.4	13.4	N 8 50.0	10.9	55.8
01	194 24.7	39.1	174 26.8	13.4	9 00.9	10.9	55.8
02	209 24.9	40.1	188 59.2	13.3	9 11.8	10.8	55.9
03	224 25.1	.. 41.0	203 31.5	13.3	9 22.6	10.8	55.9
04	239 25.3	42.0	218 03.8	13.2	9 33.4	10.8	55.9
05	254 25.5	42.9	232 36.0	13.1	9 44.2	10.7	55.9
06	269 25.6	N 6 43.9	247 08.1	13.2	N 9 54.9	10.7	55.9
07	284 25.8	44.8	261 40.3	13.0	10 05.6	10.7	55.9
S 08	299 26.0	45.7	276 12.3	13.0	10 16.3	10.6	56.0
U 09	314 26.2	.. 46.7	290 44.3	13.0	10 26.9	10.6	56.0
N 10	329 26.3	47.6	305 16.3	12.8	10 37.5	10.5	56.0
D 11	344 26.5	48.6	319 48.1	12.9	10 48.0	10.5	56.0
A 12	359 26.7	N 6 49.5	334 20.0	12.8	N10 58.5	10.4	56.0
Y 13	14 26.8	50.4	348 51.8	12.7	11 08.9	10.4	56.1
14	29 27.0	51.4	3 23.5	12.6	11 19.3	10.4	56.1
15	44 27.2	.. 52.3	17 55.1	12.7	11 29.7	10.3	56.1
16	59 27.4	53.3	32 26.8	12.5	11 40.0	10.2	56.1
17	74 27.5	54.2	46 58.3	12.5	11 50.2	10.2	56.1
18	89 27.7	N 6 55.1	61 29.8	12.4	N12 00.4	10.2	56.2
19	104 27.9	56.1	76 01.2	12.4	12 10.6	10.1	56.2
20	119 28.1	57.0	90 32.6	12.3	12 20.7	10.1	56.2
21	134 28.2	.. 58.0	105 03.9	12.3	12 30.8	10.0	56.2
22	149 28.4	58.9	119 35.2	12.1	12 40.8	9.9	56.2
23	164 28.6	6 59.8	134 06.3	12.2	12 50.7	9.9	56.3
8 00	179 28.8	N 7 00.8	148 37.5	12.0	N13 00.6	9.8	56.3
01	194 28.9	01.7	163 08.5	12.0	13 10.4	9.8	56.3
02	209 29.1	02.6	177 39.5	12.0	13 20.2	9.7	56.3
03	224 29.3	.. 03.6	192 10.5	11.9	13 29.9	9.7	56.3
04	239 29.5	04.5	206 41.4	11.8	13 39.6	9.6	56.4
05	254 29.6	05.5	221 12.2	11.7	13 49.2	9.6	56.4
06	269 29.8	N 7 06.4	235 42.9	11.7	N13 58.8	9.4	56.4
07	284 30.0	07.3	250 13.6	11.6	14 08.2	9.5	56.4
M 08	299 30.1	08.3	264 44.2	11.6	14 17.7	9.3	56.4
O 09	314 30.3	.. 09.2	279 14.8	11.5	14 27.0	9.3	56.5
N 10	329 30.5	10.1	293 45.3	11.4	14 36.3	9.2	56.5
D 11	344 30.7	11.1	308 15.7	11.3	14 45.5	9.2	56.5
A 12	359 30.8	N 7 12.0	322 46.0	11.3	N14 54.7	9.1	56.5
Y 13	14 31.0	12.9	337 16.3	11.2	15 03.8	9.0	56.6
14	29 31.2	13.9	351 46.5	11.2	15 12.8	8.9	56.6
15	44 31.4	.. 14.8	6 16.7	11.1	15 21.7	8.9	56.6
16	59 31.5	15.8	20 46.8	11.0	15 30.6	8.8	56.6
17	74 31.7	16.7	35 16.8	10.9	15 39.4	8.7	56.6
18	89 31.9	N 7 17.6	49 46.7	10.9	N15 48.1	8.7	56.7
19	104 32.0	18.6	64 16.6	10.8	15 56.8	8.6	56.7
20	119 32.2	19.5	78 46.4	10.8	16 05.4	8.5	56.7
21	134 32.4	.. 20.4	93 16.2	10.6	16 13.9	8.4	56.7
22	149 32.6	21.4	107 45.8	10.6	16 22.3	8.4	56.7
23	164 32.7	22.3	122 15.4	10.6	16 30.7	8.2	56.8
9 00	179 32.9	N 7 23.2	136 45.0	10.4	N16 38.9	8.2	56.8
01	194 33.1	24.2	151 14.4	10.4	16 47.1	8.1	56.8
02	209 33.2	25.1	165 43.8	10.4	16 55.2	8.0	56.8
03	224 33.4	.. 26.0	180 13.2	10.2	17 03.2	8.0	56.9
04	239 33.6	27.0	194 42.4	10.2	17 11.2	7.8	56.9
05	254 33.8	27.9	209 11.6	10.1	17 19.0	7.8	56.9
06	269 33.9	N 7 28.8	223 40.7	10.1	N17 26.8	7.7	56.9
07	284 34.1	29.7	238 09.8	9.9	17 34.5	7.6	56.9
T 08	299 34.3	30.7	252 38.7	9.9	17 42.1	7.5	57.0
U 09	314 34.4	.. 31.6	267 07.6	9.9	17 49.6	7.4	57.0
E 10	329 34.6	32.5	281 36.5	9.7	17 57.0	7.3	57.0
S 11	344 34.8	33.5	296 05.2	9.7	18 04.3	7.2	57.0
D 12	359 34.9	N 7 34.4	310 33.9	9.7	N18 11.5	7.2	57.0
A 13	14 35.1	35.3	325 02.6	9.5	18 18.7	7.0	57.1
Y 14	29 35.3	36.3	339 31.1	9.5	18 25.7	7.0	57.1
15	44 35.5	.. 37.2	353 59.6	9.4	18 32.7	6.8	57.1
16	59 35.6	38.1	8 28.0	9.4	18 39.5	6.8	57.1
17	74 35.8	39.0	22 56.4	9.3	18 46.3	6.6	57.2
18	89 36.0	N 7 40.0	37 24.7	9.2	N18 52.9	6.6	57.2
19	104 36.1	40.9	51 52.9	9.1	18 59.5	6.4	57.2
20	119 36.3	41.8	66 21.0	9.1	19 05.9	6.4	57.2
21	134 36.5	.. 42.8	80 49.1	9.0	19 12.3	6.2	57.2
22	149 36.6	43.7	95 17.1	8.9	19 18.5	6.2	57.3
23	164 36.8	44.6	109 45.0	8.9	N19 24.7	6.0	57.3
	SD 16.0	d 0.9	SD 15.3		15.4		15.5

Lat.	Twilight Naut.	Twilight Civil	Sunrise	Moonrise 7	8	9	10
°	h m	h m	h m	h m	h m	h m	h m
N 72	////	02 57	04 20	05 23	05 01	04 17	▭
N 70	01 14	03 20	04 32	05 38	05 27	05 10	04 26
68	02 02	03 38	04 41	05 50	05 47	05 43	05 40
66	02 32	03 52	04 49	06 00	06 03	06 07	06 18
64	02 54	04 03	04 55	06 09	06 16	06 27	06 45
62	03 11	04 13	05 01	06 16	06 27	06 42	07 05
60	03 25	04 21	05 05	06 22	06 36	06 55	07 22
N 58	03 36	04 28	05 10	06 28	06 45	07 07	07 36
56	03 46	04 35	05 13	06 33	06 52	07 17	07 49
54	03 55	04 40	05 17	06 37	06 59	07 25	07 59
52	04 02	04 45	05 20	06 41	07 05	07 33	08 09
50	04 09	04 49	05 23	06 45	07 10	07 40	08 18
45	04 23	04 59	05 29	06 53	07 22	07 56	08 36
N 40	04 33	05 06	05 34	07 00	07 32	08 08	08 51
35	04 42	05 12	05 38	07 05	07 40	08 19	09 03
30	04 49	05 17	05 42	07 10	07 47	08 28	09 14
20	05 00	05 26	05 48	07 19	08 00	08 45	09 33
N 10	05 08	05 32	05 54	07 27	08 12	08 59	09 50
0	05 14	05 38	05 59	07 35	08 22	09 12	10 06
S 10	05 18	05 43	06 04	07 42	08 33	09 26	10 21
20	05 21	05 47	06 09	07 50	08 44	09 40	10 38
30	05 23	05 51	06 15	08 00	08 58	09 57	10 57
35	05 23	05 53	06 18	08 05	09 05	10 07	11 09
40	05 23	05 54	06 22	08 11	09 14	10 18	11 22
45	05 22	05 56	06 26	08 18	09 25	10 31	11 37
S 50	05 21	05 59	06 31	08 27	09 37	10 47	11 56
52	05 20	05 59	06 33	08 31	09 43	10 55	12 05
54	05 19	06 00	06 36	08 35	09 49	11 04	12 15
56	05 18	06 01	06 39	08 40	09 57	11 13	12 27
58	05 17	06 02	06 42	08 46	10 05	11 24	12 40
S 60	05 15	06 03	06 45	08 52	10 14	11 37	12 56

Lat.	Sunset	Twilight Civil	Twilight Naut.	Moonset 7	8	9	10
°	h m	h m	h m	h m	h m	h m	h m
N 72	19 47	21 12	////	23 00	25 26	01 26	▭
N 70	19 35	20 48	23 04	22 35	24 34	00 34	03 08
68	19 26	20 29	22 08	22 17	24 02	00 02	01 54
66	19 18	20 15	21 36	22 02	23 39	25 17	01 17
64	19 11	20 03	21 14	21 50	23 20	24 51	00 51
62	19 05	19 53	20 56	21 40	23 06	24 30	00 30
60	19 00	19 45	20 42	21 31	22 53	24 14	00 14
N 58	18 56	19 37	20 30	21 23	22 42	24 00	00 00
56	18 52	19 31	20 20	21 17	22 33	23 48	24 59
54	18 48	19 25	20 11	21 11	22 25	23 38	24 47
52	18 45	19 20	20 03	21 05	22 17	23 29	24 37
50	18 42	19 16	19 56	21 00	22 11	23 20	24 27
45	18 36	19 06	19 42	20 50	21 56	23 03	24 07
N 40	18 31	18 59	19 32	20 41	21 45	22 49	23 51
35	18 27	18 52	19 23	20 34	21 35	22 36	23 38
30	18 23	18 47	19 16	20 27	21 26	22 26	23 26
20	18 16	18 38	19 04	20 16	21 11	22 08	23 06
N 10	18 10	18 32	18 56	20 06	20 58	21 52	22 48
0	18 05	18 26	18 50	19 57	20 46	21 38	22 32
S 10	18 00	18 21	18 46	19 48	20 34	21 23	22 16
20	17 55	18 17	18 43	19 38	20 21	21 07	21 58
30	17 49	18 13	18 41	19 27	20 06	20 49	21 38
35	17 45	18 11	18 40	19 21	19 58	20 39	21 26
40	17 42	18 09	18 40	19 14	19 48	20 27	21 13
45	17 37	18 07	18 41	19 06	19 37	20 13	20 57
S 50	17 32	18 04	18 42	18 55	19 23	19 56	20 37
52	17 30	18 04	18 43	18 51	19 17	19 48	20 28
54	17 27	18 03	18 43	18 46	19 10	19 39	20 18
56	17 24	18 02	18 44	18 40	19 02	19 29	20 06
58	17 21	18 01	18 46	18 34	18 53	19 18	19 52
S 60	17 18	17 59	18 47	18 27	18 43	19 05	19 37

Day	Eqn. of Time 00ʰ	Eqn. of Time 12ʰ	Mer. Pass.	Mer. Pass. Upper	Mer. Pass. Lower	Age	Phase
d	m s	m s	h m	h m	h m	d	%
7	02 22	02 14	12 02	13 46	01 23	02	5
8	02 05	01 57	12 02	14 34	02 10	03	10
9	01 49	01 41	12 02	15 25	02 59	04	17

© British Crown Copyright 2018. All rights reserved.

UT	ARIES GHA	VENUS −3.9 GHA	Dec	MARS +1.5 GHA	Dec	JUPITER −2.3 GHA	Dec	SATURN +0.5 GHA	Dec	Star Name	SHA	Dec
10 00	197 56.1	209 19.2	S 6 14.8	133 32.5	N22 20.4	294 03.7	S22 40.9	266 09.5	S21 31.1	Acamar	315 15.7	S40 14.0
01	212 58.6	224 18.8	13.7	148 33.2	20.7	309 06.1	40.9	281 11.8	31.0	Achernar	335 24.4	S57 08.6
02	228 01.0	239 18.5	12.6	163 33.9	21.0	324 08.6	40.9	296 14.2	31.0	Acrux	173 04.2	S63 12.4
03	243 03.5	254 18.1	.. 11.5	178 34.6	.. 21.3	339 11.0	.. 40.9	311 16.6	.. 31.0	Adhara	255 09.5	S29 00.2
04	258 06.0	269 17.8	10.4	193 35.4	21.6	354 13.5	40.9	326 19.0	31.0	Aldebaran	290 45.1	N16 32.6
05	273 08.4	284 17.4	09.3	208 36.1	21.9	9 15.9	40.9	341 21.3	31.0			
W 06	288 10.9	299 17.0	S 6 08.2	223 36.8	N22 22.2	24 18.4	S22 40.9	356 23.7	S21 31.0	Alioth	166 16.7	N55 51.4
E 07	303 13.4	314 16.7	07.1	238 37.5	22.5	39 20.9	40.9	11 26.1	31.0	Alkaid	152 55.3	N49 13.1
D 08	318 15.8	329 16.3	06.0	253 38.2	22.8	54 23.3	40.9	26 28.5	31.0	Alnair	27 39.1	S46 52.0
N 09	333 18.3	344 15.9	.. 04.9	268 38.9	.. 23.1	69 25.8	.. 40.9	41 30.9	.. 31.0	Alnilam	275 42.5	S 1 11.7
E 10	348 20.8	359 15.6	03.7	283 39.6	23.4	84 28.3	40.9	56 33.2	30.9	Alphard	217 52.1	S 8 44.7
S 11	3 23.2	14 15.2	02.6	298 40.3	23.6	99 30.7	40.9	71 35.6	30.9			
D 12	18 25.7	29 14.9	S 6 01.5	313 41.1	N22 23.9	114 33.2	S22 40.9	86 38.0	S21 30.9	Alphecca	126 07.4	N26 39.0
A 13	33 28.2	44 14.5	6 00.4	328 41.8	24.2	129 35.6	40.9	101 40.4	30.9	Alpheratz	357 39.8	N29 11.5
Y 14	48 30.6	59 14.1	5 59.3	343 42.5	24.5	144 38.1	40.9	116 42.8	30.9	Altair	62 04.4	N 8 55.0
15	63 33.1	74 13.8	.. 58.2	358 43.2	.. 24.8	159 40.6	.. 40.9	131 45.1	.. 30.9	Ankaa	353 12.2	S42 12.2
16	78 35.5	89 13.4	57.1	13 43.9	25.1	174 43.0	40.9	146 47.5	30.9	Antares	112 21.2	S26 28.3
17	93 38.0	104 13.0	56.0	28 44.6	25.4	189 45.5	40.9	161 49.9	30.9			
18	108 40.5	119 12.7	S 5 54.9	43 45.3	N22 25.7	204 48.0	S22 40.9	176 52.3	S21 30.9	Arcturus	145 51.8	N19 04.9
19	123 42.9	134 12.3	53.8	58 46.0	26.0	219 50.4	40.9	191 54.7	30.9	Atria	107 19.1	S69 03.4
20	138 45.4	149 12.0	52.7	73 46.8	26.3	234 52.9	40.9	206 57.0	30.8	Avior	234 16.3	S59 34.6
21	153 47.9	164 11.6	.. 51.6	88 47.5	.. 26.6	249 55.3	.. 40.9	221 59.4	.. 30.8	Bellatrix	278 27.9	N 6 21.8
22	168 50.3	179 11.2	50.5	103 48.2	26.9	264 57.8	40.9	237 01.8	30.8	Betelgeuse	270 57.2	N 7 24.4
23	183 52.8	194 10.9	49.3	118 48.9	27.2	280 00.3	40.9	252 04.2	30.8			
11 00	198 55.3	209 10.5	S 5 48.2	133 49.6	N22 27.4	295 02.7	S22 40.9	267 06.6	S21 30.8	Canopus	263 54.5	S52 42.8
01	213 57.7	224 10.2	47.1	148 50.3	27.7	310 05.2	40.9	282 08.9	30.8	Capella	280 28.9	N46 01.0
02	229 00.2	239 09.8	46.0	163 51.0	28.0	325 07.7	40.9	297 11.3	30.8	Deneb	49 28.9	N45 20.7
03	244 02.6	254 09.4	.. 44.9	178 51.7	.. 28.3	340 10.1	.. 40.9	312 13.7	.. 30.8	Denebola	182 29.4	N14 27.9
04	259 05.1	269 09.1	43.8	193 52.4	28.6	355 12.6	40.9	327 16.1	30.8	Diphda	348 52.3	S17 53.1
05	274 07.6	284 08.7	42.7	208 53.2	28.9	10 15.1	40.9	342 18.5	30.8			
T 06	289 10.0	299 08.4	S 5 41.6	223 53.9	N22 29.2	25 17.6	S22 40.9	357 20.9	S21 30.7	Dubhe	193 46.3	N61 39.0
H 07	304 12.5	314 08.0	40.5	238 54.6	29.5	40 20.0	40.9	12 23.2	30.7	Elnath	278 07.8	N28 37.3
U 08	319 15.0	329 07.6	39.3	253 55.3	29.7	55 22.5	40.9	27 25.6	30.7	Eltanin	90 44.1	N51 29.0
R 09	334 17.4	344 07.3	.. 38.2	268 56.0	.. 30.0	70 25.0	.. 40.9	42 28.0	.. 30.7	Enif	33 43.4	N 9 57.6
S 10	349 19.9	359 06.9	37.1	283 56.7	30.3	85 27.4	40.9	57 30.4	30.7	Fomalhaut	15 19.9	S29 31.3
D 11	4 22.4	14 06.6	36.0	298 57.4	30.6	100 29.9	40.9	72 32.8	30.7			
A 12	19 24.8	29 06.2	S 5 34.9	313 58.1	N22 30.9	115 32.4	S22 40.9	87 35.2	S21 30.7	Gacrux	171 55.9	S57 13.3
Y 13	34 27.3	44 05.9	33.8	328 58.8	31.2	130 34.8	40.9	102 37.5	30.7	Gienah	175 47.9	S17 39.0
14	49 29.8	59 05.5	32.7	343 59.5	31.5	145 37.3	40.9	117 39.9	30.7	Hadar	148 41.6	S60 27.8
15	64 32.2	74 05.1	.. 31.6	359 00.3	.. 31.7	160 39.8	.. 40.9	132 42.3	.. 30.7	Hamal	327 56.6	N23 32.9
16	79 34.7	89 04.8	30.4	14 01.0	32.0	175 42.3	40.9	147 44.7	30.7	Kaus Aust.	83 38.5	S34 22.3
17	94 37.1	104 04.4	29.3	29 01.7	32.3	190 44.7	40.9	162 47.1	30.6			
18	109 39.6	119 04.1	S 5 28.2	44 02.4	N22 32.6	205 47.2	S22 40.9	177 49.5	S21 30.6	Kochab	137 19.0	N74 04.6
19	124 42.1	134 03.7	27.1	59 03.1	32.9	220 49.7	40.9	192 51.9	30.6	Markab	13 34.7	N15 18.3
20	139 44.5	149 03.4	26.0	74 03.8	33.2	235 52.2	40.9	207 54.2	30.6	Menkar	314 11.2	N 4 09.6
21	154 47.0	164 03.0	.. 24.9	89 04.5	.. 33.5	250 54.6	.. 40.9	222 56.6	.. 30.6	Menkent	148 02.5	S36 27.8
22	169 49.5	179 02.7	23.7	104 05.2	33.7	265 57.1	40.9	237 59.0	30.6	Miaplacidus	221 38.5	S69 48.1
23	184 51.9	194 02.3	22.6	119 05.9	34.0	280 59.6	40.9	253 01.4	30.6			
12 00	199 54.4	209 01.9	S 5 21.5	134 06.6	N22 34.3	296 02.0	S22 40.9	268 03.8	S21 30.6	Mirfak	308 35.1	N49 55.6
01	214 56.9	224 01.6	20.4	149 07.3	34.6	311 04.5	40.9	283 06.2	30.6	Nunki	75 53.4	S26 16.2
02	229 59.3	239 01.2	19.3	164 08.1	34.9	326 07.0	40.9	298 08.6	30.6	Peacock	53 13.2	S56 40.1
03	245 01.8	254 00.9	.. 18.2	179 08.8	.. 35.1	341 09.5	.. 40.9	313 10.9	.. 30.5	Pollux	243 22.9	N27 58.7
04	260 04.3	269 00.5	17.0	194 09.5	35.4	356 12.0	40.9	328 13.3	30.5	Procyon	244 55.6	N 5 10.4
05	275 06.7	284 00.2	15.9	209 10.2	35.7	11 14.4	40.9	343 15.7	30.5			
06	290 09.2	298 59.8	S 5 14.8	224 10.9	N22 36.0	26 16.9	S22 40.9	358 18.1	S21 30.5	Rasalhague	96 02.6	N12 32.7
F 07	305 11.6	313 59.5	13.7	239 11.6	36.3	41 19.4	40.9	13 20.5	30.5	Regulus	207 39.1	N11 52.3
R 08	320 14.1	328 59.1	12.6	254 12.3	36.5	56 21.9	40.9	28 22.9	30.5	Rigel	281 08.4	S 8 11.1
I 09	335 16.6	343 58.8	.. 11.4	269 13.0	.. 36.8	71 24.3	.. 40.9	43 25.3	.. 30.5	Rigil Kent.	139 45.8	S60 54.7
D 10	350 19.0	358 58.4	10.3	284 13.7	37.1	86 26.8	40.9	58 27.6	30.5	Sabik	102 07.8	S15 44.8
A 11	5 21.5	13 58.0	09.2	299 14.4	37.4	101 29.3	40.9	73 30.0	30.5			
Y 12	20 24.0	28 57.7	S 5 08.1	314 15.1	N22 37.7	116 31.8	S22 40.9	88 32.4	S21 30.5	Schedar	349 36.6	N56 38.3
13	35 26.4	43 57.3	07.0	329 15.9	37.9	131 34.3	40.9	103 34.8	30.5	Shaula	96 16.4	S37 06.8
14	50 28.9	58 57.0	05.8	344 16.6	38.2	146 36.7	40.9	118 37.2	30.4	Sirius	258 30.3	S16 44.9
15	65 31.4	73 56.6	.. 04.7	359 17.3	.. 38.5	161 39.2	.. 40.9	133 39.6	.. 30.4	Spica	158 26.8	S11 15.7
16	80 33.8	88 56.3	03.6	14 18.0	38.8	176 41.7	40.9	148 42.0	30.4	Suhail	222 49.4	S43 30.9
17	95 36.3	103 55.9	02.5	29 18.7	39.0	191 44.2	40.9	163 44.4	30.4			
18	110 38.8	118 55.6	S 5 01.4	44 19.4	N22 39.3	206 46.7	S22 40.9	178 46.8	S21 30.4	Vega	80 36.2	N38 47.9
19	125 41.2	133 55.2	5 00.2	59 20.1	39.6	221 49.1	40.9	193 49.1	30.4	Zuben'ubi	137 00.7	S16 07.2
20	140 43.7	148 54.9	4 59.1	74 20.8	39.9	236 51.6	40.9	208 51.5	30.4			
21	155 46.1	163 54.5	.. 58.0	89 21.5	.. 40.1	251 54.1	.. 40.9	223 53.9	.. 30.4		SHA	Mer. Pass.
22	170 48.6	178 54.2	56.9	104 22.2	40.4	266 56.6	40.9	238 56.3	30.4	Venus	10 15.3	10 04
23	185 51.1	193 53.8	55.7	119 22.9	40.7	281 59.1	40.9	253 58.7	30.4	Mars	294 54.3	15 04
Mer.Pass. 10 42.6		v −0.4 d 1.1		v 0.7 d 0.3		v 2.5 d 0.0		v 2.4 d 0.0		Jupiter	96 07.5	4 19
										Saturn	68 11.3	6 11

© British Crown Copyright 2018. All rights reserved.

UT	SUN GHA	SUN Dec	MOON GHA	v	Dec	d	HP
d h	° ′	° ′	° ′	′	° ′	′	′
10 00	179 37.0	N 7 45.5	124 12.9	8.8	N19 30.7	5.9	57.3
01	194 37.1	46.5	138 40.7	8.7	19 36.6	5.9	57.3
02	209 37.3	47.4	153 08.4	8.7	19 42.5	5.7	57.4
03	224 37.5	.. 48.3	167 36.1	8.6	19 48.2	5.6	57.4
04	239 37.7	49.3	182 03.7	8.5	19 53.8	5.5	57.4
05	254 37.8	50.2	196 31.2	8.5	19 59.3	5.4	57.4
W 06	269 38.0	N 7 51.1	210 58.7	8.4	N20 04.7	5.3	57.5
E 07	284 38.2	52.0	225 26.1	8.4	20 10.0	5.2	57.5
D 08	299 38.3	53.0	239 53.5	8.2	20 15.2	5.0	57.5
N 09	314 38.5	.. 53.9	254 20.7	8.2	20 20.2	5.0	57.5
E 10	329 38.7	54.8	268 47.9	8.2	20 25.2	4.8	57.5
S 11	344 38.8	55.7	283 15.1	8.1	20 30.0	4.7	57.6
D 12	359 39.0	N 7 56.7	297 42.2	8.0	N20 34.7	4.6	57.6
A 13	14 39.2	57.6	312 09.2	8.0	20 39.3	4.5	57.6
Y 14	29 39.3	58.5	326 36.2	7.9	20 43.8	4.4	57.6
15	44 39.5	7 59.4	341 03.1	7.8	20 48.2	4.2	57.7
16	59 39.7	8 00.4	355 29.9	7.8	20 52.4	4.1	57.7
17	74 39.8	01.3	9 56.7	7.8	20 56.5	4.1	57.7
18	89 40.0	N 8 02.2	24 23.5	7.6	N21 00.6	3.8	57.7
19	104 40.2	03.1	38 50.1	7.6	21 04.4	3.8	57.7
20	119 40.3	04.0	53 16.7	7.6	21 08.2	3.6	57.8
21	134 40.5	.. 05.0	67 43.3	7.5	21 11.8	3.5	57.8
22	149 40.7	05.9	82 09.8	7.5	21 15.3	3.4	57.8
23	164 40.8	06.8	96 36.3	7.3	21 18.7	3.3	57.8
11 00	179 41.0	N 8 07.7	111 02.6	7.4	N21 22.0	3.1	57.9
01	194 41.2	08.7	125 29.0	7.3	21 25.1	3.1	57.9
02	209 41.3	09.6	139 55.3	7.2	21 28.2	2.8	57.9
03	224 41.5	.. 10.5	154 21.5	7.2	21 31.0	2.8	57.9
04	239 41.7	11.4	168 47.7	7.1	21 33.8	2.6	58.0
05	254 41.8	12.3	183 13.8	7.1	21 36.4	2.5	58.0
T 06	269 42.0	N 8 13.3	197 39.9	7.1	N21 38.9	2.4	58.0
H 07	284 42.2	14.2	212 06.0	7.0	21 41.3	2.2	58.0
U 08	299 42.3	15.1	226 32.0	6.9	21 43.5	2.1	58.0
R 09	314 42.5	.. 16.0	240 57.9	6.9	21 45.6	2.0	58.1
S 10	329 42.6	16.9	255 23.8	6.9	21 47.6	1.8	58.1
D 11	344 42.8	17.9	269 49.7	6.8	21 49.4	1.8	58.1
A 12	359 43.0	N 8 18.8	284 15.5	6.8	N21 51.2	1.5	58.1
Y 13	14 43.1	19.7	298 41.3	6.7	21 52.7	1.5	58.2
14	29 43.3	20.6	313 07.0	6.7	21 54.2	1.3	58.2
15	44 43.5	.. 21.5	327 32.7	6.7	21 55.5	1.1	58.2
16	59 43.6	22.5	341 58.4	6.6	21 56.6	1.1	58.2
17	74 43.8	23.4	356 24.0	6.6	21 57.7	0.9	58.3
18	89 44.0	N 8 24.3	10 49.6	6.5	N21 58.6	0.7	58.3
19	104 44.1	25.2	25 15.1	6.6	21 59.3	0.7	58.3
20	119 44.3	26.1	39 40.7	6.5	22 00.0	0.4	58.3
21	134 44.5	.. 27.0	54 06.2	6.4	22 00.4	0.4	58.3
22	149 44.6	28.0	68 31.6	6.4	22 00.8	0.2	58.4
23	164 44.8	28.9	82 57.0	6.4	22 01.0	0.1	58.4
12 00	179 44.9	N 8 29.8	97 22.4	6.4	N22 01.1	0.1	58.4
01	194 45.1	30.7	111 47.8	6.3	22 01.0	0.2	58.4
02	209 45.3	31.6	126 13.1	6.3	22 00.8	0.3	58.5
03	224 45.4	.. 32.5	140 38.4	6.3	22 00.5	0.5	58.5
04	239 45.6	33.5	155 03.7	6.3	22 00.0	0.7	58.5
05	254 45.8	34.4	169 29.0	6.2	21 59.3	0.7	58.5
F 06	269 45.9	N 8 35.3	183 54.2	6.3	N21 58.6	0.9	58.6
R 07	284 46.1	36.2	198 19.5	6.2	21 57.7	1.1	58.6
I 08	299 46.2	37.1	212 44.7	6.1	21 56.6	1.2	58.6
D 09	314 46.4	.. 38.0	227 09.8	6.2	21 55.4	1.3	58.6
A 10	329 46.6	38.9	241 35.0	6.2	21 54.1	1.5	58.6
Y 11	344 46.7	39.9	256 00.2	6.1	21 52.6	1.6	58.7
12	359 46.9	N 8 40.8	270 25.3	6.1	N21 51.0	1.7	58.7
13	14 47.1	41.7	284 50.4	6.1	21 49.3	1.9	58.7
14	29 47.2	42.6	299 15.5	6.0	21 47.4	2.1	58.7
15	44 47.4	.. 43.5	313 40.6	6.1	21 45.3	2.1	58.8
16	59 47.5	44.4	328 05.7	6.1	21 43.2	2.4	58.8
17	74 47.7	45.3	342 30.8	6.1	21 40.8	2.4	58.8
18	89 47.9	N 8 46.2	356 55.9	6.0	N21 38.4	2.6	58.8
19	104 48.0	47.1	11 20.9	6.1	21 35.8	2.8	58.8
20	119 48.2	48.1	25 46.0	6.1	21 33.0	2.8	58.9
21	134 48.3	.. 49.0	40 11.1	6.0	21 30.2	3.1	58.9
22	149 48.5	49.9	54 36.1	6.1	21 27.1	3.1	58.9
23	164 48.7	50.8	69 01.2	6.0	N21 24.0	3.3	58.9
	SD 16.0	d 0.9	SD 15.7	15.8			16.0

Lat.	Twilight Naut.	Twilight Civil	Sunrise	Moonrise 10	11	12	13
°	h m	h m	h m	h m	h m	h m	h m
N 72	////	02 35	04 04	⬜	⬜	⬜	⬜
N 70	////	03 02	04 17	04 26	⬜	⬜	⬜
68	01 36	03 23	04 28	05 40	05 40	06 15	08 10
66	02 13	03 39	04 37	06 18	06 41	07 32	08 57
64	02 39	03 52	04 44	06 45	07 16	08 09	09 27
62	02 58	04 02	04 51	07 05	07 41	08 36	09 50
60	03 13	04 12	04 56	07 22	08 01	08 56	10 09
N 58	03 26	04 19	05 01	07 36	08 17	09 13	10 24
56	03 37	04 26	05 06	07 49	08 31	09 27	10 37
54	03 46	04 32	05 10	07 59	08 43	09 40	10 48
52	03 54	04 38	05 13	08 09	08 54	09 51	10 58
50	04 02	04 43	05 16	08 18	09 04	10 00	11 07
45	04 17	04 53	05 23	08 36	09 24	10 21	11 26
N 40	04 28	05 01	05 29	08 51	09 40	10 37	11 41
35	04 37	05 08	05 34	09 03	09 54	10 51	11 54
30	04 45	05 14	05 38	09 14	10 06	11 03	12 05
20	04 57	05 23	05 46	09 33	10 27	11 24	12 25
N 10	05 06	05 31	05 52	09 50	10 45	11 42	12 41
0	05 13	05 37	05 58	10 06	11 01	11 59	12 57
S 10	05 18	05 42	06 04	10 21	11 18	12 16	13 13
20	05 22	05 47	06 10	10 38	11 36	12 34	13 29
30	05 25	05 52	06 16	10 57	11 57	12 55	13 49
35	05 25	05 55	06 20	11 09	12 09	13 07	14 00
40	05 26	05 57	06 25	11 22	12 23	13 21	14 13
45	05 26	06 00	06 30	11 37	12 40	13 37	14 28
S 50	05 26	06 03	06 36	11 56	13 01	13 58	14 46
52	05 25	06 04	06 38	12 05	13 11	14 08	14 55
54	05 25	06 06	06 41	12 15	13 22	14 18	15 05
56	05 24	06 07	06 45	12 27	13 34	14 31	15 15
58	05 23	06 09	06 48	12 40	13 49	14 45	15 28
S 60	05 22	06 10	06 52	12 56	14 06	15 02	15 43

Lat.	Sunset	Twilight Civil	Twilight Naut.	Moonset 10	11	12	13
°	h m	h m	h m	h m	h m	h m	h m
N 72	20 02	21 33	////	⬜	⬜	⬜	⬜
N 70	19 48	21 04	////	03 08	⬜	⬜	⬜
68	19 37	20 43	22 35	01 54	03 49	05 14	05 21
66	19 28	20 27	21 54	01 17	02 48	03 57	04 33
64	19 20	20 13	21 28	00 51	02 14	03 20	04 02
62	19 13	20 02	21 08	00 30	01 49	02 53	03 39
60	19 08	19 53	20 52	00 14	01 29	02 32	03 21
N 58	19 02	19 45	20 39	00 00	01 13	02 15	03 05
56	18 58	19 38	20 27	24 59	00 59	02 01	02 52
54	18 54	19 31	20 18	24 47	00 47	01 49	02 40
52	18 50	19 26	20 09	24 37	00 37	01 38	02 30
50	18 47	19 21	20 02	24 27	00 27	01 28	02 21
45	18 40	19 10	19 47	24 07	00 07	01 08	02 01
N 40	18 34	19 02	19 35	23 51	24 51	00 51	01 46
35	18 29	18 55	19 26	23 38	24 37	00 37	01 32
30	18 25	18 49	19 18	23 26	24 25	00 25	01 21
20	18 17	18 39	19 06	23 06	24 04	00 04	01 01
N 10	18 10	18 32	18 56	22 48	23 46	24 43	00 43
0	18 04	18 25	18 50	22 32	23 29	24 27	00 27
S 10	17 59	18 20	18 44	22 16	23 12	24 10	00 10
20	17 52	18 15	18 40	21 58	22 53	23 53	24 54
30	17 45	18 09	18 37	21 38	22 32	23 32	24 36
35	17 41	18 07	18 36	21 26	22 20	23 20	24 25
40	17 37	18 04	18 36	21 13	22 06	23 07	24 13
45	17 32	18 01	18 35	20 57	21 49	22 50	23 59
S 50	17 26	17 58	18 36	20 37	21 28	22 30	23 41
52	17 23	17 57	18 36	20 28	21 19	22 21	23 33
54	17 20	17 56	18 37	20 18	21 07	22 10	23 23
56	17 17	17 54	18 37	20 06	20 55	21 58	23 13
58	17 13	17 53	18 38	19 52	20 40	21 43	23 01
S 60	17 09	17 51	18 39	19 37	20 23	21 27	22 46

Day	SUN Eqn. of Time 00h	SUN Eqn. of Time 12h	Mer. Pass.	MOON Mer. Pass. Upper	MOON Mer. Pass. Lower	Age	Phase
d	m s	m s	h m	h m	h m	d %	
10	01 32	01 24	12 01	16 19	03 51	05 26	
11	01 16	01 08	12 01	17 15	04 47	06 36	◑
12	01 01	00 53	12 01	18 13	05 44	07 47	

© British Crown Copyright 2018. All rights reserved.

2019 APRIL 13, 14, 15 (SAT., SUN., MON.)

78

UT	ARIES GHA	VENUS −3.9 GHA	Dec	MARS +1.5 GHA	Dec	JUPITER −2.3 GHA	Dec	SATURN +0.5 GHA	Dec
13 00	200 53.5	208 53.5	S 4 54.6	134 23.6	N22 41.0	297 01.6	S22 40.9	269 01.1	S21 30.4
01	215 56.0	223 53.1	53.5	149 24.3	41.2	312 04.0	40.9	284 03.5	30.4
02	230 58.5	238 52.8	52.4	164 25.1	41.5	327 06.5	40.9	299 05.9	30.3
03	246 00.9	253 52.4	.. 51.2	179 25.8	.. 41.8	342 09.0	.. 40.9	314 08.3	.. 30.3
04	261 03.4	268 52.1	50.1	194 26.5	42.1	357 11.5	40.9	329 10.7	30.3
05	276 05.9	283 51.7	49.0	209 27.2	42.3	12 14.0	40.9	344 13.0	30.3
S 06	291 08.3	298 51.4	S 4 47.9	224 27.9	N22 42.6	27 16.5	S22 40.9	359 15.4	S21 30.3
A 07	306 10.8	313 51.0	46.7	239 28.6	42.9	42 18.9	40.9	14 17.8	30.3
T 08	321 13.2	328 50.7	45.6	254 29.3	43.2	57 21.4	40.9	29 20.2	30.3
U 09	336 15.7	343 50.3	.. 44.5	269 30.0	.. 43.4	72 23.9	.. 40.9	44 22.6	.. 30.3
R 10	351 18.2	358 50.0	43.4	284 30.7	43.7	87 26.4	40.9	59 25.0	30.3
D 11	6 20.6	13 49.6	42.2	299 31.4	44.0	102 28.9	40.9	74 27.4	30.3
A 12	21 23.1	28 49.3	S 4 41.1	314 32.1	N22 44.2	117 31.4	S22 40.9	89 29.8	S21 30.3
Y 13	36 25.6	43 48.9	40.0	329 32.8	44.5	132 33.9	40.9	104 32.2	30.3
14	51 28.0	58 48.6	38.9	344 33.5	44.8	147 36.4	40.9	119 34.6	30.2
15	66 30.5	73 48.2	.. 37.7	359 34.2	.. 45.0	162 38.8	.. 40.9	134 37.0	.. 30.2
16	81 33.0	88 47.9	36.6	14 34.9	45.3	177 41.3	40.9	149 39.4	30.2
17	96 35.4	103 47.5	35.5	29 35.7	45.6	192 43.8	40.9	164 41.8	30.2
18	111 37.9	118 47.2	S 4 34.3	44 36.4	N22 45.9	207 46.3	S22 40.9	179 44.2	S21 30.2
19	126 40.4	133 46.8	33.2	59 37.1	46.1	222 48.8	40.8	194 46.5	30.2
20	141 42.8	148 46.5	32.1	74 37.8	46.4	237 51.3	40.8	209 48.9	30.2
21	156 45.3	163 46.1	.. 31.0	89 38.5	.. 46.7	252 53.8	.. 40.8	224 51.3	.. 30.2
22	171 47.7	178 45.8	29.8	104 39.2	46.9	267 56.3	40.8	239 53.7	30.2
23	186 50.2	193 45.4	28.7	119 39.9	47.2	282 58.8	40.8	254 56.1	30.2
14 00	201 52.7	208 45.1	S 4 27.6	134 40.6	N22 47.5	298 01.3	S22 40.8	269 58.5	S21 30.2
01	216 55.1	223 44.7	26.4	149 41.3	47.7	313 03.8	40.8	285 00.9	30.2
02	231 57.6	238 44.4	25.3	164 42.0	48.0	328 06.2	40.8	300 03.3	30.1
03	247 00.1	253 44.0	.. 24.2	179 42.7	.. 48.3	343 08.7	.. 40.8	315 05.7	.. 30.1
04	262 02.5	268 43.7	23.0	194 43.4	48.5	358 11.2	40.8	330 08.1	30.1
05	277 05.0	283 43.3	21.9	209 44.1	48.8	13 13.7	40.8	345 10.5	30.1
S 06	292 07.5	298 43.0	S 4 20.8	224 44.8	N22 49.1	28 16.2	S22 40.8	0 12.9	S21 30.1
U 07	307 09.9	313 42.7	19.6	239 45.5	49.3	43 18.7	40.8	15 15.3	30.1
N 08	322 12.4	328 42.3	18.5	254 46.2	49.6	58 21.2	40.8	30 17.7	30.1
D 09	337 14.9	343 42.0	.. 17.4	269 46.9	.. 49.8	73 23.7	.. 40.8	45 20.1	.. 30.1
A 10	352 17.3	358 41.6	16.3	284 47.7	50.1	88 26.2	40.8	60 22.5	30.1
Y 11	7 19.8	13 41.3	15.1	299 48.4	50.4	103 28.7	40.8	75 24.9	30.1
12	22 22.2	28 40.9	S 4 14.0	314 49.1	N22 50.6	118 31.2	S22 40.8	90 27.3	S21 30.1
13	37 24.7	43 40.6	12.9	329 49.8	50.9	133 33.7	40.8	105 29.7	30.1
14	52 27.2	58 40.2	11.7	344 50.5	51.2	148 36.2	40.8	120 32.1	30.0
15	67 29.6	73 39.9	.. 10.6	359 51.2	.. 51.4	163 38.7	.. 40.8	135 34.5	.. 30.0
16	82 32.1	88 39.5	09.5	14 51.9	51.7	178 41.2	40.8	150 36.9	30.0
17	97 34.6	103 39.2	08.3	29 52.6	51.9	193 43.7	40.8	165 39.2	30.0
18	112 37.0	118 38.9	S 4 07.2	44 53.3	N22 52.2	208 46.2	S22 40.8	180 41.6	S21 30.0
19	127 39.5	133 38.5	06.1	59 54.0	52.5	223 48.7	40.8	195 44.0	30.0
20	142 42.0	148 38.2	04.9	74 54.7	52.7	238 51.2	40.8	210 46.4	30.0
21	157 44.4	163 37.8	.. 03.8	89 55.4	.. 53.0	253 53.7	.. 40.8	225 48.8	.. 30.0
22	172 46.9	178 37.5	02.6	104 56.1	53.2	268 56.2	40.8	240 51.2	30.0
23	187 49.4	193 37.1	01.5	119 56.8	53.5	283 58.7	40.8	255 53.6	30.0
15 00	202 51.8	208 36.8	S 4 00.4	134 57.5	N22 53.8	299 01.2	S22 40.8	270 56.0	S21 30.0
01	217 54.3	223 36.4	3 59.2	149 58.2	54.0	314 03.7	40.8	285 58.4	30.0
02	232 56.7	238 36.1	58.1	164 58.9	54.3	329 06.2	40.8	301 00.8	30.0
03	247 59.2	253 35.8	.. 57.0	179 59.6	.. 54.5	344 08.7	.. 40.8	316 03.2	.. 30.0
04	263 01.7	268 35.4	55.8	195 00.3	54.8	359 11.2	40.8	331 05.6	29.9
05	278 04.1	283 35.1	54.7	210 01.0	55.0	14 13.7	40.8	346 08.0	29.9
M 06	293 06.6	298 34.7	S 3 53.6	225 01.7	N22 55.3	29 16.2	S22 40.8	1 10.4	S21 29.9
O 07	308 09.1	313 34.4	52.4	240 02.4	55.6	44 18.7	40.8	16 12.8	29.9
N 08	323 11.5	328 34.0	51.3	255 03.1	55.8	59 21.2	40.8	31 15.2	29.9
D 09	338 14.0	343 33.7	.. 50.1	270 03.9	.. 56.1	74 23.7	.. 40.8	46 17.6	.. 29.9
A 10	353 16.5	358 33.4	49.0	285 04.6	56.3	89 26.2	40.8	61 20.0	29.9
Y 11	8 18.9	13 33.0	47.9	300 05.3	56.6	104 28.7	40.8	76 22.4	29.9
12	23 21.4	28 32.7	S 3 46.7	315 06.0	N22 56.8	119 31.2	S22 40.8	91 24.8	S21 29.9
13	38 23.8	43 32.3	45.6	330 06.7	57.1	134 33.7	40.8	106 27.2	29.9
14	53 26.3	58 32.0	44.5	345 07.4	57.3	149 36.2	40.8	121 29.6	29.9
15	68 28.8	73 31.6	.. 43.3	0 08.1	.. 57.6	164 38.7	.. 40.8	136 32.0	.. 29.9
16	83 31.2	88 31.3	42.2	15 08.8	57.9	179 41.2	40.8	151 34.4	29.9
17	98 33.7	103 31.0	41.0	30 09.5	58.1	194 43.7	40.8	166 36.8	29.8
18	113 36.2	118 30.6	S 3 39.9	45 10.2	N22 58.4	209 46.2	S22 40.8	181 39.2	S21 29.8
19	128 38.6	133 30.3	38.8	60 10.9	58.6	224 48.7	40.8	196 41.6	29.8
20	143 41.1	148 29.9	37.6	75 11.6	58.9	239 51.2	40.8	211 44.0	29.8
21	158 43.6	163 29.6	.. 36.5	90 12.3	.. 59.1	254 53.8	.. 40.8	226 46.4	.. 29.8
22	173 46.0	178 29.3	35.3	105 13.0	59.4	269 56.3	40.8	241 48.9	29.8
23	188 48.5	193 28.9	34.2	120 13.7	59.6	284 58.8	40.8	256 51.3	29.8
Mer.Pass.	10 30.8	v −0.3	d 1.1	v 0.7	d 0.3	v 2.5	d 0.0	v 2.4	d 0.0

STARS

Name	SHA	Dec
Acamar	315 15.7	S40 14.0
Achernar	335 24.4	S57 08.5
Acrux	173 04.2	S63 12.4
Adhara	255 09.5	S29 00.2
Aldebaran	290 45.1	N16 32.6
Alioth	166 16.7	N55 51.4
Alkaid	152 55.3	N49 13.1
Alnair	27 39.0	S46 52.0
Alnilam	275 42.5	S 1 11.7
Alphard	217 52.1	S 8 44.7
Alphecca	126 07.3	N26 39.0
Alpheratz	357 39.7	N29 11.5
Altair	62 04.4	N 8 55.0
Ankaa	353 12.2	S42 12.2
Antares	112 21.1	S26 28.3
Arcturus	145 51.8	N19 05.0
Atria	107 19.0	S69 03.4
Avior	234 16.3	S59 34.6
Bellatrix	278 27.9	N 6 21.8
Betelgeuse	270 57.2	N 7 24.4
Canopus	263 54.6	S52 42.8
Capella	280 28.9	N46 01.0
Deneb	49 28.9	N45 20.7
Denebola	182 29.4	N14 27.9
Diphda	348 52.2	S17 53.1
Dubhe	193 46.4	N61 39.0
Elnath	278 07.8	N28 37.3
Eltanin	90 44.1	N51 29.0
Enif	33 43.4	N 9 57.6
Fomalhaut	15 19.9	S29 31.3
Gacrux	171 55.9	S57 13.3
Gienah	175 47.9	S17 39.0
Hadar	148 41.6	S60 27.8
Hamal	327 56.6	N23 32.9
Kaus Aust.	83 38.4	S34 22.3
Kochab	137 19.0	N74 04.6
Markab	13 34.6	N15 18.3
Menkar	314 11.2	N 4 09.6
Menkent	148 02.5	S36 27.8
Miaplacidus	221 38.5	S69 48.1
Mirfak	308 35.1	N49 55.6
Nunki	75 53.4	S26 16.2
Peacock	53 13.1	S56 40.1
Pollux	243 22.9	N27 58.7
Procyon	244 55.6	N 5 10.4
Rasalhague	96 02.6	N12 32.7
Regulus	207 39.1	N11 52.3
Rigel	281 08.4	S 8 11.1
Rigil Kent.	139 45.7	S60 54.7
Sabik	102 07.8	S15 44.8
Schedar	349 36.6	N56 38.3
Shaula	96 16.3	S37 06.8
Sirius	258 30.3	S16 44.9
Spica	158 26.8	S11 15.7
Suhail	222 49.4	S43 30.9
Vega	80 36.2	N38 47.9
Zuben'ubi	137 00.7	S16 07.2

	SHA	Mer.Pass.
Venus	6 52.4	10 05
Mars	292 47.9	15 01
Jupiter	96 08.6	4 07
Saturn	68 05.8	5 59

© British Crown Copyright 2018. All rights reserved.

UT	SUN GHA	SUN Dec	MOON GHA	v	Dec	d	HP
d h	° ′	° ′	° ′	′	° ′	′	′
13 00	179 48.8	N 8 51.7	83 26.2	6.1	N21 20.7	3.5	59.0
01	194 49.0	52.6	97 51.3	6.0	21 17.2	3.6	59.0
02	209 49.1	53.5	112 16.3	6.1	21 13.6	3.7	59.0
03	224 49.3 ..	54.4	126 41.4	6.1	21 09.9	3.9	59.0
04	239 49.5	55.3	141 06.5	6.0	21 06.0	4.0	59.0
05	254 49.6	56.2	155 31.5	6.1	21 02.0	4.1	59.1
06	269 49.8	N 8 57.2	169 56.6	6.1	N20 57.9	4.3	59.1
07	284 49.9	58.1	184 21.7	6.1	20 53.6	4.4	59.1
S 08	299 50.1	59.0	198 46.8	6.1	20 49.2	4.6	59.1
A 09	314 50.3	8 59.9	213 11.9	6.1	20 44.6	4.7	59.1
T 10	329 50.4	9 00.8	227 37.0	6.1	20 39.9	4.8	59.2
U 11	344 50.6	01.7	242 02.1	6.1	20 35.1	5.0	59.2
R 12	359 50.7	N 9 02.6	256 27.2	6.2	N20 30.1	5.1	59.2
D 13	14 50.9	03.5	270 52.4	6.2	20 25.0	5.3	59.2
A 14	29 51.1	04.4	285 17.6	6.1	20 19.7	5.3	59.2
Y 15	44 51.2 ..	05.3	299 42.7	6.2	20 14.4	5.6	59.3
16	59 51.4	06.2	314 07.9	6.2	20 08.8	5.6	59.3
17	74 51.5	07.1	328 33.2	6.2	20 03.2	5.8	59.3
18	89 51.7	N 9 08.0	342 58.4	6.3	N19 57.4	5.9	59.3
19	104 51.8	08.9	357 23.7	6.2	19 51.5	6.1	59.3
20	119 52.0	09.8	11 48.9	6.3	19 45.4	6.2	59.4
21	134 52.2 ..	10.8	26 14.2	6.4	19 39.2	6.3	59.4
22	149 52.3	11.7	40 39.6	6.3	19 32.9	6.4	59.4
23	164 52.5	12.6	55 04.9	6.4	19 26.5	6.6	59.4
14 00	179 52.6	N 9 13.5	69 30.3	6.4	N19 19.9	6.7	59.4
01	194 52.8	14.4	83 55.7	6.4	19 13.2	6.8	59.5
02	209 52.9	15.3	98 21.1	6.4	19 06.4	7.0	59.5
03	224 53.1 ..	16.2	112 46.5	6.5	18 59.4	7.1	59.5
04	239 53.3	17.1	127 12.0	6.5	18 52.3	7.2	59.5
05	254 53.4	18.0	141 37.5	6.6	18 45.1	7.4	59.5
06	269 53.6	N 9 18.9	156 03.1	6.5	N18 37.7	7.4	59.6
07	284 53.7	19.8	170 28.6	6.6	18 30.3	7.6	59.6
S 08	299 53.9	20.7	184 54.2	6.6	18 22.7	7.7	59.6
U 09	314 54.0 ..	21.6	199 19.8	6.5	18 15.0	7.9	59.6
N 10	329 54.2	22.5	213 45.5	6.7	18 07.1	7.9	59.6
D 11	344 54.4	23.4	228 11.2	6.7	17 59.2	8.1	59.6
A 12	359 54.5	N 9 24.3	242 36.9	6.7	N17 51.1	8.2	59.7
Y 13	14 54.7	25.2	257 02.6	6.8	17 42.9	8.3	59.7
14	29 54.8	26.1	271 28.4	6.9	17 34.6	8.5	59.7
15	44 55.0 ..	27.0	285 54.3	6.8	17 26.1	8.5	59.7
16	59 55.1	27.9	300 20.1	6.9	17 17.6	8.7	59.7
17	74 55.3	28.8	314 46.0	6.9	17 08.9	8.8	59.7
18	89 55.4	N 9 29.7	329 11.9	7.0	N17 00.1	8.9	59.8
19	104 55.6	30.6	343 37.9	7.0	16 51.2	9.0	59.8
20	119 55.7	31.5	358 03.9	7.0	16 42.2	9.1	59.8
21	134 55.9 ..	32.4	12 29.9	7.1	16 33.1	9.3	59.8
22	149 56.1	33.3	26 56.0	7.1	16 23.8	9.3	59.8
23	164 56.2	34.2	41 22.1	7.2	16 14.5	9.5	59.8
15 00	179 56.4	N 9 35.1	55 48.3	7.1	N16 05.0	9.5	59.9
01	194 56.5	36.0	70 14.4	7.3	15 55.5	9.7	59.9
02	209 56.7	36.9	84 40.7	7.3	15 45.8	9.8	59.9
03	224 56.8 ..	37.8	99 06.9	7.3	15 36.0	9.8	59.9
04	239 57.0	38.7	113 33.2	7.4	15 26.2	10.0	59.9
05	254 57.1	39.5	127 59.6	7.4	15 16.2	10.1	59.9
06	269 57.3	N 9 40.4	142 26.0	7.4	N15 06.1	10.2	59.9
07	284 57.4	41.3	156 52.4	7.5	14 55.9	10.2	59.9
08	299 57.6	42.2	171 18.9	7.5	14 45.7	10.4	60.0
M 09	314 57.7 ..	43.1	185 45.4	7.5	14 35.3	10.5	60.0
O 10	329 57.9	44.0	200 11.9	7.6	14 24.8	10.6	60.0
N 11	344 58.0	44.9	214 38.5	7.6	14 14.2	10.6	60.0
D 12	359 58.2	N 9 45.8	229 05.1	7.7	N14 03.6	10.8	60.0
A 13	14 58.3	46.7	243 31.8	7.7	13 52.8	10.8	60.0
Y 14	29 58.5	47.6	257 58.5	7.7	13 42.0	11.0	60.0
15	44 58.7 ..	48.5	272 25.2	7.8	13 31.0	11.0	60.0
16	59 58.8	49.4	286 52.0	7.8	13 20.0	11.1	60.0
17	74 59.0	50.3	301 18.8	7.9	13 08.9	11.2	60.1
18	89 59.1	N 9 51.2	315 45.7	7.9	N12 57.7	11.3	60.1
19	104 59.3	52.1	330 12.6	7.9	12 46.4	11.4	60.1
20	119 59.4	52.9	344 39.5	8.0	12 35.0	11.4	60.1
21	134 59.6 ..	53.8	359 06.5	8.0	12 23.6	11.6	60.1
22	149 59.7	54.7	13 33.5	8.1	12 12.0	11.6	60.1
23	164 59.9	55.6	28 00.6	8.1	N12 00.4	11.7	60.1
	SD 16.0	d 0.9	SD 16.1		16.3		16.3

Lat.	Twilight Naut.	Twilight Civil	Sunrise	Moonrise 13	Moonrise 14	Moonrise 15	Moonrise 16
°	h m	h m	h m	h m	h m	h m	h m
N 72	////	02 10	03 47	□	□	11 22	13 46
N 70	////	02 43	04 02	□	09 30	11 52	14 00
68	01 01	03 07	04 15	08 10	10 13	12 14	14 11
66	01 52	03 25	04 25	08 57	10 41	12 31	14 21
64	02 22	03 40	04 34	09 27	11 03	12 45	14 29
62	02 44	03 52	04 41	09 50	11 20	12 56	14 35
60	03 01	04 02	04 47	10 09	11 34	13 06	14 41
N 58	03 16	04 10	04 53	10 24	11 46	13 15	14 46
56	03 28	04 18	04 58	10 37	11 57	13 22	14 51
54	03 38	04 25	05 02	10 48	12 06	13 29	14 55
52	03 47	04 31	05 06	10 58	12 14	13 35	14 58
50	03 54	04 36	05 10	11 07	12 21	13 41	15 02
45	04 11	04 47	05 18	11 26	12 37	13 52	15 09
N 40	04 23	04 56	05 24	11 41	12 50	14 02	15 15
35	04 33	05 04	05 30	11 54	13 01	14 10	15 20
30	04 41	05 10	05 35	12 05	13 11	14 17	15 24
20	04 54	05 21	05 43	12 25	13 27	14 30	15 32
N 10	05 04	05 29	05 50	12 41	13 41	14 41	15 39
0	05 12	05 36	05 57	12 57	13 55	14 51	15 45
S 10	05 18	05 42	06 04	13 13	14 08	15 01	15 51
20	05 23	05 48	06 11	13 29	14 22	15 11	15 58
30	05 26	05 54	06 18	13 49	14 38	15 24	16 06
35	05 28	05 57	06 23	14 00	14 48	15 31	16 10
40	05 29	06 00	06 28	14 13	14 58	15 39	16 15
45	05 30	06 04	06 33	14 28	15 11	15 48	16 21
S 50	05 30	06 07	06 40	14 46	15 26	15 59	16 28
52	05 30	06 09	06 43	14 55	15 33	16 04	16 31
54	05 30	06 11	06 47	15 05	15 41	16 10	16 34
56	05 30	06 13	06 51	15 15	15 50	16 16	16 38
58	05 29	06 15	06 55	15 28	16 00	16 23	16 42
S 60	05 29	06 17	07 00	15 43	16 11	16 31	16 47

Lat.	Sunset	Twilight Civil	Twilight Naut.	Moonset 13	Moonset 14	Moonset 15	Moonset 16
°	h m	h m	h m	h m	h m	h m	h m
N 72	20 18	21 58	////	□	□	06 11	05 42
N 70	20 01	21 22	////	□	06 02	05 39	05 25
68	19 48	20 58	23 15	05 21	05 19	05 16	05 12
66	19 38	20 39	22 15	04 33	04 50	04 57	05 01
64	19 29	20 24	21 43	04 02	04 27	04 42	04 52
62	19 21	20 11	21 20	03 39	04 10	04 30	04 44
60	19 15	20 01	21 02	03 21	03 55	04 19	04 37
N 58	19 09	19 52	20 48	03 05	03 42	04 09	04 31
56	19 04	19 44	20 35	02 52	03 31	04 01	04 25
54	19 00	19 37	20 25	02 40	03 21	03 54	04 20
52	18 55	19 31	20 16	02 30	03 13	03 47	04 16
50	18 52	19 26	20 08	02 21	03 05	03 41	04 12
45	18 44	19 14	19 51	02 01	02 48	03 28	04 03
N 40	18 37	19 05	19 39	01 46	02 34	03 17	03 56
35	18 31	18 57	19 28	01 32	02 23	03 08	03 49
30	18 26	18 51	19 20	01 21	02 12	03 00	03 43
20	18 18	18 40	19 07	01 01	01 55	02 46	03 34
N 10	18 11	18 32	18 57	00 43	01 39	02 33	03 25
0	18 04	18 25	18 49	00 27	01 25	02 21	03 17
S 10	17 57	18 18	18 43	00 10	01 10	02 10	03 08
20	17 50	18 12	18 38	24 54	00 54	01 57	02 59
30	17 42	18 06	18 33	24 36	00 36	01 42	02 49
35	17 38	18 03	18 33	24 25	00 25	01 34	02 43
40	17 33	18 00	18 31	24 13	00 13	01 24	02 36
45	17 27	17 56	18 30	23 59	25 12	01 12	02 28
S 50	17 20	17 52	18 30	23 41	24 58	00 58	02 19
52	17 17	17 51	18 30	23 33	24 52	00 52	02 14
54	17 13	17 49	18 30	23 23	24 44	00 44	02 09
56	17 09	17 47	18 30	23 13	24 36	00 36	02 04
58	17 05	17 45	18 30	23 01	24 27	00 27	01 58
S 60	17 00	17 43	18 31	22 46	24 16	00 16	01 51

Day	SUN Eqn. of Time 00h	SUN Eqn. of Time 12h	SUN Mer. Pass.	MOON Mer. Pass. Upper	MOON Mer. Pass. Lower	Age	Phase
d	m s	m s	h m	h m	h m	d	%
13	00 45	00 37	12 01	19 11	06 42	08	58
14	00 30	00 22	12 00	20 08	07 40	09	69
15	00 15	00 08	12 00	21 04	08 36	10	79

© British Crown Copyright 2018. All rights reserved.

UT	ARIES	VENUS −3.9		MARS +1.6		JUPITER −2.4		SATURN +0.5		STARS		
	GHA	GHA	Dec	GHA	Dec	GHA	Dec	GHA	Dec	Name	SHA	Dec
d h	° ′	° ′	° ′	° ′	° ′	° ′	° ′	° ′	° ′		° ′	° ′
16 00	203 51.0	208 28.6	S 3 33.1	135 14.4	N22 59.9	300 01.3	S22 40.8	271 53.7	S21 29.8	Acamar	315 15.7	S40 14.0
01	218 53.4	223 28.2	31.9	150 15.1	23 00.1	315 03.8	40.8	286 56.1	29.8	Achernar	335 24.4	S57 08.5
02	233 55.9	238 27.9	30.8	165 15.8	00.4	330 06.3	40.8	301 58.5	29.8	Acrux	173 04.2	S63 12.4
03	248 58.3	253 27.6	. . 29.6	180 16.5	. . 00.6	345 08.8	. . 40.8	317 00.9	. . 29.8	Adhara	255 09.5	S29 00.2
04	264 00.8	268 27.2	28.5	195 17.2	00.9	0 11.3	40.8	332 03.3	29.8	Aldebaran	290 45.1	N16 32.7
05	279 03.3	283 26.9	27.3	210 17.9	01.1	15 13.8	40.8	347 05.7	29.8			
06	294 05.7	298 26.5	S 3 26.2	225 18.6	N23 01.4	30 16.3	S22 40.8	2 08.1	S21 29.8	Alioth	166 16.7	N55 51.4
07	309 08.2	313 26.2	25.1	240 19.3	01.6	45 18.9	40.8	17 10.5	29.8	Alkaid	152 55.3	N49 13.1
T 08	324 10.7	328 25.9	23.9	255 20.0	01.9	60 21.4	40.8	32 12.9	29.7	Alnair	27 39.0	S46 52.0
U 09	339 13.1	343 25.5	. . 22.8	270 20.7	. . 02.1	75 23.9	. . 40.8	47 15.3	. . 29.7	Alnilam	275 42.5	S 1 11.6
E 10	354 15.6	358 25.2	21.6	285 21.4	02.4	90 26.4	40.8	62 17.7	29.7	Alphard	217 52.1	S 8 44.7
S 11	9 18.1	13 24.8	20.5	300 22.1	02.6	105 28.9	40.8	77 20.1	29.7			
D 12	24 20.5	28 24.5	S 3 19.3	315 22.8	N23 02.9	120 31.4	S22 40.8	92 22.5	S21 29.7	Alphecca	126 07.3	N26 39.0
A 13	39 23.0	43 24.2	18.2	330 23.5	03.1	135 33.9	40.8	107 24.9	29.7	Alpheratz	357 39.7	N29 11.5
Y 14	54 25.4	58 23.8	17.1	345 24.2	03.3	150 36.4	40.7	122 27.3	29.7	Altair	62 04.4	N 8 55.1
15	69 27.9	73 23.5	. . 15.9	0 24.9	. . 03.6	165 39.0	. . 40.7	137 29.7	. . 29.7	Ankaa	353 12.2	S42 12.2
16	84 30.4	88 23.1	14.8	15 25.6	03.8	180 41.5	40.7	152 32.1	29.7	Antares	112 21.1	S26 28.3
17	99 32.8	103 22.8	13.6	30 26.3	04.1	195 44.0	40.7	167 34.5	29.7			
18	114 35.3	118 22.5	S 3 12.5	45 27.0	N23 04.3	210 46.5	S22 40.7	182 36.9	S21 29.7	Arcturus	145 51.8	N19 05.0
19	129 37.8	133 22.1	11.3	60 27.7	04.6	225 49.0	40.7	197 39.3	29.7	Atria	107 19.0	S69 03.4
20	144 40.2	148 21.8	10.2	75 28.4	04.8	240 51.5	40.7	212 41.8	29.7	Avior	234 16.4	S59 34.6
21	159 42.7	163 21.4	. . 09.0	90 29.1	. . 05.1	255 54.0	. . 40.7	227 44.2	. . 29.7	Bellatrix	278 28.0	N 6 21.8
22	174 45.2	178 21.1	07.9	105 29.8	05.3	270 56.6	40.7	242 46.6	29.7	Betelgeuse	270 57.2	N 7 24.4
23	189 47.6	193 20.8	06.8	120 30.5	05.6	285 59.1	40.7	257 49.0	29.6			
17 00	204 50.1	208 20.4	S 3 05.6	135 31.2	N23 05.8	301 01.6	S22 40.7	272 51.4	S21 29.6	Canopus	263 54.6	S52 42.8
01	219 52.6	223 20.1	04.5	150 31.9	06.0	316 04.1	40.7	287 53.8	29.6	Capella	280 28.9	N46 01.0
02	234 55.0	238 19.8	03.3	165 32.6	06.3	331 06.6	40.7	302 56.2	29.6	Deneb	49 28.9	N45 20.7
03	249 57.5	253 19.4	. . 02.2	180 33.3	. . 06.5	346 09.1	. . 40.7	317 58.6	. . 29.6	Denebola	182 29.4	N14 27.9
04	264 59.9	268 19.1	3 01.0	195 34.0	06.8	1 11.7	40.7	333 01.0	29.6	Diphda	348 52.2	S17 53.1
05	280 02.4	283 18.7	2 59.9	210 34.7	07.0	16 14.2	40.7	348 03.4	29.6			
06	295 04.9	298 18.4	S 2 58.7	225 35.4	N23 07.2	31 16.7	S22 40.7	3 05.8	S21 29.6	Dubhe	193 46.4	N61 39.0
W 07	310 07.3	313 18.1	57.6	240 36.1	07.5	46 19.2	40.7	18 08.2	29.6	Elnath	278 07.8	N28 37.3
E 08	325 09.8	328 17.7	56.4	255 36.8	07.7	61 21.7	40.7	33 10.6	29.6	Eltanin	90 44.0	N51 29.0
D 09	340 12.3	343 17.4	. . 55.3	270 37.5	. . 08.0	76 24.3	. . 40.7	48 13.1	. . 29.6	Enif	33 43.4	N 9 57.6
N 10	355 14.7	358 17.1	54.1	285 38.2	08.2	91 26.8	40.7	63 15.5	29.6	Fomalhaut	15 19.9	S29 31.3
E 11	10 17.2	13 16.7	53.0	300 39.0	08.4	106 29.3	40.7	78 17.9	29.6			
S 12	25 19.7	28 16.4	S 2 51.8	315 39.7	N23 08.7	121 31.8	S22 40.7	93 20.3	S21 29.6	Gacrux	171 55.9	S57 13.3
D 13	40 22.1	43 16.0	50.7	330 40.4	08.9	136 34.3	40.7	108 22.7	29.6	Gienah	175 47.9	S17 39.0
A 14	55 24.6	58 15.7	49.6	345 41.1	09.2	151 36.9	40.7	123 25.1	29.6	Hadar	148 41.6	S60 27.8
Y 15	70 27.1	73 15.4	. . 48.4	0 41.8	. . 09.4	166 39.4	. . 40.7	138 27.5	. . 29.5	Hamal	327 56.6	N23 32.9
16	85 29.5	88 15.0	47.3	15 42.5	09.6	181 41.9	40.7	153 29.9	29.5	Kaus Aust.	83 38.4	S34 22.3
17	100 32.0	103 14.7	46.1	30 43.2	09.9	196 44.4	40.7	168 32.3	29.5			
18	115 34.4	118 14.4	S 2 45.0	45 43.9	N23 10.1	211 47.0	S22 40.7	183 34.7	S21 29.5	Kochab	137 19.0	N74 04.6
19	130 36.9	133 14.0	43.8	60 44.6	10.4	226 49.5	40.7	198 37.2	29.5	Markab	13 34.6	N15 18.3
20	145 39.4	148 13.7	42.7	75 45.3	10.6	241 52.0	40.7	213 39.6	29.5	Menkar	314 11.2	N 4 09.6
21	160 41.8	163 13.4	. . 41.5	90 46.0	. . 10.8	256 54.5	. . 40.7	228 42.0	. . 29.5	Menkent	148 02.5	S36 27.8
22	175 44.3	178 13.0	40.4	105 46.7	11.1	271 57.1	40.7	243 44.4	29.5	Miaplacidus	221 38.6	S69 48.1
23	190 46.8	193 12.7	39.2	120 47.4	11.3	286 59.6	40.7	258 46.8	29.5			
18 00	205 49.2	208 12.3	S 2 38.1	135 48.1	N23 11.5	302 02.1	S22 40.7	273 49.2	S21 29.5	Mirfak	308 35.1	N49 55.6
01	220 51.7	223 12.0	36.9	150 48.8	11.8	317 04.6	40.7	288 51.6	29.5	Nunki	75 53.3	S26 16.2
02	235 54.2	238 11.7	35.8	165 49.5	12.0	332 07.2	40.7	303 54.0	29.5	Peacock	53 13.1	S56 40.1
03	250 56.6	253 11.3	. . 34.6	180 50.2	. . 12.2	347 09.7	. . 40.7	318 56.4	. . 29.5	Pollux	243 22.9	N27 58.7
04	265 59.1	268 11.0	33.5	195 50.8	12.5	2 12.2	40.7	333 58.9	29.5	Procyon	244 55.6	N 5 10.4
05	281 01.5	283 10.7	32.3	210 51.5	12.7	17 14.7	40.7	349 01.3	29.5			
06	296 04.0	298 10.3	S 2 31.2	225 52.2	N23 12.9	32 17.3	S22 40.7	4 03.7	S21 29.5	Rasalhague	96 02.6	N12 32.7
07	311 06.5	313 10.0	30.0	240 52.9	13.2	47 19.8	40.7	19 06.1	29.5	Regulus	207 39.1	N11 52.3
T 08	326 08.9	328 09.7	28.9	255 53.6	13.4	62 22.3	40.7	34 08.5	29.5	Rigel	281 08.5	S 8 11.1
H 09	341 11.4	343 09.3	. . 27.7	270 54.3	. . 13.6	77 24.9	. . 40.7	49 10.9	. . 29.4	Rigil Kent.	139 45.7	S60 54.7
U 10	356 13.9	358 09.0	26.5	285 55.0	13.9	92 27.4	40.7	64 13.3	29.4	Sabik	102 07.8	S15 44.8
R 11	11 16.3	13 08.7	25.4	300 55.7	14.1	107 29.9	40.6	79 15.8	29.4			
S 12	26 18.8	28 08.3	S 2 24.2	315 56.4	N23 14.3	122 32.4	S22 40.6	94 18.2	S21 29.4	Schedar	349 36.6	N56 38.3
D 13	41 21.3	43 08.0	23.1	330 57.1	14.6	137 35.0	40.6	109 20.6	29.4	Shaula	96 16.3	S37 06.8
A 14	56 23.7	58 07.7	21.9	345 57.8	14.8	152 37.5	40.6	124 23.0	29.4	Sirius	258 30.3	S16 44.9
Y 15	71 26.2	73 07.3	. . 20.8	0 58.5	. . 15.0	167 40.0	. . 40.6	139 25.4	. . 29.4	Spica	158 26.8	S11 15.7
16	86 28.7	88 07.0	19.6	15 59.2	15.2	182 42.6	40.6	154 27.8	29.4	Suhail	222 49.4	S43 30.9
17	101 31.1	103 06.7	18.5	30 59.9	15.5	197 45.1	40.6	169 30.2	29.4			
18	116 33.6	118 06.3	S 2 17.3	46 00.6	N23 15.7	212 47.6	S22 40.6	184 32.7	S21 29.4	Vega	80 36.1	N38 47.9
19	131 36.0	133 06.0	16.2	61 01.3	15.9	227 50.2	40.6	199 35.1	29.4	Zuben'ubi	137 00.7	S16 07.2
20	146 38.5	148 05.6	15.0	76 02.0	16.2	242 52.7	40.6	214 37.5	29.4		SHA	Mer. Pass.
21	161 41.0	163 05.3	. . 13.9	91 02.7	. . 16.4	257 55.2	. . 40.6	229 39.9	. . 29.4		° ′	h m
22	176 43.4	178 05.0	12.7	106 03.4	16.6	272 57.8	40.6	244 42.3	29.4	Venus	3 30.3	10 07
23	191 45.9	193 04.6	11.6	121 04.1	16.8	288 00.3	40.6	259 44.7	29.4	Mars	290 41.2	14 57
	h m									Jupiter	96 11.5	3 55
Mer. Pass. 10 19.0		v −0.3	d 1.1	v 0.7	d 0.2	v 2.5	d 0.0	v 2.4	d 0.0	Saturn	68 01.3	5 48

© British Crown Copyright 2018. All rights reserved.

SUN and MOON

UT	SUN GHA	SUN Dec	MOON GHA	v	MOON Dec	d	HP
16 00	180 00.0	N 9 56.5	42 27.7	8.1	N11 48.7	11.7	60.1
01	195 00.2	57.4	56 54.8	8.2	11 37.0	11.9	60.1
02	210 00.3	58.3	71 22.0	8.2	11 25.1	11.9	60.1
03	225 00.5	9 59.2	85 49.2	8.3	11 13.2	12.0	60.1
04	240 00.6	10 00.1	100 16.5	8.2	11 01.2	12.1	60.1
05	255 00.8	01.0	114 43.7	8.4	10 49.1	12.1	60.1
06	270 00.9	N10 01.8	129 11.1	8.3	N10 37.0	12.2	60.2
T 07	285 01.1	02.7	143 38.4	8.4	10 24.8	12.3	60.2
U 08	300 01.2	03.6	158 05.8	8.5	10 12.5	12.3	60.2
E 09	315 01.4	04.5	172 33.3	8.5	10 00.2	12.4	60.2
S 10	330 01.5	05.4	187 00.8	8.5	9 47.8	12.5	60.2
D 11	345 01.7	06.3	201 28.3	8.5	9 35.3	12.5	60.2
A 12	0 01.8	N10 07.2	215 55.8	8.6	N 9 22.8	12.6	60.2
Y 13	15 02.0	08.1	230 23.4	8.6	9 10.2	12.6	60.2
14	30 02.1	08.9	244 51.0	8.7	8 57.6	12.7	60.2
15	45 02.2	09.8	259 18.7	8.7	8 44.9	12.7	60.2
16	60 02.4	10.7	273 46.4	8.7	8 32.2	12.9	60.2
17	75 02.5	11.6	288 14.1	8.8	8 19.3	12.8	60.2
18	90 02.7	N10 12.5	302 41.9	8.8	N 8 06.5	12.9	60.2
19	105 02.8	13.4	317 09.7	8.8	7 53.6	13.0	60.2
20	120 03.0	14.3	331 37.5	8.8	7 40.6	13.0	60.2
21	135 03.1	15.1	346 05.3	8.9	7 27.6	13.0	60.2
22	150 03.3	16.0	0 33.2	8.9	7 14.6	13.1	60.2
23	165 03.4	16.9	15 01.1	9.0	7 01.5	13.2	60.2
17 00	180 03.6	N10 17.8	29 29.1	9.0	N 6 48.3	13.2	60.2
01	195 03.7	18.7	43 57.1	9.0	6 35.1	13.2	60.2
02	210 03.9	19.6	58 25.1	9.0	6 21.9	13.2	60.2
03	225 04.0	20.4	72 53.1	9.1	6 08.7	13.3	60.2
04	240 04.2	21.3	87 21.2	9.1	5 55.4	13.3	60.2
05	255 04.3	22.2	101 49.3	9.1	5 42.0	13.3	60.2
06	270 04.4	N10 23.1	116 17.4	9.1	N 5 28.7	13.4	60.2
W 07	285 04.6	24.0	130 45.5	9.2	5 15.3	13.5	60.2
E 08	300 04.7	24.8	145 13.7	9.2	5 01.8	13.4	60.2
D 09	315 04.9	25.7	159 41.9	9.3	4 48.4	13.5	60.2
N 10	330 05.0	26.6	174 10.2	9.2	4 34.9	13.5	60.2
E 11	345 05.2	27.5	188 38.4	9.3	4 21.4	13.6	60.2
S 12	0 05.3	N10 28.4	203 06.7	9.3	N 4 07.8	13.5	60.2
D 13	15 05.5	29.2	217 35.0	9.3	3 54.3	13.6	60.2
A 14	30 05.6	30.1	232 03.3	9.3	3 40.7	13.6	60.2
Y 15	45 05.8	31.0	246 31.6	9.4	3 27.1	13.6	60.2
16	60 05.9	31.9	261 00.0	9.4	3 13.5	13.7	60.1
17	75 06.0	32.8	275 28.4	9.4	2 59.8	13.6	60.1
18	90 06.2	N10 33.6	289 56.8	9.4	N 2 46.2	13.7	60.1
19	105 06.3	34.5	304 25.2	9.5	2 32.5	13.7	60.1
20	120 06.5	35.4	318 53.7	9.5	2 18.8	13.6	60.1
21	135 06.6	36.3	333 22.2	9.5	2 05.2	13.7	60.1
22	150 06.8	37.1	347 50.7	9.5	1 51.5	13.8	60.1
23	165 06.9	38.0	2 19.2	9.5	1 37.7	13.7	60.1
18 00	180 07.0	N10 38.9	16 47.7	9.5	N 1 24.0	13.7	60.1
01	195 07.2	39.8	31 16.2	9.6	1 10.3	13.7	60.1
02	210 07.3	40.6	45 44.8	9.5	0 56.6	13.7	60.1
03	225 07.5	41.5	60 13.3	9.6	0 42.9	13.8	60.0
04	240 07.6	42.4	74 41.9	9.6	0 29.1	13.7	60.0
05	255 07.8	43.3	89 10.5	9.6	0 15.4	13.7	60.0
06	270 07.9	N10 44.1	103 39.1	9.7	N 0 01.7	13.7	60.0
T 07	285 08.0	45.0	118 07.8	9.6	S 0 12.0	13.7	60.0
H 08	300 08.2	45.9	132 36.4	9.7	0 25.7	13.7	60.0
U 09	315 08.3	46.8	147 05.1	9.6	0 39.4	13.7	60.0
R 10	330 08.5	47.6	161 33.7	9.7	0 53.1	13.7	60.0
S 11	345 08.6	48.5	176 02.4	9.7	1 06.8	13.7	59.9
D 12	0 08.7	N10 49.4	190 31.1	9.7	S 1 20.5	13.6	59.9
A 13	15 08.9	50.3	204 59.8	9.7	1 34.1	13.6	59.9
Y 14	30 09.0	51.1	219 28.5	9.7	1 47.7	13.7	59.9
15	45 09.2	52.0	233 57.2	9.7	2 01.4	13.6	59.9
16	60 09.3	52.9	248 25.9	9.7	2 15.0	13.6	59.9
17	75 09.4	53.7	262 54.6	9.7	2 28.6	13.5	59.9
18	90 09.6	N10 54.6	277 23.3	9.8	S 2 42.1	13.6	59.8
19	105 09.7	55.5	291 52.1	9.7	2 55.7	13.5	59.8
20	120 09.9	56.3	306 20.8	9.8	3 09.2	13.5	59.8
21	135 10.0	57.2	320 49.6	9.7	3 22.7	13.4	59.8
22	150 10.1	58.1	335 18.3	9.8	3 36.1	13.5	59.8
23	165 10.3	59.0	349 47.1	9.7	S 3 49.6	13.4	59.7
SD	16.0	d 0.9	SD 16.4		16.4		16.3

Twilight, Sunrise and Moonrise

Lat.	Naut.	Civil	Sunrise	Moonrise 16	17	18	19
N 72	////	01 41	03 29	13 46	15 58	18 06	20 16
N 70	////	02 23	03 48	14 00	16 02	18 02	20 02
68	////	02 50	04 02	14 11	16 06	17 59	19 51
66	01 27	03 11	04 14	14 21	16 09	17 56	19 42
64	02 04	03 27	04 23	14 29	16 12	17 54	19 35
62	02 30	03 41	04 32	14 35	16 14	17 52	19 28
60	02 49	03 52	04 39	14 41	16 16	17 50	19 23
N 58	03 05	04 02	04 45	14 46	16 18	17 48	19 18
56	03 18	04 10	04 50	14 51	16 19	17 47	19 14
54	03 29	04 17	04 55	14 55	16 20	17 46	19 10
52	03 39	04 24	05 00	14 58	16 22	17 44	19 06
50	03 47	04 30	05 04	15 02	16 23	17 43	19 03
45	04 05	04 42	05 13	15 09	16 25	17 41	18 56
N 40	04 18	04 52	05 20	15 15	16 27	17 39	18 51
35	04 29	05 00	05 26	15 20	16 29	17 38	18 46
30	04 38	05 07	05 31	15 24	16 31	17 36	18 41
20	04 52	05 18	05 41	15 32	16 33	17 34	18 34
N 10	05 03	05 27	05 49	15 39	16 36	17 32	18 28
0	05 11	05 35	05 56	15 45	16 38	17 30	18 22
S 10	05 18	05 42	06 04	15 51	16 40	17 28	18 16
20	05 23	05 49	06 11	15 58	16 43	17 26	18 10
30	05 28	05 56	06 20	16 06	16 45	17 24	18 03
35	05 30	05 59	06 25	16 10	16 47	17 23	17 59
40	05 32	06 03	06 31	16 15	16 49	17 21	17 54
45	05 33	06 07	06 37	16 21	16 51	17 20	17 49
S 50	05 34	06 12	06 45	16 28	16 53	17 18	17 43
52	05 35	06 14	06 48	16 31	16 54	17 17	17 40
54	05 35	06 16	06 52	16 34	16 56	17 16	17 37
56	05 35	06 18	06 57	16 38	16 57	17 15	17 33
58	05 35	06 21	07 01	16 42	16 59	17 14	17 30
S 60	05 35	06 24	07 07	16 47	17 00	17 13	17 25

Sunset, Twilight and Moonset

Lat.	Sunset	Civil	Naut.	Moonset 16	17	18	19
N 72	20 34	22 28	////	05 42	05 22	05 04	04 47
N 70	20 15	21 42	////	05 25	05 14	05 04	04 54
68	20 00	21 13	////	05 12	05 08	05 04	05 00
66	19 48	20 52	22 41	05 01	05 03	05 04	05 05
64	19 38	20 35	22 00	04 52	04 58	05 04	05 09
62	19 30	20 21	21 33	04 44	04 55	05 04	05 13
60	19 22	20 09	21 13	04 37	04 51	05 04	05 16
N 58	19 16	20 00	20 57	04 31	04 48	05 04	05 19
56	19 10	19 51	20 43	04 25	04 45	05 04	05 22
54	19 05	19 44	20 32	04 20	04 43	05 04	05 24
52	19 01	19 37	20 22	04 16	04 41	05 04	05 26
50	18 56	19 31	20 14	04 12	04 39	05 04	05 28
45	18 48	19 18	19 56	04 03	04 34	05 03	05 32
N 40	18 40	19 08	19 42	03 56	04 30	05 03	05 36
35	18 34	19 00	19 31	03 49	04 27	05 03	05 39
30	18 28	18 53	19 22	03 43	04 24	05 03	05 42
20	18 19	18 41	19 08	03 34	04 19	05 03	05 47
N 10	18 11	18 32	18 57	03 25	04 15	05 03	05 51
0	18 03	18 24	18 48	03 17	04 10	05 03	05 55
S 10	17 56	18 17	18 41	03 08	04 06	05 03	05 59
20	17 48	18 10	18 36	02 59	04 01	05 02	06 03
30	17 39	18 03	18 31	02 49	03 56	05 02	06 08
35	17 34	17 59	18 29	02 43	03 53	05 02	06 10
40	17 28	17 56	18 27	02 36	03 49	05 02	06 13
45	17 22	17 51	18 25	02 28	03 45	05 01	06 17
S 50	17 14	17 47	18 24	02 19	03 40	05 01	06 21
52	17 10	17 44	18 24	02 14	03 38	05 01	06 23
54	17 06	17 42	18 23	02 09	03 35	05 01	06 26
56	17 02	17 40	18 23	02 04	03 32	05 01	06 28
58	16 57	17 37	18 23	01 58	03 29	05 00	06 31
S 60	16 52	17 34	18 23	01 51	03 26	05 00	06 34

SUN and MOON

Day	Eqn. of Time 00ʰ	12ʰ	Mer. Pass.	Mer. Pass. Upper	Lower	Age	Phase
	m s	m s	h m	h m	h m	d	%
16	00 00	00 07	12 00	21 58	09 31	11	88
17	00 14	00 21	12 00	22 50	10 24	12	95
18	00 28	00 35	11 59	23 42	11 16	13	99

© British Crown Copyright 2018. All rights reserved.

UT	ARIES GHA	VENUS −3.9 GHA	Dec	MARS +1.6 GHA	Dec	JUPITER −2.4 GHA	Dec	SATURN +0.5 GHA	Dec	STARS Name	SHA	Dec
19 00	206 48.4	208 04.3	S 2 10.4	136 04.8	N23 17.1	303 02.8	S22 40.6	274 47.1	S21 29.4	Acamar	315 15.7	S40 13.9
01	221 50.8	223 04.0	09.3	151 05.5	17.3	318 05.4	40.6	289 49.6	29.4	Achernar	335 24.4	S57 08.5
02	236 53.3	238 03.6	08.1	166 06.2	17.5	333 07.9	40.6	304 52.0	29.4	Acrux	173 04.2	S63 12.4
03	251 55.8	253 03.3 ..	06.9	181 06.9 ..	17.8	348 10.4 ..	40.6	319 54.4 ..	29.4	Adhara	255 09.5	S29 00.2
04	266 58.2	268 03.0	05.8	196 07.6	18.0	3 13.0	40.6	334 56.8	29.3	Aldebaran	290 45.1	N16 32.6
05	282 00.7	283 02.6	04.6	211 08.3	18.2	18 15.5	40.6	349 59.2	29.3			
06	297 03.1	298 02.3	S 2 03.5	226 09.0	N23 18.4	33 18.0	S22 40.6	5 01.6	S21 29.3	Alioth	166 16.7	N55 51.5
07	312 05.6	313 02.0	02.3	241 09.7	18.7	48 20.6	40.6	20 04.1	29.3	Alkaid	152 55.3	N49 13.1
08	327 08.1	328 01.6	01.2	256 10.4	18.9	63 23.1	40.6	35 06.5	29.3	Alnair	27 39.0	S46 52.0
F 09	342 10.5	343 01.3	2 00.0	271 11.1 ..	19.1	78 25.6 ..	40.6	50 08.9 ..	29.3	Alnilam	275 42.5	S 1 11.6
R 10	357 13.0	358 01.0	1 58.9	286 11.8	19.3	93 28.2	40.6	65 11.3	29.3	Alphard	217 52.1	S 8 44.7
I 11	12 15.5	13 00.6	57.7	301 12.5	19.6	108 30.7	40.6	80 13.7	29.3			
D 12	27 17.9	28 00.3	S 1 56.5	316 13.2	N23 19.8	123 33.3	S22 40.6	95 16.1	S21 29.3	Alphecca	126 07.3	N26 39.0
A 13	42 20.4	43 00.0	55.4	331 13.9	20.0	138 35.8	40.6	110 18.6	29.3	Alpheratz	357 39.7	N29 11.5
Y 14	57 22.9	57 59.6	54.2	346 14.6	20.2	153 38.3	40.6	125 21.0	29.3	Altair	62 04.4	N 8 55.1
15	72 25.3	72 59.3 ..	53.1	1 15.3 ..	20.4	168 40.9 ..	40.6	140 23.4 ..	29.3	Ankaa	353 12.2	S42 12.2
16	87 27.8	87 59.0	51.9	16 16.0	20.7	183 43.4	40.6	155 25.8	29.3	Antares	112 21.1	S26 28.3
17	102 30.3	102 58.7	50.8	31 16.7	20.9	198 46.0	40.6	170 28.2	29.3			
18	117 32.7	117 58.3	S 1 49.6	46 17.4	N23 21.1	213 48.5	S22 40.6	185 30.7	S21 29.3	Arcturus	145 51.8	N19 05.0
19	132 35.2	132 58.0	48.5	61 18.1	21.3	228 51.0	40.6	200 33.1	29.3	Atria	107 19.0	S69 03.4
20	147 37.6	147 57.7	47.3	76 18.8	21.5	243 53.6	40.6	215 35.5	29.3	Avior	234 16.4	S59 34.6
21	162 40.1	162 57.3 ..	46.1	91 19.5 ..	21.8	258 56.1 ..	40.6	230 37.9 ..	29.3	Bellatrix	278 28.0	N 6 21.8
22	177 42.6	177 57.0	45.0	106 20.2	22.0	273 58.7	40.6	245 40.3	29.3	Betelgeuse	270 57.2	N 7 24.4
23	192 45.0	192 56.7	43.8	121 20.9	22.2	289 01.2	40.6	260 42.8	29.3			
20 00	207 47.5	207 56.3	S 1 42.7	136 21.6	N23 22.4	304 03.7	S22 40.5	275 45.2	S21 29.3	Canopus	263 54.6	S52 42.7
01	222 50.0	222 56.0	41.5	151 22.3	22.6	319 06.3	40.5	290 47.6	29.2	Capella	280 28.9	N46 01.0
02	237 52.4	237 55.7	40.3	166 23.0	22.9	334 08.8	40.5	305 50.0	29.2	Deneb	49 28.9	N45 20.7
03	252 54.9	252 55.3 ..	39.2	181 23.7 ..	23.1	349 11.4 ..	40.5	320 52.4 ..	29.2	Denebola	182 29.4	N14 27.9
04	267 57.4	267 55.0	38.0	196 24.4	23.3	4 13.9	40.5	335 54.9	29.2	Diphda	348 52.2	S17 53.1
05	282 59.8	282 54.7	36.9	211 25.1	23.5	19 16.5	40.5	350 57.3	29.2			
06	298 02.3	297 54.3	S 1 35.7	226 25.8	N23 23.7	34 19.0	S22 40.5	5 59.7	S21 29.2	Dubhe	193 46.4	N61 39.0
07	313 04.7	312 54.0	34.6	241 26.5	24.0	49 21.5	40.5	21 02.1	29.2	Elnath	278 07.9	N28 37.3
S 08	328 07.2	327 53.7	33.4	256 27.1	24.2	64 24.1	40.5	36 04.5	29.2	Eltanin	90 44.0	N51 29.0
A 09	343 09.7	342 53.3 ..	32.2	271 27.8 ..	24.4	79 26.6 ..	40.5	51 07.0 ..	29.2	Enif	33 43.4	N 9 57.6
T 10	358 12.1	357 53.0	31.1	286 28.5	24.6	94 29.2	40.5	66 09.4	29.2	Fomalhaut	15 19.9	S29 31.3
U 11	13 14.6	12 52.7	29.9	301 29.2	24.8	109 31.7	40.5	81 11.8	29.2			
R 12	28 17.1	27 52.3	S 1 28.8	316 29.9	N23 25.0	124 34.3	S22 40.5	96 14.2	S21 29.2	Gacrux	171 56.0	S57 13.3
D 13	43 19.5	42 52.0	27.6	331 30.6	25.2	139 36.8	40.5	111 16.7	29.2	Gienah	175 47.9	S17 39.0
A 14	58 22.0	57 51.7	26.4	346 31.3	25.5	154 39.4	40.5	126 19.1	29.2	Hadar	148 41.6	S60 27.8
Y 15	73 24.5	72 51.3 ..	25.3	1 32.0 ..	25.7	169 41.9 ..	40.5	141 21.5 ..	29.2	Hamal	327 56.6	N23 32.9
16	88 26.9	87 51.0	24.1	16 32.7	25.9	184 44.5	40.5	156 23.9	29.2	Kaus Aust.	83 38.4	S34 22.3
17	103 29.4	102 50.7	23.0	31 33.4	26.1	199 47.0	40.5	171 26.3	29.2			
18	118 31.9	117 50.4	S 1 21.8	46 34.1	N23 26.3	214 49.6	S22 40.5	186 28.8	S21 29.2	Kochab	137 19.0	N74 04.6
19	133 34.3	132 50.0	20.6	61 34.8	26.5	229 52.1	40.5	201 31.2	29.2	Markab	13 34.6	N15 18.3
20	148 36.8	147 49.7	19.5	76 35.5	26.7	244 54.7	40.5	216 33.6	29.2	Menkar	314 11.2	N 4 09.6
21	163 39.2	162 49.4 ..	18.3	91 36.2 ..	27.0	259 57.2 ..	40.5	231 36.0 ..	29.2	Menkent	148 02.5	S36 27.8
22	178 41.7	177 49.0	17.2	106 36.9	27.2	274 59.8	40.5	246 38.5	29.2	Miaplacidus	221 38.6	S69 48.1
23	193 44.2	192 48.7	16.0	121 37.6	27.4	290 02.3	40.5	261 40.9	29.2			
21 00	208 46.6	207 48.4	S 1 14.8	136 38.3	N23 27.6	305 04.9	S22 40.5	276 43.3	S21 29.1	Mirfak	308 35.1	N49 55.6
01	223 49.1	222 48.0	13.7	151 39.0	27.8	320 07.4	40.5	291 45.7	29.1	Nunki	75 53.3	S26 16.2
02	238 51.6	237 47.7	12.5	166 39.7	28.0	335 10.0	40.5	306 48.2	29.1	Peacock	53 13.1	S56 40.1
03	253 54.0	252 47.4 ..	11.4	181 40.4 ..	28.2	350 12.5 ..	40.5	321 50.6 ..	29.1	Pollux	243 22.9	N27 58.7
04	268 56.5	267 47.0	10.2	196 41.1	28.4	5 15.1	40.5	336 53.0	29.1	Procyon	244 55.6	N 5 10.4
05	283 59.0	282 46.7	09.0	211 41.8	28.6	20 17.6	40.5	351 55.4	29.1			
06	299 01.4	297 46.4	S 1 07.9	226 42.5	N23 28.9	35 20.2	S22 40.5	6 57.9	S21 29.1	Rasalhague	96 02.6	N12 32.7
07	314 03.9	312 46.1	06.7	241 43.2	29.1	50 22.7	40.5	22 00.3	29.1	Regulus	207 39.2	N11 52.3
08	329 06.4	327 45.7	05.6	256 43.9	29.3	65 25.3	40.4	37 02.7	29.1	Rigel	281 08.5	S 8 11.1
S 09	344 08.8	342 45.4 ..	04.4	271 44.5 ..	29.5	80 27.8 ..	40.4	52 05.1 ..	29.1	Rigil Kent.	139 45.7	S60 54.7
U 10	359 11.3	357 45.1	03.2	286 45.2	29.7	95 30.4	40.4	67 07.6	29.1	Sabik	102 07.8	S15 44.8
N 11	14 13.7	12 44.7	02.1	301 45.9	29.9	110 32.9	40.4	82 10.0	29.1			
D 12	29 16.2	27 44.4	S 1 00.9	316 46.6	N23 30.1	125 35.5	S22 40.5	97 12.4	S21 29.1	Schedar	349 36.5	N56 38.3
A 13	44 18.7	42 44.1	0 59.7	331 47.3	30.3	140 38.0	40.4	112 14.8	29.1	Shaula	96 16.3	S37 06.8
Y 14	59 21.1	57 43.7	58.6	346 48.0	30.5	155 40.6	40.4	127 17.3	29.1	Sirius	258 30.4	S16 44.9
15	74 23.6	72 43.4 ..	57.4	1 48.7 ..	30.7	170 43.1 ..	40.4	142 19.7 ..	29.1	Spica	158 26.8	S11 15.7
16	89 26.1	87 43.1	56.3	16 49.4	30.9	185 45.7	40.4	157 22.1	29.1	Suhail	222 49.4	S43 30.9
17	104 28.5	102 42.7	55.1	31 50.1	31.1	200 48.3	40.4	172 24.6	29.1			
18	119 31.0	117 42.4	S 0 53.9	46 50.8	N23 31.3	215 50.8	S22 40.4	187 27.0	S21 29.1	Vega	80 36.1	N38 47.9
19	134 33.5	132 42.1	52.8	61 51.5	31.5	230 53.4	40.4	202 29.4	29.1	Zuben'ubi	137 00.7	S16 07.2
20	149 35.9	147 41.8	51.6	76 52.2	31.7	245 55.9	40.4	217 31.8	29.1		SHA	Mer.Pass.
21	164 38.4	162 41.4 ..	50.4	91 52.9 ..	32.0	260 58.5 ..	40.4	232 34.3 ..	29.1			
22	179 40.8	177 41.1	49.3	106 53.6	32.2	276 01.0	40.4	247 36.7	29.1	Venus	0 08.8	10 08
23	194 43.3	192 40.8	48.1	121 54.3	32.4	291 03.6	40.4	262 39.1	29.1	Mars	288 34.1	14 54
	h m									Jupiter	96 16.2	3 43
Mer.Pass. 10 07.2	*v* −0.3	*d* 1.2		*v* 0.7	*d* 0.2	*v* 2.5	*d* 0.0	*v* 2.4	*d* 0.0	Saturn	67 57.7	5 36

© British Crown Copyright 2018. All rights reserved.

UT	SUN GHA	SUN Dec	MOON GHA	v	MOON Dec	d	HP
19 00	180 10.4	N10 59.8	4 15.8	9.8	S 4 03.0	13.4	59.7
01	195 10.6	11 00.7	18 44.6	9.7	4 16.4	13.3	59.7
02	210 10.7	01.6	33 13.3	9.8	4 29.7	13.3	59.7
03	225 10.8	.. 02.4	47 42.1	9.8	4 43.0	13.3	59.7
04	240 11.0	03.3	62 10.9	9.7	4 56.3	13.2	59.6
05	255 11.1	04.2	76 39.6	9.8	5 09.5	13.2	59.6
06	270 11.2	N11 05.0	91 08.4	9.7	S 5 22.7	13.2	59.6
07	285 11.4	05.9	105 37.1	9.8	5 35.9	13.1	59.6
F 08	300 11.5	06.8	120 05.9	9.8	5 49.0	13.1	59.6
R 09	315 11.7	.. 07.6	134 34.7	9.7	6 02.1	13.0	59.5
I 10	330 11.8	08.5	149 03.4	9.8	6 15.1	13.0	59.5
11	345 11.9	09.4	163 32.2	9.7	6 28.1	12.9	59.5
D 12	0 12.1	N11 10.2	178 00.9	9.8	S 6 41.0	12.9	59.5
A 13	15 12.2	11.1	192 29.7	9.7	6 53.9	12.9	59.4
Y 14	30 12.3	11.9	206 58.4	9.8	7 06.8	12.8	59.4
15	45 12.5	.. 12.8	221 27.2	9.7	7 19.6	12.7	59.4
16	60 12.6	13.7	235 55.9	9.7	7 32.3	12.7	59.4
17	75 12.7	14.5	250 24.6	9.8	7 45.0	12.6	59.4
18	90 12.9	N11 15.4	264 53.4	9.7	S 7 57.6	12.6	59.3
19	105 13.0	16.3	279 22.1	9.7	8 10.2	12.5	59.3
20	120 13.2	17.1	293 50.8	9.7	8 22.7	12.5	59.3
21	135 13.3	.. 18.0	308 19.5	9.7	8 35.2	12.4	59.3
22	150 13.4	18.8	322 48.2	9.7	8 47.6	12.3	59.2
23	165 13.6	19.7	337 16.9	9.7	8 59.9	12.3	59.2
20 00	180 13.7	N11 20.6	351 45.6	9.7	S 9 12.2	12.2	59.2
01	195 13.8	21.4	6 14.3	9.7	9 24.4	12.2	59.1
02	210 14.0	22.3	20 43.0	9.6	9 36.6	12.1	59.1
03	225 14.1	.. 23.1	35 11.6	9.7	9 48.7	12.0	59.1
04	240 14.2	24.0	49 40.3	9.6	10 00.7	11.9	59.1
05	255 14.4	24.9	64 08.9	9.7	10 12.6	11.9	59.0
06	270 14.5	N11 25.7	78 37.6	9.6	S10 24.5	11.8	59.0
07	285 14.6	26.6	93 06.2	9.6	10 36.3	11.8	59.0
S 08	300 14.8	27.4	107 34.8	9.6	10 48.1	11.6	59.0
A 09	315 14.9	.. 28.3	122 03.4	9.6	10 59.7	11.6	58.9
T 10	330 15.0	29.2	136 32.0	9.6	11 11.3	11.5	58.9
U 11	345 15.2	30.0	151 00.6	9.6	11 22.8	11.5	58.9
R 12	0 15.3	N11 30.9	165 29.2	9.5	S11 34.3	11.4	58.8
D 13	15 15.4	31.7	179 57.7	9.6	11 45.7	11.2	58.8
A 14	30 15.6	32.6	194 26.3	9.5	11 56.9	11.3	58.8
Y 15	45 15.7	.. 33.4	208 54.8	9.6	12 08.2	11.1	58.7
16	60 15.8	34.3	223 23.4	9.5	12 19.3	11.0	58.7
17	75 15.9	35.2	237 51.9	9.5	12 30.3	11.0	58.7
18	90 16.1	N11 36.0	252 20.4	9.5	S12 41.3	10.9	58.7
19	105 16.2	36.9	266 48.9	9.5	12 52.2	10.8	58.6
20	120 16.3	37.7	281 17.4	9.5	13 03.0	10.7	58.6
21	135 16.5	.. 38.6	295 45.9	9.4	13 13.7	10.6	58.6
22	150 16.6	39.4	310 14.3	9.5	13 24.3	10.5	58.5
23	165 16.7	40.3	324 42.8	9.4	13 34.8	10.5	58.5
21 00	180 16.9	N11 41.1	339 11.2	9.4	S13 45.3	10.4	58.5
01	195 17.0	42.0	353 39.6	9.5	13 55.7	10.2	58.4
02	210 17.1	42.8	8 08.1	9.4	14 05.9	10.2	58.4
03	225 17.3	.. 43.7	22 36.5	9.4	14 16.1	10.1	58.4
04	240 17.4	44.5	37 04.9	9.3	14 26.2	10.0	58.3
05	255 17.5	45.4	51 33.2	9.4	14 36.2	9.9	58.3
06	270 17.6	N11 46.2	66 01.6	9.4	S14 46.1	9.8	58.3
07	285 17.8	47.1	80 30.0	9.3	14 55.9	9.7	58.2
08	300 17.9	47.9	94 58.3	9.4	15 05.6	9.6	58.2
S 09	315 18.0	.. 48.8	109 26.7	9.3	15 15.2	9.5	58.2
U 10	330 18.2	49.6	123 55.0	9.3	15 24.7	9.4	58.1
N 11	345 18.3	50.5	138 23.3	9.3	15 34.1	9.4	58.1
D 12	0 18.4	N11 51.3	152 51.6	9.3	S15 43.5	9.2	58.1
A 13	15 18.5	52.2	167 19.9	9.3	15 52.7	9.1	58.0
Y 14	30 18.7	53.0	181 48.2	9.3	16 01.8	9.0	58.0
15	45 18.8	.. 53.9	196 16.5	9.2	16 10.8	8.9	58.0
16	60 18.9	54.7	210 44.7	9.3	16 19.7	8.9	57.9
17	75 19.0	55.6	225 13.0	9.2	16 28.6	8.7	57.9
18	90 19.2	N11 56.4	239 41.2	9.3	S16 37.3	8.6	57.9
19	105 19.3	57.3	254 09.5	9.2	16 45.9	8.5	57.8
20	120 19.4	58.1	268 37.7	9.2	16 54.4	8.4	57.8
21	135 19.5	.. 59.0	283 05.9	9.2	17 02.8	8.3	57.8
22	150 19.7	11 59.8	297 34.1	9.3	17 11.1	8.2	57.7
23	165 19.8	N12 00.7	312 02.4	9.1	S17 19.3	8.1	57.7
	SD 15.9	d 0.9	SD 16.2		16.0		15.8

Lat.	Naut.	Civil	Sunrise	Moonrise 19	20	21	22
N 72	////	01 01	03 11	20 16	22 34	25 44	01 44
N 70	////	02 00	03 32	20 02	22 05	24 18	00 18
68	////	02 33	03 49	19 51	21 44	23 39	25 36
66	00 53	02 57	04 02	19 42	21 28	23 12	24 52
64	01 45	03 15	04 13	19 35	21 15	22 52	24 23
62	02 15	03 30	04 22	19 28	21 03	22 36	24 01
60	02 37	03 42	04 30	19 23	20 54	22 22	23 43
N 58	02 54	03 53	04 37	19 18	20 46	22 10	23 28
56	03 08	04 02	04 43	19 14	20 38	22 00	23 16
54	03 20	04 10	04 48	19 10	20 32	21 51	23 05
52	03 31	04 17	04 53	19 06	20 26	21 43	22 55
50	03 40	04 23	04 58	19 03	20 21	21 36	22 46
45	03 59	04 36	05 08	18 56	20 10	21 21	22 28
N 40	04 13	04 47	05 16	18 51	20 01	21 08	22 13
35	04 25	04 56	05 22	18 46	19 53	20 58	22 00
30	04 34	05 04	05 28	18 41	19 46	20 49	21 49
20	04 49	05 16	05 39	18 34	19 34	20 33	21 30
N 10	05 01	05 26	05 47	18 28	19 23	20 19	21 14
0	05 10	05 35	05 56	18 22	19 14	20 06	20 59
S 10	05 18	05 42	06 04	18 16	19 04	19 54	20 44
20	05 24	05 50	06 12	18 10	18 54	19 40	20 28
30	05 30	05 58	06 22	18 03	18 43	19 25	20 09
35	05 32	06 02	06 27	17 59	18 36	19 16	19 59
40	05 34	06 06	06 34	17 54	18 29	19 06	19 47
45	05 37	06 11	06 41	17 49	18 20	18 54	19 32
S 50	05 39	06 16	06 49	17 43	18 10	18 40	19 15
52	05 39	06 19	06 53	17 40	18 05	18 33	19 07
54	05 40	06 21	06 58	17 37	17 59	18 26	18 57
56	05 41	06 24	07 03	17 33	17 54	18 18	18 47
58	05 41	06 27	07 08	17 30	17 47	18 08	18 35
S 60	05 42	06 31	07 14	17 25	17 40	17 58	18 22

Lat.	Sunset	Civil	Naut.	Moonset 19	20	21	22
N 72	20 51	23 15	////	04 47	04 27	03 59	02 39
N 70	20 29	22 05	////	04 54	04 43	04 29	04 06
68	20 12	21 30	////	05 00	04 56	04 51	04 46
66	19 59	21 05	23 21	05 05	05 06	05 09	05 14
64	19 47	20 46	22 20	05 09	05 15	05 23	05 35
62	19 38	20 31	21 47	05 13	05 23	05 35	05 52
60	19 30	20 18	21 25	05 16	05 30	05 46	06 06
N 58	19 23	20 07	21 07	05 19	05 36	05 55	06 19
56	19 16	19 58	20 52	05 22	05 41	06 03	06 29
54	19 11	19 50	20 39	05 24	05 46	06 10	06 39
52	19 06	19 42	20 29	05 26	05 50	06 16	06 47
50	19 01	19 36	20 19	05 28	05 54	06 22	06 55
45	18 51	19 22	20 01	05 32	06 02	06 35	07 11
N 40	18 43	19 12	19 46	05 36	06 09	06 45	07 24
35	18 36	19 03	19 34	05 39	06 16	06 54	07 35
30	18 30	18 55	19 24	05 42	06 21	07 02	07 45
20	18 20	18 42	19 09	05 47	06 30	07 16	08 03
N 10	18 11	18 32	18 57	05 51	06 39	07 28	08 17
0	18 02	18 23	18 48	05 55	06 47	07 39	08 32
S 10	17 54	18 15	18 40	05 59	06 54	07 50	08 46
20	17 45	18 08	18 34	06 03	07 03	08 02	09 01
30	17 36	18 00	18 28	06 08	07 12	08 16	09 18
35	17 30	17 56	18 25	06 10	07 18	08 24	09 28
40	17 24	17 51	18 23	06 13	07 24	08 33	09 40
45	17 17	17 46	18 21	06 17	07 31	08 44	09 53
S 50	17 08	17 41	18 19	06 21	07 40	08 57	10 10
52	17 04	17 38	18 18	06 23	07 44	09 03	10 18
54	16 59	17 36	18 17	06 26	07 49	09 10	10 27
56	16 55	17 33	18 16	06 28	07 54	09 17	10 36
58	16 49	17 30	18 15	06 31	08 00	09 26	10 48
S 60	16 43	17 26	18 15	06 34	08 06	09 36	11 01

	SUN			MOON			
Day	Eqn. of Time 00h	12h	Mer. Pass.	Mer. Pass. Upper	Lower	Age	Phase
d	m s	m s	h m	h m	h m	d	%
19	00 41	00 48	11 59	24 34	12 08	14	100
20	00 55	01 01	11 59	00 34	13 00	15	98
21	01 07	01 13	11 59	01 26	13 53	16	95

© British Crown Copyright 2018. All rights reserved.

UT	ARIES GHA	VENUS −3.9 GHA	Dec	MARS +1.6 GHA	Dec	JUPITER −2.4 GHA	Dec	SATURN +0.5 GHA	Dec	STARS Name	SHA	Dec
22 00	209 45.8	207 40.4	S 0 47.0	136 55.0	N23 32.6	306 06.2	S22 40.4	277 41.6	S21 29.1	Acamar	315 15.7	S40 13.9
01	224 48.2	222 40.1	45.8	151 55.7	32.8	321 08.7	40.4	292 44.0	29.1	Achernar	335 24.4	S57 08.5
02	239 50.7	237 39.8	44.6	166 56.4	33.0	336 11.3	40.4	307 46.4	29.1	Acrux	173 04.2	S63 12.4
03	254 53.2	252 39.4	43.5	181 57.1	33.2	351 13.8	40.4	322 48.8	29.1	Adhara	255 09.5	S29 00.2
04	269 55.6	267 39.1	42.3	196 57.7	33.4	6 16.4	40.4	337 51.3	29.0	Aldebaran	290 45.1	N16 32.6
05	284 58.1	282 38.8	41.1	211 58.4	33.6	21 19.0	40.4	352 53.7	29.0			
06	300 00.6	297 38.5	S 0 40.0	226 59.1	N23 33.8	36 21.5	S22 40.4	7 56.1	S21 29.0	Alioth	166 16.7	N55 51.5
07	315 03.0	312 38.1	38.8	241 59.8	34.0	51 24.1	40.4	22 58.6	29.0	Alkaid	152 55.3	N49 13.1
08	330 05.5	327 37.8	37.6	257 00.5	34.2	66 26.6	40.4	38 01.0	29.0	Al Na'ir	27 39.0	S46 51.9
M 09	345 08.0	342 37.5	36.5	272 01.2	34.4	81 29.2	40.4	53 03.4	29.0	Alnilam	275 42.6	S 1 11.6
O 10	0 10.4	357 37.1	35.3	287 01.9	34.6	96 31.8	40.4	68 05.9	29.0	Alphard	217 52.1	S 8 44.7
N 11	15 12.9	12 36.8	34.2	302 02.6	34.8	111 34.3	40.4	83 08.3	29.0			
D 12	30 15.3	27 36.5	S 0 33.0	317 03.3	N23 35.0	126 36.9	S22 40.4	98 10.7	S21 29.0	Alphecca	126 07.3	N26 39.0
A 13	45 17.8	42 36.1	31.8	332 04.0	35.2	141 39.5	40.3	113 13.1	29.0	Alpheratz	357 39.7	N29 11.5
Y 14	60 20.3	57 35.8	30.7	347 04.7	35.4	156 42.0	40.3	128 15.6	29.0	Altair	62 04.3	N 8 55.1
15	75 22.7	72 35.5	29.5	2 05.4	35.6	171 44.6	40.3	143 18.0	29.0	Ankaa	353 12.2	S42 12.2
16	90 25.2	87 35.2	28.3	17 06.1	35.8	186 47.1	40.3	158 20.4	29.0	Antares	112 21.1	S26 28.3
17	105 27.7	102 34.8	27.2	32 06.8	36.0	201 49.7	40.3	173 22.9	29.0			
18	120 30.1	117 34.5	S 0 26.0	47 07.5	N23 36.2	216 52.3	S22 40.3	188 25.3	S21 29.0	Arcturus	145 51.8	N19 05.0
19	135 32.6	132 34.2	24.8	62 08.2	36.4	231 54.8	40.3	203 27.7	29.0	Atria	107 18.9	S69 03.4
20	150 35.1	147 33.8	23.7	77 08.9	36.6	246 57.4	40.3	218 30.2	29.0	Avior	234 16.4	S59 34.6
21	165 37.5	162 33.5	22.5	92 09.5	36.8	262 00.0	40.3	233 32.6	29.0	Bellatrix	278 28.0	N 6 21.8
22	180 40.0	177 33.2	21.3	107 10.2	36.9	277 02.5	40.3	248 35.0	29.0	Betelgeuse	270 57.2	N 7 24.4
23	195 42.5	192 32.9	20.2	122 10.9	37.1	292 05.1	40.3	263 37.5	29.0			
23 00	210 44.9	207 32.5	S 0 19.0	137 11.6	N23 37.3	307 07.7	S22 40.3	278 39.9	S21 29.0	Canopus	263 54.6	S52 42.7
01	225 47.4	222 32.2	17.8	152 12.3	37.5	322 10.2	40.3	293 42.3	29.0	Capella	280 28.9	N46 00.9
02	240 49.8	237 31.9	16.7	167 13.0	37.7	337 12.8	40.3	308 44.8	29.0	Deneb	49 28.8	N45 20.7
03	255 52.3	252 31.5	15.5	182 13.7	37.9	352 15.4	40.3	323 47.2	29.0	Denebola	182 29.4	N14 27.9
04	270 54.8	267 31.2	14.4	197 14.4	38.1	7 17.9	40.3	338 49.6	29.0	Diphda	348 52.2	S17 53.0
05	285 57.2	282 30.9	13.2	212 15.1	38.3	22 20.5	40.3	353 52.1	29.0			
06	300 59.7	297 30.5	S 0 12.0	227 15.8	N23 38.5	37 23.1	S22 40.3	8 54.5	S21 29.0	Dubhe	193 46.4	N61 39.0
07	316 02.2	312 30.2	10.9	242 16.5	38.7	52 25.6	40.3	23 56.9	29.0	Elnath	278 07.9	N28 37.3
T 08	331 04.6	327 29.9	09.7	257 17.2	38.9	67 28.2	40.3	38 59.4	29.0	Eltanin	90 44.0	N51 29.0
U 09	346 07.1	342 29.6	08.5	272 17.9	39.1	82 30.8	40.3	54 01.8	29.0	Enif	33 43.4	N 9 57.6
E 10	1 09.6	357 29.2	07.4	287 18.6	39.3	97 33.4	40.3	69 04.2	29.0	Fomalhaut	15 19.8	S29 31.2
S 11	16 12.0	12 28.9	06.2	302 19.2	39.5	112 35.9	40.3	84 06.7	29.0			
D 12	31 14.5	27 28.6	S 0 05.0	317 19.9	N23 39.7	127 38.5	S22 40.3	99 09.1	S21 29.0	Gacrux	171 56.0	S57 13.3
A 13	46 17.0	42 28.2	03.9	332 20.6	39.8	142 41.1	40.3	114 11.5	29.0	Gienah	175 47.9	S17 39.0
Y 14	61 19.4	57 27.9	02.7	347 21.3	40.0	157 43.6	40.3	129 14.0	29.0	Hadar	148 41.6	S60 27.9
15	76 21.9	72 27.6	01.5	2 22.0	40.2	172 46.2	40.2	144 16.4	29.0	Hamal	327 56.6	N23 32.9
16	91 24.3	87 27.3 S	00.4	17 22.7	40.4	187 48.8	40.2	159 18.9	29.0	Kaus Aust.	83 38.4	S34 22.3
17	106 26.8	102 26.9 N	00.8	32 23.4	40.6	202 51.4	40.2	174 21.3	28.9			
18	121 29.3	117 26.6	N 0 02.0	47 24.1	N23 40.8	217 53.9	S22 40.2	189 23.7	S21 28.9	Kochab	137 18.9	N74 04.6
19	136 31.7	132 26.3	03.1	62 24.8	41.0	232 56.5	40.2	204 26.2	28.9	Markab	13 34.6	N15 18.3
20	151 34.2	147 25.9	04.3	77 25.5	41.2	247 59.1	40.2	219 28.6	28.9	Menkar	314 11.2	N 4 09.6
21	166 36.7	162 25.6	05.5	92 26.2	41.4	263 01.6	40.2	234 31.0	28.9	Menkent	148 02.5	S36 27.8
22	181 39.1	177 25.3	06.6	107 26.9	41.6	278 04.2	40.2	249 33.5	28.9	Miaplacidus	221 38.7	S69 48.1
23	196 41.6	192 24.9	07.8	122 27.6	41.7	293 06.8	40.2	264 35.9	28.9			
24 00	211 44.1	207 24.6	N 0 09.0	137 28.3	N23 41.9	308 09.4	S22 40.2	279 38.3	S21 28.9	Mirfak	308 35.1	N49 55.6
01	226 46.5	222 24.3	10.1	152 28.9	42.1	323 11.9	40.2	294 40.8	28.9	Nunki	75 53.3	S26 16.2
02	241 49.0	237 24.0	11.3	167 29.6	42.3	338 14.5	40.2	309 43.2	28.9	Peacock	53 13.0	S56 40.1
03	256 51.4	252 23.6	12.5	182 30.3	42.5	353 17.1	40.2	324 45.7	28.9	Pollux	243 23.0	N27 58.7
04	271 53.9	267 23.3	13.6	197 31.0	42.7	8 19.7	40.2	339 48.1	28.9	Procyon	244 55.7	N 5 10.4
05	286 56.4	282 23.0	14.8	212 31.7	42.9	23 22.3	40.2	354 50.5	28.9			
06	301 58.8	297 22.6	N 0 16.0	227 32.4	N23 43.0	38 24.8	S22 40.2	9 53.0	S21 28.9	Rasalhague	96 02.6	N12 32.7
W 07	317 01.3	312 22.3	17.1	242 33.1	43.2	53 27.4	40.2	24 55.4	28.9	Regulus	207 39.2	N11 52.4
E 08	332 03.8	327 22.0	18.3	257 33.8	43.4	68 30.0	40.2	39 57.9	28.9	Rigel	281 08.5	S 8 11.1
D 09	347 06.2	342 21.6	19.5	272 34.5	43.6	83 32.6	40.2	55 00.3	28.9	Rigil Kent.	139 45.7	S60 54.7
N 10	2 08.7	357 21.3	20.6	287 35.2	43.8	98 35.1	40.2	70 02.7	28.9	Sabik	102 07.7	S15 44.8
E 11	17 11.2	12 21.0	21.8	302 35.9	44.0	113 37.7	40.2	85 05.2	28.9			
S 12	32 13.6	27 20.7	N 0 23.0	317 36.6	N23 44.1	128 40.3	S22 40.2	100 07.6	S21 28.9	Schedar	349 36.5	N56 38.3
D 13	47 16.1	42 20.3	24.2	332 37.2	44.3	143 42.9	40.2	115 10.1	28.9	Shaula	96 16.3	S37 06.8
A 14	62 18.6	57 20.0	25.3	347 37.9	44.5	158 45.5	40.2	130 12.5	28.9	Sirius	258 30.4	S16 44.9
Y 15	77 21.0	72 19.7	26.5	2 38.6	44.7	173 48.0	40.2	145 14.9	28.9	Spica	158 26.8	S11 15.7
16	92 23.5	87 19.3	27.7	17 39.3	44.9	188 50.6	40.1	160 17.4	28.9	Suhail	222 49.4	S43 30.9
17	107 25.9	102 19.0	28.8	32 40.0	45.1	203 53.2	40.1	175 19.8	28.9			
18	122 28.4	117 18.7	N 0 30.0	47 40.7	N23 45.2	218 55.8	S22 40.1	190 22.3	S21 28.9	Vega	80 36.1	N38 47.9
19	137 30.9	132 18.4	31.2	62 41.4	45.4	233 58.4	40.1	205 24.7	28.9	Zuben'ubi	137 00.7	S16 07.2
20	152 33.3	147 18.0	32.3	77 42.1	45.6	249 00.9	40.1	220 27.1	28.9		SHA	Mer.Pass.
21	167 35.8	162 17.7	33.5	92 42.8	45.8	264 03.5	40.1	235 29.6	28.9			h m
22	182 38.3	177 17.4	34.7	107 43.5	46.0	279 06.1	40.1	250 32.0	28.9	Venus	356 47.6	10 10
23	197 40.7	192 17.0	35.8	122 44.2	46.1	294 08.7	40.1	265 34.5	28.9	Mars	286 26.7	14 51
Mer.Pass.	h m 9 55.4	v −0.3	d 1.2	v 0.7	d 0.2	v 2.6	d 0.0	v 2.4	d 0.0	Jupiter	96 22.8	3 31
										Saturn	67 55.0	5 24

© British Crown Copyright 2018. All rights reserved.

SUN and MOON

UT	SUN GHA	SUN Dec	MOON GHA	v	MOON Dec	d	HP
d h	° ′	° ′	° ′	′	° ′	′	′
22 00	180 19.9	N12 01.5	326 30.5	9.2	S17 27.4	7.9	57.7
01	195 20.0	02.3	340 58.7	9.2	17 35.3	7.9	57.6
02	210 20.2	03.2	355 26.9	9.2	17 43.2	7.8	57.6
03	225 20.3	.. 04.0	9 55.1	9.2	17 51.0	7.6	57.6
04	240 20.4	04.9	24 23.3	9.1	17 58.6	7.5	57.5
05	255 20.5	05.7	38 51.4	9.2	18 06.1	7.5	57.5
06	270 20.7	N12 06.6	53 19.6	9.1	S18 13.6	7.3	57.5
07	285 20.8	07.4	67 47.7	9.2	18 20.9	7.2	57.4
M 08	300 20.9	08.2	82 15.9	9.1	18 28.1	7.1	57.4
O 09	315 21.0	.. 09.1	96 44.0	9.2	18 35.2	7.0	57.4
N 10	330 21.2	09.9	111 12.2	9.1	18 42.2	6.8	57.3
11	345 21.3	10.8	125 40.3	9.2	18 49.0	6.8	57.3
D 12	0 21.4	N12 11.6	140 08.5	9.1	S18 55.8	6.6	57.3
A 13	15 21.5	12.4	154 36.6	9.1	19 02.4	6.6	57.2
Y 14	30 21.7	13.3	169 04.7	9.2	19 09.0	6.4	57.2
15	45 21.8	.. 14.1	183 32.9	9.1	19 15.4	6.3	57.2
16	60 21.9	15.0	198 01.0	9.1	19 21.7	6.2	57.1
17	75 22.0	15.8	212 29.1	9.2	19 27.9	6.0	57.1
18	90 22.1	N12 16.6	226 57.3	9.1	S19 33.9	6.0	57.1
19	105 22.3	17.5	241 25.4	9.1	19 39.9	5.8	57.0
20	120 22.4	18.3	255 53.5	9.2	19 45.7	5.8	57.0
21	135 22.5	.. 19.2	270 21.7	9.1	19 51.5	5.6	56.9
22	150 22.6	20.0	284 49.8	9.1	19 57.1	5.5	56.9
23	165 22.7	20.8	299 17.9	9.2	20 02.6	5.3	56.9
23 00	180 22.9	N12 21.7	313 46.1	9.1	S20 07.9	5.3	56.8
01	195 23.0	22.5	328 14.2	9.2	20 13.2	5.1	56.8
02	210 23.1	23.3	342 42.4	9.2	20 18.3	5.0	56.8
03	225 23.2	.. 24.2	357 10.5	9.2	20 23.3	4.9	56.7
04	240 23.3	25.0	11 38.7	9.2	20 28.2	4.8	56.7
05	255 23.5	25.8	26 06.9	9.2	20 33.0	4.7	56.7
06	270 23.6	N12 26.7	40 35.1	9.2	S20 37.7	4.6	56.6
07	285 23.7	27.5	55 03.3	9.2	20 42.3	4.4	56.6
T 08	300 23.8	28.3	69 31.5	9.2	20 46.7	4.3	56.6
U 09	315 23.9	.. 29.2	83 59.7	9.2	20 51.0	4.2	56.5
E 10	330 24.1	30.0	98 27.9	9.2	20 55.2	4.1	56.5
S 11	345 24.2	30.8	112 56.1	9.3	20 59.3	3.9	56.5
D 12	0 24.3	N12 31.7	127 24.4	9.2	S21 03.2	3.9	56.5
A 13	15 24.4	32.5	141 52.6	9.3	21 07.1	3.7	56.4
Y 14	30 24.5	33.3	156 20.9	9.3	21 10.8	3.6	56.4
15	45 24.7	.. 34.2	170 49.2	9.3	21 14.4	3.5	56.4
16	60 24.8	35.0	185 17.5	9.3	21 17.9	3.3	56.3
17	75 24.9	35.8	199 45.8	9.3	21 21.2	3.3	56.3
18	90 25.0	N12 36.7	214 14.1	9.3	S21 24.5	3.1	56.3
19	105 25.1	37.5	228 42.4	9.4	21 27.6	3.0	56.2
20	120 25.2	38.3	243 10.8	9.4	21 30.6	2.9	56.2
21	135 25.4	.. 39.2	257 39.2	9.4	21 33.5	2.8	56.2
22	150 25.5	40.0	272 07.6	9.4	21 36.3	2.6	56.1
23	165 25.6	40.8	286 36.0	9.4	21 38.9	2.6	56.1
24 00	180 25.7	N12 41.6	301 04.4	9.5	S21 41.5	2.4	56.1
01	195 25.8	42.5	315 32.9	9.4	21 43.9	2.3	56.0
02	210 25.9	43.3	330 01.3	9.5	21 46.2	2.2	56.0
03	225 26.0	.. 44.1	344 29.8	9.5	21 48.4	2.0	56.0
04	240 26.2	44.9	358 58.3	9.6	21 50.4	2.0	56.0
05	255 26.3	45.8	13 26.9	9.5	21 52.4	1.8	55.9
06	270 26.4	N12 46.6	27 55.4	9.6	S21 54.2	1.7	55.9
W 07	285 26.5	47.4	42 24.0	9.6	21 55.9	1.6	55.9
E 08	300 26.6	48.2	56 52.6	9.7	21 57.5	1.5	55.8
D 09	315 26.7	.. 49.1	71 21.3	9.6	21 59.0	1.3	55.8
N 10	330 26.8	49.9	85 49.9	9.7	22 00.3	1.3	55.8
E 11	345 27.0	50.7	100 18.6	9.8	22 01.6	1.1	55.7
S 12	0 27.1	N12 51.5	114 47.4	9.7	S22 02.7	1.0	55.7
D 13	15 27.2	52.4	129 16.1	9.8	22 03.7	0.9	55.7
A 14	30 27.3	53.2	143 44.9	9.8	22 04.6	0.8	55.7
Y 15	45 27.4	.. 54.0	158 13.7	9.8	22 05.4	0.6	55.6
16	60 27.5	54.8	172 42.5	9.9	22 06.0	0.6	55.6
17	75 27.6	55.7	187 11.4	9.9	22 06.6	0.4	55.6
18	90 27.7	N12 56.5	201 40.3	9.9	S22 07.0	0.3	55.6
19	105 27.9	57.3	216 09.2	10.0	22 07.3	0.2	55.5
20	120 28.0	58.1	230 38.2	10.0	22 07.5	0.1	55.5
21	135 28.1	.. 58.9	245 07.2	10.0	22 07.6	0.0	55.5
22	150 28.2	12 59.8	259 36.2	10.1	22 07.6	0.1	55.4
23	165 28.3	N13 00.6	274 05.3	10.1	S22 07.5	0.3	55.4
	SD 15.9	d 0.8	SD 15.6		15.4		15.2

Twilight / Sunrise / Moonrise

Lat.	Naut.	Civil	Sunrise	Moonrise 22	23	24	25
°	h m	h m	h m	h m	h m	h m	h m
N 72	////	////	02 53	01 44	■■■■	■■■■	■■■■
N 70	////	01 33	03 17	00 18	■■■■	■■■■	■■■■
68	////	02 14	03 35	25 36	01 36	03 47	■■■■
66	////	02 42	03 50	24 52	00 52	02 19	03 18
64	01 21	03 02	04 02	24 23	00 23	01 41	02 38
62	01 58	03 19	04 13	24 01	00 01	01 14	02 11
60	02 23	03 32	04 21	23 43	24 54	00 54	01 50
N 58	02 43	03 44	04 29	23 28	24 37	00 37	01 32
56	02 59	03 54	04 36	23 16	24 22	00 22	01 18
54	03 12	04 02	04 42	23 05	24 10	00 10	01 05
52	03 23	04 10	04 47	22 55	23 59	24 54	00 54
50	03 33	04 17	04 52	22 46	23 49	24 44	00 44
45	03 53	04 31	05 03	22 28	23 29	24 23	00 23
N 40	04 08	04 43	05 11	22 13	23 13	24 06	00 06
35	04 21	04 52	05 19	22 00	22 59	23 52	24 40
30	04 31	05 00	05 25	21 49	22 47	23 40	24 28
20	04 47	05 14	05 36	21 30	22 26	23 19	24 08
N 10	04 59	05 24	05 46	21 14	22 08	23 01	23 50
0	05 09	05 34	05 55	20 59	21 52	22 44	23 34
S 10	05 18	05 42	06 04	20 44	21 35	22 27	23 17
20	05 25	05 51	06 13	20 28	21 17	22 08	23 00
30	05 31	05 59	06 24	20 09	20 57	21 47	22 40
35	05 34	06 04	06 30	19 59	20 45	21 35	22 28
40	05 37	06 09	06 37	19 47	20 32	21 21	22 14
45	05 40	06 14	06 45	19 32	20 16	21 04	21 58
S 50	05 43	06 21	06 54	19 15	19 56	20 44	21 38
52	05 44	06 23	06 58	19 07	19 47	20 34	21 28
54	05 45	06 26	07 03	18 57	19 36	20 23	21 18
56	05 46	06 30	07 08	18 47	19 24	20 11	21 06
58	05 47	06 33	07 14	18 35	19 11	19 56	20 52
S 60	05 48	06 37	07 21	18 22	18 55	19 39	20 35

Sunset / Twilight / Moonset

Lat.	Sunset	Civil	Naut.	Moonset 22	23	24	25
°	h m	h m	h m	h m	h m	h m	h m
N 72	21 09	////	////	02 39	■■■■	■■■■	■■■■
N 70	20 44	22 33	////	04 06	■■■■	■■■■	■■■■
68	20 24	21 48	////	04 46	04 39	04 19	■■■■
66	20 09	21 19	////	05 14	05 24	05 47	06 35
64	19 57	20 58	22 44	05 35	05 54	06 25	07 14
62	19 46	20 41	22 03	05 52	06 16	06 52	07 42
60	19 37	20 27	21 37	06 06	06 34	07 13	08 03
N 58	19 29	20 15	21 17	06 19	06 49	07 30	08 20
56	19 22	20 05	21 01	06 29	07 02	07 44	08 35
54	19 16	19 56	20 47	06 39	07 14	07 57	08 48
52	19 11	19 48	20 35	06 47	07 24	08 08	08 59
50	19 06	19 41	20 25	06 55	07 33	08 17	09 09
45	18 55	19 27	20 05	07 11	07 52	08 38	09 29
N 40	18 46	19 15	19 49	07 24	08 07	08 55	09 46
35	18 39	19 05	19 37	07 35	08 20	09 09	10 00
30	18 32	18 57	19 27	07 45	08 32	09 21	10 12
20	18 21	18 43	19 10	08 03	08 51	09 42	10 33
N 10	18 11	18 32	18 58	08 17	09 08	10 00	10 51
0	18 02	18 23	18 48	08 32	09 24	10 17	11 08
S 10	17 53	18 14	18 39	08 46	09 40	10 34	11 25
20	17 43	18 06	18 32	09 01	09 57	10 52	11 43
30	17 33	17 57	18 25	09 18	10 17	11 13	12 04
35	17 27	17 52	18 22	09 28	10 29	11 25	12 16
40	17 20	17 47	18 19	09 40	10 42	11 39	12 30
45	17 12	17 42	18 16	09 53	10 58	11 55	12 46
S 50	17 02	17 35	18 13	10 10	11 17	12 16	13 06
52	16 58	17 33	18 12	10 18	11 26	12 26	13 16
54	16 53	17 29	18 10	10 27	11 36	12 37	13 27
56	16 47	17 26	18 10	10 36	11 48	12 49	13 39
58	16 41	17 23	18 08	10 48	12 01	13 04	13 53
S 60	16 35	17 18	18 07	11 01	12 17	13 21	14 10

SUN / MOON

Day	Eqn. of Time 00ʰ	Eqn. of Time 12ʰ	Mer. Pass.	Mer. Pass. Upper	Mer. Pass. Lower	Age	Phase
d	m s	m s	h m	h m	h m	d	%
22	01 19	01 25	11 59	02 19	14 45	17	89
23	01 31	01 37	11 58	03 12	15 38	18	81
24	01 43	01 48	11 58	04 04	16 30	19	73

© British Crown Copyright 2018. All rights reserved.

UT	ARIES GHA	VENUS −3.9 GHA	Dec	MARS +1.6 GHA	Dec	JUPITER −2.4 GHA	Dec	SATURN +0.5 GHA	Dec	STARS Name	SHA	Dec
25 00	212 43.2	207 16.7	N 0 37.0	137 44.9	N23 46.3	309 11.3	S22 40.1	280 36.9	S21 28.9	Acamar	315 15.7	S40 13.9
01	227 45.7	222 16.4	.. 38.2	152 45.5	46.5	324 13.9	40.1	295 39.3	28.9	Achernar	335 24.4	S57 08.5
02	242 48.1	237 16.0	39.3	167 46.2	46.7	339 16.4	40.1	310 41.8	28.9	Acrux	173 04.2	S63 12.4
03	257 50.6	252 15.7	.. 40.5	182 46.9	.. 46.9	354 19.0	.. 40.1	325 44.2	.. 28.9	Adhara	255 09.6	S29 00.2
04	272 53.1	267 15.4	41.7	197 47.6	47.0	9 21.6	40.1	340 46.7	28.9	Aldebaran	290 45.1	N16 32.6
05	287 55.5	282 15.1	42.8	212 48.3	47.2	24 24.2	40.1	355 49.1	28.9			
06	302 58.0	297 14.7	N 0 44.0	227 49.0	N23 47.4	39 26.8	S22 40.1	10 51.6	S21 28.9	Alioth	166 16.7	N55 51.5
07	318 00.4	312 14.4	45.2	242 49.7	47.6	54 29.4	40.1	25 54.0	28.9	Alkaid	152 55.3	N49 13.1
T 08	333 02.9	327 14.1	46.3	257 50.4	47.7	69 32.0	40.1	40 56.4	28.9	Alnair	27 38.9	S46 51.9
H 09	348 05.4	342 13.7	.. 47.5	272 51.1	.. 47.9	84 34.5	.. 40.1	55 58.9	.. 28.9	Alnilam	275 42.6	S 1 11.6
U 10	3 07.8	357 13.4	48.7	287 51.8	48.1	99 37.1	40.1	71 01.3	28.9	Alphard	217 52.1	S 8 44.7
R 11	18 10.3	12 13.1	49.9	302 52.5	48.3	114 39.7	40.1	86 03.8	28.9			
S 12	33 12.8	27 12.7	N 0 51.0	317 53.1	N23 48.4	129 42.3	S22 40.1	101 06.2	S21 28.9	Alphecca	126 07.3	N26 39.0
D 13	48 15.2	42 12.4	52.2	332 53.8	48.6	144 44.9	40.1	116 08.7	28.9	Alpheratz	357 39.7	N29 11.5
A 14	63 17.7	57 12.1	53.4	347 54.5	48.8	159 47.5	40.0	131 11.1	28.9	Altair	62 04.3	N 8 55.1
Y 15	78 20.2	72 11.8	.. 54.5	2 55.2	.. 49.0	174 50.1	.. 40.0	146 13.5	.. 28.9	Ankaa	353 12.1	S42 12.2
16	93 22.6	87 11.4	55.7	17 55.9	49.1	189 52.6	40.0	161 16.0	28.9	Antares	112 21.1	S26 28.3
17	108 25.1	102 11.1	56.9	32 56.6	49.3	204 55.2	40.0	176 18.4	28.9			
18	123 27.6	117 10.8	N 0 58.0	47 57.3	N23 49.5	219 57.8	S22 40.0	191 20.9	S21 28.9	Arcturus	145 51.8	N19 05.0
19	138 30.0	132 10.4	0 59.2	62 58.0	49.7	235 00.4	40.0	206 23.3	28.9	Atria	107 18.9	S69 03.4
20	153 32.5	147 10.1	1 00.4	77 58.7	49.8	250 03.0	40.0	221 25.8	28.9	Avior	234 16.4	S59 34.6
21	168 34.9	162 09.8	.. 01.5	92 59.4	.. 50.0	265 05.6	.. 40.0	236 28.2	.. 28.9	Bellatrix	278 28.0	N 6 21.8
22	183 37.4	177 09.4	02.7	108 00.0	50.2	280 08.2	40.0	251 30.7	28.9	Betelgeuse	270 57.2	N 7 24.4
23	198 39.9	192 09.1	03.9	123 00.7	50.4	295 10.8	40.0	266 33.1	28.9			
26 00	213 42.3	207 08.8	N 1 05.0	138 01.4	N23 50.5	310 13.4	S22 40.0	281 35.6	S21 28.9	Canopus	263 54.7	S52 42.7
01	228 44.8	222 08.5	06.2	153 02.1	50.7	325 16.0	40.0	296 38.0	28.9	Capella	280 28.9	N46 00.9
02	243 47.3	237 08.1	07.4	168 02.8	50.9	340 18.6	40.0	311 40.4	28.9	Deneb	49 28.8	N45 20.7
03	258 49.7	252 07.8	.. 08.6	183 03.5	.. 51.0	355 21.1	.. 40.0	326 42.9	.. 28.9	Denebola	182 29.4	N14 27.9
04	273 52.2	267 07.5	09.7	198 04.2	51.2	10 23.7	40.0	341 45.3	28.9	Diphda	348 52.2	S17 53.0
05	288 54.7	282 07.1	10.9	213 04.9	51.4	25 26.3	40.0	356 47.8	28.9			
06	303 57.1	297 06.8	N 1 12.1	228 05.6	N23 51.5	40 28.9	S22 40.0	11 50.2	S21 28.9	Dubhe	193 46.4	N61 39.1
07	318 59.6	312 06.5	13.2	243 06.3	51.7	55 31.5	40.0	26 52.7	28.9	Elnath	278 07.9	N28 37.3
F 08	334 02.1	327 06.1	14.4	258 07.0	51.9	70 34.1	40.0	41 55.1	28.9	Eltanin	90 44.0	N51 29.0
R 09	349 04.5	342 05.8	.. 15.6	273 07.6	.. 52.0	85 36.7	.. 40.0	56 57.6	.. 28.9	Enif	33 43.3	N 9 57.6
I 10	4 07.0	357 05.5	16.7	288 08.3	52.2	100 39.3	40.0	72 00.0	28.9	Fomalhaut	15 19.8	S29 31.2
D 11	19 09.4	12 05.1	17.9	303 09.0	52.4	115 41.9	40.0	87 02.5	28.9			
A 12	34 11.9	27 04.8	N 1 19.1	318 09.7	N23 52.5	130 44.5	S22 39.9	102 04.9	S21 28.9	Gacrux	171 56.0	S57 13.3
Y 13	49 14.4	42 04.5	20.2	333 10.4	52.7	145 47.1	39.9	117 07.4	28.9	Gienah	175 47.9	S17 39.0
14	64 16.8	57 04.2	21.4	348 11.1	52.9	160 49.7	39.9	132 09.8	28.9	Hadar	148 41.6	S60 27.9
15	79 19.3	72 03.8	.. 22.6	3 11.8	.. 53.0	175 52.3	.. 39.9	147 12.3	.. 28.9	Hamal	327 56.6	N23 32.9
16	94 21.8	87 03.5	23.8	18 12.5	53.2	190 54.9	39.9	162 14.7	28.9	Kaus Aust.	83 38.3	S34 22.3
17	109 24.2	102 03.2	24.9	33 13.2	53.4	205 57.5	39.9	177 17.2	28.9			
18	124 26.7	117 02.8	N 1 26.1	48 13.8	N23 53.5	221 00.1	S22 39.9	192 19.6	S21 28.9	Kochab	137 18.9	N74 04.7
19	139 29.2	132 02.5	27.3	63 14.5	53.7	236 02.7	39.9	207 22.1	28.9	Markab	13 34.6	N15 18.3
20	154 31.6	147 02.2	28.4	78 15.2	53.9	251 05.3	39.9	222 24.5	28.9	Menkar	314 11.2	N 4 09.6
21	169 34.1	162 01.8	.. 29.6	93 15.9	.. 54.0	266 07.9	.. 39.9	237 27.0	.. 28.9	Menkent	148 02.5	S36 27.8
22	184 36.5	177 01.5	30.8	108 16.6	54.2	281 10.5	39.9	252 29.4	28.9	Miaplacidus	221 38.7	S69 48.1
23	199 39.0	192 01.2	31.9	123 17.3	54.4	296 13.1	39.9	267 31.9	28.9			
27 00	214 41.5	207 00.8	N 1 33.1	138 18.0	N23 54.5	311 15.7	S22 39.9	282 34.3	S21 28.9	Mirfak	308 35.1	N49 55.6
01	229 43.9	222 00.5	34.3	153 18.7	54.7	326 18.3	39.9	297 36.8	28.9	Nunki	75 53.3	S26 16.2
02	244 46.4	237 00.2	35.4	168 19.4	54.9	341 20.9	39.9	312 39.2	28.9	Peacock	53 13.0	S56 40.1
03	259 48.9	251 59.9	.. 36.6	183 20.1	.. 55.0	356 23.5	.. 39.9	327 41.7	.. 28.9	Pollux	243 23.0	N27 58.7
04	274 51.3	266 59.5	37.8	198 20.7	55.2	11 26.1	39.9	342 44.1	28.9	Procyon	244 55.7	N 5 10.4
05	289 53.8	281 59.2	39.0	213 21.4	55.3	26 28.7	39.9	357 46.6	28.9			
06	304 56.3	296 58.9	N 1 40.1	228 22.1	N23 55.5	41 31.3	S22 39.9	12 49.0	S21 28.9	Rasalhague	96 02.5	N12 32.7
07	319 58.7	311 58.5	41.3	243 22.8	55.7	56 33.9	39.9	27 51.5	28.9	Regulus	207 39.2	N11 52.4
S 08	335 01.2	326 58.2	42.5	258 23.5	55.8	71 36.5	39.8	42 53.9	28.9	Rigel	281 08.5	S 8 11.1
A 09	350 03.7	341 57.9	.. 43.6	273 24.2	.. 56.0	86 39.1	.. 39.8	57 56.4	.. 28.9	Rigil Kent.	139 45.7	S60 54.7
T 10	5 06.1	356 57.5	44.8	288 24.9	56.1	101 41.7	39.8	72 58.8	28.9	Sabik	102 07.7	S15 44.8
U 11	20 08.6	11 57.2	46.0	303 25.6	56.3	116 44.3	39.8	88 01.3	28.9			
R 12	35 11.0	26 56.9	N 1 47.1	318 26.3	N23 56.5	131 46.9	S22 39.8	103 03.7	S21 28.9	Schedar	349 36.5	N56 38.3
D 13	50 13.5	41 56.5	48.3	333 26.9	56.6	146 49.5	39.8	118 06.2	28.9	Shaula	96 16.2	S37 06.8
A 14	65 16.0	56 56.2	49.5	348 27.6	56.8	161 52.1	39.8	133 08.6	28.9	Sirius	258 30.4	S16 44.9
Y 15	80 18.4	71 55.9	.. 50.6	3 28.3	.. 56.9	176 54.7	.. 39.8	148 11.1	.. 28.9	Spica	158 26.7	S11 15.7
16	95 20.9	86 55.5	51.8	18 29.0	57.1	191 57.3	39.8	163 13.5	28.9	Suhail	222 49.5	S43 30.9
17	110 23.4	101 55.2	53.0	33 29.7	57.2	206 59.9	39.8	178 16.0	28.9			
18	125 25.8	116 54.9	N 1 54.1	48 30.4	N23 57.4	222 02.5	S22 39.8	193 18.5	S21 28.9	Vega	80 36.1	N38 47.9
19	140 28.3	131 54.5	55.3	63 31.1	57.6	237 05.1	39.8	208 20.9	28.9	Zuben'ubi	137 00.7	S16 07.2
20	155 30.8	146 54.2	56.5	78 31.8	57.7	252 07.7	39.8	223 23.4	28.9		SHA	Mer.Pass.
21	170 33.2	161 53.9	.. 57.7	93 32.4	.. 57.9	267 10.3	.. 39.8	238 25.8	.. 28.9		° ′	h m
22	185 35.7	176 53.5	1 58.8	108 33.1	58.0	282 12.9	39.8	253 28.3	28.9	Venus	353 26.4	10 12
23	200 38.2	191 53.2	N 2 00.0	123 33.8	58.2	297 15.5	39.8	268 30.7	28.9	Mars	284 19.1	14 47
Mer.Pass.	h m 9 43.6	v −0.3	d 1.2	v 0.7	d 0.2	v 2.6	d 0.0	v 2.4	d 0.0	Jupiter	96 31.0	3 19
										Saturn	67 53.2	5 13

© British Crown Copyright 2018. All rights reserved.

UT	SUN GHA	SUN Dec	MOON GHA	v	Dec	d	HP
d h	° '	° '	° '	'	° '	'	'
25 00	180 28.4	N13 01.4	288 34.4	10.1	S22 07.2	0.4	55.4
01	195 28.5	02.2	303 03.5	10.2	22 06.8	0.4	55.4
02	210 28.6	03.0	317 32.7	10.2	22 06.4	0.6	55.3
03	225 28.7 ..	03.9	332 01.9	10.2	22 05.8	0.7	55.3
04	240 28.8	04.7	346 31.1	10.3	22 05.1	0.8	55.3
05	255 29.0	05.5	1 00.4	10.3	22 04.3	0.9	55.3
06	270 29.1	N13 06.3	15 29.7	10.4	S22 03.4	1.1	55.2
07	285 29.2	07.1	29 59.1	10.3	22 02.3	1.1	55.2
T 08	300 29.3	07.9	44 28.4	10.5	22 01.2	1.2	55.2
H 09	315 29.4 ..	08.8	58 57.9	10.5	22 00.0	1.4	55.2
U 10	330 29.5	09.6	73 27.4	10.5	21 58.6	1.5	55.1
R 11	345 29.6	10.4	87 56.9	10.5	21 57.1	1.5	55.1
S 12	0 29.7	N13 11.2	102 26.4	10.6	S21 55.6	1.7	55.1
D 13	15 29.8	12.0	116 56.0	10.7	21 53.9	1.8	55.1
A 14	30 29.9	12.8	131 25.7	10.6	21 52.1	1.9	55.1
Y 15	45 30.0 ..	13.6	145 55.3	10.8	21 50.2	2.0	55.0
16	60 30.1	14.5	160 25.1	10.7	21 48.2	2.1	55.0
17	75 30.3	15.3	174 54.8	10.8	21 46.1	2.2	55.0
18	90 30.4	N13 16.1	189 24.6	10.9	S21 43.9	2.3	55.0
19	105 30.5	16.9	203 54.5	10.9	21 41.6	2.4	54.9
20	120 30.6	17.7	218 24.4	10.9	21 39.2	2.6	54.9
21	135 30.7 ..	18.5	232 54.3	11.0	21 36.6	2.6	54.9
22	150 30.8	19.3	247 24.3	11.0	21 34.0	2.7	54.9
23	165 30.9	20.1	261 54.3	11.1	21 31.3	2.9	54.9
26 00	180 31.0	N13 20.9	276 24.4	11.1	S21 28.4	2.9	54.8
01	195 31.1	21.8	290 54.5	11.2	21 25.5	3.0	54.8
02	210 31.2	22.6	305 24.7	11.2	21 22.5	3.1	54.8
03	225 31.3 ..	23.4	319 54.9	11.2	21 19.4	3.3	54.8
04	240 31.4	24.2	334 25.1	11.3	21 16.1	3.3	54.8
05	255 31.5	25.0	348 55.4	11.2	21 12.8	3.4	54.8
06	270 31.6	N13 25.8	3 25.8	11.4	S21 09.4	3.6	54.7
07	285 31.7	26.6	17 56.2	11.4	21 05.8	3.6	54.7
08	300 31.8	27.4	32 26.6	11.5	21 02.2	3.7	54.7
F 09	315 31.9 ..	28.2	46 57.1	11.6	20 58.5	3.9	54.7
R 10	330 32.0	29.0	61 27.7	11.5	20 54.6	3.9	54.7
I 11	345 32.1	29.8	75 58.2	11.7	20 50.7	4.0	54.6
D 12	0 32.2	N13 30.6	90 28.9	11.7	S20 46.7	4.1	54.6
A 13	15 32.3	31.4	104 59.6	11.7	20 42.6	4.2	54.6
Y 14	30 32.4	32.2	119 30.3	11.8	20 38.4	4.3	54.6
15	45 32.5 ..	33.1	134 01.1	11.8	20 34.1	4.4	54.6
16	60 32.6	33.9	148 31.9	11.9	20 29.7	4.5	54.6
17	75 32.8	34.7	163 02.8	11.9	20 25.2	4.5	54.6
18	90 32.9	N13 35.5	177 33.7	11.9	S20 20.7	4.7	54.5
19	105 33.0	36.3	192 04.6	12.1	20 16.0	4.8	54.5
20	120 33.1	37.1	206 35.7	12.0	20 11.2	4.8	54.5
21	135 33.2 ..	37.9	221 06.7	12.1	20 06.4	5.0	54.5
22	150 33.3	38.7	235 37.8	12.2	20 01.4	5.0	54.5
23	165 33.4	39.5	250 09.0	12.2	19 56.4	5.1	54.5
27 00	180 33.5	N13 40.3	264 40.2	12.3	S19 51.3	5.2	54.5
01	195 33.6	41.1	279 11.5	12.3	19 46.1	5.3	54.4
02	210 33.7	41.9	293 42.8	12.3	19 40.8	5.4	54.4
03	225 33.8 ..	42.7	308 14.1	12.4	19 35.4	5.5	54.4
04	240 33.9	43.5	322 45.5	12.5	19 29.9	5.5	54.4
05	255 34.0	44.3	337 17.0	12.5	19 24.4	5.7	54.4
06	270 34.1	N13 45.1	351 48.5	12.5	S19 18.7	5.7	54.4
07	285 34.1	45.9	6 20.0	12.6	19 13.0	5.8	54.4
S 08	300 34.2	46.7	20 51.6	12.6	19 07.2	5.9	54.4
A 09	315 34.3 ..	47.5	35 23.2	12.7	19 01.3	6.0	54.4
T 10	330 34.4	48.3	49 54.9	12.8	18 55.3	6.0	54.3
U 11	345 34.5	49.1	64 26.7	12.8	18 49.3	6.2	54.3
R 12	0 34.6	N13 49.9	78 58.5	12.8	S18 43.1	6.2	54.3
D 13	15 34.7	50.7	93 30.3	12.9	18 36.9	6.3	54.3
A 14	30 34.8	51.4	108 02.2	12.9	18 30.6	6.4	54.3
Y 15	45 34.9 ..	52.2	122 34.1	12.9	18 24.2	6.4	54.3
16	60 35.0	53.0	137 06.0	13.1	18 17.8	6.6	54.3
17	75 35.1	53.8	151 38.1	13.0	18 11.2	6.6	54.3
18	90 35.2	N13 54.6	166 10.1	13.1	S18 04.6	6.7	54.3
19	105 35.3	55.4	180 42.2	13.2	17 57.9	6.7	54.3
20	120 35.4	56.2	195 14.4	13.2	17 51.2	6.9	54.3
21	135 35.5 ..	57.0	209 46.6	13.2	17 44.3	6.9	54.3
22	150 35.6	57.8	224 18.8	13.3	17 37.4	7.0	54.3
23	165 35.7	58.6	238 51.1	13.3	S17 30.4	7.1	54.3
	SD 15.9	d 0.8	SD 15.0		14.9		14.8

Lat.	Twilight Naut.	Twilight Civil	Sunrise	Moonrise 25	26	27	28
°	h m	h m	h m	h m	h m	h m	h m
N 72	////	////	02 33	▬▬	▬▬	▬▬	05 49
N 70	////	00 57	03 01	▬▬	▬▬	05 36	05 01
68	////	01 54	03 22	▬▬	04 44	04 36	04 30
66	////	02 26	03 38	03 18	03 48	04 01	04 07
64	00 50	02 49	03 52	02 38	03 15	03 36	03 49
62	01 40	03 08	04 03	02 11	02 50	03 16	03 34
60	02 10	03 22	04 13	01 50	02 31	03 00	03 21
N 58	02 31	03 35	04 21	01 32	02 15	02 47	03 10
56	02 49	03 46	04 29	01 18	02 01	02 35	03 01
54	03 03	03 55	04 35	01 05	01 49	02 24	02 52
52	03 15	04 03	04 41	00 54	01 39	02 15	02 45
50	03 26	04 11	04 46	00 44	01 29	02 07	02 38
45	03 47	04 26	04 58	00 23	01 10	01 49	02 23
N 40	04 03	04 38	05 07	00 06	00 54	01 35	02 11
35	04 17	04 49	05 15	24 40	00 40	01 23	02 01
30	04 27	04 57	05 22	24 28	00 28	01 12	01 51
20	04 45	05 11	05 34	24 08	00 08	00 54	01 36
N 10	04 58	05 23	05 45	23 50	24 37	00 37	01 22
0	05 09	05 33	05 54	23 34	24 22	00 22	01 09
S 10	05 18	05 43	06 04	23 17	24 07	00 07	00 56
20	05 26	05 52	06 14	23 00	23 51	24 42	00 42
30	05 33	06 01	06 26	22 40	23 33	24 26	00 26
35	05 36	06 06	06 32	22 28	23 22	24 17	00 17
40	05 40	06 12	06 40	22 14	23 09	24 06	00 06
45	05 43	06 18	06 48	21 58	22 55	23 54	24 54
S 50	05 47	06 25	06 59	21 38	22 37	23 39	24 42
52	05 48	06 28	07 03	21 28	22 23	23 31	24 36
54	05 50	06 31	07 09	21 18	22 19	23 23	24 30
56	05 51	06 35	07 14	21 06	22 08	23 14	24 23
58	05 53	06 39	07 21	20 52	21 55	23 04	24 16
S 60	05 55	06 44	07 28	20 35	21 41	22 53	24 07

Lat.	Sunset	Twilight Civil	Twilight Naut.	Moonset 25	26	27	28
°	h m	h m	h m	h m	h m	h m	h m
N 72	21 28	////	////	▬▬	▬▬	▬▬	09 05
N 70	20 59	23 15	////	▬▬	▬▬	07 42	09 52
68	20 37	22 08	////	▬▬	06 53	08 41	10 22
66	20 20	21 34	////	06 35	07 49	09 15	10 44
64	20 06	21 10	23 20	07 14	08 22	09 39	11 01
62	19 54	20 51	22 21	07 42	08 46	09 59	11 16
60	19 45	20 35	21 50	08 03	09 05	10 14	11 28
N 58	19 36	20 23	21 27	08 20	09 21	10 28	11 38
56	19 29	20 12	21 09	08 35	09 34	10 39	11 47
54	19 22	20 02	20 55	08 48	09 46	10 49	11 55
52	19 16	19 54	20 42	08 59	09 56	10 58	12 02
50	19 10	19 46	20 32	09 09	10 05	11 06	12 09
45	18 59	19 31	20 10	09 29	10 25	11 23	12 23
N 40	18 49	19 18	19 53	09 46	10 40	11 37	12 34
35	18 41	19 08	19 40	10 00	10 54	11 48	12 44
30	18 34	18 59	19 29	10 12	11 05	11 58	12 52
20	18 22	18 45	19 11	10 33	11 25	12 16	13 06
N 10	18 11	18 33	18 58	10 51	11 42	12 31	13 19
0	18 01	18 23	18 47	11 08	11 58	12 45	13 31
S 10	17 52	18 13	18 38	11 25	12 13	12 59	13 42
20	17 41	18 04	18 30	11 43	12 30	13 14	13 55
30	17 30	17 54	18 22	12 04	12 50	13 31	14 09
35	17 23	17 49	18 19	12 16	13 01	13 41	14 17
40	17 16	17 43	18 15	12 30	13 14	13 52	14 26
45	17 07	17 37	18 12	12 46	13 29	14 06	14 37
S 50	16 56	17 30	18 08	13 06	13 48	14 22	14 50
52	16 52	17 27	18 07	13 16	13 56	14 29	14 56
54	16 46	17 23	18 05	13 27	14 06	14 38	15 03
56	16 40	17 20	18 03	13 39	14 17	14 47	15 10
58	16 34	17 15	18 02	13 53	14 30	14 58	15 18
S 60	16 26	17 11	18 00	14 10	14 45	15 10	15 28

Day	SUN Eqn. of Time 00h	SUN Eqn. of Time 12h	SUN Mer. Pass.	MOON Mer. Pass. Upper	MOON Mer. Pass. Lower	Age	Phase
d	m s	m s	h m	h m	h m	d	%
25	01 53	01 59	11 58	04 56	17 21	20	64
26	02 04	02 09	11 58	05 46	18 10	21	54
27	02 14	02 18	11 58	06 34	18 57	22	45

© British Crown Copyright 2018. All rights reserved.

UT	ARIES GHA	VENUS −3.8 GHA	Dec	MARS +1.6 GHA	Dec	JUPITER −2.4 GHA	Dec	SATURN +0.5 GHA	Dec	STARS Name	SHA	Dec
28 00	215 40.6	206 52.9	N 2 01.2	138 34.5	N23 58.3	312 18.1	S22 39.8	283 33.2	S21 28.9	Acamar	315 15.7	S40 13.9
01	230 43.1	221 52.5	02.3	153 35.2	58.5	327 20.7	39.8	298 35.6	28.9	Achernar	335 24.4	S57 08.5
02	245 45.5	236 52.2	03.5	168 35.9	58.7	342 23.4	39.8	313 38.1	28.9	Acrux	173 04.2	S63 12.5
03	260 48.0	251 51.9	.. 04.7	183 36.6	.. 58.8	357 26.0	.. 39.7	328 40.5	.. 28.9	Adhara	255 09.6	S29 00.2
04	275 50.5	266 51.5	05.8	198 37.3	59.0	12 28.6	39.7	343 43.0	28.9	Aldebaran	290 45.1	N16 32.7
05	290 52.9	281 51.2	07.0	213 38.0	59.1	27 31.2	39.7	358 45.5	28.9			
06	305 55.4	296 50.9	N 2 08.2	228 38.6	N23 59.3	42 33.8	S22 39.7	13 47.9	S21 28.9	Alioth	166 16.7	N55 51.5
07	320 57.9	311 50.5	09.3	243 39.3	59.4	57 36.4	39.7	28 50.4	28.9	Alkaid	152 55.3	N49 13.2
08	336 00.3	326 50.2	10.5	258 40.0	59.6	72 39.0	39.7	43 52.8	28.9	Alnair	27 38.9	S46 51.9
S 09	351 02.8	341 49.9	.. 11.7	273 40.7	.. 59.7	87 41.6	.. 39.7	58 55.3	.. 28.9	Alnilam	275 42.6	S 1 11.6
U 10	6 05.3	356 49.5	12.9	288 41.4	23 59.9	102 44.2	39.7	73 57.7	28.9	Alphard	217 52.1	S 8 44.7
N 11	21 07.7	11 49.2	14.0	303 42.1	24 00.0	117 46.8	39.7	89 00.2	28.9			
D 12	36 10.2	26 48.9	N 2 15.2	318 42.8	N24 00.2	132 49.4	S22 39.7	104 02.7	S21 28.9	Alphecca	126 07.3	N26 39.0
A 13	51 12.6	41 48.5	16.4	333 43.5	00.3	147 52.1	39.7	119 05.1	28.9	Alpheratz	357 39.7	N29 11.5
Y 14	66 15.1	56 48.2	17.5	348 44.1	00.5	162 54.7	39.7	134 07.6	28.9	Altair	62 04.3	N 8 55.1
15	81 17.6	71 47.9	.. 18.7	3 44.8	.. 00.6	177 57.3	.. 39.7	149 10.0	.. 28.9	Ankaa	353 12.1	S42 12.1
16	96 20.0	86 47.5	19.9	18 45.5	00.8	192 59.9	39.7	164 12.5	28.9	Antares	112 21.1	S26 28.3
17	111 22.5	101 47.2	21.0	33 46.2	00.9	208 02.5	39.7	179 14.9	28.9			
18	126 25.0	116 46.9	N 2 22.2	48 46.9	N24 01.1	223 05.1	S22 39.7	194 17.4	S21 28.9	Arcturus	145 51.8	N19 05.0
19	141 27.4	131 46.5	23.4	63 47.6	01.2	238 07.7	39.7	209 19.9	28.9	Atria	107 18.8	S69 03.4
20	156 29.9	146 46.2	24.5	78 48.3	01.4	253 10.3	39.7	224 22.3	28.9	Avior	234 16.5	S59 34.6
21	171 32.4	161 45.9	.. 25.7	93 49.0	.. 01.5	268 13.0	.. 39.7	239 24.8	.. 28.9	Bellatrix	278 28.0	N 6 21.8
22	186 34.8	176 45.5	26.9	108 49.7	01.7	283 15.6	39.6	254 27.2	28.9	Betelgeuse	270 57.2	N 7 24.4
23	201 37.3	191 45.2	28.0	123 50.3	01.8	298 18.2	39.6	269 29.7	28.9			
29 00	216 39.8	206 44.9	N 2 29.2	138 51.0	N24 02.0	313 20.8	S22 39.6	284 32.2	S21 28.9	Canopus	263 54.7	S52 42.7
01	231 42.2	221 44.5	30.4	153 51.7	02.1	328 23.4	39.6	299 34.6	28.9	Capella	280 28.9	N46 00.9
02	246 44.7	236 44.2	31.5	168 52.4	02.3	343 26.0	39.6	314 37.1	28.9	Deneb	49 28.8	N45 20.7
03	261 47.1	251 43.9	.. 32.7	183 53.1	.. 02.4	358 28.7	.. 39.6	329 39.5	.. 28.9	Denebola	182 09.4	N14 27.9
04	276 49.6	266 43.5	33.9	198 53.8	02.5	13 31.3	39.6	344 42.0	28.9	Diphda	348 52.2	S17 53.0
05	291 52.1	281 43.2	35.1	213 54.5	02.7	28 33.9	39.6	359 44.5	28.9			
06	306 54.5	296 42.9	N 2 36.2	228 55.2	N24 02.8	43 36.5	S22 39.6	14 46.9	S21 28.9	Dubhe	193 46.4	N61 39.1
07	321 57.0	311 42.5	37.4	243 55.8	03.0	58 39.1	39.6	29 49.4	28.9	Elnath	278 07.9	N28 37.3
08	336 59.5	326 42.2	38.6	258 56.5	03.1	73 41.7	39.6	44 51.8	28.9	Eltanin	90 43.9	N51 29.0
M 09	352 01.9	341 41.9	.. 39.7	273 57.2	.. 03.3	88 44.4	.. 39.6	59 54.3	.. 28.9	Enif	33 43.3	N 9 57.6
O 10	7 04.4	356 41.5	40.9	288 57.9	03.4	103 47.0	39.6	74 56.8	28.9	Fomalhaut	15 19.8	S29 31.2
N 11	22 06.9	11 41.2	42.1	303 58.6	03.6	118 49.6	39.6	89 59.2	28.9			
D 12	37 09.3	26 40.9	N 2 43.2	318 59.3	N24 03.7	133 52.2	S22 39.6	105 01.7	S21 28.9	Gacrux	171 56.0	S57 13.4
A 13	52 11.8	41 40.5	44.4	334 00.0	03.8	148 54.8	39.6	120 04.1	28.9	Gienah	175 47.9	S17 39.0
Y 14	67 14.2	56 40.2	45.6	349 00.7	04.0	163 57.5	39.6	135 06.6	28.9	Hadar	148 41.6	S60 27.9
15	82 16.7	71 39.8	.. 46.7	4 01.3	.. 04.1	179 00.1	.. 39.5	150 09.1	.. 28.9	Hamal	327 56.6	N23 32.9
16	97 19.2	86 39.5	47.9	19 02.0	04.3	194 02.7	39.5	165 11.5	28.9	Kaus Aust.	83 38.3	S34 22.3
17	112 21.6	101 39.2	49.1	34 02.7	04.4	209 05.3	39.5	180 14.0	28.9			
18	127 24.1	116 38.8	N 2 50.2	49 03.4	N24 04.5	224 07.9	S22 39.5	195 16.4	S21 28.9	Kochab	137 18.9	N74 04.7
19	142 26.6	131 38.5	51.4	64 04.1	04.7	239 10.6	39.5	210 18.9	28.9	Markab	13 34.6	N15 18.3
20	157 29.0	146 38.2	52.6	79 04.8	04.8	254 13.2	39.5	225 21.4	28.9	Menkar	314 11.2	N 4 09.6
21	172 31.5	161 37.8	.. 53.7	94 05.5	.. 05.0	269 15.8	.. 39.5	240 23.8	.. 28.9	Menkent	148 02.5	S36 27.8
22	187 34.0	176 37.5	54.9	109 06.1	05.1	284 18.4	39.5	255 26.3	28.9	Miaplacidus	221 38.8	S69 48.1
23	202 36.4	191 37.2	56.1	124 06.8	05.2	299 21.0	39.5	270 28.8	28.9			
30 00	217 38.9	206 36.8	N 2 57.2	139 07.5	N24 05.4	314 23.7	S22 39.5	285 31.2	S21 28.9	Mirfak	308 35.1	N49 55.6
01	232 41.4	221 36.5	58.4	154 08.2	05.5	329 26.3	39.5	300 33.7	28.9	Nunki	75 53.2	S26 16.2
02	247 43.8	236 36.1	2 59.6	169 08.9	05.7	344 28.9	39.5	315 36.2	28.9	Peacock	53 12.9	S56 40.1
03	262 46.3	251 35.8	3 00.7	184 09.6	.. 05.8	359 31.5	.. 39.5	330 38.6	.. 28.9	Pollux	243 23.0	N27 58.7
04	277 48.7	266 35.5	01.9	199 10.3	05.9	14 34.2	39.5	345 41.1	28.9	Procyon	244 55.7	N 5 10.4
05	292 51.2	281 35.1	03.1	214 11.0	06.1	29 36.8	39.5	0 43.5	28.9			
06	307 53.7	296 34.8	N 3 04.2	229 11.6	N24 06.2	44 39.4	S22 39.5	15 46.0	S21 28.9	Rasalhague	96 02.5	N12 32.8
07	322 56.1	311 34.5	05.4	244 12.3	06.3	59 42.0	39.5	30 48.5	28.9	Regulus	207 39.2	N11 52.4
T 08	337 58.6	326 34.1	06.6	259 13.0	06.5	74 44.7	39.4	45 50.9	28.9	Rigel	281 08.5	S 8 11.0
U 09	353 01.1	341 33.8	.. 07.7	274 13.7	.. 06.6	89 47.3	.. 39.4	60 53.4	.. 28.9	Rigil Kent.	139 45.7	S60 54.7
E 10	8 03.5	356 33.5	08.9	289 14.4	06.8	104 49.9	39.4	75 55.9	28.9	Sabik	102 07.7	S15 44.8
S 11	23 06.0	11 33.1	10.1	304 15.1	06.9	119 52.5	39.4	90 58.3	28.9			
D 12	38 08.5	26 32.8	N 3 11.2	319 15.8	N24 07.0	134 55.2	S22 39.4	106 00.8	S21 28.9	Schedar	349 36.5	N56 38.3
A 13	53 10.9	41 32.4	12.4	334 16.4	07.2	149 57.8	39.4	121 03.3	28.9	Shaula	96 16.2	S37 06.8
Y 14	68 13.4	56 32.1	13.6	349 17.1	07.3	165 00.4	39.4	136 05.7	28.9	Sirius	258 30.4	S16 44.8
15	83 15.9	71 31.8	.. 14.7	4 17.8	.. 07.4	180 03.0	.. 39.4	151 08.2	.. 28.9	Spica	158 26.7	S11 15.7
16	98 18.3	86 31.4	15.9	19 18.5	07.6	195 05.7	39.4	166 10.7	28.9	Suhail	222 49.5	S43 30.9
17	113 20.8	101 31.1	17.1	34 19.2	07.7	210 08.3	39.4	181 13.1	28.9			
18	128 23.2	116 30.8	N 3 18.2	49 19.9	N24 07.8	225 10.9	S22 39.4	196 15.6	S21 28.9	Vega	80 36.0	N38 47.9
19	143 25.7	131 30.4	19.4	64 20.6	08.0	240 13.6	39.4	211 18.1	28.9	Zuben'ubi	137 00.7	S16 07.2
20	158 28.2	146 30.1	20.6	79 21.3	08.1	255 16.2	39.4	226 20.5	29.0		SHA	Mer. Pass.
21	173 30.6	161 29.7	.. 21.7	94 21.9	.. 08.2	270 18.8	.. 39.4	241 23.0	.. 29.0	Venus	350 05.1	10 13
22	188 33.1	176 29.4	22.9	109 22.6	08.4	285 21.4	39.4	256 25.5	29.0	Mars	282 11.3	14 44
23	203 35.6	191 29.1	24.1	124 23.3	08.5	300 24.1	39.4	271 27.9	29.0	Jupiter	96 41.1	3 06
Mer. Pass. 9 31.8		v −0.3	d 1.2	v 0.7	d 0.1	v 2.6	d 0.0	v 2.5	d 0.0	Saturn	67 52.4	5 01

© British Crown Copyright 2018. All rights reserved.

UT	SUN GHA	SUN Dec	MOON GHA	v	MOON Dec	d	HP
d h	° '	° '	° '	'	° '	'	'
28 00	180 35.8	N13 59.4	253 23.4	13.4	S17 23.3	7.1	54.2
01	195 35.9	14 00.2	267 55.8	13.4	17 16.2	7.3	54.2
02	210 36.0	01.0	282 28.2	13.5	17 08.9	7.3	54.2
03	225 36.1	.. 01.8	297 00.7	13.5	17 01.6	7.3	54.2
04	240 36.2	02.5	311 33.2	13.5	16 54.3	7.5	54.2
05	255 36.3	03.3	326 05.7	13.6	16 46.8	7.5	54.2
06	270 36.3	N14 04.1	340 38.3	13.7	S16 39.3	7.6	54.2
07	285 36.4	04.9	355 11.0	13.6	16 31.7	7.6	54.2
S 08	300 36.5	05.7	9 43.6	13.7	16 24.1	7.7	54.2
U 09	315 36.6	.. 06.5	24 16.3	13.8	16 16.4	7.8	54.2
N 10	330 36.7	07.3	38 49.1	13.8	16 08.6	7.9	54.2
11	345 36.8	08.1	53 21.9	13.8	16 00.7	7.9	54.2
D 12	0 36.9	N14 08.9	67 54.7	13.9	S15 52.8	8.0	54.2
A 13	15 37.0	09.6	82 27.6	13.9	15 44.8	8.0	54.2
Y 14	30 37.1	10.4	97 00.5	14.0	15 36.8	8.2	54.2
15	45 37.2	.. 11.2	111 33.5	14.0	15 28.6	8.2	54.2
16	60 37.3	12.0	126 06.5	14.0	15 20.4	8.2	54.2
17	75 37.4	12.8	140 39.5	14.1	15 12.2	8.3	54.2
18	90 37.4	N14 13.6	155 12.6	14.1	S15 03.9	8.4	54.2
19	105 37.5	14.3	169 45.7	14.1	14 55.5	8.5	54.2
20	120 37.6	15.1	184 18.8	14.2	14 47.0	8.5	54.2
21	135 37.7	.. 15.9	198 52.0	14.2	14 38.5	8.5	54.2
22	150 37.8	16.7	213 25.2	14.2	14 30.0	8.7	54.2
23	165 37.9	17.5	227 58.4	14.3	14 21.3	8.7	54.2
29 00	180 38.0	N14 18.3	242 31.7	14.3	S14 12.6	8.7	54.2
01	195 38.1	19.0	257 05.0	14.4	14 03.9	8.8	54.2
02	210 38.2	19.8	271 38.4	14.4	13 55.1	8.9	54.2
03	225 38.3	.. 20.6	286 11.8	14.4	13 46.2	8.9	54.2
04	240 38.3	21.4	300 45.2	14.4	13 37.3	9.0	54.2
05	255 38.4	22.2	315 18.6	14.5	13 28.3	9.1	54.2
06	270 38.5	N14 22.9	329 52.1	14.5	S13 19.2	9.1	54.2
07	285 38.6	23.7	344 25.6	14.5	13 10.1	9.1	54.2
08	300 38.7	24.5	358 59.1	14.6	13 01.0	9.2	54.2
M 09	315 38.8	.. 25.3	13 32.7	14.6	12 51.8	9.3	54.2
O 10	330 38.9	26.1	28 06.3	14.6	12 42.5	9.3	54.2
N 11	345 39.0	26.8	42 39.9	14.7	12 33.2	9.4	54.2
D 12	0 39.0	N14 27.6	57 13.6	14.7	S12 23.8	9.4	54.2
A 13	15 39.1	28.4	71 47.3	14.7	12 14.4	9.5	54.2
Y 14	30 39.2	29.2	86 21.0	14.7	12 04.9	9.5	54.3
15	45 39.3	.. 29.9	100 54.7	14.8	11 55.4	9.6	54.3
16	60 39.4	30.7	115 28.5	14.8	11 45.8	9.7	54.3
17	75 39.5	31.5	130 02.3	14.8	11 36.1	9.6	54.3
18	90 39.5	N14 32.3	144 36.1	14.8	S11 26.5	9.8	54.3
19	105 39.6	33.0	159 09.9	14.8	11 16.7	9.8	54.3
20	120 39.7	33.8	173 43.7	14.9	11 06.9	9.8	54.3
21	135 39.8	.. 34.6	188 17.6	14.9	10 57.1	9.9	54.3
22	150 39.9	35.4	202 51.5	14.9	10 47.2	9.9	54.3
23	165 40.0	36.1	217 25.4	15.0	10 37.3	10.0	54.3
30 00	180 40.1	N14 36.9	231 59.4	15.0	S10 27.3	10.0	54.3
01	195 40.1	37.7	246 33.4	14.9	10 17.3	10.1	54.3
02	210 40.2	38.4	261 07.3	15.0	10 07.2	10.1	54.3
03	225 40.3	.. 39.2	275 41.3	15.1	9 57.1	10.1	54.3
04	240 40.4	40.0	290 15.4	15.0	9 47.0	10.2	54.4
05	255 40.5	40.8	304 49.4	15.0	9 36.8	10.3	54.4
06	270 40.5	N14 41.5	319 23.4	15.1	S 9 26.5	10.3	54.4
07	285 40.6	42.3	333 57.5	15.1	9 16.2	10.3	54.4
T 08	300 40.7	43.1	348 31.6	15.1	9 05.9	10.4	54.4
U 09	315 40.8	.. 43.8	3 05.7	15.1	8 55.5	10.4	54.4
E 10	330 40.9	44.6	17 39.8	15.1	8 45.1	10.4	54.4
S 11	345 41.0	45.4	32 13.9	15.2	8 34.7	10.5	54.4
D 12	0 41.0	N14 46.1	46 48.1	15.2	S 8 24.2	10.5	54.4
A 13	15 41.1	46.9	61 22.2	15.2	8 13.7	10.6	54.4
Y 14	30 41.2	47.7	75 56.4	15.1	8 03.1	10.6	54.5
15	45 41.3	.. 48.4	90 30.5	15.2	7 52.5	10.6	54.5
16	60 41.4	49.2	105 04.7	15.2	7 41.9	10.7	54.5
17	75 41.4	50.0	119 38.9	15.2	7 31.2	10.7	54.5
18	90 41.5	N14 50.7	134 13.1	15.2	S 7 20.5	10.8	54.5
19	105 41.6	51.5	148 47.3	15.2	7 09.7	10.8	54.5
20	120 41.7	52.3	163 21.5	15.3	6 58.9	10.8	54.5
21	135 41.8	.. 53.0	177 55.8	15.2	6 48.1	10.9	54.5
22	150 41.8	53.8	192 30.0	15.2	6 37.2	10.8	54.6
23	165 41.9	54.5	207 04.2	15.3	S 6 26.4	11.0	54.6
	SD 15.9	d 0.8	SD 14.8		14.8		14.8

Lat.	Twilight Naut.	Twilight Civil	Sunrise	Moonrise 28	29	30	1
°	h m	h m	h m	h m	h m	h m	h m
N 72	////	////	02 11	05 49	05 10	04 48	04 31
N 70	////	////	02 44	05 01	04 45	04 33	04 23
68	////	01 30	03 08	04 30	04 26	04 21	04 17
66	////	02 09	03 27	04 07	04 10	04 11	04 11
64	////	02 36	03 42	03 49	03 57	04 03	04 07
62	01 19	02 56	03 54	03 34	03 46	03 55	04 03
60	01 55	03 13	04 04	03 21	03 37	03 49	04 00
N 58	02 20	03 26	04 14	03 10	03 29	03 44	03 57
56	02 39	03 38	04 22	03 01	03 21	03 39	03 54
54	02 54	03 48	04 29	02 52	03 15	03 34	03 51
52	03 07	03 57	04 35	02 45	03 09	03 30	03 49
50	03 19	04 05	04 41	02 38	03 04	03 27	03 47
45	03 41	04 21	04 53	02 23	02 52	03 19	03 43
N 40	03 59	04 34	05 03	02 11	02 43	03 12	03 39
35	04 13	04 45	05 12	02 01	02 35	03 06	03 36
30	04 24	04 54	05 19	01 51	02 27	03 01	03 33
20	04 42	05 09	05 32	01 36	02 15	02 52	03 28
N 10	04 56	05 22	05 44	01 22	02 04	02 44	03 24
0	05 08	05 33	05 54	01 09	01 54	02 37	03 20
S 10	05 18	05 43	06 04	00 56	01 43	02 30	03 15
20	05 26	05 53	06 15	00 42	01 32	02 22	03 11
30	05 35	06 03	06 27	00 26	01 20	02 13	03 06
35	05 39	06 08	06 35	00 17	01 12	02 08	03 03
40	05 43	06 14	06 43	00 06	01 04	02 02	03 00
45	05 47	06 21	06 52	24 54	00 54	01 55	02 56
S 50	05 51	06 29	07 03	24 42	00 42	01 46	02 51
52	05 53	06 33	07 08	24 36	00 36	01 43	02 49
54	05 55	06 36	07 14	24 30	00 30	01 38	02 47
56	05 57	06 41	07 20	24 23	00 23	01 34	02 44
58	05 59	06 45	07 27	24 16	00 16	01 28	02 42
S 60	06 01	06 50	07 35	24 07	00 07	01 22	02 38

Lat.	Sunset	Twilight Civil	Twilight Naut.	Moonset 28	29	30	1
°	h m	h m	h m	h m	h m	h m	h m
N 72	21 50	////	////	09 05	11 16	13 08	14 55
N 70	21 15	////	////	09 52	11 40	13 21	15 00
68	20 50	22 33	////	10 22	11 58	13 31	15 04
66	20 31	21 50	////	10 44	12 12	13 40	15 07
64	20 16	21 22	////	11 01	12 24	13 47	15 10
62	20 03	21 01	22 43	11 16	12 34	13 53	15 13
60	19 52	20 44	22 04	11 28	12 43	13 59	15 15
N 58	19 43	20 31	21 38	11 38	12 50	14 03	15 17
56	19 35	20 19	21 19	11 47	12 57	14 07	15 19
54	19 27	20 08	21 03	11 55	13 03	14 11	15 20
52	19 21	19 59	20 49	12 02	13 08	14 15	15 22
50	19 15	19 51	20 38	12 09	13 13	14 18	15 23
45	19 03	19 35	20 15	12 23	13 23	14 24	15 26
N 40	18 52	19 21	19 57	12 34	13 32	14 30	15 28
35	18 44	19 10	19 43	12 44	13 39	14 34	15 30
30	18 36	19 01	19 31	12 52	13 45	14 38	15 32
20	18 23	18 46	19 13	13 06	13 56	14 46	15 35
N 10	18 11	18 33	18 59	13 19	14 06	14 52	15 38
0	18 01	18 22	18 47	13 31	14 15	14 58	15 40
S 10	17 50	18 12	18 37	13 42	14 24	15 03	15 42
20	17 39	18 02	18 28	13 55	14 33	15 09	15 45
30	17 27	17 52	18 20	14 09	14 44	15 16	15 48
35	17 20	17 46	18 16	14 17	14 50	15 20	15 49
40	17 12	17 40	18 12	14 26	14 57	15 25	15 51
45	17 02	17 33	18 08	14 37	15 05	15 30	15 53
S 50	16 51	17 25	18 03	14 50	15 14	15 36	15 56
52	16 46	17 21	18 01	14 56	15 19	15 39	15 57
54	16 40	17 18	17 59	15 03	15 24	15 42	15 58
56	16 34	17 13	17 57	15 10	15 29	15 45	16 00
58	16 27	17 09	17 55	15 18	15 35	15 49	16 01
S 60	16 18	17 04	17 53	15 28	15 42	15 53	16 03

Day	SUN Eqn. of Time 00h	SUN Eqn. of Time 12h	SUN Mer. Pass.	MOON Mer. Pass. Upper	MOON Mer. Pass. Lower	Age	Phase
d	m s	m s	h m	h m	h m	d %	
28	02 23	02 27	11 58	07 20	19 42	23 35	
29	02 32	02 36	11 57	08 04	20 26	24 27	
30	02 40	02 44	11 57	08 47	21 09	25 19	

© British Crown Copyright 2018. All rights reserved.

UT	ARIES GHA	VENUS −3.8 GHA	Dec	MARS +1.6 GHA	Dec	JUPITER −2.5 GHA	Dec	SATURN +0.5 GHA	Dec	STARS Name	SHA	Dec
1 00	218 38.0	206 28.7	N 3 25.2	139 24.0	N24 08.6	315 26.7	S22 39.4	286 30.4	S21 29.0	Acamar	315 15.7	S40 13.9
01	233 40.5	221 28.4	26.4	154 24.7	08.7	330 29.3	39.3	301 32.9	29.0	Achernar	335 24.4	S57 08.4
02	248 43.0	236 28.0	27.6	169 25.4	08.9	345 32.0	39.3	316 35.3	29.0	Acrux	173 04.2	S63 12.5
03	263 45.4	251 27.7 ..	28.7	184 26.1 ..	09.0	0 34.6 ..	39.3	331 37.8 ..	29.0	Adhara	255 09.6	S29 00.2
04	278 47.9	266 27.4	29.9	199 26.7	09.1	15 37.2	39.3	346 40.3	29.0	Aldebaran	290 45.1	N16 32.7
05	293 50.3	281 27.0	31.1	214 27.4	09.3	30 39.9	39.3	1 42.7	29.0			
06	308 52.8	296 26.7	N 3 32.2	229 28.1	N24 09.4	45 42.5	S22 39.3	16 45.2	S21 29.0	Alioth	166 16.7	N55 51.5
W 07	323 55.3	311 26.3	33.4	244 28.8	09.5	60 45.1	39.3	31 47.7	29.0	Alkaid	152 55.3	N49 13.2
E 08	338 57.7	326 26.0	34.5	259 29.5	09.6	75 47.8	39.3	46 50.2	29.0	Alnair	27 38.9	S46 51.9
D 09	354 00.2	341 25.7 ..	35.7	274 30.2 ..	09.8	90 50.4 ..	39.3	61 52.6 ..	29.0	Alnilam	275 42.6	S 1 11.6
N 10	9 02.7	356 25.3	36.9	289 30.9	09.9	105 53.0	39.3	76 55.1	29.0	Alphard	217 52.1	S 8 44.7
E 11	24 05.1	11 25.0	38.0	304 31.5	10.0	120 55.7	39.3	91 57.6	29.0			
S 12	39 07.6	26 24.6	N 3 39.2	319 32.2	N24 10.2	135 58.3	S22 39.3	107 00.0	S21 29.0	Alphecca	126 07.3	N26 39.0
D 13	54 10.1	41 24.3	40.4	334 32.9	10.3	151 00.9	39.3	122 02.5	29.0	Alpheratz	357 39.7	N29 11.5
A 14	69 12.5	56 24.0	41.5	349 33.6	10.4	166 03.6	39.3	137 05.0	29.0	Altair	62 04.3	N 8 55.1
Y 15	84 15.0	71 23.6 ..	42.7	4 34.3 ..	10.5	181 06.2 ..	39.3	152 07.4 ..	29.0	Ankaa	353 12.1	S42 12.1
16	99 17.5	86 23.3	43.9	19 35.0	10.6	196 08.8	39.2	167 09.9	29.0	Antares	112 21.0	S26 28.3
17	114 19.9	101 22.9	45.0	34 35.7	10.8	211 11.5	39.2	182 12.4	29.0			
18	129 22.4	116 22.6	N 3 46.2	49 36.3	N24 10.9	226 14.1	S22 39.2	197 14.9	S21 29.0	Arcturus	145 51.8	N19 05.0
19	144 24.8	131 22.3	47.4	64 37.0	11.0	241 16.8	39.2	212 17.3	29.0	Atria	107 18.8	S69 03.4
20	159 27.3	146 21.9	48.5	79 37.7	11.2	256 19.4	39.2	227 19.8	29.0	Avior	234 16.5	S59 34.6
21	174 29.8	161 21.6 ..	49.7	94 38.4 ..	11.3	271 22.0 ..	39.2	242 22.3 ..	29.0	Bellatrix	278 28.0	N 6 21.8
22	189 32.2	176 21.2	50.8	109 39.1	11.4	286 24.7	39.2	257 24.7	29.0	Betelgeuse	270 57.2	N 7 24.4
23	204 34.7	191 20.9	52.0	124 39.8	11.5	301 27.3	39.2	272 27.2	29.0			
2 00	219 37.2	206 20.6	N 3 53.2	139 40.5	N24 11.6	316 29.9	S22 39.2	287 29.7	S21 29.0	Canopus	263 54.7	S52 42.7
01	234 39.6	221 20.2	54.3	154 41.1	11.8	331 32.6	39.2	302 32.2	29.0	Capella	280 28.9	N46 00.9
02	249 42.1	236 19.9	55.5	169 41.8	11.9	346 35.2	39.2	317 34.6	29.0	Deneb	49 28.7	N45 20.7
03	264 44.6	251 19.5 ..	56.7	184 42.5 ..	12.0	1 37.9 ..	39.2	332 37.1 ..	29.0	Denebola	182 29.4	N14 27.9
04	279 47.0	266 19.2	57.8	199 43.2	12.1	16 40.5	39.2	347 39.6	29.0	Diphda	348 52.2	S17 53.0
05	294 49.5	281 18.8	3 59.0	214 43.9	12.3	31 43.1	39.2	2 42.1	29.0			
06	309 51.9	296 18.5	N 4 00.1	229 44.6	N24 12.4	46 45.8	S22 39.2	17 44.5	S21 29.0	Dubhe	193 46.5	N61 39.1
T 07	324 54.4	311 18.2	01.3	244 45.3	12.5	61 48.4	39.2	32 47.0	29.0	Elnath	278 07.9	N28 37.3
H 08	339 56.9	326 17.8	02.5	259 45.9	12.6	76 51.1	39.1	47 49.5	29.0	Eltanin	90 43.9	N51 29.0
U 09	354 59.3	341 17.5 ..	03.6	274 46.6 ..	12.7	91 53.7 ..	39.1	62 51.9 ..	29.1	Enif	33 43.3	N 9 57.6
R 10	10 01.8	356 17.1	04.8	289 47.3	12.9	106 56.3	39.1	77 54.4	29.1	Fomalhaut	15 19.8	S29 31.2
S 11	25 04.3	11 16.8	06.0	304 48.0	13.0	121 59.0	39.1	92 56.9	29.1			
D 12	40 06.7	26 16.4	N 4 07.1	319 48.7	N24 13.1	137 01.6	S22 39.1	107 59.4	S21 29.1	Gacrux	171 56.0	S57 13.4
A 13	55 09.2	41 16.1	08.3	334 49.4	13.2	152 04.3	39.1	123 01.8	29.1	Gienah	175 47.9	S17 39.0
Y 14	70 11.7	56 15.8	09.4	349 50.1	13.3	167 06.9	39.1	138 04.3	29.1	Hadar	148 41.6	S60 27.9
15	85 14.1	71 15.4 ..	10.6	4 50.7 ..	13.4	182 09.5 ..	39.1	153 06.8 ..	29.1	Hamal	327 56.6	N23 32.9
16	100 16.6	86 15.1	11.8	19 51.4	13.6	197 12.2	39.1	168 09.3	29.1	Kaus Aust.	83 38.3	S34 22.3
17	115 19.1	101 14.7	12.9	34 52.1	13.7	212 14.8	39.1	183 11.7	29.1			
18	130 21.5	116 14.4	N 4 14.1	49 52.8	N24 13.8	227 17.5	S22 39.1	198 14.2	S21 29.1	Kochab	137 18.9	N74 04.7
19	145 24.0	131 14.0	15.3	64 53.5	13.9	242 20.1	39.1	213 16.7	29.1	Markab	13 34.5	N15 18.3
20	160 26.4	146 13.7	16.4	79 54.2	14.0	257 22.8	39.1	228 19.2	29.1	Menkar	314 11.2	N 4 09.6
21	175 28.9	161 13.4 ..	17.6	94 54.9 ..	14.1	272 25.4 ..	39.1	243 21.6 ..	29.1	Menkent	148 02.5	S36 27.8
22	190 31.4	176 13.0	18.7	109 55.5	14.3	287 28.1	39.0	258 24.1	29.1	Miaplacidus	221 38.8	S69 48.1
23	205 33.8	191 12.7	19.9	124 56.2	14.4	302 30.7	39.0	273 26.6	29.1			
3 00	220 36.3	206 12.3	N 4 21.1	139 56.9	N24 14.5	317 33.4	S22 39.0	288 29.1	S21 29.1	Mirfak	308 35.1	N49 55.6
01	235 38.8	221 12.0	22.3	154 57.6	14.6	332 36.0	39.0	303 31.6	29.1	Nunki	75 53.2	S26 16.2
02	250 41.2	236 11.6	23.4	169 58.3	14.7	347 38.6	39.0	318 34.0	29.1	Peacock	53 12.9	S56 40.1
03	265 43.7	251 11.3 ..	24.5	184 59.0 ..	14.8	2 41.3 ..	39.0	333 36.5 ..	29.1	Pollux	243 23.0	N27 58.7
04	280 46.2	266 10.9	25.7	199 59.7	14.9	17 43.9	39.0	348 39.0	29.1	Procyon	244 55.7	N 5 10.4
05	295 48.6	281 10.6	26.9	215 00.3	15.0	32 46.6	39.0	3 41.5	29.1			
06	310 51.1	296 10.2	N 4 28.0	230 01.0	N24 15.2	47 49.2	S22 39.0	18 43.9	S21 29.1	Rasalhague	96 02.5	N12 32.8
07	325 53.6	311 09.9	29.2	245 01.7	15.3	62 51.9	39.0	33 46.4	29.1	Regulus	207 39.2	N11 52.4
08	340 56.0	326 09.6	30.3	260 02.4	15.4	77 54.5	39.0	48 48.9	29.1	Rigel	281 08.5	S 8 11.0
F 09	355 58.5	341 09.2 ..	31.5	275 03.1 ..	15.5	92 57.2 ..	39.0	63 51.4 ..	29.1	Rigil Kent.	139 45.7	S60 54.8
R 10	11 00.9	356 08.9	32.7	290 03.8	15.6	107 59.8	39.0	78 53.9	29.1	Sabik	102 07.7	S15 44.8
I 11	26 03.4	11 08.5	33.8	305 04.4	15.7	123 02.5	39.0	93 56.3	29.1			
D 12	41 05.9	26 08.2	N 4 35.0	320 05.1	N24 15.8	138 05.1	S22 39.0	108 58.8	S21 29.1	Schedar	349 36.5	N56 38.3
A 13	56 08.3	41 07.8	36.1	335 05.8	15.9	153 07.8	38.9	124 01.3	29.2	Shaula	96 16.2	S37 06.9
Y 14	71 10.8	56 07.5	37.3	350 06.5	16.0	168 10.4	38.9	139 03.8	29.2	Sirius	258 30.4	S16 44.8
15	86 13.3	71 07.1 ..	38.5	5 07.2 ..	16.2	183 13.1 ..	38.9	154 06.2 ..	29.2	Spica	158 26.8	S11 15.7
16	101 15.7	86 06.8	39.6	20 07.9	16.3	198 15.7	38.9	169 08.7	29.2	Suhail	222 49.5	S43 30.9
17	116 18.2	101 06.4	40.8	35 08.6	16.4	213 18.4	38.9	184 11.2	29.2			
18	131 20.7	116 06.1	N 4 41.9	50 09.2	N24 16.5	228 21.0	S22 38.9	199 13.7	S21 29.2	Vega	80 36.0	N38 47.9
19	146 23.1	131 05.7	43.1	65 09.9	16.6	243 23.7	38.9	214 16.2	29.2	Zuben'ubi	137 00.7	S16 07.2
20	161 25.6	146 05.4	44.3	80 10.6	16.7	258 26.3	38.9	229 18.6	29.2		SHA	Mer. Pass.
21	176 28.0	161 05.0 ..	45.4	95 11.3 ..	16.8	273 29.0 ..	38.9	244 21.1 ..	29.2		° ′	h m
22	191 30.5	176 04.7	46.6	110 12.0	16.9	288 31.6	38.9	259 23.6	29.2	Venus	346 43.4	10 15
23	206 33.0	191 04.3	47.7	125 12.7	17.0	303 34.3	38.9	274 26.1	29.2	Mars	280 03.3	14 41
	h m									Jupiter	96 52.8	2 53
Mer. Pass.	9 20.0	v −0.3	d 1.2	v 0.7	d 0.1	v 2.6	d 0.0	v 2.5	d 0.0	Saturn	67 52.5	4 49

© British Crown Copyright 2018. All rights reserved.

SUN / MOON

UT	SUN GHA	SUN Dec	MOON GHA	v	Dec	d	HP
d h	° '	° '	° '	'	° '	'	'
1 00	180 42.0	N14 55.3	221 38.5	15.2	S 6 15.4	10.9	54.6
01	195 42.1	56.1	236 12.7	15.2	6 04.5	11.0	54.6
02	210 42.1	56.8	250 46.9	15.3	5 53.5	11.0	54.6
03	225 42.2	.. 57.6	265 21.2	15.2	5 42.5	11.0	54.6
04	240 42.3	58.3	279 55.4	15.3	5 31.5	11.1	54.6
05	255 42.4	59.1	294 29.7	15.2	5 20.4	11.1	54.7
06	270 42.4	N14 59.9	309 03.9	15.3	S 5 09.3	11.1	54.7
W 07	285 42.5	15 00.6	323 38.2	15.2	4 58.2	11.2	54.7
E 08	300 42.6	01.4	338 12.4	15.2	4 47.0	11.2	54.7
D 09	315 42.7	.. 02.1	352 46.6	15.3	4 35.8	11.2	54.7
N 10	330 42.8	02.9	7 20.9	15.2	4 24.6	11.2	54.7
E 11	345 42.8	03.7	21 55.1	15.2	4 13.4	11.3	54.7
S 12	0 42.9	N15 04.4	36 29.3	15.2	S 4 02.1	11.3	54.8
D 13	15 43.0	05.2	51 03.5	15.3	3 50.8	11.3	54.8
A 14	30 43.0	05.9	65 37.8	15.2	3 39.5	11.3	54.8
Y 15	45 43.1	.. 06.7	80 12.0	15.2	3 28.2	11.3	54.8
16	60 43.2	07.4	94 46.2	15.2	3 16.9	11.4	54.8
17	75 43.3	08.2	109 20.4	15.1	3 05.5	11.4	54.8
18	90 43.3	N15 08.9	123 54.5	15.2	S 2 54.1	11.4	54.9
19	105 43.4	09.7	138 28.7	15.2	2 42.7	11.5	54.9
20	120 43.5	10.5	153 02.9	15.1	2 31.2	11.4	54.9
21	135 43.6	.. 11.2	167 37.0	15.2	2 19.8	11.5	54.9
22	150 43.6	12.0	182 11.2	15.1	2 08.3	11.5	54.9
23	165 43.7	12.7	196 45.3	15.1	1 56.8	11.5	54.9
2 00	180 43.8	N15 13.5	211 19.4	15.1	S 1 45.3	11.5	55.0
01	195 43.9	14.2	225 53.5	15.1	1 33.8	11.5	55.0
02	210 43.9	15.0	240 27.6	15.0	1 22.3	11.6	55.0
03	225 44.0	.. 15.7	255 01.6	15.1	1 10.7	11.5	55.0
04	240 44.1	16.5	269 35.7	15.0	0 59.2	11.6	55.0
05	255 44.1	17.2	284 09.7	15.0	0 47.6	11.6	55.1
06	270 44.2	N15 18.0	298 43.7	15.0	S 0 36.0	11.6	55.1
T 07	285 44.3	18.7	313 17.7	15.0	0 24.4	11.6	55.1
H 08	300 44.3	19.5	327 51.7	14.9	0 12.8	11.6	55.1
U 09	315 44.4	.. 20.2	342 25.6	14.9	S 0 01.2	11.6	55.1
R 10	330 44.5	21.0	356 59.5	15.0	N 0 10.4	11.7	55.1
S 11	345 44.6	21.7	11 33.5	14.8	0 22.1	11.6	55.2
D 12	0 44.6	N15 22.4	26 07.3	14.9	N 0 33.7	11.7	55.2
A 13	15 44.7	23.2	40 41.2	14.8	0 45.4	11.6	55.2
Y 14	30 44.8	23.9	55 15.0	14.8	0 57.0	11.7	55.2
15	45 44.8	.. 24.7	69 48.8	14.8	1 08.7	11.7	55.2
16	60 44.9	25.4	84 22.6	14.8	1 20.4	11.6	55.3
17	75 45.0	26.2	98 56.4	14.7	1 32.0	11.7	55.3
18	90 45.0	N15 26.9	113 30.1	14.7	N 1 43.7	11.7	55.3
19	105 45.1	27.7	128 03.8	14.6	1 55.4	11.7	55.3
20	120 45.2	28.4	142 37.4	14.7	2 07.1	11.7	55.3
21	135 45.2	.. 29.1	157 11.1	14.6	2 18.8	11.6	55.4
22	150 45.3	29.9	171 44.7	14.6	2 30.4	11.7	55.4
23	165 45.4	30.6	186 18.3	14.5	2 42.1	11.7	55.4
3 00	180 45.4	N15 31.4	200 51.8	14.5	N 2 53.8	11.7	55.4
01	195 45.5	32.1	215 25.3	14.5	3 05.5	11.6	55.5
02	210 45.6	32.9	229 58.8	14.4	3 17.1	11.7	55.5
03	225 45.6	.. 33.6	244 32.2	14.4	3 28.8	11.7	55.5
04	240 45.7	34.3	259 05.6	14.4	3 40.5	11.6	55.5
05	255 45.8	35.1	273 39.0	14.3	3 52.1	11.7	55.5
06	270 45.8	N15 35.8	288 12.3	14.3	N 4 03.8	11.6	55.6
F 07	285 45.9	36.5	302 45.6	14.3	4 15.4	11.7	55.6
R 08	300 46.0	37.3	317 18.9	14.2	4 27.1	11.6	55.6
I 09	315 46.0	.. 38.0	331 52.1	14.1	4 38.7	11.6	55.6
D 10	330 46.1	38.8	346 25.2	14.2	4 50.3	11.6	55.6
A 11	345 46.2	39.5	0 58.4	14.1	5 01.9	11.6	55.7
Y 12	0 46.2	N15 40.2	15 31.5	14.0	N 5 13.5	11.6	55.7
13	15 46.3	41.0	30 04.5	14.0	5 25.1	11.6	55.7
14	30 46.3	41.7	44 37.5	14.0	5 36.7	11.5	55.7
15	45 46.4	.. 42.4	59 10.5	13.9	5 48.2	11.6	55.8
16	60 46.5	43.2	73 43.4	13.9	5 59.8	11.5	55.8
17	75 46.5	43.9	88 16.3	13.8	6 11.3	11.5	55.8
18	90 46.6	N15 44.6	102 49.1	13.8	N 6 22.8	11.5	55.8
19	105 46.7	45.4	117 21.9	13.7	6 34.3	11.4	55.8
20	120 46.7	46.1	131 54.6	13.7	6 45.7	11.5	55.9
21	135 46.8	.. 46.8	146 27.3	13.6	6 57.2	11.4	55.9
22	150 46.8	47.6	160 59.9	13.6	7 08.6	11.4	55.9
23	165 46.9	48.3	175 32.5	13.5	N 7 20.0	11.4	55.9
	SD 15.9	d 0.7	SD 14.9		15.0		15.2

Twilight / Sunrise / Moonrise

Lat.	Twilight Naut.	Twilight Civil	Sunrise	Moonrise 1	2	3	4
°	h m	h m	h m	h m	h m	h m	h m
N 72	////	////	01 47	04 31	04 15	03 59	03 42
N 70	////	////	02 27	04 23	04 14	04 04	03 54
68	////	00 59	02 54	04 17	04 12	04 08	04 04
66	////	01 51	03 15	04 11	04 11	04 11	04 12
64	////	02 22	03 31	04 07	04 11	04 14	04 19
62	00 52	02 45	03 45	04 03	04 10	04 17	04 25
60	01 39	03 03	03 56	04 00	04 09	04 19	04 30
N 58	02 07	03 18	04 06	03 57	04 09	04 21	04 34
56	02 28	03 30	04 15	03 54	04 08	04 23	04 38
54	02 45	03 41	04 22	03 51	04 08	04 24	04 42
52	03 00	03 50	04 29	03 49	04 07	04 26	04 45
50	03 12	03 59	04 35	03 47	04 07	04 27	04 49
45	03 36	04 16	04 49	03 43	04 06	04 30	04 55
N 40	03 54	04 30	04 59	03 39	04 06	04 32	05 01
35	04 09	04 42	05 09	03 36	04 05	04 35	05 06
30	04 21	04 51	05 17	03 33	04 04	04 36	05 10
20	04 40	05 07	05 31	03 28	04 04	04 40	05 17
N 10	04 55	05 21	05 42	03 24	04 03	04 43	05 24
0	05 07	05 32	05 54	03 20	04 02	04 45	05 30
S 10	05 18	05 43	06 05	03 15	04 01	04 48	05 37
20	05 27	05 53	06 16	03 11	04 01	04 51	05 43
30	05 36	06 05	06 29	03 06	04 00	04 55	05 51
35	05 41	06 11	06 37	03 03	03 59	04 57	05 56
40	05 45	06 17	06 45	03 00	03 59	04 59	06 01
45	05 50	06 25	06 56	02 56	03 58	05 02	06 07
S 50	05 55	06 33	07 08	02 51	03 57	05 05	06 14
52	05 57	06 37	07 13	02 49	03 57	05 06	06 17
54	05 59	06 41	07 19	02 47	03 57	05 08	06 21
56	06 02	06 46	07 26	02 44	03 56	05 10	06 25
58	06 04	06 51	07 34	02 42	03 56	05 12	06 30
S 60	06 07	06 57	07 43	02 38	03 55	05 14	06 35

Sunset / Twilight / Moonset

Lat.	Sunset	Twilight Civil	Twilight Naut.	Moonset 1	2	3	4
°	h m	h m	h m	h m	h m	h m	h m
N 72	22 15	////	////	14 55	16 40	18 30	20 28
N 70	21 32	////	////	15 00	16 38	18 20	20 08
68	21 03	23 07	////	15 04	16 37	18 13	19 53
66	20 42	22 08	////	15 07	16 36	18 06	19 40
64	20 25	21 36	////	15 10	16 34	18 01	19 30
62	20 11	21 12	23 13	15 13	16 33	17 56	19 21
60	20 00	20 54	22 20	15 15	16 33	17 52	19 14
N 58	19 49	20 39	21 50	15 17	16 32	17 49	19 07
56	19 41	20 26	21 28	15 19	16 31	17 45	19 02
54	19 33	20 15	21 11	15 20	16 31	17 43	18 56
52	19 26	20 05	20 56	15 22	16 30	17 40	18 52
50	19 20	19 57	20 44	15 23	16 30	17 38	18 48
45	19 06	19 39	20 19	15 26	16 28	17 33	18 38
N 40	18 55	19 25	20 01	15 28	16 28	17 28	18 31
35	18 46	19 13	19 46	15 30	16 27	17 25	18 25
30	18 38	19 03	19 34	15 32	16 26	17 22	18 19
20	18 24	18 47	19 14	15 35	16 25	17 16	18 09
N 10	18 12	18 34	18 59	15 38	16 24	17 11	18 01
0	18 00	18 22	18 47	15 40	16 23	17 07	17 53
S 10	17 49	18 11	18 36	15 42	16 22	17 02	17 45
20	17 38	18 00	18 27	15 45	16 21	16 57	17 36
30	17 24	17 49	18 18	15 48	16 19	16 52	17 26
35	17 17	17 43	18 13	15 49	16 19	16 49	17 21
40	17 08	17 36	18 08	15 51	16 18	16 45	17 15
45	16 58	17 29	18 04	15 53	16 17	16 41	17 07
S 50	16 46	17 20	17 58	15 56	16 16	16 36	16 59
52	16 40	17 16	17 56	15 57	16 15	16 34	16 55
54	16 34	17 12	17 54	15 58	16 15	16 31	16 50
56	16 27	17 07	17 52	16 00	16 14	16 29	16 45
58	16 19	17 02	17 49	16 01	16 13	16 26	16 40
S 60	16 11	16 56	17 46	16 03	16 12	16 22	16 34

SUN / MOON

Day	SUN Eqn. of Time 00h	SUN Eqn. of Time 12h	SUN Mer. Pass.	MOON Mer. Pass. Upper	MOON Mer. Pass. Lower	Age	Phase
d	m s	m s	h m	h m	h m	d	%
1	02 48	02 51	11 57	09 30	21 51	26	12
2	02 55	02 58	11 57	10 12	22 34	27	6
3	03 02	03 05	11 57	10 56	23 18	28	2

© British Crown Copyright 2018. All rights reserved.

UT (d h)	ARIES GHA	VENUS −3.8 GHA	Dec	MARS +1.7 GHA	Dec	JUPITER −2.5 GHA	Dec	SATURN +0.4 GHA	Dec	STARS Name	SHA	Dec
4 00	221 35.4	206 04.0	N 4 48.9	140 13.4	N24 17.1	318 36.9	S22 38.9	289 28.6	S21 29.2	Acamar	315 15.7	S40 13.9
01	236 37.9	221 03.7	50.0	155 14.0	17.2	333 39.6	38.9	304 31.0	29.2	Achernar	335 24.4	S57 08.4
02	251 40.4	236 03.3	51.2	170 14.7	17.3	348 42.2	38.8	319 33.5	29.2	Acrux	173 04.3	S63 12.5
03	266 42.8	251 03.0	.. 52.4	185 15.4	.. 17.4	3 44.9	.. 38.8	334 36.0	.. 29.2	Adhara	255 09.6	S29 00.2
04	281 45.3	266 02.6	53.5	200 16.1	17.5	18 47.6	38.8	349 38.5	29.2	Aldebaran	290 45.1	N16 32.7
05	296 47.8	281 02.3	54.7	215 16.8	17.6	33 50.2	38.8	4 41.0	29.2			
06	311 50.2	296 01.9	N 4 55.8	230 17.5	N24 17.8	48 52.9	S22 38.8	19 43.5	S21 29.2	Alioth	166 16.7	N55 51.5
07	326 52.7	311 01.6	57.0	245 18.1	17.9	63 55.5	38.8	34 45.9	29.2	Alkaid	152 55.3	N49 13.2
S 08	341 55.2	326 01.2	58.1	260 18.8	18.0	78 58.2	38.8	49 48.4	29.2	Alnair	27 38.9	S46 51.9
A 09	356 57.6	341 00.9	4 59.3	275 19.5	.. 18.1	94 00.8	.. 38.8	64 50.9	.. 29.2	Alnilam	275 42.6	S 1 11.6
T 10	12 00.1	356 00.5	5 00.5	290 20.2	18.2	109 03.5	38.8	79 53.4	29.2	Alphard	217 52.2	S 8 44.7
U 11	27 02.5	11 00.2	01.6	305 20.9	18.3	124 06.1	38.8	94 55.9	29.2			
R 12	42 05.0	25 59.8	N 5 02.8	320 21.6	N24 18.4	139 08.8	S22 38.8	109 58.4	S21 29.2	Alphecca	126 07.3	N26 39.0
D 13	57 07.5	40 59.5	04.0	335 22.3	18.5	154 11.5	38.8	125 00.8	29.3	Alpheratz	357 39.6	N29 11.5
A 14	72 09.9	55 59.1	05.1	350 22.9	18.6	169 14.1	38.8	140 03.3	29.3	Altair	62 04.2	N 8 55.1
Y 15	87 12.4	70 58.8	.. 06.2	5 23.6	.. 18.7	184 16.8	.. 38.8	155 05.8	.. 29.3	Ankaa	353 12.1	S42 12.1
16	102 14.9	85 58.4	07.4	20 24.3	18.8	199 19.4	38.7	170 08.3	29.3	Antares	112 21.0	S26 28.3
17	117 17.3	100 58.1	08.5	35 25.0	18.9	214 22.1	38.7	185 10.8	29.3			
18	132 19.8	115 57.7	N 5 09.7	50 25.7	N24 19.0	229 24.8	S22 38.7	200 13.3	S21 29.3	Arcturus	145 51.8	N19 05.0
19	147 22.3	130 57.4	10.9	65 26.4	19.1	244 27.4	38.7	215 15.7	29.3	Atria	107 18.8	S69 03.4
20	162 24.7	145 57.0	12.0	80 27.0	19.2	259 30.1	38.7	230 18.2	29.3	Avior	234 16.5	S59 34.6
21	177 27.2	160 56.7	.. 13.2	95 27.7	.. 19.3	274 32.7	.. 38.7	245 20.7	.. 29.3	Bellatrix	278 28.0	N 6 21.8
22	192 29.6	175 56.3	14.3	110 28.4	19.4	289 35.4	38.7	260 23.2	29.3	Betelgeuse	270 57.2	N 7 24.4
23	207 32.1	190 55.9	15.5	125 29.1	19.5	304 38.0	38.7	275 25.7	29.3			
5 00	222 34.6	205 55.6	N 5 16.6	140 29.8	N24 19.6	319 40.7	S22 38.7	290 28.2	S21 29.3	Canopus	263 54.7	S52 42.7
01	237 37.0	220 55.2	17.8	155 30.5	19.7	334 43.4	38.7	305 30.6	29.3	Capella	280 29.0	N46 00.9
02	252 39.5	235 54.9	18.9	170 31.2	19.8	349 46.0	38.7	320 33.1	29.3	Deneb	49 28.7	N45 20.7
03	267 42.0	250 54.5	.. 20.1	185 31.8	.. 19.9	4 48.7	.. 38.7	335 35.6	.. 29.3	Denebola	182 29.4	N14 27.9
04	282 44.4	265 54.2	21.2	200 32.5	20.0	19 51.4	38.7	350 38.1	29.3	Diphda	348 52.2	S17 53.0
05	297 46.9	280 53.8	22.4	215 33.2	20.1	34 54.0	38.6	5 40.6	29.3			
06	312 49.4	295 53.5	N 5 23.5	230 33.9	N24 20.1	49 56.7	S22 38.6	20 43.1	S21 29.3	Dubhe	193 46.5	N61 39.1
07	327 51.8	310 53.1	24.7	245 34.6	20.2	64 59.3	38.6	35 45.6	29.3	Elnath	278 07.9	N28 37.3
S 08	342 54.3	325 52.8	25.9	260 35.3	20.3	80 02.0	38.6	50 48.1	29.3	Eltanin	90 43.9	N51 29.1
U 09	357 56.8	340 52.4	.. 27.0	275 35.9	.. 20.4	95 04.7	.. 38.6	65 50.5	.. 29.3	Enif	33 43.3	N 9 57.6
N 10	12 59.2	355 52.1	28.2	290 36.6	20.5	110 07.3	38.6	80 53.0	29.4	Fomalhaut	15 19.8	S29 31.2
D 11	28 01.7	10 51.7	29.3	305 37.3	20.6	125 10.0	38.6	95 55.5	29.4			
A 12	43 04.1	25 51.4	N 5 30.5	320 38.0	N24 20.7	140 12.7	S22 38.6	110 58.0	S21 29.4	Gacrux	171 56.0	S57 13.4
Y 13	58 06.6	40 51.0	31.6	335 38.7	20.8	155 15.3	38.6	126 00.5	29.4	Gienah	175 48.0	S17 39.0
14	73 09.1	55 50.7	32.8	350 39.4	20.9	170 18.0	38.6	141 03.0	29.4	Hadar	148 41.6	S60 27.9
15	88 11.5	70 50.3	.. 33.9	5 40.1	.. 21.0	185 20.7	.. 38.6	156 05.5	.. 29.4	Hamal	327 56.6	N23 32.9
16	103 14.0	85 49.9	35.1	20 40.7	21.1	200 23.3	38.6	171 08.0	29.4	Kaus Aust.	83 38.3	S34 22.3
17	118 16.5	100 49.6	36.2	35 41.4	21.2	215 26.0	38.6	186 10.4	29.4			
18	133 18.9	115 49.2	N 5 37.4	50 42.1	N24 21.3	230 28.6	S22 38.5	201 12.9	S21 29.4	Kochab	137 18.9	N74 04.7
19	148 21.4	130 48.9	38.5	65 42.8	21.4	245 31.3	38.5	216 15.4	29.4	Markab	13 34.5	N15 18.3
20	163 23.9	145 48.5	39.7	80 43.5	21.5	260 34.0	38.5	231 17.9	29.4	Menkar	314 11.2	N 4 09.7
21	178 26.3	160 48.2	.. 40.8	95 44.2	.. 21.5	275 36.6	.. 38.5	246 20.4	.. 29.4	Menkent	148 02.5	S36 27.9
22	193 28.8	175 47.8	42.0	110 44.8	21.6	290 39.3	38.5	261 22.9	29.4	Miaplacidus	221 38.8	S69 48.1
23	208 31.3	190 47.5	43.1	125 45.5	21.7	305 42.0	38.5	276 25.4	29.4			
6 00	223 33.7	205 47.1	N 5 44.3	140 46.2	N24 21.8	320 44.6	S22 38.5	291 27.9	S21 29.4	Mirfak	308 35.1	N49 55.5
01	238 36.2	220 46.7	45.4	155 46.9	21.9	335 47.3	38.5	306 30.4	29.4	Nunki	75 53.2	S26 16.2
02	253 38.6	235 46.4	46.6	170 47.6	22.0	350 50.0	38.5	321 32.8	29.4	Peacock	53 12.9	S56 40.1
03	268 41.1	250 46.0	.. 47.7	185 48.3	.. 22.1	5 52.7	.. 38.5	336 35.3	.. 29.4	Pollux	243 23.0	N27 58.7
04	283 43.6	265 45.7	48.9	200 48.9	22.2	20 55.3	38.5	351 37.8	29.4	Procyon	244 55.7	N 5 10.4
05	298 46.0	280 45.3	50.0	215 49.6	22.3	35 58.0	38.5	6 40.3	29.5			
06	313 48.5	295 45.0	N 5 51.2	230 50.3	N24 22.3	51 00.7	S22 38.4	21 42.8	S21 29.5	Rasalhague	96 02.5	N12 32.8
07	328 51.0	310 44.6	52.3	245 51.0	22.4	66 03.3	38.4	36 45.3	29.5	Regulus	207 39.2	N11 52.4
08	343 53.4	325 44.2	53.5	260 51.7	22.5	81 06.0	38.4	51 47.8	29.5	Rigel	281 08.5	S 8 11.0
M 09	358 55.9	340 43.9	.. 54.6	275 52.4	.. 22.6	96 08.7	.. 38.4	66 50.3	.. 29.5	Rigil Kent.	139 45.7	S60 54.8
O 10	13 58.4	355 43.5	55.8	290 53.1	22.7	111 11.3	38.4	81 52.8	29.5	Sabik	102 07.7	S15 44.8
N 11	29 00.8	10 43.2	56.9	305 53.7	22.8	126 14.0	38.4	96 55.3	29.5			
D 12	44 03.3	25 42.8	N 5 58.1	320 54.4	N24 22.9	141 16.7	S22 38.4	111 57.8	S21 29.5	Schedar	349 36.4	N56 38.2
A 13	59 05.8	40 42.5	5 59.2	335 55.1	23.0	156 19.4	38.4	127 00.2	29.5	Shaula	96 16.2	S37 06.9
Y 14	74 08.2	55 42.1	6 00.4	350 55.8	23.0	171 22.0	38.4	142 02.7	29.5	Sirius	258 30.4	S16 44.8
15	89 10.7	70 41.7	.. 01.5	5 56.5	.. 23.1	186 24.7	.. 38.4	157 05.2	.. 29.5	Spica	158 26.8	S11 15.7
16	104 13.1	85 41.4	02.7	20 57.2	23.2	201 27.4	38.4	172 07.7	29.5	Suhail	222 49.5	S43 30.9
17	119 15.6	100 41.0	03.8	35 57.8	23.3	216 30.0	38.4	187 10.2	29.5			
18	134 18.1	115 40.7	N 6 04.9	50 58.5	N24 23.4	231 32.7	S22 38.4	202 12.7	S21 29.5	Vega	80 36.0	N38 48.0
19	149 20.5	130 40.3	06.1	65 59.2	23.5	246 35.4	38.3	217 15.2	29.5	Zuben'ubi	137 00.7	S16 07.2
20	164 23.0	145 39.9	07.2	80 59.9	23.5	261 38.1	38.3	232 17.7	29.5		SHA	Mer.Pass.
21	179 25.5	160 39.6	.. 08.4	96 00.6	.. 23.6	276 40.7	.. 38.3	247 20.2	.. 29.5			
22	194 27.9	175 39.2	09.5	111 01.3	23.7	291 43.4	38.3	262 22.7	29.6	Venus	343 21.0	10 17
23	209 30.4	190 38.9	10.7	126 02.0	23.8	306 46.1	38.3	277 25.2	29.6	Mars	277 55.2	14 37
Mer. Pass.	9 08.2	v −0.4	d 1.2	v 0.7	d 0.1	v 2.7	d 0.0	v 2.5	d 0.0	Jupiter	97 06.1	2 41
										Saturn	67 53.6	4 37

© British Crown Copyright 2018. All rights reserved.

UT	SUN GHA	SUN Dec	MOON GHA	v	MOON Dec	d	HP
d h	° ′	° ′	° ′	′	° ′	′	′
4 00	180 47.0	N15 49.0	190 05.0	13.5	N 7 31.4	11.3	56.0
01	195 47.0	49.7	204 37.5	13.4	7 42.7	11.4	56.0
02	210 47.1	50.5	219 09.9	13.4	7 54.1	11.3	56.0
03	225 47.1	.. 51.2	233 42.3	13.3	8 05.4	11.3	56.0
04	240 47.2	51.9	248 14.6	13.3	8 16.7	11.2	56.0
05	255 47.3	52.7	262 46.9	13.2	8 27.9	11.2	56.1
06	270 47.3	N15 53.4	277 19.1	13.1	N 8 39.1	11.2	56.1
07	285 47.4	54.1	291 51.2	13.2	8 50.3	11.2	56.1
S 08	300 47.4	54.8	306 23.4	13.0	9 01.5	11.1	56.1
A 09	315 47.5	.. 55.6	320 55.4	13.0	9 12.6	11.1	56.2
T 10	330 47.6	56.3	335 27.4	12.9	9 23.7	11.1	56.2
U 11	345 47.6	57.0	349 59.3	12.9	9 34.8	11.0	56.2
R 12	0 47.7	N15 57.7	4 31.2	12.8	N 9 45.8	11.0	56.2
D 13	15 47.7	58.5	19 03.0	12.8	9 56.8	10.9	56.3
A 14	30 47.8	59.2	33 34.8	12.6	10 07.7	11.0	56.3
Y 15	45 47.8	15 59.9	48 06.4	12.7	10 18.7	10.8	56.3
16	60 47.9	16 00.6	62 38.1	12.6	10 29.5	10.9	56.3
17	75 48.0	01.4	77 09.7	12.5	10 40.4	10.8	56.3
18	90 48.0	N16 02.1	91 41.2	12.4	N10 51.2	10.7	56.4
19	105 48.1	02.8	106 12.6	12.4	11 01.9	10.7	56.4
20	120 48.1	03.5	120 44.0	12.3	11 12.6	10.7	56.4
21	135 48.2	.. 04.2	135 15.3	12.3	11 23.3	10.6	56.4
22	150 48.2	05.0	149 46.6	12.2	11 33.9	10.6	56.5
23	165 48.3	05.7	164 17.8	12.1	11 44.5	10.5	56.5
5 00	180 48.3	N16 06.4	178 48.9	12.0	N11 55.0	10.5	56.5
01	195 48.4	07.1	193 19.9	12.0	12 05.5	10.4	56.5
02	210 48.4	07.8	207 50.9	12.0	12 15.9	10.4	56.5
03	225 48.5	.. 08.6	222 21.9	11.8	12 26.3	10.3	56.6
04	240 48.6	09.3	236 52.7	11.8	12 36.6	10.3	56.6
05	255 48.6	10.0	251 23.5	11.8	12 46.9	10.2	56.6
06	270 48.7	N16 10.7	265 54.3	11.6	N12 57.1	10.2	56.6
07	285 48.7	11.4	280 24.9	11.6	13 07.3	10.1	56.7
S 08	300 48.8	12.1	294 55.5	11.5	13 17.4	10.0	56.7
U 09	315 48.8	.. 12.9	309 26.0	11.5	13 27.4	10.0	56.7
N 10	330 48.9	13.6	323 56.5	11.3	13 37.4	9.9	56.7
11	345 48.9	14.3	338 26.8	11.4	13 47.3	9.9	56.8
D 12	0 49.0	N16 15.0	352 57.2	11.2	N13 57.2	9.8	56.8
A 13	15 49.0	15.7	7 27.4	11.2	14 07.0	9.7	56.8
Y 14	30 49.1	16.4	21 57.6	11.1	14 16.7	9.7	56.8
15	45 49.1	.. 17.1	36 27.7	11.0	14 26.4	9.6	56.8
16	60 49.2	17.9	50 57.7	10.9	14 36.0	9.5	56.9
17	75 49.2	18.6	65 27.6	10.9	14 45.5	9.5	56.9
18	90 49.3	N16 19.3	79 57.5	10.8	N14 55.0	9.4	56.9
19	105 49.3	20.0	94 27.3	10.8	15 04.4	9.3	56.9
20	120 49.4	20.7	108 57.1	10.6	15 13.7	9.3	57.0
21	135 49.4	.. 21.4	123 26.7	10.6	15 23.0	9.2	57.0
22	150 49.5	22.1	137 56.3	10.5	15 32.2	9.1	57.0
23	165 49.5	22.8	152 25.8	10.5	15 41.3	9.0	57.0
6 00	180 49.6	N16 23.5	166 55.3	10.3	N15 50.3	9.0	57.0
01	195 49.6	24.2	181 24.6	10.3	15 59.3	8.9	57.1
02	210 49.7	24.9	195 53.9	10.3	16 08.2	8.8	57.1
03	225 49.7	.. 25.7	210 23.2	10.1	16 17.0	8.7	57.1
04	240 49.8	26.4	224 52.3	10.1	16 25.7	8.6	57.1
05	255 49.8	27.1	239 21.4	10.0	16 34.3	8.6	57.2
06	270 49.9	N16 27.8	253 50.4	9.9	N16 42.9	8.5	57.2
07	285 49.9	28.5	268 19.3	9.9	16 51.4	8.4	57.2
08	300 50.0	29.2	282 48.2	9.7	16 59.8	8.3	57.2
M 09	315 50.0	.. 29.9	297 16.9	9.7	17 08.1	8.2	57.2
O 10	330 50.1	30.6	311 45.6	9.7	17 16.3	8.1	57.3
N 11	345 50.1	31.3	326 14.3	9.5	17 24.4	8.1	57.3
D 12	0 50.2	N16 32.0	340 42.8	9.5	N17 32.5	7.9	57.3
A 13	15 50.2	32.7	355 11.3	9.4	17 40.4	7.9	57.3
Y 14	30 50.2	33.4	9 39.7	9.4	17 48.3	7.7	57.4
15	45 50.3	.. 34.1	24 08.1	9.2	17 56.0	7.7	57.4
16	60 50.3	34.8	38 36.3	9.2	18 03.7	7.6	57.4
17	75 50.4	35.5	53 04.5	9.2	18 11.3	7.5	57.4
18	90 50.4	N16 36.2	67 32.7	9.0	N18 18.8	7.4	57.4
19	105 50.5	36.9	82 00.7	9.0	18 26.2	7.3	57.5
20	120 50.5	37.6	96 28.7	8.9	18 33.5	7.1	57.5
21	135 50.6	.. 38.3	110 56.6	8.8	18 40.6	7.1	57.5
22	150 50.6	39.0	125 24.4	8.8	18 47.7	7.0	57.5
23	165 50.6	39.7	139 52.2	8.7	N18 54.7	6.9	57.5
	SD 15.9	d 0.7	SD 15.3		15.5		15.6

Lat.	Twilight Naut.	Civil	Sunrise	Moonrise 4	5	6	7
°	h m	h m	h m	h m	h m	h m	h m
N 72	////	////	01 17	03 42	03 21	02 47	▭
N 70	////	////	02 09	03 54	03 43	03 27	02 56
68	////	////	02 40	04 04	04 00	03 55	03 50
66	////	01 31	03 03	04 12	04 13	04 16	04 24
64	////	02 08	03 21	04 19	04 25	04 33	04 48
62	////	02 33	03 36	04 25	04 34	04 48	05 07
60	01 21	02 53	03 48	04 30	04 43	05 00	05 23
N 58	01 54	03 09	03 59	04 34	04 50	05 10	05 37
56	02 18	03 22	04 08	04 38	04 57	05 19	05 49
54	02 37	03 34	04 16	04 42	05 03	05 27	05 59
52	02 52	03 44	04 24	04 45	05 08	05 35	06 08
50	03 05	03 53	04 30	04 49	05 13	05 41	06 16
45	03 31	04 11	04 44	04 55	05 23	05 55	06 34
N 40	03 50	04 26	04 56	05 01	05 32	06 07	06 48
35	04 05	04 38	05 06	05 06	05 39	06 17	07 00
30	04 18	04 49	05 14	05 10	05 46	06 26	07 11
20	04 38	05 06	05 29	05 17	05 58	06 41	07 29
N 10	04 54	05 20	05 42	05 24	06 08	06 55	07 46
0	05 07	05 32	05 53	05 30	06 17	07 08	08 01
S 10	05 18	05 43	06 05	05 37	06 27	07 20	08 16
20	05 28	05 54	06 17	05 43	06 38	07 34	08 32
30	05 38	06 06	06 31	05 51	06 49	07 50	08 51
35	05 43	06 13	06 39	05 56	06 56	07 59	09 02
40	05 48	06 20	06 48	06 01	07 04	08 09	09 15
45	05 53	06 28	06 59	06 07	07 14	08 22	09 30
S 50	05 59	06 37	07 12	06 14	07 25	08 37	09 48
52	06 01	06 42	07 18	06 17	07 30	08 44	09 57
54	06 04	06 46	07 25	06 21	07 36	08 52	10 07
56	06 07	06 51	07 32	06 25	07 42	09 01	10 18
58	06 10	06 57	07 40	06 30	07 50	09 11	10 31
S 60	06 13	07 03	07 50	06 35	07 58	09 22	10 45

Lat.	Sunset	Twilight Civil	Naut.	Moonset 4	5	6	7
°	h m	h m	h m	h m	h m	h m	h m
N 72	22 47	////	////	20 28	22 45	▭	▭
N 70	21 50	////	////	20 08	22 06	24 26	00 26
68	21 17	////	////	19 53	21 39	23 32	25 34
66	20 53	22 29	////	19 40	21 18	23 00	24 38
64	20 35	21 50	////	19 30	21 02	22 36	24 05
62	20 20	21 23	////	19 21	20 49	22 17	23 40
60	20 07	21 03	22 39	19 14	20 38	22 02	23 21
N 58	19 56	20 47	22 03	19 07	20 28	21 49	23 05
56	19 47	20 33	21 38	19 02	20 19	21 37	22 52
54	19 38	20 21	21 19	18 56	20 12	21 27	22 40
52	19 31	20 11	21 03	18 52	20 05	21 19	22 30
50	19 24	20 02	20 50	18 48	19 59	21 11	22 22
45	19 10	19 43	20 24	18 38	19 46	20 54	22 01
N 40	18 58	19 28	20 04	18 31	19 35	20 41	21 45
35	18 48	19 16	19 49	18 25	19 26	20 29	21 32
30	18 40	19 05	19 36	18 19	19 18	20 19	21 20
20	18 25	18 48	19 16	18 09	19 04	20 02	21 00
N 10	18 12	18 34	19 01	18 01	18 52	19 47	20 43
0	18 00	18 22	18 47	17 53	18 41	19 33	20 27
S 10	17 48	18 10	18 35	17 45	18 30	19 19	20 11
20	17 36	17 59	18 25	17 36	18 18	19 04	19 54
30	17 22	17 47	18 15	17 26	18 04	18 47	19 34
35	17 14	17 40	18 10	17 21	17 56	18 37	19 23
40	17 05	17 33	18 05	17 15	17 48	18 25	19 09
45	16 54	17 25	18 00	17 07	17 37	18 12	18 54
S 50	16 41	17 15	17 54	16 59	17 25	17 56	18 35
52	16 35	17 11	17 51	16 55	17 19	17 48	18 26
54	16 28	17 06	17 49	16 50	17 12	17 40	18 16
56	16 21	17 01	17 46	16 45	17 05	17 31	18 04
58	16 12	16 56	17 43	16 40	16 57	17 20	17 51
S 60	16 03	16 48	17 40	16 34	16 48	17 08	17 36

Day	SUN Eqn. of Time 00ʰ	12ʰ	Mer. Pass.	MOON Mer. Pass. Upper	Lower	Age	Phase
d	m s	m s	h m	h m	h m	d	%
4	03 08	03 11	11 57	11 41	24 05	29	0
5	03 13	03 16	11 57	12 29	00 05	01	0
6	03 18	03 21	11 57	13 20	00 54	02	3

© British Crown Copyright 2018. All rights reserved.

UT	ARIES GHA	VENUS −3.8 GHA	Dec	MARS +1.7 GHA	Dec	JUPITER −2.5 GHA	Dec	SATURN +0.4 GHA	Dec	STARS Name	SHA	Dec
7 00	224 32.9	205 38.5	N 6 11.8	141 02.6	N24 23.9	321 48.8	S22 38.3	292 27.7	S21 29.6	Acamar	315 15.7	S40 13.9
01	239 35.3	220 38.1	13.0	156 03.3	23.9	336 51.4	38.3	307 30.2	29.6	Achernar	335 24.3	S57 08.4
02	254 37.8	235 37.8	14.1	171 04.0	24.0	351 54.1	38.3	322 32.7	29.6	Acrux	173 04.3	S63 12.5
03	269 40.2	250 37.4 ..	15.3	186 04.7 ..	24.1	6 56.8 ..	38.3	337 35.1 ..	29.6	Adhara	255 09.6	S29 00.2
04	284 42.7	265 37.0	16.4	201 05.4	24.2	21 59.5	38.3	352 37.6	29.6	Aldebaran	290 45.1	N16 32.7
05	299 45.2	280 36.7	17.5	216 06.1	24.3	37 02.1	38.3	7 40.1	29.6			
06	314 47.6	295 36.3	N 6 18.7	231 06.7	N24 24.3	52 04.8	S22 38.3	22 42.6	S21 29.6	Alioth	166 16.7	N55 51.5
07	329 50.1	310 36.0	19.8	246 07.4	24.4	67 07.5	38.2	37 45.1	29.6	Alkaid	152 55.3	N49 13.2
T 08	344 52.6	325 35.6	21.0	261 08.1	24.5	82 10.2	38.2	52 47.6	29.6	Alnair	27 38.8	S46 51.9
U 09	359 55.0	340 35.2 ..	22.1	276 08.8 ..	24.6	97 12.8 ..	38.2	67 50.1 ..	29.6	Alnilam	275 42.6	S 1 11.6
E 10	14 57.5	355 34.9	23.3	291 09.5	24.7	112 15.5	38.2	82 52.6	29.6	Alphard	217 52.2	S 8 44.7
S 11	30 00.0	10 34.5	24.4	306 10.2	24.7	127 18.2	38.2	97 55.1	29.6			
D 12	45 02.4	25 34.1	N 6 25.6	321 10.8	N24 24.8	142 20.9	S22 38.2	112 57.6	S21 29.6	Alphecca	126 07.3	N26 39.1
A 13	60 04.9	40 33.8	26.7	336 11.5	24.9	157 23.6	38.2	128 00.1	29.6	Alpheratz	357 39.6	N29 11.5
Y 14	75 07.4	55 33.4	27.8	351 12.2	25.0	172 26.2	38.2	143 02.6	29.7	Altair	62 04.2	N 8 55.1
15	90 09.8	70 33.1 ..	29.0	6 12.9 ..	25.0	187 28.9 ..	38.2	158 05.1 ..	29.7	Ankaa	353 12.1	S42 12.1
16	105 12.3	85 32.7	30.1	21 13.6	25.1	202 31.6	38.2	173 07.6	29.7	Antares	112 21.0	S26 28.3
17	120 14.7	100 32.3	31.3	36 14.3	25.2	217 34.3	38.2	188 10.1	29.7			
18	135 17.2	115 32.0	N 6 32.4	51 15.0	N24 25.3	232 37.0	S22 38.1	203 12.6	S21 29.7	Arcturus	145 51.8	N19 05.0
19	150 19.7	130 31.6	33.6	66 15.6	25.4	247 39.6	38.1	218 15.1	29.7	Atria	107 18.7	S69 03.4
20	165 22.1	145 31.2	34.7	81 16.3	25.4	262 42.3	38.1	233 17.6	29.7	Avior	234 16.6	S59 34.6
21	180 24.6	160 30.9 ..	35.8	96 17.0 ..	25.5	277 45.0 ..	38.1	248 20.1 ..	29.7	Bellatrix	278 28.0	N 6 21.8
22	195 27.1	175 30.5	37.0	111 17.7	25.6	292 47.7	38.1	263 22.6	29.7	Betelgeuse	270 57.2	N 7 24.4
23	210 29.5	190 30.1	38.1	126 18.4	25.6	307 50.4	38.1	278 25.1	29.7			
8 00	225 32.0	205 29.8	N 6 39.3	141 19.1	N24 25.7	322 53.0	S22 38.1	293 27.6	S21 29.7	Canopus	263 54.8	S52 42.7
01	240 34.5	220 29.4	40.4	156 19.7	25.8	337 55.7	38.1	308 30.1	29.7	Capella	280 29.0	N46 00.9
02	255 36.9	235 29.0	41.5	171 20.4	25.9	352 58.4	38.1	323 32.6	29.7	Deneb	49 28.7	N45 20.7
03	270 39.4	250 28.7 ..	42.7	186 21.1 ..	25.9	8 01.1 ..	38.1	338 35.1 ..	29.7	Denebola	182 29.4	N14 27.9
04	285 41.9	265 28.3	43.8	201 21.8	26.0	23 03.8	38.1	353 37.6	29.7	Diphda	348 52.2	S17 53.0
05	300 44.3	280 27.9	45.0	216 22.5	26.1	38 06.5	38.1	8 40.1	29.7			
06	315 46.8	295 27.6	N 6 46.1	231 23.2	N24 26.2	53 09.1	S22 38.0	23 42.6	S21 29.8	Dubhe	193 46.5	N61 39.1
W 07	330 49.2	310 27.2	47.2	246 23.8	26.2	68 11.8	38.0	38 45.1	29.8	Elnath	278 07.9	N28 37.3
E 08	345 51.7	325 26.8	48.4	261 24.5	26.3	83 14.5	38.0	53 47.6	29.8	Eltanin	90 43.9	N51 29.1
D 09	0 54.2	340 26.5 ..	49.5	276 25.2 ..	26.4	98 17.2 ..	38.0	68 50.1 ..	29.8	Enif	33 43.2	N 9 57.7
N 10	15 56.6	355 26.1	50.7	291 25.9	26.4	113 19.9	38.0	83 52.6	29.8	Fomalhaut	15 19.7	S29 31.2
E 11	30 59.1	10 25.7	51.8	306 26.6	26.5	128 22.6	38.0	98 55.1	29.8			
S 12	46 01.6	25 25.4	N 6 52.9	321 27.3	N24 26.6	143 25.2	S22 38.0	113 57.6	S21 29.8	Gacrux	171 56.0	S57 13.4
D 13	61 04.0	40 25.0	54.1	336 28.0	26.6	158 27.9	38.0	129 00.1	29.8	Gienah	175 48.0	S17 39.0
A 14	76 06.5	55 24.6	55.2	351 28.6	26.7	173 30.6	38.0	144 02.6	29.8	Hadar	148 41.6	S60 27.9
Y 15	91 09.0	70 24.3 ..	56.3	6 29.3 ..	26.8	188 33.3 ..	38.0	159 05.1 ..	29.8	Hamal	327 56.6	N23 32.9
16	106 11.4	85 23.9	57.5	21 30.0	26.8	203 36.0	38.0	174 07.6	29.8	Kaus Aust.	83 38.2	S34 22.3
17	121 13.9	100 23.5	58.6	36 30.7	26.9	218 38.7	37.9	189 10.1	29.8			
18	136 16.4	115 23.2	N 6 59.8	51 31.4	N24 27.0	233 41.4	S22 37.9	204 12.6	S21 29.8	Kochab	137 18.9	N74 04.7
19	151 18.8	130 22.8	7 00.9	66 32.1	27.1	248 44.0	37.9	219 15.1	29.8	Markab	13 34.5	N15 18.3
20	166 21.3	145 22.4	02.0	81 32.7	27.1	263 46.7	37.9	234 17.6	29.9	Menkar	314 11.2	N 4 09.7
21	181 23.7	160 22.1 ..	03.2	96 33.4 ..	27.2	278 49.4 ..	37.9	249 20.1 ..	29.9	Menkent	148 02.5	S36 27.9
22	196 26.2	175 21.7	04.3	111 34.1	27.3	293 52.1	37.9	264 22.6	29.9	Miaplacidus	221 38.9	S69 48.1
23	211 28.7	190 21.3	05.4	126 34.8	27.3	308 54.8	37.9	279 25.1	29.9			
9 00	226 31.1	205 20.9	N 7 06.6	141 35.5	N24 27.4	323 57.5	S22 37.9	294 27.6	S21 29.9	Mirfak	308 35.1	N49 55.5
01	241 33.6	220 20.6	07.7	156 36.2	27.4	339 00.2	37.9	309 30.1	29.9	Nunki	75 53.2	S26 16.2
02	256 36.1	235 20.2	08.8	171 36.9	27.5	354 02.9	37.9	324 32.6	29.9	Peacock	53 12.8	S56 40.1
03	271 38.5	250 19.8 ..	10.0	186 37.5 ..	27.6	9 05.6 ..	37.9	339 35.1 ..	29.9	Pollux	243 23.0	N27 58.7
04	286 41.0	265 19.5	11.1	201 38.2	27.6	24 08.2	37.8	354 37.6	29.9	Procyon	244 55.7	N 5 10.4
05	301 43.5	280 19.1	12.2	216 38.9	27.7	39 10.9	37.8	9 40.1	29.9			
06	316 45.9	295 18.7	N 7 13.4	231 39.6	N24 27.8	54 13.6	S22 37.8	24 42.6	S21 29.9	Rasalhague	96 02.5	N12 32.8
07	331 48.4	310 18.3	14.5	246 40.3	27.8	69 16.3	37.8	39 45.1	29.9	Regulus	207 39.2	N11 52.4
T 08	346 50.9	325 18.0	15.6	261 41.0	27.9	84 19.0	37.8	54 47.6	29.9	Rigel	281 08.5	S 8 11.0
H 09	1 53.3	340 17.6 ..	16.8	276 41.6 ..	28.0	99 21.7 ..	37.8	69 50.1 ..	30.0	Rigil Kent.	139 45.7	S60 54.8
U 10	16 55.8	355 17.2	17.9	291 42.3	28.0	114 24.4	37.8	84 52.6	30.0	Sabik	102 07.7	S15 44.8
R 11	31 58.2	10 16.8	19.0	306 43.0	28.1	129 27.1	37.8	99 55.1	30.0			
S 12	47 00.7	25 16.5	N 7 20.2	321 43.7	N24 28.1	144 29.8	S22 37.8	114 57.6	S21 30.0	Schedar	349 36.4	N56 38.2
D 13	62 03.2	40 16.1	21.3	336 44.4	28.2	159 32.5	37.8	130 00.1	30.0	Shaula	96 16.2	S37 06.9
A 14	77 05.6	55 15.7	22.4	351 45.1	28.3	174 35.2	37.8	145 02.6	30.0	Sirius	258 30.4	S16 44.8
Y 15	92 08.1	70 15.4 ..	23.6	6 45.7 ..	28.3	189 37.8 ..	37.7	160 05.1 ..	30.0	Spica	158 26.7	S11 15.7
16	107 10.6	85 15.0	24.7	21 46.4	28.4	204 40.5	37.7	175 07.6	30.0	Suhail	222 49.5	S43 30.9
17	122 13.0	100 14.6	25.8	36 47.1	28.4	219 43.2	37.7	190 10.1	30.0			
18	137 15.5	115 14.2	N 7 27.0	51 47.8	N24 28.5	234 45.9	S22 37.7	205 12.6	S21 30.0	Vega	80 36.0	N38 48.0
19	152 18.0	130 13.9	28.1	66 48.5	28.6	249 48.6	37.7	220 15.1	30.0	Zuben'ubi	137 00.7	S16 07.2
20	167 20.4	145 13.5	29.2	81 49.2	28.6	264 51.3	37.7	235 17.7	30.0			
21	182 22.9	160 13.1 ..	30.3	96 49.9 ..	28.7	279 54.0 ..	37.7	250 20.2 ..	30.0		SHA	Mer.Pass.
22	197 25.3	175 12.7	31.5	111 50.5	28.7	294 56.7	37.7	265 22.7	30.1	Venus	339 57.8	10 18
23	212 27.8	190 12.3	32.6	126 51.2	28.8	309 59.4	37.7	280 25.2	30.1	Mars	275 47.1	14 34
	h m									Jupiter	97 21.0	2 28
Mer.Pass.	8 56.4	v −0.4	d 1.1	v 0.7	d 0.1	v 2.7	d 0.0	v 2.5	d 0.0	Saturn	67 55.6	4 25

© British Crown Copyright 2018. All rights reserved.

UT	SUN GHA	SUN Dec	MOON GHA	MOON v	MOON Dec	MOON d	MOON HP
d h	° ′	° ′	° ′	′	° ′	′	′
7 00	180 50.7	N16 40.4	154 19.9	8.6	N19 01.6	6.8	57.6
01	195 50.7	41.1	168 47.5	8.6	19 08.4	6.7	57.6
02	210 50.8	41.8	183 15.1	8.4	19 15.1	6.5	57.6
03	225 50.8	.. 42.5	197 42.5	8.5	19 21.6	6.5	57.6
04	240 50.9	43.2	212 10.0	8.3	19 28.1	6.3	57.6
05	255 50.9	43.9	226 37.3	8.3	19 34.4	6.3	57.7
06	270 50.9	N16 44.5	241 04.6	8.2	N19 40.7	6.1	57.7
07	285 51.0	45.2	255 31.8	8.1	19 46.8	6.0	57.7
08	300 51.0	45.9	269 58.9	8.1	19 52.8	5.9	57.7
09	315 51.1	.. 46.6	284 26.0	8.0	19 58.7	5.8	57.7
10	330 51.1	47.3	298 53.0	8.0	20 04.5	5.7	57.8
11	345 51.1	48.0	313 20.0	7.9	20 10.2	5.6	57.8
12	0 51.2	N16 48.7	327 46.9	7.8	N20 15.8	5.4	57.8
13	15 51.2	49.4	342 13.7	7.8	20 21.2	5.4	57.8
14	30 51.3	50.1	356 40.5	7.7	20 26.6	5.2	57.8
15	45 51.3	.. 50.8	11 07.2	7.6	20 31.8	5.1	57.8
16	60 51.3	51.5	25 33.8	7.6	20 36.9	5.0	57.9
17	75 51.4	52.1	40 00.4	7.5	20 41.9	4.8	57.9
18	90 51.4	N16 52.8	54 26.9	7.4	N20 46.7	4.8	57.9
19	105 51.5	53.5	68 53.3	7.4	20 51.5	4.6	57.9
20	120 51.5	54.2	83 19.7	7.4	20 56.1	4.5	57.9
21	135 51.5	.. 54.9	97 46.1	7.3	21 00.6	4.3	58.0
22	150 51.6	55.6	112 12.4	7.2	21 04.9	4.3	58.0
23	165 51.6	56.3	126 38.6	7.2	21 09.2	4.1	58.0
8 00	180 51.6	N16 56.9	141 04.8	7.1	N21 13.3	4.0	58.0
01	195 51.7	57.6	155 30.9	7.1	21 17.3	3.8	58.0
02	210 51.7	58.3	169 57.0	7.0	21 21.1	3.8	58.0
03	225 51.8	.. 59.0	184 23.0	7.0	21 24.9	3.6	58.1
04	240 51.8	16 59.7	198 49.0	6.9	21 28.5	3.4	58.1
05	255 51.8	17 00.4	213 14.9	6.9	21 31.9	3.4	58.1
06	270 51.9	N17 01.0	227 40.8	6.8	N21 35.3	3.2	58.1
07	285 51.9	01.7	242 06.6	6.8	21 38.5	3.0	58.1
08	300 51.9	02.4	256 32.4	6.7	21 41.5	3.0	58.2
09	315 52.0	.. 03.1	270 58.1	6.7	21 44.5	2.8	58.2
10	330 52.0	03.8	285 23.8	6.7	21 47.3	2.7	58.2
11	345 52.0	04.4	299 49.5	6.6	21 50.0	2.5	58.2
12	0 52.1	N17 05.1	314 15.1	6.6	N21 52.5	2.4	58.2
13	15 52.1	05.8	328 40.7	6.5	21 54.9	2.3	58.2
14	30 52.1	06.5	343 06.2	6.5	21 57.2	2.1	58.3
15	45 52.2	.. 07.2	357 31.7	6.4	21 59.3	2.0	58.3
16	60 52.2	07.8	11 57.1	6.5	22 01.3	1.9	58.3
17	75 52.2	08.5	26 22.6	6.4	22 03.2	1.7	58.3
18	90 52.3	N17 09.2	40 48.0	6.3	N22 04.9	1.6	58.3
19	105 52.3	09.9	55 13.3	6.3	22 06.5	1.4	58.3
20	120 52.3	10.5	69 38.6	6.3	22 07.9	1.3	58.4
21	135 52.4	.. 11.2	84 03.9	6.3	22 09.2	1.2	58.4
22	150 52.4	11.9	98 29.2	6.3	22 10.4	1.0	58.4
23	165 52.4	12.6	112 54.5	6.2	22 11.4	0.9	58.4
9 00	180 52.5	N17 13.2	127 19.7	6.2	N22 12.3	0.8	58.4
01	195 52.5	13.9	141 44.9	6.1	22 13.1	0.6	58.4
02	210 52.5	14.6	156 10.0	6.2	22 13.7	0.4	58.4
03	225 52.6	.. 15.3	170 35.2	6.1	22 14.1	0.4	58.5
04	240 52.6	15.9	185 00.3	6.1	22 14.5	0.1	58.5
05	255 52.6	16.6	199 25.4	6.1	22 14.6	0.1	58.5
06	270 52.7	N17 17.3	213 50.5	6.1	N22 14.7	0.3	58.5
07	285 52.7	17.9	228 15.6	6.0	22 14.6	0.3	58.5
08	300 52.7	18.6	242 40.6	6.1	22 14.3	0.4	58.5
09	315 52.7	.. 19.3	257 05.7	6.0	22 13.9	0.5	58.6
10	330 52.8	19.9	271 30.7	6.1	22 13.4	0.7	58.6
11	345 52.8	20.6	285 55.8	6.0	22 12.7	0.8	58.6
12	0 52.8	N17 21.3	300 20.8	5.9	N22 11.9	1.0	58.6
13	15 52.9	21.9	314 45.8	6.0	22 10.9	1.1	58.6
14	30 52.9	22.6	329 10.8	6.0	22 09.8	1.2	58.6
15	45 52.9	.. 23.3	343 35.8	6.0	22 08.6	1.4	58.6
16	60 52.9	23.9	358 00.8	6.0	22 07.2	1.5	58.7
17	75 53.0	24.6	12 25.8	6.0	22 05.7	1.7	58.7
18	90 53.0	N17 25.3	26 50.8	6.0	N22 04.0	1.8	58.7
19	105 53.0	25.9	41 15.8	5.9	22 02.2	2.0	58.7
20	120 53.1	26.6	55 40.7	6.0	22 00.2	2.1	58.7
21	135 53.1	.. 27.3	70 05.7	6.0	21 58.1	2.2	58.7
22	150 53.1	27.9	84 30.7	6.0	21 55.9	2.4	58.7
23	165 53.1	28.6	98 55.7	6.1	N21 53.5	2.5	58.7
	SD 15.9	d 0.7	SD 15.7		15.9		16.0

Days: TUESDAY (7), WEDNESDAY (8), THURSDAY (9)

Moonrise

Lat.	Twilight Naut.	Twilight Civil	Sunrise	7	8	9	10
°	h m	h m	h m	h m	h m	h m	h m
N 72	////	////	00 33	▭	▭	▭	▭
N 70	////	////	01 49	02 56	▭	▭	▭
68	////	////	02 25	03 50	03 44	▭	05 35
66	////	01 07	02 51	04 24	04 40	05 20	06 36
64	////	01 52	03 11	04 48	05 14	05 59	07 11
62	////	02 21	03 27	05 07	05 38	06 27	07 36
60	00 59	02 43	03 40	05 23	05 58	06 48	07 55
N 58	01 41	03 00	03 52	05 37	06 14	07 05	08 12
56	02 07	03 15	04 02	05 49	06 28	07 20	08 26
54	02 28	03 27	04 10	05 59	06 40	07 32	08 38
52	02 44	03 38	04 18	06 08	06 50	07 44	08 48
50	02 58	03 47	04 25	06 16	07 00	07 53	08 57
45	03 25	04 07	04 40	06 34	07 20	08 14	09 17
N 40	03 46	04 22	04 52	06 48	07 36	08 31	09 33
35	04 02	04 35	05 03	07 00	07 50	08 45	09 47
30	04 15	04 46	05 12	07 11	08 01	08 58	09 59
20	04 36	05 04	05 27	07 29	08 22	09 19	10 19
N 10	04 53	05 19	05 41	07 46	08 40	09 37	10 36
0	05 06	05 31	05 53	08 01	08 57	09 54	10 53
S 10	05 18	05 43	06 05	08 16	09 13	10 12	11 09
20	05 29	05 55	06 18	08 32	09 31	10 30	11 26
30	05 39	06 08	06 33	08 51	09 52	10 51	11 46
35	05 45	06 15	06 42	09 02	10 04	11 04	11 58
40	05 50	06 23	06 51	09 15	10 18	11 18	12 12
45	05 56	06 31	07 03	09 30	10 35	11 35	12 28
S 50	06 03	06 41	07 16	09 48	10 56	11 56	12 47
52	06 05	06 46	07 23	09 57	11 05	12 06	12 56
54	06 08	06 51	07 30	10 07	11 17	12 17	13 07
56	06 11	06 56	07 38	10 18	11 29	12 30	13 18
58	06 15	07 03	07 47	10 31	11 44	12 45	13 32
S 60	06 18	07 09	07 57	10 45	12 01	13 03	13 47

Moonset

Lat.	Sunset	Twilight Civil	Twilight Naut.	7	8	9	10
°	h m	h m	h m	h m	h m	h m	h m
N 72	▭	▭	▭	▭	▭	▭	▭
N 70	22 11	////	////	00 26	▭	▭	▭
68	21 32	////	////	25 34	01 34	▭	03 45
66	21 05	22 55	////	24 38	00 38	01 58	02 43
64	20 44	22 05	////	24 05	00 05	01 19	02 09
62	20 28	21 35	////	23 40	24 51	00 51	01 43
60	20 14	21 12	23 02	23 21	24 30	00 30	01 23
N 58	20 03	20 55	22 16	23 05	24 13	00 13	01 07
56	19 53	20 40	21 48	22 52	23 58	24 53	00 53
54	19 44	20 27	21 28	22 40	23 46	24 41	00 41
52	19 36	20 16	21 11	22 30	23 34	24 30	00 30
50	19 29	20 07	20 57	22 20	23 25	24 20	00 20
45	19 14	19 47	20 29	22 01	23 04	24 00	00 00
N 40	19 01	19 31	20 08	21 45	22 47	23 44	24 34
35	18 51	19 18	19 52	21 32	22 33	23 30	24 22
30	18 42	19 07	19 38	21 20	22 21	23 18	24 11
20	18 26	18 49	19 17	21 00	21 59	22 57	23 52
N 10	18 13	18 35	19 00	20 43	21 41	22 39	23 36
0	18 00	18 22	18 47	20 27	21 24	22 22	23 20
S 10	17 48	18 10	18 35	20 11	21 07	22 05	23 05
20	17 34	17 57	18 24	19 54	20 49	21 47	22 48
30	17 20	17 45	18 13	19 34	20 27	21 26	22 29
35	17 11	17 38	18 08	19 23	20 15	21 14	22 17
40	17 01	17 30	18 02	19 09	20 01	21 00	22 04
45	16 50	17 21	17 56	18 54	19 44	20 43	21 49
S 50	16 36	17 11	17 50	18 35	19 23	20 22	21 30
52	16 30	17 06	17 47	18 26	19 13	20 12	21 21
54	16 23	17 01	17 44	18 16	19 02	20 01	21 11
56	16 15	16 56	17 41	18 04	18 49	19 48	21 00
58	16 06	16 50	17 37	17 51	18 35	19 33	20 47
S 60	15 56	16 43	17 34	17 36	18 17	19 16	20 31

Day	SUN Eqn. of Time 00h	SUN Eqn. of Time 12h	SUN Mer. Pass.	MOON Mer. Pass. Upper	MOON Mer. Pass. Lower	Age	Phase
d	m s	m s	h m	h m	h m	d	%
7	03 23	03 25	11 57	14 14	01 47	03	7
8	03 27	03 28	11 57	15 10	02 42	04	14
9	03 30	03 31	11 56	16 08	03 39	05	23

© British Crown Copyright 2018. All rights reserved.

UT	ARIES GHA	VENUS −3.8 GHA / Dec	MARS +1.7 GHA / Dec	JUPITER −2.5 GHA / Dec	SATURN +0.4 GHA / Dec
10 FRIDAY					
00	227 30.3	205 12.0 N 7 33.7	141 51.9 N24 28.8	325 02.1 S22 37.7	295 27.7 S21 30.1
01	242 32.7	220 11.6 34.9	156 52.6 28.9	340 04.8 37.7	310 30.2 30.1
02	257 35.2	235 11.2 36.0	171 53.3 29.0	355 07.5 37.6	325 32.7 30.1
03	272 37.7	250 10.8 .. 37.1	186 54.0 .. 29.0	10 10.2 .. 37.6	340 35.2 .. 30.1
04	287 40.1	265 10.5 38.3	201 54.6 29.1	25 12.9 37.6	355 37.7 30.1
05	302 42.6	280 10.1 39.4	216 55.3 29.1	40 15.6 37.6	10 40.2 30.1
06	317 45.1	295 09.7 N 7 40.5	231 56.0 N24 29.2	55 18.3 S22 37.6	25 42.7 S21 30.1
07	332 47.5	310 09.3 41.6	246 56.7 29.2	70 21.0 37.6	40 45.2 30.1
08	347 50.0	325 09.0 42.8	261 57.4 29.3	85 23.7 37.6	55 47.7 30.1
09	2 52.5	340 08.6 .. 43.9	276 58.1 .. 29.3	100 26.4 .. 37.6	70 50.2 .. 30.1
10	17 54.9	355 08.2 45.0	291 58.8 29.4	115 29.1 37.6	85 52.8 30.1
11	32 57.4	10 07.8 46.1	306 59.4 29.4	130 31.8 37.6	100 55.3 30.2
12	47 59.8	25 07.4 N 7 47.3	322 00.1 N24 29.5	145 34.5 S22 37.6	115 57.8 S21 30.2
13	63 02.3	40 07.1 48.4	337 00.8 29.6	160 37.2 37.5	131 00.3 30.2
14	78 04.8	55 06.7 49.5	352 01.5 29.6	175 39.8 37.5	146 02.8 30.2
15	93 07.2	70 06.3 .. 50.6	7 02.2 .. 29.7	190 42.5 .. 37.5	161 05.3 .. 30.2
16	108 09.7	85 05.9 51.8	22 02.9 29.7	205 45.2 37.5	176 07.8 30.2
17	123 12.2	100 05.5 52.9	37 03.6 29.8	220 47.9 37.5	191 10.3 30.2
18	138 14.6	115 05.2 N 7 54.0	52 04.2 N24 29.8	235 50.6 S22 37.5	206 12.8 S21 30.2
19	153 17.1	130 04.8 55.1	67 04.9 29.9	250 53.3 37.5	221 15.3 30.2
20	168 19.6	145 04.4 56.3	82 05.6 29.9	265 56.0 37.5	236 17.8 30.2
21	183 22.0	160 04.0 .. 57.4	97 06.3 .. 30.0	280 58.7 .. 37.5	251 20.4 .. 30.2
22	198 24.5	175 03.6 58.5	112 07.0 30.0	296 01.4 37.5	266 22.9 30.2
23	213 27.0	190 03.2 7 59.6	127 07.7 30.1	311 04.2 37.4	281 25.4 30.3
11 SATURDAY					
00	228 29.4	205 02.9 N 8 00.8	142 08.3 N24 30.1	326 06.9 S22 37.4	296 27.9 S21 30.3
01	243 31.9	220 02.5 01.9	157 09.0 30.2	341 09.6 37.4	311 30.4 30.3
02	258 34.3	235 02.1 03.0	172 09.7 30.2	356 12.3 37.4	326 32.9 30.3
03	273 36.8	250 01.7 .. 04.1	187 10.4 .. 30.3	11 15.0 .. 37.4	341 35.4 .. 30.3
04	288 39.3	265 01.3 05.2	202 11.1 30.3	26 17.7 37.4	356 37.9 30.3
05	303 41.7	280 01.0 06.4	217 11.8 30.3	41 20.4 37.4	11 40.4 30.3
06	318 44.2	295 00.6 N 8 07.5	232 12.5 N24 30.4	56 23.1 S22 37.4	26 43.0 S21 30.3
07	333 46.7	310 00.2 08.6	247 13.1 30.4	71 25.8 37.4	41 45.5 30.3
08	348 49.1	324 59.8 09.7	262 13.8 30.5	86 28.5 37.4	56 48.0 30.3
09	3 51.6	339 59.4 .. 10.9	277 14.5 .. 30.5	101 31.2 .. 37.3	71 50.5 .. 30.3
10	18 54.1	354 59.0 12.0	292 15.2 30.6	116 33.9 37.3	86 53.0 30.3
11	33 56.5	9 58.6 13.1	307 15.9 30.6	131 36.6 37.3	101 55.5 30.4
12	48 59.0	24 58.3 N 8 14.2	322 16.6 N24 30.7	146 39.3 S22 37.3	116 58.0 S21 30.4
13	64 01.5	39 57.9 15.3	337 17.3 30.7	161 42.0 37.3	132 00.5 30.4
14	79 03.9	54 57.5 16.4	352 17.9 30.8	176 44.7 37.3	147 03.1 30.4
15	94 06.4	69 57.1 .. 17.6	7 18.6 .. 30.8	191 47.4 .. 37.3	162 05.6 .. 30.4
16	109 08.8	84 56.7 18.7	22 19.3 30.8	206 50.1 37.3	177 08.1 30.4
17	124 11.3	99 56.3 19.8	37 20.0 30.9	221 52.8 37.3	192 10.6 30.4
18	139 13.8	114 55.9 N 8 20.9	52 20.7 N24 30.9	236 55.5 S22 37.3	207 13.1 S21 30.4
19	154 16.2	129 55.6 22.0	67 21.4 31.0	251 58.2 37.2	222 15.6 30.4
20	169 18.7	144 55.2 23.2	82 22.0 31.0	267 00.9 37.2	237 18.1 30.4
21	184 21.2	159 54.8 .. 24.3	97 22.7 .. 31.1	282 03.6 .. 37.2	252 20.7 .. 30.4
22	199 23.6	174 54.4 25.4	112 23.4 31.1	297 06.4 37.2	267 23.2 30.5
23	214 26.1	189 54.0 26.5	127 24.1 31.1	312 09.1 37.2	282 25.7 30.5
12 SUNDAY					
00	229 28.6	204 53.6 N 8 27.6	142 24.8 N24 31.2	327 11.8 S22 37.2	297 28.2 S21 30.5
01	244 31.0	219 53.2 28.7	157 25.5 31.2	342 14.5 37.2	312 30.7 30.5
02	259 33.5	234 52.8 29.9	172 26.2 31.3	357 17.2 37.2	327 33.2 30.5
03	274 35.9	249 52.5 .. 31.0	187 26.8 .. 31.3	12 19.9 .. 37.2	342 35.7 .. 30.5
04	289 38.4	264 52.1 32.1	202 27.5 31.3	27 22.6 37.2	357 38.3 30.5
05	304 40.9	279 51.7 33.2	217 28.2 31.4	42 25.3 37.1	12 40.8 30.5
06	319 43.3	294 51.3 N 8 34.3	232 28.9 N24 31.4	57 28.0 S22 37.1	27 43.3 S21 30.5
07	334 45.8	309 50.9 35.4	247 29.6 31.5	72 30.7 37.1	42 45.8 30.5
08	349 48.3	324 50.5 36.5	262 30.3 31.5	87 33.4 37.1	57 48.3 30.5
09	4 50.7	339 50.1 .. 37.6	277 31.0 .. 31.5	102 36.2 .. 37.1	72 50.8 .. 30.6
10	19 53.2	354 49.7 38.8	292 31.6 31.6	117 38.9 37.1	87 53.4 30.6
11	34 55.7	9 49.3 39.9	307 32.3 31.6	132 41.6 37.1	102 55.9 30.6
12	49 58.1	24 48.9 N 8 41.0	322 33.0 N24 31.6	147 44.3 S22 37.1	117 58.4 S21 30.6
13	65 00.6	39 48.5 42.1	337 33.7 31.7	162 47.0 37.1	133 00.9 30.6
14	80 03.1	54 48.2 43.2	352 34.4 31.7	177 49.7 37.1	148 03.4 30.6
15	95 05.5	69 47.8 .. 44.3	7 35.1 .. 31.7	192 52.4 .. 37.0	163 05.9 .. 30.6
16	110 08.0	84 47.4 45.4	22 35.8 31.8	207 55.1 37.0	178 08.5 30.6
17	125 10.4	99 47.0 46.5	37 36.4 31.8	222 57.8 37.0	193 11.0 30.6
18	140 12.9	114 46.6 N 8 47.7	52 37.1 N24 31.9	238 00.6 S22 37.0	208 13.5 S21 30.6
19	155 15.4	129 46.2 48.8	67 37.8 31.9	253 03.3 37.0	223 16.0 30.7
20	170 17.8	144 45.8 49.9	82 38.5 31.9	268 06.0 37.0	238 18.5 30.7
21	185 20.3	159 45.4 .. 51.0	97 39.2 .. 32.0	283 08.7 .. 37.0	253 21.0 .. 30.7
22	200 22.8	174 45.0 52.1	112 39.9 32.0	298 11.4 37.0	268 23.6 30.7
23	215 25.5	189 44.6 53.2	127 40.6 32.0	313 14.1 37.0	283 26.1 30.7
Mer. Pass.	h m 8 44.6	v −0.4 d 1.1	v 0.7 d 0.0	v 2.7 d 0.0	v 2.5 d 0.0

STARS

Name	SHA	Dec
Acamar	315 15.7	S40 13.8
Achernar	335 24.3	S57 08.4
Acrux	173 04.3	S63 12.5
Adhara	255 09.6	S29 00.2
Aldebaran	290 45.1	N16 32.7
Alioth	166 16.7	N55 51.5
Alkaid	152 55.3	N49 13.2
Alnair	27 38.8	S46 51.9
Alnilam	275 42.6	S 1 11.6
Alphard	217 52.2	S 8 44.7
Alphecca	126 07.2	N26 39.1
Alpheratz	357 39.6	N29 11.5
Altair	62 04.2	N 8 55.1
Ankaa	353 12.0	S42 12.1
Antares	112 21.0	S26 28.3
Arcturus	145 51.8	N19 05.0
Atria	107 18.7	S69 03.5
Avior	234 16.6	S59 34.6
Bellatrix	278 28.0	N 6 21.8
Betelgeuse	270 57.2	N 7 24.4
Canopus	263 54.8	S52 42.7
Capella	280 29.0	N46 00.9
Deneb	49 28.7	N45 20.7
Denebola	182 29.4	N14 27.9
Diphda	348 52.1	S17 53.0
Dubhe	193 46.5	N61 39.1
Elnath	278 07.9	N28 37.3
Eltanin	90 43.9	N51 29.1
Enif	33 43.2	N 9 57.7
Fomalhaut	15 19.7	S29 31.2
Gacrux	171 56.0	S57 13.4
Gienah	175 48.0	S17 39.0
Hadar	148 41.6	S60 27.9
Hamal	327 56.6	N23 32.9
Kaus Aust.	83 38.2	S34 22.3
Kochab	137 18.9	N74 04.7
Markab	13 34.5	N15 18.3
Menkar	314 11.2	N 4 09.7
Menkent	148 02.5	S36 27.9
Miaplacidus	221 38.9	S69 48.1
Mirfak	308 35.1	N49 55.5
Nunki	75 53.1	S26 16.2
Peacock	53 12.8	S56 40.1
Pollux	243 23.0	N27 58.7
Procyon	244 55.7	N 5 10.4
Rasalhague	96 02.5	N12 32.8
Regulus	207 39.2	N11 52.4
Rigel	281 08.5	S 8 11.0
Rigil Kent.	139 45.6	S60 54.8
Sabik	102 07.6	S15 44.8
Schedar	349 36.4	N56 38.2
Shaula	96 16.1	S37 06.9
Sirius	258 30.4	S16 44.8
Spica	158 26.7	S11 15.7
Suhail	222 49.6	S43 30.9
Vega	80 36.0	N38 48.0
Zuben'ubi	137 00.6	S16 07.2

	SHA	Mer. Pass.
		h m
Venus	336 33.5	10 20
Mars	273 38.9	14 31
Jupiter	97 37.4	2 15
Saturn	67 58.5	4 13

© British Crown Copyright 2018. All rights reserved.

UT	SUN GHA	SUN Dec	MOON GHA	v	MOON Dec	d	HP
	° ′	° ′	° ′	′	° ′	′	′
10 00	180 53.2	N17 29.2	113 20.8	6.0	N21 51.0	2.7	58.8
01	195 53.2	29.9	127 45.8	6.0	21 48.3	2.8	58.8
02	210 53.2	30.6	142 10.8	6.1	21 45.5	3.0	58.8
03	225 53.2 ..	31.2	156 35.9	6.0	21 42.5	3.1	58.8
04	240 53.3	31.9	171 00.9	6.1	21 39.4	3.2	58.8
05	255 53.3	32.5	185 26.0	6.1	21 36.2	3.4	58.8
06	270 53.3	N17 33.2	199 51.1	6.1	N21 32.8	3.5	58.8
07	285 53.3	33.8	214 16.2	6.1	21 29.3	3.7	58.8
08	300 53.4	34.5	228 41.3	6.1	21 25.6	3.7	58.9
F 09	315 53.4 ..	35.2	243 06.4	6.2	21 21.9	4.0	58.9
R 10	330 53.4	35.8	257 31.6	6.1	21 17.9	4.0	58.9
I 11	345 53.4	36.5	271 56.7	6.2	21 13.9	4.3	58.9
D 12	0 53.5	N17 37.1	286 21.9	6.3	N21 09.6	4.3	58.9
A 13	15 53.5	37.8	300 47.2	6.2	21 05.3	4.5	58.9
Y 14	30 53.5	38.4	315 12.4	6.3	21 00.8	4.6	58.9
15	45 53.5 ..	39.1	329 37.7	6.3	20 56.2	4.8	58.9
16	60 53.5	39.7	344 03.0	6.3	20 51.4	4.8	59.0
17	75 53.6	40.4	358 28.3	6.3	20 46.6	5.1	59.0
18	90 53.6	N17 41.0	12 53.6	6.4	N20 41.5	5.1	59.0
19	105 53.6	41.7	27 19.0	6.4	20 36.4	5.3	59.0
20	120 53.6	42.3	41 44.4	6.5	20 31.1	5.4	59.0
21	135 53.6 ..	43.0	56 09.9	6.5	20 25.7	5.6	59.0
22	150 53.7	43.6	70 35.4	6.5	20 20.1	5.7	59.0
23	165 53.7	44.3	85 00.9	6.5	20 14.4	5.8	59.0
11 00	180 53.7	N17 44.9	99 26.4	6.6	N20 08.6	5.9	59.0
01	195 53.7	45.6	113 52.0	6.6	20 02.7	6.1	59.0
02	210 53.7	46.2	128 17.6	6.6	19 56.6	6.2	59.1
03	225 53.8 ..	46.9	142 43.2	6.7	19 50.4	6.4	59.1
04	240 53.8	47.5	157 08.9	6.7	19 44.0	6.4	59.1
05	255 53.8	48.2	171 34.6	6.8	19 37.6	6.6	59.1
06	270 53.8	N17 48.8	186 00.4	6.8	N19 31.0	6.7	59.1
S 07	285 53.8	49.5	200 26.2	6.8	19 24.3	6.8	59.1
A 08	300 53.9	50.1	214 52.0	6.9	19 17.5	7.0	59.1
T 09	315 53.9 ..	50.8	229 17.9	7.0	19 10.5	7.1	59.1
U 10	330 53.9	51.4	243 43.9	6.9	19 03.4	7.2	59.1
R 11	345 53.9	52.0	258 09.8	7.0	18 56.2	7.3	59.1
D 12	0 53.9	N17 52.7	272 35.8	7.1	N18 48.9	7.5	59.2
A 13	15 53.9	53.3	287 01.9	7.1	18 41.4	7.5	59.2
Y 14	30 54.0	54.0	301 28.0	7.1	18 33.9	7.7	59.2
15	45 54.0 ..	54.6	315 54.1	7.2	18 26.2	7.8	59.2
16	60 54.0	55.2	330 20.3	7.2	18 18.4	7.9	59.2
17	75 54.0	55.9	344 46.5	7.3	18 10.5	8.0	59.2
18	90 54.0	N17 56.5	359 12.8	7.3	N18 02.5	8.2	59.2
19	105 54.0	57.2	13 39.1	7.4	17 54.3	8.2	59.2
20	120 54.1	57.8	28 05.5	7.4	17 46.1	8.4	59.2
21	135 54.1 ..	58.4	42 31.9	7.5	17 37.7	8.5	59.2
22	150 54.1	59.1	56 58.4	7.5	17 29.2	8.6	59.2
23	165 54.1	17 59.7	71 24.9	7.5	17 20.6	8.7	59.2
12 00	180 54.1	N18 00.3	85 51.4	7.6	N17 11.9	8.8	59.2
01	195 54.1	01.0	100 18.0	7.7	17 03.1	8.9	59.3
02	210 54.1	01.6	114 44.7	7.7	16 54.2	9.0	59.3
03	225 54.2 ..	02.3	129 11.4	7.7	16 45.2	9.1	59.3
04	240 54.2	02.9	143 38.1	7.8	16 36.1	9.3	59.3
05	255 54.2	03.5	158 04.9	7.9	16 26.8	9.3	59.3
06	270 54.2	N18 04.1	172 31.8	7.9	N16 17.5	9.4	59.3
07	285 54.2	04.8	186 58.7	7.9	16 08.1	9.5	59.3
08	300 54.2	05.4	201 25.6	8.0	15 58.6	9.7	59.3
S 09	315 54.2 ..	06.0	215 52.6	8.0	15 48.9	9.7	59.3
U 10	330 54.2	06.7	230 19.6	8.1	15 39.2	9.8	59.3
N 11	345 54.3	07.3	244 46.7	8.2	15 29.4	9.9	59.3
D 12	0 54.3	N18 07.9	259 13.9	8.1	N15 19.5	10.1	59.3
A 13	15 54.3	08.6	273 41.0	8.3	15 09.4	10.1	59.3
Y 14	30 54.3	09.2	288 08.3	8.3	14 59.3	10.2	59.3
15	45 54.3 ..	09.8	302 35.6	8.3	14 49.1	10.3	59.3
16	60 54.3	10.4	317 02.9	8.4	14 38.8	10.3	59.3
17	75 54.3	11.1	331 30.3	8.4	14 28.5	10.5	59.4
18	90 54.3	N18 11.7	345 57.7	8.5	N14 18.0	10.6	59.4
19	105 54.3	12.3	0 25.2	8.5	14 07.4	10.6	59.4
20	120 54.4	13.0	14 52.7	8.6	13 56.8	10.7	59.4
21	135 54.4 ..	13.6	29 20.3	8.6	13 46.1	10.8	59.4
22	150 54.4	14.2	43 47.9	8.7	13 35.3	10.9	59.4
23	165 54.4	14.8	58 15.6	8.7	N13 24.4	11.0	59.4
	SD 15.9	d 0.6	SD 16.0		16.1		16.2

Lat.	Twilight Naut.	Twilight Civil	Sunrise	Moonrise 10	11	12	13
°	h m	h m	h m	h m	h m	h m	h m
N 72	▭	▭		▭		08 35	11 07
N 70	////	////	01 26	▭	06 41	09 16	11 26
68	////	////	02 10	05 35	07 42	09 44	11 41
66	////	00 30	02 39	06 36	08 17	10 05	11 53
64	////	01 36	03 01	07 11	08 42	10 22	12 03
62	////	02 09	03 18	07 36	09 01	10 35	12 12
60	00 27	02 33	03 33	07 55	09 17	10 47	12 19
N 58	01 26	02 52	03 45	08 12	09 31	10 57	12 25
56	01 57	03 08	03 56	08 26	09 42	11 05	12 31
54	02 19	03 21	04 05	08 38	09 52	11 13	12 36
52	02 37	03 32	04 13	08 48	10 01	11 20	12 41
50	02 52	03 42	04 21	08 57	10 09	11 26	12 45
45	03 20	04 03	04 36	09 17	10 26	11 39	12 54
N 40	03 42	04 19	04 49	09 33	10 40	11 50	13 01
35	03 59	04 32	05 00	09 47	10 52	12 00	13 07
30	04 13	04 44	05 10	09 59	11 03	12 08	13 13
20	04 35	05 02	05 26	10 19	11 20	12 22	13 23
N 10	04 52	05 18	05 40	10 36	11 36	12 34	13 31
0	05 06	05 31	05 53	10 53	11 50	12 45	13 39
S 10	05 18	05 44	06 06	11 09	12 04	12 57	13 47
20	05 30	05 56	06 20	11 26	12 19	13 09	13 55
30	05 41	06 10	06 35	11 46	12 37	13 23	14 04
35	05 47	06 17	06 44	11 58	12 47	13 31	14 10
40	05 53	06 25	06 54	12 12	12 59	13 40	14 16
45	05 59	06 35	07 06	12 28	13 12	13 50	14 23
S 50	06 06	06 45	07 21	12 47	13 29	14 03	14 32
52	06 09	06 50	07 27	12 56	13 37	14 09	14 36
54	06 13	06 56	07 35	13 07	13 45	14 15	14 40
56	06 16	07 02	07 43	13 18	13 55	14 23	14 45
58	06 20	07 08	07 53	13 32	14 06	14 31	14 50
S 60	06 24	07 15	08 04	13 47	14 18	14 40	14 56

Lat.	Sunset	Twilight Civil	Twilight Naut.	Moonset 10	11	12	13
°	h m	h m	h m	h m	h m	h m	h m
N 72	▭	▭	▭	▭		04 45	04 06
N 70	22 35	////	////	▭	04 40	04 02	03 45
68	21 47	////	////	03 45	03 38	03 33	03 29
66	21 17	////	////	02 43	03 03	03 11	03 15
64	20 54	22 22	////	02 09	02 37	02 54	03 04
62	20 36	21 47	////	01 43	02 17	02 39	02 54
60	20 22	21 22	////	01 23	02 01	02 27	02 46
N 58	20 09	21 03	22 32	01 07	01 47	02 16	02 38
56	19 59	20 47	21 59	00 53	01 35	02 07	02 32
54	19 49	20 34	21 36	00 41	01 24	01 59	02 26
52	19 41	20 22	21 18	00 30	01 15	01 51	02 21
50	19 33	20 12	21 03	00 20	01 07	01 45	02 16
45	19 17	19 51	20 34	00 00	00 49	01 30	02 05
N 40	19 04	19 35	20 12	24 34	00 34	01 18	01 57
35	18 53	19 21	19 55	24 22	00 22	01 08	01 49
30	18 44	19 10	19 41	24 11	00 11	00 59	01 42
20	18 27	18 51	19 18	23 52	24 43	00 43	01 31
N 10	18 13	18 35	19 01	23 36	24 29	00 29	01 21
0	18 00	18 22	18 47	23 20	24 17	00 17	01 11
S 10	17 47	18 09	18 34	23 05	24 04	00 04	01 01
20	17 33	17 56	18 23	22 48	23 50	24 51	00 51
30	17 17	17 43	18 11	22 29	23 33	24 39	00 39
35	17 08	17 35	18 05	22 17	23 24	24 32	00 32
40	16 58	17 27	18 00	22 04	23 13	24 24	00 24
45	16 46	17 18	17 53	21 49	23 01	24 15	00 15
S 50	16 32	17 07	17 46	21 30	22 45	24 03	00 03
52	16 25	17 02	17 43	21 21	22 38	23 58	25 19
54	16 17	16 56	17 39	21 11	22 30	23 52	25 16
56	16 09	16 51	17 36	21 00	22 21	23 46	25 12
58	15 59	16 44	17 32	20 47	22 10	23 38	25 07
S 60	15 49	16 37	17 28	20 31	21 58	23 30	25 02

Day	SUN Eqn. of Time 00h	12h	SUN Mer. Pass.	MOON Mer. Pass. Upper	Lower	Age	Phase
d	m s	m s	h m	h m	h m	d %	
10	03 33	03 34	11 56	17 06	04 37	06 33	
11	03 35	03 36	11 56	18 03	05 35	07 44	
12	03 36	03 37	11 56	18 58	06 31	08 55	

© British Crown Copyright 2018. All rights reserved.

UT	ARIES	VENUS −3.8		MARS +1.7		JUPITER −2.5		SATURN +0.4		STARS		
	GHA	GHA	Dec	GHA	Dec	GHA	Dec	GHA	Dec	Name	SHA	Dec
d h	° ′	° ′	° ′	° ′	° ′	° ′	° ′	° ′	° ′		° ′	° ′
13 00	230 27.7	204 44.2	N 8 54.3	142 41.2	N24 32.1	328 16.8	S22 37.0	298 28.6	S21 30.7	Acamar	315 15.7	S40 13.8
01	245 30.2	219 43.8	55.4	157 41.9	32.1	343 19.5	36.9	313 31.1	30.7	Achernar	335 24.3	S57 08.4
02	260 32.6	234 43.4	56.5	172 42.6	32.1	358 22.3	36.9	328 33.6	30.7	Acrux	173 04.3	S63 12.5
03	275 35.1	249 43.0 ..	57.6	187 43.3 ..	32.1	13 25.0 ..	36.9	343 36.2 ..	30.7	Adhara	255 09.6	S29 00.2
04	290 37.6	264 42.6	58.7	202 44.0	32.2	28 27.7	36.9	358 38.7	30.7	Aldebaran	290 45.1	N16 32.7
05	305 40.0	279 42.2	8 59.8	217 44.7	32.2	43 30.4	36.9	13 41.2	30.8			
06	320 42.5	294 41.8	N 9 01.0	232 45.4	N24 32.2	58 33.1	S22 36.9	28 43.7	S21 30.8	Alioth	166 16.7	N55 51.6
07	335 44.9	309 41.4	02.1	247 46.0	32.3	73 35.8	36.9	43 46.2	30.8	Alkaid	152 55.3	N49 13.2
08	350 47.4	324 41.0	03.2	262 46.7	32.3	88 38.6	36.9	58 48.8	30.8	Alnair	27 38.8	S46 51.9
M 09	5 49.9	339 40.6 ..	04.3	277 47.4 ..	32.3	103 41.3 ..	36.9	73 51.3 ..	30.8	Alnilam	275 42.6	S 1 11.6
O 10	20 52.3	354 40.2	05.4	292 48.1	32.4	118 44.0	36.8	88 53.8	30.8	Alphard	217 52.2	S 8 44.7
N 11	35 54.8	9 39.8	06.5	307 48.8	32.4	133 46.7	36.8	103 56.3	30.8			
D 12	50 57.3	24 39.4	N 9 07.6	322 49.5	N24 32.4	148 49.4	S22 36.8	118 58.8	S21 30.8	Alphecca	126 07.2	N26 39.1
A 13	65 59.7	39 39.1	08.7	337 50.2	32.4	163 52.1	36.8	134 01.4	30.8	Alpheratz	357 39.6	N29 11.5
Y 14	81 02.2	54 38.7	09.8	352 50.9	32.5	178 54.9	36.8	149 03.9	30.8	Altair	62 04.2	N 8 55.1
15	96 04.7	69 38.3 ..	10.9	7 51.5 ..	32.5	193 57.6 ..	36.8	164 06.4 ..	30.9	Ankaa	353 12.0	S42 12.1
16	111 07.1	84 37.9	12.0	22 52.2	32.5	209 00.3	36.8	179 08.9	30.9	Antares	112 21.0	S26 28.4
17	126 09.6	99 37.5	13.1	37 52.9	32.6	224 03.0	36.8	194 11.5	30.9			
18	141 12.0	114 37.1	N 9 14.2	52 53.6	N24 32.6	239 05.7	S22 36.8	209 14.0	S21 30.9	Arcturus	145 51.8	N19 05.0
19	156 14.5	129 36.7	15.3	67 54.3	32.6	254 08.4	36.8	224 16.5	30.9	Atria	107 18.7	S69 03.5
20	171 17.0	144 36.3	16.4	82 55.0	32.6	269 11.2	36.7	239 19.0	30.9	Avior	234 16.6	S59 34.6
21	186 19.4	159 35.8 ..	17.5	97 55.7 ..	32.7	284 13.9 ..	36.7	254 21.5 ..	30.9	Bellatrix	278 28.0	N 6 21.8
22	201 21.9	174 35.4	18.6	112 56.3	32.7	299 16.6	36.7	269 24.1	30.9	Betelgeuse	270 57.2	N 7 24.4
23	216 24.4	189 35.0	19.7	127 57.0	32.7	314 19.3	36.7	284 26.6	30.9			
14 00	231 26.8	204 34.6	N 9 20.8	142 57.7	N24 32.7	329 22.0	S22 36.7	299 29.1	S21 30.9	Canopus	263 54.8	S52 42.7
01	246 29.3	219 34.2	21.9	157 58.4	32.8	344 24.8	36.7	314 31.6	31.0	Capella	280 29.0	N46 00.9
02	261 31.8	234 33.8	23.0	172 59.1	32.8	359 27.5	36.7	329 34.2	31.0	Deneb	49 28.6	N45 20.7
03	276 34.2	249 33.4 ..	24.1	187 59.8 ..	32.8	14 30.2 ..	36.7	344 36.7 ..	31.0	Denebola	182 29.4	N14 27.9
04	291 36.7	264 33.0	25.2	203 00.5	32.8	29 32.9	36.7	359 39.2	31.0	Diphda	348 52.1	S17 53.0
05	306 39.2	279 32.6	26.3	218 01.2	32.8	44 35.6	36.6	14 41.7	31.0			
06	321 41.6	294 32.2	N 9 27.4	233 01.8	N24 32.9	59 38.4	S22 36.6	29 44.3	S21 31.0	Dubhe	193 46.6	N61 39.1
07	336 44.1	309 31.8	28.5	248 02.5	32.9	74 41.1	36.6	44 46.8	31.0	Elnath	278 07.9	N28 37.3
T 08	351 46.5	324 31.4	29.6	263 03.2	32.9	89 43.8	36.6	59 49.3	31.0	Eltanin	90 43.8	N51 29.1
U 09	6 49.0	339 31.0 ..	30.7	278 03.9 ..	32.9	104 46.5 ..	36.6	74 51.8 ..	31.0	Enif	33 43.2	N 9 57.7
E 10	21 51.5	354 30.6	31.8	293 04.6	33.0	119 49.3	36.6	89 54.3	31.0	Fomalhaut	15 19.7	S29 31.2
S 11	36 53.9	9 30.2	32.9	308 05.3	33.0	134 52.0	36.6	104 56.9	31.1			
D 12	51 56.4	24 29.8	N 9 34.0	323 06.0	N24 33.0	149 54.7	S22 36.6	119 59.4	S21 31.1	Gacrux	171 56.0	S57 13.4
A 13	66 58.9	39 29.4	35.1	338 06.6	33.0	164 57.4	36.6	135 01.9	31.1	Gienah	175 48.0	S17 39.0
Y 14	82 01.3	54 29.0	36.2	353 07.3	33.0	180 00.2	36.5	150 04.5	31.1	Hadar	148 41.6	S60 28.0
15	97 03.8	69 28.6 ..	37.3	8 08.0 ..	33.1	195 02.9 ..	36.5	165 07.0 ..	31.1	Hamal	327 56.6	N23 32.9
16	112 06.3	84 28.2	38.4	23 08.7	33.1	210 05.6	36.5	180 09.5	31.1	Kaus Aust.	83 38.2	S34 22.3
17	127 08.7	99 27.8	39.5	38 09.4	33.1	225 08.3	36.5	195 12.0	31.1			
18	142 11.2	114 27.4	N 9 40.6	53 10.1	N24 33.1	240 11.0	S22 36.5	210 14.6	S21 31.1	Kochab	137 18.9	N74 04.7
19	157 13.7	129 26.9	41.7	68 10.8	33.1	255 13.8	36.5	225 17.1	31.1	Markab	13 34.5	N15 18.3
20	172 16.1	144 26.5	42.8	83 11.5	33.1	270 16.5	36.5	240 19.6	31.2	Menkar	314 11.2	N 4 09.7
21	187 18.6	159 26.1 ..	43.8	98 12.1 ..	33.2	285 19.2 ..	36.5	255 22.1 ..	31.2	Menkent	148 02.5	S36 27.9
22	202 21.0	174 25.7	44.9	113 12.8	33.2	300 21.9	36.5	270 24.7	31.2	Miaplacidus	221 39.0	S69 48.1
23	217 23.5	189 25.3	46.0	128 13.5	33.2	315 24.7	36.4	285 27.2	31.2			
15 00	232 26.0	204 24.9	N 9 47.1	143 14.2	N24 33.2	330 27.4	S22 36.4	300 29.7	S21 31.2	Mirfak	308 35.1	N49 55.5
01	247 28.4	219 24.5	48.2	158 14.9	33.2	345 30.1	36.4	315 32.2	31.2	Nunki	75 53.1	S26 16.2
02	262 30.9	234 24.1	49.3	173 15.6	33.2	0 32.9	36.4	330 34.8	31.2	Peacock	53 12.8	S56 40.1
03	277 33.4	249 23.7 ..	50.4	188 16.3 ..	33.3	15 35.6 ..	36.4	345 37.3 ..	31.2	Pollux	243 23.0	N27 58.7
04	292 35.8	264 23.3	51.5	203 17.0	33.3	30 38.3	36.4	0 39.8	31.2	Procyon	244 55.7	N 5 10.4
05	307 38.3	279 22.9	52.6	218 17.6	33.3	45 41.0	36.4	15 42.4	31.3			
06	322 40.8	294 22.4	N 9 53.7	233 18.3	N24 33.3	60 43.8	S22 36.4	30 44.9	S21 31.3	Rasalhague	96 02.4	N12 32.8
W 07	337 43.2	309 22.0	54.8	248 19.0	33.3	75 46.5	36.4	45 47.4	31.3	Regulus	207 39.2	N11 52.4
E 08	352 45.7	324 21.6	55.8	263 19.7	33.3	90 49.2	36.3	60 49.9	31.3	Rigel	281 08.5	S 8 11.0
D 09	7 48.1	339 21.2 ..	56.9	278 20.4 ..	33.3	105 51.9 ..	36.3	75 52.5 ..	31.3	Rigil Kent.	139 45.6	S60 54.8
N 10	22 50.6	354 20.8	58.0	293 21.1	33.4	120 54.7	36.3	90 55.0	31.3	Sabik	102 07.6	S15 44.8
E 11	37 53.1	9 20.4	9 59.1	308 21.8	33.4	135 57.4	36.3	105 57.5	31.3			
S 12	52 55.5	24 20.0	N10 00.2	323 22.5	N24 33.4	151 00.1	S22 36.3	121 00.1	S21 31.3	Schedar	349 36.4	N56 38.2
D 13	67 58.0	39 19.6	01.3	338 23.1	33.4	166 02.9	36.3	136 02.6	31.3	Shaula	96 16.1	S37 06.9
A 14	83 00.5	54 19.1	02.4	353 23.8	33.4	181 05.6	36.3	151 05.1	31.4	Sirius	258 30.4	S16 44.8
Y 15	98 02.9	69 18.7 ..	03.5	8 24.5 ..	33.4	196 08.3 ..	36.3	166 07.6 ..	31.4	Spica	158 26.7	S11 15.7
16	113 05.4	84 18.3	04.5	23 25.2	33.4	211 11.0	36.3	181 10.2	31.4	Suhail	222 49.6	S43 30.9
17	128 07.9	99 17.9	05.6	38 25.9	33.4	226 13.8	36.2	196 12.7	31.4			
18	143 10.3	114 17.5	N10 06.7	53 26.6	N24 33.4	241 16.5	S22 36.2	211 15.2	S21 31.4	Vega	80 35.9	N38 48.0
19	158 12.8	129 17.1	07.8	68 27.3	33.5	256 19.2	36.2	226 17.8	31.4	Zuben'ubi	137 00.6	S16 07.2
20	173 15.3	144 16.7	08.9	83 28.0	33.5	271 22.0	36.2	241 20.3	31.4		SHA	Mer. Pass.
21	188 17.7	159 16.2 ..	10.0	98 28.6 ..	33.5	286 24.7 ..	36.2	256 22.8 ..	31.4		° ′	h m
22	203 20.2	174 15.8	11.1	113 29.3	33.5	301 27.4	36.2	271 25.4	31.4	Venus	333 07.8	10 22
23	218 22.6	189 15.4	12.1	128 30.0	33.5	316 30.2	36.2	286 27.9	31.5	Mars	271 30.9	14 27
	h m									Jupiter	97 55.2	2 02
Mer. Pass.	8 32.8	v −0.4	d 1.1	v 0.7	d 0.0	v 2.7	d 0.0	v 2.5	d 0.0	Saturn	68 02.3	4 01

© British Crown Copyright 2018. All rights reserved.

UT	SUN GHA	SUN Dec	MOON GHA	v	MOON Dec	d	HP
d h	° ′	° ′	° ′	′	° ′	′	′
13 00	180 54.4	N18 15.4	72 43.3	8.8	N13 13.4	11.1	59.4
01	195 54.4	16.1	87 11.1	8.8	13 02.3	11.1	59.4
02	210 54.4	16.7	101 38.9	8.8	12 51.2	11.2	59.4
03	225 54.4	.. 17.3	116 06.7	8.9	12 40.0	11.3	59.4
04	240 54.4	17.9	130 34.6	9.0	12 28.7	11.4	59.4
05	255 54.4	18.6	145 02.6	9.0	12 17.3	11.4	59.4
06	270 54.4	N18 19.2	159 30.6	9.0	N12 05.9	11.5	59.4
07	285 58.6	19.8	173 58.6	9.1	11 54.4	11.6	59.4
08	300 54.4	20.4	188 26.7	9.1	11 42.8	11.6	59.4
M 09	315 54.5	.. 21.0	202 54.8	9.2	11 31.2	11.7	59.4
O 10	330 54.5	21.6	217 23.0	9.2	11 19.5	11.8	59.4
N 11	345 54.5	22.3	231 51.2	9.3	11 07.7	11.9	59.4
D 12	0 54.5	N18 22.9	246 19.5	9.3	N10 55.8	11.9	59.4
A 13	15 54.5	23.5	260 47.8	9.3	10 43.9	12.0	59.4
Y 14	30 54.5	24.1	275 16.1	9.4	10 31.9	12.0	59.4
15	45 54.5	.. 24.7	289 44.5	9.4	10 19.9	12.1	59.4
16	60 54.5	25.3	304 12.9	9.5	10 07.8	12.2	59.4
17	75 54.5	26.0	318 41.4	9.5	9 55.6	12.2	59.4
18	90 54.5	N18 26.6	333 09.9	9.5	N 9 43.4	12.3	59.4
19	105 54.5	27.2	347 38.4	9.6	9 31.1	12.3	59.4
20	120 54.5	27.8	2 07.0	9.6	9 18.8	12.4	59.4
21	135 54.5	.. 28.4	16 35.6	9.6	9 06.4	12.4	59.4
22	150 54.5	29.0	31 04.2	9.7	8 54.0	12.5	59.4
23	165 54.5	29.6	45 32.9	9.8	8 41.5	12.5	59.4
14 00	180 54.5	N18 30.2	60 01.7	9.7	N 8 29.0	12.6	59.4
01	195 54.5	30.8	74 30.4	9.8	8 16.4	12.7	59.4
02	210 54.5	31.5	88 59.2	9.8	8 03.7	12.7	59.4
03	225 54.5	.. 32.1	103 28.0	9.9	7 51.0	12.7	59.4
04	240 54.5	32.7	117 56.9	9.9	7 38.3	12.8	59.4
05	255 54.5	33.3	132 25.8	9.9	7 25.5	12.8	59.4
06	270 54.5	N18 33.9	146 54.7	10.0	N 7 12.7	12.8	59.4
07	285 54.5	34.5	161 23.7	10.0	6 59.9	12.9	59.4
T 08	300 54.5	35.1	175 52.7	10.0	6 47.0	12.9	59.4
U 09	315 54.5	.. 35.7	190 21.7	10.1	6 34.1	13.0	59.4
E 10	330 54.5	36.3	204 50.8	10.0	6 21.1	13.0	59.4
S 11	345 54.5	36.9	219 19.8	10.1	6 08.1	13.1	59.4
D 12	0 54.5	N18 37.5	233 48.9	10.2	N 5 55.0	13.0	59.4
A 13	15 54.5	38.1	248 18.1	10.1	5 42.0	13.1	59.4
Y 14	30 54.5	38.7	262 47.2	10.2	5 28.9	13.2	59.4
15	45 54.5	.. 39.3	277 16.4	10.2	5 15.7	13.1	59.4
16	60 54.5	39.9	291 45.6	10.3	5 02.6	13.2	59.4
17	75 54.5	40.5	306 14.9	10.2	4 49.4	13.2	59.4
18	90 54.5	N18 41.1	320 44.1	10.3	N 4 36.2	13.3	59.4
19	105 54.5	41.7	335 13.4	10.3	4 22.9	13.3	59.4
20	120 54.5	42.3	349 42.7	10.3	4 09.6	13.2	59.4
21	135 54.5	.. 42.9	4 12.0	10.4	3 56.4	13.4	59.4
22	150 54.5	43.5	18 41.4	10.3	3 43.0	13.3	59.4
23	165 54.5	44.1	33 10.7	10.4	3 29.7	13.3	59.4
15 00	180 54.5	N18 44.7	47 40.1	10.4	N 3 16.4	13.4	59.4
01	195 54.5	45.3	62 09.5	10.5	3 03.0	13.4	59.3
02	210 54.5	45.9	76 39.0	10.4	2 49.6	13.3	59.3
03	225 54.5	.. 46.5	91 08.4	10.4	2 36.2	13.4	59.3
04	240 54.5	47.1	105 37.8	10.5	2 22.8	13.4	59.3
05	255 54.5	47.7	120 07.3	10.5	2 09.4	13.4	59.3
06	270 54.5	N18 48.3	134 36.8	10.5	N 1 56.0	13.5	59.3
W 07	285 54.5	48.9	149 06.3	10.5	1 42.5	13.4	59.3
E 08	300 54.5	49.5	163 35.8	10.5	1 29.1	13.4	59.3
D 09	315 54.5	.. 50.1	178 05.3	10.6	1 15.7	13.5	59.3
N 10	330 54.5	50.7	192 34.9	10.5	1 02.2	13.5	59.3
E 11	345 54.5	51.2	207 04.4	10.6	0 48.7	13.4	59.3
S 12	0 54.5	N18 51.8	221 34.0	10.5	N 0 35.3	13.5	59.3
D 13	15 54.5	52.4	236 03.5	10.6	0 21.8	13.4	59.3
A 14	30 54.5	53.0	250 33.1	10.6	N 0 08.4	13.5	59.3
Y 15	45 54.5	.. 53.6	265 02.7	10.6	S 0 05.1	13.5	59.3
16	60 54.4	54.2	279 32.3	10.6	0 18.6	13.4	59.2
17	75 54.4	54.8	294 01.9	10.6	0 32.0	13.5	59.2
18	90 54.4	N18 55.4	308 31.5	10.6	S 0 45.5	13.4	59.2
19	105 54.4	56.0	323 01.1	10.6	0 58.9	13.4	59.2
20	120 54.4	56.5	337 30.7	10.6	1 12.3	13.4	59.2
21	135 54.4	.. 57.1	352 00.3	10.6	1 25.7	13.5	59.2
22	150 54.4	57.7	6 29.9	10.6	1 39.2	13.4	59.2
23	165 54.4	58.3	20 59.5	10.7	S 1 52.6	13.3	59.2
	SD 15.9	d 0.6	SD 16.2		16.2		16.2

Lat.	Twilight Naut.	Civil	Sunrise	Moonrise 13	14	15	16
°	h m	h m	h m	h m	h m	h m	h m
N 72	▭	▭	▭	11 07	13 19	15 25	17 30
N 70	////	////	00 57	11 26	13 27	15 24	17 21
68	////	////	01 54	11 41	13 34	15 24	17 14
66	////	////	02 27	11 53	13 39	15 24	17 08
64	////	01 17	02 51	12 03	13 44	15 23	17 02
62	////	01 57	03 10	12 12	13 48	15 23	16 58
60	////	02 23	03 26	12 19	13 51	15 23	16 54
N 58	01 09	02 44	03 39	12 25	13 54	15 23	16 51
56	01 45	03 01	03 50	12 31	13 57	15 23	16 48
54	02 10	03 14	04 00	12 36	14 00	15 23	16 45
52	02 29	03 26	04 08	12 41	14 02	15 22	16 43
50	02 45	03 37	04 16	12 45	14 04	15 22	16 40
45	03 16	03 59	04 33	12 54	14 08	15 22	16 36
N 40	03 38	04 16	04 46	13 01	14 12	15 22	16 32
35	03 56	04 30	04 58	13 07	14 15	15 22	16 28
30	04 10	04 41	05 08	13 13	14 18	15 22	16 25
20	04 33	05 01	05 25	13 23	14 22	15 21	16 20
N 10	04 51	05 19	05 39	13 31	14 27	15 21	16 16
0	05 06	05 31	05 53	13 39	14 31	15 21	16 11
S 10	05 19	05 44	06 06	13 47	14 34	15 21	16 07
20	05 31	05 57	06 21	13 55	14 39	15 21	16 03
30	05 43	06 12	06 37	14 04	14 43	15 21	15 58
35	05 49	06 19	06 46	14 10	14 46	15 21	15 55
40	05 55	06 28	06 57	14 16	14 49	15 21	15 52
45	06 02	06 38	07 10	14 23	14 53	15 21	15 49
S 50	06 10	06 49	07 25	14 32	14 57	15 21	15 44
52	06 13	06 55	07 32	14 36	14 59	15 21	15 42
54	06 17	07 00	07 40	14 40	15 01	15 21	15 40
56	06 21	07 06	07 49	14 45	15 03	15 21	15 38
58	06 25	07 13	07 59	14 50	15 06	15 21	15 35
S 60	06 29	07 21	08 10	14 56	15 09	15 21	15 32

Lat.	Sunset	Twilight Civil	Naut.	Moonset 13	14	15	16
°	h m	h m	h m	h m	h m	h m	h m
N 72	▭	▭	▭	04 06	03 44	03 25	03 08
N 70	23 07	////	////	03 45	03 33	03 22	03 12
68	22 03	////	////	03 29	03 24	03 20	03 15
66	21 28	////	////	03 15	03 17	03 17	03 18
64	21 04	22 41	////	03 04	03 10	03 15	03 20
62	20 45	21 59	////	02 54	03 05	03 14	03 22
60	20 29	21 32	////	02 46	03 00	03 12	03 24
N 58	20 16	21 11	22 49	02 38	02 56	03 11	03 25
56	20 04	20 54	22 10	02 32	02 52	03 10	03 27
54	19 54	20 40	21 45	02 26	02 49	03 09	03 28
52	19 45	20 28	21 25	02 21	02 46	03 08	03 29
50	19 38	20 17	21 09	02 16	02 43	03 07	03 30
45	19 21	19 55	20 38	02 05	02 36	03 05	03 33
N 40	19 07	19 38	20 16	01 57	02 31	03 03	03 35
35	18 56	19 24	19 58	01 49	02 27	03 02	03 36
30	18 46	19 12	19 43	01 42	02 23	03 01	03 38
20	18 28	18 52	19 20	01 31	02 16	02 59	03 41
N 10	18 14	18 36	19 02	01 21	02 09	02 57	03 43
0	18 00	18 22	18 47	01 11	02 04	02 55	03 45
S 10	17 46	18 08	18 34	01 01	01 58	02 53	03 47
20	17 32	17 55	18 22	00 51	01 51	02 51	03 49
30	17 15	17 41	18 10	00 39	01 44	02 48	03 52
35	17 06	17 33	18 03	00 32	01 40	02 47	03 54
40	16 55	17 24	17 57	00 24	01 35	02 45	03 55
45	16 43	17 14	17 50	00 15	01 29	02 43	03 57
S 50	16 27	17 03	17 42	00 03	01 22	02 41	03 59
52	16 20	16 58	17 39	25 19	01 19	02 40	04 01
54	16 12	16 52	17 35	25 16	01 16	02 39	04 02
56	16 03	16 46	17 31	25 12	01 12	02 38	04 03
58	15 53	16 39	17 27	25 07	01 07	02 36	04 04
S 60	15 42	16 31	17 23	25 02	01 02	02 35	04 06

Day	SUN Eqn. of Time 00ʰ	12ʰ	Mer. Pass.	MOON Mer. Pass. Upper	Lower	Age	Phase
d	m s	m s	h m	h m	h m	d %	
13	03 38	03 38	11 56	19 51	07 25	09 67	
14	03 38	03 38	11 56	20 43	08 17	10 77	◑
15	03 38	03 38	11 56	21 33	09 08	11 86	

© British Crown Copyright 2018. All rights reserved.

UT	ARIES GHA	VENUS −3·8 GHA	Dec	MARS +1·7 GHA	Dec	JUPITER −2·5 GHA	Dec	SATURN +0·4 GHA	Dec	STARS Name	SHA	Dec
16 00	233 25.1	204 15.0	N10 13.2	143 30.7	N24 33.5	331 32.9	S22 36.2	301 30.4	S21 31.5	Acamar	315 15.7	S40 13.8
01	248 27.6	219 14.6	14.3	158 31.4	33.5	346 35.6	36.2	316 32.9	31.5	Achernar	335 24.3	S57 08.3
02	263 30.0	234 14.2	15.4	173 32.1	33.5	1 38.4	36.1	331 35.5	31.5	Acrux	173 04.3	S63 12.5
03	278 32.5	249 13.7 ..	16.5	188 32.8 ..	33.5	16 41.1 ..	36.1	346 38.0 ..	31.5	Adhara	255 09.6	S29 00.2
04	293 35.0	264 13.3	17.6	203 33.5	33.5	31 43.8	36.1	1 40.5	31.5	Aldebaran	290 45.1	N16 32.7
05	308 37.4	279 12.9	18.6	218 34.2	33.5	46 43.1	36.1	16 43.1	31.5			
06	323 39.9	294 12.5	N10 19.7	233 34.8	N24 33.5	61 49.3	S22 36.1	31 45.6	S21 31.5	Alioth	166 16.7	N55 51.6
07	338 42.4	309 12.1	20.8	248 35.5	33.5	76 52.0	36.1	46 48.1	31.5	Alkaid	152 55.3	N49 13.2
T 08	353 44.8	324 11.6	21.9	263 36.2	33.5	91 54.8	36.1	61 50.7	31.6	Alnair	27 38.7	S46 51.9
H 09	8 47.3	339 11.2 ..	23.0	278 36.9 ..	33.5	106 57.5 ..	36.1	76 53.2 ..	31.6	Alnilam	275 42.6	S 1 11.6
U 10	23 49.7	354 10.8	24.0	293 37.6	33.6	122 00.2	36.0	91 55.7	31.6	Alphard	217 52.2	S 8 44.7
R 11	38 52.2	9 10.4	25.1	308 38.3	33.6	137 03.0	36.0	106 58.3	31.6			
S 12	53 54.7	24 10.0	N10 26.2	323 39.0	N24 33.6	152 05.7	S22 36.0	122 00.8	S21 31.6	Alphecca	126 07.2	N26 39.1
D 13	68 57.1	39 09.5	27.3	338 39.7	33.6	167 08.4	36.0	137 03.3	31.6	Alpheratz	357 39.6	N29 11.5
A 14	83 59.6	54 09.1	28.3	353 40.3	33.6	182 11.2	36.0	152 05.9	31.6	Altair	62 04.2	N 8 55.1
Y 15	99 02.1	69 08.7 ..	29.4	8 41.0 ..	33.6	197 13.9 ..	36.0	167 08.4 ..	31.6	Ankaa	353 12.0	S42 12.1
16	114 04.5	84 08.3	30.5	23 41.7	33.6	212 16.6	36.0	182 10.9	31.7	Antares	112 21.0	S26 28.4
17	129 07.0	99 07.8	31.6	38 42.4	33.6	227 19.4	36.0	197 13.5	31.7			
18	144 09.5	114 07.4	N10 32.7	53 43.1	N24 33.6	242 22.1	S22 36.0	212 16.0	S21 31.7	Arcturus	145 51.8	N19 05.0
19	159 11.9	129 07.0	33.7	68 43.8	33.6	257 24.8	35.9	227 18.5	31.7	Atria	107 18.6	S69 03.5
20	174 14.4	144 06.6	34.8	83 44.5	33.6	272 27.6	35.9	242 21.1	31.7	Avior	234 16.6	S59 34.6
21	189 16.9	159 06.2 ..	35.9	98 45.2 ..	33.6	287 30.3 ..	35.9	257 23.6 ..	31.7	Bellatrix	278 28.0	N 6 21.8
22	204 19.3	174 05.7	37.0	113 45.9	33.6	302 33.0	35.9	272 26.1	31.7	Betelgeuse	270 57.2	N 7 24.4
23	219 21.8	189 05.3	38.0	128 46.5	33.6	317 35.8	35.9	287 28.7	31.7			
17 00	234 24.2	204 04.9	N10 39.1	143 47.2	N24 33.6	332 38.5	S22 35.9	302 31.2	S21 31.7	Canopus	263 54.8	S52 42.7
01	249 26.7	219 04.5	40.2	158 47.9	33.6	347 41.3	35.9	317 33.7	31.8	Capella	280 29.0	N46 00.9
02	264 29.2	234 04.0	41.3	173 48.6	33.6	2 44.0	35.9	332 36.3	31.8	Deneb	49 28.6	N45 20.7
03	279 31.6	249 03.6 ..	42.3	188 49.3 ..	33.6	17 46.7 ..	35.8	347 38.8 ..	31.8	Denebola	182 29.4	N14 27.9
04	294 34.1	264 03.2	43.4	203 50.0	33.6	32 49.5	35.8	2 41.4	31.8	Diphda	348 52.1	S17 53.0
05	309 36.6	279 02.7	44.5	218 50.7	33.6	47 52.2	35.8	17 43.9	31.8			
06	324 39.0	294 02.3	N10 45.5	233 51.4	N24 33.6	62 54.9	S22 35.8	32 46.4	S21 31.8	Dubhe	193 46.6	N61 39.1
07	339 41.5	309 01.9	46.6	248 52.1	33.6	77 57.7	35.8	47 49.0	31.8	Elnath	278 07.9	N28 37.2
08	354 44.0	324 01.5	47.7	263 52.8	33.6	93 00.4	35.8	62 51.5	31.8	Eltanin	90 43.8	N51 29.1
F 09	9 46.4	339 01.0 ..	48.8	278 53.4 ..	33.6	108 03.2 ..	35.8	77 54.0 ..	31.9	Enif	33 43.2	N 9 57.7
R 10	24 48.9	354 00.6	49.8	293 54.1	33.6	123 05.9	35.8	92 56.6	31.9	Fomalhaut	15 19.7	S29 31.2
I 11	39 51.4	9 00.2	50.9	308 54.8	33.6	138 08.6	35.7	107 59.1	31.9			
D 12	54 53.8	23 59.8	N10 52.0	323 55.5	N24 33.5	153 11.4	S22 35.7	123 01.6	S21 31.9	Gacrux	171 56.0	S57 13.4
A 13	69 56.3	38 59.3	53.0	338 56.2	33.5	168 14.1	35.7	138 04.2	31.9	Gienah	175 48.0	S17 39.0
Y 14	84 58.7	53 58.9	54.1	353 56.9	33.5	183 16.9	35.7	153 06.7	31.9	Hadar	148 41.6	S60 28.0
15	100 01.2	68 58.5 ..	55.2	8 57.6 ..	33.5	198 19.6 ..	35.7	168 09.3 ..	31.9	Hamal	327 56.5	N23 32.9
16	115 03.7	83 58.0	56.2	23 58.3	33.5	213 22.3	35.7	183 11.8	31.9	Kaus Aust.	83 38.2	S34 22.3
17	130 06.1	98 57.6	57.3	38 59.0	33.5	228 25.1	35.7	198 14.3	32.0			
18	145 08.6	113 57.2	N10 58.4	53 59.6	N24 33.5	243 27.8	S22 35.7	213 16.9	S21 32.0	Kochab	137 19.0	N74 04.8
19	160 11.1	128 56.7	10 59.4	69 00.3	33.5	258 30.6	35.7	228 19.4	32.0	Markab	13 34.4	N15 18.3
20	175 13.5	143 56.3	11 00.5	84 01.0	33.5	273 33.3	35.6	243 21.9	32.0	Menkar	314 11.2	N 4 09.7
21	190 16.0	158 55.9 ..	01.6	99 01.7 ..	33.5	288 36.0 ..	35.6	258 24.5 ..	32.0	Menkent	148 02.5	S36 27.9
22	205 18.5	173 55.4	02.6	114 02.4	33.5	303 38.8	35.6	273 27.0	32.0	Miaplacidus	221 39.0	S69 48.1
23	220 20.9	188 55.0	03.7	129 03.1	33.5	318 41.5	35.6	288 29.6	32.0			
18 00	235 23.4	203 54.6	N11 04.8	144 03.8	N24 33.5	333 44.3	S22 35.6	303 32.1	S21 32.0	Mirfak	308 35.1	N49 55.5
01	250 25.8	218 54.1	05.8	159 04.5	33.5	348 47.0	35.6	318 34.6	32.1	Nunki	75 53.1	S26 16.2
02	265 28.3	233 53.7	06.9	174 05.2	33.5	3 49.8	35.6	333 37.2	32.1	Peacock	53 12.7	S56 40.1
03	280 30.8	248 53.3 ..	08.0	189 05.9 ..	33.4	18 52.5 ..	35.6	348 39.7 ..	32.1	Pollux	243 23.0	N27 58.7
04	295 33.2	263 52.8	09.0	204 06.5	33.4	33 55.2	35.5	3 42.3	32.1	Procyon	244 55.7	N 5 10.4
05	310 35.7	278 52.4	10.1	219 07.2	33.4	48 58.0	35.5	18 44.8	32.1			
06	325 38.2	293 52.0	N11 11.1	234 07.9	N24 33.4	64 00.7	S22 35.5	33 47.3	S21 32.1	Rasalhague	96 02.4	N12 32.8
07	340 40.6	308 51.5	12.2	249 08.6	33.4	79 03.5	35.5	48 49.9	32.1	Regulus	207 39.2	N11 52.4
S 08	355 43.1	323 51.1	13.3	264 09.3	33.4	94 06.2	35.5	63 52.4	32.1	Rigel	281 08.5	S 8 11.0
A 09	10 45.6	338 50.7 ..	14.3	279 10.0 ..	33.4	109 09.0 ..	35.5	78 55.0 ..	32.2	Rigil Kent.	139 45.6	S60 54.8
T 10	25 48.0	353 50.2	15.4	294 10.7	33.4	124 11.7	35.5	93 57.5	32.2	Sabik	102 07.6	S15 44.8
U 11	40 50.5	8 49.8	16.4	309 11.4	33.4	139 14.5	35.5	109 00.0	32.2			
R 12	55 53.0	23 49.3	N11 17.5	324 12.1	N24 33.3	154 17.2	S22 35.4	124 02.6	S21 32.2	Schedar	349 36.3	N56 38.2
D 13	70 55.4	38 48.9	18.6	339 12.8	33.3	169 19.9	35.4	139 05.1	32.2	Shaula	96 16.1	S37 06.9
A 14	85 57.9	53 48.5	19.6	354 13.5	33.3	184 22.7	35.4	154 07.7	32.2	Sirius	258 30.5	S16 44.8
Y 15	101 00.3	68 48.0 ..	20.7	9 14.1 ..	33.3	199 25.4 ..	35.4	169 10.2 ..	32.2	Spica	158 26.8	S11 15.7
16	116 02.8	83 47.6	21.7	24 14.8	33.3	214 28.2	35.4	184 12.8	32.2	Suhail	222 49.6	S43 30.9
17	131 05.3	98 47.2	22.8	39 15.5	33.3	229 30.9	35.4	199 15.3	32.3			
18	146 07.7	113 46.7	N11 23.8	54 16.2	N24 33.3	244 33.7	S22 35.4	214 17.8	S21 32.3	Vega	80 35.9	N38 48.0
19	161 10.2	128 46.3	24.9	69 16.9	33.3	259 36.4	35.4	229 20.4	32.3	Zuben'ubi	137 00.6	S16 07.2
20	176 12.7	143 45.8	26.0	84 17.6	33.2	274 39.2	35.3	244 22.9	32.3		SHA	Mer.Pass.
21	191 15.1	158 45.4 ..	27.0	99 18.3 ..	33.2	289 41.9 ..	35.3	259 25.5 ..	32.3	Venus	329 40.6	10 24
22	206 17.6	173 45.0	28.1	114 19.0	33.2	304 44.7	35.3	274 28.0	32.3	Mars	269 23.0	14 24
23	221 20.1	188 44.5	29.1	129 19.7	33.2	319 47.4	35.3	289 30.5	32.3	Jupiter	98 14.3	1 49
Mer. Pass. 8 21.0		v −0.4	d 1.1	v 0.7	d 0.0	v 2.7	d 0.0	v 2.5	d 0.0	Saturn	68 07.0	3 49

© British Crown Copyright 2018. All rights reserved.

UT	SUN GHA	SUN Dec	MOON GHA	v	MOON Dec	d	HP
d h	° ′	° ′	° ′	′	° ′	′	′
16 00	180 54.4	N18 58.9	35 29.2	10.6	S 2 05.9	13.4	59.2
01	195 54.4	18 59.5	49 58.8	10.6	2 19.3	13.4	59.2
02	210 54.4	19 00.0	64 28.4	10.6	2 32.7	13.3	59.1
03	225 54.4	.. 00.6	78 58.0	10.6	2 46.0	13.3	59.1
04	240 54.3	01.2	93 27.6	10.6	2 59.3	13.3	59.1
05	255 54.3	01.8	107 57.2	10.6	3 12.6	13.3	59.1
06	270 54.3	N19 02.4	122 26.8	10.7	S 3 25.9	13.2	59.1
07	285 54.3	02.9	136 56.5	10.6	3 39.1	13.2	59.1
T 08	300 54.3	03.5	151 26.1	10.6	3 52.3	13.2	59.1
H 09	315 54.3	.. 04.1	165 55.7	10.5	4 05.5	13.2	59.1
U 10	330 54.3	04.7	180 25.2	10.6	4 18.7	13.2	59.0
R 11	345 54.3	05.3	194 54.8	10.6	4 31.9	13.1	59.0
S 12	0 54.3	N19 05.8	209 24.4	10.6	S 4 45.0	13.1	59.0
D 13	15 54.2	06.4	223 54.0	10.5	4 58.1	13.0	59.0
A 14	30 54.2	07.0	238 23.5	10.6	5 11.1	13.0	59.0
Y 15	45 54.2	.. 07.6	252 53.1	10.5	5 24.1	13.0	59.0
16	60 54.2	08.1	267 22.6	10.6	5 37.1	12.9	59.0
17	75 54.2	08.7	281 52.2	10.5	5 50.0	13.0	59.0
18	90 54.2	N19 09.3	296 21.7	10.5	S 6 03.0	12.8	58.9
19	105 54.2	09.9	310 51.2	10.5	6 15.8	12.9	58.9
20	120 54.2	10.4	325 20.7	10.5	6 28.7	12.7	58.9
21	135 54.1	.. 11.0	339 50.2	10.5	6 41.4	12.8	58.9
22	150 54.1	11.6	354 19.7	10.4	6 54.2	12.7	58.9
23	165 54.1	12.1	8 49.1	10.5	7 06.9	12.7	58.9
17 00	180 54.1	N19 12.7	23 18.6	10.4	S 7 19.6	12.6	58.8
01	195 54.1	13.3	37 48.0	10.4	7 32.2	12.5	58.8
02	210 54.1	13.9	52 17.4	10.4	7 44.7	12.6	58.8
03	225 54.1	.. 14.4	66 46.8	10.4	7 57.3	12.4	58.8
04	240 54.0	15.0	81 16.2	10.4	8 09.7	12.4	58.8
05	255 54.0	15.6	95 45.6	10.3	8 22.1	12.4	58.8
06	270 54.0	N19 16.1	110 14.9	10.4	S 8 34.5	12.3	58.7
07	285 54.0	16.7	124 44.3	10.3	8 46.8	12.3	58.7
08	300 54.0	17.3	139 13.6	10.3	8 59.1	12.2	58.7
F 09	315 54.0	.. 17.8	153 42.9	10.3	9 11.3	12.1	58.7
R 10	330 53.9	18.4	168 12.2	10.2	9 23.4	12.1	58.7
I 11	345 53.9	18.9	182 41.4	10.3	9 35.5	12.0	58.6
D 12	0 53.9	N19 19.5	197 10.7	10.2	S 9 47.5	12.0	58.6
A 13	15 53.9	20.1	211 39.9	10.2	9 59.5	11.9	58.6
Y 14	30 53.9	20.6	226 09.1	10.2	10 11.4	11.8	58.6
15	45 53.9	.. 21.2	240 38.3	10.1	10 23.2	11.8	58.6
16	60 53.8	21.8	255 07.4	10.1	10 35.0	11.7	58.5
17	75 53.8	22.3	269 36.6	10.1	10 46.7	11.6	58.5
18	90 53.8	N19 22.9	284 05.7	10.1	S10 58.3	11.6	58.5
19	105 53.8	23.4	298 34.8	10.1	11 09.9	11.5	58.5
20	120 53.8	24.0	313 03.9	10.0	11 21.4	11.5	58.5
21	135 53.7	.. 24.6	327 32.9	10.1	11 32.9	11.3	58.4
22	150 53.7	25.1	342 02.0	10.0	11 44.2	11.3	58.4
23	165 53.7	25.7	356 31.0	9.9	11 55.5	11.2	58.4
18 00	180 53.7	N19 26.2	10 59.9	10.0	S12 06.7	11.2	58.4
01	195 53.7	26.8	25 28.9	9.9	12 17.9	11.0	58.4
02	210 53.6	27.3	39 57.8	10.0	12 28.9	11.0	58.3
03	225 53.6	.. 27.9	54 26.8	9.9	12 39.9	10.9	58.3
04	240 53.6	28.4	68 55.7	9.8	12 50.8	10.9	58.3
05	255 53.6	29.0	83 24.5	9.9	13 01.7	10.7	58.3
06	270 53.6	N19 29.6	97 53.4	9.8	S13 12.4	10.7	58.2
07	285 53.5	30.1	112 22.2	9.8	13 23.1	10.6	58.2
S 08	300 53.5	30.7	126 51.0	9.8	13 33.7	10.5	58.2
A 09	315 53.5	.. 31.2	141 19.8	9.7	13 44.2	10.4	58.2
T 10	330 53.5	31.8	155 48.5	9.7	13 54.6	10.4	58.2
U 11	345 53.4	32.3	170 17.2	9.7	14 05.0	10.2	58.1
R 12	0 53.4	N19 32.9	184 45.9	9.7	S14 15.2	10.2	58.1
D 13	15 53.4	33.4	199 14.6	9.7	14 25.4	10.1	58.1
A 14	30 53.4	34.0	213 43.3	9.6	14 35.5	10.0	58.1
Y 15	45 53.4	.. 34.5	228 11.9	9.6	14 45.5	9.9	58.0
16	60 53.3	35.0	242 40.5	9.6	14 55.4	9.8	58.0
17	75 53.3	35.6	257 09.1	9.5	15 05.2	9.7	58.0
18	90 53.3	N19 36.1	271 37.6	9.6	S15 14.9	9.6	58.0
19	105 53.3	36.7	286 06.2	9.5	15 24.5	9.5	57.9
20	120 53.2	37.2	300 34.7	9.5	15 34.0	9.5	57.9
21	135 53.2	.. 37.8	315 03.2	9.4	15 43.5	9.3	57.9
22	150 53.2	38.3	329 31.6	9.5	15 52.8	9.3	57.9
23	165 53.2	38.9	344 00.1	9.4	S16 02.1	9.1	57.8
	SD 15.8	d 0.6	SD 16.1		16.0		15.8

Lat.	Twilight Naut.	Twilight Civil	Sunrise	Moonrise 16	17	18	19
°	h m	h m	h m	h m	h m	h m	h m
N 72	□	□	□	17 30	19 41	22 11	■■
N 70	□	□	□	17 21	19 21	21 27	24 01
68	////	////	01 37	17 14	19 05	20 58	22 56
66	////	////	02 15	17 08	18 52	20 37	22 21
64	////	00 55	02 42	17 02	18 41	20 20	21 55
62	////	01 44	03 02	16 58	18 32	20 06	21 35
60	////	02 14	03 19	16 54	18 25	19 54	21 19
N 58	00 49	02 36	03 32	16 51	18 18	19 44	21 06
56	01 34	02 54	03 44	16 48	18 12	19 35	20 54
54	02 01	03 09	03 55	16 45	18 07	19 27	20 44
52	02 22	03 21	04 04	16 43	18 02	19 20	20 35
50	02 39	03 32	04 12	16 40	17 58	19 14	20 27
45	03 11	03 55	04 29	16 36	17 49	19 00	20 10
N 40	03 34	04 13	04 43	16 32	17 41	18 49	19 56
35	03 53	04 27	04 55	16 28	17 34	18 40	19 44
30	04 08	04 39	05 06	16 25	17 29	18 32	19 34
20	04 32	05 00	05 23	16 20	17 19	18 18	19 16
N 10	04 50	05 16	05 39	16 16	17 10	18 05	19 01
0	05 06	05 31	05 53	16 11	17 02	17 54	18 46
S 10	05 19	05 45	06 07	16 07	16 54	17 42	18 32
20	05 32	05 59	06 22	16 03	16 46	17 30	18 17
30	05 44	06 13	06 39	15 58	16 36	17 17	18 00
35	05 51	06 22	06 49	15 55	16 31	17 09	17 50
40	05 58	06 31	07 00	15 52	16 25	17 00	17 39
45	06 05	06 41	07 13	15 49	16 18	16 49	17 25
S 50	06 13	06 53	07 29	15 44	16 09	16 37	17 09
52	06 17	06 59	07 36	15 42	16 05	16 31	17 02
54	06 21	07 05	07 45	15 40	16 01	16 25	16 53
56	06 25	07 11	07 54	15 38	15 56	16 18	16 44
58	06 30	07 19	08 05	15 35	15 51	16 10	16 33
S 60	06 34	07 27	08 17	15 32	15 45	16 01	16 21

Lat.	Sunset	Twilight Civil	Twilight Naut.	Moonset 16	17	18	19
°	h m	h m	h m	h m	h m	h m	h m
N 72	□	□	□	03 08	02 49	02 25	01 44
N 70	□	□	□	03 12	03 01	02 48	02 29
68	22 21	////	////	03 15	03 10	03 05	02 59
66	21 41	////	////	03 18	03 18	03 19	03 22
64	21 13	23 06	////	03 20	03 25	03 31	03 40
62	20 53	22 13	////	03 22	03 31	03 41	03 55
60	20 36	21 42	////	03 24	03 36	03 50	04 07
N 58	20 22	21 19	23 11	03 25	03 40	03 57	04 18
56	20 10	21 01	22 22	03 27	03 45	04 04	04 28
54	19 59	20 46	21 54	03 28	03 48	04 10	04 36
52	19 50	20 33	21 32	03 29	03 51	04 16	04 44
50	19 42	20 22	21 15	03 30	03 55	04 21	04 50
45	19 24	19 59	20 43	03 33	04 01	04 31	05 05
N 40	19 10	19 41	20 19	03 35	04 07	04 40	05 17
35	18 58	19 26	20 01	03 36	04 11	04 48	05 28
30	18 47	19 14	19 45	03 38	04 15	04 55	05 37
20	18 30	18 53	19 21	03 41	04 23	05 07	05 52
N 10	18 14	18 37	19 03	03 43	04 29	05 17	06 06
0	18 00	18 22	18 47	03 45	04 36	05 27	06 19
S 10	17 46	18 08	18 34	03 47	04 42	05 36	06 32
20	17 31	17 54	18 21	03 49	04 48	05 47	06 46
30	17 14	17 39	18 08	03 52	04 56	05 59	07 01
35	17 04	17 31	18 02	03 54	05 00	06 07	07 11
40	16 53	17 22	17 55	03 55	05 05	06 14	07 21
45	16 39	17 11	17 47	03 57	05 10	06 23	07 34
S 50	16 23	16 59	17 39	03 59	05 17	06 34	07 49
52	16 16	16 54	17 37	04 01	05 20	06 39	07 56
54	16 08	16 48	17 31	04 02	05 24	06 45	08 04
56	15 58	16 41	17 27	04 03	05 28	06 52	08 13
58	15 48	16 34	17 23	04 04	05 32	06 59	08 23
S 60	15 35	16 25	17 18	04 06	05 37	07 07	08 35

Day	SUN Eqn. of Time 00ʰ	12ʰ	SUN Mer. Pass.	MOON Mer. Pass. Upper	Lower	Age	Phase
d	m s	m s	h m	h m	h m	d	%
16	03 38	03 37	11 56	22 23	09 58	12	93
17	03 36	03 36	11 56	23 14	10 49	13	97
18	03 35	03 34	11 56	24 06	11 40	14	100

© British Crown Copyright 2018. All rights reserved.

UT	ARIES GHA	VENUS −3.8 GHA	Dec	MARS +1.7 GHA	Dec	JUPITER −2.6 GHA	Dec	SATURN +0.4 GHA	Dec	STARS Name	SHA	Dec
19 00	236 22.5	203 44.1	N11 30.2	144 20.4	N24 33.2	334 50.2	S22 35.3	304 33.1	S21 32.3	Acamar	315 15.7	S40 13.8
01	251 25.0	218 43.6	31.2	159 21.0	33.2	349 52.9	35.3	319 35.6	32.4	Achernar	335 24.3	S57 08.3
02	266 27.5	233 43.2	32.3	174 21.7	33.1	4 55.6	35.3	334 38.2	32.4	Acrux	173 04.3	S63 12.5
03	281 29.9	248 42.7 ..	33.3	189 22.4 ..	33.1	19 58.4 ..	35.3	349 40.7 ..	32.4	Adhara	255 09.6	S29 00.2
04	296 32.4	263 42.3	34.4	204 23.1	33.1	35 01.1	35.2	4 43.3	32.4	Aldebaran	290 45.1	N16 32.7
05	311 34.8	278 41.9	35.4	219 23.8	33.1	50 03.9	35.2	19 45.8	32.4			
06	326 37.3	293 41.4	N11 36.5	234 24.5	N24 33.1	65 06.6	S22 35.2	34 48.4	S21 32.4	Alioth	166 16.8	N55 51.6
07	341 39.8	308 41.0	37.5	249 25.2	33.0	80 09.4	35.2	49 50.9	32.4	Alkaid	152 55.3	N49 13.2
08	356 42.2	323 40.5	38.6	264 25.9	33.0	95 12.1	35.2	64 53.4	32.5	Alnair	27 38.7	S46 51.9
S 09	11 44.7	338 40.1 ..	39.6	279 26.6 ..	33.0	110 14.9 ..	35.2	79 56.0 ..	32.5	Alnilam	275 42.6	S 1 11.6
U 10	26 47.2	353 39.6	40.7	294 27.3	33.0	125 17.6	35.2	94 58.5	32.5	Alphard	217 52.2	S 8 44.7
N 11	41 49.6	8 39.2	41.7	309 28.0	33.0	140 20.4	35.2	110 01.1	32.5			
D 12	56 52.1	23 38.7	N11 42.8	324 28.7	N24 32.9	155 23.1	S22 35.1	125 03.6	S21 32.5	Alphecca	126 07.2	N26 39.1
A 13	71 54.6	38 38.3	43.8	339 29.3	32.9	170 25.9	35.1	140 06.2	32.5	Alpheratz	357 39.5	N29 11.5
Y 14	86 57.0	53 37.8	44.9	354 30.0	32.9	185 28.6	35.1	155 08.7	32.5	Altair	62 04.1	N 8 55.1
15	101 59.5	68 37.4 ..	45.9	9 30.7 ..	32.9	200 31.4 ..	35.1	170 11.3 ..	32.5	Ankaa	353 12.0	S42 12.0
16	117 02.0	83 36.9	47.0	24 31.4	32.9	215 34.1	35.1	185 13.8	32.6	Antares	112 21.0	S26 28.4
17	132 04.4	98 36.5	48.0	39 32.1	32.8	230 36.9	35.1	200 16.3	32.6			
18	147 06.9	113 36.0	N11 49.1	54 32.8	N24 32.8	245 39.6	S22 35.1	215 18.9	S21 32.6	Arcturus	145 51.8	N19 05.0
19	162 09.3	128 35.6	50.1	69 33.5	32.8	260 42.4	35.0	230 21.4	32.6	Atria	107 18.6	S69 03.5
20	177 11.8	143 35.2	51.2	84 34.2	32.8	275 45.1	35.0	245 24.0	32.6	Avior	234 16.7	S59 34.6
21	192 14.3	158 34.7 ..	52.2	99 34.9 ..	32.7	290 47.9 ..	35.0	260 26.5 ..	32.6	Bellatrix	278 28.0	N 6 21.8
22	207 16.7	173 34.3	53.3	114 35.6	32.7	305 50.6	35.0	275 29.1	32.6	Betelgeuse	270 57.2	N 7 24.4
23	222 19.2	188 33.8	54.3	129 36.3	32.7	320 53.4	35.0	290 31.6	32.7			
20 00	237 21.7	203 33.3	N11 55.3	144 37.0	N24 32.7	335 56.2	S22 35.0	305 34.2	S21 32.7	Canopus	263 54.8	S52 42.7
01	252 24.1	218 32.9	56.4	159 37.6	32.7	350 58.9	35.0	320 36.7	32.7	Capella	280 29.0	N46 00.9
02	267 26.6	233 32.4	57.4	174 38.3	32.6	6 01.7	35.0	335 39.3	32.7	Deneb	49 28.6	N45 20.7
03	282 29.1	248 32.0 ..	58.5	189 39.0 ..	32.6	21 04.4 ..	34.9	350 41.8 ..	32.7	Denebola	182 29.4	N14 27.9
04	297 31.5	263 31.5	11 59.5	204 39.7	32.6	36 07.2	34.9	5 44.4	32.7	Diphda	348 52.1	S17 52.9
05	312 34.0	278 31.1	12 00.5	219 40.4	32.5	51 09.9	34.9	20 46.9	32.7			
06	327 36.4	293 30.6	N12 01.6	234 41.1	N24 32.5	66 12.7	S22 34.9	35 49.5	S21 32.8	Dubhe	193 46.6	N61 39.1
07	342 38.9	308 30.2	02.6	249 41.8	32.5	81 15.4	34.9	50 52.0	32.8	Elnath	278 07.9	N28 37.2
08	357 41.4	323 29.7	03.7	264 42.5	32.5	96 18.2	34.9	65 54.6	32.8	Eltanin	90 43.8	N51 29.1
M 09	12 43.8	338 29.3 ..	04.7	279 43.2 ..	32.4	111 20.9 ..	34.9	80 57.1 ..	32.8	Enif	33 43.2	N 9 57.7
O 10	27 46.3	353 28.8	05.7	294 43.9	32.4	126 23.7	34.9	95 59.7	32.8	Fomalhaut	15 19.6	S29 31.1
N 11	42 48.8	8 28.4	06.8	309 44.6	32.4	141 26.4	34.8	111 02.2	32.8			
D 12	57 51.2	23 27.9	N12 07.8	324 45.3	N24 32.4	156 29.2	S22 34.8	126 04.7	S21 32.8	Gacrux	171 56.0	S57 13.4
A 13	72 53.7	38 27.5	08.9	339 46.0	32.3	171 32.0	34.8	141 07.3	32.9	Gienah	175 48.0	S17 39.0
Y 14	87 56.2	53 27.0	09.9	354 46.6	32.3	186 34.7	34.8	156 09.8	32.9	Hadar	148 41.6	S60 28.0
15	102 58.6	68 26.5 ..	10.9	9 47.3 ..	32.3	201 37.5 ..	34.8	171 12.4 ..	32.9	Hamal	327 56.5	N23 32.9
16	118 01.1	83 26.1	12.0	24 48.0	32.3	216 40.2	34.8	186 14.9	32.9	Kaus Aust.	83 38.2	S34 22.3
17	133 03.6	98 25.6	13.0	39 48.7	32.2	231 43.0	34.8	201 17.5	32.9			
18	148 06.0	113 25.2	N12 14.0	54 49.4	N24 32.2	246 45.7	S22 34.7	216 20.0	S21 32.9	Kochab	137 19.0	N74 04.8
19	163 08.5	128 24.7	15.1	69 50.1	32.1	261 48.5	34.7	231 22.6	32.9	Markab	13 34.4	N15 18.3
20	178 10.9	143 24.2	16.1	84 50.8	32.1	276 51.2	34.7	246 25.1	32.9	Menkar	314 11.2	N 4 09.7
21	193 13.4	158 23.8 ..	17.1	99 51.5 ..	32.1	291 54.0 ..	34.7	261 27.7 ..	33.0	Menkent	148 02.5	S36 27.9
22	208 15.9	173 23.3	18.2	114 52.2	32.1	306 56.8	34.7	276 30.2	33.0	Miaplacidus	221 39.1	S69 48.1
23	223 18.3	188 22.9	19.2	129 52.9	32.0	321 59.5	34.7	291 32.8	33.0			
21 00	238 20.8	203 22.4	N12 20.2	144 53.6	N24 32.0	337 02.3	S22 34.7	306 35.3	S21 33.0	Mirfak	308 35.1	N49 55.5
01	253 23.3	218 22.0	21.3	159 54.3	32.0	352 05.0	34.7	321 37.9	33.0	Nunki	75 53.1	S26 16.2
02	268 25.7	233 21.5	22.3	174 55.0	31.9	7 07.8	34.6	336 40.5	33.0	Peacock	53 12.7	S56 40.1
03	283 28.2	248 21.0 ..	23.3	189 55.7 ..	31.9	22 10.5 ..	34.6	351 43.0 ..	33.0	Pollux	243 23.1	N27 58.7
04	298 30.7	263 20.6	24.4	204 56.4	31.9	37 13.3	34.6	6 45.6	33.1	Procyon	244 55.7	N 5 10.4
05	313 33.1	278 20.1	25.4	219 57.0	31.8	52 16.1	34.6	21 48.1	33.1			
06	328 35.6	293 19.6	N12 26.4	234 57.7	N24 31.8	67 18.8	S22 34.6	36 50.7	S21 33.1	Rasalhague	96 02.4	N12 32.8
07	343 38.1	308 19.2	27.4	249 58.4	31.7	82 21.6	34.6	51 53.2	33.1	Regulus	207 39.2	N11 52.4
08	358 40.5	323 18.7	28.5	264 59.1	31.7	97 24.3	34.6	66 55.8	33.1	Rigel	281 08.5	S 8 11.0
T 09	13 43.0	338 18.3 ..	29.5	279 59.8 ..	31.7	112 27.1 ..	34.5	81 58.3 ..	33.1	Rigil Kent.	139 45.6	S60 54.8
U 10	28 45.4	353 17.8	30.5	295 00.5	31.6	127 29.9	34.5	97 00.9	33.1	Sabik	102 07.6	S15 44.8
E 11	43 47.9	8 17.3	31.6	310 01.2	31.6	142 32.6	34.5	112 03.4	33.2			
S 12	58 50.4	23 16.9	N12 32.6	325 01.9	N24 31.6	157 35.4	S22 34.5	127 06.0	S21 33.2	Schedar	349 36.3	N56 38.2
D 13	73 52.8	38 16.4	33.6	340 02.6	31.5	172 38.1	34.5	142 08.5	33.2	Shaula	96 16.1	S37 06.9
A 14	88 55.3	53 15.9	34.6	355 03.3	31.5	187 40.9	34.5	157 11.1	33.2	Sirius	258 30.5	S16 44.8
Y 15	103 57.8	68 15.5 ..	35.7	10 04.0 ..	31.5	202 43.7 ..	34.5	172 13.6 ..	33.2	Spica	158 26.8	S11 15.7
16	119 00.2	83 15.0	36.7	25 04.7	31.4	217 46.4	34.5	187 16.2	33.2	Suhail	222 49.6	S43 30.9
17	134 02.7	98 14.5	37.7	40 05.4	31.4	232 49.2	34.4	202 18.7	33.3			
18	149 05.2	113 14.1	N12 38.7	55 06.1	N24 31.3	247 51.9	S22 34.4	217 21.3	S21 33.3	Vega	80 35.9	N38 48.0
19	164 07.6	128 13.6	39.8	70 06.8	31.3	262 54.7	34.4	232 23.8	33.3	Zuben'ubi	137 00.6	S16 07.2
20	179 10.1	143 13.1	40.8	85 07.5	31.3	277 57.5	34.4	247 26.4	33.3		SHA	Mer.Pass.
21	194 12.6	158 12.7 ..	41.8	100 08.1 ..	31.2	293 00.2 ..	34.4	262 29.0 ..	33.3			h m
22	209 15.0	173 12.2	42.8	115 08.8	31.2	308 03.0	34.4	277 31.5	33.3	Venus	326 11.7	10 26
23	224 17.5	188 11.7	43.8	130 09.5	31.1	323 05.7	34.4	292 34.1	33.3	Mars	267 15.3	14 21
	h m									Jupiter	98 34.5	1 36
Mer. Pass.	8 09.2	v −0.5	d 1.0	v 0.7	d 0.0	v 2.8	d 0.0	v 2.5	d 0.0	Saturn	68 12.5	3 37

© British Crown Copyright 2018. All rights reserved.

SUN and MOON

UT	SUN GHA	SUN Dec	MOON GHA	v	MOON Dec	d	HP
19 00	180 53.1	N19 39.4	358 28.5	9.4	S16 11.2	9.1	57.8
01	195 53.1	39.9	12 56.9	9.4	16 20.3	8.9	57.8
02	210 53.1	40.5	27 25.3	9.3	16 29.2	8.9	57.8
03	225 53.0	.. 41.0	41 53.6	9.4	16 38.1	8.7	57.7
04	240 53.0	41.6	56 22.0	9.3	16 46.8	8.7	57.7
05	255 53.0	42.1	70 50.3	9.3	16 55.5	8.5	57.7
06	270 53.0	N19 42.6	85 18.6	9.2	S17 04.0	8.5	57.7
07	285 52.9	43.2	99 46.8	9.3	17 12.5	8.3	57.6
S 08	300 52.9	43.7	114 15.1	9.2	17 20.8	8.2	57.6
U 09	315 52.9	.. 44.3	128 43.3	9.2	17 29.0	8.2	57.6
N 10	330 52.9	44.8	143 11.5	9.2	17 37.2	8.0	57.5
D 11	345 52.8	45.3	157 39.7	9.2	17 45.2	7.9	57.5
A 12	0 52.8	N19 45.9	172 07.9	9.2	S17 53.1	7.8	57.5
Y 13	15 52.8	46.4	186 36.1	9.1	18 00.9	7.7	57.5
14	30 52.7	46.9	201 04.2	9.1	18 08.6	7.6	57.5
15	45 52.7	.. 47.5	215 32.3	9.1	18 16.2	7.5	57.4
16	60 52.7	48.0	230 00.4	9.1	18 23.7	7.4	57.4
17	75 52.6	48.5	244 28.5	9.1	18 31.1	7.3	57.4
18	90 52.6	N19 49.1	258 56.6	9.0	S18 38.4	7.1	57.3
19	105 52.6	49.6	273 24.6	9.1	18 45.5	7.1	57.3
20	120 52.6	50.1	287 52.7	9.0	18 52.6	6.9	57.3
21	135 52.5	.. 50.7	302 20.7	9.0	18 59.5	6.8	57.3
22	150 52.5	51.2	316 48.7	9.0	19 06.3	6.7	57.2
23	165 52.5	51.7	331 16.7	9.0	19 13.0	6.6	57.2
20 00	180 52.4	N19 52.3	345 44.7	9.0	S19 19.6	6.5	57.2
01	195 52.4	52.8	0 12.7	9.0	19 26.1	6.4	57.2
02	210 52.4	53.3	14 40.7	8.9	19 32.5	6.2	57.1
03	225 52.3	.. 53.8	29 08.6	9.0	19 38.7	6.1	57.1
04	240 52.3	54.4	43 36.6	8.9	19 44.8	6.1	57.1
05	255 52.3	54.9	58 04.5	8.9	19 50.9	5.9	57.0
06	270 52.2	N19 55.4	72 32.4	9.0	S19 56.8	5.7	57.0
07	285 52.2	55.9	87 00.4	8.9	20 02.5	5.7	57.0
08	300 52.2	56.5	101 28.3	8.9	20 08.2	5.6	57.0
M 09	315 52.1	.. 57.0	115 56.2	8.9	20 13.8	5.4	56.9
O 10	330 52.1	57.5	130 24.1	8.9	20 19.2	5.3	56.9
N 11	345 52.1	58.0	144 52.0	8.9	20 24.5	5.2	56.9
D 12	0 52.0	N19 58.5	159 19.9	8.9	S20 29.7	5.1	56.8
A 13	15 52.0	59.1	173 47.8	8.9	20 34.8	4.9	56.8
Y 14	30 52.0	19 59.6	188 15.7	8.9	20 39.7	4.9	56.8
15	45 51.9	20 00.1	202 43.6	8.9	20 44.6	4.7	56.8
16	60 51.9	00.6	217 11.5	8.8	20 49.3	4.6	56.7
17	75 51.9	01.1	231 39.3	8.9	20 53.9	4.5	56.7
18	90 51.8	N20 01.7	246 07.2	8.9	S20 58.4	4.3	56.7
19	105 51.8	02.2	260 35.1	8.9	21 02.7	4.3	56.7
20	120 51.8	02.7	275 03.0	8.9	21 07.0	4.1	56.6
21	135 51.7	.. 03.2	289 30.9	8.9	21 11.1	4.0	56.6
22	150 51.7	03.7	303 58.8	8.9	21 15.1	3.8	56.6
23	165 51.6	04.2	318 26.7	8.9	21 18.9	3.8	56.6
21 00	180 51.6	N20 04.8	332 54.7	8.9	S21 22.7	3.6	56.5
01	195 51.6	05.3	347 22.6	8.9	21 26.3	3.5	56.5
02	210 51.5	05.8	1 50.5	9.0	21 29.8	3.4	56.5
03	225 51.5	.. 06.3	16 18.5	8.9	21 33.2	3.3	56.4
04	240 51.5	06.8	30 46.4	9.0	21 36.5	3.1	56.4
05	255 51.4	07.3	45 14.4	8.9	21 39.6	3.0	56.4
06	270 51.4	N20 07.8	59 42.3	9.0	S21 42.6	2.9	56.3
07	285 51.3	08.3	74 10.3	9.0	21 45.5	2.8	56.3
T 08	300 51.3	08.9	88 38.3	9.0	21 48.3	2.7	56.3
U 09	315 51.3	.. 09.4	103 06.3	9.1	21 51.0	2.5	56.3
E 10	330 51.2	09.9	117 34.4	9.0	21 53.5	2.4	56.2
S 11	345 51.2	10.4	132 02.4	9.1	21 55.9	2.3	56.2
D 12	0 51.1	N20 10.9	146 30.5	9.0	S21 58.2	2.2	56.2
A 13	15 51.1	11.4	160 58.5	9.1	22 00.4	2.0	56.2
Y 14	30 51.1	11.9	175 26.6	9.1	22 02.4	2.0	56.1
15	45 51.0	.. 12.4	189 54.7	9.2	22 04.4	1.8	56.1
16	60 51.0	12.9	204 22.9	9.1	22 06.2	1.7	56.1
17	75 50.9	13.4	218 51.0	9.2	22 07.9	1.5	56.0
18	90 50.9	N20 13.9	233 19.2	9.2	S22 09.4	1.5	56.0
19	105 50.8	14.4	247 47.4	9.2	22 10.9	1.3	56.0
20	120 50.8	14.9	262 15.6	9.3	22 12.2	1.2	56.0
21	135 50.8	.. 15.4	276 43.9	9.2	22 13.4	1.1	55.9
22	150 50.7	15.9	291 12.1	9.3	22 14.5	0.9	55.9
23	165 50.7	16.4	305 40.4	9.4	S22 15.4	0.9	55.9
	SD 15.8	d 0.5	SD 15.7		15.5		15.3

Twilight, Sunrise and Moonrise

Lat.	Twilight Naut.	Twilight Civil	Sunrise	Moonrise 19	20	21	22
N 72	▭	▭	▭	■	■	■	■
N 70	▭	▭	▭	■	■	■	■
68	////	////	01 19	22 56	25 02	01 02	■
66	////	////	02 03	22 21	23 57	25 13	01 13
64	////	00 20	02 32	21 55	23 22	24 31	00 31
62	////	01 31	02 54	21 35	22 56	24 03	00 03
60	////	02 04	03 12	21 19	22 37	23 41	24 29
N 58	00 18	02 28	03 27	21 06	22 20	23 23	24 12
56	01 22	02 47	03 39	20 54	22 06	23 08	23 58
54	01 53	03 03	03 50	20 44	21 54	22 55	23 45
52	02 15	03 16	04 00	20 35	21 44	22 44	23 34
50	02 33	03 28	04 08	20 27	21 34	22 34	23 24
45	03 07	03 51	04 26	20 10	21 15	22 13	23 04
N 40	03 31	04 10	04 41	19 56	20 58	21 56	22 47
35	03 50	04 25	04 53	19 44	20 45	21 42	22 33
30	04 06	04 38	05 04	19 34	20 33	21 29	22 21
20	04 30	04 59	05 22	19 16	20 13	21 08	22 00
N 10	04 49	05 16	05 38	19 01	19 56	20 50	21 42
0	05 05	05 31	05 53	18 46	19 40	20 33	21 25
S 10	05 20	05 45	06 08	18 32	19 23	20 15	21 08
20	05 33	06 00	06 23	18 17	19 06	19 57	20 49
30	05 46	06 15	06 41	18 00	18 46	19 36	20 28
35	05 53	06 24	06 51	17 50	18 35	19 24	20 16
40	06 00	06 33	07 03	17 39	18 22	19 10	20 02
45	06 08	06 44	07 16	17 25	18 06	18 53	19 45
S 50	06 17	06 57	07 33	17 09	17 47	18 33	19 25
52	06 21	07 02	07 41	17 02	17 38	18 23	19 15
54	06 25	07 09	07 49	16 53	17 28	18 12	19 04
56	06 29	07 16	07 59	16 44	17 17	17 59	18 51
58	06 34	07 24	08 10	16 33	17 04	17 45	18 37
S 60	06 39	07 32	08 23	16 21	16 49	17 28	18 19

Sunset, Twilight and Moonset

Lat.	Sunset	Twilight Civil	Twilight Naut.	Moonset 19	20	21	22
N 72	▭	▭	▭	01 44	■	■	■
N 70	▭	▭	▭	02 29	01 46	■	■
68	22 41	////	////	02 59	02 52	02 37	■
66	21 53	////	////	03 22	03 28	03 43	04 17
64	21 23	////	////	03 40	03 54	04 18	04 59
62	21 01	22 27	////	03 55	04 14	04 44	05 27
60	20 43	21 52	////	04 07	04 31	05 04	05 49
N 58	20 28	21 27	////	04 18	04 45	05 21	06 07
56	20 15	21 08	22 35	04 28	04 57	05 35	06 22
54	20 04	20 52	22 03	04 36	05 08	05 47	06 35
52	19 54	20 38	21 40	04 44	05 17	05 58	06 46
50	19 46	20 26	21 21	04 50	05 26	06 07	06 56
45	19 28	20 02	20 47	05 05	05 43	06 27	07 17
N 40	19 13	19 44	20 23	05 17	05 58	06 44	07 34
35	19 00	19 29	20 03	05 28	06 11	06 58	07 48
30	18 49	19 16	19 48	05 37	06 22	07 10	08 01
20	18 31	18 55	19 23	05 52	06 40	07 30	08 22
N 10	18 15	18 37	19 04	06 06	06 57	07 48	08 41
0	18 00	18 22	18 48	06 19	07 12	08 05	08 58
S 10	17 45	18 08	18 33	06 32	07 27	08 22	09 15
20	17 30	17 53	18 20	06 46	07 44	08 40	09 33
30	17 12	17 38	18 07	07 01	08 02	09 01	09 54
35	17 02	17 29	18 00	07 10	08 14	09 13	10 07
40	16 50	17 20	17 53	07 21	08 26	09 27	10 21
45	16 36	17 09	17 45	07 34	08 41	09 43	10 38
S 50	16 20	16 56	17 36	07 49	09 00	10 03	10 59
52	16 12	16 50	17 32	07 56	09 08	10 13	11 09
54	16 03	16 44	17 28	08 04	09 18	10 24	11 20
56	15 53	16 37	17 23	08 13	09 29	10 36	11 32
58	15 42	16 29	17 18	08 23	09 42	10 51	11 47
S 60	15 29	16 20	17 13	08 35	09 56	11 08	12 04

SUN and MOON

Day	SUN Eqn. of Time 00h	12h	Mer. Pass.	MOON Mer. Pass. Upper	Lower	Age	Phase
	m s	m s	h m	h m	h m	d %	
19	03 33	03 31	11 56	00 06	12 33	15 99	◯
20	03 30	03 28	11 57	00 59	13 26	16 97	
21	03 26	03 25	11 57	01 52	14 19	17 92	

© British Crown Copyright 2018. All rights reserved.

UT	ARIES GHA	VENUS −3.8 GHA	Dec	MARS +1.7 GHA	Dec	JUPITER −2.6 GHA	Dec	SATURN +0.3 GHA	Dec	STARS Name	SHA	Dec
22 00	239 19.9	203 11.2	N12 44.9	145 10.2	N24 31.1	338 08.5	S22 34.3	307 36.6	S21 33.4	Acamar	315 15.7	S40 13.8
01	254 22.4	218 10.8	45.9	160 10.9	31.1	353 11.3	34.3	322 39.2	33.4	Achernar	335 24.2	S57 08.3
02	269 24.9	233 10.3	46.9	175 11.6	31.0	8 14.0	34.3	337 41.7	33.4	Acrux	173 04.4	S63 12.5
03	284 27.3	248 09.8 ..	47.9	190 12.3 ..	31.0	23 16.8 ..	34.3	352 44.3 ..	33.4	Adhara	255 09.7	S29 00.2
04	299 29.8	263 09.4	48.9	205 13.0	30.9	38 19.6	34.3	7 46.8	33.4	Aldebaran	290 45.1	N16 32.7
05	314 32.3	278 08.9	50.0	220 13.7	30.9	53 22.3	34.3	22 49.4	33.4			
06	329 34.7	293 08.4	N12 51.0	235 14.4	N24 30.8	68 25.1	S22 34.3	37 51.9	S21 33.4	Alioth	166 16.8	N55 51.6
W 07	344 37.2	308 07.9	52.0	250 15.1	30.8	83 27.8	34.2	52 54.5	33.5	Alkaid	152 55.3	N49 13.3
E 08	359 39.7	323 07.5	53.0	265 15.8	30.8	98 30.6	34.2	67 57.1	33.5	Alnair	27 38.7	S46 51.9
D 09	14 42.1	338 07.0 ..	54.0	280 16.5 ..	30.7	113 33.4 ..	34.2	82 59.6 ..	33.5	Alnilam	275 42.6	S 1 11.6
N 10	29 44.6	353 06.5	55.0	295 17.2	30.7	128 36.1	34.2	98 02.2	33.5	Alphard	217 52.2	S 8 44.7
E 11	44 47.1	8 06.1	56.1	310 17.9	30.6	143 38.9	34.2	113 04.7	33.5			
S 12	59 49.5	23 05.6	N12 57.1	325 18.6	N24 30.6	158 41.7	S22 34.2	128 07.3	S21 33.5	Alphecca	126 07.2	N26 39.1
D 13	74 52.0	38 05.1	58.1	340 19.3	30.5	173 44.4	34.2	143 09.8	33.5	Alpheratz	357 39.5	N29 11.5
A 14	89 54.4	53 04.6	12 59.1	355 20.0	30.5	188 47.2	34.1	158 12.4	33.6	Altair	62 04.1	N 8 55.1
Y 15	104 56.9	68 04.2	13 00.1	10 20.7 ..	30.5	203 50.0 ..	34.1	173 15.0 ..	33.6	Ankaa	353 12.0	S42 12.0
16	119 59.4	83 03.7	01.1	25 21.3	30.4	218 52.7	34.1	188 17.5	33.6	Antares	112 20.9	S26 28.4
17	135 01.8	98 03.2	02.1	40 22.0	30.4	233 55.5	34.1	203 20.1	33.6			
18	150 04.3	113 02.7	N13 03.1	55 22.7	N24 30.3	248 58.3	S22 34.1	218 22.6	S21 33.6	Arcturus	145 51.8	N19 05.1
19	165 06.8	128 02.2	04.2	70 23.4	30.3	264 01.0	34.1	233 25.2	33.6	Atria	107 18.6	S69 03.5
20	180 09.2	143 01.8	05.2	85 24.1	30.2	279 03.8	34.1	248 27.7	33.7	Avior	234 16.7	S59 34.6
21	195 11.7	158 01.3 ..	06.2	100 24.8 ..	30.2	294 06.6 ..	34.0	263 30.3 ..	33.7	Bellatrix	278 28.0	N 6 21.8
22	210 14.2	173 00.8	07.2	115 25.5	30.1	309 09.3	34.0	278 32.9	33.7	Betelgeuse	270 57.2	N 7 24.4
23	225 16.6	188 00.3	08.2	130 26.2	30.1	324 12.1	34.0	293 35.4	33.7			
23 00	240 19.1	202 59.9	N13 09.2	145 26.9	N24 30.0	339 14.9	S22 34.0	308 38.0	S21 33.7	Canopus	263 54.8	S52 42.6
01	255 21.5	217 59.4	10.2	160 27.6	30.0	354 17.6	34.0	323 40.5	33.7	Capella	280 29.0	N46 00.9
02	270 24.0	232 58.9	11.2	175 28.3	29.9	9 20.4	34.0	338 43.1	33.7	Deneb	49 28.6	N45 20.7
03	285 26.5	247 58.4 ..	12.2	190 29.0 ..	29.9	24 23.2 ..	34.0	353 45.7 ..	33.8	Denebola	182 29.4	N14 27.9
04	300 28.9	262 57.9	13.2	205 29.7	29.8	39 25.9	34.0	8 48.2	33.8	Diphda	348 52.1	S17 52.9
05	315 31.4	277 57.5	14.2	220 30.4	29.8	54 28.7	33.9	23 50.8	33.8			
06	330 33.9	292 57.0	N13 15.2	235 31.1	N24 29.7	69 31.5	S22 33.9	38 53.3	S21 33.8	Dubhe	193 46.6	N61 39.1
T 07	345 36.3	307 56.5	16.2	250 31.8	29.7	84 34.2	33.9	53 55.9	33.8	Elnath	278 07.9	N28 37.2
H 08	0 38.8	322 56.0	17.2	265 32.5	29.6	99 37.0	33.9	68 58.4	33.8	Eltanin	90 43.8	N51 29.1
U 09	15 41.3	337 55.5 ..	18.2	280 33.2 ..	29.6	114 39.8 ..	33.9	84 01.0 ..	33.9	Enif	33 43.1	N 9 57.7
R 10	30 43.7	352 55.0	19.2	295 33.9	29.5	129 42.5	33.9	99 03.6	33.9	Fomalhaut	15 19.6	S29 31.1
S 11	45 46.2	7 54.6	20.3	310 34.6	29.5	144 45.3	33.9	114 06.1	33.9			
D 12	60 48.7	22 54.1	N13 21.3	325 35.3	N24 29.4	159 48.1	S22 33.8	129 08.7	S21 33.9	Gacrux	171 56.1	S57 13.4
A 13	75 51.1	37 53.6	22.3	340 36.0	29.4	174 50.8	33.8	144 11.2	33.9	Gienah	175 48.0	S17 39.0
Y 14	90 53.6	52 53.1	23.3	355 36.7	29.3	189 53.6	33.8	159 13.8	33.9	Hadar	148 41.6	S60 28.0
15	105 56.0	67 52.6 ..	24.3	10 37.3 ..	29.3	204 56.4 ..	33.8	174 16.4 ..	33.9	Hamal	327 56.5	N23 32.9
16	120 58.5	82 52.1	25.3	25 38.0	29.2	219 59.1	33.8	189 18.9	34.0	Kaus Aust.	83 38.1	S34 22.3
17	136 01.0	97 51.6	26.3	40 38.7	29.1	235 01.9	33.8	204 21.5	34.0			
18	151 03.4	112 51.2	N13 27.3	55 39.4	N24 29.1	250 04.7	S22 33.8	219 24.1	S21 34.0	Kochab	137 19.0	N74 04.8
19	166 05.9	127 50.7	28.3	70 40.1	29.0	265 07.4	33.7	234 26.6	34.0	Markab	13 34.4	N15 18.4
20	181 08.4	142 50.2	29.2	85 40.8	29.0	280 10.2	33.7	249 29.2	34.0	Menkar	314 11.2	N 4 09.7
21	196 10.8	157 49.7 ..	30.2	100 41.5 ..	28.9	295 13.0 ..	33.7	264 31.7 ..	34.0	Menkent	148 02.5	S36 27.9
22	211 13.3	172 49.2	31.2	115 42.2	28.9	310 15.8	33.7	279 34.3	34.1	Miaplacidus	221 39.1	S69 48.1
23	226 15.8	187 48.7	32.2	130 42.9	28.8	325 18.5	33.7	294 36.9	34.1			
24 00	241 18.2	202 48.2	N13 33.2	145 43.6	N24 28.8	340 21.3	S22 33.7	309 39.4	S21 34.1	Mirfak	308 35.1	N49 55.5
01	256 20.7	217 47.7	34.2	160 44.3	28.7	355 24.1	33.6	324 42.0	34.1	Nunki	75 53.0	S26 16.2
02	271 23.2	232 47.2	35.2	175 45.0	28.6	10 26.8	33.6	339 44.5	34.1	Peacock	53 12.6	S56 40.1
03	286 25.6	247 46.8 ..	36.2	190 45.7 ..	28.6	25 29.6 ..	33.6	354 47.1 ..	34.1	Pollux	243 23.1	N27 58.7
04	301 28.1	262 46.3	37.2	205 46.4	28.5	40 32.4	33.6	9 49.7	34.2	Procyon	244 55.7	N 5 10.4
05	316 30.5	277 45.8	38.2	220 47.1	28.5	55 35.2	33.6	24 52.2	34.2			
06	331 33.0	292 45.3	N13 39.2	235 47.8	N24 28.4	70 37.9	S22 33.6	39 54.8	S21 34.2	Rasalhague	96 02.4	N12 32.8
07	346 35.5	307 44.8	40.2	250 48.5	28.3	85 40.7	33.6	54 57.4	34.2	Regulus	207 39.3	N11 52.4
08	1 37.9	322 44.3	41.2	265 49.2	28.3	100 43.5	33.5	69 59.9	34.2	Rigel	281 08.5	S 8 11.0
F 09	16 40.4	337 43.8 ..	42.2	280 49.9 ..	28.2	115 46.2 ..	33.5	85 02.5 ..	34.2	Rigil Kent.	139 45.6	S60 54.8
R 10	31 42.9	352 43.3	43.2	295 50.6	28.2	130 49.0	33.5	100 05.1	34.2	Sabik	102 07.6	S15 44.8
I 11	46 45.3	7 42.8	44.1	310 51.3	28.1	145 51.8	33.5	115 07.6	34.3			
D 12	61 47.8	22 42.3	N13 45.1	325 52.0	N24 28.0	160 54.6	S22 33.5	130 10.2	S21 34.3	Schedar	349 36.3	N56 38.2
A 13	76 50.3	37 41.8	46.1	340 52.7	28.0	175 57.3	33.5	145 12.7	34.3	Shaula	96 16.1	S37 06.9
Y 14	91 52.7	52 41.3	47.1	355 53.4	27.9	191 00.1	33.5	160 15.3	34.3	Sirius	258 30.5	S16 44.8
15	106 55.2	67 40.8 ..	48.1	10 54.1 ..	27.9	206 02.9 ..	33.4	175 17.9 ..	34.3	Spica	158 26.8	S11 15.7
16	121 57.7	82 40.3	49.1	25 54.8	27.8	221 05.7	33.4	190 20.4	34.3	Suhail	222 49.6	S43 30.9
17	137 00.1	97 39.8	50.1	40 55.5	27.7	236 08.4	33.4	205 23.0	34.4			
18	152 02.6	112 39.3	N13 51.1	55 56.2	N24 27.7	251 11.2	S22 33.4	220 25.6	S21 34.4	Vega	80 35.9	N38 48.0
19	167 05.0	127 38.8	52.0	70 56.9	27.6	266 14.0	33.4	235 28.1	34.4	Zuben'ubi	137 00.6	S16 07.2
20	182 07.5	142 38.3	53.0	85 57.6	27.5	281 16.7	33.4	250 30.7	34.4		SHA	Mer.Pass.
21	197 10.0	157 37.8 ..	54.0	100 58.3 ..	27.5	296 19.5 ..	33.4	265 33.3 ..	34.4			h m
22	212 12.4	172 37.3	55.0	115 59.0	27.4	311 22.3	33.3	280 35.8	34.4	Venus	322 40.8	10 28
23	227 14.9	187 36.8	56.0	130 59.7	27.4	326 25.1	33.3	295 38.4	34.5	Mars	265 07.8	14 18
	h m									Jupiter	98 55.8	1 23
Mer. Pass.	7 57.4	v −0.5	d 1.0	v 0.7	d 0.1	v 2.8	d 0.0	v 2.6	d 0.0	Saturn	68 18.9	3 25

© British Crown Copyright 2018. All rights reserved.

UT	SUN GHA	SUN Dec	MOON GHA	MOON v	MOON Dec	MOON d	MOON HP
d h	° ′	° ′	° ′	′	° ′	′	′
22 00	180 50.6	N20 16.9	320 08.8	9.3	S22 16.3	0.7	55.9
01	195 50.6	17.4	334 37.1	9.4	22 17.0	0.6	55.8
02	210 50.6	17.9	349 05.5	9.4	22 17.6	0.5	55.8
03	225 50.5	.. 18.4	3 33.9	9.5	22 18.1	0.4	55.8
04	240 50.5	18.9	18 02.4	9.4	22 18.5	0.2	55.8
05	255 50.4	19.4	32 30.8	9.6	22 18.7	0.2	55.7
06	270 50.4	N20 19.9	46 59.4	9.5	S22 18.9	0.0	55.7
W 07	285 50.3	20.4	61 27.9	9.6	22 18.9	0.1	55.7
E 08	300 50.3	20.9	75 56.5	9.6	22 18.8	0.2	55.7
D 09	315 50.2	.. 21.4	90 25.1	9.6	22 18.6	0.4	55.6
N 10	330 50.2	21.9	104 53.7	9.7	22 18.2	0.4	55.6
E 11	345 50.1	22.4	119 22.4	9.7	22 17.8	0.6	55.6
S 12	0 50.1	N20 22.9	133 51.1	9.8	S22 17.2	0.7	55.6
D 13	15 50.1	23.4	148 19.9	9.8	22 16.5	0.8	55.5
A 14	30 50.0	23.9	162 48.7	9.8	22 15.7	0.9	55.5
Y 15	45 50.0	.. 24.4	177 17.5	9.9	22 14.8	1.0	55.5
16	60 49.9	24.8	191 46.4	9.9	22 13.8	1.1	55.5
17	75 49.9	25.3	206 15.3	9.9	22 12.7	1.3	55.5
18	90 49.8	N20 25.8	220 44.2	10.0	S22 11.4	1.4	55.4
19	105 49.8	26.3	235 13.2	10.0	22 10.0	1.4	55.4
20	120 49.7	26.8	249 42.2	10.1	22 08.6	1.6	55.4
21	135 49.7	.. 27.3	264 11.3	10.1	22 07.0	1.7	55.3
22	150 49.6	27.8	278 40.4	10.2	22 05.3	1.8	55.3
23	165 49.6	28.3	293 09.6	10.2	22 03.5	2.0	55.3
23 00	180 49.5	N20 28.7	307 38.8	10.3	S22 01.5	2.0	55.3
01	195 49.5	29.2	322 08.1	10.3	21 59.5	2.1	55.3
02	210 49.4	29.7	336 37.4	10.3	21 57.4	2.3	55.2
03	225 49.4	.. 30.2	351 06.7	10.4	21 55.1	2.3	55.2
04	240 49.3	30.7	5 36.1	10.4	21 52.8	2.5	55.2
05	255 49.3	31.2	20 05.5	10.5	21 50.3	2.6	55.2
06	270 49.2	N20 31.6	34 35.0	10.5	S21 47.7	2.7	55.2
T 07	285 49.2	32.1	49 04.5	10.6	21 45.0	2.7	55.1
H 08	300 49.1	32.6	63 34.1	10.7	21 42.3	2.9	55.1
U 09	315 49.1	.. 33.1	78 03.8	10.6	21 39.4	3.0	55.1
R 10	330 49.0	33.6	92 33.4	10.8	21 36.4	3.1	55.1
S 11	345 49.0	34.0	107 03.2	10.7	21 33.3	3.2	55.0
D 12	0 48.9	N20 34.5	121 32.9	10.9	S21 30.1	3.3	55.0
A 13	15 48.9	35.0	136 02.8	10.9	21 26.8	3.4	55.0
Y 14	30 48.8	35.5	150 32.7	10.9	21 23.4	3.5	55.0
15	45 48.8	.. 36.0	165 02.6	11.0	21 19.9	3.6	55.0
16	60 48.7	36.4	179 32.6	11.0	21 16.3	3.8	54.9
17	75 48.7	36.9	194 02.6	11.1	21 12.5	3.8	54.9
18	90 48.6	N20 37.4	208 32.7	11.1	S21 08.7	3.9	54.9
19	105 48.6	37.9	223 02.8	11.2	21 04.8	4.0	54.9
20	120 48.5	38.3	237 33.0	11.3	21 00.8	4.1	54.9
21	135 48.5	.. 38.8	252 03.3	11.3	20 56.7	4.2	54.9
22	150 48.4	39.3	266 33.6	11.3	20 52.5	4.3	54.8
23	165 48.4	39.7	281 03.9	11.4	20 48.2	4.4	54.8
24 00	180 48.3	N20 40.2	295 34.3	11.5	S20 43.8	4.5	54.8
01	195 48.2	40.7	310 04.8	11.5	20 39.3	4.6	54.8
02	210 48.2	41.2	324 35.3	11.6	20 34.7	4.7	54.8
03	225 48.1	.. 41.6	339 05.9	11.6	20 30.0	4.7	54.8
04	240 48.1	42.1	353 36.5	11.7	20 25.3	4.9	54.7
05	255 48.0	42.6	8 07.2	11.7	20 20.4	5.0	54.7
06	270 48.0	N20 43.0	22 37.9	11.8	S20 15.4	5.0	54.7
07	285 47.9	43.5	37 08.7	11.8	20 10.4	5.2	54.7
08	300 47.9	44.0	51 39.5	11.9	20 05.2	5.2	54.7
F 09	315 47.8	.. 44.4	66 10.4	12.0	20 00.0	5.3	54.7
R 10	330 47.7	44.9	80 41.4	12.0	19 54.7	5.4	54.6
I 11	345 47.7	45.4	95 12.4	12.0	19 49.3	5.5	54.6
D 12	0 47.6	N20 45.8	109 43.4	12.1	S19 43.8	5.6	54.6
A 13	15 47.6	46.3	124 14.5	12.2	19 38.2	5.7	54.6
Y 14	30 47.5	46.7	138 45.7	12.2	19 32.5	5.8	54.6
15	45 47.5	.. 47.2	153 16.9	12.3	19 26.7	5.8	54.6
16	60 47.4	47.7	167 48.2	12.3	19 20.9	5.9	54.6
17	75 47.3	48.1	182 19.5	12.4	19 15.0	6.0	54.5
18	90 47.3	N20 48.6	196 50.9	12.5	S19 09.0	6.1	54.5
19	105 47.2	49.0	211 22.4	12.5	19 02.9	6.2	54.5
20	120 47.2	49.5	225 53.9	12.5	18 56.7	6.3	54.5
21	135 47.1	.. 50.0	240 25.4	12.6	18 50.4	6.3	54.5
22	150 47.1	50.4	254 57.0	12.7	18 44.1	6.5	54.5
23	165 47.0	50.9	269 28.7	12.7	S18 37.6	6.5	54.5
	SD 15.8	d 0.5	SD 15.1		15.0		14.9

Twilight / Sunrise / Moonrise

Lat.	Naut.	Civil	Sunrise	Moonrise 22	23	24	25
°	h m	h m	h m	h m	h m	h m	h m
N 72	▭	▭	▭	▬	▬	▬	▬
N 70	▭	▭	▭	▬	▬	▬	03 30
68	////	////	00 56	▬	03 34	02 58	02 49
66	////	////	01 51	01 13	01 56	02 14	02 21
64	////	////	02 23	00 31	01 17	01 44	02 00
62	////	01 16	02 47	00 03	00 50	01 22	01 42
60	////	01 55	03 06	24 29	00 29	01 04	01 28
N 58	////	02 21	03 21	24 12	00 12	00 49	01 16
56	01 09	02 41	03 34	23 58	24 36	00 36	01 05
54	01 44	02 58	03 46	23 45	24 25	00 25	00 56
52	02 09	03 12	03 56	23 34	24 15	00 15	00 47
50	02 28	03 24	04 05	23 24	24 06	00 06	00 40
45	03 03	03 48	04 23	23 04	23 47	24 23	00 23
N 40	03 28	04 07	04 39	22 47	23 32	24 10	00 10
35	03 48	04 23	04 51	22 33	23 19	23 59	24 34
30	04 04	04 36	05 03	22 21	23 07	23 49	24 26
20	04 29	04 58	05 22	22 00	22 48	23 32	24 12
N 10	04 49	05 15	05 38	21 42	22 31	23 17	24 00
0	05 05	05 31	05 53	21 25	22 15	23 03	23 48
S 10	05 20	05 46	06 08	21 08	21 59	22 48	23 37
20	05 34	06 01	06 24	20 49	21 42	22 33	23 24
30	05 48	06 17	06 42	20 28	21 22	22 16	23 10
35	05 55	06 26	06 53	20 16	21 11	22 06	23 02
40	06 02	06 36	07 05	20 02	20 57	21 54	22 52
45	06 11	06 47	07 19	19 45	20 42	21 41	22 41
S 50	06 20	07 00	07 37	19 25	20 22	21 24	22 27
52	06 24	07 06	07 45	19 15	20 13	21 16	22 21
54	06 28	07 13	07 54	19 04	20 03	21 07	22 14
56	06 33	07 20	08 04	18 51	19 51	20 57	22 06
58	06 38	07 28	08 16	18 37	19 38	20 46	21 57
S 60	06 44	07 38	08 29	18 19	19 22	20 33	21 47

Sunset / Twilight / Moonset

Lat.	Sunset	Civil	Naut.	Moonset 22	23	24	25
°	h m	h m	h m	h m	h m	h m	h m
N 72	▭	▭	▭	▬	▬	▬	▬
N 70	▭	▭	▭	▬	▬	▬	07 10
68	23 05	////	////	▬	▬	06 03	07 50
66	22 06	////	////	04 17	05 22	06 46	08 17
64	21 32	////	////	04 59	06 00	07 15	08 37
62	21 08	22 42	////	05 27	06 26	07 37	08 54
60	20 49	22 02	////	05 49	06 47	07 55	09 08
N 58	20 34	21 35	////	06 07	07 04	08 10	09 20
56	20 20	21 14	22 49	06 22	07 18	08 22	09 30
54	20 09	20 57	22 12	06 35	07 31	08 33	09 39
52	19 59	20 43	21 47	06 46	07 42	08 43	09 47
50	19 50	20 31	21 27	06 56	07 51	08 51	09 54
45	19 31	20 06	20 52	07 17	08 12	09 10	10 10
N 40	19 15	19 47	20 26	07 34	08 28	09 25	10 22
35	19 02	19 31	20 06	07 48	08 42	09 37	10 33
30	18 51	19 18	19 50	08 01	08 54	09 48	10 42
20	18 32	18 56	19 24	08 22	09 15	10 07	10 58
N 10	18 16	18 38	19 05	08 41	09 32	10 23	11 12
0	18 00	18 22	18 48	08 58	09 49	10 38	11 25
S 10	17 45	18 08	18 33	09 15	10 06	10 53	11 38
20	17 29	17 53	18 20	09 33	10 23	11 09	11 51
30	17 11	17 36	18 06	09 54	10 43	11 28	12 07
35	17 00	17 28	18 00	10 07	10 55	11 38	12 16
40	16 48	17 18	17 51	10 21	11 09	11 50	12 26
45	16 34	17 06	17 43	10 38	11 25	12 05	12 38
S 50	16 16	16 53	17 33	10 59	11 45	12 22	12 53
52	16 08	16 47	17 29	11 09	11 54	12 30	13 00
54	15 59	16 40	17 25	11 20	12 04	12 39	13 07
56	15 49	16 33	17 20	11 32	12 16	12 50	13 15
58	15 37	16 25	17 15	11 47	12 30	13 01	13 25
S 60	15 23	16 15	17 09	12 04	12 46	13 15	13 36

SUN / MOON

Day	Eqn. of Time 00ʰ	Eqn. of Time 12ʰ	Mer. Pass.	Mer. Pass. Upper	Mer. Pass. Lower	Age	Phase
d	m s	m s	h m	h m	h m	d	%
22	03 23	03 21	11 57	02 45	15 11	18	86
23	03 18	03 16	11 57	03 37	16 02	19	79
24	03 13	03 11	11 57	04 26	16 50	20	70

© British Crown Copyright 2018. All rights reserved.

UT	ARIES GHA	VENUS −3·8 GHA	VENUS Dec	MARS +1·7 GHA	MARS Dec	JUPITER −2·6 GHA	JUPITER Dec	SATURN +0·3 GHA	SATURN Dec	STARS Name	SHA	Dec
25 00	242 17.4	202 36.3	N13 57.0	146 00.4	N24 27.3	341 27.8	S22 33.3	310 41.0	S21 34.5	Acamar	315 15.7	S40 13.7
01	257 19.8	217 35.8	57.9	161 01.1	27.2	356 30.6	33.3	325 43.5	34.5	Achernar	335 24.2	S57 08.3
02	272 22.3	232 35.3	58.9	176 01.8	27.2	11 33.4	33.3	340 46.1	34.5	Acrux	173 04.4	S63 12.6
03	287 24.8	247 34.8	13 59.9	191 02.5 ..	27.1	26 36.2 ..	33.3	355 48.7 ..	34.5	Adhara	255 09.7	S29 00.2
04	302 27.2	262 34.3	14 00.9	206 03.2	27.0	41 38.9	33.3	10 51.2	34.5	Aldebaran	290 45.1	N16 32.7
05	317 29.7	277 33.8	01.9	221 03.9	27.0	56 41.7	33.2	25 53.8	34.6			
06	332 32.1	292 33.3	N14 02.8	236 04.6	N24 26.9	71 44.5	S22 33.2	40 56.4	S21 34.6	Alioth	166 16.8	N55 51.6
07	347 34.6	307 32.8	03.8	251 05.3	26.8	86 47.3	33.2	55 58.9	34.6	Alkaid	152 55.3	N49 13.3
S 08	2 37.1	322 32.3	04.8	266 06.0	26.8	101 50.0	33.2	71 01.5	34.6	Alnair	27 38.6	S46 51.8
A 09	17 39.5	337 31.8 ..	05.8	281 06.7 ..	26.7	116 52.8 ..	33.2	86 04.1 ..	34.6	Alnilam	275 42.6	S 1 11.6
T 10	32 42.0	352 31.3	06.8	296 07.3	26.6	131 55.6	33.2	101 06.6	34.6	Alphard	217 52.2	S 8 44.7
U 11	47 44.5	7 30.8	07.7	311 08.0	26.6	146 58.4	33.1	116 09.2	34.7			
R 12	62 46.9	22 30.3	N14 08.7	326 08.7	N24 26.5	162 01.2	S22 33.1	131 11.8	S21 34.7	Alphecca	126 07.2	N26 39.1
D 13	77 49.4	37 29.8	09.7	341 09.4	26.4	177 03.9	33.1	146 14.3	34.7	Alpheratz	357 39.5	N29 11.5
A 14	92 51.9	52 29.3	10.7	356 10.1	26.4	192 06.7	33.1	161 16.9	34.7	Altair	62 04.1	N 8 55.1
Y 15	107 54.3	67 28.8 ..	11.6	11 10.8 ..	26.3	207 09.5 ..	33.1	176 19.5 ..	34.7	Ankaa	353 11.9	S42 12.0
16	122 56.8	82 28.3	12.6	26 11.5	26.2	222 12.3	33.1	191 22.0	34.7	Antares	112 20.9	S26 28.4
17	137 59.3	97 27.8	13.6	41 12.2	26.1	237 15.0	33.1	206 24.6	34.8			
18	153 01.7	112 27.3	N14 14.5	56 12.9	N24 26.1	252 17.8	S22 33.0	221 27.2	S21 34.8	Arcturus	145 51.8	N19 05.1
19	168 04.2	127 26.8	15.5	71 13.6	26.0	267 20.6	33.0	236 29.7	34.8	Atria	107 18.5	S69 03.5
20	183 06.6	142 26.3	16.5	86 14.3	25.9	282 23.4	33.0	251 32.3	34.8	Avior	234 16.7	S59 34.6
21	198 09.1	157 25.8 ..	17.5	101 15.0 ..	25.9	297 26.2 ..	33.0	266 34.9 ..	34.8	Bellatrix	278 28.0	N 6 21.8
22	213 11.6	172 25.2	18.4	116 15.7	25.8	312 28.9	33.0	281 37.5	34.8	Betelgeuse	270 57.2	N 7 24.4
23	228 14.0	187 24.7	19.4	131 16.4	25.7	327 31.7	33.0	296 40.0	34.9			
26 00	243 16.5	202 24.2	N14 20.4	146 17.1	N24 25.6	342 34.5	S22 33.0	311 42.6	S21 34.9	Canopus	263 54.8	S52 42.6
01	258 19.0	217 23.7	21.3	161 17.8	25.6	357 37.3	32.9	326 45.2	34.9	Capella	280 28.9	N46 00.9
02	273 21.4	232 23.2	22.3	176 18.5	25.5	12 40.0	32.9	341 47.7	34.9	Deneb	49 28.5	N45 20.7
03	288 23.9	247 22.7 ..	23.3	191 19.2 ..	25.4	27 42.8 ..	32.9	356 50.3 ..	34.9	Denebola	182 29.4	N14 27.9
04	303 26.4	262 22.2	24.2	206 19.9	25.3	42 45.6	32.9	11 52.9	34.9	Diphda	348 52.0	S17 52.9
05	318 28.8	277 21.7	25.2	221 20.6	25.3	57 48.4	32.9	26 55.4	35.0			
06	333 31.3	292 21.2	N14 26.2	236 21.3	N24 25.2	72 51.2	S22 32.9	41 58.0	S21 35.0	Dubhe	193 46.7	N61 39.1
07	348 33.8	307 20.6	27.1	251 22.0	25.1	87 53.9	32.8	57 00.6	35.0	Elnath	278 07.9	N28 37.2
S 08	3 36.2	322 20.1	28.1	266 22.7	25.0	102 56.7	32.8	72 03.2	35.0	Eltanin	90 43.8	N51 29.2
U 09	18 38.7	337 19.6 ..	29.1	281 23.4 ..	25.0	117 59.5 ..	32.8	87 05.7 ..	35.0	Enif	33 43.1	N 9 57.7
N 10	33 41.1	352 19.1	30.0	296 24.1	24.9	133 02.3	32.8	102 08.3	35.0	Fomalhaut	15 19.6	S29 31.1
D 11	48 43.6	7 18.6	31.0	311 24.8	24.8	148 05.1	32.8	117 10.9	35.1			
A 12	63 46.1	22 18.1	N14 31.9	326 25.5	N24 24.7	163 07.8	S22 32.8	132 13.4	S21 35.1	Gacrux	171 56.1	S57 13.4
Y 13	78 48.5	37 17.5	32.9	341 26.2	24.7	178 10.6	32.8	147 16.0	35.1	Gienah	175 48.0	S17 39.0
14	93 51.0	52 17.0	33.9	356 26.9	24.6	193 13.4	32.7	162 18.6	35.1	Hadar	148 41.6	S60 28.0
15	108 53.5	67 16.5 ..	34.8	11 27.6 ..	24.5	208 16.2 ..	32.7	177 21.2 ..	35.1	Hamal	327 56.5	N23 32.9
16	123 55.9	82 16.0	35.8	26 28.3	24.4	223 19.0	32.7	192 23.7	35.1	Kaus Aust.	83 38.1	S34 22.3
17	138 58.4	97 15.5	36.7	41 29.0	24.4	238 21.7	32.7	207 26.3	35.2			
18	154 00.9	112 15.0	N14 37.7	56 29.7	N24 24.3	253 24.5	S22 32.7	222 28.9	S21 35.2	Kochab	137 19.0	N74 04.8
19	169 03.3	127 14.4	38.7	71 30.4	24.2	268 27.3	32.7	237 31.4	35.2	Markab	13 34.4	N15 18.4
20	184 05.8	142 13.9	39.6	86 31.1	24.1	283 30.1	32.6	252 34.0	35.2	Menkar	314 11.1	N 4 09.7
21	199 08.2	157 13.4 ..	40.6	101 31.8 ..	24.0	298 32.9 ..	32.6	267 36.6 ..	35.2	Menkent	148 02.5	S36 27.9
22	214 10.7	172 12.9	41.5	116 32.6	24.0	313 35.7	32.6	282 39.2	35.2	Miaplacidus	221 39.2	S69 48.1
23	229 13.2	187 12.4	42.5	131 33.3	23.9	328 38.4	32.6	297 41.7	35.3			
27 00	244 15.6	202 11.8	N14 43.4	146 34.0	N24 23.8	343 41.2	S22 32.6	312 44.3	S21 35.3	Mirfak	308 35.1	N49 55.5
01	259 18.1	217 11.3	44.4	161 34.7	23.7	358 44.0	32.6	327 46.9	35.3	Nunki	75 53.0	S26 16.2
02	274 20.6	232 10.8	45.3	176 35.4	23.6	13 46.8	32.6	342 49.5	35.3	Peacock	53 12.6	S56 40.1
03	289 23.0	247 10.3 ..	46.3	191 36.1 ..	23.6	28 49.6 ..	32.5	357 52.0 ..	35.3	Pollux	243 23.1	N27 58.7
04	304 25.5	262 09.8	47.2	206 36.8	23.5	43 52.4	32.5	12 54.6	35.4	Procyon	244 55.8	N 5 10.4
05	319 28.0	277 09.2	48.2	221 37.5	23.4	58 55.1	32.5	27 57.2	35.4			
06	334 30.4	292 08.7	N14 49.1	236 38.2	N24 23.3	73 57.9	S22 32.5	42 59.7	S21 35.4	Rasalhague	96 02.4	N12 32.8
07	349 32.9	307 08.2	50.1	251 38.9	23.2	89 00.7	32.5	58 02.3	35.4	Regulus	207 39.3	N11 52.4
08	4 35.4	322 07.7	51.0	266 39.6	23.1	104 03.5	32.5	73 04.9	35.4	Rigel	281 08.5	S 8 11.0
M 09	19 37.8	337 07.1 ..	52.0	281 40.3 ..	23.1	119 06.3 ..	32.4	88 07.5 ..	35.4	Rigil Kent.	139 45.6	S60 54.9
O 10	34 40.3	352 06.6	52.9	296 41.0	23.0	134 09.1	32.4	103 10.0	35.5	Sabik	102 07.6	S15 44.8
N 11	49 42.7	7 06.1	53.9	311 41.7	22.9	149 11.8	32.4	118 12.6	35.5			
D 12	64 45.2	22 05.6	N14 54.8	326 42.4	N24 22.8	164 14.6	S22 32.4	133 15.2	S21 35.5	Schedar	349 36.2	N56 38.2
A 13	79 47.7	37 05.0	55.8	341 43.1	22.7	179 17.4	32.4	148 17.8	35.5	Shaula	96 16.0	S37 06.9
Y 14	94 50.1	52 04.5	56.7	356 43.8	22.6	194 20.2	32.4	163 20.3	35.5	Sirius	258 30.5	S16 44.8
15	109 52.6	67 04.0 ..	57.7	11 44.5 ..	22.5	209 23.0 ..	32.3	178 22.9 ..	35.5	Spica	158 26.8	S11 15.7
16	124 55.1	82 03.4	58.6	26 45.2	22.5	224 25.8	32.3	193 25.5	35.6	Suhail	222 49.6	S43 30.9
17	139 57.5	97 02.9	14 59.6	41 45.9	22.4	239 28.5	32.3	208 28.1	35.6			
18	155 00.0	112 02.4	N15 00.5	56 46.6	N24 22.3	254 31.3	S22 32.3	223 30.6	S21 35.6	Vega	80 35.9	N38 48.0
19	170 02.5	127 01.9	01.4	71 47.3	22.2	269 34.1	32.3	238 33.2	35.6	Zuben'ubi	137 00.6	S16 07.2
20	185 04.9	142 01.3	02.4	86 48.0	22.1	284 36.9	32.3	253 35.8	35.6		SHA	Mer. Pass.
21	200 07.4	157 00.8 ..	03.3	101 48.7 ..	22.0	299 39.7 ..	32.3	268 38.4 ..	35.7	Venus	319 07.7	10 31
22	215 09.9	172 00.3	04.3	116 49.4	21.9	314 42.5	32.2	283 41.0	35.7	Mars	263 00.6	14 14
23	230 12.3	186 59.7	05.2	131 50.1	21.9	329 45.3	32.2	298 43.5	35.7	Jupiter	99 18.0	1 09
Mer. Pass. 7 45.6		v −0.5	d 1.0	v 0.7	d 0.1	v 2.8	d 0.0	v 2.6	d 0.0	Saturn	68 26.1	3 13

© British Crown Copyright 2018. All rights reserved.

UT	SUN GHA	SUN Dec	MOON GHA	v	MOON Dec	d	HP
25 00	180 46.9	N20 51.3	284 00.4	12.7	S18 31.1	6.6	54.5
01	195 46.9	51.8	298 32.1	12.8	18 24.5	6.6	54.5
02	210 46.8	52.2	313 03.9	12.9	18 17.9	6.8	54.4
03	225 46.8	.. 52.7	327 35.8	12.9	18 11.1	6.8	54.4
04	240 46.7	53.1	342 07.7	13.0	18 04.3	6.9	54.4
05	255 46.6	53.6	356 39.7	13.0	17 57.4	7.0	54.4
06	270 46.6	N20 54.0	11 11.7	13.1	S17 50.4	7.0	54.4
07	285 46.5	54.5	25 43.8	13.1	17 43.4	7.2	54.4
S 08	300 46.5	55.0	40 15.9	13.2	17 36.2	7.2	54.4
A 09	315 46.4	.. 55.4	54 48.1	13.2	17 29.0	7.2	54.4
T 10	330 46.3	55.9	69 20.3	13.3	17 21.8	7.4	54.4
U 11	345 46.3	56.3	83 52.6	13.3	17 14.4	7.4	54.4
R 12	0 46.2	N20 56.7	98 24.9	13.4	S17 07.0	7.5	54.4
D 13	15 46.1	57.2	112 57.3	13.4	16 59.5	7.6	54.3
A 14	30 46.1	57.6	127 29.7	13.5	16 51.9	7.6	54.3
Y 15	45 46.0	.. 58.1	142 02.2	13.5	16 44.3	7.7	54.3
16	60 46.0	58.5	156 34.7	13.6	16 36.6	7.8	54.3
17	75 45.9	59.0	171 07.3	13.6	16 28.8	7.8	54.3
18	90 45.8	N20 59.4	185 39.9	13.7	S16 21.0	7.9	54.3
19	105 45.8	20 59.9	200 12.6	13.7	16 13.1	8.0	54.3
20	120 45.7	21 00.3	214 45.3	13.8	16 05.1	8.0	54.3
21	135 45.6	.. 00.8	229 18.1	13.8	15 57.1	8.2	54.3
22	150 45.6	01.2	243 50.9	13.8	15 48.9	8.1	54.3
23	165 45.5	01.6	258 23.7	13.9	15 40.8	8.3	54.3
26 00	180 45.4	N21 02.1	272 56.6	13.9	S15 32.5	8.3	54.3
01	195 45.4	02.5	287 29.5	14.0	15 24.2	8.3	54.3
02	210 45.3	03.0	302 02.5	14.1	15 15.9	8.5	54.3
03	225 45.2	.. 03.4	316 35.6	14.0	15 07.4	8.5	54.3
04	240 45.2	03.8	331 08.6	14.2	14 58.9	8.5	54.3
05	255 45.1	04.3	345 41.8	14.1	14 50.4	8.6	54.3
06	270 45.0	N21 04.7	0 14.9	14.2	S14 41.8	8.7	54.3
07	285 45.0	05.2	14 48.1	14.2	14 33.1	8.7	54.3
S 08	300 44.9	05.6	29 21.3	14.3	14 24.4	8.8	54.3
U 09	315 44.8	.. 06.0	43 54.6	14.3	14 15.6	8.9	54.3
N 10	330 44.8	06.5	58 27.9	14.4	14 06.7	8.9	54.3
11	345 44.7	06.9	73 01.3	14.4	13 57.8	9.0	54.3
D 12	0 44.6	N21 07.3	87 34.7	14.4	S13 48.8	9.0	54.3
A 13	15 44.6	07.8	102 08.1	14.5	13 39.8	9.1	54.3
Y 14	30 44.5	08.2	116 41.6	14.5	13 30.7	9.1	54.3
15	45 44.4	.. 08.6	131 15.1	14.6	13 21.6	9.2	54.3
16	60 44.4	09.1	145 48.7	14.5	13 12.4	9.2	54.3
17	75 44.3	09.5	160 22.2	14.7	13 03.2	9.3	54.3
18	90 44.2	N21 09.9	174 55.9	14.6	S12 53.9	9.4	54.3
19	105 44.2	10.3	189 29.5	14.7	12 44.5	9.4	54.3
20	120 44.1	10.8	204 03.2	14.7	12 35.1	9.4	54.3
21	135 44.0	.. 11.2	218 36.9	14.8	12 25.7	9.6	54.3
22	150 44.0	11.6	233 10.7	14.7	12 16.1	9.5	54.3
23	165 43.9	12.1	247 44.4	14.9	12 06.6	9.6	54.3
27 00	180 43.8	N21 12.5	262 18.3	14.8	S11 57.0	9.7	54.3
01	195 43.7	12.9	276 52.1	14.9	11 47.3	9.7	54.3
02	210 43.7	13.3	291 26.0	14.9	11 37.6	9.7	54.3
03	225 43.6	.. 13.8	305 59.9	14.9	11 27.9	9.8	54.3
04	240 43.5	14.2	320 33.8	15.0	11 18.1	9.9	54.3
05	255 43.5	14.6	335 07.8	14.9	11 08.2	9.9	54.3
06	270 43.4	N21 15.0	349 41.7	15.1	S10 58.3	9.9	54.3
07	285 43.3	15.4	4 15.8	15.0	10 48.4	10.0	54.3
08	300 43.3	15.9	18 49.8	15.1	10 38.4	10.1	54.3
M 09	315 43.2	.. 16.3	33 23.9	15.0	10 28.3	10.0	54.3
O 10	330 43.1	16.7	47 57.9	15.1	10 18.3	10.2	54.3
N 11	345 43.0	17.1	62 32.0	15.2	10 08.1	10.1	54.3
D 12	0 43.0	N21 17.5	77 06.2	15.1	S 9 58.0	10.2	54.3
A 13	15 42.9	17.9	91 40.3	15.2	9 47.8	10.3	54.3
Y 14	30 42.8	18.4	106 14.5	15.2	9 37.5	10.3	54.3
15	45 42.7	.. 18.8	120 48.7	15.2	9 27.2	10.3	54.4
16	60 42.7	19.2	135 22.9	15.2	9 16.9	10.4	54.4
17	75 42.6	19.6	149 57.1	15.3	9 06.5	10.4	54.4
18	90 42.5	N21 20.0	164 31.4	15.2	S 8 56.1	10.4	54.4
19	105 42.4	20.4	179 05.6	15.3	8 45.7	10.5	54.4
20	120 42.4	20.9	193 39.9	15.3	8 35.2	10.6	54.4
21	135 42.3	.. 21.3	208 14.2	15.3	8 24.6	10.5	54.4
22	150 42.2	21.7	222 48.5	15.4	8 14.1	10.6	54.4
23	165 42.2	22.1	237 22.9	15.3	S 8 03.5	10.7	54.3
	SD 15.8	d 0.4	SD 14.8		14.8		14.8

Lat.	Twilight Naut.	Twilight Civil	Sunrise	Moonrise 25	26	27	28
N 72	▭	▭	▭	■	03 40	03 12	02 52
N 70	▭	▭	▭	03 30	03 07	02 53	02 42
68	////	////	00 23	02 49	02 43	02 38	02 33
66	////	////	01 39	02 21	02 24	02 25	02 26
64	////	////	02 15	02 00	02 09	02 15	02 19
62	////	01 00	02 40	01 42	01 56	02 06	02 14
60	////	01 45	03 00	01 28	01 45	01 59	02 09
N 58	////	02 14	03 16	01 16	01 36	01 52	02 05
56	00 54	02 35	03 30	01 05	01 28	01 46	02 01
54	01 36	02 53	03 42	00 56	01 20	01 40	01 58
52	02 02	03 07	03 52	00 47	01 14	01 36	01 55
50	02 22	03 20	04 01	00 40	01 07	01 31	01 52
45	02 59	03 45	04 21	00 23	00 54	01 22	01 46
N 40	03 25	04 05	04 37	00 10	00 44	01 14	01 41
35	03 46	04 21	04 50	24 34	00 34	01 07	01 37
30	04 02	04 35	05 01	24 26	00 26	01 01	01 33
20	04 28	04 57	05 21	24 12	00 12	00 50	01 26
N 10	04 49	05 15	05 38	24 00	00 00	00 41	01 20
0	05 05	05 31	05 53	23 48	24 32	00 32	01 15
S 10	05 21	05 46	06 09	23 37	24 23	00 23	01 09
20	05 35	06 02	06 25	23 24	24 14	00 14	01 03
30	05 49	06 18	06 44	23 10	24 03	00 03	00 56
35	05 57	06 28	06 55	23 02	23 57	24 52	00 52
40	06 04	06 38	07 08	22 52	23 50	24 48	00 48
45	06 13	06 50	07 22	22 41	23 42	24 43	00 43
S 50	06 23	07 03	07 40	22 27	23 32	24 36	00 36
52	06 27	07 10	07 49	22 21	23 27	24 33	00 33
54	06 32	07 17	07 58	22 14	23 22	24 30	00 30
56	06 37	07 24	08 09	22 06	23 16	24 27	00 27
58	06 42	07 33	08 21	21 57	23 10	24 23	00 23
S 60	06 48	07 42	08 35	21 47	23 03	24 18	00 18

Lat.	Sunset	Twilight Civil	Naut.	Moonset 25	26	27	28
N 72	▭	▭	▭	■	08 34	10 33	12 21
N 70	▭	▭	▭	07 10	09 06	10 50	12 30
68	▭	▭	▭	07 50	09 29	11 04	12 36
66	22 19	////	////	08 17	09 47	11 15	12 42
64	21 42	////	////	08 37	10 01	11 24	12 47
62	21 16	22 59	////	08 54	10 13	11 32	12 51
60	20 56	22 12	////	09 08	10 23	11 39	12 55
N 58	20 39	21 42	////	09 20	10 32	11 45	12 58
56	20 25	21 20	23 05	09 30	10 40	11 50	13 01
54	20 13	21 03	22 21	09 39	10 47	11 55	13 04
52	20 03	20 48	21 54	09 47	10 53	11 59	13 06
50	19 53	20 35	21 33	09 54	10 58	12 03	13 08
45	19 34	20 09	20 56	10 10	11 10	12 11	13 12
N 40	19 18	19 50	20 29	10 22	11 20	12 18	13 16
35	19 05	19 33	20 09	10 33	11 28	12 24	13 19
30	18 53	19 20	19 52	10 42	11 36	12 29	13 22
20	18 33	18 57	19 26	10 58	11 48	12 38	13 27
N 10	18 16	18 39	19 06	11 12	11 59	12 46	13 31
0	18 01	18 23	18 49	11 25	12 10	12 53	13 35
S 10	17 45	18 07	18 33	11 38	12 20	13 00	13 39
20	17 28	17 52	18 19	11 51	12 31	13 08	13 43
30	17 10	17 35	18 05	12 07	12 43	13 16	13 48
35	16 59	17 26	17 57	12 16	12 50	13 21	13 50
40	16 46	17 16	17 49	12 26	12 58	13 27	13 53
45	16 31	17 04	17 41	12 38	13 07	13 33	13 57
S 50	16 13	16 50	17 31	12 53	13 19	13 41	14 01
52	16 05	16 44	17 26	13 00	13 24	13 44	14 03
54	15 55	16 37	17 22	13 07	13 29	13 48	14 05
56	15 45	16 29	17 17	13 15	13 36	13 53	14 07
58	15 33	16 21	17 11	13 25	13 43	13 57	14 10
S 60	15 18	16 11	17 05	13 36	13 51	14 03	14 13

Day	SUN Eqn. of Time 00h	12h	Mer. Pass.	MOON Mer. Pass. Upper	Lower	Age	Phase
	m s	m s	h m	h m	h m	d %	
25	03 08	03 05	11 57	05 14	17 37	21 61	
26	03 02	02 59	11 57	05 59	18 21	22 52	
27	02 55	02 52	11 57	06 42	19 04	23 42	◖

© British Crown Copyright 2018. All rights reserved.

UT	ARIES GHA	VENUS −3.8 GHA	Dec	MARS +1.7 GHA	Dec	JUPITER −2.6 GHA	Dec	SATURN +0.3 GHA	Dec	STARS Name	SHA	Dec
28 00	245 14.8	201 59.2	N15 06.2	146 50.8	N24 21.8	344 48.0	S22 32.2	313 46.1	S21 35.7	Acamar	315 15.7	S40 13.7
01	260 17.2	216 58.7	07.1	161 51.5	21.7	359 50.8	32.2	328 48.7	35.7	Achernar	335 24.2	S57 08.3
02	275 19.7	231 58.1	08.0	176 52.2	21.6	14 53.6	32.2	343 51.3	35.7	Acrux	173 04.4	S63 12.6
03	290 22.2	246 57.6	.. 09.0	191 52.9	.. 21.5	29 56.4	.. 32.2	358 53.8	.. 35.8	Adhara	255 09.7	S29 00.1
04	305 24.6	261 57.1	09.9	206 53.6	21.4	44 59.2	32.1	13 56.4	35.8	Aldebaran	290 45.1	N16 32.7
05	320 27.1	276 56.5	10.8	221 54.3	21.3	60 02.0	32.1	28 59.0	35.8			
06	335 29.6	291 56.0	N15 11.8	236 55.0	N24 21.2	75 04.8	S22 32.1	44 01.6	S21 35.8	Alioth	166 16.8	N55 51.6
07	350 32.0	306 55.5	12.7	251 55.7	21.1	90 07.5	32.1	59 04.2	35.8	Alkaid	152 55.3	N49 13.3
T 08	5 34.5	321 54.9	13.6	266 56.4	21.0	105 10.3	32.1	74 06.7	35.8	Alnair	27 38.6	S46 51.8
U 09	20 37.0	336 54.4	.. 14.6	281 57.1	.. 21.0	120 13.1	.. 32.1	89 09.3	.. 35.9	Alnilam	275 42.6	S 1 11.6
E 10	35 39.4	351 53.9	15.5	296 57.8	20.9	135 15.9	32.0	104 11.9	35.9	Alphard	217 52.2	S 8 44.7
S 11	50 41.9	6 53.3	16.4	311 58.5	20.8	150 18.7	32.0	119 14.5	35.9			
D 12	65 44.3	21 52.8	N15 17.4	326 59.2	N24 20.7	165 21.5	S22 32.0	134 17.0	S21 35.9	Alphecca	126 07.2	N26 39.1
A 13	80 46.8	36 52.3	18.3	341 59.9	20.6	180 24.3	32.0	149 19.6	35.9	Alpheratz	357 39.5	N29 11.5
Y 14	95 49.3	51 51.7	19.2	357 00.6	20.5	195 27.1	32.0	164 22.2	36.0	Altair	62 04.1	N 8 55.2
15	110 51.7	66 51.2	.. 20.2	12 01.4	.. 20.4	210 29.8	.. 32.0	179 24.8	.. 36.0	Ankaa	353 11.9	S42 12.0
16	125 54.2	81 50.6	21.1	27 02.1	20.3	225 32.6	31.9	194 27.4	36.0	Antares	112 20.9	S26 28.4
17	140 56.7	96 50.1	22.0	42 02.8	20.2	240 35.4	31.9	209 29.9	36.0			
18	155 59.1	111 49.6	N15 23.0	57 03.5	N24 20.1	255 38.2	S22 31.9	224 32.5	S21 36.0	Arcturus	145 51.8	N19 05.1
19	171 01.6	126 49.0	23.9	72 04.2	20.0	270 41.0	31.9	239 35.1	36.0	Atria	107 18.5	S69 03.5
20	186 04.1	141 48.5	24.8	87 04.9	19.9	285 43.8	31.9	254 37.7	36.1	Avior	234 16.8	S59 34.6
21	201 06.5	156 47.9	.. 25.7	102 05.6	.. 19.8	300 46.6	.. 31.9	269 40.3	.. 36.1	Bellatrix	278 28.0	N 6 21.8
22	216 09.0	171 47.4	26.7	117 06.3	19.7	315 49.4	31.8	284 42.8	36.1	Betelgeuse	270 57.2	N 7 24.5
23	231 11.5	186 46.9	27.6	132 07.0	19.6	330 52.1	31.8	299 45.4	36.1			
29 00	246 13.9	201 46.3	N15 28.5	147 07.7	N24 19.5	345 54.9	S22 31.8	314 48.0	S21 36.1	Canopus	263 54.9	S52 42.6
01	261 16.4	216 45.8	29.4	162 08.4	19.4	0 57.7	31.8	329 50.6	36.2	Capella	280 28.9	N46 00.9
02	276 18.8	231 45.2	30.4	177 09.1	19.3	16 00.5	31.8	344 53.2	36.2	Deneb	49 28.5	N45 20.7
03	291 21.3	246 44.7	.. 31.3	192 09.8	.. 19.2	31 03.3	.. 31.8	359 55.7	.. 36.2	Denebola	182 29.4	N14 28.0
04	306 23.8	261 44.1	32.2	207 10.5	19.1	46 06.1	31.8	14 58.3	36.2	Diphda	348 52.0	S17 52.9
05	321 26.2	276 43.6	33.1	222 11.2	19.1	61 08.9	31.7	30 00.9	36.2			
06	336 28.7	291 43.0	N15 34.0	237 11.9	N24 19.0	76 11.7	S22 31.7	45 03.5	S21 36.3	Dubhe	193 46.7	N61 39.1
W 07	351 31.2	306 42.5	35.0	252 12.6	18.9	91 14.5	31.7	60 06.1	36.3	Elnath	278 07.9	N28 37.2
E 08	6 33.6	321 42.0	35.9	267 13.3	18.8	106 17.2	31.7	75 08.6	36.3	Eltanin	90 43.8	N51 29.2
D 09	21 36.1	336 41.4	.. 36.8	282 14.0	.. 18.7	121 20.0	.. 31.7	90 11.2	.. 36.3	Enif	33 43.1	N 9 57.7
N 10	36 38.6	351 40.9	37.7	297 14.7	18.6	136 22.8	31.7	105 13.8	36.3	Fomalhaut	15 19.6	S29 31.1
E 11	51 41.0	6 40.3	38.6	312 15.4	18.5	151 25.6	31.6	120 16.4	36.3			
S 12	66 43.5	21 39.8	N15 39.6	327 16.2	N24 18.4	166 28.4	S22 31.6	135 19.0	S21 36.4	Gacrux	171 56.1	S57 13.4
D 13	81 46.0	36 39.2	40.5	342 16.9	18.3	181 31.2	31.6	150 21.6	36.4	Gienah	175 48.0	S17 39.0
A 14	96 48.4	51 38.7	41.4	357 17.6	18.2	196 34.0	31.6	165 24.1	36.4	Hadar	148 41.6	S60 28.0
Y 15	111 50.9	66 38.1	.. 42.3	12 18.3	.. 18.1	211 36.8	.. 31.6	180 26.7	.. 36.4	Hamal	327 56.5	N23 32.9
16	126 53.3	81 37.6	43.2	27 19.0	18.0	226 39.6	31.6	195 29.3	36.4	Kaus Aust.	83 38.1	S34 22.3
17	141 55.8	96 37.0	44.1	42 19.7	17.8	241 42.4	31.5	210 31.9	36.5			
18	156 58.3	111 36.5	N15 45.0	57 20.4	N24 17.7	256 45.2	S22 31.5	225 34.5	S21 36.5	Kochab	137 19.0	N74 04.8
19	172 00.7	126 35.9	46.0	72 21.1	17.6	271 47.9	31.5	240 37.1	36.5	Markab	13 34.4	N15 18.4
20	187 03.2	141 35.4	46.9	87 21.8	17.5	286 50.7	31.5	255 39.6	36.5	Menkar	314 11.1	N 4 09.7
21	202 05.7	156 34.8	.. 47.8	102 22.5	.. 17.4	301 53.5	.. 31.5	270 42.2	.. 36.5	Menkent	148 02.5	S36 27.9
22	217 08.1	171 34.3	48.7	117 23.2	17.3	316 56.3	31.5	285 44.8	36.5	Miaplacidus	221 39.2	S69 48.1
23	232 10.6	186 33.7	49.6	132 23.9	17.2	331 59.1	31.4	300 47.4	36.6			
30 00	247 13.1	201 33.1	N15 50.5	147 24.6	N24 17.1	347 01.9	S22 31.4	315 50.0	S21 36.6	Mirfak	308 35.0	N49 55.5
01	262 15.5	216 32.6	51.4	162 25.3	17.0	2 04.7	31.4	330 52.6	36.6	Nunki	75 53.0	S26 16.2
02	277 18.0	231 32.0	52.3	177 26.0	16.9	17 07.5	31.4	345 55.1	36.6	Peacock	53 12.6	S56 40.1
03	292 20.4	246 31.5	.. 53.2	192 26.7	.. 16.8	32 10.3	.. 31.4	0 57.7	.. 36.6	Pollux	243 23.1	N27 58.7
04	307 22.9	261 30.9	54.1	207 27.4	16.7	47 13.1	31.4	16 00.3	36.7	Procyon	244 55.8	N 5 10.4
05	322 25.4	276 30.4	55.0	222 28.2	16.6	62 15.9	31.3	31 02.9	36.7			
06	337 27.8	291 29.8	N15 55.9	237 28.9	N24 16.5	77 18.7	S22 31.3	46 05.5	S21 36.7	Rasalhague	96 02.4	N12 32.8
07	352 30.3	306 29.3	56.8	252 29.6	16.4	92 21.5	31.3	61 08.1	36.7	Regulus	207 39.3	N11 52.4
T 08	7 32.8	321 28.7	57.8	267 30.3	16.3	107 24.2	31.3	76 10.6	36.7	Rigel	281 08.5	S 8 11.0
H 09	22 35.2	336 28.1	.. 58.7	282 31.0	.. 16.2	122 27.0	.. 31.3	91 13.2	.. 36.8	Rigil Kent.	139 45.7	S60 54.9
U 10	37 37.7	351 27.6	15 59.6	297 31.7	16.1	137 29.8	31.3	106 15.8	36.8	Sabik	102 07.6	S15 44.8
R 11	52 40.2	6 27.0	16 00.5	312 32.4	16.0	152 32.6	31.2	121 18.4	36.8			
S 12	67 42.6	21 26.5	N16 01.4	327 33.1	N24 15.8	167 35.4	S22 31.2	136 21.0	S21 36.8	Schedar	349 36.2	N56 38.2
D 13	82 45.1	36 25.9	02.3	342 33.8	15.7	182 38.2	31.2	151 23.6	36.8	Shaula	96 16.0	S37 06.9
A 14	97 47.6	51 25.3	03.2	357 34.5	15.6	197 41.0	31.2	166 26.2	36.8	Sirius	258 30.5	S16 44.8
Y 15	112 50.0	66 24.8	.. 04.1	12 35.2	.. 15.5	212 43.8	.. 31.2	181 28.7	.. 36.9	Spica	158 26.8	S11 15.7
16	127 52.5	81 24.2	05.0	27 35.9	15.4	227 46.6	31.2	196 31.3	36.9	Suhail	222 49.7	S43 30.9
17	142 54.9	96 23.7	05.9	42 36.6	15.3	242 49.4	31.1	211 33.9	36.9			
18	157 57.4	111 23.1	N16 06.7	57 37.3	N24 15.2	257 52.2	S22 31.1	226 36.5	S21 36.9	Vega	80 35.9	N38 48.1
19	172 59.9	126 22.5	07.6	72 38.1	15.1	272 55.0	31.1	241 39.1	36.9	Zuben'ubi	137 00.6	S16 07.2
20	188 02.3	141 22.0	08.5	87 38.8	15.0	287 57.8	31.1	256 41.7	37.0		SHA	Mer.Pass.
21	203 04.8	156 21.4	.. 09.4	102 39.5	.. 14.9	303 00.6	.. 31.1	271 44.3	.. 37.0		° ′	h m
22	218 07.3	171 20.8	10.3	117 40.2	14.7	318 03.4	31.1	286 46.8	37.0	Venus	315 32.4	10 33
23	233 09.7	186 20.3	11.2	132 40.9	14.6	333 06.1	31.0	301 49.4	37.0	Mars	260 53.8	14 11
	h m									Jupiter	99 41.0	0 56
Mer.Pass.	7 33.8	v −0.5	d 0.9	v 0.7	d 0.1	v 2.8	d 0.0	v 2.6	d 0.0	Saturn	68 34.1	3 00

© British Crown Copyright 2018. All rights reserved.

UT	SUN GHA	SUN Dec	MOON GHA	v	MOON Dec	d	HP
d h	° ′	° ′	° ′	′	° ′	′	′
28 00	180 42.1	N21 22.5	251 57.2	15.4	S 7 52.8	10.6	54.4
01	195 42.0	22.9	266 31.6	15.3	7 42.2	10.7	54.4
02	210 41.9	23.3	281 05.9	15.4	7 31.5	10.8	54.5
03	225 41.8	.. 23.7	295 40.3	15.4	7 20.7	10.8	54.5
04	240 41.8	24.1	310 14.7	15.4	7 09.9	10.8	54.5
05	255 41.7	24.5	324 49.1	15.4	6 59.1	10.8	54.5
06	270 41.6	N21 25.0	339 23.5	15.4	S 6 48.3	10.9	54.5
07	285 41.5	25.4	353 57.9	15.4	6 37.4	10.9	54.5
T 08	300 41.5	25.8	8 32.3	15.4	6 26.5	10.9	54.5
U 09	315 41.4	.. 26.2	23 06.7	15.5	6 15.6	11.0	54.5
E 10	330 41.3	26.6	37 41.2	15.4	6 04.6	11.0	54.6
S 11	345 41.2	27.0	52 15.6	15.4	5 53.6	11.0	54.6
D 12	0 41.2	N21 27.4	66 50.0	15.5	S 5 42.6	11.1	54.6
A 13	15 41.1	27.8	81 24.5	15.4	5 31.5	11.1	54.6
Y 14	30 41.0	28.2	95 58.9	15.4	5 20.4	11.1	54.6
15	45 40.9	.. 28.6	110 33.4	15.4	5 09.3	11.1	54.6
16	60 40.8	29.0	125 07.8	15.4	4 58.2	11.2	54.6
17	75 40.8	29.4	139 42.2	15.5	4 47.0	11.2	54.6
18	90 40.7	N21 29.8	154 16.7	15.4	S 4 35.8	11.2	54.7
19	105 40.6	30.2	168 51.1	15.4	4 24.6	11.3	54.7
20	120 40.5	30.6	183 25.5	15.4	4 13.3	11.3	54.7
21	135 40.5	.. 31.0	198 00.0	15.4	4 02.1	11.3	54.7
22	150 40.4	31.4	212 34.4	15.4	3 50.8	11.3	54.7
23	165 40.3	31.8	227 08.8	15.4	3 39.5	11.4	54.7
29 00	180 40.2	N21 32.2	241 43.2	15.4	S 3 28.1	11.3	54.8
01	195 40.1	32.6	256 17.6	15.4	3 16.8	11.4	54.8
02	210 40.1	33.0	270 52.0	15.4	3 05.4	11.4	54.8
03	225 40.0	.. 33.3	285 26.4	15.4	2 54.0	11.4	54.8
04	240 39.9	33.7	300 00.8	15.4	2 42.6	11.5	54.8
05	255 39.8	34.1	314 35.2	15.3	2 31.1	11.4	54.8
06	270 39.7	N21 34.5	329 09.5	15.3	S 2 19.7	11.5	54.9
W 07	285 39.6	34.9	343 43.8	15.3	2 08.2	11.5	54.9
E 08	300 39.6	35.3	358 18.2	15.3	1 56.7	11.5	54.9
D 09	315 39.5	.. 35.7	12 52.5	15.3	1 45.2	11.5	54.9
N 10	330 39.4	36.1	27 26.8	15.3	1 33.7	11.6	54.9
E 11	345 39.3	36.5	42 01.1	15.2	1 22.1	11.5	55.0
S 12	0 39.2	N21 36.9	56 35.3	15.3	S 1 10.6	11.6	55.0
D 13	15 39.2	37.2	71 09.6	15.2	0 59.0	11.6	55.0
A 14	30 39.1	37.6	85 43.8	15.2	0 47.4	11.5	55.0
Y 15	45 39.0	.. 38.0	100 18.0	15.2	0 35.9	11.7	55.0
16	60 38.9	38.4	114 52.2	15.1	0 24.2	11.6	55.1
17	75 38.8	38.8	129 26.3	15.2	0 12.6	11.6	55.1
18	90 38.7	N21 39.2	144 00.5	15.1	S 0 01.0	11.6	55.1
19	105 38.7	39.5	158 34.6	15.1	N 0 10.6	11.7	55.1
20	120 38.6	39.9	173 08.7	15.0	0 22.3	11.6	55.1
21	135 38.5	.. 40.3	187 42.7	15.1	0 33.9	11.7	55.2
22	150 38.4	40.7	202 16.8	15.0	0 45.6	11.7	55.2
23	165 38.3	41.1	216 50.8	15.0	0 57.3	11.6	55.2
30 00	180 38.2	N21 41.5	231 24.8	14.9	N 1 08.9	11.7	55.2
01	195 38.1	41.8	245 58.7	14.9	1 20.6	11.7	55.3
02	210 38.1	42.2	260 32.6	14.9	1 32.3	11.7	55.3
03	225 38.0	.. 42.6	275 06.5	14.9	1 44.0	11.7	55.3
04	240 37.9	43.0	289 40.4	14.8	1 55.7	11.7	55.3
05	255 37.8	43.3	304 14.2	14.8	2 07.4	11.7	55.3
06	270 37.7	N21 43.7	318 48.0	14.8	N 2 19.1	11.7	55.4
07	285 37.6	44.1	333 21.8	14.7	2 30.8	11.7	55.4
T 08	300 37.5	44.5	347 55.5	14.7	2 42.5	11.7	55.4
H 09	315 37.5	.. 44.8	2 29.2	14.7	2 54.2	11.7	55.4
U 10	330 37.4	45.2	17 02.9	14.6	3 05.9	11.7	55.5
R 11	345 37.3	45.6	31 36.5	14.6	3 17.6	11.7	55.5
S 12	0 37.2	N21 46.0	46 10.1	14.5	N 3 29.3	11.7	55.5
D 13	15 37.1	46.3	60 43.6	14.5	3 41.0	11.7	55.5
A 14	30 37.0	46.7	75 17.1	14.4	3 52.7	11.7	55.6
Y 15	45 36.9	.. 47.1	89 50.5	14.5	4 04.4	11.7	55.6
16	60 36.8	47.4	104 24.0	14.3	4 16.1	11.6	55.6
17	75 36.8	47.8	118 57.3	14.4	4 27.7	11.7	55.6
18	90 36.7	N21 48.2	133 30.7	14.2	N 4 39.4	11.6	55.7
19	105 36.6	48.5	148 03.9	14.3	4 51.0	11.7	55.7
20	120 36.5	48.9	162 37.2	14.2	5 02.7	11.6	55.7
21	135 36.4	.. 49.3	177 10.4	14.1	5 14.3	11.7	55.7
22	150 36.3	49.6	191 43.5	14.1	5 26.0	11.6	55.8
23	165 36.2	50.0	206 16.4	14.0	N 5 37.6	11.6	55.8
	SD 15.8	d 0.4	SD 14.9		15.0		15.1

Lat.	Twilight Naut.	Civil	Sunrise	Moonrise 28	29	30	31
°	h m	h m	h m	h m	h m	h m	h m
N 72	☐	☐	☐	02 52	02 36	02 20	02 04
N 70	☐	☐	☐	02 42	02 32	02 22	02 12
68	☐	☐	☐	02 33	02 28	02 24	02 19
66	////	////	01 27	02 26	02 25	02 25	02 25
64	////	////	02 06	02 19	02 23	02 26	02 30
62	////	00 41	02 34	02 14	02 21	02 27	02 34
60	////	01 36	02 55	02 09	02 19	02 28	02 38
N 58	////	02 07	03 12	02 05	02 17	02 29	02 41
56	00 37	02 30	03 26	02 01	02 16	02 30	02 44
54	01 27	02 48	03 38	01 58	02 14	02 30	02 47
52	01 56	03 03	03 49	01 55	02 13	02 31	02 50
50	02 18	03 16	03 59	01 52	02 12	02 32	02 52
45	02 56	03 43	04 19	01 46	02 10	02 33	02 57
N 40	03 23	04 03	04 35	01 41	02 08	02 34	03 01
35	03 44	04 20	04 49	01 37	02 06	02 35	03 05
30	04 01	04 33	05 00	01 33	02 04	02 36	03 08
20	04 28	04 56	05 20	01 26	02 01	02 37	03 14
N 10	04 48	05 15	05 38	01 20	01 59	02 38	03 19
0	05 06	05 32	05 54	01 15	01 57	02 39	03 23
S 10	05 21	05 47	06 10	01 09	01 55	02 41	03 28
20	05 36	06 03	06 27	01 03	01 52	02 42	03 33
30	05 51	06 20	06 46	00 56	01 49	02 43	03 39
35	05 58	06 29	06 57	00 52	01 48	02 44	03 42
40	06 07	06 40	07 10	00 48	01 46	02 45	03 46
45	06 16	06 52	07 25	00 43	01 44	02 47	03 51
S 50	06 26	07 06	07 44	00 36	01 42	02 48	03 56
52	06 30	07 13	07 52	00 33	01 40	02 49	03 59
54	06 35	07 20	08 02	00 30	01 39	02 49	04 01
56	06 40	07 28	08 13	00 27	01 38	02 50	04 04
58	06 46	07 37	08 26	00 23	01 36	02 51	04 08
S 60	06 52	07 47	08 41	00 18	01 35	02 52	04 12

Lat.	Sunset	Twilight Civil	Naut.	Moonset 28	29	30	31
°	h m	h m	h m	h m	h m	h m	h m
N 72	☐	☐	☐	12 21	14 06	15 54	17 47
N 70	☐	☐	☐	12 30	14 08	15 48	17 32
68	☐	☐	☐	12 36	14 09	15 43	17 21
66	22 32	////	////	12 42	14 10	15 39	17 11
64	21 51	////	////	12 47	14 10	15 35	17 03
62	21 23	23 21	////	12 51	14 11	15 32	16 56
60	21 02	22 21	////	12 55	14 11	15 30	16 50
N 58	20 44	21 50	////	12 58	14 12	15 27	16 45
56	20 30	21 26	23 25	13 01	14 12	15 25	16 41
54	20 17	21 08	22 30	13 03	14 13	15 23	16 37
52	20 07	20 52	22 00	13 06	14 13	15 22	16 33
50	19 57	20 39	21 38	13 08	14 13	15 20	16 29
45	19 37	20 13	21 00	13 12	14 14	15 17	16 22
N 40	19 20	19 52	20 32	13 16	14 14	15 14	16 16
35	19 07	19 36	20 11	13 19	14 15	15 12	16 11
30	18 55	19 22	19 54	13 22	14 15	15 10	16 06
20	18 35	18 59	19 27	13 27	14 16	15 06	15 58
N 10	18 17	18 40	19 07	13 31	14 17	15 03	15 51
0	18 01	18 23	18 49	13 35	14 17	15 00	15 45
S 10	17 45	18 08	18 34	13 39	14 18	14 57	15 39
20	17 28	17 52	18 19	13 43	14 18	14 54	15 32
30	17 09	17 35	18 04	13 48	14 19	14 51	15 24
35	16 57	17 25	17 49	13 50	14 19	14 48	15 19
40	16 45	17 14	17 48	13 53	14 20	14 46	·15 14
45	16 29	17 02	17 39	13 57	14 20	14 43	15 08
S 50	16 11	16 48	17 29	14 01	14 21	14 40	15 01
52	16 02	16 41	17 24	14 03	14 21	14 39	14 58
54	15 52	16 34	17 19	14 05	14 21	14 37	14 55
56	15 41	16 26	17 14	14 07	14 21	14 35	14 51
58	15 28	16 17	17 08	14 10	14 22	14 33	14 46
S 60	15 14	16 07	17 02	14 13	14 22	14 31	14 42

Day	SUN Eqn. of Time 00ʰ	12ʰ	Mer. Pass.	MOON Mer. Pass. Upper	Lower	Age	Phase
d	m s	m s	h m	h m	h m	d	%
28	02 48	02 45	11 57	07 25	19 46	24	33
29	02 41	02 37	11 57	08 07	20 28	25	24
30	02 33	02 29	11 58	08 50	21 12	26	16

© British Crown Copyright 2018. All rights reserved.

UT	ARIES GHA	VENUS −3.8 GHA	Dec	MARS +1.8 GHA	Dec	JUPITER −2.6 GHA	Dec	SATURN +0.3 GHA	Dec	STARS Name	SHA	Dec
31 00	248 12.2	201 19.7	N16 12.1	147 41.6	N24 14.5	348 08.9	S22 31.0	316 52.0	S21 37.0	Acamar	315 15.7	S40 13.7
01	263 14.7	216 19.2	13.0	162 42.3	14.4	3 11.7	31.0	331 54.6	37.1	Achernar	335 24.2	S57 08.3
02	278 17.1	231 18.6	13.9	177 43.0	14.3	18 14.5	31.0	346 57.2	37.1	Acrux	173 04.4	S63 12.6
03	293 19.6	246 18.0	.. 14.8	192 43.7	.. 14.2	33 17.3	.. 31.0	1 59.8	.. 37.1	Adhara	255 09.7	S29 00.1
04	308 22.0	261 17.5	15.7	207 44.4	14.1	48 20.1	30.9	17 02.4	37.1	Aldebaran	290 45.1	N16 32.7
05	323 24.5	276 16.9	16.6	222 45.1	14.0	63 22.9	30.9	32 05.0	37.1			
06	338 27.0	291 16.3	N16 17.5	237 45.8	N24 13.8	78 25.7	S22 30.9	47 07.6	S21 37.2	Alioth	166 16.8	N55 51.6
07	353 29.4	306 15.7	18.3	252 46.5	13.7	93 28.5	30.9	62 10.1	37.2	Alkaid	152 55.3	N49 13.3
08	8 31.9	321 15.2	19.2	267 47.3	13.6	108 31.3	30.9	77 12.7	37.2	Alnair	27 38.6	S46 51.8
F 09	23 34.4	336 14.6	.. 20.1	282 48.0	.. 13.5	123 34.1	.. 30.9	92 15.3	.. 37.2	Alnilam	275 42.6	S 1 11.6
R 10	38 36.8	351 14.0	21.0	297 48.7	13.4	138 36.9	30.8	107 17.9	37.2	Alphard	217 52.2	S 8 44.7
I 11	53 39.3	6 13.5	21.9	312 49.4	13.3	153 39.7	30.8	122 20.5	37.3			
D 12	68 41.8	21 12.9	N16 22.8	327 50.1	N24 13.2	168 42.5	S22 30.8	137 23.1	S21 37.3	Alphecca	126 07.2	N26 39.1
A 13	83 44.2	36 12.3	23.7	342 50.8	13.0	183 45.3	30.8	152 25.7	37.3	Alpheratz	357 39.4	N29 11.5
Y 14	98 46.7	51 11.8	24.5	357 51.5	12.9	198 48.1	30.8	167 28.3	37.3	Altair	62 04.1	N 8 55.2
15	113 49.2	66 11.2	.. 25.4	12 52.2	.. 12.8	213 50.9	.. 30.8	182 30.9	.. 37.3	Ankaa	353 11.9	S42 12.0
16	128 51.6	81 10.6	26.3	27 52.9	12.7	228 53.7	30.7	197 33.4	37.4	Antares	112 20.9	S26 28.4
17	143 54.1	96 10.0	27.2	42 53.6	12.6	243 56.5	30.7	212 36.0	37.4			
18	158 56.5	111 09.5	N16 28.1	57 54.3	N24 12.5	258 59.3	S22 30.7	227 38.6	S21 37.4	Arcturus	145 51.8	N19 05.1
19	173 59.0	126 08.9	28.9	72 55.1	12.3	274 02.1	30.7	242 41.2	37.4	Atria	107 18.5	S69 03.6
20	189 01.5	141 08.3	29.8	87 55.8	12.2	289 04.9	30.7	257 43.8	37.4	Avior	234 16.8	S59 34.6
21	204 03.9	156 07.7	.. 30.7	102 56.5	.. 12.1	304 07.7	.. 30.7	272 46.4	.. 37.4	Bellatrix	278 28.0	N 6 21.8
22	219 06.4	171 07.2	31.6	117 57.2	12.0	319 10.5	30.6	287 49.0	37.5	Betelgeuse	270 57.2	N 7 24.5
23	234 08.9	186 06.6	32.5	132 57.9	11.9	334 13.2	30.6	302 51.6	37.5			
1 00	249 11.3	201 06.0	N16 33.3	147 58.6	N24 11.7	349 16.0	S22 30.6	317 54.2	S21 37.5	Canopus	263 54.9	S52 42.6
01	264 13.8	216 05.4	34.2	162 59.3	11.6	4 18.8	30.6	332 56.8	37.5	Capella	280 28.9	N46 00.9
02	279 16.3	231 04.9	35.1	178 00.0	11.5	19 21.6	30.6	347 59.3	37.5	Deneb	49 28.5	N45 20.8
03	294 18.7	246 04.3	.. 36.0	193 00.7	.. 11.4	34 24.4	.. 30.6	3 01.9	.. 37.6	Denebola	182 29.5	N14 28.0
04	309 21.2	261 03.7	36.8	208 01.4	11.3	49 27.2	30.5	18 04.5	37.6	Diphda	348 52.0	S17 52.9
05	324 23.7	276 03.1	37.7	223 02.2	11.1	64 30.0	30.5	33 07.1	37.6			
06	339 26.1	291 02.5	N16 38.6	238 02.9	N24 11.0	79 32.8	S22 30.5	48 09.7	S21 37.6	Dubhe	193 46.7	N61 39.1
07	354 28.6	306 02.0	39.4	253 03.6	10.9	94 35.6	30.5	63 12.3	37.6	Elnath	278 07.9	N28 37.2
S 08	9 31.0	321 01.4	40.3	268 04.3	10.8	109 38.4	30.5	78 14.9	37.7	Eltanin	90 43.7	N51 29.2
A 09	24 33.5	336 00.8	.. 41.2	283 05.0	.. 10.6	124 41.2	.. 30.4	93 17.5	.. 37.7	Enif	33 43.1	N 9 57.7
T 10	39 36.0	351 00.2	42.1	298 05.7	10.5	139 44.0	30.4	108 20.1	37.7	Fomalhaut	15 19.5	S29 31.1
U 11	54 38.4	5 59.6	42.9	313 06.4	10.4	154 46.8	30.4	123 22.7	37.7			
R 12	69 40.9	20 59.1	N16 43.8	328 07.1	N24 10.3	169 49.6	S22 30.4	138 25.3	S21 37.8	Gacrux	171 56.1	S57 13.5
D 13	84 43.4	35 58.5	44.7	343 07.8	10.1	184 52.4	30.4	153 27.9	37.8	Gienah	175 48.0	S17 39.0
A 14	99 45.8	50 57.9	45.5	358 08.6	10.0	199 55.2	30.4	168 30.4	37.8	Hadar	148 41.6	S60 28.0
Y 15	114 48.3	65 57.3	.. 46.4	13 09.3	.. 09.9	214 58.0	.. 30.3	183 33.0	.. 37.8	Hamal	327 56.5	N23 32.9
16	129 50.8	80 56.7	47.3	28 10.0	09.8	230 00.8	30.3	198 35.6	37.8	Kaus Aust.	83 38.1	S34 22.3
17	144 53.2	95 56.1	48.1	43 10.7	09.6	245 03.6	30.3	213 38.2	37.8			
18	159 55.7	110 55.6	N16 49.0	58 11.4	N24 09.5	260 06.4	S22 30.3	228 40.8	S21 37.9	Kochab	137 19.1	N74 04.8
19	174 58.1	125 55.0	49.8	73 12.1	09.4	275 09.2	30.3	243 43.4	37.9	Markab	13 34.3	N15 18.4
20	190 00.6	140 54.4	50.7	88 12.8	09.3	290 12.0	30.3	258 46.0	37.9	Menkar	314 11.1	N 4 09.7
21	205 03.1	155 53.8	.. 51.6	103 13.5	.. 09.1	305 14.8	.. 30.2	273 48.6	.. 37.9	Menkent	148 02.5	S36 27.9
22	220 05.5	170 53.2	52.4	118 14.2	09.0	320 17.6	30.2	288 51.2	37.9	Miaplacidus	221 39.2	S69 48.1
23	235 08.0	185 52.6	53.3	133 15.0	08.9	335 20.4	30.2	303 53.8	38.0			
2 00	250 10.5	200 52.0	N16 54.1	148 15.7	N24 08.8	350 23.2	S22 30.2	318 56.4	S21 38.0	Mirfak	308 35.0	N49 55.5
01	265 12.9	215 51.5	55.0	163 16.4	08.6	5 26.0	30.2	333 59.0	38.0	Nunki	75 53.0	S26 16.2
02	280 15.4	230 50.9	55.9	178 17.1	08.5	20 28.8	30.1	349 01.6	38.0	Peacock	53 12.5	S56 40.1
03	295 17.9	245 50.3	.. 56.7	193 17.8	.. 08.4	35 31.6	.. 30.1	4 04.2	.. 38.0	Pollux	243 23.1	N27 58.7
04	310 20.3	260 49.7	57.6	208 18.5	08.2	50 34.4	30.1	19 06.8	38.1	Procyon	244 55.8	N 5 10.4
05	325 22.8	275 49.1	58.4	223 19.2	08.1	65 37.2	30.1	34 09.3	38.1			
06	340 25.3	290 48.5	N16 59.3	238 19.9	N24 08.0	80 40.0	S22 30.1	49 11.9	S21 38.1	Rasalhague	96 02.4	N12 32.8
07	355 27.7	305 47.9	17 00.1	253 20.7	07.9	95 42.8	30.1	64 14.5	38.1	Regulus	207 39.3	N11 52.4
08	10 30.2	320 47.3	01.0	268 21.4	07.7	110 45.6	30.0	79 17.1	38.1	Rigel	281 08.5	S 8 11.0
S 09	25 32.6	335 46.7	.. 01.8	283 22.1	.. 07.6	125 48.4	.. 30.0	94 19.7	.. 38.2	Rigil Kent.	139 45.7	S60 54.9
U 10	40 35.1	350 46.1	02.7	298 22.8	07.5	140 51.2	30.0	109 22.3	38.2	Sabik	102 07.6	S15 44.8
N 11	55 37.6	5 45.5	03.5	313 23.5	07.3	155 54.0	30.0	124 24.9	38.2			
D 12	70 40.0	20 45.0	N17 04.4	328 24.2	N24 07.2	170 56.8	S22 30.0	139 27.5	S21 38.2	Schedar	349 36.2	N56 38.2
A 13	85 42.5	35 44.4	05.2	343 24.9	07.1	185 59.6	30.0	154 30.1	38.2	Shaula	96 16.0	S37 06.9
Y 14	100 45.0	50 43.8	06.1	358 25.6	06.9	201 02.4	29.9	169 32.7	38.3	Sirius	258 30.5	S16 44.8
15	115 47.4	65 43.2	.. 06.9	13 26.4	.. 06.8	216 05.2	.. 29.9	184 35.3	.. 38.3	Spica	158 26.8	S11 15.7
16	130 49.9	80 42.6	07.8	28 27.1	06.7	231 08.0	29.9	199 37.9	38.3	Suhail	222 49.7	S43 30.9
17	145 52.4	95 42.0	08.6	43 27.8	06.5	246 10.8	29.9	214 40.5	38.3			
18	160 54.8	110 41.4	N17 09.5	58 28.5	N24 06.4	261 13.6	S22 29.9	229 43.1	S21 38.3	Vega	80 35.8	N38 48.1
19	175 57.3	125 40.8	10.3	73 29.2	06.3	276 16.4	29.8	244 45.7	38.4	Zuben'ubi	137 00.6	S16 07.2
20	190 59.8	140 40.2	11.2	88 29.9	06.1	291 19.2	29.8	259 48.3	38.4		SHA	Mer.Pass.
21	206 02.2	155 39.6	.. 12.0	103 30.6	.. 06.0	306 22.0	.. 29.8	274 50.9	.. 38.4		° '	h m
22	221 04.7	170 39.0	12.8	118 31.3	05.9	321 24.8	29.8	289 53.5	38.4	Venus	311 54.7	10 36
23	236 07.1	185 38.4	13.7	133 32.1	05.7	336 27.6	29.8	304 56.1	38.4	Mars	258 47.3	14 07
	h m									Jupiter	100 04.7	0 43
Mer.Pass.	7 22.0	v −0.6	d 0.9	v 0.7	d 0.1	v 2.8	d 0.0	v 2.6	d 0.0	Saturn	68 42.8	2 48

© British Crown Copyright 2018. All rights reserved.

UT	SUN GHA	SUN Dec	MOON GHA	v	MOON Dec	d	HP
31 00	180 36.1	N21 50.4	220 49.6	14.0	N 5 49.2	11.6	55.8
01	195 36.0	50.7	235 22.6	14.0	6 00.8	11.5	55.8
02	210 36.0	51.1	249 55.6	13.9	6 12.3	11.6	55.9
03	225 35.9	.. 51.5	264 28.5	13.8	6 23.9	11.5	55.9
04	240 35.8	51.8	279 01.3	13.8	6 35.4	11.6	55.9
05	255 35.7	52.2	293 34.1	13.7	6 47.0	11.5	55.9
06	270 35.6	N21 52.5	308 06.8	13.7	N 6 58.5	11.5	56.0
07	285 35.5	52.9	322 39.5	13.6	7 10.0	11.4	56.0
F 08	300 35.4	53.3	337 12.1	13.6	7 21.4	11.5	56.0
R 09	315 35.3	.. 53.6	351 44.7	13.5	7 32.9	11.4	56.1
I 10	330 35.2	54.0	6 17.2	13.4	7 44.3	11.4	56.1
11	345 35.1	54.3	20 49.6	13.4	7 55.7	11.4	56.1
D 12	0 35.0	N21 54.7	35 22.0	13.3	N 8 07.1	11.3	56.1
A 13	15 35.0	55.0	49 54.3	13.3	8 18.4	11.4	56.2
Y 14	30 34.9	55.4	64 26.6	13.2	8 29.8	11.3	56.2
15	45 34.8	.. 55.7	78 58.8	13.1	8 41.1	11.3	56.2
16	60 34.7	56.1	93 30.9	13.1	8 52.4	11.2	56.2
17	75 34.6	56.4	108 03.0	13.0	9 03.6	11.2	56.3
18	90 34.5	N21 56.8	122 35.0	12.9	N 9 14.8	11.2	56.3
19	105 34.4	57.1	137 06.9	12.9	9 26.0	11.2	56.3
20	120 34.3	57.5	151 38.8	12.8	9 37.2	11.1	56.4
21	135 34.2	.. 57.9	166 10.6	12.8	9 48.3	11.1	56.4
22	150 34.1	58.2	180 42.4	12.7	9 59.4	11.0	56.4
23	165 34.0	58.5	195 14.1	12.6	10 10.4	11.0	56.4
1 00	180 33.9	N21 58.9	209 45.7	12.5	N10 21.4	11.0	56.5
01	195 33.8	59.2	224 17.2	12.5	10 32.4	11.0	56.5
02	210 33.7	59.6	238 48.7	12.4	10 43.4	10.9	56.5
03	225 33.7	21 59.9	253 20.1	12.3	10 54.3	10.8	56.6
04	240 33.6	22 00.3	267 51.4	12.3	11 05.1	10.9	56.6
05	255 33.5	00.6	282 22.7	12.2	11 16.0	10.7	56.6
06	270 33.4	N22 01.0	296 53.9	12.1	N11 26.7	10.8	56.6
07	285 33.3	01.3	311 25.0	12.0	11 37.5	10.7	56.7
S 08	300 33.2	01.7	325 56.0	12.0	11 48.2	10.6	56.7
A 09	315 33.1	.. 02.0	340 27.0	11.9	11 58.8	10.6	56.7
T 10	330 33.0	02.3	354 57.9	11.8	12 09.4	10.6	56.8
U 11	345 32.9	02.7	9 28.7	11.7	12 20.0	10.5	56.8
R 12	0 32.8	N22 03.0	23 59.4	11.7	N12 30.5	10.4	56.8
D 13	15 32.7	03.4	38 30.1	11.6	12 40.9	10.4	56.8
A 14	30 32.6	03.7	53 00.7	11.5	12 51.3	10.3	56.9
Y 15	45 32.5	.. 04.0	67 31.2	11.4	13 01.6	10.3	56.9
16	60 32.4	04.4	82 01.6	11.3	13 11.9	10.3	56.9
17	75 32.3	04.7	96 31.9	11.3	13 22.2	10.1	57.0
18	90 32.2	N22 05.0	111 02.2	11.2	N13 32.3	10.2	57.0
19	105 32.1	05.4	125 32.4	11.1	13 42.5	10.0	57.0
20	120 32.0	05.7	140 02.5	11.0	13 52.5	10.0	57.0
21	135 31.9	.. 06.0	154 32.5	11.0	14 02.5	10.0	57.1
22	150 31.8	06.4	169 02.5	10.8	14 12.5	9.8	57.1
23	165 31.7	06.7	183 32.3	10.8	14 22.3	9.9	57.1
2 00	180 31.6	N22 07.0	198 02.1	10.7	N14 32.2	9.7	57.2
01	195 31.5	07.4	212 31.8	10.6	14 41.9	9.7	57.2
02	210 31.4	07.7	227 01.4	10.6	14 51.6	9.6	57.2
03	225 31.3	.. 08.0	241 31.0	10.4	15 01.2	9.6	57.2
04	240 31.2	08.4	256 00.4	10.4	15 10.8	9.4	57.3
05	255 31.1	08.7	270 29.8	10.3	15 20.2	9.4	57.3
06	270 31.0	N22 09.0	284 59.1	10.2	N15 29.6	9.4	57.3
07	285 30.9	09.4	299 28.3	10.1	15 39.0	9.2	57.4
08	300 30.8	09.7	313 57.4	10.0	15 48.2	9.2	57.4
S 09	315 30.7	.. 10.0	328 26.4	10.0	15 57.4	9.1	57.4
U 10	330 30.6	10.3	342 55.4	9.8	16 06.5	9.0	57.4
N 11	345 30.5	10.7	357 24.2	9.8	16 15.5	9.0	57.5
D 12	0 30.4	N22 11.0	11 53.0	9.7	N16 24.5	8.8	57.5
A 13	15 30.3	11.3	26 21.7	9.6	16 33.3	8.8	57.5
Y 14	30 30.2	11.6	40 50.3	9.5	16 42.1	8.7	57.6
15	45 30.1	.. 11.9	55 18.8	9.5	16 50.8	8.6	57.6
16	60 30.0	12.3	69 47.3	9.3	16 59.4	8.6	57.6
17	75 29.9	12.6	84 15.6	9.3	17 08.0	8.4	57.6
18	90 29.8	N22 12.9	98 43.9	9.2	N17 16.4	8.4	57.7
19	105 29.7	13.2	113 12.1	9.1	17 24.8	8.2	57.7
20	120 29.6	13.5	127 40.2	9.0	17 33.0	8.2	57.7
21	135 29.5	.. 13.9	142 08.2	8.9	17 41.2	8.1	57.7
22	150 29.4	14.2	156 36.1	8.8	17 49.3	8.0	57.8
23	165 29.3	14.5	171 03.9	8.8	N17 57.3	7.9	57.8
	SD 15.8	d 0.3	SD 15.3		15.5		15.7

Lat.	Twilight Naut.	Twilight Civil	Sunrise	Moonrise 31	1	2	3
N 72	☐	☐	☐	02 04	01 44	(01 17 / 23 56)	☐
N 70	☐	☐	☐	02 12	02 01	01 47	01 24
68	☐	☐	☐	02 19	02 14	02 10	02 04
66	////	////	01 14	02 25	02 25	02 27	02 32
64	////	////	01 59	02 30	02 35	02 42	02 53
62	////	00 06	02 28	02 34	02 43	02 54	03 10
60	////	01 27	02 50	02 38	02 50	03 04	03 25
N 58	////	02 01	03 08	02 41	02 56	03 13	03 37
56	00 06	02 25	03 22	02 44	03 01	03 22	03 48
54	01 19	02 44	03 35	02 47	03 06	03 29	03 57
52	01 51	03 00	03 46	02 50	03 11	03 35	04 06
50	02 13	03 14	03 56	02 52	03 15	03 41	04 13
45	02 53	03 41	04 17	02 57	03 23	03 54	04 30
N 40	03 21	04 01	04 33	03 01	03 31	04 04	04 43
35	03 42	04 18	04 47	03 05	03 37	04 13	04 54
30	04 00	04 32	05 00	03 08	03 43	04 21	05 04
20	04 27	04 56	05 20	03 14	03 53	04 35	05 22
N 10	04 48	05 15	05 38	03 19	04 01	04 47	05 37
0	05 06	05 32	05 54	03 23	04 09	04 58	05 51
S 10	05 22	05 48	06 10	03 28	04 18	05 10	06 06
20	05 37	06 04	06 28	03 33	04 26	05 22	06 21
30	05 52	06 21	06 48	03 39	04 37	05 37	06 39
35	06 00	06 31	06 59	03 42	04 42	05 45	06 49
40	06 08	06 42	07 12	03 46	04 49	05 54	07 01
45	06 18	06 55	07 28	03 51	04 57	06 05	07 15
S 50	06 28	07 09	07 47	03 56	05 07	06 19	07 32
52	06 33	07 16	07 56	03 59	05 11	06 25	07 40
54	06 38	07 23	08 06	04 01	05 16	06 32	07 50
56	06 44	07 32	08 17	04 04	05 21	06 40	08 00
58	06 50	07 41	08 30	04 08	05 27	06 49	08 12
S 60	06 56	07 51	08 46	04 12	05 34	06 59	08 25

Lat.	Sunset	Twilight Civil	Twilight Naut.	Moonset 31	1	2	3
N 72	☐	☐	☐	17 47	19 55	23 03	☐
N 70	☐	☐	☐	17 32	19 26	21 36	☐
68	☐	☐	☐	17 21	19 05	20 57	22 59
66	22 46	////	////	17 11	18 48	20 30	22 14
64	21 59	////	////	17 03	18 35	20 10	21 44
62	21 29	////	////	16 56	18 24	19 53	21 22
60	21 07	22 31	////	16 50	18 14	19 40	21 04
N 58	20 49	21 56	////	16 45	18 06	19 28	20 49
56	20 34	21 32	////	16 41	17 58	19 18	20 36
54	20 21	21 13	22 39	16 37	17 52	19 09	20 25
52	20 10	20 57	22 07	16 33	17 46	19 01	20 15
50	20 00	20 43	21 44	16 29	17 41	18 54	20 06
45	19 39	20 16	21 03	16 22	17 29	18 38	19 48
N 40	19 23	19 55	20 35	16 16	17 20	18 26	19 33
35	19 08	19 38	20 14	16 11	17 12	18 15	19 20
30	18 56	19 23	19 56	16 06	17 05	18 06	19 09
20	18 36	19 00	19 29	15 58	16 53	17 50	18 50
N 10	18 18	18 41	19 08	15 51	16 42	17 36	18 33
0	18 01	18 24	18 50	15 45	16 32	17 23	18 18
S 10	17 45	18 08	18 34	15 39	16 23	17 10	18 02
20	17 28	17 52	18 19	15 32	16 12	16 56	17 46
30	17 08	17 34	18 04	15 24	16 00	16 41	17 27
35	16 56	17 24	17 56	15 19	15 53	16 32	17 16
40	16 43	17 13	17 47	15 14	15 46	16 21	17 03
45	16 28	17 01	17 38	15 08	15 36	16 09	16 48
S 50	16 09	16 46	17 27	15 01	15 26	15 54	16 30
52	16 00	16 39	17 22	14 58	15 21	15 48	16 22
54	15 49	16 32	17 17	14 55	15 15	15 40	16 12
56	15 38	16 24	17 12	14 51	15 09	15 32	16 02
58	15 25	16 14	17 06	14 46	15 02	15 22	15 49
S 60	15 09	16 04	16 59	14 42	14 54	15 11	15 35

Day	SUN Eqn. of Time 00h	12h	Mer. Pass.	MOON Mer. Pass. Upper	Lower	Age	Phase
	m s	m s	h m	h m	h m	d	%
31	02 25	02 20	11 58	09 34	21 57	27	10
1	02 16	02 11	11 58	10 21	22 45	28	4
2	02 07	02 02	11 58	11 11	23 37	29	1

© British Crown Copyright 2018. All rights reserved.

UT	ARIES GHA	VENUS −3.8 GHA	Dec	MARS +1.8 GHA	Dec	JUPITER −2.6 GHA	Dec	SATURN +0.3 GHA	Dec	STARS Name	SHA	Dec
d h												
3 00	251 09.6	200 37.8	N17 14.5	148 32.8	N24 05.6	351 30.4	S22 29.8	319 58.7	S21 38.5	Acamar	315 15.6	S40 13.7
01	266 12.1	215 37.2	15.4	163 33.5	05.5	6 33.2	29.7	335 01.3	38.5	Achernar	335 24.1	S57 08.3
02	281 14.5	230 36.6	16.2	178 34.2	05.3	21 36.0	29.7	350 03.9	38.5	Acrux	173 04.4	S63 12.6
03	296 17.0	245 36.0 ..	17.1	193 34.9 ..	05.2	36 38.8 ..	29.7	5 06.5 ..	38.5	Adhara	255 09.7	S29 00.1
04	311 19.5	260 35.4	17.9	208 35.6	05.1	51 41.6	29.7	20 09.1	38.6	Aldebaran	290 45.1	N16 32.7
05	326 21.9	275 34.8	18.7	223 36.3	04.9	66 44.4	29.7	35 11.7	38.6			
06	341 24.4	290 34.2	N17 19.6	238 37.1	N24 04.8	81 47.2	S22 29.6	50 14.3	S21 38.6	Alioth	166 16.8	N55 51.6
07	356 26.9	305 33.6	20.4	253 37.8	04.6	96 50.0	29.6	65 16.9	38.6	Alkaid	152 55.4	N49 13.3
08	11 29.3	320 33.0	21.2	268 38.5	04.5	111 52.8	29.6	80 19.5	38.6	Alnair	27 38.5	S46 51.8
M 09	26 31.8	335 32.4 ..	22.1	283 39.2 ..	04.4	126 55.6 ..	29.6	95 22.1 ..	38.7	Alnilam	275 42.6	S 1 11.6
O 10	41 34.3	350 31.8	22.9	298 39.9	04.2	141 58.4	29.6	110 24.7	38.7	Alphard	217 52.2	S 8 44.7
N 11	56 36.7	5 31.2	23.7	313 40.6	04.1	157 01.2	29.6	125 27.3	38.7			
D 12	71 39.2	20 30.6	N17 24.6	328 41.3	N24 03.9	172 04.0	S22 29.5	140 29.9	S21 38.7	Alphecca	126 07.2	N26 39.2
A 13	86 41.6	35 30.0	25.4	343 42.1	03.8	187 06.8	29.5	155 32.4	38.7	Alpheratz	357 39.4	N29 11.6
Y 14	101 44.1	50 29.4	26.2	358 42.8	03.7	202 09.6	29.5	170 35.0	38.8	Altair	62 04.0	N 8 55.2
15	116 46.6	65 28.7 ..	27.1	13 43.5 ..	03.5	217 12.4 ..	29.5	185 37.6 ..	38.8	Ankaa	353 11.9	S42 12.0
16	131 49.0	80 28.1	27.9	28 44.2	03.4	232 15.3	29.5	200 40.2	38.8	Antares	112 20.9	S26 28.4
17	146 51.5	95 27.5	28.7	43 44.9	03.2	247 18.1	29.4	215 42.8	38.8			
18	161 54.0	110 26.9	N17 29.5	58 45.6	N24 03.1	262 20.9	S22 29.4	230 45.4	S21 38.8	Arcturus	145 51.8	N19 05.1
19	176 56.4	125 26.3	30.4	73 46.4	03.0	277 23.7	29.4	245 48.0	38.9	Atria	107 18.5	S69 03.6
20	191 58.9	140 25.7	31.2	88 47.1	02.8	292 26.5	29.4	260 50.6	38.9	Avior	234 16.8	S59 34.6
21	207 01.4	155 25.1 ..	32.0	103 47.8 ..	02.7	307 29.3 ..	29.4	275 53.2 ..	38.9	Bellatrix	278 28.0	N 6 21.8
22	222 03.8	170 24.5	32.8	118 48.5	02.5	322 32.1	29.4	290 55.8	38.9	Betelgeuse	270 57.2	N 7 24.5
23	237 06.3	185 23.9	33.7	133 49.2	02.4	337 34.9	29.3	305 58.4	38.9			
4 00	252 08.8	200 23.3	N17 34.5	148 49.9	N24 02.3	352 37.7	S22 29.3	321 01.0	S21 39.0	Canopus	263 54.9	S52 42.6
01	267 11.2	215 22.7	35.3	163 50.6	02.1	7 40.5	29.3	336 03.6	39.0	Capella	280 28.9	N46 00.9
02	282 13.7	230 22.0	36.1	178 51.4	02.0	22 43.3	29.3	351 06.2	39.0	Deneb	49 28.5	N45 20.8
03	297 16.1	245 21.4 ..	37.0	193 52.1 ..	01.8	37 46.1 ..	29.3	6 08.8 ..	39.0	Denebola	182 29.5	N14 28.0
04	312 18.6	260 20.8	37.8	208 52.8	01.7	52 48.9	29.2	21 11.4	39.1	Diphda	348 52.0	S17 52.9
05	327 21.1	275 20.2	38.6	223 53.5	01.5	67 51.7	29.2	36 14.1	39.1			
06	342 23.5	290 19.6	N17 39.4	238 54.2	N24 01.4	82 54.5	S22 29.2	51 16.7	S21 39.1	Dubhe	193 46.7	N61 39.1
07	357 26.0	305 19.0	40.2	253 54.9	01.2	97 57.3	29.2	66 19.3	39.1	Elnath	278 07.9	N28 37.2
T 08	12 28.5	320 18.4	41.1	268 55.7	01.1	113 00.1	29.2	81 21.9	39.1	Eltanin	90 43.7	N51 29.2
U 09	27 30.9	335 17.8 ..	41.9	283 56.4 ..	01.0	128 02.9 ..	29.2	96 24.5 ..	39.2	Enif	33 43.0	N 9 57.7
E 10	42 33.4	350 17.1	42.7	298 57.1	00.8	143 05.7	29.1	111 27.1	39.2	Fomalhaut	15 19.5	S29 31.1
S 11	57 35.9	5 16.5	43.5	313 57.8	00.7	158 08.5	29.1	126 29.7	39.2			
D 12	72 38.3	20 15.9	N17 44.3	328 58.5	N24 00.5	173 11.3	S22 29.1	141 32.3	S21 39.2	Gacrux	171 56.1	S57 13.5
A 13	87 40.8	35 15.3	45.1	343 59.2	00.4	188 14.1	29.1	156 34.9	39.2	Gienah	175 48.0	S17 39.0
Y 14	102 43.2	50 14.7	45.9	359 00.0	00.2	203 16.9	29.1	171 37.5	39.3	Hadar	148 41.6	S60 28.0
15	117 45.7	65 14.1 ..	46.7	14 00.7	24 00.1	218 19.7 ..	29.0	186 40.1 ..	39.3	Hamal	327 56.4	N23 33.0
16	132 48.2	80 13.4	47.6	29 01.4	23 59.9	233 22.5	29.0	201 42.7	39.3	Kaus Aust.	83 38.1	S34 22.3
17	147 50.6	95 12.8	48.4	44 02.1	59.8	248 25.3	29.0	216 45.3	39.3			
18	162 53.1	110 12.2	N17 49.2	59 02.8	N23 59.6	263 28.1	S22 29.0	231 47.9	S21 39.3	Kochab	137 19.1	N74 04.8
19	177 55.6	125 11.6	50.0	74 03.5	59.5	278 30.9	29.0	246 50.5	39.4	Markab	13 34.3	N15 18.4
20	192 58.0	140 11.0	50.8	89 04.3	59.3	293 33.8	29.0	261 53.1	39.4	Menkar	314 11.1	N 4 09.7
21	208 00.5	155 10.3 ..	51.6	104 05.0 ..	59.2	308 36.6 ..	28.9	276 55.7 ..	39.4	Menkent	148 02.5	S36 27.9
22	223 03.0	170 09.7	52.4	119 05.7	59.0	323 39.4	28.9	291 58.3	39.4	Miaplacidus	221 39.3	S69 48.1
23	238 05.4	185 09.1	53.2	134 06.4	58.9	338 42.2	28.9	307 00.9	39.5			
5 00	253 07.9	200 08.5	N17 54.0	149 07.1	N23 58.7	353 45.0	S22 28.9	322 03.5	S21 39.5	Mirfak	308 35.0	N49 55.5
01	268 10.4	215 07.9	54.8	164 07.9	58.6	8 47.8	28.9	337 06.1	39.5	Nunki	75 53.0	S26 16.2
02	283 12.8	230 07.2	55.6	179 08.6	58.4	23 50.6	28.9	352 08.7	39.5	Peacock	53 12.5	S56 40.1
03	298 15.3	245 06.6 ..	56.4	194 09.3 ..	58.3	38 53.4 ..	28.8	7 11.3 ..	39.5	Pollux	243 23.1	N27 58.7
04	313 17.7	260 06.0	57.2	209 10.0	58.1	53 56.2	28.8	22 13.9	39.6	Procyon	244 55.8	N 5 10.4
05	328 20.2	275 05.4	58.0	224 10.7	58.0	68 59.0	28.8	37 16.5	39.6			
06	343 22.7	290 04.7	N17 58.8	239 11.4	N23 57.8	84 01.8	S22 28.8	52 19.1	S21 39.6	Rasalhague	96 02.4	N12 32.9
W 07	358 25.1	305 04.1	17 59.6	254 12.2	57.7	99 04.6	28.7	67 21.7	39.6	Regulus	207 39.3	N11 52.4
E 08	13 27.6	320 03.5	18 00.4	269 12.9	57.5	114 07.4	28.7	82 24.3	39.6	Rigel	281 08.5	S 8 11.0
D 09	28 30.1	335 02.9 ..	01.2	284 13.6 ..	57.4	129 10.2 ..	28.7	97 26.9 ..	39.7	Rigil Kent.	139 45.7	S60 54.9
N 10	43 32.5	350 02.2	02.0	299 14.3	57.2	144 13.0	28.7	112 29.5	39.7	Sabik	102 07.5	S15 44.8
E 11	58 35.0	5 01.6	02.8	314 15.0	57.0	159 15.8	28.7	127 32.1	39.7			
S 12	73 37.5	20 01.0	N18 03.6	329 15.8	N23 56.9	174 18.6	S22 28.7	142 34.7	S21 39.7	Schedar	349 36.1	N56 38.2
D 13	88 39.9	35 00.3	04.4	344 16.5	56.7	189 21.4	28.6	157 37.4	39.8	Shaula	96 16.0	S37 06.9
A 14	103 42.4	49 59.7	05.2	359 17.2	56.6	204 24.2	28.6	172 40.0	39.8	Sirius	258 30.5	S16 44.8
Y 15	118 44.9	64 59.1 ..	06.0	14 17.9 ..	56.4	219 27.0 ..	28.6	187 42.6 ..	39.8	Spica	158 26.8	S11 15.7
16	133 47.3	79 58.5	06.8	29 18.6	56.3	234 29.9	28.6	202 45.2	39.8	Suhail	222 49.7	S43 30.9
17	148 49.8	94 57.8	07.6	44 19.4	56.1	249 32.7	28.6	217 47.8	39.8			
18	163 52.2	109 57.2	N18 08.4	59 20.1	N23 56.0	264 35.5	S22 28.5	232 50.4	S21 39.9	Vega	80 35.8	N38 48.1
19	178 54.7	124 56.6	09.2	74 20.8	55.8	279 38.3	28.5	247 53.0	39.9	Zuben'ubi	137 00.6	S16 07.2
20	193 57.2	139 55.9	09.9	89 21.5	55.6	294 41.1	28.5	262 55.6	39.9		SHA	Mer. Pass.
21	208 59.6	154 55.3 ..	10.7	104 22.2 ..	55.5	309 43.9 ..	28.5	277 58.2 ..	39.9	Venus	308 14.5	10 39
22	224 02.1	169 54.7	11.5	119 23.0	55.3	324 46.7	28.5	293 00.8	39.9	Mars	256 41.2	14 04
23	239 04.6	184 54.0	12.3	134 23.7	55.2	339 49.5	28.4	308 03.4	40.0	Jupiter	100 28.9	0 29
Mer. Pass.	h m 7 10.2	v −0.6	d 0.8	v 0.7	d 0.1	v 2.8	d 0.0	v 2.6	d 0.0	Saturn	68 52.3	2 35

© British Crown Copyright 2018. All rights reserved.

SUN and MOON

UT (d h)	SUN GHA	SUN Dec	MOON GHA	v	MOON Dec	d	HP
3 00	180 29.2	N22 14.8	185 31.7	8.7	N18 05.2	7.8	57.8
01	195 29.1	15.1	199 59.4	8.5	18 13.0	7.7	57.9
02	210 29.0	15.4	214 26.9	8.6	18 20.7	7.6	57.9
03	225 28.9	.. 15.8	228 54.5	8.4	18 28.3	7.5	57.9
04	240 28.8	16.1	243 21.9	8.3	18 35.8	7.4	57.9
05	255 28.7	16.4	257 49.2	8.3	18 43.2	7.3	58.0
06	270 28.6	N22 16.7	272 16.5	8.1	N18 50.5	7.2	58.0
07	285 28.5	17.0	286 43.6	8.1	18 57.7	7.1	58.0
08	300 28.4	17.3	301 10.7	8.0	19 04.8	7.0	58.0
M 09	315 28.3	.. 17.6	315 37.7	8.0	19 11.8	6.8	58.1
O 10	330 28.2	17.9	330 04.7	7.8	19 18.6	6.8	58.1
N 11	345 28.1	18.2	344 31.5	7.8	19 25.4	6.7	58.1
D 12	0 28.0	N22 18.5	358 58.3	7.7	N19 32.1	6.5	58.1
A 13	15 27.9	18.9	13 25.0	7.6	19 38.6	6.4	58.2
Y 14	30 27.8	19.2	27 51.6	7.5	19 45.0	6.4	58.2
15	45 27.7	.. 19.5	42 18.1	7.5	19 51.4	6.2	58.2
16	60 27.6	19.8	56 44.6	7.4	19 57.6	6.1	58.2
17	75 27.5	20.1	71 11.0	7.3	20 03.7	5.9	58.3
18	90 27.4	N22 20.4	85 37.3	7.2	N20 09.6	5.9	58.3
19	105 27.3	20.7	100 03.5	7.2	20 15.5	5.7	58.3
20	120 27.1	21.0	114 29.7	7.1	20 21.2	5.6	58.3
21	135 27.0	.. 21.3	128 55.8	7.0	20 26.8	5.5	58.4
22	150 26.9	21.6	143 21.8	6.9	20 32.3	5.4	58.4
23	165 26.8	21.9	157 47.7	6.9	20 37.7	5.2	58.4
4 00	180 26.7	N22 22.2	172 13.6	6.8	N20 42.9	5.2	58.4
01	195 26.6	22.5	186 39.4	6.7	20 48.1	5.0	58.4
02	210 26.5	22.8	201 05.1	6.7	20 53.1	4.8	58.5
03	225 26.4	.. 23.1	215 30.8	6.6	20 57.9	4.8	58.5
04	240 26.3	23.4	229 56.4	6.5	21 02.7	4.6	58.5
05	255 26.2	23.7	244 21.9	6.5	21 07.3	4.5	58.5
06	270 26.1	N22 24.0	258 47.4	6.4	N21 11.8	4.3	58.6
07	285 26.0	24.3	273 12.8	6.3	21 16.1	4.2	58.6
T 08	300 25.9	24.6	287 38.1	6.3	21 20.3	4.1	58.6
U 09	315 25.8	.. 24.9	302 03.4	6.3	21 24.4	4.0	58.6
E 10	330 25.7	25.1	316 28.7	6.1	21 28.4	3.8	58.6
S 11	345 25.5	25.4	330 53.8	6.1	21 32.2	3.7	58.7
D 12	0 25.4	N22 25.7	345 18.9	6.1	N21 35.9	3.5	58.7
A 13	15 25.3	26.0	359 44.0	6.0	21 39.4	3.4	58.7
Y 14	30 25.2	26.3	14 09.0	5.9	21 42.8	3.3	58.7
15	45 25.1	.. 26.6	28 33.9	5.9	21 46.1	3.1	58.7
16	60 25.0	26.9	42 58.8	5.9	21 49.2	3.0	58.8
17	75 24.9	27.2	57 23.7	5.8	21 52.2	2.9	58.8
18	90 24.8	N22 27.5	71 48.5	5.7	N21 55.1	2.7	58.8
19	105 24.7	27.7	86 13.2	5.7	21 57.8	2.5	58.8
20	120 24.6	28.0	100 37.9	5.7	22 00.3	2.5	58.8
21	135 24.5	.. 28.3	115 02.6	5.6	22 02.8	2.2	58.8
22	150 24.4	28.6	129 27.2	5.6	22 05.0	2.2	58.9
23	165 24.2	28.9	143 51.8	5.5	22 07.2	2.0	58.9
5 00	180 24.1	N22 29.2	158 16.3	5.5	N22 09.2	1.8	58.9
01	195 24.0	29.5	172 40.8	5.5	22 11.0	1.7	58.9
02	210 23.9	29.7	187 05.3	5.4	22 12.7	1.6	58.9
03	225 23.8	.. 30.0	201 29.7	5.4	22 14.3	1.4	59.0
04	240 23.7	30.3	215 54.1	5.4	22 15.7	1.2	59.0
05	255 23.6	30.6	230 18.5	5.3	22 16.9	1.2	59.0
06	270 23.5	N22 30.9	244 42.8	5.3	N22 18.1	0.9	59.0
W 07	285 23.4	31.1	259 07.1	5.3	22 19.0	0.8	59.0
E 08	300 23.3	31.4	273 31.4	5.3	22 19.8	0.7	59.0
D 09	315 23.1	.. 31.7	287 55.7	5.2	22 20.5	0.5	59.0
N 10	330 23.0	32.0	302 19.9	5.2	22 21.0	0.4	59.1
E 11	345 22.9	32.2	316 44.1	5.2	22 21.4	0.2	59.1
S 12	0 22.8	N22 32.5	331 08.3	5.2	N22 21.6	0.1	59.1
D 13	15 22.7	32.8	345 32.5	5.2	22 21.7	0.1	59.1
A 14	30 22.6	33.1	359 56.7	5.1	22 21.6	0.2	59.1
Y 15	45 22.5	.. 33.3	14 20.8	5.1	22 21.4	0.4	59.1
16	60 22.4	33.6	28 44.9	5.2	22 21.0	0.5	59.1
17	75 22.3	33.9	43 09.1	5.1	22 20.5	0.7	59.2
18	90 22.1	N22 34.2	57 33.2	5.1	N22 19.8	0.8	59.2
19	105 22.0	34.4	71 57.3	5.1	22 19.0	1.0	59.2
20	120 21.9	34.7	86 21.4	5.1	22 18.0	1.1	59.2
21	135 21.8	.. 35.0	100 45.5	5.1	22 16.9	1.3	59.2
22	150 21.7	35.2	115 09.6	5.1	22 15.6	1.4	59.2
23	165 21.6	35.5	129 33.7	5.1	N22 14.2	1.6	59.2
	SD 15.8	d 0.3	SD 15.8		16.0		16.1

Twilight — Sunrise — Moonrise

Lat.	Naut.	Civil	Sunrise	Moonrise 3	4	5	6
N 72	☐	☐	☐	☐	☐	☐	☐
N 70	☐	☐	☐	01 24	☐	☐	☐
68	☐	☐	☐	02 04	01 57	☐	02 42
66	////	////	01 01	02 32	02 43	03 12	04 16
64	////	////	01 52	02 53	03 13	03 50	04 54
62	////	////	02 23	03 10	03 36	04 18	05 21
60	////	01 19	02 46	03 25	03 55	04 39	05 42
N 58	////	01 55	03 04	03 37	04 10	04 56	05 59
56	////	02 21	03 19	03 48	04 23	05 11	06 13
54	01 12	02 41	03 33	03 57	04 35	05 24	06 26
52	01 46	02 57	03 44	04 06	04 45	05 35	06 37
50	02 09	03 11	03 54	04 13	04 54	05 45	06 47
45	02 51	03 39	04 15	04 30	05 13	06 06	07 07
N 40	03 19	04 00	04 32	04 43	05 29	06 22	07 24
35	03 41	04 17	04 47	04 54	05 42	06 37	07 38
30	03 59	04 32	04 59	05 04	05 54	06 49	07 50
20	04 27	04 56	05 20	05 22	06 14	07 10	08 11
N 10	04 48	05 15	05 38	05 37	06 31	07 29	08 29
0	05 06	05 32	05 55	05 51	06 47	07 46	08 46
S 10	05 22	05 49	06 11	06 06	07 04	08 03	09 03
20	05 38	06 05	06 29	06 21	07 21	08 22	09 21
30	05 53	06 23	06 49	06 39	07 42	08 43	09 42
35	06 01	06 33	07 01	06 49	07 53	08 56	09 54
40	06 10	06 44	07 14	07 01	08 07	09 10	10 08
45	06 20	06 57	07 30	07 15	08 23	09 27	10 24
S 50	06 31	07 12	07 50	07 32	08 44	09 49	10 45
52	06 36	07 19	07 59	07 40	08 53	09 59	10 54
54	06 41	07 26	08 09	07 50	09 04	10 10	11 05
56	06 47	07 35	08 21	08 00	09 16	10 23	11 18
58	06 53	07 44	08 35	08 12	09 30	10 38	11 32
S 60	07 00	07 55	08 51	08 25	09 47	10 56	11 49

Sunset — Twilight — Moonset

Lat.	Sunset	Civil	Naut.	Moonset 3	4	5	6
N 72	☐	☐	☐	☐	☐	☐	☐
N 70	☐	☐	☐	☐	☐	☐	☐
68	☐	☐	☐	22 59	☐	☐	02 21
66	23 00	////	////	22 14	23 47	24 47	00 47
64	22 07	////	////	21 44	23 08	24 09	00 09
62	21 35	////	////	21 22	22 41	23 42	24 23
60	21 12	22 41	////	21 04	22 20	23 21	24 05
N 58	20 53	22 03	////	20 49	22 03	23 04	23 50
56	20 38	21 37	////	20 36	21 48	22 49	23 37
54	20 25	21 17	22 47	20 25	21 36	22 37	23 25
52	20 13	21 00	22 12	20 15	21 25	22 25	23 15
50	20 03	20 46	21 48	20 06	21 15	22 16	23 06
45	19 42	20 18	21 07	19 48	20 54	21 55	22 47
N 40	19 25	19 57	20 38	19 33	20 37	21 38	22 32
35	19 10	19 40	20 16	19 20	20 23	21 24	22 19
30	18 58	19 25	19 58	19 09	20 11	21 11	22 07
20	18 37	19 01	19 30	18 50	19 50	20 50	21 48
N 10	18 19	18 42	19 09	18 33	19 32	20 32	21 30
0	18 02	18 24	18 49	18 18	19 15	20 14	21 14
S 10	17 45	18 08	18 34	18 02	18 58	19 57	20 58
20	17 28	17 51	18 19	17 46	18 40	19 39	20 40
30	17 07	17 34	18 03	17 27	18 19	19 17	20 20
35	16 56	17 24	17 55	17 16	18 07	19 05	20 08
40	16 42	17 12	17 46	17 03	17 53	18 50	19 55
45	16 26	17 00	17 37	16 48	17 36	18 33	19 39
S 50	16 07	16 45	17 27	16 30	17 16	18 12	19 19
52	15 57	16 38	17 21	16 22	17 06	18 02	19 09
54	15 47	16 30	17 15	16 12	16 55	17 50	18 59
56	15 35	16 21	17 10	16 02	16 42	17 37	18 47
58	15 22	16 12	17 04	15 49	16 28	17 22	18 33
S 60	15 06	16 01	16 57	15 35	16 11	17 04	18 16

SUN and MOON data

Day	SUN Eqn. of Time 00h	SUN Eqn. of Time 12h	SUN Mer. Pass.	MOON Mer. Pass. Upper	MOON Mer. Pass. Lower	Age	Phase
d	m s	m s	h m	h m	h m	d	%
3	01 57	01 52	11 58	12 04	24 32	00	0
4	01 47	01 42	11 58	13 01	00 32	01	1
5	01 37	01 31	11 58	14 00	01 30	02	5

© British Crown Copyright 2018. All rights reserved.

UT	ARIES GHA	VENUS −3.8 GHA Dec	MARS +1.8 GHA Dec	JUPITER −2.6 GHA Dec	SATURN +0.2 GHA Dec	STARS Name SHA Dec
6 00	254 07.0	199 53.4 N18 13.1	149 24.4 N23 55.0	354 52.3 S22 28.4	323 06.0 S21 40.0	Acamar 315 15.6 S40 13.7
01	269 09.5	214 52.8 13.9	164 25.1 54.9	9 55.1 28.4	338 08.6 40.0	Achernar 335 24.1 S57 08.2
02	284 12.0	229 52.1 14.7	179 25.8 54.7	24 57.9 28.4	353 11.2 40.0	Acrux 173 04.5 S63 12.6
03	299 14.4	244 51.5 .. 15.4	194 26.6 .. 54.5	40 00.7 .. 28.4	8 13.8 .. 40.1	Adhara 255 09.7 S29 00.1
04	314 16.9	259 50.9 16.2	209 27.3 54.4	55 03.5 28.4	23 16.4 40.1	Aldebaran 290 45.1 N16 32.7
05	329 19.4	274 50.2 17.0	224 28.0 54.2	70 06.3 28.3	38 19.1 40.1	
T 06	344 21.8	289 49.6 N18 17.8	239 28.7 N23 54.1	85 09.1 S22 28.3	53 21.7 S21 40.1	Alioth 166 16.9 N55 51.6
H 07	359 24.3	304 49.0 18.6	254 29.4 53.9	100 11.9 28.3	68 24.3 40.1	Alkaid 152 55.4 N49 13.3
U 08	14 26.7	319 48.3 19.3	269 30.2 53.7	115 14.8 28.3	83 26.9 40.2	Alnair 27 38.5 S46 51.8
R 09	29 29.2	334 47.7 .. 20.1	284 30.9 .. 53.6	130 17.6 .. 28.3	98 29.5 .. 40.2	Alnilam 275 42.6 S 1 11.6
S 10	44 31.7	349 47.0 20.9	299 31.6 53.4	145 20.4 28.2	113 32.1 40.2	Alphard 217 52.2 S 8 44.6
D 11	59 34.1	4 46.4 21.7	314 32.3 53.2	160 23.2 28.2	128 34.7 40.2	
A 12	74 36.6	19 45.8 N18 22.4	329 33.1 N23 53.1	175 26.0 S22 28.2	143 37.3 S21 40.3	Alphecca 126 07.2 N26 39.2
Y 13	89 39.1	34 45.1 23.2	344 33.8 52.9	190 28.8 28.2	158 39.9 40.3	Alpheratz 357 39.4 N29 11.6
14	104 41.5	49 44.5 24.0	359 34.5 52.8	205 31.6 28.2	173 42.5 40.3	Altair 62 04.0 N 8 55.2
15	119 44.0	64 43.8 .. 24.8	14 35.2 .. 52.6	220 34.4 .. 28.1	188 45.1 .. 40.3	Ankaa 353 11.8 S42 12.0
16	134 46.5	79 43.2 25.5	29 35.9 52.4	235 37.2 28.1	203 47.7 40.3	Antares 112 20.9 S26 28.4
17	149 48.9	94 42.6 26.3	44 36.7 52.3	250 40.0 28.1	218 50.3 40.4	
18	164 51.4	109 41.9 N18 27.1	59 37.4 N23 52.1	265 42.8 S22 28.1	233 53.0 S21 40.4	Arcturus 145 51.8 N19 05.1
19	179 53.9	124 41.3 27.9	74 38.1 51.9	280 45.6 28.1	248 55.6 40.4	Atria 107 18.5 S69 03.6
20	194 56.3	139 40.6 28.6	89 38.8 51.8	295 48.4 28.0	263 58.2 40.4	Avior 234 16.8 S59 34.6
21	209 58.8	154 40.0 .. 29.4	104 39.6 .. 51.6	310 51.2 .. 28.0	279 00.8 .. 40.4	Bellatrix 278 28.0 N 6 21.8
22	225 01.2	169 39.3 30.2	119 40.3 51.4	325 54.0 28.0	294 03.4 40.5	Betelgeuse 270 57.2 N 7 24.5
23	240 03.7	184 38.7 30.9	134 41.0 51.3	340 56.9 28.0	309 06.0 40.5	
7 00	255 06.2	199 38.1 N18 31.7	149 41.7 N23 51.1	355 59.7 S22 28.0	324 08.6 S21 40.5	Canopus 263 54.9 S52 42.6
01	270 08.6	214 37.4 32.5	164 42.4 51.0	11 02.5 28.0	339 11.2 40.5	Capella 280 28.9 N46 00.8
02	285 11.1	229 36.8 33.2	179 43.2 50.8	26 05.3 27.9	354 13.8 40.6	Deneb 49 28.4 N45 20.8
03	300 13.6	244 36.1 .. 34.0	194 43.9 .. 50.6	41 08.1 .. 27.9	9 16.4 .. 40.6	Denebola 182 29.5 N14 28.0
04	315 16.0	259 35.5 34.7	209 44.6 50.4	56 10.9 27.9	24 19.1 40.6	Diphda 348 52.0 S17 52.9
05	330 18.5	274 34.8 35.5	224 45.3 50.3	71 13.7 27.9	39 21.7 40.6	
F 06	345 21.0	289 34.2 N18 36.3	239 46.1 N23 50.1	86 16.5 S22 27.9	54 24.3 S21 40.6	Dubhe 193 46.8 N61 39.1
R 07	0 23.4	304 33.5 37.0	254 46.8 49.9	101 19.3 27.8	69 26.9 40.7	Elnath 278 07.9 N28 37.2
I 08	15 25.9	319 32.9 37.8	269 47.5 49.8	116 22.1 27.8	84 29.5 40.7	Eltanin 90 43.7 N51 29.2
D 09	30 28.4	334 32.2 .. 38.5	284 48.2 .. 49.6	131 24.9 .. 27.8	99 32.1 .. 40.7	Enif 33 43.0 N 9 57.7
A 10	45 30.8	349 31.6 39.3	299 49.0 49.4	146 27.7 27.8	114 34.7 40.7	Fomalhaut 15 19.5 S29 31.1
Y 11	60 33.3	4 30.9 40.1	314 49.7 49.3	161 30.5 27.8	129 37.3 40.8	
12	75 35.7	19 30.3 N18 40.8	329 50.4 N23 49.1	176 33.3 S22 27.7	144 39.9 S21 40.8	Gacrux 171 56.1 S57 13.5
13	90 38.2	34 29.6 41.6	344 51.1 48.9	191 36.2 27.7	159 42.5 40.8	Gienah 175 48.0 S17 39.0
14	105 40.7	49 29.0 42.3	359 51.8 48.8	206 39.0 27.7	174 45.2 40.8	Hadar 148 41.6 S60 28.0
15	120 43.1	64 28.3 .. 43.1	14 52.6 .. 48.6	221 41.8 .. 27.7	189 47.8 .. 40.8	Hamal 327 56.4 N23 33.0
16	135 45.6	79 27.7 43.8	29 53.3 48.4	236 44.6 27.7	204 50.4 40.9	Kaus Aust. 83 38.0 S34 22.3
17	150 48.1	94 27.0 44.6	44 54.0 48.2	251 47.4 27.6	219 53.0 40.9	
18	165 50.5	109 26.4 N18 45.3	59 54.7 N23 48.1	266 50.2 S22 27.6	234 55.6 S21 40.9	Kochab 137 19.1 N74 04.9
19	180 53.0	124 25.7 46.1	74 55.5 47.9	281 53.0 27.6	249 58.2 40.9	Markab 13 34.3 N15 18.4
20	195 55.5	139 25.1 46.8	89 56.2 47.7	296 55.8 27.6	265 00.8 41.0	Menkar 314 11.1 N 4 09.7
21	210 57.9	154 24.4 .. 47.6	104 56.9 .. 47.6	311 58.6 .. 27.6	280 03.4 .. 41.0	Menkent 148 02.5 S36 27.9
22	226 00.4	169 23.7 48.3	119 57.6 47.4	327 01.4 27.6	295 06.1 41.0	Miaplacidus 221 39.3 S69 48.1
23	241 02.8	184 23.1 49.1	134 58.4 47.2	342 04.2 27.5	310 08.7 41.0	
8 00	256 05.3	199 22.4 N18 49.8	149 59.1 N23 47.0	357 07.0 S22 27.5	325 11.3 S21 41.1	Mirfak 308 35.0 N49 55.5
01	271 07.8	214 21.8 50.6	164 59.8 46.9	12 09.8 27.5	340 13.9 41.1	Nunki 75 52.9 S26 16.2
02	286 10.2	229 21.1 51.3	180 00.5 46.7	27 12.7 27.5	355 16.5 41.1	Peacock 53 12.5 S56 40.1
03	301 12.7	244 20.5 .. 52.1	195 01.3 .. 46.5	42 15.5 .. 27.5	10 19.1 .. 41.1	Pollux 243 23.1 N27 58.7
04	316 15.2	259 19.8 52.8	210 02.0 46.3	57 18.3 27.4	25 21.7 41.1	Procyon 244 55.8 N 5 10.4
05	331 17.6	274 19.1 53.6	225 02.7 46.2	72 21.1 27.4	40 24.3 41.2	
S 06	346 20.1	289 18.5 N18 54.3	240 03.4 N23 46.0	87 23.9 S22 27.4	55 27.0 S21 41.2	Rasalhague 96 02.3 N12 32.9
A 07	1 22.6	304 17.8 55.0	255 04.2 45.8	102 26.7 27.4	70 29.6 41.2	Regulus 207 39.3 N11 52.4
T 08	16 25.0	319 17.2 55.8	270 04.9 45.6	117 29.5 27.4	85 32.2 41.2	Rigel 281 08.5 S 8 10.9
U 09	31 27.5	334 16.5 .. 56.5	285 05.6 .. 45.5	132 32.3 .. 27.3	100 34.8 .. 41.3	Rigil Kent. 139 45.7 S60 54.9
R 10	46 30.0	349 15.8 57.2	300 06.4 45.3	147 35.1 27.3	115 37.4 41.3	Sabik 102 07.5 S15 44.8
D 11	61 32.4	4 15.2 58.0	315 07.1 45.1	162 37.9 27.3	130 40.0 41.3	
A 12	76 34.9	19 14.5 N18 58.7	330 07.8 N23 44.9	177 40.7 S22 27.3	145 42.6 S21 41.3	Schedar 349 36.1 N56 38.2
Y 13	91 37.3	34 13.9 18 59.4	345 08.5 44.7	192 43.5 27.3	160 45.2 41.3	Shaula 96 16.0 S37 06.9
14	106 39.8	49 13.2 19 00.2	0 09.3 44.6	207 46.3 27.2	175 47.9 41.4	Sirius 258 30.5 S16 44.7
15	121 42.3	64 12.5 .. 00.9	15 10.0 .. 44.4	222 49.2 .. 27.2	190 50.5 .. 41.4	Spica 158 26.8 S11 15.7
16	136 44.7	79 11.9 01.6	30 10.7 44.2	237 52.0 27.2	205 53.1 41.4	Suhail 222 49.7 S43 30.9
17	151 47.2	94 11.2 02.4	45 11.4 44.0	252 54.8 27.2	220 55.7 41.4	
18	166 49.7	109 10.5 N19 03.1	60 12.2 N23 43.9	267 57.6 S22 27.2	235 58.3 S21 41.5	Vega 80 35.8 N38 48.1
19	181 52.1	124 09.9 03.8	75 12.9 43.7	283 00.4 27.1	251 00.9 41.5	Zuben'ubi 137 00.6 S16 07.2
20	196 54.6	139 09.2 04.6	90 13.6 43.5	298 03.2 27.1	266 03.5 41.5	
21	211 57.1	154 08.5 .. 05.3	105 14.3 .. 43.3	313 06.0 .. 27.1	281 06.2 .. 41.5	
22	226 59.5	169 07.9 06.0	120 15.1 43.1	328 08.8 27.1	296 08.8 41.5	
23	242 02.0	184 07.2 06.7	135 15.8 43.0	343 11.6 27.1	311 11.4 41.6	
Mer. Pass. h m 6 58.4		v −0.7 d 0.8	v 0.7 d 0.2	v 2.8 d 0.0	v 2.6 d 0.0	

	SHA	Mer. Pass.
Venus	304 31.9	10 42
Mars	254 35.5	14 01
Jupiter	100 53.5	0 16
Saturn	69 02.4	2 23

© British Crown Copyright 2018. All rights reserved.

UT	SUN GHA	SUN Dec	MOON GHA	v	MOON Dec	d	HP
6 00	180 21.5	N22 35.8	143 57.8	5.1	N22 12.6	1.7	59.2
01	195 21.4	36.0	158 21.9	5.1	22 10.9	1.9	59.3
02	210 21.2	36.3	172 46.0	5.1	22 09.0	2.0	59.3
03	225 21.1 ..	36.6	187 10.1	5.1	22 07.0	2.2	59.3
04	240 21.0	36.8	201 34.2	5.1	22 04.8	2.4	59.3
05	255 20.9	37.1	215 58.3	5.2	22 02.4	2.4	59.3
06	270 20.8	N22 37.3	230 22.5	5.1	N22 00.0	2.7	59.3
07	285 20.7	37.6	244 46.6	5.2	21 57.3	2.7	59.3
T 08	300 20.6	37.9	259 10.8	5.2	21 54.6	3.0	59.3
H 09	315 20.5 ..	38.1	273 35.0	5.2	21 51.6	3.0	59.3
U 10	330 20.3	38.4	287 59.2	5.2	21 48.6	3.2	59.3
R 11	345 20.2	38.7	302 23.4	5.2	21 45.4	3.4	59.4
S 12	0 20.1	N22 38.9	316 47.6	5.3	N21 42.0	3.5	59.4
D 13	15 20.0	39.2	331 11.9	5.3	21 38.5	3.7	59.4
A 14	30 19.9	39.4	345 36.2	5.3	21 34.8	3.8	59.4
Y 15	45 19.8 ..	39.7	0 00.5	5.3	21 31.0	3.9	59.4
16	60 19.7	39.9	14 24.8	5.4	21 27.1	4.1	59.4
17	75 19.5	40.2	28 49.2	5.4	21 23.0	4.3	59.4
18	90 19.4	N22 40.4	43 13.6	5.4	N21 18.7	4.3	59.4
19	105 19.3	40.7	57 38.0	5.5	21 14.4	4.6	59.4
20	120 19.2	41.0	72 02.5	5.5	21 09.8	4.6	59.4
21	135 19.1 ..	41.2	86 27.0	5.5	21 05.2	4.8	59.5
22	150 19.0	41.5	100 51.5	5.6	21 00.4	5.0	59.4
23	165 18.8	41.7	115 16.1	5.6	20 55.4	5.1	59.4
7 00	180 18.7	N22 42.0	129 40.7	5.6	N20 50.3	5.2	59.4
01	195 18.6	42.2	144 05.3	5.7	20 45.1	5.3	59.4
02	210 18.5	42.5	158 30.0	5.7	20 39.8	5.5	59.5
03	225 18.4 ..	42.7	172 54.7	5.8	20 34.3	5.7	59.5
04	240 18.3	43.0	187 19.5	5.8	20 28.6	5.8	59.5
05	255 18.1	43.2	201 44.3	5.9	20 22.8	5.9	59.5
06	270 18.0	N22 43.4	216 09.2	5.9	N20 16.9	6.0	59.5
07	285 17.9	43.7	230 34.1	5.9	20 10.9	6.2	59.5
F 08	300 17.8	43.9	244 59.0	6.0	20 04.7	6.3	59.5
R 09	315 17.7 ..	44.2	259 24.0	6.1	19 58.4	6.4	59.5
I 10	330 17.6	44.4	273 49.1	6.1	19 52.0	6.6	59.5
11	345 17.4	44.7	288 14.2	6.1	19 45.4	6.7	59.5
D 12	0 17.3	N22 44.9	302 39.3	6.2	N19 38.7	6.8	59.5
A 13	15 17.2	45.1	317 04.5	6.3	19 31.9	6.9	59.5
Y 14	30 17.1	45.4	331 29.8	6.3	19 25.0	7.1	59.5
15	45 17.0 ..	45.6	345 55.1	6.3	19 17.9	7.2	59.5
16	60 16.9	45.9	0 20.4	6.4	19 10.7	7.3	59.5
17	75 16.7	46.1	14 45.8	6.5	19 03.4	7.5	59.5
18	90 16.6	N22 46.3	29 11.3	6.5	N18 55.9	7.6	59.5
19	105 16.5	46.6	43 36.8	6.6	18 48.3	7.6	59.5
20	120 16.4	46.8	58 02.4	6.7	18 40.7	7.9	59.5
21	135 16.3 ..	47.1	72 28.1	6.7	18 32.8	7.9	59.5
22	150 16.2	47.3	86 53.8	6.7	18 24.9	8.0	59.5
23	165 16.0	47.5	101 19.5	6.8	18 16.9	8.2	59.5
8 00	180 15.9	N22 47.8	115 45.3	6.9	N18 08.7	8.3	59.5
01	195 15.8	48.0	130 11.2	7.0	18 00.4	8.3	59.5
02	210 15.7	48.2	144 37.2	7.0	17 52.1	8.5	59.5
03	225 15.6 ..	48.5	159 03.2	7.0	17 43.6	8.7	59.5
04	240 15.4	48.7	173 29.2	7.1	17 34.9	8.7	59.5
05	255 15.3	48.9	187 55.3	7.2	17 26.2	8.8	59.5
06	270 15.2	N22 49.1	202 21.5	7.3	N17 17.4	8.9	59.5
07	285 15.1	49.4	216 47.8	7.3	17 08.5	9.1	59.5
S 08	300 15.0	49.6	231 14.1	7.3	16 59.4	9.1	59.5
A 09	315 14.8 ..	49.8	245 40.4	7.5	16 50.3	9.3	59.5
T 10	330 14.7	50.1	260 06.9	7.5	16 41.0	9.4	59.5
U 11	345 14.6	50.3	274 33.4	7.5	16 31.6	9.4	59.5
R 12	0 14.5	N22 50.5	288 59.9	7.6	N16 22.2	9.6	59.5
D 13	15 14.4	50.7	303 26.5	7.7	16 12.6	9.6	59.5
A 14	30 14.2	51.0	317 53.2	7.8	16 03.0	9.8	59.5
Y 15	45 14.1 ..	51.2	332 20.0	7.8	15 53.2	9.8	59.5
16	60 14.0	51.4	346 46.8	7.9	15 43.4	10.0	59.5
17	75 13.9	51.6	1 13.7	7.9	15 33.4	10.0	59.5
18	90 13.8	N22 51.8	15 40.6	8.0	N15 23.4	10.1	59.5
19	105 13.6	52.1	30 07.6	8.1	15 13.3	10.2	59.5
20	120 13.5	52.3	44 34.7	8.1	15 03.1	10.3	59.5
21	135 13.4 ..	52.5	59 01.8	8.2	14 52.8	10.4	59.5
22	150 13.3	52.7	73 29.0	8.2	14 42.4	10.5	59.5
23	165 13.2	52.9	87 56.2	8.4	N14 31.9	10.6	59.4
	SD 15.8	d 0.2	SD 16.2		16.2		16.2

Lat.	Twilight Naut.	Twilight Civil	Sunrise	Moonrise 6	7	8	9
°	h m	h m	h m	h m	h m	h m	h m
N 72	☐	☐	☐	☐	☐	05 42	08 35
N 70	☐	☐	☐	☐	06 43	08 59	
68	☐	☐	☐	02 42	05 11	07 18	09 17
66	////	////	00 46	04 16	05 53	07 43	09 32
64	////	////	01 45	04 54	06 22	08 02	09 44
62	////	////	02 18	05 21	06 44	08 18	09 54
60	////	01 11	02 42	05 42	07 01	08 31	10 03
N 58	////	01 50	03 01	05 59	07 16	08 42	10 11
56	////	02 17	03 17	06 13	07 29	08 51	10 17
54	01 04	02 38	03 30	06 26	07 39	09 00	10 23
52	01 41	02 55	03 42	06 37	07 49	09 08	10 29
50	02 06	03 09	03 53	06 47	07 58	09 15	10 33
45	02 49	03 37	04 14	07 07	08 16	09 29	10 44
N 40	03 18	03 59	04 31	07 24	08 31	09 41	10 52
35	03 40	04 17	04 46	07 38	08 43	09 52	11 00
30	03 58	04 31	04 59	07 50	08 54	10 00	11 06
20	04 26	04 55	05 20	08 11	09 13	10 16	11 17
N 10	04 48	05 15	05 38	08 29	09 30	10 29	11 27
0	05 07	05 33	05 55	08 46	09 45	10 42	11 36
S 10	05 23	05 49	06 12	09 03	10 00	10 54	11 45
20	05 39	06 06	06 30	09 21	10 16	11 08	11 55
30	05 55	06 24	06 50	09 42	10 35	11 23	12 06
35	06 03	06 34	07 02	09 54	10 46	11 31	12 12
40	06 12	06 46	07 16	10 08	10 58	11 41	12 19
45	06 22	06 59	07 32	10 24	11 13	11 53	12 27
S 50	06 33	07 14	07 52	10 45	11 30	12 07	12 37
52	06 38	07 21	08 02	10 54	11 39	12 14	12 42
54	06 43	07 29	08 12	11 05	11 48	12 21	12 47
56	06 49	07 38	08 24	11 18	11 59	12 29	12 53
58	06 56	07 47	08 38	11 32	12 10	12 38	12 59
S 60	07 03	07 59	08 55	11 49	12 24	12 49	13 06

Lat.	Sunset	Twilight Civil	Twilight Naut.	Moonset 6	7	8	9
°	h m	h m	h m	h m	h m	h m	h m
N 72	☐	☐	☐	☐	☐	03 29	02 31
N 70	☐	☐	☐	☐	02 26	02 05	
68	☐	☐	☐	02 21	01 57	01 50	01 45
66	23 16	////	////	00 47	01 14	01 25	01 29
64	22 14	////	////	00 09	00 45	01 04	01 16
62	21 41	////	////	24 23	00 23	00 48	01 05
60	21 16	22 50	////	24 05	00 05	00 34	00 55
N 58	20 57	22 09	////	23 50	24 22	00 22	00 46
56	20 41	21 42	////	23 37	24 12	00 12	00 39
54	20 28	21 21	22 56	23 25	24 03	00 03	00 32
52	20 16	21 04	22 18	23 15	23 55	24 26	00 26
50	20 06	20 49	21 52	23 06	23 48	24 21	00 21
45	19 44	20 21	21 09	22 47	23 32	24 09	00 09
N 40	19 26	19 59	20 40	22 32	23 19	23 59	24 35
35	19 12	19 41	20 18	22 19	23 08	23 51	24 29
30	18 59	19 27	20 00	22 07	22 58	23 43	24 24
20	18 38	19 02	19 31	21 48	22 41	23 30	24 16
N 10	18 20	18 43	19 09	21 30	22 26	23 19	24 08
0	18 03	18 25	18 51	21 14	22 12	23 08	24 01
S 10	17 46	18 08	18 35	20 58	21 58	22 57	23 54
20	17 28	17 52	18 19	20 40	21 43	22 45	23 46
30	17 07	17 33	18 03	20 20	21 26	22 32	23 37
35	16 55	17 23	17 55	20 08	21 16	22 24	23 32
40	16 41	17 12	17 46	19 55	21 04	22 15	23 26
45	16 25	16 59	17 36	19 39	20 50	22 04	23 19
S 50	16 05	16 43	17 25	19 19	20 33	21 52	23 11
52	15 56	16 36	17 20	19 09	20 25	21 46	23 07
54	15 45	16 28	17 14	18 59	20 17	21 39	23 03
56	15 33	16 20	17 08	18 47	20 07	21 32	22 58
58	15 19	16 10	17 02	18 33	19 55	21 23	22 52
S 60	15 03	15 59	16 55	18 16	19 42	21 14	22 46

Day	SUN Eqn. of Time 00ʰ	SUN Eqn. of Time 12ʰ	SUN Mer. Pass.	MOON Mer. Pass. Upper	MOON Mer. Pass. Lower	Age	Phase
d	m s	m s	h m	h m	h m	d	%
6	01 26	01 21	11 59	15 00	02 30	03	12
7	01 15	01 10	11 59	15 59	03 30	04	20
8	01 04	00 58	11 59	16 55	04 27	05	30

© British Crown Copyright 2018. All rights reserved.

UT d h	ARIES GHA	VENUS −3.8 GHA	Dec	MARS +1.8 GHA	Dec	JUPITER −2.6 GHA	Dec	SATURN +0.2 GHA	Dec	STARS Name	SHA	Dec
9 00	257 04.5	199 06.5	N19 07.5	150 16.5	N23 42.8	358 14.4	S22 27.0	326 14.0	S21 41.6	Acamar	315 15.6	S40 13.7
01	272 06.9	214 05.9	08.2	165 17.3	42.6	13 17.2	27.0	341 16.6	41.6	Achernar	335 24.1	S57 08.2
02	287 09.4	229 05.2	08.9	180 18.0	42.4	28 20.0	27.0	356 19.2	41.6	Acrux	173 04.5	S63 12.6
03	302 11.8	244 04.5	.. 09.6	195 18.7	.. 42.2	43 22.9	.. 27.0	11 21.9	.. 41.7	Adhara	255 09.7	S29 00.1
04	317 14.3	259 03.9	10.4	210 19.4	42.1	58 25.7	27.0	26 24.5	41.7	Aldebaran	290 45.0	N16 32.7
05	332 16.8	274 03.2	11.1	225 20.2	41.9	73 28.5	26.9	41 27.1	41.7			
06	347 19.2	289 02.5	N19 11.8	240 20.9	N23 41.7	88 31.3	S22 26.9	56 29.7	S21 41.7	Alioth	166 16.9	N55 51.6
07	2 21.7	304 01.8	12.5	255 21.6	41.5	103 34.1	26.9	71 32.3	41.8	Alkaid	152 55.4	N49 13.3
08	17 24.2	319 01.2	13.2	270 22.4	41.3	118 36.9	26.9	86 34.9	41.8	Alnair	27 38.5	S46 51.8
S 09	32 26.6	334 00.5	.. 14.0	285 23.1	.. 41.1	133 39.7	.. 26.9	101 37.6	.. 41.8	Alnilam	275 42.6	S 1 11.6
U 10	47 29.1	348 59.8	14.7	300 23.8	41.0	148 42.5	26.9	116 40.2	41.8	Alphard	217 52.3	S 8 44.6
N 11	62 31.6	3 59.2	15.4	315 24.5	40.8	163 45.3	26.8	131 42.8	41.8			
D 12	77 34.0	18 58.5	N19 16.1	330 25.3	N23 40.6	178 48.1	S22 26.8	146 45.4	S21 41.9	Alphecca	126 07.2	N26 39.2
A 13	92 36.5	33 57.8	16.8	345 26.0	40.4	193 50.9	26.8	161 48.0	41.9	Alpheratz	357 39.4	N29 11.6
Y 14	107 39.0	48 57.1	17.5	0 26.7	40.2	208 53.7	26.8	176 50.6	41.9	Altair	62 04.0	N 8 55.2
15	122 41.4	63 56.5	.. 18.2	15 27.5	.. 40.0	223 56.6	.. 26.8	191 53.3	.. 41.9	Ankaa	353 11.8	S42 11.9
16	137 43.9	78 55.8	18.9	30 28.2	39.8	238 59.4	26.7	206 55.9	42.0	Antares	112 20.9	S26 28.4
17	152 46.3	93 55.1	19.7	45 28.9	39.7	254 02.2	26.7	221 58.5	42.0			
18	167 48.8	108 54.4	N19 20.4	60 29.6	N23 39.5	269 05.0	S22 26.7	237 01.1	S21 42.0	Arcturus	145 51.8	N19 05.1
19	182 51.3	123 53.8	21.1	75 30.4	39.3	284 07.8	26.7	252 03.7	42.0	Atria	107 18.5	S69 03.6
20	197 53.7	138 53.1	21.8	90 31.1	39.1	299 10.6	26.7	267 06.3	42.1	Avior	234 16.8	S59 34.5
21	212 56.2	153 52.4	.. 22.5	105 31.8	.. 38.9	314 13.4	.. 26.6	282 09.0	.. 42.1	Bellatrix	278 28.0	N 6 21.9
22	227 58.7	168 51.7	23.2	120 32.6	38.7	329 16.2	26.6	297 11.6	42.1	Betelgeuse	270 57.2	N 7 24.5
23	243 01.1	183 51.0	23.9	135 33.3	38.5	344 19.0	26.6	312 14.2	42.1			
10 00	258 03.6	198 50.4	N19 24.6	150 34.0	N23 38.4	359 21.8	S22 26.6	327 16.8	S21 42.1	Canopus	263 54.9	S52 42.5
01	273 06.1	213 49.7	25.3	165 34.8	38.2	14 24.6	26.6	342 19.4	42.2	Capella	280 28.9	N46 00.8
02	288 08.5	228 49.0	26.0	180 35.5	38.0	29 27.5	26.5	357 22.0	42.2	Deneb	49 28.4	N45 20.8
03	303 11.0	243 48.3	.. 26.7	195 36.2	.. 37.8	44 30.3	.. 26.5	12 24.7	.. 42.2	Denebola	182 29.5	N14 28.0
04	318 13.4	258 47.6	27.4	210 36.9	37.6	59 33.1	26.5	27 27.3	42.2	Diphda	348 51.9	S17 52.9
05	333 15.9	273 47.0	28.1	225 37.7	37.4	74 35.9	26.5	42 29.9	42.3			
06	348 18.4	288 46.3	N19 28.8	240 38.4	N23 37.2	89 38.7	S22 26.5	57 32.5	S21 42.3	Dubhe	193 46.8	N61 39.1
07	3 20.8	303 45.6	29.5	255 39.1	37.0	104 41.5	26.4	72 35.1	42.3	Elnath	278 07.9	N28 37.2
08	18 23.3	318 44.9	30.2	270 39.9	36.8	119 44.3	26.4	87 37.8	42.3	Eltanin	90 43.7	N51 29.2
M 09	33 25.8	333 44.2	.. 30.9	285 40.6	.. 36.6	134 47.1	.. 26.4	102 40.4	.. 42.4	Enif	33 43.0	N 9 57.8
O 10	48 28.2	348 43.6	31.6	300 41.3	36.5	149 49.9	26.4	117 43.0	42.4	Fomalhaut	15 19.5	S29 31.1
N 11	63 30.7	3 42.9	32.3	315 42.1	36.3	164 52.7	26.4	132 45.6	42.4			
D 12	78 33.2	18 42.2	N19 33.0	330 42.8	N23 36.1	179 55.5	S22 26.3	147 48.2	S21 42.4	Gacrux	171 56.2	S57 13.5
A 13	93 35.6	33 41.5	33.7	345 43.5	35.9	194 58.3	26.3	162 50.9	42.4	Gienah	175 48.0	S17 39.0
Y 14	108 38.1	48 40.8	34.4	0 44.3	35.7	210 01.2	26.3	177 53.5	42.5	Hadar	148 41.6	S60 28.1
15	123 40.6	63 40.1	.. 35.1	15 45.0	.. 35.5	225 04.0	.. 26.3	192 56.1	.. 42.5	Hamal	327 56.4	N23 33.0
16	138 43.0	78 39.4	35.8	30 45.7	35.3	240 06.8	26.3	207 58.7	42.5	Kaus Aust.	83 38.0	S34 22.3
17	153 45.5	93 38.8	36.4	45 46.5	35.1	255 09.6	26.2	223 01.3	42.5			
18	168 47.9	108 38.1	N19 37.1	60 47.2	N23 34.9	270 12.4	S22 26.2	238 04.0	S21 42.6	Kochab	137 19.1	N74 04.9
19	183 50.4	123 37.4	37.8	75 47.9	34.7	285 15.2	26.2	253 06.6	42.6	Markab	13 34.3	N15 18.4
20	198 52.9	138 36.7	38.5	90 48.7	34.5	300 18.0	26.2	268 09.2	42.6	Menkar	314 11.1	N 4 09.7
21	213 55.3	153 36.0	.. 39.2	105 49.4	.. 34.3	315 20.8	.. 26.2	283 11.8	.. 42.6	Menkent	148 02.5	S36 27.9
22	228 57.8	168 35.3	39.9	120 50.1	34.1	330 23.6	26.1	298 14.4	42.7	Miaplacidus	221 39.4	S69 48.1
23	244 00.3	183 34.6	40.6	135 50.9	33.9	345 26.4	26.1	313 17.1	42.7			
11 00	259 02.7	198 33.9	N19 41.2	150 51.6	N23 33.7	0 29.2	S22 26.1	328 19.7	S21 42.7	Mirfak	308 35.0	N49 55.5
01	274 05.2	213 33.2	41.9	165 52.3	33.5	15 32.0	26.1	343 22.3	42.7	Nunki	75 52.9	S26 16.2
02	289 07.7	228 32.6	42.6	180 53.1	33.3	30 34.9	26.1	358 24.9	42.8	Peacock	53 12.4	S56 40.1
03	304 10.1	243 31.9	.. 43.3	195 53.8	.. 33.1	45 37.7	.. 26.0	13 27.5	.. 42.8	Pollux	243 23.1	N27 58.7
04	319 12.6	258 31.2	44.0	210 54.5	33.0	60 40.5	26.0	28 30.2	42.8	Procyon	244 55.8	N 5 10.4
05	334 15.0	273 30.5	44.6	225 55.3	32.8	75 43.3	26.0	43 32.8	42.8			
06	349 17.5	288 29.8	N19 45.3	240 56.0	N23 32.6	90 46.1	S22 26.0	58 35.4	S21 42.8	Rasalhague	96 02.3	N12 32.9
07	4 20.0	303 29.1	46.0	255 56.7	32.4	105 48.9	26.0	73 38.0	42.9	Regulus	207 39.3	N11 52.4
T 08	19 22.4	318 28.4	46.7	270 57.5	32.2	120 51.7	25.9	88 40.6	42.9	Rigel	281 08.5	S 8 10.9
U 09	34 24.9	333 27.7	.. 47.3	285 58.2	.. 32.0	135 54.5	.. 25.9	103 43.3	.. 42.9	Rigil Kent.	139 45.7	S60 54.9
E 10	49 27.4	348 27.0	48.0	300 58.9	31.8	150 57.3	25.9	118 45.9	42.9	Sabik	102 07.5	S15 44.8
S 11	64 29.8	3 26.3	48.7	315 59.7	31.6	166 00.1	25.9	133 48.5	43.0			
D 12	79 32.3	18 25.6	N19 49.4	331 00.4	N23 31.4	181 02.9	S22 25.8	148 51.1	S21 43.0	Schedar	349 36.1	N56 38.2
A 13	94 34.8	33 24.9	50.0	346 01.1	31.2	196 05.8	25.8	163 53.8	43.0	Shaula	96 16.0	S37 06.9
Y 14	109 37.2	48 24.2	50.7	1 01.9	31.0	211 08.6	25.8	178 56.4	43.0	Sirius	258 30.5	S16 44.7
15	124 39.7	63 23.5	.. 51.4	16 02.6	.. 30.8	226 11.4	.. 25.8	193 59.0	.. 43.1	Spica	158 26.8	S11 15.7
16	139 42.2	78 22.8	52.0	31 03.3	30.6	241 14.2	25.8	209 01.6	43.1	Suhail	222 49.7	S43 30.9
17	154 44.6	93 22.1	52.7	46 04.1	30.4	256 17.0	25.8	224 04.2	43.1			
18	169 47.1	108 21.4	N19 53.4	61 04.8	N23 30.2	271 19.8	S22 25.7	239 06.9	S21 43.1	Vega	80 35.8	N38 48.1
19	184 49.5	123 20.7	54.0	76 05.5	30.0	286 22.6	25.7	254 09.5	43.2	Zuben'ubi	137 00.6	S16 07.2
20	199 52.0	138 20.0	54.7	91 06.3	29.8	301 25.4	25.7	269 12.1	43.2		SHA	Mer.Pass.
21	214 54.5	153 19.3	.. 55.4	106 07.0	.. 29.6	316 28.2	.. 25.7	284 14.7	.. 43.2		° '	h m
22	229 57.0	168 18.6	56.0	121 07.7	29.4	331 31.0	25.7	299 17.4	43.2	Venus	300 46.8	10 45
23	244 59.4	183 17.9	56.7	136 08.5	29.2	346 33.8	25.6	314 20.0	43.3	Mars	252 30.4	13 57
Mer.Pass.	h m 6 46.6	v −0.7	d 0.7	v 0.7	d 0.2	v 2.8	d 0.0	v 2.6	d 0.0	Jupiter	101 18.2	0 03
										Saturn	69 13.2	2 11

© British Crown Copyright 2018. All rights reserved.

UT	SUN		MOON				
	GHA	Dec	GHA	v	Dec	d	HP
d h	° ′	° ′	° ′	′	° ′	′	′
9 00	180 13.0	N22 53.1	102 23.6	8.3	N14 21.3	10.6	59.4
01	195 12.9	53.4	116 50.9	8.5	14 10.7	10.8	59.4
02	210 12.8	53.6	131 18.4	8.5	13 59.9	10.8	59.4
03	225 12.7	.. 53.8	145 45.9	8.5	13 49.1	10.9	59.4
04	240 12.6	54.0	160 13.4	8.7	13 38.2	11.0	59.4
05	255 12.4	54.2	174 41.1	8.7	13 27.2	11.0	59.4
06	270 12.3	N22 54.4	189 08.8	8.7	N13 16.2	11.1	59.4
07	285 12.2	54.6	203 36.5	8.8	13 05.1	11.2	59.4
08	300 12.1	54.9	218 04.3	8.9	12 53.9	11.3	59.4
S 09	315 11.9	.. 55.1	232 32.2	8.9	12 42.6	11.4	59.4
U 10	330 11.8	55.3	247 00.1	9.0	12 31.2	11.4	59.4
N 11	345 11.7	55.5	261 28.1	9.0	12 19.8	11.5	59.4
D 12	0 11.6	N22 55.7	275 56.1	9.1	N12 08.3	11.5	59.4
A 13	15 11.5	55.9	290 24.2	9.2	11 56.8	11.6	59.4
Y 14	30 11.3	56.1	304 52.4	9.2	11 45.2	11.7	59.4
15	45 11.2	.. 56.3	319 20.6	9,3	11 33.5	11.8	59.4
16	60 11.1	56.5	333 48.9	9.3	11 21.7	11.8	59.3
17	75 11.0	56.7	348 17.2	9.4	11 09.9	11.9	59.3
18	90 10.8	N22 56.9	2 45.6	9.4	N10 58.0	11.9	59.3
19	105 10.7	57.1	17 14.0	9.5	10 46.1	12.0	59.3
20	120 10.6	57.3	31 42.5	9.6	10 34.1	12.0	59.3
21	135 10.5	.. 57.5	46 11.1	9.6	10 22.1	12.1	59.3
22	150 10.3	57.7	60 39.7	9.6	10 10.0	12.1	59.3
23	165 10.2	57.9	75 08.3	9.7	9 57.8	12.2	59.3
10 00	180 10.1	N22 58.1	89 37.0	9.8	N 9 45.6	12.3	59.3
01	195 10.0	58.3	104 05.8	9.8	9 33.3	12.3	59.3
02	210 09.9	58.5	118 34.6	9.9	9 21.0	12.4	59.3
03	225 09.7	.. 58.7	133 03.5	9.9	9 08.6	12.4	59.3
04	240 09.6	58.9	147 32.4	9.9	8 56.2	12.4	59.2
05	255 09.5	59.1	162 01.3	10.0	8 43.8	12.5	59.2
06	270 09.4	N22 59.3	176 30.3	10.1	N 8 31.3	12.6	59.2
07	285 09.2	59.5	190 59.4	10.1	8 18.7	12.6	59.2
08	300 09.1	59.7	205 28.5	10.1	8 06.1	12.6	59.2
M 09	315 09.0	22 59.9	219 57.6	10.2	7 53.5	12.7	59.2
O 10	330 08.9	23 00.1	234 26.8	10.2	7 40.8	12.7	59.2
N 11	345 08.7	00.3	248 56.0	10.3	7 28.1	12.7	59.2
D 12	0 08.6	N23 00.5	263 25.3	10.3	N 7 15.4	12.8	59.2
A 13	15 08.5	00.7	277 54.6	10.4	7 02.6	12.8	59.2
Y 14	30 08.4	00.9	292 24.0	10.4	6 49.8	12.9	59.2
15	45 08.2	.. 01.1	306 53.4	10.4	6 36.9	12.8	59.1
16	60 08.1	01.2	321 22.8	10.5	6 24.1	13.0	59.1
17	75 08.0	01.4	335 52.3	10.5	6 11.1	12.9	59.1
18	90 07.9	N23 01.6	350 21.8	10.6	N 5 58.2	13.0	59.1
19	105 07.7	01.8	4 51.4	10.5	5 45.2	13.0	59.1
20	120 07.6	02.0	19 20.9	10.7	5 32.2	13.0	59.1
21	135 07.5	.. 02.2	33 50.6	10.6	5 19.2	13.0	59.1
22	150 07.4	02.4	48 20.2	10.7	5 06.2	13.1	59.1
23	165 07.2	02.5	62 49.9	10.8	4 53.1	13.1	59.1
11 00	180 07.1	N23 02.7	77 19.7	10.7	N 4 40.0	13.1	59.0
01	195 07.0	02.9	91 49.4	10.8	4 26.9	13.1	59.0
02	210 06.9	03.1	106 19.2	10.8	4 13.8	13.2	59.0
03	225 06.7	.. 03.3	120 49.0	10.9	4 00.6	13.1	59.0
04	240 06.6	03.5	135 18.9	10.8	3 47.5	13.2	59.0
05	255 06.5	03.6	149 48.7	11.0	3 34.3	13.2	59.0
06	270 06.4	N23 03.8	164 18.7	10.9	N 3 21.1	13.2	59.0
07	285 06.2	04.0	178 48.6	10.9	3 07.9	13.2	59.0
08	300 06.1	04.2	193 18.5	11.0	2 54.7	13.3	58.9
T 09	315 06.0	.. 04.3	207 48.5	11.0	2 41.4	13.2	58.9
U 10	330 05.9	04.5	222 18.5	11.1	2 28.2	13.3	58.9
E 11	345 05.7	04.7	236 48.6	11.0	2 14.9	13.2	58.9
S 12	0 05.6	N23 04.9	251 18.6	11.1	N 2 01.7	13.3	58.9
D 13	15 05.5	05.0	265 48.7	11.1	1 48.4	13.2	58.9
A 14	30 05.3	05.2	280 18.8	11.1	1 35.2	13.3	58.9
Y 15	45 05.2	.. 05.4	294 48.9	11.1	1 21.9	13.3	58.9
16	60 05.1	05.6	309 19.0	11.2	1 08.6	13.3	58.8
17	75 05.0	05.7	323 49.2	11.2	0 55.3	13.2	58.8
18	90 04.8	N23 05.9	338 19.4	11.2	N 0 42.1	13.3	58.8
19	105 04.7	06.1	352 49.6	11.2	0 28.8	13.3	58.8
20	120 04.6	06.2	7 19.8	11.2	0 15.5	13.3	58.8
21	135 04.5	.. 06.4	21 50.0	11.2	N 0 02.3	13.3	58.8
22	150 04.3	06.6	36 20.2	11.2	S 0 11.0	13.2	58.8
23	165 04.2	06.7	50 50.4	11.3	S 0 24.2	13.3	58.8
	SD 15.8	d 0.2	SD 16.2		16.1		16.0

Lat.	Twilight		Sunrise	Moonrise			
	Naut.	Civil		9	10	11	12
°	h m	h m	h m	h m	h m	h m	h m
N 72	▭	▭	▭	08 35	10 50	12 56	14 59
N 70	▭	▭	▭	08 59	11 02	12 58	14 53
68	▭	▭	▭	09 17	11 11	13 00	14 48
66	////	////	00 30	09 32	11 19	13 02	14 44
64	////	////	01 40	09 44	11 25	13 03	14 41
62	////	////	02 15	09 54	11 30	13 05	14 38
60	////	01 03	02 39	10 03	11 35	13 06	14 35
N 58	////	01 46	02 59	10 11	11 39	13 07	14 33
56	////	02 14	03 15	10 17	11 43	13 07	14 31
54	00 58	02 35	03 29	10 23	11 46	13 08	14 29
52	01 38	02 53	03 41	10 29	11 49	13 09	14 28
50	02 04	03 07	03 51	10 33	11 52	13 10	14 26
45	02 47	03 36	04 13	10 44	11 58	13 11	14 23
N 40	03 17	03 58	04 31	10 52	12 03	13 12	14 20
35	03 40	04 16	04 46	11 00	12 07	13 13	14 18
30	03 58	04 31	04 58	11 06	12 11	13 14	14 16
20	04 26	04 55	05 20	11 17	12 17	13 15	14 13
N 10	04 49	05 16	05 39	11 27	12 23	13 17	14 10
0	05 07	05 33	05 56	11 36	12 28	13 18	14 07
S 10	05 24	05 50	06 13	11 45	12 33	13 19	14 04
20	05 40	06 07	06 31	11 55	12 39	13 21	14 02
30	05 56	06 26	06 52	12 06	12 45	13 22	13 58
35	06 04	06 36	07 04	12 12	12 49	13 23	13 57
40	06 13	06 47	07 18	12 19	12 53	13 24	13 55
45	06 23	07 01	07 34	12 27	12 58	13 25	13 52
S 50	06 35	07 16	07 54	12 37	13 03	13 27	13 49
52	06 40	07 23	08 04	12 42	13 06	13 27	13 48
54	06 45	07 31	08 15	12 47	13 09	13 28	13 47
56	06 51	07 40	08 27	12 53	13 12	13 29	13 45
58	06 58	07 50	08 41	12 59	13 15	13 30	13 44
S 60	07 05	08 01	08 58	13 06	13 19	13 31	13 42

Lat.	Sunset	Twilight		Moonset			
		Civil	Naut.	9	10	11	12
°	h m	h m	h m	h m	h m	h m	h m
N 72	▭	▭	▭	02 31	02 05	01 46	01 28
N 70	▭	▭	▭	02 05	01 51	01 40	01 29
68	▭	▭	▭	01 45	01 40	01 35	01 31
66	23 35	////	////	01 29	01 31	01 31	01 32
64	22 20	////	////	01 16	01 23	01 28	01 32
62	21 45	////	////	01 05	01 16	01 25	01 33
60	21 20	22 58	////	00 55	01 10	01 23	01 34
N 58	21 01	22 14	////	00 46	01 05	01 20	01 34
56	20 44	21 45	////	00 39	01 00	01 18	01 35
54	20 30	21 24	23 03	00 32	00 56	01 16	01 35
52	20 18	21 07	22 22	00 26	00 52	01 15	01 36
50	20 08	20 52	21 56	00 21	00 49	01 13	01 36
45	19 46	20 23	21 12	00 09	00 41	01 10	01 37
N 40	19 28	20 01	20 42	24 35	00 35	01 07	01 38
35	19 13	19 43	20 19	24 29	00 29	01 05	01 38
30	19 01	19 28	20 01	24 24	00 24	01 02	01 39
20	18 39	19 03	19 33	24 16	00 16	00 59	01 40
N 10	18 20	18 43	19 10	24 08	00 08	00 55	01 41
0	18 03	18 26	18 52	24 01	00 01	00 52	01 41
S 10	17 46	18 09	18 35	23 54	24 49	00 49	01 42
20	17 28	17 52	18 19	23 46	24 45	00 45	01 43
30	17 07	17 33	18 03	23 37	24 41	00 41	01 44
35	16 55	17 23	17 54	23 32	24 39	00 39	01 44
40	16 41	17 11	17 45	23 26	24 36	00 36	01 45
45	16 25	16 58	17 35	23 19	24 33	00 33	01 45
S 50	16 04	16 42	17 24	23 11	24 29	00 29	01 46
52	15 55	16 35	17 19	23 07	24 27	00 27	01 46
54	15 44	16 27	17 13	23 03	24 25	00 25	01 47
56	15 32	16 18	17 07	22 58	24 23	00 23	01 47
58	15 17	16 08	17 01	22 52	24 21	00 21	01 48
S 60	15 00	15 57	16 53	22 46	24 18	00 18	01 48

	SUN			MOON			
Day	Eqn. of Time		Mer.	Mer. Pass.		Age	Phase
	00ʰ	12ʰ	Pass.	Upper	Lower		
d	m s	m s	h m	h m	h m	d	%
9	00 52	00 47	11 59	17 49	05 22	06	42
10	00 41	00 35	11 59	18 40	06 14	07	53
11	00 29	00 23	12 00	19 30	07 05	08	64

© British Crown Copyright 2018. All rights reserved.

UT	ARIES GHA	VENUS −3·8 GHA	Dec	MARS +1·8 GHA	Dec	JUPITER −2·6 GHA	Dec	SATURN +0·2 GHA	Dec	STARS Name	SHA	Dec
12 00	260 01.9	198 17.2	N19 57.4	151 09.2	N23 28.9	1 36.6	S22 25.6	329 22.6	S21 43.3	Acamar	315 15.6	S40 13.7
01	275 04.3	213 16.5	58.0	166 09.9	28.7	16 39.5	25.6	344 25.2	43.3	Achernar	335 24.1	S57 08.2
02	290 06.8	228 15.8	58.7	181 10.7	28.5	31 42.3	25.6	359 27.8	43.3	Acrux	173 04.5	S63 12.6
03	305 09.3	243 15.1	19 59.3	196 11.4 ..	28.3	46 45.1 ..	25.6	14 30.5 ..	43.3	Adhara	255 09.7	S29 00.1
04	320 11.7	258 14.4	20 00.0	211 12.2	28.1	61 47.9	25.5	29 33.1	43.4	Aldebaran	290 45.0	N16 32.7
05	335 14.2	273 13.7	00.6	226 12.9	27.9	76 50.7	25.5	44 35.7	43.4			
06	350 16.7	288 13.0	N20 01.3	241 13.6	N23 27.7	91 53.5	S22 25.5	59 38.3	S21 43.4	Alioth	166 16.9	N55 51.6
W 07	5 19.1	303 12.3	02.0	256 14.4	27.5	106 56.3	25.5	74 41.0	43.4	Alkaid	152 55.4	N49 13.3
E 08	20 21.6	318 11.6	02.6	271 15.1	27.3	121 59.1	25.5	89 43.6	43.5	Alnair	27 38.5	S46 51.8
D 09	35 24.0	333 10.9 ..	03.3	286 15.8 ..	27.1	137 01.9 ..	25.5	104 46.2 ..	43.5	Alnilam	275 42.6	S 1 11.5
N 10	50 26.5	348 10.2	03.9	301 16.6	26.9	152 04.7	25.4	119 48.8	43.5	Alphard	217 52.3	S 8 44.6
E 11	65 29.0	3 09.5	04.6	316 17.3	26.7	167 07.5	25.4	134 51.5	43.5			
S 12	80 31.4	18 08.8	N20 05.2	331 18.0	N23 26.5	182 10.3	S22 25.4	149 54.1	S21 43.6	Alphecca	126 07.2	N26 39.2
D 13	95 33.9	33 08.1	05.9	346 18.8	26.3	197 13.2	25.4	164 56.7	43.6	Alpheratz	357 39.3	N29 11.6
A 14	110 36.4	48 07.4	06.5	1 19.5	26.1	212 16.0	25.3	179 59.3	43.6	Altair	62 04.0	N 8 55.2
Y 15	125 38.8	63 06.7 ..	07.2	16 20.3 ..	25.9	227 18.8 ..	25.3	195 02.0 ..	43.6	Ankaa	353 11.8	S42 11.9
16	140 41.3	78 05.9	07.8	31 21.0	25.7	242 21.6	25.3	210 04.6	43.7	Antares	112 20.9	S26 28.4
17	155 43.8	93 05.2	08.5	46 21.7	25.4	257 24.4	25.3	225 07.2	43.7			
18	170 46.2	108 04.5	N20 09.1	61 22.5	N23 25.2	272 27.2	S22 25.3	240 09.8	S21 43.7	Arcturus	145 51.8	N19 05.1
19	185 48.7	123 03.8	09.7	76 23.2	25.0	287 30.0	25.2	255 12.5	43.7	Atria	107 18.5	S69 03.6
20	200 51.1	138 03.1	10.4	91 24.0	24.8	302 32.8	25.2	270 15.1	43.8	Avior	234 16.9	S59 34.5
21	215 53.6	153 02.4 ..	11.0	106 24.7 ..	24.6	317 35.6 ..	25.2	285 17.7 ..	43.8	Bellatrix	278 28.0	N 6 21.9
22	230 56.1	168 01.7	11.7	121 25.4	24.4	332 38.4	25.2	300 20.3	43.8	Betelgeuse	270 57.2	N 7 24.5
23	245 58.5	183 01.0	12.3	136 26.2	24.2	347 41.2	25.2	315 23.0	43.8			
13 00	261 01.0	198 00.3	N20 12.9	151 26.9	N23 24.0	2 44.0	S22 25.1	330 25.6	S21 43.8	Canopus	263 54.9	S52 42.5
01	276 03.5	212 59.6	13.6	166 27.6	23.8	17 46.8	25.1	345 28.2	43.9	Capella	280 28.9	N46 00.8
02	291 05.9	227 58.8	14.2	181 28.4	23.6	32 49.7	25.1	0 30.8	43.9	Deneb	49 28.4	N45 20.8
03	306 08.4	242 58.1 ..	14.9	196 29.1 ..	23.3	47 52.5 ..	25.1	15 33.5 ..	43.9	Denebola	182 29.5	N14 28.0
04	321 10.9	257 57.4	15.5	211 29.9	23.1	62 55.3	25.1	30 36.1	43.9	Diphda	348 51.9	S17 52.9
05	336 13.3	272 56.7	16.1	226 30.6	22.9	77 58.1	25.0	45 38.7	44.0			
06	351 15.8	287 56.0	N20 16.8	241 31.3	N23 22.7	93 00.9	S22 25.0	60 41.3	S21 44.0	Dubhe	193 46.8	N61 39.1
T 07	6 18.3	302 55.3	17.4	256 32.1	22.5	108 03.7	25.0	75 44.0	44.0	Elnath	278 07.9	N28 37.2
H 08	21 20.7	317 54.6	18.0	271 32.8	22.3	123 06.5	25.0	90 46.6	44.0	Eltanin	90 43.7	N51 29.3
U 09	36 23.2	332 53.8 ..	18.7	286 33.6 ..	22.1	138 09.3 ..	24.9	105 49.2 ..	44.1	Enif	33 43.0	N 9 57.8
R 10	51 25.6	347 53.1	19.3	301 34.3	21.9	153 12.1	24.9	120 51.9	44.1	Fomalhaut	15 19.4	S29 31.1
S 11	66 28.1	2 52.4	19.9	316 35.0	21.6	168 14.9	24.9	135 54.5	44.1			
D 12	81 30.6	17 51.7	N20 20.5	331 35.8	N23 21.4	183 17.7	S22 24.9	150 57.1	S21 44.1	Gacrux	171 56.2	S57 13.5
A 13	96 33.0	32 51.0	21.2	346 36.5	21.2	198 20.5	24.9	165 59.7	44.2	Gienah	175 48.0	S17 39.0
Y 14	111 35.5	47 50.2	21.8	1 37.3	21.0	213 23.3	24.8	181 02.4	44.2	Hadar	148 41.7	S60 28.1
15	126 38.0	62 49.5 ..	22.4	16 38.0 ..	20.8	228 26.2 ..	24.8	196 05.0 ..	44.2	Hamal	327 56.4	N23 33.0
16	141 40.4	77 48.8	23.0	31 38.7	20.6	243 29.0	24.8	211 07.6	44.2	Kaus Aust.	83 38.0	S34 22.3
17	156 42.9	92 48.1	23.7	46 39.5	20.4	258 31.8	24.8	226 10.2	44.3			
18	171 45.4	107 47.4	N20 24.3	61 40.2	N23 20.1	273 34.6	S22 24.8	241 12.9	S21 44.3	Kochab	137 19.2	N74 04.9
19	186 47.8	122 46.6	24.9	76 41.0	19.9	288 37.4	24.7	256 15.5	44.3	Markab	13 34.2	N15 18.4
20	201 50.3	137 45.9	25.5	91 41.7	19.7	303 40.2	24.7	271 18.1	44.3	Menkar	314 11.1	N 4 09.7
21	216 52.8	152 45.2 ..	26.1	106 42.4 ..	19.5	318 43.0 ..	24.7	286 20.8 ..	44.4	Menkent	148 02.5	S36 27.9
22	231 55.2	167 44.5	26.8	121 43.2	19.3	333 45.8	24.7	301 23.4	44.4	Miaplacidus	221 39.4	S69 48.1
23	246 57.7	182 43.8	27.4	136 43.9	19.1	348 48.6	24.7	316 26.0	44.4			
14 00	262 00.1	197 43.0	N20 28.0	151 44.7	N23 18.8	3 51.4	S22 24.6	331 28.6	S21 44.4	Mirfak	308 34.9	N49 55.5
01	277 02.6	212 42.3	28.6	166 45.4	18.6	18 54.2	24.6	346 31.3	44.5	Nunki	75 52.9	S26 16.2
02	292 05.1	227 41.6	29.2	181 46.1	18.4	33 57.0	24.6	1 33.9	44.5	Peacock	53 12.4	S56 40.1
03	307 07.5	242 40.9 ..	29.8	196 46.9 ..	18.2	48 59.8 ..	24.6	16 36.5 ..	44.5	Pollux	243 23.1	N27 58.7
04	322 10.0	257 40.1	30.4	211 47.6	18.0	64 02.6	24.6	31 39.1	44.5	Procyon	244 55.8	N 5 10.4
05	337 12.5	272 39.4	31.1	226 48.4	17.7	79 05.5	24.5	46 41.8	44.6			
06	352 14.9	287 38.7	N20 31.7	241 49.1	N23 17.5	94 08.3	S22 24.5	61 44.4	S21 44.6	Rasalhague	96 02.3	N12 32.9
07	7 17.4	302 38.0	32.3	256 49.9	17.3	109 11.1	24.5	76 47.0	44.6	Regulus	207 39.3	N11 52.4
08	22 19.9	317 37.2	32.9	271 50.6	17.1	124 13.9	24.5	91 49.7	44.6	Rigel	281 08.5	S 8 10.9
F 09	37 22.3	332 36.5 ..	33.5	286 51.3 ..	16.9	139 16.7 ..	24.5	106 52.3 ..	44.6	Rigil Kent.	139 45.7	S60 54.9
R 10	52 24.8	347 35.8	34.1	301 52.1	16.6	154 19.5	24.4	121 54.9	44.7	Sabik	102 07.5	S15 44.8
I 11	67 27.2	2 35.1	34.7	316 52.8	16.4	169 22.3	24.4	136 57.6	44.7			
D 12	82 29.7	17 34.3	N20 35.3	331 53.6	N23 16.2	184 25.1	S22 24.4	152 00.2	S21 44.7	Schedar	349 36.0	N56 38.2
A 13	97 32.2	32 33.6	35.9	346 54.3	16.0	199 27.9	24.4	167 02.8	44.7	Shaula	96 16.0	S37 06.9
Y 14	112 34.6	47 32.9	36.5	1 55.1	15.8	214 30.7	24.4	182 05.4	44.8	Sirius	258 30.5	S16 44.7
15	127 37.1	62 32.1 ..	37.1	16 55.8 ..	15.5	229 33.5 ..	24.3	197 08.1 ..	44.8	Spica	158 26.8	S11 15.7
16	142 39.6	77 31.4	37.7	31 56.5	15.3	244 36.3	24.3	212 10.7	44.8	Suhail	222 49.7	S43 30.9
17	157 42.0	92 30.7	38.3	46 57.3	15.1	259 39.1	24.3	227 13.3	44.8			
18	172 44.5	107 29.9	N20 38.9	61 58.0	N23 14.9	274 41.9	S22 24.3	242 16.0	S21 44.9	Vega	80 35.8	N38 48.1
19	187 47.0	122 29.2	39.5	76 58.8	14.6	289 44.8	24.3	257 18.6	44.9	Zuben'ubi	137 00.6	S16 07.2
20	202 49.4	137 28.5	40.1	91 59.5	14.4	304 47.6	24.2	272 21.2	44.9		SHA	Mer.Pass.
21	217 51.9	152 27.8 ..	40.7	107 00.3 ..	14.2	319 50.4 ..	24.2	287 23.8 ..	44.9			h m
22	232 54.4	167 27.0	41.3	122 01.0	14.0	334 53.2	24.2	302 26.5	45.0	Venus	296 59.3	10 48
23	247 56.8	182 26.3	41.9	137 01.7	13.7	349 56.0	24.2	317 29.1	45.0	Mars	250 25.9	13 54
Mer.Pass. h m 6 34.9		v −0.7	d 0.6	v 0.7	d 0.2	v 2.8	d 0.0	v 2.6	d 0.0	Jupiter	101 43.0	23 45
										Saturn	69 24.6	1 58

© British Crown Copyright 2018. All rights reserved.

UT		SUN GHA	SUN Dec	MOON GHA	v	MOON Dec	d	HP
d	h	° ′	° ′	° ′	′	° ′	′	′
12	00	180 04.1	N23 06.9	65 20.7	11.3	S 0 37.5	13.2	58.7
	01	195 03.9	07.1	79 51.0	11.2	0 50.7	13.2	58.7
	02	210 03.8	07.2	94 21.2	11.3	1 03.9	13.2	58.7
	03	225 03.7	. . 07.4	108 51.5	11.3	1 17.1	13.2	58.7
	04	240 03.6	07.6	123 21.8	11.3	1 30.3	13.2	58.7
	05	255 03.4	07.7	137 52.1	11.3	1 43.5	13.2	58.7
	06	270 03.3	N23 07.9	152 22.4	11.3	S 1 56.7	13.2	58.7
W	07	285 03.2	08.0	166 52.7	11.4	2 09.9	13.1	58.6
E	08	300 03.1	08.2	181 23.1	11.3	2 23.0	13.1	58.6
D	09	315 02.9	. . 08.4	195 53.4	11.3	2 36.1	13.1	58.6
N	10	330 02.8	08.5	210 23.7	11.3	2 49.2	13.1	58.6
E	11	345 02.7	08.7	224 54.0	11.4	3 02.3	13.1	58.6
S	12	0 02.5	N23 08.8	239 24.4	11.3	S 3 15.4	13.0	58.6
D	13	15 02.4	09.0	253 54.7	11.3	3 28.4	13.0	58.6
A	14	30 02.3	09.2	268 25.0	11.3	3 41.4	13.0	58.5
Y	15	45 02.2	. . 09.3	282 55.3	11.4	3 54.4	13.0	58.5
	16	60 02.0	09.5	297 25.7	11.3	4 07.4	12.9	58.5
	17	75 01.9	09.6	311 56.0	11.3	4 20.3	12.9	58.5
	18	90 01.8	N23 09.8	326 26.3	11.3	S 4 33.2	12.9	58.5
	19	105 01.6	09.9	340 56.6	11.3	4 46.1	12.8	58.5
	20	120 01.5	10.1	355 26.9	11.3	4 58.9	12.8	58.4
	21	135 01.4	. . 10.2	9 57.2	11.3	5 11.7	12.8	58.4
	22	150 01.3	10.4	24 27.5	11.3	5 24.5	12.8	58.4
	23	165 01.1	10.5	38 57.8	11.3	5 37.3	12.7	58.4
13	00	180 01.0	N23 10.7	53 28.1	11.3	S 5 50.0	12.7	58.4
	01	195 00.9	10.8	67 58.4	11.3	6 02.7	12.6	58.4
	02	210 00.7	11.0	82 28.7	11.2	6 15.3	12.6	58.3
	03	225 00.6	. . 11.1	96 58.9	11.3	6 27.9	12.5	58.3
	04	240 00.5	11.3	111 29.2	11.2	6 40.4	12.6	58.3
	05	255 00.4	11.4	125 59.4	11.2	6 53.0	12.4	58.3
	06	270 00.2	N23 11.6	140 29.6	11.2	S 7 05.4	12.5	58.3
T	07	285 00.1	11.7	154 59.8	11.2	7 17.9	12.4	58.3
H	08	300 00.0	11.8	169 30.0	11.2	7 30.3	12.3	58.2
U	09	314 59.8	. . 12.0	184 00.2	11.2	7 42.6	12.3	58.2
R	10	329 59.7	12.1	198 30.4	11.1	7 54.9	12.2	58.2
S	11	344 59.6	12.3	213 00.5	11.2	8 07.1	12.2	58.2
D	12	359 59.4	N23 12.4	227 30.7	11.1	S 8 19.3	12.2	58.2
A	13	14 59.3	12.5	242 00.8	11.1	8 31.5	12.1	58.2
Y	14	29 59.2	12.7	256 30.9	11.1	8 43.6	12.0	58.1
	15	44 59.1	. . 12.8	271 01.0	11.0	8 55.6	12.0	58.1
	16	59 58.9	13.0	285 31.0	11.1	9 07.6	12.0	58.1
	17	74 58.8	13.1	300 01.1	11.0	9 19.6	11.8	58.1
	18	89 58.7	N23 13.2	314 31.1	11.0	S 9 31.4	11.9	58.1
	19	104 58.5	13.4	329 01.1	11.0	9 43.3	11.7	58.1
	20	119 58.4	13.5	343 31.1	11.0	9 55.0	11.8	58.0
	21	134 58.3	. . 13.6	358 01.1	10.9	10 06.8	11.6	58.0
	22	149 58.1	13.8	12 31.0	10.9	10 18.4	11.6	58.0
	23	164 58.0	13.9	27 00.9	10.9	10 30.0	11.5	58.0
14	00	179 57.9	N23 14.0	41 30.8	10.9	S10 41.5	11.5	58.0
	01	194 57.8	14.2	56 00.7	10.8	10 53.0	11.4	57.9
	02	209 57.6	14.3	70 30.5	10.9	11 04.4	11.3	57.9
	03	224 57.5	. . 14.4	85 00.4	10.8	11 15.7	11.3	57.9
	04	239 57.4	14.6	99 30.2	10.8	11 27.0	11.2	57.9
	05	254 57.2	14.7	114 00.0	10.7	11 38.2	11.2	57.9
	06	269 57.1	N23 14.8	128 29.7	10.7	S11 49.4	11.0	57.9
	07	284 57.0	14.9	142 59.4	10.7	12 00.4	11.0	57.8
	08	299 56.8	15.1	157 29.1	10.7	12 11.4	11.0	57.8
F	09	314 56.7	. . 15.2	171 58.8	10.7	12 22.4	10.8	57.8
R	10	329 56.6	15.3	186 28.5	10.6	12 33.2	10.8	57.8
I	11	344 56.4	15.4	200 58.1	10.6	12 44.0	10.7	57.8
D	12	359 56.3	N23 15.6	215 27.7	10.6	S12 54.7	10.7	57.7
A	13	14 56.2	15.7	229 57.3	10.5	13 05.4	10.5	57.7
Y	14	29 56.0	15.8	244 26.8	10.5	13 15.9	10.5	57.7
	15	44 55.9	. . 15.9	258 56.3	10.5	13 26.4	10.4	57.7
	16	59 55.8	16.1	273 25.8	10.5	13 36.8	10.4	57.7
	17	74 55.7	16.2	287 55.3	10.4	13 47.2	10.2	57.6
	18	89 55.5	N23 16.3	302 24.7	10.4	S13 57.4	10.2	57.6
	19	104 55.4	16.4	316 54.1	10.4	14 07.6	10.1	57.6
	20	119 55.3	16.5	331 23.5	10.3	14 17.7	10.0	57.6
	21	134 55.1	. . 16.6	345 52.8	10.3	14 27.7	9.9	57.6
	22	149 55.0	16.8	0 22.1	10.3	14 37.6	9.8	57.5
	23	164 54.9	16.9	14 51.4	10.3	S14 47.4	9.8	57.5
		SD 15.8	d 0.1	SD 16.0		15.9		15.7

Lat.	Twilight Naut.	Twilight Civil	Sunrise	Moonrise 12	13	14	15
°	h m	h m	h m	h m	h m	h m	h m
N 72	□	□	□	14 59	17 04	19 20	■
N 70	□	□	□	14 53	16 48	18 49	21 03
68	□	□	□	14 48	16 36	18 26	20 20
66	□	□	□	14 44	16 26	18 08	19 51
64	////	////	01 36	14 41	16 17	17 54	19 29
62	////	////	02 12	14 38	16 10	17 42	19 12
60	////	00 57	02 37	14 35	16 04	17 32	18 58
N 58	////	01 43	02 57	14 33	15 59	17 23	18 46
56	////	02 12	03 14	14 31	15 54	17 16	18 35
54	00 52	02 34	03 28	14 29	15 49	17 09	18 26
52	01 35	02 51	03 40	14 28	15 46	17 03	18 18
50	02 02	03 06	03 51	14 26	15 42	16 57	18 10
45	02 46	03 36	04 13	14 23	15 35	16 45	17 54
N 40	03 16	03 58	04 31	14 20	15 28	16 35	17 42
35	03 39	04 16	04 45	14 18	15 23	16 27	17 31
30	03 58	04 31	04 58	14 16	15 18	16 20	17 21
20	04 27	04 56	05 20	14 13	15 10	16 07	17 05
N 10	04 49	05 16	05 39	14 10	15 03	15 56	16 51
0	05 08	05 34	05 56	14 07	14 56	15 46	16 38
S 10	05 25	05 51	06 14	14 04	14 50	15 36	16 24
20	05 41	06 08	06 32	14 02	14 43	15 26	16 10
30	05 57	06 27	06 53	13 58	14 35	15 14	15 55
35	06 05	06 37	07 05	13 57	14 31	15 07	15 45
40	06 15	06 49	07 19	13 55	14 26	14 59	15 35
45	06 25	07 02	07 36	13 52	14 20	14 50	15 23
S 50	06 37	07 18	07 56	13 49	14 13	14 39	15 08
52	06 42	07 25	08 06	13 48	14 10	14 33	15 01
54	06 47	07 33	08 17	13 47	14 06	14 28	14 54
56	06 53	07 42	08 30	13 45	14 02	14 22	14 45
58	07 00	07 52	08 44	13 44	13 58	14 15	14 35
S 60	07 07	08 04	09 01	13 42	13 53	14 07	14 25

Lat.	Sunset	Twilight Civil	Twilight Naut.	Moonset 12	13	14	15
°	h m	h m	h m	h m	h m	h m	h m
N 72	□	□	□	01 28	01 10	00 49	00 18
N 70	□	□	□	01 29	01 19	01 06	00 51
68	□	□	□	01 31	01 26	01 21	01 15
66	□	□	□	01 32	01 32	01 32	01 34
64	22 26	////	////	01 32	01 37	01 42	01 49
62	21 49	////	////	01 33	01 41	01 50	02 02
60	21 23	23 05	////	01 34	01 45	01 57	02 13
N 58	21 03	22 18	////	01 34	01 48	02 04	02 22
56	20 47	21 49	////	01 35	01 52	02 10	02 31
54	20 33	21 27	23 10	01 35	01 54	02 15	02 38
52	20 20	21 09	22 26	01 36	01 57	02 19	02 45
50	20 10	20 54	21 59	01 36	01 59	02 24	02 51
45	19 47	20 25	21 14	01 37	02 04	02 33	03 04
N 40	19 30	20 02	20 44	01 38	02 08	02 40	03 15
35	19 15	19 44	20 21	01 38	02 12	02 47	03 24
30	19 02	19 29	20 02	01 39	02 15	02 53	03 32
20	18 40	19 04	19 34	01 40	02 21	03 03	03 47
N 10	18 21	18 44	19 11	01 41	02 26	03 12	03 59
0	18 04	18 26	18 52	01 41	02 31	03 20	04 11
S 10	17 46	18 09	18 36	01 42	02 35	03 28	04 22
20	17 28	17 52	18 19	01 43	02 40	03 37	04 35
30	17 07	17 33	18 03	01 44	02 46	03 48	04 49
35	16 55	17 23	17 55	01 44	02 49	03 54	04 58
40	16 41	17 11	17 45	01 45	02 53	04 00	05 07
45	16 24	16 58	17 35	01 45	02 57	04 08	05 18
S 50	16 04	16 42	17 23	01 46	03 02	04 18	05 32
52	15 54	16 35	17 18	01 46	03 05	04 22	05 38
54	15 43	16 27	17 13	01 47	03 07	04 27	05 46
56	15 30	16 18	17 07	01 47	03 10	04 33	05 53
58	15 16	16 07	17 00	01 48	03 14	04 39	06 02
S 60	14 59	15 56	16 53	01 48	03 17	04 46	06 13

Day	SUN Eqn. of Time 00h	SUN Eqn. of Time 12h	SUN Mer. Pass.	MOON Mer. Pass. Upper	MOON Mer. Pass. Lower	Age	%	Phase
d	m s	m s	h m	h m	h m	d	%	
12	00 17	00 10	12 00	20 19	07 54	09	75	
13	00 04	00 02	12 00	21 08	08 43	10	84	
14	00 08	00 14	12 00	21 58	09 33	11	91	

© British Crown Copyright 2018. All rights reserved.

120   2019 JUNE 15, 16, 17 (SAT., SUN., MON.)

UT	ARIES GHA	VENUS −3.8 GHA	Dec	MARS +1.8 GHA	Dec	JUPITER −2.6 GHA	Dec	SATURN +0.2 GHA	Dec	STARS Name	SHA	Dec
15 00	262 59.3	197 25.6	N20 42.5	152 02.5	N23 13.5	4 58.8	S22 24.1	332 31.7	S21 45.0	Acamar	315 15.6	S40 13.6
01	278 01.7	212 24.8	43.1	167 03.2	13.3	20 01.6	24.1	347 34.4	45.0	Achernar	335 24.0	S57 08.2
02	293 04.2	227 24.1	43.7	182 04.0	13.1	35 04.4	24.1	2 37.0	45.1	Acrux	173 04.5	S63 12.6
03	308 06.7	242 23.3 ..	44.3	197 04.7 ..	12.8	50 07.2 ..	24.1	17 39.6 ..	45.1	Adhara	255 09.7	S29 00.1
04	323 09.1	257 22.6	44.9	212 05.5	12.6	65 10.0	24.1	32 42.3	45.1	Aldebaran	290 45.0	N16 32.7
05	338 11.6	272 21.9	45.4	227 06.2	12.4	80 12.8	24.0	47 44.9	45.1			
06	353 14.1	287 21.1	N20 46.0	242 07.0	N23 12.2	95 15.6	S22 24.0	62 47.5	S21 45.2	Alioth	166 16.9	N55 51.6
07	8 16.5	302 20.4	46.6	257 07.7	11.9	110 18.4	24.0	77 50.2	45.2	Alkaid	152 55.4	N49 13.3
08	23 19.0	317 19.7	47.2	272 08.4	11.7	125 21.2	24.0	92 52.8	45.2	Alnair	27 38.4	S46 51.8
09	38 21.5	332 18.9 ..	47.8	287 09.2 ..	11.5	140 24.0 ..	24.0	107 55.4 ..	45.2	Alnilam	275 42.6	S 1 11.5
10	53 23.9	347 18.2	48.4	302 09.9	11.3	155 26.8	23.9	122 58.1	45.3	Alphard	217 52.3	S 8 44.6
11	68 26.4	2 17.5	48.9	317 10.7	11.0	170 29.6	23.9	138 00.7	45.3			
12	83 28.9	17 16.7	N20 49.5	332 11.4	N23 10.8	185 32.5	S22 23.9	153 03.3	S21 45.3	Alphecca	126 07.2	N26 39.2
13	98 31.3	32 16.0	50.1	347 12.2	10.6	200 35.3	23.9	168 05.9	45.3	Alpheratz	357 39.3	N29 11.6
14	113 33.8	47 15.2	50.7	2 12.9	10.3	215 38.1	23.9	183 08.6	45.4	Altair	62 04.0	N 8 55.2
15	128 36.2	62 14.5 ..	51.3	17 13.7 ..	10.1	230 40.9 ..	23.8	198 11.2 ..	45.4	Ankaa	353 11.8	S42 11.9
16	143 38.7	77 13.8	51.8	32 14.4	09.9	245 43.7	23.8	213 13.8	45.4	Antares	112 20.9	S26 28.4
17	158 41.2	92 13.0	52.4	47 15.2	09.7	260 46.5	23.8	228 16.5	45.4			
18	173 43.6	107 12.3	N20 53.0	62 15.9	N23 09.4	275 49.3	S22 23.8	243 19.1	S21 45.5	Arcturus	145 51.8	N19 05.1
19	188 46.1	122 11.5	53.6	77 16.7	09.2	290 52.1	23.8	258 21.7	45.5	Atria	107 18.4	S69 03.6
20	203 48.6	137 10.8	54.1	92 17.4	09.0	305 54.9	23.7	273 24.4	45.5	Avior	234 16.9	S59 34.5
21	218 51.0	152 10.0 ..	54.7	107 18.1 ..	08.7	320 57.7 ..	23.7	288 27.0 ..	45.5	Bellatrix	278 28.0	N 6 21.9
22	233 53.5	167 09.3	55.3	122 18.9	08.5	336 00.5	23.7	303 29.6	45.6	Betelgeuse	270 57.2	N 7 24.5
23	248 56.0	182 08.6	55.9	137 19.6	08.3	351 03.3	23.7	318 32.3	45.6			
16 00	263 58.4	197 07.8	N20 56.4	152 20.4	N23 08.0	6 06.1	S22 23.7	333 34.9	S21 45.6	Canopus	263 54.9	S52 42.5
01	279 00.9	212 07.1	57.0	167 21.1	07.8	21 08.9	23.6	348 37.5	45.6	Capella	280 28.9	N46 00.8
02	294 03.4	227 06.3	57.6	182 21.9	07.6	36 11.7	23.6	3 40.2	45.7	Deneb	49 28.4	N45 20.8
03	309 05.8	242 05.6 ..	58.1	197 22.6 ..	07.3	51 14.5 ..	23.6	18 42.8 ..	45.7	Denebola	182 29.5	N14 28.0
04	324 08.3	257 04.8	58.7	212 23.4	07.1	66 17.3	23.6	33 45.4	45.7	Diphda	348 51.9	S17 52.8
05	339 10.7	272 04.1	59.3	227 24.1	06.9	81 20.1	23.6	48 48.1	45.7			
06	354 13.2	287 03.3	N20 59.8	242 24.9	N23 06.6	96 22.9	S22 23.5	63 50.7	S21 45.8	Dubhe	193 46.8	N61 39.1
07	9 15.7	302 02.6	21 00.4	257 25.6	06.4	111 25.8	23.5	78 53.3	45.8	Elnath	278 07.8	N28 37.2
08	24 18.1	317 01.8	00.9	272 26.4	06.2	126 28.6	23.5	93 56.0	45.8	Eltanin	90 43.7	N51 29.3
09	39 20.6	332 01.1 ..	01.5	287 27.1 ..	05.9	141 31.4 ..	23.5	108 58.6 ..	45.8	Enif	33 42.9	N 9 57.8
10	54 23.1	347 00.4	02.1	302 27.9	05.7	156 34.2	23.4	124 01.2	45.9	Fomalhaut	15 19.4	S29 31.1
11	69 25.5	1 59.6	02.6	317 28.6	05.5	171 37.0	23.4	139 03.9	45.9			
12	84 28.0	16 58.9	N21 03.2	332 29.4	N23 05.2	186 39.8	S22 23.4	154 06.5	S21 45.9	Gacrux	171 56.2	S57 13.5
13	99 30.5	31 58.1	03.7	347 30.1	05.0	201 42.6	23.4	169 09.1	45.9	Gienah	175 48.0	S17 39.0
14	114 32.9	46 57.4	04.3	2 30.9	04.8	216 45.4	23.4	184 11.8	46.0	Hadar	148 41.7	S60 28.1
15	129 35.4	61 56.6 ..	04.9	17 31.6 ..	04.5	231 48.2 ..	23.3	199 14.4 ..	46.0	Hamal	327 56.4	N23 33.0
16	144 37.9	76 55.9	05.4	32 32.4	04.3	246 51.0	23.3	214 17.0	46.0	Kaus Aust.	83 38.0	S34 22.3
17	159 40.3	91 55.1	06.0	47 33.1	04.0	261 53.8	23.3	229 19.7	46.0			
18	174 42.8	106 54.4	N21 06.5	62 33.9	N23 03.8	276 56.6	S22 23.3	244 22.3	S21 46.1	Kochab	137 19.2	N74 04.9
19	189 45.2	121 53.6	07.1	77 34.6	03.6	291 59.4	23.3	259 24.9	46.1	Markab	13 34.2	N15 18.4
20	204 47.7	136 52.8	07.6	92 35.4	03.3	307 02.2	23.2	274 27.6	46.1	Menkar	314 11.0	N 4 09.8
21	219 50.2	151 52.1 ..	08.2	107 36.1 ..	03.1	322 05.0 ..	23.2	289 30.2 ..	46.1	Menkent	148 02.5	S36 27.9
22	234 52.6	166 51.3	08.7	122 36.9	02.9	337 07.8	23.2	304 32.8	46.2	Miaplacidus	221 39.4	S69 48.1
23	249 55.1	181 50.6	09.3	137 37.6	02.6	352 10.6	23.2	319 35.5	46.2			
17 00	264 57.6	196 49.8	N21 09.8	152 38.4	N23 02.4	7 13.4	S22 23.2	334 38.1	S21 46.2	Mirfak	308 34.9	N49 55.5
01	280 00.0	211 49.1	10.3	167 39.1	02.1	22 16.2	23.1	349 40.7	46.2	Nunki	75 52.9	S26 16.2
02	295 02.5	226 48.3	10.9	182 39.9	01.9	37 19.0	23.1	4 43.4	46.3	Peacock	53 12.4	S56 40.1
03	310 05.0	241 47.6 ..	11.4	197 40.6 ..	01.7	52 21.8 ..	23.1	19 46.0 ..	46.3	Pollux	243 23.1	N27 58.7
04	325 07.4	256 46.8	12.0	212 41.4	01.4	67 24.6	23.1	34 48.7	46.3	Procyon	244 55.8	N 5 10.4
05	340 09.9	271 46.1	12.5	227 42.1	01.2	82 27.4	23.1	49 51.3	46.3			
06	355 12.3	286 45.3	N21 13.1	242 42.9	N23 00.9	97 30.2	S22 23.0	64 53.9	S21 46.4	Rasalhague	96 02.3	N12 32.9
07	10 14.8	301 44.5	13.6	257 43.6	00.7	112 33.1	23.0	79 56.6	46.4	Regulus	207 39.3	N11 52.4
08	25 17.3	316 43.8	14.1	272 44.4	00.4	127 35.9	23.0	94 59.2	46.4	Rigel	281 08.5	S 8 10.9
09	40 19.7	331 43.0 ..	14.7	287 45.1 ..	00.2	142 38.7 ..	23.0	110 01.8 ..	46.4	Rigil Kent.	139 45.7	S60 54.9
10	55 22.2	346 42.3	15.2	302 45.9	23 00.0	157 41.5	22.9	125 04.5	46.5	Sabik	102 07.5	S15 44.8
11	70 24.7	1 41.5	15.7	317 46.6	22 59.7	172 44.3	22.9	140 07.1	46.5			
12	85 27.1	16 40.7	N21 16.3	332 47.4	N22 59.5	187 47.1	S22 22.9	155 09.7	S21 46.5	Schedar	349 36.0	N56 38.2
13	100 29.6	31 40.0	16.8	347 48.1	59.2	202 49.9	22.9	170 12.4	46.5	Shaula	96 15.9	S37 06.9
14	115 32.1	46 39.2	17.3	2 48.9	59.0	217 52.7	22.9	185 15.0	46.6	Sirius	258 30.5	S16 44.7
15	130 34.5	61 38.5 ..	17.9	17 49.6 ..	58.7	232 55.5 ..	22.8	200 17.6 ..	46.6	Spica	158 26.8	S11 15.7
16	145 37.0	76 37.7	18.4	32 50.4	58.4	247 58.3	22.8	215 20.3	46.6	Suhail	222 49.7	S43 30.9
17	160 39.5	91 36.9	18.9	47 51.1	58.3	263 01.1	22.8	230 22.9	46.6			
18	175 41.9	106 36.2	N21 19.4	62 51.9	N22 58.0	278 03.9	S22 22.8	245 25.6	S21 46.7	Vega	80 35.8	N38 48.1
19	190 44.4	121 35.4	20.0	77 52.6	57.8	293 06.7	22.8	260 28.2	46.7	Zuben'ubi	137 00.6	S16 07.2
20	205 46.8	136 34.7	20.5	92 53.4	57.5	308 09.5	22.7	275 30.8	46.7		SHA	Mer. Pass.
21	220 49.3	151 33.9 ..	21.0	107 54.1 ..	57.3	323 12.3 ..	22.7	290 33.5 ..	46.7		° ′	h m
22	235 51.8	166 33.1	21.5	122 54.9	57.0	338 15.1	22.7	305 36.1	46.8	Venus	293 09.4	10 52
23	250 54.2	181 32.4	22.1	137 55.6	56.8	353 17.9	22.7	320 38.7	46.8	Mars	248 22.0	13 50
	h m									Jupiter	102 07.7	23 31
Mer. Pass.	6 23.1	v −0.7	d 0.6	v 0.7	d 0.2	v 2.8	d 0.0	v 2.6	d 0.0	Saturn	69 36.5	1 45

© British Crown Copyright 2018. All rights reserved.

SUN / MOON

UT	SUN GHA	SUN Dec	MOON GHA	v	MOON Dec	d	HP
d h	° ′	° ′	° ′	′	° ′	′	′
15 00	179 54.7	N23 17.0	29 20.7	10.2	S14 57.2	9.6	57.5
01	194 54.6	17.1	43 49.9	10.2	15 06.8	9.6	57.5
02	209 54.5	17.2	58 19.1	10.2	15 16.4	9.5	57.5
03	224 54.3	.. 17.3	72 48.3	10.1	15 25.9	9.4	57.4
04	239 54.2	17.4	87 17.4	10.1	15 35.3	9.3	57.4
05	254 54.1	17.6	101 46.5	10.1	15 44.6	9.3	57.4
06	269 53.9	N23 17.7	116 15.6	10.1	S15 53.9	9.1	57.4
07	284 53.8	17.8	130 44.7	10.0	16 03.0	9.0	57.4
S 08	299 53.7	17.9	145 13.7	10.0	16 12.0	9.0	57.3
A 09	314 53.5	.. 18.0	159 42.7	10.0	16 21.0	8.8	57.3
T 10	329 53.4	18.1	174 11.7	9.9	16 29.8	8.8	57.3
U 11	344 53.3	18.2	188 40.6	9.9	16 38.6	8.7	57.3
R 12	359 53.1	N23 18.3	203 09.5	9.9	S16 47.3	8.5	57.3
D 13	14 53.0	18.4	217 38.4	9.9	16 55.8	8.5	57.2
A 14	29 52.9	18.5	232 07.3	9.8	17 04.3	8.4	57.2
Y 15	44 52.7	.. 18.6	246 36.1	9.8	17 12.7	8.2	57.2
16	59 52.6	18.7	261 04.9	9.8	17 20.9	8.2	57.2
17	74 52.5	18.8	275 33.7	9.7	17 29.1	8.1	57.2
18	89 52.3	N23 18.9	290 02.4	9.8	S17 37.2	8.0	57.1
19	104 52.2	19.0	304 31.2	9.7	17 45.2	7.8	57.1
20	119 52.1	19.1	318 59.9	9.6	17 53.0	7.8	57.1
21	134 52.0	.. 19.2	333 28.5	9.7	18 00.8	7.7	57.1
22	149 51.8	19.3	347 57.2	9.6	18 08.5	7.5	57.0
23	164 51.7	19.4	2 25.8	9.6	18 16.0	7.5	57.0
16 00	179 51.6	N23 19.5	16 54.4	9.6	S18 23.5	7.3	57.0
01	194 51.4	19.6	31 23.0	9.5	18 30.8	7.3	57.0
02	209 51.3	19.7	45 51.5	9.5	18 38.1	7.1	57.0
03	224 51.2	.. 19.8	60 20.0	9.5	18 45.2	7.1	56.9
04	239 51.0	19.9	74 48.5	9.5	18 52.3	6.9	56.9
05	254 50.9	20.0	89 17.0	9.5	18 59.2	6.8	56.9
06	269 50.8	N23 20.1	103 45.5	9.4	S19 06.0	6.7	56.9
07	284 50.6	20.2	118 13.9	9.4	19 12.7	6.6	56.9
08	299 50.5	20.3	132 42.3	9.4	19 19.3	6.5	56.8
S 09	314 50.4	.. 20.4	147 10.7	9.4	19 25.8	6.4	56.8
U 10	329 50.2	20.5	161 39.1	9.3	19 32.2	6.2	56.8
N 11	344 50.1	20.6	176 07.4	9.4	19 38.4	6.2	56.8
D 12	359 50.0	N23 20.6	190 35.8	9.3	S19 44.6	6.0	56.7
A 13	14 49.8	20.7	205 04.1	9.3	19 50.6	6.0	56.7
Y 14	29 49.7	20.8	219 32.4	9.3	19 56.6	5.8	56.7
15	44 49.6	.. 20.9	234 00.7	9.2	20 02.4	5.7	56.7
16	59 49.4	21.0	248 28.9	9.3	20 08.1	5.6	56.7
17	74 49.3	21.1	262 57.2	9.2	20 13.7	5.5	56.6
18	89 49.2	N23 21.2	277 25.4	9.3	S20 19.2	5.3	56.6
19	104 49.0	21.2	291 53.7	9.2	20 24.5	5.3	56.6
20	119 48.9	21.3	306 21.9	9.2	20 29.8	5.1	56.6
21	134 48.8	.. 21.4	320 50.1	9.2	20 34.9	5.0	56.5
22	149 48.6	21.5	335 18.3	9.1	20 39.9	4.9	56.5
23	164 48.5	21.6	349 46.4	9.2	20 44.8	4.8	56.5
17 00	179 48.3	N23 21.7	4 14.6	9.2	S20 49.6	4.6	56.5
01	194 48.2	21.7	18 42.8	9.1	20 54.2	4.6	56.5
02	209 48.1	21.8	33 10.9	9.2	20 58.8	4.4	56.4
03	224 47.9	.. 21.9	47 39.1	9.1	21 03.2	4.3	56.4
04	239 47.8	22.0	62 07.2	9.1	21 07.5	4.2	56.4
05	254 47.7	22.0	76 35.3	9.1	21 11.7	4.1	56.4
06	269 47.5	N23 22.1	91 03.4	9.2	S21 15.8	3.9	56.3
07	284 47.4	22.2	105 31.6	9.1	21 19.7	3.9	56.3
08	299 47.3	22.3	119 59.7	9.1	21 23.6	3.7	56.3
M 09	314 47.1	.. 22.3	134 27.8	9.1	21 27.3	3.6	56.3
O 10	329 47.0	22.4	148 55.9	9.1	21 30.9	3.5	56.3
N 11	344 46.9	22.5	163 24.0	9.1	21 34.4	3.3	56.2
D 12	359 46.7	N23 22.6	177 52.1	9.1	S21 37.7	3.3	56.2
A 13	14 46.6	22.6	192 20.2	9.2	21 41.0	3.1	56.2
Y 14	29 46.5	22.7	206 48.4	9.1	21 44.1	3.0	56.2
15	44 46.4	.. 22.8	221 16.5	9.1	21 47.1	2.8	56.1
16	59 46.2	22.8	235 44.6	9.1	21 49.9	2.8	56.1
17	74 46.1	22.9	250 12.7	9.2	21 52.7	2.6	56.1
18	89 45.9	N23 23.0	264 40.9	9.1	S21 55.3	2.5	56.1
19	104 45.8	23.0	279 09.0	9.1	21 57.8	2.4	56.1
20	119 45.7	23.1	293 37.1	9.2	22 00.2	2.3	56.0
21	134 45.5	.. 23.2	308 05.3	9.2	22 02.5	2.2	56.0
22	149 45.4	23.2	322 33.5	9.2	22 04.7	2.0	56.0
23	164 45.3	23.3	337 01.6	9.2	S22 06.7	1.9	56.0
	SD 15.8	d 0.1	SD 15.6		15.5		15.3

Twilight — Moonrise

Lat.	Naut.	Civil	Sunrise	15	16	17	18
°	h m	h m	h m	h m	h m	h m	h m
N 72	□	□	□	■	■	■	■
N 70	□	□	□	21 03	■	■	■
68	□	□	□	20 20	22 20	■	■
66	□	□		19 51	21 31	22 58	23 56
64	////	////	01 33	19 29	21 00	22 18	23 14
62	////	////	02 10	19 12	20 37	21 50	22 46
60	////	00 52	02 36	18 58	20 18	21 28	22 24
N 58	////	01 41	02 56	18 46	20 03	21 11	22 06
56	////	02 11	03 13	18 35	19 50	20 56	21 51
54	00 48	02 33	03 27	18 26	19 38	20 43	21 38
52	01 33	02 51	03 39	18 18	19 28	20 32	21 27
50	02 00	03 06	03 50	18 10	19 19	20 22	21 17
45	02 46	03 35	04 13	17 54	19 01	20 02	20 56
N 40	03 16	03 58	04 31	17 42	18 45	19 45	20 39
35	03 39	04 16	04 46	17 31	18 32	19 31	20 25
30	03 58	04 31	04 59	17 21	18 21	19 19	20 12
20	04 27	04 56	05 21	17 05	18 02	18 58	19 51
N 10	04 49	05 16	05 39	16 51	17 45	18 39	19 32
0	05 08	05 34	05 57	16 38	17 30	18 23	19 15
S 10	05 25	05 52	06 14	16 24	17 14	18 06	18 58
20	05 41	06 09	06 33	16 10	16 58	17 48	18 39
30	05 58	06 28	06 54	15 55	16 39	17 27	18 18
35	06 06	06 38	07 06	15 45	16 28	17 15	18 06
40	06 16	06 50	07 20	15 35	16 16	17 01	17 51
45	06 26	07 03	07 37	15 23	16 01	16 45	17 35
S 50	06 38	07 19	07 58	15 08	15 43	16 25	17 14
52	06 43	07 27	08 08	15 01	15 34	16 15	17 04
54	06 49	07 35	08 19	14 54	15 25	16 04	16 52
56	06 55	07 44	08 31	14 45	15 14	15 52	16 40
58	07 02	07 54	08 46	14 35	15 02	15 38	16 25
S 60	07 09	08 06	09 03	14 25	14 48	15 22	16 07

Sunset — Twilight — Moonset

Lat.	Sunset	Civil	Naut.	15	16	17	18
°	h m	h m	h m	h m	h m	h m	h m
N 72	□	□	□	00 18	■	■	■
N 70	□	□	□	00 51	00 24	■	■
68	□	□	□	01 15	01 08	00 57	■
66	□	□	□	01 34	01 38	01 47	02 10
64	22 29	////	////	01 49	02 00	02 18	02 50
62	21 52	////	////	02 02	02 18	02 42	03 18
60	21 26	23 10	////	02 13	02 33	03 01	03 40
N 58	21 05	22 21	////	02 22	02 46	03 16	03 58
56	20 49	21 51	////	02 31	02 57	03 30	04 13
54	20 34	21 29	23 15	02 38	03 06	03 42	04 25
52	20 22	21 11	22 29	02 45	03 15	03 52	04 36
50	20 11	20 56	22 01	02 51	03 23	04 01	04 46
45	19 49	20 26	21 16	03 04	03 40	04 20	05 07
N 40	19 31	20 04	20 45	03 15	03 53	04 36	05 24
35	19 16	19 45	20 22	03 24	04 05	04 50	05 39
30	19 03	19 30	20 04	03 32	04 15	05 01	05 51
20	18 41	19 05	19 35	03 47	04 33	05 21	06 12
N 10	18 22	18 45	19 12	03 59	04 48	05 39	06 31
0	18 04	18 27	18 53	04 11	05 02	05 55	06 48
S 10	17 47	18 10	18 36	04 22	05 17	06 11	07 05
20	17 28	17 52	18 20	04 35	05 32	06 29	07 24
30	17 07	17 34	18 04	04 49	05 50	06 49	07 45
35	16 55	17 23	17 55	04 58	06 00	07 01	07 57
40	16 41	17 11	17 45	05 07	06 12	07 14	08 11
45	16 24	16 58	17 35	05 18	06 26	07 30	08 28
S 50	16 03	16 42	17 23	05 32	06 44	07 50	08 49
52	15 54	16 34	17 18	05 38	06 52	07 59	08 59
54	15 42	16 26	17 12	05 46	07 01	08 10	09 10
56	15 30	16 17	17 06	05 53	07 11	08 22	09 23
58	15 15	16 07	17 00	06 02	07 23	08 36	09 38
S 60	14 58	15 55	16 52	06 13	07 36	08 52	09 55

SUN / MOON

Day	Eqn. of Time 00h	Eqn. of Time 12h	Mer. Pass.	Mer. Pass. Upper	Mer. Pass. Lower	Age	Phase
d	m s	m s	h m	h m	h m	d	%
15	00 21	00 27	12 00	22 50	10 24	12	96
16	00 34	00 40	12 01	23 42	11 16	13	99
17	00 46	00 53	12 01	24 35	12 09	14	100

© British Crown Copyright 2018. All rights reserved.

UT	ARIES GHA	VENUS −3.8 GHA	Dec	MARS +1.8 GHA	Dec	JUPITER −2.6 GHA	Dec	SATURN +0.2 GHA	Dec
18 00	265 56.7	196 31.6	N21 22.6	152 56.4	N22 56.5	8 20.7	S22 22.7	335 41.4	S21 46.8
01	280 59.2	211 30.8	23.1	167 57.1	56.3	23 23.5	22.6	350 44.0	46.8
02	296 01.6	226 30.1	23.6	182 57.9	56.0	38 26.3	22.6	5 46.7	46.9
03	311 04.1	241 29.3 ..	24.1	197 58.6 ..	55.8	53 29.1 ..	22.6	20 49.3 ..	46.9
04	326 06.6	256 28.5	24.7	212 59.4	55.6	68 31.9	22.6	35 51.9	46.9
05	341 09.0	271 27.8	25.2	228 00.2	55.3	83 34.7	22.6	50 54.6	46.9
T 06	356 11.5	286 27.0	N21 25.7	243 00.9	N22 55.1	98 37.5	S22 22.5	65 57.2	S21 47.0
U 07	11 14.0	301 26.2	26.2	258 01.7	54.8	113 40.3	22.5	80 59.8	47.0
E 08	26 16.4	316 25.5	26.7	273 02.4	54.6	128 43.1	22.5	96 02.5	47.0
S 09	41 18.9	331 24.7 ..	27.2	288 03.2	54.3	143 45.9 ..	22.5	111 05.1 ..	47.0
D 10	56 21.3	346 23.9	27.7	303 03.9	54.1	158 48.7	22.4	126 07.8	47.1
A 11	71 23.8	1 23.2	28.3	318 04.7	53.8	173 51.5	22.4	141 10.4	47.1
Y 12	86 26.3	16 22.4	N21 28.8	333 05.4	N22 53.6	188 54.3	S22 22.4	156 13.0	S21 47.1
13	101 28.7	31 21.6	29.3	348 06.2	53.3	203 57.1	22.4	171 15.7	47.1
14	116 31.2	46 20.9	29.8	3 06.9	53.1	218 59.9	22.4	186 18.3	47.2
15	131 33.7	61 20.1 ..	30.3	18 07.7 ..	52.8	234 02.7 ..	22.3	201 20.9 ..	47.2
16	146 36.1	76 19.3	30.8	33 08.5	52.6	249 05.5	22.3	216 23.6	47.2
17	161 38.6	91 18.6	31.3	48 09.2	52.3	264 08.3	22.3	231 26.2	47.2
18	176 41.1	106 17.8	N21 31.8	63 10.0	N22 52.1	279 11.1	S22 22.3	246 28.9	S21 47.3
19	191 43.5	121 17.0	32.3	78 10.7	51.8	294 13.9	22.3	261 31.5	47.3
20	206 46.0	136 16.2	32.8	93 11.5	51.6	309 16.7	22.2	276 34.1	47.3
21	221 48.5	151 15.5 ..	33.3	108 12.2 ..	51.3	324 19.5 ..	22.2	291 36.8 ..	47.3
22	236 50.9	166 14.7	33.8	123 13.0	51.1	339 22.3	22.2	306 39.4	47.4
23	251 53.4	181 13.9	34.3	138 13.7	50.8	354 25.1	22.2	321 42.1	47.4
19 00	266 55.8	196 13.1	N21 34.8	153 14.5	N22 50.5	9 27.9	S22 22.2	336 44.7	S21 47.4
01	281 58.3	211 12.4	35.3	168 15.3	50.3	24 30.7	22.1	351 47.3	47.5
02	297 00.8	226 11.6	35.8	183 16.0	50.0	39 33.5	22.1	6 50.0	47.5
03	312 03.2	241 10.8 ..	36.3	198 16.8 ..	49.8	54 36.3 ..	22.1	21 52.6 ..	47.5
04	327 05.7	256 10.0	36.8	213 17.5	49.5	69 39.1	22.1	36 55.3	47.5
05	342 08.2	271 09.3	37.3	228 18.3	49.3	84 41.9	22.1	51 57.9	47.6
W 06	357 10.6	286 08.5	N21 37.8	243 19.0	N22 49.0	99 44.7	S22 22.0	67 00.5	S21 47.6
E 07	12 13.1	301 07.7	38.2	258 19.8	48.8	114 47.5	22.0	82 03.2	47.6
D 08	27 15.6	316 06.9	38.7	273 20.5	48.5	129 50.3	22.0	97 05.8	47.6
N 09	42 18.0	331 06.2 ..	39.2	288 21.3 ..	48.3	144 53.1 ..	22.0	112 08.5 ..	47.7
E 10	57 20.5	346 05.4	39.7	303 22.1	48.0	159 55.9	21.9	127 11.1	47.7
S 11	72 23.0	1 04.6	40.2	318 22.8	47.7	174 58.7	21.9	142 13.7	47.7
D 12	87 25.4	16 03.8	N21 40.7	333 23.6	N22 47.5	190 01.5	S22 21.9	157 16.4	S21 47.7
A 13	102 27.9	31 03.0	41.2	348 24.3	47.2	205 04.3	21.9	172 19.0	47.8
Y 14	117 30.3	46 02.3	41.6	3 25.1	47.0	220 07.1	21.9	187 21.7	47.8
15	132 32.8	61 01.5 ..	42.1	18 25.8 ..	46.7	235 09.9 ..	21.8	202 24.3 ..	47.8
16	147 35.3	76 00.7	42.6	33 26.6	46.5	250 12.7	21.8	217 26.9	47.8
17	162 37.7	90 59.9	43.1	48 27.4	46.2	265 15.5	21.8	232 29.6	47.9
18	177 40.2	105 59.1	N21 43.6	63 28.1	N22 45.9	280 18.3	S22 21.8	247 32.2	S21 47.9
19	192 42.7	120 58.4	44.0	78 28.9	45.7	295 21.1	21.8	262 34.9	47.9
20	207 45.1	135 57.6	44.5	93 29.6	45.4	310 23.9	21.7	277 37.5	47.9
21	222 47.6	150 56.8 ..	45.0	108 30.4 ..	45.2	325 26.7 ..	21.7	292 40.1 ..	48.0
22	237 50.1	165 56.0	45.5	123 31.2	44.9	340 29.5	21.7	307 42.8	48.0
23	252 52.5	180 55.2	45.9	138 31.9	44.6	355 32.3	21.7	322 45.4	48.0
20 00	267 55.0	195 54.5	N21 46.4	153 32.7	N22 44.4	10 35.1	S22 21.7	337 48.1	S21 48.0
01	282 57.4	210 53.7	46.9	168 33.4	44.1	25 37.9	21.6	352 50.7	48.1
02	297 59.9	225 52.9	47.3	183 34.2	43.9	40 40.7	21.6	7 53.3	48.1
03	313 02.4	240 52.1 ..	47.8	198 35.0 ..	43.6	55 43.5 ..	21.6	22 56.0 ..	48.1
04	328 04.8	255 51.3	48.3	213 35.7	43.3	70 46.3	21.6	37 58.6	48.1
05	343 07.3	270 50.5	48.8	228 36.5	43.1	85 49.1	21.6	53 01.3	48.2
T 06	358 09.8	285 49.7	N21 49.2	243 37.2	N22 42.8	100 51.9	S22 21.5	68 03.9	S21 48.2
H 07	13 12.2	300 49.0	49.7	258 38.0	42.5	115 54.7	21.5	83 06.5	48.2
U 08	28 14.7	315 48.2	50.1	273 38.8	42.3	130 57.5	21.5	98 09.2	48.2
R 09	43 17.2	330 47.4 ..	50.6	288 39.5 ..	42.0	146 00.3 ..	21.5	113 11.8 ..	48.3
S 10	58 19.6	345 46.6	51.1	303 40.3	41.8	161 03.1	21.4	128 14.5	48.3
D 11	73 22.1	0 45.8	51.5	318 41.0	41.5	176 05.9	21.4	143 17.1	48.3
A 12	88 24.6	15 45.0	N21 52.0	333 41.8	N22 41.1	191 08.7	S22 21.4	158 19.8	S21 48.4
Y 13	103 27.0	30 44.2	52.4	348 42.6	41.0	206 11.5	21.4	173 22.4	48.4
14	118 29.5	45 43.4	52.9	3 43.3	40.7	221 14.3	21.4	188 25.0	48.4
15	133 31.9	60 42.7 ..	53.4	18 44.1 ..	40.4	236 17.1 ..	21.3	203 27.7 ..	48.4
16	148 34.4	75 41.9	53.8	33 44.8	40.2	251 19.9	21.3	218 30.3	48.5
17	163 36.9	90 41.1	54.3	48 45.6	39.9	266 22.7	21.3	233 33.0	48.5
18	178 39.3	105 40.3	N21 54.7	63 46.4	N22 39.6	281 25.5	S22 21.3	248 35.6	S21 48.5
19	193 41.8	120 39.5	55.2	78 47.1	39.4	296 28.3	21.3	263 38.3	48.5
20	208 44.3	135 38.7	55.6	93 47.9	39.1	311 31.1	21.2	278 40.9	48.6
21	223 46.7	150 37.9 ..	56.1	108 48.6 ..	38.8	326 33.9 ..	21.2	293 43.5 ..	48.6
22	238 49.2	165 37.1	56.5	123 49.4	38.6	341 36.7	21.2	308 46.2	48.6
23	253 51.7	180 36.3	57.0	138 50.2	38.3	356 39.5	21.2	323 48.8	48.6
Mer. Pass.	h m 6 11.3	v −0.8	d 0.5	v 0.8	d 0.3	v 2.8	d 0.0	v 2.6	d 0.0

STARS

Name	SHA	Dec
Acamar	315 15.6	S40 13.6
Achernar	335 24.0	S57 08.2
Acrux	173 04.6	S63 12.6
Adhara	255 09.7	S29 00.1
Aldebaran	290 45.0	N16 32.7
Alioth	166 16.9	N55 51.7
Alkaid	152 55.4	N49 13.3
Alnair	27 38.4	S46 51.8
Alnilam	275 42.6	S 1 11.5
Alphard	217 52.3	S 8 44.6
Alphecca	126 07.2	N26 39.2
Alpheratz	357 39.3	N29 11.6
Altair	62 03.9	N 8 55.2
Ankaa	353 11.7	S42 11.9
Antares	112 20.9	S26 28.4
Arcturus	145 51.8	N19 05.1
Atria	107 18.4	S69 03.6
Avior	234 16.9	S59 34.5
Bellatrix	278 28.0	N 6 21.9
Betelgeuse	270 57.2	N 7 24.5
Canopus	263 54.9	S52 42.5
Capella	280 28.9	N46 00.8
Deneb	49 28.3	N45 20.8
Denebola	182 29.5	N14 28.0
Diphda	348 51.9	S17 52.8
Dubhe	193 46.9	N61 39.1
Elnath	278 07.8	N28 37.2
Eltanin	90 43.7	N51 29.3
Enif	33 42.9	N 9 57.8
Fomalhaut	15 19.4	S29 31.1
Gacrux	171 56.2	S57 13.5
Gienah	175 48.0	S17 39.0
Hadar	148 41.7	S60 28.1
Hamal	327 56.3	N23 33.0
Kaus Aust.	83 38.0	S34 22.3
Kochab	137 19.3	N74 04.9
Markab	13 34.2	N15 18.4
Menkar	314 11.0	N 4 09.8
Menkent	148 02.5	S36 27.9
Miaplacidus	221 39.5	S69 48.1
Mirfak	308 34.9	N49 55.5
Nunki	75 52.9	S26 16.2
Peacock	53 12.3	S56 40.1
Pollux	243 23.1	N27 58.7
Procyon	244 55.8	N 5 10.4
Rasalhague	96 02.3	N12 32.9
Regulus	207 39.3	N11 52.4
Rigel	281 08.5	S 8 10.9
Rigil Kent.	139 45.7	S60 54.9
Sabik	102 07.5	S15 44.8
Schedar	349 36.0	N56 38.2
Shaula	96 15.9	S37 06.9
Sirius	258 30.5	S16 44.7
Spica	158 26.8	S11 15.7
Suhail	222 49.7	S43 30.9
Vega	80 35.8	N38 48.2
Zuben'ubi	137 00.6	S16 07.2

	SHA	Mer. Pass.
Venus	289 17.3	h m 10 56
Mars	246 18.7	13 46
Jupiter	102 32.1	23 18
Saturn	69 48.8	1 33

© British Crown Copyright 2018. All rights reserved.

UT	SUN		MOON					Lat.	Twilight		Sunrise	Moonrise			
	GHA	Dec	GHA	v	Dec	d	HP		Naut.	Civil		18	19	20	21
d h	° ′	° ′	° ′	′	° ′	′	′	°	h m	h m	h m	h m	h m	h m	h m
18 00	179 45.1	N23 23.4	351 29.8	9.2	S22 08.6	1.8	55.9	N 72	☐	☐	☐	▬	▬	▬	▬
01	194 45.0	23.4	5 58.0	9.2	22 10.4	1.6	55.9	N 70	☐	☐	☐	▬	▬		02 04
02	209 44.9	23.5	20 26.2	9.3	22 12.0	1.6	55.9	68	☐	☐	☐	▬	▬	01 20	01 07
03	224 44.7 ..	23.6	34 54.5	9.2	22 13.6	1.4	55.9	66	////	////	01 31	23 56	24 22	00 22	00 33
04	239 44.6	23.6	49 22.7	9.3	22 15.0	1.3	55.9	64	////	////	02 09	23 14	23 49	24 08	00 08
05	254 44.5	23.7	63 51.0	9.2	22 16.3	1.2	55.8	62	////	00 50	02 36	22 46	23 24	23 49	24 05
06	269 44.3	N23 23.7	78 19.2	9.3	S22 17.5	1.1	55.8	60	////	01 40	02 56	22 24	23 04	23 33	23 52
07	284 44.2	23.8	92 47.5	9.4	22 18.6	0.9	55.8	N 58	////	01 40	02 56	22 06	22 48	23 19	23 42
08	299 44.1	23.9	107 15.9	9.3	22 19.5	0.9	55.8	56	////	02 10	03 13	21 51	22 34	23 07	23 32
09	314 43.9 ..	23.9	121 44.2	9.3	22 20.4	0.7	55.7	54	00 45	02 33	03 27	21 38	22 22	22 57	23 24
10	329 43.8	24.0	136 12.5	9.4	22 21.1	0.6	55.7	52	01 32	02 51	03 39	21 27	22 12	22 48	23 17
11	344 43.6	24.0	150 40.9	9.4	22 21.7	0.4	55.7	50	02 00	03 06	03 50	21 17	22 02	22 40	23 10
12	359 43.5	N23 24.1	165 09.3	9.5	S22 22.1	0.4	55.7	45	02 46	03 35	04 13	20 56	21 43	22 22	22 55
13	14 43.4	24.1	179 37.8	9.4	22 22.5	0.2	55.7	N 40	03 16	03 58	04 31	20 39	21 26	22 08	22 43
14	29 43.2	24.2	194 06.2	9.5	22 22.7	0.1	55.6	35	03 39	04 16	04 46	20 25	21 13	21 55	22 33
15	44 43.1 ..	24.2	208 34.7	9.5	22 22.8	0.0	55.6	30	03 58	04 32	04 59	20 12	21 01	21 45	22 24
16	59 43.0	24.3	223 03.2	9.5	22 22.8	0.1	55.6	20	04 27	04 56	05 21	19 51	20 41	21 26	22 09
17	74 42.8	24.3	237 31.7	9.6	22 22.7	0.2	55.6	N 10	04 50	05 17	05 40	19 32	20 23	21 10	21 55
18	89 42.7	N23 24.4	252 00.3	9.6	S22 22.5	0.4	55.6	0	05 09	05 35	05 58	19 15	20 06	20 55	21 42
19	104 42.6	24.4	266 28.9	9.6	22 22.1	0.5	55.5	S 10	05 26	05 52	06 15	18 58	19 50	20 40	21 30
20	119 42.4	24.5	280 57.5	9.6	22 21.6	0.6	55.5	20	05 42	06 10	06 34	18 39	19 32	20 24	21 16
21	134 42.3 ..	24.5	295 26.1	9.7	22 21.0	0.7	55.5	30	05 59	06 28	06 55	18 18	19 12	20 06	21 00
22	149 42.2	24.6	309 54.8	9.7	22 20.3	0.8	55.5	35	06 07	06 39	07 07	18 06	19 00	19 55	20 51
23	164 42.0	24.6	324 23.5	9.8	22 19.5	0.9	55.5	40	06 17	06 51	07 21	17 51	18 46	19 43	20 41
19 00	179 41.9	N23 24.7	338 52.3	9.8	S22 18.6	1.1	55.4	45	06 27	07 04	07 38	17 35	18 30	19 28	20 28
01	194 41.8	24.7	353 21.1	9.8	22 17.5	1.2	55.4	S 50	06 39	07 21	07 59	17 14	18 09	19 10	20 13
02	209 41.6	24.8	7 49.9	9.8	22 16.3	1.2	55.4	52	06 44	07 28	08 09	17 04	18 00	19 02	20 06
03	224 41.5 ..	24.8	22 18.7	9.9	22 15.1	1.4	55.4	54	06 50	07 36	08 20	16 52	17 49	18 52	19 58
04	239 41.4	24.9	36 47.6	9.9	22 13.7	1.5	55.4	56	06 56	07 45	08 33	16 40	17 37	18 41	19 50
05	254 41.2	24.9	51 16.5	10.0	22 12.2	1.7	55.3	58	07 03	07 56	08 47	16 25	17 23	18 29	19 40
06	269 41.1	N23 24.9	65 45.5	10.0	S22 10.5	1.7	55.3	S 60	07 10	08 07	09 05	16 07	17 06	18 15	19 28

								Lat.	Sunset	Twilight		Moonset			
										Civil	Naut.	18	19	20	21
07	284 40.9	25.0	80 14.5	10.1	22 08.8	1.8	55.3								
08	299 40.8	25.0	94 43.6	10.0	22 07.0	2.0	55.3	°	h m	h m	h m	h m	h m	h m	h m
09	314 40.7 ..	25.1	109 12.6	10.2	22 05.0	2.1	55.3	N 72	☐	☐	☐	▬	▬	▬	▬
10	329 40.5	25.1	123 41.8	10.1	22 02.9	2.2	55.2	N 70	☐	☐	☐	▬	▬	03 23	04 20
11	344 40.4	25.1	138 10.9	10.3	22 00.7	2.2	55.2	68	☐	☐	☐	▬	▬	03 23	05 17
12	359 40.3	N23 25.2	152 40.2	10.2	S21 58.5	2.4	55.2	66	☐	☐	☐	02 10	03 01	04 20	05 50
13	14 40.1	25.2	167 09.4	10.3	21 56.1	2.6	55.2	64	22 32	////	////	02 50	03 43	04 53	06 14
14	29 40.0	25.2	181 38.7	10.4	21 53.5	2.6	55.2	62	21 54	////	////	03 18	04 11	05 18	06 33
15	44 39.9 ..	25.3	196 08.1	10.3	21 50.9	2.7	55.1	60	21 27	23 14	////	03 40	04 33	05 37	06 49
16	59 39.7	25.3	210 37.4	10.5	21 48.2	2.8	55.1	N 58	21 07	22 23	////	03 58	04 50	05 53	07 02
17	74 39.6	25.4	225 06.9	10.5	21 45.4	3.0	55.1	56	20 50	21 53	////	04 12	05 05	06 06	07 13
18	89 39.5	N23 25.4	239 36.4	10.5	S21 42.4	3.0	55.1	54	20 36	21 30	23 18	04 25	05 18	06 18	07 23
19	104 39.3	25.4	254 05.9	10.6	21 39.4	3.2	55.1	52	20 23	21 12	22 31	04 36	05 29	06 29	07 32
20	119 39.2	25.4	268 35.5	10.6	21 36.2	3.2	55.0	50	20 12	20 57	22 03	04 46	05 39	06 38	07 40
21	134 39.1 ..	25.5	283 05.1	10.7	21 33.0	3.4	55.0	45	19 50	20 27	21 17	05 07	06 00	06 57	07 57
22	149 38.9	25.5	297 34.8	10.7	21 29.6	3.4	55.0	N 40	19 32	20 05	20 46	05 24	06 17	07 13	08 10
23	164 38.8	25.5	312 04.5	10.8	21 26.2	3.6	55.0	35	19 17	19 46	20 23	05 39	06 31	07 26	08 22
20 00	179 38.6	N23 25.6	326 34.3	10.8	S21 22.6	3.7	55.0	30	19 04	19 31	20 05	05 51	06 44	07 38	08 32
01	194 38.5	25.6	341 04.1	10.9	21 18.9	3.8	55.0	20	18 42	19 06	19 35	06 12	07 05	07 57	08 49
02	209 38.4	25.6	355 34.0	10.9	21 15.1	3.8	54.9	N 10	18 23	18 46	19 13	06 31	07 23	08 14	09 04
03	224 38.2 ..	25.7	10 03.9	11.0	21 11.3	4.0	54.9	0	18 05	18 28	18 54	06 48	07 40	08 30	09 18
04	239 38.1	25.7	24 33.9	11.0	21 07.3	4.1	54.9	S 10	17 48	18 10	18 37	07 05	07 57	08 46	09 32
05	254 38.0	25.7	39 03.9	11.1	21 03.2	4.2	54.9	20	17 29	17 53	18 21	07 24	08 15	09 03	09 47
06	269 37.8	N23 25.7	53 34.0	11.1	S20 59.0	4.2	54.9	30	17 08	17 34	18 04	07 45	08 36	09 22	10 04
07	284 37.7	25.8	68 04.1	11.2	20 54.8	4.4	54.9	35	16 55	17 24	17 55	07 57	08 48	09 34	10 14
08	299 37.6	25.8	82 34.3	11.2	20 50.4	4.5	54.8	40	16 41	17 12	17 46	08 11	09 02	09 47	10 25
09	314 37.4 ..	25.8	97 04.5	11.3	20 45.9	4.5	54.8	45	16 24	16 58	17 35	08 28	09 19	10 02	10 38
10	329 37.3	25.8	111 34.8	11.4	20 41.4	4.7	54.8	S 50	16 04	16 42	17 24	08 49	09 39	10 20	10 54
11	344 37.2	25.8	126 05.2	11.4	20 36.7	4.8	54.8	52	15 54	16 35	17 18	08 59	09 49	10 29	11 01
12	359 37.0	N23 25.9	140 35.6	11.4	S20 31.9	4.8	54.8	54	15 43	16 26	17 13	09 10	10 00	10 39	11 10
13	14 36.9	25.9	155 06.0	11.5	20 27.1	4.9	54.8	56	15 30	16 17	17 07	09 23	10 12	10 50	11 19
14	29 36.8	25.9	169 36.5	11.6	20 22.2	5.1	54.7	58	15 15	16 07	17 00	09 38	10 26	11 03	11 29
15	44 36.6 ..	25.9	184 07.1	11.6	20 17.1	5.1	54.7	S 60	14 58	15 55	16 52	09 55	10 43	11 17	11 41
16	59 36.5	25.9	198 37.7	11.7	20 12.0	5.2	54.7								
17	74 36.3	26.0	213 08.4	11.7	20 06.8	5.4	54.7			SUN			MOON		
18	89 36.2	N23 26.0	227 39.1	11.8	S20 01.4	5.4	54.7	Day	Eqn. of Time		Mer.	Mer. Pass.		Age	Phase
19	104 36.1	26.0	242 09.9	11.8	19 56.0	5.5	54.7		00ʰ	12ʰ	Pass.	Upper	Lower		
20	119 35.9	26.0	256 40.7	11.9	19 50.5	5.6	54.7	d	m s	m s	h m	h m	h m	d %	
21	134 35.8 ..	26.0	271 11.6	12.0	19 44.9	5.6	54.6	18	00 59	01 06	12 01	00 35	13 02	15 99	◯
22	149 35.7	26.0	285 42.6	12.0	19 39.3	5.8	54.6	19	01 12	01 19	12 01	01 28	13 53	16 95	
23	164 35.5	26.0	300 13.6	12.1	S19 33.5	5.8	54.6	20	01 25	01 32	12 02	02 18	14 43	17 90	
	SD 15.8	d 0.0	SD 15.2		15.0		14.9									

© British Crown Copyright 2018. All rights reserved.

2019 JUNE 21, 22, 23 (FRI., SAT., SUN.)

UT	ARIES GHA	VENUS −3·8 GHA	Dec	MARS +1·8 GHA	Dec	JUPITER −2·6 GHA	Dec	SATURN +0·1 GHA	Dec	STARS Name	SHA	Dec
21 00	268 54.1	195 35.5	N21 57.4	153 50.9	N22 38.0	11 42.2	S22 21.2	338 51.5	S21 48.7	Acamar	315 15.5	S40 13.6
01	283 56.6	210 34.7 . .	57.9	168 51.7 . .	37.8	26 45.0 . .	21.1	353 54.1 . .	48.7	Achernar	335 24.0	S57 08.2
02	298 59.1	225 34.0	58.3	183 52.5	37.5	41 47.8	21.1	8 56.8	48.7	Acrux	173 04.6	S63 12.6
03	314 01.5	240 33.2 . .	58.8	198 53.2 . .	37.2	56 50.6 . .	21.1	23 59.4 . .	48.7	Adhara	255 09.7	S29 00.0
04	329 04.0	255 32.4	59.2	213 54.0	37.0	71 53.4	21.1	39 02.0	48.8	Aldebaran	290 45.0	N16 32.7
05	344 06.4	270 31.6	21 59.6	228 54.7	36.7	86 56.2	21.0	54 04.7	48.8			
06	359 08.9	285 30.8	N22 00.1	243 55.5	N22 36.4	101 59.0	S22 21.0	69 07.3	S21 48.8	Alioth	166 16.9	N55 51.7
F 07	14 11.4	300 30.0	00.5	258 56.3	36.2	117 01.8	21.0	84 10.0	48.8	Alkaid	152 55.4	N49 13.3
R 08	29 13.8	315 29.2	01.0	273 57.0	35.9	132 04.6	21.0	99 12.6	48.9	Alnair	27 38.4	S46 51.8
I 09	44 16.3	330 28.4 . .	01.4	288 57.8 . .	35.6	147 07.4 . .	21.0	114 15.3 . .	48.9	Alnilam	275 42.5	S 1 11.5
D 10	59 18.8	345 27.6	01.8	303 58.6	35.4	162 10.2	20.9	129 17.9	48.9	Alphard	217 52.3	S 8 44.6
A 11	74 21.2	0 26.8	02.3	318 59.3	35.1	177 13.0	20.9	144 20.5	48.9			
Y 12	89 23.7	15 26.0	N22 02.7	334 00.1	N22 34.8	192 15.8	S22 20.9	159 23.2	S21 49.0	Alphecca	126 07.2	N26 39.2
13	104 26.2	30 25.2	03.1	349 00.8	34.5	207 18.6	20.9	174 25.8	49.0	Alpheratz	357 39.3	N29 11.6
14	119 28.6	45 24.4	03.6	4 01.6	34.3	222 21.4	20.9	189 28.5	49.0	Altair	62 03.9	N 8 55.2
15	134 31.1	60 23.6 . .	04.0	19 02.4 . .	34.0	237 24.2 . .	20.8	204 31.1 . .	49.1	Ankaa	353 11.7	S42 11.9
16	149 33.6	75 22.8	04.4	34 03.1	33.7	252 27.0	20.8	219 33.8	49.1	Antares	112 20.9	S26 28.4
17	164 36.0	90 22.0	04.8	49 03.9	33.5	267 29.8	20.8	234 36.4	49.1			
18	179 38.5	105 21.2	N22 05.3	64 04.7	N22 33.2	282 32.6	S22 20.8	249 39.1	S21 49.1	Arcturus	145 51.8	N19 05.1
19	194 40.9	120 20.4	05.7	79 05.4	32.9	297 35.4	20.8	264 41.7	49.2	Atria	107 18.4	S69 03.6
20	209 43.4	135 19.6	06.1	94 06.2	32.6	312 38.1	20.7	279 44.3	49.2	Avior	234 16.9	S59 34.5
21	224 45.9	150 18.8 . .	06.5	109 07.0 . .	32.4	327 40.9 . .	20.7	294 47.0 . .	49.2	Bellatrix	278 27.9	N 6 21.9
22	239 48.3	165 18.0	07.0	124 07.7	32.1	342 43.7	20.7	309 49.6	49.2	Betelgeuse	270 57.2	N 7 24.5
23	254 50.8	180 17.2	07.4	139 08.5	31.8	357 46.5	20.7	324 52.3	49.3			
22 00	269 53.3	195 16.4	N22 07.8	154 09.3	N22 31.5	12 49.3	S22 20.7	339 54.9	S21 49.3	Canopus	263 54.9	S52 42.5
01	284 55.7	210 15.6	08.2	169 10.0	31.3	27 52.1	20.6	354 57.6	49.3	Capella	280 28.9	N46 00.8
02	299 58.2	225 14.8	08.7	184 10.8	31.0	42 54.9	20.6	10 00.2	49.3	Deneb	49 28.3	N45 20.9
03	315 00.7	240 14.0 . .	09.1	199 11.5 . .	30.7	57 57.7 . .	20.6	25 02.9 . .	49.4	Denebola	182 29.5	N14 28.0
04	330 03.1	255 13.2	09.5	214 12.3	30.4	73 00.5	20.6	40 05.5	49.4	Diphda	348 51.8	S17 52.8
05	345 05.6	270 12.4	09.9	229 13.1	30.2	88 03.3	20.5	55 08.1	49.4			
06	0 08.0	285 11.6	N22 10.3	244 13.8	N22 29.9	103 06.1	S22 20.5	70 10.8	S21 49.4	Dubhe	193 46.9	N61 39.1
S 07	15 10.5	300 10.8	10.7	259 14.6	29.6	118 08.9	20.5	85 13.4	49.5	Elnath	278 07.8	N28 37.2
A 08	30 13.0	315 10.0	11.1	274 15.4	29.3	133 11.7	20.5	100 16.1	49.5	Eltanin	90 43.7	N51 29.3
T 09	45 15.4	330 09.2 . .	11.6	289 16.1 . .	29.1	148 14.5 . .	20.5	115 18.7 . .	49.5	Enif	33 42.9	N 9 57.8
U 10	60 17.9	345 08.4	12.0	304 16.9	28.8	163 17.3	20.4	130 21.4	49.6	Fomalhaut	15 19.4	S29 31.0
R 11	75 20.4	0 07.6	12.4	319 17.7	28.5	178 20.0	20.4	145 24.0	49.6			
D 12	90 22.8	15 06.8	N22 12.8	334 18.4	N22 28.2	193 22.8	S22 20.4	160 26.7	S21 49.6	Gacrux	171 56.2	S57 13.5
A 13	105 25.3	30 06.0	13.2	349 19.2	28.0	208 25.6	20.4	175 29.3	49.6	Gienah	175 48.1	S17 39.0
Y 14	120 27.8	45 05.2	13.6	4 20.0	27.7	223 28.4	20.4	190 32.0	49.7	Hadar	148 41.7	S60 28.1
15	135 30.2	60 04.4 . .	14.0	19 20.7 . .	27.4	238 31.2 . .	20.3	205 34.6 . .	49.7	Hamal	327 56.3	N23 33.0
16	150 32.7	75 03.5	14.4	34 21.5	27.1	253 34.0	20.3	220 37.2	49.7	Kaus Aust.	83 38.0	S34 22.3
17	165 35.2	90 02.7	14.8	49 22.3	26.8	268 36.8	20.3	235 39.9	49.7			
18	180 37.6	105 01.9	N22 15.2	64 23.0	N22 26.6	283 39.6	S22 20.3	250 42.5	S21 49.8	Kochab	137 19.3	N74 04.9
19	195 40.1	120 01.1	15.6	79 23.8	26.3	298 42.4	20.3	265 45.2	49.8	Markab	13 34.2	N15 18.4
20	210 42.5	135 00.3	16.0	94 24.6	26.0	313 45.2	20.2	280 47.8	49.8	Menkar	314 11.0	N 4 09.8
21	225 45.0	149 59.5 . .	16.4	109 25.3 . .	25.7	328 48.0 . .	20.2	295 50.5 . .	49.8	Menkent	148 02.5	S36 27.9
22	240 47.5	164 58.7	16.8	124 26.1	25.4	343 50.8	20.2	310 53.1	49.9	Miaplacidus	221 39.5	S69 48.0
23	255 49.9	179 57.9	17.2	139 26.9	25.2	358 53.5	20.2	325 55.8	49.9			
23 00	270 52.4	194 57.1	N22 17.6	154 27.6	N22 24.9	13 56.3	S22 20.2	340 58.4	S21 49.9	Mirfak	308 34.9	N49 55.5
01	285 54.9	209 56.3	18.0	169 28.4	24.6	28 59.1	20.1	356 01.1	49.9	Nunki	75 52.9	S26 16.2
02	300 57.3	224 55.5	18.4	184 29.2	24.3	44 01.9	20.1	11 03.7	50.0	Peacock	53 12.3	S56 40.1
03	315 59.8	239 54.6 . .	18.8	199 30.0 . .	24.0	59 04.7 . .	20.1	26 06.4 . .	50.0	Pollux	243 23.1	N27 58.7
04	331 02.3	254 53.8	19.2	214 30.7	23.8	74 07.5	20.1	41 09.0	50.0	Procyon	244 55.8	N 5 10.4
05	346 04.7	269 53.0	19.5	229 31.5	23.5	89 10.3	20.0	56 11.6	50.1			
06	1 07.2	284 52.2	N22 19.9	244 32.3	N22 23.2	104 13.1	S22 20.0	71 14.3	S21 50.1	Rasalhague	96 02.3	N12 32.9
07	16 09.7	299 51.4	20.3	259 33.0	22.9	119 15.9	20.0	86 16.9	50.1	Regulus	207 39.3	N11 52.4
08	31 12.1	314 50.6	20.7	274 33.8	22.6	134 18.7	20.0	101 19.6	50.1	Rigel	281 08.4	S 8 10.9
S 09	46 14.6	329 49.8 . .	21.1	289 34.6 . .	22.3	149 21.5 . .	20.0	116 22.2 . .	50.2	Rigil Kent.	139 45.7	S60 55.0
U 10	61 17.0	344 49.0	21.5	304 35.3	22.1	164 24.2	19.9	131 24.9	50.2	Sabik	102 07.5	S15 44.8
N 11	76 19.5	359 48.2	21.9	319 36.1	21.8	179 27.0	19.9	146 27.5	50.2			
D 12	91 22.0	14 47.3	N22 22.2	334 36.9	N22 21.5	194 29.8	S22 19.9	161 30.2	S21 50.2	Schedar	349 35.9	N56 38.2
A 13	106 24.4	29 46.5	22.6	349 37.6	21.2	209 32.6	19.9	176 32.8	50.3	Shaula	96 15.9	S37 06.9
Y 14	121 26.9	44 45.7	23.0	4 38.4	20.9	224 35.4	19.9	191 35.5	50.3	Sirius	258 30.5	S16 44.7
15	136 29.4	59 44.9 . .	23.4	19 39.2 . .	20.6	239 38.2 . .	19.8	206 38.1 . .	50.3	Spica	158 26.8	S11 15.7
16	151 31.8	74 44.1	23.8	34 40.0	20.4	254 41.0	19.8	221 40.8	50.3	Suhail	222 49.8	S43 30.8
17	166 34.3	89 43.3	24.1	49 40.7	20.1	269 43.8	19.8	236 43.4	50.4			
18	181 36.8	104 42.5	N22 24.5	64 41.5	N22 19.8	284 46.6	S22 19.8	251 46.1	S21 50.4	Vega	80 35.8	N38 48.2
19	196 39.2	119 41.6	24.9	79 42.3	19.5	299 49.3	19.8	266 48.7	50.4	Zuben'ubi	137 00.6	S16 07.2
20	211 41.7	134 40.8	25.3	94 43.0	19.2	314 52.1	19.7	281 51.4	50.4			
21	226 44.1	149 40.0 . .	25.6	109 43.8 . .	18.9	329 54.9 . .	19.7	296 54.0 . .	50.5		SHA	Mer.Pass.
22	241 46.6	164 39.2	26.0	124 44.6	18.6	344 57.7	19.7	311 56.7	50.5	Venus	285 23.1	10 59
23	256 49.1	179 38.4	26.4	139 45.3	18.3	0 00.5	19.7	326 59.3	50.5	Mars	244 16.0	13 43
Mer. Pass.	h m 5 59.5	v −0.8	d 0.4	v 0.8	d 0.3	v 2.8	d 0.0	v 2.6	d 0.0	Jupiter	102 56.1	23 04
										Saturn	70 01.7	1 20

© British Crown Copyright 2018. All rights reserved.

UT		SUN		MOON				
		GHA	Dec	GHA	v	Dec	d	HP
d h		o '	o '	o '	'	o '	'	'
21 00		179 35.4	N23 26.0	314 44.7	12.1	S19 27.7	6.0	54.6
01		194 35.3	26.1	329 15.8	12.2	19 21.7	6.0	54.6
02		209 35.1	26.1	343 47.0	12.2	19 15.7	6.1	54.6
03		224 35.0	.. 26.1	358 18.2	12.3	19 09.6	6.2	54.6
04		239 34.9	26.1	12 49.5	12.3	19 03.4	6.3	54.5
05		254 34.7	26.1	27 20.8	12.4	18 57.1	6.3	54.5
06	F	269 34.6	N23 26.1	41 52.2	12.5	S18 50.8	6.5	54.5
07	R	284 34.5	26.1	56 23.7	12.5	18 44.3	6.5	54.5
08	I	299 34.3	26.1	70 55.2	12.6	18 37.8	6.6	54.5
09	D	314 34.2	.. 26.1	85 26.8	12.6	18 31.2	6.7	54.5
10	A	329 34.0	26.1	99 58.4	12.7	18 24.5	6.7	54.5
11	Y	344 33.9	26.1	114 30.1	12.7	18 17.8	6.9	54.5
12		359 33.8	N23 26.1	129 01.8	12.8	S18 10.9	6.9	54.5
13		14 33.6	26.1	143 33.6	12.9	18 04.0	7.0	54.4
14		29 33.5	26.1	158 05.5	12.9	17 57.0	7.0	54.4
15		44 33.4	.. 26.1	172 37.4	12.9	17 50.0	7.2	54.4
16		59 33.2	26.1	187 09.3	13.0	17 42.8	7.2	54.4
17		74 33.1	26.1	201 41.3	13.1	17 35.6	7.3	54.4
18		89 33.0	N23 26.1	216 13.4	13.1	S17 28.3	7.4	54.4
19		104 32.8	26.1	230 45.5	13.2	17 20.9	7.4	54.4
20		119 32.7	26.1	245 17.7	13.2	17 13.5	7.5	54.4
21		134 32.6	.. 26.1	259 49.9	13.3	17 06.0	7.6	54.4
22		149 32.4	26.1	274 22.2	13.3	16 58.4	7.7	54.4
23		164 32.3	26.1	288 54.5	13.4	16 50.7	7.7	54.3
22 00		179 32.2	N23 26.1	303 26.9	13.4	S16 43.0	7.8	54.3
01		194 32.0	26.1	317 59.3	13.5	16 35.2	7.9	54.3
02		209 31.9	26.1	332 31.8	13.6	16 27.3	7.9	54.3
03		224 31.7	.. 26.1	347 04.4	13.6	16 19.4	8.0	54.3
04		239 31.6	26.1	1 37.0	13.6	16 11.4	8.1	54.3
05		254 31.5	26.1	16 09.6	13.7	16 03.3	8.1	54.3
06		269 31.3	N23 26.1	30 42.3	13.8	S15 55.2	8.2	54.3
07	S	284 31.2	26.1	45 15.1	13.7	15 47.0	8.2	54.3
08	A	299 31.1	26.0	59 47.8	13.9	15 38.8	8.4	54.3
09	T	314 30.9	.. 26.0	74 20.7	13.9	15 30.4	8.4	54.3
10	U	329 30.8	26.0	88 53.6	13.9	15 22.0	8.4	54.3
11	R	344 30.7	26.0	103 26.5	14.0	15 13.6	8.5	54.3
12	D	359 30.5	N23 26.0	117 59.5	14.0	S15 05.1	8.6	54.3
13	A	14 30.4	26.0	132 32.5	14.1	14 56.5	8.6	54.3
14	Y	29 30.3	26.0	147 05.6	14.2	14 47.9	8.7	54.2
15		44 30.1	.. 25.9	161 38.8	14.1	14 39.2	8.8	54.2
16		59 30.0	25.9	176 11.9	14.3	14 30.4	8.8	54.2
17		74 29.9	25.9	190 45.2	14.2	14 21.6	8.8	54.2
18		89 29.7	N23 25.9	205 18.4	14.3	S14 12.8	9.0	54.2
19		104 29.6	25.9	219 51.7	14.4	14 03.8	8.9	54.2
20		119 29.5	25.9	234 25.1	14.4	13 54.9	9.1	54.2
21		134 29.3	.. 25.8	248 58.5	14.4	13 45.8	9.1	54.2
22		149 29.2	25.8	263 31.9	14.5	13 36.7	9.1	54.2
23		164 29.0	25.8	278 05.4	14.5	13 27.6	9.2	54.2
23 00		179 28.9	N23 25.8	292 38.9	14.6	S13 18.4	9.3	54.2
01		194 28.8	25.7	307 12.5	14.6	13 09.1	9.3	54.2
02		209 28.6	25.7	321 46.1	14.6	12 59.8	9.3	54.2
03		224 28.5	.. 25.7	336 19.7	14.7	12 50.5	9.4	54.2
04		239 28.4	25.7	350 53.4	14.7	12 41.1	9.5	54.2
05		254 28.2	25.6	5 27.1	14.8	12 31.6	9.5	54.2
06		269 28.1	N23 25.6	20 00.9	14.8	S12 22.1	9.6	54.2
07		284 28.0	25.6	34 34.7	14.8	12 12.5	9.6	54.2
08		299 27.8	25.6	49 08.5	14.9	12 02.9	9.6	54.2
09	S	314 27.7	.. 25.5	63 42.4	14.9	11 53.3	9.7	54.2
10	U	329 27.6	25.5	78 16.3	15.0	11 43.6	9.8	54.2
11	N	344 27.4	25.5	92 50.3	14.9	11 33.8	9.8	54.2
12	D	359 27.3	N23 25.4	107 24.2	15.0	S11 24.0	9.8	54.2
13	A	14 27.2	25.4	121 58.2	15.0	11 14.2	9.9	54.2
14	Y	29 27.0	25.4	136 32.3	15.0	11 04.3	9.9	54.2
15		44 26.9	.. 25.3	151 06.3	15.1	10 54.4	10.0	54.2
16		59 26.8	25.3	165 40.4	15.2	10 44.4	10.0	54.2
17		74 26.6	25.3	180 14.6	15.1	10 34.4	10.1	54.2
18		89 26.5	N23 25.2	194 48.7	15.2	S10 24.3	10.1	54.2
19		104 26.4	25.2	209 22.9	15.2	10 14.2	10.1	54.2
20		119 26.2	25.2	223 57.1	15.3	10 04.1	10.2	54.2
21		134 26.1	.. 25.1	238 31.4	15.3	9 53.9	10.2	54.2
22		149 26.0	25.1	253 05.7	15.3	9 43.7	10.3	54.2
23		164 25.8	25.0	267 40.0	15.3	S 9 33.4	10.3	54.2
		SD 15.8	d 0.0	SD 14.8		14.8		14.8

Twilight / Sunrise / Moonrise

Lat.	Twilight Naut.	Twilight Civil	Sunrise	Moonrise 21	22	23	24
o	h m	h m	h m	h m	h m	h m	h m
N 72	▭	▭	▭	▬	02 14	01 36	01 14
N 70	▭	▭	▭	02 04	01 29	01 12	01 00
68	▭	▭	▭	01 07	01 00	00 54	00 49
66	▭	▭	▭	00 33	00 37	00 39	00 39
64	////	////	01 31	00 08	00 19	00 27	00 31
62	////	////	02 09	24 05	00 05	00 16	00 24
60	////	00 49	02 36	23 52	24 07	00 07	00 18
N 58	////	01 41	02 56	23 42	23 59	24 13	00 13
56	////	02 11	03 13	23 32	23 52	24 09	00 09
54	00 45	02 33	03 28	23 24	23 46	24 04	00 04
52	01 32	02 51	03 40	23 17	23 40	24 01	00 01
50	02 00	03 06	03 51	23 10	23 35	23 57	24 17
45	02 46	03 36	04 13	22 55	23 24	23 49	24 13
N 40	03 17	03 59	04 31	22 43	23 15	23 43	24 10
35	03 40	04 17	04 47	22 33	23 07	23 38	24 07
30	03 59	04 32	05 00	22 24	23 00	23 33	24 04
20	04 28	04 57	05 22	22 09	22 48	23 24	24 00
N 10	04 50	05 18	05 41	21 55	22 37	23 17	23 56
0	05 10	05 36	05 58	21 42	22 27	23 10	23 52
S 10	05 27	05 53	06 16	21 30	22 17	23 03	23 48
20	05 43	06 10	06 34	21 16	22 06	22 56	23 44
30	05 59	06 29	06 56	21 00	21 54	22 47	23 40
35	06 08	06 40	07 08	20 51	21 47	22 42	23 37
40	06 17	06 52	07 22	20 41	21 39	22 36	23 34
45	06 28	07 05	07 39	20 28	21 29	22 30	23 31
S 50	06 40	07 21	08 00	20 13	21 18	22 22	23 27
52	06 45	07 29	08 10	20 06	21 12	22 18	23 25
54	06 51	07 37	08 21	19 58	21 06	22 14	23 23
56	06 57	07 46	08 34	19 50	21 00	22 10	23 20
58	07 04	07 56	08 48	19 40	20 52	22 05	23 18
S 60	07 11	08 08	09 06	19 28	20 44	21 59	23 15

Sunset / Twilight / Moonset

Lat.	Sunset	Twilight Civil	Twilight Naut.	Moonset 21	22	23	24
o	h m	h m	h m	h m	h m	h m	h m
N 72	▭	▭	▭	▬	05 48	07 57	09 49
N 70	▭	▭	▭	04 20	06 31	08 20	10 01
68	▭	▭	▭	05 17	07 00	08 37	10 10
66	▭	▭	▭	05 50	07 21	08 51	10 18
64	22 33	////	////	06 14	07 38	09 02	10 25
62	21 54	////	////	06 33	07 52	09 12	10 30
60	21 28	23 14	////	06 49	08 04	09 20	10 35
N 58	21 07	22 23	////	07 02	08 14	09 27	10 40
56	20 51	21 53	////	07 13	08 23	09 33	10 44
54	20 36	21 31	23 18	07 23	08 31	09 39	10 47
52	20 24	21 13	22 31	07 32	08 38	09 44	10 50
50	20 13	20 58	22 03	07 40	08 44	09 49	10 53
45	19 50	20 28	21 18	07 57	08 58	09 58	10 59
N 40	19 32	20 05	20 47	08 10	09 09	10 07	11 04
35	19 17	19 47	20 24	08 22	09 18	10 14	11 09
30	19 04	19 32	20 05	08 32	09 26	10 20	11 13
20	18 42	19 07	19 36	08 49	09 40	10 30	11 19
N 10	18 23	18 46	19 13	09 04	09 53	10 39	11 25
0	18 06	18 28	18 54	09 18	10 04	10 48	11 30
S 10	17 48	18 11	18 37	09 32	10 16	10 56	11 36
20	17 30	17 54	18 21	09 47	10 28	11 05	11 41
30	17 08	17 35	18 05	10 04	10 42	11 16	11 48
35	16 56	17 24	17 56	10 15	10 49	11 22	11 51
40	16 42	17 12	17 46	10 25	10 59	11 28	11 56
45	16 25	16 59	17 36	10 38	11 09	11 36	12 00
S 50	16 04	16 43	17 24	10 54	11 22	11 45	12 06
52	15 54	16 35	17 19	11 01	11 28	11 49	12 09
54	15 43	16 27	17 13	11 10	11 34	11 54	12 11
56	15 30	16 18	17 07	11 19	11 41	11 59	12 15
58	15 16	16 08	17 00	11 29	11 49	12 05	12 18
S 60	14 58	15 56	16 53	11 41	11 58	12 11	12 22

SUN / MOON

Day	SUN Eqn. of Time 00h	12h	Mer. Pass.	MOON Mer. Pass. Upper	Lower	Age	Phase
d	m s	m s	h m	h m	h m	d	%
21	01 38	01 45	12 02	03 07	15 30	18	84
22	01 51	01 58	12 02	03 53	16 16	19	76
23	02 04	02 11	12 02	04 38	16 59	20	68

© British Crown Copyright 2018. All rights reserved.

UT	ARIES GHA	VENUS −3·8 GHA	Dec	MARS +1·8 GHA	Dec	JUPITER −2·6 GHA	Dec	SATURN +0·1 GHA	Dec	STARS Name	SHA	Dec
d h	° ′	° ′	° ′	° ′	° ′	° ′	° ′	° ′	° ′		° ′	° ′
24 00	271 51.5	194 37.6	N22 26.7	154 46.1	N22 18.1	15 03.3	S22 19.7	342 02.0	S21 50.6	Acamar	315 15.5	S40 13.6
01	286 54.0	209 36.7	27.1	169 46.9	17.8	30 06.1	19.6	357 04.6	50.6	Achernar	335 23.9	S57 08.2
02	301 56.5	224 35.9	27.5	184 47.7	17.5	45 08.9	19.6	12 07.2	50.6	Acrux	173 04.6	S63 12.6
03	316 58.9	239 35.1 ..	27.8	199 48.4 ..	17.2	60 11.6 ..	19.6	27 09.9 ..	50.6	Adhara	255 09.7	S29 00.0
04	332 01.4	254 34.3	28.2	214 49.2	16.9	75 14.4	19.6	42 12.5	50.7	Aldebaran	290 45.0	N16 32.7
05	347 03.9	269 33.5	28.6	229 50.0	16.6	90 17.2	19.5	57 15.2	50.7			
06	2 06.3	284 32.6	N22 28.9	244 50.7	N22 16.3	105 20.0	S22 19.5	72 17.8	S21 50.7	Alioth	166 17.0	N55 51.7
07	17 08.8	299 31.8	29.3	259 51.5	16.0	120 22.8	19.5	87 20.5	50.7	Alkaid	152 55.4	N49 13.4
M 08	32 11.3	314 31.0	29.6	274 52.3	15.8	135 25.6	19.5	102 23.1	50.8	Alnair	27 38.3	S46 51.8
O 09	47 13.7	329 30.2 ..	30.0	289 53.1 ..	15.5	150 28.4 ..	19.5	117 25.8 ..	50.8	Alnilam	275 42.5	S 1 11.5
N 10	62 16.2	344 29.4	30.4	304 53.8	15.2	165 31.2	19.4	132 28.4	50.8	Alphard	217 52.3	S 8 44.6
D 11	77 18.6	359 28.5	30.7	319 54.6	14.9	180 33.9	19.4	147 31.1	50.8			
A 12	92 21.1	14 27.7	N22 31.1	334 55.4	N22 14.6	195 36.7	S22 19.4	162 33.7	S21 50.9	Alphecca	126 07.2	N26 39.2
Y 13	107 23.6	29 26.9	31.4	349 56.2	14.3	210 39.5	19.4	177 36.4	50.9	Alpheratz	357 39.2	N29 11.6
14	122 26.0	44 26.1	31.8	4 56.9	14.0	225 42.3	19.4	192 39.0	50.9	Altair	62 03.9	N 8 55.2
15	137 28.5	59 25.3 ..	32.1	19 57.7 ..	13.7	240 45.1 ..	19.3	207 41.7 ..	50.9	Ankaa	353 11.7	S42 11.9
16	152 31.0	74 24.4	32.5	34 58.5	13.4	255 47.9	19.3	222 44.3	51.0	Antares	112 20.9	S26 28.4
17	167 33.4	89 23.6	32.8	49 59.2	13.1	270 50.7	19.3	237 47.0	51.0			
18	182 35.9	104 22.8	N22 33.2	65 00.0	N22 12.8	285 53.4	S22 19.3	252 49.6	S21 51.0	Arcturus	145 51.8	N19 05.1
19	197 38.4	119 22.0	33.5	80 00.8	12.5	300 56.2	19.3	267 52.3	51.1	Atria	107 18.4	S69 03.7
20	212 40.8	134 21.1	33.9	95 01.6	12.3	315 59.0	19.2	282 54.9	51.1	Avior	234 16.9	S59 34.5
21	227 43.3	149 20.3 ..	34.2	110 02.3 ..	12.0	331 01.8 ..	19.2	297 57.6 ..	51.1	Bellatrix	278 27.9	N 6 21.9
22	242 45.8	164 19.5	34.6	125 03.1	11.7	346 04.6	19.2	313 00.2	51.1	Betelgeuse	270 57.2	N 7 24.5
23	257 48.2	179 18.7	34.9	140 03.9	11.4	1 07.4	19.2	328 02.9	51.2			
25 00	272 50.7	194 17.8	N22 35.3	155 04.7	N22 11.1	16 10.2	S22 19.2	343 05.5	S21 51.2	Canopus	263 54.9	S52 42.5
01	287 53.1	209 17.0	35.6	170 05.4	10.8	31 12.9	19.1	358 08.2	51.2	Capella	280 28.8	N46 00.8
02	302 55.6	224 16.2	35.9	185 06.2	10.5	46 15.7	19.1	13 10.8	51.2	Deneb	49 28.3	N45 20.9
03	317 58.1	239 15.4 ..	36.3	200 07.0 ..	10.2	61 18.5 ..	19.1	28 13.5 ..	51.3	Denebola	182 29.5	N14 28.0
04	333 00.5	254 14.5	36.6	215 07.8	09.9	76 21.3	19.1	43 16.1	51.3	Diphda	348 51.8	S17 52.8
05	348 03.0	269 13.7	36.9	230 08.5	09.6	91 24.1	19.1	58 18.8	51.3			
06	3 05.5	284 12.9	N22 37.3	245 09.3	N22 09.3	106 26.9	S22 19.0	73 21.4	S21 51.3	Dubhe	193 46.9	N61 39.1
07	18 07.9	299 12.1	37.6	260 10.1	09.0	121 29.6	19.0	88 24.1	51.4	Elnath	278 07.8	N28 37.2
T 08	33 10.4	314 11.2	37.9	275 10.9	08.7	136 32.4	19.0	103 26.7	51.4	Eltanin	90 43.7	N51 29.3
U 09	48 12.9	329 10.4 ..	38.3	290 11.6 ..	08.4	151 35.2 ..	19.0	118 29.4 ..	51.4	Enif	33 42.9	N 9 57.8
E 10	63 15.3	344 09.6	38.6	305 12.4	08.1	166 38.0	18.9	133 32.0	51.5	Fomalhaut	15 19.3	S29 31.0
S 11	78 17.8	359 08.7	38.9	320 13.2	07.8	181 40.8	18.9	148 34.7	51.5			
D 12	93 20.2	14 07.9	N22 39.3	335 14.0	N22 07.5	196 43.6	S22 18.9	163 37.3	S21 51.5	Gacrux	171 56.3	S57 13.5
A 13	108 22.7	29 07.1	39.6	350 14.7	07.2	211 46.3	18.9	178 40.0	51.5	Gienah	175 48.1	S17 39.0
Y 14	123 25.2	44 06.3	39.9	5 15.5	06.9	226 49.1	18.9	193 42.6	51.6	Hadar	148 41.7	S60 28.1
15	138 27.6	59 05.4 ..	40.2	20 16.3 ..	06.6	241 51.9 ..	18.8	208 45.3 ..	51.6	Hamal	327 56.3	N23 33.0
16	153 30.1	74 04.6	40.6	35 17.1	06.3	256 54.7	18.8	223 47.9	51.6	Kaus Aust.	83 38.0	S34 22.4
17	168 32.6	89 03.8	40.9	50 17.8	06.0	271 57.5	18.8	238 50.6	51.6			
18	183 35.0	104 02.9	N22 41.2	65 18.6	N22 05.7	287 00.3	S22 18.8	253 53.2	S21 51.7	Kochab	137 19.3	N74 04.9
19	198 37.5	119 02.1	41.5	80 19.4	05.4	302 03.0	18.8	268 55.9	51.7	Markab	13 34.1	N15 18.5
20	213 40.0	134 01.3	41.9	95 20.2	05.1	317 05.8	18.7	283 58.5	51.7	Menkar	314 11.0	N 4 09.8
21	228 42.4	149 00.4 ..	42.2	110 21.0 ..	04.8	332 08.6 ..	18.7	299 01.2 ..	51.7	Menkent	148 02.5	S36 27.9
22	243 44.9	163 59.6	42.5	125 21.7	04.5	347 11.4	18.7	314 03.8	51.8	Miaplacidus	221 39.5	S69 48.0
23	258 47.4	178 58.8	42.8	140 22.5	04.2	2 14.2	18.7	329 06.5	51.8			
26 00	273 49.8	193 58.0	N22 43.1	155 23.3	N22 03.9	17 17.0	S22 18.7	344 09.1	S21 51.8	Mirfak	308 34.8	N49 55.5
01	288 52.3	208 57.1	43.4	170 24.1	03.6	32 19.7	18.6	359 11.8	51.9	Nunki	75 52.9	S26 16.2
02	303 54.7	223 56.3	43.8	185 24.8	03.3	47 22.5	18.6	14 14.4	51.9	Peacock	53 12.3	S56 40.1
03	318 57.2	238 55.5 ..	44.1	200 25.6 ..	03.0	62 25.3 ..	18.6	29 17.1 ..	51.9	Pollux	243 23.1	N27 58.7
04	333 59.7	253 54.6	44.4	215 26.4	02.7	77 28.1	18.6	44 19.7	51.9	Procyon	244 55.8	N 5 10.4
05	349 02.1	268 53.8	44.7	230 27.2	02.4	92 30.9	18.6	59 22.4	52.0			
06	4 04.6	283 53.0	N22 45.0	245 28.0	N22 02.1	107 33.6	S22 18.5	74 25.0	S21 52.0	Rasalhague	96 02.3	N12 32.9
W 07	19 07.1	298 52.1	45.3	260 28.7	01.8	122 36.4	18.5	89 27.7	52.0	Regulus	207 39.3	N11 52.4
E 08	34 09.5	313 51.3	45.6	275 29.5	01.5	137 39.2	18.5	104 30.3	52.0	Rigel	281 08.4	S 8 10.9
D 09	49 12.0	328 50.4 ..	45.9	290 30.3 ..	01.2	152 42.0 ..	18.5	119 33.0 ..	52.1	Rigil Kent.	139 45.8	S60 55.0
N 10	64 14.5	343 49.6	46.2	305 31.1	00.9	167 44.8	18.5	134 35.6	52.1	Sabik	102 07.5	S15 44.8
E 11	79 16.9	358 48.8	46.5	320 31.8	00.6	182 47.5	18.4	149 38.3	52.1			
S 12	94 19.4	13 47.9	N22 46.8	335 32.6	N22 00.3	197 50.3	S22 18.4	164 41.0	S21 52.1	Schedar	349 35.9	N56 38.2
D 13	109 21.9	28 47.1	47.1	350 33.4	22 00.0	212 53.1	18.4	179 43.6	52.2	Shaula	96 15.9	S37 06.9
A 14	124 24.3	43 46.3	47.4	5 34.2	21 59.7	227 55.9	18.4	194 46.3	52.2	Sirius	258 30.5	S16 44.7
Y 15	139 26.8	58 45.4 ..	47.7	20 35.0 ..	59.4	242 58.7 ..	18.3	209 48.9 ..	52.2	Spica	158 26.8	S11 15.7
16	154 29.2	73 44.6	48.0	35 35.7	59.1	258 01.4	18.3	224 51.6	52.3	Suhail	222 49.8	S43 30.8
17	169 31.7	88 43.8	48.3	50 36.5	58.8	273 04.2	18.3	239 54.2	52.3			
18	184 34.2	103 42.9	N22 48.6	65 37.3	N21 58.5	288 07.0	S22 18.3	254 56.9	S21 52.3	Vega	80 35.7	N38 48.2
19	199 36.6	118 42.1	48.9	80 38.1	58.2	303 09.8	18.3	269 59.5	52.3	Zuben'ubi	137 00.6	S16 07.2
20	214 39.1	133 41.2	49.2	95 38.9	57.9	318 12.6	18.2	285 02.2	52.4		SHA	Mer. Pass.
21	229 41.6	148 40.4 ..	49.5	110 39.6 ..	57.5	333 15.3 ..	18.2	300 04.8 ..	52.4		° ′	h m
22	244 44.0	163 39.6	49.8	125 40.4	57.2	348 18.1	18.2	315 07.5	52.4	Venus	281 27.2	11 03
23	259 46.5	178 38.7	50.1	140 41.2	56.9	3 20.9	18.2	330 10.1	52.4	Mars	242 14.0	13 39
Mer. Pass.	h m 5 47.7	v −0.8	d 0.3	v 0.8	d 0.3	v 2.8	d 0.0	v 2.7	d 0.0	Jupiter	103 19.5	22 51
										Saturn	70 14.8	1 07

© British Crown Copyright 2018. All rights reserved.

UT	SUN GHA	SUN Dec	MOON GHA	v	MOON Dec	d	HP
d h	° ′	° ′	° ′	′	° ′	′	′
24 00	179 25.7	N23 25.0	282 14.3	15.3	S 9 23.1	10.3	54.2
01	194 25.5	25.0	296 48.6	15.4	9 12.8	10.4	54.2
02	209 25.4	24.9	311 23.0	15.4	9 02.4	10.4	54.2
03	224 25.3	.. 24.9	325 57.4	15.4	8 52.0	10.5	54.3
04	239 25.1	24.8	340 31.8	15.5	8 41.5	10.5	54.3
05	254 25.0	24.8	355 06.3	15.4	8 31.0	10.5	54.3
06	269 24.9	N23 24.8	9 40.7	15.5	S 8 20.5	10.5	54.3
07	284 24.7	24.7	24 15.2	15.5	8 10.0	10.6	54.3
08	299 24.6	24.7	38 49.7	15.5	7 59.4	10.7	54.3
M 09	314 24.5	.. 24.6	53 24.2	15.5	7 48.7	10.6	54.3
O 10	329 24.3	24.6	67 58.7	15.6	7 38.1	10.7	54.3
N 11	344 24.2	24.5	82 33.3	15.5	7 27.4	10.7	54.3
D 12	359 24.1	N23 24.5	97 07.8	15.6	S 7 16.7	10.8	54.3
A 13	14 23.9	24.4	111 42.4	15.6	7 05.9	10.8	54.3
Y 14	29 23.8	24.4	126 17.0	15.6	6 55.1	10.8	54.3
15	44 23.7	.. 24.3	140 51.6	15.6	6 44.3	10.8	54.3
16	59 23.5	24.3	155 26.2	15.7	6 33.5	10.9	54.4
17	74 23.4	24.2	170 00.9	15.6	6 22.6	10.9	54.4
18	89 23.3	N23 24.2	184 35.5	15.7	S 6 11.7	10.9	54.4
19	104 23.1	24.1	199 10.2	15.6	6 00.8	11.0	54.4
20	119 23.0	24.1	213 44.8	15.7	5 49.8	11.0	54.4
21	134 22.9	.. 24.0	228 19.5	15.6	5 38.8	11.0	54.4
22	149 22.7	23.9	242 54.1	15.7	5 27.8	11.0	54.4
23	164 22.6	23.9	257 28.8	15.7	5 16.8	11.1	54.4
25 00	179 22.5	N23 23.8	272 03.5	15.7	S 5 05.7	11.1	54.4
01	194 22.3	23.8	286 38.2	15.7	4 54.6	11.1	54.4
02	209 22.2	23.7	301 12.9	15.7	4 43.5	11.1	54.5
03	224 22.1	.. 23.7	315 47.6	15.7	4 32.4	11.1	54.5
04	239 21.9	23.6	330 22.3	15.7	4 21.3	11.2	54.5
05	254 21.8	23.5	344 57.0	15.7	4 10.1	11.2	54.5
06	269 21.7	N23 23.5	359 31.7	15.7	S 3 58.9	11.2	54.5
07	284 21.5	23.4	14 06.4	15.7	3 47.7	11.3	54.5
T 08	299 21.4	23.4	28 41.1	15.7	3 36.4	11.2	54.5
U 09	314 21.3	.. 23.3	43 15.8	15.6	3 25.2	11.3	54.6
E 10	329 21.1	23.2	57 50.4	15.7	3 13.9	11.3	54.6
S 11	344 21.0	23.2	72 25.1	15.7	3 02.6	11.3	54.6
D 12	359 20.9	N23 23.1	86 59.8	15.7	S 2 51.3	11.4	54.6
A 13	14 20.7	23.0	101 34.5	15.6	2 39.9	11.3	54.6
Y 14	29 20.6	23.0	116 09.1	15.7	2 28.6	11.4	54.6
15	44 20.5	.. 22.9	130 43.8	15.6	2 17.2	11.4	54.6
16	59 20.3	22.8	145 18.4	15.7	2 05.8	11.4	54.7
17	74 20.2	22.8	159 53.1	15.6	1 54.4	11.4	54.7
18	89 20.1	N23 22.7	174 27.7	15.6	S 1 43.0	11.4	54.7
19	104 19.9	22.6	189 02.3	15.6	1 31.6	11.4	54.7
20	119 19.8	22.5	203 36.9	15.6	1 20.2	11.5	54.7
21	134 19.7	.. 22.5	218 11.5	15.6	1 08.7	11.5	54.7
22	149 19.6	22.4	232 46.1	15.5	0 57.2	11.4	54.8
23	164 19.4	22.3	247 20.6	15.6	0 45.8	11.5	54.8
26 00	179 19.3	N23 22.3	261 55.2	15.5	S 0 34.3	11.5	54.8
01	194 19.2	22.2	276 29.7	15.5	0 22.8	11.5	54.8
02	209 19.0	22.1	291 04.2	15.5	S 0 11.3	11.5	54.8
03	224 18.9	.. 22.0	305 38.7	15.4	N 0 00.2	11.6	54.9
04	239 18.8	21.9	320 13.1	15.5	0 11.8	11.5	54.9
05	254 18.6	21.9	334 47.6	15.4	0 23.3	11.5	54.9
06	269 18.5	N23 21.8	349 22.0	15.4	N 0 34.8	11.6	54.9
W 07	284 18.4	21.7	3 56.4	15.4	0 46.4	11.5	54.9
E 08	299 18.2	21.6	18 30.8	15.3	0 57.9	11.6	55.0
D 09	314 18.1	.. 21.6	33 05.1	15.3	1 09.5	11.5	55.0
N 10	329 18.0	21.5	47 39.4	15.3	1 21.0	11.6	55.0
E 11	344 17.8	21.4	62 13.7	15.3	1 32.6	11.6	55.0
S 12	359 17.7	N23 21.3	76 48.0	15.2	N 1 44.2	11.6	55.0
D 13	14 17.6	21.2	91 22.2	15.2	1 55.8	11.5	55.1
A 14	29 17.4	21.1	105 56.4	15.2	2 07.3	11.6	55.1
Y 15	44 17.3	.. 21.1	120 30.6	15.2	2 18.9	11.6	55.1
16	59 17.2	21.0	135 04.7	15.1	2 30.5	11.5	55.1
17	74 17.0	20.9	149 38.8	15.1	2 42.0	11.6	55.2
18	89 16.9	N23 20.8	164 12.9	15.0	N 2 53.6	11.6	55.2
19	104 16.8	20.7	178 46.9	15.0	3 05.2	11.6	55.2
20	119 16.7	20.6	193 20.9	15.0	3 16.8	11.5	55.2
21	134 16.5	.. 20.5	207 54.9	14.9	3 28.3	11.6	55.3
22	149 16.4	20.4	222 28.8	14.9	3 39.9	11.6	55.3
23	164 16.3	20.3	237 02.7	14.9	N 3 51.5	11.5	55.3
	SD 15.8	d 0.1	SD 14.8		14.9		15.0

Moonrise

Lat.	Twilight Naut.	Twilight Civil	Sunrise	24	25	26	27
°	h m	h m	h m	h m	h m	h m	h m
N 72	▭	▭	▭	01 14	00 56	00 40	00 24
N 70	▭	▭	▭	01 00	00 49	00 39	00 30
68	▭	▭	▭	00 49	00 44	00 39	00 34
66	▭	▭	▭	00 39	00 39	00 38	00 38
64	////	////	01 33	00 31	00 35	00 38	00 41
62	////	////	02 11	00 24	00 31	00 38	00 44
60	////	00 52	02 37	00 18	00 28	00 37	00 47
N 58	////	01 42	02 58	00 13	00 26	00 37	00 49
56	////	02 12	03 14	00 09	00 23	00 37	00 51
54	00 47	02 34	03 29	00 04	00 21	00 37	00 52
52	01 34	02 52	03 41	00 01	00 19	00 36	00 54
50	02 02	03 07	03 52	24 17	00 17	00 36	00 56
45	02 47	03 37	04 14	24 13	00 13	00 36	00 59
N 40	03 18	03 59	04 32	24 10	00 10	00 35	01 02
35	03 41	04 18	04 47	24 07	00 07	00 35	01 04
30	04 00	04 33	05 00	24 04	00 04	00 35	01 06
20	04 29	04 58	05 22	24 00	00 00	00 34	01 10
N 10	04 51	05 18	05 41	23 56	24 34	00 34	01 13
0	05 10	05 36	05 59	23 52	24 34	00 34	01 16
S 10	05 27	05 54	06 16	23 48	24 33	00 33	01 19
20	05 43	06 11	06 35	23 44	24 33	00 33	01 23
30	06 00	06 30	06 56	23 40	24 33	00 33	01 27
35	06 09	06 40	07 08	23 37	24 32	00 32	01 29
40	06 18	06 52	07 23	23 34	24 32	00 32	01 31
45	06 28	07 06	07 39	23 31	24 32	00 32	01 34
S 50	06 40	07 22	08 00	23 27	24 32	00 32	01 38
52	06 45	07 29	08 10	23 25	24 31	00 31	01 40
54	06 51	07 37	08 21	23 23	24 31	00 31	01 41
56	06 57	07 46	08 34	23 20	24 31	00 31	01 43
58	07 04	07 57	08 48	23 18	24 31	00 31	01 46
S 60	07 11	08 08	09 06	23 15	24 31	00 31	01 48

Moonset

Lat.	Sunset	Twilight Civil	Twilight Naut.	24	25	26	27
°	h m	h m	h m	h m	h m	h m	h m
N 72	▭	▭	▭	09 49	11 34	13 18	15 07
N 70	▭	▭	▭	10 01	11 38	13 16	14 56
68	▭	▭	▭	10 10	11 42	13 13	14 48
66	▭	▭	▭	10 18	11 44	13 12	14 41
64	22 32	////	////	10 25	11 47	13 10	14 35
62	21 54	////	////	10 30	11 49	13 09	14 30
60	21 28	23 13	////	10 35	11 51	13 07	14 26
N 58	21 07	22 23	////	10 40	11 53	13 06	14 22
56	20 51	21 53	////	10 44	11 54	13 06	14 19
54	20 36	21 31	23 17	10 47	11 55	13 05	14 16
52	20 24	21 13	22 31	10 50	11 57	13 04	14 13
50	20 13	20 58	22 03	10 53	11 58	13 03	14 10
45	19 51	20 28	21 18	10 59	12 00	13 02	14 05
N 40	19 33	20 06	20 47	11 04	12 02	13 00	14 00
35	19 18	19 48	20 24	11 09	12 04	12 59	13 57
30	19 05	19 32	20 06	11 12	12 05	12 58	13 53
20	18 43	19 07	19 37	11 19	12 08	12 57	13 47
N 10	18 24	18 47	19 14	11 25	12 10	12 55	13 42
0	18 06	18 29	18 55	11 30	12 12	12 54	13 37
S 10	17 49	18 12	18 38	11 36	12 14	12 53	13 32
20	17 30	17 54	18 22	11 41	12 16	12 51	13 27
30	17 09	17 36	18 05	11 48	12 19	12 49	13 21
35	16 57	17 25	17 57	11 51	12 20	12 48	13 18
40	16 43	17 13	17 47	11 56	12 21	12 47	13 14
45	16 26	17 00	17 37	12 00	12 23	12 46	13 10
S 50	16 05	16 44	17 25	12 05	12 25	12 44	13 04
52	15 55	16 36	17 20	12 09	12 26	12 44	13 02
54	15 44	16 28	17 14	12 11	12 27	12 43	12 59
56	15 32	16 19	17 08	12 15	12 29	12 42	12 57
58	15 17	16 09	17 01	12 18	12 30	12 41	12 53
S 60	14 59	15 57	16 54	12 22	12 31	12 40	12 50

	SUN			MOON			
Day	Eqn. of Time 00ʰ	Eqn. of Time 12ʰ	Mer. Pass.	Mer. Pass. Upper	Mer. Pass. Lower	Age	Phase
d	m s	m s	h m	h m	h m	d	%
24	02 17	02 23	12 02	05 20	17 41	21	59
25	02 30	02 36	12 03	06 02	18 23	22	49
26	02 43	02 49	12 03	06 44	19 05	23	40

© British Crown Copyright 2018. All rights reserved.

UT	ARIES	VENUS −3.8		MARS +1.8		JUPITER −2.6		SATURN +0.1		STARS		
d h	GHA	GHA	Dec	GHA	Dec	GHA	Dec	GHA	Dec	Name	SHA	Dec
27 00	274 49.0	193 37.9	N22 50.3	155 42.0	N21 56.6	18 23.7	S22 18.2	345 12.8	S21 52.5	Acamar	315 15.5	S40 13.6
01	289 51.4	208 37.1	50.6	170 42.8	56.3	33 26.4	18.1	0 15.4	52.5	Achernar	335 23.9	S57 08.1
02	304 53.9	223 36.2	50.9	185 43.5	56.0	48 29.2	18.1	15 18.1	52.5	Acrux	173 04.7	S63 12.6
03	319 56.3	238 35.4 ..	51.2	200 44.3 ..	55.7	63 32.0 ..	18.1	30 20.7 ..	52.6	Adhara	255 09.7	S29 00.0
04	334 58.8	253 34.5	51.5	215 45.1	55.4	78 34.8	18.1	45 23.4	52.6	Aldebaran	290 45.0	N16 32.7
05	350 01.3	268 33.7	51.8	230 45.9	55.1	93 37.6	18.1	60 26.0	52.6			
06	5 03.7	283 32.9	N22 52.1	245 46.7	N21 54.8	108 40.3	S22 18.0	75 28.7	S21 52.6	Alioth	166 17.0	N55 51.7
07	20 06.2	298 32.0	52.3	260 47.4	54.5	123 43.1	18.0	90 31.3	52.7	Alkaid	152 55.5	N49 13.4
T 08	35 08.7	313 31.2	52.6	275 48.2	54.2	138 45.9	18.0	105 34.0	52.7	Alnair	27 38.3	S46 51.8
H 09	50 11.1	328 30.3 ..	52.9	290 49.0 ..	53.8	153 48.7 ..	18.0	120 36.7 ..	52.7	Alnilam	275 42.5	S 1 11.5
U 10	65 13.6	343 29.5	53.2	305 49.8	53.5	168 51.4	18.0	135 39.3	52.7	Alphard	217 52.3	S 8 44.6
R 11	80 16.1	358 28.7	53.4	320 50.6	53.2	183 54.2	17.9	150 42.0	52.8			
S 12	95 18.5	13 27.8	N22 53.7	335 51.4	N21 52.9	198 57.0	S22 17.9	165 44.6	S21 52.8	Alphecca	126 07.2	N26 39.2
D 13	110 21.0	28 27.0	54.0	350 52.1	52.6	213 59.8	17.9	180 47.3	52.8	Alpheratz	357 39.2	N29 11.6
A 14	125 23.5	43 26.1	54.3	5 52.9	52.3	229 02.5	17.9	195 49.9	52.8	Altair	62 03.9	N 8 55.3
Y 15	140 25.9	58 25.3 ..	54.5	20 53.7 ..	52.0	244 05.3 ..	17.9	210 52.6 ..	52.9	Ankaa	353 11.6	S42 11.9
16	155 28.4	73 24.4	54.8	35 54.5	51.7	259 08.1	17.8	225 55.2	52.9	Antares	112 20.9	S26 28.4
17	170 30.8	88 23.6	55.1	50 55.3	51.4	274 10.9	17.8	240 57.9	52.9			
18	185 33.3	103 22.8	N22 55.3	65 56.1	N21 51.0	289 13.6	S22 17.8	256 00.5	S21 53.0	Arcturus	145 51.8	N19 05.1
19	200 35.8	118 21.9	55.6	80 56.8	50.7	304 16.4	17.8	271 03.2	53.0	Atria	107 18.4	S69 03.7
20	215 38.2	133 21.1	55.9	95 57.6	50.4	319 19.2	17.8	286 05.8	53.0	Avior	234 16.9	S59 34.5
21	230 40.7	148 20.2 ..	56.1	110 58.4 ..	50.1	334 22.0 ..	17.7	301 08.5 ..	53.0	Bellatrix	278 27.9	N 6 21.9
22	245 43.2	163 19.4	56.4	125 59.2	49.8	349 24.7	17.7	316 11.1	53.1	Betelgeuse	270 57.2	N 7 24.5
23	260 45.6	178 18.5	56.7	141 00.0	49.5	4 27.5	17.7	331 13.8	53.1			
28 00	275 48.1	193 17.7	N22 56.9	156 00.8	N21 49.2	19 30.3	S22 17.7	346 16.5	S21 53.1	Canopus	263 54.9	S52 42.5
01	290 50.6	208 16.8	57.2	171 01.5	48.8	34 33.1	17.7	1 19.1	53.1	Capella	280 28.8	N46 00.8
02	305 53.0	223 16.0	57.4	186 02.3	48.5	49 35.8	17.6	16 21.8	53.2	Deneb	49 28.3	N45 20.9
03	320 55.5	238 15.2 ..	57.7	201 03.1 ..	48.2	64 38.6 ..	17.6	31 24.4 ..	53.2	Denebola	182 29.5	N14 28.0
04	335 58.0	253 14.3	58.0	216 03.9	47.9	79 41.4	17.6	46 27.1	53.2	Diphda	348 51.8	S17 52.8
05	351 00.4	268 13.5	58.2	231 04.7	47.6	94 44.2	17.6	61 29.7	53.3			
06	6 02.9	283 12.6	N22 58.5	246 05.5	N21 47.3	109 46.9	S22 17.6	76 32.4	S21 53.3	Dubhe	193 46.9	N61 39.1
07	21 05.3	298 11.8	58.7	261 06.2	47.0	124 49.7	17.5	91 35.0	53.3	Elnath	278 07.8	N28 37.2
F 08	36 07.8	313 10.9	59.0	276 07.0	46.6	139 52.5	17.5	106 37.7	53.3	Eltanin	90 43.7	N51 29.3
R 09	51 10.3	328 10.1 ..	59.2	291 07.8 ..	46.3	154 55.3 ..	17.5	121 40.3 ..	53.4	Enif	33 42.9	N 9 57.8
I 10	66 12.7	343 09.2	59.5	306 08.6	46.0	169 58.0	17.5	136 43.0	53.4	Fomalhaut	15 19.3	S29 31.0
D 11	81 15.2	358 08.4	22 59.7	321 09.4	45.7	185 00.8	17.5	151 45.6	53.4			
A 12	96 17.7	13 07.5	N23 00.0	336 10.2	N21 45.4	200 03.6	S22 17.4	166 48.3	S21 53.4	Gacrux	171 56.3	S57 13.5
Y 13	111 20.1	28 06.7	00.2	351 11.0	45.0	215 06.3	17.4	181 51.0	53.5	Gienah	175 48.1	S17 39.0
14	126 22.6	43 05.8	00.4	6 11.7	44.7	230 09.1	17.4	196 53.6	53.5	Hadar	148 41.7	S60 28.1
15	141 25.1	58 05.0 ..	00.7	21 12.5 ..	44.4	245 11.9 ..	17.4	211 56.3 ..	53.5	Hamal	327 56.3	N23 33.0
16	156 27.5	73 04.1	00.9	36 13.3	44.1	260 14.7	17.3	226 58.9	53.5	Kaus Aust.	83 38.0	S34 22.4
17	171 30.0	88 03.3	01.2	51 14.1	43.8	275 17.4	17.3	242 01.6	53.6			
18	186 32.4	103 02.4	N23 01.4	66 14.9	N21 43.5	290 20.2	S22 17.3	257 04.2	S21 53.6	Kochab	137 19.4	N74 04.9
19	201 34.9	118 01.6	01.7	81 15.7	43.1	305 23.0	17.3	272 06.9	53.6	Markab	13 34.1	N15 18.5
20	216 37.4	133 00.7	01.9	96 16.5	42.8	320 25.7	17.3	287 09.5	53.7	Menkar	314 11.0	N 4 09.8
21	231 39.8	147 59.9 ..	02.1	111 17.2 ..	42.5	335 28.5 ..	17.2	302 12.2 ..	53.7	Menkent	148 02.5	S36 27.9
22	246 42.3	162 59.0	02.4	126 18.0	42.2	350 31.3	17.2	317 14.8	53.7	Miaplacidus	221 39.6	S69 48.0
23	261 44.8	177 58.2	02.6	141 18.8	41.9	5 34.1	17.2	332 17.5	53.7			
29 00	276 47.2	192 57.3	N23 02.8	156 19.6	N21 41.5	20 36.8	S22 17.2	347 20.2	S21 53.8	Mirfak	308 34.8	N49 55.5
01	291 49.7	207 56.5	03.1	171 20.4	41.2	35 39.6	17.2	2 22.8	53.8	Nunki	75 52.9	S26 16.2
02	306 52.2	222 55.6	03.3	186 21.2	40.9	50 42.4	17.1	17 25.5	53.8	Peacock	53 12.3	S56 40.1
03	321 54.6	237 54.8 ..	03.5	201 22.0 ..	40.6	65 45.1 ..	17.1	32 28.1 ..	53.8	Pollux	243 23.1	N27 58.7
04	336 57.1	252 53.9	03.8	216 22.7	40.3	80 47.9	17.1	47 30.8	53.9	Procyon	244 55.8	N 5 10.4
05	351 59.6	267 53.1	04.0	231 23.5	39.9	95 50.7	17.1	62 33.4	53.9			
06	7 02.0	282 52.2	N23 04.2	246 24.3	N21 39.6	110 53.4	S22 17.1	77 36.1	S21 53.9	Rasalhague	96 02.3	N12 32.9
07	22 04.5	297 51.4	04.4	261 25.1	39.3	125 56.2	17.0	92 38.7	54.0	Regulus	207 39.3	N11 52.4
S 08	37 06.9	312 50.5	04.7	276 25.9	39.0	140 59.0	17.0	107 41.4	54.0	Rigel	281 08.4	S 8 10.9
A 09	52 09.4	327 49.7 ..	04.9	291 26.7 ..	38.6	156 01.7 ..	17.0	122 44.1 ..	54.0	Rigil Kent.	139 45.8	S60 55.0
T 10	67 11.9	342 48.8	05.1	306 27.5	38.3	171 04.5	17.0	137 46.7	54.0	Sabik	102 07.5	S15 44.8
U 11	82 14.3	357 48.0	05.3	321 28.3	38.0	186 07.3	17.0	152 49.4	54.1			
R 12	97 16.8	12 47.1	N23 05.5	336 29.1	N21 37.7	201 10.0	S22 16.9	167 52.0	S21 54.1	Schedar	349 35.9	N56 38.2
D 13	112 19.3	27 46.3	05.8	351 29.8	37.3	216 12.8	16.9	182 54.7	54.1	Shaula	96 15.9	S37 06.9
A 14	127 21.7	42 45.4	06.0	6 30.6	37.0	231 15.6	16.9	197 57.3	54.1	Sirius	258 30.5	S16 44.7
Y 15	142 24.2	57 44.6 ..	06.2	21 31.4 ..	36.7	246 18.4 ..	16.9	213 00.0 ..	54.2	Spica	158 26.8	S11 15.7
16	157 26.7	72 43.7	06.4	36 32.2	36.4	261 21.1	16.9	228 02.6	54.2	Suhail	222 49.8	S43 30.8
17	172 29.1	87 42.8	06.6	51 33.0	36.0	276 23.9	16.8	243 05.3	54.2			
18	187 31.6	102 42.0	N23 06.8	66 33.8	N21 35.7	291 26.7	S22 16.8	258 07.9	S21 54.2	Vega	80 35.7	N38 48.2
19	202 34.1	117 41.1	07.0	81 34.6	35.4	306 29.4	16.8	273 10.6	54.3	Zuben'ubi	137 00.7	S16 07.2
20	217 36.5	132 40.3	07.2	96 35.4	35.1	321 32.2	16.8	288 13.3	54.3		SHA	Mer. Pass.
21	232 39.0	147 39.4 ..	07.5	111 36.2 ..	34.7	336 35.0 ..	16.8	303 15.9 ..	54.3			h m
22	247 41.4	162 38.6	07.7	126 36.9	34.4	351 37.7	16.7	318 18.6	54.4	Venus	277 29.6	11 07
23	262 43.9	177 37.7	07.9	141 37.7	34.1	6 40.5	16.7	333 21.2	54.4	Mars	240 12.7	13 35
	h m									Jupiter	103 42.2	22 38
Mer. Pass.	5 35.9	v −0.8	d 0.2	v 0.8	d 0.3	v 2.8	d 0.0	v 2.7	d 0.0	Saturn	70 28.4	0 55

© British Crown Copyright 2018. All rights reserved.

UT	SUN GHA	SUN Dec	MOON GHA	v	Dec	d	HP
d h	° ′	° ′	° ′	′	° ′	′	′
27 00	179 16.1	N23 20.3	251 36.6	14.8	N 4 03.0	11.6	55.3
01	194 16.0	20.2	266 10.4	14.8	4 14.6	11.5	55.4
02	209 15.9	20.1	280 44.2	14.7	4 26.1	11.5	55.4
03	224 15.7	.. 20.0	295 17.9	14.7	4 37.6	11.6	55.4
04	239 15.6	19.9	309 51.6	14.6	4 49.2	11.5	55.4
05	254 15.5	19.8	324 25.2	14.6	5 00.7	11.5	55.5
06	269 15.3	N23 19.7	338 58.8	14.5	N 5 12.2	11.5	55.5
07	284 15.2	19.6	353 32.3	14.5	5 23.7	11.5	55.5
T 08	299 15.1	19.5	8 05.8	14.5	5 35.2	11.5	55.5
H 09	314 15.0	.. 19.4	22 39.3	14.4	5 46.7	11.4	55.6
U 10	329 14.8	19.3	37 12.7	14.3	5 58.1	11.5	55.6
R 11	344 14.7	19.2	51 46.0	14.3	6 09.6	11.4	55.6
S 12	359 14.6	N23 19.1	66 19.3	14.2	N 6 21.0	11.4	55.6
D 13	14 14.4	19.0	80 52.5	14.2	6 32.4	11.4	55.7
A 14	29 14.3	18.9	95 25.7	14.2	6 43.8	11.4	55.7
Y 15	44 14.2	.. 18.8	109 58.9	14.0	6 55.2	11.4	55.7
16	59 14.0	18.7	124 31.9	14.1	7 06.6	11.3	55.8
17	74 13.9	18.6	139 05.0	13.9	7 17.9	11.4	55.8
18	89 13.8	N23 18.5	153 37.9	13.9	N 7 29.3	11.3	55.8
19	104 13.7	18.4	168 10.8	13.9	7 40.6	11.3	55.8
20	119 13.5	18.3	182 43.7	13.8	7 51.9	11.2	55.9
21	134 13.4	.. 18.2	197 16.5	13.7	8 03.1	11.3	55.9
22	149 13.3	18.1	211 49.2	13.7	8 14.4	11.2	55.9
23	164 13.1	18.0	226 21.9	13.6	8 25.6	11.2	56.0
28 00	179 13.0	N23 17.9	240 54.5	13.5	N 8 36.8	11.2	56.0
01	194 12.9	17.7	255 27.0	13.5	8 48.0	11.1	56.0
02	209 12.7	17.6	269 59.5	13.4	8 59.1	11.1	56.1
03	224 12.6	.. 17.5	284 31.9	13.3	9 10.2	11.1	56.1
04	239 12.5	17.4	299 04.2	13.3	9 21.3	11.1	56.1
05	254 12.4	17.3	313 36.5	13.2	9 32.4	11.0	56.1
06	269 12.2	N23 17.2	328 08.7	13.1	N 9 43.4	11.0	56.2
07	284 12.1	17.1	342 40.8	13.1	9 54.4	11.0	56.2
08	299 12.0	17.0	357 12.9	13.0	10 05.4	10.9	56.2
F 09	314 11.8	.. 16.8	11 44.9	12.9	10 16.3	10.9	56.3
R 10	329 11.7	16.7	26 16.8	12.9	10 27.2	10.9	56.3
I 11	344 11.6	16.6	40 48.7	12.8	10 38.1	10.8	56.3
D 12	359 11.5	N23 16.5	55 20.5	12.7	N10 48.9	10.8	56.4
A 13	14 11.3	16.4	69 52.2	12.6	10 59.7	10.7	56.4
Y 14	29 11.2	16.3	84 23.8	12.5	11 10.4	10.7	56.4
15	44 11.1	.. 16.1	98 55.3	12.5	11 21.1	10.7	56.5
16	59 10.9	16.0	113 26.8	12.4	11 31.8	10.6	56.5
17	74 10.8	15.9	127 58.2	12.3	11 42.4	10.6	56.5
18	89 10.7	N23 15.8	142 29.5	12.3	N11 53.0	10.6	56.6
19	104 10.6	15.7	157 00.8	12.1	12 03.6	10.5	56.6
20	119 10.4	15.5	171 31.9	12.1	12 14.1	10.4	56.6
21	134 10.3	.. 15.4	186 03.0	12.0	12 24.5	10.4	56.7
22	149 10.2	15.3	200 34.0	11.9	12 34.9	10.4	56.7
23	164 10.0	15.2	215 04.9	11.9	12 45.3	10.3	56.7
29 00	179 09.9	N23 15.0	229 35.8	11.7	N12 55.6	10.2	56.8
01	194 09.8	14.9	244 06.5	11.7	13 05.8	10.2	56.8
02	209 09.7	14.8	258 37.2	11.6	13 16.0	10.2	56.9
03	224 09.5	.. 14.7	273 07.8	11.5	13 26.2	10.1	56.9
04	239 09.4	14.5	287 38.3	11.4	13 36.3	10.0	56.9
05	254 09.3	14.4	302 08.7	11.3	13 46.3	10.0	57.0
06	269 09.2	N23 14.3	316 39.0	11.2	N13 56.3	9.9	57.0
07	284 09.0	14.1	331 09.2	11.2	14 06.2	9.9	57.0
S 08	299 08.9	14.0	345 39.4	11.1	14 16.1	9.8	57.0
A 09	314 08.8	.. 13.9	0 09.5	10.9	14 25.9	9.8	57.1
T 10	329 08.6	13.7	14 39.4	10.9	14 35.7	9.7	57.1
U 11	344 08.5	13.6	29 09.3	10.8	14 45.4	9.6	57.1
R 12	359 08.4	N23 13.5	43 39.1	10.7	N14 55.0	9.5	57.2
D 13	14 08.3	13.3	58 08.8	10.6	15 04.5	9.5	57.2
A 14	29 08.1	13.2	72 38.4	10.5	15 14.0	9.4	57.2
Y 15	44 08.0	.. 13.1	87 07.9	10.5	15 23.4	9.4	57.3
16	59 07.9	12.9	101 37.4	10.3	15 32.8	9.3	57.3
17	74 07.8	12.8	116 07.7	10.2	15 42.1	9.2	57.3
18	89 07.6	N23 12.7	130 35.9	10.2	N15 51.3	9.1	57.4
19	104 07.5	12.5	145 05.1	10.0	16 00.4	9.1	57.4
20	119 07.4	12.4	159 34.1	10.0	16 09.5	9.0	57.4
21	134 07.3	.. 12.2	174 03.1	9.9	16 18.5	8.9	57.5
22	149 07.1	12.1	188 32.0	9.8	16 27.4	8.8	57.5
23	164 07.0	12.0	203 00.8	9.6	N16 36.2	8.8	57.6
	SD 15.8	d 0.1	SD 15.2		15.4		15.6

Twilight / Sunrise / Moonrise

Lat.	Naut.	Civil	Sunrise	27	28	29	30
°	h m	h m	h m	h m	h m	h m	h m
N 72	▭	▭	▭	00 24	{00 02 / 23 54}		23 06
N 70	▭	▭	▭	00 30	00 19	{00 02 / 23 54}	23 10
68	▭	▭	▭	00 34	00 29	00 25	00 20
66	▭	▭	▭	00 38	00 38	00 39	00 42
64	////	////	01 36	00 41	00 45	00 51	01 00
62	////	////	02 13	00 44	00 51	01 01	01 14
60	////	00 56	02 39	00 47	00 57	01 10	01 27
N 58	////	01 45	02 59	00 49	01 02	01 17	01 38
56	////	02 14	03 16	00 51	01 06	01 24	01 47
54	00 52	02 36	03 30	00 52	01 10	01 30	01 55
52	01 36	02 54	03 42	00 54	01 13	01 36	02 03
50	02 03	03 09	03 53	00 56	01 17	01 41	02 10
45	02 49	03 38	04 15	00 59	01 24	01 52	02 24
N 40	03 19	04 01	04 33	01 02	01 30	02 01	02 36
35	03 42	04 18	04 48	01 04	01 35	02 08	02 47
30	04 01	04 34	05 01	01 06	01 39	02 15	02 56
20	04 29	04 59	05 23	01 10	01 47	02 27	03 11
N 10	04 52	05 19	05 42	01 13	01 54	02 38	03 25
0	05 11	05 37	06 00	01 16	02 01	02 48	03 38
S 10	05 28	05 54	06 17	01 19	02 07	02 58	03 51
20	05 44	06 11	06 35	01 23	02 14	03 08	04 05
30	06 00	06 30	06 56	01 27	02 22	03 21	04 21
35	06 09	06 41	07 09	01 29	02 27	03 28	04 31
40	06 18	06 52	07 23	01 31	02 32	03 36	04 42
45	06 29	07 06	07 39	01 34	02 39	03 46	04 54
S 50	06 40	07 22	08 00	01 38	02 46	03 57	05 10
52	06 45	07 29	08 10	01 40	02 50	04 03	05 17
54	06 51	07 37	08 21	01 41	02 54	04 09	05 26
56	06 57	07 46	08 33	01 43	02 58	04 15	05 35
58	07 04	07 56	08 48	01 46	03 03	04 23	05 45
S 60	07 11	08 08	09 05	01 48	03 08	04 31	05 57

Sunset / Twilight / Moonset

Lat.	Sunset	Civil	Naut.	27	28	29	30
°	h m	h m	h m	h m	h m	h m	h m
N 72	▭	▭	▭	15 07	17 05	19 27	▭
N 70	▭	▭	▭	14 56	16 44	18 44	21 15
68	▭	▭	▭	14 48	16 28	18 15	20 12
66	▭	▭	▭	14 41	16 15	17 54	19 38
64	22 29	////	////	14 35	16 04	17 37	19 13
62	21 53	////	////	14 30	15 55	17 23	18 53
60	21 27	23 09	////	14 26	15 47	17 12	18 37
N 58	21 07	22 21	////	14 22	15 40	17 01	18 23
56	20 50	21 52	////	14 19	15 34	16 53	18 12
54	20 36	21 30	23 13	14 16	15 29	16 45	18 02
52	20 24	21 12	22 30	14 13	15 24	16 38	17 53
50	20 13	20 58	22 02	14 10	15 20	16 32	17 45
45	19 51	20 28	21 18	14 05	15 10	16 18	17 27
N 40	19 33	20 06	20 47	14 00	15 03	16 07	17 13
35	19 18	19 48	20 24	13 57	14 56	15 58	17 02
30	19 05	19 33	20 06	13 53	14 50	15 49	16 51
20	18 43	19 08	19 37	13 47	14 40	15 35	16 34
N 10	18 24	18 47	19 14	13 42	14 31	15 23	16 18
0	18 07	18 29	18 56	13 37	14 23	15 11	16 04
S 10	17 50	18 12	18 39	13 32	14 14	15 00	15 50
20	17 31	17 55	18 23	13 27	14 06	14 48	15 34
30	17 10	17 36	18 06	13 21	13 56	14 34	15 17
35	16 58	17 26	17 58	13 18	13 50	14 25	15 07
40	16 44	17 14	17 48	13 14	13 43	14 16	14 55
45	16 27	17 01	17 38	13 10	13 36	14 06	14 41
S 50	16 06	16 45	17 26	13 04	13 27	13 53	14 25
52	15 57	16 38	17 21	13 02	13 22	13 47	14 17
54	15 46	16 29	17 16	12 59	13 18	13 40	14 08
56	15 33	16 20	17 09	12 57	13 13	13 33	13 59
58	15 19	16 10	17 03	12 53	13 07	13 25	13 48
S 60	15 01	15 59	16 55	12 50	13 01	13 15	13 35

Day	SUN Eqn. of Time 00h	SUN Eqn. of Time 12h	SUN Mer. Pass.	MOON Mer. Pass. Upper	MOON Mer. Pass. Lower	Age	Phase
d	m s	m s	h m	h m	h m	d	%
27	02 55	03 01	12 03	07 27	19 49	24	30
28	03 08	03 14	12 03	08 11	20 35	25	21
29	03 20	03 26	12 03	08 59	21 25	26	13

© British Crown Copyright 2018. All rights reserved.

UT	ARIES GHA	VENUS −3.9 GHA	Dec	MARS +1.8 GHA	Dec	JUPITER −2.6 GHA	Dec	SATURN +0.1 GHA	Dec	STARS Name	SHA	Dec
30 00	277 46.4	192 36.9	N23 08.1	156 38.5	N21 33.8	21 43.3	S22 16.7	348 23.9	S21 54.4	Acamar	315 15.5	S40 13.6
01	292 48.8	207 36.0	08.3	171 39.3	33.4	36 46.0	16.7	3 26.5	54.4	Achernar	335 23.9	S57 08.1
02	307 51.3	222 35.2	08.5	186 40.1	33.1	51 48.8	16.7	18 29.2	54.5	Acrux	173 04.7	S63 12.6
03	322 53.8	237 34.3	.. 08.7	201 40.9	.. 32.8	66 51.5	.. 16.6	33 31.9	.. 54.5	Adhara	255 09.7	S29 00.0
04	337 56.2	252 33.4	08.9	216 41.7	32.5	81 54.3	16.6	48 34.5	54.5	Aldebaran	290 45.0	N16 32.7
05	352 58.7	267 32.6	09.1	231 42.5	32.1	96 57.1	16.6	63 37.2	54.5			
06	8 01.2	282 31.7	N23 09.3	246 43.3	N21 31.8	111 59.8	S22 16.6	78 39.8	S21 54.6	Alioth	166 17.0	N55 51.7
07	23 03.6	297 30.9	09.5	261 44.1	31.5	127 02.6	16.6	93 42.5	54.6	Alkaid	152 55.5	N49 13.4
08	38 06.1	312 30.0	09.7	276 44.8	31.1	142 05.4	16.5	108 45.1	54.6	Alnair	27 38.3	S46 51.8
S 09	53 08.5	327 29.2	.. 09.9	291 45.6	.. 30.8	157 08.1	.. 16.5	123 47.8	.. 54.7	Alnilam	275 42.5	S 1 11.5
U 10	68 11.0	342 28.3	10.1	306 46.4	30.5	172 10.9	16.5	138 50.4	54.7	Alphard	217 52.3	S 8 44.6
N 11	83 13.5	357 27.4	10.3	321 47.2	30.1	187 13.7	16.5	153 53.1	54.7			
D 12	98 15.9	12 26.6	N23 10.4	336 48.0	N21 29.8	202 16.4	S22 16.5	168 55.8	S21 54.7	Alphecca	126 07.2	N26 39.2
A 13	113 18.4	27 25.7	10.6	351 48.8	29.5	217 19.2	16.4	183 58.4	54.8	Alpheratz	357 39.2	N29 11.6
Y 14	128 20.9	42 24.9	10.8	6 49.6	29.2	232 22.0	16.4	199 01.1	54.8	Altair	62 03.9	N 8 55.3
15	143 23.3	57 24.0	.. 11.0	21 50.4	.. 28.8	247 24.7	.. 16.4	214 03.7	.. 54.8	Ankaa	353 11.6	S42 11.9
16	158 25.8	72 23.1	11.2	36 51.2	28.5	262 27.5	16.4	229 06.4	54.8	Antares	112 20.9	S26 28.4
17	173 28.3	87 22.3	11.4	51 52.0	28.2	277 30.2	16.4	244 09.0	54.9			
18	188 30.7	102 21.4	N23 11.6	66 52.8	N21 27.8	292 33.0	S22 16.3	259 11.7	S21 54.9	Arcturus	145 51.8	N19 05.1
19	203 33.2	117 20.6	11.8	81 53.6	27.5	307 35.8	16.3	274 14.4	54.9	Atria	107 18.4	S69 03.7
20	218 35.7	132 19.7	11.9	96 54.4	27.2	322 38.5	16.3	289 17.0	55.0	Avior	234 16.9	S59 34.5
21	233 38.1	147 18.9	.. 12.1	111 55.1	.. 26.8	337 41.3	.. 16.3	304 19.7	.. 55.0	Bellatrix	278 27.9	N 6 21.9
22	248 40.6	162 18.0	12.3	126 55.9	26.5	352 44.1	16.3	319 22.3	55.0	Betelgeuse	270 57.2	N 7 24.5
23	263 43.0	177 17.1	12.5	141 56.7	26.2	7 46.8	16.2	334 25.0	55.0			
1 00	278 45.5	192 16.3	N23 12.7	156 57.5	N21 25.8	22 49.6	S22 16.2	349 27.6	S21 55.1	Canopus	263 54.9	S52 42.4
01	293 48.0	207 15.4	12.8	171 58.3	25.5	37 52.3	16.2	4 30.3	55.1	Capella	280 28.8	N46 00.8
02	308 50.4	222 14.6	13.0	186 59.1	25.2	52 55.1	16.2	19 33.0	55.1	Deneb	49 28.3	N45 20.9
03	323 52.9	237 13.7	.. 13.2	201 59.9	.. 24.8	67 57.9	.. 16.2	34 35.6	.. 55.1	Denebola	182 29.5	N14 28.0
04	338 55.4	252 12.8	13.4	217 00.7	24.5	83 00.6	16.2	49 38.3	55.2	Diphda	348 51.8	S17 52.8
05	353 57.8	267 12.0	13.5	232 01.5	24.2	98 03.4	16.1	64 40.9	55.2			
06	9 00.3	282 11.1	N23 13.7	247 02.3	N21 23.8	113 06.1	S22 16.1	79 43.6	S21 55.2	Dubhe	193 46.9	N61 39.1
07	24 02.8	297 10.2	13.9	262 03.1	23.5	128 08.9	16.1	94 46.2	55.2	Elnath	278 07.8	N28 37.2
08	39 05.2	312 09.4	14.0	277 03.9	23.2	143 11.7	16.1	109 48.9	55.3	Eltanin	90 43.7	N51 29.4
M 09	54 07.7	327 08.5	.. 14.2	292 04.7	.. 22.8	158 14.4	.. 16.1	124 51.6	.. 55.3	Enif	33 42.8	N 9 57.8
O 10	69 10.2	342 07.7	14.4	307 05.5	22.5	173 17.2	16.0	139 54.2	55.3	Fomalhaut	15 19.3	S29 31.0
N 11	84 12.6	357 06.8	14.5	322 06.3	22.1	188 19.9	16.0	154 56.9	55.4			
D 12	99 15.1	12 05.9	N23 14.7	337 07.1	N21 21.8	203 22.7	S22 16.0	169 59.5	S21 55.4	Gacrux	171 56.3	S57 13.5
A 13	114 17.5	27 05.1	14.9	352 07.8	21.5	218 25.5	16.0	185 02.2	55.4	Gienah	175 48.1	S17 39.0
Y 14	129 20.0	42 04.2	15.0	7 08.6	21.1	233 28.2	16.0	200 04.8	55.4	Hadar	148 41.8	S60 28.1
15	144 22.5	57 03.3	.. 15.2	22 09.4	.. 20.8	248 31.0	.. 15.9	215 07.5	.. 55.5	Hamal	327 56.2	N23 33.0
16	159 24.9	72 02.5	15.3	37 10.2	20.5	263 33.7	15.9	230 10.2	55.5	Kaus Aust.	83 37.9	S34 22.4
17	174 27.4	87 01.6	15.5	52 11.0	20.1	278 36.5	15.9	245 12.8	55.5			
18	189 29.9	102 00.8	N23 15.6	67 11.8	N21 19.8	293 39.3	S22 15.9	260 15.5	S21 55.5	Kochab	137 19.4	N74 04.9
19	204 32.3	116 59.9	15.8	82 12.6	19.4	308 42.0	15.9	275 18.1	55.6	Markab	13 34.1	N15 18.5
20	219 34.8	131 59.0	16.0	97 13.4	19.1	323 44.8	15.8	290 20.8	55.6	Menkar	314 10.9	N 4 09.8
21	234 37.3	146 58.2	.. 16.1	112 14.2	.. 18.8	338 47.5	.. 15.8	305 23.4	.. 55.6	Menkent	148 02.5	S36 27.9
22	249 39.7	161 57.3	16.3	127 15.0	18.4	353 50.3	15.8	320 26.1	55.7	Miaplacidus	221 39.6	S69 48.0
23	264 42.2	176 56.4	16.4	142 15.8	18.1	8 53.0	15.8	335 28.8	55.7			
2 00	279 44.7	191 55.6	N23 16.6	157 16.6	N21 17.8	23 55.8	S22 15.8	350 31.4	S21 55.7	Mirfak	308 34.8	N49 55.5
01	294 47.1	206 54.7	16.7	172 17.4	17.4	38 58.6	15.7	5 34.1	55.7	Nunki	75 52.8	S26 16.2
02	309 49.6	221 53.8	16.9	187 18.2	17.1	54 01.3	15.7	20 36.7	55.8	Peacock	53 12.2	S56 40.1
03	324 52.0	236 53.0	.. 17.0	202 19.0	.. 16.7	69 04.1	.. 15.7	35 39.4	.. 55.8	Pollux	243 23.1	N27 58.7
04	339 54.5	251 52.1	17.1	217 19.8	16.4	84 06.8	15.7	50 42.0	55.8	Procyon	244 55.8	N 5 10.4
05	354 57.0	266 51.3	17.3	232 20.6	16.0	99 09.6	15.7	65 44.7	55.8			
06	9 59.4	281 50.4	N23 17.4	247 21.4	N21 15.7	114 12.3	S22 15.6	80 47.4	S21 55.9	Rasalhague	96 02.3	N12 32.9
07	25 01.9	296 49.5	17.6	262 22.2	15.4	129 15.1	15.6	95 50.0	55.9	Regulus	207 39.3	N11 52.4
T 08	40 04.4	311 48.7	17.7	277 23.0	15.0	144 17.8	15.6	110 52.7	55.9	Rigel	281 08.4	S 8 10.9
U 09	55 06.8	326 47.8	.. 17.8	292 23.8	.. 14.7	159 20.6	.. 15.6	125 55.3	.. 56.0	Rigil Kent.	139 45.8	S60 55.0
E 10	70 09.3	341 46.9	18.0	307 24.6	14.3	174 23.4	15.6	140 58.0	56.0	Sabik	102 07.5	S15 44.8
S 11	85 11.8	356 46.1	18.1	322 25.4	14.0	189 26.1	15.5	156 00.7	56.0			
D 12	100 14.2	11 45.2	N23 18.3	337 26.2	N21 13.7	204 28.9	S22 15.5	171 03.3	S21 56.0	Schedar	349 35.8	N56 38.3
A 13	115 16.7	26 44.3	18.4	352 27.0	13.3	219 31.6	15.5	186 06.0	56.1	Shaula	96 15.9	S37 06.9
Y 14	130 19.2	41 43.5	18.5	7 27.8	13.0	234 34.4	15.5	201 08.6	56.1	Sirius	258 30.4	S16 44.7
15	145 21.6	56 42.6	.. 18.7	22 28.6	.. 12.6	249 37.1	.. 15.5	216 11.3	.. 56.1	Spica	158 26.8	S11 15.7
16	160 24.1	71 41.7	18.8	37 29.4	12.3	264 39.9	15.4	231 13.9	56.1	Suhail	222 49.8	S43 30.8
17	175 26.5	86 40.9	18.9	52 30.2	11.9	279 42.6	15.4	246 16.6	56.2			
18	190 29.0	101 40.0	N23 19.0	67 31.0	N21 11.6	294 45.4	S22 15.4	261 19.3	S21 56.2	Vega	80 35.7	N38 48.2
19	205 31.5	116 39.1	19.2	82 31.8	11.2	309 48.1	15.4	276 21.9	56.2	Zuben'ubi	137 00.7	S16 07.2
20	220 33.9	131 38.3	19.3	97 32.6	10.9	324 50.9	15.4	291 24.6	56.3		SHA	Mer.Pass.
21	235 36.4	146 37.4	.. 19.4	112 33.4	.. 10.6	339 53.6	.. 15.4	306 27.2	.. 56.3		° ′	h m
22	250 38.9	161 36.5	19.5	127 34.2	10.2	354 56.4	15.3	321 29.9	56.3	Venus	273 30.8	11 12
23	265 41.3	176 35.7	19.7	142 35.0	09.9	9 59.2	15.3	336 32.5	56.3	Mars	238 12.0	13 31
	h m									Jupiter	104 04.1	22 25
Mer.Pass.	5 24.1	v −0.9	d 0.2	v 0.6	d 0.3	v 2.8	d 0.0	v 2.7	d 0.0	Saturn	70 42.1	0 42

© British Crown Copyright 2018. All rights reserved.

UT	SUN GHA	Dec	MOON GHA	v	Dec	d	HP
d h	° ′	° ′	° ′	′	° ′	′	′
30 00	179 06.9	N23 11.8	217 29.4	9.6	N16 45.0	8.6	57.6
01	194 06.8	11.7	231 58.0	9.5	16 53.6	8.6	57.6
02	209 06.6	11.5	246 26.5	9.4	17 02.2	8.5	57.7
03	224 06.5 ..	11.4	260 54.9	9.3	17 10.7	8.5	57.7
04	239 06.4	11.2	275 23.2	9.2	17 19.2	8.3	57.7
05	254 06.3	11.1	289 51.4	9.1	17 27.5	8.3	57.8
06	269 06.1	N23 10.9	304 19.5	9.0	N17 35.8	8.1	57.8
07	284 06.0	10.8	318 47.5	8.9	17 43.9	8.1	57.8
S 08	299 05.9	10.7	333 15.4	8.9	17 52.0	8.0	57.9
U 09	314 05.8 ..	10.5	347 43.3	8.7	18 00.0	7.9	57.9
N 10	329 05.6	10.4	2 11.0	8.6	18 07.9	7.8	57.9
11	344 05.5	10.2	16 38.6	8.6	18 15.7	7.6	58.0
D 12	359 05.4	N23 10.1	31 06.2	8.4	N18 23.3	7.6	58.0
A 13	14 05.3	09.9	45 33.6	8.3	18 30.9	7.5	58.0
Y 14	29 05.1	09.8	60 00.9	8.3	18 38.4	7.5	58.1
15	44 05.0 ..	09.6	74 28.2	8.2	18 45.9	7.3	58.1
16	59 04.9	09.4	88 55.4	8.0	18 53.2	7.1	58.1
17	74 04.8	09.3	103 22.4	8.0	19 00.3	7.1	58.2
18	89 04.6	N23 09.1	117 49.4	7.9	N19 07.4	7.0	58.2
19	104 04.5	09.0	132 16.3	7.7	19 14.4	6.9	58.2
20	119 04.4	08.8	146 43.0	7.7	19 21.3	6.8	58.3
21	134 04.3 ..	08.7	161 09.7	7.6	19 28.1	6.7	58.3
22	149 04.1	08.5	175 36.3	7.5	19 34.8	6.5	58.3
23	164 04.0	08.3	190 02.8	7.4	19 41.3	6.5	58.4
1 00	179 03.9	N23 08.2	204 29.2	7.4	N19 47.8	6.3	58.4
01	194 03.8	08.0	218 55.6	7.2	19 54.1	6.2	58.4
02	209 03.7	07.9	233 21.8	7.1	20 00.3	6.1	58.5
03	224 03.5 ..	07.7	247 47.9	7.1	20 06.4	6.0	58.5
04	239 03.4	07.5	262 14.0	7.0	20 12.4	5.8	58.5
05	254 03.3	07.4	276 40.0	6.8	20 18.2	5.8	58.6
06	269 03.2	N23 07.2	291 05.8	6.8	N20 24.0	5.6	58.6
07	284 03.0	07.1	305 31.6	6.7	20 29.6	5.5	58.6
08	299 02.9	06.9	319 57.3	6.7	20 35.1	5.4	58.7
M 09	314 02.8 ..	06.7	334 23.0	6.5	20 40.5	5.3	58.7
O 10	329 02.7	06.6	348 48.5	6.4	20 45.8	5.1	58.7
N 11	344 02.6	06.4	3 13.9	6.4	20 50.9	5.0	58.8
D 12	359 02.4	N23 06.2	17 39.3	6.3	N20 55.9	4.8	58.8
A 13	14 02.3	06.1	32 04.6	6.2	21 00.7	4.8	58.8
Y 14	29 02.2	05.9	46 29.8	6.1	21 05.5	4.6	58.8
15	44 02.1 ..	05.7	60 54.9	6.1	21 10.1	4.5	58.9
16	59 01.9	05.5	75 20.0	6.0	21 14.6	4.3	58.9
17	74 01.8	05.4	89 45.0	5.9	21 18.9	4.2	58.9
18	89 01.7	N23 05.2	104 09.9	5.8	N21 23.1	4.1	59.0
19	104 01.6	05.0	118 34.7	5.7	21 27.2	4.0	59.0
20	119 01.5	04.9	132 59.4	5.7	21 31.2	3.8	59.0
21	134 01.3 ..	04.7	147 24.1	5.6	21 35.0	3.6	59.1
22	149 01.2	04.5	161 48.7	5.6	21 38.6	3.6	59.1
23	164 01.1	04.3	176 13.3	5.4	21 42.2	3.3	59.1
2 00	179 01.0	N23 04.2	190 37.7	5.5	N21 45.5	3.3	59.1
01	194 00.9	04.0	205 02.2	5.3	21 48.8	3.1	59.2
02	209 00.7	03.8	219 26.5	5.3	21 51.9	2.9	59.2
03	224 00.6 ..	03.6	233 50.8	5.2	21 54.8	2.8	59.2
04	239 00.5	03.4	248 15.0	5.1	21 57.6	2.7	59.2
05	254 00.4	03.3	262 39.1	5.1	22 00.3	2.5	59.3
06	269 00.3	N23 03.1	277 03.2	5.1	N22 02.8	2.4	59.3
07	284 00.1	02.9	291 27.3	5.0	22 05.2	2.2	59.3
T 08	299 00.0	02.7	305 51.3	4.9	22 07.4	2.1	59.4
U 09	313 59.9 ..	02.5	320 15.2	4.9	22 09.5	1.9	59.4
E 10	328 59.8	02.4	334 39.1	4.8	22 11.4	1.8	59.4
S 11	343 59.7	02.2	349 02.9	4.8	22 13.2	1.7	59.4
D 12	358 59.5	N23 02.0	3 26.7	4.7	N22 14.9	1.4	59.5
A 13	13 59.4	01.8	17 50.4	4.7	22 16.3	1.4	59.5
Y 14	28 59.3	01.6	32 14.1	4.7	22 17.7	1.1	59.5
15	43 59.2 ..	01.4	46 37.8	4.6	22 18.8	1.0	59.5
16	58 59.1	01.2	61 01.4	4.5	22 19.8	0.9	59.6
17	73 58.9	01.1	75 24.9	4.5	N22 20.7	0.7	59.6
18	88 58.8	N23 00.9					
19	103 58.7	00.7					
20	118 58.6	00.5					
21	133 58.5 ..	00.3					
22	148 58.4	23 00.1					
23	163 58.2	N22 59.9					
	SD 15.8	d 0.2	SD 15.8		16.0		16.2

Lat.	Twilight Naut.	Twilight Civil	Sunrise	Moonrise 30	1	2	3
°	h m	h m	h m	h m	h m	h m	h m
N 72	☐	☐	☐	☐	☐	☐	☐
N 70	☐	☐	☐	23 10	☐	☐	☐
68	☐	☐	☐	00 20	00 14	00 03	☐
66	////	////	00 16	00 42	00 49	01 08	01 54
64	////	////	01 41	01 00	01 15	01 43	02 35
62	////	////	02 16	01 14	01 35	02 09	03 03
60	////	01 02	02 42	01 27	01 52	02 29	03 24
N 58	////	01 48	03 02	01 38	02 06	02 45	03 42
56	////	02 17	03 18	01 47	02 18	03 00	03 57
54	00 57	02 38	03 32	01 55	02 28	03 12	04 09
52	01 39	02 56	03 44	02 03	02 38	03 23	04 21
50	02 06	03 11	03 55	02 10	02 46	03 32	04 30
45	02 50	03 40	04 17	02 24	03 04	03 53	04 51
N 40	03 21	04 02	04 35	02 36	03 19	04 09	05 08
35	03 43	04 20	04 50	02 47	03 31	04 23	05 23
30	04 02	04 35	05 02	02 56	03 42	04 35	05 35
20	04 30	05 00	05 24	03 11	04 01	04 56	05 56
N 10	04 53	05 20	05 43	03 25	04 17	05 14	06 15
0	05 12	05 38	06 00	03 38	04 33	05 31	06 32
S 10	05 28	05 55	06 17	03 51	04 48	05 48	06 49
20	05 44	06 12	06 36	04 05	05 05	06 07	07 08
30	06 00	06 30	06 57	04 21	05 24	06 28	07 29
35	06 09	06 41	07 09	04 31	05 36	06 40	07 42
40	06 18	06 52	07 23	04 42	05 49	06 55	07 56
45	06 28	07 06	07 39	04 54	06 04	07 11	08 13
S 50	06 40	07 21	08 00	05 10	06 23	07 32	08 34
52	06 45	07 29	08 09	05 17	06 32	07 43	08 44
54	06 51	07 37	08 20	05 26	06 42	07 54	08 56
56	06 57	07 46	08 33	05 35	06 54	08 07	09 08
58	07 03	07 56	08 47	05 45	07 07	08 22	09 23
S 60	07 11	08 07	09 04	05 57	07 22	08 39	09 41

Lat.	Sunset	Twilight Civil	Twilight Naut.	Moonset 30	1	2	3
°	h m	h m	h m	h m	h m	h m	h m
N 72	☐	☐	☐	21 15	☐	☐	☐
N 70	☐	☐	☐	20 12	22 23	☐	☐
68	☐	☐	☐	19 38	21 19	22 38	23 19
66	23 42	////	////	19 13	20 44	21 58	22 45
64	22 26	////	////	18 53	20 18	21 30	22 21
62	21 50	////	////	18 37	19 58	21 08	22 01
60	21 25	23 03	////	18 23	19 42	20 51	21 45
N 58	21 05	22 19	////	18 12	19 28	20 36	21 31
56	20 49	21 50	////	18 02	19 16	20 23	21 19
54	20 35	21 29	23 08	17 53	19 06	20 12	21 08
52	20 23	21 11	22 27	17 45	18 56	20 02	20 59
50	20 13	20 57	22 01	17 27	18 36	19 41	20 39
45	19 50	20 28	21 17	17 13	18 20	19 24	20 23
N 40	19 33	20 05	20 47	17 02	18 06	19 10	20 09
35	19 18	19 48	20 24	16 51	17 55	18 57	19 57
30	19 05	19 33	20 06	16 34	17 34	18 36	19 36
20	18 43	19 08	19 37	16 18	17 17	18 17	19 18
N 10	18 25	18 48	19 15	16 04	17 00	18 00	19 01
0	18 08	18 30	18 56	15 50	16 44	17 43	18 44
S 10	17 50	18 13	18 39	15 34	16 26	17 24	18 26
20	17 32	17 56	18 23	15 17	16 06	17 03	18 05
30	17 11	17 37	18 07	15 07	15 54	16 50	17 53
35	16 59	17 27	17 59	14 55	15 41	16 36	17 39
40	16 45	17 16	17 50	14 41	15 25	16 19	17 22
45	16 29	17 02	17 39	14 25	15 05	15 57	17 01
S 50	16 08	16 46	17 28	14 17	14 56	15 47	16 51
52	15 59	16 39	17 23	14 08	14 46	15 36	16 40
54	15 48	16 31	17 17	13 59	14 34	15 23	16 28
56	15 35	16 22	17 11	13 48	14 21	15 08	16 13
58	15 21	16 12	17 05	13 35	14 05	14 50	15 55
S 60	15 04	16 01	16 57				

A total eclipse of the Sun occurs on this date. See page 5.

	SUN			MOON			
Day	Eqn. of Time 00h	12h	Mer. Pass.	Mer. Pass. Upper	Lower	Age	Phase
d	m s	m s	h m	h m	h m	d	%
30	03 32	03 38	12 04	09 51	22 18	27	7
1	03 44	03 50	12 04	10 47	23 16	28	2
2	03 56	04 02	12 04	11 46	24 16	29	0

© British Crown Copyright 2018. All rights reserved.

UT	ARIES	VENUS −3·9		MARS +1·8		JUPITER −2·6		SATURN +0·1		STARS		
d h	GHA	GHA	Dec	GHA	Dec	GHA	Dec	GHA	Dec	Name	SHA	Dec
3 00	280 43.8	191 34.8	N23 19.8	157 35.8	N21 09.5	25 01.9	S22 15.3	351 35.2	S21 56.4	Acamar	315 15.4	S40 13.5
01	295 46.3	206 33.9	19.9	172 36.6	09.2	40 04.7	15.3	6 37.9	56.4	Achernar	335 23.8	S57 08.1
02	310 48.7	221 33.1	20.0	187 37.4	08.8	55 07.4	15.3	21 40.5	56.4	Acrux	173 04.7	S63 12.6
03	325 51.2	236 32.2 ..	20.1	202 38.2 ..	08.5	70 10.2 ..	15.2	36 43.2 ..	56.4	Adhara	255 09.7	S29 00.0
04	340 53.7	251 31.3	20.3	217 39.0	08.1	85 12.9	15.2	51 45.8	56.5	Aldebaran	290 44.9	N16 32.7
05	355 56.1	266 30.5	20.4	232 39.8	07.8	100 15.7	15.2	66 48.5	56.5			
06	10 58.6	281 29.6	N23 20.5	247 40.6	N21 07.4	115 18.4	S22 15.2	81 51.2	S21 56.5	Alioth	166 17.0	N55 51.7
W 07	26 01.0	296 28.7	20.6	262 41.4	07.1	130 21.2	15.2	96 53.8	56.6	Alkaid	152 55.5	N49 13.4
E 08	41 03.5	311 27.8	20.7	277 42.2	06.7	145 23.9	15.1	111 56.5	56.6	Alnair	27 38.2	S46 51.8
D 09	56 06.0	326 27.0 ..	20.8	292 43.0 ..	06.4	160 26.7 ..	15.1	126 59.1 ..	56.6	Alnilam	275 42.5	S 1 11.5
N 10	71 08.4	341 26.1	20.9	307 43.8	06.0	175 29.4	15.1	142 01.8	56.6	Alphard	217 52.3	S 8 44.6
E 11	86 10.9	356 25.2	21.0	322 44.6	05.7	190 32.2	15.1	157 04.5	56.7			
S 12	101 13.4	11 24.4	N23 21.1	337 45.4	N21 05.3	205 34.9	S22 15.1	172 07.1	S21 56.7	Alphecca	126 07.2	N26 39.2
D 13	116 15.8	26 23.5	21.2	352 46.2	05.0	220 37.7	15.0	187 09.8	56.7	Alpheratz	357 39.2	N29 11.6
A 14	131 18.3	41 22.6	21.4	7 47.0	04.6	235 40.4	15.0	202 12.4	56.7	Altair	62 03.9	N 8 55.3
Y 15	146 20.8	56 21.8 ..	21.5	22 47.8 ..	04.3	250 43.2 ..	15.0	217 15.1 ..	56.8	Ankaa	353 11.6	S42 11.9
16	161 23.2	71 20.9	21.6	37 48.6	03.9	265 45.9	15.0	232 17.7	56.8	Antares	112 20.9	S26 28.4
17	176 25.7	86 20.0	21.7	52 49.4	03.6	280 48.7	15.0	247 20.4	56.8			
18	191 28.2	101 19.2	N23 21.8	67 50.2	N21 03.2	295 51.4	S22 15.0	262 23.1	S21 56.9	Arcturus	145 51.8	N19 05.1
19	206 30.6	116 18.3	21.9	82 51.0	02.9	310 54.2	14.9	277 25.7	56.9	Atria	107 18.4	S69 03.7
20	221 33.1	131 17.4	22.0	97 51.8	02.5	325 56.9	14.9	292 28.4	56.9	Avior	234 17.0	S59 34.5
21	236 35.5	146 16.5 ..	22.1	112 52.6 ..	02.2	340 59.6 ..	14.9	307 31.0 ..	56.9	Bellatrix	278 27.9	N 6 21.9
22	251 38.0	161 15.7	22.1	127 53.4	01.8	356 02.4	14.9	322 33.7	57.0	Betelgeuse	270 57.2	N 7 24.5
23	266 40.5	176 14.8	22.2	142 54.2	01.5	11 05.1	14.9	337 36.4	57.0			
4 00	281 42.9	191 13.9	N23 22.3	157 55.0	N21 01.1	26 07.9	S22 14.9	352 39.0	S21 57.0	Canopus	263 54.9	S52 42.4
01	296 45.4	206 13.1	22.4	172 55.8	00.8	41 10.6	14.8	7 41.7	57.0	Capella	280 28.8	N46 00.8
02	311 47.9	221 12.2	22.5	187 56.6	00.4	56 13.4	14.8	22 44.3	57.1	Deneb	49 28.2	N45 20.9
03	326 50.3	236 11.3 ..	22.6	202 57.4	21 00.1	71 16.1 ..	14.8	37 47.0 ..	57.1	Denebola	182 29.5	N14 28.0
04	341 52.8	251 10.4	22.7	217 58.2	20 59.7	86 18.9	14.8	52 49.7	57.1	Diphda	348 51.7	S17 52.8
05	356 55.3	266 09.6	22.8	232 59.0	59.4	101 21.6	14.7	67 52.3	57.1			
06	11 57.7	281 08.7	N23 22.9	247 59.8	N20 59.0	116 24.4	S22 14.7	82 55.0	S21 57.2	Dubhe	193 47.0	N61 39.1
07	27 00.2	296 07.8	23.0	263 00.6	58.7	131 27.1	14.7	97 57.6	57.2	Elnath	278 07.8	N28 37.2
T 08	42 02.6	311 07.0	23.0	278 01.4	58.3	146 29.9	14.7	113 00.3	57.2	Eltanin	90 43.7	N51 29.4
H 09	57 05.1	326 06.1 ..	23.1	293 02.2 ..	58.0	161 32.6 ..	14.7	128 03.0 ..	57.3	Enif	33 42.8	N 9 57.8
U 10	72 07.6	341 05.2	23.2	308 03.0	57.6	176 35.3	14.7	143 05.6	57.3	Fomalhaut	15 19.2	S29 31.0
R 11	87 10.0	356 04.4	23.3	323 03.8	57.2	191 38.1	14.6	158 08.3	57.3			
S 12	102 12.5	11 03.5	N23 23.3	338 04.7	N20 56.9	206 40.8	S22 14.6	173 10.9	S21 57.3	Gacrux	171 56.3	S57 13.5
D 13	117 15.0	26 02.6	23.4	353 05.5	56.5	221 43.6	14.6	188 13.6	57.4	Gienah	175 48.1	S17 39.0
A 14	132 17.4	41 01.7	23.5	8 06.3	56.2	236 46.3	14.6	203 16.3	57.4	Hadar	148 41.8	S60 28.1
Y 15	147 19.9	56 00.9 ..	23.6	23 07.1 ..	55.8	251 49.1 ..	14.6	218 18.9 ..	57.4	Hamal	327 56.2	N23 33.0
16	162 22.4	71 00.0	23.6	38 07.9	55.5	266 51.8	14.5	233 21.6	57.4	Kaus Aust.	83 37.9	S34 22.4
17	177 24.8	85 59.1	23.7	53 08.7	55.1	281 54.6	14.5	248 24.2	57.5			
18	192 27.3	100 58.2	N23 23.8	68 09.5	N20 54.8	296 57.3	S22 14.5	263 26.9	S21 57.5	Kochab	137 19.5	N74 04.9
19	207 29.8	115 57.4	23.9	83 10.3	54.4	312 00.0	14.5	278 29.5	57.5	Markab	13 34.1	N15 18.5
20	222 32.2	130 56.5	23.9	98 11.1	54.0	327 02.8	14.5	293 32.2	57.6	Menkar	314 10.9	N 4 09.8
21	237 34.7	145 55.6 ..	24.0	113 11.9 ..	53.7	342 05.5 ..	14.4	308 34.9 ..	57.6	Menkent	148 02.5	S36 27.9
22	252 37.1	160 54.8	24.1	128 12.7	53.3	357 08.3	14.4	323 37.5	57.6	Miaplacidus	221 39.6	S69 48.0
23	267 39.6	175 53.9	24.1	143 13.5	53.0	12 11.0	14.4	338 40.2	57.6			
5 00	282 42.1	190 53.0	N23 24.2	158 14.3	N20 52.6	27 13.8	S22 14.4	353 42.8	S21 57.7	Mirfak	308 34.8	N49 55.5
01	297 44.5	205 52.1	24.3	173 15.1	52.3	42 16.5	14.4	8 45.5	57.7	Nunki	75 52.8	S26 16.2
02	312 47.0	220 51.3	24.3	188 15.9	51.9	57 19.2	14.4	23 48.2	57.7	Peacock	53 12.2	S56 40.1
03	327 49.5	235 50.4 ..	24.4	203 16.7 ..	51.5	72 22.0 ..	14.3	38 50.8 ..	57.7	Pollux	243 23.1	N27 58.7
04	342 51.9	250 49.5	24.4	218 17.6	51.2	87 24.7	14.3	53 53.5	57.8	Procyon	244 55.8	N 5 10.4
05	357 54.4	265 48.6	24.5	233 18.4	50.8	102 27.5	14.3	68 56.1	57.8			
06	12 56.9	280 47.8	N23 24.6	248 19.2	N20 50.5	117 30.2	S22 14.3	83 58.8	S21 57.8	Rasalhague	96 02.3	N12 32.9
07	27 59.3	295 46.9	24.6	263 20.0	50.1	132 32.9	14.3	99 01.5	57.9	Regulus	207 39.3	N11 52.4
08	43 01.8	310 46.0	24.7	278 20.8	49.7	147 35.7	14.2	114 04.1	57.9	Rigel	281 08.4	S 8 10.9
F 09	58 04.3	325 45.2 ..	24.7	293 21.6 ..	49.4	162 38.4 ..	14.2	129 06.8 ..	57.9	Rigil Kent.	139 45.8	S60 55.0
R 10	73 06.7	340 44.3	24.8	308 22.4	49.0	177 41.2	14.2	144 09.4	57.9	Sabik	102 07.5	S15 44.8
I 11	88 09.2	355 43.4	24.8	323 23.2	48.7	192 43.9	14.2	159 12.1	58.0			
D 12	103 11.6	10 42.5	N23 24.9	338 24.0	N20 48.3	207 46.6	S22 14.2	174 14.8	S21 58.0	Schedar	349 35.8	N56 38.3
A 13	118 14.1	25 41.7	24.9	353 24.8	47.9	222 49.4	14.2	189 17.4	58.0	Shaula	96 15.9	S37 06.9
Y 14	133 16.6	40 40.8	25.0	8 25.6	47.6	237 52.1	14.1	204 20.1	58.0	Sirius	258 30.4	S16 44.7
15	148 19.0	55 39.9 ..	25.0	23 26.4 ..	47.2	252 54.9 ..	14.1	219 22.7 ..	58.1	Spica	158 26.8	S11 15.7
16	163 21.5	70 39.0	25.1	38 27.2	46.8	267 57.6	14.1	234 25.4	58.1	Suhail	222 49.8	S43 30.8
17	178 24.0	85 38.2	25.1	53 28.1	46.5	283 00.3	14.1	249 28.1	58.1			
18	193 26.4	100 37.3	N23 25.1	68 28.9	N20 46.1	298 03.1	S22 14.1	264 30.7	S21 58.2	Vega	80 35.7	N38 48.2
19	208 28.9	115 36.4	25.2	83 29.7	45.8	313 05.8	14.0	279 33.4	58.2	Zuben'ubi	137 00.7	S16 07.2
20	223 31.4	130 35.5	25.2	98 30.5	45.4	328 08.5	14.0	294 36.0	58.2		SHA	Mer.Pass.
21	238 33.8	145 34.7 ..	25.3	113 31.3 ..	45.0	343 11.3 ..	14.0	309 38.7 ..	58.2	Venus	269 31.0	11 16
22	253 36.3	160 33.8	25.3	128 32.1	44.7	358 14.0	14.0	324 41.4	58.3	Mars	236 12.1	13 28
23	268 38.8	175 32.9	25.3	143 32.9	44.3	13 16.8	14.0	339 44.0	58.3	Jupiter	104 25.0	22 11
Mer.Pass. 5 12.3		v −0.9	d 0.1	v 0.8	d 0.4	v 2.7	d 0.0	v 2.7	d 0.0	Saturn	70 56.1	0 29

© British Crown Copyright 2018. All rights reserved.

UT	SUN GHA	SUN Dec	MOON GHA	v	MOON Dec	d	HP
3 00	178 58.1	N22 59.7	176 08.9	4.3	N22 22.4	0.4	59.7
01	193 58.0	59.5	190 32.2	4.3	22 22.0	0.5	59.7
02	208 57.9	59.3	204 55.5	4.3	22 21.5	0.7	59.8
03	223 57.8	.. 59.1	219 18.8	4.3	22 20.8	0.8	59.8
04	238 57.7	58.9	233 42.1	4.2	22 20.0	1.0	59.8
05	253 57.5	58.7	248 05.3	4.2	22 19.0	1.2	59.8
06	268 57.4	N22 58.6	262 28.5	4.2	N22 17.8	1.3	59.8
W 07	283 57.3	58.4	276 51.7	4.3	22 16.5	1.5	59.9
E 08	298 57.2	58.2	291 15.0	4.1	22 15.0	1.7	59.9
D 09	313 57.1	.. 58.0	305 38.1	4.2	22 13.3	1.8	59.9
N 10	328 57.0	57.8	320 01.3	4.2	22 11.5	1.9	59.9
E 11	343 56.8	57.6	334 24.5	4.2	22 09.6	2.1	59.9
S 12	358 56.7	N22 57.4	348 47.7	4.2	N22 07.5	2.3	60.0
D 13	13 56.6	57.2	3 10.9	4.2	22 05.2	2.4	60.0
A 14	28 56.5	56.9	17 34.1	4.2	22 02.8	2.6	60.0
Y 15	43 56.4	.. 56.7	31 57.3	4.2	22 00.2	2.8	60.0
16	58 56.3	56.5	46 20.5	4.2	21 57.4	2.9	60.0
17	73 56.1	56.3	60 43.7	4.2	21 54.5	3.0	60.0
18	88 56.0	N22 56.1	75 06.9	4.2	N21 51.5	3.3	60.0
19	103 55.9	55.9	89 30.1	4.2	21 48.2	3.3	60.1
20	118 55.8	55.7	103 53.3	4.3	21 44.9	3.6	60.1
21	133 55.7	.. 55.5	118 16.6	4.3	21 41.3	3.6	60.1
22	148 55.6	55.3	132 39.9	4.3	21 37.7	3.9	60.1
23	163 55.4	55.1	147 03.2	4.3	21 33.8	4.0	60.1
4 00	178 55.3	N22 54.9	161 26.5	4.3	N21 29.8	4.1	60.1
01	193 55.2	54.7	175 49.8	4.4	21 25.7	4.3	60.1
02	208 55.1	54.5	190 13.2	4.4	21 21.4	4.4	60.1
03	223 55.0	.. 54.3	204 36.6	4.4	21 17.0	4.6	60.2
04	238 54.9	54.0	219 00.0	4.4	21 12.4	4.8	60.2
05	253 54.8	53.8	233 23.4	4.5	21 07.6	4.9	60.2
06	268 54.7	N22 53.6	247 46.9	4.5	N21 02.7	5.0	60.2
T 07	283 54.5	53.4	262 10.4	4.5	20 57.7	5.2	60.2
H 08	298 54.4	53.2	276 33.9	4.6	20 52.5	5.4	60.2
U 09	313 54.3	.. 53.0	290 57.5	4.6	20 47.1	5.5	60.2
R 10	328 54.2	52.8	305 21.1	4.7	20 41.6	5.6	60.2
S 11	343 54.1	52.5	319 44.8	4.7	20 36.0	5.8	60.2
D 12	358 54.0	N22 52.3	334 08.5	4.7	N20 30.2	5.9	60.2
A 13	13 53.9	52.1	348 32.2	4.8	20 24.3	6.1	60.2
Y 14	28 53.7	51.9	2 56.0	4.8	20 18.2	6.2	60.2
15	43 53.6	.. 51.7	17 19.8	4.9	20 12.0	6.4	60.2
16	58 53.5	51.4	31 43.7	4.9	20 05.6	6.5	60.3
17	73 53.4	51.2	46 07.6	5.0	19 59.1	6.6	60.3
18	88 53.3	N22 51.0	60 31.6	5.0	N19 52.5	6.8	60.3
19	103 53.2	50.8	74 55.6	5.1	19 45.7	6.9	60.3
20	118 53.1	50.6	89 19.7	5.1	19 38.8	7.0	60.3
21	133 53.0	.. 50.3	103 43.8	5.2	19 31.8	7.2	60.3
22	148 52.9	50.1	118 08.0	5.3	19 24.6	7.3	60.3
23	163 52.7	49.9	132 32.3	5.3	19 17.3	7.5	60.3
5 00	178 52.6	N22 49.7	146 56.6	5.3	N19 09.8	7.5	60.3
01	193 52.5	49.4	161 20.9	5.4	19 02.3	7.7	60.3
02	208 52.4	49.2	175 45.3	5.5	18 54.6	7.9	60.3
03	223 52.3	.. 49.0	190 09.8	5.5	18 46.7	7.9	60.3
04	238 52.2	48.7	204 34.3	5.6	18 38.8	8.1	60.3
05	253 52.1	48.5	218 58.9	5.7	18 30.7	8.2	60.3
06	268 52.0	N22 48.3	233 23.6	5.7	N18 22.5	8.4	60.3
F 07	283 51.9	48.0	247 48.3	5.8	18 14.1	8.4	60.3
R 08	298 51.7	47.8	262 13.1	5.9	18 05.7	8.6	60.3
I 09	313 51.6	.. 47.6	276 38.0	5.9	17 57.1	8.7	60.3
D 10	328 51.5	47.4	291 02.9	6.0	17 48.4	8.8	60.3
A 11	343 51.4	47.1	305 27.9	6.0	17 39.6	9.0	60.3
Y 12	358 51.3	N22 46.9	319 52.9	6.1	N17 30.6	9.0	60.3
13	13 51.2	46.6	334 18.0	6.2	17 21.6	9.2	60.3
14	28 51.1	46.4	348 43.2	6.3	17 12.4	9.3	60.3
15	43 51.0	.. 46.2	3 08.5	6.3	17 03.1	9.4	60.3
16	58 50.9	45.9	17 33.8	6.4	16 53.7	9.5	60.3
17	73 50.8	45.7	31 59.2	6.4	16 44.2	9.6	60.3
18	88 50.7	N22 45.5	46 24.6	6.6	N16 34.6	9.7	60.2
19	103 50.5	45.2	60 50.2	6.6	16 24.9	9.8	60.2
20	118 50.4	45.0	75 15.8	6.6	16 15.1	9.9	60.2
21	133 50.3	.. 44.7	89 41.4	6.8	16 05.2	10.0	60.2
22	148 50.2	44.5	104 07.2	6.8	15 55.2	10.2	60.2
23	163 50.1	44.3	118 33.0	6.9	N15 45.0	10.2	60.2
	SD 15.8	d 0.2	SD 16.3		16.4		16.4

Lat.	Twilight Naut.	Twilight Civil	Sunrise	Moonrise 3	4	5	6
N 72	▭	▭	▭				05 53
N 70	▭	▭	▭	▭		03 55	06 25
68	▭	▭	▭	▭	02 27	04 42	06 48
66	////	////	00 40	01 54	03 22	05 13	07 06
64	////	////	02 08	02 35	03 56	05 35	07 21
62	////	////	02 21	03 03	04 20	05 53	07 33
60	////	01 10	02 45	03 24	04 39	06 08	07 43
N 58	////	01 53	03 05	03 42	04 55	06 21	07 52
56	////	02 20	03 21	03 57	05 09	06 32	08 00
54	01 04	02 41	03 34	04 09	05 20	06 41	08 06
52	01 44	02 58	03 46	04 21	05 31	06 50	08 13
50	02 09	03 13	03 57	04 30	05 40	06 57	08 18
45	02 53	03 42	04 19	04 51	05 59	07 14	08 30
N 40	03 22	04 04	04 36	05 08	06 15	07 27	08 40
35	03 45	04 21	04 51	05 23	06 29	07 38	08 48
30	04 03	04 36	05 04	05 35	06 40	07 48	08 56
20	04 32	05 01	05 25	05 56	07 00	08 05	09 09
N 10	04 54	05 21	05 44	06 15	07 17	08 19	09 20
0	05 12	05 38	06 01	06 32	07 33	08 33	09 30
S 10	05 29	05 55	06 18	06 49	07 49	08 47	09 40
20	05 45	06 12	06 36	07 08	08 07	09 01	09 51
30	06 01	06 30	06 56	07 29	08 26	09 18	10 04
35	06 09	06 41	07 09	07 42	08 38	09 28	10 11
40	06 18	06 52	07 22	07 56	08 51	09 39	10 19
45	06 28	07 05	07 39	08 13	09 07	09 52	10 29
S 50	06 39	07 21	07 59	08 34	09 26	10 07	10 41
52	06 44	07 28	08 08	08 44	09 35	10 14	10 46
54	06 50	07 36	08 18	08 56	09 45	10 23	10 52
56	06 56	07 44	08 31	09 08	09 56	10 32	10 58
58	07 02	07 54	08 45	09 23	10 09	10 42	11 05
S 60	07 09	08 05	09 02	09 41	10 24	10 54	11 14

Lat.	Sunset	Twilight Civil	Twilight Naut.	Moonset 3	4	5	6
N 72	▭	▭	▭	▭	▭	▭	00 58
N 70	▭	▭	▭	▭		00 54	00 25
68	▭	▭	▭	▭	00 15	00 06	(00 00 / 23 55)
66	23 24	////	////	23 19	23 35	23 41	23 44
64	22 21	////	////	22 45	23 11	23 25	23 34
62	21 47	////	////	22 21	22 52	23 12	23 26
60	21 23	22 56	////	22 01	22 37	23 01	23 19
N 58	21 03	22 15	////	21 45	22 24	22 52	23 12
56	20 47	21 48	////	21 31	22 12	22 43	23 07
54	20 34	21 27	23 02	21 19	22 02	22 35	23 02
52	20 22	21 10	22 24	21 08	21 53	22 29	22 57
50	20 12	20 55	21 59	20 59	21 45	22 22	22 53
45	19 50	20 27	21 15	20 39	21 28	22 09	22 44
N 40	19 32	20 05	20 46	20 23	21 14	21 58	22 36
35	19 18	19 47	20 24	20 09	21 02	21 48	22 30
30	19 05	19 32	20 05	19 57	20 51	21 40	22 24
20	18 44	19 08	19 37	19 36	20 33	21 25	22 14
N 10	18 25	18 48	19 15	19 18	20 17	21 13	22 05
0	18 08	18 30	18 57	19 01	20 02	21 01	21 56
S 10	17 51	18 14	18 40	18 44	19 47	20 48	21 48
20	17 33	17 57	18 24	18 26	19 31	20 35	21 38
30	17 12	17 39	18 08	18 05	19 12	20 20	21 28
35	17 00	17 28	18 00	17 53	19 01	20 12	21 22
40	16 47	17 17	17 51	17 39	18 49	20 01	21 15
45	16 30	17 04	17 41	17 22	18 34	19 50	21 06
S 50	16 10	16 48	17 30	17 01	18 15	19 35	20 56
52	16 01	16 41	17 25	16 51	18 07	19 28	20 52
54	15 50	16 33	17 19	16 40	17 57	19 21	20 47
56	15 38	16 25	17 13	16 28	17 46	19 12	20 41
58	15 24	16 15	17 07	16 13	17 33	19 03	20 35
S 60	15 07	16 04	17 00	15 55	17 19	18 52	20 27

	SUN Eqn. of Time 00h	SUN Eqn. of Time 12h	SUN Mer. Pass.	MOON Mer. Pass. Upper	MOON Mer. Pass. Lower	Age	Phase
Day	m s	m s	h m	h m	h m	d	%
3	04 07	04 13	12 04	12 47	00 16	01	1
4	04 18	04 24	12 04	13 48	01 17	02	4
5	04 29	04 35	12 05	14 47	02 18	03	10

© British Crown Copyright 2018. All rights reserved.

UT	ARIES GHA	VENUS −3·9 GHA	Dec	MARS +1·8 GHA	Dec	JUPITER −2·6 GHA	Dec	SATURN +0·1 GHA	Dec	STARS Name	SHA	Dec
6 00	283 41.2	190 32.0	N23 25.4	158 33.7	N20 43.9	28 19.5	S22 14.0	354 46.7	S21 58.3	Acamar	315 15.4	S40 13.5
01	298 43.7	205 31.2	25.4	173 34.5	43.6	43 22.2	13.9	9 49.3	58.3	Achernar	335 23.8	S57 08.1
02	313 46.1	220 30.3	25.4	188 35.3	43.2	58 25.0	13.9	24 52.0	58.4	Acrux	173 04.7	S63 12.6
03	328 48.6	235 29.4 ..	25.5	203 36.2 ..	42.8	73 27.7 ..	13.9	39 54.7 ..	58.4	Adhara	255 09.7	S29 00.0
04	343 51.1	250 28.5	25.5	218 37.0	42.5	88 30.4	13.9	54 57.3	58.4	Aldebaran	290 44.9	N16 32.7
05	358 53.5	265 27.7	25.5	233 37.8	42.1	103 33.2	13.9	70 00.0	58.5			
06	13 56.0	280 26.8	N23 25.6	248 38.6	N20 41.7	118 35.9	S22 13.8	85 02.6	S21 58.5	Alioth	166 17.0	N55 51.7
07	28 58.5	295 25.9	25.6	263 39.4	41.4	133 38.6	13.8	100 05.3	58.5	Alkaid	152 55.5	N49 13.4
S 08	44 00.9	310 25.1	25.6	278 40.2	41.0	148 41.4	13.8	115 08.0	58.5	Alnair	27 38.2	S46 51.8
A 09	59 03.4	325 24.2 ..	25.6	293 41.0 ..	40.6	163 44.1 ..	13.8	130 10.6 ..	58.6	Alnilam	275 42.5	S 1 11.5
T 10	74 05.9	340 23.3	25.7	308 41.8	40.3	178 46.8	13.8	145 13.3	58.6	Alphard	217 52.3	S 8 44.6
U 11	89 08.3	355 22.4	25.7	323 42.6	39.9	193 49.6	13.8	160 15.9	58.6			
R 12	104 10.8	10 21.6	N23 25.7	338 43.5	N20 39.5	208 52.3	S22 13.7	175 18.6	S21 58.6	Alphecca	126 07.3	N26 39.3
D 13	119 13.2	25 20.7	25.7	353 44.3	39.2	223 55.0	13.7	190 21.3	58.7	Alpheratz	357 39.1	N29 11.7
A 14	134 15.7	40 19.8	25.7	8 45.1	38.8	238 57.8	13.7	205 23.9	58.7	Altair	62 03.9	N 8 55.3
Y 15	149 18.2	55 18.9 ..	25.8	23 45.9 ..	38.4	254 00.5 ..	13.7	220 26.6 ..	58.7	Ankaa	353 11.5	S42 11.9
16	164 20.6	70 18.1	25.8	38 46.7	38.1	269 03.2	13.7	235 29.2	58.8	Antares	112 20.9	S26 28.4
17	179 23.1	85 17.2	25.8	53 47.5	37.7	284 06.0	13.7	250 31.9	58.8			
18	194 25.6	100 16.3	N23 25.8	68 48.3	N20 37.3	299 08.7	S22 13.6	265 34.6	S21 58.8	Arcturus	145 51.8	N19 05.1
19	209 28.0	115 15.4	25.8	83 49.1	37.0	314 11.4	13.6	280 37.2	58.8	Atria	107 18.4	S69 03.7
20	224 30.5	130 14.6	25.8	98 50.0	36.6	329 14.2	13.6	295 39.9	58.9	Avior	234 17.0	S59 34.4
21	239 33.0	145 13.7 ..	25.8	113 50.8 ..	36.2	344 16.9 ..	13.6	310 42.5 ..	58.9	Bellatrix	278 27.9	N 6 21.9
22	254 35.4	160 12.8	25.8	128 51.6	35.9	359 19.6	13.6	325 45.2	58.9	Betelgeuse	270 57.1	N 7 24.5
23	269 37.9	175 11.9	25.9	143 52.4	35.5	14 22.4	13.5	340 47.9	58.9			
7 00	284 40.4	190 11.0	N23 25.9	158 53.2	N20 35.1	29 25.1	S22 13.5	355 50.5	S21 59.0	Canopus	263 54.9	S52 42.4
01	299 42.8	205 10.2	25.9	173 54.0	34.8	44 27.8	13.5	10 53.2	59.0	Capella	280 28.8	N46 00.8
02	314 45.3	220 09.3	25.9	188 54.8	34.4	59 30.6	13.5	25 55.9	59.0	Deneb	49 28.2	N45 20.9
03	329 47.7	235 08.4 ..	25.9	203 55.7 ..	34.0	74 33.3 ..	13.5	40 58.5 ..	59.1	Denebola	182 29.5	N14 28.0
04	344 50.2	250 07.5	25.9	218 56.5	33.6	89 36.0	13.5	56 01.2	59.1	Diphda	348 51.7	S17 52.8
05	359 52.7	265 06.7	25.9	233 57.3	33.3	104 38.7	13.4	71 03.8	59.1			
06	14 55.1	280 05.8	N23 25.9	248 58.1	N20 32.9	119 41.5	S22 13.4	86 06.5	S21 59.1	Dubhe	193 47.0	N61 39.1
07	29 57.6	295 04.9	25.9	263 58.9	32.5	134 44.2	13.4	101 09.2	59.2	Elnath	278 07.7	N28 37.2
S 08	45 00.1	310 04.0	25.9	278 59.7	32.1	149 46.9	13.4	116 11.8	59.2	Eltanin	90 43.7	N51 29.4
U 09	60 02.5	325 03.2 ..	25.9	294 00.5 ..	31.8	164 49.7 ..	13.4	131 14.5 ..	59.2	Enif	33 42.8	N 9 57.9
N 10	75 05.0	340 02.3	25.9	309 01.4	31.4	179 52.4	13.4	146 17.1	59.2	Fomalhaut	15 19.2	S29 31.0
D 11	90 07.5	355 01.4	25.9	324 02.2	31.0	194 55.1	13.3	161 19.8	59.3			
A 12	105 09.9	10 00.5	N23 25.8	339 03.0	N20 30.7	209 57.8	S22 13.3	176 22.5	S21 59.3	Gacrux	171 56.3	S57 13.5
Y 13	120 12.4	24 59.7	25.8	354 03.8	30.3	225 00.6	13.3	191 25.1	59.3	Gienah	175 48.1	S17 39.0
14	135 14.9	39 58.8	25.8	9 04.6	29.9	240 03.3	13.3	206 27.8	59.4	Hadar	148 41.8	S60 28.1
15	150 17.3	54 57.9 ..	25.8	24 05.4 ..	29.5	255 06.0 ..	13.3	221 30.4 ..	59.4	Hamal	327 56.2	N23 33.0
16	165 19.8	69 57.0	25.8	39 06.2	29.2	270 08.8	13.2	236 33.1	59.4	Kaus Aust.	83 37.9	S34 22.4
17	180 22.2	84 56.2	25.8	54 07.1	28.8	285 11.5	13.2	251 35.8	59.4			
18	195 24.7	99 55.3	N23 25.8	69 07.9	N20 28.4	300 14.2	S22 13.2	266 38.4	S21 59.5	Kochab	137 19.5	N74 04.9
19	210 27.2	114 54.4	25.8	84 08.7	28.0	315 16.9	13.2	281 41.1	59.5	Markab	13 34.0	N15 18.5
20	225 29.6	129 53.5	25.7	99 09.5	27.7	330 19.7	13.2	296 43.7	59.5	Menkar	314 10.9	N 4 09.8
21	240 32.1	144 52.7 ..	25.7	114 10.3 ..	27.3	345 22.4 ..	13.2	311 46.4 ..	59.5	Menkent	148 02.6	S36 27.9
22	255 34.6	159 51.8	25.7	129 11.1	26.9	0 25.1	13.1	326 49.1	59.6	Miaplacidus	221 39.6	S69 48.0
23	270 37.0	174 50.9	25.7	144 12.0	26.5	15 27.8	13.1	341 51.7	59.6			
8 00	285 39.5	189 50.0	N23 25.7	159 12.8	N20 26.2	30 30.6	S22 13.1	356 54.4	S21 59.6	Mirfak	308 34.7	N49 55.5
01	300 42.0	204 49.2	25.6	174 13.6	25.8	45 33.3	13.1	11 57.0	59.7	Nunki	75 52.8	S26 16.2
02	315 44.4	219 48.3	25.6	189 14.4	25.4	60 36.0	13.1	26 59.7	59.7	Peacock	53 12.2	S56 40.1
03	330 46.9	234 47.4 ..	25.6	204 15.2 ..	25.0	75 38.7 ..	13.1	42 02.4 ..	59.7	Pollux	243 23.1	N27 58.7
04	345 49.3	249 46.5	25.6	219 16.0	24.7	90 41.5	13.0	57 05.0	59.7	Procyon	244 55.7	N 5 10.5
05	0 51.8	264 45.7	25.5	234 16.9	24.3	105 44.2	13.0	72 07.7	59.8			
06	15 54.3	279 44.8	N23 25.5	249 17.7	N20 23.9	120 46.9	S22 13.0	87 10.3	S21 59.8	Rasalhague	96 02.3	N12 33.0
07	30 56.7	294 43.9	25.5	264 18.5	23.5	135 49.6	13.0	102 13.0	59.8	Regulus	207 39.4	N11 52.4
08	45 59.2	309 43.0	25.4	279 19.3	23.1	150 52.4	13.0	117 15.7	59.8	Rigel	281 08.4	S 8 10.8
M 09	61 01.7	324 42.2 ..	25.4	294 20.1 ..	22.8	165 55.1 ..	13.0	132 18.3 ..	59.9	Rigil Kent.	139 45.8	S60 55.0
O 10	76 04.1	339 41.3	25.4	309 21.0	22.4	180 57.8	12.9	147 21.0	59.9	Sabik	102 07.5	S15 44.8
N 11	91 06.6	354 40.4	25.3	324 21.8	22.0	196 00.5	12.9	162 23.7	59.9			
D 12	106 09.1	9 39.5	N23 25.3	339 22.6	N20 21.6	211 03.2	S22 12.9	177 26.3	S21 59.9	Schedar	349 35.8	N56 38.3
A 13	121 11.5	24 38.6	25.3	354 23.4	21.2	226 06.0	12.9	192 29.0	22 00.0	Shaula	96 15.9	S37 06.9
Y 14	136 14.0	39 37.8	25.2	9 24.2	20.9	241 08.7	12.9	207 31.6	00.0	Sirius	258 30.4	S16 44.6
15	151 16.5	54 36.9 ..	25.2	24 25.0 ..	20.5	256 11.4 ..	12.8	222 34.3 ..	00.0	Spica	158 26.8	S11 15.7
16	166 18.9	69 36.0	25.1	39 25.9	20.1	271 14.1	12.8	237 37.0	00.1	Suhail	222 49.8	S43 30.8
17	181 21.4	84 35.1	25.1	54 26.7	19.7	286 16.9	12.8	252 39.6	00.1			
18	196 23.8	99 34.3	N23 25.1	69 27.5	N20 19.3	301 19.6	S22 12.8	267 42.3	S22 00.1	Vega	80 35.7	N38 48.3
19	211 26.3	114 33.4	25.0	84 28.3	19.0	316 22.3	12.8	282 44.9	00.1	Zuben'ubi	137 00.7	S16 07.2
20	226 28.8	129 32.5	25.0	99 29.1	18.6	331 25.0	12.8	297 47.6	00.2		SHA	Mer.Pass.
21	241 31.2	144 31.6 ..	24.9	114 30.0 ..	18.2	346 27.7 ..	12.7	312 50.3 ..	00.2		° ′	h m
22	256 33.7	159 30.8	24.9	129 30.8	17.8	1 30.5	12.7	327 52.9	00.2	Venus	265 30.7	11 20
23	271 36.2	174 29.9	24.8	144 31.6	17.4	16 33.2	12.7	342 55.6	00.2	Mars	234 12.9	13 24
	h m									Jupiter	104 44.7	21 58
Mer.Pass.	5 00.5	v −0.9	d 0.0	v 0.8　d 0.4		v 2.7　d 0.0		v 2.7　d 0.0		Saturn	71 10.2	0 17

© British Crown Copyright 2018. All rights reserved.

UT	SUN GHA	SUN Dec	MOON GHA	v	MOON Dec	d	HP
6 00	178 50.0	N22 44.0	132 58.9	6.9	N15 34.8	10.3	60.2
01	193 49.9	43.8	147 24.8	7.1	15 24.5	10.4	60.2
02	208 49.8	43.5	161 50.9	7.1	15 14.1	10.5	60.2
03	223 49.7	.. 43.3	176 17.0	7.2	15 03.6	10.6	60.2
04	238 49.6	43.0	190 43.2	7.2	14 53.0	10.7	60.2
05	253 49.5	42.8	205 09.4	7.3	14 42.3	10.8	60.2
06	268 49.4	N22 42.5	219 35.7	7.4	N14 31.5	10.9	60.2
S 07	283 49.3	42.3	234 02.1	7.5	14 20.6	10.9	60.2
A 08	298 49.2	42.1	248 28.6	7.5	14 09.7	11.1	60.2
T 09	313 49.1	.. 41.8	262 55.1	7.6	13 58.6	11.1	60.1
U 10	328 48.9	41.6	277 21.7	7.7	13 47.5	11.2	60.1
R 11	343 48.8	41.3	291 48.4	7.8	13 36.3	11.3	60.1
D 12	358 48.7	N22 41.1	306 15.2	7.8	N13 25.0	11.3	60.1
A 13	13 48.6	40.8	320 42.0	7.9	13 13.7	11.5	60.1
Y 14	28 48.5	40.5	335 08.9	7.9	13 02.2	11.5	60.1
15	43 48.4	.. 40.3	349 35.8	8.1	12 50.7	11.6	60.1
16	58 48.3	40.0	4 02.9	8.1	12 39.1	11.7	60.1
17	73 48.2	39.8	18 30.0	8.2	12 27.4	11.7	60.1
18	88 48.1	N22 39.5	32 57.2	8.2	N12 15.7	11.8	60.0
19	103 48.0	39.3	47 24.4	8.3	12 03.9	11.9	60.0
20	118 47.9	39.0	61 51.7	8.4	11 52.0	11.9	60.0
21	133 47.8	.. 38.8	76 19.1	8.4	11 40.1	12.0	60.0
22	148 47.7	38.5	90 46.5	8.6	11 28.1	12.1	60.0
23	163 47.6	38.2	105 14.1	8.6	11 16.0	12.1	60.0
7 00	178 47.5	N22 38.0	119 41.7	8.6	N11 03.9	12.2	60.0
01	193 47.4	37.7	134 09.3	8.7	10 51.7	12.2	59.9
02	208 47.3	37.5	148 37.0	8.8	10 39.5	12.3	59.9
03	223 47.2	.. 37.2	163 04.8	8.9	10 27.2	12.4	59.9
04	238 47.1	36.9	177 32.7	8.9	10 14.8	12.4	59.9
05	253 47.0	36.7	192 00.6	9.0	10 02.4	12.5	59.9
06	268 46.9	N22 36.4	206 28.6	9.0	N 9 49.9	12.5	59.9
S 07	283 46.8	36.2	220 56.6	9.1	9 37.4	12.6	59.9
U 08	298 46.7	35.9	235 24.7	9.2	9 24.8	12.6	59.8
N 09	313 46.6	.. 35.6	249 52.9	9.2	9 12.2	12.6	59.8
D 10	328 46.5	35.4	264 21.1	9.3	8 59.6	12.7	59.8
A 11	343 46.4	35.1	278 49.4	9.4	8 46.9	12.8	59.8
Y 12	358 46.3	N22 34.8	293 17.8	9.4	N 8 34.1	12.8	59.8
13	13 46.2	34.6	307 46.2	9.5	8 21.3	12.8	59.8
14	28 46.1	34.3	322 14.7	9.5	8 08.5	12.9	59.7
15	43 46.0	.. 34.0	336 43.2	9.6	7 55.6	12.9	59.7
16	58 45.9	33.8	351 11.8	9.6	7 42.7	12.9	59.7
17	73 45.8	33.5	5 40.4	9.7	7 29.8	13.0	59.7
18	88 45.7	N22 33.2	20 09.1	9.8	N 7 16.8	13.0	59.7
19	103 45.6	32.9	34 37.9	9.8	7 03.8	13.0	59.7
20	118 45.5	32.7	49 06.7	9.8	6 50.8	13.1	59.6
21	133 45.4	.. 32.4	63 35.5	9.9	6 37.7	13.1	59.6
22	148 45.3	32.1	78 04.4	10.0	6 24.6	13.1	59.6
23	163 45.2	31.8	92 33.4	10.0	6 11.5	13.2	59.6
8 00	178 45.1	N22 31.6	107 02.4	10.1	N 5 58.3	13.2	59.6
01	193 45.0	31.3	121 31.5	10.1	5 45.1	13.2	59.5
02	208 44.9	31.0	136 00.6	10.2	5 31.9	13.2	59.5
03	223 44.8	.. 30.7	150 29.8	10.2	5 18.7	13.2	59.5
04	238 44.7	30.5	164 59.0	10.2	5 05.5	13.3	59.5
05	253 44.6	30.2	179 28.2	10.4	4 52.2	13.2	59.5
06	268 44.5	N22 29.9	193 57.6	10.3	N 4 39.0	13.3	59.4
07	283 44.4	29.6	208 26.9	10.4	4 25.7	13.4	59.4
08	298 44.3	29.3	222 56.3	10.4	4 12.3	13.3	59.4
M 09	313 44.2	.. 29.1	237 25.7	10.5	3 59.0	13.3	59.4
O 10	328 44.1	28.8	251 55.2	10.5	3 45.7	13.4	59.3
N 11	343 44.0	28.5	266 24.7	10.6	3 32.3	13.3	59.3
D 12	358 43.9	N22 28.2	280 54.3	10.6	N 3 19.0	13.4	59.3
A 13	13 43.8	27.9	295 23.9	10.6	3 05.6	13.4	59.3
Y 14	28 43.7	27.6	309 53.5	10.7	2 52.3	13.4	59.3
15	43 43.6	.. 27.4	324 23.2	10.7	2 38.9	13.4	59.2
16	58 43.5	27.1	338 52.9	10.8	2 25.5	13.4	59.2
17	73 43.4	26.8	353 22.7	10.7	2 12.1	13.4	59.2
18	88 43.3	N22 26.5	7 52.4	10.8	N 1 58.7	13.3	59.2
19	103 43.2	26.2	22 22.2	10.9	1 45.4	13.4	59.2
20	118 43.1	25.9	36 52.1	10.9	1 32.0	13.4	59.1
21	133 43.0	.. 25.6	51 22.0	10.9	1 18.6	13.4	59.1
22	148 42.9	25.3	65 51.9	10.9	1 05.2	13.4	59.1
23	163 42.8	25.1	80 21.8	11.0	N 0 51.8	13.3	59.1
	SD 15.8	d 0.3	SD 16.4		16.3		16.2

Twilight / Sunrise / Moonrise

Lat.	Naut.	Civil	Sunrise	6	7	8	9
N 72	◻	◻	◻	05 53	08 20	10 30	12 34
N 70	◻	◻	◻	06 25	08 35	10 35	12 31
68	◻	◻	◻	06 48	08 47	10 39	12 28
66	////	////	00 56	07 06	08 57	10 43	12 26
64	////	////	01 53	07 21	09 05	10 46	12 24
62	////	////	02 26	07 33	09 12	10 48	12 22
60	////	01 19	02 49	07 43	09 18	10 50	12 21
N 58	////	01 58	03 08	07 52	09 23	10 52	12 20
56	////	02 24	03 24	08 00	09 28	10 54	12 18
54	01 12	02 45	03 37	08 06	09 32	10 56	12 17
52	01 49	03 02	03 49	08 13	09 36	10 57	12 17
50	02 13	03 16	03 59	08 18	09 39	10 58	12 16
45	02 56	03 44	04 21	08 30	09 46	11 01	12 14
N 40	03 25	04 06	04 38	08 40	09 53	11 03	12 13
35	03 47	04 23	04 52	08 48	09 58	11 05	12 11
30	04 05	04 38	05 05	08 56	10 02	11 07	12 10
20	04 33	05 02	05 26	09 09	10 10	11 10	12 08
N 10	04 55	05 21	05 44	09 20	10 18	11 13	12 07
0	05 13	05 39	06 01	09 30	10 24	11 15	12 05
S 10	05 29	05 55	06 18	09 40	10 31	11 18	12 04
20	05 45	06 12	06 36	09 51	10 38	11 21	12 02
30	06 00	06 30	06 56	10 04	10 46	11 24	12 00
35	06 09	06 40	07 08	10 11	10 50	11 26	11 59
40	06 18	06 51	07 22	10 19	10 55	11 28	11 58
45	06 27	07 04	07 38	10 29	11 01	11 30	11 57
S 50	06 38	07 20	07 57	10 41	11 08	11 33	11 56
52	06 43	07 27	08 07	10 46	11 12	11 34	11 55
54	06 49	07 34	08 17	10 52	11 15	11 35	11 54
56	06 54	07 43	08 29	10 58	11 19	11 37	11 53
58	07 01	07 52	08 43	11 05	11 23	11 39	11 53
S 60	07 08	08 03	08 59	11 14	11 28	11 40	11 52

Sunset / Twilight / Moonset

Lat.	Sunset	Civil	Naut.	6	7	8	9
N 72	◻	◻	◻	00 58	00 26	(00 05 / 23 47)	23 29
N 70	◻	◻	◻	00 25	(23 57)	23 46	23 35
68	◻	◻	◻	(00 00 / 23 55)	23 50	23 45	23 40
66	23 09	////	////	23 44	23 45	23 45	23 45
64	22 15	////	////	23 34	23 40	23 44	23 49
62	21 43	////	////	23 26	23 36	23 44	23 52
60	21 19	22 49	////	23 19	23 32	23 44	23 55
N 58	21 01	22 10	////	23 12	23 29	23 43	23 57
56	20 45	21 44	////	23 07	23 26	23 43	24 00
54	20 32	21 24	22 55	23 02	23 23	23 43	24 02
52	20 20	21 08	22 20	22 57	23 21	23 43	24 04
50	20 10	20 53	21 56	22 53	23 19	23 42	24 05
45	19 49	20 25	21 14	22 44	23 14	23 42	24 09
N 40	19 32	20 04	20 45	22 36	23 10	23 42	24 12
35	19 17	19 47	20 23	22 30	23 07	23 41	24 15
30	19 05	19 32	20 05	22 24	23 04	23 41	24 18
20	18 44	19 08	19 37	22 14	22 58	23 40	24 21
N 10	18 25	18 48	19 15	22 05	22 53	23 40	24 25
0	18 09	18 31	18 57	21 56	22 49	23 39	24 29
S 10	17 52	18 15	18 41	21 48	22 44	23 39	24 32
20	17 34	17 58	18 25	21 38	22 39	23 38	24 36
30	17 14	17 40	18 10	21 28	22 34	23 37	24 40
35	17 02	17 30	18 01	21 22	22 30	23 37	24 42
40	16 48	17 19	17 52	21 15	22 26	23 37	24 45
45	16 32	17 06	17 43	21 06	22 22	23 36	24 48
S 50	16 13	16 51	17 32	20 56	22 17	23 35	24 52
52	16 03	16 44	17 27	20 52	22 14	23 35	24 54
54	15 53	16 36	17 21	20 47	22 12	23 35	24 56
56	15 41	16 27	17 16	20 41	22 09	23 34	24 58
58	15 27	16 18	17 09	20 35	22 05	23 34	25 00
S 60	15 11	16 07	17 02	20 27	22 02	23 33	25 03

	SUN			MOON			
Day	Eqn. of Time 00h	Eqn. of Time 12h	Mer. Pass.	Mer. Pass. Upper	Mer. Pass. Lower	Age	Phase
d	m s	m s	h m	h m	h m	d	%
6	04 40	04 45	12 05	15 43	03 15	04	18
7	04 50	04 55	12 05	16 36	04 10	05	28
8	05 00	05 04	12 05	17 27	05 02	06	39

© British Crown Copyright 2018. All rights reserved.

UT	ARIES GHA	VENUS −3.9 GHA	Dec	MARS +1.8 GHA	Dec	JUPITER −2.5 GHA	Dec	SATURN +0.1 GHA	Dec
9 00	286 38.6	189 29.0	N23 24.8	159 32.4	N20 17.1	31 35.9	S22 12.7	357 58.2	S22 00.3
01	301 41.1	204 28.1	24.7	174 33.2	16.7	46 38.6	12.7	13 00.9	00.3
02	316 43.6	219 27.3	24.7	189 34.1	16.3	61 41.3	12.7	28 03.6	00.3
03	331 46.0	234 26.4	.. 24.6	204 34.9	.. 15.9	76 44.0	.. 12.6	43 06.2	.. 00.4
04	346 48.5	249 25.5	24.6	219 35.7	15.5	91 46.8	12.6	58 08.9	00.4
05	1 51.0	264 24.6	24.5	234 36.5	15.1	106 49.5	12.6	73 11.5	00.4
06	16 53.4	279 23.8	N23 24.4	249 37.4	N20 14.8	121 52.2	S22 12.6	88 14.2	S22 00.4
07	31 55.9	294 22.9	24.4	264 38.2	14.4	136 54.9	12.6	103 16.9	00.5
08	46 58.3	309 22.0	24.3	279 39.0	14.0	151 57.6	12.6	118 19.5	00.5
09	62 00.8	324 21.1	.. 24.3	294 39.8	.. 13.6	167 00.4	.. 12.5	133 22.2	.. 00.5
10	77 03.3	339 20.3	24.2	309 40.6	13.2	182 03.1	12.5	148 24.9	00.5
11	92 05.7	354 19.4	24.1	324 41.5	12.8	197 05.8	12.5	163 27.5	00.6
12	107 08.2	9 18.5	N23 24.1	339 42.3	N20 12.5	212 08.5	S22 12.5	178 30.2	S22 00.6
13	122 10.7	24 17.6	24.0	354 43.1	12.1	227 11.2	12.5	193 32.8	00.6
14	137 13.1	39 16.8	23.9	9 43.9	11.7	242 13.9	12.5	208 35.5	00.7
15	152 15.6	54 15.9	.. 23.9	24 44.8	.. 11.3	257 16.7	.. 12.4	223 38.2	.. 00.7
16	167 18.1	69 15.0	23.8	39 45.6	10.9	272 19.4	12.4	238 40.8	00.7
17	182 20.5	84 14.1	23.7	54 46.4	10.5	287 22.1	12.4	253 43.5	00.7
18	197 23.0	99 13.3	N23 23.6	69 47.2	N20 10.1	302 24.8	S22 12.4	268 46.1	S22 00.8
19	212 25.4	114 12.4	23.6	84 48.0	09.8	317 27.5	12.4	283 48.8	00.8
20	227 27.9	129 11.5	23.5	99 48.9	09.4	332 30.2	12.4	298 51.5	00.8
21	242 30.4	144 10.6	.. 23.4	114 49.7	.. 09.0	347 32.9	.. 12.3	313 54.1	.. 00.8
22	257 32.8	159 09.8	23.3	129 50.5	08.6	2 35.7	12.3	328 56.8	00.9
23	272 35.3	174 08.9	23.3	144 51.3	08.2	17 38.4	12.3	343 59.4	00.9
10 00	287 37.8	189 08.0	N23 23.2	159 52.2	N20 07.8	32 41.1	S22 12.3	359 02.1	S22 00.9
01	302 40.2	204 07.1	23.1	174 53.0	07.4	47 43.8	12.3	14 04.8	00.9
02	317 42.7	219 06.3	23.0	189 53.8	07.0	62 46.5	12.3	29 07.4	01.0
03	332 45.2	234 05.4	.. 22.9	204 54.6	.. 06.6	77 49.2	.. 12.2	44 10.1	.. 01.0
04	347 47.6	249 04.5	22.9	219 55.5	06.3	92 51.9	12.2	59 12.7	01.0
05	2 50.1	264 03.6	22.8	234 56.3	05.9	107 54.6	12.2	74 15.4	01.1
06	17 52.6	279 02.8	N23 22.7	249 57.1	N20 05.5	122 57.4	S22 12.2	89 18.1	S22 01.1
07	32 55.0	294 01.9	22.6	264 57.9	05.1	138 00.1	12.2	104 20.7	01.1
08	47 57.5	309 01.0	22.5	279 58.8	04.7	153 02.8	12.2	119 23.4	01.1
09	62 59.9	324 00.1	.. 22.4	294 59.6	.. 04.3	168 05.5	.. 12.2	134 26.1	.. 01.2
10	78 02.4	338 59.3	22.3	310 00.4	03.9	183 08.2	12.1	149 28.7	01.2
11	93 04.9	353 58.4	22.2	325 01.2	03.5	198 10.9	12.1	164 31.4	01.2
12	108 07.3	8 57.5	N23 22.1	340 02.1	N20 03.1	213 13.6	S22 12.1	179 34.0	S22 01.2
13	123 09.8	23 56.6	22.0	355 02.9	02.7	228 16.3	12.1	194 36.7	01.3
14	138 12.3	38 55.8	21.9	10 03.7	02.4	243 19.0	12.1	209 39.4	01.3
15	153 14.7	53 54.9	.. 21.8	25 04.5	.. 02.0	258 21.7	.. 12.1	224 42.0	.. 01.3
16	168 17.2	68 54.0	21.7	40 05.4	01.6	273 24.5	12.0	239 44.7	01.4
17	183 19.7	83 53.1	21.6	55 06.2	01.2	288 27.2	12.0	254 47.3	01.4
18	198 22.1	98 52.3	N23 21.5	70 07.0	N20 00.8	303 29.9	S22 12.0	269 50.0	S22 01.4
19	213 24.6	113 51.4	21.4	85 07.8	00.4	318 32.6	12.0	284 52.7	01.4
20	228 27.1	128 50.5	21.3	100 08.7	20 00.0	333 35.3	12.0	299 55.3	01.5
21	243 29.5	143 49.6	.. 21.2	115 09.5	19 59.6	348 38.0	.. 12.0	314 58.0	.. 01.5
22	258 32.0	158 48.8	21.1	130 10.3	59.2	3 40.7	11.9	330 00.6	01.5
23	273 34.4	173 47.9	21.0	145 11.2	58.8	18 43.4	11.9	345 03.3	01.5
11 00	288 36.9	188 47.0	N23 20.9	160 12.0	N19 58.4	33 46.1	S22 11.9	0 06.0	S22 01.6
01	303 39.4	203 46.2	20.8	175 12.8	58.0	48 48.8	11.9	15 08.6	01.6
02	318 41.8	218 45.3	20.7	190 13.6	57.6	63 51.5	11.9	30 11.3	01.6
03	333 44.3	233 44.4	.. 20.6	205 14.5	.. 57.2	78 54.2	.. 11.9	45 13.9	.. 01.6
04	348 46.8	248 43.5	20.5	220 15.3	56.9	93 56.9	11.8	60 16.6	01.7
05	3 49.2	263 42.7	20.4	235 16.1	56.5	108 59.6	11.8	75 19.3	01.7
06	18 51.7	278 41.8	N23 20.3	250 17.0	N19 56.1	124 02.4	S22 11.8	90 21.9	S22 01.7
07	33 54.2	293 40.9	20.1	265 17.8	55.7	139 05.1	11.8	105 24.6	01.8
08	48 56.6	308 40.0	20.0	280 18.6	55.3	154 07.8	11.8	120 27.2	01.8
09	63 59.1	323 39.2	.. 19.9	295 19.4	.. 54.9	169 10.5	.. 11.8	135 29.9	.. 01.8
10	79 01.5	338 38.3	19.8	310 20.3	54.5	184 13.2	11.8	150 32.6	01.8
11	94 04.0	353 37.4	19.6	325 21.1	54.1	199 15.9	11.7	165 35.2	01.9
12	109 06.5	8 36.5	N23 19.5	340 21.9	N19 53.7	214 18.6	S22 11.7	180 37.9	S22 01.9
13	124 08.9	23 35.7	19.4	355 22.8	53.3	229 21.3	11.7	195 40.6	01.9
14	139 11.4	38 34.8	19.3	10 23.6	52.9	244 24.0	11.7	210 43.2	01.9
15	154 13.9	53 33.9	.. 19.1	25 24.4	.. 52.5	259 26.7	.. 11.7	225 45.9	.. 02.0
16	169 16.3	68 33.1	19.0	40 25.2	52.1	274 29.4	11.7	240 48.5	02.0
17	184 18.8	83 32.2	18.9	55 26.1	51.7	289 32.1	11.6	255 51.2	02.0
18	199 21.3	98 31.3	N23 18.8	70 26.9	N19 51.3	304 34.8	S22 11.6	270 53.9	S22 02.1
19	214 23.7	113 30.4	18.6	85 27.7	50.9	319 37.5	11.6	285 56.5	02.1
20	229 26.2	128 29.6	18.5	100 28.6	50.5	334 40.2	11.6	300 59.2	02.1
21	244 28.7	143 28.7	.. 18.4	115 29.4	.. 50.1	349 42.9	.. 11.6	316 01.8	.. 02.1
22	259 31.1	158 27.8	18.2	130 30.2	49.7	4 45.6	11.6	331 04.5	02.2
23	274 33.6	173 27.0	18.1	145 31.1	49.3	19 48.3	11.6	346 07.2	02.2
Mer.Pass. 4 48.7		v −0.9 d 0.1		v 0.8 d 0.4		v 2.7 d 0.0		v 2.7 d 0.0	

Tuesday = 9; Wednesday = 10; Thursday = 11

STARS

Name	SHA	Dec
Acamar	315 15.4	S40 13.5
Achernar	335 23.8	S57 08.1
Acrux	173 04.8	S63 12.6
Adhara	255 09.7	S29 00.0
Aldebaran	290 44.9	N16 32.7
Alioth	166 17.1	N55 51.7
Alkaid	152 55.5	N49 13.4
Alnair	27 38.2	S46 51.8
Alnilam	275 42.5	S 1 11.5
Alphard	217 52.3	S 8 44.6
Alphecca	126 07.3	N26 39.3
Alpheratz	357 39.1	N29 11.7
Altair	62 03.9	N 8 55.3
Ankaa	353 11.5	S42 11.9
Antares	112 20.9	S26 28.4
Arcturus	145 51.9	N19 05.2
Atria	107 18.5	S69 03.7
Avior	234 17.0	S59 34.4
Bellatrix	278 27.9	N 6 21.9
Betelgeuse	270 57.1	N 7 24.5
Canopus	263 54.9	S52 42.4
Capella	280 28.7	N46 00.8
Deneb	49 28.2	N45 21.0
Denebola	182 29.6	N14 28.0
Diphda	348 51.7	S17 52.8
Dubhe	193 47.0	N61 39.1
Elnath	278 07.7	N28 37.2
Eltanin	90 43.7	N51 29.4
Enif	33 42.8	N 9 57.9
Fomalhaut	15 19.2	S29 31.0
Gacrux	171 56.4	S57 13.5
Gienah	175 48.1	S17 39.0
Hadar	148 41.8	S60 28.1
Hamal	327 56.2	N23 33.0
Kaus Aust.	83 37.9	S34 22.4
Kochab	137 19.6	N74 05.0
Markab	13 34.0	N15 18.5
Menkar	314 10.9	N 4 09.8
Menkent	148 02.6	S36 27.9
Miaplacidus	221 39.7	S69 48.0
Mirfak	308 34.7	N49 55.5
Nunki	75 52.8	S26 16.2
Peacock	53 12.2	S56 40.1
Pollux	243 23.1	N27 58.7
Procyon	244 55.7	N 5 10.5
Rasalhague	96 02.3	N12 33.0
Regulus	207 39.4	N11 52.4
Rigel	281 08.4	S 8 10.8
Rigil Kent.	139 45.9	S60 55.0
Sabik	102 07.5	S15 44.8
Schedar	349 35.7	N56 38.3
Shaula	96 15.9	S37 07.0
Sirius	258 30.4	S16 44.6
Spica	158 26.9	S11 15.7
Suhail	222 49.8	S43 30.8
Vega	80 35.7	N38 48.3
Zuben'ubi	137 00.7	S16 07.2

	SHA	Mer.Pass.
Venus	261 30.2	11 24
Mars	232 14.4	13 20
Jupiter	105 03.3	21 45
Saturn	71 24.3	0 04

© British Crown Copyright 2018. All rights reserved.

UT	SUN GHA	SUN Dec	MOON GHA	v	MOON Dec	d	HP
9 00	178 42.7	N22 24.8	94 51.8	11.0	N 0 38.5	13.4	59.0
01	193 42.6	24.5	109 21.8	11.0	0 25.1	13.3	59.0
02	208 42.5	24.2	123 51.8	11.1	N 0 11.8	13.4	59.0
03	223 42.4 ..	23.9	138 21.9	11.0	S 0 01.6	13.3	59.0
04	238 42.3	23.6	152 51.9	11.1	0 14.9	13.3	59.0
05	253 42.3	23.3	167 22.0	11.2	0 28.2	13.4	58.9
06	268 42.2	N22 23.0	181 52.2	11.1	S 0 41.6	13.2	58.9
07	283 42.1	22.7	196 22.3	11.2	0 54.8	13.3	58.9
T 08	298 42.0	22.4	210 52.5	11.2	1 08.1	13.3	58.9
U 09	313 41.9 ..	22.1	225 22.7	11.2	1 21.4	13.2	58.8
E 10	328 41.8	21.8	239 52.9	11.2	1 34.6	13.3	58.8
S 11	343 41.7	21.5	254 23.1	11.3	1 47.9	13.2	58.8
D 12	358 41.6	N22 21.2	268 53.4	11.2	S 2 01.1	13.1	58.8
A 13	13 41.5	20.9	283 23.6	11.3	2 14.2	13.2	58.7
Y 14	28 41.4	20.6	297 53.9	11.3	2 27.4	13.2	58.7
15	43 41.3 ..	20.3	312 24.2	11.3	2 40.6	13.1	58.7
16	58 41.2	20.0	326 54.5	11.3	2 53.7	13.1	58.7
17	73 41.1	19.7	341 24.8	11.3	3 06.8	13.0	58.6
18	88 41.1	N22 19.4	355 55.1	11.4	S 3 19.8	13.1	58.6
19	103 41.0	19.1	10 25.5	11.3	3 32.9	13.0	58.6
20	118 40.9	18.8	24 55.8	11.4	3 45.9	12.9	58.6
21	133 40.8 ..	18.5	39 26.2	11.4	3 58.8	13.0	58.6
22	148 40.7	18.2	53 56.6	11.4	4 11.8	12.9	58.5
23	163 40.6	17.9	68 27.0	11.4	4 24.7	12.9	58.5
10 00	178 40.5	N22 17.6	82 57.4	11.3	S 4 37.6	12.8	58.5
01	193 40.4	17.3	97 27.7	11.4	4 50.4	12.8	58.5
02	208 40.3	16.9	111 58.1	11.5	5 03.2	12.8	58.4
03	223 40.2 ..	16.6	126 28.6	11.4	5 16.0	12.7	58.4
04	238 40.1	16.3	140 59.0	11.4	5 28.7	12.7	58.4
05	253 40.1	16.0	155 29.4	11.4	5 41.4	12.7	58.4
06	268 40.0	N22 15.7	169 59.8	11.4	S 5 54.1	12.6	58.3
W 07	283 39.9	15.4	184 30.2	11.4	6 06.7	12.6	58.3
E 08	298 39.8	15.1	199 00.6	11.4	6 19.3	12.5	58.3
D 09	313 39.7 ..	14.8	213 31.0	11.4	6 31.8	12.5	58.3
N 10	328 39.6	14.4	228 01.4	11.4	6 44.3	12.4	58.2
E 11	343 39.5	14.1	242 31.8	11.5	6 56.7	12.4	58.2
S 12	358 39.4	N22 13.8	257 02.3	11.4	S 7 09.1	12.4	58.2
D 13	13 39.3	13.5	271 32.7	11.4	7 21.5	12.3	58.2
A 14	28 39.3	13.2	286 03.1	11.4	7 33.8	12.3	58.1
Y 15	43 39.2 ..	12.9	300 33.5	11.3	7 46.1	12.2	58.1
16	58 39.1	12.6	315 03.8	11.4	7 58.3	12.1	58.1
17	73 39.0	12.2	329 34.2	11.4	8 10.4	12.1	58.1
18	88 38.9	N22 11.9	344 04.6	11.4	S 8 22.5	12.1	58.1
19	103 38.8	11.6	358 35.0	11.3	8 34.6	12.0	58.0
20	118 38.7	11.3	13 05.3	11.4	8 46.6	11.9	58.0
21	133 38.7 ..	10.9	27 35.7	11.3	8 58.5	11.9	58.0
22	148 38.6	10.6	42 06.0	11.3	9 10.4	11.8	58.0
23	163 38.5	10.3	56 36.3	11.4	9 22.2	11.8	57.9
11 00	178 38.4	N22 10.0	71 06.7	11.3	S 9 34.0	11.7	57.9
01	193 38.3	09.7	85 37.0	11.3	9 45.7	11.7	57.9
02	208 38.2	09.3	100 07.3	11.2	9 57.4	11.5	57.9
03	223 38.1 ..	09.0	114 37.5	11.3	10 08.9	11.6	57.8
04	238 38.1	08.7	129 07.8	11.3	10 20.5	11.5	57.8
05	253 38.0	08.4	143 38.1	11.2	10 32.0	11.4	57.8
06	268 37.9	N22 08.0	158 08.3	11.2	S10 43.4	11.3	57.8
07	283 37.8	07.7	172 38.5	11.2	10 54.7	11.3	57.7
T 08	298 37.7	07.4	187 08.7	11.2	11 06.0	11.2	57.7
H 09	313 37.6 ..	07.0	201 38.9	11.2	11 17.2	11.1	57.7
U 10	328 37.6	06.7	216 09.1	11.1	11 28.3	11.1	57.7
R 11	343 37.5	06.4	230 39.2	11.2	11 39.4	11.0	57.6
S 12	358 37.4	N22 06.0	245 09.4	11.1	S11 50.4	11.0	57.6
D 13	13 37.3	05.7	259 39.5	11.1	12 01.4	10.8	57.6
A 14	28 37.2	05.4	274 09.6	11.1	12 12.2	10.8	57.6
Y 15	43 37.1 ..	05.0	288 39.7	11.0	12 23.0	10.8	57.5
16	58 37.1	04.7	303 09.7	11.1	12 33.8	10.6	57.5
17	73 37.0	04.4	317 39.8	11.0	12 44.4	10.6	57.5
18	88 36.9	N22 04.0	332 09.8	11.0	S12 55.0	10.5	57.5
19	103 36.8	03.7	346 39.8	11.0	13 05.5	10.4	57.5
20	118 36.7	03.4	1 09.8	10.9	13 15.9	10.4	57.4
21	133 36.6 ..	03.0	15 39.7	11.0	13 26.3	10.3	57.4
22	148 36.6	02.7	30 09.7	10.9	13 36.6	10.1	57.4
23	163 36.5	02.4	44 39.6	10.8	S13 46.7	10.2	57.4
	SD 15.8	d 0.3	SD 16.0		15.9		15.7

Lat.	Twilight Naut.	Twilight Civil	Sunrise	Moonrise 9	10	11	12
N 72	☐	☐	☐	12 34	14 37	16 47	19 26
N 70	☐	☐	☐	12 31	14 25	16 22	18 28
68	☐	☐	☐	12 28	14 15	16 03	17 54
66	////	////	01 11	12 26	14 07	15 48	17 30
64	////	////	02 01	12 24	14 00	15 36	17 11
62	////	////	02 31	12 22	13 55	15 26	16 55
60	////	01 28	02 54	12 21	13 50	15 17	16 42
N 58	////	02 04	03 12	12 20	13 45	15 09	16 31
56	////	02 29	03 28	12 18	13 41	15 02	16 22
54	01 21	02 49	03 41	12 17	13 38	14 56	16 13
52	01 54	03 05	03 52	12 17	13 35	14 51	16 06
50	02 18	03 19	04 02	12 16	13 32	14 46	15 59
45	02 59	03 47	04 23	12 14	13 25	14 36	15 44
N 40	03 27	04 08	04 40	12 13	13 20	14 27	15 33
35	03 49	04 25	04 54	12 11	13 16	14 20	15 23
30	04 06	04 39	05 06	12 10	13 12	14 13	15 14
20	04 34	05 03	05 27	12 08	13 05	14 02	14 59
N 10	04 55	05 22	05 45	12 07	13 00	13 52	14 46
0	05 13	05 39	06 02	12 05	12 54	13 43	14 33
S 10	05 29	05 56	06 18	12 04	12 49	13 34	14 21
20	05 45	06 12	06 36	12 02	12 43	13 25	14 08
30	06 00	06 30	06 56	12 00	12 37	13 14	13 54
35	06 08	06 40	07 07	11 59	12 33	13 08	13 45
40	06 17	06 51	07 21	11 58	12 29	13 01	13 35
45	06 26	07 03	07 36	11 57	12 24	12 53	13 24
S 50	06 37	07 18	07 54	11 56	12 19	12 43	13 11
52	06 42	07 25	08 05	11 55	12 16	12 39	13 04
54	06 47	07 32	08 15	11 54	12 13	12 34	12 57
56	06 53	07 41	08 27	11 53	12 10	12 28	12 50
58	06 59	07 50	08 40	11 53	12 07	12 22	12 41
S 60	07 06	08 01	08 56	11 52	12 03	12 16	12 31

Lat.	Sunset	Twilight Civil	Twilight Naut.	Moonset 9	10	11	12
N 72	☐	☐	☐	23 29	23 09	22 43	21 49
N 70	☐	☐	☐	23 35	23 24	23 10	22 49
68	☐	☐	☐	23 40	23 35	23 30	23 24
66	22 56	////	////	23 45	23 45	23 46	23 49
64	22 08	////	////	23 49	23 53	24 00	00 00
62	21 38	////	////	23 52	24 00	00 00	00 11
60	21 16	22 40	////	23 55	24 07	00 07	00 20
N 58	20 57	22 05	////	23 57	24 12	00 12	00 29
56	20 42	21 40	////	24 00	00 00	00 17	00 36
54	20 29	21 21	22 48	24 02	00 02	00 21	00 43
52	20 18	21 05	22 15	24 04	00 04	00 25	00 49
50	20 08	20 51	21 52	24 05	00 05	00 29	00 55
45	19 47	20 24	21 11	24 09	00 09	00 37	01 07
N 40	19 30	20 03	20 43	24 12	00 12	00 43	01 16
35	19 16	19 46	20 22	24 15	00 15	00 49	01 25
30	19 04	19 31	20 04	24 17	00 17	00 54	01 32
20	18 43	19 08	19 37	24 21	00 21	01 03	01 45
N 10	18 26	18 48	19 15	24 25	00 25	01 10	01 56
0	18 09	18 31	18 57	24 29	00 29	01 18	02 07
S 10	17 53	18 15	18 41	24 32	00 32	01 25	02 18
20	17 35	17 59	18 26	24 36	00 36	01 33	02 29
30	17 15	17 41	18 11	24 40	00 40	01 41	02 42
35	17 04	17 31	18 03	24 42	00 42	01 47	02 50
40	16 50	17 20	17 54	24 45	00 45	01 52	02 59
45	16 35	17 08	17 45	24 48	00 48	01 59	03 09
S 50	16 15	16 53	17 34	24 52	00 52	02 07	03 21
52	16 06	16 46	17 29	24 54	00 54	02 11	03 27
54	15 56	16 39	17 24	24 56	00 56	02 15	03 33
56	15 44	16 30	17 18	24 58	00 58	02 20	03 40
58	15 31	16 21	17 12	25 00	01 00	02 25	03 48
S 60	15 15	16 10	17 06	25 03	01 03	02 31	03 57

	SUN			MOON			
Day	Eqn. of Time 00h	12h	Mer. Pass.	Mer. Pass. Upper	Lower	Age	Phase
	m s	m s	h m	h m	h m	d	%
9	05 09	05 13	12 05	18 17	05 52	07	51
10	05 18	05 22	12 05	19 06	06 41	08	62
11	05 26	05 30	12 06	19 55	07 30	09	72

© British Crown Copyright 2018. All rights reserved.

UT	ARIES GHA	VENUS −3.9 GHA	Dec	MARS +1.8 GHA	Dec	JUPITER −2.5 GHA	Dec	SATURN +0.1 GHA	Dec	STARS Name	SHA	Dec
12 00	289 36.0	188 26.1	N23 18.0	160 31.9	N19 48.9	34 51.0	S22 11.5	1 09.8	S22 02.2	Acamar	315 15.4	S40 13.5
01	304 38.5	203 25.2	17.8	175 32.7	48.5	49 53.7	11.5	16 12.5	02.2	Achernar	335 23.7	S57 08.1
02	319 41.0	218 24.3	17.7	190 33.5	48.1	64 56.4	11.5	31 15.1	02.3	Acrux	173 04.8	S63 12.6
03	334 43.4	233 23.5 ..	17.5	205 34.4 ..	47.7	79 59.1 ..	11.5	46 17.8 ..	02.3	Adhara	255 09.7	S29 00.0
04	349 45.9	248 22.6	17.4	220 35.2	47.3	95 01.8	11.5	61 20.5	02.3	Aldebaran	290 44.9	N16 32.7
05	4 48.4	263 21.7	17.2	235 36.0	46.9	110 04.5	11.5	76 23.1	02.3			
06	19 50.8	278 20.8	N23 17.1	250 36.9	N19 46.5	125 07.2	S22 11.4	91 25.8	S22 02.4	Alioth	166 17.1	N55 51.7
07	34 53.3	293 20.0	17.0	265 37.7	46.1	140 09.9	11.4	106 28.4	02.4	Alkaid	152 55.5	N49 13.4
08	49 55.8	308 19.1	16.8	280 38.5	45.7	155 12.6	11.4	121 31.1	02.4	Alnair	27 38.2	S46 51.8
F 09	64 58.2	323 18.2 ..	16.7	295 39.4 ..	45.3	170 15.3 ..	11.4	136 33.8 ..	02.5	Alnilam	275 42.5	S 1 11.5
R 10	80 00.7	338 17.4	16.5	310 40.2	44.9	185 18.0	11.4	151 36.4	02.5	Alphard	217 52.3	S 8 44.6
I 11	95 03.2	353 16.5	16.4	325 41.0	44.5	200 20.7	11.4	166 39.1	02.5			
D 12	110 05.6	8 15.6	N23 16.2	340 41.9	N19 44.1	215 23.4	S22 11.4	181 41.7	S22 02.5	Alphecca	126 07.3	N26 39.3
A 13	125 08.1	23 14.8	16.1	355 42.7	43.7	230 26.1	11.3	196 44.4	02.6	Alpheratz	357 39.1	N29 11.7
Y 14	140 10.5	38 13.9	15.9	10 43.5	43.3	245 28.8	11.3	211 47.1	02.6	Altair	62 03.9	N 8 55.3
15	155 13.0	53 13.0 ..	15.8	25 44.4 ..	42.9	260 31.5 ..	11.3	226 49.7 ..	02.6	Ankaa	353 11.5	S42 11.9
16	170 15.5	68 12.1	15.6	40 45.2	42.5	275 34.2	11.3	241 52.4	02.6	Antares	112 20.9	S26 28.4
17	185 17.9	83 11.3	15.4	55 46.0	42.1	290 36.9	11.3	256 55.0	02.7			
18	200 20.4	98 10.4	N23 15.3	70 46.9	N19 41.7	305 39.6	S22 11.3	271 57.7	S22 02.7	Arcturus	145 51.9	N19 05.2
19	215 22.9	113 09.5	15.1	85 47.7	41.3	320 42.3	11.2	287 00.4	02.7	Atria	107 18.5	S69 03.7
20	230 25.3	128 08.7	15.0	100 48.5	40.9	335 45.0	11.2	302 03.0	02.7	Avior	234 17.0	S59 34.4
21	245 27.8	143 07.8 ..	14.8	115 49.4 ..	40.5	350 47.7 ..	11.2	317 05.7 ..	02.8	Bellatrix	278 27.9	N 6 21.9
22	260 30.3	158 06.9	14.6	130 50.2	40.1	5 50.3	11.2	332 08.3	02.8	Betelgeuse	270 57.1	N 7 24.5
23	275 32.7	173 06.1	14.5	145 51.0	39.7	20 53.0	11.2	347 11.0	02.8			
13 00	290 35.2	188 05.2	N23 14.3	160 51.9	N19 39.3	35 55.7	S22 11.2	2 13.7	S22 02.9	Canopus	263 54.8	S52 42.4
01	305 37.6	203 04.3	14.1	175 52.7	38.9	50 58.4	11.2	17 16.3	02.9	Capella	280 28.7	N46 00.8
02	320 40.1	218 03.4	14.0	190 53.5	38.4	66 01.1	11.1	32 19.0	02.9	Deneb	49 28.2	N45 21.0
03	335 42.6	233 02.6 ..	13.8	205 54.4 ..	38.0	81 03.8 ..	11.1	47 21.7 ..	02.9	Denebola	182 29.6	N14 28.0
04	350 45.0	248 01.7	13.6	220 55.2	37.6	96 06.5	11.1	62 24.3	03.0	Diphda	348 51.7	S17 52.7
05	5 47.5	263 00.8	13.5	235 56.0	37.2	111 09.2	11.1	77 27.0	03.0			
06	20 50.0	278 00.0	N23 13.3	250 56.9	N19 36.8	126 11.9	S22 11.1	92 29.6	S22 03.0	Dubhe	193 47.0	N61 39.1
07	35 52.4	292 59.1	13.1	265 57.7	36.4	141 14.6	11.1	107 32.3	03.0	Elnath	278 07.7	N28 37.2
S 08	50 54.9	307 58.2	12.9	280 58.6	36.0	156 17.3	11.1	122 35.0	03.1	Eltanin	90 43.7	N51 29.4
A 09	65 57.4	322 57.4 ..	12.8	295 59.4 ..	35.6	171 20.0 ..	11.0	137 37.6 ..	03.1	Enif	33 42.8	N 9 57.9
T 10	80 59.8	337 56.5	12.6	311 00.2	35.2	186 22.7	11.0	152 40.3	03.1	Fomalhaut	15 19.2	S29 31.0
U 11	96 02.3	352 55.6	12.4	326 01.1	34.8	201 25.4	11.0	167 42.9	03.1			
R 12	111 04.8	7 54.8	N23 12.2	341 01.9	N19 34.4	216 28.0	S22 11.0	182 45.6	S22 03.2	Gacrux	171 56.4	S57 13.5
D 13	126 07.2	22 53.9	12.0	356 02.7	34.0	231 30.7	11.0	197 48.3	03.2	Gienah	175 48.1	S17 39.0
A 14	141 09.7	37 53.0	11.9	11 03.6	33.6	246 33.4	11.0	212 50.9	03.2	Hadar	148 41.8	S60 28.1
Y 15	156 12.1	52 52.2 ..	11.7	26 04.4 ..	33.2	261 36.1 ..	11.0	227 53.6 ..	03.3	Hamal	327 56.1	N23 33.0
16	171 14.6	67 51.3	11.5	41 05.2	32.7	276 38.8	10.9	242 56.2	03.3	Kaus Aust.	83 37.9	S34 22.4
17	186 17.1	82 50.4	11.3	56 06.1	32.3	291 41.5	10.9	257 58.9	03.3			
18	201 19.5	97 49.6	N23 11.1	71 06.9	N19 31.9	306 44.2	S22 10.9	273 01.6	S22 03.3	Kochab	137 19.6	N74 05.0
19	216 22.0	112 48.7	10.9	86 07.8	31.5	321 46.9	10.9	288 04.2	03.4	Markab	13 34.0	N15 18.5
20	231 24.5	127 47.8	10.7	101 08.6	31.1	336 49.6	10.9	303 06.9	03.4	Menkar	314 10.9	N 4 09.8
21	246 26.9	142 47.0 ..	10.5	116 09.4 ..	30.7	351 52.3 ..	10.9	318 09.5 ..	03.4	Menkent	148 02.6	S36 27.9
22	261 29.4	157 46.1	10.4	131 10.3	30.3	6 54.9	10.9	333 12.2	03.4	Miaplacidus	221 39.7	S69 48.0
23	276 31.9	172 45.2	10.2	146 11.1	29.9	21 57.6	10.8	348 14.9	03.5			
14 00	291 34.3	187 44.4	N23 10.0	161 11.9	N19 29.5	37 00.3	S22 10.8	3 17.5	S22 03.5	Mirfak	308 34.7	N49 55.5
01	306 36.8	202 43.5	09.8	176 12.8	29.1	52 03.0	10.8	18 20.2	03.5	Nunki	75 52.8	S26 16.2
02	321 39.3	217 42.6	09.6	191 13.6	28.6	67 05.7	10.8	33 22.8	03.5	Peacock	53 12.1	S56 40.2
03	336 41.7	232 41.8 ..	09.4	206 14.5 ..	28.2	82 08.4 ..	10.8	48 25.5 ..	03.6	Pollux	243 23.1	N27 58.7
04	351 44.2	247 40.9	09.2	221 15.3	27.8	97 11.1	10.8	63 28.2	03.6	Procyon	244 55.7	N 5 10.5
05	6 46.6	262 40.0	09.0	236 16.1	27.4	112 13.7	10.8	78 30.8	03.6			
06	21 49.1	277 39.2	N23 08.8	251 17.0	N19 27.0	127 16.4	S22 10.7	93 33.5	S22 03.7	Rasalhague	96 02.3	N12 33.0
07	36 51.6	292 38.3	08.6	266 17.8	26.6	142 19.1	10.7	108 36.1	03.7	Regulus	207 39.4	N11 52.4
08	51 54.0	307 37.4	08.4	281 18.7	26.2	157 21.8	10.7	123 38.8	03.7	Rigel	281 08.4	S 8 10.8
S 09	66 56.5	322 36.6 ..	08.2	296 19.5 ..	25.8	172 24.5 ..	10.7	138 41.5 ..	03.7	Rigil Kent.	139 45.9	S60 55.0
U 10	81 59.0	337 35.7	08.0	311 20.3	25.4	187 27.2	10.7	153 44.1	03.8	Sabik	102 07.5	S15 44.8
N 11	97 01.4	352 34.8	07.7	326 21.2	24.9	202 29.9	10.7	168 46.8	03.8			
D 12	112 03.9	7 34.0	N23 07.5	341 22.0	N19 24.5	217 32.5	S22 10.7	183 49.4	S22 03.8	Schedar	349 35.7	N56 38.3
A 13	127 06.4	22 33.1	07.3	356 22.9	24.1	232 35.2	10.6	198 52.1	03.8	Shaula	96 15.9	S37 07.0
Y 14	142 08.8	37 32.2	07.1	11 23.7	23.7	247 37.9	10.6	213 54.8	03.9	Sirius	258 30.4	S16 44.6
15	157 11.3	52 31.4 ..	06.9	26 24.5 ..	23.3	262 40.6 ..	10.6	228 57.4 ..	03.9	Spica	158 26.9	S11 15.7
16	172 13.8	67 30.5	06.7	41 25.4	22.9	277 43.3	10.6	244 00.1	03.9	Suhail	222 49.8	S43 30.8
17	187 16.2	82 29.6	06.5	56 26.2	22.5	292 46.0	10.6	259 02.7	03.9			
18	202 18.7	97 28.8	N23 06.3	71 27.1	N19 22.0	307 48.6	S22 10.6	274 05.4	S22 04.0	Vega	80 35.7	N38 48.3
19	217 21.1	112 27.9	06.0	86 27.9	21.6	322 51.3	10.6	289 08.0	04.0	Zuben'ubi	137 00.7	S16 07.2
20	232 23.6	127 27.1	05.8	101 28.7	21.2	337 54.0	10.5	304 10.7	04.0			
21	247 26.1	142 26.2 ..	05.6	116 29.6 ..	20.8	352 56.7 ..	10.5	319 13.4 ..	04.1		SHA	Mer. Pass.
22	262 28.5	157 25.3	05.4	131 30.4	20.4	7 59.4	10.5	334 16.0	04.1	Venus	257 30.0	11 28
23	277 31.0	172 24.5	05.2	146 31.3	20.0	23 02.1	10.5	349 18.7	04.1	Mars	230 16.7	13 16
										Jupiter	105 20.6	21 32
Mer. Pass. 4 36.9		v −0.9 d 0.2		v 0.8 d 0.4		v 2.7 d 0.0		v 2.7 d 0.0		Saturn	71 38.5	23 47

© British Crown Copyright 2018. All rights reserved.

UT	SUN GHA	SUN Dec	MOON GHA	v	MOON Dec	d	HP
d h	° '	° '	° '	'	° '	'	'
12 00	178 36.4	N22 02.0	59 09.4	10.9	S13 56.9	10.0	57.3
01	193 36.3	01.7	73 39.3	10.8	14 06.9	10.0	57.3
02	208 36.2	01.3	88 09.1	10.9	14 16.9	9.8	57.3
03	223 36.2	.. 01.0	102 39.0	10.8	14 26.7	9.8	57.3
04	238 36.1	00.7	117 08.8	10.7	14 36.5	9.7	57.2
05	253 36.0	00.3	131 38.5	10.8	14 46.2	9.7	57.2
06	268 35.9	N22 00.0	146 08.3	10.7	S14 55.9	9.5	57.2
07	283 35.8	21 59.6	160 38.0	10.7	15 05.4	9.5	57.2
08	298 35.8	59.3	175 07.7	10.7	15 14.9	9.3	57.2
F 09	313 35.7	.. 58.9	189 37.4	10.6	15 24.2	9.3	57.1
R 10	328 35.6	58.6	204 07.0	10.6	15 33.5	9.2	57.1
I 11	343 35.5	58.2	218 36.6	10.6	15 42.7	9.1	57.1
D 12	358 35.4	N21 57.9	233 06.2	10.6	S15 51.8	9.0	57.1
A 13	13 35.4	57.5	247 35.8	10.5	16 00.8	9.0	57.0
Y 14	28 35.3	57.2	262 05.3	10.5	16 09.8	8.8	57.0
15	43 35.2	.. 56.8	276 34.8	10.5	16 18.6	8.8	57.0
16	58 35.1	56.5	291 04.3	10.5	16 27.4	8.6	57.0
17	73 35.1	56.1	305 33.8	10.4	16 36.0	8.6	56.9
18	88 35.0	N21 55.8	320 03.2	10.4	S16 44.6	8.4	56.9
19	103 34.9	55.4	334 32.6	10.4	16 53.0	8.4	56.9
20	118 34.8	55.1	349 02.0	10.4	17 01.4	8.3	56.9
21	133 34.8	.. 54.7	3 31.4	10.3	17 09.7	8.2	56.9
22	148 34.7	54.4	18 00.7	10.4	17 17.9	8.1	56.8
23	163 34.6	54.0	32 30.1	10.2	17 26.0	7.9	56.8
13 00	178 34.5	N21 53.7	46 59.3	10.3	S17 33.9	7.9	56.8
01	193 34.4	53.3	61 28.6	10.2	17 41.8	7.8	56.8
02	208 34.4	53.0	75 57.8	10.3	17 49.6	7.7	56.7
03	223 34.3	.. 52.6	90 27.1	10.1	17 57.3	7.6	56.7
04	238 34.2	52.3	104 56.2	10.2	18 04.9	7.5	56.7
05	253 34.1	51.9	119 25.4	10.2	18 12.4	7.4	56.7
06	268 34.1	N21 51.5	133 54.6	10.1	S18 19.8	7.3	56.7
07	283 34.0	51.2	148 23.7	10.1	18 27.1	7.2	56.6
S 08	298 33.9	50.8	162 52.8	10.0	18 34.3	7.1	56.6
A 09	313 33.9	.. 50.5	177 21.8	10.1	18 41.4	6.9	56.6
T 10	328 33.8	50.1	191 50.9	10.0	18 48.3	6.9	56.6
U 11	343 33.7	49.7	206 19.9	10.0	18 55.2	6.8	56.5
R 12	358 33.6	N21 49.4	220 48.9	10.0	S19 02.0	6.7	56.5
D 13	13 33.6	49.0	235 17.9	9.9	19 08.7	6.5	56.5
A 14	28 33.5	48.6	249 46.8	10.0	19 15.2	6.5	56.5
Y 15	43 33.4	.. 48.3	264 15.8	9.9	19 21.7	6.3	56.5
16	58 33.3	47.9	278 44.7	9.9	19 28.0	6.3	56.4
17	73 33.3	47.5	293 13.6	9.9	19 34.3	6.1	56.4
18	88 33.2	N21 47.2	307 42.5	9.8	S19 40.4	6.0	56.4
19	103 33.1	46.8	322 11.3	9.9	19 46.4	5.9	56.4
20	118 33.1	46.4	336 40.2	9.8	19 52.3	5.8	56.4
21	133 33.0	.. 46.1	351 09.0	9.8	19 58.1	5.7	56.3
22	148 32.9	45.7	5 37.8	9.8	20 03.8	5.6	56.3
23	163 32.8	45.3	20 06.6	9.7	20 09.4	5.5	56.3
14 00	178 32.8	N21 45.0	34 35.3	9.8	S20 14.9	5.4	56.3
01	193 32.7	44.6	49 04.1	9.7	20 20.3	5.2	56.2
02	208 32.6	44.2	63 32.8	9.7	20 25.5	5.2	56.2
03	223 32.6	.. 43.8	78 01.5	9.7	20 30.7	5.0	56.2
04	238 32.5	43.5	92 30.2	9.7	20 35.7	4.9	56.2
05	253 32.4	43.1	106 58.9	9.7	20 40.6	4.8	56.2
06	268 32.3	N21 42.7	121 27.6	9.6	S20 45.4	4.7	56.1
07	283 32.3	42.4	135 56.2	9.7	20 50.1	4.6	56.1
08	298 32.2	42.0	150 24.9	9.6	20 54.7	4.5	56.1
S 09	313 32.1	.. 41.6	164 53.5	9.7	20 59.2	4.3	56.1
U 10	328 32.1	41.2	179 22.2	9.6	21 03.5	4.2	56.1
N 11	343 32.0	40.8	193 50.8	9.6	21 07.7	4.2	56.0
D 12	358 31.9	N21 40.5	208 19.4	9.6	S21 11.9	4.0	56.0
A 13	13 31.9	40.1	222 48.0	9.6	21 15.9	3.9	56.0
Y 14	28 31.8	39.7	237 16.6	9.6	21 19.8	3.7	56.0
15	43 31.7	.. 39.3	251 45.2	9.5	21 23.5	3.7	56.0
16	58 31.7	38.9	266 13.7	9.6	21 27.2	3.5	55.9
17	73 31.6	38.6	280 42.3	9.6	21 30.7	3.5	55.9
18	88 31.5	N21 38.2	295 10.9	9.5	S21 34.2	3.3	55.9
19	103 31.5	37.8	309 39.4	9.6	21 37.5	3.2	55.9
20	118 31.4	37.4	324 08.0	9.6	21 40.7	3.0	55.9
21	133 31.3	.. 37.0	338 36.6	9.5	21 43.7	3.0	55.8
22	148 31.3	36.6	353 05.1	9.6	21 46.7	2.8	55.8
23	163 31.2	36.3	7 33.7	9.5	S21 49.5	2.8	55.8
	SD 15.8	d 0.4	SD 15.5		15.4		15.3

Lat.	Twilight Naut.	Twilight Civil	Sunrise	Moonrise 12	13	14	15
°	h m	h m	h m	h m	h m	h m	h m
N 72	☐	☐	☐	19 26	■	■	■
N 70	☐	☐	☐	18 28	■	■	■
68	☐	☐	☐	17 54	19 49	22 04	■
66	////	////	01 25	17 30	19 09	20 41	21 51
64	////	////	02 09	17 11	18 42	20 04	21 08
62	////	00 27	02 37	16 55	18 21	19 37	20 39
60	////	01 37	02 59	16 42	18 04	19 17	20 17
N 58	////	02 11	03 17	16 31	17 49	19 00	20 00
56	00 25	02 34	03 32	16 22	17 37	18 46	19 45
54	01 29	02 53	03 44	16 13	17 26	18 33	19 32
52	02 00	03 09	03 55	16 06	17 17	18 23	19 20
50	02 22	03 22	04 05	15 59	17 09	18 13	19 10
45	03 02	03 49	04 25	15 44	16 51	17 53	18 49
N 40	03 30	04 10	04 42	15 33	16 36	17 37	18 32
35	03 51	04 27	04 56	15 23	16 24	17 23	18 18
30	04 08	04 41	05 08	15 14	16 13	17 11	18 05
20	04 35	05 04	05 28	14 59	15 55	16 50	17 44
N 10	04 56	05 23	05 46	14 46	15 39	16 33	17 25
0	05 14	05 40	06 02	14 33	15 24	16 16	17 08
S 10	05 30	05 56	06 18	14 21	15 10	16 00	16 51
20	05 45	06 12	06 35	14 08	14 54	15 42	16 33
30	06 00	06 29	06 55	13 54	14 36	15 22	16 11
35	06 07	06 39	07 06	13 45	14 26	15 10	15 59
40	06 16	06 49	07 19	13 35	14 14	14 57	15 45
45	06 25	07 02	07 35	13 24	14 00	14 41	15 28
S 50	06 35	07 16	07 54	13 11	13 43	14 21	15 07
52	06 40	07 23	08 02	13 04	13 35	14 12	14 57
54	06 45	07 30	08 12	12 57	13 26	14 02	14 46
56	06 50	07 38	08 24	12 50	13 16	13 50	14 33
58	06 56	07 47	08 37	12 41	13 05	13 37	14 19
S 60	07 03	07 58	08 52	12 31	12 52	13 21	14 01

Lat.	Sunset	Twilight Civil	Twilight Naut.	Moonset 12	13	14	15
°	h m	h m	h m	h m	h m	h m	h m
N 72	☐	☐	☐	21 49	■	■	■
N 70	☐	☐	☐	22 49	■	■	■
68	☐	☐	☐	23 24	23 15	22 49	■
66	22 43	////	////	23 49	23 56	24 12	■
64	22 00	////	////	00 00	00 09	00 24	00 12
62	21 32	23 34	////	00 11	00 25	00 45	00 50
60	21 11	22 31	////	00 20	00 38	01 03	01 37
N 58	20 54	21 59	////	00 29	00 50	01 17	01 54
56	20 39	21 36	23 37	00 36	01 00	01 30	02 08
54	20 27	21 17	22 40	00 43	01 09	01 41	02 21
52	20 16	21 02	22 10	00 49	01 17	01 51	02 32
50	20 06	20 48	21 48	00 55	01 24	02 00	02 42
45	19 46	20 22	21 09	01 06	01 40	02 18	03 02
N 40	19 29	20 01	20 41	01 16	01 53	02 33	03 19
35	19 15	19 44	20 20	01 25	02 04	02 46	03 33
30	19 03	19 30	20 03	01 32	02 13	02 57	03 45
20	18 43	19 07	19 36	01 45	02 30	03 17	04 06
N 10	18 26	18 48	19 15	01 56	02 44	03 33	04 24
0	18 09	18 32	18 58	02 07	02 58	03 49	04 41
S 10	17 53	18 16	18 42	02 18	03 11	04 05	04 58
20	17 36	18 00	18 27	02 29	03 26	04 22	05 16
30	17 17	17 43	18 12	02 42	03 42	04 41	05 37
35	17 05	17 33	18 04	02 50	03 52	04 52	05 50
40	16 52	17 22	17 56	02 59	04 03	05 05	06 04
45	16 37	17 10	17 47	03 09	04 16	05 21	06 20
S 50	16 18	16 56	17 36	03 21	04 32	05 40	06 41
52	16 09	16 49	17 32	03 27	04 40	05 49	06 51
54	15 59	16 42	17 27	03 33	04 48	05 59	07 02
56	15 48	16 34	17 21	03 40	04 58	06 10	07 14
58	15 35	16 25	17 16	03 48	05 09	06 23	07 29
S 60	15 20	16 14	17 09	03 57	05 21	06 39	07 46

Day	SUN Eqn. of Time 00h	SUN Eqn. of Time 12h	SUN Mer. Pass.	MOON Mer. Pass. Upper	MOON Mer. Pass. Lower	Age	Phase
d	m s	m s	h m	h m	h m	d	%
12	05 34	05 38	12 06	20 45	08 20	10	81
13	05 42	05 45	12 06	21 37	09 11	11	89
14	05 49	05 52	12 06	22 29	10 03	12	94

© British Crown Copyright 2018. All rights reserved.

UT	ARIES GHA	VENUS −3.9 GHA	Dec	MARS +1.8 GHA	Dec	JUPITER −2.5 GHA	Dec	SATURN +0.1 GHA	Dec	STARS Name	SHA	Dec
15 00	292 33.5	187 23.6	N23 04.9	161 32.1	N19 19.5	38 04.7	S22 10.5	4 21.3	S22 04.1	Acamar	315 15.3	S40 13.5
01	307 35.9	202 22.7	04.7	176 32.9	19.1	53 07.4	10.5	19 24.0	04.2	Achernar	335 23.7	S57 08.1
02	322 38.4	217 21.9	04.5	191 33.8	18.7	68 10.1	10.5	34 26.7	04.2	Acrux	173 04.8	S63 12.6
03	337 40.9	232 21.0	.. 04.3	206 34.6	.. 18.3	83 12.8	.. 10.4	49 29.3	.. 04.2	Adhara	255 09.6	S28 59.9
04	352 43.3	247 20.1	04.0	221 35.5	17.9	98 15.5	10.4	64 32.0	04.2	Aldebaran	290 44.9	N16 32.7
05	7 45.8	262 19.3	03.8	236 36.3	17.5	113 18.1	10.4	79 34.6	04.3			
06	22 48.3	277 18.4	N23 03.6	251 37.2	N19 17.0	128 20.8	S22 10.4	94 37.3	S22 04.3	Alioth	166 17.1	N55 51.7
07	37 50.7	292 17.6	03.4	266 38.0	16.6	143 23.5	10.4	109 40.0	04.3	Alkaid	152 55.6	N49 13.4
M 08	52 53.2	307 16.7	03.1	281 38.8	16.2	158 26.2	10.4	124 42.6	04.3	Alnair	27 38.1	S46 51.8
O 09	67 55.6	322 15.8	.. 02.9	296 39.7	.. 15.8	173 28.8	.. 10.4	139 45.3	.. 04.4	Alnilam	275 42.4	S 1 11.5
N 10	82 58.1	337 15.0	02.7	311 40.5	15.4	188 31.5	10.4	154 47.9	04.4	Alphard	217 52.3	S 8 44.6
D 11	98 00.6	352 14.1	02.4	326 41.4	15.0	203 34.2	10.3	169 50.6	04.4			
A 12	113 03.0	7 13.3	N23 02.2	341 42.2	N19 14.5	218 36.9	S22 10.3	184 53.3	S22 04.4	Alphecca	126 07.3	N26 39.3
Y 13	128 05.5	22 12.4	01.9	356 43.1	14.1	233 39.6	10.3	199 55.9	04.5	Alpheratz	357 39.1	N29 11.7
14	143 08.0	37 11.5	01.7	11 43.9	13.7	248 42.2	10.3	214 58.6	04.5	Altair	62 03.8	N 8 55.3
15	158 10.4	52 10.7	.. 01.5	26 44.7	.. 13.3	263 44.9	.. 10.3	230 01.2	.. 04.5	Ankaa	353 11.5	S42 11.8
16	173 12.9	67 09.8	01.2	41 45.6	12.9	278 47.6	10.3	245 03.9	04.6	Antares	112 20.9	S26 28.4
17	188 15.4	82 08.9	01.0	56 46.4	12.4	293 50.3	10.3	260 06.6	04.6			
18	203 17.8	97 08.1	N23 00.7	71 47.3	N19 12.0	308 52.9	S22 10.2	275 09.2	S22 04.6	Arcturus	145 51.9	N19 05.2
19	218 20.3	112 07.2	00.5	86 48.1	11.6	323 55.6	10.2	290 11.9	04.6	Atria	107 18.5	S69 03.7
20	233 22.7	127 06.4	00.2	101 49.0	11.2	338 58.3	10.2	305 14.5	04.7	Avior	234 17.0	S59 34.4
21	248 25.2	142 05.5	23 00.0	116 49.8	.. 10.8	354 01.0	.. 10.2	320 17.2	.. 04.7	Bellatrix	278 27.8	N 6 21.9
22	263 27.7	157 04.7	22 59.7	131 50.6	10.3	9 03.6	10.2	335 19.9	04.7	Betelgeuse	270 57.1	N 7 24.5
23	278 30.1	172 03.8	59.5	146 51.5	09.9	24 06.3	10.2	350 22.5	04.7			
16 00	293 32.6	187 02.9	N22 59.2	161 52.3	N19 09.5	39 09.0	S22 10.2	5 25.2	S22 04.8	Canopus	263 54.8	S52 42.4
01	308 35.1	202 02.1	59.0	176 53.2	09.1	54 11.7	10.2	20 27.8	04.8	Capella	280 28.7	N46 00.8
02	323 37.5	217 01.2	58.7	191 54.0	08.7	69 14.3	10.1	35 30.5	04.8	Deneb	49 28.2	N45 21.0
03	338 40.0	232 00.4	.. 58.5	206 54.9	.. 08.2	84 17.0	.. 10.1	50 33.1	.. 04.8	Denebola	182 29.6	N14 28.0
04	353 42.5	246 59.5	58.2	221 55.7	07.8	99 19.7	10.1	65 35.8	04.9	Diphda	348 51.6	S17 52.7
05	8 44.9	261 58.6	58.0	236 56.6	07.4	114 22.4	10.1	80 38.5	04.9			
06	23 47.4	276 57.8	N22 57.7	251 57.4	N19 07.0	129 25.0	S22 10.1	95 41.1	S22 04.9	Dubhe	193 47.0	N61 39.1
07	38 49.9	291 56.9	57.5	266 58.3	06.5	144 27.7	10.1	110 43.8	04.9	Elnath	278 07.7	N28 37.2
T 08	53 52.3	306 56.1	57.2	281 59.1	06.1	159 30.4	10.1	125 46.4	05.0	Eltanin	90 43.7	N51 29.4
U 09	68 54.8	321 55.2	.. 56.9	296 59.9	.. 05.7	174 33.0	.. 10.1	140 49.1	.. 05.0	Enif	33 42.8	N 9 57.9
E 10	83 57.2	336 54.4	56.7	312 00.8	05.3	189 35.7	10.0	155 51.8	05.0	Fomalhaut	15 19.2	S29 31.0
S 11	98 59.7	351 53.5	56.4	327 01.6	04.8	204 38.4	10.0	170 54.4	05.1			
D 12	114 02.2	6 52.6	N22 56.1	342 02.5	N19 04.4	219 41.1	S22 10.0	185 57.1	S22 05.1	Gacrux	171 56.4	S57 13.5
A 13	129 04.6	21 51.8	55.9	357 03.3	04.0	234 43.7	10.0	200 59.7	05.1	Gienah	175 48.1	S17 39.0
Y 14	144 07.1	36 50.9	55.6	12 04.2	03.6	249 46.4	10.0	216 02.4	05.1	Hadar	148 41.9	S60 28.1
15	159 09.6	51 50.1	.. 55.3	27 05.0	.. 03.1	264 49.1	.. 10.0	231 05.0	.. 05.2	Hamal	327 56.1	N23 33.0
16	174 12.0	66 49.2	55.1	42 05.9	02.7	279 51.7	10.0	246 07.7	05.2	Kaus Aust.	83 37.9	S34 22.4
17	189 14.5	81 48.4	54.8	57 06.7	02.3	294 54.4	09.9	261 10.4	05.2			
18	204 17.0	96 47.5	N22 54.5	72 07.6	N19 01.9	309 57.1	S22 09.9	276 13.0	S22 05.2	Kochab	137 19.7	N74 05.0
19	219 19.4	111 46.6	54.2	87 08.4	01.4	324 59.7	09.9	291 15.7	05.3	Markab	13 34.0	N15 18.5
20	234 21.9	126 45.8	54.0	102 09.3	01.0	340 02.4	09.9	306 18.3	05.3	Menkar	314 10.8	N 4 09.8
21	249 24.4	141 44.9	.. 53.7	117 10.1	.. 00.6	355 05.1	.. 09.9	321 21.0	.. 05.3	Menkent	148 02.6	S36 27.9
22	264 26.8	156 44.1	53.4	132 11.0	19 00.2	10 07.7	09.9	336 23.7	05.3	Miaplacidus	221 39.7	S69 47.9
23	279 29.3	171 43.2	53.1	147 11.8	18 59.7	25 10.4	09.9	351 26.3	05.4			
17 00	294 31.7	186 42.4	N22 52.9	162 12.7	N18 59.3	40 13.1	S22 09.9	6 29.0	S22 05.4	Mirfak	308 34.6	N49 55.5
01	309 34.2	201 41.5	52.6	177 13.5	58.9	55 15.7	09.8	21 31.6	05.4	Nunki	75 52.8	S26 16.2
02	324 36.7	216 40.7	52.3	192 14.4	58.5	70 18.4	09.8	36 34.3	05.4	Peacock	53 12.1	S56 40.2
03	339 39.1	231 39.8	.. 52.0	207 15.2	.. 58.0	85 21.1	.. 09.8	51 37.0	.. 05.5	Pollux	243 23.0	N27 58.7
04	354 41.6	246 39.0	51.7	222 16.1	57.6	100 23.7	09.8	66 39.6	05.5	Procyon	244 55.7	N 5 10.5
05	9 44.1	261 38.1	51.4	237 16.9	57.2	115 26.4	09.8	81 42.3	05.5			
06	24 46.5	276 37.2	N22 51.2	252 17.7	N18 56.7	130 29.1	S22 09.8	96 44.9	S22 05.6	Rasalhague	96 02.3	N12 33.0
W 07	39 49.0	291 36.4	50.9	267 18.6	56.3	145 31.7	09.8	111 47.6	05.6	Regulus	207 39.4	N11 52.4
E 08	54 51.5	306 35.5	50.6	282 19.4	55.9	160 34.4	09.8	126 50.2	05.6	Rigel	281 08.3	S 8 10.8
D 09	69 53.9	321 34.7	.. 50.3	297 20.3	.. 55.5	175 37.1	.. 09.8	141 52.9	.. 05.6	Rigil Kent.	139 45.9	S60 55.0
N 10	84 56.4	336 33.8	50.0	312 21.1	55.0	190 39.7	09.7	156 55.6	05.7	Sabik	102 07.5	S15 44.8
E 11	99 58.9	351 33.0	49.7	327 22.0	54.6	205 42.4	09.7	171 58.2	05.7			
S 12	115 01.3	6 32.1	N22 49.4	342 22.8	N18 54.2	220 45.1	S22 09.7	187 00.9	S22 05.7	Schedar	349 35.6	N56 38.3
D 13	130 03.8	21 31.3	49.1	357 23.7	53.7	235 47.7	09.7	202 03.5	05.7	Shaula	96 15.9	S37 07.0
A 14	145 06.2	36 30.4	48.8	12 24.5	53.3	250 50.4	09.7	217 06.2	05.8	Sirius	258 30.4	S16 44.6
Y 15	160 08.7	51 29.6	.. 48.5	27 25.4	.. 52.9	265 53.1	.. 09.7	232 08.8	.. 05.8	Spica	158 26.9	S11 15.7
16	175 11.2	66 28.7	48.2	42 26.2	52.5	280 55.7	09.7	247 11.5	05.8	Suhail	222 49.8	S43 30.7
17	190 13.6	81 27.9	47.9	57 27.1	52.0	295 58.4	09.7	262 14.2	05.8			
18	205 16.1	96 27.0	N22 47.6	72 27.9	N18 51.6	311 01.0	S22 09.6	277 16.8	S22 05.9	Vega	80 35.7	N38 48.3
19	220 18.6	111 26.2	47.3	87 28.8	51.2	326 03.7	09.6	292 19.5	05.9	Zuben'ubi	137 00.7	S16 07.2
20	235 21.0	126 25.3	47.0	102 29.7	50.7	341 06.4	09.6	307 22.1	05.9		SHA	Mer.Pass.
21	250 23.5	141 24.5	.. 46.7	117 30.5	.. 50.3	356 09.0	.. 09.6	322 24.8	.. 05.9			
22	265 26.0	156 23.6	46.4	132 31.4	49.9	11 11.7	09.6	337 27.5	06.0	Venus	253 30.3	11 32
23	280 28.4	171 22.8	46.1	147 32.2	49.4	26 14.3	09.6	352 30.1	06.0	Mars	228 19.7	13 12
Mer. Pass.	h m 4 25.1	v −0.9	d 0.3	v 0.8	d 0.4	v 2.7	d 0.0	v 2.7	d 0.0	Jupiter	105 36.4	21 20
										Saturn	71 52.6	23 34

© British Crown Copyright 2018. All rights reserved.

SUN and MOON

UT	SUN GHA	SUN Dec	MOON GHA	v	MOON Dec	d	HP
15 00	178 31.1	N21 35.9	22 02.2	9.6	S21 52.3	2.6	55.8
01	193 31.1	35.5	36 30.8	9.5	21 54.9	2.5	55.8
02	208 31.0	35.1	50 59.3	9.6	21 57.4	2.3	55.7
03	223 30.9	.. 34.7	65 27.9	9.5	21 59.7	2.3	55.7
04	238 30.9	34.3	79 56.4	9.6	22 02.0	2.1	55.7
05	253 30.8	33.9	94 25.0	9.6	22 04.1	2.0	55.7
M 06	268 30.7	N21 33.5	108 53.6	9.6	S22 06.1	1.9	55.7
O 07	283 30.7	33.2	123 22.2	9.5	22 08.0	1.8	55.6
N 08	298 30.6	32.8	137 50.7	9.6	22 09.8	1.7	55.6
D 09	313 30.6	.. 32.4	152 19.3	9.6	22 11.5	1.5	55.6
A 10	328 30.5	32.0	166 47.9	9.6	22 13.0	1.5	55.6
Y 11	343 30.4	31.6	181 16.5	9.7	22 14.5	1.3	55.6
12	358 30.4	N21 31.2	195 45.2	9.6	S22 15.8	1.2	55.6
13	13 30.3	30.8	210 13.8	9.6	22 17.0	1.1	55.5
14	28 30.2	30.4	224 42.4	9.7	22 18.1	0.9	55.5
15	43 30.2	.. 30.0	239 11.1	9.7	22 19.0	0.9	55.5
16	58 30.1	29.6	253 39.8	9.7	22 19.9	0.7	55.5
17	73 30.1	29.2	268 08.5	9.7	22 20.6	0.6	55.5
18	88 30.0	N21 28.8	282 37.2	9.7	S22 21.2	0.5	55.4
19	103 29.9	28.4	297 05.9	9.7	22 21.7	0.4	55.4
20	118 29.9	28.0	311 34.6	9.8	22 22.1	0.2	55.4
21	133 29.8	.. 27.6	326 03.4	9.7	22 22.3	0.2	55.4
22	148 29.8	27.2	340 32.1	9.8	22 22.5	0.0	55.4
23	163 29.7	26.8	355 00.9	9.8	22 22.5	0.1	55.4
16 00	178 29.6	N21 26.4	9 29.7	9.9	S22 22.4	0.2	55.3
01	193 29.6	26.0	23 58.6	9.8	22 22.2	0.3	55.3
02	208 29.5	25.6	38 27.4	9.9	22 21.9	0.5	55.3
03	223 29.5	.. 25.2	52 56.3	9.9	22 21.4	0.5	55.3
04	238 29.4	24.8	67 25.2	10.0	22 20.9	0.7	55.3
05	253 29.3	24.4	81 54.2	9.9	22 20.2	0.8	55.2
T 06	268 29.3	N21 24.0	96 23.1	10.0	S22 19.4	0.9	55.2
U 07	283 29.2	23.6	110 52.1	10.0	22 18.5	1.0	55.2
E 08	298 29.2	23.2	125 21.1	10.1	22 17.5	1.1	55.2
S 09	313 29.1	.. 22.8	139 50.2	10.0	22 16.4	1.2	55.2
D 10	328 29.0	22.4	154 19.2	10.1	22 15.2	1.4	55.2
A 11	343 29.0	22.0	168 48.3	10.2	22 13.8	1.5	55.1
Y 12	358 28.9	N21 21.6	183 17.5	10.1	S22 12.3	1.5	55.1
13	13 28.9	21.2	197 46.6	10.2	22 10.8	1.7	55.1
14	28 28.8	20.7	212 15.8	10.3	22 09.1	1.8	55.1
15	43 28.8	.. 20.3	226 45.1	10.2	22 07.3	1.9	55.1
16	58 28.7	19.9	241 14.3	10.3	22 05.4	2.0	55.1
17	73 28.6	19.5	255 43.6	10.4	22 03.4	2.2	55.0
18	88 28.6	N21 19.1	270 13.0	10.3	S22 01.2	2.2	55.0
19	103 28.5	18.7	284 42.3	10.4	21 59.0	2.4	55.0
20	118 28.5	18.3	299 11.7	10.5	21 56.6	2.4	55.0
21	133 28.4	.. 17.9	313 41.2	10.5	21 54.2	2.6	55.0
22	148 28.4	17.4	328 10.7	10.5	21 51.6	2.7	55.0
23	163 28.3	17.0	342 40.2	10.6	21 48.9	2.7	54.9
17 00	178 28.3	N21 16.6	357 09.8	10.6	S21 46.2	2.9	54.9
01	193 28.2	16.2	11 39.4	10.6	21 43.3	3.0	54.9
02	208 28.1	15.8	26 09.0	10.7	21 40.3	3.1	54.9
03	223 28.1	.. 15.4	40 38.7	10.7	21 37.2	3.2	54.9
04	238 28.0	14.9	55 08.4	10.8	21 34.0	3.3	54.9
05	253 28.0	14.5	69 38.2	10.8	21 30.7	3.4	54.9
W 06	268 27.9	N21 14.1	84 08.0	10.9	S21 27.3	3.5	54.8
E 07	283 27.9	13.7	98 37.9	10.9	21 23.8	3.7	54.8
D 08	298 27.8	13.3	113 07.8	10.9	21 20.1	3.7	54.8
N 09	313 27.8	.. 12.8	127 37.7	11.0	21 16.4	3.8	54.8
E 10	328 27.7	12.4	142 07.7	11.1	21 12.6	3.9	54.8
S 11	343 27.7	12.0	156 37.8	11.1	21 08.7	4.1	54.8
D 12	358 27.6	N21 11.6	171 07.9	11.1	S21 04.6	4.1	54.8
A 13	13 27.6	11.1	185 38.0	11.2	21 00.5	4.2	54.7
Y 14	28 27.5	10.7	200 08.2	11.2	20 56.3	4.3	54.7
15	43 27.5	.. 10.3	214 38.4	11.3	20 52.0	4.4	54.7
16	58 27.4	09.9	229 08.7	11.3	20 47.6	4.6	54.7
17	73 27.4	09.4	243 39.0	11.4	20 43.0	4.6	54.7
18	88 27.3	N21 09.0	258 09.4	11.4	S20 38.4	4.7	54.7
19	103 27.3	08.6	272 39.8	11.5	20 33.7	4.8	54.7
20	118 27.2	08.2	287 10.3	11.6	20 28.9	4.9	54.6
21	133 27.2	.. 07.7	301 40.9	11.5	20 24.0	5.0	54.6
22	148 27.1	07.3	316 11.4	11.7	20 19.0	5.1	54.6
23	163 27.1	06.9	330 42.1	11.6	S20 13.9	5.2	54.6
	SD 15.8	d 0.4	SD 15.1		15.0		14.9

Twilight, Sunrise, Moonrise

Lat.	Naut.	Civil	Sunrise	Moonrise 15	16	17	18
N 72	■	■	■	■	■	■	■
N 70	■	■	■	■	■	■	23 51
68	■	■	■	■	23 46	23 23	23 15
66	////	////	01 38	21 51	22 27	22 42	22 48
64	////	////	02 17	21 08	21 50	22 14	22 28
62	////	00 55	02 44	20 39	21 24	21 53	22 12
60	////	01 47	03 05	20 17	21 03	21 35	21 58
N 58		02 18	03 22	20 00	20 46	21 21	21 46
56	00 50	02 40	03 36	19 45	20 32	21 08	21 36
54	01 38	02 58	03 48	19 32	20 19	20 57	21 27
52	02 06	03 13	03 59	19 20	20 08	20 47	21 19
50	02 28	03 26	04 08	19 10	19 59	20 39	21 11
45	03 06	03 52	04 28	18 49	19 38	20 20	20 56
N 40	03 33	04 12	04 44	18 32	19 22	20 05	20 43
35	03 53	04 29	04 58	18 18	19 08	19 52	20 32
30	04 10	04 43	05 09	18 05	18 55	19 41	20 22
20	04 37	05 05	05 29	17 44	18 35	19 22	20 05
N 10	04 57	05 24	05 47	17 25	18 16	19 05	19 51
0	05 14	05 40	06 02	17 08	18 00	18 49	19 37
S 10	05 30	05 56	06 18	16 51	17 43	18 34	19 23
20	05 44	06 11	06 35	16 33	17 24	18 17	19 09
30	05 59	06 28	06 54	16 11	17 04	17 58	18 52
35	06 06	06 38	07 05	15 59	16 51	17 46	18 42
40	06 15	06 50	07 18	15 45	16 37	17 33	18 31
45	06 23	07 00	07 33	15 28	16 21	17 18	18 18
S 50	06 34	07 14	07 51	15 07	16 00	16 59	18 01
52	06 38	07 20	08 00	14 57	15 50	16 50	17 54
54	06 43	07 28	08 09	14 46	15 39	16 40	17 45
56	06 48	07 35	08 20	14 33	15 27	16 28	17 36
58	06 54	07 44	08 33	14 19	15 12	16 15	17 25
S 60	07 00	07 54	08 47	14 01	14 55	16 00	17 12

Sunset, Twilight, Moonset

Lat.	Sunset	Civil	Naut.	Moonset 15	16	17	18
N 72	■	■	■	■	■	■	■
N 70	■	■	■	■	■	■	■
68	■	■	■	■	■	00 42	02 48
66	22 30	////	////	00 12	00 51	02 00	03 28
64	21 52	////	////	00 50	01 33	02 37	03 55
62	21 26	23 11	////	01 16	02 02	03 03	04 16
60	21 06	22 22	////	01 37	02 24	03 24	04 33
N 58	20 49	21 53	////	01 54	02 42	03 41	04 48
56	20 35	21 31	23 16	02 08	02 57	03 55	05 00
54	20 23	21 13	22 31	02 21	03 10	04 07	05 11
52	20 13	20 58	22 04	02 32	03 21	04 18	05 20
50	20 03	20 45	21 43	02 42	03 31	04 27	05 28
45	19 43	20 19	21 06	03 02	03 52	04 47	05 46
N 40	19 27	19 59	20 39	03 19	04 09	05 04	06 01
35	19 14	19 42	20 14	03 33	04 24	05 17	06 13
30	19 02	19 29	20 02	03 45	04 36	05 29	06 24
20	18 43	19 07	19 35	04 06	04 57	05 50	06 42
N 10	18 26	18 48	19 15	04 24	05 16	06 07	06 58
0	18 10	18 32	18 58	04 41	05 33	06 24	07 13
S 10	17 54	18 16	18 42	04 58	05 50	06 40	07 27
20	17 37	18 01	18 28	05 16	06 09	06 58	07 43
30	17 18	17 44	18 14	05 37	06 30	07 18	08 01
35	17 07	17 35	18 06	05 50	06 42	07 30	08 12
40	16 55	17 24	17 58	06 04	06 56	07 43	08 23
45	16 40	17 13	17 49	06 20	07 13	07 59	08 37
S 50	16 21	16 58	17 39	06 41	07 34	08 18	08 54
52	16 13	16 52	17 35	06 51	07 44	08 27	09 02
54	16 03	16 45	17 30	07 02	07 55	08 38	09 11
56	15 52	16 37	17 25	07 14	08 08	08 49	09 21
58	15 40	16 28	17 19	07 29	08 22	09 03	09 33
S 60	15 25	16 19	17 13	07 46	08 40	09 18	09 46

SUN / MOON

Day	Eqn. of Time 00h	Eqn. of Time 12h	Mer. Pass.	Mer. Pass. Upper	Mer. Pass. Lower	Age	Phase
	m s	m s	h m	h m	h m	d %	
15	05 55	05 58	12 06	23 21	10 55	13 98	
16	06 01	06 04	12 06	24 12	11 46	14 100	○
17	06 07	06 09	12 06	00 12	12 37	15 100	

© British Crown Copyright 2018. All rights reserved.

UT	ARIES GHA	VENUS −3.9 GHA	Dec	MARS +1.8 GHA	Dec	JUPITER −2.5 GHA	Dec	SATURN +0.1 GHA	Dec	STARS Name	SHA	Dec
18 00	295 30.9	186 21.9	N22 45.8	162 33.1	N18 49.0	41 17.0	S22 09.6	7 32.8	S22 06.0	Acamar	315 15.3	S40 13.5
01	310 33.4	201 21.1	.. 45.5	177 33.9	.. 48.6	56 19.7	.. 09.6	22 35.4	.. 06.0	Achernar	335 23.6	S57 08.1
02	325 35.8	216 20.2	.. 45.2	192 34.8	.. 48.1	71 22.3	.. 09.5	37 38.1	.. 06.1	Acrux	173 04.8	S63 12.6
03	340 38.3	231 19.4	.. 44.9	207 35.6	.. 47.7	86 25.0	.. 09.5	52 40.7	.. 06.1	Adhara	255 09.6	S28 59.9
04	355 40.7	246 18.5	.. 44.6	222 36.5	.. 47.3	101 27.6	.. 09.5	67 43.4	.. 06.1	Aldebaran	290 44.8	N16 32.7
05	10 43.2	261 17.7	.. 44.3	237 37.3	.. 46.8	116 30.3	.. 09.5	82 46.1	.. 06.2			
06	25 45.7	276 16.8	N22 43.9	252 38.2	N18 46.4	131 33.0	S22 09.5	97 48.7	S22 06.2	Alioth	166 17.1	N55 51.7
07	40 48.1	291 16.0	.. 43.6	267 39.0	.. 46.0	146 35.6	.. 09.5	112 51.4	.. 06.2	Alkaid	152 55.6	N49 13.4
08	55 50.6	306 15.1	.. 43.3	282 39.9	.. 45.5	161 38.3	.. 09.5	127 54.0	.. 06.2	Alnair	27 38.1	S46 51.8
09	70 53.1	321 14.3	.. 43.0	297 40.7	.. 45.1	176 40.9	.. 09.5	142 56.7	.. 06.3	Alnilam	275 42.4	S 1 11.4
10	85 55.5	336 13.4	.. 42.7	312 41.6	.. 44.7	191 43.6	.. 09.5	157 59.3	.. 06.3	Alphard	217 52.3	S 8 44.6
11	100 58.0	351 12.6	.. 42.4	327 42.4	.. 44.2	206 46.3	.. 09.4	173 02.0	.. 06.3			
12	116 00.5	6 11.7	N22 42.0	342 43.3	N18 43.8	221 48.9	S22 09.4	188 04.7	S22 06.3	Alphecca	126 07.3	N26 39.3
13	131 02.9	21 10.9	.. 41.7	357 44.1	.. 43.4	236 51.6	.. 09.4	203 07.3	.. 06.4	Alpheratz	357 39.0	N29 11.7
14	146 05.4	36 10.0	.. 41.4	12 45.0	.. 42.9	251 54.2	.. 09.4	218 10.0	.. 06.4	Altair	62 03.8	N 8 55.3
15	161 07.8	51 09.2	.. 41.1	27 45.8	.. 42.5	266 56.9	.. 09.4	233 12.6	.. 06.4	Ankaa	353 11.4	S42 11.8
16	176 10.3	66 08.4	.. 40.7	42 46.7	.. 42.1	281 59.5	.. 09.4	248 15.3	.. 06.4	Antares	112 20.9	S26 28.4
17	191 12.8	81 07.5	.. 40.4	57 47.6	.. 41.6	297 02.2	.. 09.4	263 17.9	.. 06.5			
18	206 15.2	96 06.7	N22 40.1	72 48.4	N18 41.2	312 04.8	S22 09.4	278 20.6	S22 06.5	Arcturus	145 51.9	N19 05.2
19	221 17.7	111 05.8	.. 39.7	87 49.3	.. 40.8	327 07.5	.. 09.4	293 23.3	.. 06.5	Atria	107 18.5	S69 03.8
20	236 20.2	126 05.0	.. 39.4	102 50.1	.. 40.3	342 10.1	.. 09.3	308 25.9	.. 06.5	Avior	234 17.0	S59 34.4
21	251 22.6	141 04.1	.. 39.1	117 51.0	.. 39.9	357 12.8	.. 09.3	323 28.6	.. 06.6	Bellatrix	278 27.8	N 6 21.9
22	266 25.1	156 03.3	.. 38.8	132 51.8	.. 39.4	12 15.5	.. 09.3	338 31.2	.. 06.6	Betelgeuse	270 57.1	N 7 24.5
23	281 27.6	171 02.4	.. 38.4	147 52.7	.. 39.0	27 18.1	.. 09.3	353 33.9	.. 06.6			
19 00	296 30.0	186 01.6	N22 38.1	162 53.5	N18 38.6	42 20.8	S22 09.3	8 36.5	S22 06.6	Canopus	263 54.8	S52 42.3
01	311 32.5	201 00.8	.. 37.7	177 54.4	.. 38.1	57 23.4	.. 09.3	23 39.2	.. 06.7	Capella	280 28.7	N46 00.8
02	326 35.0	215 59.9	.. 37.4	192 55.2	.. 37.7	72 26.1	.. 09.3	38 41.9	.. 06.7	Deneb	49 28.2	N45 21.0
03	341 37.4	230 59.1	.. 37.1	207 56.1	.. 37.3	87 28.7	.. 09.3	53 44.5	.. 06.7	Denebola	182 29.6	N14 28.0
04	356 39.9	245 58.2	.. 36.7	222 57.0	.. 36.8	102 31.4	.. 09.2	68 47.2	.. 06.7	Diphda	348 51.6	S17 52.7
05	11 42.3	260 57.4	.. 36.4	237 57.8	.. 36.4	117 34.0	.. 09.2	83 49.8	.. 06.8			
06	26 44.8	275 56.5	N22 36.0	252 58.7	N18 35.9	132 36.7	S22 09.2	98 52.5	S22 06.8	Dubhe	193 47.0	N61 39.1
07	41 47.3	290 55.7	.. 35.7	267 59.5	.. 35.5	147 39.3	.. 09.2	113 55.1	.. 06.8	Elnath	278 07.7	N28 37.2
08	56 49.7	305 54.9	.. 35.4	283 00.4	.. 35.1	162 42.0	.. 09.2	128 57.8	.. 06.9	Eltanin	90 43.7	N51 29.4
09	71 52.2	320 54.0	.. 35.0	298 01.2	.. 34.6	177 44.6	.. 09.2	144 00.4	.. 06.9	Enif	33 42.7	N 9 57.9
10	86 54.7	335 53.2	.. 34.7	313 02.1	.. 34.2	192 47.3	.. 09.2	159 03.1	.. 06.9	Fomalhaut	15 19.1	S29 31.0
11	101 57.1	350 52.3	.. 34.3	328 03.0	.. 33.7	207 49.9	.. 09.2	174 05.8	.. 06.9			
12	116 59.6	5 51.5	N22 34.0	343 03.8	N18 33.3	222 52.6	S22 09.2	189 08.4	S22 07.0	Gacrux	171 56.4	S57 13.5
13	132 02.1	20 50.6	.. 33.6	358 04.7	.. 32.9	237 55.2	.. 09.2	204 11.1	.. 07.0	Gienah	175 48.1	S17 39.0
14	147 04.5	35 49.8	.. 33.3	13 05.5	.. 32.4	252 57.9	.. 09.1	219 13.7	.. 07.0	Hadar	148 41.9	S60 28.1
15	162 07.0	50 49.0	.. 32.9	28 06.4	.. 32.0	268 00.5	.. 09.1	234 16.4	.. 07.0	Hamal	327 56.1	N23 33.1
16	177 09.5	65 48.1	.. 32.6	43 07.2	.. 31.5	283 03.2	.. 09.1	249 19.0	.. 07.1	Kaus Aust.	83 37.9	S34 22.4
17	192 11.9	80 47.3	.. 32.2	58 08.1	.. 31.1	298 05.8	.. 09.1	264 21.7	.. 07.1			
18	207 14.4	95 46.4	N22 31.9	73 09.0	N18 30.7	313 08.5	S22 09.1	279 24.4	S22 07.1	Kochab	137 19.7	N74 05.0
19	222 16.8	110 45.6	.. 31.5	88 09.8	.. 30.2	328 11.1	.. 09.1	294 27.0	.. 07.1	Markab	13 34.0	N15 18.5
20	237 19.3	125 44.8	.. 31.1	103 10.7	.. 29.8	343 13.8	.. 09.1	309 29.7	.. 07.2	Menkar	314 10.8	N 4 09.8
21	252 21.8	140 43.9	.. 30.8	118 11.5	.. 29.3	358 16.4	.. 09.1	324 32.3	.. 07.2	Menkent	148 02.6	S36 27.9
22	267 24.2	155 43.1	.. 30.4	133 12.4	.. 28.9	13 19.1	.. 09.1	339 35.0	.. 07.2	Miaplacidus	221 39.7	S69 47.9
23	282 26.7	170 42.3	.. 30.1	148 13.2	.. 28.5	28 21.7	.. 09.0	354 37.6	.. 07.2			
20 00	297 29.2	185 41.4	N22 29.7	163 14.1	N18 28.0	43 24.3	S22 09.0	9 40.3	S22 07.3	Mirfak	308 34.6	N49 55.5
01	312 31.6	200 40.6	.. 29.3	178 15.0	.. 27.6	58 27.0	.. 09.0	24 42.9	.. 07.3	Nunki	75 52.8	S26 16.2
02	327 34.1	215 39.7	.. 29.0	193 15.8	.. 27.1	73 29.6	.. 09.0	39 45.6	.. 07.3	Peacock	53 12.1	S56 40.2
03	342 36.6	230 38.9	.. 28.6	208 16.7	.. 26.7	88 32.3	.. 09.0	54 48.3	.. 07.3	Pollux	243 23.0	N27 58.7
04	357 39.0	245 38.1	.. 28.2	223 17.5	.. 26.2	103 34.9	.. 09.0	69 50.9	.. 07.4	Procyon	244 55.7	N 5 10.5
05	12 41.5	260 37.2	.. 27.9	238 18.4	.. 25.8	118 37.6	.. 09.0	84 53.6	.. 07.4			
06	27 43.9	275 36.4	N22 27.5	253 19.3	N18 25.4	133 40.2	S22 09.0	99 56.2	S22 07.4	Rasalhague	96 02.3	N12 33.0
07	42 46.4	290 35.6	.. 27.1	268 20.1	.. 24.9	148 42.9	.. 09.0	114 58.9	.. 07.4	Regulus	207 39.4	N11 52.4
08	57 48.9	305 34.7	.. 26.7	283 21.0	.. 24.5	163 45.5	.. 09.0	130 01.5	.. 07.5	Rigel	281 08.3	S 8 10.8
09	72 51.3	320 33.9	.. 26.4	298 21.8	.. 24.0	178 48.1	.. 08.9	145 04.2	.. 07.5	Rigil Kent.	139 45.9	S60 55.0
10	87 53.8	335 33.0	.. 26.0	313 22.7	.. 23.6	193 50.8	.. 08.9	160 06.8	.. 07.5	Sabik	102 07.5	S15 44.8
11	102 56.3	350 32.2	.. 25.6	328 23.6	.. 23.1	208 53.4	.. 08.9	175 09.5	.. 07.5			
12	117 58.7	5 31.4	N22 25.2	343 24.4	N18 22.7	223 56.1	S22 08.9	190 12.2	S22 07.6	Schedar	349 35.6	N56 38.3
13	133 01.2	20 30.5	.. 24.9	358 25.3	.. 22.2	238 58.7	.. 08.9	205 14.8	.. 07.6	Shaula	96 15.9	S37 07.0
14	148 03.7	35 29.7	.. 24.5	13 26.1	.. 21.8	254 01.4	.. 08.9	220 17.5	.. 07.6	Sirius	258 30.4	S16 44.6
15	163 06.1	50 28.9	.. 24.1	28 27.0	.. 21.3	269 04.0	.. 08.9	235 20.1	.. 07.6	Spica	158 26.9	S11 15.7
16	178 08.6	65 28.0	.. 23.7	43 27.9	.. 20.9	284 06.6	.. 08.9	250 22.8	.. 07.7	Suhail	222 49.8	S43 30.7
17	193 11.1	80 27.2	.. 23.3	58 28.7	.. 20.5	299 09.3	.. 08.9	265 25.4	.. 07.7			
18	208 13.5	95 26.4	N22 23.0	73 29.6	N18 20.0	314 11.9	S22 08.8	280 28.1	S22 07.7	Vega	80 35.7	N38 48.3
19	223 16.0	110 25.5	.. 22.6	88 30.4	.. 19.6	329 14.6	.. 08.8	295 30.7	.. 07.8	Zuben'ubi	137 00.7	S16 07.2
20	238 18.4	125 24.7	.. 22.2	103 31.3	.. 19.1	344 17.2	.. 08.8	310 33.4	.. 07.8		SHA	Mer.Pass.
21	253 20.9	140 23.9	.. 21.8	118 32.2	.. 18.7	359 19.8	.. 08.8	325 36.1	.. 07.8	Venus	249 31.6	11 37
22	268 23.4	155 23.0	.. 21.4	133 33.0	.. 18.2	14 22.5	.. 08.8	340 38.7	.. 07.8	Mars	226 23.5	13 08
23	283 25.8	170 22.2	.. 21.0	148 33.9	.. 17.8	29 25.1	.. 08.8	355 41.4	.. 07.9	Jupiter	105 50.7	21 07
Mer.Pass.	4 13.3	v −0.8	d 0.3	v 0.9	d 0.4	v 2.6	d 0.0	v 2.7	d 0.0	Saturn	72 06.5	23 21

© British Crown Copyright 2018. All rights reserved.

UT	SUN GHA	SUN Dec	MOON GHA	v	Dec	d	HP
d h	° '	° '	° '	'	° '	'	'
18 00	178 27.0	N21 06.4	345 12.7	11.8	S20 08.7	5.2	54.6
01	193 27.0	06.0	359 43.5	11.8	20 03.5	5.4	54.6
02	208 26.9	05.6	14 14.3	11.8	19 58.1	5.5	54.6
03	223 26.9	.. 05.1	28 45.1	11.9	19 52.6	5.5	54.5
04	238 26.8	04.7	43 16.0	11.9	19 47.1	5.7	54.5
05	253 26.8	04.3	57 46.9	12.0	19 41.4	5.7	54.5
06	268 26.7	N21 03.8	72 17.9	12.1	S19 35.7	5.8	54.5
07	283 26.7	03.4	86 49.0	12.1	19 29.9	5.9	54.5
T 08	298 26.6	03.0	101 20.1	12.1	19 24.0	6.0	54.5
H 09	313 26.6	.. 02.5	115 51.2	12.2	19 18.0	6.1	54.5
U 10	328 26.5	02.1	130 22.4	12.3	19 11.9	6.1	54.5
R 11	343 26.5	01.6	144 53.7	12.3	19 05.8	6.3	54.5
S 12	358 26.4	N21 01.2	159 25.0	12.4	S18 59.5	6.3	54.4
D 13	13 26.4	00.8	173 56.4	12.4	18 53.2	6.4	54.4
A 14	28 26.3	21 00.3	188 27.8	12.5	18 46.8	6.5	54.4
Y 15	43 26.3	20 59.9	202 59.3	12.5	18 40.3	6.6	54.4
16	58 26.2	59.4	217 30.8	12.6	18 33.7	6.6	54.4
17	73 26.2	59.0	232 02.4	12.6	18 27.1	6.8	54.4
18	88 26.2	N20 58.6	246 34.0	12.7	S18 20.3	6.8	54.4
19	103 26.1	58.1	261 05.7	12.8	18 13.5	6.9	54.4
20	118 26.1	57.7	275 37.5	12.8	18 06.6	6.9	54.4
21	133 26.0	.. 57.2	290 09.3	12.8	17 59.7	7.1	54.3
22	148 26.0	56.8	304 41.1	12.9	17 52.6	7.1	54.3
23	163 25.9	56.3	319 13.0	13.0	17 45.5	7.2	54.3
19 00	178 25.9	N20 55.9	333 45.0	13.0	S17 38.3	7.3	54.3
01	193 25.8	55.5	348 17.0	13.1	17 31.0	7.3	54.3
02	208 25.8	55.0	2 49.1	13.1	17 23.7	7.5	54.3
03	223 25.8	.. 54.6	17 21.2	13.2	17 16.2	7.5	54.3
04	238 25.7	54.1	31 53.4	13.2	17 08.7	7.5	54.3
05	253 25.7	53.7	46 25.6	13.3	17 01.2	7.7	54.3
06	268 25.6	N20 53.2	60 57.9	13.3	S16 53.5	7.7	54.3
07	283 25.6	52.8	75 30.2	13.4	16 45.8	7.8	54.3
08	298 25.5	52.3	90 02.6	13.4	16 38.0	7.8	54.2
F 09	313 25.5	.. 51.9	104 35.0	13.5	16 30.2	7.9	54.2
R 10	328 25.5	51.4	119 07.5	13.5	16 22.3	8.0	54.2
I 11	343 25.4	51.0	133 40.0	13.6	16 14.3	8.1	54.2
D 12	358 25.4	N20 50.5	148 12.6	13.6	S16 06.2	8.1	54.2
A 13	13 25.3	50.0	162 45.2	13.7	15 58.1	8.2	54.2
Y 14	28 25.3	49.6	177 17.9	13.8	15 49.9	8.3	54.2
15	43 25.3	.. 49.1	191 50.7	13.8	15 41.6	8.3	54.2
16	58 25.2	48.7	206 23.5	13.8	15 33.3	8.4	54.2
17	73 25.2	48.2	220 56.3	13.9	15 24.9	8.4	54.2
18	88 25.1	N20 47.8	235 29.2	13.9	S15 16.5	8.5	54.2
19	103 25.1	47.3	250 02.1	14.0	15 08.0	8.6	54.2
20	118 25.1	46.8	264 35.1	14.0	14 59.4	8.6	54.2
21	133 25.0	.. 46.4	279 08.1	14.1	14 50.8	8.7	54.2
22	148 25.0	45.9	293 41.2	14.1	14 42.1	8.7	54.2
23	163 24.9	45.5	308 14.3	14.2	14 33.4	8.8	54.1
20 00	178 24.9	N20 45.0	322 47.5	14.2	S14 24.6	8.9	54.1
01	193 24.9	44.5	337 20.7	14.3	14 15.7	8.9	54.1
02	208 24.8	44.1	351 54.0	14.3	14 06.8	9.0	54.1
03	223 24.8	.. 43.6	6 27.3	14.4	13 57.8	9.0	54.1
04	238 24.8	43.2	21 00.7	14.4	13 48.8	9.1	54.1
05	253 24.7	42.7	35 34.1	14.4	13 39.7	9.1	54.1
06	268 24.7	N20 42.2	50 07.5	14.5	S13 30.6	9.2	54.1
S 07	283 24.6	41.8	64 41.0	14.5	13 21.4	9.3	54.1
A 08	298 24.6	41.3	79 14.5	14.6	13 12.1	9.3	54.1
T 09	313 24.6	.. 40.8	93 48.1	14.6	13 02.8	9.3	54.1
U 10	328 24.5	40.4	108 21.7	14.7	12 53.5	9.4	54.1
R 11	343 24.5	39.9	122 55.4	14.7	12 44.1	9.5	54.1
D 12	358 24.5	N20 39.4	137 29.1	14.7	S12 34.6	9.5	54.1
A 13	13 24.4	39.0	152 02.8	14.8	12 25.1	9.5	54.1
Y 14	28 24.4	38.5	166 36.6	14.8	12 15.6	9.6	54.1
15	43 24.4	.. 38.0	181 10.5	14.8	12 06.0	9.7	54.1
16	58 24.3	37.6	195 44.3	14.9	11 56.3	9.7	54.1
17	73 24.3	37.1	210 18.2	14.9	11 46.6	9.7	54.1
18	88 24.3	N20 36.6	224 52.1	15.0	S11 36.9	9.8	54.1
19	103 24.2	36.1	239 26.1	15.0	11 27.1	9.8	54.1
20	118 24.2	35.7	254 00.1	15.1	11 17.3	9.9	54.1
21	133 24.2	.. 35.2	268 34.2	15.1	11 07.4	9.9	54.1
22	148 24.1	34.7	283 08.3	15.1	10 57.5	10.0	54.1
23	163 24.1	34.2	297 42.4	15.1	S10 47.5	10.0	54.1
SD 15.8	d 0.5	SD 14.8		14.8		14.7	

Lat.	Twilight Naut.	Civil	Sunrise	Moonrise 18	19	20	21
°	h m	h m	h m	h m	h m	h m	h m
N 72	□	□	□	■	00 58	{00 00 / 23 34}	23 15
N 70	□	□	□	23 51	23 30	23 17	23 06
68	////	////	00 42	23 15	23 08	23 03	22 58
66	////	////	01 51	22 48	22 51	22 52	22 51
64	////	////	02 26	22 28	22 37	22 42	22 46
62	////	01 13	02 51	22 12	22 25	22 34	22 41
60	////	01 57	03 11	21 58	22 14	22 27	22 37
N 58	////	02 25	03 27	21 46	22 05	22 21	22 33
56	01 07	02 46	03 40	21 36	21 58	22 15	22 30
54	01 47	03 03	03 52	21 27	21 50	22 10	22 27
52	02 13	03 18	04 03	21 19	21 44	22 06	22 24
50	02 33	03 30	04 12	21 11	21 38	22 01	22 22
45	03 10	03 56	04 31	20 56	21 26	21 53	22 17
N 40	03 36	04 15	04 47	20 43	21 16	21 45	22 12
35	03 56	04 31	05 00	20 32	21 07	21 39	22 08
30	04 12	04 44	05 11	20 22	20 59	21 33	22 05
20	04 38	05 06	05 31	20 05	20 46	21 23	21 59
N 10	04 58	05 25	05 47	19 51	20 34	21 14	21 53
0	05 15	05 41	06 03	19 37	20 23	21 06	21 48
S 10	05 30	05 56	06 18	19 23	20 12	20 58	21 43
20	05 44	06 11	06 34	19 09	20 00	20 49	21 38
30	05 58	06 27	06 53	18 52	19 46	20 39	21 32
35	06 05	06 36	07 04	18 42	19 38	20 34	21 28
40	06 13	06 46	07 16	18 31	19 29	20 27	21 24
45	06 22	06 58	07 31	18 18	19 18	20 19	21 20
S 50	06 31	07 11	07 48	18 01	19 05	20 10	21 14
52	06 35	07 18	07 57	17 54	18 59	20 06	21 12
54	06 40	07 24	08 06	17 45	18 53	20 01	21 09
56	06 45	07 32	08 16	17 36	18 45	19 56	21 06
58	06 50	07 40	08 28	17 25	18 37	19 50	21 02
S 60	06 56	07 50	08 42	17 12	18 27	19 43	20 58

Lat.	Sunset	Twilight Civil	Naut.	Moonset 18	19	20	21
°	h m	h m	h m	h m	h m	h m	h m
N 72	□	□	□	■	02 53	05 24	07 20
N 70	□	□	□	■	03 58	05 52	07 35
68	23 20	////	////	02 48	04 34	06 13	07 48
66	22 18	////	////	03 28	04 59	06 30	07 58
64	21 44	////	////	03 55	05 19	06 43	08 06
62	21 19	22 54	////	04 16	05 35	06 54	08 13
60	21 00	22 13	////	04 33	05 48	07 04	08 19
N 58	20 44	21 46	////	04 48	05 59	07 12	08 25
56	20 31	21 25	23 01	05 00	06 09	07 19	08 29
54	20 19	21 08	22 23	05 11	06 17	07 25	08 34
52	20 09	20 54	21 58	05 20	06 25	07 31	08 37
50	20 00	20 41	21 38	05 28	06 32	07 36	08 41
45	19 41	20 16	21 02	05 46	06 47	07 48	08 48
N 40	19 26	19 57	20 36	06 01	06 59	07 57	08 55
35	19 13	19 41	20 15	06 13	07 09	08 05	09 00
30	19 01	19 28	20 00	06 24	07 18	08 12	09 05
20	18 42	19 06	19 34	06 42	07 34	08 24	09 13
N 10	18 25	18 48	19 14	06 58	07 47	08 34	09 20
0	18 10	18 32	18 58	07 13	07 59	08 44	09 27
S 10	17 55	18 17	18 43	07 27	08 12	08 54	09 33
20	17 38	18 02	18 29	07 43	08 25	09 04	09 40
30	17 20	17 46	18 15	08 01	08 40	09 15	09 48
35	17 09	17 37	18 08	08 12	08 49	09 22	09 53
40	16 57	17 27	18 01	08 23	08 59	09 30	09 58
45	16 42	17 15	17 51	08 37	09 10	09 39	10 04
S 50	16 25	17 02	17 42	08 54	09 24	09 49	10 11
52	16 16	16 55	17 38	09 02	09 31	09 54	10 14
54	16 07	16 49	17 33	09 11	09 39	09 59	10 18
56	15 57	16 41	17 28	09 21	09 46	10 05	10 21
58	15 45	16 33	17 23	09 33	09 55	10 12	10 26
S 60	15 31	16 23	17 17	09 46	10 05	10 19	10 31

Day	SUN Eqn. of Time 00h	12h	Mer. Pass.	MOON Mer. Pass. Upper	Lower	Age	Phase
d	m s	m s	h m	h m	h m	d	%
18	06 12	06 14	12 06	01 01	13 25	16	98
19	06 16	06 18	12 06	01 48	14 11	17	94
20	06 20	06 22	12 06	02 33	14 55	18	88

© British Crown Copyright 2018. All rights reserved.

UT	ARIES GHA	VENUS −3.9 GHA	Dec	MARS +1.8 GHA	Dec	JUPITER −2.5 GHA	Dec	SATURN +0.1 GHA	Dec	STARS Name	SHA	Dec
21 00	298 28.3	185 21.4	N22 20.6	163 34.7	N18 17.3	44 27.8	S22 08.8	10 44.0	S22 07.9	Acamar	315 15.3	S40 13.5
01	313 30.8	200 20.5	20.2	178 35.6	16.9	59 30.4	08.8	25 46.7	07.9	Achernar	335 23.6	S57 08.1
02	328 33.2	215 19.7	19.9	193 36.5	16.4	74 33.0	08.8	40 49.3	07.9	Acrux	173 04.9	S63 12.6
03	343 35.7	230 18.9 ..	19.5	208 37.3 ..	16.0	89 35.7 ..	08.8	55 52.0 ..	08.0	Adhara	255 09.6	S28 59.9
04	358 38.2	245 18.1	19.1	223 38.2	15.5	104 38.3	08.8	70 54.6	08.0	Aldebaran	290 44.8	N16 32.7
05	13 40.6	260 17.2	18.7	238 39.1	15.1	119 40.9	08.8	85 57.3	08.0			
06	28 43.1	275 16.4	N22 18.3	253 39.9	N18 14.6	134 43.6	S22 08.7	100 59.9	S22 08.0	Alioth	166 17.1	N55 51.7
07	43 45.6	290 15.6	17.9	268 40.8	14.2	149 46.2	08.7	116 02.6	08.1	Alkaid	152 55.6	N49 13.4
08	58 48.0	305 14.7	17.5	283 41.6	13.7	164 48.9	08.7	131 05.3	08.1	Alnair	27 38.1	S46 51.8
S 09	73 50.5	320 13.9 ..	17.1	298 42.5 ..	13.3	179 51.5 ..	08.7	146 07.9 ..	08.1	Alnilam	275 42.4	S 1 11.4
U 10	88 52.9	335 13.1	16.7	313 43.4	12.8	194 54.1	08.7	161 10.6	08.1	Alphard	217 52.3	S 8 44.6
N 11	103 55.4	350 12.2	16.3	328 44.2	12.4	209 56.8	08.7	176 13.2	08.2			
D 12	118 57.9	5 11.4	N22 15.9	343 45.1	N18 11.9	224 59.4	S22 08.7	191 15.9	S22 08.2	Alphecca	126 07.3	N26 39.3
A 13	134 00.3	20 10.6	15.5	358 46.0	11.5	240 02.0	08.7	206 18.5	08.2	Alpheratz	357 39.0	N29 11.7
Y 14	149 02.8	35 09.8	15.1	13 46.8	11.0	255 04.7	08.7	221 21.2	08.2	Altair	62 03.8	N 8 55.3
15	164 05.3	50 08.9 ..	14.6	28 47.7 ..	10.6	270 07.3 ..	08.6	236 23.8 ..	08.3	Ankaa	353 11.4	S42 11.8
16	179 07.7	65 08.1	14.2	43 48.5	10.1	285 09.9	08.6	251 26.5	08.3	Antares	112 20.9	S26 28.4
17	194 10.2	80 07.3	13.8	58 49.4	09.7	300 12.6	08.6	266 29.1	08.3			
18	209 12.7	95 06.5	N22 13.4	73 50.3	N18 09.2	315 15.2	S22 08.6	281 31.8	S22 08.3	Arcturus	145 51.9	N19 05.2
19	224 15.1	110 05.6	13.0	88 51.1	08.8	330 17.8	08.6	296 34.4	08.4	Atria	107 18.5	S69 03.8
20	239 17.6	125 04.8	12.6	103 52.0	08.3	345 20.5	08.6	311 37.1	08.4	Avior	234 17.0	S59 34.4
21	254 20.0	140 04.0 ..	12.2	118 52.9 ..	07.9	0 23.1 ..	08.6	326 39.8 ..	08.4	Bellatrix	278 27.8	N 6 21.9
22	269 22.5	155 03.1	11.8	133 53.7	07.4	15 25.7	08.6	341 42.4	08.4	Betelgeuse	270 57.1	N 7 24.5
23	284 25.0	170 02.3	11.3	148 54.6	07.0	30 28.4	08.6	356 45.1	08.5			
22 00	299 27.4	185 01.5	N22 10.9	163 55.5	N18 06.5	45 31.0	S22 08.6	11 47.7	S22 08.5	Canopus	263 54.8	S52 42.3
01	314 29.9	200 00.7	10.5	178 56.3	06.1	60 33.6	08.6	26 50.4	08.5	Capella	280 28.7	N46 00.8
02	329 32.4	214 59.8	10.1	193 57.2	05.6	75 36.3	08.5	41 53.0	08.5	Deneb	49 28.2	N45 21.0
03	344 34.8	229 59.0 ..	09.7	208 58.1 ..	05.2	90 38.9 ..	08.5	56 55.7 ..	08.6	Denebola	182 29.6	N14 28.0
04	359 37.3	244 58.2	09.2	223 58.9	04.7	105 41.5	08.5	71 58.3	08.6	Diphda	348 51.6	S17 52.7
05	14 39.8	259 57.4	08.8	238 59.8	04.3	120 44.1	08.5	87 01.0	08.6			
06	29 42.2	274 56.6	N22 08.4	254 00.7	N18 03.8	135 46.8	S22 08.5	102 03.6	S22 08.6	Dubhe	193 47.1	N61 39.0
07	44 44.7	289 55.7	08.0	269 01.5	03.3	150 49.4	08.5	117 06.3	08.7	Elnath	278 07.6	N28 37.2
08	59 47.2	304 54.9	07.5	284 02.4	02.9	165 52.0	08.5	132 08.9	08.7	Eltanin	90 43.7	N51 29.4
M 09	74 49.6	319 54.1 ..	07.1	299 03.3 ..	02.4	180 54.7 ..	08.5	147 11.6 ..	08.7	Enif	33 42.7	N 9 57.9
O 10	89 52.1	334 53.3	06.7	314 04.1	02.0	195 57.3	08.5	162 14.3	08.7	Fomalhaut	15 19.1	S29 31.0
N 11	104 54.5	349 52.4	06.3	329 05.0	01.5	210 59.9	08.5	177 16.9	08.8			
D 12	119 57.0	4 51.6	N22 05.8	344 05.9	N18 01.1	226 02.5	S22 08.5	192 19.6	S22 08.8	Gacrux	171 56.5	S57 13.5
A 13	134 59.5	19 50.8	05.4	359 06.7	00.6	241 05.2	08.4	207 22.2	08.8	Gienah	175 48.1	S17 38.9
Y 14	150 01.9	34 50.0	05.0	14 07.6	18 00.2	256 07.8	08.4	222 24.9	08.8	Hadar	148 41.9	S60 28.1
15	165 04.4	49 49.2 ..	04.5	29 08.5	17 59.7	271 10.4 ..	08.4	237 27.5 ..	08.9	Hamal	327 56.1	N23 33.1
16	180 06.9	64 48.3	04.1	44 09.3	59.2	286 13.0	08.4	252 30.2	08.9	Kaus Aust.	83 37.9	S34 22.4
17	195 09.3	79 47.5	03.7	59 10.2	58.8	301 15.7	08.4	267 32.8	08.9			
18	210 11.8	94 46.7	N22 03.2	74 11.1	N17 58.3	316 18.3	S22 08.4	282 35.5	S22 08.9	Kochab	137 19.8	N74 05.0
19	225 14.3	109 45.9	02.8	89 11.9	57.9	331 20.9	08.4	297 38.1	09.0	Markab	13 33.9	N15 18.6
20	240 16.7	124 45.1	02.3	104 12.8	57.4	346 23.6	08.4	312 40.8	09.0	Menkar	314 10.8	N 4 09.9
21	255 19.2	139 44.2 ..	01.9	119 13.7 ..	57.0	1 26.2 ..	08.4	327 43.4 ..	09.0	Menkent	148 02.6	S36 27.9
22	270 21.6	154 43.4	01.5	134 14.5	56.5	16 28.8	08.4	342 46.1	09.0	Miaplacidus	221 39.7	S69 47.9
23	285 24.1	169 42.6	01.0	149 15.4	56.1	31 31.4	08.4	357 48.7	09.1			
23 00	300 26.6	184 41.8	N22 00.6	164 16.3	N17 55.6	46 34.0	S22 08.4	12 51.4	S22 09.1	Mirfak	308 34.6	N49 55.5
01	315 29.0	199 41.0	22 00.1	179 17.1	55.1	61 36.7	08.3	27 54.0	09.1	Nunki	75 52.8	S26 16.2
02	330 31.5	214 40.2	21 59.7	194 18.0	54.7	76 39.3	08.3	42 56.7	09.1	Peacock	53 12.1	S56 40.2
03	345 34.0	229 39.3 ..	59.2	209 18.9 ..	54.2	91 41.9 ..	08.3	57 59.4 ..	09.2	Pollux	243 23.0	N27 58.7
04	0 36.4	244 38.5	58.8	224 19.7	53.8	106 44.5	08.3	73 02.0	09.2	Procyon	244 55.7	N 5 10.5
05	15 38.9	259 37.7	58.3	239 20.6	53.3	121 47.2	08.3	88 04.7	09.2			
06	30 41.4	274 36.9	N21 57.9	254 21.5	N17 52.8	136 49.8	S22 08.3	103 07.3	S22 09.2	Rasalhague	96 02.3	N12 33.0
07	45 43.8	289 36.1	57.4	269 22.3	52.4	151 52.4	08.3	118 10.0	09.3	Regulus	207 39.4	N11 52.4
T 08	60 46.3	304 35.3	57.0	284 23.2	51.9	166 55.0	08.3	133 12.6	09.3	Rigel	281 08.3	S 8 10.8
U 09	75 48.8	319 34.4 ..	56.5	299 24.1 ..	51.5	181 57.6 ..	08.3	148 15.3 ..	09.3	Rigil Kent.	139 45.9	S60 55.0
E 10	90 51.2	334 33.6	56.1	314 25.0	51.0	197 00.3	08.3	163 17.9	09.3	Sabik	102 07.5	S15 44.8
S 11	105 53.7	349 32.8	55.6	329 25.8	50.5	212 02.9	08.3	178 20.6	09.4			
D 12	120 56.1	4 32.0	N21 55.2	344 26.7	N17 50.1	227 05.5	S22 08.3	193 23.2	S22 09.4	Schedar	349 35.6	N56 38.3
A 13	135 58.6	19 31.2	54.7	359 27.6	49.6	242 08.1	08.2	208 25.9	09.4	Shaula	96 15.9	S37 07.0
Y 14	151 01.1	34 30.4	54.2	14 28.4	49.2	257 10.7	08.2	223 28.5	09.4	Sirius	258 30.4	S16 44.6
15	166 03.5	49 29.6 ..	53.8	29 29.3 ..	48.7	272 13.4 ..	08.2	238 31.2 ..	09.5	Spica	158 26.9	S11 15.7
16	181 06.0	64 28.8	53.3	44 30.2	48.2	287 16.0	08.2	253 33.8	09.5	Suhail	222 49.8	S43 30.7
17	196 08.5	79 27.9	52.8	59 31.0	47.8	302 18.6	08.2	268 36.5	09.5			
18	211 10.9	94 27.1	N21 52.4	74 31.9	N17 47.3	317 21.2	S22 08.2	283 39.1	S22 09.5	Vega	80 35.7	N38 48.3
19	226 13.4	109 26.3	51.9	89 32.8	46.9	332 23.8	08.2	298 41.8	09.6	Zuben'ubi	137 00.7	S16 07.2
20	241 15.9	124 25.5	51.4	104 33.7	46.4	347 26.5	08.2	313 44.4	09.6		SHA	Mer. Pass.
21	256 18.3	139 24.7 ..	51.0	119 34.5 ..	45.9	2 29.1 ..	08.2	328 47.1 ..	09.6		° ′	h m
22	271 20.8	154 23.9	50.5	134 35.4	45.5	17 31.7	08.2	343 49.7	09.6	Venus	245 34.1	11 41
23	286 23.3	169 23.1	50.0	149 36.3	45.0	32 34.3	08.2	358 52.4	09.7	Mars	224 28.0	13 04
	h m									Jupiter	106 03.6	20 54
Mer. Pass.	4 01.5	v −0.8	d 0.4	v 0.9	d 0.5	v 2.6	d 0.0	v 2.7	d 0.0	Saturn	72 20.3	23 09

© British Crown Copyright 2018. All rights reserved.

UT	SUN GHA	SUN Dec	MOON GHA	v	MOON Dec	d	HP
d h	° ′	° ′	° ′	′	° ′	′	′
21 00	178 24.1	N20 33.8	312 16.5	15.2	S10 37.5	10.0	54.1
01	193 24.0	33.3	326 50.7	15.2	10 27.5	10.1	54.1
02	208 24.0	32.8	341 24.9	15.3	10 17.4	10.1	54.1
03	223 24.0	.. 32.3	355 59.2	15.3	10 07.3	10.2	54.1
04	238 23.9	31.9	10 33.5	15.3	9 57.1	10.2	54.1
05	253 23.9	31.4	25 07.8	15.3	9 46.9	10.2	54.1
06	268 23.9	N20 30.9	39 42.1	15.4	S 9 36.7	10.3	54.1
07	283 23.8	30.4	54 16.5	15.4	9 26.4	10.3	54.1
08	298 23.8	30.0	68 50.9	15.4	9 16.1	10.3	54.1
S 09	313 23.8	.. 29.5	83 25.3	15.5	9 05.8	10.4	54.1
U 10	328 23.8	29.0	97 59.8	15.4	8 55.4	10.4	54.1
N 11	343 23.7	28.5	112 34.2	15.5	8 45.0	10.5	54.1
D 12	358 23.7	N20 28.0	127 08.7	15.6	S 8 34.5	10.5	54.1
A 13	13 23.7	27.5	141 43.3	15.5	8 24.0	10.5	54.1
Y 14	28 23.6	27.1	156 17.8	15.6	8 13.5	10.6	54.1
15	43 23.6	.. 26.6	170 52.4	15.6	8 02.9	10.5	54.1
16	58 23.6	26.1	185 27.0	15.6	7 52.4	10.7	54.1
17	73 23.6	25.6	200 01.6	15.7	7 41.7	10.6	54.1
18	88 23.5	N20 25.1	214 36.3	15.6	S 7 31.1	10.7	54.1
19	103 23.5	24.6	229 10.9	15.7	7 20.4	10.7	54.1
20	118 23.5	24.1	243 45.6	15.7	7 09.7	10.7	54.1
21	133 23.4	.. 23.7	258 20.3	15.8	6 59.0	10.8	54.1
22	148 23.4	23.2	272 55.1	15.7	6 48.2	10.8	54.1
23	163 23.4	22.7	287 29.8	15.8	6 37.4	10.8	54.1
22 00	178 23.4	N20 22.2	302 04.6	15.7	S 6 26.6	10.8	54.1
01	193 23.3	21.7	316 39.3	15.8	6 15.8	10.9	54.2
02	208 23.3	21.2	331 14.1	15.8	6 04.9	10.9	54.2
03	223 23.3	.. 20.7	345 48.9	15.8	5 54.0	10.9	54.2
04	238 23.3	20.2	0 23.7	15.9	5 43.1	11.0	54.2
05	253 23.2	19.7	14 58.6	15.8	5 32.1	11.0	54.2
06	268 23.2	N20 19.2	29 33.4	15.9	S 5 21.2	11.0	54.2
07	283 23.2	18.8	44 08.3	15.8	5 10.2	11.0	54.2
08	298 23.2	18.3	58 43.1	15.9	4 59.2	11.1	54.2
M 09	313 23.1	.. 17.8	73 18.0	15.9	4 48.1	11.0	54.2
O 10	328 23.1	17.3	87 52.9	15.9	4 37.1	11.1	54.2
N 11	343 23.1	16.8	102 27.8	15.9	4 26.0	11.1	54.2
D 12	358 23.1	N20 16.3	117 02.7	15.9	S 4 14.9	11.1	54.2
A 13	13 23.0	15.8	131 37.6	15.9	4 03.8	11.2	54.2
Y 14	28 23.0	15.3	146 12.5	15.9	3 52.6	11.1	54.3
15	43 23.0	.. 14.8	160 47.4	15.9	3 41.5	11.2	54.3
16	58 23.0	14.3	175 22.3	15.9	3 30.3	11.2	54.3
17	73 22.9	13.8	189 57.2	15.9	3 19.1	11.2	54.3
18	88 22.9	N20 13.3	204 32.1	15.9	S 3 07.9	11.2	54.3
19	103 22.9	12.8	219 07.0	16.0	2 56.7	11.2	54.3
20	118 22.9	12.3	233 42.0	15.9	2 45.5	11.3	54.3
21	133 22.9	.. 11.8	248 16.9	15.9	2 34.2	11.2	54.3
22	148 22.8	11.3	262 51.8	15.9	2 23.0	11.3	54.3
23	163 22.8	10.8	277 26.7	15.9	2 11.7	11.3	54.4
23 00	178 22.8	N20 10.3	292 01.6	15.9	S 2 00.4	11.3	54.4
01	193 22.8	09.8	306 36.5	15.9	1 49.1	11.3	54.4
02	208 22.7	09.3	321 11.4	15.9	1 37.8	11.3	54.4
03	223 22.7	.. 08.8	335 46.3	15.9	1 26.5	11.4	54.4
04	238 22.7	08.3	350 21.2	15.9	1 15.1	11.3	54.4
05	253 22.7	07.7	4 56.1	15.8	1 03.8	11.4	54.4
06	268 22.7	N20 07.2	19 30.9	15.9	S 0 52.4	11.3	54.4
07	283 22.7	06.7	34 05.8	15.8	0 41.1	11.4	54.5
08	298 22.6	06.2	48 40.6	15.9	0 29.7	11.4	54.5
T 09	313 22.6	.. 05.7	63 15.5	15.8	0 18.3	11.4	54.5
U 10	328 22.6	05.2	77 50.3	15.8	S 0 06.9	11.4	54.5
E 11	343 22.6	04.7	92 25.1	15.8	N 0 04.5	11.4	54.5
S 12	358 22.6	N20 04.2	106 59.9	15.8	N 0 15.9	11.4	54.5
D 13	13 22.5	03.7	121 34.7	15.8	0 27.3	11.4	54.5
A 14	28 22.5	03.2	136 09.5	15.7	0 38.7	11.4	54.6
Y 15	43 22.5	.. 02.6	150 44.2	15.7	0 50.1	11.4	54.6
16	58 22.5	02.1	165 18.9	15.7	1 01.5	11.4	54.6
17	73 22.5	01.6	179 53.6	15.7	1 12.9	11.4	54.6
18	88 22.5	N20 01.1	194 28.3	15.7	N 1 24.3	11.4	54.6
19	103 22.4	00.6	209 03.0	15.6	1 35.7	11.5	54.6
20	118 22.4	20 00.1	223 37.6	15.7	1 47.2	11.4	54.7
21	133 22.4	19 59.6	238 12.3	15.6	1 58.6	11.4	54.7
22	148 22.4	59.0	252 46.9	15.5	2 10.0	11.4	54.7
23	163 22.4	58.5	267 21.4	15.6	N 2 21.4	11.4	54.7
	SD 15.8	d 0.5	SD 14.7		14.8		14.9

Moonrise

Lat.	Twilight Naut.	Twilight Civil	Sunrise	21	22	23	24
°	h m	h m	h m	h m	h m	h m	h m
N 72	▨	▨	▨	23 15	22 59	22 43	22 26
N 70	▨	▨	▨	23 06	22 56	22 46	22 36
68	////	////	01 12	22 58	22 53	22 48	22 44
66	////	////	02 04	22 51	22 51	22 50	22 50
64	////	////	02 36	22 46	22 49	22 52	22 56
62	////	01 29	02 59	22 41	22 47	22 54	23 00
60	////	02 07	03 17	22 37	22 46	22 55	23 04
N 58		02 32	03 32	22 33	22 45	22 56	23 08
56	01 22	02 52	03 45	22 30	22 44	22 57	23 12
54	01 56	03 09	03 57	22 27	22 43	22 58	23 15
52	02 20	03 23	04 07	22 24	22 42	22 59	23 17
50	02 39	03 35	04 15	22 22	22 41	23 00	23 20
45	03 14	03 59	04 34	22 17	22 39	23 02	23 25
N 40	03 39	04 18	04 49	22 12	22 38	23 03	23 30
35	03 58	04 33	05 02	22 08	22 36	23 05	23 34
30	04 14	04 46	05 13	22 05	22 35	23 06	23 37
20	04 39	05 08	05 32	21 59	22 33	23 08	23 43
N 10	04 59	05 25	05 48	21 53	22 31	23 10	23 49
0	05 15	05 41	06 03	21 48	22 30	23 11	23 54
S 10	05 30	05 55	06 18	21 43	22 28	23 13	23 59
20	05 43	06 10	06 34	21 38	22 26	23 15	24 05
30	05 57	06 26	06 52	21 32	22 24	23 17	24 11
35	06 04	06 35	07 02	21 28	22 23	23 18	24 15
40	06 11	06 44	07 14	21 24	22 22	23 20	24 19
45	06 19	06 56	07 28	21 20	22 20	23 21	24 24
S 50	06 29	07 09	07 45	21 14	22 19	23 23	24 30
52	06 33	07 15	07 53	21 12	22 18	23 24	24 32
54	06 37	07 21	08 02	21 09	22 17	23 25	24 35
56	06 42	07 28	08 12	21 06	22 16	23 27	24 39
58	06 47	07 36	08 23	21 02	22 15	23 28	24 42
S 60	06 52	07 45	08 37	20 58	22 13	23 29	24 47

Moonset

Lat.	Sunset	Twilight Civil	Twilight Naut.	21	22	23	24
°	h m	h m	h m	h m	h m	h m	h m
N 72	▨	▨	▨	07 20	09 06	10 49	12 34
N 70	▨	▨	▨	07 35	09 13	10 49	12 27
68	22 54	////	////	07 48	09 19	10 49	12 21
66	22 06	////	////	07 58	09 24	10 49	12 16
64	21 35	////	////	08 06	09 28	10 50	12 12
62	21 12	22 39	////	08 13	09 31	10 50	12 09
60	20 54	22 04	////	08 19	09 34	10 50	12 06
N 58	20 39	21 38	////	08 25	09 37	10 50	12 03
56	20 26	21 19	22 47	08 29	09 39	10 50	12 01
54	20 15	21 03	22 14	08 34	09 41	10 50	11 59
52	20 05	20 49	21 51	08 37	09 43	10 50	11 57
50	19 57	20 37	21 33	08 41	09 45	10 50	11 55
45	19 38	20 13	20 58	08 48	09 49	10 50	11 51
N 40	19 23	19 55	20 33	08 55	09 52	10 50	11 48
35	19 11	19 39	20 14	09 00	09 55	10 50	11 45
30	19 00	19 26	19 58	09 05	09 57	10 50	11 43
20	18 41	19 05	19 33	09 13	10 01	10 50	11 39
N 10	18 25	18 47	19 14	09 20	10 04	10 50	11 35
0	18 10	18 32	18 58	09 27	10 08	10 50	11 32
S 10	17 55	18 18	18 43	09 33	10 12	10 50	11 28
20	17 39	18 03	18 30	09 40	10 15	10 50	11 24
30	17 22	17 47	18 16	09 48	10 19	10 49	11 20
35	17 11	17 38	18 09	09 53	10 21	10 49	11 18
40	16 59	17 29	18 02	09 58	10 24	10 49	11 15
45	16 45	17 18	17 54	10 04	10 27	10 49	11 12
S 50	16 28	17 05	17 45	10 11	10 30	10 49	11 08
52	16 20	16 59	17 41	10 14	10 32	10 49	11 07
54	16 11	16 52	17 37	10 18	10 34	10 49	11 05
56	16 01	16 45	17 32	10 21	10 36	10 49	11 03
58	15 50	16 37	17 27	10 26	10 38	10 49	11 00
S 60	15 37	16 28	17 21	10 31	10 40	10 49	10 58

Day	SUN Eqn. of Time 00ʰ	SUN Eqn. of Time 12ʰ	SUN Mer. Pass.	MOON Mer. Pass. Upper	MOON Mer. Pass. Lower	Age	Phase
d	m s	m s	h m	h m	h m	d	%
21	06 24	06 25	12 06	03 17	15 38	19	82
22	06 27	06 28	12 06	03 58	16 19	20	74
23	06 29	06 30	12 06	04 40	17 00	21	65

© British Crown Copyright 2018. All rights reserved.

UT	ARIES GHA	VENUS −3.9 GHA	Dec	MARS +1.8 GHA	Dec	JUPITER −2.5 GHA	Dec	SATURN +0.1 GHA	Dec
24 00	301 25.7	184 22.3	N21 49.6	164 37.1	N17 44.5	47 36.9	S22 08.2	13 55.0	S22 09.7
01	316 28.2	199 21.5	49.1	179 38.0	44.1	62 39.5	08.1	28 57.7	09.7
02	331 30.6	214 20.6	48.6	194 38.9	43.6	77 42.2	08.1	44 00.3	09.7
03	346 33.1	229 19.8 ..	48.1	209 39.8 ..	43.2	92 44.8 ..	08.1	59 03.0 ..	09.8
04	1 35.6	244 19.0	47.7	224 40.6	42.7	107 47.4	08.1	74 05.6	09.8
05	16 38.0	259 18.2	47.2	239 41.5	42.2	122 50.0	08.1	89 08.3	09.8
06	31 40.5	274 17.4	N21 46.7	254 42.4	N17 41.8	137 52.6	S22 08.1	104 10.9	S22 09.8
W 07	46 43.0	289 16.6	46.2	269 43.2	41.3	152 55.2	08.1	119 13.6	09.9
E 08	61 45.4	304 15.8	45.7	284 44.1	40.8	167 57.8	08.1	134 16.2	09.9
D 09	76 47.9	319 15.0 ..	45.3	299 45.0 ..	40.4	183 00.5 ..	08.1	149 18.9 ..	09.9
N 10	91 50.4	334 14.2	44.8	314 45.9	39.9	198 03.1	08.1	164 21.5	09.9
E 11	106 52.8	349 13.4	44.3	329 46.7	39.4	213 05.7	08.1	179 24.2	10.0
S 12	121 55.3	4 12.6	N21 43.8	344 47.6	N17 39.0	228 08.3	S22 08.1	194 26.8	S22 10.0
D 13	136 57.7	19 11.8	43.3	359 48.5	38.5	243 10.9	08.1	209 29.5	10.0
A 14	152 00.2	34 11.0	42.8	14 49.4	38.0	258 13.5	08.1	224 32.1	10.0
Y 15	167 02.7	49 10.2 ..	42.4	29 50.2 ..	37.6	273 16.1 ..	08.0	239 34.8 ..	10.1
16	182 05.1	64 09.4	41.9	44 51.1	37.1	288 18.7	08.0	254 37.4	10.1
17	197 07.6	79 08.5	41.4	59 52.0	36.7	303 21.3	08.0	269 40.1	10.1
18	212 10.1	94 07.7	N21 40.9	74 52.8	N17 36.2	318 24.0	S22 08.0	284 42.7	S22 10.1
19	227 12.5	109 06.9	40.4	89 53.7	35.7	333 26.6	08.0	299 45.4	10.2
20	242 15.0	124 06.1	39.9	104 54.6	35.3	348 29.2	08.0	314 48.1	10.2
21	257 17.5	139 05.3 ..	39.4	119 55.5 ..	34.8	3 31.8 ..	08.0	329 50.7 ..	10.2
22	272 19.9	154 04.5	38.9	134 56.3	34.3	18 34.4	08.0	344 53.4	10.2
23	287 22.4	169 03.7	38.4	149 57.2	33.9	33 37.0	08.0	359 56.0	10.3
25 00	302 24.9	184 02.9	N21 37.9	164 58.1	N17 33.4	48 39.6	S22 08.0	14 58.6	S22 10.3
01	317 27.3	199 02.1	37.4	179 59.0	32.9	63 42.2	08.0	30 01.3	10.3
02	332 29.8	214 01.3	36.9	194 59.8	32.4	78 44.8	08.0	45 03.9	10.3
03	347 32.2	229 00.5 ..	36.4	210 00.7 ..	32.0	93 47.4 ..	08.0	60 06.6 ..	10.4
04	2 34.7	243 59.7	35.9	225 01.6	31.5	108 50.0	08.0	75 09.2	10.4
05	17 37.2	258 58.9	35.4	240 02.5	31.0	123 52.7	07.9	90 11.9	10.4
06	32 39.6	273 58.1	N21 34.9	255 03.3	N17 30.6	138 55.3	S22 07.9	105 14.5	S22 10.4
T 07	47 42.1	288 57.3	34.4	270 04.2	30.1	153 57.9	07.9	120 17.2	10.5
H 08	62 44.6	303 56.5	33.9	285 05.1	29.6	169 00.5	07.9	135 19.8	10.5
U 09	77 47.0	318 55.7 ..	33.4	300 06.0 ..	29.2	184 03.1 ..	07.9	150 22.5 ..	10.5
R 10	92 49.5	333 54.9	32.9	315 06.8	28.7	199 05.7	07.9	165 25.1	10.5
S 11	107 52.0	348 54.1	32.4	330 07.7	28.2	214 08.3	07.9	180 27.8	10.6
D 12	122 54.4	3 53.3	N21 31.9	345 08.6	N17 27.7	229 10.9	S22 07.9	195 30.4	S22 10.6
A 13	137 56.9	18 52.5	31.3	0 09.5	27.3	244 13.5	07.9	210 33.1	10.6
Y 14	152 59.4	33 51.7	30.8	15 10.4	26.8	259 16.1	07.9	225 35.7	10.6
15	168 01.8	48 50.9 ..	30.3	30 11.2 ..	26.3	274 18.7 ..	07.9	240 38.4 ..	10.7
16	183 04.3	63 50.1	29.8	45 12.1	25.9	289 21.3	07.9	255 41.0	10.7
17	198 06.7	78 49.3	29.3	60 13.0	25.4	304 23.9	07.9	270 43.7	10.7
18	213 09.2	93 48.6	N21 28.8	75 13.9	N17 24.9	319 26.5	S22 07.9	285 46.3	S22 10.7
19	228 11.7	108 47.8	28.2	90 14.7	24.5	334 29.1	07.9	300 49.0	10.8
20	243 14.1	123 47.0	27.7	105 15.6	24.0	349 31.7	07.8	315 51.6	10.8
21	258 16.6	138 46.2 ..	27.2	120 16.5 ..	23.5	4 34.3 ..	07.8	330 54.3 ..	10.8
22	273 19.1	153 45.4	26.7	135 17.4	23.0	19 36.9	07.8	345 56.9	10.8
23	288 21.5	168 44.6	26.2	150 18.2	22.6	34 39.5	07.8	0 59.6	10.9
26 00	303 24.0	183 43.8	N21 25.6	165 19.1	N17 22.1	49 42.1	S22 07.8	16 02.2	S22 10.9
01	318 26.5	198 43.0	25.1	180 20.0	21.6	64 44.7	07.8	31 04.9	10.9
02	333 28.9	213 42.2	24.6	195 20.9	21.2	79 47.3	07.8	46 07.5	10.9
03	348 31.4	228 41.4 ..	24.1	210 21.8 ..	20.7	94 49.9 ..	07.8	61 10.2 ..	10.9
04	3 33.8	243 40.6	23.5	225 22.6	20.2	109 52.5	07.8	76 12.8	11.0
05	18 36.3	258 39.8	23.0	240 23.5	19.7	124 55.1	07.8	91 15.5	11.0
06	33 38.8	273 39.0	N21 22.5	255 24.4	N17 19.3	139 57.7	S22 07.8	106 18.1	S22 11.0
07	48 41.2	288 38.2	21.9	270 25.3	18.8	155 00.3	07.8	121 20.8	11.0
08	63 43.7	303 37.5	21.4	285 26.2	18.3	170 02.9	07.8	136 23.4	11.1
F 09	78 46.2	318 36.7 ..	20.9	300 27.0 ..	17.8	185 05.5 ..	07.8	151 26.1 ..	11.1
R 10	93 48.6	333 35.9	20.3	315 27.9	17.4	200 08.1	07.8	166 28.7	11.1
I 11	108 51.1	348 35.1	19.8	330 28.8	16.9	215 10.7	07.8	181 31.4	11.1
D 12	123 53.6	3 34.3	N21 19.3	345 29.7	N17 16.4	230 13.3	S22 07.7	196 34.0	S22 11.2
A 13	138 56.0	18 33.5	18.7	0 30.5	15.9	245 15.9	07.7	211 36.6	11.2
Y 14	153 58.5	33 32.7	18.2	15 31.4	15.5	260 18.5	07.7	226 39.3	11.2
15	169 01.0	48 31.9 ..	17.6	30 32.3 ..	15.0	275 21.1 ..	07.7	241 41.9 ..	11.2
16	184 03.4	63 31.1	17.1	45 33.2	14.5	290 23.7	07.7	256 44.6	11.3
17	199 05.9	78 30.4	16.6	60 34.1	14.0	305 26.3	07.7	271 47.2	11.3
18	214 08.3	93 29.6	N21 16.0	75 34.9	N17 13.6	320 28.9	S22 07.7	286 49.9	S22 11.3
19	229 10.8	108 28.8	15.5	90 35.8	13.1	335 31.5	07.7	301 52.5	11.3
20	244 13.3	123 28.0	14.9	105 36.7	12.6	350 34.1	07.7	316 55.2	11.4
21	259 15.7	138 27.2 ..	14.4	120 37.6 ..	12.1	5 36.7 ..	07.7	331 57.8 ..	11.4
22	274 18.2	153 26.4	13.8	135 38.5	11.7	20 39.3	07.7	347 00.5	11.4
23	289 20.7	168 25.6	13.3	150 39.3	11.2	35 41.8	07.7	2 03.1	11.4
Mer. Pass.	h m 3 49.7	v −0.8	d 0.5	v 0.9	d 0.5	v 2.6	d 0.0	v 2.6	d 0.0

STARS

Name	SHA	Dec
Acamar	315 15.3	S40 13.5
Achernar	335 23.6	S57 08.1
Acrux	173 04.9	S63 12.6
Adhara	255 09.6	S28 59.9
Aldebaran	290 44.8	N16 32.7
Alioth	166 17.2	N55 51.6
Alkaid	152 55.6	N49 13.4
Alnair	27 38.1	S46 51.8
Alnilam	275 42.4	S 1 11.4
Alphard	217 52.3	S 8 44.5
Alphecca	126 07.3	N26 39.3
Alpheratz	357 39.0	N29 11.7
Altair	62 03.8	N 8 55.3
Ankaa	353 11.4	S42 11.8
Antares	112 20.9	S26 28.4
Arcturus	145 51.9	N19 05.2
Atria	107 18.6	S69 03.8
Avior	234 17.0	S59 34.3
Bellatrix	278 27.8	N 6 21.9
Betelgeuse	270 57.1	N 7 24.6
Canopus	263 54.8	S52 42.3
Capella	280 28.6	N46 00.8
Deneb	49 28.2	N45 21.0
Denebola	182 29.6	N14 28.0
Diphda	348 51.6	S17 52.7
Dubhe	193 47.1	N61 39.0
Elnath	278 07.6	N28 37.2
Eltanin	90 43.7	N51 29.5
Enif	33 42.7	N 9 57.9
Fomalhaut	15 19.1	S29 31.0
Gacrux	171 56.5	S57 13.5
Gienah	175 48.2	S17 38.9
Hadar	148 41.9	S60 28.1
Hamal	327 56.0	N23 33.1
Kaus Aust.	83 37.9	S34 22.4
Kochab	137 19.8	N74 05.0
Markab	13 33.9	N15 18.6
Menkar	314 10.8	N 4 09.9
Menkent	148 02.6	S36 27.9
Miaplacidus	221 39.8	S69 47.9
Mirfak	308 34.5	N49 55.5
Nunki	75 52.8	S26 16.2
Peacock	53 12.1	S56 40.2
Pollux	243 23.0	N27 58.7
Procyon	244 55.7	N 5 10.5
Rasalhague	96 02.3	N12 33.0
Regulus	207 39.4	N11 52.4
Rigel	281 08.3	S 8 10.8
Rigil Kent.	139 46.0	S60 55.0
Sabik	102 07.5	S15 44.8
Schedar	349 35.6	N56 38.3
Shaula	96 15.9	S37 07.0
Sirius	258 30.4	S16 44.6
Spica	158 26.9	S11 15.7
Suhail	222 49.8	S43 30.7
Vega	80 35.7	N38 48.3
Zuben'ubi	137 00.7	S16 07.2

	SHA	Mer. Pass.
Venus	241 38.1	h m 11 44
Mars	222 33.2	12 59
Jupiter	106 14.8	20 42
Saturn	72 33.8	22 56

© British Crown Copyright 2018. All rights reserved.

UT	SUN GHA	SUN Dec	MOON GHA	v	Dec	d	HP
d h	° ′	° ′	° ′	′	° ′	′	′
24 00	178 22.4	N19 58.0	281 56.0	15.5	N 2 32.8	11.4	54.7
01	193 22.3	57.5	296 30.5	15.5	2 44.2	11.4	54.8
02	208 22.3	57.0	311 05.0	15.5	2 55.6	11.5	54.8
03	223 22.3 ..	56.5	325 39.5	15.4	3 07.1	11.4	54.8
04	238 22.3	55.9	340 13.9	15.4	3 18.5	11.4	54.8
05	253 22.3	55.4	354 48.3	15.4	3 29.9	11.3	54.8
06	268 22.3	N19 54.9	9 22.7	15.3	N 3 41.2	11.4	54.9
W 07	283 22.3	54.4	23 57.0	15.3	3 52.6	11.4	54.9
E 08	298 22.3	53.8	38 31.3	15.3	4 04.0	11.4	54.9
D 09	313 22.2 ..	53.3	53 05.6	15.3	4 15.4	11.3	54.9
N 10	328 22.2	52.8	67 39.9	15.2	4 26.7	11.4	54.9
E 11	343 22.2	52.3	82 14.1	15.1	4 38.1	11.3	55.0
S 12	358 22.2	N19 51.8	96 48.2	15.1	N 4 49.4	11.4	55.0
D 13	13 22.2	51.2	111 22.3	15.1	5 00.8	11.3	55.0
A 14	28 22.2	50.7	125 56.4	15.1	5 12.1	11.3	55.0
Y 15	43 22.2 ..	50.2	140 30.5	15.0	5 23.4	11.3	55.1
16	58 22.2	49.7	155 04.5	14.9	5 34.7	11.3	55.1
17	73 22.1	49.1	169 38.4	15.0	5 46.0	11.2	55.1
18	88 22.1	N19 48.6	184 12.4	14.8	N 5 57.2	11.3	55.1
19	103 22.1	48.1	198 46.2	14.9	6 08.5	11.2	55.2
20	118 22.1	47.5	213 20.1	14.8	6 19.7	11.2	55.2
21	133 22.1 ...	47.0	227 53.9	14.7	6 30.9	11.3	55.2
22	148 22.1	46.5	242 27.6	14.7	6 42.2	11.1	55.2
23	163 22.1	45.9	257 01.3	14.6	6 53.3	11.2	55.3
25 00	178 22.1	N19 45.4	271 34.9	14.6	N 7 04.5	11.2	55.3
01	193 22.1	44.9	286 08.5	14.5	7 15.7	11.1	55.3
02	208 22.1	44.4	300 42.0	14.5	7 26.8	11.1	55.3
03	223 22.1 ..	43.8	315 15.5	14.5	7 37.9	11.1	55.4
04	238 22.0	43.3	329 49.0	14.4	7 49.0	11.0	55.4
05	253 22.0	42.8	344 22.4	14.3	8 00.0	11.1	55.4
06	268 22.0	N19 42.2	358 55.7	14.2	N 8 11.1	11.0	55.5
T 07	283 22.0	41.7	13 28.9	14.3	8 22.1	11.0	55.5
H 08	298 22.0	41.1	28 02.2	14.1	8 33.1	11.0	55.5
U 09	313 22.0 ..	40.6	42 35.3	14.1	8 44.1	10.9	55.5
R 10	328 22.0	40.1	57 08.4	14.1	8 55.0	10.9	55.5
S 11	343 22.0	39.5	71 41.5	13.9	9 05.9	10.9	55.6
D 12	358 22.0	N19 39.0	86 14.4	13.9	N 9 16.8	10.9	55.6
A 13	13 22.0	38.5	100 47.3	13.9	9 27.7	10.8	55.6
Y 14	28 22.0	37.9	115 20.2	13.8	9 38.5	10.8	55.7
15	43 22.0 ..	37.4	129 53.0	13.7	9 49.3	10.8	55.7
16	58 22.0	36.8	144 25.7	13.7	10 00.1	10.7	55.7
17	73 22.0	36.3	158 58.4	13.6	10 10.8	10.7	55.8
18	88 22.0	N19 35.8	173 31.0	13.5	N10 21.5	10.6	55.8
19	103 22.0	35.2	188 03.5	13.4	10 32.1	10.7	55.8
20	118 21.9	34.7	202 35.9	13.4	10 42.8	10.6	55.8
21	133 21.9 ..	34.1	217 08.3	13.4	10 53.4	10.5	55.9
22	148 21.9	33.6	231 40.7	13.2	11 03.9	10.5	55.9
23	163 21.9	33.0	246 12.9	13.2	11 14.4	10.5	55.9
26 00	178 21.9	N19 32.5	260 45.1	13.1	N11 24.9	10.5	56.0
01	193 21.9	31.9	275 17.2	13.0	11 35.4	10.4	56.0
02	208 21.9	31.4	289 49.2	13.0	11 45.8	10.3	56.0
03	223 21.9 ..	30.9	304 21.2	12.9	11 56.1	10.3	56.1
04	238 21.9	30.3	318 53.1	12.8	12 06.4	10.3	56.1
05	253 21.9	29.8	333 24.9	12.7	12 16.7	10.2	56.1
06	268 21.9	N19 29.2	347 56.6	12.7	N12 26.9	10.2	56.2
07	283 21.9	28.7	2 28.3	12.5	12 37.1	10.2	56.2
08	298 21.9	28.1	16 59.8	12.5	12 47.3	10.0	56.2
F 09	313 21.9 ..	27.6	31 31.3	12.4	12 57.3	10.1	56.3
R 10	328 21.9	27.0	46 02.7	12.4	13 07.4	10.0	56.3
I 11	343 21.9	26.5	60 34.1	12.2	13 17.4	9.9	56.3
D 12	358 21.9	N19 25.9	75 05.3	12.2	N13 27.3	9.9	56.4
A 13	13 21.9	25.4	89 36.5	12.1	13 37.2	9.8	56.4
Y 14	28 21.9	24.8	104 07.6	12.0	13 47.0	9.8	56.4
15	43 21.9 ..	24.3	118 38.6	11.9	13 56.8	9.7	56.5
16	58 21.9	23.7	133 09.5	11.8	14 06.5	9.7	56.5
17	73 21.9	23.1	147 40.3	11.8	14 16.2	9.6	56.5
18	88 21.9	N19 22.6	162 11.1	11.6	N14 25.8	9.6	56.6
19	103 21.9	22.0	176 41.7	11.6	14 35.4	9.4	56.6
20	118 21.9	21.5	191 12.3	11.5	14 44.8	9.5	56.6
21	133 21.9 ..	20.9	205 42.8	11.4	14 54.3	9.3	56.7
22	148 21.9	20.4	220 13.2	11.3	15 03.6	9.4	56.7
23	163 21.9	19.8	234 43.5	11.2	N15 13.0	9.2	56.8
	SD 15.8	d 0.5	SD 15.0		15.2		15.4

Twilight / Sunrise / Moonrise

Lat.	Twilight Naut.	Twilight Civil	Sunrise	Moonrise 24	25	26	27
°	h m	h m	h m	h m	h m	h m	h m
N 72	[]	[]	[]	22 26	22 07	21 39	[]
N 70	[]	[]	[]	22 36	22 25	22 10	21 47
68	////	////	01 33	22 44	22 39	22 34	22 28
66	////	////	02 16	22 50	22 50	22 52	22 57
64	////	00 40	02 45	22 56	23 00	23 07	23 18
62	////	01 44	03 06	23 00	23 08	23 19	23 36
60	////	02 16	03 24	23 04	23 16	23 30	23 50
N 58	00 36	02 40	03 38	23 08	23 22	23 39	24 03
56	01 35	02 59	03 51	23 12	23 28	23 48	24 14
54	02 05	03 14	04 01	23 15	23 33	23 55	24 23
52	02 27	03 28	04 11	23 17	23 38	24 02	00 02
50	02 45	03 39	04 19	23 20	23 42	24 08	00 08
45	03 18	04 02	04 37	23 25	23 51	24 20	00 20
N 40	03 42	04 21	04 52	23 30	23 59	24 31	00 31
35	04 01	04 36	05 04	23 34	24 05	00 05	00 40
30	04 16	04 48	05 15	23 37	24 11	00 11	00 48
20	04 41	05 09	05 33	23 43	24 21	00 21	01 02
N 10	05 00	05 26	05 48	23 49	24 30	00 30	01 15
0	05 15	05 41	06 03	23 54	24 39	00 39	01 26
S 10	05 29	05 55	06 17	23 59	24 47	00 47	01 38
20	05 43	06 09	06 33	24 05	00 05	00 56	01 51
30	05 55	06 25	06 50	24 11	00 11	01 07	02 05
35	06 02	06 33	07 00	24 15	00 15	01 13	02 14
40	06 09	06 42	07 12	24 19	00 19	01 20	02 23
45	06 17	06 53	07 25	24 24	00 24	01 28	02 35
S 50	06 26	07 05	07 41	24 30	00 30	01 38	02 48
52	06 29	07 11	07 49	24 32	00 32	01 43	02 55
54	06 33	07 17	07 58	24 35	00 35	01 48	03 02
56	06 38	07 24	08 07	24 39	00 39	01 53	03 10
58	06 42	07 32	08 18	24 42	00 42	01 59	03 19
S 60	06 48	07 40	08 31	24 47	00 47	02 07	03 30

Sunset / Twilight / Moonset

Lat.	Sunset	Twilight Civil	Twilight Naut.	Moonset 24	25	26	27
°	h m	h m	h m	h m	h m	h m	h m
N 72	[]	[]	[]	12 34	14 25	16 30	[]
N 70	[]	[]	[]	12 27	14 09	16 00	18 08
68	22 34	////	////	12 21	13 57	15 38	17 28
66	21 53	////	////	12 16	13 46	15 21	17 01
64	21 26	23 22	////	12 12	13 38	15 07	16 40
62	21 05	22 25	////	12 09	13 31	14 55	16 23
60	20 48	21 54	////	12 06	13 24	14 45	16 09
N 58	20 33	21 31	23 26	12 03	13 19	14 37	15 57
56	20 21	21 13	22 35	12 01	13 14	14 29	15 47
54	20 11	20 57	22 06	11 59	13 10	14 23	15 38
52	20 01	20 44	21 44	11 57	13 06	14 17	15 30
50	19 53	20 33	21 27	11 55	13 02	14 11	15 22
45	19 35	20 10	20 54	11 51	12 54	14 00	15 07
N 40	19 21	19 52	20 30	11 48	12 48	13 50	14 54
35	19 09	19 37	20 11	11 45	12 42	13 42	14 43
30	18 58	19 24	19 56	11 43	12 38	13 35	14 34
20	18 40	19 04	19 32	11 39	12 29	13 22	14 18
N 10	18 25	18 47	19 13	11 35	12 22	13 11	14 04
0	18 10	18 32	18 58	11 32	12 15	13 01	13 51
S 10	17 56	18 18	18 44	11 28	12 08	12 51	13 38
20	17 41	18 04	18 31	11 24	12 01	12 40	13 24
30	17 23	17 49	18 18	11 20	11 53	12 28	13 08
35	17 13	17 40	18 11	11 18	11 48	12 21	12 58
40	17 02	17 31	18 04	11 15	11 43	12 13	12 48
45	16 48	17 21	17 56	11 12	11 36	12 04	12 36
S 50	16 32	17 08	17 48	11 08	11 29	11 52	12 21
52	16 24	17 03	17 44	11 07	11 26	11 47	12 14
54	16 16	16 56	17 40	11 05	11 22	11 42	12 06
56	16 06	16 50	17 36	11 03	11 18	11 35	11 58
58	15 55	16 42	17 31	11 00	11 13	11 28	11 48
S 60	15 43	16 33	17 26	10 58	11 08	11 20	11 37

SUN / MOON

Day	Eqn. of Time 00h	Eqn. of Time 12h	Mer. Pass.	Mer. Pass. Upper	Mer. Pass. Lower	Age	Phase
d	m s	m s	h m	h m	h m	d	%
24	06 31	06 31	12 07	05 21	17 43	22	56
25	06 32	06 32	12 07	06 04	18 27	23	46
26	06 32	06 32	12 07	06 50	19 14	24	36

© British Crown Copyright 2018. All rights reserved.

2019 JULY 27, 28, 29 (SAT., SUN., MON.)

UT	ARIES GHA	VENUS −3·9 GHA	Dec	MARS +1·8 GHA	Dec	JUPITER −2·4 GHA	Dec	SATURN +0·1 GHA	Dec	STARS Name	SHA	Dec
27 00	304 23.1	183 24.9	N21 12.7	165 40.2	N17 10.7	50 44.4	S22 07.7	17 05.8	S22 11.5	Acamar	315 15.2	S40 13.5
01	319 25.6	198 24.1	12.2	180 41.1	10.2	65 47.0	07.7	32 08.4	11.5	Achernar	335 23.5	S57 08.1
02	334 28.1	213 23.3	11.6	195 42.0	09.8	80 49.6	07.7	47 11.1	11.5	Acrux	173 04.9	S63 12.6
03	349 30.5	228 22.5 ..	11.1	210 42.9 ..	09.3	95 52.2 ..	07.7	62 13.7 ..	11.5	Adhara	255 09.6	S28 59.9
04	4 33.0	243 21.7	10.5	225 43.8	08.8	110 54.8	07.7	77 16.4	11.6	Aldebaran	290 44.8	N16 32.7
05	19 35.5	258 20.9	10.0	240 44.6	08.3	125 57.4	07.7	92 19.0	11.6			
06	34 37.9	273 20.2	N21 09.4	255 45.5	N17 07.8	141 00.0	S22 07.7	107 21.6	S22 11.6	Alioth	166 17.2	N55 51.6
07	49 40.4	288 19.4	08.9	270 46.4	07.4	156 02.6	07.6	122 24.3	11.6	Alkaid	152 55.6	N49 13.4
S 08	64 42.8	303 18.6	08.3	285 47.3	06.9	171 05.2	07.6	137 26.9	11.7	Alnair	27 38.1	S46 51.8
A 09	79 45.3	318 17.8 ..	07.7	300 48.2 ..	06.4	186 07.8 ..	07.6	152 29.6 ..	11.7	Alnilam	275 42.4	S 1 11.4
T 10	94 47.8	333 17.0	07.2	315 49.0	05.9	201 10.4	07.6	167 32.2	11.7	Alphard	217 52.3	S 8 44.5
U 11	109 50.2	348 16.3	06.6	330 49.9	05.4	216 12.9	07.6	182 34.9	11.7			
R 12	124 52.7	3 15.5	N21 06.1	345 50.8	N17 05.0	231 15.5	S22 07.6	197 37.5	S22 11.7	Alphecca	126 07.3	N26 39.3
D 13	139 55.2	18 14.7	05.5	0 51.7	04.5	246 18.1	07.6	212 40.2	11.8	Alpheratz	357 39.0	N29 11.7
A 14	154 57.6	33 13.9	04.9	15 52.6	04.0	261 20.7	07.6	227 42.8	11.8	Altair	62 03.8	N 8 55.4
Y 15	170 00.1	48 13.1 ..	04.4	30 53.5 ..	03.5	276 23.3 ..	07.6	242 45.5 ..	11.8	Ankaa	353 11.4	S42 11.8
16	185 02.6	63 12.4	03.8	45 54.3	03.0	291 25.9	07.6	257 48.1	11.8	Antares	112 20.9	S26 28.4
17	200 05.0	78 11.6	03.2	60 55.2	02.6	306 28.5	07.6	272 50.8	11.9			
18	215 07.5	93 10.8	N21 02.7	75 56.1	N17 02.1	321 31.1	S22 07.6	287 53.4	S22 11.9	Arcturus	145 51.9	N19 05.2
19	230 09.9	108 10.0	02.1	90 57.0	01.6	336 33.6	07.6	302 56.0	11.9	Atria	107 18.6	S69 03.8
20	245 12.4	123 09.2	01.5	105 57.9	01.1	351 36.2	07.6	317 58.7	11.9	Avior	234 17.0	S59 34.3
21	260 14.9	138 08.5 ..	00.9	120 58.8 ..	00.6	6 38.8 ..	07.6	333 01.3 ..	12.0	Bellatrix	278 27.8	N 6 21.9
22	275 17.3	153 07.7	21 00.4	135 59.6	17 00.2	21 41.4	07.6	348 04.0	12.0	Betelgeuse	270 57.0	N 7 24.6
23	290 19.8	168 06.9	20 59.8	151 00.5	16 59.7	36 44.0	07.6	3 06.6	12.0			
28 00	305 22.3	183 06.1	N20 59.2	166 01.4	N16 59.2	51 46.6	S22 07.6	18 09.3	S22 12.0	Canopus	263 54.8	S52 42.3
01	320 24.7	198 05.4	58.6	181 02.3	58.7	66 49.2	07.6	33 11.9	12.1	Capella	280 28.6	N46 00.8
02	335 27.2	213 04.6	58.0	196 03.2	58.2	81 51.7	07.6	48 14.6	12.1	Deneb	49 28.2	N45 21.1
03	350 29.7	228 03.8 ..	57.5	211 04.1 ..	57.8	96 54.3 ..	07.5	63 17.2 ..	12.1	Denebola	182 29.6	N14 28.0
04	5 32.1	243 03.0	56.9	226 04.9	57.3	111 56.9	07.5	78 19.8	12.1	Diphda	348 51.6	S17 52.7
05	20 34.6	258 02.3	56.3	241 05.8	56.8	126 59.5	07.5	93 22.5	12.2			
06	35 37.1	273 01.5	N20 55.7	256 06.7	N16 56.3	142 02.1	S22 07.5	108 25.1	S22 12.2	Dubhe	193 47.1	N61 39.0
07	50 39.5	288 00.7	55.2	271 07.6	55.8	157 04.7	07.5	123 27.8	12.2	Elnath	278 07.6	N28 37.2
08	65 42.0	303 00.0	54.6	286 08.5	55.3	172 07.2	07.5	138 30.4	12.2	Eltanin	90 43.8	N51 29.5
S 09	80 44.4	317 59.2 ..	54.0	301 09.4 ..	54.9	187 09.8 ..	07.5	153 33.1 ..	12.2	Enif	33 42.7	N 9 57.9
U 10	95 46.9	332 58.4	53.4	316 10.3	54.4	202 12.4	07.5	168 35.7	12.3	Fomalhaut	15 19.1	S29 31.0
N 11	110 49.4	347 57.6	52.8	331 11.1	53.9	217 15.0	07.5	183 38.4	12.3			
D 12	125 51.8	2 56.9	N20 52.2	346 12.0	N16 53.4	232 17.6	S22 07.5	198 41.0	S22 12.3	Gacrux	171 56.5	S57 13.5
A 13	140 54.3	17 56.1	51.6	1 12.9	52.9	247 20.1	07.5	213 43.6	12.3	Gienah	175 48.2	S17 38.9
Y 14	155 56.8	32 55.3	51.1	16 13.8	52.4	262 22.7	07.5	228 46.3	12.4	Hadar	148 42.0	S60 28.1
15	170 59.2	47 54.6 ..	50.5	31 14.7 ..	51.9	277 25.3 ..	07.5	243 48.9 ..	12.4	Hamal	327 56.0	N23 33.1
16	186 01.7	62 53.8	49.9	46 15.6	51.5	292 27.9	07.5	258 51.6	12.4	Kaus Aust.	83 37.9	S34 22.4
17	201 04.2	77 53.0	49.3	61 16.5	51.0	307 30.5	07.5	273 54.2	12.4			
18	216 06.6	92 52.3	N20 48.7	76 17.3	N16 50.5	322 33.0	S22 07.5	288 56.9	S22 12.5	Kochab	137 19.9	N74 05.0
19	231 09.1	107 51.5	48.1	91 18.2	50.0	337 35.6	07.5	303 59.5	12.5	Markab	13 33.9	N15 18.6
20	246 11.6	122 50.7	47.5	106 19.1	49.5	352 38.2	07.5	319 02.2	12.5	Menkar	314 10.7	N 4 09.9
21	261 14.0	137 49.9 ..	46.9	121 20.0 ..	49.0	7 40.8 ..	07.5	334 04.8 ..	12.5	Menkent	148 02.6	S36 27.9
22	276 16.5	152 49.2	46.3	136 20.9	48.6	22 43.4	07.5	349 07.4	12.6	Miaplacidus	221 39.8	S69 47.9
23	291 18.9	167 48.4	45.7	151 21.8	48.1	37 45.9	07.5	4 10.1	12.6			
29 00	306 21.4	182 47.7	N20 45.1	166 22.7	N16 47.6	52 48.5	S22 07.5	19 12.7	S22 12.6	Mirfak	308 34.5	N49 55.5
01	321 23.9	197 46.9	44.5	181 23.6	47.1	67 51.1	07.5	34 15.4	12.6	Nunki	75 52.8	S26 16.2
02	336 26.3	212 46.1	43.9	196 24.4	46.6	82 53.7	07.5	49 18.0	12.7	Peacock	53 12.1	S56 40.2
03	351 28.8	227 45.4 ..	43.3	211 25.3 ..	46.1	97 56.2 ..	07.4	64 20.7 ..	12.7	Pollux	243 23.0	N27 58.7
04	6 31.3	242 44.6	42.7	226 26.2	45.6	112 58.8	07.4	79 23.3	12.7	Procyon	244 55.7	N 5 10.5
05	21 33.7	257 43.8	42.1	241 27.1	45.1	128 01.4	07.4	94 25.9	12.7			
06	36 36.2	272 43.1	N20 41.5	256 28.0	N16 44.7	143 04.0	S22 07.4	109 28.6	S22 12.7	Rasalhague	96 02.3	N12 33.0
07	51 38.7	287 42.3	40.9	271 28.9	44.2	158 06.5	07.4	124 31.2	12.8	Regulus	207 39.4	N11 52.4
08	66 41.1	302 41.5	40.3	286 29.8	43.7	173 09.1	07.4	139 33.9	12.8	Rigel	281 08.3	S 8 10.8
M 09	81 43.6	317 40.8 ..	39.6	301 30.7 ..	43.2	188 11.7 ..	07.4	154 36.5 ..	12.8	Rigil Kent.	139 46.0	S60 55.0
O 10	96 46.1	332 40.0	39.0	316 31.5	42.7	203 14.3	07.4	169 39.2	12.8	Sabik	102 07.5	S15 44.8
N 11	111 48.5	347 39.3	38.4	331 32.4	42.2	218 16.8	07.4	184 41.8	12.9			
D 12	126 51.0	2 38.5	N20 37.8	346 33.3	N16 41.7	233 19.4	S22 07.4	199 44.4	S22 12.9	Schedar	349 35.5	N56 38.3
A 13	141 53.4	17 37.7	37.2	1 34.2	41.2	248 22.0	07.4	214 47.1	12.9	Shaula	96 15.9	S37 07.0
Y 14	156 55.9	32 37.0	36.6	16 35.1	40.7	263 24.6	07.4	229 49.7	12.9	Sirius	258 30.4	S16 44.6
15	171 58.4	47 36.2 ..	36.0	31 36.0 ..	40.3	278 27.1 ..	07.4	244 52.4 ..	13.0	Spica	158 26.9	S11 15.6
16	187 00.8	62 35.5	35.3	46 36.9	39.8	293 29.7	07.4	259 55.0	13.0	Suhail	222 49.8	S43 30.7
17	202 03.3	77 34.7	34.7	61 37.8	39.3	308 32.3	07.4	274 57.7	13.0			
18	217 05.8	92 33.9	N20 34.1	76 38.7	N16 38.8	323 34.8	S22 07.4	290 00.3	S22 13.0	Vega	80 35.7	N38 48.3
19	232 08.2	107 33.2	33.5	91 39.5	38.3	338 37.4	07.4	305 02.9	13.1	Zuben'ubi	137 00.7	S16 07.2
20	247 10.7	122 32.4	32.9	106 40.4	37.8	353 40.0	07.4	320 05.6	13.1		SHA	Mer.Pass.
21	262 13.2	137 31.7 ..	32.2	121 41.3 ..	37.3	8 42.6 ..	07.4	335 08.2 ..	13.1		° ′	h m
22	277 15.6	152 30.9	31.6	136 42.2	36.8	23 45.1	07.4	350 10.9	13.1	Venus	237 43.9	11 48
23	292 18.1	167 30.1	31.0	151 43.1	36.3	38 47.7	07.4	5 13.5	13.1	Mars	220 39.1	12 55
	h m									Jupiter	106 24.3	20 29
Mer. Pass.	3 37.9	v −0.8	d 0.6	v 0.9	d 0.5	v 2.6	d 0.0	v 2.6	d 0.0	Saturn	72 47.0	22 43

© British Crown Copyright 2018. All rights reserved.

UT	SUN		MOON					Lat.	Twilight		Sunrise	Moonrise			
	GHA	Dec	GHA	v	Dec	d	HP		Naut.	Civil		27	28	29	30
d h	° ′	° ′	° ′	′	° ′	′	′	°	h m	h m	h m	h m	h m	h m	h m
27 00	178 21.9	N19 19.2	249 13.7	11.2	N15 22.2	9.2	56.8	N 70	////	////	00 27	21 47	▭	▭	▭
01	193 21.9	18.7	263 43.9	11.0	15 31.4	9.1	56.8	68	////	////	01 51	22 28	22 21	▭	23 21
02	208 21.9	18.1	278 13.9	10.9	15 40.5	9.0	56.9	66	////	////	02 28	22 57	23 08	23 38	24 46
03	223 21.9 ..	17.6	292 43.8	10.9	15 49.5	9.0	56.9	64	////	01 10	02 54	23 18	23 39	24 17	00 17
04	238 21.9	17.0	307 13.7	10.7	15 58.5	8.9	56.9	62	////	01 57	03 14	23 36	24 02	00 02	00 44
05	253 22.0	16.4	321 43.4	10.7	16 07.4	8.8	57.0	60	////	02 26	03 31	23 50	24 20	00 20	01 06
06	268 22.0	N19 15.9	336 13.1	10.6	N16 16.2	8.8	57.0	N 58	01 04	02 48	03 44	24 03	00 03	00 36	01 23
07	283 22.0	15.3	350 42.7	10.5	16 25.0	8.7	57.0	56	01 47	03 06	03 56	24 14	00 14	00 49	01 38
S 08	298 22.0	14.8	5 12.2	10.3	16 33.7	8.6	57.1	54	02 14	03 20	04 06	24 23	00 23	01 01	01 51
A 09	313 22.0 ..	14.2	19 41.5	10.3	16 42.3	8.5	57.1	52	02 34	03 33	04 15	00 02	00 32	01 11	02 02
T 10	328 22.0	13.6	34 10.8	10.2	16 50.8	8.5	57.2	50	02 51	03 44	04 23	00 08	00 39	01 20	02 12
U 11	343 22.0	13.1	48 40.0	10.1	16 59.3	8.4	57.2	45	03 22	04 06	04 40	00 20	00 56	01 39	02 33
R 12	358 22.0	N19 12.5	63 09.1	10.0	N17 07.7	8.3	57.2	N 40	03 46	04 24	04 54	00 31	01 09	01 55	02 50
D 13	13 22.0	11.9	77 38.1	9.9	17 16.0	8.2	57.3	35	04 04	04 38	05 06	00 40	01 21	02 08	03 04
A 14	28 22.0	11.4	92 07.0	9.8	17 24.2	8.1	57.3	30	04 19	04 50	05 16	00 48	01 31	02 20	03 16
Y 15	43 22.0 ..	10.8	106 35.8	9.7	17 32.3	8.1	57.3	20	04 42	05 10	05 34	01 02	01 48	02 40	03 38
16	58 22.0	10.2	121 04.5	9.6	17 40.4	7.9	57.4	N 10	05 00	05 27	05 49	01 15	02 04	02 58	03 56
17	73 22.0	09.7	135 33.1	9.6	17 48.3	7.9	57.4	0	05 16	05 41	06 03	01 26	02 18	03 14	04 13
18	88 22.0	N19 09.1	150 01.7	9.4	N17 56.2	7.8	57.5	S 10	05 29	05 55	06 17	01 38	02 33	03 30	04 31
19	103 22.0	08.5	164 30.1	9.3	18 04.0	7.7	57.5	20	05 42	06 08	06 32	01 51	02 48	03 48	04 49
20	118 22.0	08.0	178 58.4	9.2	18 11.7	7.6	57.5	30	05 54	06 23	06 48	02 05	03 06	04 09	05 11
21	133 22.1 ..	07.4	193 26.6	9.1	18 19.3	7.5	57.6	35	06 00	06 31	06 58	02 14	03 16	04 20	05 23
22	148 22.1	06.8	207 54.7	9.0	18 26.8	7.5	57.6	40	06 07	06 40	07 09	02 23	03 28	04 34	05 38
23	163 22.1	06.3	222 22.7	9.0	18 34.3	7.3	57.7	45	06 14	06 50	07 22	02 35	03 43	04 51	05 55
28 00	178 22.1	N19 05.7	236 50.7	8.8	N18 41.6	7.3	57.7	S 50	06 22	07 02	07 38	02 48	04 00	05 11	06 17
01	193 22.1	05.1	251 18.5	8.7	18 48.9	7.1	57.7	52	06 26	07 07	07 45	02 55	04 08	05 20	06 27
02	208 22.1	04.5	265 46.2	8.7	18 56.0	7.0	57.8	54	06 30	07 13	07 53	03 02	04 18	05 31	06 38
03	223 22.1 ..	04.0	280 13.9	8.5	19 03.0	7.0	57.8	56	06 34	07 20	08 02	03 10	04 28	05 44	06 51
04	238 22.1	03.4	294 41.4	8.4	19 10.0	6.8	57.8	58	06 38	07 27	08 13	03 19	04 40	05 58	07 06
05	253 22.1	02.8	309 08.8	8.3	19 16.8	6.8	57.9	S 60	06 43	07 35	08 24	03 30	04 54	06 15	07 24

UT	SUN		MOON					Lat.	Twilight		Moonset			
	GHA	Dec	GHA	v	Dec	d	HP		Sunset	Civil	Naut.	27	28	29	30
d h	° ′	° ′	° ′	′	° ′	′	′	°	h m	h m	h m	h m	h m	h m	h m
06	268 22.1	N19 02.2	323 36.1	8.3	N19 23.6	6.6	57.9								
07	283 22.1	01.7	338 03.4	8.1	19 30.2	6.6	58.0	N 72	▭	▭	▭	▭	▭	▭	▭
08	298 22.2	01.1	352 30.5	8.1	19 36.8	6.4	58.0	N 70	23 25	////	////	18 08	▭	▭	▭
S 09	313 22.2	19 00.5	6 57.6	7.9	19 43.2	6.3	58.0	68	22 17	////	////	17 28	19 29	▭	22 40
U 10	328 22.2	18 59.9	21 24.5	7.8	19 49.5	6.2	58.1	66	21 41	////	////	17 01	18 43	20 15	21 15
N 11	343 22.2	59.4	35 51.3	7.8	19 55.7	6.1	58.1	64	21 16	22 56	////	16 40	18 12	19 36	20 37
D 12	358 22.2	N18 58.8	50 18.1	7.6	N20 01.8	6.0	58.2	62	20 57	22 12	////	16 23	17 50	19 09	20 10
A 13	13 22.2	58.2	64 44.7	7.6	20 07.8	5.9	58.2	60	20 41	21 44	////	16 09	17 32	18 47	19 49
Y 14	28 22.2	57.6	79 11.3	7.5	20 13.7	5.8	58.2	N 58	20 27	21 23	23 03	15 57	17 16	18 30	19 32
15	43 22.2 ..	57.0	93 37.8	7.3	20 19.5	5.6	58.3	56	20 16	21 06	22 23	15 47	17 04	18 16	19 17
16	58 22.3	56.5	108 04.1	7.3	20 25.1	5.5	58.3	54	20 06	20 51	21 57	15 38	16 52	18 03	19 05
17	73 22.3	55.9	122 30.4	7.2	20 30.6	5.5	58.4	52	19 57	20 39	21 37	15 30	16 42	17 52	18 54
18	88 22.3	N18 55.3	136 56.6	7.1	N20 36.1	5.2	58.4	50	19 49	20 28	21 21	15 22	16 34	17 42	18 44
19	103 22.3	54.7	151 22.7	7.0	20 41.3	5.2	58.4	45	19 32	20 06	20 50	15 07	16 15	17 21	18 23
20	118 22.3	54.1	165 48.7	6.9	20 46.5	5.1	58.5	N 40	19 18	19 49	20 27	14 54	16 00	17 05	18 06
21	133 22.3 ..	53.5	180 14.6	6.8	20 51.6	4.9	58.5	35	19 06	19 35	20 09	14 43	15 47	16 50	17 52
22	148 22.3	53.0	194 40.4	6.7	20 56.5	4.8	58.5	30	18 56	19 22	19 54	14 34	15 36	16 38	17 39
23	163 22.4	52.4	209 06.1	6.6	21 01.3	4.7	58.6	20	18 39	19 03	19 31	14 18	15 16	16 17	17 18
29 00	178 22.4	N18 51.8	223 31.7	6.5	N21 06.0	4.6	58.6	N 10	18 24	18 46	19 12	14 04	15 00	15 59	17 00
01	193 22.4	51.2	237 57.2	6.5	21 10.6	4.4	58.7	0	18 10	18 32	18 57	13 51	14 44	15 42	16 43
02	208 22.4	50.6	252 22.7	6.4	21 15.0	4.3	58.7	S 10	17 56	18 18	18 44	13 38	14 29	15 25	16 25
03	223 22.4 ..	50.0	266 48.1	6.2	21 19.3	4.2	58.7	20	17 42	18 05	18 32	13 24	14 12	15 07	16 07
04	238 22.4	49.5	281 13.3	6.2	21 23.5	4.0	58.8	30	17 25	17 50	18 19	13 08	13 53	14 46	15 45
05	253 22.4	48.9	295 38.5	6.1	21 27.5	3.9	58.8	35	17 15	17 42	18 13	12 58	13 42	14 33	15 33
06	268 22.5	N18 48.3	310 03.6	6.0	N21 31.4	3.8	58.9	40	17 04	17 34	18 06	12 48	13 29	14 19	15 18
07	283 22.5	47.7	324 28.6	6.0	21 35.2	3.6	58.9	45	16 52	17 23	17 59	12 36	13 15	14 03	15 01
08	298 22.5	47.1	338 53.6	5.8	21 38.8	3.5	58.9	S 50	16 36	17 12	17 51	12 21	12 56	13 42	14 40
M 09	313 22.5 ..	46.5	353 18.4	5.8	21 42.3	3.4	59.0	52	16 29	17 06	17 48	12 14	12 48	13 32	14 30
O 10	328 22.5	45.9	7 43.2	5.7	21 45.7	3.2	59.0	54	16 21	17 01	17 44	12 06	12 38	13 21	14 19
N 11	343 22.6	45.3	22 07.9	5.6	21 48.9	3.1	59.0	56	16 11	16 54	17 40	11 58	12 27	13 09	14 05
D 12	358 22.6	N18 44.7	36 32.5	5.6	N21 52.0	2.9	59.1	58	16 01	16 47	17 36	11 48	12 15	12 54	13 50
A 13	13 22.6	44.1	50 57.1	5.5	21 54.9	2.8	59.1	S 60	15 49	16 39	17 31	11 37	12 01	12 37	13 32
Y 14	28 22.6	43.6	65 21.6	5.4	21 57.7	2.7	59.1								
15	43 22.6 ..	43.0	79 46.0	5.3	22 00.4	2.5	59.2				SUN			MOON	
16	58 22.6	42.4	94 10.3	5.2	22 02.9	2.4	59.2								
17	73 22.7	41.8	108 34.5	5.2	22 05.3	2.2	59.3								
18	88 22.7	N18 41.2	122 58.7	5.1	N22 07.5	2.1	59.3	Day	Eqn. of Time		Mer.	Mer. Pass.		Age	Phase
19	103 22.7	40.6	137 22.8	5.1	22 09.6	1.9	59.3		00ʰ	12ʰ	Pass.	Upper	Lower		
20	118 22.7	40.0	151 46.9	5.0	22 11.5	1.8	59.4	d	m s	m s	h m	h m	h m	d %	
21	133 22.7 ..	39.4	166 10.9	4.9	22 13.3	1.6	59.4	27	06 32	06 32	12 07	07 38	20 04	25 26	
22	148 22.8	38.8	180 34.8	4.8	22 14.9	1.5	59.4	28	06 32	06 31	12 07	08 31	20 59	26 17	
23	163 22.8	38.2	194 58.6	4.8	N22 16.4	1.3	59.5	29	06 31	06 30	12 06	09 28	21 58	27 10	
	SD 15.8	d 0.6	SD 15.6		15.8		16.1									

© British Crown Copyright 2018. All rights reserved.

UT	ARIES GHA	VENUS −3.9 GHA	Dec	MARS +1.8 GHA	Dec	JUPITER −2.4 GHA	Dec	SATURN +0.2 GHA	Dec	STARS Name	SHA	Dec
30 00	307 20.6	182 29.4	N20 30.4	166 44.0	N16 35.8	53 50.3	S22 07.4	20 16.1	S22 13.2	Acamar	315 15.2	S40 13.5
01	322 23.0	197 28.6	29.7	181 44.9	35.4	68 52.8	07.4	35 18.8	13.2	Achernar	335 23.5	S57 08.1
02	337 25.5	212 27.9	29.1	196 45.8	34.9	83 55.4	07.4	50 21.4	13.2	Acrux	173 04.9	S63 12.6
03	352 27.9	227 27.1 ..	28.5	211 46.7 ..	34.4	98 58.0 ..	07.4	65 24.1 ..	13.2	Adhara	255 09.6	S28 59.9
04	7 30.4	242 26.4	27.9	226 47.6	33.9	114 00.5	07.4	80 26.7	13.3	Aldebaran	290 44.7	N16 32.8
05	22 32.9	257 25.6	27.2	241 48.4	33.4	129 03.1	07.4	95 29.4	13.3			
06	37 35.3	272 24.9	N20 26.6	256 49.3	N16 32.9	144 05.7	S22 07.4	110 32.0	S22 13.3	Alioth	166 17.2	N55 51.6
07	52 37.8	287 24.1	26.0	271 50.2	32.4	159 08.2	07.4	125 34.6	13.3	Alkaid	152 55.7	N49 13.4
T 08	67 40.3	302 23.4	25.3	286 51.1	31.9	174 10.8	07.4	140 37.3	13.4	Alnair	27 38.0	S46 51.8
U 09	82 42.7	317 22.6 ..	24.7	301 52.0 ..	31.4	189 13.4 ..	07.4	155 39.9 ..	13.4	Alnilam	275 42.4	S 1 11.4
E 10	97 45.2	332 21.9	24.1	316 52.9	30.9	204 15.9	07.3	170 42.6	13.4	Alphard	217 52.3	S 8 44.5
S 11	112 47.7	347 21.1	23.4	331 53.8	30.4	219 18.5	07.3	185 45.2	13.4			
D 12	127 50.1	2 20.3	N20 22.8	346 54.7	N16 29.9	234 21.1	S22 07.3	200 47.8	S22 13.4	Alphecca	126 07.3	N26 39.3
A 13	142 52.6	17 19.6	22.1	1 55.6	29.4	249 23.6	07.3	215 50.5	13.5	Alpheratz	357 38.9	N29 11.7
Y 14	157 55.1	32 18.8	21.5	16 56.5	29.0	264 26.2	07.3	230 53.1	13.5	Altair	62 03.8	N 8 55.4
15	172 57.5	47 18.1 ..	20.9	31 57.4 ..	28.5	279 28.8 ..	07.3	245 55.8 ..	13.5	Ankaa	353 11.3	S42 11.8
16	188 00.0	62 17.3	20.2	46 58.3	28.0	294 31.3	07.3	260 58.4	13.5	Antares	112 20.9	S26 28.4
17	203 02.4	77 16.6	19.6	61 59.1	27.5	309 33.9	07.3	276 01.0	13.6			
18	218 04.9	92 15.9	N20 18.9	77 00.0	N16 27.0	324 36.5	S22 07.3	291 03.7	S22 13.6	Arcturus	145 51.9	N19 05.2
19	233 07.4	107 15.1	18.3	92 00.9	26.5	339 39.0	07.3	306 06.3	13.6	Atria	107 18.6	S69 03.8
20	248 09.8	122 14.4	17.6	107 01.8	26.0	354 41.6	07.3	321 09.0	13.6	Avior	234 17.0	S59 34.3
21	263 12.3	137 13.6 ..	17.0	122 02.7 ..	25.5	9 44.1 ..	07.3	336 11.6 ..	13.7	Bellatrix	278 27.7	N 6 22.0
22	278 14.8	152 12.9	16.4	137 03.6	25.0	24 46.7	07.3	351 14.2	13.7	Betelgeuse	270 57.0	N 7 24.6
23	293 17.2	167 12.1	15.7	152 04.5	24.5	39 49.3	07.3	6 16.9	13.7			
31 00	308 19.7	182 11.4	N20 15.1	167 05.4	N16 24.0	54 51.8	S22 07.3	21 19.5	S22 13.7	Canopus	263 54.8	S52 42.3
01	323 22.2	197 10.6	14.4	182 06.3	23.5	69 54.4	07.3	36 22.2	13.8	Capella	280 28.6	N46 00.8
02	338 24.6	212 09.9	13.8	197 07.2	23.0	84 56.9	07.3	51 24.8	13.8	Deneb	49 28.2	N45 21.1
03	353 27.1	227 09.1 ..	13.1	212 08.1 ..	22.5	99 59.5 ..	07.3	66 27.4 ..	13.8	Denebola	182 29.6	N14 28.0
04	8 29.5	242 08.4	12.4	227 09.0	22.0	115 02.1	07.3	81 30.1	13.8	Diphda	348 51.5	S17 52.7
05	23 32.0	257 07.6	11.8	242 09.9	21.5	130 04.6	07.3	96 32.7	13.8			
06	38 34.5	272 06.9	N20 11.1	257 10.8	N16 21.0	145 07.2	S22 07.3	111 35.3	S22 13.9	Dubhe	193 47.1	N61 39.0
W 07	53 36.9	287 06.2	10.5	272 11.7	20.5	160 09.7	07.3	126 38.0	13.9	Elnath	278 07.6	N28 37.2
E 08	68 39.4	302 05.4	09.8	287 12.5	20.0	175 12.3	07.3	141 40.6	13.9	Eltanin	90 43.8	N51 29.5
D 09	83 41.9	317 04.7 ..	09.2	302 13.4 ..	19.5	190 14.9 ..	07.3	156 43.3 ..	13.9	Enif	33 42.7	N 9 57.9
N 10	98 44.3	332 03.9	08.5	317 14.3	19.0	205 17.4	07.3	171 45.9	14.0	Fomalhaut	15 19.1	S29 31.0
E 11	113 46.8	347 03.2	07.8	332 15.2	18.5	220 20.0	07.3	186 48.5	14.0			
S 12	128 49.3	2 02.4	N20 07.2	347 16.1	N16 18.1	235 22.5	S22 07.3	201 51.2	S22 14.0	Gacrux	171 56.5	S57 13.4
D 13	143 51.7	17 01.7	06.5	2 17.0	17.6	250 25.1	07.3	216 53.8	14.0	Gienah	175 48.2	S17 38.9
A 14	158 54.2	32 01.0	05.9	17 17.9	17.1	265 27.6	07.3	231 56.5	14.0	Hadar	148 42.0	S60 28.1
Y 15	173 56.7	47 00.2 ..	05.2	32 18.8 ..	16.6	280 30.2 ..	07.3	246 59.1 ..	14.1	Hamal	327 56.0	N23 33.1
16	188 59.1	61 59.5	04.5	47 19.7	16.1	295 32.8	07.3	262 01.7	14.1	Kaus Aust.	83 37.9	S34 22.4
17	204 01.6	76 58.7	03.9	62 20.6	15.6	310 35.3	07.3	277 04.4	14.1			
18	219 04.0	91 58.0	N20 03.2	77 21.5	N16 15.1	325 37.9	S22 07.3	292 07.0	S22 14.1	Kochab	137 20.0	N74 05.0
19	234 06.5	106 57.3	02.5	92 22.4	14.6	340 40.4	07.3	307 09.6	14.2	Markab	13 33.9	N15 18.6
20	249 09.0	121 56.5	01.8	107 23.3	14.1	355 43.0	07.3	322 12.3	14.2	Menkar	314 10.7	N 4 09.9
21	264 11.4	136 55.8 ..	01.2	122 24.2 ..	13.6	10 45.5 ..	07.3	337 14.9 ..	14.2	Menkent	148 02.7	S36 27.9
22	279 13.9	151 55.1	20 00.5	137 25.1	13.1	25 48.1	07.3	352 17.6	14.2	Miaplacidus	221 39.8	S69 47.9
23	294 16.4	166 54.3	19 59.8	152 26.0	12.6	40 50.6	07.3	7 20.2	14.3			
1 00	309 18.8	181 53.6	N19 59.2	167 26.9	N16 12.1	55 53.2	S22 07.3	22 22.8	S22 14.3	Mirfak	308 34.5	N49 55.5
01	324 21.3	196 52.9	58.5	182 27.8	11.6	70 55.7	07.3	37 25.5	14.3	Nunki	75 52.8	S26 16.2
02	339 23.8	211 52.1	57.8	197 28.7	11.1	85 58.3	07.3	52 28.1	14.3	Peacock	53 12.0	S56 40.2
03	354 26.2	226 51.4 ..	57.1	212 29.6 ..	10.6	101 00.8 ..	07.3	67 30.7 ..	14.3	Pollux	243 23.0	N27 58.7
04	9 28.7	241 50.7	56.5	227 30.5	10.1	116 03.4	07.3	82 33.4	14.4	Procyon	244 55.7	N 5 10.5
05	24 31.2	256 49.9	55.8	242 31.4	09.6	131 05.9	07.3	97 36.0	14.4			
06	39 33.6	271 49.2	N19 55.1	257 32.3	N16 09.1	146 08.5	S22 07.3	112 38.7	S22 14.4	Rasalhague	96 02.3	N12 33.0
07	54 36.1	286 48.5	54.4	272 33.1	08.6	161 11.0	07.3	127 41.3	14.4	Regulus	207 39.4	N11 52.4
T 08	69 38.5	301 47.7	53.7	287 34.0	08.1	176 13.6	07.3	142 43.9	14.5	Rigel	281 08.2	S 8 10.8
H 09	84 41.0	316 47.0 ..	53.0	302 34.9 ..	07.6	191 16.1 ..	07.3	157 46.6 ..	14.5	Rigil Kent.	139 46.0	S60 55.0
U 10	99 43.5	331 46.3	52.4	317 35.8	07.1	206 18.7	07.3	172 49.2	14.5	Sabik	102 07.5	S15 44.8
R 11	114 45.9	346 45.5	51.7	332 36.7	06.6	221 21.2	07.3	187 51.8	14.5			
S 12	129 48.4	1 44.8	N19 51.0	347 37.6	N16 06.1	236 23.8	S22 07.3	202 54.5	S22 14.6	Schedar	349 35.5	N56 38.4
D 13	144 50.9	16 44.1	50.3	2 38.5	05.6	251 26.3	07.3	217 57.1	14.6	Shaula	96 15.9	S37 07.0
A 14	159 53.3	31 43.3	49.6	17 39.4	05.0	266 28.9	07.3	232 59.7	14.6	Sirius	258 30.3	S16 44.6
Y 15	174 55.8	46 42.6 ..	48.9	32 40.3 ..	04.5	281 31.4 ..	07.3	248 02.4 ..	14.6	Spica	158 26.9	S11 15.6
16	189 58.3	61 41.9	48.2	47 41.2	04.0	296 34.0	07.3	263 05.0	14.6	Suhail	222 49.8	S43 30.7
17	205 00.7	76 41.1	47.5	62 42.1	03.5	311 36.5	07.3	278 07.7	14.7			
18	220 03.2	91 40.4	N19 46.9	77 43.0	N16 03.0	326 39.1	S22 07.3	293 10.3	S22 14.7	Vega	80 35.7	N38 48.4
19	235 05.7	106 39.7	46.2	92 43.9	02.5	341 41.6	07.3	308 12.9	14.7	Zuben'ubi	137 00.7	S16 07.2
20	250 08.1	121 39.0	45.5	107 44.8	02.0	356 44.2	07.3	323 15.6	14.7		SHA	Mer. Pass.
21	265 10.6	136 38.2 ..	44.8	122 45.7 ..	01.5	11 46.7 ..	07.3	338 18.2 ..	14.8	Venus	233 51.7	11 52
22	280 13.0	151 37.5	44.1	137 46.6	01.0	26 49.3	07.3	353 20.8	14.8	Mars	218 45.7	12 51
23	295 15.5	166 36.8	43.4	152 47.5	00.5	41 51.8	07.3	8 23.5	14.8	Jupiter	106 32.1	20 17
Mer. Pass. 3 26.1		v −0.7 d 0.7		v 0.9 d 0.5		v 2.6 d 0.0		v 2.6 d 0.0		Saturn	72 59.8	22 31

© British Crown Copyright 2018. All rights reserved.

SUN and MOON

UT	SUN GHA	SUN Dec	MOON GHA	v	Dec	d	HP
d h	° ′	° ′	° ′	′	° ′	′	′
30 00	178 22.8	N18 37.6	209 22.4	4.8	N22 17.7	1.2	59.5
01	193 22.8	37.0	223 46.2	4.7	22 18.9	1.1	59.5
02	208 22.9	36.4	238 09.9	4.6	22 20.0	0.8	59.6
03	223 22.9	.. 35.8	252 33.5	4.6	22 20.8	0.8	59.6
04	238 22.9	35.2	266 57.1	4.5	22 21.6	0.5	59.6
05	253 22.9	34.6	281 20.6	4.5	22 22.1	0.5	59.7
06	268 22.9	N18 34.0	295 44.1	4.4	N22 22.6	0.2	59.7
T 07	283 23.0	33.4	310 07.5	4.4	22 22.8	0.1	59.7
U 08	298 23.0	32.8	324 30.9	4.3	22 22.9	0.0	59.8
E 09	313 23.0	.. 32.2	338 54.2	4.3	22 22.9	0.2	59.8
S 10	328 23.0	31.6	353 17.5	4.2	22 22.7	0.4	59.8
D 11	343 23.1	31.0	7 40.7	4.3	22 22.3	0.5	59.9
A 12	358 23.1	N18 30.4	22 04.0	4.1	N22 21.8	0.7	59.9
Y 13	13 23.1	29.8	36 27.1	4.2	22 21.1	0.9	59.9
14	28 23.1	29.2	50 50.3	4.1	22 20.2	1.0	60.0
15	43 23.2	.. 28.6	65 13.4	4.1	22 19.2	1.1	60.0
16	58 23.2	28.0	79 36.5	4.0	22 18.1	1.4	60.0
17	73 23.2	27.4	93 59.5	4.0	22 16.7	1.4	60.0
18	88 23.2	N18 26.8	108 22.5	4.0	N22 15.3	1.7	60.1
19	103 23.3	26.1	122 45.5	4.0	22 13.6	1.8	60.1
20	118 23.3	25.5	137 08.5	3.9	22 11.8	2.0	60.1
21	133 23.3	.. 24.9	151 31.4	4.0	22 09.8	2.1	60.2
22	148 23.3	24.3	165 54.4	3.9	22 07.7	2.3	60.2
23	163 23.4	23.7	180 17.3	3.9	22 05.4	2.4	60.2
31 00	178 23.4	N18 23.1	194 40.2	3.9	N22 03.0	2.6	60.2
01	193 23.4	22.5	209 03.1	3.9	22 00.4	2.8	60.3
02	208 23.5	21.9	223 26.0	3.8	21 57.6	2.9	60.3
03	223 23.5	.. 21.3	237 48.8	3.9	21 54.7	3.1	60.3
04	238 23.5	20.7	252 11.7	3.8	21 51.6	3.3	60.3
05	253 23.5	20.0	266 34.5	3.9	21 48.3	3.4	60.4
06	268 23.6	N18 19.4	280 57.4	3.9	N21 44.9	3.6	60.4
W 07	283 23.6	18.8	295 20.3	3.8	21 41.3	3.7	60.4
E 08	298 23.6	18.2	309 43.1	3.9	21 37.6	3.9	60.4
D 09	313 23.7	.. 17.6	324 06.0	3.8	21 33.7	4.0	60.5
N 10	328 23.7	17.0	338 28.8	3.9	21 29.7	4.2	60.5
E 11	343 23.7	16.4	352 51.7	3.9	21 25.5	4.4	60.5
S 12	358 23.7	N18 15.7	7 14.6	3.9	N21 21.1	4.5	60.5
D 13	13 23.8	15.1	21 37.5	3.9	21 16.6	4.7	60.6
A 14	28 23.8	14.5	36 00.4	3.9	21 11.9	4.9	60.6
Y 15	43 23.8	.. 13.9	50 23.3	3.9	21 07.0	5.0	60.6
16	58 23.9	13.3	64 46.2	4.0	21 02.0	5.1	60.6
17	73 23.9	12.6	79 09.2	3.9	20 56.9	5.3	60.6
18	88 23.9	N18 12.0	93 32.1	4.0	N20 51.6	5.5	60.7
19	103 24.0	11.4	107 55.1	4.0	20 46.1	5.6	60.7
20	118 24.0	10.8	122 18.1	4.1	20 40.5	5.8	60.7
21	133 24.0	.. 10.2	136 41.2	4.1	20 34.7	5.9	60.7
22	148 24.1	09.5	151 04.3	4.1	20 28.8	6.1	60.7
23	163 24.1	08.9	165 27.4	4.1	20 22.7	6.2	60.7
1 00	178 24.1	N18 08.3	179 50.5	4.1	N20 16.5	6.4	60.8
01	193 24.2	07.7	194 13.6	4.2	20 10.1	6.5	60.8
02	208 24.2	07.1	208 36.8	4.3	20 03.6	6.7	60.8
03	223 24.2	.. 06.4	223 00.1	4.2	19 56.9	6.8	60.8
04	238 24.3	05.8	237 23.3	4.3	19 50.1	6.9	60.8
05	253 24.3	05.2	251 46.6	4.4	19 43.2	7.1	60.8
06	268 24.3	N18 04.6	266 10.0	4.4	N19 36.1	7.3	60.8
T 07	283 24.4	03.9	280 33.4	4.4	19 28.8	7.4	60.9
H 08	298 24.4	03.3	294 56.8	4.5	19 21.4	7.5	60.9
U 09	313 24.5	.. 02.7	309 20.3	4.5	19 13.9	7.7	60.9
R 10	328 24.5	02.0	323 43.8	4.6	19 06.2	7.8	60.9
S 11	343 24.5	01.4	338 07.4	4.6	18 58.4	8.0	60.9
D 12	358 24.6	N18 00.8	352 31.0	4.7	N18 50.4	8.1	60.9
A 13	13 24.6	18 00.2	6 54.7	4.7	18 42.3	8.2	60.9
Y 14	28 24.6	17 59.5	21 18.4	4.7	18 34.1	8.3	60.9
15	43 24.7	.. 58.9	35 42.1	4.9	18 25.8	8.5	60.9
16	58 24.7	58.3	50 06.0	4.8	18 17.3	8.7	61.0
17	73 24.8	57.6	64 29.8	5.0	18 08.6	8.7	61.0
18	88 24.8	N17 57.0	78 53.8	5.0	N17 59.9	8.9	61.0
19	103 24.8	56.4	93 17.8	5.0	17 51.0	9.0	61.0
20	118 24.9	55.7	107 41.8	5.1	17 42.0	9.1	61.0
21	133 24.9	.. 55.1	122 05.9	5.2	17 32.9	9.3	61.0
22	148 24.9	54.5	136 30.1	5.2	17 23.6	9.4	61.0
23	163 25.0	53.8	150 54.3	5.3	N17 14.2	9.5	61.0
SD	15.8	d 0.6	SD 16.3		16.5		16.6

Twilight, Sunrise, Moonrise

Lat.	Naut.	Civil	Sunrise	Moonrise 30	31	1	2
°	h m	h m	h m	h m	h m	h m	h m
N 72	////	////	□	□	□	□	02 44
N 70	////	////	01 14	□	□	□	03 33
68	////	////	02 08	23 21	25 51	01 51	04 04
66	////	////	02 40	24 46	00 46	02 30	04 27
64	////	01 31	03 04	00 17	01 24	02 58	04 45
62	////	02 10	03 22	00 44	01 51	03 19	04 59
60	////	02 36	03 37	01 06	02 12	03 36	05 12
N 58	01 23	02 56	03 50	01 23	02 29	03 51	05 22
56	01 58	03 12	04 01	01 38	02 43	04 03	05 31
54	02 22	03 26	04 11	01 51	02 56	04 14	05 40
52	02 41	03 38	04 20	02 02	03 06	04 23	05 47
50	02 57	03 48	04 27	02 12	03 16	04 32	05 53
45	03 27	04 10	04 44	02 33	03 37	04 49	06 07
N 40	03 49	04 27	04 57	02 50	03 53	05 04	06 19
35	04 07	04 40	05 08	03 04	04 07	05 16	06 29
30	04 21	04 52	05 18	03 16	04 19	05 27	06 37
20	04 44	05 11	05 35	03 38	04 40	05 46	06 52
N 10	05 01	05 27	05 49	03 56	04 58	06 02	07 05
0	05 16	05 41	06 03	04 13	05 15	06 17	07 17
S 10	05 29	05 54	06 16	04 31	05 32	06 32	07 29
20	05 41	06 07	06 30	04 49	05 50	06 48	07 41
30	05 52	06 21	06 46	05 11	06 11	07 06	07 56
35	05 58	06 29	06 56	05 23	06 23	07 17	08 04
40	06 05	06 37	07 06	05 38	06 37	07 29	08 14
45	06 11	06 47	07 18	05 55	06 53	07 43	08 25
S 50	06 19	06 58	07 33	06 17	07 14	08 00	08 38
52	06 22	07 03	07 40	06 27	07 23	08 09	08 44
54	06 25	07 09	07 48	06 38	07 34	08 18	08 51
56	06 29	07 15	07 57	06 51	07 46	08 28	08 59
58	06 33	07 22	08 07	07 06	08 00	08 40	09 08
S 60	06 38	07 29	08 18	07 24	08 17	08 53	09 17

Sunset, Twilight, Moonset

Lat.	Sunset	Civil	Naut.	Moonset 30	31	1	2
°	h m	h m	h m	h m	h m	h m	h m
N 72	□	□	□	□	□	23 37	22 49
N 70	22 50	////	////	□	□	22 47	22 27
68	22 00	////	////	22 40	22 21	22 14	22 09
66	21 29	////	////	21 15	21 40	21 50	21 54
64	21 07	22 36	////	20 37	21 12	21 31	21 42
62	20 49	22 00	////	20 10	20 51	21 16	21 32
60	20 34	21 34	////	19 49	20 33	21 03	21 23
N 58	20 21	21 15	22 45	19 32	20 18	20 51	21 16
56	20 10	20 59	22 12	19 17	20 05	20 42	21 09
54	20 01	20 45	21 48	19 05	19 54	20 33	21 03
52	19 52	20 34	21 30	18 54	19 45	20 25	20 57
50	19 45	20 23	21 14	18 44	19 36	20 18	20 52
45	19 28	20 02	20 45	18 23	19 17	20 03	20 41
N 40	19 15	19 46	20 23	18 06	19 02	19 50	20 32
35	19 04	19 32	20 06	17 52	18 49	19 39	20 24
30	18 54	19 20	19 52	17 39	18 37	19 30	20 17
20	18 38	19 01	19 29	17 18	18 18	19 13	20 05
N 10	18 23	18 45	19 11	17 00	18 01	18 59	19 54
0	18 10	18 32	18 57	16 43	17 44	18 46	19 44
S 10	17 57	18 19	18 44	16 25	17 28	18 32	19 34
20	17 43	18 06	18 32	16 07	17 11	18 17	19 23
30	17 27	17 52	18 21	15 45	16 51	18 00	19 10
35	17 18	17 44	18 15	15 33	16 39	17 50	19 03
40	17 07	17 36	18 09	15 18	16 26	17 39	18 55
45	16 55	17 26	18 02	15 01	16 10	17 26	18 45
S 50	16 40	17 15	17 55	14 40	15 50	17 09	18 33
52	16 33	17 10	17 51	14 30	15 41	17 02	18 27
54	16 25	17 05	17 48	14 18	15 30	16 53	18 21
56	16 17	16 59	17 44	14 05	15 18	16 43	18 14
58	16 07	16 52	17 40	13 50	15 04	16 32	18 06
S 60	15 56	16 44	17 36	13 32	14 48	16 19	17 57

SUN and MOON

Day	SUN Eqn. of Time 00h	12h	Mer. Pass.	MOON Mer. Pass. Upper	Lower	Age	Phase
d	m s	m s	h m	h m	h m	d	%
30	06 29	06 28	12 06	10 28	22 59	28	4
31	06 26	06 25	12 06	11 30	24 01	29	1
1	06 24	06 22	12 06	12 31	00 01	00	0

© British Crown Copyright 2018. All rights reserved.

UT	ARIES GHA	VENUS −4.0 GHA	Dec	MARS +1.8 GHA	Dec	JUPITER −2.4 GHA	Dec	SATURN +0.2 GHA	Dec	Star Name	SHA	Dec
2 00	310 18.0	181 36.1	N19 42.7	167 48.4	N16 00.0	56 54.4	S22 07.3	23 26.1	S22 14.8	Acamar	315 15.2	S40 13.4
01	325 20.4	196 35.3	42.0	182 49.3	15 59.5	71 56.9	07.3	38 28.7	14.8	Achernar	335 23.5	S57 08.1
02	340 22.9	211 34.6	41.3	197 50.2	59.0	86 59.4	07.3	53 31.4	14.9	Acrux	173 05.0	S63 12.6
03	355 25.4	226 33.9	.. 40.6	212 51.1	.. 58.5	102 02.0	.. 07.3	68 34.0	.. 14.9	Adhara	255 09.6	S28 59.9
04	10 27.8	241 33.2	39.9	227 52.0	58.0	117 04.5	07.3	83 36.6	14.9	Aldebaran	290 44.7	N16 32.8
05	25 30.3	256 32.4	39.2	242 52.9	57.5	132 07.1	07.3	98 39.3	14.9			
06	40 32.8	271 31.7	N19 38.5	257 53.8	N15 57.0	147 09.6	S22 07.3	113 41.9	S22 15.0	Alioth	166 17.2	N55 51.6
07	55 35.2	286 31.0	37.8	272 54.7	56.5	162 12.2	07.3	128 44.6	15.0	Alkaid	152 55.7	N49 13.4
08	70 37.7	301 30.3	37.1	287 55.6	56.0	177 14.7	07.3	143 47.2	15.0	Alnair	27 38.0	S46 51.8
F 09	85 40.1	316 29.6	.. 36.4	302 56.5	.. 55.5	192 17.2	.. 07.3	158 49.8	.. 15.0	Alnilam	275 42.3	S 1 11.4
R 10	100 42.6	331 28.8	35.7	317 57.4	55.0	207 19.8	07.3	173 52.5	15.0	Alphard	217 52.3	S 8 44.5
I 11	115 45.1	346 28.1	34.9	332 58.3	54.5	222 22.3	07.3	188 55.1	15.1			
D 12	130 47.5	1 27.4	N19 34.2	347 59.2	N15 54.0	237 24.9	S22 07.3	203 57.7	S22 15.1	Alphecca	126 07.3	N26 39.3
A 13	145 50.0	16 26.7	33.5	3 00.1	53.4	252 27.4	07.3	219 00.4	15.1	Alpheratz	357 38.9	N29 11.8
Y 14	160 52.5	31 26.0	32.8	18 01.0	52.9	267 29.9	07.3	234 03.0	15.1	Altair	62 03.8	N 8 55.4
15	175 54.9	46 25.2	.. 32.1	33 01.9	.. 52.4	282 32.5	.. 07.3	249 05.6	.. 15.2	Ankaa	353 11.3	S42 11.8
16	190 57.4	61 24.5	31.4	48 02.8	51.9	297 35.0	07.3	264 08.3	15.2	Antares	112 20.9	S26 28.4
17	205 59.9	76 23.8	30.7	63 03.7	51.4	312 37.6	07.3	279 10.9	15.2			
18	221 02.3	91 23.1	N19 30.0	78 04.6	N15 50.9	327 40.1	S22 07.3	294 13.5	S22 15.2	Arcturus	145 51.9	N19 05.2
19	236 04.8	106 22.4	29.2	93 05.5	50.4	342 42.6	07.3	309 16.2	15.3	Atria	107 18.6	S69 03.8
20	251 07.3	121 21.7	28.5	108 06.4	49.9	357 45.2	07.3	324 18.8	15.3	Avior	234 17.0	S59 34.3
21	266 09.7	136 20.9	.. 27.8	123 07.3	.. 49.4	12 47.7	.. 07.3	339 21.4	.. 15.3	Bellatrix	278 27.7	N 6 22.0
22	281 12.2	151 20.2	27.1	138 08.2	48.9	27 50.2	07.3	354 24.1	15.3	Betelgeuse	270 57.0	N 7 24.6
23	296 14.6	166 19.5	26.4	153 09.1	48.4	42 52.8	07.3	9 26.7	15.3			
3 00	311 17.1	181 18.8	N19 25.7	168 10.0	N15 47.9	57 55.3	S22 07.3	24 29.3	S22 15.4	Canopus	263 54.7	S52 42.3
01	326 19.6	196 18.1	24.9	183 10.9	47.4	72 57.9	07.3	39 32.0	15.4	Capella	280 28.5	N46 00.8
02	341 22.0	211 17.4	24.2	198 11.8	46.8	88 00.4	07.3	54 34.6	15.4	Deneb	49 28.2	N45 21.1
03	356 24.5	226 16.7	.. 23.5	213 12.8	.. 46.3	103 02.9	.. 07.3	69 37.2	.. 15.4	Denebola	182 29.6	N14 28.0
04	11 27.0	241 15.9	22.8	228 13.7	45.8	118 05.5	07.3	84 39.9	15.5	Diphda	348 51.5	S17 52.7
05	26 29.4	256 15.2	22.0	243 14.6	45.3	133 08.0	07.3	99 42.5	15.5			
06	41 31.9	271 14.5	N19 21.3	258 15.5	N15 44.8	148 10.5	S22 07.3	114 45.1	S22 15.5	Dubhe	193 47.1	N61 39.0
07	56 34.4	286 13.8	20.6	273 16.4	44.3	163 13.1	07.3	129 47.8	15.5	Elnath	278 07.6	N28 37.2
S 08	71 36.8	301 13.1	19.9	288 17.3	43.8	178 15.6	07.3	144 50.4	15.5	Eltanin	90 43.8	N51 29.5
A 09	86 39.3	316 12.4	.. 19.1	303 18.2	.. 43.3	193 18.1	.. 07.3	159 53.0	.. 15.6	Enif	33 42.7	N 9 57.9
T 10	101 41.8	331 11.7	18.4	318 19.1	42.8	208 20.7	07.3	174 55.6	15.6	Fomalhaut	15 19.0	S29 31.0
U 11	116 44.2	346 11.0	17.7	333 20.0	42.3	223 23.2	07.3	189 58.3	15.6			
R 12	131 46.7	1 10.3	N19 16.9	348 20.9	N15 41.7	238 25.7	S22 07.3	205 00.9	S22 15.6	Gacrux	171 56.5	S57 13.4
D 13	146 49.1	16 09.5	16.2	3 21.8	41.2	253 28.3	07.3	220 03.5	15.7	Gienah	175 48.2	S17 38.9
A 14	161 51.6	31 08.8	15.5	18 22.7	40.7	268 30.8	07.3	235 06.2	15.7	Hadar	148 42.0	S60 28.1
Y 15	176 54.1	46 08.1	.. 14.7	33 23.6	.. 40.2	283 33.3	.. 07.3	250 08.8	.. 15.7	Hamal	327 56.0	N23 33.1
16	191 56.5	61 07.4	14.0	48 24.5	39.7	298 35.9	07.3	265 11.4	15.7	Kaus Aust.	83 37.9	S34 22.4
17	206 59.0	76 06.7	13.3	63 25.4	39.2	313 38.4	07.3	280 14.1	15.7			
18	222 01.5	91 06.0	N19 12.5	78 26.3	N15 38.7	328 40.9	S22 07.3	295 16.7	S22 15.8	Kochab	137 20.0	N74 05.0
19	237 03.9	106 05.3	11.8	93 27.2	38.2	343 43.4	07.3	310 19.3	15.8	Markab	13 33.9	N15 18.6
20	252 06.4	121 04.6	11.0	108 28.1	37.7	358 46.0	07.3	325 22.0	15.8	Menkar	314 10.7	N 4 09.9
21	267 08.9	136 03.9	.. 10.3	123 29.0	.. 37.1	13 48.5	.. 07.3	340 24.6	.. 15.8	Menkent	148 02.7	S36 27.9
22	282 11.3	151 03.2	09.6	138 29.9	36.6	28 51.0	07.3	355 27.2	15.8	Miaplacidus	221 39.8	S69 47.9
23	297 13.8	166 02.5	08.8	153 30.8	36.1	43 53.6	07.3	10 29.9	15.9			
4 00	312 16.2	181 01.8	N19 08.1	168 31.7	N15 35.6	58 56.1	S22 07.3	25 32.5	S22 15.9	Mirfak	308 34.4	N49 55.5
01	327 18.7	196 01.1	07.3	183 32.6	35.1	73 58.6	07.3	40 35.1	15.9	Nunki	75 52.8	S26 16.2
02	342 21.2	211 00.4	06.6	198 33.5	34.6	89 01.1	07.3	55 37.7	15.9	Peacock	53 12.0	S56 40.2
03	357 23.6	225 59.7	.. 05.8	213 34.5	.. 34.1	104 03.7	.. 07.3	70 40.4	.. 16.0	Pollux	243 23.0	N27 58.7
04	12 26.1	240 59.0	05.1	228 35.4	33.6	119 06.2	07.3	85 43.0	16.0	Procyon	244 55.7	N 5 10.5
05	27 28.6	255 58.3	04.3	243 36.3	33.0	134 08.7	07.3	100 45.6	16.0			
06	42 31.0	270 57.6	N19 03.6	258 37.2	N15 32.5	149 11.3	S22 07.3	115 48.3	S22 16.0	Rasalhague	96 02.3	N12 33.0
07	57 33.5	285 56.9	02.8	273 38.1	32.0	164 13.8	07.3	130 50.9	16.0	Regulus	207 39.4	N11 52.4
08	72 36.0	300 56.2	02.1	288 39.0	31.5	179 16.3	07.3	145 53.5	16.1	Rigel	281 08.2	S 8 10.8
S 09	87 38.4	315 55.5	.. 01.3	303 39.9	.. 31.0	194 18.8	.. 07.3	160 56.2	.. 16.1	Rigil Kent.	139 46.0	S60 55.0
U 10	102 40.9	330 54.8	19 00.6	318 40.8	30.5	209 21.4	07.3	175 58.8	16.1	Sabik	102 07.5	S15 44.8
N 11	117 43.4	345 54.1	18 59.8	333 41.7	30.0	224 23.9	07.3	191 01.4	16.1			
D 12	132 45.8	0 53.4	N18 59.1	348 42.6	N15 29.4	239 26.4	S22 07.3	206 04.0	S22 16.2	Schedar	349 35.5	N56 38.4
A 13	147 48.3	15 52.7	58.3	3 43.5	28.9	254 28.9	07.3	221 06.7	16.2	Shaula	96 15.9	S37 07.0
Y 14	162 50.7	30 52.0	57.6	18 44.4	28.4	269 31.4	07.3	236 09.3	16.2	Sirius	258 30.3	S16 44.5
15	177 53.2	45 51.3	.. 56.8	33 45.3	.. 27.9	284 34.0	.. 07.3	251 11.9	.. 16.2	Spica	158 26.9	S11 15.6
16	192 55.7	60 50.6	56.0	48 46.2	27.4	299 36.5	07.3	266 14.6	16.2	Suhail	222 49.8	S43 30.7
17	207 58.1	75 49.9	55.3	63 47.1	26.9	314 39.0	07.3	281 17.2	16.3			
18	223 00.6	90 49.2	N18 54.5	78 48.1	N15 26.3	329 41.5	S22 07.3	296 19.8	S22 16.3	Vega	80 35.8	N38 48.4
19	238 03.1	105 48.5	53.8	93 49.0	25.8	344 44.1	07.3	311 22.5	16.3	Zuben'ubi	137 00.7	S16 07.2
20	253 05.5	120 47.8	53.0	108 49.9	25.3	359 46.6	07.3	326 25.1	16.3		SHA	Mer.Pass.
21	268 08.0	135 47.1	.. 52.2	123 50.8	.. 24.8	14 49.1	.. 07.3	341 27.7	.. 16.4			h m
22	283 10.5	150 46.4	51.5	138 51.7	24.3	29 51.6	07.3	356 30.3	16.4	Venus	230 01.7	11 55
23	298 12.9	165 45.7	50.7	153 52.6	23.8	44 54.1	07.3	11 33.0	16.4	Mars	216 52.9	12 47
	h m									Jupiter	106 38.2	20 05
Mer. Pass.	3 14.3	v −0.7	d 0.7	v 0.9	d 0.5	v 2.5	d 0.0	v 2.6	d 0.0	Saturn	73 12.2	22 18

© British Crown Copyright 2018. All rights reserved.

SUN and MOON

UT (d h)	SUN GHA	SUN Dec	MOON GHA	v	Dec	d	HP
2 00	178 25.0	N17 53.2	165 18.6	5.3	N17 04.7	9.6	61.0
01	193 25.1	52.6	179 42.9	5.4	16 55.1	9.7	61.0
02	208 25.1	51.9	194 07.3	5.5	16 45.4	9.9	61.0
03	223 25.2 ..	51.3	208 31.8	5.5	16 35.5	10.0	61.0
04	238 25.2	50.7	222 56.3	5.6	16 25.5	10.1	61.0
05	253 25.2	50.0	237 20.9	5.7	16 15.4	10.2	61.0
06	268 25.3	N17 49.4	251 45.6	5.7	N16 05.2	10.3	61.0
07	283 25.3	48.7	266 10.3	5.8	15 54.9	10.4	61.0
08	298 25.4	48.1	280 35.1	5.9	15 44.5	10.5	61.0
F 09	313 25.4 ..	47.5	295 00.0	5.9	15 34.0	10.7	61.0
R 10	328 25.4	46.8	309 24.9	6.0	15 23.3	10.7	61.0
I 11	343 25.5	46.2	323 49.9	6.1	15 12.6	10.8	61.0
D 12	358 25.5	N17 45.5	338 15.0	6.1	N15 01.8	11.0	61.0
A 13	13 25.6	44.9	352 40.1	6.2	14 50.8	11.0	61.0
Y 14	28 25.6	44.3	7 05.3	6.3	14 39.8	11.1	61.0
15	43 25.7 ..	43.6	21 30.6	6.3	14 28.7	11.3	61.0
16	58 25.7	43.0	35 55.9	6.4	14 17.4	11.3	61.0
17	73 25.8	42.3	50 21.3	6.5	14 06.1	11.4	61.0
18	88 25.8	N17 41.7	64 46.8	6.5	N13 54.7	11.5	61.0
19	103 25.8	41.0	79 12.3	6.7	13 43.2	11.6	61.0
20	118 25.9	40.4	93 38.0	6.6	13 31.6	11.7	61.0
21	133 25.9 ..	39.8	108 03.6	6.8	13 19.9	11.8	61.0
22	148 26.0	39.1	122 29.4	6.8	13 08.1	11.8	61.0
23	163 26.0	38.5	136 55.2	6.9	12 56.3	11.9	60.9
3 00	178 26.1	N17 37.8	151 21.1	7.0	N12 44.4	12.1	60.9
01	193 26.1	37.2	165 47.1	7.0	12 32.3	12.0	60.9
02	208 26.2	36.5	180 13.1	7.1	12 20.3	12.2	60.9
03	223 26.2 ..	35.9	194 39.2	7.2	12 08.1	12.3	60.9
04	238 26.3	35.2	209 05.4	7.3	11 55.8	12.3	60.9
05	253 26.3	34.6	223 31.7	7.3	11 43.5	12.3	60.9
06	268 26.4	N17 33.9	237 58.0	7.3	N11 31.2	12.5	60.9
07	283 26.4	33.3	252 24.3	7.5	11 18.7	12.5	60.9
S 08	298 26.5	32.6	266 50.8	7.5	11 06.2	12.6	60.9
A 09	313 26.5 ..	32.0	281 17.3	7.6	10 53.6	12.7	60.8
T 10	328 26.6	31.3	295 43.9	7.7	10 40.9	12.7	60.8
U 11	343 26.6	30.7	310 10.6	7.7	10 28.2	12.7	60.8
R 12	358 26.7	N17 30.0	324 37.3	7.8	N10 15.5	12.9	60.8
D 13	13 26.7	29.4	339 04.1	7.8	10 02.6	12.8	60.8
A 14	28 26.8	28.7	353 30.9	7.9	9 49.8	13.0	60.8
Y 15	43 26.8 ..	28.0	7 57.8	8.0	9 36.8	13.0	60.8
16	58 26.9	27.4	22 24.8	8.1	9 23.8	13.0	60.7
17	73 26.9	26.7	36 51.9	8.1	9 10.8	13.1	60.7
18	88 27.0	N17 26.1	51 19.0	8.2	N 8 57.7	13.2	60.7
19	103 27.0	25.4	65 46.2	8.2	8 44.5	13.1	60.7
20	118 27.1	24.8	80 13.4	8.3	8 31.4	13.3	60.7
21	133 27.1 ..	24.1	94 40.7	8.4	8 18.1	13.3	60.7
22	148 27.2	23.5	109 08.1	8.4	8 04.8	13.3	60.6
23	163 27.2	22.8	123 35.5	8.5	7 51.5	13.3	60.6
4 00	178 27.3	N17 22.1	138 03.0	8.6	N 7 38.2	13.4	60.6
01	193 27.3	21.5	152 30.6	8.6	7 24.8	13.5	60.6
02	208 27.4	20.8	166 58.2	8.7	7 11.3	13.4	60.6
03	223 27.4 ..	20.2	181 25.9	8.7	6 57.9	13.5	60.5
04	238 27.5	19.5	195 53.6	8.8	6 44.4	13.5	60.5
05	253 27.5	18.8	210 21.4	8.9	6 30.9	13.6	60.5
06	268 27.6	N17 18.2	224 49.3	8.9	N 6 17.3	13.6	60.5
07	283 27.7	17.5	239 17.2	8.9	6 03.7	13.6	60.5
08	298 27.7	16.8	253 45.1	9.0	5 50.1	13.6	60.4
S 09	313 27.8 ..	16.2	268 13.1	9.1	5 36.5	13.7	60.4
U 10	328 27.8	15.5	282 41.2	9.1	5 22.8	13.7	60.4
N 11	343 27.9	14.9	297 09.3	9.2	5 09.1	13.7	60.4
D 12	358 27.9	N17 14.2	311 37.5	9.3	N 4 55.4	13.7	60.3
A 13	13 28.0	13.5	326 05.8	9.2	4 41.7	13.7	60.3
Y 14	28 28.0	12.9	340 34.0	9.4	4 28.0	13.7	60.3
15	43 28.1 ..	12.2	355 02.4	9.4	4 14.3	13.8	60.3
16	58 28.2	11.5	9 30.8	9.4	4 00.5	13.8	60.3
17	73 28.2	10.9	23 59.2	9.5	3 46.7	13.7	60.2
18	88 28.3	N17 10.2	38 27.7	9.5	N 3 33.0	13.8	60.2
19	103 28.3	09.5	52 56.2	9.6	3 19.2	13.8	60.2
20	118 28.4	08.9	67 24.8	9.6	3 05.4	13.8	60.2
21	133 28.5 ..	08.2	81 53.4	9.7	2 51.6	13.8	60.1
22	148 28.5	07.5	96 22.1	9.7	2 37.8	13.8	60.1
23	163 28.6	06.9	110 50.8	9.7	N 2 24.0	13.9	60.1
	SD 15.8	d 0.7	SD 16.6		16.6		16.4

Twilight — Sunrise — Moonrise

Lat.	Naut.	Civil	Sunrise	Moonrise 2	3	4	5
N 72	□	□	□	02 44	05 33	07 53	10 03
N 70	////	////	01 40	03 33	05 54	08 02	10 03
68	////	////	02 23	04 04	06 10	08 09	10 03
66	////	00 49	02 52	04 27	06 23	08 15	10 02
64	////	01 49	03 13	04 45	06 33	08 19	10 02
62	////	02 22	03 30	04 59	06 42	08 24	10 02
60	00 44	02 45	03 45	05 12	06 50	08 27	10 02
N 58	01 39	03 04	03 57	05 22	06 57	08 30	10 01
56	02 09	03 19	04 07	05 31	07 03	08 33	10 01
54	02 31	03 32	04 16	05 40	07 08	08 36	10 01
52	02 48	03 43	04 24	05 47	07 13	08 38	10 01
50	03 03	03 53	04 32	05 53	07 17	08 40	10 01
45	03 31	04 14	04 47	06 07	07 27	08 45	10 01
N 40	03 53	04 30	05 00	06 19	07 34	08 49	10 01
35	04 09	04 43	05 11	06 29	07 41	08 52	10 01
30	04 23	04 54	05 20	06 37	07 47	08 55	10 00
20	04 45	05 13	05 36	06 52	07 57	09 00	10 00
N 10	05 02	05 28	05 50	07 05	08 06	09 04	10 00
0	05 16	05 41	06 03	07 17	08 14	09 08	10 00
S 10	05 28	05 54	06 15	07 29	08 22	09 12	10 00
20	05 39	06 06	06 29	07 41	08 31	09 17	10 00
30	05 50	06 19	06 44	07 56	08 41	09 21	10 00
35	05 56	06 26	06 53	08 04	08 46	09 24	10 00
40	06 02	06 34	07 03	08 14	08 53	09 28	10 00
45	06 08	06 43	07 15	08 25	09 00	09 31	10 00
S 50	06 15	06 54	07 29	08 38	09 09	09 36	10 00
52	06 18	06 59	07 36	08 44	09 13	09 38	10 00
54	06 21	07 04	07 43	08 51	09 18	09 40	10 00
56	06 24	07 10	07 51	08 59	09 23	09 42	10 00
58	06 28	07 16	08 00	09 08	09 28	09 45	10 00
S 60	06 32	07 23	08 11	09 17	09 35	09 48	10 00

Sunset — Twilight — Moonset

Lat.	Sunset	Civil	Naut.	Moonset 2	3	4	5
N 72	□	□	□	22 49	22 24	22 05	21 47
N 70	22 25	////	////	22 27	22 13	21 51	21 54
68	21 45	////	////	22 09	22 04	21 59	21 57
66	21 18	23 12	////	21 54	21 56	21 57	21 59
64	20 57	22 19	////	21 42	21 50	21 55	21 59
62	20 40	21 48	////	21 32	21 44	21 53	22 01
60	20 26	21 25	23 18	21 23	21 39	21 51	22 03
N 58	20 14	21 07	22 29	21 16	21 34	21 50	22 05
56	20 04	20 52	22 01	21 09	21 30	21 49	22 06
54	19 55	20 39	21 39	21 03	21 27	21 48	22 07
52	19 47	20 28	21 22	20 57	21 24	21 47	22 08
50	19 40	20 18	21 08	20 52	21 21	21 46	22 10
45	19 25	19 58	20 40	20 41	21 14	21 44	22 12
N 40	19 12	19 42	20 19	20 32	21 09	21 42	22 14
35	19 01	19 29	20 02	20 24	21 04	21 41	22 16
30	18 52	19 18	19 49	20 17	21 00	21 39	22 17
20	18 36	19 00	19 27	20 05	20 53	21 37	22 20
N 10	18 22	18 45	19 11	19 54	20 46	21 35	22 22
0	18 10	18 31	18 57	19 44	20 40	21 33	22 24
S 10	17 57	18 19	18 44	19 34	20 34	21 31	22 26
20	17 44	18 07	18 33	19 23	20 27	21 29	22 29
30	17 29	17 54	18 22	19 10	20 19	21 26	22 31
35	17 20	17 46	18 17	19 03	20 15	21 25	22 33
40	17 10	17 39	18 11	18 55	20 10	21 23	22 34
45	16 58	17 30	18 05	18 45	20 04	21 21	22 36
S 50	16 44	17 19	17 58	18 33	19 57	21 19	22 39
52	16 37	17 14	17 55	18 27	19 53	21 18	22 40
54	16 30	17 09	17 52	18 21	19 50	21 16	22 41
56	16 22	17 04	17 49	18 14	19 46	21 15	22 42
58	16 13	16 57	17 45	18 06	19 41	21 14	22 44
S 60	16 02	16 50	17 41	17 57	19 36	21 12	22 45

SUN and MOON

Day	SUN Eqn. of Time 00h	12h	Mer. Pass.	MOON Mer. Pass. Upper	Lower	Age	Phase
d	m s	m s	h m	h m	h m	d	%
2	06 20	06 18	12 06	13 31	01 01	01	3
3	06 16	06 13	12 06	14 27	01 59	02	8
4	06 11	06 08	12 06	15 21	02 54	03	16

© British Crown Copyright 2018. All rights reserved.

UT	ARIES GHA	VENUS −4·0 GHA	Dec	MARS +1·8 GHA	Dec	JUPITER −2·4 GHA	Dec	SATURN +0·2 GHA	Dec	STARS Name	SHA	Dec
5 00	313 15.4	180 45.0	N18 49.9	168 53.5	N15 23.3	59 56.7	S22 07.3	26 35.6	S22 16.4	Acamar	315 15.2	S40 13.4
01	328 17.8	195 44.3	49.2	183 54.4	22.7	74 59.2	07.3	41 38.2	16.4	Achernar	335 23.4	S57 08.1
02	343 20.3	210 43.7	48.4	198 55.3	22.2	90 01.7	07.3	56 40.8	16.5	Acrux	173 05.0	S63 12.5
03	358 22.8	225 43.0	.. 47.6	213 56.2	.. 21.7	105 04.2	.. 07.3	71 43.5	.. 16.5	Adhara	255 09.6	S28 59.9
04	13 25.2	240 42.3	46.9	228 57.1	21.2	120 06.7	07.3	86 46.1	16.5	Aldebaran	290 44.7	N16 32.8
05	28 27.7	255 41.6	46.1	243 58.0	20.7	135 09.3	07.3	101 48.7	16.5			
06	43 30.2	270 40.9	N18 45.3	258 59.0	N15 20.1	150 11.8	S22 07.3	116 51.4	S22 16.5	Alioth	166 17.2	N55 51.6
07	58 32.6	285 40.2	44.5	273 59.9	19.6	165 14.3	07.3	131 54.0	16.6	Alkaid	152 55.7	N49 13.4
08	73 35.1	300 39.5	43.8	289 00.8	19.1	180 16.8	07.3	146 56.6	16.6	Alnair	27 38.0	S46 51.8
M 09	88 37.6	315 38.8	.. 43.0	304 01.7	.. 18.6	195 19.3	.. 07.3	161 59.2	.. 16.6	Alnilam	275 42.3	S 1 11.4
O 10	103 40.0	330 38.1	42.2	319 02.6	18.1	210 21.8	07.3	177 01.9	16.6	Alphard	217 52.3	S 8 44.5
N 11	118 42.5	345 37.5	41.4	334 03.5	17.6	225 24.4	07.3	192 04.5	16.7			
D 12	133 45.0	0 36.8	N18 40.7	349 04.4	N15 17.0	240 26.9	S22 07.3	207 07.1	S22 16.7	Alphecca	126 07.4	N26 39.3
A 13	148 47.4	15 36.1	39.9	4 05.3	16.5	255 29.4	07.3	222 09.8	16.7	Alpheratz	357 38.9	N29 11.8
Y 14	163 49.9	30 35.4	39.1	19 06.2	16.0	270 31.9	07.3	237 12.4	16.7	Altair	62 03.8	N 8 55.4
15	178 52.3	45 34.7	.. 38.3	34 07.1	.. 15.5	285 34.4	.. 07.3	252 15.0	.. 16.7	Ankaa	353 11.3	S42 11.8
16	193 54.8	60 34.0	37.6	49 08.1	15.0	300 36.9	07.4	267 17.6	16.8	Antares	112 20.9	S26 28.4
17	208 57.3	75 33.3	36.8	64 09.0	14.4	315 39.4	07.4	282 20.3	16.8			
18	223 59.7	90 32.7	N18 36.0	79 09.9	N15 13.9	330 42.0	S22 07.4	297 22.9	S22 16.8	Arcturus	145 51.9	N19 05.2
19	239 02.2	105 32.0	35.2	94 10.8	13.4	345 44.5	07.4	312 25.5	16.8	Atria	107 18.7	S69 03.8
20	254 04.7	120 31.3	34.4	109 11.7	12.9	0 47.0	07.4	327 28.1	16.8	Avior	234 17.0	S59 34.3
21	269 07.1	135 30.6	.. 33.6	124 12.6	.. 12.4	15 49.5	.. 07.4	342 30.8	.. 16.9	Bellatrix	278 27.7	N 6 22.0
22	284 09.6	150 29.9	32.8	139 13.5	11.8	30 52.0	07.4	357 33.4	16.9	Betelgeuse	270 57.0	N 7 24.6
23	299 12.1	165 29.2	32.1	154 14.4	11.3	45 54.5	07.4	12 36.0	16.9			
6 00	314 14.5	180 28.6	N18 31.3	169 15.3	N15 10.8	60 57.0	S22 07.4	27 38.6	S22 16.9	Canopus	263 54.7	S52 42.2
01	329 17.0	195 27.9	30.5	184 16.3	10.3	75 59.5	07.4	42 41.3	17.0	Capella	280 28.5	N46 00.8
02	344 19.5	210 27.2	29.7	199 17.2	09.8	91 02.1	07.4	57 43.9	17.0	Deneb	49 28.2	N45 21.1
03	359 21.9	225 26.5	.. 28.9	214 18.1	.. 09.2	106 04.6	.. 07.4	72 46.5	.. 17.0	Denebola	182 29.6	N14 28.0
04	14 24.4	240 25.8	28.1	229 19.0	08.7	121 07.1	07.4	87 49.1	17.0	Diphda	348 51.5	S17 52.7
05	29 26.8	255 25.2	27.3	244 19.9	08.2	136 09.6	07.4	102 51.8	17.0			
06	44 29.3	270 24.5	N18 26.5	259 20.8	N15 07.7	151 12.1	S22 07.4	117 54.4	S22 17.1	Dubhe	193 47.1	N61 39.0
07	59 31.8	285 23.8	25.7	274 21.7	07.1	166 14.6	07.4	132 57.0	17.1	Elnath	278 07.5	N28 37.2
T 08	74 34.2	300 23.1	24.9	289 22.6	06.6	181 17.1	07.4	147 59.6	17.1	Eltanin	90 43.8	N51 29.5
U 09	89 36.7	315 22.5	.. 24.1	304 23.6	.. 06.1	196 19.6	.. 07.4	163 02.3	.. 17.1	Enif	33 42.7	N 9 58.0
E 10	104 39.2	330 21.8	23.3	319 24.5	05.6	211 22.1	07.4	178 04.9	17.1	Fomalhaut	15 19.0	S29 31.0
S 11	119 41.6	345 21.1	22.5	334 25.4	05.1	226 24.6	07.4	193 07.5	17.2			
D 12	134 44.1	0 20.4	N18 21.7	349 26.3	N15 04.5	241 27.2	S22 07.4	208 10.1	S22 17.2	Gacrux	171 56.6	S57 13.4
A 13	149 46.6	15 19.8	20.9	4 27.2	04.0	256 29.7	07.4	223 12.8	17.2	Gienah	175 48.2	S17 38.9
Y 14	164 49.0	30 19.1	20.1	19 28.1	03.5	271 32.2	07.4	238 15.4	17.2	Hadar	148 42.0	S60 28.1
15	179 51.5	45 18.4	.. 19.3	34 29.0	.. 03.0	286 34.7	.. 07.4	253 18.0	.. 17.2	Hamal	327 55.9	N23 33.1
16	194 53.9	60 17.7	18.5	49 29.9	02.4	301 37.2	07.4	268 20.6	17.3	Kaus Aust.	83 37.9	S34 22.4
17	209 56.4	75 17.1	17.7	64 30.9	01.9	316 39.7	07.4	283 23.3	17.3			
18	224 58.9	90 16.4	N18 16.9	79 31.8	N15 01.4	331 42.2	S22 07.4	298 25.9	S22 17.3	Kochab	137 20.1	N74 05.0
19	240 01.3	105 15.7	16.1	94 32.7	00.9	346 44.7	07.4	313 28.5	17.3	Markab	13 33.9	N15 18.6
20	255 03.8	120 15.0	15.3	109 33.6	15 00.3	1 47.2	07.4	328 31.1	17.4	Menkar	314 10.7	N 4 09.9
21	270 06.3	135 14.4	.. 14.5	124 34.5	14 59.8	16 49.7	.. 07.4	343 33.8	.. 17.4	Menkent	148 02.7	S36 27.9
22	285 08.7	150 13.7	13.7	139 35.4	59.3	31 52.2	07.4	358 36.4	17.4	Miaplacidus	221 39.8	S69 47.8
23	300 11.2	165 13.0	12.9	154 36.3	58.8	46 54.7	07.5	13 39.0	17.4			
7 00	315 13.7	180 12.4	N18 12.1	169 37.3	N14 58.2	61 57.2	S22 07.5	28 41.6	S22 17.4	Mirfak	308 34.4	N49 55.5
01	330 16.1	195 11.7	11.3	184 38.2	57.7	76 59.7	07.5	43 44.2	17.5	Nunki	75 52.8	S26 16.2
02	345 18.6	210 11.0	10.5	199 39.1	57.2	92 02.2	07.5	58 46.9	17.5	Peacock	53 12.0	S56 40.2
03	0 21.1	225 10.4	.. 09.7	214 40.0	.. 56.7	107 04.7	.. 07.5	73 49.5	.. 17.5	Pollux	243 23.0	N27 58.7
04	15 23.5	240 09.7	08.8	229 40.9	56.1	122 07.2	07.5	88 52.1	17.5	Procyon	244 55.7	N 5 10.5
05	30 26.0	255 09.0	08.0	244 41.8	55.6	137 09.7	07.5	103 54.7	17.5			
06	45 28.4	270 08.4	N18 07.2	259 42.7	N14 55.1	152 12.2	S22 07.5	118 57.4	S22 17.6	Rasalhague	96 02.3	N12 33.0
W 07	60 30.9	285 07.7	06.4	274 43.7	54.6	167 14.7	07.5	134 00.0	17.6	Regulus	207 39.4	N11 52.4
E 08	75 33.4	300 07.0	05.6	289 44.6	54.0	182 17.2	07.5	149 02.6	17.6	Rigel	281 08.2	S 8 10.8
D 09	90 35.8	315 06.4	.. 04.8	304 45.5	.. 53.5	197 19.7	.. 07.5	164 05.2	.. 17.6	Rigil Kent.	139 46.1	S60 55.0
N 10	105 38.3	330 05.7	03.9	319 46.4	53.0	212 22.2	07.5	179 07.9	17.6	Sabik	102 07.5	S15 44.8
E 11	120 40.8	345 05.0	03.1	334 47.3	52.5	227 24.7	07.5	194 10.5	17.7			
S 12	135 43.2	0 04.4	N18 02.3	349 48.2	N14 51.9	242 27.2	S22 07.5	209 13.1	S22 17.7	Schedar	349 35.4	N56 38.4
D 13	150 45.7	15 03.7	01.5	4 49.2	51.4	257 29.7	07.5	224 15.7	17.7	Shaula	96 15.9	S37 07.0
A 14	165 48.2	30 03.0	18 00.7	19 50.1	50.9	272 32.2	07.5	239 18.3	17.7	Sirius	258 30.3	S16 44.5
Y 15	180 50.6	45 02.4	17 59.8	34 51.0	.. 50.4	287 34.7	.. 07.5	254 21.0	.. 17.8	Spica	158 26.9	S11 15.6
16	195 53.1	60 01.7	59.0	49 51.9	49.8	302 37.2	07.5	269 23.6	17.8	Suhail	222 49.8	S43 30.6
17	210 55.6	75 01.0	58.2	64 52.8	49.3	317 39.7	07.5	284 26.2	17.8			
18	225 58.0	90 00.4	N17 57.4	79 53.7	N14 48.8	332 42.2	S22 07.5	299 28.8	S22 17.8	Vega	80 35.8	N38 48.4
19	241 00.5	104 59.7	56.5	94 54.7	48.2	347 44.7	07.5	314 31.4	17.8	Zuben'ubi	137 00.8	S16 07.2
20	256 02.9	119 59.1	55.7	109 55.6	47.7	2 47.2	07.5	329 34.1	17.9		SHA	Mer.Pass.
21	271 05.4	134 58.4	.. 54.9	124 56.5	.. 47.2	17 49.7	.. 07.5	344 36.7	.. 17.9	Venus	226 14.0	11 59
22	286 07.9	149 57.8	54.0	139 57.4	46.7	32 52.2	07.5	359 39.3	17.9	Mars	215 00.8	12 42
23	301 10.3	164 57.1	53.2	154 58.3	46.1	47 54.7	07.6	14 41.9	17.9	Jupiter	106 42.5	19 53
Mer.Pass. 3 02.5		v −0.7	d 0.8	v 0.9	d 0.5	v 2.5	d 0.0	v 2.6	d 0.0	Saturn	73 24.1	22 06

© British Crown Copyright 2018. All rights reserved.

UT	SUN GHA	SUN Dec	MOON GHA	v	MOON Dec	d	HP
d h	° ′	° ′	° ′	′	° ′	′	′
5 00	178 28.6	N17 06.2	125 19.5	9.8	N 2 10.1	13.8	60.0
01	193 28.7	05.5	139 48.3	9.9	1 56.3	13.8	60.0
02	208 28.7	04.8	154 17.2	9.9	1 42.5	13.8	60.0
03	223 28.8	.. 04.2	168 46.1	9.9	1 28.7	13.8	60.0
04	238 28.9	03.5	183 15.0	9.9	1 14.9	13.7	59.9
05	253 28.9	02.8	197 43.9	10.0	1 01.2	13.8	59.9
06	268 29.0	N17 02.1	212 12.9	10.1	N 0 47.4	13.8	59.9
07	283 29.1	01.5	226 42.0	10.0	0 33.6	13.8	59.9
M 08	298 29.1	00.8	241 11.0	10.1	0 19.8	13.7	59.8
O 09	313 29.2	17 00.1	255 40.1	10.2	N 0 06.1	13.7	59.8
N 10	328 29.2	16 59.4	270 09.3	10.2	S 0 07.6	13.8	59.8
D 11	343 29.3	58.8	284 38.5	10.2	0 21.4	13.7	59.7
A 12	358 29.4	N16 58.1	299 07.7	10.2	S 0 35.1	13.7	59.7
Y 13	13 29.4	57.4	313 36.9	10.3	0 48.8	13.6	59.7
14	28 29.5	56.7	328 06.2	10.3	1 02.4	13.7	59.6
15	43 29.6	.. 56.1	342 35.5	10.3	1 16.1	13.6	59.6
16	58 29.6	55.4	357 04.8	10.4	1 29.7	13.6	59.6
17	73 29.7	54.7	11 34.2	10.4	1 43.3	13.6	59.6
18	88 29.7	N16 54.0	26 03.6	10.4	S 1 56.9	13.5	59.5
19	103 29.8	53.4	40 33.0	10.4	2 10.4	13.5	59.5
20	118 29.9	52.7	55 02.4	10.5	2 24.0	13.5	59.5
21	133 29.9	.. 52.0	69 31.9	10.5	2 37.5	13.4	59.4
22	148 30.0	51.3	84 01.4	10.5	2 50.9	13.5	59.4
23	163 30.1	50.6	98 30.9	10.5	3 04.4	13.4	59.4
6 00	178 30.1	N16 49.9	113 00.4	10.6	S 3 17.8	13.4	59.3
01	193 30.2	49.3	127 30.0	10.6	3 31.2	13.3	59.3
02	208 30.3	48.6	141 59.6	10.6	3 44.5	13.3	59.3
03	223 30.3	.. 47.9	156 29.2	10.6	3 57.8	13.3	59.2
04	238 30.4	47.2	170 58.8	10.6	4 11.1	13.2	59.2
05	253 30.5	46.5	185 28.4	10.7	4 24.3	13.2	59.2
06	268 30.5	N16 45.8	199 58.1	10.6	S 4 37.5	13.2	59.2
07	283 30.6	45.2	214 27.7	10.7	4 50.7	13.1	59.1
T 08	298 30.7	44.5	228 57.4	10.7	5 03.8	13.1	59.1
U 09	313 30.7	.. 43.8	243 27.1	10.7	5 16.9	13.0	59.1
E 10	328 30.8	43.1	257 56.8	10.8	5 29.9	13.0	59.0
S 11	343 30.9	42.4	272 26.6	10.7	5 42.9	12.9	59.0
D 12	358 31.0	N16 41.7	286 56.3	10.8	S 5 55.8	12.9	59.0
A 13	13 31.0	41.0	301 26.1	10.7	6 08.7	12.9	58.9
Y 14	28 31.1	40.4	315 55.8	10.8	6 21.6	12.7	58.9
15	43 31.2	.. 39.7	330 25.6	10.8	6 34.3	12.8	58.9
16	58 31.2	39.0	344 55.4	10.8	6 47.1	12.7	58.8
17	73 31.3	38.3	359 25.2	10.8	6 59.8	12.6	58.8
18	88 31.4	N16 37.6	13 55.0	10.8	S 7 12.4	12.6	58.8
19	103 31.4	36.9	28 24.8	10.8	7 25.0	12.6	58.7
20	118 31.5	36.2	42 54.6	10.8	7 37.6	12.4	58.7
21	133 31.6	.. 35.5	57 24.4	10.8	7 50.0	12.5	58.7
22	148 31.7	34.8	71 54.2	10.9	8 02.5	12.3	58.6
23	163 31.7	34.1	86 24.1	10.8	8 14.8	12.3	58.6
7 00	178 31.8	N16 33.4	100 53.9	10.8	S 8 27.1	12.3	58.6
01	193 31.9	32.7	115 23.7	10.9	8 39.4	12.2	58.5
02	208 31.9	32.1	129 53.6	10.8	8 51.6	12.1	58.5
03	223 32.0	.. 31.4	144 23.4	10.8	9 03.7	12.1	58.5
04	238 32.1	30.7	158 53.2	10.9	9 15.8	12.0	58.4
05	253 32.2	30.0	173 23.1	10.8	9 27.8	11.9	58.4
06	268 32.2	N16 29.3	187 52.9	10.8	S 9 39.7	11.9	58.4
W 07	283 32.3	28.6	202 22.7	10.9	9 51.6	11.8	58.3
E 08	298 32.4	27.9	216 52.6	10.8	10 03.4	11.7	58.3
D 09	313 32.5	.. 27.2	231 22.4	10.8	10 15.1	11.7	58.3
N 10	328 32.5	26.5	245 52.2	10.8	10 26.8	11.6	58.2
E 11	343 32.6	25.8	260 22.0	10.9	10 38.4	11.6	58.2
S 12	358 32.7	N16 25.1	274 51.9	10.8	S10 50.0	11.4	58.2
D 13	13 32.8	24.4	289 21.7	10.8	11 01.4	11.4	58.1
A 14	28 32.8	23.7	303 51.5	10.8	11 12.8	11.4	58.1
Y 15	43 32.9	.. 23.0	318 21.3	10.8	11 24.2	11.2	58.1
16	58 33.0	22.3	332 51.1	10.8	11 35.4	11.2	58.0
17	73 33.1	21.6	347 20.9	10.7	11 46.6	11.1	58.0
18	88 33.2	N16 20.9	1 50.6	10.8	S11 57.7	11.0	58.0
19	103 33.2	20.2	16 20.4	10.8	12 08.7	11.0	57.9
20	118 33.3	19.5	30 50.2	10.7	12 19.7	10.8	57.9
21	133 33.4	.. 18.8	45 19.9	10.8	12 30.5	10.8	57.9
22	148 33.4	18.1	59 49.7	10.7	12 41.3	10.8	57.8
23	163 33.5	17.4	74 19.4	10.8	S12 52.1	10.6	57.8
	SD 15.8	d 0.7	SD 16.3		16.1		15.9

Lat.	Twilight Naut.	Twilight Civil	Sunrise	Moonrise 5	6	7	8
°	h m	h m	h m	h m	h m	h m	h m
N 72	////	////	00 52	10 03	12 10	14 19	16 45
N 70	////	////	02 02	10 03	12 00	13 58	16 02
68	////	////	02 38	10 03	11 53	13 43	15 33
66	////	01 21	03 03	10 02	11 47	13 30	15 12
64	////	02 05	03 23	10 02	11 42	13 19	14 55
62	////	02 33	03 39	10 02	11 37	13 10	14 41
60	01 13	02 55	03 52	10 02	11 33	13 03	14 30
N 58	01 53	03 12	04 03	10 01	11 30	12 56	14 20
56	02 19	03 26	04 13	10 01	11 27	12 50	14 11
54	02 39	03 38	04 21	10 01	11 24	12 45	14 03
52	02 55	03 49	04 29	10 01	11 22	12 40	13 56
50	03 09	03 58	04 36	10 01	11 20	12 36	13 50
45	03 36	04 17	04 51	10 01	11 15	12 27	13 37
N 40	03 56	04 33	05 03	10 01	11 11	12 19	13 26
35	04 12	04 45	05 13	10 01	11 07	12 13	13 16
30	04 25	04 56	05 22	10 00	11 04	12 07	13 08
20	04 46	05 14	05 37	10 00	10 59	11 57	12 54
N 10	05 02	05 28	05 50	10 00	10 55	11 48	12 42
0	05 16	05 41	06 02	10 00	10 51	11 40	12 31
S 10	05 27	05 53	06 15	10 00	10 46	11 33	12 19
20	05 38	06 04	06 27	10 00	10 42	11 24	12 07
30	05 48	06 17	06 42	10 00	10 37	11 15	11 54
35	05 54	06 24	06 50	10 00	10 34	11 09	11 46
40	05 59	06 31	07 00	10 00	10 31	11 03	11 37
45	06 05	06 40	07 11	10 00	10 27	10 56	11 27
S 50	06 11	06 50	07 24	10 00	10 23	10 47	11 14
52	06 13	06 54	07 30	10 00	10 21	10 44	11 08
54	06 16	06 59	07 37	10 00	10 19	10 39	11 02
56	06 19	07 04	07 45	10 00	10 17	10 35	10 55
58	06 23	07 10	07 54	10 00	10 14	10 29	10 47
S 60	06 26	07 17	08 03	10 00	10 11	10 23	10 38

Lat.	Sunset	Twilight Civil	Twilight Naut.	Moonset 5	6	7	8
°	h m	h m	h m	h m	h m	h m	h m
N 72	23 05	////	////	21 47	21 28	21 04	20 24
N 70	22 04	////	////	21 51	21 39	21 26	21 08
68	21 30	////	////	21 54	21 49	21 44	21 37
66	21 06	22 44	////	21 57	21 57	21 58	22 00
64	20 47	22 03	////	21 59	22 04	22 09	22 17
62	20 31	21 36	////	22 01	22 10	22 19	22 32
60	20 18	21 15	22 53	22 03	22 15	22 28	22 44
N 58	20 07	20 58	22 15	22 05	22 19	22 36	22 55
56	19 58	20 44	21 50	22 06	22 23	22 42	23 05
54	19 49	20 32	21 31	22 07	22 27	22 48	23 13
52	19 42	20 22	21 15	22 08	22 30	22 54	23 20
50	19 35	20 13	21 01	22 10	22 33	22 59	23 27
45	19 21	19 54	20 35	22 12	22 40	23 09	23 42
N 40	19 09	19 38	20 15	22 14	22 45	23 18	23 54
35	18 58	19 26	19 59	22 16	22 50	23 26	24 04
30	18 50	19 15	19 46	22 17	22 54	23 33	24 13
20	18 35	18 58	19 25	22 20	23 02	23 44	24 28
N 10	18 22	18 44	19 09	22 22	23 08	23 55	24 42
0	18 09	18 31	18 56	22 24	23 14	24 04	00 04
S 10	17 57	18 19	18 45	22 26	23 20	24 14	00 14
20	17 45	18 08	18 34	22 29	23 27	24 24	00 24
30	17 30	17 55	18 24	22 31	23 34	24 36	00 36
35	17 22	17 48	18 19	22 33	23 39	24 43	00 43
40	17 13	17 41	18 13	22 34	23 44	24 51	00 51
45	17 02	17 33	18 08	22 36	23 49	25 00	01 00
S 50	16 48	17 23	18 02	22 39	23 56	25 11	01 11
52	16 42	17 19	17 59	22 40	23 59	25 17	01 17
54	16 35	17 14	17 56	22 41	24 03	00 03	01 22
56	16 28	17 09	17 53	22 42	24 07	00 07	01 29
58	16 19	17 03	17 50	22 44	24 11	00 11	01 36
S 60	16 09	16 56	17 47	22 45	24 16	00 16	01 44

Day	SUN Eqn. of Time 00h	SUN Eqn. of Time 12h	Mer. Pass.	MOON Mer. Pass. Upper	MOON Mer. Pass. Lower	Age	Phase
d	m s	m s	h m	h m	h m	d %	
5	06 06	06 03	12 06	16 12	03 47	04 26	
6	06 00	05 56	12 06	17 02	04 37	05 37	
7	05 53	05 49	12 06	17 52	05 27	06 48	

© British Crown Copyright 2018. All rights reserved.

UT	ARIES GHA	VENUS −4.0 GHA	Dec	MARS +1.8 GHA	Dec	JUPITER −2.4 GHA	Dec	SATURN +0.2 GHA	Dec	Name	SHA	Dec
8 00	316 12.8	179 56.4	N17 52.4	169 59.2	N14 45.6	62 57.2	S22 07.6	29 44.5	S22 17.9	Acamar	315 15.1	S40 13.4
01	331 15.3	194 55.8	51.6	185 00.2	45.1	77 59.7	07.6	44 47.2	18.0	Achernar	335 23.4	S57 08.1
02	346 17.7	209 55.1	50.7	200 01.1	44.5	93 02.2	07.6	59 49.8	18.0	Acrux	173 05.0	S63 12.5
03	1 20.2	224 54.5 ..	49.9	215 02.0 ..	44.0	108 04.7 ..	07.6	74 52.4 ..	18.0	Adhara	255 09.5	S28 59.8
04	16 22.7	239 53.8	49.1	230 02.9	43.5	123 07.2	07.6	89 55.0	18.0	Aldebaran	290 44.7	N16 32.8
05	31 25.1	254 53.1	48.2	245 03.8	43.0	138 09.7	07.6	104 57.6	18.0			
06	46 27.6	269 52.5	N17 47.4	260 04.7	N14 42.4	153 12.2	S22 07.6	120 00.3	S22 18.1	Alioth	166 17.3	N55 51.6
07	61 30.0	284 51.8	46.5	275 05.7	41.9	168 14.6	07.6	135 02.9	18.1	Alkaid	152 55.7	N49 13.4
08	76 32.5	299 51.2	45.7	290 06.6	41.4	183 17.1	07.6	150 05.5	18.1	Alnair	27 38.0	S46 51.8
09	91 35.0	314 50.5 ..	44.9	305 07.5 ..	40.8	198 19.6 ..	07.6	165 08.1 ..	18.1	Alnilam	275 42.3	S 1 11.4
10	106 37.4	329 49.9	44.0	320 08.4	40.3	213 22.1	07.6	180 10.7	18.1	Alphard	217 52.3	S 8 44.5
11	121 39.9	344 49.2	43.2	335 09.3	39.8	228 24.6	07.6	195 13.4	18.2			
12	136 42.4	359 48.6	N17 42.4	350 10.3	N14 39.2	243 27.1	S22 07.6	210 16.0	S22 18.2	Alphecca	126 07.4	N26 39.3
13	151 44.8	14 47.9	41.5	5 11.2	38.7	258 29.6	07.6	225 18.6	18.2	Alpheratz	357 38.9	N29 11.8
14	166 47.3	29 47.3	40.7	20 12.1	38.2	273 32.1	07.6	240 21.2	18.2	Altair	62 03.8	N 8 55.4
15	181 49.8	44 46.6 ..	39.8	35 13.0 ..	37.6	288 34.6 ..	07.6	255 23.8 ..	18.2	Ankaa	353 11.3	S42 11.8
16	196 52.2	59 46.0	39.0	50 13.9	37.1	303 37.1	07.6	270 26.5	18.3	Antares	112 20.9	S26 28.4
17	211 54.7	74 45.3	38.1	65 14.8	36.6	318 39.5	07.6	285 29.1	18.3			
18	226 57.2	89 44.7	N17 37.3	80 15.8	N14 36.1	333 42.0	S22 07.6	300 31.7	S22 18.3	Arcturus	145 52.0	N19 05.2
19	241 59.6	104 44.0	36.4	95 16.7	35.5	348 44.5	07.7	315 34.3	18.3	Atria	107 18.7	S69 03.8
20	257 02.1	119 43.4	35.6	110 17.6	35.0	3 47.0	07.7	330 36.9	18.3	Avior	234 17.0	S59 34.3
21	272 04.5	134 42.7 ..	34.7	125 18.5 ..	34.5	18 49.5 ..	07.7	345 39.6 ..	18.4	Bellatrix	278 27.7	N 6 22.0
22	287 07.0	149 42.1	33.9	140 19.4	33.9	33 52.0	07.7	0 42.2	18.4	Betelgeuse	270 57.0	N 7 24.6
23	302 09.5	164 41.4	33.0	155 20.4	33.4	48 54.5	07.7	15 44.8	18.4			
9 00	317 11.9	179 40.8	N17 32.2	170 21.3	N14 32.9	63 57.0	S22 07.7	30 47.4	S22 18.4	Canopus	263 54.7	S52 42.2
01	332 14.4	194 40.1	31.3	185 22.2	32.3	78 59.4	07.7	45 50.0	18.4	Capella	280 28.5	N46 00.8
02	347 16.9	209 39.5	30.5	200 23.1	31.8	94 01.9	07.7	60 52.6	18.5	Deneb	49 28.2	N45 21.1
03	2 19.3	224 38.8 ..	29.6	215 24.0 ..	31.3	109 04.4 ..	07.7	75 55.3 ..	18.5	Denebola	182 29.6	N14 28.0
04	17 21.8	239 38.2	28.8	230 25.0	30.7	124 06.9	07.7	90 57.9	18.5	Diphda	348 51.5	S17 52.7
05	32 24.3	254 37.5	27.9	245 25.9	30.2	139 09.4	07.7	106 00.5	18.5			
06	47 26.7	269 36.9	N17 27.1	260 26.8	N14 29.7	154 11.9	S22 07.7	121 03.1	S22 18.6	Dubhe	193 47.1	N61 39.0
07	62 29.2	284 36.3	26.2	275 27.7	29.1	169 14.4	07.7	136 05.7	18.6	Elnath	278 07.5	N28 37.2
08	77 31.7	299 35.6	25.3	290 28.7	28.6	184 16.8	07.7	151 08.3	18.6	Eltanin	90 43.8	N51 29.5
09	92 34.1	314 35.0 ..	24.5	305 29.6 ..	28.1	199 19.3 ..	07.7	166 11.0 ..	18.6	Enif	33 42.7	N 9 58.0
10	107 36.6	329 34.3	23.6	320 30.5	27.5	214 21.8	07.7	181 13.6	18.6	Fomalhaut	15 19.0	S29 31.0
11	122 39.0	344 33.7	22.8	335 31.4	27.0	229 24.3	07.7	196 16.2	18.7			
12	137 41.5	359 33.0	N17 21.9	350 32.3	N14 26.5	244 26.8	S22 07.8	211 18.8	S22 18.7	Gacrux	171 56.6	S57 13.4
13	152 44.0	14 32.4	21.0	5 33.3	25.9	259 29.3	07.8	226 21.4	18.7	Gienah	175 48.2	S17 38.9
14	167 46.4	29 31.8	20.2	20 34.2	25.4	274 31.7	07.8	241 24.0	18.7	Hadar	148 42.1	S60 28.1
15	182 48.9	44 31.1 ..	19.3	35 35.1 ..	24.8	289 34.2 ..	07.8	256 26.7 ..	18.7	Hamal	327 55.9	N23 33.1
16	197 51.4	59 30.5	18.4	50 36.0	24.3	304 36.7	07.8	271 29.3	18.8	Kaus Aust.	83 37.9	S34 22.4
17	212 53.8	74 29.8	17.6	65 36.9	23.8	319 39.2	07.8	286 31.9	18.8			
18	227 56.3	89 29.2	N17 16.7	80 37.9	N14 23.2	334 41.7	S22 07.8	301 34.5	S22 18.8	Kochab	137 20.1	N74 05.0
19	242 58.8	104 28.6	15.8	95 38.8	22.7	349 44.1	07.8	316 37.1	18.8	Markab	13 33.9	N15 18.6
20	258 01.2	119 27.9	15.0	110 39.7	22.2	4 46.6	07.8	331 39.7	18.8	Menkar	314 10.7	N 4 09.9
21	273 03.7	134 27.3 ..	14.1	125 40.6 ..	21.6	19 49.1 ..	07.8	346 42.4 ..	18.9	Menkent	148 02.7	S36 27.9
22	288 06.1	149 26.7	13.2	140 41.6	21.1	34 51.6	07.8	1 45.0	18.9	Miaplacidus	221 39.8	S69 47.8
23	303 08.6	164 26.0	12.4	155 42.5	20.6	49 54.1	07.8	16 47.6	18.9			
10 00	318 11.1	179 25.4	N17 11.5	170 43.4	N14 20.0	64 56.5	S22 07.8	31 50.2	S22 18.9	Mirfak	308 34.4	N49 55.5
01	333 13.5	194 24.8	10.6	185 44.3	19.5	79 59.0	07.8	46 52.8	18.9	Nunki	75 52.8	S26 16.2
02	348 16.0	209 24.1	09.8	200 45.3	19.0	95 01.5	07.8	61 55.4	19.0	Peacock	53 12.0	S56 40.2
03	3 18.5	224 23.5 ..	08.9	215 46.2 ..	18.4	110 04.0 ..	07.8	76 58.0 ..	19.0	Pollux	243 23.0	N27 58.7
04	18 20.9	239 22.8	08.0	230 47.1	17.9	125 06.4	07.9	92 00.7	19.0	Procyon	244 55.6	N 5 10.5
05	33 23.4	254 22.2	07.1	245 48.0	17.3	140 08.9	07.9	107 03.3	19.0			
06	48 25.9	269 21.6	N17 06.3	260 48.9	N14 16.8	155 11.4	S22 07.9	122 05.9	S22 19.0	Rasalhague	96 02.3	N12 33.0
07	63 28.3	284 21.0	05.4	275 49.9	16.3	170 13.9	07.9	137 08.5	19.1	Regulus	207 39.4	N11 52.4
08	78 30.8	299 20.3	04.5	290 50.8	15.7	185 16.4	07.9	152 11.1	19.1	Rigel	281 08.2	S 8 10.7
09	93 33.3	314 19.7 ..	03.6	305 51.7 ..	15.2	200 18.8 ..	07.9	167 13.7 ..	19.1	Rigil Kent.	139 46.1	S60 55.0
10	108 35.7	329 19.1	02.7	320 52.6	14.7	215 21.3	07.9	182 16.3	19.1	Sabik	102 07.5	S15 44.8
11	123 38.2	344 18.4	01.9	335 53.6	14.1	230 23.8	07.9	197 19.0	19.1			
12	138 40.6	359 17.8	N17 01.0	350 54.5	N14 13.6	245 26.3	S22 07.9	212 21.6	S22 19.2	Schedar	349 35.4	N56 38.4
13	153 43.1	14 17.2	17 00.1	5 55.4	13.0	260 28.7	07.9	227 24.2	19.2	Shaula	96 15.9	S37 07.0
14	168 45.6	29 16.5	16 59.2	20 56.3	12.5	275 31.2	07.9	242 26.8	19.2	Sirius	258 30.3	S16 44.5
15	183 48.0	44 15.9 ..	58.3	35 57.3 ..	12.0	290 33.7 ..	07.9	257 29.4 ..	19.2	Spica	158 26.9	S11 15.6
16	198 50.5	59 15.3	57.4	50 58.2	11.4	305 36.1	07.9	272 32.0	19.2	Suhail	222 49.8	S43 30.6
17	213 53.0	74 14.7	56.6	65 59.1	10.9	320 38.6	07.9	287 34.6	19.2			
18	228 55.4	89 14.0	N16 55.7	81 00.0	N14 10.3	335 41.1	S22 07.9	302 37.2	S22 19.3	Vega	80 35.8	N38 48.4
19	243 57.9	104 13.4	54.8	96 01.0	09.8	350 43.6	08.0	317 39.9	19.3	Zuben'ubi	137 00.8	S16 07.2
20	259 00.4	119 12.8	53.9	111 01.9	09.3	5 46.0	08.0	332 42.5	19.3		SHA	Mer.Pass.
21	274 02.8	134 12.2 ..	53.0	126 02.8 ..	08.7	20 48.5 ..	08.0	347 45.1 ..	19.3	Venus	222 28.8	12 02
22	289 05.3	149 11.5	52.1	141 03.7	08.2	35 51.0	08.0	2 47.7	19.3	Mars	213 09.3	12 38
23	304 07.8	164 10.9	51.2	156 04.7	07.6	50 53.4	08.0	17 50.3	19.4	Jupiter	106 45.0	19 41
Mer. Pass. 2 50.7	v −0.6 d 0.9	v 0.9 d 0.5		v 2.5 d 0.0		v 2.6 d 0.0				Saturn	73 35.5	21 53

© British Crown Copyright 2018. All rights reserved.

UT	SUN GHA	Dec	MOON GHA	v	Dec	d	HP
d h	o ′	o ′	o ′	′	o ′	′	′
8 00	178 33.6	N16 16.7	88 49.2	10.7	S13 02.7	10.6	57.8
01	193 33.7	16.0	103 18.9	10.7	13 13.3	10.4	57.8
02	208 33.8	15.3	117 48.6	10.7	13 23.7	10.4	57.7
03	223 33.9	.. 14.6	132 18.3	10.6	13 34.1	10.3	57.7
04	238 33.9	13.9	146 47.9	10.7	13 44.4	10.3	57.7
05	253 34.0	13.1	161 17.6	10.7	13 54.7	10.1	57.6
06	268 34.1	N16 12.4	175 47.3	10.6	S14 04.8	10.1	57.6
T 07	283 34.2	11.7	190 16.9	10.6	14 14.9	10.0	57.6
H 08	298 34.3	11.0	204 46.5	10.7	14 24.9	9.8	57.5
U 09	313 34.3	.. 10.3	219 16.2	10.6	14 34.7	9.8	57.5
R 10	328 34.4	09.6	233 45.8	10.5	14 44.5	9.8	57.5
S 11	343 34.5	08.9	248 15.3	10.6	14 54.3	9.6	57.4
D 12	358 34.6	N16 08.2	262 44.9	10.6	S15 03.9	9.5	57.4
A 13	13 34.7	07.5	277 14.5	10.5	15 13.4	9.5	57.4
Y 14	28 34.7	06.8	291 44.0	10.5	15 22.9	9.3	57.3
15	43 34.8	.. 06.1	306 13.5	10.6	15 32.2	9.3	57.3
16	58 34.9	05.3	320 43.1	10.5	15 41.5	9.2	57.3
17	73 35.0	04.6	335 12.6	10.4	15 50.7	9.0	57.3
18	88 35.1	N16 03.9	349 42.0	10.5	S15 59.7	9.0	57.2
19	103 35.2	03.2	4 11.5	10.5	16 08.7	8.9	57.2
20	118 35.2	02.5	18 41.0	10.4	16 17.6	8.8	57.2
21	133 35.3	.. 01.8	33 10.4	10.4	16 26.4	8.7	57.1
22	148 35.4	01.1	47 39.8	10.4	16 35.1	8.6	57.1
23	163 35.5	16 00.4	62 09.2	10.4	16 43.7	8.5	57.1
9 00	178 35.6	N15 59.6	76 38.6	10.4	S16 52.2	8.5	57.0
01	193 35.7	58.9	91 08.0	10.3	17 00.7	8.3	57.0
02	208 35.8	58.2	105 37.3	10.4	17 09.0	8.2	57.0
03	223 35.8	.. 57.5	120 06.7	10.3	17 17.2	8.1	57.0
04	238 35.9	56.8	134 36.0	10.3	17 25.3	8.0	56.9
05	253 36.0	56.1	149 05.3	10.3	17 33.3	8.0	56.9
06	268 36.1	N15 55.3	163 34.6	10.2	S17 41.3	7.8	56.9
07	283 36.2	54.6	178 03.8	10.3	17 49.1	7.7	56.8
F 08	298 36.3	53.9	192 33.1	10.2	17 56.8	7.6	56.8
R 09	313 36.4	.. 53.2	207 02.3	10.3	18 04.4	7.5	56.8
I 10	328 36.5	52.5	221 31.6	10.2	18 11.9	7.5	56.8
D 11	343 36.5	51.7	236 00.8	10.2	18 19.4	7.3	56.7
A 12	358 36.6	N15 51.0	250 30.0	10.1	S18 26.7	7.2	56.7
Y 13	13 36.7	50.3	264 59.1	10.2	18 33.9	7.1	56.7
14	28 36.8	49.6	279 28.3	10.1	18 41.0	7.0	56.6
15	43 36.9	.. 48.9	293 57.4	10.2	18 48.0	6.9	56.6
16	58 37.0	48.1	308 26.6	10.1	18 54.9	6.8	56.6
17	73 37.1	47.4	322 55.7	10.1	19 01.7	6.6	56.6
18	88 37.2	N15 46.7	337 24.8	10.1	S19 08.3	6.6	56.5
19	103 37.3	46.0	351 53.9	10.0	19 14.9	6.5	56.5
20	118 37.3	45.3	6 22.9	10.1	19 21.4	6.3	56.5
21	133 37.4	.. 44.5	20 52.0	10.1	19 27.7	6.3	56.4
22	148 37.5	43.8	35 21.1	10.0	19 34.0	6.1	56.4
23	163 37.6	43.1	49 50.1	10.0	19 40.1	6.1	56.4
10 00	178 37.7	N15 42.4	64 19.1	10.0	S19 46.2	5.9	56.4
01	193 37.8	41.6	78 48.1	10.0	19 52.1	5.8	56.3
02	208 37.9	40.9	93 17.1	10.0	19 57.9	5.7	56.3
03	223 38.0	.. 40.2	107 46.1	10.0	20 03.6	5.6	56.3
04	238 38.1	39.4	122 15.1	9.9	20 09.2	5.5	56.3
05	253 38.2	38.7	136 44.0	10.0	20 14.7	5.4	56.2
06	268 38.3	N15 38.0	151 13.0	9.9	S20 20.1	5.3	56.2
S 07	283 38.4	37.3	165 41.9	9.9	20 25.4	5.1	56.2
A 08	298 38.4	36.5	180 10.8	9.9	20 30.5	5.1	56.2
T 09	313 38.5	.. 35.8	194 39.7	10.0	20 35.6	4.9	56.1
U 10	328 38.6	35.1	209 08.7	9.9	20 40.5	4.8	56.1
R 11	343 38.7	34.3	223 37.6	9.9	20 45.3	4.7	56.1
D 12	358 38.8	N15 33.6	238 06.5	9.8	S20 50.0	4.6	56.1
A 13	13 38.9	32.9	252 35.3	9.9	20 54.6	4.5	56.0
Y 14	28 39.0	32.2	267 04.2	9.9	20 59.1	4.4	56.0
15	43 39.1	.. 31.4	281 33.1	9.9	21 03.5	4.2	56.0
16	58 39.2	30.7	296 02.0	9.8	21 07.7	4.1	56.0
17	73 39.3	30.0	310 30.8	9.9	21 11.8	4.1	55.9
18	88 39.4	N15 29.2	324 59.7	9.8	S21 15.9	3.9	55.9
19	103 39.5	28.5	339 28.5	9.9	21 19.8	3.8	55.9
20	118 39.6	27.8	353 57.4	9.8	21 23.6	3.7	55.9
21	133 39.7	.. 27.0	8 26.2	9.9	21 27.3	3.5	55.8
22	148 39.8	26.3	22 55.1	9.8	21 30.8	3.5	55.8
23	163 39.9	25.6	37 23.9	9.8	S21 34.3	3.3	55.8
	SD 15.8	d 0.7	SD 15.6		15.4		15.3

Lat.	Twilight Naut.	Civil	Sunrise	Moonrise 8	9	10	11
o	h m	h m	h m	h m	h m	h m	h m
N 72	////	////	01 32	16 45	■■■	■■■	■■■
N 70	////	////	02 21	16 02	18 29	■■■	■■■
68	////	00 12	02 52	15 33	17 27	19 30	■■■
66	////	01 43	03 14	15 12	16 53	18 28	19 46
64	////	02 19	03 32	14 55	16 28	17 53	19 03
62	00 11	02 44	03 47	14 41	16 09	17 28	18 35
60	01 33	03 04	03 59	14 30	15 53	17 08	18 13
N 58	02 06	03 20	04 09	14 20	15 39	16 52	17 55
56	02 29	03 33	04 18	14 11	15 28	16 38	17 40
54	02 47	03 44	04 27	14 03	15 18	16 27	17 27
52	03 02	03 54	04 34	13 56	15 09	16 16	17 16
50	03 15	04 03	04 40	13 50	15 01	16 07	17 06
45	03 41	04 21	04 54	13 37	14 44	15 47	16 45
N 40	04 00	04 36	05 05	13 26	14 30	15 31	16 28
35	04 15	04 48	05 15	13 16	14 18	15 18	16 13
30	04 28	04 58	05 24	13 08	14 08	15 06	16 01
20	04 48	05 15	05 38	12 54	13 51	14 46	15 40
N 10	05 03	05 29	05 51	12 42	13 35	14 29	15 21
0	05 16	05 41	06 02	12 31	13 21	14 13	15 04
S 10	05 27	05 52	06 14	12 19	13 07	13 57	14 47
20	05 37	06 03	06 26	12 07	12 52	13 39	14 29
30	05 46	06 15	06 39	11 54	12 35	13 20	14 08
35	05 51	06 21	06 47	11 46	12 25	13 08	13 56
40	05 56	06 28	06 56	11 37	12 14	12 55	13 41
45	06 01	06 36	07 07	11 27	12 01	12 40	13 25
S 50	06 06	06 45	07 19	11 14	11 45	12 21	13 04
52	06 09	06 49	07 25	11 08	11 37	12 12	12 54
54	06 11	06 53	07 32	11 02	11 29	12 02	12 43
56	06 14	06 58	07 39	10 55	11 20	11 51	12 31
58	06 17	07 04	07 47	10 47	11 09	11 38	12 16
S 60	06 20	07 10	07 56	10 38	10 57	11 23	11 59

Lat.	Sunset	Twilight Civil	Naut.	Moonset 8	9	10	11
o	h m	h m	h m	h m	h m	h m	h m
N 72	22 31	////	////	20 24	■■■	■■■	■■■
N 70	21 45	////	////	21 08	20 28	■■■	■■■
68	21 16	00 00	////	21 37	21 30	21 14	■■■
66	20 54	22 22	////	22 00	22 05	22 17	22 46
64	20 37	21 48	////	22 17	22 30	22 52	23 29
62	20 22	21 24	00 01	22 32	22 50	23 17	23 58
60	20 11	21 05	22 33	22 44	23 07	23 37	24 20
N 58	20 00	20 50	22 02	22 55	23 20	23 54	24 37
56	19 51	20 37	21 40	23 05	23 32	24 08	00 08
54	19 43	20 25	21 22	23 13	23 43	24 20	00 20
52	19 36	20 16	21 07	23 20	23 52	24 30	00 30
50	19 30	20 07	20 54	23 27	24 00	00 00	00 40
45	19 16	19 49	20 29	23 42	24 18	00 18	01 00
N 40	19 05	19 34	20 10	23 54	24 33	00 33	01 16
35	18 55	19 23	19 55	24 04	00 04	00 45	01 30
30	18 47	19 13	19 43	24 13	00 13	00 56	01 42
20	18 33	18 56	19 23	24 28	00 28	01 14	02 03
N 10	18 20	18 42	19 08	24 42	00 42	01 31	02 21
0	18 09	18 30	18 55	00 04	00 55	01 46	02 37
S 10	17 58	18 19	18 45	00 14	01 08	02 01	02 54
20	17 46	18 08	18 35	00 24	01 21	02 17	03 12
30	17 32	17 57	18 25	00 36	01 37	02 36	03 33
35	17 24	17 51	18 21	00 43	01 46	02 47	03 45
40	17 15	17 44	18 16	00 51	01 57	03 00	03 59
45	17 05	17 36	18 11	01 00	02 09	03 14	04 15
S 50	16 52	17 27	18 05	01 11	02 24	03 33	04 35
52	16 47	17 23	18 03	01 16	02 31	03 41	04 45
54	16 40	17 18	18 01	01 22	02 39	03 51	04 56
56	16 33	17 14	17 58	01 29	02 48	04 02	05 08
58	16 25	17 08	17 55	01 36	02 58	04 14	05 23
S 60	16 16	17 02	17 52	01 44	03 09	04 29	05 40

Day	SUN Eqn. of Time 00h	12h	Mer. Pass.	MOON Mer. Pass. Upper	Lower	Age	Phase
d	m s	m s	h m	h m	h m	d	%
8	05 46	05 42	12 06	18 43	06 17	07	58
9	05 38	05 34	12 06	19 34	07 08	08	69
10	05 29	05 25	12 05	20 25	07 59	09	78

© British Crown Copyright 2018. All rights reserved.

UT	ARIES GHA	VENUS −4.0 GHA	Dec	MARS +1.8 GHA	Dec	JUPITER −2.3 GHA	Dec	SATURN +0.2 GHA	Dec	STARS Name	SHA	Dec
11 00	319 10.2	179 10.3	N16 50.3	171 05.6	N14 07.1	65 55.9	S22 08.0	32 52.9	S22 19.4	Acamar	315 15.1	S40 13.4
01	334 12.7	194 09.7	49.4	186 06.5	06.6	80 58.4	08.0	47 55.5	19.4	Achernar	335 23.4	S57 08.1
02	349 15.1	209 09.0	48.5	201 07.4	06.0	96 00.9	08.0	62 58.1	19.4	Acrux	173 05.0	S63 12.5
03	4 17.6	224 08.4 ..	47.7	216 08.4 ..	05.5	111 03.3 ..	08.0	78 00.8 ..	19.4	Adhara	255 09.5	S28 59.8
04	19 20.1	239 07.8	46.8	231 09.3	04.9	126 05.8	08.0	93 03.4	19.5	Aldebaran	290 44.7	N16 32.8
05	34 22.5	254 07.2	45.9	246 10.2	04.4	141 08.3	08.0	108 06.0	19.5			
06	49 25.0	269 06.5	N16 45.0	261 11.2	N14 03.9	156 10.7	S22 08.0	123 08.6	S22 19.5	Alioth	166 17.3	N55 51.6
07	64 27.5	284 05.9	44.1	276 12.1	03.3	171 13.2	08.0	138 11.2	19.5	Alkaid	152 55.7	N49 13.4
08	79 29.9	299 05.3	43.2	291 13.0	02.8	186 15.7	08.1	153 13.8	19.5	Alnair	27 38.0	S46 51.9
S 09	94 32.4	314 04.7 ..	42.3	306 13.9 ..	02.2	201 18.1 ..	08.1	168 16.4 ..	19.6	Alnilam	275 42.3	S 1 11.4
U 10	109 34.9	329 04.1	41.4	321 14.9	01.7	216 20.6	08.1	183 19.0	19.6	Alphard	217 52.3	S 8 44.5
N 11	124 37.3	344 03.4	40.5	336 15.8	01.1	231 23.1	08.1	198 21.6	19.6			
D 12	139 39.8	359 02.8	N16 39.6	351 16.7	N14 00.6	246 25.5	S22 08.1	213 24.3	S22 19.6	Alphecca	126 07.4	N26 39.3
A 13	154 42.3	14 02.2	38.7	6 17.6	14 00.1	261 28.0	08.1	228 26.9	19.6	Alpheratz	357 38.9	N29 11.8
Y 14	169 44.7	29 01.6	37.8	21 18.6	13 59.5	276 30.5	08.1	243 29.5	19.7	Altair	62 03.8	N 8 55.4
15	184 47.2	44 01.0 ..	36.9	36 19.5 ..	59.0	291 32.9 ..	08.1	258 32.1 ..	19.7	Ankaa	353 11.2	S42 11.8
16	199 49.6	59 00.4	36.0	51 20.4	58.4	306 35.4	08.1	273 34.7	19.7	Antares	112 21.0	S26 28.4
17	214 52.1	73 59.7	35.1	66 21.4	57.9	321 37.9	08.1	288 37.3	19.7			
18	229 54.6	88 59.1	N16 34.1	81 22.3	N13 57.4	336 40.3	S22 08.1	303 39.9	S22 19.7	Arcturus	145 52.0	N19 05.2
19	244 57.0	103 58.5	33.2	96 23.2	56.8	351 42.8	08.1	318 42.5	19.8	Atria	107 18.7	S69 03.8
20	259 59.5	118 57.9	32.3	111 24.1	56.3	6 45.2	08.1	333 45.1	19.8	Avior	234 17.0	S59 34.2
21	275 02.0	133 57.3 ..	31.4	126 25.1 ..	55.7	21 47.7 ..	08.2	348 47.7 ..	19.8	Bellatrix	278 27.7	N 6 22.0
22	290 04.4	148 56.7	30.5	141 26.0	55.2	36 50.2	08.2	3 50.4	19.8	Betelgeuse	270 56.9	N 7 24.6
23	305 06.9	163 56.1	29.6	156 26.9	54.6	51 52.6	08.2	18 53.0	19.8			
12 00	320 09.4	178 55.4	N16 28.7	171 27.8	N13 54.1	66 55.1	S22 08.2	33 55.6	S22 19.9	Canopus	263 54.7	S52 42.2
01	335 11.8	193 54.8	27.8	186 28.8	53.5	81 57.6	08.2	48 58.2	19.9	Capella	280 28.5	N46 00.8
02	350 14.3	208 54.2	26.9	201 29.7	53.0	97 00.0	08.2	64 00.8	19.9	Deneb	49 28.2	N45 21.1
03	5 16.8	223 53.6 ..	26.0	216 30.6 ..	52.5	112 02.5 ..	08.2	79 03.4 ..	19.9	Denebola	182 29.6	N14 28.0
04	20 19.2	238 53.0	25.0	231 31.6	51.9	127 04.9	08.2	94 06.0	19.9	Diphda	348 51.4	S17 52.7
05	35 21.7	253 52.4	24.1	246 32.5	51.4	142 07.4	08.2	109 08.6	19.9			
06	50 24.1	268 51.8	N16 23.2	261 33.4	N13 50.8	157 09.9	S22 08.2	124 11.2	S22 20.0	Dubhe	193 47.1	N61 39.0
07	65 26.6	283 51.2	22.3	276 34.4	50.3	172 12.3	08.2	139 13.8	20.0	Elnath	278 07.5	N28 37.2
08	80 29.1	298 50.6	21.4	291 35.3	49.7	187 14.8	08.2	154 16.4	20.0	Eltanin	90 43.8	N51 29.5
M 09	95 31.5	313 49.9 ..	20.5	306 36.2 ..	49.2	202 17.2 ..	08.3	169 19.0 ..	20.0	Enif	33 42.7	N 9 58.0
O 10	110 34.0	328 49.3	19.5	321 37.1	48.6	217 19.7	08.3	184 21.7	20.0	Fomalhaut	15 19.0	S29 31.0
N 11	125 36.5	343 48.7	18.6	336 38.1	48.1	232 22.1	08.3	199 24.3	20.1			
D 12	140 38.9	358 48.1	N16 17.7	351 39.0	N13 47.6	247 24.6	S22 08.3	214 26.9	S22 20.1	Gacrux	171 56.6	S57 13.4
A 13	155 41.4	13 47.5	16.8	6 39.9	47.0	262 27.1	08.3	229 29.5	20.1	Gienah	175 48.2	S17 38.9
Y 14	170 43.9	28 46.9	15.9	21 40.9	46.5	277 29.5	08.3	244 32.1	20.1	Hadar	148 42.1	S60 28.1
15	185 46.3	43 46.3 ..	14.9	36 41.8 ..	45.9	292 32.0 ..	08.3	259 34.7 ..	20.1	Hamal	327 55.9	N23 33.1
16	200 48.8	58 45.7	14.0	51 42.7	45.4	307 34.4	08.3	274 37.3	20.2	Kaus Aust.	83 37.9	S34 22.4
17	215 51.2	73 45.1	13.1	66 43.7	44.8	322 36.9	08.3	289 39.9	20.2			
18	230 53.7	88 44.5	N16 12.2	81 44.6	N13 44.3	337 39.3	S22 08.3	304 42.5	S22 20.2	Kochab	137 20.2	N74 05.0
19	245 56.2	103 43.9	11.2	96 45.5	43.7	352 41.8	08.3	319 45.1	20.2	Markab	13 33.8	N15 18.6
20	260 58.6	118 43.3	10.3	111 46.4	43.2	7 44.3	08.3	334 47.7	20.2	Menkar	314 10.6	N 4 09.9
21	276 01.1	133 42.7 ..	09.4	126 47.4 ..	42.6	22 46.7 ..	08.4	349 50.3 ..	20.3	Menkent	148 02.7	S36 27.9
22	291 03.6	148 42.1	08.5	141 48.3	42.1	37 49.2	08.4	4 52.9	20.3	Miaplacidus	221 39.8	S69 47.8
23	306 06.0	163 41.5	07.5	156 49.2	41.5	52 51.6	08.4	19 55.5	20.3			
13 00	321 08.5	178 40.9	N16 06.6	171 50.2	N13 41.0	67 54.1	S22 08.4	34 58.2	S22 20.3	Mirfak	308 34.3	N49 55.5
01	336 11.0	193 40.3	05.7	186 51.1	40.4	82 56.5	08.4	50 00.8	20.3	Nunki	75 52.8	S26 16.2
02	351 13.4	208 39.7	04.8	201 52.0	39.9	97 59.0	08.4	65 03.4	20.3	Peacock	53 12.0	S56 40.3
03	6 15.9	223 39.1 ..	03.8	216 53.0 ..	39.3	113 01.4 ..	08.4	80 06.0 ..	20.4	Pollux	243 22.9	N27 58.7
04	21 18.4	238 38.5	02.9	231 53.9	38.8	128 03.9	08.4	95 08.6	20.4	Procyon	244 55.6	N 5 10.5
05	36 20.8	253 37.9	01.9	246 54.8	38.2	143 06.3	08.4	110 11.2	20.4			
06	51 23.3	268 37.3	N16 01.0	261 55.8	N13 37.7	158 08.8	S22 08.4	125 13.8	S22 20.4	Rasalhague	96 02.3	N12 33.0
07	66 25.7	283 36.7	16 00.1	276 56.7	37.2	173 11.2	08.4	140 16.4	20.4	Regulus	207 39.4	N11 52.4
T 08	81 28.2	298 36.1	15 59.1	291 57.6	36.6	188 13.7	08.5	155 19.0	20.5	Rigel	281 08.2	S 8 10.7
U 09	96 30.7	313 35.5 ..	58.2	306 58.6 ..	36.1	203 16.1 ..	08.5	170 21.6 ..	20.5	Rigil Kent.	139 46.1	S60 55.0
E 10	111 33.1	328 34.9	57.3	321 59.5	35.5	218 18.6	08.5	185 24.2	20.5	Sabik	102 07.5	S15 44.8
S 11	126 35.6	343 34.3	56.3	337 00.4	35.0	233 21.0	08.5	200 26.8	20.5			
D 12	141 38.1	358 33.7	N15 55.4	352 01.3	N13 34.4	248 23.5	S22 08.5	215 29.4	S22 20.5	Schedar	349 35.4	N56 38.4
A 13	156 40.5	13 33.1	54.4	7 02.3	33.9	263 25.9	08.5	230 32.0	20.6	Shaula	96 15.9	S37 07.0
Y 14	171 43.0	28 32.5	53.5	22 03.2	33.3	278 28.4	08.5	245 34.6	20.6	Sirius	258 30.3	S16 44.5
15	186 45.5	43 31.9 ..	52.6	37 04.1 ..	32.8	293 30.8 ..	08.5	260 37.2 ..	20.6	Spica	158 26.9	S11 15.6
16	201 47.9	58 31.3	51.6	52 05.1	32.2	308 33.3	08.5	275 39.8	20.6	Suhail	222 49.8	S43 30.6
17	216 50.4	73 30.7	50.7	67 06.0	31.7	323 35.7	08.5	290 42.4	20.6			
18	231 52.9	88 30.1	N15 49.7	82 06.9	N13 31.1	338 38.2	S22 08.6	305 45.0	S22 20.7	Vega	80 35.8	N38 48.4
19	246 55.3	103 29.5	48.8	97 07.9	30.6	353 40.6	08.6	320 47.6	20.7	Zuben'ubi	137 00.8	S16 07.2
20	261 57.8	118 28.9	47.8	112 08.8	30.0	8 43.1	08.6	335 50.2	20.7		SHA	Mer.Pass.
21	277 00.2	133 28.4 ..	46.9	127 09.7 ..	29.5	23 45.5 ..	08.6	350 52.9 ..	20.7	Venus	218 46.1	12 05
22	292 02.7	148 27.8	46.0	142 10.7	28.9	38 48.0	08.6	5 55.5	20.7	Mars	211 18.5	12 33
23	307 05.2	163 27.2	45.0	157 11.6	28.4	53 50.4	08.6	20 58.1	20.7	Jupiter	106 45.7	19 29
Mer.Pass. 2 38.9		v −0.6	d 0.9	v 0.9	d 0.5	v 2.5	d 0.0	v 2.6	d 0.0	Saturn	73 46.2	21 41

© British Crown Copyright 2018. All rights reserved.

UT	SUN GHA	SUN Dec	MOON GHA	v	MOON Dec	d	HP
d h	° '	° '	° '	'	° '	'	'
11 00	178 40.0	N15 24.8	51 52.7	9.9	S21 37.6	3.2	55.8
01	193 40.1	24.1	66 21.6	9.8	21 40.8	3.1	55.8
02	208 40.2	23.3	80 50.4	9.9	21 43.9	3.0	55.7
03	223 40.3	.. 22.6	95 19.3	9.8	21 46.9	2.9	55.7
04	238 40.4	21.9	109 48.1	9.9	21 49.8	2.8	55.7
05	253 40.5	21.1	124 17.0	9.8	21 52.6	2.6	55.7
06	268 40.6	N15 20.4	138 45.8	9.9	S21 55.2	2.5	55.6
07	283 40.7	19.7	153 14.7	9.8	21 57.7	2.5	55.6
08	298 40.8	18.9	167 43.5	9.9	22 00.2	2.2	55.6
S 09	313 40.9	.. 18.2	182 12.4	9.8	22 02.4	2.2	55.6
U 10	328 41.0	17.4	196 41.2	9.9	22 04.6	2.1	55.6
N 11	343 41.1	16.7	211 10.1	9.9	22 06.7	1.9	55.5
D 12	358 41.2	N15 16.0	225 39.0	9.9	S22 08.6	1.9	55.5
A 13	13 41.3	15.2	240 07.9	9.9	22 10.5	1.7	55.5
Y 14	28 41.4	14.5	254 36.8	9.9	22 12.2	1.6	55.5
15	43 41.5	.. 13.7	269 05.7	9.9	22 13.8	1.5	55.4
16	58 41.6	13.0	283 34.6	9.9	22 15.3	1.3	55.4
17	73 41.7	12.2	298 03.5	10.0	22 16.6	1.3	55.4
18	88 41.8	N15 11.5	312 32.5	9.9	S22 17.9	1.1	55.4
19	103 41.9	10.8	327 01.4	10.0	22 19.0	1.1	55.4
20	118 42.0	10.0	341 30.4	9.9	22 20.1	0.9	55.3
21	133 42.1	.. 09.3	355 59.3	10.0	22 21.0	0.8	55.3
22	148 42.2	08.5	10 28.3	10.0	22 21.8	0.6	55.3
23	163 42.3	07.8	24 57.3	10.1	22 22.4	0.6	55.3
12 00	178 42.4	N15 07.0	39 26.4	10.0	S22 23.0	0.4	55.3
01	193 42.5	06.3	53 55.4	10.0	22 23.4	0.4	55.2
02	208 42.6	05.5	68 24.4	10.1	22 23.8	0.2	55.2
03	223 42.7	.. 04.8	82 53.5	10.1	22 24.0	0.1	55.2
04	238 42.8	04.0	97 22.6	10.1	22 24.1	0.0	55.2
05	253 42.9	03.3	111 51.7	10.2	22 24.1	0.2	55.2
06	268 43.0	N15 02.6	126 20.9	10.1	S22 23.9	0.2	55.2
07	283 43.1	01.8	140 50.0	10.2	22 23.7	0.4	55.1
08	298 43.2	01.1	155 19.2	10.2	22 23.3	0.4	55.1
M 09	313 43.3	15 00.3	169 48.4	10.2	22 22.9	0.6	55.1
O 10	328 43.4	14 59.6	184 17.6	10.2	22 22.3	0.7	55.1
N 11	343 43.5	58.8	198 46.8	10.3	22 21.6	0.8	55.1
D 12	358 43.7	N14 58.1	213 16.1	10.3	S22 20.8	0.9	55.0
A 13	13 43.8	57.3	227 45.4	10.3	22 19.9	1.1	55.0
Y 14	28 43.9	56.6	242 14.7	10.4	22 18.8	1.1	55.0
15	43 44.0	.. 55.8	256 44.1	10.3	22 17.7	1.3	55.0
16	58 44.1	55.0	271 13.4	10.4	22 16.4	1.3	55.0
17	73 44.2	54.3	285 42.8	10.5	22 15.1	1.5	55.0
18	88 44.3	N14 53.5	300 12.3	10.4	S22 13.6	1.6	54.9
19	103 44.4	52.8	314 41.7	10.5	22 12.0	1.7	54.9
20	118 44.5	52.0	329 11.2	10.6	22 10.3	1.8	54.9
21	133 44.6	.. 51.3	343 40.8	10.5	22 08.5	1.9	54.9
22	148 44.7	50.5	358 10.3	10.6	22 06.6	2.0	54.9
23	163 44.8	49.8	12 39.9	10.6	22 04.6	2.2	54.9
13 00	178 44.9	N14 49.0	27 09.5	10.7	S22 02.4	2.2	54.8
01	193 45.1	48.3	41 39.2	10.7	22 00.2	2.4	54.8
02	208 45.2	47.5	56 08.9	10.7	21 57.8	2.4	54.8
03	223 45.3	.. 46.7	70 38.6	10.7	21 55.4	2.6	54.8
04	238 45.4	46.0	85 08.3	10.8	21 52.8	2.6	54.8
05	253 45.5	45.2	99 38.1	10.9	21 50.2	2.8	54.8
06	268 45.6	N14 44.5	114 08.0	10.8	S21 47.4	2.9	54.8
07	283 45.7	43.7	128 37.8	10.9	21 44.5	3.0	54.7
T 08	298 45.8	43.0	143 07.7	11.0	21 41.5	3.1	54.7
U 09	313 45.9	.. 42.2	157 37.7	11.0	21 38.4	3.2	54.7
E 10	328 46.1	41.4	172 07.7	11.0	21 35.2	3.3	54.7
S 11	343 46.2	40.7	186 37.7	11.1	21 31.9	3.4	54.7
D 12	358 46.3	N14 39.9	201 07.8	11.1	S21 28.5	3.5	54.7
A 13	13 46.4	39.2	215 37.9	11.1	21 25.0	3.6	54.7
Y 14	28 46.5	38.4	230 08.0	11.2	21 21.4	3.7	54.6
15	43 46.6	.. 37.6	244 38.2	11.2	21 17.7	3.8	54.6
16	58 46.7	36.9	259 08.4	11.3	21 13.9	3.9	54.6
17	73 46.8	36.1	273 38.7	11.3	21 10.0	4.0	54.6
18	88 47.0	N14 35.3	288 09.0	11.3	S21 06.0	4.1	54.6
19	103 47.1	34.6	302 39.3	11.4	21 01.9	4.2	54.6
20	118 47.2	33.8	317 09.7	11.5	20 57.7	4.3	54.5
21	133 47.3	.. 33.1	331 40.2	11.5	20 53.4	4.5	54.5
22	148 47.4	32.3	346 10.7	11.5	20 49.0	4.5	54.5
23	163 47.5	31.5	0 41.2	11.6	S20 44.5	4.6	54.5
SD	15.8	d 0.8	SD 15.1		15.0		14.9

Lat.	Twilight Naut.	Twilight Civil	Sunrise	Moonrise 11	12	13	14
°	h m	h m	h m	h m	h m	h m	h m
N 72	////	////	01 59	▨	▨	▨	▨
N 70	////	////	02 38	▨	▨	▨	22 14
68	////	01 13	03 05	▨	▨	21 40	21 29
66	////	02 02	03 25	19 46	20 32	20 51	20 59
64	////	02 33	03 42	19 03	19 52	20 20	20 37
62	01 05	02 55	03 55	18 35	19 24	19 57	20 18
60	01 50	03 13	04 06	18 13	19 02	19 38	20 03
N 58	02 18	03 27	04 16	17 55	18 45	19 23	19 51
56	02 38	03 40	04 24	17 40	18 30	19 10	19 40
54	02 55	03 50	04 32	17 27	18 18	18 58	19 30
52	03 09	04 00	04 39	17 16	18 06	18 48	19 21
50	03 21	04 08	04 45	17 06	17 56	18 39	19 13
45	03 45	04 25	04 58	16 45	17 36	18 19	18 57
N 40	04 03	04 39	05 08	16 28	17 19	18 04	18 43
35	04 18	04 50	05 17	16 13	17 04	17 50	18 31
30	04 30	05 00	05 25	16 01	16 52	17 39	18 21
20	04 49	05 16	05 39	15 40	16 31	17 19	18 03
N 10	05 03	05 29	05 51	15 21	16 13	17 02	17 48
0	05 15	05 40	06 02	15 04	15 55	16 45	17 34
S 10	05 26	05 51	06 12	14 47	15 38	16 29	17 19
20	05 35	06 01	06 24	14 29	15 20	16 12	17 04
30	05 44	06 12	06 37	14 08	14 59	15 52	16 46
35	05 48	06 18	06 44	13 56	14 46	15 40	16 35
40	05 52	06 24	06 53	13 41	14 32	15 27	16 24
45	05 57	06 32	07 02	13 25	14 15	15 11	16 09
S 50	06 02	06 40	07 14	13 04	13 54	14 51	15 52
52	06 04	06 44	07 20	12 54	13 45	14 42	15 44
54	06 06	06 48	07 26	12 43	13 33	14 31	15 35
56	06 08	06 52	07 32	12 31	13 21	14 19	15 25
58	06 11	06 57	07 40	12 16	13 06	14 06	15 13
S 60	06 13	07 03	07 48	11 59	12 48	13 50	15 00

Lat.	Sunset	Twilight Civil	Twilight Naut.	Moonset 11	12	13	14
°	h m	h m	h m	h m	h m	h m	h m
N 72	22 04	////	////	▨	▨	▨	▨
N 70	21 27	////	////	▨	▨	▨	▨
68	21 02	22 48	////	▨	▨	▨	00 22
66	20 42	22 03	////	22 46	23 47	25 10	01 10
64	20 26	21 34	////	23 29	24 26	00 26	01 40
62	20 13	21 12	22 57	23 58	24 54	00 54	02 03
60	20 02	20 55	22 16	24 20	00 20	01 15	02 22
N 58	19 53	20 41	21 49	24 37	00 37	01 32	02 37
56	19 45	20 29	21 29	00 08	00 52	01 47	02 50
54	19 37	20 18	21 13	00 20	01 05	02 00	03 01
52	19 31	20 09	20 59	00 30	01 17	02 11	03 11
50	19 25	20 01	20 47	00 40	01 27	02 21	03 20
45	19 12	19 44	20 24	01 00	01 48	02 41	03 39
N 40	19 01	19 30	20 06	01 16	02 05	02 58	03 54
35	18 52	19 19	19 52	01 30	02 19	03 12	04 07
30	18 44	19 10	19 40	01 42	02 32	03 24	04 18
20	18 31	18 54	19 21	02 03	02 53	03 45	04 37
N 10	18 19	18 41	19 07	02 21	03 12	04 03	04 53
0	18 08	18 30	18 55	02 37	03 29	04 20	05 09
S 10	17 58	18 19	18 45	02 54	03 46	04 36	05 24
20	17 47	18 09	18 35	03 12	04 05	04 54	05 41
30	17 34	17 58	18 27	03 33	04 26	05 15	05 59
35	17 26	17 53	18 23	03 45	04 38	05 27	06 10
40	17 18	17 46	18 18	03 59	04 53	05 41	06 23
45	17 08	17 39	18 14	04 15	05 10	05 57	06 37
S 50	16 57	17 31	18 09	04 35	05 30	06 17	06 55
52	16 51	17 27	18 07	04 45	05 40	06 27	07 04
54	16 45	17 23	18 05	04 56	05 52	06 37	07 13
56	16 39	17 19	18 03	05 08	06 04	06 49	07 24
58	16 31	17 14	18 01	05 23	06 19	07 03	07 36
S 60	16 23	17 08	17 58	05 40	06 37	07 20	07 50

Day	SUN Eqn. of Time 00h	SUN Eqn. of Time 12h	SUN Mer. Pass.	MOON Mer. Pass. Upper	MOON Mer. Pass. Lower	Age	Phase
d	m s	m s	h m	h m	h m	d	%
11	05 20	05 16	12 05	21 17	08 51	10	86
12	05 11	05 06	12 05	22 08	09 42	11	92
13	05 00	04 55	12 05	22 57	10 33	12	96

© British Crown Copyright 2018. All rights reserved.

UT	ARIES GHA	VENUS −4.0 GHA	Dec	MARS +1.8 GHA	Dec	JUPITER −2.3 GHA	Dec	SATURN +0.2 GHA	Dec	STARS Name	SHA	Dec
14 00	322 07.6	178 26.6	N15 44.1	172 12.5	N13 27.8	68 52.8	S22 08.6	36 00.7	S22 20.8	Acamar	315 15.1	S40 13.4
01	337 10.1	193 26.0	43.1	187 13.5	27.3	83 55.3	08.6	51 03.3	20.8	Achernar	335 23.3	S57 08.1
02	352 12.6	208 25.4	42.2	202 14.4	26.7	98 57.7	08.6	66 05.9	20.8	Acrux	173 05.1	S63 12.5
03	7 15.0	223 24.8 ..	41.2	217 15.4 ..	26.1	114 00.2 ..	08.6	81 08.5 ..	20.8	Adhara	255 09.5	S28 59.8
04	22 17.5	238 24.2	40.3	232 16.3	25.6	129 02.6	08.7	96 11.1	20.8	Aldebaran	290 44.6	N16 32.8
05	37 20.0	253 23.6	39.3	247 17.2	25.0	144 05.1	08.7	111 13.7	20.9			
06	52 22.4	268 23.0	N15 38.4	262 18.2	N13 24.5	159 07.5	S22 08.7	126 16.3	S22 20.9	Alioth	166 17.3	N55 51.6
W 07	67 24.9	283 22.5	37.4	277 19.1	23.9	174 10.0	08.7	141 18.9	20.9	Alkaid	152 55.7	N49 13.4
E 08	82 27.3	298 21.9	36.5	292 20.0	23.4	189 12.4	08.7	156 21.5	20.9	Alnair	27 38.0	S46 51.9
D 09	97 29.8	313 21.3 ..	35.5	307 21.0 ..	22.8	204 14.8 ..	08.7	171 24.1 ..	20.9	Alnilam	275 42.3	S 1 11.4
N 10	112 32.3	328 20.7	34.5	322 21.9	22.3	219 17.3	08.7	186 26.7	20.9	Alphard	217 52.3	S 8 44.5
E 11	127 34.7	343 20.1	33.6	337 22.8	21.7	234 19.7	08.7	201 29.3	21.0			
S 12	142 37.2	358 19.5	N15 32.6	352 23.8	N13 21.2	249 22.2	S22 08.7	216 31.9	S22 21.0	Alphecca	126 07.4	N26 39.3
D 13	157 39.7	13 18.9	31.7	7 24.7	20.6	264 24.6	08.7	231 34.5	21.0	Alpheratz	357 38.9	N29 11.8
A 14	172 42.1	28 18.4	30.7	22 25.6	20.1	279 27.0	08.8	246 37.1	21.0	Altair	62 03.8	N 8 55.4
Y 15	187 44.6	43 17.8 ..	29.8	37 26.6 ..	19.5	294 29.5 ..	08.8	261 39.7 ..	21.0	Ankaa	353 11.2	S42 11.8
16	202 47.1	58 17.2	28.8	52 27.5	19.0	309 31.9	08.8	276 42.3	21.1	Antares	112 21.0	S26 28.4
17	217 49.5	73 16.6	27.8	67 28.4	18.4	324 34.4	08.8	291 44.9	21.1			
18	232 52.0	88 16.0	N15 26.9	82 29.4	N13 17.9	339 36.8	S22 08.8	306 47.5	S22 21.1	Arcturus	145 52.0	N19 05.2
19	247 54.5	103 15.5	25.9	97 30.3	17.3	354 39.2	08.8	321 50.1	21.1	Atria	107 18.7	S69 03.8
20	262 56.9	118 14.9	24.9	112 31.2	16.8	9 41.7	08.8	336 52.7	21.1	Avior	234 16.9	S59 34.2
21	277 59.4	133 14.3 ..	24.0	127 32.2 ..	16.2	24 44.1 ..	08.8	351 55.3 ..	21.1	Bellatrix	278 27.6	N 6 22.0
22	293 01.8	148 13.7	23.0	142 33.1	15.6	39 46.6	08.8	6 57.9	21.2	Betelgeuse	270 56.9	N 7 24.6
23	308 04.3	163 13.1	22.1	157 34.1	15.1	54 49.0	08.9	22 00.5	21.2			
15 00	323 06.8	178 12.6	N15 21.1	172 35.0	N13 14.5	69 51.4	S22 08.9	37 03.1	S22 21.2	Canopus	263 54.7	S52 42.2
01	338 09.2	193 12.0	20.1	187 35.9	14.0	84 53.9	08.9	52 05.7	21.2	Capella	280 28.4	N46 00.8
02	353 11.7	208 11.4	19.2	202 36.9	13.4	99 56.3	08.9	67 08.3	21.2	Deneb	49 28.2	N45 21.1
03	8 14.2	223 10.8 ..	18.2	217 37.8 ..	12.9	114 58.7 ..	08.9	82 10.9 ..	21.3	Denebola	182 29.6	N14 28.0
04	23 16.6	238 10.2	17.2	232 38.7	12.3	130 01.2	08.9	97 13.5	21.3	Diphda	348 51.4	S17 52.7
05	38 19.1	253 09.7	16.2	247 39.7	11.8	145 03.6	08.9	112 16.1	21.3			
06	53 21.6	268 09.1	N15 15.3	262 40.6	N13 11.2	160 06.0	S22 08.9	127 18.7	S22 21.3	Dubhe	193 47.1	N61 39.0
07	68 24.0	283 08.5	14.3	277 41.5	10.6	175 08.5	08.9	142 21.3	21.3	Elnath	278 07.5	N28 37.2
T 08	83 26.5	298 07.9	13.3	292 42.5	10.1	190 10.9	09.0	157 23.9	21.3	Eltanin	90 43.9	N51 29.5
H 09	98 29.0	313 07.4 ..	12.4	307 43.4 ..	09.5	205 13.3 ..	09.0	172 26.5 ..	21.4	Enif	33 42.7	N 9 58.0
U 10	113 31.4	328 06.8	11.4	322 44.4	09.0	220 15.8	09.0	187 29.1	21.4	Fomalhaut	15 19.0	S29 31.0
R 11	128 33.9	343 06.2	10.4	337 45.3	08.4	235 18.2	09.0	202 31.7	21.4			
S 12	143 36.3	358 05.6	N15 09.4	352 46.2	N13 07.9	250 20.6	S22 09.0	217 34.3	S22 21.4	Gacrux	171 56.6	S57 13.4
D 13	158 38.8	13 05.1	08.5	7 47.2	07.3	265 23.1	09.0	232 36.9	21.4	Gienah	175 48.2	S17 38.9
A 14	173 41.3	28 04.5	07.5	22 48.1	06.8	280 25.5	09.0	247 39.5	21.5	Hadar	148 42.1	S60 28.1
Y 15	188 43.7	43 03.9 ..	06.5	37 49.1 ..	06.2	295 27.9 ..	09.0	262 42.1 ..	21.5	Hamal	327 55.9	N23 33.1
16	203 46.2	58 03.3	05.5	52 50.0	05.6	310 30.4	09.0	277 44.7	21.5	Kaus Aust.	83 37.9	S34 22.4
17	218 48.7	73 02.8	04.6	67 50.9	05.1	325 32.8	09.1	292 47.3	21.5			
18	233 51.1	88 02.2	N15 03.6	82 51.9	N13 04.5	340 35.2	S22 09.1	307 49.9	S22 21.5	Kochab	137 20.2	N74 04.9
19	248 53.6	103 01.6	02.6	97 52.8	04.0	355 37.7	09.1	322 52.5	21.5	Markab	13 33.8	N15 18.6
20	263 56.1	118 01.1	01.6	112 53.7	03.4	10 40.1	09.1	337 55.1	21.6	Menkar	314 10.6	N 4 09.9
21	278 58.5	133 00.5	15 00.6	127 54.7 ..	02.9	25 42.5 ..	09.1	352 57.7 ..	21.6	Menkent	148 02.7	S36 27.9
22	294 01.0	147 59.9	14 59.7	142 55.6	02.3	40 45.0	09.1	8 00.3	21.6	Miaplacidus	221 39.8	S69 47.8
23	309 03.4	162 59.4	58.7	157 56.6	01.7	55 47.4	09.1	23 02.9	21.6			
16 00	324 05.9	177 58.8	N14 57.7	172 57.5	N13 01.2	70 49.8	S22 09.1	38 05.5	S22 21.6	Mirfak	308 34.3	N49 55.5
01	339 08.4	192 58.2	56.7	187 58.4	00.6	85 52.2	09.1	53 08.0	21.7	Nunki	75 52.8	S26 16.2
02	354 10.8	207 57.7	55.7	202 59.4	13 00.1	100 54.7	09.2	68 10.6	21.7	Peacock	53 12.0	S56 40.3
03	9 13.3	222 57.1 ..	54.7	218 00.3	12 59.5	115 57.1 ..	09.2	83 13.2 ..	21.7	Pollux	243 22.9	N27 58.7
04	24 15.8	237 56.5	53.8	233 01.3	58.9	130 59.5	09.2	98 15.8	21.7	Procyon	244 55.6	N 5 10.5
05	39 18.2	252 56.0	52.8	248 02.2	58.4	146 02.0	09.2	113 18.4	21.7			
06	54 20.7	267 55.4	N14 51.8	263 03.1	N12 57.8	161 04.4	S22 09.2	128 21.0	S22 21.7	Rasalhague	96 02.3	N12 33.0
07	69 23.2	282 54.8	50.8	278 04.1	57.3	176 06.8	09.2	143 23.6	21.8	Regulus	207 39.3	N11 52.4
08	84 25.6	297 54.3	49.8	293 05.0	56.7	191 09.2	09.2	158 26.2	21.8	Rigel	281 08.1	S 8 10.7
F 09	99 28.1	312 53.7 ..	48.8	308 06.0 ..	56.2	206 11.7 ..	09.2	173 28.8 ..	21.8	Rigil Kent.	139 46.2	S60 55.0
R 10	114 30.6	327 53.1	47.8	323 06.9	55.6	221 14.1	09.3	188 31.4	21.8	Sabik	102 07.5	S15 44.8
I 11	129 33.0	342 52.6	46.8	338 07.8	55.0	236 16.5	09.3	203 34.0	21.8			
D 12	144 35.5	357 52.0	N14 45.8	353 08.8	N12 54.5	251 18.9	S22 09.3	218 36.6	S22 21.9	Schedar	349 35.3	N56 38.4
A 13	159 37.9	12 51.4	44.9	8 09.7	53.9	266 21.4	09.3	233 39.2	21.9	Shaula	96 16.0	S37 07.0
Y 14	174 40.4	27 50.9	43.9	23 10.7	53.4	281 23.8	09.3	248 41.8	21.9	Sirius	258 30.3	S16 44.5
15	189 42.9	42 50.3 ..	42.9	38 11.6 ..	52.8	296 26.2 ..	09.3	263 44.4 ..	21.9	Spica	158 27.0	S11 15.6
16	204 45.3	57 49.8	41.9	53 12.5	52.2	311 28.6	09.3	278 47.0	21.9	Suhail	222 49.8	S43 30.6
17	219 47.8	72 49.2	40.9	68 13.5	51.7	326 31.0	09.3	293 49.6	21.9			
18	234 50.3	87 48.6	N14 39.9	83 14.4	N12 51.1	341 33.5	S22 09.3	308 52.2	S22 22.0	Vega	80 35.8	N38 48.4
19	249 52.7	102 48.1	38.9	98 15.4	50.6	356 35.9	09.4	323 54.8	22.0	Zuben'ubi	137 00.8	S16 07.2
20	264 55.2	117 47.5	37.9	113 16.3	50.0	11 38.3	09.4	338 57.4	22.0		SHA	Mer.Pass.
21	279 57.7	132 47.0 ..	36.9	128 17.2 ..	49.4	26 40.7 ..	09.4	354 00.0 ..	22.0			
22	295 00.1	147 46.4	35.9	143 18.2	48.9	41 43.2	09.4	9 02.5	22.0	Venus	215 05.8	12 08
23	310 02.6	162 45.8	34.9	158 19.1	48.3	56 45.6	09.4	24 05.1	22.0	Mars	209 28.2	12 29
	h m									Jupiter	106 44.7	19 17
Mer. Pass. 2 27.1	*v* −0.6 *d* 1.0			*v* 0.9 *d* 0.6		*v* 2.4 *d* 0.0		*v* 2.6 *d* 0.0		Saturn	73 56.3	21 28

© British Crown Copyright 2018. All rights reserved.

UT	SUN GHA	SUN Dec	MOON GHA	v	MOON Dec	d	HP
14 00	178 47.6	N14 30.8	15 11.8	11.6	S20 39.9	4.7	54.5
01	193 47.8	30.0	29 42.4	11.7	20 35.2	4.8	54.5
02	208 47.9	29.2	44 13.1	11.7	20 30.4	4.9	54.5
03	223 48.0	.. 28.5	58 43.8	11.8	20 25.5	5.0	54.5
04	238 48.1	27.7	73 14.6	11.8	20 20.5	5.0	54.5
05	253 48.2	26.9	87 45.4	11.8	20 15.5	5.2	54.5
06	268 48.3	N14 26.2	102 16.2	11.9	S20 10.3	5.3	54.4
W 07	283 48.5	25.4	116 47.1	12.0	20 05.0	5.3	54.4
E 08	298 48.6	24.6	131 18.1	12.0	19 59.7	5.4	54.4
D 09	313 48.7	.. 23.9	145 49.1	12.0	19 54.3	5.6	54.4
N 10	328 48.8	23.1	160 20.1	12.1	19 48.7	5.6	54.4
E 11	343 48.9	22.3	174 51.2	12.2	19 43.1	5.7	54.4
S 12	358 49.0	N14 21.5	189 22.4	12.1	S19 37.4	5.8	54.4
D 13	13 49.2	20.8	203 53.5	12.3	19 31.6	5.9	54.4
A 14	28 49.3	20.0	218 24.8	12.3	19 25.7	5.9	54.4
Y 15	43 49.4	.. 19.2	232 56.1	12.3	19 19.8	6.1	54.3
16	58 49.5	18.5	247 27.4	12.4	19 13.7	6.1	54.3
17	73 49.6	17.7	261 58.8	12.4	19 07.6	6.3	54.3
18	88 49.8	N14 16.9	276 30.2	12.5	S19 01.3	6.3	54.3
19	103 49.9	16.1	291 01.7	12.6	18 55.0	6.4	54.3
20	118 50.0	15.4	305 33.3	12.6	18 48.6	6.4	54.3
21	133 50.1	.. 14.6	320 04.9	12.6	18 42.2	6.6	54.3
22	148 50.2	13.8	334 36.5	12.7	18 35.6	6.6	54.3
23	163 50.4	13.0	349 08.2	12.7	18 29.0	6.8	54.3
15 00	178 50.5	N14 12.3	3 39.9	12.8	S18 22.2	6.8	54.3
01	193 50.6	11.5	18 11.7	12.9	18 15.4	6.8	54.2
02	208 50.7	10.7	32 43.6	12.8	18 08.6	7.0	54.2
03	223 50.8	.. 09.9	47 15.4	13.0	18 01.6	7.0	54.2
04	238 51.0	09.2	61 47.4	13.0	17 54.6	7.2	54.2
05	253 51.1	08.4	76 19.4	13.0	17 47.4	7.1	54.2
06	268 51.2	N14 07.6	90 51.4	13.1	S17 40.3	7.3	54.2
T 07	283 51.3	06.8	105 23.5	13.1	17 33.0	7.4	54.2
H 08	298 51.5	06.1	119 55.6	13.2	17 25.6	7.4	54.2
U 09	313 51.6	.. 05.3	134 27.8	13.2	17 18.2	7.5	54.2
R 10	328 51.7	04.5	149 00.0	13.3	17 10.7	7.5	54.2
S 11	343 51.8	03.7	163 32.3	13.4	17 03.2	7.7	54.2
D 12	358 52.0	N14 02.9	178 04.7	13.3	S16 55.5	7.7	54.2
A 13	13 52.1	02.2	192 37.0	13.5	16 47.8	7.7	54.1
Y 14	28 52.2	01.4	207 09.5	13.5	16 40.1	7.9	54.1
15	43 52.3	14 00.6	221 42.0	13.5	16 32.2	7.9	54.1
16	58 52.4	13 59.8	236 14.5	13.6	16 24.3	8.0	54.1
17	73 52.6	59.0	250 47.1	13.6	16 16.3	8.1	54.1
18	88 52.7	N13 58.3	265 19.7	13.7	S16 08.2	8.1	54.1
19	103 52.8	57.5	279 52.4	13.7	16 00.1	8.2	54.1
20	118 52.9	56.7	294 25.1	13.8	15 51.9	8.2	54.1
21	133 53.1	.. 55.9	308 57.9	13.8	15 43.7	8.3	54.1
22	148 53.2	55.1	323 30.7	13.8	15 35.4	8.4	54.1
23	163 53.3	54.3	338 03.5	14.0	15 27.0	8.5	54.1
16 00	178 53.5	N13 53.6	352 36.5	13.9	S15 18.5	8.5	54.1
01	193 53.6	52.8	7 09.4	14.0	15 10.0	8.5	54.1
02	208 53.7	52.0	21 42.4	14.1	15 01.5	8.7	54.1
03	223 53.8	.. 51.2	36 15.5	14.1	14 52.8	8.7	54.1
04	238 54.0	50.4	50 48.6	14.1	14 44.1	8.7	54.1
05	253 54.1	49.6	65 21.7	14.2	14 35.4	8.8	54.0
06	268 54.2	N13 48.8	79 54.9	14.2	S14 26.6	8.9	54.0
F 07	283 54.3	48.1	94 28.1	14.3	14 17.7	8.9	54.0
R 08	298 54.5	47.3	109 01.4	14.3	14 08.8	9.0	54.0
I 09	313 54.6	.. 46.5	123 34.7	14.4	13 59.8	9.1	54.0
10	328 54.7	45.7	138 08.1	14.4	13 50.7	9.1	54.0
11	343 54.9	44.9	152 41.5	14.4	13 41.6	9.1	54.0
D 12	358 55.0	N13 44.1	167 14.9	14.5	S13 32.5	9.2	54.0
A 13	13 55.1	43.3	181 48.4	14.6	13 23.3	9.3	54.0
Y 14	28 55.2	42.5	196 22.0	14.5	13 14.0	9.3	54.0
15	43 55.4	.. 41.8	210 55.5	14.7	13 04.7	9.4	54.0
16	58 55.5	41.0	225 29.2	14.6	12 55.3	9.4	54.0
17	73 55.6	40.2	240 02.8	14.7	12 45.9	9.5	54.0
18	88 55.8	N13 39.4	254 36.5	14.7	S12 36.4	9.5	54.0
19	103 55.9	38.6	269 10.2	14.8	12 26.9	9.6	54.0
20	118 56.0	37.8	283 44.0	14.8	12 17.3	9.6	54.0
21	133 56.2	.. 37.0	298 17.8	14.9	12 07.7	9.7	54.0
22	148 56.3	36.2	312 51.7	14.9	11 58.0	9.7	54.0
23	163 56.4	35.4	327 25.6	14.9	S11 48.3	9.7	54.0
	SD 15.8	d 0.8	SD 14.8		14.8		14.7

Lat.	Twilight Naut.	Civil	Sunrise	Moonrise 14	15	16	17
N 72	////	////	02 22	■■■	22 24	21 53	21 32
N 70	////	////	02 55	22 14	21 48	21 33	21 21
68	////	01 41	03 18	21 29	21 22	21 16	21 11
66	////	02 19	03 36	20 59	21 02	21 03	21 03
64	////	02 46	03 51	20 37	20 46	20 52	20 56
62	01 30	03 06	04 03	20 18	20 33	20 43	20 51
60	02 04	03 22	04 13	20 03	20 21	20 35	20 46
N 58	02 29	03 35	04 22	19 51	20 11	20 28	20 41
56	02 48	03 47	04 30	19 40	20 03	20 21	20 37
54	03 03	03 56	04 37	19 30	19 55	20 15	20 33
52	03 16	04 05	04 43	19 21	19 48	20 11	20 30
50	03 27	04 13	04 49	19 13	19 42	20 06	20 27
45	03 50	04 29	05 01	18 57	19 28	19 56	20 21
N 40	04 07	04 42	05 11	18 43	19 17	19 47	20 15
35	04 21	04 53	05 20	18 31	19 07	19 40	20 10
30	04 32	05 02	05 27	18 21	18 59	19 34	20 06
20	04 50	05 17	05 40	18 03	18 44	19 23	19 59
N 10	05 04	05 29	05 51	17 48	18 32	19 13	19 52
0	05 15	05 40	06 01	17 34	18 20	19 04	19 46
S 10	05 25	05 50	06 11	17 19	18 08	18 55	19 40
20	05 33	05 59	06 22	17 04	17 55	18 45	19 34
30	05 41	06 09	06 34	16 46	17 40	18 34	19 26
35	05 45	06 15	06 41	16 35	17 31	18 27	19 22
40	05 49	06 21	06 49	16 24	17 21	18 20	19 17
45	05 53	06 27	06 58	16 09	17 10	18 11	19 12
S 50	05 57	06 35	07 09	15 52	16 56	18 00	19 05
52	05 59	06 38	07 14	15 44	16 49	17 55	19 02
54	06 00	06 42	07 19	15 35	16 42	17 50	18 58
56	06 02	06 46	07 26	15 25	16 34	17 44	18 54
58	06 04	06 51	07 32	15 13	16 25	17 37	18 50
S 60	06 06	06 55	07 40	15 00	16 14	17 30	18 45

Lat.	Sunset	Twilight Civil	Naut.	Moonset 14	15	16	17
N 72	21 41	////	////	■■■	■■■	02 53	04 55
N 70	21 10	23 41	////	■■■	01 27	03 28	05 14
68	20 48	22 21	////	00 22	02 11	03 53	05 28
66	20 30	21 45	////	01 10	02 41	04 11	05 40
64	20 16	21 20	23 44	01 40	03 03	04 27	05 50
62	20 04	21 01	22 33	02 03	03 20	04 39	05 59
60	19 54	20 45	22 01	02 22	03 35	04 50	06 06
N 58	19 45	20 32	21 37	02 37	03 47	04 59	06 12
56	19 38	20 21	21 19	02 50	03 57	05 07	06 18
54	19 31	20 11	21 04	03 01	04 07	05 15	06 23
52	19 25	20 03	20 51	03 11	04 15	05 21	06 27
50	19 19	19 55	20 40	03 20	04 23	05 27	06 31
45	19 07	19 39	20 18	03 39	04 38	05 39	06 40
N 40	18 57	19 26	20 01	03 54	04 51	05 50	06 47
35	18 49	19 16	19 48	04 07	05 02	05 58	06 54
30	18 42	19 07	19 36	04 18	05 12	06 06	06 59
20	18 29	18 52	19 19	04 37	05 28	06 19	07 09
N 10	18 18	18 40	19 05	04 53	05 43	06 31	07 17
0	18 08	18 29	18 54	05 09	05 56	06 41	07 24
S 10	17 58	18 20	18 44	05 24	06 09	06 52	07 32
20	17 47	18 10	18 36	05 41	06 23	07 03	07 40
30	17 35	18 00	18 28	05 59	06 40	07 16	07 49
35	17 29	17 55	18 25	06 10	06 49	07 23	07 55
40	17 21	17 49	18 21	06 23	06 59	07 32	08 01
45	17 12	17 42	18 17	06 37	07 12	07 41	08 07
S 50	17 01	17 35	18 13	06 55	07 27	07 53	08 16
52	16 56	17 31	18 11	07 04	07 34	07 59	08 19
54	16 50	17 28	18 10	07 13	07 42	08 04	08 24
56	16 44	17 24	18 08	07 24	07 50	08 11	08 28
58	16 38	17 19	18 06	07 36	08 00	08 18	08 33
S 60	16 30	17 15	18 04	07 50	08 11	08 27	08 39

Day	SUN Eqn. of Time 00h	12h	Mer. Pass.	MOON Mer. Pass. Upper	Lower	Age	Phase
d	m s	m s	h m	h m	h m	d %	
14	04 50	04 44	12 05	23 45	11 21	13 99	
15	04 38	04 32	12 05	24 30	12 08	14 100	◯
16	04 26	04 20	12 04	00 30	12 53	15 99	

© British Crown Copyright 2018. All rights reserved.

UT	ARIES GHA	VENUS −4·0 GHA	Dec	MARS +1·8 GHA	Dec	JUPITER −2·3 GHA	Dec	SATURN +0·3 GHA	Dec	STARS Name	SHA	Dec
17 00	325 05.1	177 45.3	N14 33.9	173 20.1	N12 47.7	71 48.0	S22 09.4	39 07.7	S22 22.1	Acamar	315 15.1	S40 13.4
01	340 07.5	192 44.7	32.9	188 21.0	47.2	86 50.4	09.4	54 10.3	22.1	Achernar	335 23.3	S57 08.1
02	355 10.0	207 44.2	31.9	203 21.9	46.6	101 52.8	09.4	69 12.9	22.1	Acrux	173 05.1	S63 12.5
03	10 12.4	222 43.6	.. 30.9	218 22.9	.. 46.1	116 55.3	.. 09.5	84 15.5	.. 22.1	Adhara	255 09.5	S28 59.8
04	25 14.9	237 43.1	29.9	233 23.8	45.5	131 57.7	09.5	99 18.1	22.1	Aldebaran	290 44.6	N16 32.8
05	40 17.4	252 42.5	28.9	248 24.8	44.9	147 00.1	09.5	114 20.7	22.1			
06	55 19.8	267 41.9	N14 27.9	263 25.7	N12 44.4	162 02.5	S22 09.5	129 23.3	S22 22.2	Alioth	166 17.3	N55 51.6
07	70 22.3	282 41.4	26.9	278 26.7	43.8	177 04.9	09.5	144 25.9	22.2	Alkaid	152 55.8	N49 13.3
S 08	85 24.8	297 40.8	25.9	293 27.6	43.3	192 07.4	09.5	159 28.5	22.2	Alnair	27 37.9	S46 51.9
A 09	100 27.2	312 40.3	.. 24.9	308 28.5	.. 42.7	207 09.8	.. 09.5	174 31.1	.. 22.2	Alnilam	275 42.2	S 1 11.4
T 10	115 29.7	327 39.7	23.9	323 29.5	42.1	222 12.2	09.6	189 33.7	22.2	Alphard	217 52.3	S 8 44.5
U 11	130 32.2	342 39.2	22.8	338 30.4	41.6	237 14.6	09.6	204 36.3	22.3			
R 12	145 34.6	357 38.6	N14 21.8	353 31.4	N12 41.0	252 17.0	S22 09.6	219 38.8	S22 22.3	Alphecca	126 07.4	N26 39.3
D 13	160 37.1	12 38.1	20.8	8 32.3	40.4	267 19.4	09.6	234 41.4	22.3	Alpheratz	357 38.8	N29 11.8
A 14	175 39.5	27 37.5	19.8	23 33.3	39.9	282 21.9	09.6	249 44.0	22.3	Altair	62 03.8	N 8 55.4
Y 15	190 42.0	42 37.0	.. 18.8	38 34.2	.. 39.3	297 24.3	.. 09.6	264 46.6	.. 22.3	Ankaa	353 11.2	S42 11.8
16	205 44.5	57 36.4	17.8	53 35.1	38.7	312 26.7	09.6	279 49.2	22.3	Antares	112 21.0	S26 28.4
17	220 46.9	72 35.9	16.8	68 36.1	38.2	327 29.1	09.6	294 51.8	22.4			
18	235 49.4	87 35.3	N14 15.8	83 37.0	N12 37.6	342 31.5	S22 09.7	309 54.4	S22 22.4	Arcturus	145 52.0	N19 05.2
19	250 51.9	102 34.8	14.8	98 38.0	37.1	357 33.9	09.7	324 57.0	22.4	Atria	107 18.8	S69 03.8
20	265 54.3	117 34.2	13.7	113 38.9	36.5	12 36.3	09.7	339 59.6	22.4	Avior	234 16.9	S59 34.2
21	280 56.8	132 33.7	.. 12.7	128 39.9	.. 35.9	27 38.8	.. 09.7	355 02.2	.. 22.4	Bellatrix	278 27.6	N 6 22.0
22	295 59.3	147 33.1	11.7	143 40.8	35.4	42 41.2	09.7	10 04.8	22.4	Betelgeuse	270 56.9	N 7 24.6
23	311 01.7	162 32.6	10.7	158 41.7	34.8	57 43.6	09.7	25 07.3	22.5			
18 00	326 04.2	177 32.0	N14 09.7	173 42.7	N12 34.2	72 46.0	S22 09.7	40 09.9	S22 22.5	Canopus	263 54.6	S52 42.2
01	341 06.7	192 31.5	08.7	188 43.6	33.7	87 48.4	09.7	55 12.5	22.5	Capella	280 28.4	N46 00.8
02	356 09.1	207 30.9	07.7	203 44.6	33.1	102 50.8	09.8	70 15.1	22.5	Deneb	49 28.2	N45 21.2
03	11 11.6	222 30.4	.. 06.6	218 45.5	.. 32.5	117 53.2	.. 09.8	85 17.7	.. 22.5	Denebola	182 29.6	N14 28.0
04	26 14.0	237 29.9	05.6	233 46.5	32.0	132 55.6	09.8	100 20.3	22.5	Diphda	348 51.4	S17 52.7
05	41 16.5	252 29.3	04.6	248 47.4	31.4	147 58.0	09.8	115 22.9	22.6			
06	56 19.0	267 28.8	N14 03.6	263 48.3	N12 30.8	163 00.5	S22 09.8	130 25.5	S22 22.6	Dubhe	193 47.1	N61 38.9
07	71 21.4	282 28.2	02.6	278 49.3	30.3	178 02.9	09.8	145 28.1	22.6	Elnath	278 07.4	N28 37.2
08	86 23.9	297 27.7	01.5	293 50.2	29.7	193 05.3	09.8	160 30.7	22.6	Eltanin	90 43.9	N51 29.5
S 09	101 26.4	312 27.1	14 00.5	308 51.2	.. 29.1	208 07.7	.. 09.9	175 33.2	.. 22.6	Enif	33 42.7	N 9 58.0
U 10	116 28.8	327 26.6	13 59.5	323 52.1	28.6	223 10.1	09.9	190 35.8	22.6	Fomalhaut	15 19.0	S29 31.0
N 11	131 31.3	342 26.1	58.5	338 53.1	28.0	238 12.5	09.9	205 38.4	22.7			
D 12	146 33.8	357 25.5	N13 57.4	353 54.0	N12 27.4	253 14.9	S22 09.9	220 41.0	S22 22.7	Gacrux	171 56.6	S57 13.4
A 13	161 36.2	12 25.0	56.4	8 55.0	26.9	268 17.3	09.9	235 43.6	22.7	Gienah	175 48.2	S17 38.9
Y 14	176 38.7	27 24.4	55.4	23 55.9	26.3	283 19.7	09.9	250 46.2	22.7	Hadar	148 42.1	S60 28.1
15	191 41.1	42 23.9	.. 54.4	38 56.9	.. 25.7	298 22.1	.. 09.9	265 48.8	.. 22.7	Hamal	327 55.9	N23 33.1
16	206 43.6	57 23.3	53.3	53 57.8	25.2	313 24.5	10.0	280 51.4	22.7	Kaus Aust.	83 37.9	S34 22.4
17	221 46.1	72 22.8	52.3	68 58.7	24.6	328 26.9	10.0	295 53.9	22.8			
18	236 48.5	87 22.3	N13 51.3	83 59.7	N12 24.0	343 29.4	S22 10.0	310 56.5	S22 22.8	Kochab	137 20.3	N74 04.9
19	251 51.0	102 21.7	50.2	99 00.6	23.5	358 31.8	10.0	325 59.1	22.8	Markab	13 33.8	N15 18.7
20	266 53.5	117 21.2	49.2	114 01.6	22.9	13 34.2	10.0	341 01.7	22.8	Menkar	314 10.6	N 4 09.9
21	281 55.9	132 20.7	.. 48.2	129 02.5	.. 22.3	28 36.6	.. 10.0	356 04.3	.. 22.8	Menkent	148 02.7	S36 27.9
22	296 58.4	147 20.1	47.2	144 03.5	21.8	43 39.0	10.0	11 06.9	22.8	Miaplacidus	221 39.8	S69 47.8
23	312 00.9	162 19.6	46.1	159 04.4	21.2	58 41.4	10.0	26 09.5	22.9			
19 00	327 03.3	177 19.0	N13 45.1	174 05.4	N12 20.6	73 43.8	S22 10.1	41 12.1	S22 22.9	Mirfak	308 34.3	N49 55.5
01	342 05.8	192 18.5	44.1	189 06.3	20.1	88 46.2	10.1	56 14.6	22.9	Nunki	75 52.8	S26 16.2
02	357 08.3	207 18.0	43.0	204 07.3	19.5	103 48.6	10.1	71 17.2	22.9	Peacock	53 12.0	S56 40.3
03	12 10.7	222 17.4	.. 42.0	219 08.2	.. 18.9	118 51.0	.. 10.1	86 19.8	.. 22.9	Pollux	243 22.9	N27 58.7
04	27 13.2	237 16.9	41.0	234 09.1	18.4	133 53.4	10.1	101 22.4	22.9	Procyon	244 55.6	N 5 10.5
05	42 15.6	252 16.4	39.9	249 10.1	17.8	148 55.8	10.1	116 25.0	23.0			
06	57 18.1	267 15.8	N13 38.9	264 11.0	N12 17.2	163 58.2	S22 10.1	131 27.6	S22 23.0	Rasalhague	96 02.4	N12 33.0
07	72 20.6	282 15.3	37.9	279 12.0	16.7	179 00.6	10.2	146 30.2	23.0	Regulus	207 39.3	N11 52.4
08	87 23.0	297 14.8	36.8	294 12.9	16.1	194 03.0	10.2	161 32.7	23.0	Rigel	281 08.1	S 8 10.7
M 09	102 25.5	312 14.2	.. 35.8	309 13.9	.. 15.5	209 05.4	.. 10.2	176 35.3	.. 23.0	Rigil Kent.	139 46.2	S60 55.0
O 10	117 28.0	327 13.7	34.7	324 14.8	15.0	224 07.8	10.2	191 37.9	23.0	Sabik	102 07.5	S15 44.8
N 11	132 30.4	342 13.2	33.7	339 15.8	14.4	239 10.2	10.2	206 40.5	23.1			
D 12	147 32.9	357 12.6	N13 32.7	354 16.7	N12 13.8	254 12.6	S22 10.2	221 43.1	S22 23.1	Schedar	349 35.3	N56 38.4
A 13	162 35.4	12 12.1	31.6	9 17.7	13.2	269 15.0	10.3	236 45.7	23.1	Shaula	96 16.0	S37 07.0
Y 14	177 37.8	27 11.6	30.6	24 18.6	12.7	284 17.4	10.3	251 48.3	23.1	Sirius	258 30.2	S16 44.5
15	192 40.3	42 11.1	.. 29.5	39 19.6	.. 12.1	299 19.8	.. 10.3	266 50.8	.. 23.1	Spica	158 27.0	S11 15.6
16	207 42.8	57 10.5	28.5	54 20.5	11.5	314 22.2	10.3	281 53.4	23.1	Suhail	222 49.8	S43 30.6
17	222 45.2	72 10.0	27.4	69 21.5	11.0	329 24.6	10.3	296 56.0	23.2			
18	237 47.7	87 09.5	N13 26.4	84 22.4	N12 10.4	344 27.0	S22 10.3	311 58.6	S22 23.2	Vega	80 35.8	N38 48.4
19	252 50.1	102 08.9	25.4	99 23.4	09.8	359 29.4	10.3	327 01.2	23.2	Zuben'ubi	137 00.8	S16 07.2
20	267 52.6	117 08.4	24.3	114 24.3	09.3	14 31.8	10.4	342 03.8	23.2		SHA	Mer.Pass.
21	282 55.1	132 07.9	.. 23.3	129 25.3	.. 08.7	29 34.2	.. 10.4	357 06.3	.. 23.2	Venus	211 27.8	12 10
22	297 57.5	147 07.4	22.2	144 26.2	08.1	44 36.6	10.4	12 08.9	23.2	Mars	207 38.5	12 24
23	313 00.0	162 06.8	21.2	159 27.1	07.5	59 39.0	10.4	27 11.5	23.3	Jupiter	106 41.8	19 06
Mer. Pass. 2 15.4		v −0.5 d 1.0		v 0.9 d 0.6		v 2.4 d 0.0		v 2.6 d 0.0		Saturn	74 05.7	21 16

© British Crown Copyright 2018. All rights reserved.

UT	SUN GHA	SUN Dec	MOON GHA	v	Dec	d	HP
d h	° ′	° ′	° ′	′	° ′	′	′
17 00	178 56.6	N13 34.6	341 59.5	15.0	S11 38.6	9.8	54.0
01	193 56.7	33.8	356 33.5	15.0	11 28.8	9.9	54.0
02	208 56.8	33.0	11 07.5	15.0	11 18.9	9.9	54.0
03	223 57.0	.. 32.2	25 41.5	15.1	11 09.0	9.9	54.0
04	238 57.1	31.5	40 15.6	15.1	10 59.1	10.0	54.0
05	253 57.2	30.7	54 49.7	15.1	10 49.1	10.0	54.0
06	268 57.4	N13 29.9	69 23.8	15.2	S10 39.1	10.1	54.0
S 07	283 57.5	29.1	83 58.0	15.2	10 29.0	10.1	54.0
A 08	298 57.6	28.3	98 32.2	15.2	10 18.9	10.2	54.0
T 09	313 57.8	.. 27.5	113 06.4	15.3	10 08.7	10.1	54.0
U 10	328 57.9	26.7	127 40.7	15.3	9 58.6	10.3	54.0
R 11	343 58.0	25.9	142 15.0	15.3	9 48.3	10.2	54.0
D 12	358 58.2	N13 25.1	156 49.3	15.4	S 9 38.1	10.3	54.0
A 13	13 58.3	24.3	171 23.7	15.4	9 27.8	10.4	54.0
Y 14	28 58.4	23.5	185 58.1	15.4	9 17.4	10.4	54.0
15	43 58.6	.. 22.7	200 32.5	15.5	9 07.0	10.4	54.0
16	58 58.7	21.9	215 07.0	15.5	8 56.6	10.4	54.0
17	73 58.8	21.1	229 41.5	15.5	8 46.2	10.5	54.0
18	88 59.0	N13 20.3	244 16.0	15.5	S 8 35.7	10.5	54.0
19	103 59.1	19.5	258 50.5	15.5	8 25.2	10.6	54.0
20	118 59.2	18.7	273 25.0	15.6	8 14.6	10.5	54.0
21	133 59.4	.. 17.9	287 59.6	15.6	8 04.1	10.7	54.0
22	148 59.5	17.1	302 34.2	15.7	7 53.4	10.6	54.0
23	163 59.6	16.3	317 08.9	15.6	7 42.8	10.7	54.0
18 00	178 59.8	N13 15.5	331 43.5	15.7	S 7 32.1	10.7	54.0
01	193 59.9	14.7	346 18.2	15.7	7 21.4	10.7	54.0
02	209 00.1	13.9	0 52.9	15.7	7 10.7	10.8	54.0
03	224 00.2	.. 13.1	15 27.6	15.7	6 59.9	10.8	54.0
04	239 00.3	12.3	30 02.3	15.8	6 49.1	10.8	54.0
05	254 00.5	11.5	44 37.1	15.8	6 38.3	10.8	54.0
06	269 00.6	N13 10.7	59 11.9	15.8	S 6 27.5	10.9	54.0
07	284 00.8	09.9	73 46.7	15.8	6 16.6	10.9	54.0
08	299 00.9	09.1	88 21.5	15.8	6 05.7	10.9	54.0
S 09	314 01.0	.. 08.2	102 56.3	15.9	5 54.8	10.9	54.0
U 10	329 01.2	07.4	117 31.2	15.8	5 43.9	11.0	54.0
N 11	344 01.3	06.6	132 06.0	15.9	5 32.9	11.0	54.0
D 12	359 01.4	N13 05.8	146 40.9	15.9	S 5 21.9	11.0	54.0
A 13	14 01.6	05.0	161 15.8	15.9	5 10.9	11.0	54.0
Y 14	29 01.7	04.2	175 50.7	15.9	4 59.9	11.1	54.0
15	44 01.9	.. 03.4	190 25.6	15.9	4 48.8	11.0	54.0
16	59 02.0	02.6	205 00.5	16.0	4 37.8	11.1	54.1
17	74 02.1	01.8	219 35.5	15.9	4 26.7	11.1	54.1
18	89 02.3	N13 01.0	234 10.4	16.0	S 4 15.6	11.2	54.1
19	104 02.4	13 00.2	248 45.4	16.0	4 04.4	11.1	54.1
20	119 02.6	12 59.4	263 20.4	15.9	3 53.3	11.2	54.1
21	134 02.7	.. 58.6	277 55.3	16.0	3 42.1	11.1	54.1
22	149 02.9	57.7	292 30.3	16.0	3 31.0	11.2	54.1
23	164 03.0	56.9	307 05.3	16.0	3 19.8	11.2	54.1
19 00	179 03.1	N12 56.1	321 40.3	16.0	S 3 08.6	11.3	54.1
01	194 03.3	55.3	336 15.3	16.0	2 57.3	11.2	54.1
02	209 03.4	54.5	350 50.3	16.0	2 46.1	11.2	54.1
03	224 03.6	.. 53.7	5 25.3	16.0	2 34.9	11.3	54.1
04	239 03.7	52.9	20 00.3	16.0	2 23.6	11.3	54.1
05	254 03.9	52.1	34 35.3	16.1	2 12.3	11.3	54.1
06	269 04.0	N12 51.3	49 10.4	16.0	S 2 01.0	11.2	54.2
07	284 04.1	50.4	63 45.4	16.0	1 49.8	11.3	54.2
08	299 04.3	49.6	78 20.4	16.0	1 38.5	11.4	54.2
M 09	314 04.4	.. 48.8	92 55.4	16.0	1 27.1	11.3	54.2
O 10	329 04.6	48.0	107 30.4	16.0	1 15.8	11.3	54.2
N 11	344 04.7	47.2	122 05.4	16.0	1 04.5	11.3	54.2
D 12	359 04.9	N12 46.4	136 40.4	16.0	S 0 53.2	11.4	54.2
A 13	14 05.0	45.6	151 15.4	16.0	0 41.8	11.3	54.3
Y 14	29 05.2	44.7	165 50.4	16.0	0 30.5	11.4	54.3
15	44 05.3	.. 43.9	180 25.4	16.0	0 19.1	11.4	54.3
16	59 05.4	43.1	195 00.4	15.9	S 0 07.7	11.3	54.3
17	74 05.6	42.3	209 35.3	16.0	N 0 03.6	11.4	54.3
18	89 05.7	N12 41.5	224 10.3	16.0	N 0 15.0	11.3	54.3
19	104 05.9	40.7	238 45.3	15.9	0 26.3	11.4	54.3
20	119 06.0	39.8	253 20.2	15.9	0 37.7	11.4	54.3
21	134 06.2	.. 39.0	267 55.1	16.0	0 49.1	11.4	54.3
22	149 06.3	38.2	282 30.1	15.9	1 00.5	11.3	54.3
23	164 06.5	37.4	297 05.0	15.9	N 1 11.8	11.4	54.3
SD 15.8	d 0.8		SD 14.7		14.7		14.8

Lat.	Twilight Naut.	Twilight Civil	Sunrise	Moonrise 17	18	19	20
°	h m	h m	h m	h m	h m	h m	h m
N 72	////	////	02 42	21 32	21 15	20 59	20 43
N 70	////	01 09	03 10	21 21	21 10	21 00	20 50
68	////	02 03	03 30	21 11	21 06	21 01	20 56
66	////	02 35	03 47	21 03	21 03	21 02	21 01
64	01 00	02 58	04 00	20 56	21 00	21 02	21 05
62	01 49	03 16	04 11	20 51	20 57	21 03	21 09
60	02 18	03 30	04 21	20 46	20 55	21 03	21 12
N 58	02 39	03 43	04 29	20 41	20 53	21 04	21 15
56	02 56	03 53	04 36	20 37	20 51	21 04	21 18
54	03 11	04 02	04 42	20 33	20 49	21 05	21 20
52	03 23	04 11	04 48	20 30	20 48	21 05	21 22
50	03 33	04 18	04 54	20 27	20 46	21 05	21 24
45	03 54	04 33	05 05	20 21	20 43	21 06	21 28
N 40	04 10	04 45	05 14	20 15	20 41	21 06	21 32
35	04 23	04 55	05 22	20 10	20 39	21 07	21 35
30	04 34	05 04	05 29	20 06	20 37	21 07	21 38
20	04 51	05 18	05 41	19 59	20 33	21 08	21 42
N 10	05 04	05 29	05 51	19 52	20 31	21 08	21 47
0	05 15	05 39	06 01	19 46	20 28	21 09	21 51
S 10	05 24	05 48	06 10	19 40	20 25	21 10	21 55
20	05 31	05 57	06 20	19 34	20 22	21 10	21 59
30	05 38	06 07	06 31	19 26	20 19	21 11	22 04
35	05 42	06 11	06 37	19 22	20 17	21 11	22 07
40	05 45	06 16	06 45	19 17	20 15	21 12	22 10
45	05 48	06 23	06 53	19 12	20 12	21 13	22 14
S 50	05 52	06 30	07 03	19 05	20 09	21 13	22 18
52	05 53	06 33	07 08	19 02	20 08	21 14	22 21
54	05 55	06 36	07 13	18 58	20 06	21 14	22 23
56	05 56	06 40	07 19	18 54	20 04	21 15	22 25
58	05 57	06 44	07 25	18 50	20 02	21 15	22 28
S 60	05 59	06 48	07 32	18 45	20 00	21 15	22 32

Lat.	Sunset	Twilight Civil	Twilight Naut.	Moonset 17	18	19	20
°	h m	h m	h m	h m	h m	h m	h m
N 72	21 21	////	////	04 55	06 43	08 27	10 10
N 70	20 54	22 48	////	05 14	06 53	08 29	10 06
68	20 34	21 59	////	05 28	07 01	08 31	10 02
66	20 19	21 29	////	05 40	07 07	08 33	09 59
64	20 06	21 07	22 57	05 50	07 13	08 34	09 56
62	19 55	20 50	22 14	05 59	07 17	08 35	09 54
60	19 46	20 35	21 46	06 06	07 21	08 36	09 52
N 58	19 38	20 23	21 26	06 12	07 25	08 37	09 50
56	19 30	20 13	21 09	06 18	07 28	08 38	09 48
54	19 24	20 04	20 55	06 23	07 31	08 39	09 47
52	19 18	19 56	20 43	06 27	07 33	08 39	09 46
50	19 13	19 49	20 33	06 31	07 36	08 40	09 45
45	19 02	19 34	20 12	06 40	07 41	08 41	09 42
N 40	18 53	19 22	19 57	06 47	07 45	08 42	09 40
35	18 45	19 12	19 44	06 54	07 49	08 43	09 38
30	18 38	19 03	19 33	06 59	07 52	08 44	09 36
20	18 27	18 50	19 16	07 09	07 57	08 45	09 34
N 10	18 17	18 38	19 04	07 17	08 02	08 47	09 31
0	18 07	18 28	18 53	07 24	08 06	08 48	09 29
S 10	17 58	18 19	18 44	07 32	08 11	08 49	09 27
20	17 48	18 11	18 37	07 40	08 15	08 50	09 24
30	17 37	18 02	18 30	07 49	08 21	08 51	09 21
35	17 31	17 57	18 27	07 55	08 24	08 52	09 20
40	17 24	17 51	18 23	08 01	08 27	08 53	09 18
45	17 15	17 46	18 20	08 07	08 31	08 53	09 16
S 50	17 05	17 39	18 17	08 16	08 36	08 55	09 13
52	17 01	17 36	18 15	08 19	08 38	08 55	09 12
54	16 56	17 33	18 14	08 24	08 40	08 56	09 11
56	16 50	17 29	18 13	08 28	08 43	08 56	09 09
58	16 44	17 25	18 11	08 33	08 46	08 57	09 08
S 60	16 37	17 21	18 10	08 39	08 49	08 58	09 06

Day	SUN Eqn. of Time 00h	12h	SUN Mer. Pass.	MOON Mer. Pass. Upper	Lower	Age	Phase
d	m s	m s	h m	h m	h m	d %	
17	04 14	04 08	12 04	01 14	13 35	16 96	
18	04 01	03 54	12 04	01 56	14 17	17 92	
19	03 48	03 41	12 04	02 38	14 58	18 86	◐

© British Crown Copyright 2018. All rights reserved.

UT	ARIES GHA	VENUS −4.0 GHA	Dec	MARS +1.8 GHA	Dec	JUPITER −2.3 GHA	Dec	SATURN +0.3 GHA	Dec	STARS Name	SHA	Dec
20 00	328 02.5	177 06.3	N13 20.1	174 28.1	N12 07.0	74 41.4	S22 10.4	42 14.1	S22 23.3	Acamar	315 15.0	S40 13.4
01	343 04.9	192 05.8	19.1	189 29.0	06.4	89 43.8	10.4	57 16.7	23.3	Achernar	335 23.3	S57 08.1
02	358 07.4	207 05.2	18.0	204 30.0	05.8	104 46.2	10.4	72 19.3	23.3	Acrux	173 05.1	S63 12.5
03	13 09.9	222 04.7	.. 17.0	219 30.9	.. 05.3	119 48.6	.. 10.5	87 21.8	.. 23.3	Adhara	255 09.5	S28 59.8
04	28 12.3	237 04.2	15.9	234 31.9	04.7	134 51.0	10.5	102 24.4	23.3	Aldebaran	290 44.6	N16 32.8
05	43 14.8	252 03.7	14.9	249 32.8	04.1	149 53.4	10.5	117 27.0	23.4			
06	58 17.2	267 03.2	N13 13.8	264 33.8	N12 03.5	164 55.7	S22 10.5	132 29.6	S22 23.4	Alioth	166 17.3	N55 51.6
T 07	73 19.7	282 02.6	12.8	279 34.7	03.0	179 58.1	10.5	147 32.2	23.4	Alkaid	152 55.8	N49 13.3
U 08	88 22.2	297 02.1	11.7	294 35.7	02.4	195 00.5	10.5	162 34.8	23.4	Alnair	27 37.9	S46 51.9
E 09	103 24.6	312 01.6	.. 10.7	309 36.6	.. 01.8	210 02.9	.. 10.5	177 37.3	.. 23.4	Alnilam	275 42.2	S 1 11.4
S 10	118 27.1	327 01.1	09.6	324 37.6	01.2	225 05.3	10.6	192 39.9	23.4	Alphard	217 52.3	S 8 44.5
D 11	133 29.6	342 00.5	08.6	339 38.5	00.7	240 07.7	10.6	207 42.5	23.5			
A 12	148 32.0	357 00.0	N13 07.5	354 39.5	N12 00.1	255 10.1	S22 10.6	222 45.1	S22 23.5	Alphecca	126 07.4	N26 39.3
Y 13	163 34.5	11 59.5	06.5	9 40.4	11 59.5	270 12.5	10.6	237 47.7	23.5	Alpheratz	357 38.8	N29 11.8
14	178 37.0	26 59.0	05.4	24 41.4	59.0	285 14.9	10.6	252 50.2	23.5	Altair	62 03.8	N 8 55.4
15	193 39.4	41 58.5	.. 04.3	39 42.3	.. 58.4	300 17.3	.. 10.6	267 52.8	.. 23.5	Ankaa	353 11.2	S42 11.8
16	208 41.9	56 57.9	03.3	54 43.3	57.8	315 19.7	10.7	282 55.4	23.5	Antares	112 21.0	S26 28.4
17	223 44.4	71 57.4	02.2	69 44.2	57.2	330 22.1	10.7	297 58.0	23.6			
18	238 46.8	86 56.9	N13 01.2	84 45.2	N11 56.7	345 24.4	S22 10.7	313 00.6	S22 23.6	Arcturus	145 52.0	N19 05.2
19	253 49.3	101 56.4	13 00.1	99 46.1	56.1	0 26.8	10.7	328 03.2	23.6	Atria	107 18.8	S69 03.8
20	268 51.7	116 55.9	12 59.0	114 47.1	55.5	15 29.2	10.7	343 05.7	23.6	Avior	234 16.9	S59 34.2
21	283 54.2	131 55.3	.. 58.0	129 48.0	.. 54.9	30 31.6	.. 10.7	358 08.3	.. 23.6	Bellatrix	278 27.6	N 6 22.0
22	298 56.7	146 54.8	56.9	144 49.0	54.4	45 34.0	10.8	13 10.9	23.6	Betelgeuse	270 56.9	N 7 24.6
23	313 59.1	161 54.3	55.9	159 49.9	53.8	60 36.4	10.8	28 13.5	23.7			
21 00	329 01.6	176 53.8	N12 54.8	174 50.9	N11 53.2	75 38.8	S22 10.8	43 16.1	S22 23.7	Canopus	263 54.6	S52 42.2
01	344 04.1	191 53.3	53.7	189 51.8	52.6	90 41.2	10.8	58 18.6	23.7	Capella	280 28.4	N46 00.8
02	359 06.5	206 52.8	52.7	204 52.8	52.1	105 43.6	10.8	73 21.2	23.7	Deneb	49 28.2	N45 21.2
03	14 09.0	221 52.3	.. 51.6	219 53.7	.. 51.5	120 45.9	.. 10.8	88 23.8	.. 23.7	Denebola	182 29.6	N14 28.0
04	29 11.5	236 51.7	50.5	234 54.7	50.9	135 48.3	10.9	103 26.4	23.7	Diphda	348 51.4	S17 52.7
05	44 13.9	251 51.2	49.5	249 55.6	50.3	150 50.7	10.9	118 29.0	23.7			
06	59 16.4	266 50.7	N12 48.4	264 56.6	N11 49.8	165 53.1	S22 10.9	133 31.5	S22 23.8	Dubhe	193 47.1	N61 38.9
W 07	74 18.8	281 50.2	47.3	279 57.5	49.2	180 55.5	10.9	148 34.1	23.8	Elnath	278 07.4	N28 37.2
E 08	89 21.3	296 49.7	46.3	294 58.5	48.6	195 57.9	10.9	163 36.7	23.8	Eltanin	90 43.9	N51 29.6
D 09	104 23.8	311 49.2	.. 45.2	309 59.4	.. 48.0	211 00.3	.. 10.9	178 39.3	.. 23.8	Enif	33 42.6	N 9 58.0
N 10	119 26.2	326 48.7	44.1	325 00.4	47.5	226 02.6	10.9	193 41.8	23.8	Fomalhaut	15 19.0	S29 31.0
E 11	134 28.7	341 48.1	43.1	340 01.3	46.9	241 05.0	11.0	208 44.4	23.8			
S 12	149 31.2	356 47.6	N12 42.0	355 02.3	N11 46.3	256 07.4	S22 11.0	223 47.0	S22 23.9	Gacrux	171 56.6	S57 13.4
D 13	164 33.6	11 47.1	40.9	10 03.2	45.7	271 09.8	11.0	238 49.6	23.9	Gienah	175 48.2	S17 38.9
A 14	179 36.1	26 46.6	39.9	25 04.2	45.2	286 12.2	11.0	253 52.2	23.9	Hadar	148 42.2	S60 28.1
Y 15	194 38.6	41 46.1	.. 38.8	40 05.2	.. 44.6	301 14.6	.. 11.0	268 54.7	.. 23.9	Hamal	327 55.8	N23 33.1
16	209 41.0	56 45.6	37.7	55 06.1	44.0	316 16.9	11.0	283 57.3	23.9	Kaus Aust.	83 38.0	S34 22.4
17	224 43.5	71 45.1	36.6	70 07.1	43.4	331 19.3	11.1	298 59.9	23.9			
18	239 46.0	86 44.6	N12 35.6	85 08.0	N11 42.9	346 21.7	S22 11.1	314 02.5	S22 24.0	Kochab	137 20.3	N74 04.9
19	254 48.4	101 44.1	34.5	100 09.0	42.3	1 24.1	11.1	329 05.0	24.0	Markab	13 33.8	N15 18.7
20	269 50.9	116 43.6	33.4	115 09.9	41.7	16 26.5	11.1	344 07.6	24.0	Menkar	314 10.6	N 4 09.9
21	284 53.3	131 43.1	.. 32.3	130 10.9	.. 41.1	31 28.8	.. 11.1	359 10.2	.. 24.0	Menkent	148 02.8	S36 27.9
22	299 55.8	146 42.5	31.3	145 11.8	40.6	46 31.2	11.1	14 12.8	24.0	Miaplacidus	221 39.8	S69 47.8
23	314 58.3	161 42.0	30.2	160 12.8	40.0	61 33.6	11.2	29 15.4	24.0			
22 00	330 00.7	176 41.5	N12 29.1	175 13.7	N11 39.4	76 36.0	S22 11.2	44 17.9	S22 24.0	Mirfak	308 34.2	N49 55.5
01	345 03.2	191 41.0	28.0	190 14.7	38.8	91 38.4	11.2	59 20.5	24.1	Nunki	75 52.8	S26 16.2
02	0 05.7	206 40.5	27.0	205 15.6	38.2	106 40.7	11.2	74 23.1	24.1	Peacock	53 12.0	S56 40.3
03	15 08.1	221 40.0	.. 25.9	220 16.6	.. 37.7	121 43.1	.. 11.2	89 25.7	.. 24.1	Pollux	243 22.9	N27 58.7
04	30 10.6	236 39.5	24.8	235 17.5	37.1	136 45.5	11.2	104 28.2	24.1	Procyon	244 55.6	N 5 10.5
05	45 13.1	251 39.0	23.7	250 18.5	36.5	151 47.9	11.3	119 30.8	24.1			
06	60 15.5	266 38.5	N12 22.6	265 19.4	N11 35.9	166 50.3	S22 11.3	134 33.4	S22 24.1	Rasalhague	96 02.4	N12 33.0
T 07	75 18.0	281 38.0	21.6	280 20.4	35.4	181 52.6	11.3	149 36.0	24.2	Regulus	207 39.3	N11 52.4
H 08	90 20.5	296 37.5	20.5	295 21.3	34.8	196 55.0	11.3	164 38.5	24.2	Rigel	281 08.1	S 8 10.7
U 09	105 22.9	311 37.0	.. 19.4	310 22.3	.. 34.2	211 57.4	.. 11.3	179 41.1	.. 24.2	Rigil Kent.	139 46.2	S60 55.0
R 10	120 25.4	326 36.5	18.3	325 23.3	33.6	226 59.8	11.3	194 43.7	24.2	Sabik	102 07.6	S15 44.8
S 11	135 27.8	341 36.0	17.2	340 24.2	33.0	242 02.1	11.4	209 46.3	24.2			
D 12	150 30.3	356 35.5	N12 16.1	355 25.2	N11 32.5	257 04.5	S22 11.4	224 48.8	S22 24.2	Schedar	349 35.3	N56 38.5
A 13	165 32.8	11 35.0	15.1	10 26.1	31.9	272 06.9	11.4	239 51.4	24.2	Shaula	96 16.0	S37 07.0
Y 14	180 35.2	26 34.5	14.0	25 27.1	31.3	287 09.3	11.4	254 54.0	24.3	Sirius	258 30.2	S16 44.5
15	195 37.7	41 34.0	.. 12.9	40 28.0	.. 30.7	302 11.6	.. 11.4	269 56.6	.. 24.3	Spica	158 27.0	S11 15.6
16	210 40.2	56 33.5	11.8	55 29.0	30.1	317 14.0	11.4	284 59.1	24.3	Suhail	222 49.8	S43 30.6
17	225 42.6	71 33.0	10.7	70 29.9	29.6	332 16.4	11.5	300 01.7	24.3			
18	240 45.1	86 32.5	N12 09.6	85 30.9	N11 29.0	347 18.8	S22 11.5	315 04.3	S22 24.3	Vega	80 35.8	N38 48.4
19	255 47.6	101 32.0	08.5	100 31.8	28.4	2 21.1	11.5	330 06.8	24.3	Zuben'ubi	137 00.8	S16 07.2
20	270 50.0	116 31.5	07.5	115 32.8	27.8	17 23.5	11.5	345 09.4	24.4		SHA	Mer.Pass.
21	285 52.5	131 31.0	.. 06.4	130 33.8	.. 27.2	32 25.9	.. 11.5	0 12.0	.. 24.4			
22	300 54.9	146 30.5	05.3	145 34.7	26.7	47 28.2	11.5	15 14.6	24.4	Venus	207 52.2	12 13
23	315 57.4	161 30.0	04.2	160 35.7	26.1	62 30.6	11.6	30 17.1	24.4	Mars	205 49.3	12 20
Mer.Pass.	h m 2 03.6	v −0.5	d 1.1	v 1.0	d 0.6	v 2.4	d 0.0	v 2.6	d 0.0	Jupiter	106 37.2	18 54
										Saturn	74 14.5	21 03

© British Crown Copyright 2018. All rights reserved.

UT	SUN GHA	SUN Dec	MOON GHA	v	MOON Dec	d	HP
d h	° ′	° ′	° ′	′	° ′	′	′
20 00	179 06.6	N12 36.6	311 39.9	15.8	N 1 23.2	11.4	54.3
01	194 06.8	35.7	326 14.7	15.9	1 34.6	11.4	54.4
02	209 06.9	34.9	340 49.6	15.8	1 46.0	11.3	54.4
03	224 07.1	.. 34.1	355 24.4	15.9	1 57.3	11.4	54.4
04	239 07.2	33.3	9 59.3	15.8	2 08.7	11.4	54.4
05	254 07.4	32.5	24 34.1	15.8	2 20.1	11.3	54.4
06	269 07.5	N12 31.6	39 08.9	15.7	N 2 31.4	11.4	54.4
07	284 07.6	30.8	53 43.6	15.8	2 42.8	11.3	54.4
T 08	299 07.8	30.0	68 18.4	15.7	2 54.1	11.4	54.4
U 09	314 07.9	.. 29.2	82 53.1	15.7	3 05.5	11.3	54.5
E 10	329 08.1	28.4	97 27.8	15.7	3 16.8	11.3	54.5
S 11	344 08.2	27.5	112 02.5	15.7	3 28.1	11.4	54.5
D 12	359 08.4	N12 26.7	126 37.2	15.6	N 3 39.5	11.3	54.5
A 13	14 08.5	25.9	141 11.8	15.6	3 50.8	11.3	54.5
Y 14	29 08.7	25.1	155 46.4	15.6	4 02.1	11.3	54.5
15	44 08.8	.. 24.2	170 21.0	15.6	4 13.4	11.3	54.6
16	59 09.0	23.4	184 55.5	15.6	4 24.7	11.2	54.6
17	74 09.1	22.6	199 30.1	15.5	4 35.9	11.3	54.6
18	89 09.3	N12 21.8	214 04.6	15.4	N 4 47.2	11.2	54.6
19	104 09.4	20.9	228 39.0	15.5	4 58.4	11.3	54.6
20	119 09.6	20.1	243 13.5	15.4	5 09.7	11.2	54.6
21	134 09.7	.. 19.3	257 47.9	15.3	5 20.9	11.2	54.7
22	149 09.9	18.5	272 22.2	15.4	5 32.1	11.2	54.7
23	164 10.1	17.6	286 56.6	15.3	5 43.3	11.1	54.7
21 00	179 10.2	N12 16.8	301 30.9	15.2	N 5 54.4	11.2	54.7
01	194 10.4	16.0	316 05.1	15.3	6 05.6	11.1	54.7
02	209 10.5	15.1	330 39.4	15.2	6 16.7	11.2	54.7
03	224 10.7	.. 14.3	345 13.6	15.1	6 27.9	11.1	54.8
04	239 10.8	13.5	359 47.7	15.1	6 39.0	11.0	54.8
05	254 11.0	12.7	14 21.8	15.1	6 50.0	11.1	54.8
06	269 11.1	N12 11.8	28 55.9	15.0	N 7 01.1	11.0	54.8
W 07	284 11.3	11.0	43 29.9	15.0	7 12.1	11.1	54.8
E 08	299 11.4	10.2	58 03.9	15.0	7 23.2	10.9	54.9
D 09	314 11.6	.. 09.3	72 37.9	14.9	7 34.1	11.0	54.9
N 10	329 11.7	08.5	87 11.8	14.8	7 45.1	11.0	54.9
E 11	344 11.9	07.7	101 45.6	14.9	7 56.1	10.9	54.9
S 12	359 12.0	N12 06.8	116 19.5	14.7	N 8 07.0	10.9	54.9
D 13	14 12.2	06.0	130 53.2	14.7	8 17.9	10.9	55.0
A 14	29 12.4	05.2	145 26.9	14.7	8 28.8	10.8	55.0
Y 15	44 12.5	.. 04.3	160 00.6	14.6	8 39.6	10.8	55.0
16	59 12.7	03.5	174 34.2	14.6	8 50.4	10.8	55.0
17	74 12.8	02.7	189 07.8	14.5	9 01.2	10.8	55.1
18	89 13.0	N12 01.8	203 41.3	14.5	N 9 12.0	10.7	55.1
19	104 13.1	01.0	218 14.8	14.4	9 22.7	10.7	55.1
20	119 13.3	12 00.2	232 48.2	14.4	9 33.4	10.6	55.1
21	134 13.4	11 59.3	247 21.6	14.3	9 44.0	10.7	55.1
22	149 13.6	58.5	261 54.9	14.3	9 54.7	10.6	55.2
23	164 13.8	57.7	276 28.2	14.2	10 05.3	10.5	55.2
22 00	179 13.9	N11 56.8	291 01.4	14.1	N10 15.8	10.6	55.2
01	194 14.1	56.0	305 34.5	14.1	10 26.4	10.5	55.2
02	209 14.2	55.2	320 07.6	14.0	10 36.9	10.4	55.3
03	224 14.4	.. 54.3	334 40.6	14.0	10 47.3	10.4	55.3
04	239 14.5	53.5	349 13.6	13.9	10 57.7	10.4	55.3
05	254 14.7	52.7	3 46.5	13.8	11 08.1	10.4	55.3
06	269 14.9	N11 51.8	18 19.3	13.8	N11 18.5	10.3	55.4
07	284 15.0	51.0	32 52.1	13.8	11 28.8	10.2	55.4
T 08	299 15.2	50.1	47 24.9	13.6	11 39.0	10.3	55.4
H 09	314 15.3	.. 49.3	61 57.5	13.6	11 49.3	10.1	55.4
U 10	329 15.5	48.5	76 30.1	13.5	11 59.4	10.2	55.5
R 11	344 15.6	47.6	91 02.6	13.5	12 09.6	10.1	55.5
S 12	359 15.8	N11 46.8	105 35.1	13.4	N12 19.7	10.0	55.5
D 13	14 16.0	46.0	120 07.5	13.3	12 29.7	10.0	55.6
A 14	29 16.1	45.1	134 39.8	13.3	12 39.7	10.0	55.6
Y 15	44 16.3	.. 44.3	149 12.1	13.2	12 49.7	9.9	55.6
16	59 16.4	43.4	163 44.3	13.1	12 59.6	9.8	55.6
17	74 16.6	42.6	178 16.4	13.1	13 09.4	9.8	55.7
18	89 16.8	N11 41.7	192 48.5	12.9	N13 19.2	9.8	55.7
19	104 16.9	40.9	207 20.4	12.9	13 29.0	9.7	55.7
20	119 17.1	40.1	221 52.3	12.9	13 38.7	9.6	55.8
21	134 17.2	.. 39.2	236 24.2	12.7	13 48.3	9.6	55.8
22	149 17.4	38.4	250 55.9	12.7	13 57.9	9.6	55.8
23	164 17.6	37.5	265 27.6	12.6	N14 07.5	9.5	55.8
	SD 15.8	d 0.8	SD 14.9		15.0		15.1

Lat.	Twilight Naut.	Twilight Civil	Sunrise	Moonrise 20	21	22	23
°	h m	h m	h m	h m	h m	h m	h m
N 72	////	////	03 00	20 43	20 25	20 01	19 16
N 70	////	01 41	03 24	20 50	20 40	20 27	20 08
68	////	02 22	03 43	20 56	20 51	20 46	20 40
66	////	02 49	03 57	21 01	21 01	21 02	21 04
64	01 29	03 09	04 09	21 05	21 09	21 15	21 23
62	02 05	03 25	04 19	21 09	21 16	21 26	21 39
60	02 30	03 39	04 28	21 12	21 22	21 35	21 52
N 58	02 49	03 50	04 35	21 15	21 28	21 43	22 03
56	03 05	04 00	04 42	21 18	21 33	21 50	22 13
54	03 18	04 09	04 48	21 20	21 37	21 57	22 22
52	03 29	04 16	04 53	21 22	21 41	22 03	22 29
50	03 39	04 23	04 58	21 24	21 45	22 08	22 36
45	03 59	04 37	05 08	21 28	21 53	22 20	22 52
N 40	04 14	04 48	05 17	21 32	21 59	22 29	23 04
35	04 26	04 58	05 24	21 35	22 05	22 38	23 15
30	04 36	05 06	05 31	21 38	22 10	22 45	23 24
20	04 52	05 19	05 42	21 42	22 19	22 58	23 40
N 10	05 04	05 30	05 51	21 47	22 26	23 09	23 54
0	05 14	05 39	06 00	21 51	22 34	23 19	24 08
S 10	05 22	05 47	06 09	21 55	22 41	23 30	24 21
20	05 29	05 55	06 18	21 59	22 49	23 41	24 36
30	05 36	06 04	06 28	22 04	22 58	23 54	24 52
35	05 38	06 08	06 34	22 07	23 03	24 02	00 02
40	05 41	06 13	06 41	22 10	23 09	24 10	00 10
45	05 44	06 18	06 48	22 14	23 16	24 21	00 21
S 50	05 46	06 24	06 57	22 18	23 25	24 33	00 33
52	05 47	06 27	07 02	22 21	23 29	24 39	00 39
54	05 49	06 30	07 06	22 23	23 33	24 45	00 45
56	05 50	06 33	07 11	22 25	23 38	24 52	00 52
58	05 51	06 36	07 17	22 28	23 43	25 00	01 00
S 60	05 52	06 40	07 24	22 32	23 49	25 09	01 09

Lat.	Sunset	Twilight Civil	Twilight Naut.	Moonset 20	21	22	23
°	h m	h m	h m	h m	h m	h m	h m
N 72	21 01	23 46	////	10 10	11 57	13 54	16 18
N 70	20 38	22 17	////	10 06	11 45	13 30	15 27
68	20 21	21 40	////	10 02	11 35	13 12	14 56
66	20 07	21 14	23 48	09 59	11 26	12 58	14 33
64	19 55	20 54	22 30	09 56	11 19	12 46	14 15
62	19 45	20 38	21 57	09 54	11 14	12 36	14 00
60	19 37	20 25	21 33	09 52	11 08	12 27	13 48
N 58	19 30	20 14	21 14	09 50	11 04	12 20	13 37
56	19 23	20 05	20 59	09 48	11 00	12 13	13 28
54	19 17	19 56	20 46	09 47	10 56	12 07	13 20
52	19 12	19 49	20 36	09 46	10 53	12 02	13 12
50	19 07	19 42	20 26	09 45	10 50	11 57	13 06
45	18 57	19 28	20 07	09 42	10 44	11 47	12 52
N 40	18 49	19 17	19 52	09 40	10 38	11 38	12 40
35	18 42	19 08	19 40	09 38	10 34	11 31	12 30
30	18 35	19 00	19 30	09 36	10 30	11 25	12 22
20	18 25	18 47	19 14	09 34	10 23	11 14	12 07
N 10	18 15	18 37	19 02	09 31	10 17	11 04	11 54
0	18 07	18 28	18 52	09 29	10 11	10 55	11 42
S 10	17 58	18 19	18 44	09 27	10 05	10 46	11 30
20	17 49	18 11	18 37	09 24	09 59	10 37	11 17
30	17 39	18 03	18 31	09 21	09 53	10 26	11 03
35	17 33	17 59	18 28	09 20	09 49	10 20	10 54
40	17 26	17 54	18 26	09 18	09 44	10 13	10 45
45	17 19	17 49	18 23	09 16	09 39	10 04	10 33
S 50	17 10	17 43	18 21	09 13	09 33	09 55	10 20
52	17 05	17 40	18 20	09 12	09 30	09 50	10 14
54	17 01	17 38	18 19	09 11	09 27	09 45	10 07
56	16 56	17 34	18 18	09 09	09 24	09 40	09 59
58	16 50	17 31	18 17	09 08	09 20	09 33	09 50
S 60	16 44	17 27	18 16	09 06	09 16	09 26	09 40

	SUN			MOON			
Day	Eqn. of Time 00ʰ	12ʰ	Mer. Pass.	Mer. Pass. Upper	Lower	Age	Phase
d	m s	m s	h m	h m	h m	d %	
20	03 34	03 27	12 03	03 19	15 40	19 79	
21	03 19	03 12	12 03	04 01	16 22	20 71	
22	03 05	02 57	12 03	04 44	17 07	21 61	

© British Crown Copyright 2018. All rights reserved.

UT	ARIES GHA	VENUS −4.0 GHA	Dec	MARS +1.8 GHA	Dec	JUPITER −2.3 GHA	Dec	SATURN +0.3 GHA	Dec	STARS Name	SHA	Dec
23 00	330 59.9	176 29.5	N12 03.1	175 36.6	N11 25.5	77 33.0	S22 11.6	45 19.7	S22 24.4	Acamar	315 15.0	S40 13.4
01	346 02.3	191 29.0	02.0	190 37.6	24.9	92 35.4	11.6	60 22.3	24.4	Achernar	335 23.2	S57 08.1
02	1 04.8	206 28.5	12 00.9	205 38.5	24.3	107 37.7	11.6	75 24.9	24.4	Acrux	173 05.1	S63 12.5
03	16 07.3	221 28.0	11 59.8	220 39.5	.. 23.8	122 40.1	.. 11.6	90 27.4	.. 24.5	Adhara	255 09.5	S28 59.8
04	31 09.7	236 27.5	58.7	235 40.4	23.2	137 42.5	11.6	105 30.0	24.5	Aldebaran	290 44.6	N16 32.8
05	46 12.2	251 27.0	57.6	250 41.4	22.6	152 44.8	11.7	120 32.6	24.5			
06	61 14.7	266 26.5	N11 56.5	265 42.3	N11 22.0	167 47.2	S22 11.7	135 35.1	S22 24.5	Alioth	166 17.3	N55 51.6
07	76 17.1	281 26.0	55.4	280 43.3	21.4	182 49.6	11.7	150 37.7	24.5	Alkaid	152 55.8	N49 13.3
08	91 19.6	296 25.5	54.3	295 44.3	20.9	197 51.9	11.7	165 40.3	24.5	Alnair	27 37.9	S46 51.9
F 09	106 22.1	311 25.0	.. 53.2	310 45.2	.. 20.3	212 54.3	.. 11.7	180 42.9	.. 24.5	Alnilam	275 42.2	S 1 11.4
R 10	121 24.5	326 24.5	52.2	325 46.2	19.7	227 56.7	11.8	195 45.4	24.6	Alphard	217 52.3	S 8 44.5
I 11	136 27.0	341 24.1	51.1	340 47.1	19.1	242 59.1	11.8	210 48.0	24.6			
D 12	151 29.4	356 23.6	N11 50.0	355 48.1	N11 18.5	258 01.4	S22 11.8	225 50.6	S22 24.6	Alphecca	126 07.4	N26 39.3
A 13	166 31.9	11 23.1	48.9	10 49.0	17.9	273 03.8	11.8	240 53.1	24.6	Alpheratz	357 38.8	N29 11.8
Y 14	181 34.4	26 22.6	47.8	25 50.0	17.4	288 06.2	11.8	255 55.7	24.6	Altair	62 03.8	N 8 55.4
15	196 36.8	41 22.1	.. 46.7	40 50.9	.. 16.8	303 08.5	.. 11.8	270 58.3	.. 24.6	Ankaa	353 11.2	S42 11.9
16	211 39.3	56 21.6	45.6	55 51.9	16.2	318 10.9	11.9	286 00.9	24.7	Antares	112 21.0	S26 28.4
17	226 41.8	71 21.1	44.5	70 52.9	15.6	333 13.3	11.9	301 03.4	24.7			
18	241 44.2	86 20.6	N11 43.4	85 53.8	N11 15.0	348 15.6	S22 11.9	316 06.0	S22 24.7	Arcturus	145 52.0	N19 05.2
19	256 46.7	101 20.1	42.3	100 54.8	14.4	3 18.0	11.9	331 08.6	24.7	Atria	107 18.9	S69 03.8
20	271 49.2	116 19.6	41.2	115 55.7	13.9	18 20.3	11.9	346 11.1	24.7	Avior	234 16.9	S59 34.2
21	286 51.6	131 19.2	.. 40.1	130 56.7	.. 13.3	33 22.7	.. 12.0	1 13.7	.. 24.7	Bellatrix	278 27.6	N 6 22.0
22	301 54.1	146 18.7	38.9	145 57.6	12.7	48 25.1	12.0	16 16.3	24.7	Betelgeuse	270 56.9	N 7 24.6
23	316 56.6	161 18.2	37.8	160 58.6	12.1	63 27.4	12.0	31 18.8	24.8			
24 00	331 59.0	176 17.7	N11 36.7	175 59.6	N11 11.5	78 29.8	S22 12.0	46 21.4	S22 24.8	Canopus	263 54.6	S52 42.2
01	347 01.5	191 17.2	35.6	191 00.5	10.9	93 32.2	12.0	61 24.0	24.8	Capella	280 28.3	N46 00.8
02	2 03.9	206 16.7	34.5	206 01.5	10.4	108 34.5	12.0	76 26.6	24.8	Deneb	49 28.2	N45 21.2
03	17 06.4	221 16.2	.. 33.4	221 02.4	.. 09.8	123 36.9	.. 12.1	91 29.1	.. 24.8	Denebola	182 29.6	N14 28.0
04	32 08.9	236 15.7	32.3	236 03.4	09.2	138 39.3	12.1	106 31.7	24.8	Diphda	348 51.4	S17 52.7
05	47 11.3	251 15.3	31.2	251 04.3	08.6	153 41.6	12.1	121 34.3	24.8			
06	62 13.8	266 14.8	N11 30.1	266 05.3	N11 08.0	168 44.0	S22 12.1	136 36.8	S22 24.9	Dubhe	193 47.1	N61 38.9
07	77 16.3	281 14.3	29.0	281 06.3	07.4	183 46.3	12.1	151 39.4	24.9	Elnath	278 07.4	N28 37.2
S 08	92 18.7	296 13.8	27.9	296 07.2	06.9	198 48.7	12.2	166 42.0	24.9	Eltanin	90 43.9	N51 29.6
A 09	107 21.2	311 13.3	.. 26.8	311 08.2	.. 06.3	213 51.1	.. 12.2	181 44.5	.. 24.9	Enif	33 42.6	N 9 58.0
T 10	122 23.7	326 12.8	25.7	326 09.1	05.7	228 53.4	12.2	196 47.1	24.9	Fomalhaut	15 18.9	S29 31.0
U 11	137 26.1	341 12.3	24.6	341 10.1	05.1	243 55.8	12.2	211 49.7	24.9			
R 12	152 28.6	356 11.9	N11 23.4	356 11.0	N11 04.5	258 58.1	S22 12.2	226 52.2	S22 25.0	Gacrux	171 56.7	S57 13.4
D 13	167 31.0	11 11.4	22.3	11 12.0	03.9	274 00.5	12.2	241 54.8	25.0	Gienah	175 48.2	S17 38.9
A 14	182 33.5	26 10.9	21.2	26 13.0	03.4	289 02.9	12.3	256 57.4	25.0	Hadar	148 42.2	S60 28.1
Y 15	197 36.0	41 10.4	.. 20.1	41 13.9	.. 02.8	304 05.2	.. 12.3	271 59.9	.. 25.0	Hamal	327 55.8	N23 33.2
16	212 38.4	56 09.9	19.0	56 14.9	02.2	319 07.6	12.3	287 02.5	25.0	Kaus Aust.	83 38.0	S34 22.4
17	227 40.9	71 09.5	17.9	71 15.8	01.6	334 09.9	12.3	302 05.1	25.0			
18	242 43.4	86 09.0	N11 16.8	86 16.8	N11 01.0	349 12.3	S22 12.3	317 07.6	S22 25.0	Kochab	137 20.4	N74 04.9
19	257 45.8	101 08.5	15.7	101 17.7	11 00.4	4 14.6	12.4	332 10.2	25.0	Markab	13 33.8	N15 18.7
20	272 48.3	116 08.0	14.5	116 18.7	10 59.8	19 17.0	12.4	347 12.8	25.1	Menkar	314 10.5	N 4 09.9
21	287 50.8	131 07.5	.. 13.4	131 19.7	.. 59.3	34 19.4	.. 12.4	2 15.3	.. 25.1	Menkent	148 02.8	S36 27.9
22	302 53.2	146 07.1	12.3	146 20.6	58.7	49 21.7	12.4	17 17.9	25.1	Miaplacidus	221 39.8	S69 47.7
23	317 55.7	161 06.6	11.2	161 21.6	58.1	64 24.1	12.4	32 20.5	25.1			
25 00	332 58.2	176 06.1	N11 10.1	176 22.5	N10 57.5	79 26.4	S22 12.5	47 23.0	S22 25.1	Mirfak	308 34.2	N49 55.5
01	348 00.6	191 05.6	09.0	191 23.5	56.9	94 28.8	12.5	62 25.6	25.1	Nunki	75 52.8	S26 16.2
02	3 03.1	206 05.1	07.8	206 24.5	56.3	109 31.1	12.5	77 28.2	25.2	Peacock	53 12.0	S56 40.3
03	18 05.5	221 04.7	.. 06.7	221 25.4	.. 55.7	124 33.5	.. 12.5	92 30.7	.. 25.2	Pollux	243 22.9	N27 58.7
04	33 08.0	236 04.2	05.6	236 26.4	55.1	139 35.8	12.5	107 33.3	25.2	Procyon	244 55.6	N 5 10.5
05	48 10.5	251 03.7	04.5	251 27.3	54.6	154 38.2	12.5	122 35.8	25.2			
06	63 12.9	266 03.2	N11 03.4	266 28.3	N10 54.0	169 40.6	S22 12.6	137 38.4	S22 25.2	Rasalhague	96 02.4	N12 33.1
07	78 15.4	281 02.8	02.2	281 29.3	53.4	184 42.9	12.6	152 41.0	25.2	Regulus	207 39.3	N11 52.4
08	93 17.9	296 02.3	01.1	296 30.2	52.9	199 45.3	12.6	167 43.5	25.2	Rigel	281 08.1	S 8 10.7
S 09	108 20.3	311 01.8	11 00.0	311 31.2	.. 52.2	214 47.6	.. 12.6	182 46.1	.. 25.3	Rigil Kent.	139 46.2	S60 55.0
U 10	123 22.8	326 01.3	10 58.9	326 32.1	51.6	229 50.0	12.6	197 48.7	25.3	Sabik	102 07.6	S15 44.8
N 11	138 25.3	341 00.9	57.7	341 33.1	51.0	244 52.3	12.7	212 51.2	25.3			
D 12	153 27.7	356 00.4	N10 56.6	356 34.1	N10 50.5	259 54.7	S22 12.7	227 53.8	S22 25.3	Schedar	349 35.3	N56 38.5
A 13	168 30.2	10 59.9	55.5	11 35.0	49.9	274 57.0	12.7	242 56.4	25.3	Shaula	96 16.0	S37 07.0
Y 14	183 32.7	25 59.4	54.4	26 36.0	49.3	289 59.4	12.7	257 58.9	25.3	Sirius	258 30.2	S16 44.5
15	198 35.1	40 59.0	.. 53.2	41 36.9	.. 48.7	305 01.7	.. 12.7	273 01.5	.. 25.3	Spica	158 27.0	S11 15.6
16	213 37.6	55 58.5	52.1	56 37.9	48.1	320 04.1	12.8	288 04.0	25.3	Suhail	222 49.8	S43 30.6
17	228 40.0	70 58.0	51.0	71 38.9	47.5	335 06.4	12.8	303 06.6	25.4			
18	243 42.5	85 57.5	N10 49.9	86 39.8	N10 46.9	350 08.8	S22 12.8	318 09.2	S22 25.4	Vega	80 35.8	N38 48.4
19	258 45.0	100 57.1	48.7	101 40.8	46.3	5 11.1	12.8	333 11.7	25.4	Zuben'ubi	137 00.8	S16 07.2
20	273 47.4	115 56.6	47.6	116 41.7	45.7	20 13.5	12.8	348 14.3	25.4		SHA	Mer.Pass.
21	288 49.9	130 56.1	.. 46.5	131 42.7	.. 45.2	35 15.8	.. 12.9	3 16.9	.. 25.4	Venus	204 18.7	12 15
22	303 52.4	145 55.7	45.4	146 43.7	44.6	50 18.2	12.9	18 19.4	25.4	Mars	204 00.5	12 15
23	318 54.8	160 55.2	44.2	161 44.6	44.0	65 20.5	12.9	33 22.0	25.4	Jupiter	106 30.8	18 43
Mer.Pass. 1 51.8		v −0.5	d 1.1	v 1.0	d 0.6	v 2.4	d 0.0	v 2.6	d 0.0	Saturn	74 22.4	20 51

© British Crown Copyright 2018. All rights reserved.

UT	SUN GHA	SUN Dec	MOON GHA	v	MOON Dec	d	HP
d h	° '	° '	° '	'	° '	'	'
23 00	179 17.7	N11 36.7	279 59.2	12.6	N14 17.0	9.4	55.9
01	194 17.9	35.9	294 30.8	12.4	14 26.4	9.4	55.9
02	209 18.0	35.0	309 02.2	12.4	14 35.8	9.3	55.9
03	224 18.2	.. 34.2	323 33.6	12.3	14 45.1	9.2	56.0
04	239 18.4	33.3	338 04.9	12.2	14 54.3	9.2	56.0
05	254 18.5	32.5	352 36.1	12.2	15 03.5	9.2	56.0
06	269 18.7	N11 31.6	7 07.3	12.1	N15 12.7	9.0	56.1
07	284 18.9	30.8	21 38.4	11.9	15 21.7	9.1	56.1
08	299 19.0	29.9	36 09.3	11.9	15 30.8	8.9	56.1
F 09	314 19.2	.. 29.1	50 40.2	11.9	15 39.7	8.9	56.2
R 10	329 19.3	28.2	65 11.1	11.7	15 48.6	8.8	56.2
I 11	344 19.5	27.4	79 41.8	11.7	15 57.4	8.7	56.2
D 12	359 19.7	N11 26.6	94 12.5	11.5	N16 06.1	8.7	56.2
A 13	14 19.8	25.7	108 43.0	11.5	16 14.8	8.6	56.3
Y 14	29 20.0	24.9	123 13.5	11.4	16 23.4	8.6	56.3
15	44 20.2	.. 24.0	137 43.9	11.3	16 32.0	8.4	56.3
16	59 20.3	23.2	152 14.2	11.3	16 40.4	8.4	56.4
17	74 20.5	22.3	166 44.5	11.1	16 48.8	8.3	56.4
18	89 20.7	N11 21.5	181 14.6	11.1	N16 57.1	8.3	56.4
19	104 20.8	20.6	195 44.7	11.0	17 05.4	8.2	56.5
20	119 21.0	19.8	210 14.7	10.8	17 13.6	8.0	56.5
21	134 21.2	.. 18.9	224 44.5	10.8	17 21.6	8.1	56.6
22	149 21.3	18.1	239 14.3	10.8	17 29.7	7.9	56.6
23	164 21.5	17.2	253 44.1	10.6	17 37.6	7.8	56.6
24 00	179 21.6	N11 16.4	268 13.7	10.5	N17 45.4	7.8	56.7
01	194 21.8	15.5	282 43.2	10.4	17 53.2	7.7	56.7
02	209 22.0	14.7	297 12.6	10.4	18 00.9	7.6	56.7
03	224 22.1	.. 13.8	311 42.0	10.3	18 08.5	7.5	56.8
04	239 22.3	13.0	326 11.3	10.1	18 16.0	7.5	56.8
05	254 22.5	12.1	340 40.4	10.1	18 23.5	7.3	56.8
06	269 22.6	N11 11.3	355 09.5	10.0	N18 30.8	7.3	56.9
07	284 22.8	10.4	9 38.5	9.9	18 38.1	7.1	56.9
S 08	299 23.0	09.5	24 07.4	9.8	18 45.2	7.1	56.9
A 09	314 23.1	.. 08.7	38 36.2	9.7	18 52.3	7.0	57.0
T 10	329 23.3	07.8	53 04.9	9.7	18 59.3	6.9	57.0
U 11	344 23.5	07.0	67 33.6	9.5	19 06.2	6.8	57.1
R 12	359 23.6	N11 06.1	82 02.1	9.4	N19 13.0	6.7	57.1
D 13	14 23.8	05.3	96 30.5	9.4	19 19.7	6.6	57.1
A 14	29 24.0	04.4	110 58.9	9.2	19 26.3	6.5	57.2
Y 15	44 24.2	.. 03.6	125 27.1	9.2	19 32.8	6.4	57.2
16	59 24.3	02.7	139 55.3	9.1	19 39.2	6.3	57.2
17	74 24.5	01.9	154 23.4	9.0	19 45.5	6.2	57.3
18	89 24.7	N11 01.0	168 51.4	8.8	N19 51.7	6.1	57.3
19	104 24.8	11 00.1	183 19.2	8.8	19 57.8	6.0	57.4
20	119 25.0	10 59.3	197 47.0	8.8	20 03.8	5.9	57.4
21	134 25.2	.. 58.4	212 14.8	8.6	20 09.7	5.8	57.4
22	149 25.3	57.6	226 42.4	8.5	20 15.5	5.7	57.5
23	164 25.5	56.7	241 09.9	8.4	20 21.2	5.6	57.5
25 00	179 25.7	N10 55.9	255 37.3	8.4	N20 26.8	5.4	57.5
01	194 25.8	55.0	270 04.7	8.2	20 32.2	5.4	57.6
02	209 26.0	54.1	284 31.9	8.2	20 37.6	5.2	57.6
03	224 26.2	.. 53.3	298 59.1	8.1	20 42.8	5.2	57.7
04	239 26.4	52.4	313 26.2	7.9	20 48.0	5.0	57.7
05	254 26.5	51.6	327 53.1	7.9	20 53.0	4.9	57.7
06	269 26.7	N10 50.7	342 20.0	7.8	N20 57.9	4.8	57.8
07	284 26.9	49.8	356 46.8	7.8	21 02.7	4.6	57.8
08	299 27.0	49.0	11 13.6	7.6	21 07.3	4.6	57.9
S 09	314 27.2	.. 48.1	25 40.2	7.5	21 11.9	4.4	57.9
U 10	329 27.4	47.3	40 06.7	7.5	21 16.3	4.3	57.9
N 11	344 27.5	46.4	54 33.2	7.4	21 20.6	4.2	58.0
D 12	359 27.7	N10 45.5	68 59.6	7.2	N21 24.8	4.1	58.0
A 13	14 27.9	44.7	83 25.8	7.2	21 28.9	3.9	58.1
Y 14	29 28.1	43.8	97 52.0	7.2	21 32.8	3.8	58.1
15	44 28.2	.. 42.9	112 18.2	7.0	21 36.6	3.7	58.1
16	59 28.4	42.1	126 44.2	6.9	21 40.3	3.6	58.2
17	74 28.6	41.2	141 10.1	6.9	21 43.9	3.4	58.2
18	89 28.8	N10 40.4	155 36.0	6.8	N21 47.3	3.3	58.3
19	104 28.9	39.5	170 01.8	6.7	21 50.6	3.1	58.3
20	119 29.1	38.6	184 27.5	6.6	21 53.7	3.1	58.3
21	134 29.3	.. 37.8	198 53.1	6.6	21 56.8	2.9	58.4
22	149 29.4	36.9	213 18.7	6.4	21 59.7	2.7	58.4
23	164 29.6	36.0	227 44.1	6.4	N22 02.4	2.7	58.5
	SD 15.8	d 0.9	SD 15.3		15.6		15.8

Lat.	Twilight Naut.	Twilight Civil	Sunrise	Moonrise 23	24	25	26
°	h m	h m	h m	h m	h m	h m	h m
N 72	////	01 10	03 18	19 16	▭	▭	▭
N 70	////	02 06	03 38	20 08	19 16	▭	▭
68	////	02 39	03 54	20 40	20 33	20 18	▭
66	01 00	03 02	04 07	21 04	21 11	21 29	22 16
64	01 50	03 20	04 18	21 23	21 38	22 06	22 57
62	02 20	03 35	04 27	21 39	21 59	22 32	23 25
60	02 42	03 47	04 35	21 52	22 16	22 52	23 47
N 58	02 59	03 58	04 42	22 03	22 30	23 09	24 05
56	03 13	04 07	04 48	22 13	22 43	23 24	24 20
54	03 25	04 14	04 53	22 22	22 53	23 36	24 32
52	03 36	04 21	04 58	22 29	23 03	23 47	24 44
50	03 45	04 28	05 02	22 36	23 12	23 57	24 54
45	04 03	04 41	05 12	22 52	23 30	24 17	00 17
N 40	04 17	04 51	05 20	23 04	23 45	24 34	00 34
35	04 29	05 00	05 26	23 15	23 58	24 48	00 48
30	04 38	05 08	05 32	23 24	24 09	00 09	01 00
20	04 53	05 20	05 42	23 40	24 28	00 28	01 21
N 10	05 05	05 30	05 51	23 54	24 45	00 45	01 39
0	05 14	05 38	05 59	24 08	00 08	01 00	01 56
S 10	05 21	05 46	06 07	24 21	00 21	01 16	02 14
20	05 27	05 53	06 15	24 36	00 36	01 33	02 32
30	05 33	06 00	06 25	24 52	00 52	01 52	02 53
35	05 35	06 04	06 30	00 02	01 02	02 04	03 06
40	05 37	06 09	06 36	00 10	01 13	02 17	03 20
45	05 39	06 13	06 43	00 21	01 26	02 33	03 37
S 50	05 41	06 19	06 52	00 33	01 42	02 52	03 58
52	05 42	06 21	06 55	00 39	01 50	03 01	04 08
54	05 42	06 23	07 00	00 45	01 58	03 11	04 20
56	05 43	06 26	07 04	00 52	02 08	03 23	04 33
58	05 43	06 29	07 09	01 00	02 19	03 36	04 48
S 60	05 44	06 32	07 15	01 09	02 31	03 52	05 06

Lat.	Sunset	Twilight Civil	Naut.	Moonset 23	24	25	26
°	h m	h m	h m	h m	h m	h m	h m
N 72	20 43	22 42	////	16 18	▭	▭	▭
N 70	20 23	21 52	////	15 27	18 06	▭	▭
68	20 08	21 22	////	14 56	16 49	19 00	▭
66	19 55	20 59	22 53	14 33	16 12	17 49	19 05
64	19 45	20 42	22 09	14 15	15 46	17 13	18 24
62	19 36	20 27	21 41	14 00	15 26	16 47	17 56
60	19 28	20 16	21 20	13 48	15 09	16 27	17 34
N 58	19 22	20 05	21 03	13 37	14 55	16 10	17 16
56	19 16	19 57	20 49	13 28	14 43	15 56	17 01
54	19 10	19 49	20 38	13 20	14 33	15 44	16 48
52	19 06	19 42	20 28	13 12	14 24	15 33	16 37
50	19 01	19 36	20 19	13 06	14 15	15 23	16 27
45	18 52	19 23	20 01	12 52	13 58	15 03	16 06
N 40	18 44	19 13	19 47	12 40	13 44	14 47	15 49
35	18 38	19 04	19 35	12 30	13 31	14 33	15 34
30	18 32	18 57	19 26	12 22	13 21	14 21	15 22
20	18 22	18 45	19 11	12 07	13 03	14 01	15 00
N 10	18 14	18 35	19 00	11 54	12 47	13 43	14 42
0	18 06	18 27	18 51	11 42	12 32	13 27	14 24
S 10	17 58	18 19	18 44	11 30	12 18	13 10	14 07
20	17 50	18 12	18 38	11 17	12 02	12 52	13 48
30	17 40	18 05	18 33	11 03	11 44	12 32	13 27
35	17 35	18 01	18 30	10 54	11 34	12 20	13 14
40	17 29	17 57	18 28	10 45	11 22	12 07	13 00
45	17 22	17 52	18 26	10 33	11 08	11 50	12 43
S 50	17 14	17 47	18 25	10 20	10 51	11 31	12 21
52	17 10	17 45	18 24	10 14	10 43	11 21	12 11
54	17 06	17 42	18 24	10 07	10 34	11 11	12 00
56	17 01	17 40	18 23	09 59	10 24	10 59	11 47
58	16 56	17 37	18 23	09 50	10 13	10 45	11 31
S 60	16 51	17 34	18 22	09 40	10 00	10 29	11 13

Day	SUN Eqn. of Time 00h	12h	Mer. Pass.	MOON Mer. Pass. Upper	Lower	Age	Phase
d	m s	m s	h m	h m	h m	d	%
23	02 49	02 42	12 03	05 31	17 55	22	51
24	02 34	02 26	12 02	06 20	18 46	23	41
25	02 18	02 09	12 02	07 13	19 41	24	31

© British Crown Copyright 2018. All rights reserved.

UT	ARIES	VENUS −3.9		MARS +1.7		JUPITER −2.2		SATURN +0.3		STARS		
d h	GHA	GHA	Dec	GHA	Dec	GHA	Dec	GHA	Dec	Name	SHA	Dec
26 00	333 57.3	175 54.7	N10 43.1	176 45.6	N10 43.4	80 22.9	S22 12.9	48 24.5	S22 25.5	Acamar	315 15.0	S40 13.4
01	348 59.8	190 54.2	42.0	191 46.5	42.8	95 25.2	12.9	63 27.1	25.5	Achernar	335 23.2	S57 08.1
02	4 02.2	205 53.8	40.8	206 47.5	42.2	110 27.5	13.0	78 29.7	25.5	Acrux	173 05.1	S63 12.5
03	19 04.7	220 53.3 ..	39.7	221 48.5 ..	41.6	125 29.9 ..	13.0	93 32.2 ..	25.5	Adhara	255 09.4	S28 59.8
04	34 07.2	235 52.8	38.6	236 49.4	41.0	140 32.2	13.0	108 34.8	25.5	Aldebaran	290 44.5	N16 32.8
05	49 09.6	250 52.4	37.4	251 50.4	40.4	155 34.6	13.0	123 37.3	25.5			
06	64 12.1	265 51.9	N10 36.3	266 51.3	N10 39.9	170 36.9	S22 13.0	138 39.9	S22 25.5	Alioth	166 17.4	N55 51.6
07	79 14.5	280 51.4	35.2	281 52.3	39.3	185 39.3	13.1	153 42.5	25.6	Alkaid	152 55.8	N49 13.3
08	94 17.0	295 51.0	34.0	296 53.3	38.7	200 41.6	13.1	168 45.0	25.6	Alnair	27 37.9	S46 51.9
M 09	109 19.5	310 50.5 ..	32.9	311 54.2 ..	38.1	215 44.0 ..	13.1	183 47.6 ..	25.6	Alnilam	275 42.2	S 1 11.4
O 10	124 21.9	325 50.0	31.8	326 55.2	37.5	230 46.3	13.1	198 50.2	25.6	Alphard	217 52.2	S 8 44.5
N 11	139 24.4	340 49.6	30.6	341 56.1	36.9	245 48.7	13.1	213 52.7	25.6			
D 12	154 26.9	355 49.1	N10 29.5	356 57.1	N10 36.3	260 51.0	S22 13.2	228 55.3	S22 25.6	Alphecca	126 07.5	N26 39.3
A 13	169 29.3	10 48.6	28.4	11 58.1	35.7	275 53.3	13.2	243 57.8	25.6	Alpheratz	357 38.8	N29 11.9
Y 14	184 31.8	25 48.2	27.2	26 59.0	35.1	290 55.7	13.2	259 00.4	25.7	Altair	62 03.8	N 8 55.4
15	199 34.3	40 47.7 ..	26.1	42 00.0 ..	34.5	305 58.0 ..	13.2	274 02.9 ..	25.7	Ankaa	353 11.1	S42 11.9
16	214 36.7	55 47.2	25.0	57 01.0	33.9	321 00.4	13.2	289 05.5	25.7	Antares	112 21.0	S26 28.4
17	229 39.2	70 46.8	23.8	72 01.9	33.4	336 02.7	13.3	304 08.1	25.7			
18	244 41.6	85 46.3	N10 22.7	87 02.9	N10 32.8	351 05.0	S22 13.3	319 10.6	S22 25.7	Arcturus	145 52.0	N19 05.2
19	259 44.1	100 45.9	21.5	102 03.8	32.2	6 07.4	13.3	334 13.2	25.7	Atria	107 18.9	S69 03.8
20	274 46.6	115 45.4	20.4	117 04.8	31.6	21 09.7	13.3	349 15.7	25.7	Avior	234 16.9	S59 34.2
21	289 49.0	130 44.9 ..	19.3	132 05.8 ..	31.0	36 12.1 ..	13.3	4 18.3 ..	25.8	Bellatrix	278 27.6	N 6 22.0
22	304 51.5	145 44.5	18.1	147 06.7	30.4	51 14.4	13.4	19 20.9	25.8	Betelgeuse	270 56.8	N 7 24.6
23	319 54.0	160 44.0	17.0	162 07.7	29.8	66 16.8	13.4	34 23.4	25.8			
27 00	334 56.4	175 43.5	N10 15.8	177 08.7	N10 29.2	81 19.1	S22 13.4	49 26.0	S22 25.8	Canopus	263 54.6	S52 42.2
01	349 58.9	190 43.1	14.7	192 09.6	28.6	96 21.4	13.4	64 28.5	25.8	Capella	280 28.3	N46 00.8
02	5 01.4	205 42.6	13.6	207 10.6	28.0	111 23.8	13.4	79 31.1	25.8	Deneb	49 28.2	N45 21.2
03	20 03.8	220 42.2 ..	12.4	222 11.5 ..	27.4	126 26.1 ..	13.5	94 33.6 ..	25.8	Denebola	182 29.6	N14 28.0
04	35 06.3	235 41.7	11.3	237 12.5	26.8	141 28.4	13.5	109 36.2	25.8	Diphda	348 51.4	S17 52.7
05	50 08.8	250 41.2	10.1	252 13.5	26.3	156 30.8	13.5	124 38.8	25.9			
06	65 11.2	265 40.8	N10 09.0	267 14.4	N10 25.7	171 33.1	S22 13.5	139 41.3	S22 25.9	Dubhe	193 47.1	N61 38.9
07	80 13.7	280 40.3	07.8	282 15.4	25.1	186 35.5	13.5	154 43.9	25.9	Elnath	278 07.4	N28 37.2
T 08	95 16.1	295 39.9	06.7	297 16.4	24.5	201 37.8	13.6	169 46.4	25.9	Eltanin	90 43.9	N51 29.6
U 09	110 18.6	310 39.4 ..	05.5	312 17.3 ..	23.9	216 40.1 ..	13.6	184 49.0 ..	25.9	Enif	33 42.6	N 9 58.0
E 10	125 21.1	325 39.0	04.4	327 18.3	23.3	231 42.5	13.6	199 51.5	25.9	Fomalhaut	15 18.9	S29 31.0
S 11	140 23.5	340 38.5	03.2	342 19.2	22.7	246 44.8	13.6	214 54.1	25.9			
D 12	155 26.0	355 38.0	N10 02.1	357 20.2	N10 22.1	261 47.1	S22 13.6	229 56.7	S22 26.0	Gacrux	171 56.7	S57 13.4
A 13	170 28.5	10 37.6	10 01.0	12 21.2	21.5	276 49.5	13.7	244 59.2	26.0	Gienah	175 48.2	S17 38.9
Y 14	185 30.9	25 37.1	9 59.8	27 22.1	20.9	291 51.8	13.7	260 01.8	26.0	Hadar	148 42.2	S60 28.1
15	200 33.4	40 36.7 ..	58.7	42 23.1 ..	20.3	306 54.1 ..	13.7	275 04.3 ..	26.0	Hamal	327 55.8	N23 33.2
16	215 35.9	55 36.2	57.5	57 24.1	19.7	321 56.5	13.7	290 06.9	26.0	Kaus Aust.	83 38.0	S34 22.4
17	230 38.3	70 35.8	56.4	72 25.0	19.1	336 58.8	13.8	305 09.4	26.0			
18	245 40.8	85 35.3	N 9 55.2	87 26.0	N10 18.5	352 01.1	S22 13.8	320 12.0	S22 26.0	Kochab	137 20.5	N74 04.9
19	260 43.3	100 34.8	54.1	102 27.0	17.9	7 03.5	13.8	335 14.5	26.0	Markab	13 33.8	N15 18.7
20	275 45.7	115 34.4	52.9	117 27.9	17.4	22 05.8	13.8	350 17.1	26.1	Menkar	314 10.5	N 4 09.9
21	290 48.2	130 33.9 ..	51.8	132 28.9 ..	16.8	37 08.1 ..	13.8	5 19.6 ..	26.1	Menkent	148 02.8	S36 27.9
22	305 50.6	145 33.5	50.6	147 29.9	16.2	52 10.5	13.9	20 22.2	26.1	Miaplacidus	221 39.7	S69 47.7
23	320 53.1	160 33.0	49.4	162 30.8	15.6	67 12.8	13.9	35 24.8	26.1			
28 00	335 55.6	175 32.6	N 9 48.3	177 31.8	N10 15.0	82 15.1	S22 13.9	50 27.3	S22 26.1	Mirfak	308 34.2	N49 55.5
01	350 58.0	190 32.1	47.1	192 32.7	14.4	97 17.5	13.9	65 29.9	26.1	Nunki	75 52.8	S26 16.2
02	6 00.5	205 31.7	46.0	207 33.7	13.8	112 19.8	13.9	80 32.4	26.1	Peacock	53 12.0	S56 40.3
03	21 03.0	220 31.2 ..	44.8	222 34.7 ..	13.2	127 22.1 ..	14.0	95 35.0 ..	26.2	Pollux	243 22.8	N27 58.7
04	36 05.4	235 30.8	43.7	237 35.6	12.6	142 24.5	14.0	110 37.5	26.2	Procyon	244 55.6	N 5 10.5
05	51 07.9	250 30.3	42.5	252 36.6	12.0	157 26.8	14.0	125 40.1	26.2			
06	66 10.4	265 29.9	N 9 41.4	267 37.6	N10 11.4	172 29.1	S22 14.0	140 42.6	S22 26.2	Rasalhague	96 02.4	N12 33.1
W 07	81 12.8	280 29.4	40.2	282 38.5	10.8	187 31.4	14.1	155 45.2	26.2	Regulus	207 39.3	N11 52.4
E 08	96 15.3	295 29.0	39.1	297 39.5	10.2	202 33.8	14.1	170 47.7	26.2	Rigel	281 08.1	S 8 10.7
D 09	111 17.8	310 28.5 ..	37.9	312 40.5 ..	09.6	217 36.1 ..	14.1	185 50.3 ..	26.2	Rigil Kent.	139 46.3	S60 55.0
N 10	126 20.2	325 28.1	36.7	327 41.4	09.0	232 38.4	14.1	200 52.8	26.2	Sabik	102 07.6	S15 44.8
E 11	141 22.7	340 27.6	35.6	342 42.4	08.4	247 40.8	14.1	215 55.4	26.3			
S 12	156 25.1	355 27.2	N 9 34.4	357 43.4	N10 07.8	262 43.1	S22 14.2	230 57.9	S22 26.3	Schedar	349 35.2	N56 38.5
D 13	171 27.6	10 26.7	33.3	12 44.3	07.2	277 45.4	14.2	246 00.5	26.3	Shaula	96 16.0	S37 07.0
A 14	186 30.1	25 26.3	32.1	27 45.3	06.6	292 47.7	14.2	261 03.0	26.3	Sirius	258 30.2	S16 44.5
Y 15	201 32.5	40 25.8 ..	30.9	42 46.3 ..	06.0	307 50.1 ..	14.2	276 05.6 ..	26.3	Spica	158 27.0	S11 15.6
16	216 35.0	55 25.4	29.8	57 47.2	05.4	322 52.4	14.2	291 08.2	26.3	Suhail	222 49.8	S43 30.6
17	231 37.5	70 24.9	28.6	72 48.2	04.8	337 54.7	14.3	306 10.7	26.3			
18	246 39.9	85 24.5	N 9 27.5	87 49.2	N10 04.3	352 57.0	S22 14.3	321 13.3	S22 26.3	Vega	80 35.8	N38 48.4
19	261 42.4	100 24.0	26.3	102 50.1	03.7	7 59.4	14.3	336 15.8	26.4	Zuben'ubi	137 00.8	S16 07.2
20	276 44.9	115 23.6	25.1	117 51.1	03.1	23 01.7	14.3	351 18.4	26.4		SHA	Mer.Pass.
21	291 47.3	130 23.1 ..	24.0	132 52.1 ..	02.5	38 04.0 ..	14.4	6 20.9 ..	26.4		° ′	h m
22	306 49.8	145 22.7	22.8	147 53.0	01.9	53 06.3	14.4	21 23.5	26.4	Venus	200 47.1	12 17
23	321 52.2	160 22.2	21.6	162 54.0	01.3	68 08.7	14.4	36 26.0	26.4	Mars	202 12.2	12 11
	h m									Jupiter	106 22.7	18 32
Mer. Pass.	1 40.0	v −0.5	d 1.1	v 1.0	d 0.6	v 2.3	d 0.0	v 2.6	d 0.0	Saturn	74 29.5	20 39

© British Crown Copyright 2018. All rights reserved.

SUN / MOON

UT	SUN GHA	Dec	MOON GHA	v	Dec	d	HP
26 00	179 29.8	N10 35.2	242 09.5	6.4	N22 05.1	2.5	58.5
01	194 30.0	34.3	256 34.9	6.2	22 07.6	2.3	58.5
02	209 30.3	33.4	271 00.1	6.2	22 09.9	2.3	58.6
03	224 30.3	.. 32.6	285 25.3	6.1	22 12.2	2.0	58.6
04	239 30.5	31.7	299 50.4	6.0	22 14.2	2.0	58.7
05	254 30.7	30.8	314 15.4	6.0	22 16.2	1.8	58.7
06	269 30.8	N10 30.0	328 40.4	5.9	N22 18.0	1.6	58.7
07	284 31.0	29.1	343 05.3	5.8	22 19.6	1.6	58.8
M 08	299 31.2	28.2	357 30.1	5.7	22 21.2	1.3	58.8
O 09	314 31.4	.. 27.4	11 54.8	5.7	22 22.5	1.3	58.9
N 10	329 31.5	26.5	26 19.5	5.6	22 23.8	1.0	58.9
D 11	344 31.7	25.6	40 44.1	5.6	22 24.8	1.0	58.9
A 12	359 31.9	N10 24.8	55 08.7	5.5	N22 25.8	0.8	59.0
Y 13	14 32.1	23.9	69 33.2	5.5	22 26.6	0.6	59.0
14	29 32.2	23.0	83 57.7	5.3	22 27.2	0.5	59.1
15	44 32.4	.. 22.1	98 22.0	5.4	22 27.7	0.4	59.1
16	59 32.6	21.3	112 46.4	5.2	22 28.1	0.2	59.1
17	74 32.8	20.4	127 10.6	5.3	22 28.3	0.0	59.2
18	89 33.0	N10 19.5	141 34.9	5.1	N22 28.3	0.1	59.2
19	104 33.1	18.7	155 59.0	5.1	22 28.2	0.2	59.2
20	119 33.3	17.8	170 23.1	5.1	22 28.0	0.5	59.3
21	134 33.5	.. 16.9	184 47.2	5.0	22 27.5	0.5	59.3
22	149 33.7	16.1	199 11.2	5.2	22 27.0	0.7	59.4
23	164 33.8	15.2	213 35.2	4.9	22 26.3	0.9	59.4
27 00	179 34.0	N10 14.3	227 59.1	4.9	N22 25.4	1.0	59.4
01	194 34.2	13.4	242 23.0	4.8	22 24.4	1.2	59.5
02	209 34.4	12.6	256 46.8	4.8	22 23.2	1.3	59.5
03	224 34.5	.. 11.7	271 10.6	4.8	22 21.9	1.5	59.6
04	239 34.7	10.8	285 34.4	4.7	22 20.4	1.6	59.6
05	254 34.9	09.9	299 58.1	4.7	22 18.8	1.8	59.6
06	269 35.1	N10 09.1	314 21.8	4.7	N22 17.0	2.0	59.7
07	284 35.3	08.2	328 45.5	4.6	22 15.0	2.1	59.7
T 08	299 35.4	07.3	343 09.1	4.6	22 12.9	2.2	59.7
U 09	314 35.6	.. 06.4	357 32.7	4.6	22 10.7	2.5	59.8
E 10	329 35.8	05.6	11 56.3	4.5	22 08.2	2.5	59.8
S 11	344 36.0	04.7	26 19.8	4.5	22 05.7	2.8	59.8
D 12	359 36.2	N10 03.8	40 43.3	4.5	N22 02.9	2.9	59.9
A 13	14 36.3	02.9	55 06.8	4.5	22 00.0	3.0	59.9
Y 14	29 36.5	02.1	69 30.3	4.5	21 57.0	3.2	59.9
15	44 36.7	.. 01.2	83 53.8	4.4	21 53.8	3.4	60.0
16	59 36.9	10 00.3	98 17.2	4.4	21 50.4	3.5	60.0
17	74 37.1	9 59.4	112 40.6	4.4	21 46.9	3.7	60.1
18	89 37.2	N 9 58.6	127 04.0	4.4	N21 43.2	3.8	60.1
19	104 37.4	57.7	141 27.4	4.4	21 39.4	4.0	60.1
20	119 37.6	56.8	155 50.8	4.4	21 35.4	4.2	60.2
21	134 37.8	.. 55.9	170 14.2	4.4	21 31.2	4.3	60.2
22	149 38.0	55.0	184 37.6	4.3	21 26.9	4.5	60.2
23	164 38.1	54.2	199 00.9	4.4	21 22.4	4.6	60.3
28 00	179 38.3	N 9 53.3	213 24.3	4.3	N21 17.8	4.8	60.3
01	194 38.5	52.4	227 47.6	4.4	21 13.0	4.9	60.3
02	209 38.7	51.5	242 11.0	4.4	21 08.1	5.1	60.3
03	224 38.9	.. 50.7	256 34.4	4.3	21 03.0	5.2	60.4
04	239 39.1	49.8	270 57.7	4.4	20 57.8	5.4	60.4
05	254 39.2	48.9	285 21.1	4.3	20 52.4	5.6	60.4
06	269 39.4	N 9 48.0	299 44.4	4.4	N20 46.8	5.7	60.5
W 07	284 39.6	47.1	314 07.8	4.4	20 41.1	5.8	60.5
E 08	299 39.8	46.2	328 31.2	4.4	20 35.3	6.0	60.5
D 09	314 40.0	.. 45.4	342 54.6	4.4	20 29.3	6.2	60.6
N 10	329 40.2	44.5	357 18.0	4.4	20 23.1	6.3	60.6
E 11	344 40.3	43.6	11 41.4	4.5	20 16.8	6.5	60.6
S 12	359 40.5	N 9 42.7	26 04.9	4.4	N20 10.3	6.6	60.6
D 13	14 40.7	41.8	40 28.3	4.5	20 03.7	6.8	60.7
A 14	29 40.9	41.0	54 51.8	4.5	19 56.9	6.9	60.7
Y 15	44 41.1	.. 40.1	69 15.3	4.5	19 50.0	7.0	60.7
16	59 41.3	39.2	83 38.8	4.6	19 43.0	7.3	60.7
17	74 41.4	38.3	98 02.4	4.5	19 35.7	7.3	60.8
18	89 41.6	N 9 37.4	112 25.9	4.6	N19 28.4	7.5	60.8
19	104 41.8	36.5	126 49.5	4.7	19 20.9	7.6	60.8
20	119 42.0	35.7	141 13.2	4.6	19 13.3	7.8	60.8
21	134 42.2	.. 34.8	155 36.8	4.7	19 05.5	8.0	60.9
22	149 42.4	33.9	170 00.5	4.7	18 57.5	8.0	60.9
23	164 42.5	33.0	184 24.2	4.7	N18 49.5	8.2	60.9
	SD 15.9	d 0.9	SD 16.1		16.3		16.5

Twilight / Sunrise / Moonrise

Lat.	Naut.	Civil	Sunrise	26	27	28	29
N 72	////	01 46	03 34	⬜	⬜	⬜	⬜
N 70	////	02 27	03 52	⬜	⬜	⬜	00 19
68	////	02 55	04 06	⬜	22 47	25 07	01 07
66	01 32	03 15	04 17	22 16	23 44	25 37	01 37
64	02 08	03 31	04 27	22 57	24 18	00 18	02 00
62	02 34	03 44	04 35	23 25	24 42	00 42	02 18
60	02 53	03 55	04 42	23 47	25 02	01 02	02 33
N 58	03 08	04 05	04 48	24 05	00 05	01 18	02 45
56	03 21	04 13	04 54	24 20	00 20	01 31	02 56
54	03 32	04 20	04 59	24 32	00 32	01 43	03 06
52	03 42	04 27	05 03	24 44	00 44	01 54	03 14
50	03 50	04 33	05 07	24 54	00 54	02 03	03 22
45	04 07	04 45	05 15	00 17	01 15	02 22	03 38
N 40	04 21	04 54	05 23	00 34	01 32	02 38	03 51
35	04 31	05 03	05 29	00 48	01 46	02 52	04 03
30	04 40	05 09	05 34	01 00	01 59	03 03	04 12
20	04 54	05 21	05 43	01 21	02 20	03 23	04 29
N 10	05 05	05 30	05 51	01 39	02 38	03 41	04 44
0	05 13	05 37	05 58	01 56	02 56	03 57	04 57
S 10	05 20	05 44	06 05	02 14	03 13	04 13	05 11
20	05 25	05 51	06 13	02 32	03 32	04 30	05 26
30	05 29	05 57	06 21	02 53	03 53	04 50	05 42
35	05 31	06 01	06 26	03 06	04 06	05 02	05 52
40	05 33	06 04	06 32	03 20	04 20	05 15	06 03
45	05 34	06 08	06 38	03 37	04 37	05 30	06 16
S 50	05 35	06 13	06 46	03 58	04 58	05 50	06 31
52	05 36	06 15	06 49	04 08	05 08	05 59	06 39
54	05 36	06 17	06 53	04 20	05 20	06 09	06 47
56	05 36	06 19	06 57	04 33	05 33	06 20	06 56
58	05 36	06 21	07 02	04 48	05 48	06 33	07 06
S 60	05 36	06 24	07 07	05 06	06 06	06 48	07 18

Sunset / Twilight / Moonset

Lat.	Sunset	Civil	Naut.	26	27	28	29
N 72	20 25	22 09	////	⬜	⬜	⬜	⬜
N 70	20 08	21 31	////	⬜	⬜	21 18	20 47
68	19 55	21 05	23 39	⬜	20 41	20 30	20 23
66	19 43	20 45	22 24	19 05	19 44	19 58	20 04
64	19 34	20 29	21 50	18 24	19 10	19 35	19 49
62	19 26	20 17	21 26	17 56	18 45	19 16	19 36
60	19 19	20 06	21 07	17 34	18 25	19 01	19 25
N 58	19 13	19 56	20 52	17 16	18 09	18 48	19 16
56	19 08	19 48	20 40	17 01	17 55	18 36	19 07
54	19 03	19 41	20 29	16 48	17 43	18 26	19 00
52	18 59	19 35	20 20	16 37	17 32	18 17	18 53
50	18 55	19 29	20 12	16 27	17 23	18 09	18 47
45	18 47	19 18	19 55	16 06	17 03	17 52	18 34
N 40	18 40	19 08	19 42	15 49	16 46	17 38	18 23
35	18 34	19 00	19 31	15 34	16 32	17 26	18 15
30	18 29	18 53	19 22	15 22	16 20	17 15	18 05
20	18 20	18 42	19 09	15 00	16 00	16 57	17 50
N 10	18 12	18 33	18 58	14 42	15 42	16 41	17 38
0	18 05	18 26	18 50	14 24	15 25	16 26	17 26
S 10	17 58	18 19	18 44	14 07	15 08	16 11	17 14
20	17 50	18 13	18 39	13 48	14 50	15 54	17 01
30	17 42	18 06	18 34	13 27	14 29	15 36	16 46
35	17 37	18 03	18 32	13 14	14 16	15 25	16 37
40	17 32	17 59	18 31	13 00	14 02	15 12	16 27
45	17 26	17 56	18 30	12 43	13 45	14 57	16 15
S 50	17 18	17 51	18 29	12 21	13 24	14 39	16 01
52	17 15	17 49	18 29	12 11	13 14	14 30	15 54
54	17 11	17 47	18 28	12 00	13 03	14 20	15 47
56	17 07	17 45	18 28	11 47	12 50	14 09	15 38
58	17 03	17 43	18 28	11 31	12 36	13 57	15 29
S 60	16 58	17 40	18 29	11 13	12 18	13 42	15 15

SUN / MOON

Day	Eqn. of Time 00h	Eqn. of Time 12h	Mer. Pass.	Mer. Pass. Upper	Mer. Pass. Lower	Age	Phase
	m s	m s	h m	h m	h m	d	%
26	02 01	01 53	12 02	08 10	20 40	25	21
27	01 44	01 36	12 02	09 10	21 41	26	12
28	01 27	01 18	12 01	10 11	22 42	27	6

© British Crown Copyright 2018. All rights reserved.

UT	ARIES GHA	VENUS −3.9 GHA	Dec	MARS +1.7 GHA	Dec	JUPITER −2.2 GHA	Dec	SATURN +0.3 GHA	Dec	STARS Name	SHA	Dec
d h	° ′	° ′	° ′	° ′	° ′	° ′	° ′	° ′	° ′		° ′	° ′
29 00	336 54.7	175 21.8	N 9 20.5	177 54.9	N10 00.7	83 11.0	S22 14.4	51 28.6	S22 26.4	Acamar	315 14.9	S40 13.4
01	351 57.2	190 21.3	19.3	192 55.9	10 00.1	98 13.3	14.4	66 31.1	26.4	Achernar	335 23.2	S57 08.1
02	6 59.6	205 20.9	18.2	207 56.9	9 59.5	113 15.6	14.5	81 33.7	26.5	Acrux	173 05.2	S63 12.5
03	22 02.1	220 20.5	.. 17.0	222 57.8	.. 58.9	128 18.0	.. 14.5	96 36.2	.. 26.5	Adhara	255 09.4	S28 59.8
04	37 04.6	235 20.0	15.8	237 58.8	58.3	143 20.3	14.5	111 38.8	26.5	Aldebaran	290 44.5	N16 32.8
05	52 07.0	250 19.6	14.7	252 59.8	57.7	158 22.6	14.5	126 41.3	26.5			
06	67 09.5	265 19.1	N 9 13.5	268 00.7	N 9 57.1	173 24.9	S22 14.6	141 43.9	S22 26.5	Alioth	166 17.4	N55 51.5
07	82 12.0	280 18.7	12.3	283 01.7	56.5	188 27.2	14.6	156 46.4	26.5	Alkaid	152 55.8	N49 13.3
08	97 14.4	295 18.2	11.2	298 02.7	55.9	203 29.6	14.6	171 48.9	26.5	Alnair	27 37.9	S46 51.9
09	112 16.9	310 17.8	.. 10.0	313 03.6	.. 55.3	218 31.9	.. 14.6	186 51.5	.. 26.5	Alnilam	275 42.2	S 1 11.4
10	127 19.4	325 17.4	08.8	328 04.6	54.7	233 34.2	14.6	201 54.0	26.6	Alphard	217 52.5	S 8 44.5
11	142 21.8	340 16.9	07.7	343 05.6	54.1	248 36.5	14.7	216 56.6	26.6			
12	157 24.3	355 16.5	N 9 06.5	358 06.5	N 9 53.5	263 38.8	S22 14.7	231 59.1	S22 26.6	Alphecca	126 07.5	N26 39.3
13	172 26.7	10 16.0	05.3	13 07.5	52.9	278 41.2	14.7	247 01.7	26.6	Alpheratz	357 38.8	N29 11.9
14	187 29.2	25 15.6	04.1	28 08.5	52.3	293 43.5	14.7	262 04.2	26.6	Altair	62 03.8	N 8 55.4
15	202 31.7	40 15.1	.. 03.0	43 09.5	.. 51.7	308 45.8	.. 14.8	277 06.8	.. 26.6	Ankaa	353 11.1	S42 11.9
16	217 34.1	55 14.7	01.8	58 10.4	51.1	323 48.1	14.8	292 09.3	26.6	Antares	112 21.0	S26 28.4
17	232 36.6	70 14.3	9 00.6	73 11.4	50.5	338 50.4	14.8	307 11.9	26.6			
18	247 39.1	85 13.8	N 8 59.5	88 12.4	N 9 49.9	353 52.8	S22 14.8	322 14.4	S22 26.7	Arcturus	145 52.0	N19 05.2
19	262 41.5	100 13.4	58.3	103 13.3	49.3	8 55.1	14.8	337 17.0	26.7	Atria	107 18.9	S69 03.8
20	277 44.0	115 12.9	57.1	118 14.3	48.7	23 57.4	14.9	352 19.5	26.7	Avior	234 16.9	S59 34.2
21	292 46.5	130 12.5	.. 55.9	133 15.3	.. 48.1	38 59.7	.. 14.9	7 22.1	.. 26.7	Bellatrix	278 27.5	N 6 22.0
22	307 48.9	145 12.1	54.8	148 16.2	47.5	54 02.0	14.9	22 24.6	26.7	Betelgeuse	270 56.8	N 7 24.6
23	322 51.4	160 11.6	53.6	163 17.2	46.9	69 04.3	14.9	37 27.2	26.7			
30 00	337 53.9	175 11.2	N 8 52.4	178 18.2	N 9 46.3	84 06.6	S22 15.0	52 29.7	S22 26.7	Canopus	263 54.5	S52 42.2
01	352 56.3	190 10.8	51.2	193 19.1	45.7	99 09.0	15.0	67 32.2	26.7	Capella	280 28.3	N46 00.8
02	7 58.8	205 10.3	50.1	208 20.1	45.1	114 11.3	15.0	82 34.8	26.8	Deneb	49 28.2	N45 21.2
03	23 01.2	220 09.9	.. 48.9	223 21.1	.. 44.5	129 13.6	.. 15.0	97 37.3	.. 26.8	Denebola	182 29.6	N14 28.0
04	38 03.7	235 09.4	47.7	238 22.0	43.9	144 15.9	15.1	112 39.9	26.8	Diphda	348 51.3	S17 52.7
05	53 06.2	250 09.0	46.5	253 23.0	43.3	159 18.2	15.1	127 42.4	26.8			
06	68 08.6	265 08.6	N 8 45.4	268 24.0	N 9 42.7	174 20.5	S22 15.1	142 45.0	S22 26.8	Dubhe	193 47.1	N61 38.9
07	83 11.1	280 08.1	44.2	283 24.9	42.1	189 22.8	15.1	157 47.5	26.8	Elnath	278 07.3	N28 37.3
08	98 13.6	295 07.7	43.0	298 25.9	41.5	204 25.2	15.1	172 50.1	26.8	Eltanin	90 44.0	N51 29.6
09	113 16.0	310 07.3	.. 41.8	313 26.9	.. 40.9	219 27.5	.. 15.2	187 52.6	.. 26.8	Enif	33 42.6	N 9 58.0
10	128 18.5	325 06.8	40.7	328 27.8	40.3	234 29.8	15.2	202 55.2	26.9	Fomalhaut	15 18.9	S29 31.0
11	143 21.0	340 06.4	39.5	343 28.8	39.7	249 32.1	15.2	217 57.7	26.9			
12	158 23.4	355 06.0	N 8 38.3	358 29.8	N 9 39.1	264 34.4	S22 15.2	233 00.2	S22 26.9	Gacrux	171 56.7	S57 13.3
13	173 25.9	10 05.5	37.1	13 30.7	38.5	279 36.7	15.3	248 02.8	26.9	Gienah	175 48.2	S17 38.9
14	188 28.3	25 05.1	35.9	28 31.7	37.9	294 39.0	15.3	263 05.3	26.9	Hadar	148 42.2	S60 28.1
15	203 30.8	40 04.7	.. 34.8	43 32.7	.. 37.3	309 41.3	.. 15.3	278 07.9	.. 26.9	Hamal	327 55.8	N23 33.2
16	218 33.3	55 04.2	33.6	58 33.7	36.7	324 43.7	15.3	293 10.4	26.9	Kaus Aust.	83 38.0	S34 22.4
17	233 35.7	70 03.8	32.4	73 34.6	36.1	339 46.0	15.4	308 13.0	26.9			
18	248 38.2	85 03.4	N 8 31.2	88 35.6	N 9 35.5	354 48.3	S22 15.4	323 15.5	S22 26.9	Kochab	137 20.5	N74 04.9
19	263 40.7	100 02.9	30.0	103 36.6	34.9	9 50.6	15.4	338 18.0	27.0	Markab	13 33.8	N15 18.7
20	278 43.1	115 02.5	28.8	118 37.5	34.3	24 52.9	15.4	353 20.6	27.0	Menkar	314 10.5	N 4 10.0
21	293 45.6	130 02.1	.. 27.7	133 38.5	.. 33.7	39 55.2	.. 15.4	8 23.1	.. 27.0	Menkent	148 02.8	S36 27.9
22	308 48.1	145 01.6	26.5	148 39.5	33.1	54 57.5	15.5	23 25.7	27.0	Miaplacidus	221 39.7	S69 47.7
23	323 50.5	160 01.2	25.3	163 40.4	32.5	69 59.8	15.5	38 28.2	27.0			
31 00	338 53.0	175 00.8	N 8 24.1	178 41.4	N 9 31.9	85 02.1	S22 15.5	53 30.8	S22 27.0	Mirfak	308 34.1	N49 55.5
01	353 55.5	190 00.3	22.9	193 42.4	31.3	100 04.4	15.5	68 33.3	27.0	Nunki	75 52.8	S26 16.2
02	8 57.9	204 59.9	21.7	208 43.4	30.7	115 06.7	15.6	83 35.8	27.0	Peacock	53 12.0	S56 40.3
03	24 00.4	219 59.5	.. 20.6	223 44.3	.. 30.1	130 09.0	.. 15.6	98 38.4	.. 27.1	Pollux	243 22.8	N27 58.7
04	39 02.8	234 59.1	19.4	238 45.3	29.5	145 11.3	15.6	113 40.9	27.1	Procyon	244 55.5	N 5 10.5
05	54 05.3	249 58.6	18.2	253 46.3	28.9	160 13.7	15.6	128 43.5	27.1			
06	69 07.8	264 58.2	N 8 17.0	268 47.2	N 9 28.3	175 16.0	S22 15.7	143 46.0	S22 27.1	Rasalhague	96 02.4	N12 33.1
07	84 10.2	279 57.8	15.8	283 48.2	27.7	190 18.3	15.7	158 48.5	27.1	Regulus	207 39.3	N11 52.4
08	99 12.7	294 57.3	14.6	298 49.2	27.1	205 20.6	15.7	173 51.1	27.1	Rigel	281 08.0	S 8 10.7
09	114 15.2	309 56.9	.. 13.4	313 50.1	.. 26.5	220 22.9	.. 15.7	188 53.6	.. 27.1	Rigil Kent.	139 46.3	S60 55.0
10	129 17.6	324 56.5	12.2	328 51.1	25.9	235 25.2	15.8	203 56.2	27.1	Sabik	102 07.6	S15 44.8
11	144 20.1	339 56.1	11.1	343 52.1	25.2	250 27.5	15.8	218 58.7	27.2			
12	159 22.6	354 55.6	N 8 09.9	358 53.1	N 9 24.6	265 29.8	S22 15.8	234 01.2	S22 27.2	Schedar	349 35.2	N56 38.5
13	174 25.0	9 55.2	08.7	13 54.0	24.0	280 32.1	15.8	249 03.8	27.2	Shaula	96 16.0	S37 07.0
14	189 27.5	24 54.8	07.5	28 55.0	23.4	295 34.4	15.9	264 06.3	27.2	Sirius	258 30.2	S16 44.5
15	204 30.0	39 54.3	.. 06.3	43 56.0	.. 22.8	310 36.7	.. 15.9	279 08.9	.. 27.2	Spica	158 27.0	S11 15.6
16	219 32.4	54 53.9	05.1	58 56.9	22.2	325 39.0	15.9	294 11.4	27.2	Suhail	222 49.8	S43 30.5
17	234 34.9	69 53.5	03.9	73 57.9	21.6	340 41.3	15.9	309 13.9	27.2			
18	249 37.3	84 53.1	N 8 02.7	88 58.9	N 9 21.0	355 43.6	S22 15.9	324 16.5	S22 27.2	Vega	80 35.9	N38 48.5
19	264 39.8	99 52.6	01.5	103 59.8	20.4	10 45.9	16.0	339 19.0	27.2	Zuben'ubi	137 00.8	S16 07.2
20	279 42.3	114 52.2	8 00.3	119 00.8	19.8	25 48.2	16.0	354 21.6	27.3		SHA	Mer. Pass.
21	294 44.7	129 51.8	7 59.2	134 01.8	.. 19.2	40 50.5	.. 16.0	9 24.1	.. 27.3		° ′	h m
22	309 47.2	144 51.4	58.0	149 02.8	18.6	55 52.8	16.0	24 26.6	27.3	Venus	197 17.3	12 20
23	324 49.7	159 50.9	56.8	164 03.7	18.0	70 55.1	16.1	39 29.2	27.3	Mars	200 24.3	12 06
	h m									Jupiter	106 12.8	18 21
Mer. Pass.	1 28.2	v −0.4	d 1.2	v 1.0	d 0.6	v 2.3	d 0.0	v 2.5	d 0.0	Saturn	74 35.9	20 27

© British Crown Copyright 2018. All rights reserved.

UT	SUN GHA	SUN Dec	MOON GHA	v	Dec	d	HP
d h	° ′	° ′	° ′	′	° ′	′	′
29 00	179 42.7	N 9 32.1	198 47.9	4.8	N18 41.3	8.4	60.9
01	194 42.9	31.2	213 11.7	4.8	18 32.9	8.5	61.0
02	209 43.1	30.3	227 35.5	4.9	18 24.4	8.6	61.0
03	224 43.3	.. 29.5	241 59.4	4.8	18 15.8	8.8	61.0
04	239 43.5	28.6	256 23.2	4.9	18 07.0	8.8	61.0
05	254 43.7	27.7	270 47.1	5.0	17 58.2	9.1	61.0
06	269 43.8	N 9 26.8	285 11.1	5.0	N17 49.1	9.1	61.1
07	284 44.0	25.9	299 35.1	5.0	17 40.0	9.3	61.1
T 08	299 44.2	25.0	313 59.1	5.1	17 30.7	9.4	61.1
H 09	314 44.4	.. 24.1	328 23.2	5.1	17 21.3	9.6	61.1
U 10	329 44.6	23.2	342 47.3	5.2	17 11.7	9.6	61.1
R 11	344 44.8	22.4	357 11.5	5.2	17 02.1	9.8	61.1
S 12	359 45.0	N 9 21.5	11 35.7	5.3	N16 52.3	10.0	61.2
D 13	14 45.2	20.6	26 00.0	5.3	16 42.3	10.0	61.2
A 14	29 45.3	19.7	40 24.3	5.3	16 32.3	10.2	61.2
Y 15	44 45.5	.. 18.8	54 48.6	5.4	16 22.1	10.3	61.2
16	59 45.7	17.9	69 13.0	5.5	16 11.8	10.4	61.2
17	74 45.9	17.0	83 37.5	5.5	16 01.4	10.5	61.2
18	89 46.1	N 9 16.1	98 02.0	5.5	N15 50.9	10.6	61.3
19	104 46.3	15.2	112 26.5	5.6	15 40.3	10.8	61.3
20	119 46.5	14.3	126 51.1	5.7	15 29.5	10.8	61.3
21	134 46.7	.. 13.5	141 15.8	5.7	15 18.7	11.0	61.3
22	149 46.8	12.6	155 40.5	5.7	15 07.7	11.1	61.3
23	164 47.0	11.7	170 05.2	5.8	14 56.6	11.1	61.3
30 00	179 47.2	N 9 10.8	184 30.0	5.9	N14 45.5	11.3	61.3
01	194 47.4	09.9	198 54.9	5.9	14 34.2	11.4	61.3
02	209 47.6	09.0	213 19.8	5.9	14 22.8	11.5	61.3
03	224 47.8	.. 08.1	227 44.7	6.1	14 11.3	11.6	61.3
04	239 48.0	07.2	242 09.8	6.0	13 59.7	11.7	61.3
05	254 48.2	06.3	256 34.8	6.2	13 48.0	11.8	61.3
06	269 48.4	N 9 05.4	271 00.0	6.1	N13 36.2	11.9	61.4
07	284 48.5	04.5	285 25.1	6.3	13 24.3	12.0	61.4
08	299 48.7	03.6	299 50.4	6.3	13 12.3	12.0	61.4
F 09	314 48.9	.. 02.7	314 15.7	6.3	13 00.3	12.2	61.4
R 10	329 49.1	01.9	328 41.0	6.4	12 48.1	12.3	61.4
I 11	344 49.3	01.0	343 06.4	6.5	12 35.8	12.3	61.4
D 12	359 49.5	N 9 00.1	357 31.9	6.5	N12 23.5	12.4	61.4
A 13	14 49.7	8 59.2	11 57.4	6.6	12 11.1	12.5	61.4
Y 14	29 49.9	58.3	26 23.0	6.6	11 58.6	12.6	61.4
15	44 50.1	.. 57.4	40 48.6	6.7	11 46.0	12.7	61.4
16	59 50.3	56.5	55 14.3	6.7	11 33.3	12.7	61.4
17	74 50.5	55.6	69 40.0	6.8	11 20.6	12.8	61.4
18	89 50.6	N 8 54.7	84 05.8	6.9	N11 07.8	12.9	61.4
19	104 50.8	53.8	98 31.7	6.9	10 54.9	13.0	61.4
20	119 51.0	52.9	112 57.6	6.9	10 41.9	13.0	61.4
21	134 51.2	.. 52.0	127 23.5	7.1	10 28.9	13.1	61.4
22	149 51.4	51.1	141 49.6	7.0	10 15.8	13.2	61.4
23	164 51.6	50.2	156 15.6	7.2	10 02.6	13.2	61.4
31 00	179 51.8	N 8 49.3	170 41.8	7.2	N 9 49.4	13.3	61.4
01	194 52.0	48.4	185 08.0	7.2	9 36.1	13.3	61.4
02	209 52.2	47.5	199 34.2	7.3	9 22.8	13.5	61.4
03	224 52.4	.. 46.6	214 00.5	7.3	9 09.3	13.4	61.4
04	239 52.6	45.7	228 26.8	7.4	8 55.9	13.6	61.3
05	254 52.8	44.8	242 53.2	7.5	8 42.3	13.5	61.3
06	269 53.0	N 8 43.9	257 19.7	7.5	N 8 28.8	13.7	61.3
07	284 53.1	43.0	271 46.2	7.6	8 15.1	13.6	61.3
S 08	299 53.3	42.1	286 12.8	7.6	8 01.5	13.8	61.3
A 09	314 53.5	.. 41.2	300 39.4	7.6	7 47.7	13.7	61.3
T 10	329 53.7	40.3	315 06.0	7.8	7 34.0	13.8	61.3
U 11	344 53.9	39.4	329 32.8	7.7	7 20.2	13.9	61.2
R 12	359 54.1	N 8 38.5	343 59.5	7.8	N 7 06.3	13.9	61.2
D 13	14 54.3	37.6	358 26.3	7.9	6 52.4	13.9	61.2
A 14	29 54.5	36.7	12 53.2	7.9	6 38.5	14.0	61.2
Y 15	44 54.7	.. 35.8	27 20.1	8.0	6 24.5	14.0	61.2
16	59 54.9	34.9	41 47.1	8.0	6 10.5	14.0	61.2
17	74 55.1	34.0	56 14.1	8.1	5 56.5	14.1	61.2
18	89 55.3	N 8 33.1	70 41.2	8.1	N 5 42.4	14.1	61.2
19	104 55.5	32.2	85 08.3	8.2	5 28.3	14.1	61.2
20	119 55.7	31.3	99 35.5	8.2	5 14.2	14.2	61.2
21	134 55.9	.. 30.4	114 02.7	8.2	5 00.0	14.2	61.1
22	149 56.1	29.5	128 29.9	8.3	4 45.8	14.2	61.1
23	164 56.3	28.6	142 57.2	8.4	N 4 31.6	14.2	61.1
	SD 15.9	d 0.9	SD 16.7		16.7		16.7

Lat.	Twilight Naut.	Twilight Civil	Sunrise	Moonrise 29	30	31	1
°	h m	h m	h m	h m	h m	h m	h m
N 72	////	02 13	03 50	⊂⊃	02 25	04 59	07 17
N 70	////	02 46	04 05	00 19	02 56	05 12	07 20
68	01 05	03 09	04 17	01 07	03 18	05 23	07 23
66	01 54	03 27	04 27	01 37	03 36	05 32	07 25
64	02 24	03 42	04 36	02 00	03 50	05 40	07 27
62	02 46	03 53	04 43	02 18	04 01	05 46	07 29
60	03 03	04 04	04 49	02 33	04 11	05 52	07 31
N 58	03 17	04 12	04 55	02 45	04 20	05 57	07 32
56	03 29	04 20	05 00	02 56	04 28	06 01	07 33
54	03 39	04 26	05 04	03 06	04 34	06 05	07 34
52	03 48	04 32	05 08	03 14	04 41	06 08	07 35
50	03 56	04 37	05 11	03 22	04 46	06 12	07 36
45	04 12	04 49	05 19	03 38	04 58	06 18	07 38
N 40	04 24	04 57	05 25	03 51	05 07	06 24	07 40
35	04 34	05 05	05 31	04 03	05 16	06 29	07 41
30	04 42	05 11	05 36	04 12	05 23	06 33	07 42
20	04 55	05 21	05 44	04 29	05 36	06 41	07 44
N 10	05 05	05 30	05 51	04 44	05 46	06 47	07 46
0	05 12	05 36	05 57	04 57	05 57	06 53	07 48
S 10	05 18	05 43	06 04	05 11	06 07	06 59	07 50
20	05 23	05 48	06 11	05 26	06 18	07 06	07 52
30	05 26	05 54	06 18	05 42	06 30	07 13	07 54
35	05 27	05 57	06 22	05 52	06 37	07 18	07 55
40	05 28	06 00	06 27	06 03	06 45	07 22	07 57
45	05 29	06 03	06 33	06 16	06 54	07 28	07 58
S 50	05 29	06 07	06 39	06 31	07 06	07 34	08 00
52	05 29	06 08	06 42	06 39	07 11	07 38	08 01
54	05 29	06 10	06 46	06 47	07 17	07 41	08 02
56	05 29	06 12	06 49	06 56	07 23	07 44	08 03
58	05 28	06 14	06 53	07 06	07 30	07 49	08 04
S 60	05 28	06 16	06 58	07 18	07 38	07 53	08 06

Lat.	Sunset	Twilight Civil	Twilight Naut.	Moonset 29	30	31	1
°	h m	h m	h m	h m	h m	h m	h m
N 72	20 08	21 42	////	21 20	20 47	20 24	20 05
N 70	19 53	21 11	////	20 47	20 31	20 18	20 06
68	19 42	20 48	22 45	20 23	20 17	20 12	20 06
66	19 32	20 31	22 01	20 04	20 07	20 07	20 07
64	19 24	20 17	21 33	19 49	19 58	20 03	20 08
62	19 17	20 06	21 12	19 36	19 50	20 00	20 08
60	19 11	19 56	20 55	19 25	19 43	19 57	20 09
N 58	19 05	19 48	20 42	19 16	19 37	19 54	20 09
56	19 01	19 40	20 30	19 07	19 31	19 52	20 09
54	18 56	19 34	20 20	19 00	19 27	19 49	20 10
52	18 52	19 28	20 12	18 53	19 22	19 47	20 10
50	18 49	19 23	20 04	18 47	19 18	19 45	20 10
45	18 42	19 12	19 49	18 34	19 10	19 41	20 11
N 40	18 35	19 03	19 36	18 23	19 02	19 38	20 11
35	18 30	18 56	19 27	18 13	18 56	19 35	20 11
30	18 25	18 50	19 18	18 05	18 50	19 32	20 12
20	18 17	18 40	19 06	17 50	18 41	19 28	20 12
N 10	18 10	18 32	18 56	17 38	18 32	19 23	20 13
0	18 04	18 25	18 49	17 26	18 24	19 19	20 13
S 10	17 58	18 19	18 44	17 14	18 16	19 15	20 14
20	17 51	18 13	18 39	17 01	18 07	19 11	20 14
30	17 44	18 08	18 36	16 46	17 57	19 06	20 14
35	17 40	18 05	18 34	16 37	17 51	19 03	20 15
40	17 35	18 02	18 34	16 27	17 44	19 00	20 15
45	17 29	17 59	18 33	16 15	17 36	18 56	20 15
S 50	17 23	17 56	18 33	16 01	17 26	18 52	20 15
52	17 20	17 54	18 33	15 54	17 22	18 50	20 16
54	17 17	17 52	18 33	15 47	17 17	18 47	20 16
56	17 13	17 51	18 34	15 38	17 11	18 45	20 16
58	17 09	17 49	18 34	15 29	17 05	18 42	20 16
S 60	17 04	17 47	18 35	15 18	16 58	18 38	20 16

Day	SUN Eqn. of Time 00h	12h	Mer. Pass.	MOON Mer. Pass. Upper	Lower	Age	Phase
d	m s	m s	h m	h m	h m	d	%
29	01 09	01 01	12 01	11 12	23 41	28	1
30	00 51	00 42	12 01	12 10	24 39	00	0
31	00 33	00 24	12 00	13 06	00 39	01	2

© British Crown Copyright 2018. All rights reserved.

UT	ARIES GHA	VENUS −3.9 GHA	Dec	MARS +1.7 GHA	Dec	JUPITER −2.2 GHA	Dec	SATURN +0.3 GHA	Dec	STARS Name	SHA	Dec
1 00	339 52.1	174 50.5 N 7	55.6	179 04.7 N 9	17.4	85 57.4 S22	16.1	54 31.7 S22	27.3	Acamar	315 14.9	S40 13.4
01	354 54.6	189 50.1	54.4	194 05.7	16.8	100 59.7	16.1	69 34.3	27.3	Achernar	335 23.2	S57 08.1
02	9 57.1	204 49.7	53.2	209 06.6	16.2	116 02.0	16.1	84 36.8	27.3	Acrux	173 05.2	S63 12.4
03	24 59.5	219 49.2 ..	52.0	224 07.6 ..	15.6	131 04.3 ..	16.2	99 39.3 ..	27.3	Adhara	255 09.4	S28 59.8
04	40 02.0	234 48.8	50.8	239 08.6	15.0	146 06.6	16.2	114 41.9	27.4	Aldebaran	290 44.5	N16 32.8
05	55 04.4	249 48.4	49.6	254 09.6	14.4	161 08.9	16.2	129 44.4	27.4			
06	70 06.9	264 48.0 N 7	48.4	269 10.5 N 9	13.8	176 11.2 S22	16.2	144 46.9 S22	27.4	Alioth	166 17.4	N55 51.5
07	85 09.4	279 47.6	47.2	284 11.5	13.2	191 13.5	16.3	159 49.5	27.4	Alkaid	152 55.8	N49 13.3
08	100 11.8	294 47.1	46.0	299 12.5	12.6	206 15.8	16.3	174 52.0	27.4	Alnair	27 37.9	S46 51.9
S 09	115 14.3	309 46.7 ..	44.8	314 13.5 ..	11.9	221 18.1 ..	16.3	189 54.5 ..	27.4	Alnilam	275 42.1	S 1 11.4
U 10	130 16.8	324 46.3	43.6	329 14.4	11.3	236 20.4	16.3	204 57.1	27.4	Alphard	217 52.2	S 8 44.5
N 11	145 19.2	339 45.9	42.4	344 15.4	10.7	251 22.7	16.4	219 59.6	27.4			
D 12	160 21.7	354 45.5 N 7	41.2	359 16.4 N 9	10.1	266 25.0 S22	16.4	235 02.2 S22	27.4	Alphecca	126 07.5	N26 39.3
A 13	175 24.2	9 45.0	40.0	14 17.3	09.5	281 27.3	16.4	250 04.7	27.5	Alpheratz	357 38.8	N29 11.9
Y 14	190 26.6	24 44.6	38.8	29 18.3	08.9	296 29.6	16.4	265 07.2	27.5	Altair	62 03.9	N 8 55.4
15	205 29.1	39 44.2 ..	37.6	44 19.3 ..	08.3	311 31.9 ..	16.5	280 09.8 ..	27.5	Ankaa	353 11.1	S42 11.9
16	220 31.6	54 43.8	36.4	59 20.3	07.7	326 34.2	16.5	295 12.3	27.5	Antares	112 21.0	S26 28.4
17	235 34.0	69 43.4	35.2	74 21.2	07.1	341 36.5	16.5	310 14.8	27.5			
18	250 36.5	84 42.9 N 7	34.0	89 22.2 N 9	06.5	356 38.7 S22	16.5	325 17.4 S22	27.5	Arcturus	145 52.0	N19 05.2
19	265 38.9	99 42.5	32.8	104 23.2	05.9	11 41.0	16.6	340 19.9	27.5	Atria	107 19.0	S69 03.8
20	280 41.4	114 42.1	31.6	119 24.1	05.3	26 43.3	16.6	355 22.4	27.5	Avior	234 16.8	S59 34.1
21	295 43.9	129 41.7 ..	30.4	134 25.1 ..	04.7	41 45.6 ..	16.6	10 25.0 ..	27.5	Bellatrix	278 27.5	N 6 22.0
22	310 46.3	144 41.3	29.2	149 26.1	04.1	56 47.9	16.6	25 27.5	27.6	Betelgeuse	270 56.8	N 7 24.6
23	325 48.8	159 40.8	28.0	164 27.1	03.5	71 50.2	16.7	40 30.0	27.6			
2 00	340 51.3	174 40.4 N 7	26.8	179 28.0 N 9	02.9	86 52.5 S22	16.7	55 32.6 S22	27.6	Canopus	263 54.5	S52 42.1
01	355 53.7	189 40.0	25.6	194 29.0	02.2	101 54.8	16.7	70 35.1	27.6	Capella	280 28.2	N46 00.8
02	10 56.2	204 39.6	24.4	209 30.0	01.6	116 57.1	16.7	85 37.6	27.6	Deneb	49 28.2	N45 21.2
03	25 58.7	219 39.2 ..	23.2	224 31.0 ..	01.0	131 59.4 ..	16.8	100 40.2 ..	27.6	Denebola	182 29.6	N14 28.0
04	41 01.1	234 38.8	22.0	239 31.9	9 00.4	147 01.7	16.8	115 42.7	27.6	Diphda	348 51.3	S17 52.7
05	56 03.6	249 38.3	20.8	254 32.9	8 59.8	162 04.0	16.8	130 45.2	27.6			
06	71 06.0	264 37.9 N 7	19.6	269 33.9 N 8	59.2	177 06.2 S22	16.8	145 47.8 S22	27.6	Dubhe	193 47.1	N61 38.9
07	86 08.5	279 37.5	18.4	284 34.9	58.6	192 08.5	16.9	160 50.3	27.7	Elnath	278 07.3	N28 37.3
08	101 11.0	294 37.1	17.2	299 35.8	58.0	207 10.8	16.9	175 52.8	27.7	Eltanin	90 44.0	N51 29.6
M 09	116 13.4	309 36.7 ..	16.0	314 36.8 ..	57.4	222 13.1 ..	16.9	190 55.4 ..	27.7	Enif	33 42.6	N 9 58.0
O 10	131 15.9	324 36.3	14.8	329 37.8	56.8	237 15.4	16.9	205 57.9	27.7	Fomalhaut	15 18.9	S29 31.0
N 11	146 18.4	339 35.9	13.6	344 38.7	56.2	252 17.7	17.0	221 00.4	27.7			
D 12	161 20.8	354 35.4 N 7	12.4	359 39.7 N 8	55.6	267 20.0 S22	17.0	236 03.0 S22	27.7	Gacrux	171 56.7	S57 13.3
A 13	176 23.3	9 35.0	11.2	14 40.7	55.0	282 22.3	17.0	251 05.5	27.7	Gienah	175 48.2	S17 38.9
Y 14	191 25.8	24 34.6	09.9	29 41.7	54.3	297 24.6	17.0	266 08.0	27.7	Hadar	148 42.3	S60 28.1
15	206 28.2	39 34.2 ..	08.7	44 42.6 ..	53.7	312 26.8 ..	17.1	281 10.6 ..	27.7	Hamal	327 55.8	N23 33.2
16	221 30.7	54 33.8	07.5	59 43.6	53.1	327 29.1	17.1	296 13.1	27.8	Kaus Aust.	83 38.0	S34 22.4
17	236 33.2	69 33.4	06.3	74 44.6	52.5	342 31.4	17.1	311 15.6	27.8			
18	251 35.6	84 33.0 N 7	05.1	89 45.6 N 8	51.9	357 33.7 S22	17.1	326 18.2 S22	27.8	Kochab	137 20.6	N74 04.9
19	266 38.1	99 32.6	03.9	104 46.5	51.3	12 36.0	17.2	341 20.7	27.8	Markab	13 33.8	N15 18.7
20	281 40.5	114 32.1	02.7	119 47.5	50.7	27 38.3	17.2	356 23.2	27.8	Menkar	314 10.5	N 4 10.0
21	296 43.0	129 31.7 ..	01.5	134 48.5 ..	50.1	42 40.6 ..	17.2	11 25.7 ..	27.8	Menkent	148 02.8	S36 27.9
22	311 45.5	144 31.3	7 00.3	149 49.5	49.5	57 42.8	17.2	26 28.3	27.8	Miaplacidus	221 39.7	S69 47.7
23	326 47.9	159 30.9	6 59.1	164 50.4	48.9	72 45.1	17.3	41 30.8	27.8			
3 00	341 50.4	174 30.5 N 6	57.9	179 51.4 N 8	48.3	87 47.4 S22	17.3	56 33.3 S22	27.8	Mirfak	308 34.1	N49 55.5
01	356 52.9	189 30.1	56.6	194 52.4	47.6	102 49.7	17.3	71 35.9	27.8	Nunki	75 52.8	S26 16.2
02	11 55.3	204 29.7	55.3	209 53.4	47.0	117 52.0	17.3	86 38.4	27.9	Peacock	53 12.1	S56 40.3
03	26 57.8	219 29.3 ..	54.2	224 54.3 ..	46.4	132 54.3 ..	17.4	101 40.9 ..	27.9	Pollux	243 22.8	N27 58.7
04	42 00.3	234 28.9	53.0	239 55.3	45.8	147 56.5	17.4	116 43.4	27.9	Procyon	244 55.5	N 5 10.5
05	57 02.7	249 28.4	51.8	254 56.3	45.2	162 58.8	17.4	131 46.0	27.9			
06	72 05.2	264 28.0 N 6	50.6	269 57.3 N 8	44.6	178 01.1 S22	17.4	146 48.5 S22	27.9	Rasalhague	96 02.4	N12 33.1
07	87 07.6	279 27.6	49.4	284 58.2	44.0	193 03.4	17.5	161 51.0	27.9	Regulus	207 39.3	N11 52.4
T 08	102 10.1	294 27.2	48.2	299 59.2	43.4	208 05.7	17.5	176 53.6	27.9	Rigel	281 08.0	S 8 10.7
U 09	117 12.6	309 26.8 ..	46.9	315 00.2 ..	42.8	223 08.0 ..	17.5	191 56.1 ..	27.9	Rigil Kent.	139 46.3	S60 55.0
E 10	132 15.0	324 26.4	45.7	330 01.2	42.2	238 10.2	17.5	206 58.6	27.9	Sabik	102 07.6	S15 44.8
S 11	147 17.5	339 26.0	44.5	345 02.1	41.5	253 12.5	17.6	222 01.1	28.0			
D 12	162 20.0	354 25.6 N 6	43.3	0 03.1 N 8	40.9	268 14.8 S22	17.6	237 03.7 S22	28.0	Schedar	349 35.2	N56 38.5
A 13	177 22.4	9 25.2	42.1	15 04.1	40.3	283 17.1	17.6	252 06.2	28.0	Shaula	96 16.0	S37 07.0
Y 14	192 24.9	24 24.8	40.9	30 05.1	39.7	298 19.4	17.6	267 08.7	28.0	Sirius	258 30.2	S16 44.5
15	207 27.4	39 24.4 ..	39.7	45 06.0 ..	39.1	313 21.6 ..	17.7	282 11.3 ..	28.0	Spica	158 27.0	S11 15.6
16	222 29.8	54 23.9	38.4	60 07.0	38.5	328 23.9	17.7	297 13.8	28.0	Suhail	222 49.8	S43 30.5
17	237 32.3	69 23.5	37.2	75 08.0	37.9	343 26.2	17.7	312 16.3	28.0			
18	252 34.8	84 23.1 N 6	36.0	90 09.0 N 8	37.3	358 28.5 S22	17.7	327 18.8 S22	28.0	Vega	80 35.9	N38 48.5
19	267 37.2	99 22.7	34.8	105 09.9	36.7	13 30.8	17.8	342 21.4	28.0	Zuben'ubi	137 00.9	S16 07.2
20	282 39.7	114 22.3	33.6	120 10.9	36.0	28 33.0	17.8	357 23.9	28.0		SHA	Mer.Pass.
21	297 42.1	129 21.9 ..	32.4	135 11.9 ..	35.4	43 35.3 ..	17.8	12 26.4 ..	28.1		° ′	h m
22	312 44.6	144 21.5	31.1	150 12.9	34.8	58 37.6	17.9	27 28.9	28.1	Venus	193 49.2	12 22
23	327 47.1	159 21.1	29.9	165 13.9	34.2	73 39.9	17.9	42 31.5	28.1	Mars	198 36.8	12 01
	h m									Jupiter	106 01.2	18 10
Mer. Pass.	1 16.4	v −0.4	d 1.2	v 1.0	d 0.6	v 2.3	d 0.0	v 2.5	d 0.0	Saturn	74 41.3	20 14

© British Crown Copyright 2018. All rights reserved.

SUN and MOON

UT	SUN GHA	SUN Dec	MOON GHA	v	MOON Dec	d	HP
d h	° '	° '	° '	'	° '	'	'
1 00	179 56.5	N 8 27.7	157 24.6	8.3	N 4 17.4	14.2	61.1
01	194 56.6	26.8	171 51.9	8.5	4 03.2	14.3	61.1
02	209 56.8	25.9	186 19.4	8.5	3 48.9	14.2	61.1
03	224 57.0	.. 25.0	200 46.9	8.5	3 34.7	14.3	61.0
04	239 57.2	24.1	215 14.4	8.5	3 20.4	14.3	61.0
05	254 57.4	23.2	229 41.9	8.6	3 06.1	14.3	61.0
06	269 57.6	N 8 22.3	244 09.5	8.7	N 2 51.8	14.3	61.0
07	284 57.8	21.4	258 37.2	8.6	2 37.5	14.3	61.0
08	299 58.0	20.5	273 04.8	8.8	2 23.2	14.3	60.9
S 09	314 58.2	.. 19.5	287 32.6	8.7	2 08.9	14.3	60.9
U 10	329 58.4	18.6	302 00.3	8.8	1 54.6	14.3	60.9
N 11	344 58.6	17.7	316 28.1	8.8	1 40.3	14.4	60.9
D 12	359 58.8	N 8 16.8	330 55.9	8.9	N 1 25.9	14.3	60.8
A 13	14 59.0	15.9	345 23.8	8.9	1 11.6	14.3	60.8
Y 14	29 59.2	15.0	359 51.7	9.0	0 57.3	14.3	60.8
15	44 59.4	.. 14.1	14 19.7	8.9	0 43.0	14.3	60.8
16	59 59.6	13.2	28 47.6	9.0	0 28.7	14.2	60.7
17	74 59.8	12.3	43 15.6	9.1	0 14.5	14.3	60.7
18	90 00.0	N 8 11.4	57 43.7	9.0	N 0 00.2	14.3	60.7
19	105 00.2	10.5	72 11.7	9.1	S 0 14.1	14.2	60.7
20	120 00.4	09.6	86 39.8	9.2	0 28.3	14.3	60.6
21	135 00.6	.. 08.7	101 08.0	9.1	0 42.6	14.2	60.6
22	150 00.8	07.8	115 36.1	9.2	0 56.8	14.2	60.6
23	165 01.0	06.8	130 04.3	9.2	1 11.0	14.1	60.6
2 00	180 01.2	N 8 05.9	144 32.5	9.3	S 1 25.1	14.2	60.5
01	195 01.4	05.0	159 00.8	9.3	1 39.3	14.1	60.5
02	210 01.6	04.1	173 29.1	9.3	1 53.4	14.1	60.5
03	225 01.8	.. 03.2	187 57.4	9.3	2 07.5	14.1	60.4
04	240 02.0	02.3	202 25.7	9.3	2 21.6	14.0	60.4
05	255 02.2	01.4	216 54.0	9.4	2 35.6	14.0	60.4
06	270 02.4	N 8 00.5	231 22.4	9.4	S 2 49.6	14.0	60.4
07	285 02.6	7 59.6	245 50.8	9.4	3 03.6	14.0	60.3
08	300 02.8	58.7	260 19.2	9.5	3 17.6	13.9	60.3
M 09	315 03.0	.. 57.7	274 47.7	9.4	3 31.5	13.8	60.3
O 10	330 03.2	56.8	289 16.1	9.5	3 45.3	13.9	60.2
N 11	345 03.4	55.9	303 44.6	9.5	3 59.2	13.8	60.2
D 12	0 03.6	N 7 55.0	318 13.1	9.5	S 4 13.0	13.7	60.2
A 13	15 03.8	54.1	332 41.6	9.6	4 26.7	13.8	60.1
Y 14	30 04.0	53.2	347 10.2	9.5	4 40.5	13.6	60.1
15	45 04.2	.. 52.3	1 38.7	9.6	4 54.1	13.7	60.1
16	60 04.4	51.4	16 07.3	9.6	5 07.8	13.6	60.0
17	75 04.6	50.4	30 35.9	9.6	5 21.4	13.5	60.0
18	90 04.8	N 7 49.5	45 04.5	9.6	S 5 34.9	13.5	60.0
19	105 05.0	48.6	59 33.1	9.7	5 48.4	13.4	59.9
20	120 05.2	47.7	74 01.8	9.6	6 01.8	13.4	59.9
21	135 05.4	.. 46.8	88 30.4	9.7	6 15.2	13.4	59.9
22	150 05.6	45.9	102 59.1	9.7	6 28.6	13.3	59.8
23	165 05.8	45.0	117 27.8	9.6	6 41.9	13.2	59.8
3 00	180 06.0	N 7 44.1	131 56.4	9.7	S 6 55.1	13.2	59.8
01	195 06.2	43.1	146 25.1	9.7	7 08.3	13.1	59.7
02	210 06.4	42.2	160 53.8	9.8	7 21.4	13.0	59.7
03	225 06.6	.. 41.3	175 22.6	9.7	7 34.4	13.0	59.7
04	240 06.8	40.4	189 51.3	9.7	7 47.4	13.0	59.6
05	255 07.0	39.5	204 20.0	9.8	8 00.4	12.9	59.6
06	270 07.2	N 7 38.6	218 48.8	9.7	S 8 13.3	12.8	59.5
07	285 07.4	37.6	233 17.5	9.8	8 26.1	12.7	59.5
T 08	300 07.6	36.7	247 46.3	9.7	8 38.8	12.7	59.5
U 09	315 07.8	.. 35.8	262 15.0	9.8	8 51.5	12.6	59.4
E 10	330 08.0	34.9	276 43.8	9.8	9 04.1	12.6	59.4
S 11	345 08.2	34.0	291 12.6	9.8	9 16.7	12.4	59.4
D 12	0 08.4	N 7 33.1	305 41.4	9.7	S 9 29.1	12.5	59.3
A 13	15 08.6	32.1	320 10.1	9.8	9 41.6	12.3	59.3
Y 14	30 08.8	31.2	334 38.9	9.8	9 53.9	12.3	59.2
15	45 09.0	.. 30.3	349 07.7	9.8	10 06.2	12.2	59.2
16	60 09.2	29.4	3 36.5	9.8	10 18.4	12.1	59.2
17	75 09.5	28.5	18 05.3	9.8	10 30.5	12.0	59.1
18	90 09.7	N 7 27.6	32 34.1	9.8	S10 42.5	12.0	59.1
19	105 09.9	26.6	47 02.9	9.8	10 54.5	11.9	59.1
20	120 10.1	25.7	61 31.7	9.8	11 06.4	11.8	59.0
21	135 10.3	.. 24.8	76 00.5	9.8	11 18.2	11.7	59.0
22	150 10.5	23.9	90 29.3	9.8	11 29.9	11.7	58.9
23	165 10.7	23.0	104 58.1	9.8	S11 41.6	11.6	58.9
	SD 15.9	d 0.9	SD 16.6		16.4		16.2

Twilight, Sunrise and Moonrise

Lat.	Twilight Naut.	Twilight Civil	Sunrise	Moonrise 1	Moonrise 2	Moonrise 3	Moonrise 4
°	h m	h m	h m	h m	h m	h m	h m
N 72	////	02 36	04 05	07 17	09 29	11 42	14 04
N 70	////	03 03	04 18	07 20	09 24	11 26	13 31
68	01 37	03 23	04 28	07 23	09 19	11 13	13 08
66	02 14	03 39	04 37	07 25	09 15	11 03	12 50
64	02 39	03 52	04 45	07 27	09 12	10 55	12 35
62	02 58	04 02	04 51	07 29	09 09	10 47	12 23
60	03 13	04 11	04 56	07 31	09 07	10 41	12 12
N 58	03 26	04 19	05 01	07 32	09 05	10 36	12 03
56	03 37	04 26	05 05	07 33	09 03	10 31	11 55
54	03 46	04 32	05 09	07 34	09 01	10 26	11 48
52	03 54	04 37	05 13	07 35	09 00	10 22	11 42
50	04 01	04 42	05 16	07 36	08 59	10 19	11 37
45	04 16	04 52	05 23	07 38	08 56	10 11	11 24
N 40	04 27	05 01	05 28	07 40	08 53	10 05	11 15
35	04 37	05 07	05 33	07 41	08 51	09 59	11 06
30	04 44	05 13	05 37	07 42	08 49	09 55	10 59
20	04 56	05 22	05 45	07 44	08 46	09 47	10 46
N 10	05 05	05 30	05 51	07 46	08 43	09 39	10 35
0	05 11	05 36	05 56	07 48	08 41	09 33	10 24
S 10	05 16	05 41	06 02	07 50	08 38	09 26	10 14
20	05 20	05 46	06 08	07 52	08 36	09 19	10 03
30	05 23	05 51	06 15	07 54	08 33	09 11	09 51
35	05 24	05 53	06 18	07 55	08 31	09 07	09 44
40	05 24	05 55	06 23	07 57	08 29	09 02	09 36
45	05 24	05 58	06 27	07 58	08 27	08 56	09 27
S 50	05 23	06 01	06 33	08 00	08 24	08 49	09 15
52	05 23	06 02	06 36	08 01	08 23	08 46	09 10
54	05 22	06 03	06 39	08 02	08 22	08 42	09 05
56	05 21	06 04	06 42	08 03	08 21	08 38	08 58
58	05 21	06 06	06 45	08 04	08 19	08 34	08 51
S 60	05 19	06 07	06 49	08 06	08 17	08 29	08 43

Sunset, Twilight and Moonset

Lat.	Sunset	Twilight Civil	Twilight Naut.	Moonset 1	Moonset 2	Moonset 3	Moonset 4
°	h m	h m	h m	h m	h m	h m	h m
N 72	19 52	21 18	////	20 05	19 46	19 23	18 50
N 70	19 39	20 52	23 23	20 06	19 55	19 41	19 24
68	19 29	20 33	22 15	20 07	20 01	19 56	19 49
66	19 20	20 18	21 41	20 07	20 07	20 08	20 09
64	19 13	20 05	21 17	20 08	20 12	20 18	20 25
62	19 07	19 55	20 59	20 08	20 17	20 26	20 38
60	19 02	19 46	20 44	20 09	20 21	20 33	20 49
N 58	18 57	19 39	20 31	20 09	20 24	20 40	20 59
56	18 53	19 32	20 21	20 09	20 27	20 46	21 07
54	18 49	19 26	20 12	20 10	20 30	20 51	21 15
52	18 46	19 21	20 04	20 10	20 32	20 56	21 22
50	18 43	19 16	19 57	20 10	20 35	21 00	21 28
45	18 36	19 06	19 42	20 11	20 40	21 09	21 41
N 40	18 31	18 58	19 31	20 11	20 44	21 17	21 52
35	18 26	18 52	19 22	20 11	20 47	21 24	22 02
30	18 22	18 46	19 15	20 12	20 50	21 30	22 10
20	18 15	18 37	19 03	20 12	20 56	21 40	22 25
N 10	18 09	18 30	18 55	20 13	21 01	21 49	22 37
0	18 03	18 24	18 48	20 13	21 06	21 57	22 49
S 10	17 58	18 19	18 43	20 14	21 10	22 06	23 01
20	17 52	18 14	18 40	20 14	21 15	22 15	23 14
30	17 45	18 09	18 37	20 14	21 21	22 25	23 29
35	17 42	18 07	18 37	20 15	21 24	22 31	23 37
40	17 38	18 05	18 36	20 15	21 28	22 38	23 47
45	17 33	18 02	18 36	20 15	21 32	22 46	23 58
S 50	17 27	18 00	18 37	20 15	21 37	22 56	24 12
52	17 25	17 59	18 38	20 16	21 39	23 01	24 19
54	17 22	17 57	18 38	20 16	21 42	23 06	24 26
56	17 19	17 56	18 39	20 16	21 45	23 11	24 34
58	17 15	17 55	18 40	20 16	21 48	23 17	24 43
S 60	17 11	17 53	18 42	20 16	21 52	23 24	24 54

SUN and MOON data

Day	SUN Eqn. of Time 00h	SUN Eqn. of Time 12h	SUN Mer. Pass.	MOON Mer. Pass. Upper	MOON Mer. Pass. Lower	Age	Phase
d	m s	m s	h m	h m	h m	d %	
1	00 15	00 05	12 00	14 01	01 34	02 7	
2	00 04	00 14	12 00	14 53	02 27	03 14	
3	00 24	00 33	11 59	15 45	03 19	04 23	

© British Crown Copyright 2018. All rights reserved.

UT	ARIES GHA	VENUS −3.9 GHA	Dec	MARS +1.7 GHA	Dec	JUPITER −2.2 GHA	Dec	SATURN +0.4 GHA	Dec	STARS Name	SHA	Dec
4 00	342 49.5	174 20.7	N 6 28.7	180 14.8	N 8 33.6	88 42.1	S22 17.9	57 34.0	S22 28.1	Acamar	315 14.9	S40 13.4
01	357 52.0	189 20.3	27.5	195 15.8	33.0	103 44.4	17.9	72 36.5	28.1	Achernar	335 23.1	S57 08.1
02	12 54.5	204 19.9	26.3	210 16.8	32.4	118 46.7	18.0	87 39.0	28.1	Acrux	173 05.2	S63 12.4
03	27 56.9	219 19.5 ..	25.0	225 17.8 ..	31.8	133 49.0 ..	18.0	102 41.6 ..	28.1	Adhara	255 09.4	S28 59.8
04	42 59.4	234 19.1	23.8	240 18.7	31.2	148 51.2	18.0	117 44.1	28.1	Aldebaran	290 44.5	N16 32.8
05	58 01.9	249 18.7	22.6	255 19.7	30.5	163 53.5	18.0	132 46.6	28.1			
06	73 04.3	264 18.3	N 6 21.4	270 20.7	N 8 29.9	178 55.8	S22 18.1	147 49.1	S22 28.2	Alioth	166 17.4	N55 51.5
W 07	88 06.8	279 17.9	20.2	285 21.7	29.3	193 58.1	18.1	162 51.7	28.2	Alkaid	152 55.8	N49 13.3
E 08	103 09.3	294 17.5	18.9	300 22.6	28.7	209 00.3	18.1	177 54.2	28.2	Alnair	27 37.9	S46 51.9
D 09	118 11.7	309 17.1 ..	17.7	315 23.6 ..	28.1	224 02.6 ..	18.1	192 56.7 ..	28.2	Alnilam	275 42.1	S 1 11.4
N 10	133 14.2	324 16.7	16.5	330 24.6	27.5	239 04.9	18.2	207 59.2	28.2	Alphard	217 52.2	S 8 44.5
E 11	148 16.6	339 16.3	15.3	345 25.6	26.9	254 07.2	18.2	223 01.8	28.2			
S 12	163 19.1	354 15.9	N 6 14.0	0 26.5	N 8 26.3	269 09.4	S22 18.2	238 04.3	S22 28.2	Alphecca	126 07.5	N26 39.3
D 13	178 21.6	9 15.5	12.8	15 27.5	25.6	284 11.7	18.2	253 06.8	28.2	Alpheratz	357 38.8	N29 11.9
A 14	193 24.0	24 15.1	11.6	30 28.5	25.0	299 14.0	18.3	268 09.3	28.2	Altair	62 03.9	N 8 55.4
Y 15	208 26.5	39 14.7 ..	10.4	45 29.5 ..	24.4	314 16.3 ..	18.3	283 11.9 ..	28.2	Ankaa	353 11.1	S42 11.9
16	223 29.0	54 14.2	09.2	60 30.5	23.8	329 18.5	18.3	298 14.4	28.3	Antares	112 21.1	S26 28.4
17	238 31.4	69 13.8	07.9	75 31.4	23.2	344 20.8	18.4	313 16.9	28.3			
18	253 33.9	84 13.4	N 6 06.7	90 32.4	N 8 22.6	359 23.1	S22 18.4	328 19.4	S22 28.3	Arcturus	145 52.1	N19 05.2
19	268 36.4	99 13.0	05.5	105 33.4	22.0	14 25.3	18.4	343 21.9	28.3	Atria	107 19.0	S69 03.8
20	283 38.8	114 12.6	04.3	120 34.4	21.3	29 27.6	18.4	358 24.5	28.3	Avior	234 16.8	S59 34.1
21	298 41.3	129 12.2 ..	03.0	135 35.3 ..	20.7	44 29.9 ..	18.5	13 27.0 ..	28.3	Bellatrix	278 27.5	N 6 22.0
22	313 43.7	144 11.8	01.8	150 36.3	20.1	59 32.1	18.5	28 29.5	28.3	Betelgeuse	270 56.8	N 7 24.6
23	328 46.2	159 11.4	6 00.6	165 37.3	19.5	74 34.4	18.5	43 32.0	28.3			
5 00	343 48.7	174 11.0	N 5 59.4	180 38.3	N 8 18.9	89 36.7	S22 18.5	58 34.6	S22 28.3	Canopus	263 54.5	S52 42.1
01	358 51.1	189 10.6	58.1	195 39.3	18.3	104 39.0	18.6	73 37.1	28.3	Capella	280 28.2	N46 00.8
02	13 53.6	204 10.2	56.9	210 40.2	17.7	119 41.2	18.6	88 39.6	28.4	Deneb	49 28.2	N45 21.2
03	28 56.1	219 09.8 ..	55.7	225 41.2 ..	17.1	134 43.5 ..	18.6	103 42.1 ..	28.4	Denebola	182 29.6	N14 28.0
04	43 58.5	234 09.4	54.5	240 42.2	16.4	149 45.8	18.6	118 44.6	28.4	Diphda	348 51.3	S17 52.7
05	59 01.0	249 09.0	53.2	255 43.2	15.8	164 48.0	18.7	133 47.2	28.4			
06	74 03.5	264 08.7	N 5 52.0	270 44.1	N 8 15.2	179 50.3	S22 18.7	148 49.7	S22 28.4	Dubhe	193 47.1	N61 38.8
T 07	89 05.9	279 08.3	50.8	285 45.1	14.6	194 52.6	18.7	163 52.2	28.4	Elnath	278 07.3	N28 37.3
H 08	104 08.4	294 07.9	49.5	300 46.1	14.0	209 54.8	18.8	178 54.7	28.4	Eltanin	90 44.0	N51 29.6
U 09	119 10.9	309 07.5 ..	48.3	315 47.1 ..	13.4	224 57.1 ..	18.8	193 57.2 ..	28.4	Enif	33 42.6	N 9 58.0
R 10	134 13.3	324 07.1	47.1	330 48.1	12.8	239 59.4	18.8	208 59.8	28.4	Fomalhaut	15 18.9	S29 31.0
S 11	149 15.8	339 06.7	45.9	345 49.0	12.1	255 01.6	18.8	224 02.3	28.4			
D 12	164 18.2	354 06.3	N 5 44.6	0 50.0	N 8 11.5	270 03.9	S22 18.9	239 04.8	S22 28.4	Gacrux	171 56.7	S57 13.3
A 13	179 20.7	9 05.9	43.4	15 51.0	10.9	285 06.2	18.9	254 07.3	28.5	Gienah	175 48.2	S17 38.9
Y 14	194 23.2	24 05.5	42.2	30 52.0	10.3	300 08.4	18.9	269 09.8	28.5	Hadar	148 42.3	S60 28.1
15	209 25.6	39 05.1 ..	40.9	45 52.9 ..	09.7	315 10.7 ..	18.9	284 12.4 ..	28.5	Hamal	327 55.7	N23 33.2
16	224 28.1	54 04.7	39.7	60 53.9	09.1	330 12.9	19.0	299 14.9	28.5	Kaus Aust.	83 38.0	S34 22.4
17	239 30.6	69 04.3	38.5	75 54.9	08.4	345 15.2	19.0	314 17.4	28.5			
18	254 33.0	84 03.9	N 5 37.2	90 55.9	N 8 07.8	0 17.5	S22 19.0	329 19.9	S22 28.5	Kochab	137 20.6	N74 04.9
19	269 35.5	99 03.5	36.0	105 56.9	07.2	15 19.7	19.1	344 22.4	28.5	Markab	13 33.8	N15 18.7
20	284 38.0	114 03.1	34.8	120 57.8	06.6	30 22.0	19.1	359 24.9	28.5	Menkar	314 10.5	N 4 10.0
21	299 40.4	129 02.7 ..	33.5	135 58.8 ..	06.0	45 24.3 ..	19.1	14 27.5 ..	28.5	Menkent	148 02.8	S36 27.9
22	314 42.9	144 02.3	32.3	150 59.8	05.4	60 26.5	19.1	29 30.0	28.5	Miaplacidus	221 39.7	S69 47.7
23	329 45.4	159 01.9	31.1	166 00.8	04.8	75 28.8	19.2	44 32.5	28.6			
6 00	344 47.8	174 01.5	N 5 29.9	181 01.8	N 8 04.1	90 31.0	S22 19.2	59 35.0	S22 28.6	Mirfak	308 34.1	N49 55.5
01	359 50.3	189 01.1	28.6	196 02.7	03.5	105 33.3	19.2	74 37.5	28.6	Nunki	75 52.9	S26 16.2
02	14 52.7	204 00.7	27.4	211 03.7	02.9	120 35.6	19.2	89 40.0	28.6	Peacock	53 12.1	S56 40.3
03	29 55.2	219 00.3 ..	26.2	226 04.7 ..	02.3	135 37.8 ..	19.3	104 42.6 ..	28.6	Pollux	243 22.8	N27 58.7
04	44 57.7	233 59.9	24.9	241 05.7	01.7	150 40.1	19.3	119 45.1	28.6	Procyon	244 55.5	N 5 10.5
05	60 00.1	248 59.5	23.7	256 06.7	01.1	165 42.4	19.3	134 47.6	28.6			
06	75 02.6	263 59.2	N 5 22.4	271 07.6	N 8 00.4	180 44.6	S22 19.4	149 50.1	S22 28.6	Rasalhague	96 02.4	N12 33.1
07	90 05.1	278 58.8	21.2	286 08.6	7 59.8	195 46.9	19.4	164 52.6	28.6	Regulus	207 39.3	N11 52.4
08	105 07.5	293 58.4	20.0	301 09.6	59.2	210 49.1	19.4	179 55.1	28.6	Rigel	281 08.0	S 8 10.7
F 09	120 10.0	308 58.0 ..	18.7	316 10.6 ..	58.6	225 51.4 ..	19.4	194 57.7 ..	28.6	Rigil Kent.	139 46.3	S60 55.0
R 10	135 12.5	323 57.6	17.5	331 11.6	58.0	240 53.6	19.5	210 00.2	28.7	Sabik	102 07.6	S15 44.8
I 11	150 14.9	338 57.2	16.3	346 12.5	57.4	255 55.9	19.5	225 02.7	28.7			
D 12	165 17.4	353 56.8	N 5 15.0	1 13.5	N 7 56.7	270 58.2	S22 19.5	240 05.2	S22 28.7	Schedar	349 35.2	N56 38.5
A 13	180 19.8	8 56.4	13.8	16 14.5	56.1	286 00.4	19.6	255 07.7	28.7	Shaula	96 16.1	S37 07.0
Y 14	195 22.3	23 56.0	12.6	31 15.5	55.5	301 02.7	19.6	270 10.2	28.7	Sirius	258 30.1	S16 44.5
15	210 24.8	38 55.6 ..	11.3	46 16.5 ..	54.9	316 04.9 ..	19.6	285 12.7 ..	28.7	Spica	158 27.0	S11 15.6
16	225 27.2	53 55.2	10.1	61 17.4	54.3	331 07.2	19.6	300 15.3	28.7	Suhail	222 49.7	S43 30.5
17	240 29.7	68 54.8	08.9	76 18.4	53.7	346 09.4	19.7	315 17.8	28.7			
18	255 32.2	83 54.4	N 5 07.6	91 19.4	N 7 53.0	1 11.7	S22 19.7	330 20.3	S22 28.7	Vega	80 35.9	N38 48.5
19	270 34.6	98 54.1	06.4	106 20.4	52.4	16 14.0	19.7	345 22.8	28.7	Zuben'ubi	137 00.9	S16 07.2
20	285 37.1	113 53.7	05.1	121 21.4	51.8	31 16.2	19.7	0 25.3	28.7		SHA	Mer.Pass.
21	300 39.6	128 53.3 ..	03.9	136 22.3 ..	51.2	46 18.5 ..	19.8	15 27.8 ..	28.8			h m
22	315 42.0	143 52.9	02.7	151 23.3	50.6	61 20.7	19.8	30 30.3	28.8	Venus	190 22.4	12 24
23	330 44.5	158 52.5	01.4	166 24.3	49.9	76 23.0	19.8	45 32.9	28.8	Mars	196 49.6	11 57
	h m									Jupiter	105 48.0	17 59
Mer. Pass.	1 04.6	v −0.4	d 1.2	v 1.0	d 0.6	v 2.3	d 0.0	v 2.5	d 0.0	Saturn	74 45.9	20 02

© British Crown Copyright 2018. All rights reserved.

UT	SUN GHA	SUN Dec	MOON GHA	v	Dec	d	HP
d h	° ′	° ′	° ′	′	° ′	′	′
4 00	180 10.9	N 7 22.0	119 26.9	9.7	S11 53.2	11.4	58.9
01	195 11.1	21.1	133 55.6	9.8	12 04.6	11.4	58.8
02	210 11.3	20.2	148 24.4	9.8	12 16.0	11.4	58.8
03	225 11.5	.. 19.3	162 53.2	9.8	12 27.4	11.2	58.7
04	240 11.7	18.4	177 22.0	9.8	12 38.6	11.2	58.7
05	255 11.9	17.4	191 50.8	9.8	12 49.8	11.0	58.7
06	270 12.1	N 7 16.5	206 19.6	9.7	S13 00.8	11.0	58.6
W 07	285 12.3	15.6	220 48.3	9.8	13 11.8	10.9	58.6
E 08	300 12.5	14.7	235 17.1	9.8	13 22.7	10.8	58.6
D 09	315 12.7	.. 13.8	249 45.9	9.7	13 33.5	10.7	58.5
N 10	330 12.9	12.8	264 14.6	9.8	13 44.2	10.6	58.5
E 11	345 13.1	11.9	278 43.4	9.8	13 54.8	10.6	58.4
S 12	0 13.3	N 7 11.0	293 12.2	9.7	S14 05.4	10.4	58.4
D 13	15 13.6	10.1	307 40.9	9.7	14 15.8	10.3	58.4
A 14	30 13.8	09.2	322 09.6	9.8	14 26.1	10.3	58.3
Y 15	45 14.0	.. 08.2	336 38.4	9.7	14 36.4	10.2	58.3
16	60 14.2	07.3	351 07.1	9.7	14 46.6	10.0	58.2
17	75 14.4	06.4	5 35.8	9.8	14 56.6	10.0	58.2
18	90 14.6	N 7 05.5	20 04.6	9.7	S15 06.6	9.8	58.2
19	105 14.8	04.5	34 33.3	9.7	15 16.4	9.8	58.1
20	120 15.0	03.6	49 02.0	9.7	15 26.2	9.7	58.1
21	135 15.2	.. 02.7	63 30.7	9.7	15 35.9	9.6	58.1
22	150 15.4	01.8	77 59.4	9.6	15 45.5	9.4	58.0
23	165 15.6	7 00.8	92 28.0	9.7	15 54.9	9.4	58.0
5 00	180 15.8	N 6 59.9	106 56.7	9.7	S16 04.3	9.3	57.9
01	195 16.0	59.0	121 25.4	9.6	16 13.6	9.1	57.9
02	210 16.2	58.1	135 54.0	9.7	16 22.7	9.1	57.9
03	225 16.5	.. 57.1	150 22.7	9.7	16 31.8	9.0	57.8
04	240 16.7	56.2	164 51.4	9.6	16 40.8	8.8	57.8
05	255 16.9	55.3	179 20.0	9.6	16 49.6	8.8	57.8
06	270 17.1	N 6 54.4	193 48.6	9.7	S16 58.4	8.7	57.7
T 07	285 17.3	53.4	208 17.3	9.6	17 07.1	8.5	57.7
H 08	300 17.5	52.5	222 45.9	9.6	17 15.6	8.4	57.6
U 09	315 17.7	.. 51.6	237 14.5	9.6	17 24.0	8.4	57.6
R 10	330 17.9	50.7	251 43.1	9.6	17 32.4	8.2	57.6
S 11	345 18.1	49.7	266 11.7	9.6	17 40.6	8.1	57.5
D 12	0 18.3	N 6 48.8	280 40.3	9.6	S17 48.7	8.1	57.5
A 13	15 18.5	47.9	295 08.9	9.5	17 56.8	7.9	57.5
Y 14	30 18.8	47.0	309 37.4	9.6	18 04.7	7.8	57.4
15	45 19.0	.. 46.0	324 06.0	9.6	18 12.5	7.6	57.4
16	60 19.2	45.1	338 34.6	9.5	18 20.1	7.6	57.3
17	75 19.4	44.2	353 03.1	9.6	18 27.7	7.5	57.3
18	90 19.6	N 6 43.3	7 31.7	9.5	S18 35.2	7.4	57.3
19	105 19.8	42.3	22 00.2	9.6	18 42.6	7.2	57.2
20	120 20.0	41.4	36 28.8	9.5	18 49.8	7.1	57.2
21	135 20.2	.. 40.5	50 57.3	9.5	18 56.9	7.1	57.2
22	150 20.4	39.5	65 25.8	9.6	19 04.0	6.9	57.1
23	165 20.6	38.6	79 54.4	9.5	19 10.9	6.8	57.1
6 00	180 20.8	N 6 37.7	94 22.9	9.5	S19 17.7	6.7	57.1
01	195 21.1	36.8	108 51.4	9.5	19 24.4	6.5	57.0
02	210 21.3	35.8	123 19.9	9.5	19 30.9	6.5	57.0
03	225 21.5	.. 34.9	137 48.4	9.5	19 37.4	6.3	56.9
04	240 21.7	34.0	152 16.9	9.5	19 43.7	6.3	56.9
05	255 21.9	33.0	166 45.4	9.5	19 50.0	6.1	56.9
06	270 22.1	N 6 32.1	181 13.9	9.5	S19 56.1	6.0	56.8
07	285 22.3	31.2	195 42.4	9.5	20 02.1	5.9	56.8
08	300 22.5	30.2	210 10.9	9.5	20 08.0	5.8	56.8
F 09	315 22.7	.. 29.3	224 39.4	9.5	20 13.8	5.6	56.7
R 10	330 23.0	28.4	239 07.9	9.5	20 19.4	5.6	56.7
I 11	345 23.2	27.5	253 36.4	9.5	20 25.0	5.4	56.7
D 12	0 23.4	N 6 26.5	268 04.9	9.5	S20 30.4	5.3	56.6
A 13	15 23.6	25.6	282 33.4	9.5	20 35.7	5.2	56.6
Y 14	30 23.8	24.7	297 01.9	9.5	20 40.9	5.1	56.6
15	45 24.0	.. 23.7	311 30.4	9.5	20 46.0	4.9	56.5
16	60 24.2	22.8	325 58.9	9.5	20 50.9	4.9	56.5
17	75 24.4	21.9	340 27.4	9.5	20 55.8	4.7	56.5
18	90 24.6	N 6 20.9	354 55.9	9.5	S21 00.5	4.6	56.4
19	105 24.9	20.0	9 24.4	9.5	21 05.1	4.5	56.4
20	120 25.1	19.1	23 52.9	9.5	21 09.6	4.3	56.4
21	135 25.3	.. 18.1	38 21.4	9.5	21 13.9	4.3	56.3
22	150 25.5	17.2	52 49.9	9.5	21 18.2	4.1	56.3
23	165 25.7	16.3	67 18.4	9.5	S21 22.3	4.0	56.3
	SD 15.9	d 0.9	SD 15.9		15.7		15.4

Twilight — Sunrise — Moonrise

Lat.	Naut.	Civil	Sunrise	Moonrise 4	5	6	7
°	h m	h m	h m	h m	h m	h m	h m
N 72	////	02 56	04 19	14 04	■■■	■■■	■■■
N 70	01 13	03 19	04 30	13 31	15 51	■■■	■■■
68	02 01	03 36	04 39	13 08	15 04	17 08	■■■
66	02 30	03 50	04 47	12 50	14 34	16 15	17 41
64	02 52	04 02	04 53	12 35	14 12	15 42	16 59
62	03 09	04 11	04 59	12 23	13 54	15 18	16 30
60	03 23	04 19	05 03	12 12	13 39	15 00	16 08
N 58	03 34	04 26	05 08	12 03	13 27	14 44	15 51
56	03 44	04 32	05 11	11 55	13 16	14 31	15 36
54	03 53	04 38	05 15	11 48	13 07	14 19	15 23
52	04 00	04 43	05 18	11 42	12 58	14 09	15 12
50	04 07	04 47	05 20	11 37	12 51	14 00	15 02
45	04 20	04 56	05 26	11 24	12 35	13 41	14 41
N 40	04 31	05 03	05 31	11 15	12 22	13 25	14 24
35	04 39	05 10	05 35	11 06	12 10	13 12	14 09
30	04 46	05 15	05 39	10 59	12 01	13 01	13 57
20	04 57	05 23	05 45	10 46	11 44	12 41	13 36
N 10	05 05	05 29	05 51	10 35	11 30	12 24	13 18
0	05 11	05 35	05 56	10 24	11 16	12 08	13 01
S 10	05 15	05 39	06 00	10 14	11 03	11 53	12 44
20	05 18	05 43	06 05	10 03	10 49	11 36	12 25
30	05 19	05 47	06 11	09 51	10 33	11 17	12 05
35	05 20	05 49	06 14	09 44	10 23	11 06	11 52
40	05 19	05 51	06 18	09 36	10 13	10 53	11 38
45	05 19	05 53	06 22	09 27	10 00	10 38	11 22
S 50	05 17	05 54	06 27	09 15	09 45	10 20	11 01
52	05 16	05 55	06 29	09 10	09 38	10 12	10 52
54	05 15	05 56	06 31	09 05	09 30	10 02	10 41
56	05 14	05 57	06 34	08 58	09 22	09 51	10 29
58	05 12	05 58	06 37	08 51	09 12	09 39	10 14
S 60	05 11	05 59	06 40	08 43	09 01	09 25	09 57

Sunset — Twilight — Moonset

Lat.	Sunset	Civil	Naut.	Moonset 4	5	6	7
°	h m	h m	h m	h m	h m	h m	h m
N 72	19 35	20 57	////	18 50	■■■	■■■	■■■
N 70	19 24	20 35	22 34	19 24	18 54	■■■	■■■
68	19 16	20 18	21 51	19 49	19 41	19 27	■■■
66	19 09	20 05	21 23	20 09	20 12	20 21	20 43
64	19 02	19 54	21 02	20 25	20 35	20 53	21 25
62	18 57	19 44	20 46	20 38	20 54	21 18	21 54
60	18 53	19 36	20 32	20 49	21 09	21 37	22 16
N 58	18 49	19 30	20 21	20 59	21 22	21 53	22 34
56	18 45	19 24	20 12	21 07	21 33	22 06	22 49
54	18 42	19 18	20 03	21 15	21 43	22 18	23 02
52	18 39	19 14	19 56	21 22	21 52	22 29	23 13
50	18 36	19 09	19 50	21 28	22 00	22 38	23 23
45	18 31	19 00	19 36	21 41	22 17	22 58	23 44
N 40	18 26	18 53	19 26	21 52	22 31	23 14	24 01
35	18 22	18 47	19 18	22 02	22 43	23 27	24 16
30	18 18	18 42	19 11	22 10	22 53	23 39	24 28
20	18 12	18 34	19 00	22 25	23 11	23 59	24 50
N 10	18 07	18 28	18 53	22 37	23 27	24 17	00 17
0	18 02	18 23	18 47	22 49	23 41	24 34	00 34
S 10	17 57	18 18	18 43	23 01	23 56	24 50	00 50
20	17 52	18 14	18 40	23 14	24 12	00 12	01 08
30	17 47	18 11	18 39	23 29	24 30	00 30	01 28
35	17 44	18 09	18 39	23 37	24 40	00 40	01 40
40	17 40	18 08	18 39	23 47	24 52	00 52	01 54
45	17 36	18 06	18 40	23 58	25 07	01 07	02 10
S 50	17 32	18 04	18 41	24 12	00 12	01 24	02 30
52	17 29	18 03	18 42	24 19	00 19	01 32	02 39
54	17 27	18 03	18 43	24 26	00 26	01 42	02 50
56	17 24	18 02	18 45	24 34	00 34	01 52	03 02
58	17 22	18 01	18 46	24 43	00 43	02 04	03 16
S 60	17 18	18 00	18 48	24 54	00 54	02 18	03 33

SUN — MOON

Day	Eqn. of Time 00h	Eqn. of Time 12h	Mer. Pass.	Mer. Pass. Upper	Mer. Pass. Lower	Age	Phase
d	m s	m s	h m	h m	h m	d	%
4	00 43	00 53	11 59	16 37	04 11	05	33
5	01 03	01 13	11 59	17 29	05 03	06	43
6	01 23	01 33	11 58	18 21	05 55	07	54

© British Crown Copyright 2018. All rights reserved.

UT d h	ARIES GHA	VENUS −3.9 GHA	Dec	MARS +1.7 GHA	Dec	JUPITER −2.2 GHA	Dec	SATURN +0.4 GHA	Dec	STARS Name	SHA	Dec
7 00	345 47.0	173 52.1 N 5	00.2	181 25.3 N 7	49.3	91 25.2 S22	19.9	60 35.4 S22	28.8	Acamar	315 14.9	S40 13.4
01	0 49.4	188 51.7	4 58.9	196 26.3	48.7	106 27.5	19.9	75 37.9	28.8	Achernar	335 23.1	S57 08.1
02	15 51.9	203 51.3	57.7	211 27.2	48.1	121 29.7	19.9	90 40.4	28.8	Acrux	173 05.2	S63 12.4
03	30 54.3	218 50.9 ..	56.5	226 28.2 ..	47.5	136 32.0 ..	19.9	105 42.9 ..	28.8	Adhara	255 09.4	S28 59.8
04	45 56.8	233 50.5	55.2	241 29.2	46.9	151 34.2	20.0	120 45.4	28.8	Aldebaran	290 44.5	N16 32.8
05	60 59.3	248 50.2	54.0	256 30.2	46.2	166 36.5	20.0	135 47.9	28.8			
06	76 01.7	263 49.8 N 4	52.7	271 31.2 N 7	45.6	181 38.7 S22	20.0	150 50.4 S22	28.8	Alioth	166 17.4	N55 51.5
07	91 04.2	278 49.4	51.5	286 32.1	45.0	196 41.0	20.1	165 53.0	28.8	Alkaid	152 55.9	N49 13.3
S 08	106 06.7	293 49.0	50.3	301 33.1	44.4	211 43.3	20.1	180 55.5	28.9	Alnair	27 37.9	S46 51.9
A 09	121 09.1	308 48.6 ..	49.0	316 34.1 ..	43.8	226 45.5 ..	20.1	195 58.0 ..	28.9	Alnilam	275 42.1	S 1 11.4
T 10	136 11.6	323 48.2	47.8	331 35.1	43.1	241 47.8	20.1	211 00.5	28.9	Alphard	217 52.2	S 8 44.5
U 11	151 14.1	338 47.8	46.5	346 36.1	42.5	256 50.0	20.2	226 03.0	28.9			
R 12	166 16.5	353 47.4 N 4	45.3	1 37.0 N 7	41.9	271 52.3 S22	20.2	241 05.5 S22	28.9	Alphecca	126 07.5	N26 39.3
D 13	181 19.0	8 47.1	44.1	16 38.0	41.3	286 54.5	20.2	256 08.0	28.9	Alpheratz	357 38.8	N29 11.9
A 14	196 21.5	23 46.7	42.8	31 39.0	40.7	301 56.8	20.3	271 10.5	28.9	Altair	62 03.9	N 8 55.4
Y 15	211 23.9	38 46.3 ..	41.6	46 40.0 ..	40.1	316 59.0 ..	20.3	286 13.0 ..	28.9	Ankaa	353 11.1	S42 11.9
16	226 26.4	53 45.9	40.3	61 41.0	39.4	332 01.3	20.3	301 15.5	28.9	Antares	112 21.1	S26 28.4
17	241 28.8	68 45.5	39.1	76 42.0	38.8	347 03.5	20.3	316 18.1	28.9			
18	256 31.3	83 45.1 N 4	37.8	91 42.9 N 7	38.2	2 05.8 S22	20.4	331 20.6 S22	28.9	Arcturus	145 52.1	N19 05.1
19	271 33.8	98 44.7	36.6	106 43.9	37.6	17 08.0	20.4	346 23.1	29.0	Atria	107 19.0	S69 03.8
20	286 36.2	113 44.3	35.4	121 44.9	37.0	32 10.2	20.4	1 25.6	29.0	Avior	234 16.8	S59 34.1
21	301 38.7	128 44.0 ..	34.1	136 45.9 ..	36.3	47 12.5 ..	20.5	16 28.1 ..	29.0	Bellatrix	278 27.5	N 6 22.0
22	316 41.2	143 43.6	32.9	151 46.9	35.7	62 14.7	20.5	31 30.6	29.0	Betelgeuse	270 56.8	N 7 24.6
23	331 43.6	158 43.2	31.6	166 47.8	35.1	77 17.0	20.5	46 33.1	29.0			
8 00	346 46.1	173 42.8 N 4	30.4	181 48.8 N 7	34.5	92 19.2 S22	20.5	61 35.6 S22	29.0	Canopus	263 54.4	S52 42.1
01	1 48.6	188 42.4	29.1	196 49.8	33.9	107 21.5	20.6	76 38.1	29.0	Capella	280 28.2	N46 00.8
02	16 51.0	203 42.0	27.9	211 50.8	33.2	122 23.7	20.6	91 40.6	29.0	Deneb	49 28.2	N45 21.3
03	31 53.5	218 41.6 ..	26.6	226 51.8 ..	32.6	137 26.0 ..	20.6	106 43.1 ..	29.0	Denebola	182 29.6	N14 28.0
04	46 56.0	233 41.3	25.4	241 52.8	32.0	152 28.2	20.7	121 45.7	29.0	Diphda	348 51.3	S17 52.7
05	61 58.4	248 40.9	24.2	256 53.7	31.4	167 30.5	20.7	136 48.2	29.0			
06	77 00.9	263 40.5 N 4	22.9	271 54.7 N 7	30.8	182 32.7 S22	20.7	151 50.7 S22	29.0	Dubhe	193 47.1	N61 38.8
07	92 03.3	278 40.1	21.7	286 55.7	30.1	197 35.0	20.7	166 53.2	29.1	Elnath	278 07.3	N28 37.3
S 08	107 05.8	293 39.7	20.4	301 56.7	29.5	212 37.2	20.8	181 55.7	29.1	Eltanin	90 44.0	N51 29.6
U 09	122 08.3	308 39.3 ..	19.2	316 57.7 ..	28.9	227 39.4 ..	20.8	196 58.2 ..	29.1	Enif	33 42.6	N 9 58.0
N 10	137 10.7	323 39.0	17.9	331 58.7	28.3	242 41.7	20.8	212 00.7	29.1	Fomalhaut	15 18.9	S29 31.0
D 11	152 13.2	338 38.6	16.7	346 59.6	27.6	257 43.9	20.9	227 03.2	29.1			
A 12	167 15.7	353 38.2 N 4	15.4	2 00.6 N 7	27.0	272 46.2 S22	20.9	242 05.7 S22	29.1	Gacrux	171 56.7	S57 13.3
Y 13	182 18.1	8 37.8	14.2	17 01.6	26.4	287 48.4	20.9	257 08.2	29.1	Gienah	175 48.2	S17 38.9
14	197 20.6	23 37.4	12.9	32 02.6	25.8	302 50.7	20.9	272 10.7	29.1	Hadar	148 42.3	S60 28.0
15	212 23.1	38 37.0 ..	11.7	47 03.6 ..	25.2	317 52.9 ..	21.0	287 13.2 ..	29.1	Hamal	327 55.7	N23 33.2
16	227 25.5	53 36.7	10.4	62 04.5	24.5	332 55.1	21.0	302 15.7	29.1	Kaus Aust.	83 38.0	S34 22.4
17	242 28.0	68 36.3	09.2	77 05.5	23.9	347 57.4	21.0	317 18.2	29.1			
18	257 30.4	83 35.9 N 4	07.9	92 06.5 N 7	23.3	2 59.6 S22	21.1	332 20.7 S22	29.1	Kochab	137 20.7	N74 04.9
19	272 32.9	98 35.5	06.7	107 07.5	22.7	18 01.9	21.1	347 23.3	29.2	Markab	13 33.8	N15 18.7
20	287 35.4	113 35.1	05.4	122 08.5	22.1	33 04.1	21.1	2 25.8	29.2	Menkar	314 10.4	N 4 10.0
21	302 37.8	128 34.7 ..	04.2	137 09.5 ..	21.4	48 06.3 ..	21.1	17 28.3 ..	29.2	Menkent	148 02.8	S36 27.9
22	317 40.3	143 34.4	02.9	152 10.4	20.8	63 08.6	21.2	32 30.8	29.2	Miaplacidus	221 39.7	S69 47.7
23	332 42.8	158 34.0	01.7	167 11.4	20.2	78 10.8	21.2	47 33.3	29.2			
9 00	347 45.2	173 33.6 N 4	00.4	182 12.4 N 7	19.6	93 13.1 S22	21.2	62 35.8 S22	29.2	Mirfak	308 34.1	N49 55.6
01	2 47.7	188 33.2	3 59.2	197 13.4	19.0	108 15.3	21.3	77 38.3	29.2	Nunki	75 52.9	S26 16.2
02	17 50.2	203 32.8	57.9	212 14.4	18.3	123 17.5	21.3	92 40.8	29.2	Peacock	53 12.1	S56 40.3
03	32 52.6	218 32.5 ..	56.7	227 15.4 ..	17.7	138 19.8 ..	21.3	107 43.3 ..	29.2	Pollux	243 22.8	N27 58.7
04	47 55.1	233 32.1	55.4	242 16.3	17.1	153 22.0	21.4	122 45.8	29.2	Procyon	244 55.5	N 5 10.5
05	62 57.6	248 31.7	54.2	257 17.3	16.5	168 24.3	21.4	137 48.3	29.2			
06	78 00.0	263 31.3 N 3	52.9	272 18.3 N 7	15.8	183 26.5 S22	21.4	152 50.8 S22	29.2	Rasalhague	96 02.4	N12 33.1
07	93 02.5	278 30.9	51.7	287 19.3	15.2	198 28.7	21.4	167 53.3	29.3	Regulus	207 39.3	N11 52.4
M 08	108 04.9	293 30.5	50.4	302 20.3	14.6	213 31.0	21.5	182 55.8	29.3	Rigel	281 08.0	S 8 10.7
O 09	123 07.4	308 30.2 ..	49.2	317 21.3 ..	14.0	228 33.2 ..	21.5	197 58.3 ..	29.3	Rigil Kent.	139 46.4	S60 54.9
N 10	138 09.9	323 29.8	47.9	332 22.2	13.4	243 35.4	21.5	213 00.8	29.3	Sabik	102 07.6	S15 44.8
N 11	153 12.3	338 29.4	46.7	347 23.2	12.7	258 37.7	21.6	228 03.3	29.3			
D 12	168 14.8	353 29.0 N 3	45.4	2 24.2 N 7	12.1	273 39.9 S22	21.6	243 05.8 S22	29.3	Schedar	349 35.2	N56 38.5
A 13	183 17.3	8 28.6	44.2	17 25.2	11.5	288 42.1	21.6	258 08.3	29.3	Shaula	96 16.1	S37 07.0
Y 14	198 19.7	23 28.3	42.9	32 26.2	10.9	303 44.4	21.6	273 10.8	29.3	Sirius	258 30.1	S16 44.5
15	213 22.2	38 27.9 ..	41.7	47 27.2 ..	10.2	318 46.6 ..	21.7	288 13.3 ..	29.3	Spica	158 27.0	S11 15.6
16	228 24.7	53 27.5	40.4	62 28.1	09.6	333 48.9	21.7	303 15.8	29.3	Suhail	222 49.7	S43 30.5
17	243 27.1	68 27.1	39.2	77 29.1	09.0	348 51.1	21.7	318 18.3	29.3			
18	258 29.6	83 26.7 N 3	37.9	92 30.1 N 7	08.4	3 53.3 S22	21.8	333 20.8 S22	29.3	Vega	80 35.9	N38 48.5
19	273 32.1	98 26.4	36.6	107 31.1	07.7	18 55.6	21.8	348 23.3	29.4	Zuben'ubi	137 00.9	S16 07.2
20	288 34.5	113 26.0	35.4	122 32.1	07.1	33 57.8	21.8	3 25.8	29.4		SHA	Mer.Pass.
21	303 37.0	128 25.6 ..	34.1	137 33.1 ..	06.5	49 00.0 ..	21.9	18 28.3 ..	29.4			h m
22	318 39.4	143 25.2	32.9	152 34.1	05.9	64 02.3	21.9	33 30.8	29.4	Venus	186 56.7	12 25
23	333 41.9	158 24.9	31.6	167 35.0	05.2	79 04.5	21.9	48 33.3	29.4	Mars	195 02.7	11 52
	h m									Jupiter	105 33.1	17 48
Mer. Pass.	0 52.8	v −0.4	d 1.2	v 1.0	d 0.6	v 2.2	d 0.0	v 2.5	d 0.0	Saturn	74 49.5	19 50

© British Crown Copyright 2018. All rights reserved.

Day	UT (d h)	SUN GHA (° ′)	SUN Dec (° ′)	MOON GHA (° ′)	v (′)	MOON Dec (° ′)	d (′)	HP (′)
SATURDAY	7 00	180 25.9	N 6 15.3	81 46.9	9.6	S21 26.3	3.9	56.3
	01	195 26.1	14.4	96 15.5	9.5	21 30.2	3.8	56.2
	02	210 26.3	13.5	110 44.0	9.5	21 34.0	3.7	56.2
	03	225 26.6	. . 12.5	125 12.5	9.6	21 37.7	3.5	56.2
	04	240 26.8	11.6	139 41.1	9.5	21 41.2	3.4	56.1
	05	255 27.0	10.7	154 09.6	9.6	21 44.6	3.3	56.1
	06	270 27.2	N 6 09.7	168 38.2	9.6	S21 47.9	3.2	56.1
	07	285 27.4	08.8	183 06.8	9.6	21 51.1	3.1	56.0
	08	300 27.6	07.9	197 35.4	9.5	21 54.2	2.9	56.0
	09	315 27.8	. . 06.9	212 03.9	9.7	21 57.1	2.9	56.0
	10	330 28.1	06.0	226 32.6	9.6	22 00.0	2.7	56.0
	11	345 28.3	05.1	241 01.2	9.6	22 02.7	2.6	55.9
	12	0 28.5	N 6 04.1	255 29.8	9.6	S22 05.3	2.4	55.9
	13	15 28.7	03.2	269 58.4	9.7	22 07.7	2.4	55.9
	14	30 28.9	02.3	284 27.1	9.7	22 10.1	2.2	55.8
	15	45 29.1	. . 01.3	298 55.8	9.7	22 12.3	2.2	55.8
	16	60 29.3	6 00.4	313 24.5	9.7	22 14.5	2.0	55.8
	17	75 29.6	5 59.5	327 53.2	9.7	22 16.5	1.8	55.8
	18	90 29.8	N 5 58.5	342 21.9	9.7	S22 18.3	1.8	55.7
	19	105 30.0	57.6	356 50.6	9.7	22 20.1	1.6	55.7
	20	120 30.2	56.6	11 19.3	9.8	22 21.7	1.6	55.7
	21	135 30.4	. . 55.7	25 48.1	9.8	22 23.3	1.4	55.6
	22	150 30.6	54.8	40 16.9	9.8	22 24.7	1.3	55.6
	23	165 30.8	53.8	54 45.7	9.8	22 26.0	1.1	55.6
SUNDAY	8 00	180 31.1	N 5 52.9	69 14.5	9.9	S22 27.1	1.1	55.6
	01	195 31.3	52.0	83 43.4	9.8	22 28.2	0.9	55.5
	02	210 31.5	51.0	98 12.2	9.9	22 29.1	0.9	55.5
	03	225 31.7	. . 50.1	112 41.1	9.9	22 30.0	0.7	55.5
	04	240 31.9	49.1	127 10.0	10.0	22 30.7	0.6	55.5
	05	255 32.1	48.2	141 39.0	9.9	22 31.3	0.4	55.4
	06	270 32.3	N 5 47.3	156 07.9	10.0	S22 31.7	0.4	55.4
	07	285 32.6	46.3	170 36.9	10.0	22 32.1	0.2	55.4
	08	300 32.8	45.4	185 05.9	10.1	22 32.3	0.2	55.4
	09	315 33.0	. . 44.5	199 35.0	10.0	22 32.5	0.0	55.3
	10	330 33.2	43.5	214 04.0	10.1	22 32.5	0.1	55.3
	11	345 33.4	42.6	228 33.1	10.1	22 32.4	0.2	55.3
	12	0 33.6	N 5 41.6	243 02.2	10.1	S22 32.2	0.4	55.3
	13	15 33.9	40.7	257 31.3	10.2	22 31.8	0.4	55.3
	14	30 34.1	39.8	272 00.5	10.2	22 31.4	0.6	55.2
	15	45 34.3	. . 38.8	286 29.7	10.2	22 30.8	0.7	55.2
	16	60 34.5	37.9	300 58.9	10.3	22 30.1	0.7	55.2
	17	75 34.7	36.9	315 28.2	10.3	22 29.4	0.9	55.2
	18	90 34.9	N 5 36.0	329 57.5	10.3	S22 28.5	1.0	55.1
	19	105 35.1	35.1	344 26.8	10.4	22 27.5	1.2	55.1
	20	120 35.4	34.1	358 56.2	10.3	22 26.3	1.2	55.1
	21	135 35.6	. . 33.2	13 25.5	10.5	22 25.1	1.4	55.1
	22	150 35.8	32.2	27 55.0	10.4	22 23.7	1.4	55.1
	23	165 36.0	31.3	42 24.4	10.5	22 22.3	1.6	55.0
MONDAY	9 00	180 36.2	N 5 30.4	56 53.9	10.5	S22 20.7	1.7	55.0
	01	195 36.4	29.4	71 23.4	10.6	22 19.0	1.8	55.0
	02	210 36.7	28.5	85 53.0	10.6	22 17.2	1.9	55.0
	03	225 36.9	. . 27.5	100 22.6	10.6	22 15.3	2.0	54.9
	04	240 37.1	26.6	114 52.2	10.7	22 13.3	2.1	54.9
	05	255 37.3	25.6	129 21.9	10.7	22 11.2	2.2	54.9
	06	270 37.5	N 5 24.7	143 51.6	10.7	S22 09.0	2.3	54.9
	07	285 37.7	23.8	158 21.3	10.8	22 06.7	2.5	54.9
	08	300 38.0	22.8	172 51.1	10.8	22 04.2	2.5	54.9
	09	315 38.2	. . 21.9	187 20.9	10.9	22 01.7	2.7	54.8
	10	330 38.4	20.9	201 50.8	10.9	21 59.0	2.7	54.8
	11	345 38.6	20.0	216 20.7	10.9	21 56.3	2.9	54.8
	12	0 38.8	N 5 19.0	230 50.6	11.0	S21 53.4	3.0	54.8
	13	15 39.1	18.1	245 20.6	11.0	21 50.4	3.0	54.8
	14	30 39.3	17.2	259 50.6	11.1	21 47.4	3.2	54.7
	15	45 39.5	. . 16.2	274 20.7	11.1	21 44.2	3.3	54.7
	16	60 39.7	15.3	288 50.8	11.1	21 40.9	3.4	54.7
	17	75 39.9	14.3	303 20.9	11.2	21 37.5	3.5	54.7
	18	90 40.1	N 5 13.4	317 51.1	11.3	S21 34.0	3.6	54.7
	19	105 40.4	12.4	332 21.4	11.2	21 30.4	3.6	54.7
	20	120 40.6	11.5	346 51.6	11.3	21 26.8	3.8	54.6
	21	135 40.8	. . 10.6	1 21.9	11.4	21 23.0	3.9	54.6
	22	150 41.0	09.6	15 52.3	11.4	21 19.1	4.0	54.6
	23	165 41.2	08.7	30 22.7	11.5	S21 15.1	4.1	54.6
		SD 15.9	d 0.9	SD 15.2		15.1		14.9

Lat. (°)	Twilight Naut. (h m)	Twilight Civil (h m)	Sunrise (h m)	Moonrise 7 (h m)	Moonrise 8 (h m)	Moonrise 9 (h m)	Moonrise 10 (h m)
N 72	00 25	03 14	04 33	▬	▬	▬	▬
N 70	01 45	03 34	04 43	▬	▬	▬	20 47
68	02 21	03 49	04 50	▬	▬	20 03	19 46
66	02 46	04 01	04 57	17 41	18 37	19 02	19 11
64	03 05	04 11	05 02	16 59	17 54	18 27	18 46
62	03 20	04 20	05 07	16 30	17 25	18 02	18 26
60	03 32	04 27	05 10	16 08	17 03	17 42	18 10
N 58	03 42	04 33	05 14	15 51	16 45	17 26	17 56
56	03 51	04 39	05 17	15 36	16 30	17 12	17 44
54	03 59	04 44	05 20	15 23	16 17	17 00	17 34
52	04 06	04 48	05 22	15 12	16 05	16 49	17 24
50	04 12	04 52	05 25	15 02	15 55	16 40	17 16
45	04 24	05 00	05 30	14 41	15 34	16 20	16 58
N 40	04 34	05 06	05 34	14 24	15 17	16 03	16 44
35	04 42	05 12	05 37	14 09	15 02	15 49	16 32
30	04 48	05 16	05 41	13 57	14 50	15 38	16 21
20	04 58	05 24	05 46	13 36	14 28	15 17	16 02
N 10	05 05	05 29	05 50	13 18	14 10	14 59	15 46
0	05 10	05 34	05 55	13 01	13 52	14 42	15 31
S 10	05 13	05 37	05 59	12 44	13 35	14 26	15 16
20	05 15	05 41	06 03	12 25	13 16	14 08	15 00
30	05 16	05 43	06 07	12 05	12 55	13 47	14 41
35	05 15	05 45	06 10	11 52	12 42	13 35	14 30
40	05 15	05 46	06 13	11 38	12 28	13 21	14 18
45	05 13	05 47	06 16	11 22	12 11	13 05	14 03
S 50	05 11	05 48	06 20	11 01	11 50	12 45	13 45
52	05 10	05 48	06 22	10 52	11 40	12 35	13 36
54	05 08	05 49	06 24	10 41	11 28	12 24	13 26
56	05 06	05 49	06 26	10 29	11 15	12 12	13 15
58	05 04	05 50	06 29	10 14	11 00	11 57	13 03
S 60	05 02	05 50	06 31	09 57	10 43	11 41	12 48

Lat. (°)	Sunset (h m)	Twilight Civil (h m)	Twilight Naut. (h m)	Moonset 7 (h m)	Moonset 8 (h m)	Moonset 9 (h m)	Moonset 10 (h m)
N 72	19 19	20 37	23 05	▬	▬	▬	▬
N 70	19 10	20 18	22 03	▬	▬	▬	22 48
68	19 03	20 03	21 29	▬	▬	21 51	23 48
66	18 57	19 52	21 06	20 43	21 33	22 52	24 23
64	18 52	19 42	20 48	21 25	22 16	23 27	24 47
62	18 47	19 34	20 33	21 54	22 45	23 52	25 07
60	18 44	19 27	20 21	22 16	23 08	24 11	00 11
N 58	18 40	19 21	20 11	22 34	23 25	24 27	00 27
56	18 37	19 15	20 02	22 49	23 40	24 41	00 41
54	18 34	19 11	19 55	23 02	23 53	24 53	00 53
52	18 32	19 06	19 48	23 13	24 05	00 05	01 03
50	18 30	19 03	19 42	23 23	24 15	00 15	01 13
45	18 25	18 55	19 30	23 44	24 36	00 36	01 32
N 40	18 21	18 48	19 21	24 01	00 01	00 53	01 48
35	18 18	18 43	19 13	24 16	00 16	01 07	02 01
30	18 15	18 39	19 07	24 28	00 28	01 20	02 13
20	18 09	18 32	18 57	24 50	00 50	01 41	02 33
N 10	18 05	18 26	18 51	00 17	01 08	01 59	02 50
0	18 01	18 22	18 46	00 34	01 26	02 17	03 06
S 10	17 57	18 18	18 43	00 50	01 43	02 34	03 22
20	17 53	18 15	18 41	01 08	02 01	02 52	03 39
30	17 49	18 13	18 40	01 28	02 23	03 13	03 59
35	17 46	18 11	18 41	01 40	02 35	03 25	04 10
40	17 43	18 10	18 42	01 54	02 50	03 39	04 23
45	17 40	18 09	18 43	02 10	03 07	03 56	04 38
S 50	17 36	18 08	18 46	02 30	03 28	04 17	04 57
52	17 34	18 08	18 47	02 39	03 38	04 27	05 06
54	17 32	18 08	18 49	02 50	03 49	04 38	05 16
56	17 30	18 07	18 51	03 02	04 02	04 50	05 27
58	17 28	18 07	18 53	03 16	04 17	05 05	05 40
S 60	17 25	18 07	18 55	03 33	04 35	05 22	05 55

Day (d)	SUN Eqn. of Time 00^h (m s)	SUN Eqn. of Time 12^h (m s)	SUN Mer. Pass. (h m)	MOON Mer. Pass. Upper (h m)	MOON Mer. Pass. Lower (h m)	MOON Age (d)	MOON Phase (%)
7	01 43	01 53	11 58	19 13	06 47	08	64
8	02 04	02 14	11 58	20 04	07 39	09	73
9	02 24	02 35	11 57	20 54	08 30	10	81

© British Crown Copyright 2018. All rights reserved.

UT	ARIES	VENUS −3.9		MARS +1.7		JUPITER −2.2		SATURN +0.4		STARS		
	GHA	GHA	Dec	GHA	Dec	GHA	Dec	GHA	Dec	Name	SHA	Dec
d h	° ′	° ′	° ′	° ′	° ′	° ′	° ′	° ′	° ′		° ′	° ′
10 00	348 44.4	173 24.5 N 3 30.4		182 36.0 N 7 04.6		94 06.7 S22 21.9		63 35.8 S22 29.4		Acamar	315 14.9	S40 13.4
01	3 46.8	188 24.1	29.1	197 37.0	04.0	109 08.9	22.0	78 38.3	29.4	Achernar	335 23.1	S57 08.1
02	18 49.3	203 23.7	27.9	212 38.0	03.4	124 11.2	22.0	93 40.8	29.4	Acrux	173 05.2	S63 12.4
03	33 51.8	218 23.3 . .	26.6	227 39.0 . .	02.8	139 13.4 . .	22.0	108 43.3 . .	29.4	Adhara	255 09.3	S28 59.7
04	48 54.2	233 23.0	25.4	242 40.0	02.1	154 15.6	22.1	123 45.8	29.4	Aldebaran	290 44.4	N16 32.8
05	63 56.7	248 22.6	24.1	257 40.9	01.5	169 17.9	22.1	138 48.3	29.4			
06	78 59.2	263 22.2 N 3 22.8		272 41.9 N 7 00.9		184 20.1 S22 22.1		153 50.8 S22 29.4		Alioth	166 17.4	N55 51.5
07	94 01.6	278 21.8	21.6	287 42.9	7 00.3	199 22.3	22.2	168 53.3	29.4	Alkaid	152 55.9	N49 13.3
08	109 04.1	293 21.5	20.3	302 43.9	6 59.6	214 24.6	22.2	183 55.8	29.5	Alnair	27 37.9	S46 51.9
09	124 06.5	308 21.1 . .	19.1	317 44.9 . .	59.0	229 26.8 . .	22.2	198 58.3 . .	29.5	Alnilam	275 42.1	S 1 11.3
10	139 09.0	323 20.7	17.8	332 45.9	58.4	244 29.0	22.2	214 00.8	29.5	Alphard	217 52.2	S 8 44.5
11	154 11.5	338 20.3	16.6	347 46.9	57.8	259 31.2	22.3	229 03.3	29.5			
12	169 13.9	353 19.9 N 3 15.3		2 47.8 N 6 57.1		274 33.5 S22 22.3		244 05.8 S22 29.5		Alphecca	126 07.5	N26 39.3
13	184 16.4	8 19.6	14.0	17 48.8	56.5	289 35.7	22.3	259 08.3	29.5	Alpheratz	357 38.7	N29 11.9
14	199 18.9	23 19.2	12.8	32 49.8	55.9	304 37.9	22.4	274 10.8	29.5	Altair	62 03.9	N 8 55.4
15	214 21.3	38 18.8 . .	11.5	47 50.8 . .	55.3	319 40.2 . .	22.4	289 13.3 . .	29.5	Ankaa	353 11.1	S42 11.9
16	229 23.8	53 18.4	10.3	62 51.8	54.6	334 42.4	22.4	304 15.8	29.5	Antares	112 21.1	S26 28.4
17	244 26.3	68 18.1	09.0	77 52.8	54.0	349 44.6	22.5	319 18.3	29.5			
18	259 28.7	83 17.7 N 3 07.8		92 53.7 N 6 53.4		4 46.8 S22 22.5		334 20.8 S22 29.5		Arcturus	145 52.1	N19 05.1
19	274 31.2	98 17.3	06.5	107 54.7	52.8	19 49.1	22.5	349 23.3	29.5	Atria	107 19.1	S69 03.8
20	289 33.7	113 16.9	05.2	122 55.7	52.1	34 51.3	22.5	4 25.8	29.5	Avior	234 16.8	S59 34.1
21	304 36.1	128 16.6 . .	04.0	137 56.7 . .	51.5	49 53.5 . .	22.6	19 28.3 . .	29.5	Bellatrix	278 27.4	N 6 22.0
22	319 38.6	143 16.2	02.7	152 57.7	50.9	64 55.7	22.6	34 30.8	29.6	Betelgeuse	270 56.7	N 7 24.6
23	334 41.0	158 15.8	01.5	167 58.7	50.3	79 58.0	22.6	49 33.3	29.6			
11 00	349 43.5	173 15.4 N 3 00.2		182 59.7 N 6 49.6		95 00.2 S22 22.7		64 35.8 S22 29.6		Canopus	263 54.4	S52 42.1
01	4 46.0	188 15.1	2 58.9	198 00.6	49.0	110 02.4	22.7	79 38.3	29.6	Capella	280 28.1	N46 00.8
02	19 48.4	203 14.7	57.7	213 01.6	48.4	125 04.6	22.7	94 40.8	29.6	Deneb	49 28.2	N45 21.3
03	34 50.9	218 14.3 . .	56.4	228 02.6 . .	47.8	140 06.9 . .	22.8	109 43.3 . .	29.6	Denebola	182 29.6	N14 28.0
04	49 53.4	233 13.9	55.2	243 03.6	47.1	155 09.1	22.8	124 45.8	29.6	Diphda	348 51.3	S17 52.7
05	64 55.8	248 13.6	53.9	258 04.6	46.5	170 11.3	22.8	139 48.3	29.6			
06	79 58.3	263 13.2 N 2 52.6		273 05.6 N 6 45.9		185 13.5 S22 22.8		154 50.7 S22 29.6		Dubhe	193 47.1	N61 38.8
07	95 00.8	278 12.8	51.4	288 06.6	45.3	200 15.8	22.9	169 53.2	29.6	Elnath	278 07.2	N28 37.3
08	110 03.2	293 12.4	50.1	303 07.5	44.6	215 18.0	22.9	184 55.7	29.6	Eltanin	90 44.1	N51 29.6
09	125 05.7	308 12.1 . .	48.9	318 08.5 . .	44.0	230 20.2 . .	22.9	199 58.2 . .	29.6	Enif	33 42.6	N 9 58.0
10	140 08.2	323 11.7	47.6	333 09.5	43.4	245 22.4	23.0	215 00.7	29.6	Fomalhaut	15 18.9	S29 31.0
11	155 10.6	338 11.3	46.3	348 10.5	42.8	260 24.6	23.0	230 03.2	29.7			
12	170 13.1	353 10.9 N 2 45.1		3 11.5 N 6 42.1		275 26.9 S22 23.0		245 05.7 S22 29.7		Gacrux	171 56.7	S57 13.3
13	185 15.5	8 10.6	43.8	18 12.5	41.5	290 29.1	23.1	260 08.2	29.7	Gienah	175 48.2	S17 38.9
14	200 18.0	23 10.2	42.6	33 13.5	40.9	305 31.3	23.1	275 10.7	29.7	Hadar	148 42.3	S60 28.0
15	215 20.5	38 09.8 . .	41.3	48 14.4 . .	40.2	320 33.5 . .	23.1	290 13.2 . .	29.7	Hamal	327 55.7	N23 33.2
16	230 22.9	53 09.4	40.0	63 15.4	39.6	335 35.8	23.2	305 15.7	29.7	Kaus Aust.	83 38.0	S34 22.4
17	245 25.4	68 09.1	38.8	78 16.4	39.0	350 38.0	23.2	320 18.2	29.7			
18	260 27.9	83 08.7 N 2 37.5		93 17.4 N 6 38.4		5 40.2 S22 23.2		335 20.7 S22 29.7		Kochab	137 20.7	N74 04.9
19	275 30.3	98 08.3	36.3	108 18.4	37.7	20 42.4	23.2	350 23.2	29.7	Markab	13 33.8	N15 18.7
20	290 32.8	113 08.0	35.0	123 19.4	37.1	35 44.6	23.3	5 25.7	29.7	Menkar	314 10.4	N 4 10.0
21	305 35.3	128 07.6 . .	33.7	138 20.4 . .	36.5	50 46.8 . .	23.3	20 28.1 . .	29.7	Menkent	148 02.8	S36 27.9
22	320 37.7	143 07.2	32.5	153 21.4	35.9	65 49.1	23.3	35 30.6	29.7	Miaplacidus	221 39.7	S69 47.7
23	335 40.2	158 06.8	31.2	168 22.3	35.2	80 51.3	23.4	50 33.1	29.7			
12 00	350 42.6	173 06.5 N 2 29.9		183 23.3 N 6 34.6		95 53.5 S22 23.4		65 35.6 S22 29.7		Mirfak	308 34.0	N49 55.6
01	5 45.1	188 06.1	28.7	198 24.3	34.0	110 55.7	23.4	80 38.1	29.8	Nunki	75 52.9	S26 16.2
02	20 47.6	203 05.7	27.4	213 25.3	33.4	125 57.9	23.5	95 40.6	29.8	Peacock	53 12.1	S56 40.4
03	35 50.0	218 05.3 . .	26.2	228 26.3 . .	32.7	141 00.2 . .	23.5	110 43.1 . .	29.8	Pollux	243 22.7	N27 58.6
04	50 52.5	233 05.0	24.9	243 27.3	32.1	156 02.4	23.5	125 45.6	29.8	Procyon	244 55.5	N 5 10.5
05	65 55.0	248 04.6	23.6	258 28.3	31.5	171 04.6	23.6	140 48.1	29.8			
06	80 57.4	263 04.2 N 2 22.4		273 29.2 N 6 30.8		186 06.8 S22 23.6		155 50.6 S22 29.8		Rasalhague	96 02.5	N12 33.1
07	95 59.9	278 03.9	21.1	288 30.2	30.2	201 09.0	23.6	170 53.1	29.8	Regulus	207 39.3	N11 52.4
08	111 02.4	293 03.5	19.8	303 31.2	29.6	216 11.2	23.6	185 55.5	29.8	Rigel	281 08.0	S 8 10.7
09	126 04.8	308 03.1 . .	18.6	318 32.2 . .	29.0	231 13.4 . .	23.7	200 58.0 . .	29.8	Rigil Kent.	139 46.4	S60 54.9
10	141 07.3	323 02.7	17.3	333 33.2	28.3	246 15.7	23.7	216 00.5	29.8	Sabik	102 07.6	S15 44.8
11	156 09.8	338 02.4	16.0	348 34.2	27.7	261 17.9	23.7	231 03.0	29.8			
12	171 12.2	353 02.0 N 2 14.8		3 35.2 N 6 27.1		276 20.1 S22 23.8		246 05.5 S22 29.8		Schedar	349 35.2	N56 38.6
13	186 14.7	8 01.6	13.5	18 36.2	26.4	291 22.3	23.8	261 08.0	29.8	Shaula	96 16.1	S37 07.0
14	201 17.1	23 01.3	12.2	33 37.1	25.8	306 24.5	23.8	276 10.5	29.8	Sirius	258 30.1	S16 44.5
15	216 19.6	38 00.9 . .	11.0	48 38.1 . .	25.2	321 26.7 . .	23.9	291 13.0 . .	29.8	Spica	158 27.0	S11 15.6
16	231 22.1	53 00.5	09.7	63 39.1	24.6	336 28.9	23.9	306 15.5	29.9	Suhail	222 49.7	S43 30.5
17	246 24.5	68 00.1	08.4	78 40.1	23.9	351 31.2	23.9	321 17.9	29.9			
18	261 27.0	82 59.8 N 2 07.2		93 41.1 N 6 23.3		6 33.4 S22 24.0		336 20.4 S22 29.9		Vega	80 35.9	N38 48.5
19	276 29.5	97 59.4	05.9	108 42.1	22.7	21 35.6	24.0	351 22.9	29.9	Zuben'ubi	137 00.9	S16 07.2
20	291 31.9	112 59.0	04.7	123 43.1	22.0	36 37.8	24.0	6 25.4	29.9			SHA Mer. Pass.
21	306 34.4	127 58.7 . .	03.4	138 44.0 . .	21.4	51 40.0 . .	24.0	21 27.9 . .	29.9			° ′ h m
22	321 36.9	142 58.3	02.1	153 45.0	20.8	66 42.2	24.1	36 30.4	29.9	Venus	183 31.9	12 27
23	336 39.3	157 57.9	00.9	168 46.0	20.2	81 44.4	24.1	51 32.9	29.9	Mars	193 16.1	11 47
	h m									Jupiter	105 16.7	17 37
Mer. Pass. 0 41.0		v −0.4	d 1.3	v 1.0	d 0.6	v 2.2	d 0.0	v 2.5	d 0.0	Saturn	74 52.3	19 38

© British Crown Copyright 2018. All rights reserved.

UT	SUN GHA	SUN Dec	MOON GHA	v	MOON Dec	d	HP
d h	o '	o '	o '	'	o '	'	'
10 00	180 41.5	N 5 07.7	44 53.2	11.5	S21 11.0	4.2	54.6
01	195 41.7	06.8	59 23.7	11.5	21 06.8	4.3	54.6
02	210 41.9	05.8	73 54.2	11.6	21 02.5	4.4	54.5
03	225 42.1	.. 04.9	88 24.8	11.6	20 58.1	4.4	54.5
04	240 42.3	03.9	102 55.4	11.7	20 53.7	4.6	54.5
05	255 42.5	03.0	117 26.1	11.8	20 49.1	4.7	54.5
06	270 42.8	N 5 02.0	131 56.9	11.7	S20 44.4	4.7	54.5
07	285 43.0	01.1	146 27.6	11.9	20 39.7	4.9	54.5
T 08	300 43.2	5 00.2	160 58.5	11.8	20 34.8	5.0	54.5
U 09	315 43.4	4 59.2	175 29.3	11.9	20 29.8	5.0	54.4
E 10	330 43.6	58.3	190 00.2	12.0	20 24.8	5.2	54.4
S 11	345 43.9	57.3	204 31.2	12.0	20 19.6	5.2	54.4
D 12	0 44.1	N 4 56.4	219 02.2	12.1	S20 14.4	5.3	54.4
A 13	15 44.3	55.4	233 33.3	12.1	20 09.1	5.4	54.4
Y 14	30 44.5	54.5	248 04.4	12.2	20 03.7	5.5	54.4
15	45 44.7	.. 53.5	262 35.6	12.2	19 58.2	5.6	54.4
16	60 45.0	52.6	277 06.8	12.2	19 52.6	5.7	54.4
17	75 45.2	51.6	291 38.0	12.3	19 46.9	5.8	54.3
18	90 45.4	N 4 50.7	306 09.3	12.4	S19 41.1	5.8	54.3
19	105 45.6	49.7	320 40.7	12.4	19 35.3	6.0	54.3
20	120 45.8	48.8	335 12.1	12.4	19 29.3	6.0	54.3
21	135 46.1	.. 47.8	349 43.5	12.5	19 23.3	6.2	54.3
22	150 46.3	46.9	4 15.0	12.6	19 17.1	6.2	54.3
23	165 46.5	45.9	18 46.6	12.5	19 10.9	6.2	54.3
11 00	180 46.7	N 4 45.0	33 18.1	12.7	S19 04.7	6.4	54.3
01	195 46.9	44.1	47 49.8	12.7	18 58.3	6.5	54.3
02	210 47.2	43.1	62 21.5	12.7	18 51.8	6.5	54.2
03	225 47.4	.. 42.2	76 53.2	12.8	18 45.3	6.6	54.2
04	240 47.6	41.2	91 25.0	12.9	18 38.7	6.7	54.2
05	255 47.8	40.3	105 56.9	12.8	18 32.0	6.8	54.2
06	270 48.0	N 4 39.3	120 28.7	13.0	S18 25.2	6.9	54.2
W 07	285 48.3	38.4	135 00.7	13.0	18 18.3	6.9	54.2
E 08	300 48.5	37.4	149 32.7	13.0	18 11.4	7.1	54.2
D 09	315 48.7	.. 36.5	164 04.7	13.1	18 04.3	7.1	54.2
N 10	330 48.9	35.5	178 36.8	13.1	17 57.2	7.1	54.2
E 11	345 49.1	34.6	193 08.9	13.2	17 50.1	7.3	54.2
S 12	0 49.4	N 4 33.6	207 41.1	13.2	S17 42.8	7.3	54.2
D 13	15 49.6	32.7	222 13.3	13.3	17 35.5	7.4	54.1
A 14	30 49.8	31.7	236 45.6	13.3	17 28.1	7.5	54.1
Y 15	45 50.0	.. 30.8	251 17.9	13.4	17 20.6	7.5	54.1
16	60 50.2	29.8	265 50.3	13.4	17 13.1	7.7	54.1
17	75 50.5	28.9	280 22.7	13.5	17 05.4	7.7	54.1
18	90 50.7	N 4 27.9	294 55.2	13.5	S16 57.7	7.7	54.1
19	105 50.9	27.0	309 27.7	13.5	16 50.0	7.9	54.1
20	120 51.1	26.0	324 00.2	13.6	16 42.1	7.9	54.1
21	135 51.3	.. 25.1	338 32.8	13.7	16 34.2	8.0	54.1
22	150 51.6	24.1	353 05.5	13.7	16 26.2	8.0	54.1
23	165 51.8	23.2	7 38.2	13.7	16 18.2	8.1	54.1
12 00	180 52.0	N 4 22.2	22 10.9	13.8	S16 10.1	8.2	54.1
01	195 52.2	21.2	36 43.7	13.9	16 01.9	8.3	54.1
02	210 52.5	20.3	51 16.6	13.8	15 53.6	8.3	54.1
03	225 52.7	.. 19.3	65 49.4	14.0	15 45.3	8.4	54.1
04	240 52.9	18.4	80 22.4	13.9	15 36.9	8.4	54.0
05	255 53.1	17.4	94 55.3	14.1	15 28.5	8.5	54.0
06	270 53.3	N 4 16.5	109 28.4	14.0	S15 20.0	8.6	54.0
07	285 53.6	15.5	124 01.4	14.1	15 11.4	8.7	54.0
T 08	300 53.8	14.6	138 34.5	14.2	15 02.7	8.7	54.0
H 09	315 54.0	.. 13.6	153 07.7	14.1	14 54.0	8.7	54.0
U 10	330 54.2	12.7	167 40.8	14.3	14 45.3	8.8	54.0
R 11	345 54.4	11.7	182 14.1	14.3	14 36.5	8.9	54.0
S 12	0 54.7	N 4 10.8	196 47.4	14.3	S14 27.6	9.0	54.0
D 13	15 54.9	09.8	211 20.7	14.3	14 18.6	9.0	54.0
A 14	30 55.1	08.9	225 54.0	14.4	14 09.6	9.0	54.0
Y 15	45 55.3	.. 07.9	240 27.4	14.5	14 00.6	9.1	54.0
16	60 55.6	07.0	255 00.9	14.5	13 51.5	9.2	54.0
17	75 55.8	06.0	269 34.4	14.5	13 42.3	9.2	54.0
18	90 56.0	N 4 05.1	284 07.9	14.5	S13 33.1	9.3	54.0
19	105 56.2	04.1	298 41.4	14.6	13 23.8	9.4	54.0
20	120 56.4	03.1	313 15.0	14.7	13 14.4	9.4	54.0
21	135 56.7	.. 02.2	327 48.7	14.6	13 05.0	9.5	54.0
22	150 56.9	01.2	342 22.3	14.8	12 55.6	9.5	54.0
23	165 57.1	00.3	356 56.1	14.7	S12 46.1	9.6	54.0
	SD 15.9	d 0.9	SD 14.8		14.8		14.7

Lat.	Twilight Naut.	Twilight Civil	Sunrise	Moonrise 10	11	12	13
o	h m	h m	h m	h m	h m	h m	h m
N 72	01 23	03 32	04 47	▨	20 54	20 14	19 51
N 70	02 10	03 48	04 55	20 47	20 08	19 50	19 36
68	02 39	04 01	05 01	19 46	19 37	19 31	19 25
66	03 00	04 12	05 06	19 11	19 15	19 16	19 15
64	03 16	04 21	05 11	18 46	18 57	19 03	19 07
62	03 30	04 28	05 14	18 26	18 42	18 53	19 01
60	03 41	04 35	05 18	18 10	18 29	18 43	18 54
N 58	03 50	04 40	05 20	17 56	18 18	18 35	18 49
56	03 58	04 45	05 23	17 44	18 09	18 28	18 44
54	04 05	04 49	05 25	17 34	18 00	18 22	18 40
52	04 11	04 53	05 27	17 24	17 53	18 16	18 36
50	04 17	04 56	05 29	17 16	17 46	18 11	18 33
45	04 28	05 04	05 33	16 58	17 31	18 00	18 25
N 40	04 37	05 09	05 37	16 44	17 19	17 50	18 19
35	04 44	05 14	05 40	16 32	17 09	17 42	18 13
30	04 50	05 18	05 42	16 21	17 00	17 35	18 08
20	04 58	05 24	05 46	16 02	16 44	17 23	18 00
N 10	05 05	05 29	05 50	15 46	16 30	17 12	17 52
0	05 09	05 33	05 53	15 31	16 18	17 02	17 45
S 10	05 11	05 36	05 57	15 16	16 05	16 52	17 38
20	05 12	05 38	06 00	15 00	15 51	16 41	17 30
30	05 12	05 40	06 04	14 41	15 35	16 29	17 22
35	05 11	05 41	06 06	14 30	15 26	16 21	17 17
40	05 10	05 41	06 08	14 18	15 15	16 13	17 11
45	05 08	05 41	06 11	14 03	15 03	16 03	17 04
S 50	05 04	05 42	06 14	13 45	14 48	15 52	16 56
52	05 03	05 42	06 15	13 36	14 40	15 46	16 53
54	05 01	05 42	06 17	13 26	14 32	15 40	16 49
56	04 58	05 42	06 18	13 15	14 24	15 34	16 44
58	04 56	05 41	06 20	13 03	14 13	15 26	16 39
S 60	04 53	05 41	06 22	12 48	14 02	15 17	16 33

Lat.	Sunset	Twilight Civil	Twilight Naut.	Moonset 10	11	12	13
o	h m	h m	h m	h m	h m	h m	h m
N 72	19 03	20 18	22 19	▨	▨	00 18	02 30
N 70	18 56	20 02	21 38	22 48	25 03	01 03	02 53
68	18 50	19 49	21 10	23 48	25 32	01 32	03 10
66	18 45	19 39	20 50	24 23	00 23	01 54	03 24
64	18 41	19 30	20 34	24 47	00 47	02 12	03 36
62	18 38	19 23	20 21	25 07	01 07	02 26	03 45
60	18 34	19 17	20 10	00 11	01 23	02 38	03 54
N 58	18 32	19 12	20 01	00 27	01 36	02 48	04 01
56	18 29	19 07	19 53	00 41	01 47	02 57	04 07
54	18 27	19 03	19 47	00 53	01 58	03 05	04 13
52	18 25	18 59	19 41	01 03	02 06	03 12	04 18
50	18 23	18 56	19 35	01 13	02 14	03 18	04 23
45	18 19	18 49	19 24	01 32	02 31	03 32	04 33
N 40	18 16	18 43	19 15	01 48	02 45	03 43	04 41
35	18 13	18 39	19 09	02 01	02 57	03 53	04 48
30	18 11	18 35	19 03	02 13	03 07	04 01	04 54
20	18 07	18 29	18 55	02 33	03 24	04 15	05 05
N 10	18 03	18 24	18 49	02 50	03 40	04 28	05 14
0	18 00	18 21	18 45	03 06	03 54	04 39	05 23
S 10	17 57	18 18	18 42	03 22	04 08	04 51	05 32
20	17 54	18 16	18 41	03 39	04 23	05 03	05 41
30	17 50	18 14	18 42	03 59	04 40	05 17	05 51
35	17 48	18 13	18 43	04 10	04 50	05 25	05 57
40	17 46	18 13	18 44	04 23	05 01	05 34	06 04
45	17 43	18 13	18 46	04 38	05 14	05 45	06 12
S 50	17 40	18 13	18 50	04 57	05 30	05 58	06 21
52	17 39	18 13	18 52	05 06	05 38	06 04	06 25
54	17 38	18 13	18 54	05 16	05 46	06 10	06 30
56	17 36	18 13	18 56	05 27	05 56	06 18	06 35
58	17 34	18 13	18 59	05 40	06 06	06 26	06 41
S 60	17 32	18 14	19 02	05 55	06 18	06 35	06 48

Day	SUN Eqn. of Time 00h	SUN Eqn. of Time 12h	SUN Mer. Pass.	MOON Mer. Pass. Upper	MOON Mer. Pass. Lower	Age	Phase
d	m s	m s	h m	h m	h m	d	%
10	02 45	02 56	11 57	21 42	09 19	11	88
11	03 06	03 17	11 57	22 28	10 06	12	94
12	03 28	03 38	11 56	23 13	10 51	13	97

© British Crown Copyright 2018. All rights reserved.

UT	ARIES GHA	VENUS −3.9 GHA	Dec	MARS +1.8 GHA	Dec	JUPITER −2.1 GHA	Dec	SATURN +0.4 GHA	Dec	STARS Name	SHA	Dec
13 00	351 41.8	172 57.5	N 1 59.6	183 47.0	N 6 19.5	96 46.6	S22 24.1	66 35.4	S22 29.9	Acamar	315 14.8	S40 13.4
01	6 44.3	187 57.2	58.3	198 48.0	18.9	111 48.9	24.2	81 37.8	29.9	Achernar	335 23.1	S57 08.1
02	21 46.7	202 56.8	57.1	213 49.0	18.3	126 51.1	24.2	96 40.3	29.9	Acrux	173 05.2	S63 12.4
03	36 49.2	217 56.4	.. 55.8	228 50.0	.. 17.6	141 53.3	.. 24.2	111 42.8	.. 29.9	Adhara	255 09.3	S28 59.7
04	51 51.6	232 56.1	54.5	243 51.0	17.0	156 55.5	24.3	126 45.3	29.9	Aldebaran	290 44.4	N16 32.8
05	66 54.1	247 55.7	53.3	258 51.9	16.4	171 57.7	24.3	141 47.8	29.9			
06	81 56.6	262 55.3	N 1 52.0	273 52.9	N 6 15.8	186 59.9	S22 24.3	156 50.3	S22 29.9	Alioth	166 17.4	N55 51.5
07	96 59.0	277 55.0	50.7	288 53.9	15.1	202 02.1	24.4	171 52.8	30.0	Alkaid	152 55.9	N49 13.3
08	112 01.5	292 54.6	49.5	303 54.9	14.5	217 04.3	24.4	186 55.3	30.0	Alnair	27 37.9	S46 52.0
F 09	127 04.0	307 54.2	.. 48.2	318 55.9	.. 13.9	232 06.5	.. 24.4	201 57.7	.. 30.0	Alnilam	275 42.1	S 1 11.3
R 10	142 06.4	322 53.8	46.9	333 56.9	13.2	247 08.7	24.5	217 00.2	30.0	Alphard	217 52.2	S 8 44.5
I 11	157 08.9	337 53.5	45.7	348 57.9	12.6	262 10.9	24.5	232 02.7	30.0			
D 12	172 11.4	352 53.1	N 1 44.4	3 58.9	N 6 12.0	277 13.1	S22 24.6	247 05.2	S22 30.0	Alphecca	126 07.5	N26 39.3
A 13	187 13.8	7 52.7	43.1	18 59.9	11.4	292 15.4	24.6	262 07.7	30.0	Alpheratz	357 38.7	N29 11.9
Y 14	202 16.3	22 52.4	41.9	34 00.8	10.7	307 17.6	24.6	277 10.2	30.0	Altair	62 03.9	N 8 55.4
15	217 18.7	37 52.0	.. 40.6	49 01.8	.. 10.1	322 19.8	.. 24.6	292 12.6	.. 30.0	Ankaa	353 11.0	S42 11.9
16	232 21.2	52 51.6	39.3	64 02.8	09.5	337 22.0	24.6	307 15.1	30.0	Antares	112 21.1	S26 28.4
17	247 23.7	67 51.3	38.0	79 03.8	08.8	352 24.2	24.7	322 17.6	30.0			
18	262 26.1	82 50.9	N 1 36.8	94 04.8	N 6 08.2	7 26.4	S22 24.7	337 20.1	S22 30.0	Arcturus	145 52.1	N19 05.1
19	277 28.6	97 50.5	35.5	109 05.8	07.6	22 28.6	24.7	352 22.6	30.0	Atria	107 19.1	S69 03.8
20	292 31.1	112 50.1	34.2	124 06.8	06.9	37 30.8	24.8	7 25.1	30.0	Avior	234 16.8	S59 34.1
21	307 33.5	127 49.8	.. 33.0	139 07.8	.. 06.3	52 33.0	.. 24.8	22 27.5	.. 30.0	Bellatrix	278 27.4	N 6 22.0
22	322 36.0	142 49.4	31.7	154 08.7	05.7	67 35.2	24.8	37 30.0	30.0	Betelgeuse	270 56.7	N 7 24.6
23	337 38.5	157 49.0	30.4	169 09.7	05.1	82 37.4	24.9	52 32.5	30.1			
14 00	352 40.9	172 48.7	N 1 29.2	184 10.7	N 6 04.4	97 39.6	S22 24.9	67 35.0	S22 30.1	Canopus	263 54.4	S52 42.1
01	7 43.4	187 48.3	27.9	199 11.7	03.8	112 41.8	24.9	82 37.5	30.1	Capella	280 28.1	N46 00.8
02	22 45.9	202 47.9	26.6	214 12.7	03.2	127 44.0	25.0	97 40.0	30.1	Deneb	49 28.3	N45 21.3
03	37 48.3	217 47.6	.. 25.4	229 13.7	.. 02.5	142 46.2	.. 25.0	112 42.4	.. 30.1	Denebola	182 29.6	N14 28.0
04	52 50.8	232 47.2	24.1	244 14.7	01.9	157 48.4	25.0	127 44.9	30.1	Diphda	348 51.3	S17 52.7
05	67 53.2	247 46.8	22.8	259 15.7	01.3	172 50.6	25.1	142 47.4	30.1			
06	82 55.7	262 46.5	N 1 21.6	274 16.7	N 6 00.6	187 52.8	S22 25.1	157 49.9	S22 30.1	Dubhe	193 47.1	N61 38.8
07	97 58.2	277 46.1	20.3	289 17.6	6 00.0	202 55.0	25.1	172 52.4	30.1	Elnath	278 07.2	N28 37.3
08	113 00.6	292 45.7	19.0	304 18.6	5 59.4	217 57.2	25.2	187 54.9	30.1	Eltanin	90 44.1	N51 29.6
S 09	128 03.1	307 45.4	.. 17.7	319 19.6	.. 58.7	232 59.4	.. 25.2	202 57.3	.. 30.1	Enif	33 42.6	N 9 58.0
A 10	143 05.6	322 45.0	16.5	334 20.6	58.1	248 01.6	25.2	217 59.8	30.1	Fomalhaut	15 18.9	S29 31.0
T 11	158 08.0	337 44.6	15.2	349 21.6	57.5	263 03.8	25.2	233 02.3	30.1			
U 12	173 10.5	352 44.2	N 1 13.9	4 22.6	N 5 56.9	278 06.0	S22 25.3	248 04.8	S22 30.1	Gacrux	171 56.7	S57 13.3
R 13	188 13.0	7 43.9	12.7	19 23.6	56.2	293 08.2	25.3	263 07.3	30.1	Gienah	175 48.2	S17 38.9
D 14	203 15.4	22 43.5	11.4	34 24.6	55.6	308 10.4	25.3	278 09.7	30.1	Hadar	148 42.3	S60 28.0
A 15	218 17.9	37 43.1	.. 10.1	49 25.6	.. 55.0	323 12.6	.. 25.4	293 12.2	.. 30.1	Hamal	327 55.7	N23 33.2
Y 16	233 20.3	52 42.8	08.9	64 26.5	54.3	338 14.8	25.4	308 14.7	30.2	Kaus Aust.	83 38.0	S34 22.5
17	248 22.8	67 42.4	07.6	79 27.5	53.7	353 17.0	25.4	323 17.2	30.2			
18	263 25.3	82 42.0	N 1 06.3	94 28.5	N 5 53.1	8 19.2	S22 25.5	338 19.7	S22 30.2	Kochab	137 20.8	N74 04.9
19	278 27.7	97 41.7	05.0	109 29.5	52.4	23 21.4	25.5	353 22.1	30.2	Markab	13 33.8	N15 18.7
20	293 30.2	112 41.3	03.8	124 30.5	51.8	38 23.6	25.5	8 24.6	30.2	Menkar	314 10.4	N 4 10.0
21	308 32.7	127 40.9	.. 02.5	139 31.5	.. 51.2	53 25.8	.. 25.6	23 27.1	.. 30.2	Menkent	148 02.8	S36 27.9
22	323 35.1	142 40.6	01.2	154 32.5	50.5	68 28.0	25.6	38 29.6	30.2	Miaplacidus	221 39.6	S69 47.6
23	338 37.6	157 40.2	1 00.0	169 33.5	49.9	83 30.2	25.6	53 32.1	30.2			
15 00	353 40.1	172 39.8	N 0 58.7	184 34.5	N 5 49.3	98 32.4	S22 25.7	68 34.5	S22 30.2	Mirfak	308 34.0	N49 55.6
01	8 42.5	187 39.5	57.4	199 35.4	48.6	113 34.6	25.7	83 37.0	30.2	Nunki	75 52.9	S26 16.2
02	23 45.0	202 39.1	56.1	214 36.4	48.0	128 36.8	25.7	98 39.5	30.2	Peacock	53 12.1	S56 40.4
03	38 47.5	217 38.7	.. 54.9	229 37.4	.. 47.4	143 39.0	.. 25.8	113 42.0	.. 30.2	Pollux	243 22.7	N27 58.6
04	53 49.9	232 38.4	53.6	244 38.4	46.7	158 41.2	25.8	128 44.4	30.2	Procyon	244 55.4	N 5 10.5
05	68 52.4	247 38.0	52.3	259 39.4	46.1	173 43.4	25.8	143 46.9	30.2			
06	83 54.8	262 37.6	N 0 51.1	274 40.4	N 5 45.5	188 45.6	S22 25.9	158 49.4	S22 30.2	Rasalhague	96 02.5	N12 33.1
07	98 57.3	277 37.3	49.8	289 41.4	44.8	203 47.8	25.9	173 51.9	30.2	Regulus	207 39.3	N11 52.4
08	113 59.8	292 36.9	48.5	304 42.4	44.2	218 50.0	25.9	188 54.3	30.2	Rigel	281 07.9	S 8 10.7
S 09	129 02.2	307 36.5	.. 47.2	319 43.4	.. 43.6	233 52.2	.. 26.0	203 56.8	.. 30.2	Rigil Kent.	139 46.4	S60 54.9
U 10	144 04.7	322 36.2	46.0	334 44.3	42.9	248 54.4	26.0	218 59.3	30.3	Sabik	102 07.7	S15 44.8
N 11	159 07.2	337 35.8	44.7	349 45.3	42.3	263 56.6	26.0	234 01.8	30.3			
D 12	174 09.6	352 35.4	N 0 43.4	4 46.3	N 5 41.7	278 58.7	S22 26.1	249 04.3	S22 30.3	Schedar	349 35.1	N56 38.6
A 13	189 12.1	7 35.1	42.2	19 47.3	41.1	294 00.9	26.1	264 06.7	30.3	Shaula	96 16.1	S37 07.0
Y 14	204 14.6	22 34.7	40.9	34 48.3	40.4	309 03.1	26.1	279 09.2	30.3	Sirius	258 30.1	S16 44.5
15	219 17.0	37 34.3	.. 39.6	49 49.3	.. 39.8	324 05.3	.. 26.1	294 11.7	.. 30.3	Spica	158 27.0	S11 15.6
16	234 19.5	52 34.0	38.3	64 50.3	39.2	339 07.5	26.2	309 14.2	30.3	Suhail	222 49.7	S43 30.5
17	249 21.9	67 33.6	37.1	79 51.3	38.5	354 09.7	26.2	324 16.6	30.3			
18	264 24.4	82 33.2	N 0 35.8	94 52.3	N 5 37.9	9 11.9	S22 26.2	339 19.1	S22 30.3	Vega	80 35.9	N38 48.5
19	279 26.9	97 32.9	34.5	109 53.3	37.3	24 14.1	26.3	354 21.6	30.3	Zuben'ubi	137 00.9	S16 07.2
20	294 29.3	112 32.5	33.2	124 54.2	36.6	39 16.3	26.3	9 24.1	30.3		SHA	Mer.Pass.
21	309 31.8	127 32.1	.. 32.0	139 55.2	.. 36.0	54 18.5	.. 26.3	24 26.5	.. 30.3		° ′	h m
22	324 34.3	142 31.8	30.7	154 56.2	35.4	69 20.7	26.4	39 29.0	30.3	Venus	180 07.7	12 29
23	339 36.7	157 31.4	29.4	169 57.2	34.7	84 22.9	26.4	54 31.5	30.3	Mars	191 29.8	11 43
	h m									Jupiter	104 58.7	17 27
Mer.Pass.	0 29.2	v −0.4	d 1.3	v 1.0	d 0.6	v 2.2	d 0.0	v 2.5	d 0.0	Saturn	74 54.1	19 26

© British Crown Copyright 2018. All rights reserved.

UT	SUN GHA	SUN Dec	MOON GHA	v	Dec	d	HP
13 00	180 57.3	N 3 59.3	11 29.8	14.8	S12 36.5	9.6	54.0
01	195 57.6	58.4	26 03.6	14.8	12 26.9	9.6	54.0
02	210 57.8	57.4	40 37.4	14.9	12 17.3	9.7	54.0
03	225 58.0	.. 56.5	55 11.3	14.9	12 07.6	9.8	54.0
04	240 58.2	55.5	69 45.2	14.9	11 57.8	9.8	54.0
05	255 58.4	54.6	84 19.1	15.0	11 48.0	9.8	54.0
06	270 58.7	N 3 53.6	98 53.1	15.0	S11 38.2	9.9	54.0
F 07	285 58.9	52.6	113 27.1	15.0	11 28.3	9.9	54.0
R 08	300 59.1	51.7	128 01.1	15.1	11 18.4	10.0	54.0
I 09	315 59.3	.. 50.7	142 35.2	15.1	11 08.4	10.0	54.0
D 10	330 59.6	49.8	157 09.3	15.1	10 58.4	10.1	54.0
A 11	345 59.8	48.8	171 43.4	15.2	10 48.3	10.1	54.0
Y 12	1 00.0	N 3 47.9	186 17.6	15.2	S10 38.2	10.2	54.0
13	16 00.2	46.9	200 51.8	15.2	10 28.0	10.2	54.0
14	31 00.5	46.0	215 26.0	15.3	10 17.8	10.2	54.0
15	46 00.7	.. 45.0	230 00.3	15.3	10 07.6	10.3	54.0
16	61 00.9	44.0	244 34.6	15.3	9 57.3	10.3	54.0
17	76 01.1	43.1	259 08.9	15.3	9 47.0	10.4	54.0
18	91 01.3	N 3 42.1	273 43.2	15.4	S 9 36.6	10.4	54.0
19	106 01.6	41.2	288 17.6	15.4	9 26.2	10.4	54.0
20	121 01.8	40.2	302 52.0	15.4	9 15.8	10.5	54.0
21	136 02.0	.. 39.3	317 26.4	15.5	9 05.3	10.5	54.0
22	151 02.2	38.3	332 00.9	15.5	8 54.8	10.6	54.0
23	166 02.5	37.3	346 35.4	15.5	8 44.2	10.6	54.0
14 00	181 02.7	N 3 36.4	1 09.9	15.5	S 8 33.6	10.6	54.0
01	196 02.9	35.4	15 44.4	15.5	8 23.0	10.6	54.0
02	211 03.1	34.5	30 18.9	15.6	8 12.4	10.7	54.0
03	226 03.3	.. 33.5	44 53.5	15.6	8 01.7	10.7	54.0
04	241 03.6	32.6	59 28.1	15.6	7 51.0	10.8	54.0
05	256 03.8	31.6	74 02.7	15.7	7 40.2	10.8	54.0
06	271 04.0	N 3 30.6	88 37.4	15.6	S 7 29.4	10.8	54.0
S 07	286 04.2	29.7	103 12.0	15.7	7 18.6	10.8	54.0
A 08	301 04.5	28.7	117 46.7	15.7	7 07.8	10.9	54.0
T 09	316 04.7	.. 27.8	132 21.4	15.7	6 56.9	10.9	54.0
U 10	331 04.9	26.8	146 56.1	15.8	6 46.0	10.9	54.0
R 11	346 05.1	25.8	161 30.9	15.7	6 35.1	11.0	54.0
D 12	1 05.4	N 3 24.9	176 05.6	15.8	S 6 24.1	10.9	54.0
A 13	16 05.6	23.9	190 40.4	15.8	6 13.2	11.1	54.0
Y 14	31 05.8	23.0	205 15.2	15.8	6 02.1	11.0	54.0
15	46 06.0	.. 22.0	219 50.0	15.8	5 51.1	11.0	54.0
16	61 06.3	21.1	234 24.8	15.8	5 40.1	11.1	54.0
17	76 06.5	20.1	248 59.6	15.9	5 29.0	11.1	54.0
18	91 06.7	N 3 19.1	263 34.5	15.8	S 5 17.9	11.1	54.0
19	106 06.9	18.2	278 09.3	15.9	5 06.8	11.2	54.0
20	121 07.1	17.2	292 44.2	15.9	4 55.6	11.2	54.0
21	136 07.4	.. 16.3	307 19.1	15.8	4 44.4	11.1	54.0
22	151 07.6	15.3	321 53.9	16.0	4 33.3	11.2	54.0
23	166 07.8	14.3	336 28.9	15.9	4 22.1	11.3	54.0
15 00	181 08.0	N 3 13.4	351 03.8	15.9	S 4 10.8	11.2	54.0
01	196 08.3	12.4	5 38.7	15.9	3 59.6	11.3	54.0
02	211 08.5	11.5	20 13.6	15.9	3 48.3	11.3	54.1
03	226 08.7	.. 10.5	34 48.5	16.0	3 37.0	11.3	54.1
04	241 08.9	09.5	49 23.5	15.9	3 25.7	11.3	54.1
05	256 09.2	08.6	63 58.4	16.0	3 14.4	11.3	54.1
06	271 09.4	N 3 07.6	78 33.4	15.9	S 3 03.1	11.3	54.1
07	286 09.6	06.7	93 08.3	16.0	2 51.8	11.4	54.1
08	301 09.8	05.7	107 43.3	16.0	2 40.4	11.3	54.1
S 09	316 10.1	.. 04.7	122 18.3	15.9	2 29.1	11.4	54.1
U 10	331 10.3	03.8	136 53.2	16.0	2 17.7	11.4	54.1
N 11	346 10.5	02.8	151 28.2	16.0	2 06.3	11.4	54.1
D 12	1 10.7	N 3 01.9	166 03.2	15.9	S 1 54.9	11.4	54.1
A 13	16 11.0	3 00.9	180 38.1	16.0	1 43.5	11.4	54.1
Y 14	31 11.2	2 59.9	195 13.1	16.0	1 32.1	11.5	54.1
15	46 11.4	.. 59.0	209 48.1	15.9	1 20.6	11.4	54.1
16	61 11.6	58.0	224 23.0	16.0	1 09.2	11.5	54.2
17	76 11.8	57.0	238 58.0	16.0	0 57.7	11.4	54.2
18	91 12.1	N 2 56.1	253 33.0	15.9	S 0 46.3	11.5	54.2
19	106 12.3	55.1	268 07.9	16.0	0 34.8	11.4	54.2
20	121 12.5	54.2	282 42.9	15.9	0 23.4	11.5	54.2
21	136 12.7	.. 53.2	297 17.8	15.9	0 11.9	11.5	54.2
22	151 13.0	52.2	311 52.7	16.0	S 0 00.4	11.4	54.2
23	166 13.2	51.3	326 27.7	15.9	N 0 11.0	11.5	54.2
	SD 15.9	d 1.0	SD 14.7		14.7		14.7

Lat.	Twilight Naut.	Twilight Civil	Sunrise	Moonrise 13	14	15	16
	h m	h m	h m	h m	h m	h m	h m
N 72	01 56	03 48	05 01	19 51	19 32	19 16	18 59
N 70	02 31	04 02	05 07	19 36	19 25	19 15	19 05
68	02 55	04 13	05 12	19 25	19 19	19 14	19 09
66	03 13	04 22	05 16	19 15	19 15	19 14	19 13
64	03 28	04 30	05 19	19 07	19 11	19 13	19 16
62	03 39	04 36	05 22	19 01	19 07	19 13	19 18
60	03 49	04 42	05 25	18 54	19 04	19 12	19 21
N 58	03 58	04 47	05 27	18 49	19 01	19 12	19 23
56	04 05	04 51	05 29	18 44	18 59	19 12	19 25
54	04 11	04 55	05 31	18 40	18 56	19 11	19 27
52	04 17	04 58	05 32	18 36	18 54	19 11	19 28
50	04 22	05 01	05 34	18 33	18 52	19 11	19 30
45	04 32	05 07	05 37	18 25	18 48	19 10	19 33
N 40	04 40	05 12	05 40	18 19	18 45	19 10	19 35
35	04 47	05 16	05 42	18 13	18 42	19 10	19 38
30	04 52	05 20	05 44	18 08	18 39	19 09	19 40
20	04 59	05 25	05 47	18 00	18 35	19 09	19 43
N 10	05 04	05 29	05 50	17 52	18 31	19 08	19 47
0	05 08	05 32	05 52	17 45	18 27	19 08	19 50
S 10	05 09	05 34	05 55	17 38	18 23	19 08	19 53
20	05 10	05 35	05 57	17 30	18 19	19 07	19 56
30	05 08	05 36	06 00	17 22	18 14	19 07	20 00
35	05 07	05 36	06 02	17 17	18 12	19 07	20 02
40	05 05	05 36	06 03	17 11	18 09	19 06	20 04
45	05 02	05 36	06 05	17 04	18 05	19 06	20 07
S 50	04 58	05 35	06 07	16 56	18 01	19 06	20 11
52	04 56	05 35	06 08	16 53	17 59	19 05	20 12
54	04 53	05 34	06 09	16 49	17 57	19 05	20 14
56	04 50	05 34	06 11	16 44	17 54	19 05	20 16
58	04 47	05 33	06 12	16 39	17 52	19 05	20 18
S 60	04 44	05 32	06 13	16 33	17 49	19 04	20 20

Lat.	Sunset	Twilight Civil	Naut.	Moonset 13	14	15	16
	h m	h m	h m	h m	h m	h m	h m
N 72	18 48	20 00	21 48	02 30	04 22	06 07	07 51
N 70	18 42	19 46	21 15	02 53	04 34	06 12	07 48
68	18 37	19 35	20 52	03 10	04 44	06 15	07 46
66	18 34	19 27	20 35	03 24	04 52	06 18	07 45
64	18 30	19 19	20 21	03 36	04 59	06 21	07 43
62	18 28	19 13	20 09	03 45	05 05	06 23	07 42
60	18 25	19 08	20 00	03 54	05 10	06 25	07 41
N 58	18 23	19 03	19 52	04 01	05 14	06 27	07 40
56	18 21	18 59	19 44	04 07	05 18	06 28	07 39
54	18 20	18 55	19 38	04 13	05 21	06 30	07 38
52	18 18	18 52	19 33	04 18	05 25	06 31	07 37
50	18 17	18 49	19 28	04 23	05 27	06 32	07 37
45	18 14	18 43	19 18	04 33	05 34	06 34	07 35
N 40	18 11	18 38	19 10	04 41	05 39	06 36	07 34
35	18 09	18 34	19 04	04 48	05 43	06 38	07 33
30	18 07	18 31	18 59	04 54	05 47	06 40	07 32
20	18 04	18 26	18 52	05 05	05 54	06 42	07 31
N 10	18 01	18 22	18 47	05 14	06 00	06 45	07 29
0	17 59	18 20	18 44	05 23	06 05	06 47	07 28
S 10	17 57	18 18	18 42	05 32	06 11	06 49	07 27
20	17 54	18 16	18 42	05 41	06 16	06 51	07 25
30	17 52	18 16	18 43	05 51	06 23	06 54	07 24
35	17 50	18 16	18 45	05 57	06 27	06 55	07 23
40	17 49	18 16	18 47	06 04	06 31	06 57	07 22
45	17 47	18 16	18 50	06 12	06 36	06 58	07 20
S 50	17 45	18 17	18 55	06 21	06 42	07 01	07 19
52	17 44	18 18	18 57	06 25	06 44	07 02	07 18
54	17 43	18 18	19 00	06 30	06 47	07 03	07 18
56	17 42	18 19	19 02	06 35	06 50	07 04	07 17
58	17 41	18 20	19 06	06 41	06 54	07 05	07 16
S 60	17 39	18 21	19 09	06 48	06 58	07 07	07 15

Day	SUN Eqn. of Time 00h	12h	Mer. Pass.	MOON Mer. Pass. Upper	Lower	Age	Phase
d	m s	m s	h m	h m	h m	d %	
13	03 49	04 00	11 56	23 55	11 34	14 99	
14	04 10	04 21	11 56	24 37	12 16	15 100	○
15	04 32	04 42	11 55	00 37	12 57	16 98	

© British Crown Copyright 2018. All rights reserved.

UT	ARIES GHA	VENUS −3.9 GHA	Dec	MARS +1.8 GHA	Dec	JUPITER −2.1 GHA	Dec	SATURN +0.4 GHA	Dec	Name	SHA	Dec
16 00	354 39.2	172 31.0 N 0	28.2	184 58.2 N 5	34.1	99 25.0 S22	26.4	69 34.0 S22	30.3	Acamar	315 14.8	S40 13.4
01	9 41.7	187 30.7	26.9	199 59.2	33.5	114 27.2	26.5	84 36.4	30.3	Achernar	335 23.0	S57 08.1
02	24 44.1	202 30.3	25.6	215 00.2	32.8	129 29.4	26.5	99 38.9	30.3	Acrux	173 05.2	S63 12.4
03	39 46.6	217 29.9 ..	24.3	230 01.2 ..	32.2	144 31.6 ..	26.5	114 41.4 ..	30.3	Adhara	255 09.3	S28 59.7
04	54 49.1	232 29.6	23.1	245 02.2	31.6	159 33.8	26.6	129 43.9	30.3	Aldebaran	290 44.4	N16 32.8
05	69 51.5	247 29.2	21.8	260 03.2	30.9	174 36.0	26.6	144 46.3	30.3			
06	84 54.0	262 28.8 N 0	20.5	275 04.1 N 5	30.3	189 38.2 S22	26.6	159 48.8 S22	30.4	Alioth	166 17.4	N55 51.5
07	99 56.4	277 28.5	19.2	290 05.1	29.7	204 40.4	26.7	174 51.3	30.4	Alkaid	152 55.9	N49 13.2
08	114 58.9	292 28.1	18.0	305 06.1	29.0	219 42.6	26.7	189 53.7	30.4	Alnair	27 37.9	S46 52.0
M 09	130 01.4	307 27.7 ..	16.7	320 07.1 ..	28.4	234 44.7 ..	26.7	204 56.2 ..	30.4	Alnilam	275 42.0	S 1 11.3
O 10	145 03.8	322 27.4	15.4	335 08.1	27.7	249 46.9	26.8	219 58.7	30.4	Alphard	217 52.2	S 8 44.5
N 11	160 06.3	337 27.0	14.1	350 09.1	27.1	264 49.1	26.8	235 01.2	30.4			
D 12	175 08.8	352 26.6 N 0	12.9	5 10.1 N 5	26.5	279 51.3 S22	26.8	250 03.6 S22	30.4	Alphecca	126 07.6	N26 39.3
A 13	190 11.2	7 26.3	11.6	20 11.1	25.8	294 53.5	26.9	265 06.1	30.4	Alpheratz	357 38.7	N29 11.9
Y 14	205 13.7	22 25.9	10.3	35 12.1	25.2	309 55.7	26.9	280 08.6	30.4	Altair	62 03.9	N 8 55.4
15	220 16.2	37 25.5 ..	09.1	50 13.1 ..	24.6	324 57.9 ..	26.9	295 11.0 ..	30.4	Ankaa	353 11.0	S42 11.9
16	235 18.6	52 25.2	07.8	65 14.0	23.9	340 00.0	27.0	310 13.5	30.4	Antares	112 21.1	S26 28.4
17	250 21.1	67 24.8	06.5	80 15.0	23.3	355 02.2	27.0	325 16.0	30.4			
18	265 23.5	82 24.4 N 0	05.2	95 16.0 N 5	22.7	10 04.4 S22	27.0	340 18.5 S22	30.4	Arcturus	145 52.1	N19 05.1
19	280 26.0	97 24.1	04.0	110 17.0	22.0	25 06.6	27.1	355 20.9	30.4	Atria	107 19.2	S69 03.8
20	295 28.5	112 23.7	02.7	125 18.0	21.4	40 08.8	27.1	10 23.4	30.4	Avior	234 16.7	S59 34.1
21	310 30.9	127 23.3 ..	01.4	140 19.0 ..	20.8	55 11.0 ..	27.1	25 25.9 ..	30.4	Bellatrix	278 27.4	N 6 22.0
22	325 33.4	142 23.0 N	00.1	155 20.0	20.1	70 13.1	27.2	40 28.3	30.4	Betelgeuse	270 56.7	N 7 24.6
23	340 35.9	157 22.6 S	01.1	170 21.0	19.5	85 15.3	27.2	55 30.8	30.4			
17 00	355 38.3	172 22.2 S 0	02.4	185 22.0 N 5	18.9	100 17.5 S22	27.2	70 33.3 S22	30.4	Canopus	263 54.4	S52 42.1
01	10 40.8	187 21.9	03.7	200 23.0	18.2	115 19.7	27.3	85 35.7	30.5	Capella	280 28.1	N46 00.8
02	25 43.3	202 21.5	05.0	215 24.0	17.6	130 21.9	27.3	100 38.2	30.5	Deneb	49 28.3	N45 21.3
03	40 45.7	217 21.1 ..	06.2	230 24.9 ..	17.0	145 24.1 ..	27.3	115 40.7 ..	30.5	Denebola	182 29.6	N14 28.0
04	55 48.2	232 20.8	07.5	245 25.9	16.3	160 26.2	27.4	130 43.2	30.5	Diphda	348 51.3	S17 52.7
05	70 50.7	247 20.4	08.8	260 26.9	15.7	175 28.4	27.4	145 45.6	30.5			
06	85 53.1	262 20.0 S 0	10.1	275 27.9 N 5	15.1	190 30.6 S22	27.4	160 48.1 S22	30.5	Dubhe	193 47.1	N61 38.8
07	100 55.6	277 19.7	11.3	290 28.9	14.4	205 32.8	27.5	175 50.6	30.5	Elnath	278 07.2	N28 37.3
T 08	115 58.0	292 19.3	12.6	305 29.9	13.8	220 35.0	27.5	190 53.0	30.5	Eltanin	90 44.1	N51 29.6
U 09	131 00.5	307 18.9 ..	13.9	320 30.9 ..	13.1	235 37.1 ..	27.5	205 55.5 ..	30.5	Enif	33 42.7	N 9 58.0
E 10	146 03.0	322 18.6	15.2	335 31.9	12.5	250 39.3	27.6	220 58.0	30.5	Fomalhaut	15 18.9	S29 31.1
S 11	161 05.4	337 18.2	16.4	350 32.9	11.9	265 41.5	27.6	236 00.4	30.5			
D 12	176 07.9	352 17.8 S 0	17.7	5 33.9 N 5	11.2	280 43.7 S22	27.6	251 02.9 S22	30.5	Gacrux	171 56.7	S57 13.3
A 13	191 10.4	7 17.5	19.0	20 34.8	10.6	295 45.9	27.7	266 05.4	30.5	Gienah	175 48.2	S17 38.8
Y 14	206 12.8	22 17.1	20.3	35 35.8	10.0	310 48.0	27.7	281 07.8	30.5	Hadar	148 42.4	S60 28.0
15	221 15.3	37 16.7 ..	21.5	50 36.8 ..	09.3	325 50.2 ..	27.7	296 10.3 ..	30.5	Hamal	327 55.7	N23 33.2
16	236 17.8	52 16.4	22.8	65 37.8	08.7	340 52.4	27.8	311 12.8	30.5	Kaus Aust.	83 38.1	S34 22.5
17	251 20.2	67 16.0	24.1	80 38.8	08.1	355 54.6	27.8	326 15.2	30.5			
18	266 22.7	82 15.6 S 0	25.4	95 39.8 N 5	07.4	10 56.8 S22	27.8	341 17.7 S22	30.5	Kochab	137 20.8	N74 04.9
19	281 25.2	97 15.3	26.6	110 40.8	06.8	25 58.9	27.9	356 20.2	30.5	Markab	13 33.8	N15 18.7
20	296 27.6	112 14.9	27.9	125 41.8	06.2	41 01.1	27.9	11 22.6	30.5	Menkar	314 10.4	N 4 10.0
21	311 30.1	127 14.5 ..	29.2	140 42.8 ..	05.5	56 03.3 ..	27.9	26 25.1 ..	30.5	Menkent	148 02.9	S36 27.9
22	326 32.5	142 14.2	30.5	155 43.8	04.9	71 05.5	28.0	41 27.6	30.5	Miaplacidus	221 39.6	S69 47.6
23	341 35.0	157 13.8	31.7	170 44.8	04.2	86 07.6	28.0	56 30.0	30.6			
18 00	356 37.5	172 13.4 S 0	33.0	185 45.8 N 5	03.6	101 09.8 S22	28.0	71 32.5 S22	30.6	Mirfak	308 34.0	N49 55.6
01	11 39.9	187 13.1	34.3	200 46.7	03.0	116 12.0	28.1	86 35.0	30.6	Nunki	75 52.9	S26 16.2
02	26 42.4	202 12.7	35.6	215 47.7	02.3	131 14.2	28.1	101 37.4	30.6	Peacock	53 12.1	S56 40.4
03	41 44.9	217 12.3 ..	36.8	230 48.7 ..	01.7	146 16.3 ..	28.1	116 39.9 ..	30.6	Pollux	243 22.7	N27 58.6
04	56 47.3	232 12.0	38.1	245 49.7	01.1	161 18.5	28.2	131 42.4	30.6	Procyon	244 55.4	N 5 10.5
05	71 49.8	247 11.6	39.4	260 50.7 5	00.4	176 20.7	28.2	146 44.8	30.6			
06	86 52.3	262 11.2 S 0	40.7	275 51.7 N 4	59.8	191 22.9 S22	28.2	161 47.3 S22	30.6	Rasalhague	96 02.5	N12 33.1
W 07	101 54.7	277 10.9	41.9	290 52.7	59.2	206 25.0	28.3	176 49.7	30.6	Regulus	207 39.3	N11 52.4
E 08	116 57.2	292 10.5	43.2	305 53.7	58.5	221 27.2	28.3	191 52.2	30.6	Rigel	281 07.9	S 8 10.7
D 09	131 59.6	307 10.1 ..	44.5	320 54.7 ..	57.9	236 29.4 ..	28.3	206 54.7 ..	30.6	Rigil Kent.	139 46.4	S60 54.9
N 10	147 02.1	322 09.8	45.8	335 55.7	57.2	251 31.6	28.4	221 57.1	30.6	Sabik	102 07.7	S15 44.8
E 11	162 04.6	337 09.4	47.0	350 56.7	56.6	266 33.7	28.4	236 59.6	30.6			
S 12	177 07.0	352 09.0 S 0	48.3	5 57.6 N 4	56.0	281 35.9 S22	28.5	252 02.1 S22	30.6	Schedar	349 35.1	N56 38.6
D 13	192 09.5	7 08.6	49.6	20 58.6	55.3	296 38.1	28.5	267 04.5	30.6	Shaula	96 16.1	S37 07.0
A 14	207 12.0	22 08.3	50.9	35 59.6	54.7	311 40.3	28.5	282 07.0	30.6	Sirius	258 30.1	S16 44.5
Y 15	222 14.4	37 07.9 ..	52.1	51 00.6 ..	54.1	326 42.4 ..	28.5	297 09.5 ..	30.6	Spica	158 27.0	S11 15.6
16	237 16.9	52 07.5	53.4	66 01.6	53.4	341 44.6	28.6	312 11.9	30.6	Suhail	222 49.7	S43 30.5
17	252 19.4	67 07.2	54.7	81 02.6	52.8	356 46.8	28.6	327 14.4	30.6			
18	267 21.8	82 06.8 S 0	56.0	96 03.6 N 4	52.1	11 48.9 S22	28.6	342 16.8 S22	30.6	Vega	80 36.0	N38 48.5
19	282 24.3	97 06.4	57.2	111 04.6	51.5	26 51.1	28.7	357 19.3	30.6	Zuben'ubi	137 00.9	S16 07.2
20	297 26.8	112 06.1	58.5	126 05.6	50.9	41 53.3	28.7	12 21.8	30.6		SHA	Mer.Pass.
21	312 29.2	127 05.7 0	59.8	141 06.6 ..	50.2	56 55.5 ..	28.7	27 24.2 ..	30.6		° ′	h m
22	327 31.7	142 05.3 1	01.1	156 07.6	49.6	72 57.6	28.8	42 26.7	30.6	Venus	176 43.9	12 31
23	342 34.1	157 05.0 S 1	02.3	171 08.6	49.0	86 59.8	28.8	57 29.1	30.7	Mars	189 43.6	11 38
Mer. Pass.	h m 0 17.4	v −0.4	d 1.3	v 1.0	d 0.6	v 2.2	d 0.0	v 2.5	d 0.0	Jupiter	104 39.2	17 16
										Saturn	74 54.9	19 15

© British Crown Copyright 2018. All rights reserved.

UT	SUN GHA	SUN Dec	MOON GHA	v	MOON Dec	d	HP
d h	° ′	° ′	° ′	′	° ′	′	′
16 00	181 13.4	N 2 50.3	341 02.6	15.9	N 0 22.5	11.5	54.2
01	196 13.6	49.3	355 37.5	15.9	0 34.0	11.5	54.2
02	211 13.9	48.4	10 12.4	15.9	0 45.5	11.5	54.2
03	226 14.1	.. 47.4	24 47.3	15.9	0 57.0	11.5	54.2
04	241 14.3	46.5	39 22.2	15.9	1 08.5	11.4	54.3
05	256 14.5	45.5	53 57.1	15.8	1 19.9	11.5	54.3
06	271 14.8	N 2 44.5	68 31.9	15.9	N 1 31.4	11.5	54.3
07	286 15.0	43.6	83 06.8	15.8	1 42.9	11.5	54.3
08	301 15.2	42.6	97 41.6	15.8	1 54.4	11.4	54.3
M 09	316 15.4	.. 41.6	112 16.4	15.8	2 05.8	11.5	54.3
O 10	331 15.7	40.7	126 51.2	15.8	2 17.3	11.5	54.3
N 11	346 15.9	39.7	141 26.0	15.8	2 28.8	11.4	54.3
D 12	1 16.1	N 2 38.8	156 00.8	15.7	N 2 40.2	11.5	54.3
A 13	16 16.3	37.8	170 35.5	15.8	2 51.7	11.4	54.3
Y 14	31 16.6	36.8	185 10.3	15.7	3 03.1	11.5	54.4
15	46 16.8	.. 35.9	199 45.0	15.7	3 14.6	11.4	54.4
16	61 17.0	34.9	214 19.7	15.6	3 26.0	11.4	54.4
17	76 17.2	33.9	228 54.3	15.7	3 37.4	11.4	54.4
18	91 17.5	N 2 33.0	243 29.0	15.6	N 3 48.8	11.4	54.4
19	106 17.7	32.0	258 03.6	15.6	4 00.2	11.4	54.4
20	121 17.9	31.0	272 38.2	15.6	4 11.6	11.4	54.4
21	136 18.1	.. 30.1	287 12.8	15.6	4 23.0	11.4	54.4
22	151 18.3	29.1	301 47.4	15.5	4 34.4	11.3	54.5
23	166 18.6	28.2	316 21.9	15.5	4 45.7	11.4	54.5
17 00	181 18.8	N 2 27.2	330 56.4	15.5	N 4 57.1	11.3	54.5
01	196 19.0	26.2	345 30.9	15.4	5 08.4	11.3	54.5
02	211 19.2	25.3	0 05.3	15.4	5 19.7	11.3	54.5
03	226 19.5	.. 24.3	14 39.7	15.4	5 31.0	11.2	54.5
04	241 19.7	23.3	29 14.1	15.4	5 42.2	11.3	54.5
05	256 19.9	22.4	43 48.5	15.3	5 53.5	11.2	54.5
06	271 20.1	N 2 21.4	58 22.8	15.3	N 6 04.7	11.3	54.6
07	286 20.4	20.4	72 57.1	15.3	6 16.0	11.2	54.6
T 08	301 20.6	19.5	87 31.4	15.2	6 27.2	11.1	54.6
U 09	316 20.8	.. 18.5	102 05.6	15.2	6 38.3	11.2	54.6
E 10	331 21.0	17.5	116 39.8	15.2	6 49.5	11.1	54.6
S 11	346 21.3	16.6	131 14.0	15.1	7 00.6	11.1	54.6
D 12	1 21.5	N 2 15.6	145 48.1	15.1	N 7 11.7	11.1	54.6
A 13	16 21.7	14.6	160 22.2	15.1	7 22.8	11.1	54.7
Y 14	31 21.9	13.7	174 56.3	15.0	7 33.9	11.0	54.7
15	46 22.2	.. 12.7	189 30.3	15.0	7 44.9	11.1	54.7
16	61 22.4	11.7	204 04.3	14.9	7 56.0	10.9	54.7
17	76 22.6	10.8	218 38.2	14.9	8 06.9	11.0	54.7
18	91 22.8	N 2 09.8	233 12.1	14.9	N 8 17.9	10.9	54.7
19	106 23.1	08.9	247 46.0	14.8	8 28.8	10.9	54.8
20	121 23.3	07.9	262 19.8	14.8	8 39.7	10.9	54.8
21	136 23.5	.. 06.9	276 53.6	14.7	8 50.6	10.9	54.8
22	151 23.7	06.0	291 27.3	14.7	9 01.5	10.8	54.8
23	166 23.9	05.0	306 01.0	14.6	9 12.3	10.7	54.8
18 00	181 24.2	N 2 04.0	320 34.6	14.6	N 9 23.0	10.8	54.8
01	196 24.4	03.1	335 08.2	14.6	9 33.8	10.7	54.9
02	211 24.6	02.1	349 41.8	14.5	9 44.5	10.7	54.9
03	226 24.8	.. 01.1	4 15.3	14.5	9 55.2	10.6	54.9
04	241 25.1	2 00.2	18 48.8	14.4	10 05.8	10.6	54.9
05	256 25.3	1 59.2	33 22.2	14.3	10 16.4	10.6	54.9
06	271 25.5	N 1 58.2	47 55.5	14.3	N10 27.0	10.5	54.9
W 07	286 25.7	57.3	62 28.8	14.3	10 37.5	10.5	55.0
E 08	301 26.0	56.3	77 02.1	14.2	10 48.0	10.5	55.0
D 09	316 26.2	.. 55.3	91 35.3	14.2	10 58.5	10.4	55.0
N 10	331 26.4	54.4	106 08.5	14.1	11 08.9	10.4	55.0
E 11	346 26.6	53.4	120 41.6	14.0	11 19.3	10.3	55.0
S 12	1 26.9	N 1 52.4	135 14.6	14.0	N11 29.6	10.3	55.1
D 13	16 27.1	51.5	149 47.6	14.0	11 39.9	10.3	55.1
A 14	31 27.3	50.5	164 20.6	13.8	11 50.2	10.2	55.1
Y 15	46 27.5	.. 49.5	178 53.4	13.9	12 00.4	10.1	55.1
16	61 27.8	48.5	193 26.3	13.8	12 10.5	10.1	55.1
17	76 28.0	47.6	207 59.1	13.7	12 20.6	10.0	55.2
18	91 28.2	N 1 46.6	222 31.8	13.6	N12 30.7	10.0	55.2
19	106 28.4	45.6	237 04.4	13.6	12 40.7	10.0	55.2
20	121 28.7	44.7	251 37.0	13.6	12 50.7	9.9	55.2
21	136 28.9	.. 43.7	266 09.6	13.4	13 00.6	9.9	55.2
22	151 29.1	42.7	280 42.0	13.5	13 10.5	9.8	55.3
23	166 29.3	41.8	295 14.5	13.3	N13 20.3	9.8	55.3
	SD 15.9	d 1.0	SD 14.8		14.9		15.0

Lat.	Twilight Naut.	Twilight Civil	Sunrise	Moonrise 16	17	18	19
°	h m	h m	h m	h m	h m	h m	h m
N 72	02 21	04 03	05 14	18 59	18 41	18 19	17 43
N 70	02 49	04 15	05 19	19 05	18 54	18 41	18 24
68	03 10	04 25	05 22	19 09	19 03	18 58	18 51
66	03 26	04 33	05 25	19 13	19 12	19 12	19 13
64	03 38	04 39	05 28	19 16	19 19	19 23	19 30
62	03 49	04 45	05 30	19 18	19 25	19 33	19 44
60	03 58	04 49	05 32	19 21	19 30	19 41	19 56
N 58	04 05	04 54	05 33	19 23	19 35	19 49	20 06
56	04 12	04 57	05 35	19 25	19 39	19 55	20 15
54	04 18	05 00	05 36	19 27	19 43	20 01	20 23
52	04 23	05 03	05 37	19 28	19 46	20 06	20 31
50	04 27	05 06	05 38	19 30	19 49	20 11	20 37
45	04 36	05 11	05 40	19 33	19 56	20 22	20 51
N 40	04 43	05 15	05 42	19 35	20 02	20 31	21 03
35	04 49	05 19	05 44	19 38	20 07	20 38	21 13
30	04 53	05 21	05 45	19 40	20 11	20 45	21 22
20	05 00	05 26	05 48	19 43	20 19	20 56	21 37
N 10	05 04	05 29	05 50	19 47	20 26	21 07	21 50
0	05 07	05 31	05 51	19 50	20 32	21 16	22 03
S 10	05 08	05 32	05 53	19 53	20 38	21 26	22 16
20	05 07	05 33	05 55	19 56	20 45	21 36	22 29
30	05 05	05 32	05 56	20 00	20 53	21 48	22 45
35	05 03	05 32	05 57	20 02	20 58	21 55	22 54
40	05 00	05 31	05 58	20 04	21 03	22 03	23 05
45	04 56	05 30	05 59	20 07	21 09	22 12	23 17
S 50	04 51	05 29	06 01	20 11	21 17	22 24	23 32
52	04 48	05 28	06 01	20 12	21 20	22 29	23 39
54	04 46	05 27	06 02	20 14	21 24	22 35	23 47
56	04 42	05 26	06 03	20 16	21 28	22 41	23 56
58	04 39	05 24	06 03	20 18	21 32	22 49	24 06
S 60	04 34	05 23	06 04	20 20	21 38	22 57	24 17

Lat.	Sunset	Twilight Civil	Twilight Naut.	Moonset 16	17	18	19
°	h m	h m	h m	h m	h m	h m	h m
N 72	18 32	19 42	21 22	07 51	09 37	11 30	13 42
N 70	18 28	19 31	20 55	07 48	09 27	11 10	13 03
68	18 25	19 22	20 36	07 46	09 19	10 54	12 36
66	18 22	19 14	20 20	07 45	09 12	10 42	12 16
64	18 20	19 08	20 08	07 43	09 06	10 32	11 59
62	18 18	19 03	19 58	07 42	09 01	10 23	11 46
60	18 16	18 58	19 49	07 41	08 57	10 15	11 35
N 58	18 15	18 54	19 42	07 40	08 54	10 09	11 25
56	18 13	18 51	19 36	07 39	08 50	10 03	11 17
54	18 12	18 48	19 30	07 38	08 47	09 58	11 09
52	18 11	18 45	19 25	07 37	08 45	09 53	11 02
50	18 10	18 42	19 21	07 37	08 42	09 49	10 56
45	18 08	18 37	19 12	07 35	08 37	09 39	10 43
N 40	18 06	18 33	19 05	07 34	08 32	09 32	10 33
35	18 05	18 30	19 00	07 33	08 29	09 25	10 23
30	18 03	18 27	18 55	07 32	08 25	09 20	10 15
20	18 01	18 23	18 49	07 31	08 20	09 10	10 02
N 10	17 59	18 20	18 45	07 29	08 15	09 01	09 50
0	17 58	18 18	18 43	07 28	08 10	08 53	09 38
S 10	17 56	18 17	18 42	07 27	08 05	08 45	09 27
20	17 55	18 17	18 42	07 25	08 00	08 36	09 15
30	17 53	18 17	18 45	07 24	07 54	08 27	09 02
35	17 52	18 18	18 47	07 23	07 51	08 21	08 54
40	17 52	18 19	18 50	07 22	07 47	08 15	08 45
45	17 51	18 20	18 54	07 20	07 43	08 07	08 35
S 50	17 49	18 22	18 59	07 19	07 38	07 59	08 22
52	17 49	18 22	19 02	07 18	07 36	07 55	08 16
54	17 48	18 23	19 05	07 18	07 33	07 50	08 10
56	17 48	18 25	19 08	07 17	07 30	07 45	08 03
58	17 47	18 26	19 12	07 16	07 27	07 40	07 55
S 60	17 46	18 28	19 17	07 15	07 24	07 34	07 46

Day	SUN Eqn. of Time 00h	SUN Eqn. of Time 12h	Mer. Pass.	MOON Mer. Pass. Upper	MOON Mer. Pass. Lower	Age	Phase
d	m s	m s	h m	h m	h m	d	%
16	04 53	05 04	11 55	01 18	13 39	17	95
17	05 15	05 25	11 55	02 00	14 21	18	90
18	05 36	05 47	11 54	02 42	15 05	19	84

© British Crown Copyright 2018. All rights reserved.

UT	ARIES GHA	VENUS −3.9 GHA	Dec	MARS +1.8 GHA	Dec	JUPITER −2.1 GHA	Dec	SATURN +0.4 GHA	Dec	STARS Name	SHA	Dec
d h	° ′	° ′	° ′	° ′	° ′	° ′	° ′	° ′	° ′		° ′	° ′
19 00	357 36.6	172 04.6	S 1 03.6	186 09.5	N 4 48.3	102 02.0	S22 28.8	72 31.6	S22 30.7	Acamar	315 14.8	S40 13.4
01	12 39.1	187 04.2	04.9	201 10.5	47.7	117 04.1	28.9	87 34.1	30.7	Achernar	335 23.0	S57 08.2
02	27 41.5	202 03.9	06.2	216 11.5	47.0	132 06.3	28.9	102 36.5	30.7	Acrux	173 05.2	S63 12.4
03	42 44.0	217 03.5 ..	07.4	231 12.5 ..	46.4	147 08.5 ..	28.9	117 39.0 ..	30.7	Adhara	255 09.3	S28 59.7
04	57 46.5	232 03.1	08.7	246 13.5	45.8	162 10.6	29.0	132 41.5	30.7	Aldebaran	290 44.4	N16 32.8
05	72 48.9	247 02.8	10.0	261 14.5	45.1	177 12.8	29.0	147 43.9	30.7			
06	87 51.4	262 02.4	S 1 11.3	276 15.5	N 4 44.5	192 15.0	S22 29.0	162 46.4	S22 30.7	Alioth	166 17.4	N55 51.4
07	102 53.9	277 02.0	12.5	291 16.5	43.9	207 17.1	29.1	177 48.8	30.7	Alkaid	152 55.9	N49 13.2
T 08	117 56.3	292 01.7	13.8	306 17.5	43.2	222 19.3	29.1	192 51.3	30.7	Alnair	27 37.9	S46 52.0
H 09	132 58.8	307 01.3 ..	15.1	321 18.5 ..	42.6	237 21.5 ..	29.1	207 53.7 ..	30.7	Alnilam	275 42.0	S 1 11.3
U 10	148 01.2	322 00.9	16.4	336 19.5	41.9	252 23.6	29.2	222 56.2	30.7	Alphard	217 52.2	S 8 44.5
R 11	163 03.7	337 00.6	17.6	351 20.5	41.3	267 25.8	29.2	237 58.7	30.7			
S 12	178 06.2	352 00.2	S 1 18.9	6 21.4	N 4 40.7	282 28.0	S22 29.2	253 01.1	S22 30.7	Alphecca	126 07.6	N26 39.3
D 13	193 08.6	6 59.8	20.2	21 22.4	40.0	297 30.1	29.3	268 03.6	30.7	Alpheratz	357 38.7	N29 11.9
A 14	208 11.1	21 59.5	21.5	36 23.4	39.4	312 32.3	29.3	283 06.0	30.7	Altair	62 03.9	N 8 55.4
Y 15	223 13.6	36 59.1 ..	22.7	51 24.4 ..	38.8	327 34.5 ..	29.3	298 08.5 ..	30.7	Ankaa	353 11.0	S42 11.9
16	238 16.0	51 58.7	24.0	66 25.4	38.1	342 36.6	29.4	313 11.0	30.7	Antares	112 21.1	S26 28.4
17	253 18.5	66 58.4	25.3	81 26.4	37.5	357 38.8	29.4	328 13.4	30.7			
18	268 21.0	81 58.0	S 1 26.6	96 27.4	N 4 36.8	12 41.0	S22 29.4	343 15.9	S22 30.7	Arcturus	145 52.1	N19 05.1
19	283 23.4	96 57.6	27.8	111 28.4	36.2	27 43.1	29.5	358 18.3	30.7	Atria	107 19.2	S69 03.8
20	298 25.9	111 57.3	29.1	126 29.4	35.6	42 45.3	29.5	13 20.8	30.7	Avior	234 16.7	S59 34.1
21	313 28.4	126 56.9 ..	30.4	141 30.4 ..	34.9	57 47.5 ..	29.5	28 23.2 ..	30.7	Bellatrix	278 27.4	N 6 22.0
22	328 30.8	141 56.5	31.7	156 31.4	34.3	72 49.6	29.6	43 25.7	30.7	Betelgeuse	270 56.7	N 7 24.6
23	343 33.3	156 56.1	32.9	171 32.4	33.6	87 51.8	29.6	58 28.2	30.7			
20 00	358 35.7	171 55.8	S 1 34.2	186 33.4	N 4 33.0	102 53.9	S22 29.6	73 30.6	S22 30.7	Canopus	263 54.3	S52 42.1
01	13 38.2	186 55.4	35.5	201 34.3	32.4	117 56.1	29.7	88 33.1	30.7	Capella	280 28.1	N46 00.8
02	28 40.7	201 55.0	36.8	216 35.3	31.7	132 58.3	29.7	103 35.5	30.8	Deneb	49 28.3	N45 21.3
03	43 43.1	216 54.7 ..	38.0	231 36.3 ..	31.1	148 00.4 ..	29.7	118 38.0 ..	30.8	Denebola	182 29.6	N14 27.9
04	58 45.6	231 54.3	39.3	246 37.3	30.4	163 02.6	29.8	133 40.4	30.8	Diphda	348 51.3	S17 52.7
05	73 48.1	246 53.9	40.6	261 38.3	29.8	178 04.8	29.8	148 42.9	30.8			
06	88 50.5	261 53.6	S 1 41.9	276 39.3	N 4 29.2	193 06.9	S22 29.8	163 45.4	S22 30.8	Dubhe	193 47.1	N61 38.8
07	103 53.0	276 53.2	43.1	291 40.3	28.5	208 09.1	29.9	178 47.8	30.8	Elnath	278 07.2	N28 37.3
08	118 55.5	291 52.8	44.4	306 41.3	27.9	223 11.2	29.9	193 50.3	30.8	Eltanin	90 44.1	N51 29.6
F 09	133 57.9	306 52.5 ..	45.7	321 42.3 ..	27.3	238 13.4 ..	29.9	208 52.7 ..	30.8	Enif	33 42.7	N 9 58.1
R 10	149 00.4	321 52.1	47.0	336 43.3	26.6	253 15.6	30.0	223 55.2	30.8	Fomalhaut	15 18.9	S29 31.1
I 11	164 02.9	336 51.7	48.2	351 44.3	26.0	268 17.7	30.0	238 57.6	30.8			
D 12	179 05.3	351 51.4	S 1 49.5	6 45.3	N 4 25.3	283 19.9	S22 30.0	254 00.1	S22 30.8	Gacrux	171 56.7	S57 13.3
A 13	194 07.8	6 51.0	50.8	21 46.3	24.7	298 22.0	30.1	269 02.5	30.8	Gienah	175 48.2	S17 38.8
Y 14	209 10.2	21 50.6	52.1	36 47.2	24.1	313 24.2	30.1	284 05.0	30.8	Hadar	148 42.4	S60 28.0
15	224 12.7	36 50.2 ..	53.3	51 48.2 ..	23.4	328 26.4 ..	30.1	299 07.4 ..	30.8	Hamal	327 55.7	N23 33.2
16	239 15.2	51 49.9	54.6	66 49.2	22.8	343 28.5	30.2	314 09.9	30.8	Kaus Aust.	83 38.1	S34 22.5
17	254 17.6	66 49.5	55.9	81 50.2	22.1	358 30.7	30.2	329 12.3	30.8			
18	269 20.1	81 49.1	S 1 57.2	96 51.2	N 4 21.5	13 32.8	S22 30.3	344 14.8	S22 30.8	Kochab	137 20.9	N74 04.8
19	284 22.6	96 48.8	58.4	111 52.2	20.9	28 35.0	30.3	359 17.3	30.8	Markab	13 33.8	N15 18.7
20	299 25.0	111 48.4	1 59.7	126 53.2	20.2	43 37.1	30.3	14 19.7	30.8	Menkar	314 10.4	N 4 10.0
21	314 27.5	126 48.0 ..	2 01.0	141 54.2 ..	19.6	58 39.3 ..	30.4	29 22.2 ..	30.8	Menkent	148 02.9	S36 27.8
22	329 30.0	141 47.7	02.3	156 55.2	18.9	73 41.5	30.4	44 24.6	30.8	Miaplacidus	221 39.6	S69 47.6
23	344 32.4	156 47.3	03.5	171 56.2	18.3	88 43.6	30.4	59 27.1	30.8			
21 00	359 34.9	171 46.9	S 2 04.8	186 57.2	N 4 17.7	103 45.8	S22 30.5	74 29.5	S22 30.8	Mirfak	308 33.9	N49 55.6
01	14 37.3	186 46.6	06.1	201 58.2	17.0	118 47.9	30.5	89 32.0	30.8	Nunki	75 52.9	S26 16.2
02	29 39.8	201 46.2	07.4	216 59.2	16.4	133 50.1	30.5	104 34.4	30.8	Peacock	53 12.1	S56 40.4
03	44 42.3	216 45.8 ..	08.6	232 00.1 ..	15.7	148 52.2 ..	30.6	119 36.9 ..	30.8	Pollux	243 22.7	N27 58.6
04	59 44.7	231 45.4	09.9	247 01.1	15.1	163 54.4	30.6	134 39.3	30.8	Procyon	244 55.4	N 5 10.5
05	74 47.2	246 45.1	11.2	262 02.1	14.5	178 56.5	30.6	149 41.8	30.8			
06	89 49.7	261 44.7	S 2 12.5	277 03.1	N 4 13.8	193 58.7	S22 30.7	164 44.2	S22 30.8	Rasalhague	96 02.5	N12 33.1
07	104 52.1	276 44.3	13.7	292 04.1	13.2	209 00.9	30.7	179 46.7	30.8	Regulus	207 39.3	N11 52.4
S 08	119 54.6	291 44.0	15.0	307 05.1	12.5	224 03.0	30.7	194 49.1	30.8	Rigel	281 07.9	S 8 10.7
A 09	134 57.1	306 43.6 ..	16.3	322 06.1 ..	11.9	239 05.2 ..	30.8	209 51.6 ..	30.8	Rigil Kent.	139 46.5	S60 54.9
T 10	149 59.5	321 43.2	17.5	337 07.1	11.2	254 07.3	30.8	224 54.0	30.9	Sabik	102 07.7	S15 44.8
U 11	165 02.0	336 42.8	18.8	352 08.1	10.6	269 09.5	30.8	239 56.5	30.9			
R 12	180 04.5	351 42.5	S 2 20.1	7 09.1	N 4 10.0	284 11.6	S22 30.9	254 58.9	S22 30.9	Schedar	349 35.1	N56 38.6
D 13	195 06.9	6 42.1	21.4	22 10.1	09.3	299 13.8	30.9	270 01.4	30.9	Shaula	96 16.1	S37 07.0
A 14	210 09.4	21 41.7	22.6	37 11.1	08.7	314 15.9	30.9	285 03.8	30.9	Sirius	258 30.0	S16 44.5
Y 15	225 11.8	36 41.4 ..	23.9	52 12.1 ..	08.0	329 18.1 ..	31.0	300 06.3 ..	30.9	Spica	158 27.0	S11 15.6
16	240 14.3	51 41.0	25.2	67 13.1	07.4	344 20.2	31.0	315 08.7	30.9	Suhail	222 49.7	S43 30.5
17	255 16.8	66 40.6	26.5	82 14.0	06.8	359 22.4	31.0	330 11.2	30.9			
18	270 19.2	81 40.2	S 2 27.7	97 15.0	N 4 06.1	14 24.5	S22 31.1	345 13.6	S22 30.9	Vega	80 36.0	N38 48.5
19	285 21.7	96 39.9	29.0	112 16.0	05.5	29 26.7	31.1	0 16.1	30.9	Zuben'ubi	137 00.9	S16 07.2
20	300 24.2	111 39.5	30.3	127 17.0	04.8	44 28.8	31.1	15 18.5	30.9		SHA	Mer.Pass.
21	315 26.6	126 39.1 ..	31.6	142 18.0 ..	04.2	59 31.0 ..	31.2	30 21.0 ..	30.9		° ′	h m
22	330 29.1	141 38.8	32.8	157 19.0	03.6	74 33.1	31.2	45 23.4	30.9	Venus	173 20.0	12 33
23	345 31.6	156 38.4	34.1	172 20.0	02.9	89 35.3	31.3	60 25.9	30.9	Mars	187 57.6	11 33
	h m									Jupiter	104 18.2	17 06
Mer.Pass.	0 05.6	v −0.4	d 1.3	v 1.0	d 0.6	v 2.2	d 0.0	v 2.5	d 0.0	Saturn	74 54.9	19 03

© British Crown Copyright 2018. All rights reserved.

UT	SUN GHA	SUN Dec	MOON GHA	v	Dec	d	HP
d h	° ′	° ′	° ′	′	° ′	′	′
19 00	181 29.5	N 1 40.8	309 46.8	13.3	N13 30.1	9.7	55.3
01	196 29.8	39.8	324 19.1	13.2	13 39.8	9.6	55.3
02	211 30.0	38.9	338 51.3	13.2	13 49.4	9.6	55.4
03	226 30.2	.. 37.9	353 23.5	13.1	13 59.0	9.6	55.4
04	241 30.4	36.9	7 55.6	13.1	14 08.6	9.5	55.4
05	256 30.7	36.0	22 27.7	12.9	14 18.1	9.4	55.4
06	271 30.9	N 1 35.0	36 59.6	12.9	N14 27.5	9.4	55.4
07	286 31.1	34.0	51 31.5	12.9	14 36.9	9.3	55.5
T 08	301 31.3	33.1	66 03.4	12.8	14 46.2	9.3	55.5
H 09	316 31.6	.. 32.1	80 35.2	12.7	14 55.5	9.2	55.5
U 10	331 31.8	31.1	95 06.9	12.6	15 04.7	9.1	55.5
R 11	346 32.0	30.2	109 38.5	12.6	15 13.8	9.1	55.6
S 12	1 32.2	N 1 29.2	124 10.1	12.5	N15 22.9	9.0	55.6
D 13	16 32.5	28.2	138 41.6	12.4	15 31.9	8.9	55.6
A 14	31 32.7	27.2	153 13.0	12.4	15 40.8	8.9	55.6
Y 15	46 32.9	.. 26.3	167 44.4	12.3	15 49.7	8.8	55.7
16	61 33.1	25.3	182 15.7	12.2	15 58.5	8.8	55.7
17	76 33.3	24.3	196 46.9	12.1	16 07.3	8.6	55.7
18	91 33.6	N 1 23.4	211 18.0	12.1	N16 15.9	8.6	55.7
19	106 33.8	22.4	225 49.1	12.0	16 24.5	8.6	55.8
20	121 34.0	21.4	240 20.1	11.9	16 33.1	8.4	55.8
21	136 34.2	.. 20.5	254 51.0	11.9	16 41.5	8.4	55.8
22	151 34.5	19.5	269 21.9	11.8	16 49.9	8.4	55.8
23	166 34.7	18.5	283 52.7	11.7	16 58.3	8.2	55.9
20 00	181 34.9	N 1 17.6	298 23.4	11.6	N17 06.5	8.2	55.9
01	196 35.1	16.6	312 54.0	11.6	17 14.7	8.1	55.9
02	211 35.4	15.6	327 24.6	11.4	17 22.8	8.0	55.9
03	226 35.6	.. 14.6	341 55.0	11.5	17 30.8	7.9	56.0
04	241 35.8	13.7	356 25.5	11.3	17 38.7	7.9	56.0
05	256 36.0	12.7	10 55.8	11.2	17 46.6	7.8	56.0
06	271 36.2	N 1 11.7	25 26.0	11.2	N17 54.4	7.6	56.0
07	286 36.5	10.8	39 56.2	11.1	18 02.0	7.7	56.1
08	301 36.7	09.8	54 26.3	11.0	18 09.7	7.5	56.1
F 09	316 36.9	.. 08.8	68 56.3	11.0	18 17.2	7.4	56.1
R 10	331 37.1	07.9	83 26.3	10.9	18 24.6	7.4	56.2
I 11	346 37.4	06.9	97 56.2	10.7	18 32.0	7.3	56.2
D 12	1 37.6	N 1 05.9	112 25.9	10.8	N18 39.3	7.2	56.2
A 13	16 37.8	04.9	126 55.7	10.6	18 46.5	7.1	56.2
Y 14	31 38.0	04.0	141 25.3	10.5	18 53.6	7.0	56.3
15	46 38.2	.. 03.0	155 54.8	10.5	19 00.6	6.9	56.3
16	61 38.5	02.0	170 24.3	10.4	19 07.5	6.8	56.3
17	76 38.7	01.1	184 53.7	10.3	19 14.3	6.8	56.4
18	91 38.9	N 1 00.1	199 23.0	10.3	N19 21.1	6.6	56.4
19	106 39.1	0 59.1	213 52.3	10.1	19 27.7	6.6	56.4
20	121 39.4	58.2	228 21.4	10.1	19 34.3	6.4	56.5
21	136 39.6	.. 57.2	242 50.5	10.0	19 40.7	6.4	56.5
22	151 39.8	56.2	257 19.5	10.0	19 47.1	6.2	56.5
23	166 40.0	55.2	271 48.5	9.8	19 53.3	6.2	56.5
21 00	181 40.3	N 0 54.3	286 17.3	9.8	N19 59.5	6.1	56.6
01	196 40.5	53.3	300 46.1	9.7	20 05.6	5.9	56.6
02	211 40.7	52.3	315 14.8	9.6	20 11.5	5.9	56.6
03	226 40.9	.. 51.4	329 43.4	9.5	20 17.4	5.8	56.7
04	241 41.1	50.4	344 11.9	9.4	20 23.2	5.6	56.7
05	256 41.4	49.4	358 40.3	9.4	20 28.8	5.6	56.7
06	271 41.6	N 0 48.4	13 08.7	9.3	N20 34.4	5.4	56.8
07	286 41.8	47.5	27 37.0	9.2	20 39.8	5.4	56.8
S 08	301 42.0	46.5	42 05.2	9.2	20 45.2	5.2	56.8
A 09	316 42.2	.. 45.5	56 33.4	9.0	20 50.4	5.1	56.9
T 10	331 42.5	44.6	71 01.4	9.0	20 55.5	5.0	56.9
U 11	346 42.7	43.6	85 29.4	8.9	21 00.5	4.9	56.9
R 12	1 42.9	N 0 42.6	99 57.3	8.9	N21 05.4	4.8	57.0
D 13	16 43.1	41.6	114 25.2	8.7	21 10.2	4.7	57.0
A 14	31 43.4	40.7	128 52.9	8.7	21 14.9	4.6	57.0
Y 15	46 43.6	.. 39.7	143 20.6	8.6	21 19.5	4.4	57.1
16	61 43.8	38.7	157 48.2	8.5	21 23.9	4.4	57.1
17	76 44.0	37.8	172 15.7	8.5	21 28.3	4.2	57.1
18	91 44.2	N 0 36.8	186 43.2	8.4	N21 32.5	4.1	57.2
19	106 44.5	35.8	201 10.6	8.3	21 36.6	4.0	57.2
20	121 44.7	34.8	215 37.9	8.2	21 40.6	3.8	57.2
21	136 44.9	.. 33.9	230 05.1	8.2	21 44.4	3.8	57.3
22	151 45.1	32.9	244 32.3	8.0	21 48.2	3.6	57.3
23	166 45.4	31.9	258 59.3	8.1	N21 51.8	3.5	57.3
	SD 16.0	d 1.0	SD 15.1		15.3		15.5

Lat.	Twilight Naut.	Civil	Sunrise	Moonrise 19	20	21	22
°	h m	h m	h m	h m	h m	h m	h m
N 72	02 43	04 18	05 28	17 43	▭	▭	▭
N 70	03 06	04 28	05 31	18 24	17 49	▭	▭
68	03 24	04 36	05 33	18 51	18 43	18 28	▭
66	03 37	04 43	05 35	19 13	19 16	19 27	19 57
64	03 49	04 48	05 36	19 30	19 41	20 01	20 40
62	03 58	04 53	05 37	19 44	20 00	20 26	21 09
60	04 06	04 57	05 39	19 56	20 16	20 46	21 31
N 58	04 13	05 00	05 40	20 06	20 30	21 02	21 49
56	04 18	05 03	05 41	20 15	20 41	21 16	22 04
54	04 23	05 06	05 41	20 23	20 51	21 28	22 17
52	04 28	05 08	05 42	20 31	21 01	21 39	22 29
50	04 32	05 10	05 43	20 37	21 09	21 49	22 39
45	04 40	05 15	05 44	20 51	21 26	22 09	23 00
N 40	04 46	05 18	05 45	21 03	21 41	22 25	23 17
35	04 51	05 21	05 46	21 13	21 53	22 39	23 32
30	04 55	05 23	05 47	21 22	22 03	22 51	23 45
20	05 01	05 26	05 48	21 37	22 22	23 11	23 45
N 10	05 04	05 28	05 49	21 50	22 38	23 29	24 25
0	05 06	05 30	05 50	22 03	22 53	23 46	24 43
S 10	05 06	05 30	05 51	22 16	23 08	24 03	00 03
20	05 04	05 30	05 52	22 29	23 24	24 21	00 21
30	05 01	05 29	05 53	22 45	23 43	24 42	00 42
35	04 58	05 28	05 53	22 54	23 54	24 55	00 55
40	04 55	05 26	05 53	23 05	24 07	00 07	01 09
45	04 50	05 24	05 54	23 17	24 22	00 22	01 26
S 50	04 44	05 22	05 54	23 32	24 40	00 40	01 46
52	04 41	05 21	05 54	23 39	24 49	00 49	01 56
54	04 38	05 19	05 55	23 47	24 59	00 59	02 08
56	04 34	05 18	05 55	23 56	25 10	01 10	02 20
58	04 30	05 16	05 55	24 06	00 06	01 23	02 35
S 60	04 25	05 14	05 55	24 17	00 17	01 37	02 53

Lat.	Sunset	Twilight Civil	Naut.	Moonset 19	20	21	22
°	h m	h m	h m	h m	h m	h m	h m
N 72	18 17	19 25	20 59	13 42	▭	▭	▭
N 70	18 14	19 16	20 37	13 03	15 19	▭	▭
68	18 12	19 08	20 20	12 36	14 25	16 29	▭
66	18 11	19 02	20 07	12 16	13 53	15 31	16 57
64	18 09	18 57	19 56	11 59	13 29	14 57	16 14
62	18 08	18 53	19 47	11 46	13 10	14 32	15 45
60	18 07	18 49	19 39	11 35	12 55	14 13	15 23
N 58	18 06	18 45	19 33	11 25	12 42	13 57	15 05
56	18 05	18 42	19 27	11 17	12 31	13 43	14 50
54	18 05	18 40	19 22	11 09	12 21	13 32	14 37
52	18 04	18 38	19 18	11 02	12 12	13 21	14 26
50	18 03	18 36	19 14	10 56	12 05	13 12	14 16
45	18 02	18 31	19 06	10 43	11 48	12 52	13 54
N 40	18 01	18 28	19 00	10 33	11 34	12 36	13 37
35	18 00	18 26	18 55	10 23	11 23	12 23	13 23
30	18 00	18 23	18 51	10 15	11 13	12 11	13 10
20	17 58	18 20	18 46	10 02	10 56	11 52	12 49
N 10	17 58	18 18	18 43	09 50	10 41	11 34	12 30
0	17 57	18 17	18 41	09 38	10 27	11 18	12 13
S 10	17 56	18 17	18 41	09 27	10 13	11 02	11 56
20	17 56	18 17	18 43	09 15	09 58	10 45	11 37
30	17 55	18 19	18 47	09 02	09 41	10 25	11 15
35	17 55	18 20	18 49	08 54	09 31	10 14	11 03
40	17 54	18 21	18 53	08 45	09 21	10 00	10 48
45	17 54	18 23	18 58	08 35	09 06	09 45	10 31
S 50	17 54	18 26	19 04	08 22	08 50	09 26	10 10
52	17 54	18 27	19 07	08 16	08 43	09 17	10 00
54	17 54	18 29	19 11	08 10	08 35	09 06	09 49
56	17 53	18 31	19 14	08 03	08 25	08 55	09 36
58	17 53	18 33	19 19	07 55	08 15	08 42	09 21
S 60	17 53	18 35	19 24	07 46	08 03	08 27	09 03

Day	SUN Eqn. of Time 00h	12h	Mer. Pass.	MOON Mer. Pass. Upper	Lower	Age	Phase
d	m s	m s	h m	h m	h m	d	%
19	05 58	06 08	11 54	03 27	15 51	20	76
20	06 19	06 30	11 54	04 15	16 40	21	67
21	06 41	06 51	11 53	05 06	17 32	22	57

© British Crown Copyright 2018. All rights reserved.

UT	ARIES GHA	VENUS −3.9 GHA	VENUS Dec	MARS +1.8 GHA	MARS Dec	JUPITER −2.1 GHA	JUPITER Dec	SATURN +0.4 GHA	SATURN Dec	STARS Name	SHA	Dec
22 00	0 34.0	171 38.0	S 2 35.4	187 21.0	N 4 02.3	104 37.4	S22 31.3	75 28.3	S22 30.9	Acamar	315 14.8	S40 13.4
01	15 36.5	186 37.6	36.6	202 22.0	01.6	119 39.6	31.3	90 30.8	30.9	Achernar	335 23.0	S57 08.2
02	30 39.0	201 37.3	37.9	217 23.0	01.0	134 41.7	31.4	105 33.2	30.9	Acrux	173 05.2	S63 12.4
03	45 41.4	216 36.9	.. 39.2	232 24.0	4 00.4	149 43.9	.. 31.4	120 35.7	.. 30.9	Adhara	255 09.3	S28 59.7
04	60 43.9	231 36.5	40.5	247 25.0	3 59.7	164 46.0	31.4	135 38.1	30.9	Aldebaran	290 44.3	N16 32.8
05	75 46.3	246 36.2	41.7	262 26.0	59.1	179 48.2	31.5	150 40.5	30.9			
06	90 48.8	261 35.8	S 2 43.0	277 26.9	N 3 58.4	194 50.3	S22 31.5	165 43.0	S22 30.9	Alioth	166 17.4	N55 51.4
07	105 51.3	276 35.4	44.3	292 27.9	57.8	209 52.5	31.5	180 45.4	30.9	Alkaid	152 55.9	N49 13.2
08	120 53.7	291 35.0	45.6	307 28.9	57.1	224 54.6	31.6	195 47.9	30.9	Alnair	27 37.9	S46 52.0
S 09	135 56.2	306 34.7	.. 46.8	322 29.9	56.5	239 56.8	.. 31.6	210 50.3	.. 30.9	Alnilam	275 42.0	S 1 11.3
U 10	150 58.7	321 34.3	48.1	337 30.9	55.9	254 58.9	31.6	225 52.8	30.9	Alphard	217 52.1	S 8 44.5
N 11	166 01.1	336 33.9	49.4	352 31.9	55.2	270 01.1	31.7	240 55.2	30.9			
D 12	181 03.6	351 33.5	S 2 50.6	7 32.9	N 3 54.6	285 03.2	S22 31.7	255 57.7	S22 30.9	Alphecca	126 07.6	N26 39.3
A 13	196 06.1	6 33.2	51.9	22 33.9	53.9	300 05.4	31.7	271 00.1	30.9	Alpheratz	357 38.7	N29 12.0
Y 14	211 08.5	21 32.8	53.2	37 34.9	53.3	315 07.5	31.8	286 02.6	30.9	Altair	62 03.9	N 8 55.4
15	226 11.0	36 32.4	.. 54.5	52 35.9	.. 52.7	330 09.7	.. 31.8	301 05.0	.. 30.9	Ankaa	353 11.0	S42 11.9
16	241 13.5	51 32.1	55.7	67 36.9	52.0	345 11.8	31.8	316 07.4	30.9	Antares	112 21.1	S26 28.4
17	256 15.9	66 31.7	57.0	82 37.9	51.4	0 13.9	31.9	331 09.9	30.9			
18	271 18.4	81 31.3	S 2 58.3	97 38.9	N 3 50.7	15 16.1	S22 31.9	346 12.3	S22 30.9	Arcturus	145 52.1	N19 05.1
19	286 20.8	96 30.9	2 59.6	112 39.9	50.1	30 18.2	31.9	1 14.8	30.9	Atria	107 19.2	S69 03.8
20	301 23.3	111 30.6	3 00.8	127 40.9	49.4	45 20.4	32.0	16 17.2	30.9	Avior	234 16.7	S59 34.1
21	316 25.8	126 30.2	.. 02.1	142 41.8	.. 48.8	60 22.5	.. 32.0	31 19.7	.. 30.9	Bellatrix	278 27.4	N 6 22.0
22	331 28.2	141 29.8	03.4	157 42.8	48.2	75 24.7	32.1	46 22.1	30.9	Betelgeuse	270 56.7	N 7 24.6
23	346 30.7	156 29.4	04.6	172 43.8	47.5	90 26.8	32.1	61 24.6	30.9			
23 00	1 33.2	171 29.1	S 3 05.9	187 44.8	N 3 46.9	105 28.9	S22 32.1	76 27.0	S22 30.9	Canopus	263 54.3	S52 42.1
01	16 35.6	186 28.7	07.2	202 45.8	46.2	120 31.1	32.2	91 29.4	30.9	Capella	280 28.0	N46 00.8
02	31 38.1	201 28.3	08.5	217 46.8	45.6	135 33.2	32.2	106 31.9	30.9	Deneb	49 28.3	N45 21.3
03	46 40.6	216 27.9	.. 09.7	232 47.8	.. 44.9	150 35.4	.. 32.2	121 34.3	.. 31.0	Denebola	182 29.6	N14 27.9
04	61 43.0	231 27.6	11.0	247 48.8	44.3	165 37.5	32.3	136 36.8	31.0	Diphda	348 51.3	S17 52.7
05	76 45.5	246 27.2	12.3	262 49.8	43.7	180 39.7	32.3	151 39.2	31.0			
06	91 47.9	261 26.8	S 3 13.5	277 50.8	N 3 43.0	195 41.8	S22 32.3	166 41.7	S22 31.0	Dubhe	193 47.1	N61 38.8
07	106 50.4	276 26.4	14.8	292 51.8	42.4	210 43.9	32.4	181 44.1	31.0	Elnath	278 07.2	N28 37.3
08	121 52.9	291 26.1	16.1	307 52.8	41.7	225 46.1	32.4	196 46.5	31.0	Eltanin	90 44.2	N51 29.6
M 09	136 55.3	306 25.7	.. 17.3	322 53.8	.. 41.1	240 48.2	.. 32.4	211 49.0	.. 31.0	Enif	33 42.7	N 9 58.1
O 10	151 57.8	321 25.3	18.6	337 54.8	40.4	255 50.4	32.5	226 51.4	31.0	Fomalhaut	15 18.9	S29 31.1
N 11	167 00.3	336 24.9	19.9	352 55.7	39.8	270 52.5	32.5	241 53.9	31.0			
D 12	182 02.7	351 24.6	S 3 21.2	7 56.7	N 3 39.2	285 54.6	S22 32.5	256 56.3	S22 31.0	Gacrux	171 56.7	S57 13.2
A 13	197 05.2	6 24.2	22.4	22 57.7	38.5	300 56.8	32.6	271 58.7	31.0	Gienah	175 48.2	S17 38.8
Y 14	212 07.7	21 23.8	23.7	37 58.7	37.9	315 58.9	32.6	287 01.2	31.0	Hadar	148 42.4	S60 28.0
15	227 10.1	36 23.4	.. 25.0	52 59.7	.. 37.2	331 01.1	.. 32.6	302 03.6	.. 31.0	Hamal	327 55.6	N23 33.2
16	242 12.6	51 23.1	26.2	68 00.7	36.6	346 03.2	32.7	317 06.1	31.0	Kaus Aust.	83 38.1	S34 22.5
17	257 15.1	66 22.7	27.5	83 01.7	35.9	1 05.3	32.7	332 08.5	31.0			
18	272 17.5	81 22.3	S 3 28.8	98 02.7	N 3 35.3	16 07.5	S22 32.8	347 10.9	S22 31.0	Kochab	137 20.9	N74 04.8
19	287 20.0	96 21.9	30.0	113 03.7	34.7	31 09.6	32.8	2 13.4	31.0	Markab	13 33.8	N15 18.8
20	302 22.4	111 21.6	31.3	128 04.7	34.0	46 11.8	32.8	17 15.8	31.0	Menkar	314 10.3	N 4 10.0
21	317 24.9	126 21.2	.. 32.6	143 05.7	.. 33.4	61 13.9	.. 32.9	32 18.3	.. 31.0	Menkent	148 02.9	S36 27.8
22	332 27.4	141 20.8	33.9	158 06.7	32.7	76 16.0	32.9	47 20.7	31.0	Miaplacidus	221 39.5	S69 47.6
23	347 29.8	156 20.4	35.1	173 07.7	32.1	91 18.2	32.9	62 23.1	31.0			
24 00	2 32.3	171 20.0	S 3 36.4	188 08.7	N 3 31.4	106 20.3	S22 33.0	77 25.6	S22 31.0	Mirfak	308 33.9	N49 55.6
01	17 34.8	186 19.7	37.7	203 09.7	30.8	121 22.4	33.0	92 28.0	31.0	Nunki	75 52.9	S26 16.2
02	32 37.2	201 19.3	38.9	218 10.6	30.2	136 24.6	33.0	107 30.5	31.0	Peacock	53 12.2	S56 40.4
03	47 39.7	216 18.9	.. 40.2	233 11.6	.. 29.5	151 26.7	.. 33.1	122 32.9	.. 31.0	Pollux	243 22.7	N27 58.6
04	62 42.2	231 18.5	41.5	248 12.6	28.9	166 28.8	33.1	137 35.3	31.0	Procyon	244 55.4	N 5 10.5
05	77 44.6	246 18.2	42.7	263 13.6	28.2	181 31.0	33.1	152 37.8	31.0			
06	92 47.1	261 17.8	S 3 44.0	278 14.6	N 3 27.6	196 33.1	S22 33.2	167 40.2	S22 31.0	Rasalhague	96 02.5	N12 33.1
07	107 49.6	276 17.4	45.3	293 15.6	26.9	211 35.3	33.2	182 42.6	31.0	Regulus	207 39.2	N11 52.4
T 08	122 52.0	291 17.0	46.5	308 16.6	26.3	226 37.4	33.2	197 45.1	31.0	Rigel	281 07.9	S 8 10.7
U 09	137 54.5	306 16.6	.. 47.8	323 17.6	.. 25.6	241 39.5	.. 33.3	212 47.5	.. 31.0	Rigil Kent.	139 46.5	S60 54.9
E 10	152 56.9	321 16.3	49.1	338 18.6	25.0	256 41.7	33.3	227 50.0	31.0	Sabik	102 07.7	S15 44.8
S 11	167 59.4	336 15.9	50.3	353 19.6	24.4	271 43.8	33.4	242 52.4	31.0			
D 12	183 01.9	351 15.5	S 3 51.6	8 20.6	N 3 23.7	286 45.9	S22 33.4	257 54.8	S22 31.0	Schedar	349 35.1	N56 38.6
A 13	198 04.3	6 15.1	52.9	23 21.6	23.1	301 48.1	33.4	272 57.3	31.0	Shaula	96 16.1	S37 07.0
Y 14	213 06.8	21 14.8	54.2	38 22.6	22.4	316 50.2	33.5	287 59.7	31.0	Sirius	258 30.0	S16 44.5
15	228 09.3	36 14.4	.. 55.4	53 23.6	.. 21.8	331 52.3	.. 33.5	303 02.1	.. 31.0	Spica	158 27.0	S11 15.6
16	243 11.7	51 14.0	56.7	68 24.6	21.1	346 54.5	33.5	318 04.6	31.0	Suhail	222 49.6	S43 30.5
17	258 14.2	66 13.6	58.0	83 25.5	20.5	1 56.6	33.6	333 07.0	31.0			
18	273 16.7	81 13.2	S 3 59.2	98 26.5	N 3 19.9	16 58.7	S22 33.6	348 09.4	S22 31.0	Vega	80 36.0	N38 48.5
19	288 19.1	96 12.9	4 00.5	113 27.5	19.2	32 00.9	33.6	3 11.9	31.0	Zuben'ubi	137 00.9	S16 07.2
20	303 21.6	111 12.5	01.8	128 28.5	18.6	47 03.0	33.7	18 14.3	31.0			
21	318 24.1	126 12.1	.. 03.0	143 29.5	.. 17.9	62 05.1	.. 33.7	33 16.8	.. 31.0		SHA	Mer. Pass.
22	333 26.5	141 11.7	04.3	158 30.5	17.3	77 07.2	33.7	48 19.2	31.0	Venus	169 55.9	12 34
23	348 29.0	156 11.3	05.6	173 31.5	16.6	92 09.4	33.8	63 21.6	31.0	Mars	186 11.7	11 28
	h m									Jupiter	103 55.8	16 56
Mer. Pass.	23 49.9	v −0.4	d 1.3	v 1.0	d 0.6	v 2.1	d 0.0	v 2.4	d 0.0	Saturn	74 53.8	18 51

© British Crown Copyright 2018. All rights reserved.

UT	SUN GHA	SUN Dec	MOON GHA	v	MOON Dec	d	HP
d h	° ′	° ′	° ′	′	° ′	′	′
22 00	181 45.6	N 0 31.0	273 26.4	7.9	N21 55.3	3.4	57.4
01	196 45.8	30.0	287 53.3	7.9	21 58.7	3.3	57.4
02	211 46.0	29.0	302 20.2	7.8	22 02.0	3.1	57.5
03	226 46.2	.. 28.0	316 47.0	7.7	22 05.1	3.0	57.5
04	241 46.5	27.1	331 13.7	7.7	22 08.1	2.9	57.5
05	256 46.7	26.1	345 40.4	7.6	22 11.0	2.7	57.5
06	271 46.9	N 0 25.1	0 07.0	7.5	N22 13.7	2.7	57.6
07	286 47.1	24.2	14 33.5	7.5	22 16.4	2.5	57.6
S 08	301 47.3	23.2	29 00.0	7.4	22 18.9	2.3	57.6
U 09	316 47.6	.. 22.2	43 26.4	7.3	22 21.2	2.3	57.7
N 10	331 47.8	21.2	57 52.7	7.3	22 23.5	2.1	57.7
D 11	346 48.0	20.3	72 19.0	7.2	22 25.6	2.0	57.7
A 12	1 48.2	N 0 19.3	86 45.2	7.1	N22 27.6	1.8	57.8
Y 13	16 48.4	18.3	101 11.3	7.1	22 29.4	1.7	57.8
14	31 48.7	17.3	115 37.4	7.1	22 31.1	1.6	57.9
15	46 48.9	.. 16.4	130 03.5	6.9	22 32.7	1.4	57.9
16	61 49.1	15.4	144 29.4	6.9	22 34.1	1.3	57.9
17	76 49.3	14.4	158 55.3	6.9	22 35.4	1.2	58.0
18	91 49.5	N 0 13.5	173 21.2	6.8	N22 36.6	1.0	58.0
19	106 49.8	12.5	187 47.0	6.7	22 37.6	0.9	58.0
20	121 50.0	11.5	202 12.7	6.7	22 38.5	0.8	58.1
21	136 50.2	.. 10.5	216 38.4	6.7	22 39.3	0.6	58.1
22	151 50.4	09.6	231 04.1	6.5	22 39.9	0.5	58.1
23	166 50.6	08.6	245 29.6	6.6	22 40.4	0.3	58.2
23 00	181 50.9	N 0 07.6	259 55.2	6.5	N22 40.7	0.2	58.2
01	196 51.1	06.6	274 20.7	6.4	22 40.9	0.0	58.2
02	211 51.3	05.7	288 46.1	6.4	22 40.9	0.1	58.3
03	226 51.5	.. 04.7	303 11.5	6.3	22 40.8	0.2	58.3
04	241 51.7	03.7	317 36.8	6.3	22 40.6	0.4	58.4
05	256 52.0	02.8	332 02.1	6.3	22 40.2	0.5	58.4
06	271 52.2	N 0 01.8	346 27.4	6.2	N22 39.7	0.7	58.4
07	286 52.4	N 00.8	0 52.6	6.1	22 39.0	0.8	58.5
M 08	301 52.6	S 00.2	15 17.7	6.2	22 38.2	0.9	58.5
O 09	316 52.8	.. 01.1	29 42.9	6.1	22 37.3	1.1	58.5
N 10	331 53.1	02.1	44 08.0	6.0	22 36.2	1.3	58.6
D 11	346 53.3	03.1	58 33.0	6.0	22 34.9	1.4	58.6
A 12	1 53.5	S 0 04.1	72 58.0	6.0	N22 33.5	1.5	58.6
Y 13	16 53.7	05.0	87 23.0	6.0	22 32.0	1.7	58.7
14	31 53.9	06.0	101 48.0	5.9	22 30.3	1.8	58.7
15	46 54.2	.. 07.0	116 12.9	5.9	22 28.5	2.0	58.8
16	61 54.4	07.9	130 37.8	5.8	22 26.5	2.1	58.8
17	76 54.6	08.9	145 02.6	5.8	22 24.4	2.3	58.8
18	91 54.8	S 0 09.9	159 27.4	5.8	N22 22.1	2.4	58.9
19	106 55.0	10.9	173 52.2	5.8	22 19.7	2.6	58.9
20	121 55.3	11.8	188 17.0	5.8	22 17.1	2.7	58.9
21	136 55.5	.. 12.8	202 41.8	5.7	22 14.4	2.9	59.0
22	151 55.7	13.8	217 06.5	5.7	22 11.5	3.0	59.0
23	166 55.9	14.8	231 31.2	5.7	22 08.5	3.2	59.0
24 00	181 56.1	S 0 15.7	245 55.9	5.6	N22 05.3	3.3	59.1
01	196 56.3	16.7	260 20.5	5.7	22 02.0	3.5	59.1
02	211 56.6	17.7	274 45.2	5.6	21 58.5	3.6	59.2
03	226 56.8	.. 18.7	289 09.8	5.6	21 54.9	3.8	59.2
04	241 57.0	19.6	303 34.4	5.6	21 51.1	3.9	59.2
05	256 57.2	20.6	317 59.0	5.6	21 47.2	4.1	59.3
06	271 57.4	S 0 21.6	332 23.6	5.6	N21 43.1	4.2	59.3
07	286 57.7	22.5	346 48.2	5.6	21 38.9	4.3	59.3
T 08	301 57.9	23.5	1 12.8	5.6	21 34.6	4.5	59.4
U 09	316 58.1	.. 24.5	15 37.3	5.6	21 30.1	4.7	59.4
E 10	331 58.3	25.5	30 01.9	5.5	21 25.4	4.8	59.4
S 11	346 58.5	26.4	44 26.4	5.5	21 20.6	5.0	59.5
D 12	1 58.7	S 0 27.4	58 50.9	5.6	N21 15.6	5.1	59.5
A 13	16 59.0	28.4	73 15.5	5.5	21 10.5	5.2	59.5
Y 14	31 59.2	29.4	87 40.0	5.6	21 05.3	5.4	59.6
15	46 59.4	.. 30.3	102 04.6	5.5	20 59.9	5.6	59.6
16	61 59.6	31.3	116 29.1	5.5	20 54.3	5.7	59.6
17	76 59.8	32.3	130 53.6	5.6	20 48.6	5.8	59.7
18	92 00.0	S 0 33.3	145 18.2	5.5	N20 42.8	6.0	59.7
19	107 00.3	34.2	159 42.7	5.6	20 36.8	6.1	59.7
20	122 00.5	35.2	174 07.3	5.5	20 30.7	6.3	59.8
21	137 00.7	.. 36.2	188 31.8	5.5	20 24.4	6.4	59.8
22	152 00.9	37.2	202 56.4	5.5	20 18.0	6.6	59.8
23	167 01.1	38.1	217 20.9	5.6	N20 11.4	6.7	59.9
	SD 16.0	d 1.0	SD 15.7		16.0		16.2

Lat.	Twilight Naut.	Twilight Civil	Sunrise	Moonrise 22	Moonrise 23	Moonrise 24	Moonrise 25
°	h m	h m	h m	h m	h m	h m	h m
N 72	03 02	04 33	05 41	☐	☐	☐	22 56
N 70	03 22	04 41	05 42	☐	☐	☐	23 50
68	03 37	04 47	05 43	☐	☐	22 08	24 22
66	03 49	04 53	05 44	19 57	21 07	22 50	24 45
64	03 59	04 57	05 45	20 40	21 46	23 18	25 04
62	04 07	05 01	05 45	21 09	22 14	23 40	25 19
60	04 14	05 04	05 46	21 31	22 35	23 57	25 31
N 58	04 20	05 07	05 46	21 49	22 53	24 12	00 12
56	04 25	05 09	05 46	22 04	23 07	24 24	00 24
54	04 29	05 11	05 47	22 17	23 20	24 35	00 35
52	04 33	05 13	05 47	22 29	23 31	24 45	00 45
50	04 37	05 15	05 47	22 39	23 41	24 54	00 54
45	04 44	05 18	05 48	23 00	24 02	00 02	01 12
N 40	04 49	05 21	05 48	23 17	24 18	00 18	01 27
35	04 54	05 23	05 48	23 32	24 32	00 32	01 39
30	04 57	05 25	05 49	23 45	24 45	00 45	01 50
20	05 01	05 27	05 49	24 06	00 06	01 06	02 09
N 10	05 04	05 28	05 49	24 25	00 25	01 24	02 25
0	05 05	05 29	05 49	24 43	00 43	01 41	02 40
S 10	05 04	05 28	05 49	00 03	01 00	01 58	02 55
20	05 01	05 27	05 49	00 21	01 19	02 16	03 11
30	04 57	05 25	05 49	00 42	01 41	02 37	03 30
35	04 54	05 23	05 49	00 55	01 54	02 49	03 40
40	04 50	05 21	05 48	01 09	02 08	03 03	03 53
45	04 44	05 19	05 48	01 26	02 26	03 20	04 07
S 50	04 37	05 15	05 48	01 46	02 47	03 40	04 25
52	04 34	05 14	05 47	01 56	02 58	03 50	04 33
54	04 30	05 12	05 47	02 08	03 09	04 01	04 42
56	04 26	05 10	05 47	02 20	03 23	04 13	04 53
58	04 21	05 07	05 46	02 35	03 38	04 28	05 04
S 60	04 15	05 05	05 46	02 53	03 57	04 45	05 18

Lat.	Sunset	Twilight Civil	Naut.	Moonset 22	Moonset 23	Moonset 24	Moonset 25
°	h m	h m	h m	h m	h m	h m	h m
N 72	18 01	19 09	20 38	☐	☐	☐	20 08
N 70	18 00	19 01	20 19	☐	☐	☐	19 14
68	18 00	18 55	20 05	☐	☐	18 51	18 40
66	17 59	18 50	19 53	16 57	17 48	18 08	18 16
64	17 59	18 46	19 44	16 14	17 08	17 39	17 56
62	17 58	18 42	19 36	15 45	16 40	17 17	17 40
60	17 58	18 39	19 29	15 23	16 19	16 59	17 27
N 58	17 58	18 37	19 23	15 05	16 01	16 44	17 16
56	17 57	18 34	19 18	14 50	15 47	16 31	17 06
54	17 57	18 32	19 14	14 37	15 34	16 20	16 57
52	17 57	18 31	19 10	14 26	15 23	16 10	16 49
50	17 57	18 29	19 07	14 16	15 13	16 01	16 41
45	17 56	18 26	19 00	13 54	14 52	15 42	16 26
N 40	17 56	18 23	18 55	13 37	14 35	15 27	16 13
35	17 56	18 21	18 51	13 23	14 20	15 14	16 02
30	17 56	18 20	18 47	13 10	14 08	15 02	15 53
20	17 56	18 18	18 43	12 49	13 46	14 42	15 36
N 10	17 56	18 16	18 41	12 30	13 28	14 25	15 22
0	17 56	18 16	18 40	12 13	13 10	14 09	15 08
S 10	17 56	18 17	18 41	11 56	12 53	13 53	14 54
20	17 56	18 18	18 44	11 37	12 34	13 35	14 39
30	17 57	18 20	18 48	11 15	12 12	13 15	14 22
35	17 57	18 22	18 52	11 03	12 00	13 03	14 12
40	17 57	18 24	18 56	10 48	11 45	12 50	14 01
45	17 58	18 27	19 01	10 31	11 28	12 34	13 47
S 50	17 58	18 31	19 09	10 10	11 06	12 14	13 30
52	17 59	18 32	19 12	10 00	10 56	12 04	13 23
54	17 59	18 34	19 16	09 49	10 44	11 53	13 14
56	17 59	18 36	19 21	09 36	10 31	11 41	13 04
58	18 00	18 39	19 26	09 21	10 15	11 27	12 53
S 60	18 00	18 42	19 32	09 03	09 57	11 11	12 40

Day	SUN Eqn. of Time 00h	SUN Eqn. of Time 12h	SUN Mer. Pass.	MOON Mer. Pass. Upper	MOON Mer. Pass. Lower	Age	Phase
d	m s	m s	h m	h m	h m	d	%
22	07 02	07 12	11 53	06 00	18 28	23	46
23	07 23	07 34	11 52	06 56	19 26	24	35
24	07 44	07 55	11 52	07 55	20 24	25	25

© British Crown Copyright 2018. All rights reserved.

UT	ARIES GHA	VENUS −3.9 GHA	Dec	MARS +1.8 GHA	Dec	JUPITER −2.1 GHA	Dec	SATURN +0.5 GHA	Dec	STARS Name	SHA	Dec
25 00	3 31.4	171 11.0	S 4 06.8	188 32.5	N 3 16.0	107 11.5	S22 33.8	78 24.1	S22 31.0	Acamar	315 14.8	S40 13.4
01	18 33.9	186 10.6	.. 08.1	203 33.5	.. 15.3	122 13.6	.. 33.8	93 26.5	.. 31.0	Achernar	335 23.0	S57 08.2
02	33 36.4	201 10.2	.. 09.4	218 34.5	.. 14.7	137 15.8	.. 33.9	108 28.9	.. 31.0	Acrux	173 05.2	S63 12.3
03	48 38.8	216 09.8	.. 10.6	233 35.5	.. 14.1	152 17.9	.. 33.9	123 31.4	.. 31.0	Adhara	255 09.2	S28 59.7
04	63 41.3	231 09.4	.. 11.9	248 36.5	.. 13.4	167 20.0	.. 34.0	138 33.8	.. 31.0	Aldebaran	290 44.3	N16 32.8
05	78 43.8	246 09.0	.. 13.2	263 37.5	.. 12.8	182 22.2	.. 34.0	153 36.2	.. 31.0			
W 06	93 46.2	261 08.7	S 4 14.4	278 38.5	N 3 12.1	197 24.3	S22 34.0	168 38.7	S22 31.0	Alioth	166 17.4	N55 51.4
E 07	108 48.7	276 08.3	.. 15.7	293 39.5	.. 11.5	212 26.4	.. 34.1	183 41.1	.. 31.0	Alkaid	152 55.9	N49 13.2
D 08	123 51.2	291 07.9	.. 16.9	308 40.4	.. 10.8	227 28.5	.. 34.1	198 43.5	.. 31.0	Alnair	27 37.9	S46 52.0
N 09	138 53.6	306 07.5	.. 18.2	323 41.4	.. 10.2	242 30.7	.. 34.1	213 46.0	.. 31.0	Alnilam	275 42.0	S 1 11.3
E 10	153 56.1	321 07.1	.. 19.5	338 42.4	.. 09.5	257 32.8	.. 34.2	228 48.4	.. 31.0	Alphard	217 52.1	S 8 44.5
S 11	168 58.5	336 06.8	.. 20.7	353 43.4	.. 08.9	272 34.9	.. 34.2	243 50.8	.. 31.0			
D 12	184 01.0	351 06.4	S 4 22.0	8 44.4	N 3 08.3	287 37.0	S22 34.2	258 53.3	S22 31.0	Alphecca	126 07.6	N26 39.3
A 13	199 03.5	6 06.0	.. 23.3	23 45.4	.. 07.6	302 39.2	.. 34.3	273 55.7	.. 31.0	Alpheratz	357 38.7	N29 12.0
Y 14	214 05.9	21 05.6	.. 24.5	38 46.4	.. 07.0	317 41.3	.. 34.3	288 58.1	.. 31.0	Altair	62 03.9	N 8 55.4
15	229 08.4	36 05.2	.. 25.8	53 47.4	.. 06.3	332 43.4	.. 34.3	304 00.5	.. 31.0	Ankaa	353 11.0	S42 11.9
16	244 10.9	51 04.8	.. 27.1	68 48.4	.. 05.7	347 45.6	.. 34.4	319 03.0	.. 31.0	Antares	112 21.2	S26 28.4
17	259 13.3	66 04.5	.. 28.3	83 49.4	.. 05.0	2 47.7	.. 34.4	334 05.4	.. 31.0			
18	274 15.8	81 04.1	S 4 29.6	98 50.4	N 3 04.4	17 49.8	S22 34.5	349 07.8	S22 31.0	Arcturus	145 52.1	N19 05.1
19	289 18.3	96 03.7	.. 30.9	113 51.4	.. 03.7	32 51.9	.. 34.5	4 10.3	.. 31.1	Atria	107 19.3	S69 03.8
20	304 20.7	111 03.3	.. 32.1	128 52.4	.. 03.1	47 54.1	.. 34.5	19 12.7	.. 31.1	Avior	234 16.6	S59 34.1
21	319 23.2	126 02.9	.. 33.4	143 53.4	.. 02.4	62 56.2	.. 34.6	34 15.1	.. 31.1	Bellatrix	278 27.3	N 6 22.0
22	334 25.7	141 02.5	.. 34.6	158 54.4	.. 01.8	77 58.3	.. 34.6	49 17.6	.. 31.1	Betelgeuse	270 56.6	N 7 24.6
23	349 28.1	156 02.2	.. 35.9	173 55.3	.. 01.2	93 00.4	.. 34.6	64 20.0	.. 31.1			
26 00	4 30.6	171 01.8	S 4 37.2	188 56.3	N 3 00.5	108 02.6	S22 34.7	79 22.4	S22 31.1	Canopus	263 54.3	S52 42.1
01	19 33.0	186 01.4	.. 38.4	203 57.3	2 59.9	123 04.7	.. 34.7	94 24.9	.. 31.1	Capella	280 28.0	N46 00.8
02	34 35.5	201 01.0	.. 39.7	218 58.3	.. 59.2	138 06.8	.. 34.7	109 27.3	.. 31.1	Deneb	49 28.3	N45 21.3
03	49 38.0	216 00.6	.. 41.0	233 59.3	.. 58.6	153 08.9	.. 34.8	124 29.7	.. 31.1	Denebola	182 29.6	N14 27.9
04	64 40.4	231 00.2	.. 42.2	249 00.3	.. 57.9	168 11.0	.. 34.8	139 32.1	.. 31.1	Diphda	348 51.2	S17 52.7
05	79 42.9	245 59.9	.. 43.5	264 01.3	.. 57.3	183 13.2	.. 34.8	154 34.6	.. 31.1			
T 06	94 45.4	260 59.5	S 4 44.7	279 02.3	N 2 56.6	198 15.3	S22 34.9	169 37.0	S22 31.1	Dubhe	193 47.0	N61 38.7
H 07	109 47.8	275 59.1	.. 46.0	294 03.3	.. 56.0	213 17.4	.. 34.9	184 39.4	.. 31.1	Elnath	278 07.1	N28 37.3
U 08	124 50.3	290 58.7	.. 47.3	309 04.3	.. 55.3	228 19.5	.. 35.0	199 41.9	.. 31.1	Eltanin	90 44.2	N51 29.6
R 09	139 52.8	305 58.3	.. 48.5	324 05.3	.. 54.7	243 21.7	.. 35.0	214 44.3	.. 31.1	Enif	33 42.7	N 9 58.1
S 10	154 55.2	320 57.9	.. 49.8	339 06.3	.. 54.1	258 23.8	.. 35.0	229 46.7	.. 31.1	Fomalhaut	15 18.9	S29 31.1
D 11	169 57.7	335 57.5	.. 51.1	354 07.3	.. 53.4	273 25.9	.. 35.1	244 49.1	.. 31.1			
A 12	185 00.2	350 57.2	S 4 52.3	9 08.3	N 2 52.8	288 28.0	S22 35.1	259 51.6	S22 31.1	Gacrux	171 56.7	S57 13.2
Y 13	200 02.6	5 56.8	.. 53.6	24 09.3	.. 52.1	303 30.1	.. 35.1	274 54.0	.. 31.1	Gienah	175 48.2	S17 38.8
14	215 05.1	20 56.4	.. 54.8	39 10.2	.. 51.5	318 32.3	.. 35.2	289 56.4	.. 31.1	Hadar	148 42.4	S60 28.0
15	230 07.5	35 56.0	.. 56.1	54 11.2	.. 50.8	333 34.4	.. 35.2	304 58.9	.. 31.1	Hamal	327 55.6	N23 33.2
16	245 10.0	50 55.6	.. 57.4	69 12.2	.. 50.2	348 36.5	.. 35.2	320 01.3	.. 31.1	Kaus Aust.	83 38.1	S34 22.5
17	260 12.5	65 55.2	.. 58.6	84 13.2	.. 49.5	3 38.6	.. 35.3	335 03.7	.. 31.1			
18	275 14.9	80 54.8	S 4 59.9	99 14.2	N 2 48.9	18 40.7	S22 35.3	350 06.1	S22 31.1	Kochab	137 20.9	N74 04.8
19	290 17.4	95 54.4	5 01.1	114 15.2	.. 48.2	33 42.9	.. 35.3	5 08.6	.. 31.1	Markab	13 33.8	N15 18.8
20	305 19.9	110 54.1	.. 02.4	129 16.2	.. 47.6	48 45.0	.. 35.4	20 11.0	.. 31.1	Menkar	314 10.3	N 4 10.0
21	320 22.3	125 53.7	.. 03.7	144 17.2	.. 47.0	63 47.1	.. 35.4	35 13.4	.. 31.1	Menkent	148 02.9	S36 27.8
22	335 24.8	140 53.3	.. 04.9	159 18.2	.. 46.3	78 49.2	.. 35.5	50 15.8	.. 31.1	Miaplacidus	221 39.5	S69 47.6
23	350 27.3	155 52.9	.. 06.2	174 19.2	.. 45.7	93 51.3	.. 35.5	65 18.3	.. 31.1			
27 00	5 29.7	170 52.5	S 5 07.4	189 20.2	N 2 45.0	108 53.5	S22 35.5	80 20.7	S22 31.1	Mirfak	308 33.9	N49 55.6
01	20 32.2	185 52.1	.. 08.7	204 21.2	.. 44.4	123 55.6	.. 35.6	95 23.1	.. 31.1	Nunki	75 52.9	S26 16.2
02	35 34.6	200 51.7	.. 10.0	219 22.2	.. 43.7	138 57.7	.. 35.6	110 25.5	.. 31.1	Peacock	53 12.2	S56 40.4
03	50 37.1	215 51.3	.. 11.2	234 23.2	.. 43.1	153 59.8	.. 35.6	125 28.0	.. 31.1	Pollux	243 22.6	N27 58.6
04	65 39.6	230 50.9	.. 12.5	249 24.2	.. 42.4	169 01.9	.. 35.7	140 30.4	.. 31.1	Procyon	244 55.4	N 5 10.5
05	80 42.0	245 50.6	.. 13.7	264 25.1	.. 41.8	184 04.0	.. 35.7	155 32.8	.. 31.1			
F 06	95 44.5	260 50.2	S 5 15.0	279 26.1	N 2 41.1	199 06.2	S22 35.7	170 35.2	S22 31.1	Rasalhague	96 02.5	N12 33.1
R 07	110 47.0	275 49.8	.. 16.2	294 27.1	.. 40.5	214 08.3	.. 35.8	185 37.7	.. 31.1	Regulus	207 39.2	N11 52.4
I 08	125 49.4	290 49.4	.. 17.5	309 28.1	.. 39.8	229 10.4	.. 35.8	200 40.1	.. 31.1	Rigel	281 07.9	S 8 10.7
D 09	140 51.9	305 49.0	.. 18.8	324 29.1	.. 39.2	244 12.5	.. 35.8	215 42.5	.. 31.1	Rigil Kent.	139 46.5	S60 54.9
A 10	155 54.4	320 48.6	.. 20.0	339 30.1	.. 38.6	259 14.6	.. 35.9	230 44.9	.. 31.1	Sabik	102 07.7	S15 44.8
Y 11	170 56.8	335 48.2	.. 21.3	354 31.1	.. 37.9	274 16.7	.. 35.9	245 47.4	.. 31.1			
12	185 59.3	350 47.8	S 5 22.5	9 32.1	N 2 37.3	289 18.8	S22 36.0	260 49.8	S22 31.1	Schedar	349 35.1	N56 38.6
13	201 01.8	5 47.4	.. 23.8	24 33.1	.. 36.6	304 21.0	.. 36.0	275 52.2	.. 31.1	Shaula	96 16.2	S37 07.0
14	216 04.2	20 47.0	.. 25.0	39 34.1	.. 36.0	319 23.1	.. 36.0	290 54.6	.. 31.1	Sirius	258 30.0	S16 44.5
15	231 06.7	35 46.7	.. 26.3	54 35.1	.. 35.3	334 25.2	.. 36.1	305 57.0	.. 31.1	Spica	158 27.0	S11 15.6
16	246 09.1	50 46.3	.. 27.6	69 36.1	.. 34.7	349 27.3	.. 36.1	320 59.5	.. 31.1	Suhail	222 49.6	S43 30.5
17	261 11.6	65 45.9	.. 28.8	84 37.1	.. 34.0	4 29.4	.. 36.1	336 01.9	.. 31.1			
18	276 14.1	80 45.5	S 5 30.1	99 38.1	N 2 33.4	19 31.5	S22 36.2	351 04.3	S22 31.1	Vega	80 36.0	N38 48.5
19	291 16.5	95 45.1	.. 31.3	114 39.1	.. 32.7	34 33.6	.. 36.2	6 06.7	.. 31.1	Zuben'ubi	137 00.9	S16 07.2
20	306 19.0	110 44.7	.. 32.6	129 40.0	.. 32.1	49 35.8	.. 36.2	21 09.2	.. 31.1			
21	321 21.5	125 44.3	.. 33.8	144 41.0	.. 31.4	64 37.9	.. 36.3	36 11.6	.. 31.1			
22	336 23.9	140 43.9	.. 35.1	159 42.0	.. 30.8	79 40.0	.. 36.3	51 14.0	.. 31.1			
23	351 26.4	155 43.5	.. 36.4	174 43.0	.. 30.1	94 42.1	.. 36.4	66 16.4	.. 31.1			
Mer.Pass. 23 38.1		v −0.4	d 1.3	v 1.0	d 0.6	v 2.1	d 0.0	v 2.4	d 0.0			

	SHA	Mer.Pass.
	° '	h m
Venus	166 31.2	12 36
Mars	184 25.8	11 23
Jupiter	103 32.0	16 45
Saturn	74 51.8	18 39

© British Crown Copyright 2018. All rights reserved.

UT	SUN GHA	SUN Dec	MOON GHA	v	MOON Dec	d	HP
d h	° '	° '	° '	'	° '	'	'
25 00	182 01.3	S 0 39.1	231 45.5	5.6	N20 04.7	6.8	59.9
01	197 01.6	40.1	246 10.1	5.6	19 57.9	7.0	59.9
02	212 01.8	41.0	260 34.7	5.6	19 50.9	7.1	60.0
03	227 02.0	.. 42.0	274 59.3	5.7	19 43.8	7.3	60.0
04	242 02.2	43.0	289 24.0	5.6	19 36.5	7.4	60.0
05	257 02.4	44.0	303 48.6	5.7	19 29.1	7.6	60.1
06	272 02.6	S 0 44.9	318 13.3	5.7	N19 21.5	7.7	60.1
W 07	287 02.9	45.9	332 38.0	5.7	19 13.8	7.8	60.1
E 08	302 03.1	46.9	347 02.7	5.7	19 06.0	8.0	60.2
D 09	317 03.3	.. 47.9	1 27.4	5.8	18 58.0	8.1	60.2
N 10	332 03.5	48.8	15 52.1	5.8	18 49.9	8.2	60.2
E 11	347 03.7	49.8	30 16.9	5.8	18 41.7	8.4	60.3
S 12	2 03.9	S 0 50.8	44 41.7	5.8	N18 33.3	8.5	60.3
D 13	17 04.2	51.8	59 06.5	5.8	18 24.8	8.6	60.3
A 14	32 04.4	52.7	73 31.3	5.9	18 16.2	8.8	60.3
Y 15	47 04.6	.. 53.7	87 56.2	5.9	18 07.4	8.9	60.4
16	62 04.8	54.7	102 21.1	5.9	17 58.5	9.0	60.4
17	77 05.0	55.7	116 46.0	5.9	17 49.5	9.2	60.4
18	92 05.2	S 0 56.6	131 10.9	6.0	N17 40.3	9.2	60.5
19	107 05.4	57.6	145 35.9	5.9	17 31.1	9.4	60.5
20	122 05.7	58.6	160 00.8	6.1	17 21.7	9.6	60.5
21	137 05.9	0 59.5	174 25.9	6.0	17 12.1	9.6	60.5
22	152 06.1	1 00.5	188 50.9	6.1	17 02.5	9.8	60.6
23	167 06.3	01.5	203 16.0	6.1	16 52.7	9.9	60.6
26 00	182 06.5	S 1 02.5	217 41.1	6.1	N16 42.8	10.1	60.6
01	197 06.7	03.4	232 06.2	6.2	16 32.7	10.1	60.6
02	212 07.0	04.4	246 31.4	6.2	16 22.6	10.3	60.7
03	227 07.2	.. 05.4	260 56.6	6.3	16 12.3	10.4	60.7
04	242 07.4	06.4	275 21.9	6.2	16 01.9	10.5	60.7
05	257 07.6	07.3	289 47.1	6.3	15 51.4	10.6	60.7
06	272 07.8	S 1 08.3	304 12.4	6.4	N15 40.8	10.7	60.8
T 07	287 08.0	09.3	318 37.8	6.4	15 30.1	10.9	60.8
H 08	302 08.2	10.3	333 03.2	6.4	15 19.2	10.9	60.8
U 09	317 08.5	.. 11.2	347 28.6	6.4	15 08.3	11.1	60.8
R 10	332 08.7	12.2	1 54.0	6.5	14 57.2	11.1	60.8
S 11	347 08.9	13.2	16 19.5	6.5	14 46.1	11.3	60.9
D 12	2 09.1	S 1 14.2	30 45.0	6.6	N14 34.8	11.4	60.9
A 13	17 09.3	15.1	45 10.6	6.6	14 23.4	11.5	60.9
Y 14	32 09.5	16.1	59 36.2	6.6	14 11.9	11.6	60.9
15	47 09.7	.. 17.1	74 01.8	6.7	14 00.3	11.6	60.9
16	62 10.0	18.0	88 27.5	6.7	13 48.7	11.8	61.0
17	77 10.2	19.0	102 53.2	6.7	13 36.9	11.9	61.0
18	92 10.4	S 1 20.0	117 18.9	6.8	N13 25.0	12.0	61.0
19	107 10.6	21.0	131 44.7	6.8	13 13.0	12.1	61.0
20	122 10.8	21.9	146 10.5	6.9	13 00.9	12.1	61.0
21	137 11.0	.. 22.9	160 36.4	6.9	12 48.8	12.3	61.0
22	152 11.2	23.9	175 02.3	6.9	12 36.5	12.4	61.1
23	167 11.4	24.9	189 28.2	7.0	12 24.1	12.4	61.1
27 00	182 11.7	S 1 25.8	203 54.2	7.0	N12 11.7	12.5	61.1
01	197 11.9	26.8	218 20.2	7.1	11 59.2	12.6	61.1
02	212 12.1	27.8	232 46.3	7.0	11 46.6	12.7	61.1
03	227 12.3	.. 28.8	247 12.3	7.2	11 33.9	12.8	61.1
04	242 12.5	29.7	261 38.5	7.1	11 21.1	12.9	61.1
05	257 12.7	30.7	276 04.6	7.2	11 08.2	12.9	61.2
06	272 12.9	S 1 31.7	290 30.8	7.3	N10 55.3	13.0	61.2
07	287 13.1	32.7	304 57.1	7.2	10 42.3	13.1	61.2
08	302 13.4	33.6	319 23.3	7.4	10 29.2	13.1	61.2
F 09	317 13.6	.. 34.6	333 49.7	7.3	10 16.1	13.3	61.2
R 10	332 13.8	35.6	348 16.0	7.4	10 02.8	13.3	61.2
I 11	347 14.0	36.5	2 42.4	7.4	9 49.5	13.4	61.2
D 12	2 14.2	S 1 37.5	17 08.8	7.5	N 9 36.1	13.4	61.2
A 13	17 14.4	38.5	31 35.3	7.5	9 22.7	13.5	61.2
Y 14	32 14.6	39.5	46 01.8	7.5	9 09.2	13.6	61.2
15	47 14.8	.. 40.4	60 28.3	7.6	8 55.6	13.6	61.3
16	62 15.1	41.4	74 54.9	7.6	8 42.0	13.7	61.3
17	77 15.3	42.4	89 21.5	7.6	8 28.3	13.7	61.3
18	92 15.5	S 1 43.4	103 48.1	7.7	N 8 14.6	13.8	61.3
19	107 15.7	44.3	118 14.8	7.7	8 00.8	13.9	61.3
20	122 15.9	45.3	132 41.5	7.8	7 46.9	13.9	61.3
21	137 16.1	.. 46.3	147 08.3	7.8	7 33.0	13.9	61.3
22	152 16.3	47.3	161 35.1	7.8	7 19.1	14.0	61.3
23	167 16.5	48.2	176 01.9	7.8	N 7 05.1	14.1	61.3
	SD 16.0	d 1.0	SD 16.4		16.6		16.7

Lat.	Twilight Naut.	Twilight Civil	Sunrise	Moonrise 25	26	27	28
°	h m	h m	h m	h m	h m	h m	h m
N 72	03 20	04 47	05 55	22 56	25 51	01 51	04 17
N 70	03 37	04 53	05 54	23 50	26 13	02 13	04 25
68	03 50	04 58	05 54	24 22	00 22	02 29	04 32
66	04 00	05 02	05 54	24 45	00 45	02 42	04 38
64	04 08	05 06	05 53	25 04	01 04	02 53	04 43
62	04 16	05 09	05 53	25 19	01 19	03 02	04 47
60	04 22	05 11	05 53	25 31	01 31	03 10	04 50
N 58	04 27	05 13	05 52	00 12	01 42	03 17	04 54
56	04 31	05 15	05 52	00 24	01 52	03 23	04 56
54	04 35	05 17	05 52	00 35	02 00	03 29	04 59
52	04 39	05 18	05 52	00 45	02 07	03 34	05 01
50	04 42	05 19	05 52	00 54	02 14	03 38	05 03
45	04 48	05 22	05 51	01 12	02 28	03 47	05 08
N 40	04 52	05 24	05 51	01 27	02 40	03 55	05 12
35	04 56	05 25	05 51	01 39	02 50	04 02	05 15
30	04 59	05 26	05 50	01 50	02 58	04 08	05 18
20	05 02	05 28	05 50	02 09	03 13	04 18	05 23
N 10	05 04	05 28	05 49	02 25	03 26	04 27	05 27
0	05 03	05 27	05 48	02 40	03 38	04 35	05 31
S 10	05 02	05 26	05 47	02 55	03 51	04 44	05 35
20	04 59	05 24	05 46	03 11	04 03	04 53	05 39
30	04 53	05 21	05 45	03 30	04 18	05 03	05 44
35	04 49	05 19	05 44	03 40	04 27	05 08	05 47
40	04 45	05 16	05 43	03 53	04 38	05 15	05 50
45	04 38	05 13	05 42	04 07	04 48	05 23	05 54
S 50	04 30	05 09	05 41	04 25	05 01	05 32	05 58
52	04 26	05 07	05 40	04 33	05 08	05 36	06 00
54	04 22	05 04	05 40	04 42	05 14	05 40	06 03
56	04 17	05 02	05 39	04 53	05 22	05 46	06 05
58	04 11	04 59	05 38	05 04	05 31	05 51	06 08
S 60	04 05	04 55	05 37	05 18	05 41	05 58	06 11

Lat.	Sunset	Twilight Civil	Twilight Naut.	Moonset 25	26	27	28
°	h m	h m	h m	h m	h m	h m	h m
N 72	17 46	18 53	20 19	20 08	19 15	18 47	18 26
N 70	17 46	18 47	20 03	19 14	18 51	18 36	18 23
68	17 47	18 42	19 50	18 40	18 33	18 27	18 21
66	17 48	18 38	19 40	18 16	18 18	18 19	18 19
64	17 48	18 35	19 32	17 56	18 06	18 12	18 17
62	17 48	18 32	19 25	17 40	17 56	18 07	18 15
60	17 49	18 30	19 19	17 27	17 47	18 01	18 14
N 58	17 49	18 28	19 14	17 16	17 39	17 57	18 13
56	17 49	18 26	19 10	17 06	17 32	17 53	18 11
54	17 50	18 25	19 06	16 57	17 26	17 49	18 10
52	17 50	18 23	19 03	16 49	17 20	17 46	18 10
50	17 50	18 22	19 00	16 41	17 15	17 43	18 09
45	17 51	18 20	18 54	16 26	17 04	17 37	18 07
N 40	17 51	18 18	18 50	16 13	16 54	17 31	18 05
35	17 52	18 17	18 46	16 02	16 46	17 26	18 04
30	17 52	18 16	18 44	15 53	16 39	17 22	18 03
20	17 53	18 15	18 40	15 36	16 27	17 15	18 00
N 10	17 54	18 15	18 39	15 22	16 16	17 08	17 59
0	17 55	18 15	18 39	15 08	16 06	17 02	17 57
S 10	17 56	18 17	18 41	14 54	15 55	16 56	17 55
20	17 57	18 19	18 44	14 39	15 44	16 49	17 53
30	17 58	18 22	18 50	14 22	15 31	16 41	17 50
35	17 59	18 24	18 54	14 12	15 24	16 37	17 49
40	18 00	18 27	18 59	14 01	15 15	16 31	17 47
45	18 01	18 31	19 05	13 47	15 05	16 25	17 46
S 50	18 03	18 35	19 14	13 30	14 53	16 18	17 43
52	18 04	18 37	19 18	13 23	14 47	16 15	17 42
54	18 04	18 40	19 22	13 14	14 41	16 11	17 41
56	18 05	18 43	19 27	13 04	14 34	16 07	17 40
58	18 06	18 46	19 33	12 53	14 26	16 02	17 39
S 60	18 07	18 49	19 40	12 40	14 17	15 57	17 37

	SUN			MOON			
Day	Eqn. of Time 00h	Eqn. of Time 12h	Mer. Pass.	Mer. Pass. Upper	Mer. Pass. Lower	Age	Phase
d	m s	m s	h m	h m	h m	d	%
25	08 05	08 15	11 52	08 54	21 23	26	15
26	08 26	08 36	11 51	09 52	22 21	27	8
27	08 46	08 56	11 51	10 49	23 16	28	3

© British Crown Copyright 2018. All rights reserved.

UT	ARIES GHA	VENUS −3.9 GHA	Dec	MARS +1.8 GHA	Dec	JUPITER −2.0 GHA	Dec	SATURN +0.5 GHA	Dec	STARS Name	SHA	Dec
28 00	6 28.9	170 43.1	S 5 37.6	189 44.0	N 2 29.5	109 44.2	S22 36.4	81 18.8	S22 31.1	Acamar	315 14.7	S40 13.5
01	21 31.3	185 42.7	38.9	204 45.0	28.9	124 46.3	36.4	96 21.3	31.1	Achernar	335 23.0	S57 08.2
02	36 33.8	200 42.3	40.1	219 46.0	28.2	139 48.4	36.5	111 23.7	31.1	Acrux	173 05.2	S63 12.3
03	51 36.2	215 41.9	.. 41.4	234 47.0	.. 27.6	154 50.5	.. 36.5	126 26.1	.. 31.1	Adhara	255 09.2	S28 59.7
04	66 38.7	230 41.6	42.6	249 48.0	26.9	169 52.6	36.5	141 28.5	31.1	Aldebaran	290 44.3	N16 32.8
05	81 41.2	245 41.2	43.9	264 49.0	26.3	184 54.8	36.6	156 30.9	31.1			
06	96 43.6	260 40.8	S 5 45.1	279 50.0	N 2 25.6	199 56.9	S22 36.6	171 33.4	S22 31.1	Alioth	166 17.4	N55 51.4
07	111 46.1	275 40.4	46.4	294 51.0	25.0	214 59.0	36.6	186 35.8	31.1	Alkaid	152 55.9	N49 13.2
S 08	126 48.6	290 40.0	47.6	309 52.0	24.3	230 01.1	36.7	201 38.2	31.1	Alnair	27 37.9	S46 52.0
A 09	141 51.0	305 39.6	.. 48.9	324 53.0	.. 23.7	245 03.2	.. 36.7	216 40.6	.. 31.1	Alnilam	275 41.9	S 1 11.3
T 10	156 53.5	320 39.2	50.1	339 54.0	23.0	260 05.3	36.7	231 43.0	31.1	Alphard	217 52.1	S 8 44.5
U 11	171 56.0	335 38.8	51.4	354 55.0	22.4	275 07.4	36.8	246 45.5	31.1			
R 12	186 58.4	350 38.4	S 5 52.7	9 55.9	N 2 21.7	290 09.5	S22 36.8	261 47.9	S22 31.1	Alphecca	126 07.6	N26 39.3
D 13	202 00.9	5 38.0	53.9	24 56.9	21.1	305 11.6	36.9	276 50.3	31.1	Alpheratz	357 38.7	N29 12.0
A 14	217 03.4	20 37.6	55.2	39 57.9	20.4	320 13.7	36.9	291 52.7	31.1	Altair	62 03.9	N 8 55.4
Y 15	232 05.8	35 37.2	.. 56.4	54 58.9	.. 19.8	335 15.8	.. 36.9	306 55.1	.. 31.1	Ankaa	353 11.0	S42 11.9
16	247 08.3	50 36.8	57.7	69 59.9	19.2	350 18.0	37.0	321 57.6	31.1	Antares	112 21.2	S26 28.4
17	262 10.7	65 36.4	5 58.9	85 00.9	18.5	5 20.1	37.0	337 00.0	31.1			
18	277 13.2	80 36.0	S 6 00.2	100 01.9	N 2 17.9	20 22.2	S22 37.0	352 02.4	S22 31.1	Arcturus	145 52.1	N19 05.1
19	292 15.7	95 35.6	01.4	115 02.9	17.2	35 24.3	37.1	7 04.8	31.1	Atria	107 19.3	S69 03.8
20	307 18.1	110 35.2	02.7	130 03.9	16.6	50 26.4	37.1	22 07.2	31.1	Avior	234 16.6	S59 34.1
21	322 20.6	125 34.8	.. 03.9	145 04.9	.. 15.9	65 28.5	.. 37.1	37 09.6	.. 31.1	Bellatrix	278 27.3	N 6 22.0
22	337 23.1	140 34.4	05.2	160 05.9	15.3	80 30.6	37.2	52 12.1	31.1	Betelgeuse	270 56.6	N 7 24.6
23	352 25.5	155 34.0	06.4	175 06.9	14.6	95 32.7	37.2	67 14.5	31.1			
29 00	7 28.0	170 33.6	S 6 07.7	190 07.9	N 2 14.0	110 34.8	S22 37.3	82 16.9	S22 31.1	Canopus	263 54.2	S52 42.1
01	22 30.5	185 33.2	08.9	205 08.9	13.3	125 36.9	37.3	97 19.3	31.1	Capella	280 28.0	N46 00.8
02	37 32.9	200 32.8	10.2	220 09.9	12.7	140 39.0	37.3	112 21.7	31.1	Deneb	49 28.3	N45 21.3
03	52 35.4	215 32.4	.. 11.4	235 10.8	.. 12.0	155 41.1	.. 37.4	127 24.1	.. 31.1	Denebola	182 29.6	N14 27.9
04	67 37.8	230 32.0	12.7	250 11.8	11.4	170 43.2	37.4	142 26.6	31.1	Diphda	348 51.2	S17 52.7
05	82 40.3	245 31.6	13.9	265 12.8	10.7	185 45.3	37.4	157 29.0	31.1			
06	97 42.8	260 31.2	S 6 15.2	280 13.8	N 2 10.1	200 47.4	S22 37.5	172 31.4	S22 31.1	Dubhe	193 47.0	N61 38.7
07	112 45.2	275 30.8	16.4	295 14.8	09.4	215 49.5	37.5	187 33.8	31.1	Elnath	278 07.1	N28 37.3
08	127 47.7	290 30.4	17.7	310 15.8	08.8	230 51.6	37.5	202 36.2	31.1	Eltanin	90 44.2	N51 29.6
S 09	142 50.2	305 30.0	.. 18.9	325 16.8	.. 08.1	245 53.7	.. 37.6	217 38.6	.. 31.1	Enif	33 42.7	N 9 58.1
U 10	157 52.6	320 29.6	20.2	340 17.8	07.5	260 55.8	37.6	232 41.1	31.1	Fomalhaut	15 18.9	S29 31.1
N 11	172 55.1	335 29.2	21.4	355 18.8	06.8	275 57.9	37.7	247 43.5	31.1			
D 12	187 57.6	350 28.8	S 6 22.6	10 19.8	N 2 06.2	291 00.1	S22 37.7	262 45.9	S22 31.1	Gacrux	171 56.7	S57 13.2
A 13	203 00.0	5 28.4	23.9	25 20.8	05.6	306 02.2	37.7	277 48.3	31.1	Gienah	175 48.2	S17 38.8
Y 14	218 02.5	20 28.0	25.1	40 21.8	04.9	321 04.3	37.8	292 50.7	31.1	Hadar	148 42.4	S60 28.0
15	233 05.0	35 27.6	.. 26.4	55 22.8	.. 04.3	336 06.4	.. 37.8	307 53.1	.. 31.1	Hamal	327 55.6	N23 33.3
16	248 07.4	50 27.2	27.6	70 23.8	03.6	351 08.5	37.8	322 55.5	31.1	Kaus Aust.	83 38.1	S34 22.5
17	263 09.9	65 26.8	28.9	85 24.8	03.0	6 10.6	37.9	337 57.9	31.1			
18	278 12.3	80 26.4	S 6 30.1	100 25.7	N 2 02.3	21 12.7	S22 37.9	353 00.4	S22 31.1	Kochab	137 21.0	N74 04.8
19	293 14.8	95 26.0	31.4	115 26.7	01.7	36 14.8	37.9	8 02.8	31.1	Markab	13 33.8	N15 18.8
20	308 17.3	110 25.6	32.6	130 27.7	01.0	51 16.9	38.0	23 05.2	31.1	Menkar	314 10.3	N 4 10.0
21	323 19.7	125 25.2	.. 33.9	145 28.7	2 00.4	66 19.0	.. 38.0	38 07.6	.. 31.1	Menkent	148 02.9	S36 27.8
22	338 22.2	140 24.8	35.1	160 29.7	1 59.7	81 21.1	38.1	53 10.0	31.1	Miaplacidus	221 39.5	S69 47.6
23	353 24.7	155 24.4	36.4	175 30.7	59.1	96 23.2	38.1	68 12.4	31.1			
30 00	8 27.1	170 24.0	S 6 37.6	190 31.7	N 1 58.4	111 25.3	S22 38.1	83 14.8	S22 31.1	Mirfak	308 33.9	N49 55.6
01	23 29.6	185 23.6	38.8	205 32.7	57.8	126 27.4	38.2	98 17.3	31.1	Nunki	75 53.0	S26 16.3
02	38 32.1	200 23.2	40.1	220 33.7	57.1	141 29.5	38.2	113 19.7	31.1	Peacock	53 12.2	S56 40.4
03	53 34.5	215 22.8	.. 41.3	235 34.7	.. 56.5	156 31.6	.. 38.2	128 22.1	.. 31.1	Pollux	243 22.6	N27 58.6
04	68 37.0	230 22.4	42.6	250 35.7	55.8	171 33.7	38.3	143 24.5	31.0	Procyon	244 55.4	N 5 10.5
05	83 39.4	245 22.0	43.8	265 36.7	55.2	186 35.8	38.3	158 26.9	31.0			
06	98 41.9	260 21.6	S 6 45.1	280 37.7	N 1 54.5	201 37.9	S22 38.3	173 29.3	S22 31.0	Rasalhague	96 02.5	N12 33.1
07	113 44.3	275 21.2	46.3	295 38.7	53.9	216 39.9	38.4	188 31.7	31.0	Regulus	207 39.2	N11 52.4
08	128 46.8	290 20.8	47.5	310 39.6	53.2	231 42.0	38.4	203 34.1	31.0	Rigel	281 07.8	S 8 10.7
M 09	143 49.3	305 20.4	.. 48.8	325 40.6	.. 52.6	246 44.1	.. 38.4	218 36.5	.. 31.0	Rigil Kent.	139 46.5	S60 54.9
O 10	158 51.8	320 20.0	50.0	340 41.6	51.9	261 46.2	38.5	233 39.0	31.0	Sabik	102 07.7	S15 44.8
N 11	173 54.2	335 19.6	51.3	355 42.6	51.3	276 48.3	38.5	248 41.4	31.0			
D 12	188 56.7	350 19.2	S 6 52.5	10 43.6	N 1 50.7	291 50.4	S22 38.6	263 43.8	S22 31.0	Schedar	349 35.1	N56 38.7
A 13	203 59.2	5 18.8	53.8	25 44.6	50.0	306 52.5	38.6	278 46.2	31.0	Shaula	96 16.2	S37 07.0
Y 14	219 01.6	20 18.3	55.0	40 45.6	49.3	321 54.6	38.6	293 48.6	31.0	Sirius	258 30.0	S16 44.5
15	234 04.1	35 17.9	.. 56.2	55 46.6	.. 48.7	336 56.7	.. 38.7	308 51.0	.. 31.0	Spica	158 27.0	S11 15.6
16	249 06.6	50 17.5	57.5	70 47.6	48.1	351 58.8	38.7	323 53.4	31.0	Suhail	222 49.6	S43 30.4
17	264 09.0	65 17.1	6 58.7	85 48.6	47.4	7 00.9	38.7	338 55.8	31.0			
18	279 11.5	80 16.7	S 7 00.0	100 49.6	N 1 46.8	22 03.0	S22 38.8	353 58.2	S22 31.0	Vega	80 36.0	N38 48.5
19	294 13.9	95 16.3	01.2	115 50.6	46.1	37 05.1	38.8	9 00.6	31.0	Zuben'ubi	137 00.9	S16 07.2
20	309 16.4	110 15.9	02.4	130 51.6	45.5	52 07.2	38.8	24 03.0	31.0		SHA	Mer.Pass.
21	324 18.9	125 15.5	.. 03.7	145 52.6	.. 44.8	67 09.3	.. 38.9	39 05.5	.. 31.0			
22	339 21.3	140 15.1	04.9	160 53.6	44.2	82 11.4	38.9	54 07.9	31.0	Venus	163 05.6	12 38
23	354 23.8	155 14.7	06.2	175 54.5	43.5	97 13.5	39.0	69 10.3	31.0	Mars	182 39.9	11 19
Mer.Pass.	23 26.3	v −0.4	d 1.2	v 1.0	d 0.6	v 2.1	d 0.0	v 2.4	d 0.0	Jupiter	103 06.8	16 35
										Saturn	74 48.9	18 28

© British Crown Copyright 2018. All rights reserved.

UT	SUN GHA	SUN Dec	MOON GHA	v	MOON Dec	d	HP
28 00	182 16.7	S 1 49.2	190 28.7	7.9	N 6 51.0	14.1	61.3
01	197 16.9	50.2	204 55.6	7.9	6 36.9	14.1	61.3
02	212 17.2	51.1	219 22.5	7.9	6 22.8	14.2	61.3
03	227 17.4	.. 52.1	233 49.4	8.0	6 08.6	14.2	61.3
04	242 17.6	53.1	248 16.4	8.0	5 54.4	14.3	61.3
05	257 17.8	54.1	262 43.4	8.1	5 40.1	14.3	61.3
06	272 18.0	S 1 55.0	277 10.5	8.0	N 5 25.8	14.3	61.3
07	287 18.2	56.0	291 37.5	8.1	5 11.5	14.4	61.3
S 08	302 18.4	57.0	306 04.6	8.2	4 57.1	14.4	61.3
A 09	317 18.6	.. 58.0	320 31.8	8.1	4 42.7	14.5	61.3
T 10	332 18.8	58.9	334 58.9	8.2	4 28.3	14.4	61.3
U 11	347 19.0	1 59.9	349 26.1	8.2	4 13.9	14.5	61.3
R 12	2 19.3	S 2 00.9	3 53.3	8.2	N 3 59.4	14.5	61.3
D 13	17 19.5	01.8	18 20.5	8.3	3 44.9	14.5	61.3
A 14	32 19.7	02.8	32 47.8	8.3	3 30.4	14.6	61.2
Y 15	47 19.9	.. 03.8	47 15.1	8.3	3 15.8	14.5	61.2
16	62 20.1	04.8	61 42.4	8.3	3 01.3	14.6	61.2
17	77 20.3	05.7	76 09.7	8.4	2 46.7	14.6	61.2
18	92 20.5	S 2 06.7	90 37.1	8.4	N 2 32.1	14.6	61.2
19	107 20.7	07.7	105 04.5	8.4	2 17.5	14.6	61.2
20	122 20.9	08.7	119 31.9	8.4	2 02.9	14.6	61.2
21	137 21.1	.. 09.6	133 59.3	8.5	1 48.3	14.6	61.2
22	152 21.3	10.6	148 26.8	8.4	1 33.7	14.6	61.2
23	167 21.6	11.6	162 54.2	8.5	1 19.1	14.6	61.2
29 00	182 21.8	S 2 12.5	177 21.7	8.5	N 1 04.5	14.7	61.2
01	197 22.0	13.5	191 49.2	8.6	0 49.8	14.6	61.1
02	212 22.2	14.5	206 16.8	8.5	0 35.2	14.6	61.1
03	227 22.4	.. 15.5	220 44.3	8.6	0 20.6	14.6	61.1
04	242 22.6	16.4	235 11.9	8.6	N 0 06.0	14.7	61.1
05	257 22.8	17.4	249 39.5	8.6	S 0 08.7	14.6	61.1
06	272 23.0	S 2 18.4	264 07.1	8.6	S 0 23.3	14.6	61.1
07	287 23.2	19.4	278 34.7	8.6	0 37.9	14.5	61.1
S 08	302 23.4	20.3	293 02.3	8.7	0 52.4	14.6	61.0
U 09	317 23.6	.. 21.3	307 30.0	8.7	1 07.0	14.6	61.0
N 10	332 23.8	22.3	321 57.7	8.6	1 21.6	14.5	61.0
D 11	347 24.0	23.2	336 25.3	8.7	1 36.1	14.5	61.0
A 12	2 24.3	S 2 24.2	350 53.0	8.8	S 1 50.6	14.5	61.0
Y 13	17 24.5	25.2	5 20.8	8.7	2 05.1	14.5	60.9
14	32 24.7	26.2	19 48.5	8.7	2 19.6	14.5	60.9
15	47 24.9	.. 27.1	34 16.2	8.7	2 34.1	14.4	60.9
16	62 25.1	28.1	48 43.9	8.8	2 48.5	14.4	60.9
17	77 25.3	29.1	63 11.7	8.8	3 02.9	14.4	60.9
18	92 25.5	S 2 30.0	77 39.5	8.7	S 3 17.3	14.3	60.8
19	107 25.7	31.0	92 07.2	8.8	3 31.6	14.4	60.8
20	122 25.9	32.0	106 35.0	8.8	3 46.0	14.2	60.8
21	137 26.1	.. 33.0	121 02.8	8.8	4 00.2	14.3	60.8
22	152 26.3	33.9	135 30.6	8.8	4 14.5	14.2	60.8
23	167 26.5	34.9	149 58.4	8.8	4 28.7	14.2	60.7
30 00	182 26.7	S 2 35.9	164 26.2	8.8	S 4 42.9	14.1	60.7
01	197 26.9	36.8	178 54.0	8.8	4 57.0	14.1	60.7
02	212 27.1	37.8	193 21.8	8.9	5 11.1	14.0	60.7
03	227 27.3	.. 38.8	207 49.7	8.8	5 25.1	14.0	60.6
04	242 27.6	39.8	222 17.5	8.8	5 39.1	14.0	60.6
05	257 27.8	40.7	236 45.3	8.9	5 53.1	13.9	60.6
06	272 28.0	S 2 41.7	251 13.2	8.8	S 6 07.0	13.8	60.6
07	287 28.2	42.7	265 41.0	8.9	6 20.8	13.8	60.5
08	302 28.4	43.6	280 08.9	8.8	6 34.6	13.8	60.5
M 09	317 28.6	.. 44.6	294 36.7	8.8	6 48.4	13.7	60.5
O 10	332 28.8	45.6	309 04.5	8.9	7 02.1	13.6	60.4
N 11	347 29.0	46.6	323 32.4	8.8	7 15.7	13.6	60.4
D 12	2 29.2	S 2 47.5	338 00.2	8.9	S 7 29.3	13.6	60.4
A 13	17 29.4	48.5	352 28.1	8.8	7 42.9	13.4	60.4
Y 14	32 29.6	49.5	6 55.9	8.9	7 56.3	13.4	60.3
15	47 29.8	.. 50.4	21 23.8	8.8	8 09.7	13.4	60.3
16	62 30.0	51.4	35 51.6	8.8	8 23.1	13.2	60.3
17	77 30.2	52.4	50 19.4	8.9	8 36.3	13.3	60.2
18	92 30.4	S 2 53.4	64 47.3	8.8	S 8 49.6	13.1	60.2
19	107 30.6	54.3	79 15.1	8.9	9 02.7	13.1	60.2
20	122 30.8	55.3	93 43.0	8.8	9 15.8	13.0	60.1
21	137 31.0	.. 56.3	108 10.8	8.7	9 28.8	12.9	60.1
22	152 31.2	57.2	122 38.6	8.8	9 41.7	12.9	60.1
23	167 31.4	58.2	137 06.4	8.8	S 9 54.6	12.8	60.0
	SD 16.0	d 1.0	SD 16.7		16.6		16.5

Lat.	Twilight Naut.	Twilight Civil	Sunrise	Moonrise 28	29	30	1
N 72	03 37	05 01	06 08	04 17	06 33	08 49	11 11
N 70	03 51	05 05	06 06	04 25	06 32	08 38	10 47
68	04 02	05 09	06 04	04 32	06 32	08 30	10 29
66	04 11	05 12	06 03	04 38	06 31	08 23	10 14
64	04 18	05 14	06 02	04 43	06 30	08 17	10 02
62	04 24	05 17	06 01	04 47	06 30	08 12	09 52
60	04 29	05 18	06 00	04 50	06 30	08 07	09 43
N 58	04 34	05 20	05 59	04 54	06 29	08 03	09 36
56	04 38	05 21	05 58	04 56	06 29	08 00	09 29
54	04 41	05 22	05 57	04 59	06 29	07 57	09 23
52	04 44	05 23	05 57	05 01	06 28	07 54	09 18
50	04 46	05 24	05 56	05 03	06 28	07 52	09 13
45	04 52	05 26	05 55	05 08	06 28	07 46	09 03
N 40	04 55	05 27	05 54	05 12	06 27	07 42	08 55
35	04 58	05 28	05 53	05 15	06 27	07 38	08 47
30	05 00	05 28	05 52	05 18	06 26	07 34	08 41
20	05 03	05 28	05 50	05 23	06 26	07 28	08 30
N 10	05 03	05 28	05 49	05 27	06 25	07 23	08 21
0	05 02	05 26	05 47	05 31	06 25	07 19	08 12
S 10	05 00	05 24	05 45	05 35	06 25	07 14	08 03
20	04 56	05 22	05 44	05 39	06 24	07 09	07 54
30	04 49	05 17	05 41	05 44	06 24	07 03	07 44
35	04 45	05 15	05 40	05 47	06 24	07 00	07 38
40	04 39	05 11	05 38	05 50	06 24	06 57	07 31
45	04 32	05 07	05 37	05 54	06 23	06 53	07 23
S 50	04 23	05 02	05 34	05 58	06 23	06 48	07 13
52	04 19	04 59	05 33	06 00	06 23	06 45	07 09
54	04 14	04 57	05 32	06 03	06 23	06 43	07 04
56	04 08	04 53	05 31	06 05	06 23	06 40	06 59
58	04 02	04 50	05 29	06 08	06 23	06 37	06 53
S 60	03 54	04 46	05 28	06 11	06 22	06 34	06 47

Lat.	Sunset	Twilight Civil	Twilight Naut.	Moonset 28	29	30	1
N 72	17 30	18 37	20 00	18 26	18 06	17 45	17 16
N 70	17 33	18 33	19 47	18 23	18 11	17 58	17 42
68	17 35	18 30	19 36	18 21	18 15	18 09	18 02
66	17 36	18 27	19 28	18 19	18 18	18 17	18 17
64	17 37	18 25	19 22	18 17	18 21	18 25	18 31
62	17 39	18 23	19 15	18 15	18 23	18 32	18 42
60	17 40	18 21	19 10	18 14	18 25	18 37	18 51
N 58	17 41	18 20	19 06	18 13	18 27	18 42	19 00
56	17 41	18 18	19 02	18 11	18 29	18 47	19 07
54	17 42	18 17	18 59	18 10	18 30	18 51	19 14
52	17 43	18 16	18 56	18 10	18 32	18 55	19 20
50	17 44	18 16	18 53	18 09	18 33	18 58	19 25
45	17 45	18 14	18 48	18 07	18 36	19 06	19 37
N 40	17 46	18 13	18 45	18 05	18 38	19 12	19 47
35	17 47	18 13	18 42	18 04	18 40	19 17	19 55
30	17 48	18 12	18 40	18 03	18 42	19 22	20 03
20	17 50	18 12	18 38	18 00	18 45	19 30	20 16
N 10	17 52	18 13	18 37	17 59	18 48	19 37	20 27
0	17 54	18 14	18 38	17 57	18 50	19 44	20 37
S 10	17 55	18 16	18 41	17 55	18 53	19 51	20 48
20	17 58	18 20	18 45	17 53	18 56	19 58	20 59
30	18 00	18 24	18 52	17 50	18 59	20 06	21 12
35	18 01	18 27	18 56	17 49	19 01	20 11	21 20
40	18 03	18 30	19 02	17 47	19 03	20 17	21 29
45	18 05	18 35	19 09	17 46	19 05	20 23	21 39
S 50	18 07	18 40	19 19	17 43	19 08	20 31	21 51
52	18 09	18 43	19 23	17 42	19 09	20 34	21 57
54	18 10	18 45	19 28	17 41	19 10	20 38	22 03
56	18 11	18 49	19 34	17 40	19 12	20 42	22 10
58	18 13	18 52	19 41	17 39	19 14	20 47	22 18
S 60	18 14	18 57	19 48	17 37	19 16	20 53	22 27

Day	SUN Eqn. of Time 00h	12h	Mer. Pass.	MOON Mer. Pass. Upper	Lower	Age	Phase
	m s	m s	h m	h m	h m	d	%
28	09 07	09 17	11 51	11 44	24 11	29	0
29	09 27	09 37	11 50	12 38	00 11	01	1
30	09 47	09 56	11 50	13 31	01 05	02	5

© British Crown Copyright 2018. All rights reserved.

2019 OCTOBER 1, 2, 3 (TUES., WED., THURS.)

UT	ARIES GHA	VENUS −3·9 GHA	Dec	MARS +1·8 GHA	Dec	JUPITER −2·0 GHA	Dec	SATURN +0·5 GHA	Dec	STARS Name	SHA	Dec
d h	° ′	° ′	° ′	° ′	° ′	° ′	° ′	° ′	° ′		° ′	° ′
1 00	9 26.3	170 14.3 S 7 07.4		190 55.5 N 1 42.9		112 15.6 S22 39.0		84 12.7 S22 31.0		Acamar	315 14.7	S40 13.5
01	24 28.7	185 13.9	08.6	205 56.5	42.2	127 17.7	39.0	99 15.1	31.0	Achernar	335 23.0	S57 08.2
02	39 31.2	200 13.4	09.9	220 57.5	41.6	142 19.8	39.1	114 17.5	31.0	Acrux	173 05.2	S63 12.3
03	54 33.7	215 13.0 . .	11.1	235 58.5 . .	40.9	157 21.9 . .	39.1	129 19.9 . .	31.0	Adhara	255 09.2	S28 59.7
04	69 36.1	230 12.6	12.4	250 59.5	40.3	172 23.9	39.1	144 22.3	31.0	Aldebaran	290 44.3	N16 32.8
05	84 38.6	245 12.2	13.6	266 00.5	39.6	187 26.0	39.1	159 24.7	31.0			
06	99 41.1	260 11.8 S 7 14.8		281 01.5 N 1 39.0		202 28.1 S22 39.2		174 27.1 S22 31.0		Alioth	166 17.4	N55 51.4
07	114 43.5	275 11.4	16.1	296 02.5	38.3	217 30.2	39.2	189 29.5	31.0	Alkaid	152 55.9	N49 13.2
08	129 46.0	290 11.0	17.3	311 03.5	37.7	232 32.3	39.3	204 31.9	31.0	Alnair	27 38.0	S46 52.0
T 09	144 48.4	305 10.6 . .	18.5	326 04.5 . .	37.0	247 34.4 . .	39.3	219 34.3 . .	31.0	Alnilam	275 41.9	S 1 11.3
U 10	159 50.9	320 10.2	19.8	341 05.5	36.4	262 36.5	39.4	234 36.7	31.0	Alphard	217 52.1	S 8 44.5
E 11	174 53.4	335 09.8	21.0	356 06.5	35.7	277 38.6	39.4	249 39.1	31.0			
S 12	189 55.8	350 09.3 S 7 22.2		11 07.5 N 1 35.1		292 40.7 S22 39.4		264 41.6 S22 31.0		Alphecca	126 07.6	N26 39.3
D 13	204 58.3	5 08.9	23.5	26 08.4	34.4	307 42.8	39.5	279 44.0	31.0	Alpheratz	357 38.7	N29 12.0
A 14	220 00.8	20 08.5	24.7	41 09.4	33.8	322 44.9	39.5	294 46.4	31.0	Altair	62 04.0	N 8 55.5
Y 15	235 03.2	35 08.1 . .	25.9	56 10.4 . .	33.1	337 46.9 . .	39.5	309 48.8 . .	31.0	Ankaa	353 11.0	S42 12.0
16	250 05.7	50 07.7	27.2	71 11.4	32.5	352 49.0	39.6	324 51.2	31.0	Antares	112 21.2	S26 28.4
17	265 08.2	65 07.3	28.4	86 12.4	31.8	7 51.1	39.6	339 53.6	31.0			
18	280 10.6	80 06.9 S 7 29.6		101 13.4 N 1 31.2		22 53.2 S22 39.7		354 56.0 S22 31.0		Arcturus	145 52.1	N19 05.1
19	295 13.1	95 06.4	30.9	116 14.4	30.5	37 55.3	39.7	9 58.4	31.0	Atria	107 19.4	S69 03.8
20	310 15.5	110 06.0	32.1	131 15.4	29.9	52 57.4	39.7	25 00.8	31.0	Avior	234 16.6	S59 34.0
21	325 18.0	125 05.6 . .	33.3	146 16.4 . .	29.2	67 59.5 . .	39.8	40 03.2 . .	31.0	Bellatrix	278 27.3	N 6 22.0
22	340 20.5	140 05.2	34.6	161 17.4	28.6	83 01.6	39.8	55 05.6	31.0	Betelgeuse	270 56.6	N 7 24.6
23	355 22.9	155 04.8	35.8	176 18.4	27.9	98 03.7	39.8	70 08.0	31.0			
2 00	10 25.4	170 04.4 S 7 37.0		191 19.4 N 1 27.3		113 05.7 S22 39.9		85 10.4 S22 31.0		Canopus	263 54.2	S52 42.1
01	25 27.9	185 04.0	38.3	206 20.4	26.6	128 07.8	39.9	100 12.8	31.0	Capella	280 27.9	N46 00.8
02	40 30.3	200 03.5	39.5	221 21.4	26.0	143 09.9	39.9	115 15.2	31.0	Deneb	49 28.4	N45 21.3
03	55 32.8	215 03.1 . .	40.7	236 22.3 . .	25.3	158 12.0 . .	40.0	130 17.6 . .	31.0	Denebola	182 29.6	N14 27.9
04	70 35.3	230 02.7	42.0	251 23.3	24.7	173 14.1	40.0	145 20.0	31.0	Diphda	348 51.2	S17 52.7
05	85 37.7	245 02.3	43.2	266 24.3	24.0	188 16.2	40.1	160 22.4	31.0			
06	100 40.2	260 01.9 S 7 44.4		281 25.3 N 1 23.4		203 18.3 S22 40.1		175 24.8 S22 31.0		Dubhe	193 47.0	N61 38.7
W 07	115 42.7	275 01.5	45.7	296 26.3	22.7	218 20.3	40.1	190 27.2	31.0	Elnath	278 07.1	N28 37.3
E 08	130 45.1	290 01.0	46.9	311 27.3	22.1	233 22.4	40.2	205 29.6	31.0	Eltanin	90 44.2	N51 29.6
D 09	145 47.6	305 00.6 . .	48.1	326 28.3 . .	21.4	248 24.5 . .	40.2	220 32.0 . .	31.0	Enif	33 42.7	N 9 58.1
N 10	160 50.0	320 00.2	49.4	341 29.3	20.8	263 26.6	40.2	235 34.4	31.0	Fomalhaut	15 18.9	S29 31.1
E 11	175 52.5	334 59.8	50.6	356 30.3	20.1	278 28.7	40.3	250 36.8	31.0			
S 12	190 55.0	349 59.4 S 7 51.8		11 31.3 N 1 19.5		293 30.8 S22 40.3		265 39.2 S22 31.0		Gacrux	171 56.7	S57 13.2
D 13	205 57.4	4 59.0	53.0	26 32.3	18.9	308 32.9	40.3	280 41.6	31.0	Gienah	175 48.2	S17 38.8
A 14	220 59.9	19 58.5	54.3	41 33.3	18.2	323 34.9	40.4	295 44.0	31.0	Hadar	148 42.4	S60 28.0
Y 15	236 02.4	34 58.1 . .	55.5	56 34.3 . .	17.6	338 37.0 . .	40.4	310 46.4 . .	31.0	Hamal	327 55.6	N23 33.3
16	251 04.8	49 57.7	56.7	71 35.3	16.9	353 39.1	40.5	325 48.8	31.0	Kaus Aust.	83 38.1	S34 22.5
17	266 07.3	64 57.3	58.0	86 36.2	16.3	8 41.2	40.5	340 51.2	31.0			
18	281 09.8	79 56.9 S 7 59.2		101 37.2 N 1 15.6		23 43.3 S22 40.5		355 53.6 S22 31.0		Kochab	137 21.0	N74 04.8
19	296 12.2	94 56.4 8 00.4		116 38.2	15.0	38 45.4	40.6	10 56.0	30.9	Markab	13 33.8	N15 18.8
20	311 14.7	109 56.0	01.6	131 39.2	14.3	53 47.4	40.6	25 58.4	30.9	Menkar	314 10.3	N 4 10.0
21	326 17.2	124 55.6 . .	02.9	146 40.2 . .	13.7	68 49.5 . .	40.6	41 00.8 . .	30.9	Menkent	148 02.9	S36 27.8
22	341 19.6	139 55.2	04.1	161 41.2	13.0	83 51.6	40.7	56 03.2	30.9	Miaplacidus	221 39.4	S69 47.6
23	356 22.1	154 54.7	05.3	176 42.2	12.4	98 53.7	40.7	71 05.6	30.9			
3 00	11 24.5	169 54.3 S 8 06.5		191 43.2 N 1 11.7		113 55.8 S22 40.7		86 08.0 S22 30.9		Mirfak	308 33.8	N49 55.6
01	26 27.0	184 53.9	07.8	206 44.2	11.1	128 57.8	40.8	101 10.4	30.9	Nunki	75 53.0	S26 16.3
02	41 29.5	199 53.5	09.0	221 45.2	10.4	143 59.9	40.8	116 12.8	30.9	Peacock	53 12.2	S56 40.4
03	56 31.9	214 53.1 . .	10.2	236 46.2 . .	09.8	159 02.0 . .	40.9	131 15.2 . .	30.9	Pollux	243 22.6	N27 58.6
04	71 34.4	229 52.6	11.4	251 47.2	09.1	174 04.1	40.9	146 17.6	30.9	Procyon	244 55.3	N 5 10.5
05	86 36.9	244 52.2	12.7	266 48.2	08.5	189 06.2	40.9	161 20.0	30.9			
06	101 39.3	259 51.8 S 8 13.9		281 49.2 N 1 07.8		204 08.3 S22 41.0		176 22.4 S22 30.9		Rasalhague	96 02.6	N12 33.1
07	116 41.8	274 51.4	15.1	296 50.1	07.2	219 10.3	41.0	191 24.8	30.9	Regulus	207 39.2	N11 52.4
T 08	131 44.3	289 50.9	16.3	311 51.1	06.5	234 12.4	41.0	206 27.2	30.9	Rigel	281 07.8	S 8 10.7
H 09	146 46.7	304 50.5 . .	17.5	326 52.1 . .	05.9	249 14.5 . .	41.1	221 29.6 . .	30.9	Rigil Kent.	139 46.5	S60 54.9
U 10	161 49.2	319 50.1	18.8	341 53.1	05.2	264 16.6	41.1	236 32.0	30.9	Sabik	102 07.7	S15 44.8
R 11	176 51.6	334 49.7	20.0	356 54.1	04.6	279 18.7	41.1	251 34.4	30.9			
S 12	191 54.1	349 49.2 S 8 21.2		11 55.1 N 1 03.9		294 20.7 S22 41.2		266 36.8 S22 30.9		Schedar	349 35.1	N56 38.7
D 13	206 56.6	4 48.8	22.4	26 56.1	03.3	309 22.8	41.2	281 39.2	30.9	Shaula	96 16.2	S37 07.0
A 14	221 59.0	19 48.4	23.7	41 57.1	02.6	324 24.9	41.3	296 41.6	30.9	Sirius	258 29.9	S16 44.5
Y 15	237 01.5	34 48.0 . .	24.9	56 58.1 . .	02.0	339 27.0 . .	41.3	311 44.0 . .	30.9	Spica	158 27.0	S11 15.6
16	252 04.0	49 47.5	26.1	71 59.1	01.3	354 29.0	41.3	326 46.4	30.9	Suhail	222 49.6	S43 30.4
17	267 06.4	64 47.1	27.3	87 00.1	00.7	9 31.1	41.4	341 48.8	30.9			
18	282 08.9	79 46.7 S 8 28.5		102 01.1 N 1 00.0		24 33.2 S22 41.4		356 51.2 S22 30.9		Vega	80 36.1	N38 48.5
19	297 11.4	94 46.3	29.8	117 02.1	0 59.4	39 35.3	41.4	11 53.6	30.9	Zuben'ubi	137 00.9	S16 07.2
20	312 13.8	109 45.8	31.0	132 03.0	58.7	54 37.4	41.5	26 56.0	30.9		SHA	Mer. Pass.
21	327 16.3	124 45.4 . .	32.2	147 04.0 . .	58.1	69 39.4 . .	41.5	41 58.4 . .	30.9		° ′	h m
22	342 18.8	139 45.0	33.4	162 05.0	57.4	84 41.5	41.6	57 00.8	30.9	Venus	159 39.0	12 40
23	357 21.2	154 44.6	34.6	177 06.0	56.8	99 43.6	41.6	72 03.2	30.9	Mars	180 54.0	11 14
	h m									Jupiter	102 40.3	16 25
Mer. Pass. 23 14.5		v −0.4 d 1.2		v 1.0 d 0.6		v 2.1 d 0.0		v 2.4 d 0.0		Saturn	74 45.0	18 16

© British Crown Copyright 2018. All rights reserved.

UT	SUN GHA	SUN Dec	MOON GHA	v	MOON Dec	d	HP
1 00	182 31.6	S 2 59.2	151 34.2	8.9	S10 07.4	12.7	60.0
01	197 31.8	3 00.2	166 02.1	8.8	10 20.1	12.6	60.0
02	212 32.0	01.1	180 29.9	8.8	10 32.7	12.6	59.9
03	227 32.2	.. 02.1	194 57.7	8.8	10 45.3	12.5	59.9
04	242 32.4	03.1	209 25.5	8.8	10 57.8	12.4	59.9
05	257 32.6	04.0	223 53.3	8.7	11 10.2	12.3	59.8
06	272 32.9	S 3 05.0	238 21.0	8.8	S11 22.5	12.2	59.8
07	287 33.1	06.0	252 48.8	8.8	11 34.7	12.2	59.8
08	302 33.3	06.9	267 16.6	8.7	11 46.9	12.0	59.7
09	317 33.5	.. 07.9	281 44.3	8.8	11 58.9	12.0	59.7
10	332 33.7	08.9	296 12.1	8.7	12 10.9	11.9	59.7
11	347 33.9	09.9	310 39.8	8.8	12 22.8	11.8	59.6
12	2 34.1	S 3 10.8	325 07.6	8.7	S12 34.6	11.7	59.6
13	17 34.3	11.8	339 35.3	8.7	12 46.3	11.7	59.5
14	32 34.5	12.8	354 03.0	8.8	12 58.0	11.5	59.5
15	47 34.7	.. 13.7	8 30.8	8.7	13 09.5	11.4	59.5
16	62 34.9	14.7	22 58.5	8.7	13 20.9	11.4	59.4
17	77 35.1	15.7	37 26.2	8.7	13 32.3	11.2	59.4
18	92 35.3	S 3 16.6	51 53.9	8.7	S13 43.5	11.2	59.4
19	107 35.5	17.6	66 21.6	8.6	13 54.7	11.1	59.3
20	122 35.7	18.6	80 49.2	8.7	14 05.8	10.9	59.3
21	137 35.9	.. 19.5	95 16.9	8.7	14 16.7	10.9	59.2
22	152 36.1	20.5	109 44.6	8.6	14 27.6	10.7	59.2
23	167 36.3	21.5	124 12.2	8.6	14 38.3	10.7	59.2
2 00	182 36.5	S 3 22.5	138 39.8	8.7	S14 49.0	10.6	59.1
01	197 36.7	23.4	153 07.5	8.6	14 59.6	10.4	59.1
02	212 36.9	24.4	167 35.1	8.6	15 10.0	10.4	59.1
03	227 37.1	.. 25.4	182 02.7	8.6	15 20.4	10.2	59.0
04	242 37.3	26.3	196 30.3	8.6	15 30.6	10.2	59.0
05	257 37.5	27.3	210 57.9	8.6	15 40.8	10.0	58.9
06	272 37.7	S 3 28.3	225 25.5	8.6	S15 50.8	10.0	58.9
07	287 37.9	29.2	239 53.1	8.6	16 00.8	9.8	58.9
08	302 38.1	30.2	254 20.7	8.5	16 10.6	9.7	58.8
09	317 38.3	.. 31.2	268 48.2	8.6	16 20.3	9.6	58.8
10	332 38.5	32.1	283 15.8	8.6	16 29.9	9.5	58.7
11	347 38.7	33.1	297 43.4	8.5	16 39.4	9.4	58.7
12	2 38.9	S 3 34.1	312 10.9	8.5	S16 48.8	9.3	58.7
13	17 39.1	35.0	326 38.4	8.6	16 58.1	9.1	58.6
14	32 39.3	36.0	341 06.0	8.5	17 07.2	9.1	58.6
15	47 39.5	.. 37.0	355 33.5	8.5	17 16.3	8.9	58.5
16	62 39.7	37.9	10 01.0	8.5	17 25.2	8.9	58.5
17	77 39.9	38.9	24 28.5	8.5	17 34.1	8.7	58.5
18	92 40.1	S 3 39.9	38 56.0	8.5	S17 42.8	8.6	58.4
19	107 40.3	40.9	53 23.5	8.5	17 51.4	8.4	58.4
20	122 40.5	41.8	67 51.0	8.5	17 59.8	8.4	58.3
21	137 40.6	.. 42.8	82 18.5	8.5	18 08.2	8.2	58.3
22	152 40.8	43.8	96 46.0	8.5	18 16.4	8.2	58.3
23	167 41.0	44.7	111 13.5	8.5	18 24.6	8.0	58.2
3 00	182 41.2	S 3 45.7	125 41.0	8.4	S18 32.6	7.9	58.2
01	197 41.4	46.7	140 08.4	8.5	18 40.5	7.7	58.1
02	212 41.6	47.6	154 35.9	8.5	18 48.2	7.7	58.1
03	227 41.8	.. 48.6	169 03.4	8.4	18 55.9	7.5	58.1
04	242 42.0	49.6	183 30.8	8.5	19 03.4	7.4	58.0
05	257 42.2	50.5	197 58.3	8.5	19 10.8	7.3	58.0
06	272 42.4	S 3 51.5	212 25.8	8.4	S19 18.1	7.2	57.9
07	287 42.6	52.5	226 53.2	8.5	19 25.3	7.0	57.9
08	302 42.8	53.4	241 20.7	8.5	19 32.3	7.0	57.9
09	317 43.0	.. 54.4	255 48.2	8.4	19 39.3	6.8	57.8
10	332 43.2	55.4	270 15.6	8.5	19 46.1	6.6	57.8
11	347 43.4	56.3	284 43.1	8.5	19 52.7	6.6	57.7
12	2 43.6	S 3 57.3	299 10.6	8.4	S19 59.3	6.4	57.7
13	17 43.8	58.3	313 38.0	8.5	20 05.7	6.3	57.7
14	32 44.0	3 59.2	328 05.5	8.5	20 12.0	6.2	57.6
15	47 44.2	4 00.2	342 33.0	8.5	20 18.2	6.1	57.6
16	62 44.4	01.2	357 00.5	8.4	20 24.3	5.9	57.5
17	77 44.6	02.1	11 27.9	8.5	20 30.2	5.8	57.5
18	92 44.8	S 4 03.1	25 55.4	8.5	S20 36.0	5.7	57.5
19	107 45.0	04.1	40 22.9	8.5	20 41.7	5.6	57.4
20	122 45.2	05.0	54 50.4	8.5	20 47.3	5.4	57.4
21	137 45.4	.. 06.0	69 17.9	8.5	20 52.7	5.3	57.4
22	152 45.5	06.9	83 45.4	8.6	20 58.0	5.2	57.3
23	167 45.7	07.9	98 13.0	8.5	S21 03.2	5.1	57.3
	SD 16.0	d 1.0	SD 16.2		16.0		15.7

Row labels (left margin): TUESDAY (1), WEDNESDAY (2), THURSDAY (3)

Lat.	Twilight Naut.	Twilight Civil	Sunrise	Moonrise 1	2	3	4
N 72	03 52	05 14	06 22	11 11	14 09	■■■■	■■■■
N 70	04 04	05 17	06 18	10 47	13 05	■■■■	■■■■
68	04 13	05 20	06 15	10 29	12 30	14 37	■■■■
66	04 21	05 22	06 13	10 14	12 05	13 53	15 31
64	04 27	05 23	06 10	10 02	11 45	13 23	14 50
62	04 32	05 24	06 09	09 52	11 29	13 01	14 21
60	04 37	05 25	06 07	09 43	11 16	12 43	14 00
N 58	04 41	05 26	06 05	09 36	11 05	12 28	13 42
56	04 44	05 27	06 04	09 29	10 55	12 16	13 27
54	04 47	05 28	06 03	09 23	10 47	12 05	13 15
52	04 49	05 28	06 02	09 18	10 39	11 55	13 03
50	04 51	05 29	06 01	09 13	10 32	11 46	12 53
45	04 55	05 29	05 59	09 03	10 18	11 28	12 33
N 40	04 58	05 30	05 57	08 55	10 06	11 13	12 16
35	05 01	05 30	05 55	08 47	09 55	11 01	12 02
30	05 02	05 30	05 54	08 41	09 46	10 50	11 49
20	05 03	05 29	05 51	08 30	09 31	10 31	11 28
N 10	05 03	05 28	05 49	08 21	09 18	10 15	11 10
0	05 01	05 25	05 46	08 12	09 06	10 00	10 53
S 10	04 58	05 23	05 44	08 03	08 53	09 44	10 36
20	04 53	05 19	05 41	07 54	08 40	09 28	10 19
30	04 46	05 14	05 38	07 44	08 26	09 10	09 58
35	04 41	05 10	05 36	07 38	08 17	09 00	09 46
40	04 34	05 06	05 33	07 31	08 07	08 47	09 32
45	04 26	05 01	05 31	07 23	07 56	08 33	09 16
S 50	04 16	04 55	05 28	07 13	07 42	08 16	08 56
52	04 11	04 52	05 26	07 09	07 36	08 08	08 46
54	04 06	04 49	05 25	07 04	07 29	07 59	08 36
56	04 00	04 45	05 23	06 59	07 21	07 49	08 23
58	03 52	04 41	05 21	06 53	07 13	07 37	08 10
S 60	03 44	04 36	05 19	06 47	07 03	07 24	07 53

Lat.	Sunset	Twilight Civil	Twilight Naut.	Moonset 1	2	3	4
N 72	17 15	18 22	19 43	17 16	16 11	■■■■	■■■■
N 70	17 19	18 19	19 32	17 42	17 16	■■■■	■■■■
68	17 22	18 17	19 23	18 02	17 53	17 39	■■■■
66	17 25	18 15	19 16	18 17	18 19	18 23	18 37
64	17 27	18 14	19 10	18 31	18 39	18 53	19 19
62	17 29	18 13	19 05	18 42	18 56	19 16	19 47
60	17 31	18 12	19 00	18 51	19 09	19 34	20 09
N 58	17 32	18 11	18 57	19 00	19 21	19 49	20 27
56	17 34	18 11	18 54	19 07	19 32	20 02	20 42
54	17 35	18 10	18 51	19 14	19 41	20 14	20 55
52	17 36	18 10	18 49	19 20	19 49	20 24	21 06
50	17 37	18 09	18 47	19 25	19 56	20 33	21 16
45	17 39	18 09	18 43	19 37	20 12	20 52	21 37
N 40	17 41	18 08	18 40	19 47	20 25	21 08	21 55
35	17 43	18 08	18 38	19 55	20 36	21 21	22 09
30	17 45	18 09	18 36	20 03	20 46	21 32	22 22
20	17 48	18 10	18 35	20 16	21 03	21 52	22 43
N 10	17 50	18 11	18 36	20 27	21 18	22 09	23 02
0	17 53	18 13	18 37	20 37	21 31	22 25	23 19
S 10	17 55	18 16	18 41	20 48	21 45	22 41	23 36
20	17 58	18 20	18 46	20 59	22 00	22 59	23 55
30	18 02	18 26	18 54	21 12	22 17	23 19	24 16
35	18 04	18 29	18 59	21 20	22 27	23 30	24 29
40	18 06	18 33	19 05	21 29	22 38	23 44	24 43
45	18 09	18 38	19 13	21 39	22 52	23 59	25 01
S 50	18 12	18 45	19 24	21 51	23 08	24 19	00 19
52	18 14	18 48	19 29	21 57	23 16	24 28	00 28
54	18 15	18 51	19 35	22 03	23 24	24 39	00 39
56	18 17	18 55	19 41	22 10	23 34	24 50	00 50
58	18 19	18 59	19 48	22 18	23 45	25 04	01 04
S 60	18 22	19 04	19 57	22 27	23 58	25 20	01 20

Day	SUN Eqn. of Time 00ʰ	SUN Eqn. of Time 12ʰ	Mer. Pass.	MOON Mer. Pass. Upper	Lower	Age	Phase
d	m s	m s	h m	h m	h m	d	%
1	10 06	10 16	11 50	14 25	01 58	03	11
2	10 25	10 35	11 49	15 18	02 52	04	19
3	10 45	10 54	11 49	16 12	03 45	05	28

© British Crown Copyright 2018. All rights reserved.

2019 OCTOBER 4, 5, 6 (FRI., SAT., SUN.)

UT	ARIES GHA	VENUS −3.9 GHA	Dec	MARS +1.8 GHA	Dec	JUPITER −2.0 GHA	Dec	SATURN +0.5 GHA	Dec	STARS Name	SHA	Dec
d h	° ′	° ′	° ′	° ′	° ′	° ′	° ′	° ′	° ′		° ′	° ′
4 00	12 23.7	169 44.1	S 8 35.8	192 07.0	N 0 56.1	114 45.7	S22 41.6	87 05.6	S22 30.9	Acamar	315 14.7	S40 13.5
01	27 26.1	184 43.7	37.1	207 08.0	55.5	129 47.7	41.7	102 07.9	30.9	Achernar	335 23.0	S57 08.2
02	42 28.6	199 43.3	38.3	222 09.0	54.8	144 49.8	41.7	117 10.3	30.9	Acrux	173 05.2	S63 12.3
03	57 31.1	214 42.8	.. 39.5	237 10.0	.. 54.2	159 51.9	.. 41.7	132 12.7	.. 30.9	Adhara	255 09.2	S28 59.7
04	72 33.5	229 42.4	40.7	252 11.0	53.5	174 54.0	41.8	147 15.1	30.9	Aldebaran	290 44.3	N16 32.8
05	87 36.0	244 42.0	41.9	267 12.0	52.9	189 56.0	41.8	162 17.5	30.9			
06	102 38.5	259 41.5	S 8 43.1	282 13.0	N 0 52.2	204 58.1	S22 41.8	177 19.9	S22 30.9	Alioth	166 17.4	N55 51.4
07	117 40.9	274 41.1	44.4	297 14.0	51.6	220 00.2	41.9	192 22.3	30.9	Alkaid	152 55.9	N49 13.2
08	132 43.4	289 40.7	45.6	312 15.0	50.9	235 02.3	41.9	207 24.7	30.9	Alnair	27 38.0	S46 52.0
F 09	147 45.9	304 40.3	.. 46.8	327 15.9	.. 50.3	250 04.3	.. 42.0	222 27.1	.. 30.9	Alnilam	275 41.9	S 1 11.3
R 10	162 48.3	319 39.8	48.0	342 16.9	49.6	265 06.4	42.0	237 29.5	30.8	Alphard	217 52.1	S 8 44.5
I 11	177 50.8	334 39.4	49.2	357 17.9	49.0	280 08.5	42.0	252 31.9	30.8			
D 12	192 53.3	349 39.0	S 8 50.4	12 18.9	N 0 48.3	295 10.6	S22 42.1	267 34.3	S22 30.8	Alphecca	126 07.6	N26 39.2
A 13	207 55.7	4 38.5	51.6	27 19.9	47.7	310 12.6	42.1	282 36.7	30.8	Alpheratz	357 38.7	N29 12.0
Y 14	222 58.2	19 38.1	52.9	42 20.9	47.0	325 14.7	42.1	297 39.1	30.8	Altair	62 04.0	N 8 55.5
15	238 00.6	34 37.7	.. 54.1	57 21.9	.. 46.4	340 16.8	.. 42.2	312 41.5	.. 30.8	Ankaa	353 11.0	S42 12.0
16	253 03.1	49 37.2	55.3	72 22.9	45.7	355 18.8	42.2	327 43.8	30.8	Antares	112 21.2	S26 28.4
17	268 05.6	64 36.8	56.5	87 23.9	45.1	10 20.9	42.2	342 46.2	30.8			
18	283 08.0	79 36.4	S 8 57.7	102 24.9	N 0 44.4	25 23.0	S22 42.3	357 48.6	S22 30.8	Arcturus	145 52.1	N19 05.1
19	298 10.5	94 35.9	8 58.9	117 25.9	43.8	40 25.1	42.3	12 51.0	30.8	Atria	107 19.4	S69 03.8
20	313 13.0	109 35.5	9 00.1	132 26.9	43.1	55 27.1	42.4	27 53.4	30.8	Avior	234 16.5	S59 34.0
21	328 15.4	124 35.1	.. 01.3	147 27.8	.. 42.5	70 29.2	.. 42.4	42 55.8	.. 30.8	Bellatrix	278 27.3	N 6 22.0
22	343 17.9	139 34.6	02.6	162 28.8	41.8	85 31.3	42.4	57 58.2	30.8	Betelgeuse	270 56.6	N 7 24.6
23	358 20.4	154 34.2	03.8	177 29.8	41.2	100 33.3	42.5	73 00.6	30.8			
5 00	13 22.8	169 33.7	S 9 05.0	192 30.8	N 0 40.5	115 35.4	S22 42.5	88 03.0	S22 30.8	Canopus	263 54.2	S52 42.1
01	28 25.3	184 33.3	06.2	207 31.8	39.9	130 37.5	42.5	103 05.4	30.8	Capella	280 27.9	N46 00.8
02	43 27.8	199 32.9	07.4	222 32.8	39.2	145 39.6	42.6	118 07.8	30.8	Deneb	49 28.4	N45 21.3
03	58 30.2	214 32.4	.. 08.6	237 33.8	.. 38.6	160 41.6	.. 42.6	133 10.1	.. 30.8	Denebola	182 29.6	N14 27.9
04	73 32.7	229 32.0	09.8	252 34.8	37.9	175 43.7	42.6	148 12.5	30.8	Diphda	348 51.2	S17 52.7
05	88 35.1	244 31.6	11.0	267 35.8	37.3	190 45.8	42.7	163 14.9	30.8			
06	103 37.6	259 31.1	S 9 12.2	282 36.8	N 0 36.6	205 47.8	S22 42.7	178 17.3	S22 30.8	Dubhe	193 47.0	N61 38.7
07	118 40.1	274 30.7	13.4	297 37.8	36.0	220 49.9	42.8	193 19.7	30.8	Elnath	278 07.1	N28 37.3
S 08	133 42.5	289 30.2	14.6	312 38.8	35.3	235 52.0	42.8	208 22.1	30.8	Eltanin	90 44.3	N51 29.6
A 09	148 45.0	304 29.8	.. 15.8	327 39.7	.. 34.7	250 54.0	.. 42.8	223 24.5	.. 30.8	Enif	33 42.7	N 9 58.1
T 10	163 47.5	319 29.4	17.0	342 40.7	34.0	265 56.1	42.9	238 26.9	30.8	Fomalhaut	15 18.9	S29 31.1
U 11	178 49.9	334 28.9	18.3	357 41.7	33.4	280 58.2	42.9	253 29.3	30.8			
R 12	193 52.4	349 28.5	S 9 19.5	12 42.7	N 0 32.7	296 00.2	S22 42.9	268 31.6	S22 30.8	Gacrux	171 56.7	S57 13.2
D 13	208 54.9	4 28.0	20.7	27 43.7	32.1	311 02.3	43.0	283 34.0	30.8	Gienah	175 48.2	S17 38.8
A 14	223 57.3	19 27.6	21.9	42 44.7	31.4	326 04.4	43.0	298 36.4	30.8	Hadar	148 42.4	S60 27.9
Y 15	238 59.8	34 27.2	.. 23.1	57 45.7	.. 30.8	341 06.4	.. 43.1	313 38.8	.. 30.8	Hamal	327 55.6	N23 33.3
16	254 02.3	49 26.7	24.3	72 46.7	30.1	356 08.5	43.1	328 41.2	30.8	Kaus Aust.	83 38.2	S34 22.5
17	269 04.7	64 26.3	25.5	87 47.7	29.5	11 10.6	43.1	343 43.6	30.7			
18	284 07.2	79 25.8	S 9 26.7	102 48.7	N 0 28.8	26 12.6	S22 43.2	358 46.0	S22 30.7	Kochab	137 21.1	N74 04.8
19	299 09.6	94 25.4	27.9	117 49.7	28.2	41 14.7	43.2	13 48.4	30.7	Markab	13 33.8	N15 18.8
20	314 12.1	109 25.0	29.1	132 50.7	27.5	56 16.8	43.2	28 50.7	30.7	Menkar	314 10.3	N 4 10.0
21	329 14.6	124 24.5	.. 30.3	147 51.6	.. 26.9	71 18.8	.. 43.3	43 53.1	.. 30.7	Menkent	148 02.9	S36 27.8
22	344 17.0	139 24.1	31.5	162 52.6	26.2	86 20.9	43.3	58 55.5	30.7	Miaplacidus	221 39.4	S69 47.6
23	359 19.5	154 23.6	32.7	177 53.6	25.6	101 23.0	43.3	73 57.9	30.7			
6 00	14 22.0	169 23.2	S 9 33.9	192 54.6	N 0 24.9	116 25.0	S22 43.4	89 00.3	S22 30.7	Mirfak	308 33.8	N49 55.6
01	29 24.4	184 22.7	35.1	207 55.6	24.3	131 27.1	43.4	104 02.7	30.7	Nunki	75 53.0	S26 16.3
02	44 26.9	199 22.3	36.3	222 56.6	23.6	146 29.2	43.5	119 05.1	30.7	Peacock	53 12.2	S56 40.4
03	59 29.4	214 21.9	.. 37.5	237 57.6	.. 23.0	161 31.2	.. 43.5	134 07.4	.. 30.7	Pollux	243 22.6	N27 58.6
04	74 31.8	229 21.4	38.7	252 58.6	22.3	176 33.3	43.5	149 09.8	30.7	Procyon	244 55.3	N 5 10.5
05	89 34.3	244 21.0	39.9	267 59.6	21.7	191 35.3	43.6	164 12.2	30.7			
06	104 36.7	259 20.5	S 9 41.1	283 00.6	N 0 21.0	206 37.4	S22 43.6	179 14.6	S22 30.7	Rasalhague	96 02.6	N12 33.1
07	119 39.2	274 20.1	42.3	298 01.6	20.4	221 39.5	43.6	194 17.0	30.7	Regulus	207 39.2	N11 52.4
08	134 41.7	289 19.6	43.5	313 02.6	19.7	236 41.5	43.7	209 19.4	30.7	Rigel	281 07.8	S 8 10.7
S 09	149 44.1	304 19.2	.. 44.7	328 03.5	.. 19.1	251 43.6	.. 43.7	224 21.7	.. 30.7	Rigil Kent.	139 46.5	S60 54.9
U 10	164 46.6	319 18.7	45.9	343 04.5	18.4	266 45.7	43.7	239 24.1	30.7	Sabik	102 07.7	S15 44.8
N 11	179 49.1	334 18.3	47.1	358 05.5	17.8	281 47.7	43.8	254 26.5	30.7			
D 12	194 51.5	349 17.8	S 9 48.3	13 06.5	N 0 17.1	296 49.8	S22 43.8	269 28.9	S22 30.7	Schedar	349 35.1	N56 38.7
A 13	209 54.0	4 17.4	49.5	28 07.5	16.5	311 51.8	43.9	284 31.3	30.7	Shaula	96 16.2	S37 07.0
Y 14	224 56.5	19 16.9	50.7	43 08.5	15.8	326 53.9	43.9	299 33.7	30.7	Sirius	258 29.9	S16 44.5
15	239 58.9	34 16.5	.. 51.9	58 09.5	.. 15.2	341 56.0	.. 43.9	314 36.1	.. 30.7	Spica	158 27.0	S11 15.6
16	255 01.4	49 16.0	53.1	73 10.5	14.5	356 58.0	44.0	329 38.4	30.7	Suhail	222 49.6	S43 30.4
17	270 03.9	64 15.6	54.3	88 11.5	13.9	12 00.1	44.0	344 40.8	30.7			
18	285 06.3	79 15.1	S 9 55.4	103 12.5	N 0 13.2	27 02.2	S22 44.0	359 43.2	S22 30.7	Vega	80 36.1	N38 48.5
19	300 08.8	94 14.7	56.6	118 13.5	12.6	42 04.2	44.1	14 45.6	30.7	Zuben'ubi	137 00.9	S16 07.2
20	315 11.2	109 14.2	57.8	133 14.4	11.9	57 06.3	44.1	29 48.0	30.6		SHA	Mer.Pass.
21	330 13.7	124 13.8	9 59.0	148 15.4	.. 11.2	72 08.3	.. 44.2	44 50.3	.. 30.6		° ′	h m
22	345 16.2	139 13.3	10 00.2	163 16.4	10.6	87 10.4	44.2	59 52.7	30.6	Venus	156 10.9	12 42
23	0 18.6	154 12.9	S10 01.4	178 17.4	09.9	102 12.5	44.2	74 55.1	30.6	Mars	179 08.0	11 09
	h m									Jupiter	102 12.6	16 15
Mer.Pass. 23 02.7		v −0.4	d 1.2	v 1.0	d 0.7	v 2.1	d 0.0	v 2.4	d 0.0	Saturn	74 40.1	18 05

© British Crown Copyright 2018. All rights reserved.

UT	SUN GHA	SUN Dec	MOON GHA	v	MOON Dec	d	HP
d h	° ′	° ′	° ′	′	° ′	′	′
4 00	182 45.9	S 4 08.9	112 40.5	8.5	S21 08.3	4.9	57.2
01	197 46.1	09.8	127 08.0	8.6	21 13.2	4.8	57.2
02	212 46.3	10.8	141 35.6	8.6	21 18.0	4.7	57.1
03	227 46.5	.. 11.8	156 03.2	8.5	21 22.7	4.5	57.1
04	242 46.7	12.7	170 30.7	8.6	21 27.2	4.4	57.1
05	257 46.9	13.7	184 58.3	8.6	21 31.6	4.3	57.0
06	272 47.1	S 4 14.7	199 25.9	8.6	S21 35.9	4.2	57.0
07	287 47.3	15.6	213 53.5	8.7	21 40.1	4.1	57.0
08	302 47.5	16.6	228 21.2	8.6	21 44.2	3.9	56.9
F 09	317 47.7	.. 17.6	242 48.8	8.7	21 48.1	3.8	56.9
R 10	332 47.9	18.5	257 16.5	8.6	21 51.9	3.6	56.8
I 11	347 48.1	19.5	271 44.1	8.7	21 55.5	3.6	56.8
D 12	2 48.2	S 4 20.5	286 11.8	8.7	S21 59.1	3.4	56.8
A 13	17 48.4	21.4	300 39.5	8.8	22 02.5	3.3	56.7
Y 14	32 48.6	22.4	315 07.3	8.7	22 05.8	3.1	56.7
15	47 48.8	.. 23.3	329 35.0	8.8	22 08.9	3.1	56.7
16	62 49.0	24.3	344 02.8	8.8	22 12.0	2.9	56.6
17	77 49.2	25.3	358 30.6	8.8	22 14.9	2.7	56.6
18	92 49.4	S 4 26.2	12 58.4	8.8	S22 17.6	2.7	56.6
19	107 49.6	27.2	27 26.2	8.8	22 20.3	2.5	56.5
20	122 49.8	28.2	41 54.0	8.9	22 22.8	2.4	56.5
21	137 50.0	.. 29.1	56 21.9	8.9	22 25.2	2.3	56.5
22	152 50.2	30.1	70 49.8	8.9	22 27.5	2.2	56.4
23	167 50.4	31.1	85 17.7	9.0	22 29.7	2.0	56.4
5 00	182 50.5	S 4 32.0	99 45.7	9.0	S22 31.7	1.9	56.3
01	197 50.7	33.0	114 13.7	9.0	22 33.6	1.8	56.3
02	212 50.9	33.9	128 41.7	9.0	22 35.4	1.6	56.3
03	227 51.1	.. 34.9	143 09.7	9.1	22 37.0	1.5	56.2
04	242 51.3	35.9	157 37.8	9.1	22 38.5	1.4	56.2
05	257 51.5	36.8	172 05.9	9.1	22 39.9	1.3	56.2
06	272 51.7	S 4 37.8	186 34.0	9.1	S22 41.2	1.2	56.1
07	287 51.9	38.8	201 02.1	9.2	22 42.4	1.0	56.1
S 08	302 52.1	39.7	215 30.3	9.2	22 43.4	0.9	56.1
A 09	317 52.3	.. 40.7	229 58.5	9.3	22 44.3	0.8	56.0
T 10	332 52.4	41.6	244 26.8	9.3	22 45.1	0.7	56.0
U 11	347 52.6	42.6	258 55.1	9.3	22 45.8	0.5	56.0
R 12	2 52.8	S 4 43.6	273 23.4	9.3	S22 46.3	0.5	56.0
D 13	17 53.0	44.5	287 51.7	9.4	22 46.8	0.3	55.9
A 14	32 53.2	45.5	302 20.1	9.4	22 47.1	0.1	55.9
Y 15	47 53.4	.. 46.5	316 48.5	9.5	22 47.2	0.1	55.9
16	62 53.6	47.4	331 17.0	9.5	22 47.3	0.1	55.8
17	77 53.8	48.4	345 45.5	9.5	22 47.2	0.1	55.8
18	92 53.9	S 4 49.3	0 14.0	9.6	S22 47.1	0.3	55.8
19	107 54.1	50.3	14 42.6	9.6	22 46.8	0.4	55.7
20	122 54.3	51.3	29 11.2	9.6	22 46.4	0.6	55.7
21	137 54.5	.. 52.2	43 39.8	9.7	22 45.8	0.6	55.7
22	152 54.7	53.2	58 08.5	9.7	22 45.2	0.8	55.6
23	167 54.9	54.1	72 37.3	9.7	22 44.4	0.9	55.6
6 00	182 55.1	S 4 55.1	87 06.0	9.9	S22 43.5	1.0	55.6
01	197 55.3	56.1	101 34.9	9.8	22 42.5	1.1	55.6
02	212 55.4	57.0	116 03.7	9.9	22 41.4	1.2	55.5
03	227 55.6	.. 58.0	130 32.6	10.0	22 40.2	1.4	55.5
04	242 55.8	58.9	145 01.6	10.0	22 38.8	1.5	55.5
05	257 56.0	4 59.9	159 30.6	10.0	22 37.3	1.5	55.5
06	272 56.2	S 5 00.9	173 59.6	10.1	S22 35.8	1.7	55.4
07	287 56.4	01.8	188 28.7	10.1	22 34.1	1.8	55.4
08	302 56.6	02.8	202 57.8	10.2	22 32.3	2.0	55.4
S 09	317 56.7	.. 03.7	217 27.0	10.2	22 30.3	2.0	55.3
U 10	332 56.9	04.7	231 56.2	10.2	22 28.3	2.1	55.3
N 11	347 57.1	05.7	246 25.4	10.4	22 26.2	2.3	55.3
D 12	2 57.3	S 5 06.6	260 54.8	10.3	S22 23.9	2.3	55.3
A 13	17 57.5	07.6	275 24.1	10.4	22 21.6	2.5	55.2
Y 14	32 57.7	08.5	289 53.5	10.5	22 19.1	2.6	55.2
15	47 57.9	.. 09.5	304 23.0	10.5	22 16.5	2.7	55.2
16	62 58.0	10.5	318 52.5	10.5	22 13.8	2.8	55.2
17	77 58.2	11.4	333 22.0	10.7	22 11.0	2.9	55.1
18	92 58.4	S 5 12.4	347 51.7	10.6	S22 08.1	3.0	55.1
19	107 58.6	13.3	2 21.3	10.7	22 05.1	3.1	55.1
20	122 58.8	14.3	16 51.0	10.8	22 02.0	3.3	55.1
21	137 59.0	.. 15.2	31 20.8	10.8	21 58.7	3.3	55.0
22	152 59.2	16.2	45 50.6	10.9	21 55.4	3.4	55.0
23	167 59.3	17.2	60 20.5	10.9	S21 52.0	3.6	55.0
	SD 16.0	d 1.0	SD 15.5		15.2		15.1

Lat.	Twilight Naut.	Twilight Civil	Sunrise	Moonrise 4	5	6	7
°	h m	h m	h m	h m	h m	h m	h m
N 72	04 07	05 28	06 35	████	████	████	████
N 70	04 17	05 29	06 30	████	████	████	████
68	04 25	05 30	06 26	████	████	████	18 09
66	04 31	05 31	06 22	15 31	16 43	17 15	17 26
64	04 36	05 32	06 19	14 50	15 55	16 35	16 57
62	04 41	05 32	06 16	14 21	15 24	16 07	16 34
60	04 44	05 33	06 14	14 00	15 01	15 46	16 16
N 58	04 47	05 33	06 12	13 42	14 42	15 28	16 02
56	04 50	05 33	06 10	13 27	14 27	15 13	15 49
54	04 52	05 33	06 08	13 15	14 13	15 01	15 37
52	04 54	05 33	06 07	13 03	14 02	14 49	15 28
50	04 56	05 33	06 05	12 53	13 51	14 40	15 19
45	04 59	05 33	06 02	12 33	13 30	14 19	15 00
N 40	05 01	05 33	06 00	12 16	13 12	14 02	14 44
35	05 03	05 32	05 57	12 02	12 57	13 47	14 31
30	05 04	05 31	05 55	11 49	12 45	13 35	14 20
20	05 04	05 30	05 52	11 28	12 23	13 14	14 01
N 10	05 03	05 27	05 48	11 10	12 04	12 55	13 44
0	05 00	05 24	05 45	10 53	11 46	12 38	13 28
S 10	04 56	05 21	05 42	10 36	11 29	12 21	13 12
20	04 50	05 16	05 38	10 19	11 10	12 02	12 55
30	04 42	05 10	05 34	09 58	10 48	11 41	12 35
35	04 36	05 06	05 31	09 46	10 36	11 29	12 24
40	04 29	05 01	05 29	09 32	10 21	11 14	12 10
45	04 20	04 56	05 25	09 16	10 04	10 57	11 55
S 50	04 09	04 48	05 21	08 56	09 43	10 36	11 35
52	04 04	04 45	05 19	08 46	09 32	10 26	11 26
54	03 58	04 41	05 15	08 36	09 21	10 15	11 16
56	03 51	04 37	05 15	08 23	09 08	10 02	11 04
58	03 43	04 32	05 12	08 10	08 53	09 47	10 51
S 60	03 33	04 27	05 10	07 53	08 35	09 29	10 35

Lat.	Sunset	Twilight Civil	Twilight Naut.	Moonset 4	5	6	7
°	h m	h m	h m	h m	h m	h m	h m
N 72	17 00	18 07	19 26	████	████	████	████
N 70	17 05	18 06	19 17	████	████	████	████
68	17 09	18 05	19 10	████	████	████	21 19
66	17 13	18 04	19 04	18 37	19 16	20 30	22 01
64	17 16	18 04	18 59	19 19	20 04	21 10	22 30
62	17 19	18 03	18 55	19 47	20 34	21 37	22 51
60	17 22	18 03	18 51	20 09	20 57	21 59	23 09
N 58	17 24	18 03	18 48	20 27	21 16	22 16	23 23
56	17 26	18 03	18 46	20 42	21 32	22 30	23 36
54	17 28	18 03	18 44	20 55	21 45	22 43	23 47
52	17 29	18 03	18 42	21 06	21 57	22 54	23 56
50	17 31	18 03	18 40	21 16	22 07	23 04	24 05
45	17 34	18 03	18 37	21 37	22 29	23 24	24 23
N 40	17 37	18 04	18 35	21 55	22 46	23 41	24 38
35	17 39	18 04	18 34	22 09	23 01	23 55	24 50
30	17 41	18 05	18 33	22 22	23 13	24 07	00 07
20	17 45	18 07	18 33	22 43	23 35	24 28	00 28
N 10	17 48	18 09	18 34	23 02	23 54	24 46	00 46
0	17 52	18 12	18 37	23 19	24 12	00 12	01 02
S 10	17 55	18 16	18 41	23 36	24 29	00 29	01 19
20	17 59	18 21	18 47	23 55	24 48	00 48	01 37
30	18 03	18 28	18 56	24 16	00 16	01 09	01 57
35	18 06	18 32	19 02	24 29	00 29	01 22	02 09
40	18 09	18 36	19 09	24 43	00 43	01 36	02 23
45	18 13	18 42	19 18	25 01	01 01	01 54	02 39
S 50	18 17	18 50	19 29	00 19	01 22	02 15	02 59
52	18 19	18 53	19 35	00 28	01 32	02 25	03 08
54	18 21	18 57	19 41	00 39	01 43	02 36	03 18
56	18 23	19 01	19 48	00 50	01 56	02 49	03 30
58	18 26	19 06	19 56	01 04	02 11	03 05	03 44
S 60	18 29	19 12	20 06	01 20	02 29	03 23	04 00

	SUN		MOON			
Day	Eqn. of Time 00ʰ	Eqn. of Time 12ʰ	Mer. Pass.	Mer. Pass. Upper	Lower	Age	Phase
d	m s	m s	h m	h m	h m	d %	
4	11 03	11 13	11 49	17 06	04 39	06 38	
5	11 22	11 31	11 48	17 59	05 33	07 48	◐
6	11 40	11 49	11 48	18 50	06 25	08 58	

© British Crown Copyright 2018. All rights reserved.

UT	ARIES GHA	VENUS −3.9 GHA	Dec	MARS +1.8 GHA	Dec	JUPITER −2.0 GHA	Dec	SATURN +0.5 GHA	Dec	STARS Name	SHA	Dec
7 00	15 21.1	169 12.4	S10 02.6	193 18.4	N 0 09.3	117 14.5	S22 44.3	89 57.5	S22 30.6	Acamar	315 14.7	S40 13.5
01	30 23.6	184 12.0	03.8	208 19.4	08.6	132 16.6	44.3	104 59.9	30.6	Achernar	335 22.9	S57 08.2
02	45 26.0	199 11.5	05.0	223 20.4	08.0	147 18.6	44.3	120 02.3	30.6	Acrux	173 05.2	S63 12.3
03	60 28.5	214 11.1 ..	06.2	238 21.4 ..	07.3	162 20.7 ..	44.4	135 04.6 ..	30.6	Adhara	255 09.1	S28 59.7
04	75 31.0	229 10.6	07.4	253 22.4	06.7	177 22.7	44.4	150 07.0	30.6	Aldebaran	290 44.2	N16 32.8
05	90 33.4	244 10.2	08.6	268 23.4	06.0	192 24.8	44.4	165 09.4	30.6			
06	105 35.9	259 09.7	S10 09.7	283 24.4	N 0 05.4	207 26.9	S22 44.5	180 11.8	S22 30.6	Alioth	166 17.4	N55 51.3
07	120 38.4	274 09.3	10.9	298 25.3	04.7	222 28.9	44.5	195 14.2	30.6	Alkaid	152 55.9	N49 13.1
08	135 40.8	289 08.8	12.1	313 26.3	04.1	237 31.0	44.6	210 16.5	30.6	Alnair	27 38.0	S46 52.0
M 09	150 43.3	304 08.4 ..	13.3	328 27.3 ..	03.4	252 33.0 ..	44.6	225 18.9 ..	30.6	Alnilam	275 41.9	S 1 11.3
O 10	165 45.7	319 07.9	14.5	343 28.3	02.8	267 35.1	44.6	240 21.3	30.6	Alphard	217 52.1	S 8 44.5
N 11	180 48.2	334 07.4	15.7	358 29.3	02.1	282 37.2	44.7	255 23.7	30.6			
D 12	195 50.7	349 07.0	S10 16.9	13 30.3	N 0 01.5	297 39.2	S22 44.7	270 26.1	S22 30.6	Alphecca	126 07.6	N26 39.2
A 13	210 53.1	4 06.5	18.1	28 31.3	00.8	312 41.3	44.7	285 28.4	30.6	Alpheratz	357 38.7	N29 12.0
Y 14	225 55.6	19 06.1	19.2	43 32.3	N 00.2	327 43.3	44.8	300 30.8	30.6	Altair	62 04.0	N 8 55.5
15	240 58.1	34 05.6 ..	20.4	58 33.3	S 00.5	342 45.4 ..	44.8	315 33.2 ..	30.6	Ankaa	353 11.0	S42 12.0
16	256 00.5	49 05.2	21.6	73 34.3	01.1	357 47.4	44.8	330 35.6	30.6	Antares	112 21.2	S26 28.4
17	271 03.0	64 04.7	22.8	88 35.3	01.8	12 49.5	44.9	345 38.0	30.6			
18	286 05.5	79 04.2	S10 24.0	103 36.2	S 0 02.4	27 51.5	S22 44.9	0 40.3	S22 30.6	Arcturus	145 52.1	N19 05.1
19	301 07.9	94 03.8	25.2	118 37.2	03.1	42 53.6	45.0	15 42.7	30.6	Atria	107 19.4	S69 03.8
20	316 10.4	109 03.3	26.4	133 38.2	03.7	57 55.7	45.0	30 45.1	30.5	Avior	234 16.5	S59 34.0
21	331 12.8	124 02.9 ..	27.5	148 39.2 ..	04.4	72 57.7 ..	45.0	45 47.5 ..	30.5	Bellatrix	278 27.3	N 6 22.0
22	346 15.3	139 02.4	28.7	163 40.2	05.0	87 59.8	45.1	60 49.8	30.5	Betelgeuse	270 56.5	N 7 24.6
23	1 17.8	154 02.0	29.9	178 41.2	05.7	103 01.8	45.1	75 52.2	30.5			
8 00	16 20.2	169 01.5	S10 31.1	193 42.2	S 0 06.3	118 03.9	S22 45.1	90 54.6	S22 30.5	Canopus	263 54.1	S52 42.1
01	31 22.7	184 01.0	32.3	208 43.2	07.0	133 05.9	45.2	105 57.0	30.5	Capella	280 27.9	N46 00.8
02	46 25.2	199 00.6	33.4	223 44.2	07.6	148 08.0	45.2	120 59.4	30.5	Deneb	49 28.4	N45 21.3
03	61 27.6	214 00.1 ..	34.6	238 45.2 ..	08.3	163 10.0 ..	45.2	136 01.7 ..	30.5	Denebola	182 29.6	N14 27.9
04	76 30.1	228 59.6	35.8	253 46.1	08.9	178 12.1	45.3	151 04.1	30.5	Diphda	348 51.2	S17 52.7
05	91 32.6	243 59.2	37.0	268 47.1	09.6	193 14.1	45.3	166 06.5	30.5			
06	106 35.0	258 58.7	S10 38.2	283 48.1	S 0 10.2	208 16.2	S22 45.4	181 08.9	S22 30.5	Dubhe	193 47.0	N61 38.7
07	121 37.5	273 58.3	39.3	298 49.1	10.9	223 18.2	45.4	196 11.2	30.5	Elnath	278 07.0	N28 37.3
T 08	136 40.0	288 57.8	40.5	313 50.1	11.5	238 20.3	45.4	211 13.6	30.5	Eltanin	90 44.3	N51 29.6
U 09	151 42.4	303 57.3 ..	41.7	328 51.1 ..	12.2	253 22.3 ..	45.5	226 16.0 ..	30.5	Enif	33 42.7	N 9 58.1
E 10	166 44.9	318 56.9	42.9	343 52.1	12.8	268 24.4	45.5	241 18.4	30.5	Fomalhaut	15 18.9	S29 31.1
S 11	181 47.3	333 56.4	44.1	358 53.1	13.5	283 26.4	45.5	256 20.7	30.5			
D 12	196 49.8	348 55.9	S10 45.2	13 54.1	S 0 14.1	298 28.5	S22 45.6	271 23.1	S22 30.5	Gacrux	171 56.7	S57 13.2
A 13	211 52.3	3 55.5	46.4	28 55.1	14.8	313 30.5	45.6	286 25.5	30.5	Gienah	175 48.2	S17 38.8
Y 14	226 54.7	18 55.0	47.6	43 56.0	15.4	328 32.6	45.6	301 27.9	30.5	Hadar	148 42.4	S60 27.9
15	241 57.2	33 54.5 ..	48.8	58 57.0 ..	16.1	343 34.6 ..	45.7	316 30.2 ..	30.5	Hamal	327 55.6	N23 33.3
16	256 59.7	48 54.1	49.9	73 58.0	16.7	358 36.7	45.7	331 32.6	30.5	Kaus Aust.	83 38.2	S34 22.5
17	272 02.1	63 53.6	51.1	88 59.0	17.4	13 38.7	45.8	346 35.0	30.5			
18	287 04.6	78 53.1	S10 52.3	104 00.0	S 0 18.0	28 40.8	S22 45.8	1 37.4	S22 30.4	Kochab	137 21.1	N74 04.7
19	302 07.1	93 52.7	53.5	119 01.0	18.7	43 42.8	45.8	16 39.7	30.4	Markab	13 33.8	N15 18.8
20	317 09.5	108 52.2	54.6	134 02.0	19.3	58 44.9	45.9	31 42.1	30.4	Menkar	314 10.3	N 4 10.0
21	332 12.0	123 51.7 ..	55.8	149 03.0 ..	20.0	73 46.9 ..	45.9	46 44.5 ..	30.4	Menkent	148 02.9	S36 27.8
22	347 14.5	138 51.3	57.0	164 04.0	20.6	88 49.0	45.9	61 46.9	30.4	Miaplacidus	221 39.3	S69 47.6
23	2 16.9	153 50.8	58.2	179 05.0	21.3	103 51.0	46.0	76 49.2	30.4			
9 00	17 19.4	168 50.3	S10 59.3	194 05.9	S 0 21.9	118 53.1	S22 46.0	91 51.6	S22 30.4	Mirfak	308 33.8	N49 55.7
01	32 21.8	183 49.9	11 00.5	209 06.9	22.6	133 55.1	46.1	106 54.0	30.4	Nunki	75 53.0	S26 16.3
02	47 24.3	198 49.4	01.7	224 07.9	23.2	148 57.2	46.1	121 56.3	30.4	Peacock	53 12.3	S56 40.4
03	62 26.8	213 48.9 ..	02.8	239 08.9 ..	23.9	163 59.2 ..	46.1	136 58.7 ..	30.4	Pollux	243 22.5	N27 58.6
04	77 29.2	228 48.5	04.0	254 09.9	24.5	179 01.3	46.2	152 01.1	30.4	Procyon	244 55.3	N 5 10.5
05	92 31.7	243 48.0	05.2	269 10.9	25.2	194 03.3	46.2	167 03.5	30.4			
06	107 34.2	258 47.5	S11 06.3	284 11.9	S 0 25.8	209 05.4	S22 46.2	182 05.8	S22 30.4	Rasalhague	96 02.6	N12 33.0
W 07	122 36.6	273 47.0	07.5	299 12.9	26.5	224 07.4	46.3	197 08.2	30.4	Regulus	207 39.2	N11 52.4
E 08	137 39.1	288 46.6	08.7	314 13.9	27.1	239 09.5	46.3	212 10.6	30.4	Rigel	281 07.8	S 8 10.7
D 09	152 41.6	303 46.1 ..	09.9	329 14.8 ..	27.8	254 11.5 ..	46.3	227 13.0 ..	30.4	Rigil Kent.	139 46.5	S60 54.8
N 10	167 44.0	318 45.6	11.0	344 15.8	28.4	269 13.6	46.4	242 15.3	30.4	Sabik	102 07.8	S15 44.8
E 11	182 46.5	333 45.2	12.2	359 16.8	29.1	284 15.6	46.4	257 17.7	30.4			
S 12	197 48.9	348 44.7	S11 13.4	14 17.8	S 0 29.7	299 17.7	S22 46.5	272 20.1	S22 30.4	Schedar	349 35.1	N56 38.7
D 13	212 51.4	3 44.2	14.5	29 18.8	30.4	314 19.7	46.5	287 22.4	30.4	Shaula	96 16.2	S37 07.0
A 14	227 53.9	18 43.7	15.7	44 19.8	31.0	329 21.7	46.5	302 24.8	30.3	Sirius	258 29.9	S16 44.5
Y 15	242 56.3	33 43.3 ..	16.9	59 20.8 ..	31.7	344 23.8 ..	46.6	317 27.2 ..	30.3	Spica	158 27.0	S11 15.6
16	257 58.8	48 42.8	18.0	74 21.8	32.3	359 25.8	46.6	332 29.5	30.3	Suhail	222 49.5	S43 30.4
17	273 01.3	63 42.3	19.2	89 22.8	33.0	14 27.9	46.6	347 31.9	30.3			
18	288 03.7	78 41.8	S11 20.3	104 23.7	S 0 33.6	29 29.9	S22 46.7	2 34.3	S22 30.3	Vega	80 36.1	N38 48.5
19	303 06.2	93 41.4	21.5	119 24.7	34.3	44 32.0	46.7	17 36.7	30.3	Zuben'ubi	137 00.9	S16 07.2
20	318 08.7	108 40.9	22.7	134 25.7	34.9	59 34.0	46.7	32 39.0	30.3		SHA	Mer.Pass.
21	333 11.1	123 40.4 ..	23.8	149 26.7 ..	35.6	74 36.1 ..	46.8	47 41.4 ..	30.3			h m
22	348 13.6	138 39.9	25.0	164 27.7	36.2	89 38.1	46.8	62 43.8	30.3	Venus	152 41.3	12 44
23	3 16.1	153 39.5	26.2	179 28.7	36.9	104 40.1	46.9	77 46.1	30.3	Mars	177 21.9	11 04
	h m									Jupiter	101 43.6	16 06
Mer.Pass. 22 50.9	*v* −0.5 *d* 1.2			*v* 1.0 *d* 0.7		*v* 2.1 *d* 0.0		*v* 2.4 *d* 0.0		Saturn	74 34.4	17 54

© British Crown Copyright 2018. All rights reserved.

UT	SUN GHA	SUN Dec	MOON GHA	v	MOON Dec	d	HP
d h	° ′	° ′	° ′	′	° ′	′	′
7 00	182 59.5	S 5 18.1	74 50.4	10.9	S21 48.4	3.6	55.0
01	197 59.7	19.1	89 20.3	11.1	21 44.8	3.8	55.0
02	212 59.9	20.0	103 50.4	11.0	21 41.0	3.8	54.9
03	228 00.1	.. 21.0	118 20.4	11.1	21 37.2	4.0	54.9
04	243 00.2	22.0	132 50.5	11.2	21 33.2	4.0	54.9
05	258 00.4	22.9	147 20.7	11.3	21 29.2	4.2	54.9
06	273 00.6	S 5 23.9	161 51.0	11.2	S21 25.0	4.2	54.9
07	288 00.8	24.8	176 21.2	11.4	21 20.8	4.4	54.8
M 08	303 01.0	25.8	190 51.6	11.4	21 16.4	4.4	54.8
O 09	318 01.1	.. 26.7	205 22.0	11.4	21 12.0	4.6	54.8
N 10	333 01.3	27.7	219 52.4	11.5	21 07.4	4.6	54.8
D 11	348 01.5	28.7	234 22.9	11.6	21 02.8	4.8	54.8
A 12	3 01.7	S 5 29.6	248 53.5	11.6	S20 58.0	4.8	54.7
Y 13	18 01.9	30.6	263 24.1	11.6	20 53.2	4.9	54.7
14	33 02.0	31.5	277 54.7	11.8	20 48.3	5.1	54.7
15	48 02.2	.. 32.5	292 25.5	11.7	20 43.2	5.1	54.7
16	63 02.4	33.4	306 56.2	11.9	20 38.1	5.2	54.7
17	78 02.6	34.4	321 27.1	11.8	20 32.9	5.3	54.6
18	93 02.8	S 5 35.3	335 57.9	12.0	S20 27.6	5.4	54.6
19	108 02.9	36.3	350 28.9	12.0	20 22.2	5.5	54.6
20	123 03.1	37.3	4 59.9	12.0	20 16.7	5.6	54.6
21	138 03.3	.. 38.2	19 30.9	12.1	20 11.1	5.6	54.6
22	153 03.5	39.2	34 02.0	12.2	20 05.5	5.8	54.6
23	168 03.7	40.1	48 33.2	12.2	19 59.7	5.8	54.5
8 00	183 03.8	S 5 41.1	63 04.4	12.3	S19 53.9	6.0	54.5
01	198 04.0	42.0	77 35.7	12.3	19 47.9	6.0	54.5
02	213 04.2	43.0	92 07.0	12.4	19 41.9	6.1	54.5
03	228 04.4	.. 43.9	106 38.4	12.4	19 35.8	6.2	54.5
04	243 04.6	44.9	121 09.8	12.5	19 29.6	6.3	54.5
05	258 04.7	45.8	135 41.3	12.5	19 23.3	6.4	54.4
06	273 04.9	S 5 46.8	150 12.8	12.6	S19 16.9	6.4	54.4
07	288 05.1	47.8	164 44.4	12.6	19 10.5	6.5	54.4
T 08	303 05.3	48.7	179 16.0	12.8	19 04.0	6.7	54.4
U 09	318 05.4	.. 49.7	193 47.8	12.7	18 57.3	6.7	54.4
E 10	333 05.6	50.6	208 19.5	12.8	18 50.6	6.7	54.4
S 11	348 05.8	51.6	222 51.3	12.9	18 43.9	6.9	54.4
D 12	3 06.0	S 5 52.5	237 23.2	12.9	S18 37.0	6.9	54.4
A 13	18 06.2	53.5	251 55.1	13.0	18 30.1	7.1	54.3
Y 14	33 06.3	54.4	266 27.1	13.0	18 23.0	7.1	54.3
15	48 06.5	.. 55.4	280 59.1	13.1	18 15.9	7.1	54.3
16	63 06.7	56.3	295 31.2	13.1	18 08.8	7.3	54.3
17	78 06.9	57.3	310 03.3	13.2	18 01.5	7.3	54.3
18	93 07.0	S 5 58.2	324 35.5	13.2	S17 54.2	7.4	54.3
19	108 07.2	5 59.2	339 07.7	13.3	17 46.8	7.5	54.3
20	123 07.4	6 00.1	353 40.0	13.3	17 39.3	7.5	54.3
21	138 07.6	.. 01.1	8 12.3	13.4	17 31.8	7.7	54.2
22	153 07.7	02.0	22 44.7	13.4	17 24.1	7.7	54.2
23	168 07.9	03.0	37 17.1	13.5	17 16.4	7.7	54.2
9 00	183 08.1	S 6 04.0	51 49.6	13.5	S17 08.7	7.9	54.2
01	198 08.3	04.9	66 22.1	13.6	17 00.8	7.9	54.2
02	213 08.4	05.9	80 54.7	13.7	16 52.9	8.0	54.2
03	228 08.6	.. 06.8	95 27.4	13.6	16 44.9	8.1	54.2
04	243 08.8	07.8	110 00.0	13.8	16 36.8	8.1	54.2
05	258 09.0	08.7	124 32.8	13.8	16 28.7	8.2	54.2
06	273 09.1	S 6 09.7	139 05.6	13.8	S16 20.5	8.2	54.2
W 07	288 09.3	10.6	153 38.4	13.9	16 12.3	8.4	54.2
E 08	303 09.5	11.6	168 11.3	13.9	16 03.9	8.4	54.1
D 09	318 09.6	.. 12.5	182 44.2	14.0	15 55.5	8.4	54.1
N 10	333 09.8	13.5	197 17.2	14.0	15 47.1	8.5	54.1
E 11	348 10.0	14.4	211 50.2	14.0	15 38.6	8.6	54.1
S 12	3 10.2	S 6 15.4	226 23.2	14.1	S15 30.0	8.7	54.1
D 13	18 10.3	16.3	240 56.3	14.2	15 21.3	8.7	54.1
A 14	33 10.5	17.3	255 29.5	14.2	15 12.6	8.8	54.1
Y 15	48 10.7	.. 18.2	270 02.7	14.2	15 03.8	8.8	54.1
16	63 10.9	19.2	284 35.9	14.3	14 55.0	8.9	54.1
17	78 11.0	20.1	299 09.2	14.4	14 46.1	9.0	54.1
18	93 11.2	S 6 21.1	313 42.6	14.3	S14 37.1	9.0	54.1
19	108 11.4	22.0	328 15.9	14.4	14 28.1	9.1	54.1
20	123 11.5	23.0	342 49.3	14.5	14 19.0	9.1	54.1
21	138 11.7	.. 23.9	357 22.8	14.5	14 09.9	9.2	54.1
22	153 11.9	24.9	11 56.3	14.4	14 00.7	9.2	54.1
23	168 12.0	25.8	26 29.8	14.6	S13 51.5	9.4	54.1
	SD 16.0	d 1.0	SD 14.9		14.8		14.7

Moonrise

Lat.	Twilight Naut.	Twilight Civil	Sunrise	7	8	9	10
°	h m	h m	h m	h m	h m	h m	h m
N 72	04 22	05 41	06 49	■■■	19 47	18 40	18 12
N 70	04 30	05 41	06 42	■■■	18 34	18 10	17 54
68	04 36	05 41	06 37	18 09	17 56	17 47	17 41
66	04 41	05 41	06 32	17 26	17 29	17 30	17 29
64	04 45	05 40	06 28	16 57	17 08	17 15	17 20
62	04 49	05 40	06 24	16 34	16 52	17 03	17 11
60	04 51	05 40	06 21	16 16	16 38	16 53	17 04
N 58	04 54	05 39	06 19	16 02	16 26	16 44	16 58
56	04 56	05 39	06 16	15 49	16 15	16 36	16 53
54	04 58	05 39	06 14	15 37	16 06	16 29	16 48
52	04 59	05 38	06 12	15 28	15 58	16 22	16 43
50	05 00	05 38	06 10	15 19	15 50	16 17	16 39
45	05 03	05 37	06 06	15 00	15 34	16 04	16 30
N 40	05 04	05 36	06 03	14 44	15 21	15 54	16 22
35	05 05	05 35	06 00	14 31	15 10	15 45	16 16
30	05 06	05 33	05 57	14 20	15 00	15 37	16 10
20	05 05	05 30	05 53	14 01	14 44	15 23	16 00
N 10	05 03	05 27	05 48	13 44	14 29	15 11	15 52
0	04 59	05 24	05 44	13 28	14 15	15 00	15 44
S 10	04 55	05 19	05 40	13 12	14 01	14 49	15 35
20	04 48	05 14	05 36	12 55	13 46	14 37	15 27
30	04 38	05 06	05 30	12 35	13 29	14 23	15 16
35	04 32	05 02	05 27	12 24	13 19	14 15	15 11
40	04 24	04 56	05 24	12 10	13 08	14 06	15 04
45	04 14	04 50	05 20	11 55	12 54	13 55	14 56
S 50	04 02	04 42	05 15	11 35	12 38	13 42	14 47
52	03 56	04 38	05 12	11 26	12 30	13 36	14 43
54	03 49	04 34	05 10	11 16	12 22	13 29	14 38
56	03 42	04 29	05 07	11 04	12 12	13 22	14 33
58	03 33	04 23	05 04	10 51	12 01	13 13	14 27
S 60	03 23	04 17	05 01	10 35	11 48	13 04	14 20

Moonset

Lat.	Sunset	Twilight Civil	Twilight Naut.	7	8	9	10
°	h m	h m	h m	h m	h m	h m	h m
N 72	16 44	17 52	19 10	■■■	21 19	23 59	25 57
N 70	16 51	17 52	19 03	■■■	22 32	24 28	00 28
68	16 57	17 53	18 57	21 19	23 09	24 49	00 49
66	17 02	17 53	18 52	22 01	23 34	25 06	01 06
64	17 06	17 53	18 48	22 30	23 54	25 19	01 19
62	17 10	17 54	18 45	22 51	24 10	00 10	01 30
60	17 13	17 54	18 42	23 09	24 24	00 24	01 40
N 58	17 15	17 55	18 40	23 23	24 35	00 35	01 48
56	17 18	17 55	18 38	23 36	24 45	00 45	01 56
54	17 20	17 56	18 36	23 47	24 54	00 54	02 02
52	17 22	17 56	18 35	23 56	25 02	01 02	02 08
50	17 24	17 56	18 34	24 05	00 05	01 09	02 13
45	17 28	17 58	18 32	24 23	00 23	01 24	02 25
N 40	17 32	17 59	18 30	24 38	00 38	01 36	02 34
35	17 35	18 00	18 29	24 50	00 50	01 46	02 42
30	17 38	18 02	18 29	00 07	01 01	01 55	02 49
20	17 42	18 04	18 30	00 28	01 20	02 11	03 01
N 10	17 47	18 08	18 32	00 46	01 36	02 24	03 12
0	17 51	18 12	18 36	01 02	01 51	02 37	03 21
S 10	17 55	18 16	18 41	01 19	02 06	02 50	03 31
20	18 00	18 22	18 48	01 37	02 22	03 03	03 41
30	18 05	18 29	18 58	01 57	02 40	03 18	03 53
35	18 08	18 34	19 04	02 09	02 50	03 27	04 00
40	18 12	18 40	19 12	02 23	03 02	03 37	04 07
45	18 16	18 46	19 22	02 39	03 17	03 49	04 16
S 50	18 21	18 55	19 35	02 59	03 34	04 03	04 27
52	18 24	18 59	19 41	03 08	03 42	04 09	04 32
54	18 26	19 03	19 48	03 18	03 51	04 17	04 37
56	18 29	19 08	19 55	03 30	04 01	04 25	04 43
58	18 33	19 13	20 05	03 44	04 13	04 34	04 50
S 60	18 36	19 20	20 15	04 00	04 26	04 44	04 57

Day	SUN Eqn. of Time 00h	SUN Eqn. of Time 12h	SUN Mer. Pass.	MOON Mer. Pass. Upper	MOON Mer. Pass. Lower	Age	Phase
d	m s	m s	h m	h m	h m	d	%
7	11 58	12 06	11 48	19 39	07 15	09	67
8	12 15	12 24	11 48	20 26	08 03	10	76
9	12 32	12 40	11 47	21 11	08 49	11	84

© British Crown Copyright 2018. All rights reserved.

UT	ARIES GHA	VENUS −3.9 GHA	Dec	MARS +1.8 GHA	Dec	JUPITER −2.0 GHA	Dec	SATURN +0.5 GHA	Dec	STARS Name	SHA	Dec
10 00	18 18.5	168 39.0	S11 27.3	194 29.7	S 0 37.5	119 42.2	S22 46.9	92 48.5	S22 30.3	Acamar	315 14.7	S40 13.5
01	33 21.0	183 38.5	28.5	209 30.7	38.2	134 44.2	46.9	107 50.9	30.3	Achernar	335 22.9	S57 08.2
02	48 23.4	198 38.0	29.6	224 31.7	38.8	149 46.3	47.0	122 53.2	30.3	Acrux	173 05.2	S63 12.3
03	63 25.9	213 37.5	.. 30.8	239 32.6	.. 39.5	164 48.3	.. 47.0	137 55.6	.. 30.3	Adhara	255 09.1	S28 59.7
04	78 28.4	228 37.1	32.0	254 33.6	40.1	179 50.4	47.0	152 58.0	30.3	Aldebaran	290 44.2	N16 32.8
05	93 30.8	243 36.6	33.1	269 34.6	40.8	194 52.4	47.1	168 00.3	30.3			
06	108 33.3	258 36.1	S11 34.3	284 35.6	S 0 41.4	209 54.4	S22 47.1	183 02.7	S22 30.3	Alioth	166 17.4	N55 51.3
07	123 35.8	273 35.6	35.4	299 36.6	42.1	224 56.5	47.1	198 05.1	30.3	Alkaid	152 55.9	N49 13.1
T 08	138 38.2	288 35.1	36.6	314 37.6	42.7	239 58.5	47.2	213 07.4	30.2	Alnair	27 38.0	S46 52.0
H 09	153 40.7	303 34.7	.. 37.7	329 38.6	.. 43.4	255 00.6	.. 47.2	228 09.8	.. 30.2	Alnilam	275 41.9	S 1 11.3
U 10	168 43.2	318 34.2	38.9	344 39.6	44.0	270 02.6	47.3	243 12.2	30.2	Alphard	217 52.0	S 8 44.5
R 11	183 45.6	333 33.7	40.1	359 40.6	44.7	285 04.7	47.3	258 14.6	30.2			
S 12	198 48.1	348 33.2	S11 41.2	14 41.5	S 0 45.3	300 06.7	S22 47.3	273 16.9	S22 30.2	Alphecca	126 07.6	N26 39.2
D 13	213 50.5	3 32.7	42.4	29 42.5	46.0	315 08.7	47.4	288 19.3	30.2	Alpheratz	357 38.7	N29 12.0
A 14	228 53.0	18 32.2	43.5	44 43.5	46.6	330 10.8	47.4	303 21.7	30.2	Altair	62 04.0	N 8 55.4
Y 15	243 55.5	33 31.8	.. 44.7	59 44.5	.. 47.3	345 12.8	.. 47.4	318 24.0	.. 30.2	Ankaa	353 11.0	S42 12.0
16	258 57.9	48 31.3	45.8	74 45.5	47.9	0 14.9	47.5	333 26.4	30.2	Antares	112 21.2	S26 28.4
17	274 00.4	63 30.8	47.0	89 46.5	48.6	15 16.9	47.5	348 28.7	30.2			
18	289 02.9	78 30.3	S11 48.1	104 47.5	S 0 49.2	30 18.9	S22 47.5	3 31.1	S22 30.2	Arcturus	145 52.1	N19 05.1
19	304 05.3	93 29.8	49.3	119 48.5	49.9	45 21.0	47.6	18 33.5	30.2	Atria	107 19.5	S69 03.8
20	319 07.8	108 29.3	50.4	134 49.4	50.5	60 23.0	47.6	33 35.8	30.2	Avior	234 16.5	S59 34.0
21	334 10.3	123 28.8	.. 51.6	149 50.4	.. 51.2	75 25.0	.. 47.7	48 38.2	.. 30.2	Bellatrix	278 27.2	N 6 22.0
22	349 12.7	138 28.4	52.7	164 51.4	51.8	90 27.1	47.7	63 40.6	30.2	Betelgeuse	270 56.5	N 7 24.6
23	4 15.2	153 27.9	53.9	179 52.4	52.5	105 29.1	47.7	78 42.9	30.2			
11 00	19 17.7	168 27.4	S11 55.0	194 53.4	S 0 53.1	120 31.2	S22 47.8	93 45.3	S22 30.2	Canopus	263 54.1	S52 42.1
01	34 20.1	183 26.9	56.2	209 54.4	53.8	135 33.2	47.8	108 47.7	30.2	Capella	280 27.8	N46 00.8
02	49 22.6	198 26.4	57.3	224 55.4	54.4	150 35.2	47.8	123 50.0	30.1	Deneb	49 28.4	N45 21.3
03	64 25.0	213 25.9	.. 58.5	239 56.4	.. 55.1	165 37.3	.. 47.9	138 52.4	.. 30.1	Denebola	182 29.6	N14 27.9
04	79 27.5	228 25.4	11 59.6	254 57.4	55.7	180 39.3	47.9	153 54.8	30.1	Diphda	348 51.2	S17 52.7
05	94 30.0	243 24.9	12 00.8	269 58.3	56.4	195 41.3	47.9	168 57.1	30.1			
06	109 32.4	258 24.4	S12 01.9	284 59.3	S 0 57.1	210 43.4	S22 48.0	183 59.5	S22 30.1	Dubhe	193 46.9	N61 38.7
07	124 34.9	273 24.0	03.1	300 00.3	57.7	225 45.4	48.0	199 01.9	30.1	Elnath	278 07.0	N28 37.3
F 08	139 37.4	288 23.5	04.2	315 01.3	58.4	240 47.5	48.0	214 04.2	30.1	Eltanin	90 44.3	N51 29.6
R 09	154 39.8	303 23.0	.. 05.4	330 02.3	.. 59.0	255 49.5	.. 48.1	229 06.6	.. 30.1	Enif	33 42.7	N 9 58.1
I 10	169 42.3	318 22.5	06.5	345 03.3	0 59.7	270 51.5	48.1	244 08.9	30.1	Fomalhaut	15 18.9	S29 31.1
D 11	184 44.8	333 22.0	07.7	0 04.3	1 00.3	285 53.6	48.2	259 11.3	30.1			
A 12	199 47.2	348 21.5	S12 08.8	15 05.3	S 1 01.0	300 55.6	S22 48.2	274 13.7	S22 30.1	Gacrux	171 56.7	S57 13.2
Y 13	214 49.7	3 21.0	09.9	30 06.2	01.6	315 57.6	48.2	289 16.0	30.1	Gienah	175 48.2	S17 38.8
14	229 52.1	18 20.5	11.1	45 07.2	02.3	330 59.7	48.3	304 18.4	30.1	Hadar	148 42.4	S60 27.9
15	244 54.6	33 20.0	.. 12.2	60 08.2	.. 02.9	346 01.7	.. 48.3	319 20.8	.. 30.1	Hamal	327 55.6	N23 33.3
16	259 57.1	48 19.5	13.4	75 09.2	03.6	1 03.7	48.3	334 23.1	30.1	Kaus Aust.	83 38.2	S34 22.5
17	274 59.5	63 19.0	14.5	90 10.2	04.2	16 05.8	48.4	349 25.5	30.1			
18	290 02.0	78 18.5	S12 15.7	105 11.2	S 1 04.9	31 07.8	S22 48.4	4 27.8	S22 30.0	Kochab	137 21.1	N74 04.7
19	305 04.5	93 18.0	16.8	120 12.2	05.5	46 09.8	48.4	19 30.2	30.0	Markab	13 33.8	N15 18.8
20	320 06.9	108 17.5	17.9	135 13.2	06.2	61 11.9	48.5	34 32.6	30.0	Menkar	314 10.3	N 4 10.0
21	335 09.4	123 17.0	.. 19.1	150 14.1	.. 06.8	76 13.9	.. 48.5	49 34.9	.. 30.0	Menkent	148 02.9	S36 27.8
22	350 11.9	138 16.5	20.2	165 15.1	07.5	91 15.9	48.6	64 37.3	30.0	Miaplacidus	221 39.3	S69 47.6
23	5 14.3	153 16.1	21.3	180 16.1	08.1	106 18.0	48.6	79 39.6	30.0			
12 00	20 16.8	168 15.6	S12 22.5	195 17.1	S 1 08.8	121 20.0	S22 48.6	94 42.0	S22 30.0	Mirfak	308 33.8	N49 55.7
01	35 19.3	183 15.1	23.6	210 18.1	09.4	136 22.0	48.7	109 44.4	30.0	Nunki	75 53.0	S26 16.3
02	50 21.7	198 14.6	24.8	225 19.1	10.1	151 24.1	48.7	124 46.7	30.0	Peacock	53 12.3	S56 40.4
03	65 24.2	213 14.1	.. 25.9	240 20.1	.. 10.7	166 26.1	.. 48.7	139 49.1	.. 30.0	Pollux	243 22.5	N27 58.6
04	80 26.6	228 13.6	27.0	255 21.0	11.4	181 28.1	48.8	154 51.4	30.0	Procyon	244 55.3	N 5 10.5
05	95 29.1	243 13.1	28.2	270 22.0	12.0	196 30.2	48.8	169 53.8	30.0			
06	110 31.6	258 12.6	S12 29.3	285 23.0	S 1 12.7	211 32.2	S22 48.8	184 56.2	S22 30.0	Rasalhague	96 02.6	N12 33.0
07	125 34.0	273 12.1	30.4	300 24.0	13.3	226 34.2	48.9	199 58.5	30.0	Regulus	207 39.2	N11 52.4
S 08	140 36.5	288 11.6	31.6	315 25.0	14.0	241 36.3	48.9	215 00.9	30.0	Rigel	281 07.7	S 8 10.7
A 09	155 39.0	303 11.1	.. 32.7	330 26.0	.. 14.6	256 38.3	.. 49.0	230 03.2	.. 30.0	Rigil Kent.	139 46.5	S60 54.8
T 10	170 41.4	318 10.6	33.8	345 27.0	15.3	271 40.3	49.0	245 05.6	29.9	Sabik	102 07.8	S15 44.8
U 11	185 43.9	333 10.1	35.0	0 28.0	15.9	286 42.4	49.0	260 08.0	29.9			
R 12	200 46.4	348 09.6	S12 36.1	15 28.9	S 1 16.6	300 44.4	S22 49.1	275 10.3	S22 29.9	Schedar	349 35.1	N56 38.7
D 13	215 48.8	3 09.0	37.2	30 29.9	17.2	316 46.4	49.1	290 12.7	29.9	Shaula	96 16.2	S37 07.0
A 14	230 51.3	18 08.5	38.4	45 30.9	17.9	331 48.4	49.1	305 15.0	29.9	Sirius	258 29.9	S16 44.5
Y 15	245 53.8	33 08.0	.. 39.5	60 31.9	.. 18.5	346 50.5	.. 49.2	320 17.4	.. 29.9	Spica	158 27.0	S11 15.6
16	260 56.2	48 07.5	40.6	75 32.9	19.2	1 52.5	49.2	335 19.8	29.9	Suhail	222 49.5	S43 30.4
17	275 58.7	63 07.0	41.8	90 33.9	19.8	16 54.5	49.2	350 22.1	29.9			
18	291 01.1	78 06.5	S12 42.9	105 34.9	S 1 20.5	31 56.6	S22 49.3	5 24.5	S22 29.9	Vega	80 36.1	N38 48.5
19	306 03.6	93 06.0	44.0	120 35.8	21.1	46 58.6	49.3	20 26.8	29.9	Zuben'ubi	137 01.0	S16 07.2
20	321 06.1	108 05.5	45.1	135 36.8	21.8	62 00.6	49.3	35 29.2	29.9		SHA	Mer.Pass.
21	336 08.5	123 05.0	.. 46.3	150 37.8	.. 22.4	77 02.7	.. 49.4	50 31.5	.. 29.9	Venus	149 09.7	12 47
22	351 11.0	138 04.5	47.4	165 38.8	23.1	92 04.7	49.4	65 33.9	29.9	Mars	175 35.7	11 00
23	6 13.5	153 04.0	48.5	180 39.8	23.7	107 06.7	49.5	80 36.3	29.9	Jupiter	101 13.5	15 56
Mer.Pass. 22 39.1		v −0.5	d 1.1	v 1.0	d 0.7	v 2.0	d 0.0	v 2.4	d 0.0	Saturn	74 27.7	17 42

© British Crown Copyright 2018. All rights reserved.

UT	SUN GHA	SUN Dec	MOON GHA	v	MOON Dec	d	HP
d h	° ′	° ′	° ′	′	° ′	′	′
10 00	183 12.2	S 6 26.7	41 03.4	14.6	S13 42.1	9.3	54.1
01	198 12.4	27.7	55 37.0	14.7	13 32.8	9.4	54.1
02	213 12.6	28.6	70 10.7	14.7	13 23.4	9.5	54.0
03	228 12.7 ..	29.6	84 44.4	14.7	13 13.9	9.5	54.0
04	243 12.9	30.5	99 18.1	14.8	13 04.4	9.6	54.0
05	258 13.1	31.5	113 51.9	14.8	12 54.8	9.6	54.0
06	273 13.2	S 6 32.4	128 25.7	14.9	S12 45.2	9.7	54.0
T 07	288 13.4	33.4	142 59.6	14.9	12 35.5	9.8	54.0
H 08	303 13.6	34.3	157 33.5	14.9	12 25.7	9.7	54.0
U 09	318 13.7 ..	35.3	172 07.4	14.9	12 16.0	9.9	54.0
R 10	333 13.9	36.2	186 41.3	15.0	12 06.1	9.9	54.0
S 11	348 14.1	37.2	201 15.3	15.0	11 56.2	9.9	54.0
D 12	3 14.2	S 6 38.1	215 49.3	15.1	S11 46.3	10.0	54.0
A 13	18 14.4	39.1	230 23.4	15.1	11 36.3	10.0	54.0
Y 14	33 14.6	40.0	244 57.5	15.1	11 26.3	10.1	54.0
15	48 14.7 ..	41.0	259 31.6	15.2	11 16.2	10.1	54.0
16	63 14.9	41.9	274 05.8	15.2	11 06.1	10.1	54.0
17	78 15.1	42.8	288 40.0	15.2	10 56.0	10.2	54.0
18	93 15.2	S 6 43.8	303 14.2	15.2	S10 45.8	10.3	54.0
19	108 15.4	44.7	317 48.4	15.3	10 35.5	10.3	54.0
20	123 15.6	45.7	332 22.7	15.3	10 25.2	10.3	54.0
21	138 15.7 ..	46.6	346 57.0	15.3	10 14.9	10.4	54.0
22	153 15.9	47.6	1 31.3	15.4	10 04.5	10.4	54.0
23	168 16.1	48.5	16 05.7	15.4	9 54.1	10.5	54.0
11 00	183 16.2	S 6 49.5	30 40.1	15.4	S 9 43.6	10.5	54.0
01	198 16.4	50.4	45 14.5	15.4	9 33.1	10.5	54.0
02	213 16.6	51.3	59 48.9	15.5	9 22.6	10.6	54.0
03	228 16.7 ..	52.3	74 23.4	15.5	9 12.0	10.6	54.0
04	243 16.9	53.2	88 57.9	15.5	9 01.4	10.7	54.0
05	258 17.1	54.2	103 32.4	15.5	8 50.7	10.6	54.0
06	273 17.2	S 6 55.1	118 06.9	15.6	S 8 40.1	10.8	54.0
07	288 17.4	56.1	132 41.5	15.5	8 29.3	10.7	54.0
08	303 17.6	57.0	147 16.0	15.6	8 18.6	10.8	54.0
F 09	318 17.7 ..	57.9	161 50.6	15.6	8 07.8	10.8	54.0
R 10	333 17.9	58.9	176 25.2	15.7	7 57.0	10.9	54.0
I 11	348 18.0	6 59.8	190 59.9	15.6	7 46.1	10.9	54.0
D 12	3 18.2	S 7 00.8	205 34.5	15.7	S 7 35.2	10.9	54.1
A 13	18 18.4	01.7	220 09.2	15.7	7 24.3	11.0	54.1
Y 14	33 18.5	02.7	234 43.9	15.7	7 13.3	11.0	54.1
15	48 18.7 ..	03.6	249 18.6	15.7	7 02.3	11.0	54.1
16	63 18.9	04.5	263 53.3	15.8	6 51.3	11.0	54.1
17	78 19.0	05.5	278 28.1	15.7	6 40.3	11.1	54.1
18	93 19.2	S 7 06.4	293 02.8	15.8	S 6 29.2	11.1	54.1
19	108 19.3	07.4	307 37.6	15.8	6 18.1	11.1	54.1
20	123 19.5	08.3	322 12.4	15.8	6 07.0	11.2	54.1
21	138 19.7 ..	09.3	336 47.2	15.8	5 55.8	11.2	54.1
22	153 19.8	10.2	351 22.0	15.8	5 44.6	11.2	54.1
23	168 20.0	11.1	5 56.8	15.9	5 33.4	11.2	54.1
12 00	183 20.1	S 7 12.1	20 31.7	15.8	S 5 22.2	11.3	54.1
01	198 20.3	13.0	35 06.5	15.8	5 10.9	11.3	54.1
02	213 20.5	14.0	49 41.3	15.9	4 59.6	11.3	54.1
03	228 20.6 ..	14.9	64 16.2	15.9	4 48.3	11.3	54.1
04	243 20.8	15.8	78 51.1	15.8	4 37.0	11.3	54.1
05	258 20.9	16.8	93 25.9	15.9	4 25.7	11.4	54.1
06	273 21.1	S 7 17.7	108 00.8	15.9	S 4 14.3	11.4	54.1
07	288 21.3	18.6	122 35.7	15.9	4 02.9	11.4	54.1
S 08	303 21.4	19.6	137 10.6	15.9	3 51.5	11.4	54.2
A 09	318 21.6 ..	20.5	151 45.5	15.9	3 40.1	11.4	54.2
T 10	333 21.7	21.5	166 20.4	15.9	3 28.7	11.5	54.2
U 11	348 21.9	22.4	180 55.3	15.9	3 17.2	11.5	54.2
R 12	3 22.0	S 7 23.3	195 30.2	15.9	S 3 05.7	11.5	54.2
D 13	18 22.2	24.3	210 05.1	15.9	2 54.2	11.5	54.2
A 14	33 22.4	25.2	224 40.0	15.9	2 42.7	11.5	54.2
Y 15	48 22.5 ..	26.2	239 14.9	15.9	2 31.2	11.5	54.2
16	63 22.7	27.1	253 49.8	15.9	2 19.7	11.6	54.2
17	78 22.8	28.0	268 24.7	15.9	2 08.1	11.5	54.2
18	93 23.0	S 7 29.0	282 59.6	15.9	S 1 56.6	11.6	54.2
19	108 23.1	29.9	297 34.5	15.9	1 45.0	11.6	54.2
20	123 23.3	30.8	312 09.4	15.9	1 33.4	11.6	54.2
21	138 23.5 ..	31.8	326 44.3	15.9	1 21.8	11.6	54.3
22	153 23.6	32.7	341 19.2	15.9	1 10.2	11.6	54.3
23	168 23.8	33.7	355 54.1	15.9	S 0 58.6	11.6	54.3
	SD 16.0	d 0.9	SD 14.7		14.7		14.8

Twilight / Sunrise / Moonrise

Lat.	Naut.	Civil	Sunrise	Moonrise 10	11	12	13
°	h m	h m	h m	h m	h m	h m	h m
N 72	04 36	05 54	07 03	18 12	17 51	17 34	17 17
N 70	04 42	05 53	06 55	17 54	17 42	17 31	17 20
68	04 47	05 51	06 48	17 41	17 34	17 28	17 23
66	04 51	05 50	06 42	17 29	17 28	17 26	17 25
64	04 54	05 49	06 37	17 20	17 23	17 27	17 27
62	04 56	05 48	06 32	17 11	17 18	17 23	17 29
60	04 59	05 47	06 29	17 04	17 14	17 22	17 30
N 58	05 00	05 46	06 25	16 58	17 10	17 21	17 31
56	05 02	05 45	06 22	16 53	17 07	17 20	17 33
54	05 03	05 44	06 20	16 48	17 04	17 19	17 34
52	05 04	05 43	06 17	16 43	17 01	17 18	17 35
50	05 05	05 42	06 15	16 39	16 59	17 17	17 36
45	05 07	05 41	06 10	16 30	16 53	17 16	17 38
N 40	05 07	05 39	06 06	16 22	16 49	17 14	17 39
35	05 08	05 37	06 02	16 16	16 45	17 13	17 41
30	05 07	05 35	05 59	16 10	16 42	17 12	17 42
20	05 06	05 31	05 53	16 00	16 36	17 10	17 44
N 10	05 03	05 27	05 48	15 52	16 30	17 08	17 46
0	04 59	05 23	05 44	15 44	16 26	17 07	17 48
S 10	04 53	05 17	05 39	15 35	16 21	17 05	17 50
20	04 45	05 11	05 33	15 27	16 15	17 04	17 52
30	04 34	05 03	05 27	15 16	16 09	17 02	17 55
35	04 27	04 58	05 23	15 11	16 06	17 01	17 56
40	04 19	04 52	05 19	15 04	16 02	17 00	17 58
45	04 08	04 44	05 14	14 56	15 57	16 58	18 00
S 50	03 55	04 35	05 08	14 47	15 52	16 57	18 02
52	03 48	04 31	05 06	14 43	15 49	16 56	18 03
54	03 41	04 26	05 03	14 38	15 46	16 55	18 04
56	03 32	04 21	04 59	14 33	15 43	16 54	18 05
58	03 23	04 15	04 56	14 27	15 40	16 53	18 07
S 60	03 11	04 08	04 52	14 20	15 36	16 52	18 08

Sunset / Twilight / Moonset

Lat.	Sunset	Civil	Naut.	Moonset 10	11	12	13
°	h m	h m	h m	h m	h m	h m	h m
N 72	16 28	17 37	18 55	25 57	01 57	03 45	05 30
N 70	16 37	17 39	18 49	00 28	02 12	03 52	05 29
68	16 44	17 40	18 45	00 49	02 25	03 57	05 29
66	16 50	17 42	18 41	01 06	02 35	04 02	05 29
64	16 56	17 43	18 38	01 19	02 43	04 06	05 29
62	17 00	17 44	18 36	01 30	02 50	04 09	05 29
60	17 04	17 46	18 34	01 40	02 56	04 12	05 28
N 58	17 07	17 47	18 32	01 48	03 02	04 15	05 28
56	17 10	17 48	18 30	01 56	03 07	04 17	05 28
54	17 13	17 48	18 29	02 02	03 11	04 19	05 28
52	17 16	17 49	18 28	02 08	03 15	04 21	05 28
50	17 18	17 50	18 28	02 13	03 18	04 23	05 28
45	17 23	17 52	18 26	02 25	03 26	04 27	05 28
N 40	17 27	17 54	18 26	02 34	03 32	04 30	05 28
35	17 31	17 56	18 26	02 42	03 37	04 32	05 28
30	17 34	17 58	18 28	02 49	03 42	04 35	05 27
20	17 40	18 02	18 28	03 01	03 50	04 39	05 27
N 10	17 45	18 06	18 31	03 12	03 57	04 42	05 27
0	17 50	18 11	18 35	03 21	04 04	04 46	05 27
S 10	17 55	18 16	18 41	03 31	04 10	04 49	05 27
20	18 01	18 23	18 49	03 41	04 17	04 52	05 26
30	18 07	18 31	19 00	03 53	04 25	04 56	05 26
35	18 11	18 37	19 07	04 00	04 30	04 58	05 26
40	18 15	18 43	19 16	04 07	04 35	05 01	05 26
45	18 20	18 50	19 26	04 16	04 41	05 04	05 26
S 50	18 26	19 00	19 40	04 27	04 48	05 07	05 25
52	18 29	19 04	19 47	04 32	04 51	05 09	05 25
54	18 32	19 09	19 54	04 37	04 55	05 10	05 25
56	18 36	19 15	20 03	04 43	04 59	05 12	05 25
58	18 39	19 21	20 13	04 50	05 03	05 14	05 25
S 60	18 44	19 28	20 25	04 57	05 08	05 16	05 25

SUN / MOON

Day	Eqn. of Time 00ʰ	12ʰ	Mer. Pass.	Mer. Pass. Upper	Lower	Age	Phase
d	m s	m s	h m	h m	h m	d	%
10	12 49	12 57	11 47	21 54	09 32	12	90
11	13 05	13 12	11 47	22 36	10 15	13	95
12	13 20	13 28	11 47	23 17	10 56	14	98

© British Crown Copyright 2018. All rights reserved.

2019 OCTOBER 13, 14, 15 (SUN., MON., TUES.)

UT	ARIES GHA	VENUS −3.8 GHA	Dec	MARS +1.8 GHA	Dec	JUPITER −2.0 GHA	Dec	SATURN +0.5 GHA	Dec	STARS Name	SHA	Dec
13 00	21 15.9	168 03.5	S12 49.6	195 40.8	S 1 24.4	122 08.7	S22 49.5	95 38.6	S22 29.9	Acamar	315 14.7	S40 13.5
01	36 18.4	183 03.0	50.8	210 41.8	25.0	137 10.8	49.5	110 41.0	29.8	Achernar	335 22.9	S57 08.3
02	51 20.9	198 02.5	51.9	225 42.7	25.7	152 12.8	49.6	125 43.3	29.8	Acrux	173 05.2	S63 12.3
03	66 23.3	213 02.0 ..	53.0	240 43.7 ..	26.3	167 14.8 ..	49.6	140 45.7 ..	29.8	Adhara	255 09.1	S28 59.7
04	81 25.8	228 01.5	54.1	255 44.7	27.0	182 16.8	49.6	155 48.0	29.8	Aldebaran	290 44.2	N16 32.8
05	96 28.2	243 00.9	55.3	270 45.7	27.6	197 18.9	49.7	170 50.4	29.8			
06	111 30.7	258 00.4	S12 56.4	285 46.7	S 1 28.3	212 20.9	S22 49.7	185 52.7	S22 29.8	Alioth	166 17.4	N55 51.3
07	126 33.2	272 59.9	57.5	300 47.7	28.9	227 22.9	49.7	200 55.1	29.8	Alkaid	152 55.9	N49 13.1
08	141 35.6	287 59.4	58.6	315 48.7	29.6	242 25.0	49.8	215 57.5	29.8	Alnair	27 38.0	S46 52.1
S 09	156 38.1	302 58.9	12 59.7	330 49.6 ..	30.2	257 27.0 ..	49.8	230 59.8 ..	29.8	Alnilam	275 41.8	S 1 11.3
U 10	171 40.6	317 58.4	13 00.9	345 50.6	30.9	272 29.0	49.8	246 02.2	29.8	Alphard	217 52.0	S 8 44.5
N 11	186 43.0	332 57.9	02.0	0 51.6	31.5	287 31.0	49.9	261 04.5	29.8			
D 12	201 45.5	347 57.4	S13 03.1	15 52.6	S 1 32.2	302 33.1	S22 49.9	276 06.9	S22 29.8	Alphecca	126 07.7	N26 39.2
A 13	216 48.0	2 56.8	04.2	30 53.6	32.8	317 35.1	50.0	291 09.2	29.8	Alpheratz	357 38.7	N29 12.0
Y 14	231 50.4	17 56.3	05.3	45 54.6	33.5	332 37.1	50.0	306 11.6	29.8	Altair	62 04.0	N 8 55.4
15	246 52.9	32 55.8 ..	06.5	60 55.6 ..	34.1	347 39.1 ..	50.0	321 13.9 ..	29.8	Ankaa	353 11.0	S42 12.0
16	261 55.4	47 55.3	07.6	75 56.5	34.8	2 41.2	50.1	336 16.3	29.7	Antares	112 21.2	S26 28.4
17	276 57.8	62 54.8	08.7	90 57.5	35.4	17 43.2	50.1	351 18.6	29.7			
18	292 00.3	77 54.3	S13 09.8	105 58.5	S 1 36.1	32 45.2	S22 50.1	6 21.0	S22 29.7	Arcturus	145 52.1	N19 05.1
19	307 02.7	92 53.8	10.9	120 59.5	36.7	47 47.2	50.2	21 23.3	29.7	Atria	107 19.5	S69 03.8
20	322 05.2	107 53.2	12.0	136 00.5	37.4	62 49.2	50.2	36 25.7	29.7	Avior	234 16.4	S59 34.0
21	337 07.7	122 52.7 ..	13.1	151 01.5 ..	38.0	77 51.3 ..	50.2	51 28.1 ..	29.7	Bellatrix	278 27.2	N 6 22.0
22	352 10.1	137 52.2	14.3	166 02.5	38.7	92 53.3	50.3	66 30.4	29.7	Betelgeuse	270 56.5	N 7 24.6
23	7 12.6	152 51.7	15.4	181 03.4	39.3	107 55.3	50.3	81 32.8	29.7			
14 00	22 15.1	167 51.2	S13 16.5	196 04.4	S 1 40.0	122 57.3	S22 50.3	96 35.1	S22 29.7	Canopus	263 54.1	S52 42.1
01	37 17.5	182 50.7	17.6	211 05.4	40.6	137 59.4	50.4	111 37.5	29.7	Capella	280 27.8	N46 00.8
02	52 20.0	197 50.1	18.7	226 06.4	41.3	153 01.4	50.4	126 39.8	29.7	Deneb	49 28.4	N45 21.4
03	67 22.5	212 49.6 ..	19.8	241 07.4 ..	41.9	168 03.4 ..	50.5	141 42.2 ..	29.7	Denebola	182 29.6	N14 27.9
04	82 24.9	227 49.1	20.9	256 08.4	42.5	183 05.4	50.5	156 44.5	29.7	Diphda	348 51.2	S17 52.7
05	97 27.4	242 48.6	22.0	271 09.4	43.2	198 07.5	50.5	171 46.9	29.6			
06	112 29.8	257 48.1	S13 23.1	286 10.3	S 1 43.8	213 09.5	S22 50.6	186 49.2	S22 29.6	Dubhe	193 46.9	N61 38.6
07	127 32.3	272 47.5	24.3	301 11.3	44.5	228 11.5	50.6	201 51.6	29.6	Elnath	278 07.0	N28 37.3
08	142 34.8	287 47.0	25.4	316 12.3	45.1	243 13.5	50.6	216 53.9	29.6	Eltanin	90 44.3	N51 29.6
M 09	157 37.2	302 46.5 ..	26.5	331 13.3	45.8	258 15.5 ..	50.7	231 56.3 ..	29.6	Enif	33 42.7	N 9 58.1
O 10	172 39.7	317 46.0	27.6	346 14.3	46.4	273 17.6	50.7	246 58.6	29.6	Fomalhaut	15 18.9	S29 31.1
N 11	187 42.2	332 45.4	28.7	1 15.3	47.1	288 19.6	50.7	262 01.0	29.6			
D 12	202 44.6	347 44.9	S13 29.8	16 16.2	S 1 47.7	303 21.6	S22 50.8	277 03.3	S22 29.6	Gacrux	171 56.7	S57 13.2
A 13	217 47.1	2 44.4	30.9	31 17.2	48.4	318 23.6	50.8	292 05.7	29.6	Gienah	175 48.2	S17 38.8
Y 14	232 49.6	17 43.9	32.0	46 18.2	49.0	333 25.6	50.8	307 08.0	29.6	Hadar	148 42.4	S60 27.9
15	247 52.0	32 43.3 ..	33.1	61 19.2 ..	49.7	348 27.7 ..	50.9	322 10.4 ..	29.6	Hamal	327 55.6	N23 33.3
16	262 54.5	47 42.8	34.2	76 20.2	50.3	3 29.7	50.9	337 12.7	29.6	Kaus Aust.	83 38.2	S34 22.5
17	277 57.0	62 42.3	35.3	91 21.2	51.0	18 31.7	51.0	352 15.1	29.6			
18	292 59.4	77 41.8	S13 36.4	106 22.1	S 1 51.6	33 33.7	S22 51.0	7 17.4	S22 29.6	Kochab	137 21.1	N74 04.7
19	308 01.9	92 41.2	37.5	121 23.1	52.3	48 35.7	51.0	22 19.8	29.5	Markab	13 33.8	N15 18.8
20	323 04.3	107 40.7	38.6	136 24.1	52.9	63 37.8	51.1	37 22.1	29.5	Menkar	314 10.2	N 4 10.0
21	338 06.8	122 40.2 ..	39.7	151 25.1 ..	53.6	78 39.8 ..	51.1	52 24.5 ..	29.5	Menkent	148 02.9	S36 27.8
22	353 09.3	137 39.7	40.8	166 26.1	54.2	93 41.8	51.1	67 26.8	29.5	Miaplacidus	221 39.3	S69 47.5
23	8 11.7	152 39.1	41.9	181 27.1	54.9	108 43.8	51.2	82 29.2	29.5			
15 00	23 14.2	167 38.6	S13 43.0	196 28.1	S 1 55.5	123 45.8	S22 51.2	97 31.5	S22 29.5	Mirfak	308 33.8	N49 55.7
01	38 16.7	182 38.1	44.1	211 29.0	56.2	138 47.8	51.2	112 33.9	29.5	Nunki	75 53.0	S26 16.3
02	53 19.1	197 37.5	45.2	226 30.0	56.8	153 49.9	51.3	127 36.2	29.5	Peacock	53 12.3	S56 40.4
03	68 21.6	212 37.0 ..	46.3	241 31.0 ..	57.5	168 51.9 ..	51.3	142 38.6 ..	29.5	Pollux	243 22.5	N27 58.6
04	83 24.1	227 36.5	47.4	256 32.0	58.1	183 53.9	51.3	157 40.9	29.5	Procyon	244 55.2	N 5 10.5
05	98 26.5	242 35.9	48.5	271 33.0	58.8	198 55.9	51.4	172 43.2	29.5			
06	113 29.0	257 35.4	S13 49.6	286 34.0	S 1 59.4	213 57.9	S22 51.4	187 45.6	S22 29.5	Rasalhague	96 02.6	N12 33.0
07	128 31.4	272 34.9	50.7	301 34.9	2 00.1	228 59.9	51.5	202 47.9	29.5	Regulus	207 39.1	N11 52.4
08	143 33.9	287 34.4	51.8	316 35.9	00.7	244 02.0	51.5	217 50.3	29.4	Rigel	281 07.7	S 8 10.7
T 09	158 36.4	302 33.8 ..	52.9	331 36.9	01.4	259 04.0 ..	51.5	232 52.6 ..	29.4	Rigil Kent.	139 46.6	S60 54.8
U 10	173 38.8	317 33.3	54.0	346 37.9	02.0	274 06.0	51.6	247 55.0	29.4	Sabik	102 07.8	S15 44.8
E 11	188 41.3	332 32.8	55.1	1 38.9	02.7	289 08.0	51.6	262 57.3	29.4			
S 12	203 43.8	347 32.2	S13 56.2	16 39.9	S 2 03.3	304 10.0	S22 51.6	277 59.7	S22 29.4	Schedar	349 35.1	N56 38.7
D 13	218 46.2	2 31.7	57.3	31 40.8	04.0	319 12.0	51.7	293 02.0	29.4	Shaula	96 16.3	S37 07.0
A 14	233 48.7	17 31.1	58.3	46 41.8	04.6	334 14.1	51.7	308 04.4	29.4	Sirius	258 29.9	S16 44.5
Y 15	248 51.2	32 30.6	13 59.4	61 42.8 ..	05.2	349 16.1 ..	51.7	323 06.7 ..	29.4	Spica	158 27.0	S11 15.6
16	263 53.6	47 30.1	14 00.5	76 43.8	05.9	4 18.1	51.8	338 09.1	29.4	Suhail	222 49.5	S43 30.4
17	278 56.1	62 29.5	01.6	91 44.8	06.6	19 20.1	51.8	353 11.4	29.4			
18	293 58.6	77 29.0	S14 02.7	106 45.8	S 2 07.2	34 22.1	S22 51.8	8 13.7	S22 29.4	Vega	80 36.1	N38 48.5
19	309 01.0	92 28.5	03.8	121 46.7	07.9	49 24.1	51.9	23 16.1	29.4	Zuben'ubi	137 01.0	S16 07.2
20	324 03.5	107 27.9	04.9	136 47.7	08.5	64 26.1	51.9	38 18.4	29.3		SHA	Mer. Pass.
21	339 05.9	122 27.4 ..	06.0	151 48.7 ..	09.2	79 28.2 ..	51.9	53 20.8 ..	29.3		° ′	h m
22	354 08.4	137 26.8	07.0	166 49.7	09.8	94 30.2	52.0	68 23.1	29.3	Venus	145 36.1	12 49
23	9 10.9	152 26.3	08.1	181 50.7	10.5	109 32.2	52.0	83 25.5	29.3	Mars	173 49.4	10 55
	h m									Jupiter	100 42.3	15 46
Mer. Pass.	22 27.3	v −0.5	d 1.1	v 1.0	d 0.6	v 2.0	d 0.0	v 2.4	d 0.0	Saturn	74 20.0	17 31

© British Crown Copyright 2018. All rights reserved.

UT	SUN GHA	SUN Dec	MOON GHA	v	MOON Dec	d	HP
d h	° ′	° ′	° ′	′	° ′	′	′
13 00	183 23.9	S 7 34.6	10 29.0	15.8	S 0 47.0	11.7	54.3
01	198 24.1	35.5	25 03.8	15.9	0 35.3	11.6	54.3
02	213 24.2	36.5	39 38.7	15.8	0 23.7	11.6	54.3
03	228 24.4	.. 37.4	54 13.5	15.9	0 12.1	11.7	54.3
04	243 24.5	38.3	68 48.4	15.8	S 0 00.4	11.6	54.3
05	258 24.7	39.3	83 23.2	15.8	N 0 11.2	11.7	54.3
06	273 24.8	S 7 40.2	97 58.0	15.9	N 0 22.9	11.7	54.3
07	288 25.0	41.1	112 32.9	15.7	0 34.6	11.6	54.3
08	303 25.2	42.1	127 07.6	15.8	0 46.2	11.7	54.4
S 09	318 25.3	.. 43.0	141 42.4	15.8	0 57.9	11.7	54.4
U 10	333 25.5	43.9	156 17.2	15.8	1 09.6	11.6	54.4
N 11	348 25.6	44.9	170 52.0	15.7	1 21.2	11.7	54.4
D 12	3 25.8	S 7 45.8	185 26.7	15.7	N 1 32.9	11.6	54.4
A 13	18 25.9	46.7	200 01.4	15.7	1 44.5	11.7	54.4
Y 14	33 26.1	47.7	214 36.1	15.7	1 56.2	11.7	54.4
15	48 26.2	.. 48.6	229 10.8	15.7	2 07.9	11.6	54.4
16	63 26.4	49.5	243 45.5	15.6	2 19.5	11.7	54.4
17	78 26.5	50.5	258 20.1	15.7	2 31.2	11.6	54.4
18	93 26.7	S 7 51.4	272 54.8	15.6	N 2 42.8	11.7	54.5
19	108 26.8	52.3	287 29.4	15.6	2 54.5	11.6	54.5
20	123 27.0	53.3	302 04.0	15.5	3 06.1	11.6	54.5
21	138 27.1	.. 54.2	316 38.5	15.6	3 17.7	11.7	54.5
22	153 27.3	55.1	331 13.1	15.5	3 29.4	11.6	54.5
23	168 27.4	56.1	345 47.6	15.5	3 41.0	11.6	54.5
14 00	183 27.6	S 7 57.0	0 22.1	15.5	N 3 52.6	11.6	54.5
01	198 27.7	57.9	14 56.6	15.4	4 04.2	11.6	54.5
02	213 27.9	58.9	29 31.0	15.5	4 15.8	11.6	54.6
03	228 28.0	7 59.8	44 05.5	15.4	4 27.4	11.5	54.6
04	243 28.2	8 00.7	58 39.9	15.3	4 38.9	11.6	54.6
05	258 28.3	01.7	73 14.2	15.4	4 50.5	11.5	54.6
06	273 28.5	S 8 02.6	87 48.6	15.3	N 5 02.0	11.5	54.6
07	288 28.6	03.5	102 22.9	15.2	5 13.5	11.5	54.6
08	303 28.8	04.4	116 57.1	15.3	5 25.0	11.5	54.6
M 09	318 28.9	.. 05.4	131 31.4	15.2	5 36.5	11.5	54.6
O 10	333 29.1	06.3	146 05.6	15.2	5 48.0	11.4	54.7
N 11	348 29.2	07.2	160 39.8	15.1	5 59.4	11.5	54.7
D 12	3 29.4	S 8 08.2	175 13.9	15.2	N 6 10.9	11.4	54.7
A 13	18 29.5	09.1	189 48.1	15.1	6 22.3	11.4	54.7
Y 14	33 29.6	10.0	204 22.2	15.0	6 33.7	11.4	54.7
15	48 29.8	.. 11.0	218 56.2	15.0	6 45.1	11.3	54.7
16	63 29.9	11.9	233 30.2	15.0	6 56.4	11.4	54.7
17	78 30.1	12.8	248 04.2	14.9	7 07.8	11.3	54.8
18	93 30.2	S 8 13.7	262 38.1	14.9	N 7 19.1	11.3	54.8
19	108 30.4	14.7	277 12.0	14.9	7 30.4	11.3	54.8
20	123 30.5	15.6	291 45.9	14.8	7 41.6	11.3	54.8
21	138 30.7	.. 16.5	306 19.7	14.8	7 52.9	11.2	54.8
22	153 30.8	17.4	320 53.5	14.8	8 04.1	11.1	54.8
23	168 31.0	18.4	335 27.3	14.7	8 15.2	11.2	54.8
15 00	183 31.1	S 8 19.3	350 01.0	14.6	N 8 26.4	11.1	54.9
01	198 31.2	20.2	4 34.6	14.6	8 37.5	11.1	54.9
02	213 31.4	21.2	19 08.2	14.6	8 48.6	11.1	54.9
03	228 31.5	.. 22.1	33 41.8	14.5	8 59.7	11.0	54.9
04	243 31.7	23.0	48 15.3	14.5	9 10.7	11.0	54.9
05	258 31.8	23.9	62 48.8	14.5	9 21.7	11.0	54.9
06	273 32.0	S 8 24.9	77 22.3	14.4	N 9 32.7	10.9	54.9
07	288 32.1	25.8	91 55.7	14.3	9 43.6	10.9	55.0
T 08	303 32.2	26.7	106 29.0	14.3	9 54.5	10.9	55.0
U 09	318 32.4	.. 27.6	121 02.3	14.3	10 05.4	10.8	55.0
E 10	333 32.5	28.6	135 35.6	14.2	10 16.2	10.8	55.0
S 11	348 32.7	29.5	150 08.8	14.1	10 27.0	10.7	55.0
D 12	3 32.8	S 8 30.4	164 41.9	14.1	N10 37.7	10.7	55.1
A 13	18 32.9	31.3	179 15.0	14.1	10 48.4	10.7	55.1
Y 14	33 33.1	32.3	193 48.1	14.0	10 59.1	10.6	55.1
15	48 33.2	.. 33.2	208 21.1	13.9	11 09.7	10.6	55.1
16	63 33.4	34.1	222 54.0	13.9	11 20.3	10.6	55.1
17	78 33.5	35.0	237 26.9	13.9	11 30.9	10.5	55.1
18	93 33.6	S 8 36.0	251 59.8	13.8	N11 41.4	10.4	55.1
19	108 33.8	36.9	266 32.6	13.7	11 51.8	10.4	55.2
20	123 33.9	37.8	281 05.3	13.7	12 02.2	10.4	55.2
21	138 34.1	.. 38.7	295 38.0	13.6	12 12.6	10.3	55.2
22	153 34.2	39.6	310 10.6	13.6	12 22.9	10.3	55.2
23	168 34.3	40.6	324 43.2	13.5	N12 33.2	10.2	55.2
	SD 16.1	d 0.9	SD 14.8		14.9		15.0

Lat.	Twilight Naut.	Twilight Civil	Sunrise	Moonrise 13	14	15	16
°	h m	h m	h m	h m	h m	h m	h m
N 72	04 49	06 08	07 18	17 17	16 59	16 37	16 05
N 70	04 54	06 04	07 07	17 20	17 08	16 56	16 39
68	04 57	06 02	06 59	17 23	17 17	17 10	17 03
66	05 00	05 59	06 52	17 25	17 23	17 22	17 22
64	05 02	05 57	06 46	17 27	17 29	17 33	17 38
62	05 04	05 55	06 40	17 29	17 34	17 41	17 51
60	05 06	05 54	06 36	17 30	17 39	17 49	18 02
N 58	05 07	05 52	06 32	17 31	17 43	17 55	18 11
56	05 08	05 51	06 28	17 33	17 46	18 01	18 20
54	05 09	05 50	06 25	17 34	17 49	18 07	18 27
52	05 09	05 48	06 22	17 35	17 52	18 11	18 34
50	05 10	05 47	06 20	17 36	17 55	18 16	18 40
45	05 10	05 44	06 14	17 38	18 01	18 25	18 53
N 40	05 10	05 42	06 09	17 39	18 05	18 33	19 04
35	05 10	05 39	06 05	17 41	18 10	18 40	19 14
30	05 09	05 37	06 01	17 42	18 13	18 46	19 22
20	05 06	05 32	05 54	17 44	18 20	18 57	19 36
N 10	05 03	05 27	05 48	17 46	18 25	19 06	19 49
0	04 58	05 22	05 43	17 48	18 31	19 15	20 01
S 10	04 51	05 16	05 37	17 50	18 36	19 24	20 13
20	04 42	05 08	05 31	17 52	18 42	19 33	20 26
30	04 31	04 59	05 24	17 55	18 49	19 44	20 40
35	04 23	04 53	05 19	17 56	18 53	19 50	20 49
40	04 14	04 47	05 14	17 58	18 57	19 57	20 59
45	04 02	04 39	05 09	18 00	19 02	20 06	21 11
S 50	03 48	04 29	05 02	18 02	19 08	20 16	21 25
52	03 41	04 24	04 59	18 03	19 11	20 21	21 31
54	03 32	04 18	04 55	18 04	19 14	20 26	21 39
56	03 23	04 12	04 52	18 05	19 18	20 32	21 47
58	03 13	04 06	04 47	18 07	19 22	20 38	21 56
S 60	03 00	03 58	04 43	18 08	19 26	20 46	22 07

Lat.	Sunset	Twilight Civil	Twilight Naut.	Moonset 13	14	15	16
°	h m	h m	h m	h m	h m	h m	h m
N 72	16 13	17 22	18 40	05 30	07 16	09 08	11 14
N 70	16 23	17 26	18 36	05 29	07 08	08 51	10 42
68	16 32	17 29	18 33	05 29	07 02	08 38	10 19
66	16 39	17 31	18 30	05 29	06 57	08 27	10 01
64	16 45	17 33	18 28	05 29	06 52	08 18	09 46
62	16 50	17 35	18 26	05 29	06 49	08 10	09 34
60	16 55	17 37	18 25	05 28	06 45	08 04	09 24
N 58	16 59	17 39	18 24	05 28	06 43	07 58	09 15
56	17 03	17 40	18 23	05 28	06 40	07 53	09 07
54	17 06	17 42	18 22	05 28	06 38	07 48	09 00
52	17 09	17 43	18 22	05 28	06 36	07 44	08 54
50	17 12	17 44	18 22	05 28	06 34	07 41	08 49
45	17 18	17 47	18 21	05 28	06 30	07 33	08 37
N 40	17 23	17 50	18 21	05 28	06 26	07 26	08 27
35	17 27	17 52	18 22	05 28	06 23	07 20	08 18
30	17 31	17 55	18 23	05 27	06 21	07 15	08 11
20	17 38	18 00	18 25	05 27	06 16	07 06	07 58
N 10	17 44	18 05	18 29	05 27	06 12	06 59	07 47
0	17 49	18 10	18 34	05 27	06 09	06 52	07 37
S 10	17 55	18 17	18 41	05 27	06 05	06 45	07 26
20	18 02	18 24	18 50	05 26	06 01	06 37	07 15
30	18 09	18 33	19 02	05 26	05 57	06 28	07 03
35	18 13	18 39	19 10	05 26	05 54	06 23	06 55
40	18 18	18 46	19 19	05 26	05 51	06 18	06 47
45	18 24	18 54	19 31	05 26	05 48	06 11	06 38
S 50	18 31	19 05	19 46	05 25	05 44	06 05	06 26
52	18 34	19 10	19 53	05 25	05 42	06 00	06 21
54	18 38	19 15	20 01	05 25	05 40	05 56	06 15
56	18 42	19 21	20 11	05 25	05 38	05 52	06 08
58	18 46	19 28	20 22	05 25	05 35	05 47	06 01
S 60	18 51	19 36	20 35	05 25	05 33	05 42	05 53

Day	SUN Eqn. of Time 00h	SUN Eqn. of Time 12h	SUN Mer. Pass.	MOON Mer. Pass. Upper	MOON Mer. Pass. Lower	Age	Phase
d	m s	m s	h m	h m	h m	d	%
13	13 35	13 43	11 46	23 58	11 38	15	100
14	13 50	13 57	11 46	24 41	12 20	16	99
15	14 04	14 11	11 46	00 41	13 03	17	97

© British Crown Copyright 2018. All rights reserved.

UT	ARIES GHA	VENUS −3.8 GHA	Dec	MARS +1.8 GHA	Dec	JUPITER −2.0 GHA	Dec	SATURN +0.5 GHA	Dec	STARS Name	SHA	Dec
16 00	24 13.3	167 25.8	S14 09.2	196 51.6	S 2 11.1	124 34.2	S22 52.1	98 27.8	S22 29.3	Acamar	315 14.7	S40 13.5
01	39 15.8	182 25.2	10.3	211 52.6	11.8	139 36.2	52.1	113 30.2	29.3	Achernar	335 22.9	S57 08.3
02	54 18.3	197 24.7	11.4	226 53.6	12.4	154 38.2	52.1	128 32.5	29.3	Acrux	173 05.2	S63 12.2
03	69 20.7	212 24.1	.. 12.5	241 54.6	.. 13.1	169 40.2	.. 52.2	143 34.8	.. 29.3	Adhara	255 09.1	S28 59.7
04	84 23.2	227 23.6	13.6	256 55.6	13.7	184 42.2	52.2	158 37.2	29.3	Aldebaran	290 44.2	N16 32.8
05	99 25.7	242 23.1	14.6	271 56.6	14.4	199 44.3	52.2	173 39.5	29.3			
06	114 28.1	257 22.5	S14 15.7	286 57.5	S 2 15.0	214 46.3	S22 52.3	188 41.9	S22 29.3	Alioth	166 17.4	N55 51.3
W 07	129 30.6	272 22.0	16.8	301 58.5	15.7	229 48.3	52.3	203 44.2	29.3	Alkaid	152 56.0	N49 13.1
E 08	144 33.1	287 21.4	17.9	316 59.5	16.3	244 50.3	52.3	218 46.6	29.2	Alnair	27 38.0	S46 52.1
D 09	159 35.5	302 20.9	.. 19.0	332 00.5	.. 17.0	259 52.3	.. 52.4	233 48.9	.. 29.2	Alnilam	275 41.8	S 1 11.4
N 10	174 38.0	317 20.3	20.0	347 01.5	17.6	274 54.3	52.4	248 51.2	29.2	Alphard	217 52.0	S 8 44.5
E 11	189 40.4	332 19.8	21.1	2 02.5	18.3	289 56.3	52.4	263 53.6	29.2			
S 12	204 42.9	347 19.2	S14 22.2	17 03.4	S 2 18.9	304 58.3	S22 52.5	278 55.9	S22 29.2	Alphecca	126 07.7	N26 39.2
D 13	219 45.4	2 18.7	23.3	32 04.4	19.6	320 00.3	52.5	293 58.3	29.2	Alpheratz	357 38.7	N29 12.0
A 14	234 47.8	17 18.2	24.3	47 05.4	20.2	335 02.4	52.5	309 00.6	29.2	Altair	62 04.0	N 8 55.4
Y 15	249 50.3	32 17.6	.. 25.4	62 06.4	.. 20.8	350 04.4	.. 52.6	324 03.0	.. 29.2	Ankaa	353 11.0	S42 12.0
16	264 52.8	47 17.1	26.5	77 07.4	21.5	5 06.4	52.6	339 05.3	29.2	Antares	112 21.2	S26 28.4
17	279 55.2	62 16.5	27.6	92 08.3	22.1	20 08.4	52.7	354 07.6	29.2			
18	294 57.7	77 16.0	S14 28.6	107 09.3	S 2 22.8	35 10.4	S22 52.7	9 10.0	S22 29.2	Arcturus	145 52.1	N19 05.1
19	310 00.2	92 15.4	29.7	122 10.3	23.4	50 12.4	52.7	24 12.3	29.2	Atria	107 19.5	S69 03.8
20	325 02.6	107 14.9	30.8	137 11.3	24.1	65 14.4	52.8	39 14.7	29.1	Avior	234 16.4	S59 34.0
21	340 05.1	122 14.3	.. 31.9	152 12.3	.. 24.7	80 16.4	.. 52.8	54 17.0	.. 29.1	Bellatrix	278 27.2	N 6 22.0
22	355 07.5	137 13.8	32.9	167 13.3	25.4	95 18.4	52.8	69 19.3	29.1	Betelgeuse	270 56.5	N 7 24.6
23	10 10.0	152 13.2	34.0	182 14.2	26.0	110 20.4	52.9	84 21.7	29.1			
17 00	25 12.5	167 12.7	S14 35.1	197 15.2	S 2 26.7	125 22.4	S22 52.9	99 24.0	S22 29.1	Canopus	263 54.1	S52 42.1
01	40 14.9	182 12.1	36.1	212 16.2	27.3	140 24.5	52.9	114 26.4	29.1	Capella	280 27.8	N46 00.8
02	55 17.4	197 11.6	37.2	227 17.2	28.0	155 26.5	53.0	129 28.7	29.1	Deneb	49 28.5	N45 21.4
03	70 19.9	212 11.0	.. 38.3	242 18.2	.. 28.6	170 28.5	.. 53.0	144 31.0	.. 29.1	Denebola	182 29.6	N14 27.9
04	85 22.3	227 10.5	39.3	257 19.1	29.3	185 30.5	53.0	159 33.4	29.1	Diphda	348 51.2	S17 52.7
05	100 24.8	242 09.9	40.4	272 20.1	29.9	200 32.5	53.1	174 35.7	29.1			
06	115 27.3	257 09.3	S14 41.5	287 21.1	S 2 30.6	215 34.5	S22 53.1	189 38.1	S22 29.1	Dubhe	193 46.9	N61 38.6
T 07	130 29.7	272 08.8	42.5	302 22.1	31.2	230 36.5	53.1	204 40.4	29.1	Elnath	278 07.0	N28 37.3
H 08	145 32.2	287 08.2	43.6	317 23.1	31.9	245 38.5	53.2	219 42.7	29.0	Eltanin	90 44.4	N51 29.6
U 09	160 34.7	302 07.7	.. 44.7	332 24.0	.. 32.5	260 40.5	.. 53.2	234 45.1	.. 29.0	Enif	33 42.7	N 9 58.1
R 10	175 37.1	317 07.1	45.7	347 25.0	33.2	275 42.5	53.2	249 47.4	29.0	Fomalhaut	15 18.9	S29 31.1
S 11	190 39.6	332 06.6	46.8	2 26.0	33.8	290 44.5	53.3	264 49.8	29.0			
D 12	205 42.0	347 06.0	S14 47.9	17 27.0	S 2 34.5	305 46.5	S22 53.3	279 52.1	S22 29.0	Gacrux	171 56.7	S57 13.2
A 13	220 44.5	2 05.4	48.9	32 28.0	35.1	320 48.5	53.4	294 54.4	29.0	Gienah	175 48.2	S17 38.8
Y 14	235 47.0	17 04.9	50.0	47 28.9	35.8	335 50.5	53.4	309 56.8	29.0	Hadar	148 42.4	S60 27.9
15	250 49.4	32 04.3	.. 51.1	62 29.9	.. 36.4	350 52.5	.. 53.4	324 59.1	.. 29.0	Hamal	327 55.5	N23 33.3
16	265 51.9	47 03.8	52.1	77 30.9	37.1	5 54.5	53.5	340 01.4	29.0	Kaus Aust.	83 38.2	S34 22.5
17	280 54.4	62 03.2	53.2	92 31.9	37.7	20 56.6	53.5	355 03.8	29.0			
18	295 56.8	77 02.7	S14 54.2	107 32.9	S 2 38.4	35 58.6	S22 53.5	10 06.1	S22 29.0	Kochab	137 21.2	N74 04.7
19	310 59.3	92 02.1	55.3	122 33.8	39.0	51 00.6	53.6	25 08.4	28.9	Markab	13 33.8	N15 18.8
20	326 01.8	107 01.5	56.3	137 34.8	39.6	66 02.6	53.6	40 10.8	28.9	Menkar	314 10.2	N 4 10.0
21	341 04.2	122 01.0	.. 57.4	152 35.8	.. 40.3	81 04.6	.. 53.6	55 13.1	.. 28.9	Menkent	148 02.9	S36 27.8
22	356 06.7	137 00.4	58.5	167 36.8	40.9	96 06.6	53.7	70 15.5	28.9	Miaplacidus	221 39.2	S69 47.5
23	11 09.2	151 59.8	14 59.5	182 37.8	41.6	111 08.6	53.7	85 17.8	28.9			
18 00	26 11.6	166 59.3	S15 00.6	197 38.7	S 2 42.2	126 10.6	S22 53.7	100 20.1	S22 28.9	Mirfak	308 33.7	N49 55.7
01	41 14.1	181 58.7	01.6	212 39.7	42.9	141 12.6	53.8	115 22.5	28.9	Nunki	75 53.0	S26 16.3
02	56 16.5	196 58.2	02.7	227 40.7	43.5	156 14.6	53.8	130 24.8	28.9	Peacock	53 12.3	S56 40.4
03	71 19.0	211 57.6	.. 03.7	242 41.7	.. 44.2	171 16.6	.. 53.8	145 27.1	.. 28.9	Pollux	243 22.5	N27 58.6
04	86 21.5	226 57.0	04.8	257 42.7	44.8	186 18.6	53.9	160 29.5	28.9	Procyon	244 55.2	N 5 10.5
05	101 23.9	241 56.5	05.8	272 43.6	45.5	201 20.6	53.9	175 31.8	28.9			
06	116 26.4	256 55.9	S15 06.9	287 44.6	S 2 46.1	216 22.6	S22 53.9	190 34.1	S22 28.8	Rasalhague	96 02.6	N12 33.0
07	131 28.9	271 55.3	07.9	302 45.6	46.8	231 24.6	54.0	205 36.5	28.8	Regulus	207 39.1	N11 52.3
08	146 31.3	286 54.8	09.0	317 46.6	47.4	246 26.6	54.0	220 38.8	28.8	Rigel	281 07.7	S 8 10.7
F 09	161 33.8	301 54.2	.. 10.0	332 47.6	.. 48.1	261 28.6	.. 54.0	235 41.1	.. 28.8	Rigil Kent.	139 46.6	S60 54.8
R 10	176 36.3	316 53.6	11.1	347 48.5	48.7	276 30.6	54.1	250 43.5	28.8	Sabik	102 07.8	S15 44.8
I 11	191 38.7	331 53.1	12.1	2 49.5	49.4	291 32.6	54.1	265 45.8	28.8			
D 12	206 41.2	346 52.5	S15 13.2	17 50.5	S 2 50.0	306 34.6	S22 54.1	280 48.1	S22 28.8	Schedar	349 35.1	N56 38.8
A 13	221 43.6	1 51.9	14.2	32 51.5	50.7	321 36.6	54.2	295 50.5	28.8	Shaula	96 16.3	S37 07.0
Y 14	236 46.1	16 51.3	15.3	47 52.5	51.3	336 38.6	54.2	310 52.8	28.8	Sirius	258 29.8	S16 44.5
15	251 48.6	31 50.8	.. 16.3	62 53.4	.. 52.0	351 40.6	.. 54.3	325 55.2	.. 28.8	Spica	158 27.0	S11 15.6
16	266 51.0	46 50.2	17.4	77 54.4	52.6	6 42.6	54.3	340 57.5	28.8	Suhail	222 49.5	S43 30.4
17	281 53.5	61 49.6	18.4	92 55.4	53.3	21 44.6	54.3	355 59.8	28.7			
18	296 56.0	76 49.1	S15 19.5	107 56.4	S 2 53.9	36 46.6	S22 54.4	11 02.1	S22 28.7	Vega	80 36.2	N38 48.5
19	311 58.4	91 48.5	20.5	122 57.4	54.5	51 48.6	54.4	26 04.5	28.7	Zuben'ubi	137 01.0	S16 07.2
20	327 00.9	106 47.9	21.5	137 58.3	55.2	66 50.6	54.4	41 06.8	28.7		SHA	Mer.Pass.
21	342 03.4	121 47.3	.. 22.6	152 59.3	.. 55.8	81 52.6	.. 54.5	56 09.1	.. 28.7	Venus	142 00.2	12 52
22	357 05.8	136 46.8	23.6	168 00.3	56.5	96 54.6	54.5	71 11.5	28.7	Mars	172 02.7	10 50
23	12 08.3	151 46.2	24.7	183 01.3	57.1	111 56.6	54.5	86 13.8	28.7	Jupiter	100 10.0	15 36
Mer.Pass. 22 15.5		v −0.6	d 1.1	v 1.0	d 0.6	v 2.0	d 0.0	v 2.3	d 0.0	Saturn	74 11.5	17 20

© British Crown Copyright 2018. All rights reserved.

UT	SUN GHA	SUN Dec	MOON GHA	v	MOON Dec	d	HP
d h	° ′	° ′	° ′	′	° ′	′	′
16 00	183 34.5	S 8 41.5	339 15.7	13.5	N12 43.4	10.2	55.2
01	198 34.6	42.4	353 48.2	13.4	12 53.6	10.1	55.3
02	213 34.8	43.3	8 20.6	13.3	13 03.7	10.1	55.3
03	228 34.9	.. 44.3	22 52.9	13.3	13 13.8	10.0	55.3
04	243 35.0	45.2	37 25.2	13.2	13 23.8	9.9	55.3
05	258 35.2	46.1	51 57.4	13.2	13 33.7	10.0	55.3
06	273 35.3	S 8 47.0	66 29.6	13.1	N13 43.7	9.8	55.3
W 07	288 35.4	47.9	81 01.7	13.1	13 53.5	9.8	55.4
E 08	303 35.6	48.9	95 33.8	13.0	14 03.3	9.7	55.4
D 09	318 35.7	.. 49.8	110 05.8	12.9	14 13.0	9.7	55.4
N 10	333 35.8	50.7	124 37.7	12.8	14 22.7	9.6	55.4
E 11	348 36.0	51.6	139 09.5	12.8	14 32.3	9.6	55.4
S 12	3 36.1	S 8 52.5	153 41.3	12.8	N14 41.9	9.5	55.5
D 13	18 36.3	53.5	168 13.1	12.7	14 51.4	9.4	55.5
A 14	33 36.4	54.4	182 44.8	12.6	15 00.8	9.4	55.5
Y 15	48 36.5	.. 55.3	197 16.4	12.5	15 10.2	9.3	55.5
16	63 36.7	56.2	211 47.9	12.5	15 19.5	9.2	55.5
17	78 36.8	57.1	226 19.4	12.4	15 28.7	9.2	55.5
18	93 36.9	S 8 58.0	240 50.8	12.4	N15 37.9	9.1	55.6
19	108 37.1	59.0	255 22.2	12.3	15 47.0	9.1	55.6
20	123 37.2	8 59.9	269 53.5	12.2	15 56.1	8.9	55.6
21	138 37.3	9 00.8	284 24.7	12.1	16 05.0	8.9	55.6
22	153 37.5	01.7	298 55.8	12.1	16 13.9	8.9	55.6
23	168 37.6	02.6	313 26.9	12.0	16 22.8	8.7	55.7
17 00	183 37.7	S 9 03.6	327 57.9	12.0	N16 31.5	8.7	55.7
01	198 37.9	04.5	342 28.9	11.9	16 40.2	8.6	55.7
02	213 38.0	05.4	356 59.8	11.8	16 48.8	8.6	55.7
03	228 38.1	.. 06.3	11 30.6	11.8	16 57.4	8.4	55.7
04	243 38.2	07.2	26 01.4	11.6	17 05.8	8.4	55.8
05	258 38.4	08.1	40 32.0	11.6	17 14.2	8.3	55.8
06	273 38.5	S 9 09.0	55 02.6	11.6	N17 22.5	8.3	55.8
T 07	288 38.6	10.0	69 33.2	11.5	17 30.8	8.1	55.8
H 08	303 38.8	10.9	84 03.7	11.4	17 38.9	8.1	55.8
U 09	318 38.9	.. 11.8	98 34.1	11.3	17 47.0	8.0	55.9
R 10	333 39.0	12.7	113 04.4	11.3	17 55.0	7.9	55.9
S 11	348 39.2	13.6	127 34.7	11.2	18 02.9	7.8	55.9
D 12	3 39.3	S 9 14.5	142 04.9	11.1	N18 10.7	7.8	55.9
A 13	18 39.4	15.5	156 35.0	11.1	18 18.5	7.6	55.9
Y 14	33 39.5	16.4	171 05.1	11.0	18 26.1	7.6	56.0
15	48 39.7	.. 17.3	185 35.1	10.9	18 33.7	7.5	56.0
16	63 39.8	18.2	200 05.0	10.8	18 41.2	7.4	56.0
17	78 39.9	19.1	214 34.8	10.8	18 48.6	7.3	56.0
18	93 40.0	S 9 20.0	229 04.6	10.7	N18 55.9	7.2	56.1
19	108 40.2	20.9	243 34.3	10.7	19 03.1	7.1	56.1
20	123 40.3	21.8	258 04.0	10.5	19 10.2	7.0	56.1
21	138 40.4	.. 22.8	272 33.5	10.5	19 17.2	7.0	56.1
22	153 40.6	23.7	287 03.0	10.5	19 24.2	6.8	56.1
23	168 40.7	24.6	301 32.5	10.3	19 31.0	6.8	56.2
18 00	183 40.8	S 9 25.5	316 01.8	10.3	N19 37.8	6.6	56.2
01	198 40.9	26.4	330 31.1	10.3	19 44.4	6.6	56.2
02	213 41.1	27.3	345 00.4	10.1	19 51.0	6.4	56.2
03	228 41.2	.. 28.2	359 29.5	10.1	19 57.4	6.4	56.3
04	243 41.3	29.1	13 58.6	10.0	20 03.8	6.2	56.3
05	258 41.4	30.0	28 27.6	10.0	20 10.0	6.2	56.3
06	273 41.6	S 9 31.0	42 56.6	9.8	N20 16.2	6.0	56.3
07	288 41.7	31.9	57 25.4	9.8	20 22.2	6.0	56.3
08	303 41.8	32.8	71 54.2	9.8	20 28.2	5.8	56.4
F 09	318 41.9	.. 33.7	86 23.0	9.7	20 34.0	5.8	56.4
R 10	333 42.1	34.6	100 51.7	9.6	20 39.8	5.6	56.4
I 11	348 42.2	35.5	115 20.3	9.5	20 45.4	5.6	56.4
D 12	3 42.3	S 9 36.4	129 48.8	9.5	N20 51.0	5.4	56.5
A 13	18 42.4	37.3	144 17.3	9.4	20 56.4	5.3	56.5
Y 14	33 42.5	38.2	158 45.7	9.3	21 01.7	5.2	56.5
15	48 42.7	.. 39.1	173 14.0	9.3	21 06.9	5.1	56.5
16	63 42.8	40.0	187 42.3	9.2	21 12.0	5.0	56.6
17	78 42.9	40.9	202 10.5	9.1	21 17.0	4.9	56.6
18	93 43.0	S 9 41.9	216 38.6	9.1	N21 21.9	4.7	56.6
19	108 43.1	42.8	231 06.7	9.0	21 26.6	4.7	56.6
20	123 43.3	43.7	245 34.7	9.0	21 31.3	4.5	56.7
21	138 43.4	.. 44.6	260 02.7	8.9	21 35.8	4.5	56.7
22	153 43.5	45.5	274 30.6	8.8	21 40.3	4.3	56.7
23	168 43.6	46.4	288 58.4	8.8	N21 44.6	4.2	56.7
	SD 16.1	d 0.9	SD 15.1		15.2		15.4

Lat.	Naut.	Civil	Sunrise	Moonrise 16	17	18	19
°	h m	h m	h m	h m	h m	h m	h m
N 72	05 02	06 21	07 32	16 05	▭	▭	▭
N 70	05 05	06 16	07 20	16 39	16 10	▭	▭
68	05 08	06 12	07 10	17 03	16 54	16 38	▭
66	05 09	06 09	07 02	17 22	17 24	17 30	17 49
64	05 11	06 06	06 55	17 38	17 46	18 02	18 32
62	05 12	06 03	06 49	17 51	18 04	18 26	19 01
60	05 13	06 01	06 43	18 02	18 19	18 45	19 24
N 58	05 13	05 59	06 39	18 11	18 32	19 01	19 42
56	05 14	05 57	06 35	18 20	18 43	19 15	19 57
54	05 14	05 55	06 31	18 27	18 53	19 26	20 10
52	05 14	05 53	06 27	18 34	19 02	19 37	20 22
50	05 14	05 52	06 24	18 40	19 10	19 46	20 32
45	05 14	05 48	06 18	18 53	19 26	20 06	20 53
N 40	05 13	05 45	06 12	19 04	19 40	20 22	21 11
35	05 12	05 42	06 07	19 14	19 52	20 35	21 25
30	05 11	05 39	06 03	19 22	20 02	20 47	21 38
20	05 07	05 33	05 55	19 36	20 20	21 07	22 00
N 10	05 03	05 27	05 49	19 49	20 35	21 25	22 19
0	04 57	05 21	05 42	20 01	20 50	21 42	22 36
S 10	04 49	05 14	05 36	20 13	21 05	21 59	22 54
20	04 40	05 06	05 28	20 26	21 20	22 16	23 13
30	04 27	04 56	05 20	20 40	21 38	22 37	23 35
35	04 19	04 49	05 15	20 49	21 49	22 49	23 48
40	04 09	04 42	05 09	20 59	22 01	23 03	24 03
45	03 56	04 33	05 04	21 11	22 16	23 20	24 20
S 50	03 40	04 22	04 56	21 25	22 33	23 40	24 42
52	03 33	04 17	04 52	21 31	22 42	23 50	24 53
54	03 24	04 11	04 48	21 39	22 51	24 01	00 01
56	03 14	04 04	04 44	21 47	23 02	24 14	00 14
58	03 02	03 57	04 39	21 56	23 14	24 28	00 28
S 60	02 48	03 48	04 34	22 07	23 28	24 45	00 45

Lat.	Sunset	Civil	Naut.	Moonset 16	17	18	19
°	h m	h m	h m	h m	h m	h m	h m
N 72	15 57	17 08	18 26	11 14	▭	▭	▭
N 70	16 09	17 13	18 23	10 42	12 51	▭	▭
68	16 19	17 17	18 21	10 19	12 08	14 10	▭
66	16 28	17 20	18 20	10 01	11 39	13 19	14 52
64	16 35	17 24	18 18	09 46	11 17	12 47	14 09
62	16 41	17 26	18 17	09 34	11 00	12 23	13 40
60	16 46	17 29	18 17	09 24	10 45	12 05	13 18
N 58	16 51	17 31	18 16	09 15	10 33	11 49	13 00
56	16 55	17 33	18 16	09 07	10 22	11 36	12 45
54	16 59	17 35	18 16	09 00	10 13	11 25	12 32
52	17 02	17 37	18 16	08 54	10 05	11 14	12 20
50	17 06	17 38	18 16	08 49	09 57	11 05	12 10
45	17 12	17 42	18 16	08 37	09 42	10 46	11 49
N 40	17 18	17 45	18 17	08 27	09 29	10 31	11 32
35	17 23	17 49	18 18	08 18	09 18	10 18	11 17
30	17 27	17 52	18 19	08 11	09 08	10 07	11 05
20	17 35	17 57	18 23	07 58	08 52	09 47	10 44
N 10	17 42	18 03	18 28	07 47	08 37	09 30	10 25
0	17 49	18 10	18 34	07 37	08 24	09 14	10 08
S 10	17 55	18 17	18 42	07 26	08 11	08 59	09 50
20	18 03	18 25	18 51	07 15	07 57	08 42	09 32
30	18 11	18 36	19 04	07 03	07 40	08 23	09 11
35	18 16	18 42	19 13	06 55	07 31	08 11	08 58
40	18 22	18 50	19 23	06 47	07 20	07 59	08 44
45	18 28	18 59	19 36	06 38	07 08	07 44	08 27
S 50	18 36	19 10	19 52	06 26	06 52	07 25	08 06
52	18 40	19 15	20 00	06 21	06 45	07 16	07 56
54	18 44	19 21	20 09	06 15	06 38	07 07	07 45
56	18 48	19 28	20 19	06 08	06 29	06 56	07 32
58	18 53	19 36	20 31	06 01	06 19	06 43	07 17
S 60	18 59	19 45	20 45	05 53	06 08	06 28	06 59

Day	SUN Eqn. of Time 00h	12h	Mer. Pass.	MOON Mer. Pass. Upper	Lower	Age	Phase
d	m s	m s	h m	h m	h m	d	%
16	14 18	14 24	11 46	01 26	13 49	18	93
17	14 31	14 37	11 45	02 12	14 37	19	88
18	14 43	14 49	11 45	03 02	15 28	20	80

© British Crown Copyright 2018. All rights reserved.

UT	ARIES GHA	VENUS −3.8 GHA	VENUS Dec	MARS +1.8 GHA	MARS Dec	JUPITER −1.9 GHA	JUPITER Dec	SATURN +0.5 GHA	SATURN Dec	STARS Name	SHA	Dec
19 00	27 10.8	166 45.6	S15 25.7	198 02.2	S 2 57.8	126 58.6	S22 54.6	101 16.1	S22 28.7	Acamar	315 14.6	S40 13.5
01	42 13.2	181 45.0	26.7	213 03.2	58.4	142 00.6	54.6	116 18.5	28.7	Achernar	335 22.9	S57 08.3
02	57 15.7	196 44.5	27.8	228 04.2	59.1	157 02.6	54.6	131 20.8	28.7	Acrux	173 05.1	S63 12.2
03	72 18.1	211 43.9	.. 28.8	243 05.2	2 59.7	172 04.6	.. 54.7	146 23.1	.. 28.6	Adhara	255 09.0	S28 59.7
04	87 20.6	226 43.3	29.9	258 06.2	3 00.4	187 06.6	54.7	161 25.5	28.6	Aldebaran	290 44.2	N16 32.8
05	102 23.1	241 42.7	30.9	273 07.1	01.0	202 08.6	54.7	176 27.8	28.6			
S 06	117 25.5	256 42.2	S15 31.9	288 08.1	S 3 01.7	217 10.6	S22 54.8	191 30.1	S22 28.6	Alioth	166 17.4	N55 51.3
A 07	132 28.0	271 41.6	33.0	303 09.1	02.3	232 12.6	54.8	206 32.5	28.6	Alkaid	152 55.9	N49 13.1
T 08	147 30.5	286 41.0	34.0	318 10.1	03.0	247 14.6	54.8	221 34.8	28.6	Alnair	27 38.0	S46 52.1
U 09	162 32.9	301 40.4	.. 35.0	333 11.0	.. 03.6	262 16.6	.. 54.9	236 37.1	.. 28.6	Alnilam	275 41.8	S 1 11.4
R 10	177 35.4	316 39.8	36.1	348 12.0	04.3	277 18.6	54.9	251 39.5	28.6	Alphard	217 52.0	S 8 44.5
D 11	192 37.9	331 39.3	37.1	3 13.0	04.9	292 20.6	54.9	266 41.8	28.6			
A 12	207 40.3	346 38.7	S15 38.1	18 14.0	S 3 05.6	307 22.6	S22 55.0	281 44.1	S22 28.6	Alphecca	126 07.7	N26 39.2
Y 13	222 42.8	1 38.1	39.2	33 15.0	06.2	322 24.6	55.0	296 46.4	28.5	Alpheratz	357 38.7	N29 12.0
14	237 45.3	16 37.5	40.2	48 15.9	06.8	337 26.6	55.0	311 48.8	28.5	Altair	62 04.0	N 8 55.4
15	252 47.7	31 36.9	.. 41.2	63 16.9	.. 07.5	352 28.6	.. 55.1	326 51.1	.. 28.5	Ankaa	353 11.0	S42 12.0
16	267 50.2	46 36.3	42.2	78 17.9	08.1	7 30.6	55.1	341 53.4	28.5	Antares	112 21.2	S26 28.4
17	282 52.6	61 35.8	43.3	93 18.9	08.8	22 32.5	55.1	356 55.8	28.5			
18	297 55.1	76 35.2	S15 44.3	108 19.8	S 3 09.4	37 34.5	S22 55.2	11 58.1	S22 28.5	Arcturus	145 52.1	N19 05.0
19	312 57.6	91 34.6	45.3	123 20.8	10.1	52 36.5	55.2	27 00.4	28.5	Atria	107 19.5	S69 03.8
20	328 00.0	106 34.0	46.4	138 21.8	10.7	67 38.5	55.3	42 02.7	28.5	Avior	234 16.4	S59 34.0
21	343 02.5	121 33.4	.. 47.4	153 22.8	.. 11.4	82 40.5	.. 55.3	57 05.1	.. 28.5	Bellatrix	278 27.2	N 6 22.0
22	358 05.0	136 32.8	48.4	168 23.8	12.0	97 42.5	55.3	72 07.4	28.5	Betelgeuse	270 56.5	N 7 24.6
23	13 07.4	151 32.2	49.4	183 24.7	12.7	112 44.5	55.4	87 09.7	28.5			
20 00	28 09.9	166 31.7	S15 50.4	198 25.7	S 3 13.3	127 46.5	S22 55.4	102 12.1	S22 28.4	Canopus	263 54.0	S52 42.1
01	43 12.4	181 31.1	51.5	213 26.7	14.0	142 48.5	55.4	117 14.4	28.4	Capella	280 27.8	N46 00.8
02	58 14.8	196 30.5	52.5	228 27.7	14.6	157 50.5	55.5	132 16.7	28.4	Deneb	49 28.5	N45 21.4
03	73 17.3	211 29.9	.. 53.5	243 28.6	.. 15.3	172 52.5	.. 55.5	147 19.0	.. 28.4	Denebola	182 29.5	N14 27.9
04	88 19.8	226 29.3	54.5	258 29.6	15.9	187 54.5	55.5	162 21.4	28.4	Diphda	348 51.2	S17 52.7
05	103 22.2	241 28.7	55.6	273 30.6	16.5	202 56.5	55.6	177 23.7	28.4			
S 06	118 24.7	256 28.1	S15 56.6	288 31.6	S 3 17.2	217 58.5	S22 55.6	192 26.0	S22 28.4	Dubhe	193 46.9	N61 38.6
U 07	133 27.1	271 27.5	57.6	303 32.5	17.8	233 00.5	55.6	207 28.4	28.4	Elnath	278 06.9	N28 37.3
N 08	148 29.6	286 26.9	58.6	318 33.5	18.5	248 02.5	55.7	222 30.7	28.4	Eltanin	90 44.4	N51 29.6
D 09	163 32.1	301 26.4	15 59.6	333 34.5	.. 19.1	263 04.4	.. 55.7	237 33.0	.. 28.3	Enif	33 42.7	N 9 58.1
A 10	178 34.5	316 25.8	16 00.6	348 35.5	19.8	278 06.4	55.7	252 35.3	28.3	Fomalhaut	15 18.9	S29 31.1
Y 11	193 37.0	331 25.2	01.7	3 36.4	20.4	293 08.4	55.8	267 37.7	28.3			
12	208 39.5	346 24.6	S16 02.7	18 37.4	S 3 21.1	308 10.4	S22 55.8	282 40.0	S22 28.3	Gacrux	171 56.7	S57 13.1
13	223 41.9	1 24.0	03.7	33 38.4	21.7	323 12.4	55.8	297 42.3	28.3	Gienah	175 48.2	S17 38.8
14	238 44.4	16 23.4	04.7	48 39.4	22.4	338 14.4	55.9	312 44.6	28.3	Hadar	148 42.4	S60 27.9
15	253 46.9	31 22.8	.. 05.7	63 40.4	.. 23.0	353 16.4	.. 55.9	327 47.0	.. 28.3	Hamal	327 55.5	N23 33.3
16	268 49.3	46 22.2	06.7	78 41.3	23.7	8 18.4	55.9	342 49.3	28.3	Kaus Aust.	83 38.2	S34 22.5
17	283 51.8	61 21.6	07.7	93 42.3	24.3	23 20.4	56.0	357 51.6	28.3			
18	298 54.3	76 21.0	S16 08.7	108 43.3	S 3 24.9	38 22.4	S22 56.0	12 53.9	S22 28.3	Kochab	137 21.2	N74 04.7
19	313 56.7	91 20.4	09.8	123 44.3	25.6	53 24.4	56.0	27 56.3	28.2	Markab	13 33.8	N15 18.8
20	328 59.2	106 19.8	10.8	138 45.2	26.2	68 26.4	56.1	42 58.6	28.2	Menkar	314 10.2	N 4 10.0
21	344 01.6	121 19.2	.. 11.8	153 46.2	.. 26.9	83 28.3	.. 56.1	58 00.9	.. 28.2	Menkent	148 02.9	S36 27.8
22	359 04.1	136 18.6	12.8	168 47.2	27.5	98 30.3	56.1	73 03.2	28.2	Miaplacidus	221 39.2	S69 47.5
23	14 06.6	151 18.0	13.8	183 48.2	28.2	113 32.3	56.2	88 05.6	28.2			
21 00	29 09.0	166 17.4	S16 14.8	198 49.1	S 3 28.8	128 34.3	S22 56.2	103 07.9	S22 28.2	Mirfak	308 33.7	N49 55.7
01	44 11.5	181 16.8	15.8	213 50.1	29.5	143 36.3	56.2	118 10.2	28.2	Nunki	75 53.1	S26 16.3
02	59 14.0	196 16.2	16.8	228 51.1	30.1	158 38.3	56.3	133 12.5	28.2	Peacock	53 12.4	S56 40.4
03	74 16.4	211 15.6	.. 17.8	243 52.1	.. 30.8	173 40.3	.. 56.3	148 14.9	.. 28.2	Pollux	243 22.4	N27 58.6
04	89 18.9	226 15.0	18.8	258 53.0	31.4	188 42.3	56.3	163 17.2	28.2	Procyon	244 55.2	N 5 10.5
05	104 21.4	241 14.4	19.8	273 54.0	32.1	203 44.3	56.4	178 19.5	28.1			
06	119 23.8	256 13.8	S16 20.8	288 55.0	S 3 32.7	218 46.2	S22 56.4	193 21.8	S22 28.1	Rasalhague	96 02.6	N12 33.0
07	134 26.3	271 13.2	21.8	303 56.0	33.3	233 48.2	56.4	208 24.1	28.1	Regulus	207 39.1	N11 52.3
08	149 28.7	286 12.6	22.8	318 56.9	34.0	248 50.2	56.5	223 26.5	28.1	Rigel	281 07.7	S 8 10.7
M 09	164 31.2	301 12.0	.. 23.8	333 57.9	.. 34.6	263 52.2	.. 56.5	238 28.8	.. 28.1	Rigil Kent.	139 46.6	S60 54.8
O 10	179 33.7	316 11.4	24.8	348 58.9	35.3	278 54.2	56.5	253 31.1	28.1	Sabik	102 07.8	S15 44.8
N 11	194 36.1	331 10.8	25.8	3 59.9	35.9	293 56.2	56.6	268 33.4	28.1			
D 12	209 38.6	346 10.2	S16 26.8	19 00.8	S 3 36.6	308 58.2	S22 56.6	283 35.8	S22 28.1	Schedar	349 35.1	N56 38.8
A 13	224 41.1	1 09.6	27.8	34 01.8	37.2	324 00.2	56.6	298 38.1	28.1	Shaula	96 16.3	S37 07.0
Y 14	239 43.5	16 09.0	28.8	49 02.8	37.9	339 02.1	56.7	313 40.4	28.0	Sirius	258 29.8	S16 44.5
15	254 46.0	31 08.4	.. 29.8	64 03.8	.. 38.5	354 04.1	.. 56.7	328 42.7	.. 28.0	Spica	158 27.0	S11 15.6
16	269 48.5	46 07.8	30.8	79 04.7	39.2	9 06.1	56.7	343 45.0	28.0	Suhail	222 49.4	S43 30.4
17	284 50.9	61 07.1	31.8	94 05.7	39.8	24 08.1	56.8	358 47.4	28.0			
18	299 53.4	76 06.5	S16 32.8	109 06.7	S 3 40.4	39 10.1	S22 56.8	13 49.7	S22 28.0	Vega	80 36.2	N38 48.5
19	314 55.9	91 05.9	33.8	124 07.6	41.1	54 12.1	56.8	28 52.0	28.0	Zuben'ubi	137 01.0	S16 07.2
20	329 58.3	106 05.3	34.8	139 08.6	41.7	69 14.1	56.9	43 54.3	28.0		SHA	Mer.Pass.
21	345 00.8	121 04.7	.. 35.8	154 09.6	.. 42.4	84 16.0	.. 56.9	58 56.6	.. 28.0		° ′	h m
22	0 03.2	136 04.1	36.8	169 10.6	43.0	99 18.0	56.9	73 59.0	28.0	Venus	138 21.8	12 54
23	15 05.7	151 03.5	37.8	184 11.5	43.7	114 20.0	57.0	89 01.3	27.9	Mars	170 15.8	10 46
	h m									Jupiter	99 36.6	15 27
Mer.Pass.	22 03.7	v −0.6	d 1.0	v 1.0	d 0.6	v 2.0	d 0.0	v 2.3	d 0.0	Saturn	74 02.2	17 09

© British Crown Copyright 2018. All rights reserved.

UT	SUN GHA	SUN Dec	MOON GHA	v	MOON Dec	d	HP
19 00	183 43.7	S 9 47.3	303 26.2	8.7	N21 48.8	4.0	56.8
01	198 43.9	48.2	317 53.9	8.6	21 52.8	4.0	56.8
02	213 44.0	49.1	332 21.5	8.6	21 56.8	3.8	56.8
03	228 44.1	.. 50.0	346 49.1	8.5	22 00.6	3.7	56.8
04	243 44.2	50.9	1 16.6	8.5	22 04.3	3.6	56.9
05	258 44.3	51.8	15 44.1	8.4	22 07.9	3.5	56.9
06	273 44.5	S 9 52.7	30 11.5	8.3	N22 11.4	3.3	56.9
S 07	288 44.6	53.6	44 38.8	8.3	22 14.7	3.3	56.9
A 08	303 44.7	54.5	59 06.1	8.3	22 18.0	3.1	57.0
T 09	318 44.8	.. 55.4	73 33.4	8.2	22 21.1	3.0	57.0
U 10	333 44.9	56.3	88 00.6	8.1	22 24.1	2.8	57.0
R 11	348 45.0	57.2	102 27.7	8.1	22 26.9	2.7	57.0
D 12	3 45.2	S 9 58.1	116 54.8	8.0	N22 29.6	2.6	57.1
A 13	18 45.3	59.0	131 21.8	7.9	22 32.2	2.5	57.1
Y 14	33 45.4	9 59.9	145 48.7	8.0	22 34.7	2.4	57.1
15	48 45.5	10 00.8	160 15.7	7.8	22 37.1	2.2	57.1
16	63 45.6	01.7	174 42.5	7.7	22 39.3	2.1	57.2
17	78 45.7	02.6	189 09.4	7.7	22 41.4	1.9	57.2
18	93 45.8	S10 03.5	203 36.1	7.7	N22 43.3	1.9	57.2
19	108 46.0	04.4	218 02.8	7.7	22 45.2	1.7	57.2
20	123 46.1	05.4	232 29.5	7.5	22 46.9	1.5	57.3
21	138 46.2	.. 06.3	246 56.2	7.5	22 48.4	1.5	57.3
22	153 46.3	07.2	261 22.7	7.6	22 49.9	1.3	57.3
23	168 46.4	08.1	275 49.3	7.5	22 51.2	1.1	57.4
20 00	183 46.5	S10 09.0	290 15.8	7.4	N22 52.3	1.1	57.4
01	198 46.6	09.8	304 42.2	7.5	22 53.4	0.9	57.4
02	213 46.7	10.7	319 08.7	7.3	22 54.3	0.7	57.4
03	228 46.9	.. 11.6	333 35.0	7.4	22 55.0	0.7	57.5
04	243 47.0	12.5	348 01.4	7.3	22 55.7	0.5	57.5
05	258 47.1	13.4	2 27.7	7.2	22 56.2	0.3	57.5
06	273 47.2	S10 14.3	16 53.9	7.3	N22 56.5	0.2	57.5
07	288 47.3	15.2	31 20.2	7.2	22 56.7	0.1	57.6
S 08	303 47.4	16.1	45 46.4	7.1	22 56.8	0.0	57.6
U 09	318 47.5	.. 17.0	60 12.5	7.1	22 56.8	0.2	57.6
N 10	333 47.6	17.9	74 38.6	7.1	22 56.6	0.3	57.7
D 11	348 47.7	18.8	89 04.7	7.1	22 56.3	0.5	57.7
A 12	3 47.8	S10 19.7	103 30.8	7.1	N22 55.8	0.6	57.7
Y 13	18 48.0	20.6	117 56.9	7.0	22 55.2	0.8	57.7
14	33 48.1	21.5	132 22.9	6.9	22 54.4	0.8	57.8
15	48 48.2	.. 22.4	146 48.8	7.0	22 53.6	1.1	57.8
16	63 48.3	23.3	161 14.8	6.9	22 52.5	1.1	57.8
17	78 48.4	24.2	175 40.7	6.9	22 51.4	1.3	57.8
18	93 48.5	S10 25.1	190 06.6	6.9	N22 50.1	1.5	57.9
19	108 48.6	26.0	204 32.5	6.9	22 48.6	1.6	57.9
20	123 48.7	26.9	218 58.4	6.8	22 47.0	1.7	57.9
21	138 48.8	.. 27.8	233 24.2	6.9	22 45.3	1.9	58.0
22	153 48.9	28.7	247 50.1	6.8	22 43.4	2.0	58.0
23	168 49.0	29.6	262 15.9	6.8	22 41.4	2.1	58.0
21 00	183 49.1	S10 30.5	276 41.7	6.8	N22 39.3	2.3	58.0
01	198 49.2	31.4	291 07.5	6.7	22 37.0	2.4	58.1
02	213 49.3	32.3	305 33.2	6.8	22 34.6	2.6	58.1
03	228 49.5	.. 33.1	319 59.0	6.7	22 32.0	2.7	58.1
04	243 49.6	34.0	334 24.7	6.7	22 29.3	2.9	58.2
05	258 49.7	34.9	348 50.4	6.7	22 26.4	3.0	58.2
06	273 49.8	S10 35.8	3 16.1	6.8	N22 23.4	3.1	58.2
07	288 49.9	36.7	17 41.9	6.7	22 20.3	3.3	58.3
08	303 50.0	37.6	32 07.6	6.7	22 17.0	3.4	58.3
M 09	318 50.1	.. 38.5	46 33.3	6.6	22 13.6	3.6	58.3
O 10	333 50.2	39.4	60 58.9	6.7	22 10.0	3.7	58.3
N 11	348 50.3	40.3	75 24.6	6.7	22 06.3	3.8	58.4
D 12	3 50.4	S10 41.2	89 50.3	6.7	N22 02.5	4.0	58.4
A 13	18 50.5	42.1	104 16.0	6.7	21 58.5	4.1	58.4
Y 14	33 50.6	42.9	118 41.7	6.6	21 54.4	4.3	58.4
15	48 50.7	.. 43.8	133 07.3	6.7	21 50.1	4.4	58.5
16	63 50.8	44.7	147 33.0	6.7	21 45.7	4.5	58.5
17	78 50.9	45.6	161 58.7	6.7	21 41.2	4.7	58.5
18	93 51.0	S10 46.5	176 24.4	6.7	N21 36.5	4.8	58.6
19	108 51.1	47.4	190 50.1	6.7	21 31.7	5.0	58.6
20	123 51.2	48.3	205 15.8	6.7	21 26.7	5.1	58.6
21	138 51.3	.. 49.2	219 41.5	6.7	21 21.6	5.2	58.6
22	153 51.4	50.1	234 07.2	6.7	21 16.4	5.4	58.7
23	168 51.5	50.9	248 32.9	6.7	N21 11.0	5.5	58.7
	SD 16.1	d 0.9	SD 15.5		15.7		15.9

Lat.	Twilight Naut.	Twilight Civil	Sunrise	Moonrise 19	20	21	22
N 72	05 15	06 34	07 47	░░	░░	░░	
N 70	05 17	06 28	07 33	░░	░░	░░	20 47
68	05 18	06 23	07 21	░░	░░	19 15	21 35
66	05 19	06 18	07 12	17 49	18 42	20 16	22 06
64	05 19	06 14	07 04	18 32	19 27	20 50	22 29
62	05 19	06 11	06 57	19 01	19 57	21 15	22 47
60	05 20	06 08	06 51	19 24	20 20	21 34	23 02
N 58	05 20	06 05	06 45	19 42	20 38	21 50	23 14
56	05 20	06 03	06 41	19 57	20 54	22 04	23 25
54	05 19	06 00	06 37	20 10	21 07	22 16	23 35
52	05 19	05 58	06 33	20 22	21 18	22 26	23 43
50	05 19	05 56	06 29	20 32	21 29	22 36	23 51
45	05 18	05 52	06 22	20 53	21 50	22 55	24 07
N 40	05 16	05 48	06 15	21 11	22 07	23 11	24 20
35	05 15	05 44	06 10	21 25	22 22	23 25	24 32
30	05 13	05 41	06 05	21 38	22 35	23 36	24 41
20	05 08	05 34	05 56	22 00	22 56	23 56	24 58
N 10	05 03	05 27	05 49	22 19	23 15	24 14	00 14
0	04 56	05 20	05 41	22 36	23 33	24 30	00 30
S 10	04 48	05 13	05 34	22 54	23 50	24 46	00 46
20	04 37	05 04	05 26	23 13	24 09	00 09	01 03
30	04 23	04 52	05 17	23 35	24 31	00 31	01 23
35	04 15	04 46	05 12	23 48	24 44	00 44	01 35
40	04 04	04 37	05 06	24 03	00 03	00 58	01 48
45	03 50	04 28	04 58	24 20	00 20	01 15	02 04
S 50	03 33	04 16	04 50	24 42	00 42	01 37	02 23
52	03 25	04 10	04 46	24 53	00 53	01 47	02 32
54	03 15	04 03	04 41	00 01	01 05	01 59	02 42
56	03 04	03 56	04 37	00 14	01 18	02 12	02 53
58	02 52	03 48	04 31	00 28	01 34	02 27	03 06
S 60	02 36	03 38	04 25	00 45	01 53	02 45	03 22

Lat.	Sunset	Twilight Civil	Twilight Naut.	Moonset 19	20	21	22
N 72	15 41	16 54	18 12	░░	░░	░░	░░
N 70	15 55	17 00	18 11	░░	░░	░░	17 50
68	16 07	17 05	18 10	░░	░░	17 22	17 01
66	16 17	17 10	18 09	14 52	15 56	16 22	16 30
64	16 25	17 14	18 09	14 09	15 10	15 47	16 06
62	16 32	17 17	18 09	13 40	14 40	15 22	15 47
60	16 38	17 21	18 09	13 18	14 18	15 02	15 32
N 58	16 43	17 23	18 09	13 00	13 59	14 45	15 19
56	16 48	17 26	18 09	12 45	13 44	14 31	15 07
54	16 52	17 28	18 09	12 32	13 30	14 19	14 57
52	16 56	17 30	18 10	12 20	13 19	14 08	14 48
50	17 00	17 32	18 10	12 10	13 09	13 59	14 40
45	17 07	17 37	18 11	11 49	12 47	13 38	14 23
N 40	17 14	17 41	18 13	11 32	12 29	13 22	14 09
35	17 19	17 45	18 14	11 17	12 15	13 08	13 57
30	17 24	17 49	18 16	11 05	12 02	12 56	13 46
20	17 33	17 55	18 21	10 44	11 40	12 35	13 28
N 10	17 41	18 02	18 27	10 25	11 21	12 17	13 12
0	17 48	18 09	18 34	10 08	11 03	12 00	12 57
S 10	17 56	18 17	18 42	09 50	10 45	11 43	12 42
20	18 04	18 26	18 53	09 32	10 26	11 25	12 26
30	18 13	18 38	19 16	09 11	10 04	11 07	12 07
35	18 19	18 45	19 16	08 58	09 51	10 51	11 56
40	18 25	18 53	19 27	08 44	09 37	10 37	11 43
45	18 32	19 03	19 40	08 27	09 19	10 20	11 29
S 50	18 41	19 15	19 58	08 06	08 57	09 59	11 10
52	18 45	19 21	20 06	07 56	08 46	09 49	11 01
54	18 49	19 28	20 16	07 45	08 34	09 37	10 52
56	18 54	19 35	20 27	07 32	08 21	09 24	10 41
58	19 00	19 44	20 41	07 17	08 05	09 09	10 28
S 60	19 06	19 53	20 57	06 59	07 46	08 51	10 13

	SUN			MOON			
Day	Eqn. of Time 00ʰ	12ʰ	Mer. Pass.	Mer. Pass. Upper	Lower	Age	Phase
	m s	m s	h m	h m	h m	d	%
19	14 55	15 00	11 45	03 55	16 22	21	71
20	15 06	15 11	11 45	04 50	17 18	22	61
21	15 16	15 21	11 45	05 46	18 15	23	50

© British Crown Copyright 2018. All rights reserved.

UT	ARIES GHA	VENUS −3.8 GHA	Dec	MARS +1.8 GHA	Dec	JUPITER −1.9 GHA	Dec	SATURN +0.5 GHA	Dec	Star Name	SHA	Dec
22 00	30 08.2	166 02.9	S16 38.7	199 12.5	S 3 44.3	129 22.0	S22 57.0	104 03.6	S22 27.9	Acamar	315 14.6	S40 13.5
01	45 10.6	181 02.3	39.7	214 13.5	45.0	144 24.0	57.0	119 05.9	27.9	Achernar	335 22.9	S57 08.3
02	60 13.1	196 01.6	40.7	229 14.5	45.6	159 26.0	57.1	134 08.2	27.9	Acrux	173 05.1	S63 12.2
03	75 15.6	211 01.0 ..	41.7	244 15.4 ..	46.3	174 28.0 ..	57.1	149 10.6 ..	27.9	Adhara	255 09.0	S28 59.8
04	90 18.0	226 00.4	42.7	259 16.4	46.9	189 29.9	57.1	164 12.9	27.9	Aldebaran	290 44.1	N16 32.8
05	105 20.5	240 59.8	43.7	274 17.4	47.5	204 31.9	57.2	179 15.2	27.9			
06	120 23.0	255 59.2	S16 44.7	289 18.4	S 3 48.2	219 33.9	S22 57.2	194 17.5	S22 27.9	Alioth	166 17.4	N55 51.3
07	135 25.4	270 58.6	45.6	304 19.3	48.8	234 35.9	57.2	209 19.8	27.9	Alkaid	152 55.9	N49 13.1
08	150 27.9	285 58.0	46.6	319 20.3	49.5	249 37.9	57.3	224 22.2	27.8	Alnair	27 38.0	S46 52.1
09	165 30.4	300 57.3 ..	47.6	334 21.3 ..	50.1	264 39.9 ..	57.3	239 24.5 ..	27.8	Alnilam	275 41.8	S 1 11.4
10	180 32.8	315 56.7	48.6	349 22.2	50.8	279 41.8	57.3	254 26.8	27.8	Alphard	217 52.0	S 8 44.5
11	195 35.3	330 56.1	49.6	4 23.2	51.4	294 43.8	57.4	269 29.1	27.8			
12	210 37.7	345 55.5	S16 50.6	19 24.2	S 3 52.1	309 45.8	S22 57.4	284 31.4	S22 27.8	Alphecca	126 07.7	N26 39.2
13	225 40.2	0 54.9	51.5	34 25.2	52.7	324 47.8	57.4	299 33.8	27.8	Alpheratz	357 38.7	N29 12.0
14	240 42.7	15 54.2	52.5	49 26.1	53.3	339 49.8	57.5	314 36.1	27.8	Altair	62 04.0	N 8 55.4
15	255 45.1	30 53.6 ..	53.5	64 27.1 ..	54.0	354 51.8 ..	57.5	329 38.4 ..	27.8	Ankaa	353 11.0	S42 12.0
16	270 47.6	45 53.0	54.5	79 28.1	54.6	9 53.7	57.5	344 40.7	27.8	Antares	112 21.2	S26 28.4
17	285 50.1	60 52.4	55.4	94 29.1	55.3	24 55.7	57.6	359 43.0	27.7			
18	300 52.5	75 51.8	S16 56.4	109 30.0	S 3 55.9	39 57.7	S22 57.6	14 45.3	S22 27.7	Arcturus	145 52.1	N19 05.0
19	315 55.0	90 51.1	57.4	124 31.0	56.6	54 59.7	57.6	29 47.7	27.7	Atria	107 19.6	S69 03.8
20	330 57.5	105 50.5	58.4	139 32.0	57.2	70 01.7	57.7	44 50.0	27.7	Avior	234 16.3	S59 34.0
21	345 59.9	120 49.9	16 59.3	154 32.9 ..	57.9	85 03.6 ..	57.7	59 52.3 ..	27.7	Bellatrix	278 27.2	N 6 22.0
22	1 02.4	135 49.3	17 00.3	169 33.9	58.5	100 05.6	57.7	74 54.6	27.7	Betelgeuse	270 56.4	N 7 24.6
23	16 04.8	150 48.6	01.3	184 34.9	59.1	115 07.6	57.8	89 56.9	27.7			
23 00	31 07.3	165 48.0	S17 02.3	199 35.9	S 3 59.8	130 09.6	S22 57.8	104 59.2	S22 27.7	Canopus	263 54.0	S52 42.1
01	46 09.8	180 47.4	03.2	214 36.8	4 00.4	145 11.6	57.8	120 01.6	27.7	Capella	280 27.7	N46 00.8
02	61 12.2	195 46.8	04.2	229 37.8	01.1	160 13.5	57.9	135 03.9	27.6	Deneb	49 28.5	N45 21.4
03	76 14.7	210 46.1 ..	05.2	244 38.8 ..	01.7	175 15.5 ..	57.9	150 06.2 ..	27.6	Denebola	182 29.5	N14 27.9
04	91 17.2	225 45.5	06.1	259 39.7	02.4	190 17.5	57.9	165 08.5	27.6	Diphda	348 51.2	S17 52.7
05	106 19.6	240 44.9	07.1	274 40.7	03.0	205 19.5	58.0	180 10.8	27.6			
06	121 22.1	255 44.3	S17 08.1	289 41.7	S 4 03.7	220 21.5	S22 58.0	195 13.1	S22 27.6	Dubhe	193 46.8	N61 38.6
07	136 24.6	270 43.6	09.0	304 42.7	04.3	235 23.4	58.0	210 15.5	27.6	Elnath	278 06.9	N28 37.3
08	151 27.0	285 43.0	10.0	319 43.6	04.9	250 25.4	58.1	225 17.8	27.6	Eltanin	90 44.4	N51 29.5
09	166 29.5	300 42.4 ..	11.0	334 44.6 ..	05.6	265 27.4 ..	58.1	240 20.1 ..	27.6	Enif	33 42.7	N 9 58.1
10	181 32.0	315 41.7	11.9	349 45.6	06.2	280 29.4	58.1	255 22.4	27.6	Fomalhaut	15 18.9	S29 31.1
11	196 34.4	330 41.1	12.9	4 46.5	06.9	295 31.4	58.2	270 24.7	27.5			
12	211 36.9	345 40.5	S17 13.9	19 47.5	S 4 07.5	310 33.3	S22 58.2	285 27.0	S22 27.5	Gacrux	171 56.7	S57 13.1
13	226 39.3	0 39.9	14.8	34 48.5	08.2	325 35.3	58.2	300 29.3	27.5	Gienah	175 48.2	S17 38.8
14	241 41.8	15 39.2	15.8	49 49.5	08.8	340 37.3	58.3	315 31.7	27.5	Hadar	148 42.4	S60 27.9
15	256 44.3	30 38.6 ..	16.7	64 50.4 ..	09.5	355 39.3 ..	58.3	330 34.0 ..	27.5	Hamal	327 55.5	N23 33.3
16	271 46.7	45 38.0	17.7	79 51.4	10.1	10 41.2	58.3	345 36.3	27.5	Kaus Aust.	83 38.2	S34 22.5
17	286 49.2	60 37.3	18.7	94 52.4	10.7	25 43.2	58.4	0 38.6	27.5			
18	301 51.7	75 36.7	S17 19.6	109 53.3	S 4 11.4	40 45.2	S22 58.4	15 40.9	S22 27.5	Kochab	137 21.2	N74 04.7
19	316 54.1	90 36.1	20.6	124 54.3	12.0	55 47.2	58.4	30 43.2	27.4	Markab	13 33.8	N15 18.8
20	331 56.6	105 35.4	21.5	139 55.3	12.7	70 49.2	58.5	45 45.5	27.4	Menkar	314 10.2	N 4 10.0
21	346 59.1	120 34.8 ..	22.5	154 56.3 ..	13.3	85 51.1 ..	58.5	60 47.8 ..	27.4	Menkent	148 02.9	S36 27.8
22	2 01.5	135 34.1	23.4	169 57.2	14.0	100 53.1	58.5	75 50.2	27.4	Miaplacidus	221 39.1	S69 47.5
23	17 04.0	150 33.5	24.4	184 58.2	14.6	115 55.1	58.6	90 52.5	27.4			
24 00	32 06.5	165 32.9	S17 25.3	199 59.2	S 4 15.2	130 57.1	S22 58.6	105 54.8	S22 27.4	Mirfak	308 33.7	N49 55.7
01	47 08.9	180 32.2	26.3	215 00.1	15.9	145 59.0	58.6	120 57.1	27.4	Nunki	75 53.1	S26 16.3
02	62 11.4	195 31.6	27.2	230 01.1	16.5	161 01.0	58.7	135 59.4	27.4	Peacock	53 12.4	S56 40.4
03	77 13.8	210 31.0 ..	28.2	245 02.1 ..	17.2	176 03.0 ..	58.7	151 01.7 ..	27.4	Pollux	243 22.4	N27 58.6
04	92 16.3	225 30.3	29.1	260 03.0	17.8	191 05.0	58.7	166 04.0	27.3	Procyon	244 55.2	N 5 10.5
05	107 18.8	240 29.7	30.1	275 04.0	18.5	206 06.9	58.8	181 06.3	27.3			
06	122 21.2	255 29.0	S17 31.0	290 05.0	S 4 19.1	221 08.9	S22 58.8	196 08.7	S22 27.3	Rasalhague	96 02.6	N12 33.0
07	137 23.7	270 28.4	32.0	305 05.9	19.7	236 10.9	58.8	211 11.0	27.3	Regulus	207 39.1	N11 52.3
08	152 26.2	285 27.8	32.9	320 06.9	20.4	251 12.9	58.9	226 13.3	27.3	Rigel	281 07.7	S 8 10.7
09	167 28.6	300 27.1 ..	33.9	335 07.9 ..	21.0	266 14.8 ..	58.9	241 15.6 ..	27.3	Rigil Kent.	139 46.6	S60 54.8
10	182 31.1	315 26.5	34.8	350 08.9	21.7	281 16.8	58.9	256 17.9	27.3	Sabik	102 07.8	S15 44.8
11	197 33.6	330 25.8	35.8	5 09.8	22.3	296 18.8	59.0	271 20.2	27.3			
12	212 36.0	345 25.2	S17 36.7	20 10.8	S 4 23.0	311 20.8	S22 59.0	286 22.5	S22 27.2	Schedar	349 35.1	N56 38.8
13	227 38.5	0 24.5	37.7	35 11.8	23.6	326 22.7	59.0	301 24.8	27.2	Shaula	96 16.3	S37 07.0
14	242 40.9	15 23.9	38.6	50 12.7	24.2	341 24.7	59.1	316 27.1	27.2	Sirius	258 29.8	S16 44.5
15	257 43.4	30 23.2 ..	39.5	65 13.7 ..	24.9	356 26.7 ..	59.1	331 29.4 ..	27.2	Spica	158 27.0	S11 15.6
16	272 45.9	45 22.6	40.5	80 14.7	25.5	11 28.7	59.1	346 31.8	27.2	Suhail	222 49.4	S43 30.4
17	287 48.3	60 22.0	41.4	95 15.6	26.2	26 30.6	59.2	1 34.1	27.2			
18	302 50.8	75 21.3	S17 42.4	110 16.6	S 4 26.8	41 32.6	S22 59.2	16 36.4	S22 27.2	Vega	80 36.2	N38 48.5
19	317 53.3	90 20.7	43.3	125 17.6	27.5	56 34.6	59.2	31 38.7	27.2	Zuben'ubi	137 01.0	S16 07.2
20	332 55.7	105 20.0	44.2	140 18.5	28.1	71 36.5	59.3	46 41.0	27.1		SHA	Mer.Pass.
21	347 58.2	120 19.4 ..	45.2	155 19.5 ..	28.7	86 38.5 ..	59.3	61 43.3 ..	27.1			
22	3 00.7	135 18.7	46.1	170 20.5	29.4	101 40.5	59.3	76 45.6	27.1	Venus	134 40.7	12 57
23	18 03.1	150 18.1	47.0	185 21.5	30.0	116 42.5	59.4	91 47.9	27.1	Mars	168 28.5	10 41
Mer.Pass.	21 51.9	v −0.6	d 1.0	v 1.0	d 0.6	v 2.0	d 0.0	v 2.3	d 0.0	Jupiter	99 02.3	15 17
										Saturn	73 51.9	16 57

© British Crown Copyright 2018. All rights reserved.

SUN and MOON

UT (d h)	SUN GHA ° '	SUN Dec ° '	MOON GHA ° '	v '	MOON Dec ° '	d '	HP '
22 00	183 51.6	S10 51.8	262 58.6	6.8	N21 05.5	5.7	58.7
01	198 51.7	52.7	277 24.4	6.7	20 59.8	5.8	58.8
02	213 51.8	53.6	291 50.1	6.8	20 54.0	5.9	58.8
03	228 51.9	.. 54.5	306 15.9	6.7	20 48.1	6.1	58.8
04	243 52.0	55.4	320 41.6	6.8	20 42.0	6.2	58.8
05	258 52.1	56.3	335 07.4	6.8	20 35.8	6.3	58.9
06	273 52.2	S10 57.1	349 33.2	6.8	N20 29.5	6.5	58.9
07	288 52.3	58.0	3 59.0	6.8	20 23.0	6.6	58.9
08	303 52.4	58.9	18 24.8	6.9	20 16.4	6.7	59.0
09	318 52.5	10 59.8	32 50.7	6.8	20 09.7	6.9	59.0
10	333 52.6	11 00.7	47 16.5	6.9	20 02.8	7.0	59.0
11	348 52.6	01.6	61 42.4	6.9	19 55.8	7.1	59.0
12	3 52.7	S11 02.4	76 08.3	6.9	N19 48.7	7.3	59.1
13	18 52.8	03.3	90 34.2	7.0	19 41.4	7.4	59.1
14	33 52.9	04.2	105 00.2	6.9	19 34.0	7.5	59.1
15	48 53.0	.. 05.1	119 26.1	7.0	19 26.5	7.6	59.1
16	63 53.1	06.0	133 52.1	7.0	19 18.9	7.8	59.2
17	78 53.2	06.9	148 18.1	7.1	19 11.1	7.9	59.2
18	93 53.3	S11 07.7	162 44.2	7.0	N19 03.2	8.1	59.2
19	108 53.4	08.6	177 10.2	7.1	18 55.1	8.1	59.3
20	123 53.5	09.5	191 36.3	7.1	18 47.0	8.3	59.3
21	138 53.6	.. 10.4	206 02.4	7.1	18 38.7	8.4	59.3
22	153 53.7	11.3	220 28.5	7.1	18 30.3	8.5	59.3
23	168 53.8	12.1	234 54.6	7.2	18 21.8	8.7	59.4
23 00	183 53.9	S11 13.0	249 20.8	7.2	N18 13.1	8.8	59.4
01	198 53.9	13.9	263 47.0	7.3	18 04.3	8.9	59.4
02	213 54.0	14.8	278 13.3	7.3	17 55.4	9.0	59.4
03	228 54.1	.. 15.7	292 39.5	7.3	17 46.4	9.1	59.5
04	243 54.2	16.5	307 05.8	7.3	17 37.3	9.3	59.5
05	258 54.3	17.4	321 32.1	7.4	17 28.0	9.4	59.5
06	273 54.4	S11 18.3	335 58.5	7.3	N17 18.6	9.5	59.5
07	288 54.5	19.2	350 24.8	7.4	17 09.1	9.6	59.6
08	303 54.6	20.1	4 51.2	7.4	16 59.5	9.7	59.6
09	318 54.7	.. 20.9	19 17.6	7.5	16 49.8	9.8	59.6
10	333 54.8	21.8	33 44.1	7.5	16 40.0	10.0	59.7
11	348 54.8	22.7	48 10.6	7.5	16 30.0	10.0	59.7
12	3 54.9	S11 23.6	62 37.1	7.6	N16 20.0	10.2	59.7
13	18 55.0	24.4	77 03.7	7.5	16 09.8	10.3	59.7
14	33 55.1	25.3	91 30.2	7.6	15 59.5	10.4	59.7
15	48 55.2	.. 26.2	105 56.8	7.7	15 49.1	10.5	59.8
16	63 55.3	27.1	120 23.5	7.7	15 38.6	10.6	59.8
17	78 55.4	27.9	134 50.2	7.7	15 28.0	10.7	59.8
18	93 55.4	S11 28.8	149 16.9	7.7	N15 17.3	10.8	59.8
19	108 55.5	29.7	163 43.6	7.8	15 06.5	10.9	59.9
20	123 55.6	30.6	178 10.4	7.8	14 55.6	11.0	59.9
21	138 55.7	.. 31.4	192 37.2	7.8	14 44.6	11.1	59.9
22	153 55.8	32.3	207 04.0	7.8	14 33.5	11.3	59.9
23	168 55.9	33.2	221 30.8	7.9	14 22.2	11.3	60.0
24 00	183 56.0	S11 34.1	235 57.7	8.0	N14 10.9	11.4	60.0
01	198 56.1	34.9	250 24.7	7.9	13 59.5	11.5	60.0
02	213 56.1	35.8	264 51.6	8.0	13 48.0	11.6	60.0
03	228 56.2	.. 36.7	279 18.6	8.0	13 36.4	11.7	60.0
04	243 56.3	37.5	293 45.6	8.0	13 24.7	11.7	60.1
05	258 56.4	38.4	308 12.6	8.1	13 13.0	11.9	60.1
06	273 56.5	S11 39.3	322 39.7	8.1	N13 01.1	12.0	60.1
07	288 56.5	40.2	337 06.8	8.2	12 49.1	12.0	60.1
08	303 56.6	41.0	351 34.0	8.1	12 37.1	12.2	60.1
09	318 56.7	.. 41.9	6 01.1	8.2	12 24.9	12.2	60.2
10	333 56.8	42.8	20 28.3	8.2	12 12.7	12.3	60.2
11	348 56.9	43.6	34 55.5	8.3	12 00.4	12.4	60.2
12	3 56.9	S11 44.5	49 22.8	8.3	N11 48.0	12.5	60.2
13	18 57.0	45.4	63 50.1	8.3	11 35.5	12.5	60.2
14	33 57.1	46.3	78 17.4	8.3	11 23.0	12.6	60.3
15	48 57.2	.. 47.1	92 44.7	8.4	11 10.4	12.7	60.3
16	63 57.3	48.0	107 12.1	8.4	10 57.7	12.8	60.3
17	78 57.3	48.9	121 39.5	8.4	10 44.9	12.9	60.3
18	93 57.4	S11 49.7	136 06.9	8.5	N10 32.0	12.9	60.3
19	108 57.5	50.6	150 34.4	8.4	10 19.1	13.0	60.3
20	123 57.6	51.5	165 01.8	8.5	10 06.1	13.0	60.4
21	138 57.6	.. 52.3	179 29.3	8.6	9 53.1	13.2	60.4
22	153 57.7	53.2	193 56.9	8.5	9 39.9	13.2	60.4
23	168 57.8	54.1	208 24.4	8.6	N 9 26.7	13.2	60.4
	SD 16.1	d 0.9	SD 16.1		16.3		16.4

(Day-of-week markers: 22 = TUESDAY, 23 = WEDNESDAY, 24 = THURSDAY)

Twilight, Sunrise and Moonrise

Lat.	Naut.	Civil	Sunrise	Moonrise 22	23	24	25
N 72	05 28	06 47	08 03	▯▯▯▯	22 48	25 18	01 18
N 70	05 28	06 39	07 46	20 47	23 19	25 32	01 32
68	05 28	06 33	07 33	21 35	23 42	25 44	01 44
66	05 28	06 28	07 22	22 06	24 00	00 00	01 53
64	05 27	06 23	07 13	22 29	24 14	00 14	02 01
62	05 27	06 19	07 05	22 47	24 26	00 26	02 07
60	05 26	06 15	06 58	23 02	24 36	00 36	02 13
N 58	05 26	06 12	06 52	23 14	24 45	00 45	02 18
56	05 25	06 09	06 47	23 25	24 52	00 52	02 22
54	05 25	06 06	06 42	23 35	24 59	00 59	02 26
52	05 24	06 03	06 38	23 43	25 05	01 05	02 30
50	05 23	06 01	06 34	23 51	25 11	01 11	02 33
45	05 21	05 56	06 26	24 07	00 07	01 23	02 40
N 40	05 19	05 51	06 19	24 20	00 20	01 33	02 46
35	05 17	05 47	06 12	24 32	00 32	01 41	02 51
30	05 15	05 43	06 07	24 41	00 41	01 48	02 56
20	05 09	05 35	05 57	24 58	00 58	02 01	03 03
N 10	05 03	05 28	05 41	00 14	01 13	02 12	03 10
0	04 55	05 20	05 33	00 30	01 27	02 22	03 16
S 10	04 46	05 11	05 33	00 46	01 40	02 32	03 23
20	04 35	05 01	05 24	01 03	01 55	02 43	03 29
30	04 20	04 49	05 14	01 23	02 11	02 56	03 37
35	04 10	04 42	05 08	01 35	02 21	03 03	03 41
40	03 59	04 33	05 01	01 48	02 32	03 11	03 46
45	03 45	04 22	04 53	02 04	02 45	03 20	03 52
S 50	03 26	04 09	04 44	02 23	03 00	03 32	03 58
52	03 17	04 03	04 39	02 32	03 08	03 37	04 01
54	03 07	03 56	04 35	02 42	03 16	03 42	04 05
56	02 55	03 48	04 29	02 53	03 25	03 49	04 09
58	02 41	03 39	04 23	03 06	03 35	03 56	04 13
S 60	02 23	03 29	04 16	03 22	03 46	04 04	04 17

Sunset, Twilight and Moonset

Lat.	Sunset	Civil	Naut.	Moonset 22	23	24	25
N 72	15 24	16 40	17 58	▯▯▯▯	17 49	17 13	16 50
N 70	15 41	16 48	17 59	17 50	17 15	16 57	16 43
68	15 54	16 54	17 59	17 01	16 51	16 44	16 37
66	16 05	17 00	17 59	16 30	16 32	16 33	16 32
64	16 15	17 05	18 00	16 06	16 17	16 23	16 27
62	16 22	17 09	18 00	15 47	16 04	16 15	16 24
60	16 29	17 13	18 01	15 32	15 53	16 08	16 21
N 58	16 35	17 16	18 02	15 19	15 43	16 02	16 18
56	16 41	17 19	18 02	15 07	15 35	15 57	16 15
54	16 45	17 22	18 03	14 57	15 27	15 52	16 13
52	16 50	17 24	18 04	14 48	15 21	15 47	16 11
50	16 54	17 27	18 04	14 40	15 14	15 43	16 09
45	17 02	17 32	18 07	14 23	15 01	15 34	16 04
N 40	17 10	17 37	18 09	14 09	14 50	15 27	16 01
35	17 16	17 42	18 11	13 57	14 41	15 21	15 58
30	17 21	17 46	18 14	13 46	14 32	15 15	15 55
20	17 31	17 53	18 19	13 28	14 18	15 05	15 50
N 10	17 40	18 01	18 26	13 12	14 05	14 56	15 46
0	17 48	18 09	18 33	12 57	13 53	14 48	15 42
S 10	17 56	18 17	18 43	12 42	13 41	14 40	15 37
20	18 05	18 28	18 54	12 26	13 28	14 31	15 33
30	18 15	18 40	19 09	12 07	13 13	14 20	15 28
35	18 21	18 48	19 19	11 56	13 04	14 14	15 25
40	18 28	18 57	19 31	11 43	12 54	14 07	15 21
45	18 36	19 07	19 45	11 29	12 43	13 59	15 17
S 50	18 46	19 21	20 04	11 10	12 28	13 50	15 13
52	18 50	19 27	20 13	11 01	12 21	13 45	15 10
54	18 55	19 34	20 24	10 52	12 14	13 40	15 08
56	19 01	19 42	20 36	10 41	12 06	13 35	15 05
58	19 07	19 52	20 51	10 28	11 56	13 28	15 02
S 60	19 14	20 02	21 08	10 13	11 45	13 21	14 59

SUN and MOON

Day	Eqn. of Time 00h	Eqn. of Time 12h	Mer. Pass.	Mer. Pass. Upper	Lower	Age	Phase
	m s	m s	h m	h m	h m	d %	
22	15 26	15 31	11 44	06 43	19 12	24 39	
23	15 35	15 40	11 44	07 40	20 08	25 28	
24	15 44	15 48	11 44	08 35	21 02	26 19	

© British Crown Copyright 2018. All rights reserved.

UT	ARIES GHA	VENUS −3.8 GHA	Dec	MARS +1.8 GHA	Dec	JUPITER −1.9 GHA	Dec	SATURN +0.6 GHA	Dec	Name (STARS)	SHA	Dec
25 00	33 05.6	165 17.4	S17 48.0	200 22.4	S 4 30.7	131 44.4	S22 59.4	106 50.2	S22 27.1	Acamar	315 14.6	S40 13.5
01	48 08.1	180 16.8	48.9	215 23.4	31.3	146 46.4	59.4	121 52.5	27.1	Achernar	335 22.9	S57 08.3
02	63 10.5	195 16.1	49.8	230 24.4	32.0	161 48.4	59.5	136 54.8	27.1	Acrux	173 05.1	S63 12.2
03	78 13.0	210 15.5	.. 50.8	245 25.3	.. 32.6	176 50.4	.. 59.5	151 57.2	.. 27.1	Adhara	255 09.0	S28 59.8
04	93 15.4	225 14.8	51.7	260 26.3	33.2	191 52.3	59.5	166 59.5	27.1	Aldebaran	290 44.1	N16 32.8
05	108 17.9	240 14.2	52.6	275 27.3	33.9	206 54.3	59.5	182 01.8	27.0			
06	123 20.4	255 13.5	S17 53.6	290 28.2	S 4 34.5	221 56.3	S22 59.6	197 04.1	S22 27.0	Alioth	166 17.4	N55 51.2
07	138 22.8	270 12.8	54.5	305 29.2	35.2	236 58.2	59.6	212 06.4	27.0	Alkaid	152 55.9	N49 13.0
08	153 25.3	285 12.2	55.4	320 30.2	35.8	252 00.2	59.6	227 08.7	27.0	Alnair	27 38.1	S46 52.1
F 09	168 27.8	300 11.5	.. 56.3	335 31.1	.. 36.4	267 02.2	.. 59.7	242 11.0	.. 27.0	Alnilam	275 41.8	S 1 11.4
R 10	183 30.2	315 10.9	57.3	350 32.1	37.1	282 04.1	59.7	257 13.3	27.0	Alphard	217 51.9	S 8 44.5
I 11	198 32.7	330 10.2	58.2	5 33.1	37.7	297 06.1	59.7	272 15.6	27.0			
D 12	213 35.2	345 09.6	S17 59.1	20 34.0	S 4 38.4	312 08.1	S22 59.8	287 17.9	S22 27.0	Alphecca	126 07.7	N26 39.2
A 13	228 37.6	0 08.9	18 00.0	35 35.0	39.0	327 10.1	59.8	302 20.2	26.9	Alpheratz	357 38.7	N29 12.1
Y 14	243 40.1	15 08.3	01.0	50 36.0	39.7	342 12.0	59.8	317 22.5	26.9	Altair	62 04.1	N 8 55.4
15	258 42.6	30 07.6	.. 01.9	65 36.9	.. 40.3	357 14.0	.. 59.9	332 24.8	.. 26.9	Ankaa	353 11.0	S42 12.0
16	273 45.0	45 06.9	02.8	80 37.9	40.9	12 16.0	59.9	347 27.1	26.9	Antares	112 21.3	S26 28.4
17	288 47.5	60 06.3	03.7	95 38.9	41.6	27 17.9	22 59.9	2 29.4	26.9			
18	303 49.9	75 05.6	S18 04.7	110 39.8	S 4 42.2	42 19.9	S23 00.0	17 31.8	S22 26.9	Arcturus	145 52.1	N19 05.0
19	318 52.4	90 05.0	05.6	125 40.8	42.9	57 21.9	00.0	32 34.1	26.9	Atria	107 19.6	S69 03.8
20	333 54.9	105 04.3	06.5	140 41.8	43.5	72 23.8	00.0	47 36.4	26.8	Avior	234 16.3	S59 34.0
21	348 57.3	120 03.6	.. 07.4	155 42.7	.. 44.1	87 25.8	.. 00.1	62 38.7	.. 26.8	Bellatrix	278 27.1	N 6 22.0
22	3 59.8	135 03.0	08.3	170 43.7	44.8	102 27.8	00.1	77 41.0	26.8	Betelgeuse	270 56.4	N 7 24.6
23	19 02.3	150 02.3	09.2	185 44.7	45.4	117 29.7	00.1	92 43.3	26.8			
26 00	34 04.7	165 01.6	S18 10.2	200 45.6	S 4 46.1	132 31.7	S23 00.2	107 45.6	S22 26.8	Canopus	263 54.0	S52 42.1
01	49 07.2	180 01.0	11.1	215 46.6	46.7	147 33.7	00.2	122 47.9	26.8	Capella	280 27.7	N46 00.8
02	64 09.7	195 00.3	12.0	230 47.6	47.4	162 35.6	00.2	137 50.2	26.8	Deneb	49 28.5	N45 21.4
03	79 12.1	209 59.6	.. 12.9	245 48.5	.. 48.0	177 37.6	.. 00.3	152 52.5	.. 26.8	Denebola	182 29.5	N14 27.9
04	94 14.6	224 59.0	13.8	260 49.5	48.6	192 39.6	00.3	167 54.8	26.7	Diphda	348 51.2	S17 52.7
05	109 17.0	239 58.3	14.7	275 50.5	49.3	207 41.5	00.3	182 57.1	26.7			
06	124 19.5	254 57.7	S18 15.6	290 51.4	S 4 49.9	222 43.5	S23 00.3	197 59.4	S22 26.7	Dubhe	193 46.8	N61 38.6
07	139 22.0	269 57.0	16.5	305 52.4	50.6	237 45.5	00.4	213 01.7	26.7	Elnath	278 06.9	N28 37.3
S 08	154 24.4	284 56.3	17.4	320 53.4	51.2	252 47.4	00.4	228 04.0	26.7	Eltanin	90 44.4	N51 29.5
A 09	169 26.9	299 55.6	.. 18.3	335 54.3	.. 51.8	267 49.4	.. 00.4	243 06.3	.. 26.7	Enif	33 42.8	N 9 58.1
T 10	184 29.4	314 55.0	19.3	350 55.3	52.5	282 51.4	00.5	258 08.6	26.7	Fomalhaut	15 19.0	S29 31.1
U 11	199 31.8	329 54.3	20.2	5 56.3	53.1	297 53.3	00.5	273 10.9	26.7			
R 12	214 34.3	344 53.6	S18 21.1	20 57.2	S 4 53.8	312 55.3	S23 00.5	288 13.2	S22 26.6	Gacrux	171 56.6	S57 13.1
D 13	229 36.8	359 53.0	22.0	35 58.2	54.4	327 57.3	00.6	303 15.5	26.6	Gienah	175 48.1	S17 38.8
A 14	244 39.2	14 52.3	22.9	50 59.2	55.0	342 59.2	00.6	318 17.8	26.6	Hadar	148 42.4	S60 27.9
Y 15	259 41.7	29 51.6	.. 23.8	66 00.1	.. 55.7	358 01.2	.. 00.6	333 20.1	.. 26.6	Hamal	327 55.5	N23 33.3
16	274 44.2	44 51.0	24.7	81 01.1	56.3	13 03.2	00.7	348 22.4	26.6	Kaus Aust.	83 38.3	S34 22.5
17	289 46.6	59 50.3	25.6	96 02.0	57.0	28 05.1	00.7	3 24.7	26.6			
18	304 49.1	74 49.6	S18 26.5	111 03.0	S 4 57.6	43 07.1	S23 00.7	18 27.0	S22 26.6	Kochab	137 21.2	N74 04.6
19	319 51.5	89 48.9	27.4	126 04.0	58.2	58 09.1	00.8	33 29.3	26.6	Markab	13 33.8	N15 18.8
20	334 54.0	104 48.3	28.3	141 04.9	58.9	73 11.0	00.8	48 31.6	26.5	Menkar	314 10.2	N 4 10.0
21	349 56.5	119 47.6	.. 29.2	156 05.9	4 59.5	88 13.0	.. 00.8	63 33.9	.. 26.5	Menkent	148 02.9	S36 27.8
22	4 58.9	134 46.9	30.1	171 06.9	5 00.2	103 14.9	00.9	78 36.2	26.5	Miaplacidus	221 39.1	S69 47.5
23	20 01.4	149 46.2	31.0	186 07.8	00.8	118 16.9	00.9	93 38.5	26.5			
27 00	35 03.9	164 45.6	S18 31.8	201 08.8	S 5 01.4	133 18.9	S23 00.9	108 40.8	S22 26.5	Mirfak	308 33.7	N49 55.7
01	50 06.3	179 44.9	32.7	216 09.8	02.1	148 20.8	01.0	123 43.1	26.5	Nunki	75 53.1	S26 16.3
02	65 08.8	194 44.2	33.6	231 10.7	02.7	163 22.8	01.0	138 45.5	26.4	Peacock	53 12.4	S56 40.4
03	80 11.3	209 43.5	.. 34.5	246 11.7	.. 03.4	178 24.8	.. 01.0	153 47.8	.. 26.4	Pollux	243 22.4	N27 58.6
04	95 13.7	224 42.8	35.4	261 12.7	04.0	193 26.7	01.0	168 50.1	26.4	Procyon	244 55.2	N 5 10.5
05	110 16.2	239 42.2	36.3	276 13.6	04.6	208 28.7	01.1	183 52.4	26.4			
06	125 18.6	254 41.5	S18 37.2	291 14.6	S 5 05.3	223 30.7	S23 01.1	198 54.7	S22 26.4	Rasalhague	96 02.7	N12 33.0
07	140 21.1	269 40.8	38.1	306 15.6	05.9	238 32.6	01.1	213 57.0	26.4	Regulus	207 39.1	N11 52.3
08	155 23.6	284 40.1	39.0	321 16.5	06.6	253 34.6	01.2	228 59.3	26.4	Rigel	281 07.7	S 8 10.7
S 09	170 26.0	299 39.4	.. 39.9	336 17.5	.. 07.2	268 36.5	.. 01.2	244 01.6	.. 26.4	Rigil Kent.	139 46.6	S60 54.8
U 10	185 28.5	314 38.8	40.7	351 18.4	07.8	283 38.5	01.2	259 03.8	26.4	Sabik	102 07.8	S15 44.8
N 11	200 31.0	329 38.1	41.6	6 19.4	08.5	298 40.5	01.3	274 06.1	26.3			
D 12	215 33.4	344 37.4	S18 42.5	21 20.4	S 5 09.1	313 42.4	S23 01.3	289 08.4	S22 26.3	Schedar	349 35.1	N56 38.8
A 13	230 35.9	359 36.7	43.4	36 21.3	09.8	328 44.4	01.3	304 10.7	26.3	Shaula	96 16.3	S37 07.0
Y 14	245 38.4	14 36.0	44.3	51 22.3	10.4	343 46.3	01.4	319 13.0	26.3	Sirius	258 29.8	S16 44.5
15	260 40.8	29 35.4	.. 45.2	66 23.3	.. 11.0	358 48.3	.. 01.4	334 15.3	.. 26.3	Spica	158 27.0	S11 15.6
16	275 43.3	44 34.7	46.0	81 24.2	11.7	13 50.3	01.4	349 17.6	26.3	Suhail	222 49.4	S43 30.4
17	290 45.8	59 34.0	46.9	96 25.2	12.3	28 52.2	01.5	4 19.9	26.3			
18	305 48.2	74 33.3	S18 47.8	111 26.1	S 5 13.0	43 54.2	S23 01.5	19 22.2	S22 26.2	Vega	80 36.2	N38 48.5
19	320 50.7	89 32.6	48.7	126 27.1	13.6	58 56.1	01.5	34 24.5	26.2	Zuben'ubi	137 01.0	S16 07.2
20	335 53.1	104 31.9	49.6	141 28.1	14.2	73 58.1	01.5	49 26.8	26.2		SHA	Mer.Pass.
21	350 55.6	119 31.2	.. 50.4	156 29.0	.. 14.9	89 00.1	.. 01.6	64 29.1	.. 26.2		° ′	h m
22	5 58.1	134 30.5	51.3	171 30.0	15.5	104 02.0	01.6	79 31.4	26.2	Venus	130 56.9	13 00
23	21 00.5	149 29.9	52.2	186 31.0	16.2	119 04.0	01.6	94 33.7	26.2	Mars	166 40.9	10 36
	h m									Jupiter	98 27.0	15 08
Mer.Pass. 21 40.1	v −0.7 d 0.9	v 1.0	d 0.6	v 2.0	d 0.0	v 2.3	d 0.0			Saturn	73 40.9	16 46

© British Crown Copyright 2018. All rights reserved.

UT	SUN GHA	Dec	MOON GHA	v	Dec	d	HP
	° '	° '	° '	'	° '	'	'
25 00	183 57.9	S11 54.9	222 52.0	8.6	N 9 13.5	13.4	60.4
01	198 58.0	55.8	237 19.6	8.6	9 00.1	13.4	60.4
02	213 58.0	56.7	251 47.2	8.7	8 46.7	13.4	60.5
03	228 58.1	.. 57.5	266 14.9	8.6	8 33.3	13.5	60.5
04	243 58.2	58.4	280 42.5	8.7	8 19.8	13.6	60.5
05	258 58.3	11 59.2	295 10.2	8.8	8 06.2	13.6	60.5
06	273 58.3	S12 00.1	309 38.0	8.7	N 7 52.6	13.7	60.5
07	288 58.4	01.0	324 05.7	8.8	7 38.9	13.7	60.5
08	303 58.5	01.8	338 33.5	8.7	7 25.2	13.8	60.5
F 09	318 58.6	.. 02.7	353 01.2	8.8	7 11.4	13.8	60.5
R 10	333 58.6	03.6	7 29.0	8.9	6 57.6	13.9	60.6
I 11	348 58.7	04.4	21 56.9	8.8	6 43.7	14.0	60.6
D 12	3 58.8	S12 05.3	36 24.7	8.9	N 6 29.7	13.9	60.6
A 13	18 58.8	06.1	50 52.6	8.8	6 15.8	14.0	60.6
Y 14	33 58.9	07.0	65 20.4	8.9	6 01.8	14.1	60.6
15	48 59.0	.. 07.9	79 48.3	8.9	5 47.7	14.1	60.6
16	63 59.1	08.7	94 16.2	9.0	5 33.6	14.1	60.6
17	78 59.1	09.6	108 44.2	8.9	5 19.5	14.2	60.6
18	93 59.2	S12 10.5	123 12.1	8.9	N 5 05.3	14.2	60.6
19	108 59.3	11.3	137 40.0	9.0	4 51.1	14.3	60.6
20	123 59.3	12.2	152 08.0	9.0	4 36.8	14.2	60.6
21	138 59.4	.. 13.0	166 36.0	9.0	4 22.6	14.4	60.6
22	153 59.5	13.9	181 04.0	9.0	4 08.2	14.3	60.7
23	168 59.5	14.7	195 32.0	9.0	3 53.9	14.4	60.7
26 00	183 59.6	S12 15.6	210 00.0	9.0	N 3 39.5	14.3	60.7
01	198 59.7	16.5	224 28.0	9.1	3 25.2	14.5	60.7
02	213 59.8	17.3	238 56.1	9.0	3 10.7	14.4	60.7
03	228 59.8	.. 18.2	253 24.1	9.1	2 56.3	14.4	60.7
04	243 59.9	19.0	267 52.2	9.1	2 41.9	14.5	60.7
05	259 00.0	19.9	282 20.3	9.0	2 27.4	14.5	60.7
06	274 00.0	S12 20.7	296 48.3	9.1	N 2 12.9	14.5	60.7
07	289 00.1	21.6	311 16.4	9.1	1 58.4	14.5	60.7
S 08	304 00.2	22.5	325 44.5	9.1	1 43.9	14.6	60.7
A 09	319 00.2	.. 23.3	340 12.6	9.1	1 29.3	14.5	60.7
T 10	334 00.3	24.2	354 40.7	9.1	1 14.8	14.6	60.7
U 11	349 00.4	25.0	9 08.8	9.1	1 00.2	14.5	60.7
R 12	4 00.4	S12 25.9	23 36.9	9.1	N 0 45.7	14.6	60.7
D 13	19 00.5	26.7	38 05.0	9.1	0 31.1	14.6	60.7
A 14	34 00.5	27.6	52 33.1	9.1	0 16.5	14.5	60.7
Y 15	49 00.6	.. 28.4	67 01.2	9.1	N 0 02.0	14.6	60.7
16	64 00.7	29.3	81 29.3	9.2	S 0 12.6	14.6	60.7
17	79 00.7	30.1	95 57.5	9.1	0 27.2	14.5	60.7
18	94 00.8	S12 31.0	110 25.6	9.1	S 0 41.7	14.6	60.7
19	109 00.9	31.8	124 53.7	9.1	0 56.3	14.6	60.7
20	124 00.9	32.7	139 21.8	9.1	1 10.8	14.6	60.7
21	139 01.0	.. 33.5	153 49.9	9.1	1 25.4	14.5	60.7
22	154 01.1	34.4	168 18.0	9.1	1 39.9	14.5	60.7
23	169 01.1	35.2	182 46.1	9.1	1 54.4	14.6	60.7
27 00	184 01.2	S12 36.1	197 14.2	9.1	S 2 09.0	14.5	60.6
01	199 01.2	36.9	211 42.3	9.1	2 23.5	14.4	60.6
02	214 01.3	37.8	226 10.4	9.1	2 37.9	14.5	60.6
03	229 01.4	.. 38.6	240 38.5	9.0	2 52.4	14.4	60.6
04	244 01.4	39.5	255 06.5	9.1	3 06.8	14.5	60.6
05	259 01.5	40.3	269 34.6	9.1	3 21.3	14.4	60.6
06	274 01.5	S12 41.2	284 02.7	9.0	S 3 35.7	14.3	60.6
07	289 01.6	42.0	298 30.7	9.1	3 50.0	14.4	60.6
08	304 01.7	42.9	312 58.8	9.0	4 04.4	14.3	60.6
S 09	319 01.7	.. 43.7	327 26.8	9.0	4 18.7	14.3	60.6
U 10	334 01.8	44.6	341 54.8	9.0	4 33.0	14.2	60.6
N 11	349 01.8	45.4	356 22.8	9.0	4 47.2	14.3	60.5
D 12	4 01.9	S12 46.3	10 50.8	9.0	S 5 01.5	14.1	60.5
A 13	19 01.9	47.1	25 18.8	9.0	5 15.6	14.2	60.5
Y 14	34 02.0	48.0	39 46.8	9.0	5 29.8	14.1	60.5
15	49 02.1	.. 48.8	54 14.8	8.9	5 43.9	14.1	60.5
16	64 02.1	49.7	68 42.7	8.9	5 58.0	14.0	60.5
17	79 02.2	50.5	83 10.6	9.0	6 12.0	14.0	60.5
18	94 02.2	S12 51.3	97 38.6	8.9	S 6 26.0	13.9	60.5
19	109 02.3	52.2	112 06.5	8.8	6 39.9	13.9	60.4
20	124 02.3	53.0	126 34.3	8.9	6 53.8	13.9	60.4
21	139 02.4	.. 53.9	141 02.2	8.9	7 07.7	13.8	60.4
22	154 02.4	54.7	155 30.1	8.8	7 21.5	13.7	60.4
23	169 02.5	55.6	169 57.9	8.8	S 7 35.2	13.7	60.4
	SD 16.1	d 0.9	SD 16.5		16.5		16.5

Lat.	Twilight Naut.	Civil	Sunrise	Moonrise 25	26	27	28
°	h m	h m	h m	h m	h m	h m	h m
N 72	05 40	07 01	08 19	01 18	03 35	05 50	08 08
N 70	05 39	06 51	08 00	01 32	03 39	05 44	07 52
68	05 38	06 43	07 45	01 44	03 42	05 40	07 39
66	05 37	06 37	07 32	01 53	03 45	05 36	07 28
64	05 36	06 31	07 22	02 01	03 47	05 33	07 20
62	05 34	06 26	07 13	02 07	03 49	05 30	07 12
60	05 33	06 22	07 06	02 13	03 51	05 28	07 06
N 58	05 32	06 18	06 59	02 18	03 52	05 26	07 00
56	05 31	06 15	06 53	02 22	03 53	05 24	06 55
54	05 30	06 11	06 48	02 26	03 54	05 23	06 51
52	05 29	06 08	06 43	02 30	03 56	05 21	06 47
50	05 28	06 06	06 39	02 33	03 57	05 20	06 43
45	05 25	05 59	06 30	02 40	03 59	05 17	06 35
N 40	05 22	05 54	06 22	02 46	04 00	05 15	06 29
35	05 20	05 49	06 15	02 51	04 02	05 13	06 23
30	05 17	05 45	06 09	02 56	04 03	05 11	06 18
20	05 10	05 36	05 59	03 03	04 06	05 08	06 10
N 10	05 03	05 28	05 49	03 10	04 08	05 05	06 02
0	04 55	05 19	05 41	03 16	04 10	05 02	05 56
S 10	04 45	05 10	05 32	03 23	04 11	05 00	05 49
20	04 33	04 59	05 22	03 29	04 14	04 57	05 42
30	04 17	04 46	05 11	03 37	04 16	04 55	05 34
35	04 07	04 38	05 05	03 41	04 17	04 53	05 29
40	03 54	04 29	04 57	03 46	04 19	04 51	05 24
45	03 39	04 17	04 49	03 52	04 21	04 49	05 18
S 50	03 19	04 03	04 38	03 58	04 23	04 46	05 11
52	03 09	03 56	04 33	04 01	04 24	04 45	05 08
54	02 58	03 49	04 28	04 05	04 25	04 44	05 04
56	02 45	03 40	04 22	04 09	04 26	04 43	05 00
58	02 30	03 30	04 15	04 13	04 27	04 41	04 56
S 60	02 10	03 19	04 08	04 17	04 29	04 40	04 51

Lat.	Sunset	Twilight Civil	Naut.	Moonset 25	26	27	28
°	h m	h m	h m	h m	h m	h m	h m
N 72	15 07	16 26	17 45	16 50	16 29	16 08	15 42
N 70	15 26	16 35	17 47	16 43	16 30	16 16	16 01
68	15 42	16 43	17 48	16 37	16 30	16 23	16 16
66	15 54	16 50	17 50	16 32	16 30	16 29	16 28
64	16 05	16 55	17 51	16 27	16 31	16 34	16 38
62	16 13	17 00	17 52	16 24	16 31	16 39	16 47
60	16 21	17 05	17 53	16 21	16 31	16 42	16 55
N 58	16 28	17 09	17 55	16 18	16 32	16 46	17 01
56	16 34	17 12	17 56	16 15	16 32	16 49	17 07
54	16 39	17 16	17 57	16 13	16 32	16 52	17 13
52	16 44	17 19	17 58	16 11	16 32	16 54	17 18
50	16 48	17 22	17 59	16 09	16 33	16 56	17 22
45	16 58	17 28	18 02	16 04	16 33	17 01	17 32
N 40	17 06	17 33	18 05	16 01	16 33	17 06	17 40
35	17 12	17 38	18 08	15 58	16 33	17 09	17 46
30	17 18	17 43	18 11	15 55	16 34	17 12	17 53
20	17 29	17 52	18 17	15 50	16 34	17 18	18 03
N 10	17 38	18 00	18 25	15 46	16 34	17 23	18 12
0	17 47	18 09	18 33	15 42	16 35	17 28	18 21
S 10	17 56	18 18	18 43	15 37	16 35	17 32	18 30
20	18 06	18 29	18 56	15 33	16 35	17 37	18 39
30	18 17	18 42	19 12	15 28	16 35	17 43	18 50
35	18 24	18 50	19 22	15 25	16 35	17 46	18 56
40	18 31	19 00	19 35	15 21	16 36	17 50	19 04
45	18 40	19 12	19 50	15 17	16 36	17 54	19 12
S 50	18 51	19 26	20 10	15 13	16 36	17 59	19 22
52	18 56	19 33	20 20	15 10	16 36	18 02	19 27
54	19 01	19 41	20 32	15 08	16 36	18 04	19 32
56	19 07	19 50	20 45	15 05	16 36	18 07	19 37
58	19 14	20 00	21 01	15 02	16 36	18 10	19 44
S 60	19 22	20 11	21 21	14 59	16 36	18 14	19 51

Day	SUN Eqn. of Time 00ʰ	12ʰ	Mer. Pass.	MOON Mer. Pass. Upper	Lower	Age	Phase
d	m s	m s	h m	h m	h m	d	%
25	15 51	15 55	11 44	09 29	21 56	27	10
26	15 58	16 02	11 44	10 22	22 49	28	4
27	16 05	16 07	11 44	11 15	23 42	29	1

© British Crown Copyright 2018. All rights reserved.

UT	ARIES GHA	VENUS −3.8 GHA	Dec	MARS +1.8 GHA	Dec	JUPITER −1.9 GHA	Dec	SATURN +0.6 GHA	Dec	STARS Name	SHA	Dec
28 00	36 03.0	164 29.2	S18 53.1	201 31.9	S 5 16.8	134 05.9	S23 01.7	109 36.0	S22 26.2	Acamar	315 14.6	S40 13.6
01	51 05.5	179 28.5	53.9	216 32.9	17.4	149 07.9	01.7	124 38.3	26.1	Achernar	335 22.9	S57 08.3
02	66 07.9	194 27.8	54.8	231 33.8	18.1	164 09.9	01.7	139 40.6	26.1	Acrux	173 05.1	S63 12.2
03	81 10.4	209 27.1	.. 55.7	246 34.8	.. 18.7	179 11.8	.. 01.8	154 42.9	.. 26.1	Adhara	255 09.0	S28 59.8
04	96 12.9	224 26.4	56.5	261 35.8	19.3	194 13.8	01.8	169 45.2	26.1	Aldebaran	290 44.1	N16 32.8
05	111 15.3	239 25.7	57.4	276 36.7	20.0	209 15.7	01.8	184 47.5	26.1			
06	126 17.8	254 25.0	S18 58.3	291 37.7	S 5 20.6	224 17.7	S23 01.9	199 49.8	S22 26.1	Alioth	166 17.4	N55 51.2
07	141 20.2	269 24.3	18 59.2	306 38.7	21.3	239 19.7	01.9	214 52.1	26.1	Alkaid	152 55.9	N49 13.0
M 08	156 22.7	284 23.6	19 00.0	321 39.6	21.9	254 21.6	01.9	229 54.4	26.0	Alnair	27 38.1	S46 52.1
O 09	171 25.2	299 22.9	.. 00.9	336 40.6	.. 22.5	269 23.6	.. 01.9	244 56.7	.. 26.0	Alnilam	275 41.7	S 1 11.4
N 10	186 27.6	314 22.2	01.7	351 41.5	23.2	284 25.5	02.0	259 59.0	26.0	Alphard	217 51.9	S 8 44.5
D 11	201 30.1	329 21.5	02.6	6 42.5	23.8	299 27.5	02.0	275 01.3	26.0			
A 12	216 32.6	344 20.9	S19 03.5	21 43.5	S 5 24.5	314 29.4	S23 02.0	290 03.6	S22 26.0	Alphecca	126 07.7	N26 39.2
Y 13	231 35.0	359 20.2	04.3	36 44.4	25.1	329 31.4	02.1	305 05.9	26.0	Alpheratz	357 38.7	N29 12.1
14	246 37.5	14 19.5	05.2	51 45.4	25.7	344 33.4	02.1	320 08.2	26.0	Altair	62 04.1	N 8 55.4
15	261 40.0	29 18.8	.. 06.1	66 46.4	.. 26.4	359 35.3	.. 02.1	335 10.5	.. 26.0	Ankaa	353 11.0	S42 12.1
16	276 42.4	44 18.1	06.9	81 47.3	27.0	14 37.3	02.2	350 12.8	25.9	Antares	112 21.3	S26 28.4
17	291 44.9	59 17.4	07.8	96 48.3	27.6	29 39.2	02.2	5 15.1	25.9			
18	306 47.4	74 16.7	S19 08.6	111 49.2	S 5 28.3	44 41.2	S23 02.2	20 17.3	S22 25.9	Arcturus	145 52.1	N19 05.0
19	321 49.8	89 16.0	09.5	126 50.2	28.9	59 43.1	02.3	35 19.6	25.9	Atria	107 19.6	S69 03.7
20	336 52.3	104 15.3	10.4	141 51.2	29.6	74 45.1	02.3	50 21.9	25.9	Avior	234 16.3	S59 34.0
21	351 54.7	119 14.6	.. 11.2	156 52.1	.. 30.2	89 47.1	.. 02.3	65 24.2	.. 25.9	Bellatrix	278 27.1	N 6 22.0
22	6 57.2	134 13.9	12.1	171 53.1	30.8	104 49.0	02.3	80 26.5	25.9	Betelgeuse	270 56.4	N 7 24.6
23	21 59.7	149 13.2	12.9	186 54.0	31.5	119 51.0	02.4	95 28.8	25.8			
29 00	37 02.1	164 12.5	S19 13.8	201 55.0	S 5 32.1	134 52.9	S23 02.4	110 31.1	S22 25.8	Canopus	263 53.9	S52 42.2
01	52 04.6	179 11.8	14.6	216 56.0	32.7	149 54.9	02.4	125 33.4	25.8	Capella	280 27.7	N46 00.8
02	67 07.1	194 11.1	15.5	231 56.9	33.4	164 56.8	02.5	140 35.7	25.8	Deneb	49 28.5	N45 21.4
03	82 09.5	209 10.4	.. 16.3	246 57.9	.. 34.0	179 58.8	.. 02.5	155 38.0	.. 25.8	Denebola	182 29.5	N14 27.8
04	97 12.0	224 09.6	17.2	261 58.8	34.7	195 00.7	02.5	170 40.3	25.8	Diphda	348 51.2	S17 52.8
05	112 14.5	239 08.9	18.0	276 59.8	35.3	210 02.7	02.6	185 42.6	25.8			
06	127 16.9	254 08.2	S19 18.9	292 00.8	S 5 35.9	225 04.6	S23 02.6	200 44.9	S22 25.7	Dubhe	193 46.8	N61 38.6
07	142 19.4	269 07.5	19.7	307 01.7	36.6	240 06.6	02.6	215 47.2	25.7	Elnath	278 06.9	N28 37.3
T 08	157 21.9	284 06.8	20.6	322 02.7	37.2	255 08.6	02.6	230 49.4	25.7	Eltanin	90 44.5	N51 29.5
U 09	172 24.3	299 06.1	.. 21.4	337 03.6	.. 37.8	270 10.5	.. 02.7	245 51.7	.. 25.7	Enif	33 42.8	N 9 58.1
E 10	187 26.8	314 05.4	22.2	352 04.6	38.5	285 12.5	02.7	260 54.0	25.7	Fomalhaut	15 19.0	S29 31.2
S 11	202 29.2	329 04.7	23.1	7 05.6	39.1	300 14.4	02.7	275 56.3	25.7			
D 12	217 31.7	344 04.0	S19 23.9	22 06.5	S 5 39.8	315 16.4	S23 02.8	290 58.6	S22 25.7	Gacrux	171 56.6	S57 13.1
A 13	232 34.2	359 03.3	24.8	37 07.5	40.4	330 18.3	02.8	306 00.9	25.6	Gienah	175 48.1	S17 38.8
Y 14	247 36.6	14 02.6	25.6	52 08.4	41.0	345 20.3	02.8	321 03.2	25.6	Hadar	148 42.4	S60 27.8
15	262 39.1	29 01.9	.. 26.4	67 09.4	.. 41.7	0 22.2	.. 02.9	336 05.5	.. 25.6	Hamal	327 55.5	N23 33.3
16	277 41.6	44 01.2	27.3	82 10.4	42.3	15 24.2	02.9	351 07.8	25.6	Kaus Aust.	83 38.3	S34 22.5
17	292 44.0	59 00.4	28.1	97 11.3	42.9	30 26.1	02.9	6 10.1	25.6			
18	307 46.5	73 59.7	S19 29.0	112 12.3	S 5 43.6	45 28.1	S23 03.0	21 12.4	S22 25.6	Kochab	137 21.2	N74 04.6
19	322 49.0	88 59.0	29.8	127 13.2	44.2	60 30.0	03.0	36 14.7	25.5	Markab	13 33.8	N15 18.8
20	337 51.4	103 58.3	30.6	142 14.2	44.9	75 32.0	03.0	51 16.9	25.5	Menkar	314 10.2	N 4 10.0
21	352 53.9	118 57.6	.. 31.5	157 15.1	.. 45.5	90 33.9	.. 03.0	66 19.2	.. 25.5	Menkent	148 02.9	S36 27.8
22	7 56.4	133 56.9	32.3	172 16.1	46.1	105 35.9	03.1	81 21.5	25.5	Miaplacidus	221 39.0	S69 47.5
23	22 58.8	148 56.2	33.1	187 17.1	46.8	120 37.8	03.1	96 23.8	25.5			
30 00	38 01.3	163 55.4	S19 34.0	202 18.0	S 5 47.4	135 39.8	S23 03.1	111 26.1	S22 25.5	Mirfak	308 33.7	N49 55.7
01	53 03.7	178 54.7	34.8	217 19.0	48.0	150 41.7	03.2	126 28.4	25.5	Nunki	75 53.1	S26 16.3
02	68 06.2	193 54.0	35.6	232 19.9	48.7	165 43.7	03.2	141 30.7	25.4	Peacock	53 12.4	S56 40.4
03	83 08.7	208 53.3	.. 36.4	247 20.9	.. 49.3	180 45.6	.. 03.2	156 33.0	.. 25.4	Pollux	243 22.4	N27 58.6
04	98 11.1	223 52.6	37.3	262 21.9	49.9	195 47.6	03.3	171 35.3	25.4	Procyon	244 55.1	N 5 10.5
05	113 13.6	238 51.9	38.1	277 22.8	50.6	210 49.5	03.3	186 37.6	25.4			
06	128 16.1	253 51.1	S19 38.9	292 23.8	S 5 51.2	225 51.5	S23 03.3	201 39.8	S22 25.4	Rasalhague	96 02.7	N12 33.0
W 07	143 18.5	268 50.4	39.8	307 24.7	51.8	240 53.4	03.3	216 42.1	25.4	Regulus	207 39.0	N11 52.3
E 08	158 21.0	283 49.7	40.6	322 25.7	52.5	255 55.4	03.4	231 44.4	25.4	Rigel	281 07.6	S 8 10.7
D 09	173 23.5	298 49.0	.. 41.4	337 26.6	.. 53.1	270 57.3	.. 03.4	246 46.7	.. 25.3	Rigil Kent.	139 46.6	S60 54.8
N 10	188 25.9	313 48.3	42.2	352 27.6	53.8	285 59.3	03.4	261 49.0	25.3	Sabik	102 07.8	S15 44.8
E 11	203 28.4	328 47.5	43.0	7 28.6	54.4	301 01.2	03.5	276 51.3	25.3			
S 12	218 30.8	343 46.8	S19 43.9	22 29.5	S 5 55.0	316 03.2	S23 03.5	291 53.6	S22 25.3	Schedar	349 35.1	N56 38.8
D 13	233 33.3	358 46.1	44.7	37 30.5	55.7	331 05.1	03.5	306 55.9	25.3	Shaula	96 16.3	S37 07.0
A 14	248 35.8	13 45.4	45.5	52 31.4	56.3	346 07.1	03.6	321 58.1	25.3	Sirius	258 29.8	S16 44.5
Y 15	263 38.2	28 44.7	.. 46.3	67 32.4	.. 56.9	1 09.0	.. 03.6	337 00.4	.. 25.3	Spica	158 27.0	S11 15.6
16	278 40.7	43 43.9	47.1	82 33.3	57.6	16 11.0	03.6	352 02.7	25.2	Suhail	222 49.4	S43 30.4
17	293 43.2	58 43.2	47.9	97 34.3	58.2	31 12.9	03.6	7 05.0	25.2			
18	308 45.6	73 42.5	S19 48.8	112 35.3	S 5 58.8	46 14.9	S23 03.7	22 07.3	S22 25.2	Vega	80 36.2	N38 48.5
19	323 48.1	88 41.8	49.6	127 36.2	5 59.5	61 16.8	03.7	37 09.6	25.2	Zuben'ubi	137 01.0	S16 07.2
20	338 50.6	103 41.0	50.4	142 37.2	6 00.1	76 18.8	03.7	52 11.9	25.2		SHA	Mer.Pass.
21	353 53.0	118 40.3	.. 51.2	157 38.1	.. 00.7	91 20.7	.. 03.8	67 14.2	.. 25.2			h m
22	8 55.5	133 39.6	52.0	172 39.1	01.4	106 22.7	03.8	82 16.4	25.1	Venus	127 10.3	13 04
23	23 58.0	148 38.9	52.8	187 40.0	02.0	121 24.6	03.8	97 18.7	25.1	Mars	164 52.9	10 32
	h m									Jupiter	97 50.8	14 59
Mer. Pass.	21 28.3	v −0.7	d 0.8	v 1.0	d 0.6	v 2.0	d 0.0	v 2.3	d 0.0	Saturn	73 29.0	16 35

© British Crown Copyright 2018. All rights reserved.

UT	SUN GHA	SUN Dec	MOON GHA	v	MOON Dec	d	HP
28 00	184 02.5	S12 56.4	184 25.7	8.8	S 7 48.9	13.6	60.4
01	199 02.6	57.2	198 53.5	8.8	8 02.5	13.6	60.3
02	214 02.7	58.1	213 21.3	8.8	8 16.1	13.5	60.3
03	229 02.7	.. 58.9	227 49.1	8.7	8 29.6	13.5	60.3
04	244 02.8	12 59.8	242 16.8	8.8	8 43.1	13.4	60.3
05	259 02.8	13 00.6	256 44.6	8.7	8 56.5	13.4	60.3
06	274 02.9	S13 01.4	271 12.3	8.7	S 9 09.9	13.2	60.2
07	289 02.9	02.3	285 40.0	8.6	9 23.1	13.2	60.2
M 08	304 03.0	03.1	300 07.6	8.7	9 36.3	13.2	60.2
O 09	319 03.0	.. 04.0	314 35.3	8.6	9 49.5	13.1	60.2
N 10	334 03.1	04.8	329 02.9	8.6	10 02.6	13.0	60.2
11	349 03.1	05.6	343 30.5	8.6	10 15.6	12.9	60.1
D 12	4 03.2	S13 06.5	357 58.1	8.6	S10 28.5	12.9	60.1
A 13	19 03.2	07.3	12 25.7	8.5	10 41.4	12.8	60.1
Y 14	34 03.3	08.1	26 53.2	8.5	10 54.2	12.7	60.1
15	49 03.3	.. 09.0	41 20.7	8.5	11 06.9	12.6	60.0
16	64 03.4	09.8	55 48.2	8.5	11 19.5	12.6	60.0
17	79 03.4	10.7	70 15.7	8.5	11 32.1	12.5	60.0
18	94 03.4	S13 11.5	84 43.2	8.4	S11 44.6	12.4	60.0
19	109 03.5	12.3	99 10.6	8.4	11 57.0	12.3	60.0
20	124 03.5	13.2	113 38.0	8.4	12 09.3	12.2	59.9
21	139 03.6	.. 14.0	128 05.4	8.3	12 21.5	12.1	59.9
22	154 03.6	14.8	142 32.7	8.4	12 33.6	12.1	59.9
23	169 03.7	15.7	157 00.1	8.3	12 45.7	12.0	59.8
29 00	184 03.7	S13 16.5	171 27.4	8.3	S12 57.7	11.9	59.8
01	199 03.8	17.3	185 54.7	8.2	13 09.6	11.7	59.8
02	214 03.8	18.2	200 21.9	8.3	13 21.3	11.7	59.8
03	229 03.9	.. 19.0	214 49.2	8.2	13 33.0	11.7	59.7
04	244 03.9	19.8	229 16.4	8.2	13 44.7	11.5	59.7
05	259 04.0	20.7	243 43.6	8.2	13 56.2	11.4	59.7
06	274 04.0	S13 21.5	258 10.8	8.1	S14 07.6	11.3	59.7
07	289 04.0	22.3	272 37.9	8.2	14 18.9	11.2	59.6
T 08	304 04.1	23.2	287 05.1	8.1	14 30.1	11.1	59.6
U 09	319 04.1	.. 24.0	301 32.2	8.1	14 41.2	11.1	59.6
E 10	334 04.2	24.8	315 59.3	8.0	14 52.3	10.9	59.5
S 11	349 04.2	25.6	330 26.3	8.1	15 03.2	10.8	59.5
D 12	4 04.3	S13 26.5	344 53.4	8.0	S15 14.0	10.7	59.5
A 13	19 04.3	27.3	359 20.4	8.0	15 24.7	10.6	59.4
Y 14	34 04.3	28.1	13 47.4	7.9	15 35.3	10.5	59.4
15	49 04.4	.. 29.0	28 14.3	8.0	15 45.8	10.4	59.4
16	64 04.4	29.8	42 41.3	7.9	15 56.2	10.3	59.3
17	79 04.5	30.6	57 08.2	7.9	16 06.5	10.2	59.3
18	94 04.5	S13 31.4	71 35.1	7.9	S16 16.7	10.0	59.3
19	109 04.5	32.3	86 02.0	7.9	16 26.7	10.0	59.3
20	124 04.6	33.1	100 28.9	7.9	16 36.7	9.8	59.2
21	139 04.6	.. 33.9	114 55.8	7.8	16 46.5	9.8	59.2
22	154 04.6	34.7	129 22.6	7.8	16 56.3	9.6	59.2
23	169 04.7	35.6	143 49.4	7.8	17 05.9	9.5	59.1
30 00	184 04.7	S13 36.4	158 16.2	7.8	S17 15.4	9.4	59.1
01	199 04.8	37.2	172 43.0	7.7	17 24.8	9.3	59.0
02	214 04.8	38.0	187 09.7	7.8	17 34.1	9.1	59.0
03	229 04.8	.. 38.9	201 36.5	7.7	17 43.2	9.0	59.0
04	244 04.9	39.7	216 03.2	7.7	17 52.2	9.0	58.9
05	259 04.9	40.5	230 29.9	7.7	18 01.2	8.7	58.9
06	274 04.9	S13 41.3	244 56.6	7.7	S18 09.9	8.7	58.9
W 07	289 05.0	42.2	259 23.3	7.7	18 18.6	8.6	58.8
E 08	304 05.0	43.0	273 50.0	7.6	18 27.2	8.4	58.8
D 09	319 05.0	.. 43.8	288 16.6	7.6	18 35.6	8.3	58.8
N 10	334 05.1	44.6	302 43.2	7.7	18 43.9	8.2	58.7
E 11	349 05.1	45.4	317 09.9	7.6	18 52.1	8.0	58.7
S 12	4 05.1	S13 46.3	331 36.5	7.6	S19 00.1	8.0	58.7
D 13	19 05.2	47.1	346 03.1	7.6	19 08.1	7.8	58.6
A 14	34 05.2	47.9	0 29.7	7.6	19 15.9	7.7	58.6
Y 15	49 05.2	.. 48.7	14 56.3	7.5	19 23.6	7.5	58.6
16	64 05.3	49.5	29 22.8	7.6	19 31.1	7.4	58.5
17	79 05.3	50.4	43 49.4	7.6	19 38.5	7.3	58.5
18	94 05.3	S13 51.2	58 16.0	7.5	S19 45.8	7.2	58.4
19	109 05.4	52.0	72 42.5	7.6	19 53.0	7.1	58.4
20	124 05.4	52.8	87 09.1	7.5	20 00.1	6.9	58.4
21	139 05.4	.. 53.6	101 35.6	7.6	20 07.0	6.7	58.3
22	154 05.5	54.4	116 02.2	7.5	20 13.7	6.7	58.3
23	169 05.5	55.3	130 28.7	7.5	S20 20.4	6.5	58.3
	SD 16.1	d 0.8	SD 16.4		16.2		16.0

Lat.	Twilight Naut.	Twilight Civil	Sunrise	Moonrise 28	29	30	31
°	h m	h m	h m	h m	h m	h m	h m
N 72	05 53	07 14	08 37	08 08	10 44	▓▓	▓▓
N 70	05 50	07 03	08 14	07 52	10 07	12 50	▓▓
68	05 48	06 54	07 57	07 39	09 41	11 50	14 31
66	05 46	06 46	07 43	07 28	09 22	11 15	13 05
64	05 44	06 40	07 32	07 20	09 06	10 51	12 28
62	05 42	06 34	07 22	07 12	08 53	10 31	12 01
60	05 40	06 29	07 14	07 06	08 42	10 15	11 41
N 58	05 38	06 25	07 06	07 00	08 33	10 02	11 24
56	05 37	06 21	07 00	06 55	08 25	09 51	11 10
54	05 35	06 17	06 54	06 51	08 17	09 41	10 57
52	05 34	06 13	06 49	06 47	08 11	09 32	10 46
50	05 32	06 10	06 44	06 43	08 05	09 24	10 37
45	05 29	06 03	06 34	06 35	07 52	09 07	10 17
N 40	05 25	05 57	06 25	06 29	07 42	08 53	10 00
35	05 22	05 52	06 18	06 23	07 33	08 41	09 47
30	05 19	05 47	06 11	06 18	07 25	08 31	09 35
20	05 11	05 37	06 00	06 10	07 12	08 14	09 14
N 10	05 03	05 28	05 50	06 02	07 00	07 59	08 57
0	04 54	05 19	05 40	05 56	06 50	07 45	08 40
S 10	04 44	05 09	05 31	05 49	06 39	07 31	08 24
20	04 31	04 57	05 20	05 42	06 28	07 16	08 06
30	04 14	04 43	05 08	05 34	06 15	06 59	07 47
35	04 03	04 35	05 01	05 29	06 08	06 49	07 35
40	03 50	04 24	04 53	05 24	05 59	06 38	07 22
45	03 33	04 12	04 44	05 18	05 50	06 25	07 06
S 50	03 12	03 57	04 33	05 11	05 38	06 09	06 47
52	03 02	03 50	04 27	05 08	05 33	06 02	06 38
54	02 49	03 41	04 21	05 04	05 27	05 54	06 28
56	02 35	03 32	04 15	05 00	05 20	05 45	06 16
58	02 18	03 21	04 08	04 56	05 13	05 34	06 03
S 60	01 57	03 09	03 59	04 51	05 05	05 23	05 48

Lat.	Sunset	Twilight Civil	Naut.	Moonset 28	29	30	31
°	h m	h m	h m	h m	h m	h m	h m
N 72	14 49	16 12	17 33	15 42	15 02	▓▓	▓▓
N 70	15 12	16 23	17 36	16 01	15 40	14 52	▓▓
68	15 29	16 32	17 38	16 16	16 07	15 54	15 09
66	15 43	16 40	17 40	16 28	16 28	16 29	16 35
64	15 55	16 46	17 43	16 38	16 44	16 54	17 13
62	16 04	16 52	17 44	16 47	16 58	17 15	17 40
60	16 13	16 57	17 46	16 55	17 10	17 31	18 01
N 58	16 20	17 02	17 48	17 01	17 20	17 45	18 18
56	16 27	17 06	17 50	17 07	17 29	17 57	18 33
54	16 33	17 10	17 51	17 13	17 37	18 07	18 45
52	16 38	17 13	17 53	17 18	17 44	18 17	18 56
50	16 43	17 16	17 54	17 22	17 51	18 25	19 06
45	16 53	17 23	17 58	17 32	18 05	18 43	19 27
N 40	17 02	17 30	18 01	17 40	18 17	18 58	19 44
35	17 09	17 35	18 05	17 46	18 26	19 10	19 58
30	17 16	17 40	18 09	17 53	18 35	19 21	20 10
20	17 27	17 50	18 16	18 03	18 50	19 40	20 31
N 10	17 37	17 59	18 24	18 12	19 03	19 56	20 50
0	17 47	18 08	18 33	18 21	19 16	20 11	21 07
S 10	17 57	18 19	18 44	18 30	19 28	20 27	21 24
20	18 07	18 30	18 57	18 39	19 42	20 43	21 42
30	18 20	18 45	19 15	18 50	19 57	21 02	22 04
35	18 27	18 53	19 26	18 56	20 06	21 13	22 16
40	18 35	19 04	19 39	19 04	20 16	21 26	22 30
45	18 44	19 16	19 55	19 12	20 28	21 41	22 47
S 50	18 56	19 32	20 17	19 22	20 43	21 59	23 08
52	19 01	19 39	20 28	19 27	20 49	22 08	23 18
54	19 07	19 48	20 40	19 32	20 57	22 17	23 29
56	19 14	19 57	20 55	19 37	21 06	22 29	23 42
58	19 21	20 08	21 12	19 44	21 15	22 41	23 57
S 60	19 30	20 21	21 35	19 51	21 26	22 56	24 15

Day	SUN Eqn. of Time 00ʰ	12ʰ	Mer. Pass.	MOON Mer. Pass. Upper	Lower	Age	Phase
d	m s	m s	h m	h m	h m	d	%
28	16 10	16 13	11 44	12 08	24 35	00	0
29	16 15	16 17	11 44	13 03	00 35	01	3
30	16 19	16 21	11 44	13 58	01 30	02	7

© British Crown Copyright 2018. All rights reserved.

UT	ARIES GHA	VENUS −3.8 GHA	Dec	MARS +1.8 GHA	Dec	JUPITER −1.9 GHA	Dec	SATURN +0.6 GHA	Dec	Name	SHA	Dec
31 00	39 00.4	163 38.1	S19 53.6	202 41.0	S 6 02.6	136 26.6	S23 03.8	112 21.0	S22 25.1	Acamar	315 14.6	S40 13.6
01	54 02.9	178 37.4	54.4	217 42.0	03.3	151 28.5	03.9	127 23.3	25.1	Achernar	335 22.9	S57 08.3
02	69 05.3	193 36.7	55.2	232 42.9	03.9	166 30.5	03.9	142 25.6	25.1	Acrux	173 05.1	S63 12.2
03	84 07.8	208 35.9 ..	56.1	247 43.9 ..	04.5	181 32.4 ..	03.9	157 27.9 ..	25.1	Adhara	255 09.0	S28 59.8
04	99 10.3	223 35.2	56.9	262 44.8	05.2	196 34.4	04.0	172 30.2	25.1	Aldebaran	290 44.1	N16 32.8
05	114 12.7	238 34.5	57.7	277 45.8	05.8	211 36.3	04.0	187 32.4	25.0			
06	129 15.2	253 33.7	S19 58.5	292 46.7	S 6 06.5	226 38.3	S23 04.0	202 34.7	S22 25.0	Alioth	166 17.3	N55 51.2
07	144 17.7	268 33.0	19 59.3	307 47.7	07.1	241 40.2	04.1	217 37.0	25.0	Alkaid	152 55.9	N49 13.0
T 08	159 20.1	283 32.3	20 00.1	322 48.6	07.7	256 42.1	04.1	232 39.3	25.0	Alnair	27 38.1	S46 52.1
H 09	174 22.6	298 31.5 ..	00.9	337 49.6 ..	08.4	271 44.1 ..	04.1	247 41.6 ..	25.0	Alnilam	275 41.7	S 1 11.4
U 10	189 25.1	313 30.8	01.7	352 50.6	09.0	286 46.0	04.1	262 43.9	25.0	Alphard	217 51.9	S 8 44.5
R 11	204 27.5	328 30.1	02.5	7 51.5	09.6	301 48.0	04.2	277 46.1	24.9			
S 12	219 30.0	343 29.3	S20 03.3	22 52.5	S 6 10.3	316 49.9	S23 04.2	292 48.4	S22 24.9	Alphecca	126 07.7	N26 39.2
D 13	234 32.5	358 28.6	04.1	37 53.4	10.9	331 51.9	04.2	307 50.7	24.9	Alpheratz	357 38.7	N29 12.1
A 14	249 34.9	13 27.9	04.9	52 54.4	11.5	346 53.8	04.3	322 53.0	24.9	Altair	62 04.1	N 8 55.4
Y 15	264 37.4	28 27.1 ..	05.7	67 55.3 ..	12.2	1 55.8 ..	04.3	337 55.3 ..	24.9	Ankaa	353 11.0	S42 12.1
16	279 39.8	43 26.4	06.4	82 56.3	12.8	16 57.7	04.3	352 57.6	24.9	Antares	112 21.3	S26 28.4
17	294 42.3	58 25.7	07.2	97 57.2	13.4	31 59.7	04.3	7 59.9	24.9			
18	309 44.8	73 24.9	S20 08.0	112 58.2	S 6 14.1	47 01.6	S23 04.4	23 02.1	S22 24.8	Arcturus	145 52.1	N19 05.0
19	324 47.2	88 24.2	08.8	127 59.2	14.7	62 03.5	04.4	38 04.4	24.8	Atria	107 19.6	S69 03.7
20	339 49.7	103 23.5	09.6	143 00.1	15.3	77 05.5	04.4	53 06.7	24.8	Avior	234 16.2	S59 34.0
21	354 52.2	118 22.7 ..	10.4	158 01.1 ..	16.0	92 07.4 ..	04.5	68 09.0 ..	24.8	Bellatrix	278 27.1	N 6 22.0
22	9 54.6	133 22.0	11.2	173 02.0	16.6	107 09.4	04.5	83 11.3	24.8	Betelgeuse	270 56.4	N 7 24.6
23	24 57.1	148 21.2	12.0	188 03.0	17.2	122 11.3	04.5	98 13.6	24.8			
1 00	39 59.6	163 20.5	S20 12.8	203 03.9	S 6 17.9	137 13.3	S23 04.5	113 15.8	S22 24.7	Canopus	263 53.9	S52 42.2
01	55 02.0	178 19.8	13.5	218 04.9	18.5	152 15.2	04.6	128 18.1	24.7	Capella	280 27.7	N46 00.8
02	70 04.5	193 19.0	14.3	233 05.8	19.1	167 17.2	04.6	143 20.4	24.7	Deneb	49 28.6	N45 21.4
03	85 07.0	208 18.3 ..	15.1	248 06.8 ..	19.8	182 19.1 ..	04.6	158 22.7 ..	24.7	Denebola	182 29.5	N14 27.8
04	100 09.4	223 17.5	15.9	263 07.7	20.4	197 21.0	04.7	173 25.0	24.7	Diphda	348 51.2	S17 52.8
05	115 11.9	238 16.8	16.7	278 08.7	21.0	212 23.0	04.7	188 27.2	24.7			
06	130 14.3	253 16.0	S20 17.5	293 09.6	S 6 21.7	227 24.9	S23 04.7	203 29.5	S22 24.6	Dubhe	193 46.7	N61 38.5
07	145 16.8	268 15.3	18.2	308 10.6	22.3	242 26.9	04.8	218 31.8	24.6	Elnath	278 06.8	N28 37.3
F 08	160 19.3	283 14.6	19.0	323 11.6	22.9	257 28.8	04.8	233 34.1	24.6	Eltanin	90 44.5	N51 29.5
R 09	175 21.7	298 13.8 ..	19.8	338 12.5 ..	23.6	272 30.7 ..	04.8	248 36.4 ..	24.6	Enif	33 42.8	N 9 58.1
I 10	190 24.2	313 13.1	20.6	353 13.5	24.2	287 32.7	04.8	263 38.7	24.6	Fomalhaut	15 19.0	S29 31.2
D 11	205 26.7	328 12.3	21.3	8 14.4	24.8	302 34.6	04.9	278 40.9	24.6			
A 12	220 29.1	343 11.6	S20 22.1	23 15.4	S 6 25.5	317 36.6	S23 04.9	293 43.2	S22 24.6	Gacrux	171 56.6	S57 13.1
Y 13	235 31.6	358 10.8	22.9	38 16.3	26.1	332 38.5	04.9	308 45.5	24.5	Gienah	175 48.1	S17 38.8
14	250 34.1	13 10.1	23.7	53 17.3	26.7	347 40.5	05.0	323 47.8	24.5	Hadar	148 42.4	S60 27.8
15	265 36.5	28 09.3 ..	24.4	68 18.2 ..	27.3	2 42.4 ..	05.0	338 50.1 ..	24.5	Hamal	327 55.5	N23 33.3
16	280 39.0	43 08.6	25.2	83 19.2	28.0	17 44.3	05.0	353 52.3	24.5	Kaus Aust.	83 38.3	S34 22.4
17	295 41.4	58 07.8	26.0	98 20.1	28.6	32 46.3	05.0	8 54.6	24.5			
18	310 43.9	73 07.1	S20 26.7	113 21.1	S 6 29.2	47 48.2	S23 05.1	23 56.9	S22 24.5	Kochab	137 21.2	N74 04.6
19	325 46.4	88 06.3	27.5	128 22.0	29.9	62 50.2	05.1	38 59.2	24.4	Markab	13 33.8	N15 18.8
20	340 48.8	103 05.6	28.3	143 23.0	30.5	77 52.1	05.1	54 01.5	24.4	Menkar	314 10.2	N 4 10.0
21	355 51.3	118 04.8 ..	29.0	158 23.9 ..	31.1	92 54.0 ..	05.2	69 03.7 ..	24.4	Menkent	148 02.9	S36 27.8
22	10 53.8	133 04.1	29.8	173 24.9	31.8	107 56.0	05.2	84 06.0	24.4	Miaplacidus	221 39.0	S69 47.5
23	25 56.2	148 03.3	30.6	188 25.8	32.4	122 57.9	05.2	99 08.3	24.4			
2 00	40 58.7	163 02.6	S20 31.3	203 26.8	S 6 33.0	137 59.9	S23 05.2	114 10.6	S22 24.4	Mirfak	308 33.6	N49 55.7
01	56 01.2	178 01.8	32.1	218 27.7	33.7	153 01.8	05.3	129 12.8	24.3	Nunki	75 53.1	S26 16.3
02	71 03.6	193 01.1	32.9	233 28.7	34.3	168 03.7	05.3	144 15.1	24.3	Peacock	53 12.4	S56 40.4
03	86 06.1	208 00.3 ..	33.6	248 29.6 ..	34.9	183 05.7 ..	05.3	159 17.4 ..	24.3	Pollux	243 22.3	N27 58.6
04	101 08.6	222 59.5	34.4	263 30.6	35.6	198 07.6	05.4	174 19.7	24.3	Procyon	244 55.1	N 5 10.5
05	116 11.0	237 58.8	35.1	278 31.6	36.2	213 09.6	05.4	189 22.0	24.3			
06	131 13.5	252 58.0	S20 35.9	293 32.5	S 6 36.8	228 11.5	S23 05.4	204 24.2	S22 24.3	Rasalhague	96 02.7	N12 33.0
07	146 15.9	267 57.3	36.7	308 33.5	37.5	243 13.4	05.4	219 26.5	24.2	Regulus	207 39.0	N11 52.3
S 08	161 18.4	282 56.5	37.5	323 34.4	38.1	258 15.4	05.5	234 28.8	24.2	Rigel	281 07.6	S 8 10.7
A 09	176 20.9	297 55.8 ..	38.2	338 35.4 ..	38.7	273 17.3 ..	05.5	249 31.1 ..	24.2	Rigil Kent.	139 46.5	S60 54.8
T 10	191 23.3	312 55.0	38.9	353 36.3	39.3	288 19.3	05.5	264 33.4	24.2	Sabik	102 07.8	S15 44.8
U 11	206 25.8	327 54.2	39.7	8 37.3	40.0	303 21.2	05.5	279 35.6	24.2			
R 12	221 28.3	342 53.5	S20 40.4	23 38.2	S 6 40.6	318 23.1	S23 05.6	294 37.9	S22 24.2	Schedar	349 35.1	N56 38.8
D 13	236 30.7	357 52.7	41.2	38 39.2	41.2	333 25.1	05.6	309 40.2	24.2	Shaula	96 16.3	S37 07.0
A 14	251 33.2	12 52.0	41.9	53 40.1	41.9	348 27.0	05.6	324 42.5	24.1	Sirius	258 29.7	S16 44.5
Y 15	266 35.7	27 51.2 ..	42.7	68 41.1 ..	42.5	3 28.9 ..	05.7	339 44.7 ..	24.1	Spica	158 27.0	S11 15.6
16	281 38.1	42 50.4	43.4	83 42.0	43.1	18 30.9	05.7	354 47.0	24.1	Suhail	222 49.3	S43 30.4
17	296 40.6	57 49.7	44.2	98 43.0	43.8	33 32.8	05.7	9 49.3	24.1			
18	311 43.1	72 48.9	S20 44.9	113 43.9	S 6 44.4	48 34.8	S23 05.7	24 51.6	S22 24.1	Vega	80 36.2	N38 48.5
19	326 45.5	87 48.2	45.6	128 44.9	45.0	63 36.7	05.8	39 53.8	24.1	Zuben'ubi	137 01.0	S16 07.2
20	341 48.0	102 47.4	46.4	143 45.8	45.7	78 38.6	05.8	54 56.1	24.0		SHA	Mer.Pass.
21	356 50.4	117 46.6 ..	47.1	158 46.8 ..	46.3	93 40.6 ..	05.8	69 58.4 ..	24.0			h m
22	11 52.9	132 45.9	47.9	173 47.7	46.9	108 42.5	05.9	85 00.7	24.0	Venus	123 20.9	13 07
23	26 55.4	147 45.1	48.6	188 48.7	47.5	123 44.4	05.9	100 02.9	24.0	Mars	163 04.4	10 27
	h m									Jupiter	97 13.7	14 49
Mer. Pass. 21 16.5	v −0.7 d 0.8			v 1.0 d 0.6		v 1.9 d 0.0		v 2.3 d 0.0		Saturn	73 16.3	16 24

© British Crown Copyright 2018. All rights reserved.

SUN and MOON

UT	SUN GHA	SUN Dec	MOON GHA	v	MOON Dec	d	HP
31 00	184 05.5	S13 56.1	144 55.2	7.6	S20 26.9	6.4	58.2
01	199 05.6	56.9	159 21.8	7.5	20 33.3	6.3	58.2
02	214 05.6	57.7	173 48.3	7.5	20 39.6	6.1	58.2
03	229 05.6	.. 58.5	188 14.8	7.5	20 45.7	6.0	58.1
04	244 05.6	13 59.3	202 41.3	7.6	20 51.7	5.8	58.1
05	259 05.7	14 00.1	217 07.9	7.5	20 57.5	5.8	58.0
T 06	274 05.7	S14 01.0	231 34.4	7.6	S21 03.3	5.5	58.0
H 07	289 05.7	01.8	246 01.0	7.5	21 08.8	5.5	58.0
U 08	304 05.7	02.6	260 27.5	7.5	21 14.3	5.3	57.9
R 09	319 05.8	.. 03.4	274 54.0	7.6	21 19.6	5.2	57.9
S 10	334 05.8	04.2	289 20.6	7.6	21 24.8	5.1	57.9
D 11	349 05.8	05.0	303 47.2	7.5	21 29.9	4.9	57.8
A 12	4 05.9	S14 05.8	318 13.7	7.6	S21 34.8	4.8	57.8
Y 13	19 05.9	06.6	332 40.3	7.6	21 39.6	4.6	57.7
14	34 05.9	07.4	347 06.9	7.6	21 44.2	4.6	57.7
15	49 05.9	.. 08.3	1 33.5	7.6	21 48.8	4.3	57.7
16	64 06.0	09.1	16 00.1	7.7	21 53.1	4.3	57.6
17	79 06.0	09.9	30 26.8	7.6	21 57.4	4.1	57.6
18	94 06.0	S14 10.7	44 53.4	7.7	S22 01.5	4.0	57.6
19	109 06.0	11.5	59 20.1	7.6	22 05.5	3.8	57.5
20	124 06.0	12.3	73 46.7	7.7	22 09.3	3.7	57.5
21	139 06.1	.. 13.1	88 13.4	7.7	22 13.0	3.6	57.4
22	154 06.1	13.9	102 40.1	7.8	22 16.6	3.5	57.4
23	169 06.1	14.7	117 06.9	7.7	22 20.1	3.3	57.4
1 00	184 06.1	S14 15.5	131 33.6	7.8	S22 23.4	3.1	57.3
01	199 06.2	16.3	146 00.4	7.8	22 26.5	3.1	57.3
02	214 06.2	17.1	160 27.2	7.8	22 29.6	2.9	57.3
03	229 06.2	.. 17.9	174 54.0	7.9	22 32.5	2.7	57.2
04	244 06.2	18.7	189 20.9	7.8	22 35.2	2.7	57.2
05	259 06.2	19.5	203 47.7	7.9	22 37.9	2.5	57.1
F 06	274 06.3	S14 20.3	218 14.6	7.9	S22 40.4	2.3	57.1
R 07	289 06.3	21.2	232 41.5	8.0	22 42.7	2.3	57.1
I 08	304 06.3	22.0	247 08.5	8.0	22 45.0	2.0	57.0
D 09	319 06.3	.. 22.8	261 35.5	8.0	22 47.0	2.0	57.0
A 10	334 06.3	23.6	276 02.5	8.0	22 49.0	1.8	57.0
Y 11	349 06.3	24.4	290 29.5	8.1	22 50.8	1.7	56.9
12	4 06.4	S14 25.2	304 56.6	8.1	S22 52.5	1.6	56.9
13	19 06.4	26.0	319 23.7	8.2	22 54.1	1.4	56.9
14	34 06.4	26.8	333 50.9	8.1	22 55.5	1.3	56.8
15	49 06.4	.. 27.6	348 18.0	8.3	22 56.8	1.2	56.8
16	64 06.4	28.4	2 45.3	8.2	22 58.0	1.1	56.7
17	79 06.4	29.2	17 12.5	8.3	22 59.1	0.9	56.7
18	94 06.5	S14 30.0	31 39.8	8.3	S23 00.0	0.7	56.7
19	109 06.5	30.8	46 07.1	8.4	23 00.7	0.7	56.6
20	124 06.5	31.6	60 34.5	8.4	23 01.4	0.5	56.6
21	139 06.5	.. 32.4	75 01.9	8.5	23 01.9	0.4	56.6
22	154 06.5	33.2	89 29.4	8.5	23 02.3	0.3	56.5
23	169 06.5	33.9	103 56.9	8.5	23 02.6	0.1	56.5
2 00	184 06.5	S14 34.7	118 24.4	8.6	S23 02.7	0.0	56.5
01	199 06.6	35.5	132 52.0	8.6	23 02.7	0.1	56.4
02	214 06.6	36.3	147 19.6	8.7	23 02.6	0.3	56.4
03	229 06.6	.. 37.1	161 47.3	8.7	23 02.3	0.3	56.4
04	244 06.6	37.9	176 15.0	8.8	23 02.0	0.5	56.3
05	259 06.6	38.7	190 42.8	8.8	23 01.5	0.7	56.3
S 06	274 06.6	S14 39.5	205 10.6	8.8	S23 00.8	0.7	56.3
A 07	289 06.6	40.3	219 38.4	9.0	23 00.1	0.9	56.2
T 08	304 06.6	41.1	234 06.4	8.9	22 59.2	1.0	56.2
U 09	319 06.7	.. 41.9	248 34.3	9.0	22 58.2	1.1	56.2
R 10	334 06.7	42.7	263 02.3	9.1	22 57.1	1.2	56.1
D 11	349 06.7	43.5	277 30.4	9.1	22 55.9	1.4	56.1
A 12	4 06.7	S14 44.3	291 58.5	9.2	S22 54.5	1.5	56.1
Y 13	19 06.7	45.1	306 26.7	9.2	22 53.0	1.6	56.0
14	34 06.7	45.9	320 54.9	9.3	22 51.4	1.7	56.0
15	49 06.7	.. 46.6	335 23.2	9.4	22 49.7	1.8	56.0
16	64 06.7	47.4	349 51.6	9.4	22 47.9	2.0	55.9
17	79 06.7	48.2	4 20.0	9.4	22 45.9	2.1	55.9
18	94 06.7	S14 49.0	18 48.4	9.5	S22 43.8	2.2	55.9
19	109 06.7	49.8	33 16.9	9.6	22 41.6	2.3	55.8
20	124 06.7	50.6	47 45.5	9.6	22 39.3	2.4	55.8
21	139 06.7	.. 51.4	62 14.1	9.7	22 36.9	2.6	55.8
22	154 06.8	52.2	76 42.8	9.7	22 34.3	2.6	55.8
23	169 06.8	52.9	91 11.5	9.8	S22 31.7	2.8	55.7
	SD 16.1	d 0.8	SD 15.7		15.5		15.3

Twilight, Sunrise and Moonrise

Lat.	Naut.	Civil	Sunrise	Moonrise 31	1	2	3
N 72	06 05	07 28	08 55	▬▬▬	▬▬▬	▬▬▬	▬▬▬
N 70	06 01	07 15	08 29	▬▬▬	▬▬▬	▬▬▬	▬▬▬
68	05 57	07 04	08 09	14 31	▬▬▬	▬▬▬	16 42
66	05 54	06 56	07 54	13 05	14 38	15 27	15 41
64	05 51	06 48	07 41	12 28	13 47	14 39	15 06
62	05 49	06 42	07 30	12 01	13 15	14 08	14 41
60	05 47	06 36	07 21	11 41	12 52	13 45	14 21
N 58	05 45	06 31	07 13	11 24	12 33	13 26	14 05
56	05 42	06 27	07 06	11 10	12 17	13 11	13 51
54	05 41	06 22	07 00	10 57	12 03	12 57	13 39
52	05 39	06 19	06 54	10 46	11 52	12 46	13 28
50	05 37	06 15	06 49	10 37	11 41	12 35	13 19
45	05 33	06 07	06 38	10 17	11 19	12 13	12 59
N 40	05 29	06 00	06 29	10 00	11 02	11 56	12 42
35	05 25	05 54	06 21	09 47	10 47	11 41	12 28
30	05 21	05 49	06 14	09 35	10 34	11 28	12 16
20	05 12	05 39	06 01	09 14	10 12	11 06	11 56
N 10	05 04	05 29	05 50	08 57	09 53	10 47	11 38
0	04 54	05 19	05 40	08 40	09 35	10 29	11 21
S 10	04 43	05 08	05 30	08 24	09 18	10 12	11 04
20	04 29	04 56	05 19	08 06	08 59	09 53	10 46
30	04 10	04 40	05 06	07 47	08 37	09 31	10 26
35	03 59	04 31	04 58	07 35	08 25	09 18	10 14
40	03 45	04 20	04 49	07 22	08 10	09 03	10 00
45	03 28	04 07	04 39	07 06	07 53	08 46	09 43
S 50	03 05	03 51	04 27	06 47	07 32	08 24	09 23
52	02 54	03 43	04 21	06 38	07 21	08 14	09 13
54	02 41	03 34	04 15	06 28	07 10	08 02	09 02
56	02 25	03 24	04 08	06 16	06 57	07 48	08 49
58	02 06	03 13	04 00	06 03	06 42	07 33	08 35
S 60	01 42	02 59	03 51	05 48	06 24	07 14	08 18

Sunset, Twilight and Moonset

Lat.	Sunset	Civil	Naut.	Moonset 31	1	2	3
N 72	14 31	15 58	17 21	▬▬▬	▬▬▬	▬▬▬	▬▬▬
N 70	14 57	16 11	17 25	▬▬▬	▬▬▬	▬▬▬	▬▬▬
68	15 17	16 21	17 28	15 09	▬▬▬	▬▬▬	18 31
66	15 32	16 30	17 32	16 35	16 57	18 00	19 32
64	15 45	16 38	17 34	17 13	17 49	18 48	20 06
62	15 56	16 44	17 37	17 40	18 20	19 19	20 31
60	16 05	16 50	17 39	18 01	18 44	19 42	20 51
N 58	16 13	16 55	17 42	18 18	19 03	20 00	21 07
56	16 20	17 00	17 44	18 33	19 19	20 16	21 20
54	16 27	17 04	17 46	18 45	19 32	20 29	21 32
52	16 32	17 08	17 48	18 56	19 44	20 40	21 43
50	16 37	17 11	17 50	19 06	19 55	20 51	21 52
45	16 49	17 19	17 54	19 27	20 17	21 12	22 11
N 40	16 58	17 26	17 58	19 44	20 35	21 30	22 27
35	17 06	17 32	18 02	19 58	20 50	21 44	22 41
30	17 13	17 38	18 06	20 10	21 03	21 57	22 52
20	17 26	17 48	18 14	20 31	21 25	22 18	23 12
N 10	17 37	17 58	18 23	20 50	21 44	22 37	23 29
0	17 47	18 08	18 33	21 07	22 02	22 55	23 45
S 10	17 58	18 19	18 45	21 24	22 19	23 12	24 01
20	18 09	18 32	18 59	21 42	22 38	23 30	24 18
30	18 22	18 47	19 15	22 04	23 00	23 52	24 37
35	18 30	18 57	19 29	22 16	23 13	24 04	00 04
40	18 38	19 08	19 43	22 30	23 28	24 19	00 19
45	18 49	19 21	20 01	22 47	23 46	24 35	00 35
S 50	19 01	19 37	20 24	23 08	24 08	00 08	00 56
52	19 07	19 45	20 35	23 18	24 18	00 18	01 06
54	19 13	19 54	20 49	23 29	24 30	00 30	01 17
56	19 21	20 05	21 04	23 42	24 43	00 43	01 30
58	19 29	20 16	21 24	23 57	24 59	00 59	01 45
S 60	19 38	20 30	21 50	24 15	00 15	01 17	02 02

SUN and MOON

Day	SUN Eqn. of Time 00ʰ	12ʰ	Mer. Pass.	MOON Mer. Pass. Upper	Lower	Age	Phase
31	16 22	16 23	11 44	14 54	02 26	03	14%
1	16 24	16 25	11 44	15 49	03 21	04	22%
2	16 26	16 27	11 44	16 42	04 16	05	31%

© British Crown Copyright 2018. All rights reserved.

UT	ARIES GHA	VENUS −3.8 GHA	Dec	MARS +1.8 GHA	Dec	JUPITER −1.9 GHA	Dec	SATURN +0.6 GHA	Dec	STARS Name	SHA	Dec
3 00	41 57.8	162 44.3	S20 49.4	203 49.6	S 6 48.2	138 46.4	S23 05.9	115 05.2	S22 24.0	Acamar	315 14.6	S40 13.6
01	57 00.3	177 43.6	50.1	218 50.6	48.8	153 48.3	05.9	130 07.5	24.0	Achernar	335 22.9	S57 08.4
02	72 02.8	192 42.8	50.8	233 51.5	49.4	168 50.2	06.0	145 09.8	23.9	Acrux	173 05.0	S63 12.2
03	87 05.2	207 42.0	.. 51.6	248 52.5	.. 50.1	183 52.2	.. 06.0	160 12.0	.. 23.9	Adhara	255 08.9	S28 59.8
04	102 07.7	222 41.3	52.3	263 53.4	50.7	198 54.1	06.0	175 14.3	23.9	Aldebaran	290 44.1	N16 32.8
05	117 10.2	237 40.5	53.1	278 54.4	51.3	213 56.1	06.1	190 16.6	23.9			
06	132 12.6	252 39.7	S20 53.8	293 55.3	S 6 51.9	228 58.0	S23 06.1	205 18.9	S22 23.9	Alioth	166 17.3	N55 51.2
07	147 15.1	267 39.0	54.5	308 56.3	52.6	243 59.9	06.1	220 21.1	23.9	Alkaid	152 55.9	N49 13.0
08	162 17.6	282 38.2	55.2	323 57.2	53.2	259 01.9	06.1	235 23.4	23.8	Alnair	27 38.1	S46 52.1
S 09	177 20.0	297 37.4	.. 56.0	338 58.2	.. 53.8	274 03.8	.. 06.2	250 25.7	.. 23.8	Alnilam	275 41.7	S 1 11.4
U 10	192 22.5	312 36.6	56.7	353 59.1	54.5	289 05.7	06.2	265 28.0	23.8	Alphard	217 51.9	S 8 44.5
N 11	207 24.9	327 35.9	57.4	9 00.1	55.1	304 07.7	06.2	280 30.2	23.8			
D 12	222 27.4	342 35.1	S20 58.1	24 01.0	S 6 55.7	319 09.6	S23 06.2	295 32.5	S22 23.8	Alphecca	126 07.7	N26 39.1
A 13	237 29.9	357 34.3	58.9	39 01.9	56.4	334 11.5	06.3	310 34.8	23.8	Alpheratz	357 38.7	N29 12.1
Y 14	252 32.3	12 33.6	20 59.6	54 02.9	57.0	349 13.5	06.3	325 37.1	23.7	Altair	62 04.1	N 8 55.4
15	267 34.8	27 32.8	21 00.3	69 03.8	.. 57.6	4 15.4	.. 06.3	340 39.3	.. 23.7	Ankaa	353 11.0	S42 12.1
16	282 37.3	42 32.0	01.0	84 04.8	58.2	19 17.3	06.4	355 41.6	23.7	Antares	112 21.3	S26 28.4
17	297 39.7	57 31.2	01.8	99 05.7	58.9	34 19.3	06.4	10 43.9	23.7			
18	312 42.2	72 30.5	S21 02.5	114 06.7	S 6 59.5	49 21.2	S23 06.4	25 46.2	S22 23.7	Arcturus	145 52.1	N19 05.0
19	327 44.7	87 29.7	03.2	129 07.6	7 00.1	64 23.1	06.4	40 48.4	23.6	Atria	107 19.6	S69 03.7
20	342 47.1	102 28.9	03.9	144 08.6	00.8	79 25.1	06.5	55 50.7	23.6	Avior	234 16.2	S59 34.0
21	357 49.6	117 28.1	.. 04.6	159 09.5	.. 01.4	94 27.0	.. 06.5	70 53.0	.. 23.6	Bellatrix	278 27.1	N 6 22.0
22	12 52.0	132 27.4	05.4	174 10.5	02.0	109 28.9	06.5	85 55.2	23.6	Betelgeuse	270 56.4	N 7 24.6
23	27 54.5	147 26.6	06.1	189 11.4	02.6	124 30.9	06.5	100 57.5	23.6			
4 00	42 57.0	162 25.8	S21 06.8	204 12.4	S 7 03.3	139 32.8	S23 06.6	115 59.8	S22 23.6	Canopus	263 53.9	S52 42.2
01	57 59.4	177 25.0	07.5	219 13.3	03.9	154 34.7	06.6	131 02.1	23.5	Capella	280 27.6	N46 00.8
02	73 01.9	192 24.2	08.2	234 14.3	04.5	169 36.7	06.6	146 04.3	23.5	Deneb	49 28.6	N45 21.4
03	88 04.4	207 23.5	.. 08.9	249 15.2	.. 05.2	184 38.6	.. 06.7	161 06.6	.. 23.5	Denebola	182 29.5	N14 27.8
04	103 06.8	222 22.7	09.6	264 16.2	05.8	199 40.5	06.7	176 08.9	23.5	Diphda	348 51.2	S17 52.8
05	118 09.3	237 21.9	10.3	279 17.1	06.4	214 42.5	06.7	191 11.2	23.5			
06	133 11.8	252 21.1	S21 11.1	294 18.1	S 7 07.0	229 44.4	S23 06.7	206 13.4	S22 23.5	Dubhe	193 46.7	N61 38.5
07	148 14.2	267 20.3	11.8	309 19.0	07.7	244 46.3	06.8	221 15.7	23.4	Elnath	278 06.8	N28 37.3
08	163 16.7	282 19.6	12.5	324 19.9	08.3	259 48.3	06.8	236 18.0	23.4	Eltanin	90 44.5	N51 29.5
M 09	178 19.2	297 18.8	.. 13.2	339 20.9	.. 08.9	274 50.2	.. 06.8	251 20.2	.. 23.4	Enif	33 42.8	N 9 58.1
O 10	193 21.6	312 18.0	.13.9	354 21.8	09.5	289 52.1	06.8	266 22.5	23.4	Fomalhaut	15 19.0	S29 31.2
N 11	208 24.1	327 17.2	14.6	9 22.8	10.2	304 54.0	06.9	281 24.8	23.4			
D 12	223 26.5	342 16.4	S21 15.3	24 23.7	S 7 10.8	319 56.0	S23 06.9	296 27.0	S22 23.4	Gacrux	171 56.6	S57 13.1
A 13	238 29.0	357 15.6	16.0	39 24.7	11.4	334 57.9	06.9	311 29.3	23.3	Gienah	175 48.1	S17 38.8
Y 14	253 31.5	12 14.9	16.7	54 25.6	12.1	349 59.8	07.0	326 31.6	23.3	Hadar	148 42.4	S60 27.8
15	268 33.9	27 14.1	.. 17.4	69 26.6	.. 12.7	5 01.8	.. 07.0	341 33.9	.. 23.3	Hamal	327 55.5	N23 33.3
16	283 36.4	42 13.3	18.1	84 27.5	13.3	20 03.7	07.0	356 36.1	23.3	Kaus Aust.	83 38.3	S34 22.4
17	298 38.9	57 12.5	18.8	99 28.5	13.9	35 05.6	07.0	11 38.4	23.3			
18	313 41.3	72 11.7	S21 19.5	114 29.4	S 7 14.6	50 07.6	S23 07.1	26 40.7	S22 23.3	Kochab	137 21.3	N74 04.6
19	328 43.8	87 10.9	20.2	129 30.4	15.2	65 09.5	07.1	41 42.9	23.2	Markab	13 33.8	N15 18.8
20	343 46.3	102 10.1	20.9	144 31.3	15.8	80 11.4	07.1	56 45.2	23.2	Menkar	314 10.2	N 4 10.0
21	358 48.7	117 09.4	.. 21.6	159 32.2	.. 16.4	95 13.3	.. 07.1	71 47.5	.. 23.2	Menkent	148 02.9	S36 27.8
22	13 51.2	132 08.6	22.3	174 33.2	17.1	110 15.3	07.2	86 49.7	23.2	Miaplacidus	221 38.9	S69 47.5
23	28 53.7	147 07.8	22.9	189 34.1	17.7	125 17.2	07.2	101 52.0	23.2			
5 00	43 56.1	162 07.0	S21 23.6	204 35.1	S 7 18.3	140 19.1	S23 07.2	116 54.3	S22 23.1	Mirfak	308 33.6	N49 55.7
01	58 58.6	177 06.2	24.3	219 36.0	18.9	155 21.1	07.3	131 56.5	23.1	Nunki	75 53.1	S26 16.3
02	74 01.0	192 05.4	25.0	234 37.0	19.6	170 23.0	07.3	146 58.8	23.1	Peacock	53 12.5	S56 40.4
03	89 03.5	207 04.6	.. 25.7	249 37.9	.. 20.2	185 24.9	.. 07.3	162 01.1	.. 23.1	Pollux	243 22.3	N27 58.6
04	104 06.0	222 03.8	26.4	264 38.9	20.8	200 26.9	07.3	177 03.4	23.1	Procyon	244 55.1	N 5 10.5
05	119 08.4	237 03.0	27.1	279 39.8	21.4	215 28.8	07.4	192 05.6	23.1			
06	134 10.9	252 02.2	S21 27.8	294 40.7	S 7 22.1	230 30.7	S23 07.4	207 07.9	S22 23.0	Rasalhague	96 02.7	N12 33.0
07	149 13.4	267 01.4	28.4	309 41.7	22.7	245 32.6	07.4	222 10.2	23.0	Regulus	207 39.0	N11 52.3
T 08	164 15.8	282 00.7	29.1	324 42.6	23.3	260 34.6	07.4	237 12.4	23.0	Rigel	281 07.6	S 8 10.7
U 09	179 18.3	296 59.9	.. 29.8	339 43.6	.. 24.0	275 36.5	.. 07.5	252 14.7	.. 23.0	Rigil Kent.	139 46.5	S60 54.7
E 10	194 20.8	311 59.1	30.5	354 44.5	24.6	290 38.4	07.5	267 17.0	23.0	Sabik	102 07.8	S15 44.8
S 11	209 23.2	326 58.3	31.2	9 45.5	25.2	305 40.3	07.5	282 19.2	23.0			
D 12	224 25.7	341 57.5	S21 31.8	24 46.4	S 7 25.8	320 42.3	S23 07.5	297 21.5	S22 22.9	Schedar	349 35.1	N56 38.8
A 13	239 28.2	356 56.7	32.5	39 47.4	26.5	335 44.2	07.6	312 23.8	22.9	Shaula	96 16.3	S37 07.0
Y 14	254 30.6	11 55.9	33.2	54 48.3	27.1	350 46.1	07.6	327 26.0	22.9	Sirius	258 29.7	S16 44.5
15	269 33.1	26 55.1	.. 33.9	69 49.2	.. 27.7	5 48.1	.. 07.6	342 28.3	.. 22.9	Spica	158 27.0	S11 15.6
16	284 35.5	41 54.3	34.5	84 50.2	28.3	20 50.0	07.6	357 30.6	22.9	Suhail	222 49.3	S43 30.4
17	299 38.0	56 53.5	35.2	99 51.1	29.0	35 51.9	07.7	12 32.8	22.8			
18	314 40.5	71 52.7	S21 35.9	114 52.1	S 7 29.6	50 53.8	S23 07.7	27 35.1	S22 22.8	Vega	80 36.3	N38 48.4
19	329 42.9	86 51.9	36.6	129 53.0	30.2	65 55.8	07.7	42 37.4	22.8	Zuben'ubi	137 00.9	S16 07.2
20	344 45.4	101 51.1	37.2	144 54.0	30.8	80 57.7	07.8	57 39.6	22.8		SHA	Mer.Pass.
21	359 47.9	116 50.3	.. 37.9	159 54.9	.. 31.5	95 59.6	.. 07.8	72 41.9	.. 22.8			
22	14 50.3	131 49.5	38.6	174 55.8	32.1	111 01.5	07.8	87 44.2	22.8	Venus	119 28.8	13 11
23	29 52.8	146 48.7	39.2	189 56.8	32.7	126 03.5	07.8	102 46.4	22.7	Mars	161 15.4	10 23
Mer. Pass. 21 04.7		v −0.8	d 0.7	v 0.9	d 0.6	v 1.9	d 0.0	v 2.3	d 0.0	Jupiter	96 35.8	14 40
										Saturn	73 02.8	16 14

© British Crown Copyright 2018. All rights reserved.

UT	SUN GHA	SUN Dec	MOON GHA	v	MOON Dec	d	HP
d h	° ′	° ′	° ′	′	° ′	′	′
3 00	184 06.8	S14 53.7	105 40.3	9.9	S22 28.9	2.9	55.7
01	199 06.8	54.5	120 09.2	9.9	22 26.0	3.0	55.7
02	214 06.8	55.3	134 38.1	10.0	22 23.0	3.1	55.6
03	229 06.8	.. 56.1	149 07.1	10.0	22 19.9	3.2	55.6
04	244 06.8	56.9	163 36.1	10.1	22 16.7	3.3	55.6
05	259 06.8	57.7	178 05.2	10.2	22 13.4	3.5	55.6
06	274 06.8	S14 58.4	192 34.4	10.2	S22 09.9	3.5	55.5
07	289 06.8	14 59.2	207 03.6	10.3	22 06.4	3.7	55.5
08	304 06.8	15 00.0	221 32.9	10.4	22 02.7	3.7	55.5
S 09	319 06.8	.. 00.8	236 02.3	10.4	21 59.0	3.9	55.4
U 10	334 06.8	01.6	250 31.7	10.5	21 55.1	4.0	55.4
N 11	349 06.8	02.4	265 01.2	10.5	21 51.1	4.0	55.4
D 12	4 06.8	S15 03.1	279 30.7	10.6	S21 47.1	4.2	55.4
A 13	19 06.8	03.9	294 00.3	10.7	21 42.9	4.3	55.3
Y 14	34 06.8	04.7	308 30.0	10.8	21 38.6	4.4	55.3
15	49 06.8	.. 05.5	322 59.8	10.8	21 34.2	4.5	55.3
16	64 06.8	06.3	337 29.6	10.8	21 29.7	4.6	55.3
17	79 06.8	07.0	351 59.4	11.0	21 25.1	4.7	55.2
18	94 06.8	S15 07.8	6 29.4	11.0	S21 20.4	4.8	55.2
19	109 06.8	08.6	20 59.4	11.0	21 15.6	4.9	55.2
20	124 06.8	09.4	35 29.4	11.2	21 10.7	4.9	55.2
21	139 06.8	.. 10.1	49 59.6	11.2	21 05.8	5.1	55.1
22	154 06.8	10.9	64 29.8	11.2	21 00.7	5.2	55.1
23	169 06.8	11.7	79 00.0	11.3	20 55.5	5.3	55.1
4 00	184 06.8	S15 12.5	93 30.3	11.4	S20 50.2	5.4	55.1
01	199 06.8	13.3	108 00.7	11.5	20 44.8	5.4	55.0
02	214 06.8	14.0	122 31.2	11.5	20 39.4	5.6	55.0
03	229 06.8	.. 14.8	137 01.7	11.6	20 33.8	5.7	55.0
04	244 06.8	15.6	151 32.3	11.6	20 28.1	5.7	55.0
05	259 06.8	16.4	166 02.9	11.8	20 22.4	5.9	54.9
06	274 06.8	S15 17.1	180 33.7	11.7	S20 16.5	5.9	54.9
07	289 06.8	17.9	195 04.4	11.9	20 10.6	6.0	54.9
08	304 06.7	18.7	209 35.3	11.9	20 04.6	6.1	54.9
M 09	319 06.7	.. 19.4	224 06.2	12.0	19 58.5	6.2	54.9
O 10	334 06.7	20.2	238 37.2	12.0	19 52.3	6.3	54.8
N 11	349 06.7	21.0	253 08.2	12.1	19 46.0	6.4	54.8
D 12	4 06.7	S15 21.8	267 39.3	12.2	S19 39.6	6.4	54.8
A 13	19 06.7	22.5	282 10.5	12.2	19 33.2	6.6	54.8
Y 14	34 06.7	23.3	296 41.7	12.3	19 26.6	6.6	54.8
15	49 06.7	.. 24.1	311 13.0	12.4	19 20.0	6.7	54.7
16	64 06.7	24.8	325 44.4	12.4	19 13.3	6.8	54.7
17	79 06.7	25.6	340 15.8	12.5	19 06.5	6.9	54.7
18	94 06.7	S15 26.4	354 47.3	12.6	S18 59.6	6.9	54.7
19	109 06.7	27.1	9 18.9	12.6	18 52.7	7.0	54.7
20	124 06.6	27.9	23 50.5	12.7	18 45.7	7.2	54.7
21	139 06.6	.. 28.7	38 22.2	12.7	18 38.5	7.1	54.6
22	154 06.6	29.4	52 53.9	12.8	18 31.4	7.3	54.6
23	169 06.6	30.2	67 25.7	12.9	18 24.1	7.4	54.6
5 00	184 06.6	S15 31.0	81 57.6	12.9	S18 16.7	7.4	54.6
01	199 06.6	31.7	96 29.5	13.0	18 09.3	7.5	54.6
02	214 06.6	32.5	111 01.5	13.0	18 01.8	7.6	54.6
03	229 06.6	.. 33.3	125 33.5	13.1	17 54.2	7.6	54.5
04	244 06.6	34.0	140 05.6	13.2	17 46.6	7.8	54.5
05	259 06.5	34.8	154 37.8	13.2	17 38.8	7.8	54.5
06	274 06.5	S15 35.6	169 10.0	13.3	S17 31.0	7.8	54.5
07	289 06.5	36.3	183 42.3	13.3	17 23.2	8.0	54.5
08	304 06.5	37.1	198 14.6	13.4	17 15.2	8.0	54.5
T 09	319 06.5	.. 37.8	212 47.0	13.5	17 07.2	8.1	54.5
U 10	334 06.5	38.6	227 19.5	13.5	16 59.1	8.1	54.4
E 11	349 06.5	39.4	241 52.0	13.5	16 51.0	8.2	54.4
S 12	4 06.4	S15 40.1	256 24.5	13.7	S16 42.8	8.3	54.4
D 13	19 06.4	40.9	270 57.2	13.6	16 34.5	8.4	54.4
A 14	34 06.4	41.6	285 29.8	13.8	16 26.1	8.4	54.4
Y 15	49 06.4	.. 42.4	300 02.6	13.8	16 17.7	8.5	54.4
16	64 06.4	43.2	314 35.4	13.8	16 09.2	8.6	54.4
17	79 06.4	43.9	329 08.2	13.9	16 00.6	8.6	54.4
18	94 06.3	S15 44.7	343 41.1	14.0	S15 52.0	8.7	54.3
19	109 06.3	45.4	358 14.1	14.0	15 43.3	8.7	54.3
20	124 06.3	46.2	12 47.1	14.0	15 34.6	8.8	54.3
21	139 06.3	.. 46.9	27 20.1	14.1	15 25.8	8.9	54.3
22	154 06.3	47.7	41 53.2	14.2	15 16.9	8.9	54.3
23	169 06.2	48.5	56 26.4	14.2	S15 08.0	9.0	54.3
	SD 16.2	d 0.8	SD 15.1		14.9		14.8

Lat.	Twilight Naut.	Twilight Civil	Sunrise	Moonrise 3	Moonrise 4	Moonrise 5	Moonrise 6
°	h m	h m	h m	h m	h m	h m	h m
N 72	06 17	07 41	09 14	▪	▪	17 14	16 36
N 70	06 11	07 27	08 44	▪	17 11	16 34	16 15
68	06 07	07 15	08 22	16 42	16 18	16 06	15 58
66	06 03	07 05	08 05	15 41	15 45	15 45	15 44
64	05 59	06 57	07 51	15 06	15 21	15 28	15 33
62	05 56	06 49	07 39	14 41	15 01	15 14	15 23
60	05 53	06 43	07 29	14 21	14 46	15 02	15 15
N 58	05 51	06 37	07 20	14 05	14 32	14 52	15 07
56	05 48	06 32	07 13	13 51	14 21	14 43	15 01
54	05 46	06 28	07 06	13 39	14 11	14 35	14 55
52	05 43	06 24	07 00	13 28	14 01	14 28	14 50
50	05 41	06 20	06 54	13 19	13 53	14 21	14 45
45	05 36	06 11	06 42	12 59	13 36	14 07	14 34
N 40	05 32	06 04	06 32	12 42	13 22	13 56	14 26
35	05 27	05 57	06 23	12 28	13 10	13 46	14 18
30	05 23	05 51	06 16	12 16	12 59	13 37	14 12
20	05 14	05 40	06 03	11 56	12 41	13 22	14 00
N 10	05 04	05 29	05 51	11 38	12 25	13 09	13 50
0	04 54	05 19	05 40	11 21	12 10	12 56	13 41
S 10	04 42	05 07	05 29	11 04	11 55	12 44	13 31
20	04 27	04 54	05 17	10 46	11 39	12 31	13 21
30	04 08	04 38	05 03	10 26	11 21	12 15	13 09
35	03 56	04 28	04 55	10 14	11 10	12 07	13 02
40	03 41	04 17	04 46	10 00	10 58	11 56	12 55
45	03 22	04 03	04 35	09 43	10 43	11 44	12 46
S 50	02 58	03 45	04 22	09 23	10 25	11 30	12 35
52	02 46	03 37	04 16	09 13	10 17	11 23	12 30
54	02 32	03 27	04 09	09 02	10 07	11 15	12 24
56	02 15	03 17	04 01	08 49	09 57	11 07	12 18
58	01 54	03 04	03 53	08 35	09 44	10 57	12 11
S 60	01 26	02 49	03 43	08 18	09 30	10 46	12 03

Lat.	Sunset	Twilight Civil	Twilight Naut.	Moonset 3	Moonset 4	Moonset 5	Moonset 6
°	h m	h m	h m	h m	h m	h m	h m
N 72	14 12	15 44	17 09	▪	▪	21 17	23 25
N 70	14 42	15 59	17 14	▪	19 44	21 56	23 45
68	15 04	16 11	17 19	18 31	20 36	22 22	24 01
66	15 21	16 21	17 23	19 32	21 08	22 42	24 13
64	15 35	16 29	17 27	20 06	21 32	22 58	24 23
62	15 47	16 37	17 30	20 31	21 51	23 12	24 32
60	15 57	16 43	17 33	20 51	22 06	23 23	24 40
N 58	16 06	16 49	17 36	21 07	22 19	23 32	24 46
56	16 14	16 54	17 38	21 20	22 30	23 41	24 52
54	16 21	16 59	17 41	21 32	22 40	23 48	24 57
52	16 27	17 03	17 43	21 43	22 48	23 55	25 02
50	16 32	17 07	17 45	21 52	22 56	24 01	00 01
45	16 45	17 15	17 50	22 11	23 12	24 14	00 14
N 40	16 55	17 23	17 55	22 27	23 26	24 25	00 25
35	17 03	17 30	18 00	22 41	23 37	24 34	00 34
30	17 11	17 36	18 04	22 52	23 47	24 42	00 42
20	17 24	17 47	18 13	23 12	24 04	00 04	00 55
N 10	17 36	17 58	18 23	23 29	24 19	00 19	01 07
0	17 47	18 08	18 33	23 45	24 33	00 33	01 18
S 10	17 58	18 20	18 46	24 01	00 01	00 46	01 29
20	18 10	18 33	19 01	24 18	00 18	01 01	01 41
30	18 24	18 50	19 20	24 37	00 37	01 18	01 54
35	18 32	19 00	19 32	00 04	00 49	01 27	02 01
40	18 42	19 11	19 47	00 19	01 02	01 38	02 10
45	18 53	19 25	20 05	00 35	01 17	01 50	02 20
S 50	19 06	19 43	20 30	00 56	01 35	02 07	02 32
52	19 12	19 52	20 43	01 06	01 44	02 14	02 38
54	19 19	20 01	20 57	01 17	01 54	02 22	02 44
56	19 27	20 12	21 15	01 30	02 05	02 32	02 51
58	19 36	20 25	21 37	01 45	02 18	02 41	02 59
S 60	19 46	20 40	22 06	02 02	02 32	02 53	03 07

Day	SUN Eqn. of Time 00ʰ	SUN Eqn. of Time 12ʰ	SUN Mer. Pass.	MOON Mer. Pass. Upper	MOON Mer. Pass. Lower	Age	Phase
d	m s	m s	h m	h m	h m	d	%
3	16 27	16 27	11 44	17 33	05 08	06	41
4	16 27	16 27	11 44	18 22	05 58	07	51
5	16 26	16 26	11 44	19 07	06 45	08	60

© British Crown Copyright 2018. All rights reserved.

UT	ARIES GHA	VENUS −3.8 GHA	Dec	MARS +1.8 GHA	Dec	JUPITER −1.9 GHA	Dec	SATURN +0.6 GHA	Dec	STARS Name	SHA	Dec
6 00	44 55.3	161 47.9	S21 39.9	204 57.7	S 7 33.3	141 05.4	S23 07.9	117 48.7	S22 22.7	Acamar	315 14.6	S40 13.6
01	59 57.7	176 47.1	40.6	219 58.7	33.9	156 07.3	07.9	132 51.0	22.7	Achernar	335 22.9	S57 08.4
02	75 00.2	191 46.3	41.2	234 59.6	34.6	171 09.2	07.9	147 53.2	22.7	Acrux	173 05.0	S63 12.2
03	90 02.6	206 45.5 ..	41.9	250 00.6 ..	35.2	186 11.2 ..	07.9	162 55.5 ..	22.7	Adhara	255 08.9	S28 59.8
04	105 05.1	221 44.7	42.5	265 01.5	35.8	201 13.1	08.0	177 57.7	22.6	Aldebaran	290 44.1	N16 32.8
05	120 07.6	236 43.9	43.2	280 02.4	36.4	216 15.0	08.0	193 00.0	22.6			
W 06	135 10.0	251 43.1	S21 43.9	295 03.4	S 7 37.1	231 16.9	S23 08.0	208 02.3	S22 22.6	Alioth	166 17.3	N55 51.2
E 07	150 12.5	266 42.3	44.5	310 04.3	37.7	246 18.9	08.0	223 04.5	22.6	Alkaid	152 55.9	N49 13.0
D 08	165 15.0	281 41.5	45.2	325 05.3	38.3	261 20.8	08.1	238 06.8	22.6	Alnair	27 38.1	S46 52.1
N 09	180 17.4	296 40.7 ..	45.8	340 06.2 ..	38.9	276 22.7 ..	08.1	253 09.1 ..	22.6	Alnilam	275 41.7	S 1 11.4
E 10	195 19.9	311 39.8	46.5	355 07.1	39.6	291 24.6	08.1	268 11.3	22.5	Alphard	217 51.8	S 8 44.5
S 11	210 22.4	326 39.0	47.1	10 08.1	40.2	306 26.6	08.1	283 13.6	22.5			
D 12	225 24.8	341 38.2	S21 47.8	25 09.0	S 7 40.8	321 28.5	S23 08.2	298 15.9	S22 22.5	Alphecca	126 07.7	N26 39.1
A 13	240 27.3	356 37.4	48.4	40 10.0	41.4	336 30.4	08.2	313 18.1	22.5	Alpheratz	357 38.7	N29 12.1
Y 14	255 29.8	11 36.6	49.1	55 10.9	42.1	351 32.3	08.2	328 20.4	22.5	Altair	62 04.1	N 8 55.4
15	270 32.2	26 35.8 ..	49.7	70 11.8 ..	42.7	6 34.3 ..	08.2	343 22.6 ..	22.4	Ankaa	353 11.0	S42 12.1
16	285 34.7	41 35.0	50.4	85 12.8	43.3	21 36.2	08.3	358 24.9	22.4	Antares	112 21.3	S26 28.4
17	300 37.1	56 34.2	51.0	100 13.7	43.9	36 38.1	08.3	13 27.2	22.4			
18	315 39.6	71 33.4	S21 51.7	115 14.7	S 7 44.5	51 40.0	S23 08.3	28 29.4	S22 22.4	Arcturus	145 52.1	N19 05.0
19	330 42.1	86 32.6	52.3	130 15.6	45.2	66 42.0	08.3	43 31.7	22.4	Atria	107 19.7	S69 03.7
20	345 44.5	101 31.8	53.0	145 16.6	45.8	81 43.9	08.4	58 34.0	22.4	Avior	234 16.2	S59 34.1
21	0 47.0	116 30.9 ..	53.6	160 17.5 ..	46.4	96 45.8 ..	08.4	73 36.2 ..	22.3	Bellatrix	278 27.1	N 6 22.0
22	15 49.5	131 30.1	54.3	175 18.4	47.0	111 47.7	08.4	88 38.5	22.3	Betelgeuse	270 56.3	N 7 24.6
23	30 51.9	146 29.3	54.9	190 19.4	47.7	126 49.6	08.4	103 40.7	22.3			
7 00	45 54.4	161 28.5	S21 55.5	205 20.3	S 7 48.3	141 51.6	S23 08.5	118 43.0	S22 22.3	Canopus	263 53.9	S52 42.2
01	60 56.9	176 27.7	56.2	220 21.3	48.9	156 53.5	08.5	133 45.3	22.3	Capella	280 27.6	N46 00.9
02	75 59.3	191 26.9	56.8	235 22.2	49.5	171 55.4	08.5	148 47.5	22.2	Deneb	49 28.6	N45 21.4
03	91 01.8	206 26.1 ..	57.4	250 23.1 ..	50.1	186 57.3 ..	08.5	163 49.8 ..	22.2	Denebola	182 29.4	N14 27.8
04	106 04.2	221 25.2	58.1	265 24.1	50.8	201 59.3	08.6	178 52.1	22.2	Diphda	348 51.2	S17 52.8
05	121 06.7	236 24.4	58.7	280 25.0	51.4	217 01.2	08.6	193 54.3	22.2			
T 06	136 09.2	251 23.6	S21 59.3	295 25.9	S 7 52.0	232 03.1	S23 08.6	208 56.6	S22 22.2	Dubhe	193 46.7	N61 38.5
H 07	151 11.6	266 22.8	22 00.0	310 26.9	52.6	247 05.0	08.7	223 58.8	22.2	Elnath	278 06.8	N28 37.3
U 08	166 14.1	281 22.0	00.6	325 27.8	53.3	262 06.9	08.7	239 01.1	22.1	Eltanin	90 44.5	N51 29.5
R 09	181 16.6	296 21.2 ..	01.2	340 28.8 ..	53.9	277 08.9 ..	08.7	254 03.4 ..	22.1	Enif	33 42.8	N 9 58.1
S 10	196 19.0	311 20.3	01.9	355 29.7	54.5	292 10.8	08.7	269 05.6	22.1	Fomalhaut	15 19.0	S29 31.2
D 11	211 21.5	326 19.5	02.5	10 30.6	55.1	307 12.7	08.8	284 07.9	22.1			
A 12	226 24.0	341 18.7	S22 03.1	25 31.6	S 7 55.7	322 14.6	S23 08.8	299 10.1	S22 22.1	Gacrux	171 56.5	S57 13.1
Y 13	241 26.4	356 17.9	03.7	40 32.5	56.4	337 16.5	08.8	314 12.4	22.0	Gienah	175 48.1	S17 38.8
14	256 28.9	11 17.1	04.4	55 33.5	57.0	352 18.5	08.8	329 14.7	22.0	Hadar	148 42.4	S60 27.8
15	271 31.4	26 16.3 ..	05.0	70 34.4 ..	57.6	7 20.4 ..	08.9	344 16.9 ..	22.0	Hamal	327 55.5	N23 33.3
16	286 33.8	41 15.4	05.6	85 35.3	58.2	22 22.3	08.9	359 19.2	22.0	Kaus Aust.	83 38.3	S34 22.4
17	301 36.3	56 14.6	06.2	100 36.3	58.8	37 24.2	08.9	14 21.4	22.0			
18	316 38.7	71 13.8	S22 06.9	115 37.2	S 7 59.5	52 26.1	S23 08.9	29 23.7	S22 21.9	Kochab	137 21.3	N74 04.6
19	331 41.2	86 13.0	07.5	130 38.1	8 00.1	67 28.1	09.0	44 26.0	21.9	Markab	13 33.8	N15 18.8
20	346 43.7	101 12.1	08.1	145 39.1	00.7	82 30.0	09.0	59 28.2	21.9	Menkar	314 10.2	N 4 10.0
21	1 46.1	116 11.3 ..	08.7	160 40.0 ..	01.3	97 31.9 ..	09.0	74 30.5 ..	21.9	Menkent	148 02.8	S36 27.8
22	16 48.6	131 10.5	09.3	175 41.0	02.0	112 33.8	09.0	89 32.7	21.9	Miaplacidus	221 38.9	S69 47.5
23	31 51.1	146 09.7	09.9	190 41.9	02.6	127 35.7	09.1	104 35.0	21.9			
8 00	46 53.5	161 08.8	S22 10.6	205 42.8	S 8 03.2	142 37.7	S23 09.1	119 37.3	S22 21.8	Mirfak	308 33.6	N49 55.8
01	61 56.0	176 08.0	11.2	220 43.8	03.8	157 39.6	09.1	134 39.5	21.8	Nunki	75 53.1	S26 16.3
02	76 58.5	191 07.2	11.8	235 44.7	04.4	172 41.5	09.1	149 41.8	21.8	Peacock	53 12.5	S56 40.4
03	92 00.9	206 06.4 ..	12.4	250 45.6 ..	05.1	187 43.4 ..	09.1	164 44.0 ..	21.8	Pollux	243 22.3	N27 58.6
04	107 03.4	221 05.5	13.0	265 46.6	05.7	202 45.3	09.2	179 46.3	21.8	Procyon	244 55.1	N 5 10.5
05	122 05.9	236 04.7	13.6	280 47.5	06.3	217 47.3	09.2	194 48.6	21.7			
F 06	137 08.3	251 03.9	S22 14.2	295 48.5	S 8 06.9	232 49.2	S23 09.2	209 50.8	S22 21.7	Rasalhague	96 02.7	N12 33.0
R 07	152 10.8	266 03.1	14.8	310 49.4	07.5	247 51.1	09.2	224 53.1	21.7	Regulus	207 39.0	N11 52.3
I 08	167 13.2	281 02.2	15.4	325 50.3	08.2	262 53.0	09.3	239 55.3	21.7	Rigel	281 07.6	S 8 10.7
D 09	182 15.7	296 01.4 ..	16.0	340 51.3 ..	08.8	277 54.9 ..	09.3	254 57.6 ..	21.7	Rigil Kent.	139 46.5	S60 54.7
A 10	197 18.2	311 00.6	16.6	355 52.2	09.4	292 56.8	09.3	269 59.8	21.6	Sabik	102 07.8	S15 44.8
Y 11	212 20.6	325 59.8	17.2	10 53.1	10.0	307 58.8	09.3	285 02.1	21.6			
12	227 23.1	340 58.9	S22 17.8	25 54.1	S 8 10.6	323 00.7	S23 09.4	300 04.4	S22 21.6	Schedar	349 35.1	N56 38.9
13	242 25.6	355 58.1	18.4	40 55.0	11.2	338 02.6	09.4	315 06.6	21.6	Shaula	96 16.3	S37 07.0
14	257 28.0	10 57.3	19.0	55 55.9	11.9	353 04.5	09.4	330 08.9	21.6	Sirius	258 29.7	S16 44.5
15	272 30.5	25 56.4 ..	19.6	70 56.9 ..	12.5	8 06.4 ..	09.4	345 11.1 ..	21.5	Spica	158 27.0	S11 15.6
16	287 33.0	40 55.6	20.2	85 57.8	13.1	23 08.3	09.5	0 13.4	21.5	Suhail	222 49.3	S43 30.4
17	302 35.4	55 54.8	20.8	100 58.8	13.7	38 10.3	09.5	15 15.6	21.5			
18	317 37.9	70 53.9	S22 21.4	115 59.7	S 8 14.3	53 12.2	S23 09.5	30 17.9	S22 21.5	Vega	80 36.3	N38 48.4
19	332 40.3	85 53.1	22.0	131 00.6	15.0	68 14.1	09.5	45 20.2	21.5	Zuben'ubi	137 00.9	S16 07.2
20	347 42.8	100 52.3	22.6	146 01.6	15.6	83 16.0	09.6	60 22.4	21.4		SHA	Mer.Pass.
21	2 45.3	115 51.4 ..	23.2	161 02.5 ..	16.2	98 17.9 ..	09.6	75 24.7 ..	21.4		° '	h m
22	17 47.7	130 50.6	23.8	176 03.4	16.8	113 19.8	09.6	90 26.9	21.4	Venus	115 34.1	13 15
23	32 50.2	145 49.8	24.4	191 04.4	17.4	128 21.8	09.6	105 29.2	21.4	Mars	159 25.9	10 18
	h m									Jupiter	95 57.2	14 31
Mer.Pass. 20 52.9		v −0.8	d 0.6	v 0.9	d 0.6	v 1.9	d 0.0	v 2.3	d 0.0	Saturn	72 48.6	16 03

© British Crown Copyright 2018. All rights reserved.

UT	SUN GHA	SUN Dec	MOON GHA	v	MOON Dec	d	HP
d h	° ′	° ′	° ′	′	° ′	′	′
6 00	184 06.2	S15 49.2	70 59.6	14.2	S14 59.0	9.1	54.3
01	199 06.2	50.0	85 32.8	14.3	14 49.9	9.1	54.3
02	214 06.2	50.7	100 06.1	14.4	14 40.8	9.1	54.3
03	229 06.2	.. 51.5	114 39.5	14.4	14 31.7	9.3	54.3
04	244 06.1	52.2	129 12.9	14.4	14 22.4	9.3	54.2
05	259 06.1	53.0	143 46.3	14.5	14 13.1	9.3	54.2
06	274 06.1	S15 53.7	158 19.8	14.6	S14 03.8	9.4	54.2
W 07	289 06.1	54.5	172 53.4	14.5	13 54.4	9.4	54.2
E 08	304 06.0	55.2	187 26.9	14.7	13 45.0	9.5	54.2
D 09	319 06.0	.. 56.0	202 00.6	14.6	13 35.5	9.6	54.2
N 10	334 06.0	56.7	216 34.2	14.8	13 25.9	9.6	54.2
E 11	349 06.0	57.5	231 08.0	14.7	13 16.3	9.7	54.2
S 12	4 06.0	S15 58.2	245 41.7	14.8	S13 06.6	9.7	54.2
D 13	19 05.9	59.0	260 15.5	14.9	12 56.9	9.7	54.2
A 14	34 05.9	15 59.7	274 49.4	14.8	12 47.2	9.9	54.2
Y 15	49 05.9	16 00.5	289 23.2	15.0	12 37.3	9.8	54.2
16	64 05.9	01.2	303 57.2	14.9	12 27.5	9.9	54.2
17	79 05.8	02.0	318 31.1	15.0	12 17.6	10.0	54.2
18	94 05.8	S16 02.7	333 05.1	15.1	S12 07.6	10.0	54.2
19	109 05.8	03.5	347 39.2	15.0	11 57.6	10.1	54.2
20	124 05.7	04.2	2 13.2	15.1	11 47.5	10.1	54.2
21	139 05.7	.. 05.0	16 47.3	15.2	11 37.4	10.1	54.2
22	154 05.7	05.7	31 21.5	15.2	11 27.3	10.2	54.2
23	169 05.7	06.4	45 55.7	15.2	11 17.1	10.3	54.1
7 00	184 05.6	S16 07.2	60 29.9	15.2	S11 06.8	10.3	54.1
01	199 05.6	07.9	75 04.1	15.3	10 56.5	10.3	54.1
02	214 05.6	08.7	89 38.4	15.3	10 46.2	10.3	54.1
03	229 05.5	.. 09.4	104 12.7	15.4	10 35.9	10.5	54.1
04	244 05.5	10.2	118 47.1	15.3	10 25.4	10.4	54.1
05	259 05.5	10.9	133 21.4	15.4	10 15.0	10.5	54.1
06	274 05.5	S16 11.6	147 55.8	15.5	S10 04.5	10.5	54.1
T 07	289 05.4	12.4	162 30.3	15.4	9 54.0	10.6	54.1
H 08	304 05.4	13.1	177 04.7	15.5	9 43.4	10.6	54.1
U 09	319 05.4	.. 13.9	191 39.2	15.5	9 32.8	10.7	54.1
R 10	334 05.3	14.6	206 13.7	15.6	9 22.1	10.7	54.1
S 11	349 05.3	15.3	220 48.3	15.5	9 11.4	10.7	54.1
D 12	4 05.3	S16 16.1	235 22.8	15.6	S 9 00.7	10.8	54.1
A 13	19 05.2	16.8	249 57.4	15.7	8 49.9	10.8	54.1
Y 14	34 05.2	17.5	264 32.1	15.6	8 39.1	10.8	54.1
15	49 05.2	.. 18.3	279 06.7	15.7	8 28.3	10.9	54.1
16	64 05.1	19.0	293 41.4	15.6	8 17.4	10.9	54.1
17	79 05.1	19.8	308 16.0	15.7	8 06.5	10.9	54.1
18	94 05.1	S16 20.5	322 50.7	15.8	S 7 55.6	11.0	54.1
19	109 05.0	21.2	337 25.5	15.7	7 44.6	11.0	54.1
20	124 05.0	22.0	352 00.2	15.8	7 33.6	11.0	54.2
21	139 05.0	.. 22.7	6 35.0	15.7	7 22.6	11.1	54.2
22	154 04.9	23.4	21 09.7	15.8	7 11.5	11.0	54.2
23	169 04.9	24.2	35 44.5	15.8	7 00.5	11.2	54.2
8 00	184 04.8	S16 24.9	50 19.3	15.9	S 6 49.3	11.1	54.2
01	199 04.8	25.6	64 54.2	15.8	6 38.2	11.2	54.2
02	214 04.8	26.4	79 29.0	15.8	6 27.0	11.2	54.2
03	229 04.7	.. 27.1	94 03.8	15.9	6 15.8	11.2	54.2
04	244 04.7	27.8	108 38.7	15.9	6 04.6	11.3	54.2
05	259 04.7	28.5	123 13.6	15.9	5 53.3	11.3	54.2
06	274 04.6	S16 29.3	137 48.5	15.9	S 5 42.0	11.3	54.2
07	289 04.6	30.0	152 23.4	15.9	5 30.7	11.3	54.2
08	304 04.5	30.7	166 58.3	15.9	5 19.4	11.4	54.2
F 09	319 04.5	.. 31.5	181 33.2	15.9	5 08.0	11.4	54.2
R 10	334 04.5	32.2	196 08.1	16.0	4 56.6	11.4	54.2
I 11	349 04.4	32.9	210 43.1	15.9	4 45.2	11.4	54.2
D 12	4 04.4	S16 33.6	225 18.0	15.9	S 4 33.8	11.5	54.2
A 13	19 04.3	34.4	239 52.9	16.0	4 22.3	11.5	54.2
Y 14	34 04.3	35.1	254 27.9	15.9	4 10.8	11.4	54.2
15	49 04.2	.. 35.8	269 02.8	16.0	3 59.4	11.6	54.2
16	64 04.2	36.5	283 37.8	15.9	3 47.8	11.5	54.3
17	79 04.2	37.3	298 12.7	16.0	3 36.3	11.5	54.3
18	94 04.1	S16 38.0	312 47.7	16.0	S 3 24.8	11.6	54.3
19	109 04.1	38.7	327 22.7	15.9	3 13.2	11.6	54.3
20	124 04.0	39.4	341 57.6	16.0	3 01.6	11.6	54.3
21	139 04.0	.. 40.2	356 32.6	15.9	2 50.0	11.6	54.3
22	154 03.9	40.9	11 07.5	16.0	2 38.4	11.6	54.3
23	169 03.9	41.6	25 42.5	15.9	S 2 26.8	11.7	54.3
	SD 16.2	d 0.7	SD 14.8		14.8		14.8

Twilight / Moonrise

Lat.	Naut.	Civil	Sunrise	Moonrise 6	7	8	9
°	h m	h m	h m	h m	h m	h m	h m
N 72	06 28	07 55	09 35	16 36	16 13	15 54	15 36
N 70	06 22	07 39	09 00	16 15	16 01	15 49	15 37
68	06 16	07 25	08 35	15 58	15 51	15 44	15 38
66	06 11	07 14	08 16	15 44	15 43	15 41	15 39
64	06 07	07 05	08 00	15 33	15 36	15 38	15 39
62	06 03	06 57	07 48	15 23	15 30	15 35	15 40
60	06 00	06 50	07 37	15 15	15 24	15 32	15 40
N 58	05 57	06 44	07 27	15 07	15 20	15 30	15 41
56	05 54	06 38	07 19	15 01	15 15	15 28	15 41
54	05 51	06 33	07 12	14 55	15 12	15 27	15 41
52	05 48	06 29	07 05	14 50	15 08	15 25	15 42
50	05 46	06 24	06 59	14 45	15 05	15 24	15 42
45	05 40	06 15	06 46	14 34	14 58	15 21	15 42
N 40	05 35	06 07	06 35	14 26	14 53	15 18	15 43
35	05 30	06 00	06 26	14 18	14 48	15 16	15 43
30	05 25	05 53	06 18	14 12	14 43	15 14	15 44
20	05 15	05 41	06 04	14 00	14 36	15 10	15 44
N 10	05 05	05 30	05 52	13 50	14 29	15 07	15 45
0	04 54	05 19	05 40	13 41	14 23	15 04	15 46
S 10	04 41	05 06	05 28	13 31	14 17	15 01	15 46
20	04 25	04 52	05 16	13 21	14 10	14 58	15 47
30	04 05	04 35	05 01	13 09	14 02	14 55	15 48
35	03 52	04 25	04 52	13 02	13 58	14 53	15 48
40	03 37	04 13	04 43	12 55	13 53	14 51	15 49
45	03 17	03 58	04 31	12 46	13 47	14 48	15 49
S 50	02 52	03 40	04 17	12 35	13 40	14 45	15 50
52	02 39	03 31	04 10	12 30	13 37	14 43	15 50
54	02 23	03 21	04 03	12 24	13 33	14 42	15 51
56	02 05	03 09	03 55	12 18	13 29	14 40	15 51
58	01 41	02 56	03 46	12 11	13 24	14 38	15 52
S 60	01 07	02 40	03 35	12 03	13 19	14 36	15 52

Sunset / Twilight / Moonset

Lat.	Sunset	Civil	Naut.	Moonset 6	7	8	9
°	h m	h m	h m	h m	h m	h m	h m
N 72	13 51	15 31	16 57	23 25	25 16	01 16	03 02
N 70	14 26	15 47	17 04	23 45	25 26	01 26	03 05
68	14 51	16 01	17 10	24 01	00 01	01 35	03 07
66	15 10	16 12	17 15	24 13	00 13	01 41	03 08
64	15 26	16 21	17 19	24 23	00 23	01 47	03 10
62	15 39	16 29	17 23	24 32	00 32	01 52	03 11
60	15 50	16 36	17 27	24 40	00 40	01 56	03 12
N 58	15 59	16 43	17 30	24 46	00 46	02 00	03 13
56	16 08	16 48	17 33	24 52	00 52	02 03	03 14
54	16 15	16 53	17 36	24 57	00 57	02 06	03 15
52	16 22	16 58	17 38	25 02	01 02	02 09	03 15
50	16 28	17 02	17 41	00 01	01 06	02 11	03 16
45	16 41	17 12	17 47	00 14	01 15	02 16	03 17
N 40	16 51	17 20	17 52	00 25	01 23	02 21	03 18
35	17 01	17 27	17 57	00 34	01 29	02 24	03 19
30	17 09	17 34	18 02	00 42	01 35	02 28	03 20
20	17 23	17 46	18 12	00 55	01 45	02 33	03 22
N 10	17 35	17 57	18 22	01 07	01 53	02 38	03 23
0	17 47	18 09	18 34	01 18	02 01	02 43	03 24
S 10	17 59	18 21	18 47	01 29	02 09	02 47	03 25
20	18 12	18 35	19 03	01 41	02 17	02 52	03 26
30	18 27	18 52	19 23	01 54	02 27	02 58	03 28
35	18 35	19 03	19 36	02 01	02 32	03 01	03 29
40	18 45	19 15	19 51	02 10	02 38	03 04	03 29
45	18 57	19 30	20 11	02 20	02 46	03 09	03 30
S 50	19 11	19 49	20 37	02 32	02 54	03 13	03 32
52	19 18	19 58	20 51	02 38	02 58	03 16	03 32
54	19 25	20 08	21 06	02 44	03 02	03 18	03 33
56	19 34	20 20	21 25	02 51	03 07	03 21	03 33
58	19 43	20 34	21 50	02 59	03 12	03 24	03 34
S 60	19 54	20 50	22 26	03 07	03 18	03 27	03 35

SUN / MOON

Day	Eqn. of Time 00h	12h	Mer. Pass.	Mer. Pass. Upper	Lower	Age	Phase
d	m s	m s	h m	h m	h m	d	%
6	16 25	16 24	11 44	19 51	07 29	09	69
7	16 23	16 21	11 44	20 33	08 12	10	78
8	16 19	16 18	11 44	21 14	08 54	11	85

© British Crown Copyright 2018. All rights reserved.

UT	ARIES GHA	VENUS −3.8 GHA	Dec	MARS +1.8 GHA	Dec	JUPITER −1.9 GHA	Dec	SATURN +0.6 GHA	Dec	STARS Name	SHA	Dec
9 00	47 52.7	160 48.9	S22 24.9	206 05.3	S 8 18.1	143 23.7	S23 09.7	120 31.4	S22 21.4	Acamar	315 14.6	S40 13.6
01	62 55.1	175 48.1	25.5	221 06.2	18.7	158 25.6	09.7	135 33.7	21.4	Achernar	335 22.9	S57 08.4
02	77 57.6	190 47.3	26.1	236 07.2	19.3	173 27.5	09.7	150 35.9	21.3	Acrux	173 05.0	S63 12.2
03	93 00.1	205 46.4 ..	26.7	251 08.1 ..	19.9	188 29.4 ..	09.7	165 38.2 ..	21.3	Adhara	255 08.9	S28 59.8
04	108 02.5	220 45.6	27.3	266 09.0	20.5	203 31.3	09.8	180 40.5	21.3	Aldebaran	290 44.0	N16 32.8
05	123 05.0	235 44.7	27.9	281 10.0	21.1	218 33.3	09.8	195 42.7	21.3			
06	138 07.5	250 43.9	S22 28.4	296 10.9	S 8 21.8	233 35.2	S23 09.8	210 45.0	S22 21.3	Alioth	166 17.3	N55 51.1
07	153 09.9	265 43.1	29.0	311 11.8	22.4	248 37.1	09.8	225 47.2	21.2	Alkaid	152 55.9	N49 13.0
S 08	168 12.4	280 42.2	29.6	326 12.8	23.0	263 39.0	09.9	240 49.5	21.2	Alnair	27 38.1	S46 52.1
A 09	183 14.8	295 41.4 ..	30.2	341 13.7 ..	23.6	278 40.9 ..	09.9	255 51.7 ..	21.2	Alnilam	275 41.7	S 1 11.4
T 10	198 17.3	310 40.6	30.7	356 14.6	24.2	293 42.8	09.9	270 54.0	21.2	Alphard	217 51.8	S 8 44.5
U 11	213 19.8	325 39.7	31.3	11 15.6	24.8	308 44.7	09.9	285 56.2	21.2			
R 12	228 22.2	340 38.9	S22 31.9	26 16.5	S 8 25.5	323 46.7	S23 09.9	300 58.5	S22 21.1	Alphecca	126 07.7	N26 39.1
D 13	243 24.7	355 38.0	32.5	41 17.4	26.1	338 48.6	10.0	316 00.7	21.1	Alpheratz	357 38.7	N29 12.1
A 14	258 27.2	10 37.2	33.0	56 18.4	26.7	353 50.5	10.0	331 03.0	21.1	Altair	62 04.1	N 8 55.4
Y 15	273 29.6	25 36.3 ..	33.6	71 19.3 ..	27.3	8 52.4 ..	10.0	346 05.2 ..	21.1	Ankaa	353 11.0	S42 12.1
16	288 32.1	40 35.5	34.2	86 20.2	27.9	23 54.3	10.0	1 07.5	21.1	Antares	112 21.3	S26 28.4
17	303 34.6	55 34.7	34.7	101 21.2	28.5	38 56.2	10.1	16 09.8	21.0			
18	318 37.0	70 33.8	S22 35.3	116 22.1	S 8 29.2	53 58.1	S23 10.1	31 12.0	S22 21.0	Arcturus	145 52.1	N19 05.0
19	333 39.5	85 33.0	35.9	131 23.0	29.8	69 00.1	10.1	46 14.3	21.0	Atria	107 19.7	S69 03.7
20	348 41.9	100 32.1	36.4	146 24.0	30.4	84 02.0	10.1	61 16.5	21.0	Avior	234 16.1	S59 34.1
21	3 44.4	115 31.3 ..	37.0	161 24.9 ..	31.0	99 03.9 ..	10.2	76 18.8 ..	21.0	Bellatrix	278 27.0	N 6 22.0
22	18 46.9	130 30.4	37.6	176 25.8	31.6	114 05.8	10.2	91 21.0	20.9	Betelgeuse	270 56.3	N 7 24.6
23	33 49.3	145 29.6	38.1	191 26.8	32.2	129 07.7	10.2	106 23.3	20.9			
10 00	48 51.8	160 28.8	S22 38.7	206 27.7	S 8 32.9	144 09.6	S23 10.2	121 25.5	S22 20.9	Canopus	263 53.8	S52 42.2
01	63 54.3	175 27.9	39.2	221 28.6	33.5	159 11.5	10.3	136 27.8	20.9	Capella	280 27.6	N46 00.9
02	78 56.7	190 27.1	39.8	236 29.6	34.1	174 13.4	10.3	151 30.0	20.9	Deneb	49 28.6	N45 21.4
03	93 59.2	205 26.2 ..	40.4	251 30.5 ..	34.7	189 15.4 ..	10.3	166 32.3 ..	20.8	Denebola	182 29.4	N14 27.8
04	109 01.7	220 25.4	40.9	266 31.4	35.3	204 17.3	10.3	181 34.5	20.8	Diphda	348 51.2	S17 52.8
05	124 04.1	235 24.5	41.5	281 32.4	35.9	219 19.2	10.3	196 36.8	20.8			
06	139 06.6	250 23.7	S22 42.0	296 33.3	S 8 36.6	234 21.1	S23 10.4	211 39.0	S22 20.8	Dubhe	193 46.6	N61 38.5
07	154 09.1	265 22.8	42.6	311 34.2	37.2	249 23.0	10.4	226 41.3	20.8	Elnath	278 06.8	N28 37.3
S 08	169 11.5	280 22.0	43.1	326 35.1	37.8	264 24.9	10.4	241 43.5	20.7	Eltanin	90 44.5	N51 29.5
U 09	184 14.0	295 21.1 ..	43.7	341 36.1 ..	38.4	279 26.8 ..	10.4	256 45.8 ..	20.7	Enif	33 42.8	N 9 58.1
N 10	199 16.4	310 20.3	44.2	356 37.0	39.0	294 28.7	10.5	271 48.0	20.7	Fomalhaut	15 19.0	S29 31.2
D 11	214 18.9	325 19.4	44.8	11 37.9	39.6	309 30.7	10.5	286 50.3	20.7			
A 12	229 21.4	340 18.6	S22 45.3	26 38.9	S 8 40.2	324 32.6	S23 10.5	301 52.5	S22 20.7	Gacrux	171 56.5	S57 13.1
Y 13	244 23.8	355 17.7	45.9	41 39.8	40.9	339 34.5	10.5	316 54.8	20.6	Gienah	175 48.1	S17 38.8
14	259 26.3	10 16.9	46.4	56 40.7	41.5	354 36.4	10.6	331 57.0	20.6	Hadar	148 42.4	S60 27.8
15	274 28.8	25 16.0 ..	46.9	71 41.7 ..	42.1	9 38.3 ..	10.6	346 59.3 ..	20.6	Hamal	327 55.5	N23 33.3
16	289 31.2	40 15.2	47.5	86 42.6	42.7	24 40.2	10.6	2 01.5	20.6	Kaus Aust.	83 38.3	S34 22.4
17	304 33.7	55 14.3	48.0	101 43.5	43.3	39 42.1	10.6	17 03.8	20.6			
18	319 36.2	70 13.5	S22 48.6	116 44.4	S 8 43.9	54 44.0	S23 10.6	32 06.0	S22 20.5	Kochab	137 21.3	N74 04.5
19	334 38.6	85 12.6	49.1	131 45.4	44.5	69 45.9	10.7	47 08.3	20.5	Markab	13 33.8	N15 18.8
20	349 41.1	100 11.7	49.6	146 46.3	45.2	84 47.8	10.7	62 10.5	20.5	Menkar	314 10.2	N 4 10.0
21	4 43.6	115 10.9 ..	50.2	161 47.2 ..	45.8	99 49.8 ..	10.7	77 12.8 ..	20.5	Menkent	148 02.8	S36 27.7
22	19 46.0	130 10.0	50.7	176 48.2	46.4	114 51.7	10.7	92 15.0	20.5	Miaplacidus	221 38.8	S69 47.5
23	34 48.5	145 09.2	51.2	191 49.1	47.0	129 53.6	10.8	107 17.3	20.4			
11 00	49 50.9	160 08.3	S22 51.8	206 50.0	S 8 47.6	144 55.5	S23 10.8	122 19.5	S22 20.4	Mirfak	308 33.6	N49 55.8
01	64 53.4	175 07.5	52.3	221 51.0	48.2	159 57.4	10.8	137 21.8	20.4	Nunki	75 53.1	S26 16.3
02	79 55.9	190 06.6	52.8	236 51.9	48.8	174 59.3	10.8	152 24.0	20.4	Peacock	53 12.5	S56 40.4
03	94 58.3	205 05.8 ..	53.4	251 52.8 ..	49.5	190 01.2 ..	10.8	167 26.3 ..	20.4	Pollux	243 22.3	N27 58.6
04	110 00.8	220 04.9	53.9	266 53.7	50.1	205 03.1	10.9	182 28.5	20.3	Procyon	244 55.0	N 5 10.4
05	125 03.3	235 04.0	54.4	281 54.7	50.7	220 05.0	10.9	197 30.8	20.3			
06	140 05.7	250 03.2	S22 54.9	296 55.6	S 8 51.3	235 06.9	S23 10.9	212 33.0	S22 20.3	Rasalhague	96 02.7	N12 33.0
07	155 08.2	265 02.3	55.5	311 56.5	51.9	250 08.9	10.9	227 35.3	20.3	Regulus	207 39.0	N11 52.3
08	170 10.7	280 01.5	56.0	326 57.4	52.5	265 10.8	11.0	242 37.5	20.2	Rigel	281 07.6	S 8 10.7
M 09	185 13.1	295 00.6 ..	56.5	341 58.4 ..	53.1	280 12.7 ..	11.0	257 39.8 ..	20.2	Rigil Kent.	139 46.5	S60 54.7
O 10	200 15.6	309 59.7	57.0	356 59.3	53.8	295 14.6	11.0	272 42.0	20.2	Sabik	102 07.8	S15 44.8
N 11	215 18.0	324 58.9	57.6	12 00.2	54.4	310 16.5	11.0	287 44.3	20.2			
D 12	230 20.5	339 58.0	S22 58.1	27 01.2	S 8 55.0	325 18.4	S23 11.0	302 46.5	S22 20.2	Schedar	349 35.1	N56 38.9
A 13	245 23.0	354 57.2	58.6	42 02.1	55.6	340 20.3	11.1	317 48.8	20.1	Shaula	96 16.3	S37 07.0
Y 14	260 25.4	9 56.3	59.1	57 03.0	56.2	355 22.2	11.1	332 51.0	20.1	Sirius	258 29.7	S16 44.5
15	275 27.9	24 55.4	22 59.6	72 03.9 ..	56.8	10 24.1 ..	11.1	347 53.3 ..	20.1	Spica	158 27.0	S11 15.6
16	290 30.4	39 54.6	23 00.1	87 04.9	57.4	25 26.0	11.1	2 55.5	20.1	Suhail	222 49.2	S43 30.4
17	305 32.8	54 53.7	00.6	102 05.8	58.0	40 27.9	11.2	17 57.8	20.1			
18	320 35.3	69 52.8	S23 01.2	117 06.7	S 8 58.7	55 29.8	S23 11.2	33 00.0	S22 20.0	Vega	80 36.3	N38 48.4
19	335 37.8	84 52.0	01.7	132 07.7	59.3	70 31.7	11.2	48 02.3	20.0	Zuben'ubi	137 00.9	S16 07.2
20	350 40.2	99 51.1	02.2	147 08.6	8 59.9	85 33.7	11.2	63 04.5	20.0		SHA	Mer. Pass.
21	5 42.7	114 50.3 ..	02.7	162 09.5	9 00.5	100 35.6 ..	11.2	78 06.7 ..	20.0			h m
22	20 45.2	129 49.4	03.2	177 10.4	01.1	115 37.5	11.3	93 09.0	20.0	Venus	111 36.9	13 19
23	35 47.6	144 48.5	03.7	192 11.4	01.7	130 39.4	11.3	108 11.2	19.9	Mars	157 35.9	10 14
	h m									Jupiter	95 17.8	14 22
Mer. Pass.	20 41.1	v −0.9	d 0.5	v 0.9	d 0.6	v 1.9	d 0.0	v 2.3	d 0.0	Saturn	72 33.7	15 52

© British Crown Copyright 2018. All rights reserved.

UT	SUN GHA	SUN Dec	MOON GHA	v	MOON Dec	d	HP
d h	° ′	° ′	° ′	′	° ′	′	′
9 00	184 03.8	S16 42.3	40 17.4	16.0	S 2 15.1	11.7	54.3
01	199 03.8	43.0	54 52.4	15.9	2 03.4	11.6	54.3
02	214 03.7	43.8	69 27.3	15.9	1 51.8	11.7	54.3
03	229 03.7 ..	44.5	84 02.2	16.0	1 40.1	11.7	54.4
04	244 03.7	45.2	98 37.2	15.9	1 28.4	11.7	54.4
05	259 03.6	45.9	113 12.1	15.9	1 16.7	11.7	54.4
06	274 03.6	S16 46.6	127 47.0	15.9	S 1 05.0	11.8	54.4
S 07	289 03.5	47.3	142 21.9	15.9	0 53.2	11.7	54.4
A 08	304 03.5	48.1	156 56.8	15.9	0 41.5	11.8	54.4
T 09	319 03.4 ..	48.8	171 31.7	15.8	0 29.7	11.7	54.4
U 10	334 03.4	49.5	186 06.5	15.9	0 18.0	11.8	54.4
R 11	349 03.3	50.2	200 41.4	15.8	S 0 06.2	11.8	54.4
D 12	4 03.3	S16 50.9	215 16.2	15.9	N 0 05.6	11.7	54.4
A 13	19 03.2	51.6	229 51.1	15.8	0 17.3	11.8	54.5
Y 14	34 03.2	52.3	244 25.9	15.8	0 29.1	11.8	54.5
15	49 03.1 ..	53.1	259 00.7	15.7	0 40.9	11.8	54.5
16	64 03.1	53.8	273 35.4	15.8	0 52.7	11.8	54.5
17	79 03.0	54.5	288 10.2	15.7	1 04.5	11.8	54.5
18	94 03.0	S16 55.2	302 44.9	15.8	N 1 16.3	11.8	54.5
19	109 02.9	55.9	317 19.7	15.7	1 28.1	11.8	54.5
20	124 02.9	56.6	331 54.4	15.7	1 39.9	11.8	54.5
21	139 02.8 ..	57.3	346 29.1	15.6	1 51.7	11.8	54.6
22	154 02.7	58.0	1 03.7	15.7	2 03.5	11.8	54.6
23	169 02.7	58.7	15 38.4	15.6	2 15.3	11.8	54.6
10 00	184 02.6	S16 59.5	30 13.0	15.6	N 2 27.1	11.8	54.6
01	199 02.6	17 00.2	44 47.6	15.5	2 38.9	11.8	54.6
02	214 02.5	00.9	59 22.1	15.6	2 50.7	11.7	54.6
03	229 02.5 ..	01.6	73 56.7	15.5	3 02.4	11.8	54.6
04	244 02.4	02.3	88 31.2	15.5	3 14.2	11.8	54.7
05	259 02.4	03.0	103 05.7	15.4	3 26.0	11.8	54.7
06	274 02.3	S17 03.7	117 40.1	15.5	N 3 37.8	11.7	54.7
07	289 02.2	04.4	132 14.6	15.4	3 49.5	11.8	54.7
S 08	304 02.2	05.1	146 49.0	15.4	4 01.3	11.7	54.7
U 09	319 02.1 ..	05.8	161 23.4	15.3	4 13.0	11.8	54.7
N 10	334 02.1	06.5	175 57.7	15.3	4 24.8	11.7	54.7
D 11	349 02.0	07.2	190 32.0	15.3	4 36.5	11.7	54.8
A 12	4 02.0	S17 07.9	205 06.3	15.2	N 4 48.2	11.7	54.8
Y 13	19 01.9	08.6	219 40.5	15.2	4 59.9	11.7	54.8
14	34 01.8	09.3	234 14.7	15.2	5 11.6	11.7	54.8
15	49 01.8 ..	10.0	248 48.9	15.1	5 23.3	11.6	54.8
16	64 01.7	10.7	263 23.0	15.1	5 34.9	11.7	54.8
17	79 01.7	11.4	277 57.1	15.1	5 46.6	11.6	54.9
18	94 01.6	S17 12.1	292 31.2	15.0	N 5 58.2	11.6	54.9
19	109 01.5	12.8	307 05.2	15.0	6 09.8	11.6	54.9
20	124 01.5	13.5	321 39.2	15.0	6 21.4	11.6	54.9
21	139 01.4 ..	14.2	336 13.2	14.9	6 33.0	11.6	54.9
22	154 01.3	14.9	350 47.1	14.8	6 44.6	11.5	54.9
23	169 01.3	15.6	5 20.9	14.8	6 56.1	11.6	54.9
11 00	184 01.2	S17 16.3	19 54.7	14.8	N 7 07.7	11.5	55.0
01	199 01.2	17.0	34 28.5	14.8	7 19.2	11.4	55.0
02	214 01.1	17.7	49 02.3	14.6	7 30.6	11.5	55.0
03	229 01.0 ..	18.4	63 35.9	14.7	7 42.1	11.4	55.0
04	244 01.0	19.1	78 09.6	14.6	7 53.5	11.4	55.0
05	259 00.9	19.8	92 43.2	14.5	8 04.9	11.4	55.1
06	274 00.8	S17 20.5	107 16.7	14.5	N 8 16.3	11.4	55.1
07	289 00.8	21.2	121 50.2	14.5	8 27.7	11.3	55.1
08	304 00.7	21.9	136 23.7	14.4	8 39.0	11.3	55.1
M 09	319 00.6 ..	22.6	150 57.1	14.4	8 50.3	11.2	55.1
O 10	334 00.6	23.2	165 30.5	14.3	9 01.5	11.3	55.1
N 11	349 00.5	23.9	180 03.8	14.2	9 12.8	11.2	55.2
D 12	4 00.4	S17 24.6	194 37.0	14.2	N 9 24.0	11.2	55.2
A 13	19 00.4	25.3	209 10.2	14.2	9 35.2	11.1	55.2
Y 14	34 00.3	26.0	223 43.4	14.1	9 46.3	11.1	55.2
15	49 00.2 ..	26.7	238 16.5	14.1	9 57.4	11.1	55.2
16	64 00.2	27.4	252 49.6	13.9	10 08.5	11.0	55.2
17	79 00.1	28.1	267 22.5	14.0	10 19.5	11.0	55.3
18	94 00.0	S17 28.8	281 55.5	13.9	N10 30.5	11.0	55.3
19	108 59.9	29.4	296 28.4	13.8	10 41.5	10.9	55.3
20	123 59.9	30.1	311 01.2	13.8	10 52.4	10.9	55.3
21	138 59.8 ..	30.8	325 34.0	13.7	11 03.3	10.8	55.3
22	153 59.7	31.5	340 06.7	13.6	11 14.1	10.9	55.4
23	168 59.7	32.2	354 39.3	13.6	N11 25.0	10.7	55.4
	SD 16.2	d 0.7	SD 14.8		14.9		15.0

Lat.	Twilight Naut.	Twilight Civil	Sunrise	Moonrise 9	Moonrise 10	Moonrise 11	Moonrise 12
°	h m	h m	h m	h m	h m	h m	h m
N 72	06 40	08 09	09 59	15 36	15 18	14 58	14 30
N 70	06 32	07 50	09 17	15 37	15 26	15 13	14 57
68	06 25	07 36	08 48	15 38	15 32	15 25	15 18
66	06 19	07 23	08 27	15 39	15 37	15 35	15 34
64	06 14	07 13	08 10	15 39	15 41	15 44	15 48
62	06 10	07 05	07 56	15 40	15 45	15 51	15 59
60	06 06	06 57	07 44	15 40	15 48	15 57	16 09
N 58	06 02	06 50	07 34	15 41	15 51	16 03	16 17
56	05 59	06 44	07 25	15 41	15 54	16 08	16 25
54	05 56	06 39	07 17	15 41	15 56	16 13	16 32
52	05 53	06 34	07 10	15 42	15 58	16 17	16 38
50	05 50	06 29	07 04	15 42	16 00	16 21	16 43
45	05 44	06 19	06 50	15 42	16 05	16 29	16 55
N 40	05 38	06 10	06 39	15 43	16 08	16 35	17 05
35	05 32	06 03	06 29	15 43	16 11	16 41	17 14
30	05 27	05 56	06 21	15 44	16 14	16 47	17 22
20	05 16	05 43	06 06	15 44	16 19	16 56	17 35
N 10	05 05	05 31	05 53	15 45	16 24	17 04	17 46
0	04 54	05 19	05 40	15 46	16 28	17 11	17 57
S 10	04 40	05 06	05 28	15 46	16 32	17 19	18 08
20	04 24	04 51	05 14	15 47	16 36	17 27	18 20
30	04 02	04 33	04 59	15 48	16 41	17 37	18 33
35	03 49	04 22	04 50	15 48	16 44	17 42	18 41
40	03 33	04 10	04 39	15 49	16 48	17 48	18 50
45	03 12	03 54	04 27	15 49	16 52	17 55	19 01
S 50	02 45	03 34	04 12	15 50	16 56	18 04	19 14
52	02 31	03 25	04 05	15 50	16 59	18 08	19 20
54	02 15	03 14	03 57	15 51	17 01	18 13	19 26
56	01 54	03 02	03 49	15 51	17 04	18 18	19 34
58	01 27	02 47	03 39	15 52	17 07	18 23	19 42
S 60	00 45	02 30	03 27	15 52	17 10	18 30	19 52

Lat.	Sunset	Twilight Civil	Twilight Naut.	Moonset 9	Moonset 10	Moonset 11	Moonset 12
°	h m	h m	h m	h m	h m	h m	h m
N 72	13 27	15 17	16 47	03 02	04 48	06 39	08 41
N 70	14 10	15 36	16 55	03 05	04 43	06 25	08 15
68	14 38	15 51	17 01	03 07	04 39	06 15	07 56
66	15 00	16 03	17 07	03 08	04 36	06 06	07 40
64	15 17	16 13	17 12	03 10	04 34	05 59	07 28
62	15 31	16 22	17 17	03 11	04 31	05 53	07 18
60	15 43	16 30	17 21	03 12	04 29	05 48	07 09
N 58	15 53	16 37	17 24	03 13	04 27	05 43	07 01
56	16 02	16 43	17 28	03 14	04 26	05 39	06 54
54	16 10	16 48	17 31	03 15	04 24	05 35	06 48
52	16 17	16 53	17 34	03 15	04 23	05 32	06 42
50	16 23	16 58	17 37	03 16	04 22	05 29	06 37
45	16 37	17 08	17 43	03 17	04 19	05 22	06 27
N 40	16 48	17 17	17 49	03 18	04 17	05 17	06 18
35	16 58	17 25	17 55	03 19	04 15	05 12	06 10
30	17 07	17 32	18 01	03 20	04 13	05 08	06 04
20	17 22	17 45	18 11	03 22	04 11	05 01	05 52
N 10	17 35	17 57	18 22	03 23	04 08	04 54	05 42
0	17 47	18 09	18 34	03 24	04 06	04 48	05 33
S 10	18 00	18 22	18 48	03 25	04 03	04 42	05 24
20	18 14	18 37	19 04	03 26	04 01	04 36	05 14
30	18 29	18 55	19 26	03 28	03 58	04 29	05 03
35	18 38	19 06	19 39	03 29	03 56	04 25	04 56
40	18 49	19 19	19 56	03 29	03 54	04 20	04 49
45	19 01	19 35	20 17	03 30	03 52	04 15	04 40
S 50	19 16	19 55	20 44	03 32	03 50	04 09	04 30
52	19 24	20 04	20 59	03 32	03 49	04 06	04 25
54	19 32	20 15	21 15	03 33	03 47	04 03	04 20
56	19 40	20 28	21 37	03 33	03 46	04 00	04 14
58	19 51	20 43	22 05	03 34	03 44	03 55	04 08
S 60	20 02	21 00	22 51	03 35	03 43	03 51	04 01

Day	SUN Eqn. of Time 00h	SUN Eqn. of Time 12h	SUN Mer. Pass.	MOON Mer. Pass. Upper	MOON Mer. Pass. Lower	Age	Phase
d	m s	m s	h m	h m	h m	d	%
9	16 15	16 13	11 44	21 56	09 35	12	91
10	16 11	16 08	11 44	22 38	10 17	13	96
11	16 05	16 02	11 44	23 22	11 00	14	99

© British Crown Copyright 2018. All rights reserved.

UT	ARIES GHA	VENUS −3.8 GHA	Dec	MARS +1.8 GHA	Dec	JUPITER −1.9 GHA	Dec	SATURN +0.6 GHA	Dec	STARS Name	SHA	Dec
12 00	50 50.1	159 47.7	S23 04.2	207 12.3	S 9 02.3	145 41.3	S23 11.3	123 13.5	S22 19.9	Acamar	315 14.6	S40 13.6
01	65 52.5	174 46.8	04.7	222 13.2	02.9	160 43.2	11.3	138 15.7	19.9	Achernar	335 22.9	S57 08.4
02	80 55.0	189 45.9	05.2	237 14.1	03.5	175 45.1	11.4	153 18.0	19.9	Acrux	173 04.9	S63 12.2
03	95 57.5	204 45.1 ..	05.7	252 15.1 ..	04.2	190 47.0 ..	11.4	168 20.2 ..	19.9	Adhara	255 08.9	S28 59.8
04	110 59.9	219 44.2	06.2	267 16.0	04.8	205 48.9	11.4	183 22.5	19.8	Aldebaran	290 44.0	N16 32.8
05	126 02.4	234 43.3	06.7	282 16.9	05.4	220 50.8	11.4	198 24.7	19.8			
06	141 04.9	249 42.5	S23 07.2	297 17.8	S 9 06.0	235 52.7	S23 11.4	213 27.0	S22 19.8	Alioth	166 17.3	N55 51.1
07	156 07.3	264 41.6	07.7	312 18.8	06.6	250 54.6	11.5	228 29.2	19.8	Alkaid	152 55.9	N49 12.9
T 08	171 09.8	279 40.7	08.2	327 19.7	07.2	265 56.5	11.5	243 31.4	19.7	Alnair	27 38.2	S46 52.1
U 09	186 12.3	294 39.8 ..	08.7	342 20.6 ..	07.8	280 58.4 ..	11.5	258 33.7 ..	19.7	Alnilam	275 41.7	S 1 11.4
E 10	201 14.7	309 39.0	09.2	357 21.5	08.4	296 00.3	11.5	273 35.9	19.7	Alphard	217 51.8	S 8 44.5
S 11	216 17.2	324 38.1	09.7	12 22.5	09.0	311 02.2	11.6	288 38.2	19.7			
D 12	231 19.7	339 37.2	S23 10.2	27 23.4	S 9 09.7	326 04.1	S23 11.6	303 40.4	S22 19.7	Alphecca	126 07.7	N26 39.1
A 13	246 22.1	354 36.4	10.7	42 24.3	10.3	341 06.1	11.6	318 42.7	19.6	Alpheratz	357 38.8	N29 12.1
Y 14	261 24.6	9 35.5	11.1	57 25.2	10.9	356 08.0	11.6	333 44.9	19.6	Altair	62 04.1	N 8 55.4
15	276 27.0	24 34.6 ..	11.6	72 26.2 ..	11.5	11 09.9 ..	11.6	348 47.2 ..	19.6	Ankaa	353 11.1	S42 12.1
16	291 29.5	39 33.8	12.1	87 27.1	12.1	26 11.8	11.7	3 49.4	19.6	Antares	112 21.3	S26 28.4
17	306 32.0	54 32.9	12.6	102 28.0	12.7	41 13.7	11.7	18 51.6	19.6			
18	321 34.4	69 32.0	S23 13.1	117 28.9	S 9 13.3	56 15.6	S23 11.7	33 53.9	S22 19.5	Arcturus	145 52.1	N19 04.9
19	336 36.9	84 31.1	13.6	132 29.9	13.9	71 17.5	11.7	48 56.1	19.5	Atria	107 19.7	S69 03.7
20	351 39.4	99 30.3	14.1	147 30.8	14.5	86 19.4	11.7	63 58.4	19.5	Avior	234 16.1	S59 34.1
21	6 41.8	114 29.4 ..	14.5	162 31.7 ..	15.1	101 21.3 ..	11.8	79 00.6 ..	19.5	Bellatrix	278 27.0	N 6 22.0
22	21 44.3	129 28.5	15.0	177 32.6	15.7	116 23.2	11.8	94 02.9	19.4	Betelgeuse	270 56.3	N 7 24.6
23	36 46.8	144 27.6	15.5	192 33.5	16.4	131 25.1	11.8	109 05.1	19.4			
13 00	51 49.2	159 26.8	S23 16.0	207 34.5	S 9 17.0	146 27.0	S23 11.8	124 07.4	S22 19.4	Canopus	263 53.8	S52 42.2
01	66 51.7	174 25.9	16.4	222 35.4	17.6	161 28.9	11.9	139 09.6	19.4	Capella	280 27.6	N46 00.9
02	81 54.1	189 25.0	16.9	237 36.3	18.2	176 30.8	11.9	154 11.8	19.4	Deneb	49 28.6	N45 21.4
03	96 56.6	204 24.1 ..	17.4	252 37.2 ..	18.8	191 32.7 ..	11.9	169 14.1 ..	19.3	Denebola	182 29.4	N14 27.8
04	111 59.1	219 23.3	17.9	267 38.2	19.4	206 34.6	11.9	184 16.3	19.3	Diphda	348 51.2	S17 52.8
05	127 01.5	234 22.4	18.3	282 39.1	20.0	221 36.5	11.9	199 18.6	19.3			
06	142 04.0	249 21.5	S23 18.8	297 40.0	S 9 20.6	236 38.4	S23 12.0	214 20.8	S22 19.3	Dubhe	193 46.6	N61 38.5
W 07	157 06.5	264 20.6	19.3	312 40.9	21.2	251 40.3	12.0	229 23.1	19.3	Elnath	278 06.8	N28 37.3
E 08	172 08.9	279 19.7	19.7	327 41.9	21.8	266 42.2	12.0	244 25.3	19.2	Eltanin	90 44.5	N51 29.5
D 09	187 11.4	294 18.9 ..	20.2	342 42.8 ..	22.4	281 44.1 ..	12.0	259 27.5 ..	19.2	Enif	33 42.8	N 9 58.1
N 10	202 13.9	309 18.0	20.7	357 43.7	23.1	296 46.0	12.0	274 29.8	19.2	Fomalhaut	15 19.0	S29 31.2
E 11	217 16.3	324 17.1	21.1	12 44.6	23.7	311 47.9	12.1	289 32.0	19.2			
S 12	232 18.8	339 16.2	S23 21.6	27 45.5	S 9 24.3	326 49.8	S23 12.1	304 34.3	S22 19.1	Gacrux	171 56.5	S57 13.1
D 13	247 21.3	354 15.4	22.1	42 46.5	24.9	341 51.7	12.1	319 36.5	19.1	Gienah	175 48.0	S17 38.8
A 14	262 23.7	9 14.5	22.5	57 47.4	25.5	356 53.6	12.1	334 38.7	19.1	Hadar	148 42.3	S60 27.8
Y 15	277 26.2	24 13.6 ..	23.0	72 48.3 ..	26.1	11 55.5 ..	12.1	349 41.0 ..	19.1	Hamal	327 55.5	N23 33.3
16	292 28.6	39 12.7	23.4	87 49.2	26.7	26 57.4	12.2	4 43.2	19.1	Kaus Aust.	83 38.3	S34 22.4
17	307 31.1	54 11.8	23.9	102 50.1	27.3	41 59.3	12.2	19 45.5	19.0			
18	322 33.6	69 10.9	S23 24.3	117 51.1	S 9 27.9	57 01.2	S23 12.2	34 47.7	S22 19.0	Kochab	137 21.3	N74 04.5
19	337 36.0	84 10.1	24.8	132 52.0	28.5	72 03.1	12.2	49 49.9	19.0	Markab	13 33.9	N15 18.8
20	352 38.5	99 09.2	25.2	147 52.9	29.1	87 05.0	12.2	64 52.2	19.0	Menkar	314 10.2	N 4 10.0
21	7 41.0	114 08.3 ..	25.7	162 53.8 ..	29.7	102 06.9 ..	12.3	79 54.4 ..	19.0	Menkent	148 02.8	S36 27.7
22	22 43.4	129 07.4	26.2	177 54.7	30.3	117 08.8	12.3	94 56.7	18.9	Miaplacidus	221 38.8	S69 47.5
23	37 45.9	144 06.5	26.6	192 55.7	30.9	132 10.7	12.3	109 58.9	18.9			
14 00	52 48.4	159 05.6	S23 27.0	207 56.6	S 9 31.6	147 12.6	S23 12.3	125 01.1	S22 18.9	Mirfak	308 33.6	N49 55.8
01	67 50.8	174 04.8	27.5	222 57.5	32.2	162 14.6	12.3	140 03.4	18.9	Nunki	75 53.1	S26 16.3
02	82 53.3	189 03.9	27.9	237 58.4	32.8	177 16.5	12.4	155 05.6	18.8	Peacock	53 12.5	S56 40.4
03	97 55.8	204 03.0 ..	28.4	252 59.3 ..	33.4	192 18.4 ..	12.4	170 07.9 ..	18.8	Pollux	243 22.2	N27 58.6
04	112 58.2	219 02.1	28.8	268 00.3	34.0	207 20.3	12.4	185 10.1	18.8	Procyon	244 55.0	N 5 10.4
05	128 00.7	234 01.2	29.3	283 01.2	34.6	222 22.2	12.4	200 12.3	18.8			
06	143 03.1	249 00.3	S23 29.7	298 02.1	S 9 35.2	237 24.1	S23 12.5	215 14.6	S22 18.8	Rasalhague	96 02.7	N12 33.0
07	158 05.6	263 59.4	30.2	313 03.0	35.8	252 26.0	12.5	230 16.8	18.7	Regulus	207 38.9	N11 52.3
T 08	173 08.1	278 58.6	30.6	328 03.9	36.4	267 27.9	12.5	245 19.1	18.7	Rigel	281 07.6	S 8 10.8
H 09	188 10.5	293 57.7 ..	31.0	343 04.9 ..	37.0	282 29.8 ..	12.5	260 21.3 ..	18.7	Rigil Kent.	139 46.5	S60 54.7
U 10	203 13.0	308 56.8	31.5	358 05.8	37.6	297 31.7	12.5	275 23.5	18.7	Sabik	102 07.9	S15 44.8
R 11	218 15.5	323 55.9	31.9	13 06.7	38.2	312 33.5	12.6	290 25.8	18.6			
S 12	233 17.9	338 55.0	S23 32.3	28 07.6	S 9 38.8	327 35.4	S23 12.6	305 28.0	S22 18.6	Schedar	349 35.1	N56 38.9
D 13	248 20.4	353 54.1	32.8	43 08.5	39.4	342 37.3	12.6	320 30.3	18.6	Shaula	96 16.4	S37 07.0
A 14	263 22.9	8 53.2	33.2	58 09.5	40.0	357 39.2	12.6	335 32.5	18.6	Sirius	258 29.6	S16 44.5
Y 15	278 25.3	23 52.3 ..	33.6	73 10.4 ..	40.6	12 41.1 ..	12.6	350 34.7 ..	18.6	Spica	158 26.9	S11 15.6
16	293 27.8	38 51.5	34.1	88 11.3	41.2	27 43.0	12.7	5 37.0	18.5	Suhail	222 49.2	S43 30.4
17	308 30.3	53 50.6	34.5	103 12.2	41.8	42 44.9	12.7	20 39.2	18.5			
18	323 32.7	68 49.7	S23 34.9	118 13.1	S 9 42.5	57 46.8	S23 12.7	35 41.4	S22 18.5	Vega	80 36.3	N38 48.4
19	338 35.2	83 48.8	35.3	133 14.0	43.1	72 48.7	12.7	50 43.7	18.5	Zuben'ubi	137 00.9	S16 07.2
20	353 37.6	98 47.9	35.8	148 15.0	43.7	87 50.6	12.7	65 45.9	18.4		SHA	Mer. Pass.
21	8 40.1	113 47.0 ..	36.2	163 15.9 ..	44.3	102 52.5 ..	12.8	80 48.2 ..	18.4	Venus	107 37.5	13 23
22	23 42.6	128 46.1	36.6	178 16.8	44.9	117 54.4	12.8	95 50.4	18.4	Mars	155 45.3	10 09
23	38 45.0	143 45.2	37.0	193 17.7	45.5	132 56.3	12.8	110 52.6	18.4	Jupiter	94 37.8	14 12
Mer. Pass. 20 29.4		v −0.9	d 0.5	v 0.9	d 0.6	v 1.9	d 0.0	v 2.2	d 0.0	Saturn	72 18.1	15 41

© British Crown Copyright 2018. All rights reserved.

SUN and MOON

UT	SUN GHA	SUN Dec	MOON GHA	v	MOON Dec	d	HP
d h	° ′	° ′	° ′	′	° ′	′	′
12 00	183 59.6	S17 32.9	9 11.9	13.6	N11 35.7	10.7	55.4
01	198 59.5	33.5	23 44.5	13.5	11 46.4	10.7	55.4
02	213 59.4	34.2	38 17.0	13.4	11 57.1	10.6	55.4
03	228 59.4	.. 34.9	52 49.4	13.3	12 07.7	10.6	55.5
04	243 59.3	35.6	67 21.7	13.3	12 18.3	10.6	55.5
05	258 59.2	36.3	81 54.0	13.3	12 28.9	10.4	55.5
06	273 59.1	S17 37.0	96 26.3	13.1	N12 39.3	10.5	55.5
07	288 59.1	37.6	110 58.4	13.1	12 49.8	10.4	55.5
T 08	303 59.0	38.3	125 30.5	13.1	13 00.2	10.3	55.5
U 09	318 58.9	.. 39.0	140 02.6	13.0	13 10.5	10.3	55.6
E 10	333 58.8	39.7	154 34.6	12.9	13 20.8	10.2	55.6
S 11	348 58.8	40.4	169 06.5	12.8	13 31.0	10.2	55.6
D 12	3 58.7	S17 41.0	183 38.3	12.8	N13 41.2	10.1	55.6
A 13	18 58.6	41.7	198 10.1	12.7	13 51.3	10.1	55.6
Y 14	33 58.5	42.4	212 41.8	12.7	14 01.4	10.0	55.7
15	48 58.5	.. 43.1	227 13.5	12.6	14 11.4	9.9	55.7
16	63 58.4	43.7	241 45.1	12.5	14 21.3	9.9	55.7
17	78 58.3	44.4	256 16.6	12.5	14 31.2	9.9	55.7
18	93 58.2	S17 45.1	270 48.1	12.3	N14 41.1	9.7	55.7
19	108 58.1	45.8	285 19.4	12.4	14 50.8	9.7	55.8
20	123 58.1	46.4	299 50.8	12.2	15 00.5	9.7	55.8
21	138 58.0	.. 47.1	314 22.0	12.2	15 10.2	9.5	55.8
22	153 57.9	47.8	328 53.2	12.1	15 19.7	9.6	55.8
23	168 57.8	48.4	343 24.3	12.0	15 29.3	9.4	55.8
13 00	183 57.7	S17 49.1	357 55.3	12.0	N15 38.7	9.4	55.9
01	198 57.7	49.8	12 26.3	11.9	15 48.1	9.3	55.9
02	213 57.6	50.5	26 57.2	11.8	15 57.4	9.2	55.9
03	228 57.5	.. 51.1	41 28.0	11.8	16 06.6	9.2	55.9
04	243 57.4	51.8	55 58.8	11.6	16 15.8	9.1	55.9
05	258 57.3	52.5	70 29.4	11.7	16 24.9	9.0	56.0
06	273 57.3	S17 53.1	85 00.1	11.5	N16 33.9	8.9	56.0
W 07	288 57.2	53.8	99 30.6	11.5	16 42.8	8.9	56.0
E 08	303 57.1	54.5	114 01.1	11.4	16 51.7	8.8	56.0
D 09	318 57.0	.. 55.1	128 31.5	11.3	17 00.5	8.7	56.0
N 10	333 56.9	55.8	143 01.8	11.2	17 09.2	8.7	56.1
E 11	348 56.8	56.5	157 32.0	11.2	17 17.9	8.5	56.1
S 12	3 56.7	S17 57.1	172 02.2	11.1	N17 26.4	8.5	56.1
D 13	18 56.7	57.8	186 32.3	11.1	17 34.9	8.4	56.1
A 14	33 56.6	58.5	201 02.4	10.9	17 43.3	8.3	56.1
Y 15	48 56.5	.. 59.1	215 32.3	10.9	17 51.6	8.3	56.2
16	63 56.4	17 59.8	230 02.2	10.8	17 59.9	8.1	56.2
17	78 56.3	18 00.4	244 32.0	10.8	18 08.0	8.1	56.2
18	93 56.2	S18 01.1	259 01.8	10.6	N18 16.1	7.9	56.2
19	108 56.1	01.8	273 31.4	10.6	18 24.0	7.9	56.2
20	123 56.1	02.4	288 01.0	10.6	18 31.9	7.8	56.3
21	138 56.0	.. 03.1	302 30.6	10.4	18 39.7	7.7	56.3
22	153 55.9	03.7	317 00.0	10.4	18 47.4	7.6	56.3
23	168 55.8	04.4	331 29.4	10.3	18 55.0	7.6	56.3
14 00	183 55.7	S18 05.1	345 58.7	10.2	N19 02.6	7.4	56.3
01	198 55.6	05.7	0 27.9	10.2	19 10.0	7.3	56.4
02	213 55.5	06.4	14 57.1	10.1	19 17.3	7.3	56.4
03	228 55.4	.. 07.0	29 26.2	10.0	19 24.6	7.1	56.4
04	243 55.3	07.7	43 55.2	10.0	19 31.7	7.0	56.4
05	258 55.2	08.3	58 24.2	9.8	19 38.7	7.0	56.5
06	273 55.1	S18 09.0	72 53.0	9.8	N19 45.7	6.8	56.5
07	288 55.1	09.7	87 21.8	9.8	19 52.5	6.8	56.5
T 08	303 55.0	10.3	101 50.6	9.5	19 59.3	6.6	56.5
H 09	318 54.9	.. 11.0	116 19.2	9.6	20 05.9	6.6	56.5
U 10	333 54.8	11.6	130 47.8	9.6	20 12.5	6.4	56.6
R 11	348 54.7	12.3	145 16.4	9.4	20 18.9	6.3	56.6
S 12	3 54.6	S18 12.9	159 44.8	9.4	N20 25.2	6.3	56.6
D 13	18 54.5	13.6	174 13.2	9.3	20 31.5	6.1	56.6
A 14	33 54.4	14.2	188 41.5	9.3	20 37.6	6.0	56.6
Y 15	48 54.3	.. 14.9	203 09.8	9.2	20 43.6	5.9	56.7
16	63 54.2	15.5	217 38.0	9.1	20 49.5	5.8	56.7
17	78 54.1	16.2	232 06.1	9.0	20 55.3	5.7	56.7
18	93 54.0	S18 16.8	246 34.1	9.0	N21 01.0	5.5	56.7
19	108 53.9	17.5	261 02.1	8.9	21 06.5	5.5	56.7
20	123 53.8	18.1	275 30.0	8.9	21 12.0	5.3	56.8
21	138 53.7	.. 18.8	289 57.9	8.8	21 17.3	5.3	56.8
22	153 53.6	19.4	304 25.7	8.7	21 22.6	5.1	56.8
23	168 53.5	20.0	318 53.4	8.7	N21 27.7	5.0	56.8
	SD 16.2	d 0.7	SD 15.2		15.3		15.4

Twilight, Sunrise and Moonrise

Lat.	Naut.	Civil	Sunrise	Moonrise 12	13	14	15
°	h m	h m	h m	h m	h m	h m	h m
N 72	06 51	08 23	10 29	14 30	13 29	▭	▭
N 70	06 42	08 02	09 34	14 57	14 32	▭	▭
68	06 34	07 46	09 02	15 18	15 08	14 53	▭
66	06 28	07 33	08 38	15 34	15 34	15 37	15 48
64	06 22	07 21	08 20	15 48	15 54	16 06	16 30
62	06 17	07 12	08 05	15 59	16 11	16 29	16 59
60	06 12	07 04	07 52	16 09	16 24	16 47	17 21
N 58	06 08	06 56	07 41	16 17	16 36	17 02	17 39
56	06 04	06 50	07 32	16 25	16 46	17 15	17 54
54	06 01	06 44	07 23	16 32	16 56	17 26	18 07
52	05 58	06 39	07 16	16 38	17 04	17 36	18 18
50	05 54	06 34	07 09	16 43	17 11	17 45	18 28
45	05 47	06 23	06 54	16 55	17 27	18 04	18 50
N 40	05 41	06 13	06 42	17 05	17 40	18 20	19 07
35	05 35	06 05	06 32	17 14	17 51	18 33	19 21
30	05 29	05 58	06 23	17 22	18 01	18 44	19 34
20	05 18	05 44	06 07	17 35	18 17	19 04	19 56
N 10	05 06	05 32	05 54	17 46	18 32	19 22	20 15
0	04 54	05 19	05 41	17 57	18 46	19 38	20 32
S 10	04 39	05 05	05 28	18 08	19 00	19 54	20 50
20	04 22	04 50	05 13	18 20	19 15	20 11	21 09
30	04 00	04 31	04 57	18 33	19 32	20 32	21 31
35	03 46	04 20	04 48	18 41	19 42	20 43	21 44
40	03 29	04 06	04 37	18 50	19 54	20 57	21 59
45	03 08	03 50	04 24	19 01	20 07	21 13	22 16
S 50	02 39	03 29	04 08	19 14	20 24	21 33	22 38
52	02 24	03 19	04 00	19 20	20 32	21 43	22 49
54	02 06	03 08	03 52	19 26	20 41	21 53	23 01
56	01 43	02 55	03 43	19 34	20 51	22 06	23 14
58	01 12	02 39	03 32	19 42	21 02	22 20	23 30
S 60	00 10	02 20	03 20	19 52	21 15	22 36	23 49

Sunset, Twilight and Moonset

Lat.	Sunset	Civil	Naut.	Moonset 12	13	14	15
°	h m	h m	h m	h m	h m	h m	h m
N 72	12 58	15 04	16 36	08 41	11 21	▭	▭
N 70	13 53	15 25	16 45	08 15	10 19	▭	▭
68	14 26	15 41	16 53	07 56	09 44	11 45	▭
66	14 49	15 55	17 00	07 40	09 19	11 02	12 43
64	15 08	16 06	17 06	07 28	09 00	10 33	12 01
62	15 23	16 16	17 11	07 18	08 44	10 11	11 33
60	15 36	16 24	17 15	07 09	08 31	09 54	11 11
N 58	15 47	16 31	17 20	07 01	08 20	09 39	10 53
56	15 56	16 38	17 23	06 54	08 10	09 26	10 38
54	16 05	16 44	17 27	06 48	08 02	09 15	10 26
52	16 12	16 49	17 30	06 42	07 54	09 06	10 14
50	16 19	16 54	17 33	06 37	07 47	08 57	10 04
45	16 34	17 05	17 41	06 27	07 33	08 39	09 44
N 40	16 46	17 15	17 47	06 18	07 21	08 24	09 27
35	16 56	17 23	17 53	06 10	07 10	08 11	09 12
30	17 05	17 30	17 59	06 04	07 01	08 01	09 00
20	17 21	17 44	18 10	05 52	06 46	07 42	08 39
N 10	17 35	17 57	18 22	05 42	06 33	07 26	08 21
0	17 48	18 09	18 35	05 33	06 20	07 10	08 04
S 10	18 01	18 23	18 49	05 24	06 08	06 55	07 47
20	18 15	18 39	19 06	05 14	05 54	06 39	07 28
30	18 32	18 58	19 29	05 03	05 39	06 21	07 07
35	18 41	19 09	19 43	04 56	05 31	06 10	06 55
40	18 52	19 23	20 00	04 49	05 21	05 58	06 41
45	19 06	19 39	20 22	04 40	05 09	05 43	06 24
S 50	19 22	20 00	20 51	04 30	04 55	05 25	06 04
52	19 29	20 10	21 07	04 25	04 48	05 17	05 54
54	19 37	20 22	21 25	04 20	04 41	05 08	05 43
56	19 47	20 36	21 48	04 14	04 33	04 57	05 30
58	19 58	20 51	22 21	04 08	04 24	04 46	05 16
S 60	20 10	21 11	////	04 01	04 14	04 32	04 59

Day	SUN Eqn. of Time 00h	12h	Mer. Pass.	MOON Mer. Pass. Upper	Lower	Age	Phase
d	m s	m s	h m	h m	h m	d %	
12	15 58	15 55	11 44	24 09	11 45	15 100	○
13	15 51	15 47	11 44	00 09	12 33	16 99	
14	15 43	15 39	11 44	00 58	13 24	17 96	

© British Crown Copyright 2018. All rights reserved.

UT (d h)	ARIES GHA	VENUS −3.9 GHA	Dec	MARS +1.7 GHA	Dec	JUPITER −1.9 GHA	Dec	SATURN +0.6 GHA	Dec	STARS Name	SHA	Dec
15 00	53 47.5	158 44.3	S23 37.4	208 18.6	S 9 46.1	147 58.2	S23 12.8	125 54.9	S22 18.4	Acamar	315 14.6	S40 13.6
01	68 50.0	173 43.4	37.9	223 19.5	46.7	163 00.1	12.8	140 57.1	18.3	Achernar	335 23.0	S57 08.4
02	83 52.4	188 42.5	38.3	238 20.5	47.3	178 02.0	12.8	155 59.3	18.3	Acrux	173 04.9	S63 12.2
03	98 54.9	203 41.6 ..	38.7	253 21.4	47.9	193 03.9 ..	12.9	171 01.6 ..	18.3	Adhara	255 08.8	S28 59.8
04	113 57.4	218 40.7	39.1	268 22.3	48.5	208 05.8	12.9	186 03.8	18.3	Aldebaran	290 44.0	N16 32.8
05	128 59.8	233 39.9	39.5	283 23.2	49.1	223 07.7	12.9	201 06.1	18.2			
06	144 02.3	248 39.0	S23 39.9	298 24.1	S 9 49.7	238 09.6	S23 12.9	216 08.3	S22 18.2	Alioth	166 17.2	N55 51.1
07	159 04.7	263 38.1	40.3	313 25.0	50.3	253 11.5	12.9	231 10.5	18.2	Alkaid	152 55.9	N49 12.9
08	174 07.2	278 37.2	40.8	328 26.0	50.9	268 13.4	13.0	246 12.8	18.2	Alnair	27 38.2	S46 52.1
F 09	189 09.7	293 36.3 ..	41.2	343 26.9	51.5	283 15.3 ..	13.0	261 15.0 ..	18.2	Alnilam	275 41.6	S 1 11.4
R 10	204 12.1	308 35.4	41.6	358 27.8	52.1	298 17.2	13.0	276 17.2	18.1	Alphard	217 51.8	S 8 44.5
I 11	219 14.6	323 34.5	42.0	13 28.7	52.7	313 19.1	13.0	291 19.5	18.1			
D 12	234 17.1	338 33.6	S23 42.4	28 29.6	S 9 53.3	328 21.0	S23 13.0	306 21.7	S22 18.1	Alphecca	126 07.7	N26 39.1
A 13	249 19.5	353 32.7	42.8	43 30.5	53.9	343 22.9	13.1	321 23.9	18.1	Alpheratz	357 38.8	N29 12.1
Y 14	264 22.0	8 31.8	43.2	58 31.5	54.5	358 24.8	13.1	336 26.2	18.0	Altair	62 04.1	N 8 55.4
15	279 24.5	23 30.9 ..	43.6	73 32.4 ..	55.1	13 26.7 ..	13.1	351 28.4 ..	18.0	Ankaa	353 11.1	S42 12.1
16	294 26.9	38 30.0	44.0	88 33.3	55.7	28 28.6	13.1	6 30.7	18.0	Antares	112 21.3	S26 28.3
17	309 29.4	53 29.1	44.4	103 34.2	56.3	43 30.5	13.1	21 32.9	18.0			
18	324 31.9	68 28.2	S23 44.8	118 35.1	S 9 56.9	58 32.4	S23 13.2	36 35.1	S22 17.9	Arcturus	145 52.1	N19 04.9
19	339 34.3	83 27.3	45.2	133 36.0	57.5	73 34.3	13.2	51 37.4	17.9	Atria	107 19.7	S69 03.7
20	354 36.8	98 26.4	45.6	148 36.9	58.1	88 36.2	13.2	66 39.6	17.9	Avior	234 16.0	S59 34.1
21	9 39.2	113 25.5 ..	46.0	163 37.9 ..	58.7	103 38.1 ..	13.2	81 41.8 ..	17.9	Bellatrix	278 27.0	N 6 22.0
22	24 41.7	128 24.6	46.4	178 38.8	59.3	118 40.0	13.2	96 44.1	17.9	Betelgeuse	270 56.3	N 7 24.6
23	39 44.2	143 23.7	46.8	193 39.7	9 59.9	133 41.8	13.3	111 46.3	17.8			
16 00	54 46.6	158 22.8	S23 47.1	208 40.6	S10 00.5	148 43.7	S23 13.3	126 48.5	S22 17.8	Canopus	263 53.8	S52 42.2
01	69 49.1	173 21.9	47.5	223 41.5	01.1	163 45.6	13.3	141 50.8	17.8	Capella	280 27.5	N46 00.9
02	84 51.6	188 21.0	47.9	238 42.4	01.8	178 47.5	13.3	156 53.0	17.8	Deneb	49 28.7	N45 21.4
03	99 54.0	203 20.1 ..	48.3	253 43.3	02.4	193 49.4 ..	13.3	171 55.2	17.7	Denebola	182 29.4	N14 27.8
04	114 56.5	218 19.2	48.7	268 44.3	03.0	208 51.3	13.3	186 57.5	17.7	Diphda	348 51.2	S17 52.8
05	129 59.0	233 18.3	49.1	283 45.2	03.6	223 53.2	13.4	201 59.7	17.7			
06	145 01.4	248 17.4	S23 49.5	298 46.1	S10 04.2	238 55.1	S23 13.4	217 01.9	S22 17.7	Dubhe	193 46.6	N61 38.5
07	160 03.9	263 16.5	49.8	313 47.0	04.8	253 57.0	13.4	232 04.2	17.7	Elnath	278 06.7	N28 37.3
S 08	175 06.4	278 15.6	50.2	328 47.9	05.4	268 58.9	13.4	247 06.4	17.6	Eltanin	90 44.6	N51 29.5
A 09	190 08.8	293 14.7 ..	50.6	343 48.8 ..	06.0	284 00.8 ..	13.4	262 08.6 ..	17.6	Enif	33 42.8	N 9 58.1
T 10	205 11.3	308 13.8	51.0	358 49.7	06.6	299 02.7	13.5	277 10.9	17.6	Fomalhaut	15 19.0	S29 31.2
U 11	220 13.7	323 12.9	51.4	13 50.6	07.2	314 04.6	13.5	292 13.1	17.6			
R 12	235 16.2	338 12.0	S23 51.7	28 51.6	S10 07.8	329 06.5	S23 13.5	307 15.3	S22 17.5	Gacrux	171 56.5	S57 13.1
D 13	250 18.7	353 11.1	52.1	43 52.5	08.4	344 08.4	13.5	322 17.6	17.5	Gienah	175 48.0	S17 38.8
A 14	265 21.1	8 10.2	52.5	58 53.4	09.0	359 10.3	13.5	337 19.8	17.5	Hadar	148 42.3	S60 27.8
Y 15	280 23.6	23 09.3 ..	52.8	73 54.3 ..	09.6	14 12.2 ..	13.6	352 22.0 ..	17.5	Hamal	327 55.5	N23 33.3
16	295 26.1	38 08.3	53.2	88 55.2	10.2	29 14.0	13.6	7 24.3	17.4	Kaus Aust.	83 38.3	S34 22.4
17	310 28.5	53 07.4	53.6	103 56.1	10.8	44 15.9	13.6	22 26.5	17.4			
18	325 31.0	68 06.5	S23 54.0	118 57.0	S10 11.4	59 17.8	S23 13.6	37 28.7	S22 17.4	Kochab	137 21.3	N74 04.5
19	340 33.5	83 05.6	54.3	133 57.9	12.0	74 19.7	13.6	52 31.0	17.4	Markab	13 33.9	N15 18.8
20	355 35.9	98 04.7	54.7	148 58.8	12.6	89 21.6	13.6	67 33.2	17.4	Menkar	314 10.1	N 4 10.0
21	10 38.4	113 03.8 ..	55.1	163 59.8 ..	13.2	104 23.5 ..	13.7	82 35.4 ..	17.3	Menkent	148 02.8	S36 27.7
22	25 40.9	128 02.9	55.4	179 00.7	13.8	119 25.4	13.7	97 37.6	17.3	Miaplacidus	221 38.7	S69 47.5
23	40 43.3	143 02.0	55.8	194 01.6	14.4	134 27.3	13.7	112 39.9	17.3			
17 00	55 45.8	158 01.1	S23 56.1	209 02.5	S10 15.0	149 29.2	S23 13.7	127 42.1	S22 17.3	Mirfak	308 33.6	N49 55.8
01	70 48.2	173 00.2	56.5	224 03.4	15.6	164 31.1	13.7	142 44.3	17.2	Nunki	75 53.2	S26 16.3
02	85 50.7	187 59.3	56.9	239 04.3	16.1	178 33.0	13.8	157 46.6	17.2	Peacock	53 12.6	S56 40.4
03	100 53.2	202 58.4 ..	57.2	254 05.2	16.7	194 34.9 ..	13.8	172 48.8 ..	17.2	Pollux	243 22.2	N27 58.6
04	115 55.6	217 57.5	57.6	269 06.1	17.3	209 36.8	13.8	187 51.0	17.2	Procyon	244 55.0	N 5 10.4
05	130 58.1	232 56.5	57.9	284 07.0	17.9	224 38.7	13.8	202 53.3	17.1			
06	146 00.6	247 55.6	S23 58.3	299 08.0	S10 18.5	239 40.5	S23 13.8	217 55.5	S22 17.1	Rasalhague	96 02.7	N12 33.0
07	161 03.0	262 54.7	58.6	314 08.9	19.1	254 42.4	13.8	232 57.7	17.1	Regulus	207 38.9	N11 52.3
08	176 05.5	277 53.8	59.0	329 09.8	19.7	269 44.3	13.9	248 00.0	17.1	Rigel	281 07.5	S 8 10.8
S 09	191 08.0	292 52.9 ..	59.3	344 10.7 ..	20.3	284 46.2 ..	13.9	263 02.2 ..	17.0	Rigil Kent.	139 46.5	S60 54.7
U 10	206 10.4	307 52.0	23 59.7	359 11.6	20.9	299 48.1	13.9	278 04.4	17.0	Sabik	102 07.8	S15 44.8
N 11	221 12.9	322 51.1	24 00.0	14 12.5	21.5	314 50.0	13.9	293 06.6	17.0			
D 12	236 15.4	337 50.2	S24 00.4	29 13.4	S10 22.1	329 51.9	S23 13.9	308 08.9	S22 17.0	Schedar	349 35.1	N56 38.9
A 13	251 17.8	352 49.3	00.7	44 14.3	22.7	344 53.8	13.9	323 11.1	17.0	Shaula	96 16.4	S37 07.0
Y 14	266 20.3	7 48.3	01.1	59 15.2	23.3	359 55.7	14.0	338 13.3	16.9	Sirius	258 29.6	S16 44.5
15	281 22.7	22 47.4 ..	01.4	74 16.1 ..	23.9	14 57.6 ..	14.0	353 15.6 ..	16.9	Spica	158 26.9	S11 15.6
16	296 25.2	37 46.5	01.7	89 17.0	24.5	29 59.5	14.0	8 17.8	16.9	Suhail	222 49.2	S43 30.5
17	311 27.7	52 45.6	02.1	104 17.9	25.1	45 01.3	14.0	23 20.0	16.9			
18	326 30.1	67 44.7	S24 02.4	119 18.9	S10 25.7	60 03.2	S23 14.0	38 22.3	S22 16.8	Vega	80 36.3	N38 48.4
19	341 32.6	82 43.8	02.8	134 19.8	26.3	75 05.1	14.1	53 24.5	16.8	Zuben'ubi	137 00.9	S16 07.2
20	356 35.1	97 42.9	03.1	149 20.7	26.9	90 07.0	14.1	68 26.7	16.8			
21	11 37.5	112 42.0 ..	03.4	164 21.6	27.5	105 08.9 ..	14.1	83 28.9 ..	16.8		SHA	Mer.Pass.
22	26 40.0	127 41.0	03.8	179 22.5	28.1	120 10.8	14.1	98 31.2	16.7	Venus	103 36.2	13 27
23	41 42.5	142 40.1	04.1	194 23.4	28.7	135 12.7	14.1	113 33.4	16.7	Mars	153 54.0	10 05
Mer.Pass. 20 17.6		v −0.9	d 0.4	v 0.9	d 0.6	v 1.9	d 0.0	v 2.2	d 0.0	Jupiter	93 57.1	14 03
										Saturn	72 01.9	15 30

© British Crown Copyright 2018. All rights reserved.

UT	SUN GHA	SUN Dec	MOON GHA	v	MOON Dec	d	HP
d h	° ′	° ′	° ′	′	° ′	′	′
15 00	183 53.4	S18 20.7	333 21.1	8.6	N21 32.7	4.9	56.8
01	198 53.3	21.3	347 48.7	8.5	21 37.6	4.7	56.9
02	213 53.2	22.0	2 16.2	8.5	21 42.3	4.7	56.9
03	228 53.1	.. 22.6	16 43.7	8.5	21 47.0	4.5	56.9
04	243 53.0	23.3	31 11.2	8.3	21 51.5	4.4	56.9
05	258 52.9	23.9	45 38.5	8.3	21 55.9	4.3	56.9
06	273 52.8	S18 24.6	60 05.8	8.3	N22 00.2	4.1	57.0
07	288 52.7	25.2	74 33.1	8.2	22 04.3	4.1	57.0
08	303 52.6	25.8	89 00.3	8.1	22 08.4	3.9	57.0
F 09	318 52.5	.. 26.5	103 27.4	8.1	22 12.3	3.8	57.0
R 10	333 52.4	27.1	117 54.5	8.0	22 16.1	3.7	57.0
I 11	348 52.3	27.8	132 21.5	8.0	22 19.8	3.5	57.1
D 12	3 52.2	S18 28.4	146 48.5	7.9	N22 23.3	3.4	57.1
A 13	18 52.1	29.0	161 15.4	7.9	22 26.7	3.3	57.1
Y 14	33 52.0	29.7	175 42.3	7.8	22 30.0	3.2	57.1
15	48 51.9	.. 30.3	190 09.1	7.8	22 33.2	3.0	57.1
16	63 51.8	30.9	204 35.9	7.7	22 36.2	2.9	57.2
17	78 51.7	31.6	219 02.6	7.7	22 39.1	2.8	57.2
18	93 51.6	S18 32.2	233 29.3	7.6	N22 41.9	2.6	57.2
19	108 51.5	32.8	247 55.9	7.6	22 44.5	2.5	57.2
20	123 51.4	33.5	262 22.5	7.6	22 47.0	2.4	57.2
21	138 51.3	.. 34.1	276 49.1	7.5	22 49.4	2.2	57.3
22	153 51.2	34.7	291 15.6	7.5	22 51.6	2.1	57.3
23	168 51.1	35.4	305 42.1	7.4	22 53.7	2.0	57.3
16 00	183 50.9	S18 36.0	320 08.5	7.4	N22 55.7	1.8	57.3
01	198 50.8	36.6	334 34.9	7.3	22 57.5	1.7	57.3
02	213 50.7	37.3	349 01.2	7.3	22 59.2	1.6	57.4
03	228 50.6	.. 37.9	3 27.5	7.3	23 00.8	1.4	57.4
04	243 50.5	38.5	17 53.8	7.2	23 02.2	1.3	57.4
05	258 50.4	39.2	32 20.0	7.3	23 03.5	1.2	57.4
06	273 50.3	S18 39.8	46 46.3	7.1	N23 04.7	1.0	57.4
S 07	288 50.2	40.4	61 12.4	7.2	23 05.7	0.9	57.5
A 08	303 50.1	41.0	75 38.6	7.1	23 06.6	0.8	57.5
T 09	318 50.0	.. 41.7	90 04.7	7.1	23 07.4	0.6	57.5
U 10	333 49.8	42.3	104 30.8	7.0	23 08.0	0.5	57.5
R 11	348 49.7	42.9	118 56.8	7.1	23 08.5	0.3	57.5
D 12	3 49.6	S18 43.5	133 22.9	7.0	N23 08.8	0.2	57.6
A 13	18 49.5	44.2	147 48.9	7.0	23 09.0	0.0	57.6
Y 14	33 49.4	44.8	162 14.9	7.0	23 09.0	0.0	57.6
15	48 49.3	.. 45.4	176 40.9	6.9	23 09.0	0.3	57.6
16	63 49.2	46.0	191 06.8	6.9	23 08.7	0.3	57.6
17	78 49.1	46.6	205 32.7	6.9	23 08.4	0.5	57.7
18	93 48.9	S18 47.3	219 58.6	6.9	N23 07.9	0.7	57.7
19	108 48.8	47.9	234 24.5	6.9	23 07.2	0.8	57.7
20	123 48.7	48.5	248 50.4	6.9	23 06.4	0.9	57.7
21	138 48.6	.. 49.1	263 16.3	6.8	23 05.5	1.1	57.7
22	153 48.5	49.7	277 42.1	6.9	23 04.4	1.2	57.7
23	168 48.4	50.4	292 08.0	6.8	23 03.2	1.3	57.8
17 00	183 48.2	S18 51.0	306 33.8	6.8	N23 01.9	1.5	57.8
01	198 48.1	51.6	320 59.6	6.9	23 00.4	1.7	57.8
02	213 48.0	52.2	335 25.5	6.8	22 58.7	1.7	57.8
03	228 47.9	.. 52.8	349 51.3	6.8	22 57.0	1.9	57.8
04	243 47.8	53.5	4 17.1	6.8	22 55.1	2.1	57.9
05	258 47.7	54.1	18 42.9	6.8	22 53.0	2.2	57.9
06	273 47.5	S18 54.7	33 08.7	6.8	N22 50.8	2.3	57.9
07	288 47.4	55.3	47 34.5	6.8	22 48.5	2.5	57.9
08	303 47.3	55.9	62 00.3	6.8	22 46.0	2.6	57.9
S 09	318 47.2	.. 56.5	76 26.1	6.8	22 43.4	2.8	58.0
U 10	333 47.1	57.1	90 51.9	6.8	22 40.6	2.9	58.0
N 11	348 46.9	57.7	105 17.7	6.8	22 37.7	3.0	58.0
D 12	3 46.8	S18 58.4	119 43.5	6.8	N22 34.7	3.2	58.0
A 13	18 46.7	59.0	134 09.3	6.8	22 31.5	3.4	58.0
Y 14	33 46.6	18 59.6	148 35.1	6.9	22 28.1	3.4	58.1
15	48 46.5	19 00.2	163 01.0	6.8	22 24.7	3.6	58.1
16	63 46.3	00.8	177 26.8	6.9	22 21.1	3.8	58.1
17	78 46.2	01.4	191 52.7	6.8	22 17.3	3.8	58.1
18	93 46.1	S19 02.0	206 18.5	6.9	N22 13.5	4.1	58.1
19	108 46.0	02.6	220 44.5	6.9	22 09.4	4.1	58.1
20	123 45.8	03.2	235 10.3	6.9	22 05.3	4.3	58.2
21	138 45.7	.. 03.8	249 36.2	6.9	22 01.0	4.4	58.2
22	153 45.6	04.4	264 02.1	7.0	21 56.6	4.6	58.2
23	168 45.5	05.0	278 28.1	6.9	N21 52.0	4.7	58.2
	SD 16.2 d 0.6		SD 15.6	15.7			15.8

Lat.	Twilight Naut.	Twilight Civil	Sunrise	Moonrise 15	16	17	18
°	h m	h m	h m	h m	h m	h m	h m
N 72	07 02	08 37	11 18	▭	▭	▭	▭
N 70	06 51	08 14	09 54	▭	▭	▭	17 30
68	06 43	07 56	09 16	▭	▭	▭	19 01
66	06 35	07 42	08 50	15 48	16 26	17 51	19 39
64	06 29	07 29	08 29	16 30	17 16	18 31	20 06
62	06 23	07 19	08 13	16 59	17 48	18 59	20 27
60	06 18	07 10	08 00	17 21	18 11	19 20	20 44
N 58	06 14	07 02	07 48	17 39	18 30	19 38	20 58
56	06 10	06 55	07 38	17 54	18 46	19 52	21 10
54	06 06	06 49	07 29	18 07	19 00	20 05	21 20
52	06 02	06 43	07 21	18 18	19 11	20 16	21 30
50	05 59	06 38	07 14	18 28	19 22	20 26	21 38
45	05 51	06 27	06 58	18 50	19 44	20 47	21 56
N 40	05 44	06 17	06 46	19 07	20 02	21 03	22 10
35	05 37	06 08	06 35	19 21	20 16	21 17	22 22
30	05 31	06 00	06 26	19 34	20 29	21 30	22 33
20	05 19	05 46	06 09	19 56	20 51	21 50	22 51
N 10	05 07	05 33	05 55	20 15	21 11	22 08	23 07
0	04 54	05 19	05 41	20 32	21 29	22 25	23 22
S 10	04 39	05 05	05 27	20 50	21 46	22 42	23 36
20	04 21	04 49	05 13	21 09	22 06	23 00	23 52
30	03 58	04 29	04 56	21 31	22 28	23 21	24 10
35	03 44	04 18	04 46	21 44	22 41	23 33	24 20
40	03 26	04 03	04 34	21 59	22 56	23 47	24 32
45	03 03	03 46	04 20	22 16	23 14	24 04	00 04
S 50	02 33	03 25	04 04	22 38	23 36	24 24	00 24
52	02 17	03 14	03 56	22 49	23 46	24 34	00 34
54	01 57	03 02	03 47	23 01	23 58	24 44	00 44
56	01 32	02 48	03 37	23 14	24 12	00 12	00 57
58	00 55	02 31	03 26	23 30	24 28	00 28	01 11
S 60	////	02 10	03 13	23 49	24 47	00 47	01 27

Lat.	Sunset	Twilight Civil	Twilight Naut.	Moonset 15	16	17	18
°	h m	h m	h m	h m	h m	h m	h m
N 72	12 10	14 51	16 26	▭	▭	▭	▭
N 70	13 35	15 14	16 37	▭	▭	▭	16 56
68	14 13	15 32	16 46	▭	▭	▭	15 24
66	14 39	15 47	16 53	12 43	14 01	14 35	14 45
64	14 59	15 59	16 59	12 01	13 11	13 55	14 18
62	15 15	16 09	17 05	11 33	12 40	13 27	13 56
60	15 29	16 18	17 10	11 11	12 16	13 05	13 39
N 58	15 41	16 26	17 15	10 53	11 58	12 48	13 24
56	15 51	16 33	17 19	10 38	11 42	12 33	13 12
54	16 00	16 40	17 23	10 26	11 28	12 20	13 01
52	16 08	16 45	17 27	10 14	11 16	12 09	12 51
50	16 15	16 51	17 30	10 04	11 06	11 59	12 42
45	16 31	17 02	17 38	09 44	10 44	11 38	12 24
N 40	16 43	17 12	17 45	09 27	10 26	11 21	12 09
35	16 54	17 21	17 52	09 12	10 11	11 06	11 56
30	17 04	17 29	17 58	09 00	09 58	10 54	11 45
20	17 20	17 43	18 10	08 39	09 36	10 32	11 25
N 10	17 35	17 57	18 22	08 21	09 17	10 13	11 08
0	17 48	18 10	18 35	08 04	08 59	09 56	10 52
S 10	18 02	18 24	18 51	07 47	08 41	09 38	10 36
20	18 17	18 41	19 09	07 28	08 22	09 19	10 19
30	18 34	19 00	19 32	07 07	08 00	08 57	09 59
35	18 44	19 12	19 46	06 55	07 47	08 45	09 48
40	18 56	19 27	20 04	06 41	07 32	08 30	09 34
45	19 10	19 44	20 27	06 24	07 14	08 12	09 18
S 50	19 27	20 06	20 58	06 04	06 52	07 50	08 59
52	19 34	20 17	21 15	05 54	06 41	07 40	08 50
54	19 43	20 29	21 35	05 43	06 29	07 28	08 39
56	19 53	20 43	22 01	05 30	06 15	07 15	08 27
58	20 05	21 00	22 40	05 16	05 59	06 59	08 13
S 60	20 18	21 22	////	04 59	05 40	06 40	07 57

Day	SUN Eqn. of Time 00h	SUN Eqn. of Time 12h	SUN Mer. Pass.	MOON Mer. Pass. Upper	MOON Mer. Pass. Lower	Age	Phase
d	m s	m s	h m	h m	h m	d	%
15	15 34	15 29	11 45	01 51	14 18	18	91
16	15 24	15 19	11 45	02 46	15 14	19	84
17	15 13	15 08	11 45	03 42	16 11	20	75

© British Crown Copyright 2018. All rights reserved.

UT	ARIES	VENUS −3.9		MARS +1.7		JUPITER −1.9		SATURN +0.6		STARS		
	GHA	GHA	Dec	GHA	Dec	GHA	Dec	GHA	Dec	Name	SHA	Dec
d h	° ′	° ′	° ′	° ′	° ′	° ′	° ′	° ′	° ′		° ′	° ′
18 00	56 44.9	157 39.2	S24 04.4	209 24.3	S10 29.3	150 14.6	S23 14.1	128 35.6	S22 16.7	Acamar	315 14.6	S40 13.7
01	71 47.4	172 38.3	04.8	224 25.2	29.9	165 16.5	14.2	143 37.9	16.7	Achernar	335 23.0	S57 08.4
02	86 49.8	187 37.4	05.1	239 26.1	30.5	180 18.4	14.2	158 40.1	16.6	Acrux	173 04.9	S63 12.2
03	101 52.3	202 36.5 ..	05.4	254 27.0 ..	31.1	195 20.2 ..	14.2	173 42.3 ..	16.6	Adhara	255 08.8	S28 59.8
04	116 54.8	217 35.5	05.7	269 27.9	31.7	210 22.1	14.2	188 44.5	16.6	Aldebaran	290 44.0	N16 32.8
05	131 57.2	232 34.6	06.1	284 28.8	32.3	225 24.0	14.2	203 46.8	16.6			
06	146 59.7	247 33.7	S24 06.4	299 29.7	S10 32.9	240 25.9	S23 14.2	218 49.0	S22 16.5	Alioth	166 17.2	N55 51.1
07	162 02.2	262 32.8	06.7	314 30.7	33.5	255 27.8	14.3	233 51.2	16.5	Alkaid	152 55.8	N49 12.9
08	177 04.6	277 31.9	07.0	329 31.6	34.1	270 29.7	14.3	248 53.5	16.5	Alnair	27 38.2	S46 52.1
M 09	192 07.1	292 31.0 ..	07.3	344 32.5 ..	34.7	285 31.6 ..	14.3	263 55.7 ..	16.5	Alnilam	275 41.6	S 1 11.4
O 10	207 09.6	307 30.0	07.7	359 33.4	35.2	300 33.5	14.3	278 57.9	16.5	Alphard	217 51.8	S 8 44.5
N 11	222 12.0	322 29.1	08.0	14 34.3	35.8	315 35.4	14.3	294 00.1	16.4			
D 12	237 14.5	337 28.2	S24 08.3	29 35.2	S10 36.4	330 37.2	S23 14.3	309 02.4	S22 16.4	Alphecca	126 07.7	N26 39.1
A 13	252 17.0	352 27.3	08.6	44 36.1	37.0	345 39.1	14.4	324 04.6	16.4	Alpheratz	357 38.8	N29 12.1
Y 14	267 19.4	7 26.4	08.9	59 37.0	37.6	0 41.0	14.4	339 06.8	16.4	Altair	62 04.1	N 8 55.4
15	282 21.9	22 25.5 ..	09.2	74 37.9 ..	38.2	15 42.9 ..	14.4	354 09.0 ..	16.3	Ankaa	353 11.1	S42 12.1
16	297 24.3	37 24.5	09.6	89 38.8	38.8	30 44.8	14.4	9 11.3	16.3	Antares	112 21.3	S26 28.3
17	312 26.8	52 23.6	09.9	104 39.7	39.4	45 46.7	14.4	24 13.5	16.3			
18	327 29.3	67 22.7	S24 10.2	119 40.6	S10 40.0	60 48.6	S23 14.4	39 15.7	S22 16.3	Arcturus	145 52.1	N19 04.9
19	342 31.7	82 21.8	10.5	134 41.5	40.6	75 50.5	14.5	54 17.9	16.2	Atria	107 19.7	S69 03.7
20	357 34.2	97 20.9	10.8	149 42.4	41.2	90 52.3	14.5	69 20.2	16.2	Avior	234 16.0	S59 34.1
21	12 36.7	112 19.9 ..	11.1	164 43.3 ..	41.8	105 54.2 ..	14.5	84 22.4 ..	16.2	Bellatrix	278 27.0	N 6 22.0
22	27 39.1	127 19.0	11.4	179 44.2	42.4	120 56.1	14.5	99 24.6	16.2	Betelgeuse	270 56.3	N 7 24.6
23	42 41.6	142 18.1	11.7	194 45.1	43.0	135 58.0	14.5	114 26.8	16.1			
19 00	57 44.1	157 17.2	S24 12.0	209 46.0	S10 43.6	150 59.9	S23 14.5	129 29.1	S22 16.1	Canopus	263 53.8	S52 42.2
01	72 46.5	172 16.2	12.3	224 46.9	44.2	166 01.8	14.6	144 31.3	16.1	Capella	280 27.5	N46 00.9
02	87 49.0	187 15.3	12.6	239 47.8	44.7	181 03.7	14.6	159 33.5	16.1	Deneb	49 28.7	N45 21.4
03	102 51.5	202 14.4 ..	12.9	254 48.7 ..	45.3	196 05.6 ..	14.6	174 35.8 ..	16.0	Denebola	182 29.4	N14 27.8
04	117 53.9	217 13.5	13.2	269 49.7	45.9	211 07.4	14.6	189 38.0	16.0	Diphda	348 51.2	S17 52.8
05	132 56.4	232 12.6	13.5	284 50.6	46.5	226 09.3	14.6	204 40.2	16.0			
06	147 58.8	247 11.6	S24 13.8	299 51.5	S10 47.1	241 11.2	S23 14.6	219 42.4	S22 16.0	Dubhe	193 46.5	N61 38.5
07	163 01.3	262 10.7	14.1	314 52.4	47.7	256 13.1	14.7	234 44.7	15.9	Elnath	278 06.7	N28 37.3
08	178 03.8	277 09.8	14.4	329 53.3	48.3	271 15.0	14.7	249 46.9	15.9	Eltanin	90 44.6	N51 29.4
T 09	193 06.2	292 08.9 ..	14.6	344 54.2 ..	48.9	286 16.9 ..	14.7	264 49.1 ..	15.9	Enif	33 42.8	N 9 58.1
U 10	208 08.7	307 07.9	14.9	359 55.1	49.5	301 18.8	14.7	279 51.3	15.9	Fomalhaut	15 19.0	S29 31.2
E 11	223 11.2	322 07.0	15.2	14 56.0	50.1	316 20.6	14.7	294 53.6	15.8			
S 12	238 13.6	337 06.1	S24 15.5	29 56.9	S10 50.7	331 22.5	S23 14.7	309 55.8	S22 15.8	Gacrux	171 56.4	S57 13.1
D 13	253 16.1	352 05.2	15.8	44 57.8	51.3	346 24.4	14.8	324 58.0	15.8	Gienah	175 48.0	S17 38.9
A 14	268 18.6	7 04.2	16.1	59 58.7	51.9	1 26.3	14.8	340 00.2	15.8	Hadar	148 42.3	S60 27.8
Y 15	283 21.0	22 03.3 ..	16.4	74 59.6 ..	52.4	16 28.2 ..	14.8	355 02.4 ..	15.7	Hamal	327 55.5	N23 33.3
16	298 23.5	37 02.4	16.6	90 00.5	53.0	31 30.1	14.8	10 04.7	15.7	Kaus Aust.	83 38.3	S34 22.4
17	313 26.0	52 01.5	16.9	105 01.4	53.6	46 32.0	14.8	25 06.9	15.7			
18	328 28.4	67 00.5	S24 17.2	120 02.3	S10 54.2	61 33.8	S23 14.8	40 09.1	S22 15.7	Kochab	137 21.2	N74 04.5
19	343 30.9	81 59.6	17.5	135 03.2	54.8	76 35.7	14.9	55 11.3	15.7	Markab	13 33.9	N15 18.8
20	358 33.3	96 58.7	17.8	150 04.1	55.4	91 37.6	14.9	70 13.6	15.6	Menkar	314 10.1	N 4 10.0
21	13 35.8	111 57.8 ..	18.0	165 05.0 ..	56.0	106 39.5 ..	14.9	85 15.8 ..	15.6	Menkent	148 02.8	S36 27.7
22	28 38.3	126 56.8	18.3	180 05.9	56.6	121 41.4	14.9	100 18.0	15.6	Miaplacidus	221 38.7	S69 47.6
23	43 40.7	141 55.9	18.6	195 06.8	57.2	136 43.3	14.9	115 20.2	15.6			
20 00	58 43.2	156 55.0	S24 18.8	210 07.7	S10 57.8	151 45.1	S23 14.9	130 22.5	S22 15.5	Mirfak	308 33.6	N49 55.8
01	73 45.7	171 54.1	19.1	225 08.6	58.4	166 47.0	15.0	145 24.7	15.5	Nunki	75 53.2	S26 16.3
02	88 48.1	186 53.1	19.4	240 09.5	58.9	181 48.9	15.0	160 26.9	15.5	Peacock	53 12.6	S56 40.4
03	103 50.6	201 52.2 ..	19.6	255 10.4	10 59.5	196 50.8 ..	15.0	175 29.1 ..	15.5	Pollux	243 22.2	N27 58.6
04	118 53.1	216 51.3	19.9	270 11.3	11 00.1	211 52.7	15.0	190 31.3	15.4	Procyon	244 55.0	N 5 10.4
05	133 55.5	231 50.3	20.2	285 12.2	00.7	226 54.6	15.0	205 33.6	15.4			
06	148 58.0	246 49.4	S24 20.4	300 13.1	S11 01.3	241 56.5	S23 15.0	220 35.8	S22 15.4	Rasalhague	96 02.7	N12 33.0
W 07	164 00.4	261 48.5	20.7	315 14.0	01.9	256 58.3	15.0	235 38.0	15.4	Regulus	207 38.9	N11 52.3
E 08	179 02.9	276 47.6	21.0	330 14.9	02.5	272 00.2	15.1	250 40.2	15.3	Rigel	281 07.5	S 8 10.8
D 09	194 05.4	291 46.6 ..	21.2	345 15.8 ..	03.1	287 02.1 ..	15.1	265 42.5 ..	15.3	Rigil Kent.	139 46.5	S60 54.7
N 10	209 07.8	306 45.7	21.5	0 16.7	03.7	302 04.0	15.1	280 44.7	15.3	Sabik	102 07.8	S15 44.8
E 11	224 10.3	321 44.8	21.7	15 17.6	04.3	317 05.9	15.1	295 46.9	15.3			
S 12	239 12.8	336 43.8	S24 22.0	30 18.5	S11 04.8	332 07.8	S23 15.1	310 49.1	S22 15.2	Schedar	349 35.1	N56 38.9
D 13	254 15.2	351 42.9	22.2	45 19.4	05.4	347 09.6	15.1	325 51.3	15.2	Shaula	96 16.3	S37 07.0
A 14	269 17.7	6 42.0	22.5	60 20.3	06.0	2 11.5	15.2	340 53.6	15.2	Sirius	258 29.6	S16 44.6
Y 15	284 20.2	21 41.1 ..	22.8	75 21.2 ..	06.6	17 13.4 ..	15.2	355 55.8 ..	15.2	Spica	158 26.9	S11 15.6
16	299 22.6	36 40.1	23.0	90 22.1	07.2	32 15.3	15.2	10 58.0	15.1	Suhail	222 49.2	S43 30.5
17	314 25.1	51 39.2	23.3	105 23.0	07.8	47 17.2	15.2	26 00.2	15.1			
18	329 27.6	66 38.3	S24 23.5	120 23.9	S11 08.4	62 19.1	S23 15.2	41 02.5	S22 15.1	Vega	80 36.3	N38 48.4
19	344 30.0	81 37.3	23.7	135 24.8	09.0	77 20.9	15.2	56 04.7	15.1	Zuben'ubi	137 00.9	S16 07.2
20	359 32.5	96 36.4	24.0	150 25.7	09.5	92 22.8	15.2	71 06.9	15.0		SHA	Mer.Pass.
21	14 34.9	111 35.5 ..	24.2	165 26.6 ..	10.1	107 24.7 ..	15.3	86 09.1 ..	15.0		° ′	h m
22	29 37.4	126 34.5	24.5	180 27.5	10.7	122 26.6	15.3	101 11.3	15.0	Venus	99 33.1	13 32
23	44 39.9	141 33.6	24.7	195 28.4	11.3	137 28.5	15.3	116 13.6	15.0	Mars	152 02.0	10 00
	h m									Jupiter	93 15.8	13 54
Mer.Pass. 20 05.8		v −0.9	d 0.3	v 0.9	d 0.6	v 1.9	d 0.0	v 2.2	d 0.0	Saturn	71 45.0	15 20

© British Crown Copyright 2018. All rights reserved.

UT	SUN GHA	SUN Dec	MOON GHA	v	MOON Dec	d	HP
d h	° ′	° ′	° ′	′	° ′	′	′
18 00	183 45.3	S19 05.6	292 54.0	7.0	N21 47.3	4.9	58.2
01	198 45.2	06.2	307 20.0	7.0	21 42.4	4.9	58.3
02	213 45.1	06.8	321 46.0	7.0	21 37.5	5.1	58.3
03	228 45.0 . .	07.4	336 12.0	7.1	21 32.4	5.3	58.3
04	243 44.8	08.0	350 38.1	7.1	21 27.1	5.4	58.3
05	258 44.7	08.6	5 04.2	7.1	21 21.7	5.5	58.3
06	273 44.6	S19 09.2	19 30.3	7.1	N21 16.2	5.6	58.4
07	288 44.5	09.8	33 56.4	7.1	21 10.6	5.8	58.4
08	303 44.3	10.4	48 22.5	7.2	21 04.8	5.9	58.4
M 09	318 44.2 . .	11.0	62 48.7	7.2	20 58.9	6.1	58.4
O 10	333 44.1	11.6	77 14.9	7.2	20 52.8	6.1	58.4
N 11	348 43.9	12.2	91 41.1	7.3	20 46.7	6.3	58.4
D 12	3 43.8	S19 12.8	106 07.4	7.3	N20 40.4	6.5	58.5
A 13	18 43.7	13.4	120 33.7	7.3	20 33.9	6.5	58.5
Y 14	33 43.5	14.0	135 00.0	7.3	20 27.4	6.7	58.5
15	48 43.4 . .	14.6	149 26.3	7.4	20 20.7	6.8	58.5
16	63 43.3	15.2	163 52.7	7.4	20 13.9	7.0	58.5
17	78 43.2	15.8	178 19.1	7.5	20 06.9	7.1	58.5
18	93 43.0	S19 16.4	192 45.6	7.4	N19 59.8	7.2	58.6
19	108 42.9	17.0	207 12.0	7.6	19 52.6	7.3	58.6
20	123 42.8	17.6	221 38.6	7.5	19 45.3	7.4	58.6
21	138 42.6 . .	18.2	236 05.1	7.6	19 37.9	7.6	58.6
22	153 42.5	18.8	250 31.7	7.6	19 30.3	7.7	58.6
23	168 42.4	19.4	264 58.3	7.7	19 22.6	7.8	58.7
19 00	183 42.2	S19 19.9	279 25.0	7.7	N19 14.8	7.9	58.7
01	198 42.1	20.5	293 51.7	7.7	19 06.9	8.1	58.7
02	213 41.9	21.1	308 18.4	7.8	18 58.8	8.1	58.7
03	228 41.8 . .	21.7	322 45.2	7.8	18 50.7	8.3	58.7
04	243 41.7	22.3	337 12.0	7.8	18 42.4	8.4	58.7
05	258 41.5	22.9	351 38.8	7.9	18 34.0	8.5	58.8
06	273 41.4	S19 23.5	6 05.7	7.9	N18 25.5	8.7	58.8
07	288 41.3	24.1	20 32.6	8.0	18 16.8	8.7	58.8
T 08	303 41.1	24.6	34 59.6	8.0	18 08.1	8.9	58.8
U 09	318 41.0 . .	25.2	49 26.6	8.1	17 59.2	8.9	58.8
E 10	333 40.9	25.8	63 53.7	8.0	17 50.3	9.1	58.8
S 11	348 40.7	26.4	78 20.7	8.2	17 41.2	9.2	58.9
D 12	3 40.6	S19 27.0	92 47.9	8.1	N17 32.0	9.3	58.9
A 13	18 40.4	27.5	107 15.0	8.2	17 22.7	9.4	58.9
Y 14	33 40.3	28.1	121 42.2	8.3	17 13.3	9.5	58.9
15	48 40.2 . .	28.7	136 09.5	8.3	17 03.8	9.7	58.9
16	63 40.0	29.3	150 36.8	8.3	16 54.1	9.7	58.9
17	78 39.9	29.9	165 04.1	8.4	16 44.4	9.8	59.0
18	93 39.7	S19 30.4	179 31.5	8.4	N16 34.6	10.0	59.0
19	108 39.6	31.0	193 58.9	8.5	16 24.6	10.0	59.0
20	123 39.5	31.6	208 26.4	8.5	16 14.6	10.1	59.0
21	138 39.3 . .	32.2	222 53.9	8.5	16 04.5	10.3	59.0
22	153 39.2	32.8	237 21.4	8.6	15 54.2	10.3	59.0
23	168 39.0	33.3	251 49.0	8.6	15 43.9	10.5	59.1
20 00	183 38.9	S19 33.9	266 16.6	8.6	N15 33.4	10.5	59.1
01	198 38.7	34.5	280 44.2	8.7	15 22.9	10.6	59.1
02	213 38.6	35.1	295 11.9	8.8	15 12.3	10.7	59.1
03	228 38.5 . .	35.6	309 39.7	8.8	15 01.6	10.9	59.1
04	243 38.3	36.2	324 07.5	8.8	14 50.7	10.9	59.1
05	258 38.2	36.8	338 35.3	8.9	14 39.8	11.0	59.1
06	273 38.0	S19 37.3	353 03.2	8.9	N14 28.8	11.1	59.2
W 07	288 37.9	37.9	7 31.1	8.9	14 17.7	11.1	59.2
E 08	303 37.7	38.5	21 59.0	9.0	14 06.6	11.3	59.2
D 09	318 37.6 . .	39.1	36 27.0	9.0	13 55.3	11.4	59.2
N 10	333 37.4	39.6	50 55.0	9.0	13 43.9	11.4	59.2
E 11	348 37.3	40.2	65 23.0	9.1	13 32.5	11.5	59.2
S 12	3 37.1	S19 40.8	79 51.1	9.2	N13 21.0	11.6	59.2
D 13	18 37.0	41.3	94 19.3	9.1	13 09.4	11.7	59.3
A 14	33 36.8	41.9	108 47.4	9.2	12 57.7	11.8	59.3
Y 15	48 36.7 . .	42.5	123 15.6	9.3	12 45.9	11.8	59.3
16	63 36.5	43.0	137 43.9	9.3	12 34.1	12.0	59.3
17	78 36.4	43.6	152 12.2	9.3	12 22.1	12.0	59.3
18	93 36.2	S19 44.1	166 40.5	9.3	N12 10.1	12.0	59.3
19	108 36.1	44.7	181 08.8	9.4	11 58.1	12.2	59.3
20	123 35.9	45.3	195 37.2	9.4	11 45.9	12.2	59.4
21	138 35.8 . .	45.8	210 05.6	9.5	11 33.7	12.3	59.4
22	153 35.6	46.4	224 34.1	9.5	11 21.4	12.4	59.4
23	168 35.5	47.0	239 02.6	9.5	N11 09.0	12.4	59.4
	SD 16.2	d 0.6	SD 15.9		16.0		16.1

Lat.	Twilight Naut.	Twilight Civil	Sunrise	Moonrise 18	Moonrise 19	Moonrise 20	Moonrise 21
°	h m	h m		h m	h m	h m	h m
N 72	07 12	08 52	▬▬	▭	19 55	22 35	24 51
N 70	07 01	08 26	10 15	17 30	20 40	22 54	24 59
68	06 51	08 06	09 30	19 01	21 10	23 10	25 05
66	06 43	07 50	09 01	19 39	21 31	23 22	25 11
64	06 36	07 37	08 39	20 06	21 49	23 32	25 15
62	06 30	07 26	08 21	20 27	22 03	23 41	25 19
60	06 24	07 17	08 07	20 44	22 15	23 48	25 22
N 58	06 19	07 08	07 55	20 58	22 25	23 55	25 25
56	06 15	07 01	07 44	21 10	22 34	24 00	00 00
54	06 10	06 54	07 34	21 20	22 42	24 06	00 06
52	06 06	06 48	07 26	21 30	22 49	24 10	00 10
50	06 03	06 42	07 19	21 38	22 55	24 14	00 14
45	05 54	06 30	07 02	21 56	23 09	24 23	00 23
N 40	05 47	06 20	06 49	22 10	23 20	24 31	00 31
35	05 40	06 11	06 38	22 22	23 29	24 37	00 37
30	05 33	06 03	06 28	22 33	23 38	24 43	00 43
20	05 21	05 48	06 11	22 51	23 52	24 53	00 53
N 10	05 08	05 34	05 56	23 07	24 04	00 04	01 01
0	04 54	05 20	05 42	23 22	24 16	00 16	01 09
S 10	04 39	05 05	05 27	23 36	24 28	00 28	01 17
20	04 20	04 48	05 12	23 52	24 40	00 40	01 25
30	03 56	04 28	04 54	24 10	00 10	00 54	01 35
35	03 41	04 16	04 44	24 20	00 20	01 02	01 40
40	03 23	04 01	04 32	24 32	00 32	01 12	01 47
45	02 59	03 43	04 18	00 04	00 46	01 22	01 54
S 50	02 27	03 20	04 00	00 24	01 03	01 35	02 02
52	02 10	03 09	03 52	00 34	01 11	01 41	02 06
54	01 49	02 56	03 43	00 44	01 20	01 48	02 11
56	01 21	02 41	03 32	00 57	01 30	01 55	02 15
58	00 34	02 23	03 20	01 11	01 41	02 04	02 21
S 60	////	02 01	03 06	01 27	01 54	02 13	02 27

Lat.	Sunset	Twilight Civil	Twilight Naut.	Moonset 18	Moonset 19	Moonset 20	Moonset 21
°	h m	h m	h m	h m	h m	h m	h m
N 72	▬▬	14 38	16 17	▭	16 28	15 40	15 13
N 70	13 14	15 04	16 29	16 56	15 41	15 18	15 03
68	13 59	15 24	16 39	15 24	15 11	15 01	14 54
66	14 29	15 39	16 47	14 45	14 48	14 48	14 46
64	14 51	15 53	16 54	14 18	14 29	14 36	14 40
62	15 08	16 04	17 00	13 56	14 14	14 26	14 35
60	15 23	16 13	17 06	13 39	14 02	14 18	14 30
N 58	15 35	16 22	17 11	13 24	13 51	14 10	14 26
56	15 46	16 29	17 15	13 12	13 41	14 04	14 22
54	15 56	16 36	17 20	13 01	13 33	13 58	14 18
52	16 04	16 42	17 24	12 51	13 25	13 52	14 15
50	16 12	16 48	17 27	12 42	13 18	13 47	14 13
45	16 28	17 00	17 36	12 24	13 03	13 37	14 06
N 40	16 41	17 10	17 43	12 09	12 51	13 28	14 01
35	16 52	17 19	17 50	11 56	12 40	13 20	13 57
30	17 02	17 28	17 57	11 45	12 31	13 13	13 53
20	17 20	17 43	18 10	11 25	12 15	13 02	13 46
N 10	17 35	17 57	18 23	11 08	12 01	12 51	13 39
0	17 49	18 11	18 36	10 52	11 48	12 41	13 34
S 10	18 03	18 26	18 52	10 36	11 34	12 32	13 28
20	18 19	18 43	19 11	10 19	11 20	12 21	13 21
30	18 37	19 03	19 35	09 59	11 04	12 09	13 14
35	18 47	19 16	19 50	09 48	10 54	12 02	13 10
40	18 59	19 30	20 09	09 34	10 43	11 54	13 05
45	19 14	19 48	20 33	09 18	10 30	11 44	12 59
S 50	19 31	20 11	21 05	08 59	10 14	11 32	12 52
52	19 40	20 23	21 23	08 50	10 06	11 27	12 49
54	19 49	20 36	21 44	08 39	09 58	11 21	12 46
56	20 00	20 51	22 14	08 27	09 49	11 14	12 42
58	20 12	21 09	23 05	08 13	09 38	11 07	12 37
S 60	20 26	21 33	////	07 57	09 25	10 58	12 33

	SUN			MOON			
Day	Eqn. of Time 00ʰ	Eqn. of Time 12ʰ	Mer. Pass.	Mer. Pass. Upper	Mer. Pass. Lower	Age	Phase
d	m s	m s	h m	h m	h m	d	%
18	15 02	14 55	11 45	04 39	17 07	21	65
19	14 49	14 43	11 45	05 35	18 02	22	54
20	14 36	14 29	11 46	06 29	18 55	23	43

© British Crown Copyright 2018. All rights reserved.

2019 NOVEMBER 21, 22, 23 (THURS., FRI., SAT.)

UT	ARIES GHA	VENUS −3.9 GHA	Dec	MARS +1.7 GHA	Dec	JUPITER −1.9 GHA	Dec	SATURN +0.6 GHA	Dec	STARS Name	SHA	Dec
21 00	59 42.3	156 32.7	S24 25.0	210 29.3	S11 11.9	152 30.3	S23 15.3	131 15.8	S22 14.9	Acamar	315 14.6	S40 13.7
01	74 44.8	171 31.7	25.2	225 30.2	12.5	167 32.2	15.3	146 18.0	14.9	Achernar	335 23.0	S57 08.4
02	89 47.3	186 30.8	25.4	240 31.1	13.1	182 34.1	15.3	161 20.2	14.9	Acrux	173 04.8	S63 12.2
03	104 49.7	201 29.9 ..	25.7	255 31.9 ..	13.7	197 36.0 ..	15.3	176 22.4 ..	14.9	Adhara	255 08.8	S28 59.8
04	119 52.2	216 28.9	25.9	270 32.8	14.2	212 37.9	15.4	191 24.7	14.8	Aldebaran	290 44.0	N16 32.8
05	134 54.7	231 28.0	26.1	285 33.7	14.8	227 39.8	15.4	206 26.9	14.8			
06	149 57.1	246 27.1	S24 26.4	300 34.6	S11 15.4	242 41.6	S23 15.4	221 29.1	S22 14.8	Alioth	166 17.2	N55 51.1
T 07	164 59.6	261 26.1	26.6	315 35.5	16.0	257 43.5	15.4	236 31.3	14.8	Alkaid	152 55.8	N49 12.9
H 08	180 02.1	276 25.2	26.8	330 36.4	16.6	272 45.4	15.4	251 33.5	14.7	Alnair	27 38.2	S46 52.1
U 09	195 04.5	291 24.3 ..	27.1	345 37.3 ..	17.2	287 47.3 ..	15.4	266 35.8 ..	14.7	Alnilam	275 41.6	S 1 11.4
R 10	210 07.0	306 23.3	27.3	0 38.2	17.8	302 49.2	15.4	281 38.0	14.7	Alphard	217 51.7	S 8 44.5
S 11	225 09.4	321 22.4	27.5	15 39.1	18.4	317 51.0	15.5	296 40.2	14.6			
D 12	240 11.9	336 21.5	S24 27.7	30 40.0	S11 18.9	332 52.9	S23 15.5	311 42.4	S22 14.6	Alphecca	126 07.7	N26 39.1
A 13	255 14.4	351 20.5	28.0	45 40.9	19.5	347 54.8	15.5	326 44.6	14.6	Alpheratz	357 38.8	N29 12.1
Y 14	270 16.8	6 19.6	28.2	60 41.8	20.1	2 56.7	15.5	341 46.8	14.6	Altair	62 04.2	N 8 55.4
15	285 19.3	21 18.7 ..	28.4	75 42.7 ..	20.7	17 58.6 ..	15.5	356 49.1 ..	14.5	Ankaa	353 11.1	S42 12.1
16	300 21.8	36 17.7	28.6	90 43.6	21.3	33 00.4	15.5	11 51.3	14.5	Antares	112 21.3	S26 28.3
17	315 24.2	51 16.8	28.9	105 44.5	21.9	48 02.3	15.5	26 53.5	14.5			
18	330 26.7	66 15.9	S24 29.1	120 45.4	S11 22.5	63 04.2	S23 15.6	41 55.7	S22 14.5	Arcturus	145 52.0	N19 04.9
19	345 29.2	81 14.9	29.3	135 46.3	23.0	78 06.1	15.6	56 57.9	14.4	Atria	107 19.7	S69 03.6
20	0 31.6	96 14.0	29.5	150 47.2	23.6	93 08.0	15.6	72 00.2	14.4	Avior	234 16.0	S59 34.1
21	15 34.1	111 13.0 ..	29.7	165 48.1 ..	24.2	108 09.8 ..	15.6	87 02.4 ..	14.4	Bellatrix	278 27.0	N 6 22.0
22	30 36.5	126 12.1	29.9	180 49.0	24.8	123 11.7	15.6	102 04.6	14.4	Betelgeuse	270 56.2	N 7 24.6
23	45 39.0	141 11.2	30.1	195 49.9	25.4	138 13.6	15.6	117 06.8	14.3			
22 00	60 41.5	156 10.2	S24 30.3	210 50.7	S11 26.0	153 15.5	S23 15.6	132 09.0	S22 14.3	Canopus	263 53.7	S52 42.3
01	75 43.9	171 09.3	30.6	225 51.6	26.5	168 17.4	15.7	147 11.2	14.3	Capella	280 27.5	N46 00.9
02	90 46.4	186 08.4	30.8	240 52.5	27.1	183 19.2	15.7	162 13.5	14.3	Deneb	49 28.7	N45 21.3
03	105 48.9	201 07.4 ..	31.0	255 53.4 ..	27.7	198 21.1 ..	15.7	177 15.7 ..	14.2	Denebola	182 29.3	N14 27.8
04	120 51.3	216 06.5	31.2	270 54.3	28.3	213 23.0	15.7	192 17.9	14.2	Diphda	348 51.3	S17 52.8
05	135 53.8	231 05.5	31.4	285 55.2	28.9	228 24.9	15.7	207 20.1	14.2			
06	150 56.3	246 04.6	S24 31.6	300 56.1	S11 29.5	243 26.8	S23 15.7	222 22.3	S22 14.2	Dubhe	193 46.5	N61 38.5
07	165 58.7	261 03.7	31.8	315 57.0	30.0	258 28.6	15.7	237 24.5	14.1	Elnath	278 06.7	N28 37.3
08	181 01.2	276 02.7	32.0	330 57.9	30.6	273 30.5	15.8	252 26.8	14.1	Eltanin	90 44.6	N51 29.4
F 09	196 03.7	291 01.8 ..	32.2	345 58.8 ..	31.2	288 32.4 ..	15.8	267 29.0 ..	14.1	Enif	33 42.9	N 9 58.1
R 10	211 06.1	306 00.9	32.4	0 59.7	31.8	303 34.3	15.8	282 31.2	14.1	Fomalhaut	15 19.1	S29 31.2
I 11	226 08.6	320 59.9	32.6	16 00.6	32.4	318 36.2	15.8	297 33.4	14.0			
D 12	241 11.0	335 59.0	S24 32.8	31 01.5	S11 33.0	333 38.0	S23 15.8	312 35.6	S22 14.0	Gacrux	171 56.4	S57 13.1
A 13	256 13.5	350 58.0	33.0	46 02.3	33.5	348 39.9	15.8	327 37.8	14.0	Gienah	175 48.0	S17 38.9
Y 14	271 16.0	5 57.1	33.2	61 03.2	34.1	3 41.8	15.8	342 40.1	14.0	Hadar	148 42.3	S60 27.8
15	286 18.4	20 56.2 ..	33.3	76 04.1 ..	34.7	18 43.7 ..	15.9	357 42.3 ..	13.9	Hamal	327 55.5	N23 33.3
16	301 20.9	35 55.2	33.5	91 05.0	35.3	33 45.5	15.9	12 44.5	13.9	Kaus Aust.	83 38.3	S34 22.4
17	316 23.4	50 54.3	33.7	106 05.9	35.9	48 47.4	15.9	27 46.7	13.9			
18	331 25.8	65 53.3	S24 33.9	121 06.8	S11 36.5	63 49.3	S23 15.9	42 48.9	S22 13.9	Kochab	137 21.2	N74 04.5
19	346 28.3	80 52.4	34.1	136 07.7	37.0	78 51.2	15.9	57 51.1	13.8	Markab	13 33.9	N15 18.8
20	1 30.8	95 51.5	34.3	151 08.6	37.6	93 53.1	15.9	72 53.4	13.8	Menkar	314 10.1	N 4 10.0
21	16 33.2	110 50.5 ..	34.5	166 09.5 ..	38.2	108 54.9 ..	15.9	87 55.6 ..	13.8	Menkent	148 02.8	S36 27.7
22	31 35.7	125 49.6	34.6	181 10.4	38.8	123 56.8	15.9	102 57.8	13.7	Miaplacidus	221 38.6	S69 47.6
23	46 38.1	140 48.6	34.8	196 11.3	39.4	138 58.7	16.0	118 00.0	13.7			
23 00	61 40.6	155 47.7	S24 35.0	211 12.1	S11 39.9	154 00.6	S23 16.0	133 02.2	S22 13.7	Mirfak	308 33.6	N49 55.8
01	76 43.1	170 46.8	35.2	226 13.0	40.5	169 02.4	16.0	148 04.4	13.7	Nunki	75 53.2	S26 16.3
02	91 45.5	185 45.8	35.4	241 13.9	41.1	184 04.3	16.0	163 06.6	13.6	Peacock	53 12.6	S56 40.4
03	106 48.0	200 44.9 ..	35.5	256 14.8 ..	41.7	199 06.2 ..	16.0	178 08.9 ..	13.6	Pollux	243 22.2	N27 58.6
04	121 50.5	215 43.9	35.7	271 15.7	42.3	214 08.1	16.0	193 11.1	13.6	Procyon	244 54.9	N 5 10.4
05	136 52.9	230 43.0	35.9	286 16.6	42.9	229 09.9	16.0	208 13.3	13.6			
06	151 55.4	245 42.1	S24 36.0	301 17.5	S11 43.4	244 11.8	S23 16.1	223 15.5	S22 13.5	Rasalhague	96 02.7	N12 33.0
S 07	166 57.9	260 41.1	36.2	316 18.4	44.0	259 13.7	16.1	238 17.7	13.5	Regulus	207 38.9	N11 52.2
A 08	182 00.3	275 40.2	36.4	331 19.3	44.6	274 15.6	16.1	253 19.9	13.5	Rigel	281 07.5	S 8 10.8
T 09	197 02.8	290 39.2 ..	36.5	346 20.2 ..	45.2	289 17.5 ..	16.1	268 22.1 ..	13.5	Rigil Kent.	139 46.4	S60 54.7
U 10	212 05.3	305 38.3	36.7	1 21.0	45.8	304 19.3	16.1	283 24.4	13.4	Sabik	102 07.8	S15 44.8
R 11	227 07.7	320 37.3	36.9	16 21.9	46.3	319 21.2	16.1	298 26.6	13.4			
D 12	242 10.2	335 36.4	S24 37.0	31 22.8	S11 47.0	334 23.1	S23 16.1	313 28.8	S22 13.4	Schedar	349 35.2	N56 38.9
A 13	257 12.6	350 35.5	37.2	46 23.7	47.5	349 25.0	16.1	328 31.0	13.4	Shaula	96 16.4	S37 07.0
Y 14	272 15.1	5 34.5	37.4	61 24.6	48.1	4 26.8	16.2	343 33.2	13.3	Sirius	258 29.6	S16 44.6
15	287 17.6	20 33.6 ..	37.5	76 25.5 ..	48.7	19 28.7 ..	16.2	358 35.4 ..	13.3	Spica	158 26.9	S11 15.6
16	302 20.0	35 32.6	37.7	91 26.4	49.2	34 30.6	16.2	13 37.6	13.3	Suhail	222 49.1	S43 30.5
17	317 22.5	50 31.7	37.8	106 27.3	49.8	49 32.5	16.2	28 39.9	13.2			
18	332 25.0	65 30.7	S24 38.0	121 28.1	S11 50.4	64 34.3	S23 16.2	43 42.1	S22 13.2	Vega	80 36.3	N38 48.4
19	347 27.4	80 29.8	38.2	136 29.0	51.0	79 36.2	16.2	58 44.3	13.2	Zuben'ubi	137 00.9	S16 07.2
20	2 29.9	95 28.9	38.3	151 29.9	51.5	94 38.1	16.2	73 46.5	13.2		SHA	Mer.Pass.
21	17 32.4	110 27.9 ..	38.5	166 30.8 ..	52.1	109 40.0 ..	16.2	88 48.7 ..	13.1			
22	32 34.8	125 27.0	38.6	181 31.7	52.7	124 41.8	16.3	103 50.9	13.1	Venus	95 28.8	13 36
23	47 37.3	140 26.0	38.8	196 32.6	53.3	139 43.7	16.3	118 53.1	13.1	Mars	150 09.3	9 56
Mer.Pass. 19 54.0		v −0.9	d 0.2	v 0.9	d 0.6	v 1.9	d 0.0	v 2.2	d 0.0	Jupiter	92 34.0	13 45
										Saturn	71 27.5	15 09

© British Crown Copyright 2018. All rights reserved.

UT	SUN GHA	SUN Dec	MOON GHA	v	MOON Dec	d	HP
d h	° ′	° ′	° ′	′	° ′	′	′
21 00	183 35.3	S19 47.5	253 31.1	9.5	N10 56.6	12.5	59.4
01	198 35.2	48.1	267 59.6	9.6	10 44.1	12.6	59.4
02	213 35.0	48.6	282 28.2	9.6	10 31.5	12.6	59.4
03	228 34.9 . .	49.2	296 56.8	9.6	10 18.9	12.7	59.4
04	243 34.7	49.8	311 25.4	9.7	10 06.2	12.8	59.5
05	258 34.6	50.3	325 54.1	9.7	9 53.4	12.8	59.5
06	273 34.4	S19 50.9	340 22.8	9.7	N 9 40.6	12.9	59.5
T 07	288 34.3	51.4	354 51.5	9.8	9 27.7	13.0	59.5
H 08	303 34.1	52.0	9 20.3	9.8	9 14.7	13.0	59.5
U 09	318 34.0 . .	52.5	23 49.1	9.8	9 01.7	13.0	59.5
R 10	333 33.8	53.1	38 17.9	9.8	8 48.7	13.2	59.5
S 11	348 33.7	53.6	52 46.7	9.8	8 35.5	13.1	59.5
D 12	3 33.5	S19 54.2	67 15.6	9.9	N 8 22.4	13.2	59.5
A 13	18 33.3	54.7	81 44.5	9.9	8 09.2	13.3	59.6
Y 14	33 33.2	55.3	96 13.4	9.9	7 55.9	13.4	59.6
15	48 33.0 . .	55.8	110 42.3	10.0	7 42.5	13.3	59.6
16	63 32.9	56.4	125 11.3	9.9	7 29.2	13.4	59.6
17	78 32.7	56.9	139 40.2	10.0	7 15.8	13.5	59.6
18	93 32.6	S19 57.5	154 09.2	10.1	N 7 02.3	13.5	59.6
19	108 32.4	58.0	168 38.3	10.0	6 48.8	13.6	59.6
20	123 32.2	58.6	183 07.3	10.0	6 35.2	13.6	59.6
21	138 32.1 . .	59.1	197 36.3	10.1	6 21.6	13.6	59.6
22	153 31.9	19 59.7	212 05.4	10.1	6 08.0	13.7	59.6
23	168 31.8	20 00.2	226 34.5	10.1	5 54.3	13.7	59.7
22 00	183 31.6	S20 00.8	241 03.6	10.1	N 5 40.6	13.8	59.7
01	198 31.4	01.3	255 32.7	10.2	5 26.8	13.8	59.7
02	213 31.3	01.9	270 01.9	10.1	5 13.0	13.8	59.7
03	228 31.1 . .	02.4	284 31.0	10.2	4 59.2	13.8	59.7
04	243 30.9	02.9	299 00.2	10.1	4 45.4	13.9	59.7
05	258 30.8	03.5	313 29.3	10.2	4 31.5	13.9	59.7
06	273 30.6	S20 04.0	327 58.5	10.2	N 4 17.6	14.0	59.7
07	288 30.5	04.6	342 27.7	10.2	4 03.6	14.0	59.7
08	303 30.3	05.1	356 56.9	10.2	3 49.6	14.0	59.7
F 09	318 30.1 . .	05.6	11 26.1	10.3	3 35.6	14.0	59.7
R 10	333 30.0	06.2	25 55.4	10.2	3 21.6	14.0	59.7
I 11	348 29.8	06.7	40 24.6	10.2	3 07.6	14.1	59.7
D 12	3 29.6	S20 07.3	54 53.8	10.3	N 2 53.5	14.1	59.7
A 13	18 29.5	07.8	69 23.1	10.2	2 39.4	14.1	59.7
Y 14	33 29.3	08.3	83 52.3	10.3	2 25.3	14.1	59.8
15	48 29.1 . .	08.9	98 21.6	10.2	2 11.2	14.1	59.8
16	63 29.0	09.4	112 50.8	10.3	1 57.1	14.2	59.8
17	78 28.8	09.9	127 20.1	10.2	1 42.9	14.1	59.8
18	93 28.6	S20 10.5	141 49.3	10.3	N 1 28.8	14.2	59.8
19	108 28.5	11.0	156 18.6	10.2	1 14.6	14.2	59.8
20	123 28.3	11.5	170 47.8	10.3	1 00.4	14.2	59.8
21	138 28.1 . .	12.1	185 17.1	10.2	0 46.2	14.2	59.8
22	153 28.0	12.6	199 46.3	10.3	0 32.0	14.2	59.8
23	168 27.8	13.1	214 15.6	10.2	0 17.8	14.2	59.8
23 00	183 27.6	S20 13.7	228 44.8	10.3	N 0 03.6	14.2	59.8
01	198 27.5	14.2	243 14.1	10.2	S 0 10.6	14.2	59.8
02	213 27.3	14.7	257 43.3	10.2	0 24.8	14.2	59.8
03	228 27.1 . .	15.2	272 12.5	10.3	0 39.0	14.2	59.8
04	243 27.0	15.8	286 41.8	10.2	0 53.2	14.3	59.8
05	258 26.8	16.3	301 11.0	10.2	1 07.5	14.2	59.8
06	273 26.6	S20 16.8	315 40.2	10.2	S 1 21.7	14.2	59.8
S 07	288 26.4	17.3	330 09.4	10.2	1 35.9	14.1	59.8
A 08	303 26.3	17.9	344 38.6	10.1	1 50.0	14.2	59.8
T 09	318 26.1 . .	18.4	359 07.7	10.2	2 04.2	14.2	59.8
U 10	333 25.9	18.9	13 36.9	10.1	2 18.4	14.1	59.8
R 11	348 25.8	19.4	28 06.0	10.2	2 32.5	14.2	59.8
D 12	3 25.6	S20 20.0	42 35.2	10.1	S 2 46.7	14.1	59.8
A 13	18 25.4	20.5	57 04.3	10.1	3 00.8	14.1	59.8
Y 14	33 25.2	21.0	71 33.4	10.1	3 14.9	14.1	59.8
15	48 25.1 . .	21.5	86 02.5	10.1	3 29.0	14.1	59.8
16	63 24.9	22.0	100 31.6	10.0	3 43.1	14.1	59.8
17	78 24.7	22.6	115 00.6	10.1	3 57.2	14.0	59.8
18	93 24.5	S20 23.1	129 29.7	10.0	S 4 11.2	14.0	59.8
19	108 24.4	23.6	143 58.7	10.0	4 25.2	14.0	59.8
20	123 24.2	24.1	158 27.7	10.0	4 39.2	13.9	59.8
21	138 24.0 . .	24.6	172 56.7	9.9	4 53.1	14.0	59.8
22	153 23.8	25.1	187 25.6	10.0	5 07.1	13.9	59.8
23	168 23.7	25.7	201 54.6	9.9	S 5 21.0	13.8	59.8
	SD 16.2	d 0.5	SD 16.2		16.3		16.3

Lat.	Twilight Naut.	Twilight Civil	Sunrise	Moonrise 21	22	23	24
°	h m	h m	h m	h m	h m	h m	h m
N 72	07 22	09 06	▬	24 51	00 51	03 01	05 13
N 70	07 10	08 37	10 42	24 59	00 59	03 00	05 03
68	06 59	08 16	09 45	25 05	01 05	02 59	04 54
66	06 50	07 59	09 12	25 11	01 11	02 58	04 47
64	06 43	07 45	08 48	25 15	01 15	02 58	04 41
62	06 36	07 33	08 30	25 19	01 19	02 57	04 36
60	06 30	07 23	08 14	25 22	01 22	02 57	04 32
N 58	06 24	07 14	08 01	25 25	01 25	02 56	04 28
56	06 19	07 06	07 50	00 00	01 28	02 56	04 24
54	06 15	06 59	07 40	00 06	01 30	02 56	04 21
52	06 11	06 53	07 31	00 10	01 33	02 55	04 18
50	06 07	06 47	07 23	00 14	01 35	02 55	04 16
45	05 58	06 34	07 06	00 23	01 39	02 54	04 10
N 40	05 50	06 23	06 53	00 31	01 42	02 54	04 06
35	05 43	06 14	06 41	00 37	01 45	02 53	04 02
30	05 36	06 05	06 30	00 43	01 48	02 53	03 58
20	05 22	05 49	06 13	00 53	01 53	02 52	03 53
N 10	05 09	05 35	05 57	01 01	01 57	02 52	03 48
0	04 55	05 20	05 42	01 09	02 01	02 52	03 43
S 10	04 39	05 05	05 28	01 17	02 04	02 51	03 38
20	04 19	04 48	05 12	01 25	02 08	02 51	03 33
30	03 55	04 27	04 53	01 35	02 13	02 50	03 28
35	03 39	04 14	04 42	01 40	02 16	02 50	03 24
40	03 20	03 59	04 30	01 47	02 19	02 50	03 21
45	02 55	03 40	04 15	01 54	02 22	02 49	03 17
S 50	02 21	03 16	03 57	02 02	02 26	02 49	03 12
52	02 03	03 04	03 48	02 06	02 28	02 49	03 09
54	01 40	02 51	03 38	02 11	02 30	02 48	03 07
56	01 08	02 35	03 27	02 15	02 32	02 48	03 04
58	////	02 16	03 15	02 21	02 35	02 48	03 01
S 60	////	01 51	03 00	02 27	02 38	02 48	02 58

Lat.	Sunset	Twilight Civil	Twilight Naut.	Moonset 21	22	23	24
°	h m	h m	h m	h m	h m	h m	h m
N 72	▬	14 25	16 08	15 13	14 52	14 31	14 08
N 70	12 50	14 54	16 21	15 03	14 49	14 36	14 21
68	13 46	15 15	16 32	14 54	14 47	14 40	14 32
66	14 19	15 32	16 41	14 46	14 45	14 43	14 41
64	14 43	15 46	16 49	14 40	14 43	14 46	14 49
62	15 02	15 58	16 55	14 35	14 42	14 48	14 55
60	15 17	16 08	17 02	14 30	14 40	14 50	15 01
N 58	15 30	16 17	17 07	14 26	14 39	14 52	15 06
56	15 42	16 25	17 12	14 22	14 38	14 54	15 11
54	15 52	16 32	17 16	14 18	14 37	14 55	15 15
52	16 00	16 39	17 21	14 15	14 36	14 57	15 18
50	16 08	16 45	17 25	14 13	14 36	14 58	15 22
45	16 25	16 58	17 34	14 06	14 34	15 01	15 29
N 40	16 39	17 09	17 42	14 01	14 33	15 03	15 35
35	16 51	17 18	17 49	13 57	14 31	15 05	15 41
30	17 01	17 27	17 56	13 53	14 30	15 07	15 45
20	17 19	17 43	18 09	13 46	14 28	15 10	15 53
N 10	17 35	17 57	18 23	13 39	14 26	15 13	16 01
0	17 50	18 12	18 37	13 34	14 25	15 16	16 07
S 10	18 05	18 27	18 53	13 28	14 23	15 18	16 14
20	18 21	18 45	19 13	13 21	14 21	15 21	16 22
30	18 39	19 06	19 38	13 14	14 19	15 24	16 30
35	18 50	19 19	19 54	13 10	14 18	15 26	16 35
40	19 03	19 34	20 13	13 05	14 16	15 28	16 40
45	19 18	19 53	20 38	12 59	14 15	15 30	16 46
S 50	19 36	20 17	21 12	12 52	14 13	15 33	16 54
52	19 45	20 29	21 31	12 49	14 12	15 35	16 58
54	19 55	20 42	21 54	12 46	14 11	15 36	17 02
56	20 06	20 59	22 28	12 42	14 10	15 38	17 06
58	20 19	21 18	////	12 37	14 08	15 39	17 11
S 60	20 34	21 44	////	12 33	14 07	15 41	17 16

Day	SUN Eqn. of Time 00h	SUN Eqn. of Time 12h	SUN Mer. Pass.	MOON Mer. Pass. Upper	MOON Mer. Pass. Lower	Age	Phase
d	m s	m s	h m	h m	h m	d %	
21	14 22	14 14	11 46	07 21	19 47	24 32	
22	14 07	13 59	11 46	08 13	20 38	25 22	
23	13 51	13 43	11 46	09 04	21 29	26 13	

© British Crown Copyright 2018. All rights reserved.

UT	ARIES GHA	VENUS −3.9 GHA	Dec	MARS +1.7 GHA	Dec	JUPITER −1.8 GHA	Dec	SATURN +0.6 GHA	Dec	STARS Name	SHA	Dec
24 00	62 39.8	155 25.1	S24 38.9	211 33.5	S11 53.9	154 45.6	S23 16.3	133 55.3	S22 13.1	Acamar	315 14.6	S40 13.7
01	77 42.2	170 24.1	39.1	226 34.4	54.4	169 47.5	16.3	148 57.6	13.0	Achernar	335 23.0	S57 08.4
02	92 44.7	185 23.2	39.2	241 35.2	55.0	184 49.3	16.3	163 59.8	13.0	Acrux	173 04.8	S63 12.1
03	107 47.1	200 22.2	.. 39.3	256 36.1	.. 55.6	199 51.2	.. 16.3	179 02.0	.. 13.0	Adhara	255 08.8	S28 59.9
04	122 49.6	215 21.3	39.5	271 37.0	56.2	214 53.1	16.3	194 04.2	13.0	Aldebaran	290 44.0	N16 32.8
05	137 52.1	230 20.4	39.6	286 37.9	56.7	229 55.0	16.3	209 06.4	12.9			
06	152 54.5	245 19.4	S24 39.8	301 38.8	S11 57.3	244 56.8	S23 16.4	224 08.6	S22 12.9	Alioth	166 17.2	N55 51.1
07	167 57.0	260 18.5	39.9	316 39.7	57.9	259 58.7	16.4	239 10.8	12.9	Alkaid	152 55.8	N49 12.9
08	182 59.5	275 17.5	40.0	331 40.6	58.5	275 00.6	16.4	254 13.0	12.8	Alnair	27 38.2	S46 52.1
S 09	198 01.9	290 16.6	.. 40.2	346 41.4	.. 59.1	290 02.5	.. 16.4	269 15.2	.. 12.8	Alnilam	275 41.6	S 1 11.4
U 10	213 04.4	305 15.6	40.3	1 42.3	11 59.6	305 04.3	16.4	284 17.5	12.8	Alphard	217 51.7	S 8 44.6
N 11	228 06.9	320 14.7	40.4	16 43.2	12 00.2	320 06.2	16.4	299 19.7	12.8			
D 12	243 09.3	335 13.7	S24 40.6	31 44.1	S12 00.8	335 08.1	S23 16.4	314 21.9	S22 12.7	Alphecca	126 07.7	N26 39.0
A 13	258 11.8	350 12.8	40.7	46 45.0	01.4	350 10.0	16.4	329 24.1	12.7	Alpheratz	357 38.8	N29 12.1
Y 14	273 14.2	5 11.9	40.8	61 45.9	01.9	5 11.8	16.4	344 26.3	12.7	Altair	62 04.2	N 8 55.4
15	288 16.7	20 10.9	.. 41.0	76 46.7	.. 02.5	20 13.7	.. 16.5	359 28.5	.. 12.7	Ankaa	353 11.1	S42 12.2
16	303 19.2	35 10.0	41.1	91 47.6	03.1	35 15.6	16.5	14 30.7	12.6	Antares	112 21.2	S26 28.3
17	318 21.6	50 09.0	41.2	106 48.5	03.7	50 17.4	16.5	29 32.9	12.6			
18	333 24.1	65 08.1	S24 41.3	121 49.4	S12 04.2	65 19.3	S23 16.5	44 35.1	S22 12.6	Arcturus	145 52.0	N19 04.9
19	348 26.6	80 07.1	41.5	136 50.3	04.8	80 21.2	16.5	59 37.4	12.6	Atria	107 19.7	S69 03.6
20	3 29.0	95 06.2	41.6	151 51.2	05.4	95 23.1	16.5	74 39.6	12.5	Avior	234 15.9	S59 34.1
21	18 31.5	110 05.2	.. 41.7	166 52.1	.. 06.0	110 24.9	.. 16.5	89 41.8	.. 12.5	Bellatrix	278 27.0	N 6 22.0
22	33 34.0	125 04.3	41.8	181 52.9	06.5	125 26.8	16.5	104 44.0	12.5	Betelgeuse	270 56.2	N 7 24.6
23	48 36.4	140 03.3	41.9	196 53.8	07.1	140 28.7	16.6	119 46.2	12.4			
25 00	63 38.9	155 02.4	S24 42.1	211 54.7	S12 07.7	155 30.6	S23 16.6	134 48.4	S22 12.4	Canopus	263 53.7	S52 42.3
01	78 41.4	170 01.4	42.2	226 55.6	08.3	170 32.4	16.6	149 50.6	12.4	Capella	280 27.5	N46 00.9
02	93 43.8	185 00.5	42.3	241 56.5	08.8	185 34.3	16.6	164 52.8	12.4	Deneb	49 28.7	N45 21.3
03	108 46.3	199 59.6	.. 42.4	256 57.3	.. 09.4	200 36.2	.. 16.6	179 55.0	.. 12.3	Denebola	182 29.3	N14 27.7
04	123 48.7	214 58.6	42.5	271 58.2	10.0	215 38.0	16.6	194 57.2	12.3	Diphda	348 51.3	S17 52.8
05	138 51.2	229 57.7	42.6	286 59.1	10.6	230 39.9	16.6	209 59.5	12.3			
06	153 53.7	244 56.7	S24 42.7	302 00.0	S12 11.1	245 41.8	S23 16.6	225 01.7	S22 12.3	Dubhe	193 46.4	N61 38.4
07	168 56.1	259 55.8	42.8	317 00.9	11.7	260 43.7	16.6	240 03.9	12.2	Elnath	278 06.7	N28 37.3
08	183 58.6	274 54.8	43.0	332 01.8	12.3	275 45.5	16.7	255 06.1	12.2	Eltanin	90 44.6	N51 29.4
M 09	199 01.1	289 53.9	.. 43.1	347 02.6	.. 12.9	290 47.4	.. 16.7	270 08.3	.. 12.2	Enif	33 42.9	N 9 58.1
O 10	214 03.5	304 52.9	43.2	2 03.5	13.4	305 49.3	16.7	285 10.5	12.1	Fomalhaut	15 19.1	S29 31.2
N 11	229 06.0	319 52.0	43.3	17 04.4	14.0	320 51.2	16.7	300 12.7	12.1			
D 12	244 08.5	334 51.0	S24 43.4	32 05.3	S12 14.6	335 53.0	S23 16.7	315 14.9	S22 12.1	Gacrux	171 56.4	S57 13.1
A 13	259 10.9	349 50.1	43.5	47 06.2	15.1	350 54.9	16.7	330 17.1	12.1	Gienah	175 48.0	S17 38.9
Y 14	274 13.4	4 49.1	43.6	62 07.0	15.7	5 56.8	16.7	345 19.3	12.0	Hadar	148 42.2	S60 27.8
15	289 15.9	19 48.2	.. 43.7	77 07.9	.. 16.3	20 58.6	.. 16.7	0 21.5	.. 12.0	Hamal	327 55.5	N23 33.3
16	304 18.3	34 47.2	43.8	92 08.8	16.9	36 00.5	16.7	15 23.7	12.0	Kaus Aust.	83 38.3	S34 22.4
17	319 20.8	49 46.3	43.9	107 09.7	17.4	51 02.4	16.7	30 26.0	12.0			
18	334 23.2	64 45.3	S24 43.9	122 10.6	S12 18.0	66 04.3	S23 16.8	45 28.2	S22 11.9	Kochab	137 21.2	N74 04.4
19	349 25.7	79 44.4	44.0	137 11.5	18.6	81 06.1	16.8	60 30.4	11.9	Markab	13 33.9	N15 18.8
20	4 28.2	94 43.4	44.1	152 12.3	19.2	96 08.0	16.8	75 32.6	11.9	Menkar	314 10.1	N 4 10.0
21	19 30.6	109 42.5	.. 44.2	167 13.2	.. 19.7	111 09.9	.. 16.8	90 34.8	.. 11.8	Menkent	148 02.8	S36 27.7
22	34 33.1	124 41.6	44.3	182 14.1	20.3	126 11.7	16.8	105 37.0	11.8	Miaplacidus	221 38.5	S69 47.6
23	49 35.6	139 40.6	44.4	197 15.0	20.9	141 13.6	16.8	120 39.2	11.8			
26 00	64 38.0	154 39.7	S24 44.5	212 15.8	S12 21.4	156 15.5	S23 16.8	135 41.4	S22 11.8	Mirfak	308 33.6	N49 55.8
01	79 40.5	169 38.7	44.6	227 16.7	22.0	171 17.3	16.8	150 43.6	11.7	Nunki	75 53.2	S26 16.3
02	94 43.0	184 37.8	44.6	242 17.6	22.6	186 19.2	16.8	165 45.8	11.7	Peacock	53 12.6	S56 40.4
03	109 45.4	199 36.8	.. 44.7	257 18.5	.. 23.2	201 21.1	.. 16.9	180 48.0	.. 11.7	Pollux	243 22.1	N27 58.5
04	124 47.9	214 35.9	44.8	272 19.4	23.7	216 23.0	16.9	195 50.2	11.6	Procyon	244 54.9	N 5 10.4
05	139 50.4	229 34.9	44.9	287 20.2	24.3	231 24.8	16.9	210 52.4	11.6			
06	154 52.8	244 34.0	S24 45.0	302 21.1	S12 24.9	246 26.7	S23 16.9	225 54.6	S22 11.6	Rasalhague	96 02.7	N12 32.9
07	169 55.3	259 33.0	45.0	317 22.0	25.4	261 28.6	16.9	240 56.9	11.6	Regulus	207 38.8	N11 52.2
T 08	184 57.7	274 32.1	45.1	332 22.9	26.0	276 30.4	16.9	255 59.1	11.5	Rigel	281 07.5	S 8 10.8
U 09	200 00.2	289 31.1	.. 45.2	347 23.8	.. 26.6	291 32.3	.. 16.9	271 01.3	.. 11.5	Rigil Kent.	139 46.4	S60 54.7
E 10	215 02.7	304 30.2	45.3	2 24.6	27.1	306 34.2	16.9	286 03.5	11.5	Sabik	102 07.8	S15 44.8
S 11	230 05.1	319 29.2	45.3	17 25.5	27.7	321 36.0	16.9	301 05.7	11.5			
D 12	245 07.6	334 28.3	S24 45.4	32 26.4	S12 28.3	336 37.9	S23 16.9	316 07.9	S22 11.4	Schedar	349 35.2	N56 38.9
A 13	260 10.1	349 27.3	45.5	47 27.3	28.9	351 39.8	17.0	331 10.1	11.4	Shaula	96 16.4	S37 07.0
Y 14	275 12.5	4 26.4	45.5	62 28.1	29.4	6 41.7	17.0	346 12.3	11.4	Sirius	258 29.6	S16 44.6
15	290 15.0	19 25.4	.. 45.6	77 29.0	.. 30.0	21 43.5	.. 17.0	1 14.5	.. 11.3	Spica	158 26.9	S11 15.6
16	305 17.5	34 24.5	45.7	92 29.9	30.6	36 45.4	17.0	16 16.7	11.3	Suhail	222 49.1	S43 30.5
17	320 19.9	49 23.5	45.7	107 30.8	31.1	51 47.3	17.0	31 18.9	11.3			
18	335 22.4	64 22.6	S24 45.8	122 31.7	S12 31.7	66 49.1	S23 17.0	46 21.1	S22 11.3	Vega	80 36.3	N38 48.4
19	350 24.8	79 21.6	45.9	137 32.5	32.3	81 51.0	17.0	61 23.3	11.2	Zuben'ubi	137 00.9	S16 07.2
20	5 27.3	94 20.7	45.9	152 33.4	32.8	96 52.9	17.0	76 25.5	11.2		SHA	Mer.Pass.
21	20 29.8	109 19.7	.. 46.0	167 34.3	.. 33.4	111 54.7	.. 17.0	91 27.7	.. 11.2		° ′	h m
22	35 32.2	124 18.8	46.0	182 35.2	34.0	126 56.6	17.0	106 29.9	11.1	Venus	91 23.5	13 41
23	50 34.7	139 17.8	46.1	197 36.0	34.5	141 58.5	17.1	121 32.1	11.1	Mars	148 15.8	9 52
	h m									Jupiter	91 51.7	13 36
Mer.Pass.	19 42.2	v −0.9	d 0.1	v 0.9	d 0.6	v 1.9	d 0.0	v 2.2	d 0.0	Saturn	71 09.5	14 59

© British Crown Copyright 2018. All rights reserved.

UT	SUN GHA	SUN Dec	MOON GHA	v	Dec	d	HP
d h	° ′	° ′	° ′	′	° ′	′	′
24 00	183 23.5	S20 26.2	216 23.5	9.9	S 5 34.8	13.9	59.8
01	198 23.3	26.7	230 52.4	9.8	5 48.7	13.8	59.7
02	213 23.1	27.2	245 21.2	9.9	6 02.5	13.7	59.7
03	228 22.9	.. 27.7	259 50.1	9.8	6 16.2	13.7	59.7
04	243 22.8	28.2	274 18.9	9.8	6 29.9	13.7	59.7
05	258 22.6	28.7	288 47.7	9.8	6 43.6	13.7	59.7
06	273 22.4	S20 29.2	303 16.5	9.7	S 6 57.3	13.6	59.7
07	288 22.2	29.8	317 45.2	9.7	7 10.9	13.5	59.7
08	303 22.1	30.3	332 13.9	9.7	7 24.4	13.6	59.7
S 09	318 21.9	.. 30.8	346 42.6	9.6	7 38.0	13.4	59.7
U 10	333 21.7	31.3	1 11.2	9.7	7 51.4	13.5	59.7
N 11	348 21.5	31.8	15 39.9	9.6	8 04.9	13.3	59.7
D 12	3 21.3	S20 32.3	30 08.5	9.5	S 8 18.2	13.4	59.7
A 13	18 21.1	32.8	44 37.0	9.6	8 31.6	13.2	59.7
Y 14	33 21.0	33.3	59 05.6	9.5	8 44.8	13.2	59.7
15	48 20.8	.. 33.8	73 34.1	9.4	8 58.0	13.2	59.7
16	63 20.6	34.3	88 02.5	9.5	9 11.2	13.1	59.6
17	78 20.4	34.8	102 31.0	9.4	9 24.3	13.1	59.6
18	93 20.2	S20 35.3	116 59.4	9.4	S 9 37.4	13.0	59.6
19	108 20.1	35.8	131 27.8	9.3	9 50.4	12.9	59.6
20	123 19.9	36.3	145 56.1	9.3	10 03.3	12.8	59.6
21	138 19.7	.. 36.8	160 24.4	9.3	10 16.1	12.8	59.6
22	153 19.5	37.3	174 52.7	9.2	10 28.9	12.8	59.6
23	168 19.3	37.8	189 20.9	9.2	10 41.7	12.7	59.6
25 00	183 19.1	S20 38.3	203 49.1	9.2	S10 54.4	12.6	59.5
01	198 18.9	38.8	218 17.3	9.1	11 07.0	12.5	59.5
02	213 18.8	39.3	232 45.4	9.1	11 19.5	12.5	59.5
03	228 18.6	.. 39.8	247 13.5	9.1	11 32.0	12.3	59.5
04	243 18.4	40.3	261 41.6	9.0	11 44.3	12.4	59.5
05	258 18.2	40.8	276 09.6	9.0	11 56.7	12.2	59.5
06	273 18.0	S20 41.3	290 37.6	8.9	S12 08.9	12.2	59.5
07	288 17.8	41.8	305 05.5	8.9	12 21.1	12.1	59.4
08	303 17.6	42.3	319 33.4	8.9	12 33.2	12.0	59.4
M 09	318 17.4	.. 42.8	334 01.3	8.8	12 45.2	11.9	59.4
O 10	333 17.3	43.3	348 29.1	8.8	12 57.1	11.8	59.4
N 11	348 17.1	43.8	2 56.9	8.8	13 08.9	11.8	59.4
D 12	3 16.9	S20 44.2	17 24.7	8.7	S13 20.7	11.7	59.4
A 13	18 16.7	44.7	31 52.4	8.7	13 32.4	11.6	59.3
Y 14	33 16.5	45.2	46 20.1	8.6	13 44.0	11.5	59.3
15	48 16.3	.. 45.7	60 47.7	8.6	13 55.5	11.4	59.3
16	63 16.1	46.2	75 15.3	8.6	14 06.9	11.3	59.3
17	78 15.9	46.7	89 42.9	8.5	14 18.2	11.2	59.3
18	93 15.7	S20 47.2	104 10.4	8.5	S14 29.4	11.2	59.2
19	108 15.5	47.7	118 37.9	8.5	14 40.6	11.0	59.2
20	123 15.4	48.1	133 05.4	8.4	14 51.6	11.0	59.2
21	138 15.2	.. 48.6	147 32.8	8.4	15 02.6	10.8	59.2
22	153 15.0	49.1	162 00.2	8.3	15 13.4	10.8	59.2
23	168 14.8	49.6	176 27.5	8.3	15 24.2	10.7	59.2
26 00	183 14.6	S20 50.1	190 54.8	8.3	S15 34.9	10.5	59.1
01	198 14.4	50.6	205 22.1	8.2	15 45.4	10.5	59.1
02	213 14.2	51.0	219 49.3	8.2	15 55.9	10.3	59.1
03	228 14.0	.. 51.5	234 16.5	8.2	16 06.2	10.3	59.1
04	243 13.8	52.0	248 43.7	8.1	16 16.5	10.1	59.1
05	258 13.6	52.5	263 10.8	8.1	16 26.6	10.1	59.0
06	273 13.4	S20 53.0	277 37.9	8.0	S16 36.7	9.9	59.0
07	288 13.2	53.4	292 04.9	8.0	16 46.6	9.9	59.0
08	303 13.0	53.9	306 31.9	8.0	16 56.5	9.7	59.0
T 09	318 12.8	.. 54.4	320 58.9	8.0	17 06.2	9.6	58.9
U 10	333 12.6	54.9	335 25.9	7.9	17 15.8	9.5	58.9
E 11	348 12.4	55.3	349 52.8	7.8	17 25.3	9.4	58.9
S 12	3 12.2	S20 55.8	4 19.6	7.9	S17 34.7	9.2	58.9
D 13	18 12.0	56.3	18 46.5	7.8	17 43.9	9.2	58.9
A 14	33 11.8	56.8	33 13.3	7.8	17 53.1	9.0	58.8
Y 15	48 11.6	.. 57.2	47 40.1	7.7	18 02.1	9.0	58.8
16	63 11.4	57.7	62 06.8	7.7	18 11.1	8.8	58.8
17	78 11.2	58.2	76 33.5	7.7	18 19.9	8.7	58.8
18	93 11.0	S20 58.6	91 00.2	7.7	S18 28.6	8.6	58.7
19	108 10.8	59.1	105 26.9	7.6	18 37.2	8.4	58.7
20	123 10.6	20 59.6	119 53.5	7.6	18 45.6	8.3	58.7
21	138 10.4	21 00.0	134 20.1	7.6	18 53.9	8.2	58.7
22	153 10.2	00.5	148 46.7	7.6	19 02.1	8.1	58.6
23	168 10.0	01.0	163 13.3	7.5	S19 10.2	8.0	58.6
	SD 16.2	d 0.5	SD 16.3		16.2		16.0

Lat.	Twilight Naut.	Twilight Civil	Sunrise	Moonrise 24	25	26	27
°	h m	h m	h m	h m	h m	h m	h m
N 72	07 32	09 20	■■■	05 13	07 35	10 46	■■■
N 70	07 18	08 48	11 23	05 03	07 11	09 34	■■■
68	07 07	08 25	10 01	04 54	06 52	08 57	11 15
66	06 57	08 07	09 24	04 47	06 38	08 31	10 25
64	06 49	07 52	08 58	04 41	06 26	08 11	09 54
62	06 42	07 40	08 38	04 36	06 16	07 55	09 31
60	06 35	07 29	08 21	04 32	06 07	07 42	09 12
N 58	06 29	07 20	08 07	04 28	05 59	07 30	08 57
56	06 24	07 11	07 56	04 24	05 53	07 20	08 44
54	06 19	07 04	07 45	04 21	05 47	07 12	08 32
52	06 15	06 57	07 36	04 18	05 42	07 04	08 22
50	06 11	06 51	07 28	04 16	05 37	06 57	08 14
45	06 01	06 38	07 10	04 10	05 26	06 42	07 55
N 40	05 53	06 26	06 56	04 06	05 18	06 30	07 39
35	05 45	06 16	06 44	04 02	05 11	06 19	07 27
30	05 38	06 07	06 33	03 58	05 04	06 10	07 15
20	05 24	05 51	06 15	03 53	04 53	05 55	06 56
N 10	05 10	05 36	05 58	03 48	04 44	05 41	06 40
0	04 55	05 21	05 43	03 43	04 35	05 29	06 24
S 10	04 39	05 05	05 28	03 38	04 26	05 17	06 09
20	04 19	04 47	05 11	03 33	04 17	05 03	05 53
30	03 53	04 26	04 52	03 28	04 07	04 48	05 34
35	03 37	04 12	04 41	03 24	04 01	04 40	05 23
40	03 17	03 57	04 28	03 21	03 54	04 30	05 11
45	02 52	03 37	04 13	03 17	03 46	04 19	04 56
S 50	02 16	03 13	03 54	03 12	03 36	04 05	04 39
52	01 57	03 00	03 45	03 09	03 32	03 58	04 30
54	01 32	02 46	03 34	03 07	03 27	03 51	04 21
56	00 55	02 29	03 23	03 04	03 22	03 43	04 11
58	////	02 09	03 10	03 01	03 16	03 35	03 59
S 60	////	01 42	02 54	02 58	03 10	03 25	03 45

Lat.	Sunset	Twilight Civil	Twilight Naut.	Moonset 24	25	26	27
°	h m	h m	h m	h m	h m	h m	h m
N 72	■■■	14 13	16 01	14 08	13 37	12 21	■■■
N 70	12 10	14 44	16 15	14 21	14 03	13 34	■■■
68	13 32	15 08	16 26	14 32	14 24	14 12	13 51
66	14 09	15 26	16 36	14 41	14 40	14 39	14 41
64	14 35	15 41	16 44	14 49	14 53	15 00	15 13
62	14 56	15 53	16 51	14 55	15 04	15 17	15 36
60	15 12	16 04	16 58	15 01	15 14	15 31	15 55
N 58	15 26	16 14	17 04	15 06	15 22	15 43	16 11
56	15 38	16 22	17 09	15 11	15 30	15 54	16 25
54	15 48	16 29	17 14	15 15	15 36	16 03	16 36
52	15 57	16 36	17 18	15 18	15 42	16 11	16 47
50	16 06	16 42	17 23	15 22	15 48	16 19	16 56
45	16 23	16 56	17 32	15 29	16 00	16 35	17 16
N 40	16 38	17 07	17 40	15 35	16 10	16 48	17 32
35	16 50	17 17	17 48	15 41	16 18	16 59	17 45
30	17 01	17 26	17 56	15 45	16 26	17 09	17 57
20	17 19	17 43	18 10	15 53	16 39	17 26	18 17
N 10	17 35	17 58	18 24	16 01	16 50	17 41	18 35
0	17 51	18 13	18 38	16 07	17 01	17 55	18 51
S 10	18 06	18 29	18 55	16 14	17 11	18 09	19 08
20	18 23	18 47	19 15	16 22	17 23	18 24	19 25
30	18 42	19 09	19 41	16 30	17 36	18 42	19 46
35	18 53	19 22	19 57	16 35	17 43	18 52	19 57
40	19 06	19 38	20 17	16 40	17 52	19 03	20 11
45	19 22	19 57	20 43	16 46	18 02	19 17	20 27
S 50	19 41	20 22	21 19	16 54	18 15	19 34	20 47
52	19 50	20 35	21 39	16 58	18 21	19 41	20 57
54	20 00	20 49	22 05	17 02	18 27	19 50	21 08
56	20 12	21 06	22 43	17 06	18 34	20 00	21 20
58	20 25	21 27	////	17 11	18 42	20 11	21 34
S 60	20 41	21 55	////	17 16	18 51	20 24	21 51

Day	SUN Eqn. of Time 00h	SUN Eqn. of Time 12h	SUN Mer. Pass.	MOON Mer. Pass. Upper	MOON Mer. Pass. Lower	Age	Phase
d	m s	m s	h m	h m	h m	d %	
24	13 34	13 26	11 47	09 55	22 21	27 6	
25	13 17	13 08	11 47	10 48	23 15	28 2	●
26	12 59	12 49	11 47	11 42	24 10	29 0	

© British Crown Copyright 2018. All rights reserved.

UT	ARIES GHA	VENUS −3.9 GHA	Dec	MARS +1.7 GHA	Dec	JUPITER −1.8 GHA	Dec	SATURN +0.6 GHA	Dec	STARS Name	SHA	Dec
d h	° ′	° ′	° ′	° ′	° ′	° ′	° ′	° ′	° ′		° ′	° ′
27 00	65 37.2	154 16.9	S24 46.1	212 36.9	S12 35.1	157 00.3	S23 17.1	136 34.4	S22 11.1	Acamar	315 14.6	S40 13.7
01	80 39.6	169 15.9	46.2	227 37.8	35.7	172 02.2	17.1	151 36.6	11.1	Achernar	335 23.0	S57 08.5
02	95 42.1	184 15.0	46.2	242 38.7	36.2	187 04.1	17.1	166 38.8	11.0	Acrux	173 04.7	S63 12.1
03	110 44.6	199 14.0 ..	46.3	257 39.5 ..	36.8	202 05.9 ..	17.1	181 41.0 ..	11.0	Adhara	255 08.8	S28 59.9
04	125 47.0	214 13.1	46.3	272 40.4	37.4	217 07.8	17.1	196 43.2	11.0	Aldebaran	290 44.0	N16 32.8
05	140 49.5	229 12.1	46.4	287 41.3	37.9	232 09.7	17.1	211 45.4	10.9			
06	155 52.0	244 11.2	S24 46.4	302 42.2	S12 38.5	247 11.6	S23 17.1	226 47.6	S22 10.9	Alioth	166 17.1	N55 51.0
W 07	170 54.4	259 10.2	46.5	317 43.0	39.1	262 13.4	17.1	241 49.8	10.9	Alkaid	152 55.8	N49 12.9
E 08	185 56.9	274 09.3	46.5	332 43.9	39.6	277 15.3	17.1	256 52.0	10.9	Alnair	27 38.2	S46 52.1
D 09	200 59.3	289 08.3 ..	46.6	347 44.8 ..	40.2	292 17.2 ..	17.1	271 54.2 ..	10.8	Alnilam	275 41.6	S 1 11.4
N 10	216 01.8	304 07.4	46.6	2 45.7	40.8	307 19.0	17.2	286 56.4	10.8	Alphard	217 51.7	S 8 44.6
E 11	231 04.3	319 06.4	46.7	17 46.5	41.3	322 20.9	17.2	301 58.6	10.8			
S 12	246 06.7	334 05.5	S24 46.7	32 47.4	S12 41.9	337 22.8	S23 17.2	317 00.8	S22 10.7	Alphecca	126 07.6	N26 39.0
D 13	261 09.2	349 04.5	46.7	47 48.3	42.5	352 24.6	17.2	332 03.0	10.7	Alpheratz	357 38.8	N29 12.1
A 14	276 11.7	4 03.6	46.8	62 49.2	43.0	7 26.5	17.2	347 05.2	10.7	Altair	62 04.2	N 8 55.4
Y 15	291 14.1	19 02.6 ..	46.8	77 50.0 ..	43.6	22 28.4 ..	17.2	2 07.4 ..	10.7	Ankaa	353 11.1	S42 12.2
16	306 16.6	34 01.7	46.8	92 50.9	44.2	37 30.2	17.2	17 09.6	10.6	Antares	112 21.2	S26 28.3
17	321 19.1	49 00.7	46.9	107 51.8	44.7	52 32.1	17.2	32 11.8	10.6			
18	336 21.5	63 59.8	S24 46.9	122 52.6	S12 45.3	67 34.0	S23 17.2	47 14.0	S22 10.6	Arcturus	145 52.0	N19 04.9
19	351 24.0	78 58.8	46.9	137 53.5	45.9	82 35.8	17.2	62 16.2	10.6	Atria	107 19.7	S69 03.6
20	6 26.5	93 57.9	47.0	152 54.4	46.4	97 37.7	17.2	77 18.4	10.5	Avior	234 15.9	S59 34.1
21	21 28.9	108 56.9 ..	47.0	167 55.3 ..	47.0	112 39.6 ..	17.3	92 20.6 ..	10.5	Bellatrix	278 27.0	N 6 22.0
22	36 31.4	123 56.0	47.0	182 56.1	47.6	127 41.4	17.3	107 22.8	10.5	Betelgeuse	270 56.2	N 7 24.6
23	51 33.8	138 55.0	47.0	197 57.0	48.1	142 43.3	17.3	122 25.0	10.4			
28 00	66 36.3	153 54.1	S24 47.1	212 57.9	S12 48.7	157 45.2	S23 17.3	137 27.2	S22 10.4	Canopus	263 53.7	S52 42.3
01	81 38.8	168 53.2	47.1	227 58.8	49.3	172 47.0	17.3	152 29.4	10.4	Capella	280 27.5	N46 00.9
02	96 41.2	183 52.2	47.1	242 59.6	49.8	187 48.9	17.3	167 31.6	10.4	Deneb	49 28.7	N45 21.3
03	111 43.7	198 51.3 ..	47.1	258 00.5 ..	50.4	202 50.8 ..	17.3	182 33.8 ..	10.3	Denebola	182 29.3	N14 27.7
04	126 46.2	213 50.3	47.1	273 01.4	51.0	217 52.6	17.3	197 36.1	10.3	Diphda	348 51.3	S17 52.8
05	141 48.6	228 49.4	47.1	288 02.2	51.5	232 54.5	17.3	212 38.3	10.3			
06	156 51.1	243 48.4	S24 47.2	303 03.1	S12 52.1	247 56.4	S23 17.3	227 40.5	S22 10.2	Dubhe	193 46.4	N61 38.4
T 07	171 53.6	258 47.5	47.2	318 04.0	52.6	262 58.2	17.3	242 42.7	10.2	Elnath	278 06.7	N28 37.3
H 08	186 56.0	273 46.5	47.2	333 04.9	53.2	278 00.1	17.4	257 44.9	10.2	Eltanin	90 44.6	N51 29.4
U 09	201 58.5	288 45.6 ..	47.2	348 05.7 ..	53.8	293 02.0 ..	17.4	272 47.1 ..	10.1	Enif	33 42.9	N 9 58.1
R 10	217 01.0	303 44.6	47.2	3 06.6	54.3	308 03.8	17.4	287 49.3	10.1	Fomalhaut	15 19.1	S29 31.2
S 11	232 03.4	318 43.7	47.2	18 07.5	54.9	323 05.7	17.4	302 51.5	10.1			
D 12	247 05.9	333 42.7	S24 47.2	33 08.3	S12 55.5	338 07.6	S23 17.4	317 53.7	S22 10.1	Gacrux	171 56.3	S57 13.1
A 13	262 08.3	348 41.8	47.2	48 09.2	56.0	353 09.4	17.4	332 55.9	10.0	Gienah	175 47.9	S17 38.9
Y 14	277 10.8	3 40.8	47.2	63 10.1	56.6	8 11.3	17.4	347 58.1	10.0	Hadar	148 42.2	S60 27.8
15	292 13.3	18 39.9 ..	47.2	78 10.9 ..	57.1	23 13.1 ..	17.4	3 00.3 ..	10.0	Hamal	327 55.5	N23 33.4
16	307 15.7	33 38.9	47.2	93 11.8	57.7	38 15.0	17.4	18 02.5	09.9	Kaus Aust.	83 38.3	S34 22.4
17	322 18.2	48 38.0	47.2	108 12.7	58.3	53 16.9	17.4	33 04.7	09.9			
18	337 20.7	63 37.0	S24 47.2	123 13.6	S12 58.8	68 18.7	S23 17.4	48 06.9	S22 09.9	Kochab	137 21.2	N74 04.4
19	352 23.1	78 36.1	47.2	138 14.4	12 59.4	83 20.6	17.4	63 09.1	09.9	Markab	13 33.9	N15 18.8
20	7 25.6	93 35.1	47.2	153 15.3	13 00.0	98 22.5	17.4	78 11.3	09.8	Menkar	314 10.1	N 4 10.0
21	22 28.1	108 34.2 ..	47.2	168 16.2 ..	00.5	113 24.3 ..	17.5	93 13.5 ..	09.8	Menkent	148 02.7	S36 27.7
22	37 30.5	123 33.2	47.2	183 17.0	01.1	128 26.2	17.5	108 15.7	09.8	Miaplacidus	221 38.5	S69 47.6
23	52 33.0	138 32.3	47.2	198 17.9	01.6	143 28.1	17.5	123 17.9	09.7			
29 00	67 35.5	153 31.3	S24 47.2	213 18.8	S13 02.2	158 29.9	S23 17.5	138 20.1	S22 09.7	Mirfak	308 33.5	N49 55.8
01	82 37.9	168 30.4	47.1	228 19.6	02.8	173 31.8	17.5	153 22.3	09.7	Nunki	75 53.2	S26 16.3
02	97 40.4	183 29.4	47.2	243 20.5	03.3	188 33.7	17.5	168 24.5	09.7	Peacock	53 12.6	S56 40.4
03	112 42.8	198 28.5 ..	47.2	258 21.4 ..	03.9	203 35.5 ..	17.5	183 26.7 ..	09.6	Pollux	243 22.1	N27 58.5
04	127 45.3	213 27.5	47.2	273 22.2	04.4	218 37.4	17.5	198 28.9	09.6	Procyon	244 54.9	N 5 10.4
05	142 47.8	228 26.6	47.2	288 23.1	05.0	233 39.3	17.5	213 31.1	09.6			
06	157 50.2	243 25.6	S24 47.1	303 24.0	S13 05.6	248 41.1	S23 17.5	228 33.3	S22 09.5	Rasalhague	96 02.7	N12 32.9
07	172 52.7	258 24.7	47.1	318 24.8	06.1	263 43.0	17.5	243 35.5	09.5	Regulus	207 38.8	N11 52.2
08	187 55.2	273 23.7	47.1	333 25.7	06.7	278 44.8	17.5	258 37.7	09.5	Rigel	281 07.5	S 8 10.8
F 09	202 57.6	288 22.8 ..	47.1	348 26.6 ..	07.2	293 46.7 ..	17.5	273 39.9 ..	09.5	Rigil Kent.	139 46.4	S60 54.7
R 10	218 00.1	303 21.8	47.1	3 27.4	07.8	308 48.6	17.6	288 42.1	09.4	Sabik	102 07.8	S15 44.8
I 11	233 02.6	318 20.9	47.0	18 28.3	08.4	323 50.4	17.6	303 44.3	09.4			
D 12	248 05.0	333 19.9	S24 47.0	33 29.2	S13 08.9	338 52.3	S23 17.6	318 46.5	S22 09.4	Schedar	349 35.2	N56 38.9
A 13	263 07.5	348 19.0	47.0	48 30.0	09.5	353 54.2	17.6	333 48.7	09.3	Shaula	96 16.3	S37 06.9
Y 14	278 10.0	3 18.0	47.0	63 30.9	10.0	8 56.0	17.6	348 50.9	09.3	Sirius	258 29.6	S16 44.6
15	293 12.4	18 17.1 ..	46.9	78 31.8 ..	10.6	23 57.9 ..	17.6	3 53.1 ..	09.3	Spica	158 26.9	S11 15.7
16	308 14.9	33 16.1	46.9	93 32.6	11.1	38 59.8	17.6	18 55.3	09.2	Suhail	222 49.1	S43 30.5
17	323 17.3	48 15.2	46.9	108 33.5	11.7	54 01.6	17.6	33 57.5	09.2			
18	338 19.8	63 14.2	S24 46.8	123 34.4	S13 12.3	69 03.5	S23 17.6	48 59.7	S22 09.2	Vega	80 36.4	N38 48.4
19	353 22.3	78 13.3	46.8	138 35.2	12.8	84 05.3	17.6	64 01.9	09.2	Zuben'ubi	137 00.9	S16 07.2
20	8 24.7	93 12.3	46.8	153 36.1	13.4	99 07.2	17.6	79 04.1	09.1		SHA	Mer.Pass.
21	23 27.2	108 11.4 ..	46.7	168 37.0 ..	13.9	114 09.1 ..	17.6	94 06.3 ..	09.1	Venus	87 17.8	13 45
22	38 29.7	123 10.4	46.7	183 37.8	14.5	129 10.9	17.6	109 08.5	09.1	Mars	146 21.6	9 48
23	53 32.1	138 09.5	46.7	198 38.7	15.0	144 12.8	17.6	124 10.7	09.0	Jupiter	91 08.8	13 27
Mer.Pass.	19 30.4	v −0.9	d 0.0	v 0.9	d 0.6	v 1.9	d 0.0	v 2.2	d 0.0	Saturn	70 50.9	14 48

© British Crown Copyright 2018. All rights reserved.

UT	SUN GHA	SUN Dec	MOON GHA	v	MOON Dec	d	HP
d h	° ′	° ′	° ′	′	° ′	′	′
27 00	183 09.8	S21 01.4	177 39.8	7.5	S19 18.2	7.8	58.6
01	198 09.6	01.9	192 06.3	7.4	19 26.0	7.8	58.6
02	213 09.4	02.4	206 32.7	7.5	19 33.8	7.5	58.5
03	228 09.2	.. 02.8	220 59.2	7.4	19 41.3	7.5	58.5
04	243 09.0	03.3	235 25.6	7.4	19 48.8	7.3	58.5
05	258 08.8	03.8	249 52.0	7.4	19 56.1	7.2	58.4
W 06	273 08.6	S21 04.2	264 18.4	7.4	S20 03.3	7.1	58.4
E 07	288 08.4	04.7	278 44.8	7.3	20 10.4	7.0	58.4
D 08	303 08.2	05.1	293 11.1	7.4	20 17.4	6.8	58.4
N 09	318 08.0	.. 05.6	307 37.5	7.3	20 24.2	6.7	58.3
E 10	333 07.8	06.1	322 03.8	7.3	20 30.9	6.5	58.3
S 11	348 07.6	06.5	336 30.1	7.2	20 37.4	6.5	58.3
D 12	3 07.4	S21 07.0	350 56.3	7.3	S20 43.9	6.3	58.2
A 13	18 07.2	07.4	5 22.6	7.3	20 50.2	6.1	58.2
Y 14	33 07.0	07.9	19 48.9	7.2	20 56.3	6.0	58.2
15	48 06.8	.. 08.3	34 15.1	7.2	21 02.3	5.9	58.2
16	63 06.6	08.8	48 41.3	7.3	21 08.2	5.8	58.1
17	78 06.4	09.3	63 07.6	7.2	21 14.0	5.6	58.1
18	93 06.2	S21 09.7	77 33.8	7.2	S21 19.6	5.5	58.1
19	108 06.0	10.2	92 00.0	7.2	21 25.1	5.4	58.0
20	123 05.8	10.6	106 26.2	7.2	21 30.5	5.2	58.0
21	138 05.6	.. 11.1	120 52.4	7.2	21 35.7	5.1	58.0
22	153 05.3	11.5	135 18.6	7.2	21 40.8	4.9	58.0
23	168 05.1	12.0	149 44.8	7.1	21 45.7	4.8	57.9
28 00	183 04.9	S21 12.4	164 10.9	7.2	S21 50.5	4.7	57.9
01	198 04.7	12.9	178 37.1	7.2	21 55.2	4.5	57.9
02	213 04.5	13.3	193 03.3	7.2	21 59.7	4.4	57.8
03	228 04.3	.. 13.8	207 29.5	7.2	22 04.1	4.3	57.8
04	243 04.1	14.2	221 55.7	7.2	22 08.4	4.1	57.8
05	258 03.9	14.7	236 21.9	7.2	22 12.5	4.0	57.7
T 06	273 03.7	S21 15.1	250 48.1	7.2	S22 16.5	3.8	57.7
H 07	288 03.5	15.5	265 14.3	7.2	22 20.3	3.7	57.7
U 08	303 03.3	16.0	279 40.5	7.3	22 24.0	3.6	57.6
R 09	318 03.0	.. 16.4	294 06.8	7.2	22 27.6	3.4	57.6
S 10	333 02.8	16.9	308 33.0	7.2	22 31.0	3.3	57.6
D 11	348 02.6	17.3	322 59.2	7.3	22 34.3	3.2	57.6
A 12	3 02.4	S21 17.8	337 25.5	7.3	S22 37.5	3.0	57.5
Y 13	18 02.2	18.2	351 51.8	7.3	22 40.5	2.8	57.5
14	33 02.0	18.6	6 18.1	7.3	22 43.3	2.8	57.5
15	48 01.8	.. 19.1	20 44.4	7.3	22 46.1	2.6	57.4
16	63 01.6	19.5	35 10.7	7.4	22 48.7	2.4	57.4
17	78 01.3	20.0	49 37.1	7.4	22 51.1	2.4	57.4
18	93 01.1	S21 20.4	64 03.5	7.3	S22 53.5	2.1	57.3
19	108 00.9	20.8	78 29.8	7.5	22 55.6	2.1	57.3
20	123 00.7	21.3	92 56.3	7.4	22 57.7	1.9	57.3
21	138 00.5	.. 21.7	107 22.7	7.5	22 59.6	1.8	57.2
22	153 00.3	22.1	121 49.2	7.5	23 01.4	1.6	57.2
23	168 00.1	22.6	136 15.7	7.5	23 03.0	1.5	57.2
29 00	182 59.8	S21 23.0	150 42.2	7.6	S23 04.5	1.3	57.1
01	197 59.6	23.4	165 08.8	7.5	23 05.8	1.3	57.1
02	212 59.4	23.9	179 35.3	7.7	23 07.1	1.0	57.1
03	227 59.2	.. 24.3	194 02.0	7.6	23 08.1	1.0	57.0
04	242 59.0	24.7	208 28.6	7.7	23 09.1	0.8	57.0
05	257 58.8	25.1	222 55.3	7.7	23 09.9	0.7	57.0
F 06	272 58.5	S21 25.6	237 22.0	7.8	S23 10.6	0.5	57.0
R 07	287 58.3	26.0	251 48.8	7.8	23 11.1	0.4	56.9
I 08	302 58.1	26.4	266 15.6	7.8	23 11.5	0.3	56.9
D 09	317 57.9	.. 26.9	280 42.4	7.9	23 11.8	0.2	56.9
A 10	332 57.7	27.3	295 09.3	7.9	23 12.0	0.0	56.8
Y 11	347 57.4	27.7	309 36.2	8.0	23 12.0	0.2	56.8
12	2 57.2	S21 28.1	324 03.2	8.0	S23 11.8	0.2	56.8
13	17 57.0	28.6	338 30.2	8.0	23 11.6	0.4	56.7
14	32 56.8	29.0	352 57.2	8.1	23 11.2	0.5	56.7
15	47 56.6	.. 29.4	7 24.3	8.2	23 10.7	0.7	56.7
16	62 56.3	29.8	21 51.5	8.2	23 10.0	0.8	56.6
17	77 56.1	30.2	36 18.7	8.2	23 09.2	0.9	56.6
18	92 55.9	S21 30.7	50 45.9	8.3	S23 08.3	1.0	56.6
19	107 55.7	31.1	65 13.2	8.3	23 07.3	1.2	56.5
20	122 55.5	31.5	79 40.5	8.4	23 06.1	1.3	56.5
21	137 55.2	.. 31.9	94 07.9	8.5	23 04.8	1.4	56.5
22	152 55.0	32.3	108 35.4	8.5	23 03.4	1.5	56.4
23	167 54.8	32.7	123 02.9	8.5	S23 01.9	1.7	56.4
	SD 16.2	d 0.4	SD 15.9		15.7		15.5

Lat.	Twilight Naut.	Civil	Sunrise	Moonrise 27	28	29	30
°	h m	h m	h m	h m	h m	h m	h m
N 72	07 41	09 35	▬▬▬	▬▬▬	▬▬▬	▬▬▬	▬▬▬
N 70	07 26	08 59	▬▬▬	▬▬▬	▬▬▬	▬▬▬	▬▬▬
68	07 14	08 34	10 17	11 15	▬▬▬	▬▬▬	▬▬▬
66	07 04	08 15	09 35	10 25	12 13	13 29	13 54
64	06 55	07 59	09 07	09 54	11 26	12 33	13 12
62	06 47	07 46	08 45	09 31	10 55	12 01	12 43
60	06 40	07 35	08 28	09 12	10 33	11 36	12 21
N 58	06 34	07 25	08 13	08 57	10 14	11 17	12 03
56	06 29	07 16	08 01	08 44	09 59	11 01	11 48
54	06 24	07 08	07 50	08 32	09 46	10 47	11 35
52	06 19	07 01	07 41	08 22	09 34	10 35	11 24
50	06 15	06 55	07 32	08 14	09 24	10 24	11 13
45	06 05	06 41	07 14	07 55	09 02	10 02	10 52
N 40	05 56	06 29	06 59	07 39	08 45	09 44	10 35
35	05 48	06 19	06 46	07 27	08 30	09 29	10 21
30	05 40	06 10	06 35	07 15	08 18	09 16	10 08
20	05 26	05 53	06 16	06 56	07 56	08 53	09 46
N 10	05 11	05 37	06 00	06 40	07 38	08 34	09 28
0	04 56	05 22	05 44	06 24	07 20	08 16	09 10
S 10	04 39	05 06	05 28	06 09	07 03	07 58	08 53
20	04 19	04 47	05 11	05 53	06 45	07 39	08 34
30	03 52	04 25	04 52	05 34	06 24	07 17	08 12
35	03 36	04 11	04 40	05 23	06 11	07 04	08 00
40	03 16	03 55	04 27	05 11	05 57	06 49	07 45
45	02 49	03 35	04 11	04 56	05 40	06 31	07 28
S 50	02 11	03 09	03 51	04 39	05 20	06 09	07 06
52	01 51	02 57	03 42	04 30	05 10	05 59	06 56
54	01 24	02 42	03 31	04 21	04 59	05 47	06 44
56	00 40	02 24	03 19	04 11	04 46	05 33	06 31
58	////	02 02	03 05	03 59	04 32	05 17	06 16
S 60	////	01 33	02 49	03 45	04 15	04 59	05 57

Lat.	Sunset	Twilight Civil	Naut.	Moonset 27	28	29	30
°	h m	h m	h m	h m	h m	h m	h m
N 72	▬▬▬	14 00	15 53	▬▬▬	▬▬▬	▬▬▬	▬▬▬
N 70	▬▬▬	14 36	16 09	▬▬▬	▬▬▬	▬▬▬	▬▬▬
68	13 18	15 01	16 21	13 51	▬▬▬	▬▬▬	▬▬▬
66	14 00	15 20	16 31	14 41	14 51	15 30	16 57
64	14 28	15 36	16 40	15 13	15 38	16 26	17 39
62	14 50	15 49	16 48	15 36	16 08	16 59	18 07
60	15 07	16 00	16 55	15 55	16 32	17 23	18 29
N 58	15 22	16 10	17 01	16 11	16 50	17 42	18 46
56	15 35	16 19	17 06	16 25	17 06	17 58	19 01
54	15 45	16 27	17 12	16 36	17 19	18 12	19 14
52	15 55	16 34	17 16	16 47	17 31	18 24	19 25
50	16 03	16 40	17 21	16 56	17 41	18 35	19 35
45	16 21	16 54	17 31	17 16	18 03	18 57	19 56
N 40	16 36	17 06	17 40	17 32	18 21	19 15	20 13
35	16 49	17 17	17 48	17 45	18 36	19 30	20 27
30	17 00	17 26	17 55	17 57	18 48	19 43	20 39
20	17 19	17 43	18 10	18 17	19 10	20 05	21 00
N 10	17 36	17 58	18 24	18 35	19 29	20 24	21 18
0	17 51	18 14	18 40	18 51	19 47	20 42	21 35
S 10	18 07	18 30	18 57	19 08	20 05	21 00	21 52
20	18 24	18 49	19 17	19 25	20 24	21 19	22 10
30	18 44	19 11	19 44	19 46	20 46	21 41	22 31
35	18 56	19 25	20 00	19 57	20 59	21 54	22 43
40	19 09	19 41	20 21	20 11	21 14	22 09	22 56
45	19 26	20 01	20 48	20 27	21 31	22 27	23 13
S 50	19 45	20 27	21 26	20 47	21 53	22 48	23 33
52	19 55	20 40	21 47	20 57	22 04	22 59	23 42
54	20 05	20 55	22 15	21 08	22 15	23 10	23 53
56	20 18	21 13	23 02	21 20	22 29	23 24	24 05
58	20 32	21 36	////	21 34	22 45	23 39	24 18
S 60	20 48	22 06	////	21 51	23 03	23 58	24 35

	SUN			MOON			
Day	Eqn. of Time 00h	12h	Mer. Pass.	Mer. Pass. Upper	Lower	Age	Phase
d	m s	m s	h m	h m	h m	d	%
27	12 40	12 30	11 47	12 38	00 10	01	1
28	12 20	12 10	11 48	13 34	01 06	02	4
29	12 00	11 49	11 48	14 29	02 02	03	10

© British Crown Copyright 2018. All rights reserved.

UT	ARIES GHA	VENUS −3.9 GHA	Dec	MARS +1.7 GHA	Dec	JUPITER −1.8 GHA	Dec	SATURN +0.6 GHA	Dec
30 00	68 34.6	153 08.6	S24 46.6	213 39.6	S13 15.6	159 14.7	S23 17.7	139 12.8	S22 09.0
01	83 37.1	168 07.6	46.6	228 40.4	16.2	174 16.5	17.7	154 15.0	09.0
02	98 39.5	183 06.7	46.5	243 41.3	16.7	189 18.4	17.7	169 17.2	09.0
03	113 42.0	198 05.7	.. 46.5	258 42.2	.. 17.3	204 20.2	.. 17.7	184 19.4	.. 08.9
04	128 44.4	213 04.8	46.4	273 43.0	17.8	219 22.1	17.7	199 21.6	08.9
05	143 46.9	228 03.8	46.4	288 43.9	18.4	234 24.0	17.7	214 23.8	08.9
06	158 49.4	243 02.9	S24 46.4	303 44.8	S13 18.9	249 25.8	S23 17.7	229 26.0	S22 08.8
07	173 51.8	258 01.9	46.3	318 45.6	19.5	264 27.7	17.7	244 28.2	08.8
S 08	188 54.3	273 01.0	46.3	333 46.5	20.1	279 29.6	17.7	259 30.4	08.8
A 09	203 56.8	288 00.0	.. 46.2	348 47.3	.. 20.6	294 31.4	.. 17.7	274 32.6	.. 08.7
T 10	218 59.2	302 59.1	46.1	3 48.2	21.2	309 33.3	17.7	289 34.8	08.7
U 11	234 01.7	317 58.1	46.1	18 49.1	21.7	324 35.1	17.7	304 37.0	08.7
R 12	249 04.2	332 57.2	S24 46.0	33 49.9	S13 22.3	339 37.0	S23 17.7	319 39.2	S22 08.7
D 13	264 06.6	347 56.2	46.0	48 50.8	22.8	354 38.9	17.7	334 41.4	08.6
A 14	279 09.1	2 55.3	45.9	63 51.7	23.4	9 40.7	17.7	349 43.6	08.6
Y 15	294 11.6	17 54.3	.. 45.9	78 52.5	.. 23.9	24 42.6	.. 17.8	4 45.8	.. 08.6
16	309 14.0	32 53.4	45.8	93 53.4	24.5	39 44.4	17.8	19 48.0	08.5
17	324 16.5	47 52.5	45.7	108 54.2	25.1	54 46.3	17.8	34 50.2	08.5
18	339 18.9	62 51.5	S24 45.7	123 55.1	S13 25.6	69 48.2	S23 17.8	49 52.4	S22 08.5
19	354 21.4	77 50.6	45.6	138 56.0	26.2	84 50.0	17.8	64 54.6	08.5
20	9 23.9	92 49.6	45.5	153 56.8	26.7	99 51.9	17.8	79 56.8	08.4
21	24 26.3	107 48.7	.. 45.5	168 57.7	.. 27.3	114 53.8	.. 17.8	94 59.0	.. 08.4
22	39 28.8	122 47.7	45.4	183 58.6	27.8	129 55.6	17.8	110 01.2	08.4
23	54 31.3	137 46.8	45.3	198 59.4	28.4	144 57.5	17.8	125 03.4	08.3
1 00	69 33.7	152 45.8	S24 45.3	214 00.3	S13 28.9	159 59.3	S23 17.8	140 05.6	S22 08.3
01	84 36.2	167 44.9	45.2	229 01.1	29.5	175 01.2	17.8	155 07.8	08.3
02	99 38.7	182 43.9	45.1	244 02.0	30.0	190 03.1	17.8	170 10.0	08.2
03	114 41.1	197 43.0	.. 45.0	259 02.9	.. 30.6	205 04.9	.. 17.8	185 12.2	.. 08.2
04	129 43.6	212 42.0	45.0	274 03.7	31.1	220 06.8	17.8	200 14.4	08.2
05	144 46.1	227 41.1	44.9	289 04.6	31.7	235 08.6	17.8	215 16.5	08.2
06	159 48.5	242 40.2	S24 44.8	304 05.4	S13 32.2	250 10.5	S23 17.8	230 18.7	S22 08.1
07	174 51.0	257 39.2	44.7	319 06.3	32.8	265 12.4	17.9	245 20.9	08.1
S 08	189 53.4	272 38.3	44.7	334 07.2	33.3	280 14.2	17.9	260 23.1	08.1
U 09	204 55.9	287 37.3	.. 44.6	349 08.0	.. 33.9	295 16.1	.. 17.9	275 25.3	.. 08.0
N 10	219 58.4	302 36.4	44.5	4 08.9	34.4	310 17.9	17.9	290 27.5	08.0
D 11	235 00.8	317 35.4	44.4	19 09.7	35.0	325 19.8	17.9	305 29.7	08.0
A 12	250 03.3	332 34.5	S24 44.3	34 10.6	S13 35.6	340 21.7	S23 17.9	320 31.9	S22 07.9
Y 13	265 05.8	347 33.5	44.2	49 11.5	36.1	355 23.5	17.9	335 34.1	07.9
14	280 08.2	2 32.6	44.1	64 12.3	36.7	10 25.4	17.9	350 36.3	07.9
15	295 10.7	17 31.7	.. 44.0	79 13.2	.. 37.2	25 27.2	.. 17.9	5 38.5	.. 07.9
16	310 13.2	32 30.7	44.0	94 14.0	37.8	40 29.1	17.9	20 40.7	07.8
17	325 15.6	47 29.8	43.9	109 14.9	38.3	55 31.0	17.9	35 42.9	07.8
18	340 18.1	62 28.8	S24 43.8	124 15.8	S13 38.9	70 32.8	S23 17.9	50 45.1	S22 07.8
19	355 20.6	77 27.9	43.7	139 16.6	39.4	85 34.7	17.9	65 47.3	07.7
20	10 23.0	92 26.9	43.6	154 17.5	40.0	100 36.5	17.9	80 49.5	07.7
21	25 25.5	107 26.0	.. 43.5	169 18.3	.. 40.5	115 38.4	.. 17.9	95 51.7	.. 07.7
22	40 27.9	122 25.0	43.4	184 19.2	41.1	130 40.3	17.9	110 53.9	07.6
23	55 30.4	137 24.1	43.3	199 20.0	41.6	145 42.1	17.9	125 56.0	07.6
2 00	70 32.9	152 23.2	S24 43.2	214 20.9	S13 42.2	160 44.0	S23 17.9	140 58.2	S22 07.6
01	85 35.3	167 22.2	43.1	229 21.8	42.7	175 45.8	17.9	156 00.4	07.5
02	100 37.8	182 21.3	43.0	244 22.6	43.3	190 47.7	18.0	171 02.6	07.5
03	115 40.3	197 20.3	.. 42.9	259 23.5	.. 43.8	205 49.6	.. 18.0	186 04.8	.. 07.5
04	130 42.7	212 19.4	42.7	274 24.3	44.3	220 51.4	18.0	201 07.0	07.5
05	145 45.2	227 18.4	42.6	289 25.2	44.9	235 53.3	18.0	216 09.2	07.4
06	160 47.7	242 17.5	S24 42.5	304 26.0	S13 45.4	250 55.1	S23 18.0	231 11.4	S22 07.4
07	175 50.1	257 16.6	42.4	319 26.9	46.0	265 57.0	18.0	246 13.6	07.4
M 08	190 52.6	272 15.6	42.3	334 27.8	46.5	280 58.8	18.0	261 15.8	07.3
O 09	205 55.0	287 14.7	.. 42.2	349 28.6	.. 47.1	296 00.7	.. 18.0	276 18.0	.. 07.3
N 10	220 57.5	302 13.7	42.1	4 29.5	47.6	311 02.6	18.0	291 20.2	07.3
D 11	236 00.0	317 12.8	42.0	19 30.3	48.2	326 04.4	18.0	306 22.4	07.2
A 12	251 02.4	332 11.9	S24 41.8	34 31.2	S13 48.7	341 06.3	S23 18.0	321 24.6	S22 07.2
Y 13	266 04.9	347 10.9	41.7	49 32.0	49.3	356 08.1	18.0	336 26.8	07.2
14	281 07.4	2 10.0	41.6	64 32.9	49.8	11 10.0	18.0	351 28.9	07.2
15	296 09.8	17 09.0	.. 41.5	79 33.7	.. 50.4	26 11.9	.. 18.0	6 31.1	.. 07.1
16	311 12.3	32 08.1	41.4	94 34.6	50.9	41 13.7	18.0	21 33.3	07.1
17	326 14.8	47 07.2	41.2	109 35.5	51.5	56 15.6	18.0	36 35.5	07.1
18	341 17.2	62 06.2	S24 41.1	124 36.3	S13 52.0	71 17.4	S23 18.0	51 37.7	S22 07.0
19	356 19.7	77 05.3	41.0	139 37.2	52.6	86 19.3	18.0	66 39.9	07.0
20	11 22.2	92 04.3	40.8	154 38.0	53.1	101 21.1	18.0	81 42.1	07.0
21	26 24.6	107 03.4	.. 40.7	169 38.9	.. 53.7	116 23.0	.. 18.0	96 44.3	.. 06.9
22	41 27.1	122 02.4	40.6	184 39.7	54.2	131 24.9	18.0	111 46.5	06.9
23	56 29.5	137 01.5	40.5	199 40.6	54.7	146 26.7	18.0	126 48.7	06.9
Mer.Pass. 19 18.6		v −0.9	d 0.1	v 0.9	d 0.6	v 1.9	d 0.0	v 2.2	d 0.0

STARS

Name	SHA	Dec
Acamar	315 14.6	S40 13.7
Achernar	335 23.0	S57 08.5
Acrux	173 04.7	S63 12.1
Adhara	255 08.7	S28 59.9
Aldebaran	290 44.0	N16 32.8
Alioth	166 17.1	N55 51.0
Alkaid	152 55.8	N49 12.8
Alnair	27 38.3	S46 52.1
Alnilam	275 41.6	S 1 11.4
Alphard	217 51.7	S 8 44.6
Alphecca	126 07.6	N26 39.0
Alpheratz	357 38.8	N29 12.1
Altair	62 04.2	N 8 55.4
Ankaa	353 11.1	S42 12.2
Antares	112 21.2	S26 28.3
Arcturus	145 52.0	N19 04.9
Atria	107 19.6	S69 03.6
Avior	234 15.9	S59 34.1
Bellatrix	278 26.9	N 6 22.0
Betelgeuse	270 56.2	N 7 24.6
Canopus	263 53.7	S52 42.3
Capella	280 27.4	N46 00.9
Deneb	49 28.7	N45 21.3
Denebola	182 29.3	N14 27.7
Diphda	348 51.3	S17 52.8
Dubhe	193 46.3	N61 38.4
Elnath	278 06.7	N28 37.3
Eltanin	90 44.6	N51 29.4
Enif	33 42.9	N 9 58.1
Fomalhaut	15 19.1	S29 31.2
Gacrux	171 56.3	S57 13.1
Gienah	175 47.9	S17 38.9
Hadar	148 42.2	S60 27.8
Hamal	327 55.5	N23 33.4
Kaus Aust.	83 38.3	S34 22.4
Kochab	137 21.2	N74 04.4
Markab	13 33.9	N15 18.8
Menkar	314 10.1	N 4 10.0
Menkent	148 02.7	S36 27.7
Miaplacidus	221 38.4	S69 47.6
Mirfak	308 33.5	N49 55.8
Nunki	75 53.2	S26 16.3
Peacock	53 12.6	S56 40.4
Pollux	243 22.1	N27 58.5
Procyon	244 54.9	N 5 10.4
Rasalhague	96 02.7	N12 32.9
Regulus	207 38.8	N11 52.2
Rigel	281 07.5	S 8 10.8
Rigil Kent.	139 46.4	S60 54.7
Sabik	102 07.8	S15 44.8
Schedar	349 35.2	N56 38.9
Shaula	96 16.3	S37 06.9
Sirius	258 29.5	S16 44.6
Spica	158 26.8	S11 15.7
Suhail	222 49.0	S43 30.5
Vega	80 36.4	N38 48.3
Zuben'ubi	137 00.8	S16 07.2

	SHA	Mer.Pass.
	° ′	h m
Venus	83 12.1	13 50
Mars	144 26.5	9 43
Jupiter	90 25.6	13 18
Saturn	70 31.8	14 37

© British Crown Copyright 2018. All rights reserved.

SUN and MOON

UT	SUN GHA	SUN Dec	MOON GHA	v	MOON Dec	d	HP
d h	° '	° '	° '	'	° '	'	'
30 00	182 54.6	S21 33.2	137 30.4	8.7	S23 00.2	1.8	56.4
01	197 54.3	33.6	151 58.1	8.6	22 58.4	1.9	56.4
02	212 54.1	34.0	166 25.7	8.8	22 56.5	2.1	56.3
03	227 53.9	.. 34.4	180 53.5	8.7	22 54.4	2.1	56.3
04	242 53.7	34.8	195 21.2	8.9	22 52.3	2.3	56.3
05	257 53.5	35.2	209 49.1	8.9	22 50.0	2.4	56.2
06	272 53.2	S21 35.6	224 17.0	9.0	S22 47.6	2.6	56.2
07	287 53.0	36.1	238 45.0	9.0	22 45.0	2.6	56.2
S 08	302 52.8	36.5	253 13.0	9.1	22 42.4	2.8	56.1
A 09	317 52.6	.. 36.9	267 41.1	9.1	22 39.6	2.9	56.1
T 10	332 52.3	37.3	282 09.2	9.3	22 36.7	3.0	56.1
U 11	347 52.1	37.7	296 37.5	9.2	22 33.7	3.1	56.1
R 12	2 51.9	S21 38.1	311 05.7	9.4	S22 30.6	3.3	56.0
D 13	17 51.6	38.5	325 34.1	9.4	22 27.3	3.3	56.0
A 14	32 51.4	38.9	340 02.5	9.5	22 24.0	3.5	56.0
Y 15	47 51.2	.. 39.3	354 31.0	9.5	22 20.5	3.6	55.9
16	62 51.0	39.7	8 59.5	9.6	22 16.9	3.7	55.9
17	77 50.7	40.1	23 28.1	9.7	22 13.2	3.8	55.9
18	92 50.5	S21 40.5	37 56.8	9.8	S22 09.4	3.9	55.9
19	107 50.3	40.9	52 25.6	9.8	22 05.5	4.1	55.8
20	122 50.1	41.3	66 54.4	9.9	22 01.4	4.1	55.8
21	137 49.8	.. 41.7	81 23.3	9.9	21 57.3	4.3	55.8
22	152 49.6	42.1	95 52.2	10.0	21 53.0	4.3	55.7
23	167 49.4	42.5	110 21.2	10.1	21 48.7	4.5	55.7
1 00	182 49.1	S21 42.9	124 50.3	10.2	S21 44.2	4.6	55.7
01	197 48.9	43.3	139 19.5	10.2	21 39.6	4.6	55.7
02	212 48.7	43.7	153 48.7	10.3	21 35.0	4.8	55.6
03	227 48.4	.. 44.1	168 18.0	10.4	21 30.2	4.9	55.6
04	242 48.2	44.5	182 47.4	10.5	21 25.3	5.0	55.6
05	257 48.0	44.9	197 16.9	10.5	21 20.3	5.1	55.6
06	272 47.8	S21 45.3	211 46.4	10.6	S21 15.2	5.2	55.5
07	287 47.5	45.7	226 16.0	10.6	21 10.0	5.3	55.5
S 08	302 47.3	46.1	240 45.6	10.8	21 04.7	5.4	55.5
U 09	317 47.1	.. 46.5	255 15.4	10.8	20 59.3	5.4	55.4
N 10	332 46.8	46.9	269 45.2	10.9	20 53.9	5.6	55.4
11	347 46.6	47.3	284 15.1	10.9	20 48.3	5.7	55.4
D 12	2 46.4	S21 47.7	298 45.0	11.1	S20 42.6	5.8	55.4
A 13	17 46.1	48.0	313 15.1	11.1	20 36.8	5.9	55.3
Y 14	32 45.9	48.4	327 45.2	11.1	20 30.9	5.9	55.3
15	47 45.7	.. 48.8	342 15.3	11.3	20 25.0	6.1	55.3
16	62 45.4	49.2	356 45.6	11.3	20 18.9	6.2	55.3
17	77 45.2	49.6	11 15.9	11.4	20 12.7	6.2	55.3
18	92 45.0	S21 50.0	25 46.3	11.4	S20 06.5	6.3	55.2
19	107 44.7	50.4	40 16.7	11.6	20 00.2	6.5	55.2
20	122 44.5	50.7	54 47.3	11.6	19 53.7	6.5	55.2
21	137 44.3	.. 51.1	69 17.9	11.7	19 47.2	6.6	55.2
22	152 44.0	51.5	83 48.6	11.7	19 40.6	6.7	55.1
23	167 43.8	51.9	98 19.3	11.9	19 33.9	6.7	55.1
2 00	182 43.5	S21 52.3	112 50.2	11.9	S19 27.2	6.9	55.1
01	197 43.3	52.7	127 21.1	11.9	19 20.3	6.9	55.1
02	212 43.1	53.0	141 52.0	12.1	19 13.4	7.1	55.0
03	227 42.8	.. 53.4	156 23.1	12.1	19 06.3	7.1	55.0
04	242 42.6	53.8	170 54.2	12.2	18 59.2	7.2	55.0
05	257 42.4	54.2	185 25.4	12.2	18 52.0	7.2	55.0
06	272 42.1	S21 54.5	199 56.6	12.3	S18 44.8	7.4	55.0
07	287 41.9	54.9	214 27.9	12.4	18 37.4	7.4	54.9
08	302 41.6	55.3	228 59.3	12.5	18 30.0	7.5	54.9
M 09	317 41.4	.. 55.7	243 30.8	12.5	18 22.5	7.6	54.9
O 10	332 41.2	56.0	258 02.3	12.6	18 14.9	7.7	54.9
N 11	347 40.9	56.4	272 33.9	12.7	18 07.2	7.7	54.9
D 12	2 40.7	S21 56.8	287 05.6	12.8	S17 59.5	7.8	54.8
A 13	17 40.5	57.2	301 37.4	12.8	17 51.7	7.9	54.8
Y 14	32 40.2	57.5	316 09.2	12.8	17 43.8	8.0	54.8
15	47 40.0	.. 57.9	330 41.0	13.0	17 35.8	8.0	54.8
16	62 39.7	58.3	345 13.0	13.0	17 27.8	8.1	54.8
17	77 39.5	58.6	359 45.0	13.1	17 19.7	8.2	54.7
18	92 39.2	S21 59.0	14 17.1	13.1	S17 11.5	8.3	54.7
19	107 39.0	59.4	28 49.2	13.2	17 03.2	8.3	54.7
20	122 38.8	21 59.7	43 21.4	13.3	16 54.9	8.4	54.7
21	137 38.5	22 00.1	57 53.7	13.3	16 46.5	8.4	54.7
22	152 38.3	00.5	72 26.0	13.4	16 38.1	8.5	54.7
23	167 38.0	00.8	86 58.4	13.5	S16 29.6	8.6	54.6
	SD 16.2	d 0.4	SD 15.3		15.1		14.9

Twilight, Sunrise, Moonrise

Lat.	Twilight Naut.	Twilight Civil	Sunrise	Moonrise 30	1	2	3
°	h m	h m	h m	h m	h m	h m	h m
N 72	07 50	09 49	▮	▮	▮	16 06	15 05
N 70	07 34	09 10	▮	▮	▮	15 02	14 37
68	07 21	08 43	10 34	▮	14 43	14 26	14 16
66	07 10	08 22	09 46	13 54	14 00	14 00	13 59
64	07 01	08 06	09 15	13 12	13 31	13 40	13 46
62	06 52	07 52	08 52	12 43	13 09	13 24	13 34
60	06 45	07 40	08 34	12 21	12 51	13 10	13 24
N 58	06 39	07 30	08 19	12 03	12 36	12 59	13 15
56	06 33	07 21	08 06	11 48	12 23	12 48	13 08
54	06 28	07 13	07 55	11 35	12 12	12 39	13 01
52	06 23	07 05	07 45	11 24	12 02	12 31	12 55
50	06 18	06 59	07 36	11 13	11 53	12 24	12 49
45	06 08	06 44	07 17	10 52	11 34	12 08	12 37
N 40	05 59	06 32	07 02	10 35	11 18	11 55	12 27
35	05 50	06 21	06 49	10 21	11 05	11 44	12 18
30	05 42	06 12	06 38	10 08	10 54	11 35	12 11
20	05 27	05 55	06 18	09 46	10 34	11 18	11 58
N 10	05 13	05 39	06 01	09 28	10 17	11 03	11 46
0	04 57	05 23	05 45	09 10	10 01	10 50	11 35
S 10	04 40	05 06	05 29	08 53	09 46	10 36	11 24
20	04 19	04 47	05 12	08 34	09 28	10 21	11 13
30	03 52	04 24	04 51	08 12	09 09	10 05	10 59
35	03 35	04 10	04 39	08 00	08 57	09 55	10 52
40	03 14	03 54	04 26	07 45	08 44	09 44	10 43
45	02 46	03 33	04 09	07 28	08 28	09 30	10 32
S 50	02 07	03 07	03 49	07 06	08 09	09 14	10 20
52	01 45	02 53	03 39	06 56	08 00	09 06	10 14
54	01 16	02 38	03 28	06 44	07 49	08 58	10 07
56	00 20	02 19	03 16	06 31	07 38	08 48	10 00
58	////	01 56	03 01	06 16	07 24	08 37	09 52
S 60	////	01 24	02 44	05 57	07 08	08 25	09 43

Sunset, Twilight, Moonset

Lat.	Sunset	Twilight Civil	Twilight Naut.	Moonset 30	1	2	3
°	h m	h m	h m	h m	h m	h m	h m
N 72	▮	13 48	15 47	▮	▮	18 11	20 45
N 70	▮	14 27	16 03	▮	▮	19 14	21 12
68	13 03	14 54	16 16	▮	17 54	19 49	21 32
66	13 52	15 15	16 27	16 57	18 36	20 14	21 47
64	14 22	15 32	16 37	17 39	19 05	20 33	22 00
62	14 45	15 45	16 45	18 07	19 26	20 49	22 11
60	15 03	15 57	16 52	18 29	19 44	21 02	22 20
N 58	15 18	16 08	16 59	18 46	19 58	21 13	22 28
56	15 31	16 17	17 04	19 01	20 11	21 22	22 35
54	15 42	16 25	17 10	19 14	20 21	21 31	22 41
52	15 52	16 32	17 15	19 25	20 31	21 39	22 46
50	16 01	16 39	17 20	19 35	20 40	21 46	22 51
45	16 20	16 53	17 30	19 56	20 58	22 00	23 02
N 40	16 35	17 05	17 39	20 13	21 12	22 12	23 11
35	16 48	17 16	17 47	20 27	21 25	22 22	23 19
30	17 00	17 26	17 55	20 39	21 36	22 31	23 25
20	17 19	17 43	18 10	21 00	21 54	22 46	23 37
N 10	17 36	17 59	18 25	21 18	22 10	23 00	23 47
0	17 53	18 15	18 41	21 35	22 25	23 12	23 56
S 10	18 09	18 32	18 58	21 52	22 40	23 24	24 06
20	18 26	18 51	19 19	22 10	22 56	23 37	24 16
30	18 47	19 14	19 46	22 31	23 14	23 52	24 27
35	18 59	19 28	20 04	22 43	23 24	24 01	00 01
40	19 13	19 45	20 25	22 56	23 36	24 11	00 11
45	19 29	20 05	20 53	23 13	23 51	24 22	00 22
S 50	19 50	20 32	21 32	23 33	24 08	00 08	00 36
52	19 59	20 46	21 54	23 42	24 16	00 16	00 42
54	20 10	21 01	22 25	23 53	24 25	00 25	00 49
56	20 23	21 20	23 28	24 05	00 05	00 35	00 57
58	20 38	21 44	////	24 18	00 18	00 46	01 06
S 60	20 55	22 17	////	24 35	00 35	00 59	01 06

SUN / MOON

Day	SUN Eqn. of Time 00ʰ	12ʰ	Mer. Pass.	MOON Mer. Pass. Upper	Lower	Age	Phase
d	m s	m s	h m	h m	h m	d	%
30	11 39	11 28	11 49	15 23	02 56	04	16
1	11 17	11 06	11 49	16 13	03 48	05	25
2	10 55	10 43	11 49	17 01	04 38	06	33

© British Crown Copyright 2018. All rights reserved.

UT	ARIES	VENUS −3.9		MARS +1.7		JUPITER −1.8		SATURN +0.6		STARS		
d h	GHA	GHA	Dec	GHA	Dec	GHA	Dec	GHA	Dec	Name	SHA	Dec
3 00	71 32.0	152 00.6	S24 40.3	214 41.4	S13 55.3	161 28.6	S23 18.0	141 50.9	S22 06.8	Acamar	315 14.6	S40 13.7
01	86 34.5	166 59.6	40.2	229 42.3	55.8	176 30.4	18.1	156 53.1	06.8	Achernar	335 23.0	S57 08.5
02	101 36.9	181 58.7	40.0	244 43.1	56.4	191 32.3	18.1	171 55.2	06.8	Acrux	173 04.7	S63 12.1
03	116 39.4	196 57.8	.. 39.9	259 44.0	.. 56.9	206 34.2	.. 18.1	186 57.4	.. 06.8	Adhara	255 08.7	S28 59.9
04	131 41.9	211 56.8	39.8	274 44.8	57.5	221 36.0	18.1	201 59.6	06.7	Aldebaran	290 44.0	N16 32.8
05	146 44.3	226 55.9	39.6	289 45.7	58.0	236 37.9	18.1	217 01.8	06.7			
06	161 46.8	241 54.9	S24 39.5	304 46.5	S13 58.6	251 39.7	S23 18.1	232 04.0	S22 06.7	Alioth	166 17.1	N55 51.0
07	176 49.3	256 54.0	39.3	319 47.4	59.1	266 41.6	18.1	247 06.2	06.6	Alkaid	152 55.7	N49 12.8
08	191 51.7	271 53.1	39.2	334 48.3	13 59.6	281 43.4	18.1	262 08.4	06.6	Alnair	27 38.3	S46 52.1
T 09	206 54.2	286 52.1	.. 39.1	349 49.1	14 00.2	296 45.3	.. 18.1	277 10.6	.. 06.6	Alnilam	275 41.5	S 1 11.4
U 10	221 56.7	301 51.2	38.9	4 50.0	00.7	311 47.2	18.1	292 12.8	06.5	Alphard	217 51.6	S 8 44.6
E 11	236 59.1	316 50.2	38.8	19 50.8	01.3	326 49.0	18.1	307 15.0	06.5			
S 12	252 01.6	331 49.3	S24 38.6	34 51.7	S14 01.8	341 50.9	S23 18.1	322 17.2	S22 06.5	Alphecca	126 07.6	N26 39.0
D 13	267 04.0	346 48.4	38.5	49 52.5	02.4	356 52.7	18.1	337 19.3	06.4	Alpheratz	357 38.8	N29 12.1
A 14	282 06.5	1 47.4	38.3	64 53.4	02.9	11 54.6	18.1	352 21.5	06.4	Altair	62 04.2	N 8 55.4
Y 15	297 09.0	16 46.5	.. 38.2	79 54.2	.. 03.4	26 56.4	.. 18.1	7 23.7	.. 06.4	Ankaa	353 11.1	S42 12.2
16	312 11.4	31 45.6	38.0	94 55.1	04.0	41 58.3	18.1	22 25.9	06.3	Antares	112 21.2	S26 28.3
17	327 13.9	46 44.6	37.8	109 55.9	04.5	57 00.1	18.1	37 28.1	06.3			
18	342 16.4	61 43.7	S24 37.7	124 56.8	S14 05.1	72 02.0	S23 18.1	52 30.3	S22 06.3	Arcturus	145 52.0	N19 04.8
19	357 18.8	76 42.7	37.5	139 57.6	05.6	87 03.9	18.1	67 32.5	06.3	Atria	107 19.6	S69 03.6
20	12 21.3	91 41.8	37.4	154 58.5	06.2	102 05.7	18.1	82 34.7	06.2	Avior	234 15.8	S59 34.1
21	27 23.8	106 40.9	.. 37.2	169 59.3	.. 06.7	117 07.6	.. 18.1	97 36.9	.. 06.2	Bellatrix	278 26.9	N 6 22.0
22	42 26.2	121 39.9	37.0	185 00.2	07.2	132 09.4	18.1	112 39.1	06.2	Betelgeuse	270 56.2	N 7 24.5
23	57 28.7	136 39.0	36.9	200 01.0	07.8	147 11.3	18.1	127 41.2	06.1			
4 00	72 31.2	151 38.1	S24 36.7	215 01.9	S14 08.3	162 13.1	S23 18.1	142 43.4	S22 06.1	Canopus	263 53.7	S52 42.3
01	87 33.6	166 37.1	36.5	230 02.7	08.9	177 15.0	18.1	157 45.6	06.1	Capella	280 27.4	N46 00.9
02	102 36.1	181 36.2	36.4	245 03.6	09.4	192 16.9	18.1	172 47.8	06.0	Deneb	49 28.8	N45 21.3
03	117 38.5	196 35.3	.. 36.2	260 04.4	.. 09.9	207 18.7	.. 18.1	187 50.0	.. 06.0	Denebola	182 29.2	N14 27.7
04	132 41.0	211 34.3	36.0	275 05.3	10.5	222 20.6	18.1	202 52.2	06.0	Diphda	348 51.3	S17 52.8
05	147 43.5	226 33.4	35.9	290 06.1	11.0	237 22.4	18.1	217 54.4	05.9			
06	162 45.9	241 32.5	S24 35.7	305 07.0	S14 11.6	252 24.3	S23 18.2	232 56.6	S22 05.9	Dubhe	193 46.3	N61 38.4
W 07	177 48.4	256 31.5	35.5	320 07.8	12.1	267 26.1	18.2	247 58.8	05.9	Elnath	278 06.6	N28 37.3
E 08	192 50.9	271 30.6	35.3	335 08.7	12.6	282 28.0	18.2	263 00.9	05.8	Eltanin	90 44.6	N51 29.4
D 09	207 53.3	286 29.7	.. 35.2	350 09.5	.. 13.2	297 29.8	.. 18.2	278 03.1	.. 05.8	Enif	33 42.9	N 9 58.0
N 10	222 55.8	301 28.7	35.0	5 10.4	13.7	312 31.7	18.2	293 05.3	05.8	Fomalhaut	15 19.1	S29 31.2
E 11	237 58.3	316 27.8	34.8	20 11.2	14.3	327 33.6	18.2	308 07.5	05.8			
S 12	253 00.7	331 26.9	S24 34.6	35 12.0	S14 14.8	342 35.4	S23 18.2	323 09.7	S22 05.7	Gacrux	171 56.3	S57 13.1
D 13	268 03.2	346 25.9	34.5	50 12.9	15.3	357 37.3	18.2	338 11.9	05.7	Gienah	175 47.9	S17 38.9
A 14	283 05.6	1 25.0	34.3	65 13.7	15.9	12 39.1	18.2	353 14.1	05.7	Hadar	148 42.1	S60 27.7
Y 15	298 08.1	16 24.1	.. 34.1	80 14.6	.. 16.4	27 41.0	.. 18.2	8 16.3	.. 05.6	Hamal	327 55.5	N23 33.4
16	313 10.6	31 23.1	33.9	95 15.4	17.0	42 42.8	18.2	23 18.5	05.6	Kaus Aust.	83 38.3	S34 22.4
17	328 13.0	46 22.2	33.7	110 16.3	17.5	57 44.7	18.2	38 20.6	05.6			
18	343 15.5	61 21.3	S24 33.5	125 17.1	S14 18.0	72 46.5	S23 18.2	53 22.8	S22 05.5	Kochab	137 21.1	N74 04.4
19	358 18.0	76 20.3	33.3	140 18.0	18.6	87 48.4	18.2	68 25.0	05.5	Markab	13 33.9	N15 18.8
20	13 20.4	91 19.4	33.1	155 18.8	19.1	102 50.2	18.2	83 27.2	05.5	Menkar	314 10.1	N 4 10.0
21	28 22.9	106 18.5	.. 33.0	170 19.7	.. 19.6	117 52.1	.. 18.2	98 29.4	.. 05.4	Menkent	148 02.7	S36 27.7
22	43 25.4	121 17.5	32.8	185 20.5	20.2	132 54.0	18.2	113 31.6	05.4	Miaplacidus	221 38.4	S69 47.6
23	58 27.8	136 16.6	32.6	200 21.4	20.7	147 55.8	18.2	128 33.8	05.4			
5 00	73 30.3	151 15.7	S24 32.4	215 22.2	S14 21.3	162 57.7	S23 18.2	143 36.0	S22 05.3	Mirfak	308 33.5	N49 55.9
01	88 32.8	166 14.7	32.2	230 23.1	21.8	177 59.5	18.2	158 38.1	05.3	Nunki	75 53.2	S26 16.3
02	103 35.2	181 13.8	32.0	245 23.9	22.3	193 01.4	18.2	173 40.3	05.3	Peacock	53 12.7	S56 40.4
T 03	118 37.7	196 12.9	.. 31.8	260 24.7	.. 22.9	208 03.2	.. 18.2	188 42.5	.. 05.2	Pollux	243 22.1	N27 58.5
H 04	133 40.1	211 12.0	31.6	275 25.6	23.4	223 05.1	18.2	203 44.7	05.2	Procyon	244 54.9	N 5 10.4
U 05	148 42.6	226 11.0	31.4	290 26.4	23.9	238 06.9	18.2	218 46.9	05.2			
R 06	163 45.1	241 10.1	S24 31.2	305 27.3	S14 24.5	253 08.8	S23 18.2	233 49.1	S22 05.2	Rasalhague	96 02.7	N12 32.9
S 07	178 47.5	256 09.2	31.0	320 28.1	25.0	268 10.6	18.2	248 51.3	05.1	Regulus	207 38.8	N11 52.2
08	193 50.0	271 08.2	30.8	335 29.0	25.6	283 12.5	18.2	263 53.5	05.1	Rigel	281 07.5	S 8 10.8
T 09	208 52.5	286 07.3	.. 30.5	350 29.8	.. 26.1	298 14.4	.. 18.2	278 55.6	.. 05.1	Rigil Kent.	139 46.3	S60 54.7
H 10	223 54.9	301 06.4	30.3	5 30.7	26.6	313 16.2	18.2	293 57.8	05.0	Sabik	102 07.8	S15 44.8
U 11	238 57.4	316 05.5	30.1	20 31.5	27.2	328 18.1	18.2	309 00.0	05.0			
R 12	253 59.9	331 04.5	S24 29.9	35 32.3	S14 27.7	343 19.9	S23 18.2	324 02.2	S22 05.0	Schedar	349 35.2	N56 38.9
S 13	269 02.3	346 03.6	29.7	50 33.2	28.2	358 21.8	18.2	339 04.4	04.9	Shaula	96 16.3	S37 06.9
D 14	284 04.8	1 02.7	29.5	65 34.0	28.8	13 23.6	18.2	354 06.6	04.9	Sirius	258 29.5	S16 44.6
A 15	299 07.2	16 01.7	.. 29.3	80 34.9	.. 29.3	28 25.5	.. 18.2	9 08.8	.. 04.9	Spica	158 26.8	S11 15.7
Y 16	314 09.7	31 00.8	29.1	95 35.7	29.8	43 27.3	18.2	24 10.9	04.8	Suhail	222 49.0	S43 30.5
17	329 12.2	45 59.9	28.8	110 36.6	30.4	58 29.2	18.2	39 13.1	04.8			
18	344 14.6	60 59.0	S24 28.6	125 37.4	S14 30.9	73 31.0	S23 18.2	54 15.3	S22 04.8	Vega	80 36.4	N38 48.3
19	359 17.1	75 58.0	28.4	140 38.2	31.4	88 32.9	18.2	69 17.5	04.7	Zuben'ubi	137 00.8	S16 07.2
20	14 19.6	90 57.1	28.2	155 39.1	32.0	103 34.7	18.2	84 19.7	04.7		SHA	Mer.Pass.
21	29 22.0	105 56.2	.. 28.0	170 39.9	.. 32.5	118 36.6	.. 18.2	99 21.9	.. 04.7		° ′	h m
22	44 24.5	120 55.3	27.7	185 40.8	33.0	133 38.5	18.2	114 24.1	04.6	Venus	79 06.9	13 54
23	59 27.0	135 54.3	27.5	200 41.6	33.6	148 40.3	18.2	129 26.2	04.6	Mars	142 30.7	9 39
Mer. Pass.	h m 19 06.8	v −0.9	d 0.2	v 0.8	d 0.5	v 1.9	d 0.0	v 2.2	d 0.0	Jupiter Saturn	89 42.0 70 12.3	13 09 14 27

© British Crown Copyright 2018. All rights reserved.

UT	SUN GHA	SUN Dec	MOON GHA	v	MOON Dec	d	HP
d h	° ′	° ′	° ′	′	° ′	′	′
3 00	182 37.8	S22 01.2	101 30.9	13.5	S16 21.0	8.7	54.6
01	197 37.6	01.6	116 03.4	13.6	16 12.3	8.7	54.6
02	212 37.3	01.9	130 36.0	13.7	16 03.6	8.7	54.6
03	227 37.1	.. 02.3	145 08.7	13.7	15 54.9	8.9	54.6
04	242 36.8	02.6	159 41.4	13.7	15 46.0	8.9	54.6
05	257 36.6	03.0	174 14.1	13.9	15 37.1	9.0	54.6
06	272 36.3	S22 03.4	188 47.0	13.9	S15 28.1	9.0	54.5
07	287 36.1	03.7	203 19.9	13.9	15 19.1	9.1	54.5
08	302 35.8	04.1	217 52.8	14.0	15 10.0	9.1	54.5
09	317 35.6	.. 04.4	232 25.8	14.1	15 00.9	9.2	54.5
10	332 35.4	04.8	246 58.9	14.1	14 51.7	9.3	54.5
11	347 35.1	05.1	261 32.0	14.2	14 42.4	9.3	54.5
12	2 34.9	S22 05.5	276 05.2	14.2	S14 33.1	9.4	54.5
13	17 34.6	05.9	290 38.4	14.3	14 23.7	9.4	54.5
14	32 34.4	06.2	305 11.7	14.3	14 14.3	9.5	54.4
15	47 34.1	.. 06.6	319 45.0	14.4	14 04.8	9.5	54.4
16	62 33.9	06.9	334 18.4	14.5	13 55.3	9.6	54.4
17	77 33.6	07.3	348 51.9	14.5	13 45.7	9.6	54.4
18	92 33.4	S22 07.6	3 25.4	14.5	S13 36.1	9.7	54.4
19	107 33.1	08.0	17 58.9	14.6	13 26.4	9.8	54.4
20	122 32.9	08.3	32 32.5	14.7	13 16.6	9.8	54.4
21	137 32.6	.. 08.7	47 06.2	14.7	13 06.8	9.8	54.4
22	152 32.4	09.0	61 39.9	14.7	12 57.0	9.9	54.4
23	167 32.1	09.4	76 13.6	14.8	12 47.1	9.9	54.3
4 00	182 31.9	S22 09.7	90 47.4	14.8	S12 37.2	10.0	54.3
01	197 31.7	10.0	105 21.2	14.9	12 27.2	10.1	54.3
02	212 31.4	10.4	119 55.1	14.9	12 17.1	10.0	54.3
03	227 31.2	.. 10.7	134 29.0	15.0	12 07.1	10.2	54.3
04	242 30.9	11.1	149 03.0	15.0	11 56.9	10.1	54.3
05	257 30.7	11.4	163 37.0	15.1	11 46.8	10.3	54.3
06	272 30.4	S22 11.8	178 11.1	15.1	S11 36.5	10.2	54.3
07	287 30.2	12.1	192 45.2	15.1	11 26.3	10.3	54.3
08	302 29.9	12.4	207 19.3	15.2	11 16.0	10.4	54.3
09	317 29.7	.. 12.8	221 53.5	15.3	11 05.6	10.4	54.3
10	332 29.4	13.1	236 27.8	15.2	10 55.2	10.4	54.3
11	347 29.2	13.4	251 02.0	15.3	10 44.8	10.4	54.3
12	2 28.9	S22 13.8	265 36.3	15.3	S10 34.4	10.6	54.3
13	17 28.6	14.1	280 10.6	15.4	10 23.8	10.5	54.3
14	32 28.4	14.5	294 45.0	15.4	10 13.3	10.6	54.2
15	47 28.1	.. 14.8	309 19.4	15.5	10 02.7	10.6	54.2
16	62 27.9	15.1	323 53.9	15.4	9 52.1	10.7	54.2
17	77 27.6	15.5	338 28.3	15.6	9 41.4	10.7	54.2
18	92 27.4	S22 15.8	353 02.9	15.5	S 9 30.7	10.7	54.2
19	107 27.1	16.1	7 37.4	15.6	9 20.0	10.8	54.2
20	122 26.9	16.5	22 12.0	15.6	9 09.2	10.8	54.2
21	137 26.6	.. 16.8	36 46.6	15.6	8 58.4	10.8	54.2
22	152 26.4	17.1	51 21.2	15.7	8 47.6	10.9	54.2
23	167 26.1	17.4	65 55.9	15.7	8 36.7	10.9	54.2
5 00	182 25.9	S22 17.8	80 30.6	15.7	S 8 25.8	10.9	54.2
01	197 25.6	18.1	95 05.3	15.7	8 14.9	11.0	54.2
02	212 25.4	18.4	109 40.0	15.8	8 03.9	11.0	54.2
03	227 25.1	.. 18.7	124 14.8	15.8	7 52.9	11.0	54.2
04	242 24.8	19.1	138 49.6	15.8	7 41.9	11.1	54.2
05	257 24.6	19.4	153 24.4	15.8	7 30.8	11.1	54.2
06	272 24.3	S22 19.7	167 59.2	15.9	S 7 19.7	11.1	54.2
07	287 24.1	20.0	182 34.1	15.8	7 08.6	11.1	54.2
08	302 23.8	20.4	197 08.9	15.9	6 57.5	11.2	54.2
09	317 23.6	.. 20.7	211 43.8	16.0	6 46.3	11.2	54.2
10	332 23.3	21.0	226 18.8	15.9	6 35.1	11.2	54.2
11	347 23.0	21.3	240 53.7	15.9	6 23.9	11.3	54.2
12	2 22.8	S22 21.6	255 28.6	16.0	S 6 12.6	11.3	54.2
13	17 22.5	22.0	270 03.6	16.0	6 01.3	11.3	54.2
14	32 22.3	22.3	284 38.6	16.0	5 50.0	11.3	54.2
15	47 22.0	.. 22.6	299 13.6	16.0	5 38.7	11.3	54.2
16	62 21.8	22.9	313 48.6	16.0	5 27.4	11.4	54.2
17	77 21.5	23.2	328 23.6	16.0	5 16.0	11.4	54.2
18	92 21.2	S22 23.5	342 58.6	16.1	S 5 04.6	11.4	54.2
19	107 21.0	23.8	357 33.7	16.0	4 53.2	11.5	54.2
20	122 20.7	24.2	12 08.7	16.1	4 41.7	11.4	54.3
21	137 20.5	.. 24.5	26 43.8	16.1	4 30.3	11.5	54.3
22	152 20.2	24.8	41 18.9	16.1	4 18.8	11.5	54.3
23	167 19.9	25.1	55 54.0	16.0	S 4 07.3	11.5	54.3
SD	16.3	d 0.3	SD 14.8		14.8		14.8

Lat.	Twilight Naut.	Twilight Civil	Sunrise	Moonrise 3	4	5	6
°	h m	h m	h m	h m	h m	h m	h m
N 72	07 58	10 02	■■■	15 05	14 37	14 16	13 58
N 70	07 41	09 19	■■■	14 37	14 21	14 08	13 56
68	07 27	08 51	10 53	14 16	14 08	14 01	13 54
66	07 16	08 29	09 56	13 59	13 58	13 55	13 53
64	07 06	08 12	09 23	13 46	13 49	13 51	13 52
62	06 57	07 57	08 59	13 34	13 41	13 46	13 51
60	06 50	07 45	08 40	13 24	13 34	13 43	13 50
N 58	06 43	07 34	08 24	13 15	13 29	13 40	13 50
56	06 37	07 25	08 11	13 08	13 23	13 37	13 49
54	06 31	07 17	07 59	13 01	13 19	13 34	13 49
52	06 26	07 09	07 49	12 55	13 14	13 32	13 48
50	06 21	07 02	07 40	12 49	13 11	13 30	13 48
45	06 11	06 48	07 21	12 37	13 02	13 25	13 47
N 40	06 01	06 35	07 05	12 27	12 55	13 21	13 46
35	05 53	06 24	06 52	12 18	12 49	13 17	13 45
30	05 45	06 14	06 40	12 11	12 44	13 14	13 44
20	05 29	05 56	06 20	11 58	12 34	13 09	13 43
N 10	05 14	05 40	06 03	11 46	12 26	13 05	13 42
0	04 58	05 24	05 46	11 35	12 18	13 00	13 41
S 10	04 40	05 07	05 30	11 24	12 11	12 56	13 40
20	04 19	04 48	05 12	11 13	12 02	12 51	13 39
30	03 51	04 24	04 51	10 59	11 53	12 46	13 38
35	03 34	04 10	04 39	10 52	11 48	12 43	13 38
40	03 12	03 53	04 25	10 43	11 41	12 39	13 37
45	02 44	03 32	04 08	10 32	11 34	12 35	13 36
S 50	02 03	03 04	03 47	10 20	11 25	12 30	13 35
52	01 40	02 51	03 37	10 14	11 21	12 28	13 35
54	01 08	02 34	03 26	10 07	11 17	12 25	13 34
56	////	02 15	03 13	10 00	11 12	12 23	13 34
58	////	01 50	02 58	09 52	11 06	12 20	13 33
S 60	////	01 15	02 40	09 43	11 00	12 16	13 32

Lat.	Sunset	Twilight Civil	Twilight Naut.	Moonset 3	4	5	6
°	h m	h m	h m	h m	h m	h m	h m
N 72	■■■	13 37	15 42	20 45	22 43	24 30	00 30
N 70	■■■	14 20	15 59	21 12	22 57	24 36	00 36
68	12 47	14 49	16 13	21 32	23 08	24 40	00 40
66	13 44	15 11	16 24	21 47	23 17	24 44	00 44
64	14 17	15 28	16 34	22 00	23 24	24 47	00 47
62	14 41	15 42	16 42	22 11	23 31	24 50	00 50
60	15 00	15 55	16 50	22 20	23 37	24 53	00 53
N 58	15 15	16 05	16 57	22 28	23 41	24 55	00 55
56	15 29	16 15	17 03	22 35	23 46	24 57	00 57
54	15 40	16 23	17 08	22 41	23 50	24 58	00 58
52	15 51	16 31	17 14	22 46	23 53	25 00	01 00
50	16 00	16 37	17 18	22 51	23 57	25 01	01 01
45	16 19	16 52	17 29	23 02	24 03	00 03	01 04
N 40	16 35	17 05	17 39	23 11	24 09	00 09	01 07
35	16 48	17 16	17 47	23 19	24 14	00 14	01 09
30	17 00	17 26	17 55	23 25	24 19	00 19	01 11
20	17 20	17 44	18 11	23 37	24 26	00 26	01 14
N 10	17 37	18 00	18 26	23 47	24 33	00 33	01 17
0	17 54	18 16	18 42	23 56	24 39	00 39	01 20
S 10	18 10	18 33	19 00	24 06	00 06	00 45	01 23
20	18 28	18 53	19 22	24 16	00 16	00 51	01 25
30	18 49	19 16	19 49	24 27	00 27	00 58	01 29
35	19 01	19 31	20 07	00 01	00 33	01 03	01 30
40	19 16	19 48	20 28	00 11	00 40	01 07	01 32
45	19 33	20 09	20 57	00 22	00 49	01 13	01 35
S 50	19 54	20 37	21 38	00 36	00 59	01 19	01 37
52	20 04	20 50	22 01	00 42	01 04	01 22	01 39
54	20 15	21 07	22 35	00 49	01 09	01 25	01 40
56	20 28	21 26	////	00 57	01 14	01 29	01 42
58	20 43	21 52	////	01 06	01 21	01 33	01 43
S 60	21 02	22 28	////	01 16	01 28	01 37	01 45

Day	SUN Eqn. of Time 00h	SUN Eqn. of Time 12h	SUN Mer. Pass.	MOON Mer. Pass. Upper	MOON Mer. Pass. Lower	Age	Phase
d	m s	m s	h m	h m	h m	d	%
3	10 32	10 20	11 50	17 46	05 24	07	43
4	10 08	09 56	11 50	18 29	06 07	08	52
5	09 44	09 32	11 50	19 10	06 49	09	61

© British Crown Copyright 2018. All rights reserved.

UT	ARIES GHA	VENUS −3.9 GHA	Dec	MARS +1.7 GHA	Dec	JUPITER −1.8 GHA	Dec	SATURN +0.6 GHA	Dec	STARS Name	SHA	Dec
6 00	74 29.4	150 53.4	S24 27.3	215 42.5	S14 34.1	163 42.2	S23 18.2	144 28.4	S22 04.6	Acamar	315 14.6	S40 13.7
01	89 31.9	165 52.5	27.0	230 43.3	34.6	178 44.0	18.2	159 30.6	04.5	Achernar	335 23.0	S57 08.5
02	104 34.4	180 51.6	26.8	245 44.1	35.2	193 45.9	18.2	174 32.8	04.5	Acrux	173 04.6	S63 12.1
03	119 36.8	195 50.6	.. 26.6	260 45.0	.. 35.7	208 47.7	.. 18.2	189 35.0	.. 04.5	Adhara	255 08.7	S28 59.9
04	134 39.3	210 49.7	26.4	275 45.8	36.2	223 49.6	18.2	204 37.2	04.4	Aldebaran	290 43.9	N16 32.8
05	149 41.7	225 48.8	26.1	290 46.7	36.8	238 51.4	18.2	219 39.4	04.4			
06	164 44.2	240 47.9	S24 25.9	305 47.5	S14 37.3	253 53.3	S23 18.2	234 41.5	S22 04.4	Alioth	166 17.0	N55 51.0
07	179 46.7	255 46.9	25.7	320 48.3	37.8	268 55.1	18.2	249 43.7	04.3	Alkaid	152 55.7	N49 12.8
08	194 49.1	270 46.0	25.4	335 49.2	38.4	283 57.0	18.2	264 45.9	04.3	Alnair	27 38.3	S46 52.1
F 09	209 51.6	285 45.1	.. 25.2	350 50.0	.. 38.9	298 58.8	.. 18.2	279 48.1	.. 04.3	Alnilam	275 41.5	S 1 11.4
R 10	224 54.1	300 44.2	24.9	5 50.9	39.4	314 00.7	18.2	294 50.3	04.3	Alphard	217 51.6	S 8 44.6
I 11	239 56.5	315 43.2	24.7	20 51.7	39.9	329 02.5	18.2	309 52.5	04.2			
D 12	254 59.0	330 42.3	S24 24.5	35 52.5	S14 40.5	344 04.4	S23 18.2	324 54.7	S22 04.2	Alphecca	126 07.6	N26 39.0
A 13	270 01.5	345 41.4	24.2	50 53.4	41.0	359 06.2	18.2	339 56.8	04.2	Alpheratz	357 38.8	N29 12.1
Y 14	285 03.9	0 40.5	24.0	65 54.2	41.5	14 08.1	18.2	354 59.0	04.1	Altair	62 04.2	N 8 55.4
15	300 06.4	15 39.6	.. 23.7	80 55.1	.. 42.1	29 09.9	.. 18.2	10 01.2	.. 04.1	Ankaa	353 11.1	S42 12.2
16	315 08.9	30 38.6	23.5	95 55.9	42.6	44 11.8	18.2	25 03.4	04.1	Antares	112 21.2	S26 28.3
17	330 11.3	45 37.7	23.2	110 56.7	43.1	59 13.7	18.2	40 05.6	04.0			
18	345 13.8	60 36.8	S24 23.0	125 57.6	S14 43.7	74 15.5	S23 18.2	55 07.8	S22 04.0	Arcturus	145 52.0	N19 04.8
19	0 16.2	75 35.9	22.7	140 58.4	44.2	89 17.4	18.2	70 09.9	04.0	Atria	107 19.6	S69 03.6
20	15 18.7	90 35.0	22.5	155 59.3	44.7	104 19.2	18.2	85 12.1	03.9	Avior	234 15.8	S59 34.2
21	30 21.2	105 34.0	.. 22.2	171 00.1	.. 45.2	119 21.1	.. 18.2	100 14.3	.. 03.9	Bellatrix	278 26.9	N 6 22.0
22	45 23.6	120 33.1	22.0	186 00.9	45.8	134 22.9	18.2	115 16.5	03.9	Betelgeuse	270 56.2	N 7 24.5
23	60 26.1	135 32.2	21.7	201 01.8	46.3	149 24.8	18.2	130 18.7	03.8			
7 00	75 28.6	150 31.3	S24 21.4	216 02.6	S14 46.8	164 26.6	S23 18.2	145 20.9	S22 03.8	Canopus	263 53.7	S52 42.3
01	90 31.0	165 30.4	21.2	231 03.5	47.4	179 28.5	18.2	160 23.0	03.8	Capella	280 27.4	N46 00.9
02	105 33.5	180 29.4	20.9	246 04.3	47.9	194 30.3	18.2	175 25.2	03.7	Deneb	49 28.8	N45 21.3
03	120 36.0	195 28.5	.. 20.7	261 05.1	.. 48.4	209 32.2	.. 18.2	190 27.4	.. 03.7	Denebola	182 29.2	N14 27.7
04	135 38.4	210 27.6	20.4	276 06.0	48.9	224 34.0	18.2	205 29.6	03.7	Diphda	348 51.3	S17 52.8
05	150 40.9	225 26.7	20.1	291 06.8	49.5	239 35.9	18.2	220 31.8	03.6			
06	165 43.3	240 25.8	S24 19.9	306 07.6	S14 50.0	254 37.7	S23 18.2	235 34.0	S22 03.6	Dubhe	193 46.3	N61 38.4
07	180 45.8	255 24.9	19.6	321 08.5	50.5	269 39.6	18.2	250 36.1	03.6	Elnath	278 06.6	N28 37.3
S 08	195 48.3	270 23.9	19.3	336 09.3	51.1	284 41.4	18.2	265 38.3	03.5	Eltanin	90 44.6	N51 29.3
A 09	210 50.7	285 23.0	.. 19.1	351 10.1	.. 51.6	299 43.3	.. 18.2	280 40.5	.. 03.5	Enif	33 42.9	N 9 58.0
T 10	225 53.2	300 22.1	18.8	6 11.0	52.1	314 45.1	18.2	295 42.7	03.5	Fomalhaut	15 19.1	S29 31.2
U 11	240 55.7	315 21.2	18.5	21 11.8	52.6	329 47.0	18.2	310 44.9	03.4			
R 12	255 58.1	330 20.3	S24 18.3	36 12.7	S14 53.2	344 48.8	S23 18.2	325 47.1	S22 03.4	Gacrux	171 56.2	S57 13.1
D 13	271 00.6	345 19.4	18.0	51 13.5	53.7	359 50.7	18.2	340 49.2	03.4	Gienah	175 47.9	S17 38.9
A 14	286 03.1	0 18.4	17.7	66 14.3	54.2	14 52.5	18.2	355 51.4	03.3	Hadar	148 42.1	S60 27.7
Y 15	301 05.5	15 17.5	.. 17.4	81 15.2	.. 54.7	29 54.4	.. 18.2	10 53.6	.. 03.3	Hamal	327 55.5	N23 33.4
16	316 08.0	30 16.6	17.1	96 16.0	55.3	44 56.2	18.2	25 55.8	03.3	Kaus Aust.	83 38.3	S34 22.4
17	331 10.5	45 15.7	16.9	111 16.8	55.8	59 58.1	18.2	40 58.0	03.2			
18	346 12.9	60 14.8	S24 16.6	126 17.7	S14 56.3	74 59.9	S23 18.2	56 00.2	S22 03.2	Kochab	137 21.1	N74 04.4
19	1 15.4	75 13.9	16.3	141 18.5	56.8	90 01.8	18.2	71 02.3	03.2	Markab	13 33.9	N15 18.8
20	16 17.8	90 13.0	16.0	156 19.3	57.4	105 03.6	18.2	86 04.5	03.1	Menkar	314 10.1	N 4 09.9
21	31 20.3	105 12.1	.. 15.7	171 20.2	.. 57.9	120 05.5	.. 18.2	101 06.7	.. 03.1	Menkent	148 02.7	S36 27.7
22	46 22.8	120 11.1	15.4	186 21.0	58.4	135 07.3	18.2	116 08.9	03.1	Miaplacidus	221 38.4	S69 47.6
23	61 25.2	135 10.2	15.2	201 21.8	58.9	150 09.2	18.2	131 11.1	03.0			
8 00	76 27.7	150 09.3	S24 14.9	216 22.7	S14 59.5	165 11.0	S23 18.2	146 13.2	S22 03.0	Mirfak	308 33.5	N49 55.9
01	91 30.2	165 08.4	14.6	231 23.5	15 00.0	180 12.9	18.2	161 15.4	03.0	Nunki	75 53.2	S26 16.3
02	106 32.6	180 07.5	14.3	246 24.3	00.5	195 14.7	18.2	176 17.6	02.9	Peacock	53 12.7	S56 40.4
03	121 35.1	195 06.6	.. 14.0	261 25.2	.. 01.0	210 16.6	.. 18.2	191 19.8	.. 02.9	Pollux	243 22.0	N27 58.5
04	136 37.6	210 05.7	13.7	276 26.0	01.6	225 18.4	18.2	206 22.0	02.9	Procyon	244 54.8	N 5 10.4
05	151 40.0	225 04.8	13.4	291 26.8	02.1	240 20.3	18.2	221 24.2	02.8			
06	166 42.5	240 03.9	S24 13.1	306 27.7	S15 02.6	255 22.1	S23 18.2	236 26.3	S22 02.8	Rasalhague	96 02.7	N12 32.9
07	181 45.0	255 02.9	12.8	321 28.5	03.1	270 24.0	18.2	251 28.5	02.8	Regulus	207 38.7	N11 52.2
08	196 47.4	270 02.0	12.5	336 29.3	03.7	285 25.8	18.2	266 30.7	02.7	Rigel	281 07.5	S 8 10.8
S 09	211 49.9	285 01.1	.. 12.2	351 30.1	.. 04.2	300 27.7	.. 18.2	281 32.9	.. 02.7	Rigil Kent.	139 46.3	S60 54.6
U 10	226 52.3	300 00.2	11.9	6 31.0	04.7	315 29.5	18.2	296 35.1	02.7	Sabik	102 07.8	S15 44.8
N 11	241 54.8	314 59.3	11.6	21 31.8	05.2	330 31.4	18.2	311 37.2	02.6			
D 12	256 57.3	329 58.4	S24 11.3	36 32.7	S15 05.7	345 33.2	S23 18.2	326 39.4	S22 02.6	Schedar	349 35.2	N56 38.9
A 13	271 59.7	344 57.5	11.0	51 33.5	06.3	0 35.1	18.2	341 41.6	02.6	Shaula	96 16.3	S37 06.9
Y 14	287 02.2	359 56.6	10.7	66 34.3	06.8	15 36.9	18.2	356 43.8	02.5	Sirius	258 29.5	S16 44.6
15	302 04.7	14 55.7	.. 10.4	81 35.2	.. 07.3	30 38.8	.. 18.2	11 46.0	.. 02.5	Spica	158 26.8	S11 15.7
16	317 07.1	29 54.8	10.1	96 36.0	07.8	45 40.6	18.2	26 48.1	02.5	Suhail	222 49.0	S43 30.5
17	332 09.6	44 53.9	09.8	111 36.8	08.4	60 42.5	18.2	41 50.3	02.4			
18	347 12.1	59 53.0	S24 09.5	126 37.7	S15 08.9	75 44.3	S23 18.2	56 52.5	S22 02.4	Vega	80 36.4	N38 48.3
19	2 14.5	74 52.0	09.2	141 38.5	09.4	90 46.2	18.2	71 54.7	02.4	Zuben'ubi	137 00.8	S16 07.2
20	17 17.0	89 51.1	08.8	156 39.3	09.9	105 48.0	18.2	86 56.9	02.3		SHA	Mer.Pass.
21	32 19.4	104 50.2	.. 08.5	171 40.1	.. 10.4	120 49.9	.. 18.2	101 59.0	.. 02.3			h m
22	47 21.9	119 49.3	08.2	186 41.0	11.0	135 51.7	18.2	117 01.2	02.3	Venus	75 02.7	13 59
23	62 24.4	134 48.4	07.9	201 41.8	11.5	150 53.6	18.2	132 03.4	02.2	Mars	140 34.1	9 35
	h m									Jupiter	88 58.1	13 01
Mer.Pass. 18 55.0	v −0.9	d 0.3	v 0.8	d 0.5	v 1.9	d 0.0	v 2.2	d 0.0	Saturn	69 52.3	14 17

© British Crown Copyright 2018. All rights reserved.

UT	SUN GHA	SUN Dec	MOON GHA	v	MOON Dec	d	HP
6 00	182 19.7	S22 25.4	70 29.0	16.1	S 3 55.8	11.5	54.3
01	197 19.4	25.7	85 04.1	16.1	3 44.3	11.6	54.3
02	212 19.2	26.0	99 39.2	16.1	3 32.7	11.6	54.3
03	227 18.9	.. 26.3	114 14.3	16.1	3 21.1	11.6	54.3
04	242 18.6	26.6	128 49.4	16.1	3 09.5	11.6	54.3
05	257 18.4	26.9	143 24.5	16.1	2 57.9	11.6	54.3
06	272 18.1	S22 27.2	157 59.6	16.1	S 2 46.3	11.6	54.3
07	287 17.9	27.6	172 34.7	16.1	2 34.7	11.6	54.3
F 08	302 17.6	27.9	187 09.8	16.1	2 23.1	11.7	54.3
R 09	317 17.3	.. 28.2	201 44.9	16.1	2 11.4	11.7	54.3
I 10	332 17.1	28.5	216 20.0	16.1	1 59.7	11.7	54.3
11	347 16.8	28.8	230 55.1	16.1	1 48.0	11.6	54.4
D 12	2 16.5	S22 29.1	245 30.2	16.0	S 1 36.4	11.8	54.4
A 13	17 16.3	29.4	260 05.2	16.1	1 24.6	11.7	54.4
Y 14	32 16.0	29.7	274 40.3	16.1	1 12.9	11.7	54.4
15	47 15.8	.. 30.0	289 15.4	16.0	1 01.2	11.7	54.4
16	62 15.5	30.3	303 50.4	16.1	0 49.5	11.8	54.4
17	77 15.2	30.6	318 25.5	16.0	0 37.7	11.7	54.4
18	92 15.0	S22 30.8	333 00.5	16.0	S 0 26.0	11.8	54.4
19	107 14.7	31.1	347 35.5	16.0	0 14.2	11.7	54.4
20	122 14.4	31.4	2 10.5	16.0	S 0 02.5	11.8	54.4
21	137 14.2	.. 31.7	16 45.5	16.0	N 0 09.3	11.8	54.5
22	152 13.9	32.0	31 20.5	16.0	0 21.1	11.8	54.5
23	167 13.6	32.3	45 55.5	15.9	0 32.9	11.8	54.5
7 00	182 13.4	S22 32.6	60 30.4	16.0	N 0 44.7	11.8	54.5
01	197 13.1	32.9	75 05.4	15.9	0 56.5	11.7	54.5
02	212 12.8	33.2	89 40.3	15.9	1 08.2	11.8	54.5
03	227 12.6	.. 33.5	104 15.2	15.9	1 20.0	11.8	54.5
04	242 12.3	33.8	118 50.1	15.8	1 31.8	11.8	54.5
05	257 12.0	34.0	133 24.9	15.8	1 43.6	11.8	54.6
06	272 11.8	S22 34.3	147 59.7	15.9	N 1 55.4	11.8	54.6
07	287 11.5	34.6	162 34.6	15.7	2 07.2	11.8	54.6
S 08	302 11.2	34.9	177 09.3	15.8	2 19.0	11.8	54.6
A 09	317 11.0	.. 35.2	191 44.1	15.7	2 30.8	11.8	54.6
T 10	332 10.7	35.5	206 18.8	15.7	2 42.6	11.8	54.6
U 11	347 10.4	35.8	220 53.5	15.7	2 54.4	11.8	54.7
R 12	2 10.2	S22 36.0	235 28.2	15.7	N 3 06.2	11.8	54.7
D 13	17 09.9	36.3	250 02.9	15.6	3 18.0	11.7	54.7
A 14	32 09.6	36.6	264 37.5	15.6	3 29.7	11.8	54.7
Y 15	47 09.4	.. 36.9	279 12.1	15.6	3 41.5	11.8	54.7
16	62 09.1	37.2	293 46.7	15.5	3 53.3	11.7	54.7
17	77 08.8	37.4	308 21.2	15.5	4 05.0	11.8	54.7
18	92 08.6	S22 37.7	322 55.7	15.5	N 4 16.8	11.7	54.8
19	107 08.3	38.0	337 30.2	15.4	4 28.5	11.8	54.8
20	122 08.0	38.3	352 04.6	15.4	4 40.3	11.7	54.8
21	137 07.8	.. 38.5	6 39.0	15.3	4 52.0	11.7	54.8
22	152 07.5	38.8	21 13.3	15.4	5 03.7	11.7	54.8
23	167 07.2	39.1	35 47.7	15.2	5 15.4	11.7	54.8
8 00	182 06.9	S22 39.4	50 21.9	15.3	N 5 27.1	11.6	54.9
01	197 06.7	39.6	64 56.2	15.2	5 38.7	11.7	54.9
02	212 06.4	39.9	79 30.4	15.1	5 50.4	11.6	54.9
03	227 06.1	.. 40.2	94 04.5	15.2	6 02.0	11.7	54.9
04	242 05.9	40.4	108 38.7	15.0	6 13.7	11.6	54.9
05	257 05.6	40.7	123 12.7	15.1	6 25.3	11.6	54.9
06	272 05.3	S22 41.0	137 46.8	14.9	N 6 36.9	11.6	55.0
07	287 05.0	41.3	152 20.7	15.0	6 48.5	11.5	55.0
S 08	302 04.8	41.5	166 54.7	14.9	7 00.0	11.6	55.0
U 09	317 04.5	.. 41.8	181 28.6	14.8	7 11.6	11.5	55.0
N 10	332 04.2	42.0	196 02.4	14.8	7 23.1	11.5	55.1
D 11	347 04.0	42.3	210 36.2	14.8	7 34.6	11.5	55.1
A 12	2 03.7	S22 42.6	225 10.0	14.7	N 7 46.1	11.4	55.1
Y 13	17 03.4	42.8	239 43.7	14.6	7 57.5	11.5	55.1
14	32 03.1	43.1	254 17.3	14.6	8 09.0	11.4	55.1
15	47 02.9	.. 43.4	268 50.9	14.6	8 20.4	11.4	55.2
16	62 02.6	43.6	283 24.5	14.5	8 31.8	11.3	55.2
17	77 02.3	43.9	297 58.0	14.4	8 43.1	11.3	55.2
18	92 02.0	S22 44.1	312 31.4	14.4	N 8 54.4	11.3	55.2
19	107 01.8	44.4	327 04.8	14.3	9 05.7	11.3	55.3
20	122 01.5	44.7	341 38.1	14.3	9 17.0	11.3	55.3
21	137 01.2	.. 44.9	356 11.4	14.2	9 28.3	11.2	55.3
22	152 00.9	45.2	10 44.6	14.1	9 39.5	11.2	55.3
23	167 00.7	45.4	25 17.7	14.1	N 9 50.7	11.1	55.3
	SD 16.3	d 0.3	SD 14.8		14.9		15.0

Twilight / Sunrise / Moonrise

Lat.	Naut.	Civil	Sunrise	Moonrise 6	7	8	9
°	h m	h m	h m	h m	h m	h m	h m
N 72	08 05	10 16	▨	13 58	13 40	13 20	12 56
N 70	07 47	09 28	▨	13 56	13 44	13 32	13 17
68	07 33	08 58	11 16	13 54	13 48	13 41	13 34
66	07 21	08 35	10 06	13 53	13 51	13 49	13 47
64	07 10	08 17	09 30	13 52	13 54	13 56	13 59
62	07 02	08 02	09 05	13 51	13 56	14 01	14 08
60	06 54	07 50	08 45	13 50	13 58	14 06	14 16
N 58	06 47	07 39	08 29	13 50	14 00	14 11	14 24
56	06 41	07 29	08 15	13 49	14 01	14 15	14 30
54	06 35	07 20	08 04	13 49	14 03	14 18	14 36
52	06 30	07 13	07 53	13 48	14 04	14 22	14 41
50	06 25	07 06	07 44	13 48	14 05	14 25	14 46
45	06 14	06 50	07 24	13 47	14 08	14 31	14 56
N 40	06 04	06 38	07 08	13 46	14 10	14 36	15 05
35	05 55	06 26	06 54	13 45	14 12	14 41	15 12
30	05 47	06 16	06 42	13 44	14 14	14 45	15 19
20	05 31	05 58	06 22	13 43	14 17	14 53	15 30
N 10	05 15	05 42	06 04	13 42	14 20	14 59	15 41
0	04 59	05 25	05 48	13 41	14 23	15 05	15 50
S 10	04 41	05 08	05 31	13 40	14 25	15 11	16 00
20	04 19	04 48	05 12	13 39	14 28	15 18	16 10
30	03 51	04 24	04 51	13 38	14 31	15 25	16 22
35	03 33	04 10	04 39	13 38	14 33	15 30	16 29
40	03 11	03 52	04 25	13 37	14 35	15 35	16 36
45	02 42	03 31	04 07	13 36	14 38	15 41	16 46
S 50	02 00	03 03	03 46	13 35	14 41	15 48	16 57
52	01 36	02 48	03 36	13 35	14 42	15 51	17 02
54	01 01	02 32	03 24	13 34	14 43	15 54	17 08
56	////	02 12	03 11	13 34	14 45	15 58	17 14
58	////	01 45	02 55	13 33	14 47	16 03	17 21
S 60	////	01 07	02 36	13 32	14 49	16 08	17 29

Sunset / Twilight / Moonset

Lat.	Sunset	Civil	Naut.	Moonset 6	7	8	9
°	h m	h m	h m	h m	h m	h m	h m
N 72	▨	13 26	15 37	00 30	02 15	04 03	05 59
N 70	▨	14 14	15 55	00 36	02 14	03 54	05 39
68	12 26	14 44	16 10	00 40	02 12	03 46	05 24
66	13 36	15 07	16 22	00 44	02 11	03 40	05 12
64	14 12	15 25	16 32	00 47	02 10	03 35	05 02
62	14 37	15 40	16 41	00 50	02 10	03 30	04 54
60	14 57	15 53	16 48	00 53	02 09	03 26	04 46
N 58	15 13	16 04	16 55	00 55	02 08	03 23	04 40
56	15 27	16 13	17 02	00 57	02 08	03 20	04 34
54	15 39	16 22	17 07	00 58	02 07	03 17	04 29
52	15 49	16 30	17 13	01 00	02 07	03 15	04 25
50	15 59	16 37	17 18	01 01	02 06	03 13	04 20
45	16 18	16 52	17 29	01 04	02 06	03 08	04 12
N 40	16 35	17 05	17 39	01 07	02 05	03 04	04 04
35	16 48	17 16	17 48	01 09	02 04	03 00	03 58
30	17 00	17 26	17 56	01 11	02 04	02 57	03 52
20	17 20	17 44	18 12	01 14	02 03	02 52	03 43
N 10	17 38	18 01	18 27	01 17	02 02	02 47	03 34
0	17 55	18 17	18 44	01 20	02 01	02 43	03 26
S 10	18 12	18 35	19 02	01 23	02 00	02 38	03 19
20	18 30	18 55	19 24	01 25	01 59	02 34	03 10
30	18 51	19 19	19 52	01 29	01 58	02 29	03 01
35	19 04	19 33	20 10	01 30	01 58	02 26	02 55
40	19 18	19 51	20 32	01 32	01 57	02 22	02 49
45	19 36	20 12	21 01	01 35	01 56	02 18	02 42
S 50	19 57	20 41	21 43	01 37	01 55	02 14	02 33
52	20 08	20 55	22 08	01 39	01 55	02 11	02 30
54	20 19	21 12	22 45	01 40	01 54	02 09	02 25
56	20 33	21 32	////	01 42	01 54	02 06	02 20
58	20 48	21 59	////	01 43	01 53	02 04	02 15
S 60	21 07	22 38	////	01 45	01 53	02 00	02 09

	SUN			MOON			
Day	Eqn. of Time 00ʰ	12ʰ	Mer. Pass.	Mer. Pass. Upper	Lower	Age	Phase
d	m s	m s	h m	h m	h m	d	%
6	09 19	09 07	11 51	19 51	07 31	10	70
7	08 54	08 41	11 51	20 33	08 12	11	79
8	08 28	08 15	11 52	21 16	08 54	12	86

© British Crown Copyright 2018. All rights reserved.

UT (d h)	ARIES GHA	VENUS −3.9 GHA	Dec	MARS +1.7 GHA	Dec	JUPITER −1.8 GHA	Dec	SATURN +0.6 GHA	Dec	STARS Name	SHA	Dec
9 00	77 26.8	149 47.5	S24 07.6	216 42.6	S15 12.0	165 55.4	S23 18.2	147 05.6	S22 02.2	Acamar	315 14.6	S40 13.7
01	92 29.3	164 46.6	07.3	231 43.5	12.5	180 57.3	18.2	162 07.8	02.2	Achernar	335 23.1	S57 08.5
02	107 31.8	179 45.7	06.9	246 44.3	13.0	195 59.1	18.2	177 09.9	02.1	Acrux	173 04.6	S63 12.1
03	122 34.2	194 44.8 ..	06.6	261 45.1 ..	13.6	211 01.0 ..	18.2	192 12.1 ..	02.1	Adhara	255 08.7	S28 59.9
04	137 36.7	209 43.9	06.3	276 46.0	14.1	226 02.8	18.2	207 14.3	02.1	Aldebaran	290 43.9	N16 32.8
05	152 39.2	224 43.0	06.0	291 46.8	14.6	241 04.7	18.2	222 16.5	02.0			
06	167 41.6	239 42.1	S24 05.6	306 47.6	S15 15.1	256 06.5	S23 18.2	237 18.7	S22 02.0	Alioth	166 17.0	N55 51.0
07	182 44.1	254 41.2	05.3	321 48.4	15.6	271 08.4	18.2	252 20.8	02.0	Alkaid	152 55.7	N49 12.8
08	197 46.6	269 40.3	05.0	336 49.3	16.1	286 10.2	18.2	267 23.0	01.9	Alnair	27 38.3	S46 52.1
09	212 49.0	284 39.4 ..	04.7	351 50.1 ..	16.7	301 12.1 ..	18.2	282 25.2 ..	01.9	Alnilam	275 41.5	S 1 11.5
10	227 51.5	299 38.5	04.3	6 50.9	17.2	316 13.9	18.2	297 27.4	01.9	Alphard	217 51.6	S 8 44.6
11	242 53.9	314 37.6	04.0	21 51.8	17.7	331 15.8	18.2	312 29.6	01.8			
M 12	257 56.4	329 36.7	S24 03.7	36 52.6	S15 18.2	346 17.6	S23 18.2	327 31.7	S22 01.8	Alphecca	126 07.6	N26 39.0
O 13	272 58.9	344 35.8	03.3	51 53.4	18.7	1 19.5	18.2	342 33.9	01.8	Alpheratz	357 38.8	N29 12.1
N 14	288 01.3	359 34.9	03.0	66 54.2	19.3	16 21.3	18.2	357 36.1	01.7	Altair	62 04.2	N 8 55.4
D 15	303 03.8	14 34.0 ..	02.6	81 55.1 ..	19.8	31 23.2 ..	18.2	12 38.3 ..	01.7	Ankaa	353 11.2	S42 12.2
A 16	318 06.3	29 33.1	02.3	96 55.9	20.3	46 25.0	18.2	27 40.5	01.7	Antares	112 21.2	S26 28.3
Y 17	333 08.7	44 32.2	02.0	111 56.7	20.8	61 26.9	18.2	42 42.6	01.6			
18	348 11.2	59 31.3	S24 01.6	126 57.5	S15 21.3	76 28.7	S23 18.2	57 44.8	S22 01.6	Arcturus	145 51.9	N19 04.8
19	3 13.7	74 30.4	01.3	141 58.4	21.8	91 30.6	18.2	72 47.0	01.6	Atria	107 19.6	S69 03.6
20	18 16.1	89 29.5	00.9	156 59.2	22.3	106 32.4	18.2	87 49.2	01.5	Avior	234 15.8	S59 34.2
21	33 18.6	104 28.6 ..	00.6	172 00.0 ..	22.9	121 34.3 ..	18.2	102 51.4 ..	01.5	Bellatrix	278 26.9	N 6 21.9
22	48 21.1	119 27.7	24 00.2	187 00.8	23.4	136 36.1	18.2	117 53.5	01.5	Betelgeuse	270 56.2	N 7 24.5
23	63 23.5	134 26.8	23 59.9	202 01.7	23.9	151 38.0	18.2	132 55.7	01.4			
10 00	78 26.0	149 25.9	S23 59.5	217 02.5	S15 24.4	166 39.8	S23 18.2	147 57.9	S22 01.4	Canopus	263 53.6	S52 42.4
01	93 28.4	164 25.0	59.2	232 03.3	24.9	181 41.7	18.1	163 00.1	01.4	Capella	280 27.4	N46 00.9
02	108 30.9	179 24.1	58.8	247 04.1	25.4	196 43.5	18.1	178 02.2	01.3	Deneb	49 28.8	N45 21.3
03	123 33.4	194 23.2 ..	58.5	262 05.0 ..	26.0	211 45.3 ..	18.1	193 04.4 ..	01.3	Denebola	182 29.2	N14 27.7
04	138 35.8	209 22.3	58.1	277 05.8	26.5	226 47.2	18.1	208 06.6	01.3	Diphda	348 51.3	S17 52.8
05	153 38.3	224 21.4	57.8	292 06.6	27.0	241 49.0	18.1	223 08.8	01.2			
06	168 40.8	239 20.5	S23 57.4	307 07.4	S15 27.5	256 50.9	S23 18.1	238 11.0	S22 01.2	Dubhe	193 46.2	N61 38.4
07	183 43.2	254 19.7	57.1	322 08.3	28.0	271 52.7	18.1	253 13.1	01.2	Elnath	278 06.6	N28 37.3
T 08	198 45.7	269 18.8	56.7	337 09.1	28.5	286 54.6	18.1	268 15.3	01.1	Eltanin	90 44.6	N51 29.3
U 09	213 48.2	284 17.9 ..	56.4	352 09.9 ..	29.0	301 56.4 ..	18.1	283 17.5 ..	01.1	Enif	33 42.9	N 9 58.0
E 10	228 50.6	299 17.0	56.0	7 10.7	29.6	316 58.3	18.1	298 19.7	01.1	Fomalhaut	15 19.1	S29 31.2
S 11	243 53.1	314 16.1	55.6	22 11.6	30.1	332 00.1	18.1	313 21.8	01.0			
D 12	258 55.5	329 15.2	S23 55.3	37 12.4	S15 30.6	347 02.0	S23 18.1	328 24.0	S22 01.0	Gacrux	171 56.2	S57 13.1
A 13	273 58.0	344 14.3	54.9	52 13.2	31.1	2 03.8	18.1	343 26.2	00.9	Gienah	175 47.8	S17 38.9
Y 14	289 00.5	359 13.4	54.5	67 14.0	31.6	17 05.7	18.1	358 28.4	00.9	Hadar	148 42.1	S60 27.7
15	304 02.9	14 12.5 ..	54.2	82 14.9 ..	32.1	32 07.5 ..	18.1	13 30.6 ..	00.9	Hamal	327 55.5	N23 33.4
16	319 05.4	29 11.6	53.8	97 15.7	32.6	47 09.4	18.1	28 32.7	00.8	Kaus Aust.	83 38.3	S34 22.4
17	334 07.9	44 10.7	53.4	112 16.5	33.1	62 11.2	18.1	43 34.9	00.8			
18	349 10.3	59 09.8	S23 53.1	127 17.3	S15 33.7	77 13.1	S23 18.1	58 37.1	S22 00.8	Kochab	137 21.1	N74 04.4
19	4 12.8	74 09.0	52.7	142 18.2	34.2	92 14.9	18.1	73 39.3	00.7	Markab	13 33.9	N15 18.8
20	19 15.3	89 08.1	52.3	157 19.0	34.7	107 16.8	18.1	88 41.4	00.7	Menkar	314 10.1	N 4 09.9
21	34 17.7	104 07.2 ..	51.9	172 19.8 ..	35.2	122 18.6 ..	18.1	103 43.6 ..	00.7	Menkent	148 02.6	S36 27.7
22	49 20.2	119 06.3	51.6	187 20.6	35.7	137 20.5	18.1	118 45.8	00.6	Miaplacidus	221 38.3	S69 47.6
23	64 22.7	134 05.4	51.2	202 21.4	36.2	152 22.3	18.1	133 48.0	00.6			
11 00	79 25.1	149 04.5	S23 50.8	217 22.3	S15 36.7	167 24.1	S23 18.1	148 50.1	S22 00.6	Mirfak	308 33.5	N49 55.9
01	94 27.6	164 03.6	50.4	232 23.1	37.2	182 26.0	18.1	163 52.3	00.5	Nunki	75 53.2	S26 16.2
02	109 30.0	179 02.7	50.0	247 23.9	37.7	197 27.8	18.1	178 54.5	00.5	Peacock	53 12.7	S56 40.4
03	124 32.5	194 01.9 ..	49.7	262 24.7 ..	38.3	212 29.7 ..	18.1	193 56.7 ..	00.5	Pollux	243 22.0	N27 58.5
04	139 35.0	209 01.0	49.3	277 25.5	38.8	227 31.5	18.1	208 58.9	00.4	Procyon	244 54.8	N 5 10.4
05	154 37.4	224 00.1	48.9	292 26.4	39.3	242 33.4	18.0	224 01.0	00.4			
06	169 39.9	238 59.2	S23 48.5	307 27.2	S15 39.8	257 35.2	S23 18.0	239 03.2	S22 00.4	Rasalhague	96 02.7	N12 32.9
W 07	184 42.4	253 58.3	48.1	322 28.0	40.3	272 37.1	18.0	254 05.4	00.3	Regulus	207 38.7	N11 52.2
E 08	199 44.8	268 57.4	47.7	337 28.8	40.8	287 38.9	18.0	269 07.6	00.3	Rigel	281 07.5	S 8 10.8
D 09	214 47.3	283 56.5 ..	47.3	352 29.6 ..	41.3	302 40.8 ..	18.0	284 09.7 ..	00.3	Rigil Kent.	139 46.3	S60 54.6
N 10	229 49.8	298 55.7	47.0	7 30.5	41.8	317 42.6	18.0	299 11.9	00.2	Sabik	102 07.8	S15 44.8
E 11	244 52.2	313 54.8	46.6	22 31.3	42.3	332 44.5	18.0	314 14.1	00.2			
S 12	259 54.7	328 53.9	S23 46.2	37 32.1	S15 42.8	347 46.3	S23 18.0	329 16.3	S22 00.2	Schedar	349 35.3	N56 38.9
D 13	274 57.2	343 53.0	45.8	52 32.9	43.3	2 48.2	18.0	344 18.4	00.1	Shaula	96 16.3	S37 06.9
A 14	289 59.6	358 52.1	45.4	67 33.7	43.9	17 50.0	18.0	359 20.6	00.1	Sirius	258 29.5	S16 44.6
Y 15	305 02.1	13 51.3 ..	45.0	82 34.6 ..	44.4	32 51.8 ..	18.0	14 22.8 ..	00.1	Spica	158 26.8	S11 15.7
16	320 04.5	28 50.4	44.6	97 35.4	44.9	47 53.7	18.0	29 25.0	00.0	Suhail	222 49.0	S43 30.5
17	335 07.0	43 49.5	44.2	112 36.2	45.4	62 55.5	18.0	44 27.1	22 00.0			
18	350 09.5	58 48.6	S23 43.8	127 37.0	S15 45.9	77 57.4	S23 18.0	59 29.3	S21 59.9	Vega	80 36.4	N38 48.3
19	5 11.9	73 47.7	43.4	142 37.8	46.4	92 59.2	18.0	74 31.5	59.9	Zuben'ubi	137 00.8	S16 07.2
20	20 14.4	88 46.8	43.0	157 38.7	46.9	108 01.1	18.0	89 33.7	59.9		SHA	Mer.Pass.
21	35 16.9	103 46.0 ..	42.6	172 39.5 ..	47.4	123 02.9 ..	18.0	104 35.8 ..	59.8	Venus	70 59.9	14 03
22	50 19.3	118 45.1	42.2	187 40.3	47.9	138 04.8	18.0	119 38.0 ·	59.8	Mars	138 36.5	9 31
23	65 21.8	133 44.2	41.8	202 41.1	48.4	153 06.6	18.0	134 40.2	59.8	Jupiter	88 13.8	12 52
Mer.Pass. 18 43.2		v −0.9	d 0.4	v 0.8	d 0.5	v 1.8	d 0.0	v 2.2	d 0.0	Saturn	69 31.9	14 06

© British Crown Copyright 2018. All rights reserved.

UT	SUN GHA	SUN Dec	MOON GHA	v	Dec	d	HP
d h	° ′	° ′	° ′	′	° ′	′	′
9 00	182 00.4	S22 45.7	39 50.8	14.1	N10 01.8	11.1	55.4
01	197 00.1	45.9	54 23.9	13.9	10 12.9	11.1	55.4
02	211 59.8	46.2	68 56.8	14.0	10 24.0	11.1	55.4
03	226 59.6	.. 46.4	83 29.8	13.8	10 35.1	11.0	55.4
04	241 59.3	46.7	98 02.6	13.8	10 46.1	11.0	55.4
05	256 59.0	46.9	112 35.4	13.7	10 57.1	10.9	55.5
06	271 58.7	S22 47.2	127 08.1	13.7	N11 08.0	10.9	55.5
07	286 58.5	47.4	141 40.8	13.6	11 18.9	10.9	55.5
08	301 58.2	47.7	156 13.4	13.5	11 29.8	10.8	55.5
M 09	316 57.9	.. 47.9	170 45.9	13.5	11 40.6	10.8	55.6
O 10	331 57.6	48.2	185 18.4	13.4	11 51.4	10.7	55.6
N 11	346 57.4	48.4	199 50.8	13.3	12 02.1	10.7	55.6
D 12	1 57.1	S22 48.7	214 23.1	13.2	N12 12.8	10.6	55.6
A 13	16 56.8	48.9	228 55.3	13.2	12 23.4	10.6	55.7
Y 14	31 56.5	49.2	243 27.5	13.2	12 34.0	10.6	55.7
15	46 56.2	.. 49.4	257 59.7	13.0	12 44.6	10.5	55.7
16	61 56.0	49.6	272 31.7	13.0	12 55.1	10.5	55.7
17	76 55.7	49.9	287 03.7	12.9	13 05.6	10.4	55.8
18	91 55.4	S22 50.1	301 35.6	12.8	N13 16.0	10.3	55.8
19	106 55.1	50.4	316 07.4	12.8	13 26.3	10.3	55.8
20	121 54.9	50.6	330 39.2	12.7	13 36.6	10.3	55.8
21	136 54.6	.. 50.8	345 10.9	12.6	13 46.9	10.2	55.9
22	151 54.3	51.1	359 42.5	12.5	13 57.1	10.1	55.9
23	166 54.0	51.3	14 14.0	12.5	14 07.2	10.1	55.9
10 00	181 53.7	S22 51.5	28 45.5	12.3	N14 17.3	10.1	55.9
01	196 53.5	51.8	43 16.8	12.3	14 27.4	9.9	55.9
02	211 53.2	52.0	57 48.1	12.3	14 37.3	9.9	56.0
03	226 52.9	.. 52.2	72 19.4	12.1	14 47.2	9.9	56.0
04	241 52.6	52.5	86 50.5	12.1	14 57.1	9.8	56.0
05	256 52.3	52.7	101 21.6	12.0	15 06.9	9.7	56.1
06	271 52.1	S22 52.9	115 52.6	11.9	N15 16.6	9.7	56.1
07	286 51.8	53.2	130 23.5	11.9	15 26.3	9.6	56.1
T 08	301 51.5	53.4	144 54.4	11.7	15 35.9	9.5	56.1
U 09	316 51.2	.. 53.6	159 25.1	11.7	15 45.4	9.5	56.2
E 10	331 50.9	53.9	173 55.8	11.6	15 54.9	9.4	56.2
S 11	346 50.6	54.1	188 26.4	11.5	16 04.3	9.3	56.2
D 12	1 50.4	S22 54.3	202 56.9	11.4	N16 13.6	9.3	56.2
A 13	16 50.1	54.5	217 27.3	11.4	16 22.9	9.1	56.3
Y 14	31 49.8	54.8	231 57.7	11.3	16 32.0	9.2	56.3
15	46 49.5	.. 55.0	246 28.0	11.2	16 41.2	9.0	56.3
16	61 49.2	55.2	260 58.2	11.1	16 50.2	9.0	56.3
17	76 49.0	55.4	275 28.3	11.0	16 59.2	8.9	56.4
18	91 48.7	S22 55.6	289 58.3	10.9	N17 08.1	8.8	56.4
19	106 48.4	55.9	304 28.2	10.9	17 16.9	8.7	56.4
20	121 48.1	56.1	318 58.1	10.8	17 25.6	8.6	56.4
21	136 47.8	.. 56.3	333 27.9	10.7	17 34.2	8.6	56.5
22	151 47.5	56.5	347 57.6	10.6	17 42.8	8.5	56.5
23	166 47.3	56.7	2 27.2	10.5	17 51.3	8.4	56.5
11 00	181 47.0	S22 57.0	16 56.7	10.4	N17 59.7	8.3	56.5
01	196 46.7	57.2	31 26.1	10.4	18 08.0	8.2	56.6
02	211 46.4	57.4	45 55.5	10.3	18 16.2	8.2	56.6
03	226 46.1	.. 57.6	60 24.8	10.2	18 24.4	8.0	56.6
04	241 45.8	57.8	74 54.0	10.1	18 32.4	8.0	56.6
05	256 45.5	58.0	89 23.1	10.0	18 40.4	7.9	56.7
06	271 45.3	S22 58.2	103 52.1	10.0	N18 48.3	7.8	56.7
W 07	286 45.0	58.5	118 21.1	9.8	18 56.1	7.7	56.7
E 08	301 44.7	58.7	132 49.9	9.8	19 03.8	7.6	56.7
D 09	316 44.4	.. 58.9	147 18.7	9.7	19 11.4	7.5	56.8
N 10	331 44.1	59.1	161 47.4	9.6	19 18.9	7.4	56.8
E 11	346 43.8	59.3	176 16.0	9.5	19 26.3	7.3	56.8
S 12	1 43.5	S22 59.5	190 44.5	9.5	N19 33.6	7.2	56.8
D 13	16 43.3	59.7	205 13.0	9.3	19 40.8	7.1	56.9
A 14	31 43.0	22 59.9	219 41.3	9.3	19 47.9	7.0	56.9
Y 15	46 42.7	23 00.1	234 09.6	9.2	19 54.9	6.9	56.9
16	61 42.4	00.3	248 37.8	9.1	20 01.8	6.8	56.9
17	76 42.1	00.5	263 05.9	9.1	20 08.6	6.7	57.0
18	91 41.8	S23 00.7	277 34.0	8.9	N20 15.3	6.6	57.0
19	106 41.5	00.9	292 01.9	8.9	20 21.9	6.4	57.0
20	121 41.3	01.1	306 29.8	8.8	20 28.3	6.4	57.0
21	136 41.0	.. 01.3	320 57.6	8.7	20 34.7	6.3	57.1
22	151 40.7	01.5	335 25.3	8.7	20 41.0	6.1	57.1
23	166 40.4	01.7	349 53.0	8.6	N20 47.1	6.1	57.1
	SD 16.3	d 0.2	SD 15.2		15.3		15.5

Lat.	Twilight Naut.	Twilight Civil	Sunrise	Moonrise 9	10	11	12
°	h m	h m	h m	h m	h m	h m	h m
N 72	08 11	10 28	▨	12 56	12 17	▭	▭
N 70	07 53	09 36	▨	13 17	12 57	12 13	▭
68	07 38	09 04	▨	13 34	13 25	13 13	12 38
66	07 25	08 41	10 15	13 47	13 46	13 48	13 54
64	07 15	08 22	09 37	13 59	14 04	14 13	14 31
62	07 06	08 07	09 11	14 08	14 18	14 33	14 57
60	06 58	07 54	08 50	14 16	14 30	14 49	15 18
N 58	06 50	07 42	08 34	14 24	14 40	15 03	15 35
56	06 44	07 33	08 19	14 30	14 49	15 15	15 50
54	06 38	07 24	08 07	14 36	14 58	15 25	16 02
52	06 33	07 16	07 56	14 41	15 05	15 35	16 13
50	06 27	07 09	07 47	14 46	15 11	15 43	16 23
45	06 16	06 53	07 27	14 56	15 26	16 01	16 44
N 40	06 06	06 40	07 10	15 05	15 37	16 15	17 00
35	05 57	06 29	06 57	15 12	15 47	16 28	17 15
30	05 49	06 18	06 45	15 19	15 56	16 39	17 27
20	05 33	06 00	06 24	15 30	16 12	16 57	17 48
N 10	05 17	05 43	06 06	15 41	16 25	17 14	18 07
0	05 00	05 26	05 49	15 50	16 38	17 29	18 24
S 10	04 42	05 09	05 32	16 00	16 51	17 45	18 41
20	04 20	04 49	05 13	16 10	17 04	18 01	19 00
30	03 51	04 24	04 52	16 22	17 20	18 20	19 21
35	03 33	04 10	04 39	16 29	17 29	18 32	19 34
40	03 11	03 52	04 24	16 36	17 40	18 45	19 48
45	02 41	03 30	04 07	16 46	17 52	19 00	20 06
S 50	01 58	03 01	03 45	16 57	18 08	19 19	20 27
52	01 32	02 47	03 35	17 02	18 15	19 28	20 38
54	00 54	02 30	03 23	17 08	18 23	19 38	20 49
56	////	02 09	03 09	17 14	18 31	19 49	21 02
58	////	01 41	02 53	17 21	18 42	20 02	21 18
S 60	////	01 00	02 34	17 29	18 53	20 17	21 36

Lat.	Sunset	Twilight Civil	Twilight Naut.	Moonset 9	10	11	12
°	h m	h m	h m	h m	h m	h m	h m
N 72	▨	13 17	15 33	05 59	08 16	▭	▭
N 70	▨	14 08	15 52	05 39	07 37	10 06	▭
68	▨	14 41	16 07	05 24	07 10	09 07	11 34
66	13 30	15 04	16 20	05 12	06 50	08 33	10 18
64	14 08	15 23	16 30	05 02	06 33	08 08	09 41
62	14 34	15 38	16 39	04 54	06 20	07 49	09 15
60	14 55	15 51	16 47	04 46	06 09	07 33	08 55
N 58	15 11	16 03	16 55	04 40	05 59	07 20	08 38
56	15 26	16 12	17 01	04 34	05 51	07 08	08 24
54	15 38	16 21	17 07	04 29	05 43	06 58	08 12
52	15 49	16 29	17 12	04 25	05 36	06 49	08 01
50	15 58	16 36	17 18	04 20	05 30	06 41	07 52
45	16 18	16 52	17 29	04 12	05 17	06 25	07 31
N 40	16 35	17 05	17 39	04 04	05 07	06 11	07 15
35	16 48	17 16	17 48	03 58	04 57	05 59	07 01
30	17 00	17 27	17 57	03 52	04 49	05 49	06 50
20	17 21	17 45	18 13	03 43	04 36	05 31	06 29
N 10	17 39	18 02	18 28	03 34	04 24	05 16	06 11
0	17 56	18 19	18 45	03 26	04 13	05 02	05 55
S 10	18 14	18 37	19 04	03 19	04 01	04 48	05 39
20	18 32	18 57	19 26	03 10	03 50	04 33	05 21
30	18 54	19 21	19 54	03 01	03 36	04 16	05 01
35	19 06	19 36	20 13	02 55	03 28	04 06	04 49
40	19 21	19 54	20 35	02 49	03 19	03 54	04 35
45	19 39	20 16	21 05	02 42	03 09	03 41	04 19
S 50	20 00	20 44	21 48	02 33	02 57	03 25	04 00
52	20 11	20 59	22 14	02 30	02 51	03 17	03 51
54	20 23	21 16	22 54	02 25	02 44	03 08	03 40
56	20 37	21 37	////	02 20	02 37	02 58	03 28
58	20 53	22 05	////	02 15	02 29	02 48	03 15
S 60	21 12	22 48	////	02 09	02 20	02 36	02 59

Day	SUN Eqn. of Time 00ʰ	12ʰ	Mer. Pass.	MOON Mer. Pass. Upper	Lower	Age	Phase
d	m s	m s	h m	h m	h m	d	%
9	08 02	07 49	11 52	22 01	09 38	13	92
10	07 35	07 22	11 53	22 50	10 25	14	97
11	07 08	06 55	11 53	23 42	11 15	15	99

© British Crown Copyright 2018. All rights reserved.

UT	ARIES	VENUS −3·9		MARS +1·7		JUPITER −1·8		SATURN +0·6		STARS		
d h	GHA	GHA	Dec	GHA	Dec	GHA	Dec	GHA	Dec	Name	SHA	Dec
12 00	80 24.3	148 43.3	S23 41.3	217 41.9	S15 48.9	168 08.5	S23 18.0	149 42.4	S21 59.7	Acamar	315 14.6	S40 13.8
01	95 26.7	163 42.5	40.9	232 42.7	49.4	183 10.3	18.0	164 44.5	59.7	Achernar	335 23.1	S57 08.5
02	110 29.2	178 41.6	40.5	247 43.6	49.9	198 12.1	18.0	179 46.7	59.7	Acrux	173 04.5	S63 12.1
03	125 31.7	193 40.7 ..	40.1	262 44.4 ..	50.4	213 14.0 ..	17.9	194 48.9 ..	59.6	Adhara	255 08.7	S28 59.9
04	140 34.1	208 39.8	39.7	277 45.2	50.9	228 15.8	17.9	209 51.1	59.6	Aldebaran	290 43.9	N16 32.8
05	155 36.6	223 38.9	39.3	292 46.0	51.4	243 17.7	17.9	224 53.2	59.6			
06	170 39.0	238 38.1	S23 38.9	307 46.8	S15 52.0	258 19.5	S23 17.9	239 55.4	S21 59.5	Alioth	166 17.0	N55 51.0
07	185 41.5	253 37.2	38.5	322 47.6	52.5	273 21.4	17.9	254 57.6	59.5	Alkaid	152 55.7	N49 12.8
T 08	200 44.0	268 36.3	38.0	337 48.5	53.0	288 23.2	17.9	269 59.8	59.5	Alnair	27 38.3	S46 52.1
H 09	215 46.4	283 35.4 ..	37.6	352 49.3 ..	53.5	303 25.1 ..	17.9	285 01.9 ..	59.4	Alnilam	275 41.5	S 1 11.5
U 10	230 48.9	298 34.6	37.2	7 50.1	54.0	318 26.9	17.9	300 04.1	59.4	Alphard	217 51.6	S 8 44.6
R 11	245 51.4	313 33.7	36.8	22 50.9	54.5	333 28.8	17.9	315 06.3	59.4			
S 12	260 53.8	328 32.8	S23 36.4	37 51.7	S15 55.0	348 30.6	S23 17.9	330 08.5	S21 59.3	Alphecca	126 07.6	N26 39.0
D 13	275 56.3	343 32.0	35.9	52 52.5	55.5	3 32.5	17.9	345 10.6	59.3	Alpheratz	357 38.8	N29 12.1
A 14	290 58.8	358 31.1	35.5	67 53.4	56.0	18 34.3	17.9	0 12.8	59.2	Altair	62 04.2	N 8 55.4
Y 15	306 01.2	13 30.2 ..	35.1	82 54.2 ..	56.5	33 36.1 ..	17.9	15 15.0 ..	59.2	Ankaa	353 11.2	S42 12.2
16	321 03.7	28 29.3	34.6	97 55.0	57.0	48 38.0	17.9	30 17.2	59.2	Antares	112 21.2	S26 28.3
17	336 06.2	43 28.5	34.2	112 55.8	57.5	63 39.8	17.9	45 19.3	59.1			
18	351 08.6	58 27.6	S23 33.8	127 56.6	S15 58.0	78 41.7	S23 17.9	60 21.5	S21 59.1	Arcturus	145 51.9	N19 04.8
19	6 11.1	73 26.7	33.4	142 57.4	58.5	93 43.5	17.9	75 23.7	59.1	Atria	107 19.6	S69 03.6
20	21 13.5	88 25.9	32.9	157 58.2	59.0	108 45.4	17.9	90 25.8	59.0	Avior	234 15.8	S59 34.2
21	36 16.0	103 25.0 ..	32.5	172 59.0	15 59.5	123 47.2 ..	17.9	105 28.0 ..	59.0	Bellatrix	278 26.9	N 6 21.9
22	51 18.5	118 24.1	32.1	187 59.9	16 00.0	138 49.1	17.8	120 30.2	59.0	Betelgeuse	270 56.1	N 7 24.5
23	66 20.9	133 23.2	31.6	203 00.7	00.5	153 50.9	17.8	135 32.4	58.9			
13 00	81 23.4	148 22.4	S23 31.2	218 01.5	S16 01.0	168 52.7	S23 17.8	150 34.5	S21 58.9	Canopus	263 53.6	S52 42.4
01	96 25.9	163 21.5	30.7	233 02.3	01.5	183 54.6	17.8	165 36.7	58.9	Capella	280 27.4	N46 00.9
02	111 28.3	178 20.6	30.3	248 03.1	02.0	198 56.4	17.8	180 38.9	58.8	Deneb	49 28.8	N45 21.3
03	126 30.8	193 19.8 ..	29.9	263 03.9 ..	02.5	213 58.3 ..	17.8	195 41.1 ..	58.8	Denebola	182 29.2	N14 27.7
04	141 33.3	208 18.9	29.4	278 04.7	03.0	229 00.1	17.8	210 43.2	58.8	Diphda	348 51.3	S17 52.8
05	156 35.7	223 18.0	29.0	293 05.6	03.5	244 02.0	17.8	225 45.4	58.7			
06	171 38.2	238 17.2	S23 28.5	308 06.4	S16 04.0	259 03.8	S23 17.8	240 47.6	S21 58.7	Dubhe	193 46.2	N61 38.4
07	186 40.7	253 16.3	28.1	323 07.2	04.5	274 05.7	17.8	255 49.8	58.6	Elnath	278 06.6	N28 37.3
08	201 43.1	268 15.4	27.6	338 08.0	05.0	289 07.5	17.8	270 51.9	58.6	Eltanin	90 44.6	N51 29.3
F 09	216 45.6	283 14.6 ..	27.2	353 08.8 ..	05.5	304 09.3 ..	17.8	285 54.1 ..	58.6	Enif	33 42.9	N 9 58.0
R 10	231 48.0	298 13.7	26.7	8 09.6	06.0	319 11.2	17.8	300 56.3	58.5	Fomalhaut	15 19.1	S29 31.2
I 11	246 50.5	313 12.9	26.3	23 10.4	06.5	334 13.0	17.8	315 58.4	58.5			
D 12	261 53.0	328 12.0	S23 25.8	38 11.2	S16 07.0	349 14.9	S23 17.8	331 00.6	S21 58.5	Gacrux	171 56.1	S57 13.1
A 13	276 55.4	343 11.1	25.4	53 12.0	07.5	4 16.7	17.8	346 02.8	58.4	Gienah	175 47.8	S17 38.9
Y 14	291 57.9	358 10.3	24.9	68 12.9	08.0	19 18.6	17.7	1 05.0	58.4	Hadar	148 42.0	S60 27.7
15	307 00.4	13 09.4 ..	24.5	83 13.7 ..	08.5	34 20.4 ..	17.7	16 07.1 ..	58.4	Hamal	327 55.5	N23 33.4
16	322 02.8	28 08.5	24.0	98 14.5	09.0	49 22.3	17.7	31 09.3	58.3	Kaus Aust.	83 38.3	S34 22.4
17	337 05.3	43 07.7	23.6	113 15.3	09.5	64 24.1	17.7	46 11.5	58.3			
18	352 07.8	58 06.8	S23 23.1	128 16.1	S16 10.0	79 25.9	S23 17.7	61 13.7	S21 58.3	Kochab	137 21.0	N74 04.3
19	7 10.2	73 06.0	22.6	143 16.9	10.5	94 27.8	17.7	76 15.8	58.2	Markab	13 33.9	N15 18.8
20	22 12.7	88 05.1	22.2	158 17.7	11.0	109 29.6	17.7	91 18.0	58.2	Menkar	314 10.1	N 4 09.9
21	37 15.1	103 04.2 ..	21.7	173 18.5 ..	11.5	124 31.5 ..	17.7	106 20.2 ..	58.1	Menkent	148 02.6	S36 27.7
22	52 17.6	118 03.4	21.3	188 19.3	12.0	139 33.3	17.7	121 22.3	58.1	Miaplacidus	221 38.3	S69 47.6
23	67 20.1	133 02.5	20.8	203 20.1	12.5	154 35.2	17.7	136 24.5	58.1			
14 00	82 22.5	148 01.7	S23 20.3	218 20.9	S16 13.0	169 37.0	S23 17.7	151 26.7	S21 58.0	Mirfak	308 33.5	N49 55.9
01	97 25.0	163 00.8	19.9	233 21.8	13.5	184 38.9	17.7	166 28.9	58.0	Nunki	75 53.2	S26 16.2
02	112 27.5	178 00.0	19.4	248 22.6	14.0	199 40.7	17.7	181 31.0	58.0	Peacock	53 12.7	S56 40.4
03	127 29.9	192 59.1 ..	18.9	263 23.4 ..	14.5	214 42.5 ..	17.7	196 33.2 ..	57.9	Pollux	243 22.0	N27 58.5
04	142 32.4	207 58.2	18.4	278 24.2	15.0	229 44.4	17.7	211 35.4	57.9	Procyon	244 54.8	N 5 10.4
05	157 34.9	222 57.4	18.0	293 25.0	15.5	244 46.2	17.6	226 37.5	57.9			
06	172 37.3	237 56.5	S23 17.5	308 25.8	S16 16.0	259 48.1	S23 17.6	241 39.7	S21 57.8	Rasalhague	96 02.7	N12 32.9
07	187 39.8	252 55.7	17.0	323 26.6	16.5	274 49.9	17.6	256 41.9	57.8	Regulus	207 38.7	N11 52.2
S 08	202 42.3	267 54.8	16.5	338 27.4	16.9	289 51.8	17.6	271 44.1	57.8	Rigel	281 07.4	S 8 10.8
A 09	217 44.7	282 54.0 ..	16.1	353 28.2 ..	17.4	304 53.6 ..	17.6	286 46.2 ..	57.7	Rigil Kent.	139 46.2	S60 54.6
T 10	232 47.2	297 53.1	15.6	8 29.0	17.9	319 55.4	17.6	301 48.4	57.7	Sabik	102 07.8	S15 44.8
U 11	247 49.6	312 52.3	15.1	23 29.8	18.4	334 57.3	17.6	316 50.6	57.6			
R 12	262 52.1	327 51.4	S23 14.6	38 30.6	S16 18.9	349 59.1	S23 17.6	331 52.7	S21 57.6	Schedar	349 35.3	N56 39.0
D 13	277 54.6	342 50.6	14.1	53 31.4	19.4	5 01.0	17.6	346 54.9	57.6	Shaula	96 16.3	S37 06.9
A 14	292 57.0	357 49.7	13.7	68 32.3	19.9	20 02.8	17.6	1 57.1	57.5	Sirius	258 29.5	S16 44.7
Y 15	307 59.5	12 48.8 ..	13.2	83 33.1 ..	20.4	35 04.7 ..	17.6	16 59.3 ..	57.5	Spica	158 26.7	S11 15.7
16	323 02.0	27 48.0	12.7	98 33.9	20.9	50 06.5	17.6	32 01.4	57.5	Suhail	222 48.9	S43 30.6
17	338 04.4	42 47.1	12.2	113 34.7	21.4	65 08.4	17.6	47 03.6	57.4			
18	353 06.9	57 46.3	S23 11.7	128 35.5	S16 21.9	80 10.2	S23 17.6	62 05.8	S21 57.4	Vega	80 36.4	N38 48.3
19	8 09.4	72 45.4	11.2	143 36.3	22.4	95 12.0	17.5	77 07.9	57.4	Zuben'ubi	137 00.8	S16 07.2
20	23 11.8	87 44.6	10.7	158 37.1	22.9	110 13.9	17.5	92 10.1	57.3		SHA	Mer.Pass.
21	38 14.3	102 43.8 ..	10.2	173 37.9 ..	23.4	125 15.7 ..	17.5	107 12.3 ..	57.3		° '	h m
22	53 16.8	117 42.9	09.8	188 38.7	23.9	140 17.6	17.5	122 14.4	57.3	Venus	66 59.0	14 07
23	68 19.2	132 42.1	09.3	203 39.5	24.3	155 19.4	17.5	137 16.6	57.2	Mars	136 38.1	9 27
	h m									Jupiter	87 29.3	12 43
Mer.Pass. 18 31.4	v −0.9 d 0.5	v 0.8	d 0.5	v 0.8	d 0.5	v 1.8	d 0.0	v 2.2	d 0.0	Saturn	69 11.1	13 56

© British Crown Copyright 2018. All rights reserved.

UT	SUN GHA	SUN Dec	MOON GHA	v	MOON Dec	d	HP
12 00	181 40.1	S23 01.9	4 20.6	8.4	N20 53.2	5.9	57.1
01	196 39.8	02.1	18 48.0	8.5	20 59.1	5.8	57.2
02	211 39.5	02.3	33 15.5	8.3	21 04.9	5.7	57.2
03	226 39.2	.. 02.5	47 42.8	8.3	21 10.6	5.6	57.2
04	241 38.9	02.7	62 10.1	8.2	21 16.2	5.5	57.2
05	256 38.7	02.9	76 37.3	8.1	21 21.7	5.3	57.2
T 06	271 38.4	S23 03.1	91 04.4	8.0	N21 27.0	5.2	57.3
H 07	286 38.1	03.3	105 31.4	8.0	21 32.2	5.1	57.3
U 08	301 37.8	03.5	119 58.4	7.9	21 37.3	5.0	57.3
R 09	316 37.5	.. 03.7	134 25.3	7.8	21 42.3	4.9	57.4
S 10	331 37.2	03.9	148 52.1	7.8	21 47.2	4.7	57.4
D 11	346 36.9	04.0	163 18.9	7.7	21 51.9	4.6	57.4
A 12	1 36.6	S23 04.2	177 45.6	7.6	N21 56.5	4.5	57.4
Y 13	16 36.3	04.4	192 12.2	7.6	22 01.0	4.4	57.5
14	31 36.1	04.6	206 38.8	7.5	22 05.4	4.2	57.5
15	46 35.8	.. 04.8	221 05.3	7.4	22 09.6	4.1	57.5
16	61 35.5	05.0	235 31.7	7.3	22 13.7	4.0	57.5
17	76 35.2	05.2	249 58.0	7.4	22 17.7	3.9	57.6
18	91 34.9	S23 05.3	264 24.4	7.2	N22 21.6	3.7	57.6
19	106 34.6	05.5	278 50.6	7.2	22 25.3	3.6	57.6
20	121 34.3	05.7	293 16.8	7.1	22 28.9	3.4	57.6
21	136 34.0	.. 05.9	307 42.9	7.1	22 32.3	3.3	57.6
22	151 33.7	06.1	322 09.0	7.0	22 35.6	3.2	57.7
23	166 33.4	06.3	336 35.0	6.9	22 38.8	3.1	57.7
13 00	181 33.1	S23 06.4	351 00.9	6.9	N22 41.9	2.9	57.7
01	196 32.8	06.6	5 26.8	6.9	22 44.8	2.8	57.7
02	211 32.6	06.8	19 52.7	6.8	22 47.6	2.6	57.8
03	226 32.3	.. 07.0	34 18.5	6.7	22 50.2	2.5	57.8
04	241 32.0	07.1	48 44.2	6.7	22 52.7	2.4	57.8
05	256 31.7	07.3	63 09.9	6.7	22 55.1	2.2	57.8
F 06	271 31.4	S23 07.5	77 35.6	6.6	N22 57.3	2.1	57.8
R 07	286 31.1	07.7	92 01.2	6.6	22 59.4	1.9	57.9
I 08	301 30.8	07.8	106 26.8	6.5	23 01.3	1.8	57.9
D 09	316 30.5	.. 08.0	120 52.3	6.5	23 03.1	1.7	57.9
A 10	331 30.2	08.2	135 17.8	6.4	23 04.8	1.5	57.9
Y 11	346 29.9	08.3	149 43.2	6.4	23 06.3	1.4	57.9
12	1 29.6	S23 08.5	164 08.6	6.4	N23 07.7	1.2	58.0
13	16 29.3	08.7	178 34.0	6.3	23 08.9	1.1	58.0
14	31 29.0	08.8	192 59.3	6.3	23 10.0	1.0	58.0
15	46 28.7	.. 09.0	207 24.6	6.3	23 11.0	0.8	58.0
16	61 28.5	09.2	221 49.9	6.2	23 11.8	0.6	58.0
17	76 28.2	09.3	236 15.1	6.2	23 12.4	0.5	58.1
18	91 27.9	S23 09.5	250 40.3	6.2	N23 12.9	0.4	58.1
19	106 27.6	09.7	265 05.5	6.2	23 13.3	0.2	58.1
20	121 27.3	09.8	279 30.7	6.1	23 13.5	0.1	58.1
21	136 27.0	.. 10.0	293 55.8	6.1	23 13.6	0.1	58.1
22	151 26.7	10.2	308 20.9	6.1	23 13.5	0.2	58.2
23	166 26.4	10.3	322 46.0	6.0	23 13.3	0.4	58.2
14 00	181 26.1	S23 10.5	337 11.0	6.1	N23 12.9	0.5	58.2
01	196 25.8	10.6	351 36.1	6.0	23 12.4	0.7	58.2
02	211 25.5	10.8	6 01.1	6.0	23 11.7	0.8	58.2
03	226 25.2	.. 11.0	20 26.1	6.1	23 10.9	1.0	58.3
04	241 24.9	11.1	34 51.2	6.0	23 09.9	1.1	58.3
05	256 24.6	11.3	49 16.1	6.0	23 08.8	1.3	58.3
S 06	271 24.3	S23 11.4	63 41.1	6.0	N23 07.5	1.4	58.3
A 07	286 24.0	11.6	78 06.1	6.0	23 06.1	1.5	58.3
T 08	301 23.7	11.7	92 31.1	6.0	23 04.6	1.7	58.3
U 09	316 23.4	.. 11.9	106 56.1	5.9	23 02.9	1.9	58.4
R 10	331 23.1	12.0	121 21.0	6.0	23 01.0	2.0	58.4
D 11	346 22.8	12.2	135 46.0	5.9	22 59.0	2.1	58.4
A 12	1 22.5	S23 12.3	150 10.9	6.0	N22 56.9	2.3	58.4
Y 13	16 22.2	12.5	164 35.9	6.0	22 54.6	2.5	58.4
14	31 21.9	12.6	179 00.9	5.9	22 52.1	2.6	58.4
15	46 21.7	.. 12.8	193 25.8	6.0	22 49.5	2.7	58.5
16	61 21.4	12.9	207 50.8	6.0	22 46.8	2.9	58.5
17	76 21.1	13.1	222 15.8	6.0	22 43.9	3.0	58.5
18	91 20.8	S23 13.2	236 40.8	6.0	N22 40.9	3.2	58.5
19	106 20.5	13.4	251 05.8	6.0	22 37.7	3.3	58.5
20	121 20.2	13.5	265 30.8	6.1	22 34.4	3.5	58.5
21	136 19.9	.. 13.6	279 55.9	6.0	22 30.9	3.6	58.5
22	151 19.6	13.8	294 20.9	6.1	22 27.3	3.8	58.6
23	166 19.3	13.9	308 46.0	6.1	N22 23.5	3.9	58.6
	SD 16.3	d 0.2	SD 15.6		15.8		15.9

Lat.	Twilight Naut.	Twilight Civil	Sunrise	Moonrise 12	Moonrise 13	Moonrise 14	Moonrise 15
N 72	08 17	10 39	████	▭	▭	▭	▭
N 70	07 57	09 43	████	▭	▭	▭	▭
68	07 42	09 10	████	12 38	▭	▭	16 26
66	07 29	08 45	10 22	13 54	14 18	15 29	17 15
64	07 18	08 26	09 43	14 31	15 08	16 14	17 46
62	07 09	08 11	09 15	14 57	15 39	16 44	18 09
60	07 01	07 57	08 54	15 18	16 03	17 07	18 28
N 58	06 53	07 46	08 37	15 35	16 22	17 25	18 43
56	06 47	07 36	08 23	15 50	16 38	17 41	18 56
54	06 41	07 27	08 10	16 02	16 51	17 54	19 08
52	06 35	07 19	08 00	16 13	17 03	18 05	19 18
50	06 30	07 12	07 50	16 23	17 14	18 16	19 27
45	06 19	06 56	07 29	16 44	17 36	18 37	19 46
N 40	06 08	06 42	07 13	17 00	17 54	18 54	20 01
35	05 59	06 31	06 59	17 15	18 08	19 09	20 14
30	05 51	06 20	06 47	17 27	18 21	19 22	20 25
20	05 34	06 02	06 26	17 48	18 44	19 43	20 45
N 10	05 18	05 45	06 07	18 07	19 03	20 02	21 01
0	05 02	05 28	05 50	18 24	19 21	20 19	21 17
S 10	04 43	05 10	05 33	18 41	19 39	20 37	21 33
20	04 21	04 50	05 14	19 00	19 58	20 55	21 49
30	03 52	04 25	04 52	19 21	20 21	21 17	22 08
35	03 33	04 10	04 40	19 34	20 34	21 30	22 19
40	03 11	03 52	04 25	19 48	20 49	21 44	22 32
45	02 41	03 30	04 07	20 06	21 07	22 01	22 47
S 50	01 56	03 01	03 45	20 27	21 30	22 22	23 05
52	01 30	02 46	03 34	20 38	21 40	22 33	23 14
54	00 48	02 28	03 22	20 49	21 52	22 44	23 24
56	////	02 07	03 08	21 02	22 06	22 57	23 34
58	////	01 39	02 52	21 18	22 23	23 12	23 47
S 60	////	00 53	02 32	21 36	22 42	23 30	24 01

Lat.	Sunset	Twilight Civil	Twilight Naut.	Moonset 12	Moonset 13	Moonset 14	Moonset 15
N 72	████	13 08	15 31	▭	▭	▭	▭
N 70	████	14 05	15 50	▭	▭	▭	▭
68	████	14 38	16 06	11 34	▭	▭	13 48
66	13 26	15 02	16 19	10 18	11 52	12 43	12 58
64	14 05	15 22	16 29	09 41	11 03	11 57	12 26
62	14 33	15 37	16 39	09 15	10 31	11 27	12 03
60	14 53	15 51	16 47	08 55	10 08	11 04	11 44
N 58	15 11	16 02	16 54	08 38	09 49	10 46	11 28
56	15 25	16 12	17 01	08 24	09 33	10 30	11 14
54	15 37	16 21	17 07	08 12	09 20	10 17	11 03
52	15 48	16 29	17 13	08 01	09 08	10 05	10 52
50	15 58	16 36	17 18	07 52	08 57	09 55	10 43
45	16 18	16 52	17 29	07 31	08 35	09 33	10 23
N 40	16 35	17 06	17 40	07 15	08 18	09 16	10 07
35	16 49	17 17	17 49	07 01	08 03	09 01	09 54
30	17 01	17 28	17 57	06 50	07 50	08 48	09 42
20	17 22	17 46	18 14	06 29	07 28	08 26	09 21
N 10	17 41	18 03	18 30	06 11	07 09	08 07	09 04
0	17 58	18 20	18 46	05 55	06 51	07 49	08 47
S 10	18 15	18 38	19 05	05 39	06 33	07 31	08 30
20	18 34	18 58	19 28	05 21	06 14	07 12	08 12
30	18 56	19 23	19 56	05 01	05 52	06 49	07 52
35	19 09	19 38	20 15	04 49	05 39	06 36	07 39
40	19 23	19 56	20 38	04 35	05 24	06 21	07 25
45	19 41	20 18	21 08	04 19	05 07	06 03	07 09
S 50	20 03	20 48	21 52	04 00	04 45	05 41	06 48
52	20 14	21 03	22 19	03 51	04 34	05 30	06 38
54	20 26	21 20	23 02	03 40	04 23	05 18	06 27
56	20 40	21 42	////	03 28	04 09	05 04	06 14
58	20 57	22 11	////	03 15	03 53	04 48	06 00
S 60	21 17	22 57	////	02 59	03 35	04 29	05 42

Day	SUN Eqn. of Time 00h	SUN Eqn. of Time 12h	SUN Mer. Pass.	MOON Mer. Pass. Upper	MOON Mer. Pass. Lower	Age	Phase
	m s	m s	h m	h m	h m	d %	
12	06 41	06 27	11 54	24 37	12 09	16 100	◯
13	06 13	05 59	11 54	00 37	13 06	17 98	
14	05 45	05 31	11 54	01 35	14 04	18 94	

© British Crown Copyright 2018. All rights reserved.

UT	ARIES	VENUS −3.9		MARS +1.6		JUPITER −1.8		SATURN +0.6		STARS		
d h	GHA	GHA	Dec	GHA	Dec	GHA	Dec	GHA	Dec	Name	SHA	Dec
15 00	83 21.7	147 41.2	S23 08.8	218 40.3	S16 24.8	170 21.3	S23 17.5	152 18.8	S21 57.2	Acamar	315 14.6	S40 13.8
01	98 24.1	162 40.4	08.3	233 41.1	25.3	185 23.1	17.5	167 21.0	57.1	Achernar	335 23.1	S57 08.5
02	113 26.6	177 39.5	07.8	248 41.9	25.8	200 24.9	17.5	182 23.1	57.1	Acrux	173 04.5	S63 12.2
03	128 29.1	192 38.7	.. 07.3	263 42.7	.. 26.3	215 26.8	.. 17.5	197 25.3	.. 57.1	Adhara	255 08.7	S29 00.0
04	143 31.5	207 37.8	06.8	278 43.5	26.8	230 28.6	17.5	212 27.5	57.0	Aldebaran	290 43.9	N16 32.8
05	158 34.0	222 37.0	06.3	293 44.3	27.3	245 30.5	17.5	227 29.6	57.0			
06	173 36.5	237 36.1	S23 05.8	308 45.1	S16 27.8	260 32.3	S23 17.5	242 31.8	S21 57.0	Alioth	166 16.9	N55 51.0
07	188 38.9	252 35.3	05.3	323 45.9	28.3	275 34.2	17.5	257 34.0	56.9	Alkaid	152 55.6	N49 12.8
08	203 41.4	267 34.4	04.8	338 46.7	28.8	290 36.0	17.5	272 36.2	56.9	Alnair	27 38.3	S46 52.1
S 09	218 43.9	282 33.6	.. 04.3	353 47.5	.. 29.3	305 37.8	.. 17.4	287 38.3	.. 56.9	Alnilam	275 41.5	S 1 11.5
U 10	233 46.3	297 32.8	03.8	8 48.3	29.7	320 39.7	17.4	302 40.5	56.8	Alphard	217 51.5	S 8 44.6
N 11	248 48.8	312 31.9	03.2	23 49.1	30.2	335 41.5	17.4	317 42.7	56.8			
D 12	263 51.3	327 31.1	S23 02.7	38 49.9	S16 30.7	350 43.4	S23 17.4	332 44.8	S21 56.7	Alphecca	126 07.6	N26 38.9
A 13	278 53.7	342 30.2	02.2	53 50.7	31.2	5 45.2	17.4	347 47.0	56.7	Alpheratz	357 38.8	N29 12.1
Y 14	293 56.2	357 29.4	01.7	68 51.6	31.7	20 47.1	17.4	2 49.2	56.7	Altair	62 04.2	N 8 55.4
15	308 58.6	12 28.6	.. 01.2	83 52.4	.. 32.2	35 48.9	.. 17.4	17 51.3	.. 56.6	Ankaa	353 11.2	S42 12.2
16	324 01.1	27 27.7	00.7	98 53.2	32.7	50 50.7	17.4	32 53.5	56.6	Antares	112 21.2	S26 28.3
17	339 03.6	42 26.9	23 00.2	113 54.0	33.2	65 52.6	17.4	47 55.7	56.6			
18	354 06.0	57 26.0	S22 59.7	128 54.8	S16 33.7	80 54.4	S23 17.4	62 57.8	S21 56.5	Arcturus	145 51.9	N19 04.8
19	9 08.5	72 25.2	59.1	143 55.6	34.1	95 56.3	17.3	78 00.0	56.5	Atria	107 19.5	S69 03.5
20	24 11.0	87 24.4	58.6	158 56.4	34.6	110 58.1	17.3	93 02.2	56.5	Avior	234 15.7	S59 34.2
21	39 13.4	102 23.5	.. 58.1	173 57.2	.. 35.1	126 00.0	.. 17.3	108 04.4	.. 56.4	Bellatrix	278 26.9	N 6 21.9
22	54 15.9	117 22.7	57.6	188 58.0	35.6	141 01.8	17.3	123 06.5	56.4	Betelgeuse	270 56.1	N 7 24.5
23	69 18.4	132 21.9	57.1	203 58.8	36.1	156 03.6	17.3	138 08.7	56.3			
16 00	84 20.8	147 21.0	S22 56.5	218 59.6	S16 36.6	171 05.5	S23 17.3	153 10.9	S21 56.3	Canopus	263 53.6	S52 42.4
01	99 23.3	162 20.2	56.0	234 00.4	37.1	186 07.3	17.3	168 13.0	56.3	Capella	280 27.4	N46 00.9
02	114 25.8	177 19.3	55.5	249 01.2	37.6	201 09.2	17.3	183 15.2	56.2	Deneb	49 28.8	N45 21.3
03	129 28.2	192 18.5	.. 55.0	264 02.0	.. 38.0	216 11.0	.. 17.3	198 17.4	.. 56.2	Denebola	182 29.1	N14 27.7
04	144 30.7	207 17.7	54.4	279 02.8	38.5	231 12.8	17.3	213 19.5	56.2	Diphda	348 51.3	S17 52.9
05	159 33.1	222 16.8	53.9	294 03.6	39.0	246 14.7	17.3	228 21.7	56.1			
06	174 35.6	237 16.0	S22 53.4	309 04.4	S16 39.5	261 16.5	S23 17.3	243 23.9	S21 56.1	Dubhe	193 46.1	N61 38.4
07	189 38.1	252 15.2	52.8	324 05.2	40.0	276 18.4	17.2	258 26.0	56.1	Elnath	278 06.6	N28 37.3
08	204 40.5	267 14.3	52.3	339 06.0	40.5	291 20.2	17.2	273 28.2	56.0	Eltanin	90 44.6	N51 29.3
M 09	219 43.0	282 13.5	.. 51.8	354 06.8	.. 40.9	306 22.1	.. 17.2	288 30.4	.. 56.0	Enif	33 42.9	N 9 58.0
O 10	234 45.5	297 12.7	51.2	9 07.6	41.4	321 23.9	17.2	303 32.5	55.9	Fomalhaut	15 19.1	S29 31.2
N 11	249 47.9	312 11.9	50.7	24 08.4	41.9	336 25.7	17.2	318 34.7	55.9			
D 12	264 50.4	327 11.0	S22 50.2	39 09.1	S16 42.4	351 27.6	S23 17.2	333 36.9	S21 55.9	Gacrux	171 56.1	S57 13.1
A 13	279 52.9	342 10.2	49.6	54 09.9	42.9	6 29.4	17.2	348 39.1	55.8	Gienah	175 47.8	S17 38.9
Y 14	294 55.3	357 09.4	49.1	69 10.7	43.4	21 31.3	17.2	3 41.2	55.8	Hadar	148 42.0	S60 27.7
15	309 57.8	12 08.5	.. 48.5	84 11.5	.. 43.9	36 33.1	.. 17.2	18 43.4	.. 55.8	Hamal	327 55.5	N23 33.4
16	325 00.3	27 07.7	48.0	99 12.3	44.3	51 34.9	17.2	33 45.6	55.7	Kaus Aust.	83 38.3	S34 22.4
17	340 02.7	42 06.9	47.5	114 13.1	44.8	66 36.8	17.1	48 47.7	55.7			
18	355 05.2	57 06.1	S22 46.9	129 13.9	S16 45.3	81 38.6	S23 17.1	63 49.9	S21 55.6	Kochab	137 21.0	N74 04.3
19	10 07.6	72 05.2	46.4	144 14.7	45.8	96 40.5	17.1	78 52.1	55.6	Markab	13 34.0	N15 18.8
20	25 10.1	87 04.4	45.8	159 15.5	46.3	111 42.3	17.1	93 54.2	55.6	Menkar	314 10.1	N 4 09.9
21	40 12.6	102 03.6	.. 45.3	174 16.3	.. 46.8	126 44.2	.. 17.1	108 56.4	.. 55.5	Menkent	148 02.6	S36 27.7
22	55 15.0	117 02.7	44.7	189 17.1	47.2	141 46.0	17.1	123 58.6	55.5	Miaplacidus	221 38.2	S69 47.6
23	70 17.5	132 01.9	44.2	204 17.9	47.7	156 47.8	17.1	139 00.7	55.5			
17 00	85 20.0	147 01.1	S22 43.6	219 18.7	S16 48.2	171 49.7	S23 17.1	154 02.9	S21 55.4	Mirfak	308 33.5	N49 55.9
01	100 22.4	162 00.3	43.1	234 19.5	48.7	186 51.5	17.1	169 05.1	55.4	Nunki	75 53.2	S26 16.2
02	115 24.9	176 59.5	42.5	249 20.3	49.2	201 53.4	17.1	184 07.2	55.4	Peacock	53 12.7	S56 40.4
03	130 27.4	191 58.6	.. 42.0	264 21.1	.. 49.6	216 55.2	.. 17.1	199 09.4	.. 55.3	Pollux	243 22.0	N27 58.5
04	145 29.8	206 57.8	41.4	279 21.9	50.1	231 57.0	17.0	214 11.6	55.3	Procyon	244 54.8	N 5 10.4
05	160 32.3	221 57.0	40.8	294 22.7	50.6	246 58.9	17.0	229 13.7	55.2			
06	175 34.7	236 56.2	S22 40.3	309 23.5	S16 51.1	262 00.7	S23 17.0	244 15.9	S21 55.2	Rasalhague	96 02.7	N12 32.9
07	190 37.2	251 55.3	39.7	324 24.3	51.6	277 02.6	17.0	259 18.1	55.2	Regulus	207 38.7	N11 52.2
T 08	205 39.7	266 54.5	39.2	339 25.1	52.0	292 04.4	17.0	274 20.2	55.1	Rigel	281 07.4	S 8 10.8
U 09	220 42.1	281 53.7	.. 38.6	354 25.9	.. 52.5	307 06.3	.. 17.0	289 22.4	.. 55.1	Rigil Kent.	139 46.2	S60 54.6
E 10	235 44.6	296 52.9	38.0	9 26.7	53.0	322 08.1	17.0	304 24.6	55.1	Sabik	102 07.8	S15 44.8
S 11	250 47.1	311 52.1	37.5	24 27.5	53.5	337 09.9	17.0	319 26.7	55.0			
D 12	265 49.5	326 51.2	S22 36.9	39 28.2	S16 54.0	352 11.8	S23 17.0	334 28.9	S21 55.0	Schedar	349 35.3	N56 39.0
A 13	280 52.0	341 50.4	36.3	54 29.0	54.4	7 13.6	16.9	349 31.1	54.9	Shaula	96 16.3	S37 06.9
Y 14	295 54.5	356 49.6	35.8	69 29.8	54.9	22 15.5	16.9	4 33.2	54.9	Sirius	258 29.5	S16 44.7
15	310 56.9	11 48.8	.. 35.2	84 30.6	.. 55.4	37 17.3	.. 16.9	19 35.4	.. 54.9	Spica	158 26.7	S11 15.7
16	325 59.4	26 48.0	34.6	99 31.4	55.9	52 19.1	16.9	34 37.6	54.8	Suhail	222 48.9	S43 30.6
17	341 01.9	41 47.2	34.1	114 32.2	56.4	67 21.0	16.9	49 39.7	54.8			
18	356 04.3	56 46.3	S22 33.5	129 33.0	S16 56.8	82 22.8	S23 16.9	64 41.9	S21 54.7	Vega	80 36.4	N38 48.3
19	11 06.8	71 45.5	32.9	144 33.8	57.3	97 24.7	16.9	79 44.1	54.7	Zuben'ubi	137 00.8	S16 07.2
20	26 09.2	86 44.7	32.4	159 34.6	57.8	112 26.5	16.9	94 46.2	54.7		SHA	Mer. Pass.
21	41 11.7	101 43.9	.. 31.8	174 35.4	.. 58.3	127 28.3	.. 16.9	109 48.4	.. 54.6		° ′	h m
22	56 14.2	116 43.1	31.2	189 36.2	58.7	142 30.2	16.9	124 50.6	54.6	Venus	63 00.2	14 11
23	71 16.6	131 42.3	30.6	204 37.0	59.2	157 32.0	16.8	139 52.7	54.6	Mars	134 38.7	9 24
	h m									Jupiter	86 44.7	12 34
Mer. Pass.	18 19.6	v −0.8	d 0.5	v 0.8	d 0.5	v 1.8	d 0.0	v 2.2	d 0.0	Saturn	68 50.0	13 45

© British Crown Copyright 2018. All rights reserved.

UT	SUN GHA	SUN Dec	MOON GHA	v	Dec	d	HP
d h	o '	o '	o '	'	o '	'	'
15 00	181 19.0	S23 14.1	323 11.1	6.1	N22 19.6	4.0	58.6
01	196 18.7	14.2	337 36.2	6.1	22 15.6	4.2	58.6
02	211 18.4	14.3	352 01.3	6.2	22 11.4	4.4	58.6
03	226 18.1	.. 14.5	6 26.5	6.1	22 07.0	4.5	58.6
04	241 17.8	14.6	20 51.6	6.2	22 02.5	4.6	58.7
05	256 17.5	14.8	35 16.8	6.3	21 57.9	4.7	58.7
06	271 17.2	S23 14.9	49 42.1	6.2	N21 53.2	4.9	58.7
07	286 16.9	15.0	64 07.3	6.3	21 48.3	5.1	58.7
S 08	301 16.6	15.2	78 32.6	6.3	21 43.2	5.2	58.7
U 09	316 16.3	.. 15.3	92 57.9	6.4	21 38.0	5.3	58.7
N 10	331 16.0	15.4	107 23.3	6.3	21 32.7	5.5	58.7
D 11	346 15.7	15.6	121 48.6	6.4	21 27.2	5.6	58.7
A 12	1 15.4	S23 15.7	136 14.0	6.5	N21 21.6	5.7	58.8
Y 13	16 15.1	15.8	150 39.5	6.5	21 15.9	5.9	58.8
14	31 14.8	15.9	165 05.0	6.5	21 10.0	6.0	58.8
15	46 14.5	.. 16.1	179 30.5	6.6	21 04.0	6.2	58.8
16	61 14.2	16.2	193 56.1	6.6	20 57.8	6.2	58.8
17	76 13.9	16.3	208 21.7	6.6	20 51.6	6.4	58.8
18	91 13.6	S23 16.5	222 47.3	6.7	N20 45.2	6.6	58.8
19	106 13.3	16.6	237 13.0	6.7	20 38.6	6.7	58.8
20	121 13.0	16.7	251 38.7	6.8	20 31.9	6.8	58.9
21	136 12.7	.. 16.8	266 04.5	6.8	20 25.1	6.9	58.9
22	151 12.4	16.9	280 30.3	6.8	20 18.2	7.1	58.9
23	166 12.1	17.1	294 56.1	6.9	20 11.1	7.2	58.9
16 00	181 11.8	S23 17.2	309 22.0	7.0	N20 03.9	7.3	58.9
01	196 11.5	17.3	323 48.0	7.0	19 56.6	7.5	58.9
02	211 11.2	17.4	338 14.0	7.0	19 49.1	7.5	58.9
03	226 10.9	.. 17.6	352 40.0	7.1	19 41.6	7.7	58.9
04	241 10.6	17.7	7 06.1	7.2	19 33.9	7.8	58.9
05	256 10.3	17.8	21 32.3	7.2	19 26.1	8.0	58.9
06	271 10.0	S23 17.9	35 58.5	7.2	N19 18.1	8.0	59.0
07	286 09.7	18.0	50 24.7	7.3	19 10.1	8.2	59.0
M 08	301 09.4	18.1	64 51.0	7.3	19 01.9	8.3	59.0
O 09	316 09.1	.. 18.2	79 17.3	7.4	18 53.6	8.5	59.0
N 10	331 08.8	18.4	93 43.7	7.5	18 45.1	8.5	59.0
D 11	346 08.5	18.5	108 10.2	7.5	18 36.6	8.6	59.0
A 12	1 08.2	S23 18.6	122 36.7	7.6	N18 28.0	8.8	59.0
Y 13	16 07.8	18.7	137 03.3	7.6	18 19.2	8.9	59.0
14	31 07.5	18.8	151 29.9	7.6	18 10.3	9.0	59.0
15	46 07.2	.. 18.9	165 56.5	7.8	18 01.3	9.1	59.0
16	61 06.9	19.0	180 23.3	7.7	17 52.2	9.2	59.0
17	76 06.6	19.1	194 50.0	7.9	17 43.0	9.3	59.0
18	91 06.3	S23 19.2	209 16.9	7.9	N17 33.7	9.5	59.0
19	106 06.0	19.3	223 43.8	7.9	17 24.2	9.5	59.0
20	121 05.7	19.4	238 10.7	8.0	17 14.7	9.6	59.1
21	136 05.4	.. 19.5	252 37.7	8.0	17 05.1	9.8	59.1
22	151 05.1	19.7	267 04.7	8.2	16 55.3	9.8	59.1
23	166 04.8	19.8	281 31.9	8.1	16 45.5	10.0	59.1
17 00	181 04.5	S23 19.9	295 59.0	8.2	N16 35.5	10.0	59.1
01	196 04.2	20.0	310 26.2	8.3	16 25.5	10.2	59.1
02	211 03.9	20.1	324 53.5	8.4	16 15.3	10.2	59.1
03	226 03.6	.. 20.2	339 20.9	8.3	16 05.1	10.4	59.1
04	241 03.3	20.3	353 48.2	8.5	15 54.7	10.4	59.1
05	256 03.0	20.4	8 15.7	8.5	15 44.3	10.5	59.1
06	271 02.7	S23 20.4	22 43.2	8.6	N15 33.8	10.7	59.1
07	286 02.4	20.5	37 10.8	8.6	15 23.1	10.7	59.1
T 08	301 02.1	20.6	51 38.4	8.6	15 12.4	10.9	59.1
U 09	316 01.8	.. 20.7	66 06.0	8.8	15 01.6	10.9	59.1
E 10	331 01.5	20.8	80 33.8	8.7	14 50.7	11.0	59.1
S 11	346 01.2	20.9	95 01.5	8.9	14 39.7	11.1	59.1
D 12	1 00.9	S23 21.0	109 29.4	8.9	N14 28.6	11.1	59.2
A 13	16 00.6	21.1	123 57.3	8.9	14 17.5	11.3	59.2
Y 14	31 00.3	21.2	138 25.2	9.0	14 06.2	11.3	59.2
15	45 59.9	.. 21.3	152 53.2	9.0	13 54.9	11.4	59.2
16	60 59.6	21.4	167 21.2	9.2	13 43.5	11.5	59.2
17	75 59.3	21.5	181 49.4	9.1	13 32.0	11.5	59.2
18	90 59.0	S23 21.5	196 17.5	9.2	N13 20.5	11.7	59.2
19	105 58.7	21.6	210 45.7	9.3	13 08.8	11.7	59.2
20	120 58.4	21.7	225 14.0	9.3	12 57.1	11.8	59.2
21	135 58.1	.. 21.8	239 42.3	9.4	12 45.3	11.9	59.2
22	150 57.8	21.9	254 10.7	9.4	12 33.4	11.9	59.2
23	165 57.5	22.0	268 39.1	9.4	N12 21.5	12.0	59.2
	SD 16.3	d 0.1	SD 16.0		16.1		16.1

Lat.	Twilight Naut.	Twilight Civil	Sunrise	Moonrise 15	16	17	18
o	h m	h m	h m	h m	h m	h m	h m
N 72	08 21	10 48	■■	▭	16 51	20 02	22 21
N 70	08 01	09 49	■■	▭	18 05	20 27	22 33
68	07 45	09 14	■■	16 26	18 43	20 46	22 42
66	07 32	08 49	10 28	17 15	19 09	21 01	22 49
64	07 21	08 30	09 47	17 46	19 29	21 13	22 55
62	07 12	08 14	09 19	18 09	19 45	21 23	23 01
60	07 04	08 00	08 58	18 28	19 59	21 32	23 05
N 58	06 56	07 49	08 40	18 43	20 10	21 40	23 10
56	06 49	07 39	08 26	18 56	20 20	21 47	23 13
54	06 43	07 29	08 13	19 08	20 29	21 53	23 16
52	06 38	07 21	08 02	19 18	20 37	21 58	23 19
50	06 32	07 14	07 52	19 27	20 44	22 03	23 22
45	06 21	06 58	07 32	19 46	20 59	22 13	23 28
N 40	06 10	06 44	07 15	20 01	21 11	22 22	23 33
35	06 01	06 33	07 01	20 14	21 22	22 29	23 37
30	05 52	06 22	06 49	20 25	21 31	22 36	23 41
20	05 36	06 03	06 28	20 45	21 46	22 47	23 47
N 10	05 20	05 46	06 09	21 01	22 00	22 57	23 52
0	05 03	05 29	05 52	21 17	22 13	23 06	23 58
S 10	04 44	05 11	05 34	21 33	22 25	23 15	24 03
20	04 22	04 51	05 15	21 49	22 39	23 25	24 08
30	03 53	04 26	04 53	22 08	22 54	23 36	24 15
35	03 34	04 11	04 40	22 19	23 03	23 43	24 18
40	03 11	03 53	04 25	22 32	23 14	23 50	24 22
45	02 41	03 30	04 08	22 47	23 26	23 58	24 27
S 50	01 56	03 01	03 45	23 05	23 40	24 08	00 08
52	01 28	02 46	03 34	23 14	23 47	24 13	00 13
54	00 44	02 28	03 22	23 24	23 54	24 18	00 18
56	////	02 06	03 08	23 34	24 02	00 02	00 23
58	////	01 37	02 51	23 47	24 11	00 11	00 30
S 60	////	00 48	02 31	24 01	00 01	00 22	00 37

Lat.	Sunset	Twilight Civil	Twilight Naut.	Moonset 15	16	17	18
o	h m	h m	h m	h m	h m	h m	h m
N 72	■■	13 02	15 30	▭	15 23	14 06	13 35
N 70	■■	14 02	15 50	▭	14 07	13 39	13 21
68	■■	14 37	16 05	13 48	13 29	13 18	13 10
66	13 22	15 02	16 18	12 58	13 02	13 02	13 01
64	14 04	15 21	16 29	12 26	12 41	12 48	12 53
62	14 32	15 37	16 39	12 03	12 24	12 37	12 46
60	14 53	15 50	16 47	11 44	12 10	12 27	12 40
N 58	15 10	16 02	16 55	11 28	11 57	12 19	12 35
56	15 25	16 12	17 01	11 14	11 47	12 11	12 30
54	15 38	16 21	17 08	11 03	11 37	12 04	12 26
52	15 49	16 29	17 13	10 52	11 29	11 58	12 22
50	15 58	16 37	17 18	10 43	11 21	11 53	12 19
45	16 19	16 53	17 30	10 23	11 05	11 41	12 11
N 40	16 36	17 06	17 40	10 07	10 52	11 31	12 05
35	16 50	17 18	17 50	09 54	10 41	11 22	11 59
30	17 02	17 29	17 58	09 42	10 31	11 14	11 54
20	17 23	17 47	18 15	09 21	10 13	11 01	11 46
N 10	17 42	18 05	18 31	09 04	09 58	10 49	11 38
0	17 59	18 22	18 48	08 47	09 44	10 39	11 31
S 10	18 17	18 40	19 07	08 30	09 30	10 27	11 24
20	18 36	19 00	19 29	08 12	09 14	10 16	11 16
30	18 58	19 25	19 58	07 52	08 56	10 02	11 07
35	19 11	19 40	20 17	07 39	08 46	09 54	11 02
40	19 26	19 58	20 40	07 25	08 34	09 45	10 56
45	19 43	20 21	21 10	07 09	08 20	09 34	10 49
S 50	20 06	20 50	21 56	06 48	08 03	09 21	10 40
52	20 17	21 05	22 23	06 38	07 54	09 15	10 37
54	20 29	21 23	23 08	06 27	07 45	09 08	10 32
56	20 43	21 45	////	06 14	07 35	09 01	10 28
58	21 00	22 15	////	06 00	07 23	08 52	10 22
S 60	21 20	23 04	////	05 42	07 09	08 42	10 16

Day	SUN Eqn. of Time 00h	SUN Eqn. of Time 12h	SUN Mer. Pass.	MOON Mer. Pass. Upper	MOON Mer. Pass. Lower	Age	Phase
d	m s	m s	h m	h m	h m	d	%
15	05 16	05 02	11 55	02 33	15 02	19	87
16	04 48	04 33	11 55	03 30	15 58	20	79
17	04 19	04 04	11 56	04 26	16 52	21	69

© British Crown Copyright 2018. All rights reserved.

UT	ARIES GHA	VENUS −3.9 GHA	Dec	MARS +1.6 GHA	Dec	JUPITER −1.8 GHA	Dec	SATURN +0.6 GHA	Dec	STARS Name	SHA	Dec
18 00	86 19.1	146 41.5	S22 30.0	219 37.8	S16 59.7	172 33.9	S23 16.8	154 54.9	S21 54.5	Acamar	315 14.6	S40 13.8
01	101 21.6	161 40.7	29.5	234 38.5	17 00.2	187 35.7	16.8	169 57.1	54.5	Achernar	335 23.1	S57 08.5
02	116 24.0	176 39.8	28.9	249 39.3	00.6	202 37.5	16.8	184 59.2	54.5	Acrux	173 04.5	S63 12.2
03	131 26.5	191 39.0 ··	28.3	264 40.1 ··	01.1	217 39.4 ··	16.8	200 01.4 ··	54.4	Adhara	255 08.7	S29 00.0
04	146 29.0	206 38.2	27.7	279 40.9	01.6	232 41.2	16.8	215 03.6	54.4	Aldebaran	290 43.9	N16 32.8
05	161 31.4	221 37.4	27.1	294 41.7	02.1	247 43.1	16.8	230 05.7	54.3			
06	176 33.9	236 36.6	S22 26.5	309 42.5	S17 02.5	262 44.9	S23 16.8	245 07.9	S21 54.3	Alioth	166 16.9	N55 51.0
W 07	191 36.4	251 35.8	26.0	324 43.3	03.0	277 46.8	16.8	260 10.1	54.3	Alkaid	152 55.6	N49 12.7
E 08	206 38.8	266 35.0	25.4	339 44.1	03.5	292 48.6	16.7	275 12.2	54.2	Alnair	27 38.3	S46 52.1
D 09	221 41.3	281 34.2 ··	24.8	354 44.9 ··	04.0	307 50.4 ··	16.7	290 14.4 ··	54.2	Alnilam	275 41.5	S 1 11.5
N 10	236 43.7	296 33.4	24.2	9 45.7	04.4	322 52.3	16.7	305 16.6	54.2	Alphard	217 51.5	S 8 44.6
E 11	251 46.2	311 32.6	23.6	24 46.4	04.9	337 54.1	16.7	320 18.7	54.1			
S 12	266 48.7	326 31.8	S22 23.0	39 47.2	S17 05.4	352 56.0	S23 16.7	335 20.9	S21 54.1	Alphecca	126 07.5	N26 38.9
D 13	281 51.1	341 31.0	22.4	54 48.0	05.9	7 57.8	16.7	350 23.1	54.0	Alpheratz	357 38.9	N29 12.1
A 14	296 53.6	356 30.2	21.8	69 48.8	06.3	22 59.6	16.7	5 25.2	54.0	Altair	62 04.2	N 8 55.3
Y 15	311 56.1	11 29.3 ··	21.2	84 49.6 ··	06.8	38 01.5 ··	16.7	20 27.4 ··	54.0	Ankaa	353 11.2	S42 12.2
16	326 58.5	26 28.5	20.6	99 50.4	07.3	53 03.3	16.7	35 29.6	53.9	Antares	112 21.1	S26 28.3
17	342 01.0	41 27.7	20.0	114 51.2	07.8	68 05.2	16.6	50 31.7	53.9			
18	357 03.5	56 26.9	S22 19.4	129 52.0	S17 08.2	83 07.0	S23 16.6	65 33.9	S21 53.9	Arcturus	145 51.9	N19 04.8
19	12 05.9	71 26.1	18.8	144 52.8	08.7	98 08.8	16.6	80 36.0	53.8	Atria	107 19.5	S69 03.5
20	27 08.4	86 25.3	18.2	159 53.5	09.2	113 10.7	16.6	95 38.2	53.8	Avior	234 15.7	S59 34.2
21	42 10.8	101 24.5 ··	17.6	174 54.3 ··	09.7	128 12.5 ··	16.6	110 40.4 ··	53.7	Bellatrix	278 26.9	N 6 21.9
22	57 13.3	116 23.7	17.0	189 55.1	10.1	143 14.4	16.6	125 42.5	53.7	Betelgeuse	270 56.1	N 7 24.5
23	72 15.8	131 22.9	16.4	204 55.9	10.6	158 16.2	16.6	140 44.7	53.7			
19 00	87 18.2	146 22.1	S22 15.8	219 56.7	S17 11.1	173 18.0	S23 16.6	155 46.9	S21 53.6	Canopus	263 53.6	S52 42.4
01	102 20.7	161 21.3	15.2	234 57.5	11.5	188 19.9	16.5	170 49.0	53.6	Capella	280 27.4	N46 01.0
02	117 23.2	176 20.5	14.6	249 58.3	12.0	203 21.7	16.5	185 51.2	53.6	Deneb	49 28.8	N45 21.3
03	132 25.6	191 19.7 ··	14.0	264 59.1 ··	12.5	218 23.6 ··	16.5	200 53.4 ··	53.5	Denebola	182 29.1	N14 27.7
04	147 28.1	206 18.9	13.4	279 59.8	12.9	233 25.4	16.5	215 55.5	53.5	Diphda	348 51.3	S17 52.9
05	162 30.6	221 18.1	12.8	295 00.6	13.4	248 27.2	16.5	230 57.7	53.4			
06	177 33.0	236 17.3	S22 12.2	310 01.4	S17 13.9	263 29.1	S23 16.5	245 59.9	S21 53.4	Dubhe	193 46.1	N61 38.4
T 07	192 35.5	251 16.6	11.5	325 02.2	14.4	278 30.9	16.5	261 02.0	53.4	Elnath	278 06.6	N28 37.3
H 08	207 38.0	266 15.8	10.9	340 03.0	14.8	293 32.8	16.5	276 04.2	53.3	Eltanin	90 44.6	N51 29.3
U 09	222 40.4	281 15.0 ··	10.3	355 03.8 ··	15.3	308 34.6 ··	16.4	291 06.4 ··	53.3	Enif	33 42.9	N 9 58.0
R 10	237 42.9	296 14.2	09.7	10 04.6	15.8	323 36.4	16.4	306 08.5	53.3	Fomalhaut	15 19.1	S29 31.2
S 11	252 45.3	311 13.4	09.1	25 05.3	16.2	338 38.3	16.4	321 10.7	53.2			
D 12	267 47.8	326 12.6	S22 08.5	40 06.1	S17 16.7	353 40.1	S23 16.4	336 12.8	S21 53.2	Gacrux	171 56.1	S57 13.1
A 13	282 50.3	341 11.8	07.8	55 06.9	17.2	8 42.0	16.4	351 15.0	53.1	Gienah	175 47.8	S17 38.9
Y 14	297 52.7	356 11.0	07.2	70 07.7	17.6	23 43.8	16.4	6 17.2	53.1	Hadar	148 42.0	S60 27.7
15	312 55.2	11 10.2 ··	06.6	85 08.5 ··	18.1	38 45.6 ··	16.4	21 19.3 ··	53.1	Hamal	327 55.5	N23 33.4
16	327 57.7	26 09.4	06.0	100 09.3	18.6	53 47.5	16.4	36 21.5	53.0	Kaus Aust.	83 38.3	S34 22.4
17	343 00.1	41 08.6	05.3	115 10.0	19.0	68 49.3	16.4	51 23.7	53.0			
18	358 02.6	56 07.8	S22 04.7	130 10.8	S17 19.5	83 51.2	S23 16.3	66 25.8	S21 52.9	Kochab	137 21.0	N74 04.3
19	13 05.1	71 07.0	04.1	145 11.6	20.0	98 53.0	16.3	81 28.0	52.9	Markab	13 34.0	N15 18.8
20	28 07.5	86 06.3	03.5	160 12.4	20.4	113 54.8	16.3	96 30.2	52.9	Menkar	314 10.1	N 4 09.9
21	43 10.0	101 05.5 ··	02.8	175 13.2 ··	20.9	128 56.7 ··	16.3	111 32.3 ··	52.8	Menkent	148 02.6	S36 27.7
22	58 12.5	116 04.7	02.2	190 14.0	21.4	143 58.5	16.3	126 34.5	52.8	Miaplacidus	221 38.2	S69 47.7
23	73 14.9	131 03.9	01.6	205 14.7	21.8	159 00.4	16.3	141 36.6	52.8			
20 00	88 17.4	146 03.1	S22 00.9	220 15.5	S17 22.3	174 02.2	S23 16.3	156 38.8	S21 52.7	Mirfak	308 33.5	N49 55.9
01	103 19.8	161 02.3	22 00.3	235 16.3	22.8	189 04.0	16.2	171 41.0	52.7	Nunki	75 53.2	S26 16.2
02	118 22.3	176 01.5	21 59.7	250 17.1	23.2	204 05.9	16.2	186 43.1	52.6	Peacock	53 12.7	S56 40.4
03	133 24.8	191 00.7 ··	59.0	265 17.9 ··	23.7	219 07.7 ··	16.2	201 45.3 ··	52.6	Pollux	243 22.0	N27 58.5
04	148 27.2	206 00.0	58.4	280 18.7	24.2	234 09.6	16.2	216 47.5	52.6	Procyon	244 54.8	N 5 10.4
05	163 29.7	220 59.2	57.8	295 19.4	24.6	249 11.4	16.2	231 49.6	52.5			
06	178 32.2	235 58.4	S21 57.1	310 20.2	S17 25.1	264 13.2	S23 16.2	246 51.8	S21 52.5	Rasalhague	96 02.7	N12 32.9
07	193 34.6	250 57.6	56.5	325 21.0	25.6	279 15.1	16.2	261 54.0	52.5	Regulus	207 38.6	N11 52.2
08	208 37.1	265 56.8	55.8	340 21.8	26.0	294 16.9	16.2	276 56.1	52.4	Rigel	281 07.4	S 8 10.9
F 09	223 39.6	280 56.0 ··	55.2	355 22.6 ··	26.5	309 18.7 ··	16.1	291 58.3 ··	52.4	Rigil Kent.	139 46.2	S60 54.6
R 10	238 42.0	295 55.3	54.5	10 23.3	27.0	324 20.6	16.1	307 00.4	52.3	Sabik	102 07.8	S15 44.8
I 11	253 44.5	310 54.5	53.9	25 24.1	27.4	339 22.4	16.1	322 02.6	52.3			
D 12	268 46.9	325 53.7	S21 53.3	40 24.9	S17 27.9	354 24.3	S23 16.1	337 04.8	S21 52.3	Schedar	349 35.3	N56 39.0
A 13	283 49.4	340 52.9	52.6	55 25.7	28.3	9 26.1	16.1	352 06.9	52.2	Shaula	96 16.3	S37 06.9
Y 14	298 51.9	355 52.1	52.0	70 26.5	28.8	24 27.9	16.1	7 09.1	52.2	Sirius	258 29.5	S16 44.7
15	313 54.3	10 51.4 ··	51.3	85 27.2 ··	29.3	39 29.8 ··	16.1	22 11.3 ··	52.1	Spica	158 26.7	S11 15.7
16	328 56.8	25 50.6	50.7	100 28.0	29.7	54 31.6	16.0	37 13.4	52.1	Suhail	222 48.9	S43 30.6
17	343 59.3	40 49.8	50.0	115 28.8	30.2	69 33.5	16.0	52 15.6	52.1			
18	359 01.7	55 49.0	S21 49.4	130 29.6	S17 30.7	84 35.3	S23 16.0	67 17.7	S21 52.0	Vega	80 36.4	N38 48.3
19	14 04.2	70 48.3	48.8	145 30.4	31.1	99 37.1	16.0	82 19.9	52.0	Zuben'ubi	137 00.7	S16 07.2
20	29 06.7	85 47.5	48.1	160 31.1	31.6	114 39.0	16.0	97 22.1	52.0		SHA	Mer.Pass.
21	44 09.1	100 46.7 ··	47.4	175 31.9 ··	32.0	129 40.8 ··	16.0	112 24.2 ··	51.9		° ′	h m
22	59 11.6	115 45.9	46.7	190 32.7	32.5	144 42.7	16.0	127 26.4	51.9	Venus	59 03.9	14 15
23	74 14.1	130 45.2	46.1	205 33.5	33.0	159 44.5	16.0	142 28.6	51.8	Mars	132 38.5	9 20
	h m									Jupiter	85 59.8	12 25
Mer.Pass. 18 07.8	v −0.8 d 0.6	v 0.8 d 0.5		v 1.8 d 0.0		v 2.2 d 0.0				Saturn	68 28.6	13 35

© British Crown Copyright 2018. All rights reserved.

UT	SUN		MOON					Lat.	Twilight		Sunrise	Moonrise			
									Naut.	Civil		18	19	20	21
	GHA	Dec	GHA	v	Dec	d	HP	°	h m	h m	h m	h m	h m	h m	h m
d h	° ′	° ′	° ′	′	° ′	′	′	N 72	08 24	10 55	▬▬	22 21	24 30	00 30	02 37
18 00	180 57.2	S23 22.1	283 07.5	9.5	N12 09.5	12.1	59.2	N 70	08 04	09 52	▬▬	22 33	24 32	00 32	02 30
01	195 56.9	22.1	297 36.0	9.6	11 57.4	12.1	59.2	68	07 48	09 17	▬▬	22 42	24 34	00 34	02 25
02	210 56.6	22.2	312 04.6	9.6	11 45.3	12.3	59.2	66	07 35	08 52	10 33	22 49	24 35	00 35	02 20
03	225 56.3	.. 22.3	326 33.2	9.7	11 33.0	12.2	59.2	64	07 24	08 32	09 50	22 55	24 36	00 36	02 16
04	240 56.0	22.4	341 01.9	9.7	11 20.8	12.4	59.2	62	07 14	08 16	09 22	23 01	24 37	00 37	02 13
05	255 55.7	22.5	355 30.6	9.7	11 08.4	12.4	59.2	60	07 06	08 03	09 00	23 05	24 38	00 38	02 10
06	270 55.4	S23 22.5	9 59.3	9.8	N10 56.0	12.5	59.2	N 58	06 58	07 51	08 43	23 10	24 39	00 39	02 07
W 07	285 55.0	22.6	24 28.1	9.9	10 43.5	12.5	59.2	56	06 52	07 41	08 28	23 13	24 39	00 39	02 05
E 08	300 54.7	22.7	38 57.0	9.9	10 31.0	12.6	59.2	54	06 45	07 32	08 15	23 16	24 40	00 40	02 03
D 09	315 54.4	.. 22.8	53 25.9	9.9	10 18.4	12.6	59.2	52	06 40	07 23	08 04	23 19	24 40	00 40	02 01
N 10	330 54.1	22.8	67 54.8	10.0	10 05.8	12.8	59.2	50	06 34	07 16	07 54	23 22	24 41	00 41	01 59
E 11	345 53.8	22.9	82 23.8	10.0	9 53.0	12.7	59.2	45	06 23	07 00	07 34	23 28	24 42	00 42	01 56
S 12	0 53.5	S23 23.0	96 52.8	10.1	N 9 40.3	12.8	59.2	N 40	06 12	06 46	07 17	23 33	24 43	00 43	01 53
D 13	15 53.2	23.0	111 21.9	10.1	9 27.5	12.9	59.2	35	06 03	06 35	07 03	23 37	24 44	00 44	01 50
A 14	30 52.9	23.1	125 51.0	10.1	9 14.6	12.9	59.2	30	05 54	06 24	06 50	23 41	24 44	00 44	01 48
Y 15	45 52.6	.. 23.2	140 20.1	10.2	9 01.7	13.0	59.2	20	05 38	06 05	06 29	23 47	24 45	00 45	01 44
16	60 52.3	23.3	154 49.3	10.2	8 48.7	13.0	59.2	N 10	05 21	05 48	06 11	23 52	24 47	00 47	01 40
17	75 52.0	23.3	169 18.5	10.3	8 35.7	13.1	59.2	0	05 04	05 31	05 53	23 58	24 48	00 48	01 37
18	90 51.7	S23 23.4	183 47.8	10.3	N 8 22.6	13.1	59.2	S 10	04 45	05 13	05 36	24 03	00 03	00 49	01 34
19	105 51.4	23.5	198 17.1	10.3	8 09.5	13.1	59.2	20	04 23	04 52	05 17	24 08	00 08	00 50	01 31
20	120 51.1	23.5	212 46.4	10.4	7 56.4	13.2	59.2	30	03 54	04 27	04 55	24 15	00 15	00 51	01 27
21	135 50.7	.. 23.6	227 15.8	10.4	7 43.2	13.3	59.2	35	03 35	04 12	04 42	24 18	00 18	00 52	01 25
22	150 50.4	23.7	241 45.2	10.4	7 29.9	13.3	59.2	40	03 12	03 54	04 26	24 22	00 22	00 53	01 23
23	165 50.1	23.7	256 14.6	10.5	7 16.6	13.3	59.2	45	02 41	03 31	04 08	24 27	00 27	00 54	01 20
19 00	180 49.8	S23 23.8	270 44.1	10.5	N 7 03.3	13.3	59.2	S 50	01 56	03 01	03 46	00 08	00 32	00 55	01 17
01	195 49.5	23.8	285 13.6	10.6	6 50.0	13.4	59.2	52	01 28	02 46	03 35	00 13	00 35	00 55	01 15
02	210 49.2	23.9	299 43.2	10.5	6 36.6	13.5	59.2	54	00 41	02 28	03 23	00 18	00 38	00 56	01 13
03	225 48.9	.. 24.0	314 12.7	10.6	6 23.1	13.4	59.2	56	////	02 06	03 08	00 23	00 41	00 56	01 12
04	240 48.6	24.0	328 42.3	10.6	6 09.7	13.5	59.2	58	////	01 36	02 52	00 30	00 44	00 57	01 10
05	255 48.3	24.1	343 11.9	10.7	5 56.2	13.6	59.2	S 60	////	00 46	02 31	00 37	00 48	00 58	01 07

06	270 48.0	S23 24.1	357 41.6	10.7	N 5 42.6	13.5	59.2	Lat.	Sunset	Twilight		Moonset			
07	285 47.7	24.2	12 11.3	10.7	5 29.1	13.6	59.2			Civil	Naut.	18	19	20	21
T 08	300 47.4	24.3	26 41.0	10.7	5 15.5	13.6	59.2								
H 09	315 47.1	.. 24.3	41 10.7	10.8	5 01.9	13.7	59.2	°	h m	h m	h m	h m	h m	h m	h m
U 10	330 46.7	24.4	55 40.5	10.8	4 48.2	13.6	59.2	N 72	▬▬	12 59	15 30	13 35	13 12	12 52	12 31
R 11	345 46.4	24.4	70 10.3	10.8	4 34.6	13.7	59.2	N 70	▬▬	14 01	15 50	13 21	13 07	12 54	12 40
S 12	0 46.1	S23 24.5	84 40.1	10.8	N 4 20.9	13.8	59.2	68	▬▬	14 36	16 06	13 10	13 03	12 56	12 48
D 13	15 45.8	24.5	99 09.9	10.8	4 07.1	13.7	59.2	66	13 21	15 02	16 19	13 01	12 59	12 57	12 55
A 14	30 45.5	24.6	113 39.7	10.9	3 53.4	13.8	59.2	64	14 03	15 21	16 30	12 53	12 56	12 58	13 01
Y 15	45 45.2	.. 24.6	128 09.6	10.9	3 39.6	13.7	59.2	62	14 32	15 38	16 40	12 46	12 53	12 59	13 06
16	60 44.9	24.7	142 39.5	10.9	3 25.9	13.8	59.2	60	14 53	15 51	16 48	12 40	12 51	13 00	13 10
17	75 44.6	24.7	157 09.4	10.9	3 12.1	13.8	59.2								
18	90 44.3	S23 24.8	171 39.3	10.9	N 2 58.3	13.9	59.2	N 58	15 11	16 03	16 55	12 35	12 49	13 01	13 14
19	105 44.0	24.8	186 09.2	11.0	2 44.4	13.8	59.2	56	15 26	16 13	17 02	12 30	12 47	13 02	13 17
20	120 43.7	24.9	200 39.2	11.0	2 30.6	13.9	59.2	54	15 38	16 22	17 08	12 26	12 45	13 03	13 20
21	135 43.3	.. 24.9	215 09.2	10.9	2 16.7	13.8	59.2	52	15 49	16 30	17 14	12 22	12 43	13 03	13 23
22	150 43.0	25.0	229 39.1	11.0	2 02.9	13.9	59.2	50	15 59	16 38	17 19	12 19	12 42	13 04	13 26
23	165 42.7	25.0	244 09.1	11.0	1 49.0	13.9	59.2	45	16 20	16 54	17 31	12 11	12 39	13 05	13 31
20 00	180 42.4	S23 25.0	258 39.1	11.0	N 1 35.1	13.9	59.2	N 40	16 37	17 07	17 42	12 05	12 36	13 06	13 36
01	195 42.1	25.1	273 09.1	11.1	1 21.2	13.9	59.2	35	16 51	17 19	17 51	11 59	12 34	13 07	13 40
02	210 41.8	25.1	287 39.2	11.0	1 07.3	13.9	59.2	30	17 03	17 30	18 02	11 54	12 31	13 08	13 44
03	225 41.5	.. 25.2	302 09.2	11.0	0 53.4	13.9	59.2	20	17 25	17 49	18 16	11 46	12 28	13 09	13 50
04	240 41.2	25.2	316 39.2	11.1	0 39.5	13.9	59.2	N 10	17 43	18 06	18 32	11 38	12 25	13 10	13 56
05	255 40.9	25.2	331 09.3	11.0	0 25.6	13.9	59.2	0	18 01	18 23	18 49	11 31	12 21	13 11	14 01
06	270 40.6	S23 25.3	345 39.3	11.1	N 0 11.7	13.9	59.2	S 10	18 18	18 41	19 08	11 24	12 18	13 12	14 06
07	285 40.2	25.3	0 09.4	11.0	S 0 02.2	13.9	59.1	20	18 37	19 02	19 31	11 16	12 15	13 13	14 12
08	300 39.9	25.4	14 39.4	11.1	0 16.1	13.9	59.1	30	18 59	19 27	20 00	11 07	12 11	13 15	14 18
F 09	315 39.6	.. 25.4	29 09.5	11.0	0 30.0	13.9	59.1	35	19 12	19 42	20 19	11 02	12 09	13 15	14 22
R 10	330 39.3	25.4	43 39.5	11.1	0 43.9	13.9	59.1	40	19 27	20 00	20 42	10 56	12 06	13 16	14 26
I 11	345 39.0	25.5	58 09.6	11.0	0 57.8	13.9	59.1	45	19 45	20 23	21 13	10 49	12 03	13 17	14 31
D 12	0 38.7	S23 25.5	72 39.6	11.1	S 1 11.7	13.8	59.1	S 50	20 08	20 53	21 58	10 40	12 00	13 18	14 37
A 13	15 38.4	25.5	87 09.7	11.1	1 25.5	13.9	59.1	52	20 19	21 08	22 26	10 37	11 58	13 19	14 39
Y 14	30 38.1	25.6	101 39.8	11.0	1 39.4	13.9	59.1	54	20 31	21 26	23 13	10 32	11 56	13 19	14 42
15	45 37.8	.. 25.6	116 09.8	11.1	1 53.3	13.8	59.1	56	20 45	21 48	////	10 28	11 54	13 20	14 46
16	60 37.5	25.6	130 39.9	11.0	2 07.1	13.8	59.1	58	21 02	22 18	////	10 22	11 52	13 21	14 49
17	75 37.1	25.6	145 09.9	11.0	2 20.9	13.9	59.1	S 60	21 23	23 09	////	10 16	11 49	13 21	14 53

18	90 36.8	S23 25.7	159 39.9	11.1	S 2 34.8	13.8	59.1		SUN			MOON			
19	105 36.5	25.7	174 10.0	11.0	2 48.6	13.7	59.1	Day	Eqn. of Time		Mer.	Mer. Pass.		Age	Phase
20	120 36.2	25.7	188 40.0	11.0	3 02.3	13.8	59.1		00ʰ	12ʰ	Pass.	Upper	Lower		
21	135 35.9	.. 25.8	203 10.0	11.0	3 16.1	13.8	59.1	d	m s	m s	h m	h m	h m	d	%
22	150 35.6	25.8	217 40.0	11.0	3 29.9	13.7	59.1	18	03 49	03 35	11 56	05 19	17 44	22	58
23	165 35.3	25.8	232 10.0	11.0	S 3 43.6	13.7	59.1	19	03 20	03 05	11 57	06 10	18 35	23	47
	SD 16.3	d 0.1	SD 16.1		16.1		16.1	20	02 50	02 35	11 57	06 59	19 24	24	36

© British Crown Copyright 2018. All rights reserved.

UT	ARIES GHA	VENUS −3·9 GHA	Dec	MARS +1·6 GHA	Dec	JUPITER −1·8 GHA	Dec	SATURN +0·6 GHA	Dec	Name	SHA	Dec
21 00	89 16.5	145 44.4	S21 45.4	220 34.3	S17 33.4	174 46.3	S23 15.9	157 30.7	S21 51.8	Acamar	315 14.6	S40 13.8
01	104 19.0	160 43.6	44.8	235 35.0	33.9	189 48.2	15.9	172 32.9	51.8	Achernar	335 23.1	S57 08.5
02	119 21.4	175 42.8	44.1	250 35.8	34.3	204 50.0	15.9	187 35.0	51.7	Acrux	173 04.4	S63 12.2
03	134 23.9	190 42.1 ..	43.4	265 36.6 ..	34.8	219 51.9 ..	15.9	202 37.2 ..	51.7	Adhara	255 08.6	S29 00.0
04	149 26.4	205 41.3	42.8	280 37.4	35.3	234 53.7	15.9	217 39.4	51.6	Aldebaran	290 43.9	N16 32.8
05	164 28.8	220 40.5	42.1	295 38.1	35.7	249 55.5	15.9	232 41.5	51.6			
06	179 31.3	235 39.8	S21 41.4	310 38.9	S17 36.2	264 57.4	S23 15.9	247 43.7	S21 51.5	Alioth	166 16.9	N55 50.9
07	194 33.8	250 39.0	40.8	325 39.7	36.6	279 59.2	15.8	262 45.9	51.5	Alkaid	152 55.6	N49 12.7
S 08	209 36.2	265 38.2	40.1	340 40.5	37.1	295 01.0	15.8	277 48.0	51.5	Alnair	27 38.4	S46 52.1
A 09	224 38.7	280 37.4 ..	39.4	355 41.3 ..	37.6	310 02.9 ..	15.8	292 50.2 ..	51.4	Alnilam	275 41.5	S 1 11.5
T 10	239 41.2	295 36.7	38.8	10 42.0	38.0	325 04.7	15.8	307 52.3	51.4	Alphard	217 51.5	S 8 44.7
U 11	254 43.6	310 35.9	38.1	25 42.8	38.5	340 06.6	15.8	322 54.5	51.4			
R 12	269 46.1	325 35.1	S21 37.4	40 43.6	S17 38.9	355 08.4	S23 15.8	337 56.7	S21 51.3	Alphecca	126 07.5	N26 38.9
D 13	284 48.6	340 34.4	36.8	55 44.4	39.4	10 10.2	15.8	352 58.8	51.3	Alpheratz	357 38.9	N29 12.1
A 14	299 51.0	355 33.6	36.1	70 45.1	39.9	25 12.1	15.7	8 01.0	51.3	Altair	62 04.2	N 8 55.3
Y 15	314 53.5	10 32.8 ..	35.4	85 45.9 ..	40.3	40 13.9 ..	15.7	23 03.2 ..	51.2	Ankaa	353 11.2	S42 12.2
16	329 55.9	25 32.1	34.7	100 46.7	40.8	55 15.8	15.7	38 05.3	51.2	Antares	112 21.1	S26 28.3
17	344 58.4	40 31.3	34.1	115 47.5	41.2	70 17.6	15.7	53 07.5	51.1			
18	0 00.9	55 30.6	S21 33.4	130 48.2	S17 41.7	85 19.4	S23 15.7	68 09.6	S21 51.1	Arcturus	145 51.9	N19 04.8
19	15 03.3	70 29.8	32.7	145 49.0	42.1	100 21.3	15.7	83 11.8	51.1	Atria	107 19.5	S69 03.5
20	30 05.8	85 29.0	32.0	160 49.8	42.6	115 23.1	15.6	98 14.0	51.0	Avior	234 15.7	S59 34.2
21	45 08.3	100 28.3 ..	31.3	175 50.6 ..	43.1	130 25.0 ..	15.6	113 16.1 ..	51.0	Bellatrix	278 26.9	N 6 21.9
22	60 10.7	115 27.5	30.6	190 51.3	43.5	145 26.8	15.6	128 18.3	50.9	Betelgeuse	270 56.1	N 7 24.5
23	75 13.2	130 26.7	30.0	205 52.1	44.0	160 28.6	15.6	143 20.4	50.9			
22 00	90 15.7	145 26.0	S21 29.3	220 52.9	S17 44.4	175 30.5	S23 15.6	158 22.6	S21 50.9	Canopus	263 53.6	S52 42.4
01	105 18.1	160 25.2	28.6	235 53.7	44.9	190 32.3	15.6	173 24.8	50.8	Capella	280 27.4	N46 01.0
02	120 20.6	175 24.5	27.9	250 54.4	45.3	205 34.1	15.6	188 26.9	50.8	Deneb	49 28.8	N45 21.3
03	135 23.0	190 23.7 ..	27.2	265 55.2 ..	45.8	220 36.0 ..	15.5	203 29.1 ..	50.7	Denebola	182 29.1	N14 27.6
04	150 25.5	205 22.9	26.5	280 56.0	46.2	235 37.8	15.5	218 31.3	50.7	Diphda	348 51.3	S17 52.9
05	165 28.0	220 22.2	25.8	295 56.8	46.7	250 39.7	15.5	233 33.4	50.7			
06	180 30.4	235 21.4	S21 25.1	310 57.5	S17 47.1	265 41.5	S23 15.5	248 35.6	S21 50.6	Dubhe	193 46.0	N61 38.4
07	195 32.9	250 20.7	24.5	325 58.3	47.6	280 43.3	15.5	263 37.7	50.6	Elnath	278 06.6	N28 37.3
08	210 35.4	265 19.9	23.8	340 59.1	48.1	295 45.2	15.5	278 39.9	50.6	Eltanin	90 44.6	N51 29.3
S 09	225 37.8	280 19.2 ..	23.1	355 59.8 ..	48.5	310 47.0 ..	15.5	293 42.1 ..	50.5	Enif	33 42.9	N 9 58.0
U 10	240 40.3	295 18.4	22.4	11 00.6	49.0	325 48.9	15.4	308 44.2	50.5	Fomalhaut	15 19.2	S29 31.2
N 11	255 42.8	310 17.7	21.7	26 01.4	49.4	340 50.7	15.4	323 46.4	50.4			
D 12	270 45.2	325 16.9	S21 21.0	41 02.2	S17 49.9	355 52.5	S23 15.4	338 48.5	S21 50.4	Gacrux	171 56.0	S57 13.1
A 13	285 47.7	340 16.1	20.3	56 02.9	50.3	10 54.4	15.4	353 50.7	50.4	Gienah	175 47.7	S17 38.9
Y 14	300 50.2	355 15.4	19.6	71 03.7	50.8	25 56.2	15.4	8 52.9	50.3	Hadar	148 41.9	S60 27.7
15	315 52.6	10 14.6 ..	18.9	86 04.5 ..	51.2	40 58.0 ..	15.4	23 55.0 ..	50.3	Hamal	327 55.5	N23 33.4
16	330 55.1	25 13.9	18.2	101 05.2	51.7	55 59.9	15.3	38 57.2	50.2	Kaus Aust.	83 38.3	S34 22.4
17	345 57.5	40 13.1	17.5	116 06.0	52.1	71 01.7	15.3	53 59.3	50.2			
18	1 00.0	55 12.4	S21 16.8	131 06.8	S17 52.6	86 03.6	S23 15.3	69 01.5	S21 50.2	Kochab	137 20.9	N74 04.3
19	16 02.5	70 11.6	16.1	146 07.6	53.0	101 05.4	15.3	84 03.7	50.1	Markab	13 34.0	N15 18.8
20	31 04.9	85 10.9	15.4	161 08.3	53.5	116 07.2	15.3	99 05.8	50.1	Menkar	314 10.1	N 4 09.9
21	46 07.4	100 10.1 ..	14.7	176 09.1 ..	53.9	131 09.1 ..	15.3	114 08.0 ..	50.0	Menkent	148 02.5	S36 27.7
22	61 09.9	115 09.4	13.9	191 09.9	54.4	146 10.9	15.2	129 10.1	50.0	Miaplacidus	221 38.2	S69 47.7
23	76 12.3	130 08.7	13.2	206 10.6	54.8	161 12.7	15.2	144 12.3	50.0			
23 00	91 14.8	145 07.9	S21 12.5	221 11.4	S17 55.3	176 14.6	S23 15.2	159 14.5	S21 49.9	Mirfak	308 33.5	N49 55.9
01	106 17.3	160 07.2	11.8	236 12.2	55.7	191 16.4	15.2	174 16.6	49.9	Nunki	75 53.2	S26 16.2
02	121 19.7	175 06.4	11.1	251 12.9	56.2	206 18.3	15.2	189 18.8	49.8	Peacock	53 12.7	S56 40.4
03	136 22.2	190 05.7 ..	10.4	266 13.7 ..	56.6	221 20.1 ..	15.2	204 20.9 ..	49.8	Pollux	243 21.9	N27 58.5
04	151 24.7	205 04.9	09.7	281 14.5	57.1	236 21.9	15.2	219 23.1	49.8	Procyon	244 54.8	N 5 10.3
05	166 27.1	220 04.2	09.0	296 15.3	57.5	251 23.8	15.1	234 25.3	49.7			
06	181 29.6	235 03.4	S21 08.2	311 16.0	S17 58.0	266 25.6	S23 15.1	249 27.4	S21 49.7	Rasalhague	96 02.7	N12 32.8
07	196 32.0	250 02.7	07.5	326 16.8	58.4	281 27.5	15.1	264 29.6	49.6	Regulus	207 38.6	N11 52.2
08	211 34.5	265 02.0	06.8	341 17.6	58.9	296 29.3	15.1	279 31.7	49.6	Rigel	281 07.4	S 8 10.9
M 09	226 37.0	280 01.2 ..	06.1	356 18.3 ..	59.3	311 31.1 ..	15.1	294 33.9 ..	49.6	Rigil Kent.	139 46.1	S60 54.6
O 10	241 39.4	295 00.5	05.4	11 19.1	17 59.8	326 33.0	15.1	309 36.1	49.5	Sabik	102 07.8	S15 44.8
N 11	256 41.9	309 59.7	04.6	26 19.9	18 00.2	341 34.8	15.0	324 38.2	49.5			
D 12	271 44.4	324 59.0	S21 03.9	41 20.6	S18 00.7	356 36.6	S23 15.0	339 40.4	S21 49.4	Schedar	349 35.3	N56 39.0
A 13	286 46.8	339 58.3	03.2	56 21.4	01.1	11 38.5	15.0	354 42.5	49.4	Shaula	96 16.3	S37 06.9
Y 14	301 49.3	354 57.5	02.5	71 22.2	01.5	26 40.3	15.0	9 44.7	49.4	Sirius	258 29.4	S16 44.7
15	316 51.8	9 56.8 ..	01.7	86 22.9 ..	02.0	41 42.2 ..	15.0	24 46.9 ..	49.3	Spica	158 26.7	S11 15.7
16	331 54.2	24 56.0	01.0	101 23.7	02.4	56 44.0	15.0	39 49.0	49.3	Suhail	222 48.9	S43 30.6
17	346 56.7	39 55.3	21 00.3	116 24.5	02.9	71 45.8	14.9	54 51.2	49.2			
18	1 59.2	54 54.6	S20 59.6	131 25.2	S18 03.3	86 47.7	S23 14.9	69 53.3	S21 49.2	Vega	80 36.4	N38 48.2
19	17 01.6	69 53.8	58.8	146 26.0	03.8	101 49.5	14.9	84 55.5	49.2	Zuben'ubi	137 00.7	S16 07.2
20	32 04.1	84 53.1	58.1	161 26.8	04.2	116 51.3	14.9	99 57.7	49.1			
21	47 06.5	99 52.4 ..	57.4	176 27.5 ..	04.7	131 53.2 ..	14.9	114 59.8 ..	49.1		SHA	Mer. Pass.
22	62 09.0	114 51.6	56.6	191 28.3	05.1	146 55.0	14.9	130 02.0	49.1	Venus	55 10.3	14 19
23	77 11.5	129 50.9	55.9	206 29.1	05.6	161 56.9	14.8	145 04.1	49.0	Mars	130 37.2	9 16
Mer. Pass. 17 56.0		v −0.8	d 0.7	v 0.8	d 0.5	v 1.8	d 0.0	v 2.2	d 0.0	Jupiter	85 14.8	12 16
										Saturn	68 07.0	13 25

© British Crown Copyright 2018. All rights reserved.

UT		SUN		MOON				
		GHA	Dec	GHA	v	Dec	d	HP
d h		° ′	° ′	° ′	′	° ′	′	′
21 00		180 35.0	S23 25.8	246 40.0	10.9	S 3 57.3	13.7	59.1
01		195 34.7	25.9	261 09.9	11.0	4 11.0	13.6	59.0
02		210 34.3	25.9	275 39.9	10.9	4 24.6	13.7	59.0
03		225 34.0	.. 25.9	290 09.8	11.0	4 38.3	13.6	59.0
04		240 33.7	25.9	304 39.8	10.9	4 51.9	13.5	59.0
05		255 33.4	25.9	319 09.7	10.9	5 05.4	13.6	59.0
06		270 33.1	S23 26.0	333 39.6	10.8	S 5 19.0	13.5	59.0
07		285 32.8	26.0	348 09.4	10.9	5 32.5	13.5	59.0
S 08		300 32.5	26.0	2 39.3	10.8	5 46.0	13.4	59.0
A 09		315 32.2	.. 26.0	17 09.1	10.8	5 59.4	13.4	59.0
T 10		330 31.9	26.0	31 38.9	10.8	6 12.8	13.4	59.0
U 11		345 31.5	26.0	46 08.7	10.8	6 26.2	13.3	59.0
R 12		0 31.2	S23 26.1	60 38.5	10.7	S 6 39.5	13.3	59.0
D 13		15 30.9	26.1	75 08.2	10.8	6 52.8	13.3	59.0
A 14		30 30.6	26.1	89 38.0	10.7	7 06.1	13.2	58.9
Y 15		45 30.3	.. 26.1	104 07.7	10.7	7 19.3	13.2	58.9
16		60 30.0	26.1	118 37.4	10.6	7 32.5	13.1	58.9
17		75 29.7	26.1	133 07.0	10.6	7 45.6	13.1	58.9
18		90 29.4	S23 26.1	147 36.6	10.6	S 7 58.7	13.1	58.9
19		105 29.1	26.1	162 06.2	10.6	8 11.8	13.0	58.9
20		120 28.7	26.1	176 35.8	10.5	8 24.8	12.9	58.9
21		135 28.4	.. 26.1	191 05.3	10.6	8 37.7	12.9	58.9
22		150 28.1	26.1	205 34.9	10.4	8 50.6	12.9	58.9
23		165 27.8	26.1	220 04.3	10.5	9 03.5	12.7	58.9
22 00		180 27.5	S23 26.2	234 33.8	10.4	S 9 16.2	12.8	58.9
01		195 27.2	26.2	249 03.2	10.4	9 29.0	12.7	58.8
02		210 26.9	26.2	263 32.6	10.4	9 41.7	12.6	58.8
03		225 26.6	.. 26.2	278 02.0	10.3	9 54.3	12.6	58.8
04		240 26.3	26.2	292 31.3	10.3	10 06.9	12.5	58.8
05		255 25.9	26.2	307 00.6	10.2	10 19.4	12.4	58.8
06		270 25.6	S23 26.2	321 29.8	10.2	S10 31.8	12.4	58.8
07		285 25.3	26.2	335 59.0	10.2	10 44.2	12.3	58.8
S 08		300 25.0	26.2	350 28.2	10.2	10 56.5	12.3	58.8
U 09		315 24.7	.. 26.2	4 57.4	10.1	11 08.8	12.2	58.8
N 10		330 24.4	26.1	19 26.5	10.1	11 21.0	12.1	58.7
D 11		345 24.1	26.1	33 55.6	10.0	11 33.1	12.1	58.7
A 12		0 23.8	S23 26.1	48 24.6	10.0	S11 45.2	12.0	58.7
Y 13		15 23.5	26.1	62 53.6	10.0	11 57.2	11.9	58.7
14		30 23.1	26.1	77 22.6	9.9	12 09.1	11.9	58.7
15		45 22.8	.. 26.1	91 51.5	9.9	12 21.0	11.8	58.7
16		60 22.5	26.1	106 20.4	9.8	12 32.8	11.7	58.7
17		75 22.2	26.1	120 49.2	9.8	12 44.5	11.6	58.7
18		90 21.9	S23 26.1	135 18.0	9.8	S12 56.1	11.6	58.6
19		105 21.6	26.1	149 46.8	9.7	13 07.7	11.4	58.6
20		120 21.3	26.1	164 15.5	9.7	13 19.1	11.4	58.6
21		135 21.0	.. 26.0	178 44.2	9.6	13 30.5	11.4	58.6
22		150 20.6	26.0	193 12.8	9.6	13 41.9	11.2	58.6
23		165 20.3	26.0	207 41.4	9.6	13 53.1	11.2	58.6
23 00		180 20.0	S23 26.0	222 10.0	9.5	S14 04.3	11.0	58.6
01		195 19.7	26.0	236 38.5	9.5	14 15.3	11.0	58.6
02		210 19.4	26.0	251 07.0	9.4	14 26.3	10.9	58.5
03		225 19.1	.. 26.0	265 35.4	9.4	14 37.2	10.9	58.5
04		240 18.8	25.9	280 03.8	9.4	14 48.1	10.7	58.5
05		255 18.5	25.9	294 32.2	9.3	14 58.8	10.6	58.5
06		270 18.1	S23 25.9	309 00.5	9.2	S15 09.4	10.6	58.5
07		285 17.8	25.9	323 28.7	9.2	15 20.0	10.4	58.5
M 08		300 17.5	25.8	337 56.9	9.2	15 30.4	10.4	58.5
O 09		315 17.2	.. 25.8	352 25.1	9.2	15 40.8	10.3	58.4
N 10		330 16.9	25.8	6 53.3	9.0	15 51.1	10.2	58.4
11		345 16.6	25.8	21 21.3	9.1	16 01.3	10.0	58.4
D 12		0 16.3	S23 25.8	35 49.4	9.0	S16 11.3	10.0	58.4
A 13		15 16.0	25.7	50 17.4	9.0	16 21.3	9.9	58.4
Y 14		30 15.7	25.7	64 45.4	8.9	16 31.2	9.8	58.4
15		45 15.3	.. 25.7	79 13.3	8.9	16 41.0	9.7	58.3
16		60 15.0	25.6	93 41.2	8.8	16 50.7	9.6	58.3
17		75 14.7	25.6	108 09.0	8.8	17 00.3	9.5	58.3
18		90 14.4	S23 25.6	122 36.8	8.8	S17 09.8	9.4	58.3
19		105 14.1	25.5	137 04.6	8.7	17 19.2	9.2	58.3
20		120 13.8	25.5	151 32.3	8.7	17 28.4	9.2	58.2
21		135 13.5	.. 25.5	166 00.0	8.6	17 37.6	9.1	58.2
22		150 13.2	25.5	180 27.6	8.6	17 46.7	8.9	58.2
23		165 12.8	25.4	194 55.2	8.5	S17 55.6	8.9	58.2
		SD 16.3	d 0.0	SD 16.1		16.0		15.9

Lat.	Twilight		Sunrise	Moonrise			
	Naut.	Civil		21	22	23	24
°	h m	h m	h m	h m	h m	h m	h m
N 72	08 26	10 58	■	02 37	04 50	07 22	■
N 70	08 06	09 55	■	02 30	04 32	06 43	09 31
68	07 50	09 19	■	02 25	04 18	06 16	08 23
66	07 37	08 54	10 35	02 20	04 06	05 55	07 47
64	07 26	08 34	09 52	02 16	03 57	05 39	07 21
62	07 16	08 18	09 24	02 13	03 49	05 26	07 01
60	07 08	08 04	09 02	02 10	03 42	05 15	06 45
N 58	07 00	07 53	08 45	02 07	03 36	05 05	06 32
56	06 53	07 42	08 30	02 05	03 31	04 56	06 20
54	06 47	07 33	08 17	02 03	03 26	04 49	06 10
52	06 41	07 25	08 06	02 01	03 22	04 42	06 01
50	06 36	07 18	07 56	01 59	03 18	04 36	05 53
45	06 24	07 02	07 35	01 56	03 09	04 23	05 35
N 40	06 14	06 48	07 19	01 53	03 02	04 12	05 21
35	06 04	06 36	07 04	01 50	02 57	04 03	05 10
30	05 56	06 26	06 52	01 48	02 51	03 55	04 59
20	05 39	06 07	06 31	01 44	02 42	03 42	04 42
N 10	05 23	05 49	06 12	01 40	02 35	03 30	04 26
0	05 06	05 32	05 55	01 37	02 27	03 19	04 12
S 10	04 47	05 14	05 37	01 34	02 20	03 08	03 58
20	04 24	04 53	05 18	01 31	02 13	02 56	03 43
30	03 55	04 28	04 56	01 27	02 04	02 43	03 26
35	03 36	04 13	04 43	01 25	01 59	02 36	03 16
40	03 13	03 55	04 28	01 23	01 53	02 27	03 05
45	02 42	03 32	04 10	01 20	01 47	02 17	02 51
S 50	01 57	03 02	03 47	01 17	01 39	02 05	02 35
52	01 29	02 47	03 36	01 15	01 36	02 00	02 28
54	00 42	02 29	03 24	01 13	01 32	01 53	02 20
56	////	02 07	03 10	01 12	01 28	01 47	02 10
58	////	01 37	02 53	01 10	01 23	01 39	02 00
S 60	////	00 46	02 32	01 07	01 18	01 31	01 48

Lat.	Sunset	Twilight		Moonset			
		Civil	Naut.	21	22	23	24
°	h m	h m	h m	h m	h m	h m	h m
N 72	■	12 59	15 31	12 31	12 04	11 21	■
N 70	■	14 02	15 51	12 40	12 24	12 02	11 06
68	■	14 37	16 07	12 48	12 40	12 30	12 15
66	13 22	15 03	16 20	12 55	12 53	12 52	12 52
64	14 04	15 23	16 31	13 01	13 04	13 09	13 18
62	14 33	15 39	16 41	13 06	13 13	13 24	13 39
60	14 55	15 52	16 49	13 10	13 21	13 36	13 56
N 58	15 12	16 04	16 57	13 14	13 28	13 46	14 10
56	15 27	16 14	17 04	13 17	13 35	13 55	14 22
54	15 40	16 23	17 10	13 20	13 40	14 04	14 33
52	15 51	16 32	17 15	13 23	13 45	14 11	14 42
50	16 01	16 39	17 21	13 26	13 50	14 18	14 51
45	16 21	16 55	17 33	13 31	14 00	14 32	15 09
N 40	16 38	17 09	17 43	13 36	14 08	14 44	15 24
35	16 52	17 21	17 52	13 40	14 15	14 54	15 36
30	17 05	17 31	18 01	13 44	14 22	15 03	15 47
20	17 26	17 50	18 18	13 50	14 33	15 18	16 06
N 10	17 45	18 08	18 34	13 56	14 43	15 31	16 23
0	18 02	18 25	18 51	14 01	14 52	15 44	16 38
S 10	18 20	18 43	19 10	14 06	15 01	15 57	16 54
20	18 39	19 03	19 33	14 12	15 11	16 10	17 10
30	19 01	19 28	20 02	14 18	15 22	16 26	17 29
35	19 14	19 44	20 20	14 22	15 28	16 35	17 41
40	19 29	20 02	20 44	14 26	15 36	16 45	17 53
45	19 47	20 25	21 14	14 31	15 44	16 58	18 09
S 50	20 10	20 54	22 00	14 37	15 55	17 13	18 27
52	20 21	21 09	22 28	14 39	16 00	17 20	18 36
54	20 33	21 27	23 15	14 42	16 05	17 27	18 46
56	20 47	21 50	////	14 46	16 11	17 36	18 57
58	21 04	22 20	////	14 49	16 18	17 46	19 10
S 60	21 25	23 11	////	14 53	16 26	17 57	19 26

	SUN			MOON			
Day	Eqn. of Time		Mer.	Mer. Pass.		Age	Phase
	00ʰ	12ʰ	Pass.	Upper	Lower		
d	m s	m s	h m	h m	h m	d	%
21	02 21	02 06	11 58	07 49	20 14	25	25
22	01 51	01 36	11 58	08 39	21 05	26	16
23	01 21	01 06	11 59	09 31	21 58	27	9

© British Crown Copyright 2018. All rights reserved.

UT	ARIES GHA	VENUS −3.9 GHA	Dec	MARS +1.6 GHA	Dec	JUPITER −1.8 GHA	Dec	SATURN +0.6 GHA	Dec	STARS Name	SHA	Dec
24 00	92 13.9	144 50.2	S20 55.2	221 29.8	S18 06.0	176 58.7	S23 14.8	160 06.3	S21 49.0	Acamar	315 14.6	S40 13.8
01	107 16.4	159 49.4	54.4	236 30.6	06.4	192 00.5	14.8	175 08.5	48.9	Achernar	335 23.2	S57 08.5
02	122 18.9	174 48.7	53.7	251 31.4	06.9	207 02.4	14.8	190 10.6	48.9	Acrux	173 04.4	S63 12.2
03	137 21.3	189 48.0 ..	52.9	266 32.1 ..	07.3	222 04.2 ..	14.8	205 12.8 ..	48.9	Adhara	255 08.6	S29 00.0
04	152 23.8	204 47.2	52.2	281 32.9	07.8	237 06.0	14.8	220 14.9	48.8	Aldebaran	290 43.9	N16 32.8
05	167 26.3	219 46.5	51.5	296 33.6	08.2	252 07.9	14.7	235 17.1	48.8			
06	182 28.7	234 45.8	S20 50.7	311 34.4	S18 08.7	267 09.7	S23 14.7	250 19.2	S21 48.7	Alioth	166 16.8	N55 50.9
07	197 31.2	249 45.1	50.0	326 35.2	09.1	282 11.6	14.7	265 21.4	48.7	Alkaid	152 55.6	N49 12.7
T 08	212 33.6	264 44.3	49.2	341 35.9	09.5	297 13.4	14.7	280 23.6	48.7	Alnair	27 38.4	S46 52.1
U 09	227 36.1	279 43.6 ..	48.5	356 36.7 ..	10.0	312 15.2 ..	14.7	295 25.7 ..	48.6	Alnilam	275 41.5	S 1 11.5
E 10	242 38.6	294 42.9	47.8	11 37.5	10.4	327 17.1	14.6	310 27.9	48.6	Alphard	217 51.5	S 8 44.7
S 11	257 41.0	309 42.1	47.0	26 38.2	10.9	342 18.9	14.6	325 30.0	48.5			
D 12	272 43.5	324 41.4	S20 46.3	41 39.0	S18 11.3	357 20.8	S23 14.6	340 32.2	S21 48.5	Alphecca	126 07.5	N26 38.9
A 13	287 46.0	339 40.7	45.5	56 39.8	11.7	12 22.6	14.6	355 34.4	48.5	Alpheratz	357 38.9	N29 12.1
Y 14	302 48.4	354 40.0	44.8	71 40.5	12.2	27 24.4	14.6	10 36.5	48.4	Altair	62 04.2	N 8 55.3
15	317 50.9	9 39.2 ..	44.0	86 41.3 ..	12.6	42 26.3 ..	14.6	25 38.7 ..	48.4	Ankaa	353 11.2	S42 12.2
16	332 53.4	24 38.5	43.3	101 42.0	13.1	57 28.1	14.5	40 40.8	48.3	Antares	112 21.1	S26 28.3
17	347 55.8	39 37.8	42.5	116 42.8	13.5	72 29.9	14.5	55 43.0	48.3			
18	2 58.3	54 37.1	S20 41.8	131 43.6	S18 13.9	87 31.8	S23 14.5	70 45.1	S21 48.3	Arcturus	145 51.8	N19 04.8
19	18 00.8	69 36.4	41.0	146 44.3	14.4	102 33.6	14.5	85 47.3	48.2	Atria	107 19.5	S69 03.5
20	33 03.2	84 35.6	40.2	161 45.1	14.8	117 35.5	14.5	100 49.5	48.2	Avior	234 15.7	S59 34.3
21	48 05.7	99 34.9 ..	39.5	176 45.9 ..	15.3	132 37.3 ..	14.5	115 51.6 ..	48.1	Bellatrix	278 26.9	N 6 21.9
22	63 08.1	114 34.2	38.7	191 46.6	15.7	147 39.1	14.4	130 53.8	48.1	Betelgeuse	270 56.1	N 7 24.5
23	78 10.6	129 33.5	38.0	206 47.4	16.1	162 41.0	14.4	145 55.9	48.1			
25 00	93 13.1	144 32.8	S20 37.2	221 48.1	S18 16.6	177 42.8	S23 14.4	160 58.1	S21 48.0	Canopus	263 53.6	S52 42.4
01	108 15.5	159 32.0	36.4	236 48.9	17.0	192 44.6	14.4	176 00.3	48.0	Capella	280 27.4	N46 01.0
02	123 18.0	174 31.3	35.7	251 49.7	17.5	207 46.5	14.4	191 02.4	47.9	Deneb	49 28.8	N45 21.2
03	138 20.5	189 30.6 ..	34.9	266 50.4 ..	17.9	222 48.3 ..	14.3	206 04.6 ..	47.9	Denebola	182 29.1	N14 27.6
04	153 22.9	204 29.9	34.2	281 51.2	18.3	237 50.2	14.3	221 06.7	47.9	Diphda	348 51.3	S17 52.9
05	168 25.4	219 29.2	33.4	296 51.9	18.8	252 52.0	14.3	236 08.9	47.8			
06	183 27.9	234 28.5	S20 32.6	311 52.7	S18 19.2	267 53.8	S23 14.3	251 11.0	S21 47.8	Dubhe	193 46.0	N61 38.4
W 07	198 30.3	249 27.8	31.9	326 53.5	19.6	282 55.7	14.3	266 13.2	47.7	Elnath	278 06.6	N28 37.3
E 08	213 32.8	264 27.0	31.1	341 54.2	20.1	297 57.5	14.3	281 15.4	47.7	Eltanin	90 44.6	N51 29.2
D 09	228 35.3	279 26.3 ..	30.3	356 55.0 ..	20.5	312 59.3 ..	14.2	296 17.5 ..	47.6	Enif	33 42.9	N 9 58.0
N 10	243 37.7	294 25.6	29.6	11 55.7	21.0	328 01.2	14.2	311 19.7	47.6	Fomalhaut	15 19.2	S29 31.2
E 11	258 40.2	309 24.9	28.8	26 56.5	21.4	343 03.0	14.2	326 21.8	47.6			
S 12	273 42.6	324 24.2	S20 28.0	41 57.3	S18 21.8	358 04.9	S23 14.2	341 24.0	S21 47.5	Gacrux	171 56.0	S57 13.1
D 13	288 45.1	339 23.5	27.2	56 58.0	22.3	13 06.7	14.2	356 26.1	47.5	Gienah	175 47.7	S17 39.0
A 14	303 47.6	354 22.8	26.5	71 58.8	22.7	28 08.5	14.1	11 28.3	47.4	Hadar	148 41.9	S60 27.7
Y 15	318 50.0	9 22.1 ..	25.7	86 59.5 ..	23.1	43 10.4 ..	14.1	26 30.5 ..	47.4	Hamal	327 55.5	N23 33.4
16	333 52.5	24 21.4	24.9	102 00.3	23.6	58 12.2	14.1	41 32.6	47.4	Kaus Aust.	83 38.3	S34 22.4
17	348 55.0	39 20.6	24.1	117 01.0	24.0	73 14.0	14.1	56 34.8	47.3			
18	3 57.4	54 19.9	S20 23.4	132 01.8	S18 24.4	88 15.9	S23 14.1	71 36.9	S21 47.3	Kochab	137 20.9	N74 04.3
19	18 59.9	69 19.2	22.6	147 02.6	24.9	103 17.7	14.0	86 39.1	47.2	Markab	13 34.0	N15 18.8
20	34 02.4	84 18.5	21.8	162 03.3	25.3	118 19.6	14.0	101 41.3	47.2	Menkar	314 10.1	N 4 09.9
21	49 04.8	99 17.8 ..	21.0	177 04.1 ..	25.7	133 21.4 ..	14.0	116 43.4 ..	47.2	Menkent	148 02.5	S36 27.8
22	64 07.3	114 17.1	20.2	192 04.8	26.2	148 23.2	14.0	131 45.6	47.1	Miaplacidus	221 38.1	S69 47.7
23	79 09.8	129 16.4	19.5	207 05.6	26.6	163 25.1	14.0	146 47.7	47.1			
26 00	94 12.2	144 15.7	S20 18.7	222 06.3	S18 27.0	178 26.9	S23 14.0	161 49.9	S21 47.0	Mirfak	308 33.5	N49 55.9
01	109 14.7	159 15.0	17.9	237 07.1	27.5	193 28.7	13.9	176 52.0	47.0	Nunki	75 53.2	S26 16.2
02	124 17.1	174 14.3	17.1	252 07.9	27.9	208 30.6	13.9	191 54.2	47.0	Peacock	53 12.7	S56 40.4
03	139 19.6	189 13.6 ..	16.3	267 08.6 ..	28.3	223 32.4 ..	13.9	206 56.4 ..	46.9	Pollux	243 21.9	N27 58.5
04	154 22.1	204 12.9	15.5	282 09.4	28.8	238 34.2	13.9	221 58.5	46.9	Procyon	244 54.7	N 5 10.3
05	169 24.5	219 12.2	14.7	297 10.1	29.2	253 36.1	13.9	237 00.7	46.8			
06	184 27.0	234 11.5	S20 13.9	312 10.9	S18 29.6	268 37.9	S23 13.8	252 02.8	S21 46.8	Rasalhague	96 02.6	N12 32.8
07	199 29.5	249 10.8	13.2	327 11.6	30.1	283 39.8	13.8	267 05.0	46.8	Regulus	207 38.6	N11 52.1
T 08	214 31.9	264 10.1	12.4	342 12.4	30.5	298 41.6	13.8	282 07.1	46.7	Rigel	281 07.4	S 8 10.9
H 09	229 34.4	279 09.4 ..	11.6	357 13.1 ..	30.9	313 43.4 ..	13.8	297 09.3 ..	46.7	Rigil Kent.	139 46.1	S60 54.6
U 10	244 36.9	294 08.7	10.8	12 13.9	31.3	328 45.3	13.8	312 11.4	46.6	Sabik	102 07.8	S15 44.8
R 11	259 39.3	309 08.0	10.0	27 14.7	31.8	343 47.1	13.7	327 13.6	46.6			
S 12	274 41.8	324 07.3	S20 09.2	42 15.4	S18 32.2	358 48.9	S23 13.7	342 15.8	S21 46.6	Schedar	349 35.4	N56 39.0
D 13	289 44.3	339 06.6	08.4	57 16.2	32.6	13 50.8	13.7	357 17.9	46.5	Shaula	96 16.3	S37 06.9
A 14	304 46.7	354 05.9	07.6	72 16.9	33.1	28 52.6	13.7	12 20.1	46.5	Sirius	258 29.4	S16 44.7
Y 15	319 49.2	9 05.2 ..	06.8	87 17.7 ..	33.5	43 54.5 ..	13.7	27 22.2 ..	46.4	Spica	158 26.6	S11 15.7
16	334 51.6	24 04.5	06.0	102 18.4	33.9	58 56.3	13.6	42 24.4	46.4	Suhail	222 48.8	S43 30.6
17	349 54.1	39 03.8	05.2	117 19.2	34.3	73 58.1	13.6	57 26.5	46.4			
18	4 56.6	54 03.1	S20 04.4	132 19.9	S18 34.8	89 00.0	S23 13.6	72 28.7	S21 46.3	Vega	80 36.4	N38 48.2
19	19 59.0	69 02.5	03.6	147 20.7	35.2	104 01.8	13.6	87 30.9	46.3	Zuben'ubi	137 00.7	S16 07.3
20	35 01.5	84 01.8	02.8	162 21.4	35.6	119 03.6	13.6	102 33.0	46.2		SHA	Mer.Pass.
21	50 04.0	99 01.1 ..	02.0	177 22.2 ..	36.1	134 05.5 ..	13.5	117 35.2 ..	46.2			h m
22	65 06.4	114 00.4	01.2	192 22.9	36.5	149 07.3	13.5	132 37.3	46.1	Venus	51 19.7	14 23
23	80 08.9	128 59.7	00.4	207 23.7	36.9	164 09.2	13.5	147 39.5	46.1	Mars	128 35.1	9 12
	h m									Jupiter	84 29.7	12 08
Mer.Pass. 17 44.2	v −0.7 d 0.8			v 0.8 d 0.4		v 1.8 d 0.0		v 2.2 d 0.0		Saturn	67 45.0	13 14

© British Crown Copyright 2018. All rights reserved.

UT	SUN GHA	SUN Dec	MOON GHA	v	MOON Dec	d	HP
d h	° '	° '	° '	'	° '	'	'
24 00	180 12.5	S23 25.4	209 22.7	8.6	S18 04.5	8.7	58.2
01	195 12.2	25.3	223 50.3	8.4	18 13.2	8.7	58.2
02	210 11.9	25.3	238 17.7	8.5	18 21.9	8.5	58.2
03	225 11.6 ..	25.3	252 45.2	8.4	18 30.4	8.4	58.1
04	240 11.3	25.2	267 12.6	8.3	18 38.8	8.3	58.1
05	255 11.0	25.2	281 39.9	8.3	18 47.1	8.2	58.1
06	270 10.7	S23 25.2	296 07.2	8.3	S18 55.3	8.0	58.1
07	285 10.3	25.1	310 34.5	8.3	19 03.3	8.0	58.1
T 08	300 10.0	25.1	325 01.8	8.2	19 11.3	7.8	58.0
U 09	315 09.7 ..	25.0	339 29.0	8.2	19 19.1	7.7	58.0
E 10	330 09.4	25.0	353 56.2	8.1	19 26.8	7.6	58.0
S 11	345 09.1	24.9	8 23.3	8.1	19 34.4	7.5	58.0
D 12	0 08.8	S23 24.9	22 50.4	8.1	S19 41.9	7.4	58.0
A 13	15 08.5	24.8	37 17.5	8.1	19 49.3	7.2	58.0
Y 14	30 08.2	24.8	51 44.6	8.0	19 56.5	7.1	57.9
15	45 07.9 ..	24.8	66 11.6	8.0	20 03.6	7.0	57.9
16	60 07.5	24.7	80 38.6	7.9	20 10.6	6.9	57.9
17	75 07.2	24.7	95 05.5	7.9	20 17.5	6.7	57.9
18	90 06.9	S23 24.6	109 32.4	7.9	S20 24.2	6.7	57.9
19	105 06.6	24.6	123 59.3	7.9	20 30.9	6.5	57.8
20	120 06.3	24.5	138 26.2	7.8	20 37.4	6.3	57.8
21	135 06.0 ..	24.5	152 53.0	7.8	20 43.7	6.3	57.8
22	150 05.7	24.4	167 19.8	7.8	20 50.0	6.1	57.8
23	165 05.4	24.3	181 46.6	7.8	20 56.1	6.0	57.8
25 00	180 05.0	S23 24.3	196 13.4	7.8	S21 02.1	5.8	57.7
01	195 04.7	24.2	210 40.2	7.7	21 07.9	5.8	57.7
02	210 04.4	24.2	225 06.9	7.7	21 13.7	5.6	57.7
03	225 04.1 ..	24.1	239 33.6	7.7	21 19.3	5.4	57.7
04	240 03.8	24.1	254 00.3	7.6	21 24.7	5.4	57.6
05	255 03.5	24.0	268 26.9	7.7	21 30.1	5.2	57.6
06	270 03.2	S23 23.9	282 53.6	7.6	S21 35.3	5.1	57.6
W 07	285 02.9	23.9	297 20.2	7.6	21 40.4	4.9	57.6
E 08	300 02.6	23.8	311 46.8	7.6	21 45.3	4.9	57.6
D 09	315 02.2 ..	23.8	326 13.4	7.6	21 50.2	4.6	57.5
N 10	330 01.9	23.7	340 40.0	7.6	21 54.8	4.6	57.5
E 11	345 01.6	23.6	355 06.6	7.5	21 59.4	4.4	57.5
S 12	0 01.3	S23 23.6	9 33.1	7.6	S22 03.8	4.3	57.5
D 13	15 01.0	23.5	23 59.7	7.5	22 08.1	4.1	57.4
A 14	30 00.7	23.4	38 26.2	7.6	22 12.2	4.1	57.4
Y 15	45 00.4 ..	23.4	52 52.8	7.5	22 16.3	3.8	57.4
16	60 00.1	23.3	67 19.3	7.5	22 20.1	3.8	57.4
17	74 59.8	23.2	81 45.8	7.5	22 23.9	3.6	57.4
18	89 59.4	S23 23.2	96 12.3	7.6	S22 27.5	3.5	57.3
19	104 59.1	23.1	110 38.9	7.5	22 31.0	3.3	57.3
20	119 58.8	23.0	125 05.4	7.5	22 34.3	3.2	57.3
21	134 58.5 ..	22.9	139 31.9	7.5	22 37.5	3.1	57.3
22	149 58.2	22.9	153 58.4	7.5	22 40.6	2.9	57.2
23	164 57.9	22.8	168 24.9	7.6	S22 43.5	2.8	57.2
26 00	179 57.6	S23 22.7					
01	194 57.3	22.7					
02	209 57.0	22.6	An annular eclipse of				
03	224 56.6 ..	22.5	the Sun occurs on this				
04	239 56.3	22.4	date. See page 5.				
05	254 56.0	22.3					
06	269 55.7	S23 22.3	269 30.8	7.6	S23 00.2	1.9	57.1
07	284 55.4	22.2	283 57.4	7.6	23 02.1	1.7	57.0
T 08	299 55.1	22.1	298 24.0	7.6	23 03.8	1.5	57.0
H 09	314 54.8 ..	22.0	312 50.6	7.7	23 05.3	1.5	57.0
U 10	329 54.5	21.9	327 17.3	7.6	23 06.8	1.3	57.0
R 11	344 54.2	21.9	341 43.9	7.7	23 08.1	1.1	56.9
S 12	359 53.8	S23 21.8	356 10.6	7.7	S23 09.2	1.1	56.9
D 13	14 53.5	21.7	10 37.3	7.7	23 10.3	0.8	56.9
A 14	29 53.2	21.6	25 04.0	7.8	23 11.1	0.8	56.9
Y 15	44 52.9 ..	21.5	39 30.8	7.8	23 11.9	0.6	56.8
16	59 52.6	21.4	53 57.6	7.8	23 12.5	0.5	56.8
17	74 52.3	21.3	68 24.4	7.8	23 13.0	0.4	56.8
18	89 52.0	S23 21.2	82 51.2	7.8	S23 13.4	0.2	56.8
19	104 51.7	21.2	97 18.0	7.9	23 13.6	0.1	56.7
20	119 51.4	21.1	111 44.9	8.0	23 13.7	0.1	56.7
21	134 51.1 ..	21.0	126 11.9	7.9	23 13.8	0.2	56.7
22	149 50.7	20.9	140 38.8	8.0	23 13.6	0.3	56.7
23	164 50.4	20.8	155 05.8	8.0	S23 13.1	0.4	56.6
	SD 16.3	d 0.1	SD 15.8		15.7		15.5

Lat.	Twilight Naut.	Twilight Civil	Sunrise	Moonrise 24	25	26	27
°	h m	h m	h m	h m	h m	h m	h m
N 72	08 27	10 57	■■	■■	■■	■■	■■
N 70	08 07	09 55	■■	09 31	■■	■■	■■
68	07 51	09 20	■■	08 23	■■	■■	■■
66	07 38	08 55	10 35	07 47	09 38	11 13	12 00
64	07 27	08 35	09 53	07 21	08 58	10 18	11 10
62	07 17	08 19	09 25	07 01	08 31	09 46	10 39
60	07 09	08 06	09 03	06 45	08 10	09 22	10 15
N 58	07 01	07 54	08 46	06 32	07 53	09 02	09 56
56	06 54	07 44	08 31	06 20	07 38	08 46	09 40
54	06 48	07 35	08 18	06 10	07 26	08 32	09 27
52	06 43	07 26	08 07	06 01	07 15	08 20	09 15
50	06 37	07 19	07 57	05 53	07 05	08 10	09 04
45	06 26	07 03	07 37	05 35	06 45	07 48	08 42
N 40	06 15	06 49	07 20	05 21	06 28	07 30	08 25
35	06 06	06 38	07 06	05 10	06 14	07 15	08 10
30	05 57	06 27	06 53	04 59	06 02	07 02	07 57
20	05 41	06 08	06 32	04 42	05 41	06 40	07 35
N 10	05 24	05 51	06 14	04 26	05 24	06 20	07 15
0	05 07	05 34	05 56	04 12	05 07	06 03	06 58
S 10	04 48	05 15	05 39	03 58	04 51	05 45	06 40
20	04 26	04 55	05 20	03 43	04 33	05 26	06 21
30	03 57	04 30	04 58	03 26	04 13	05 04	05 58
35	03 38	04 15	04 45	03 16	04 01	04 51	05 45
40	03 15	03 57	04 29	03 05	03 48	04 36	05 31
45	02 44	03 34	04 11	02 51	03 32	04 19	05 13
S 50	01 59	03 04	03 49	02 35	03 12	03 57	04 51
52	01 31	02 49	03 38	02 28	03 03	03 47	04 40
54	00 44	02 31	03 26	02 20	02 53	03 35	04 29
56	////	02 09	03 11	02 10	02 41	03 22	04 15
58	////	01 39	02 55	02 00	02 28	03 07	03 59
S 60	////	00 48	02 34	01 48	02 12	02 48	03 40

Lat.	Sunset	Twilight Civil	Twilight Naut.	Moonset 24	25	26	27
°	h m	h m	h m	h m	h m	h m	h m
N 72	■■	13 03	15 33	■■	■■	■■	■■
N 70	■■	14 05	15 53	11 06	■■	■■	■■
68	■■	14 40	16 09	12 15	■■	■■	■■
66	13 25	15 05	16 22	12 52	12 57	13 17	14 24
64	14 07	15 25	16 33	13 18	13 36	14 12	15 14
62	14 35	15 41	16 43	13 39	14 04	14 45	15 45
60	14 57	15 54	16 51	13 56	14 25	15 09	16 09
N 58	15 14	16 06	16 59	14 10	14 43	15 28	16 27
56	15 29	16 16	17 05	14 22	14 58	15 44	16 43
54	15 41	16 25	17 12	14 33	15 10	15 58	16 57
52	15 53	16 33	17 17	14 42	15 22	16 10	17 08
50	16 02	16 41	17 22	14 51	15 32	16 21	17 19
45	16 23	16 57	17 34	15 09	15 53	16 43	17 40
N 40	16 40	17 11	17 45	15 24	16 10	17 01	17 58
35	16 54	17 22	17 54	15 36	16 24	17 16	18 13
30	17 06	17 33	18 03	15 47	16 36	17 29	18 25
20	17 28	17 52	18 19	16 06	16 58	17 52	18 47
N 10	17 46	18 09	18 35	16 23	17 16	18 11	19 06
0	18 04	18 26	18 52	16 38	17 34	18 29	19 23
S 10	18 21	18 44	19 11	16 54	17 51	18 47	19 41
20	18 40	19 05	19 34	17 10	18 10	19 06	19 59
30	19 02	19 30	20 03	17 29	18 31	19 29	20 21
35	19 15	19 45	20 22	17 41	18 44	19 42	20 33
40	19 30	20 03	20 45	17 53	18 58	19 57	20 48
45	19 48	20 26	21 15	18 09	19 15	20 14	21 05
S 50	20 11	20 55	22 01	18 27	19 36	20 36	21 26
52	20 22	21 10	22 29	18 36	19 47	20 47	21 36
54	20 34	21 28	23 15	18 46	19 58	21 00	21 47
56	20 48	21 51	////	18 57	20 11	21 12	22 00
58	21 05	22 20	////	19 10	20 26	21 28	22 15
S 60	21 25	23 10	////	19 26	20 44	21 47	22 32

Day	SUN Eqn. of Time 00h	12h	SUN Mer. Pass.	MOON Mer. Pass. Upper	Lower	Age	Phase
d	m s	m s	h m	h m	h m	d	%
24	00 51	00 36	11 59	10 25	22 53	28	3
25	00 21	00 06	12 00	11 20	23 48	29	1
26	00 09	00 24	12 00	12 16	24 43	00	0

© British Crown Copyright 2018. All rights reserved.

UT	ARIES GHA	VENUS −3.9 GHA	Dec	MARS +1.6 GHA	Dec	JUPITER −1.8 GHA	Dec	SATURN +0.6 GHA	Dec
27 00	95 11.4	143 59.0	S19 59.6	222 24.5	S18 37.3	179 11.0	S23 13.5	162 41.6	S21 46.1
01	110 13.8	158 58.3	58.8	237 25.2	37.8	194 12.8	13.5	177 43.8	46.0
02	125 16.3	173 57.6	57.9	252 26.0	38.2	209 14.7	13.4	192 46.0	46.0
03	140 18.8	188 56.9 ..	57.1	267 26.7 ..	38.6	224 16.5 ..	13.4	207 48.1 ..	45.9
04	155 21.2	203 56.3	56.3	282 27.5	39.0	239 18.3	13.4	222 50.3	45.9
05	170 23.7	218 55.6	55.5	297 28.2	39.5	254 20.2	13.4	237 52.4	45.9
06	185 26.1	233 54.9	S19 54.7	312 29.0	S18 39.9	269 22.0	S23 13.4	252 54.6	S21 45.8
F 07	200 28.6	248 54.2	53.9	327 29.7	40.3	284 23.8	13.3	267 56.7	45.8
R 08	215 31.1	263 53.5	53.1	342 30.5	40.7	299 25.7	13.3	282 58.9	45.7
I 09	230 33.5	278 52.8 ..	52.3	357 31.2 ..	41.2	314 27.5 ..	13.3	298 01.0 ..	45.7
D 10	245 36.0	293 52.1	51.4	12 32.0	41.6	329 29.4	13.3	313 03.2	45.7
A 11	260 38.5	308 51.5	50.6	27 32.7	42.0	344 31.2	13.3	328 05.4	45.6
Y 12	275 40.9	323 50.8	S19 49.8	42 33.5	S18 42.4	359 33.0	S23 13.2	343 07.5	S21 45.6
13	290 43.4	338 50.1	49.0	57 34.2	42.9	14 34.9	13.2	358 09.7	45.5
14	305 45.9	353 49.4	48.2	72 35.0	43.3	29 36.7	13.2	13 11.8	45.5
15	320 48.3	8 48.7 ..	47.3	87 35.7 ..	43.7	44 38.5 ..	13.2	28 14.0 ..	45.4
16	335 50.8	23 48.1	46.5	102 36.5	44.1	59 40.4	13.1	43 16.1	45.4
17	350 53.2	38 47.4	45.7	117 37.2	44.6	74 42.2	13.1	58 18.3	45.4
18	5 55.7	53 46.7	S19 44.9	132 38.0	S18 45.0	89 44.1	S23 13.1	73 20.4	S21 45.3
19	20 58.2	68 46.0	44.0	147 38.7	45.4	104 45.9	13.0	88 22.6	45.3
20	36 00.6	83 45.4	43.2	162 39.5	45.8	119 47.8	13.0	103 24.8	45.2
21	51 03.1	98 44.7 ..	42.4	177 40.2 ..	46.2	134 49.6 ..	13.0	118 26.9 ..	45.2
22	66 05.6	113 44.0	41.6	192 41.0	46.7	149 51.5	13.0	133 29.1	45.2
23	81 08.0	128 43.3	40.7	207 41.7	47.1	164 53.3	13.0	148 31.2	45.1
28 00	96 10.5	143 42.7	S19 39.9	222 42.5	S18 47.5	179 55.1	S23 13.0	163 33.4	S21 45.1
01	111 13.0	158 42.0	39.1	237 43.2	47.9	194 57.0	13.0	178 35.5	45.0
02	126 15.4	173 41.3	38.2	252 44.0	48.3	209 58.8	12.9	193 37.7	45.0
03	141 17.9	188 40.6 ..	37.4	267 44.7 ..	48.8	225 00.6 ..	12.9	208 39.8 ..	45.0
04	156 20.4	203 40.0	36.6	282 45.4	49.2	240 02.5	12.9	223 42.0	44.9
05	171 22.8	218 39.3	35.7	297 46.2	49.6	255 04.3	12.9	238 44.2	44.9
06	186 25.3	233 38.6	S19 34.9	312 46.9	S18 50.0	270 06.1	S23 12.9	253 46.3	S21 44.8
S 07	201 27.7	248 38.0	34.1	327 47.7	50.4	285 08.0	12.8	268 48.5	44.8
A 08	216 30.2	263 37.3	33.2	342 48.4	50.9	300 09.8	12.8	283 50.6	44.7
T 09	231 32.7	278 36.6 ..	32.4	357 49.2 ..	51.3	315 11.6 ..	12.8	298 52.8 ..	44.7
U 10	246 35.1	293 35.9	31.5	12 49.9	51.7	330 13.5	12.8	313 54.9	44.7
R 11	261 37.6	308 35.3	30.7	27 50.7	52.1	345 15.3	12.8	328 57.1	44.6
D 12	276 40.1	323 34.6	S19 29.9	42 51.4	S18 52.5	0 17.2	S23 12.7	343 59.2	S21 44.6
A 13	291 42.5	338 33.9	29.0	57 52.2	52.9	15 19.0	12.7	359 01.4	44.5
Y 14	306 45.0	353 33.3	28.2	72 52.9	53.4	30 20.8	12.7	14 03.6	44.5
15	321 47.5	8 32.6 ..	27.3	87 53.7 ..	53.8	45 22.7 ..	12.7	29 05.7 ..	44.5
16	336 49.9	23 32.0	26.5	102 54.4	54.2	60 24.5	12.7	44 07.9	44.4
17	351 52.4	38 31.3	25.6	117 55.2	54.6	75 26.3	12.6	59 10.0	44.4
18	6 54.9	53 30.6	S19 24.8	132 55.9	S18 55.0	90 28.2	S23 12.6	74 12.2	S21 44.3
19	21 57.3	68 30.0	23.9	147 56.6	55.4	105 30.0	12.6	89 14.3	44.3
20	36 59.8	83 29.3	23.1	162 57.4	55.9	120 31.9	12.6	104 16.5	44.2
21	52 02.2	98 28.6 ..	22.2	177 58.1 ..	56.3	135 33.7 ..	12.5	119 18.6 ..	44.2
22	67 04.7	113 28.0	21.4	192 58.9	56.7	150 35.5	12.5	134 20.8	44.2
23	82 07.2	128 27.3	20.5	207 59.6	57.1	165 37.4	12.5	149 22.9	44.1
29 00	97 09.6	143 26.7	S19 19.7	223 00.4	S18 57.5	180 39.2	S23 12.5	164 25.1	S21 44.1
01	112 12.1	158 26.0	18.8	238 01.1	57.9	195 41.0	12.5	179 27.3	44.0
02	127 14.6	173 25.3	18.0	253 01.9	58.4	210 42.9	12.4	194 29.4	44.0
03	142 17.0	188 24.7 ..	17.1	268 02.6 ..	58.8	225 44.7 ..	12.4	209 31.6 ..	44.0
04	157 19.5	203 24.0	16.3	283 03.3	59.2	240 46.6	12.4	224 33.7	43.9
05	172 22.0	218 23.4	15.4	298 04.1	18 59.6	255 48.4	12.4	239 35.9	43.9
06	187 24.4	233 22.7	S19 14.6	313 04.8	S19 00.0	270 50.2	S23 12.3	254 38.0	S21 43.8
07	202 26.9	248 22.1	13.7	328 05.6	00.4	285 52.1	12.3	269 40.2	43.8
S 08	217 29.4	263 21.4	12.8	343 06.3	00.9	300 53.9	12.3	284 42.3	43.8
U 09	232 31.8	278 20.8 ..	12.0	358 07.1 ..	01.2	315 55.7 ..	12.3	299 44.5 ..	43.7
N 10	247 34.3	293 20.1	11.1	13 07.8	01.7	330 57.6	12.3	314 46.6	43.7
D 11	262 36.7	308 19.5	10.3	28 08.5	02.1	345 59.4	12.2	329 48.8	43.6
A 12	277 39.2	323 18.8	S19 09.4	43 09.3	S19 02.5	1 01.2	S23 12.2	344 51.0	S21 43.6
Y 13	292 41.7	338 18.1	08.5	58 10.0	02.9	16 03.1	12.2	359 53.1	43.5
14	307 44.1	353 17.5	07.7	73 10.8	03.3	31 04.9	12.2	14 55.3	43.5
15	322 46.6	8 16.8 ..	06.8	88 11.5 ..	03.7	46 06.8 ..	12.1	29 57.4 ..	43.5
16	337 49.1	23 16.2	05.9	103 12.2	04.1	61 08.6	12.1	44 59.6	43.4
17	352 51.5	38 15.6	05.1	118 13.0	04.5	76 10.4	12.1	60 01.7	43.4
18	7 54.0	53 14.9	S19 04.2	133 13.7	S19 04.9	91 12.3	S23 12.1	75 03.9	S21 43.3
19	22 56.5	68 14.3	03.3	148 14.5	05.4	106 14.1	12.1	90 06.0	43.3
20	37 58.9	83 13.6	02.4	163 15.2	05.8	121 15.9	12.0	105 08.2	43.2
21	53 01.4	98 13.0 ..	01.6	178 15.9 ..	06.2	136 17.8 ..	12.0	120 10.3 ..	43.2
22	68 03.9	113 12.3	19 00.7	193 16.7	06.6	151 19.6	12.0	135 12.5	43.2
23	83 06.3	128 11.7	S18 59.8	208 17.4	07.0	166 21.5	12.0	150 14.7	43.1
Mer. Pass.	17 32.4	v −0.7	d 0.8	v 0.7	d 0.4	v 1.8	d 0.0	v 2.2	d 0.0

STARS

Name	SHA	Dec
Acamar	315 14.6	S40 13.8
Achernar	335 23.2	S57 08.5
Acrux	173 04.3	S63 12.2
Adhara	255 08.6	S29 00.0
Aldebaran	290 43.9	N16 32.8
Alioth	166 16.8	N55 50.9
Alkaid	152 55.5	N49 12.7
Alnair	27 38.4	S46 52.1
Alnilam	275 41.5	S 1 11.5
Alphard	217 51.5	S 8 44.7
Alphecca	126 07.5	N26 38.9
Alpheratz	357 38.9	N29 12.1
Altair	62 04.2	N 8 55.3
Ankaa	353 11.2	S42 12.2
Antares	112 21.1	S26 28.4
Arcturus	145 51.8	N19 04.7
Atria	107 19.4	S69 03.5
Avior	234 15.6	S59 34.3
Bellatrix	278 26.9	N 6 21.9
Betelgeuse	270 56.1	N 7 24.5
Canopus	263 53.6	S52 42.5
Capella	280 27.3	N46 01.0
Deneb	49 28.8	N45 21.2
Denebola	182 29.0	N14 27.6
Diphda	348 51.3	S17 52.9
Dubhe	193 45.9	N61 38.4
Elnath	278 06.6	N28 37.3
Eltanin	90 44.5	N51 29.2
Enif	33 42.9	N 9 58.0
Fomalhaut	15 19.2	S29 31.2
Gacrux	171 55.9	S57 13.1
Gienah	175 47.7	S17 39.0
Hadar	148 41.8	S60 27.7
Hamal	327 55.5	N23 33.4
Kaus Aust.	83 38.3	S34 22.4
Kochab	137 20.8	N74 04.3
Markab	13 34.0	N15 18.8
Menkar	314 10.1	N 4 09.9
Menkent	148 02.5	S36 27.8
Miaplacidus	221 38.1	S69 47.7
Mirfak	308 33.5	N49 55.9
Nunki	75 53.1	S26 16.2
Peacock	53 12.7	S56 40.4
Pollux	243 21.9	N27 58.5
Procyon	244 54.7	N 5 10.3
Rasalhague	96 02.6	N12 32.8
Regulus	207 38.6	N11 52.1
Rigel	281 07.4	S 8 10.9
Rigil Kent.	139 46.0	S60 54.6
Sabik	102 07.7	S15 44.8
Schedar	349 35.4	N56 39.0
Shaula	96 16.2	S37 06.9
Sirius	258 29.4	S16 44.7
Spica	158 26.6	S11 15.7
Suhail	222 48.8	S43 30.6
Vega	80 36.4	N38 48.2
Zuben'ubi	137 00.7	S16 07.3

	SHA	Mer. Pass.
		h m
Venus	47 32.2	14 26
Mars	126 32.0	9 09
Jupiter	83 44.6	11 59
Saturn	67 22.9	13 04

© British Crown Copyright 2018. All rights reserved.

UT	SUN GHA	SUN Dec	MOON GHA	v	MOON Dec	d	HP
d h	° ′	° ′	° ′	′	° ′	′	′
27 00	179 50.1	S23 20.7	169 32.8	8.1	S23 12.7	0.6	56.6
01	194 49.8	20.6	183 59.9	8.1	23 12.1	0.7	56.6
02	209 49.5	20.5	198 27.0	8.1	23 11.4	0.9	56.6
03	224 49.2	.. 20.4	212 54.1	8.2	23 10.5	0.9	56.5
04	239 48.9	20.3	227 21.3	8.2	23 09.6	1.1	56.5
05	254 48.6	20.2	241 48.5	8.3	23 08.5	1.3	56.5
06	269 48.3	S23 20.1	256 15.8	8.3	S23 07.2	1.3	56.5
07	284 48.0	20.0	270 43.1	8.3	23 05.9	1.5	56.4
F 08	299 47.7	19.9	285 10.4	8.4	23 04.4	1.6	56.4
R 09	314 47.3	.. 19.8	299 37.8	8.4	23 02.8	1.8	56.4
I 10	329 47.0	19.7	314 05.2	8.5	23 01.0	1.8	56.4
11	344 46.7	19.6	328 32.7	8.6	22 59.2	2.0	56.3
D 12	359 46.4	S23 19.5	343 00.3	8.6	S22 57.2	2.1	56.3
A 13	14 46.1	19.4	357 27.9	8.6	22 55.1	2.3	56.3
Y 14	29 45.8	19.3	11 55.5	8.7	22 52.8	2.4	56.3
15	44 45.5	.. 19.2	26 23.2	8.7	22 50.4	2.4	56.2
16	59 45.2	19.1	40 50.9	8.8	22 48.0	2.7	56.2
17	74 44.9	19.0	55 18.7	8.9	22 45.3	2.7	56.2
18	89 44.6	S23 18.9	69 46.6	8.9	S22 42.6	2.8	56.2
19	104 44.3	18.8	84 14.5	9.0	22 39.8	3.0	56.1
20	119 43.9	18.6	98 42.5	9.0	22 36.8	3.1	56.1
21	134 43.6	.. 18.5	113 10.5	9.1	22 33.7	3.2	56.1
22	149 43.3	18.4	127 38.6	9.1	22 30.5	3.4	56.1
23	164 43.0	18.3	142 06.7	9.2	22 27.1	3.4	56.0
28 00	179 42.7	S23 18.2	156 34.9	9.3	S22 23.7	3.6	56.0
01	194 42.4	18.1	171 03.2	9.3	22 20.1	3.7	56.0
02	209 42.1	18.0	185 31.5	9.4	22 16.4	3.8	56.0
03	224 41.8	.. 17.9	199 59.9	9.4	22 12.6	3.9	55.9
04	239 41.5	17.7	214 28.3	9.5	22 08.7	4.0	55.9
05	254 41.2	17.6	228 56.8	9.6	22 04.7	4.2	55.9
06	269 40.9	S23 17.5	243 25.4	9.7	S22 00.5	4.2	55.9
S 07	284 40.6	17.4	257 54.1	9.7	21 56.3	4.4	55.8
A 08	299 40.3	17.3	272 22.8	9.8	21 51.9	4.5	55.8
T 09	314 39.9	.. 17.1	286 51.6	9.8	21 47.4	4.5	55.8
U 10	329 39.6	17.0	301 20.4	9.9	21 42.9	4.7	55.8
R 11	344 39.3	16.9	315 49.3	10.0	21 38.2	4.8	55.7
D 12	359 39.0	S23 16.8	330 18.3	10.0	S21 33.4	4.9	55.7
A 13	14 38.7	16.6	344 47.3	10.1	21 28.5	5.1	55.7
Y 14	29 38.4	16.5	359 16.4	10.2	21 23.4	5.1	55.7
15	44 38.1	.. 16.4	13 45.6	10.3	21 18.3	5.2	55.7
16	59 37.8	16.3	28 14.9	10.3	21 13.1	5.3	55.6
17	74 37.5	16.1	42 44.2	10.4	21 07.8	5.4	55.6
18	89 37.2	S23 16.0	57 13.6	10.4	S21 02.4	5.6	55.6
19	104 36.9	15.9	71 43.0	10.6	20 56.8	5.6	55.6
20	119 36.6	15.8	86 12.6	10.6	20 51.2	5.7	55.5
21	134 36.3	.. 15.6	100 42.2	10.7	20 45.5	5.9	55.5
22	149 36.0	15.5	115 11.9	10.7	20 39.6	5.9	55.5
23	164 35.6	15.4	129 41.6	10.8	20 33.7	6.0	55.5
29 00	179 35.3	S23 15.2	144 11.4	10.9	S20 27.7	6.1	55.4
01	194 35.0	15.1	158 41.3	11.0	20 21.6	6.2	55.4
02	209 34.7	15.0	173 11.3	11.0	20 15.4	6.3	55.4
03	224 34.4	.. 14.8	187 41.3	11.1	20 09.1	6.4	55.4
04	239 34.1	14.7	202 11.4	11.2	20 02.7	6.5	55.4
05	254 33.8	14.6	216 41.6	11.3	19 56.2	6.6	55.3
06	269 33.5	S23 14.4	231 11.9	11.3	S19 49.6	6.7	55.3
07	284 33.2	14.3	245 42.2	11.4	19 42.9	6.7	55.3
08	299 32.9	14.1	260 12.6	11.5	19 36.2	6.9	55.3
S 09	314 32.6	.. 14.0	274 43.1	11.5	19 29.3	6.9	55.2
U 10	329 32.3	13.9	289 13.6	11.6	19 22.4	7.1	55.2
N 11	344 32.0	13.7	303 44.2	11.7	19 15.3	7.1	55.2
D 12	359 31.7	S23 13.6	318 14.9	11.8	S19 08.2	7.2	55.2
A 13	14 31.4	13.4	332 45.7	11.8	19 01.0	7.2	55.2
Y 14	29 31.1	13.3	347 16.5	11.9	18 53.8	7.4	55.1
15	44 30.8	.. 13.1	1 47.4	12.0	18 46.4	7.4	55.1
16	59 30.5	13.0	16 18.4	12.1	18 39.0	7.6	55.1
17	74 30.2	12.8	30 49.5	12.1	18 31.4	7.6	55.1
18	89 29.8	S23 12.7	45 20.6	12.2	S18 23.8	7.7	55.1
19	104 29.5	12.5	59 51.8	12.3	18 16.1	7.7	55.0
20	119 29.2	12.4	74 23.1	12.3	18 08.4	7.9	55.0
21	134 28.9	.. 12.2	88 54.4	12.4	18 00.5	7.9	55.0
22	149 28.6	12.1	103 25.8	12.5	17 52.6	8.0	55.0
23	164 28.3	11.9	117 57.3	12.6	S17 44.6	8.0	55.0
	SD 16.3	d 0.1	SD 15.3		15.2		15.0

Lat.	Twilight Naut.	Twilight Civil	Sunrise	Moonrise 27	28	29	30
°	h m	h m	h m	h m	h m	h m	h m
N 72	08 27	10 53	■	■	■	■	13 37
N 70	08 07	09 54	■	■	■	13 36	12 59
68	07 51	09 20	■	■	13 13	12 46	12 33
66	07 38	08 55	10 34	12 00	12 11	12 14	12 13
64	07 27	08 35	09 53	11 10	11 37	11 50	11 57
62	07 18	08 19	09 25	10 39	11 11	11 31	11 43
60	07 09	08 06	09 03	10 15	10 51	11 15	11 31
N 58	07 02	07 54	08 46	09 56	10 35	11 02	11 21
56	06 55	07 44	08 32	09 40	10 21	10 51	11 13
54	06 49	07 35	08 19	09 27	10 09	10 40	11 05
52	06 44	07 27	08 08	09 15	09 58	10 32	10 58
50	06 38	07 20	07 58	09 04	09 49	10 23	10 51
45	06 27	07 04	07 38	08 42	09 28	10 06	10 38
N 40	06 16	06 50	07 21	08 25	09 12	09 52	10 26
35	06 07	06 39	07 07	08 10	08 58	09 40	10 17
30	05 58	06 28	06 55	07 57	08 46	09 30	10 08
20	05 42	06 09	06 33	07 35	08 25	09 12	09 53
N 10	05 26	05 52	06 15	07 15	08 07	08 56	09 40
0	05 09	05 35	05 58	06 58	07 51	08 41	09 28
S 10	04 50	05 17	05 40	06 40	07 34	08 26	09 16
20	04 28	04 57	05 21	06 21	07 16	08 10	09 03
30	03 59	04 32	04 59	05 58	06 55	07 52	08 48
35	03 40	04 17	04 46	05 45	06 43	07 41	08 39
40	03 17	03 59	04 31	05 31	06 29	07 29	08 29
45	02 47	03 36	04 13	05 13	06 12	07 14	08 18
S 50	02 01	03 07	03 51	04 51	05 52	06 57	08 03
52	01 34	02 52	03 40	04 40	05 42	06 48	07 57
54	00 49	02 34	03 28	04 29	05 31	06 39	07 49
56	////	02 12	03 14	04 15	05 18	06 28	07 41
58	////	01 42	02 57	03 59	05 04	06 16	07 31
S 60	////	00 54	02 37	03 40	04 46	06 02	07 21

Lat.	Sunset	Twilight Civil	Twilight Naut.	Moonset 27	28	29	30
°	h m	h m	h m	h m	h m	h m	h m
N 72	■	13 10	15 36	■	■	■	17 59
N 70	■	14 09	15 56	■	■	16 21	18 35
68	■	14 43	16 12	■	15 01	17 11	19 00
66	13 29	15 08	16 25	14 24	16 02	17 43	19 19
64	14 10	15 28	16 36	15 14	16 36	18 06	19 35
62	14 38	15 43	16 45	15 45	17 01	18 24	19 47
60	14 59	15 57	16 54	16 09	17 21	18 39	19 58
N 58	15 17	16 08	17 01	16 27	17 37	18 52	20 07
56	15 31	16 19	17 08	16 43	17 51	19 03	20 16
54	15 44	16 28	17 14	16 57	18 02	19 12	20 23
52	15 55	16 36	17 19	17 08	18 13	19 21	20 29
50	16 05	16 43	17 25	17 19	18 22	19 28	20 35
45	16 25	16 59	17 36	17 40	18 42	19 45	20 48
N 40	16 42	17 12	17 47	17 58	18 57	19 58	20 58
35	16 56	17 24	17 56	18 13	19 11	20 09	21 07
30	17 08	17 35	18 05	18 25	19 22	20 19	21 15
20	17 29	17 53	18 21	18 47	19 42	20 36	21 28
N 10	17 48	18 11	18 37	19 06	19 59	20 50	21 39
0	18 05	18 28	18 54	19 23	20 15	21 04	21 50
S 10	18 23	18 46	19 13	19 41	20 31	21 18	22 01
20	18 41	19 06	19 35	19 59	20 48	21 32	22 12
30	19 03	19 31	20 04	20 21	21 07	21 48	22 25
35	19 16	19 46	20 23	20 33	21 19	21 58	22 32
40	19 31	20 04	20 46	20 48	21 32	22 09	22 41
45	19 49	20 26	21 16	21 05	21 47	22 21	22 50
S 50	20 11	20 56	22 01	21 26	22 05	22 37	23 02
52	20 22	21 11	22 28	21 36	22 14	22 44	23 08
54	20 34	21 29	23 12	21 47	22 24	22 52	23 14
56	20 48	21 50	////	22 00	22 35	23 01	23 20
58	21 05	22 20	////	22 15	22 48	23 11	23 28
S 60	21 25	23 07	////	22 32	23 02	23 22	23 36

	SUN Eqn. of Time 00h	SUN Eqn. of Time 12h	SUN Mer. Pass.	MOON Mer. Pass. Upper	MOON Mer. Pass. Lower	Age	Phase
Day	m s	m s	h m	h m	h m	d	%
27	00 39	00 54	12 01	13 11	00 43	01	2
28	01 09	01 23	12 01	14 03	01 37	02	6
29	01 38	01 53	12 02	14 53	02 28	03	11

© British Crown Copyright 2018. All rights reserved.

UT	ARIES GHA	VENUS −4.0 GHA	VENUS Dec	MARS +1.6 GHA	MARS Dec	JUPITER −1.8 GHA	JUPITER Dec	SATURN +0.5 GHA	SATURN Dec	STARS Name	SHA	Dec
30 00	98 08.8	143 11.0	S18 59.0	223 18.2	S19 07.4	181 23.3	S23 11.9	165 16.8	S21 43.1	Acamar	315 14.6	S40 13.8
01	113 11.2	158 10.4	58.1	238 18.9	07.8	196 25.1	11.9	180 19.0	43.0	Achernar	335 23.2	S57 08.5
02	128 13.7	173 09.7	57.2	253 19.6	08.2	211 27.0	11.9	195 21.1	43.0	Acrux	173 04.3	S63 12.2
03	143 16.2	188 09.1 ..	56.3	268 20.4 ..	08.6	226 28.8 ..	11.9	210 23.3 ..	43.0	Adhara	255 08.6	S29 00.0
04	158 18.6	203 08.5	55.4	283 21.1	09.0	241 30.6	11.8	225 25.4	42.9	Aldebaran	290 43.9	N16 32.8
05	173 21.1	218 07.8	54.6	298 21.9	09.4	256 32.5	11.8	240 27.6	42.9			
M 06	188 23.6	233 07.2	S18 53.7	313 22.6	S19 09.8	271 34.3	S23 11.8	255 29.7	S21 42.8	Alioth	166 16.8	N55 50.9
O 07	203 26.0	248 06.5	52.8	328 23.3	10.3	286 36.2	11.8	270 31.9	42.8	Alkaid	152 55.5	N49 12.7
N 08	218 28.5	263 05.9	51.9	343 24.1	10.7	301 38.0	11.8	285 34.0	42.7	Alnair	27 38.4	S46 52.1
D 09	233 31.0	278 05.3 ..	51.0	358 24.8 ..	11.1	316 39.8 ..	11.7	300 36.2 ..	42.7	Alnilam	275 41.5	S 1 11.5
A 10	248 33.4	293 04.6	50.2	13 25.6	11.5	331 41.7	11.7	315 38.3	42.7	Alphard	217 51.4	S 8 44.7
Y 11	263 35.9	308 04.0	49.3	28 26.3	11.9	346 43.5	11.7	330 40.5	42.6			
12	278 38.3	323 03.4	S18 48.4	43 27.0	S19 12.3	1 45.3	S23 11.7	345 42.7	S21 42.6	Alphecca	126 07.5	N26 38.9
13	293 40.8	338 02.7	47.5	58 27.8	12.7	16 47.2	11.6	0 44.8	42.5	Alpheratz	357 38.9	N29 12.1
14	308 43.3	353 02.1	46.6	73 28.5	13.1	31 49.0	11.6	15 47.0	42.5	Altair	62 04.2	N 8 55.3
15	323 45.7	8 01.4 ..	45.7	88 29.2 ..	13.5	46 50.9 ..	11.6	30 49.1 ..	42.4	Ankaa	353 11.3	S42 12.2
16	338 48.2	23 00.8	44.8	103 30.0	13.9	61 52.7	11.6	45 51.3	42.4	Antares	112 21.1	S26 28.4
17	353 50.7	38 00.2	43.9	118 30.7	14.3	76 54.5	11.5	60 53.4	42.4			
18	8 53.1	52 59.5	S18 43.1	133 31.5	S19 14.7	91 56.4	S23 11.5	75 55.6	S21 42.3	Arcturus	145 51.8	N19 04.7
19	23 55.6	67 58.9	42.2	148 32.2	15.1	106 58.2	11.5	90 57.7	42.3	Atria	107 19.4	S69 03.5
20	38 58.1	82 58.3	41.3	163 32.9	15.5	122 00.1	11.5	105 59.9	42.2	Avior	234 15.6	S59 34.3
21	54 00.5	97 57.7 ..	40.4	178 33.7 ..	15.9	137 01.9 ..	11.4	121 02.0 ..	42.2	Bellatrix	278 26.9	N 6 21.9
22	69 03.0	112 57.0	39.5	193 34.4	16.3	152 03.7	11.4	136 04.2	42.2	Betelgeuse	270 56.1	N 7 24.5
23	84 05.5	127 56.4	38.6	208 35.1	16.7	167 05.6	11.4	151 06.3	42.1			
31 00	99 07.9	142 55.8	S18 37.7	223 35.9	S19 17.1	182 07.4	S23 11.4	166 08.5	S21 42.1	Canopus	263 53.6	S52 42.5
01	114 10.4	157 55.1	36.8	238 36.6	17.5	197 09.2	11.3	181 10.6	42.0	Capella	280 27.3	N46 01.0
02	129 12.8	172 54.5	35.9	253 37.3	17.9	212 11.1	11.3	196 12.8	42.0	Deneb	49 28.9	N45 21.2
03	144 15.3	187 53.9 ..	35.0	268 38.1 ..	18.3	227 12.9 ..	11.3	211 15.0 ..	41.9	Denebola	182 29.0	N14 27.6
04	159 17.8	202 53.3	34.1	283 38.8	18.7	242 14.8	11.3	226 17.1	41.9	Diphda	348 51.4	S17 52.9
05	174 20.2	217 52.6	33.2	298 39.5	19.1	257 16.6	11.3	241 19.3	41.9			
T 06	189 22.7	232 52.0	S18 32.3	313 40.3	S19 19.5	272 18.4	S23 11.2	256 21.4	S21 41.8	Dubhe	193 45.9	N61 38.4
U 07	204 25.2	247 51.4	31.4	328 41.0	19.9	287 20.3	11.2	271 23.6	41.8	Elnath	278 06.6	N28 37.3
E 08	219 27.6	262 50.8	30.5	343 41.7	20.3	302 22.1	11.2	286 25.7	41.7	Eltanin	90 44.6	N51 29.2
S 09	234 30.1	277 50.1 ..	29.6	358 42.5 ..	20.7	317 23.9 ..	11.2	301 27.9 ..	41.7	Enif	33 43.0	N 9 58.0
D 10	249 32.6	292 49.5	28.7	13 43.2	21.1	332 25.8	11.1	316 30.0	41.6	Fomalhaut	15 19.2	S29 31.2
A 11	264 35.0	307 48.9	27.8	28 44.0	21.5	347 27.6	11.1	331 32.2	41.6			
Y 12	279 37.5	322 48.3	S18 26.9	43 44.7	S19 21.9	2 29.5	S23 11.1	346 34.3	S21 41.5	Gacrux	171 55.9	S57 13.1
13	294 40.0	337 47.7	26.0	58 45.4	22.3	17 31.3	11.1	1 36.5	41.5	Gienah	175 47.7	S17 39.0
14	309 42.4	352 47.0	25.1	73 46.2	22.7	32 33.1	11.0	16 38.6	41.5	Hadar	148 41.8	S60 27.7
15	324 44.9	7 46.4 ..	24.1	88 46.9 ..	23.1	47 35.0 ..	11.0	31 40.8 ..	41.4	Hamal	327 55.5	N23 33.4
16	339 47.3	22 45.8	23.2	103 47.6	23.5	62 36.8	11.0	46 42.9	41.4	Kaus Aust.	83 38.3	S34 22.4
17	354 49.8	37 45.2	22.3	118 48.3	23.9	77 38.6	11.0	61 45.1	41.3			
18	9 52.3	52 44.6	S18 21.4	133 49.1	S19 24.3	92 40.5	S23 10.9	76 47.2	S21 41.3	Kochab	137 20.8	N74 04.2
19	24 54.7	67 43.9	20.5	148 49.8	24.7	107 42.3	10.9	91 49.4	41.3	Markab	13 34.0	N15 18.8
20	39 57.2	82 43.3	19.6	163 50.5	25.1	122 44.2	10.9	106 51.6	41.2	Menkar	314 10.1	N 4 09.9
21	54 59.7	97 42.7 ..	18.7	178 51.3 ..	25.5	137 46.0 ..	10.9	121 53.7 ..	41.2	Menkent	148 02.5	S36 27.8
22	70 02.1	112 42.1	17.8	193 52.0	25.9	152 47.8	10.8	136 55.9	41.1	Miaplacidus	221 38.0	S69 47.7
23	85 04.6	127 41.5	16.8	208 52.7	26.3	167 49.7	10.8	151 58.0	41.1			
1 00	100 07.1	142 40.9	S18 15.9	223 53.5	S19 26.7	182 51.5	S23 10.8	167 00.2	S21 41.1	Mirfak	308 33.6	N49 55.9
01	115 09.5	157 40.3	15.0	238 54.2	27.1	197 53.3	10.8	182 02.3	41.0	Nunki	75 53.1	S26 16.2
02	130 12.0	172 39.6	14.1	253 54.9	27.5	212 55.2	10.7	197 04.5	41.0	Peacock	53 12.7	S56 40.3
03	145 14.4	187 39.0 ..	13.2	268 55.7 ..	27.9	227 57.0 ..	10.7	212 06.6 ..	40.9	Pollux	243 21.9	N27 58.5
04	160 16.9	202 38.4	12.2	283 56.4	28.3	242 58.9	10.7	227 08.8	40.9	Procyon	244 54.7	N 5 10.3
05	175 19.4	217 37.8	11.3	298 57.1	28.7	258 00.7	10.7	242 10.9	40.8			
W 06	190 21.8	232 37.2	S18 10.4	313 57.9	S19 29.1	273 02.5	S23 10.6	257 13.1	S21 40.8	Rasalhague	96 02.6	N12 32.8
E 07	205 24.3	247 36.6	09.5	328 58.6	29.5	288 04.4	10.6	272 15.2	40.8	Regulus	207 38.5	N11 52.1
D 08	220 26.8	262 36.0	08.6	343 59.3	29.9	303 06.2	10.6	287 17.4	40.7	Rigel	281 07.4	S 8 10.9
N 09	235 29.2	277 35.4 ..	07.6	359 00.0 ..	30.3	318 08.1 ..	10.6	302 19.5 ..	40.7	Rigil Kent.	139 46.0	S60 54.6
E 10	250 31.7	292 34.8	06.7	14 00.8	30.6	333 09.9	10.5	317 21.7	40.6	Sabik	102 07.7	S15 44.8
S 11	265 34.2	307 34.2	05.8	29 01.5	31.0	348 11.7	10.5	332 23.8	40.6			
D 12	280 36.6	322 33.6	S18 04.9	44 02.2	S19 31.4	3 13.6	S23 10.5	347 26.0	S21 40.5	Schedar	349 35.4	N56 39.0
A 13	295 39.1	337 33.0	03.9	59 03.0	31.8	18 15.4	10.5	2 28.1	40.5	Shaula	96 16.2	S37 06.9
Y 14	310 41.6	352 32.3	03.0	74 03.7	32.2	33 17.2	10.4	17 30.3	40.5	Sirius	258 29.4	S16 44.7
15	325 44.0	7 31.7 ..	02.1	89 04.4 ..	32.6	48 19.1 ..	10.4	32 32.5 ..	40.4	Spica	158 26.6	S11 15.8
16	340 46.5	22 31.1	01.1	104 05.2	33.0	63 20.9	10.4	47 34.6	40.4	Suhail	222 48.8	S43 30.7
17	355 48.9	37 30.5	18 00.2	119 05.9	33.4	78 22.8	10.4	62 36.8	40.3			
18	10 51.4	52 29.9	S17 59.3	134 06.6	S19 33.8	93 24.6	S23 10.3	77 38.9	S21 40.3	Vega	80 36.4	N38 48.2
19	25 53.9	67 29.3	58.3	149 07.3	34.2	108 26.4	10.3	92 41.1	40.2	Zuben'ubi	137 00.6	S16 07.3
20	40 56.3	82 28.7	57.4	164 08.1	34.6	123 28.3	10.3	107 43.2	40.2			
21	55 58.8	97 28.1 ..	56.5	179 08.8 ..	35.0	138 30.1 ..	10.2	122 45.4 ..	40.2		SHA	Mer.Pass.
22	71 01.3	112 27.5	55.5	194 09.5	35.3	153 31.9	10.2	137 47.5	40.1	Venus	43 47.8	14 29
23	86 03.7	127 26.9	54.6	209 10.2	35.7	168 33.8	10.2	152 49.7	40.1	Mars	124 28.0	9 05
										Jupiter	82 59.5	11 50
Mer.Pass. 17 20.6		v −0.6	d 0.9	v 0.7	d 0.4	v 1.8	d 0.0	v 2.2	d 0.0	Saturn	67 00.6	12 54

© British Crown Copyright 2018. All rights reserved.

UT	SUN GHA	SUN Dec	MOON GHA	v	MOON Dec	d	HP
d h	° '	° '	° '	'	° '	'	'
30 00	179 28.0	S23 11.8	132 28.9	12.6	S17 36.6	8.2	54.9
01	194 27.7	11.6	147 00.5	12.7	17 28.4	8.2	54.9
02	209 27.4	11.5	161 32.2	12.7	17 20.2	8.3	54.9
03	224 27.1	.. 11.3	176 03.9	12.9	17 11.9	8.3	54.9
04	239 26.8	11.2	190 35.8	12.9	17 03.6	8.4	54.9
05	254 26.5	11.0	205 07.7	12.9	16 55.2	8.5	54.9
06	269 26.2	S23 10.9	219 39.6	13.1	S16 46.7	8.6	54.8
07	284 25.9	10.7	234 11.7	13.1	16 38.1	8.6	54.8
M 08	299 25.6	10.5	248 43.8	13.2	16 29.5	8.7	54.8
O 09	314 25.3	.. 10.4	263 16.0	13.2	16 20.8	8.8	54.8
N 10	329 25.0	10.2	277 48.2	13.3	16 12.0	8.8	54.8
D 11	344 24.7	10.1	292 20.5	13.4	16 03.2	8.9	54.7
A 12	359 24.4	S23 09.9	306 52.9	13.4	S15 54.3	9.0	54.7
Y 13	14 24.1	09.7	321 25.3	13.5	15 45.3	9.0	54.7
14	29 23.8	09.6	335 57.8	13.6	15 36.3	9.1	54.7
15	44 23.5	.. 09.4	350 30.4	13.6	15 27.2	9.1	54.7
16	59 23.2	09.2	5 03.0	13.7	15 18.1	9.2	54.7
17	74 22.9	09.1	19 35.7	13.7	15 08.9	9.2	54.7
18	89 22.6	S23 08.9	34 08.4	13.9	S14 59.7	9.4	54.6
19	104 22.3	08.7	48 41.3	13.8	14 50.3	9.3	54.6
20	119 22.0	08.6	63 14.1	14.0	14 41.0	9.5	54.6
21	134 21.7	.. 08.4	77 47.1	14.0	14 31.5	9.4	54.6
22	149 21.4	08.2	92 20.1	14.0	14 22.1	9.6	54.6
23	164 21.1	08.1	106 53.1	14.1	14 12.5	9.6	54.6
31 00	179 20.8	S23 07.9	121 26.2	14.2	S14 02.9	9.6	54.6
01	194 20.5	07.7	135 59.4	14.3	13 53.3	9.7	54.5
02	209 20.2	07.5	150 32.7	14.2	13 43.6	9.8	54.5
03	224 19.9	.. 07.4	165 05.9	14.4	13 33.8	9.8	54.5
04	239 19.6	07.2	179 39.3	14.4	13 24.0	9.8	54.5
05	254 19.3	07.0	194 12.7	14.4	13 14.2	9.9	54.5
06	269 19.0	S23 06.8	208 46.1	14.6	S13 04.3	10.0	54.5
07	284 18.7	06.7	223 19.7	14.5	12 54.3	10.0	54.5
T 08	299 18.4	06.5	237 53.2	14.6	12 44.3	10.0	54.4
U 09	314 18.1	.. 06.3	252 26.8	14.7	12 34.3	10.1	54.4
E 10	329 17.8	06.1	267 00.5	14.7	12 24.2	10.1	54.4
S 11	344 17.5	06.0	281 34.2	14.8	12 14.1	10.2	54.4
D 12	359 17.2	S23 05.8	296 08.0	14.8	S12 03.9	10.2	54.4
A 13	14 16.9	05.6	310 41.8	14.9	11 53.7	10.3	54.4
Y 14	29 16.6	05.4	325 15.7	14.9	11 43.4	10.3	54.4
15	44 16.3	.. 05.2	339 49.6	15.0	11 33.1	10.4	54.4
16	59 16.0	05.0	354 23.6	15.0	11 22.7	10.4	54.4
17	74 15.7	04.8	8 57.6	15.1	11 12.3	10.4	54.4
18	89 15.4	S23 04.7	23 31.7	15.1	S11 01.9	10.5	54.3
19	104 15.1	04.5	38 05.8	15.1	10 51.4	10.5	54.3
20	119 14.8	04.3	52 39.9	15.2	10 40.9	10.5	54.3
21	134 14.5	.. 04.1	67 14.1	15.2	10 30.4	10.6	54.3
22	149 14.2	03.9	81 48.3	15.3	10 19.8	10.6	54.3
23	164 13.9	03.7	96 22.6	15.3	10 09.2	10.7	54.3
1 00	179 13.6	S23 03.5	110 56.9	15.4	S 9 58.5	10.7	54.3
01	194 13.3	03.3	125 31.3	15.4	9 47.8	10.7	54.3
02	209 13.0	03.1	140 05.7	15.4	9 37.1	10.8	54.3
03	224 12.7	.. 03.0	154 40.1	15.5	9 26.3	10.8	54.3
04	239 12.4	02.8	169 14.6	15.5	9 15.5	10.8	54.3
05	254 12.1	02.6	183 49.1	15.6	9 04.7	10.9	54.3
06	269 11.8	S23 02.4	198 23.7	15.6	S 8 53.8	10.9	54.3
W 07	284 11.5	02.2	212 58.3	15.6	8 42.9	10.9	54.2
E 08	299 11.2	02.0	227 32.9	15.6	8 32.0	11.0	54.2
D 09	314 10.9	.. 01.8	242 07.5	15.7	8 21.0	11.0	54.2
N 10	329 10.6	01.6	256 42.2	15.7	8 10.0	11.0	54.2
E 11	344 10.3	01.4	271 16.9	15.8	7 59.0	11.0	54.2
S 12	359 10.0	S23 01.2	285 51.7	15.8	S 7 48.0	11.1	54.2
D 13	14 09.7	01.0	300 26.5	15.8	7 36.9	11.1	54.2
A 14	29 09.4	00.8	315 01.3	15.8	7 25.8	11.1	54.2
Y 15	44 09.1	.. 00.6	329 36.1	15.9	7 14.7	11.2	54.2
16	59 08.8	00.4	344 11.0	15.9	7 03.5	11.2	54.2
17	74 08.5	00.2	358 45.9	15.9	6 52.3	11.2	54.2
18	89 08.2	S23 00.0	13 20.8	15.9	S 6 41.1	11.2	54.2
19	104 07.9	22 59.7	27 55.7	16.0	6 29.9	11.2	54.2
20	119 07.6	59.5	42 30.7	16.0	6 18.7	11.3	54.2
21	134 07.3	.. 59.3	57 05.7	16.0	6 07.4	11.3	54.2
22	149 07.1	59.1	71 40.7	16.0	5 56.1	11.3	54.2
23	164 06.8	58.9	86 15.7	16.1	S 5 44.8	11.4	54.2
	SD 16.3	d 0.2	SD 14.9		14.8		14.8

Lat.	Twilight Naut.	Twilight Civil	Sunrise	Moonrise 30	Moonrise 31	Moonrise 1	Moonrise 2
°	h m	h m	h m	h m	h m	h m	h m
N 72	08 25	10 46	■■■■	13 37	13 00	12 37	12 18
N 70	08 06	09 51	■■■■	12 59	12 40	12 26	12 14
68	07 50	09 18	■■■■	12 33	12 24	12 17	12 10
66	07 38	08 54	10 30	12 13	12 11	12 09	12 07
64	07 27	08 35	09 51	11 57	12 00	12 03	12 04
62	07 18	08 19	09 24	11 43	11 51	11 57	12 02
60	07 09	08 06	09 03	11 31	11 43	11 52	12 00
N 58	07 02	07 54	08 46	11 21	11 36	11 48	11 58
56	06 56	07 44	08 31	11 13	11 30	11 44	11 57
54	06 50	07 36	08 19	11 05	11 24	11 40	11 55
52	06 44	07 28	08 08	10 58	11 19	11 37	11 54
50	06 39	07 20	07 59	10 51	11 14	11 34	11 53
45	06 27	07 04	07 38	10 38	11 04	11 28	11 50
N 40	06 17	06 51	07 22	10 26	10 56	11 23	11 48
35	06 08	06 40	07 08	10 17	10 49	11 18	11 46
30	05 59	06 29	06 55	10 08	10 43	11 14	11 44
20	05 43	06 11	06 35	09 53	10 32	11 07	11 41
N 10	05 27	05 54	06 16	09 40	10 22	11 01	11 39
0	05 10	05 37	05 59	09 28	10 13	10 55	11 36
S 10	04 52	05 19	05 42	09 16	10 04	10 49	11 34
20	04 29	04 59	05 23	09 03	09 54	10 43	11 31
30	04 01	04 34	05 01	08 48	09 43	10 36	11 28
35	03 42	04 19	04 48	08 39	09 36	10 32	11 27
40	03 19	04 01	04 34	08 29	09 29	10 27	11 25
45	02 49	03 39	04 16	08 18	09 20	10 22	11 22
S 50	02 05	03 10	03 54	08 03	09 10	10 15	11 20
52	01 38	02 55	03 43	07 57	09 05	10 12	11 19
54	00 56	02 37	03 31	07 49	08 59	10 09	11 17
56	////	02 16	03 17	07 41	08 53	10 05	11 16
58	////	01 47	03 01	07 31	08 47	10 01	11 14
S 60	////	01 02	02 41	07 21	08 39	09 56	11 12

Lat.	Sunset	Twilight Civil	Twilight Naut.	Moonset 30	Moonset 31	Moonset 1	Moonset 2
°	h m	h m	h m	h m	h m	h m	h m
N 72	■■■■	13 20	15 41	17 59	20 06	21 57	23 42
N 70	■■■■	14 15	16 00	18 35	20 25	22 06	23 44
68	■■■■	14 48	16 16	19 00	20 39	22 13	23 45
66	13 36	15 12	16 28	19 19	20 51	22 19	23 46
64	14 15	15 31	16 39	19 35	21 01	22 25	23 47
62	14 42	15 47	16 48	19 47	21 09	22 29	23 47
60	15 03	16 00	16 56	19 58	21 16	22 33	23 48
N 58	15 20	16 11	17 04	20 07	21 22	22 36	23 49
56	15 34	16 21	17 10	20 16	21 28	22 39	23 49
54	15 47	16 30	17 16	20 23	21 33	22 42	23 50
52	15 58	16 38	17 22	20 29	21 37	22 44	23 50
50	16 07	16 46	17 27	20 35	21 41	22 46	23 51
45	16 28	17 01	17 39	20 48	21 50	22 51	23 52
N 40	16 44	17 15	17 49	20 58	21 57	22 55	23 52
35	16 58	17 26	17 58	21 07	22 03	22 58	23 53
30	17 10	17 37	18 06	21 15	22 08	23 01	23 53
20	17 31	17 55	18 23	21 28	22 18	23 06	23 54
N 10	17 49	18 12	18 38	21 39	22 26	23 11	23 55
0	18 07	18 29	18 55	21 50	22 33	23 15	23 56
S 10	18 24	18 47	19 14	22 01	22 41	23 19	23 57
20	18 43	19 07	19 36	22 12	22 49	23 24	23 57
30	19 04	19 32	20 05	22 25	22 58	23 28	23 58
35	19 17	19 47	20 23	22 32	23 03	23 31	23 58
40	19 32	20 05	20 46	22 41	23 09	23 34	23 59
45	19 50	20 27	21 16	22 50	23 15	23 38	24 00
S 50	20 12	20 56	22 00	23 02	23 24	23 42	24 00
52	20 22	21 10	22 26	23 08	23 27	23 44	24 01
54	20 34	21 28	23 07	23 14	23 31	23 47	24 01
56	20 48	21 49	////	23 20	23 36	23 49	24 01
58	21 04	22 18	////	23 28	23 41	23 52	24 02
S 60	21 24	23 02	////	23 36	23 46	23 55	24 02

Day	SUN Eqn. of Time 00h	SUN Eqn. of Time 12h	SUN Mer. Pass.	MOON Mer. Pass. Upper	MOON Mer. Pass. Lower	Age	Phase
d	m s	m s	h m	h m	h m	d	%
30	02 07	02 22	12 02	15 39	03 16	04	18
31	02 36	02 51	12 03	16 23	04 01	05	26
1	03 05	03 19	12 03	17 05	04 44	06	34

© British Crown Copyright 2018. All rights reserved.

EXPLANATION

PRINCIPLE AND ARRANGEMENT

1. *Object.* The object of this Almanac is to provide, in a convenient form, the data required for the practice of astronomical navigation at sea.

2. *Principle.* The main contents of the Almanac consist of data from which the *Greenwich Hour Angle* (GHA) and the *Declination* (Dec) of all the bodies used for navigation can be obtained for any instant of *Universal Time* (UT, specifically UT1, or previously Greenwich Mean Time (GMT)).

The *Local Hour Angle* (LHA) can then be obtained by means of the formula:

$$\text{LHA} = \text{GHA} \genfrac{}{}{0pt}{}{-\text{ west}}{+\text{ east}} \text{ longitude}$$

The remaining data consist of: times of rising and setting of the Sun and Moon, and times of twilight; miscellaneous calendarial and planning data and auxiliary tables, including a list of Standard Times; corrections to be applied to observed altitude.

For the Sun, Moon, and planets, the GHA and Dec are tabulated directly for each hour of UT throughout the year. For the stars, the *Sidereal Hour Angle* (SHA) is given, and the GHA is obtained from:

$$\text{GHA Star} = \text{GHA Aries} + \text{SHA Star}$$

The SHA and Dec of the stars change slowly and may be regarded as constant over periods of several days. GHA Aries, or the Greenwich Hour Angle of the first point of Aries (the Vernal Equinox), is tabulated for each hour. Permanent tables give the appropriate increments and corrections to the tabulated hourly values of GHA and Dec for the minutes and seconds of UT.

The six-volume series of *Sight Reduction Tables for Marine Navigation* (published in U.S.A. as Pub. No. 229) has been designed for the solution of the navigational triangle and is intended for use with *The Nautical Almanac*.

Two alternative procedures for sight reduction are described on pages 277–318. The first requires the use of programmable calculators or computers, while the second uses a set of concise tables that is given on pages 286–317.

The tabular accuracy is $0\!\cdot\!1$ throughout. The time argument on the daily pages of this Almanac is UT1 denoted throughout by UT. This scale may differ from the broadcast time signals (UTC) by an amount which, if ignored, will introduce an error of up to $0\!\cdot\!2$ in longitude determined from astronomical observations. The difference arises because the time argument depends on the variable rate of rotation of the Earth while the broadcast time signals are based on an atomic time-scale. Step adjustments of exactly one second are made to the time signals as required (normally at 24^{h} on December 31 and June 30) so that the difference between the time signals and UT, as used in this Almanac, may not exceed $0\!\cdot\!9$. Those who require to reduce observations to a precision of better than 1^{s} must therefore obtain the correction (DUT1) to the time signals from coding in the signal, or from other sources; the required time is given by UT1=UTC+DUT1 to a precision of $0\!\cdot\!1$. Alternatively, the longitude, when determined from astronomical observations, may be corrected by the corresponding amount shown in the following table:

Correction to time signals	Correction to longitude
$-0\!\cdot\!9$ to $-0\!\cdot\!7$	$0\!\cdot\!2$ to east
$-0\!\cdot\!6$ to $-0\!\cdot\!3$	$0\!\cdot\!1$ to east
$-0\!\cdot\!2$ to $+0\!\cdot\!2$	no correction
$+0\!\cdot\!3$ to $+0\!\cdot\!6$	$0\!\cdot\!1$ to west
$+0\!\cdot\!7$ to $+0\!\cdot\!9$	$0\!\cdot\!2$ to west

© British Crown Copyright 2018. All rights reserved.

3. *Lay-out.* The ephemeral data for three days are presented on an opening of two pages: the left-hand page contains the data for the planets and stars; the right-hand page contains the data for the Sun and Moon, together with times of twilight, sunrise, sunset, moonrise and moonset.

The remaining contents are arranged as follows: for ease of reference the altitude-correction tables are given on pages A2, A3, A4, xxxiv and xxxv; calendar, Moon's phases, eclipses, and planet notes (i.e. data of general interest) precede the main tabulations. The Explanation is followed by information on standard times, star charts and list of star positions, sight reduction procedures and concise sight reduction tables, polar phenomena information and graphs, tables of increments and corrections and other auxiliary tables that are frequently used.

MAIN DATA

4. *Daily pages.* The daily pages give the GHA of Aries, the GHA and Dec of the Sun, Moon, and the four navigational planets, for each hour of UT. For the Moon, values of v and d are also tabulated for each hour to facilitate the correction of GHA and Dec to intermediate times; v and d for the Sun and planets change so slowly that they are given, at the foot of the appropriate columns, once only on the page; v is zero for Aries and negligible for the Sun, and is omitted. The SHA and Dec of the 57 selected stars, arranged in alphabetical order of proper name, are also given.

5. *Stars.* The SHA and Dec of 173 stars, including the 57 selected stars, are tabulated for each month on pages 268–273; no interpolation is required and the data can be used in precisely the same way as those for the selected stars on the daily pages. The stars are arranged in order of SHA.

The list of 173 includes all stars down to magnitude 3·0, together with a few fainter ones to fill the larger gaps. The 57 selected stars have been chosen from amongst these on account of brightness and distribution in the sky; they will suffice for the majority of observations.

The 57 selected stars are known by their proper names, but they are also numbered in descending order of SHA. In the list of 173 stars, the constellation names are always given on the left-hand page; on the facing page proper names are given where well-known names exist. Numbers for the selected stars are given in both columns.

An index to the selected stars, containing lists in both alphabetical and numerical order, is given on page xxxiii and is also reprinted on the bookmark.

6. *Increments and corrections.* The tables printed on tinted paper (pages ii–xxxi) at the back of the Almanac provide the increments and corrections for minutes and seconds to be applied to the hourly values of GHA and Dec. They consist of sixty tables, one for each minute, separated into two parts: increments to GHA for Sun and planets, Aries, and Moon for every minute and second; and, for each minute, corrections to be applied to GHA and Dec corresponding to the values of v and d given on the daily pages.

The increments are based on the following adopted hourly rates of increase of the GHA: Sun and planets, $15°$ precisely; Aries, $15°\ 02'\!.46$; Moon, $14°\ 19'\!.0$. The values of v on the daily pages are the excesses of the actual hourly motions over the adopted values; they are generally positive, except for Venus. The tabulated hourly values of the Sun's GHA have been adjusted to reduce to a minimum the error caused by treating v as negligible. The values of d on the daily pages are the hourly differences of the Dec. For the Moon, the true values of v and d are given for each hour; otherwise mean values are given for the three days on the page.

7. *Method of entry.* The UT of an observation is expressed as a day and hour, followed by a number of minutes and seconds. The tabular values of GHA and Dec, and, where necessary, the corresponding values of v and d, are taken directly from the daily pages for the day and hour of UT; this hour is always *before* the time of observation. SHA and Dec of the selected stars are also taken from the daily pages.

© British Crown Copyright 2018. All rights reserved.

The table of Increments and Corrections for the minute of UT is then selected. For the GHA, the increment for minutes and seconds is taken from the appropriate column opposite the seconds of UT; the v-correction is taken from the second part of the same table opposite the value of v as given on the daily pages. Both increment and v-correction are to be added to the GHA, except for Venus when v is prefixed by a minus sign and the v-correction is to be subtracted. For the Dec there is no increment, but a d-correction is applied in the same way as the v-correction; d is given without sign on the daily pages and the sign of the correction is to be supplied by inspection of the Dec column. In many cases the correction may be applied mentally.

8. *Examples.* (a) Sun and Moon. Required the GHA and Dec of the Sun and Moon on 2019 March 15 at $15^h 47^m 13^s$ UT.

		SUN			MOON			
		GHA	Dec	d	GHA	v	Dec	d
		° ′	° ′	′	° ′	′	° ′	′
Daily page, March 15^d 15^h		42 45·4	S 2 05·4	1·0	297 15·8	5·8	N 21 45·0	0·4
Increments for	47^m 13^s	11 48·3			11 16·0			
v or d corrections for	47^m		−0·8			+4·6	+0·3	
Sum for March 15^d 15^h 47^m 13^s		54 33·7	S 2 04·6		308 36·4		N 21 45·3	

(b) Planets. Required the LHA and Dec of (i) Venus on 2019 March 15 at $10^h 55^m 15^s$ UT in longitude W 82° 18′; (ii) Mars on 2019 March 15 at $13^h 56^m 51^s$ UT in longitude E 73° 36′.

		VENUS				MARS			
		GHA	v	Dec	d	GHA	v	Dec	d
		° ′	′	° ′	′	° ′	′	° ′	′
Daily page, Mar. 15^d	(10^h)	3 55·2	−0·5	S15 59·9	0·8	(13^h) 320 58·1	0·8	N18 22·9	0·5
Increments (planets)	(55^m 15^s)	13 48·8				(56^m 51^s) 14 12·8			
v or d corrections	(55^m)		−0·5	−0·7		(56^m)	+0·8	+0·5	
Sum = GHA and Dec.		17 43·5		S15 59·2		335 11·7		N18 23·4	
Longitude	(west)	− 82 18·0				(east) + 73 36·0			
Multiples of 360°		+360				−360			
LHA planet		295 25·5				48 47·7			

(c) Stars. Required the GHA and Dec of (i) *Aldebaran* on 2019 March 15 at $20^h 28^m 04^s$ UT; (ii) *Vega* on 2019 March 15 at $7^h 02^m 16^s$ UT.

		Aldebaran			*Vega*		
		GHA	Dec		GHA	Dec	
		° ′	° ′		° ′	° ′	
Daily page (SHA and Dec)		290 45·0	N 16 32·7		80 36·4	N 38 47·9	
Daily page (GHA Aries)	(20^h)	113 07·8		(7^h)	277 35·8		
Increments (Aries)	(28^m 04^s)	7 02·2		(02^m 16^s)	0 34·1		
Sum = GHA star		410 55·0			358 46·3		
Multiples of 360°		−360					
GHA star		50 55·0			358 46·3		

9. *Polaris (Pole Star) tables.* The tables on pages 274–276 provide means by which the latitude can be deduced from an observed altitude of *Polaris*, and they also give its azimuth; their use is explained and illustrated on those pages. They are based on the following formula:

$$\text{Latitude} - H_O = -p\cos h + \tfrac{1}{2}p\sin p \sin^2 h \tan(\text{latitude})$$

where

H_O = Apparent altitude (corrected for refraction)

p = polar distance of *Polaris* = 90° − Dec

h = local hour angle of *Polaris* = LHA Aries + SHA

a_0, which is a function of LHA Aries only, is the value of both terms of the above formula calculated for mean values of the SHA (315° 56′) and Dec (N 89° 20·7) of *Polaris*, for a mean latitude of 50°, and adjusted by the addition of a constant (58·8).

© British Crown Copyright 2018. All rights reserved.

a_1, which is a function of LHA Aries and latitude, is the excess of the value of the second term over its mean value for latitude 50°, increased by a constant (0′.6) to make it always positive. a_2, which is a function of LHA Aries and date, is the correction to the first term for the variation of *Polaris* from its adopted mean position; it is increased by a constant (0′.6) to make it positive. The sum of the added constants is 1°, so that:

$$\text{Latitude} = \text{Apparent altitude (corrected for refraction)} - 1° + a_0 + a_1 + a_2$$

RISING AND SETTING PHENOMENA

10. *General.* On the right-hand daily pages are given the times of sunrise and sunset, of the beginning and end of civil and nautical twilights, and of moonrise and moonset for a range of latitudes from N 72° to S 60°. These times, which are given to the nearest minute, are strictly the UT of the phenomena on the Greenwich meridian; they are given for every day for moonrise and moonset, but only for the middle day of the three on each page for the solar phenomena.

They are approximately the Local Mean Times (LMT) of the corresponding phenomena on other meridians; they can be formally interpolated if desired. The UT of a phenomenon is obtained from the LMT by:

$$\text{UT} = \text{LMT} \begin{array}{l} + \text{ west} \\ - \text{ east} \end{array} \text{longitude}$$

in which the longitude must first be converted to time by the table on page i or otherwise. Interpolation for latitude can be done mentally or with the aid of Table I on page xxxii.

The following symbols are used to indicate the conditions under which, in high latitudes, some of the phenomena do not occur:

⬜ Sun or Moon remains continuously above the horizon;

⬛ Sun or Moon remains continuously below the horizon;

//// twilight lasts all night.

Basis of the tabulations. At sunrise and sunset 16′ is allowed for semi-diameter and 34′ for horizontal refraction, so that at the times given the Sun's upper limb is on the visible horizon; all times refer to phenomena as seen from sea level with a clear horizon.

At the times given for the beginning and end of twilight, the Sun's zenith distance is 96° for civil, and 102° for nautical twilight. The degree of illumination at the times given for civil twilight (in good conditions and in the absence of other illumination) is such that the brightest stars are visible and the horizon is clearly defined. At the times given for nautical twilight, the horizon is in general not visible, and it is too dark for observation with a marine sextant.

Times corresponding to other depressions of the Sun may be obtained by interpolation or, for depressions of more than 12°, less reliably, by extrapolation; times so obtained will be subject to considerable uncertainty near extreme conditions.

At moonrise and moonset, allowance is made for semi-diameter, parallax, and refraction (34′), so that at the times given the Moon's upper limb is on the visible horizon as seen from sea level.

Polar phenomena. Information and graphs concerning the rising and setting of the Sun and Moon and the duration of civil twilight for high latitudes are given on pages 320–325.

11. *Sunrise, sunset, twilight.* The tabulated times may be regarded, without serious error, as the LMT of the phenomena on any of the three days on the page and in any longitude. Precise times may normally be obtained by interpolating the tabular values for latitude and to the correct day and longitude, the latter being expressed as a fraction of a day by dividing it by 360°, positive for west and negative for east longitudes. In the extreme conditions near ⬜, ⬛ or //// interpolation may not be possible in one direction, but accurate times are of little value in these circumstances.

Examples. Required the UT of (a) the beginning of morning twilights and sunrise on 2019 January 13 for latitude S 48° 55′, longitude E 75° 18′; (b) sunset and the end of evening twilights on 2019 January 15 for latitude N 67° 10′, longitude W 168° 05′.

© British Crown Copyright 2018. All rights reserved.

	(a)	Twilight Nautical	Civil	Sunrise	(b)	Sunset	Twilight Civil	Nautical
		d h m	d h m	d h m		d h m	d h m	d h m
From p. 19								
LMT for Lat	S 45°	13 03 09	13 03 55	13 04 31	N 66°	15 14 22	15 15 42	15 16 53
Corr. to	S 48° 55′	−30	−20	−16	N 67° 10′	−22	−12	−6
(p. xxxii, Table I)								
Long (p. i)	E 75° 18′	−5 01	−5 01	−5 01	W 168° 05′	+11 12	+11 12	+11 12
UT		12 21 38	12 22 34	12 23 14		16 01 12	16 02 42	16 03 59

The LMT are strictly for January 14 (middle date on page) and 0° longitude; for more precise times it is necessary to interpolate, but rounding errors may accumulate to about 2^m.

(a) to January $13^d - 75°/360° =$ Jan. 12^d8, i.e. $\frac{1}{3}(1\cdot2) = 0\cdot4$ backwards towards the data for the same latitude interpolated similarly from page 17; the corrections are -2^m to nautical twilight, -2^m to civil twilight and -1^m to sunrise.

(b) to January $15^d + 168°/360° =$ Jan. 15^d5, i.e. $\frac{1}{3}(1\cdot5) = 0\cdot5$ forwards towards the data for the same latitude interpolated similarly from page 21; the corrections are $+7^m$ to sunset, $+4^m$ to civil twilight, and $+4^m$ to nautical twilight.

12. *Moonrise, moonset.* Precise times of moonrise and moonset are rarely needed; a glance at the tables will generally give sufficient indication of whether the Moon is available for observation and of the hours of rising and setting. If needed, precise times may be obtained as follows. Interpolate for latitude, using Table I on page xxxii, on the day wanted and also on the preceding day in east longitudes or the following day in west longitudes; take the difference between these times and interpolate for longitude by applying to the time for the day wanted the correction from Table II on page xxxii, so that the resulting time is between the two times used. In extreme conditions near □ or ■ interpolation for latitude or longitude may be possible only in one direction; accurate times are of little value in these circumstances.

To facilitate this interpolation, the times of moonrise and moonset are given for four days on each page; where no phenomenon occurs during a particular day (as happens once a month) the time of the phenomenon on the following day, increased by 24^h, is given; extra care must be taken when interpolating between two values, when one of those values exceeds 24^h. In practice it suffices to use the daily difference between the times for the nearest tabular latitude, and generally, to enter Table II with the nearest tabular arguments as in the examples below.

Examples. Required the UT of moonrise and moonset in latitude S 47° 10′, longitudes E 124° 00′ and W 78° 31′ on 2019 January 17.

	Longitude E 124° 00′ Moonrise	Moonset	Longitude W 78° 31′ Moonrise	Moonset
	d h m	d h m	d h m	d h m
LMT for Lat. S 45°	17 15 59	17 01 04	17 15 59	17 01 04
Lat correction (p. xxxii, Table I)	+07	−07	+07	−07
Long correction (p. xxxii, Table II)	−23	−10	+16	+09
Correct LMT	17 15 43	17 00 47	17 16 22	17 01 06
Longitude (p. i)	−8 16	−8 16	+5 14	+5 14
UT	17 07 27	16 16 31	17 21 36	17 06 20

ALTITUDE CORRECTION TABLES

13. *General.* In general, two corrections are given for application to altitudes observed with a marine sextant; additional corrections are required for Venus and Mars and also for very low altitudes.

Tables of the correction for dip of the horizon, due to height of eye above sea level, are given on pages A2 and xxxiv. Strictly this correction should be applied first and subtracted from the sextant altitude to give apparent altitude, which is the correct argument for the other tables.

© British Crown Copyright 2018. All rights reserved.

Separate tables are given of the second correction for the Sun, for stars and planets (on pages A2 and A3), and for the Moon (on pages xxxiv and xxxv). For the Sun, values are given for both lower and upper limbs, for two periods of the year. The star tables are used for the planets, but additional corrections for parallax (page A2) are required for Venus and Mars. The Moon tables are in two parts: the main correction is a function of apparent altitude only and is tabulated for the lower limb (30′ must be subtracted to obtain the correction for the upper limb); the other, which is given for both lower and upper limbs, depends also on the horizontal parallax, which has to be taken from the daily pages.

An additional correction, given on page A4, is required for the change in the refraction, due to variations of pressure and temperature from the adopted standard conditions; it may generally be ignored for altitudes greater than 10°, except possibly in extreme conditions. The correction tables for the Sun, stars, and planets are in two parts; only those for altitudes greater than 10° are reprinted on the bookmark.

14. *Critical tables.* Some of the altitude correction tables are arranged as critical tables. In these, an interval of apparent altitude (or height of eye) corresponds to a single value of the correction; no interpolation is required. At a "critical" entry the upper of the two possible values of the correction is to be taken. For example, in the table of dip, a correction of −4′.1 corresponds to all values of the height of eye from 5·3 to 5·5 metres (17·5 to 18·3 feet) inclusive.

15. *Examples.* The following examples illustrate the use of the altitude correction tables; the sextant altitudes given are assumed to be taken on 2019 August 9 with a marine sextant at height 5·4 metres (18 feet), temperature −3°C and pressure 982 mb, the Moon sights being taken at about 10^h UT.

	SUN lower limb	SUN upper limb	MOON lower limb	MOON upper limb	VENUS	*Polaris*
	° ′	° ′	° ′	° ′	° ′	° ′
Sextant altitude	21 19·7	3 20·2	33 27·6	26 06·7	4 32·6	49 36·5
Dip, height 5·4 metres (18 feet)	−4·1	−4·1	−4·1	−4·1	−4·1	−4·1
Main correction	+13·6	−29·3	+57·4	+60·5	−10·8	−0·8
−30′ for upper limb (Moon)	—	—	—	−30·0	—	—
L, U correction for Moon	—	—	+4·0	+3·1	—	—
Additional correction for Venus	—	—	—	—	+0·1	—
Additional refraction correction	−0·1	−0·6	−0·1	−0·1	−0·5	0·0
Corrected sextant altitude	21 29·1	2 46·2	34 24·8	26 36·1	4 17·3	49 31·6

The main corrections have been taken out with apparent altitude (sextant altitude corrected for index error and dip) as argument, interpolating where possible. These refinements are rarely necessary.

16. *Composition of the Corrections.* The table for the dip of the sea horizon is based on the formula:

$$\text{Correction for dip} = -1'.76\sqrt{(\text{height of eye in metres})} = -0'.97\sqrt{(\text{height of eye in feet})}$$

The correction table for the Sun includes the effects of semi-diameter, parallax and mean refraction.

The correction tables for the stars and planets allow for the effect of mean refraction.

The phase correction for Venus has been incorporated in the tabulations for GHA and Dec, and no correction for phase is required. The additional corrections for Venus and Mars allow for parallax. Alternatively, the correction for parallax may be calculated from $p \cos H$, where p is the parallax and H is the altitude. In 2019 the values for p are:

	Jan. 1	Feb. 15	Dec. 31
Venus	0′.2	0′.1	

	Jan. 1	Dec. 31
Mars	0′.1	

The correction table for the Moon includes the effect of semi-diameter, parallax, augmentation and mean refraction.

© British Crown Copyright 2018. All rights reserved.

Mean refraction is calculated for a temperature of 10°C (50°F), a pressure of 1010 mb (29·83 inches), humidity of 80% and wavelength 0·50169 μm.

17. *Bubble sextant observations.* When observing with a bubble sextant, no correction is necessary for dip, semi-diameter, or augmentation. The altitude corrections for the stars and planets on page A2 and on the bookmark should be used for the Sun as well as for the stars and planets; for the Moon, it is easiest to take the mean of the corrections for lower and upper limbs and subtract 15′ from the altitude; the correction for dip must not be applied.

AUXILIARY AND PLANNING DATA

18. *Sun and Moon.* On the daily pages are given: hourly values of the horizontal parallax of the Moon; the semi-diameters and the times of meridian passage of both Sun and Moon over the Greenwich meridian; the equation of time; the age of the Moon, the percent (%) illuminated and a symbol indicating the phase. The times of the phases of the Moon are given in UT on page 4. For the Moon, the semi-diameters for each of the three days are given at the foot of the column; for the Sun a single value is sufficient. Table II on page xxxii may be used for interpolating the time of the Moon's meridian passage for longitude. The equation of time is given daily at 00^h and 12^h UT. The sign is *positive* for unshaded values and *negative* for shaded values. To obtain apparent time add the equation of time to mean time when the sign is *positive*. Subtract the equation of time from mean time when the sign is *negative*. At 12^h UT, when the sign is *positive*, meridian passage of the Sun occurs *before* 12^h UT, otherwise it occurs *after* 12^h UT.

19. *Planets.* The magnitudes of the planets are given immediately following their names in the headings on the daily pages; also given, for the middle day of the three on the page, are their SHA at 00^h UT and their times of meridian passage.

The planet notes and diagram on pages 8 and 9 provide descriptive information as to the suitability of the planets for observation during the year, and of their positions and movements.

20. *Stars.* The time of meridian passage of the first point of Aries over the Greenwich meridian is given on the daily pages, for the middle day of the three on the page, to 0^m1. The interval between successive meridian passages is $23^h 56^m1$ (24^h less 3^m9), so that times for intermediate days and other meridians can readily be derived. If a precise time is required, it may be obtained by finding the UT at which LHA Aries is zero.

The meridian passage of a star occurs when its LHA is zero, that is when LHA Aries + SHA = 360°. An approximate time can be obtained from the planet diagram on page 9.

The star charts on pages 266 and 267 are intended to assist identification. They show the relative positions of the stars in the sky as seen from the Earth and include all 173 stars used in the Almanac, together with a few others to complete the main constellation configurations. The local meridian at any time may be located on the chart by means of its SHA which is 360° − LHA Aries, or west longitude − GHA Aries.

21. *Star globe.* To set a star globe on which is printed a scale of LHA Aries, first set the globe for latitude and then rotate about the polar axis until the scale under the edge of the meridian circle reads LHA Aries.

To mark the positions of the Sun, Moon, and planets on the star globe, take the difference GHA Aries − GHA body and use this along the LHA Aries scale, in conjunction with the declination, to plot the position. GHA Aries − GHA body is most conveniently found by taking the difference when the GHA of the body is small (less than 15°), which happens once a day.

22. *Calendar.* On page 4 are given lists of ecclesiastical festivals, and of the principal anniversaries and holidays in the United Kingdom and the United States of America. The calendar on page 5 includes the day of the year as well as the day of the week.

© British Crown Copyright 2018. All rights reserved.

Brief particulars are given, at the foot of page 5, of the solar and lunar eclipses occurring during the year; the times given are in UT. The principal features of the more important solar eclipses are shown on the maps on pages 6 and 7.

23. *Standard times.* The lists on pages 262–265 give the standard times used in most countries. In general no attempt is made to give details of the beginning and end of summer time, since they are liable to frequent changes at short notice. For the latest information consult Admiralty List of Radio Signals Volume 2 (NP 282) corrected by Section VI of the weekly edition of Admiralty Notices to Mariners.

The Date or Calendar Line is an arbitrary line, on either side of which the date differs by one day; when crossing this line on a westerly course, the date must be advanced one day; when crossing it on an easterly course, the date must be put back one day. The line is a modification of the line of the 180th meridian, and is drawn so as to include, as far as possible, islands of any one group, etc., on the same side of the line. It may be traced by starting at the South Pole and joining up to the following positions:

Lat	S 51·0	S 45·0	S 15·0	S 5·0	N 48·0	N 53·0	N 65·5
Long	180·0	W 172·5	W 172·5	180·0	180·0	E 170·0	W 169·0

thence through the middle of the Diomede Islands to Lat N 68°·0, Long W 169°·0, passing east of Ostrov Vrangelya (Wrangel Island) to Lat N 75°·0, Long 180°·0, and thence to the North Pole.

ACCURACY

24. *Main data.* The quantities tabulated in this Almanac are generally correct to the nearest 0'·1; the exception is the Sun's GHA which is deliberately adjusted by up to 0'·15 to reduce the error due to ignoring the v-correction. The GHA and Dec at intermediate times cannot be obtained to this precision, since at least two quantities must be added; moreover, the v- and d-corrections are based on mean values of v and d and are taken from tables for the whole minute only. The largest error that can occur in the GHA or Dec of any body other than the Sun or Moon is less than 0'·2; it may reach 0'·25 for the GHA of the Sun and 0'·3 for that of the Moon.

In practice, it may be expected that only one third of the values of GHA and Dec taken out will have errors larger than 0'·05 and less than one tenth will have errors larger than 0'·1.

25. *Altitude corrections.* The errors in the altitude corrections are nominally of the same order as those in GHA and Dec, as they result from the addition of several quantities each correctly rounded off to 0'·1. But the actual values of the dip and of the refraction at low altitudes may, in extreme atmospheric conditions, differ considerably from the mean values used in the tables.

USE OF THIS ALMANAC IN 2020

This Almanac may be used for the Sun and stars in 2020 in the following manner.

For the Sun, take out the GHA and Dec for the same date but, for January and February (for February 29 use March 1), for a time $5^h 48^m 00^s$ *earlier* and, for March to December, for a time $18^h 12^m 00^s$ *later* than the UT of observation; in both cases *add* 87° 00' to the GHA so obtained. The error, mainly due to planetary perturbations of the Earth, is unlikely to exceed 0'·4.

For the stars, calculate the GHA and Dec for the same date and the same time, but for January and February (for February 29 use March 1) *subtract* 15'·1 and for March to December *add* 44'·0 to the GHA so found. The error due to incomplete correction for precession and nutation is unlikely to exceed 0'·4. If preferred, the same result can be obtained by using a time $5^h 48^m 00^s$ earlier for January and February (for February 29 use March 1) and $18^h 12^m 00^s$ later for March to December, than the UT of observation (as for the Sun) and adding 86° 59'·2 to the GHA (or adding 87° as for the Sun and subtracting 0'·8, for precession, from the SHA of the star).

The Almanac cannot be so used for the Moon or planets.

© British Crown Copyright 2018. All rights reserved.

LIST I — PLACES FAST ON UTC (mainly those EAST OF GREENWICH)

The times given ⎱ *added* to UTC to give Standard Time
below should be ⎰ *subtracted* from Standard Time to give UTC.

	h	m
Admiralty Islands	10	
Afghanistan	04	30
Albania*	01	
Algeria	01	
Amirante Islands	04	
Andaman Islands	05	30
Angola	01	
Armenia	04	
Australia		
Australian Capital Territory*	10	
New South Wales*[1]	10	
Northern Territory	09	30
Queensland	10	
South Australia*	09	30
Tasmania*	10	
Victoria*	10	
Western Australia	08	
Whitsunday Islands	10	
Austria*†	01	
Azerbaijan	04	
Bahrain	03	
Balearic Islands*†	01	
Bangladesh	06	
Belarus	03	
Belgium*†	01	
Benin	01	
Bosnia and Herzegovina*	01	
Botswana, Republic of	02	
Brunei	08	
Bulgaria*†	02	
Burma (Myanmar)	06	30
Burundi	02	
Cambodia	07	
Cameroon Republic	01	
Caroline Islands[2]	10	
Central African Republic	01	
Chad	01	
Chagos Archipelago & Diego Garcia	06	
Chatham Islands*	12	45
China, People's Republic of	08	
Christmas Island, Indian Ocean ...	07	
Cocos (Keeling) Islands	06	30
Comoro Islands (Comoros)	03	
Congo, Democratic Republic		
West: Kinshasa, Equateur	01	
East: Orientale, Kasai, Kivu, Shaba	02	
Congo Republic	01	
Corsica*†	01	
Crete*†	02	
Croatia*†	01	
Cyprus†: Ercan*, Larnaca*	02	
Czech Republic*†	01	

	h	m
Denmark*†	01	
Djibouti	03	
Egypt, Arab Republic of	02	
Equatorial Guinea, Republic of	01	
Bioko	01	
Eritrea	03	
Estonia*†	02	
Ethiopia	03	
Fiji*	12	
Finland*†	02	
France*†	01	
Gabon	01	
Georgia	04	
Germany*†	01	
Gibraltar*	01	
Greece*†	02	
Guam	10	
Hong Kong	08	
Hungary*†	01	
India	05	30
Indonesia, Republic of		
Bangka, Billiton, Java, West and		
Central Kalimantan, Madura, Sumatra	07	
Bali, Flores, South, North and East		
Kalimantan, Lombok, Sulawesi,		
Sumba, Sumbawa, West Timor ...	08	
Aru, Irian Jaya, Kai, Moluccas		
Tanimbar	09	
Iran*	03	30
Iraq	03	
Israel*	02	
Italy*†	01	
Jan Mayen Island*	01	
Japan	09	
Jordan*	02	
Kazakhstan		
Western: Aktau, Uralsk, Atyrau ...	05	
Eastern & Central: Kzyl-Orda, Astana	06	
Kenya	03	
Kerguelen Islands	05	
Kiribati Republic		
Gilbert Islands	12	
Phoenix Islands[3]	13	
Line Islands[3]	14	
Korea, North	08	30
Korea, South	09	
Kuwait	03	
Kyrgyzstan	06	
Laccadive Islands	05	30
Laos	07	

* Daylight-saving time may be kept in these places.   † For Summer time dates see List II footnotes.
[1] Except Broken Hill Area* which keeps 09^h 30^m.
[2] Except Pohnpei, Pingelap and Kosrae which keep 11^h and Palau which keeps 09^h.
[3] The Line and Phoenix Is. not part of the Kiribati Republic may keep other time zones.

© British Crown Copyright 2018. All rights reserved.

LIST I — (*continued*)

	h	m		h	m
Latvia*†	02		Norilsk, Krasnoyarsk, Dikson,		
Lebanon*	02		Novosibirsk, Tomsk	07	
Lesotho	02		Irkutsk, Bratsk, Ulan-Ude	08	
Libya	02		Tiksi, Yakutsk, Chita	09	
Liechtenstein*	01		Vladivostok, Khabarovsk, Okhotsk	10	
Lithuania*†	02		Severo-Kurilsk, Magadan,		
Lord Howe Island*	10	30	Sakhalin Island	11	
Luxembourg*†	01		Petropavlovsk-K., Anadyr	12	
			Rwanda	02	
Macau	08		Ryukyu Islands	09	
Macedonia*, former Yugoslav Republic	01				
Madagascar, Democratic Republic of	03		Samoa*	13	
Malawi	02		Santa Cruz Islands	11	
Malaysia, Malaya, Sabah, Sarawak ...	08		Sardinia*†	01	
Maldives, Republic of The	05		Saudi Arabia	03	
Malta*†	01		Schouten Islands	09	
Mariana Islands	10		Serbia*	01	
Marshall Islands	12		Seychelles	04	
Mauritius	04		Sicily*†	01	
Moldova*	02		Singapore	08	
Monaco*	01		Slovakia*†	01	
Mongolia	08		Slovenia*†	01	
Montenegro*	01		Socotra	03	
Mozambique	02		Solomon Islands	11	
			Somalia Republic	03	
Namibia	02		South Africa, Republic of	02	
Nauru	12		South Sudan	03	
Nepal	05	45	Spain*†	01	
Netherlands, The*†	01		Spanish Possessions in North Africa*	01	
New Caledonia	11		Spitsbergen (Svalbard)*	01	
New Zealand*	12		Sri Lanka	05	30
Nicobar Islands	05	30	Sudan, Republic of	02	
Niger	01		Swaziland	02	
Nigeria, Republic of	01		Sweden*†	01	
Norfolk Island	11		Switzerland*	01	
Norway*	01		Syria (Syrian Arab Republic)*	02	
Novaya Zemlya	03				
			Taiwan	08	
Okinawa	09		Tajikistan	05	
Oman	04		Tanzania	03	
			Thailand	07	
Pagalu (Annobon Islands)	01		Timor-Leste	09	
Pakistan	05		Tonga	13	
Palau Islands	09		Tunisia	01	
Papua New Guinea[4]	10		Turkey	03	
Pescadores Islands	08		Turkmenistan	05	
Philippine Republic	08		Tuvalu	12	
Poland*†	01				
			Uganda	03	
Qatar	03		Ukraine*	02	
			United Arab Emirates	04	
Reunion	04		Uzbekistan	05	
Romania*†	02				
Russia[5]			Vanuatu, Republic of	11	
Kaliningrad	02		Vietnam, Socialist Republic of	07	
Moscow, St. Petersburg, Volgograd,					
Arkhangelsk	03		Yemen	03	
Samara, Astrakhan, Saratov	04				
Ekaterinburg, Ufa, Perm, Novyy Port	05		Zambia, Republic of	02	
Omsk	06		Zimbabwe	02	

* Daylight-saving time may be kept in these places.   † For Summer time dates see List II footnotes.
[4] Excluding the Autonomous Region of Bougainville which keeps 11ʰ.
[5] The boundaries between the zones are irregular; listed are chief towns in each zone.

© British Crown Copyright 2018. All rights reserved.

LIST II — PLACES NORMALLY KEEPING UTC

Ascension Island	Ghana	Irish Republic*†	Morocco*	Sierra Leone
Burkina-Faso	Great Britain†	Ivory Coast	Portugal*†	Togo Republic
Canary Islands*†	Guinea-Bissau	Liberia	Principe	Tristan da Cunha
Channel Islands†	Guinea Republic	Madeira*†	St. Helena	
Faeroes*, The	Iceland	Mali	São Tomé	
Gambia, The	Ireland, Northern†	Mauritania	Senegal	

* Daylight-saving time may be kept in these places.

† Summer time (daylight-saving time), one hour in advance of UTC, will be kept from 2019 March 31^d 01^h to October 27^d 01^h UTC (Ninth Summer Time Directive of the European Union). Ratification by member countries has not been verified.

LIST III — PLACES SLOW ON UTC (WEST OF GREENWICH)

The times given ⎱ *subtracted* from UTC to give Standard Time
below should be ⎰ *added* to Standard Time to give UTC.

	h	m		h	m
American Samoa	11		Canada (*continued*)		
Argentina	03		Prince Edward Island*	04	
Austral (Tubuai) Islands[1]	10		Quebec, east of long. W. 63°	04	
Azores*†	01		west of long. W. 63°* ...	05	
			Saskatchewan	06	
Bahamas*	05		Yukon*	08	
Barbados	04		Cape Verde Islands	01	
Belize	06		Cayman Islands	05	
Bermuda*	04		Chile		
Bolivia	04		General*	04	
Brazil			Magallanes and Chilean Antarctic ...	03	
Fernando de Noronha I., Trindade I.,			Colombia	05	
Oceanic Is.	02		Cook Islands	10	
N and NE coastal states, Tocantins,			Costa Rica	06	
Minas Gerais*, Goiás*, Brasilia*,			Cuba*	05	
S and E coastal states*	03		Curaçao Island	04	
Amazonas[2], Mato Grosso do Sul*,					
Mato Grosso*, Rondônia, Roraima	04		Dominican Republic	04	
Acre	05				
British Antarctic Territory[3,4]	03		Easter Island (I. de Pascua)*	06	
			Ecuador	05	
Canada[4‡]			El Salvador	06	
Alberta*	07				
British Columbia*	08		Falkland Islands	03	
Labrador*	04		Fernando de Noronha Island	02	
Manitoba*	06		French Guiana	03	
New Brunswick*	04				
Newfoundland*	03 30		Galápagos Islands	06	
Nunavut*			Greenland		
east of long. W. 85°	05		Danmarkshavn, Mesters Vig	00	
long. W. 85° to W. 102°	06		General*	03	
west of long. W. 102°	07		Scoresby Sound*	01	
Northwest Territories*	07		Thule*, Pituffik*	04	
Nova Scotia*	04		Grenada	04	
Ontario, east of long. W. 90°*	05		Guadeloupe	04	
Ontario, west of long. W. 90°* ...	06		Guatemala	06	
			Guyana, Republic of	04	

* Daylight-saving time may be kept in these places.   ‡ Dates for DST are given at the end of List III.
[1] This is the legal standard time, but local mean time is generally used.
[2] Except the cities of Eirunepe, Benjamin Constant and Tabatinga which keep 05^h.
[3] Stations may use UTC.
[4] Some areas may keep another time zone.

© British Crown Copyright 2018. All rights reserved.

LIST III — (*continued*)

	h	m		h	m
Haiti*	05		United States of America‡(*continued*)		
Honduras	06		Idaho, southern part	07	
			northern part	08	
Jamaica	05		Illinois	06	
Johnston Island	10		Indiana⁶	05	
Juan Fernandez Islands*	04		Iowa	06	
			Kansas⁶	06	
Leeward Islands	04		Kentucky, eastern part	05	
			western part	06	
Marquesas Islands	09	30	Louisiana	06	
Martinique	04		Maine	05	
Mexico			Maryland	05	
General*	06		Massachusetts	05	
Quintana Roo	05		Michigan⁶	05	
Baja California Sur*, Chihuahua*			Minnesota	06	
Nayarit*, Sinaloa* and Sonara ...	07		Mississippi	06	
Baja California Norte*	08		Missouri	06	
Midway Islands	11		Montana	07	
			Nebraska, eastern part	06	
Nicaragua	06		western part	07	
Niue	11		Nevada	08	
			New Hampshire	05	
Panama, Republic of	05		New Jersey	05	
Paraguay*	04		New Mexico	07	
Peru	05		New York	05	
Pitcairn Island	08		North Carolina	05	
Puerto Rico	04		North Dakota, eastern part	06	
			western part	07	
St. Pierre and Miquelon*	03		Ohio	05	
Society Islands	10		Oklahoma	06	
South Georgia	02		Oregon⁶	08	
Suriname	03		Pennsylvania	05	
			Rhode Island	05	
Trindade Island, South Atlantic ...	02		South Carolina	05	
Trinidad and Tobago	04		South Dakota, eastern part	06	
Tuamotu Archipelago	10		western part	07	
Tubuai (Austral) Islands	10		Tennessee, eastern part	05	
Turks and Caicos Islands*	05		western part	06	
			Texas⁶	06	
United States of America‡			Utah	07	
Alabama	06		Vermont	05	
Alaska	09		Virginia	05	
Aleutian Islands, east of W. 169° 30'	09		Washington D.C.	05	
Aleutian Islands, west of W. 169° 30'	10		Washington	08	
Arizona⁵	07		West Virginia	05	
Arkansas	06		Wisconsin	06	
California	08		Wyoming	07	
Colorado	07		Uruguay	03	
Connecticut	05				
Delaware	05		Venezuela	04	
District of Columbia	05		Virgin Islands	04	
Florida⁶	05				
Georgia	05		Windward Islands	04	
Hawaii⁵	10				

* Daylight-saving time may be kept in these places.

‡ Daylight-saving (Summer) time, one hour fast on the time given, is kept during 2019 from March 10 (second Sunday) to November 3 (first Sunday), changing at 02ʰ 00ᵐ local clock time.

⁵ Exempt from keeping daylight-saving time, except for a portion of Arizona.

⁶ A small portion of the state is in another time zone.

© British Crown Copyright 2018. All rights reserved.

STAR CHARTS

NORTHERN STARS

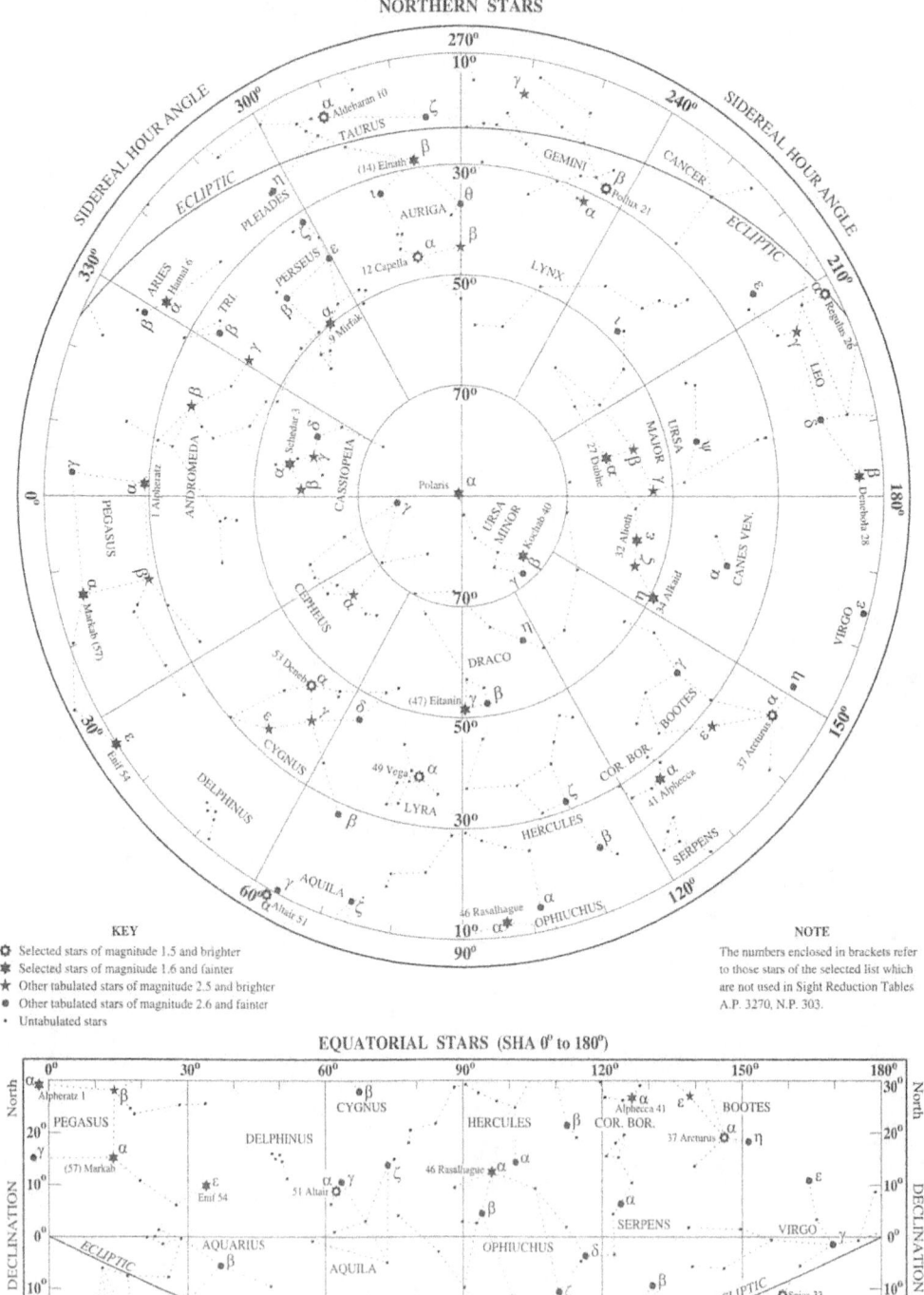

© British Crown Copyright 2018. All rights reserved.

SOUTHERN STARS

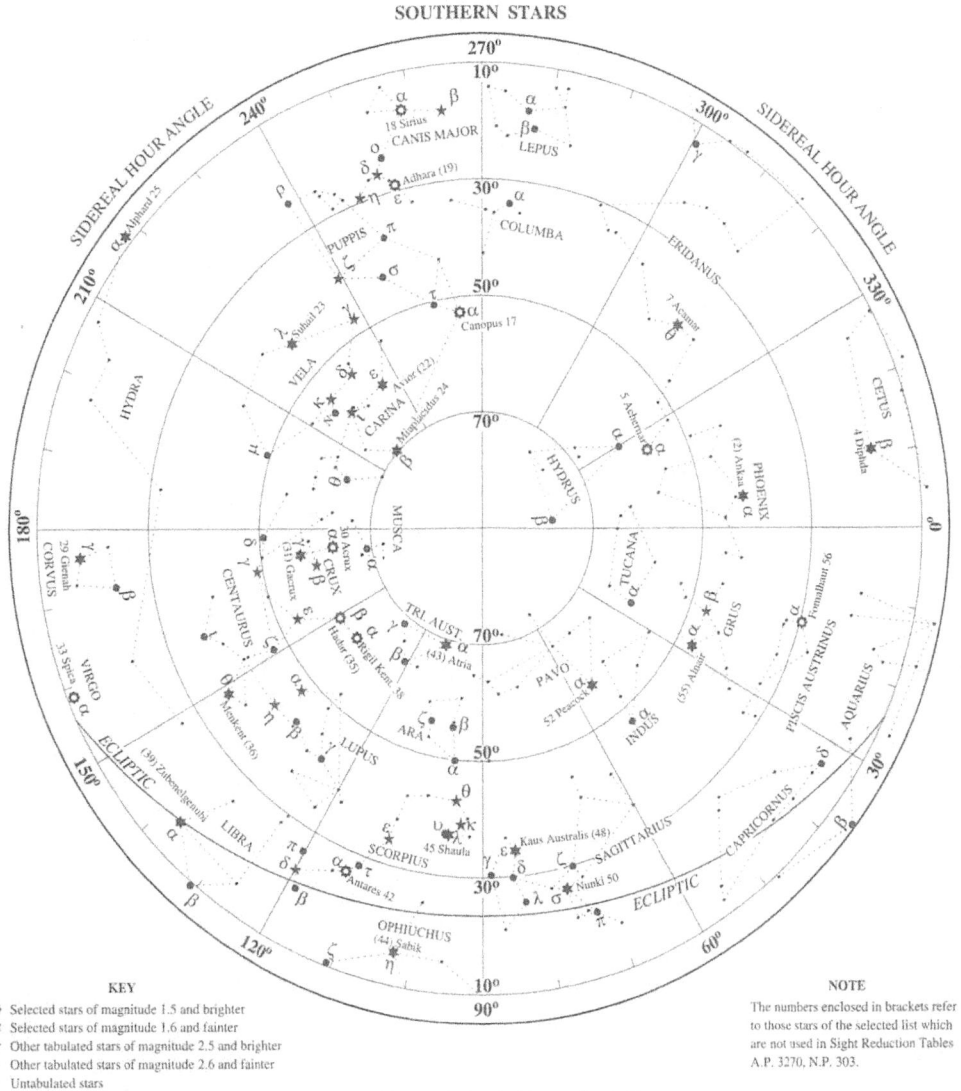

KEY

✿ Selected stars of magnitude 1.5 and brighter
✳ Selected stars of magnitude 1.6 and fainter
★ Other tabulated stars of magnitude 2.5 and brighter
● Other tabulated stars of magnitude 2.6 and fainter
· Untabulated stars

NOTE

The numbers enclosed in brackets refer
to those stars of the selected list which
are not used in Sight Reduction Tables
A.P. 3270, N.P. 303.

EQUATORIAL STARS (SHA 180° to 360°)

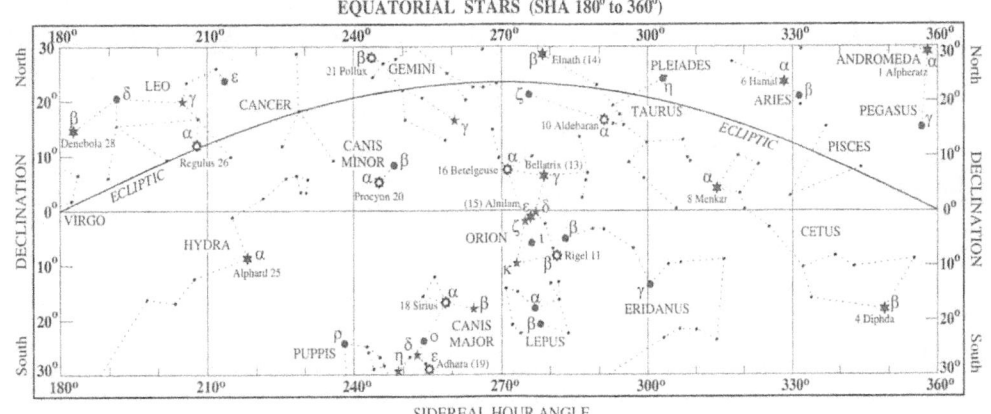

© British Crown Copyright 2018. All rights reserved.

Mag.	Name and Number	No.	SHA °	JAN.	FEB.	MAR.	APR.	MAY	JUNE	Dec.	JAN.	FEB.	MAR.	APR.	MAY	JUNE
3·2	γ Cephei		4	58·4	58·9	59·1	58·9	58·3	57·5	N 77	44·5	44·4	44·2	44·1	44·0	44·0
2·5	α Pegasi	57	13	34·8	34·8	34·8	34·6	34·5	34·2	N 15	18·4	18·4	18·3	18·3	18·3	18·4
2·4	β Pegasi		13	49·9	50·0	49·9	49·8	49·6	49·4	N 28	11·2	11·1	11·0	11·0	11·0	11·1
1·2	α Piscis Aust.	56	15	20·0	20·1	20·0	19·9	19·7	19·4	S 29	31·5	31·5	31·4	31·3	31·2	31·1
2·1	β Gruis		19	03·7	03·8	03·7	03·5	03·3	02·9	S 46	47·4	47·3	47·1	47·0	46·9	46·8
2·9	α Tucanæ		25	04·1	04·1	04·0	03·7	03·4	02·9	S 60	10·1	10·0	09·8	09·7	09·6	09·5
1·7	α Gruis	55	27	39·4	39·4	39·3	39·0	38·8	38·4	S 46	52·3	52·2	52·1	52·0	51·9	51·8
2·9	δ Capricorni		32	59·2	59·2	59·1	58·9	58·7	58·5	S 16	02·6	02·5	02·5	02·4	02·4	02·3
2·4	ε Pegasi	54	33	43·7	43·7	43·6	43·4	43·2	43·0	N 9	57·7	57·7	57·6	57·6	57·7	57·8
2·9	β Aquarii		36	52·1	52·1	52·0	51·8	51·6	51·4	S 5	29·3	29·3	29·3	29·3	29·2	29·1
2·4	α Cephei		40	15·2	15·2	15·1	14·7	14·4	14·0	N 62	40·1	39·9	39·8	39·7	39·7	39·8
2·5	ε Cygni		48	15·8	15·7	15·6	15·4	15·2	14·9	N 34	02·6	02·4	02·3	02·3	02·3	02·5
1·3	α Cygni	53	49	29·3	29·3	29·2	28·9	28·6	28·4	N 45	21·0	20·8	20·7	20·7	20·7	20·8
3·1	α Indi		50	17·4	17·3	17·1	16·8	16·5	16·1	S 47	13·5	13·4	13·3	13·3	13·2	13·2
1·9	α Pavonis	52	53	13·9	13·7	13·5	13·1	12·7	12·4	S 56	40·4	40·3	40·2	40·1	40·1	40·1
2·2	γ Cygni		54	16·9	16·8	16·7	16·4	16·2	15·9	N 40	19·1	19·0	18·9	18·8	18·9	19·0
0·8	α Aquilæ	51	62	04·9	04·8	04·6	04·4	04·2	04·0	N 8	55·2	55·1	55·0	55·1	55·1	55·2
2·7	γ Aquilæ		63	13·1	13·0	12·8	12·6	12·4	12·2	N 10	39·6	39·5	39·5	39·5	39·6	39·7
2·9	δ Cygni		63	37·0	36·9	36·8	36·5	36·2	36·0	N 45	10·7	10·5	10·4	10·4	10·5	10·6
3·1	β Cygni		67	08·2	08·1	07·9	07·7	07·5	07·3	N 27	60·0	59·9	59·8	59·8	59·9	60·0
2·9	π Sagittarii		72	17·2	17·1	16·9	16·6	16·4	16·2	S 20	59·5	59·5	59·5	59·5	59·4	59·4
3·0	ζ Aquilæ		73	26·3	26·1	26·0	25·7	25·5	25·3	N 13	53·6	53·5	53·4	53·4	53·5	53·6
2·6	ζ Sagittarii		74	03·4	03·2	03·0	02·7	02·5	02·3	S 29	51·1	51·0	51·0	51·0	51·0	51·0
2·0	σ Sagittarii	50	75	54·0	53·8	53·6	53·3	53·1	52·9	S 26	16·3	16·3	16·2	16·2	16·2	16·2
0·0	α Lyræ	49	80	36·8	36·6	36·4	36·2	35·9	35·8	N 38	48·1	48·0	47·9	47·9	48·0	48·1
2·8	λ Sagittarii		82	43·5	43·3	43·1	42·8	42·6	42·4	S 25	24·5	24·5	24·5	24·5	24·5	24·5
1·9	ε Sagittarii	48	83	39·2	39·0	38·7	38·4	38·2	38·0	S 34	22·4	22·3	22·3	22·3	22·3	22·3
2·7	δ Sagittarii		84	27·5	27·3	27·0	26·8	26·5	26·4	S 29	49·0	49·0	49·0	49·0	49·0	49·0
3·0	γ Sagittarii		88	15·2	15·0	14·7	14·5	14·2	14·1	S 30	25·2	25·2	25·2	25·2	25·2	25·3
2·2	γ Draconis	47	90	44·9	44·7	44·4	44·1	43·8	43·7	N 51	29·2	29·0	29·0	29·0	29·1	29·3
2·8	β Ophiuchi		93	54·3	54·1	53·9	53·7	53·5	53·4	N 4	33·7	33·6	33·5	33·6	33·6	33·7
2·4	κ Scorpii		94	03·6	03·4	03·1	02·8	02·6	02·4	S 39	02·1	02·1	02·1	02·1	02·2	02·2
1·9	θ Scorpii		95	20·4	20·1	19·8	19·5	19·3	19·1	S 43	00·3	00·3	00·3	00·3	00·4	00·4
2·1	α Ophiuchi	46	96	03·2	03·0	02·8	02·6	02·4	02·3	N 12	32·8	32·7	32·7	32·7	32·8	32·9
1·6	λ Scorpii	45	96	17·1	16·9	16·6	16·3	16·1	16·0	S 37	06·8	06·8	06·8	06·8	06·9	06·9
3·0	α Aræ		96	41·1	40·8	40·4	40·1	39·8	39·6	S 49	53·2	53·1	53·1	53·2	53·2	53·3
2·7	υ Scorpii		96	59·8	59·5	59·3	59·0	58·7	58·6	S 37	18·4	18·4	18·4	18·4	18·5	18·5
2·8	β Draconis		97	17·6	17·4	17·1	16·8	16·6	16·5	N 52	17·1	17·1	17·0	17·0	17·2	17·3
2·8	β Aræ		98	17·6	17·2	16·9	16·5	16·2	16·0	S 55	32·5	32·5	32·5	32·5	32·6	32·7
Var.‡	α Herculis		101	07·8	07·6	07·3	07·1	07·0	06·9	N 14	22·2	22·1	22·0	22·1	22·1	22·2
2·4	η Ophiuchi	44	102	08·5	08·3	08·0	07·8	07·6	07·5	S 15	44·7	44·8	44·8	44·8	44·8	44·8
3·1	ζ Aræ		104	57·8	57·4	57·1	56·7	56·4	56·3	S 56	00·8	00·8	00·8	00·9	01·0	01·1
2·3	ε Scorpii		107	09·6	09·3	09·1	08·8	08·6	08·5	S 34	19·4	19·4	19·4	19·5	19·5	19·6
1·9	α Triang. Aust.	43	107	20·7	20·2	19·6	19·0	18·7	18·5	S 69	03·3	03·3	03·3	03·4	03·5	03·6
2·8	ζ Herculis		109	30·4	30·2	29·9	29·7	29·6	29·5	N 31	34·1	34·0	33·9	34·0	34·1	34·2
2·6	ζ Ophiuchi		110	27·4	27·1	26·9	26·7	26·6	26·5	S 10	36·2	36·2	36·3	36·3	36·3	36·2
2·8	τ Scorpii		110	44·5	44·2	44·0	43·7	43·6	43·5	S 28	15·1	15·1	15·1	15·2	15·2	15·2
2·8	β Herculis		112	14·9	14·7	14·4	14·2	14·1	14·0	N 21	26·9	26·8	26·8	26·8	26·9	27·0
1·0	α Scorpii	42	112	21·9	21·6	21·4	21·1	21·0	20·9	S 26	28·2	28·2	28·3	28·3	28·4	28·4
2·7	η Draconis		113	56·8	56·5	56·1	55·8	55·6	55·6	N 61	28·1	28·0	28·0	28·1	28·2	28·4
2·7	δ Ophiuchi		116	10·3	10·1	09·8	09·6	09·5	09·4	S 3	44·5	44·5	44·6	44·6	44·5	44·5
2·6	β Scorpii		118	22·3	22·0	21·8	21·6	21·5	21·4	S 19	51·2	51·3	51·3	51·4	51·4	51·4
2·3	δ Scorpii		119	38·5	38·3	38·1	37·8	37·7	37·6	S 22	40·3	40·4	40·4	40·5	40·5	40·5
2·9	π Scorpii		119	60·4	60·1	59·9	59·7	59·5	59·5	S 26	09·9	09·9	10·0	10·0	10·1	10·1
2·8	β Trianguli Aust.		120	48·2	47·8	47·3	46·9	46·7	46·6	S 63	28·9	28·9	29·0	29·1	29·2	29·3
2·6	α Serpentis		123	42·3	42·1	41·9	41·7	41·6	41·5	N 6	22·0	22·0	21·9	21·9	22·0	22·0
2·8	γ Lupi		125	54·3	54·0	53·7	53·5	53·3	53·3	S 41	13·5	13·5	13·6	13·7	13·8	13·8
2·2	α Coronæ Bor.	41	126	08·0	07·7	07·5	07·3	07·2	07·2	N 26	39·0	38·9	38·9	39·0	39·1	39·2

‡ 2·9 — 3·6

© British Crown Copyright 2018. All rights reserved.

Mag.	Name and Number		SHA °	JULY	AUG.	SEPT.	OCT.	NOV.	DEC.	Declination °	JULY	AUG.	SEPT.	OCT.	NOV.	DEC.
3·2	γ Cephei		4	56·8	56·2	56·0	56·1	56·6	57·2	N 77	44·1	44·3	44·4	44·6	44·8	44·8
2·5	*Markab*	57	13	34·0	33·8	33·8	33·8	33·9	34·0	N 15	18·5	18·6	18·7	18·8	18·8	18·8
2·4	*Scheat*		13	49·1	49·0	48·9	48·9	49·0	49·1	N 28	11·2	11·3	11·4	11·5	11·6	11·6
1·2	*Fomalhaut*	56	15	19·2	19·0	18·9	18·9	19·0	19·1	S 29	31·0	31·0	31·0	31·1	31·2	31·2
2·1	β Gruis		19	02·6	02·4	02·3	02·4	02·5	02·7	S 46	46·8	46·8	46·9	47·0	47·1	47·1
2·9	α Tucanæ		25	02·6	02·3	02·3	02·4	02·6	02·9	S 60	09·5	09·6	09·7	09·9	09·9	09·9
1·7	*Alnair*	55	27	38·2	38·0	37·9	38·0	38·2	38·3	S 46	51·8	51·9	52·0	52·1	52·1	52·1
2·9	δ Capricorni		32	58·2	58·1	58·1	58·2	58·3	58·4	S 16	02·2	02·2	02·2	02·2	02·3	02·3
2·4	*Enif*	54	33	42·8	42·7	42·6	42·7	42·8	42·9	N 9	57·9	58·0	58·0	58·1	58·1	58·0
2·9	β Aquarii		36	51·2	51·1	51·1	51·1	51·3	51·3	S 5	29·0	29·0	29·0	29·0	29·0	29·0
2·4	*Alderamin*		40	13·7	13·7	13·8	14·0	14·4	14·7	N 62	40·0	40·1	40·3	40·4	40·5	40·4
2·5	ε Cygni		48	14·8	14·7	14·8	14·9	15·1	15·2	N 34	02·6	02·8	02·9	02·9	02·9	02·9
1·3	*Deneb*	53	49	28·2	28·2	28·3	28·4	28·6	28·8	N 45	21·0	21·1	21·3	21·4	21·4	21·3
3·1	α Indi		50	15·9	15·8	15·9	16·0	16·2	16·3	S 47	13·2	13·3	13·4	13·5	13·5	13·4
1·9	*Peacock*	52	53	12·1	12·0	12·1	12·3	12·6	12·7	S 56	40·2	40·3	40·4	40·4	40·4	40·4
2·2	γ Cygni		54	15·8	15·7	15·8	16·0	16·2	16·3	N 40	19·2	19·3	19·4	19·5	19·5	19·4
0·8	*Altair*	51	62	03·8	03·8	03·9	04·0	04·1	04·2	N 8	55·3	55·4	55·4	55·4	55·4	55·4
2·7	γ Aquilæ		63	12·1	12·0	12·1	12·2	12·4	12·4	N 10	39·8	39·9	39·9	39·9	39·9	39·8
2·9	δ Cygni		63	35·9	35·9	36·0	36·2	36·5	36·6	N 45	10·8	10·9	11·0	11·1	11·0	10·9
3·1	*Albireo*		67	07·2	07·2	07·3	07·4	07·6	07·7	N 28	00·2	00·3	00·4	00·4	00·3	00·2
2·9	π Sagittarii		72	16·1	16·0	16·1	16·3	16·4	16·4	S 20	59·4	59·4	59·4	59·4	59·4	59·5
3·0	ζ Aquilæ		73	25·3	25·3	25·4	25·5	25·6	25·7	N 13	53·8	53·8	53·8	53·8	53·8	53·7
2·6	ζ Sagittarii		74	02·1	02·1	02·2	02·4	02·5	02·5	S 29	51·0	51·0	51·0	51·1	51·1	51·0
2·0	*Nunki*	50	75	52·8	52·8	52·9	53·0	53·2	53·2	S 26	16·2	16·2	16·2	16·3	16·3	16·2
0·0	*Vega*	49	80	35·7	35·8	36·0	36·1	36·3	36·4	N 38	48·3	48·4	48·5	48·5	48·4	48·3
2·8	λ Sagittarii		82	42·3	42·3	42·4	42·6	42·7	42·7	S 25	24·5	24·5	24·5	24·6	24·5	24·5
1·9	*Kaus Australis*	48	83	37·9	37·9	38·1	38·2	38·3	38·3	S 34	22·4	22·4	22·5	22·5	22·4	22·4
2·7	δ Sagittarii		84	26·3	26·3	26·4	26·6	26·7	26·7	S 29	49·0	49·1	49·1	49·1	49·1	49·1
3·0	γ Sagittarii		88	14·0	14·0	14·1	14·3	14·4	14·4	S 30	25·3	25·3	25·3	25·3	25·3	25·3
2·2	*Eltanin*	47	90	43·7	43·8	44·1	44·3	44·6	44·6	N 51	29·4	29·5	29·6	29·6	29·5	29·3
2·8	β Ophiuchi		93	53·4	53·4	53·5	53·7	53·7	53·7	N 4	33·8	33·8	33·8	33·8	33·8	33·7
2·4	κ Scorpii		94	02·3	02·4	02·5	02·7	02·8	02·8	S 39	02·3	02·3	02·3	02·3	02·3	02·3
1·9	θ Scorpii		95	19·1	19·1	19·3	19·5	19·6	19·5	S 43	00·5	00·6	00·6	00·6	00·5	00·5
2·1	*Rasalhague*	46	96	02·3	02·3	02·5	02·6	02·7	02·7	N 12	33·0	33·0	33·1	33·0	33·0	32·9
1·6	*Shaula*	45	96	15·9	16·0	16·1	16·3	16·4	16·3	S 37	07·0	07·0	07·0	07·0	07·0	06·9
3·0	α Aræ		96	39·6	39·7	39·9	40·1	40·2	40·1	S 49	53·4	53·5	53·5	53·5	53·4	53·3
2·7	υ Scorpii		96	58·5	58·6	58·8	58·9	59·0	59·0	S 37	18·6	18·6	18·6	18·6	18·6	18·5
2·8	β Draconis		97	16·5	16·7	16·9	17·2	17·4	17·4	N 52	17·6	17·6	17·6	17·6	17·5	17·3
2·8	β Aræ		98	16·0	16·1	16·3	16·5	16·7	16·6	S 55	32·8	32·9	32·9	32·9	32·8	32·7
Var.‡	α Herculis		101	06·8	06·9	07·0	07·2	07·3	07·2	N 14	22·3	22·4	22·4	22·4	22·3	22·2
2·4	*Sabik*	44	102	07·5	07·5	07·7	07·8	07·8	07·8	S 15	44·8	44·8	44·8	44·8	44·8	44·8
3·1	ζ Aræ		104	56·2	56·4	56·6	56·8	56·9	56·9	S 56	01·2	01·2	01·3	01·2	01·1	01·0
2·3	ε Scorpii		107	08·5	08·6	08·7	08·9	08·9	08·9	S 34	19·6	19·6	19·6	19·6	19·6	19·5
1·9	*Atria*	43	107	18·5	18·7	19·1	19·5	19·7	19·6	S 69	03·7	03·8	03·8	03·8	03·7	03·6
2·8	ζ Herculis		109	29·5	29·7	29·8	30·0	30·1	30·0	N 31	34·3	34·4	34·4	34·4	34·2	34·1
2·6	ζ Ophiuchi		110	26·5	26·5	26·7	26·8	26·8	26·7	S 10	36·2	36·2	36·2	36·2	36·2	36·3
2·8	τ Scorpii		110	43·5	43·6	43·7	43·8	43·9	43·8	S 28	15·3	15·3	15·3	15·3	15·2	15·2
2·8	β Herculis		112	14·0	14·1	14·3	14·4	14·5	14·4	N 21	27·1	27·2	27·2	27·1	27·0	26·9
1·0	*Antares*	42	112	20·9	21·0	21·1	21·2	21·3	21·2	S 26	28·4	28·4	28·4	28·4	28·3	28·3
2·7	η Draconis		113	55·7	56·0	56·3	56·6	56·8	56·8	N 61	28·5	28·6	28·6	28·5	28·3	28·2
2·7	δ Ophiuchi		116	09·5	09·5	09·7	09·8	09·8	09·7	S 3	44·5	44·4	44·4	44·4	44·5	44·6
2·6	β Scorpii		118	21·4	21·5	21·6	21·7	21·7	21·6	S 19	51·4	51·4	51·4	51·4	51·4	51·4
2·3	*Dschubba*		119	37·7	37·7	37·9	38·0	38·0	37·9	S 22	40·5	40·5	40·5	40·5	40·5	40·5
2·9	π Scorpii		119	59·5	59·6	59·7	59·8	59·8	59·7	S 26	10·1	10·1	10·1	10·1	10·1	10·0
2·8	β Trianguli Aust.		120	46·7	46·9	47·2	47·5	47·5	47·4	S 63	29·4	29·5	29·5	29·4	29·3	29·2
2·6	α Serpentis		123	41·6	41·7	41·8	41·9	41·9	41·8	N 6	22·1	22·1	22·1	22·1	22·0	21·9
2·8	γ Lupi		125	53·3	53·4	53·6	53·7	53·7	53·6	S 41	13·9	13·9	13·9	13·8	13·8	13·7
2·2	*Alphecca*	41	126	07·3	07·4	07·5	07·7	07·7	07·6	N 26	39·3	39·3	39·3	39·2	39·1	38·9

‡ 2·9 — 3·6

© British Crown Copyright 2018. All rights reserved.

Mag.	Name and Number		SHA							Declination					
			JAN.	FEB.	MAR.	APR.	MAY	JUNE		JAN.	FEB.	MAR.	APR.	MAY	JUNE
		°	′	′	′	′	′	′	°	′	′	′	′	′	′
2·9	γ Trianguli Aust.	129	50·0	49·4	48·9	48·5	48·3	48·3	S 68	44·5	44·5	44·6	44·7	44·9	45·0
3·1	γ Ursæ Minoris	129	50·0	49·4	48·9	48·5	48·4	48·5	N 71	45·8	45·7	45·8	45·9	46·0	46·2
2·6	β Libræ	130	29·9	29·6	29·4	29·3	29·2	29·1	S 9	27·0	27·1	27·1	27·2	27·2	27·1
2·7	β Lupi	135	03·6	03·3	03·0	02·8	02·7	02·7	S 43	12·3	12·3	12·4	12·5	12·6	12·7
2·8	α Libræ 39	137	01·3	01·1	00·9	00·7	00·6	00·6	S 16	07·0	07·1	07·2	07·2	07·2	07·2
2·1	β Ursæ Minoris 40	137	20·6	19·9	19·4	19·0	18·9	19·2	N 74	04·5	04·4	04·5	04·6	04·7	04·9
2·4	ε Bootis	138	33·1	32·8	32·6	32·5	32·4	32·4	N 26	59·7	59·6	59·6	59·6	59·7	59·8
2·3	α Lupi	139	12·3	12·0	11·7	11·5	11·4	11·4	S 47	27·8	27·9	28·0	28·1	28·2	28·3
−0·3	α Centauri 38	139	46·7	46·3	46·0	45·7	45·6	45·7	S 60	54·4	54·4	54·5	54·7	54·8	54·9
2·3	η Centauri	140	49·5	49·2	49·0	48·8	48·7	48·7	S 42	14·1	14·2	14·3	14·4	14·5	14·6
3·0	γ Bootis	141	47·7	47·4	47·2	47·0	47·0	47·0	N 38	13·4	13·3	13·4	13·5	13·6	13·7
0·0	α Bootis 37	145	52·3	52·1	51·9	51·8	51·8	51·8	N 19	05·0	04·9	04·9	05·0	05·0	05·1
2·1	θ Centauri 36	148	03·1	02·9	02·7	02·5	02·5	02·5	S 36	27·5	27·6	27·7	27·8	27·9	27·9
0·6	β Centauri 35	148	42·6	42·1	41·8	41·6	41·6	41·7	S 60	27·4	27·5	27·7	27·8	28·0	28·1
2·6	ζ Centauri	150	49·2	48·9	48·7	48·5	48·5	48·5	S 47	22·5	22·6	22·8	22·9	23·0	23·1
2·7	η Bootis	151	06·4	06·2	06·0	05·9	05·9	05·9	N 18	18·1	18·1	18·1	18·1	18·2	18·3
1·9	η Ursæ Majoris 34	152	56·0	55·6	55·4	55·3	55·3	55·4	N 49	12·9	12·9	13·0	13·1	13·2	13·3
2·3	ε Centauri	154	43·6	43·3	43·0	42·9	42·9	43·0	S 53	33·4	33·5	33·6	33·8	33·9	34·0
1·0	α Virginis 33	158	27·2	27·0	26·8	26·8	26·7	26·8	S 11	15·5	15·6	15·6	15·7	15·7	15·7
2·3	ζ Ursæ Majoris	158	49·9	49·6	49·3	49·2	49·3	49·4	N 54	49·4	49·4	49·4	49·6	49·7	49·8
2·8	ι Centauri	159	35·1	34·8	34·6	34·5	34·5	34·6	S 36	48·5	48·6	48·7	48·8	48·9	48·9
2·8	ε Virginis	164	13·3	13·1	13·0	12·9	12·9	13·0	N 10	51·4	51·4	51·3	51·4	51·4	51·5
2·9	α Canum Venat.	165	46·5	46·2	46·0	46·0	46·0	46·1	N 38	12·8	12·8	12·8	12·9	13·0	13·1
1·8	ε Ursæ Majoris 32	166	17·3	16·9	16·7	16·7	16·7	16·9	N 55	51·2	51·2	51·3	51·4	51·6	51·6
1·3	β Crucis	167	47·3	47·0	46·8	46·7	46·8	46·9	S 59	47·2	47·3	47·5	47·6	47·8	47·8
2·9	γ Virginis	169	20·8	20·6	20·4	20·4	20·4	20·5	S 1	33·2	33·3	33·3	33·3	33·3	33·3
2·2	γ Centauri	169	21·4	21·1	21·0	20·9	21·0	21·1	S 49	03·5	03·7	03·8	04·0	04·1	04·1
2·7	α Muscæ	170	24·8	24·3	24·0	24·0	24·1	24·4	S 69	14·0	14·1	14·3	14·5	14·6	14·7
2·7	β Corvi	171	09·2	09·0	08·9	08·9	08·9	09·0	S 23	29·9	30·0	30·1	30·2	30·3	30·3
1·6	γ Crucis 31	171	56·5	56·2	56·0	55·9	56·0	56·2	S 57	12·8	13·0	13·1	13·3	13·4	13·5
1·3	α Crucis 30	173	04·8	04·4	04·2	04·2	04·3	04·5	S 63	11·9	12·0	12·2	12·4	12·5	12·6
2·6	γ Corvi 29	175	48·3	48·1	48·0	47·9	48·0	48·0	S 17	38·7	38·8	38·9	39·0	39·0	39·0
2·6	δ Centauri	177	39·7	39·4	39·3	39·3	39·3	39·5	S 50	49·4	49·5	49·7	49·8	49·9	50·0
2·4	γ Ursæ Majoris	181	17·7	17·4	17·3	17·3	17·4	17·6	N 53	35·1	35·2	35·3	35·4	35·5	35·6
2·1	β Leonis 28	182	29·7	29·5	29·4	29·4	29·4	29·5	N 14	27·9	27·8	27·8	27·9	27·9	28·0
2·6	δ Leonis	191	13·3	13·1	13·0	13·0	13·1	13·2	N 20	25·1	25·0	25·1	25·1	25·2	25·2
3·0	ψ Ursæ Majoris	192	19·1	18·9	18·8	18·9	19·0	19·1	N 44	23·5	23·6	23·7	23·8	23·8	23·9
1·8	α Ursæ Majoris 27	193	46·7	46·4	46·3	46·4	46·6	46·8	N 61	38·7	38·8	38·9	39·0	39·1	39·1
2·4	β Ursæ Majoris	194	15·3	15·1	15·0	15·0	15·2	15·4	N 56	16·6	16·7	16·8	16·9	17·0	17·0
2·7	μ Velorum	198	05·9	05·7	05·7	05·8	05·9	06·1	S 49	31·0	31·2	31·4	31·5	31·6	31·6
2·8	θ Carinæ	199	04·9	04·7	04·7	04·8	05·1	05·4	S 64	29·4	29·6	29·8	29·9	30·0	30·0
2·3	γ Leonis	204	44·7	44·6	44·5	44·6	44·7	44·8	N 19	44·6	44·6	44·6	44·6	44·7	44·7
1·4	α Leonis 26	207	39·2	39·1	39·1	39·1	39·2	39·3	N 11	52·4	52·3	52·3	52·3	52·4	52·4
3·0	ε Leonis	213	16·0	15·9	15·9	16·0	16·1	16·2	N 23	41·1	41·1	41·1	41·1	41·2	41·2
3·1	N Velorum	217	02·5	02·4	02·5	02·7	02·9	03·2	S 57	07·0	07·2	07·3	07·4	07·5	07·4
2·0	α Hydræ 25	217	52·1	52·0	52·0	52·1	52·2	52·3	S 8	44·5	44·6	44·7	44·7	44·7	44·6
2·5	κ Velorum	219	19·0	18·9	19·0	19·2	19·4	19·7	S 55	05·4	05·6	05·8	05·9	05·9	05·8
2·2	ι Carinæ	220	35·4	35·4	35·5	35·7	36·0	36·3	S 59	21·2	21·4	21·5	21·7	21·7	21·6
1·7	β Carinæ 24	221	38·0	37·9	38·1	38·5	39·0	39·4	S 69	47·6	47·8	48·0	48·1	48·1	48·1
2·2	λ Velorum 23	222	49·2	49·2	49·2	49·4	49·6	49·7	S 43	30·5	30·7	30·8	30·9	30·9	30·9
3·1	ι Ursæ Majoris	224	52·4	52·2	52·3	52·4	52·6	52·7	N 47	57·8	57·9	58·0	58·1	58·1	58·1
2·0	δ Velorum	228	41·0	41·0	41·2	41·4	41·7	41·9	S 54	46·7	46·9	47·0	47·1	47·1	47·0
1·9	ε Carinæ 22	234	15·8	15·8	16·0	16·3	16·6	16·9	S 59	34·2	34·4	34·6	34·6	34·6	34·5
1·8	γ Velorum	237	27·8	27·8	27·9	28·2	28·4	28·5	S 47	23·6	23·8	23·9	23·9	23·9	23·8
2·8	ρ Puppis	237	54·5	54·5	54·5	54·7	54·8	54·9	S 24	21·7	21·8	21·9	21·9	21·9	21·8
2·3	ζ Puppis	238	55·9	55·9	56·0	56·2	56·4	56·5	S 40	03·5	03·6	03·7	03·8	03·8	03·7
1·1	β Geminorum 21	243	22·7	22·7	22·8	22·9	23·0	23·1	N 27	58·6	58·7	58·7	58·7	58·7	58·7
0·4	α Canis Minoris 20	244	55·4	55·4	55·5	55·6	55·7	55·8	N 5	10·4	10·4	10·3	10·4	10·4	10·4

© British Crown Copyright 2018. All rights reserved.

Mag.	Name and Number	SHA °	JULY	AUG.	SEPT.	OCT.	NOV.	DEC.	Dec.	JULY	AUG.	SEPT.	OCT.	NOV.	DEC.
2·9	γ Trianguli Aust.	129	48·5	48·8	49·2	49·5	49·5	49·2	S 68	45·1	45·2	45·1	45·0	44·9	44·8
3·1	γ Ursæ Minoris	129	48·9	49·4	49·9	50·3	50·4	50·3	N 71	46·3	46·3	46·2	46·1	45·9	45·7
2·6	β Libræ	130	29·2	29·3	29·4	29·5	29·5	29·3	S 9	27·1	27·1	27·1	27·1	27·1	27·2
2·7	β Lupi	135	02·8	02·9	03·1	03·2	03·2	03·0	S 43	12·7	12·7	12·7	12·6	12·5	12·5
2·8	Zubenelgenubi 39	137	00·7	00·8	00·9	01·0	00·9	00·8	S 16	07·2	07·2	07·2	07·2	07·2	07·2
2·1	Kochab 40	137	19·7	20·2	20·8	21·1	21·3	21·0	N 74	05·0	05·0	04·9	04·7	04·5	04·3
2·4	ε Bootis	138	32·5	32·6	32·8	32·8	32·8	32·7	N 26	59·9	59·9	59·9	59·8	59·7	59·5
2·3	α Lupi	139	11·5	11·7	11·9	12·0	11·9	11·7	S 47	28·3	28·3	28·3	28·2	28·1	28·1
−0·3	Rigil Kent. 38	139	45·9	46·1	46·4	46·6	46·5	46·2	S 60	55·0	55·0	54·9	54·8	54·7	54·6
2·3	η Centauri	140	48·8	48·9	49·1	49·2	49·1	48·9	S 42	14·6	14·6	14·5	14·5	14·4	14·4
3·0	γ Bootis	141	47·1	47·3	47·4	47·5	47·5	47·3	N 38	13·8	13·8	13·7	13·6	13·4	13·3
0·0	Arcturus 37	145	51·9	52·0	52·1	52·1	52·1	51·9	N 19	05·2	05·2	05·1	05·1	04·9	04·8
2·1	Menkent 36	148	02·6	02·7	02·8	02·9	02·8	02·6	S 36	27·9	27·9	27·9	27·8	27·7	27·7
0·6	Hadar 35	148	41·8	42·1	42·3	42·4	42·3	42·0	S 60	28·1	28·1	28·0	27·9	27·8	27·7
2·6	ζ Centauri	150	48·7	48·8	49·0	49·0	48·9	48·7	S 47	23·1	23·1	23·0	22·9	22·8	22·8
2·7	η Bootis	151	06·0	06·1	06·2	06·2	06·1	05·9	N 18	18·3	18·3	18·3	18·2	18·1	17·9
1·9	Alkaid 34	152	55·6	55·7	55·9	55·9	55·9	55·7	N 49	13·4	13·4	13·3	13·1	12·9	12·8
2·3	ε Centauri	154	43·1	43·3	43·5	43·5	43·4	43·1	S 53	34·0	34·0	33·9	33·8	33·7	33·7
1·0	Spica 33	158	26·9	27·0	27·0	27·0	26·9	26·7	S 11	15·7	15·6	15·6	15·6	15·6	15·7
2·3	Mizar	158	49·6	49·8	50·0	50·0	49·9	49·6	N 54	49·8	49·8	49·7	49·5	49·3	49·2
2·8	ι Centauri	159	34·7	34·8	34·9	35·0	34·8	34·6	S 36	48·9	48·9	48·8	48·7	48·7	48·7
2·8	ε Virginis	164	13·0	13·1	13·2	13·2	13·1	12·9	N 10	51·5	51·5	51·5	51·4	51·3	51·2
2·9	Cor Caroli	165	46·2	46·3	46·4	46·4	46·3	46·0	N 38	13·2	13·1	13·0	12·9	12·7	12·6
1·8	Alioth 32	166	17·1	17·3	17·4	17·4	17·3	17·0	N 55	51·7	51·6	51·5	51·3	51·1	51·0
1·3	Mimosa	167	47·1	47·4	47·5	47·5	47·3	47·0	S 59	47·9	47·8	47·7	47·5	47·5	47·4
2·9	γ Virginis	169	20·5	20·6	20·7	20·6	20·5	20·3	S 1	33·2	33·2	33·2	33·2	33·3	33·4
2·2	Muhlifain	169	21·2	21·4	21·5	21·5	21·3	21·0	S 49	04·1	04·0	03·9	03·8	03·8	03·8
2·7	α Muscæ	170	24·8	25·1	25·4	25·4	25·1	24·6	S 69	14·7	14·7	14·6	14·4	14·3	14·3
2·7	β Corvi	171	09·0	09·1	09·2	09·2	09·0	08·8	S 23	30·2	30·2	30·1	30·1	30·1	30·1
1·6	Gacrux 31	171	56·4	56·6	56·7	56·7	56·5	56·1	S 57	13·5	13·4	13·3	13·2	13·1	13·1
1·3	Acrux 30	173	04·8	05·1	05·2	05·2	04·9	04·5	S 63	12·6	12·5	12·4	12·3	12·2	12·1
2·6	Gienah 29	175	48·1	48·2	48·2	48·2	48·0	47·8	S 17	39·0	38·9	38·9	38·8	38·8	38·9
2·6	δ Centauri	177	39·7	39·8	39·9	39·8	39·6	39·3	S 50	50·0	49·9	49·8	49·7	49·6	49·6
2·4	Phecda	181	17·8	17·9	17·9	17·8	17·6	17·3	N 53	35·5	35·5	35·3	35·2	35·0	34·9
2·1	Denebola 28	182	29·6	29·6	29·6	29·6	29·4	29·2	N 14	28·0	28·0	28·0	27·9	27·8	27·7
2·6	δ Leonis	191	13·3	13·3	13·3	13·2	13·0	12·7	N 20	25·2	25·2	25·2	25·1	25·0	24·8
3·0	ψ Ursæ Majoris	192	19·2	19·3	19·3	19·2	18·9	18·6	N 44	23·9	23·8	23·7	23·5	23·4	23·3
1·8	Dubhe 27	193	47·0	47·1	47·1	46·9	46·6	46·1	N 61	39·1	39·0	38·8	38·6	38·5	38·4
2·4	Merak	194	15·6	15·7	15·6	15·5	15·2	14·8	N 56	17·0	16·9	16·7	16·6	16·4	16·3
2·7	μ Velorum	198	06·3	06·3	06·3	06·2	05·9	05·6	S 49	31·5	31·4	31·3	31·2	31·1	31·2
2·8	θ Carinæ	199	05·7	05·9	05·9	05·7	05·3	04·8	S 64	30·0	29·8	29·7	29·5	29·5	29·5
2·3	Algieba	204	44·8	44·8	44·8	44·6	44·4	44·1	N 19	44·7	44·7	44·7	44·6	44·5	44·4
1·4	Regulus 26	207	39·4	39·3	39·3	39·1	38·9	38·7	N 11	52·4	52·4	52·4	52·4	52·3	52·2
3·0	ε Leonis	213	16·2	16·2	16·1	15·9	15·7	15·4	N 23	41·2	41·2	41·1	41·0	40·9	40·9
3·1	N Velorum	217	03·3	03·4	03·3	03·1	02·7	02·4	S 57	07·3	07·2	07·0	06·9	06·9	07·0
2·0	Alphard 25	217	52·3	52·3	52·2	52·0	51·8	51·6	S 8	44·6	44·5	44·5	44·5	44·5	44·6
2·5	κ Velorum	219	19·8	19·8	19·7	19·5	19·1	18·8	S 55	05·6	05·6	05·5	05·4	05·4	05·5
2·2	ι Carinæ	220	36·4	36·5	36·4	36·1	35·7	35·4	S 59	21·5	21·4	21·2	21·1	21·1	21·2
1·7	Miaplacidus 24	221	39·7	39·8	39·6	39·3	38·7	38·2	S 69	48·0	47·8	47·6	47·5	47·5	47·6
2·2	Suhail 23	222	49·8	49·8	49·7	49·5	49·2	48·9	S 43	30·8	30·6	30·5	30·4	30·5	30·6
3·1	ι Ursæ Majoris	224	52·8	52·7	52·5	52·3	51·9	51·6	N 47	58·0	57·9	57·8	57·7	57·6	57·6
2·0	δ Velorum	228	42·0	42·0	41·8	41·5	41·2	40·9	S 54	46·9	46·7	46·6	46·5	46·6	46·7
1·9	Avior 22	234	17·0	16·9	16·8	16·4	16·1	15·7	S 59	34·4	34·2	34·1	34·0	34·1	34·2
1·8	γ Velorum	237	28·6	28·5	28·3	28·1	27·8	27·5	S 47	23·7	23·5	23·4	23·4	23·4	23·6
2·8	ρ Puppis	237	54·9	54·8	54·7	54·5	54·2	54·0	S 24	21·7	21·6	21·5	21·5	21·5	21·6
2·3	ζ Puppis	238	56·5	56·4	56·3	56·0	55·8	55·5	S 40	03·5	03·4	03·3	03·2	03·3	03·4
1·1	Pollux 21	243	23·0	22·9	22·7	22·5	22·2	22·0	N 27	58·7	58·7	58·6	58·6	58·6	58·5
0·4	Procyon 20	244	55·7	55·6	55·4	55·2	55·0	54·8	N 5	10·5	10·5	10·5	10·5	10·4	10·4

© British Crown Copyright 2018. All rights reserved.

Mag.	Name and Number		SHA								Declination					
		°	JAN.	FEB.	MAR.	APR.	MAY	JUNE		°	JAN.	FEB.	MAR.	APR.	MAY	JUNE
1·6	α Geminorum	246	02·8	02·7	02·8	03·0	03·1	03·1	N 31	50·6	50·6	50·7	50·7	50·7	50·7
3·3	σ Puppis	247	32·1	32·2	32·3	32·5	32·7	32·8	S 43	20·5	20·7	20·8	20·8	20·7	20·6
2·9	β Canis Minoris	247	57·2	57·1	57·2	57·4	57·5	57·5	N 8	14·9	14·9	14·8	14·9	14·9	14·9
2·4	η Canis Majoris	248	47·0	47·1	47·2	47·3	47·5	47·6	S 29	20·6	20·7	20·8	20·8	20·7	20·6
2·7	π Puppis	250	32·5	32·5	32·7	32·8	33·0	33·1	S 37	08·0	08·2	08·3	08·3	08·2	08·1
1·8	δ Canis Majoris	252	42·3	42·3	42·4	42·6	42·7	42·8	S 26	25·6	25·7	25·8	25·8	25·7	25·6
3·0	o Canis Majoris	254	02·5	02·5	02·7	02·8	02·9	03·0	S 23	51·8	52·0	52·0	52·0	52·0	51·9
1·5	ε Canis Majoris 19	255	09·2	09·2	09·3	09·5	09·6	09·7	S 29	00·1	00·2	00·2	00·2	00·2	00·1
2·9	τ Puppis	257	23·4	23·5	23·7	24·0	24·2	24·3	S 50	38·4	38·6	38·6	38·6	38·6	38·4
−1·5	α Canis Majoris 18	258	30·0	30·1	30·2	30·3	30·4	30·5	S 16	44·7	44·8	44·9	44·9	44·8	44·7
1·9	γ Geminorum	260	17·8	17·8	17·9	18·0	18·1	18·1	N 16	22·8	22·8	22·8	22·8	22·8	22·8
−0·7	α Carinæ 17	263	53·9	54·1	54·3	54·6	54·8	54·9	S 52	42·6	42·7	42·8	42·8	42·7	42·5
2·0	β Canis Majoris	264	06·8	06·8	06·9	07·1	07·2	07·2	S 17	58·1	58·2	58·3	58·3	58·2	58·1
2·6	θ Aurigæ	269	44·6	44·7	44·8	45·0	45·1	45·0	N 37	12·7	12·7	12·7	12·7	12·7	12·7
1·9	β Aurigæ	269	46·0	46·1	46·2	46·4	46·5	46·5	N 44	56·8	56·9	56·9	56·9	56·9	56·8
Var.‡	α Orionis 16	270	56·9	56·9	57·0	57·2	57·2	57·2	N 7	24·4	24·4	24·4	24·4	24·4	24·5
2·1	κ Orionis	272	50·0	50·1	50·2	50·3	50·4	50·4	S 9	40·0	40·1	40·1	40·1	40·0	39·9
1·9	ζ Orionis	274	34·1	34·2	34·3	34·4	34·5	34·5	S 1	56·2	56·2	56·2	56·2	56·2	56·1
2·6	α Columbæ	274	54·7	54·8	55·0	55·2	55·3	55·3	S 34	04·1	04·2	04·2	04·2	04·1	04·0
3·0	ζ Tauri	275	18·2	18·2	18·4	18·5	18·6	18·5	N 21	09·1	09·1	09·1	09·1	09·1	09·1
1·7	ε Orionis 15	275	42·2	42·3	42·4	42·5	42·6	42·6	S 1	11·6	11·7	11·7	11·7	11·6	11·5
2·8	ι Orionis	275	54·4	54·5	54·6	54·8	54·8	54·8	S 5	54·1	54·1	54·2	54·1	54·1	54·0
2·6	α Leporis	276	36·3	36·4	36·5	36·7	36·8	36·7	S 17	48·8	48·9	48·9	48·8	48·8	48·7
2·2	δ Orionis	276	45·2	45·3	45·4	45·5	45·6	45·6	S 0	17·3	17·4	17·4	17·4	17·3	17·3
2·8	β Leporis	277	43·9	44·0	44·2	44·3	44·4	44·4	S 20	44·9	45·0	45·0	45·0	44·9	44·8
1·7	β Tauri 14	278	07·5	07·6	07·7	07·8	07·9	07·8	N 28	37·3	37·3	37·3	37·3	37·3	37·2
1·6	γ Orionis 13	278	27·6	27·7	27·8	27·9	28·0	28·0	N 6	21·8	21·8	21·8	21·8	21·8	21·9
0·1	α Aurigæ 12	280	28·4	28·5	28·7	28·9	29·0	28·9	N 46	00·9	01·0	01·0	01·0	00·9	00·8
0·1	β Orionis 11	281	08·1	08·2	08·3	08·4	08·5	08·5	S 8	11·0	11·1	11·1	11·1	11·0	10·9
2·8	β Eridani	282	48·1	48·2	48·3	48·5	48·5	48·5	S 5	04·0	04·0	04·0	04·0	03·9	03·9
2·7	ι Aurigæ	285	26·4	26·5	26·6	26·8	26·8	26·8	N 33	11·6	11·7	11·7	11·6	11·6	11·6
0·9	α Tauri 10	290	44·8	44·8	45·0	45·1	45·1	45·0	N 16	32·7	32·7	32·7	32·7	32·7	32·7
2·9	ε Persei	300	12·9	13·1	13·2	13·4	13·4	13·2	N 40	03·8	03·9	03·8	03·8	03·7	03·7
3·0	γ Eridani	300	16·2	16·3	16·5	16·6	16·6	16·5	S 13	27·6	27·6	27·6	27·6	27·5	27·4
2·9	ζ Persei	301	10·0	10·1	10·3	10·4	10·4	10·3	N 31	56·3	56·3	56·3	56·2	56·2	56·2
2·9	η Tauri	302	50·7	50·8	51·0	51·1	51·1	50·9	N 24	09·7	09·7	09·7	09·7	09·6	09·6
1·8	α Persei 9	308	34·6	34·8	35·0	35·1	35·1	34·9	N 49	55·7	55·7	55·7	55·6	55·5	55·5
Var.§	β Persei	312	38·8	39·0	39·1	39·2	39·2	39·0	N 41	01·7	01·7	01·7	01·6	01·5	01·5
2·5	α Ceti 8	314	10·9	11·0	11·2	11·2	11·2	11·0	N 4	09·6	09·6	09·6	09·6	09·7	09·7
3·2	θ Eridani 7	315	15·3	15·5	15·6	15·7	15·7	15·6	S 40	14·1	14·1	14·1	14·0	13·8	13·6
2·0	α Ursæ Minoris	315	55·2	68·4	80·5	87·9	87·5	79·8	N 89	20·8	20·9	20·8	20·7	20·5	20·4
3·0	β Trianguli	327	19·9	20·0	20·1	20·2	20·1	19·9	N 35	04·6	04·6	04·5	04·5	04·4	04·4
2·0	α Arietis 6	327	56·4	56·5	56·6	56·6	56·6	56·4	N 23	33·1	33·0	33·0	32·9	32·9	33·0
2·3	γ Andromedæ	328	44·0	44·2	44·3	44·3	44·2	44·0	N 42	25·3	25·2	25·2	25·1	25·0	25·0
2·9	α Hydri	330	09·6	09·9	10·1	10·2	10·2	09·9	S 61	29·1	29·1	29·0	28·8	28·6	28·4
2·6	β Arietis	331	04·7	04·9	04·9	05·0	04·9	04·7	N 20	54·0	53·9	53·9	53·9	53·9	53·9
0·5	α Eridani 5	335	23·9	24·2	24·3	24·4	24·3	24·0	S 57	08·9	08·8	08·7	08·5	08·4	08·2
2·7	δ Cassiopeiæ	338	14·0	14·3	14·4	14·5	14·3	14·0	N 60	20·2	20·1	20·0	19·9	19·8	19·8
2·1	β Andromedæ	342	18·2	18·3	18·4	18·4	18·2	18·0	N 35	43·3	43·2	43·2	43·1	43·1	43·1
Var.‖	γ Cassiopeiæ	345	32·1	32·4	32·5	32·5	32·3	32·0	N 60	49·3	49·3	49·1	49·0	48·9	48·9
2·0	β Ceti 4	348	52·2	52·2	52·3	52·2	52·1	51·9	S 17	53·2	53·2	53·2	53·1	53·0	52·8
2·2	α Cassiopeiæ 3	349	36·3	36·5	36·6	36·6	36·4	36·0	N 56	38·6	38·5	38·4	38·3	38·2	38·2
2·4	α Phœnicis 2	353	12·1	12·2	12·2	12·2	12·0	11·8	S 42	12·5	12·5	12·4	12·2	12·1	11·9
2·8	β Hydri	353	20·0	20·5	20·8	20·7	20·3	19·6	S 77	09·3	09·2	09·0	08·8	08·6	08·5
2·8	γ Pegasi	356	27·0	27·1	27·1	27·1	26·9	26·7	N 15	17·3	17·2	17·2	17·2	17·2	17·3
2·3	β Cassiopeiæ	357	27·3	27·5	27·6	27·5	27·2	26·8	N 59	15·4	15·3	15·2	15·1	15·0	15·0
2·1	α Andromedæ 1	357	39·7	39·8	39·8	39·7	39·6	39·3	N 29	11·7	11·7	11·6	11·5	11·5	11·6

‡ 0·1 — 1·2   § 2·1 — 3·4   ‖ Irregular variable; 2017 mag. 2·2

© British Crown Copyright 2018. All rights reserved.

Mag.	Name and Number		SHA							Declination					
		°	JULY	AUG.	SEPT.	OCT.	NOV.	DEC.	°	JULY	AUG.	SEPT.	OCT.	NOV.	DEC.
1·6	*Castor*	246	03·1	02·9	02·7	02·5	02·2	02·0	N 31	50·7	50·6	50·6	50·5	50·5	50·5
3·3	σ Puppis	247	32·8	32·7	32·5	32·3	32·0	31·8	S 43	20·5	20·3	20·2	20·2	20·3	20·4
2·9	β Canis Minoris	247	57·5	57·3	57·1	56·9	56·7	56·5	N 8	15·0	15·0	15·0	15·0	14·9	14·9
2·4	η Canis Majoris	248	47·5	47·4	47·2	47·0	46·8	46·6	S 29	20·5	20·4	20·3	20·3	20·4	20·5
2·7	π Puppis	250	33·1	33·0	32·8	32·5	32·3	32·1	S 37	08·0	07·8	07·7	07·7	07·8	07·9
1·8	*Wezen*	252	42·8	42·6	42·5	42·2	42·0	41·8	S 26	25·5	25·4	25·3	25·3	25·4	25·5
3·0	o Canis Majoris	254	02·9	02·8	02·6	02·4	02·2	02·0	S 23	51·7	51·6	51·6	51·5	51·6	51·7
1·5	*Adhara* 19	255	09·6	09·5	09·3	09·1	08·9	08·7	S 28	59·9	59·8	59·7	59·7	59·8	59·9
2·9	τ Puppis	257	24·3	24·2	23·9	23·6	23·3	23·1	S 50	38·3	38·1	38·0	38·0	38·1	38·3
−1·5	*Sirius* 18	258	30·4	30·3	30·1	29·9	29·6	29·5	S 16	44·6	44·5	44·5	44·5	44·5	44·7
1·9	*Alhena*	260	18·0	17·9	17·7	17·4	17·2	17·0	N 16	22·8	22·9	22·9	22·9	22·8	22·8
−0·7	*Canopus* 17	263	54·8	54·7	54·4	54·1	53·8	53·6	S 52	42·4	42·2	42·1	42·1	42·2	42·4
2·0	*Mirzam*	264	07·1	07·0	06·8	06·6	06·3	06·2	S 17	58·0	57·9	57·8	57·8	57·9	58·0
2·6	θ Aurigæ	269	44·9	44·7	44·4	44·1	43·9	43·7	N 37	12·6	12·6	12·6	12·6	12·6	12·7
1·9	*Menkalinan*	269	46·3	46·1	45·8	45·5	45·2	45·0	N 44	56·7	56·7	56·7	56·7	56·7	56·8
Var.‡	*Betelgeuse* 16	270	57·1	56·9	56·7	56·5	56·3	56·1	N 7	24·5	24·6	24·6	24·6	24·6	24·5
2·1	κ Orionis	272	50·3	50·1	49·9	49·7	49·5	49·3	S 9	39·8	39·7	39·7	39·7	39·8	39·9
1·9	*Alnitak*	274	34·4	34·2	34·0	33·8	33·6	33·4	S 1	56·0	55·9	55·9	55·9	56·0	56·0
2·6	*Phact*	274	55·2	55·0	54·8	54·5	54·3	54·2	S 34	03·8	03·7	03·6	03·7	03·8	03·9
3·0	ζ Tauri	275	18·4	18·2	18·0	17·7	17·5	17·4	N 21	09·1	09·1	09·1	09·2	09·2	09·1
1·7	*Alnilam* 15	275	42·5	42·3	42·0	41·8	41·6	41·5	S 1	11·5	11·4	11·3	11·3	11·4	11·5
2·8	ι Orionis	275	54·7	54·5	54·3	54·1	53·9	53·8	S 5	53·9	53·8	53·8	53·8	53·8	53·9
2·6	α Leporis	276	36·6	36·4	36·2	36·0	35·8	35·7	S 17	48·5	48·4	48·4	48·4	48·5	48·6
2·2	δ Orionis	276	45·5	45·3	45·0	44·8	44·6	44·5	S 0	17·2	17·1	17·1	17·1	17·1	17·2
2·8	β Leporis	277	44·3	44·1	43·9	43·6	43·5	43·3	S 20	44·7	44·6	44·5	44·5	44·6	44·7
1·7	*Elnath* 14	278	07·7	07·5	07·2	07·0	06·8	06·6	N 28	37·2	37·2	37·3	37·3	37·3	37·3
1·6	*Bellatrix* 13	278	27·8	27·6	27·4	27·2	27·0	26·9	N 6	21·9	22·0	22·0	22·0	22·0	21·9
0·1	*Capella* 12	280	28·7	28·4	28·1	27·8	27·6	27·4	N 46	00·8	00·8	00·8	00·8	00·9	00·9
0·1	*Rigel* 11	281	08·3	08·2	07·9	07·7	07·5	07·4	S 8	10·8	10·7	10·7	10·7	10·8	10·8
2·8	β Eridani	282	48·3	48·1	47·9	47·7	47·5	47·4	S 5	03·8	03·7	03·6	03·6	03·7	03·8
2·7	ι Aurigæ	285	26·6	26·3	26·1	25·8	25·6	25·5	N 33	11·6	11·6	11·6	11·7	11·7	11·7
0·9	*Aldebaran* 10	290	44·9	44·6	44·4	44·2	44·0	43·9	N 16	32·7	32·8	32·8	32·8	32·8	32·8
2·9	ε Persei	300	13·0	12·7	12·4	12·2	12·0	11·9	N 40	03·7	03·7	03·8	03·8	03·9	04·0
3·0	γ Eridani	300	16·3	16·1	15·9	15·7	15·6	15·5	S 13	27·2	27·1	27·1	27·1	27·2	27·3
2·9	ζ Persei	301	10·0	09·8	09·5	09·3	09·2	09·1	N 31	56·2	56·3	56·3	56·4	56·4	56·5
2·9	*Alcyone*	302	50·7	50·5	50·2	50·1	49·9	49·8	N 24	09·7	09·7	09·8	09·8	09·9	09·9
1·8	*Mirfak* 9	308	34·6	34·3	34·0	33·7	33·6	33·5	N 49	55·5	55·5	55·6	55·7	55·8	55·9
Var.§	*Algol*	312	38·8	38·5	38·2	38·0	37·9	37·8	N 41	01·5	01·6	01·6	01·7	01·8	01·9
2·5	*Menkar* 8	314	10·8	10·6	10·4	10·2	10·2	10·1	N 4	09·8	09·9	10·0	10·0	10·0	09·9
3·2	*Acamar* 7	315	15·4	15·1	14·8	14·7	14·6	14·6	S 40	13·5	13·4	13·4	13·5	13·6	13·8
2·0	*Polaris*	315	66·9	52·0	38·3	28·2	23·5	27·3	N 89	20·4	20·4	20·5	20·6	20·8	21·0
3·0	β Trianguli	327	19·6	19·4	19·1	19·0	18·9	19·0	N 35	04·5	04·6	04·7	04·8	04·8	04·9
2·0	*Hamal* 6	327	56·1	55·9	55·7	55·6	55·5	55·5	N 23	33·0	33·1	33·2	33·3	33·3	33·4
2·3	*Almach*	328	43·7	43·4	43·2	43·1	43·0	43·0	N 42	25·1	25·1	25·3	25·4	25·5	25·6
2·9	α Hydri	330	09·6	09·2	08·8	08·7	08·7	08·8	S 61	28·3	28·3	28·3	28·5	28·6	28·8
2·6	*Sheratan*	331	04·4	04·2	04·0	03·9	03·8	03·9	N 20	54·0	54·1	54·2	54·2	54·3	54·3
0·5	*Achernar* 5	335	23·7	23·3	23·1	22·9	22·9	23·1	S 57	08·1	08·1	08·1	08·3	08·4	08·5
2·7	*Ruchbah*	338	13·6	13·2	12·9	12·8	12·8	12·9	N 60	19·8	19·9	20·0	20·2	20·3	20·5
2·1	*Mirach*	342	17·7	17·5	17·3	17·2	17·2	17·3	N 35	43·1	43·3	43·4	43·5	43·6	43·6
Var.‖	γ Cassiopeiæ	345	31·6	31·2	31·0	30·9	30·9	31·1	N 60	48·9	49·1	49·2	49·4	49·5	49·6
2·0	*Diphda* 4	348	51·7	51·4	51·3	51·2	51·2	51·3	S 17	52·7	52·7	52·7	52·7	52·8	52·8
2·2	*Schedar* 3	349	35·7	35·3	35·1	35·1	35·1	35·3	N 56	38·3	38·4	38·6	38·7	38·9	39·0
2·4	*Ankaa* 2	353	11·5	11·2	11·0	11·0	11·1	11·2	S 42	11·8	11·8	12·0	12·1	12·1	12·2
2·8	β Hydri	353	18·8	18·0	17·6	17·5	17·8	18·4	S 77	08·5	08·5	08·6	08·8	08·9	09·0
2·8	*Algenib*	356	26·5	26·3	26·1	26·1	26·1	26·2	N 15	17·4	17·5	17·6	17·6	17·7	17·7
2·3	*Caph*	357	26·5	26·2	26·0	26·0	26·1	26·3	N 59	15·1	15·2	15·4	15·6	15·7	15·8
2·1	*Alpheratz* 1	357	39·1	38·9	38·7	38·7	38·8	38·8	N 29	11·7	11·8	11·9	12·0	12·1	12·1

‡ 0·1 — 1·2   § 2·1 — 3·4   ‖ Irregular variable; 2017 mag. 2·2

© British Crown Copyright 2018. All rights reserved.

POLARIS (POLE STAR) TABLES, 2019
FOR DETERMINING LATITUDE FROM SEXTANT ALTITUDE AND FOR AZIMUTH

LHA ARIES	0° – 9°	10° – 19°	20° – 29°	30° – 39°	40° – 49°	50° – 59°	60° – 69°	70° – 79°	80° – 89°	90° – 99°	100° – 109°	110° – 119°
°	a_0	a_0	a_0	a_0	a_0	a_0	a_0	a_0	a_0	a_0	a_0	a_0
	° ′	° ′	° ′	° ′	° ′	° ′	° ′	° ′	° ′	° ′	° ′	° ′
0	0 30·7	0 26·3	0 23·0	0 20·7	0 19·6	0 19·7	0 21·0	0 23·5	0 27·1	0 31·6	0 37·0	0 43·0
1	30·2	25·9	22·7	20·5	19·6	19·8	21·2	23·8	27·5	32·1	37·5	43·6
2	29·7	25·6	22·4	20·4	19·5	19·9	21·4	24·1	27·9	32·6	38·1	44·3
3	29·3	25·2	22·2	20·2	19·5	20·0	21·7	24·5	28·3	33·1	38·7	44·9
4	28·8	24·9	21·9	20·1	19·5	20·1	21·9	24·8	28·8	33·7	39·3	45·6
5	0 28·4	0 24·5	0 21·7	0 20·0	0 19·5	0 20·2	0 22·1	0 25·2	0 29·2	0 34·2	0 39·9	0 46·2
6	28·0	24·2	21·5	19·9	19·5	20·4	22·4	25·5	29·7	34·7	40·5	46·9
7	27·5	23·9	21·3	19·8	19·6	20·5	22·6	25·9	30·2	35·3	41·1	47·5
8	27·1	23·5	21·1	19·7	19·6	20·7	22·9	26·3	30·6	35·8	41·7	48·2
9	26·7	23·2	20·9	19·7	19·6	20·8	23·2	26·7	31·1	36·4	42·4	48·8
10	0 26·3	0 23·0	0 20·7	0 19·6	0 19·7	0 21·0	0 23·5	0 27·1	0 31·6	0 37·0	0 43·0	0 49·5

Lat.	a_1	a_1	a_1	a_1	a_1	a_1	a_1	a_1	a_1	a_1	a_1	a_1
°	′	′	′	′	′	′	′	′	′	′	′	′
0	0·5	0·5	0·6	0·6	0·6	0·6	0·6	0·5	0·5	0·4	0·4	0·4
10	·5	·5	·6	·6	·6	·6	·6	·5	·5	·5	·4	·4
20	·5	·6	·6	·6	·6	·6	·6	·6	·5	·5	·5	·4
30	·5	·6	·6	·6	·6	·6	·6	·6	·6	·5	·5	·5
40	0·6	0·6	0·6	0·6	0·6	0·6	0·6	0·6	0·6	0·6	0·5	0·5
45	·6	·6	·6	·6	·6	·6	·6	·6	·6	·6	·6	·6
50	·6	·6	·6	·6	·6	·6	·6	·6	·6	·6	·6	·6
55	·6	·6	·6	·6	·6	·6	·6	·6	·6	·6	·6	·6
60	·6	·6	·6	·6	·6	·6	·6	·6	·7	·7	·7	·7
62	0·7	0·6	0·6	0·6	0·6	0·6	0·6	0·6	0·7	0·7	0·7	0·7
64	·7	·6	·6	·6	·6	·6	·6	·7	·7	·7	·7	·8
66	·7	·7	·6	·6	·6	·6	·6	·7	·7	·7	·8	·8
68	0·7	0·7	0·6	0·6	0·6	0·6	0·6	0·7	0·7	0·8	0·8	0·9

Month	a_2	a_2	a_2	a_2	a_2	a_2	a_2	a_2	a_2	a_2	a_2	a_2
	′	′	′	′	′	′	′	′	′	′	′	′
Jan.	0·7	0·7	0·7	0·7	0·7	0·7	0·7	0·7	0·7	0·7	0·7	0·6
Feb.	·6	·7	·7	·7	·8	·8	·8	·8	·8	·8	·8	·8
Mar.	·5	·6	·6	·7	·7	·8	·8	·8	·9	·9	·9	·9
Apr.	0·4	0·4	0·5	0·5	0·6	0·7	0·7	0·8	0·8	0·9	0·9	0·9
May	·2	·3	·3	·4	·4	·5	·6	·6	·7	·8	·8	·9
June	·2	·2	·2	·3	·3	·4	·4	·5	·6	·6	·7	·8
July	0·3	0·2	0·2	0·2	0·3	0·3	0·3	0·4	0·4	0·5	0·5	0·6
Aug.	·4	·3	·3	·3	·3	·3	·3	·3	·3	·4	·4	·5
Sept.	·6	·5	·5	·4	·4	·3	·3	·3	·3	·3	·3	·3
Oct.	0·7	0·7	0·6	0·6	0·5	0·5	0·4	0·4	0·3	0·3	0·3	0·3
Nov.	0·9	0·9	0·8	·8	·7	·6	·6	·5	·4	·4	·3	·3
Dec.	1·0	1·0	1·0	0·9	0·9	0·8	0·7	0·7	0·6	0·5	0·5	0·4

Lat.	AZIMUTH											
°	°	°	°	°	°	°	°	°	°	°	°	°
0	0·4	0·3	0·2	0·1	0·0	359·9	359·8	359·7	359·6	359·5	359·4	359·4
20	0·4	0·3	0·2	0·1	0·0	359·9	359·7	359·6	359·5	359·5	359·4	359·3
40	0·5	0·4	0·3	0·1	0·0	359·8	359·7	359·6	359·4	359·3	359·2	359·2
50	0·6	0·5	0·3	0·2	0·0	359·8	359·6	359·5	359·3	359·2	359·1	359·0
55	0·7	0·6	0·4	0·2	0·0	359·8	359·6	359·4	359·2	359·1	359·0	358·9
60	0·8	0·6	0·4	0·2	0·0	359·7	359·5	359·3	359·1	359·0	358·8	358·8
65	1·0	0·8	0·5	0·3	0·0	359·7	359·4	359·2	359·0	358·8	358·6	358·5

Latitude = Apparent altitude (corrected for refraction) $-1° + a_0 + a_1 + a_2$

The table is entered with LHA Aries to determine the column to be used; each column refers to a range of 10°. a_0 is taken, with mental interpolation, from the upper table with the units of LHA Aries in degrees as argument; a_1, a_2 are taken, without interpolation, from the second and third tables with arguments latitude and month respectively. a_0, a_1, a_2, are always positive. The final table gives the azimuth of *Polaris*.

© British Crown Copyright 2018. All rights reserved.

FOR DETERMINING LATITUDE FROM SEXTANT ALTITUDE AND FOR AZIMUTH

LHA ARIES	120° – 129°	130° – 139°	140° – 149°	150° – 159°	160° – 169°	170° – 179°	180° – 189°	190° – 199°	200° – 209°	210° – 219°	220° – 229°	230° – 239°
	a_0	a_0	a_0	a_0	a_0	a_0	a_0	a_0	a_0	a_0	a_0	a_0
°	° ′	° ′	° ′	° ′	° ′	° ′	° ′	° ′	° ′	° ′	° ′	° ′
0	0 49·5	0 56·3	1 03·1	1 09·8	1 16·2	1 22·0	1 27·2	1 31·4	1 34·7	1 36·9	1 38·0	1 37·9
1	50·2	57·0	03·8	10·5	16·8	22·6	27·6	31·8	35·0	37·1	38·0	37·8
2	50·8	57·7	04·5	11·1	17·4	23·1	28·1	32·2	35·3	37·2	38·1	37·7
3	51·5	58·3	05·2	11·8	18·0	23·7	28·5	32·5	35·5	37·4	38·1	37·6
4	52·2	59·0	05·8	12·4	18·6	24·2	29·0	32·9	35·7	37·5	38·1	37·5
5	0 52·9	0 59·7	1 06·5	1 13·1	1 19·2	1 24·7	1 29·4	1 33·2	1 36·0	1 37·6	1 38·1	1 37·4
6	53·5	1 00·4	07·2	13·7	19·8	25·2	29·8	33·5	36·2	37·7	38·1	37·3
7	54·2	01·1	07·9	14·3	20·4	25·7	30·3	33·9	36·4	37·8	38·0	37·1
8	54·9	01·8	08·5	15·0	20·9	26·2	30·7	34·2	36·6	37·9	38·0	37·0
9	55·6	02·4	09·2	15·6	21·5	26·7	31·1	34·4	36·8	37·9	38·0	36·8
10	0 56·3	1 03·1	1 09·8	1 16·2	1 22·0	1 27·2	1 31·4	1 34·7	1 36·9	1 38·0	1 37·9	1 36·6

Lat.	a_1	a_1	a_1	a_1	a_1	a_1	a_1	a_1	a_1	a_1	a_1	a_1
°	′	′	′	′	′	′	′	′	′	′	′	′
0	0·3	0·3	0·3	0·4	0·4	0·4	0·5	0·5	0·6	0·6	0·6	0·6
10	·4	·4	·4	·4	·4	·5	·5	·5	·6	·6	·6	·6
20	·4	·4	·4	·4	·5	·5	·5	·6	·6	·6	·6	·6
30	·5	·5	·5	·5	·5	·5	·5	·6	·6	·6	·6	·6
40	0·5	0·5	0·5	0·5	0·5	0·6	0·6	0·6	0·6	0·6	0·6	0·6
45	·6	·6	·6	·6	·6	·6	·6	·6	·6	·6	·6	·6
50	·6	·6	·6	·6	·6	·6	·6	·6	·6	·6	·6	·6
55	·7	·7	·7	·6	·6	·6	·6	·6	·6	·6	·6	·6
60	·7	·7	·7	·7	·7	·7	·6	·6	·6	·6	·6	·6
62	0·8	0·8	0·7	0·7	0·7	0·7	0·7	0·6	0·6	0·6	0·6	0·6
64	·8	·8	·8	·8	·7	·7	·7	·6	·6	·6	·6	·6
66	·8	·8	·8	·8	·8	·7	·7	·7	·6	·6	·6	·6
68	0·9	0·9	0·9	0·9	0·8	0·8	0·7	0·7	0·6	0·6	0·6	0·6

Month	a_2	a_2	a_2	a_2	a_2	a_2	a_2	a_2	a_2	a_2	a_2	a_2
	′	′	′	′	′	′	′	′	′	′	′	′
Jan.	0·6	0·6	0·6	0·5	0·5	0·5	0·5	0·5	0·5	0·5	0·5	0·5
Feb.	·8	·7	·7	·7	·6	·6	·6	·5	·5	·5	·4	·4
Mar.	0·9	0·9	0·9	·8	·8	·7	·7	·6	·6	·5	·5	·4
Apr.	1·0	1·0	1·0	0·9	0·9	0·9	0·8	0·8	0·7	0·7	0·6	0·5
May	0·9	1·0	1·0	1·0	1·0	1·0	1·0	0·9	0·9	·8	·8	·7
June	·8	0·9	0·9	1·0	1·0	1·0	1·0	1·0	1·0	0·9	·9	·8
July	0·7	0·7	0·8	0·8	0·9	0·9	0·9	1·0	1·0	1·0	0·9	0·9
Aug.	·5	·6	·6	·7	·7	·8	·8	0·9	0·9	0·9	·9	·9
Sept.	·4	·4	·4	·5	·5	·6	·6	·7	·7	·8	·8	·9
Oct.	0·3	0·3	0·3	0·3	0·4	0·4	0·5	0·5	0·6	0·6	0·7	0·7
Nov.	·3	·2	·2	·2	·2	·2	·3	·3	·4	·4	·5	·6
Dec.	0·3	0·3	0·2	0·2	0·2	0·2	0·2	0·2	0·2	0·3	0·3	0·4

Lat.	AZIMUTH											
°	°	°	°	°	°	°	°	°	°	°	°	°
0	359·4	359·3	359·4	359·4	359·4	359·5	359·6	359·7	359·8	359·9	0·0	0·1
20	359·3	359·3	359·3	359·3	359·4	359·5	359·6	359·7	359·8	359·9	0·0	0·1
40	359·2	359·1	359·2	359·2	359·3	359·4	359·5	359·6	359·7	359·9	0·0	0·2
50	359·0	359·0	359·0	359·1	359·1	359·2	359·4	359·5	359·7	359·8	0·0	0·2
55	358·9	358·9	358·9	358·9	359·0	359·1	359·3	359·5	359·6	359·8	0·0	0·2
60	358·7	358·7	358·7	358·8	358·9	359·0	359·2	359·4	359·6	359·8	0·0	0·2
65	358·5	358·5	358·5	358·6	358·7	358·8	359·0	359·3	359·5	359·8	0·0	0·3

ILLUSTRATION				
	From the daily pages:	° ′	H_0	49 31·6
On 2019 April 21 at	GHA Aries (23ʰ)	194 43·3	a_0 (argument 162° 14′)	1 17·5
23ʰ 18ᵐ 56ˢ UT in longitude	Increment (18ᵐ 56ˢ)	4 44·8	a_1 (Lat 50° approx.)	0·6
W 37° 14′, the apparent altitude	Longitude (west)	−37 14	a_2 (April)	0·9
(corrected for refraction), H_0, of				
Polaris was 49° 31′·6	LHA Aries	162 14	Sum − 1° = Lat =	49 50·6

© British Crown Copyright 2018. All rights reserved.

POLARIS (POLE STAR) TABLES, 2019
FOR DETERMINING LATITUDE FROM SEXTANT ALTITUDE AND FOR AZIMUTH

LHA ARIES	240°– 249°	250°– 259°	260°– 269°	270°– 279°	280°– 289°	290°– 299°	300°– 309°	310°– 319°	320°– 329°	330°– 339°	340°– 349°	350°– 359°
°	a_0	a_0	a_0	a_0	a_0	a_0	a_0	a_0	a_0	a_0	a_0	a_0
	° ′	° ′	° ′	° ′	° ′	° ′	° ′	° ′	° ′	° ′	° ′	° ′
0	1 36·6	1 34·2	1 30·7	1 26·3	1 21·0	1 15·0	1 08·6	1 01·9	0 55·0	0 48·3	0 41·8	0 35·9
1	36·4	33·9	30·3	25·8	20·4	14·4	07·9	01·2	54·3	47·6	41·2	35·4
2	36·2	33·6	29·9	25·3	19·9	13·8	07·3	1 00·5	53·6	46·9	40·6	34·8
3	36·0	33·3	29·5	24·8	19·3	13·2	06·6	0 59·8	53·0	46·3	40·0	34·3
4	35·8	32·9	29·0	24·3	18·7	12·5	05·9	59·1	52·3	45·6	39·4	33·7
5	1 35·5	1 32·6	1 28·6	1 23·7	1 18·1	1 11·9	1 05·3	0 58·4	0 51·6	0 45·0	0 38·8	0 33·2
6	35·3	32·2	28·2	23·2	17·5	11·2	04·6	57·7	50·9	44·4	38·2	32·7
7	35·0	31·9	27·7	22·7	16·9	10·6	03·9	57·1	50·3	43·7	37·6	32·2
8	34·8	31·5	27·2	22·1	16·3	09·9	03·2	56·4	49·6	43·1	37·0	31·7
9	34·5	31·1	26·8	21·6	15·7	09·3	02·5	55·7	48·9	42·5	36·5	31·2
10	1 34·2	1 30·7	1 26·3	1 21·0	1 15·0	1 08·6	1 01·9	0 55·0	0 48·3	0 41·8	0 35·9	0 30·7

Lat.	a_1	a_1	a_1	a_1	a_1	a_1	a_1	a_1	a_1	a_1	a_1	a_1
°	′	′	′	′	′	′	′	′	′	′	′	′
0	0·6	0·5	0·5	0·4	0·4	0·4	0·3	0·3	0·3	0·4	0·4	0·4
10	·6	·5	·5	·5	·4	·4	·4	·4	·4	·4	·4	·5
20	·6	·6	·5	·5	·5	·4	·4	·4	·4	·4	·5	·5
30	·6	·6	·5	·5	·5	·5	·5	·5	·5	·5	·5	·5
40	0·6	0·6	0·6	0·6	0·5	0·5	0·5	0·5	0·5	0·5	0·5	0·6
45	·6	·6	·6	·6	·6	·6	·6	·6	·6	·6	·6	·6
50	·6	·6	·6	·6	·6	·6	·6	·6	·6	·6	·6	·6
55	·6	·6	·6	·6	·6	·6	·7	·7	·7	·6	·6	·6
60	·6	·6	·7	·7	·7	·7	·7	·7	·7	·7	·7	·7
62	0·6	0·6	0·7	0·7	0·7	0·7	0·8	0·8	0·7	0·7	0·7	0·7
64	·6	·7	·7	·7	·7	·8	·8	·8	·8	·8	·7	·7
66	·6	·7	·7	·7	·8	·8	·8	·8	·8	·8	·8	·7
68	0·6	0·7	0·7	0·8	0·8	0·9	0·9	0·9	0·9	0·9	0·8	0·8

Month	a_2	a_2	a_2	a_2	a_2	a_2	a_2	a_2	a_2	a_2	a_2	a_2
	′	′	′	′	′	′	′	′	′	′	′	′
Jan.	0·5	0·5	0·5	0·5	0·5	0·6	0·6	0·6	0·6	0·7	0·7	0·7
Feb.	·4	·4	·4	·4	·4	·4	·4	·5	·5	·5	·6	·6
Mar.	·4	·4	·3	·3	·3	·3	·3	·3	·3	·4	·4	·5
Apr.	0·5	0·4	0·4	0·3	0·3	0·3	0·2	0·2	0·2	0·3	0·3	0·3
May	·6	·6	·5	·4	·4	·3	·3	·2	·2	·2	·2	·2
June	·8	·7	·6	·6	·5	·4	·4	·3	·3	·2	·2	·2
July	0·9	0·8	0·8	0·7	0·7	0·6	0·5	0·5	0·4	0·4	0·3	0·3
Aug.	·9	·9	·9	·8	·8	·7	·7	·6	·6	·5	·5	·4
Sept.	·9	·9	·9	·9	·9	·9	·8	·8	·8	·7	·7	·6
Oct.	0·8	0·8	0·9	0·9	0·9	0·9	0·9	0·9	0·9	0·9	0·8	0·8
Nov.	·6	·7	·8	·8	·9	·9	·9	1·0	1·0	1·0	1·0	1·0
Dec.	0·5	0·5	0·6	0·7	0·7	0·8	0·9	0·9	1·0	1·0	1·0	1·0

Lat.	AZIMUTH											
°	°	°	°	°	°	°	°	°	°	°	°	°
0	0·2	0·3	0·4	0·5	0·6	0·6	0·6	0·7	0·6	0·6	0·6	0·5
20	0·2	0·4	0·5	0·5	0·6	0·7	0·7	0·7	0·7	0·7	0·6	0·5
40	0·3	0·4	0·6	0·7	0·7	0·8	0·8	0·9	0·8	0·8	0·7	0·7
50	0·4	0·5	0·7	0·8	0·9	1·0	1·0	1·0	1·0	1·0	0·9	0·8
55	0·4	0·6	0·7	0·9	1·0	1·1	1·1	1·1	1·1	1·1	1·0	0·9
60	0·5	0·7	0·8	1·0	1·1	1·2	1·3	1·3	1·3	1·2	1·1	1·0
65	0·5	0·8	1·0	1·2	1·3	1·5	1·5	1·6	1·5	1·5	1·3	1·2

Latitude = Apparent altitude (corrected for refraction) $-1° + a_0 + a_1 + a_2$

The table is entered with LHA Aries to determine the column to be used; each column refers to a range of 10°. a_0 is taken, with mental interpolation, from the upper table with the units of LHA Aries in degrees as argument; a_1, a_2 are taken, without interpolation, from the second and third tables with arguments latitude and month respectively. a_0, a_1, a_2, are always positive. The final table gives the azimuth of *Polaris*.

© British Crown Copyright 2018. All rights reserved.

SIGHT REDUCTION PROCEDURES
METHODS AND FORMULAE FOR DIRECT COMPUTATION

1. *Introduction.* In this section, formulae and methods are provided for *calculating* position at sea from observed altitudes taken with a marine sextant using a computer or programmable calculator.

The method uses analogous concepts and similar terminology as that used in *manual* methods of astro-navigation, where position is found by plotting position lines from their intercept and azimuth on a marine chart.

The algorithms are presented in standard algebra suitable for translating into the programming language of the user's computer. The basic ephemeris data may be taken directly from the main tabular pages of a current version of *The Nautical Almanac.* Formulae are given for calculating altitude and azimuth from the *GHA* and *Dec* of a body, and the estimated position of the observer. Formulae are also given for reducing sextant observations to observed altitudes by applying the corrections for dip, refraction, parallax and semi-diameter.

The intercept and azimuth obtained from each observation determine a position line, and the observer should lie on or close to each position line. The method of least squares is used to calculate the fix by finding the position where the sum of the squares of the distances from the position lines is a minimum. The use of least squares has other advantages. For example, it is possible to improve the estimated position at the time of fix by repeating the calculation. It is also possible to include more observations in the solution and to reject doubtful ones.

2. *Notation.*

GHA = Greenwich hour angle. The range of GHA is from $0°$ to $360°$ starting at $0°$ on the Greenwich meridian increasing to the west, back to $360°$ on the Greenwich meridian.

SHA = sidereal hour angle. The range is $0°$ to $360°$.

Dec = declination. The sign convention for declination is north is positive, south is negative. The range is from $-90°$ at the south celestial pole to $+90°$ at the north celestial pole.

$Long$ = longitude. The sign convention is east is positive, west is negative. The range is $-180°$ to $+180°$.

Lat = latitude. The sign convention is north is positive, south is negative. The range is from $-90°$ to $+90°$.

LHA = $GHA + Long$ = local hour angle. The LHA increases to the west from $0°$ on the local meridian to $360°$.

H_C = calculated altitude. Above the horizon is positive, below the horizon is negative. The range is from $-90°$ in the nadir to $+90°$ in the zenith.

H_S = sextant altitude.

H = apparent altitude = sextant altitude corrected for instrumental error and dip.

H_O = observed altitude = apparent altitude corrected for refraction and, in appropriate cases, corrected for parallax and semi-diameter.

Z = Z_n = true azimuth. Z is measured from true north through east, south, west and back to north. The range is from $0°$ to $360°$.

I = sextant index error.

D = dip of horizon.

R = atmospheric refraction.

© British Crown Copyright 2018. All rights reserved.

HP = horizontal parallax of the Sun, Moon, Venus or Mars.
PA = parallax in altitude of the Sun, Moon, Venus or Mars.
SD = semi-diameter of the Sun or Moon.
p = intercept = $H_O - H_C$. Towards is positive, away is negative.
T = course or track, measured as for azimuth from the north.
V = speed in knots.

3. *Entering Basic Data.* When quantities such as GHA are entered, which in *The Nautical Almanac* are given in degrees and minutes, convert them to degrees and decimals of a degree by dividing the minutes by 60 and adding to the degrees; for example, if $GHA = 123° 45\!.6$, enter the two numbers 123 and 45·6 into the memory and set $GHA = 123 + 45·6/60 = 123°7600$. Although four decimal places of a degree are shown in the examples, it is assumed that full precision is maintained in the calculations.

When using a computer or programmable calculator, write a subroutine to convert degrees and minutes to degrees and decimals. Scientific calculators usually have a special key for this purpose. For quantities like *Dec* which require a minus sign for southern declination, change the sign from plus to minus after the value has been converted to degrees and decimals, *e.g.* $Dec = S 0° 12\!.3 = S 0°2050 = -0°2050$. Other quantities which require conversion are semi-diameter, horizontal parallax, longitude and latitude.

4. *Interpolation of GHA and Dec* The GHA and *Dec* of the Sun, Moon and planets are interpolated to the time of observation by direct calculation as follows: If the universal time is $a^h b^m c^s$, form the interpolation factor $x = b/60 + c/3600$. Enter the tabular value GHA_0 for the preceding hour (a) and the tabular value GHA_1 for the following hour ($a + 1$) then the interpolated value GHA is given by

$$GHA = GHA_0 + x(GHA_1 - GHA_0)$$

If the GHA passes through 360° between tabular values, add 360° to GHA_1 before interpolation. If the interpolated value exceeds 360°, subtract 360° from GHA.

Similarly for declination, enter the tabular value Dec_0 for the preceding hour (a) and the tabular value Dec_1 for the following hour ($a + 1$), then the interpolated value *Dec* is given by

$$Dec = Dec_0 + x(Dec_1 - Dec_0)$$

5. *Example.* (a) Find the GHA and *Dec* of the Sun on 2019 February 16 at $14^h 47^m 13^s$ UT.

The interpolation factor $x = 47/60 + 13/3600 = 0^h7869$

page 41 14^h $GHA_0 = 26° 28\!.9 = 26°4817$

15^h $GHA_1 = 41° 28\!.9 = 41°4817$

14^h7869 $GHA = 26·4817 + 0·7869(41·4817 - 26·4817) = 38°2858$

14^h $Dec_0 = S 12° 18\!.3 = -12°3050$

15^h $Dec_1 = S 12° 17\!.4 = -12°2900$

14^h7869 $Dec = -12·3050 + 0·7869(-12·2900 + 12·3050) = -12°2932$

GHA Aries is interpolated in the same way as GHA of a body. For a star the SHA and *Dec* are taken from the tabular page and do not require interpolation, then

$$GHA = GHA \text{ Aries} + SHA$$

where GHA Aries is interpolated to the time of observation.

© British Crown Copyright 2018. All rights reserved.

(b) Find the *GHA* and *Dec* of *Vega* on 2019 February 16 at $14^h\ 47^m\ 13^s$ UT.

The interpolation factor $x = 0^h\!.7869$ as in the previous example

page 40 14^h *GHA* Aries$_0$ = 356° 16$'$.3 = 356°.2717

15^h *GHA* Aries$_1$ = 11° 18$'$.8 = 371°.3133   (360° added)

$14^h\!.7869$ *GHA* Aries = $356\cdot2717 + 0\cdot7869(371\cdot3133 - 356\cdot2717) = 368°\!.1086$

$SHA = 80°\ 36'\!.6 = 80°\!.6100$

$GHA = GHA$ Aries $+ SHA = 88°\!.7186$ (multiple of 360° removed)

$Dec = $ N 38° 48$'$.0 $= +38°\!.8000$

6. *The calculated altitude and azimuth.* The calculated altitude H_C and true azimuth Z are determined from the *GHA* and *Dec* interpolated to the time of observation and from the *Long* and *Lat* estimated at the time of observation as follows:

Step 1.   Calculate the local hour angle

$$LHA = GHA + Long$$

Add or subtract multiples of 360° to set *LHA* in the range 0° to 360°.

Step 2.   Calculate *S*, *C* and the altitude H_C from

$$S = \sin Dec$$
$$C = \cos Dec \cos LHA$$
$$H_C = \sin^{-1}(S\ \sin Lat + C\ \cos Lat)$$

where $\sin^{-1}$ is the inverse function of sine.

Step 3.   Calculate *X* and *A* from

$$X = (S\ \cos Lat - C\ \sin Lat)/\cos H_C$$
If $X > +1$ set $X = +1$
If $X < -1$ set $X = -1$
$$A = \cos^{-1} X$$

where $\cos^{-1}$ is the inverse function of cosine.

Step 4.   Determine the azimuth *Z*

If $LHA > 180°$ then $Z = A$
Otherwise $Z = 360° - A$

7. *Example.* Find the calculated altitude H_C and azimuth *Z* when

$$GHA = 53°\quad Dec = \text{S}\ 15°\quad Lat = \text{N}\ 32°\quad Long = \text{W}\ 16°$$

For the calculation

$GHA = 53°\!.0000\quad Dec = -15°\!.0000\quad Lat = +32°\!.0000\quad Long = -16°\!.0000$

Step 1. $LHA = 53\cdot0000 - 16\cdot0000 = 37\cdot0000$
Step 2. $S = -0\cdot2588$
$C = +0\cdot9659 \times 0\cdot7986 = 0\cdot7714$
$\sin H_C = -0\cdot2588 \times 0\cdot5299 + 0\cdot7714 \times 0\cdot8480 = 0\cdot5171$
$H_C = 31°\!.1346$

© British Crown Copyright 2018. All rights reserved.

Step 3. $X = (-0{\cdot}2588 \times 0{\cdot}8480 - 0{\cdot}7714 \times 0{\cdot}5299)/0{\cdot}8560 = -0{\cdot}7340$

                   $A = 137{\overset{\circ}{\cdot}}2239$

Step 4.   Since $LHA \leq 180°$ then $Z = 360° - A = 222{\overset{\circ}{\cdot}}7761$

8. *Reduction from sextant altitude to observed altitude.*   The sextant altitude H_S is corrected for both dip and index error to produce the apparent altitude. The observed altitude H_O is calculated by applying a correction for refraction. For the Sun, Moon, Venus and Mars a correction for parallax is also applied to H, and for the Sun and Moon a further correction for semi-diameter is required. The corrections are calculated as follows:

Step 1.   Calculate dip

$$D = 0{\overset{\circ}{\cdot}}0293 \sqrt{h}$$

where h is the height of eye above the horizon in metres.

Step 2.   Calculate apparent altitude

$$H = H_S + I - D$$

where I is the sextant index error.

Step 3.   Calculate refraction (R) at a standard temperature of 10° Celsius (C) and pressure of 1010 millibars (mb)

$$R_0 = 0{\overset{\circ}{\cdot}}0167/ \tan (H + 7{\cdot}32/(H + 4{\cdot}32))$$

If the temperature $T°\,C$ and pressure P mb are known calculate the refraction from

$$R = f R_0 \qquad \text{where} \qquad f = 0{\cdot}28 P/(T + 273)$$

otherwise set $R = R_0$

Step 4.   Calculate the parallax in altitude (PA) from the horizontal parallax (HP) and the apparent altitude (H) for the Sun, Moon, Venus and Mars as follows:

$$PA = HP \cos H$$

For the Sun $HP = 0{\overset{\circ}{\cdot}}0024$. This correction is very small and could be ignored.

For the Moon HP is taken for the nearest hour from the main tabular page and converted to degrees.

For Venus and Mars the HP is taken from the critical table at the bottom of page 259 and converted to degrees.

For the navigational stars and the remaining planets, Jupiter and Saturn set $PA = 0$.

If an error of $0{\overset{\prime}{\cdot}}2$ is significant the expression for the parallax in altitude for the Moon should include a small correction OB for the oblateness of the Earth as follows:

$$PA = HP \cos H + OB$$

where $OB = -0{\overset{\circ}{\cdot}}0032 \sin^2 Lat \cos H + 0{\overset{\circ}{\cdot}}0032 \sin (2Lat) \cos Z \sin H$

At mid-latitudes and for altitudes of the Moon below 60° a simple approximation to OB is

$$OB = -0{\overset{\circ}{\cdot}}0017 \cos H$$

© British Crown Copyright 2018. All rights reserved.

Step 5. Calculate the semi-diameter for the Sun and Moon as follows:

Sun: *SD* is taken from the main tabular page and converted to degrees.

Moon: $SD = 0°2724HP$ where *HP* is taken for the nearest hour from the main tabular page and converted to degrees.

Step 6. Calculate the observed altitude

$$H_O = H - R + PA \pm SD$$

where the plus sign is used if the lower limb of the Sun or Moon was observed and the minus sign if the upper limb was observed.

9. *Example.* The following example illustrates how to use a calculator to reduce the sextant altitude (H_S) to observed altitude (H_O); the sextant altitudes given are assumed to be taken on 2019 August 9 with a marine sextant, zero index error, at height 5·4 m, temperature $-3°$ C and pressure 982 mb, the Moon sights are assumed to be taken at 10^h UT.

Body limb	Sun lower	Sun upper	Moon lower	Moon upper	Venus —	*Polaris* —
Sextant altitude: H_S	21·3283	3·3367	33·4600	26·1117	4·5433	49·6083
Step 1. Dip: $D = 0·0293\sqrt{h}$	0·0681	0·0681	0·0681	0·0681	0·0681	0·0681
Step 2. Apparent altitude: $H = H_S + I - D$	21·2602	3·2686	33·3919	26·0436	4·4752	49·5402
Step 3. Refraction: R_0	0·0423	0·2256	0·0251	0·0338	0·1798	0·0142
f	1·0184	1·0184	1·0184	1·0184	1·0184	1·0184
$R = fR_0$	0·0431	0·2298	0·0256	0·0344	0·1831	0·0144
Step 4. Parallax: HP	0·0024	0·0024	(56′8) 0·9467	(56′8) 0·9467	(0′1) 0·0017	—
Parallax in altitude: $PA = HP\cos H$	0·0022	0·0024	0·7904	0·8505	0·0017	—
Step 5. Semi-diameter: Sun : $SD = 15·8/60$	0·2633	0·2633	—	—	—	—
Moon : $SD = 0·2724HP$	—	—	0·2579	0·2579	—	—
Step 6. Observed altitude: $H_O = H - R + PA \pm SD$	21·4827	2·7779	34·4146	26·6018	4·2938	49·5258

Note that for the Moon the correction for the oblateness of the Earth of about $-0°0017\cos H$, which equals $-0°0014$ for the lower limb and $-0°0015$ for the upper limb, has been ignored in the above calculation.

10. *Position from intercept and azimuth using a chart.* An estimate is made of the position at the adopted time of fix. The position at the time of observation is then calculated by dead reckoning from the time of fix. For example, if the course (track) *T* and the speed *V* (in knots) of the observer are constant, then *Long* and *Lat* at the time of observation are calculated from

© British Crown Copyright 2018. All rights reserved.

$$Long = L_F + t\,(V/60)\sin T / \cos B_F$$
$$Lat = B_F + t\,(V/60)\cos T$$

where L_F and B_F are the estimated longitude and latitude at the time of fix and t is the time interval in hours from the time of fix to the time of observation, t is positive if the time of observation is after the time of fix and negative if it was before.

The position line of an observation is plotted on a chart using the intercept

$$p = H_O - H_C$$

and azimuth Z with origin at the calculated position ($Long, Lat$) at the time of observation, where H_C and Z are calculated using the method in section 6, page 279. Starting from this calculated position a line is drawn on the chart along the direction of the azimuth to the body. Convert p to nautical miles by multiplying by 60. The position line is drawn at right angles to the azimuth line, distance p from ($Long, Lat$) towards the body if p is positive and distance p away from the body if p is negative. Provided there are no gross errors, the navigator should be somewhere on or near the position line at the time of observation. Two or more position lines are required to determine a fix.

11. *Position from intercept and azimuth by calculation.* The position of the fix may be calculated from two or more sextant observations as follows.

If p_1, Z_1, are the intercept and azimuth of the first observation, p_2, Z_2, of the second observation and so on, form the summations

$$A = \cos^2 Z_1 + \cos^2 Z_2 + \cdots$$
$$B = \cos Z_1 \sin Z_1 + \cos Z_2 \sin Z_2 + \cdots$$
$$C = \sin^2 Z_1 + \sin^2 Z_2 + \cdots$$
$$D = p_1 \cos Z_1 + p_2 \cos Z_2 + \cdots$$
$$E = p_1 \sin Z_1 + p_2 \sin Z_2 + \cdots$$

where the number of terms in each summation is equal to the number of observations.

With $G = A C - B^2$, an improved estimate of the position at the time of fix (L_I, B_I) is given by

$$L_I = L_F + (A E - B D)/(G \cos B_F), \qquad B_I = B_F + (C D - B E)/G$$

Calculate the distance d between the initial estimated position (L_F, B_F) at the time of fix and the improved estimated position (L_I, B_I) in nautical miles from

$$d = 60 \sqrt{((L_I - L_F)^2 \cos^2 B_F + (B_I - B_F)^2)}$$

If d exceeds about 20 nautical miles set $L_F = L_I$, $B_F = B_I$ and repeat the calculation until d, the distance between the position at the previous estimate and the improved estimate, is less than about 20 nautical miles.

12. *Example of direct computation.* Using the method described above, calculate the position of a ship on 2019 July 4 at $21^h\,00^m\,00^s$ UT from the marine sextant observations of the three stars *Regulus* (No. 26) at $20^h\,39^m\,23^s$ UT, *Antares* (No. 42) at $20^h\,45^m\,47^s$ UT and *Kochab* (No. 40) at $21^h\,10^m\,34^s$ UT, where the observed altitudes of the three stars corrected for the effects of refraction, dip and instrumental error, are $27°2789$, $25°8539$ and $47°5472$ respectively. The ship was travelling at a constant speed of 20 knots on a course of 325° during the period of observation, and the position of the ship at the time of fix $21^h\,00^m\,00^s$ UT is only known to the nearest whole degree W 15°, N 32°.

© British Crown Copyright 2018. All rights reserved.

Intermediate values for the first iteration are shown in the table. *GHA* Aries was interpolated from the nearest tabular values on page 132. For the first iteration set $L_F = -15°0000$, $B_F = +32°0000$ at the time of fix at $21^h\ 00^m\ 00^s$ UT.

First Iteration

Body	Regulus	Antares	Kochab
No.	26	42	40
time of observation	$20^h\ 39^m\ 23^s$	$20^h\ 45^m\ 47^s$	$21^h\ 10^m\ 34^s$
H_O	27·2789	25·8539	47·5472
interpolation factor	0·6564	0·7631	0·1761
GHA Aries	232·4098	234·0143	240·2270
SHA (page 132)	207·6550	112·3483	137·3250
GHA	80·0648	346·3626	17·5520
Dec (page 132)	+11·8733	−26·4733	+74·0817
t	−0·3436	−0·2369	+0·1761
Long	−14·9225	−14·9466	−15·0397
Lat	+31·9062	+31·9353	+32·0481
Z	267·2430	151·6608	358·9716
H_C	27·2558	25·5481	47·9473
p	+0·0231	+0·3058	−0·4001

$$A = 1·7767 \quad B = -0·3877 \quad C = 1·2233 \quad D = -0·6703 \quad E = 0·1293 \quad G = 2·0231$$
$$(AE - BD)/(G\cos B_F) = -0·0176, \qquad (CD - BE)/G = -0·3805$$

An improved estimate of the position at the time of fix is

$$L_I = L_F - 0·0176 = -15·0176 \quad \text{and} \quad B_I = B_F - 0·3805 = +31·6195$$

Since the distance between the previous estimated position and the improved estimate is $d = 22·8$ nautical miles, set $L_F = -15·0176$, and $B_F = +31·6195$ and repeat the calculation. The table shows the intermediate values of the calculation for the second iteration. In each iteration the quantities H_O, *GHA*, *Dec* and t do not change.

Second Iteration

Body	Regulus	Antares	Kochab
No.	26	42	40
Long	−14·9405	−14·9644	−15·0571
Lat	+31·5256	+31·5548	+31·6675
Z	267·4292	151·5579	358·9861
H_C	27·2887	25·8756	47·5671
p	−0·0098	−0·0218	−0·0199

$$A = 1·7749 \quad B = -0·3917 \quad C = 1·2251 \quad D = -0·0003 \quad E = -0·0002 \quad G = 2·0210$$
$$(AE - BD)/(G\cos B_F) = -0·0003, \qquad (CD - BE)/G = -0·0002$$

An improved estimate of the position at the time of fix is

$$L_I = L_F - 0·0003 = -15·0179 \quad \text{and} \quad B_I = B_F - 0·0002 = +31·6192$$

The distance between the previous estimated position and the improved estimated position, $d = 0·02$ nautical miles, is so small that a third iteration would produce a negligible improvement to the estimate of the position.

© British Crown Copyright 2018. All rights reserved.

USE OF CONCISE SIGHT REDUCTION TABLES

1. *Introduction.* The concise sight reduction tables given on pages 286 to 317 are intended for use when neither more extensive tables nor electronic computing aids are available. These "NAO sight reduction tables" provide for the reduction of the local hour angle and declination of a celestial object to azimuth and altitude, referred to an assumed position on the Earth, for use in the intercept method of celestial navigation which is now standard practice.

2. *Form of tables.* Entries in the reduction table are at a fixed interval of one degree for all latitudes and hour angles. A compact arrangement results from division of the navigational triangle into two right spherical triangles, so that the table has to be entered twice. Assumed latitude and local hour angle are the arguments for the first entry. The reduction table responds with the intermediate arguments A, B, and Z_1, where A is used as one of the arguments for the second entry to the table, B has to be incremented by the declination to produce the quantity F, and Z_1 is a component of the azimuth angle. The reduction table is then reentered with A and F and yields H, P, and Z_2 where H is the altitude, P is the complement of the parallactic angle, and Z_2 is the second component of the azimuth angle. It is usually necessary to adjust the tabular altitude for the fractional parts of the intermediate entering arguments to derive computed altitude, and an auxiliary table is provided for the purpose. Rules governing signs of the quantities which must be added or subtracted are given in the instructions and summarized on each tabular page. Azimuth angle is the sum of two components and is converted to true azimuth by familiar rules, repeated at the bottom of the tabular pages.

Tabular altitude and intermediate quantities are given to the nearest minute of arc, although errors of $2'$ in computed altitude may accrue during adjustment for the minutes parts of entering arguments. Components of azimuth angle are stated to $0°1$; for derived true azimuth, only whole degrees are warranted. Since objects near the zenith are difficult to observe with a marine sextant, they should be avoided; altitudes greater than about $80°$ are not suited to reduction by this method.

In many circumstances, the accuracy provided by these tables is sufficient. However, to maintain the full accuracy ($0°1$) of the ephemeral data in the almanac throughout their reduction to altitude and azimuth, more extensive tables or a calculator should be used.

3. *Use of Tables.*

Step 1. Determine the Greenwich hour angle (GHA) and Declination (Dec) of the body from the almanac. Select an assumed latitude (Lat) of integral degrees nearest to the estimated latitude. Choose an assumed longitude nearest to the estimated longitude such that the local hour angle

$$LHA = GHA \begin{array}{l} - \text{ west} \\ + \text{ east} \end{array} \text{longitude}$$

has integral degrees.

Step 2. Enter the reduction table with Lat and LHA as arguments. Record the quantities A, B and Z_1. Apply the rules for the sign of B and Z_1: B is minus if $90° < LHA < 270°$: Z_1 has the same sign as B. Set $A° =$ nearest whole degree of A and $A' =$ minutes part of A. This step may be repeated for all reductions before leaving the latitude opening of the table.

Step 3. Record the declination Dec. Apply the rules for the sign of Dec: Dec is minus if the name of Dec (*i.e.* N or S) is contrary to latitude. Add B and Dec algebraically to produce F. If F is negative, the object is below the horizon (in sight reduction, this can occur when the objects are close to the horizon). Regard F as positive until step 7. Set $F° =$ nearest whole degree of F and $F' =$ minutes part of F.

© British Crown Copyright 2018. All rights reserved.

Step 4.   Enter the reduction table a second time with $A°$ and $F°$ as arguments and record H, P, and Z_2. Set $P° =$ nearest whole degree of P and $Z_2° =$ nearest whole degree of Z_2.

Step 5.   Enter the auxiliary table with F' and $P°$ as arguments to obtain $corr_1$ to H for F'. Apply the rule for the sign of $corr_1$: $corr_1$ is minus if $F < 90°$ and $F' > 29'$ or if $F > 90°$ and $F' < 30'$, otherwise $corr_1$ is plus.

Step 6.   Enter the auxiliary table with A' and $Z_2°$ as arguments to obtain $corr_2$ to H for A'. Apply the rule for the sign of $corr_2$: $corr_2$ is minus if $A' < 30'$, otherwise $corr_2$ is plus.

Step 7.   Calculate the computed altitude H_C as the sum of H, $corr_1$ and $corr_2$. Apply the rule for the sign of H_C: H_C is minus if F is negative.

Step 8.   Apply the rule for the sign of Z_2: Z_2 is minus if $F > 90°$. If F is negative, replace Z_2 by $180° - Z_2$. Set the azimuth angle Z equal to the algebraic sum of Z_1 and Z_2 and ignore the resulting sign. Obtain the true azimuth Z_n from the rules

$$
\begin{aligned}
\text{For N latitude, if} \quad LHA &> 180° &\quad Z_n &= Z \\
\text{if} \quad LHA &< 180° &\quad Z_n &= 360° - Z \\
\\
\text{For S latitude, if} \quad LHA &> 180° &\quad Z_n &= 180° - Z \\
\text{if} \quad LHA &< 180° &\quad Z_n &= 180° + Z
\end{aligned}
$$

Observed altitude H_O is compared with H_C to obtain the altitude difference, which, with Z_n, is used to plot the position line.

4. *Example.*   (a) Required the altitude and azimuth of *Schedar* on 2019 February 4 at UT 06^h 32^m from the estimated position N 53°, E 5°.

1. Assumed latitude $Lat =$ 53° N
   From the almanac $GHA =$ 221° 45′
   Assumed longitude   5° 15′ E
   Local hour angle $LHA =$ 227

2. Reduction table, 1st entry
   $(Lat, LHA) = (53, 227)$ $A =$ 26 07 $A° = 26, A' = 7$
                                $B = -27$ 12 $Z_1 = -49·4$, $90° < LHA < 270°$
3. From the almanac $Dec = +56$ 39   *Lat* and *Dec* same
   Sum $= B + Dec$ $F = +29$ 27 $F° = 29, F' = 27$

4. Reduction table, 2nd entry
   $(A°, F°) = (26, 29)$ $H =$ 25 50 $P° = 61$
                                                $Z_2 = 76·3, Z_2° = 76$

5. Auxiliary table, 1st entry
   $(F', P°) = (27, 61)$ $corr_1 = \underline{\quad +24}$ $F < 90°, F' < 29'$
   Sum   26 14
6. Auxiliary table, 2nd entry
   $(A', Z_2°) = (7, 76)$ $corr_2 = \underline{\quad -2}$ $A' < 30'$
7. Sum $=$ computed altitude $H_C = +26°$ 12′ $F > 0°$

8. Azimuth, first component $Z_1 = -49·4$ same sign as B
             second component $Z_2 = \underline{+76·3}$ $F < 90°, F > 0°$
   Sum $=$ azimuth angle $Z =$ 26·9

   True azimuth $Z_n =$ 027°   N *Lat*, $LHA > 180°$

continued on page 318

© British Crown Copyright 2018. All rights reserved.

SIGHT REDUCTION TABLE

Z₁: same sign as B
Z₂: (−) for F > 90°

B: (−) for 90° < LHA < 270°
Dec: (−) for Lat. contrary name

LHA/F	0° A/H	0° B/P	0° Z₁/Z₂	1° A/H	1° B/P	1° Z₁/Z₂	2° A/H	2° B/P	2° Z₁/Z₂	3° A/H	3° B/P	3° Z₁/Z₂	4° A/H	4° B/P	4° Z₁/Z₂	5° A/H	5° B/P	5° Z₁/Z₂	LHA/A
0 / 180	0 00	90 00	90·0	0 00	89 00	90·0	0 00	88 00	90·0	0 00	87 00	90·0	0 00	86 00	90·0	0 00	85 00	90·0	180 / 360
1 / 179	1 00	90 00	90·0	1 00	89 00	90·0	1 00	88 00	90·0	1 00	87 00	89·9	1 00	86 00	89·9	1 00	85 00	89·9	181 / 359
2 / 178	2 00	90 00	90·0	2 00	89 00	90·0	2 00	88 00	89·9	2 00	87 00	89·9	2 00	86 00	89·9	2 00	85 00	89·8	182 / 358
3 / 177	3 00	90 00	90·0	3 00	89 00	89·9	3 00	88 00	89·9	3 00	87 00	89·8	2 59	86 00	89·8	2 59	85 00	89·7	183 / 357
4 / 176	4 00	90 00	90·0	4 00	89 00	89·9	4 00	88 00	89·9	4 00	87 00	89·8	3 59	85 59	89·7	3 59	84 59	89·6	184 / 356
5 / 175	5 00	90 00	90·0	5 00	89 00	89·9	5 00	88 00	89·8	5 00	86 59	89·7	4 59	85 59	89·7	4 59	84 59	89·5	185 / 355
6 / 174	6 00	90 00	90·0	6 00	89 00	89·9	6 00	87 59	89·8	6 00	86 59	89·6	5 59	85 59	89·6	5 59	84 58	89·4	186 / 354
7 / 173	7 00	90 00	90·0	7 00	89 00	89·9	7 00	87 59	89·8	6 59	86 59	89·6	6 59	85 59	89·5	6 58	84 58	89·3	187 / 353
8 / 172	8 00	90 00	90·0	8 00	88 59	89·9	8 00	87 59	89·7	7 59	86 58	89·5	7 59	85 59	89·5	7 58	84 57	89·2	188 / 352
9 / 171	9 00	90 00	90·0	9 00	88 59	89·9	9 00	87 59	89·7	8 59	86 58	89·5	8 58	85 58	89·4	8 58	84 56	89·0	189 / 351
10 / 170	10 00	90 00	90·0	10 00	88 59	89·8	10 00	87 59	89·6	9 59	86 58	89·4	9 58	85 58	89·3	9 57	84 54	88·9	190 / 350
11 / 169	11 00	90 00	90·0	11 00	88 59	89·8	11 00	87 58	89·6	10 59	86 57	89·4	10 58	85 57	89·3	10 57	84 53	88·8	191 / 349
12 / 168	12 00	90 00	90·0	12 00	88 59	89·8	12 00	87 57	89·6	11 59	86 56	89·3	11 58	85 56	89·2	11 57	84 51	88·7	192 / 348
13 / 167	13 00	90 00	90·0	13 00	88 58	89·8	12 59	87 57	89·5	12 59	86 55	89·3	12 58	85 55	89·1	12 56	84 49	88·6	193 / 347
14 / 166	14 00	90 00	90·0	14 00	88 58	89·8	13 59	87 57	89·5	13 59	86 54	89·2	13 58	85 54	89·0	13 56	84 48	88·5	194 / 346
15 / 165	15 00	90 00	90·0	15 00	88 58	89·7	14 59	87 56	89·4	14 59	86 53	89·1	14 58	85 53	89·0	14 56	84 46	88·4	195 / 345
16 / 164	16 00	90 00	90·0	16 00	88 58	89·7	15 59	87 56	89·4	15 59	86 52	89·1	15 57	85 52	88·9	15 56	84 44	88·3	196 / 344
17 / 163	17 00	90 00	90·0	17 00	88 57	89·7	16 59	87 55	89·4	16 59	86 51	89·1	16 57	85 51	88·8	16 55	84 41	88·1	197 / 343
18 / 162	18 00	90 00	90·0	18 00	88 57	89·7	17 59	87 54	89·3	17 58	86 51	89·0	17 57	85 48	88·7	17 55	84 39	88·0	198 / 342
19 / 161	19 00	90 00	90·0	19 00	88 57	89·7	18 59	87 53	89·3	18 58	86 50	89·0	18 57	85 46	88·6	18 55	84 37	87·9	199 / 341
20 / 160	20 00	90 00	90·0	20 00	88 56	89·6	19 59	87 52	89·3	19 58	86 48	88·9	19 57	85 45	88·5	19 54	84 34	87·8	200 / 340
21 / 159	21 00	90 00	90·0	21 00	88 56	89·6	20 59	87 51	89·2	20 58	86 47	88·8	20 57	85 43	88·4	20 54	84 32	87·7	201 / 339
22 / 158	22 00	90 00	90·0	22 00	88 55	89·6	21 59	87 51	89·2	21 58	86 46	88·8	21 56	85 41	88·4	21 54	84 29	87·6	202 / 338
23 / 157	23 00	90 00	90·0	23 00	88 55	89·6	22 59	87 50	89·2	22 58	86 44	88·7	22 56	85 39	88·3	22 54	84 26	87·5	203 / 337
24 / 156	24 00	90 00	90·0	24 00	88 54	89·6	23 59	87 49	89·1	23 58	86 43	88·7	23 56	85 37	88·2	23 53	84 24	87·3	204 / 336
25 / 155	25 00	90 00	90·0	25 00	88 54	89·5	24 59	87 48	89·1	24 58	86 41	88·6	24 56	85 35	88·1	24 53	84 22	87·2	205 / 335
26 / 154	26 00	90 00	90·0	26 00	88 53	89·5	25 59	87 47	89·0	25 58	86 40	88·5	25 56	85 33	88·1	25 53	84 20	87·1	206 / 334
27 / 153	27 00	90 00	90·0	27 00	88 53	89·5	26 59	87 45	89·0	26 57	86 38	88·5	26 56	85 31	88·0	26 52	84 17	87·0	207 / 333
28 / 152	28 00	90 00	90·0	28 00	88 52	89·5	27 59	87 44	89·0	27 57	86 36	88·4	27 55	85 28	87·9	27 52	84 14	86·9	208 / 332
29 / 151	29 00	90 00	90·0	29 00	88 51	89·4	28 59	87 43	88·9	28 57	86 34	88·3	28 55	85 26	87·8	28 52	84 10	86·6	209 / 331
30 / 150	30 00	90 00	90·0	30 00	88 51	89·4	29 59	87 41	88·8	29 57	86 32	88·3	29 55	85 23	87·7	29 51	84 07	86·5	210 / 330
31 / 149	31 00	90 00	90·0	31 00	88 50	89·4	30 59	87 40	88·8	30 57	86 30	88·2	30 55	85 20	87·6	30 51	84 03	86·4	211 / 329
32 / 148	32 00	90 00	90·0	32 00	88 49	89·4	31 59	87 39	88·7	31 57	86 28	88·1	31 54	85 17	87·5	31 51	83 59	86·3	212 / 328
33 / 147	33 00	90 00	90·0	33 00	88 48	89·3	32 59	87 37	88·7	32 57	86 26	88·1	32 54	85 14	87·4	32 50	83 55	86·2	213 / 327
34 / 146	34 00	90 00	90·0	34 00	88 48	89·3	33 59	87 35	88·6	33 57	86 23	88·1	33 54	85 11	87·3	33 50	83 51	86·1	214 / 326
35 / 145	35 00	90 00	90·0	35 00	88 47	89·3	34 59	87 34	88·6	34 57	86 20	87·9	34 54	85 07	87·2	34 50	83 47	86·0	215 / 325
36 / 144	36 00	90 00	90·0	36 00	88 46	89·3	35 58	87 32	88·5	35 57	86 18	87·8	35 54	85 04	87·1	35 49	83 43	85·8	216 / 324
37 / 143	37 00	90 00	90·0	37 00	88 45	89·2	36 58	87 30	88·5	36 56	86 15	87·7	36 53	85 00	87·0	36 49	83 39	85·7	217 / 323
38 / 142	38 00	90 00	90·0	38 00	88 44	89·2	37 58	87 28	88·4	37 56	86 12	87·7	37 53	84 56	86·9	37 49	83 35	85·7	218 / 322
39 / 141	39 00	90 00	90·0	39 00	88 43	89·2	38 58	87 26	88·3	38 56	86 09	87·6	38 53	84 52	86·8	38 48	83 30	85·6	219 / 321
40 / 140	40 00	90 00	90·0	40 00	88 41	89·1	39 58	87 23	88·3	39 56	86 05	87·5	39 53	84 47	86·7	39 48	83 25	85·6	220 / 320
41 / 139	41 00	90 00	90·0	41 00	88 40	89·1	40 58	87 21	88·2	40 56	86 02	87·4	40 52	84 42	86·5	40 48	83 20	85·6	221 / 319
42 / 138	42 00	90 00	90·0	42 00	88 39	89·1	41 58	87 19	88·1	41 56	85 58	87·3	41 52	84 37	86·4	41 48	83 17	85·5	222 / 318
43 / 137	43 00	90 00	90·0	43 00	88 38	89·1	42 58	87 16	88·1	42 56	85 54	87·1	42 52	84 32	86·3	42 48	83 11	85·4	223 / 317
44 / 136	44 00	90 00	90·0	43 59	88 37	89·0	43 58	87 13	88·1	43 55	85 50	87·1	43 52	84 27	86·1	43 47	83 04	85·2	224 / 316
45 / 135	45 00	90 00	90·0	44 59	88 35	89·0	44 58	87 10	88·0	44 55	85 46	87·0	44 52	84 21	86·0	44 47	82 57	85·0	225 / 315

© British Crown Copyright 2018. All rights reserved.

Lat./A LHA/F		0° A/H	0° B/P	0° Z_1/Z_2	1° A/H	1° B/P	1° Z_1/Z_2	2° A/H	2° B/P	2° Z_1/Z_2	3° A/H	3° B/P	3° Z_1/Z_2	4° A/H	4° B/P	4° Z_1/Z_2	5° A/H	5° B/P	5° Z_1/Z_2	Lat./A LHA	
45	135	45 00	90 00	90·0	44 59	88 35	89·0	44 58	87 10	88·0	44 55	85 46	87·0	44 52	84 21	86·0	44 47	82 57	85·0	225	315
46	134	46 00	90 00	90·0	45 59	88 34	89·0	45 58	87 07	87·9	45 55	85 41	86·9	45 51	84 15	85·9	45 46	82 49	84·8	226	314
47	133	47 00	90 00	90·0	46 59	88 32	88·9	46 58	87 04	87·8	46 55	85 36	86·8	46 51	84 09	85·7	46 46	82 41	84·6	227	313
48	132	48 00	90 00	90·0	47 59	88 30	88·9	47 58	87 01	87·8	47 55	85 31	86·7	47 51	84 02	85·6	47 46	82 33	84·5	228	312
49	131	49 00	90 00	90·0	48 59	88 29	88·8	48 58	86 57	87·7	48 55	85 26	86·6	48 50	83 55	85·4	48 45	82 24	84·3	229	311
50	130	50 00	90 00	90·0	49 59	88 27	88·8	49 58	86 53	87·6	49 54	85 20	86·4	49 50	83 47	85·2	49 44	82 15	84·1	230	310
51	129	51 00	90 00	90·0	50 59	88 25	88·8	50 57	86 49	87·5	50 54	85 14	86·3	50 50	83 40	85·1	50 44	82 05	83·9	231	309
52	128	52 00	90 00	90·0	51 59	88 23	88·7	51 57	86 45	87·4	51 54	85 08	86·2	51 49	83 31	84·9	51 43	81 55	83·6	232	308
53	127	53 00	90 00	90·0	52 59	88 20	88·7	52 57	86 41	87·3	52 54	85 01	86·0	52 49	83 22	84·7	52 43	81 44	83·4	233	307
54	126	54 00	90 00	90·0	53 59	88 18	88·6	53 57	86 36	87·2	53 54	84 54	85·9	53 48	83 13	84·5	53 42	81 32	83·2	234	306
55	125	55 00	90 00	90·0	54 59	88 15	88·6	54 57	86 31	87·1	54 53	84 47	85·7	54 48	83 03	84·3	54 41	81 20	82·9	235	305
56	124	56 00	90 00	90·0	55 59	88 13	88·5	55 57	86 26	87·0	55 53	84 39	85·6	55 48	82 52	84·1	55 41	81 06	82·6	236	304
57	123	57 00	90 00	90·0	56 59	88 10	88·5	56 57	86 20	86·9	56 53	84 30	85·4	56 47	82 41	83·9	56 40	80 52	82·4	237	303
58	122	58 00	90 00	90·0	57 59	88 07	88·4	57 57	86 14	86·8	57 52	84 21	85·2	57 47	82 29	83·6	57 39	80 38	82·1	238	302
59	121	59 00	90 00	90·0	58 59	88 04	88·3	58 57	86 07	86·7	58 52	84 11	85·0	58 46	82 16	83·4	58 38	80 22	81·7	239	301
60	120	60 00	90 00	90·0	59 59	88 00	88·2	59 56	86 00	86·5	59 52	84 01	84·8	59 45	82 02	83·1	59 37	80 05	81·4	240	300
61	119	61 00	90 00	90·0	60 59	87 56	88·2	60 56	85 53	86·4	60 51	83 50	84·6	60 44	81 48	82·8	60 37	79 46	81·1	241	299
62	118	62 00	90 00	90·0	61 59	87 52	88·1	61 55	85 45	86·2	61 51	83 38	84·4	61 44	81 32	82·5	61 36	79 27	80·7	242	298
63	117	63 00	90 00	90·0	62 59	87 48	88·0	62 56	85 36	86·1	62 51	83 25	84·1	62 44	81 15	82·2	62 35	79 06	80·3	243	297
64	116	64 00	90 00	90·0	63 59	87 43	88·0	63 56	85 27	85·9	63 50	83 11	83·9	63 43	80 56	81·9	63 33	78 43	79·9	244	296
65	115	65 00	90 00	90·0	64 59	87 38	87·9	64 56	85 17	85·7	64 50	82 56	83·6	64 42	80 36	81·5	64 32	78 18	79·4	245	295
66	114	66 00	90 00	90·0	65 59	87 33	87·8	65 55	85 06	85·5	65 49	82 39	83·3	65 41	80 15	81·1	65 31	77 52	78·9	246	294
67	113	67 00	90 00	90·0	66 59	87 27	87·8	66 55	84 54	85·3	66 49	82 22	83·0	66 40	79 51	80·7	66 29	77 23	78·4	247	293
68	112	68 00	90 00	90·0	67 59	87 20	87·5	67 55	84 40	85·1	67 48	82 02	82·6	67 39	79 26	80·2	67 28	76 51	77·8	248	292
69	111	69 00	90 00	90·0	68 59	87 13	87·4	68 55	84 26	84·8	68 48	81 41	82·2	68 38	78 58	79·7	68 26	76 17	77·2	249	291
70	110	70 00	90 00	90·0	69 59	87 05	87·3	69 54	84 10	84·5	69 47	81 17	81·8	69 37	78 37	79·2	69 25	75 39	76·5	250	290
71	109	71 00	90 00	90·0	70 58	86 56	87·1	70 54	83 53	84·2	70 46	80 51	81·4	70 36	77 53	78·5	70 23	74 58	75·8	251	289
72	108	72 00	90 00	90·0	71 58	86 46	86·9	71 53	83 33	83·9	71 46	80 22	80·8	71 35	77 15	77·9	71 20	74 12	75·0	252	288
73	107	73 00	90 00	90·0	72 58	86 35	86·7	72 53	83 11	83·5	72 45	79 50	80·3	72 33	76 33	77·1	72 18	73 23	74·1	253	287
74	106	74 00	90 00	90·0	73 58	86 23	86·5	73 53	82 47	83·1	73 44	79 14	79·7	73 31	75 46	76·3	73 15	72 23	73·1	254	286
75	105	75 00	90 00	90·0	74 58	86 09	86·3	74 52	82 19	82·6	74 43	78 33	78·9	74 29	74 53	75·4	74 12	71 19	72·0	255	285
76	104	76 00	90 00	90·0	75 58	85 54	86·0	75 51	81 47	82·0	75 41	77 47	78·1	75 25	73 53	74·4	75 09	70 07	70·7	256	284
77	103	77 00	90 00	90·0	76 57	85 34	85·7	76 51	81 11	81·4	76 38	76 51	77·2	76 22	72 44	73·2	76 05	68 45	69·3	257	283
78	102	78 00	90 00	90·0	77 57	85 12	85·3	77 50	80 28	80·7	77 36	75 51	76·2	77 18	71 25	71·8	77 01	67 11	67·7	258	282
79	101	79 00	90 00	90·0	78 57	84 46	84·9	78 49	79 38	79·8	78 34	74 34	74·9	78 14	69 53	70·3	77 56	65 22	65·8	259	281
80	100	80 00	90 00	90·0	79 57	84 16	84·3	79 48	78 38	78·8	79 31	73 12	73·5	79 14	68 04	68·4	78 50	63 16	63·7	260	280
81	99	81 00	90 00	90·0	80 57	83 38	83·7	80 47	77 25	77·6	80 31	71 29	71·7	80 09	65 55	66·2	79 43	60 47	61·2	261	279
82	98	82 00	90 00	90·0	81 56	82 51	82·9	81 45	75 55	76·1	81 28	69 22	69·6	81 04	63 19	63·6	80 34	57 51	58·2	262	278
83	97	83 00	90 00	90·0	82 56	81 51	81·9	82 43	74 00	74·1	82 23	66 44	66·9	81 54	60 09	60·4	81 24	54 04	54·6	263	277
84	96	84 00	90 00	90·0	83 55	80 31	80·6	83 41	71 32	71·6	83 18	63 22	63·5	82 48	56 13	56·4	82 12	50 04	50·3	264	276
85	95	85 00	90 00	90·0	84 54	78 40	78·7	84 37	68 13	68·3	84 10	58 59	59·1	83 36	51 16	51·4	82 56	44 53	45·1	265	275
86	94	86 00	90 00	90·0	85 53	75 57	76·0	85 32	63 24	63·5	85 00	53 05	53·2	84 21	44 56	45·1	83 36	38 34	38·7	266	274
87	93	87 00	90 00	90·0	86 50	71 33	71·6	86 24	56 17	56·3	85 45	44 58	45·0	85 00	36 49	36·9	84 10	30 53	31·0	267	273
88	92	88 00	90 00	90·0	87 46	63 26	63·4	87 10	44 59	45·0	86 24	33 40	33·7	85 32	26 31	26·6	84 37	21 45	21·8	268	272
89	91	89 00	90 00	90·0	88 35	45 00	45·0	87 46	26 33	26·6	86 50	18 25	18·4	85 53	14 01	14·0	84 54	11 17	11·3	269	271
90	90	90 00	90 00	0·0	89 00	0 00	0·0	88 00	0 00	0·0	87 00	0 00	0·0	86 00	0 00	0·0	85 00	0 00	0·0	270	270

N. Lat.: for LHA > 180° ... $Z_n = Z$
for LHA < 180° ... $Z_n = 360° − Z$

S. Lat.: for LHA > 180° ... $Z_n = 180° − Z$
for LHA < 180° ... $Z_n = 180° + Z$

© British Crown Copyright 2018. All rights reserved.

SIGHT REDUCTION TABLE

B: (−) for 90° < LHA < 270°
Dec:(−) for Lat. contrary name

Z1: same sign as B
Z2: (−) for F > 90°

LHA/F	Lat./A	6° A/H	6° B/P	6° Z1/Z2	7° A/H	7° B/P	7° Z1/Z2	8° A/H	8° B/P	8° Z1/Z2	9° A/H	9° B/P	9° Z1/Z2	10° A/H	10° B/P	10° Z1/Z2	11° A/H	11° B/P	11° Z1/Z2	LHA	A
0	180	0 00	84 00	90·0	0 00	83 00	90·0	0 00	82 00	90·0	0 00	81 00	90·0	0 00	80 00	90·0	0 00	79 00	90·0	180	360
1	179	1 00	84 00	89·9	1 00	83 00	89·9	0 59	82 00	89·9	0 59	81 00	89·8	0 59	80 00	89·8	0 59	79 00	89·8	181	359
2	178	1 59	84 00	89·8	1 59	83 00	89·8	1 59	82 00	89·7	1 59	81 00	89·7	1 58	80 00	89·7	1 58	79 00	89·6	182	358
3	177	2 59	84 00	89·7	2 59	83 00	89·7	2 59	81 59	89·6	2 58	80 59	89·5	2 57	79 59	89·5	2 57	78 59	89·4	183	357
4	176	3 59	83 59	89·6	3 58	82 59	89·6	3 58	81 59	89·4	3 57	80 59	89·4	3 56	79 59	89·3	3 56	78 58	89·2	184	356
5	175	4 58	83 59	89·5	4 58	82 58	89·4	4 57	81 58	89·3	4 56	80 58	89·2	4 55	79 58	89·1	4 54	78 58	89·0	185	355
6	174	5 58	83 58	89·4	5 57	82 58	89·3	5 56	81 57	89·2	5 56	80 57	89·1	5 55	79 57	89·0	5 53	78 55	88·9	186	354
7	173	6 58	83 57	89·3	6 57	82 57	89·2	6 56	81 56	89·1	6 55	80 56	89·0	6 54	79 56	88·8	6 52	78 54	88·7	187	353
8	172	7 57	83 56	89·2	7 56	82 56	89·1	7 55	81 55	89·0	7 54	80 55	88·9	7 53	79 54	88·6	7 51	78 53	88·5	188	352
9	171	8 57	83 56	89·1	8 56	82 55	89·0	8 55	81 54	88·9	8 53	80 53	88·7	8 52	79 53	88·4	8 50	78 51	88·3	189	351
10	170	9 57	83 54	89·0	9 55	82 54	88·8	9 54	81 53	88·7	9 53	80 52	88·4	9 51	79 51	88·2	9 49	78 50	88·1	190	350
11	169	10 56	83 53	88·8	10 55	82 52	88·7	10 53	81 51	88·5	10 52	80 50	88·3	10 50	79 49	88·1	10 48	78 48	87·9	191	349
12	168	11 56	83 52	88·7	11 55	82 51	88·5	11 53	81 49	88·3	11 51	80 48	88·1	11 49	79 47	87·9	11 47	78 46	87·7	192	348
13	167	12 56	83 51	88·6	12 54	82 49	88·4	12 52	81 48	88·2	12 50	80 46	88·0	12 48	79 45	87·7	12 45	78 43	87·5	193	347
14	166	13 55	83 49	88·5	13 54	82 47	88·2	13 52	81 46	88·0	13 49	80 44	87·8	13 47	79 42	87·5	13 44	78 40	87·3	194	346
15	165	14 55	83 47	88·4	14 53	82 45	88·1	14 51	81 43	87·9	14 49	80 41	87·7	14 46	79 39	87·3	14 43	78 37	87·1	195	345
16	164	15 55	83 46	88·3	15 53	82 43	88·0	15 50	81 41	87·7	15 48	80 39	87·4	15 45	79 36	87·1	15 42	78 34	86·9	196	344
17	163	16 54	83 44	88·2	16 52	82 41	87·8	16 50	81 38	87·6	16 47	80 36	87·3	16 44	79 33	87·0	16 41	78 31	86·7	197	343
18	162	17 54	83 42	88·1	17 52	82 39	87·7	17 49	81 36	87·4	17 46	80 33	87·1	17 43	79 30	86·8	17 39	78 27	86·5	198	342
19	161	18 54	83 39	87·9	18 51	82 36	87·6	18 48	81 33	87·3	18 45	80 29	86·9	18 42	79 26	86·6	18 38	78 23	86·2	199	341
20	160	19 53	83 37	87·8	19 51	82 33	87·5	19 48	81 30	87·1	19 44	80 26	86·7	19 41	79 22	86·4	19 37	78 19	86·0	200	340
21	159	20 53	83 35	87·7	20 50	82 30	87·3	20 47	81 26	86·9	20 44	80 22	86·6	20 40	79 18	86·2	20 36	78 14	85·8	201	339
22	158	21 52	83 32	87·6	21 50	82 27	87·2	21 46	81 23	86·8	21 43	80 18	86·4	21 39	79 14	86·0	21 35	78 10	85·6	202	338
23	157	22 52	83 29	87·5	22 49	82 24	87·0	22 46	81 19	86·6	22 42	80 14	86·2	22 38	79 09	85·8	22 33	78 05	85·4	203	337
24	156	23 52	83 26	87·3	23 49	82 21	86·9	23 45	81 15	86·5	23 41	80 10	86·0	23 37	79 05	85·6	23 32	77 59	85·1	204	336
25	155	24 51	83 23	87·2	24 48	82 17	86·7	24 44	81 11	86·3	24 40	80 05	85·8	24 36	78 59	85·4	24 31	77 54	84·9	205	335
26	154	25 51	83 20	87·1	25 48	82 13	86·5	25 44	81 07	86·1	25 39	80 00	85·6	25 35	78 54	85·2	25 29	77 48	84·7	206	334
27	153	26 50	83 16	87·0	26 47	82 09	86·4	26 43	81 02	85·9	26 38	79 55	85·4	26 33	78 48	84·9	26 28	77 42	84·4	207	333
28	152	27 50	83 13	86·8	27 46	82 05	86·3	27 42	80 57	85·8	27 38	79 50	85·2	27 32	78 42	84·7	27 27	77 36	84·2	208	332
29	151	28 50	83 09	86·7	28 46	82 01	86·1	28 41	80 52	85·6	28 37	79 44	85·0	28 31	78 36	84·5	28 25	77 28	84·0	209	331
30	150	29 49	83 05	86·5	29 45	81 56	86·0	29 41	80 47	85·4	29 36	79 38	84·8	29 30	78 29	84·3	29 24	77 21	83·7	210	330
31	149	30 49	83 01	86·4	30 45	81 51	85·8	30 40	80 41	85·2	30 35	79 32	84·6	30 29	78 23	84·0	30 22	77 13	83·5	211	329
32	148	31 48	82 56	86·3	31 44	81 46	85·6	31 39	80 35	85·0	31 34	79 25	84·4	31 27	78 15	83·8	31 21	77 05	83·2	212	328
33	147	32 48	82 51	86·1	32 43	81 40	85·5	32 38	80 29	84·8	32 33	79 18	84·2	32 26	78 08	83·6	32 19	76 57	82·9	213	327
34	146	33 47	82 46	86·0	33 43	81 35	85·3	33 37	80 23	84·6	33 32	79 11	84·0	33 25	78 00	83·3	33 18	76 48	82·7	214	326
35	145	34 47	82 41	85·8	34 42	81 29	85·1	34 37	80 16	84·4	34 30	79 03	83·7	34 24	77 51	83·1	34 16	76 39	82·4	215	325
36	144	35 46	82 36	85·7	35 41	81 22	84·9	35 36	80 09	84·2	35 29	78 55	83·5	35 22	77 42	82·8	35 14	76 29	82·1	216	324
37	143	36 46	82 30	85·5	36 41	81 16	84·8	36 35	80 01	84·0	36 28	78 47	83·3	36 21	77 33	82·5	36 13	76 19	81·8	217	323
38	142	37 45	82 24	85·3	37 40	81 09	84·6	37 34	79 53	83·8	37 27	78 38	83·0	37 19	77 23	82·3	37 11	76 09	81·5	218	322
39	141	38 45	82 18	85·2	38 39	81 01	84·4	38 33	79 45	83·6	38 25	78 29	82·8	38 18	77 13	82·0	38 09	75 57	81·2	219	321
40	140	39 44	82 11	85·0	39 39	80 54	84·2	39 32	79 36	83·3	39 25	78 19	82·5	39 16	77 02	81·7	39 07	75 46	80·9	220	320
41	139	40 44	82 04	84·8	40 38	80 46	84·0	40 31	79 27	83·1	40 23	78 09	82·3	40 15	76 51	81·4	40 05	75 33	80·6	221	319
42	138	41 43	81 57	84·6	41 37	80 37	83·7	41 30	79 17	82·9	41 22	77 58	82·0	41 13	76 39	81·1	41 04	75 21	80·3	222	318
43	137	42 42	81 49	84·4	42 36	80 28	83·5	42 29	79 07	82·6	42 21	77 47	81·7	42 12	76 27	80·8	42 02	75 07	79·9	223	317
44	136	43 42	81 41	84·2	43 35	80 19	83·3	43 28	78 57	82·3	43 19	77 35	81·4	43 10	76 14	80·5	43 00	74 53	79·6	224	316
45	135	44 41	81 33	84·0	44 34	80 09	83·1	44 27	78 46	82·1	44 18	77 22	81·1	44 08	76 00	80·1	43 57	74 38	79·2	225	315

© British Crown Copyright 2018. All rights reserved.

Lat./A	LHA/F	6° A/H	6° B/P	6° Z₁/Z₂	7° A/H	7° B/P	7° Z₁/Z₂	8° A/H	8° B/P	8° Z₁/Z₂	9° A/H	9° B/P	9° Z₁/Z₂	10° A/H	10° B/P	10° Z₁/Z₂	11° A/H	11° B/P	11° Z₁/Z₂	Lat./A	LHA
45	135	44 41	81 33	84·0	44 34	80 09	83·1	44 27	78 46	82·1	44 18	77 22	81·1	44 08	76 00	80·1	43 57	74 38	79·2	225	315
46	134	45 41	81 24	83·8	45 34	80 01	82·8	45 26	78 34	81·8	45 16	77 09	80·8	45 06	75 45	79·8	44 55	74 22	78·8	226	314
47	133	46 40	81 14	83·6	46 33	79 48	82·6	46 24	78 21	81·5	46 15	76 56	80·5	46 04	75 30	79·5	45 53	74 05	78·4	227	313
48	132	47 39	81 04	83·4	47 32	79 36	82·3	47 23	78 08	81·2	47 13	76 41	80·1	47 03	75 14	79·1	46 51	73 48	78·0	228	312
49	131	48 38	80 54	83·1	48 31	79 24	82·0	48 22	77 55	80·9	48 12	76 26	79·8	48 01	74 57	78·7	47 48	73 30	77·6	229	311
50	130	49 38	80 43	82·9	49 30	79 11	81·7	49 20	77 40	80·6	49 10	76 09	79·4	48 58	74 40	78·3	48 46	73 10	77·2	230	310
51	129	50 37	80 31	82·6	50 29	78 58	81·4	50 19	77 25	80·2	50 08	75 52	79·1	49 56	74 21	77·9	49 43	72 50	76·7	231	309
52	128	51 36	80 19	82·4	51 27	78 43	81·1	51 18	77 08	79·9	51 06	75 34	78·7	50 54	74 01	77·5	50 40	72 29	76·3	232	308
53	127	52 35	80 06	82·1	52 26	78 28	80·8	52 16	76 51	79·5	52 05	75 15	78·3	51 52	73 40	77·0	51 37	72 06	75·8	233	307
54	126	53 34	79 52	81·8	53 25	78 12	80·5	53 14	76 33	79·2	53 02	74 55	77·8	52 49	73 18	76·6	52 35	71 42	75·3	234	306
55	125	54 33	79 37	81·5	54 24	77 55	80·1	54 12	76 14	78·8	54 00	74 34	77·4	53 47	72 55	76·1	53 31	71 17	74·8	235	305
56	124	55 32	79 21	81·2	55 22	77 37	79·8	55 11	75 54	78·3	54 58	74 11	76·9	54 44	72 30	75·6	54 28	70 50	74·2	236	304
57	123	56 31	79 05	80·9	56 21	77 18	79·4	56 09	75 32	77·9	55 56	73 47	76·5	55 41	72 04	75·0	55 25	70 22	73·6	237	303
58	122	57 30	78 47	80·5	57 19	76 57	79·0	57 07	75 09	77·4	56 53	73 22	75·9	56 38	71 36	74·5	56 21	69 51	73·0	238	302
59	121	58 29	78 28	80·1	58 18	76 35	78·5	58 05	74 44	77·0	57 51	72 56	75·4	57 35	71 06	73·9	57 17	69 19	72·4	239	301
60	120	59 28	78 08	79·7	59 16	76 12	78·1	59 03	74 18	76·4	58 48	72 25	74·8	58 32	70 34	73·3	58 13	68 45	71·7	240	300
61	119	60 26	77 46	79·3	60 14	75 47	77·6	60 01	73 50	75·9	59 45	71 54	74·2	59 28	70 01	72·6	59 09	68 09	71·0	241	299
62	118	61 25	77 23	78·9	61 12	75 21	77·1	60 58	73 20	75·3	60 42	71 21	73·6	60 24	69 25	71·9	60 05	67 31	70·3	242	298
63	117	62 23	76 58	78·4	62 10	74 52	76·5	61 56	72 48	74·7	61 39	70 46	72·9	61 20	68 46	71·2	61 00	66 49	69·5	243	297
64	116	63 22	76 31	77·9	63 08	74 21	76·0	62 53	72 13	74·1	62 35	70 08	72·2	62 16	68 05	70·4	61 55	66 05	68·6	244	296
65	115	64 20	76 02	77·4	64 06	73 48	75·4	63 50	71 36	73·4	63 32	69 27	71·5	63 12	67 21	69·6	62 50	65 18	67·7	245	295
66	114	65 18	75 31	76·8	65 01	73 12	74·7	64 48	70 56	72·6	64 28	68 56	70·6	64 07	66 34	68·7	63 44	64 27	66·8	246	294
67	113	66 16	74 57	76·2	66 01	72 33	74·0	65 43	70 13	71·8	65 23	67 56	69·8	65 02	65 43	67·8	64 38	63 33	65·8	247	293
68	112	67 14	74 20	75·5	66 58	71 51	73·2	66 40	69 26	71·0	66 19	67 05	68·8	65 56	64 48	66·7	65 32	62 35	64·7	248	292
69	111	68 12	73 39	74·8	67 55	71 05	72·4	67 36	68 35	70·1	67 14	66 09	67·8	66 50	63 48	65·7	66 25	61 31	63·6	249	291
70	110	69 09	72 55	74·0	68 51	70 15	71·5	68 31	67 40	69·1	68 09	65 09	66·7	67 44	62 44	64·5	67 17	60 23	62·3	250	290
71	109	70 07	72 06	73·1	69 48	69 20	70·5	69 27	66 39	68·0	69 03	64 03	65·6	68 37	61 34	63·2	68 09	59 10	61·0	251	289
72	108	71 03	71 13	72·2	70 44	68 20	69·4	70 21	65 33	66·8	69 57	62 53	64·3	69 29	60 17	61·9	69 00	57 50	59·6	252	288
73	107	72 00	70 14	71·1	71 39	67 13	68·3	71 16	64 20	65·5	70 50	61 33	62·9	70 21	58 54	60·4	69 50	56 23	58·0	253	287
74	106	72 56	69 08	70·0	72 34	65 59	67·0	72 09	62 59	64·1	71 42	60 07	61·4	71 12	57 24	58·8	70 40	54 49	56·4	254	286
75	105	73 52	67 54	68·7	73 29	64 37	65·5	73 03	61 30	62·6	72 34	58 32	59·7	72 02	55 44	57·1	71 28	53 06	54·5	255	285
76	104	74 48	66 31	67·3	74 23	63 05	64·0	73 55	59 51	60·8	73 24	56 47	57·9	72 52	53 55	55·1	72 16	51 13	52·6	256	284
77	103	75 42	64 57	65·6	75 16	61 22	62·2	74 46	58 00	58·9	74 14	54 51	55·9	73 39	51 55	53·1	73 02	49 10	50·4	257	283
78	102	76 36	63 11	63·8	76 08	59 26	60·2	75 37	55 57	56·8	75 02	52 42	53·6	74 26	49 42	50·8	73 47	46 56	48·1	258	282
79	101	77 29	61 09	61·7	76 59	57 14	57·9	76 26	53 38	54·4	75 49	50 18	51·2	75 11	47 16	48·2	74 30	44 28	45·5	259	281
80	100	78 21	58 49	59·3	77 49	54 44	55·3	77 13	51 01	51·7	76 35	47 38	48·4	75 54	44 34	45·4	75 11	41 47	42·7	260	280
81	99	79 12	56 06	56·6	78 37	51 52	52·4	77 59	48 04	48·7	77 18	44 39	45·4	76 35	41 35	42·4	75 49	38 50	39·7	261	279
82	98	80 01	52 56	53·4	79 23	48 35	49·1	78 42	44 43	45·3	77 59	41 18	41·9	77 13	38 17	39·0	76 26	35 36	36·4	262	278
83	97	80 47	49 13	49·6	80 07	44 51	45·2	79 21	40 56	41·4	78 37	37 35	38·1	77 50	34 39	35·3	77 00	32 18	32·8	263	277
84	96	81 31	44 51	45·2	80 47	40 24	40·8	80 01	36 38	37·1	79 12	33 25	33·9	78 21	30 40	31·2	77 29	28 16	28·8	264	276
85	95	82 12	39 40	39·9	81 24	35 38	35·7	80 34	31 48	32·2	79 43	28 39	29·2	78 50	26 18	26·7	77 56	24 09	24·6	265	275
86	94	82 48	33 34	33·8	81 57	29 36	29·8	81 04	26 24	26·7	80 09	23 46	24·1	79 14	21 35	21·9	78 18	19 44	20·1	266	274
87	93	83 18	26 28	26·6	82 23	23 05	23·3	81 28	20 25	20·6	80 31	18 17	18·5	79 34	16 32	16·8	78 36	15 04	15·4	267	273
88	92	83 41	18 22	18·5	82 43	15 52	16·0	81 45	13 57	14·1	80 47	12 26	12·6	79 48	11 12	11·4	78 49	10 11	10·4	268	272
89	91	83 55	9 26	9·5	82 56	8 08	8·2	81 56	7 05	7·1	80 57	6 17	6·4	79 57	5 39	5·7	78 57	5 08	5·2	269	271
90	90	84 00	0 00	0·0	83 00	0 00	0·0	82 00	0 00	0·0	81 00	0 00	0·0	80 00	0 00	0·0	79 00	0 00	0·0	270	270

N. Lat.: for LHA > 180° ... Zₙ = Z
for LHA < 180° ... Zₙ = 360° − Z

S. Lat.: for LHA > 180° ... Zₙ = 180° − Z
for LHA < 180° ... Zₙ = 180° + Z

© British Crown Copyright 2018. All rights reserved.

SIGHT REDUCTION TABLE

B: (−) for 90° < LHA < 270°
Dec:(−) for Lat. contrary name

Z_1: same sign as B
Z_2 : (−) for F > 90°

LHA/F	A	12° A/H	12° B/P	12° Z_1/Z_2	13° A/H	13° B/P	13° Z_1/Z_2	14° A/H	14° B/P	14° Z_1/Z_2	15° A/H	15° B/P	15° Z_1/Z_2	16° A/H	16° B/P	16° Z_1/Z_2	17° A/H	17° B/P	17° Z_1/Z_2	A	LHA
0	180	0 00	78 00	90·0	0 00	77 00	90·0	0 00	76 00	90·0	0 00	75 00	90·0	0 00	74 00	90·0	0 00	73 00	90·0	180	360
1	179	0 59	78 00	89·8	0 58	77 00	89·8	0 58	76 00	89·8	0 58	75 00	89·7	0 58	74 00	89·7	0 57	73 00	89·7	181	359
2	178	1 57	78 00	89·6	1 57	77 00	89·5	1 56	76 00	89·5	1 56	74 59	89·5	1 55	73 59	89·4	1 55	72 59	89·4	182	358
3	177	2 56	77 59	89·4	2 55	76 59	89·3	2 54	75 59	89·3	2 54	74 59	89·2	2 53	73 59	89·2	2 52	72 59	89·1	183	357
4	176	3 55	77 58	89·2	3 54	76 58	89·1	3 52	75 58	89·1	3 52	74 58	89·0	3 51	73 58	88·9	3 49	72 58	88·8	184	356
5	175	4 53	77 57	89·0	4 52	76 57	88·9	4 50	75 57	88·8	4 50	74 57	88·7	4 48	73 57	88·6	4 47	72 56	88·5	185	355
6	174	5 52	77 56	88·7	5 51	76 56	88·6	5 49	75 56	88·5	5 48	74 55	88·4	5 46	73 55	88·3	5 44	72 55	88·2	186	354
7	173	6 51	77 55	88·5	6 49	76 54	88·4	6 47	75 54	88·4	6 46	74 54	88·2	6 44	73 54	88·1	6 42	72 54	87·9	187	353
8	172	7 49	77 53	88·3	7 48	76 53	88·2	7 45	75 52	88·2	7 44	74 52	88·0	7 41	73 51	87·8	7 39	72 51	87·6	188	352
9	171	8 48	77 51	88·1	8 46	76 51	88·0	8 43	75 50	88·0	8 41	74 49	87·7	8 39	73 49	87·5	8 36	72 48	87·3	189	351
10	170	9 47	77 49	87·9	9 44	76 48	87·7	9 41	75 48	87·7	9 39	74 47	87·4	9 37	73 46	87·2	9 34	72 45	87·0	190	350
11	169	10 45	77 47	87·7	10 43	76 46	87·5	10 39	75 45	87·5	10 37	74 44	87·1	10 34	73 43	86·9	10 31	72 42	86·7	191	349
12	168	11 44	77 44	87·5	11 41	76 43	87·3	11 38	75 42	87·3	11 35	74 41	86·9	11 32	73 40	86·6	11 28	72 39	86·4	192	348
13	167	12 43	77 42	87·3	12 40	76 40	87·0	12 36	75 39	87·0	12 33	74 37	86·6	12 29	73 36	86·1	12 25	72 36	86·1	193	347
14	166	13 41	77 39	87·0	13 38	76 37	86·8	13 34	75 35	86·8	13 31	74 34	86·3	13 27	73 32	85·8	13 23	72 31	85·8	194	346
15	165	14 40	77 36	86·8	14 36	76 33	86·6	14 32	75 32	86·5	14 29	74 30	86·0	14 24	73 28	85·5	14 20	72 26	85·5	195	345
16	164	15 38	77 32	86·6	15 35	76 30	86·3	15 30	75 28	86·3	15 26	74 26	85·8	15 22	73 23	85·2	15 17	72 21	85·2	196	344
17	163	16 37	77 28	86·4	16 33	76 26	86·1	16 28	75 23	86·0	16 24	74 21	85·5	16 19	73 19	84·9	16 14	72 16	84·9	197	343
18	162	17 36	77 24	86·1	17 31	76 21	85·8	17 26	75 19	85·8	17 22	74 16	85·2	17 17	73 13	84·3	17 11	72 11	84·6	198	342
19	161	18 34	77 20	85·9	18 30	76 17	85·6	18 24	75 14	85·6	18 20	74 11	84·9	18 14	73 08	84·0	18 08	72 05	84·3	199	341
20	160	19 33	77 15	85·7	19 28	76 12	85·3	19 22	75 08	85·3	19 17	74 05	84·6	19 12	73 02	83·7	19 05	71 59	83·9	200	340
21	159	20 31	77 10	85·4	20 26	76 07	85·1	20 20	75 03	85·1	20 15	73 59	84·3	20 09	72 56	83·0	20 03	71 52	83·6	201	339
22	158	21 30	77 05	85·2	21 24	76 01	84·8	21 18	74 57	84·8	21 13	73 53	84·0	21 06	72 49	82·7	21 00	71 45	83·3	202	338
23	157	22 28	77 00	85·0	22 23	75 55	84·5	22 16	74 51	84·5	22 10	73 46	83·7	22 04	72 42	82·3	21 56	71 38	82·9	203	337
24	156	23 27	76 54	84·7	23 21	75 49	84·3	23 14	74 44	84·3	23 08	73 39	83·4	23 01	72 34	82·0	22 53	71 30	82·6	204	336
25	155	24 25	76 48	84·5	24 19	75 43	84·0	24 12	74 37	84·0	24 06	73 32	83·1	23 58	72 27	81·7	23 50	71 22	82·2	205	335
26	154	25 23	76 42	84·2	25 17	75 36	83·7	25 10	74 30	83·9	25 03	73 24	82·8	24 55	72 18	81·3	24 47	71 13	81·9	206	334
27	153	26 22	76 35	84·0	26 15	75 28	83·5	26 08	74 22	83·6	26 01	73 16	82·5	25 52	72 10	81·0	25 44	71 04	81·5	207	333
28	152	27 20	76 28	83·7	27 13	75 21	83·2	27 06	74 14	83·3	26 58	73 07	82·2	26 50	72 00	80·6	26 41	70 54	81·2	208	332
29	151	28 18	76 20	83·4	28 11	75 13	82·9	28 03	74 05	83·0	27 55	72 58	81·8	27 47	71 51	80·2	27 37	70 44	80·8	209	331
30	150	29 17	76 13	83·2	29 09	75 04	82·6	29 01	73 56	82·7	28 53	72 48	81·5	28 44	71 41	79·9	28 34	70 33	80·4	210	330
31	149	30 15	76 05	82·9	30 07	74 56	82·3	29 59	73 47	82·4	29 50	72 38	81·2	29 41	71 30	79·5	29 30	70 22	80·0	211	329
32	148	31 13	75 56	82·6	31 05	74 46	82·0	30 57	73 37	82·0	30 47	72 28	80·8	30 37	71 19	79·1	30 27	70 11	79·6	212	328
33	147	32 11	75 47	82·3	32 03	74 37	81·7	31 54	73 27	81·7	31 44	72 17	80·5	31 34	71 07	78·7	31 23	69 59	79·2	213	327
34	146	33 10	75 37	82·0	33 01	74 26	81·4	32 52	73 16	81·4	32 42	72 05	80·1	32 31	70 55	78·3	32 20	69 45	78·8	214	326
35	145	34 08	75 27	81·7	33 59	74 16	81·0	33 49	73 04	81·0	33 39	71 53	79·7	33 28	70 42	77·8	33 16	69 32	78·4	215	325
36	144	35 06	75 17	81·4	34 56	74 04	80·7	34 46	72 52	80·7	34 36	71 40	79·4	34 24	70 29	77·4	34 12	69 18	78·0	216	324
37	143	36 04	75 06	81·1	35 54	73 54	80·3	35 44	72 40	80·3	35 33	71 27	79·0	35 21	70 15	77·0	35 08	69 03	77·6	217	323
38	142	37 02	74 54	80·8	36 52	73 40	80·0	36 41	72 27	80·0	36 29	71 13	78·6	36 17	70 00	76·5	36 04	68 48	77·1	218	322
39	141	38 00	74 42	80·4	37 49	73 27	79·7	37 38	72 13	79·7	37 26	70 59	78·2	37 14	69 45	76·1	37 00	68 32	76·7	219	321
40	140	38 57	74 30	80·1	38 47	73 14	79·3	38 35	71 58	79·3	38 23	70 43	77·8	38 10	69 29	75·6	37 56	68 15	76·2	220	320
41	139	39 55	74 16	79·8	39 44	72 59	78·9	39 32	71 43	78·9	39 19	70 27	77·3	39 06	69 12	75·1	38 51	67 57	75·7	221	319
42	138	40 53	74 02	79·4	40 41	72 45	78·5	40 29	71 27	78·5	40 16	70 10	76·9	40 02	68 54	74·6	39 47	67 38	75·3	222	318
43	137	41 51	73 48	79·0	41 39	72 29	78·2	41 26	71 11	78·1	41 12	69 54	76·4	40 58	68 35	74·6	40 42	67 19	74·7	223	317
44	136	42 48	73 32	78·6	42 36	72 12	77·7	42 23	70 53	77·7	42 09	69 34	76·0	41 54	68 16	75·1	41 38	66 58	74·2	224	316
45	135	43 46	73 16	78·3	43 33	71 55	77·3	43 19	70 35	77·3	43 05	69 15	75·5	42 49	67 56	74·6	42 33	66 37	73·7	225	315

© British Crown Copyright 2018. All rights reserved.

Lat./A		12°			13°			14°			15°			16°			17°			Lat./A
A	LHA/F	A/H	B/P	Z_1/Z_2	A/H	B/P	Z_1/Z_2	A/H	B/P	Z_1/Z_2	A/H	B/P	Z_1/Z_2	A/H	B/P	Z_1/Z_2	A/H	B/P	Z_1/Z_2	LHA
135	45	43 46	73 16	78·3	43 33	71 55	77·3	43 19	70 35	76·4	43 05	69 15	75·5	42 49	67 56	74·6	42 33	66 37	73·7	225
134	46	44 43	72 59	77·8	44 30	71 37	76·9	44 16	70 15	75·9	44 01	68 54	75·0	43 45	67 34	74·1	43 28	66 15	73·2	226
133	47	45 40	72 41	77·4	45 27	71 18	76·4	45 12	69 55	75·5	44 57	68 33	74·5	44 40	67 12	73·5	44 23	65 51	72·6	227
132	48	46 38	72 23	77·0	46 24	70 58	76·0	46 09	69 34	75·0	45 53	68 11	74·0	45 35	66 48	73·0	45 17	65 27	72·0	228
131	49	47 35	72 03	76·5	47 20	70 37	75·5	47 05	69 11	74·4	46 48	67 47	73·4	46 30	66 23	72·4	46 12	65 01	71·4	229
130	50	48 32	71 42	76·1	48 17	70 15	75·0	48 01	68 48	73·9	47 44	67 22	72·9	47 25	65 58	71·8	47 06	64 34	70·8	230
129	51	49 29	71 20	75·6	49 13	69 51	74·5	48 57	68 23	73·4	48 39	66 56	72·3	48 20	65 30	71·2	48 00	64 05	70·1	231
128	52	50 25	70 57	75·1	50 09	69 27	73·9	49 52	67 57	72·8	49 34	66 29	71·7	49 15	65 02	70·6	48 54	63 35	69·5	232
127	53	51 22	70 33	74·6	51 06	69 01	73·4	50 48	67 30	72·2	50 29	66 01	71·0	50 09	64 31	69·9	49 48	63 04	68·8	233
126	54	52 19	70 07	74·0	52 02	68 33	72·8	51 43	67 01	71·6	51 24	65 30	70·4	51 03	64 00	69·2	50 41	62 31	68·1	234
125	55	53 15	69 40	73·5	52 57	68 04	72·2	52 38	66 30	71·0	52 18	64 58	69·7	51 57	63 26	68·5	51 34	61 56	67·3	235
124	56	54 11	69 11	72·9	53 53	67 34	71·6	53 33	65 58	70·3	53 12	64 24	69·0	52 50	62 51	67·8	52 27	61 20	66·6	236
123	57	55 07	68 41	72·2	54 48	67 02	70·9	54 28	65 24	69·6	54 06	63 48	68·3	53 43	62 14	67·0	53 19	60 42	65·8	237
122	58	56 03	68 09	71·6	55 43	66 28	70·2	55 22	64 48	68·8	55 00	63 11	67·5	54 36	61 35	66·2	54 12	60 01	64·9	238
121	59	56 59	67 34	70·9	56 38	65 51	69·5	56 16	64 10	68·1	55 53	62 31	66·7	55 29	60 53	65·4	55 03	59 18	64·1	239
120	60	57 54	66 58	70·2	57 33	65 13	68·7	57 10	63 30	67·3	56 46	61 49	65·9	56 21	60 10	64·5	55 55	58 33	63·1	240
119	61	58 49	66 20	69·4	58 27	64 32	67·9	58 04	62 47	66·4	57 39	61 04	65·0	57 13	59 24	63·6	56 46	57 46	62·2	241
118	62	59 44	65 38	68·6	59 21	63 49	67·1	58 57	62 02	65·5	58 31	60 17	64·0	58 05	58 35	62·6	57 36	56 56	61·2	242
117	63	60 38	64 55	67·8	60 15	63 03	66·2	59 50	61 13	64·6	59 23	59 27	63·1	58 55	57 43	61·6	58 26	56 03	60·2	243
116	64	61 32	64 08	66·9	61 08	62 14	65·2	60 42	60 22	63·6	60 15	58 34	62·0	59 46	56 49	60·5	59 16	55 08	59·1	244
115	65	62 26	63 18	66·0	62 01	61 21	64·2	61 34	59 28	62·6	61 06	57 37	61·0	60 36	55 51	59·4	60 05	54 07	57·9	245
114	66	63 20	62 24	65·0	62 53	60 25	63·2	62 26	58 30	61·5	61 56	56 37	59·8	61 25	54 49	58·2	60 53	53 04	56·7	246
113	67	64 13	61 27	63·9	63 45	59 25	62·1	63 16	57 27	60·3	62 46	55 34	58·6	62 14	53 44	57·0	61 41	51 57	55·4	247
112	68	65 05	60 26	62·8	64 37	58 21	60·9	64 07	56 21	59·1	63 35	54 25	57·4	63 02	52 34	55·7	62 27	50 47	54·1	248
111	69	65 57	59 20	61·6	65 27	57 13	59·6	64 56	55 10	57·8	64 23	53 13	56·0	63 49	51 20	54·3	63 14	49 32	52·7	249
110	70	66 48	58 09	60·3	66 18	55 59	58·3	65 45	53 55	56·4	65 11	51 55	54·6	64 36	50 01	52·9	63 59	48 12	51·2	250
109	71	67 39	56 52	58·9	67 07	54 40	56·8	66 33	52 33	54·9	65 58	50 33	53·1	65 21	48 38	51·3	64 43	46 48	49·7	251
108	72	68 29	55 29	57·4	67 55	53 14	55·3	67 20	51 06	53·3	66 44	49 04	51·5	66 06	47 08	49·7	65 26	45 18	48·0	252
107	73	69 18	53 59	55·8	68 43	51 42	53·7	68 07	49 33	51·6	67 29	47 30	49·8	66 49	45 33	48·0	66 08	43 43	46·3	253
106	74	70 06	52 22	54·1	69 30	50 03	51·9	68 52	47 52	49·8	68 12	45 49	47·9	67 31	43 52	46·1	66 49	42 02	44·4	254
105	75	70 53	50 36	52·2	70 15	48 16	50·0	69 36	46 04	47·9	68 55	44 00	46·0	68 12	42 04	44·2	67 29	40 15	42·5	255
104	76	71 38	48 42	50·2	70 59	46 20	48·0	70 18	44 08	45·9	69 36	42 05	43·9	68 52	40 09	42·1	68 07	38 21	40·5	256
103	77	72 23	46 37	48·0	71 42	44 15	45·7	70 59	42 03	43·7	70 15	40 01	41·7	69 30	38 07	39·9	68 43	36 13	38·3	257
102	78	73 06	44 22	45·6	72 23	42 00	43·4	71 38	39 49	41·3	70 53	37 49	39·4	70 06	35 57	37·6	69 18	34 13	36·0	258
101	79	73 47	41 55	43·1	73 02	39 34	40·8	72 16	37 26	38·8	71 28	35 27	36·9	70 40	33 38	35·2	69 50	31 58	33·6	259
100	80	74 26	39 15	40·3	73 39	36 57	38·1	72 51	34 51	36·1	72 02	32 57	34·3	71 12	31 12	32·6	70 21	29 36	31·1	260
99	81	75 02	36 21	37·3	74 14	34 07	35·1	73 24	32 06	33·2	72 34	30 17	31·5	71 42	28 37	29·9	70 50	27 06	28·4	261
98	82	75 37	33 13	34·1	74 46	31 05	32·0	73 55	29 10	30·2	73 03	27 27	28·5	72 09	25 53	27·0	71 16	24 29	25·7	262
97	83	76 08	29 50	30·6	75 16	27 50	28·6	74 23	26 03	26·9	73 29	24 27	25·4	72 34	23 02	24·0	71 39	21 44	22·8	263
96	84	76 36	26 11	26·8	75 42	24 22	25·0	74 48	22 45	23·5	73 52	21 19	22·1	72 56	20 02	20·9	72 00	18 53	19·8	264
95	85	77 01	22 18	22·8	76 05	20 41	21·3	75 09	19 16	19·9	74 12	18 01	18·7	73 15	16 54	17·8	72 18	15 55	16·7	265
94	86	77 22	18 10	18·6	76 25	16 49	17·3	75 27	15 38	16·1	74 29	14 36	15·1	73 31	13 40	14·2	72 33	12 51	13·5	266
93	87	77 38	13 50	14·1	76 40	12 46	13·1	75 41	11 51	12·2	74 43	11 03	11·4	73 44	10 21	10·8	72 45	9 43	10·2	267
92	88	77 50	9 19	9·5	76 51	8 36	8·8	75 52	7 58	8·2	74 52	7 25	7·7	73 53	6 56	7·2	72 53	6 31	6·8	268
91	89	77 58	4 42	4·8	76 58	4 19	4·4	75 58	4 00	4·1	74 58	3 44	3·9	73 58	3 29	3·6	72 58	3 16	3·4	269
90	90	78 00	0 00	0·0	77 00	0 00	0·0	76 00	0 00	0·0	75 00	0 00	0·0	74 00	0 00	0·0	73 00	0 00	0·0	270

N. Lat.: for LHA $> 180°$ .... $Z_n = Z$
for LHA $< 180°$ .... $Z_n = 360° - Z$

S. Lat.: for LHA $> 180°$ .... $Z_n = 180° - Z$
for LHA $< 180°$ .... $Z_n = 180° + Z$

© British Crown Copyright 2018. All rights reserved.

SIGHT REDUCTION TABLE

B: (−) for 90° < LHA < 270°
Dec:(−) for Lat. contrary name

Z1: same sign as B
Z2: (−) for F > 90°

Lat./A		18°			19°			20°			21°			22°			23°			Lat./A	
LHA/F	A	A/H	B/P	Z1/Z2	A/H	B/P	Z1/Z2	A/H	B/P	Z1/Z2	A/H	B/P	Z1/Z2	A/H	B/P	Z1/Z2	A/H	B/P	Z1/Z2	LHA	
0	180	0 00	72 00	90·0	0 00	71 00	90·0	0 00	70 00	90·0	0 00	69 00	90·0	0 00	68 00	90·0	0 00	67 00	90·0	180	360
1	179	0 57	72 00	89·7	0 57	71 00	89·7	0 56	70 00	89·7	0 56	69 00	89·7	0 56	68 00	89·6	0 55	67 00	89·6	181	359
2	178	1 54	71 59	89·4	1 53	70 59	89·3	1 53	69 59	89·3	1 52	68 59	89·3	1 51	67 59	89·3	1 50	66 59	89·2	182	358
3	177	2 51	71 59	89·0	2 50	70 58	89·0	2 49	69 58	89·0	2 48	68 58	88·9	2 47	67 58	88·9	2 46	66 58	88·8	183	357
4	176	3 48	71 58	88·8	3 47	70 57	88·7	3 46	69 57	88·6	3 44	68 57	88·6	3 42	67 57	88·5	3 41	66 57	88·4	184	356
5	175	4 45	71 56	88·5	4 44	70 56	88·4	4 42	69 56	88·3	4 40	68 56	88·2	4 38	67 55	88·1	4 36	66 55	88·0	185	355
6	174	5 42	71 54	88·1	5 40	70 54	88·0	5 38	69 54	87·9	5 36	68 54	87·8	5 34	67 53	87·7	5 31	66 53	87·7	186	354
7	173	6 39	71 52	87·8	6 37	70 52	87·6	6 35	69 52	87·6	6 32	68 51	87·5	6 29	67 51	87·4	6 26	66 51	87·3	187	353
8	172	7 36	71 50	87·5	7 34	70 50	87·4	7 31	69 49	87·2	7 28	68 49	87·1	7 25	67 48	87·0	7 22	66 48	86·9	188	352
9	171	8 33	71 47	87·2	8 30	70 47	87·0	8 27	69 46	86·9	8 24	68 46	86·8	8 20	67 45	86·6	8 17	66 45	86·5	189	351
10	170	9 30	71 44	86·9	9 27	70 44	86·7	9 23	69 43	86·5	9 20	68 43	86·4	9 16	67 42	86·2	9 12	66 41	86·1	190	350
11	169	10 27	71 41	86·6	10 24	70 40	86·4	10 20	69 39	86·2	10 16	68 39	86·0	10 11	67 38	85·8	10 07	66 37	85·7	191	349
12	168	11 24	71 37	86·2	11 20	70 36	86·0	11 16	69 35	85·8	11 12	68 34	85·6	11 07	67 33	85·4	11 02	66 32	85·4	192	348
13	167	12 21	71 33	85·9	12 17	70 32	85·7	12 12	69 31	85·5	12 07	68 30	85·3	12 02	67 29	85·1	11 57	66 28	84·8	193	347
14	166	13 18	71 29	85·6	13 13	70 28	85·3	13 08	69 26	85·1	13 03	68 25	84·9	12 58	67 24	84·7	12 52	66 22	84·4	194	346
15	165	14 15	71 24	85·3	14 10	70 23	85·0	14 05	69 21	84·8	13 59	68 20	84·5	13 53	67 18	84·3	13 47	66 17	84·0	195	345
16	164	15 12	71 19	84·9	15 06	70 18	84·7	15 01	69 16	84·4	14 55	68 14	84·1	14 48	67 12	83·9	14 42	66 10	83·6	196	344
17	163	16 09	71 14	84·6	16 03	70 12	84·3	15 57	69 10	84·0	15 50	68 08	83·7	15 44	67 06	83·5	15 37	66 04	83·2	197	343
18	162	17 05	71 08	84·3	16 59	70 06	84·0	16 53	69 03	83·7	16 46	68 01	83·4	16 39	66 59	83·1	16 32	65 57	82·8	198	342
19	161	18 02	71 02	83·9	17 56	69 59	83·6	17 49	68 57	83·3	17 42	67 54	83·0	17 34	66 52	82·7	17 26	65 49	82·3	199	341
20	160	18 59	70 56	83·6	18 52	69 53	83·2	18 45	68 50	82·9	18 37	67 47	82·6	18 29	66 44	82·2	18 21	65 41	81·9	200	340
21	159	19 56	70 49	83·2	19 48	69 45	82·9	19 41	68 42	82·5	19 33	67 39	82·2	19 24	66 36	81·8	19 16	65 33	81·5	201	339
22	158	20 52	70 41	82·9	20 45	69 38	82·5	20 37	68 34	82·1	20 28	67 31	81·8	20 19	66 27	81·4	20 10	65 24	81·0	202	338
23	157	21 49	70 33	82·5	21 41	69 29	82·1	21 32	68 26	81·7	21 24	67 21	81·4	21 14	66 18	81·0	21 05	65 15	80·6	203	337
24	156	22 45	70 25	82·2	22 37	69 21	81·8	22 28	68 17	81·3	22 19	67 12	80·9	22 09	66 09	80·5	21 59	65 05	80·1	204	336
25	155	23 42	70 17	81·8	23 33	69 12	81·4	23 24	68 07	80·9	23 14	67 03	80·5	23 04	65 58	80·1	22 54	64 54	79·7	205	335
26	154	24 38	70 07	81·4	24 29	69 02	81·0	24 20	67 57	80·5	24 09	66 52	80·1	23 58	65 48	79·6	23 48	64 44	79·2	206	334
27	153	25 35	69 58	81·1	25 25	68 52	80·6	25 15	67 47	80·1	25 05	66 42	79·7	24 53	65 36	79·2	24 42	64 32	78·7	207	333
28	152	26 31	69 48	80·7	26 21	68 42	80·2	26 11	67 36	79·7	26 00	66 30	79·2	25 48	65 25	78·7	25 36	64 19	78·3	208	332
29	151	27 27	69 37	80·3	27 17	68 31	79·8	27 06	67 24	79·3	26 55	66 18	78·8	26 43	65 12	78·3	26 30	64 07	77·8	209	331
30	150	28 24	69 26	79·9	28 13	68 19	79·4	28 01	67 12	78·8	27 50	66 06	78·3	27 37	64 59	77·8	27 24	63 53	77·3	210	330
31	149	29 20	69 14	79·5	29 09	68 07	78·9	28 57	67 00	78·4	28 44	65 53	77·8	28 31	64 46	77·3	28 18	63 39	76·8	211	329
32	148	30 16	69 02	79·1	30 04	67 54	78·5	29 52	66 46	77·9	29 39	65 39	77·4	29 26	64 32	76·8	29 12	63 25	76·3	212	328
33	147	31 12	68 49	78·7	31 00	67 41	78·1	30 47	66 32	77·5	30 34	65 24	76·9	30 20	64 17	76·3	30 05	63 09	75·8	213	327
34	146	32 08	68 36	78·2	31 55	67 27	77·6	31 42	66 18	77·0	31 28	65 09	76·4	31 14	64 01	75·8	30 59	62 53	75·2	214	326
35	145	33 04	68 22	77·8	32 51	67 12	77·2	32 37	66 03	76·5	32 23	64 54	75·9	32 08	63 45	75·3	31 52	62 36	74·7	215	325
36	144	33 59	68 07	77·3	33 46	66 57	76·7	33 32	65 47	76·0	33 17	64 37	75·4	33 01	63 28	74·8	32 45	62 19	74·2	216	324
37	143	34 55	67 52	76·9	34 41	66 41	76·2	34 26	65 30	75·5	34 11	64 20	74·9	33 55	63 11	74·2	33 38	62 01	73·6	217	323
38	142	35 50	67 36	76·4	35 36	66 24	75·7	35 21	65 13	75·0	35 05	64 02	74·4	34 48	62 51	73·7	34 31	61 41	73·0	218	322
39	141	36 46	67 19	76·0	36 31	66 06	75·2	36 15	64 54	74·5	35 59	63 43	73·8	35 41	62 32	73·1	35 24	61 21	72·4	219	321
40	140	37 41	67 01	75·5	37 26	65 48	74·7	37 10	64 35	74·0	36 53	63 23	73·3	36 35	62 12	72·6	36 17	61 01	71·8	220	320
41	139	38 36	66 42	75·0	38 20	65 29	74·2	38 04	64 15	73·4	37 46	63 02	72·7	37 28	61 50	72·0	37 09	60 39	71·2	221	319
42	138	39 31	66 23	74·5	39 15	65 08	73·7	38 58	63 54	72·9	38 40	62 41	72·1	38 21	61 28	71·4	38 01	60 16	70·6	222	318
43	137	40 26	66 03	74·0	40 09	64 48	73·1	39 51	63 33	72·3	39 33	62 18	71·5	39 13	61 05	70·7	38 53	59 52	70·0	223	317
44	136	41 21	65 42	73·4	41 03	64 25	72·5	40 45	63 10	71·7	40 26	61 55	70·9	40 06	60 41	70·1	39 45	59 27	69·3	224	316
45	135	42 16	65 19	72·8	41 57	64 02	72·0	41 38	62 46	71·1	41 19	61 30	70·3	40 58	60 15	69·5	40 37	59 01	68·7	225	315

© British Crown Copyright 2018. All rights reserved.

LHA/F	18° A/H	18° B/P	18° Z1/Z2	19° A/H	19° B/P	19° Z1/Z2	20° A/H	20° B/P	20° Z1/Z2	21° A/H	21° B/P	21° Z1/Z2	22° A/H	22° B/P	22° Z1/Z2	23° A/H	23° B/P	23° Z1/Z2	LHA
45	42 16	65 19	72.8	41 57	64 02	72.0	41 38	62 46	71.1	41 19	61 30	70.3	40 58	60 15	69.5	40 37	59 01	68.7	225
46	43 10	64 56	72.3	42 51	63 38	71.4	42 32	62 21	70.5	42 11	61 05	69.6	41 50	59 49	68.8	41 28	58 34	68.0	226
47	44 04	64 32	71.7	43 45	63 13	70.8	43 25	61 55	69.9	43 04	60 38	69.0	42 42	59 21	68.1	42 19	58 06	67.3	227
48	44 58	64 06	71.1	44 38	62 46	70.1	44 18	61 27	69.2	43 56	60 09	68.3	43 33	58 53	67.4	43 10	57 37	66.5	228
49	45 52	63 39	70.4	45 32	62 18	69.5	45 10	60 59	68.5	44 48	59 40	67.6	44 24	58 22	66.7	44 00	57 06	65.8	229
50	46 46	63 11	69.8	46 25	61 49	68.8	46 03	60 29	67.8	45 39	59 09	66.9	45 15	57 51	65.9	44 50	56 34	65.0	230
51	47 39	62 42	69.1	47 17	61 19	68.1	46 55	59 57	67.1	46 31	58 37	66.1	46 06	57 18	65.2	45 40	56 00	64.2	231
52	48 33	62 11	68.4	48 10	60 47	67.4	47 46	59 25	66.4	47 22	58 03	65.4	46 56	56 44	64.4	46 30	55 25	63.4	232
53	49 25	61 38	67.7	49 02	60 13	66.6	48 38	58 50	65.6	48 13	57 28	64.6	47 46	56 07	63.6	47 19	54 48	62.6	233
54	50 18	61 04	67.0	49 54	59 38	65.9	49 29	58 14	64.8	49 03	56 51	63.7	48 36	55 30	62.7	48 08	54 10	61.7	234
55	51 10	60 28	66.2	50 46	59 01	65.1	50 20	57 36	64.0	49 53	56 13	62.9	49 25	54 50	61.9	48 56	53 30	60.8	235
56	52 03	59 50	65.4	51 37	58 23	64.2	51 10	56 56	63.1	50 43	55 32	62.0	50 14	54 09	61.0	49 44	52 48	59.9	236
57	52 54	59 11	64.6	52 28	57 42	63.4	52 00	56 15	62.2	51 32	54 49	61.1	51 02	53 26	60.0	50 32	52 04	59.0	237
58	53 46	58 29	63.7	53 18	56 59	62.5	52 50	55 31	61.3	52 21	54 05	60.2	51 50	52 41	59.1	51 19	51 18	58.0	238
59	54 37	57 45	62.8	54 08	56 14	61.5	53 39	54 45	60.4	53 09	53 18	59.2	52 38	51 53	58.1	52 06	50 30	57.0	239
60	55 27	56 59	61.8	54 58	55 27	60.6	54 28	53 57	59.4	53 57	52 29	58.2	53 25	51 04	57.0	52 52	49 40	55.9	240
61	56 17	56 10	60.9	55 47	54 37	59.6	55 16	53 06	58.3	54 44	51 38	57.1	54 11	50 12	55.9	53 37	48 48	54.8	241
62	57 07	55 19	59.8	56 36	53 45	58.5	56 04	52 12	57.2	55 31	50 44	56.0	54 57	49 17	54.8	54 22	47 53	53.7	242
63	57 56	54 25	58.8	57 24	52 49	57.4	56 51	51 17	56.1	56 17	49 47	54.9	55 42	48 20	53.7	55 06	46 55	52.5	243
64	58 44	53 27	57.6	58 12	51 51	56.3	57 38	50 18	55.0	57 03	48 48	53.7	56 27	47 20	52.5	55 50	45 55	51.3	244
65	59 32	52 27	56.5	58 58	50 50	55.1	58 24	49 16	53.7	57 47	47 45	52.5	57 10	46 17	51.2	56 32	44 52	50.0	245
66	60 19	51 23	55.3	59 45	49 45	53.8	59 09	48 11	52.5	58 32	46 39	51.2	57 54	45 11	49.9	57 14	43 46	48.7	246
67	61 06	50 15	53.9	60 30	48 37	52.5	59 53	47 02	51.1	59 15	45 30	49.8	58 36	44 02	48.6	57 55	42 38	47.4	247
68	61 52	49 04	52.6	61 15	47 25	51.1	60 36	45 50	49.8	59 57	44 18	48.4	59 17	42 50	47.2	58 36	41 26	46.0	248
69	62 37	47 48	51.2	61 58	46 09	49.7	61 19	44 33	48.3	60 39	43 02	47.0	59 57	41 34	45.7	59 15	40 10	44.5	249
70	63 21	46 28	49.7	62 41	44 48	48.2	62 01	43 13	46.8	61 19	41 42	45.4	60 36	40 15	44.2	59 53	38 52	43.0	250
71	64 04	45 03	48.1	63 23	43 24	46.6	62 41	41 49	45.2	61 58	40 18	43.9	61 15	38 52	42.6	60 30	37 29	41.4	251
72	64 45	43 34	46.4	64 04	41 54	44.9	63 21	40 20	43.5	62 37	38 50	42.2	61 52	37 25	40.9	61 06	36 03	39.7	252
73	65 26	41 59	44.7	64 43	40 20	43.2	63 59	38 46	41.8	63 14	37 18	40.5	62 27	35 53	39.2	61 41	34 34	38.0	253
74	66 06	40 19	42.9	65 21	38 41	41.4	64 36	37 08	40.0	63 49	35 41	38.7	63 02	34 18	37.4	62 14	33 00	36.3	254
75	66 44	38 32	40.9	65 58	36 56	39.5	65 11	35 25	38.1	64 23	33 59	36.8	63 35	32 39	35.6	62 46	31 22	34.4	255
76	67 20	36 40	38.9	66 33	35 05	37.4	65 45	33 37	36.1	64 56	32 12	34.8	64 07	30 55	33.6	63 16	29 41	32.5	256
77	67 55	34 42	36.8	67 07	33 09	35.3	66 18	31 43	34.0	65 27	30 22	32.8	64 37	29 06	31.6	63 45	27 55	30.6	257
78	68 29	32 37	34.5	67 39	31 07	33.0	66 48	29 44	31.9	65 57	28 26	30.7	65 05	27 14	29.6	64 13	26 06	28.5	258
79	69 00	30 25	32.2	68 09	29 00	30.8	67 17	27 40	29.6	66 25	26 26	28.5	65 32	25 15	27.4	64 38	24 12	26.4	259
80	69 29	28 07	29.7	68 37	26 46	28.4	67 44	25 30	27.3	66 50	24 20	26.2	65 56	23 15	25.2	65 02	22 15	24.3	260
81	69 57	25 43	27.1	69 03	24 26	25.9	68 09	23 15	24.8	67 14	22 10	23.8	66 19	21 10	22.9	65 23	20 14	22.1	261
82	70 21	23 11	24.5	69 27	22 00	23.3	68 31	20 56	22.3	67 36	19 56	21.4	66 40	19 00	20.6	65 43	18 09	19.8	262
83	70 44	20 34	21.7	69 48	19 29	20.7	68 51	18 31	19.7	67 55	17 37	18.9	66 58	16 47	18.1	66 01	16 01	17.4	263
84	71 03	17 50	18.8	70 07	16 53	17.9	69 09	16 01	17.1	68 12	15 14	16.3	67 14	14 30	15.7	66 16	13 50	15.1	264
85	71 20	15 01	15.8	70 23	14 12	15.0	69 25	13 28	14.3	68 26	12 48	13.7	67 28	12 10	13.1	66 29	11 36	12.6	265
86	71 35	12 07	12.8	70 36	11 27	12.1	69 37	10 51	11.6	68 38	10 18	11.0	67 39	9 48	10.6	66 40	9 20	10.1	266
87	71 46	9 09	9.6	70 46	8 39	9.1	69 47	8 11	8.7	68 48	7 46	8.3	67 48	7 23	8.0	66 49	7 02	7.6	267
88	71 54	6 08	6.4	70 54	5 47	6.1	69 54	5 29	5.8	68 55	5 12	5.6	67 55	4 56	5.3	66 55	4 42	5.1	268
89	71 58	3 04	3.2	70 58	2 54	3.1	69 59	2 45	2.9	68 59	2 36	2.8	67 59	2 28	2.7	66 59	2 21	2.6	269
90	72 00	0 00	0.0	71 00	0 00	0.0	70 00	0 00	0.0	69 00	0 00	0.0	68 00	0 00	0.0	67 00	0 00	0.0	270

N. Lat.: for LHA > 180° ... $Z_n = Z$
for LHA < 180° ... $Z_n = 360° − Z$

S. Lat.: for LHA > 180° ... $Z_n = 180° − Z$
for LHA < 180° ... $Z_n = 180° + Z$

© British Crown Copyright 2018. All rights reserved.

SIGHT REDUCTION TABLE

B: (−) for 90° < LHA < 270°
Dec:(−) for Lat. contrary name

Z₁: same sign as B
Z₂: (−) for F > 90°

Lat./A LHA/F	A	24° A/H	24° B/P	24° Z_1/Z_2	25° A/H	25° B/P	25° Z_1/Z_2	26° A/H	26° B/P	26° Z_1/Z_2	27° A/H	27° B/P	27° Z_1/Z_2	28° A/H	28° B/P	28° Z_1/Z_2	29° A/H	29° B/P	29° Z_1/Z_2	A	Lat./A LHA
0	180	0 00	66 00	90·0	0 00	65 00	90·0	0 00	64 00	90·0	0 00	63 00	90·0	0 00	62 00	90·0	0 00	61 00	90·0	180	360
1	179	0 55	66 00	89·6	0 54	65 00	89·6	0 54	64 00	89·6	0 53	63 00	89·5	0 53	62 00	89·5	0 52	61 00	89·5	181	359
2	178	1 50	65 59	89·2	1 49	64 59	89·2	1 48	63 59	89·1	1 47	62 59	89·1	1 46	61 59	89·1	1 45	60 59	89·0	182	358
3	177	2 44	65 58	88·8	2 43	64 58	88·7	2 42	63 58	88·7	2 40	62 58	88·6	2 39	61 58	88·6	2 37	60 58	88·5	183	357
4	176	3 39	65 57	88·4	3 37	64 57	88·3	3 36	63 57	88·2	3 34	62 57	88·2	3 32	61 57	88·1	3 30	60 56	88·1	184	356
5	175	4 34	65 55	88·0	4 32	64 55	87·9	4 30	63 55	87·8	4 27	62 55	87·7	4 25	61 55	87·6	4 22	60 54	87·6	185	355
6	174	5 29	65 53	87·6	5 26	64 53	87·5	5 23	63 53	87·4	5 21	62 52	87·3	5 18	61 52	87·2	5 15	60 52	87·1	186	354
7	173	6 24	65 50	87·1	6 20	64 50	87·0	6 17	63 50	86·9	6 14	62 50	86·8	6 11	61 49	86·7	6 07	60 49	86·6	187	353
8	172	7 18	65 47	86·7	7 15	64 47	86·6	7 11	63 47	86·5	7 07	62 46	86·3	7 04	61 46	86·2	6 59	60 46	86·1	188	352
9	171	8 13	65 44	86·3	8 09	64 44	86·2	8 05	63 43	86·0	8 01	62 43	85·9	7 56	61 42	85·7	7 52	60 42	85·6	189	351
10	170	9 08	65 40	85·9	9 03	64 40	85·7	8 59	63 39	85·6	8 54	62 39	85·4	8 49	61 38	85·3	8 44	60 38	85·1	190	350
11	169	10 02	65 36	85·5	9 57	64 35	85·3	9 52	63 35	85·1	9 47	62 34	85·0	9 42	61 33	84·8	9 36	60 33	84·6	191	349
12	168	10 57	65 32	85·1	10 52	64 31	84·9	10 46	63 30	84·7	10 41	62 29	84·5	10 35	61 28	84·3	10 29	60 28	84·1	192	348
13	167	11 52	65 27	84·6	11 46	64 26	84·4	11 40	63 25	84·2	11 34	62 24	84·0	11 27	61 23	83·8	11 21	60 22	83·6	193	347
14	166	12 46	65 21	84·2	12 40	64 20	84·0	12 34	63 19	83·8	12 27	62 18	83·5	12 20	61 17	83·3	12 13	60 16	83·1	194	346
15	165	13 41	65 15	83·8	13 34	64 14	83·5	13 27	63 13	83·3	13 20	62 11	83·1	13 13	61 10	82·8	13 05	60 09	82·6	195	345
16	164	14 35	65 09	83·3	14 28	64 07	83·1	14 21	63 06	82·8	14 13	62 04	82·6	14 05	61 03	82·3	13 57	60 02	82·1	196	344
17	163	15 29	65 02	82·9	15 22	64 00	82·6	15 14	62 59	82·4	15 06	61 57	82·1	14 58	60 56	81·8	14 49	59 54	81·6	197	343
18	162	16 24	64 55	82·5	16 16	63 53	82·2	16 08	62 51	81·9	15 59	61 49	81·6	15 50	60 47	81·3	15 41	59 46	81·0	198	342
19	161	17 18	64 47	82·0	17 10	63 45	81·7	17 01	62 43	81·4	16 52	61 41	81·1	16 42	60 39	80·8	16 33	59 37	80·5	199	341
20	160	18 12	64 39	81·6	18 03	63 36	81·3	17 54	62 34	80·9	17 45	61 31	80·6	17 35	60 30	80·3	17 24	59 28	80·0	200	340
21	159	19 07	64 30	81·1	18 57	63 28	80·8	18 47	62 25	80·4	18 37	61 23	80·1	18 27	60 20	79·8	18 16	59 18	79·5	201	339
22	158	20 01	64 21	80·7	19 51	63 18	80·3	19 41	62 15	80·0	19 30	61 13	79·6	19 19	60 10	79·3	19 08	59 08	78·9	202	338
23	157	20 55	64 11	80·2	20 44	63 08	79·8	20 34	62 05	79·5	20 22	61 02	79·1	20 11	59 59	78·7	19 59	58 57	78·4	203	337
24	156	21 49	64 01	79·7	21 38	62 58	79·3	21 27	61 54	79·0	21 15	60 51	78·6	21 03	59 48	78·2	20 50	58 45	77·8	204	336
25	155	22 43	63 50	79·3	22 31	62 46	78·9	22 19	61 43	78·4	22 07	60 39	78·0	21 55	59 36	77·7	21 42	58 33	77·3	205	335
26	154	23 36	63 39	78·8	23 25	62 35	78·4	23 12	61 31	78·0	22 59	60 27	77·5	22 46	59 24	77·1	22 33	58 20	76·7	206	334
27	153	24 30	63 27	78·3	24 18	62 22	77·8	24 05	61 18	77·4	23 52	60 14	77·0	23 38	59 10	76·5	23 24	58 07	76·1	207	333
28	152	25 23	63 14	77·8	25 11	62 10	77·3	24 57	61 05	76·9	24 44	60 01	76·4	24 29	58 57	76·0	24 15	57 53	75·5	208	332
29	151	26 17	63 01	77·3	26 04	61 56	76·8	25 50	60 51	76·3	25 36	59 47	75·9	25 21	58 42	75·4	25 05	57 38	74·9	209	331
30	150	27 11	62 48	76·8	26 57	61 42	76·3	26 42	60 37	75·8	26 27	59 32	75·3	26 12	58 27	74·8	25 56	57 23	74·4	210	330
31	149	28 04	62 33	76·3	27 50	61 27	75·8	27 35	60 22	75·2	27 19	59 16	74·7	27 03	58 11	74·2	26 46	57 07	73·8	211	329
32	148	28 57	62 18	75·7	28 42	61 12	75·2	28 27	60 06	74·7	28 10	59 00	74·2	27 54	57 55	73·7	27 37	56 50	73·1	212	328
33	147	29 50	62 02	75·2	29 35	60 56	74·7	29 19	59 49	74·1	29 02	58 43	73·6	28 45	57 37	73·0	28 27	56 32	72·5	213	327
34	146	30 43	61 46	74·7	30 27	60 39	74·1	30 10	59 32	73·5	29 53	58 26	73·0	29 35	57 20	72·4	29 17	56 14	71·9	214	326
35	145	31 36	61 28	74·1	31 19	60 21	73·5	31 02	59 14	72·9	30 44	58 07	72·4	30 26	57 01	71·8	30 07	55 55	71·2	215	325
36	144	32 29	61 10	73·5	32 11	60 02	72·9	31 53	58 55	72·3	31 35	57 48	71·7	31 16	56 41	71·2	30 56	55 35	70·6	216	324
37	143	33 21	60 51	73·0	33 03	59 43	72·3	32 45	58 35	71·7	32 26	57 28	71·1	32 06	56 21	70·5	31 46	55 14	69·9	217	323
38	142	34 13	60 32	72·4	33 55	59 23	71·7	33 36	58 15	71·1	33 16	57 07	70·5	32 56	56 00	69·9	32 35	54 53	69·3	218	322
39	141	35 06	60 11	71·8	34 47	59 02	71·1	34 27	57 53	70·5	34 06	56 45	69·8	33 45	55 37	69·2	33 24	54 30	68·6	219	321
40	140	35 58	59 50	71·2	35 38	58 38	70·5	35 17	57 31	69·8	34 57	56 22	69·1	34 34	55 14	68·5	34 12	54 07	67·9	220	320
41	139	36 49	59 28	70·5	36 29	58 17	69·8	36 08	57 08	69·1	35 46	55 59	68·5	35 24	54 50	67·8	35 01	53 42	67·1	221	319
42	138	37 41	59 04	69·9	37 20	57 54	69·2	36 58	56 43	68·5	36 36	55 34	67·8	36 13	54 25	67·1	35 49	53 17	66·4	222	318
43	137	38 32	58 40	69·2	38 11	57 29	68·5	37 48	56 18	67·8	37 25	55 08	67·1	37 02	53 59	66·4	36 37	52 50	65·7	223	317
44	136	39 23	58 15	68·6	39 01	57 03	67·8	38 38	55 52	67·1	38 14	54 41	66·3	37 50	53 32	65·7	37 25	52 23	64·9	224	316
45	135	40 14	57 48	67·9	39 51	56 36	67·1	39 28	55 24	66·3	39 03	54 13	65·6	38 38	53 04	64·9	38 12	51 54	64·1	225	315

© British Crown Copyright 2018. All rights reserved.

Lat./A		24°			25°			26°			27°			28°			29°			Lat./A	
LHA/F		A/H	B/P	Z_1/Z_2	A/H	B/P	Z_1/Z_2	A/H	B/P	Z_1/Z_2	A/H	B/P	Z_1/Z_2	A/H	B/P	Z_1/Z_2	A/H	B/P	Z_1/Z_2	**LHA**	
45	135	40 14	57 48	67·9	39 51	56 36	67·1	39 28	55 24	66·3	39 03	54 13	65·6	38 38	53 04	64·9	38 12	51 54	64·1	225	315
46	134	41 05	57 21	67·2	40 41	56 08	66·4	40 17	54 56	65·6	39 52	53 44	64·8	39 26	52 34	64·1	38 59	51 25	63·3	226	314
47	133	41 55	56 52	66·4	41 31	55 38	65·6	41 06	54 26	64·8	40 40	53 14	64·0	40 13	52 04	63·3	39 46	50 54	62·5	227	313
48	132	42 45	56 22	65·7	42 20	55 08	64·9	41 54	53 55	64·0	41 28	52 43	63·2	41 00	51 32	62·5	40 32	50 22	61·7	228	312
49	131	43 35	55 50	64·9	43 09	54 36	64·1	42 43	53 23	63·2	42 15	52 10	62·4	41 47	51 00	61·6	41 18	49 48	60·9	229	311
50	130	44 25	55 17	64·1	43 58	54 02	63·3	43 31	52 49	62·4	43 03	51 36	61·6	42 34	50 24	60·8	42 04	49 14	60·0	230	310
51	129	45 14	54 43	63·3	44 47	53 28	62·4	44 18	52 13	61·6	43 49	51 00	60·7	43 20	49 48	59·9	42 49	48 38	59·1	231	309
52	128	46 03	54 08	62·5	45 35	52 54	61·6	45 06	51 37	60·7	44 36	50 23	59·8	44 05	49 11	59·0	43 34	48 00	58·2	232	308
53	127	46 51	53 30	61·6	46 22	52 14	60·7	45 52	50 59	59·8	45 22	49 45	58·9	44 51	48 32	58·1	44 18	47 21	57·2	233	307
54	126	47 39	52 51	60·8	47 09	51 34	59·8	46 39	50 19	58·9	46 07	49 05	58·0	45 35	47 52	57·1	45 02	46 41	56·3	234	306
55	125	48 27	52 11	59·8	47 56	50 53	58·9	47 25	49 37	58·0	46 53	48 23	57·0	46 19	47 10	56·2	45 45	45 59	55·3	235	305
56	124	49 14	51 28	58·9	48 43	50 11	57·9	48 10	48 54	57·0	47 37	47 40	56·1	47 03	46 27	55·2	46 29	45 15	54·3	236	304
57	123	50 01	50 44	57·9	49 28	49 26	56·9	48 55	48 09	56·0	48 21	46 54	55·0	47 46	45 41	54·1	47 11	44 30	53·3	237	303
58	122	50 47	49 58	56·9	50 14	48 39	55·9	49 40	47 22	54·9	49 05	46 07	54·0	48 29	44 54	53·1	47 53	43 43	52·2	238	302
59	121	51 33	49 09	55·9	50 58	47 51	54·9	50 23	46 34	53·9	49 48	45 18	52·9	49 11	44 05	52·0	48 34	42 54	51·1	239	301
60	120	52 18	48 19	54·8	51 43	47 00	53·8	51 07	45 43	52·8	50 30	44 28	51·8	49 53	43 14	50·9	49 14	42 03	50·0	240	300
61	119	53 02	47 26	53·7	52 26	46 07	52·7	51 49	44 50	51·7	51 12	43 35	50·7	50 33	42 22	49·7	49 54	41 10	48·8	241	299
62	118	53 46	46 31	52·6	53 09	45 12	51·5	52 31	43 54	50·5	51 53	42 39	49·5	51 13	41 27	48·6	50 33	40 16	47·6	242	298
63	117	54 29	45 33	51·4	53 51	44 14	50·3	53 13	42 57	49·3	52 33	41 42	48·3	51 53	40 30	47·3	51 12	39 19	46·4	243	297
64	116	55 12	44 30	50·2	54 33	43 14	49·1	53 53	41 57	48·1	53 13	40 42	47·1	52 31	39 30	46·1	51 49	38 20	45·2	244	296
65	115	55 53	43 30	48·9	55 13	42 06	47·8	54 33	40 55	46·8	53 51	39 40	45·8	53 09	38 29	44·8	52 26	37 19	43·9	245	295
66	114	56 34	42 25	47·6	55 53	41 06	46·5	55 12	39 50	45·4	54 29	38 36	44·4	53 46	37 25	43·5	53 02	36 11	42·6	246	294
67	113	57 14	41 16	46·2	56 32	39 58	45·1	55 50	38 42	44·1	55 06	37 29	43·1	54 22	36 19	42·1	53 37	35 11	41·2	247	293
68	112	57 53	40 05	44·8	57 10	38 47	43·7	56 27	37 32	42·7	55 42	36 19	41·7	54 57	35 10	40·7	54 11	34 03	39·8	248	292
69	111	58 32	38 50	43·3	57 47	37 33	42·2	57 03	36 18	41·2	56 17	35 07	40·2	55 31	33 59	39·3	54 44	32 53	38·4	249	291
70	110	59 09	37 32	41·8	58 24	36 16	40·7	57 38	35 02	39·7	56 51	33 52	38·7	56 04	32 45	37·8	55 16	31 41	36·9	250	290
71	109	59 45	36 11	40·2	58 58	34 55	39·2	58 12	33 43	38·1	57 24	32 35	37·2	56 36	31 29	36·3	55 47	30 26	35·4	251	289
72	108	60 19	34 46	38·6	59 32	33 32	37·6	58 44	32 21	36·5	57 56	31 14	35·6	57 07	30 10	34·7	56 17	29 08	33·8	252	288
73	107	60 53	33 18	36·9	60 05	32 05	35·9	59 16	30 56	34·9	58 26	29 51	34·0	57 36	28 48	33·1	56 46	27 49	32·2	253	287
74	106	61 25	31 46	35·2	60 36	30 35	34·2	59 46	29 28	33·2	58 55	28 25	32·3	58 05	27 24	31·4	57 13	26 26	30·6	254	286
75	105	61 56	30 10	33·4	61 06	29 02	32·4	60 15	27 57	31·4	59 23	26 56	30·5	58 31	25 57	29·7	57 39	25 02	28·9	255	285
76	104	62 26	28 31	31·5	61 34	27 25	30·5	60 42	26 23	29·6	59 50	25 26	28·8	58 57	24 28	28·0	58 04	23 28	27·2	256	284
77	103	62 53	26 48	29·6	62 01	25 45	28·6	61 08	24 46	27·8	60 15	23 49	27·0	59 21	22 56	26·2	58 27	22 05	25·5	257	283
78	102	63 20	25 02	27·6	62 26	24 02	26·7	61 32	23 05	25·9	60 38	22 12	25·1	59 45	21 21	24·4	58 49	20 34	23·7	258	282
79	101	63 44	23 12	25·5	62 50	22 15	24·7	61 55	21 22	23·9	61 00	20 32	23·2	60 06	19 44	22·5	59 09	19 00	21·8	259	281
80	100	64 07	21 18	23·4	63 12	20 25	22·6	62 16	19 36	21·9	61 20	18 49	21·2	60 24	18 05	20·6	59 28	17 24	20·0	260	280
81	99	64 28	19 22	21·3	63 32	18 33	20·5	62 35	17 47	19·9	61 39	17 04	19·2	60 42	16 24	18·6	59 45	15 46	18·1	261	279
82	98	64 47	17 22	19·1	63 53	16 39	18·4	62 53	15 56	17·8	61 56	15 17	17·2	60 58	14 40	16·7	60 01	14 06	16·2	262	278
83	97	65 03	15 18	16·8	64 06	14 39	16·2	63 08	14 02	15·6	62 10	13 27	15·1	61 14	12 55	14·7	60 14	12 24	14·2	263	277
84	96	65 18	13 13	14·5	64 20	12 38	14·0	63 22	12 06	13·5	62 23	11 36	13·0	61 25	11 07	12·6	60 26	10 41	12·2	264	276
85	95	65 31	11 05	12·1	64 32	10 35	11·7	63 33	10 08	11·3	62 35	9 42	10·9	61 36	9 19	10·6	60 37	8 56	10·2	265	275
86	94	65 41	8 54	9·8	64 42	8 30	9·4	63 43	8 08	9·1	62 44	7 48	8·8	61 44	7 28	8·5	60 45	7 10	8·2	266	274
87	93	65 49	6 42	7·3	64 50	6 24	7·1	63 50	6 07	6·8	62 51	5 52	6·6	61 51	5 37	6·4	60 52	5 24	6·2	267	273
88	92	65 55	4 29	4·9	64 56	4 17	4·7	63 56	4 06	4·6	62 56	3 55	4·4	61 56	3 45	4·3	60 56	3 36	4·1	268	272
89	91	65 59	2 15	2·4	64 59	2 09	2·4	63 59	2 03	2·3	62 59	1 58	2·2	61 59	1 53	2·1	60 59	1 48	2·1	269	271
90	90	66 00	0 00	0·0	65 00	0 00	0·0	64 00	0 00	0·0	63 00	0 00	0·0	62 00	0 00	0·0	61 00	0 00	0·0	270	270

N. Lat: for LHA > 180° ... $Z_n = Z$
for LHA < 180° ... $Z_n = 360° - Z$

S. Lat: for LHA > 180° ... $Z_n = 180° - Z$
for LHA < 180° ... $Z_n = 180° + Z$

© British Crown Copyright 2018. All rights reserved.

SIGHT REDUCTION TABLE

B: (−) for 90° < LHA < 270°
Dec:(−) for Lat. contrary name

Z₁: same sign as B
Z₂: (−) for F > 90°

LHA/F	A	30° A/H	30° B/P	30° Z₁/Z₂	31° A/H	31° B/P	31° Z₁/Z₂	32° A/H	32° B/P	32° Z₁/Z₂	33° A/H	33° B/P	33° Z₁/Z₂	34° A/H	34° B/P	34° Z₁/Z₂	35° A/H	35° B/P	35° Z₁/Z₂	LHA	A
0	180	0 00	60 00	90.0	0 00	59 00	90.0	0 00	58 00	90.0	0 00	57 00	90.0	0 00	56 00	90.0	0 00	55 00	90.0	180	360
1	179	0 52	60 00	89.5	0 51	59 00	89.5	0 51	58 00	89.5	0 50	57 00	89.5	0 50	56 00	89.4	0 49	55 00	89.4	181	359
2	178	1 44	59 59	89.0	1 43	58 59	89.0	1 42	57 59	89.0	1 41	56 59	88.9	1 39	55 59	88.9	1 38	54 59	88.9	182	358
3	177	2 36	59 58	88.5	2 34	58 58	88.5	2 33	57 58	88.4	2 31	56 58	88.4	2 29	55 58	88.3	2 27	54 58	88.3	183	357
4	176	3 28	59 56	88.0	3 26	58 56	87.9	3 23	57 56	87.9	3 21	56 56	87.8	3 19	55 56	87.8	3 17	54 56	87.7	184	356
5	175	4 20	59 54	87.5	4 17	58 54	87.4	4 14	57 54	87.3	4 12	56 54	87.3	4 09	55 54	87.2	4 06	54 54	87.1	185	355
6	174	5 12	59 52	87.0	5 08	58 52	86.9	5 05	57 52	86.8	5 02	56 51	86.7	4 58	55 51	86.6	4 55	54 51	86.6	186	354
7	173	6 04	59 49	86.5	6 00	58 49	86.4	5 56	57 48	86.3	5 52	56 48	86.2	5 48	55 48	86.1	5 44	54 48	86.0	187	353
8	172	6 55	59 45	86.0	6 51	58 45	85.9	6 47	57 45	85.7	6 42	56 45	85.7	6 38	55 44	85.5	6 33	54 44	85.4	188	352
9	171	7 47	59 42	85.5	7 42	58 41	85.3	7 37	57 41	85.2	7 32	56 40	85.1	7 27	55 40	84.9	7 22	54 40	84.8	189	351
10	170	8 39	59 37	85.0	8 34	58 37	84.8	8 28	57 36	84.6	8 22	56 36	84.5	8 17	55 36	84.3	8 11	54 35	84.2	190	350
11	169	9 31	59 32	84.4	9 25	58 32	84.3	9 19	57 31	84.1	9 13	56 31	84.0	9 06	55 30	83.8	9 00	54 30	83.6	191	349
12	168	10 22	59 27	83.9	10 16	58 26	83.8	10 09	57 26	83.6	10 03	56 25	83.4	9 56	55 25	83.2	9 48	54 24	83.0	192	348
13	167	11 14	59 21	83.4	11 07	58 20	83.2	11 00	57 20	83.0	10 52	56 19	82.8	10 45	55 18	82.6	10 37	54 18	82.4	193	347
14	166	12 06	59 15	82.9	11 58	58 14	82.7	11 50	57 13	82.5	11 42	56 12	82.3	11 34	55 12	82.1	11 26	54 11	81.9	194	346
15	165	12 57	59 08	82.4	12 49	58 07	82.1	12 41	57 06	81.9	12 32	56 05	81.7	12 23	55 04	81.5	12 14	54 04	81.3	195	345
16	164	13 49	59 01	81.8	13 40	58 00	81.6	13 31	56 58	81.4	13 22	55 58	81.1	13 13	54 57	80.9	13 03	53 56	80.7	196	344
17	163	14 40	58 53	81.3	14 31	57 51	81.1	14 21	56 50	80.8	14 12	55 49	80.5	14 02	54 48	80.3	13 51	53 47	80.1	197	343
18	162	15 31	58 44	80.8	15 22	57 43	80.5	15 12	56 42	80.2	15 01	55 40	80.0	14 51	54 39	79.7	14 40	53 38	79.4	198	342
19	161	16 23	58 35	80.2	16 12	57 34	79.9	16 02	56 32	79.7	15 51	55 31	79.4	15 40	54 30	79.1	15 28	53 29	78.8	199	341
20	160	17 14	58 26	79.7	17 03	57 24	79.4	16 52	56 23	79.1	16 40	55 21	78.8	16 28	54 21	78.5	16 16	53 19	78.2	200	340
21	159	18 05	58 16	79.1	17 53	57 14	78.8	17 42	56 12	78.5	17 29	55 11	78.2	17 17	54 09	77.9	17 04	53 08	77.6	201	339
22	158	18 56	58 05	78.6	18 44	57 03	78.2	18 31	56 01	77.9	18 19	55 00	77.6	18 06	53 58	77.3	17 52	52 56	77.0	202	338
23	157	19 47	57 54	78.0	19 34	56 52	77.7	19 21	55 50	77.3	19 08	54 48	77.0	18 54	53 46	76.6	18 40	52 44	76.3	203	337
24	156	20 37	57 42	77.4	20 24	56 40	77.1	20 11	55 38	76.7	19 57	54 36	76.4	19 42	53 34	76.0	19 28	52 32	75.7	204	336
25	155	21 28	57 30	76.9	21 14	56 27	76.5	21 00	55 25	76.1	20 46	54 23	75.7	20 31	53 21	75.4	20 15	52 19	75.0	205	335
26	154	22 19	57 17	76.3	22 04	56 14	75.9	21 49	55 12	75.5	21 35	54 10	75.1	21 19	53 07	74.7	21 03	52 05	74.4	206	334
27	153	23 09	57 03	75.7	22 54	56 00	75.3	22 39	54 57	74.9	22 23	53 55	74.5	22 07	52 52	74.1	21 50	51 50	73.7	207	333
28	152	23 59	56 49	75.1	23 44	55 46	74.7	23 28	54 43	74.3	23 11	53 40	73.8	22 54	52 37	73.4	22 37	51 35	73.0	208	332
29	151	24 50	56 34	74.5	24 33	55 31	74.1	24 17	54 27	73.6	23 59	53 24	73.2	23 42	52 21	72.8	23 23	51 19	72.4	209	331
30	150	25 40	56 19	73.9	25 23	55 15	73.4	25 05	54 11	73.0	24 48	53 08	72.5	24 29	52 05	72.1	24 11	51 03	71.7	210	330
31	149	26 29	56 02	73.3	26 12	54 58	72.8	25 54	53 54	72.3	25 35	52 51	71.9	25 17	51 48	71.4	24 57	50 45	71.0	211	329
32	148	27 19	55 45	72.6	27 01	54 41	72.2	26 42	53 37	71.7	26 23	52 33	71.2	26 04	51 30	70.7	25 44	50 27	70.3	212	328
33	147	28 09	55 27	72.0	27 50	54 23	71.5	27 31	53 19	71.0	27 11	52 15	70.5	26 51	51 12	70.0	26 30	50 08	69.6	213	327
34	146	28 58	55 09	71.4	28 38	54 04	70.8	28 19	53 00	70.3	27 58	51 56	69.8	27 37	50 52	69.3	27 16	49 49	68.8	214	326
35	145	29 47	54 49	70.7	29 27	53 44	70.2	29 06	52 40	69.6	28 45	51 36	69.1	28 24	50 32	68.6	28 01	49 29	68.1	215	325
36	144	30 36	54 29	70.0	30 15	53 24	69.5	29 54	52 19	68.9	29 32	51 15	68.4	29 10	50 11	67.9	28 47	49 07	67.4	216	324
37	143	31 25	54 08	69.4	31 03	53 04	68.8	30 41	51 58	68.2	30 19	50 53	67.7	29 56	49 49	67.2	29 32	48 45	66.6	217	323
38	142	32 13	53 46	68.7	31 51	52 40	68.1	31 28	51 35	67.5	31 05	50 30	66.9	30 41	49 26	66.4	30 17	48 23	65.9	218	322
39	141	33 02	53 23	68.0	32 39	52 17	67.4	32 15	51 12	66.8	31 51	50 07	66.2	31 27	49 03	65.6	31 02	48 01	65.1	219	321
40	140	33 50	53 00	67.2	33 26	51 53	66.6	33 02	50 48	66.0	32 37	49 43	65.4	32 12	48 38	64.9	31 46	47 34	64.3	220	320
41	139	34 37	52 35	66.5	34 13	51 29	65.9	33 48	50 23	65.3	33 23	49 17	64.7	32 57	48 13	64.1	32 30	47 09	63.5	221	319
42	138	35 25	52 09	65.8	35 00	51 03	65.1	34 34	49 56	64.5	34 08	48 51	63.9	33 42	47 46	63.3	33 14	46 42	62.7	222	318
43	137	36 12	51 43	65.0	35 46	50 38	64.3	35 20	49 30	63.7	34 53	48 25	63.1	34 26	47 19	62.5	33 58	46 15	61.9	223	317
44	136	36 59	51 15	64.2	36 33	50 08	63.6	36 06	49 01	62.9	35 38	47 58	62.3	35 10	46 51	61.6	34 41	45 46	61.0	224	316
45	135	37 46	50 46	63.4	37 19	49 39	62.7	36 51	48 32	62.1	36 22	47 26	61.4	35 53	46 21	60.8	35 24	45 17	60.2	225	315

© British Crown Copyright 2018. All rights reserved.

Lat./A		30°			31°			32°			33°			34°			35°			Lat./A	
	LHA/F	A/H	B/P	Z₁/Z₂	A/H	B/P	Z₁/Z₂	A/H	B/P	Z₁/Z₂	A/H	B/P	Z₁/Z₂	A/H	B/P	Z₁/Z₂	A/H	B/P	Z₁/Z₂	LHA	
135	45	37 46	50 46	63·4	37 19	49 39	62·7	36 51	48 32	62·1	36 22	47 26	61·4	35 53	46 21	60·8	35 24	45 17	60·2	315	225
134	46	38 32	50 16	62·6	38 04	49 08	61·9	37 36	48 02	61·2	37 06	46 56	60·6	36 37	45 51	59·9	36 06	44 46	59·3	314	226
133	47	39 18	49 45	61·8	38 49	48 37	61·1	38 20	47 30	60·4	37 50	46 24	59·7	37 19	45 19	59·1	36 48	44 15	58·4	313	227
132	48	40 04	49 13	61·0	39 34	48 05	60·2	39 04	46 58	59·5	38 33	45 51	58·8	38 02	44 46	58·2	37 30	43 42	57·5	312	228
131	49	40 49	48 39	60·1	40 19	47 31	59·4	39 48	46 24	58·6	39 16	45 18	57·9	38 44	44 12	57·2	38 11	43 08	56·6	311	229
130	50	41 34	48 04	59·2	41 03	46 56	58·5	40 31	45 49	57·7	39 59	44 42	57·0	39 26	43 37	56·3	38 52	42 33	55·6	310	230
129	51	42 18	47 28	58·3	41 46	46 20	57·5	41 14	45 12	56·8	40 41	44 06	56·1	40 07	43 01	55·4	39 32	41 57	54·7	309	231
128	52	43 02	46 50	57·4	42 29	45 42	56·6	41 56	44 34	55·9	41 22	43 28	55·1	40 47	42 23	54·4	40 12	41 19	53·7	308	232
127	53	43 46	46 11	56·4	43 12	45 03	55·6	42 38	43 55	54·9	42 03	42 49	54·1	41 28	41 44	53·4	40 52	40 41	52·7	307	233
126	54	44 29	45 31	55·5	43 54	44 22	54·7	43 19	43 15	53·9	42 44	42 09	53·1	42 07	41 04	52·4	41 30	40 01	51·7	306	234
125	55	45 11	44 49	54·5	44 36	43 40	53·7	44 00	42 33	52·9	43 24	41 27	52·1	42 46	40 23	51·4	42 09	39 19	50·7	305	235
124	56	45 53	44 05	53·5	45 17	42 57	52·6	44 40	41 50	51·8	44 03	40 44	51·1	43 25	39 40	50·3	42 46	38 37	49·6	304	236
123	57	46 35	43 20	52·4	45 58	42 11	51·6	45 20	41 05	50·8	44 42	39 59	50·0	44 03	38 55	49·3	43 24	37 53	48·5	303	237
122	58	47 16	42 33	51·3	46 38	41 25	50·5	45 59	40 18	49·7	45 20	39 13	48·9	44 40	38 09	48·2	44 00	37 07	47·5	302	238
121	59	47 56	41 44	50·2	47 17	40 36	49·4	46 38	39 30	48·6	45 58	38 25	47·8	45 17	37 22	47·1	44 36	36 20	46·3	301	239
120	60	48 35	40 54	49·1	47 56	39 46	48·3	47 16	38 40	47·5	46 35	37 36	46·7	45 53	36 34	45·9	45 11	35 32	45·2	300	240
119	61	49 14	40 01	47·9	48 34	38 54	47·1	47 53	37 48	46·3	47 11	36 45	45·5	46 29	35 42	44·7	45 46	34 42	44·0	299	241
118	62	49 53	39 07	46·8	49 11	38 00	45·9	48 29	36 55	45·1	47 46	35 52	44·3	47 03	34 50	43·6	46 19	33 50	42·8	298	242
117	63	50 30	38 11	45·5	49 48	37 04	44·7	49 05	36 00	43·9	48 21	34 57	43·1	47 37	33 57	42·3	46 53	32 57	41·6	297	243
116	64	51 07	37 13	44·3	50 23	36 07	43·4	49 40	35 03	42·6	48 55	34 01	41·8	48 10	33 01	41·1	47 25	32 03	40·4	296	244
115	65	51 43	36 12	43·0	50 58	35 07	42·2	50 14	34 04	41·3	49 28	33 03	40·6	48 43	32 04	39·8	47 56	31 07	39·1	295	245
114	66	52 18	35 10	41·7	51 33	34 05	40·8	50 47	33 03	40·0	50 01	32 04	39·3	49 14	31 05	38·5	48 27	30 09	37·8	294	246
113	67	52 52	34 05	40·3	52 06	33 02	39·5	51 19	32 01	38·7	50 32	31 02	37·9	49 44	30 05	37·2	48 56	29 10	36·5	293	247
112	68	53 25	32 59	38·9	52 38	31 56	38·1	51 50	30 57	37·3	51 02	29 59	36·6	50 14	29 03	35·8	49 25	28 09	35·2	292	248
111	69	53 57	31 50	37·5	53 09	30 49	36·7	52 20	29 50	35·9	51 32	28 53	35·2	50 43	27 59	34·5	49 53	27 06	33·8	291	249
110	70	54 28	30 39	36·1	53 39	29 39	35·2	52 50	28 41	34·5	52 00	27 46	33·8	51 10	26 53	33·1	50 20	26 02	32·4	290	250
109	71	54 58	29 25	34·6	54 08	28 27	33·8	53 18	27 31	33·0	52 28	26 38	32·3	51 37	25 46	31·6	50 46	24 56	31·0	289	251
108	72	55 27	28 09	33·0	54 37	27 13	32·2	53 46	26 19	31·5	52 54	25 27	30·8	52 03	24 37	30·2	51 10	23 49	29·5	288	252
107	73	55 55	26 51	31·4	55 03	25 57	30·7	54 12	25 04	30·0	53 19	24 14	29·3	52 27	23 26	28·7	51 34	22 40	28·1	287	253
106	74	56 21	25 31	29·8	55 29	24 39	29·1	54 36	23 48	28·4	53 43	23 00	27·8	52 50	22 14	27·1	51 57	21 29	26·6	286	254
105	75	56 46	24 09	28·2	55 53	23 18	27·5	55 00	22 30	26·8	54 06	21 44	26·2	53 12	21 00	25·6	52 18	20 17	25·0	285	255
104	76	57 10	22 44	26·5	56 16	21 56	25·8	55 22	21 10	25·2	54 27	20 26	24·6	53 33	19 44	24·0	52 38	19 04	23·5	284	256
103	77	57 33	21 17	24·8	56 38	20 31	24·1	55 43	19 48	23·5	54 48	19 06	23·0	53 53	18 27	22·4	52 57	17 49	21·9	283	257
102	78	57 54	19 48	23·0	56 59	19 05	22·4	56 03	18 24	21·9	55 07	17 45	21·3	54 11	17 08	20·8	53 15	16 32	20·3	282	258
101	79	58 13	18 17	21·2	57 17	17 37	20·7	56 21	16 59	20·1	55 25	16 22	19·6	54 28	15 48	19·2	53 31	15 15	18·7	281	259
100	80	58 32	16 44	19·4	57 35	16 07	18·9	56 38	15 32	18·4	55 41	14 58	17·9	54 44	14 26	17·5	53 47	13 56	17·1	280	260
99	81	58 48	15 10	17·6	57 51	14 36	17·1	56 53	14 03	16·6	55 56	13 33	16·2	54 58	13 03	15·8	54 00	12 36	15·4	279	261
98	82	59 03	13 33	15·7	58 05	13 02	15·3	57 07	12 33	14·9	56 09	12 06	14·5	55 11	11 40	14·1	54 13	11 14	13·8	278	262
97	83	59 16	11 55	13·8	58 18	11 28	13·4	57 19	11 02	13·0	56 21	10 38	12·7	55 22	10 14	12·4	54 24	9 52	12·1	277	263
96	84	59 28	10 16	11·9	58 29	9 52	11·5	57 30	9 30	11·2	56 31	9 09	10·9	55 32	8 49	10·6	54 33	8 29	10·4	276	264
95	85	59 37	8 35	9·9	58 38	8 15	9·6	57 39	7 56	9·4	56 40	7 39	9·1	55 41	7 22	8·9	54 41	7 06	8·7	275	265
94	86	59 46	6 53	8·0	58 46	6 37	7·7	57 47	6 22	7·5	56 47	6 08	7·3	55 48	5 54	7·1	54 48	5 41	7·0	274	266
93	87	59 52	5 11	6·0	58 52	4 59	5·8	57 52	4 47	5·6	56 53	4 36	5·5	55 53	4 26	5·4	54 53	4 16	5·2	273	267
92	88	59 56	3 28	4·0	58 57	3 19	3·9	57 57	3 12	3·8	56 57	3 05	3·7	55 57	2 58	3·6	54 57	2 51	3·5	272	268
91	89	59 59	1 44	2·0	58 59	1 40	1·9	57 59	1 36	1·9	56 59	1 32	1·8	55 59	1 29	1·8	54 59	1 26	1·7	271	269
90	90	60 00	0 00	0·0	59 00	0 00	0·0	58 00	0 00	0·0	57 00	0 00	0·0	56 00	0 00	0·0	55 00	0 00	0·0	270	270

N. Lat: for LHA > 180° .... $Z_n = Z$
for LHA < 180° .... $Z_n = 360° - Z$

S. Lat.: for LHA > 180° .... $Z_n = 180° - Z$
for LHA < 180° .... $Z_n = 180° + Z$

© British Crown Copyright 2018. All rights reserved.

SIGHT REDUCTION TABLE

B: (—) for 90° < LHA < 270°
Dec:(—) for Lat. contrary name

Z₁: same sign as B
Z₂: (—) for F > 90°

		36°			37°			38°			39°			40°			41°			
LHA/F	A	A/H	B/P	Z₁/Z₂	A/H	B/P	Z₁/Z₂	A/H	B/P	Z₁/Z₂	A/H	B/P	Z₁/Z₂	A/H	B/P	Z₁/Z₂	A/H	B/P	Z₁/Z₂	Lat./A	LHA
0	180	0 00	54 00	90·0	0 00	53 00	90·0	0 00	52 00	90·0	0 00	51 00	90·0	0 00	50 00	90·0	0 00	49 00	90·0	180	360
1	179	0 49	54 00	89·4	0 48	53 00	89·4	0 47	52 00	89·4	0 47	51 00	89·4	0 46	50 00	89·4	0 45	49 00	89·3	181	359
2	178	1 37	53 59	88·8	1 36	52 59	88·8	1 35	51 59	88·8	1 33	50 59	88·7	1 32	49 59	88·7	1 31	48 59	88·7	182	358
3	177	2 26	53 58	88·2	2 24	52 58	88·2	2 22	51 59	88·2	2 20	50 58	88·1	2 18	49 58	88·1	2 16	48 58	88·0	183	357
4	176	3 14	53 56	87·6	3 12	52 56	87·6	3 09	51 56	87·6	3 06	50 56	87·5	3 04	49 56	87·5	3 01	48 56	87·4	184	356
5	175	4 03	53 54	87·1	3 59	52 54	87·0	3 56	51 54	86·9	3 53	50 54	86·8	3 50	49 54	86·8	3 46	48 54	86·7	185	355
6	174	4 51	53 51	86·5	4 47	52 51	86·4	4 43	51 51	86·3	4 40	50 51	86·2	4 36	49 51	86·1	4 31	48 51	86·1	186	354
7	173	5 39	53 48	85·9	5 35	52 48	85·8	5 31	51 48	85·7	5 26	50 48	85·6	5 21	49 47	85·5	5 17	48 47	85·4	187	353
8	172	6 28	53 44	85·3	6 23	52 44	85·2	6 18	51 44	85·1	6 13	50 44	84·9	6 07	49 43	84·8	6 02	48 43	84·7	188	352
9	171	7 16	53 40	84·7	7 11	52 39	84·6	7 05	51 39	84·4	6 59	50 39	84·3	6 53	49 39	84·2	6 47	48 39	84·1	189	351
10	170	8 05	53 35	84·1	7 58	52 35	84·0	7 52	51 34	83·8	7 45	50 34	83·6	7 39	49 34	83·5	7 32	48 34	83·4	190	350
11	169	8 53	53 30	83·5	8 46	52 29	83·3	8 39	51 29	83·2	8 32	50 29	83·0	8 24	49 29	82·9	8 17	48 28	82·7	191	349
12	168	9 41	53 24	82·9	9 33	52 23	82·7	9 26	51 23	82·5	9 18	50 23	82·4	9 10	49 23	82·2	9 02	48 22	82·1	192	348
13	167	10 29	53 17	82·3	10 21	52 17	82·1	10 13	51 17	81·9	10 04	50 16	81·7	9 55	49 16	81·6	9 46	48 16	81·4	193	347
14	166	11 17	53 10	81·7	11 08	52 10	81·5	10 59	51 10	81·3	10 50	50 09	81·0	10 41	49 09	80·9	10 31	48 09	80·7	194	346
15	165	12 05	53 03	81·0	11 56	52 02	80·8	11 46	51 02	80·6	11 36	50 02	80·4	11 26	49 01	80·2	11 16	48 01	80·0	195	345
16	164	12 53	52 55	80·4	12 43	51 54	80·2	12 33	50 54	80·0	12 22	49 54	79·8	12 11	48 53	79·6	12 00	47 53	79·3	196	344
17	163	13 41	52 46	79·8	13 30	51 46	79·6	13 19	50 45	79·3	13 08	49 45	79·1	12 57	48 44	78·9	12 45	47 44	78·7	197	343
18	162	14 29	52 37	79·2	14 17	51 37	78·9	14 06	50 36	78·7	13 54	49 35	78·4	13 42	48 35	78·2	13 29	47 34	78·0	198	342
19	161	15 16	52 28	78·6	15 04	51 27	78·3	14 52	50 26	78·0	14 39	49 25	77·8	14 27	48 25	77·5	14 13	47 24	77·3	199	341
20	160	16 04	52 17	77·9	15 51	51 16	77·6	15 38	50 16	77·4	15 25	49 15	77·1	15 11	48 14	76·8	14 58	47 14	76·6	200	340
21	159	16 51	52 07	77·3	16 38	51 05	77·0	16 24	50 05	76·7	16 10	49 04	76·4	15 56	48 03	76·1	15 42	47 03	75·9	201	339
22	158	17 39	51 55	76·6	17 24	50 54	76·3	17 10	49 53	76·0	16 56	48 52	75·7	16 41	47 51	75·4	16 25	46 51	75·2	202	338
23	157	18 26	51 43	76·0	18 11	50 42	75·7	17 56	49 41	75·4	17 41	48 40	75·0	17 25	47 39	74·7	17 09	46 38	74·4	203	337
24	156	19 13	51 30	75·3	18 57	50 29	75·0	18 42	49 28	74·7	18 26	48 27	74·3	18 09	47 26	74·0	17 53	46 25	73·7	204	336
25	155	20 00	51 17	74·7	19 44	50 15	74·3	19 27	49 14	74·0	19 10	48 13	73·6	18 53	47 12	73·3	18 36	46 12	73·0	205	335
26	154	20 46	51 03	74·0	20 30	50 01	73·6	20 13	49 00	73·3	19 55	47 59	72·9	19 37	46 58	72·6	19 19	45 58	72·3	206	334
27	153	21 33	50 48	73·3	21 15	49 47	73·0	20 58	48 45	72·6	20 39	47 44	72·2	20 21	46 43	71·9	20 02	45 42	71·5	207	333
28	152	22 19	50 33	72·6	22 01	49 31	72·3	21 43	48 30	71·9	21 24	47 28	71·5	21 05	46 28	71·1	20 45	45 27	70·8	208	332
29	151	23 06	50 17	72·0	22 47	49 15	71·6	22 28	48 14	71·2	22 08	47 12	70·8	21 48	46 11	70·4	21 28	45 11	70·0	209	331
30	150	23 52	50 00	71·3	23 32	48 58	70·8	23 12	47 57	70·4	22 52	46 56	70·0	22 31	45 54	69·6	22 10	44 54	69·3	210	330
31	149	24 37	49 43	70·5	24 17	48 41	70·1	23 57	47 39	69·7	23 36	46 38	69·3	23 14	45 37	68·9	22 52	44 36	68·5	211	329
32	148	25 23	49 25	69·8	25 02	48 23	69·4	24 41	47 21	68·9	24 19	46 19	68·5	23 57	45 18	68·1	23 34	44 17	67·7	212	328
33	147	26 09	49 06	69·1	25 47	48 04	68·7	25 25	47 02	68·2	25 02	46 00	67·7	24 39	44 59	67·3	24 16	43 58	66·9	213	327
34	146	26 54	48 46	68·4	26 32	47 44	67·9	26 09	46 42	67·4	25 45	45 40	67·0	25 22	44 39	66·6	24 58	43 39	66·1	214	326
35	145	27 39	48 26	67·6	27 16	47 23	67·1	26 52	46 21	66·7	26 28	45 20	66·2	26 04	44 19	65·8	25 39	43 18	65·3	215	325
36	144	28 24	48 04	66·9	28 00	47 02	66·4	27 36	46 00	65·9	27 11	44 58	65·4	26 46	43 57	65·0	26 20	42 57	64·5	216	324
37	143	29 08	47 42	66·1	28 44	46 40	65·6	28 19	45 38	65·1	27 53	44 36	64·6	27 27	43 36	64·2	27 01	42 36	63·7	217	323
38	142	29 52	47 19	65·3	29 27	46 17	64·8	29 01	45 15	64·3	28 35	44 13	63·8	28 08	43 12	63·3	27 41	42 12	62·9	218	322
39	141	30 36	46 56	64·5	30 10	45 53	64·0	29 44	44 51	63·5	29 17	43 49	63·0	28 49	42 48	62·5	28 21	41 48	62·0	219	321
40	140	31 20	46 31	63·7	30 53	45 28	63·2	30 26	44 26	62·7	29 58	43 24	62·2	29 30	42 24	61·7	29 01	41 23	61·2	220	320
41	139	32 03	46 05	62·9	31 36	45 03	62·4	31 08	44 01	61·8	30 39	42 59	61·3	30 10	41 58	60·8	29 41	40 58	60·3	221	319
42	138	32 46	45 39	62·1	32 18	44 36	61·5	31 49	43 34	61·0	31 20	42 33	60·5	30 50	41 32	59·9	30 20	40 32	59·4	222	318
43	137	33 29	45 11	61·3	33 00	44 09	60·7	32 30	43 07	60·1	32 00	42 06	59·6	31 30	41 05	59·1	30 59	40 04	58·5	223	317
44	136	34 12	44 43	60·4	33 42	43 40	59·8	33 11	42 38	59·3	32 40	41 37	58·7	32 09	40 36	58·2	31 37	39 36	57·6	224	316
45	135	34 54	44 13	59·6	34 23	43 11	59·0	33 52	42 09	58·4	33 20	41 08	57·8	32 48	40 07	57·3	32 15	39 08	56·7	225	315

© British Crown Copyright 2018. All rights reserved.

LHA	F	36° A/H	36° B/P	36° Z₁/Z₂	37° A/H	37° B/P	37° Z₁/Z₂	38° A/H	38° B/P	38° Z₁/Z₂	39° A/H	39° B/P	39° Z₁/Z₂	40° A/H	40° B/P	40° Z₁/Z₂	41° A/H	41° B/P	41° Z₁/Z₂	LHA	LHA
45	135	34 54	44 13	59·6	34 23	43 11	59·0	33 52	42 09	58·4	33 20	41 08	57·8	32 48	40 07	57·3	32 15	39 08	56·7	225	315
46	134	35 35	43 43	58·7	35 04	42 40	58·1	34 32	41 38	57·5	33 59	40 37	56·9	33 26	39 37	56·4	32 53	38 38	55·8	226	314
47	133	36 17	43 11	57·8	35 44	42 09	57·2	35 12	41 07	56·6	34 38	40 06	56·0	34 04	39 06	55·5	33 30	38 07	54·9	227	313
48	132	36 57	42 39	56·9	36 24	41 36	56·2	35 51	40 35	55·6	35 17	39 34	55·0	34 42	38 34	54·5	34 07	37 35	53·9	228	312
49	131	37 38	42 05	56·0	37 04	41 03	55·3	36 30	40 01	54·7	35 55	39 01	54·1	35 19	38 01	53·5	34 43	37 03	53·0	229	311
50	130	38 18	41 30	55·0	37 43	40 28	54·4	37 08	39 27	53·7	36 32	38 27	53·1	35 56	37 27	52·5	35 19	36 29	52·0	230	310
51	129	38 57	40 54	54·0	38 22	39 52	53·4	37 46	38 51	52·8	37 09	37 51	52·1	36 32	36 52	51·6	35 55	35 54	51·0	231	309
52	128	39 36	40 17	53·0	39 00	39 15	52·4	38 23	38 14	51·8	37 46	37 15	51·1	37 08	36 16	50·6	36 30	35 18	50·0	232	308
53	127	40 15	39 38	52·0	39 38	38 37	51·4	39 00	37 36	50·8	38 22	36 37	50·1	37 43	35 39	49·5	37 04	34 42	49·0	233	307
54	126	40 53	38 58	51·0	40 15	37 57	50·4	39 36	36 57	49·7	38 57	35 58	49·1	38 18	35 01	48·5	37 38	34 04	47·9	234	306
55	125	41 30	38 17	50·0	40 52	37 17	49·3	40 12	36 17	48·7	39 32	35 18	48·1	38 52	34 21	47·4	38 11	33 25	46·9	235	305
56	124	42 07	37 35	48·9	41 28	36 35	48·2	40 47	35 36	47·6	40 07	34 38	47·0	39 26	33 41	46·4	38 44	32 45	45·8	236	304
57	123	42 44	36 51	47·9	42 03	35 51	47·2	41 22	34 53	46·5	40 41	33 55	45·9	39 59	32 59	45·3	39 16	32 04	44·7	237	303
58	122	43 19	36 06	46·8	42 38	35 07	46·1	41 56	34 09	45·4	41 14	33 12	44·8	40 31	32 16	44·2	39 48	31 22	43·6	238	302
59	121	43 54	35 20	45·6	43 12	34 21	45·0	42 29	33 24	44·3	41 46	32 27	43·7	41 03	31 32	43·1	40 19	30 39	42·5	239	301
60	120	44 29	34 32	44·5	43 46	33 34	43·9	43 02	32 37	43·2	42 18	31 42	42·5	41 34	30 47	41·9	40 49	29 54	41·3	240	300
61	119	45 02	33 43	43·3	44 18	32 45	42·7	43 34	31 49	42·0	42 49	30 56	41·4	42 04	30 01	40·8	41 18	29 09	40·2	241	299
62	118	45 35	32 52	42·1	44 51	31 55	41·5	44 05	31 00	40·8	43 20	30 06	40·2	42 34	29 14	39·6	41 47	28 22	39·0	242	298
63	117	46 07	32 00	40·9	45 22	31 04	40·3	44 36	30 10	39·6	43 49	29 17	39·0	43 03	28 25	38·4	42 15	27 35	37·8	243	297
64	116	46 39	31 06	39·7	45 52	30 11	39·0	45 06	29 18	38·4	44 18	28 26	37·8	43 31	27 35	37·2	42 43	26 46	36·6	244	296
65	115	47 09	30 11	38·4	46 22	29 17	37·8	45 35	28 25	37·1	44 47	27 34	36·5	43 58	26 44	36·0	43 09	25 56	35·4	245	295
66	114	47 39	29 14	37·1	46 51	28 21	36·5	46 03	27 30	35·9	45 14	26 40	35·3	44 25	25 52	34·7	43 35	25 05	34·2	246	294
67	113	48 08	28 16	35·8	47 19	27 24	35·2	46 30	26 34	34·6	45 40	25 45	34·0	44 50	24 58	33·4	44 00	24 12	32·9	247	293
68	112	48 36	27 17	34·5	47 46	26 26	33·9	46 56	25 37	33·3	46 06	24 50	32·7	45 15	24 03	32·2	44 24	23 19	31·6	248	292
69	111	49 03	26 15	33·1	48 13	25 26	32·5	47 22	24 38	31·9	46 31	23 52	31·4	45 39	23 08	30·8	44 48	22 24	30·3	249	291
70	110	49 29	25 15	31·8	48 38	24 25	31·1	47 46	23 39	30·6	46 55	22 54	30·0	46 03	22 11	29·5	45 10	21 29	29·0	250	290
71	109	49 54	24 08	30·4	49 02	23 22	29·8	48 10	22 37	29·2	47 17	21 54	28·7	46 25	21 12	28·2	45 32	20 32	27·7	251	289
72	108	50 18	23 02	29·0	49 25	22 18	28·4	48 33	21 35	27·8	47 39	20 53	27·3	46 46	20 13	26·8	45 52	19 34	26·3	252	288
73	107	50 41	21 55	27·5	49 48	21 12	26·9	48 54	20 31	26·4	48 00	19 51	25·9	47 06	19 13	25·4	46 12	18 35	25·0	253	287
74	106	51 03	20 47	26·0	50 09	20 06	25·5	49 15	19 26	25·0	48 20	18 48	24·5	47 25	18 11	24·0	46 30	17 36	23·6	254	286
75	105	51 24	19 36	24·5	50 29	18 57	24·0	49 34	18 20	23·5	48 39	17 43	23·1	47 44	17 09	22·6	46 48	16 35	22·2	255	285
76	104	51 43	18 25	23·0	50 48	17 48	22·5	49 52	17 12	22·0	48 57	16 37	21·6	48 01	16 05	21·2	47 05	15 33	20·8	256	284
77	103	52 02	17 12	21·4	51 06	16 37	21·0	50 09	16 04	20·6	49 13	15 31	20·1	48 17	15 00	19·8	47 20	14 31	19·4	257	283
78	102	52 19	15 58	19·9	51 22	15 25	19·5	50 25	14 54	19·0	49 29	14 24	18·7	48 32	13 55	18·3	47 35	13 27	18·0	258	282
79	101	52 35	14 43	18·3	51 37	14 13	17·9	50 40	13 43	17·5	49 43	13 16	17·2	48 46	12 49	16·8	47 48	12 23	16·5	259	281
80	100	52 49	13 27	16·7	51 52	12 59	16·3	50 54	12 32	16·0	49 56	12 06	15·7	48 58	11 42	15·3	48 01	11 18	15·0	260	280
81	99	53 02	12 09	15·1	52 04	11 44	14·7	51 06	11 19	14·4	50 08	10 56	14·1	49 10	10 34	13·8	48 12	10 12	13·6	261	279
82	98	53 14	10 51	13·4	52 16	10 28	13·1	51 18	10 06	12·9	50 19	9 45	12·6	49 20	9 25	12·3	48 21	9 06	12·1	262	278
83	97	53 25	9 31	11·8	52 26	9 11	11·5	51 27	8 52	11·3	50 29	8 34	11·0	49 30	8 16	10·8	48 31	7 59	10·6	263	277
84	96	53 34	8 11	10·1	52 35	7 54	9·9	51 36	7 37	9·7	50 37	7 21	9·5	49 38	7 06	9·3	48 38	6 51	9·1	264	276
85	95	53 42	6 50	8·5	52 42	6 36	8·3	51 43	6 22	8·1	50 44	6 09	7·9	49 44	5 56	7·8	48 45	5 44	7·6	265	275
86	94	53 49	5 29	6·8	52 49	5 17	6·6	51 49	5 06	6·5	50 50	4 55	6·3	49 50	4 45	6·2	48 50	4 35	6·1	266	274
87	93	53 54	4 07	5·1	52 54	3 58	5·0	51 54	3 50	4·9	50 54	3 42	4·8	49 54	3 34	4·7	48 54	3 27	4·6	267	273
88	92	53 57	2 45	3·4	52 57	2 39	3·3	51 57	2 33	3·2	50 57	2 28	3·2	49 57	2 23	3·1	48 57	2 18	3·0	268	272
89	91	53 59	1 23	1·7	52 59	1 20	1·7	51 59	1 17	1·6	50 59	1 14	1·6	49 59	1 11	1·6	48 59	1 09	1·5	269	271
90	90	54 00	0 00	0·0	53 00	0 00	0·0	52 00	0 00	0·0	51 00	0 00	0·0	50 00	0 00	0·0	49 00	0 00	0·0	270	270

N. Lat.: for LHA > 180° .... Zₙ = Z
for LHA < 180° .... Zₙ = 360° − Z

S. Lat.: for LHA > 180° .... Zₙ = 180° − Z
for LHA < 180° .... Zₙ = 180° + Z

© British Crown Copyright 2018. All rights reserved.

SIGHT REDUCTION TABLE

B: (–) for 90° < LHA < 270°
Dec:(–) for Lat. contrary name

Z₁: same sign as B
Z₂: (–) for F > 90°

LHA/F	A	42° A/H	42° B/P	42° Z₁/Z₂	43° A/H	43° B/P	43° Z₁/Z₂	44° A/H	44° B/P	44° Z₁/Z₂	45° A/H	45° B/P	45° Z₁/Z₂	46° A/H	46° B/P	46° Z₁/Z₂	47° A/H	47° B/P	47° Z₁/Z₂	A	LHA
0	180	0 00	48 00	90·0	0 00	47 00	90·0	0 00	46 00	90·0	0 00	45 00	90·0	0 00	44 00	90·0	0 00	43 00	90·0	180	360
1	179	0 45	48 00	89·3	0 44	47 00	89·3	0 43	46 00	89·3	0 42	45 00	89·3	0 42	44 00	89·3	0 41	43 00	89·3	181	359
2	178	1 29	47 59	88·7	1 28	46 59	88·6	1 26	45 59	88·6	1 25	44 59	88·6	1 23	43 59	88·6	1 22	42 59	88·5	182	358
3	177	2 14	47 58	88·0	2 12	46 58	88·0	2 09	45 58	87·9	2 07	44 58	87·9	2 05	43 58	87·8	2 03	42 58	87·8	183	357
4	176	2 58	47 56	87·3	2 55	46 56	87·3	2 53	45 56	87·2	2 50	44 56	87·2	2 47	43 56	87·1	2 44	42 56	87·1	184	356
5	175	3 43	47 53	86·6	3 39	46 53	86·6	3 36	45 53	86·5	3 32	44 53	86·5	3 28	43 53	86·4	3 24	42 53	86·3	185	355
6	174	4 27	47 51	86·0	4 23	46 51	85·9	4 19	45 51	85·8	4 14	44 51	85·7	4 10	43 51	85·7	4 05	42 51	85·6	186	354
7	173	5 12	47 47	85·3	5 07	46 47	85·2	5 02	45 47	85·1	4 57	44 47	85·0	4 51	43 47	85·0	4 46	42 47	84·9	187	353
8	172	5 56	47 43	84·6	5 51	46 43	84·6	5 45	45 43	84·4	5 39	44 43	84·3	5 33	43 43	84·2	5 27	42 43	84·1	188	352
9	171	6 41	47 39	84·0	6 34	46 39	84·0	6 28	45 39	83·7	6 21	44 39	83·6	6 14	43 39	83·5	6 07	42 39	83·4	189	351
10	170	7 25	47 34	83·3	7 18	46 34	83·3	7 11	45 34	83·0	7 03	44 34	82·9	6 56	43 34	82·8	6 48	42 34	82·7	190	350
11	169	8 09	47 28	82·6	8 01	46 28	82·6	7 53	45 28	82·3	7 45	44 28	82·2	7 37	43 28	82·0	7 29	42 28	81·9	191	349
12	168	8 53	47 22	81·9	8 45	46 22	81·8	8 36	45 22	81·6	8 27	44 22	81·5	8 18	43 22	81·3	8 09	42 22	81·2	192	348
13	167	9 37	47 16	81·2	9 28	46 15	81·1	9 19	45 15	80·9	9 09	44 15	80·7	8 59	43 15	80·6	8 49	42 16	80·4	193	347
14	166	10 21	47 08	80·5	10 11	46 08	80·5	10 01	45 08	80·2	9 51	44 08	80·0	9 40	43 08	79·8	9 30	42 08	79·7	194	346
15	165	11 05	47 01	79·8	10 55	46 00	79·8	10 44	45 00	79·5	10 33	44 00	79·3	10 21	43 00	79·1	10 10	42 01	78·9	195	345
16	164	11 49	46 52	79·1	11 38	45 52	79·1	11 26	44 52	78·7	11 14	43 52	78·5	11 02	42 52	78·3	10 50	41 52	78·2	196	344
17	163	12 33	46 43	78·4	12 21	45 43	78·2	12 08	44 43	78·0	11 56	43 43	77·8	11 43	42 43	77·6	11 30	41 44	77·4	197	343
18	162	13 17	46 34	77·7	13 04	45 34	77·5	12 51	44 34	77·3	12 37	43 34	77·1	12 24	42 34	76·8	12 10	41 34	76·6	198	342
19	161	14 00	46 24	77·0	13 46	45 24	76·8	13 33	44 24	76·5	13 19	43 24	76·3	13 04	42 24	76·1	12 50	41 24	75·9	199	341
20	160	14 43	46 13	76·3	14 29	45 13	76·1	14 15	44 13	75·8	14 00	43 13	75·6	13 45	42 13	75·3	13 29	41 14	75·1	200	340
21	159	15 27	46 02	75·6	15 12	45 02	75·3	14 56	44 02	75·1	14 41	43 02	74·8	14 25	42 02	74·6	14 09	41 03	74·3	201	339
22	158	16 10	45 50	74·9	15 54	44 50	74·6	15 38	43 50	74·3	15 22	42 50	74·1	15 05	41 50	73·8	14 48	40 51	73·5	202	338
23	157	16 53	45 38	74·1	16 36	44 38	73·9	16 19	43 38	73·6	16 02	42 38	73·3	15 45	41 38	73·0	15 27	40 39	72·8	203	337
24	156	17 36	45 25	73·4	17 18	44 25	73·1	17 01	43 25	72·8	16 43	42 25	72·5	16 25	41 25	72·2	16 06	40 26	72·0	204	336
25	155	18 18	45 11	72·7	18 00	44 11	72·4	17 42	43 11	72·1	17 23	42 11	71·8	17 04	41 12	71·5	16 45	40 12	71·2	205	335
26	154	19 01	44 57	71·9	18 42	43 57	71·6	18 23	42 57	71·3	18 03	41 57	71·0	17 44	40 57	70·7	17 24	39 58	70·4	206	334
27	153	19 43	44 42	71·2	19 24	43 42	70·8	19 04	42 42	70·5	18 43	41 42	70·2	18 23	40 43	69·9	18 02	39 43	69·6	207	333
28	152	20 25	44 26	70·4	20 05	43 26	70·1	19 44	42 26	69·7	19 23	41 27	69·4	19 02	40 27	69·1	18 40	39 28	68·8	208	332
29	151	21 07	44 10	69·6	20 46	43 10	69·3	20 25	42 10	68·9	20 03	41 10	68·6	19 41	40 11	68·3	19 18	39 12	67·9	209	331
30	150	21 49	43 53	68·9	21 27	42 53	68·5	21 05	41 53	68·1	20 42	40 54	67·8	20 20	39 54	67·4	19 56	38 55	67·1	210	330
31	149	22 30	43 35	68·1	22 08	42 35	67·7	21 45	41 36	67·3	21 21	40 36	67·0	20 58	39 37	66·6	20 34	38 38	66·3	211	329
32	148	23 11	43 17	67·3	22 48	42 17	66·9	22 24	41 17	66·5	22 00	40 18	66·2	21 36	39 19	65·8	21 11	38 20	65·4	212	328
33	147	23 53	42 58	66·5	23 28	41 58	66·1	23 04	40 58	65·7	22 39	39 59	65·3	22 14	39 00	65·0	21 48	38 02	64·6	213	327
34	146	24 33	42 38	65·7	24 08	41 38	65·3	23 43	40 39	64·9	23 17	39 40	64·5	22 51	38 41	64·1	22 25	37 42	63·7	214	326
35	145	25 14	42 18	64·9	24 48	41 18	64·5	24 22	40 18	64·1	23 56	39 19	63·7	23 29	38 21	63·3	23 02	37 23	62·9	215	325
36	144	25 54	41 56	64·1	25 28	40 57	63·6	25 01	39 57	63·2	24 34	38 58	62·8	24 06	38 00	62·4	23 38	37 02	62·0	216	324
37	143	26 34	41 34	63·2	26 07	40 35	62·8	25 39	39 35	62·4	25 11	38 38	61·9	24 43	37 38	61·5	24 14	36 41	61·1	217	323
38	142	27 14	41 11	62·4	26 46	40 12	61·9	26 17	39 13	61·5	25 48	38 14	61·1	25 19	37 16	60·7	24 50	36 19	60·3	218	322
39	141	27 53	40 48	61·5	27 24	39 48	61·1	26 55	38 50	60·7	26 25	37 51	60·2	25 55	36 53	59·8	25 25	35 56	59·4	219	321
40	140	28 32	40 23	60·7	28 02	39 24	60·2	27 32	38 26	59·8	27 02	37 27	59·3	26 31	36 29	58·9	26 00	35 32	58·5	220	320
41	139	29 11	39 58	59·8	28 40	38 59	59·3	28 10	38 01	58·9	27 38	37 03	58·4	27 07	36 05	58·0	26 35	35 08	57·6	221	319
42	138	29 49	39 32	58·9	29 18	38 33	58·4	28 46	37 35	58·0	28 14	36 37	57·5	27 42	35 40	57·1	27 09	34 43	56·6	222	318
43	137	30 27	39 05	58·0	29 55	38 06	57·5	29 23	37 08	57·1	28 50	36 11	56·6	28 17	35 14	56·1	27 43	34 18	55·7	223	317
44	136	31 05	38 37	57·1	30 32	37 39	56·6	29 59	36 41	56·1	29 25	35 44	55·7	28 51	34 47	55·2	28 17	33 53	54·8	224	316
45	135	31 42	38 09	56·2	31 08	37 10	55·7	30 34	36 13	55·2	30 00	35 16	54·7	29 25	34 20	54·3	28 50	33 24	53·8	225	315

© British Crown Copyright 2018. All rights reserved.

Lat./A	LHA/F	42° A/H	42° B/P	42° Z₁/Z₂	43° A/H	43° B/P	43° Z₁/Z₂	44° A/H	44° B/P	44° Z₁/Z₂	45° A/H	45° B/P	45° Z₁/Z₂	46° A/H	46° B/P	46° Z₁/Z₂	47° A/H	47° B/P	47° Z₁/Z₂	LHA	Lat./A
135	45	31 42	38 09	56·2	31 08	37 10	55·7	30 34	36 13	55·2	30 00	35 16	54·7	29 25	34 20	54·3	28 50	33 24	53·8	225	315
134	46	32 19	37 39	55·3	31 45	36 41	54·8	31 10	35 44	54·3	30 34	34 47	53·8	29 59	33 51	53·3	29 23	32 56	52·9	226	314
133	47	32 55	37 08	54·3	32 20	36 11	53·8	31 45	35 14	53·3	31 08	34 18	52·8	30 32	33 22	52·4	29 55	32 27	51·9	227	313
132	48	33 31	36 37	53·4	32 55	35 40	52·9	32 19	34 43	52·3	31 42	33 47	51·9	31 05	32 52	51·4	30 27	31 58	50·9	228	312
131	49	34 07	36 05	52·4	33 30	35 08	51·9	32 53	34 11	51·4	32 15	33 16	50·9	31 37	32 21	50·4	30 59	31 27	49·9	229	311
130	50	34 42	35 31	51·4	34 04	34 35	50·9	33 26	33 39	50·4	32 48	32 44	49·9	32 09	31 50	49·4	31 30	30 56	48·9	230	310
129	51	35 17	34 57	50·4	34 38	34 01	49·9	33 59	33 05	49·4	33 20	32 11	48·9	32 40	31 17	48·4	32 00	30 24	47·9	231	309
128	52	35 51	34 22	49·4	35 11	33 26	48·9	34 32	32 31	48·4	33 52	31 37	47·9	33 11	30 44	47·4	32 30	29 52	46·9	232	308
127	53	36 24	33 45	48·4	35 44	32 50	47·9	35 04	31 56	47·3	34 23	31 02	46·8	33 42	30 10	46·3	33 00	29 18	45·9	233	307
126	54	36 57	33 08	47·4	36 17	32 13	46·8	35 35	31 20	46·3	34 54	30 27	45·8	34 12	29 35	45·3	33 29	28 44	44·8	234	306
125	55	37 30	32 30	46·3	36 48	31 35	45·8	36 06	30 43	45·2	35 24	29 50	44·7	34 41	28 59	44·2	33 58	28 08	43·8	235	305
124	56	38 02	31 51	45·2	37 19	30 57	44·7	36 37	30 04	44·2	35 53	29 13	43·6	35 10	28 22	43·2	34 26	27 32	42·7	236	304
123	57	38 33	31 10	44·1	37 50	30 17	43·6	37 06	29 25	43·1	36 22	28 34	42·6	35 38	27 45	42·1	34 53	26 56	41·6	237	303
122	58	39 04	30 29	43·0	38 20	29 36	42·5	37 36	28 45	42·0	36 51	27 55	41·5	36 06	27 06	41·0	35 20	26 18	40·5	238	302
121	59	39 34	29 46	41·9	38 49	28 55	41·4	38 04	28 04	40·9	37 19	27 15	40·4	36 33	26 27	39·9	35 46	25 39	39·4	239	301
120	60	40 04	29 03	40·8	39 18	28 12	40·2	38 32	27 22	39·7	37 46	26 34	39·2	36 59	25 46	38·8	36 12	25 00	38·3	240	300
119	61	40 32	28 18	39·6	39 46	27 28	39·1	38 59	26 39	38·6	38 12	25 52	38·1	37 25	25 05	37·6	36 37	24 20	37·2	241	299
118	62	41 00	27 32	38·5	40 13	26 43	37·9	39 26	25 56	37·4	38 38	25 09	36·9	37 50	24 23	36·5	37 02	23 39	36·0	242	298
117	63	41 28	26 45	37·3	40 40	25 58	36·8	39 52	25 11	36·3	39 03	24 25	35·8	38 14	23 40	35·3	37 25	22 56	34·9	243	297
116	64	41 54	25 58	36·1	41 06	25 11	35·6	40 17	24 25	35·1	39 28	23 40	34·6	38 38	22 57	34·1	37 48	22 14	33·7	244	296
115	65	42 20	25 09	34·9	41 31	24 23	34·4	40 41	23 38	33·9	39 51	22 55	33·4	39 01	22 12	33·0	38 11	21 31	32·5	245	295
114	66	42 45	24 19	33·6	41 55	23 34	33·1	41 05	22 50	32·7	40 14	22 08	32·2	39 23	21 27	31·8	38 32	20 46	31·3	246	294
113	67	43 10	23 28	32·4	42 19	22 44	31·9	41 28	22 02	31·4	40 37	21 21	31·0	39 45	20 40	30·5	38 53	20 01	30·1	247	293
112	68	43 33	22 35	31·1	42 42	21 53	30·6	41 50	21 12	30·2	40 58	20 32	29·7	40 06	19 53	29·3	39 13	19 15	28·9	248	292
111	69	43 56	21 42	29·8	43 04	21 01	29·4	42 11	20 22	28·9	41 19	19 43	28·5	40 26	19 05	28·1	39 33	18 29	27·7	249	291
110	70	44 18	20 48	28·5	43 25	20 08	28·1	42 32	19 30	27·7	41 38	18 53	27·2	40 45	18 17	26·8	39 51	17 41	26·5	250	290
109	71	44 38	19 53	27·2	43 45	19 15	26·8	42 51	18 38	26·4	41 57	18 02	26·0	41 03	17 27	25·6	40 09	16 53	25·2	251	289
108	72	44 58	18 57	25·9	44 04	18 20	25·5	43 10	17 45	25·1	42 16	17 10	24·7	41 21	16 37	24·3	40 26	16 05	24·0	252	288
107	73	45 17	17 59	24·6	44 23	17 24	24·1	43 28	16 51	23·8	42 33	16 18	23·4	41 38	15 46	23·0	40 42	15 15	22·7	253	287
106	74	45 35	17 01	23·2	44 40	16 28	22·8	43 45	15 56	22·4	42 49	15 25	22·1	41 54	14 54	21·7	40 58	14 25	21·4	254	286
105	75	45 53	16 02	21·8	44 57	15 31	21·4	44 01	15 00	21·1	43 05	14 31	20·8	42 09	14 02	20·4	41 12	13 34	20·1	255	285
104	76	46 09	15 02	20·4	45 12	14 33	20·1	44 16	14 04	19·7	43 19	13 36	19·4	42 23	13 09	19·1	41 26	12 43	18·8	256	284
103	77	46 24	14 02	19·0	45 27	13 34	18·7	44 30	13 07	18·4	43 33	12 41	18·1	42 36	12 15	17·8	41 39	11 51	17·5	257	283
102	78	46 38	13 00	17·6	45 40	12 34	17·3	44 43	12 09	17·0	43 46	11 45	16·7	42 48	11 21	16·5	41 51	10 58	16·2	258	282
101	79	46 51	11 58	16·2	45 53	11 34	15·9	44 55	11 11	15·6	43 57	10 48	15·4	43 00	10 26	15·1	42 02	10 05	14·9	259	281
100	80	47 03	10 55	14·8	46 04	10 33	14·5	45 06	10 12	14·2	44 08	9 51	14·0	43 10	9 31	13·8	42 12	9 12	13·6	260	280
99	81	47 13	9 51	13·3	46 15	9 31	13·1	45 16	9 12	12·8	44 18	8 53	12·6	43 19	8 35	12·4	42 21	8 18	12·2	261	279
98	82	47 23	8 47	11·9	46 24	8 29	11·6	45 26	8 12	11·4	44 27	7 55	11·2	43 28	7 39	11·1	42 30	7 24	10·9	262	278
97	83	47 32	7 42	10·4	46 33	7 27	10·2	45 34	7 12	10·0	44 34	6 57	9·9	43 35	6 43	9·7	42 36	6 29	9·5	263	277
96	84	47 39	6 37	8·9	46 40	6 24	8·8	45 41	6 11	8·6	44 41	5 58	8·5	43 42	5 46	8·3	42 42	5 34	8·1	264	276
95	85	47 46	5 32	7·4	46 46	5 20	7·3	45 46	5 11	7·2	44 47	4 59	7·1	43 47	4 49	6·9	42 47	4 39	6·8	265	275
94	86	47 51	4 26	6·0	46 51	4 17	5·9	45 51	4 08	5·7	44 52	3 59	5·6	43 52	3 51	5·6	42 52	3 43	5·5	266	274
93	87	47 55	3 20	4·5	46 55	3 13	4·4	45 55	3 06	4·3	44 55	3 00	4·2	43 55	2 54	4·2	42 56	2 48	4·1	267	273
92	88	47 58	2 13	3·0	46 58	2 09	2·9	45 58	2 04	2·9	44 58	2 00	2·8	43 58	1 56	2·8	42 58	1 52	2·7	268	272
91	89	47 59	1 07	1·5	46 59	1 04	1·5	45 59	1 02	1·4	44 59	1 00	1·4	43 59	0 58	1·4	43 00	0 56	1·4	269	271
90	90	48 00	0 00	0·0	47 00	0 00	0·0	46 00	0 00	0·0	45 00	0 00	0·0	44 00	0 00	0·0	43 00	0 00	0·0	270	270

N. Lat: for LHA > 180° ... Zₙ = Z
for LHA < 180° ... Zₙ = 360° − Z

S. Lat: for LHA > 180° ... Zₙ = 180° − Z
for LHA < 180° ... Zₙ = 180° + Z

© British Crown Copyright 2018. All rights reserved.

SIGHT REDUCTION TABLE

B: (−) for 90° < LHA < 270°
Dec:(−) for Lat. contrary name

Z₁: same sign as B
Z₂:(−) for F > 90°

LHA/F	A	48° A/H	48° B/P	48° Z_1/Z_2	49° A/H	49° B/P	49° Z_1/Z_2	50° A/H	50° B/P	50° Z_1/Z_2	51° A/H	51° B/P	51° Z_1/Z_2	52° A/H	52° B/P	52° Z_1/Z_2	53° A/H	53° B/P	53° Z_1/Z_2	LHA
0	180	0 00	42 00	90·0	0 00	41 00	90·0	0 00	40 00	90·0	0 00	39 00	90·0	0 00	38 00	90·0	0 00	37 00	90·0	180 360
1	179	0 40	42 00	89·3	0 39	41 00	89·3	0 39	40 00	89·3	0 38	39 00	89·3	0 37	38 00	89·2	0 36	37 00	89·2	181 359
2	178	1 20	41 59	88·5	1 19	40 59	88·5	1 17	39 59	88·5	1 16	38 59	88·5	1 14	37 59	88·4	1 12	36 59	88·4	182 358
3	177	2 01	41 58	87·8	1 58	40 58	87·7	1 56	39 58	87·7	1 53	38 58	87·7	1 51	37 58	87·6	1 48	36 58	87·6	183 357
4	176	2 41	41 56	87·0	2 37	40 56	87·0	2 34	39 56	86·9	2 31	38 56	86·9	2 28	37 56	86·8	2 24	36 56	86·8	184 356
5	175	3 21	41 53	86·3	3 17	40 54	86·2	3 13	39 54	86·2	3 09	38 54	86·1	3 05	37 54	86·1	3 00	36 54	86·0	185 355
6	174	4 01	41 51	85·5	3 56	40 51	85·5	3 51	39 51	85·4	3 46	38 51	85·4	3 41	37 51	85·3	3 36	36 51	85·2	186 354
7	173	4 41	41 47	84·7	4 35	40 47	84·7	4 30	39 47	84·6	4 24	38 48	84·6	4 18	37 48	84·5	4 12	36 48	84·4	187 353
8	172	5 21	41 43	84·0	5 14	40 43	83·9	5 08	39 43	83·9	5 01	38 44	83·8	4 55	37 44	83·7	4 48	36 44	83·6	188 352
9	171	6 01	41 39	83·3	5 53	40 39	83·2	5 46	39 39	83·1	5 39	38 39	83·0	5 32	37 39	82·9	5 24	36 40	82·8	189 351
10	170	6 40	41 34	82·5	6 32	40 34	82·4	6 25	39 34	82·3	6 16	38 34	82·2	6 08	37 35	82·1	6 00	36 35	82·0	190 350
11	169	7 20	41 28	81·8	7 11	40 28	81·7	7 03	39 29	81·5	6 54	38 29	81·4	6 45	37 29	81·3	6 36	36 29	81·2	191 349
12	168	8 00	41 22	81·0	7 50	40 22	80·9	7 41	39 23	80·8	7 31	38 23	80·6	7 21	37 23	80·5	7 11	36 24	80·4	192 348
13	167	8 39	41 16	80·3	8 29	40 16	80·1	8 19	39 16	80·0	8 08	38 16	79·8	7 58	37 17	79·7	7 47	36 17	79·6	193 347
14	166	9 19	41 09	79·5	9 08	40 09	79·3	8 57	39 09	79·2	8 45	38 09	79·0	8 34	37 10	78·9	8 22	36 10	78·7	194 346
15	165	9 58	41 01	78·7	9 47	40 01	78·6	9 35	39 02	78·4	9 22	38 02	78·2	9 10	37 02	78·1	8 58	36 03	77·9	195 345
16	164	10 38	40 53	78·0	10 25	39 53	77·8	10 12	38 54	77·6	9 59	37 54	77·4	9 46	36 54	77·3	9 33	35 55	77·1	196 344
17	163	11 17	40 44	77·2	11 04	39 44	77·0	10 50	38 45	76·8	10 36	37 45	76·6	10 22	36 46	76·5	10 08	35 47	76·3	197 343
18	162	11 56	40 34	76·4	11 42	39 35	76·2	11 27	38 35	76·0	11 13	37 36	75·8	10 58	36 37	75·6	10 43	35 38	75·5	198 342
19	161	12 35	40 25	75·6	12 20	39 25	75·4	12 05	38 26	75·2	11 49	37 26	75·0	11 34	36 27	74·8	11 18	35 28	74·6	199 341
20	160	13 14	40 14	74·9	12 58	39 15	74·6	12 42	38 16	74·4	12 26	37 16	74·2	12 09	36 17	74·0	11 53	35 18	73·8	200 340
21	159	13 52	40 03	74·1	13 36	39 04	73·8	13 19	38 04	73·6	13 02	37 05	73·4	12 45	36 06	73·2	12 27	35 08	73·0	201 339
22	158	14 31	39 51	73·3	14 14	38 52	73·0	13 56	37 53	72·8	13 38	36 54	72·6	13 20	35 55	72·3	13 02	34 57	72·1	202 338
23	157	15 09	39 39	72·5	14 51	38 40	72·2	14 33	37 41	72·0	14 14	36 42	71·7	13 55	35 43	71·5	13 36	34 45	71·3	203 337
24	156	15 48	39 26	71·7	15 29	38 27	71·4	15 09	37 28	71·2	14 50	36 30	70·9	14 30	35 31	70·7	14 10	34 33	70·4	204 336
25	155	16 26	39 13	70·9	16 06	38 14	70·6	15 46	37 14	70·3	15 25	36 17	70·1	15 05	35 18	69·8	14 44	34 20	69·6	205 335
26	154	17 03	38 59	70·1	16 43	38 00	69·8	16 22	37 01	69·5	16 01	36 03	69·2	15 39	35 05	69·0	15 18	34 07	68·7	206 334
27	153	17 41	38 44	69·3	17 20	37 46	69·0	16 58	36 47	68·7	16 36	35 49	68·4	16 14	34 51	68·1	15 51	33 53	67·9	207 333
28	152	18 19	38 29	68·4	17 56	37 30	68·1	17 34	36 32	67·8	17 11	35 34	67·5	16 48	34 36	67·3	16 25	33 38	67·0	208 332
29	151	18 56	38 13	67·6	18 33	37 15	67·3	18 09	36 16	67·0	17 46	35 18	66·7	17 22	34 21	66·4	16 58	33 23	66·1	209 331
30	150	19 33	37 57	66·8	19 09	36 58	66·5	18 45	36 00	66·1	18 20	35 03	65·8	17 56	34 05	65·5	17 31	33 08	65·2	210 330
31	149	20 10	37 40	65·9	19 45	36 41	65·6	19 20	35 44	65·3	18 55	34 46	65·0	18 29	33 49	64·7	18 03	32 52	64·4	211 329
32	148	20 46	37 22	65·1	20 21	36 24	64·8	19 55	35 26	64·4	19 29	34 29	64·1	19 02	33 32	63·8	18 36	32 35	63·5	212 328
33	147	21 22	37 03	64·2	20 56	36 06	63·9	20 30	35 08	63·6	20 03	34 11	63·2	19 35	33 14	62·9	19 08	32 18	62·6	213 327
34	146	21 58	36 44	63·4	21 31	35 47	63·0	21 04	34 49	62·7	20 36	33 53	62·3	20 08	32 56	62·0	19 40	32 00	61·7	214 326
35	145	22 34	36 25	62·5	22 06	35 27	62·1	21 38	34 30	61·8	21 10	33 33	61·4	20 41	32 37	61·1	20 12	31 41	60·8	215 325
36	144	23 10	36 04	61·6	22 41	35 07	61·3	22 12	34 10	60·9	21 43	33 14	60·5	21 13	32 18	60·2	20 43	31 22	59·9	216 324
37	143	23 45	35 43	60·8	23 15	34 46	60·4	22 45	33 49	60·0	22 15	32 53	59·6	21 45	31 58	59·3	21 14	31 02	59·0	217 323
38	142	24 20	35 21	59·9	23 49	34 25	59·5	23 19	33 28	59·1	22 48	32 31	58·7	22 16	31 37	58·4	21 45	30 42	58·0	218 322
39	141	24 54	34 59	59·0	24 23	34 02	58·6	23 52	33 07	58·2	23 20	32 11	57·8	22 48	31 16	57·5	22 15	30 21	57·1	219 321
40	140	25 28	34 36	58·1	24 57	33 40	57·7	24 24	32 44	57·3	23 52	31 49	56·9	23 19	30 54	56·5	22 45	30 00	56·2	220 320
41	139	26 02	34 12	57·1	25 30	33 16	56·7	24 57	32 21	56·3	24 23	31 26	56·0	23 49	30 32	55·6	23 15	29 38	55·2	221 319
42	138	26 36	33 47	56·2	26 02	32 52	55·8	25 28	31 57	55·4	24 54	31 02	55·0	24 20	30 08	54·6	23 45	29 15	54·3	222 318
43	137	27 09	33 22	55·3	26 35	32 27	54·9	26 00	31 32	54·5	25 25	30 38	54·1	24 50	29 45	53·7	24 14	28 52	53·4	223 317
44	136	27 42	32 56	54·3	27 07	32 01	53·9	26 31	31 07	53·5	25 55	30 13	53·1	25 19	29 20	52·7	24 43	28 28	52·4	224 316
45	135	28 14	32 29	53·4	27 38	31 35	53·0	27 02	30 41	52·5	26 25	29 48	52·1	25 48	28 55	51·8	25 11	28 03	51·4	225 315

© British Crown Copyright 2018. All rights reserved.

LHA	A	48° A/H	48° B/P	48° Z_1/Z_2	49° A/H	49° B/P	49° Z_1/Z_2	50° A/H	50° B/P	50° Z_1/Z_2	51° A/H	51° B/P	51° Z_1/Z_2	52° A/H	52° B/P	52° Z_1/Z_2	53° A/H	53° B/P	53° Z_1/Z_2	LHA	A
45	135	28 14	32 29	53.4	27 38	31 35	53.0	27 02	30 41	52.5	26 25	29 48	52.1	25 48	28 55	51.8	25 11	28 03	51.4	225	315
46	134	28 46	32 01	52.4	28 10	31 08	52.0	27 32	30 14	51.6	26 55	29 22	51.2	26 17	28 29	50.8	25 39	27 38	50.4	226	314
47	133	29 18	31 33	51.4	28 40	30 40	51.0	28 02	29 47	50.6	27 24	28 55	50.2	26 46	28 03	49.8	26 07	27 12	49.4	227	313
48	132	29 49	31 04	50.5	29 11	30 11	50.0	28 32	29 19	49.6	27 53	28 27	49.2	27 14	27 36	48.8	26 34	26 46	48.4	228	312
49	131	30 20	30 34	49.5	29 41	29 42	49.0	29 01	28 50	48.6	28 21	27 59	48.2	27 41	27 08	47.8	27 01	26 18	47.4	229	311
50	130	30 50	30 04	48.5	30 10	29 12	48.0	29 30	28 20	47.6	28 49	27 30	47.2	28 08	26 40	46.8	27 27	25 51	46.4	230	310
51	129	31 20	29 32	47.5	30 39	28 41	47.0	29 58	27 50	46.6	29 17	27 00	46.2	28 35	26 11	45.8	27 53	25 22	45.4	231	309
52	128	31 49	29 00	46.4	31 08	28 09	46.0	30 26	27 19	45.6	29 44	26 30	45.2	29 01	25 41	44.8	28 19	24 53	44.4	232	308
53	127	32 18	28 27	45.4	31 36	27 37	45.0	30 53	26 48	44.5	30 10	25 59	44.1	29 27	25 11	43.7	28 44	24 24	43.3	233	307
54	126	32 46	27 53	44.4	32 03	27 04	43.9	31 20	26 15	43.5	30 36	25 27	43.1	29 52	24 40	42.7	29 08	23 53	42.3	234	306
55	125	33 14	27 19	43.3	32 30	26 30	42.9	31 46	25 42	42.4	31 02	24 55	42.0	30 17	24 08	41.6	29 32	23 23	41.2	235	305
56	124	33 42	26 44	42.2	32 57	25 56	41.8	32 12	25 08	41.4	31 27	24 22	41.0	30 41	23 36	40.6	29 56	22 51	40.2	236	304
57	123	34 08	26 07	41.1	33 23	25 20	40.7	32 37	24 34	40.3	31 51	23 48	39.9	31 05	23 03	39.5	30 19	22 19	39.1	237	303
58	122	34 34	25 30	40.1	33 48	24 44	39.6	33 02	23 58	39.2	32 15	23 14	38.8	31 28	22 29	38.4	30 41	21 46	38.0	238	302
59	121	35 00	24 53	39.0	34 13	24 07	38.5	33 26	23 22	38.1	32 39	22 38	37.7	31 51	21 55	37.3	31 03	21 13	37.0	239	301
60	120	35 25	24 15	37.8	34 37	23 29	37.4	33 50	22 46	37.0	33 02	22 03	36.6	32 13	21 20	36.2	31 25	20 39	35.9	240	300
61	119	35 49	23 35	36.7	35 01	22 51	36.3	34 12	22 08	35.9	33 24	21 26	35.5	32 35	20 45	35.1	31 46	20 04	34.8	241	299
62	118	36 13	22 55	35.6	35 24	22 11	35.2	34 35	21 30	34.8	33 45	20 49	34.4	32 56	20 09	34.0	32 06	19 29	33.7	242	298
63	117	36 36	22 14	34.4	35 46	21 32	34.0	34 56	20 51	33.6	34 06	20 11	33.3	33 16	19 32	32.9	32 26	18 53	32.5	243	297
64	116	36 58	21 32	33.3	36 08	20 52	32.9	35 17	20 12	32.5	34 27	19 33	32.1	33 36	18 54	31.8	32 45	18 17	31.4	244	296
65	115	37 20	20 50	32.1	36 29	20 10	31.7	35 38	19 32	31.3	34 47	18 54	31.0	33 55	18 16	30.6	33 03	17 40	30.3	245	295
66	114	37 41	20 07	30.9	36 50	19 28	30.5	35 58	18 51	30.2	35 06	18 14	29.8	34 14	17 38	29.5	33 21	17 02	29.1	246	294
67	113	38 01	19 23	29.7	37 09	18 46	29.4	36 17	18 09	29.0	35 24	17 33	28.6	34 31	16 59	28.3	33 38	16 24	28.0	247	293
68	112	38 21	18 38	28.5	37 28	18 02	28.2	36 35	17 27	27.8	35 42	16 53	27.5	34 48	16 19	27.1	33 55	15 46	26.8	248	292
69	111	38 40	17 53	27.3	37 46	17 18	27.0	36 53	16 44	26.6	35 59	16 11	26.3	35 05	15 38	26.0	34 11	15 07	25.7	249	291
70	110	38 58	17 07	26.1	38 04	16 33	25.7	37 10	16 01	25.4	36 15	15 29	25.1	35 21	14 58	24.8	34 26	14 27	24.5	250	290
71	109	39 15	16 20	24.9	38 20	15 48	24.5	37 26	15 17	24.2	36 31	14 46	23.9	35 36	14 16	23.6	34 41	13 47	23.3	251	289
72	108	39 31	15 33	23.6	38 36	15 02	23.3	37 41	14 32	23.0	36 46	14 03	22.7	35 50	13 34	22.4	34 55	13 07	22.1	252	288
73	107	39 47	14 45	22.4	38 51	14 16	22.1	37 56	13 47	21.8	37 00	13 19	21.5	36 04	12 52	21.2	35 08	12 25	20.9	253	287
74	106	40 02	13 56	21.1	39 06	13 28	20.8	38 10	13 01	20.5	37 13	12 35	20.3	36 17	12 09	20.0	35 21	11 44	19.8	254	286
75	105	40 16	13 07	19.8	39 19	12 41	19.5	38 23	12 15	19.3	37 26	11 50	19.0	36 29	11 26	18.8	35 33	11 02	18.5	255	285
76	104	40 29	12 17	18.5	39 32	11 53	18.3	38 35	11 28	18.0	37 38	11 05	17.8	36 41	10 42	17.6	35 44	10 20	17.3	256	284
77	103	40 41	11 27	17.3	39 44	11 04	17.0	38 47	10 41	16.8	37 49	10 19	16.5	36 52	9 58	16.3	35 54	9 37	16.1	257	283
78	102	40 53	10 36	16.0	39 55	10 15	15.7	38 57	9 54	15.5	38 00	9 33	15.3	37 02	9 14	15.1	36 04	8 54	14.9	258	282
79	101	41 04	9 45	14.7	40 05	9 25	14.4	39 07	9 06	14.2	38 09	8 47	14.0	37 11	8 30	13.9	36 13	8 11	13.7	259	281
80	100	41 13	8 53	13.3	40 15	8 35	13.2	39 16	8 17	13.0	38 18	8 00	12.8	37 19	7 44	12.6	36 21	7 27	12.5	260	280
81	99	41 22	8 01	12.0	40 23	7 45	11.9	39 25	7 29	11.7	38 26	7 13	11.5	37 27	6 58	11.4	36 28	6 43	11.2	261	279
82	98	41 30	7 09	10.7	40 31	6 54	10.5	39 32	6 40	10.4	38 33	6 26	10.3	37 34	6 12	10.1	36 35	5 59	10.0	262	278
83	97	41 37	6 16	9.4	40 38	6 03	9.2	39 39	5 50	9.1	38 39	5 38	9.0	37 41	5 26	8.9	36 41	5 15	8.7	263	277
84	96	41 43	5 23	8.1	40 44	5 12	7.9	39 44	5 01	7.8	38 45	4 50	7.7	37 45	4 40	7.6	36 46	4 30	7.5	264	276
85	95	41 48	4 29	6.7	40 49	4 20	6.6	39 49	4 11	6.5	38 49	4 02	6.4	37 50	3 54	6.3	36 50	3 45	6.3	265	275
86	94	41 52	3 36	5.4	40 53	3 28	5.3	39 53	3 21	5.2	38 53	3 14	5.1	37 53	3 07	5.1	36 54	3 01	5.0	266	274
87	93	41 56	2 42	4.0	40 56	2 36	4.0	39 56	2 31	3.9	38 56	2 26	3.9	37 56	2 20	3.8	36 56	2 16	3.8	267	273
88	92	41 58	1 48	2.7	40 58	1 44	2.6	39 58	1 41	2.6	38 58	1 37	2.6	37 58	1 34	2.5	36 58	1 30	2.5	268	272
89	91	42 00	0 54	1.3	41 00	0 52	1.3	40 00	0 50	1.3	39 00	0 49	1.3	38 00	0 47	1.3	37 00	0 45	1.3	269	271
90	90	42 00	0 00	0.0	41 00	0 00	0.0	40 00	0 00	0.0	39 00	0 00	0.0	38 00	0 00	0.0	37 00	0 00	0.0	270	270

N. Lat.: for LHA > 180° ... $Z_n = Z$
for LHA < 180° ... $Z_n = 360° - Z$

S. Lat.: for LHA > 180° ... $Z_n = 180° - Z$
for LHA < 180° ... $Z_n = 180° + Z$

© British Crown Copyright 2018. All rights reserved.

B: (−) for 90° < LHA < 270°
Dec:(−) for Lat. contrary name

Z₁: same sign as B
Z₂: (−) for F > 90°

SIGHT REDUCTION TABLE

LHA/F	A	54° A/H	54° B/P	54° Z₁/Z₂	55° A/H	55° B/P	55° Z₁/Z₂	56° A/H	56° B/P	56° Z₁/Z₂	57° A/H	57° B/P	57° Z₁/Z₂	58° A/H	58° B/P	58° Z₁/Z₂	59° A/H	59° B/P	59° Z₁/Z₂	A	LHA
0	180	0 00	36 00	90.0	0 00	35 00	90.0	0 00	34 00	90.0	0 00	33 00	90.0	0 00	32 00	90.0	0 00	31 00	90.0	360	180
1	179	0 35	36 00	89.2	0 34	35 00	89.2	0 34	34 00	89.2	0 33	33 00	89.2	0 32	32 00	89.2	0 31	31 00	89.1	359	181
2	178	1 11	35 59	88.4	1 09	34 59	88.4	1 07	33 59	88.3	1 05	32 59	88.3	1 04	31 59	88.3	1 02	30 59	88.3	358	182
3	177	1 46	35 58	87.6	1 43	34 58	87.5	1 41	33 58	87.5	1 38	32 58	87.5	1 35	31 58	87.5	1 33	30 58	87.4	357	183
4	176	2 21	35 56	86.8	2 18	34 56	86.7	2 14	33 56	86.6	2 11	32 56	86.6	2 07	31 56	86.6	2 04	30 56	86.6	356	184
5	175	2 56	35 54	86.0	2 52	34 54	85.9	2 48	33 54	85.8	2 43	32 54	85.8	2 39	31 54	85.8	2 34	30 54	85.7	355	185
6	174	3 31	35 51	85.1	3 26	34 51	85.1	3 21	33 51	85.0	3 16	32 51	85.0	3 11	31 52	84.9	3 05	30 52	84.9	354	186
7	173	4 06	35 48	84.3	4 00	34 48	84.3	3 55	33 48	84.2	3 48	32 48	84.2	3 42	31 48	84.1	3 36	30 49	84.0	353	187
8	172	4 42	35 44	83.5	4 35	34 44	83.4	4 28	33 44	83.4	4 21	32 45	83.3	4 14	31 45	83.2	4 07	30 45	83.1	352	188
9	171	5 17	35 40	82.7	5 09	34 40	82.6	5 01	33 40	82.5	4 53	32 41	82.4	4 45	31 41	82.3	4 37	30 41	82.3	351	189
10	170	5 51	35 35	81.9	5 43	34 35	81.8	5 35	33 36	81.7	5 26	32 36	81.6	5 17	31 36	81.5	5 08	30 37	81.4	350	190
11	169	6 26	35 30	81.1	6 17	34 30	81.0	6 08	33 31	80.8	5 58	32 31	80.7	5 48	31 31	80.6	5 38	30 32	80.5	349	191
12	168	7 01	35 24	80.2	6 51	34 24	80.1	6 41	33 25	80.0	6 30	32 25	79.9	6 20	31 26	79.8	6 09	30 27	79.7	348	192
13	167	7 36	35 18	79.4	7 25	34 18	79.3	7 14	33 19	79.2	7 02	32 19	79.0	6 51	31 20	78.9	6 39	30 21	78.8	347	193
14	166	8 11	35 11	78.6	7 59	34 12	78.5	7 46	33 12	78.3	7 34	32 13	78.2	7 22	31 14	78.1	7 09	30 15	77.9	346	194
15	165	8 45	35 04	77.8	8 32	34 04	77.6	8 19	33 05	77.5	8 06	32 06	77.3	7 53	31 07	77.2	7 40	30 08	77.1	345	195
16	164	9 20	34 56	76.9	9 06	33 57	76.8	8 52	32 58	76.6	8 38	31 58	76.5	8 24	31 00	76.3	8 10	30 01	76.2	344	196
17	163	9 54	34 47	76.1	9 39	33 48	75.9	9 25	32 49	75.8	9 10	31 50	75.6	8 55	30 52	75.5	8 40	29 53	75.3	343	197
18	162	10 28	34 39	75.3	10 13	33 40	75.1	9 57	32 41	74.9	9 41	31 42	74.8	9 25	30 43	74.6	9 09	29 45	74.4	342	198
19	161	11 02	34 29	74.4	10 46	33 30	74.2	10 29	32 32	74.1	10 13	31 33	73.9	9 56	30 35	73.7	9 39	29 36	73.6	341	199
20	160	11 36	34 19	73.6	11 19	33 21	73.4	11 02	32 22	73.2	10 44	31 24	73.0	10 27	30 25	72.8	10 09	29 27	72.7	340	200
21	159	12 10	34 09	72.7	11 52	33 10	72.5	11 34	32 12	72.3	11 15	31 14	72.2	10 57	30 15	72.0	10 38	29 17	71.8	339	201
22	158	12 43	33 58	71.9	12 24	33 00	71.7	12 06	32 01	71.5	11 46	31 03	71.3	11 27	30 05	71.1	11 07	29 07	70.9	338	202
23	157	13 17	33 46	71.0	12 57	32 48	70.8	12 37	31 50	70.6	12 17	30 52	70.4	11 57	29 54	70.2	11 37	28 57	70.0	337	203
24	156	13 50	33 34	70.3	13 29	32 36	70.0	13 09	31 38	69.7	12 48	30 41	69.5	12 27	29 43	69.3	12 06	28 46	69.1	336	204
25	155	14 23	33 22	69.4	14 02	32 24	69.1	13 40	31 26	68.9	13 18	30 29	68.6	12 56	29 31	68.4	12 34	28 34	68.2	335	205
26	154	14 56	33 09	68.5	14 34	32 11	68.2	14 11	31 14	68.0	13 49	30 16	67.8	13 26	29 19	67.5	13 03	28 22	67.3	334	206
27	153	15 29	32 55	67.6	15 06	31 58	67.3	14 42	31 00	67.1	14 19	30 03	66.9	13 55	29 06	66.6	13 31	28 10	66.4	333	207
28	152	16 01	32 41	66.7	15 37	31 44	66.5	15 13	30 47	66.2	14 49	29 50	66.0	14 24	28 53	65.7	14 00	27 57	65.5	332	208
29	151	16 33	32 26	65.8	16 09	31 29	65.6	15 44	30 32	65.3	15 19	29 36	65.1	14 53	28 39	64.8	14 28	27 43	64.6	331	209
30	150	17 05	32 11	65.0	16 40	31 14	64.7	16 14	30 17	64.4	15 48	29 21	64.2	15 22	28 25	63.9	14 55	27 29	63.7	330	210
31	149	17 37	31 55	64.1	17 11	30 58	63.8	16 44	30 02	63.5	16 17	29 06	63.3	15 50	28 10	63.0	15 23	27 15	62.7	329	211
32	148	18 09	31 38	63.2	17 42	30 42	62.9	17 14	29 46	62.6	16 47	28 51	62.3	16 19	27 55	62.1	15 50	27 00	61.8	328	212
33	147	18 40	31 21	62.3	18 12	30 25	62.0	17 43	29 29	61.7	17 15	28 34	61.4	16 47	27 39	61.2	16 17	26 45	60.9	327	213
34	146	19 11	31 04	61.4	18 42	30 08	61.1	18 13	29 13	60.8	17 44	28 18	60.5	17 14	27 23	60.2	16 44	26 29	60.0	326	214
35	145	19 42	30 46	60.5	19 12	29 50	60.2	18 42	28 55	59.9	18 12	28 01	59.6	17 42	27 06	59.3	17 11	26 12	59.0	325	215
36	144	20 13	30 27	59.6	19 42	29 32	59.2	19 11	28 37	59.0	18 40	27 43	58.6	18 09	26 49	58.4	17 37	25 55	58.1	324	216
37	143	20 43	30 07	58.6	20 11	29 13	58.3	19 40	28 19	58.0	19 08	27 25	57.8	18 36	26 31	57.4	18 03	25 38	57.1	323	217
38	142	21 13	29 48	57.7	20 41	28 53	57.4	20 08	27 59	57.1	19 35	27 06	56.8	19 02	26 13	56.5	18 29	25 20	56.2	322	218
39	141	21 42	29 27	56.8	21 10	28 33	56.4	20 36	27 40	56.2	20 03	26 47	55.8	19 29	25 54	55.5	18 55	25 02	55.2	321	219
40	140	22 12	29 06	55.8	21 38	28 13	55.5	21 04	27 20	55.2	20 30	26 27	54.9	19 55	25 35	54.6	19 20	24 43	54.3	320	220
41	139	22 41	28 44	54.9	22 06	27 51	54.5	21 31	26 59	54.3	20 56	26 07	53.9	20 21	25 15	53.6	19 45	24 24	53.3	319	221
42	138	23 10	28 22	53.9	22 34	27 29	53.6	21 58	26 37	53.3	21 22	25 46	53.0	20 46	24 55	52.6	20 10	24 04	52.3	318	222
43	137	23 38	27 59	53.0	23 02	27 07	52.6	22 25	26 15	52.4	21 48	25 24	52.0	21 11	24 34	51.7	20 34	23 43	51.4	317	223
44	136	24 06	27 36	52.0	23 29	26 44	51.7	22 51	25 53	51.4	22 14	25 02	51.0	21 36	24 12	50.7	20 58	23 23	50.4	316	224
45	135	24 34	27 11	51.0	23 56	26 20	50.7	23 17	25 30	50.4	22 39	24 40	50.0	22 00	23 50	49.7	21 21	23 01	49.4	315	225

© British Crown Copyright 2018. All rights reserved.

Lat. / A	54°			55°			56°			57°			58°			59°			Lat. / A	
LHA/F	A/H	B/P	Z₁/Z₂	A/H	B/P	Z₁/Z₂	A/H	B/P	Z₁/Z₂	A/H	B/P	Z₁/Z₂	A/H	B/P	Z₁/Z₂	A/H	B/P	Z₁/Z₂	A	LHA
45	24 34	27 11	51.0	23 56	26 20	50.7	23 17	25 30	50.3	22 39	24 40	50.0	22 00	23 50	49.7	21 21	23 01	49.4	315	225
46	25 01	26 47	50.0	24 22	25 56	49.7	23 43	25 06	49.4	23 04	24 17	49.0	22 24	23 28	48.7	21 45	22 39	48.4	314	226
47	25 28	26 22	49.1	24 48	25 32	48.7	24 08	24 42	48.4	23 28	23 53	48.0	22 48	23 05	47.7	22 08	22 17	47.4	313	227
48	25 54	25 56	48.1	25 14	25 06	47.7	24 33	24 17	47.4	23 53	23 29	47.0	23 11	22 41	46.7	22 30	21 54	46.4	312	228
49	26 20	25 30	47.1	25 39	24 40	46.7	24 58	23 51	46.4	24 16	23 03	46.0	23 34	22 17	45.7	22 52	21 31	45.4	311	229
50	26 46	25 02	46.0	26 04	24 14	45.7	25 22	23 26	45.3	24 40	22 39	45.0	23 57	21 53	44.7	23 14	21 07	44.4	310	230
51	27 11	24 34	45.0	26 28	23 47	44.7	25 45	23 00	44.3	25 02	22 14	44.0	24 19	21 28	43.7	23 36	20 43	43.4	309	231
52	27 36	24 06	44.0	26 52	23 19	43.6	26 09	22 33	43.3	25 25	21 48	43.0	24 41	21 03	42.7	23 57	20 18	42.3	308	232
53	28 00	23 37	43.0	27 16	22 51	42.6	26 32	22 06	42.3	25 47	21 21	41.9	25 02	20 37	41.6	24 17	19 53	41.3	307	233
54	28 24	23 07	41.9	27 39	22 22	41.6	26 54	21 38	41.2	26 09	20 54	40.9	25 23	20 10	40.6	24 37	19 27	40.3	306	234
55	28 47	22 37	40.9	28 02	21 53	40.5	27 17	21 09	40.2	26 30	20 26	39.9	25 44	19 43	39.5	24 57	19 01	39.2	305	235
56	29 10	22 07	39.8	28 24	21 23	39.5	27 38	20 40	39.1	26 50	19 57	38.8	26 04	19 16	38.5	25 17	18 34	38.2	304	236
57	29 32	21 35	38.8	28 45	20 52	38.4	27 58	20 10	38.1	27 11	19 29	37.8	26 23	18 48	37.4	25 35	18 07	37.1	303	237
58	29 54	21 03	37.7	29 06	20 21	37.3	28 19	19 40	37.0	27 31	18 59	36.7	26 42	18 19	36.4	25 54	17 40	36.1	302	238
59	30 15	20 31	36.6	29 27	19 50	36.3	28 38	19 09	35.9	27 50	18 30	35.6	27 01	17 50	35.3	26 12	17 12	35.0	301	239
60	30 36	19 58	35.5	29 47	19 18	35.2	28 58	18 38	34.9	28 09	17 59	34.5	27 19	17 21	34.2	26 30	16 43	34.0	300	240
61	30 56	19 24	34.4	30 07	18 45	34.1	29 17	18 06	33.8	28 27	17 29	33.5	27 37	16 51	33.2	26 46	16 14	32.9	299	241
62	31 16	18 50	33.3	30 26	18 12	33.0	29 35	17 34	32.7	28 45	16 57	32.4	27 54	16 21	32.1	27 03	15 45	31.8	298	242
63	31 35	18 15	32.2	30 44	17 38	31.9	29 53	17 02	31.6	29 02	16 26	31.3	28 10	15 50	31.0	27 19	15 15	30.7	297	243
64	31 53	17 40	31.1	31 02	17 04	30.8	30 10	16 28	30.5	29 19	15 53	30.2	28 27	15 19	29.9	27 35	14 45	29.6	296	244
65	32 11	17 04	30.0	31 19	16 29	29.7	30 27	15 55	29.4	29 35	15 21	29.1	28 42	14 48	28.8	27 50	14 15	28.5	295	245
66	32 29	16 28	28.8	31 36	15 54	28.5	30 43	15 21	28.2	29 50	14 48	28.0	28 58	14 16	27.7	28 04	13 44	27.4	294	246
67	32 45	15 51	27.7	31 52	15 18	27.4	30 59	14 46	27.1	30 05	14 14	26.8	29 12	13 43	26.6	28 18	13 13	26.3	293	247
68	33 01	15 14	26.5	32 08	14 42	26.3	31 14	14 11	26.0	30 20	13 40	25.7	29 26	13 10	25.5	28 31	12 41	25.2	292	248
69	33 17	14 36	25.4	32 23	14 05	25.1	31 28	13 35	24.8	30 34	13 06	24.6	29 39	12 37	24.4	28 44	12 09	24.1	291	249
70	33 32	13 58	24.2	32 37	13 28	24.0	31 42	12 59	23.7	30 47	12 31	23.5	29 52	12 04	23.2	28 57	11 37	23.0	290	250
71	33 46	13 18	23.1	32 51	12 51	22.8	31 55	12 23	22.6	31 00	11 56	22.3	30 04	11 30	22.1	29 09	11 04	21.9	289	251
72	33 59	12 39	21.9	33 04	12 13	21.6	32 08	11 46	21.4	31 12	11 21	21.2	30 16	10 56	21.0	29 20	10 31	20.8	288	252
73	34 12	12 00	20.7	33 16	11 34	20.5	32 20	11 09	20.2	31 23	10 45	20.0	30 27	10 21	19.8	29 30	9 58	19.6	287	253
74	34 24	11 19	19.5	33 28	10 55	19.3	32 31	10 32	19.1	31 34	10 09	18.9	30 37	9 46	18.7	29 41	9 24	18.5	286	254
75	34 36	10 39	18.3	33 39	10 16	18.1	32 42	9 54	17.9	31 44	9 32	17.7	30 47	9 11	17.5	29 50	8 50	17.4	285	255
76	34 46	9 58	17.1	33 49	9 37	16.9	32 52	9 16	16.7	31 54	8 56	16.6	30 56	8 36	16.4	29 59	8 16	16.2	284	256
77	34 56	9 17	15.9	33 59	8 57	15.7	33 01	8 38	15.6	32 03	8 19	15.4	31 05	8 00	15.2	30 07	7 42	15.1	283	257
78	35 06	8 35	14.7	34 08	8 17	14.5	33 10	7 59	14.4	32 11	7 41	14.2	31 13	7 24	14.1	30 15	7 07	13.9	282	258
79	35 14	7 54	13.5	34 16	7 37	13.3	33 18	7 20	13.2	32 19	7 04	13.0	31 21	6 48	12.9	30 22	6 32	12.8	281	259
80	35 22	7 11	12.3	34 24	6 56	12.1	33 25	6 41	12.0	32 26	6 26	11.9	31 27	6 12	11.7	30 29	5 57	11.6	280	260
81	35 29	6 29	11.1	34 30	6 15	10.9	33 32	6 01	10.8	32 33	5 48	10.7	31 34	5 35	10.6	30 35	5 22	10.5	279	261
82	35 36	5 46	9.9	34 37	5 34	9.7	33 38	5 22	9.6	32 38	5 10	9.5	31 39	4 58	9.4	30 40	4 47	9.3	278	262
83	35 41	5 04	8.6	34 42	4 53	8.5	33 43	4 42	8.4	32 43	4 32	8.3	31 44	4 21	8.2	30 45	4 11	8.2	277	263
84	35 46	4 21	7.4	34 47	4 11	7.3	33 47	4 02	7.2	32 48	3 53	7.1	31 48	3 44	7.1	30 49	3 36	7.0	276	264
85	35 51	3 37	6.2	34 51	3 30	6.1	33 51	3 22	6.0	32 52	3 14	6.0	31 52	3 07	5.9	30 52	3 00	5.8	275	265
86	35 54	2 54	4.9	34 54	2 48	4.9	33 54	2 42	4.8	32 55	2 36	4.8	31 55	2 30	4.7	30 55	2 24	4.7	274	266
87	35 57	2 11	3.7	34 57	2 06	3.7	33 57	2 01	3.6	32 57	1 57	3.6	31 57	1 52	3.5	30 57	1 48	3.5	273	267
88	35 58	1 27	2.5	34 59	1 24	2.4	33 59	1 21	2.4	32 59	1 18	2.4	31 59	1 15	2.4	30 59	1 12	2.3	272	268
89	36 00	0 44	1.2	35 00	0 42	1.2	34 00	0 40	1.2	33 00	0 39	1.2	32 00	0 37	1.2	31 00	0 36	1.2	271	269
90	36 00	0 00	0.0	35 00	0 00	0.0	34 00	0 00	0.0	33 00	0 00	0.0	32 00	0 00	0.0	31 00	0 00	0.0	270	270

N. Lat.: for LHA > 180° ... Zn = Z
for LHA < 180° ... Zn = 360° − Z

S. Lat.: for LHA > 180° ... Zn = 180° − Z
for LHA < 180° ... Zn = 180° + Z

© British Crown Copyright 2018. All rights reserved.

SIGHT REDUCTION TABLE

B: (−) for 90° < LHA < 270°
Dec:(−) for Lat. contrary name

Z₁: same sign as B → Z_1: same sign as B
Z_2: (−) for F > 90°

LHA/F	A	60° A/H	60° B/P	60° Z_1/Z_2	61° A/H	61° B/P	61° Z_1/Z_2	62° A/H	62° B/P	62° Z_1/Z_2	63° A/H	63° B/P	63° Z_1/Z_2	64° A/H	64° B/P	64° Z_1/Z_2	65° A/H	65° B/P	65° Z_1/Z_2	A	LHA
0	180	0 00	30 00	90·0	0 00	29 00	90·0	0 00	28 00	90·0	0 00	27 00	90·0	0 00	26 00	90·0	0 00	25 00	90·0	360	180
1	179	0 30	30 00	89·1	0 29	29 00	89·1	0 28	28 00	89·1	0 27	27 00	89·1	0 26	26 00	89·1	0 25	25 00	89·1	359	181
2	178	1 00	29 59	88·3	0 58	28 59	88·3	0 56	27 59	88·2	0 54	26 59	88·2	0 53	25 59	88·2	0 51	24 59	88·2	358	182
3	177	1 30	29 58	87·4	1 27	28 58	87·4	1 24	27 58	87·4	1 22	26 58	87·3	1 19	25 58	87·3	1 16	24 58	87·3	357	183
4	176	2 00	29 56	86·5	1 56	28 56	86·5	1 53	27 57	86·5	1 49	26 57	86·4	1 45	25 57	86·4	1 41	24 57	86·4	356	184
5	175	2 30	29 54	85·7	2 25	28 54	85·7	2 21	27 55	85·6	2 16	26 55	85·5	2 11	25 55	85·5	2 07	24 55	85·5	355	185
6	174	3 00	29 52	84·8	2 54	28 52	84·8	2 49	27 52	84·7	2 43	26 52	84·6	2 38	25 53	84·6	2 32	24 53	84·6	354	186
7	173	3 30	29 49	83·9	3 23	28 49	83·9	3 17	27 49	83·9	3 10	26 49	83·8	3 04	25 50	83·7	2 57	24 50	83·7	353	187
8	172	3 59	29 45	83·1	3 52	28 46	83·1	3 45	27 46	83·0	3 37	26 46	82·9	3 30	25 47	82·8	3 22	24 47	82·7	352	188
9	171	4 29	29 42	82·2	4 21	28 42	82·2	4 13	27 42	82·1	4 04	26 43	82·0	3 56	25 43	81·9	3 47	24 44	81·8	351	189
10	170	4 59	29 37	81·3	4 50	28 38	81·3	4 41	27 38	81·2	4 31	26 39	81·1	4 22	25 39	81·0	4 13	24 40	80·9	350	190
11	169	5 28	29 33	80·4	5 18	28 33	80·4	5 08	27 34	80·4	4 58	26 34	80·2	4 48	25 35	80·1	4 38	24 36	80·0	349	191
12	168	5 58	29 27	79·6	5 47	28 28	79·6	5 36	27 29	79·5	5 25	26 29	79·3	5 14	25 30	79·2	5 02	24 31	79·1	348	192
13	167	6 27	29 22	78·7	6 16	28 22	78·6	6 04	27 23	78·6	5 52	26 24	78·4	5 40	25 25	78·3	5 27	24 26	78·2	347	193
14	166	6 57	29 15	77·8	6 44	28 16	77·7	6 31	27 17	77·7	6 18	26 18	77·5	6 05	25 20	77·4	5 52	24 21	77·3	346	194
15	165	7 26	29 09	76·9	7 13	28 10	76·8	6 59	27 11	76·8	6 45	26 12	76·6	6 31	25 14	76·5	6 17	24 15	76·4	345	195
16	164	7 55	29 02	76·1	7 41	28 03	75·9	7 26	27 04	75·9	7 11	26 06	75·8	6 56	25 07	75·5	6 41	24 09	75·4	344	196
17	163	8 24	28 54	75·2	8 09	27 56	75·0	7 53	26 57	75·0	7 38	25 59	74·8	7 22	25 00	74·6	7 06	24 02	74·5	343	197
18	162	8 53	28 46	74·3	8 37	27 48	74·1	8 20	26 50	74·1	8 04	25 51	73·9	7 47	24 53	73·7	7 30	23 55	73·6	342	198
19	161	9 22	28 38	73·4	9 05	27 40	73·2	8 48	26 41	73·2	8 30	25 43	72·9	8 12	24 45	72·8	7 55	23 48	72·7	341	199
20	160	9 51	28 29	72·5	9 33	27 31	72·3	9 14	26 33	72·3	8 56	25 35	72·0	8 37	24 37	71·9	8 19	23 40	71·7	340	200
21	159	10 19	28 19	71·6	10 00	27 22	71·4	9 41	26 24	71·4	9 22	25 26	71·1	9 02	24 29	71·0	8 43	23 32	70·8	339	201
22	158	10 48	28 10	70·7	10 28	27 12	70·5	10 08	26 15	70·5	9 48	25 17	70·2	9 27	24 20	70·0	9 07	23 23	69·8	338	202
23	157	11 16	27 59	69·8	10 55	27 02	69·6	10 34	26 05	69·6	10 13	25 08	69·3	9 52	24 11	69·1	9 30	23 14	69·0	337	203
24	156	11 44	27 49	68·9	11 22	26 51	68·7	11 00	25 54	68·7	10 38	24 58	68·4	10 16	24 01	68·2	9 54	23 04	68·0	336	204
25	155	12 12	27 37	68·0	11 49	26 40	67·8	11 27	25 44	67·8	11 04	24 47	67·4	10 41	23 51	67·3	10 17	22 55	67·1	335	205
26	154	12 40	27 26	67·1	12 16	26 29	66·9	11 53	25 33	66·8	11 29	24 36	66·5	11 05	23 40	66·3	10 41	22 44	66·2	334	206
27	153	13 07	27 13	66·2	12 43	26 17	66·0	12 18	25 21	66·0	11 54	24 25	65·6	11 29	23 29	65·4	11 04	22 34	65·2	333	207
28	152	13 35	27 01	65·3	13 09	26 05	65·1	12 44	25 09	65·1	12 18	24 13	64·7	11 53	23 18	64·5	11 27	22 22	64·3	332	208
29	151	14 02	26 48	64·4	13 36	25 52	64·1	13 09	24 56	64·1	12 43	24 01	63·7	12 16	23 06	63·5	11 49	22 11	63·3	331	209
30	150	14 28	26 34	63·4	14 02	25 39	63·2	13 35	24 43	63·2	13 07	23 49	62·8	12 40	22 54	62·6	12 12	21 59	62·4	330	210
31	149	14 55	26 20	62·5	14 28	25 25	62·3	14 00	24 30	62·2	13 31	23 36	61·8	13 03	22 41	61·6	12 34	21 47	61·4	329	211
32	148	15 22	26 05	61·6	14 53	25 11	61·3	14 24	24 16	61·3	13 55	23 22	60·9	13 26	22 28	60·7	12 56	21 35	60·5	328	212
33	147	15 48	25 50	60·6	15 19	24 56	60·4	14 49	24 02	60·3	14 19	23 08	59·9	13 49	22 15	59·7	13 18	21 22	59·5	327	213
34	146	16 14	25 35	59·7	15 44	24 41	59·5	15 13	23 47	59·4	14 42	22 54	59·0	14 11	22 01	58·8	13 40	21 08	58·6	326	214
35	145	16 40	25 19	58·8	16 09	24 25	58·5	15 37	23 32	58·4	15 06	22 39	58·0	14 34	21 47	57·8	14 02	20 54	57·6	325	215
36	144	17 05	25 02	57·8	16 33	24 09	57·6	16 01	23 17	57·4	15 29	22 24	57·1	14 56	21 32	56·9	14 23	20 40	56·6	324	216
37	143	17 31	24 45	56·9	16 58	23 53	56·6	16 25	23 00	56·4	15 51	22 09	56·1	15 18	21 17	55·9	14 44	20 26	55·7	323	217
38	142	17 56	24 28	55·9	17 22	23 36	55·7	16 48	22 44	55·4	16 14	21 53	55·2	15 39	21 01	54·9	15 05	20 11	54·7	322	218
39	141	18 21	24 10	55·0	17 46	23 18	54·7	17 11	22 27	54·4	16 36	21 36	54·2	16 01	20 46	54·0	15 25	19 55	53·7	321	219
40	140	18 45	23 52	54·0	18 09	23 00	53·7	17 34	22 10	53·5	16 58	21 19	53·2	16 22	20 30	53·0	15 46	19 39	52·7	320	220
41	139	19 09	23 33	53·0	18 33	22 42	52·8	17 56	21 52	52·5	17 20	21 02	52·2	16 43	20 13	52·0	16 06	19 23	51·8	319	221
42	138	19 33	23 13	52·1	18 56	22 23	51·8	18 19	21 34	51·5	17 41	20 44	51·3	17 03	19 55	51·0	16 26	19 07	50·8	318	222
43	137	19 56	22 54	51·1	19 18	22 04	50·8	18 40	21 15	50·5	18 02	20 26	50·3	17 24	19 38	50·0	16 45	18 50	49·8	317	223
44	136	20 19	22 33	50·1	19 41	21 44	49·8	19 02	20 56	49·5	18 23	20 08	49·3	17 44	19 20	49·0	17 04	18 33	48·8	316	224
45	135	20 42	22 12	49·1	20 03	21 24	48·8	19 23	20 36	48·6	18 43	19 49	48·3	18 03	19 02	48·1	17 23	18 15	47·8	315	225

© British Crown Copyright 2018. All rights reserved.

Lat./A	LHA/F	60° A/H	60° B/P	60° Z₁/Z₂	61° A/H	61° B/P	61° Z₁/Z₂	62° A/H	62° B/P	62° Z₁/Z₂	63° A/H	63° B/P	63° Z₁/Z₂	64° A/H	64° B/P	64° Z₁/Z₂	65° A/H	65° B/P	65° Z₁/Z₂	LHA	Lat./A
135	45	20 42	22 12	49·1	20 03	21 24	48·8	19 23	20 36	48·6	18 43	19 49	48·3	18 03	19 02	48·1	17 23	18 15	47·8	225	315
134	46	21 05	21 51	48·1	20 25	21 04	47·8	19 44	20 16	47·6	19 04	19 29	47·3	18 23	18 43	47·1	17 42	17 57	46·8	226	314
133	47	21 27	21 30	47·1	20 46	20 43	46·8	20 05	19 56	46·6	19 24	19 10	46·3	18 42	18 24	46·1	18 00	17 39	45·8	227	313
132	48	21 49	21 07	46·1	21 07	20 21	45·8	20 25	19 35	45·6	19 43	18 50	45·3	19 01	18 04	45·1	18 18	17 20	44·8	228	312
131	49	22 10	20 45	45·1	21 28	19 59	44·8	20 45	19 14	44·6	20 02	18 29	44·3	19 19	17 45	44·1	18 36	17 01	43·8	229	311
130	50	22 31	20 22	44·1	21 48	19 37	43·8	21 05	18 52	43·5	20 21	18 08	43·3	19 37	17 24	43·0	18 53	16 41	42·8	230	310
129	51	22 52	19 58	43·1	22 08	19 14	42·8	21 24	18 30	42·5	20 40	17 47	42·3	19 55	17 04	42·0	19 10	16 21	41·8	231	309
128	52	23 12	19 34	42·1	22 28	18 51	41·8	21 43	18 08	41·5	20 58	17 25	41·2	20 13	16 43	41·0	19 27	16 01	40·8	232	308
127	53	23 32	19 10	41·0	22 47	18 27	40·7	22 01	17 45	40·5	21 15	17 03	40·2	20 30	16 21	40·0	19 44	15 41	39·7	233	307
126	54	23 52	18 45	40·0	23 06	18 03	39·7	22 19	17 21	39·4	21 33	16 40	39·2	20 46	16 00	39·0	20 00	15 20	38·7	234	306
125	55	24 11	18 19	39·0	23 24	17 38	38·7	22 37	16 58	38·4	21 50	16 17	38·2	21 03	15 38	37·9	20 15	14 58	37·7	235	305
124	56	24 29	17 54	37·9	23 42	17 13	37·6	22 54	16 34	37·4	22 07	15 54	37·1	21 19	15 15	36·9	20 31	14 37	36·7	236	304
123	57	24 48	17 27	36·9	23 59	16 48	36·6	23 11	16 09	36·3	22 23	15 31	36·1	21 34	14 53	35·8	20 46	14 15	35·6	237	303
122	58	25 05	17 01	35·8	24 17	16 22	35·5	23 28	15 44	35·3	22 39	15 07	35·0	21 49	14 29	34·8	21 00	13 53	34·6	238	302
121	59	25 24	16 34	34·8	24 33	15 56	34·5	23 44	15 19	34·2	22 54	14 42	34·0	22 04	14 06	33·8	21 14	13 30	33·5	239	301
120	60	25 40	16 06	33·7	24 50	15 29	33·4	23 59	14 53	33·2	23 09	14 18	32·9	22 19	13 42	32·7	21 28	13 07	32·5	240	300
119	61	25 56	15 38	32·6	25 05	15 02	32·4	24 15	14 27	32·1	23 24	13 53	31·9	22 33	13 18	31·7	21 42	12 44	31·5	241	299
118	62	26 12	15 10	31·5	25 21	14 35	31·3	24 29	14 01	31·0	23 38	13 27	30·8	22 46	12 54	30·6	21 55	12 21	30·4	242	298
117	63	26 27	14 41	30·5	25 36	14 08	30·2	24 44	13 34	30·0	23 52	13 01	29·8	22 59	12 29	29·5	22 07	11 57	29·3	243	297
116	64	26 42	14 12	29·4	25 50	13 39	29·1	24 57	13 07	28·9	24 05	12 35	28·7	23 12	12 04	28·5	22 19	11 33	28·3	244	296
115	65	26 57	13 43	28·3	26 04	13 11	28·1	25 11	12 40	27·8	24 18	12 09	27·6	23 25	11 39	27·4	22 31	11 09	27·2	245	295
114	66	27 11	13 13	27·2	26 17	12 42	27·0	25 24	12 12	26·8	24 30	11 43	26·6	23 37	11 13	26·4	22 43	10 44	26·2	246	294
113	67	27 24	12 43	26·1	26 30	12 13	25·9	25 36	11 44	25·7	24 42	11 16	25·5	23 48	10 47	25·3	22 54	10 20	25·1	247	293
112	68	27 37	12 12	25·0	26 43	11 44	24·8	25 48	11 16	24·6	24 54	10 48	24·4	23 59	10 21	24·2	23 04	9 55	24·0	248	292
111	69	27 50	11 41	23·9	26 55	11 14	23·7	26 00	10 47	23·5	25 05	10 21	23·3	24 09	9 55	23·1	23 14	9 29	23·0	249	291
110	70	28 01	11 10	22·8	27 06	10 44	22·6	26 11	10 18	22·4	25 15	9 53	22·2	24 20	9 28	22·0	23 24	9 04	21·9	250	290
109	71	28 13	10 39	21·7	27 17	10 14	21·5	26 21	9 49	21·3	25 25	9 25	21·1	24 29	9 01	21·0	23 33	8 38	20·8	251	289
108	72	28 24	10 07	20·6	27 27	9 43	20·4	26 31	9 20	20·2	25 35	8 57	20·0	24 38	8 34	19·9	23 42	8 12	19·7	252	288
107	73	28 34	9 35	19·4	27 37	9 12	19·3	26 41	8 50	19·1	25 44	8 28	18·9	24 47	8 07	18·8	23 50	7 46	18·6	253	287
106	74	28 44	9 03	18·3	27 47	8 41	18·2	26 50	8 20	18·0	25 52	8 00	17·8	24 55	7 39	17·7	23 58	7 19	17·6	254	286
105	75	28 53	8 30	17·2	27 55	8 10	17·0	26 58	7 50	16·9	26 01	7 31	16·7	25 03	7 12	16·6	24 06	6 53	16·5	255	285
104	76	29 01	7 57	16·1	28 04	7 57	15·9	27 06	7 20	15·8	26 08	7 02	15·6	25 10	6 44	15·5	24 13	6 26	15·4	256	284
103	77	29 09	7 24	14·9	28 11	7 06	14·8	27 13	6 49	14·7	26 15	6 32	14·5	25 17	6 16	14·4	24 19	5 59	14·3	257	283
102	78	29 17	6 51	13·8	28 18	6 34	13·7	27 20	6 19	13·5	26 22	6 03	13·4	25 23	5 47	13·3	24 25	5 32	13·2	258	282
101	79	29 24	6 17	12·7	28 25	6 02	12·5	27 27	5 48	12·4	26 28	5 33	12·3	25 29	5 19	12·2	24 31	5 05	12·1	259	281
100	80	29 30	5 44	11·5	28 31	5 30	11·4	27 32	5 17	11·3	26 33	5 03	11·2	25 35	4 50	11·1	24 36	4 38	11·0	260	280
99	81	29 36	5 10	10·4	28 37	4 57	10·3	27 38	4 45	10·2	26 38	4 33	10·1	25 39	4 22	10·0	24 40	4 10	9·9	261	279
98	82	29 41	4 36	9·2	28 41	4 25	9·1	27 42	4 14	9·0	26 43	4 03	9·0	25 44	3 53	8·9	24 44	3 43	8·8	262	278
97	83	29 45	4 01	8·1	28 46	3 52	8·0	27 46	3 42	7·9	26 47	3 33	7·8	25 48	3 24	7·8	24 48	3 15	7·7	263	277
96	84	29 49	3 27	6·9	28 50	3 19	6·9	27 50	3 11	6·8	26 50	3 03	6·7	25 51	2 55	6·7	24 51	2 47	6·6	264	276
95	85	29 52	2 53	5·8	28 53	2 46	5·7	27 53	2 39	5·7	26 53	2 33	5·6	25 54	2 26	5·6	24 54	2 20	5·5	265	275
94	86	29 55	2 18	4·6	28 55	2 13	4·6	27 56	2 07	4·5	26 56	2 02	4·5	25 56	1 57	4·4	24 56	1 52	4·4	266	274
93	87	29 57	1 44	3·5	28 57	1 40	3·4	27 57	1 36	3·4	26 58	1 32	3·4	25 58	1 28	3·3	24 58	1 24	3·3	267	273
92	88	29 59	1 09	2·3	28 59	1 06	2·3	27 59	1 04	2·3	26 59	1 01	2·2	25 59	0 59	2·2	24 59	0 56	2·2	268	272
91	89	30 00	0 35	1·2	29 00	0 33	1·1	28 00	0 32	1·1	27 00	0 31	1·1	26 00	0 29	1·1	25 00	0 28	1·1	269	271
90	90	30 00	0 00	0·0	29 00	0 00	0·0	28 00	0 00	0·0	27 00	0 00	0·0	26 00	0 00	0·0	25 00	0 00	0·0	270	270

N. Lat.: for LHA > 180° ... Zₙ = Z
for LHA < 180° ... Zₙ = 360° − Z

S. Lat.: for LHA > 180° ... Zₙ = 180° − Z
for LHA < 180° ... Zₙ = 180° + Z

© British Crown Copyright 2018. All rights reserved.

SIGHT REDUCTION TABLE

B: (−) for 90° < LHA < 270°
Dec:† (−) for Lat. contrary name

Z_1: same sign as B
Z_2: (−) for F > 90°

Lat./A	LHA/F	66° A/H	66° B/P	66° Z_1/Z_2	67° A/H	67° B/P	67° Z_1/Z_2	68° A/H	68° B/P	68° Z_1/Z_2	69° A/H	69° B/P	69° Z_1/Z_2	70° A/H	70° B/P	70° Z_1/Z_2	71° A/H	71° B/P	71° Z_1/Z_2	Lat./A	LHA
180	0	0 00	24 00	90·0	0 00	23 00	90·0	0 00	22 00	90·0	0 00	21 00	90·0	0 00	20 00	90·0	0 00	19 00	90·0	180	360
179	1	0 24	24 00	89·1	0 23	23 00	89·1	0 22	22 00	89·1	0 21	21 00	89·1	0 21	20 00	89·1	0 20	19 00	89·1	181	359
178	2	0 49	23 59	88·2	0 47	22 59	88·2	0 45	21 59	88·1	0 43	20 59	88·1	0 41	19 59	88·1	0 39	18 59	88·1	182	358
177	3	1 13	23 58	87·3	1 10	22 58	87·2	1 07	21 58	87·2	1 04	20 58	87·2	1 02	19 59	87·2	0 59	18 59	87·2	183	357
176	4	1 38	23 57	86·3	1 34	22 57	86·3	1 30	21 57	86·3	1 26	20 57	86·3	1 22	19 57	86·2	1 18	18 57	86·2	184	356
175	5	2 02	23 55	85·4	1 57	22 55	85·4	1 52	21 55	85·4	1 47	20 56	85·4	1 42	19 56	85·3	1 38	18 56	85·3	185	355
174	6	2 26	23 53	84·5	2 20	22 53	84·5	2 15	21 53	84·4	2 09	20 54	84·4	2 03	19 54	84·4	1 57	18 54	84·3	186	354
173	7	2 50	23 50	83·6	2 44	22 50	83·6	2 37	21 51	83·5	2 30	20 51	83·5	2 23	19 51	83·4	2 16	18 52	83·4	187	353
172	8	3 15	23 47	82·7	3 07	22 48	82·6	3 00	21 48	82·6	2 52	20 49	82·6	2 44	19 49	82·5	2 36	18 50	82·4	188	352
171	9	3 39	23 44	81·8	3 30	22 45	81·7	3 22	21 45	81·6	3 13	20 46	81·6	3 04	19 46	81·5	2 55	18 47	81·5	189	351
170	10	4 03	23 40	80·8	3 53	22 41	80·8	3 44	21 42	80·7	3 35	20 43	80·7	3 24	19 43	80·6	3 14	18 44	80·5	190	350
169	11	4 27	23 36	79·9	4 17	22 37	79·9	4 06	21 38	79·7	3 55	20 39	79·7	3 45	19 40	79·6	3 34	18 41	79·6	191	349
168	12	4 51	23 32	79·0	4 40	22 33	78·9	4 28	21 34	78·8	4 16	20 35	78·8	4 05	19 36	78·7	3 53	18 37	78·6	192	348
167	13	5 15	23 27	78·1	5 03	22 28	78·0	4 50	21 29	77·9	4 37	20 31	77·8	4 25	19 32	77·8	4 12	18 33	77·7	193	347
166	14	5 39	23 22	77·2	5 26	22 23	77·1	5 12	21 24	77·0	4 58	20 26	76·9	4 45	19 27	76·8	4 31	18 28	76·7	194	346
165	15	6 03	23 16	76·2	5 48	22 18	76·1	5 34	21 19	76·0	5 19	20 21	76·0	5 05	19 22	75·9	4 50	18 24	75·8	195	345
164	16	6 26	23 10	75·3	6 11	22 12	75·2	5 56	21 13	75·1	5 40	20 15	75·0	5 25	19 17	74·9	5 09	18 19	74·8	196	344
163	17	6 50	23 04	74·4	6 34	22 06	74·3	6 17	21 08	74·2	6 01	20 09	74·1	5 44	19 11	74·0	5 28	18 14	73·9	197	343
162	18	7 13	22 57	73·5	6 56	21 59	73·3	6 39	21 01	73·2	6 21	20 03	73·1	6 04	19 06	73·0	5 46	18 08	72·9	198	342
161	19	7 37	22 50	72·5	7 19	21 52	72·4	7 00	20 54	72·3	6 42	19 57	72·2	6 24	18 59	72·1	6 05	18 02	72·0	199	341
160	20	8 00	22 42	71·6	7 41	21 45	71·5	7 22	20 47	71·4	7 02	19 50	71·2	6 43	18 53	71·1	6 24	17 56	71·0	200	340
159	21	8 23	22 34	70·7	8 03	21 37	70·5	7 43	20 40	70·4	7 23	19 43	70·3	7 02	18 46	70·2	6 42	17 49	70·1	201	339
158	22	8 46	22 26	69·7	8 25	21 29	69·6	8 04	20 32	69·5	7 43	19 36	69·3	7 22	18 39	69·2	7 00	17 42	69·1	202	338
157	23	9 09	22 17	68·8	8 47	21 21	68·7	8 25	20 24	68·5	8 03	19 28	68·4	7 41	18 31	68·3	7 19	17 35	68·1	203	337
156	24	9 31	22 08	67·9	9 09	21 12	67·7	8 46	20 16	67·6	8 23	19 20	67·4	8 00	18 24	67·3	7 37	17 28	67·2	204	336
155	25	9 54	21 58	66·9	9 30	21 03	66·8	9 07	20 07	66·6	8 43	19 11	66·5	8 19	18 15	66·3	7 55	17 20	66·2	205	335
154	26	10 16	21 49	66·0	9 52	20 53	65·8	9 27	19 57	65·7	9 02	19 02	65·5	8 37	18 07	65·4	8 13	17 12	65·2	206	334
153	27	10 38	21 38	65·0	10 13	20 43	64·9	9 48	19 48	64·7	9 22	18 53	64·6	8 56	17 58	64·4	8 30	17 03	64·3	207	333
152	28	11 00	21 28	64·1	10 34	20 33	63·9	10 08	19 38	63·8	9 41	18 44	63·6	9 14	17 49	63·5	8 48	16 55	63·3	208	332
151	29	11 22	21 17	63·1	10 55	20 22	63·0	10 28	19 28	62·8	10 00	18 34	62·6	9 33	17 39	62·5	9 05	16 46	62·3	209	331
150	30	11 44	21 05	62·2	11 16	20 11	62·0	10 48	19 17	61·8	10 19	18 24	61·7	9 51	17 30	61·5	9 22	16 36	61·3	210	330
149	31	12 06	20 53	61·2	11 37	20 00	61·1	11 07	19 06	60·9	10 38	18 13	60·8	10 09	17 20	60·5	9 39	16 27	60·4	211	329
148	32	12 27	20 41	60·3	11 57	19 48	60·1	11 27	18 55	59·9	10 57	18 02	59·8	10 27	17 09	59·6	9 56	16 17	59·4	212	328
147	33	12 48	20 29	59·3	12 17	19 36	59·1	11 46	18 43	58·9	11 15	17 51	58·8	10 44	16 58	58·6	10 13	16 06	58·4	213	327
146	34	13 09	20 16	58·4	12 37	19 23	58·2	12 06	18 31	58·0	11 34	17 39	57·9	11 02	16 47	57·6	10 29	15 56	57·5	214	326
145	35	13 29	20 02	57·4	12 57	19 10	57·2	12 24	18 19	57·0	11 52	17 28	56·9	11 19	16 36	56·7	10 46	15 45	56·5	215	325
144	36	13 50	19 49	56·4	13 17	18 57	56·2	12 43	18 06	56·0	12 10	17 15	55·9	11 36	16 24	55·7	11 02	15 34	55·5	216	324
143	37	14 10	19 34	55·5	13 36	18 44	55·3	13 02	17 53	55·1	12 28	17 03	54·9	11 53	16 12	54·7	11 18	15 23	54·5	217	323
142	38	14 30	19 20	54·5	13 55	18 30	54·3	13 20	17 40	54·1	12 45	16 50	53·9	12 09	16 00	53·7	11 34	15 11	53·5	218	322
141	39	14 50	19 05	53·5	14 14	18 15	53·3	13 38	17 26	53·1	13 02	16 37	52·9	12 26	15 48	52·7	11 49	14 59	52·6	219	321
140	40	15 09	18 50	52·5	14 33	18 01	52·3	13 56	17 12	52·1	13 19	16 24	51·9	12 42	15 35	51·7	12 05	14 47	51·6	220	320
139	41	15 29	18 34	51·5	14 51	17 46	51·3	14 14	16 57	51·1	13 36	16 10	50·9	12 58	15 22	50·8	12 20	14 34	50·6	221	319
138	42	15 48	18 18	50·6	15 09	17 30	50·3	14 31	16 43	50·1	13 52	15 56	49·9	13 14	15 08	49·8	12 35	14 21	49·6	222	318
137	43	16 06	18 02	49·6	15 27	17 15	49·4	14 48	16 28	49·2	14 09	15 41	49·0	13 29	14 54	48·8	12 50	14 08	48·6	223	317
136	44	16 25	17 46	48·6	15 45	16 59	48·4	15 05	16 12	48·2	14 25	15 26	48·0	13 45	14 40	47·8	13 04	13 55	47·6	224	316
135	45	16 43	17 29	47·6	16 02	16 42	47·4	15 22	15 57	47·2	14 41	15 11	47·0	14 00	14 26	46·8	13 19	13 41	46·6	225	315

© British Crown Copyright 2018. All rights reserved.

Lat./A LHA/F	66° A/H	66° B/P	66° Z_1/Z_2	67° A/H	67° B/P	67° Z_1/Z_2	68° A/H	68° B/P	68° Z_1/Z_2	69° A/H	69° B/P	69° Z_1/Z_2	70° A/H	70° B/P	70° Z_1/Z_2	71° A/H	71° B/P	71° Z_1/Z_2	Lat./A LHA
45	16 43	17 29	47.6	16 02	16 42	47.4	15 22	15 57	47.2	14 41	15 11	47.0	14 00	14 26	46.8	13 19	13 41	46.6	315 / 225
46	17 01	17 11	46.6	16 19	16 26	46.4	15 38	15 41	46.2	14 56	14 56	46.0	14 15	14 11	45.8	13 33	13 27	45.6	314 / 226
47	17 18	16 53	45.6	16 36	16 09	45.4	15 54	15 24	45.2	15 12	14 40	45.0	14 29	13 56	44.8	13 46	13 13	44.6	313 / 227
48	17 36	16 35	44.6	16 53	15 51	44.4	16 10	15 08	44.2	15 27	14 24	44.0	14 43	13 41	43.8	14 00	12 58	43.6	312 / 228
49	17 53	16 17	43.6	17 09	15 34	43.4	16 25	14 51	43.2	15 42	14 08	43.0	14 58	13 26	42.8	14 13	12 44	42.6	311 / 229
50	18 09	15 58	42.6	17 25	15 16	42.4	16 41	14 33	42.1	15 56	13 52	41.9	15 11	13 10	41.8	14 27	12 29	41.6	310 / 230
51	18 26	15 39	41.6	17 41	14 57	41.3	16 56	14 16	41.1	16 10	13 35	40.9	15 25	12 54	40.8	14 39	12 14	40.6	309 / 231
52	18 42	15 20	40.5	17 56	14 39	40.3	17 10	13 58	40.1	16 24	13 18	39.9	15 38	12 38	39.7	14 52	11 58	39.6	308 / 232
53	18 57	15 00	39.5	18 11	14 20	39.3	17 24	13 40	39.1	16 38	13 00	38.9	15 51	12 21	38.7	15 04	11 42	38.6	307 / 233
54	19 13	14 40	38.5	18 26	14 01	38.3	17 39	13 22	38.1	16 51	12 43	37.9	16 04	12 05	37.7	15 16	11 26	37.6	306 / 234
55	19 28	14 20	37.5	18 40	13 41	37.3	17 52	13 03	37.1	17 04	12 25	36.9	16 16	11 48	36.7	15 28	11 10	36.5	305 / 235
56	19 42	13 59	36.4	18 54	13 21	36.2	18 06	12 44	36.0	17 17	12 07	35.8	16 28	11 30	35.7	15 40	10 54	35.5	304 / 236
57	19 57	13 38	35.4	19 08	13 01	35.2	18 19	12 25	35.0	17 29	11 49	34.8	16 40	11 13	34.6	15 51	10 37	34.5	303 / 237
58	20 11	13 17	34.4	19 21	12 41	34.2	18 31	12 05	34.0	17 42	11 30	33.8	16 52	10 55	33.6	16 02	10 20	33.5	302 / 238
59	20 24	12 55	33.3	19 34	12 20	33.1	18 44	11 45	32.9	17 53	11 11	32.8	17 04	10 37	32.6	16 13	10 03	32.4	301 / 239
60	20 37	12 33	32.3	19 47	11 59	32.1	18 56	11 25	31.9	18 05	10 52	31.7	17 14	10 19	31.6	16 23	9 46	31.4	300 / 240
61	20 50	12 11	31.2	19 59	11 38	31.1	19 08	11 05	30.9	18 16	10 33	30.7	17 24	10 00	30.5	16 33	9 29	30.4	299 / 241
62	21 03	11 48	30.2	20 11	11 16	30.0	19 19	10 44	29.8	18 27	10 13	29.7	17 35	9 42	29.5	16 42	9 11	29.4	298 / 242
63	21 15	11 26	29.2	20 22	10 54	29.0	19 30	10 24	28.8	18 37	9 53	28.6	17 45	9 23	28.5	16 52	8 53	28.3	297 / 243
64	21 27	11 03	28.1	20 34	10 32	27.9	19 41	10 03	27.7	18 47	9 33	27.6	17 54	9 04	27.4	17 01	8 35	27.3	296 / 244
65	21 38	10 39	27.0	20 45	10 10	26.9	19 51	9 41	26.7	18 57	9 13	26.5	18 03	8 45	26.4	17 10	8 17	26.3	295 / 245
66	21 49	10 16	26.0	20 55	9 48	25.8	20 01	9 20	25.7	19 07	8 52	25.5	18 12	8 25	25.4	17 18	7 58	25.2	294 / 246
67	21 59	9 52	24.9	21 05	9 25	24.8	20 10	8 58	24.6	19 16	8 32	24.5	18 20	8 06	24.3	17 26	7 40	24.2	293 / 247
68	22 09	9 28	23.9	21 14	9 02	23.7	20 19	8 36	23.5	19 24	8 11	23.4	18 29	7 46	23.3	17 34	7 21	23.1	292 / 248
69	22 19	9 04	22.8	21 24	8 39	22.6	20 28	8 14	22.5	19 33	7 50	22.4	18 37	7 26	22.2	17 42	7 02	22.1	291 / 249
70	22 28	8 39	21.7	21 32	8 16	21.6	20 37	7 52	21.4	19 41	7 29	21.3	18 45	7 06	21.2	17 49	6 43	21.1	290 / 250
71	22 37	8 15	20.7	21 41	7 52	20.5	20 45	7 30	20.4	19 48	7 07	20.2	18 52	6 45	20.1	17 56	6 24	20.0	289 / 251
72	22 45	7 50	19.6	21 49	7 28	19.4	20 52	7 07	19.3	19 56	6 46	19.2	19 00	6 25	19.1	18 02	6 04	19.0	288 / 252
73	22 53	7 25	18.5	21 56	7 04	18.4	21 00	6 44	18.2	20 03	6 24	18.1	19 05	6 04	18.0	18 08	5 45	17.9	287 / 253
74	23 01	7 00	17.4	22 04	6 40	17.3	21 06	6 21	17.2	20 09	6 02	17.1	19 12	5 44	17.0	18 14	5 25	16.9	286 / 254
75	23 08	6 34	16.3	22 10	6 16	16.2	21 13	5 58	16.1	20 15	5 40	16.0	19 17	5 23	15.9	18 20	5 06	15.8	285 / 255
76	23 15	6 09	15.3	22 17	5 51	15.2	21 19	5 35	15.0	20 21	5 18	15.0	19 23	5 02	14.9	18 25	4 46	14.8	284 / 256
77	23 21	5 43	14.2	22 23	5 27	14.1	21 24	5 12	14.0	20 26	4 56	13.9	19 28	4 41	13.8	18 30	4 26	13.7	283 / 257
78	23 27	5 17	13.1	22 28	5 03	13.0	21 30	4 48	12.9	20 31	4 34	12.8	19 33	4 20	12.7	18 34	4 06	12.7	282 / 258
79	23 32	4 51	12.0	22 33	4 38	11.9	21 35	4 24	11.8	20 36	4 11	11.8	19 37	3 58	11.7	18 38	3 46	11.6	281 / 259
80	23 37	4 25	10.9	22 38	4 13	10.8	21 39	4 01	10.8	20 40	3 49	10.7	19 41	3 37	10.6	18 42	3 25	10.6	280 / 260
81	23 41	3 59	9.8	22 42	3 48	9.8	21 43	3 37	9.7	20 44	3 26	9.6	19 45	3 16	9.5	18 45	3 05	9.5	279 / 261
82	23 45	3 33	8.7	22 46	3 23	8.6	21 46	3 13	8.6	20 47	3 03	8.6	19 48	2 54	8.5	18 48	2 45	8.5	278 / 262
83	23 49	3 06	7.7	22 49	2 58	7.6	21 50	2 49	7.5	20 50	2 41	7.5	19 51	2 32	7.4	18 51	2 24	7.4	277 / 263
84	23 52	2 40	6.6	22 52	2 32	6.5	21 52	2 25	6.5	20 53	2 18	6.4	19 53	2 11	6.4	18 53	2 04	6.3	276 / 264
85	23 54	2 13	5.5	22 54	2 07	5.4	21 55	2 01	5.4	20 55	1 55	5.4	19 55	1 49	5.3	18 55	1 43	5.3	275 / 265
86	23 56	1 47	4.4	22 56	1 42	4.3	21 57	1 37	4.3	20 57	1 32	4.3	19 57	1 27	4.3	18 57	1 23	4.2	274 / 266
87	23 58	1 20	3.3	22 58	1 16	3.3	21 58	1 13	3.2	20 58	1 09	3.2	19 58	1 05	3.2	18 58	1 02	3.2	273 / 267
88	23 59	0 53	2.2	22 59	0 51	2.2	21 59	0 48	2.2	20 59	0 46	2.1	19 59	0 44	2.1	18 59	0 41	2.1	272 / 268
89	24 00	0 27	1.1	23 00	0 25	1.1	22 00	0 24	1.1	21 00	0 23	1.1	20 00	0 22	1.1	19 00	0 21	1.1	271 / 269
90	24 00	0 00	0.0	23 00	0 00	0.0	22 00	0 00	0.0	21 00	0 00	0.0	20 00	0 00	0.0	19 00	0 00	0.0	270 / 270

N. Lat: for LHA > 180° ... $Z_n = Z$, for LHA < 180° ... $Z_n = 360° - Z$

S. Lat: for LHA > 180° ... $Z_n = 180° - Z$, for LHA < 180° ... $Z_n = 180° + Z$

© British Crown Copyright 2018. All rights reserved.

SIGHT REDUCTION TABLE

B: (−) for 90° < LHA < 270°
Dec: (−) for Lat. contrary name

Z₁: same sign as B
Z₂: (−) for F > 90°

LHA/F	Lat./A	72° A/H	72° B/P	72° Z₁/Z₂	73° A/H	73° B/P	73° Z₁/Z₂	74° A/H	74° B/P	74° Z₁/Z₂	75° A/H	75° B/P	75° Z₁/Z₂	76° A/H	76° B/P	76° Z₁/Z₂	77° A/H	77° B/P	77° Z₁/Z₂	Lat./A	LHA
0	180	0 00	18 00	90·0	0 00	17 00	90·0	0 00	16 00	90·0	0 00	15 00	90·0	0 00	14 00	90·0	0 00	13 00	90·0	180	360
1	179	0 19	18 00	89·0	0 18	17 00	89·0	0 17	16 00	89·0	0 16	15 00	89·0	0 15	14 00	89·0	0 13	13 00	89·0	181	359
2	178	0 37	17 59	88·1	0 35	16 59	88·1	0 33	15 59	88·1	0 31	14 59	88·1	0 29	13 59	88·1	0 27	13 00	88·1	182	358
3	177	0 56	17 59	87·1	0 53	16 59	87·1	0 50	15 59	87·1	0 47	14 59	87·1	0 44	13 59	87·1	0 40	12 59	87·1	183	357
4	176	1 14	17 58	86·2	1 10	16 58	86·2	1 06	15 58	86·2	1 02	14 58	86·1	0 58	13 58	86·1	0 54	12 58	86·1	184	356
5	175	1 33	17 56	85·2	1 28	16 56	85·2	1 23	15 57	85·2	1 18	14 57	85·2	1 12	13 57	85·1	1 07	12 57	85·1	185	355
6	174	1 51	17 54	84·3	1 45	16 55	84·3	1 39	15 55	84·2	1 33	14 55	84·2	1 27	13 56	84·2	1 21	12 56	84·2	186	354
7	173	2 09	17 52	83·3	2 03	16 53	83·3	1 56	15 53	83·3	1 48	14 54	83·2	1 41	13 54	83·2	1 34	12 54	83·2	187	353
8	172	2 28	17 50	82·4	2 20	16 51	82·3	2 12	15 51	82·3	2 04	14 52	82·3	1 56	13 52	82·3	1 48	12 53	82·2	188	352
9	171	2 46	17 48	81·4	2 37	16 48	81·4	2 28	15 49	81·3	2 19	14 49	81·3	2 10	13 50	81·3	2 01	12 51	81·2	189	351
10	170	3 05	17 45	80·5	2 55	16 45	80·4	2 45	15 46	80·4	2 35	14 47	80·3	2 24	13 48	80·3	2 14	12 49	80·3	190	350
11	169	3 23	17 41	79·5	3 12	16 42	79·5	3 01	15 43	79·4	2 50	14 44	79·4	2 39	13 45	79·3	2 28	12 46	79·3	191	349
12	168	3 41	17 38	78·6	3 29	16 39	78·5	3 17	15 40	78·5	3 05	14 41	78·4	2 53	13 42	78·3	2 41	12 44	78·3	192	348
13	167	3 59	17 34	77·6	3 46	16 35	77·5	3 33	15 37	77·5	3 20	14 38	77·4	3 07	13 39	77·4	2 54	12 41	77·3	193	347
14	166	4 17	17 30	76·7	4 03	16 31	76·6	3 49	15 33	76·5	3 35	14 34	76·5	3 21	13 36	76·4	3 07	12 38	76·3	194	346
15	165	4 35	17 25	75·7	4 20	16 27	75·6	4 05	15 29	75·6	3 50	14 31	75·5	3 35	13 32	75·4	3 20	12 34	75·4	195	345
16	164	4 53	17 21	74·7	4 37	16 23	74·7	4 21	15 25	74·6	4 05	14 27	74·5	3 49	13 29	74·5	3 33	12 31	74·4	196	344
17	163	5 11	17 16	73·8	4 54	16 18	73·7	4 37	15 20	73·6	4 20	14 22	73·5	4 03	13 25	73·5	3 46	12 27	73·4	197	343
18	162	5 29	17 10	72·8	5 11	16 13	72·7	4 53	15 15	72·7	4 35	14 18	72·6	4 17	13 20	72·6	3 59	12 23	72·4	198	342
19	161	5 46	17 05	71·9	5 28	16 07	71·8	5 09	15 10	71·7	4 50	14 13	71·6	4 31	13 16	71·6	4 12	12 19	71·5	199	341
20	160	6 04	16 59	70·9	5 44	16 02	70·8	5 25	15 05	70·7	5 05	14 08	70·6	4 45	13 11	70·6	4 25	12 14	70·5	200	340
21	159	6 21	16 52	69·9	6 01	15 56	69·8	5 40	14 59	69·7	5 19	14 03	69·7	4 58	13 06	69·6	4 37	12 10	69·5	201	339
22	158	6 39	16 46	69·0	6 17	15 50	68·9	5 56	14 53	68·8	5 34	13 57	68·7	5 12	13 01	68·6	4 50	12 05	68·5	202	338
23	157	6 56	16 39	68·0	6 34	15 43	67·9	6 11	14 47	67·8	5 48	13 51	67·7	5 25	12 56	67·6	5 03	12 00	67·5	203	337
24	156	7 13	16 32	67·1	6 50	15 36	66·9	6 26	14 41	66·8	6 03	13 45	66·7	5 39	12 50	66·6	5 15	11 55	66·5	204	336
25	155	7 30	16 24	66·1	7 06	15 29	66·0	6 41	14 34	65·9	6 17	13 39	65·8	5 52	12 44	65·7	5 27	11 49	65·6	205	335
26	154	7 47	16 17	65·1	7 22	15 22	65·0	6 56	14 27	64·9	6 31	13 32	64·8	6 05	12 38	64·7	5 40	11 43	64·6	206	334
27	153	8 04	16 09	64·1	7 38	15 14	64·0	7 11	14 20	63·9	6 45	13 26	63·8	6 18	12 32	63·7	5 52	11 37	63·6	207	333
28	152	8 20	16 00	63·2	7 53	15 06	63·0	7 26	14 12	62·9	6 59	13 19	62·8	6 31	12 25	62·7	6 04	11 31	62·6	208	332
29	151	8 37	15 52	62·2	8 09	14 58	62·1	7 41	14 05	61·9	7 13	13 11	61·8	6 44	12 18	61·7	6 16	11 25	61·6	209	331
30	150	8 53	15 43	61·2	8 24	14 50	61·1	7 55	13 57	61·0	7 26	13 04	60·9	6 57	12 11	60·7	6 27	11 18	60·6	210	330
31	149	9 09	15 34	60·3	8 40	14 41	60·1	8 10	13 49	60·0	7 40	12 56	59·9	7 09	12 04	59·8	6 39	11 12	59·7	211	329
32	148	9 25	15 24	59·3	8 55	14 32	59·1	8 24	13 40	59·0	7 53	12 48	58·9	7 22	11 56	58·8	6 51	11 05	58·7	212	328
33	147	9 41	15 15	58·3	9 10	14 23	58·2	8 38	13 31	58·0	8 06	12 40	57·9	7 34	11 49	57·8	7 02	10 57	57·7	213	327
34	146	9 57	15 05	57·3	9 25	14 13	57·2	8 52	13 22	57·0	8 19	12 31	56·9	7 46	11 41	56·8	7 14	10 50	56·7	214	326
35	145	10 13	14 54	56·3	9 39	14 04	56·2	9 06	13 13	56·1	8 32	12 23	55·9	7 59	11 33	55·8	7 25	10 43	55·7	215	325
36	144	10 28	14 44	55·4	9 54	13 54	55·2	9 19	13 04	55·1	8 45	12 14	54·9	8 11	11 24	54·8	7 36	10 35	54·7	216	324
37	143	10 43	14 33	54·4	10 08	13 43	54·2	9 33	12 54	54·1	8 58	12 05	53·9	8 22	11 16	53·8	7 47	10 27	53·7	217	323
38	142	10 58	14 23	53·4	10 22	13 33	53·2	9 46	12 44	53·1	9 10	11 55	53·0	8 34	11 07	52·8	7 58	10 19	52·7	218	322
39	141	11 13	14 10	52·4	10 36	13 22	52·2	9 59	12 34	52·1	9 22	11 46	52·0	8 45	10 58	51·8	8 08	10 10	51·7	219	321
40	140	11 27	13 59	51·4	10 50	13 11	51·3	10 12	12 24	51·1	9 35	11 36	51·0	8 57	10 49	50·8	8 19	10 02	50·7	220	320
41	139	11 42	13 47	50·4	11 04	13 00	50·3	10 25	12 13	50·1	9 47	11 26	50·0	9 08	10 39	49·9	8 29	9 53	49·7	221	319
42	138	11 56	13 34	49·4	11 17	12 48	49·3	10 38	12 02	49·1	9 58	11 16	49·0	9 19	10 30	48·9	8 39	9 44	48·7	222	318
43	137	12 10	13 22	48·4	11 30	12 36	48·3	10 50	11 51	48·1	10 10	11 05	48·0	9 30	10 20	47·9	8 49	9 35	47·7	223	317
44	136	12 24	13 09	47·4	11 43	12 24	47·3	11 02	11 39	47·1	10 21	10 55	47·0	9 40	10 10	46·9	8 59	9 26	46·7	224	316
45	135	12 37	12 56	46·4	11 56	12 12	46·3	11 14	11 28	46·1	10 33	10 44	46·0	9 51	10 00	45·9	9 09	9 16	45·7	225	315

© British Crown Copyright 2018. All rights reserved.

Lat. / A LHA/F	72° A/H	72° B/P	72° Z₁/Z₂	73° A/H	73° B/P	73° Z₁/Z₂	74° A/H	74° B/P	74° Z₁/Z₂	75° A/H	75° B/P	75° Z₁/Z₂	76° A/H	76° B/P	76° Z₁/Z₂	77° A/H	77° B/P	77° Z₁/Z₂	LHA Lat. / A
45 / 135	12 37	12 56	46·4	11 56	12 12	46·3	11 14	11 28	46·1	10 33	10 44	46·0	9 51	10 00	45·9	9 09	9 16	45·7	225 / 315
46 / 134	12 51	12 43	45·4	12 08	11 59	45·3	11 26	11 16	45·1	10 44	10 33	45·0	10 01	9 50	44·9	9 19	9 07	44·7	226 / 314
47 / 133	13 04	12 30	44·4	12 21	11 47	44·3	11 38	11 04	44·1	10 55	10 21	44·0	10 11	9 39	43·9	9 28	8 57	43·7	227 / 313
48 / 132	13 17	12 16	43·4	12 33	11 34	43·3	11 49	10 52	43·1	11 05	10 10	43·0	10 21	9 28	42·9	9 37	8 47	42·7	228 / 312
49 / 131	13 29	12 02	42·4	12 45	11 21	42·3	12 00	10 39	42·1	11 16	9 58	42·0	10 31	9 17	41·9	9 46	8 37	41·7	229 / 311
50 / 130	13 42	11 48	41·4	12 57	11 07	41·3	12 11	10 27	41·1	11 26	9 46	41·0	10 41	9 06	40·9	9 55	8 26	40·7	230 / 310
51 / 129	13 54	11 33	40·4	13 08	10 53	40·3	12 22	10 14	40·1	11 36	9 34	40·0	10 50	8 55	39·8	10 04	8 16	39·7	231 / 309
52 / 128	14 06	11 19	39·4	13 19	10 40	39·2	12 33	10 01	39·1	11 46	9 22	39·0	10 59	8 44	38·8	10 13	8 05	38·7	232 / 308
53 / 127	14 17	11 04	38·4	13 30	10 26	38·2	12 43	9 47	38·1	11 56	9 10	38·0	11 08	8 32	37·8	10 21	7 55	37·7	233 / 307
54 / 126	14 29	10 49	37·4	13 41	10 11	37·2	12 53	9 34	37·2	12 05	8 57	36·9	11 17	8 20	36·8	10 29	7 44	36·7	234 / 306
55 / 125	14 40	10 33	36·4	13 51	9 57	36·2	13 03	9 20	36·1	12 14	8 44	35·9	11 26	8 08	35·8	10 37	7 33	35·8	235 / 305
56 / 124	14 51	10 18	35·3	14 02	9 42	35·2	13 13	9 07	35·1	12 23	8 31	34·9	11 34	7 56	34·8	10 45	7 21	34·7	236 / 304
57 / 123	15 01	10 02	34·3	14 12	9 27	34·2	13 22	8 53	34·2	12 32	8 18	33·9	11 42	7 44	33·8	10 52	7 10	33·7	237 / 303
58 / 122	15 12	9 46	33·3	14 21	9 12	33·2	13 31	8 38	33·0	12 41	8 05	32·9	11 50	7 32	32·8	11 00	6 58	32·7	238 / 302
59 / 121	15 22	9 30	32·3	14 31	8 57	32·1	13 40	8 24	32·0	12 49	7 51	31·9	11 58	7 19	31·8	11 07	6 47	31·7	239 / 301
60 / 120	15 31	9 14	31·3	14 40	8 41	31·1	13 49	8 10	31·0	12 57	7 38	30·9	12 06	7 06	30·8	11 14	6 35	30·6	240 / 300
61 / 119	15 41	8 57	30·2	14 49	8 26	30·1	13 57	7 55	29·9	13 05	7 24	29·8	12 13	6 54	29·7	11 21	6 23	29·6	241 / 299
62 / 118	15 50	8 40	29·2	14 58	8 10	29·1	14 05	7 40	28·9	13 13	7 10	28·8	12 20	6 41	28·7	11 27	6 11	28·6	242 / 298
63 / 117	15 59	8 23	28·2	15 06	7 54	28·0	14 13	7 25	27·9	13 20	6 56	27·8	12 27	6 27	27·7	11 34	5 59	27·6	243 / 297
64 / 116	16 08	8 06	27·2	15 14	7 38	27·0	14 21	7 10	26·9	13 27	6 42	26·8	12 34	6 14	26·7	11 40	5 47	26·6	244 / 296
65 / 115	16 16	7 49	26·1	15 22	7 22	26·0	14 28	6 55	25·9	13 34	6 28	25·7	12 40	6 01	25·7	11 46	5 34	25·6	245 / 295
66 / 114	16 24	7 32	25·1	15 29	7 05	25·0	14 35	6 39	24·9	13 41	6 13	24·7	12 46	5 47	24·6	11 52	5 22	24·6	246 / 294
67 / 113	16 32	7 14	24·1	15 37	6 49	24·0	14 42	6 24	23·8	13 47	5 59	23·7	12 52	5 34	23·6	11 57	5 09	23·5	247 / 293
68 / 112	16 39	6 56	23·0	15 44	6 32	22·9	14 48	6 08	22·8	13 53	5 44	22·7	12 58	5 20	22·6	12 02	4 57	22·5	248 / 292
69 / 111	16 46	6 38	22·0	15 50	6 15	21·9	14 55	5 52	21·8	13 59	5 29	21·7	13 03	5 06	21·6	12 07	4 44	21·5	249 / 291
70 / 110	16 53	6 20	20·9	15 57	5 58	20·8	15 01	5 36	20·7	14 05	5 14	20·6	13 08	4 52	20·6	12 12	4 31	20·5	250 / 290
71 / 109	16 59	6 02	19·9	16 03	5 41	19·8	15 06	5 20	19·7	14 10	4 59	19·6	13 13	4 38	19·5	12 17	4 18	19·5	251 / 289
72 / 108	17 05	5 44	18·9	16 09	5 24	18·8	15 12	5 04	18·7	14 15	4 44	18·6	13 18	4 24	18·5	12 21	4 05	18·4	252 / 288
73 / 107	17 11	5 26	17·8	16 14	5 06	17·8	15 17	4 48	17·6	14 20	4 29	17·6	13 23	4 10	17·5	12 25	3 52	17·4	253 / 287
74 / 106	17 17	5 07	16·8	16 19	4 49	16·7	15 22	4 31	16·6	14 24	4 13	16·5	13 27	3 56	16·5	12 29	3 38	16·4	254 / 286
75 / 105	17 22	4 48	15·7	16 24	4 31	15·7	15 26	4 15	15·6	14 29	3 58	15·5	13 31	3 42	15·4	12 33	3 25	15·4	255 / 285
76 / 104	17 27	4 30	14·7	16 29	4 13	14·6	15 31	3 58	14·5	14 33	3 43	14·5	13 35	3 27	14·4	12 36	3 12	14·3	256 / 284
77 / 103	17 31	4 11	13·6	16 33	3 56	13·6	15 35	3 41	13·5	14 36	3 27	13·4	13 38	3 13	13·3	12 40	2 58	13·3	257 / 283
78 / 102	17 36	3 53	12·6	16 37	3 38	12·5	15 39	3 25	12·5	14 40	3 11	12·4	13 41	2 58	12·4	12 43	2 45	12·3	258 / 282
79 / 101	17 39	3 33	11·6	16 41	3 20	11·5	15 42	3 08	11·4	14 43	2 56	11·4	13 44	2 43	11·3	12 45	2 31	11·3	259 / 281
80 / 100	17 43	3 14	10·5	16 44	3 02	10·4	15 45	2 51	10·4	14 46	2 40	10·3	13 47	2 29	10·3	12 48	2 18	10·3	260 / 280
81 / 99	17 46	2 55	9·5	16 47	2 44	9·4	15 48	2 34	9·4	14 49	2 24	9·3	13 49	2 14	9·3	12 50	2 04	9·2	261 / 279
82 / 98	17 49	2 36	8·4	16 50	2 26	8·4	15 50	2 17	8·3	14 51	2 08	8·3	13 52	1 59	8·2	12 52	1 50	8·2	262 / 278
83 / 97	17 52	2 16	7·4	16 52	2 08	7·3	15 53	2 00	7·3	14 53	1 52	7·2	13 54	1 44	7·2	12 54	1 37	7·2	263 / 277
84 / 96	17 54	1 57	6·3	16 54	1 50	6·3	15 55	1 43	6·2	14 55	1 36	6·2	13 55	1 30	6·2	12 56	1 23	6·2	264 / 276
85 / 95	17 56	1 37	5·3	16 56	1 32	5·2	15 56	1 26	5·2	14 57	1 20	5·2	13 57	1 15	5·1	12 57	1 09	5·1	265 / 275
86 / 94	17 57	1 18	4·2	16 57	1 13	4·2	15 58	1 09	4·2	14 58	1 04	4·1	13 57	1 00	4·1	12 58	0 55	4·1	266 / 274
87 / 93	17 58	0 58	3·2	16 59	0 55	3·1	15 59	0 52	3·1	14 59	0 48	3·1	13 59	0 45	3·1	12 59	0 42	3·1	267 / 273
88 / 92	17 59	0 39	2·1	16 59	0 37	2·1	15 59	0 34	2·1	14 59	0 32	2·1	13 59	0 30	2·1	13 00	0 28	2·1	268 / 272
89 / 91	18 00	0 19	1·1	17 00	0 18	1·0	16 00	0 17	1·0	15 00	0 16	1·0	14 00	0 15	1·0	13 00	0 14	1·0	269 / 271
90 / 90	18 00	0 00	0·0	17 00	0 00	0·0	16 00	0 00	0·0	15 00	0 00	0·0	14 00	0 00	0·0	13 00	0 00	0·0	270 / 270

N. Lat.: for LHA > 180° ... Zₙ = Z / for LHA < 180° ... Zₙ = 360° − Z

S. Lat.: for LHA > 180° ... Zₙ = 180° − Z / for LHA < 180° ... Zₙ = 180° + Z

© British Crown Copyright 2018. All rights reserved.

SIGHT REDUCTION TABLE

B: (−) for 90° < LHA < 270°
Dec:(−) for Lat. contrary name

Z₁: same sign as B
Z₂: (−) for F > 90°

LHA/F	Lat./A	78° A/H	78° B/P	78° Z₁/Z₂	79° A/H	79° B/P	79° Z₁/Z₂	80° A/H	80° B/P	80° Z₁/Z₂	81° A/H	81° B/P	81° Z₁/Z₂	82° A/H	82° B/P	82° Z₁/Z₂	83° A/H	83° B/P	83° Z₁/Z₂	Lat./A	LHA
0	180	0 00	12 00	90.0	0 00	11 00	90.0	0 00	10 00	90.0	0 00	9 00	90.0	0 00	8 00	90.0	0 00	7 00	90.0	180	360
1	179	0 12	12 00	89.0	0 11	11 00	89.0	0 10	10 00	89.0	0 09	9 00	89.0	0 08	8 00	89.0	0 07	7 00	89.0	181	359
2	178	0 25	12 00	88.0	0 23	11 00	88.0	0 21	10 00	88.0	0 19	9 00	88.0	0 17	8 00	88.0	0 15	7 00	88.0	182	358
3	177	0 37	11 59	87.1	0 34	10 59	87.1	0 31	9 59	87.1	0 28	8 59	87.0	0 25	7 59	87.0	0 22	6 59	87.0	183	357
4	176	0 50	11 58	86.1	0 46	10 58	86.1	0 42	9 59	86.1	0 38	8 59	86.0	0 33	7 59	86.0	0 29	6 59	86.0	184	356
5	175	1 02	11 57	85.1	0 57	10 58	85.1	0 52	9 58	85.1	0 47	8 58	85.1	0 42	7 58	85.0	0 37	6 58	85.0	185	355
6	174	1 15	11 56	84.1	1 09	10 56	84.1	1 02	9 57	84.1	0 56	8 57	84.1	0 50	7 57	84.1	0 44	6 58	84.0	186	354
7	173	1 27	11 55	83.2	1 20	10 55	83.1	1 13	9 56	83.1	1 06	8 56	83.1	0 58	7 56	83.1	0 51	6 57	83.1	187	353
8	172	1 39	11 54	82.2	1 31	10 54	82.2	1 23	9 54	82.1	1 15	8 55	82.1	1 07	7 55	82.1	0 58	6 56	82.1	188	352
9	171	1 52	11 51	81.2	1 43	10 52	81.2	1 33	9 53	81.2	1 24	8 53	81.1	1 15	7 54	81.1	1 06	6 54	81.1	189	351
10	170	2 04	11 49	80.2	1 54	10 50	80.2	1 44	9 51	80.2	1 33	8 52	80.1	1 23	7 53	80.1	1 13	6 53	80.1	190	350
11	169	2 16	11 47	79.2	2 05	10 48	79.2	1 54	9 49	79.2	1 43	8 50	79.1	1 31	7 51	79.1	1 20	6 52	79.1	191	349
12	168	2 29	11 45	78.3	2 16	10 46	78.2	2 04	9 47	78.2	1 52	8 48	78.1	1 39	7 50	78.1	1 27	6 51	78.1	192	348
13	167	2 41	11 42	77.3	2 28	10 43	77.2	2 14	9 45	77.2	2 01	8 46	77.2	1 48	7 48	77.1	1 34	6 49	77.1	193	347
14	166	2 53	11 39	76.3	2 39	10 41	76.2	2 24	9 43	76.2	2 10	8 44	76.2	1 56	7 46	76.1	1 41	6 48	76.1	194	346
15	165	3 05	11 36	75.3	2 50	10 38	75.3	2 35	9 40	75.2	2 19	8 42	75.2	2 04	7 44	75.1	1 48	6 46	75.1	195	345
16	164	3 17	11 33	74.3	3 01	10 35	74.3	2 45	9 37	74.2	2 28	8 39	74.2	2 12	7 42	74.2	1 56	6 44	74.1	196	344
17	163	3 29	11 29	73.4	3 12	10 32	73.3	2 55	9 34	73.3	2 37	8 37	73.2	2 20	7 39	73.2	2 03	6 42	73.1	197	343
18	162	3 41	11 26	72.4	3 23	10 28	72.3	3 05	9 31	72.3	2 46	8 34	72.2	2 28	7 37	72.2	2 09	6 40	72.1	198	342
19	161	3 53	11 22	71.4	3 34	10 25	71.4	3 14	9 28	71.3	2 55	8 31	71.2	2 36	7 34	71.2	2 16	6 37	71.1	199	341
20	160	4 05	11 18	70.4	3 45	10 21	70.4	3 24	9 24	70.3	3 04	8 28	70.2	2 44	7 31	70.2	2 23	6 35	70.1	200	340
21	159	4 16	11 13	69.4	3 55	10 17	69.4	3 34	9 21	69.3	3 13	8 25	69.3	2 52	7 28	69.2	2 30	6 32	69.1	201	339
22	158	4 28	11 09	68.4	4 06	10 13	68.4	3 44	9 17	68.3	3 22	8 21	68.3	2 59	7 25	68.2	2 37	6 30	68.1	202	338
23	157	4 40	11 04	67.5	4 17	10 09	67.4	3 53	9 13	67.3	3 30	8 18	67.3	3 07	7 22	67.2	2 44	6 27	67.2	203	337
24	156	4 51	10 59	66.5	4 27	10 04	66.5	4 03	9 09	66.3	3 39	8 14	66.3	3 15	7 19	66.2	2 50	6 24	66.2	204	336
25	155	5 03	10 54	65.5	4 38	9 59	65.5	4 13	9 05	65.4	3 47	8 10	65.3	3 22	7 16	65.2	2 57	6 21	65.2	205	335
26	154	5 14	10 49	64.5	4 48	9 55	64.5	4 22	9 00	64.4	3 56	8 06	64.3	3 30	7 12	64.2	3 04	6 18	64.2	206	334
27	153	5 25	10 43	63.5	4 58	9 50	63.5	4 31	8 56	63.4	4 04	8 02	63.3	3 37	7 08	63.2	3 10	6 15	63.2	207	333
28	152	5 36	10 38	62.5	5 08	9 44	62.5	4 41	8 51	62.4	4 13	7 58	62.3	3 45	7 04	62.2	3 17	6 11	62.2	208	332
29	151	5 47	10 32	61.5	5 18	9 39	61.5	4 50	8 46	61.4	4 21	7 53	61.3	3 52	7 00	61.2	3 23	6 08	61.2	209	331
30	150	5 58	10 26	60.5	5 28	9 33	60.5	4 59	8 41	60.4	4 29	7 49	60.3	3 59	6 56	60.2	3 30	6 04	60.2	210	330
31	149	6 09	10 20	59.6	5 38	9 28	59.5	5 08	8 36	59.5	4 37	7 44	59.3	4 07	6 52	59.2	3 36	6 00	59.2	211	329
32	148	6 20	10 13	58.6	5 48	9 22	58.6	5 17	8 30	58.5	4 45	7 39	58.3	4 14	6 48	58.3	3 42	5 57	58.2	212	328
33	147	6 30	10 06	57.6	5 58	9 16	57.6	5 26	8 25	57.5	4 53	7 34	57.3	4 21	6 43	57.3	3 48	5 53	57.2	213	327
34	146	6 41	10 00	56.6	6 08	9 09	56.6	5 34	8 19	56.5	5 01	7 29	56.4	4 28	6 39	56.3	3 54	5 49	56.2	214	326
35	145	6 51	9 53	55.6	6 17	9 03	55.6	5 43	8 13	55.5	5 09	7 24	55.4	4 35	6 34	55.3	4 00	5 45	55.2	215	325
36	144	7 01	9 45	54.6	6 26	8 56	54.6	5 51	8 07	54.5	5 17	7 18	54.4	4 42	6 29	54.3	4 06	5 40	54.2	216	324
37	143	7 11	9 38	53.6	6 36	8 49	53.6	6 00	8 01	53.5	5 24	7 13	53.4	4 48	6 24	53.3	4 12	5 36	53.2	217	323
38	142	7 21	9 31	52.6	6 45	8 43	52.6	6 08	7 55	52.5	5 32	7 07	52.4	4 55	6 19	52.3	4 18	5 32	52.2	218	322
39	141	7 31	9 23	51.6	6 54	8 35	51.6	6 16	7 48	51.5	5 39	7 01	51.4	5 01	6 14	51.3	4 24	5 27	51.2	219	321
40	140	7 41	9 15	50.6	7 03	8 28	50.6	6 24	7 42	50.5	5 46	6 55	50.4	5 08	6 09	50.3	4 30	5 22	50.2	220	320
41	139	7 50	9 07	49.6	7 11	8 21	49.6	6 32	7 35	49.5	5 53	6 49	49.4	5 14	6 03	49.3	4 35	5 18	49.2	221	319
42	138	8 00	8 59	48.6	7 20	8 13	48.6	6 40	7 28	48.5	6 01	6 43	48.4	5 21	5 58	48.3	4 41	5 13	48.2	222	318
43	137	8 09	8 50	47.6	7 29	8 05	47.6	6 48	7 21	47.5	6 07	6 36	47.4	5 27	5 52	47.3	4 46	5 08	47.2	223	317
44	136	8 18	8 42	46.6	7 37	7 58	46.6	6 56	7 14	46.5	6 14	6 30	46.4	5 33	5 46	46.3	4 51	5 03	46.2	224	316
45	135	8 27	8 33	45.6	7 45	7 50	45.6	7 03	7 06	45.5	6 21	6 23	45.4	5 39	5 41	45.3	4 57	4 58	45.2	225	315

© British Crown Copyright 2018. All rights reserved.

LHA/F	A	78° A/H	78° B/P	78° Z_1/Z_2	79° A/H	79° B/P	79° Z_1/Z_2	80° A/H	80° B/P	80° Z_1/Z_2	81° A/H	81° B/P	81° Z_1/Z_2	82° A/H	82° B/P	82° Z_1/Z_2	83° A/H	83° B/P	83° Z_1/Z_2	A	LHA
45	135	8 27	8 33	45·6	7 45	7 50	45·5	7 03	7 06	45·4	6 21	6 23	45·4	5 39	5 41	45·3	4 57	4 58	45·2	315	225
46	134	8 36	8 24	44·6	7 53	7 41	44·5	7 11	6 59	44·4	6 28	6 17	44·4	5 45	5 35	44·3	5 02	4 53	44·2	314	226
47	133	8 45	8 15	43·6	8 01	7 33	43·5	7 18	6 51	43·4	6 34	6 10	43·4	5 51	5 28	43·3	5 07	4 47	43·2	313	227
48	132	8 53	8 06	42·6	8 09	7 25	42·5	7 25	6 44	42·4	6 41	6 03	42·4	5 56	5 22	42·3	5 12	4 42	42·2	312	228
49	131	9 02	7 56	41·6	8 17	7 16	41·5	7 32	6 36	41·4	6 47	5 56	41·4	6 02	5 16	41·3	5 17	4 36	41·2	311	229
50	130	9 10	7 47	40·6	8 24	7 07	40·5	7 39	6 28	40·4	6 53	5 49	40·3	6 07	5 10	40·3	5 21	4 31	40·2	310	230
51	129	9 18	7 37	39·6	8 32	6 58	39·5	7 45	6 20	39·4	6 59	5 42	39·3	6 13	5 03	39·3	5 26	4 25	39·3	309	231
52	128	9 26	7 27	38·6	8 39	6 49	38·5	7 52	6 12	38·4	7 05	5 34	38·3	6 18	4 57	38·3	5 31	4 19	38·2	308	232
53	127	9 33	7 17	37·6	8 46	6 40	37·5	7 58	6 03	37·4	7 11	5 27	37·3	6 23	4 50	37·3	5 35	4 14	37·2	307	233
54	126	9 41	7 07	36·6	8 53	6 31	36·5	8 05	5 55	36·4	7 16	5 19	36·3	6 28	4 43	36·3	5 39	4 08	36·2	306	234
55	125	9 48	6 57	35·6	9 00	6 22	35·5	8 11	5 47	35·4	7 22	5 11	35·3	6 33	4 37	35·3	5 44	4 02	35·2	305	235
56	124	9 56	6 47	34·6	9 06	6 12	34·5	8 17	5 38	34·4	7 27	5 04	34·3	6 38	4 30	34·3	5 48	3 56	34·2	304	236
57	123	10 03	6 36	33·6	9 13	6 03	33·5	8 22	5 29	33·4	7 32	4 56	33·3	6 42	4 23	33·3	5 52	3 50	33·2	303	237
58	122	10 09	6 26	32·6	9 19	5 53	32·5	8 28	5 20	32·4	7 37	4 48	32·3	6 47	4 16	32·3	5 56	3 43	32·2	302	238
59	121	10 16	6 15	31·6	9 25	5 43	31·5	8 34	5 11	31·4	7 42	4 40	31·3	6 51	4 08	31·2	6 00	3 37	31·2	301	239
60	120	10 22	6 04	30·5	9 31	5 33	30·5	8 39	5 02	30·4	7 47	4 32	30·3	6 55	4 01	30·2	6 04	3 31	30·2	300	240
61	119	10 29	5 53	29·5	9 36	5 23	29·5	8 44	4 53	29·4	7 52	4 24	29·3	6 59	3 54	29·2	6 07	3 24	29·2	299	241
62	118	10 35	5 42	28·5	9 42	5 13	28·4	8 49	4 44	28·4	7 56	4 15	28·3	7 04	3 46	28·2	6 11	3 18	28·2	298	242
63	117	10 41	5 31	27·5	9 47	5 03	27·4	8 54	4 35	27·4	8 01	4 07	27·3	7 07	3 39	27·3	6 14	3 11	27·2	297	243
64	116	10 46	5 19	26·5	9 52	4 52	26·4	8 59	4 25	26·3	8 05	3 58	26·3	7 11	3 32	26·2	6 17	3 05	26·2	296	244
65	115	10 52	5 08	25·5	9 57	4 42	25·4	9 03	4 16	25·3	8 09	3 50	25·3	7 15	3 24	25·2	6 20	2 58	25·2	295	245
66	114	10 57	4 56	24·5	10 02	4 31	24·4	9 08	4 06	24·3	8 13	3 41	24·3	7 18	3 16	24·2	6 24	2 52	24·2	294	246
67	113	11 02	4 44	23·5	10 07	4 21	23·4	9 12	3 56	23·3	8 17	3 32	23·3	7 22	3 09	23·2	6 26	2 45	23·2	293	247
68	112	11 07	4 33	22·4	10 11	4 10	22·4	9 16	3 47	22·3	8 20	3 24	22·2	7 25	3 01	22·2	6 29	2 38	22·1	292	248
69	111	11 12	4 21	21·4	10 16	3 59	21·4	9 20	3 37	21·3	8 24	3 15	21·2	7 28	2 53	21·2	6 32	2 31	21·1	291	249
70	110	11 16	4 09	20·4	10 20	3 48	20·4	9 23	3 27	20·3	8 27	3 06	20·2	7 31	2 45	20·2	6 35	2 24	20·1	290	250
71	109	11 20	3 58	19·4	10 24	3 37	19·3	9 27	3 17	19·3	8 30	2 57	19·2	7 34	2 37	19·2	6 37	2 17	19·1	289	251
72	108	11 24	3 45	18·4	10 27	3 26	18·3	9 30	3 07	18·3	8 33	2 48	18·2	7 36	2 29	18·2	6 39	2 10	18·1	288	252
73	107	11 28	3 33	17·4	10 31	3 15	17·3	9 34	2 57	17·3	8 36	2 39	17·2	7 39	2 21	17·2	6 42	2 03	17·1	287	253
74	106	11 32	3 21	16·3	10 34	3 04	16·3	9 37	2 47	16·2	8 39	2 30	16·2	7 41	2 13	16·1	6 44	1 56	16·1	286	254
75	105	11 35	3 09	15·3	10 37	2 53	15·3	9 39	2 37	15·2	8 41	2 21	15·2	7 44	2 05	15·1	6 46	1 49	15·1	285	255
76	104	11 38	2 57	14·3	10 40	2 41	14·3	9 42	2 26	14·2	8 44	2 12	14·2	7 46	1 57	14·1	6 47	1 42	14·1	284	256
77	103	11 41	2 44	13·3	10 43	2 30	13·2	9 44	2 16	13·2	8 46	2 02	13·2	7 48	1 49	13·1	6 49	1 35	13·1	283	257
78	102	11 44	2 32	12·3	10 45	2 19	12·2	9 47	2 06	12·2	8 48	1 53	12·1	7 49	1 40	12·1	6 51	1 28	12·1	282	258
79	101	11 47	2 19	11·2	10 48	2 07	11·2	9 49	1 56	11·2	8 50	1 44	11·1	7 51	1 32	11·1	6 52	1 21	11·1	281	259
80	100	11 49	2 07	10·2	10 50	1 56	10·2	9 51	1 45	10·2	8 52	1 35	10·1	7 53	1 24	10·1	6 54	1 13	10·1	280	260
81	99	11 51	1 54	9·2	10 52	1 45	9·2	9 53	1 35	9·1	8 53	1 25	9·1	7 54	1 16	9·1	6 55	1 06	9·1	279	261
82	98	11 53	1 42	8·2	10 54	1 33	8·1	9 54	1 24	8·1	8 55	1 16	8·1	7 56	1 07	8·1	6 56	0 59	8·1	278	262
83	97	11 55	1 29	7·2	10 55	1 21	7·1	9 56	1 14	7·1	8 56	1 06	7·1	7 57	0 59	7·1	6 57	0 51	7·1	277	263
84	96	11 56	1 16	6·1	10 56	1 10	6·1	9 57	1 03	6·1	8 57	0 57	6·1	7 57	0 50	6·0	6 58	0 44	6·0	276	264
85	95	11 57	1 03	5·1	10 57	0 58	5·1	9 58	0 53	5·1	8 58	0 47	5·1	7 58	0 42	5·0	6 58	0 37	5·0	275	265
86	94	11 58	0 51	4·1	10 58	0 47	4·1	9 59	0 42	4·1	8 59	0 38	4·0	7 59	0 34	4·0	6 59	0 29	4·0	274	266
87	93	11 59	0 38	3·1	10 59	0 35	3·1	9 59	0 32	3·0	8 59	0 28	3·0	7 59	0 25	3·0	6 59	0 22	3·0	273	267
88	92	12 00	0 26	2·0	11 00	0 23	2·0	10 00	0 21	2·0	9 00	0 19	2·0	8 00	0 17	2·0	7 00	0 15	2·0	272	268
89	91	12 00	0 13	1·0	11 00	0 12	1·0	10 00	0 11	1·0	9 00	0 10	1·0	8 00	0 08	1·0	7 00	0 07	1·0	271	269
90	90	12 00	0 00	0·0	11 00	0 00	0·0	10 00	0 00	0·0	9 00	0 00	0·0	8 00	0 00	0·0	7 00	0 00	0·0	270	270

N. Lat.: for LHA > 180° ... $Z_n = Z$
for LHA < 180° ... $Z_n = 360° - Z$

S. Lat.: for LHA > 180° ... $Z_n = 180° - Z$
for LHA < 180° ... $Z_n = 180° + Z$

© British Crown Copyright 2018. All rights reserved.

SIGHT REDUCTION TABLE

B: (−) for 90° < LHA < 270°
Dec:(−) for Lat. contrary name

Z₁ : same sign as B
Z₂ : (−) for F > 90°

LHA/F	84° A/H	B/P	Z₁/Z₂	85° A/H	B/P	Z₁/Z₂	86° A/H	B/P	Z₁/Z₂	87° A/H	B/P	Z₁/Z₂	88° A/H	B/P	Z₁/Z₂	89° A/H	B/P	Z₁/Z₂	Z₁/Z₂	LHA
0 / 180	0 00	6 00	90·0	0 00	5 00	90·0	0 00	4 00	90·0	0 00	3 00	90·0	0 00	2 00	90·0	0 00	1 00	90·0	90·0	180 / 360
1 / 179	0 06	6 00	89·0	0 05	5 00	89·0	0 04	4 00	89·0	0 03	3 00	89·0	0 02	2 00	89·0	0 01	1 00	89·0	89·0	181 / 359
2 / 178	0 13	6 00	88·0	0 10	5 00	88·0	0 08	4 00	88·0	0 06	3 00	88·0	0 04	2 00	88·0	0 02	1 00	88·0	88·0	182 / 358
3 / 177	0 19	6 00	87·0	0 16	5 00	87·0	0 13	4 00	87·0	0 09	3 00	87·0	0 06	2 00	87·0	0 03	1 00	87·0	87·0	183 / 357
4 / 176	0 25	5 59	86·0	0 21	5 00	86·0	0 17	4 00	86·0	0 13	3 00	86·0	0 08	2 00	86·0	0 04	1 00	86·0	86·0	184 / 356
5 / 175	0 31	5 59	85·0	0 26	4 59	85·0	0 21	3 59	85·0	0 16	2 59	85·0	0 10	2 00	85·0	0 05	1 00	85·0	85·0	185 / 355
6 / 174	0 38	5 58	84·0	0 31	4 58	84·0	0 25	3 59	84·0	0 19	2 59	84·0	0 13	1 59	84·0	0 06	1 00	84·0	84·0	186 / 354
7 / 173	0 44	5 57	83·0	0 37	4 58	83·0	0 29	3 58	83·0	0 22	2 59	83·0	0 15	1 59	83·0	0 07	1 00	83·0	83·0	187 / 353
8 / 172	0 50	5 57	82·0	0 42	4 57	82·0	0 33	3 58	82·0	0 25	2 58	82·0	0 17	1 59	82·0	0 08	0 59	82·0	82·0	188 / 352
9 / 171	0 56	5 56	81·0	0 47	4 56	81·0	0 38	3 57	81·0	0 28	2 58	81·0	0 19	1 59	81·0	0 09	0 59	81·0	81·0	189 / 351
10 / 170	1 02	5 55	80·1	0 52	4 55	80·1	0 42	3 56	80·0	0 31	2 57	80·0	0 21	1 58	80·0	0 10	0 59	80·0	80·0	190 / 350
11 / 169	1 09	5 53	79·1	0 57	4 55	79·1	0 46	3 56	79·0	0 34	2 57	79·0	0 23	1 58	79·0	0 11	0 59	79·0	79·0	191 / 349
12 / 168	1 15	5 52	78·1	1 02	4 53	78·1	0 50	3 55	78·0	0 37	2 56	78·0	0 25	1 57	78·0	0 12	0 59	78·0	78·0	192 / 348
13 / 167	1 21	5 51	77·1	1 07	4 52	77·1	0 54	3 54	77·0	0 40	2 55	77·0	0 27	1 57	77·0	0 13	0 58	77·0	77·0	193 / 347
14 / 166	1 27	5 49	76·1	1 12	4 51	76·1	0 58	3 53	76·0	0 44	2 55	76·0	0 29	1 56	76·0	0 15	0 58	76·0	76·0	194 / 346
15 / 165	1 33	5 48	75·1	1 18	4 50	75·1	1 02	3 52	75·0	0 47	2 54	75·0	0 31	1 56	75·0	0 16	0 58	75·0	75·0	195 / 345
16 / 164	1 39	5 46	74·1	1 23	4 48	74·1	1 06	3 51	74·0	0 50	2 53	74·0	0 33	1 55	74·0	0 17	0 58	74·0	74·0	196 / 344
17 / 163	1 45	5 44	73·1	1 28	4 47	73·1	1 10	3 50	73·0	0 53	2 52	73·0	0 35	1 55	73·0	0 18	0 57	73·0	73·0	197 / 343
18 / 162	1 51	5 42	72·1	1 33	4 45	72·1	1 14	3 48	72·0	0 56	2 51	72·0	0 37	1 54	72·0	0 19	0 57	72·0	72·0	198 / 342
19 / 161	1 57	5 41	71·1	1 38	4 44	71·1	1 18	3 47	71·0	0 59	2 50	71·0	0 39	1 53	71·0	0 20	0 57	71·0	71·0	199 / 341
20 / 160	2 03	5 38	70·1	1 42	4 42	70·1	1 22	3 46	70·0	1 02	2 49	70·0	0 41	1 53	70·0	0 21	0 56	70·0	70·0	200 / 340
21 / 159	2 09	5 36	69·1	1 47	4 40	69·1	1 26	3 44	69·0	1 04	2 48	69·0	0 43	1 52	69·0	0 22	0 56	69·0	69·0	201 / 339
22 / 158	2 15	5 34	68·1	1 52	4 38	68·1	1 30	3 43	68·0	1 07	2 47	68·0	0 45	1 51	68·0	0 22	0 56	68·0	68·0	202 / 338
23 / 157	2 20	5 32	67·1	1 57	4 36	67·1	1 34	3 41	67·0	1 10	2 46	67·0	0 47	1 50	67·0	0 23	0 55	67·0	67·0	203 / 337
24 / 156	2 26	5 29	66·1	2 02	4 34	66·1	1 38	3 39	66·1	1 13	2 44	66·0	0 49	1 50	66·0	0 24	0 55	66·0	66·0	204 / 336
25 / 155	2 32	5 26	65·1	2 07	4 32	65·1	1 41	3 38	65·1	1 16	2 43	65·0	0 51	1 49	65·0	0 25	0 54	65·0	65·0	205 / 335
26 / 154	2 38	5 24	64·1	2 11	4 30	64·1	1 45	3 36	64·1	1 19	2 42	64·0	0 53	1 48	64·0	0 26	0 54	64·0	64·0	206 / 334
27 / 153	2 43	5 21	63·1	2 16	4 27	63·1	1 49	3 34	63·1	1 22	2 40	63·0	0 54	1 47	63·0	0 27	0 53	63·0	63·0	207 / 333
28 / 152	2 49	5 18	62·1	2 21	4 25	62·1	1 53	3 32	62·1	1 24	2 39	62·0	0 56	1 46	62·0	0 28	0 53	62·0	62·0	208 / 332
29 / 151	2 54	5 15	61·1	2 25	4 23	61·1	1 56	3 30	61·1	1 27	2 37	61·0	0 58	1 45	61·0	0 29	0 52	61·0	61·0	209 / 331
30 / 150	3 00	5 12	60·1	2 30	4 20	60·1	2 00	3 28	60·1	1 30	2 36	60·0	1 00	1 44	60·0	0 30	0 52	60·0	60·0	210 / 330
31 / 149	3 05	5 09	59·1	2 34	4 17	59·1	2 03	3 26	59·1	1 33	2 34	59·0	1 02	1 43	59·0	0 31	0 51	59·0	59·0	211 / 329
32 / 148	3 11	5 06	58·1	2 39	4 15	58·1	2 07	3 24	58·1	1 35	2 33	58·0	1 04	1 42	58·0	0 32	0 51	58·0	58·0	212 / 328
33 / 147	3 16	5 02	57·1	2 43	4 12	57·1	2 11	3 21	57·1	1 38	2 31	57·0	1 05	1 41	57·0	0 33	0 50	57·0	57·0	213 / 327
34 / 146	3 21	4 59	56·1	2 48	4 09	56·1	2 14	3 19	56·1	1 41	2 29	56·0	1 07	1 39	56·0	0 34	0 50	56·0	56·0	214 / 326
35 / 145	3 26	4 55	55·1	2 52	4 06	55·1	2 18	3 17	55·1	1 43	2 27	55·0	1 09	1 38	55·0	0 34	0 49	55·0	55·0	215 / 325
36 / 144	3 31	4 52	54·1	2 56	4 03	54·1	2 21	3 14	54·1	1 46	2 26	54·0	1 11	1 37	54·0	0 35	0 49	54·0	54·0	216 / 324
37 / 143	3 36	4 48	53·2	3 00	4 00	53·1	2 24	3 12	53·1	1 48	2 24	53·0	1 12	1 36	53·0	0 36	0 48	53·0	53·0	217 / 323
38 / 142	3 41	4 44	52·2	3 05	3 57	52·1	2 28	3 09	52·1	1 51	2 22	52·0	1 14	1 35	52·0	0 37	0 47	52·0	52·0	218 / 322
39 / 141	3 46	4 40	51·2	3 09	3 53	51·1	2 31	3 07	51·1	1 53	2 20	51·0	1 16	1 33	51·0	0 38	0 47	51·0	51·0	219 / 321
40 / 140	3 51	4 36	50·2	3 13	3 50	50·2	2 34	3 04	50·1	1 56	2 18	50·0	1 17	1 32	50·0	0 39	0 46	50·0	50·0	220 / 320
41 / 139	3 56	4 32	49·2	3 17	3 47	49·1	2 37	3 01	49·1	1 58	2 16	49·0	1 19	1 31	49·0	0 39	0 45	49·0	49·0	221 / 319
42 / 138	4 01	4 28	48·2	3 21	3 43	48·1	2 41	2 58	48·1	2 00	2 14	48·0	1 20	1 29	48·0	0 40	0 45	48·0	48·0	222 / 318
43 / 137	4 05	4 24	47·2	3 24	3 40	47·1	2 44	2 56	47·1	2 03	2 12	47·0	1 22	1 28	47·0	0 41	0 44	47·0	47·0	223 / 317
44 / 136	4 10	4 19	46·2	3 28	3 36	46·1	2 47	2 53	46·1	2 05	2 10	46·0	1 23	1 26	46·0	0 42	0 43	46·0	46·0	224 / 316
45 / 135	4 14	4 15	45·2	3 32	3 32	45·1	2 50	2 50	45·1	2 07	2 07	45·0	1 25	1 25	45·0	0 42	0 42	45·0	45·0	225 / 315

© British Crown Copyright 2018. All rights reserved.

Lat./A	LHA	89°			88°			87°			86°			85°			84°			Lat./A	LHA/F
		A/H	B/P	Z_1/Z_2	A/H	B/P	Z_1/Z_2	A/H	B/P	Z_1/Z_2	A/H	B/P	Z_1/Z_2	A/H	B/P	Z_1/Z_2	A/H	B/P	Z_1/Z_2		
225	315	0 42	0 42	45·0	1 25	1 25	45·0	2 07	2 07	45·0	2 50	2 50	45·1	3 32	3 32	45·1	4 14	4 15	45·2	45	135
226	314	0 43	0 42	44·0	1 26	1 23	44·0	2 09	2 05	44·0	2 53	2 47	44·1	3 36	3 29	44·1	4 19	4 11	44·2	46	134
227	313	0 44	0 41	43·0	1 28	1 22	43·0	2 12	2 03	43·0	2 55	2 44	43·1	3 39	3 25	43·1	4 23	4 06	43·2	47	133
228	312	0 45	0 40	42·0	1 29	1 20	42·0	2 14	2 01	42·0	2 58	2 41	42·1	3 43	3 21	42·1	4 27	4 01	42·2	48	132
229	311	0 45	0 39	41·0	1 31	1 19	41·0	2 16	1 58	41·0	3 01	2 38	41·1	3 46	3 17	41·1	4 31	3 57	41·2	49	131
230	310	0 46	0 39	40·0	1 32	1 17	40·0	2 18	1 56	40·0	3 04	2 34	40·1	3 50	3 13	40·1	4 36	3 52	40·2	50	130
231	309	0 47	0 38	39·0	1 33	1 16	39·0	2 20	1 53	39·0	3 06	2 31	39·1	3 53	3 09	39·1	4 40	3 47	39·2	51	129
232	308	0 47	0 37	38·0	1 35	1 14	38·0	2 22	1 51	38·0	3 09	2 28	38·1	3 56	3 05	38·1	4 43	3 42	38·2	52	128
233	307	0 48	0 36	37·0	1 36	1 12	37·0	2 24	1 48	37·0	3 12	2 25	37·1	3 59	3 01	37·1	4 47	3 37	37·2	53	127
234	306	0 49	0 35	36·0	1 37	1 11	36·0	2 26	1 46	36·0	3 14	2 21	36·1	4 03	2 57	36·1	4 51	3 32	36·1	54	126
235	305	0 49	0 34	35·0	1 38	1 09	35·0	2 27	1 43	35·0	3 17	2 18	35·1	4 06	2 52	35·1	4 55	3 27	35·1	55	125
236	304	0 50	0 34	34·0	1 39	1 07	34·0	2 29	1 41	34·0	3 19	2 14	34·1	4 09	2 48	34·1	4 58	3 22	34·1	56	124
237	303	0 50	0 33	33·0	1 41	1 05	33·0	2 31	1 38	33·0	3 21	2 11	33·1	4 12	2 44	33·1	5 02	3 17	33·1	57	123
238	302	0 51	0 32	32·0	1 42	1 04	32·0	2 33	1 35	32·0	3 23	2 07	32·1	4 14	2 39	32·1	5 05	3 11	32·1	58	122
239	301	0 51	0 31	31·0	1 43	1 02	31·0	2 34	1 33	31·0	3 26	2 04	31·1	4 17	2 35	31·1	5 08	3 06	31·1	59	121
240	300	0 52	0 30	30·0	1 44	1 00	30·0	2 36	1 30	30·0	3 28	2 00	30·1	4 20	2 30	30·1	5 12	3 00	30·1	60	120
241	299	0 52	0 29	29·0	1 45	0 58	29·0	2 37	1 27	29·0	3 30	1 56	29·1	4 22	2 26	29·1	5 15	2 55	29·1	61	119
242	298	0 53	0 28	28·0	1 46	0 56	28·0	2 39	1 25	28·0	3 32	1 53	28·1	4 25	2 21	28·1	5 18	2 49	28·1	62	118
243	297	0 53	0 27	27·0	1 47	0 54	27·0	2 40	1 22	27·0	3 34	1 49	27·1	4 27	2 16	27·1	5 21	2 44	27·1	63	117
244	296	0 54	0 26	26·0	1 48	0 53	26·0	2 42	1 19	26·0	3 36	1 45	26·1	4 30	2 12	26·1	5 23	2 38	26·1	64	116
245	295	0 54	0 25	25·0	1 49	0 51	25·0	2 43	1 16	25·0	3 37	1 42	25·1	4 32	2 07	25·1	5 26	2 33	25·1	65	115
246	294	0 55	0 24	24·0	1 50	0 49	24·0	2 44	1 13	24·0	3 39	1 38	24·1	4 34	2 02	24·1	5 29	2 27	24·1	66	114
247	293	0 55	0 23	23·0	1 50	0 47	23·0	2 46	1 10	23·0	3 41	1 34	23·1	4 36	1 57	23·1	5 31	2 21	23·1	67	113
248	292	0 56	0 22	22·0	1 51	0 45	22·0	2 47	1 07	22·0	3 42	1 30	22·0	4 38	1 53	22·1	5 34	2 15	22·1	68	112
249	291	0 56	0 21	21·0	1 52	0 43	21·0	2 48	1 05	21·0	3 44	1 26	21·1	4 40	1 48	21·1	5 36	2 09	21·1	69	111
250	290	0 56	0 20	20·0	1 53	0 41	20·0	2 49	1 02	20·0	3 46	1 22	20·1	4 42	1 43	20·1	5 38	2 04	20·1	70	110
251	289	0 57	0 19	19·0	1 53	0 39	19·0	2 50	0 59	19·0	3 47	1 18	19·1	4 44	1 38	19·1	5 40	1 58	19·1	71	109
252	288	0 57	0 18	18·0	1 54	0 37	18·0	2 51	0 56	18·0	3 48	1 14	18·1	4 45	1 33	18·1	5 42	1 52	18·1	72	108
253	287	0 57	0 17	17·0	1 55	0 35	17·0	2 52	0 53	17·0	3 49	1 10	17·0	4 47	1 28	17·1	5 44	1 46	17·1	73	107
254	286	0 58	0 16	16·0	1 55	0 33	16·0	2 53	0 50	16·0	3 51	1 06	16·0	4 48	1 23	16·1	5 46	1 40	16·1	74	106
255	285	0 58	0 15	15·0	1 56	0 31	15·0	2 54	0 47	15·0	3 52	1 02	15·0	4 50	1 18	15·1	5 48	1 33	15·1	75	105
256	284	0 58	0 14	14·0	1 57	0 29	14·0	2 55	0 44	14·0	3 53	0 58	14·0	4 51	1 13	14·1	5 49	1 27	14·1	76	104
257	283	0 58	0 13	13·0	1 57	0 27	13·0	2 56	0 41	13·0	3 54	0 54	13·0	4 52	1 08	13·0	5 51	1 21	13·1	77	103
258	282	0 59	0 12	12·0	1 58	0 25	12·0	2 57	0 37	12·0	3 55	0 50	12·0	4 53	1 03	12·0	5 52	1 15	12·1	78	102
259	281	0 59	0 11	11·0	1 58	0 23	11·0	2 58	0 34	11·0	3 56	0 46	11·0	4 54	0 57	11·0	5 54	1 09	11·1	79	101
260	280	0 59	0 10	10·0	1 58	0 21	10·0	2 58	0 31	10·0	3 56	0 42	10·0	4 55	0 52	10·0	5 55	1 03	10·1	80	100
261	279	0 59	0 09	9·0	1 59	0 19	9·0	2 58	0 28	9·0	3 57	0 38	9·0	4 56	0 47	9·0	5 56	0 57	9·0	81	99
262	278	0 59	0 08	8·0	1 59	0 17	8·0	2 58	0 25	8·0	3 58	0 33	8·0	4 57	0 42	8·0	5 56	0 50	8·0	82	98
263	277	1 00	0 07	7·0	1 59	0 15	7·0	2 59	0 22	7·0	3 58	0 29	7·0	4 58	0 37	7·0	5 57	0 44	7·0	83	97
264	276	1 00	0 06	6·0	1 59	0 13	6·0	2 59	0 19	6·0	3 59	0 25	6·0	4 58	0 31	6·0	5 58	0 38	6·0	84	96
265	275	1 00	0 05	5·0	2 00	0 10	5·0	2 59	0 16	5·0	3 59	0 21	5·0	4 59	0 26	5·0	5 59	0 31	5·0	85	95
266	274	1 00	0 04	4·0	2 00	0 08	4·0	2 59	0 13	4·0	3 59	0 17	4·0	4 59	0 21	4·0	5 59	0 25	4·0	86	94
267	273	1 00	0 03	3·0	2 00	0 06	3·0	3 00	0 09	3·0	4 00	0 13	3·0	5 00	0 16	3·0	6 00	0 19	3·0	87	93
268	272	1 00	0 02	2·0	2 00	0 04	2·0	3 00	0 06	2·0	4 00	0 08	2·0	5 00	0 10	2·0	6 00	0 13	2·0	88	92
269	271	1 00	0 01	1·0	2 00	0 02	1·0	3 00	0 03	1·0	4 00	0 04	1·0	5 00	0 05	1·0	6 00	0 06	1·0	89	91
270	270	1 00	0 00	0·0	2 00	0 00	0·0	3 00	0 00	0·0	4 00	0 00	0·0	5 00	0 00	0·0	6 00	0 00	0·0	90	90

S. Lat.: for LHA > 180° ... $Z_n = 180° - Z$
for LHA < 180° ... $Z_n = 180° + Z$

N. Lat.: for LHA > 180° ... $Z_n = Z$
for LHA < 180° ... $Z_n = 360° - Z$

© British Crown Copyright 2018. All rights reserved.

AUXILIARY TABLE

Sign for corr₂ for A'. →

Sign of corr₁ for F'. →   *Reverse sign if F > 90°.*

Z° (+A'−)	30	29 / 31	28 / 32	27 / 33	26 / 34	25 / 35	24 / 36	23 / 37	22 / 38	21 / 39	20 / 40	19 / 41	18 / 42	17 / 43	16 / 44	15 / 45	14 / 46	13 / 47	12 / 48	11 / 49	10 / 50	9 / 51	8 / 52	7 / 53	6 / 54	5 / 55	4 / 56	3 / 57	2 / 58	1 / 59	P° (F' +/−)
89	ˏ	ˏ	ˏ	ˏ	ˏ	ˏ	ˏ	ˏ	ˏ	ˏ	ˏ	ˏ	ˏ	ˏ	ˏ	ˏ	ˏ	ˏ	ˏ	ˏ	ˏ	ˏ	ˏ	ˏ	ˏ	ˏ	ˏ	ˏ	ˏ	ˏ	1
88	1	1	0	0	0	0	0	0	0	0	0	0	0	0	0	0	0	0	0	0	0	0	0	0	0	0	0	0	0	0	2
87	1	1	1	1	1	1	1	1	1	1	1	1	1	1	1	1	0	0	0	0	0	0	0	0	0	0	0	0	0	0	3
86	2	2	1	1	1	1	1	1	1	1	1	1	1	1	1	1	1	1	1	1	1	1	1	0	0	0	0	0	0	0	4
85	3	3	2	2	2	2	2	2	2	2	2	2	1	1	1	1	1	1	1	1	1	1	1	1	1	0	0	0	0	0	5
84	3	3	3	3	3	3	3	3	3	2	2	2	2	2	2	2	1	2	1	1	1	1	1	1	1	1	0	0	0	0	6
83	4	4	3	3	3	3	3	3	3	3	2	2	2	2	2	2	2	2	1	2	1	1	1	1	1	1	1	1	0	0	7
82	4	4	3	4	4	4	4	4	3	3	3	3	3	2	2	2	2	2	2	2	2	2	1	1	1	1	1	1	1	0	8
81	5	5	4	4	4	4	4	4	4	4	3	3	3	3	3	2	2	2	2	2	2	2	2	1	1	1	1	1	1	0	9
80	5	5	5	5	5	4	4	4	4	4	4	4	3	3	3	3	3	3	2	2	2	2	2	2	1	1	1	1	1	0	10
79	6	6	5	5	5	5	5	4	4	4	4	4	4	4	3	3	3	3	3	2	2	2	2	2	2	1	1	1	1	0	11
78	6	6	6	6	5	5	5	5	5	5	4	4	4	4	4	3	3	3	3	3	2	2	2	2	2	1	1	1	1	0	12
77	7	7	6	6	6	6	6	5	5	5	5	5	4	4	4	4	4	3	3	3	3	3	2	2	2	2	1	1	1	0	13
76	7	7	6	7	7	6	6	6	6	5	5	5	5	4	4	4	4	4	4	3	3	3	2	2	2	2	2	1	1	0	14
75	8	8	7	7	7	6	6	6	6	6	5	5	5	5	5	4	4	4	4	4	3	3	3	2	2	2	2	1	1	0	15
74	8	8	8	7	7	7	7	6	6	6	6	5	5	5	5	5	5	4	4	4	4	3	3	3	2	2	1	1	1	0	16
73	9	8	8	8	8	7	7	7	7	6	6	6	6	5	5	5	5	5	4	4	4	3	3	3	2	2	2	1	1	0	17
72	9	9	9	9	8	8	7	7	7	7	6	6	6	6	5	5	5	5	4	4	4	4	3	3	3	2	2	1	1	0	18
71	10	9	9	9	9	8	8	8	7	7	7	6	6	6	6	5	5	5	4	4	4	4	3	3	3	2	2	1	1	0	19
70	10	10	10	9	9	9	8	8	8	7	7	7	7	6	6	6	5	5	5	5	4	4	3	3	3	2	2	1	1	0	20
69	11	10	10	10	9	9	9	8	8	8	7	7	7	6	6	6	6	5	5	5	4	4	4	3	3	2	2	1	1	0	21
68	11	11	11	10	10	10	9	9	9	8	7	8	7	7	6	6	6	5	5	5	5	4	4	3	3	2	2	1	1	0	22
67	12	11	11	11	11	10	9	9	9	9	8	8	7	7	7	6	6	6	5	5	5	4	4	3	3	2	2	1	1	0	23
66	12	12	11	11	11	10	10	10	9	9	8	8	8	7	7	6	6	6	5	5	5	4	4	3	3	2	2	1	1	0	24
65	13	12	12	11	12	11	10	10	9	9	9	8	8	8	7	6	6	6	5	5	5	4	4	3	3	2	2	1	1	0	25
64	13	13	12	12	13	11	11	10	10	9	9	8	8	9	7	7	7	6	6	5	5	4	4	3	3	2	2	1	1	0	26
63	14	13	13	12	14	12	11	11	10	10	9	9	8	9	7	7	7	6	6	5	5	4	4	3	3	2	2	1	1	0	27
62	15	14	13	13	13	12	12	11	11	10	10	9	9	9	8	7	7	7	6	6	5	5	4	4	3	2	2	2	1	0	28
61	15	14	14	13	15	13	12	12	11	11	10	10	9	10	8	8	7	7	6	6	6	5	4	4	3	3	2	2	1	0	29
60	15	14	14	13	15	13	13	12	11	11	10	10	10	10	8	8	8	7	6	6	6	5	5	4	3	3	2	2	1	0	30
59	15	15	14	14	15	13	14	12	12	11	11	10	10	10	9	8	8	7	7	6	6	5	5	4	3	3	2	2	1	1	31
58	16	15	15	15	16	14	14	13	13	12	12	11	11	10	9	8	8	8	7	6	6	5	5	4	3	3	2	2	1	1	32
57	16	16	15	15	16	15	14	14	13	13	12	11	11	11	9	8	8	8	7	7	6	5	5	4	4	3	2	2	1	1	33
56	17	16	16	15	17	16	15	14	14	13	12	12	11	11	10	9	9	8	7	7	6	6	5	4	4	3	2	2	1	1	34
55	17	17	16	16	17	16	15	15	14	13	13	12	12	11	10	9	9	8	8	7	6	6	5	4	4	3	3	2	1	1	35
54	18	17	16	16	18	15	14	14	13	13	12	12	11	10	9	9	8	8	7	6	6	5	4	4	4	3	2	2	1	1	36
53	18	17	17	17	18	16	15	14	14	13	13	12	11	11	10	9	8	8	7	7	6	5	5	4	4	3	2	2	1	1	37
52	18	18	18	17	18	16	15	15	14	14	13	12	12	11	10	9	9	8	8	7	6	5	5	4	4	3	3	2	1	1	38
51	19	18	18	17	19	16	15	15	14	14	13	13	12	11	10	9	9	8	8	7	6	6	5	4	4	3	3	2	1	1	39
50	19	19	18	17	19	16	15	15	14	13	13	12	12	11	10	10	9	8	8	7	6	6	5	4	4	3	3	2	1	1	40

© British Crown Copyright 2018. All rights reserved.

Note: For Z₂ < 10°, use 10°

Note: For P > 80°, use 80°

−A' / Z²	F' / P°	30/□	29/31	28/32	27/33	26/34	25/35	24/36	23/37	22/38	21/39	20/40	19/41	18/42	17/43	16/44	15/45	14/46	13/47	12/48	11/49	10/50	9/51	8/52	7/53	6/54	5/55	4/56	3/57	2/58	1/59
49	41	20	19	18	18	17	16	16	15	14	14	13	12	12	11	10	10	9	9	8	7	7	6	5	5	4	3	3	2	1	1
48	42	20	19	19	18	18	17	16	15	15	14	13	13	12	11	11	10	9	9	8	7	7	6	5	5	4	3	3	2	1	1
47	43	20	20	19	18	18	17	16	16	15	14	14	13	12	12	11	10	10	9	8	8	7	6	5	5	4	3	3	2	1	1
46	44	21	20	19	19	18	18	17	16	15	15	14	13	13	12	11	10	10	9	8	8	7	6	6	5	4	3	3	2	1	1
45	45	21	21	20	19	18	18	17	16	16	15	14	14	13	12	12	11	10	9	8	8	7	6	6	5	4	4	3	2	2	1
44	46	22	21	20	19	19	18	17	17	16	15	14	14	13	12	12	11	10	9	9	8	7	6	6	5	4	4	3	2	1	1
43	47	22	21	20	20	19	18	18	17	16	15	15	14	13	13	12	11	10	10	9	8	7	7	6	5	4	4	3	2	1	1
42	48	22	22	21	20	19	19	18	17	17	16	15	14	13	13	12	11	11	10	9	8	8	7	6	5	4	4	3	2	2	1
41	49	23	22	21	21	20	19	18	18	17	16	15	15	14	13	13	11	11	10	9	8	8	7	6	6	5	4	3	2	2	1
40	50	23	22	21	21	20	19	18	18	17	16	15	15	14	13	13	11	11	10	9	8	8	7	6	6	5	4	3	2	2	2
39	51	23	23	22	21	20	19	19	18	17	16	16	15	14	13	13	12	11	10	9	9	8	7	6	6	5	4	3	2	2	1
38	52	24	23	22	21	21	20	19	18	18	17	16	15	14	14	13	12	11	11	10	9	8	7	6	6	5	4	3	2	2	1
37	53	24	23	23	22	21	20	19	19	18	17	16	15	15	14	13	12	12	11	10	9	9	7	7	6	5	4	3	3	2	1
36	54	24	23	23	22	21	20	19	19	18	17	16	16	15	14	14	12	12	11	10	9	9	7	7	6	5	4	3	3	2	2
35	55	25	24	23	22	21	20	20	19	18	17	16	16	15	14	14	12	12	11	10	10	9	7	7	6	5	5	4	3	2	2
34	56	25	24	23	22	22	21	20	19	18	17	17	16	15	14	13	12	12	11	10	9	8	7	6	6	4	4	3	3	2	1
33	57	25	25	24	23	22	21	20	20	19	18	17	16	15	15	14	13	12	11	10	9	9	8	7	6	5	4	4	3	2	2
32	58	26	25	24	23	22	21	21	20	19	18	17	16	15	15	14	13	12	12	10	10	9	8	7	6	5	4	4	3	2	2
31	59	26	25	24	23	23	22	21	20	19	18	17	16	15	15	14	13	13	12	10	10	9	8	7	6	5	4	4	3	2	2
30	60	26	25	24	23	23	22	21	20	20	18	18	17	16	15	14	13	13	12	10	10	9	8	7	6	5	5	4	3	3	2
29	61	26	26	24	24	23	22	21	20	20	18	17	17	16	15	14	13	12	12	10	10	9	8	7	6	5	4	3	3	2	2
28	62	26	26	25	24	23	22	21	21	20	19	18	17	16	16	15	13	13	12	11	10	9	8	7	6	5	4	4	3	2	2
27	63	27	26	25	24	23	22	22	21	20	19	18	17	16	16	15	13	13	12	11	10	10	8	7	7	5	4	4	3	3	2
26	64	27	26	25	24	24	23	22	21	21	19	18	18	16	16	15	14	13	13	11	10	10	8	7	7	6	5	4	3	3	2
25	65	27	26	25	24	24	23	22	21	21	19	18	18	16	16	15	14	13	13	11	10	10	8	8	7	6	5	4	3	3	2
24	66	27	26	26	24	23	22	22	21	21	19	18	17	16	15	15	13	13	12	11	10	9	8	7	6	5	5	4	3	2	2
23	67	28	27	26	25	24	23	22	22	21	19	18	18	17	16	15	14	13	13	11	10	10	8	7	7	6	5	4	3	3	2
22	68	28	27	26	25	24	23	23	22	21	20	19	18	17	16	16	14	13	13	11	11	10	8	7	7	6	5	4	3	3	2
21	69	28	27	26	25	24	23	23	22	21	20	19	18	17	16	16	14	14	13	11	11	10	8	8	7	6	5	4	3	3	2
20	70	28	27	26	25	24	23	23	22	22	20	19	18	17	16	16	14	14	13	11	11	10	8	8	7	6	5	4	3	3	2
19	71	28	27	26	25	24	23	23	22	21	20	19	18	17	16	15	14	13	13	11	10	10	8	7	7	6	5	4	3	2	2
18	72	29	28	27	26	25	24	23	22	22	20	19	18	17	16	16	14	14	13	11	11	10	9	8	7	6	5	4	3	3	2
17	73	29	28	27	26	25	24	23	22	22	21	20	19	17	16	16	15	14	13	12	11	10	9	8	7	6	5	4	3	3	2
16	74	29	28	27	26	25	24	24	23	22	21	20	19	18	17	16	15	14	14	12	11	11	9	8	7	6	5	4	3	3	2
15	75	29	28	27	26	25	24	24	23	22	21	20	19	18	17	16	15	14	14	12	11	11	9	8	7	6	5	4	3	3	2
14	76	29	28	27	26	25	24	23	22	21	20	19	18	17	16	16	15	14	13	11	11	10	9	8	7	6	5	4	3	2	2
13	77	29	28	27	26	25	24	23	22	22	21	20	19	18	17	16	15	14	14	12	11	10	9	8	7	6	5	4	3	3	2
12	78	29	28	27	26	25	24	23	22	22	21	20	19	18	17	16	15	14	14	12	11	11	9	8	7	6	5	4	3	3	2
11	79	30	29	28	26	25	24	24	23	22	21	20	19	18	17	17	15	14	14	12	11	11	9	8	7	6	5	4	3	3	2
10	80	30	29	28	26	25	24	24	23	22	21	20	19	18	17	17	15	14	14	12	11	11	9	8	7	6	5	4	3	3	2

© British Crown Copyright 2018. All rights reserved.

USE OF CONCISE SIGHT REDUCTION TABLES (continued)

4. *Example.* (b) Required the altitude and azimuth of *Vega* on 2019 July 29 at UT 04^h 50^m from the estimated position S $15°$, W $152°$.

1. Assumed latitude $\quad\quad\quad Lat = \quad 15° \text{ S}$
    From the almanac $\quad\quad\quad GHA = \quad 99° \quad 39'$
    Assumed longitude $\quad\quad\quad\quad\quad\quad 151° \quad 39' \text{ W}$

    Local hour angle $\quad\quad\quad LHA = \quad 308$

2. Reduction table, 1st entry
    $(Lat, LHA) = (15, 308)$ $\quad\quad A = \quad 49 \quad 34 \quad\quad A° = 50, A' = 34$
    $\quad\quad\quad\quad\quad\quad\quad\quad\quad\quad\quad\quad B = +66 \quad 29 \quad\quad Z_1 = +71{\cdot}7, \quad\quad\quad\quad\quad LHA > 270°$
3. From the almanac $\quad\quad\quad Dec = -38 \quad 48 \quad\quad\quad\quad\quad\quad\quad\quad Lat \text{ and } Dec \text{ contrary}$

    $\text{Sum} = B + Dec \quad\quad\quad F = +27 \quad 41 \quad\quad F° = 28, F' = 41$

4. Reduction table, 2nd entry
    $(A°, F°) = (50, 28)$ $\quad\quad\quad H = \quad 17 \quad 34 \quad\quad P° = 37$
    $\quad\quad\quad\quad\quad\quad\quad\quad\quad\quad\quad\quad\quad\quad\quad\quad\quad\quad\quad\quad\quad Z_2 = 67{\cdot}8, Z_2° = 68$

5. Auxiliary table, 1st entry
    $(F', P°) = (41, 37)$ $\quad\quad\quad corr_1 = \quad\quad -11 \quad\quad\quad\quad\quad\quad\quad F < 90°, F' > 29'$
    $\text{Sum} \quad\quad\quad\quad\quad\quad\quad\quad\quad\quad\quad\quad\quad 17 \quad 23$
6. Auxiliary table, 2nd entry
    $(A', Z_2°) = (34, 68)$ $\quad\quad corr_2 = \quad\quad +10 \quad\quad\quad\quad\quad\quad\quad\quad A' > 30'$
7. $\text{Sum} = \text{computed altitude} \quad H_c = +17° \quad 33' \quad\quad\quad\quad\quad\quad F > 0°$

8. Azimuth, first component $\quad Z_1 = +71{\cdot}7 \quad\quad\quad\quad\quad\quad \text{same sign as } B$
    $\quad\quad\quad\quad$ second component $\quad Z_2 = +67{\cdot}8 \quad\quad\quad\quad\quad\quad F < 90°, F > 0°$

    $\text{Sum} = \text{azimuth angle} \quad\quad Z = \quad 139{\cdot}5$

    True azimuth $\quad\quad\quad\quad\quad Z_n = \quad 040° \quad\quad\quad\quad\quad\quad S\ Lat, LHA > 180°$

5. *Form for use with the Concise Sight Reduction Tables.*   The form on the following page lays out the procedure explained on pages 284-285. Each step is shown, with notes and rules to ensure accuracy, rather than speed, throughout the calculation. The form is mainly intended for the calculation of star positions. It therefore includes the formation of the Greenwich hour of Aries (*GHA* Aries), and thus the Greenwich hour angle of the star (*GHA*) from its tabular sidereal hour angle (*SHA*). These calculations, included in step 1 of the form, can easily be replaced by the interpolation of *GHA* and *Dec* for the Sun, Moon or planets.

The form may be freely copied; however, acknowledgement of the source is requested.

© British Crown Copyright 2018. All rights reserved.

Date & UT of observation		Body	Estimated Latitude & Longitude
h m s			° ' ° '

Step	Calculate Altitude & Azimuth		Summary of Rules & Notes
Assumed latitude	$Lat =$ °		Nearest estimated latitude, integral number of degrees.
Assumed longitude	$Long =$ ° '		Choose $Long$ so that LHA has integral number of degrees.
1. From the almanac:	$Dec =$ ° '		Record the Dec for use in Step 3.
GHA Aries ^{h}	$=$ ° '		Needed if using SHA. Tabular value.
Increment ^{m} ^{s}	$=$ ° '		for minutes and seconds of time.
SHA	$SHA =$ ° '		
$GHA = GHA\ Aries + SHA$	$GHA =$ ° '		Remove multiples of 360°.
Assumed longitude	$Long =$ ° '		West longitudes are negative.
$LHA = GHA + Long$	$LHA =$ °		Remove multiples of 360°.
2. Reduction table, 1st entry			
$(Lat, LHA) = ($ °, °$)$	$A =$ ° '	$A° =$ °	nearest whole degree of A.
record A, B and Z_1.		$A' =$ '	minutes part of A.
	$B =$ ° '		B is minus if $90° < LHA < 270°$.
		$Z_1 =$ °	Z_1 has the same sign as B.
3. From step 1	$Dec =$ ° '		Dec is minus if contrary to Lat.
$F = B + Dec$	$F =$ ° '		Regard F as positive until step 7.
		$F° =$ °	nearest whole degree of F.
		$F' =$ '	minutes part of F.
4. Reduction table, 2nd entry			
$(A°, F°) = ($ °, °$)$	$H =$ ° '	$P° =$ °	nearest whole degree of P.
record H, P and Z_2.		$Z_2 =$ °	
5. Auxiliary table, 1st entry			
$(F', P°) = ($ ', °$)$	$corr_1 =$ '		$corr_1$ is minus if $F < 90°$ & $F' > 29'$,
record $corr_1$			or if $F > 90°$ & $F' < 30'$.
6. Auxiliary table, 2nd entry			$Z_2°$ nearest whole degree of Z_2.
$(A', Z_2°) = ($ ', °$)$	$corr_2 =$ '		$corr_2$ is minus if $A' < 30'$.
record $corr_2$			
7. Calculated altitude $=$	$H_C =$ ° '		H_C is minus if F is negative, and
$H_C = H + corr_1 + corr_2$			object is below the horizon.
8. Azimuth, 1st component	$Z_1 =$ °		Z_1 has the same sign as B.
2nd component	$Z_2 =$ °		Z_2 is minus if $F > 90°$.
			If F is negative, $Z_2 = 180° - Z_2$.
$Z = Z_1 + Z_2$	$Z =$ °		Ignore the sign of Z.
			N Lat: If $LHA > 180°$, $Z_n = Z$, or if $LHA < 180°$, $Z_n = 360° - Z$,
			S Lat: If $LHA > 180°$, $Z_n = 180° - Z$, or if $LHA < 180°$, $Z_n = 180° + Z$.
True azimuth	$Z_n =$ °		©HMNAO

For use with *The Nautical Almanac's* Concise Sight Reduction Tables pages 284-318.

© British Crown Copyright 2018. All rights reserved.

POLAR PHENOMENA

EXPLANATION

1. *Introduction.* The graphs on pages 322-325 give data concerning the rising and setting of the Sun and Moon and the duration of civil twilight for high latitudes. Graphs are given instead of tables for high latitudes because they give a clearer picture of the phenomena and of the attainable accuracy in any given case. In the regions of the graph that are difficult to read accurately, the phenomenon itself is generally uncertain.

2. *Semiduration of sunlight.* The graphs for the semiduration of sunlight (page 322) give for latitudes north of N 65° the number of hours from sunrise to meridian passage or from meridian passage to sunset. There is continuous daylight in an area marked "Sun above horizon", and no direct sunlight in an area marked "Sun below horizon". The figures near the top indicate, for several convenient dates, the local mean times of meridian passage; with the aid of the intermediate dots the LMT on any given day may be obtained to the nearest minute. The LMT of sunrise may be found by subtracting the semiduration from the time of meridian passage, and the time of sunset by adding. The equation of time is given by subtracting the time of meridian passage from noon.

Examples. (a) Estimate the time of sunrise and sunset on 2019 March 10 at latitude N 77°. The semiduration of sunlight (page 322) is about $5^h 00^m$. The time of meridian passage is $12^h 10^m$, and hence the LMT of sunrise is $07^h 10^m$, and of sunset $17^h 10^m$. (b) Estimate the dates, for the first half of 2019, when the Sun is continuously below and above the horizon at latitude N 80°. The semiduration of sunlight graph (page 322) indicates the Sun is continuously below the horizon until about February 21, and is continuously above the horizon after April 14.

3. *Duration of civil twilight.* The graphs for the duration of twilight (page 322) give the interval from the beginning of morning civil twilight (Sun 6° below the horizon) to the time of sunrise or from the time of sunset to the end of evening civil twilight. In a region marked "No twilight or sunlight", the Sun is continuously below the horizon by more than 6°. In a region marked "Continuous twilight or sunlight", the Sun never goes lower than 6° below the horizon.

Adjacent to a region marked "No twilight or sunlight" is a region in which the Sun is continuously below the horizon, but so near to the horizon during a portion of the day that there is twilight. This area is the shaded region. The value given by the graph in this shaded region is the interval from the beginning of morning twilight to meridian passage of the Sun, or from meridian passage to the end of evening twilight, the total duration of twilight being twice the value given by the graph. The border between this shaded region and the remainder of the graph indicates that the Sun only just rises at meridian passage at the date and latitude shown. The remainder of the graph gives the total duration of civil twilight.

Examples. (a) Estimate the time of the beginning of morning civil twilight at latitude N 77° on 2019 March 10. The duration of twilight (page 322) is about $1^h 30^m$. Applying this to the time of sunrise, $07^h 10^m$, found in the preceding example, the beginning of morning civil twilight is $05^h 40^m$ LMT. (b) Estimate, for the first half of 2019, the limiting dates of civil twilight and sunlight at latitude N 80°. The graphs (page 322) indicate there is no sunlight or twilight till about February 6, there is twilight but no sunlight from February 6 until February 21, sunlight and twilight till April 1, continuous twilight or sunlight till April 14, and then continuous sunlight. (c) Estimate the time of the beginning and end of civil twilight on 2019 February 14 at latitude N 80°. The graph (page 322) indicates there is no direct sunlight at this date and latitude, but three hours of twilight before and after meridian passage occurring at $12^h 14^m$. Thus civil twilight begins at about $09^h 14^m$ and ends at about $15^h 14^m$ LMT.

© British Crown Copyright 2018. All rights reserved.

4. *Semiduration of moonlight* The graphs, for each month, for the semiduration of moonlight give for the Moon the same data as the graphs for the semiduration of sunlight give for the Sun. The scale near the top gives the LMT of meridian passage. In addition, the phase symbols are placed on the graphs to show the day on which each phase occurs. Since the times of meridian passage and the semiduration change more rapidly from day to day for the Moon than for the Sun, special care will be required in reading the graphs accurately.

For most purposes, in these high latitudes, a rough idea of the time of moonrise or moonset is all that is required, and this may be obtained by a glance at the graph.

Example. Estimate the moon phase and the time of moonrise and moonset on 2019 January 28 at latitude N 71°. The phase is found from pages 323-325 to be near last quarter, and the Moon crosses the meridian at 06^h LMT. The semiduration of moonlight taken for the time of meridian passage is 4 hours, giving moonrise at 02^h LMT on January 28 and moonset at 10^h on January 28.

If greater accuracy is required, it is necessary to read the graph for the UT of each phenomenon at the desired meridian. The dates indicated on the graph are for 00^h UT, and intermediate values of the UT may be located by estimation.

Example. Required to improve the results obtained in the preceding example, assuming the observer to be in longitude W 90° (6^h) west.

The values found previously were:

			d	h			d	h	
Time of meridian passage	2019	Jan.	28	06 LMT	=	Jan.	28	12 UT	
Semiduration of moonlight				4					
Time of moonrise		Jan.	28	02 LMT	=	Jan.	28	08 UT	
Time of moonset		Jan.	28	10 LMT	=	Jan.	28	16 UT	

Returning to the graphs (pages 323-325) with these three values of the UT, the following results are obtained:

			d	h	m			d	h	m
Time of meridian passage	2019	Jan.	28	06	10 LMT	=	Jan.	28	12	10 UT
Semiduration for moonrise				03	50					
Time of moonrise		Jan.	28	02	20 LMT	=	Jan.	28	08	20 UT
Semiduration for moonset				03	30					
Time of moonset		Jan.	28	09	40 LMT	=	Jan.	28	15	40 UT

© British Crown Copyright 2018. All rights reserved.

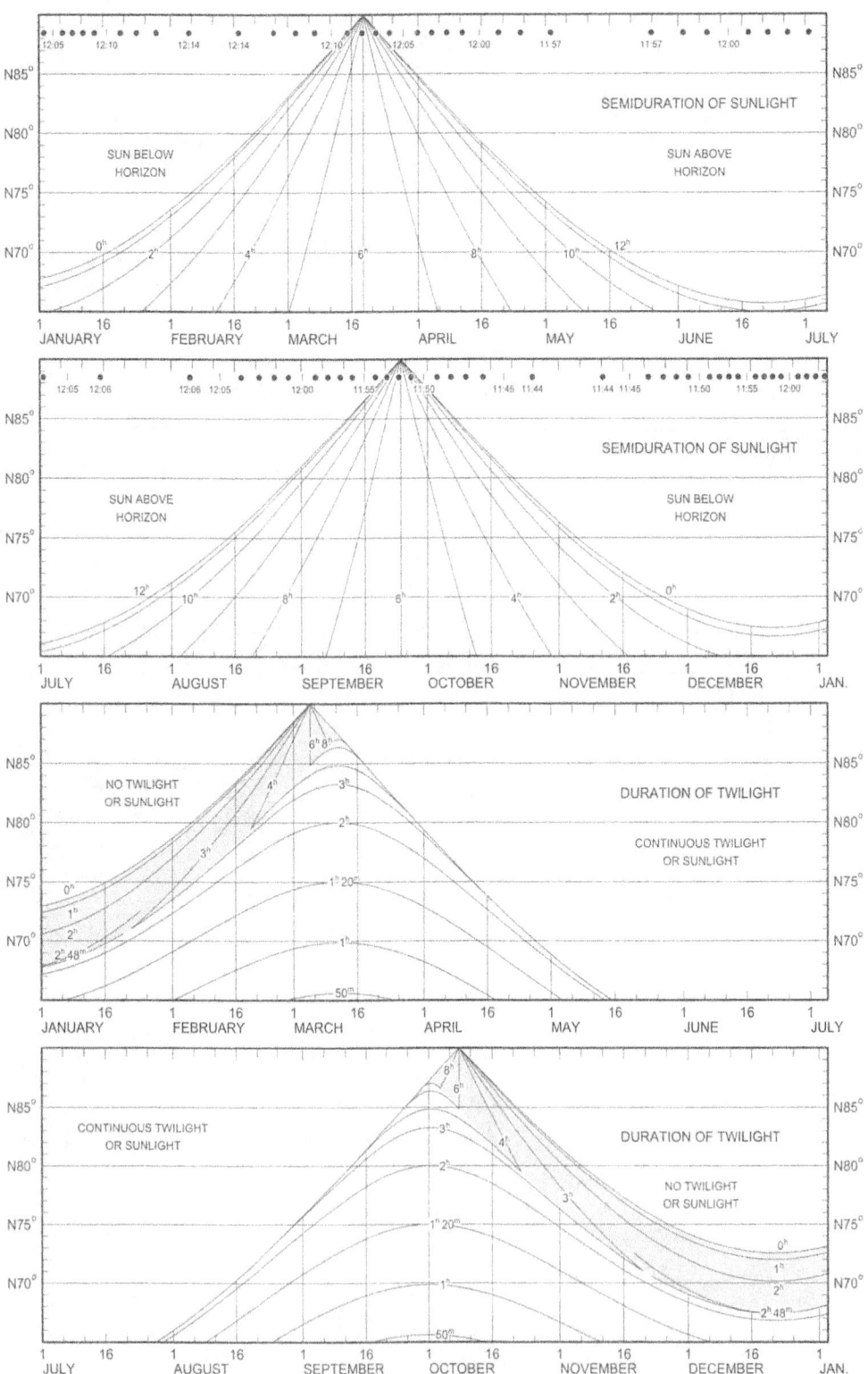

© British Crown Copyright 2018. All rights reserved.

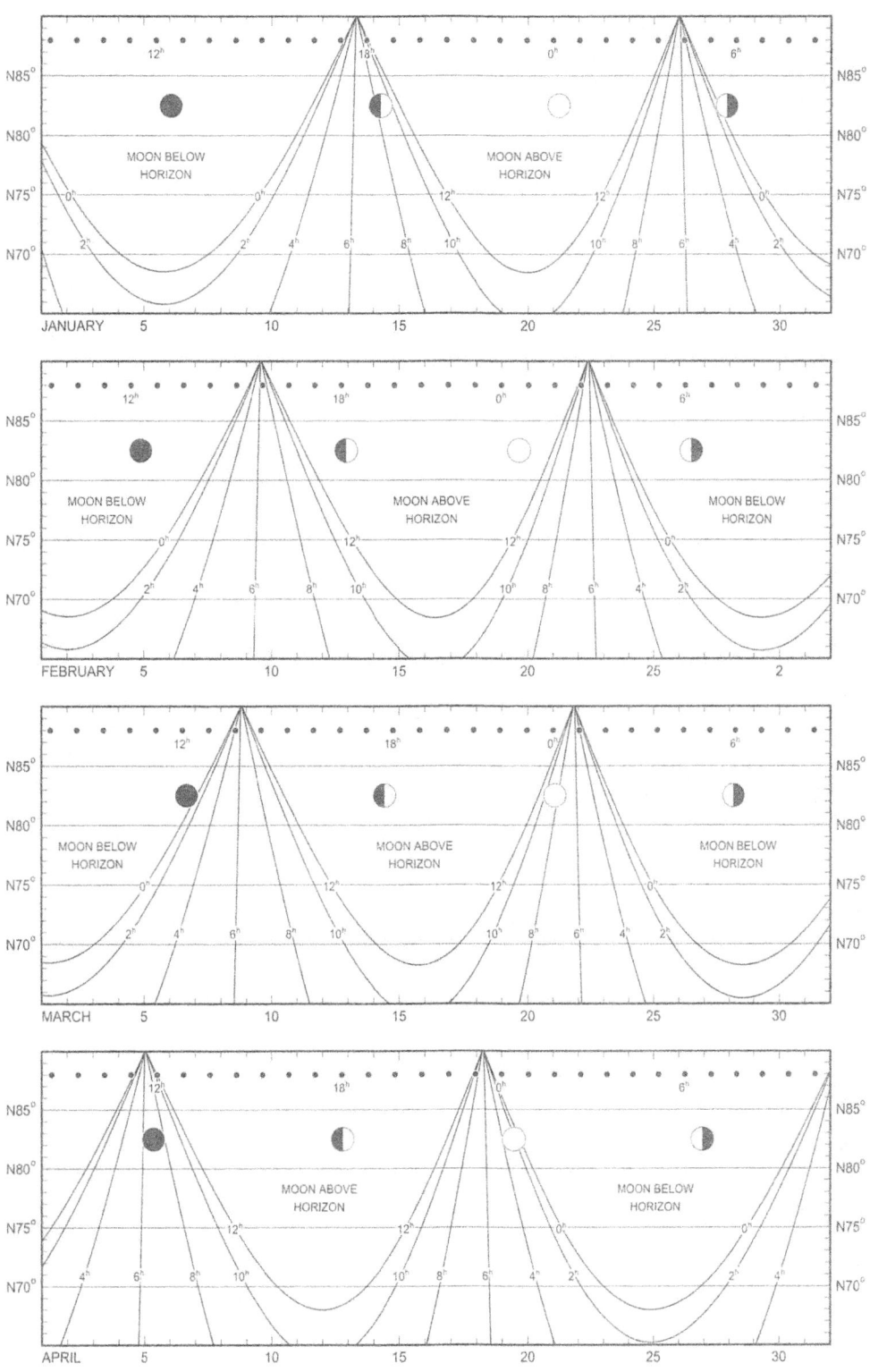

© British Crown Copyright 2018. All rights reserved.

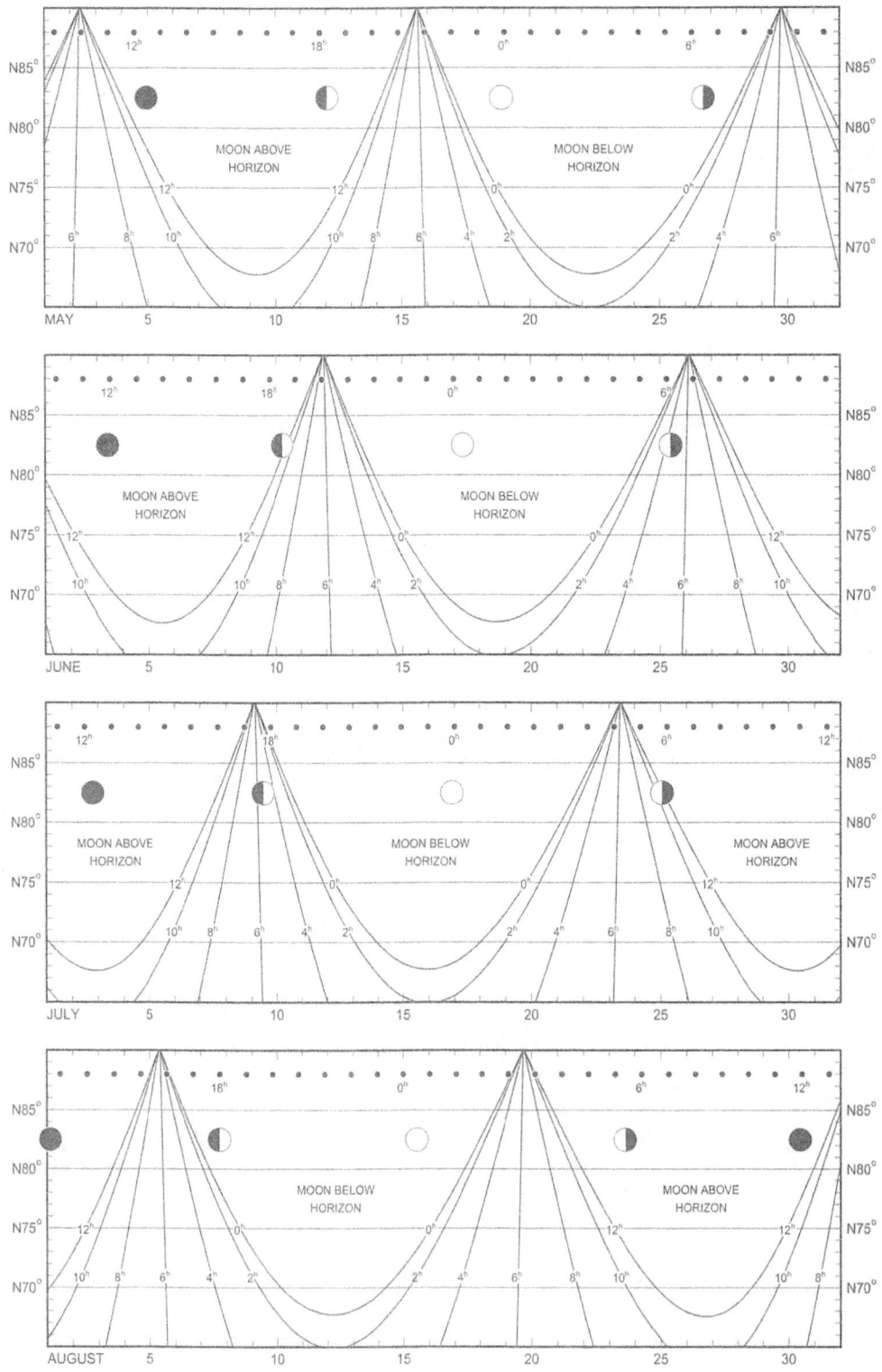

© British Crown Copyright 2018. All rights reserved.

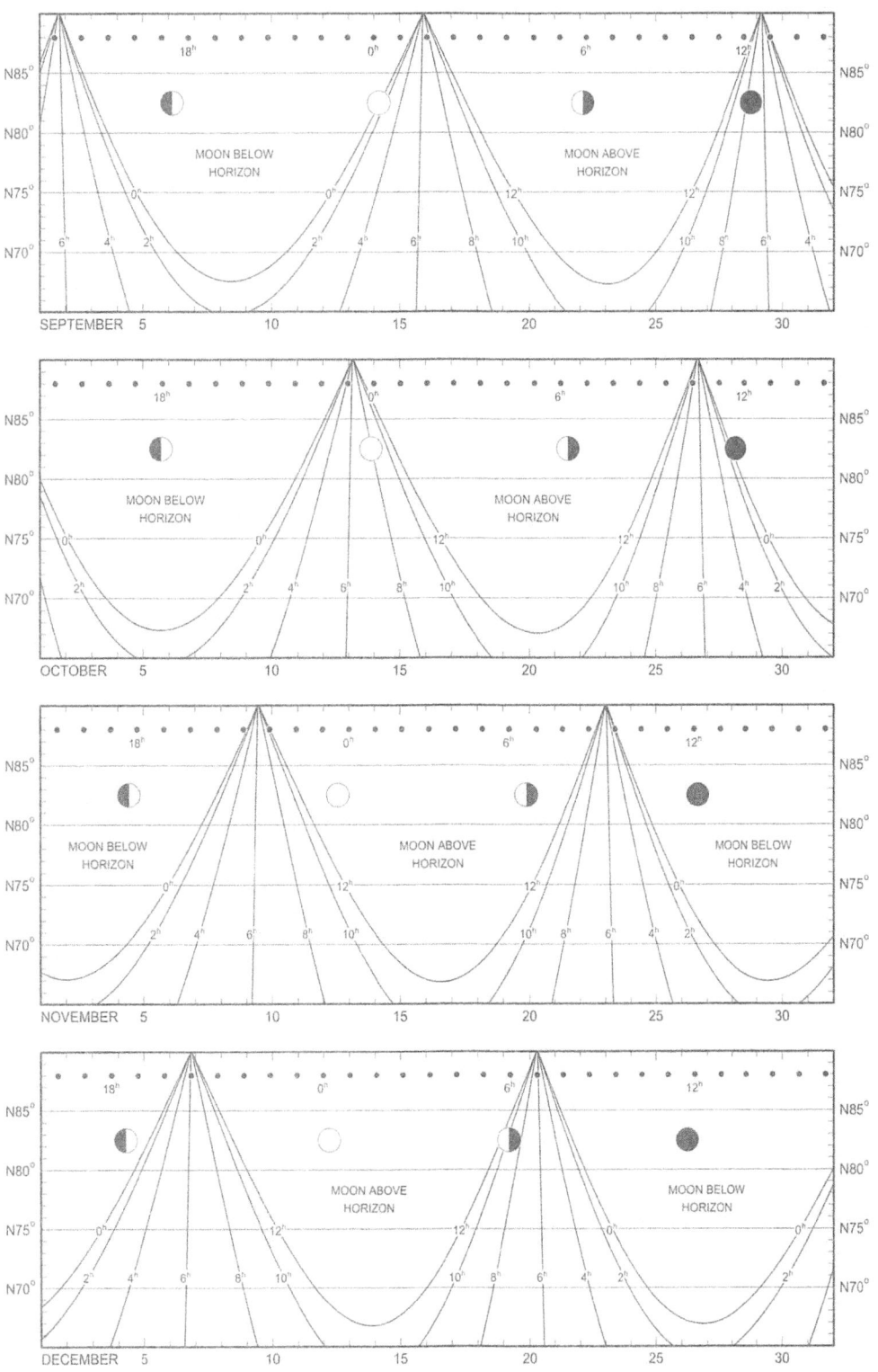

© British Crown Copyright 2018. All rights reserved.

NOTES

© British Crown Copyright 2018. All rights reserved.

CONVERSION OF ARC TO TIME

0°–59°		60°–119°		120°–179°		180°–239°		240°–299°		300°–359°			0′00	0′25	0′50	0′75
°	h m	°	h m	°	h m	°	h m	°	h m	°	h m	′	m s	m s	m s	m s
0	0 00	60	4 00	120	8 00	180	12 00	240	16 00	300	20 00	0	0 00	0 01	0 02	0 03
1	0 04	61	4 04	121	8 04	181	12 04	241	16 04	301	20 04	1	0 04	0 05	0 06	0 07
2	0 08	62	4 08	122	8 08	182	12 08	242	16 08	302	20 08	2	0 08	0 09	0 10	0 11
3	0 12	63	4 12	123	8 12	183	12 12	243	16 12	303	20 12	3	0 12	0 13	0 14	0 15
4	0 16	64	4 16	124	8 16	184	12 16	244	16 16	304	20 16	4	0 16	0 17	0 18	0 19
5	0 20	65	4 20	125	8 20	185	12 20	245	16 20	305	20 20	5	0 20	0 21	0 22	0 23
6	0 24	66	4 24	126	8 24	186	12 24	246	16 24	306	20 24	6	0 24	0 25	0 26	0 27
7	0 28	67	4 28	127	8 28	187	12 28	247	16 28	307	20 28	7	0 28	0 29	0 30	0 31
8	0 32	68	4 32	128	8 32	188	12 32	248	16 32	308	20 32	8	0 32	0 33	0 34	0 35
9	0 36	69	4 36	129	8 36	189	12 36	249	16 36	309	20 36	9	0 36	0 37	0 38	0 39
10	0 40	70	4 40	130	8 40	190	12 40	250	16 40	310	20 40	10	0 40	0 41	0 42	0 43
11	0 44	71	4 44	131	8 44	191	12 44	251	16 44	311	20 44	11	0 44	0 45	0 46	0 47
12	0 48	72	4 48	132	8 48	192	12 48	252	16 48	312	20 48	12	0 48	0 49	0 50	0 51
13	0 52	73	4 52	133	8 52	193	12 52	253	16 52	313	20 52	13	0 52	0 53	0 54	0 55
14	0 56	74	4 56	134	8 56	194	12 56	254	16 56	314	20 56	14	0 56	0 57	0 58	0 59
15	1 00	75	5 00	135	9 00	195	13 00	255	17 00	315	21 00	15	1 00	1 01	1 02	1 03
16	1 04	76	5 04	136	9 04	196	13 04	256	17 04	316	21 04	16	1 04	1 05	1 06	1 07
17	1 08	77	5 08	137	9 08	197	13 08	257	17 08	317	21 08	17	1 08	1 09	1 10	1 11
18	1 12	78	5 12	138	9 12	198	13 12	258	17 12	318	21 12	18	1 12	1 13	1 14	1 15
19	1 16	79	5 16	139	9 16	199	13 16	259	17 16	319	21 16	19	1 16	1 17	1 18	1 19
20	1 20	80	5 20	140	9 20	200	13 20	260	17 20	320	21 20	20	1 20	1 21	1 22	1 23
21	1 24	81	5 24	141	9 24	201	13 24	261	17 24	321	21 24	21	1 24	1 25	1 26	1 27
22	1 28	82	5 28	142	9 28	202	13 28	262	17 28	322	21 28	22	1 28	1 29	1 30	1 31
23	1 32	83	5 32	143	9 32	203	13 32	263	17 32	323	21 32	23	1 32	1 33	1 34	1 35
24	1 36	84	5 36	144	9 36	204	13 36	264	17 36	324	21 36	24	1 36	1 37	1 38	1 39
25	1 40	85	5 40	145	9 40	205	13 40	265	17 40	325	21 40	25	1 40	1 41	1 42	1 43
26	1 44	86	5 44	146	9 44	206	13 44	266	17 44	326	21 44	26	1 44	1 45	1 46	1 47
27	1 48	87	5 48	147	9 48	207	13 48	267	17 48	327	21 48	27	1 48	1 49	1 50	1 51
28	1 52	88	5 52	148	9 52	208	13 52	268	17 52	328	21 52	28	1 52	1 53	1 54	1 55
29	1 56	89	5 56	149	9 56	209	13 56	269	17 56	329	21 56	29	1 56	1 57	1 58	1 59
30	2 00	90	6 00	150	10 00	210	14 00	270	18 00	330	22 00	30	2 00	2 01	2 02	2 03
31	2 04	91	6 04	151	10 04	211	14 04	271	18 04	331	22 04	31	2 04	2 05	2 06	2 07
32	2 08	92	6 08	152	10 08	212	14 08	272	18 08	332	22 08	32	2 08	2 09	2 10	2 11
33	2 12	93	6 12	153	10 12	213	14 12	273	18 12	333	22 12	33	2 12	2 13	2 14	2 15
34	2 16	94	6 16	154	10 16	214	14 16	274	18 16	334	22 16	34	2 16	2 17	2 18	2 19
35	2 20	95	6 20	155	10 20	215	14 20	275	18 20	335	22 20	35	2 20	2 21	2 22	2 23
36	2 24	96	6 24	156	10 24	216	14 24	276	18 24	336	22 24	36	2 24	2 25	2 26	2 27
37	2 28	97	6 28	157	10 28	217	14 28	277	18 28	337	22 28	37	2 28	2 29	2 30	2 31
38	2 32	98	6 32	158	10 32	218	14 32	278	18 32	338	22 32	38	2 32	2 33	2 34	2 35
39	2 36	99	6 36	159	10 36	219	14 36	279	18 36	339	22 36	39	2 36	2 37	2 38	2 39
40	2 40	100	6 40	160	10 40	220	14 40	280	18 40	340	22 40	40	2 40	2 41	2 42	2 43
41	2 44	101	6 44	161	10 44	221	14 44	281	18 44	341	22 44	41	2 44	2 45	2 46	2 47
42	2 48	102	6 48	162	10 48	222	14 48	282	18 48	342	22 48	42	2 48	2 49	2 50	2 51
43	2 52	103	6 52	163	10 52	223	14 52	283	18 52	343	22 52	43	2 52	2 53	2 54	2 55
44	2 56	104	6 56	164	10 56	224	14 56	284	18 56	344	22 56	44	2 56	2 57	2 58	2 59
45	3 00	105	7 00	165	11 00	225	15 00	285	19 00	345	23 00	45	3 00	3 01	3 02	3 03
46	3 04	106	7 04	166	11 04	226	15 04	286	19 04	346	23 04	46	3 04	3 05	3 06	3 07
47	3 08	107	7 08	167	11 08	227	15 08	287	19 08	347	23 08	47	3 08	3 09	3 10	3 11
48	3 12	108	7 12	168	11 12	228	15 12	288	19 12	348	23 12	48	3 12	3 13	3 14	3 15
49	3 16	109	7 16	169	11 16	229	15 16	289	19 16	349	23 16	49	3 16	3 17	3 18	3 19
50	3 20	110	7 20	170	11 20	230	15 20	290	19 20	350	23 20	50	3 20	3 21	3 22	3 23
51	3 24	111	7 24	171	11 24	231	15 24	291	19 24	351	23 24	51	3 24	3 25	3 26	3 27
52	3 28	112	7 28	172	11 28	232	15 28	292	19 28	352	23 28	52	3 28	3 29	3 30	3 31
53	3 32	113	7 32	173	11 32	233	15 32	293	19 32	353	23 32	53	3 32	3 33	3 34	3 35
54	3 36	114	7 36	174	11 36	234	15 36	294	19 36	354	23 36	54	3 36	3 37	3 38	3 39
55	3 40	115	7 40	175	11 40	235	15 40	295	19 40	355	23 40	55	3 40	3 41	3 42	3 43
56	3 44	116	7 44	176	11 44	236	15 44	296	19 44	356	23 44	56	3 44	3 45	3 46	3 47
57	3 48	117	7 48	177	11 48	237	15 48	297	19 48	357	23 48	57	3 48	3 49	3 50	3 51
58	3 52	118	7 52	178	11 52	238	15 52	298	19 52	358	23 52	58	3 52	3 53	3 54	3 55
59	3 56	119	7 56	179	11 56	239	15 56	299	19 56	359	23 56	59	3 56	3 57	3 58	3 59

The above table is for converting expressions in arc to their equivalent in time; its main use in this Almanac is for the conversion of longitude for application to LMT (*added* if *west*, *subtracted* if *east*) to give UT or vice versa, particularly in the case of sunrise, sunset, etc.

i

© British Crown Copyright 2018. All rights reserved.

0	SUN PLANETS	ARIES	MOON	v or Corrⁿ d		v or Corrⁿ d		v or Corrⁿ d		1	SUN PLANETS	ARIES	MOON	v or Corrⁿ d		v or Corrⁿ d		v or Corrⁿ d	
s	° ′	° ′	° ′	′	′	′	′	′	′	s	° ′	° ′	° ′	′	′	′	′	′	′
00	0 00·0	0 00·0	0 00·0	0·0	0·0	6·0	0·1	12·0	0·1	00	0 15·0	0 15·0	0 14·3	0·0	0·0	6·0	0·2	12·0	0·3
01	0 00·3	0 00·3	0 00·2	0·1	0·0	6·1	0·1	12·1	0·1	01	0 15·3	0 15·3	0 14·6	0·1	0·0	6·1	0·2	12·1	0·3
02	0 00·5	0 00·5	0 00·5	0·2	0·0	6·2	0·1	12·2	0·1	02	0 15·5	0 15·5	0 14·8	0·2	0·0	6·2	0·2	12·2	0·3
03	0 00·8	0 00·8	0 00·7	0·3	0·0	6·3	0·1	12·3	0·1	03	0 15·8	0 15·8	0 15·0	0·3	0·0	6·3	0·2	12·3	0·3
04	0 01·0	0 01·0	0 01·0	0·4	0·0	6·4	0·1	12·4	0·1	04	0 16·0	0 16·0	0 15·3	0·4	0·0	6·4	0·2	12·4	0·3
05	0 01·3	0 01·3	0 01·2	0·5	0·0	6·5	0·1	12·5	0·1	05	0 16·3	0 16·3	0 15·5	0·5	0·0	6·5	0·2	12·5	0·3
06	0 01·5	0 01·5	0 01·4	0·6	0·0	6·6	0·1	12·6	0·1	06	0 16·5	0 16·5	0 15·7	0·6	0·0	6·6	0·2	12·6	0·3
07	0 01·8	0 01·8	0 01·7	0·7	0·0	6·7	0·1	12·7	0·1	07	0 16·8	0 16·8	0 16·0	0·7	0·0	6·7	0·2	12·7	0·3
08	0 02·0	0 02·0	0 01·9	0·8	0·0	6·8	0·1	12·8	0·1	08	0 17·0	0 17·0	0 16·2	0·8	0·0	6·8	0·2	12·8	0·3
09	0 02·3	0 02·3	0 02·1	0·9	0·0	6·9	0·1	12·9	0·1	09	0 17·3	0 17·3	0 16·5	0·9	0·0	6·9	0·2	12·9	0·3
10	0 02·5	0 02·5	0 02·4	1·0	0·0	7·0	0·1	13·0	0·1	10	0 17·5	0 17·5	0 16·7	1·0	0·0	7·0	0·2	13·0	0·3
11	0 02·8	0 02·8	0 02·6	1·1	0·0	7·1	0·1	13·1	0·1	11	0 17·8	0 17·8	0 16·9	1·1	0·0	7·1	0·2	13·1	0·3
12	0 03·0	0 03·0	0 02·9	1·2	0·0	7·2	0·1	13·2	0·1	12	0 18·0	0 18·0	0 17·2	1·2	0·0	7·2	0·2	13·2	0·3
13	0 03·3	0 03·3	0 03·1	1·3	0·0	7·3	0·1	13·3	0·1	13	0 18·3	0 18·3	0 17·4	1·3	0·0	7·3	0·2	13·3	0·3
14	0 03·5	0 03·5	0 03·3	1·4	0·0	7·4	0·1	13·4	0·1	14	0 18·5	0 18·6	0 17·7	1·4	0·0	7·4	0·2	13·4	0·3
15	0 03·8	0 03·8	0 03·6	1·5	0·0	7·5	0·1	13·5	0·1	15	0 18·8	0 18·8	0 17·9	1·5	0·0	7·5	0·2	13·5	0·3
16	0 04·0	0 04·0	0 03·8	1·6	0·0	7·6	0·1	13·6	0·1	16	0 19·0	0 19·1	0 18·1	1·6	0·0	7·6	0·2	13·6	0·3
17	0 04·3	0 04·3	0 04·1	1·7	0·0	7·7	0·1	13·7	0·1	17	0 19·3	0 19·3	0 18·4	1·7	0·0	7·7	0·2	13·7	0·3
18	0 04·5	0 04·5	0 04·3	1·8	0·0	7·8	0·1	13·8	0·1	18	0 19·5	0 19·6	0 18·6	1·8	0·0	7·8	0·2	13·8	0·3
19	0 04·8	0 04·8	0 04·5	1·9	0·0	7·9	0·1	13·9	0·1	19	0 19·8	0 19·8	0 18·9	1·9	0·0	7·9	0·2	13·9	0·3
20	0 05·0	0 05·0	0 04·8	2·0	0·0	8·0	0·1	14·0	0·1	20	0 20·0	0 20·1	0 19·1	2·0	0·1	8·0	0·2	14·0	0·4
21	0 05·3	0 05·3	0 05·0	2·1	0·0	8·1	0·1	14·1	0·1	21	0 20·3	0 20·3	0 19·3	2·1	0·1	8·1	0·2	14·1	0·4
22	0 05·5	0 05·5	0 05·2	2·2	0·0	8·2	0·1	14·2	0·1	22	0 20·5	0 20·6	0 19·6	2·2	0·1	8·2	0·2	14·2	0·4
23	0 05·8	0 05·8	0 05·5	2·3	0·0	8·3	0·1	14·3	0·1	23	0 20·8	0 20·8	0 19·8	2·3	0·1	8·3	0·2	14·3	0·4
24	0 06·0	0 06·0	0 05·7	2·4	0·0	8·4	0·1	14·4	0·1	24	0 21·0	0 21·1	0 20·0	2·4	0·1	8·4	0·2	14·4	0·4
25	0 06·3	0 06·3	0 06·0	2·5	0·0	8·5	0·1	14·5	0·1	25	0 21·3	0 21·3	0 20·3	2·5	0·1	8·5	0·2	14·5	0·4
26	0 06·5	0 06·5	0 06·2	2·6	0·0	8·6	0·1	14·6	0·1	26	0 21·5	0 21·6	0 20·5	2·6	0·1	8·6	0·2	14·6	0·4
27	0 06·8	0 06·8	0 06·4	2·7	0·0	8·7	0·1	14·7	0·1	27	0 21·8	0 21·8	0 20·8	2·7	0·1	8·7	0·2	14·7	0·4
28	0 07·0	0 07·0	0 06·7	2·8	0·0	8·8	0·1	14·8	0·1	28	0 22·0	0 22·1	0 21·0	2·8	0·1	8·8	0·2	14·8	0·4
29	0 07·3	0 07·3	0 06·9	2·9	0·0	8·9	0·1	14·9	0·1	29	0 22·3	0 22·3	0 21·2	2·9	0·1	8·9	0·2	14·9	0·4
30	0 07·5	0 07·5	0 07·2	3·0	0·0	9·0	0·1	15·0	0·1	30	0 22·5	0 22·6	0 21·5	3·0	0·1	9·0	0·2	15·0	0·4
31	0 07·8	0 07·8	0 07·4	3·1	0·0	9·1	0·1	15·1	0·1	31	0 22·8	0 22·8	0 21·7	3·1	0·1	9·1	0·2	15·1	0·4
32	0 08·0	0 08·0	0 07·6	3·2	0·0	9·2	0·1	15·2	0·1	32	0 23·0	0 23·1	0 22·0	3·2	0·1	9·2	0·2	15·2	0·4
33	0 08·3	0 08·3	0 07·9	3·3	0·0	9·3	0·1	15·3	0·1	33	0 23·3	0 23·3	0 22·2	3·3	0·1	9·3	0·2	15·3	0·4
34	0 08·5	0 08·5	0 08·1	3·4	0·0	9·4	0·1	15·4	0·1	34	0 23·5	0 23·6	0 22·4	3·4	0·1	9·4	0·2	15·4	0·4
35	0 08·8	0 08·8	0 08·4	3·5	0·0	9·5	0·1	15·5	0·1	35	0 23·8	0 23·8	0 22·7	3·5	0·1	9·5	0·2	15·5	0·4
36	0 09·0	0 09·0	0 08·6	3·6	0·0	9·6	0·1	15·6	0·1	36	0 24·0	0 24·1	0 22·9	3·6	0·1	9·6	0·2	15·6	0·4
37	0 09·3	0 09·3	0 08·8	3·7	0·0	9·7	0·1	15·7	0·1	37	0 24·3	0 24·3	0 23·1	3·7	0·1	9·7	0·2	15·7	0·4
38	0 09·5	0 09·5	0 09·1	3·8	0·0	9·8	0·1	15·8	0·1	38	0 24·5	0 24·6	0 23·4	3·8	0·1	9·8	0·2	15·8	0·4
39	0 09·8	0 09·8	0 09·3	3·9	0·0	9·9	0·1	15·9	0·1	39	0 24·8	0 24·8	0 23·6	3·9	0·1	9·9	0·2	15·9	0·4
40	0 10·0	0 10·0	0 09·5	4·0	0·0	10·0	0·1	16·0	0·1	40	0 25·0	0 25·1	0 23·9	4·0	0·1	10·0	0·3	16·0	0·4
41	0 10·3	0 10·3	0 09·8	4·1	0·0	10·1	0·1	16·1	0·1	41	0 25·3	0 25·3	0 24·1	4·1	0·1	10·1	0·3	16·1	0·4
42	0 10·5	0 10·5	0 10·0	4·2	0·0	10·2	0·1	16·2	0·1	42	0 25·5	0 25·6	0 24·3	4·2	0·1	10·2	0·3	16·2	0·4
43	0 10·8	0 10·8	0 10·3	4·3	0·0	10·3	0·1	16·3	0·1	43	0 25·8	0 25·8	0 24·6	4·3	0·1	10·3	0·3	16·3	0·4
44	0 11·0	0 11·0	0 10·5	4·4	0·0	10·4	0·1	16·4	0·1	44	0 26·0	0 26·1	0 24·8	4·4	0·1	10·4	0·3	16·4	0·4
45	0 11·3	0 11·3	0 10·7	4·5	0·0	10·5	0·1	16·5	0·1	45	0 26·3	0 26·3	0 25·1	4·5	0·1	10·5	0·3	16·5	0·4
46	0 11·5	0 11·5	0 11·0	4·6	0·0	10·6	0·1	16·6	0·1	46	0 26·5	0 26·6	0 25·3	4·6	0·1	10·6	0·3	16·6	0·4
47	0 11·8	0 11·8	0 11·2	4·7	0·0	10·7	0·1	16·7	0·1	47	0 26·8	0 26·8	0 25·5	4·7	0·1	10·7	0·3	16·7	0·4
48	0 12·0	0 12·0	0 11·5	4·8	0·0	10·8	0·1	16·8	0·1	48	0 27·0	0 27·1	0 25·8	4·8	0·1	10·8	0·3	16·8	0·4
49	0 12·3	0 12·3	0 11·7	4·9	0·0	10·9	0·1	16·9	0·1	49	0 27·3	0 27·3	0 26·0	4·9	0·1	10·9	0·3	16·9	0·4
50	0 12·5	0 12·5	0 11·9	5·0	0·0	11·0	0·1	17·0	0·1	50	0 27·5	0 27·6	0 26·2	5·0	0·1	11·0	0·3	17·0	0·4
51	0 12·8	0 12·8	0 12·2	5·1	0·0	11·1	0·1	17·1	0·1	51	0 27·8	0 27·8	0 26·5	5·1	0·1	11·1	0·3	17·1	0·4
52	0 13·0	0 13·0	0 12·4	5·2	0·0	11·2	0·1	17·2	0·1	52	0 28·0	0 28·1	0 26·7	5·2	0·1	11·2	0·3	17·2	0·4
53	0 13·3	0 13·3	0 12·6	5·3	0·0	11·3	0·1	17·3	0·1	53	0 28·3	0 28·3	0 27·0	5·3	0·1	11·3	0·3	17·3	0·4
54	0 13·5	0 13·5	0 12·9	5·4	0·0	11·4	0·1	17·4	0·1	54	0 28·5	0 28·6	0 27·2	5·4	0·1	11·4	0·3	17·4	0·4
55	0 13·8	0 13·8	0 13·1	5·5	0·0	11·5	0·1	17·5	0·1	55	0 28·8	0 28·8	0 27·4	5·5	0·1	11·5	0·3	17·5	0·4
56	0 14·0	0 14·0	0 13·4	5·6	0·0	11·6	0·1	17·6	0·1	56	0 29·0	0 29·1	0 27·7	5·6	0·1	11·6	0·3	17·6	0·4
57	0 14·3	0 14·3	0 13·6	5·7	0·0	11·7	0·1	17·7	0·1	57	0 29·3	0 29·3	0 27·9	5·7	0·1	11·7	0·3	17·7	0·4
58	0 14·5	0 14·5	0 13·8	5·8	0·0	11·8	0·1	17·8	0·1	58	0 29·5	0 29·6	0 28·2	5·8	0·1	11·8	0·3	17·8	0·4
59	0 14·8	0 14·8	0 14·1	5·9	0·0	11·9	0·1	17·9	0·1	59	0 29·8	0 29·8	0 28·4	5·9	0·1	11·9	0·3	17·9	0·4
60	0 15·0	0 15·0	0 14·3	6·0	0·1	12·0	0·1	18·0	0·2	60	0 30·0	0 30·1	0 28·6	6·0	0·2	12·0	0·3	18·0	0·5

ii

© British Crown Copyright 2018. All rights reserved.

2^m	SUN PLANETS	ARIES	MOON	v or d	Corr^n	v or d	Corr^n	v or d	Corr^n
s	° ′	° ′	° ′	′	′	′	′	′	′
00	0 30.0	0 30.1	0 28.6	0.0	0.0	6.0	0.3	12.0	0.5
01	0 30.3	0 30.3	0 28.9	0.1	0.0	6.1	0.3	12.1	0.5
02	0 30.5	0 30.6	0 29.1	0.2	0.0	6.2	0.3	12.2	0.5
03	0 30.8	0 30.8	0 29.3	0.3	0.0	6.3	0.3	12.3	0.5
04	0 31.0	0 31.1	0 29.6	0.4	0.0	6.4	0.3	12.4	0.5
05	0 31.3	0 31.3	0 29.8	0.5	0.0	6.5	0.3	12.5	0.5
06	0 31.5	0 31.6	0 30.1	0.6	0.0	6.6	0.3	12.6	0.5
07	0 31.8	0 31.8	0 30.3	0.7	0.0	6.7	0.3	12.7	0.5
08	0 32.0	0 32.1	0 30.5	0.8	0.0	6.8	0.3	12.8	0.5
09	0 32.3	0 32.3	0 30.8	0.9	0.0	6.9	0.3	12.9	0.5
10	0 32.5	0 32.6	0 31.0	1.0	0.0	7.0	0.3	13.0	0.5
11	0 32.8	0 32.8	0 31.3	1.1	0.0	7.1	0.3	13.1	0.5
12	0 33.0	0 33.1	0 31.5	1.2	0.1	7.2	0.3	13.2	0.6
13	0 33.3	0 33.3	0 31.7	1.3	0.1	7.3	0.3	13.3	0.6
14	0 33.5	0 33.6	0 32.0	1.4	0.1	7.4	0.3	13.4	0.6
15	0 33.8	0 33.8	0 32.2	1.5	0.1	7.5	0.3	13.5	0.6
16	0 34.0	0 34.1	0 32.5	1.6	0.1	7.6	0.3	13.6	0.6
17	0 34.3	0 34.3	0 32.7	1.7	0.1	7.7	0.3	13.7	0.6
18	0 34.5	0 34.6	0 32.9	1.8	0.1	7.8	0.3	13.8	0.6
19	0 34.8	0 34.8	0 33.2	1.9	0.1	7.9	0.3	13.9	0.6
20	0 35.0	0 35.1	0 33.4	2.0	0.1	8.0	0.3	14.0	0.6
21	0 35.3	0 35.3	0 33.6	2.1	0.1	8.1	0.3	14.1	0.6
22	0 35.5	0 35.6	0 33.9	2.2	0.1	8.2	0.3	14.2	0.6
23	0 35.8	0 35.8	0 34.1	2.3	0.1	8.3	0.3	14.3	0.6
24	0 36.0	0 36.1	0 34.4	2.4	0.1	8.4	0.3	14.4	0.6
25	0 36.3	0 36.3	0 34.6	2.5	0.1	8.5	0.4	14.5	0.6
26	0 36.5	0 36.6	0 34.8	2.6	0.1	8.6	0.4	14.6	0.6
27	0 36.8	0 36.9	0 35.1	2.7	0.1	8.7	0.4	14.7	0.6
28	0 37.0	0 37.1	0 35.3	2.8	0.1	8.8	0.4	14.8	0.6
29	0 37.3	0 37.4	0 35.6	2.9	0.1	8.9	0.4	14.9	0.6
30	0 37.5	0 37.6	0 35.8	3.0	0.1	9.0	0.4	15.0	0.6
31	0 37.8	0 37.9	0 36.0	3.1	0.1	9.1	0.4	15.1	0.6
32	0 38.0	0 38.1	0 36.3	3.2	0.1	9.2	0.4	15.2	0.6
33	0 38.3	0 38.4	0 36.5	3.3	0.1	9.3	0.4	15.3	0.6
34	0 38.5	0 38.6	0 36.7	3.4	0.1	9.4	0.4	15.4	0.6
35	0 38.8	0 38.9	0 37.0	3.5	0.1	9.5	0.4	15.5	0.6
36	0 39.0	0 39.1	0 37.2	3.6	0.2	9.6	0.4	15.6	0.7
37	0 39.3	0 39.4	0 37.5	3.7	0.2	9.7	0.4	15.7	0.7
38	0 39.5	0 39.6	0 37.7	3.8	0.2	9.8	0.4	15.8	0.7
39	0 39.8	0 39.9	0 37.9	3.9	0.2	9.9	0.4	15.9	0.7
40	0 40.0	0 40.1	0 38.2	4.0	0.2	10.0	0.4	16.0	0.7
41	0 40.3	0 40.4	0 38.4	4.1	0.2	10.1	0.4	16.1	0.7
42	0 40.5	0 40.6	0 38.7	4.2	0.2	10.2	0.4	16.2	0.7
43	0 40.8	0 40.9	0 38.9	4.3	0.2	10.3	0.4	16.3	0.7
44	0 41.0	0 41.1	0 39.1	4.4	0.2	10.4	0.4	16.4	0.7
45	0 41.3	0 41.4	0 39.4	4.5	0.2	10.5	0.4	16.5	0.7
46	0 41.5	0 41.6	0 39.6	4.6	0.2	10.6	0.4	16.6	0.7
47	0 41.8	0 41.9	0 39.8	4.7	0.2	10.7	0.4	16.7	0.7
48	0 42.0	0 42.1	0 40.1	4.8	0.2	10.8	0.5	16.8	0.7
49	0 42.3	0 42.4	0 40.3	4.9	0.2	10.9	0.5	16.9	0.7
50	0 42.5	0 42.6	0 40.6	5.0	0.2	11.0	0.5	17.0	0.7
51	0 42.8	0 42.9	0 40.8	5.1	0.2	11.1	0.5	17.1	0.7
52	0 43.0	0 43.1	0 41.0	5.2	0.2	11.2	0.5	17.2	0.7
53	0 43.3	0 43.4	0 41.3	5.3	0.2	11.3	0.5	17.3	0.7
54	0 43.5	0 43.6	0 41.5	5.4	0.2	11.4	0.5	17.4	0.7
55	0 43.8	0 43.9	0 41.8	5.5	0.2	11.5	0.5	17.5	0.7
56	0 44.0	0 44.1	0 42.0	5.6	0.2	11.6	0.5	17.6	0.7
57	0 44.3	0 44.4	0 42.2	5.7	0.2	11.7	0.5	17.7	0.7
58	0 44.5	0 44.6	0 42.5	5.8	0.2	11.8	0.5	17.8	0.7
59	0 44.8	0 44.9	0 42.7	5.9	0.2	11.9	0.5	17.9	0.7
60	0 45.0	0 45.1	0 43.0	6.0	0.3	12.0	0.5	18.0	0.8

3^m	SUN PLANETS	ARIES	MOON	v or d	Corr^n	v or d	Corr^n	v or d	Corr^n
s	° ′	° ′	° ′	′	′	′	′	′	′
00	0 45.0	0 45.1	0 43.0	0.0	0.0	6.0	0.4	12.0	0.7
01	0 45.3	0 45.4	0 43.2	0.1	0.0	6.1	0.4	12.1	0.7
02	0 45.5	0 45.6	0 43.4	0.2	0.0	6.2	0.4	12.2	0.7
03	0 45.8	0 45.9	0 43.7	0.3	0.0	6.3	0.4	12.3	0.7
04	0 46.0	0 46.1	0 43.9	0.4	0.0	6.4	0.4	12.4	0.7
05	0 46.3	0 46.4	0 44.1	0.5	0.0	6.5	0.4	12.5	0.7
06	0 46.5	0 46.6	0 44.4	0.6	0.0	6.6	0.4	12.6	0.7
07	0 46.8	0 46.9	0 44.6	0.7	0.0	6.7	0.4	12.7	0.7
08	0 47.0	0 47.1	0 44.9	0.8	0.0	6.8	0.4	12.8	0.7
09	0 47.3	0 47.4	0 45.1	0.9	0.1	6.9	0.4	12.9	0.8
10	0 47.5	0 47.6	0 45.3	1.0	0.1	7.0	0.4	13.0	0.8
11	0 47.8	0 47.9	0 45.6	1.1	0.1	7.1	0.4	13.1	0.8
12	0 48.0	0 48.1	0 45.8	1.2	0.1	7.2	0.4	13.2	0.8
13	0 48.3	0 48.4	0 46.1	1.3	0.1	7.3	0.4	13.3	0.8
14	0 48.5	0 48.6	0 46.3	1.4	0.1	7.4	0.4	13.4	0.8
15	0 48.8	0 48.9	0 46.5	1.5	0.1	7.5	0.4	13.5	0.8
16	0 49.0	0 49.1	0 46.8	1.6	0.1	7.6	0.4	13.6	0.8
17	0 49.3	0 49.4	0 47.0	1.7	0.1	7.7	0.4	13.7	0.8
18	0 49.5	0 49.6	0 47.2	1.8	0.1	7.8	0.5	13.8	0.8
19	0 49.8	0 49.9	0 47.5	1.9	0.1	7.9	0.5	13.9	0.8
20	0 50.0	0 50.1	0 47.7	2.0	0.1	8.0	0.5	14.0	0.8
21	0 50.3	0 50.4	0 48.0	2.1	0.1	8.1	0.5	14.1	0.8
22	0 50.5	0 50.6	0 48.2	2.2	0.1	8.2	0.5	14.2	0.8
23	0 50.8	0 50.9	0 48.4	2.3	0.1	8.3	0.5	14.3	0.8
24	0 51.0	0 51.1	0 48.7	2.4	0.1	8.4	0.5	14.4	0.8
25	0 51.3	0 51.4	0 48.9	2.5	0.1	8.5	0.5	14.5	0.8
26	0 51.5	0 51.6	0 49.2	2.6	0.2	8.6	0.5	14.6	0.9
27	0 51.8	0 51.9	0 49.4	2.7	0.2	8.7	0.5	14.7	0.9
28	0 52.0	0 52.1	0 49.6	2.8	0.2	8.8	0.5	14.8	0.9
29	0 52.3	0 52.4	0 49.9	2.9	0.2	8.9	0.5	14.9	0.9
30	0 52.5	0 52.6	0 50.1	3.0	0.2	9.0	0.5	15.0	0.9
31	0 52.8	0 52.9	0 50.3	3.1	0.2	9.1	0.5	15.1	0.9
32	0 53.0	0 53.1	0 50.6	3.2	0.2	9.2	0.5	15.2	0.9
33	0 53.3	0 53.4	0 50.8	3.3	0.2	9.3	0.5	15.3	0.9
34	0 53.5	0 53.6	0 51.1	3.4	0.2	9.4	0.5	15.4	0.9
35	0 53.8	0 53.9	0 51.3	3.5	0.2	9.5	0.6	15.5	0.9
36	0 54.0	0 54.1	0 51.5	3.6	0.2	9.6	0.6	15.6	0.9
37	0 54.3	0 54.4	0 51.8	3.7	0.2	9.7	0.6	15.7	0.9
38	0 54.5	0 54.6	0 52.0	3.8	0.2	9.8	0.6	15.8	0.9
39	0 54.8	0 54.9	0 52.3	3.9	0.2	9.9	0.6	15.9	0.9
40	0 55.0	0 55.2	0 52.5	4.0	0.2	10.0	0.6	16.0	0.9
41	0 55.3	0 55.4	0 52.7	4.1	0.2	10.1	0.6	16.1	0.9
42	0 55.5	0 55.7	0 53.0	4.2	0.2	10.2	0.6	16.2	0.9
43	0 55.8	0 55.9	0 53.2	4.3	0.3	10.3	0.6	16.3	1.0
44	0 56.0	0 56.2	0 53.4	4.4	0.3	10.4	0.6	16.4	1.0
45	0 56.3	0 56.4	0 53.7	4.5	0.3	10.5	0.6	16.5	1.0
46	0 56.5	0 56.7	0 53.9	4.6	0.3	10.6	0.6	16.6	1.0
47	0 56.8	0 56.9	0 54.2	4.7	0.3	10.7	0.6	16.7	1.0
48	0 57.0	0 57.2	0 54.4	4.8	0.3	10.8	0.6	16.8	1.0
49	0 57.3	0 57.4	0 54.6	4.9	0.3	10.9	0.6	16.9	1.0
50	0 57.5	0 57.7	0 54.9	5.0	0.3	11.0	0.6	17.0	1.0
51	0 57.8	0 57.9	0 55.1	5.1	0.3	11.1	0.6	17.1	1.0
52	0 58.0	0 58.2	0 55.4	5.2	0.3	11.2	0.7	17.2	1.0
53	0 58.3	0 58.4	0 55.6	5.3	0.3	11.3	0.7	17.3	1.0
54	0 58.5	0 58.7	0 55.8	5.4	0.3	11.4	0.7	17.4	1.0
55	0 58.8	0 58.9	0 56.1	5.5	0.3	11.5	0.7	17.5	1.0
56	0 59.0	0 59.2	0 56.3	5.6	0.3	11.6	0.7	17.6	1.0
57	0 59.3	0 59.4	0 56.6	5.7	0.3	11.7	0.7	17.7	1.0
58	0 59.5	0 59.7	0 56.8	5.8	0.3	11.8	0.7	17.8	1.0
59	0 59.8	0 59.9	0 57.0	5.9	0.3	11.9	0.7	17.9	1.0
60	1 00.0	1 00.2	0 57.3	6.0	0.4	12.0	0.7	18.0	1.1

iii

© British Crown Copyright 2018. All rights reserved.

4 m	SUN PLANETS	ARIES	MOON	v or Corrⁿ d		v or Corrⁿ d		v or Corrⁿ d	
s	o ′	o ′	o ′	′	′	′	′	′	′
00	1 00·0	1 00·2	0 57·3	0·0	0·0	6·0	0·5	12·0	0·9
01	1 00·3	1 00·4	0 57·5	0·1	0·0	6·1	0·5	12·1	0·9
02	1 00·5	1 00·7	0 57·7	0·2	0·0	6·2	0·5	12·2	0·9
03	1 00·8	1 00·9	0 58·0	0·3	0·0	6·3	0·5	12·3	0·9
04	1 01·0	1 01·2	0 58·2	0·4	0·0	6·4	0·5	12·4	0·9
05	1 01·3	1 01·4	0 58·5	0·5	0·0	6·5	0·5	12·5	0·9
06	1 01·5	1 01·7	0 58·7	0·6	0·0	6·6	0·5	12·6	0·9
07	1 01·8	1 01·9	0 58·9	0·7	0·1	6·7	0·5	12·7	1·0
08	1 02·0	1 02·2	0 59·2	0·8	0·1	6·8	0·5	12·8	1·0
09	1 02·3	1 02·4	0 59·4	0·9	0·1	6·9	0·5	12·9	1·0
10	1 02·5	1 02·7	0 59·7	1·0	0·1	7·0	0·5	13·0	1·0
11	1 02·8	1 02·9	0 59·9	1·1	0·1	7·1	0·5	13·1	1·0
12	1 03·0	1 03·2	1 00·1	1·2	0·1	7·2	0·5	13·2	1·0
13	1 03·3	1 03·4	1 00·4	1·3	0·1	7·3	0·5	13·3	1·0
14	1 03·5	1 03·7	1 00·6	1·4	0·1	7·4	0·6	13·4	1·0
15	1 03·8	1 03·9	1 00·8	1·5	0·1	7·5	0·6	13·5	1·0
16	1 04·0	1 04·2	1 01·1	1·6	0·1	7·6	0·6	13·6	1·0
17	1 04·3	1 04·4	1 01·3	1·7	0·1	7·7	0·6	13·7	1·0
18	1 04·5	1 04·7	1 01·6	1·8	0·1	7·8	0·6	13·8	1·0
19	1 04·8	1 04·9	1 01·8	1·9	0·1	7·9	0·6	13·9	1·0
20	1 05·0	1 05·2	1 02·0	2·0	0·2	8·0	0·6	14·0	1·1
21	1 05·3	1 05·4	1 02·3	2·1	0·2	8·1	0·6	14·1	1·1
22	1 05·5	1 05·7	1 02·5	2·2	0·2	8·2	0·6	14·2	1·1
23	1 05·8	1 05·9	1 02·8	2·3	0·2	8·3	0·6	14·3	1·1
24	1 06·0	1 06·2	1 03·0	2·4	0·2	8·4	0·6	14·4	1·1
25	1 06·3	1 06·4	1 03·2	2·5	0·2	8·5	0·6	14·5	1·1
26	1 06·5	1 06·7	1 03·5	2·6	0·2	8·6	0·6	14·6	1·1
27	1 06·8	1 06·9	1 03·7	2·7	0·2	8·7	0·7	14·7	1·1
28	1 07·0	1 07·2	1 03·9	2·8	0·2	8·8	0·7	14·8	1·1
29	1 07·3	1 07·4	1 04·2	2·9	0·2	8·9	0·7	14·9	1·1
30	1 07·5	1 07·7	1 04·4	3·0	0·2	9·0	0·7	15·0	1·1
31	1 07·8	1 07·9	1 04·7	3·1	0·2	9·1	0·7	15·1	1·1
32	1 08·0	1 08·2	1 04·9	3·2	0·2	9·2	0·7	15·2	1·1
33	1 08·3	1 08·4	1 05·1	3·3	0·2	9·3	0·7	15·3	1·1
34	1 08·5	1 08·7	1 05·4	3·4	0·3	9·4	0·7	15·4	1·2
35	1 08·8	1 08·9	1 05·6	3·5	0·3	9·5	0·7	15·5	1·2
36	1 09·0	1 09·2	1 05·9	3·6	0·3	9·6	0·7	15·6	1·2
37	1 09·3	1 09·4	1 06·1	3·7	0·3	9·7	0·7	15·7	1·2
38	1 09·5	1 09·7	1 06·3	3·8	0·3	9·8	0·7	15·8	1·2
39	1 09·8	1 09·9	1 06·6	3·9	0·3	9·9	0·7	15·9	1·2
40	1 10·0	1 10·2	1 06·8	4·0	0·3	10·0	0·8	16·0	1·2
41	1 10·3	1 10·4	1 07·0	4·1	0·3	10·1	0·8	16·1	1·2
42	1 10·5	1 10·7	1 07·3	4·2	0·3	10·2	0·8	16·2	1·2
43	1 10·8	1 10·9	1 07·5	4·3	0·3	10·3	0·8	16·3	1·2
44	1 11·0	1 11·2	1 07·8	4·4	0·3	10·4	0·8	16·4	1·2
45	1 11·3	1 11·4	1 08·0	4·5	0·3	10·5	0·8	16·5	1·2
46	1 11·5	1 11·7	1 08·2	4·6	0·3	10·6	0·8	16·6	1·2
47	1 11·8	1 11·9	1 08·5	4·7	0·4	10·7	0·8	16·7	1·3
48	1 12·0	1 12·2	1 08·7	4·8	0·4	10·8	0·8	16·8	1·3
49	1 12·3	1 12·4	1 09·0	4·9	0·4	10·9	0·8	16·9	1·3
50	1 12·5	1 12·7	1 09·2	5·0	0·4	11·0	0·8	17·0	1·3
51	1 12·8	1 12·9	1 09·4	5·1	0·4	11·1	0·8	17·1	1·3
52	1 13·0	1 13·2	1 09·7	5·2	0·4	11·2	0·8	17·2	1·3
53	1 13·3	1 13·5	1 09·9	5·3	0·4	11·3	0·8	17·3	1·3
54	1 13·5	1 13·7	1 10·2	5·4	0·4	11·4	0·9	17·4	1·3
55	1 13·8	1 14·0	1 10·4	5·5	0·4	11·5	0·9	17·5	1·3
56	1 14·0	1 14·2	1 10·6	5·6	0·4	11·6	0·9	17·6	1·3
57	1 14·3	1 14·5	1 10·9	5·7	0·4	11·7	0·9	17·7	1·3
58	1 14·5	1 14·7	1 11·1	5·8	0·4	11·8	0·9	17·8	1·3
59	1 14·8	1 15·0	1 11·3	5·9	0·4	11·9	0·9	17·9	1·3
60	1 15·0	1 15·2	1 11·6	6·0	0·5	12·0	0·9	18·0	1·4

5 m	SUN PLANETS	ARIES	MOON	v or Corrⁿ d		v or Corrⁿ d		v or Corrⁿ d	
s	o ′	o ′	o ′	′	′	′	′	′	′
00	1 15·0	1 15·2	1 11·6	0·0	0·0	6·0	0·6	12·0	1·1
01	1 15·3	1 15·5	1 11·8	0·1	0·0	6·1	0·6	12·1	1·1
02	1 15·5	1 15·7	1 12·1	0·2	0·0	6·2	0·6	12·2	1·1
03	1 15·8	1 16·0	1 12·3	0·3	0·0	6·3	0·6	12·3	1·1
04	1 16·0	1 16·2	1 12·5	0·4	0·0	6·4	0·6	12·4	1·1
05	1 16·3	1 16·5	1 12·8	0·5	0·0	6·5	0·6	12·5	1·1
06	1 16·5	1 16·7	1 13·0	0·6	0·1	6·6	0·6	12·6	1·2
07	1 16·8	1 17·0	1 13·3	0·7	0·1	6·7	0·6	12·7	1·2
08	1 17·0	1 17·2	1 13·5	0·8	0·1	6·8	0·6	12·8	1·2
09	1 17·3	1 17·5	1 13·7	0·9	0·1	6·9	0·6	12·9	1·2
10	1 17·5	1 17·7	1 14·0	1·0	0·1	7·0	0·6	13·0	1·2
11	1 17·8	1 18·0	1 14·2	1·1	0·1	7·1	0·7	13·1	1·2
12	1 18·0	1 18·2	1 14·4	1·2	0·1	7·2	0·7	13·2	1·2
13	1 18·3	1 18·5	1 14·7	1·3	0·1	7·3	0·7	13·3	1·2
14	1 18·5	1 18·7	1 14·9	1·4	0·1	7·4	0·7	13·4	1·2
15	1 18·8	1 19·0	1 15·2	1·5	0·1	7·5	0·7	13·5	1·2
16	1 19·0	1 19·2	1 15·4	1·6	0·1	7·6	0·7	13·6	1·2
17	1 19·3	1 19·5	1 15·6	1·7	0·2	7·7	0·7	13·7	1·3
18	1 19·5	1 19·7	1 15·9	1·8	0·2	7·8	0·7	13·8	1·3
19	1 19·8	1 20·0	1 16·1	1·9	0·2	7·9	0·7	13·9	1·3
20	1 20·0	1 20·2	1 16·4	2·0	0·2	8·0	0·7	14·0	1·3
21	1 20·3	1 20·5	1 16·6	2·1	0·2	8·1	0·7	14·1	1·3
22	1 20·5	1 20·7	1 16·8	2·2	0·2	8·2	0·8	14·2	1·3
23	1 20·8	1 21·0	1 17·1	2·3	0·2	8·3	0·8	14·3	1·3
24	1 21·0	1 21·2	1 17·3	2·4	0·2	8·4	0·8	14·4	1·3
25	1 21·3	1 21·5	1 17·5	2·5	0·2	8·5	0·8	14·5	1·3
26	1 21·5	1 21·7	1 17·8	2·6	0·2	8·6	0·8	14·6	1·3
27	1 21·8	1 22·0	1 18·0	2·7	0·2	8·7	0·8	14·7	1·3
28	1 22·0	1 22·2	1 18·3	2·8	0·3	8·8	0·8	14·8	1·4
29	1 22·3	1 22·5	1 18·5	2·9	0·3	8·9	0·8	14·9	1·4
30	1 22·5	1 22·7	1 18·7	3·0	0·3	9·0	0·8	15·0	1·4
31	1 22·8	1 23·0	1 19·0	3·1	0·3	9·1	0·8	15·1	1·4
32	1 23·0	1 23·2	1 19·2	3·2	0·3	9·2	0·8	15·2	1·4
33	1 23·3	1 23·5	1 19·5	3·3	0·3	9·3	0·9	15·3	1·4
34	1 23·5	1 23·7	1 19·7	3·4	0·3	9·4	0·9	15·4	1·4
35	1 23·8	1 24·0	1 19·9	3·5	0·3	9·5	0·9	15·5	1·4
36	1 24·0	1 24·2	1 20·2	3·6	0·3	9·6	0·9	15·6	1·4
37	1 24·3	1 24·5	1 20·4	3·7	0·3	9·7	0·9	15·7	1·4
38	1 24·5	1 24·7	1 20·7	3·8	0·3	9·8	0·9	15·8	1·4
39	1 24·8	1 25·0	1 20·9	3·9	0·4	9·9	0·9	15·9	1·5
40	1 25·0	1 25·2	1 21·1	4·0	0·4	10·0	0·9	16·0	1·5
41	1 25·3	1 25·5	1 21·4	4·1	0·4	10·1	0·9	16·1	1·5
42	1 25·5	1 25·7	1 21·6	4·2	0·4	10·2	0·9	16·2	1·5
43	1 25·8	1 26·0	1 21·8	4·3	0·4	10·3	0·9	16·3	1·5
44	1 26·0	1 26·2	1 22·1	4·4	0·4	10·4	1·0	16·4	1·5
45	1 26·3	1 26·5	1 22·3	4·5	0·4	10·5	1·0	16·5	1·5
46	1 26·5	1 26·7	1 22·6	4·6	0·4	10·6	1·0	16·6	1·5
47	1 26·8	1 27·0	1 22·8	4·7	0·4	10·7	1·0	16·7	1·5
48	1 27·0	1 27·2	1 23·0	4·8	0·4	10·8	1·0	16·8	1·5
49	1 27·3	1 27·5	1 23·3	4·9	0·4	10·9	1·0	16·9	1·5
50	1 27·5	1 27·7	1 23·5	5·0	0·5	11·0	1·0	17·0	1·6
51	1 27·8	1 28·0	1 23·8	5·1	0·5	11·1	1·0	17·1	1·6
52	1 28·0	1 28·2	1 24·0	5·2	0·5	11·2	1·0	17·2	1·6
53	1 28·3	1 28·5	1 24·2	5·3	0·5	11·3	1·0	17·3	1·6
54	1 28·5	1 28·7	1 24·5	5·4	0·5	11·4	1·0	17·4	1·6
55	1 28·8	1 29·0	1 24·7	5·5	0·5	11·5	1·1	17·5	1·6
56	1 29·0	1 29·2	1 24·9	5·6	0·5	11·6	1·1	17·6	1·6
57	1 29·3	1 29·5	1 25·2	5·7	0·5	11·7	1·1	17·7	1·6
58	1 29·5	1 29·7	1 25·4	5·8	0·5	11·8	1·1	17·8	1·6
59	1 29·8	1 30·0	1 25·7	5·9	0·5	11·9	1·1	17·9	1·6
60	1 30·0	1 30·2	1 25·9	6·0	0·6	12·0	1·1	18·0	1·7

iv

© British Crown Copyright 2018. All rights reserved.

6	SUN PLANETS	ARIES	MOON	v or Corrⁿ d		v or Corrⁿ d		v or Corrⁿ d	
s	o ′	o ′	o ′	′	′	′	′	′	′
00	1 30·0	1 30·2	1 25·9	0·0	0·0	6·0	0·7	12·0	1·3
01	1 30·3	1 30·5	1 26·1	0·1	0·0	6·1	0·7	12·1	1·3
02	1 30·5	1 30·7	1 26·4	0·2	0·0	6·2	0·7	12·2	1·3
03	1 30·8	1 31·0	1 26·6	0·3	0·0	6·3	0·7	12·3	1·3
04	1 31·0	1 31·2	1 26·9	0·4	0·0	6·4	0·7	12·4	1·3
05	1 31·3	1 31·5	1 27·1	0·5	0·1	6·5	0·7	12·5	1·4
06	1 31·5	1 31·8	1 27·3	0·6	0·1	6·6	0·7	12·6	1·4
07	1 31·8	1 32·0	1 27·6	0·7	0·1	6·7	0·7	12·7	1·4
08	1 32·0	1 32·3	1 27·8	0·8	0·1	6·8	0·7	12·8	1·4
09	1 32·3	1 32·5	1 28·0	0·9	0·1	6·9	0·7	12·9	1·4
10	1 32·5	1 32·8	1 28·3	1·0	0·1	7·0	0·8	13·0	1·4
11	1 32·8	1 33·0	1 28·5	1·1	0·1	7·1	0·8	13·1	1·4
12	1 33·0	1 33·3	1 28·8	1·2	0·1	7·2	0·8	13·2	1·4
13	1 33·3	1 33·5	1 29·0	1·3	0·1	7·3	0·8	13·3	1·4
14	1 33·5	1 33·8	1 29·2	1·4	0·2	7·4	0·8	13·4	1·5
15	1 33·8	1 34·0	1 29·5	1·5	0·2	7·5	0·8	13·5	1·5
16	1 34·0	1 34·3	1 29·7	1·6	0·2	7·6	0·8	13·6	1·5
17	1 34·3	1 34·5	1 30·0	1·7	0·2	7·7	0·8	13·7	1·5
18	1 34·5	1 34·8	1 30·2	1·8	0·2	7·8	0·8	13·8	1·5
19	1 34·8	1 35·0	1 30·4	1·9	0·2	7·9	0·9	13·9	1·5
20	1 35·0	1 35·3	1 30·7	2·0	0·2	8·0	0·9	14·0	1·5
21	1 35·3	1 35·5	1 30·9	2·1	0·2	8·1	0·9	14·1	1·5
22	1 35·5	1 35·8	1 31·1	2·2	0·2	8·2	0·9	14·2	1·5
23	1 35·8	1 36·0	1 31·4	2·3	0·2	8·3	0·9	14·3	1·5
24	1 36·0	1 36·3	1 31·6	2·4	0·3	8·4	0·9	14·4	1·6
25	1 36·3	1 36·5	1 31·9	2·5	0·3	8·5	0·9	14·5	1·6
26	1 36·5	1 36·8	1 32·1	2·6	0·3	8·6	0·9	14·6	1·6
27	1 36·8	1 37·0	1 32·3	2·7	0·3	8·7	0·9	14·7	1·6
28	1 37·0	1 37·3	1 32·6	2·8	0·3	8·8	1·0	14·8	1·6
29	1 37·3	1 37·5	1 32·8	2·9	0·3	8·9	1·0	14·9	1·6
30	1 37·5	1 37·8	1 33·1	3·0	0·3	9·0	1·0	15·0	1·6
31	1 37·8	1 38·0	1 33·3	3·1	0·3	9·1	1·0	15·1	1·6
32	1 38·0	1 38·3	1 33·5	3·2	0·3	9·2	1·0	15·2	1·6
33	1 38·3	1 38·5	1 33·8	3·3	0·4	9·3	1·0	15·3	1·7
34	1 38·5	1 38·8	1 34·0	3·4	0·4	9·4	1·0	15·4	1·7
35	1 38·8	1 39·0	1 34·3	3·5	0·4	9·5	1·0	15·5	1·7
36	1 39·0	1 39·3	1 34·5	3·6	0·4	9·6	1·0	15·6	1·7
37	1 39·3	1 39·5	1 34·7	3·7	0·4	9·7	1·1	15·7	1·7
38	1 39·5	1 39·8	1 35·0	3·8	0·4	9·8	1·1	15·8	1·7
39	1 39·8	1 40·0	1 35·2	3·9	0·4	9·9	1·1	15·9	1·7
40	1 40·0	1 40·3	1 35·4	4·0	0·4	10·0	1·1	16·0	1·7
41	1 40·3	1 40·5	1 35·7	4·1	0·4	10·1	1·1	16·1	1·7
42	1 40·5	1 40·8	1 35·9	4·2	0·5	10·2	1·1	16·2	1·8
43	1 40·8	1 41·0	1 36·2	4·3	0·5	10·3	1·1	16·3	1·8
44	1 41·0	1 41·3	1 36·4	4·4	0·5	10·4	1·1	16·4	1·8
45	1 41·3	1 41·5	1 36·6	4·5	0·5	10·5	1·1	16·5	1·8
46	1 41·5	1 41·8	1 36·9	4·6	0·5	10·6	1·1	16·6	1·8
47	1 41·8	1 42·0	1 37·1	4·7	0·5	10·7	1·2	16·7	1·8
48	1 42·0	1 42·3	1 37·4	4·8	0·5	10·8	1·2	16·8	1·8
49	1 42·3	1 42·5	1 37·6	4·9	0·5	10·9	1·2	16·9	1·8
50	1 42·5	1 42·8	1 37·8	5·0	0·5	11·0	1·2	17·0	1·8
51	1 42·8	1 43·0	1 38·1	5·1	0·6	11·1	1·2	17·1	1·9
52	1 43·0	1 43·3	1 38·3	5·2	0·6	11·2	1·2	17·2	1·9
53	1 43·3	1 43·5	1 38·5	5·3	0·6	11·3	1·2	17·3	1·9
54	1 43·5	1 43·8	1 38·8	5·4	0·6	11·4	1·2	17·4	1·9
55	1 43·8	1 44·0	1 39·0	5·5	0·6	11·5	1·2	17·5	1·9
56	1 44·0	1 44·3	1 39·3	5·6	0·6	11·6	1·3	17·6	1·9
57	1 44·3	1 44·5	1 39·5	5·7	0·6	11·7	1·3	17·7	1·9
58	1 44·5	1 44·8	1 39·7	5·8	0·6	11·8	1·3	17·8	1·9
59	1 44·8	1 45·0	1 40·0	5·9	0·6	11·9	1·3	17·9	1·9
60	1 45·0	1 45·3	1 40·2	6·0	0·7	12·0	1·3	18·0	2·0

7	SUN PLANETS	ARIES	MOON	v or Corrⁿ d		v or Corrⁿ d		v or Corrⁿ d	
s	o ′	o ′	o ′	′	′	′	′	′	′
00	1 45·0	1 45·3	1 40·2	0·0	0·0	6·0	0·8	12·0	1·5
01	1 45·3	1 45·5	1 40·5	0·1	0·0	6·1	0·8	12·1	1·5
02	1 45·5	1 45·8	1 40·7	0·2	0·0	6·2	0·8	12·2	1·5
03	1 45·8	1 46·0	1 40·9	0·3	0·0	6·3	0·8	12·3	1·5
04	1 46·0	1 46·3	1 41·2	0·4	0·1	6·4	0·8	12·4	1·6
05	1 46·3	1 46·5	1 41·4	0·5	0·1	6·5	0·8	12·5	1·6
06	1 46·5	1 46·8	1 41·6	0·6	0·1	6·6	0·8	12·6	1·6
07	1 46·8	1 47·0	1 41·9	0·7	0·1	6·7	0·8	12·7	1·6
08	1 47·0	1 47·3	1 42·1	0·8	0·1	6·8	0·9	12·8	1·6
09	1 47·3	1 47·5	1 42·4	0·9	0·1	6·9	0·9	12·9	1·6
10	1 47·5	1 47·8	1 42·6	1·0	0·1	7·0	0·9	13·0	1·6
11	1 47·8	1 48·0	1 42·8	1·1	0·1	7·1	0·9	13·1	1·6
12	1 48·0	1 48·3	1 43·1	1·2	0·2	7·2	0·9	13·2	1·7
13	1 48·3	1 48·5	1 43·3	1·3	0·2	7·3	0·9	13·3	1·7
14	1 48·5	1 48·8	1 43·6	1·4	0·2	7·4	0·9	13·4	1·7
15	1 48·8	1 49·0	1 43·8	1·5	0·2	7·5	0·9	13·5	1·7
16	1 49·0	1 49·3	1 44·0	1·6	0·2	7·6	1·0	13·6	1·7
17	1 49·3	1 49·5	1 44·3	1·7	0·2	7·7	1·0	13·7	1·7
18	1 49·5	1 49·8	1 44·5	1·8	0·2	7·8	1·0	13·8	1·7
19	1 49·8	1 50·1	1 44·8	1·9	0·2	7·9	1·0	13·9	1·7
20	1 50·0	1 50·3	1 45·0	2·0	0·3	8·0	1·0	14·0	1·8
21	1 50·3	1 50·6	1 45·2	2·1	0·3	8·1	1·0	14·1	1·8
22	1 50·5	1 50·8	1 45·5	2·2	0·3	8·2	1·0	14·2	1·8
23	1 50·8	1 51·1	1 45·7	2·3	0·3	8·3	1·0	14·3	1·8
24	1 51·0	1 51·3	1 45·9	2·4	0·3	8·4	1·1	14·4	1·8
25	1 51·3	1 51·6	1 46·2	2·5	0·3	8·5	1·1	14·5	1·8
26	1 51·5	1 51·8	1 46·4	2·6	0·3	8·6	1·1	14·6	1·8
27	1 51·8	1 52·1	1 46·7	2·7	0·3	8·7	1·1	14·7	1·8
28	1 52·0	1 52·3	1 46·9	2·8	0·4	8·8	1·1	14·8	1·9
29	1 52·3	1 52·6	1 47·1	2·9	0·4	8·9	1·1	14·9	1·9
30	1 52·5	1 52·8	1 47·4	3·0	0·4	9·0	1·1	15·0	1·9
31	1 52·8	1 53·1	1 47·6	3·1	0·4	9·1	1·1	15·1	1·9
32	1 53·0	1 53·3	1 47·9	3·2	0·4	9·2	1·2	15·2	1·9
33	1 53·3	1 53·6	1 48·1	3·3	0·4	9·3	1·2	15·3	1·9
34	1 53·5	1 53·8	1 48·3	3·4	0·4	9·4	1·2	15·4	1·9
35	1 53·8	1 54·1	1 48·6	3·5	0·4	9·5	1·2	15·5	1·9
36	1 54·0	1 54·3	1 48·8	3·6	0·5	9·6	1·2	15·6	2·0
37	1 54·3	1 54·6	1 49·0	3·7	0·5	9·7	1·2	15·7	2·0
38	1 54·5	1 54·8	1 49·3	3·8	0·5	9·8	1·2	15·8	2·0
39	1 54·8	1 55·1	1 49·5	3·9	0·5	9·9	1·2	15·9	2·0
40	1 55·0	1 55·3	1 49·8	4·0	0·5	10·0	1·3	16·0	2·0
41	1 55·3	1 55·6	1 50·0	4·1	0·5	10·1	1·3	16·1	2·0
42	1 55·5	1 55·8	1 50·2	4·2	0·5	10·2	1·3	16·2	2·0
43	1 55·8	1 56·1	1 50·5	4·3	0·5	10·3	1·3	16·3	2·0
44	1 56·0	1 56·3	1 50·7	4·4	0·6	10·4	1·3	16·4	2·1
45	1 56·3	1 56·6	1 51·0	4·5	0·6	10·5	1·3	16·5	2·1
46	1 56·5	1 56·8	1 51·2	4·6	0·6	10·6	1·3	16·6	2·1
47	1 56·8	1 57·1	1 51·4	4·7	0·6	10·7	1·3	16·7	2·1
48	1 57·0	1 57·3	1 51·7	4·8	0·6	10·8	1·4	16·8	2·1
49	1 57·3	1 57·6	1 51·9	4·9	0·6	10·9	1·4	16·9	2·1
50	1 57·5	1 57·8	1 52·1	5·0	0·6	11·0	1·4	17·0	2·1
51	1 57·8	1 58·1	1 52·4	5·1	0·6	11·1	1·4	17·1	2·1
52	1 58·0	1 58·3	1 52·6	5·2	0·7	11·2	1·4	17·2	2·2
53	1 58·3	1 58·6	1 52·9	5·3	0·7	11·3	1·4	17·3	2·2
54	1 58·5	1 58·8	1 53·1	5·4	0·7	11·4	1·4	17·4	2·2
55	1 58·8	1 59·1	1 53·3	5·5	0·7	11·5	1·4	17·5	2·2
56	1 59·0	1 59·3	1 53·6	5·6	0·7	11·6	1·5	17·6	2·2
57	1 59·3	1 59·6	1 53·8	5·7	0·7	11·7	1·5	17·7	2·2
58	1 59·5	1 59·8	1 54·1	5·8	0·7	11·8	1·5	17·8	2·2
59	1 59·8	2 00·1	1 54·3	5·9	0·7	11·9	1·5	17·9	2·2
60	2 00·0	2 00·3	1 54·5	6·0	0·8	12·0	1·5	18·0	2·3

V

© British Crown Copyright 2018. All rights reserved.

8ᵐ

8 s	SUN PLANETS ° '	ARIES ° '	MOON ° '	v or Corrⁿ d		v or Corrⁿ d		v or Corrⁿ d	
00	2 00·0	2 00·3	1 54·5	0·0	0·0	6·0	0·9	12·0	1·7
01	2 00·3	2 00·6	1 54·8	0·1	0·0	6·1	0·9	12·1	1·7
02	2 00·5	2 00·8	1 55·0	0·2	0·0	6·2	0·9	12·2	1·7
03	2 00·8	2 01·1	1 55·2	0·3	0·0	6·3	0·9	12·3	1·7
04	2 01·0	2 01·3	1 55·5	0·4	0·1	6·4	0·9	12·4	1·8
05	2 01·3	2 01·6	1 55·7	0·5	0·1	6·5	0·9	12·5	1·8
06	2 01·5	2 01·8	1 56·0	0·6	0·1	6·6	0·9	12·6	1·8
07	2 01·8	2 02·1	1 56·2	0·7	0·1	6·7	0·9	12·7	1·8
08	2 02·0	2 02·3	1 56·4	0·8	0·1	6·8	1·0	12·8	1·8
09	2 02·3	2 02·6	1 56·7	0·9	0·1	6·9	1·0	12·9	1·8
10	2 02·5	2 02·8	1 56·9	1·0	0·1	7·0	1·0	13·0	1·8
11	2 02·8	2 03·1	1 57·2	1·1	0·2	7·1	1·0	13·1	1·9
12	2 03·0	2 03·3	1 57·4	1·2	0·2	7·2	1·0	13·2	1·9
13	2 03·3	2 03·6	1 57·6	1·3	0·2	7·3	1·0	13·3	1·9
14	2 03·5	2 03·8	1 57·9	1·4	0·2	7·4	1·0	13·4	1·9
15	2 03·8	2 04·1	1 58·1	1·5	0·2	7·5	1·1	13·5	1·9
16	2 04·0	2 04·3	1 58·4	1·6	0·2	7·6	1·1	13·6	1·9
17	2 04·3	2 04·6	1 58·6	1·7	0·2	7·7	1·1	13·7	1·9
18	2 04·5	2 04·8	1 58·8	1·8	0·3	7·8	1·1	13·8	2·0
19	2 04·8	2 05·1	1 59·1	1·9	0·3	7·9	1·1	13·9	2·0
20	2 05·0	2 05·3	1 59·3	2·0	0·3	8·0	1·1	14·0	2·0
21	2 05·3	2 05·6	1 59·5	2·1	0·3	8·1	1·1	14·1	2·0
22	2 05·5	2 05·8	1 59·8	2·2	0·3	8·2	1·2	14·2	2·0
23	2 05·8	2 06·1	2 00·0	2·3	0·3	8·3	1·2	14·3	2·0
24	2 06·0	2 06·3	2 00·3	2·4	0·3	8·4	1·2	14·4	2·0
25	2 06·3	2 06·6	2 00·5	2·5	0·4	8·5	1·2	14·5	2·1
26	2 06·5	2 06·8	2 00·7	2·6	0·4	8·6	1·2	14·6	2·1
27	2 06·8	2 07·1	2 01·0	2·7	0·4	8·7	1·2	14·7	2·1
28	2 07·0	2 07·3	2 01·2	2·8	0·4	8·8	1·2	14·8	2·1
29	2 07·3	2 07·6	2 01·5	2·9	0·4	8·9	1·3	14·9	2·1
30	2 07·5	2 07·8	2 01·7	3·0	0·4	9·0	1·3	15·0	2·1
31	2 07·8	2 08·1	2 01·9	3·1	0·4	9·1	1·3	15·1	2·1
32	2 08·0	2 08·4	2 02·2	3·2	0·5	9·2	1·3	15·2	2·2
33	2 08·3	2 08·6	2 02·4	3·3	0·5	9·3	1·3	15·3	2·2
34	2 08·5	2 08·9	2 02·6	3·4	0·5	9·4	1·3	15·4	2·2
35	2 08·8	2 09·1	2 02·9	3·5	0·5	9·5	1·3	15·5	2·2
36	2 09·0	2 09·4	2 03·1	3·6	0·5	9·6	1·4	15·6	2·2
37	2 09·3	2 09·6	2 03·4	3·7	0·5	9·7	1·4	15·7	2·2
38	2 09·5	2 09·9	2 03·6	3·8	0·5	9·8	1·4	15·8	2·2
39	2 09·8	2 10·1	2 03·8	3·9	0·6	9·9	1·4	15·9	2·3
40	2 10·0	2 10·4	2 04·1	4·0	0·6	10·0	1·4	16·0	2·3
41	2 10·3	2 10·6	2 04·3	4·1	0·6	10·1	1·4	16·1	2·3
42	2 10·5	2 10·9	2 04·6	4·2	0·6	10·2	1·4	16·2	2·3
43	2 10·8	2 11·1	2 04·8	4·3	0·6	10·3	1·5	16·3	2·3
44	2 11·0	2 11·4	2 05·0	4·4	0·6	10·4	1·5	16·4	2·3
45	2 11·3	2 11·6	2 05·3	4·5	0·6	10·5	1·5	16·5	2·3
46	2 11·5	2 11·9	2 05·5	4·6	0·7	10·6	1·5	16·6	2·4
47	2 11·8	2 12·1	2 05·7	4·7	0·7	10·7	1·5	16·7	2·4
48	2 12·0	2 12·4	2 06·0	4·8	0·7	10·8	1·5	16·8	2·4
49	2 12·3	2 12·6	2 06·2	4·9	0·7	10·9	1·5	16·9	2·4
50	2 12·5	2 12·9	2 06·5	5·0	0·7	11·0	1·6	17·0	2·4
51	2 12·8	2 13·1	2 06·7	5·1	0·7	11·1	1·6	17·1	2·4
52	2 13·0	2 13·4	2 06·9	5·2	0·7	11·2	1·6	17·2	2·4
53	2 13·3	2 13·6	2 07·2	5·3	0·8	11·3	1·6	17·3	2·5
54	2 13·5	2 13·9	2 07·4	5·4	0·8	11·4	1·6	17·4	2·5
55	2 13·8	2 14·1	2 07·7	5·5	0·8	11·5	1·6	17·5	2·5
56	2 14·0	2 14·4	2 07·9	5·6	0·8	11·6	1·6	17·6	2·5
57	2 14·3	2 14·6	2 08·1	5·7	0·8	11·7	1·7	17·7	2·5
58	2 14·5	2 14·9	2 08·4	5·8	0·8	11·8	1·7	17·8	2·5
59	2 14·8	2 15·1	2 08·6	5·9	0·8	11·9	1·7	17·9	2·5
60	2 15·0	2 15·4	2 08·9	6·0	0·9	12·0	1·7	18·0	2·6

9ᵐ

9 s	SUN PLANETS ° '	ARIES ° '	MOON ° '	v or Corrⁿ d		v or Corrⁿ d		v or Corrⁿ d	
00	2 15·0	2 15·4	2 08·9	0·0	0·0	6·0	1·0	12·0	1·9
01	2 15·3	2 15·6	2 09·1	0·1	0·0	6·1	1·0	12·1	1·9
02	2 15·5	2 15·9	2 09·3	0·2	0·0	6·2	1·0	12·2	1·9
03	2 15·8	2 16·1	2 09·6	0·3	0·0	6·3	1·0	12·3	1·9
04	2 16·0	2 16·4	2 09·8	0·4	0·1	6·4	1·0	12·4	2·0
05	2 16·3	2 16·6	2 10·0	0·5	0·1	6·5	1·0	12·5	2·0
06	2 16·5	2 16·9	2 10·3	0·6	0·1	6·6	1·0	12·6	2·0
07	2 16·8	2 17·1	2 10·5	0·7	0·1	6·7	1·1	12·7	2·0
08	2 17·0	2 17·4	2 10·8	0·8	0·1	6·8	1·1	12·8	2·0
09	2 17·3	2 17·6	2 11·0	0·9	0·1	6·9	1·1	12·9	2·0
10	2 17·5	2 17·9	2 11·2	1·0	0·2	7·0	1·1	13·0	2·1
11	2 17·8	2 18·1	2 11·5	1·1	0·2	7·1	1·1	13·1	2·1
12	2 18·0	2 18·4	2 11·7	1·2	0·2	7·2	1·1	13·2	2·1
13	2 18·3	2 18·6	2 12·0	1·3	0·2	7·3	1·2	13·3	2·1
14	2 18·5	2 18·9	2 12·2	1·4	0·2	7·4	1·2	13·4	2·1
15	2 18·8	2 19·1	2 12·4	1·5	0·2	7·5	1·2	13·5	2·1
16	2 19·0	2 19·4	2 12·7	1·6	0·3	7·6	1·2	13·6	2·2
17	2 19·3	2 19·6	2 12·9	1·7	0·3	7·7	1·2	13·7	2·2
18	2 19·5	2 19·9	2 13·1	1·8	0·3	7·8	1·2	13·8	2·2
19	2 19·8	2 20·1	2 13·4	1·9	0·3	7·9	1·3	13·9	2·2
20	2 20·0	2 20·4	2 13·6	2·0	0·3	8·0	1·3	14·0	2·2
21	2 20·3	2 20·6	2 13·9	2·1	0·3	8·1	1·3	14·1	2·2
22	2 20·5	2 20·9	2 14·1	2·2	0·3	8·2	1·3	14·2	2·2
23	2 20·8	2 21·1	2 14·3	2·3	0·4	8·3	1·3	14·3	2·3
24	2 21·0	2 21·4	2 14·6	2·4	0·4	8·4	1·3	14·4	2·3
25	2 21·3	2 21·6	2 14·8	2·5	0·4	8·5	1·3	14·5	2·3
26	2 21·5	2 21·9	2 15·1	2·6	0·4	8·6	1·4	14·6	2·3
27	2 21·8	2 22·1	2 15·3	2·7	0·4	8·7	1·4	14·7	2·3
28	2 22·0	2 22·4	2 15·5	2·8	0·4	8·8	1·4	14·8	2·3
29	2 22·3	2 22·6	2 15·8	2·9	0·5	8·9	1·4	14·9	2·4
30	2 22·5	2 22·9	2 16·0	3·0	0·5	9·0	1·4	15·0	2·4
31	2 22·8	2 23·1	2 16·2	3·1	0·5	9·1	1·4	15·1	2·4
32	2 23·0	2 23·4	2 16·5	3·2	0·5	9·2	1·5	15·2	2·4
33	2 23·3	2 23·6	2 16·7	3·3	0·5	9·3	1·5	15·3	2·4
34	2 23·5	2 23·9	2 17·0	3·4	0·5	9·4	1·5	15·4	2·4
35	2 23·8	2 24·1	2 17·2	3·5	0·6	9·5	1·5	15·5	2·5
36	2 24·0	2 24·4	2 17·4	3·6	0·6	9·6	1·5	15·6	2·5
37	2 24·3	2 24·6	2 17·7	3·7	0·6	9·7	1·5	15·7	2·5
38	2 24·5	2 24·9	2 17·9	3·8	0·6	9·8	1·6	15·8	2·5
39	2 24·8	2 25·1	2 18·2	3·9	0·6	9·9	1·6	15·9	2·5
40	2 25·0	2 25·4	2 18·4	4·0	0·6	10·0	1·6	16·0	2·5
41	2 25·3	2 25·6	2 18·6	4·1	0·6	10·1	1·6	16·1	2·5
42	2 25·5	2 25·9	2 18·9	4·2	0·7	10·2	1·6	16·2	2·6
43	2 25·8	2 26·1	2 19·1	4·3	0·7	10·3	1·6	16·3	2·6
44	2 26·0	2 26·4	2 19·3	4·4	0·7	10·4	1·6	16·4	2·6
45	2 26·3	2 26·7	2 19·6	4·5	0·7	10·5	1·7	16·5	2·6
46	2 26·5	2 26·9	2 19·8	4·6	0·7	10·6	1·7	16·6	2·6
47	2 26·8	2 27·2	2 20·1	4·7	0·7	10·7	1·7	16·7	2·6
48	2 27·0	2 27·4	2 20·3	4·8	0·8	10·8	1·7	16·8	2·7
49	2 27·3	2 27·7	2 20·5	4·9	0·8	10·9	1·7	16·9	2·7
50	2 27·5	2 27·9	2 20·8	5·0	0·8	11·0	1·7	17·0	2·7
51	2 27·8	2 28·2	2 21·0	5·1	0·8	11·1	1·8	17·1	2·7
52	2 28·0	2 28·4	2 21·3	5·2	0·8	11·2	1·8	17·2	2·7
53	2 28·3	2 28·7	2 21·5	5·3	0·8	11·3	1·8	17·3	2·7
54	2 28·5	2 28·9	2 21·7	5·4	0·9	11·4	1·8	17·4	2·8
55	2 28·8	2 29·2	2 22·0	5·5	0·9	11·5	1·8	17·5	2·8
56	2 29·0	2 29·4	2 22·2	5·6	0·9	11·6	1·8	17·6	2·8
57	2 29·3	2 29·7	2 22·5	5·7	0·9	11·7	1·9	17·7	2·8
58	2 29·5	2 29·9	2 22·7	5·8	0·9	11·8	1·9	17·8	2·8
59	2 29·8	2 30·2	2 22·9	5·9	0·9	11·9	1·9	17·9	2·8
60	2 30·0	2 30·4	2 23·2	6·0	1·0	12·0	1·9	18·0	2·9

© British Crown Copyright 2018. All rights reserved.

10	SUN PLANETS	ARIES	MOON	v or Corrⁿ d	v or Corrⁿ d	v or Corrⁿ d
s	° ′	° ′	° ′	′ ′	′ ′	′ ′
00	2 30.0	2 30.4	2 23.2	0.0 0.0	6.0 1.1	12.0 2.1
01	2 30.3	2 30.7	2 23.4	0.1 0.0	6.1 1.1	12.1 2.1
02	2 30.5	2 30.9	2 23.6	0.2 0.0	6.2 1.1	12.2 2.1
03	2 30.8	2 31.2	2 23.9	0.3 0.1	6.3 1.1	12.3 2.2
04	2 31.0	2 31.4	2 24.1	0.4 0.1	6.4 1.1	12.4 2.2
05	2 31.3	2 31.7	2 24.4	0.5 0.1	6.5 1.1	12.5 2.2
06	2 31.5	2 31.9	2 24.6	0.6 0.1	6.6 1.2	12.6 2.2
07	2 31.8	2 32.2	2 24.8	0.7 0.1	6.7 1.2	12.7 2.2
08	2 32.0	2 32.4	2 25.1	0.8 0.1	6.8 1.2	12.8 2.2
09	2 32.3	2 32.7	2 25.3	0.9 0.2	6.9 1.2	12.9 2.3
10	2 32.5	2 32.9	2 25.6	1.0 0.2	7.0 1.2	13.0 2.3
11	2 32.8	2 33.2	2 25.8	1.1 0.2	7.1 1.2	13.1 2.3
12	2 33.0	2 33.4	2 26.0	1.2 0.2	7.2 1.3	13.2 2.3
13	2 33.3	2 33.7	2 26.3	1.3 0.2	7.3 1.3	13.3 2.3
14	2 33.5	2 33.9	2 26.5	1.4 0.2	7.4 1.3	13.4 2.3
15	2 33.8	2 34.2	2 26.7	1.5 0.3	7.5 1.3	13.5 2.4
16	2 34.0	2 34.4	2 27.0	1.6 0.3	7.6 1.3	13.6 2.4
17	2 34.3	2 34.7	2 27.2	1.7 0.3	7.7 1.3	13.7 2.4
18	2 34.5	2 34.9	2 27.5	1.8 0.3	7.8 1.4	13.8 2.4
19	2 34.8	2 35.2	2 27.7	1.9 0.3	7.9 1.4	13.9 2.4
20	2 35.0	2 35.4	2 27.9	2.0 0.4	8.0 1.4	14.0 2.5
21	2 35.3	2 35.7	2 28.2	2.1 0.4	8.1 1.4	14.1 2.5
22	2 35.5	2 35.9	2 28.4	2.2 0.4	8.2 1.4	14.2 2.5
23	2 35.8	2 36.2	2 28.7	2.3 0.4	8.3 1.5	14.3 2.5
24	2 36.0	2 36.4	2 28.9	2.4 0.4	8.4 1.5	14.4 2.5
25	2 36.3	2 36.7	2 29.1	2.5 0.4	8.5 1.5	14.5 2.5
26	2 36.5	2 36.9	2 29.4	2.6 0.5	8.6 1.5	14.6 2.6
27	2 36.8	2 37.2	2 29.6	2.7 0.5	8.7 1.5	14.7 2.6
28	2 37.0	2 37.4	2 29.8	2.8 0.5	8.8 1.5	14.8 2.6
29	2 37.3	2 37.7	2 30.1	2.9 0.5	8.9 1.6	14.9 2.6
30	2 37.5	2 37.9	2 30.3	3.0 0.5	9.0 1.6	15.0 2.6
31	2 37.8	2 38.2	2 30.6	3.1 0.5	9.1 1.6	15.1 2.6
32	2 38.0	2 38.4	2 30.8	3.2 0.6	9.2 1.6	15.2 2.7
33	2 38.3	2 38.7	2 31.0	3.3 0.6	9.3 1.6	15.3 2.7
34	2 38.5	2 38.9	2 31.3	3.4 0.6	9.4 1.6	15.4 2.7
35	2 38.8	2 39.2	2 31.5	3.5 0.6	9.5 1.7	15.5 2.7
36	2 39.0	2 39.4	2 31.8	3.6 0.6	9.6 1.7	15.6 2.7
37	2 39.3	2 39.7	2 32.0	3.7 0.6	9.7 1.7	15.7 2.7
38	2 39.5	2 39.9	2 32.2	3.8 0.7	9.8 1.7	15.8 2.8
39	2 39.8	2 40.2	2 32.5	3.9 0.7	9.9 1.7	15.9 2.8
40	2 40.0	2 40.4	2 32.7	4.0 0.7	10.0 1.8	16.0 2.8
41	2 40.3	2 40.7	2 32.9	4.1 0.7	10.1 1.8	16.1 2.8
42	2 40.5	2 40.9	2 33.2	4.2 0.7	10.2 1.8	16.2 2.8
43	2 40.8	2 41.2	2 33.4	4.3 0.8	10.3 1.8	16.3 2.9
44	2 41.0	2 41.4	2 33.7	4.4 0.8	10.4 1.8	16.4 2.9
45	2 41.3	2 41.7	2 33.9	4.5 0.8	10.5 1.8	16.5 2.9
46	2 41.5	2 41.9	2 34.1	4.6 0.8	10.6 1.9	16.6 2.9
47	2 41.8	2 42.2	2 34.4	4.7 0.8	10.7 1.9	16.7 2.9
48	2 42.0	2 42.4	2 34.6	4.8 0.8	10.8 1.9	16.8 2.9
49	2 42.3	2 42.7	2 34.9	4.9 0.9	10.9 1.9	16.9 3.0
50	2 42.5	2 42.9	2 35.1	5.0 0.9	11.0 1.9	17.0 3.0
51	2 42.8	2 43.2	2 35.3	5.1 0.9	11.1 1.9	17.1 3.0
52	2 43.0	2 43.4	2 35.6	5.2 0.9	11.2 2.0	17.2 3.0
53	2 43.3	2 43.7	2 35.8	5.3 0.9	11.3 2.0	17.3 3.0
54	2 43.5	2 43.9	2 36.1	5.4 0.9	11.4 2.0	17.4 3.0
55	2 43.8	2 44.2	2 36.3	5.5 1.0	11.5 2.0	17.5 3.1
56	2 44.0	2 44.4	2 36.5	5.6 1.0	11.6 2.0	17.6 3.1
57	2 44.3	2 44.7	2 36.8	5.7 1.0	11.7 2.0	17.7 3.1
58	2 44.5	2 45.0	2 37.0	5.8 1.0	11.8 2.1	17.8 3.1
59	2 44.8	2 45.2	2 37.2	5.9 1.0	11.9 2.1	17.9 3.1
60	2 45.0	2 45.5	2 37.5	6.0 1.1	12.0 2.1	18.0 3.2

11	SUN PLANETS	ARIES	MOON	v or Corrⁿ d	v or Corrⁿ d	v or Corrⁿ d
s	° ′	° ′	° ′	′ ′	′ ′	′ ′
00	2 45.0	2 45.5	2 37.5	0.0 0.0	6.0 1.2	12.0 2.3
01	2 45.3	2 45.7	2 37.7	0.1 0.0	6.1 1.2	12.1 2.3
02	2 45.5	2 46.0	2 38.0	0.2 0.0	6.2 1.2	12.2 2.3
03	2 45.8	2 46.2	2 38.2	0.3 0.1	6.3 1.2	12.3 2.4
04	2 46.0	2 46.5	2 38.4	0.4 0.1	6.4 1.2	12.4 2.4
05	2 46.3	2 46.7	2 38.7	0.5 0.1	6.5 1.2	12.5 2.4
06	2 46.5	2 47.0	2 38.9	0.6 0.1	6.6 1.3	12.6 2.4
07	2 46.8	2 47.2	2 39.2	0.7 0.1	6.7 1.3	12.7 2.4
08	2 47.0	2 47.5	2 39.4	0.8 0.2	6.8 1.3	12.8 2.5
09	2 47.3	2 47.7	2 39.6	0.9 0.2	6.9 1.3	12.9 2.5
10	2 47.5	2 48.0	2 39.9	1.0 0.2	7.0 1.3	13.0 2.5
11	2 47.8	2 48.2	2 40.1	1.1 0.2	7.1 1.4	13.1 2.5
12	2 48.0	2 48.5	2 40.3	1.2 0.2	7.2 1.4	13.2 2.5
13	2 48.3	2 48.7	2 40.6	1.3 0.2	7.3 1.4	13.3 2.5
14	2 48.5	2 49.0	2 40.8	1.4 0.3	7.4 1.4	13.4 2.6
15	2 48.8	2 49.2	2 41.1	1.5 0.3	7.5 1.4	13.5 2.6
16	2 49.0	2 49.5	2 41.3	1.6 0.3	7.6 1.5	13.6 2.6
17	2 49.3	2 49.7	2 41.5	1.7 0.3	7.7 1.5	13.7 2.6
18	2 49.5	2 50.0	2 41.8	1.8 0.3	7.8 1.5	13.8 2.6
19	2 49.8	2 50.2	2 42.0	1.9 0.4	7.9 1.5	13.9 2.7
20	2 50.0	2 50.5	2 42.3	2.0 0.4	8.0 1.5	14.0 2.7
21	2 50.3	2 50.7	2 42.5	2.1 0.4	8.1 1.6	14.1 2.7
22	2 50.5	2 51.0	2 42.7	2.2 0.4	8.2 1.6	14.2 2.7
23	2 50.8	2 51.2	2 43.0	2.3 0.4	8.3 1.6	14.3 2.7
24	2 51.0	2 51.5	2 43.2	2.4 0.5	8.4 1.6	14.4 2.8
25	2 51.3	2 51.7	2 43.4	2.5 0.5	8.5 1.6	14.5 2.8
26	2 51.5	2 52.0	2 43.7	2.6 0.5	8.6 1.6	14.6 2.8
27	2 51.8	2 52.2	2 43.9	2.7 0.5	8.7 1.7	14.7 2.8
28	2 52.0	2 52.5	2 44.2	2.8 0.5	8.8 1.7	14.8 2.8
29	2 52.3	2 52.7	2 44.4	2.9 0.6	8.9 1.7	14.9 2.9
30	2 52.5	2 53.0	2 44.6	3.0 0.6	9.0 1.7	15.0 2.9
31	2 52.8	2 53.2	2 44.9	3.1 0.6	9.1 1.7	15.1 2.9
32	2 53.0	2 53.5	2 45.1	3.2 0.6	9.2 1.8	15.2 2.9
33	2 53.3	2 53.7	2 45.4	3.3 0.6	9.3 1.8	15.3 2.9
34	2 53.5	2 54.0	2 45.6	3.4 0.7	9.4 1.8	15.4 3.0
35	2 53.8	2 54.2	2 45.8	3.5 0.7	9.5 1.8	15.5 3.0
36	2 54.0	2 54.5	2 46.1	3.6 0.7	9.6 1.8	15.6 3.0
37	2 54.3	2 54.7	2 46.3	3.7 0.7	9.7 1.9	15.7 3.0
38	2 54.5	2 55.0	2 46.6	3.8 0.7	9.8 1.9	15.8 3.0
39	2 54.8	2 55.2	2 46.8	3.9 0.7	9.9 1.9	15.9 3.0
40	2 55.0	2 55.5	2 47.0	4.0 0.8	10.0 1.9	16.0 3.1
41	2 55.3	2 55.7	2 47.3	4.1 0.8	10.1 1.9	16.1 3.1
42	2 55.5	2 56.0	2 47.5	4.2 0.8	10.2 2.0	16.2 3.1
43	2 55.8	2 56.2	2 47.7	4.3 0.8	10.3 2.0	16.3 3.1
44	2 56.0	2 56.5	2 48.0	4.4 0.8	10.4 2.0	16.4 3.1
45	2 56.3	2 56.7	2 48.2	4.5 0.9	10.5 2.0	16.5 3.2
46	2 56.5	2 57.0	2 48.5	4.6 0.9	10.6 2.0	16.6 3.2
47	2 56.8	2 57.2	2 48.7	4.7 0.9	10.7 2.1	16.7 3.2
48	2 57.0	2 57.5	2 48.9	4.8 0.9	10.8 2.1	16.8 3.2
49	2 57.3	2 57.7	2 49.2	4.9 0.9	10.9 2.1	16.9 3.2
50	2 57.5	2 58.0	2 49.4	5.0 1.0	11.0 2.1	17.0 3.3
51	2 57.8	2 58.2	2 49.7	5.1 1.0	11.1 2.1	17.1 3.3
52	2 58.0	2 58.5	2 49.9	5.2 1.0	11.2 2.1	17.2 3.3
53	2 58.3	2 58.7	2 50.1	5.3 1.0	11.3 2.2	17.3 3.3
54	2 58.5	2 59.0	2 50.4	5.4 1.0	11.4 2.2	17.4 3.3
55	2 58.8	2 59.2	2 50.6	5.5 1.1	11.5 2.2	17.5 3.4
56	2 59.0	2 59.5	2 50.8	5.6 1.1	11.6 2.2	17.6 3.4
57	2 59.3	2 59.7	2 51.1	5.7 1.1	11.7 2.2	17.7 3.4
58	2 59.5	3 00.0	2 51.3	5.8 1.1	11.8 2.3	17.8 3.4
59	2 59.8	3 00.2	2 51.6	5.9 1.1	11.9 2.3	17.9 3.4
60	3 00.0	3 00.5	2 51.8	6.0 1.2	12.0 2.3	18.0 3.5

© British Crown Copyright 2018. All rights reserved.

12^m

12 m/s	SUN PLANETS	ARIES	MOON	v or Corrn d	v or Corrn d	v or Corrn d
s	° ′	° ′	° ′	′ ′	′ ′	′ ′
00	3 00·0	3 00·5	2 51·8	0·0 0·0	6·0 1·3	12·0 2·5
01	3 00·3	3 00·7	2 52·0	0·1 0·0	6·1 1·3	12·1 2·5
02	3 00·5	3 01·0	2 52·3	0·2 0·0	6·2 1·3	12·2 2·5
03	3 00·8	3 01·2	2 52·5	0·3 0·1	6·3 1·3	12·3 2·6
04	3 01·0	3 01·5	2 52·8	0·4 0·1	6·4 1·3	12·4 2·6
05	3 01·3	3 01·7	2 53·0	0·5 0·1	6·5 1·4	12·5 2·6
06	3 01·5	3 02·0	2 53·2	0·6 0·1	6·6 1·4	12·6 2·6
07	3 01·8	3 02·2	2 53·5	0·7 0·1	6·7 1·4	12·7 2·6
08	3 02·0	3 02·5	2 53·7	0·8 0·2	6·8 1·4	12·8 2·7
09	3 02·3	3 02·7	2 53·9	0·9 0·2	6·9 1·4	12·9 2·7
10	3 02·5	3 03·0	2 54·2	1·0 0·2	7·0 1·5	13·0 2·7
11	3 02·8	3 03·3	2 54·4	1·1 0·2	7·1 1·5	13·1 2·7
12	3 03·0	3 03·5	2 54·7	1·2 0·3	7·2 1·5	13·2 2·8
13	3 03·3	3 03·8	2 54·9	1·3 0·3	7·3 1·5	13·3 2·8
14	3 03·5	3 04·0	2 55·1	1·4 0·3	7·4 1·5	13·4 2·8
15	3 03·8	3 04·3	2 55·4	1·5 0·3	7·5 1·6	13·5 2·8
16	3 04·0	3 04·5	2 55·6	1·6 0·3	7·6 1·6	13·6 2·8
17	3 04·3	3 04·8	2 55·9	1·7 0·4	7·7 1·6	13·7 2·9
18	3 04·5	3 05·0	2 56·1	1·8 0·4	7·8 1·6	13·8 2·9
19	3 04·8	3 05·3	2 56·3	1·9 0·4	7·9 1·6	13·9 2·9
20	3 05·0	3 05·5	2 56·6	2·0 0·4	8·0 1·7	14·0 2·9
21	3 05·3	3 05·8	2 56·8	2·1 0·4	8·1 1·7	14·1 2·9
22	3 05·5	3 06·0	2 57·0	2·2 0·5	8·2 1·7	14·2 3·0
23	3 05·8	3 06·3	2 57·3	2·3 0·5	8·3 1·7	14·3 3·0
24	3 06·0	3 06·5	2 57·5	2·4 0·5	8·4 1·8	14·4 3·0
25	3 06·3	3 06·8	2 57·8	2·5 0·5	8·5 1·8	14·5 3·0
26	3 06·5	3 07·0	2 58·0	2·6 0·5	8·6 1·8	14·6 3·0
27	3 06·8	3 07·3	2 58·2	2·7 0·6	8·7 1·8	14·7 3·1
28	3 07·0	3 07·5	2 58·5	2·8 0·6	8·8 1·8	14·8 3·1
29	3 07·3	3 07·8	2 58·7	2·9 0·6	8·9 1·9	14·9 3·1
30	3 07·5	3 08·0	2 59·0	3·0 0·6	9·0 1·9	15·0 3·1
31	3 07·8	3 08·3	2 59·2	3·1 0·6	9·1 1·9	15·1 3·1
32	3 08·0	3 08·5	2 59·4	3·2 0·7	9·2 1·9	15·2 3·2
33	3 08·3	3 08·8	2 59·7	3·3 0·7	9·3 1·9	15·3 3·2
34	3 08·5	3 09·0	2 59·9	3·4 0·7	9·4 2·0	15·4 3·2
35	3 08·8	3 09·3	3 00·2	3·5 0·7	9·5 2·0	15·5 3·2
36	3 09·0	3 09·5	3 00·4	3·6 0·8	9·6 2·0	15·6 3·3
37	3 09·3	3 09·8	3 00·6	3·7 0·8	9·7 2·0	15·7 3·3
38	3 09·5	3 10·0	3 00·9	3·8 0·8	9·8 2·0	15·8 3·3
39	3 09·8	3 10·3	3 01·1	3·9 0·8	9·9 2·1	15·9 3·3
40	3 10·0	3 10·5	3 01·3	4·0 0·8	10·0 2·1	16·0 3·3
41	3 10·3	3 10·8	3 01·6	4·1 0·9	10·1 2·1	16·1 3·4
42	3 10·5	3 11·0	3 01·8	4·2 0·9	10·2 2·1	16·2 3·4
43	3 10·8	3 11·3	3 02·1	4·3 0·9	10·3 2·1	16·3 3·4
44	3 11·0	3 11·5	3 02·3	4·4 0·9	10·4 2·2	16·4 3·4
45	3 11·3	3 11·8	3 02·5	4·5 0·9	10·5 2·2	16·5 3·4
46	3 11·5	3 12·0	3 02·8	4·6 1·0	10·6 2·2	16·6 3·5
47	3 11·8	3 12·3	3 03·0	4·7 1·0	10·7 2·2	16·7 3·5
48	3 12·0	3 12·5	3 03·3	4·8 1·0	10·8 2·3	16·8 3·5
49	3 12·3	3 12·8	3 03·5	4·9 1·0	10·9 2·3	16·9 3·5
50	3 12·5	3 13·0	3 03·7	5·0 1·0	11·0 2·3	17·0 3·5
51	3 12·8	3 13·3	3 04·0	5·1 1·1	11·1 2·3	17·1 3·6
52	3 13·0	3 13·5	3 04·2	5·2 1·1	11·2 2·3	17·2 3·6
53	3 13·3	3 13·8	3 04·4	5·3 1·1	11·3 2·4	17·3 3·6
54	3 13·5	3 14·0	3 04·7	5·4 1·1	11·4 2·4	17·4 3·6
55	3 13·8	3 14·3	3 04·9	5·5 1·1	11·5 2·4	17·5 3·6
56	3 14·0	3 14·5	3 05·2	5·6 1·2	11·6 2·4	17·6 3·7
57	3 14·3	3 14·8	3 05·4	5·7 1·2	11·7 2·4	17·7 3·7
58	3 14·5	3 15·0	3 05·6	5·8 1·2	11·8 2·5	17·8 3·7
59	3 14·8	3 15·3	3 05·9	5·9 1·2	11·9 2·5	17·9 3·7
60	3 15·0	3 15·5	3 06·1	6·0 1·3	12·0 2·5	18·0 3·8

13^m

13 m/s	SUN PLANETS	ARIES	MOON	v or Corrn d	v or Corrn d	v or Corrn d
s	° ′	° ′	° ′	′ ′	′ ′	′ ′
00	3 15·0	3 15·5	3 06·1	0·0 0·0	6·0 1·4	12·0 2·7
01	3 15·3	3 15·8	3 06·4	0·1 0·0	6·1 1·4	12·1 2·7
02	3 15·5	3 16·0	3 06·6	0·2 0·0	6·2 1·4	12·2 2·7
03	3 15·8	3 16·3	3 06·8	0·3 0·1	6·3 1·4	12·3 2·8
04	3 16·0	3 16·5	3 07·1	0·4 0·1	6·4 1·4	12·4 2·8
05	3 16·3	3 16·8	3 07·3	0·5 0·1	6·5 1·5	12·5 2·8
06	3 16·5	3 17·0	3 07·5	0·6 0·1	6·6 1·5	12·6 2·8
07	3 16·8	3 17·3	3 07·8	0·7 0·2	6·7 1·5	12·7 2·9
08	3 17·0	3 17·5	3 08·0	0·8 0·2	6·8 1·5	12·8 2·9
09	3 17·3	3 17·8	3 08·3	0·9 0·2	6·9 1·6	12·9 2·9
10	3 17·5	3 18·0	3 08·5	1·0 0·2	7·0 1·6	13·0 2·9
11	3 17·8	3 18·3	3 08·7	1·1 0·2	7·1 1·6	13·1 2·9
12	3 18·0	3 18·5	3 09·0	1·2 0·3	7·2 1·6	13·2 3·0
13	3 18·3	3 18·8	3 09·2	1·3 0·3	7·3 1·6	13·3 3·0
14	3 18·5	3 19·0	3 09·5	1·4 0·3	7·4 1·7	13·4 3·0
15	3 18·8	3 19·3	3 09·7	1·5 0·3	7·5 1·7	13·5 3·0
16	3 19·0	3 19·5	3 09·9	1·6 0·4	7·6 1·7	13·6 3·1
17	3 19·3	3 19·8	3 10·2	1·7 0·4	7·7 1·7	13·7 3·1
18	3 19·5	3 20·0	3 10·4	1·8 0·4	7·8 1·8	13·8 3·1
19	3 19·8	3 20·3	3 10·7	1·9 0·4	7·9 1·8	13·9 3·1
20	3 20·0	3 20·5	3 10·9	2·0 0·5	8·0 1·8	14·0 3·2
21	3 20·3	3 20·8	3 11·1	2·1 0·5	8·1 1·8	14·1 3·2
22	3 20·5	3 21·0	3 11·4	2·2 0·5	8·2 1·8	14·2 3·2
23	3 20·8	3 21·3	3 11·6	2·3 0·5	8·3 1·9	14·3 3·2
24	3 21·0	3 21·6	3 11·8	2·4 0·5	8·4 1·9	14·4 3·2
25	3 21·3	3 21·8	3 12·1	2·5 0·6	8·5 1·9	14·5 3·3
26	3 21·5	3 22·1	3 12·3	2·6 0·6	8·6 1·9	14·6 3·3
27	3 21·8	3 22·3	3 12·6	2·7 0·6	8·7 2·0	14·7 3·3
28	3 22·0	3 22·6	3 12·8	2·8 0·6	8·8 2·0	14·8 3·3
29	3 22·3	3 22·8	3 13·0	2·9 0·7	8·9 2·0	14·9 3·4
30	3 22·5	3 23·1	3 13·3	3·0 0·7	9·0 2·0	15·0 3·4
31	3 22·8	3 23·3	3 13·5	3·1 0·7	9·1 2·0	15·1 3·4
32	3 23·0	3 23·6	3 13·8	3·2 0·7	9·2 2·1	15·2 3·4
33	3 23·3	3 23·8	3 14·0	3·3 0·7	9·3 2·1	15·3 3·4
34	3 23·5	3 24·1	3 14·2	3·4 0·8	9·4 2·1	15·4 3·5
35	3 23·8	3 24·3	3 14·5	3·5 0·8	9·5 2·1	15·5 3·5
36	3 24·0	3 24·6	3 14·7	3·6 0·8	9·6 2·2	15·6 3·5
37	3 24·3	3 24·8	3 14·9	3·7 0·8	9·7 2·2	15·7 3·5
38	3 24·5	3 25·1	3 15·2	3·8 0·9	9·8 2·2	15·8 3·6
39	3 24·8	3 25·3	3 15·4	3·9 0·9	9·9 2·2	15·9 3·6
40	3 25·0	3 25·6	3 15·7	4·0 0·9	10·0 2·3	16·0 3·6
41	3 25·3	3 25·8	3 15·9	4·1 0·9	10·1 2·3	16·1 3·6
42	3 25·5	3 26·1	3 16·1	4·2 0·9	10·2 2·3	16·2 3·6
43	3 25·8	3 26·3	3 16·4	4·3 1·0	10·3 2·3	16·3 3·7
44	3 26·0	3 26·6	3 16·6	4·4 1·0	10·4 2·3	16·4 3·7
45	3 26·3	3 26·8	3 16·9	4·5 1·0	10·5 2·4	16·5 3·7
46	3 26·5	3 27·1	3 17·1	4·6 1·0	10·6 2·4	16·6 3·7
47	3 26·8	3 27·3	3 17·3	4·7 1·1	10·7 2·4	16·7 3·8
48	3 27·0	3 27·6	3 17·6	4·8 1·1	10·8 2·4	16·8 3·8
49	3 27·3	3 27·8	3 17·8	4·9 1·1	10·9 2·5	16·9 3·8
50	3 27·5	3 28·1	3 18·0	5·0 1·1	11·0 2·5	17·0 3·8
51	3 27·8	3 28·3	3 18·3	5·1 1·1	11·1 2·5	17·1 3·8
52	3 28·0	3 28·6	3 18·5	5·2 1·2	11·2 2·5	17·2 3·9
53	3 28·3	3 28·8	3 18·8	5·3 1·2	11·3 2·5	17·3 3·9
54	3 28·5	3 29·1	3 19·0	5·4 1·2	11·4 2·6	17·4 3·9
55	3 28·8	3 29·3	3 19·2	5·5 1·2	11·5 2·6	17·5 3·9
56	3 29·0	3 29·6	3 19·5	5·6 1·3	11·6 2·6	17·6 4·0
57	3 29·3	3 29·8	3 19·7	5·7 1·3	11·7 2·6	17·7 4·0
58	3 29·5	3 30·1	3 20·0	5·8 1·3	11·8 2·7	17·8 4·0
59	3 29·8	3 30·3	3 20·2	5·9 1·3	11·9 2·7	17·9 4·0
60	3 30·0	3 30·6	3 20·4	6·0 1·4	12·0 2·7	18·0 4·1

© British Crown Copyright 2018. All rights reserved.

14^m s	SUN PLANETS	ARIES	MOON	v or d Corrn		v or d Corrn		v or d Corrn		15^m s	SUN PLANETS	ARIES	MOON	v or d Corrn		v or d Corrn		v or d Corrn	
00	3 30·0	3 30·6	3 20·4	0·0	0·0	6·0	1·5	12·0	2·9	00	3 45·0	3 45·6	3 34·8	0·0	0·0	6·0	1·6	12·0	3·1
01	3 30·3	3 30·8	3 20·7	0·1	0·0	6·1	1·5	12·1	2·9	01	3 45·3	3 45·9	3 35·0	0·1	0·0	6·1	1·6	12·1	3·1
02	3 30·5	3 31·1	3 20·9	0·2	0·0	6·2	1·5	12·2	2·9	02	3 45·5	3 46·1	3 35·2	0·2	0·1	6·2	1·6	12·2	3·2
03	3 30·8	3 31·3	3 21·1	0·3	0·1	6·3	1·5	12·3	3·0	03	3 45·8	3 46·4	3 35·5	0·3	0·1	6·3	1·6	12·3	3·2
04	3 31·0	3 31·6	3 21·4	0·4	0·1	6·4	1·5	12·4	3·0	04	3 46·0	3 46·6	3 35·7	0·4	0·1	6·4	1·7	12·4	3·2
05	3 31·3	3 31·8	3 21·6	0·5	0·1	6·5	1·6	12·5	3·0	05	3 46·3	3 46·9	3 35·9	0·5	0·1	6·5	1·7	12·5	3·2
06	3 31·5	3 32·1	3 21·9	0·6	0·1	6·6	1·6	12·6	3·0	06	3 46·5	3 47·1	3 36·2	0·6	0·2	6·6	1·7	12·6	3·3
07	3 31·8	3 32·3	3 22·1	0·7	0·2	6·7	1·6	12·7	3·1	07	3 46·8	3 47·4	3 36·4	0·7	0·2	6·7	1·7	12·7	3·3
08	3 32·0	3 32·6	3 22·3	0·8	0·2	6·8	1·6	12·8	3·1	08	3 47·0	3 47·6	3 36·7	0·8	0·2	6·8	1·8	12·8	3·3
09	3 32·3	3 32·8	3 22·6	0·9	0·2	6·9	1·7	12·9	3·1	09	3 47·3	3 47·9	3 36·9	0·9	0·2	6·9	1·8	12·9	3·3
10	3 32·5	3 33·1	3 22·8	1·0	0·2	7·0	1·7	13·0	3·1	10	3 47·5	3 48·1	3 37·1	1·0	0·3	7·0	1·8	13·0	3·4
11	3 32·8	3 33·3	3 23·1	1·1	0·3	7·1	1·7	13·1	3·2	11	3 47·8	3 48·4	3 37·4	1·1	0·3	7·1	1·8	13·1	3·4
12	3 33·0	3 33·6	3 23·3	1·2	0·3	7·2	1·7	13·2	3·2	12	3 48·0	3 48·6	3 37·6	1·2	0·3	7·2	1·9	13·2	3·4
13	3 33·3	3 33·8	3 23·5	1·3	0·3	7·3	1·8	13·3	3·2	13	3 48·3	3 48·9	3 37·9	1·3	0·3	7·3	1·9	13·3	3·4
14	3 33·5	3 34·1	3 23·8	1·4	0·3	7·4	1·8	13·4	3·2	14	3 48·5	3 49·1	3 38·1	1·4	0·4	7·4	1·9	13·4	3·5
15	3 33·8	3 34·3	3 24·0	1·5	0·4	7·5	1·8	13·5	3·3	15	3 48·8	3 49·4	3 38·3	1·5	0·4	7·5	1·9	13·5	3·5
16	3 34·0	3 34·6	3 24·3	1·6	0·4	7·6	1·8	13·6	3·3	16	3 49·0	3 49·6	3 38·6	1·6	0·4	7·6	2·0	13·6	3·5
17	3 34·3	3 34·8	3 24·5	1·7	0·4	7·7	1·9	13·7	3·3	17	3 49·3	3 49·9	3 38·8	1·7	0·4	7·7	2·0	13·7	3·5
18	3 34·5	3 35·1	3 24·7	1·8	0·4	7·8	1·9	13·8	3·3	18	3 49·5	3 50·1	3 39·0	1·8	0·5	7·8	2·0	13·8	3·6
19	3 34·8	3 35·3	3 25·0	1·9	0·5	7·9	1·9	13·9	3·4	19	3 49·8	3 50·4	3 39·3	1·9	0·5	7·9	2·0	13·9	3·6
20	3 35·0	3 35·6	3 25·2	2·0	0·5	8·0	1·9	14·0	3·4	20	3 50·0	3 50·6	3 39·5	2·0	0·5	8·0	2·1	14·0	3·6
21	3 35·3	3 35·8	3 25·4	2·1	0·5	8·1	2·0	14·1	3·4	21	3 50·3	3 50·9	3 39·8	2·1	0·5	8·1	2·1	14·1	3·6
22	3 35·5	3 36·1	3 25·7	2·2	0·5	8·2	2·0	14·2	3·4	22	3 50·5	3 51·1	3 40·0	2·2	0·6	8·2	2·1	14·2	3·7
23	3 35·8	3 36·3	3 25·9	2·3	0·6	8·3	2·0	14·3	3·5	23	3 50·8	3 51·4	3 40·2	2·3	0·6	8·3	2·1	14·3	3·7
24	3 36·0	3 36·6	3 26·2	2·4	0·6	8·4	2·0	14·4	3·5	24	3 51·0	3 51·6	3 40·5	2·4	0·6	8·4	2·2	14·4	3·7
25	3 36·3	3 36·8	3 26·4	2·5	0·6	8·5	2·1	14·5	3·5	25	3 51·3	3 51·9	3 40·7	2·5	0·6	8·5	2·2	14·5	3·7
26	3 36·5	3 37·1	3 26·6	2·6	0·6	8·6	2·1	14·6	3·5	26	3 51·5	3 52·1	3 41·0	2·6	0·7	8·6	2·2	14·6	3·8
27	3 36·8	3 37·3	3 26·9	2·7	0·7	8·7	2·1	14·7	3·6	27	3 51·8	3 52·4	3 41·2	2·7	0·7	8·7	2·2	14·7	3·8
28	3 37·0	3 37·6	3 27·1	2·8	0·7	8·8	2·1	14·8	3·6	28	3 52·0	3 52·6	3 41·4	2·8	0·7	8·8	2·3	14·8	3·8
29	3 37·3	3 37·8	3 27·4	2·9	0·7	8·9	2·2	14·9	3·6	29	3 52·3	3 52·9	3 41·7	2·9	0·7	8·9	2·3	14·9	3·8
30	3 37·5	3 38·1	3 27·6	3·0	0·7	9·0	2·2	15·0	3·6	30	3 52·5	3 53·1	3 41·9	3·0	0·8	9·0	2·3	15·0	3·9
31	3 37·8	3 38·3	3 27·8	3·1	0·7	9·1	2·2	15·1	3·7	31	3 52·8	3 53·4	3 42·1	3·1	0·8	9·1	2·4	15·1	3·9
32	3 38·0	3 38·6	3 28·1	3·2	0·8	9·2	2·2	15·2	3·7	32	3 53·0	3 53·6	3 42·4	3·2	0·8	9·2	2·4	15·2	3·9
33	3 38·3	3 38·8	3 28·3	3·3	0·8	9·3	2·2	15·3	3·7	33	3 53·3	3 53·9	3 42·6	3·3	0·9	9·3	2·4	15·3	4·0
34	3 38·5	3 39·1	3 28·5	3·4	0·8	9·4	2·3	15·4	3·7	34	3 53·5	3 54·1	3 42·9	3·4	0·9	9·4	2·4	15·4	4·0
35	3 38·8	3 39·3	3 28·8	3·5	0·8	9·5	2·3	15·5	3·7	35	3 53·8	3 54·4	3 43·1	3·5	0·9	9·5	2·5	15·5	4·0
36	3 39·0	3 39·6	3 29·0	3·6	0·9	9·6	2·3	15·6	3·8	36	3 54·0	3 54·6	3 43·3	3·6	0·9	9·6	2·5	15·6	4·0
37	3 39·3	3 39·9	3 29·3	3·7	0·9	9·7	2·3	15·7	3·8	37	3 54·3	3 54·9	3 43·6	3·7	1·0	9·7	2·5	15·7	4·1
38	3 39·5	3 40·1	3 29·5	3·8	0·9	9·8	2·4	15·8	3·8	38	3 54·5	3 55·1	3 43·8	3·8	1·0	9·8	2·5	15·8	4·1
39	3 39·8	3 40·4	3 29·7	3·9	0·9	9·9	2·4	15·9	3·8	39	3 54·8	3 55·4	3 44·1	3·9	1·0	9·9	2·6	15·9	4·1
40	3 40·0	3 40·6	3 30·0	4·0	1·0	10·0	2·4	16·0	3·9	40	3 55·0	3 55·6	3 44·3	4·0	1·0	10·0	2·6	16·0	4·1
41	3 40·3	3 40·9	3 30·2	4·1	1·0	10·1	2·4	16·1	3·9	41	3 55·3	3 55·9	3 44·5	4·1	1·1	10·1	2·6	16·1	4·2
42	3 40·5	3 41·1	3 30·5	4·2	1·0	10·2	2·5	16·2	3·9	42	3 55·5	3 56·1	3 44·8	4·2	1·1	10·2	2·6	16·2	4·2
43	3 40·8	3 41·4	3 30·7	4·3	1·0	10·3	2·5	16·3	3·9	43	3 55·8	3 56·4	3 45·0	4·3	1·1	10·3	2·7	16·3	4·2
44	3 41·0	3 41·6	3 30·9	4·4	1·1	10·4	2·5	16·4	4·0	44	3 56·0	3 56·6	3 45·2	4·4	1·1	10·4	2·7	16·4	4·2
45	3 41·3	3 41·9	3 31·2	4·5	1·1	10·5	2·5	16·5	4·0	45	3 56·3	3 56·9	3 45·5	4·5	1·2	10·5	2·7	16·5	4·3
46	3 41·5	3 42·1	3 31·4	4·6	1·1	10·6	2·6	16·6	4·0	46	3 56·5	3 57·1	3 45·7	4·6	1·2	10·6	2·7	16·6	4·3
47	3 41·8	3 42·4	3 31·6	4·7	1·1	10·7	2·6	16·7	4·0	47	3 56·8	3 57·4	3 46·0	4·7	1·2	10·7	2·8	16·7	4·3
48	3 42·0	3 42·6	3 31·9	4·8	1·2	10·8	2·6	16·8	4·1	48	3 57·0	3 57·6	3 46·2	4·8	1·2	10·8	2·8	16·8	4·3
49	3 42·3	3 42·9	3 32·1	4·9	1·2	10·9	2·6	16·9	4·1	49	3 57·3	3 57·9	3 46·4	4·9	1·3	10·9	2·8	16·9	4·4
50	3 42·5	3 43·1	3 32·4	5·0	1·2	11·0	2·7	17·0	4·1	50	3 57·5	3 58·2	3 46·7	5·0	1·3	11·0	2·8	17·0	4·4
51	3 42·8	3 43·4	3 32·6	5·1	1·2	11·1	2·7	17·1	4·1	51	3 57·8	3 58·4	3 46·9	5·1	1·3	11·1	2·9	17·1	4·4
52	3 43·0	3 43·6	3 32·8	5·2	1·3	11·2	2·7	17·2	4·2	52	3 58·0	3 58·7	3 47·2	5·2	1·3	11·2	2·9	17·2	4·4
53	3 43·3	3 43·9	3 33·1	5·3	1·3	11·3	2·7	17·3	4·2	53	3 58·3	3 58·9	3 47·4	5·3	1·4	11·3	2·9	17·3	4·5
54	3 43·5	3 44·1	3 33·3	5·4	1·3	11·4	2·8	17·4	4·2	54	3 58·5	3 59·2	3 47·6	5·4	1·4	11·4	2·9	17·4	4·5
55	3 43·8	3 44·4	3 33·6	5·5	1·3	11·5	2·8	17·5	4·2	55	3 58·8	3 59·4	3 47·9	5·5	1·4	11·5	3·0	17·5	4·5
56	3 44·0	3 44·6	3 33·8	5·6	1·4	11·6	2·8	17·6	4·3	56	3 59·0	3 59·7	3 48·1	5·6	1·4	11·6	3·0	17·6	4·5
57	3 44·3	3 44·9	3 34·0	5·7	1·4	11·7	2·8	17·7	4·3	57	3 59·3	3 59·9	3 48·4	5·7	1·5	11·7	3·0	17·7	4·6
58	3 44·5	3 45·1	3 34·3	5·8	1·4	11·8	2·9	17·8	4·3	58	3 59·5	4 00·2	3 48·6	5·8	1·5	11·8	3·0	17·8	4·6
59	3 44·8	3 45·4	3 34·5	5·9	1·4	11·9	2·9	17·9	4·3	59	3 59·8	4 00·4	3 48·8	5·9	1·5	11·9	3·1	17·9	4·6
60	3 45·0	3 45·6	3 34·8	6·0	1·5	12·0	2·9	18·0	4·4	60	4 00·0	4 00·7	3 49·1	6·0	1·6	12·0	3·1	18·0	4·7

ix

© British Crown Copyright 2018. All rights reserved.

16	SUN PLANETS	ARIES	MOON	v or Corrⁿ d	v or Corrⁿ d	v or Corrⁿ d
s	° ′	° ′	° ′	′ ′	′ ′	′ ′
00	4 00·0	4 00·7	3 49·1	0·0 0·0	6·0 1·7	12·0 3·3
01	4 00·3	4 00·9	3 49·3	0·1 0·0	6·1 1·7	12·1 3·3
02	4 00·5	4 01·2	3 49·5	0·2 0·1	6·2 1·7	12·2 3·4
03	4 00·8	4 01·4	3 49·8	0·3 0·1	6·3 1·7	12·3 3·4
04	4 01·0	4 01·7	3 50·0	0·4 0·1	6·4 1·8	12·4 3·4
05	4 01·3	4 01·9	3 50·3	0·5 0·1	6·5 1·8	12·5 3·4
06	4 01·5	4 02·2	3 50·5	0·6 0·2	6·6 1·8	12·6 3·5
07	4 01·8	4 02·4	3 50·7	0·7 0·2	6·7 1·8	12·7 3·5
08	4 02·0	4 02·7	3 51·0	0·8 0·2	6·8 1·9	12·8 3·5
09	4 02·3	4 02·9	3 51·2	0·9 0·2	6·9 1·9	12·9 3·5
10	4 02·5	4 03·2	3 51·5	1·0 0·3	7·0 1·9	13·0 3·6
11	4 02·8	4 03·4	3 51·7	1·1 0·3	7·1 2·0	13·1 3·6
12	4 03·0	4 03·7	3 51·9	1·2 0·3	7·2 2·0	13·2 3·6
13	4 03·3	4 03·9	3 52·2	1·3 0·4	7·3 2·0	13·3 3·7
14	4 03·5	4 04·2	3 52·4	1·4 0·4	7·4 2·0	13·4 3·7
15	4 03·8	4 04·4	3 52·6	1·5 0·4	7·5 2·1	13·5 3·7
16	4 04·0	4 04·7	3 52·9	1·6 0·4	7·6 2·1	13·6 3·7
17	4 04·3	4 04·9	3 53·1	1·7 0·5	7·7 2·1	13·7 3·8
18	4 04·5	4 05·2	3 53·4	1·8 0·5	7·8 2·1	13·8 3·8
19	4 04·8	4 05·4	3 53·6	1·9 0·5	7·9 2·2	13·9 3·8
20	4 05·0	4 05·7	3 53·8	2·0 0·6	8·0 2·2	14·0 3·9
21	4 05·3	4 05·9	3 54·1	2·1 0·6	8·1 2·2	14·1 3·9
22	4 05·5	4 06·2	3 54·3	2·2 0·6	8·2 2·3	14·2 3·9
23	4 05·8	4 06·4	3 54·6	2·3 0·6	8·3 2·3	14·3 3·9
24	4 06·0	4 06·7	3 54·8	2·4 0·7	8·4 2·3	14·4 4·0
25	4 06·3	4 06·9	3 55·0	2·5 0·7	8·5 2·3	14·5 4·0
26	4 06·5	4 07·2	3 55·3	2·6 0·7	8·6 2·4	14·6 4·0
27	4 06·8	4 07·4	3 55·5	2·7 0·7	8·7 2·4	14·7 4·0
28	4 07·0	4 07·7	3 55·7	2·8 0·8	8·8 2·4	14·8 4·1
29	4 07·3	4 07·9	3 56·0	2·9 0·8	8·9 2·4	14·9 4·1
30	4 07·5	4 08·2	3 56·2	3·0 0·8	9·0 2·5	15·0 4·1
31	4 07·8	4 08·4	3 56·5	3·1 0·9	9·1 2·5	15·1 4·2
32	4 08·0	4 08·7	3 56·7	3·2 0·9	9·2 2·5	15·2 4·2
33	4 08·3	4 08·9	3 56·9	3·3 0·9	9·3 2·6	15·3 4·2
34	4 08·5	4 09·2	3 57·2	3·4 0·9	9·4 2·6	15·4 4·2
35	4 08·8	4 09·4	3 57·4	3·5 1·0	9·5 2·6	15·5 4·3
36	4 09·0	4 09·7	3 57·7	3·6 1·0	9·6 2·6	15·6 4·3
37	4 09·3	4 09·9	3 57·9	3·7 1·0	9·7 2·7	15·7 4·3
38	4 09·5	4 10·2	3 58·1	3·8 1·0	9·8 2·7	15·8 4·3
39	4 09·8	4 10·4	3 58·4	3·9 1·1	9·9 2·7	15·9 4·4
40	4 10·0	4 10·7	3 58·6	4·0 1·1	10·0 2·8	16·0 4·4
41	4 10·3	4 10·9	3 58·8	4·1 1·1	10·1 2·8	16·1 4·4
42	4 10·5	4 11·2	3 59·1	4·2 1·2	10·2 2·8	16·2 4·5
43	4 10·8	4 11·4	3 59·3	4·3 1·2	10·3 2·8	16·3 4·5
44	4 11·0	4 11·7	3 59·6	4·4 1·2	10·4 2·9	16·4 4·5
45	4 11·3	4 11·9	3 59·8	4·5 1·2	10·5 2·9	16·5 4·5
46	4 11·5	4 12·2	4 00·0	4·6 1·3	10·6 2·9	16·6 4·6
47	4 11·8	4 12·4	4 00·3	4·7 1·3	10·7 2·9	16·7 4·6
48	4 12·0	4 12·7	4 00·5	4·8 1·3	10·8 3·0	16·8 4·6
49	4 12·3	4 12·9	4 00·8	4·9 1·3	10·9 3·0	16·9 4·6
50	4 12·5	4 13·2	4 01·0	5·0 1·4	11·0 3·0	17·0 4·7
51	4 12·8	4 13·4	4 01·2	5·1 1·4	11·1 3·1	17·1 4·7
52	4 13·0	4 13·7	4 01·5	5·2 1·4	11·2 3·1	17·2 4·7
53	4 13·3	4 13·9	4 01·7	5·3 1·5	11·3 3·1	17·3 4·8
54	4 13·5	4 14·2	4 02·0	5·4 1·5	11·4 3·1	17·4 4·8
55	4 13·8	4 14·4	4 02·2	5·5 1·5	11·5 3·2	17·5 4·8
56	4 14·0	4 14·7	4 02·4	5·6 1·5	11·6 3·2	17·6 4·8
57	4 14·3	4 14·9	4 02·7	5·7 1·6	11·7 3·2	17·7 4·9
58	4 14·5	4 15·2	4 02·9	5·8 1·6	11·8 3·2	17·8 4·9
59	4 14·8	4 15·4	4 03·1	5·9 1·6	11·9 3·3	17·9 4·9
60	4 15·0	4 15·7	4 03·4	6·0 1·7	12·0 3·3	18·0 5·0

17	SUN PLANETS	ARIES	MOON	v or Corrⁿ d	v or Corrⁿ d	v or Corrⁿ d
s	° ′	° ′	° ′	′ ′	′ ′	′ ′
00	4 15·0	4 15·7	4 03·4	0·0 0·0	6·0 1·8	12·0 3·5
01	4 15·3	4 15·9	4 03·6	0·1 0·0	6·1 1·8	12·1 3·5
02	4 15·5	4 16·2	4 03·9	0·2 0·1	6·2 1·8	12·2 3·6
03	4 15·8	4 16·5	4 04·1	0·3 0·1	6·3 1·8	12·3 3·6
04	4 16·0	4 16·7	4 04·3	0·4 0·1	6·4 1·9	12·4 3·6
05	4 16·3	4 17·0	4 04·6	0·5 0·1	6·5 1·9	12·5 3·6
06	4 16·5	4 17·2	4 04·8	0·6 0·2	6·6 1·9	12·6 3·7
07	4 16·8	4 17·5	4 05·1	0·7 0·2	6·7 2·0	12·7 3·7
08	4 17·0	4 17·7	4 05·3	0·8 0·2	6·8 2·0	12·8 3·7
09	4 17·3	4 18·0	4 05·5	0·9 0·3	6·9 2·0	12·9 3·8
10	4 17·5	4 18·2	4 05·8	1·0 0·3	7·0 2·0	13·0 3·8
11	4 17·8	4 18·5	4 06·0	1·1 0·3	7·1 2·1	13·1 3·8
12	4 18·0	4 18·7	4 06·2	1·2 0·4	7·2 2·1	13·2 3·9
13	4 18·3	4 19·0	4 06·5	1·3 0·4	7·3 2·1	13·3 3·9
14	4 18·5	4 19·2	4 06·7	1·4 0·4	7·4 2·2	13·4 3·9
15	4 18·8	4 19·5	4 07·0	1·5 0·4	7·5 2·2	13·5 3·9
16	4 19·0	4 19·7	4 07·2	1·6 0·5	7·6 2·2	13·6 4·0
17	4 19·3	4 20·0	4 07·4	1·7 0·5	7·7 2·2	13·7 4·0
18	4 19·5	4 20·2	4 07·7	1·8 0·5	7·8 2·3	13·8 4·0
19	4 19·8	4 20·5	4 07·9	1·9 0·6	7·9 2·3	13·9 4·1
20	4 20·0	4 20·7	4 08·2	2·0 0·6	8·0 2·3	14·0 4·1
21	4 20·3	4 21·0	4 08·4	2·1 0·6	8·1 2·4	14·1 4·1
22	4 20·5	4 21·2	4 08·6	2·2 0·6	8·2 2·4	14·2 4·1
23	4 20·8	4 21·5	4 08·9	2·3 0·7	8·3 2·4	14·3 4·2
24	4 21·0	4 21·7	4 09·1	2·4 0·7	8·4 2·5	14·4 4·2
25	4 21·3	4 22·0	4 09·3	2·5 0·7	8·5 2·5	14·5 4·2
26	4 21·5	4 22·2	4 09·6	2·6 0·8	8·6 2·5	14·6 4·3
27	4 21·8	4 22·5	4 09·8	2·7 0·8	8·7 2·5	14·7 4·3
28	4 22·0	4 22·7	4 10·1	2·8 0·8	8·8 2·6	14·8 4·3
29	4 22·3	4 23·0	4 10·3	2·9 0·8	8·9 2·6	14·9 4·3
30	4 22·5	4 23·2	4 10·5	3·0 0·9	9·0 2·6	15·0 4·4
31	4 22·8	4 23·5	4 10·8	3·1 0·9	9·1 2·7	15·1 4·4
32	4 23·0	4 23·7	4 11·0	3·2 0·9	9·2 2·7	15·2 4·4
33	4 23·3	4 24·0	4 11·3	3·3 1·0	9·3 2·7	15·3 4·5
34	4 23·5	4 24·2	4 11·5	3·4 1·0	9·4 2·7	15·4 4·5
35	4 23·8	4 24·5	4 11·7	3·5 1·0	9·5 2·8	15·5 4·5
36	4 24·0	4 24·7	4 12·0	3·6 1·1	9·6 2·8	15·6 4·6
37	4 24·3	4 25·0	4 12·2	3·7 1·1	9·7 2·8	15·7 4·6
38	4 24·5	4 25·2	4 12·5	3·8 1·1	9·8 2·9	15·8 4·6
39	4 24·8	4 25·5	4 12·7	3·9 1·1	9·9 2·9	15·9 4·6
40	4 25·0	4 25·7	4 12·9	4·0 1·2	10·0 2·9	16·0 4·7
41	4 25·3	4 26·0	4 13·2	4·1 1·2	10·1 2·9	16·1 4·7
42	4 25·5	4 26·2	4 13·4	4·2 1·2	10·2 3·0	16·2 4·7
43	4 25·8	4 26·5	4 13·6	4·3 1·3	10·3 3·0	16·3 4·8
44	4 26·0	4 26·7	4 13·9	4·4 1·3	10·4 3·0	16·4 4·8
45	4 26·3	4 27·0	4 14·1	4·5 1·3	10·5 3·1	16·5 4·8
46	4 26·5	4 27·2	4 14·4	4·6 1·3	10·6 3·1	16·6 4·8
47	4 26·8	4 27·5	4 14·6	4·7 1·4	10·7 3·1	16·7 4·9
48	4 27·0	4 27·7	4 14·8	4·8 1·4	10·8 3·2	16·8 4·9
49	4 27·3	4 28·0	4 15·1	4·9 1·4	10·9 3·2	16·9 4·9
50	4 27·5	4 28·2	4 15·3	5·0 1·5	11·0 3·2	17·0 5·0
51	4 27·8	4 28·5	4 15·6	5·1 1·5	11·1 3·3	17·1 5·0
52	4 28·0	4 28·7	4 15·8	5·2 1·5	11·2 3·3	17·2 5·0
53	4 28·3	4 29·0	4 16·0	5·3 1·5	11·3 3·3	17·3 5·0
54	4 28·5	4 29·2	4 16·3	5·4 1·6	11·4 3·3	17·4 5·1
55	4 28·8	4 29·5	4 16·5	5·5 1·6	11·5 3·4	17·5 5·1
56	4 29·0	4 29·7	4 16·7	5·6 1·6	11·6 3·4	17·6 5·1
57	4 29·3	4 30·0	4 17·0	5·7 1·7	11·7 3·4	17·7 5·2
58	4 29·5	4 30·2	4 17·2	5·8 1·7	11·8 3·4	17·8 5·2
59	4 29·8	4 30·5	4 17·5	5·9 1·7	11·9 3·5	17·9 5·2
60	4 30·0	4 30·7	4 17·7	6·0 1·8	12·0 3·5	18·0 5·3

x

© British Crown Copyright 2018. All rights reserved.

18	SUN PLANETS	ARIES	MOON	v or Corrn d	v or Corrn d	v or Corrn d	19	SUN PLANETS	ARIES	MOON	v or Corrn d	v or Corrn d	v or Corrn d
s	° ′	° ′	° ′	′ ′	′ ′	′ ′	s	° ′	° ′	° ′	′ ′	′ ′	′ ′
00	4 30·0	4 30·7	4 17·7	0·0 0·0	6·0 1·9	12·0 3·7	00	4 45·0	4 45·8	4 32·0	0·0 0·0	6·0 2·0	12·0 3·9
01	4 30·3	4 31·0	4 17·9	0·1 0·0	6·1 1·9	12·1 3·7	01	4 45·3	4 46·0	4 32·3	0·1 0·0	6·1 2·0	12·1 3·9
02	4 30·5	4 31·2	4 18·2	0·2 0·1	6·2 1·9	12·2 3·8	02	4 45·5	4 46·3	4 32·5	0·2 0·1	6·2 2·0	12·2 4·0
03	4 30·8	4 31·5	4 18·4	0·3 0·1	6·3 1·9	12·3 3·8	03	4 45·8	4 46·5	4 32·7	0·3 0·1	6·3 2·0	12·3 4·0
04	4 31·0	4 31·7	4 18·7	0·4 0·1	6·4 2·0	12·4 3·8	04	4 46·0	4 46·8	4 33·0	0·4 0·1	6·4 2·1	12·4 4·0
05	4 31·3	4 32·0	4 18·9	0·5 0·2	6·5 2·0	12·5 3·9	05	4 46·3	4 47·0	4 33·2	0·5 0·2	6·5 2·1	12·5 4·1
06	4 31·5	4 32·2	4 19·1	0·6 0·2	6·6 2·0	12·6 3·9	06	4 46·5	4 47·3	4 33·4	0·6 0·2	6·6 2·1	12·6 4·1
07	4 31·8	4 32·5	4 19·4	0·7 0·2	6·7 2·1	12·7 3·9	07	4 46·8	4 47·5	4 33·7	0·7 0·2	6·7 2·2	12·7 4·1
08	4 32·0	4 32·7	4 19·6	0·8 0·2	6·8 2·1	12·8 3·9	08	4 47·0	4 47·8	4 33·9	0·8 0·3	6·8 2·2	12·8 4·2
09	4 32·3	4 33·0	4 19·8	0·9 0·3	6·9 2·1	12·9 4·0	09	4 47·3	4 48·0	4 34·2	0·9 0·3	6·9 2·2	12·9 4·2
10	4 32·5	4 33·2	4 20·1	1·0 0·3	7·0 2·2	13·0 4·0	10	4 47·5	4 48·3	4 34·4	1·0 0·3	7·0 2·3	13·0 4·2
11	4 32·8	4 33·5	4 20·3	1·1 0·3	7·1 2·2	13·1 4·0	11	4 47·8	4 48·5	4 34·6	1·1 0·4	7·1 2·3	13·1 4·3
12	4 33·0	4 33·7	4 20·6	1·2 0·4	7·2 2·2	13·2 4·1	12	4 48·0	4 48·8	4 34·9	1·2 0·4	7·2 2·3	13·2 4·3
13	4 33·3	4 34·0	4 20·8	1·3 0·4	7·3 2·3	13·3 4·1	13	4 48·3	4 49·0	4 35·1	1·3 0·4	7·3 2·4	13·3 4·3
14	4 33·5	4 34·2	4 21·0	1·4 0·4	7·4 2·3	13·4 4·1	14	4 48·5	4 49·3	4 35·4	1·4 0·5	7·4 2·4	13·4 4·4
15	4 33·8	4 34·5	4 21·3	1·5 0·5	7·5 2·3	13·5 4·2	15	4 48·8	4 49·5	4 35·6	1·5 0·5	7·5 2·4	13·5 4·4
16	4 34·0	4 34·8	4 21·5	1·6 0·5	7·6 2·3	13·6 4·2	16	4 49·0	4 49·8	4 35·8	1·6 0·5	7·6 2·5	13·6 4·4
17	4 34·3	4 35·0	4 21·8	1·7 0·5	7·7 2·4	13·7 4·2	17	4 49·3	4 50·0	4 36·1	1·7 0·6	7·7 2·5	13·7 4·5
18	4 34·5	4 35·3	4 22·0	1·8 0·6	7·8 2·4	13·8 4·3	18	4 49·5	4 50·3	4 36·3	1·8 0·6	7·8 2·5	13·8 4·5
19	4 34·8	4 35·5	4 22·2	1·9 0·6	7·9 2·4	13·9 4·3	19	4 49·8	4 50·5	4 36·6	1·9 0·6	7·9 2·6	13·9 4·5
20	4 35·0	4 35·8	4 22·5	2·0 0·6	8·0 2·5	14·0 4·3	20	4 50·0	4 50·8	4 36·8	2·0 0·7	8·0 2·6	14·0 4·6
21	4 35·3	4 36·0	4 22·7	2·1 0·6	8·1 2·5	14·1 4·3	21	4 50·3	4 51·0	4 37·0	2·1 0·7	8·1 2·6	14·1 4·6
22	4 35·5	4 36·3	4 22·9	2·2 0·7	8·2 2·5	14·2 4·4	22	4 50·5	4 51·3	4 37·3	2·2 0·7	8·2 2·7	14·2 4·6
23	4 35·8	4 36·5	4 23·2	2·3 0·7	8·3 2·6	14·3 4·4	23	4 50·8	4 51·5	4 37·5	2·3 0·7	8·3 2·7	14·3 4·6
24	4 36·0	4 36·8	4 23·4	2·4 0·7	8·4 2·6	14·4 4·4	24	4 51·0	4 51·8	4 37·7	2·4 0·8	8·4 2·7	14·4 4·7
25	4 36·3	4 37·0	4 23·7	2·5 0·8	8·5 2·6	14·5 4·5	25	4 51·3	4 52·0	4 38·0	2·5 0·8	8·5 2·8	14·5 4·7
26	4 36·5	4 37·3	4 23·9	2·6 0·8	8·6 2·7	14·6 4·5	26	4 51·5	4 52·3	4 38·2	2·6 0·8	8·6 2·8	14·6 4·7
27	4 36·8	4 37·5	4 24·1	2·7 0·8	8·7 2·7	14·7 4·5	27	4 51·8	4 52·5	4 38·5	2·7 0·9	8·7 2·8	14·7 4·8
28	4 37·0	4 37·8	4 24·4	2·8 0·9	8·8 2·7	14·8 4·6	28	4 52·0	4 52·8	4 38·7	2·8 0·9	8·8 2·9	14·8 4·8
29	4 37·3	4 38·0	4 24·6	2·9 0·9	8·9 2·7	14·9 4·6	29	4 52·3	4 53·1	4 38·9	2·9 0·9	8·9 2·9	14·9 4·8
30	4 37·5	4 38·3	4 24·9	3·0 0·9	9·0 2·8	15·0 4·6	30	4 52·5	4 53·3	4 39·2	3·0 1·0	9·0 2·9	15·0 4·9
31	4 37·8	4 38·5	4 25·1	3·1 1·0	9·1 2·8	15·1 4·7	31	4 52·8	4 53·6	4 39·4	3·1 1·0	9·1 3·0	15·1 4·9
32	4 38·0	4 38·8	4 25·3	3·2 1·0	9·2 2·8	15·2 4·7	32	4 53·0	4 53·8	4 39·7	3·2 1·0	9·2 3·0	15·2 4·9
33	4 38·3	4 39·0	4 25·6	3·3 1·0	9·3 2·9	15·3 4·7	33	4 53·3	4 54·1	4 39·9	3·3 1·1	9·3 3·0	15·3 5·0
34	4 38·5	4 39·3	4 25·8	3·4 1·0	9·4 2·9	15·4 4·7	34	4 53·5	4 54·3	4 40·1	3·4 1·1	9·4 3·1	15·4 5·0
35	4 38·8	4 39·5	4 26·1	3·5 1·1	9·5 2·9	15·5 4·8	35	4 53·8	4 54·6	4 40·4	3·5 1·1	9·5 3·1	15·5 5·0
36	4 39·0	4 39·8	4 26·3	3·6 1·1	9·6 3·0	15·6 4·8	36	4 54·0	4 54·8	4 40·6	3·6 1·2	9·6 3·1	15·6 5·1
37	4 39·3	4 40·0	4 26·5	3·7 1·1	9·7 3·0	15·7 4·8	37	4 54·3	4 55·1	4 40·8	3·7 1·2	9·7 3·2	15·7 5·1
38	4 39·5	4 40·3	4 26·8	3·8 1·2	9·8 3·0	15·8 4·9	38	4 54·5	4 55·3	4 41·1	3·8 1·2	9·8 3·2	15·8 5·1
39	4 39·8	4 40·5	4 27·0	3·9 1·2	9·9 3·1	15·9 4·9	39	4 54·8	4 55·6	4 41·3	3·9 1·3	9·9 3·2	15·9 5·2
40	4 40·0	4 40·8	4 27·2	4·0 1·2	10·0 3·1	16·0 4·9	40	4 55·0	4 55·8	4 41·6	4·0 1·3	10·0 3·3	16·0 5·2
41	4 40·3	4 41·0	4 27·5	4·1 1·3	10·1 3·1	16·1 5·0	41	4 55·3	4 56·1	4 41·8	4·1 1·3	10·1 3·3	16·1 5·2
42	4 40·5	4 41·3	4 27·7	4·2 1·3	10·2 3·1	16·2 5·0	42	4 55·5	4 56·3	4 42·0	4·2 1·4	10·2 3·3	16·2 5·3
43	4 40·8	4 41·5	4 28·0	4·3 1·3	10·3 3·2	16·3 5·0	43	4 55·8	4 56·6	4 42·3	4·3 1·4	10·3 3·3	16·3 5·3
44	4 41·0	4 41·8	4 28·2	4·4 1·4	10·4 3·2	16·4 5·1	44	4 56·0	4 56·8	4 42·5	4·4 1·4	10·4 3·4	16·4 5·3
45	4 41·3	4 42·0	4 28·4	4·5 1·4	10·5 3·2	16·5 5·1	45	4 56·3	4 57·1	4 42·8	4·5 1·5	10·5 3·4	16·5 5·4
46	4 41·5	4 42·3	4 28·7	4·6 1·4	10·6 3·3	16·6 5·1	46	4 56·5	4 57·3	4 43·0	4·6 1·5	10·6 3·4	16·6 5·4
47	4 41·8	4 42·5	4 28·9	4·7 1·4	10·7 3·3	16·7 5·1	47	4 56·8	4 57·6	4 43·2	4·7 1·5	10·7 3·5	16·7 5·4
48	4 42·0	4 42·8	4 29·2	4·8 1·5	10·8 3·3	16·8 5·2	48	4 57·0	4 57·8	4 43·5	4·8 1·6	10·8 3·5	16·8 5·5
49	4 42·3	4 43·0	4 29·4	4·9 1·5	10·9 3·4	16·9 5·2	49	4 57·3	4 58·1	4 43·7	4·9 1·6	10·9 3·5	16·9 5·5
50	4 42·5	4 43·3	4 29·6	5·0 1·5	11·0 3·4	17·0 5·2	50	4 57·5	4 58·3	4 43·9	5·0 1·6	11·0 3·6	17·0 5·5
51	4 42·8	4 43·5	4 29·9	5·1 1·6	11·1 3·4	17·1 5·3	51	4 57·8	4 58·6	4 44·2	5·1 1·7	11·1 3·6	17·1 5·6
52	4 43·0	4 43·8	4 30·1	5·2 1·6	11·2 3·5	17·2 5·3	52	4 58·0	4 58·8	4 44·4	5·2 1·7	11·2 3·6	17·2 5·6
53	4 43·3	4 44·0	4 30·3	5·3 1·6	11·3 3·5	17·3 5·3	53	4 58·3	4 59·1	4 44·7	5·3 1·7	11·3 3·7	17·3 5·6
54	4 43·5	4 44·3	4 30·6	5·4 1·7	11·4 3·5	17·4 5·4	54	4 58·5	4 59·3	4 44·9	5·4 1·8	11·4 3·7	17·4 5·7
55	4 43·8	4 44·5	4 30·8	5·5 1·7	11·5 3·5	17·5 5·4	55	4 58·8	4 59·6	4 45·1	5·5 1·8	11·5 3·7	17·5 5·7
56	4 44·0	4 44·8	4 31·1	5·6 1·7	11·6 3·6	17·6 5·4	56	4 59·0	4 59·8	4 45·4	5·6 1·8	11·6 3·8	17·6 5·7
57	4 44·3	4 45·0	4 31·3	5·7 1·8	11·7 3·6	17·7 5·5	57	4 59·3	5 00·1	4 45·6	5·7 1·9	11·7 3·8	17·7 5·8
58	4 44·5	4 45·3	4 31·5	5·8 1·8	11·8 3·6	17·8 5·5	58	4 59·5	5 00·3	4 45·9	5·8 1·9	11·8 3·8	17·8 5·8
59	4 44·8	4 45·5	4 31·8	5·9 1·8	11·9 3·7	17·9 5·5	59	4 59·8	5 00·6	4 46·1	5·9 1·9	11·9 3·9	17·9 5·8
60	4 45·0	4 45·8	4 32·0	6·0 1·9	12·0 3·7	18·0 5·6	60	5 00·0	5 00·8	4 46·3	6·0 2·0	12·0 3·9	18·0 5·9

xi

© British Crown Copyright 2018. All rights reserved.

20	SUN PLANETS	ARIES	MOON	v or Corrⁿ d		v or Corrⁿ d		v or Corrⁿ d	
s	° ′	° ′	° ′	′	′	′	′	′	′
00	5 00·0	5 00·8	4 46·3	0·0	0·0	6·0	2·1	12·0	4·1
01	5 00·3	5 01·1	4 46·6	0·1	0·0	6·1	2·1	12·1	4·1
02	5 00·5	5 01·3	4 46·8	0·2	0·1	6·2	2·1	12·2	4·2
03	5 00·8	5 01·6	4 47·0	0·3	0·1	6·3	2·2	12·3	4·2
04	5 01·0	5 01·8	4 47·3	0·4	0·1	6·4	2·2	12·4	4·2
05	5 01·3	5 02·1	4 47·5	0·5	0·2	6·5	2·2	12·5	4·3
06	5 01·5	5 02·3	4 47·8	0·6	0·2	6·6	2·3	12·6	4·3
07	5 01·8	5 02·6	4 48·0	0·7	0·2	6·7	2·3	12·7	4·3
08	5 02·0	5 02·8	4 48·2	0·8	0·3	6·8	2·3	12·8	4·4
09	5 02·3	5 03·1	4 48·5	0·9	0·3	6·9	2·4	12·9	4·4
10	5 02·5	5 03·3	4 48·7	1·0	0·3	7·0	2·4	13·0	4·4
11	5 02·8	5 03·6	4 49·0	1·1	0·4	7·1	2·4	13·1	4·5
12	5 03·0	5 03·8	4 49·2	1·2	0·4	7·2	2·5	13·2	4·5
13	5 03·3	5 04·1	4 49·4	1·3	0·4	7·3	2·5	13·3	4·5
14	5 03·5	5 04·3	4 49·7	1·4	0·5	7·4	2·5	13·4	4·6
15	5 03·8	5 04·6	4 49·9	1·5	0·5	7·5	2·6	13·5	4·6
16	5 04·0	5 04·8	4 50·2	1·6	0·5	7·6	2·6	13·6	4·6
17	5 04·3	5 05·1	4 50·4	1·7	0·6	7·7	2·6	13·7	4·7
18	5 04·5	5 05·3	4 50·6	1·8	0·6	7·8	2·7	13·8	4·7
19	5 04·8	5 05·6	4 50·9	1·9	0·6	7·9	2·7	13·9	4·7
20	5 05·0	5 05·8	4 51·1	2·0	0·7	8·0	2·7	14·0	4·8
21	5 05·3	5 06·1	4 51·3	2·1	0·7	8·1	2·8	14·1	4·8
22	5 05·5	5 06·3	4 51·6	2·2	0·8	8·2	2·8	14·2	4·9
23	5 05·8	5 06·6	4 51·8	2·3	0·8	8·3	2·8	14·3	4·9
24	5 06·0	5 06·8	4 52·1	2·4	0·8	8·4	2·9	14·4	4·9
25	5 06·3	5 07·1	4 52·3	2·5	0·9	8·5	2·9	14·5	5·0
26	5 06·5	5 07·3	4 52·5	2·6	0·9	8·6	2·9	14·6	5·0
27	5 06·8	5 07·6	4 52·8	2·7	0·9	8·7	3·0	14·7	5·0
28	5 07·0	5 07·8	4 53·0	2·8	1·0	8·8	3·0	14·8	5·1
29	5 07·3	5 08·1	4 53·3	2·9	1·0	8·9	3·0	14·9	5·1
30	5 07·5	5 08·3	4 53·5	3·0	1·0	9·0	3·1	15·0	5·1
31	5 07·8	5 08·6	4 53·7	3·1	1·1	9·1	3·1	15·1	5·2
32	5 08·0	5 08·8	4 54·0	3·2	1·1	9·2	3·1	15·2	5·2
33	5 08·3	5 09·1	4 54·2	3·3	1·1	9·3	3·2	15·3	5·2
34	5 08·5	5 09·3	4 54·4	3·4	1·2	9·4	3·2	15·4	5·3
35	5 08·8	5 09·6	4 54·7	3·5	1·2	9·5	3·2	15·5	5·3
36	5 09·0	5 09·8	4 54·9	3·6	1·2	9·6	3·3	15·6	5·3
37	5 09·3	5 10·1	4 55·2	3·7	1·3	9·7	3·3	15·7	5·4
38	5 09·5	5 10·3	4 55·4	3·8	1·3	9·8	3·3	15·8	5·4
39	5 09·8	5 10·6	4 55·6	3·9	1·3	9·9	3·4	15·9	5·4
40	5 10·0	5 10·8	4 55·9	4·0	1·4	10·0	3·4	16·0	5·5
41	5 10·3	5 11·1	4 56·1	4·1	1·4	10·1	3·5	16·1	5·5
42	5 10·5	5 11·4	4 56·4	4·2	1·4	10·2	3·5	16·2	5·6
43	5 10·8	5 11·6	4 56·6	4·3	1·5	10·3	3·5	16·3	5·6
44	5 11·0	5 11·9	4 56·8	4·4	1·5	10·4	3·6	16·4	5·6
45	5 11·3	5 12·1	4 57·1	4·5	1·5	10·5	3·6	16·5	5·6
46	5 11·5	5 12·4	4 57·3	4·6	1·6	10·6	3·6	16·6	5·7
47	5 11·8	5 12·6	4 57·5	4·7	1·6	10·7	3·7	16·7	5·7
48	5 12·0	5 12·9	4 57·8	4·8	1·6	10·8	3·7	16·8	5·7
49	5 12·3	5 13·1	4 58·0	4·9	1·7	10·9	3·7	16·9	5·8
50	5 12·5	5 13·4	4 58·3	5·0	1·7	11·0	3·8	17·0	5·8
51	5 12·8	5 13·6	4 58·5	5·1	1·7	11·1	3·8	17·1	5·8
52	5 13·0	5 13·9	4 58·7	5·2	1·8	11·2	3·8	17·2	5·9
53	5 13·3	5 14·1	4 59·0	5·3	1·8	11·3	3·9	17·3	5·9
54	5 13·5	5 14·4	4 59·2	5·4	1·8	11·4	3·9	17·4	5·9
55	5 13·8	5 14·6	4 59·5	5·5	1·9	11·5	3·9	17·5	6·0
56	5 14·0	5 14·9	4 59·7	5·6	1·9	11·6	4·0	17·6	6·0
57	5 14·3	5 15·1	4 59·9	5·7	1·9	11·7	4·0	17·7	6·0
58	5 14·5	5 15·4	5 00·2	5·8	2·0	11·8	4·0	17·8	6·1
59	5 14·8	5 15·6	5 00·4	5·9	2·0	11·9	4·1	17·9	6·1
60	5 15·0	5 15·9	5 00·7	6·0	2·1	12·0	4·1	18·0	6·2

21	SUN PLANETS	ARIES	MOON	v or Corrⁿ d		v or Corrⁿ d		v or Corrⁿ d	
s	° ′	° ′	° ′	′	′	′	′	′	′
00	5 15·0	5 15·9	5 00·7	0·0	0·0	6·0	2·2	12·0	4·3
01	5 15·3	5 16·1	5 00·9	0·1	0·0	6·1	2·2	12·1	4·3
02	5 15·5	5 16·4	5 01·1	0·2	0·1	6·2	2·2	12·2	4·4
03	5 15·8	5 16·6	5 01·4	0·3	0·1	6·3	2·3	12·3	4·4
04	5 16·0	5 16·9	5 01·6	0·4	0·1	6·4	2·3	12·4	4·4
05	5 16·3	5 17·1	5 01·8	0·5	0·2	6·5	2·3	12·5	4·5
06	5 16·5	5 17·4	5 02·1	0·6	0·2	6·6	2·4	12·6	4·5
07	5 16·8	5 17·6	5 02·3	0·7	0·3	6·7	2·4	12·7	4·6
08	5 17·0	5 17·9	5 02·6	0·8	0·3	6·8	2·4	12·8	4·6
09	5 17·3	5 18·1	5 02·8	0·9	0·3	6·9	2·5	12·9	4·6
10	5 17·5	5 18·4	5 03·0	1·0	0·4	7·0	2·5	13·0	4·7
11	5 17·8	5 18·6	5 03·3	1·1	0·4	7·1	2·5	13·1	4·7
12	5 18·0	5 18·9	5 03·5	1·2	0·4	7·2	2·6	13·2	4·7
13	5 18·3	5 19·1	5 03·8	1·3	0·5	7·3	2·6	13·3	4·8
14	5 18·5	5 19·4	5 04·0	1·4	0·5	7·4	2·7	13·4	4·8
15	5 18·8	5 19·6	5 04·2	1·5	0·5	7·5	2·7	13·5	4·8
16	5 19·0	5 19·9	5 04·5	1·6	0·6	7·6	2·7	13·6	4·9
17	5 19·3	5 20·1	5 04·7	1·7	0·6	7·7	2·8	13·7	4·9
18	5 19·5	5 20·4	5 04·9	1·8	0·6	7·8	2·8	13·8	4·9
19	5 19·8	5 20·6	5 05·2	1·9	0·7	7·9	2·8	13·9	5·0
20	5 20·0	5 20·9	5 05·4	2·0	0·7	8·0	2·9	14·0	5·0
21	5 20·3	5 21·1	5 05·7	2·1	0·8	8·1	2·9	14·1	5·1
22	5 20·5	5 21·4	5 05·9	2·2	0·8	8·2	2·9	14·2	5·1
23	5 20·8	5 21·6	5 06·1	2·3	0·8	8·3	3·0	14·3	5·1
24	5 21·0	5 21·9	5 06·4	2·4	0·9	8·4	3·0	14·4	5·2
25	5 21·3	5 22·1	5 06·6	2·5	0·9	8·5	3·0	14·5	5·2
26	5 21·5	5 22·4	5 06·9	2·6	0·9	8·6	3·1	14·6	5·2
27	5 21·8	5 22·6	5 07·1	2·7	1·0	8·7	3·1	14·7	5·3
28	5 22·0	5 22·9	5 07·3	2·8	1·0	8·8	3·2	14·8	5·3
29	5 22·3	5 23·1	5 07·6	2·9	1·0	8·9	3·2	14·9	5·3
30	5 22·5	5 23·4	5 07·8	3·0	1·1	9·0	3·2	15·0	5·4
31	5 22·8	5 23·6	5 08·0	3·1	1·1	9·1	3·3	15·1	5·4
32	5 23·0	5 23·9	5 08·3	3·2	1·1	9·2	3·3	15·2	5·5
33	5 23·3	5 24·1	5 08·5	3·3	1·2	9·3	3·3	15·3	5·5
34	5 23·5	5 24·4	5 08·8	3·4	1·2	9·4	3·4	15·4	5·5
35	5 23·8	5 24·6	5 09·0	3·5	1·3	9·5	3·4	15·5	5·6
36	5 24·0	5 24·9	5 09·2	3·6	1·3	9·6	3·4	15·6	5·6
37	5 24·3	5 25·1	5 09·5	3·7	1·3	9·7	3·5	15·7	5·6
38	5 24·5	5 25·4	5 09·7	3·8	1·4	9·8	3·5	15·8	5·7
39	5 24·8	5 25·6	5 10·0	3·9	1·4	9·9	3·5	15·9	5·7
40	5 25·0	5 25·9	5 10·2	4·0	1·4	10·0	3·6	16·0	5·7
41	5 25·3	5 26·1	5 10·4	4·1	1·5	10·1	3·6	16·1	5·8
42	5 25·5	5 26·4	5 10·7	4·2	1·5	10·2	3·7	16·2	5·8
43	5 25·8	5 26·6	5 10·9	4·3	1·5	10·3	3·7	16·3	5·8
44	5 26·0	5 26·9	5 11·1	4·4	1·6	10·4	3·7	16·4	5·9
45	5 26·3	5 27·1	5 11·4	4·5	1·6	10·5	3·8	16·5	5·9
46	5 26·5	5 27·4	5 11·6	4·6	1·6	10·6	3·8	16·6	5·9
47	5 26·8	5 27·6	5 11·9	4·7	1·7	10·7	3·8	16·7	6·0
48	5 27·0	5 27·9	5 12·1	4·8	1·7	10·8	3·9	16·8	6·0
49	5 27·3	5 28·1	5 12·3	4·9	1·8	10·9	3·9	16·9	6·1
50	5 27·5	5 28·4	5 12·6	5·0	1·8	11·0	3·9	17·0	6·1
51	5 27·8	5 28·6	5 12·8	5·1	1·8	11·1	4·0	17·1	6·1
52	5 28·0	5 28·9	5 13·1	5·2	1·9	11·2	4·0	17·2	6·2
53	5 28·3	5 29·1	5 13·3	5·3	1·9	11·3	4·0	17·3	6·2
54	5 28·5	5 29·4	5 13·5	5·4	1·9	11·4	4·1	17·4	6·2
55	5 28·8	5 29·7	5 13·8	5·5	2·0	11·5	4·1	17·5	6·3
56	5 29·0	5 29·9	5 14·0	5·6	2·0	11·6	4·2	17·6	6·3
57	5 29·3	5 30·2	5 14·3	5·7	2·0	11·7	4·2	17·7	6·3
58	5 29·5	5 30·4	5 14·5	5·8	2·1	11·8	4·2	17·8	6·4
59	5 29·8	5 30·7	5 14·7	5·9	2·1	11·9	4·3	17·9	6·4
60	5 30·0	5 30·9	5 15·0	6·0	2·2	12·0	4·3	18·0	6·5

© British Crown Copyright 2018. All rights reserved.

22^m	SUN PLANETS	ARIES	MOON	v or Corrn d	v or Corrn d	v or Corrn d	23^m	SUN PLANETS	ARIES	MOON	v or Corrn d	v or Corrn d	v or Corrn d
s	° ′	° ′	° ′	′ ′	′ ′	′ ′	s	° ′	° ′	° ′	′ ′	′ ′	′ ′
00	5 30·0	5 30·9	5 15·0	0·0 0·0	6·0 2·3	12·0 4·5	00	5 45·0	5 45·9	5 29·3	0·0 0·0	6·0 2·4	12·0 4·7
01	5 30·3	5 31·2	5 15·2	0·1 0·0	6·1 2·3	12·1 4·5	01	5 45·3	5 46·2	5 29·5	0·1 0·0	6·1 2·4	12·1 4·7
02	5 30·5	5 31·4	5 15·4	0·2 0·1	6·2 2·3	12·2 4·6	02	5 45·5	5 46·4	5 29·8	0·2 0·1	6·2 2·4	12·2 4·8
03	5 30·8	5 31·7	5 15·7	0·3 0·1	6·3 2·4	12·3 4·6	03	5 45·8	5 46·7	5 30·0	0·3 0·1	6·3 2·5	12·3 4·8
04	5 31·0	5 31·9	5 15·9	0·4 0·2	6·4 2·4	12·4 4·7	04	5 46·0	5 46·9	5 30·2	0·4 0·2	6·4 2·5	12·4 4·9
05	5 31·3	5 32·2	5 16·2	0·5 0·2	6·5 2·4	12·5 4·7	05	5 46·3	5 47·2	5 30·5	0·5 0·2	6·5 2·5	12·5 4·9
06	5 31·5	5 32·4	5 16·4	0·6 0·2	6·6 2·5	12·6 4·7	06	5 46·5	5 47·4	5 30·7	0·6 0·2	6·6 2·6	12·6 4·9
07	5 31·8	5 32·7	5 16·6	0·7 0·3	6·7 2·5	12·7 4·8	07	5 46·8	5 47·7	5 31·0	0·7 0·3	6·7 2·6	12·7 5·0
08	5 32·0	5 32·9	5 16·9	0·8 0·3	6·8 2·6	12·8 4·8	08	5 47·0	5 48·0	5 31·2	0·8 0·3	6·8 2·7	12·8 5·0
09	5 32·3	5 33·2	5 17·1	0·9 0·3	6·9 2·6	12·9 4·8	09	5 47·3	5 48·2	5 31·4	0·9 0·4	6·9 2·7	12·9 5·1
10	5 32·5	5 33·4	5 17·4	1·0 0·4	7·0 2·6	13·0 4·9	10	5 47·5	5 48·5	5 31·7	1·0 0·4	7·0 2·7	13·0 5·1
11	5 32·8	5 33·7	5 17·6	1·1 0·4	7·1 2·7	13·1 4·9	11	5 47·8	5 48·7	5 31·9	1·1 0·4	7·1 2·8	13·1 5·1
12	5 33·0	5 33·9	5 17·8	1·2 0·5	7·2 2·7	13·2 5·0	12	5 48·0	5 49·0	5 32·1	1·2 0·5	7·2 2·8	13·2 5·2
13	5 33·3	5 34·2	5 18·1	1·3 0·5	7·3 2·7	13·3 5·0	13	5 48·3	5 49·2	5 32·4	1·3 0·5	7·3 2·9	13·3 5·2
14	5 33·5	5 34·4	5 18·3	1·4 0·5	7·4 2·8	13·4 5·0	14	5 48·5	5 49·5	5 32·6	1·4 0·5	7·4 2·9	13·4 5·2
15	5 33·8	5 34·7	5 18·5	1·5 0·6	7·5 2·8	13·5 5·1	15	5 48·8	5 49·7	5 32·9	1·5 0·6	7·5 2·9	13·5 5·3
16	5 34·0	5 34·9	5 18·8	1·6 0·6	7·6 2·9	13·6 5·1	16	5 49·0	5 50·0	5 33·1	1·6 0·6	7·6 3·0	13·6 5·3
17	5 34·3	5 35·2	5 19·0	1·7 0·6	7·7 2·9	13·7 5·1	17	5 49·3	5 50·2	5 33·3	1·7 0·7	7·7 3·0	13·7 5·4
18	5 34·5	5 35·4	5 19·3	1·8 0·7	7·8 2·9	13·8 5·2	18	5 49·5	5 50·5	5 33·6	1·8 0·7	7·8 3·1	13·8 5·4
19	5 34·8	5 35·7	5 19·5	1·9 0·7	7·9 3·0	13·9 5·2	19	5 49·8	5 50·7	5 33·8	1·9 0·7	7·9 3·1	13·9 5·4
20	5 35·0	5 35·9	5 19·7	2·0 0·8	8·0 3·0	14·0 5·3	20	5 50·0	5 51·0	5 34·1	2·0 0·8	8·0 3·1	14·0 5·5
21	5 35·3	5 36·2	5 20·0	2·1 0·8	8·1 3·0	14·1 5·3	21	5 50·3	5 51·2	5 34·3	2·1 0·8	8·1 3·2	14·1 5·5
22	5 35·5	5 36·4	5 20·2	2·2 0·8	8·2 3·1	14·2 5·3	22	5 50·5	5 51·5	5 34·5	2·2 0·9	8·2 3·2	14·2 5·6
23	5 35·8	5 36·7	5 20·5	2·3 0·9	8·3 3·1	14·3 5·4	23	5 50·8	5 51·7	5 34·8	2·3 0·9	8·3 3·3	14·3 5·6
24	5 36·0	5 36·9	5 20·7	2·4 0·9	8·4 3·2	14·4 5·4	24	5 51·0	5 52·0	5 35·0	2·4 0·9	8·4 3·3	14·4 5·6
25	5 36·3	5 37·2	5 20·9	2·5 0·9	8·5 3·2	14·5 5·4	25	5 51·3	5 52·2	5 35·2	2·5 1·0	8·5 3·3	14·5 5·7
26	5 36·5	5 37·4	5 21·2	2·6 1·0	8·6 3·2	14·6 5·5	26	5 51·5	5 52·5	5 35·5	2·6 1·0	8·6 3·4	14·6 5·7
27	5 36·8	5 37·7	5 21·4	2·7 1·0	8·7 3·3	14·7 5·5	27	5 51·8	5 52·7	5 35·7	2·7 1·1	8·7 3·4	14·7 5·8
28	5 37·0	5 37·9	5 21·6	2·8 1·0	8·8 3·3	14·8 5·6	28	5 52·0	5 53·0	5 36·0	2·8 1·1	8·8 3·4	14·8 5·8
29	5 37·3	5 38·2	5 21·9	2·9 1·1	8·9 3·3	14·9 5·6	29	5 52·3	5 53·2	5 36·2	2·9 1·1	8·9 3·5	14·9 5·8
30	5 37·5	5 38·4	5 22·1	3·0 1·1	9·0 3·4	15·0 5·6	30	5 52·5	5 53·5	5 36·4	3·0 1·2	9·0 3·5	15·0 5·9
31	5 37·8	5 38·7	5 22·4	3·1 1·2	9·1 3·4	15·1 5·7	31	5 52·8	5 53·7	5 36·7	3·1 1·2	9·1 3·6	15·1 5·9
32	5 38·0	5 38·9	5 22·6	3·2 1·2	9·2 3·5	15·2 5·7	32	5 53·0	5 54·0	5 36·9	3·2 1·3	9·2 3·6	15·2 6·0
33	5 38·3	5 39·2	5 22·8	3·3 1·2	9·3 3·5	15·3 5·7	33	5 53·3	5 54·2	5 37·2	3·3 1·3	9·3 3·6	15·3 6·0
34	5 38·5	5 39·4	5 23·1	3·4 1·3	9·4 3·5	15·4 5·8	34	5 53·5	5 54·5	5 37·4	3·4 1·3	9·4 3·7	15·4 6·0
35	5 38·8	5 39·7	5 23·3	3·5 1·3	9·5 3·6	15·5 5·8	35	5 53·8	5 54·7	5 37·6	3·5 1·4	9·5 3·7	15·5 6·1
36	5 39·0	5 39·9	5 23·6	3·6 1·4	9·6 3·6	15·6 5·9	36	5 54·0	5 55·0	5 37·9	3·6 1·4	9·6 3·8	15·6 6·1
37	5 39·3	5 40·2	5 23·8	3·7 1·4	9·7 3·6	15·7 5·9	37	5 54·3	5 55·2	5 38·1	3·7 1·4	9·7 3·8	15·7 6·1
38	5 39·5	5 40·4	5 24·0	3·8 1·4	9·8 3·7	15·8 5·9	38	5 54·5	5 55·5	5 38·4	3·8 1·5	9·8 3·8	15·8 6·2
39	5 39·8	5 40·7	5 24·3	3·9 1·5	9·9 3·7	15·9 6·0	39	5 54·8	5 55·7	5 38·6	3·9 1·5	9·9 3·9	15·9 6·2
40	5 40·0	5 40·9	5 24·5	4·0 1·5	10·0 3·8	16·0 6·0	40	5 55·0	5 56·0	5 38·8	4·0 1·6	10·0 3·9	16·0 6·3
41	5 40·3	5 41·2	5 24·7	4·1 1·5	10·1 3·8	16·1 6·0	41	5 55·3	5 56·2	5 39·1	4·1 1·6	10·1 4·0	16·1 6·3
42	5 40·5	5 41·4	5 25·0	4·2 1·6	10·2 3·8	16·2 6·1	42	5 55·5	5 56·5	5 39·3	4·2 1·6	10·2 4·0	16·2 6·3
43	5 40·8	5 41·7	5 25·2	4·3 1·6	10·3 3·9	16·3 6·1	43	5 55·8	5 56·7	5 39·5	4·3 1·7	10·3 4·0	16·3 6·4
44	5 41·0	5 41·9	5 25·5	4·4 1·7	10·4 3·9	16·4 6·1	44	5 56·0	5 57·0	5 39·8	4·4 1·7	10·4 4·1	16·4 6·4
45	5 41·3	5 42·2	5 25·7	4·5 1·7	10·5 3·9	16·5 6·2	45	5 56·3	5 57·2	5 40·0	4·5 1·8	10·5 4·1	16·5 6·5
46	5 41·5	5 42·4	5 25·9	4·6 1·7	10·6 4·0	16·6 6·2	46	5 56·5	5 57·5	5 40·3	4·6 1·8	10·6 4·2	16·6 6·5
47	5 41·8	5 42·7	5 26·2	4·7 1·8	10·7 4·0	16·7 6·3	47	5 56·8	5 57·7	5 40·5	4·7 1·8	10·7 4·2	16·7 6·5
48	5 42·0	5 42·9	5 26·4	4·8 1·8	10·8 4·1	16·8 6·3	48	5 57·0	5 58·0	5 40·7	4·8 1·9	10·8 4·2	16·8 6·6
49	5 42·3	5 43·2	5 26·7	4·9 1·8	10·9 4·1	16·9 6·3	49	5 57·3	5 58·2	5 41·0	4·9 1·9	10·9 4·3	16·9 6·6
50	5 42·5	5 43·4	5 26·9	5·0 1·9	11·0 4·1	17·0 6·4	50	5 57·5	5 58·5	5 41·2	5·0 2·0	11·0 4·3	17·0 6·7
51	5 42·8	5 43·7	5 27·1	5·1 1·9	11·1 4·2	17·1 6·4	51	5 57·8	5 58·7	5 41·5	5·1 2·0	11·1 4·3	17·1 6·7
52	5 43·0	5 43·9	5 27·4	5·2 2·0	11·2 4·2	17·2 6·5	52	5 58·0	5 59·0	5 41·7	5·2 2·0	11·2 4·4	17·2 6·7
53	5 43·3	5 44·2	5 27·6	5·3 2·0	11·3 4·2	17·3 6·5	53	5 58·3	5 59·2	5 41·9	5·3 2·1	11·3 4·4	17·3 6·8
54	5 43·5	5 44·4	5 27·9	5·4 2·0	11·4 4·3	17·4 6·5	54	5 58·5	5 59·5	5 42·2	5·4 2·1	11·4 4·5	17·4 6·8
55	5 43·8	5 44·7	5 28·1	5·5 2·1	11·5 4·3	17·5 6·6	55	5 58·8	5 59·7	5 42·4	5·5 2·2	11·5 4·5	17·5 6·9
56	5 44·0	5 44·9	5 28·3	5·6 2·1	11·6 4·4	17·6 6·6	56	5 59·0	6 00·0	5 42·6	5·6 2·2	11·6 4·5	17·6 6·9
57	5 44·3	5 45·2	5 28·6	5·7 2·1	11·7 4·4	17·7 6·6	57	5 59·3	6 00·2	5 42·9	5·7 2·2	11·7 4·6	17·7 6·9
58	5 44·5	5 45·4	5 28·8	5·8 2·2	11·8 4·4	17·8 6·7	58	5 59·5	6 00·5	5 43·1	5·8 2·3	11·8 4·6	17·8 7·0
59	5 44·8	5 45·7	5 29·0	5·9 2·2	11·9 4·5	17·9 6·7	59	5 59·8	6 00·7	5 43·4	5·9 2·3	11·9 4·7	17·9 7·0
60	5 45·0	5 45·9	5 29·3	6·0 2·3	12·0 4·5	18·0 6·8	60	6 00·0	6 01·0	5 43·6	6·0 2·4	12·0 4·7	18·0 7·1

© British Crown Copyright 2018. All rights reserved.

24ᵐ

s	SUN PLANETS	ARIES	MOON	v or Corrⁿ d	v or Corrⁿ d	v or Corrⁿ d
	° ′	° ′	° ′	′ ′	′ ′	′ ′
00	6 00.0	6 01.0	5 43.6	0.0 0.0	6.0 2.5	12.0 4.9
01	6 00.3	6 01.2	5 43.8	0.1 0.0	6.1 2.5	12.1 4.9
02	6 00.5	6 01.5	5 44.1	0.2 0.1	6.2 2.5	12.2 5.0
03	6 00.8	6 01.7	5 44.3	0.3 0.1	6.3 2.6	12.3 5.0
04	6 01.0	6 02.0	5 44.6	0.4 0.2	6.4 2.6	12.4 5.1
05	6 01.3	6 02.2	5 44.8	0.5 0.2	6.5 2.7	12.5 5.1
06	6 01.5	6 02.5	5 45.0	0.6 0.2	6.6 2.7	12.6 5.1
07	6 01.8	6 02.7	5 45.3	0.7 0.3	6.7 2.7	12.7 5.2
08	6 02.0	6 03.0	5 45.5	0.8 0.3	6.8 2.8	12.8 5.2
09	6 02.3	6 03.2	5 45.7	0.9 0.4	6.9 2.8	12.9 5.3
10	6 02.5	6 03.5	5 46.0	1.0 0.4	7.0 2.9	13.0 5.3
11	6 02.8	6 03.7	5 46.2	1.1 0.4	7.1 2.9	13.1 5.3
12	6 03.0	6 04.0	5 46.5	1.2 0.5	7.2 2.9	13.2 5.4
13	6 03.3	6 04.2	5 46.7	1.3 0.5	7.3 3.0	13.3 5.4
14	6 03.5	6 04.5	5 46.9	1.4 0.6	7.4 3.0	13.4 5.5
15	6 03.8	6 04.7	5 47.2	1.5 0.6	7.5 3.1	13.5 5.5
16	6 04.0	6 05.0	5 47.4	1.6 0.7	7.6 3.1	13.6 5.6
17	6 04.3	6 05.2	5 47.7	1.7 0.7	7.7 3.1	13.7 5.6
18	6 04.5	6 05.5	5 47.9	1.8 0.7	7.8 3.2	13.8 5.6
19	6 04.8	6 05.7	5 48.1	1.9 0.8	7.9 3.2	13.9 5.7
20	6 05.0	6 06.0	5 48.4	2.0 0.8	8.0 3.3	14.0 5.7
21	6 05.3	6 06.3	5 48.6	2.1 0.9	8.1 3.3	14.1 5.8
22	6 05.5	6 06.5	5 48.8	2.2 0.9	8.2 3.3	14.2 5.8
23	6 05.8	6 06.8	5 49.1	2.3 0.9	8.3 3.4	14.3 5.8
24	6 06.0	6 07.0	5 49.3	2.4 1.0	8.4 3.4	14.4 5.9
25	6 06.3	6 07.3	5 49.6	2.5 1.0	8.5 3.5	14.5 5.9
26	6 06.5	6 07.5	5 49.8	2.6 1.1	8.6 3.5	14.6 6.0
27	6 06.8	6 07.8	5 50.0	2.7 1.1	8.7 3.6	14.7 6.0
28	6 07.0	6 08.0	5 50.3	2.8 1.1	8.8 3.6	14.8 6.0
29	6 07.3	6 08.3	5 50.5	2.9 1.2	8.9 3.6	14.9 6.1
30	6 07.5	6 08.5	5 50.8	3.0 1.2	9.0 3.7	15.0 6.1
31	6 07.8	6 08.8	5 51.0	3.1 1.3	9.1 3.7	15.1 6.2
32	6 08.0	6 09.0	5 51.2	3.2 1.3	9.2 3.8	15.2 6.2
33	6 08.3	6 09.3	5 51.5	3.3 1.3	9.3 3.8	15.3 6.2
34	6 08.5	6 09.5	5 51.7	3.4 1.4	9.4 3.8	15.4 6.3
35	6 08.8	6 09.8	5 52.0	3.5 1.4	9.5 3.9	15.5 6.3
36	6 09.0	6 10.0	5 52.2	3.6 1.5	9.6 3.9	15.6 6.4
37	6 09.3	6 10.3	5 52.4	3.7 1.5	9.7 4.0	15.7 6.4
38	6 09.5	6 10.5	5 52.7	3.8 1.6	9.8 4.0	15.8 6.5
39	6 09.8	6 10.8	5 52.9	3.9 1.6	9.9 4.0	15.9 6.5
40	6 10.0	6 11.0	5 53.1	4.0 1.6	10.0 4.1	16.0 6.5
41	6 10.3	6 11.3	5 53.4	4.1 1.7	10.1 4.1	16.1 6.6
42	6 10.5	6 11.5	5 53.6	4.2 1.7	10.2 4.2	16.2 6.6
43	6 10.8	6 11.8	5 53.9	4.3 1.8	10.3 4.2	16.3 6.7
44	6 11.0	6 12.0	5 54.1	4.4 1.8	10.4 4.2	16.4 6.7
45	6 11.3	6 12.3	5 54.3	4.5 1.8	10.5 4.3	16.5 6.7
46	6 11.5	6 12.5	5 54.6	4.6 1.9	10.6 4.3	16.6 6.8
47	6 11.8	6 12.8	5 54.8	4.7 1.9	10.7 4.4	16.7 6.8
48	6 12.0	6 13.0	5 55.1	4.8 2.0	10.8 4.4	16.8 6.9
49	6 12.3	6 13.3	5 55.3	4.9 2.0	10.9 4.5	16.9 6.9
50	6 12.5	6 13.5	5 55.5	5.0 2.0	11.0 4.5	17.0 6.9
51	6 12.8	6 13.8	5 55.8	5.1 2.1	11.1 4.5	17.1 7.0
52	6 13.0	6 14.0	5 56.0	5.2 2.1	11.2 4.6	17.2 7.0
53	6 13.3	6 14.3	5 56.2	5.3 2.2	11.3 4.6	17.3 7.1
54	6 13.5	6 14.5	5 56.5	5.4 2.2	11.4 4.7	17.4 7.1
55	6 13.8	6 14.8	5 56.7	5.5 2.2	11.5 4.7	17.5 7.1
56	6 14.0	6 15.0	5 57.0	5.6 2.3	11.6 4.7	17.6 7.2
57	6 14.3	6 15.3	5 57.2	5.7 2.3	11.7 4.8	17.7 7.2
58	6 14.5	6 15.5	5 57.4	5.8 2.4	11.8 4.8	17.8 7.3
59	6 14.8	6 15.8	5 57.7	5.9 2.4	11.9 4.9	17.9 7.3
60	6 15.0	6 16.0	5 57.9	6.0 2.5	12.0 4.9	18.0 7.4

25ᵐ

s	SUN PLANETS	ARIES	MOON	v or Corrⁿ d	v or Corrⁿ d	v or Corrⁿ d
	° ′	° ′	° ′	′ ′	′ ′	′ ′
00	6 15.0	6 16.0	5 57.9	0.0 0.0	6.0 2.6	12.0 5.1
01	6 15.3	6 16.3	5 58.2	0.1 0.0	6.1 2.6	12.1 5.1
02	6 15.5	6 16.5	5 58.4	0.2 0.1	6.2 2.6	12.2 5.2
03	6 15.8	6 16.8	5 58.6	0.3 0.1	6.3 2.7	12.3 5.2
04	6 16.0	6 17.0	5 58.9	0.4 0.2	6.4 2.7	12.4 5.3
05	6 16.3	6 17.3	5 59.1	0.5 0.2	6.5 2.8	12.5 5.3
06	6 16.5	6 17.5	5 59.3	0.6 0.3	6.6 2.8	12.6 5.4
07	6 16.8	6 17.8	5 59.6	0.7 0.3	6.7 2.8	12.7 5.4
08	6 17.0	6 18.0	5 59.8	0.8 0.3	6.8 2.9	12.8 5.4
09	6 17.3	6 18.3	6 00.1	0.9 0.4	6.9 2.9	12.9 5.5
10	6 17.5	6 18.5	6 00.3	1.0 0.4	7.0 3.0	13.0 5.5
11	6 17.8	6 18.8	6 00.5	1.1 0.5	7.1 3.0	13.1 5.6
12	6 18.0	6 19.0	6 00.8	1.2 0.5	7.2 3.1	13.2 5.6
13	6 18.3	6 19.3	6 01.0	1.3 0.6	7.3 3.1	13.3 5.7
14	6 18.5	6 19.5	6 01.3	1.4 0.6	7.4 3.1	13.4 5.7
15	6 18.8	6 19.8	6 01.5	1.5 0.6	7.5 3.2	13.5 5.7
16	6 19.0	6 20.0	6 01.7	1.6 0.7	7.6 3.2	13.6 5.8
17	6 19.3	6 20.3	6 02.0	1.7 0.7	7.7 3.3	13.7 5.8
18	6 19.5	6 20.5	6 02.2	1.8 0.8	7.8 3.3	13.8 5.9
19	6 19.8	6 20.8	6 02.5	1.9 0.8	7.9 3.4	13.9 5.9
20	6 20.0	6 21.0	6 02.7	2.0 0.9	8.0 3.4	14.0 6.0
21	6 20.3	6 21.3	6 02.9	2.1 0.9	8.1 3.4	14.1 6.0
22	6 20.5	6 21.5	6 03.2	2.2 0.9	8.2 3.5	14.2 6.0
23	6 20.8	6 21.8	6 03.4	2.3 1.0	8.3 3.5	14.3 6.1
24	6 21.0	6 22.0	6 03.6	2.4 1.0	8.4 3.6	14.4 6.1
25	6 21.3	6 22.3	6 03.9	2.5 1.1	8.5 3.6	14.5 6.2
26	6 21.5	6 22.5	6 04.1	2.6 1.1	8.6 3.7	14.6 6.2
27	6 21.8	6 22.8	6 04.4	2.7 1.1	8.7 3.7	14.7 6.2
28	6 22.0	6 23.0	6 04.6	2.8 1.2	8.8 3.7	14.8 6.3
29	6 22.3	6 23.3	6 04.8	2.9 1.2	8.9 3.8	14.9 6.3
30	6 22.5	6 23.5	6 05.1	3.0 1.3	9.0 3.8	15.0 6.4
31	6 22.8	6 23.8	6 05.3	3.1 1.3	9.1 3.9	15.1 6.4
32	6 23.0	6 24.0	6 05.6	3.2 1.4	9.2 3.9	15.2 6.5
33	6 23.3	6 24.3	6 05.8	3.3 1.4	9.3 4.0	15.3 6.5
34	6 23.5	6 24.5	6 06.0	3.4 1.4	9.4 4.0	15.4 6.5
35	6 23.8	6 24.8	6 06.3	3.5 1.5	9.5 4.0	15.5 6.6
36	6 24.0	6 25.1	6 06.5	3.6 1.5	9.6 4.1	15.6 6.6
37	6 24.3	6 25.3	6 06.7	3.7 1.6	9.7 4.1	15.7 6.7
38	6 24.5	6 25.6	6 07.0	3.8 1.6	9.8 4.2	15.8 6.7
39	6 24.8	6 25.8	6 07.2	3.9 1.7	9.9 4.2	15.9 6.8
40	6 25.0	6 26.1	6 07.5	4.0 1.7	10.0 4.3	16.0 6.8
41	6 25.3	6 26.3	6 07.7	4.1 1.7	10.1 4.3	16.1 6.8
42	6 25.5	6 26.6	6 07.9	4.2 1.8	10.2 4.3	16.2 6.9
43	6 25.8	6 26.8	6 08.2	4.3 1.8	10.3 4.4	16.3 6.9
44	6 26.0	6 27.1	6 08.4	4.4 1.9	10.4 4.4	16.4 7.0
45	6 26.3	6 27.3	6 08.7	4.5 1.9	10.5 4.5	16.5 7.0
46	6 26.5	6 27.6	6 08.9	4.6 2.0	10.6 4.5	16.6 7.1
47	6 26.8	6 27.8	6 09.1	4.7 2.0	10.7 4.5	16.7 7.1
48	6 27.0	6 28.1	6 09.4	4.8 2.0	10.8 4.6	16.8 7.1
49	6 27.3	6 28.3	6 09.6	4.9 2.1	10.9 4.6	16.9 7.2
50	6 27.5	6 28.6	6 09.8	5.0 2.1	11.0 4.7	17.0 7.2
51	6 27.8	6 28.8	6 10.1	5.1 2.2	11.1 4.7	17.1 7.3
52	6 28.0	6 29.1	6 10.3	5.2 2.2	11.2 4.8	17.2 7.3
53	6 28.3	6 29.3	6 10.6	5.3 2.3	11.3 4.8	17.3 7.4
54	6 28.5	6 29.6	6 10.8	5.4 2.3	11.4 4.8	17.4 7.4
55	6 28.8	6 29.8	6 11.0	5.5 2.3	11.5 4.9	17.5 7.4
56	6 29.0	6 30.1	6 11.3	5.6 2.4	11.6 4.9	17.6 7.5
57	6 29.3	6 30.3	6 11.5	5.7 2.4	11.7 5.0	17.7 7.5
58	6 29.5	6 30.6	6 11.8	5.8 2.5	11.8 5.0	17.8 7.6
59	6 29.8	6 30.8	6 12.0	5.9 2.5	11.9 5.1	17.9 7.6
60	6 30.0	6 31.1	6 12.2	6.0 2.6	12.0 5.1	18.0 7.7

© British Crown Copyright 2018. All rights reserved.

26ᵐ

m 26	SUN PLANETS	ARIES	MOON	v or d Corrⁿ	v or d Corrⁿ	v or d Corrⁿ
s	° ′	° ′	° ′	′ ′	′ ′	′ ′
00	6 30.0	6 31.1	6 12.2	0.0 0.0	6.0 2.7	12.0 5.3
01	6 30.3	6 31.3	6 12.5	0.1 0.0	6.1 2.7	12.1 5.3
02	6 30.5	6 31.6	6 12.7	0.2 0.1	6.2 2.7	12.2 5.4
03	6 30.8	6 31.8	6 12.9	0.3 0.1	6.3 2.8	12.3 5.4
04	6 31.0	6 32.1	6 13.2	0.4 0.2	6.4 2.8	12.4 5.5
05	6 31.3	6 32.3	6 13.4	0.5 0.2	6.5 2.9	12.5 5.5
06	6 31.5	6 32.6	6 13.7	0.6 0.3	6.6 2.9	12.6 5.6
07	6 31.8	6 32.8	6 13.9	0.7 0.3	6.7 3.0	12.7 5.6
08	6 32.0	6 33.1	6 14.1	0.8 0.4	6.8 3.0	12.8 5.7
09	6 32.3	6 33.3	6 14.4	0.9 0.4	6.9 3.0	12.9 5.7
10	6 32.5	6 33.6	6 14.6	1.0 0.4	7.0 3.1	13.0 5.7
11	6 32.8	6 33.8	6 14.9	1.1 0.5	7.1 3.1	13.1 5.8
12	6 33.0	6 34.1	6 15.1	1.2 0.5	7.2 3.2	13.2 5.8
13	6 33.3	6 34.3	6 15.3	1.3 0.6	7.3 3.2	13.3 5.9
14	6 33.5	6 34.6	6 15.6	1.4 0.6	7.4 3.3	13.4 5.9
15	6 33.8	6 34.8	6 15.8	1.5 0.7	7.5 3.3	13.5 6.0
16	6 34.0	6 35.1	6 16.1	1.6 0.7	7.6 3.4	13.6 6.0
17	6 34.3	6 35.3	6 16.3	1.7 0.8	7.7 3.4	13.7 6.1
18	6 34.5	6 35.6	6 16.5	1.8 0.8	7.8 3.4	13.8 6.1
19	6 34.8	6 35.8	6 16.8	1.9 0.8	7.9 3.5	13.9 6.1
20	6 35.0	6 36.1	6 17.0	2.0 0.9	8.0 3.5	14.0 6.2
21	6 35.3	6 36.3	6 17.2	2.1 0.9	8.1 3.6	14.1 6.2
22	6 35.5	6 36.6	6 17.5	2.2 1.0	8.2 3.6	14.2 6.3
23	6 35.8	6 36.8	6 17.7	2.3 1.0	8.3 3.7	14.3 6.3
24	6 36.0	6 37.1	6 18.0	2.4 1.1	8.4 3.7	14.4 6.4
25	6 36.3	6 37.3	6 18.2	2.5 1.1	8.5 3.8	14.5 6.4
26	6 36.5	6 37.6	6 18.4	2.6 1.1	8.6 3.8	14.6 6.4
27	6 36.8	6 37.8	6 18.7	2.7 1.2	8.7 3.8	14.7 6.5
28	6 37.0	6 38.1	6 18.9	2.8 1.2	8.8 3.9	14.8 6.5
29	6 37.3	6 38.3	6 19.2	2.9 1.3	8.9 3.9	14.9 6.6
30	6 37.5	6 38.6	6 19.4	3.0 1.3	9.0 4.0	15.0 6.6
31	6 37.8	6 38.8	6 19.6	3.1 1.4	9.1 4.0	15.1 6.7
32	6 38.0	6 39.1	6 19.9	3.2 1.4	9.2 4.1	15.2 6.7
33	6 38.3	6 39.3	6 20.1	3.3 1.5	9.3 4.1	15.3 6.8
34	6 38.5	6 39.6	6 20.3	3.4 1.5	9.4 4.2	15.4 6.8
35	6 38.8	6 39.8	6 20.6	3.5 1.5	9.5 4.2	15.5 6.8
36	6 39.0	6 40.1	6 20.8	3.6 1.6	9.6 4.2	15.6 6.9
37	6 39.3	6 40.3	6 21.1	3.7 1.6	9.7 4.3	15.7 6.9
38	6 39.5	6 40.6	6 21.3	3.8 1.7	9.8 4.3	15.8 7.0
39	6 39.8	6 40.8	6 21.5	3.9 1.7	9.9 4.4	15.9 7.0
40	6 40.0	6 41.1	6 21.8	4.0 1.8	10.0 4.4	16.0 7.1
41	6 40.3	6 41.3	6 22.0	4.1 1.8	10.1 4.5	16.1 7.1
42	6 40.5	6 41.6	6 22.3	4.2 1.9	10.2 4.5	16.2 7.2
43	6 40.8	6 41.8	6 22.5	4.3 1.9	10.3 4.5	16.3 7.2
44	6 41.0	6 42.1	6 22.7	4.4 1.9	10.4 4.6	16.4 7.2
45	6 41.3	6 42.3	6 23.0	4.5 2.0	10.5 4.6	16.5 7.3
46	6 41.5	6 42.6	6 23.2	4.6 2.0	10.6 4.7	16.6 7.3
47	6 41.8	6 42.8	6 23.4	4.7 2.1	10.7 4.7	16.7 7.4
48	6 42.0	6 43.1	6 23.7	4.8 2.1	10.8 4.8	16.8 7.4
49	6 42.3	6 43.4	6 23.9	4.9 2.2	10.9 4.8	16.9 7.5
50	6 42.5	6 43.6	6 24.2	5.0 2.2	11.0 4.9	17.0 7.5
51	6 42.8	6 43.9	6 24.4	5.1 2.3	11.1 4.9	17.1 7.6
52	6 43.0	6 44.1	6 24.6	5.2 2.3	11.2 4.9	17.2 7.6
53	6 43.3	6 44.4	6 24.9	5.3 2.3	11.3 5.0	17.3 7.6
54	6 43.5	6 44.6	6 25.1	5.4 2.4	11.4 5.0	17.4 7.7
55	6 43.8	6 44.9	6 25.4	5.5 2.4	11.5 5.1	17.5 7.7
56	6 44.0	6 45.1	6 25.6	5.6 2.5	11.6 5.1	17.6 7.8
57	6 44.3	6 45.4	6 25.8	5.7 2.5	11.7 5.2	17.7 7.8
58	6 44.5	6 45.6	6 26.1	5.8 2.6	11.8 5.2	17.8 7.9
59	6 44.8	6 45.9	6 26.3	5.9 2.6	11.9 5.3	17.9 7.9
60	6 45.0	6 46.1	6 26.6	6.0 2.7	12.0 5.3	18.0 8.0

27ᵐ

m 27	SUN PLANETS	ARIES	MOON	v or d Corrⁿ	v or d Corrⁿ	v or d Corrⁿ
s	° ′	° ′	° ′	′ ′	′ ′	′ ′
00	6 45.0	6 46.1	6 26.6	0.0 0.0	6.0 2.8	12.0 5.5
01	6 45.3	6 46.4	6 26.8	0.1 0.0	6.1 2.8	12.1 5.5
02	6 45.5	6 46.6	6 27.0	0.2 0.1	6.2 2.8	12.2 5.6
03	6 45.8	6 46.9	6 27.3	0.3 0.1	6.3 2.9	12.3 5.6
04	6 46.0	6 47.1	6 27.5	0.4 0.2	6.4 2.9	12.4 5.7
05	6 46.3	6 47.4	6 27.7	0.5 0.2	6.5 3.0	12.5 5.7
06	6 46.5	6 47.6	6 28.0	0.6 0.3	6.6 3.0	12.6 5.8
07	6 46.8	6 47.9	6 28.2	0.7 0.3	6.7 3.1	12.7 5.8
08	6 47.0	6 48.1	6 28.5	0.8 0.4	6.8 3.1	12.8 5.9
09	6 47.3	6 48.4	6 28.7	0.9 0.4	6.9 3.2	12.9 5.9
10	6 47.5	6 48.6	6 28.9	1.0 0.5	7.0 3.2	13.0 6.0
11	6 47.8	6 48.9	6 29.2	1.1 0.5	7.1 3.3	13.1 6.0
12	6 48.0	6 49.1	6 29.4	1.2 0.6	7.2 3.3	13.2 6.1
13	6 48.3	6 49.4	6 29.7	1.3 0.6	7.3 3.3	13.3 6.1
14	6 48.5	6 49.6	6 29.9	1.4 0.6	7.4 3.4	13.4 6.1
15	6 48.8	6 49.9	6 30.1	1.5 0.7	7.5 3.4	13.5 6.2
16	6 49.0	6 50.1	6 30.4	1.6 0.7	7.6 3.5	13.6 6.2
17	6 49.3	6 50.4	6 30.6	1.7 0.8	7.7 3.5	13.7 6.3
18	6 49.5	6 50.6	6 30.8	1.8 0.8	7.8 3.6	13.8 6.3
19	6 49.8	6 50.9	6 31.1	1.9 0.9	7.9 3.6	13.9 6.4
20	6 50.0	6 51.1	6 31.3	2.0 0.9	8.0 3.7	14.0 6.4
21	6 50.3	6 51.4	6 31.6	2.1 1.0	8.1 3.7	14.1 6.5
22	6 50.5	6 51.6	6 31.8	2.2 1.0	8.2 3.8	14.2 6.5
23	6 50.8	6 51.9	6 32.0	2.3 1.1	8.3 3.8	14.3 6.6
24	6 51.0	6 52.1	6 32.3	2.4 1.1	8.4 3.9	14.4 6.6
25	6 51.3	6 52.4	6 32.5	2.5 1.1	8.5 3.9	14.5 6.6
26	6 51.5	6 52.6	6 32.8	2.6 1.2	8.6 3.9	14.6 6.7
27	6 51.8	6 52.9	6 33.0	2.7 1.2	8.7 4.0	14.7 6.7
28	6 52.0	6 53.1	6 33.2	2.8 1.3	8.8 4.0	14.8 6.8
29	6 52.3	6 53.4	6 33.5	2.9 1.3	8.9 4.1	14.9 6.8
30	6 52.5	6 53.6	6 33.7	3.0 1.4	9.0 4.1	15.0 6.9
31	6 52.8	6 53.9	6 33.9	3.1 1.4	9.1 4.2	15.1 6.9
32	6 53.0	6 54.1	6 34.2	3.2 1.5	9.2 4.2	15.2 7.0
33	6 53.3	6 54.4	6 34.4	3.3 1.5	9.3 4.3	15.3 7.0
34	6 53.5	6 54.6	6 34.7	3.4 1.6	9.4 4.3	15.4 7.1
35	6 53.8	6 54.9	6 34.9	3.5 1.6	9.5 4.4	15.5 7.1
36	6 54.0	6 55.1	6 35.1	3.6 1.7	9.6 4.4	15.6 7.2
37	6 54.3	6 55.4	6 35.4	3.7 1.7	9.7 4.4	15.7 7.2
38	6 54.5	6 55.6	6 35.6	3.8 1.7	9.8 4.5	15.8 7.2
39	6 54.8	6 55.9	6 35.9	3.9 1.8	9.9 4.5	15.9 7.3
40	6 55.0	6 56.1	6 36.1	4.0 1.8	10.0 4.6	16.0 7.3
41	6 55.3	6 56.4	6 36.3	4.1 1.9	10.1 4.6	16.1 7.4
42	6 55.5	6 56.6	6 36.6	4.2 1.9	10.2 4.7	16.2 7.4
43	6 55.8	6 56.9	6 36.8	4.3 2.0	10.3 4.7	16.3 7.5
44	6 56.0	6 57.1	6 37.0	4.4 2.0	10.4 4.8	16.4 7.5
45	6 56.3	6 57.4	6 37.3	4.5 2.1	10.5 4.8	16.5 7.6
46	6 56.5	6 57.6	6 37.5	4.6 2.1	10.6 4.9	16.6 7.6
47	6 56.8	6 57.9	6 37.8	4.7 2.2	10.7 4.9	16.7 7.7
48	6 57.0	6 58.1	6 38.0	4.8 2.2	10.8 5.0	16.8 7.7
49	6 57.3	6 58.4	6 38.2	4.9 2.2	10.9 5.0	16.9 7.7
50	6 57.5	6 58.6	6 38.5	5.0 2.3	11.0 5.0	17.0 7.8
51	6 57.8	6 58.9	6 38.7	5.1 2.3	11.1 5.1	17.1 7.8
52	6 58.0	6 59.1	6 39.0	5.2 2.4	11.2 5.1	17.2 7.9
53	6 58.3	6 59.4	6 39.2	5.3 2.4	11.3 5.2	17.3 7.9
54	6 58.5	6 59.6	6 39.4	5.4 2.5	11.4 5.2	17.4 8.0
55	6 58.8	6 59.9	6 39.7	5.5 2.5	11.5 5.3	17.5 8.0
56	6 59.0	7 00.1	6 39.9	5.6 2.6	11.6 5.3	17.6 8.1
57	6 59.3	7 00.4	6 40.2	5.7 2.6	11.7 5.4	17.7 8.1
58	6 59.5	7 00.6	6 40.4	5.8 2.7	11.8 5.4	17.8 8.2
59	6 59.8	7 00.9	6 40.6	5.9 2.7	11.9 5.5	17.9 8.2
60	7 00.0	7 01.1	6 40.9	6.0 2.8	12.0 5.5	18.0 8.3

© British Crown Copyright 2018. All rights reserved.

28ᵐ

28 s	SUN PLANETS	ARIES	MOON	v or Corrn d		v or Corrn d		v or Corrn d	
00	7 00·0	7 01·1	6 40·9	0·0	0·0	6·0	2·9	12·0	5·7
01	7 00·3	7 01·4	6 41·1	0·1	0·0	6·1	2·9	12·1	5·7
02	7 00·5	7 01·7	6 41·3	0·2	0·1	6·2	2·9	12·2	5·8
03	7 00·8	7 01·9	6 41·6	0·3	0·1	6·3	3·0	12·3	5·8
04	7 01·0	7 02·2	6 41·8	0·4	0·2	6·4	3·0	12·4	5·9
05	7 01·3	7 02·4	6 42·1	0·5	0·2	6·5	3·1	12·5	5·9
06	7 01·5	7 02·7	6 42·3	0·6	0·3	6·6	3·1	12·6	6·0
07	7 01·8	7 02·9	6 42·5	0·7	0·3	6·7	3·2	12·7	6·0
08	7 02·0	7 03·2	6 42·8	0·8	0·4	6·8	3·2	12·8	6·1
09	7 02·3	7 03·4	6 43·0	0·9	0·4	6·9	3·3	12·9	6·1
10	7 02·5	7 03·7	6 43·3	1·0	0·5	7·0	3·3	13·0	6·2
11	7 02·8	7 03·9	6 43·5	1·1	0·5	7·1	3·4	13·1	6·2
12	7 03·0	7 04·2	6 43·7	1·2	0·6	7·2	3·4	13·2	6·3
13	7 03·3	7 04·4	6 44·0	1·3	0·6	7·3	3·5	13·3	6·3
14	7 03·5	7 04·7	6 44·2	1·4	0·7	7·4	3·5	13·4	6·4
15	7 03·8	7 04·9	6 44·4	1·5	0·7	7·5	3·6	13·5	6·4
16	7 04·0	7 05·2	6 44·7	1·6	0·8	7·6	3·6	13·6	6·5
17	7 04·3	7 05·4	6 44·9	1·7	0·8	7·7	3·7	13·7	6·5
18	7 04·5	7 05·7	6 45·2	1·8	0·9	7·8	3·7	13·8	6·6
19	7 04·8	7 05·9	6 45·4	1·9	0·9	7·9	3·8	13·9	6·6
20	7 05·0	7 06·2	6 45·6	2·0	1·0	8·0	3·8	14·0	6·7
21	7 05·3	7 06·4	6 45·9	2·1	1·0	8·1	3·8	14·1	6·7
22	7 05·5	7 06·7	6 46·1	2·2	1·0	8·2	3·9	14·2	6·7
23	7 05·8	7 06·9	6 46·4	2·3	1·1	8·3	3·9	14·3	6·8
24	7 06·0	7 07·2	6 46·6	2·4	1·1	8·4	4·0	14·4	6·8
25	7 06·3	7 07·4	6 46·8	2·5	1·2	8·5	4·0	14·5	6·9
26	7 06·5	7 07·7	6 47·1	2·6	1·2	8·6	4·1	14·6	6·9
27	7 06·8	7 07·9	6 47·3	2·7	1·3	8·7	4·1	14·7	7·0
28	7 07·0	7 08·2	6 47·5	2·8	1·3	8·8	4·2	14·8	7·0
29	7 07·3	7 08·4	6 47·8	2·9	1·4	8·9	4·2	14·9	7·1
30	7 07·5	7 08·7	6 48·0	3·0	1·4	9·0	4·3	15·0	7·1
31	7 07·8	7 08·9	6 48·3	3·1	1·5	9·1	4·3	15·1	7·2
32	7 08·0	7 09·2	6 48·5	3·2	1·5	9·2	4·4	15·2	7·2
33	7 08·3	7 09·4	6 48·7	3·3	1·6	9·3	4·4	15·3	7·3
34	7 08·5	7 09·7	6 49·0	3·4	1·6	9·4	4·5	15·4	7·3
35	7 08·8	7 09·9	6 49·2	3·5	1·7	9·5	4·5	15·5	7·4
36	7 09·0	7 10·2	6 49·5	3·6	1·7	9·6	4·6	15·6	7·4
37	7 09·3	7 10·4	6 49·7	3·7	1·8	9·7	4·6	15·7	7·5
38	7 09·5	7 10·7	6 49·9	3·8	1·8	9·8	4·7	15·8	7·5
39	7 09·8	7 10·9	6 50·2	3·9	1·9	9·9	4·7	15·9	7·6
40	7 10·0	7 11·2	6 50·4	4·0	1·9	10·0	4·8	16·0	7·6
41	7 10·3	7 11·4	6 50·6	4·1	1·9	10·1	4·8	16·1	7·7
42	7 10·5	7 11·7	6 50·9	4·2	2·0	10·2	4·8	16·2	7·7
43	7 10·8	7 11·9	6 51·1	4·3	2·0	10·3	4·9	16·3	7·7
44	7 11·0	7 12·2	6 51·4	4·4	2·1	10·4	4·9	16·4	7·8
45	7 11·3	7 12·4	6 51·6	4·5	2·1	10·5	5·0	16·5	7·8
46	7 11·5	7 12·7	6 51·8	4·6	2·2	10·6	5·0	16·6	7·9
47	7 11·8	7 12·9	6 52·1	4·7	2·2	10·7	5·1	16·7	7·9
48	7 12·0	7 13·2	6 52·3	4·8	2·3	10·8	5·1	16·8	8·0
49	7 12·3	7 13·4	6 52·6	4·9	2·3	10·9	5·2	16·9	8·0
50	7 12·5	7 13·7	6 52·8	5·0	2·4	11·0	5·2	17·0	8·1
51	7 12·8	7 13·9	6 53·0	5·1	2·4	11·1	5·3	17·1	8·1
52	7 13·0	7 14·2	6 53·3	5·2	2·5	11·2	5·3	17·2	8·2
53	7 13·3	7 14·4	6 53·5	5·3	2·5	11·3	5·4	17·3	8·2
54	7 13·5	7 14·7	6 53·8	5·4	2·6	11·4	5·4	17·4	8·3
55	7 13·8	7 14·9	6 54·0	5·5	2·6	11·5	5·5	17·5	8·3
56	7 14·0	7 15·2	6 54·2	5·6	2·7	11·6	5·5	17·6	8·4
57	7 14·3	7 15·4	6 54·5	5·7	2·7	11·7	5·6	17·7	8·4
58	7 14·5	7 15·7	6 54·7	5·8	2·8	11·8	5·6	17·8	8·5
59	7 14·8	7 15·9	6 54·9	5·9	2·8	11·9	5·7	17·9	8·5
60	7 15·0	7 16·2	6 55·2	6·0	2·9	12·0	5·7	18·0	8·6

29ᵐ

29 s	SUN PLANETS	ARIES	MOON	v or Corrn d		v or Corrn d		v or Corrn d	
00	7 15·0	7 16·2	6 55·2	0·0	0·0	6·0	3·0	12·0	5·9
01	7 15·3	7 16·4	6 55·4	0·1	0·0	6·1	3·0	12·1	5·9
02	7 15·5	7 16·7	6 55·7	0·2	0·1	6·2	3·0	12·2	6·0
03	7 15·8	7 16·9	6 55·9	0·3	0·1	6·3	3·1	12·3	6·0
04	7 16·0	7 17·2	6 56·1	0·4	0·2	6·4	3·1	12·4	6·1
05	7 16·3	7 17·4	6 56·4	0·5	0·2	6·5	3·2	12·5	6·1
06	7 16·5	7 17·7	6 56·6	0·6	0·3	6·6	3·2	12·6	6·2
07	7 16·8	7 17·9	6 56·9	0·7	0·3	6·7	3·3	12·7	6·2
08	7 17·0	7 18·2	6 57·1	0·8	0·4	6·8	3·3	12·8	6·3
09	7 17·3	7 18·4	6 57·3	0·9	0·4	6·9	3·4	12·9	6·3
10	7 17·5	7 18·7	6 57·6	1·0	0·5	7·0	3·4	13·0	6·4
11	7 17·8	7 18·9	6 57·8	1·1	0·5	7·1	3·5	13·1	6·4
12	7 18·0	7 19·2	6 58·0	1·2	0·6	7·2	3·5	13·2	6·5
13	7 18·3	7 19·4	6 58·3	1·3	0·6	7·3	3·6	13·3	6·5
14	7 18·5	7 19·7	6 58·5	1·4	0·7	7·4	3·6	13·4	6·6
15	7 18·8	7 20·0	6 58·8	1·5	0·7	7·5	3·7	13·5	6·6
16	7 19·0	7 20·2	6 59·0	1·6	0·8	7·6	3·7	13·6	6·7
17	7 19·3	7 20·5	6 59·2	1·7	0·8	7·7	3·8	13·7	6·7
18	7 19·5	7 20·7	6 59·5	1·8	0·9	7·8	3·8	13·8	6·8
19	7 19·8	7 21·0	6 59·7	1·9	0·9	7·9	3·9	13·9	6·8
20	7 20·0	7 21·2	7 00·0	2·0	1·0	8·0	3·9	14·0	6·9
21	7 20·3	7 21·5	7 00·2	2·1	1·0	8·1	4·0	14·1	6·9
22	7 20·5	7 21·7	7 00·4	2·2	1·1	8·2	4·0	14·2	7·0
23	7 20·8	7 22·0	7 00·7	2·3	1·1	8·3	4·1	14·3	7·0
24	7 21·0	7 22·2	7 00·9	2·4	1·2	8·4	4·1	14·4	7·1
25	7 21·3	7 22·5	7 01·1	2·5	1·2	8·5	4·2	14·5	7·1
26	7 21·5	7 22·7	7 01·4	2·6	1·3	8·6	4·2	14·6	7·2
27	7 21·8	7 23·0	7 01·6	2·7	1·3	8·7	4·3	14·7	7·2
28	7 22·0	7 23·2	7 01·9	2·8	1·4	8·8	4·3	14·8	7·3
29	7 22·3	7 23·5	7 02·1	2·9	1·4	8·9	4·4	14·9	7·3
30	7 22·5	7 23·7	7 02·3	3·0	1·5	9·0	4·4	15·0	7·4
31	7 22·8	7 24·0	7 02·6	3·1	1·5	9·1	4·5	15·1	7·4
32	7 23·0	7 24·2	7 02·8	3·2	1·6	9·2	4·5	15·2	7·5
33	7 23·3	7 24·5	7 03·1	3·3	1·6	9·3	4·6	15·3	7·5
34	7 23·5	7 24·7	7 03·3	3·4	1·7	9·4	4·6	15·4	7·6
35	7 23·8	7 25·0	7 03·5	3·5	1·7	9·5	4·7	15·5	7·6
36	7 24·0	7 25·2	7 03·8	3·6	1·8	9·6	4·7	15·6	7·7
37	7 24·3	7 25·5	7 04·0	3·7	1·8	9·7	4·8	15·7	7·7
38	7 24·5	7 25·7	7 04·3	3·8	1·9	9·8	4·8	15·8	7·8
39	7 24·8	7 26·0	7 04·5	3·9	1·9	9·9	4·9	15·9	7·8
40	7 25·0	7 26·2	7 04·7	4·0	2·0	10·0	4·9	16·0	7·9
41	7 25·3	7 26·5	7 05·0	4·1	2·0	10·1	5·0	16·1	7·9
42	7 25·5	7 26·7	7 05·2	4·2	2·1	10·2	5·0	16·2	8·0
43	7 25·8	7 27·0	7 05·4	4·3	2·1	10·3	5·1	16·3	8·0
44	7 26·0	7 27·2	7 05·7	4·4	2·2	10·4	5·1	16·4	8·1
45	7 26·3	7 27·5	7 05·9	4·5	2·2	10·5	5·2	16·5	8·1
46	7 26·5	7 27·7	7 06·2	4·6	2·3	10·6	5·2	16·6	8·2
47	7 26·8	7 28·0	7 06·4	4·7	2·3	10·7	5·3	16·7	8·2
48	7 27·0	7 28·2	7 06·6	4·8	2·4	10·8	5·3	16·8	8·3
49	7 27·3	7 28·5	7 06·9	4·9	2·4	10·9	5·4	16·9	8·3
50	7 27·5	7 28·7	7 07·1	5·0	2·5	11·0	5·4	17·0	8·4
51	7 27·8	7 29·0	7 07·4	5·1	2·5	11·1	5·5	17·1	8·4
52	7 28·0	7 29·2	7 07·6	5·2	2·6	11·2	5·5	17·2	8·5
53	7 28·3	7 29·5	7 07·8	5·3	2·6	11·3	5·6	17·3	8·5
54	7 28·5	7 29·7	7 08·1	5·4	2·7	11·4	5·6	17·4	8·6
55	7 28·8	7 30·0	7 08·3	5·5	2·7	11·5	5·7	17·5	8·6
56	7 29·0	7 30·2	7 08·5	5·6	2·8	11·6	5·7	17·6	8·7
57	7 29·3	7 30·5	7 08·8	5·7	2·8	11·7	5·8	17·7	8·7
58	7 29·5	7 30·7	7 09·0	5·8	2·9	11·8	5·8	17·8	8·8
59	7 29·8	7 31·0	7 09·3	5·9	2·9	11·9	5·9	17·9	8·8
60	7 30·0	7 31·2	7 09·5	6·0	3·0	12·0	5·9	18·0	8·9

© British Crown Copyright 2018. All rights reserved.

30ᵐ

30 s	SUN PLANETS	ARIES	MOON	v or Corrⁿ d	v or Corrⁿ d	v or Corrⁿ d
00	7 30·0	7 31·2	7 09·5	0·0 0·0	6·0 3·1	12·0 6·1
01	7 30·3	7 31·5	7 09·7	0·1 0·1	6·1 3·1	12·1 6·2
02	7 30·5	7 31·7	7 10·0	0·2 0·1	6·2 3·2	12·2 6·2
03	7 30·8	7 32·0	7 10·2	0·3 0·2	6·3 3·2	12·3 6·3
04	7 31·0	7 32·2	7 10·5	0·4 0·2	6·4 3·3	12·4 6·3
05	7 31·3	7 32·5	7 10·7	0·5 0·3	6·5 3·3	12·5 6·4
06	7 31·5	7 32·7	7 10·9	0·6 0·3	6·6 3·4	12·6 6·4
07	7 31·8	7 33·0	7 11·2	0·7 0·4	6·7 3·4	12·7 6·5
08	7 32·0	7 33·2	7 11·4	0·8 0·4	6·8 3·5	12·8 6·5
09	7 32·3	7 33·5	7 11·6	0·9 0·5	6·9 3·5	12·9 6·6
10	7 32·5	7 33·7	7 11·9	1·0 0·5	7·0 3·6	13·0 6·6
11	7 32·8	7 34·0	7 12·1	1·1 0·6	7·1 3·6	13·1 6·7
12	7 33·0	7 34·2	7 12·4	1·2 0·6	7·2 3·7	13·2 6·7
13	7 33·3	7 34·5	7 12·6	1·3 0·7	7·3 3·7	13·3 6·8
14	7 33·5	7 34·7	7 12·8	1·4 0·7	7·4 3·8	13·4 6·8
15	7 33·8	7 35·0	7 13·1	1·5 0·8	7·5 3·8	13·5 6·9
16	7 34·0	7 35·2	7 13·3	1·6 0·8	7·6 3·9	13·6 6·9
17	7 34·3	7 35·5	7 13·6	1·7 0·9	7·7 3·9	13·7 7·0
18	7 34·5	7 35·7	7 13·8	1·8 0·9	7·8 4·0	13·8 7·0
19	7 34·8	7 36·0	7 14·0	1·9 1·0	7·9 4·0	13·9 7·1
20	7 35·0	7 36·2	7 14·3	2·0 1·0	8·0 4·1	14·0 7·1
21	7 35·3	7 36·5	7 14·5	2·1 1·1	8·1 4·1	14·1 7·2
22	7 35·5	7 36·7	7 14·7	2·2 1·1	8·2 4·2	14·2 7·2
23	7 35·8	7 37·0	7 15·0	2·3 1·2	8·3 4·2	14·3 7·3
24	7 36·0	7 37·2	7 15·2	2·4 1·2	8·4 4·3	14·4 7·3
25	7 36·3	7 37·5	7 15·5	2·5 1·3	8·5 4·3	14·5 7·4
26	7 36·5	7 37·7	7 15·7	2·6 1·3	8·6 4·4	14·6 7·4
27	7 36·8	7 38·0	7 15·9	2·7 1·4	8·7 4·4	14·7 7·5
28	7 37·0	7 38·3	7 16·2	2·8 1·4	8·8 4·5	14·8 7·5
29	7 37·3	7 38·5	7 16·4	2·9 1·5	8·9 4·5	14·9 7·6
30	7 37·5	7 38·8	7 16·7	3·0 1·5	9·0 4·6	15·0 7·6
31	7 37·8	7 39·0	7 16·9	3·1 1·6	9·1 4·6	15·1 7·7
32	7 38·0	7 39·3	7 17·1	3·2 1·6	9·2 4·7	15·2 7·7
33	7 38·3	7 39·5	7 17·4	3·3 1·7	9·3 4·7	15·3 7·8
34	7 38·5	7 39·8	7 17·6	3·4 1·7	9·4 4·8	15·4 7·8
35	7 38·8	7 40·0	7 17·9	3·5 1·8	9·5 4·8	15·5 7·9
36	7 39·0	7 40·3	7 18·1	3·6 1·8	9·6 4·9	15·6 7·9
37	7 39·3	7 40·5	7 18·3	3·7 1·9	9·7 4·9	15·7 8·0
38	7 39·5	7 40·8	7 18·6	3·8 1·9	9·8 5·0	15·8 8·0
39	7 39·8	7 41·0	7 18·8	3·9 2·0	9·9 5·0	15·9 8·1
40	7 40·0	7 41·3	7 19·0	4·0 2·0	10·0 5·1	16·0 8·1
41	7 40·3	7 41·5	7 19·3	4·1 2·1	10·1 5·1	16·1 8·2
42	7 40·5	7 41·8	7 19·5	4·2 2·1	10·2 5·2	16·2 8·2
43	7 40·8	7 42·0	7 19·8	4·3 2·2	10·3 5·2	16·3 8·3
44	7 41·0	7 42·3	7 20·0	4·4 2·2	10·4 5·3	16·4 8·3
45	7 41·3	7 42·5	7 20·2	4·5 2·3	10·5 5·3	16·5 8·4
46	7 41·5	7 42·8	7 20·5	4·6 2·3	10·6 5·4	16·6 8·4
47	7 41·8	7 43·0	7 20·7	4·7 2·4	10·7 5·4	16·7 8·5
48	7 42·0	7 43·3	7 21·0	4·8 2·4	10·8 5·5	16·8 8·5
49	7 42·3	7 43·5	7 21·2	4·9 2·5	10·9 5·5	16·9 8·6
50	7 42·5	7 43·8	7 21·4	5·0 2·5	11·0 5·6	17·0 8·6
51	7 42·8	7 44·0	7 21·7	5·1 2·6	11·1 5·6	17·1 8·7
52	7 43·0	7 44·3	7 21·9	5·2 2·6	11·2 5·7	17·2 8·7
53	7 43·3	7 44·5	7 22·1	5·3 2·7	11·3 5·7	17·3 8·8
54	7 43·5	7 44·8	7 22·4	5·4 2·7	11·4 5·8	17·4 8·8
55	7 43·8	7 45·0	7 22·6	5·5 2·8	11·5 5·8	17·5 8·9
56	7 44·0	7 45·3	7 22·9	5·6 2·8	11·6 5·9	17·6 8·9
57	7 44·3	7 45·5	7 23·1	5·7 2·9	11·7 5·9	17·7 9·0
58	7 44·5	7 45·8	7 23·3	5·8 2·9	11·8 6·0	17·8 9·0
59	7 44·8	7 46·0	7 23·6	5·9 3·0	11·9 6·0	17·9 9·1
60	7 45·0	7 46·3	7 23·8	6·0 3·1	12·0 6·1	18·0 9·2

31ᵐ

31 s	SUN PLANETS	ARIES	MOON	v or Corrⁿ d	v or Corrⁿ d	v or Corrⁿ d
00	7 45·0	7 46·3	7 23·8	0·0 0·0	6·0 3·2	12·0 6·3
01	7 45·3	7 46·5	7 24·1	0·1 0·1	6·1 3·2	12·1 6·4
02	7 45·5	7 46·8	7 24·3	0·2 0·1	6·2 3·3	12·2 6·4
03	7 45·8	7 47·0	7 24·5	0·3 0·2	6·3 3·3	12·3 6·5
04	7 46·0	7 47·3	7 24·8	0·4 0·2	6·4 3·4	12·4 6·5
05	7 46·3	7 47·5	7 25·0	0·5 0·3	6·5 3·4	12·5 6·6
06	7 46·5	7 47·8	7 25·2	0·6 0·3	6·6 3·5	12·6 6·6
07	7 46·8	7 48·0	7 25·5	0·7 0·4	6·7 3·5	12·7 6·7
08	7 47·0	7 48·3	7 25·7	0·8 0·4	6·8 3·6	12·8 6·7
09	7 47·3	7 48·5	7 26·0	0·9 0·5	6·9 3·6	12·9 6·8
10	7 47·5	7 48·8	7 26·2	1·0 0·5	7·0 3·7	13·0 6·8
11	7 47·8	7 49·0	7 26·4	1·1 0·6	7·1 3·7	13·1 6·9
12	7 48·0	7 49·3	7 26·7	1·2 0·6	7·2 3·8	13·2 6·9
13	7 48·3	7 49·5	7 26·9	1·3 0·7	7·3 3·8	13·3 7·0
14	7 48·5	7 49·8	7 27·2	1·4 0·7	7·4 3·9	13·4 7·0
15	7 48·8	7 50·0	7 27·4	1·5 0·8	7·5 3·9	13·5 7·1
16	7 49·0	7 50·3	7 27·6	1·6 0·8	7·6 4·0	13·6 7·1
17	7 49·3	7 50·5	7 27·9	1·7 0·9	7·7 4·0	13·7 7·2
18	7 49·5	7 50·8	7 28·1	1·8 0·9	7·8 4·1	13·8 7·2
19	7 49·8	7 51·0	7 28·4	1·9 1·0	7·9 4·1	13·9 7·3
20	7 50·0	7 51·3	7 28·6	2·0 1·1	8·0 4·2	14·0 7·4
21	7 50·3	7 51·5	7 28·8	2·1 1·1	8·1 4·3	14·1 7·4
22	7 50·5	7 51·8	7 29·1	2·2 1·2	8·2 4·3	14·2 7·5
23	7 50·8	7 52·0	7 29·3	2·3 1·2	8·3 4·4	14·3 7·5
24	7 51·0	7 52·3	7 29·5	2·4 1·3	8·4 4·4	14·4 7·6
25	7 51·3	7 52·5	7 29·8	2·5 1·3	8·5 4·5	14·5 7·6
26	7 51·5	7 52·8	7 30·0	2·6 1·4	8·6 4·5	14·6 7·7
27	7 51·8	7 53·0	7 30·3	2·7 1·4	8·7 4·6	14·7 7·7
28	7 52·0	7 53·3	7 30·5	2·8 1·5	8·8 4·6	14·8 7·8
29	7 52·3	7 53·5	7 30·7	2·9 1·5	8·9 4·7	14·9 7·8
30	7 52·5	7 53·8	7 31·0	3·0 1·6	9·0 4·7	15·0 7·9
31	7 52·8	7 54·0	7 31·2	3·1 1·6	9·1 4·8	15·1 7·9
32	7 53·0	7 54·3	7 31·5	3·2 1·7	9·2 4·8	15·2 8·0
33	7 53·3	7 54·5	7 31·7	3·3 1·7	9·3 4·9	15·3 8·0
34	7 53·5	7 54·8	7 31·9	3·4 1·8	9·4 4·9	15·4 8·1
35	7 53·8	7 55·0	7 32·2	3·5 1·8	9·5 5·0	15·5 8·1
36	7 54·0	7 55·3	7 32·4	3·6 1·9	9·6 5·0	15·6 8·2
37	7 54·3	7 55·5	7 32·6	3·7 1·9	9·7 5·1	15·7 8·2
38	7 54·5	7 55·8	7 32·9	3·8 2·0	9·8 5·1	15·8 8·3
39	7 54·8	7 56·0	7 33·1	3·9 2·0	9·9 5·2	15·9 8·3
40	7 55·0	7 56·3	7 33·4	4·0 2·1	10·0 5·3	16·0 8·4
41	7 55·3	7 56·6	7 33·6	4·1 2·2	10·1 5·3	16·1 8·5
42	7 55·5	7 56·8	7 33·8	4·2 2·2	10·2 5·4	16·2 8·5
43	7 55·8	7 57·1	7 34·1	4·3 2·3	10·3 5·4	16·3 8·6
44	7 56·0	7 57·3	7 34·3	4·4 2·3	10·4 5·5	16·4 8·6
45	7 56·3	7 57·6	7 34·6	4·5 2·4	10·5 5·5	16·5 8·7
46	7 56·5	7 57·8	7 34·8	4·6 2·4	10·6 5·6	16·6 8·7
47	7 56·8	7 58·1	7 35·0	4·7 2·5	10·7 5·6	16·7 8·8
48	7 57·0	7 58·3	7 35·3	4·8 2·5	10·8 5·7	16·8 8·8
49	7 57·3	7 58·6	7 35·5	4·9 2·6	10·9 5·7	16·9 8·9
50	7 57·5	7 58·8	7 35·7	5·0 2·6	11·0 5·8	17·0 8·9
51	7 57·8	7 59·1	7 36·0	5·1 2·7	11·1 5·8	17·1 9·0
52	7 58·0	7 59·3	7 36·2	5·2 2·7	11·2 5·9	17·2 9·0
53	7 58·3	7 59·6	7 36·5	5·3 2·8	11·3 5·9	17·3 9·1
54	7 58·5	7 59·8	7 36·7	5·4 2·8	11·4 6·0	17·4 9·1
55	7 58·8	8 00·1	7 36·9	5·5 2·9	11·5 6·0	17·5 9·2
56	7 59·0	8 00·3	7 37·2	5·6 2·9	11·6 6·1	17·6 9·2
57	7 59·3	8 00·6	7 37·4	5·7 3·0	11·7 6·1	17·7 9·3
58	7 59·5	8 00·8	7 37·7	5·8 3·0	11·8 6·2	17·8 9·3
59	7 59·8	8 01·1	7 37·9	5·9 3·1	11·9 6·2	17·9 9·4
60	8 00·0	8 01·3	7 38·1	6·0 3·2	12·0 6·3	18·0 9·5

© British Crown Copyright 2018. All rights reserved.

32ᵐ

32	SUN PLANETS	ARIES	MOON	v or Corrⁿ d	v or Corrⁿ d	v or Corrⁿ d
s	° ′	° ′	° ′	′ ′	′ ′	′ ′
00	8 00·0	8 01·3	7 38·1	0·0 0·0	6·0 3·3	12·0 6·5
01	8 00·3	8 01·6	7 38·4	0·1 0·1	6·1 3·3	12·1 6·6
02	8 00·5	8 01·8	7 38·6	0·2 0·1	6·2 3·4	12·2 6·8
03	8 00·8	8 02·1	7 38·8	0·3 0·2	6·3 3·4	12·3 6·7
04	8 01·0	8 02·3	7 39·1	0·4 0·2	6·4 3·5	12·4 6·7
05	8 01·3	8 02·6	7 39·3	0·5 0·3	6·5 3·5	12·5 6·8
06	8 01·5	8 02·8	7 39·6	0·6 0·3	6·6 3·6	12·6 6·8
07	8 01·8	8 03·1	7 39·8	0·7 0·4	6·7 3·6	12·7 6·9
08	8 02·0	8 03·3	7 40·0	0·8 0·4	6·8 3·7	12·8 6·9
09	8 02·3	8 03·6	7 40·3	0·9 0·5	6·9 3·7	12·9 7·0
10	8 02·5	8 03·8	7 40·5	1·0 0·5	7·0 3·8	13·0 7·0
11	8 02·8	8 04·1	7 40·8	1·1 0·6	7·1 3·8	13·1 7·1
12	8 03·0	8 04·3	7 41·0	1·2 0·7	7·2 3·9	13·2 7·2
13	8 03·3	8 04·6	7 41·2	1·3 0·7	7·3 4·0	13·3 7·2
14	8 03·5	8 04·8	7 41·5	1·4 0·8	7·4 4·0	13·4 7·3
15	8 03·8	8 05·1	7 41·7	1·5 0·8	7·5 4·1	13·5 7·3
16	8 04·0	8 05·3	7 42·0	1·6 0·9	7·6 4·1	13·6 7·4
17	8 04·3	8 05·6	7 42·2	1·7 0·9	7·7 4·2	13·7 7·4
18	8 04·5	8 05·8	7 42·4	1·8 1·0	7·8 4·2	13·8 7·5
19	8 04·8	8 06·1	7 42·7	1·9 1·0	7·9 4·3	13·9 7·5
20	8 05·0	8 06·3	7 42·9	2·0 1·1	8·0 4·3	14·0 7·6
21	8 05·3	8 06·6	7 43·1	2·1 1·1	8·1 4·4	14·1 7·6
22	8 05·5	8 06·8	7 43·4	2·2 1·2	8·2 4·4	14·2 7·7
23	8 05·8	8 07·1	7 43·6	2·3 1·2	8·3 4·5	14·3 7·7
24	8 06·0	8 07·3	7 43·9	2·4 1·3	8·4 4·6	14·4 7·8
25	8 06·3	8 07·6	7 44·1	2·5 1·4	8·5 4·6	14·5 7·9
26	8 06·5	8 07·8	7 44·3	2·6 1·4	8·6 4·7	14·6 7·9
27	8 06·8	8 08·1	7 44·6	2·7 1·5	8·7 4·7	14·7 8·0
28	8 07·0	8 08·3	7 44·8	2·8 1·5	8·8 4·8	14·8 8·0
29	8 07·3	8 08·6	7 45·1	2·9 1·6	8·9 4·8	14·9 8·1
30	8 07·5	8 08·8	7 45·3	3·0 1·6	9·0 4·9	15·0 8·1
31	8 07·8	8 09·1	7 45·5	3·1 1·7	9·1 4·9	15·1 8·2
32	8 08·0	8 09·3	7 45·8	3·2 1·7	9·2 5·0	15·2 8·2
33	8 08·3	8 09·6	7 46·0	3·3 1·8	9·3 5·0	15·3 8·3
34	8 08·5	8 09·8	7 46·2	3·4 1·8	9·4 5·1	15·4 8·3
35	8 08·8	8 10·1	7 46·5	3·5 1·9	9·5 5·1	15·5 8·4
36	8 09·0	8 10·3	7 46·7	3·6 2·0	9·6 5·2	15·6 8·5
37	8 09·3	8 10·6	7 47·0	3·7 2·0	9·7 5·3	15·7 8·5
38	8 09·5	8 10·8	7 47·2	3·8 2·1	9·8 5·3	15·8 8·6
39	8 09·8	8 11·1	7 47·4	3·9 2·1	9·9 5·4	15·9 8·6
40	8 10·0	8 11·3	7 47·7	4·0 2·2	10·0 5·4	16·0 8·7
41	8 10·3	8 11·6	7 47·9	4·1 2·2	10·1 5·5	16·1 8·7
42	8 10·5	8 11·8	7 48·2	4·2 2·3	10·2 5·5	16·2 8·8
43	8 10·8	8 12·1	7 48·4	4·3 2·3	10·3 5·6	16·3 8·8
44	8 11·0	8 12·3	7 48·6	4·4 2·4	10·4 5·6	16·4 8·9
45	8 11·3	8 12·6	7 48·9	4·5 2·4	10·5 5·7	16·5 8·9
46	8 11·5	8 12·8	7 49·1	4·6 2·5	10·6 5·7	16·6 9·0
47	8 11·8	8 13·1	7 49·3	4·7 2·5	10·7 5·8	16·7 9·0
48	8 12·0	8 13·3	7 49·6	4·8 2·6	10·8 5·9	16·8 9·1
49	8 12·3	8 13·6	7 49·8	4·9 2·7	10·9 5·9	16·9 9·2
50	8 12·5	8 13·8	7 50·1	5·0 2·7	11·0 6·0	17·0 9·2
51	8 12·8	8 14·1	7 50·3	5·1 2·8	11·1 6·0	17·1 9·3
52	8 13·0	8 14·3	7 50·5	5·2 2·8	11·2 6·1	17·2 9·3
53	8 13·3	8 14·6	7 50·8	5·3 2·9	11·3 6·1	17·3 9·4
54	8 13·5	8 14·9	7 51·0	5·4 2·9	11·4 6·2	17·4 9·4
55	8 13·8	8 15·1	7 51·3	5·5 3·0	11·5 6·2	17·5 9·5
56	8 14·0	8 15·4	7 51·5	5·6 3·0	11·6 6·3	17·6 9·5
57	8 14·3	8 15·6	7 51·7	5·7 3·1	11·7 6·3	17·7 9·6
58	8 14·5	8 15·9	7 52·0	5·8 3·1	11·8 6·4	17·8 9·6
59	8 14·8	8 16·1	7 52·2	5·9 3·2	11·9 6·4	17·9 9·7
60	8 15·0	8 16·4	7 52·5	6·0 3·3	12·0 6·5	18·0 9·8

33ᵐ

33	SUN PLANETS	ARIES	MOON	v or Corrⁿ d	v or Corrⁿ d	v or Corrⁿ d
s	° ′	° ′	° ′	′ ′	′ ′	′ ′
00	8 15·0	8 16·4	7 52·5	0·0 0·0	6·0 3·4	12·0 6·7
01	8 15·3	8 16·6	7 52·7	0·1 0·1	6·1 3·4	12·1 6·8
02	8 15·5	8 16·9	7 52·9	0·2 0·1	6·2 3·5	12·2 6·8
03	8 15·8	8 17·1	7 53·2	0·3 0·2	6·3 3·5	12·3 6·9
04	8 16·0	8 17·4	7 53·4	0·4 0·2	6·4 3·6	12·4 6·9
05	8 16·3	8 17·6	7 53·6	0·5 0·3	6·5 3·6	12·5 7·0
06	8 16·5	8 17·9	7 53·9	0·6 0·3	6·6 3·7	12·6 7·0
07	8 16·8	8 18·1	7 54·1	0·7 0·4	6·7 3·7	12·7 7·1
08	8 17·0	8 18·4	7 54·4	0·8 0·4	6·8 3·8	12·8 7·1
09	8 17·3	8 18·6	7 54·6	0·9 0·5	6·9 3·9	12·9 7·2
10	8 17·5	8 18·9	7 54·8	1·0 0·6	7·0 3·9	13·0 7·3
11	8 17·8	8 19·1	7 55·1	1·1 0·6	7·1 4·0	13·1 7·3
12	8 18·0	8 19·4	7 55·3	1·2 0·7	7·2 4·0	13·2 7·4
13	8 18·3	8 19·6	7 55·6	1·3 0·7	7·3 4·1	13·3 7·4
14	8 18·5	8 19·9	7 55·8	1·4 0·8	7·4 4·1	13·4 7·5
15	8 18·8	8 20·1	7 56·0	1·5 0·8	7·5 4·2	13·5 7·5
16	8 19·0	8 20·4	7 56·3	1·6 0·9	7·6 4·2	13·6 7·6
17	8 19·3	8 20·6	7 56·5	1·7 0·9	7·7 4·3	13·7 7·6
18	8 19·5	8 20·9	7 56·7	1·8 1·0	7·8 4·4	13·8 7·7
19	8 19·8	8 21·1	7 57·0	1·9 1·1	7·9 4·4	13·9 7·8
20	8 20·0	8 21·4	7 57·2	2·0 1·1	8·0 4·5	14·0 7·8
21	8 20·3	8 21·6	7 57·5	2·1 1·2	8·1 4·5	14·1 7·9
22	8 20·5	8 21·9	7 57·7	2·2 1·2	8·2 4·6	14·2 7·9
23	8 20·8	8 22·1	7 57·9	2·3 1·3	8·3 4·6	14·3 8·0
24	8 21·0	8 22·4	7 58·2	2·4 1·3	8·4 4·7	14·4 8·0
25	8 21·3	8 22·6	7 58·4	2·5 1·4	8·5 4·7	14·5 8·1
26	8 21·5	8 22·9	7 58·7	2·6 1·5	8·6 4·8	14·6 8·2
27	8 21·8	8 23·1	7 58·9	2·7 1·5	8·7 4·9	14·7 8·2
28	8 22·0	8 23·4	7 59·1	2·8 1·6	8·8 4·9	14·8 8·3
29	8 22·3	8 23·6	7 59·4	2·9 1·6	8·9 5·0	14·9 8·3
30	8 22·5	8 23·9	7 59·6	3·0 1·7	9·0 5·0	15·0 8·4
31	8 22·8	8 24·1	7 59·8	3·1 1·7	9·1 5·1	15·1 8·4
32	8 23·0	8 24·4	8 00·1	3·2 1·8	9·2 5·1	15·2 8·5
33	8 23·3	8 24·6	8 00·3	3·3 1·8	9·3 5·2	15·3 8·5
34	8 23·5	8 24·9	8 00·6	3·4 1·9	9·4 5·2	15·4 8·6
35	8 23·8	8 25·1	8 00·8	3·5 2·0	9·5 5·3	15·5 8·7
36	8 24·0	8 25·4	8 01·0	3·6 2·0	9·6 5·4	15·6 8·7
37	8 24·3	8 25·6	8 01·3	3·7 2·1	9·7 5·4	15·7 8·8
38	8 24·5	8 25·9	8 01·5	3·8 2·1	9·8 5·5	15·8 8·8
39	8 24·8	8 26·1	8 01·8	3·9 2·2	9·9 5·5	15·9 8·9
40	8 25·0	8 26·4	8 02·0	4·0 2·2	10·0 5·6	16·0 8·9
41	8 25·3	8 26·6	8 02·2	4·1 2·3	10·1 5·6	16·1 9·0
42	8 25·5	8 26·9	8 02·5	4·2 2·3	10·2 5·7	16·2 9·0
43	8 25·8	8 27·1	8 02·7	4·3 2·4	10·3 5·8	16·3 9·1
44	8 26·0	8 27·4	8 02·9	4·4 2·5	10·4 5·8	16·4 9·2
45	8 26·3	8 27·6	8 03·2	4·5 2·5	10·5 5·9	16·5 9·2
46	8 26·5	8 27·9	8 03·4	4·6 2·6	10·6 5·9	16·6 9·3
47	8 26·8	8 28·1	8 03·7	4·7 2·6	10·7 6·0	16·7 9·3
48	8 27·0	8 28·4	8 03·9	4·8 2·7	10·8 6·0	16·8 9·4
49	8 27·3	8 28·6	8 04·1	4·9 2·7	10·9 6·1	16·9 9·4
50	8 27·5	8 28·9	8 04·4	5·0 2·8	11·0 6·1	17·0 9·5
51	8 27·8	8 29·1	8 04·6	5·1 2·8	11·1 6·2	17·1 9·5
52	8 28·0	8 29·4	8 04·9	5·2 2·9	11·2 6·3	17·2 9·6
53	8 28·3	8 29·6	8 05·1	5·3 3·0	11·3 6·3	17·3 9·7
54	8 28·5	8 29·9	8 05·3	5·4 3·0	11·4 6·4	17·4 9·7
55	8 28·8	8 30·1	8 05·6	5·5 3·1	11·5 6·4	17·5 9·8
56	8 29·0	8 30·4	8 05·8	5·6 3·1	11·6 6·5	17·6 9·8
57	8 29·3	8 30·6	8 06·1	5·7 3·2	11·7 6·5	17·7 9·9
58	8 29·5	8 30·9	8 06·3	5·8 3·2	11·8 6·6	17·8 9·9
59	8 29·8	8 31·1	8 06·5	5·9 3·3	11·9 6·6	17·9 10·0
60	8 30·0	8 31·4	8 06·8	6·0 3·4	12·0 6·7	18·0 10·1

© British Crown Copyright 2018. All rights reserved.

34m

34 s	SUN PLANETS	ARIES	MOON	v or Corrn d		v or Corrn d		v or Corrn d	
00	8 30.0	8 31.4	8 06.8	0.0	0.0	6.0	3.5	12.0	6.9
01	8 30.3	8 31.6	8 07.0	0.1	0.1	6.1	3.5	12.1	7.0
02	8 30.5	8 31.9	8 07.2	0.2	0.1	6.2	3.6	12.2	7.0
03	8 30.8	8 32.1	8 07.5	0.3	0.2	6.3	3.6	12.3	7.1
04	8 31.0	8 32.4	8 07.7	0.4	0.2	6.4	3.7	12.4	7.1
05	8 31.3	8 32.6	8 08.0	0.5	0.3	6.5	3.7	12.5	7.2
06	8 31.5	8 32.9	8 08.2	0.6	0.3	6.6	3.8	12.6	7.2
07	8 31.8	8 33.2	8 08.4	0.7	0.4	6.7	3.9	12.7	7.3
08	8 32.0	8 33.4	8 08.7	0.8	0.5	6.8	3.9	12.8	7.4
09	8 32.3	8 33.7	8 08.9	0.9	0.5	6.9	4.0	12.9	7.4
10	8 32.5	8 33.9	8 09.2	1.0	0.6	7.0	4.0	13.0	7.5
11	8 32.8	8 34.2	8 09.4	1.1	0.6	7.1	4.1	13.1	7.5
12	8 33.0	8 34.4	8 09.6	1.2	0.7	7.2	4.1	13.2	7.6
13	8 33.3	8 34.7	8 09.9	1.3	0.7	7.3	4.2	13.3	7.6
14	8 33.5	8 34.9	8 10.1	1.4	0.8	7.4	4.3	13.4	7.7
15	8 33.8	8 35.2	8 10.3	1.5	0.9	7.5	4.3	13.5	7.8
16	8 34.0	8 35.4	8 10.6	1.6	0.9	7.6	4.4	13.6	7.8
17	8 34.3	8 35.7	8 10.8	1.7	1.0	7.7	4.4	13.7	7.9
18	8 34.5	8 35.9	8 11.1	1.8	1.0	7.8	4.5	13.8	7.9
19	8 34.8	8 36.2	8 11.3	1.9	1.1	7.9	4.5	13.9	8.0
20	8 35.0	8 36.4	8 11.5	2.0	1.2	8.0	4.6	14.0	8.1
21	8 35.3	8 36.7	8 11.8	2.1	1.2	8.1	4.7	14.1	8.1
22	8 35.5	8 36.9	8 12.0	2.2	1.3	8.2	4.7	14.2	8.2
23	8 35.8	8 37.2	8 12.3	2.3	1.3	8.3	4.8	14.3	8.2
24	8 36.0	8 37.4	8 12.5	2.4	1.4	8.4	4.8	14.4	8.3
25	8 36.3	8 37.7	8 12.7	2.5	1.4	8.5	4.9	14.5	8.3
26	8 36.5	8 37.9	8 13.0	2.6	1.5	8.6	4.9	14.6	8.4
27	8 36.8	8 38.2	8 13.2	2.7	1.6	8.7	5.0	14.7	8.5
28	8 37.0	8 38.4	8 13.4	2.8	1.6	8.8	5.1	14.8	8.5
29	8 37.3	8 38.7	8 13.7	2.9	1.7	8.9	5.1	14.9	8.6
30	8 37.5	8 38.9	8 13.9	3.0	1.7	9.0	5.2	15.0	8.6
31	8 37.8	8 39.2	8 14.2	3.1	1.8	9.1	5.2	15.1	8.7
32	8 38.0	8 39.4	8 14.4	3.2	1.8	9.2	5.3	15.2	8.7
33	8 38.3	8 39.7	8 14.6	3.3	1.9	9.3	5.3	15.3	8.8
34	8 38.5	8 39.9	8 14.9	3.4	2.0	9.4	5.4	15.4	8.9
35	8 38.8	8 40.2	8 15.1	3.5	2.0	9.5	5.5	15.5	8.9
36	8 39.0	8 40.4	8 15.4	3.6	2.1	9.6	5.5	15.6	9.0
37	8 39.3	8 40.7	8 15.6	3.7	2.1	9.7	5.6	15.7	9.0
38	8 39.5	8 40.9	8 15.8	3.8	2.2	9.8	5.6	15.8	9.1
39	8 39.8	8 41.2	8 16.1	3.9	2.2	9.9	5.7	15.9	9.1
40	8 40.0	8 41.4	8 16.3	4.0	2.3	10.0	5.8	16.0	9.2
41	8 40.3	8 41.7	8 16.5	4.1	2.4	10.1	5.8	16.1	9.3
42	8 40.5	8 41.9	8 16.8	4.2	2.4	10.2	5.9	16.2	9.3
43	8 40.8	8 42.2	8 17.0	4.3	2.5	10.3	5.9	16.3	9.4
44	8 41.0	8 42.4	8 17.3	4.4	2.5	10.4	6.0	16.4	9.4
45	8 41.3	8 42.7	8 17.5	4.5	2.6	10.5	6.0	16.5	9.5
46	8 41.5	8 42.9	8 17.7	4.6	2.6	10.6	6.1	16.6	9.5
47	8 41.8	8 43.2	8 18.0	4.7	2.7	10.7	6.2	16.7	9.6
48	8 42.0	8 43.4	8 18.2	4.8	2.8	10.8	6.2	16.8	9.7
49	8 42.3	8 43.7	8 18.5	4.9	2.8	10.9	6.3	16.9	9.7
50	8 42.5	8 43.9	8 18.7	5.0	2.9	11.0	6.3	17.0	9.8
51	8 42.8	8 44.2	8 18.9	5.1	2.9	11.1	6.4	17.1	9.8
52	8 43.0	8 44.4	8 19.2	5.2	3.0	11.2	6.4	17.2	9.9
53	8 43.3	8 44.7	8 19.4	5.3	3.0	11.3	6.5	17.3	9.9
54	8 43.5	8 44.9	8 19.7	5.4	3.1	11.4	6.6	17.4	10.0
55	8 43.8	8 45.2	8 19.9	5.5	3.2	11.5	6.6	17.5	10.1
56	8 44.0	8 45.4	8 20.1	5.6	3.2	11.6	6.7	17.6	10.1
57	8 44.3	8 45.7	8 20.4	5.7	3.3	11.7	6.7	17.7	10.2
58	8 44.5	8 45.9	8 20.6	5.8	3.3	11.8	6.8	17.8	10.2
59	8 44.8	8 46.2	8 20.8	5.9	3.4	11.9	6.8	17.9	10.3
60	8 45.0	8 46.4	8 21.1	6.0	3.5	12.0	6.9	18.0	10.4

35m

35 s	SUN PLANETS	ARIES	MOON	v or Corrn d		v or Corrn d		v or Corrn d	
00	8 45.0	8 46.4	8 21.1	0.0	0.0	6.0	3.6	12.0	7.1
01	8 45.3	8 46.7	8 21.3	0.1	0.1	6.1	3.6	12.1	7.2
02	8 45.5	8 46.9	8 21.6	0.2	0.1	6.2	3.7	12.2	7.2
03	8 45.8	8 47.2	8 21.8	0.3	0.2	6.3	3.7	12.3	7.3
04	8 46.0	8 47.4	8 22.0	0.4	0.2	6.4	3.8	12.4	7.3
05	8 46.3	8 47.7	8 22.3	0.5	0.3	6.5	3.8	12.5	7.4
06	8 46.5	8 47.9	8 22.5	0.6	0.4	6.6	3.9	12.6	7.5
07	8 46.8	8 48.2	8 22.8	0.7	0.4	6.7	4.0	12.7	7.5
08	8 47.0	8 48.4	8 23.0	0.8	0.5	6.8	4.0	12.8	7.6
09	8 47.3	8 48.7	8 23.2	0.9	0.5	6.9	4.1	12.9	7.6
10	8 47.5	8 48.9	8 23.5	1.0	0.6	7.0	4.1	13.0	7.7
11	8 47.8	8 49.2	8 23.7	1.1	0.7	7.1	4.2	13.1	7.8
12	8 48.0	8 49.4	8 23.9	1.2	0.7	7.2	4.3	13.2	7.8
13	8 48.3	8 49.7	8 24.2	1.3	0.8	7.3	4.3	13.3	7.9
14	8 48.5	8 49.9	8 24.4	1.4	0.8	7.4	4.4	13.4	7.9
15	8 48.8	8 50.2	8 24.7	1.5	0.9	7.5	4.4	13.5	8.0
16	8 49.0	8 50.4	8 24.9	1.6	0.9	7.6	4.5	13.6	8.0
17	8 49.3	8 50.7	8 25.1	1.7	1.0	7.7	4.6	13.7	8.1
18	8 49.5	8 50.9	8 25.4	1.8	1.1	7.8	4.6	13.8	8.2
19	8 49.8	8 51.2	8 25.6	1.9	1.1	7.9	4.7	13.9	8.2
20	8 50.0	8 51.5	8 25.9	2.0	1.2	8.0	4.7	14.0	8.3
21	8 50.3	8 51.7	8 26.1	2.1	1.2	8.1	4.8	14.1	8.3
22	8 50.5	8 52.0	8 26.3	2.2	1.3	8.2	4.9	14.2	8.4
23	8 50.8	8 52.2	8 26.6	2.3	1.4	8.3	4.9	14.3	8.5
24	8 51.0	8 52.5	8 26.8	2.4	1.4	8.4	5.0	14.4	8.5
25	8 51.3	8 52.7	8 27.0	2.5	1.5	8.5	5.0	14.5	8.6
26	8 51.5	8 53.0	8 27.3	2.6	1.5	8.6	5.1	14.6	8.6
27	8 51.8	8 53.2	8 27.5	2.7	1.6	8.7	5.1	14.7	8.7
28	8 52.0	8 53.5	8 27.8	2.8	1.7	8.8	5.2	14.8	8.8
29	8 52.3	8 53.7	8 28.0	2.9	1.7	8.9	5.3	14.9	8.8
30	8 52.5	8 54.0	8 28.2	3.0	1.8	9.0	5.3	15.0	8.9
31	8 52.8	8 54.2	8 28.5	3.1	1.8	9.1	5.4	15.1	8.9
32	8 53.0	8 54.5	8 28.7	3.2	1.9	9.2	5.4	15.2	9.0
33	8 53.3	8 54.7	8 29.0	3.3	2.0	9.3	5.5	15.3	9.1
34	8 53.5	8 55.0	8 29.2	3.4	2.0	9.4	5.6	15.4	9.1
35	8 53.8	8 55.2	8 29.4	3.5	2.1	9.5	5.6	15.5	9.2
36	8 54.0	8 55.5	8 29.7	3.6	2.1	9.6	5.7	15.6	9.2
37	8 54.3	8 55.7	8 29.9	3.7	2.2	9.7	5.7	15.7	9.3
38	8 54.5	8 56.0	8 30.2	3.8	2.2	9.8	5.8	15.8	9.3
39	8 54.8	8 56.2	8 30.4	3.9	2.3	9.9	5.9	15.9	9.4
40	8 55.0	8 56.5	8 30.6	4.0	2.4	10.0	5.9	16.0	9.5
41	8 55.3	8 56.7	8 30.9	4.1	2.4	10.1	6.0	16.1	9.5
42	8 55.5	8 57.0	8 31.1	4.2	2.5	10.2	6.0	16.2	9.6
43	8 55.8	8 57.2	8 31.3	4.3	2.5	10.3	6.1	16.3	9.6
44	8 56.0	8 57.5	8 31.6	4.4	2.6	10.4	6.2	16.4	9.7
45	8 56.3	8 57.7	8 31.8	4.5	2.7	10.5	6.2	16.5	9.8
46	8 56.5	8 58.0	8 32.1	4.6	2.7	10.6	6.3	16.6	9.8
47	8 56.8	8 58.2	8 32.3	4.7	2.8	10.7	6.3	16.7	9.9
48	8 57.0	8 58.5	8 32.5	4.8	2.8	10.8	6.4	16.8	9.9
49	8 57.3	8 58.7	8 32.8	4.9	2.9	10.9	6.4	16.9	10.0
50	8 57.5	8 59.0	8 33.0	5.0	3.0	11.0	6.5	17.0	10.1
51	8 57.8	8 59.2	8 33.3	5.1	3.0	11.1	6.6	17.1	10.1
52	8 58.0	8 59.5	8 33.5	5.2	3.1	11.2	6.6	17.2	10.2
53	8 58.3	8 59.7	8 33.7	5.3	3.1	11.3	6.7	17.3	10.2
54	8 58.5	9 00.0	8 34.0	5.4	3.2	11.4	6.7	17.4	10.3
55	8 58.8	9 00.2	8 34.2	5.5	3.3	11.5	6.8	17.5	10.4
56	8 59.0	9 00.5	8 34.4	5.6	3.3	11.6	6.9	17.6	10.4
57	8 59.3	9 00.7	8 34.7	5.7	3.4	11.7	6.9	17.7	10.5
58	8 59.5	9 01.0	8 34.9	5.8	3.4	11.8	7.0	17.8	10.5
59	8 59.8	9 01.2	8 35.2	5.9	3.5	11.9	7.0	17.9	10.6
60	9 00.0	9 01.5	8 35.4	6.0	3.6	12.0	7.1	18.0	10.7

© British Crown Copyright 2018. All rights reserved.

36ᵐ

s	SUN PLANETS	ARIES	MOON	v or d	Corrⁿ	v or d	Corrⁿ	v or d	Corrⁿ
00	9 00.0	9 01.5	8 35.4	0.0	0.0	6.0	3.7	12.0	7.3
01	9 00.3	9 01.7	8 35.6	0.1	0.1	6.1	3.7	12.1	7.4
02	9 00.5	9 02.0	8 35.9	0.2	0.1	6.2	3.8	12.2	7.4
03	9 00.8	9 02.2	8 36.1	0.3	0.2	6.3	3.8	12.3	7.5
04	9 01.0	9 02.5	8 36.4	0.4	0.3	6.4	3.9	12.4	7.5
05	9 01.3	9 02.7	8 36.6	0.5	0.3	6.5	4.0	12.5	7.6
06	9 01.5	9 03.0	8 36.8	0.6	0.4	6.6	4.0	12.6	7.7
07	9 01.8	9 03.2	8 37.1	0.7	0.4	6.7	4.1	12.7	7.7
08	9 02.0	9 03.5	8 37.3	0.8	0.5	6.8	4.1	12.8	7.8
09	9 02.3	9 03.7	8 37.5	0.9	0.5	6.9	4.2	12.9	7.8
10	9 02.5	9 04.0	8 37.8	1.0	0.6	7.0	4.3	13.0	7.9
11	9 02.8	9 04.2	8 38.0	1.1	0.7	7.1	4.3	13.1	8.0
12	9 03.0	9 04.5	8 38.3	1.2	0.7	7.2	4.4	13.2	8.0
13	9 03.3	9 04.7	8 38.5	1.3	0.8	7.3	4.4	13.3	8.1
14	9 03.5	9 05.0	8 38.7	1.4	0.9	7.4	4.5	13.4	8.2
15	9 03.8	9 05.2	8 39.0	1.5	0.9	7.5	4.6	13.5	8.2
16	9 04.0	9 05.5	8 39.2	1.6	1.0	7.6	4.6	13.6	8.3
17	9 04.3	9 05.7	8 39.5	1.7	1.0	7.7	4.7	13.7	8.3
18	9 04.5	9 06.0	8 39.7	1.8	1.1	7.8	4.7	13.8	8.4
19	9 04.8	9 06.2	8 39.9	1.9	1.2	7.9	4.8	13.9	8.5
20	9 05.0	9 06.5	8 40.2	2.0	1.2	8.0	4.9	14.0	8.5
21	9 05.3	9 06.7	8 40.4	2.1	1.3	8.1	4.9	14.1	8.6
22	9 05.5	9 07.0	8 40.6	2.2	1.3	8.2	5.0	14.2	8.6
23	9 05.8	9 07.2	8 40.9	2.3	1.4	8.3	5.0	14.3	8.7
24	9 06.0	9 07.5	8 41.1	2.4	1.5	8.4	5.1	14.4	8.8
25	9 06.3	9 07.7	8 41.4	2.5	1.5	8.5	5.2	14.5	8.8
26	9 06.5	9 08.0	8 41.6	2.6	1.6	8.6	5.2	14.6	8.9
27	9 06.8	9 08.2	8 41.8	2.7	1.6	8.7	5.3	14.7	8.9
28	9 07.0	9 08.5	8 42.1	2.8	1.7	8.8	5.4	14.8	9.0
29	9 07.3	9 08.7	8 42.3	2.9	1.8	8.9	5.4	14.9	9.1
30	9 07.5	9 09.0	8 42.6	3.0	1.8	9.0	5.5	15.0	9.1
31	9 07.8	9 09.2	8 42.8	3.1	1.9	9.1	5.5	15.1	9.2
32	9 08.0	9 09.5	8 43.0	3.2	1.9	9.2	5.6	15.2	9.2
33	9 08.3	9 09.8	8 43.3	3.3	2.0	9.3	5.7	15.3	9.3
34	9 08.5	9 10.0	8 43.5	3.4	2.1	9.4	5.7	15.4	9.4
35	9 08.8	9 10.3	8 43.8	3.5	2.1	9.5	5.8	15.5	9.4
36	9 09.0	9 10.5	8 44.0	3.6	2.2	9.6	5.8	15.6	9.5
37	9 09.3	9 10.8	8 44.2	3.7	2.3	9.7	5.9	15.7	9.6
38	9 09.5	9 11.0	8 44.5	3.8	2.3	9.8	6.0	15.8	9.6
39	9 09.8	9 11.3	8 44.7	3.9	2.4	9.9	6.0	15.9	9.7
40	9 10.0	9 11.5	8 44.9	4.0	2.4	10.0	6.1	16.0	9.7
41	9 10.3	9 11.8	8 45.2	4.1	2.5	10.1	6.1	16.1	9.8
42	9 10.5	9 12.0	8 45.4	4.2	2.6	10.2	6.2	16.2	9.9
43	9 10.8	9 12.3	8 45.7	4.3	2.6	10.3	6.3	16.3	9.9
44	9 11.0	9 12.5	8 45.9	4.4	2.7	10.4	6.3	16.4	10.0
45	9 11.3	9 12.8	8 46.1	4.5	2.7	10.5	6.4	16.5	10.0
46	9 11.5	9 13.0	8 46.4	4.6	2.8	10.6	6.4	16.6	10.1
47	9 11.8	9 13.3	8 46.6	4.7	2.9	10.7	6.5	16.7	10.2
48	9 12.0	9 13.5	8 46.9	4.8	2.9	10.8	6.6	16.8	10.2
49	9 12.3	9 13.8	8 47.1	4.9	3.0	10.9	6.6	16.9	10.3
50	9 12.5	9 14.0	8 47.3	5.0	3.0	11.0	6.7	17.0	10.3
51	9 12.8	9 14.3	8 47.6	5.1	3.1	11.1	6.8	17.1	10.4
52	9 13.0	9 14.5	8 47.8	5.2	3.2	11.2	6.8	17.2	10.5
53	9 13.3	9 14.8	8 48.0	5.3	3.2	11.3	6.9	17.3	10.5
54	9 13.5	9 15.0	8 48.3	5.4	3.3	11.4	6.9	17.4	10.6
55	9 13.8	9 15.3	8 48.5	5.5	3.3	11.5	7.0	17.5	10.6
56	9 14.0	9 15.5	8 48.8	5.6	3.4	11.6	7.1	17.6	10.7
57	9 14.3	9 15.8	8 49.0	5.7	3.5	11.7	7.1	17.7	10.8
58	9 14.5	9 16.0	8 49.2	5.8	3.5	11.8	7.2	17.8	10.8
59	9 14.8	9 16.3	8 49.5	5.9	3.6	11.9	7.2	17.9	10.9
60	9 15.0	9 16.5	8 49.7	6.0	3.7	12.0	7.3	18.0	11.0

37ᵐ

s	SUN PLANETS	ARIES	MOON	v or d	Corrⁿ	v or d	Corrⁿ	v or d	Corrⁿ
00	9 15.0	9 16.5	8 49.7	0.0	0.0	6.0	3.8	12.0	7.5
01	9 15.3	9 16.8	8 50.0	0.1	0.1	6.1	3.8	12.1	7.6
02	9 15.5	9 17.0	8 50.2	0.2	0.1	6.2	3.9	12.2	7.6
03	9 15.8	9 17.3	8 50.4	0.3	0.2	6.3	3.9	12.3	7.7
04	9 16.0	9 17.5	8 50.7	0.4	0.3	6.4	4.0	12.4	7.8
05	9 16.3	9 17.8	8 50.9	0.5	0.3	6.5	4.1	12.5	7.8
06	9 16.5	9 18.0	8 51.1	0.6	0.4	6.6	4.1	12.6	7.9
07	9 16.8	9 18.3	8 51.4	0.7	0.4	6.7	4.2	12.7	7.9
08	9 17.0	9 18.5	8 51.6	0.8	0.5	6.8	4.3	12.8	8.0
09	9 17.3	9 18.8	8 51.9	0.9	0.6	6.9	4.3	12.9	8.1
10	9 17.5	9 19.0	8 52.1	1.0	0.6	7.0	4.4	13.0	8.1
11	9 17.8	9 19.3	8 52.3	1.1	0.7	7.1	4.4	13.1	8.2
12	9 18.0	9 19.5	8 52.6	1.2	0.8	7.2	4.5	13.2	8.3
13	9 18.3	9 19.8	8 52.8	1.3	0.8	7.3	4.6	13.3	8.3
14	9 18.5	9 20.0	8 53.1	1.4	0.9	7.4	4.6	13.4	8.4
15	9 18.8	9 20.3	8 53.3	1.5	0.9	7.5	4.7	13.5	8.4
16	9 19.0	9 20.5	8 53.5	1.6	1.0	7.6	4.8	13.6	8.5
17	9 19.3	9 20.8	8 53.8	1.7	1.1	7.7	4.8	13.7	8.6
18	9 19.5	9 21.0	8 54.0	1.8	1.1	7.8	4.9	13.8	8.6
19	9 19.8	9 21.3	8 54.3	1.9	1.2	7.9	4.9	13.9	8.7
20	9 20.0	9 21.5	8 54.5	2.0	1.3	8.0	5.0	14.0	8.8
21	9 20.3	9 21.8	8 54.7	2.1	1.3	8.1	5.1	14.1	8.8
22	9 20.5	9 22.0	8 55.0	2.2	1.4	8.2	5.1	14.2	8.9
23	9 20.8	9 22.3	8 55.2	2.3	1.4	8.3	5.2	14.3	8.9
24	9 21.0	9 22.5	8 55.4	2.4	1.5	8.4	5.3	14.4	9.0
25	9 21.3	9 22.8	8 55.7	2.5	1.6	8.5	5.3	14.5	9.1
26	9 21.5	9 23.0	8 55.9	2.6	1.6	8.6	5.4	14.6	9.1
27	9 21.8	9 23.3	8 56.2	2.7	1.7	8.7	5.4	14.7	9.2
28	9 22.0	9 23.5	8 56.4	2.8	1.8	8.8	5.5	14.8	9.3
29	9 22.3	9 23.8	8 56.6	2.9	1.8	8.9	5.6	14.9	9.3
30	9 22.5	9 24.0	8 56.9	3.0	1.9	9.0	5.6	15.0	9.4
31	9 22.8	9 24.3	8 57.1	3.1	1.9	9.1	5.7	15.1	9.4
32	9 23.0	9 24.5	8 57.4	3.2	2.0	9.2	5.8	15.2	9.5
33	9 23.3	9 24.8	8 57.6	3.3	2.1	9.3	5.8	15.3	9.6
34	9 23.5	9 25.0	8 57.8	3.4	2.1	9.4	5.9	15.4	9.6
35	9 23.8	9 25.3	8 58.1	3.5	2.2	9.5	5.9	15.5	9.7
36	9 24.0	9 25.5	8 58.3	3.6	2.3	9.6	6.0	15.6	9.8
37	9 24.3	9 25.8	8 58.5	3.7	2.3	9.7	6.1	15.7	9.8
38	9 24.5	9 26.0	8 58.8	3.8	2.4	9.8	6.1	15.8	9.9
39	9 24.8	9 26.3	8 59.0	3.9	2.4	9.9	6.2	15.9	9.9
40	9 25.0	9 26.5	8 59.3	4.0	2.5	10.0	6.3	16.0	10.0
41	9 25.3	9 26.8	8 59.5	4.1	2.6	10.1	6.3	16.1	10.1
42	9 25.5	9 27.0	8 59.7	4.2	2.6	10.2	6.4	16.2	10.1
43	9 25.8	9 27.3	9 00.0	4.3	2.7	10.3	6.4	16.3	10.2
44	9 26.0	9 27.5	9 00.2	4.4	2.8	10.4	6.5	16.4	10.3
45	9 26.3	9 27.8	9 00.5	4.5	2.8	10.5	6.6	16.5	10.3
46	9 26.5	9 28.1	9 00.7	4.6	2.9	10.6	6.6	16.6	10.4
47	9 26.8	9 28.3	9 00.9	4.7	2.9	10.7	6.7	16.7	10.4
48	9 27.0	9 28.6	9 01.2	4.8	3.0	10.8	6.8	16.8	10.5
49	9 27.3	9 28.8	9 01.4	4.9	3.1	10.9	6.8	16.9	10.6
50	9 27.5	9 29.1	9 01.6	5.0	3.1	11.0	6.9	17.0	10.6
51	9 27.8	9 29.3	9 01.9	5.1	3.2	11.1	6.9	17.1	10.7
52	9 28.0	9 29.6	9 02.1	5.2	3.3	11.2	7.0	17.2	10.8
53	9 28.3	9 29.8	9 02.4	5.3	3.3	11.3	7.1	17.3	10.8
54	9 28.5	9 30.1	9 02.6	5.4	3.4	11.4	7.1	17.4	10.9
55	9 28.8	9 30.3	9 02.8	5.5	3.4	11.5	7.2	17.5	10.9
56	9 29.0	9 30.6	9 03.1	5.6	3.5	11.6	7.3	17.6	11.0
57	9 29.3	9 30.8	9 03.3	5.7	3.6	11.7	7.3	17.7	11.1
58	9 29.5	9 31.1	9 03.6	5.8	3.6	11.8	7.4	17.8	11.1
59	9 29.8	9 31.3	9 03.8	5.9	3.7	11.9	7.4	17.9	11.2
60	9 30.0	9 31.6	9 04.0	6.0	3.8	12.0	7.5	18.0	11.3

© British Crown Copyright 2018. All rights reserved.

38ᵐ

38	SUN PLANETS	ARIES	MOON	v or Corrⁿ d	v or Corrⁿ d	v or Corrⁿ d
s	° ′	° ′	° ′	′ ′	′ ′	′ ′
00	9 30.0	9 31.6	9 04.0	0.0 0.0	6.0 3.9	12.0 7.7
01	9 30.3	9 31.8	9 04.3	0.1 0.1	6.1 3.9	12.1 7.8
02	9 30.5	9 32.1	9 04.5	0.2 0.1	6.2 4.0	12.2 7.8
03	9 30.8	9 32.3	9 04.7	0.3 0.2	6.3 4.0	12.3 7.9
04	9 31.0	9 32.6	9 05.0	0.4 0.3	6.4 4.1	12.4 8.0
05	9 31.3	9 32.8	9 05.2	0.5 0.3	6.5 4.2	12.5 8.0
06	9 31.5	9 33.1	9 05.5	0.6 0.4	6.6 4.2	12.6 8.1
07	9 31.8	9 33.3	9 05.7	0.7 0.4	6.7 4.3	12.7 8.1
08	9 32.0	9 33.6	9 05.9	0.8 0.5	6.8 4.4	12.8 8.2
09	9 32.3	9 33.8	9 06.2	0.9 0.6	6.9 4.4	12.9 8.3
10	9 32.5	9 34.1	9 06.4	1.0 0.6	7.0 4.5	13.0 8.3
11	9 32.8	9 34.3	9 06.7	1.1 0.7	7.1 4.6	13.1 8.4
12	9 33.0	9 34.6	9 06.9	1.2 0.8	7.2 4.6	13.2 8.5
13	9 33.3	9 34.8	9 07.1	1.3 0.8	7.3 4.7	13.3 8.5
14	9 33.5	9 35.1	9 07.4	1.4 0.9	7.4 4.7	13.4 8.6
15	9 33.8	9 35.3	9 07.6	1.5 1.0	7.5 4.8	13.5 8.7
16	9 34.0	9 35.6	9 07.9	1.6 1.0	7.6 4.9	13.6 8.7
17	9 34.3	9 35.8	9 08.1	1.7 1.1	7.7 4.9	13.7 8.8
18	9 34.5	9 36.1	9 08.3	1.8 1.2	7.8 5.0	13.8 8.9
19	9 34.8	9 36.3	9 08.6	1.9 1.2	7.9 5.1	13.9 8.9
20	9 35.0	9 36.6	9 08.8	2.0 1.3	8.0 5.1	14.0 9.0
21	9 35.3	9 36.8	9 09.0	2.1 1.3	8.1 5.2	14.1 9.0
22	9 35.5	9 37.1	9 09.3	2.2 1.4	8.2 5.3	14.2 9.1
23	9 35.8	9 37.3	9 09.5	2.3 1.5	8.3 5.3	14.3 9.2
24	9 36.0	9 37.6	9 09.8	2.4 1.5	8.4 5.4	14.4 9.2
25	9 36.3	9 37.8	9 10.0	2.5 1.6	8.5 5.5	14.5 9.3
26	9 36.5	9 38.1	9 10.2	2.6 1.7	8.6 5.5	14.6 9.4
27	9 36.8	9 38.3	9 10.5	2.7 1.7	8.7 5.6	14.7 9.4
28	9 37.0	9 38.6	9 10.7	2.8 1.8	8.8 5.6	14.8 9.5
29	9 37.3	9 38.8	9 11.0	2.9 1.9	8.9 5.7	14.9 9.6
30	9 37.5	9 39.1	9 11.2	3.0 1.9	9.0 5.8	15.0 9.6
31	9 37.8	9 39.3	9 11.4	3.1 2.0	9.1 5.8	15.1 9.7
32	9 38.0	9 39.6	9 11.7	3.2 2.1	9.2 5.9	15.2 9.8
33	9 38.3	9 39.8	9 11.9	3.3 2.1	9.3 6.0	15.3 9.8
34	9 38.5	9 40.1	9 12.1	3.4 2.2	9.4 6.0	15.4 9.9
35	9 38.8	9 40.3	9 12.4	3.5 2.2	9.5 6.1	15.5 9.9
36	9 39.0	9 40.6	9 12.6	3.6 2.3	9.6 6.2	15.6 10.0
37	9 39.3	9 40.8	9 12.9	3.7 2.4	9.7 6.2	15.7 10.1
38	9 39.5	9 41.1	9 13.1	3.8 2.4	9.8 6.3	15.8 10.1
39	9 39.8	9 41.3	9 13.3	3.9 2.5	9.9 6.4	15.9 10.2
40	9 40.0	9 41.6	9 13.6	4.0 2.6	10.0 6.4	16.0 10.3
41	9 40.3	9 41.8	9 13.8	4.1 2.6	10.1 6.5	16.1 10.3
42	9 40.5	9 42.1	9 14.1	4.2 2.7	10.2 6.5	16.2 10.4
43	9 40.8	9 42.3	9 14.3	4.3 2.8	10.3 6.6	16.3 10.5
44	9 41.0	9 42.6	9 14.5	4.4 2.8	10.4 6.7	16.4 10.5
45	9 41.3	9 42.8	9 14.8	4.5 2.9	10.5 6.7	16.5 10.6
46	9 41.5	9 43.1	9 15.0	4.6 3.0	10.6 6.8	16.6 10.7
47	9 41.8	9 43.3	9 15.2	4.7 3.0	10.7 6.9	16.7 10.7
48	9 42.0	9 43.6	9 15.5	4.8 3.1	10.8 6.9	16.8 10.8
49	9 42.3	9 43.8	9 15.7	4.9 3.1	10.9 7.0	16.9 10.8
50	9 42.5	9 44.1	9 16.0	5.0 3.2	11.0 7.1	17.0 10.9
51	9 42.8	9 44.3	9 16.2	5.1 3.3	11.1 7.1	17.1 11.0
52	9 43.0	9 44.6	9 16.4	5.2 3.3	11.2 7.2	17.2 11.0
53	9 43.3	9 44.8	9 16.7	5.3 3.4	11.3 7.3	17.3 11.1
54	9 43.5	9 45.1	9 16.9	5.4 3.5	11.4 7.3	17.4 11.2
55	9 43.8	9 45.3	9 17.2	5.5 3.5	11.5 7.4	17.5 11.2
56	9 44.0	9 45.6	9 17.4	5.6 3.6	11.6 7.4	17.6 11.3
57	9 44.3	9 45.8	9 17.6	5.7 3.7	11.7 7.5	17.7 11.4
58	9 44.5	9 46.1	9 17.9	5.8 3.7	11.8 7.6	17.8 11.4
59	9 44.8	9 46.4	9 18.1	5.9 3.8	11.9 7.6	17.9 11.5
60	9 45.0	9 46.6	9 18.4	6.0 3.9	12.0 7.7	18.0 11.6

39ᵐ

39	SUN PLANETS	ARIES	MOON	v or Corrⁿ d	v or Corrⁿ d	v or Corrⁿ d
s	° ′	° ′	° ′	′ ′	′ ′	′ ′
00	9 45.0	9 46.6	9 18.4	0.0 0.0	6.0 4.0	12.0 7.9
01	9 45.3	9 46.9	9 18.6	0.1 0.1	6.1 4.0	12.1 8.0
02	9 45.5	9 47.1	9 18.8	0.2 0.1	6.2 4.1	12.2 8.0
03	9 45.8	9 47.4	9 19.1	0.3 0.2	6.3 4.1	12.3 8.1
04	9 46.0	9 47.6	9 19.3	0.4 0.3	6.4 4.2	12.4 8.2
05	9 46.3	9 47.9	9 19.5	0.5 0.3	6.5 4.3	12.5 8.2
06	9 46.5	9 48.1	9 19.8	0.6 0.4	6.6 4.3	12.6 8.3
07	9 46.8	9 48.4	9 20.0	0.7 0.5	6.7 4.4	12.7 8.4
08	9 47.0	9 48.6	9 20.3	0.8 0.5	6.8 4.5	12.8 8.4
09	9 47.3	9 48.9	9 20.5	0.9 0.6	6.9 4.5	12.9 8.5
10	9 47.5	9 49.1	9 20.7	1.0 0.7	7.0 4.6	13.0 8.6
11	9 47.8	9 49.4	9 21.0	1.1 0.7	7.1 4.7	13.1 8.6
12	9 48.0	9 49.6	9 21.2	1.2 0.8	7.2 4.7	13.2 8.7
13	9 48.3	9 49.9	9 21.5	1.3 0.9	7.3 4.8	13.3 8.8
14	9 48.5	9 50.1	9 21.7	1.4 0.9	7.4 4.9	13.4 8.8
15	9 48.8	9 50.4	9 21.9	1.5 1.0	7.5 4.9	13.5 8.9
16	9 49.0	9 50.6	9 22.2	1.6 1.1	7.6 5.0	13.6 9.0
17	9 49.3	9 50.9	9 22.4	1.7 1.1	7.7 5.1	13.7 9.0
18	9 49.5	9 51.1	9 22.6	1.8 1.2	7.8 5.1	13.8 9.1
19	9 49.8	9 51.4	9 22.9	1.9 1.3	7.9 5.2	13.9 9.2
20	9 50.0	9 51.6	9 23.1	2.0 1.3	8.0 5.3	14.0 9.2
21	9 50.3	9 51.9	9 23.4	2.1 1.4	8.1 5.3	14.1 9.3
22	9 50.5	9 52.1	9 23.6	2.2 1.4	8.2 5.4	14.2 9.3
23	9 50.8	9 52.4	9 23.8	2.3 1.5	8.3 5.5	14.3 9.4
24	9 51.0	9 52.6	9 24.1	2.4 1.6	8.4 5.5	14.4 9.5
25	9 51.3	9 52.9	9 24.3	2.5 1.6	8.5 5.6	14.5 9.5
26	9 51.5	9 53.1	9 24.6	2.6 1.7	8.6 5.7	14.6 9.6
27	9 51.8	9 53.4	9 24.8	2.7 1.8	8.7 5.7	14.7 9.7
28	9 52.0	9 53.6	9 25.0	2.8 1.8	8.8 5.8	14.8 9.7
29	9 52.3	9 53.9	9 25.3	2.9 1.9	8.9 5.9	14.9 9.8
30	9 52.5	9 54.1	9 25.5	3.0 2.0	9.0 5.9	15.0 9.9
31	9 52.8	9 54.4	9 25.7	3.1 2.0	9.1 6.0	15.1 9.9
32	9 53.0	9 54.6	9 26.0	3.2 2.1	9.2 6.1	15.2 10.0
33	9 53.3	9 54.9	9 26.2	3.3 2.2	9.3 6.1	15.3 10.1
34	9 53.5	9 55.1	9 26.5	3.4 2.2	9.4 6.2	15.4 10.1
35	9 53.8	9 55.4	9 26.7	3.5 2.3	9.5 6.3	15.5 10.2
36	9 54.0	9 55.6	9 26.9	3.6 2.4	9.6 6.3	15.6 10.3
37	9 54.3	9 55.9	9 27.2	3.7 2.4	9.7 6.4	15.7 10.3
38	9 54.5	9 56.1	9 27.4	3.8 2.5	9.8 6.5	15.8 10.4
39	9 54.8	9 56.4	9 27.7	3.9 2.6	9.9 6.5	15.9 10.5
40	9 55.0	9 56.6	9 27.9	4.0 2.6	10.0 6.6	16.0 10.5
41	9 55.3	9 56.9	9 28.1	4.1 2.7	10.1 6.6	16.1 10.6
42	9 55.5	9 57.1	9 28.4	4.2 2.8	10.2 6.7	16.2 10.7
43	9 55.8	9 57.4	9 28.6	4.3 2.8	10.3 6.8	16.3 10.7
44	9 56.0	9 57.6	9 28.8	4.4 2.9	10.4 6.8	16.4 10.8
45	9 56.3	9 57.9	9 29.1	4.5 3.0	10.5 6.9	16.5 10.9
46	9 56.5	9 58.1	9 29.3	4.6 3.0	10.6 7.0	16.6 10.9
47	9 56.8	9 58.4	9 29.6	4.7 3.1	10.7 7.0	16.7 11.0
48	9 57.0	9 58.6	9 29.8	4.8 3.2	10.8 7.1	16.8 11.1
49	9 57.3	9 58.9	9 30.0	4.9 3.2	10.9 7.2	16.9 11.1
50	9 57.5	9 59.1	9 30.3	5.0 3.3	11.0 7.2	17.0 11.2
51	9 57.8	9 59.4	9 30.5	5.1 3.4	11.1 7.3	17.1 11.3
52	9 58.0	9 59.6	9 30.8	5.2 3.4	11.2 7.4	17.2 11.3
53	9 58.3	9 59.9	9 31.0	5.3 3.5	11.3 7.4	17.3 11.4
54	9 58.5	10 00.1	9 31.2	5.4 3.6	11.4 7.5	17.4 11.5
55	9 58.8	10 00.4	9 31.5	5.5 3.6	11.5 7.6	17.5 11.5
56	9 59.0	10 00.6	9 31.7	5.6 3.7	11.6 7.6	17.6 11.6
57	9 59.3	10 00.9	9 32.0	5.7 3.8	11.7 7.7	17.7 11.7
58	9 59.5	10 01.1	9 32.2	5.8 3.8	11.8 7.7	17.8 11.7
59	9 59.8	10 01.4	9 32.4	5.9 3.9	11.9 7.8	17.9 11.8
60	10 00.0	10 01.6	9 32.7	6.0 4.0	12.0 7.9	18.0 11.9

© British Crown Copyright 2018. All rights reserved.

40	SUN PLANETS	ARIES	MOON	v or d	Corrⁿ	v or d	Corrⁿ	v or d	Corrⁿ
s	° ′	° ′	° ′	′	′	′	′	′	′
00	10 00·0	10 01·6	9 32·7	0·0	0·0	6·0	4·1	12·0	8·1
01	10 00·3	10 01·9	9 32·9	0·1	0·1	6·1	4·1	12·1	8·2
02	10 00·5	10 02·1	9 33·1	0·2	0·1	6·2	4·2	12·2	8·2
03	10 00·8	10 02·4	9 33·4	0·3	0·2	6·3	4·3	12·3	8·3
04	10 01·0	10 02·6	9 33·6	0·4	0·3	6·4	4·3	12·4	8·4
05	10 01·3	10 02·9	9 33·9	0·5	0·3	6·5	4·4	12·5	8·4
06	10 01·5	10 03·1	9 34·1	0·6	0·4	6·6	4·5	12·6	8·5
07	10 01·8	10 03·4	9 34·3	0·7	0·5	6·7	4·5	12·7	8·6
08	10 02·0	10 03·6	9 34·6	0·8	0·5	6·8	4·6	12·8	8·6
09	10 02·3	10 03·9	9 34·8	0·9	0·6	6·9	4·7	12·9	8·7
10	10 02·5	10 04·1	9 35·1	1·0	0·7	7·0	4·7	13·0	8·8
11	10 02·8	10 04·4	9 35·3	1·1	0·7	7·1	4·8	13·1	8·8
12	10 03·0	10 04·7	9 35·5	1·2	0·8	7·2	4·9	13·2	8·9
13	10 03·3	10 04·9	9 35·8	1·3	0·9	7·3	4·9	13·3	9·0
14	10 03·5	10 05·2	9 36·0	1·4	0·9	7·4	5·0	13·4	9·0
15	10 03·8	10 05·4	9 36·2	1·5	1·0	7·5	5·1	13·5	9·1
16	10 04·0	10 05·7	9 36·5	1·6	1·1	7·6	5·1	13·6	9·2
17	10 04·3	10 05·9	9 36·7	1·7	1·1	7·7	5·2	13·7	9·2
18	10 04·5	10 06·2	9 37·0	1·8	1·2	7·8	5·3	13·8	9·3
19	10 04·8	10 06·4	9 37·2	1·9	1·3	7·9	5·3	13·9	9·4
20	10 05·0	10 06·7	9 37·4	2·0	1·4	8·0	5·4	14·0	9·5
21	10 05·3	10 06·9	9 37·7	2·1	1·4	8·1	5·5	14·1	9·5
22	10 05·5	10 07·2	9 37·9	2·2	1·5	8·2	5·5	14·2	9·6
23	10 05·8	10 07·4	9 38·2	2·3	1·6	8·3	5·6	14·3	9·7
24	10 06·0	10 07·7	9 38·4	2·4	1·6	8·4	5·7	14·4	9·7
25	10 06·3	10 07·9	9 38·6	2·5	1·7	8·5	5·7	14·5	9·8
26	10 06·5	10 08·2	9 38·9	2·6	1·8	8·6	5·8	14·6	9·9
27	10 06·8	10 08·4	9 39·1	2·7	1·8	8·7	5·9	14·7	9·9
28	10 07·0	10 08·7	9 39·3	2·8	1·9	8·8	5·9	14·8	10·0
29	10 07·3	10 08·9	9 39·6	2·9	2·0	8·9	6·0	14·9	10·1
30	10 07·5	10 09·2	9 39·8	3·0	2·0	9·0	6·1	15·0	10·1
31	10 07·8	10 09·4	9 40·1	3·1	2·1	9·1	6·1	15·1	10·2
32	10 08·0	10 09·7	9 40·3	3·2	2·2	9·2	6·2	15·2	10·3
33	10 08·3	10 09·9	9 40·5	3·3	2·2	9·3	6·3	15·3	10·3
34	10 08·5	10 10·2	9 40·8	3·4	2·3	9·4	6·3	15·4	10·4
35	10 08·8	10 10·4	9 41·0	3·5	2·4	9·5	6·4	15·5	10·5
36	10 09·0	10 10·7	9 41·3	3·6	2·4	9·6	6·5	15·6	10·5
37	10 09·3	10 10·9	9 41·5	3·7	2·5	9·7	6·5	15·7	10·6
38	10 09·5	10 11·2	9 41·7	3·8	2·6	9·8	6·6	15·8	10·7
39	10 09·8	10 11·4	9 42·0	3·9	2·6	9·9	6·7	15·9	10·7
40	10 10·0	10 11·7	9 42·2	4·0	2·7	10·0	6·8	16·0	10·8
41	10 10·3	10 11·9	9 42·4	4·1	2·8	10·1	6·8	16·1	10·9
42	10 10·5	10 12·2	9 42·7	4·2	2·8	10·2	6·9	16·2	10·9
43	10 10·8	10 12·4	9 42·9	4·3	2·9	10·3	7·0	16·3	11·0
44	10 11·0	10 12·7	9 43·2	4·4	3·0	10·4	7·0	16·4	11·1
45	10 11·3	10 12·9	9 43·4	4·5	3·0	10·5	7·1	16·5	11·1
46	10 11·5	10 13·2	9 43·6	4·6	3·1	10·6	7·2	16·6	11·2
47	10 11·8	10 13·4	9 43·9	4·7	3·2	10·7	7·2	16·7	11·3
48	10 12·0	10 13·7	9 44·1	4·8	3·2	10·8	7·3	16·8	11·3
49	10 12·3	10 13·9	9 44·4	4·9	3·3	10·9	7·4	16·9	11·4
50	10 12·5	10 14·2	9 44·6	5·0	3·4	11·0	7·4	17·0	11·5
51	10 12·8	10 14·4	9 44·8	5·1	3·4	11·1	7·5	17·1	11·5
52	10 13·0	10 14·7	9 45·1	5·2	3·5	11·2	7·6	17·2	11·6
53	10 13·3	10 14·9	9 45·3	5·3	3·6	11·3	7·6	17·3	11·7
54	10 13·5	10 15·2	9 45·6	5·4	3·6	11·4	7·7	17·4	11·7
55	10 13·8	10 15·4	9 45·8	5·5	3·7	11·5	7·8	17·5	11·8
56	10 14·0	10 15·7	9 46·0	5·6	3·8	11·6	7·8	17·6	11·9
57	10 14·3	10 15·9	9 46·3	5·7	3·8	11·7	7·9	17·7	11·9
58	10 14·5	10 16·2	9 46·5	5·8	3·9	11·8	8·0	17·8	12·0
59	10 14·8	10 16·4	9 46·7	5·9	4·0	11·9	8·0	17·9	12·1
60	10 15·0	10 16·7	9 47·0	6·0	4·1	12·0	8·1	18·0	12·2

41	SUN PLANETS	ARIES	MOON	v or d	Corrⁿ	v or d	Corrⁿ	v or d	Corrⁿ
s	° ′	° ′	° ′	′	′	′	′	′	′
00	10 15·0	10 16·7	9 47·0	0·0	0·0	6·0	4·2	12·0	8·3
01	10 15·3	10 16·9	9 47·2	0·1	0·1	6·1	4·2	12·1	8·4
02	10 15·5	10 17·2	9 47·5	0·2	0·1	6·2	4·3	12·2	8·4
03	10 15·8	10 17·4	9 47·7	0·3	0·2	6·3	4·4	12·3	8·5
04	10 16·0	10 17·7	9 47·9	0·4	0·3	6·4	4·4	12·4	8·6
05	10 16·3	10 17·9	9 48·2	0·5	0·3	6·5	4·5	12·5	8·6
06	10 16·5	10 18·2	9 48·4	0·6	0·4	6·6	4·6	12·6	8·7
07	10 16·8	10 18·4	9 48·7	0·7	0·5	6·7	4·6	12·7	8·8
08	10 17·0	10 18·7	9 48·9	0·8	0·6	6·8	4·7	12·8	8·9
09	10 17·3	10 18·9	9 49·1	0·9	0·6	6·9	4·8	12·9	8·9
10	10 17·5	10 19·2	9 49·4	1·0	0·7	7·0	4·8	13·0	9·0
11	10 17·8	10 19·4	9 49·6	1·1	0·8	7·1	4·9	13·1	9·1
12	10 18·0	10 19·7	9 49·8	1·2	0·8	7·2	5·0	13·2	9·1
13	10 18·3	10 19·9	9 50·1	1·3	0·9	7·3	5·0	13·3	9·2
14	10 18·5	10 20·2	9 50·3	1·4	1·0	7·4	5·1	13·4	9·3
15	10 18·8	10 20·4	9 50·6	1·5	1·0	7·5	5·2	13·5	9·3
16	10 19·0	10 20·7	9 50·8	1·6	1·1	7·6	5·3	13·6	9·4
17	10 19·3	10 20·9	9 51·0	1·7	1·2	7·7	5·3	13·7	9·5
18	10 19·5	10 21·2	9 51·3	1·8	1·2	7·8	5·4	13·8	9·5
19	10 19·8	10 21·4	9 51·5	1·9	1·3	7·9	5·5	13·9	9·6
20	10 20·0	10 21·7	9 51·8	2·0	1·4	8·0	5·5	14·0	9·7
21	10 20·3	10 21·9	9 52·0	2·1	1·5	8·1	5·6	14·1	9·8
22	10 20·5	10 22·2	9 52·2	2·2	1·5	8·2	5·7	14·2	9·8
23	10 20·8	10 22·4	9 52·5	2·3	1·6	8·3	5·7	14·3	9·9
24	10 21·0	10 22·7	9 52·7	2·4	1·7	8·4	5·8	14·4	10·0
25	10 21·3	10 23·0	9 52·9	2·5	1·7	8·5	5·9	14·5	10·0
26	10 21·5	10 23·2	9 53·2	2·6	1·8	8·6	5·9	14·6	10·1
27	10 21·8	10 23·5	9 53·4	2·7	1·9	8·7	6·0	14·7	10·2
28	10 22·0	10 23·7	9 53·7	2·8	1·9	8·8	6·1	14·8	10·2
29	10 22·3	10 24·0	9 53·9	2·9	2·0	8·9	6·2	14·9	10·3
30	10 22·5	10 24·2	9 54·1	3·0	2·1	9·0	6·2	15·0	10·4
31	10 22·8	10 24·5	9 54·4	3·1	2·1	9·1	6·3	15·1	10·4
32	10 23·0	10 24·7	9 54·6	3·2	2·2	9·2	6·4	15·2	10·5
33	10 23·3	10 25·0	9 54·9	3·3	2·3	9·3	6·4	15·3	10·6
34	10 23·5	10 25·2	9 55·1	3·4	2·4	9·4	6·5	15·4	10·7
35	10 23·8	10 25·5	9 55·3	3·5	2·4	9·5	6·6	15·5	10·7
36	10 24·0	10 25·7	9 55·6	3·6	2·5	9·6	6·6	15·6	10·8
37	10 24·3	10 26·0	9 55·8	3·7	2·6	9·7	6·7	15·7	10·9
38	10 24·5	10 26·2	9 56·1	3·8	2·6	9·8	6·8	15·8	10·9
39	10 24·8	10 26·5	9 56·3	3·9	2·7	9·9	6·8	15·9	11·0
40	10 25·0	10 26·7	9 56·5	4·0	2·8	10·0	6·9	16·0	11·1
41	10 25·3	10 27·0	9 56·8	4·1	2·8	10·1	7·0	16·1	11·1
42	10 25·5	10 27·2	9 57·0	4·2	2·9	10·2	7·1	16·2	11·2
43	10 25·8	10 27·5	9 57·2	4·3	3·0	10·3	7·1	16·3	11·3
44	10 26·0	10 27·7	9 57·5	4·4	3·0	10·4	7·2	16·4	11·3
45	10 26·3	10 28·0	9 57·7	4·5	3·1	10·5	7·3	16·5	11·4
46	10 26·5	10 28·2	9 58·0	4·6	3·2	10·6	7·3	16·6	11·5
47	10 26·8	10 28·5	9 58·2	4·7	3·3	10·7	7·4	16·7	11·6
48	10 27·0	10 28·7	9 58·4	4·8	3·3	10·8	7·5	16·8	11·6
49	10 27·3	10 29·0	9 58·7	4·9	3·4	10·9	7·5	16·9	11·7
50	10 27·5	10 29·2	9 58·9	5·0	3·5	11·0	7·6	17·0	11·8
51	10 27·8	10 29·5	9 59·2	5·1	3·5	11·1	7·7	17·1	11·8
52	10 28·0	10 29·7	9 59·4	5·2	3·6	11·2	7·7	17·2	11·9
53	10 28·3	10 30·0	9 59·6	5·3	3·7	11·3	7·8	17·3	12·0
54	10 28·5	10 30·2	9 59·9	5·4	3·7	11·4	7·9	17·4	12·0
55	10 28·8	10 30·5	10 00·1	5·5	3·8	11·5	8·0	17·5	12·1
56	10 29·0	10 30·7	10 00·3	5·6	3·9	11·6	8·0	17·6	12·2
57	10 29·3	10 31·0	10 00·6	5·7	3·9	11·7	8·1	17·7	12·2
58	10 29·5	10 31·2	10 00·8	5·8	4·0	11·8	8·2	17·8	12·3
59	10 29·8	10 31·5	10 01·1	5·9	4·1	11·9	8·2	17·9	12·4
60	10 30·0	10 31·7	10 01·3	6·0	4·2	12·0	8·3	18·0	12·5

xxii

© British Crown Copyright 2018. All rights reserved.

42ᵐ

42 s	SUN PLANETS	ARIES	MOON	v or Corrⁿ d		v or Corrⁿ d		v or Corrⁿ d	
00	10 30.0	10 31.7	10 01.3	0.0	0.0	6.0	4.3	12.0	8.5
01	10 30.3	10 32.0	10 01.5	0.1	0.1	6.1	4.3	12.1	8.6
02	10 30.5	10 32.2	10 01.8	0.2	0.1	6.2	4.4	12.2	8.6
03	10 30.8	10 32.5	10 02.0	0.3	0.2	6.3	4.5	12.3	8.7
04	10 31.0	10 32.7	10 02.3	0.4	0.3	6.4	4.5	12.4	8.8
05	10 31.3	10 33.0	10 02.5	0.5	0.4	6.5	4.6	12.5	8.9
06	10 31.5	10 33.2	10 02.7	0.6	0.4	6.6	4.7	12.6	8.9
07	10 31.8	10 33.5	10 03.0	0.7	0.5	6.7	4.7	12.7	9.0
08	10 32.0	10 33.7	10 03.2	0.8	0.6	6.8	4.8	12.8	9.1
09	10 32.3	10 34.0	10 03.4	0.9	0.6	6.9	4.9	12.9	9.1
10	10 32.5	10 34.2	10 03.7	1.0	0.7	7.0	5.0	13.0	9.2
11	10 32.8	10 34.5	10 03.9	1.1	0.8	7.1	5.0	13.1	9.3
12	10 33.0	10 34.7	10 04.2	1.2	0.9	7.2	5.1	13.2	9.4
13	10 33.3	10 35.0	10 04.4	1.3	0.9	7.3	5.2	13.3	9.4
14	10 33.5	10 35.2	10 04.6	1.4	1.0	7.4	5.2	13.4	9.5
15	10 33.8	10 35.5	10 04.9	1.5	1.1	7.5	5.3	13.5	9.6
16	10 34.0	10 35.7	10 05.1	1.6	1.1	7.6	5.4	13.6	9.6
17	10 34.3	10 36.0	10 05.4	1.7	1.2	7.7	5.5	13.7	9.7
18	10 34.5	10 36.2	10 05.6	1.8	1.3	7.8	5.5	13.8	9.8
19	10 34.8	10 36.5	10 05.8	1.9	1.3	7.9	5.6	13.9	9.8
20	10 35.0	10 36.7	10 06.1	2.0	1.4	8.0	5.7	14.0	9.9
21	10 35.3	10 37.0	10 06.3	2.1	1.5	8.1	5.7	14.1	10.0
22	10 35.5	10 37.2	10 06.5	2.2	1.6	8.2	5.8	14.2	10.1
23	10 35.8	10 37.5	10 06.8	2.3	1.6	8.3	5.9	14.3	10.1
24	10 36.0	10 37.7	10 07.0	2.4	1.7	8.4	6.0	14.4	10.2
25	10 36.3	10 38.0	10 07.3	2.5	1.8	8.5	6.0	14.5	10.3
26	10 36.5	10 38.2	10 07.5	2.6	1.8	8.6	6.1	14.6	10.3
27	10 36.8	10 38.5	10 07.7	2.7	1.9	8.7	6.2	14.7	10.4
28	10 37.0	10 38.7	10 08.0	2.8	2.0	8.8	6.2	14.8	10.5
29	10 37.3	10 39.0	10 08.2	2.9	2.1	8.9	6.3	14.9	10.6
30	10 37.5	10 39.2	10 08.5	3.0	2.1	9.0	6.4	15.0	10.6
31	10 37.8	10 39.5	10 08.7	3.1	2.2	9.1	6.4	15.1	10.7
32	10 38.0	10 39.7	10 08.9	3.2	2.3	9.2	6.5	15.2	10.8
33	10 38.3	10 40.0	10 09.2	3.3	2.3	9.3	6.6	15.3	10.8
34	10 38.5	10 40.2	10 09.4	3.4	2.4	9.4	6.7	15.4	10.9
35	10 38.8	10 40.5	10 09.7	3.5	2.5	9.5	6.7	15.5	11.0
36	10 39.0	10 40.7	10 09.9	3.6	2.6	9.6	6.8	15.6	11.1
37	10 39.3	10 41.0	10 10.1	3.7	2.6	9.7	6.9	15.7	11.1
38	10 39.5	10 41.3	10 10.4	3.8	2.7	9.8	6.9	15.8	11.2
39	10 39.8	10 41.5	10 10.6	3.9	2.8	9.9	7.0	15.9	11.3
40	10 40.0	10 41.8	10 10.8	4.0	2.8	10.0	7.1	16.0	11.3
41	10 40.3	10 42.0	10 11.1	4.1	2.9	10.1	7.2	16.1	11.4
42	10 40.5	10 42.3	10 11.3	4.2	3.0	10.2	7.2	16.2	11.5
43	10 40.8	10 42.5	10 11.6	4.3	3.0	10.3	7.3	16.3	11.5
44	10 41.0	10 42.8	10 11.8	4.4	3.1	10.4	7.4	16.4	11.6
45	10 41.3	10 43.0	10 12.0	4.5	3.2	10.5	7.4	16.5	11.7
46	10 41.5	10 43.3	10 12.3	4.6	3.3	10.6	7.5	16.6	11.8
47	10 41.8	10 43.5	10 12.5	4.7	3.3	10.7	7.6	16.7	11.8
48	10 42.0	10 43.8	10 12.8	4.8	3.4	10.8	7.7	16.8	11.9
49	10 42.3	10 44.0	10 13.0	4.9	3.5	10.9	7.7	16.9	12.0
50	10 42.5	10 44.3	10 13.2	5.0	3.5	11.0	7.8	17.0	12.0
51	10 42.8	10 44.5	10 13.5	5.1	3.6	11.1	7.9	17.1	12.1
52	10 43.0	10 44.8	10 13.7	5.2	3.7	11.2	7.9	17.2	12.2
53	10 43.3	10 45.0	10 13.9	5.3	3.8	11.3	8.0	17.3	12.3
54	10 43.5	10 45.3	10 14.2	5.4	3.8	11.4	8.1	17.4	12.3
55	10 43.8	10 45.5	10 14.4	5.5	3.9	11.5	8.1	17.5	12.4
56	10 44.0	10 45.8	10 14.7	5.6	4.0	11.6	8.2	17.6	12.5
57	10 44.3	10 46.0	10 14.9	5.7	4.0	11.7	8.3	17.7	12.5
58	10 44.5	10 46.3	10 15.1	5.8	4.1	11.8	8.4	17.8	12.6
59	10 44.8	10 46.5	10 15.4	5.9	4.2	11.9	8.4	17.9	12.7
60	10 45.0	10 46.8	10 15.6	6.0	4.3	12.0	8.5	18.0	12.8

43ᵐ

43 s	SUN PLANETS	ARIES	MOON	v or Corrⁿ d		v or Corrⁿ d		v or Corrⁿ d	
00	10 45.0	10 46.8	10 15.6	0.0	0.0	6.0	4.4	12.0	8.7
01	10 45.3	10 47.0	10 15.9	0.1	0.1	6.1	4.4	12.1	8.8
02	10 45.5	10 47.3	10 16.1	0.2	0.1	6.2	4.5	12.2	8.8
03	10 45.8	10 47.5	10 16.3	0.3	0.2	6.3	4.6	12.3	8.9
04	10 46.0	10 47.8	10 16.6	0.4	0.3	6.4	4.6	12.4	9.0
05	10 46.3	10 48.0	10 16.8	0.5	0.4	6.5	4.7	12.5	9.1
06	10 46.5	10 48.3	10 17.0	0.6	0.4	6.6	4.8	12.6	9.1
07	10 46.8	10 48.5	10 17.3	0.7	0.5	6.7	4.9	12.7	9.2
08	10 47.0	10 48.8	10 17.5	0.8	0.6	6.8	4.9	12.8	9.3
09	10 47.3	10 49.0	10 17.8	0.9	0.7	6.9	5.0	12.9	9.4
10	10 47.5	10 49.3	10 18.0	1.0	0.7	7.0	5.1	13.0	9.4
11	10 47.8	10 49.5	10 18.2	1.1	0.8	7.1	5.1	13.1	9.5
12	10 48.0	10 49.8	10 18.5	1.2	0.9	7.2	5.2	13.2	9.6
13	10 48.3	10 50.0	10 18.7	1.3	0.9	7.3	5.3	13.3	9.6
14	10 48.5	10 50.3	10 19.0	1.4	1.0	7.4	5.4	13.4	9.7
15	10 48.8	10 50.5	10 19.2	1.5	1.1	7.5	5.4	13.5	9.8
16	10 49.0	10 50.8	10 19.4	1.6	1.2	7.6	5.5	13.6	9.9
17	10 49.3	10 51.0	10 19.7	1.7	1.2	7.7	5.6	13.7	9.9
18	10 49.5	10 51.3	10 19.9	1.8	1.3	7.8	5.7	13.8	10.0
19	10 49.8	10 51.5	10 20.2	1.9	1.4	7.9	5.7	13.9	10.1
20	10 50.0	10 51.8	10 20.4	2.0	1.5	8.0	5.8	14.0	10.2
21	10 50.3	10 52.0	10 20.6	2.1	1.5	8.1	5.9	14.1	10.2
22	10 50.5	10 52.3	10 20.9	2.2	1.6	8.2	5.9	14.2	10.3
23	10 50.8	10 52.5	10 21.1	2.3	1.7	8.3	6.0	14.3	10.4
24	10 51.0	10 52.8	10 21.3	2.4	1.7	8.4	6.1	14.4	10.4
25	10 51.3	10 53.0	10 21.6	2.5	1.8	8.5	6.2	14.5	10.5
26	10 51.5	10 53.3	10 21.8	2.6	1.9	8.6	6.2	14.6	10.6
27	10 51.8	10 53.5	10 22.1	2.7	2.0	8.7	6.3	14.7	10.7
28	10 52.0	10 53.8	10 22.3	2.8	2.0	8.8	6.4	14.8	10.7
29	10 52.3	10 54.0	10 22.5	2.9	2.1	8.9	6.5	14.9	10.8
30	10 52.5	10 54.3	10 22.8	3.0	2.2	9.0	6.5	15.0	10.9
31	10 52.8	10 54.5	10 23.0	3.1	2.2	9.1	6.6	15.1	10.9
32	10 53.0	10 54.8	10 23.3	3.2	2.3	9.2	6.7	15.2	11.0
33	10 53.3	10 55.0	10 23.5	3.3	2.4	9.3	6.7	15.3	11.1
34	10 53.5	10 55.3	10 23.7	3.4	2.5	9.4	6.8	15.4	11.2
35	10 53.8	10 55.5	10 24.0	3.5	2.5	9.5	6.9	15.5	11.2
36	10 54.0	10 55.8	10 24.2	3.6	2.6	9.6	7.0	15.6	11.3
37	10 54.3	10 56.0	10 24.4	3.7	2.7	9.7	7.0	15.7	11.4
38	10 54.5	10 56.3	10 24.7	3.8	2.8	9.8	7.1	15.8	11.5
39	10 54.8	10 56.5	10 24.9	3.9	2.8	9.9	7.2	15.9	11.5
40	10 55.0	10 56.8	10 25.2	4.0	2.9	10.0	7.3	16.0	11.6
41	10 55.3	10 57.0	10 25.4	4.1	3.0	10.1	7.3	16.1	11.7
42	10 55.5	10 57.3	10 25.6	4.2	3.0	10.2	7.4	16.2	11.7
43	10 55.8	10 57.5	10 25.9	4.3	3.1	10.3	7.5	16.3	11.8
44	10 56.0	10 57.8	10 26.1	4.4	3.2	10.4	7.5	16.4	11.9
45	10 56.3	10 58.0	10 26.4	4.5	3.3	10.5	7.6	16.5	12.0
46	10 56.5	10 58.3	10 26.6	4.6	3.3	10.6	7.7	16.6	12.0
47	10 56.8	10 58.5	10 26.8	4.7	3.4	10.7	7.8	16.7	12.1
48	10 57.0	10 58.8	10 27.1	4.8	3.5	10.8	7.8	16.8	12.2
49	10 57.3	10 59.0	10 27.3	4.9	3.6	10.9	7.9	16.9	12.3
50	10 57.5	10 59.3	10 27.5	5.0	3.6	11.0	8.0	17.0	12.3
51	10 57.8	10 59.6	10 27.8	5.1	3.7	11.1	8.0	17.1	12.4
52	10 58.0	10 59.8	10 28.0	5.2	3.8	11.2	8.1	17.2	12.5
53	10 58.3	11 00.1	10 28.3	5.3	3.8	11.3	8.2	17.3	12.5
54	10 58.5	11 00.3	10 28.5	5.4	3.9	11.4	8.3	17.4	12.6
55	10 58.8	11 00.6	10 28.7	5.5	4.0	11.5	8.3	17.5	12.7
56	10 59.0	11 00.8	10 29.0	5.6	4.1	11.6	8.4	17.6	12.8
57	10 59.3	11 01.1	10 29.2	5.7	4.1	11.7	8.5	17.7	12.8
58	10 59.5	11 01.3	10 29.5	5.8	4.2	11.8	8.6	17.8	12.9
59	10 59.8	11 01.6	10 29.7	5.9	4.3	11.9	8.6	17.9	13.0
60	11 00.0	11 01.8	10 29.9	6.0	4.4	12.0	8.7	18.0	13.1

© British Crown Copyright 2018. All rights reserved.

44ᵐ

44	SUN PLANETS	ARIES	MOON	v or Corrⁿ / d	v or Corrⁿ / d	v or Corrⁿ / d
s	° ′	° ′	° ′	′ ′	′ ′	′ ′
00	11 00.0	11 01.8	10 29.9	0.0 0.0	6.0 4.5	12.0 8.9
01	11 00.3	11 02.1	10 30.2	0.1 0.1	6.1 4.5	12.1 9.0
02	11 00.5	11 02.3	10 30.4	0.2 0.1	6.2 4.6	12.2 9.0
03	11 00.8	11 02.6	10 30.6	0.3 0.2	6.3 4.7	12.3 9.1
04	11 01.0	11 02.8	10 30.9	0.4 0.3	6.4 4.7	12.4 9.2
05	11 01.3	11 03.1	10 31.1	0.5 0.4	6.5 4.8	12.5 9.3
06	11 01.5	11 03.3	10 31.4	0.6 0.4	6.6 4.9	12.6 9.3
07	11 01.8	11 03.6	10 31.6	0.7 0.5	6.7 5.0	12.7 9.4
08	11 02.0	11 03.8	10 31.8	0.8 0.6	6.8 5.0	12.8 9.5
09	11 02.3	11 04.1	10 32.1	0.9 0.7	6.9 5.1	12.9 9.6
10	11 02.5	11 04.3	10 32.3	1.0 0.7	7.0 5.2	13.0 9.6
11	11 02.8	11 04.6	10 32.6	1.1 0.8	7.1 5.3	13.1 9.7
12	11 03.0	11 04.8	10 32.8	1.2 0.9	7.2 5.3	13.2 9.8
13	11 03.3	11 05.1	10 33.0	1.3 1.0	7.3 5.4	13.3 9.9
14	11 03.5	11 05.3	10 33.3	1.4 1.0	7.4 5.5	13.4 9.9
15	11 03.8	11 05.6	10 33.5	1.5 1.1	7.5 5.6	13.5 10.0
16	11 04.0	11 05.8	10 33.8	1.6 1.2	7.6 5.6	13.6 10.1
17	11 04.3	11 06.1	10 34.0	1.7 1.3	7.7 5.7	13.7 10.2
18	11 04.5	11 06.3	10 34.2	1.8 1.3	7.8 5.8	13.8 10.2
19	11 04.8	11 06.6	10 34.5	1.9 1.4	7.9 5.9	13.9 10.3
20	11 05.0	11 06.8	10 34.7	2.0 1.5	8.0 5.9	14.0 10.4
21	11 05.3	11 07.1	10 34.9	2.1 1.6	8.1 6.0	14.1 10.5
22	11 05.5	11 07.3	10 35.2	2.2 1.6	8.2 6.1	14.2 10.5
23	11 05.8	11 07.6	10 35.4	2.3 1.7	8.3 6.2	14.3 10.6
24	11 06.0	11 07.8	10 35.7	2.4 1.8	8.4 6.2	14.4 10.7
25	11 06.3	11 08.1	10 35.9	2.5 1.9	8.5 6.3	14.5 10.8
26	11 06.5	11 08.3	10 36.1	2.6 1.9	8.6 6.4	14.6 10.8
27	11 06.8	11 08.6	10 36.4	2.7 2.0	8.7 6.5	14.7 10.9
28	11 07.0	11 08.8	10 36.6	2.8 2.1	8.8 6.5	14.8 11.0
29	11 07.3	11 09.1	10 36.9	2.9 2.2	8.9 6.6	14.9 11.1
30	11 07.5	11 09.3	10 37.1	3.0 2.2	9.0 6.7	15.0 11.1
31	11 07.8	11 09.6	10 37.3	3.1 2.3	9.1 6.7	15.1 11.2
32	11 08.0	11 09.8	10 37.6	3.2 2.4	9.2 6.8	15.2 11.3
33	11 08.3	11 10.1	10 37.8	3.3 2.4	9.3 6.9	15.3 11.3
34	11 08.5	11 10.3	10 38.0	3.4 2.5	9.4 7.0	15.4 11.4
35	11 08.8	11 10.6	10 38.3	3.5 2.6	9.5 7.0	15.5 11.5
36	11 09.0	11 10.8	10 38.5	3.6 2.7	9.6 7.1	15.6 11.6
37	11 09.3	11 11.1	10 38.8	3.7 2.7	9.7 7.2	15.7 11.6
38	11 09.5	11 11.3	10 39.0	3.8 2.8	9.8 7.3	15.8 11.7
39	11 09.8	11 11.6	10 39.2	3.9 2.9	9.9 7.3	15.9 11.8
40	11 10.0	11 11.8	10 39.5	4.0 3.0	10.0 7.4	16.0 11.9
41	11 10.3	11 12.1	10 39.7	4.1 3.0	10.1 7.5	16.1 11.9
42	11 10.5	11 12.3	10 40.0	4.2 3.1	10.2 7.6	16.2 12.0
43	11 10.8	11 12.6	10 40.2	4.3 3.2	10.3 7.6	16.3 12.1
44	11 11.0	11 12.8	10 40.4	4.4 3.3	10.4 7.7	16.4 12.2
45	11 11.3	11 13.1	10 40.7	4.5 3.3	10.5 7.8	16.5 12.2
46	11 11.5	11 13.3	10 40.9	4.6 3.4	10.6 7.9	16.6 12.3
47	11 11.8	11 13.6	10 41.1	4.7 3.5	10.7 7.9	16.7 12.4
48	11 12.0	11 13.8	10 41.4	4.8 3.6	10.8 8.0	16.8 12.5
49	11 12.3	11 14.1	10 41.6	4.9 3.6	10.9 8.1	16.9 12.5
50	11 12.5	11 14.3	10 41.9	5.0 3.7	11.0 8.2	17.0 12.6
51	11 12.8	11 14.6	10 42.1	5.1 3.8	11.1 8.2	17.1 12.7
52	11 13.0	11 14.8	10 42.3	5.2 3.9	11.2 8.3	17.2 12.8
53	11 13.3	11 15.1	10 42.6	5.3 3.9	11.3 8.4	17.3 12.8
54	11 13.5	11 15.3	10 42.8	5.4 4.0	11.4 8.5	17.4 12.9
55	11 13.8	11 15.6	10 43.1	5.5 4.1	11.5 8.5	17.5 13.0
56	11 14.0	11 15.8	10 43.3	5.6 4.2	11.6 8.6	17.6 13.1
57	11 14.3	11 16.1	10 43.5	5.7 4.2	11.7 8.7	17.7 13.1
58	11 14.5	11 16.3	10 43.8	5.8 4.3	11.8 8.8	17.8 13.2
59	11 14.8	11 16.6	10 44.0	5.9 4.4	11.9 8.8	17.9 13.3
60	11 15.0	11 16.8	10 44.3	6.0 4.5	12.0 8.9	18.0 13.4

45ᵐ

45	SUN PLANETS	ARIES	MOON	v or Corrⁿ / d	v or Corrⁿ / d	v or Corrⁿ / d
s	° ′	° ′	° ′	′ ′	′ ′	′ ′
00	11 15.0	11 16.8	10 44.3	0.0 0.0	6.0 4.6	12.0 9.1
01	11 15.3	11 17.1	10 44.5	0.1 0.1	6.1 4.6	12.1 9.2
02	11 15.5	11 17.3	10 44.7	0.2 0.2	6.2 4.7	12.2 9.3
03	11 15.8	11 17.6	10 45.0	0.3 0.2	6.3 4.8	12.3 9.3
04	11 16.0	11 17.9	10 45.2	0.4 0.3	6.4 4.9	12.4 9.4
05	11 16.3	11 18.1	10 45.4	0.5 0.4	6.5 4.9	12.5 9.5
06	11 16.5	11 18.4	10 45.7	0.6 0.5	6.6 5.0	12.6 9.6
07	11 16.8	11 18.6	10 45.9	0.7 0.5	6.7 5.1	12.7 9.6
08	11 17.0	11 18.9	10 46.2	0.8 0.6	6.8 5.2	12.8 9.7
09	11 17.3	11 19.1	10 46.4	0.9 0.7	6.9 5.2	12.9 9.8
10	11 17.5	11 19.4	10 46.6	1.0 0.8	7.0 5.3	13.0 9.9
11	11 17.8	11 19.6	10 46.9	1.1 0.8	7.1 5.4	13.1 9.9
12	11 18.0	11 19.9	10 47.1	1.2 0.9	7.2 5.5	13.2 10.0
13	11 18.3	11 20.1	10 47.4	1.3 1.0	7.3 5.5	13.3 10.1
14	11 18.5	11 20.4	10 47.6	1.4 1.1	7.4 5.6	13.4 10.2
15	11 18.8	11 20.6	10 47.8	1.5 1.1	7.5 5.7	13.5 10.2
16	11 19.0	11 20.9	10 48.1	1.6 1.2	7.6 5.8	13.6 10.3
17	11 19.3	11 21.1	10 48.3	1.7 1.3	7.7 5.8	13.7 10.4
18	11 19.5	11 21.4	10 48.5	1.8 1.4	7.8 5.9	13.8 10.5
19	11 19.8	11 21.6	10 48.8	1.9 1.4	7.9 6.0	13.9 10.5
20	11 20.0	11 21.9	10 49.0	2.0 1.5	8.0 6.1	14.0 10.6
21	11 20.3	11 22.1	10 49.3	2.1 1.6	8.1 6.1	14.1 10.7
22	11 20.5	11 22.4	10 49.5	2.2 1.7	8.2 6.2	14.2 10.8
23	11 20.8	11 22.6	10 49.7	2.3 1.7	8.3 6.3	14.3 10.8
24	11 21.0	11 22.9	10 50.0	2.4 1.8	8.4 6.4	14.4 10.9
25	11 21.3	11 23.1	10 50.2	2.5 1.9	8.5 6.4	14.5 11.0
26	11 21.5	11 23.4	10 50.5	2.6 2.0	8.6 6.5	14.6 11.1
27	11 21.8	11 23.6	10 50.7	2.7 2.0	8.7 6.6	14.7 11.1
28	11 22.0	11 23.9	10 50.9	2.8 2.1	8.8 6.7	14.8 11.2
29	11 22.3	11 24.1	10 51.2	2.9 2.2	8.9 6.7	14.9 11.3
30	11 22.5	11 24.4	10 51.4	3.0 2.3	9.0 6.8	15.0 11.4
31	11 22.8	11 24.6	10 51.6	3.1 2.4	9.1 6.9	15.1 11.5
32	11 23.0	11 24.9	10 51.9	3.2 2.4	9.2 7.0	15.2 11.5
33	11 23.3	11 25.1	10 52.1	3.3 2.5	9.3 7.1	15.3 11.6
34	11 23.5	11 25.4	10 52.4	3.4 2.6	9.4 7.1	15.4 11.7
35	11 23.8	11 25.6	10 52.6	3.5 2.7	9.5 7.2	15.5 11.8
36	11 24.0	11 25.9	10 52.8	3.6 2.7	9.6 7.3	15.6 11.8
37	11 24.3	11 26.1	10 53.1	3.7 2.8	9.7 7.4	15.7 11.9
38	11 24.5	11 26.4	10 53.3	3.8 2.9	9.8 7.4	15.8 12.0
39	11 24.8	11 26.6	10 53.6	3.9 3.0	9.9 7.5	15.9 12.1
40	11 25.0	11 26.9	10 53.8	4.0 3.0	10.0 7.6	16.0 12.1
41	11 25.3	11 27.1	10 54.0	4.1 3.1	10.1 7.7	16.1 12.2
42	11 25.5	11 27.4	10 54.3	4.2 3.2	10.2 7.7	16.2 12.3
43	11 25.8	11 27.6	10 54.5	4.3 3.3	10.3 7.8	16.3 12.4
44	11 26.0	11 27.9	10 54.7	4.4 3.3	10.4 7.9	16.4 12.4
45	11 26.3	11 28.1	10 55.0	4.5 3.4	10.5 8.0	16.5 12.5
46	11 26.5	11 28.4	10 55.2	4.6 3.5	10.6 8.0	16.6 12.6
47	11 26.8	11 28.6	10 55.5	4.7 3.6	10.7 8.1	16.7 12.7
48	11 27.0	11 28.9	10 55.7	4.8 3.6	10.8 8.2	16.8 12.7
49	11 27.3	11 29.1	10 55.9	4.9 3.7	10.9 8.3	16.9 12.8
50	11 27.5	11 29.4	10 56.2	5.0 3.8	11.0 8.3	17.0 12.9
51	11 27.8	11 29.6	10 56.4	5.1 3.9	11.1 8.4	17.1 13.0
52	11 28.0	11 29.9	10 56.7	5.2 3.9	11.2 8.5	17.2 13.0
53	11 28.3	11 30.1	10 56.9	5.3 4.0	11.3 8.6	17.3 13.1
54	11 28.5	11 30.4	10 57.1	5.4 4.1	11.4 8.6	17.4 13.2
55	11 28.8	11 30.6	10 57.4	5.5 4.2	11.5 8.7	17.5 13.3
56	11 29.0	11 30.9	10 57.6	5.6 4.2	11.6 8.8	17.6 13.3
57	11 29.3	11 31.1	10 57.9	5.7 4.3	11.7 8.8	17.7 13.4
58	11 29.5	11 31.4	10 58.1	5.8 4.4	11.8 8.9	17.8 13.5
59	11 29.8	11 31.6	10 58.3	5.9 4.5	11.9 9.0	17.9 13.6
60	11 30.0	11 31.9	10 58.6	6.0 4.6	12.0 9.1	18.0 13.7

© British Crown Copyright 2018. All rights reserved.

46ᵐ

s	SUN PLANETS	ARIES	MOON	v or Corrn d	v or Corrn d	v or Corrn d
00	11 30.0	11 31.9	10 58.6	0.0 0.0	6.0 4.7	12.0 9.3
01	11 30.3	11 32.1	10 58.8	0.1 0.1	6.1 4.7	12.1 9.4
02	11 30.5	11 32.4	10 59.0	0.2 0.2	6.2 4.8	12.2 9.5
03	11 30.8	11 32.6	10 59.3	0.3 0.2	6.3 4.9	12.3 9.5
04	11 31.0	11 32.9	10 59.5	0.4 0.3	6.4 5.0	12.4 9.6
05	11 31.3	11 33.1	10 59.8	0.5 0.4	6.5 5.0	12.5 9.7
06	11 31.5	11 33.4	11 00.0	0.6 0.5	6.6 5.1	12.6 9.8
07	11 31.8	11 33.6	11 00.2	0.7 0.5	6.7 5.2	12.7 9.8
08	11 32.0	11 33.9	11 00.5	0.8 0.6	6.8 5.3	12.8 9.9
09	11 32.3	11 34.1	11 00.7	0.9 0.7	6.9 5.3	12.9 10.0
10	11 32.5	11 34.4	11 01.0	1.0 0.8	7.0 5.4	13.0 10.1
11	11 32.8	11 34.6	11 01.2	1.1 0.9	7.1 5.5	13.1 10.2
12	11 33.0	11 34.9	11 01.4	1.2 0.9	7.2 5.6	13.2 10.2
13	11 33.3	11 35.1	11 01.7	1.3 1.0	7.3 5.7	13.3 10.3
14	11 33.5	11 35.4	11 01.9	1.4 1.1	7.4 5.7	13.4 10.4
15	11 33.8	11 35.6	11 02.1	1.5 1.2	7.5 5.8	13.5 10.5
16	11 34.0	11 35.9	11 02.4	1.6 1.2	7.6 5.9	13.6 10.5
17	11 34.3	11 36.2	11 02.6	1.7 1.3	7.7 6.0	13.7 10.6
18	11 34.5	11 36.4	11 02.9	1.8 1.4	7.8 6.0	13.8 10.7
19	11 34.8	11 36.7	11 03.1	1.9 1.5	7.9 6.1	13.9 10.8
20	11 35.0	11 36.9	11 03.3	2.0 1.6	8.0 6.2	14.0 10.9
21	11 35.3	11 37.2	11 03.6	2.1 1.6	8.1 6.3	14.1 10.9
22	11 35.5	11 37.4	11 03.8	2.2 1.7	8.2 6.4	14.2 11.0
23	11 35.8	11 37.7	11 04.1	2.3 1.8	8.3 6.4	14.3 11.1
24	11 36.0	11 37.9	11 04.3	2.4 1.9	8.4 6.5	14.4 11.2
25	11 36.3	11 38.2	11 04.5	2.5 1.9	8.5 6.6	14.5 11.2
26	11 36.5	11 38.4	11 04.8	2.6 2.0	8.6 6.7	14.6 11.3
27	11 36.8	11 38.7	11 05.0	2.7 2.1	8.7 6.7	14.7 11.4
28	11 37.0	11 38.9	11 05.2	2.8 2.2	8.8 6.8	14.8 11.5
29	11 37.3	11 39.2	11 05.5	2.9 2.2	8.9 6.9	14.9 11.5
30	11 37.5	11 39.4	11 05.7	3.0 2.3	9.0 7.0	15.0 11.6
31	11 37.8	11 39.7	11 06.0	3.1 2.4	9.1 7.1	15.1 11.7
32	11 38.0	11 39.9	11 06.2	3.2 2.5	9.2 7.1	15.2 11.8
33	11 38.3	11 40.2	11 06.4	3.3 2.6	9.3 7.2	15.3 11.9
34	11 38.5	11 40.4	11 06.7	3.4 2.6	9.4 7.3	15.4 11.9
35	11 38.8	11 40.7	11 06.9	3.5 2.7	9.5 7.4	15.5 12.0
36	11 39.0	11 40.9	11 07.2	3.6 2.8	9.6 7.4	15.6 12.1
37	11 39.3	11 41.2	11 07.4	3.7 2.9	9.7 7.5	15.7 12.2
38	11 39.5	11 41.4	11 07.6	3.8 2.9	9.8 7.6	15.8 12.2
39	11 39.8	11 41.7	11 07.9	3.9 3.0	9.9 7.7	15.9 12.3
40	11 40.0	11 41.9	11 08.1	4.0 3.1	10.0 7.8	16.0 12.4
41	11 40.3	11 42.2	11 08.3	4.1 3.2	10.1 7.8	16.1 12.5
42	11 40.5	11 42.4	11 08.6	4.2 3.3	10.2 7.9	16.2 12.6
43	11 40.8	11 42.7	11 08.8	4.3 3.3	10.3 8.0	16.3 12.6
44	11 41.0	11 42.9	11 09.1	4.4 3.4	10.4 8.1	16.4 12.7
45	11 41.3	11 43.2	11 09.3	4.5 3.5	10.5 8.1	16.5 12.8
46	11 41.5	11 43.4	11 09.5	4.6 3.6	10.6 8.2	16.6 12.9
47	11 41.8	11 43.7	11 09.8	4.7 3.6	10.7 8.3	16.7 12.9
48	11 42.0	11 43.9	11 10.0	4.8 3.7	10.8 8.4	16.8 13.0
49	11 42.3	11 44.2	11 10.3	4.9 3.8	10.9 8.4	16.9 13.1
50	11 42.5	11 44.4	11 10.5	5.0 3.9	11.0 8.5	17.0 13.2
51	11 42.8	11 44.7	11 10.7	5.1 4.0	11.1 8.6	17.1 13.3
52	11 43.0	11 44.9	11 11.0	5.2 4.0	11.2 8.7	17.2 13.3
53	11 43.3	11 45.2	11 11.2	5.3 4.1	11.3 8.8	17.3 13.4
54	11 43.5	11 45.4	11 11.5	5.4 4.2	11.4 8.8	17.4 13.5
55	11 43.8	11 45.7	11 11.7	5.5 4.3	11.5 8.9	17.5 13.6
56	11 44.0	11 45.9	11 11.9	5.6 4.3	11.6 9.0	17.6 13.6
57	11 44.3	11 46.2	11 12.2	5.7 4.4	11.7 9.1	17.7 13.7
58	11 44.5	11 46.4	11 12.4	5.8 4.5	11.8 9.1	17.8 13.8
59	11 44.8	11 46.7	11 12.6	5.9 4.6	11.9 9.2	17.9 13.9
60	11 45.0	11 46.9	11 12.9	6.0 4.7	12.0 9.3	18.0 14.0

47ᵐ

s	SUN PLANETS	ARIES	MOON	v or Corrn d	v or Corrn d	v or Corrn d
00	11 45.0	11 46.9	11 12.9	0.0 0.0	6.0 4.8	12.0 9.5
01	11 45.3	11 47.2	11 13.1	0.1 0.1	6.1 4.8	12.1 9.6
02	11 45.5	11 47.4	11 13.4	0.2 0.2	6.2 4.9	12.2 9.7
03	11 45.8	11 47.7	11 13.6	0.3 0.2	6.3 5.0	12.3 9.7
04	11 46.0	11 47.9	11 13.8	0.4 0.3	6.4 5.1	12.4 9.8
05	11 46.3	11 48.2	11 14.1	0.5 0.4	6.5 5.1	12.5 9.9
06	11 46.5	11 48.4	11 14.3	0.6 0.5	6.6 5.2	12.6 10.0
07	11 46.8	11 48.7	11 14.6	0.7 0.6	6.7 5.3	12.7 10.1
08	11 47.0	11 48.9	11 14.8	0.8 0.6	6.8 5.4	12.8 10.1
09	11 47.3	11 49.2	11 15.0	0.9 0.7	6.9 5.5	12.9 10.2
10	11 47.5	11 49.4	11 15.3	1.0 0.8	7.0 5.5	13.0 10.3
11	11 47.8	11 49.7	11 15.5	1.1 0.9	7.1 5.6	13.1 10.4
12	11 48.0	11 49.9	11 15.7	1.2 1.0	7.2 5.7	13.2 10.5
13	11 48.3	11 50.2	11 16.0	1.3 1.0	7.3 5.8	13.3 10.5
14	11 48.5	11 50.4	11 16.2	1.4 1.1	7.4 5.9	13.4 10.6
15	11 48.8	11 50.7	11 16.5	1.5 1.2	7.5 5.9	13.5 10.7
16	11 49.0	11 50.9	11 16.7	1.6 1.3	7.6 6.0	13.6 10.8
17	11 49.3	11 51.2	11 16.9	1.7 1.3	7.7 6.1	13.7 10.8
18	11 49.5	11 51.4	11 17.2	1.8 1.4	7.8 6.2	13.8 10.9
19	11 49.8	11 51.7	11 17.4	1.9 1.5	7.9 6.3	13.9 11.0
20	11 50.0	11 51.9	11 17.7	2.0 1.6	8.0 6.3	14.0 11.1
21	11 50.3	11 52.2	11 17.9	2.1 1.7	8.1 6.4	14.1 11.2
22	11 50.5	11 52.4	11 18.1	2.2 1.7	8.2 6.5	14.2 11.2
23	11 50.8	11 52.7	11 18.4	2.3 1.8	8.3 6.6	14.3 11.3
24	11 51.0	11 52.9	11 18.6	2.4 1.9	8.4 6.7	14.4 11.4
25	11 51.3	11 53.2	11 18.8	2.5 2.0	8.5 6.7	14.5 11.5
26	11 51.5	11 53.4	11 19.1	2.6 2.1	8.6 6.8	14.6 11.6
27	11 51.8	11 53.7	11 19.3	2.7 2.1	8.7 6.9	14.7 11.6
28	11 52.0	11 53.9	11 19.6	2.8 2.2	8.8 7.0	14.8 11.7
29	11 52.3	11 54.2	11 19.8	2.9 2.3	8.9 7.0	14.9 11.8
30	11 52.5	11 54.5	11 20.0	3.0 2.4	9.0 7.1	15.0 11.9
31	11 52.8	11 54.7	11 20.3	3.1 2.5	9.1 7.2	15.1 12.0
32	11 53.0	11 55.0	11 20.5	3.2 2.5	9.2 7.3	15.2 12.0
33	11 53.3	11 55.2	11 20.8	3.3 2.6	9.3 7.4	15.3 12.1
34	11 53.5	11 55.5	11 21.0	3.4 2.7	9.4 7.4	15.4 12.2
35	11 53.8	11 55.7	11 21.2	3.5 2.8	9.5 7.5	15.5 12.3
36	11 54.0	11 56.0	11 21.5	3.6 2.9	9.6 7.6	15.6 12.4
37	11 54.3	11 56.2	11 21.7	3.7 2.9	9.7 7.7	15.7 12.4
38	11 54.5	11 56.5	11 22.0	3.8 3.0	9.8 7.8	15.8 12.5
39	11 54.8	11 56.7	11 22.2	3.9 3.1	9.9 7.8	15.9 12.6
40	11 55.0	11 57.0	11 22.4	4.0 3.2	10.0 7.9	16.0 12.7
41	11 55.3	11 57.2	11 22.7	4.1 3.2	10.1 8.0	16.1 12.7
42	11 55.5	11 57.5	11 22.9	4.2 3.3	10.2 8.1	16.2 12.8
43	11 55.8	11 57.7	11 23.1	4.3 3.4	10.3 8.2	16.3 12.9
44	11 56.0	11 58.0	11 23.4	4.4 3.5	10.4 8.2	16.4 13.0
45	11 56.3	11 58.2	11 23.6	4.5 3.6	10.5 8.3	16.5 13.1
46	11 56.5	11 58.5	11 23.9	4.6 3.6	10.6 8.4	16.6 13.1
47	11 56.8	11 58.7	11 24.1	4.7 3.7	10.7 8.5	16.7 13.2
48	11 57.0	11 59.0	11 24.3	4.8 3.8	10.8 8.6	16.8 13.3
49	11 57.3	11 59.2	11 24.6	4.9 3.9	10.9 8.6	16.9 13.4
50	11 57.5	11 59.5	11 24.8	5.0 4.0	11.0 8.7	17.0 13.5
51	11 57.8	11 59.7	11 25.1	5.1 4.0	11.1 8.8	17.1 13.5
52	11 58.0	12 00.0	11 25.3	5.2 4.1	11.2 8.9	17.2 13.6
53	11 58.3	12 00.2	11 25.5	5.3 4.2	11.3 8.9	17.3 13.7
54	11 58.5	12 00.5	11 25.8	5.4 4.3	11.4 9.0	17.4 13.8
55	11 58.8	12 00.7	11 26.0	5.5 4.4	11.5 9.1	17.5 13.9
56	11 59.0	12 01.0	11 26.2	5.6 4.4	11.6 9.2	17.6 13.9
57	11 59.3	12 01.2	11 26.5	5.7 4.5	11.7 9.3	17.7 14.0
58	11 59.5	12 01.5	11 26.7	5.8 4.6	11.8 9.3	17.8 14.1
59	11 59.8	12 01.7	11 27.0	5.9 4.7	11.9 9.4	17.9 14.2
60	12 00.0	12 02.0	11 27.2	6.0 4.8	12.0 9.5	18.0 14.3

© British Crown Copyright 2018. All rights reserved.

48ᵐ

48 s	SUN PLANETS	ARIES	MOON	v or Corrⁿ d	v or Corrⁿ d	v or Corrⁿ d
00	12 00·0	12 02·0	11 27·2	0·0 0·0	6·0 4·9	12·0 9·7
01	12 00·3	12 02·2	11 27·4	0·1 0·1	6·1 4·9	12·1 9·8
02	12 00·5	12 02·5	11 27·7	0·2 0·2	6·2 5·0	12·2 9·9
03	12 00·8	12 02·7	11 27·9	0·3 0·2	6·3 5·1	12·3 9·9
04	12 01·0	12 03·0	11 28·2	0·4 0·3	6·4 5·2	12·4 10·0
05	12 01·3	12 03·2	11 28·4	0·5 0·4	6·5 5·3	12·5 10·1
06	12 01·5	12 03·5	11 28·6	0·6 0·5	6·6 5·3	12·6 10·2
07	12 01·8	12 03·7	11 28·9	0·7 0·6	6·7 5·4	12·7 10·3
08	12 02·0	12 04·0	11 29·1	0·8 0·6	6·8 5·5	12·8 10·3
09	12 02·3	12 04·2	11 29·3	0·9 0·7	6·9 5·6	12·9 10·4
10	12 02·5	12 04·5	11 29·6	1·0 0·8	7·0 5·7	13·0 10·5
11	12 02·8	12 04·7	11 29·8	1·1 0·9	7·1 5·7	13·1 10·6
12	12 03·0	12 05·0	11 30·1	1·2 1·0	7·2 5·8	13·2 10·7
13	12 03·3	12 05·2	11 30·3	1·3 1·1	7·3 5·9	13·3 10·8
14	12 03·5	12 05·5	11 30·5	1·4 1·1	7·4 6·0	13·4 10·8
15	12 03·8	12 05·7	11 30·8	1·5 1·2	7·5 6·1	13·5 10·9
16	12 04·0	12 06·0	11 31·0	1·6 1·3	7·6 6·1	13·6 11·0
17	12 04·3	12 06·2	11 31·3	1·7 1·4	7·7 6·2	13·7 11·1
18	12 04·5	12 06·5	11 31·5	1·8 1·5	7·8 6·3	13·8 11·2
19	12 04·8	12 06·7	11 31·7	1·9 1·5	7·9 6·4	13·9 11·2
20	12 05·0	12 07·0	11 32·0	2·0 1·6	8·0 6·5	14·0 11·3
21	12 05·3	12 07·2	11 32·2	2·1 1·7	8·1 6·5	14·1 11·4
22	12 05·5	12 07·5	11 32·4	2·2 1·8	8·2 6·6	14·2 11·5
23	12 05·8	12 07·7	11 32·7	2·3 1·9	8·3 6·7	14·3 11·6
24	12 06·0	12 08·0	11 32·9	2·4 1·9	8·4 6·8	14·4 11·6
25	12 06·3	12 08·2	11 33·2	2·5 2·0	8·5 6·9	14·5 11·7
26	12 06·5	12 08·5	11 33·4	2·6 2·1	8·6 7·0	14·6 11·8
27	12 06·8	12 08·7	11 33·6	2·7 2·2	8·7 7·0	14·7 11·9
28	12 07·0	12 09·0	11 33·9	2·8 2·3	8·8 7·1	14·8 12·0
29	12 07·3	12 09·2	11 34·1	2·9 2·3	8·9 7·2	14·9 12·0
30	12 07·5	12 09·5	11 34·4	3·0 2·4	9·0 7·3	15·0 12·1
31	12 07·8	12 09·7	11 34·6	3·1 2·5	9·1 7·4	15·1 12·2
32	12 08·0	12 10·0	11 34·8	3·2 2·6	9·2 7·4	15·2 12·3
33	12 08·3	12 10·2	11 35·1	3·3 2·7	9·3 7·5	15·3 12·4
34	12 08·5	12 10·5	11 35·3	3·4 2·7	9·4 7·6	15·4 12·4
35	12 08·8	12 10·7	11 35·6	3·5 2·8	9·5 7·7	15·5 12·5
36	12 09·0	12 11·0	11 35·8	3·6 2·9	9·6 7·8	15·6 12·6
37	12 09·3	12 11·2	11 36·0	3·7 3·0	9·7 7·8	15·7 12·7
38	12 09·5	12 11·5	11 36·3	3·8 3·1	9·8 7·9	15·8 12·8
39	12 09·8	12 11·7	11 36·5	3·9 3·2	9·9 8·0	15·9 12·9
40	12 10·0	12 12·0	11 36·7	4·0 3·2	10·0 8·1	16·0 12·9
41	12 10·3	12 12·2	11 37·0	4·1 3·3	10·1 8·2	16·1 13·0
42	12 10·5	12 12·5	11 37·2	4·2 3·4	10·2 8·2	16·2 13·1
43	12 10·8	12 12·8	11 37·5	4·3 3·5	10·3 8·3	16·3 13·2
44	12 11·0	12 13·0	11 37·7	4·4 3·6	10·4 8·4	16·4 13·3
45	12 11·3	12 13·3	11 37·9	4·5 3·6	10·5 8·5	16·5 13·3
46	12 11·5	12 13·5	11 38·2	4·6 3·7	10·6 8·6	16·6 13·4
47	12 11·8	12 13·8	11 38·4	4·7 3·8	10·7 8·6	16·7 13·5
48	12 12·0	12 14·0	11 38·7	4·8 3·9	10·8 8·7	16·8 13·6
49	12 12·3	12 14·3	11 38·9	4·9 4·0	10·9 8·8	16·9 13·7
50	12 12·5	12 14·5	11 39·1	5·0 4·0	11·0 8·9	17·0 13·7
51	12 12·8	12 14·8	11 39·4	5·1 4·1	11·1 9·0	17·1 13·8
52	12 13·0	12 15·0	11 39·6	5·2 4·2	11·2 9·1	17·2 13·9
53	12 13·3	12 15·3	11 39·8	5·3 4·3	11·3 9·1	17·3 14·0
54	12 13·5	12 15·5	11 40·1	5·4 4·4	11·4 9·2	17·4 14·1
55	12 13·8	12 15·8	11 40·3	5·5 4·4	11·5 9·3	17·5 14·1
56	12 14·0	12 16·0	11 40·6	5·6 4·5	11·6 9·4	17·6 14·2
57	12 14·3	12 16·3	11 40·8	5·7 4·6	11·7 9·5	17·7 14·3
58	12 14·5	12 16·5	11 41·0	5·8 4·7	11·8 9·5	17·8 14·4
59	12 14·8	12 16·8	11 41·3	5·9 4·8	11·9 9·6	17·9 14·5
60	12 15·0	12 17·0	11 41·5	6·0 4·9	12·0 9·7	18·0 14·6

49ᵐ

49 s	SUN PLANETS	ARIES	MOON	v or Corrⁿ d	v or Corrⁿ d	v or Corrⁿ d
00	12 15·0	12 17·0	11 41·5	0·0 0·0	6·0 5·0	12·0 9·9
01	12 15·3	12 17·3	11 41·8	0·1 0·1	6·1 5·0	12·1 10·0
02	12 15·5	12 17·5	11 42·0	0·2 0·2	6·2 5·1	12·2 10·1
03	12 15·8	12 17·8	11 42·2	0·3 0·2	6·3 5·2	12·3 10·1
04	12 16·0	12 18·0	11 42·5	0·4 0·3	6·4 5·3	12·4 10·2
05	12 16·3	12 18·3	11 42·7	0·5 0·4	6·5 5·3	12·5 10·3
06	12 16·5	12 18·5	11 42·9	0·6 0·5	6·6 5·4	12·6 10·4
07	12 16·8	12 18·8	11 43·2	0·7 0·6	6·7 5·5	12·7 10·5
08	12 17·0	12 19·0	11 43·4	0·8 0·7	6·8 5·6	12·8 10·6
09	12 17·3	12 19·3	11 43·7	0·9 0·7	6·9 5·7	12·9 10·6
10	12 17·5	12 19·5	11 43·9	1·0 0·8	7·0 5·8	13·0 10·7
11	12 17·8	12 19·8	11 44·1	1·1 0·9	7·1 5·9	13·1 10·8
12	12 18·0	12 20·0	11 44·4	1·2 1·0	7·2 5·9	13·2 10·9
13	12 18·3	12 20·3	11 44·6	1·3 1·1	7·3 6·0	13·3 11·0
14	12 18·5	12 20·5	11 44·9	1·4 1·2	7·4 6·1	13·4 11·1
15	12 18·8	12 20·8	11 45·1	1·5 1·2	7·5 6·2	13·5 11·1
16	12 19·0	12 21·0	11 45·3	1·6 1·3	7·6 6·3	13·6 11·2
17	12 19·3	12 21·3	11 45·6	1·7 1·4	7·7 6·4	13·7 11·3
18	12 19·5	12 21·5	11 45·8	1·8 1·5	7·8 6·4	13·8 11·4
19	12 19·8	12 21·8	11 46·1	1·9 1·6	7·9 6·5	13·9 11·5
20	12 20·0	12 22·0	11 46·3	2·0 1·7	8·0 6·6	14·0 11·6
21	12 20·3	12 22·3	11 46·5	2·1 1·7	8·1 6·7	14·1 11·6
22	12 20·5	12 22·5	11 46·8	2·2 1·8	8·2 6·8	14·2 11·7
23	12 20·8	12 22·8	11 47·0	2·3 1·9	8·3 6·8	14·3 11·8
24	12 21·0	12 23·0	11 47·2	2·4 2·0	8·4 6·9	14·4 11·9
25	12 21·3	12 23·3	11 47·5	2·5 2·1	8·5 7·0	14·5 12·0
26	12 21·5	12 23·5	11 47·7	2·6 2·1	8·6 7·1	14·6 12·0
27	12 21·8	12 23·8	11 48·0	2·7 2·2	8·7 7·2	14·7 12·1
28	12 22·0	12 24·0	11 48·2	2·8 2·3	8·8 7·3	14·8 12·2
29	12 22·3	12 24·3	11 48·4	2·9 2·4	8·9 7·3	14·9 12·3
30	12 22·5	12 24·5	11 48·7	3·0 2·5	9·0 7·4	15·0 12·4
31	12 22·8	12 24·8	11 48·9	3·1 2·6	9·1 7·5	15·1 12·5
32	12 23·0	12 25·0	11 49·2	3·2 2·6	9·2 7·6	15·2 12·5
33	12 23·3	12 25·3	11 49·4	3·3 2·7	9·3 7·7	15·3 12·6
34	12 23·5	12 25·5	11 49·6	3·4 2·8	9·4 7·8	15·4 12·7
35	12 23·8	12 25·8	11 49·9	3·5 2·9	9·5 7·8	15·5 12·8
36	12 24·0	12 26·0	11 50·1	3·6 3·0	9·6 7·9	15·6 12·9
37	12 24·3	12 26·3	11 50·3	3·7 3·1	9·7 8·0	15·7 13·0
38	12 24·5	12 26·5	11 50·6	3·8 3·1	9·8 8·1	15·8 13·0
39	12 24·8	12 26·8	11 50·8	3·9 3·2	9·9 8·2	15·9 13·1
40	12 25·0	12 27·0	11 51·1	4·0 3·3	10·0 8·3	16·0 13·2
41	12 25·3	12 27·3	11 51·3	4·1 3·4	10·1 8·3	16·1 13·3
42	12 25·5	12 27·5	11 51·5	4·2 3·5	10·2 8·4	16·2 13·4
43	12 25·8	12 27·8	11 51·8	4·3 3·5	10·3 8·5	16·3 13·4
44	12 26·0	12 28·0	11 52·0	4·4 3·6	10·4 8·6	16·4 13·5
45	12 26·3	12 28·3	11 52·3	4·5 3·7	10·5 8·7	16·5 13·6
46	12 26·5	12 28·5	11 52·5	4·6 3·8	10·6 8·7	16·6 13·7
47	12 26·8	12 28·8	11 52·7	4·7 3·9	10·7 8·8	16·7 13·8
48	12 27·0	12 29·0	11 53·0	4·8 4·0	10·8 8·9	16·8 13·9
49	12 27·3	12 29·3	11 53·2	4·9 4·0	10·9 9·0	16·9 13·9
50	12 27·5	12 29·5	11 53·4	5·0 4·1	11·0 9·1	17·0 14·0
51	12 27·8	12 29·8	11 53·7	5·1 4·2	11·1 9·2	17·1 14·1
52	12 28·0	12 30·0	11 53·9	5·2 4·3	11·2 9·2	17·2 14·2
53	12 28·3	12 30·3	11 54·2	5·3 4·4	11·3 9·3	17·3 14·3
54	12 28·5	12 30·5	11 54·4	5·4 4·5	11·4 9·4	17·4 14·4
55	12 28·8	12 30·8	11 54·6	5·5 4·5	11·5 9·5	17·5 14·4
56	12 29·0	12 31·1	11 54·9	5·6 4·6	11·6 9·6	17·6 14·5
57	12 29·3	12 31·3	11 55·1	5·7 4·7	11·7 9·7	17·7 14·6
58	12 29·5	12 31·6	11 55·4	5·8 4·8	11·8 9·7	17·8 14·7
59	12 29·8	12 31·8	11 55·6	5·9 4·9	11·9 9·8	17·9 14·8
60	12 30·0	12 32·1	11 55·8	6·0 5·0	12·0 9·9	18·0 14·9

© British Crown Copyright 2018. All rights reserved.

50ᵐ

s	SUN PLANETS	ARIES	MOON	v or Corrⁿ / d		v or Corrⁿ / d		v or Corrⁿ / d	
	° ′	° ′	° ′	′	′	′	′	′	′
00	12 30.0	12 32.1	11 55.8	0.0	0.0	6.0	5.1	12.0	10.1
01	12 30.3	12 32.3	11 56.1	0.1	0.1	6.1	5.1	12.1	10.2
02	12 30.5	12 32.6	11 56.3	0.2	0.2	6.2	5.2	12.2	10.3
03	12 30.8	12 32.8	11 56.5	0.3	0.3	6.3	5.3	12.3	10.4
04	12 31.0	12 33.1	11 56.8	0.4	0.3	6.4	5.4	12.4	10.4
05	12 31.3	12 33.3	11 57.0	0.5	0.4	6.5	5.5	12.5	10.5
06	12 31.5	12 33.6	11 57.3	0.6	0.5	6.6	5.6	12.6	10.6
07	12 31.8	12 33.8	11 57.5	0.7	0.6	6.7	5.6	12.7	10.7
08	12 32.0	12 34.1	11 57.7	0.8	0.7	6.8	5.7	12.8	10.8
09	12 32.3	12 34.3	11 58.0	0.9	0.8	6.9	5.8	12.9	10.9
10	12 32.5	12 34.6	11 58.2	1.0	0.8	7.0	5.9	13.0	10.9
11	12 32.8	12 34.8	11 58.5	1.1	0.9	7.1	6.0	13.1	11.0
12	12 33.0	12 35.1	11 58.7	1.2	1.0	7.2	6.1	13.2	11.1
13	12 33.3	12 35.3	11 58.9	1.3	1.1	7.3	6.1	13.3	11.2
14	12 33.5	12 35.6	11 59.2	1.4	1.2	7.4	6.2	13.4	11.3
15	12 33.8	12 35.8	11 59.4	1.5	1.3	7.5	6.3	13.5	11.4
16	12 34.0	12 36.1	11 59.7	1.6	1.3	7.6	6.4	13.6	11.4
17	12 34.3	12 36.3	11 59.9	1.7	1.4	7.7	6.5	13.7	11.5
18	12 34.5	12 36.6	12 00.1	1.8	1.5	7.8	6.6	13.8	11.6
19	12 34.8	12 36.8	12 00.4	1.9	1.6	7.9	6.6	13.9	11.7
20	12 35.0	12 37.1	12 00.6	2.0	1.7	8.0	6.7	14.0	11.8
21	12 35.3	12 37.3	12 00.8	2.1	1.8	8.1	6.8	14.1	11.9
22	12 35.5	12 37.6	12 01.1	2.2	1.9	8.2	6.9	14.2	12.0
23	12 35.8	12 37.8	12 01.3	2.3	1.9	8.3	7.0	14.3	12.0
24	12 36.0	12 38.1	12 01.6	2.4	2.0	8.4	7.1	14.4	12.1
25	12 36.3	12 38.3	12 01.8	2.5	2.1	8.5	7.2	14.5	12.2
26	12 36.5	12 38.6	12 02.0	2.6	2.2	8.6	7.2	14.6	12.3
27	12 36.8	12 38.8	12 02.3	2.7	2.3	8.7	7.3	14.7	12.4
28	12 37.0	12 39.1	12 02.5	2.8	2.4	8.8	7.4	14.8	12.5
29	12 37.3	12 39.3	12 02.8	2.9	2.4	8.9	7.5	14.9	12.5
30	12 37.5	12 39.6	12 03.0	3.0	2.5	9.0	7.6	15.0	12.6
31	12 37.8	12 39.8	12 03.2	3.1	2.6	9.1	7.7	15.1	12.7
32	12 38.0	12 40.1	12 03.5	3.2	2.7	9.2	7.7	15.2	12.8
33	12 38.3	12 40.3	12 03.7	3.3	2.8	9.3	7.8	15.3	12.9
34	12 38.5	12 40.6	12 03.9	3.4	2.9	9.4	7.9	15.4	13.0
35	12 38.8	12 40.8	12 04.2	3.5	2.9	9.5	8.0	15.5	13.0
36	12 39.0	12 41.1	12 04.4	3.6	3.0	9.6	8.1	15.6	13.1
37	12 39.3	12 41.3	12 04.7	3.7	3.1	9.7	8.2	15.7	13.2
38	12 39.5	12 41.6	12 04.9	3.8	3.2	9.8	8.2	15.8	13.3
39	12 39.8	12 41.8	12 05.1	3.9	3.3	9.9	8.3	15.9	13.4
40	12 40.0	12 42.1	12 05.4	4.0	3.4	10.0	8.4	16.0	13.5
41	12 40.3	12 42.3	12 05.6	4.1	3.5	10.1	8.5	16.1	13.6
42	12 40.5	12 42.6	12 05.9	4.2	3.5	10.2	8.6	16.2	13.6
43	12 40.8	12 42.8	12 06.1	4.3	3.6	10.3	8.7	16.3	13.7
44	12 41.0	12 43.1	12 06.3	4.4	3.7	10.4	8.8	16.4	13.8
45	12 41.3	12 43.3	12 06.6	4.5	3.8	10.5	8.8	16.5	13.9
46	12 41.5	12 43.6	12 06.8	4.6	3.9	10.6	8.9	16.6	14.0
47	12 41.8	12 43.8	12 07.0	4.7	4.0	10.7	9.0	16.7	14.1
48	12 42.0	12 44.1	12 07.3	4.8	4.0	10.8	9.1	16.8	14.1
49	12 42.3	12 44.3	12 07.5	4.9	4.1	10.9	9.2	16.9	14.2
50	12 42.5	12 44.6	12 07.8	5.0	4.2	11.0	9.3	17.0	14.3
51	12 42.8	12 44.8	12 08.0	5.1	4.3	11.1	9.3	17.1	14.4
52	12 43.0	12 45.1	12 08.2	5.2	4.4	11.2	9.4	17.2	14.5
53	12 43.3	12 45.3	12 08.5	5.3	4.5	11.3	9.5	17.3	14.6
54	12 43.5	12 45.6	12 08.7	5.4	4.5	11.4	9.6	17.4	14.6
55	12 43.8	12 45.8	12 09.0	5.5	4.6	11.5	9.7	17.5	14.7
56	12 44.0	12 46.1	12 09.2	5.6	4.7	11.6	9.8	17.6	14.8
57	12 44.3	12 46.3	12 09.4	5.7	4.8	11.7	9.8	17.7	14.9
58	12 44.5	12 46.6	12 09.7	5.8	4.9	11.8	9.9	17.8	15.0
59	12 44.8	12 46.8	12 09.9	5.9	5.0	11.9	10.0	17.9	15.1
60	12 45.0	12 47.1	12 10.2	6.0	5.1	12.0	10.1	18.0	15.2

51ᵐ

s	SUN PLANETS	ARIES	MOON	v or Corrⁿ / d		v or Corrⁿ / d		v or Corrⁿ / d	
	° ′	° ′	° ′	′	′	′	′	′	′
00	12 45.0	12 47.1	12 10.2	0.0	0.0	6.0	5.2	12.0	10.3
01	12 45.3	12 47.3	12 10.4	0.1	0.1	6.1	5.2	12.1	10.4
02	12 45.5	12 47.6	12 10.6	0.2	0.2	6.2	5.3	12.2	10.5
03	12 45.8	12 47.8	12 10.9	0.3	0.3	6.3	5.4	12.3	10.6
04	12 46.0	12 48.1	12 11.1	0.4	0.3	6.4	5.5	12.4	10.6
05	12 46.3	12 48.3	12 11.3	0.5	0.4	6.5	5.6	12.5	10.7
06	12 46.5	12 48.6	12 11.6	0.6	0.5	6.6	5.7	12.6	10.8
07	12 46.8	12 48.8	12 11.8	0.7	0.6	6.7	5.8	12.7	10.9
08	12 47.0	12 49.1	12 12.1	0.8	0.7	6.8	5.8	12.8	11.0
09	12 47.3	12 49.4	12 12.3	0.9	0.8	6.9	5.9	12.9	11.1
10	12 47.5	12 49.6	12 12.5	1.0	0.9	7.0	6.0	13.0	11.2
11	12 47.8	12 49.9	12 12.8	1.1	0.9	7.1	6.1	13.1	11.2
12	12 48.0	12 50.1	12 13.0	1.2	1.0	7.2	6.2	13.2	11.3
13	12 48.3	12 50.4	12 13.3	1.3	1.1	7.3	6.3	13.3	11.4
14	12 48.5	12 50.6	12 13.5	1.4	1.2	7.4	6.4	13.4	11.5
15	12 48.8	12 50.9	12 13.7	1.5	1.3	7.5	6.4	13.5	11.6
16	12 49.0	12 51.1	12 14.0	1.6	1.4	7.6	6.5	13.6	11.7
17	12 49.3	12 51.4	12 14.2	1.7	1.5	7.7	6.6	13.7	11.8
18	12 49.5	12 51.6	12 14.4	1.8	1.5	7.8	6.7	13.8	11.8
19	12 49.8	12 51.9	12 14.7	1.9	1.6	7.9	6.8	13.9	11.9
20	12 50.0	12 52.1	12 14.9	2.0	1.7	8.0	6.9	14.0	12.0
21	12 50.3	12 52.4	12 15.2	2.1	1.8	8.1	7.0	14.1	12.1
22	12 50.5	12 52.6	12 15.4	2.2	1.9	8.2	7.0	14.2	12.2
23	12 50.8	12 52.9	12 15.6	2.3	2.0	8.3	7.1	14.3	12.3
24	12 51.0	12 53.1	12 15.9	2.4	2.1	8.4	7.2	14.4	12.4
25	12 51.3	12 53.4	12 16.1	2.5	2.1	8.5	7.3	14.5	12.4
26	12 51.5	12 53.6	12 16.4	2.6	2.2	8.6	7.4	14.6	12.5
27	12 51.8	12 53.9	12 16.6	2.7	2.3	8.7	7.5	14.7	12.6
28	12 52.0	12 54.1	12 16.8	2.8	2.4	8.8	7.6	14.8	12.7
29	12 52.3	12 54.4	12 17.1	2.9	2.5	8.9	7.6	14.9	12.8
30	12 52.5	12 54.6	12 17.3	3.0	2.6	9.0	7.7	15.0	12.9
31	12 52.8	12 54.9	12 17.5	3.1	2.7	9.1	7.8	15.1	13.0
32	12 53.0	12 55.1	12 17.8	3.2	2.7	9.2	7.9	15.2	13.0
33	12 53.3	12 55.4	12 18.0	3.3	2.8	9.3	8.0	15.3	13.1
34	12 53.5	12 55.6	12 18.3	3.4	2.9	9.4	8.1	15.4	13.2
35	12 53.8	12 55.9	12 18.5	3.5	3.0	9.5	8.2	15.5	13.3
36	12 54.0	12 56.1	12 18.7	3.6	3.1	9.6	8.2	15.6	13.4
37	12 54.3	12 56.4	12 19.0	3.7	3.2	9.7	8.3	15.7	13.5
38	12 54.5	12 56.6	12 19.2	3.8	3.3	9.8	8.4	15.8	13.6
39	12 54.8	12 56.9	12 19.5	3.9	3.3	9.9	8.5	15.9	13.6
40	12 55.0	12 57.1	12 19.7	4.0	3.4	10.0	8.6	16.0	13.7
41	12 55.3	12 57.4	12 19.9	4.1	3.5	10.1	8.7	16.1	13.8
42	12 55.5	12 57.6	12 20.2	4.2	3.6	10.2	8.8	16.2	13.9
43	12 55.8	12 57.9	12 20.4	4.3	3.7	10.3	8.8	16.3	14.0
44	12 56.0	12 58.1	12 20.6	4.4	3.8	10.4	8.9	16.4	14.1
45	12 56.3	12 58.4	12 20.9	4.5	3.9	10.5	9.0	16.5	14.2
46	12 56.5	12 58.6	12 21.1	4.6	3.9	10.6	9.1	16.6	14.2
47	12 56.8	12 58.9	12 21.4	4.7	4.0	10.7	9.2	16.7	14.3
48	12 57.0	12 59.1	12 21.6	4.8	4.1	10.8	9.3	16.8	14.4
49	12 57.3	12 59.4	12 21.8	4.9	4.2	10.9	9.4	16.9	14.5
50	12 57.5	12 59.6	12 22.1	5.0	4.3	11.0	9.4	17.0	14.6
51	12 57.8	12 59.9	12 22.3	5.1	4.4	11.1	9.5	17.1	14.7
52	12 58.0	13 00.1	12 22.6	5.2	4.5	11.2	9.6	17.2	14.8
53	12 58.3	13 00.4	12 22.8	5.3	4.5	11.3	9.7	17.3	14.8
54	12 58.5	13 00.6	12 23.0	5.4	4.6	11.4	9.8	17.4	14.9
55	12 58.8	13 00.9	12 23.3	5.5	4.7	11.5	9.9	17.5	15.0
56	12 59.0	13 01.1	12 23.5	5.6	4.8	11.6	10.0	17.6	15.1
57	12 59.3	13 01.4	12 23.8	5.7	4.9	11.7	10.0	17.7	15.2
58	12 59.5	13 01.6	12 24.0	5.8	5.0	11.8	10.1	17.8	15.3
59	12 59.8	13 01.9	12 24.2	5.9	5.1	11.9	10.2	17.9	15.4
60	13 00.0	13 02.1	12 24.5	6.0	5.2	12.0	10.3	18.0	15.5

© British Crown Copyright 2018. All rights reserved.

52	SUN PLANETS	ARIES	MOON	v or d Corrⁿ		v or d Corrⁿ		v or d Corrⁿ	
s	° ′	° ′	° ′	′	′	′	′	′	′
00	13 00·0	13 02·1	12 24·5	0·0	0·0	6·0	5·3	12·0	10·5
01	13 00·3	13 02·4	12 24·7	0·1	0·1	6·1	5·3	12·1	10·6
02	13 00·5	13 02·6	12 24·9	0·2	0·2	6·2	5·4	12·2	10·7
03	13 00·8	13 02·9	12 25·2	0·3	0·3	6·3	5·5	12·3	10·8
04	13 01·0	13 03·1	12 25·4	0·4	0·4	6·4	5·6	12·4	10·9
05	13 01·3	13 03·4	12 25·7	0·5	0·4	6·5	5·7	12·5	10·9
06	13 01·5	13 03·6	12 25·9	0·6	0·5	6·6	5·8	12·6	11·0
07	13 01·8	13 03·9	12 26·1	0·7	0·6	6·7	5·9	12·7	11·1
08	13 02·0	13 04·1	12 26·4	0·8	0·7	6·8	6·0	12·8	11·2
09	13 02·3	13 04·4	12 26·6	0·9	0·8	6·9	6·0	12·9	11·3
10	13 02·5	13 04·6	12 26·9	1·0	0·9	7·0	6·1	13·0	11·4
11	13 02·8	13 04·9	12 27·1	1·1	1·0	7·1	6·2	13·1	11·5
12	13 03·0	13 05·1	12 27·3	1·2	1·1	7·2	6·3	13·2	11·6
13	13 03·3	13 05·4	12 27·6	1·3	1·1	7·3	6·4	13·3	11·6
14	13 03·5	13 05·6	12 27·8	1·4	1·2	7·4	6·5	13·4	11·7
15	13 03·8	13 05·9	12 28·0	1·5	1·3	7·5	6·6	13·5	11·8
16	13 04·0	13 06·1	12 28·3	1·6	1·4	7·6	6·7	13·6	11·9
17	13 04·3	13 06·4	12 28·5	1·7	1·5	7·7	6·7	13·7	12·0
18	13 04·5	13 06·6	12 28·8	1·8	1·6	7·8	6·8	13·8	12·1
19	13 04·8	13 06·9	12 29·0	1·9	1·7	7·9	6·9	13·9	12·2
20	13 05·0	13 07·1	12 29·2	2·0	1·8	8·0	7·0	14·0	12·3
21	13 05·3	13 07·4	12 29·5	2·1	1·8	8·1	7·1	14·1	12·3
22	13 05·5	13 07·7	12 29·7	2·2	1·9	8·2	7·2	14·2	12·4
23	13 05·8	13 07·9	12 30·0	2·3	2·0	8·3	7·3	14·3	12·5
24	13 06·0	13 08·2	12 30·2	2·4	2·1	8·4	7·4	14·4	12·6
25	13 06·3	13 08·4	12 30·4	2·5	2·2	8·5	7·4	14·5	12·7
26	13 06·5	13 08·7	12 30·7	2·6	2·3	8·6	7·5	14·6	12·8
27	13 06·8	13 08·9	12 30·9	2·7	2·4	8·7	7·6	14·7	12·9
28	13 07·0	13 09·2	12 31·1	2·8	2·5	8·8	7·7	14·8	13·0
29	13 07·3	13 09·4	12 31·4	2·9	2·5	8·9	7·8	14·9	13·0
30	13 07·5	13 09·7	12 31·6	3·0	2·6	9·0	7·9	15·0	13·1
31	13 07·8	13 09·9	12 31·9	3·1	2·7	9·1	8·0	15·1	13·2
32	13 08·0	13 10·2	12 32·1	3·2	2·8	9·2	8·0	15·2	13·3
33	13 08·3	13 10·4	12 32·3	3·3	2·9	9·3	8·1	15·3	13·4
34	13 08·5	13 10·7	12 32·6	3·4	3·0	9·4	8·2	15·4	13·5
35	13 08·8	13 10·9	12 32·8	3·5	3·1	9·5	8·3	15·5	13·6
36	13 09·0	13 11·2	12 33·1	3·6	3·2	9·6	8·4	15·6	13·7
37	13 09·3	13 11·4	12 33·3	3·7	3·2	9·7	8·5	15·7	13·7
38	13 09·5	13 11·7	12 33·5	3·8	3·3	9·8	8·6	15·8	13·8
39	13 09·8	13 11·9	12 33·8	3·9	3·4	9·9	8·7	15·9	13·9
40	13 10·0	13 12·2	12 34·0	4·0	3·5	10·0	8·8	16·0	14·0
41	13 10·3	13 12·4	12 34·2	4·1	3·6	10·1	8·8	16·1	14·1
42	13 10·5	13 12·7	12 34·5	4·2	3·7	10·2	8·9	16·2	14·2
43	13 10·8	13 12·9	12 34·7	4·3	3·8	10·3	9·0	16·3	14·3
44	13 11·0	13 13·2	12 35·0	4·4	3·9	10·4	9·1	16·4	14·3
45	13 11·3	13 13·4	12 35·2	4·5	3·9	10·5	9·2	16·5	14·4
46	13 11·5	13 13·7	12 35·4	4·6	4·0	10·6	9·3	16·6	14·5
47	13 11·8	13 13·9	12 35·7	4·7	4·1	10·7	9·4	16·7	14·6
48	13 12·0	13 14·2	12 35·9	4·8	4·2	10·8	9·5	16·8	14·7
49	13 12·3	13 14·4	12 36·2	4·9	4·3	10·9	9·5	16·9	14·8
50	13 12·5	13 14·7	12 36·4	5·0	4·4	11·0	9·6	17·0	14·9
51	13 12·8	13 14·9	12 36·6	5·1	4·5	11·1	9·7	17·1	15·0
52	13 13·0	13 15·2	12 36·9	5·2	4·6	11·2	9·8	17·2	15·1
53	13 13·3	13 15·4	12 37·1	5·3	4·6	11·3	9·9	17·3	15·1
54	13 13·5	13 15·7	12 37·4	5·4	4·7	11·4	10·0	17·4	15·2
55	13 13·8	13 15·9	12 37·6	5·5	4·8	11·5	10·1	17·5	15·3
56	13 14·0	13 16·2	12 37·8	5·6	4·9	11·6	10·2	17·6	15·4
57	13 14·3	13 16·4	12 38·1	5·7	5·0	11·7	10·2	17·7	15·5
58	13 14·5	13 16·7	12 38·3	5·8	5·1	11·8	10·3	17·8	15·6
59	13 14·8	13 16·9	12 38·5	5·9	5·2	11·9	10·4	17·9	15·7
60	13 15·0	13 17·2	12 38·8	6·0	5·3	12·0	10·5	18·0	15·8

53	SUN PLANETS	ARIES	MOON	v or d Corrⁿ		v or d Corrⁿ		v or d Corrⁿ	
s	° ′	° ′	° ′	′	′	′	′	′	′
00	13 15·0	13 17·2	12 38·8	0·0	0·0	6·0	5·4	12·0	10·7
01	13 15·3	13 17·4	12 39·0	0·1	0·1	6·1	5·4	12·1	10·8
02	13 15·5	13 17·7	12 39·3	0·2	0·2	6·2	5·5	12·2	10·9
03	13 15·8	13 17·9	12 39·5	0·3	0·3	6·3	5·6	12·3	11·0
04	13 16·0	13 18·2	12 39·7	0·4	0·4	6·4	5·7	12·4	11·1
05	13 16·3	13 18·4	12 40·0	0·5	0·4	6·5	5·8	12·5	11·1
06	13 16·5	13 18·7	12 40·2	0·6	0·5	6·6	5·9	12·6	11·2
07	13 16·8	13 18·9	12 40·5	0·7	0·6	6·7	6·0	12·7	11·3
08	13 17·0	13 19·2	12 40·7	0·8	0·7	6·8	6·1	12·8	11·4
09	13 17·3	13 19·4	12 40·9	0·9	0·8	6·9	6·2	12·9	11·5
10	13 17·5	13 19·7	12 41·2	1·0	0·9	7·0	6·2	13·0	11·6
11	13 17·8	13 19·9	12 41·4	1·1	1·0	7·1	6·3	13·1	11·7
12	13 18·0	13 20·2	12 41·6	1·2	1·1	7·2	6·4	13·2	11·8
13	13 18·3	13 20·4	12 41·9	1·3	1·2	7·3	6·5	13·3	11·9
14	13 18·5	13 20·7	12 42·1	1·4	1·2	7·4	6·6	13·4	11·9
15	13 18·8	13 20·9	12 42·4	1·5	1·3	7·5	6·7	13·5	12·0
16	13 19·0	13 21·2	12 42·6	1·6	1·4	7·6	6·8	13·6	12·1
17	13 19·3	13 21·4	12 42·8	1·7	1·5	7·7	6·9	13·7	12·2
18	13 19·5	13 21·7	12 43·1	1·8	1·6	7·8	7·0	13·8	12·3
19	13 19·8	13 21·9	12 43·3	1·9	1·7	7·9	7·0	13·9	12·4
20	13 20·0	13 22·2	12 43·6	2·0	1·8	8·0	7·1	14·0	12·5
21	13 20·3	13 22·4	12 43·8	2·1	1·9	8·1	7·2	14·1	12·6
22	13 20·5	13 22·7	12 44·0	2·2	2·0	8·2	7·3	14·2	12·7
23	13 20·8	13 22·9	12 44·3	2·3	2·1	8·3	7·4	14·3	12·8
24	13 21·0	13 23·2	12 44·5	2·4	2·1	8·4	7·5	14·4	12·8
25	13 21·3	13 23·4	12 44·7	2·5	2·2	8·5	7·6	14·5	12·9
26	13 21·5	13 23·7	12 45·0	2·6	2·3	8·6	7·7	14·6	13·0
27	13 21·8	13 23·9	12 45·2	2·7	2·4	8·7	7·8	14·7	13·1
28	13 22·0	13 24·2	12 45·5	2·8	2·5	8·8	7·8	14·8	13·2
29	13 22·3	13 24·4	12 45·7	2·9	2·6	8·9	7·9	14·9	13·3
30	13 22·5	13 24·7	12 45·9	3·0	2·7	9·0	8·0	15·0	13·4
31	13 22·8	13 24·9	12 46·2	3·1	2·8	9·1	8·1	15·1	13·5
32	13 23·0	13 25·2	12 46·4	3·2	2·9	9·2	8·2	15·2	13·6
33	13 23·3	13 25·4	12 46·7	3·3	2·9	9·3	8·3	15·3	13·6
34	13 23·5	13 25·7	12 46·9	3·4	3·0	9·4	8·4	15·4	13·7
35	13 23·8	13 26·0	12 47·1	3·5	3·1	9·5	8·5	15·5	13·8
36	13 24·0	13 26·2	12 47·4	3·6	3·2	9·6	8·6	15·6	13·9
37	13 24·3	13 26·5	12 47·6	3·7	3·3	9·7	8·6	15·7	14·0
38	13 24·5	13 26·7	12 47·9	3·8	3·4	9·8	8·7	15·8	14·1
39	13 24·8	13 27·0	12 48·1	3·9	3·5	9·9	8·8	15·9	14·2
40	13 25·0	13 27·2	12 48·3	4·0	3·6	10·0	8·9	16·0	14·3
41	13 25·3	13 27·5	12 48·6	4·1	3·7	10·1	9·0	16·1	14·4
42	13 25·5	13 27·7	12 48·8	4·2	3·7	10·2	9·1	16·2	14·4
43	13 25·8	13 28·0	12 49·0	4·3	3·8	10·3	9·2	16·3	14·5
44	13 26·0	13 28·2	12 49·3	4·4	3·9	10·4	9·3	16·4	14·6
45	13 26·3	13 28·5	12 49·5	4·5	4·0	10·5	9·4	16·5	14·7
46	13 26·5	13 28·7	12 49·8	4·6	4·1	10·6	9·5	16·6	14·8
47	13 26·8	13 29·0	12 50·0	4·7	4·2	10·7	9·5	16·7	14·9
48	13 27·0	13 29·2	12 50·2	4·8	4·3	10·8	9·6	16·8	15·0
49	13 27·3	13 29·5	12 50·5	4·9	4·4	10·9	9·7	16·9	15·1
50	13 27·5	13 29·7	12 50·7	5·0	4·5	11·0	9·8	17·0	15·2
51	13 27·8	13 30·0	12 51·0	5·1	4·5	11·1	9·9	17·1	15·2
52	13 28·0	13 30·2	12 51·2	5·2	4·6	11·2	10·0	17·2	15·3
53	13 28·3	13 30·5	12 51·4	5·3	4·7	11·3	10·1	17·3	15·4
54	13 28·5	13 30·7	12 51·7	5·4	4·8	11·4	10·2	17·4	15·5
55	13 28·8	13 31·0	12 51·9	5·5	4·9	11·5	10·3	17·5	15·6
56	13 29·0	13 31·2	12 52·1	5·6	5·0	11·6	10·3	17·6	15·7
57	13 29·3	13 31·5	12 52·4	5·7	5·1	11·7	10·4	17·7	15·8
58	13 29·5	13 31·7	12 52·6	5·8	5·2	11·8	10·5	17·8	15·9
59	13 29·8	13 32·0	12 52·9	5·9	5·3	11·9	10·6	17·9	16·0
60	13 30·0	13 32·2	12 53·1	6·0	5·4	12·0	10·7	18·0	16·1

© British Crown Copyright 2018. All rights reserved.

54ᵐ

54ᵐ s	SUN PLANETS ° ′	ARIES ° ′	MOON ° ′	v or d Corrⁿ	v or d Corrⁿ	v or d Corrⁿ
00	13 30.0	13 32.2	12 53.1	0.0 0.0	6.0 5.5	12.0 10.9
01	13 30.3	13 32.5	12 53.3	0.1 0.1	6.1 5.5	12.1 11.0
02	13 30.5	13 32.7	12 53.6	0.2 0.2	6.2 5.6	12.2 11.1
03	13 30.8	13 33.0	12 53.8	0.3 0.3	6.3 5.7	12.3 11.2
04	13 31.0	13 33.2	12 54.1	0.4 0.4	6.4 5.8	12.4 11.3
05	13 31.3	13 33.5	12 54.3	0.5 0.5	6.5 5.9	12.5 11.4
06	13 31.5	13 33.7	12 54.5	0.6 0.5	6.6 6.0	12.6 11.4
07	13 31.8	13 34.0	12 54.8	0.7 0.6	6.7 6.1	12.7 11.5
08	13 32.0	13 34.2	12 55.0	0.8 0.7	6.8 6.2	12.8 11.6
09	13 32.3	13 34.5	12 55.2	0.9 0.8	6.9 6.3	12.9 11.7
10	13 32.5	13 34.7	12 55.5	1.0 0.9	7.0 6.4	13.0 11.8
11	13 32.8	13 35.0	12 55.7	1.1 1.0	7.1 6.4	13.1 11.9
12	13 33.0	13 35.2	12 56.0	1.2 1.1	7.2 6.5	13.2 12.0
13	13 33.3	13 35.5	12 56.2	1.3 1.2	7.3 6.6	13.3 12.1
14	13 33.5	13 35.7	12 56.4	1.4 1.3	7.4 6.7	13.4 12.2
15	13 33.8	13 36.0	12 56.7	1.5 1.4	7.5 6.8	13.5 12.3
16	13 34.0	13 36.2	12 56.9	1.6 1.5	7.6 6.9	13.6 12.4
17	13 34.3	13 36.5	12 57.2	1.7 1.5	7.7 7.0	13.7 12.4
18	13 34.5	13 36.7	12 57.4	1.8 1.6	7.8 7.1	13.8 12.5
19	13 34.8	13 37.0	12 57.6	1.9 1.7	7.9 7.2	13.9 12.6
20	13 35.0	13 37.2	12 57.9	2.0 1.8	8.0 7.3	14.0 12.7
21	13 35.3	13 37.5	12 58.1	2.1 1.9	8.1 7.4	14.1 12.8
22	13 35.5	13 37.7	12 58.3	2.2 2.0	8.2 7.4	14.2 12.9
23	13 35.8	13 38.0	12 58.6	2.3 2.1	8.3 7.5	14.3 13.0
24	13 36.0	13 38.2	12 58.8	2.4 2.2	8.4 7.6	14.4 13.1
25	13 36.3	13 38.5	12 59.1	2.5 2.3	8.5 7.7	14.5 13.2
26	13 36.5	13 38.7	12 59.3	2.6 2.4	8.6 7.8	14.6 13.3
27	13 36.8	13 39.0	12 59.5	2.7 2.5	8.7 7.9	14.7 13.4
28	13 37.0	13 39.2	12 59.8	2.8 2.5	8.8 8.0	14.8 13.4
29	13 37.3	13 39.5	13 00.0	2.9 2.6	8.9 8.1	14.9 13.5
30	13 37.5	13 39.7	13 00.3	3.0 2.7	9.0 8.2	15.0 13.6
31	13 37.8	13 40.0	13 00.5	3.1 2.8	9.1 8.3	15.1 13.7
32	13 38.0	13 40.2	13 00.7	3.2 2.9	9.2 8.4	15.2 13.8
33	13 38.3	13 40.5	13 01.0	3.3 3.0	9.3 8.4	15.3 13.9
34	13 38.5	13 40.7	13 01.2	3.4 3.1	9.4 8.5	15.4 14.0
35	13 38.8	13 41.0	13 01.5	3.5 3.2	9.5 8.6	15.5 14.1
36	13 39.0	13 41.2	13 01.7	3.6 3.3	9.6 8.7	15.6 14.2
37	13 39.3	13 41.5	13 01.9	3.7 3.4	9.7 8.8	15.7 14.3
38	13 39.5	13 41.7	13 02.2	3.8 3.5	9.8 8.9	15.8 14.4
39	13 39.8	13 42.0	13 02.4	3.9 3.5	9.9 9.0	15.9 14.4
40	13 40.0	13 42.2	13 02.6	4.0 3.6	10.0 9.1	16.0 14.5
41	13 40.3	13 42.5	13 02.9	4.1 3.7	10.1 9.2	16.1 14.6
42	13 40.5	13 42.7	13 03.1	4.2 3.8	10.2 9.3	16.2 14.7
43	13 40.8	13 43.0	13 03.4	4.3 3.9	10.3 9.4	16.3 14.8
44	13 41.0	13 43.2	13 03.6	4.4 4.0	10.4 9.4	16.4 14.9
45	13 41.3	13 43.5	13 03.8	4.5 4.1	10.5 9.5	16.5 15.0
46	13 41.5	13 43.7	13 04.1	4.6 4.2	10.6 9.6	16.6 15.1
47	13 41.8	13 44.0	13 04.3	4.7 4.3	10.7 9.7	16.7 15.2
48	13 42.0	13 44.3	13 04.6	4.8 4.4	10.8 9.8	16.8 15.3
49	13 42.3	13 44.5	13 04.8	4.9 4.5	10.9 9.9	16.9 15.4
50	13 42.5	13 44.8	13 05.0	5.0 4.5	11.0 10.0	17.0 15.4
51	13 42.8	13 45.0	13 05.3	5.1 4.6	11.1 10.1	17.1 15.5
52	13 43.0	13 45.3	13 05.5	5.2 4.7	11.2 10.2	17.2 15.6
53	13 43.3	13 45.5	13 05.7	5.3 4.8	11.3 10.3	17.3 15.7
54	13 43.5	13 45.8	13 06.0	5.4 4.9	11.4 10.4	17.4 15.8
55	13 43.8	13 46.0	13 06.2	5.5 5.0	11.5 10.4	17.5 15.9
56	13 44.0	13 46.3	13 06.5	5.6 5.1	11.6 10.5	17.6 16.0
57	13 44.3	13 46.5	13 06.7	5.7 5.2	11.7 10.6	17.7 16.1
58	13 44.5	13 46.8	13 06.9	5.8 5.3	11.8 10.7	17.8 16.2
59	13 44.8	13 47.0	13 07.2	5.9 5.4	11.9 10.8	17.9 16.3
60	13 45.0	13 47.3	13 07.4	6.0 5.5	12.0 10.9	18.0 16.4

55ᵐ

55ᵐ s	SUN PLANETS ° ′	ARIES ° ′	MOON ° ′	v or d Corrⁿ	v or d Corrⁿ	v or d Corrⁿ
00	13 45.0	13 47.3	13 07.4	0.0 0.0	6.0 5.6	12.0 11.1
01	13 45.3	13 47.5	13 07.7	0.1 0.1	6.1 5.6	12.1 11.2
02	13 45.5	13 47.8	13 07.9	0.2 0.2	6.2 5.7	12.2 11.3
03	13 45.8	13 48.0	13 08.1	0.3 0.3	6.3 5.8	12.3 11.4
04	13 46.0	13 48.3	13 08.4	0.4 0.4	6.4 5.9	12.4 11.5
05	13 46.3	13 48.5	13 08.6	0.5 0.5	6.5 6.0	12.5 11.6
06	13 46.5	13 48.8	13 08.8	0.6 0.6	6.6 6.1	12.6 11.7
07	13 46.8	13 49.0	13 09.1	0.7 0.6	6.7 6.2	12.7 11.7
08	13 47.0	13 49.3	13 09.3	0.8 0.7	6.8 6.3	12.8 11.8
09	13 47.3	13 49.5	13 09.6	0.9 0.8	6.9 6.4	12.9 11.9
10	13 47.5	13 49.8	13 09.8	1.0 0.9	7.0 6.5	13.0 12.0
11	13 47.8	13 50.0	13 10.0	1.1 1.0	7.1 6.6	13.1 12.1
12	13 48.0	13 50.3	13 10.3	1.2 1.1	7.2 6.7	13.2 12.2
13	13 48.3	13 50.5	13 10.5	1.3 1.2	7.3 6.8	13.3 12.3
14	13 48.5	13 50.8	13 10.8	1.4 1.3	7.4 6.8	13.4 12.4
15	13 48.8	13 51.0	13 11.0	1.5 1.4	7.5 6.9	13.5 12.5
16	13 49.0	13 51.3	13 11.2	1.6 1.5	7.6 7.0	13.6 12.6
17	13 49.3	13 51.5	13 11.5	1.7 1.6	7.7 7.1	13.7 12.7
18	13 49.5	13 51.8	13 11.7	1.8 1.7	7.8 7.2	13.8 12.8
19	13 49.8	13 52.0	13 12.0	1.9 1.8	7.9 7.3	13.9 12.9
20	13 50.0	13 52.3	13 12.2	2.0 1.9	8.0 7.4	14.0 13.0
21	13 50.3	13 52.5	13 12.4	2.1 1.9	8.1 7.5	14.1 13.0
22	13 50.5	13 52.8	13 12.7	2.2 2.0	8.2 7.6	14.2 13.1
23	13 50.8	13 53.0	13 12.9	2.3 2.1	8.3 7.7	14.3 13.2
24	13 51.0	13 53.3	13 13.1	2.4 2.2	8.4 7.8	14.4 13.3
25	13 51.3	13 53.5	13 13.4	2.5 2.3	8.5 7.9	14.5 13.4
26	13 51.5	13 53.8	13 13.6	2.6 2.4	8.6 8.0	14.6 13.5
27	13 51.8	13 54.0	13 13.9	2.7 2.5	8.7 8.0	14.7 13.6
28	13 52.0	13 54.3	13 14.1	2.8 2.6	8.8 8.1	14.8 13.7
29	13 52.3	13 54.5	13 14.3	2.9 2.7	8.9 8.2	14.9 13.8
30	13 52.5	13 54.8	13 14.6	3.0 2.8	9.0 8.3	15.0 13.9
31	13 52.8	13 55.0	13 14.8	3.1 2.9	9.1 8.4	15.1 14.0
32	13 53.0	13 55.3	13 15.1	3.2 3.0	9.2 8.5	15.2 14.1
33	13 53.3	13 55.5	13 15.3	3.3 3.1	9.3 8.6	15.3 14.2
34	13 53.5	13 55.8	13 15.5	3.4 3.1	9.4 8.7	15.4 14.2
35	13 53.8	13 56.0	13 15.8	3.5 3.2	9.5 8.8	15.5 14.3
36	13 54.0	13 56.3	13 16.0	3.6 3.3	9.6 8.9	15.6 14.4
37	13 54.3	13 56.5	13 16.2	3.7 3.4	9.7 9.0	15.7 14.5
38	13 54.5	13 56.8	13 16.5	3.8 3.5	9.8 9.1	15.8 14.6
39	13 54.8	13 57.0	13 16.7	3.9 3.6	9.9 9.2	15.9 14.7
40	13 55.0	13 57.3	13 17.0	4.0 3.7	10.0 9.3	16.0 14.8
41	13 55.3	13 57.5	13 17.2	4.1 3.8	10.1 9.3	16.1 14.9
42	13 55.5	13 57.8	13 17.4	4.2 3.9	10.2 9.4	16.2 15.0
43	13 55.8	13 58.0	13 17.7	4.3 4.0	10.3 9.5	16.3 15.1
44	13 56.0	13 58.3	13 17.9	4.4 4.1	10.4 9.6	16.4 15.2
45	13 56.3	13 58.5	13 18.2	4.5 4.2	10.5 9.7	16.5 15.3
46	13 56.5	13 58.8	13 18.4	4.6 4.3	10.6 9.8	16.6 15.4
47	13 56.8	13 59.0	13 18.6	4.7 4.3	10.7 9.9	16.7 15.4
48	13 57.0	13 59.3	13 18.9	4.8 4.4	10.8 10.0	16.8 15.5
49	13 57.3	13 59.5	13 19.1	4.9 4.5	10.9 10.1	16.9 15.6
50	13 57.5	13 59.8	13 19.3	5.0 4.6	11.0 10.2	17.0 15.7
51	13 57.8	14 00.0	13 19.6	5.1 4.7	11.1 10.3	17.1 15.8
52	13 58.0	14 00.3	13 19.8	5.2 4.8	11.2 10.4	17.2 15.9
53	13 58.3	14 00.5	13 20.1	5.3 4.9	11.3 10.5	17.3 16.0
54	13 58.5	14 00.8	13 20.3	5.4 5.0	11.4 10.5	17.4 16.1
55	13 58.8	14 01.0	13 20.5	5.5 5.1	11.5 10.6	17.5 16.2
56	13 59.0	14 01.3	13 20.8	5.6 5.2	11.6 10.7	17.6 16.3
57	13 59.3	14 01.5	13 21.0	5.7 5.3	11.7 10.8	17.7 16.4
58	13 59.5	14 01.8	13 21.3	5.8 5.4	11.8 10.9	17.8 16.5
59	13 59.8	14 02.0	13 21.5	5.9 5.5	11.9 11.0	17.9 16.6
60	14 00.0	14 02.3	13 21.7	6.0 5.6	12.0 11.1	18.0 16.7

xxix

© British Crown Copyright 2018. All rights reserved.

56ᵐ

s	SUN PLANETS	ARIES	MOON	v or Corrⁿ d	v or Corrⁿ d	v or Corrⁿ d
	° ′	° ′	° ′	′ ′	′ ′	′ ′
00	14 00·0	14 02·3	13 21·7	0·0 0·0	6·0 5·7	12·0 11·3
01	14 00·3	14 02·6	13 22·0	0·1 0·1	6·1 5·7	12·1 11·4
02	14 00·5	14 02·8	13 22·2	0·2 0·2	6·2 5·8	12·2 11·5
03	14 00·8	14 03·1	13 22·4	0·3 0·3	6·3 5·9	12·3 11·6
04	14 01·0	14 03·3	13 22·7	0·4 0·4	6·4 6·0	12·4 11·7
05	14 01·3	14 03·6	13 22·9	0·5 0·5	6·5 6·1	12·5 11·8
06	14 01·5	14 03·8	13 23·2	0·6 0·6	6·6 6·2	12·6 11·9
07	14 01·8	14 04·1	13 23·4	0·7 0·7	6·7 6·3	12·7 12·0
08	14 02·0	14 04·3	13 23·6	0·8 0·8	6·8 6·4	12·8 12·1
09	14 02·3	14 04·6	13 23·9	0·9 0·8	6·9 6·5	12·9 12·1
10	14 02·5	14 04·8	13 24·1	1·0 0·9	7·0 6·6	13·0 12·2
11	14 02·8	14 05·1	13 24·4	1·1 1·0	7·1 6·7	13·1 12·3
12	14 03·0	14 05·3	13 24·6	1·2 1·1	7·2 6·8	13·2 12·4
13	14 03·3	14 05·6	13 24·8	1·3 1·2	7·3 6·9	13·3 12·5
14	14 03·5	14 05·8	13 25·1	1·4 1·3	7·4 7·0	13·4 12·6
15	14 03·8	14 06·1	13 25·3	1·5 1·4	7·5 7·1	13·5 12·7
16	14 04·0	14 06·3	13 25·6	1·6 1·5	7·6 7·2	13·6 12·8
17	14 04·3	14 06·6	13 25·8	1·7 1·6	7·7 7·3	13·7 12·9
18	14 04·5	14 06·8	13 26·0	1·8 1·7	7·8 7·3	13·8 13·0
19	14 04·8	14 07·1	13 26·3	1·9 1·8	7·9 7·4	13·9 13·1
20	14 05·0	14 07·3	13 26·5	2·0 1·9	8·0 7·5	14·0 13·2
21	14 05·3	14 07·6	13 26·7	2·1 2·0	8·1 7·6	14·1 13·4
22	14 05·5	14 07·8	13 27·0	2·2 2·1	8·2 7·7	14·2 13·4
23	14 05·8	14 08·1	13 27·2	2·3 2·2	8·3 7·8	14·3 13·5
24	14 06·0	14 08·3	13 27·5	2·4 2·3	8·4 7·9	14·4 13·6
25	14 06·3	14 08·6	13 27·7	2·5 2·4	8·5 8·0	14·5 13·7
26	14 06·5	14 08·8	13 27·9	2·6 2·4	8·6 8·1	14·6 14·0
27	14 06·8	14 09·1	13 28·2	2·7 2·5	8·7 8·2	14·7 13·8
28	14 07·0	14 09·3	13 28·4	2·8 2·6	8·8 8·3	14·8 13·9
29	14 07·3	14 09·6	13 28·7	2·9 2·7	8·9 8·4	14·9 14·0
30	14 07·5	14 09·8	13 28·9	3·0 2·8	9·0 8·5	15·0 14·1
31	14 07·8	14 10·1	13 29·1	3·1 2·9	9·1 8·6	15·1 14·2
32	14 08·0	14 10·3	13 29·4	3·2 3·0	9·2 8·7	15·2 14·3
33	14 08·3	14 10·6	13 29·6	3·3 3·1	9·3 8·8	15·3 14·4
34	14 08·5	14 10·8	13 29·8	3·4 3·2	9·4 8·9	15·4 14·5
35	14 08·8	14 11·1	13 30·1	3·5 3·3	9·5 8·9	15·5 14·6
36	14 09·0	14 11·3	13 30·3	3·6 3·4	9·6 9·0	15·6 14·7
37	14 09·3	14 11·6	13 30·6	3·7 3·5	9·7 9·1	15·7 14·8
38	14 09·5	14 11·8	13 30·8	3·8 3·6	9·8 9·2	15·8 14·9
39	14 09·8	14 12·1	13 31·0	3·9 3·7	9·9 9·3	15·9 15·0
40	14 10·0	14 12·3	13 31·3	4·0 3·8	10·0 9·4	16·0 15·1
41	14 10·3	14 12·6	13 31·5	4·1 3·9	10·1 9·5	16·1 15·2
42	14 10·5	14 12·8	13 31·8	4·2 4·0	10·2 9·6	16·2 15·3
43	14 10·8	14 13·1	13 32·0	4·3 4·0	10·3 9·7	16·3 15·3
44	14 11·0	14 13·3	13 32·2	4·4 4·1	10·4 9·8	16·4 15·4
45	14 11·3	14 13·6	13 32·5	4·5 4·2	10·5 9·9	16·5 15·5
46	14 11·5	14 13·8	13 32·7	4·6 4·3	10·6 10·0	16·6 15·6
47	14 11·8	14 14·1	13 32·9	4·7 4·4	10·7 10·1	16·7 15·7
48	14 12·0	14 14·3	13 33·2	4·8 4·5	10·8 10·2	16·8 15·8
49	14 12·3	14 14·6	13 33·4	4·9 4·6	10·9 10·3	16·9 15·9
50	14 12·5	14 14·8	13 33·7	5·0 4·7	11·0 10·4	17·0 16·0
51	14 12·8	14 15·1	13 33·9	5·1 4·8	11·1 10·5	17·1 16·1
52	14 13·0	14 15·3	13 34·1	5·2 4·9	11·2 10·5	17·2 16·2
53	14 13·3	14 15·6	13 34·4	5·3 5·0	11·3 10·6	17·3 16·3
54	14 13·5	14 15·8	13 34·6	5·4 5·1	11·4 10·7	17·4 16·4
55	14 13·8	14 16·1	13 34·8	5·5 5·2	11·5 10·8	17·5 16·5
56	14 14·0	14 16·3	13 35·1	5·6 5·3	11·6 10·9	17·6 16·6
57	14 14·3	14 16·6	13 35·3	5·7 5·4	11·7 11·0	17·7 16·7
58	14 14·5	14 16·8	13 35·6	5·8 5·5	11·8 11·1	17·8 16·8
59	14 14·8	14 17·1	13 35·8	5·9 5·6	11·9 11·2	17·9 16·9
60	14 15·0	14 17·3	13 36·1	6·0 5·7	12·0 11·3	18·0 17·0

57ᵐ

s	SUN PLANETS	ARIES	MOON	v or Corrⁿ d	v or Corrⁿ d	v or Corrⁿ d
	° ′	° ′	° ′	′ ′	′ ′	′ ′
00	14 15·0	14 17·3	13 36·1	0·0 0·0	6·0 5·8	12·0 11·5
01	14 15·3	14 17·6	13 36·3	0·1 0·1	6·1 5·8	12·1 11·6
02	14 15·5	14 17·8	13 36·5	0·2 0·2	6·2 5·9	12·2 11·7
03	14 15·8	14 18·1	13 36·8	0·3 0·3	6·3 6·0	12·3 11·8
04	14 16·0	14 18·3	13 37·0	0·4 0·4	6·4 6·1	12·4 11·9
05	14 16·3	14 18·6	13 37·2	0·5 0·5	6·5 6·2	12·5 12·0
06	14 16·5	14 18·8	13 37·5	0·6 0·6	6·6 6·3	12·6 12·1
07	14 16·8	14 19·1	13 37·7	0·7 0·7	6·7 6·4	12·7 12·2
08	14 17·0	14 19·3	13 38·0	0·8 0·8	6·8 6·5	12·8 12·3
09	14 17·3	14 19·6	13 38·2	0·9 0·9	6·9 6·6	12·9 12·4
10	14 17·5	14 19·8	13 38·4	1·0 1·0	7·0 6·7	13·0 12·5
11	14 17·8	14 20·1	13 38·7	1·1 1·1	7·1 6·8	13·1 12·6
12	14 18·0	14 20·3	13 38·9	1·2 1·2	7·2 6·9	13·2 12·7
13	14 18·3	14 20·6	13 39·2	1·3 1·2	7·3 7·0	13·3 12·7
14	14 18·5	14 20·9	13 39·4	1·4 1·3	7·4 7·1	13·4 12·8
15	14 18·8	14 21·1	13 39·6	1·5 1·4	7·5 7·2	13·5 12·9
16	14 19·0	14 21·4	13 39·9	1·6 1·5	7·6 7·3	13·6 13·0
17	14 19·3	14 21·6	13 40·1	1·7 1·6	7·7 7·4	13·7 13·1
18	14 19·5	14 21·9	13 40·3	1·8 1·7	7·8 7·5	13·8 13·2
19	14 19·8	14 22·1	13 40·6	1·9 1·8	7·9 7·6	13·9 13·3
20	14 20·0	14 22·4	13 40·8	2·0 1·9	8·0 7·7	14·0 13·4
21	14 20·3	14 22·6	13 41·1	2·1 2·0	8·1 7·8	14·1 13·5
22	14 20·5	14 22·9	13 41·3	2·2 2·1	8·2 7·9	14·2 13·6
23	14 20·8	14 23·1	13 41·5	2·3 2·2	8·3 8·0	14·3 13·7
24	14 21·0	14 23·4	13 41·8	2·4 2·3	8·4 8·1	14·4 13·8
25	14 21·3	14 23·6	13 42·0	2·5 2·4	8·5 8·1	14·5 13·9
26	14 21·5	14 23·9	13 42·3	2·6 2·5	8·6 8·2	14·6 14·0
27	14 21·8	14 24·1	13 42·5	2·7 2·6	8·7 8·3	14·7 14·1
28	14 22·0	14 24·4	13 42·7	2·8 2·7	8·8 8·4	14·8 14·2
29	14 22·3	14 24·6	13 43·0	2·9 2·8	8·9 8·5	14·9 14·3
30	14 22·5	14 24·9	13 43·2	3·0 2·9	9·0 8·6	15·0 14·4
31	14 22·8	14 25·1	13 43·4	3·1 3·0	9·1 8·7	15·1 14·5
32	14 23·0	14 25·4	13 43·7	3·2 3·1	9·2 8·8	15·2 14·6
33	14 23·3	14 25·6	13 43·9	3·3 3·2	9·3 8·9	15·3 14·7
34	14 23·5	14 25·9	13 44·2	3·4 3·3	9·4 9·0	15·4 14·8
35	14 23·8	14 26·1	13 44·4	3·5 3·4	9·5 9·1	15·5 14·9
36	14 24·0	14 26·4	13 44·6	3·6 3·5	9·6 9·2	15·6 15·0
37	14 24·3	14 26·6	13 44·9	3·7 3·5	9·7 9·3	15·7 15·0
38	14 24·5	14 26·9	13 45·1	3·8 3·6	9·8 9·4	15·8 15·1
39	14 24·8	14 27·1	13 45·4	3·9 3·7	9·9 9·5	15·9 15·2
40	14 25·0	14 27·4	13 45·6	4·0 3·8	10·0 9·6	16·0 15·3
41	14 25·3	14 27·6	13 45·8	4·1 3·9	10·1 9·7	16·1 15·4
42	14 25·5	14 27·9	13 46·1	4·2 4·0	10·2 9·8	16·2 15·5
43	14 25·8	14 28·1	13 46·3	4·3 4·1	10·3 9·9	16·3 15·6
44	14 26·0	14 28·4	13 46·5	4·4 4·2	10·4 10·0	16·4 15·7
45	14 26·3	14 28·6	13 46·8	4·5 4·3	10·5 10·1	16·5 15·8
46	14 26·5	14 28·9	13 47·0	4·6 4·4	10·6 10·2	16·6 15·9
47	14 26·8	14 29·1	13 47·3	4·7 4·5	10·7 10·3	16·7 16·0
48	14 27·0	14 29·4	13 47·5	4·8 4·6	10·8 10·4	16·8 16·1
49	14 27·3	14 29·6	13 47·7	4·9 4·7	10·9 10·4	16·9 16·2
50	14 27·5	14 29·9	13 48·0	5·0 4·8	11·0 10·5	17·0 16·3
51	14 27·8	14 30·1	13 48·2	5·1 4·9	11·1 10·6	17·1 16·4
52	14 28·0	14 30·4	13 48·5	5·2 5·0	11·2 10·7	17·2 16·5
53	14 28·3	14 30·6	13 48·7	5·3 5·1	11·3 10·8	17·3 16·6
54	14 28·5	14 30·9	13 48·9	5·4 5·2	11·4 10·9	17·4 16·7
55	14 28·8	14 31·1	13 49·2	5·5 5·3	11·5 11·0	17·5 16·8
56	14 29·0	14 31·4	13 49·4	5·6 5·4	11·6 11·1	17·6 16·9
57	14 29·3	14 31·6	13 49·7	5·7 5·5	11·7 11·2	17·7 17·0
58	14 29·5	14 31·9	13 49·9	5·8 5·6	11·8 11·3	17·8 17·1
59	14 29·8	14 32·1	13 50·1	5·9 5·7	11·9 11·4	17·9 17·2
60	14 30·0	14 32·4	13 50·4	6·0 5·8	12·0 11·5	18·0 17·3

xxx

© British Crown Copyright 2018. All rights reserved.

58ᵐ

58	SUN PLANETS	ARIES	MOON	v or Corrⁿ d	v or Corrⁿ d	v or Corrⁿ d
s	° '	° '	° '	' '	' '	' '
00	14 30·0	14 32·4	13 50·4	0·0 0·0	6·0 5·9	12·0 11·7
01	14 30·3	14 32·6	13 50·6	0·1 0·1	6·1 5·9	12·1 11·8
02	14 30·5	14 32·9	13 50·8	0·2 0·2	6·2 6·0	12·2 11·9
03	14 30·8	14 33·1	13 51·1	0·3 0·3	6·3 6·1	12·3 12·0
04	14 31·0	14 33·4	13 51·3	0·4 0·4	6·4 6·2	12·4 12·1
05	14 31·3	14 33·6	13 51·6	0·5 0·5	6·5 6·3	12·5 12·2
06	14 31·5	14 33·9	13 51·8	0·6 0·6	6·6 6·4	12·6 12·3
07	14 31·8	14 34·1	13 52·0	0·7 0·7	6·7 6·5	12·7 12·4
08	14 32·0	14 34·4	13 52·3	0·8 0·8	6·8 6·6	12·8 12·5
09	14 32·3	14 34·6	13 52·5	0·9 0·9	6·9 6·7	12·9 12·6
10	14 32·5	14 34·9	13 52·8	1·0 1·0	7·0 6·8	13·0 12·7
11	14 32·8	14 35·1	13 53·0	1·1 1·1	7·1 6·9	13·1 12·8
12	14 33·0	14 35·4	13 53·2	1·2 1·2	7·2 7·0	13·2 12·9
13	14 33·3	14 35·6	13 53·5	1·3 1·3	7·3 7·1	13·3 13·0
14	14 33·5	14 35·9	13 53·7	1·4 1·4	7·4 7·2	13·4 13·1
15	14 33·8	14 36·1	13 53·9	1·5 1·5	7·5 7·3	13·5 13·2
16	14 34·0	14 36·4	13 54·2	1·6 1·6	7·6 7·4	13·6 13·3
17	14 34·3	14 36·6	13 54·4	1·7 1·7	7·7 7·5	13·7 13·4
18	14 34·5	14 36·9	13 54·7	1·8 1·8	7·8 7·6	13·8 13·5
19	14 34·8	14 37·1	13 54·9	1·9 1·9	7·9 7·7	13·9 13·6
20	14 35·0	14 37·4	13 55·1	2·0 2·0	8·0 7·8	14·0 13·7
21	14 35·3	14 37·6	13 55·4	2·1 2·0	8·1 7·9	14·1 13·7
22	14 35·5	14 37·9	13 55·6	2·2 2·1	8·2 8·0	14·2 13·8
23	14 35·8	14 38·1	13 55·9	2·3 2·2	8·3 8·1	14·3 13·9
24	14 36·0	14 38·4	13 56·1	2·4 2·3	8·4 8·2	14·4 14·0
25	14 36·3	14 38·6	13 56·3	2·5 2·4	8·5 8·3	14·5 14·1
26	14 36·5	14 38·9	13 56·6	2·6 2·5	8·6 8·4	14·6 14·2
27	14 36·8	14 39·2	13 56·8	2·7 2·6	8·7 8·5	14·7 14·3
28	14 37·0	14 39·4	13 57·0	2·8 2·7	8·8 8·6	14·8 14·4
29	14 37·3	14 39·7	13 57·3	2·9 2·8	8·9 8·7	14·9 14·5
30	14 37·5	14 39·9	13 57·5	3·0 2·9	9·0 8·8	15·0 14·6
31	14 37·8	14 40·2	13 57·8	3·1 3·0	9·1 8·9	15·1 14·7
32	14 38·0	14 40·4	13 58·0	3·2 3·1	9·2 9·0	15·2 14·8
33	14 38·3	14 40·7	13 58·2	3·3 3·2	9·3 9·1	15·3 14·9
34	14 38·5	14 40·9	13 58·5	3·4 3·3	9·4 9·2	15·4 15·0
35	14 38·8	14 41·2	13 58·7	3·5 3·4	9·5 9·3	15·5 15·1
36	14 39·0	14 41·4	13 59·0	3·6 3·5	9·6 9·4	15·6 15·2
37	14 39·3	14 41·7	13 59·2	3·7 3·6	9·7 9·5	15·7 15·3
38	14 39·5	14 41·9	13 59·4	3·8 3·7	9·8 9·6	15·8 15·4
39	14 39·8	14 42·2	13 59·7	3·9 3·8	9·9 9·7	15·9 15·5
40	14 40·0	14 42·4	13 59·9	4·0 3·9	10·0 9·8	16·0 15·6
41	14 40·3	14 42·7	14 00·1	4·1 4·0	10·1 9·8	16·1 15·7
42	14 40·5	14 42·9	14 00·4	4·2 4·1	10·2 9·9	16·2 15·8
43	14 40·8	14 43·2	14 00·6	4·3 4·2	10·3 10·0	16·3 15·9
44	14 41·0	14 43·4	14 00·9	4·4 4·3	10·4 10·1	16·4 16·0
45	14 41·3	14 43·7	14 01·1	4·5 4·4	10·5 10·2	16·5 16·1
46	14 41·5	14 43·9	14 01·3	4·6 4·5	10·6 10·3	16·6 16·2
47	14 41·8	14 44·2	14 01·6	4·7 4·6	10·7 10·4	16·7 16·3
48	14 42·0	14 44·4	14 01·8	4·8 4·7	10·8 10·5	16·8 16·4
49	14 42·3	14 44·7	14 02·1	4·9 4·8	10·9 10·6	16·9 16·5
50	14 42·5	14 44·9	14 02·3	5·0 4·9	11·0 10·7	17·0 16·6
51	14 42·8	14 45·2	14 02·5	5·1 5·0	11·1 10·8	17·1 16·7
52	14 43·0	14 45·4	14 02·8	5·2 5·1	11·2 10·9	17·2 16·8
53	14 43·3	14 45·7	14 03·0	5·3 5·2	11·3 11·0	17·3 16·9
54	14 43·5	14 45·9	14 03·3	5·4 5·3	11·4 11·1	17·4 17·0
55	14 43·8	14 46·2	14 03·5	5·5 5·4	11·5 11·2	17·5 17·1
56	14 44·0	14 46·4	14 03·7	5·6 5·5	11·6 11·3	17·6 17·2
57	14 44·3	14 46·7	14 04·0	5·7 5·6	11·7 11·4	17·7 17·3
58	14 44·5	14 46·9	14 04·2	5·8 5·7	11·8 11·5	17·8 17·4
59	14 44·8	14 47·2	14 04·4	5·9 5·8	11·9 11·6	17·9 17·5
60	14 45·0	14 47·4	14 04·7	6·0 5·9	12·0 11·7	18·0 17·6

59ᵐ

59	SUN PLANETS	ARIES	MOON	v or Corrⁿ d	v or Corrⁿ d	v or Corrⁿ d
s	° '	° '	° '	' '	' '	' '
00	14 45·0	14 47·4	14 04·7	0·0 0·0	6·0 6·0	12·0 11·9
01	14 45·3	14 47·7	14 04·9	0·1 0·1	6·1 6·0	12·1 12·0
02	14 45·5	14 47·9	14 05·2	0·2 0·2	6·2 6·1	12·2 12·1
03	14 45·8	14 48·2	14 05·4	0·3 0·3	6·3 6·2	12·3 12·2
04	14 46·0	14 48·4	14 05·6	0·4 0·4	6·4 6·3	12·4 12·3
05	14 46·3	14 48·7	14 05·9	0·5 0·5	6·5 6·4	12·5 12·4
06	14 46·5	14 48·9	14 06·1	0·6 0·6	6·6 6·5	12·6 12·5
07	14 46·8	14 49·2	14 06·4	0·7 0·7	6·7 6·6	12·7 12·6
08	14 47·0	14 49·4	14 06·6	0·8 0·8	6·8 6·7	12·8 12·7
09	14 47·3	14 49·7	14 06·8	0·9 0·9	6·9 6·8	12·9 12·8
10	14 47·5	14 49·9	14 07·1	1·0 1·0	7·0 6·9	13·0 12·9
11	14 47·8	14 50·2	14 07·3	1·1 1·1	7·1 7·0	13·1 13·0
12	14 48·0	14 50·4	14 07·5	1·2 1·2	7·2 7·1	13·2 13·1
13	14 48·3	14 50·7	14 07·8	1·3 1·3	7·3 7·2	13·3 13·2
14	14 48·5	14 50·9	14 08·0	1·4 1·4	7·4 7·3	13·4 13·3
15	14 48·8	14 51·2	14 08·3	1·5 1·5	7·5 7·4	13·5 13·4
16	14 49·0	14 51·4	14 08·5	1·6 1·6	7·6 7·5	13·6 13·5
17	14 49·3	14 51·7	14 08·7	1·7 1·7	7·7 7·6	13·7 13·6
18	14 49·5	14 51·9	14 09·0	1·8 1·8	7·8 7·7	13·8 13·7
19	14 49·8	14 52·2	14 09·2	1·9 1·9	7·9 7·8	13·9 13·8
20	14 50·0	14 52·4	14 09·5	2·0 2·0	8·0 7·9	14·0 13·9
21	14 50·3	14 52·7	14 09·7	2·1 2·1	8·1 8·0	14·1 14·0
22	14 50·5	14 52·9	14 09·9	2·2 2·2	8·2 8·1	14·2 14·1
23	14 50·8	14 53·2	14 10·2	2·3 2·3	8·3 8·2	14·3 14·2
24	14 51·0	14 53·4	14 10·4	2·4 2·4	8·4 8·3	14·4 14·3
25	14 51·3	14 53·7	14 10·6	2·5 2·5	8·5 8·4	14·5 14·4
26	14 51·5	14 53·9	14 10·8	2·6 2·6	8·6 8·5	14·6 14·5
27	14 51·8	14 54·2	14 11·1	2·7 2·7	8·7 8·6	14·7 14·6
28	14 52·0	14 54·4	14 11·4	2·8 2·8	8·8 8·7	14·8 14·7
29	14 52·3	14 54·7	14 11·6	2·9 2·9	8·9 8·8	14·9 14·8
30	14 52·5	14 54·9	14 11·8	3·0 3·0	9·0 8·9	15·0 14·9
31	14 52·8	14 55·2	14 12·1	3·1 3·1	9·1 9·0	15·1 15·0
32	14 53·0	14 55·4	14 12·3	3·2 3·2	9·2 9·1	15·2 15·1
33	14 53·3	14 55·7	14 12·6	3·3 3·3	9·3 9·2	15·3 15·2
34	14 53·5	14 55·9	14 12·8	3·4 3·4	9·4 9·3	15·4 15·3
35	14 53·8	14 56·2	14 13·0	3·5 3·5	9·5 9·4	15·5 15·4
36	14 54·0	14 56·4	14 13·3	3·6 3·6	9·6 9·5	15·6 15·5
37	14 54·3	14 56·7	14 13·5	3·7 3·7	9·7 9·6	15·7 15·6
38	14 54·5	14 56·9	14 13·8	3·8 3·8	9·8 9·7	15·8 15·7
39	14 54·8	14 57·2	14 14·0	3·9 3·9	9·9 9·8	15·9 15·8
40	14 55·0	14 57·5	14 14·2	4·0 4·0	10·0 9·9	16·0 15·9
41	14 55·3	14 57·7	14 14·5	4·1 4·1	10·1 10·0	16·1 16·0
42	14 55·5	14 58·0	14 14·7	4·2 4·2	10·2 10·1	16·2 16·1
43	14 55·8	14 58·2	14 14·9	4·3 4·3	10·3 10·2	16·3 16·2
44	14 56·0	14 58·5	14 15·2	4·4 4·4	10·4 10·3	16·4 16·3
45	14 56·3	14 58·7	14 15·4	4·5 4·5	10·5 10·4	16·5 16·4
46	14 56·5	14 59·0	14 15·7	4·6 4·6	10·6 10·5	16·6 16·5
47	14 56·8	14 59·2	14 15·9	4·7 4·7	10·7 10·6	16·7 16·6
48	14 57·0	14 59·5	14 16·1	4·8 4·8	10·8 10·7	16·8 16·7
49	14 57·3	14 59·7	14 16·4	4·9 4·9	10·9 10·8	16·9 16·8
50	14 57·5	15 00·0	14 16·6	5·0 5·0	11·0 10·9	17·0 16·9
51	14 57·8	15 00·2	14 16·9	5·1 5·1	11·1 11·0	17·1 17·0
52	14 58·0	15 00·5	14 17·1	5·2 5·2	11·2 11·1	17·2 17·1
53	14 58·3	15 00·7	14 17·3	5·3 5·3	11·3 11·2	17·3 17·2
54	14 58·5	15 01·0	14 17·6	5·4 5·4	11·4 11·3	17·4 17·3
55	14 58·8	15 01·2	14 17·8	5·5 5·5	11·5 11·4	17·5 17·4
56	14 59·0	15 01·5	14 18·0	5·6 5·6	11·6 11·5	17·6 17·5
57	14 59·3	15 01·7	14 18·3	5·7 5·7	11·7 11·6	17·7 17·6
58	14 59·5	15 02·0	14 18·5	5·8 5·8	11·8 11·7	17·8 17·7
59	14 59·8	15 02·2	14 18·8	5·9 5·9	11·9 11·8	17·9 17·8
60	15 00·0	15 02·5	14 19·0	6·0 6·0	12·0 11·9	18·0 17·9

© British Crown Copyright 2018. All rights reserved.

TABLES FOR INTERPOLATING SUNRISE, MOONRISE, ETC.
TABLE I—FOR LATITUDE

10°	5°	2°	5m	10m	15m	20m	25m	30m	35m	40m	45m	50m	55m	60m	1h05m	1h10m	1h15m	1h20m
0 30	0 15	0 06	0	0	1	1	1	1	1	2	2	2	2	2	0 02	0 02	0 02	0 02
1 00	0 30	0 12	0	1	1	2	2	3	3	3	4	4	4	5	05	05	05	05
1 30	0 45	0 18	1	1	2	3	3	4	4	5	5	6	7	7	07	07	07	07
2 00	1 00	0 24	1	2	3	4	5	5	6	7	7	8	9	10	10	10	10	10
2 30	1 15	0 30	1	2	4	5	6	7	8	9	9	10	11	12	12	13	13	13
3 00	1 30	0 36	1	3	4	6	7	8	9	10	11	12	13	14	0 15	0 15	0 16	0 16
3 30	1 45	0 42	2	3	5	7	8	10	11	12	13	14	16	17	18	18	19	19
4 00	2 00	0 48	2	4	6	8	9	11	13	14	15	16	18	19	20	21	22	22
4 30	2 15	0 54	2	4	7	9	11	13	15	16	18	19	21	22	23	24	25	26
5 00	2 30	1 00	2	5	7	10	12	14	16	18	20	22	23	25	26	27	28	29
5 30	2 45	1 06	3	5	8	11	13	16	18	20	22	24	26	28	0 29	0 30	0 31	0 32
6 00	3 00	1 12	3	6	9	12	14	17	20	22	24	26	29	31	32	33	34	36
6 30	3 15	1 18	3	6	10	13	16	19	22	24	26	29	31	34	36	37	38	40
7 00	3 30	1 24	3	7	10	14	17	20	23	26	29	31	34	37	39	41	42	44
7 30	3 45	1 30	4	7	11	15	18	22	25	28	31	34	37	40	43	44	46	48
8 00	4 00	1 36	4	8	12	16	20	23	27	30	34	37	41	44	0 47	0 48	0 51	0 53
8 30	4 15	1 42	4	8	13	17	21	25	29	33	36	40	44	48	0 51	0 53	0 56	0 58
9 00	4 30	1 48	4	9	13	18	22	27	31	35	39	43	47	52	0 55	0 58	1 01	1 04
9 30	4 45	1 54	5	9	14	19	24	28	33	38	42	47	51	56	1 00	1 04	1 08	1 12
10 00	5 00	2 00	5	10	15	20	25	30	35	40	45	50	55	60	1 05	1 10	1 15	1 20

Table I is for interpolating the LMT of sunrise, twilight, moonrise, etc., for latitude. It is to be entered, in the appropriate column on the left, with the difference between true latitude and the nearest tabular latitude which is *less* than the true latitude; and with the argument at the top which is the nearest value of the difference between the times for the tabular latitude and the next higher one; the correction so obtained is applied to the time for the tabular latitude; the sign of the correction can be seen by inspection. It is to be noted that the interpolation is not linear, so that when using this table it is essential to take out the tabular phenomenon for the latitude *less* than the true latitude.

TABLE II—FOR LONGITUDE

Long. East or West	10m	20m	30m	40m	50m	60m	1h+ 10m	1h+ 20m	1h+ 30m	1h+ 40m	1h+ 50m	1h+ 60m	2h10m	2h20m	2h30m	2h40m	2h50m	3h00m
0	0	0	0	0	0	0	0	0	0	0	0	0	0 00	0 00	0 00	0 00	0 00	0 00
10	0	1	1	1	1	2	2	2	2	3	3	3	04	04	04	04	05	05
20	1	1	2	2	3	3	4	4	5	6	6	7	07	08	08	09	09	10
30	1	2	2	3	4	5	6	7	7	8	9	10	11	12	12	13	14	15
40	1	2	3	4	6	7	8	9	10	11	12	13	14	16	17	18	19	20
50	1	3	4	6	7	8	10	11	12	14	15	17	0 18	0 19	0 21	0 22	0 24	0 25
60	2	3	5	7	8	10	12	13	15	17	18	20	22	23	25	27	28	30
70	2	4	6	8	10	12	14	16	17	19	21	23	25	27	29	31	33	35
80	2	4	7	9	11	13	16	18	20	22	24	27	29	31	33	36	38	40
90	2	5	7	10	12	15	17	20	22	25	27	30	32	35	37	40	42	45
100	3	6	8	11	14	17	19	22	25	28	31	33	0 36	0 39	0 42	0 44	0 47	0 50
110	3	6	9	12	15	18	21	24	27	31	34	37	40	43	46	49	0 52	0 55
120	3	7	10	13	17	20	23	27	30	33	37	40	43	47	50	53	0 57	1 00
130	4	7	11	14	18	22	25	29	32	36	40	43	47	51	54	0 58	1 01	1 05
140	4	8	12	16	19	23	27	31	35	39	43	47	51	54	0 58	1 02	1 06	1 10
150	4	8	13	17	21	25	29	33	38	42	46	50	0 54	0 58	1 03	1 07	1 11	1 15
160	4	9	13	18	22	27	31	36	40	44	49	53	0 58	1 02	1 07	1 11	1 16	1 20
170	5	9	14	19	24	28	33	38	42	47	52	57	1 01	1 06	1 11	1 16	1 20	1 25
180	5	10	15	20	25	30	35	40	45	50	55	60	1 05	1 10	1 15	1 20	1 25	1 30

Table II is for interpolating the LMT of moonrise, moonset and the Moon's meridian passage for longitude. It is entered with longitude and with the difference between the times for the given date and for the preceding date (in east longitudes) or following date (in west longitudes). The correction is normally *added* for west longitudes and *subtracted* for east longitudes, but if, as occasionally happens, the times become earlier each day instead of later, the signs of the corrections must be reversed.

INDEX TO SELECTED STARS, 2019

Name	No	Mag	SHA	Dec		No	Name	Mag	SHA	Dec
				°						°
Acamar	7	3·2	315	S 40		1	Alpheratz	2·1	358	N 29
Achernar	5	0·5	335	S 57		2	Ankaa	2·4	353	S 42
Acrux	30	1·3	173	S 63		3	Schedar	2·2	350	N 57
Adhara	19	1·5	255	S 29		4	Diphda	2·0	349	S 18
Aldebaran	10	0·9	291	N 17		5	Achernar	0·5	335	S 57
Alioth	32	1·8	166	N 56		6	Hamal	2·0	328	N 24
Alkaid	34	1·9	153	N 49		7	Acamar	3·2	315	S 40
Alnair	55	1·7	28	S 47		8	Menkar	2·5	314	N 4
Alnilam	15	1·7	276	S 1		9	Mirfak	1·8	309	N 50
Alphard	25	2·0	218	S 9		10	Aldebaran	0·9	291	N 17
Alphecca	41	2·2	126	N 27		11	Rigel	0·1	281	S 8
Alpheratz	1	2·1	358	N 29		12	Capella	0·1	280	N 46
Altair	51	0·8	62	N 9		13	Bellatrix	1·6	278	N 6
Ankaa	2	2·4	353	S 42		14	Elnath	1·7	278	N 29
Antares	42	1·0	112	S 26		15	Alnilam	1·7	276	S 1
Arcturus	37	0·0	146	N 19		16	Betelgeuse	Var.*	271	N 7
Atria	43	1·9	107	S 69		17	Canopus	−0·7	264	S 53
Avior	22	1·9	234	S 60		18	Sirius	−1·5	259	S 17
Bellatrix	13	1·6	278	N 6		19	Adhara	1·5	255	S 29
Betelgeuse	16	Var.*	271	N 7		20	Procyon	0·4	245	N 5
Canopus	17	−0·7	264	S 53		21	Pollux	1·1	243	N 28
Capella	12	0·1	280	N 46		22	Avior	1·9	234	S 60
Deneb	53	1·3	49	N 45		23	Suhail	2·2	223	S 44
Denebola	28	2·1	182	N 14		24	Miaplacidus	1·7	222	S 70
Diphda	4	2·0	349	S 18		25	Alphard	2·0	218	S 9
Dubhe	27	1·8	194	N 62		26	Regulus	1·4	208	N 12
Elnath	14	1·7	278	N 29		27	Dubhe	1·8	194	N 62
Eltanin	47	2·2	91	N 51		28	Denebola	2·1	182	N 14
Enif	54	2·4	34	N 10		29	Gienah	2·6	176	S 18
Fomalhaut	56	1·2	15	S 30		30	Acrux	1·3	173	S 63
Gacrux	31	1·6	172	S 57		31	Gacrux	1·6	172	S 57
Gienah	29	2·6	176	S 18		32	Alioth	1·8	166	N 56
Hadar	35	0·6	149	S 60		33	Spica	1·0	158	S 11
Hamal	6	2·0	328	N 24		34	Alkaid	1·9	153	N 49
Kaus Australis	48	1·9	84	S 34		35	Hadar	0·6	149	S 60
Kochab	40	2·1	137	N 74		36	Menkent	2·1	148	S 36
Markab	57	2·5	14	N 15		37	Arcturus	0·0	146	N 19
Menkar	8	2·5	314	N 4		38	Rigil Kentaurus	−0·3	140	S 61
Menkent	36	2·1	148	S 36		39	Zubenelgenubi	2·8	137	S 16
Miaplacidus	24	1·7	222	S 70		40	Kochab	2·1	137	N 74
Mirfak	9	1·8	309	N 50		41	Alphecca	2·2	126	N 27
Nunki	50	2·0	76	S 26		42	Antares	1·0	112	S 26
Peacock	52	1·9	53	S 57		43	Atria	1·9	107	S 69
Pollux	21	1·1	243	N 28		44	Sabik	2·4	102	S 16
Procyon	20	0·4	245	N 5		45	Shaula	1·6	96	S 37
Rasalhague	46	2·1	96	N 13		46	Rasalhague	2·1	96	N 13
Regulus	26	1·4	208	N 12		47	Eltanin	2·2	91	N 51
Rigel	11	0·1	281	S 8		48	Kaus Australis	1·9	84	S 34
Rigil Kentaurus	38	−0·3	140	S 61		49	Vega	0·0	81	N 39
Sabik	44	2·4	102	S 16		50	Nunki	2·0	76	S 26
Schedar	3	2·2	350	N 57		51	Altair	0·8	62	N 9
Shaula	45	1·6	96	S 37		52	Peacock	1·9	53	S 57
Sirius	18	−1·5	259	S 17		53	Deneb	1·3	49	N 45
Spica	33	1·0	158	S 11		54	Enif	2·4	34	N 10
Suhail	23	2·2	223	S 44		55	Alnair	1·7	28	S 47
Vega	49	0·0	81	N 39		56	Fomalhaut	1·2	15	S 30
Zubenelgenubi	39	2·8	137	S 16		57	Markab	2·5	14	N 15

*0·1 — 1·2

xxxiii

© British Crown Copyright 2018. All rights reserved.

ALTITUDE CORRECTION TABLES 0°–35°— MOON

App. Alt.	0°–4° Corr^n	5°–9° Corr^n	10°–14° Corr^n	15°–19° Corr^n	20°–24° Corr^n	25°–29° Corr^n	30°–34° Corr^n	App. Alt.
′	° ′	° ′	° ′	° ′	° ′	° ′	° ′	′
00	0 34·5	5 58·2	10 62·1	15 62·8	20 62·2	25 60·8	30 58·9	00
10	36·5	58·5	62·2	62·8	62·2	60·8	58·8	10
20	38·3	58·7	62·2	62·8	62·1	60·7	58·8	20
30	40·0	58·9	62·3	62·8	62·1	60·6	58·7	30
40	41·5	59·1	62·3	62·8	62·0	60·6	58·6	40
50	42·9	59·3	62·4	62·7	62·0	60·6	58·5	50
00	1 44·2	6 59·5	11 62·4	16 62·7	21 62·0	26 60·5	31 58·5	00
10	45·4	59·7	62·4	62·7	61·9	60·4	58·4	10
20	46·5	59·9	62·5	62·7	61·9	60·4	58·3	20
30	47·5	60·0	62·5	62·7	61·9	60·3	58·2	30
40	48·4	60·2	62·5	62·7	61·8	60·3	58·2	40
50	49·3	60·3	62·6	62·7	61·8	60·2	58·1	50
00	2 50·1	7 60·5	12 62·6	17 62·7	22 61·7	27 60·1	32 58·0	00
10	50·8	60·6	62·6	62·6	61·7	60·1	57·9	10
20	51·5	60·7	62·6	62·6	61·6	60·0	57·8	20
30	52·2	60·9	62·7	62·6	61·6	59·9	57·8	30
40	52·8	61·0	62·7	62·6	61·6	59·9	57·7	40
50	53·4	61·1	62·7	62·6	61·5	59·8	57·6	50
00	3 53·9	8 61·2	13 62·7	18 62·5	23 61·5	28 59·7	33 57·5	00
10	54·4	61·3	62·7	62·5	61·4	59·7	57·4	10
20	54·9	61·4	62·7	62·5	61·4	59·6	57·4	20
30	55·3	61·5	62·8	62·5	61·3	59·5	57·3	30
40	55·7	61·6	62·8	62·4	61·3	59·5	57·2	40
50	56·1	61·6	62·8	62·4	61·2	59·4	57·1	50
00	4 56·4	9 61·7	14 62·8	19 62·4	24 61·2	29 59·3	34 57·0	00
10	56·8	61·8	62·8	62·4	61·1	59·3	56·9	10
20	57·1	61·9	62·8	62·3	61·1	59·2	56·9	20
30	57·4	61·9	62·8	62·3	61·0	59·1	56·8	30
40	57·7	62·0	62·8	62·3	61·0	59·1	56·7	40
50	58·0	62·1	62·8	62·2	60·9	59·0	56·6	50

HP	L	U	L	U	L	U	L	U	L	U	L	U	L	U	HP
′	′	′	′	′	′	′	′	′	′	′	′	′	′	′	′
54·0	0·3	0·9	0·3	0·9	0·4	1·0	0·5	1·1	0·6	1·2	0·7	1·3	0·9	1·5	54·0
54·3	0·7	1·1	0·7	1·2	0·8	1·2	0·8	1·3	0·9	1·4	1·1	1·5	1·2	1·7	54·3
54·6	1·1	1·4	1·1	1·4	1·1	1·4	1·2	1·5	1·3	1·6	1·4	1·7	1·5	1·8	54·6
54·9	1·4	1·6	1·5	1·6	1·5	1·6	1·6	1·7	1·6	1·8	1·8	1·9	1·9	2·0	54·9
55·2	1·8	1·8	1·8	1·8	1·9	1·8	1·9	1·9	2·0	2·0	2·1	2·1	2·2	2·2	55·2
55·5	2·2	2·0	2·2	2·0	2·3	2·1	2·3	2·1	2·4	2·2	2·4	2·3	2·5	2·4	55·5
55·8	2·6	2·2	2·6	2·2	2·6	2·3	2·7	2·3	2·7	2·4	2·8	2·4	2·9	2·5	55·8
56·1	3·0	2·4	3·0	2·5	3·0	2·5	3·0	2·5	3·1	2·6	3·1	2·6	3·2	2·7	56·1
56·4	3·3	2·7	3·4	2·7	3·4	2·7	3·4	2·7	3·4	2·8	3·5	2·8	3·5	2·9	56·4
56·7	3·7	2·9	3·7	2·9	3·8	2·9	3·8	2·9	3·8	3·0	3·8	3·0	3·9	3·0	56·7
57·0	4·1	3·1	4·1	3·1	4·1	3·1	4·1	3·1	4·2	3·2	4·2	3·2	4·2	3·2	57·0
57·3	4·5	3·3	4·5	3·3	4·5	3·3	4·5	3·3	4·5	3·3	4·5	3·4	4·6	3·4	57·3
57·6	4·9	3·5	4·9	3·5	4·9	3·5	4·9	3·5	4·9	3·5	4·9	3·5	4·9	3·6	57·6
57·9	5·3	3·8	5·3	3·8	5·3	3·8	5·2	3·8	5·2	3·7	5·2	3·7	5·2	3·7	57·9
58·2	5·6	4·0	5·6	4·0	5·6	4·0	5·6	4·0	5·6	3·9	5·6	3·9	5·6	3·9	58·2
58·5	6·0	4·2	6·0	4·2	6·0	4·2	6·0	4·2	6·0	4·1	5·9	4·1	5·9	4·1	58·5
58·8	6·4	4·4	6·4	4·4	6·4	4·4	6·3	4·4	6·3	4·3	6·3	4·3	6·2	4·2	58·8
59·1	6·8	4·6	6·8	4·6	6·7	4·6	6·7	4·6	6·7	4·5	6·6	4·5	6·6	4·4	59·1
59·4	7·2	4·8	7·1	4·8	7·1	4·8	7·1	4·8	7·0	4·7	7·0	4·7	6·9	4·6	59·4
59·7	7·5	5·1	7·5	5·0	7·5	5·0	7·5	5·0	7·4	4·9	7·3	4·8	7·2	4·8	59·7
60·0	7·9	5·3	7·9	5·3	7·9	5·2	7·8	5·2	7·8	5·1	7·7	5·0	7·6	4·9	60·0
60·3	8·3	5·5	8·3	5·5	8·2	5·4	8·2	5·4	8·1	5·3	8·0	5·2	7·9	5·1	60·3
60·6	8·7	5·7	8·7	5·7	8·6	5·7	8·6	5·6	8·5	5·5	8·4	5·4	8·2	5·3	60·6
60·9	9·1	5·9	9·0	5·9	9·0	5·9	8·9	5·8	8·8	5·7	8·7	5·6	8·6	5·4	60·9
61·2	9·5	6·2	9·4	6·1	9·4	6·1	9·3	6·0	9·2	5·9	9·1	5·8	8·9	5·6	61·2
61·5	9·8	6·4	9·8	6·3	9·7	6·3	9·7	6·2	9·5	6·1	9·4	5·9	9·2	5·8	61·5

DIP

Ht. of Eye	Corr^n	Ht. of Eye	Ht. of Eye	Corr^n	Ht. of Eye
m		ft.	m		ft.
2·4	−2·8	8·0	9·5	−5·5	31·5
2·6	−2·9	8·6	9·9	−5·6	32·7
2·8	−3·0	9·2	10·3	−5·7	33·9
3·0	−3·1	9·8	10·6	−5·8	35·1
3·2	−3·2	10·5	11·0	−5·9	36·3
3·4	−3·3	11·2	11·4	−6·0	37·6
3·6	−3·4	11·9	11·8	−6·1	38·9
3·8	−3·5	12·6	12·2	−6·2	40·1
4·0	−3·6	13·3	12·6	−6·3	41·5
4·3	−3·7	14·1	13·0	−6·4	42·8
4·5	−3·8	14·9	13·4	−6·5	44·2
4·7	−3·9	15·7	13·8	−6·6	45·5
5·0	−4·0	16·5	14·2	−6·7	46·9
5·2	−4·1	17·4	14·7	−6·8	48·4
5·5	−4·2	18·3	15·1	−6·9	49·8
5·8	−4·3	19·1	15·5	−7·0	51·3
6·1	−4·4	20·1	16·0	−7·1	52·8
6·3	−4·5	21·0	16·5	−7·2	54·3
6·6	−4·6	22·0	16·9	−7·3	55·8
6·9	−4·7	22·9	17·4	−7·4	57·4
7·2	−4·8	23·9	17·9	−7·5	58·9
7·5	−4·9	24·9	18·4	−7·6	60·5
7·9	−5·0	26·0	18·8	−7·7	62·1
8·2	−5·1	27·1	19·3	−7·8	63·8
8·5	−5·2	28·1	19·8	−7·9	65·4
8·8	−5·3	29·2	20·4	−8·0	67·1
9·2	−5·4	30·4	20·9	−8·1	68·8
9·5		31·5	21·4		70·5

MOON CORRECTION TABLE

The correction is in two parts; the first correction is taken from the upper part of the table with argument apparent altitude, and the second from the lower part, with argument HP, in the same column as that from which the first correction was taken. Separate corrections are given in the lower part for lower (L) and upper (U) limbs. All corrections are to be **added** to apparent altitude, *but 30′ is to be subtracted from the altitude of the upper limb.*

For corrections for pressure and temperature see page A4.

For bubble sextant observations ignore dip, take the mean of upper and lower limb corrections and subtract 15′ from the altitude.

App. Alt. = Apparent altitude = Sextant altitude corrected for index error and dip.

© British Crown Copyright 2018. All rights reserved.

ALTITUDE CORRECTION TABLES 35°–90°— MOON

App. Alt.	35°–39° Corrⁿ	40°–44° Corrⁿ	45°–49° Corrⁿ	50°–54° Corrⁿ	55°–59° Corrⁿ	60°–64° Corrⁿ	65°–69° Corrⁿ	70°–74° Corrⁿ	75°–79° Corrⁿ	80°–84° Corrⁿ	85°–89° Corrⁿ	App. Alt.
00	35 56.5	40 53.7	45 50.5	50 46.9	55 43.1	60 38.9	65 34.6	70 30.0	75 25.3	80 20.5	85 15.6	00
10	56.4	53.6	50.4	46.8	42.9	38.8	34.4	29.9	25.2	20.4	15.5	10
20	56.3	53.5	50.2	46.7	42.8	38.7	34.3	29.7	25.0	20.2	15.3	20
30	56.2	53.4	50.1	46.5	42.7	38.5	34.1	29.6	24.9	20.0	15.1	30
40	56.2	53.3	50.0	46.4	42.5	38.4	34.0	29.4	24.7	19.9	15.0	40
50	56.1	53.2	49.9	46.3	42.4	38.2	33.8	29.3	24.5	19.7	14.8	50
00	36 56.0	41 53.1	46 49.8	51 46.2	56 42.3	61 38.1	66 33.7	71 29.1	76 24.4	81 19.6	86 14.6	00
10	55.9	53.0	49.7	46.0	42.1	37.9	33.5	29.0	24.2	19.4	14.5	10
20	55.8	52.9	49.5	45.9	42.0	37.8	33.4	28.8	24.1	19.2	14.3	20
30	55.7	52.8	49.4	45.8	41.9	37.7	33.2	28.7	23.9	19.1	14.2	30
40	55.6	52.6	49.3	45.7	41.7	37.5	33.1	28.5	23.8	18.9	14.0	40
50	55.5	52.5	49.2	45.5	41.6	37.4	32.9	28.3	23.6	18.7	13.8	50
00	37 55.4	42 52.4	47 49.1	52 45.4	57 41.4	62 37.2	67 32.8	72 28.2	77 23.4	82 18.6	87 13.7	00
10	55.3	52.3	49.0	45.3	41.3	37.1	32.6	28.0	23.3	18.4	13.5	10
20	55.2	52.2	48.8	45.2	41.2	36.9	32.5	27.9	23.1	18.2	13.3	20
30	55.1	52.1	48.7	45.0	41.0	36.8	32.3	27.7	22.9	18.1	13.2	30
40	55.0	52.0	48.6	44.9	40.9	36.6	32.2	27.6	22.8	17.9	13.0	40
50	55.0	51.9	48.5	44.8	40.8	36.5	32.0	27.4	22.6	17.8	12.8	50
00	38 54.9	43 51.8	48 48.4	53 44.6	58 40.6	63 36.4	68 31.9	73 27.2	78 22.5	83 17.6	88 12.7	00
10	54.8	51.7	48.3	44.5	40.5	36.2	31.7	27.1	22.3	17.4	12.5	10
20	54.7	51.6	48.1	44.4	40.3	36.1	31.6	26.9	22.1	17.3	12.3	20
30	54.6	51.5	48.0	44.2	40.2	35.9	31.4	26.8	22.0	17.1	12.2	30
40	54.5	51.4	47.9	44.1	40.1	35.8	31.3	26.6	21.8	16.9	12.0	40
50	54.4	51.2	47.8	44.0	39.9	35.6	31.1	26.5	21.7	16.8	11.8	50
00	39 54.3	44 51.1	49 47.7	54 43.9	59 39.8	64 35.5	69 31.0	74 26.3	79 21.5	84 16.6	89 11.7	00
10	54.2	51.0	47.5	43.7	39.6	35.3	30.8	26.1	21.3	16.4	11.5	10
20	54.1	50.9	47.4	43.6	39.5	35.2	30.7	26.0	21.2	16.3	11.4	20
30	54.0	50.8	47.3	43.5	39.4	35.0	30.5	25.8	21.0	16.1	11.2	30
40	53.9	50.7	47.2	43.3	39.2	34.9	30.4	25.7	20.9	16.0	11.0	40
50	53.8	50.6	47.0	43.2	39.1	34.7	30.2	25.5	20.7	15.8	10.9	50

HP	L U	L U	L U	L U	L U	L U	L U	L U	L U	L U	L U	HP
54.0	1.1 1.7	1.3 1.9	1.5 2.1	1.7 2.4	2.0 2.6	2.3 2.9	2.6 3.2	2.9 3.5	3.2 3.8	3.5 4.1	3.8 4.5	54.0
54.3	1.4 1.8	1.6 2.0	1.8 2.2	2.0 2.5	2.2 2.7	2.5 3.0	2.8 3.2	3.1 3.5	3.3 3.8	3.6 4.1	3.9 4.4	54.3
54.6	1.7 2.0	1.9 2.2	2.1 2.4	2.3 2.6	2.5 2.8	2.7 3.0	3.0 3.3	3.2 3.5	3.5 3.8	3.8 4.0	4.0 4.3	54.6
54.9	2.0 2.2	2.2 2.3	2.3 2.5	2.5 2.7	2.7 2.9	2.9 3.1	3.2 3.3	3.4 3.5	3.6 3.8	3.9 4.0	4.1 4.3	54.9
55.2	2.3 2.3	2.5 2.4	2.6 2.6	2.8 2.8	3.0 2.9	3.2 3.1	3.4 3.3	3.6 3.5	3.8 3.7	4.0 4.0	4.2 4.2	55.2
55.5	2.7 2.5	2.8 2.6	2.9 2.7	3.1 2.9	3.2 3.0	3.4 3.2	3.6 3.4	3.7 3.5	3.9 3.7	4.1 3.9	4.3 4.1	55.5
55.8	3.0 2.6	3.1 2.7	3.2 2.8	3.3 3.0	3.5 3.1	3.6 3.3	3.8 3.4	3.9 3.6	4.1 3.7	4.2 3.9	4.4 4.0	55.8
56.1	3.3 2.8	3.4 2.9	3.5 3.0	3.6 3.1	3.7 3.2	3.8 3.3	4.0 3.4	4.1 3.6	4.2 3.7	4.4 3.8	4.5 4.0	56.1
56.4	3.6 2.9	3.7 3.0	3.8 3.1	3.9 3.2	3.9 3.3	4.0 3.4	4.1 3.5	4.3 3.6	4.4 3.7	4.5 3.8	4.6 3.9	56.4
56.7	3.9 3.1	4.0 3.1	4.1 3.2	4.1 3.3	4.2 3.3	4.3 3.4	4.3 3.5	4.4 3.6	4.5 3.7	4.6 3.8	4.7 3.8	56.7
57.0	4.3 3.2	4.3 3.3	4.3 3.3	4.4 3.4	4.4 3.4	4.5 3.5	4.5 3.5	4.6 3.6	4.7 3.6	4.7 3.7	4.8 3.8	57.0
57.3	4.6 3.4	4.6 3.4	4.6 3.4	4.6 3.5	4.7 3.5	4.7 3.5	4.7 3.6	4.8 3.6	4.8 3.6	4.8 3.7	4.9 3.7	57.3
57.6	4.9 3.6	4.9 3.6	4.9 3.6	4.9 3.6	4.9 3.6	4.9 3.6	4.9 3.6	5.0 3.6	5.0 3.6	5.0 3.6	5.0 3.6	57.6
57.9	5.2 3.7	5.2 3.7	5.2 3.7	5.2 3.7	5.2 3.7	5.1 3.6	5.1 3.6	5.1 3.6	5.1 3.6	5.1 3.6	5.1 3.6	57.9
58.2	5.5 3.9	5.5 3.8	5.5 3.8	5.4 3.8	5.4 3.7	5.4 3.7	5.3 3.7	5.3 3.6	5.2 3.6	5.2 3.5	5.2 3.5	58.2
58.5	5.9 4.0	5.8 4.0	5.8 3.9	5.7 3.9	5.6 3.8	5.6 3.8	5.5 3.7	5.5 3.6	5.4 3.6	5.3 3.5	5.3 3.4	58.5
58.8	6.2 4.2	6.1 4.1	6.0 4.1	6.0 4.0	5.9 3.9	5.8 3.8	5.7 3.7	5.6 3.6	5.5 3.5	5.4 3.5	5.3 3.4	58.8
59.1	6.5 4.3	6.4 4.3	6.3 4.2	6.2 4.1	6.1 4.0	6.0 3.9	5.9 3.8	5.8 3.6	5.7 3.5	5.6 3.4	5.4 3.3	59.1
59.4	6.8 4.5	6.7 4.4	6.6 4.3	6.5 4.2	6.4 4.1	6.2 3.9	6.1 3.8	6.0 3.7	5.8 3.5	5.7 3.4	5.5 3.2	59.4
59.7	7.1 4.7	7.0 4.5	6.9 4.4	6.8 4.3	6.6 4.1	6.5 4.0	6.3 3.8	6.1 3.7	6.0 3.5	5.8 3.3	5.6 3.2	59.7
60.0	7.5 4.8	7.3 4.7	7.2 4.5	7.0 4.4	6.9 4.2	6.7 4.0	6.5 3.9	6.3 3.7	6.1 3.5	5.9 3.3	5.7 3.1	60.0
60.3	7.8 5.0	7.6 4.8	7.5 4.7	7.3 4.5	7.1 4.3	6.9 4.1	6.7 3.9	6.5 3.7	6.3 3.5	6.0 3.2	5.8 3.0	60.3
60.6	8.1 5.1	7.9 5.0	7.7 4.8	7.6 4.6	7.3 4.4	7.1 4.2	6.9 3.9	6.7 3.7	6.4 3.4	6.2 3.2	5.9 2.9	60.6
60.9	8.4 5.3	8.2 5.1	8.0 4.9	7.8 4.7	7.6 4.5	7.3 4.2	7.1 4.0	6.8 3.7	6.6 3.4	6.3 3.2	6.0 2.9	60.9
61.2	8.7 5.4	8.5 5.2	8.3 5.0	8.1 4.8	7.8 4.5	7.6 4.3	7.3 4.0	7.0 3.7	6.7 3.4	6.4 3.1	6.1 2.8	61.2
61.5	9.1 5.6	8.8 5.4	8.6 5.1	8.3 4.9	8.1 4.6	7.8 4.3	7.5 4.0	7.2 3.7	6.9 3.4	6.5 3.1	6.2 2.7	61.5

XXXV

© British Crown Copyright 2018. All rights reserved.

NOTES

NOTES

NOTES

Recommended Readings

- Riches Are Your Right by Joseph Murphy

- The Money Illusion by Irving Fisher

- How To Win Friends And Influence People: A Condensation From The Book by Dale Carnegie

- Praying the Psalms by Thomas Merton

- The Magic of Believing by Claude M. Bristol

- Scientific Advertising by Claude C. Hopkins

- The Law of Success: Using the Power of Spirit to Create Health, Prosperity, and Happiness by Paramahansa Yogananda

Available at www.snowballpublishing.com

CPSIA information can be obtained
at www.ICGtesting.com
Printed in the USA
LVHW061612100119
603457LV00014B/502/P

9 781684 116485